American Cars, 1973–1980

Every Model, Year by Year

J. "KELLY" FLORY, JR.

McFarland & Company, Inc., Publishers
Jefferson, North Carolina, and London

LIBRARY OF CONGRESS CATALOGUING-IN-PUBLICATION DATA

Flory, J. "Kelly."
American cars, 1973–1980 : every model, year by year / J. "Kelly"
Flory, Jr.
p.   cm.
Includes bibliographical references and index.

ISBN 978-0-7864-4352-9
illustrated case binding : acid free paper ∞

1. Automobiles — United States — History.   2. Automobile industry
and trade — United States — History.   I. Title.
TL.23.F593 2013   629.2220973 — dc23   2012029675

BRITISH LIBRARY CATALOGUING DATA ARE AVAILABLE

Cover photograph: 1976 Oldsmobile Cutlass Supreme Brougham

Edited by Steve Wilson

Manufactured in the United States of America

McFarland & Company, Inc., Publishers
Box 611, Jefferson, North Carolina 28640
www.mcfarlandpub.com

Acknowledgments

Having been a teenager through the time period covered by this book, I was already an avid car enthusiast, and had collected hundreds of pieces of car literature, pictures and other car-related items by 1980. I had even imagined writing a book at this early stage with some preliminary draft work done, though my conservative upbringing and mindset told me that I could never make a living doing that. Fast-forward thirty years, and here I am finally writing the book on those cars that originally gave me the inspiration. Along the way, through my family's involvement in antique cars, I came to appreciate and enjoy all cars and trucks.

Most important to acknowledge are my parents, John and Mary Jean Flory, who probably thought I was a little crazy spending hours reading car books and sales literature as a teenager. Then there is my life-long friend Dan Reinheimer, who would ride with me to all the dealerships every year picking up car literature and taking pictures of cars on the dealership lot after hours. Of course in all that collecting of materials, there are always items missed, because the dealer was out of something, or they were "hiding away" their Corvette brochures. So even though I thought I had everything for writing this book, I found myself borrowing some brochures, which I would like to thank Brian Atwell for providing along with other dealer promotional materials. In my prior two books, I have borrowed materials from other people, specifically Tom Millard, a veteran of more than 50 years of collecting automotive memorabilia, and I would like to thank him for his continued support. I would also like to thank everyone who has offered their input and encouragement for my efforts.

I also need to thank Roland and Earlene Reichart, whom I've known for the past 30 years. Always avid car enthusiasts, they particularly enjoyed Route 66 history, their fine collection of award-winning Buicks, and assortment of many other unique cars, ranging from an early Willys Jeepster wagon to a 1974 Ford Pinto hatchback named "Buttercup." Roland passed away in early 2011, but before his death, I acquired part of a fabulous collection of sales literature, which proved invaluable to my research.

Finally, I want to acknowledge the person who got me started on gathering and collecting NADA price guides and the *Manual for the Identification of Automobiles* books, which are the source of much of the pricing and VIN information found within all of my books. This person is my aunt Virginia (Flory) Schrenk. Virginia spent many years working in the Kansas Motor Vehicle Department. New versions of these books came in regularly and were kept for years, but when things became computerized and offices were moved around, the old books were discarded more frequently. Having quite a few car enthusiasts in the family, including herself, Virginia kept them. Several years later, knowing my interest in literature collecting, she asked me if I wanted them, and thus began a collection of these informative books. Virginia's husband Kermit Schrenk was responsible for my dad, John Flory, purchasing his first antique car back in the 1950s, when the two of them bought and restored nearly identical 1926 Ford Model T touring cars. From my dad's antique car interest came my own enthusiasm for automobiles. Needless to say, Aunt Virginia has since passed, but I'll always remember her enjoying her 1965 Mustang convertible, restored by her husband, with a personalized license plate of "MY PONY."

Contents

Abbreviations and Terminology

Auto body related terminology

Colonnade	Frameless door glass w/B-pillar (a GM–specific term)
Conv.	Convertible or convertible coupe
Cpe.	Coupe
Dr.	Door
FBK	Fastback
HBK	Hatchback
HT/Hdtp.	Hardtop
NBK	Notchback
Pillared Hardtop	Frameless door glass w/B-pillar
Sdn.	Sedan
Spt.	Sport (Cpe. or Sdn.)
Wgn.	Wagon or station wagon
# - p.	Number of passengers vehicle is designed to carry
# - S.	Number of seats in vehicle (usually refers to wagons)

Engine related terminology

bbl.	Barrels (ports or venturi) on a carburetor
CID	Cubic inch displacement
DOHC	Dual overhead cam
Dual exhaust	Two separate exhaust outlet systems (typically each has ½ of engine exhaust)
Dual-outlet exhaust	Exhaust in single pipe off engine, but split into 2 outlets at back of car
EFI	Electronic fuel injection
FI	Fuel injection
Hemi	Hemispherical head
HO or H.O.	High output
I #	Inline engine block design
OHC	Overhead cam
OHV	Overhead valve
SFI	Sequential fuel injection
TPI	Throttle port injection
VIH	Valve in head
V #	V-shape engine block design

Measurements

Cap.	Capacity
cm	Centimeter
Cu.	Cubic
F	Front
Ft.	Foot or feet
g or gal.	gallon
in.	inch or inches
1 or L	Litre or liter
lbs.	pounds
R	Rear
WB	Wheelbase

Metric conversion

Inches to Centimeters:	1" = 2.54cm
Centimeter to Inches:	1 cm = .39"
Gallons to Liter:	1 gal. = 3.785L
Liter to Gallons:	1 L = .264 gal.
Cubic Inch to Liter:	1 cu.in. = .016L
Liter to Cubic Inch:	1 L = 61.02 cu. in.

Miscellaneous

AC or A/C	Air conditioning
BSW	Black sidewall (tire)
B/WL	Black sidewall with white letter (tire)
CAFE	Corporate Average Fuel Economy
CC	Cruise control *or* clear coat paint
DOE	Department of Energy
EC or E/C	Extra cost
EPA	Environmental Protection Agency
I/P	Instrument panel
Met.	Metallic (paint)
MPG	Miles per gallon
MSRP	Manufacturer's suggested retail price
NA or N/A	Not available
NC or N/C	No cost option
OWL	Oval white letter (tire)
PB	Power brakes
PS	Power steering
RWL or R/WL	Raised white letter tire
S or Std.	Standard equipment
$	Available at extra cost, but price not available at this time
WO	Wide Oval tire
WSW	White sidewall (tire)

Grille configurations

Crosshatch — Rectangular design; horizontal.

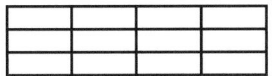

Crosshatch — Rectangular design; vertical.

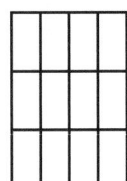

Egg-crate — Square design with all sides equal length.

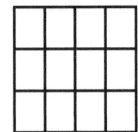

Honeycomb — Consists of multiple six-sided openings, typically each opening ¾" to 1" in size.

Mesh or wire mesh — similar to screen wire pattern, generally in an X or diamond pattern, typically each opening ⅛" to ½" in size.

Preface

For the American automobile industry, the mid to late 1970s was a period rife with government regulation, increasing foreign competition, and rising costs, bookended by both a fuel crisis and recession. The manufacturers struggled to keep up with changing consumer demands, government mandates and the difficulties of maintaining a profitable business while working within the confines of what was becoming an antiquated system of factories, design processes and corporate bureaucracy. Today, this period has come to be seen as the starting point of Detroit's path toward the crisis of 2008–2009, when government loans were required to get General Motors through bankruptcy and keep it in business, and loans were similarly needed to sustain Chrysler — something it had prior experience with during the 1979 to 1981 period. In retrospect, this is easy to see, but at the time, the manufacturers were in a continuing struggle to meet current demands, and foresight proved short as a rising tide of imported competition swept in.

Arranged year by year, this book includes all cars offered for sale in the United States by major American manufacturers in model years 1973 through 1980, to include "captive imports." For each of these model years, the reader will find an overview of developments affecting the automobile industry, followed by an annual status report of each nameplate and extensive data about every model sold that year: production numbers, pricing, specifications and dimensions, standard equipment and major options, paint color choices, running changes from the previous model year, and other information.

The term "captive import" is briefly defined as cars designed, built and manufactured overseas, with specific features included for sale under American manufacturers' nameplates, or to be marketed through their dealerships. Captive imports sold under American manufacturers' names are covered within this volume much the same as the domestic models, and include the Dodge Colt, Plymouth Arrow and Ford Fiesta. Those captive imports sold under their own name but marketed through domestic dealerships, including the Opel (Buick) and Capri and Pantera (Lincoln-Mercury), are all covered with slight variations from the other captive imports. The captive imports are not included in the price and production summaries of each make's yearly introduction. Where they appear in the model listings, no corporate siblings are listed (as none were offered in the U.S. market); nor is the percentage of the division's sales volume calculated. Also, note that for the Pantera, powertrains and options are listed within the details of the model's standard equipment section.

Trucks are not included within this book, but each year's commentary includes brief remarks on events surrounding truck production by the major car manufacturers. Models such as the International Harvester Travelall and Scout and American Motors Jeep Wagoneer and Cherokee lines are not included, despite their being sold as alternatives to station wagons and being classified as cars by the National Automobile Dealers Association. This is because they were built on truck chassis, which places them in the truck category. Interestingly, these models were considered cars while similar models such as Chevrolet's Blazer and Suburban and Ford's Bronco were considered trucks. Traditional thinking only allowed for car and truck categories, but the situation would be remedied in the early eighties when the term "sport utility vehicle" came into being.

Likewise, this book excludes details of chassis-only offerings (such as the Oldsmobile Toronado chassis built for use on the GMC motorhomes) and commercial chassis products built by the major manufacturers (such as those built for aftermarket conversion to ambulances, hearses or limousines). Products of small, independent makes of limited production (i.e., Checker, Avanti II and Bricklin, and others building fewer than 500 units per year) are not covered in the usual format, but rather are featured in Appendix I, which contains an overview of most minor manufacturers and limited production models.

1

Make and Model Listings

LISTING BY MAKE

Introduction. Each make is listed alphabetically within a yearly grouping. Following the make's name is its main advertising slogan for the year, taken directly from factory sales literature or advertising. Next is an overview of what was new for the year, including styling, powertrain and model lineup changes.

Sales, pricing and production information. This section includes sales totals for the model year (unless otherwise noted), the marque's percentage share of production in the entire industry, and its ranking amongst all American competitors. Following the sales information is pricing information that includes the make's average base price and its pricing range. Also listed is the make's month or exact date of introduction of the model year. Listed next are the various assembly plants in which the cars were manufactured as reported by the manufacturer's records, and used for decoding the Vehicle Identification Number.

Data plate identification (VIN). This section breaks down the details of the individual cars' Vehicle Identification Numbers, or VINs. For all models built in 1973–1980, the VIN plate is located on the left hand side of the upper instrument panel where it is visible through the windshield. The meaning of each digit or letter of the VIN is identified and an example of a complete VIN is given. Details of the body data plate tag, usually located on the cowl, are not included, but for most makes and models, the model number and paint codes provided within this book can be found on this tag. Variations from the above are typically seen only in the "captive imports" and details are included within the specific model or years.

Powertrains. The chart presented in this section lists all known engine and transmission combinations that were offered at the time of each model's introduction. In some cases, mid-year changes may have been made, or certain other optional equipment may have been required to order a particular engine, and whenever possible, these details are noted. Also, included are fuel mileage estimates whenever available, as they played a major role in the marketing of automobiles from 1973 onward. Further details of how the estimates are presented are included in the introduction of this book. Pricing information is given whenever an accurate price could be determined from manufacturer records. The prices listed are for the engine and transmission together. For example, if a V8 engine with automatic transmission is listed as an option for a car that had a 6-cylinder engine with 3-speed manual transmission as standard equipment, and the chart says the V8 and automatic is a $450 option, that price is for the two options combined. This amount would be added to the base price of the car. If accurate pricing is not available, that will be noted by a $ symbol with no price, indicating an extra-cost option of unknown price.

Major options. This is a chart listing the most popular or most heavily promoted options available across the full line of cars. Generally this would include air conditioning, power steering, power brakes, radio and stereos, wheel covers, and other power accessories. Certain options, such as intermittent windshield wipers, are only included when they were at the peak of popularity, or in the case of Ford Motor Company cars they are included throughout the period, because Ford developed the wiper delay system. While option packages first became a sales tool in the immediate post–World War II era, they became unbelievably numerous during the late 1970s; therefore a special section for pricing of these follows the Major Options section, and is titled "Option Groups and Packages." Appendix II of this book includes contents of each of the packages, with as much detail as possible included.

The following disclaimer applies to all optional equipment pricing within this book: Any individual item may be standard equipment, optional at different pricing, or unavailable on certain models. The option charts are only a guide.

To expand on the above comments, some options were offered at different prices depending upon the trim level or other options purchased. For example, forged aluminum wheels on a 1974 Pinto are $142, unless ordered with a luxury décor group, or accent group, and then they are $119. The proliferation of these pricing practices in the 1970s makes it virtually impossible to list all the pricing combinations. If one examines the 1973 Ford pricing lists for an example of how multiple models or trim levels could affect the pricing, and keeps in mind that in combination with other options or packages, the prices could change further, it becomes more clear why not every price and detail can be listed. Similarly, space restrictions prevent all of the various optional rear axle ratios, limited-slip differentials and suspension/handling packages from being included unless they were high profile and popular options, such as the RTS suspension system offered by Pontiac during the late 1970s. Also, numerous other options are not listed, such as floor mats, bumper guards, intermittent windshield wipers (after 1975), various body moldings, and tires of larger sizes or different types. Then there are variations on the options that *are* listed, such as tinted windshield only (rather than all glass being tinted), AM/FM radio with two speakers (rather than the AM/FM stereo with four speakers), CB radio options with an AM radio only (during the late 1970s), and so forth. The possibilities were seemingly endless during this time period, so in trying to fit in as many as possible, only the most popular or noteworthy are mentioned.

Paint colors. This is a listing of all known colors offered during the model year. Some colors were offered only on certain models; such cases are noted whenever known. While most manufacturers had moved away from the practice, it was still possible that special order, non-standard color options were available. Two-tone paint options, while not as popular as they once were due to the increasing popularity of vinyl tops, were still available, with pricing of the option listed if available. However, details of colors offered in two-tones are not given, as the variations among the numerous models available are too extensive to include. In some cases, certain colors were used only in a two-tone combination, and if that is the case it is noted with "two-tone only" after the paint color.

Model Listings

Introduction. Each model has its own section, starting at the lowest priced or smallest entry-level model, and proceeding through the highest-priced or top-of-the-line model offered by the manufacturer. Generally manufacturers promoted their models in a similar manner. This is only a general guide, and is always subject to exceptions such as the Chevrolet Corvette being listed last because it is the prestige model of the line, and Chevrolet always touted it as such. Following each model name is its main advertising slogan for the year, again taken directly from factory sales literature and advertising.

Historical overview of the model. Following the introduction is a section containing basic facts about the model, including the year the nameplate first appeared, the time span when the same basic body or chassis was used, and models that preceded and followed the current one. "Corporate siblings" are any car models manufactured by the parent company sharing most major components, including chassis and body. "Primary competition" includes any direct competition, and on occasion some models that are indirect competition; only domestic or captive import competitors are listed. Most compact and smaller cars also had import competition, but it is not included in this book. An example of indirect competition is the 1978 Dodge Challenger, a performance-oriented, front-wheel-drive, four-cylinder captive import model that was targeted at the same buyer demographic as the rear-wheel-drive Ford Mustang II that was available with engines ranging from an economy four-cylinder to a V8 engine. It also competed more directly in price with the Buick Skyhawk, which was a hatchback whereas the Challenger was a two-door hardtop. Also listed is the percentage of the manufacturer's total sales generated by this model, and then a very general description of changes for the model year in question under "Notable Changes." The phrase "Completely redesigned" indicates basically a new car from the ground up, with at least a new chassis and body, or a new body and powertrain configurations, whereas "Completely restyled" indicates a car new in appearance, but still utilizing the same chassis and main body

structure as the previous year's model with new and significant sheetmetal changes. Other changes could typically include new interior designs and possibly revised or new powertrains.

Standard equipment. This is a list of the basic features deemed as standard by the manufacturer according to factory literature. Certain equipment is considered to be standard on all models during this time period, and is not listed within this book. These features include such things as heater and defroster, two-speed windshield wipers with washers, door armrests, and mandated safety equipment. Certain items such as door armrests are listed when not standard on the base model. It is also important to note that not all models during this period had standard floor carpeting, so this is listed. Also noteworthy is that not all models came with color-keyed instrument panels, steering columns and steering wheels, with many base models, particularly early in the period, having all of these features finished in black. Whenever it is known, these features are listed as color-keyed if black was used on the base models, or had been black recently during prior model years. By the 1980 model year, nearly all but the most basic of cars had color-keyed interiors.

Models Available. This is a chart listing all models available under a model nameplate throughout the season. Some cars were offered in a six-cylinder and a V8 line, and where this is the case sometimes the larger engine was standard in specific models, such as the station wagons, while the six-cylinder engine was standard in coupes and sedans, so the price found in the Models Available chart needs to be used in conjunction with the Powertrains chart to determine the standard engine and transmission combination for the price listed. This is done to keep the listings uniform among makes. Production numbers are fairly straightforward, representing the total model year production by body style and series. During certain periods of time some manufacturers' model year production by body style was not available or does not exist, so production is given as the information is available, with footnotes explaining how the production is listed when it varies. Some manufacturers gave their two- and three-seat station wagons different model numbers but kept production as one total, and this will be noted if known. Conversely, some used the same model numbers but kept separate production totals, so this total is given if available. Model year production is not available for captive imports, and rather the model year sales were generally reported, though occasionally calendar year sales, with these differences being noted within the model listing. Chrysler production numbers through the 1975 model year include only U.S. production for domestic sales. Therefore, any production from Canadian plants built for sale in the United States is not available; this mostly affects the Dodge Dart and Plymouth Valiant models. Base Manufacturer's Suggested Retail Price

(MSRP) is listed as of the beginning of the model year, unless otherwise noted. Price changes occurred often throughout the model year, and were under government price controls well into the 1974 season, but became more frequent for 1975 and beyond. Discrepancies in introductory date prices are prevalent even within industry records, as sometimes the prices announced were changed before the cars hit the showroom floors, so readers are cautioned to use this listing as the intended introductory prices, generally taken from corporate sources for General Motors and Ford, and from industry sources for Chrysler and American Motors. The columns for change from LY (last year) on pricing and the production show the increase or decrease in each and how they affected one another. Finally the column for shipping weight reflects the weight as a car leaves the production line, and not including a full tank of fuel and such things. Curb weight (not used here) is slightly higher as it includes a full tank of fuel, oil, water and other items in its total weight.

Measurements. In general, most of the measurements given are for 4-Door Sedan models, when that model is available in a line. Otherwise measurements are for the lowest priced model in the line, or else the table specifies which model is used. For the most part measurements such as wheelbase, length, width, luggage capacity, and fuel tank capacity are the same amongst all variations of a model. Where there are significant differences, such as with station wagon models, this is listed, if available. Two measurements that frequently vary among models are headroom and legroom. By the seventies, most manufacturers had standardized these specifications, and they typically reported maximum dimensions for the front seat and minimum dimensions for the rear seat. However, a disclaimer is required as in some cases competitive pressures led to the use of maximum dimensions being advertised. Similar differences can be found in the cargo capacity given, as some manufacturers reported "usable cargo capacity" which accounts for the spare tire or other consumers of space. Other manufacturers may have reported "total cargo capacity." Cargo capacity listed for station wagon models and most hatchback models is assumed to be with the rear seat folded down. When there is a significant change in cargo capacity from year to year without significant design changes to any individual model, this usually is an indication that the spare tire was changed from a standard size wheel and tire to an inflatable tire, or vice versa. Late in the decade it could also mean a change to a compact spare tire. Details of these changes are usually not mentioned as they varied by model, series and sub-series, and would become too cumbersome to include in this book.

NOTES ON THE DATA

Aside from the previously mentioned details, certain assumptions have been made to fit the era of the vehicles in this book. Two examples are the steering and braking systems, which generally follow these assumptions. If a base model has as standard equipment manual recirculating ball or rack-and-pinion steering and manual brakes with drums front and rear, this is not always mentioned in the Major Standard Equipment section. However, if any trim level above the base model adds power-assisted steering (of either type), power drum brakes, or power front disc/rear drum brakes, this will be listed. If a base model had power-assisted steering (of either type), power drum brakes, or power front disc/rear drum brakes, this may not necessarily be listed in the Major Standard Equipment section. Confirmation of what is standard equipment can be made by referring to the Major Options section on all but the luxury makes of Cadillac, Chrysler and Lincoln, which had long used power steering and power brakes as standard equipment. Note that for the brake types shown above, "power brakes" will indicate power drum brakes, front and rear, and "power front disc brakes" will indicate power-assisted front disc and rear drum brakes. Always assume rear drum brakes are included; in the rare event a model has four-wheel disc brakes, this will be mentioned. A listing of power steering is assuming power-assisted steering, which is usually hydraulically assisted, whether it is the recirculating ball type or rack-and-pinion.

Also, many features that were optional or not even developed yet in the mid-sixties were, by 1974, standard on nearly every car sold in the United States, mainly as a result of government requirements and the overall advancement of the automobile industry and its suppliers. Below is a representative list from the 1976 American Motors brochure, giving the "SAFE-COMMAND" features that were standard equipment on all new American Motors cars:

Energy absorbing bumper system.
Single-buckle front-seat lap and shoulder belts for driver and right side passenger, with seat belt buzzer and warning reminder light, and seat belts for all rear seat passengers.
Certified flame-resistant fabrics.
Two front seat head restraints.
4-way hazard warning signals.
Lane changer turn signals.
Automatically activated backup lights.
Side of car safety marker lights.
Guard-rail doors (internal rigid structural support).
Energy-absorbing steering column.
High-strength windshield glass.
Tempered side and rear glass.
Padded sun visors.
Padded instrument panel.
Safety-shaped armrests.
Double-safety brake system (dual master cylinder).
Brake system warning light (low-fluid level).
Self-adjusting brakes.
Corrosion-resistant brake lines.
Safety rim wheels.
Tire tread wear indicators.

Captive engine mounts.
High-strength door locks and hinges.
Safety-shaped door handles (and I/P controls).
Front-seat back lock (two-doors).
Dual action hood latch.

Engines, especially the higher power V8's (e.g., 350 CID and larger), often require other optional equipment such as power steering, power front disc brakes, or heavy-duty alternators, batteries, cooling systems, or other equipment. The optional prices listed in the powertrain tables do not include these other "required" options, unless noted. For many cars through the mid–1970s, a heavy-duty or a larger transmission may have been required, or included, with the larger engines. For example, the 1974 Buick LeSabre ordered with base equipment had a 350 CID, 2-barrel, V8 engine, with a Turbo Hydra-matic 375B automatic transmission as standard. If ordered with a 455 CID, 2-barrel, V8 engine it required the Turbo Hydra-matic 400 automatic transmission, which was included in the price of the larger engine. Typically the price of a larger transmission was included in the pricing of the optional engine, but be aware that in most cases this detailed information is not noted, so it is possible to have additional costs for transmission upgrades. Also, horsepower ratings may vary by model application due to optional transmission and axle gear ratios. Typically the variance is less than 5 horsepower, and a difference will only be noted if it is more significant.

For most manufacturers, throughout this period, a required option for cars sold in California was a California Emissions Controls system. This option added equipment or required adjustments to the powertrain and exhaust system, which typically cost $20–$50 in 1973, depending upon model and manufacturer, and by 1976 would cost anywhere from $35 to $90. This was in addition to any higher cost added by other required equipment, such as a different engine or optional axle ratios. These requirements made a car sold in California generally sell from $75 to $350 higher, or more in some cases, than a standard "Federal Emissions" equipped car. Finally, all cars sold in New York state were required to have some type of rear window defroster or defogger system. Therefore, all cars sold in New York would have this option added to their base price. When both a blower-type defogger and an electric grid defroster were available, usually the lower-priced one was required for New York state delivery.

Introduction

If the American auto industry could have one wish granted allowing them to change the past, odds are that with a few exceptions, they would like to rewrite the period from 1973 to 1980, or even forget that it ever happened. Internal issues of poor quality and labor unrest developed alongside multiple external problems — inflation, gas shortages, new governmental regulations, environmental concerns, and safety issues, just to name a few. It has been argued by some that the industry devoted so much effort during this period to combating the external concerns that it brought the internal problems upon itself. Others say that the U.S. industry chose to ignore the internal problems until it was too late, while trying to resist or ignore some of the external issues. And then there is always the possibility that both groups are right, at least to some extent.

The external concerns began with events in American history that characterize the entire period. The Vietnam War and continuing racial discord had inflicted a lingering strain on the nation's mood and attitude. Inflation had first become a problem in the early 1970s, causing the government to implement price controls on many manufactured goods. By 1972, inflation was easing somewhat, helping 1973 to become one of the automobile manufacturers' best sales years ever. Then, another period of inflation started during a 1973 and 1974 stock market collapse following the first fuel crisis, and with a recovery underway by 1978 and 1979, yet another fuel crisis came along, followed by inflation in 1980, after which the nation fell into a period of deep recession through 1982. Only in 1983 did a long-term recovery finally start. Along the way came numerous government regulations and programs that imposed new demands on the manufacturers.

Internal issues troubling the car companies included union labor unrest, less than desirable build quality on the assembly lines, and some unsettling engineering qualities designed into some cars. It all led to problems, some of which manufacturers were legally mandated to meet, and others of

which the media and the public were convinced that Detroit was ignoring or avoiding.

Despite some often-critical reviews, it is not necessarily true that the industry as a whole was avoiding or ignoring every issue. As a case in point, discussions and early proposals for down-sizing efforts were underway at General Motors in 1972, before "OPEC" or "fuel crisis" were regularly used words in daily conversation. This initiative demonstrates recognition of the excessive size of American full-size cars of the period. On the safety front, Ford had long championed safety initiatives with a full-fledged safety program launched back in 1956, and both GM and Ford would produce Experimental Safety Vehicles, or "ESVs," with GM's debuting in 1972 and Ford's in 1973, both being based on their then-current full-sized models. Chrysler later introduced the RSV (Research Safety Vehicle) in 1976, based on a production Simca 1308, coincidentally Europe's "Car of the Year" and "Safety Car of the Year," and Simca being a company of which Chrysler owned a portion. The ESVs and RSV were intended to showcase all of the current and foreseeable safety equipment that could be added to cars, while the manufacturers also made a point to emphasize the down sides, such as increased costs and added weight that would result in lower fuel economy.

Efforts were also underway prior to this time toward better fuel economy and lower emissions in engineering concepts such as the Wankel rotary engine project, which GM joined in 1971, ultimately to no avail. (The rotary engine project will be further discussed later in this introduction.) Chrysler was still leaning toward the turbine engine, which it began experimenting with back in the 1950s, and rolled out a 1977 Chrysler LeBaron Turbine and a 1980 Dodge Mirada Turbine. There were also less serious efforts put out by American Motors with its 1968 Amitron and later renamed 1978 Concept Electron, which was to have total on-board electric operation, but ended up being only a rolling concept. In the end, none of these concepts made it to showroom floors, and Detroit was saddled with a reputation of not taking the issues seriously.

The Fuel of the American Economy

During the 1970s, industry economists reported that one in ten jobs in the United States was somehow directly related to the auto industry, and that any situation that affected the automakers would trickle down through the rest of the American economy. There is also a famous saying that "As GM goes, so goes the nation." The actual statement made by the chairman of General Motors, Charles Wilson, in a 1953 reporting to a Senate committee was, "For years I thought what was good for our country was good for General Motors and vice versa. The difference did not exist. Our company is too big. It goes with the welfare of the country."* Whatever economic belief one holds, there is no doubt that the automotive industry was a key player in the national economy throughout the 1970s, and it still is today. It is little wonder, then, that two significant gas crises and the inflation which they served to worsen drove the economy into recession, eventually resulting in a change of the nation's car buying habits. That shift would lead to new automotive design and engineering strategies, manufacturing practices, and marketing tactics.

The first oil crisis came in the fall of 1973 with the OPEC (Organization of Petroleum Exporting Countries) oil embargo, which was implemented over U.S. support of Israel in the Yom Kippur war. On October 16, six Middle East countries unilaterally raised posted prices by 17 percent, to $3.65 per barrel, and announced production cuts. On October 17, Arab oil producing nations announced that they would reduce oil production steadily in 5 percent increments. Then, on October 20, other countries including Saudi Arabia joined the embargo, and OPEC declared that it would no longer supply oil to the U.S. or other countries supporting Israel in the conflict. Independently, OPEC members agreed to use their leverage over the world price-setting mechanism for oil in order to stabilize their real incomes by raising world oil prices. The ensuing gas shortages, long lines at the pump and rising prices are well-documented history. Further cuts in production were promised, but within months, negotiations gained a production increase, and by March 17, 1974, an end to the embargo was announced.

In 1974, after a recovery from that crisis began, efforts were stepped up at the Federal level to put regulations into place regarding the fuel efficiency of the nation's automobile fleet. For the 1975 model year, the average fuel economy for new light duty vehicles was about 13 miles per gallon (MPG). The result of these efforts was passage of the Corporate Av-

erage Fuel Economy (CAFE) standards act by Congress in 1975. Implemented by the Environmental Protection Agency (EPA), their now familiar CAFE standards began during 1975 for all cars, foreign and domestic. The goal was to raise the average mileage incrementally to 27.5 MPG by 1986. A second oil crisis ensued in 1979 after the Iranian revolution, with the results being no less dramatic than the first crisis. The biggest difference this time was that the country knew what to expect, and was better prepared. The second crisis is well known for gasoline prices skyrocketing. In fact, on an inflation-adjusted basis, the average price of a gallon of gasoline in early 2004 was just beginning to surpass what it had been at the peak of pricing in 1980–1981, nearly 25 years later. Details of the CAFE standards, rules and other details are discussed further in the "Government Regulations" section.

Environment

The EPA had concerns other than gas mileage that greatly affected cars of this period as well. During most of the period, emphasis was placed on cleaning up the nation's air quality. The effect on manufacturers was twofold — facilities and product. For years, especially in the first half the 20th century, factories of all types were known for belching out literally tons of smoke and pollutants. Factories had created air pollution, water pollution, and other environmental damage as a result of their operations. Once established, though, many companies realized they were damaging the very environment in which they were living and which they depended upon, and as a result some became more corporately responsible, while others ignored the problem to save money. By the 1970s, those that were slow at "cleaning up" or chose to ignore the environment totally were held accountable. Many active organizations, such as the Sierra Club and Greenpeace, eventually helped raise public awareness and were able to engage world governments in helping to start cleaning up our world. Their efforts were slow in effecting change, but eventually cleaner and greener solutions were implemented.

As for the product, it was well known that automobiles were a cause of pollution in industrialized countries. The sheer volume of cars on our roads makes them easy to single out as large polluters, but jet aircraft, trains, buses, and heavy trucks also played their part in the transportation industry's clean air struggle. A lot of pollution was emitted from a single automobile exhaust pipe prior to 1975; today, after decades of work, research, the advent of catalytic converters and the development of electronic engine control systems, the internal combustion gasoline engine produces less than 10 percent as many toxic emissions. There is more to be done, but the

*New York Times, *February 24, 1953.*

future is looking brighter for both cleaner air and decreased dependence on fossil fuels.

Government Regulation

For the automotive industry, the 1970s was a period of constant introduction of new government regulations, some of them demanded by consumers, others demanded by safety and environmental activists, and all of them driving up the price of a new car. Of course, the manufacturers were required to conform to all enacted legislation within certain time frames, and for most companies this would mean delaying expenditures on new designs and other changes, and even delaying introductions of all-new cars, to be able to meet the mandated government requirements. It was a frustration for many in the auto industry, and in the end a costly period for consumers, as all the changes, coupled with inflation throughout the economy, resulted in the sharpest rise in history for automobile prices, with the average base price of a car increasing by nearly 85 percent within a relatively short eight-year time span.

Government regulation was nothing new to the automotive industry. Three decades prior, in 1940, the first legislation was signed mandating that all cars use the recently invented sealed beam headlights for added safety. The "Mulroney" sticker act, requiring prices to be posted in the window of all new automobiles, was enacted in the late 1950s. By the mid–1960s, the U.S. Congress had created several safety agencies, and regulations became more frequent. The first major legislation was the National Traffic and Motor Vehicle Safety Act of 1966. Requirements resulting from this mandate included front seat safety belts in 1966, padded instrument panels, and the 1968 safety standards requiring front seat head restraints, seat belts in all seating positions, side marker lamps, safety-designed instrument panel controls, and other changes. During 1970, the NHTSA (National Highway Traffic Safety Administration) was formed by combining several pre-existing federal government agencies.

Then a second major piece of federal legislation was enacted, the Motor Vehicle Information and Cost Savings Act of 1972. The United States Congress acted to protect consumers and provide information to new car buyers about crashworthiness and reparability of cars sold in the country. Acting under this direction from Congress, in 1973 NHTSA issued the first bumper crash standards for automobiles sold in the United States. The standard required automobiles to be capable of sustaining a 5 mph frontal impact and a 2.5 mph rear impact without damage to its safety systems. In 1974, the standard for rear crashes was raised to 5 mph. Manufacturers had to spend significant money to update existing car lines and make necessary styling changes, and of course the cost was passed on to the consumer through higher retail prices. Interestingly, the smallest manufacturer, American Motors, was the only manufacturer to offer rear bumpers meeting the 1974 standard as an option on its 1973 model cars.

Another safety requirement enacted by NHTSA for 1972 required passenger vehicles for sale in the United States to be equipped with passive restraints protecting vehicle occupants in frontal barrier crashes up to and including 30 mph, or alternatively, with a combination buzzer and warning light reminder system. With few exceptions the automobile manufacturers opted for the reminder system. The system consisted of a flashing light and buzzer, which activated continuously for at least one minute if the vehicle was placed in gear and the driver or front outboard passenger was not belted. The simple sensor system used to activate the reminder system, however, could be bypassed in a variety of ingenious ways. When it became evident that the introduction of passive restraint systems would be delayed, NHTSA moved to require seat belt ignition interlock systems on all cars as an interim measure. Effective August 15, 1973, NHTSA required in Federal Motor Vehicle Safety Standard (FMVSS) 208 that all 1974 model year passenger vehicles be equipped with an ignition interlock that allowed the vehicle to start only if the driver was seated and the belts were extended more than four inches from their normally stowed position or the belts were latched. In addition, an audible warning was activated if seat belts were unfastened after the car was started. It was assumed that the ignition interlock would increase seat belt use by eliminating two of the most popular ways of defeating the earlier belt reminder systems: leaving the belt fastened and tucking it behind the seat, or tying a knot in the belt so that it was held out of the retractor. However, the public uproar was so loud, Congress acted to require NHTSA to do something about the situation.

When Congress passed legislation, which was immediately signed by President Ford, prohibiting NHTSA from requiring either the ignition interlock or continuous buzzer systems, NHTSA changed FMVSS 208 to a less aggressive requirement. Passenger vehicles manufactured after February 1975 were required to have a warning light of four to eight seconds in duration that is activated when the ignition is turned on regardless of whether the seat belt is fastened, and a chime of similar duration that sounds unless the driver's belt is buckled. This standard would remain in effect for several years.

All of these improvements and changes caused manufacturing costs to rise astronomically. To determine how much of the cost of the required features could be reflected in increased prices of the 1973 automobiles, the Price Commission in Washington, D.C., conducted public hearings during the fall of 1972. Since nearly all cars were on sale by September, new 1973 models were introduced at prices not much greater than the 1972 models. However, after the hearings, price increases were allowed, and they occurred several times during the 1973 model year. By 1974 model introductions, prices had risen 13 percent, and then another 9 percent by the time 1975 automobiles were introduced.

Simultaneously during this time frame, government units were raising concerns over environmental issues. Smog had become so severe in such heavily populated areas as Los Angeles and southern California that the state of California formed CARB, the California Air Resources Board. This agency began implementing stringent controls on auto pollutants from all cars destined for sale in California. Automakers had adapted nearly all engines to run on low lead and no-lead fuels by 1971, which helped meet the initial requirements. Then when the federal government implemented controls on air quality, and California's rules became more strict, the auto industry had to react and quickly.

To meet the federal emission standards, automakers basically took similar approaches, all falling into three main categories: ignition systems, fuel delivery systems, and exhaust controls. Automakers had been working towards improving electronic ignition systems since the 1960s. By 1973, they were greatly improving the firing and timing of the engine through electronics, which could help burn the fuel more efficiently, thereby reducing emissions. Each manufacturer developed its own system: Chrysler's was termed "Lean Burn" ignition, General Motors' system was called "High-Energy" ignition (HEI), while Ford called their version a solid-state ignition system, and American Motors simply had an electronic ignition. When catalytic converters were introduced in 1975 (see below), General Motors' combined it with HEI to introduce the "Maximum Mileage System." Such improvements continued as the years went on, and by the early 1980s when computers became small enough and powerful enough, they were used in combination with the aforementioned fuel delivery improvements, which came in the form of advanced electronic fuel injection technology, and the carburetor would eventually become a thing of the past on new cars.

Exhaust system controls took several forms, with a few manufacturers opting to rely on their electronic systems and powertrain technology to keep emissions in check, while most also added a physical system change. Most manufacturers quickly adopted this system change, after General Motors developed a unit that could be successfully put into production. Although catalytic converters had been invented prior to 1973, getting them to work and survive in harsh environments like the undercarriages of cars proved to be a significant challenge. A team of engineering, research and development professionals at General Motors produced a behind-the-scenes engineering breakthrough that helped to overcome the effects of severe thermal, chemical and mechanical punishment of catalysts in harsh automotive exhaust gas environments. Their engineering efforts between 1973

and 1975 resulted in the adoption of the automotive catalytic converter in time for General Motors' 1975 model year. A catalytic converter provides an environment for a chemical reaction wherein toxic combustion by-products from the engine are converted to less-toxic substances being expelled through the exhaust, thereby creating less air pollution. Typically containing internal components of stainless steel, ceramic and platinum, the catalytic converter is heavy and expensive. Although it added more cost for the consumer, it was credited for creating a big environmental gain and becoming one of the auto industry's first "green" initiatives. Eventually the catalytic converter was introduced on most American cars equipped with electronic ignitions within the 1975 model year, and it remains a fixture on new gasoline and diesel powered automobiles and trucks. It should be noted that all through this period, cars destined for sale in California were required to have additional special emissions equipment and a testing certification before being sold, costing consumers an extra $30 to $100, depending upon model and year.

Then came the "big one," Corporate Average Fuel Economy, or CAFE. The rules, which have changed many times over the years, remain in force today. At times consumers have been nearly as frustrated as manufacturers when it comes to interpreting the resulting reports. The purpose of CAFE, first enacted by Congress in 1975, was to reduce energy consumption, specifically gasoline, by increasing the fuel economy of cars and light-duty trucks. The regulation of CAFE is the responsibility of NHTSA and the Environmental Protection Agency (EPA). NHTSA sets the fuel economy standards for cars and light-duty trucks sold within the United States, and the EPA calculates the average fuel economy for each manufacturer, based on testing of all models in a controlled environment, and a formula that includes the total number of each model sold and its estimated fuel mileage. By 1978, rules were in place dictating that the "corporate" average fuel economy for passenger cars had to be at least 27.5 MPG by the 1984 model year. They began with a minimum of 18.0 MPG in 1978, rising to 19.0 in 1979, then 20.0 for 1980. From that point the standard increased annually, until reaching the 1984 model year requirement, where the standard remained for most of the next 25 years.

The miles-per-gallon estimate reporting, or MPG as they are more commonly referred to, varied greatly in the early years of the program. The first publicly released estimates from a government agency began in 1973. This initial year was the startup period, prior to any signed legislation, so not all cars were tested, and publicly available reports were minimal. A more formal program was implemented in 1974 when most cars had been tested, though not in all of the possible variations, and a two- to three-page sheet was made available in limited quantities for consumer reference. These tests were the benchmarks for the actual beginning of the program for the 1975 model year. In 1976, the first pamphlets with mileage estimate information on all cars were printed. From this time on, these pamphlets were required to be displayed in all new car showrooms, and readily available to consumers.

What follows here is reprinted from the 1977 EPA Mileage Guide,* which explains how the mileage estimates are calculated.

> The city and highway fuel economy values in this Guide come from tests conducted or approved by the U.S. Environmental Protection Agency (EPA). These tests are performed on vehicles submitted by the auto industry to EPA to demonstrate compliance with the requirements of the Clean Air Act and the Energy Policy and Conservation Act. Each vehicle is tested under precisely controlled conditions by professional drivers in a laboratory on a dynamometer. The dynamometer is a machine that permits exact simulation of the vehicle's operation under various driving conditions. Temperature is controlled in the laboratory in a range of 68° to 86° F, in order to provide the same temperature conditions for all vehicles.
>
> *City Test*
> This test simulates a 7.5-mile, stop-and-go trip with a speed range of 0 to 56 MPH, and an average speed of 20 MPH. The trip takes 23 minutes and has 18 stops. Eighteen percent of the trip is spent idling, such as would be expected in the city at traffic lights or in rush-hour traffic. Two kinds of engine starts are used. One is a cold start, which is similar to starting a car in the morning after it has been parked all night. The other is a hot start, which is similar to starting a vehicle after having parked it for a short time while shopping. The information from this test is then combined to represent the fuel economy of that vehicle during a realistic mixture of hot and cold starts during urban driving conditions.
>
> *Highway Test*
> This test simulates a 10-mile, non-stop trip that begins with the vehicle warmed up. The trip has an average speed of about 50 MPH and lasts 13 minutes. The speed during the test ranges from 0 to 60 MPH. If your highway driving speed averages faster than the test's average of 50 MPH, you should expect to achieve poorer fuel economy than the highway fuel economy estimate in this Guide. The amount of this decrease is approximately 10 to 15 percent for every 10 MPH above 50 MPH.
>
> *Combined Fuel Economy*
> Combined fuel economy is a weighted average of the city and highway estimates based on Federal Highway Administration studies of average U.S. driving patterns. This value (which assumes approximately half city and half highway driving) is what the average driver can expect in overall summer driving on level roads after the car has been broken in.

The EPA further goes on to determine the size classifications for passenger automobiles to make the fuel mileage estimates easier to compare. For 1975 and 1976, the models were broken into size classifications that seemed to be based upon where the manufacturer slotted each model for sales purposes. For example, Chevrolet sold the Nova as a compact and the Chevelle Malibu and Monte Carlo as mid-size cars, so that is where they could be found in the EPA guides. All that changed in 1977, when it was decided to be fair to all manufacturers, an interior "volume rating" would be calculated for all models, and by this rating each car would be assigned to a set "size classification." The ratings were set to the values in the table below. In the end, this type of rating helped some manufacturers, while harming others. For example, after the 1977 changes, a Chevrolet Nova was still classified as a compact, while the Monte Carlo was now also considered a compact, and the Chevelle Malibu was still a mid-size car. The following is a list of classifications from the 1978 Gas Mileage Guide.†

> Passenger automobiles — Classified by car line into one of the following classes based on interior volume index or seating capacity, except for those passenger automobiles which are most appropriately classed as a special purpose vehicle (as determined by EPA Administrator and regulations):
>
> - Two seaters. A car line shall be classed as "Two Seater" if the majority of the vehicles in that car line have no more than two designated seating positions as defined by NHTSA, DOT.
> - Minicompact cars. Interior volume index less than 85 cubic feet. (Ex: Dodge Colt, Ford Pinto, Ford Mustang II, and Mercury Bobcat).
> - Subcompact cars. Interior volume index greater than or equal to 85 cubic feet but less than 100 cubic feet. (Ex: AMC Gremlin, Buick Opel, Buick Skyhawk, Chevrolet Camaro, Chevrolet Chevette, Chevrolet Monza, and Ford Fiesta).
> - Compact cars. Interior volume index greater than or equal to 100 cubic feet but less than 110 cubic feet. (Ex: AMC Concord, AMC Pacer, Cadillac Seville, Dodge Aspen, Mercury Monarch, Plymouth Horizon, and Pontiac Ventura).
> - Mid-size cars. Interior volume index greater than or equal to 110 cubic feet but less than 120 cubic feet. (Ex: AMC Matador Coupe, Buick Regal, Chevrolet Malibu, Checker, Chrysler Cordoba, Dodge Diplomat, Ford Torino, and Mercury Zephyr).
> - Large cars. Interior volume index greater than or equal to 120 cubic feet. (Ex: AMC Matador Sedan, Buick Electra, Chevrolet Impala, Chrysler Newport, and Ford LTD).
> - Small station wagons. Station wagons with interior volume index less than 130 cubic feet. (Ex: AMC Pacer and Concord, Chevrolet Vega, Dodge Colt, and Ford Pinto).
> - Mid-size station wagons. Station wagons with interior volume index greater than or equal to 130 cubic feet but less than 160 cubic feet. (Ex: Chevrolet Malibu, Chrysler LeBaron, Dodge Aspen, Ford Torino, Mercury Zephyr, and Plymouth Satellite/Fury).
> - Large station wagons. Station wagons with interior volume

*Department of Energy, publication FEA/D-76/378, "1977 Gas Mileage Guide." Washington, DC: U.S. Government Printing Office, September 1976, pp. 5, 25–26.

†Department of Energy, publication DOE/CS-0024/1, "1978 Gas Mileage Guide, Second Edition." Washington, DC: U.S. Government Printing Office, February 1978, pp. 2–3.

index greater than or equal to 160 cubic feet. (Ex: AMC Matador, Dodge Royal Monaco, Ford LTD, and Oldsmobile Custom Cruiser).

Interior volume index is calculated by the arithmetic average of the interior volume indexes of each body style in the car line. It is the sum of the front seat volume, rear seat volume and the luggage capacity or cargo volume (wagons and hatchbacks). Dimensions are determined in accordance with procedures outlined in Motor Vehicle Dimensions SAE J1100a.

A few notes are necessary about how fuel economy reporting is handled within this book. Footnotes within the powertrain charts can be used to determine what engines were, or were not, available only in California or designated high altitude areas. This mainly will be found after the 1976 model year. Also, nearly every model year saw a change in how mileage estimates were reported or calculated. The following is an overview of what can be found within the powertrain tables of each make, by year:

- *1973 and 1974:* Mileage calculated was typically an overall average that used a mix of city and highway driving. Therefore, only an "average" mpg is reported. Since not all models were tested by the EPA, some figures reported are from road tests conducted by automotive magazines or consumer magazine guides. When used, these road tests figures will be in the format of *city mpg/highway mpg* and the magazine that did the testing is in the bibliography.
- *1975:* The EPA reported this year's mileage figures, and all cars were tested. Tests were conducted by averaging mileage over several tests, and with several cars, which could have been equipped differently. Therefore, this is the only year that reporting was not broken down by transmission type, so all gas mileage figures are listed under the automatic transmission for each engine. This year an estimated city mpg and highway mpg were published, and it was the first year for separate estimates for cars built to meet California requirements. Where the California numbers are known, and differ from 49-state cars,* they are included with the notation *Calif* on the powertrain tables, in the format of city/highway MPG.
- *1976:* All cars were tested for 1976, with a slight change in publishing of the reports. The mileage guide was compiled and prepared by the EPA, while the guide was published and distributed by the Department of Energy. This was also the first year for three sets of mileage estimates to be reported: city, highway and combined estimates. All three numbers are reported

herein with the standard format of *city/highway/combined MPG.*
- *1977 and 1978:* Reporting continued as in 1976, except that estimates for cars built for sale in designated high-altitude counties† began to be reported. Being generally the same as for California cars, they are not included separately within this book.
- *1979:* The reporting this year reverted to a single number as the estimated miles per gallon. As explained in the introduction to the 1979 EPA Gas Mileage Guide pamphlet, "the Gas Mileage Guide no longer gives the values previously called the 'highway' and 'combined' mpg. The value previously named the 'city' estimate is now called the 'Estimated mpg.' Studies have shown that, of the three previously published values, the city number was the closest to average fuel economy in real driving. It thus provides the consumer with a better single estimate of average, overall performance than either of the other values."‡ It was also noted that the change was an interim measure until technical changes to testing could improve the accuracy. However, most manufacturers continued to advertise their own estimates as to highway mileage, so when that information is available, it is reported herein in the format of *city mpg/highway mpg.* Otherwise, if a single number, assume that it is the EPA overall mileage estimate.
- *1980:* The reporting continued as in 1979 with a single number, taken as the estimated mpg. And again, many manufacturers continued to advertise their own highway mileage estimates, so when that information is available, it is reported in the format of *city mpg/highway mpg.* Otherwise, if a single number, assume that it is the EPA overall mileage estimate. In some cases, particularly by the 1980 model year, Federal and California mileage estimates were sometimes the same, so only MPG is listed.

Variances occur between years for no apparent reason in these estimates, but when details are reviewed, they can be explained as in the following example. For 1977, a Dodge Aspen with a 225 CID, 6-cylinder, 1-bbl. engine with an automatic transmission was rated at 18/24/20. In 1978, the exact same combination was rated at 20/27/23. The difference was that the 1978 model had a direct-drive lock-up torque converter added on all Chrysler TorqueFlite automatics that kicked in around 35 mph, thereby increasing gas mileage. This is just one example of the advances implemented to meet and improve upon federal fuel economy requirements. Another factor playing into fuel mileage is the

*"Federal" equipped cars are also known as "49 state," meaning the cars meet all requirements for emission standards except in the state of California.
†Designated high-altitude counties are defined as counties where the majority of the area is over 4,000 ft. altitude.
‡Department of Energy, publication DOE/CS-0024/5, "1979 Gas Mileage Guide, Second Edition." Washington, DC: U.S. Government Printing Office, January 1979, p. 3.

axle ratio selected for any given car. Particularly American Motors, which did not have the luxury of funding to produce multiple engines and develop a lot of new systems to meet the requirements, would partially rely on a change of axle ratios to help meet requirements, whether for Federal or California rules. Obviously this kind of change affected performance, but it was a sacrifice American Motors chose to make.

Effects on Automobile Design and Engineering

POWERTRAINS

The design and performance of automobile engines were greatly affected by the CAFE standards and EPA emission standards. To deal with the emissions issue, nearly all manufacturers chose to run lower-compression engines with electronic ignitions and to filter the exhaust through an expensive catalytic converter as previously mentioned. The combination contributed to decreasing the power available from engines, rendering the period notable for an industry-wide lack of horsepower. One Japanese manufacturer, Honda, managed to develop and produce a low-emissions vehicle without the use of a catalytic converter in their Civic CVCC (Compound Vortex Controlled Combustion) line. Actually the label CVCC is a misnomer as there is no vortex created in the production version, but it is a stratified-charge carbureted system.

Another idea that seemed to have real promise was the rotary engine. General Motors had paid $50 million to obtain licenses to develop the Wankel engine in November of 1970. Based on the promises of performance, fuel economy and cost-savings, GM invested the money and spent several years in research and development before announcing that they could have the engine in production by October 1973, in time for introduction in the 1974 Chevrolet Vega as an option. Benefits of the Wankel engine were that it was smaller, lighter and cheaper to manufacture and assemble than a reciprocating piston engine of equal output. It also offered 100,000-mile-plus seal life, could run 24,000 miles or more between oil changes, and needed only cheaper low-grade motor oil. It was also vibrationless when running and had very low noise levels, a wide speed range, and a high speed range, up to 8,000 rpm. Everything was looking great with the rotary engine, and a new car line was planned around it. That new line would be the H-body cars, heavily based on the Vega, and introduced for 1975 as the Chevrolet Monza, and its sister cars. American Motors, which was also working on a rotary engine, was so impressed with GM's engine that it entered into a deal for GM to supply rotary engines to American Motors for a car designed specifically for

a rotary engine — the 1975 AMC Pacer. Then when October 1973 arrived, the engine didn't come out in the Vega as promised, and soon, events conspired to doom the GM rotary engine before it ever made it to the production line.

Problems with emissions are partially to blame for the rotary engine's demise at GM. General Motors had planned on introducing the electronic ignition system in the 1974 rotary-powered Vega so that they could have a cleaner burning system and also meet the 50,000-mile emissions compliance mandated by the federal government. The Wankel was indeed an internal combustion engine, and could therefore be cleaned up just like a V8 engine, but in theory the Wankel was "easier" to purify. Reliability was not an issue, at least initially, as GM had tested some rotary engines that lasted 400,000 to 500,000 miles with minimal wear. Also, the rotary had a much lower number of parts than a conventional engine, and even fewer "moving" parts, so the chances of something breaking were greatly reduced. However, as Mazda would learn with its own early rotary engines, problems in the real world appeared around 50,000 miles.

The fuel mileage problem was what really killed the Wankel engine for General Motors. The ill-timed Arab oil embargo took the wind out of the Wankel project, as consumers were now concerned more about fuel economy than how clean the emissions were. General Motors acknowledged that the fuel economy of the rotary engine was substandard and postponed production in favor of "further development." Adding to the list of reasons to drop the project was the EPA's less than optimistic reporting of fuel economy data that misrepresented the Mazda's rotary engine fuel economy. This resulted in the rotary engine being viewed unfavorably by both consumers and General Motors.

SAFETY

On the safety front, rising insurance rates had forced a decline in muscle car sales late in the 1960s. At about the same time, safety issues began to arise over convertibles and their rollover protection capabilities. There were also design concerns with maintaining structural rigidity as cars became smaller and lighter. These factors, combined with slipping sales and a rise in the popularity of sunroofs and T-tops, led to the American convertible's demise with the 1976 Cadillac Eldorado, at least temporarily. In 1982, a revived Chrysler Corporation brought out two new convertible models on the K-car platform, and Chrysler soon became the largest manufacturer of convertible models in the United States through most of the remainder of the 20th century.

As discussed previously, beginning with the 1973 model year, another safety issue came to the forefront, and it was mandated by the federal government that front bumpers had to meet a 5 mph crash test without significant damage occurring to the car. For 1974, it was the rear bumper that had to meet the 5 mph requirement. The protection system employed most often to meet this challenge was a hydraulic-based, energy absorption bumper mount. In some cases, it also meant adding swing-away grilles to minimize, or eliminate, damage to that delicate area. Of course, this added weight, which dealt a further blow to performance. Retuning the engines for emissions standards and adding the weight to meet safety requirements put a tremendous strain on engineers to meet the fuel economy standards. To resolve these issues, two tactics emerged: downsizing and front-wheel drive.

Yet another safety mandate that came into play was passive restraint systems, also mentioned previously. The electronics systems required to make the seat belt ignition starter interlock system work were not cheap, and they had an impact on prices. The conjoined lap belt/shoulder belt system that was eventually settled upon, with warning buzzers, required changes in the interior hardware of cars, and more money had to be spent on engineering this feature. Once one realizes all the little expenses involved in meeting federal requirements, it becomes clear why prices in the showroom were increasing at a rate of nearly 10 percent a year through the 1973 to 1980 period.

In 1974 General Motors introduced an Air Cushion Restraint System, or airbags as they are commonly known, on full-size Buick, Cadillac and Oldsmobile models. The optional system required many extra dollars to engineer and install, and it is doubtful that the money invested was recouped at $300 per car, when so few consumers were interested in purchasing the system.

The GM airbag system contained an airbag mounted in the steering wheel, a driver's side knee cushion, and a bag on the right side of the instrument panel, above the glove box. The system, designed to restrain front seat occupants in a front-end collision, eliminated the shoulder belts and starter interlock system.

DOWNSIZING

The term downsizing tends to carry a negative connotation. In more recent times, downsizing often refers to a corporate restructuring in which large groups of employees are released to save, or restore, the company's financial health. But in the 1970s the term was a good thing, especially when applied to cars. Some of the largest luxury cars on the road in 1973 were approaching 20 feet in length and weighed in at well over 5,000 pounds.

Some manufacturers were realizing that vehicle size had become excessive before the gas crisis occurred, given the evidence of the rising popularity of the smaller, more maneuverable Japanese cars, and they were beginning to look at making their cars smaller. American Motors, always known as the small car company, was in the process of designing the 1975 Pacer, the "first wide, small car" as it would come to be known. Designed as a roomy compact, it initially was

planned to use the Wankel rotary engine under development at GM, but when that project was dropped, AMC had to use its own heavy inline 6-cylinder engine. Although sales were good at first, consumers soon realized that the car was not so much an economy car as it was just a roomy, small car. Ford had very good luck with the new Mustang II in 1974. The timing for this new car could not have been better as it hit showrooms just as the gas crisis was in full swing. Applying some of the original Mustang formula to the new car's styling helped greatly, and shedding many pounds along the way didn't hurt. General Motors was uncharacteristically behind the curve but was working on new, smaller cars. The first to appear was the 1976 Cadillac Seville. This new smaller Cadillac proved that a luxury car didn't have to be 20 feet long to be luxurious, roomy and powerful — at least powerful in 1975 terms. The 1976 Chevy Chevette (a variant of a GM Europe T-bodied model) was an early attempt to compete with the Japanese manufacturers head-to-head, and closely followed the Seville introduction. It was somewhat successful, and it showed the capabilities were there, they just needed to be refined. Chrysler initially turned to its British organization Simca and the Japanese manufacturer Mitsubishi to supply small, economical, fun to drive cars. The Simca cars were sold through Chrysler-Plymouth dealerships as the Plymouth Cricket from 1971 through 1973, but never sold well due to their rather stodgy appearance and poor reliability. By 1973, the Mitsubishi built products (notably the Dodge Colt) proved to be the better cars and the better sellers, and were sold by Chrysler well into the 1990s. They helped lay the groundwork for Mitsubishi to launch its own dealer network in the United States by the mid–1980s.

Credit for the first true downsizing efforts has to go to General Motors. They had begun preliminary work on smaller, lighter full-size cars as early as 1972. By the time they reached the market for the 1977 model year, they were a resounding success. The plan was to begin with the largest of cars, and make them just as roomy as their predecessors while shedding unnecessary exterior bulk. The resulting weight savings would help boost both power and fuel economy. Once the plan was put into action, each line of cars would get a transformation into a smaller, more economical line of cars, with all of the space and luxury inside that the car buying public had become accustomed to having. The 1977 full-size GM line was well received and had other manufacturers taking notice. Ford and Chrysler obviously knew about these new full-size cars from GM in advance, and had competing downsized, full-size models ready for the market by the 1979 model year. Next up for GM was a downsized mid-size line in 1978, new personal luxury coupes in 1979, new front-wheel-drive compacts and Cadillac Seville in 1980 and a new subcompact line in mid–1981. Ford and Chrysler went through similar downsizing efforts after their full-size line was done to keep up with GM, but more often than not, they were based upon existing platforms. For example, the 1976 Dodge Aspen and Plymouth Volaré were the basis for the early eighties Dodge Mirada, Chrysler Cordoba, Dodge Diplomat, Plymouth Gran Fury, and Chrysler Fifth Avenue. Ford's 1978 Fairmont and Mercury Zephyr, replacements for the Maverick and Comet, were built on the corporate "Fox" platform and formed the basis for the 1979 Mustang and Capri and the 1980 line of downsized intermediate cars, including the Granada, Thunderbird, and Cougar.

FRONT-WHEEL DRIVE

While front-wheel-drive (FWD) was certainly not a new idea to the automobile industry, its use had not been widespread in the United States. The first modern day, popular application of FWD in an American car was the 1966 Oldsmobile Toronado. At the time it was designed, it seemed to be largely a marketing tool, with ads touting how it maximized interior floor space and how the car would handle and drive better in adverse driving conditions. It was not until the gas crisis and the need for smaller cars that Americans realized that FWD could provide real benefits in smaller cars. The first successful modern-day FWD small car in the U.S. turned out to be the Volkswagen Rabbit, introduced in 1974. As with the Ford Mustang II, it was a matter of timing, and the Rabbit hit the market just right.

The key to the new smaller cars was the transverse mounting of the engine, across the engine bay instead of front-to-back lengthwise, and the use of a transaxle to put the power to the road. This eliminated the need for a large transmission "hump" at the front seat, and the large drive shaft tunnel through the rest of the car. It could be accommodated in a relatively small package, allowing for a smaller and lighter car design. Most of the early designs utilized four-cylinder engines, but soon after, V6 engines were introduced.

Chrysler Corporation was the first American manufacturer to market with a successful, domestically built small front-wheel-drive car, the Dodge Omni and Plymouth Horizon. Chrysler wisely chose to copy a proven design, and the "Omni-rizon" twins resembled the popular VW Rabbit, even being powered by a VW–sourced engine for a while. A year later, 2-door coupe models were spun-off of these cars. In Chrysler's second attempt at downsizing, the 1981 K-Cars were the real winners for Chrysler, as they literally saved the company.

The next round of popular FWD cars to hit the market was the GM X-car compacts. Early in 1979, the Chevrolet Citation (Nova replacement), Pontiac Phoenix, Oldsmobile Omega and Buick Skylark were introduced and became an instant hit with car buyers. While plagued with early production problems and recalls, they sold well and provided a basis for the second and third round of downsizing that hit the mid-size A-car line in 1982, spawning the Chevrolet Celebrity and its sister cars. Following the problems encountered with the launch of the X-cars, a more cautious approach was taken with the company's new J-car sub-compact line that originally was slated for showrooms as 1981 models. With a 1982 introduction, the line sold well, but was often criticized as being overpriced and lacking power. Receiving the most criticism was the much-maligned Cadillac Cimarron. Credit Cadillac for trying, but a very thinly disguised Chevrolet Cavalier didn't win any praise with Cadillac buyers or media pundits.

Ford put its European Fiesta FWD subcompact into U.S. showrooms from 1978 through 1980, but it was a little late to the front-wheel-drive game with a domestically built car, opting for a "World Car" formula in its sub-compact Escort and Mercury Lynx introduced in 1981. It was a wise move to wait, as the Escort quickly became one of the country's best-selling cars. The Escort was already a best seller in Europe, and Ford used this car's foundation for the U.S. Escort. A spinoff pair of sporty 2-passenger coupes, the EXP and LN7, were introduced mid-year as 1982 models. Feeling that rear-wheel drive was still the best alternative for performance, Ford did not introduce another front-wheel-drive car until the 1984 Ford Tempo and Mercury Topaz.

American Motors did not get into the front-wheel-drive market until some time after their merger with Renault in 1979. It was at this time that the Alliance was under development, and AMC introduced this car for the 1983 model year. Since Renault had years of experience with front-wheel-drive, the cars were dependable and initially somewhat successful. AMC's Jeep line had been highly successful through the seventies, and AMC opted to add all-wheel-drive on its own cars as a means of distinguishing itself in the marketplace. It was a natural fit to add four-wheel-drive to cars such as the Hornet/Concord platform, to make the Eagle line of cars. Similar drivetrains were installed under the Gremlin/Spirit bodies creating the SX/4. Unfortunately this great idea was about 15 years ahead of its time. In the mid-nineties, it became more widely accepted that all-wheel-drive systems were a great performance addition under cars, as well as trucks.

ECONOMY AND LUXURY OVERTAKE POWER AND STYLING

Between government regulations and the insurance industry's concerns over high-performance cars, the end of the muscle car era came quickly. Engines once rated near 300 horsepower were rated under 200 in just a few years' time, and not long after that, they would be dropped from the line as priorities shifted from making a powerful statement in the market, to meeting government mandates. It would take at least ten years before manufacturers were truly able to bring back performance as a selling point.

Along the way, safety concerns during this period led to the discontinuation of body styles that had been at the top of their game only 10 years earlier. Convertibles reached their peak in sales during the 1966 model year, but all were gone from the domestic manufacturers lines when the 1977 models were introduced. Conventional thinking has blamed government safety regulations and rising insurance costs for the demise of the convertible. However, that is only part of the story, as rising costs of manufacturing and declining sales of convertibles in general had as much to do with the temporary disappearance of the body style as any other factors. The last AMC convertibles had been the 1968 Rebel 550 and SST models, while the 1971 Dodge Challenger and Plymouth Barracuda were the last Mopar drop-tops. Ford kept convertibles in their lineup through the 1973 model year, ending with the Ford Mustang and Mercury Cougar offerings. This left General Motors as the sole domestic manufacturer of convertibles from 1974 through 1976. In their lines, the compact and pony-car convertibles were gone by the end of the 1969 model year, and the mid-size convertibles lasted through 1972. Full-size models and the Corvette were all that remained for the 1973 model year through 1975 with the exception of the Eldorado which ran through 1976.

The announcement that the Corvette convertible and GM's full-sized convertibles (except the Cadillac Eldorado), would be discontinued at the end of the 1975 model year prompted a rise in sales for these models in their final season. With only one GM convertible left in the line, what was advertised as the last convertible from Detroit was the 1976 Cadillac Eldorado convertible. Speculators bought up Eldorado convertibles in droves, and when the announcement of a special edition "final run" of 200 cars, done in all white with "Bicentennial" red and blue paint stripes and special interior trim, was made, they were selling at two and three times the manufacturer's sticker price. However, even before convertible production ended, taking the place of factory-built convertibles was a growing aftermarket of convertible conversions. A discussion of this phenomenon is contained in Appendix VII, "Aftermarket Convertible Conversions."

With the muscle cars gone, the sporty lines of a convertible gone, and a general evolution away from uniquely styled cars, consumers now wanted economy and luxury in their cars. The former was obviously driven by the events of the 1973 fuel crisis. But the latter seemed to be driven by "baby boomers," born in the late 1940s and early 1950s, who were now of the age to have families and well-paying jobs, and willing to spend money for the finer things in life. Auto manufacturers were only too quick to oblige, as adding luxury features to cars meant easy profits. This can be confirmed by the long lists of optional equipment and option packages offered through this period. By 1976, "Brougham" signified a luxury model, but had become the most overused trim level nameplate in the industry. For example there was the Oldsmobile Cutlass Supreme Brougham, the Mercury Marquis Brougham, the Ford Gran Torino Brougham, and then cars with Brougham option packages, such as the Plymouth Valiant and AMC Matador.

The luxury features extended to a proliferation of vinyl top configurations, with the Landau top with an opera window becoming a symbol of the more luxurious models. Interior seating began using "pillow-look" stitching, and leather upholstery became a more common feature. Features formerly reserved for the middle and upper price ranges, or even exclusively to full-size models, found their way into even the smallest and most basic of cars. At one point, Pontiac Firebirds with power windows, power door locks, and canopy vinyl tops were as likely to be seen in a dealer's showroom as a Trans Am with a 400 CID V8, hood scoop, and "screaming eagle" hood decal. The shift to luxury engulfed all manufacturers, and those that did not succumb to the consumers' desires were left behind. Then when the Cadillac Seville was introduced, it opened up a whole new market for luxury compact cars that saw the introduction of models such as the Mercury Monarch Grand Ghia, the Chrysler LeBaron, the Chevrolet Concours (Nova), and the Lincoln Versailles.

The Beginning of a Downhill Slide for the American Auto Industry

Numerous cars became infamous during the 1970s because of engineering and manufacturing flaws and other undesirable qualities that attracted negative publicity. It was during this time that stories of such defective cars gave the U.S. auto industry a black eye and helped the import models to gain a strong foothold in the market. Note that some issues listed below began prior to the period of 1973 through 1980 covered by this book, but they are relevant to the period for their history and resolution.

TROUBLING CARS

1971–1975 Chevrolet Vega. The Vega's most unusual feature was its 2.3 liter (140CID) OHC four-cylinder engine. Unlike previous GM aluminum engines, the Vega block did not have cylinder liners in order to save on production costs. GM Research Labs had been working on a sleeveless aluminum block since the late 1950s. This involved a joint venture between the GM labs, Reynolds Metal Company, and Sealed Power Corporation. Reynolds came up with an alloy called "A-390" that was suitable for faster production by die casting the block. These qualities made the Vega engine block less expensive and easier to manufacture than other aluminum engines. A large bore, long stroke design provided good torque and lower engine RPM for reduced wear. A cast iron cylinder head was chosen for low cost and structural integrity, and an overhead cam was specified. By 1972, as the original Vegas were racking up miles, the experience of consumers with the cars in actual use became apparent, and it was not good. The 2300 engine's aluminum engine blocks began to warp because of the heat generated, but the cast iron cylinder heads maintained their integrity, causing coolant leaks and further contributing to heat buildup. The 1971–1973 Vegas also had rust issues in the front fenders, as they did not have fender inner liners to protect from buildup of dirt. Despite the bad press, Vegas continued to sell well, and after resolving most of the problems by the 1975 model year, GM was able to offer a 5-year, 60,000 mile limited engine warranty on new 1976 Vegas. This strong a warranty was unheard of at the time, and went a long way in restoring faith in GM powertrains. At least temporarily.

1971–1976 Ford Pinto. Ford faced strong competition in the American small-car market from Volkswagen and several Japanese companies in the 1960s. To fight the competition Ford rushed its newest car, the Pinto, into production for 1971 in much less time than is usually required to develop a car. The regular time to design, engineer, and produce an automobile at that time was 43 months, Ford took 25 months for the Pinto. Before production, however, Ford engineers discovered a major flaw in the car's design. In nearly all rear-end crash test collisions the Pinto's fuel system would rupture extremely easily. It is interesting to note that the Pinto disaster almost did not occur. In pre-production planning, engineers seriously considered using in the Pinto the same kind of gas tank that Ford of Europe used in the Capri. The Capri tank rides over the rear axle and differential housing. The technology was obviously available to make the Pinto a safer car. All that was required was an inexpensive lightweight plastic baffle placed between the front of the gas tank and the four protruding bolts on the differential housing. This piece of plastic prevents the bolts from puncturing the gas tank and was used in one of the only successful crash tests the Pinto underwent. In another successful test, a piece of steel was placed between the tank and the bumper to add support against the crumpling back end. The best method for improving the safety of the Pinto was to line the gas tank with a rubber bladder. Goodyear Tire & Rubber Corporation had developed the bladder and had demonstrated it to the automotive industry. Crash-tests were conducted and there are reports showing that the Goodyear bladder worked very well. But Ford took none of these measures, putting the Pinto into production with the original tank design. Although Ford lost a 1972 lawsuit, *Grimshaw v. Ford Motor Co.*, following a fatal Pinto rear-end collision and fire, and was ordered to pay $2.5 million in compensatory damages and $3.5 million in punitive damages, it wasn't until May of 1978 that the Department of Transportation (a division of NHTSA) announced that the Pinto fuel system had a "safety related defect" and demanded a recall. Ford agreed, and on June 9, 1978, the company recalled 1.5 million Pintos. Reportedly, Ford had corrected the situation in production models beginning in 1975, but it took nearly the full lifespan of the Pinto to bring the situation to full resolution, unfortunately after the loss of innocent lives.

1973 Chrysler Imperial. A road test of a 1973 Chrysler Imperial in the April 1973 issue of *Mechanix Illustrated* magazine came to symbolize what was wrong with the quality of product in Detroit. The famed new car road tester Tom McCahill, who was himself a long-time Imperial owner, pointed out numerous flaws in workmanship in a car that, as he put it, was "no longer as outstanding as it once was...." This was in reference to the quality as compared to when Imperial had been its own make within the Chrysler organization. An example of the decline in design workmanship was in the trunk, where McCahill stated, the Imperial "...used to have a fine finish from rug to lid. Now it's more like that of a cab." Build quality issues ranged from a power radio antenna that would not raise and lower properly to a map light that would shut off the clock when turned on. Mechanical problems included a power steering leak that necessitated a refill every two to three hours.

1976–1977 Dodge Aspen and Plymouth Volaré. Similar to what had happened to Chrysler with the highly popular 1957 "Forward Look" Chrysler models, which experienced early rust problems, the same problem would return 20 years later. The Aspen/Volaré twins were, from the start, plagued with early rust-out, driveability and reliability issues (due mainly to electronic ignition and carburetor issues). The 1976 Aspen and Volaré turned out to be the most recalled cars in history up to that time, and were among very few cars ever recalled over rust issues.

1979 Chrysler R-Body Cars: Chrysler Newport, Chrysler New Yorker and Dodge St. Regis. Lee Iacocca, who is generally credited with being the father of the Mustang, became president of Ford Division in 1964 and eventually president of Ford Motor Company. Known not to get along well with Henry Ford II, Iacocca was fired by Henry Ford II in late 1978 despite leading the company to a $2 billion profit the prior year. Once released from Ford he was quickly recruited by a failing Chrysler Corporation to help revive it using his unequalled talents. Iacocca arrived just about the same time the new R-body cars were being released. Featuring all-new bodies on the existing mid-size platform, the R-body cars were sold in 1979 as the Chrysler Newport and New Yorker and the Dodge St. Regis. The Plymouth Gran Fury R-body would arrive for 1980. When Iacocca arrived at Chrysler he rejected the top of the line New Yorker Fifth Avenue Edition he was given for personal use, saying it didn't "represent the target it was meant to." Instead he took a new Cordoba, which he felt more properly represented the right "size."

Even though initial sales were strong for the R-body cars, a spring season recession sent jitters through the public. Gasoline prices rose. Sales took a nosedive. Those R-body cars that did sell were riddled with problems. Before the first of them was built, Chrysler quality engineering had predicted an estimate of 1,077 defects for every 100 units built. That meant that each car was expected to be built with an average of 11 defects! Some cars might come down the line with four problems (defects could be anything from chipped paint to lack of an engine), while the very next car off the line would have as many as 15 defects. No one on the line or in management took any action to rectify the situation. This quality situation became known to Iacocca about the same time he became aware of a production study that predicted about 740 defects for every 100 of the upcoming new K-cars, despite millions having been spent putting robotic equipment on the production lines. Iacocca was furious. Knowing that everything depended upon the product, especially the K-car, he went straight to the vice president of quality control and production. He was especially fired up because the Aspen-Volaré twins were costing Chrysler a lot of money to make fixes that quality control engineering should have made before those cars ever hit the production line. Iacocca was also concerned about how the new Imperial would be launched, as he wanted it to be the most defect free vehicle of all. When it hit the market in 1981, it wasn't defect free, but it was a far cry from where the R-body stood at its introduction. In the end, it was suddenly quality that became the benchmark for accomplishment. As a result of Iacocca's intervention, all Chrysler lines had improved quality going forward, including the R-body vehicles.

1980 GM X-Cars: Buick Skylark, Chevrolet Citation, Oldsmobile Omega, Pontiac Phoenix. Planning for this family of compact General Motors vehicles started as early as April 1974. The first full-size prototypes were created in mid-summer 1976, and the production versions of the Citation and its corporate kin — the Phoenix, Omega and Skylark — were released in April 1979 as early 1980 models. The Citation's initial retail price was just under $6,000, making it rather pricey compared to its competitors of older design. Between the four brands four body styles were available, a 2-door coupe (in formal roof and slanting roof versions), 3-door hatchback, 4-door sedan and a 5-door hatchback. The front-wheel-drive design and hatchback bodies were a radical departure for the American industry, and GM was widely praised for the X-body's efficient packaging and smaller engines. Helped by an April 1979 release, the 1980 Citation sold more than 800,000 units and earned "Car of the Year" honors from *Motor Trend* magazine along the way, while its sister brands sold at five times or more their 1979 rate.

The X-body cars were the target of an unsuccessful lawsuit by NHTSA, which cited a tendency to lose control under heavy braking and power steering problems. The X-cars were unfortunately plagued by various teething problems and factory recalls, however, that would soon have an impact on their sales totals and their reputation with the buying public.

Some of these problems included premature rear-brake lockup during panic stops, power steering pump failures and other driveability issues. The X-body cars were recalled many times and the Citation's reputation in particular took a beating, resulting in decreasing sales every year. The 1984 and 1985 models were badged "Citation II" in a halfhearted attempt to convince consumers that the vehicle's problems had been overcome to the extent that the car deserved a new name.

THE 1977 GENERAL MOTORS ENGINE DEBACLE

After the successful launch of the new full-sized GM cars in 1977, many consumers were outraged to learn that their Oldsmobiles and Buicks had Chevrolet V8 engines in them, instead of an Oldsmobile or Buick engine that they thought they were getting. It's easy to understand the frustration consumers had, when one looks at the decades of marketing efforts by each division to promote their unique engines. As recently as 1973, the Buick showroom brochure used the following introductory line on the two pages touting their precision-built and highly tested engines: "We submit that no other engine in the world is built like a Buick engine." Consumers believed the marketing campaigns, and often in their own experiences would confirm that they were excellent engines. So it is easy to imagine that when Buick loyalists walked into a showroom to trade a trusted 1973 Estate Wagon in for a new 1978 model, they were not happy to learn that their new Buick had a Chevrolet engine installed.

Basic economics accounted for some of the switch-ups, but poor public relations and GM management's poor handling of media attention and customer unhappiness exacerbated a difficult situation.

By the beginning of the 1970s, of the four remaining corporations, only General Motors still allowed each division to engineer and build its own distinct engines. For the most part, Ford and Chrysler had shared engines or basic engine designs across their divisions since about 1955. American Motors of course built most of its own engines for most of the period, but did purchase engines from GM during the late 1970s. General Motors, on the other hand, limited the use of sharing engines. The first cases of engine sharing across divisions turned up in 1961 when the new "senior compact" Oldsmobile F-85 and Pontiac Tempest shared the Buick-built 215 CID V8 engine with the Buick Special. When these cars were enlarged to mid-size status for 1964, the 250 CID 6-cylinder Chevrolet-built engine was used in both Chevrolet Chevelle and Pontiac Tempest models. More sharing occurred along the way, including the "new" 1975 Buick-built 231 CID V6 engine being used in a variety of Buicks as well as the Oldsmobile Starfire, and for 1976 the Pontiac Sunbird. The real problems began with the 1977 models, when in order to produce a sufficient quantity of engines, it was decided

Chevrolet's engine plants had excess capacity and could provide engines to other divisions. Also, in order to meet tougher emission and fuel economy standards, some engines in the corporate lineup were certified only for the "49-state" or Federal requirements, while others were better suited to meet the more stringent California requirements. This led to complaints mostly with buyers of Buick and Oldsmobile products that had Chevrolet engines installed. A court hearing during the summer of 1977 decided that a case could be made, and eventually led to a class action lawsuit against General Motors filed on behalf of a group of Oldsmobile Delta 88 owners that was argued on September 28, 1978. Some of the details surrounding the suit are contained in the following court record information.

> Beginning in 1974, GM planners began considering the manufacturing requirements for GM cars for the 1977 model year. By 1976 various GM management committees began planning for extensive interdivisional engine exchanges. Because the Chevrolet Division had a significant surplus production capacity, GM planners decided to rely on Chevrolet produced engines to meet part of the engine requirements of GM's Buick, Oldsmobile and Pontiac Divisions.
>
> To institute the engine interchange in the Oldsmobile Division, GM used codes to identify the different engines that would be used in its 1977 Oldsmobiles. The Rocket 350 V8 produced by Oldsmobile, for example, was given the code name "L34"; the Chevrolet engine used in place of the Rocket was given the code "LM1." Moreover, GM, over some objections by the Chevrolet Division, decided to adopt a common engine color for all of its engines. Thus, the distinctive red Chevrolet engine became blue. Despite the planned Oldsmobile-Chevrolet engine change, GM's advertising, EPA gas mileage disclosures and communications to Oldsmobile dealers referred to the changes by the use of the codes.
>
> The switch from standard components to different components in Oldsmobiles was not confined to engines. GM used different components than it had used in previous years for other parts of the power train (the engine, transmission, and drive axle) in some of its Oldsmobiles. For reasons that do not appear with clarity in the record, GM decided in 1976 to install in all 1977 Oldsmobile Delta 88 coupes and sedans, the THM 200 transmission instead of the THM 350, the transmission traditionally used in those cars. The THM 200, like the THM 350, is produced by GM's Hydra-matic Division. The THM 200, originally designed for use in the subcompact Chevette, was used in all 1977 Delta 88 coupes and sedans regardless of whether they contained Oldsmobile or Chevrolet engines. The appellants maintain that GM's advertising materials nevertheless indicated that the THM 350 was standard equipment in all 1977 Deltas.*

> The proposed settlement provided that

> GM would provide to each consumer who had purchased a 1977 Oldsmobile, Buick or Pontiac equipped with a Chevrolet engine on or before April 10, 1977, $200 plus a 36-month or 36,000-mile extended warranty on the power train. In return

each purchaser would be required to sign a release of all state and federal claims concerning the substitution of engines, components, parts, and assemblies in the car. GM also agreed to disclose the source of all engines of new GM cars for the next three years. The Attorneys General, in turn, promised to secure dismissals with prejudice of all actions prosecuted by them.

Due to the above requirements, GM did indeed disclose the source of all engines for the next three years. Within this book, the distinct codes are used within the powertrain charts for each division, and a complete listing of GM engines, codes and manufacturing unit is included in Appendix V.

BADGE-ENGINEERING

From the beginning of the automobile industry, component sharing, even of major parts, has been commonplace. For example, the 1903 Ford and 1903 Cadillac shared most body parts as the design was done mostly by Henry Ford when he was working on an auto venture in 1902 that failed. When the company failed, Ford's shareholders brought in Henry Leland to catalog and sell the company's assets, and that is when Leland had the idea to buy Ford's assets and start his own company, Cadillac. Meanwhile Ford continued his work, and hit on a successful car in 1903 that used the same body design Leland was using. However, the cars are mechanically different because Ford used a twin-cylinder opposed type engine of his design, while Henry Leland over at Cadillac engaged the use of Ransom E. Olds' single-cylinder engine. For decades afterward, various engine manufacturers such as Continental, Herschell-Spillman and many others supplied engines to auto manufacturers, so that a given engine might appear in several makes at once. General Motors' Hydramatic transmissions have been used by Hudson, Lincoln, Rolls-Royce and others. Sharing of components was, and always has been, a practice used by companies to take advantage of cost efficiencies.

It should come as no surprise that corporate divisions have long shared components, and on occasion powertrains were shared among companies. Ford and Chrysler have both shared powertrain components throughout their divisions since about 1955. All of the "Big Three" automakers have also shared body shells among their respective divisions, most notably with the 1959 GM line when all five divisions shared common body designs. But it was mainly economies of scale that compelled companies to share, allowing them to hold the line on prices and increase profits. Eventually the sharing would lead to the practice that became known as "badge-engineering" — the practice of changing cosmetic features of a car, such as grille and taillights or side trim, and putting a different name on the car to sell it through another division's

---

*For more detailed information of the case settlement, and the court proceedings, visit the following website: http://openjurist.org/594/f2d/1106. The included details are covered by common license agreement as detailed at this website: http://creativecommons.org/licenses/by/3.0/us/.

dealer network. In general cars that are termed "badge-engineered" share chassis, body and powertrain features, and in most cases share basic interior design.

Prior to the 1973–1980 period, only a few cars would be considered badge-engineered, such as the Ford Maverick and Mercury Comet, the Dodge Dart and Plymouth Valiant, and the Chevrolet Nova and Pontiac Ventura II. For the most part these cars shared everything except the grille and the taillights. The Mopar compacts used different wheelbases for some models, but they were still clearly related. For 1973, GM added the compact Oldsmobile Omega and Buick Skylark to the X-body line that the Nova and Ventura were based on, creating the first "quadruplets" to be known as "badge-engineered" cars. More would follow with the Pontiac Astre based on the Chevrolet Vega, the Dodge Aspen and Plymouth Volaré, the Ford Pinto and Mercury Bobcat and the group of four GM H-body cars led by the Chevrolet Monza. Still the front styling on all of these was distinct enough to quickly distinguish them from a distance.

This was all working fine until the practice made it nearly impossible for consumers to distinguish between the various makes, and diluted the brand recognition built up over the years. When the 1978 Dodge Omni and Plymouth Horizon hatchbacks were introduced, it was not at all clear which car belonged to each division, despite their varying grille designs. Similarly the 1978 Ford Fairmont and Mercury Zephyr lines appeared to be the same. General Motors would get in the act again for 1981 when the new Pontiac T1000 mirrored the Chevrolet Chevette in all but grille and taillight design.

In the Right Place at the Right Time

In retrospect it is easy to understand how, when and why the American automobile industry fell on hard times during the 1970s, and why they have struggled ever since then to compete with foreign auto companies. While outside forces contributed, it was mainly upon the shoulders of the four remaining American companies at the time to take immediate corrective actions and rethink the way they did business. Unfortunately, they continued to follow outdated practices and methods, with some exceptions, and were slow to react to a changing world, which eventually led them to the position the three remaining companies found themselves in thirty years later. This complacency helped the eager-to-expand Japanese and later Korean manufacturers to gain a foothold in the American market that has yet to be released. At least they did recognize the growing impact of imported car sales on their businesses, and the Big Three took action by importing cars from their fully or partially owned subsidiary partner companies, who would build cars specifically for sale in the United States.

Known as "captive imports," these models fell into basically two categories. The first includes the German-built, GM–owned, Opel sold and serviced through Buick dealers, which had great success through the late 1960s and into the early 1970s. Ford, which also had some experience in selling its European built Ford's on the east and west coasts, decided to bring its German-built Ford Capri to America for 1971, selling it through Lincoln-Mercury dealerships, where it met with considerable success. The problem with these cars was that when the U.S. economy tanked in 1974, the Deutschmark began climbing in relation to the U.S. dollar, causing the German-built cars to become too expensive. The Opels were gone by 1976, with the Capri following late in 1977.

This first category is defined by the cars being sold and serviced through some, but not necessarily all, of their respective dealer networks, while retaining their unique nameplates and identity. In other words, they did not typically carry the Buick or Lincoln-Mercury name on the car. These models would include the German-built Opel and Capri, the Japanese-built Isuzu Opel, and the Italian-built, Ford-powered Pantera. Typically, the Capri and Pantera were advertised as "Imported for Lincoln-Mercury," while the Opels were advertised as "Buick's Opel." In the case of the Opel, the German-built models were imported directly from GM's European subsidiary. The later Isuzu Opels were designed by Opel in Germany and powered by Isuzu engines, with the cars being assembled in Japan and imported from there. Importation of the original German Opels began in 1958, so there was a vast amount of association with Buick, but the Buick nameplate did not actually appear on the car. This era of Opel carried the Opel insignia only. With the Isuzu-built Opels, the "Buick Opel" name actually appeared on the exterior and interior of the car, with the Buick "Tri-shield" emblem on the steering wheel hub. They also tended to be available through all dealerships, as the dealer body wanted more fuel-efficient cars to sell at that time. By the mid- to late seventies, the industry was beginning to utilize "badge-engineering," and the Isuzu Opel was one example of this type of marketing, as the same car was sold in Europe under the Opel name and in Japan under the Isuzu name. Model year sales of these models are included when available, but are not added into the manufacturer's total production or sales ranking for each model year. The reader will find the Opel listed under Buick, and the Capri and Pantera under Mercury.

That leads into the differences of the second type of captive import. Cars in this category were sold through their respective dealer networks, and each had the division's nameplate — e.g., Dodge, Ford or Plymouth — affixed to the car. Production of these cars cannot be calculated accurately as they were produced in other countries as exports, but there are records to determine model year sales through U.S. dealerships. Generally this total is available only by model, and it is not broken down by body style. Therefore, the model year sales of these captive imports are not included with the model year production of Dodge, Ford and Plymouth to determine their total production and sales ranking for each model year. Models falling into this second category include the Ford Fiesta, which was imported from Ford's European operations, and the Plymouth Cricket and Dodge Colt models introduced in 1971 to compete with the Ford Pinto and Chevrolet Vega. The English-built Cricket was gone by 1973, mostly due to a lack of interest from American consumers. The Dodge Colt, which proved far more successful than the Plymouth Cricket, was built in Japan by Chrysler's partially owned partner, Mitsubishi. The success of the Colt eventually led to the importing of the 1976 Plymouth Arrow, 1978 Dodge Challenger and Plymouth Sapporo, and 1979 Dodge Colt hatchback and Plymouth Champ, all built by Mitsubishi.

While all of these were successful in their own ways, the lessons learned from the Dodge Colt and Ford Fiesta in particular were that if you build a quality small car, consumers will buy it. Throughout the 1970s the tide of imported cars would rise as the foreign companies, Japanese in particular, learned quickly that quality sells, and they worked hard to learn what American car buyers wanted. At the beginning of the decade few Japanese importers other than Toy-

ota and Datsun were selling multiple model lines, but by the end of the decade, it seemed all manufacturers had a full line of cars and were competing head-to-head in all lines except the full-size models. Even the more basic economy lines were gussied up in the form of more luxurious cars like the larger Honda Accord, the Toyota Cressida, the Datsun 810, and the Subaru GLF hardtop. The European manufacturers were not as successful during the 1970s, with some exceptions, mainly from Germany, when Audi, BMW and Mercedes-Benz began to increase their sales by 1980.

Conclusion

In the end, no matter what regulations were implemented, no matter how bad the economy performed, the times were changing. The American automakers won the battle of the seventies despite their own internal issues by surviving two recessions and two fuel crises and, for a time at least, keeping the import competition at bay, all while keeping up with ever changing government regulation and providing consumers with cars that seemed right for the times. Their success led to record model year production in 1973, and near record totals for 1977, 1978 and 1979. Unfortunately, there were more battles to come.

1973

Aided by an improved economy, and with industry strikes resolved, the auto manufacturers were looking forward to a second year of increased sales for 1973. A plethora of new hatchback models and the newly enacted federal bumper safety standards highlighted the start of the model year. The new protection standards required that no damage occur to the car at the front end when involved in a 5 mph impact, and rear bumpers were required to withstand a 2.5 mph impact without damage. Due to the requirements, the front-end appearance of nearly every 1973 model was changed in some way, whether with a new bumper design or a new grille and bumper layout, and it also made the new cars easily recognizable, as many models wore a shelf-like bumper in front.

Surprising to auto industry analysts was the resurgence of interest in what had been called "muscle cars" or "pony-cars" prior to 1972. By 1973, engines were less powerful, insurance rates were soaring, and interest in the models seemed to be declining, so in 1972 manufacturers scaled back somewhat, with the Pontiac GTO being relegated back to option package status and the Chrysler Hemi engine being dropped. But consumers discovered that power and performance was not completely gone, just less muscular than it had been, though in some cases just the looks remained without the brawn. Regardless, the high-performance pony car and muscle car models that remained saw a large sales increase this year. Many models now used smaller engines, at least as standard equipment, and some lost some of their previous performance equipment. Still, cars like the Plymouth Road Runner, which was practically down to a trim option by 1973, had production more than double the 1972 total. Similarly the high-performance Pontiac Trans Am had a nearly four-fold increase over the prior year, and the AMC Javelin AMX doubled in sales. Yet these three cars didn't tell the whole story, as the Ford Mustang Mach I, Chevrolet Camaro, Dodge Challenger, and the Plymouth Barracuda all had sales gains in the double digits this year.

The giant General Motors had the only all-new cars

this year, with the introductions of completely redesigned mid-size models and an expansion of the X-car compact line. New mid-size models were originally planned to be introduced for 1972, but partially due to a United Auto Workers strike in 1970 that played a hand in the delay of the cars' development, and also because of the corporation's switch in 1971 to engines designed to run on low-lead fuels, and then the need to incorporate safety equipment to meet impending federal standards for the 1973 model year, the cars were delayed by a year. The new mid-size line included both the regular A-bodied cars consisting of the Chevrolet Chevelle, Pontiac LeMans, Oldsmobile Cutlass, and a newly named Buick Century replacing the Skylark nameplate, and also new "A-special" body cars that included the Chevrolet Monte Carlo and Pontiac Grand Prix. Along with these new models, sporty and luxurious top-of-the line subseries were added, bearing the names of Chevelle Laguna, Grand Am, and Century Regal. Styling for each of these mid-size models was unique and in keeping with the themes of their respective divisions, but all used the new GM–termed "Colonnade" styling. In general, colonnade refers to a series of columns, usually freestanding, and typically in a row at least twice as long as they are high. The mid-size cars' rooflines used columns, otherwise known as A-, B- and C-pillars, but as for the rest of the definition, it's unclear how the styling fit the name. Regardless, in GM's world the Colonnade design used somewhat wide center pillars on all body styles, and all door windows were frameless with rounded corners at the B-pillar post, creating a hardtop look for the doors, while the roofs were pillared like a sedan. Ford had a similar design with more slender B-pillars, and its cars were more simply named as pillared hardtops. All of the regular A-bodied coupes had a rakish rear window that provided a semi-fast-back roofline, while sedans used a more gently sloping rear window for a more formal appearance. Station wagons all used a new liftgate style tailgate with fixed rear windows, and a rear side window flip-out vent window was standard on three-seat models and optional on two-seat models. With the new body style introductions, the mid-size convertibles were dropped. Standard rooflines on coupes used a new fixed rear quarter window that was large and triangular in shape for most models, with a more rectangular vertical opera window offered for upper trim level models. All sedans used a six-window design, with a fixed window behind the rear door. For the most part the same powerplants were found underneath the hood, with a variety of V8 engines available for all models, and some of the Chevelle and LeMans models being available with an inline six-cylinder engine.

The Monte Carlo and Grand Prix coupes shared a new V-shaped rear window and rode on the longer 116-inch wheelbase used for sedans and wagons. Their new roofline included standard opera window styling, which was shared with certain regular A-bodied coupes riding on the 112-inch coupe wheelbase, such as the new Buick Century Regal, Century Luxus, and the Oldsmobile Cutlass Supreme. Stylewise the Monte Carlo and Grand Prix bore an obvious resemblance to their immediate predecessors, but were clearly all-new designs. Muscle car names returned this year, but all were relegated to trim option packages, with a few pieces of performance hardware, such as suspension upgrades, thrown in for good measure. These packages included the Chevy Chevelle SS package, the Pontiac LeMans GTO package, Oldsmobile Cutlass 4-4-2 package, and the Buick Century GS package. Customers wanting to find any type of mid-size performance car without having to buy an option package could opt for the new Pontiac Grand Am, which came standard with the Grand Prix's 400 CID V8 engine, a luxury interior that borrowed the Grand Prix cockpit-style instrument panel, and a performance-tuned suspension, and could be ordered with the Trans Am's 455 CID V8 engine. The Grand Am, available in two-door coupe and four-door sedan models, essentially replaced the GTO as Pontiac's top muscle car for 1973.

In the compact GM lines, the Chevrolet Nova and re-named Pontiac Ventura were joined by the Oldsmobile Omega and Buick Apollo. While the styling was updated for the Nova and Ventura this year to modernize front-end appearance, the coupe models' roofline was significantly altered as well, with more rounded rear quarter side windows. Another reason for changing the roofline was to add a new model, the two-door hatchback, which was offered in all four divisions' models. Some media members at the time of the 1973 X-body cars' introduction theorized that the choice of names for the Buick and Oldsmobile models was intentional to show the corporate relation of all the X-body cars creating the *N*ova, *O*mega, *V*entura, *A*pollo nameplates. That theory is not proven by any known corporate records. It is important to mention at this point that most commonly, the 1973 and 1974 Nova and its related models are grouped with the 1968 through 1972 models as a generation, though a few references group the two years as more closely related to the 1975 through 1979 models. In reality, from 1968 through 1979, all X-body cars rode on a 111-inch wheelbase and shared many common components under the skin, but visually the interior and exterior went through three variations, so for this reference, they are being listed as completely restyled versions of the "third generation" 1968 to 1972 Chevy II and Nova models, and included separately from what are commonly referred to as the "fourth generation" 1975–1979 models which represented more of a complete redesign. The most obvious linkage of the 1973 and 1974 versions to the 1968 through 1972 versions can be found in the front grille and header design. Where the earlier cars had a grille inset that extended onto the front fender ends, the new for '73 design had a body-color metal end to the outside of the headlights. Upon close inspection, one can see the break where the grille section used to be.

The rest of the GM line was not greatly changed this year, with mostly the required bumper changes affecting some models' front-end styling. The changes were most obvious on the full-size line, where all but Oldsmobile adopted full-width grilles and new bumpers. Oldsmobile stuck with its twin grille design and modified it to fit the new bumper requirements. Significant changes were found in the truck lines of General Motors, with all-new Chevrolet and GMC trucks being introduced. This new design of truck would carry through the 1987 model year for the pickups, and into 1992 for the Suburban and Chevy Blazer/GMC Jimmy models. The medium-sized Chevrolet El Camino and its twin, the GMC Sprint, were both restyled in line with the related Chevelle model, while the imported LUV (Light Utility Vehicle), introduced to the U.S. market in 1972 and built by GM's Japanese partner, Isuzu, continued into 1973 with few changes. The Vega panel wagon was also still available and was based on the Vega Kammback station wagon.

Also getting into the hatchback act this year was American Motors, which now offered the bodystyle in its popular compact Hornet line, complementing the two- and four-door sedans and the always popular Sportabout four-door wagon, the only compact station wagon built by an American manufacturer since the Ford Falcon left the market in 1970. While the Hornet received a more rounded front-end restyling, the rest of the AMC line offered only new grille patterns and the required bumper changes, some of which were met by adding bumper guards. AMC continued to widely promote its exclusive Buyer Protection Plan as a distinctive choice from the rest of the American automobile industry. It is interesting to note that of the four American manufacturers, only AMC offered optional rear bumper systems in 1973 that met the 1974 standards. There were no significant changes to AMC's Jeep line of trucks and off-road utility vehicles. This would be the final year of production for the Ambassador two-door hardtop model.

Ford Motor Company put in a big restyling effort on its full-sized Ford and Mercury lines. While not a total redesign, the new styling smoothed out the bodysides and added shelf-like front bumpers for both, and new full-width grilles for Fords. The mid-size Ford Torino and Mercury Montego, which had been completely redesigned for 1972, were given a major facelift to meet the new federal bumper standards. Similarly, the Thunderbird and Continental Mark IV, both of which were new designs in 1972, required a facelift to add new front bumpers. The Mercury Cougar and Comet and the Ford Maverick were all fitted with the new box-like shelf bumpers, while the Ford Pinto and Mustang continued with less visible changes. The 1973 model year would be the final one for Ford convertibles, as the Mustang and Cougar drop-tops would be dropped at the end of the model year. Changes for the imported Capri and Pantera are noted under the 1973 Mercury introduction. Ford's truck line, which had been completely restyled in 1967, was given another redesign for 1973. The most obvious visual changes were to move the parking/turn signal lights above the headlights and to raise the bodyside feature and trim line. The popular Ranchero car-based pickup continued with front-end styling changes in line with the Ford Torino. The imported Courier, built by Ford's Japanese partner, Mazda, continued into its second season in the U.S. market mostly unchanged.

At Chrysler, the full-size Plymouth, Dodge Polara, and Chrysler lines received noticeable front-end restyling, dispensing with their former loop-style front bumpers, in favor of a more traditional bumper and grille combination. The Dodge Monaco and Imperial retained their former designs while adding bumper guards and hidden shocks to meet the new bumper standards. The compact Plymouth Valiant and Dodge Dart models received new sheetmetal styling that moved away from the former flat looking bodysides and added more shape to the rear quarters. This design was particularly noticeable on the sporty Duster and Dart Sport coupes, where the rear quarters took on more of a "Cokebottle" shape. The Valiant and Dart also had new front-end styling using the shelf-like front bumpers, but overall the cars did not stray greatly from the clean appearance of their predecessors.

Through the rest of the line the styling was not changed greatly, and most models were able to meet the front bumper standards with the addition of bumper guards and hydraulic supports behind the bumper. In the muscle car lines, most models returned with two notable exceptions. The Dodge Challenger Rallye was no longer a separate model, but rather moved to an option package, and the Plymouth GTX, which was dropped from the line after the 1971 model year, had its name used when a 440 CID V8 engine was installed on the Road Runner. In such a case, the tape stripe on the car read "440 GTX."

The Dodge truck line, having been completely redesigned in 1972, received only minor changes for their second year on the market. In Chrysler's "captive import" line, the British-built Plymouth Cricket continued to hang on into the 1973 model year, if only briefly — most likely only to dispose of unsold 1972 models remaining in inventory. Apparently the Cricket was pulled from the U.S. market not only because of poor sales, but also to avoid spending money to redesign the bumper systems to meet 1973 requirements. On the other hand, the Japanese-built Dodge Colt, which was selling quite well and was likely stealing Cricket sales, held onto its original 1971 design for one more season.

Finally, a note on GM pricing as presented in this book: In researching prices it was found that the GM full-line introduction catalog sent to shareholders at the beginning of the model year shows pricing of all models, except the new A-body mid-size cars and some full-sized B-body station wagons, to be the same as 1972 models. Many prices are taken from these references for this book. However in reviewing many other references for an explanation as to why they would be the same, the author has concluded that the GM shareholder catalog may have been printed prior to GM's receiving confirmation that it would be allowed to increase prices under the regulations imposed by the Federal Government's Price Commission. The commission, established in 1971 and remaining in operation into 1974, was closely linked to the Office of Price Stabilization (OPS) and was designed to keep price hikes under control to keep inflation in check. Therefore, the prices shown in the model charts for 1973 are taken from the July 1973 NADA price guide, which concurs with all other references researched for confirmation of prices.

1973 Overview and Changes from Prior Year

- **Total industry model year production:** 10,628,988, up 13.7%.
- **Total estimated captive import sales:** 217,619, up 2.66%.
- **Market share by corporation:** GM 52.17%; Ford 27.89%; Chrysler 16.92%; AMC 3.02%.
- **Number of models and body types available:** 298, down from 303.
- **Highest production series:** Chevrolet BelAir/Impala/Caprice — 978,046.
- **Lowest production series:** Cadillac Fleetwood 75 — 2,060.
- **Highest individual model production:** Chevrolet Vega 2-Dr. Notchback Cpe.— 266,124.
- **Lowest individual model production:** Cadillac Fleetwood 75 4-Dr., 9-p. Sedan —1,017.

- **Industry average base price:** $3,710, up 0.35%.
- **Highest individual model base price:** Cadillac Fleetwood 75 Limousine, $12,080.
- **Lowest individual model base price:** Ford Pinto 2-Door Sedan, $2,021.
- **Highest average MPG with base powertrain:** Chevrolet Vega, 24.6 MPG.
- **Lowest average MPG with base powertrain:** Lincoln Continental, 7.9 MPG.
- **Indianapolis 500 Pace Car:** Cadillac Eldorado Convertible.
- ***Motor Trend* magazine "Car of the Year":** Chevrolet Monte Carlo Landau.

AMERICAN MOTORS

"Introducing the '73's from American Motors.
We back them better because we build them better."

Aside from the federally required changes, American Motors began the 1973 model year with only minor changes to their products and some realignment to trim levels for various models. Most important for the company this year was the "Buyer Protection Plan," introduced in 1972. The plan was designed to guarantee to the purchaser of a new American Motors car that it would be free from defects. The plan, heavily promoted in all of AMC's advertising, continued to be successful, with model year production up nearly 25 percent, outperforming the industry average production increase by more than 75 percent. This gain followed a production increase in 1972, and in both years, it was accomplished with only slightly changed product in the showrooms. To add further benefit to the plan, purchasers of 1973 AMCs could double the coverage to 24 months or 24,000 miles for only $149. This definitely caught the attention of the "Big Three," most of which were offering lesser guarantees. AMC's sales had proven the power of a good guarantee and an economical product line.

An all-new Hornet 2-Door Hatchback was added to the otherwise unchanged model line, as an attempt to capture the perceived interest of the public in hatchback body styles. All the rage in Europe, the hatchback did find some success in America. Many manufacturers would struggle to make a success out of their hatchback models, however, and they soon fell out of favor in all but the subcompact lines. In the smaller cars, the ease of access provided by an opening hatch and a larger cargo area were seen as a real benefit. But by year's end, adding a Hornet Hatchback to the line proved a wise investment for American Motors.

Most of the model lines received trim modifications, such as new striping for the Gremlin and a new grille design for the Matador. Javelin models received a new mesh grille with rectangular parking and turn signal lamps incorporated just inside the grille frame, while the AMX continued with its round lamp units set within a finely meshed grille. The Hornet line received a mildly revised front-end design in conjunction with the new 5-mph bumper, which eliminated the pan used below the bumper on earlier models. The new grille consisted of many equally spaced dark argent-colored vertical bars, highlighted with a double silver horizontal bar stretching in a continuous line between the headlamps through the center of the grille, and rounding above and below the relocated parking and turn signal lamps located just inside of the headlamps.

Other changes for 1973 included the addition of the famed Levi's custom trim option for the Gremlin and the revision of option packages such as the Gucci package for the Hornet Sportabout and the Cardin interior trim package for the Javelin. A special "Trans Am" Javelin was introduced which featured a large "Trans Am Victory Edition" decal on either fender just in front of the door. The "Trans Am Victory Editions" were usually more heavily optioned than regular production Javelins, and this package included the aforementioned decal with "SCCA 1971–72 Trans Am Champs" on it, plus 14" slot wheels with E70X14 RWL tires and space saver spare. The SST nomenclature that had designated the base Hornet, Javelin, and Ambassador lines in 1972 was dropped for the new season. The slowly fading Ambassador was pared down to the Brougham series to carry the "luxury car" banner for AMC.

Ambassador Brougham 4-Door Sedan

Gremlin 2-Door Sedan

Hornet 2-Door Sedan

Hornet 3-Door Hatchback

Hornet Sportabout optional Gucci interior

Javelin 2-Door Hardtop with
Javelin AMX 2-Door Hardtop, rear

Matador 4-Door Station Wagon

Matador 2-Door Hardtop

Model year production: 320,785, up 24.27% from 1972.

Domestic market share: 3.02% (9th place).

Base price range: $2,098 to $4,861.

American Motors average base price: $3,128, down 2.71%.

Introduction date: September 22, 1972.

Assembly plants: Kenosha, Wisconsin, and Brampton, Ontario, Canada.

Data plate identification (VIN): Thirteen digit code read as follows: First digit indicates company (A = American Motors); Second digit indicates model year (3 = 1973); Third digit is transmission code (see powertrain chart); Fourth through sixth digits indicate car line, body type and series (three-digit model number in model charts); Seventh digit is engine code (see powertrain chart); Eighth digit indicates assembly plant (1 = Kenosha, 7 = Ontario); Remaining digits are sequential with beginning number of 00001. *Example:* A3A797M100001 is a 1973 Javelin 2-Door, 304 CID V8, with Torque-Command Automatic, serial number 00001, built in Kenosha.

Powertrains

Engine displacement and intake	Net HP	Engine/ Trans. Codes[1]	Transmission Availability[1]		Gremlin	Hornet	Javelin	Matador	Ambassador
232 CID (3.8L), 1-bbl., 6-cyl.	100	E/S	3-speed manual		S	S	S (Javelin)	S (ex. wgn.)	—
				MPG:	15.6	NA	NA	NA	
		E/A	Torque-Command 3-sp. Automatic		$200	$200	$218	$226	—
				MPG:	15.9	15.5	NA	NA	—
258 CID (4.2L), 1-bbl., 6-cyl.	110	A/S	3-speed manual		$51	$51	—	S (wgn.)/ $46 (others)	—
				MPG:	NA	11.7	—	NA	
		A/A	Torque-Command 3-sp. Automatic		$251	$251	$261 (Javelin)	$272 (ex. wgn.)	—
				MPG:	13.2	14.3	NA	NA	—

Engine displacement and intake	Net HP	Engine/ Trans. Codes[1]	Transmission Availability[1]		Gremlin	Hornet	Javelin	Matador	Ambassador
304 CID (5.0L), 2-bbl., V8	150	H/S	3-speed manual		$154	$138	$94 (Javelin)/ S (AMX)	$52 (wgn.)/ $99 (others)	—
				MPG:	NA	NA	NA	NA	—
		H/A	Torque-Command 3-sp. Automatic		$373	$369	$330 (Javelin)/ $236 (AMX)	$297 (wgn.)/ $344 (others)	S
				MPG:	NA	NA	12.1	12.4	NA
360 CID (5.9L), 2-bbl., V8	175	N/A	Torque-Command 3-sp. Automatic		—	$411	$372 (Javelin)/ $278 (AMX)	$310 (wgn.)/ $356 (others)	$50
				MPG:	—	11	11.6	NA	10.8
360 CID (5.9L), 4-bbl., V8	195 (220 w/dual exhaust)[2]	P/F	4-speed manual		—	—	$273 (Javelin)/ $179 (AMX)	—	—
				MPG:	—	—	10.8	—	—
		P/A	Torque-Command 3-sp. Automatic		—	—	$382 (Javelin)/ $288 (AMX)	$330 (wgn.)/ $376 (others)	$70
				MPG:	—	—	NA	10	10.4
401 CID (6.6L), 4-bbl., V8	255[2]	Z/F	4-speed manual		—	—	$346 (Javelin)/ $249 (AMX)	—	—
				MPG:	—	—	NA	—	—
		Z/A	Torque-Command 3-sp. Automatic		—	—	$467 (Javelin)/ $371 (AMX)	$381 (wgn.)/ $427 (others)	$145
				MPG:	—	—	NA	NA	NA

[1]Unless otherwise noted: All manual transmissions are floor-shifts, except on Hornet and Matador, and all automatics, except AMX, are column-shift. Floor-shift is standard on all AMX models, and available for $20 extra on Gremlin w/automatic, Hornet Hatchback, Javelin w/V8 and automatic, and any Matador Coupe. Transmission code w/Automatic floor shift is C, w/3-speed synchronized manual is E.   [2]Dual exhaust standard on AMX and all with 401 CID V8. Available on Javelin, Matador and Ambassador with 360 CID 4-bbl. V8, for approximately $30.

Major Options

	Gremlin	Hornet	Javelin	Matador	Ambassador
All-season air conditioning	$377	$377	$377	$377	S
Adjust-O-Tilt steering wheel	$43	$43	$43	$46	$46
Cruise-Command speed control	—	—	—	$62	$62
Electric rear window defogger	—	—	$45	$48	$48
Tinted glass, all windows	$37	$40	$40	$42	S
Power windows	—	—	—	$123	$123
Front bucket seats	$131	$131	S[1]	$131[1]	$131[1]
Third row seat on station wagons	—	—	—	$108	$108
AM radio	$66	$66	$66	$75	S
AM/FM stereo	$130	$130	$196	$230	$61
Vinyl top (excluding wagon models)	—	$88	$88	$91	$109
Sunroof	$142	—	—	—	—
Power steering	$99	$99	$106	$111	S
Power brakes	$44	$44	$44	$44	S
Power front disc brakes	$79	$79	$79	$79	S
Custom wheel covers	$50	$50	$50	$53	S
Spoke style wheels	$100	$100	$100	$105	$75
Popular Option Groups & Packages					
360 "Go" package (AMX only)	—	—	$428	—	—
401 "Go" package (AMX only)	—	—	$476	—	—
Custom trim package	$80	—	—	—	—
Décor group	$37	—	—	—	—
D/L package (Sportabout only)	—	$237[2]	—	—	—
Handling package	$23	$23	$30	$30	—
Insulation group	$22	$22	$22	S	S
Interior appointment package	$19	—	—	—	—

	Gremlin	Hornet	Javelin	Matador	Ambassador
Interior groups: Gucci and Cardin[2]	—	$142	$85	—	—
Interior groups: special fabric trim	—	—	—	$69[3]	$69[4]
Levi's custom trim package	$135[5]	—	—	—	—
Light group	$28	$28	$33	$35	S
Protection group	$14	$19	$19	$20	$35
Rally-Pac instrument package	—	—	$77	—	—
Visibility group	$49	$60	$40	$60	S
"X" package	$285	$207[6]	—	—	—

—= Not Available; S = Standard equipment.   [1]Two-door hardtop models only. Floor console available on Javelin for $57 extra.   [2]Gucci available only on Hornet Sportabout, and Cardin available only on Javelin. Sportabout with D/L package is available with "Scorpio" fabric trim for $47 extra.   [3]"Tropicana" fabric available for sedan and hardtop as listed, and for $96 on wagon.   [4]"Camelot" fabric available for sedan and hardtop as listed, and for $96 on wagon.   [5]$50 with Gremlin "X" package.   [6]HBK and Sportabout only.

Paint Colors

	Code	Gremlin/Hornet	Javelin	Matador/Ambassador
Snow White	A1	x	x	x
Grasshopper Green metallic	C8	x[1,2]	x[4]	x
Cordoba Brown metallic	D4	—	x[4]	x
Trans-Am Red	D7	x[1,3]	x	x
Diamond Blue metallic	E1	x[2,3]	x	x
Olympic Blue metallic	E2	x[3]	x	x
Fairway Green metallic	E3	x[1,2]	x[4]	x
Tallyho Green metallic	E4	x[1,2]	x[4]	x
Pewter Silver metallic	E5	x	x	x
Fawn Beige	E6	x[1,2]	x[4]	x
Copper Tan metallic	E7	x[1,2,3]	x[4]	x
Mellow Yellow	E9	x[1,3]	—	—
Blarney Green	F1	x[1,3]	—	—
Maxi Blue	F2	x[3]	x[4]	
Fresh Plum metallic	F3	x[1,3]	x	—
Daisy Yellow	F4	—	x[4]	x
Vineyard Burgundy metallic	F5	—	x[4]	x
Classic Black	P1	x	x	x

Two-tone paint combinations are available on Hornet, Matador and Ambassador (except Sportabout) at $30–$35 depending upon model. Non-standard model colors are available at approximately $38 extra.   [1]Not available on Gremlin with Levi's interior package.   [2]Not available on Gremlin with "X" package.   [3]Not available on Hornet Sportabout with Gucci package.   [4]Not available on Javelin with Cardin package.

Gremlin

"An economy drive can be fun."

Nameplate year of origin: 1970.

Current bodystyle lifespan: 1970 through 1983; as Gremlin 1970 to 1978, restyled and renamed Spirit 1979 to 1982, 4WD added and re-badged Eagle SX/4 1981 to 1983.

Predecessor to this model: None.

Replacement for this model: Spirit (1979 to 1982) and Eagle SX/4 (1981 to 1983).

Percentage of division's production: 26.07%.

Corporate siblings: None; however, many components were shared with the Hornet.

Primary competition: Buick/Opel 1900, Chevrolet Vega, Dodge Colt, and Ford Pinto.

Measurements

Wheelbase	96.0"
Length	65.5"
Width	70.6"
Height	51.7"
Legroom — front	40.8"
Legroom — rear	27.8"
Headroom — front	38.1"
Headroom — rear	36.4"
Cargo capacity (cu. ft.)	6.4*
Fuel capacity (gals.)	21.0

*16.4 cu. ft. with rear seat down.

Notable changes: Minor interior trim changes.
Major standard equipment: Vinyl bench front seat with foam cushions, front door pockets, fold-down rear seat, rubber floor mats, interior lights, aluminized exhaust system, exterior pinstripes, hubcaps, and 6.45 × 14 BSW tires.

Models Available

	Model No.	Base MSRP	Change from LY	Shipping Wt. (lbs.)	Model Year Production	Change from LY
Gremlin 2-Door Sedan	46-5	$2,098	+4.05%	2642	83,625*	+35.50%
TOTALS		*Avg. price* $2,098	+4.05%	*Production*	83,625*	+35.50%

Estimated based on calendar year production.

Hornet

"We built economy into the way they run. Not the way they look."

Nameplate year of origin: 1951 (Previously used on 1951 to 1957 Hudson series).
Current bodystyle lifespan: 1970 through 1987; as Hornet 1970 to 1977, restyled and renamed Concord 1978 to 1982, 4WD added and rebadged Eagle 1980 to 1987.
Predecessor to this model: (Rambler) American (1964 to 1969).
Replacement for this model: Concord (1978 to 1982) and Eagle (1980 to 1987).
Percentage of division's production: 33.52%.
Corporate siblings: None; however, many components were shared with the Gremlin.
Primary competition: Chevrolet Nova, Dodge Dart, Ford Maverick, Plymouth Valiant, and Pontiac Ventura.
Notable changes: New front end styling and trim and detail changes. New hatchback model.
Major standard equipment: "Leo" fabric-covered front bench seat with foam cushions, full-floor carpeting, instrument panel package tray, custom steering wheel, aluminized exhaust system, exterior pinstripes, hubcaps, and 6.95 × 14 BSW tires. Hatchback adds: Flip-open rear windows, gas-charged lift-gate supports. Sportabout adds: "Striped Uganda" upholstery, hidden rear compartment lock.

Measurements

	Sedans	Hatchback	Sportabout
Wheelbase	108.0"	108.0"	108.0"
Length	184.9"	184.9"	184.9"
Width	70.6"	70.6"	70.6"
Height	51.1"	51.0"	51.3"
Legroom — front	40.8"	40.8"	40.8"
Legroom — rear	36.1"	36.1"	36.1"
Headroom — front	38.1"	38.0"	38.1"
Headroom — rear	37.5"	36.5"	37.9"
Cargo capacity (cu. ft.)	11.2	22.9*	64.6*
Fuel capacity (gals.)	16.0	16.0	16.0

Maximum with rear seat down, and space-saver spare tire on Hatchback.

Models Available

	Model No.	Base MSRP	Change from LY	Shipping Wt. (lbs.)	Model Year Production	Change from LY
Hornet 2-Door Sedan	06-7	$2,298	+4.50%	2777	*	*
Hornet 2-Door Hatchback	03-7	$2,449	NEW	2818	*	*
Hornet 4-Door Sedan	05-7	$2,343	+3.44%	2854	*	*
Hornet 4-Door Sportabout Wagon	08-7	$2,675	+3.40%	2921	*	*
TOTALS		*Avg. price* $2,441	+3.87%	*Production*	107,530*	+51.34%

Estimated based on calendar year production. Production by body style is not available.

Javelin

"A performance pair for the open road (or track)."

Nameplate year of origin: 1968.
Current bodystyle lifespan: 1971 through 1974.
Predecessor to this model: Javelin (1968 to 1970).
Replacement for this model: None.
Percentage of division's production: 9.63%.
Corporate siblings: None.
Primary competition: Chevrolet Camaro, Dodge Challenger, Ford Mustang, Plymouth Barracuda, and Pontiac Firebird.
Notable changes: New grille (Javelin) and trim and detail changes.
Major standard equipment: "Slim-shell" vinyl front bucket seats with foam cushions, aluminized exhaust system, custom steering wheel, sport hubcaps, and D78 × 14 BSW tires. AMX adds: 304 CID V8, three-spoke sport steering wheel, deck-mounted rear spoiler, specific tape stripe package, slotted 14 × 6 wheels, space saver spare tire, and E70 × 14 RWL tires.

Measurements

Wheelbase	110.0"
Length	192.3"
Width	75.2"
Height	51.2"
Legroom — front	42.5"
Legroom — rear	31.0"
Headroom — front	37.5"
Headroom — rear	35.5"
Cargo capacity (cu. ft.)	10.2
Fuel capacity (gals.)	16.0

Models Available

	Model No.	Base MSRP	Change from LY	Shipping Wt. (lbs.)	Model Year Production	Change from LY
Javelin 2-Door Hardtop	79-7	$2,889	+2.92%	2868	25,195	+7.42%
Javelin AMX 2-Door Hardtop	79-8	$3,191	+2.64%	3170	5,707	+109.12%
TOTALS		*Avg. price* $3,040	+2.77%		*Production* 30,902	+18.02%

Matador

"The roomy intermediate."

Nameplate year of origin: 1971.
Current bodystyle lifespan: 1967 through 1978 (as Rebel 1967–1970; restyled in 1969; restyled and renamed Matador in 1971; sedan and wagon restyled in 1974).
Predecessor to this model: Rebel (1967 to 1970).
Replacement for this model: Matador (1974 to 1978).
Percentage of division's production: 19.20%.
Corporate siblings: AMC Ambassador (shared components from the cowl back).
Primary competition: Chevrolet Chevelle, Dodge Coronet, Ford Torino, Plymouth Satellite, and Pontiac LeMans.
Notable changes: Revised black-finish grille; trim and detail changes.
Major standard equipment: Fabric-covered front bench seat with foam cushions, C-pillar interior lights on hardtop, dome light on sedan and wagon, aluminized exhaust system, vinyl bodyside scuff moldings, and E78 × 14 BSW tires. Wagon adds: "Uganda" perforated-vinyl trim seats, rubber cargo area mat, hidden rear compartment with lock, dual-swing tailgate, and H78 × 14 BSW tires.

Measurements

	Cars	Wagon
Wheelbase	118.0"	118.0"
Length	208.4"	208.0"
Width	77.2"	77.2"
Height	54.5"	54.5"
Legroom — front	41.0"	41.0"
Legroom — rear	37.6"	37.6"
Headroom — front	39.3"	39.3"
Headroom — rear	37.0"	37.0"
Cargo capacity (cu. ft.)	18.2	99.1
Fuel capacity (gals.)	19.5	20.0

Models Available

	Model No.	Base MSRP	Change from LY	Shipping Wt. (lbs.)	Model Year Production	Change from LY
Matador 2-Door Hardtop	19-7	$2,887	+1.24%	3314	*	*
Matador 4-Door Sedan	15-7	$2,853	+3.70%	3289	*	*

	Model No.	Base MSRP	Change from LY	Shipping Wt. (lbs.)	Model Year Production	Change from LY
Matador 4-Door Station Wagon	18-7	$3,179	+1.24%	3627	*	*
TOTALS		Avg. price $2,973	+2.02%		Production 61,605*	+12.39%

Estimated based on calendar year production. Production by body style is not available.

Ambassador Brougham

*"You get as standard equipment, the luxuries
you'd normally have to pay extra for."*

Nameplate year of origin: 1933 (from top-of-the-line Nash).
Current bodystyle lifespan: 1967 through 1974.
Predecessor to this model: Ambassador (1963 to 1966).
Replacement for this model: None.
Percentage of division's production: 11.57%.
Corporate siblings: AMC Matador (shared components from the cowl back).
Primary competition: Chevrolet BelAir/Impala/Caprice, Ford LTD, and Plymouth Fury.
Notable Changes: Minor trim and detail changes.
Major Standard Equipment: "Interlaken" fabric-covered front bench seat with foam cushions, custom steering wheel, "All-season" air conditioning, power steering, power front disc brakes, aluminized exhaust system, rear bumper guards, Ambassador-specific hubcaps, and F78 × 14 WSW tires. Wagon adds: Vinyl upholstery, roof-top luggage rack, simulated woodgrain side and rear panels, cargo area mat (carpet w/available 3rd seat), hidden rear compartment with lock, dual-swing tailgate, and H78 × 14 WSW tires.

Measurements

	Cars	Wagons
Wheelbase	122.0"	122.0"
Length	212.4"	212.0"
Width	77.2"	77.2"
Height	54.5"	54.5"
Legroom — front	41.0"	41.0"
Legroom — rear	37.6"	37.6"
Headroom — front	39.3"	39.3"
Headroom — rear	37.0"	37.0"
Cargo capacity (cu. ft.)	18.2	99.1
Fuel capacity (gals.)	19.5	20.0

Models Available

	Model No.	Base MSRP	Change from LY	Shipping Wt. (lbs.)	Model Year Production	Change from LY
Ambassador 2-Door Hardtop	89-7	$4,477	+11.42%	3774	*	*
Ambassador 4-Door Sedan	85-7	$4,461	+11.47%	3763	*	*
Ambassador 4-Door Station Wagon	88-7	$4,861	+9.56%	4054	*	*
TOTALS		Avg. price $4,600	+12.58%		Production 37,125*	-16.32%

Estimated based on calendar year production. Production by body style is not available.

BUICK

"Buick. The solid feeling."

Buick entered 1973 with a completely redesigned and renamed mid-size lineup, a facelifted line of full-size near-luxury and personal cars, and the popular German-built Opels that again were available with the sporty Manta adding a new luxury model. To top it off, in the spring of 1973, an all-new car named Apollo was introduced, bringing a compact-sized car back into showrooms, something dealers had not seen since 1961–1963 when the Buick Special was part of General Motors' initial wave of compact cars. All of this combined to increase Buick sales 20 percent over the prior year, giving Buick its second best sales year in history. But with the entire industry experiencing an extraordinary seller's market, the brand's market share was up only slightly, and Buick retained the same ranking as it held in 1972.

The Apollo was Buick's version of the X-body Chevrolet Nova, which itself was greatly restyled for 1973. While touted as having a smoother, quieter ride than most compacts, it was not really much different from a well-optioned Nova with a Buick grille. The Nova and Apollo and their corporate siblings, the Ventura and Omega, were truly the first of many "badge-engineered" cars to come from GM. Offered in the three body styles, a coupe, sedan and hatchback, the Apollo got off to a slow start in the marketplace, mostly because it was duplicated in nearly every other GM showroom.

The Century name, last used in 1958, was applied to the completely redesigned A-body mid-size line, replacing the well-known Skylark nameplate. Along with its equally new corporate siblings, the new Century carried smoother, flowing and seemingly more aerodynamic lines. Single headlamps mounted at the front fender ends with round parking lights set in between them and a chrome outlined, horizontal bar grille characterized the new Century look up front. The grille had three prominent bars with two smaller bars between each. The front bumper was full-width with the contemporary wrap-around ends that turned up slightly, and a center section that continued the grille theme into the lower area below the bumper. The new top-of-the-line Regal coupe carried a vertical bar grille divided into 10 sections with each outlined in chrome, and several smaller vertical bars within. It should also be pointed out that the new Regal model was considered a part of the Century line in Buick's sales and marketing approach through the 1977 model year, and will be presented as such in this book.

Styling features along the bodysides and rear end were a fresh take on the full-size line, restyled for the 1971 model year. Bodysides featured a body line which began at the outside leading edge of the front fender and curved slightly downward at the back edge of the fender, running onto the door, and ending midway through the rear door on four-door models, and ending near the back edge of the front door on two-doors. A second line began in a crease at the front above the parking lights, running along the hood past the cowl, a few inches below the A-pillar, and gradually tapering downward, almost imperceptibly, and ending slightly above the top of the rear bumper. The rear bumper on all coupes and sedans was a virtual clone of the LeSabre and Centurion's, rolled under the car, with raised ends and a center section capping the horizontal tail lamps. All station wagons in GM's A-body line used the same rear bumper with differing patterns on the tail lamp lens. They also shared a "liftgate" style tailgate with a fixed rear window.

Inside, the new Century and in particular the Century Regal were far more luxurious in appearance than their predecessors. Seating areas of plush looking fabrics and door panels featured mostly monochromatic colors, highlighted with thin strips of bright trim on door panels of base models, and woodgrained trim on others that also included the steering wheel and instrument panel. With the new models also came a change in the makeup of Buick's mid-size lineup. Convertibles and traditional two- and four-door hardtop models were gone, as was the Sportwagon, once a twin to the Oldsmobile Vista-Cruiser. For 1973, all coupes and sedans were known as Colonnade Hardtops, General Motors' generic name for a sedan with frameless door glass, giving the appearance of a hardtop. The new model line consisted of the base Century and Century Luxus, replacing the Skylark and Skylark Custom respectively. Each trim level offered a two- and four-door Colonnade Hardtop and a station wagon model available in 2- or 3-seat versions. The former Skylark 350 was replaced by a "350" option package for the base Century, and the "GS" was now offered as the Gran Sport option package on Century coupes.

The remainder of the Buick lineup consisted of the full-size LeSabre, Centurion, Estate Wagon and Electra 225 models, plus the Riviera personal luxury coupe. All of these "near-luxury" cars were basically carried over from 1972 with styling changes confined to those required to accommodate the new federally-mandated bumper standards, meaning an updated grille design and headlights appearing to be mounted slightly higher on the front fender. The rear of the "boat-tailed" Riviera was slightly altered to give the bumper a less pronounced point. All other features were upgraded as necessary, for example the new Exhaust Gas Recirculation (EGR) and Air Injection Reactor (AIR) emission control systems, a radiator overflow reservoir, new windshield wiper and washer systems, and the expected upholstery and detail trim changes. The only model change was the deletion of the LeSabre Custom convertible, leaving the Centurion as the sole Buick convertible.

Apollo 2-Door Hatchback

Centurion 4-Door Hardtop
with Centurion Convertible, rear

Century 350 2-Door Colonnade Hardtop
Coupe with Century 350 4-Door
Colonnade Hardtop Sedan, rear

Century Luxus 4-Door Station Wagon

Estate Wagon

Opel 1900 2-Door and 4-Door Sedans

Century Regal 2-Door
Colonnade Hardtop Coupe

LeSabre 2-Door Hardtop

Opel GT 2-Door Coupe

Electra 225 Limited 4-Door Hardtop

Riviera 2-Door Hardtop

Opel Manta Rallye 2-Door Coupe

Model year production: 821,155, up 20.82% from 1972.

Domestic market share: 7.73% (6th place).

Base price range: $2,605 to $5,221.

Buick average base price: $3,969, up 0.16%.

Introduction date: September 21, 1972; Opel introduced September 15, 1972; Apollo introduced April 12, 1973.

Assembly plants: Baltimore, MD (B); Southgate, CA (C); Doraville, GA (D); Framingham, MA (G); Flint, MI (H); Kansas City/Leeds, MO (K); Van Nuys, CA (L); Tarrytown, NY (T); Kansas City/Fairfax, KS (X); Fremont, CA (Z). *Opel:* Bochum, Germany (2); Russelsheim, Germany (5); Antwerp, Belgium (9).

Data plate identification (VIN): Thirteen digit code read as follows: First digit indicates division (4 = Buick); second through fourth digits indicate series and body style (model number in model charts); fifth digit is engine code (see powertrain chart); sixth digit indicates model year (3 = 1973); seventh digit indicates assembly plant (see list above); remaining digits are sequential with beginning number of 100001. *Example:* 4L69H3H100001 is a 1973 Buick LeSabre 4-Door Sedan, with 350 CID, 2-bbl. V8 engine, serial number 100001, built in Flint, MI.

1973 Opels use a 13-digit code read as follows: First digit is "O" for Opel; the next three digits indicate series and body style (GT=Y07, Manta=L77, 1900 2-door=L11, 1900 4-door=L69, 1900 Wagon=L15); fifth digit, "N," indicates engine code; sixth digit indicates year (C = 1973); seventh digit indicates assembly plant (see list above). Remaining digits are sequential with beginning numbers as follows: 1900 Deluxe 2-door sedan, 764367; 1900 Deluxe 4-door sedan, 764372; 1900 Deluxe 2-door wagon, 764363; GT Sport coupe, 944586; Manta coupe, 762540; Manta Rallye coupe, 762538; Manta Luxus coupe, 769102.

Powertrains

Engine	Net HP	Engine Code	Transmission Availability[1]		Opel	Apollo	Century	LeSabre & Centurion	Electra & Estate Wagon	Riviera
116 CID (1.9L), 2-bbl., 4-cyl.	75	N	4-speed manual		S	—	—	—	—	—
				MPG:	19.8	—	—	—	—	—

Major standard equipment: *1900:* Vinyl bench front seat with foam cushions, front door pockets, fold-down rear seat, rubber floor mats, interior lights, aluminized exhaust system, exterior pinstripes, hubcaps, and 6.45 × 13 BSW tires. *GT:* Vinyl bucket seats and 165 × 13 BSW tires. *Manta:* Reclining vinyl bucket seats, center console, two-spoke steering wheel, woodgrain vinyl I/P gauge cluster appliqué, and 165 × 13 BSW tires. Rallye adds: Tachometer, console mounted gauges (L to R: ampere, clock, and oil pressure), special black paint treatment on hood and bodyside stripes, firm shocks, 3.67 rear axle ratio, and 4-spoke steel wheels. Luxus adds: Corduroy upholstery, color-keyed center console, sound deadening insulation, glove box light, and exterior identification badges.

Measurements (cont.)

	GT	1900	Manta
Cargo capacity (cu. ft.)	NA	10.8*	11.5
Fuel capacity (gals.)	NA	12.0	12.0

Station Wagon, 62.6 cu. ft.

Models Available

	Model No.	Base MSRP	Change from LY	Shipping Wt. (lbs.)	Model Year Sales	Change from LY
1900 2-Door Sedan	51	$2,483	+8.19%	2063	NA	NA
1900 4-Door Sedan	53	$2,573	+8.11%	2108	NA	NA
1900 2-Door Wagon	54	$2,709	+7.71%	2152	NA	NA
Manta 2-Door Sport Coupe	57	$2,579	+7.41%	2108	NA	NA
Manta Rallye 2-Door Sport Coupe	57R	$2,758	+7.65%	2130	8,360	-21.48%
Manta Luxus 2-Door Sport Coupe	57L	$2,769	NEW	2108	17,536	NEW
GT 2-Door Coupe	77	$3,346	+5.79%	2030	11,693	-3.01%
TOTALS	*Avg. price*	$2,745	+7.55%	*Production*	68,400*	NA

Total is estimated model year sales.

Apollo

"The difference between a small car, and a small car by Buick. Introducing Apollo. By Buick."

Nameplate year of origin: 1973.
Current bodystyle lifespan: 1973 through 1974.
Predecessor to this model: None.
Replacement for this model: Apollo (1975) and Skylark (1975 to 1979).
Percentage of division's production: 3.99%.
Corporate siblings: Chevrolet Nova, Oldsmobile Omega, and Pontiac Ventura.
Primary competition: Dodge Dart and Mercury Comet.
Notable changes: All-new model based on GM's X-body platform.
Major standard equipment: Glenbrook cloth and Madrid-grain vinyl front bench seat with foam cushions, full-floor carpeting, rear quarter/rear door armrests, deluxe steering wheel, dual speed wipers w/washers, extra sound deadening insulation, roof drip moldings, front and rear wheel opening moldings, hubcaps, and E78 × 14 BSW tires. Hatchback model adds: Fold-down rear seat.

Measurements

	Coupe & HBK	Sedan
Wheelbase	111.0"	111.0"
Length	197.9"	197.9"
Width	72.4"	72.4"
Height	52.5"	53.9"
Legroom — front	41.7"	41.7"
Legroom — rear	33.4"	35.3"
Headroom — front	38.0"	39.3"
Headroom — rear	36.9"	37.3"
Cargo capacity (cu. ft.)	13.6*	13.6
Fuel capacity (gals.)	21.0	21.0

Hatchback maximum with rear seat down, 27 cu. ft.

Models Available

	Model No.	Base MSRP	Change from LY	Shipping Wt. (lbs.)	Model Year Production	Change from LY
Apollo 2-Door Coupe	B27	$2,605	NEW	3108	14,475	NEW
Apollo 2-Door Hatchback	B17	$2,754	NEW	3210	9,868	NEW

	Model No.	Base MSRP	Change from LY	Shipping Wt. (lbs.)	Model Year Production	Change from LY
Apollo 2-Door Coupe	B27	$2,605	NEW	3108	14,475	NEW
Apollo 2-Door Hatchback	B17	$2,754	NEW	3210	9,868	NEW

Century

"A new, smaller luxury car from Buick."

Nameplate year of origin: 1936.
Current bodystyle lifespan: 1973 through 1977.
Predecessor to this model: Skylark (1968 to 1972).
Replacement for this model: Century (1978 to 1981).
Percentage of division's production: 36.35%.
Corporate siblings: Chevrolet Malibu, Oldsmobile Cutlass, and Pontiac LeMans.
Primary competition: Dodge Coronet and Mercury Montego.
Notable changes: Completely redesigned, and renamed.
Major standard equipment: Caribou-grain and Madrid-grain vinyl front bench seat, full-floor carpeting, custom steering wheel, front disc brakes, wheel covers, and G78 × 14 BSW tires. Luxus adds: Genoa cloth and Madrid-grain vinyl bench seat, luxury carpeting, bright belt line moldings, lower front fender "Luxus" badge, wheel opening moldings, and rocker panel molding. Wagons add: Oxen-grain and Madrid-grain vinyl front bench seat, and H78 × 14 BSW tires. Regal adds: Oxen-grain expanded vinyl and Madrid-grain vinyl notchback seat with center armrest.

Measurements

	Coupes	Regal	Sedans	Wagons
Wheelbase	112.0"	112.0"	116.0"	116.0"
Length	208.4"	210.7"	212.4"	216.6"
Width	78.0"	78.0"	78.0"	78.0"
Height	53.7"	53.5"	54.4"	55.5"
Legroom — front	42.5"	42.5"	42.5"	42.5"
Legroom — rear	33.7"	33.4"	38.4"	36.8"
Headroom — front	37.7"	37.5"	38.3"	38.8"
Headroom — rear	37.0"	37.4"	37.5"	39.4"
Cargo capacity (cu. ft.)	15.1	15.1	14.6	85.1
Fuel capacity (gals.)	NA	NA	NA	22.0

Models Available

	Model No.	Base MSRP	Change from LY*	Shipping Wt. (lbs.)	Model Year Production	Change from LY*
Century 2-Door Colonnade HT Coupe	D37	$3,057	+2.14%	3713	56,154	+2.14%
Century 4-Door Colonnade HT Sedan	D29	$3,057	+2.83%	3780	38,202	+2.83%
Century 4-Door Station Wagon, 2-S.	F35	$3,486	+1.22%	4156	7,760	+1.22%
Century 4-Door Station Wagon, 3-S.	F45	$3,601	NEW	4192	**	NEW
Century Luxus 2-Door Colonnade HT Coupe	H57	$3,331	+2.33%	3718	71,712	+2.33%
Century Luxus 4-Door Colonnade HT Sedan	H29	$3,326	+3.04%	3797	22,438	+3.04%
Century Luxus 4-Door Station Wagon, 2-S.	K35	$3,652	NEW	4190	10,645	NEW
Century Luxus 4-Door Station Wagon, 3-S.	K45	$3,767	NEW	4227	**	NEW
Century Regal 2-Door Colonnade HT Coupe	J57	$3,470	NEW	3743	91,557	NEW
TOTALS	*Avg. price*	$3,416	+2.77%	*Production*	298,468	+32.45%

*Comparisons made to equivalent 1972 Skylark & Sportwagon models.   **Production of 3-seat wagon models included with 2-seat models.

LeSabre

*"The full-size Buick we sell more of than any other.
Which says a lot about a new LeSabre even before you look at it."*

Nameplate year of origin: 1959 (also used on 1951 GM show car).
Current bodystyle lifespan: 1971 through 1976.
Predecessor to this model: LeSabre (1969 to 1970).
Replacement for this model: LeSabre (1977 to 1985).

Measurements

Wheelbase	124.0"
Length	224.2"
Width	79.6"

Percentage of division's production: 24.02%.
Corporate siblings: Chevrolet BelAir/Impala/Caprice, Pontiac Catalina/Bonne-
ville/Grand Ville, Oldsmobile Delta 88, and Buick Centurion.
Primary competition: Chrysler Newport and Mercury Monterey.
Notable changes: Revised front and rear styling.
Major standard equipment: Gothic cloth and Madrid-grain vinyl bench seat or
Oxen-grain and Madrid-grain vinyl bench seat, full-floor carpeting, woodgrained
vinyl trim on door panels, LH outside rear view mirror, hood-mounted three-sec-
tion rectangular "venti-port" ornaments, wheel opening moldings, rocker panel
molding, and H78 × 15 BSW tires. Custom adds: Oxen-grain and Madrid-grain vinyl bench seat with pleated vinyl door panel
insets surrounded by chrome and woodgrain trim, I/P woodgrain appliqués, custom steering wheel, wide rocker panel molding,
"Custom" interior and exterior badging, and deluxe wheel covers.

Measurements (cont.)

Height	54.4"
Legroom — front	42.6"
Legroom — rear	38.8"
Headroom — front	38.9"
Headroom — rear	38.0"
Cargo capacity (cu. ft.)	NA
Fuel capacity (gals.)	NA

Models Available

	Model No.	Base MSRP	Change from LY	Shipping Wt. (lbs.)	Model Year Production	Change from LY
LeSabre 2-Door Hardtop Coupe	L57	$4,067	+1.07%	4210	14,061	+0.43%
LeSabre 4-Door Sedan	L69	$3,998	+1.01%	4234	29,649	+0.49%
LeSabre 4-Door Hardtop Sedan	L39	$4,125	+1.13%	4259	13,413	-11.52%
LeSabre Custom 2-Door Hardtop Coupe	N57	$4,154	+1.14%	4225	41,425	+13.46%
LeSabre Custom 4-Door Sedan	N69	$4,091	+1.09%	4264	42,845	+21.39%
LeSabre Custom 4-Door Hardtop Sedan	N39	$4,217	+1.18%	4284	55,879	+9.99%
TOTALS		Avg. price $4,109	+0.30%		Production 197,272	+7.62%

Centurion

*"Whether it's a family car or a very personal road car,
depends on whether your family is with you or not."*

Nameplate year of origin: 1971 (taken from 1956 Buick show car).
Current bodystyle lifespan: 1971 through 1976.
Predecessor to this model: Wildcat (1969 to 1970).
Replacement for this model: LeSabre Luxus (1974).
Percentage of division's production: 5.48%.
Corporate siblings: Chevrolet BelAir/Impala/Caprice, Pontiac Catalina/Bonneville/
Grand Ville, Oldsmobile Delta 88, and Buick Centurion.
Primary competition: Chrysler Newport Custom and Mercury Monterey Custom.
Notable changes: Revised front and rear styling.
Major standard equipment: Oxen-grain expanded vinyl and Madrid-grain vinyl
notchback seat with center fold-down armrest, full-floor carpeting, custom steering
wheel, LH rear view mirror, deluxe wheel covers, and H78 × 15 BSW tires. Convertible adds: Oxen-grain expanded vinyl and Madrid-grain vinyl 60/40 notchback
seat with center fold-down armrest, and inward-folding power-operated vinyl convertible top.

Measurements

Wheelbase	124.0"
Length	224.2"
Width	79.6"
Height	53.8"
Legroom — front	42.6"
Legroom — rear	38.8"
Headroom — front	38.4"
Headroom — rear	37.4"
Cargo capacity (cu. ft.)	NA
Fuel capacity (gals.)	NA

Models Available

	Model No.	Base MSRP	Change from LY	Shipping Wt. (lbs.)	Model Year Production	Change from LY
Centurion 2-Door Hardtop Coupe	P57	$4,336	-5.31%	4260	16,883	+19.00%
Centurion 2-Door Convertible	P67	$4,534	-1.78%	4316	5,739	+139.52%
Centurion 4-Door Hardtop Sedan	P39	$4,390	-2.62%	4390	22,354	+14.16%
TOTALS		Avg. price $4,420	-3.23%		Production 44,976	+24.36%

Estate Wagon

"The luxury car that's also a station wagon."

Nameplate year of origin: 1940 (as designation for station wagons).
Current bodystyle lifespan: 1971 through 1976.
Predecessor to this model: Estate Wagon (1970).
Replacement for this model: Estate Wagon (1977 to 1990).
Percentage of division's production: 4.36%.
Corporate siblings: Chevrolet BelAir/Impala/Caprice, Pontiac Catalina Safari/Grand Safari, and Oldsmobile Custom Cruiser.
Primary competition: Chrysler Town & Country and Mercury Colony Park.
Notable changes: Revised front and rear styling.
Major standard equipment: Oxen-grain and Madrid-grain vinyl bench seat, full-floor carpeting, Glide-Away tailgate, power tailgate window, LH and RH rear view mirrors, hood-mounted 4-section rectangular "venti-port" ornaments, deluxe wheel covers, and L78 × 15 BSW tires.

Measurements

Wheelbase	127.0"
Length	229.5"
Width	79.6"
Height	57.3"
Legroom — front	42.6"
Legroom — rear	39.9"
Headroom — front	39.6"
Headroom — rear	39.3"
Cargo capacity (cu. ft.)	106.0
Fuel capacity (gals.)	NA

Models Available

	Model No.	Base MSRP	Change from LY	Shipping Wt. (lbs.)	Model Year Production	Change from LY
Estate Wagon 4-Door, 2-S. Wagon	R35	$4,645	+1.22%	4952	12,282	+20.71%
Estate Wagon 4-Door, 3-S. Wagon	R45	$4,790	+1.31%	5021	23,513	+25.12%
TOTALS		Avg. price $4,718	+1.27%		Production 35,795	+23.57%

Electra 225

"When luxury comes to you as naturally as it does to the ultimate Buick, you don't have to shout it."

Nameplate year of origin: 1959.
Current bodystyle lifespan: 1971 through 1976.
Predecessor to this model: Electra (1969 to 1970).
Replacement for this model: Electra 225 (1977 to 1984).
Percentage of division's production: 21.65%.
Corporate siblings: Cadillac Calais, Cadillac deVille, and Oldsmobile Ninety-Eight.
Primary competition: Chrysler New Yorker and Mercury Marquis Brougham.
Notable changes: Revised front and rear styling.
Major standard equipment: Oxen-grain and Madrid-grain vinyl or Grande cloth and Madrid-grain vinyl bench seat, full-floor luxury carpeting, simulated woodgrain appliqués on door panels and instrument panel, electric clock, custom steering wheel, custom safety belts, remote-control LH rear view mirror, hood-mounted 4-section rectangular "venti-port" ornaments, wheel opening moldings, full-length rocker panel molding, rear fender skirts, super deluxe wheel covers, and J78 × 15 BSW tires. Custom adds: Oxen-grain expanded vinyl and Madrid-grain vinyl notchback seat with fold-down center armrest or Bravo cloth and Madrid-grain vinyl bench seat, door pull straps, and carpeted lower door panels.

Measurements

Wheelbase	127.0"
Length	229.8"
Width	79.3"
Height	54.9"
Legroom — front	42.6"
Legroom — rear	41.3"
Headroom — front	39.3"
Headroom — rear	38.2"
Cargo capacity (cu. ft.)	NA
Fuel capacity (gals.)	NA

Models Available

	Model No.	Base MSRP	Change from LY	Shipping Wt. (lbs.)	Model Year Production	Change from LY
Electra 225 2-Door Hardtop Coupe	T37	$4,815	+0.69%	4488	9,224	-7.40%
Electra 225 4-Door Hardtop Sedan	T39	$4,928	+0.78%	4581	17,189	-11.55%

	Model No.	Base MSRP	Change from LY	Shipping Wt. (lbs.)	Model Year Production	Change from LY
Electra 225 Custom 2-Dr. Hdtp. Cpe.	V37	$4,993	+0.83%	4505	44,328	+16.73%
Electra 225 Custom 4-Dr. Hdtp. Sdn.	V39	$5,105	+0.89%	4603	107,031	+2.17%
TOTALS		Avg. price $4,960	+0.80%		Production 177,772	+3.28%

Riviera

*"Nobody's yet been able to copy it.
Maybe because we didn't copy it in the first place."*

Nameplate year of origin: 1963 (1949 as designation for hardtop models).
Current bodystyle lifespan: 1971 through 1976.
Predecessor to this model: Riviera (1966 to 1970).
Replacement for this model: Riviera (1977 to 1978).
Percentage of division's production: 4.15%.
Corporate siblings: Cadillac Eldorado and Oldsmobile Toronado.
Primary competition: Ford Thunderbird.
Notable changes: Revised front and rear styling.
Major standard equipment: Newport knit vinyl and Madrid-grain vinyl 40/40 seats, full-floor carpeting, simulated woodgrain appliqué on door panels and I/P, tilt steering wheel, LH rear view mirror, deluxe wheel covers, and H78 × 15 BSW tires.

Measurements

Wheelbase	122.0"
Length	223.4"
Width	79.9"
Height	54.0"
Legroom — front	42.5"
Legroom — rear	35.4"
Headroom — front	38.2"
Headroom — rear	37.0"
Cargo capacity (cu. ft.)	NA
Fuel capacity (gals.)	NA

Models Available

	Model No.	Base MSRP	Change from LY	Shipping Wt. (lbs.)	Model Year Production	Change from LY
Riviera 2-Door Hardtop	Y87	$5,221	+1.40%	4486	34,084	+1.04%
TOTALS		Avg. price $5,221	+1.40%		Production 34,084	+1.04%

CADILLAC

"The special world of Cadillac 1973 — the legend and the lifestyle."

Since all Cadillac models had been restyled in 1971, the new model year brought few changes other than those required to meet the federally mandated bumper and safety changes. All models adopted a bumper that ran straight across the entire front end bisecting the grille, as opposed to the style used on 1972 models that dropped down in the center to the bottom of the grille. The grille of the personal luxury Eldorado series carried a new egg-crate design with large openings three rows high and 12 columns across above the bumper, and two rows high and 10 columns across within the lower portion of the bumper, capped by tall bumper guards. All other models used an egg-crate grille design similar to the Eldorado, but with 22 columns across giving

a more classic look to the front end. All models except the Eldorado continued the use of dual headlamps separated by oversized rectangular turn signal/parking lamps.

Other than the deletion of the vertical quarter panel windsplit molding on the Eldorado, there was not a lot to differentiate the new models from the 1972 Cadillacs in profile. The Fleetwood Sixty-Special Brougham and Fleetwood Seventy-Five models continued to share the frameless door window and single center post design, which was now being incorporated on all of the new-for-'73 GM intermediate four-doors. Inside, new "soft pillow" door panels featured a heavily padded upper portion, making a comfy armrest for those who liked to drive with their elbow on the window ledge. Also new was a crushed velour upholstery named "Medici," available on any Fleetwood model. One of the unique Cadillac accessories this year was the Deluxe robe and pillow package. Available for $85 with any Cadillac, it featured a robe and occasional pillow fashioned from Medici crushed velour and was color-coordinated with the interior color of the car. Truly the lap of luxury.

Finally, Cadillac marked two landmarks for the 1973 model year. For the first time since 1931, Cadillac was selected as the official pace car of the 57th annual Indianapolis 500

race, held on May 28. An Eldorado convertible in Cotillion white with a red leather interior was chosen to pace the race, with no replica pace car offered. It also happened to be only the second time in the history of the race that the pace car was front-wheel-drive, with the first time being in 1930 when a Cord paced the field. Then on June 27 the second landmark was reached when, after 70 years in business, the five millionth Cadillac was built. The car designated as the milestone car was a blue Sedan deVille.

Calais 2-Door Hardtop

Eldorado 2-Door Convertible

Eldorado 2-Door Hardtop

Fleetwood 60 Special Brougham 4-Door Sedan

Fleetwood 75 Limousine

deVille instrument panel

Sedan deVille 4-Door Hardtop

Model year production: 302,554, up 14.01% from 1972.
Domestic market share: 3.02% (10th place).
Base price range: $5,866 to $12,080.
Cadillac average base price: $7,945, up 1.70%.
Introduction date: September 21, 1972.
Assembly plants: Linden, NJ (E); and Detroit, MI (Q). *Note:* Both plants built the deVille, but all other series were built in Detroit.
Data plate identification (VIN): Thirteen digit code read as follows: First digit indicates division (6 = Cadillac); second

through fourth digits indicate series and body style (model number in model charts); fifth digit is engine code (see powertrain chart); sixth digit indicates model year (3 = 1973); seventh digit indicates assembly plant (see list above); remaining digits are sequential with beginning number of 100001 (Calais, 60 Special Brougham, Fleetwoods and Detroit-built deVilles), 500001 (Linden-built deVilles) or 400001 (Eldorado). *Example:* 6D49R3Q100001 is a 1973 Cadillac Sedan deVille 4-Door Hardtop, with 472 CID, 4-bbl. V8 engine, serial number 100001, built in Detroit, MI.

Powertrains

Engine	Net HP	Engine Code	Transmission Availability[1]		Calais & deVille	Fleetwood Brougham	Fleetwood Seventy-Five	Eldorado
472 CID (7.8L), 4-bbl., V8	205	R	3-speed Turbo Hydra-matic		S	S	S	—
				MPG:	8.9	8.9	8.7	—
500 CID (8.2L), 4-bbl., V8	210	S	3-speed Turbo Hydra-matic		—	—	—	S
				MPG:	—	—	—	10.4

Major Options

	Calais	deVille	Eldorado	Fleetwood Brougham	Fleetwood Seventy-Five
Automatic climate control	$523	$523	$523	$523	S
Electric rear window defogger	$62	$62	$62	$62	S
Tilt and telescope steering wheel	$92	$92	$92	$92	$92
Cruise control	$92	$92	$92	$92	$92
Twilight Sentinel	$40	$40	$40	$40	S
Soft Ray tinted glass	$57	$57	$57	$57	$57
Leather upholstery[1]	—	$169	$179	$169	—
Power front seat, 2-way	$26	S	S	S[2]	S
Power front seat, 6-way bench	$115	$89	$89	—	—
Power front seat, 6-way dual comfort, driver/passenger	—	$89/ $115	$89/ $115	$89/ $115	—
Lighted vanity mirror	$43	$43	$43	$43	$43
Power door locks	$69	$69	$69	$69	$115
AM/FM stereo, signal seeking[3]	$340	$340	$340	$340	$340
AM/FM stereo w/8-track tape[3]	$426	$426	$426	$426	$426
Remote control trunk release/lock	$56	$56	$56	$56	$56
Padded vinyl top	—	$152	$157	S	$741
Electric sunroof[4]	—	$610	$610	$610	—
Lamp monitor system	$48	$48	$48	$48	$48
Power steering	S	S	S	S	S
Power brakes, w/front disc	S	S	S	S	S
Track Master anti-skid control	$205	$205	$205	$205	$205
Automatic level control	$78	$78	$78	$78	$78

Popular Option Groups & Packages

	Calais	deVille	Eldorado	Fleetwood Brougham	Fleetwood Seventy-Five
Deluxe trim package	—	—	—	$	—
Brougham d'Elegance package	—	—	—	$750	—
Cabriolet package, coupe only	—	—	$385	—	—

—= Not Available; S = Standard equipment. [1]Standard on Eldorado convertible. Available on Calais and Seventy-Five by special order only. [2]Driver side only. [3]$20 less w/windshield antenna. [4]Requires vinyl top.

Paint Colors

	Code		Code		Code
Cotillion White	11	Sage metallic	44	Harvest Yellow	81
Georgian Silver metallic	13	Forest Green metallic	49	Shadow Taupe Firemist metallic*	90
Park Avenue Gray metallic	18	Renaissance Gold metallic	54	St. Tropez Blue Firemist metallic*	92
Sable Black	19	Laredo Tan metallic	63	Phoenix Gold Firemist metallic*	94
Antigua Blue metallic	24	Mirage Taupe metallic	64	Oceanic Teal Firemist metallic*	95
Diplomat Blue metallic	29	Burnt Sienna metallic	68	Viridian Green Firemist metallic*	96
Garganey Teal metallic	39	Dynasty Red	72	Saturn Bronze Firemist metallic*	99

*Firemist paint available for $128 extra.

Calais

"An extraordinary investment, any way you look at it."

Nameplate year of origin: 1965.
Current bodystyle lifespan: 1971 through 1976.
Predecessor to this model: Calais (1969 to 1970).
Replacement for this model: None.
Percentage of division's production: 2.64%.
Corporate siblings: Buick Electra 225, Cadillac deVille, and Oldsmobile 98.

Measurements

Wheelbase	130.0"
Length	228.5"
Width	79.8"
Height	55.5"

Primary competition: Chrysler New Yorker Brougham and Oldsmobile 98 Regency.
Notable changes: Revised front-end styling, and minor trim and detail changes.
Major standard equipment: Mayfair cloth w/vinyl bolsters and front seat center armrest, door pull assist straps, electric clock, cigar lighter (2 in front), power windows, LH remote-control rear view mirror, front cornering lights, rear wheel fender skirts, wheel opening moldings, full wheel covers, and L78 × 15 BSW tires.

Measurements (cont.)

Legroom — front	42.0"
Legroom — rear	NA
Headroom — front	39.2"
Headroom — rear	38.2"
Cargo capacity (cu. ft.)	19.3
Fuel capacity (gals.)	27.0

Models Available

	Model No.	Base MSRP	Change from LY	Shipping Wt. (lbs.)	Model Year Production	Change from LY
Calais 2-Door Hardtop	C47	$5,886	+1.65%	4900	4,202	+7.74%
Calais 4-Door Hardtop	C49	$6,038	+1.68%	4953	3,798	-1.99%
TOTALS		Avg. price $5,952	+1.67%		Production 8,000	+2.89%

deVille

"The luxury cars enjoyed by more motorists than any others."

Nameplate year of origin: 1959 (series); 1949 (as Hardtop designation).
Current bodystyle lifespan: 1971 through 1976.
Predecessor to this model: deVille (1969 to 1970).
Replacement for this model: deVille (1977 to 1984).
Percentage of division's production: 71.47%.
Corporate siblings: Buick Electra 225, Cadillac Calais, and Oldsmobile 98.
Primary competition: Chrysler Imperial and Lincoln Continental.
Notable changes: Revised front-end styling and trim and detail changes.
Major standard equipment: Medallion cloth w/vinyl bolsters and front seat center armrest, 2-way power front seat adjuster, cut-pile carpeting, door pull assist straps, courtesy lights, electric clock, cigar lighters (2 front & 2 rear), power windows, LH remote-control rear view mirror, front cornering lights, rear wheel fender skirts, wheel opening moldings, rocker panel moldings, full wheel covers, and L78 × 15 BSW tires.

Measurements

Wheelbase	130.0"
Length	228.5"
Width	79.8"
Height	55.5"
Legroom — front	42.0"
Legroom — rear	NA
Headroom — front	39.2"
Headroom — rear	38.2"
Cargo capacity (cu. ft.)	19.3
Fuel capacity (gals.)	27.0

Models Available

	Model No.	Base MSRP	Change from LY	Shipping Wt. (lbs.)	Model Year Production	Change from LY
Coupe deVille 2-Door Hardtop	D47	$6,268	+1.62%	4925	112,849	+18.44%
Sedan deVille 4-Door Hardtop	D49	$6,500	+1.72%	4985	103,394	+3.88%
TOTALS		Avg. price $6,384	+1.67%		Production 216,243	+11.00%

Eldorado

"Our most elegant personal cars.
Including the only luxury convertible built in America."

Nameplate year of origin: 1953.
Current bodystyle lifespan: 1971 through 1978.
Predecessor to this model: Fleetwood Eldorado (1967 to 1970).
Replacement for this model: Eldorado (1979 to 1985).
Percentage of division's production: 17.01%.

Measurements

Wheelbase	126.3"
Length	222.0"
Width	79.8"

Corporate siblings: Buick Riviera and Oldsmobile Toronado.
Primary competition: Lincoln Continental Mark IV.
Notable changes: Revised front and rear end styling and minor trim and detail changes.
Major standard equipment: Manchester fabric w/vinyl bolsters front bench seat w/center armrest (hardtop), leather front bench seat w/center armrest (convertible), 2-way power front seat adjuster, cut-pile carpeting, door pull assist straps, courtesy lights, electric clock, cigar lighters (2 front & 2 rear), power windows, LH remote-control rear view mirror, front cornering lights, rear wheel fender skirts, wheel opening moldings, rocker panel moldings, full wheel covers, and L78 × 15 BSW tires.

Measurements (cont.)

Height	NA
Legroom — front	43.0"
Legroom — rear	NA
Headroom — front	38.1"
Headroom — rear	37.1"
Cargo capacity (cu. ft.)	NA
Fuel capacity (gals.)	27.0

Models Available

	Model No.	Base MSRP	Change from LY	Shipping Wt. (lbs.)	Model Year Production	Change from LY
Eldorado 2-Door Hardtop	L47	$7,360	+1.80%	4880	42,136	+31.27%
Eldorado 2-Door Convertible	L67	$7,681	+1.79%	4966	9,315	+16.80%
TOTALS		Avg. price $7,521	+1.79%		Production 51,451	+28.39%

Fleetwood Sixty-Special Brougham

"Special even in the special world of Cadillac."

Nameplate year of origin: 1938.
Current bodystyle lifespan: 1971 through 1976.
Predecessor to this model: Fleetwood Sixty-Special (1969 to 1970).
Replacement for this model: Fleetwood Brougham (1977 to 1984).
Percentage of division's sales volume: 8.20%.
Corporate siblings: None.
Primary competition: None.
Notable changes: Revised front-end styling and trim and detail changes.
Major standard equipment: Magi matelasse* or Sierra grain leather dual comfort front seat, driver's side 2-way power front seat adjuster, front and rear seat fold-down center armrests, cut-pile carpeting, rear seat carpeted foot rests, door pull assist straps, front passenger reading light, courtesy lights, electric clock, cigar lighters (2 front & 2 rear), power windows, LH remote-control rear view mirror, padded vinyl roof, front cornering lights, rear wheel fender skirts, wheel opening moldings, rocker panel moldings w/upper ridge, full wheel covers, and L78 × 15 BSW tires.

*Matelasse is a French word meaning quilted, padded or cushioned. Usually refers to hand-quilted fabrics.

Measurements

Wheelbase	133.0"
Length	231.5"
Width	79.8"
Height	55.5"
Legroom — front	NA
Legroom — rear	NA
Headroom — front	NA
Headroom — rear	NA
Cargo capacity (cu. ft.)	19.3
Fuel capacity (gals.)	27.0

Models Available

	Model No.	Base MSRP	Change from LY	Shipping Wt. (lbs.)	Model Year Production	Change from LY
Fltwd. Sixty-Special Brougham 4-Dr. Sedan	B69	$7,765	+1.68%	5102	24,800	+19.52%
TOTALS		Avg. price $7,765	+1.68%		Production 24,800	+19.52%

Fleetwood Seventy-Five

"Our ultimate is yours in the Fleetwood Seventy-Five."

Nameplate year of origin: 1927 (models using Fleetwood bodies); 1935 (75 series).
Current bodystyle lifespan: 1971 through 1976.
Predecessor to this model: Fleetwood Seventy-Five (1969 to 1970).
Replacement for this model: Fleetwood Limousine (1977 to 1984).

Measurements

Wheelbase	151.5"
Length	250.0"

Percentage of division's sales volume: 0.68%.
Corporate siblings: None.
Primary competition: None.
Notable changes: Revised front-end styling and trim and detail changes.
Major standard equipment: Potomac grey cord fabric upholstery, 2-way power front seat adjuster, front and back seat fold-down center armrests, cut-pile carpeting, full-width folding seats (rearward facing for three additional passengers), rear seat carpeted foot rests, door pull assist straps, dual automatic climate control system (front and rear), courtesy lights, electric clock, cigar lighters (2 front & 4 rear), passenger control panel (controls power windows, reading lights, rear automatic climate control system, and the glass partition in the Limousine), automatic level control, LH and RH remote-control rear view mirror, front cornering lights, rear wheel fender skirts, wheel opening moldings, full-length rocker panel moldings, full wheel covers, and L78 × 15 BSW tires.

Measurements (cont.)

Width	80.0"
Height	NA
Legroom — front	NA
Legroom — rear	NA
Headroom — front	NA
Headroom — rear	NA
Cargo capacity (cu. ft.)	NA
Fuel capacity (gals.)	27.0

Models Available

	Model No.	Base MSRP	Change from LY	Shipping Wt. (lbs.)	Model Year Production	Change from LY
Fltwd. Seventy-Five 4-Door Sedan, 9-p.	F23	$11,948	+1.70%	5620	1,017	+2.21%
Fltwd. Seventy-Five 4-Door Limousine	F33	$12,080	+1.68%	5742	1,043	+8.65%
TOTALS		*Avg. price* $12,014	+1.69%	*Production*	2,060	+5.37%

CHEVROLET

"Building a better way to see the U.S.A."

New mid-size models, which were originally supposed to be introduced for 1972, were finally ready for their debut as 1973 models, and almost every car in the Chevrolet lineup had at least a few styling changes, some just to meet the new front bumper standards. Powertrain options did not change greatly, but there was a mid-year change with the slow-selling Bel Air sedan having its standard six-cylinder engine and three-speed manual transmission discontinued, and replaced by a standard V8 and automatic transmission, marking the first time ever that all full-size Chevrolets had a V8 engine standard. The compact Vega's steel head gaskets on an aluminum block were beginning to cause warranty issues, as many engines had to be replaced under the 12-month, 12,000-mile warranty. Despite the ongoing problems, sales of the Vega would continue to rise, and the Vega continued to win awards, most recently with the Vega GT being named *Motor Trend* magazine's Economy Car of the Year for 1973. Chevrolet would end the year further advancing its lead over Ford and retaining its number one position.

The all-new Chevelle line featured GM's colonnade hardtop styling on all models with coupes having a semi-fastback roofline and large triangular fixed rear quarter win-

dows being their main identifying feature in profile. For sedans, a six-window style was adopted with a small triangular fixed rear quarter window; this design replaced both the traditional four-door sedan and four-door hardtops of the past. All models including the station wagon had a fixed B-pillar post, but all door glass was frameless like a hardtop, thereby giving them the "Colonnade Hardtop" identification. The Malibu convertible was no longer in the lineup, but the SS option continued to be available on the Malibu coupe and, for one year only, on the Malibu station wagon. A total of 28,647 SS-equipped cars were sold, with no breakdown between coupe and wagon available, though it is doubtful that many SS wagons were sold. Also new, there were now three Chevelle trim levels, the base Chevelle Deluxe, the mid-level Malibu, and the new top-of-the-line "luxury" Laguna.

The Deluxe and Malibu Chevelle models shared a similar front-end design with a full-width horizontal crosshatch grille design twenty-two columns across and eight rows high through the main portion, then notching down under the single headlights to a strip seven columns wide and two rows high. All of this was topped by a chrome trim piece. Headlights were set within the end of a slightly tunneled front header panel, which created a valley between the raised center section of the hood and the raised area above the headlights. All of the lines gradually leveled out as they ran back towards the rear edge. A slightly V-shaped front bumper with parking and turn signal lights in each end below the headlights sat below the grille, which had a body-color filler pan of flexible plastic placed between the bumper and the grille. A chrome Chevy bowtie emblem was placed in the center of the grille, and the Chevelle name in capital block letters was on the lower right side of the grille.

A resilient urethane front end highlighted the unique Laguna front-end appearance. Using the single headlights of other Chevelle models, the body-color front header panel encompassed the grille and included the front bumper, which also had black rubber impact strips. The grille was rectangular and outlined in chrome, with round corners, and carrying an intricate egg-crate pattern divided horizontally by two chrome bars into three sections. At each end of the grille was a round parking and turn signal light. The Laguna was intended to be the "luxury" version of the Chevelle, but mostly due to the front-end design, it immediately became the "sporty" version of the mid-size Chevy line in 1974.

Bodysides of all the new Chevelle models were slightly rounded and carried three bodyside feature lines. An upper line at the front began where the small portion of the grille ended on the front fender, following the front fender edge up and then turning backwards creating a ridge along the front fender, with the line trailing off into the front door, and ending just past the mid-point. From the rear end, on coupes and sedans a line began off the top edge of the rear quarter panel running forward to a point near the front corner of the rear side quarter window. Wheelhouse openings were flared on all models, with a faintly visible mid-level feature line beginning near the top of the front wheel housing and running straight to the back, ending where it met the slightly pointed rear panel. The body colored rear panel held traditional dual round taillamps now set above the bumper, rather than within the bumper as previously seen. On the Malibu, the taillights had a chrome trim ring. Station wagons had a new hatchback style liftgate with a fixed rear window that was nearly full-width across the back; therefore half-moon shaped taillights were used in the rear bumper set directly below the liftgate opening.

Inside, the new Chevelle followed the pattern set by the new full-sized Chevrolets in 1971. This included the use of more plastic in areas such as on lower door panels, the instrument panel, and gauge cluster. Door panels were slightly convex, rather than flat, providing more hip room for passengers, and creating the illusion of a larger passenger compartment. Upholstery and trim materials were not greatly changed, but the base Chevelle Deluxe looked spartan compared to the Laguna, mostly due to materials, patterns and stitching used. The instrument panel used a driver's side

"cockpit" design, with all controls contained within. The speedometer was a horizontal style, with warning lights replacing most gauges, except the fuel gauge, which was placed to the left side of the panel along with a horizontal rectangular air vent and wiper and light controls. On the right from top to bottom were an optional clock, ventilation controls, and optional radio. The passenger side of the dash held two vertical rectangular vents near the center of the car, and one vertical rectangular vent at the far right end.

Chevy's other newly redesigned mid-size car was the Monte Carlo. The new Monte Carlo was part of General Motors' A-body specialty platform, shared with the equally new Pontiac Grand Prix. The specialty part was that the Monte Carlos were built on the A-body four-door chassis with a 116-inch wheelbase, as they had been since their 1970 introduction. The Monte Carlo used a unique roofline with rectangular rear quarter windows, or opera windows as they came to be known, and a rear window design that appeared to be V-shaped, but more upright than the "fastback" look of the Chevelle coupes. Inside, the Monte Carlo shared basic design elements with the Chevelle, but with a sportier and more luxurious appearance. Gauges within the instrument cluster were all round, including the speedometer, fuel gauge and clock. Seat and door panels seemed to be more heavily padded, with nicer looking fabrics and vinyls. A unique feature that was also available on Chevelle coupes was the new swing-out "Strato" bucket seats that would swivel up to ninety degrees. While Chrysler had offered this feature fourteen years earlier, Chevrolet's introduction of the swiveling bucket seat brought the feature to mainstream buyers. It was advertised as making easy entry or exit for front seat driver and passengers, but also greatly improving rear seat accessibility. Power for the Monte Carlo continued to come from a standard 350 CID V8 engine or optional 454 CID V8 engine, but the 400 CID V8 was no longer offered.

Styling of the new Monte Carlo raised the bar for its competition, both within General Motors and outside of the company. The bodyside "swoops," an identifying feature of the Monte Carlo, were more exaggerated and curved on the new cars, in comparison to the square and formal lines of the first generation Monte Carlo. The front line began on the front fender just above the lower body "tuck under" line, which ran the full length of the car between the top corners of the bumpers. The line angled forward from its start point as it moved upwards, with a slight bulge in the sheetmetal enlarging as it moved up. Near the top of the fender, it turned to follow the top edge of the front fender to a point just past the front wheel opening where it then started to flow downward, disappearing just past the center point of the door. A second matching line began in front of the rear wheel opening and ended just above the top corner of the rear bumper. This basic bodyside design would be a Monte Carlo signature feature for the next fifteen years, although in less exaggerated form as it went through two redesigns. At the front end, single round headlamps were set in the end of a tunnel design that ran into the hood, narrowing and flattening out as it continued towards the cowl. An intricate egg-crate grille pattern was set low in the front header panel with chrome trim surrounding all but the bottom edge. The front fender ends were tall and pointed, and held a two-section parking/turn signal light, which wrapped around the end. The fender ends protruded forward to about the same plane as the slight "V" point of the grille, and the front bumper conformed to the overall shape of the front end. Seven horizontal trim bars crossed the taillight lenses that were inset in the rear end panel with a chrome surround, and a chrome trim piece connected the two, running along the lower edge of the deck lid. The full-width rear bumper held a center-mounted license plate and backup lights to each side. The new Monte Carlo was well-received by the press, and *Motor Trend* magazine named the Monte Carlo Landau its 1973 "Car of the Year" winner, for its styling and for its emphasis on European-style ride and handling qualities.

Nova was the third Chevrolet line to have a major makeover for 1973. While still based on the 111-inch wheelbase chassis that had been used since 1968, it received new front end and rear quarter styling and many updates to the interior design, while most other features, such as front fenders, engines and suspensions remained unchanged. At the front end was an egg-crate grille, five rows high and eighteen columns across, set between single round headlights, all of which was surrounded by chrome trim. Large rectangular parking/turn signal lights were set in the ends of the grille next to the headlights. Vent windows were removed from the front doors, and a new hatchback body style was introduced. Four-door models still had a rear quarter window, but as with the coupes, rounder corners were used. It was the new hatchback model that necessitated redesigned rear quarter panels. Still having a slight fastback appearance for the coupe and hatchback, the rear end had more rounded edges, and new dual rectangular taillights were set into the panel between the hatch or decklid opening and the bumper. On the bodyside, the rear quarter panels had a new feature line that began near the bottom corner of the rear quarter window and ran back to the top end of the quarter panel. A new Custom series offered nicer interior trim and a few more exterior trim pieces.

The Camaro line added a new Type LT model to give the Camaro a broader appeal as muscle cars were beginning to fade, and consumers began looking for a more luxurious ride, providing more luxury features in much the same vein as its primary competitor, the Mustang Grande. All models received a new full-width blade-style bumper, with stronger supports to meet the new front bumper standards. A new horizontal crosshatch grille pattern was eight columns across and six rows high, with the fourth row down being behind the bumper. Horizontal parking and turn signal lights were mounted below the bumper, beneath the headlights. A completely different front-end appearance was created when the Rally Sport option was ordered. A horizontal crosshatch grille, twelve columns across and ten rows high, was split in the center by a thin vertical space, and the entire grille was recessed into a chrome lined housing, which was inset into a body colored resilient frame with impact-absorbing capabilities. The resilient frame eliminated the requirement for a full-width bumper, so "bumperettes" were used on each side of the grill, directly under the headlights and wrapped slightly around the front fender end. Parking lights were round units and moved to the space between the headlight and grille. Most other styling features inside and out continued as in prior years, and while the Z28 option package continued to be available, with 11,574 sold, the SS package was dropped.

For the 1973 Vega, more than 300 changes and improvements were made, but most were strictly internal. The changes included new colors inside and out, new interior trims, nameplates being changed from "Chevrolet Vega 2300" to "Vega by Chevrolet" and many similar changes. To meet the new front bumper requirements, the chrome V-shaped front bumper was extended several inches to accommodate the new supports and brackets behind it, which required a steel, body colored filler panel between the grille and bumper. Full wheel covers first used on the 1964 Corvair and Chevy II were reissued for the Vega. Major mechanical changes included new U.S.-built manual transmissions. (Opel and GM of Europe formerly supplied the manual transmissions.) After the start of the model year, the two-speed Powerglide automatic was dropped as an option, and the Turbo Hydra-matic became the sole automatic transmission option. The two-door sedan was officially renamed "Notchback," and an LX option package was introduced exclusively for it that included a vinyl top and custom interior and exterior trim. Also new was an Estate option package for the Kammback Wagon, which included woodgrained exterior trim, an Estate tailgate emblem, wheel trim rings, and custom interior trim. A unique "Hutch" option available for the Hatchback added a tentlike fabric cover that fit over the open hatchback and attached to the rear bumper, turning the rear of the Vega into sleeping quarters for camping. The same idea was later offered in the larger Nova Hatchback. On May 20, 1973, the millionth Vega was produced, and to celebrate the achievement a limited edition "Millionth Vega" option, code ZM5, was offered for $497 on Vega GT hatchbacks, with one per dealer produced between May and August 1973, or approximately 6,100 units total. See Appendix IV for option details.

Full-sized Chevrolet models gained a new front-end appearance that included new grilles and full bumpers to meet the new requirements. Impala and Bel Air models shared a grid pattern grille with eight main sections across, divided into three rows and set between dual headlights mounted at each end. Within each section of the chromed grille were three by three argent colored inserts. The upscale Caprice line used a Cadillac-style vertical crosshatch grille being three rows high and twenty-eight columns wide between the dual headlights, and a similar design carried into the headlight surrounds, all of which was chrome lined. Officially, the Caprice was renamed Caprice Classic, and the top-line series added a convertible model, which moved up from the popular Impala series. The Biscayne series was dropped for the new year, making the Bel Air the entry-level full-size car. The Bel Air sedan was the only full-size Chevrolet that was

standard with a six-cylinder engine and a three-speed manual transmission; at midyear it would move to standard V8 power and automatic transmission.

Finally, the Corvette entered 1973 with a significant front end styling change for the five-year-old design. To meet the new federal bumper standards, the blade-style front bumper was removed, and a new body color urethane front end was added, with a new die-cast aluminum grille insert. The grille had five horizontal openings across, divided into three sections, with the parking and turn signal lights mounted within the outer ends of the two outermost sections. Also added were a new domed air induction hood, standard radial tires, and upgraded suspension components.

Camaro Type LT 2-Door Coupe

Caprice Classic 4-Door Hardtop Sport Sedan

Chevelle Laguna 2-Door interior
with Swing-Out Strato-Bucket seats

Chevelle Malibu 4-Door Station Wagon
with SS package

Camaro Type LT 2-Door Coupe
with Rally Sport option

Chevelle Laguna 2-Door
Colonnade Hardtop Coupe

Chevelle Malibu 2-Door Colonnade
Hardtop Coupe with SS package

Corvette Stingray 2-Door Convertible

Caprice Classic 2-Door Convertible

Chevelle Laguna 4-Door, 3-Seat Station Wagon

Chevelle Malibu 4-Door
Colonnade Hardtop Sedan

Impala Custom Coupe 2-Door Hardtop

Impala 4-Door Station Wagon with Bel Air
4-Door Station Wagon, rear

Nova 4-Door Sedan

Monte Carlo 2-Door Hardtop Coupe

Nova Custom 2-Door Hatchback Coupe

Monte Carlo S 2-Door Hardtop Coupe

Vega 2-Door Hatchback Coupe

Vega 2-Door Kammback Wagon

Model year production: 2,579,503, up 10.63% from 1972.
Domestic market share: 24.27% (1st place).
Base price range: $2,087 to $5,635.
Chevrolet average base price: $3,445, down 0.48%.
Introduction date: September 21, 1972.
Assembly plants: Lakewood, GA (A); Baltimore, MD (B); Southgate, CA (C); Doraville, GA (D); Framingham, MA (G); Janesville, WI (J); Kansas City/Leeds, MO (K); Van Nuys, CA (L); Norwood, OH (N); Arlington, TX (R); St. Louis, MO (S); Tarrytown, NY (T); Lordstown, OH (U); Willow Run, MI (W); Wilmington, DE (Y); Fremont, CA (Z); Oshawa, Ontario, Canada (1); and Ste. Therese, Quebec, Canada (2).

Data plate identification (VIN): Thirteen digit code read as follows: First digit indicates division (1 = Chevrolet); second through fourth digits indicate series and body style (model number in model charts); fifth digit is engine code (see powertrain chart); sixth digit indicates model year (3 = 1973); seventh digit indicates assembly plant (see list above); remaining digits are sequential with beginning number of 100001, except Chevelle, Monte Carlo and Corvette which start at 400001. *Example:* 1S87H3N100001 is a 1973 Chevrolet Camaro Type LT 2-Door Sport Coupe, with 350 CID, 2-bbl. V8 engine, serial number 100001, built in Norwood, OH.

Powertrains

Engine	Net HP	Engine Code	Transmission Availability[1]		Vega	Camaro	Nova	Chevelle	Laguna & Monte Carlo	Bel Air, Impala, Caprice	Corvette
140 CID (2.3L) OHC, 1-bbl., 4-cyl.	72	A	3-speed manual		S	—	—	—	—	—	—
				MPG:	24.6	—	—	—	—	—	—
			4-speed manual		$51	—	—	—	—	—	—
				MPG:	18.1	—	—	—	—	—	—
			Powerglide		$163	—	—	—	—	—	—

Engine	Net HP	Engine Code	Transmission Availability[1]		Vega	Camaro	Nova	Chevelle	Laguna & Monte Carlo	Bel Air, Impala, Caprice	Corvette
			automatic	MPG:	20	—	—	—	—	—	—
			3-speed Turbo		$193	—	—	—	—	—	—
			Hydra-matic	MPG:	19.6	—	—	—	—	—	—
140 CID (2.3L) OHC, 2-bbl., 4-cyl.	85	B	3-speed manual		$41	—	—	—	—	—	—
				MPG:	NA	—	—	—	—	—	—
			4-speed manual		$92	—	—	—	—	—	—
				MPG:	17.4	—	—	—	—	—	—
			Powerglide automatic		$204	—	—	—	—	—	—
				MPG:	19.4	—	—	—	—	—	—
			3-speed Turbo Hydra-matic		$234	—	—	—	—	—	—
				MPG:	15.7	—	—	—	—	—	—
250 CID (4.1L) Turbo-Thrift, 1-bbl., 6-cyl.	100	D	3-speed manual		—	—	S (base)	S	S (ex. Malibu Estate)	—	S (Bel Air sdn.)	—
				MPG:	—	NA	NA	NA	—	—	—
			Powerglide automatic		—	—	$169	—	—	—	—
				MPG:	—	—	15.7	—	—	—	—
			3-speed Turbo Hydra-matic		—	$210 (base)	—	$210 (ex. Malibu Estate)	—	$210 (Bel Air sdn.)	—
				MPG:	—	15.2	—	15.7	—	—	—
307 CID (5.0L) Turbo-Fire, 2-bbl., V8	115	F	3-speed manual		—	$90 (base)	$86	S (Malibu Est.)/$111 (others)	—	—	—
				MPG:	—	NA	NA	NA	—	—	—
			3-speed Turbo Hydra-matic		—	$300 (base)	$286	$210 (Malibu Est.)/$321 (others)	—	—	—
				MPG:	—	15.2	NA	15.7	—	—	—
350 CID (5.7L) Turbo-Fire, 2-bbl., V8	145	H	3-speed manual		—	S (LT)/$116 (base)	$112	$26 (Malibu Est.)/$137 (others)	S	—	—
				MPG:	—	NA	NA	NA	NA	—	—
			4-speed manual		—	$200 (LT)/$316 (base)	—	—	—	—	—
				MPG:	—	NA	—	—	—	—	—
			3-speed Turbo Hydra-matic		—	$210 (LT)/$326 (base)	$312	$236 (Malibu Est.)/$347 (others)	$210	$334 (BelAir Sdn.)/ S (others ex. Caprice)	—
				MPG:	—	NA	9.9	9.9	9.9	10.1	—
350 CID (5.7L) Turbo-Fire, 4-bbl., V8	175	T	3-speed manual		—	$76 (LT)/$192 (base)	$188	—	—	—	—
				MPG:	—	NA	NA	—	—	—	—
			4-speed manual		—	$276 (LT)/$392 (base)	$378	$413 (coupes only)	—	—	—
				MPG:	—	NA	8.8	NA	—	—	—
			3-speed Turbo Hydra-matic		—	$286 (LT)/$402 (base)	$388	$307 (Malibu Est.)/$423 (others)	$256	$410 (BelAir)/ $76 (others ex. Caprice)	—
				MPG:	—	9.8	8.9	9.4	9.2	11.0	—
350 CID (5.7L) Turbo-Fire,	190	J	4-speed manual		—	—	—	—	—	—	S

Engine	Net HP	Engine Code	Transmission Availability[1]		Vega	Camaro	Nova	Chevelle	Laguna & Monte Carlo	Bel Air, Impala, Caprice	Corvette
4-bbl., V8				MPG:	—	—	—	—	—	—	NA
					—	—	—	—	—	—	N/C
			3-speed Turbo Hydra-matic	MPG:	—	—	—	—	—	—	NA
350 CID (5.7L) Turbo-Fire Special, 4-bbl., V8	250[2]	K	4-sp. manual or 4-sp. close ratio man.		—	—	—	—	—	—	$76
				MPG:	—	—	—	—	—	—	NA
			3-speed Turbo Hydra-matic		—	—	—	—	—	—	$173
				MPG:	—	—	—	—	—	—	12.9
400 CID (6.6L) Turbo-Fire, 2-bbl., V8	150	R	3-speed Turbo Hydra-matic		—	—	—	—	—	S (Caprice)/$127 (others ex. BelAir)	—
				MPG:	—	—	—	—	—	9.6	—
454 CID (7.4L) Turbo-Jet, 4-bbl., V8	215	X	3-speed Turbo Hydra-matic		—	—	—	—	—	$150 (Caprice)/$277 (others ex. BelAir)	—
				MPG:	—	—	—	—	—	10.8	—
454 CID (7.4L) Turbo-Jet, 4-bbl., V8	245[2]	Y	4-speed manual		—	$598 (incl. Z/28 option pkg. only)	—	$445 (coupes only)	—	—	—
				MPG:	—	—	—	NA	—	—	—
			3-speed Turbo Hydra-matic		—	$598 (incl. Z/28 option pkg. only)	—	$466 (Malibu Est.)/$577 (others)	$440	$180 (Caprice)/$307 (others ex. BelAir)	—
				MPG:	—	—	—	NA	NA	10.8	—
454 CID (7.4L) Turbo-Jet, 4-bbl., V8	275[2]	Z	4-sp. manual or 4-sp. close ratio man.		—	—	—	—	—	—	$250
				MPG:	—	—	—	—	—	—	NA
			3-speed Turbo Hydra-matic		—	—	—	—	—	—	$347
				MPG:	—	—	—	—	—	—	NA

[1]Unless otherwise specified: All 3-speed manuals are column shift. All 4-speed manuals are floor shift. All automatics are column shift, except on Vega, Camaro and Corvette. Floor shift automatic is optional on Nova, Chevelle and Monte Carlo with other specified equipment at extra cost.   [2]Includes dual exhaust.

Major Options

	Vega	Camaro	Nova	Chevelle	Monte Carlo	Full-size Chevy	Corvette
Four-season air conditioning[1]	$349	$397	$381	$397	$397	$405	$452
Comfortilt steering wheel	—	$44	$44	$44	$44	$44	S
Tilt-and-telescope steering wheel	—	—	—	—	$62	$62	$82
Speed and cruise control	—	—	—	—	$62	$62	—
Rear window defogger[2]	$52	$31	$31	$31	$31	$31	$41
Soft-Ray tinted glass, all windows	$36	$39	$39	$42	$45	$49	S
Power windows, 2-dr./4-dr.	—	$75[3]	—	$75/$113	$75	$124[4]	$83
Power door locks, 2-dr./4-dr.	—	—	—	$45/$69	$45	$45/$69	—
Power front seat, w/std. seat	—	—	—	$103	$103	$103[4]	—
Front bucket seats, w/console[5]	S	$57	$114	$190	$190	—	S
Rear facing third seat, wagons	—	—	—	$133	—	$65	—
AM radio	$59	$65	$65	$65	$65	$65	—
AM/FM stereo[6]	—	—	—	$233	$233	$233	$276
AM/FM stereo w/8-track tape	—	—	—	$363	$363	$363	—
Vinyl top, full[7]	—	$87	$82	$92	$123	$106	$62
Vinyl top, landau[8]	—	—	—	—	$	—	—
Sky Roof (sunroof), power[9]	—	—	$179	$325	$325	—	—
Power steering, variable-ratio	$92	$113	$100	$113	S	S	$113

	Vega	Camaro	Nova	Chevelle	Monte Carlo	Full-size Chevy	Corvette
Power brakes, w/front disc	—	$46	$68	$46[10]	S	S	$46[11]
Custom/Deluxe wheel covers	—	—	—	—	$15	$26	$62
Wire wheel covers	—	$82	$82	$82	—	$82	—
Rally wheels w/trim rings	$26	$44	$44	—	$30	—	S
Turbine I wheels	—	$111	—	$111	—	—	—
Turbine II aluminum wheels	—	—	—	—	$175	—	$175
WSW tires	$28	$32	$30	$32	$32	$33	$32

Popular Option Groups & Packages

	Vega	Camaro	Nova	Chevelle	Monte Carlo	Full-size Chevy	Corvette
Custom interior package	$115	—	—	—	—	—	$154
Custom exterior package	$77	—	—	—	—	—	—
Décor group	$26	—	—	—	—	—	—
Exterior décor package	—	—	$59	$34	—	—	—
Estate Wagon package	$212	—	—	—	—	—	—
GT package	$340	—	—	—	—	—	—
Interior décor/Quiet sound group	—	$35	$33	—	—	—	—
Rally Sport equipment package	—	$118[12]	—	—	—	—	—
Special instrumentation package	$62	$82	$87	$82	$67	—	S
Sports stripes, hood/deck	$46	—	—	—	—	—	—
SS package	—	—	$123	$243	—	—	—
Style trim group	—	$56	—	—	—	—	—
Z28 special equipment package	—	$598[13]	—	—	—	—	—

—= Not Available; S = Standard equipment. [1]Requires V8 engine on Bel Air, Chevelle, Camaro and Nova. [2]Blower type defogger. [3] Other select equipment required. [4] Not available on Bel Air. [5] Bucket seats standard on Vega and Camaro, with console being optional. Swivel bucket seats available on Chevelle coupes and Monte Carlo. [6]AM/FM radio (non-stereo) available on Vega for $120, and $135 on Nova and Camaro. [7] Requires optional removable top at $267 extra on Corvette convertible. Price is $138 on full-size Chevrolet wagons. Not available on Vega or Chevelle station wagons. [8] Standard on Monte Carlo Landau coupe. [9]Sky Roof pull-back vinyl sunroof opening on Nova two-door models only. Electrically operated sunroof $50 higher, and requires power windows. [10] Standard on station wagons. [11]Power front and rear disc brakes. [12]Rally Sport package price on Camaro LT is $97. [13] Z28 package on LT is $502.

Paint Colors

	Code		Code		Code
Classic White[1]	10	Elkhart Green[1]	47	Corvette Orange metallic[1]	80
Antique White	11	Midnight Green[2]	48	Beige[2]	81
Corvette Silver metallic[1]	14	Light Yellow[5]	51	Bright Orange[3]	86
Tuxedo Black[2]	19	Corvette Yellow[1]	52	Medium Orange[6]	97
Corvette Medium Blue metallic[1]	22	Corvette Yellow metallic[1]	53		
Medium Blue[3]	23	Chamois	56	
Light Blue metallic[4]	24	Light Copper metallic[4]	60	
Dark Blue metallic[4]	26	Light Orange[3]	61	
Targa Blue metallic[1]	27	Medium Bronze metallic[3]	62	
Midnight Blue metallic[4]	29	Silver metallic	64	
Medium Green metallic[3]	41	Taupe metallic[2]	66	
Dark Green metallic[4]	42	Dark Brown metallic[4]	68	
Light Green metallic[4]	44	Dark Red metallic[4]	74	
Corvette Blue-Green metallic[1]	45	Medium Red[5]	75	
Green-Gold metallic[4]	46	Mille Miglia Red[1]	76	

In two-tone combinations, the first two digits indicate lower color and the next two digits are the upper color. Two-tones are available for $31 on most Nova, Chevelle and full-size models. Colors listed with no footnotes are available on all models except Corvette. [1]Available only on Corvette. [2]Available on all models except Vega, Camaro and Corvette. [3]Available only on Vega. [4]Available on all models except Vega and Corvette. [5]Available only on Vega and Camaro. [6]Available only on Camaro.

Vega

"The award winning little car."

Nameplate year of origin: 1971.
Current bodystyle lifespan: 1971 through 1977 (some models moved to Monza series, continuing through 1979).
Predecessor to this model: Corvair (1965 to 1969).

Replacement for this model: Cavalier (1982 to 1993).
Percentage of division's production: 16.57%.
Corporate siblings: None.
Primary competition: AMC Gremlin, Dodge Colt, Ford Pinto and Plymouth Cricket.
Notable changes: Minor trim and detail changes.
Major standard equipment: Knit pattern vinyl high-back front bucket seats w/foam cushions, sliding seat adjustment for both front seats (driver's side only on Notchback), full-floor carpeting, fold-down rear seat (Hatchback and Kammback wagon), driver's door stowage well and armrest, passenger side door armrest, two-spoke steering wheel, glove box, two-speed wipers w/washers, bright front and rear window moldings, and A78 × 13 BSW tires.

Measurements

	Coupes	Wagon
Wheelbase	97.0"	97.0"
Length	173.0"	173.0"
Width	65.6"	65.6"
Height	51.9"	52.0"
Legroom — front	42.8"	42.8"
Legroom — rear	28.9"	30.1"
Headroom — front	38.4"	38.5"
Headroom — rear	38.4"	38.3"
Cargo capacity (cu. ft.)	8.7*	50.2
Fuel capacity (gals.)	11.0	11.0

Hatchback maximum with rear seat down, 27 cu. ft.

Models Available

	Model No.	Base MSRP	Change from LY	Shipping Wt. (lbs.)	Model Year Production	Change from LY
Vega 2-Door Notchback Coupe	V11	$2,087	+1.31%	2219	58,425	+4.63%
Vega 2-Door Hatchback Coupe	V77	$2,192	+1.48%	2313	266,124	+1.31%
Vega 2-Door Kammback (Wagon)	V15	$2,323	+1.66%	2327	102,751	+42.80%
TOTALS		*Avg. price* $2,201	+1.49%	*Production*	427,300	+9.43%

Camaro

"Our sporty way to see the U.S.A.
You're probably much closer to owning one than you thought."

Nameplate year of origin: 1967.
Current bodystyle lifespan: 1970 through 1981.
Predecessor to this model: Camaro (1967 to 1969).
Replacement for this model: Camaro (1982 to 1992).
Percentage of division's production: 3.75%.
Corporate siblings: Pontiac Firebird.
Primary competition: AMC Javelin, Dodge Challenger, Ford Mustang, and Plymouth Barracuda.
Notable changes: Front-end restyling and minor trim and detail changes.
Major standard equipment: Choice of mixed-tone cloth-and-vinyl or solid all-vinyl front bucket seats, deep-twist color-keyed carpeting, flat black instrument panel, four-spoke steering wheel, molded stowage compartments in door panels, dual speed wipers w/washers, bright front and rear window moldings, hubcaps, and E78 × 14 BSW tires. Type LT adds: Interior Décor/Quiet Sound group, woodgrain vinyl accents on I/P cluster and door panels, lower I/P silver finish accents, LT emblem on steering wheel, special instrumentation package, electric clock, LH remote and RH manual sport mirrors, LT identification on front and rear end panels and on roof rear quarter panel, black finished lower body rocker sills, and rally wheels.

Measurements

Wheelbase	108.0"
Length	188.4"
Width	74.4"
Height	49.1"
Legroom — front	43.9"
Legroom — rear	30.7"
Headroom — front	37.3"
Headroom — rear	36.0"
Cargo capacity (cu. ft.)	6.7
Fuel capacity (gals.)	18.0

Models Available

	Model No.	Base MSRP	Change from LY	Shipping Wt. (lbs.)	Model Year Production	Change from LY
Camaro 2-Door Sport Coupe	Q87	$2,781	+1.87%	3119	64,424	-6.16%
Camaro Type LT 2-Door Sport Coupe	S87	$3,268	NEW	3349	32,327	NEW
TOTALS		*Avg. price* $3,025	+10.79%	*Production*	96,751	+40.92%

Nova

"You get a lot to choose from. And all at a Nova price tag."

Nameplate year of origin: 1962, as top of the line Chevy II model; became series name in 1969.

Current bodystyle lifespan: 1968 through 1974; restyled in 1973.

Predecessor to this model: Chevy II (1966 to 1967).

Replacement for this model: Nova and Concours (1975 to 1979).

Percentage of division's production: 14.32%.

Corporate siblings: Buick Apollo, Oldsmobile Omega, and Pontiac Ventura.

Primary competition: AMC Hornet, Ford Maverick, and Plymouth Valiant.

Notable changes: Completely restyled; new hatchback model.

Major standard equipment: Choice of patterned cloth-and-vinyl or all-vinyl front bench seat, color-keyed rubber floor covering, vinyl covered door panels, black two-spoke steering wheel and steering column, dual speed wipers w/washers, bright front and rear window moldings, and E78 × 14 BSW tires. Hatchback model adds: Fold-down rear seat. Custom adds: Choice of patterned cloth or all-vinyl front bench seat, color-keyed deep-twist carpeting (includes cargo area on hatchback), 10" wide non-glare rearview mirror, glove compartment light, right front door courtesy light switch, luggage compartment mat, bright roof drip molding, bright parking light and taillight accents, Nova Custom nameplates on front fenders, Interior Décor/Quiet Sound group, front and rear bumper impact strips.

Measurements

	Coupe & HBK	Sedan
Wheelbase	111.0"	111.0"
Length	194.3"	194.3"
Width	72.4"	72.4"
Height	52.5"	53.9"
Legroom — front	41.7"	41.7"
Legroom — rear	33.4"	35.3"
Headroom — front	38.0"	39.3"
Headroom — rear	36.9"	37.3"
Cargo capacity (cu. ft.)	14.6*	13.8
Fuel capacity (gals.)	21.0	21.0

Hatchback maximum with rear seat down, 27.3 cu. ft.

Models Available

	Model No.	Base MSRP	Change from LY	Shipping Wt. (lbs.)	Model Year Production	Change from LY
Nova 2-Door Coupe	X27	$2,377	+1.11%	3033	135,819	-47.81%
Nova 2-Door Hatchback	X17	$2,528	NEW	3146	44,954	NEW
Nova 4-Door Sedan	X69	$2,407	+1.18%	3065	60,283	-32.66%
Nova Custom 2-Door Coupe	Y27	$2,551	NEW	3073	58,378	NEW
Nova Custom 2-Door Hatchback	Y17	$2,701	NEW	3152	46,058	NEW
Nova Custom 4-Door Sedan	Y69	$2,580	NEW	3105	24,017	NEW
TOTALS		*Avg. price* $2,524	+6.72%		*Production* 369,509	+5.65%

Chevelle

*"Redesigned this year to make it the right car
for more people than ever before."*

Nameplate year of origin: 1964.

Current bodystyle lifespan: 1973 through 1977.

Predecessor to this model: Chevelle (1968 to 1972).

Replacement for this model: Malibu (1978 to 1983).

Percentage of division's production: 14.99%.

Corporate siblings: Buick Century, Oldsmobile Cutlass, and Pontiac LeMans.

Primary competition: AMC Matador, Ford Torino, and Plymouth Satellite.

Notable changes: Completely redesigned.

Major standard equipment: Choice of cloth-and-vinyl or knit all-vinyl front bench seat, color-keyed vinyl coated rubber floor covering, door panel trim in matching vinyl, two-spoke soft-rim black steering wheel, black steering column, two-speed windshield wipers w/washers, bright front and rear

Measurements

	Coupes	Sedans	Wagons
Wheelbase	112.0"	116.0"	116.0"
Length*	202.9"	206.9"	213.3"
Width	76.6"	76.6"	76.6"
Height	53.1"	53.8"	55.2"
Legroom — front	42.1"	42.1"	42.1"
Legroom — rear	32.9"	37.0"	36.8"
Headroom — front	37.7"	38.3"	38.8"
Headroom — rear	37.0"	37.5"	39.4"
Cargo capacity (cu. ft.)	15.3	15.3	85.0**
Fuel capacity (gals.)	22.0	22.0	22.0

Overall length of Laguna models is 1" longer. **Plus 9.8 cu. ft. of hidden storage space on two-seat models.*

window moldings, bright rear quarter window trim, manual front disc brakes, and E78 × 14 BSW tires. Wagon adds: Black or saddle all-vinyl front bench seat, vinyl coated metal cargo area sidewalls, swing up tailgate w/fixed window, I/P mounted "door ajar" warning light for tailgate, power front disc brakes, and H78 × 14 BSW tires. Malibu adds: Choice of mixed pattern cloth-and-vinyl or all-vinyl front bench seat, deep-twist color-keyed carpeting, glove compartment light, bright window surround moldings, rocker panel molding, and hubcaps. Malibu wagon adds: All-vinyl front bench seat, complementing door panel and cargo area sidewall trim. Malibu Estate wagon adds: Woodgrain vinyl bodyside and tailgate panels, hood rear edge molding and wheel opening moldings. Laguna adds: Choice of patterned cloth-and-vinyl or breathable all-vinyl front bench seat, simulated Carpathian burled elm woodgrain vinyl inserts on color-keyed steering wheel, color-keyed steering column, bright accented dual-unit taillights, roof drip rail moldings, bumper impact strips, rocker panel molding, wheel opening moldings, unique Laguna urethane front end styling, front fender Laguna nameplates, and full wheel covers. Laguna wagon adds: Luxury vinyl front bench seat. Laguna Estate wagon adds: Woodgrain vinyl bodyside and tailgate panels.

Models Available

	Model No.	Base MSRP	Change from LY*	Shipping Wt. (lbs.)	Model Year Production	Change from LY*
Chevelle Deluxe 2-Door Colonnade HT Coupe	C37	$2,743	+2.77%	3423	21,377	-28.04%
Chevelle Deluxe 4-Door Colonnade HT Sedan	C29	$2,719	+3.15%	3435	20,755	+5.65%
Chevelle Deluxe 4-Door Station Wagon, 2-S.**	C35	$3,106	+6.15%	3849	10,940	+2.01%
Malibu 2-Door Colonnade HT Coupe	D37	$2,894	+2.15%	3430	168,784	-20.53%
Malibu 4-Door Colonnade HT Sedan	D29	$2,871	+2.50%	3477	60,679	+24.92%
Malibu 4-Door Station Wagon, 2-S.	D35	$3,290	+4.78%	4027	24,553	+252.01%
Malibu Estate 4-Door Station Wagon, 2-S.**	G35	$3,475	NEW	4032	9,626	NEW
Laguna 2-Door Colonnade HT Coupe	E37	$3,203	NEW	3678	42,941	NEW
Laguna 4-Door Colonnade HT Sedan	E29	$3,179	NEW	3627	13,095	NEW
Laguna 4-Door Station Wagon, 2-S.**	E35	$3,483	NEW	4110	6,619	NEW
Laguna Estate 4-Door Station Wagon, 2-S.**	H35	$3,662	+6.73%	4141	7,370	+38.25%
TOTALS	Avg. price $3,148		+2.19%	Production	386,739	-1.77%

*Comparisons made to equivalent 1972 model numbers (i.e., 1973 Chevelle Deluxe "C" models equal 1972 Chevelle "C" models and 1973 Laguna Estate "H" models equal 1972 Chevelle Concours Estate "H" models).   **Production of wagons with third seat option is included above. By model: Deluxe, 1,316; Malibu, 5,961; Malibu Estate, 4,099; Laguna, 2,200; and Laguna Estate, 3,709.

Monte Carlo

"Combining American comfort with European handling."

Nameplate year of origin: 1970.
Current bodystyle lifespan: 1973 through 1977.
Predecessor to this model: Monte Carlo (1970 to 1972).
Replacement for this model: Monte Carlo (1978 to 1987).
Percentage of division's production: 11.27%.
Corporate siblings: Pontiac Grand Prix.
Primary competition: Dodge Charger and Plymouth Satellite Sebring.
Notable changes: Completely redesigned.
Major standard equipment: Choice of rich knit cloth and soft vinyl or all-vinyl front bench seat, color-keyed deep-twist full-floor carpeting, LH outside rear view mirror, bright wheel opening moldings and rocker panel molding w/front and rear extensions, wheel covers, and G78 × 15 BSW tires. "S" adds: Simulated Carpathian burled elm vinyl trim on I/P and steering wheel, door map pockets, door pull assist straps, electric clock, and GR70 × 15 BSW tires. Landau adds: Landau vinyl roof, visor vanity mirror, Landau interior nameplates, dual sport mirrors w/LH remote, bodyside accent stripes, Landau crests on rear quarter pillar, and Turbine II wheels.

Measurements

Wheelbase	116.0"
Length	210.4"
Width	77.6"
Height	52.2"
Legroom — front	42.1"
Legroom — rear	32.9"
Headroom — front	37.5"
Headroom — rear	37.4"
Cargo capacity (cu. ft.)	14.7
Fuel capacity (gals.)	22.0

Models Available

	Model No.	Base MSRP	Change from LY	Shipping Wt. (lbs.)	Model Year Production	Change from LY
Monte Carlo 2-Door Hardtop Coupe	H57	$3,415	+1.58%	3713	4,960	-94.61%
Monte Carlo S 2-Door Hardtop Coupe	H57	$3,562	NEW	3720	177,963	NEW
Monte Carlo Landau 2-Door Hardtop Coupe	H57	$3,806	NEW	3722	107,770	NEW
TOTALS	*Avg. price*	$3,594	+6.91%	*Production*	290,693	+216.10%

Bel Air, Impala and Caprice

*"We don't just say that Chevrolet is building a better way
to see the U.S.A.— we go out of our way to prove it."*

Nameplate year of origin: 1950 (Bel Air, as hardtop model designation and 1953 as series); 1958 (Impala); and 1966 (Caprice).

Current bodystyle lifespan: 1971 through 1976.

Predecessor to this model: Biscayne/Bel Air/Impala/Caprice (1969 to 1970).

Replacement for this model: Impala and Caprice (1977 to 1990).

Percentage of division's production: 37.92%.

Corporate siblings: Buick LeSabre and Centurion, Oldsmobile Delta 88, Pontiac Catalina/Bonneville/Grand Ville.

Primary competition: AMC Ambassador, Dodge Polara, Ford Custom 500/Galaxie 500/LTD, and Plymouth Fury.

Notable changes: Revised styling.

Major standard equipment: Choice of patterned cloth-and-vinyl or all-vinyl front bench seat, deep-twist carpeting, black soft-rim steering wheel, black steering column, LH rear view mirror, dual unit tail lamps w/silver accents, rocker panel sill moldings, single horn, power steering, power front disc brakes, hubcaps, and G78 × 15 BSW tires. Wagon adds: All-vinyl front bench seat, Glide-Away tailgate w/power-operated rear window, and L78 × 15 BSW tires. Impala adds: Choice of patterned deluxe cloth-and-vinyl or all-vinyl front bench seat (all-vinyl only in wagon), color-keyed deep-twist carpeting, woodgrain vinyl accent trim on I/P and door panels, glove compartment light, luggage compartment light, triple unit taillights w/silver accents, wheel opening moldings (Custom Coupe only), and bodyside molding w/black vinyl insert (Custom Coupe only). Caprice adds: Choice of nylon knit cloth and vinyl or pattern cloth and vinyl front bench seat, fold-down center armrest (four-doors only), color-keyed steering wheel and steering column, electric clock, rear door courtesy light switches (four-doors), door pull straps on front door panels, rocker panel moldings w/rear extensions, front wheel opening moldings, rear wheel opening fender skirts, dual horns, and full wheel covers. Convertible adds: Expanded vinyl front bench seat and inward-folding power-operated vinyl convertible top. Caprice Estate wagon adds: All-vinyl interior w/cargo area color-keyed textured vinyl sidewalls, and translucent woodgrain vinyl exterior panels.

Measurements

	2-doors	4-doors	Wagons
Wheelbase	121.5"	121.5"	125.0"
Length	221.9"	221.9"	226.8"
Width	79.5"	79.5"	79.5"
Height	53.7"	54.5"	58.3"
Legroom — front	42.5"	42.5"	42.5"
Legroom — rear	35.8"	38.8"	38.9"
Headroom — front	38.1"	38.9"	39.6"
Headroom — rear	37.1"	38.0"	39.3"
Cargo capacity (cu. ft.)	19.5*	20.5	106.4
Fuel capacity (gals.)	26.0	26.0	22.0

Convertible is 14.4 cu. ft.

Models Available

	Model No.	Base MSRP	Change from LY	Shipping Wt. (lbs.)	Model Year Production	Change from LY
Bel Air 4-Door Sedan	K69	$3,247	-8.22%	3895	41,832	-0.13%
Bel Air 4-Door, 2-Seat Station Wagon	K35	$4,022	+1.34%	4717	14,549	-11.73%
Bel Air 4-Door, 3-Seat Station Wagon	K45	$4,136	+1.42%	4770	6,321	-27.07%
Impala 2-Door Hardtop Sport Coupe	L57	$3,769	+1.32%	4096	42,979	-18.43%
Impala 2-Door Hardtop Custom Coupe	L47	$3,836	+1.29%	4110	176,824	-3.63%
Impala 4-Door Sedan	L69	$3,752	+1.30%	4138	190,536	+3.22%
Impala 4-Door Hardtop Sport Sedan	L39	$3,822	+1.35%	4162	139,143	-18.30%
Impala 4-Door, 2-Seat Station Wagon	L35	$4,119	+1.55%	4742	46,940	+8.78%
Impala 4-Door, 3-Seat Station Wagon	L45	$4,233	+1.63%	4807	43,664	+8.49%
Caprice 2-Door Hardtop Coupe	N47	$4,082	+1.39%	4143	77,134	+17.74%

	Model No.	Base MSRP	Change from LY	Shipping Wt. (lbs.)	Model Year Production	Change from LY
Caprice 2-Door Convertible	N67	$4,345	NEW	4191	7,339	NEW
Caprice 4-Door Sedan	N69	$4,064	+1.37%	4176	58,126	+70.09%
Caprice 4-Door Hardtop Sport Sedan	N39	$4,134	+1.42%	4208	70,155	-10.93%
Caprice Estate 4-Door, 2-Seat Station Wagon	N35	$4,382	+1.58%	4779	22,969	+13.25%
Caprice Estate 4-Door, 3-Seat Station Wagon	N45	$4,496	+1.65%	4858	39,535	+13.86%
TOTALS		Avg. price $4,029	+2.38%		Production 978,046	-3.18%

Corvette

"A true production sports car. And made in U.S.A.
No other sports car can make that statement."

Nameplate year of origin: 1953 (also used on show car of same year).
Current bodystyle lifespan: 1968 through 1982.
Predecessor to this model: Corvette (1963 to 1967).
Replacement for this model: Corvette (1984 to 1996).
Percentage of division's production: 1.18%.
Corporate siblings: None.
Primary competition: Pantera (Imported by Lincoln-Mercury).
Notable changes: Revised front and rear styling.
Major standard equipment: All-vinyl high-back contoured bucket seats, center floor console, color-keyed cut-pile carpeting, tilt steering wheel, sports instrumentation with full gauges including tachometer, electric clock, tinted glass, LH rear view sport mirror, carpeted cargo area with light concealed behind seats, removable roof panels (coupe), hide-away folding top (convertible), domed hood w/air scoop, front and rear air spoilers, four wheel disc brakes, rally wheels w/trim rings, and GR70 × 15 BSW tires.

Measurements

Wheelbase	98.0"
Length	184.7"
Width	69.0"
Height	47.7"
Legroom — front	42.1"
Headroom — front	36.2"
Cargo capacity (cu. ft.)	NA
Fuel capacity (gals.)	18.0

Models Available

	Model No.	Base MSRP	Change from LY	Shipping Wt. (lbs.)	Model Year Production	Change from LY
Corvette Stingray 2-Door Coupe	Z37	$5,635	+2.98%	3326	24,372	+18.97%
Corvette Stingray 2-Door Convertible	Z67	$5,399	+2.92%	3333	6,093	-6.38%
TOTALS		Avg. price $5,517	+2.95%		Production 30,465	+12.86%

CHRYSLER

"It's easy to move up to Chrysler living."

Making do with what could be considered minor changes, Chrysler managed to maintain its portion of market share and increase production by more than 13 percent, just meeting the overall industry average. Although there were no earth shattering changes, the loop style front bumpers were removed for this season on the standard Chryslers, partially because of new federal safety standards, while the Imperial used the design for one final season. Also, it would be the final year for the fuselage body design introduced for the 1969 model year.

The regular Chrysler line, to include Newport, Town & Country, and New Yorker, was given a facelift to bring them in line with the required safety standards. In addition to the loop-style bumper being abandoned in favor of a more conventional bumper, a new grille of a rectangular design was introduced, with angled lower corners as it dipped slightly into the bumper line, flanked by dual headlamps in individual chrome bezels at each end. Parking lamp/turn signal lights were mounted in the front bumper below the headlamps. Two different grille patterns were used to distinguish the lower and higher priced series. The Newport series had a horizontal crosshatch grille twelve rows high and eighteen columns across with a winged Newport emblem placed in the center. The New Yorker and Town & Country wagons used a horizontal multi-bar design with a center split that jutted out about an inch. All carried the name Chrysler in block letters on the header panel above the grille, and the New Yorker added a stand-up hood ornament.

Interiors continued much the same as they were in 1972, with more luxurious designs for seats and door panels for each step up in trim level and series. The new year also saw the Newport name replace the Newport Royal, after a short two years of use, and the New Yorker base 2-door hardtop model was discontinued due to deteriorating sales. By year's end, production of the Brougham 2-door hardtop had made up for any lack of base model sales. One other change was that the 400 CID V8 engine was now the base Newport offering, and the 360 CID V8 was no longer offered in a Chrysler, but it would return to the line for the 1976 model year.

Imperial was in its third year after returning under the Chrysler nameplate, having been its own division of Chrysler from 1955 through the 1970 model year. The only styling changes were a mesh-style grille insert and the addition of front bumper guards as standard equipment in order to meet the new federal government safety standards with the loop-style bumper. The "LeBaron" designation was dropped from the Imperial's official name, but the LeBaron name was still used on the rear quarter sail panel. Imperial LeBaron would return as the official name for 1974.

Imperial 2-Door Hardtop

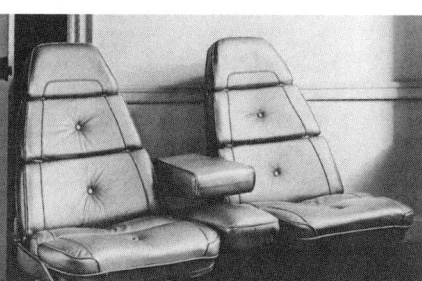

Imperial optional bucket seats with center cushion and armrest

New Yorker Brougham 4-Door Hardtop

Newport 4-Door Sedan

Newport Custom 2-Door Hardtop

Town & Country Station Wagon

Model year production: 250,958, up 13.30% from 1972.
Domestic market share: 2.36% (11th place).
Base price range: $4,181 to $7,057.
Chrysler average base price: $5,140, up 8.63%.
Introduction date: September 1972.
Assembly plants: Jefferson Ave., Detroit, MI (C); and Newark, DE (F).
Data plate identification (VIN): Thirteen digit code read as follows: First four digits indicate series and body style (model number in model charts); fifth digit indicates engine code (see powertrain chart); sixth digit indicates year (3 = 1973); seventh digit indicates assembly plant (see list above); remaining digits are sequential with beginning numbers of 100001.
Example: CL43M3C100001 is a 1973 Chrysler Newport 4-Door Hardtop, with 400 CID, 2-bbl. V8 engine, serial number 100001, built in Detroit, MI.

Powertrains

Engine	Net HP	Engine Code	Transmission Availability[1]		Newport	Town & Country	New Yorker	Imperial
400 CID (6.6L), 2-bbl., V8	185	M	3-speed Torque Flite automatic	MPG:	S 8.9	— —	— —	— —
440 CID (7.2L), 4-bbl., V8	215	T	3-speed Torque Flite automatic	MPG:	$123 9.1	S 8.9	S 9.1	S 9.1

Major Options

	Newport	Town & Country	New Yorker	Imperial
Air conditioning[1]	$421	$421	$421	S[2]
Rear seat heater and defroster	—	—	—	$78
Tilt and telescope steering wheel	$90	$90	$90	$95
Automatic speed control	$69	$69	$69	$93
Automatic headlamp dimmer	—	—	—	$51
Electric rear window defroster	$35	—	$35	$35
Tinted glass, all windows	$53	$53	$53	S
Power windows	—	$126	$126[3]	S
Power front vent window, 4-dr. HT	—	—	$66	$86
Power door locks, 2-dr./4-dr.	$47/$73	$73	$47/$73	$49/$73
Power front bench seat, 6-way	$105	$105	$105	—
Power 50/50 or bucket seat, 6-way	$196	$196	$196	$223
AM radio	$91	$91	$91	S
AM/FM stereo	$240	$240	$240	$272
AM/FM stereo w/8-track tape	$403	$403	$403	$436
Electronic digital clock	$39	$39	$39	S
Vinyl top	$127	—	$127	S
Remote control trunk release	$15	—	$15	S
Sunroof, electric[4]	$592	—	$592	$585
Security alarm system	$101	$101	$101	$101
"Sure-brake" antilock brake system	—	—	—	$344
Premier wheel covers	$40	$40	$40	S
Chrome styled road wheels	$101	$101	$101	—
White sidewall tires, std. size	$40	$40	$40	S

Popular Option Groups & Packages

	Newport	Town & Country	New Yorker	Imperial
Accessory package	—	—	—	$35
Navajo package	$	—	—	—

—= Not Available; S = Standard equipment. [1]Auto-Temp air conditioning available for $495. Dual air conditioning for Town & Country is $648, and w/Auto-Temp is $723. [2]Dual air conditioning for Imperial available for $251. [3]Standard on New Yorker Brougham. [4]Requires vinyl top. Only available on 2-door hardtop models.

Paint Colors

Code		Code		Code	
Silver Frost metallic	A5	Navajo Copper metallic	K3	Golden Haze metallic	Y6
Blue Sky	B1	Sahara Beige	L4	Tahitian Gold	JY9
True Blue metallic	B5	Coral Turquoise metallic	Q5		
Regal Blue metallic	B9	Chestnut metallic	T8	*Single tones are coded W1, W1. Two-tones are*	
Burnished Red metallic	E7	Spinnaker White	W1	*available for $44, and are coded X9, W1 where*	
Mist Green	F1	Formal Black	X9	*first two digits are accent or roof color and sec-*	
Amber Sherwood	F3	Sun Fire Yellow	Y2	*ond two digits are basic body color.*	
Forest Green metallic	F8	Honey Gold	Y3		

Newport

"Coming through with a full measure of luxury and comfort."

Nameplate year of origin: 1961 (as series); 1950 (as HT model of the T & C).
Current bodystyle lifespan: 1969 through 1973.
Predecessor to this model: Newport (1965 to 1968).
Replacement for this model: Newport (1974 to 1978).
Percentage of division's sales volume: 61.45%.
Corporate siblings: Chrysler New Yorker.
Primary competition: Buick LeSabre, Mercury Monterey, and Oldsmobile Delta 88.
Notable changes: Revised front and rear styling.
Major standard equipment: Cloth-and-vinyl front bench seat, color-keyed loop pile carpeting, trip odometer, lighted front ashtray w/two rear seat ashtrays, 12" inside day/night mirror, two-speed electric windshield wipers w/washers, full-length bodyside molding w/partial front wheel lip molding, drip rail molding, bright rear window moldings, dual horns, power brakes, power steering, deluxe wheel covers, and H78 × 15 BSW tires. Custom adds: Cloth-and-vinyl split back front seat w/fold-down center armrest, seat side shields, vinyl-insert bodyside protective moldings, front and rear wheel lip moldings, deck lid molding, belt moldings, and upper door frame moldings (4-door sedan only).

Measurements

Wheelbase	124.0"
Length	230.1"
Width	79.4"
Height	56.2"
Legroom — front	41.8"
Legroom — rear	41.5"
Headroom — front	38.7"
Headroom — rear	37.9"
Cargo capacity (cu. ft.)	22.1
Fuel capacity (gals.)	24.0

Models Available

	Model No.	Base MSRP	Change from LY	Shipping Wt. (lbs.)	Model Year Production	Change from LY
Newport 2-Door Hardtop	CL23	$4,254	+3.15%	4160	27,456	+21.73%
Newport 4-Door Sedan	CL41	$4,181	+3.21%	4200	54,147	+14.15%
Newport 4-Door Hardtop	CL43	$4,316	+3.11%	4210	20,175	+32.86%
Newport Custom 2-Door Hardtop	CM23	$4,484	+2.91%	4145	12,293	+19.05%
Newport Custom 4-Door Sedan	CM41	$4,419	+3.08%	4200	20,092	+4.22%
Newport Custom 4-Door Hardtop	CM43	$4,567	+2.98%	4225	20,050	+29.71%
TOTALS		*Avg. price* $4,370	+3.07%		*Production* 154,213	+18.35%

Town & Country

*"Chrysler makes only one station wagon ...
the best choice among luxury wagons."*

Nameplate year of origin: 1941.
Current bodystyle lifespan: 1969 through 1973.
Predecessor to this model: Town & Country (1965 to 1968).
Replacement for this model: Town & Country (1974 to 1977).
Percentage of division's sales volume: 7.99%.
Corporate siblings: Dodge Polara and Monaco, and Plymouth Fury.
Primary competition: Buick Estate Wagon, Mercury Colony Park, and Oldsmobile Custom Cruiser.
Notable changes: Revised front and rear styling.
Major standard equipment: All-vinyl 50/50 split front seat w/individual fold-down center armrests and passenger-side recliner, color-keyed loop pile carpeting, electric clock, interior lights (cargo, glove box, map/courtesy and ashtray lights), power tail-gate window, sound absorbing headliner, trip odometer, front ashtray w/two rear seat ashtrays, 12" inside day/night mirror, three-speed electric windshield wipers w/washers, concealed storage compartments in rear wheelhouse cover, "Power Auto-Lock" tailgate lock (activates when ignition turned on), fender mounted turn signal indicators, bodyside simulated woodgrain appliqués, drip rail molding, rear wheel opening skirts, roof air deflector, dual horns, power brakes, power steering, deluxe wheel covers, and L84 × 15 BSW tires.

Measurements

Wheelbase	151.5"
Wheelbase	122.0"
Length	229.6"
Width	79.4"
Height	58.1"
Legroom — front	41.8"
Legroom — rear	39.1"
Headroom — front	40.1"
Headroom — rear	40.7"
Cargo capacity (cu. ft.)	113.2
Fuel capacity (gals.)	23.0

Models Available

	Model No.	Base MSRP	Change from LY	Shipping Wt. (lbs.)	Model Year Production	Change from LY
Town & Country 4-Door, 2-S. Wagon	CP45	$5,241	+3.68%	4670	5,353	-17.30%
Town & Country 4-Door, 3-S. Wagon	CP46	$5,366	+4.42%	4725	14,687	+4.05%
TOTALS		Avg. price $5,304	+4.05%		Production 20,040	-2.67%

New Yorker

"It'll spoil you for other kinds of driving."

Nameplate year of origin: 1939.
Current bodystyle lifespan: 1969 through 1973.
Predecessor to this model: New Yorker (1965 to 1968).
Replacement for this model: New Yorker (1974 to 1978).
Percentage of division's sales volume: 23.90%.
Corporate siblings: Chrysler Newport.
Primary competition: Buick Electra 225, Mercury Marquis, and Oldsmobile Ninety-Eight.
Notable changes: Revised front and rear styling.
Major standard equipment: Cloth-and-vinyl front bench seat w/fold-down center armrest, color-keyed loop-pile carpeting, color-keyed seat belts, trip odometer, electric clock, dual front ashtrays w/two rear seat ashtrays, interior lights (glove box, map/courtesy and ashtray lights), 12" inside day/night mirror, three-speed electric windshield wipers w/washers, carpeted trunk floor, LH remote control mirror, double full-length bodyside molding w/filigree-textured insert, front wheel lip molding, drip rail molding, bright window moldings, rear bumper periphery molding, rear wheel opening skirts, fender-mounted turn signal indicators, undercoating, hood insulation pad, deluxe wheel covers, and J78 × 15 BSW tires. Brougham adds: All-vinyl bucket seats w/center cushion, fold-down armrest and passenger side recliner (2-door), cloth-and-vinyl 50/50 split bench seat w/individual fold-down center armrest and passenger side recliner (4-door), rear seat fold-down center armrest, power windows, console-type armrests on all doors, headlights-on warning signal, and headlight time-delay switch.

Measurements

Wheelbase	124.0"
Length	230.8"
Width	79.4"
Height	56.4"
Legroom — front	41.8"
Legroom — rear	41.5"
Headroom — front	38.7"
Headroom — rear	37.9"
Cargo capacity (cu. ft.)	22.1
Fuel capacity (gals.)	24.0

Models Available

	Model No.	Base MSRP	Change from LY	Shipping Wt. (lbs.)	Model Year Production	Change from LY
New Yorker 4-Door Sedan	CH41	$4,997	+2.71%	4355	7,991	+9.53%
New Yorker 4-Door Hardtop	CH43	$5,125	+2.64%	4375	7,619	-23.91%
New Yorker Brougham 2-Door Hardtop	CS23	$5,413	+2.69%	4335	9,190	+98.27%
New Yorker Brougham 4-Door Sedan	CS41	$5,384	+2.72%	4425	8,541	+22.52%
New Yorker Brougham 4-Door Hardtop	CS43	$5,492	+2.65%	4440	26,635	+31.03%
TOTALS		Avg. price $5,278	+3.44%		Production 59,976	+9.43%

Imperial

"In automotive design, engineering excellence, quality workmanship and attention to detail ... this is Chrysler Corporation's top-of-the-line entry."

Nameplate year of origin: 1926 (as series); 1924 (as Sedan model designation).
Current bodystyle lifespan: 1969 through 1973.
Predecessor to this model: Imperial (1967 to 1968).
Replacement for this model: Imperial (1974 to 1975).

Measurements

Wheelbase	127.0"
Length	235.3"

Percentage of division's sales volume: 6.67%.
Corporate siblings: None.
Primary competition: Cadillac Calais and DeVille and Lincoln Continental.
Notable changes: Revised front and rear styling.
Major standard equipment: Iraq cloth and Cologne-grain leather 50/50 split bench seat w/individual fold-down center armrest and passenger side recliner, color-keyed loop-pile carpeting, color-keyed seat belts, rear seat passenger assist straps and C-pillar pillows, trip odometer, air conditioning, electronic digital clock, power windows, tinted glass, dual front ashtrays w/two rear seat ashtrays, interior lights — (glove box, map/courtesy and ashtray lights), 12" inside day/night mirror, three-speed electric windshield wipers w/washers, carpeted trunk floor and spare tire cover, LH remote control mirror, full vinyl top, full-length bodyside molding, front and rear wheel lip molding, drip rail molding, bright window moldings, rear bumper periphery molding, fender-mounted turn signal indicators, undercoating, hood insulation pad, deluxe wheel covers, and L84 × 15 BSW tires.

Measurements (cont.)

Width	79.6"
Height	56.2"
Legroom — front	41.9"
Legroom — rear	41.2"
Headroom — front	38.3"
Headroom — rear	37.0"
Cargo capacity (cu. ft.)	18.6
Fuel capacity (gals.)	24.0

Models Available

	Model No.	Base MSRP	Change from LY	Shipping Wt. (lbs.)	Model Year Production	Change from LY
Imperial 2-Door Hardtop	YM23	$6,829	+4.26%	4905	2,563	+10.38%
Imperial 4-Door Hardtop	YM43	$7,057	+4.12%	5035	14,166	+5.15%
TOTALS		*Avg. price* $6,973	+4.19%	*Production*	16,729	+5.92%

DODGE

"Extra care in engineering makes a difference in Dodge ... Depend on it."

Dodge began its 59th year in business without having any all-new cars in the line for the third season in a row. Even in the face of the federal front bumper safety standards, the front-end styling of the mid-size Charger and Coronet was not greatly changed from the 1972 models, as the Chrysler corporate "loop-style" bumper design seemed able to meet the requirements by simply adding energy absorbing mounts and bumper guards. Similarly, the Challenger and imported Colt were fitted with only revised bumper mounts and bumper guards to meet the new requirements. Interior changes for all models consisted mainly of new upholstery designs.

Under the hood, several additions were made to improve performance and fuel economy while reducing emissions. Most important was the introduction of the electronic ignition system on all 6-cylinder and V8 engines. This system did away with points and condenser and reduced the need for timing adjustments, which eliminated the major cause of engine misfiring. Also new was an electric assist choke, an exhaust gas recirculation (EGR) system, proportional exhaust gas recirculation (PEGR) system and the orifice spark advance

control (OSAC) system. Combined they helped reduce emission output of Dodge automobiles.

The Dart and full-size Polara and Monaco lines received the most exterior styling changes for the new model year. The compact Dart, which continued to be the best selling Dodge, received its first major facelift since 1970. The most obvious change was the pointed header panel and grille which sat above an imposing front bumper, also pointed in the center. Single headlamps with horizontally mounted rectangular parking lamps were set into the ends of the crosshatch grille, which was surrounded by chrome trim. A secondary horizontal break ran across the center of the grille connecting the parking lamps. Front fenders and hood were also new, giving a squared-off appearance, as opposed to the prior year's slightly rounded styling. The new look provided the Dart with a more modern and larger look. Few other changes were made to the Dart styling except for a new, two-unit taillight design on the new Dart Sport. The Dart Sport replaced the Dart Demon nameplate in what appeared to be a wise move, as sales of the renamed Sport sky-rocketed to a 70 percent increase over the Demon, partially at the expense of the

Swinger hardtops. Still, the Dart line as a whole finished the year with a sales increase of 10 percent.

The full-size Polara and Monaco were in the final year of their current body style, but took differing approaches in the new front-end styling created to meet the new bumper standards. The Polara did away with the loop-style bumper and received a more traditional bumper that curved slightly downward under the large grille opening and jutted outward slightly under the dual headlamps, mimicking the lines of the front header panel as it ran across the car. The new grille, of a crosshatch design eight columns wide and seven rows tall, with each opening carrying a small chrome lined insert, was surrounded in chrome with "DODGE" in block letters across the top. It was a pleasing design that gave the Polara a more luxurious look, but seemed oddly similar to an Oldsmobile Delta 88, sans the split grille theme.

Monaco models continued to use the loop style bumper set low on the front with a horizontal style grille. The bumper appeared massive with pointed ends and a point in the center, with bumper guards placed between the points. A new header panel contained the concealed headlamps that were moved above the bumper, rather than within the grille as in 1972. A wide chrome trim piece was applied to the header directly above the bumper, intersecting the headlight coverings, and having "DODGE" in block letters between the headlight openings. Other changes on the outside were minimal for 1973.

The mid-size Charger and Coronet lines retained their loop-style bumpers but received new grilles, with a more refined crosshatch design on the Coronet, and a horizontal grille split by a vertical bar for the Charger, which created a look reminiscent of earlier Chargers. The Charger SE added a center horizontal bar that was chrome lined and painted red.

The Challenger line was down to a lone 2-door hardtop model with only minor updates for the new year. The convertible and Hemi engines had been dropped at the end of the 1971 model year, and the Rallye model was discontinued at the end of the 1972 model run. For 1973, a Rallye package was introduced to supplant the missing Rallye hardtop. Apparently word was spreading that the end was near for the sporty Challenger, as production and sales were up more than 20 percent from 1972, even with only one model. Finally, the imported Colt received few changes other than the addition of a new GT 2-door hardtop model. The GT featured a black-out grille, GT identification, tape stripes and rallye wheels, but no performance enhancements.

Challenger 2-Door Hardtop with Rallye package

Charger SE 2-Door Hardtop

Colt 2-Door Coupe

Coronet Crestwood 4-Door,
2-Seat Station Wagon

Dart 340 Sport 2-Door Coupe

Dart Swinger 2-Door Hardtop with
Dart Custom 4-Door Sedan, rear

Monaco 2-Door Hardtop

Monaco 4-Door, 3-Seat Station Wagon

Polara 4-Door Sedan

Model year production: 665,536, up 15.18% from 1972.
Domestic market share: 6.26% (7th place).
Base price range: $2,424 to $4,859.
Dodge average base price: $3,541, up 8.09%.
Introduction date: September 1972.
Assembly plants: Lynch Road, Detroit, MI (A); Hamtramck, MI (B); Jefferson Ave., Detroit, MI (C); Belvidere, IL (D); Newark, DE (F); and St. Louis, MO (G). *Colt manufacturer:* Mitsubishi Heavy Industries, Tokyo, Japan.
Data plate identification (VIN): Thirteen digit code read as follows: First four digits indicate series and body style (model number in model charts); fifth digit indicates engine code (see powertrain chart); sixth digit indicates year (3 = 1973);

seventh digit indicates assembly plant for all except Colt* (see list above); remaining digits are sequential with beginning numbers of 100001 for all Dodge models except Colt. Colt sequential numbers begin as follows: 2-door coupe, 306092; 2-door hardtop w/manual, 116853; 2-door hardtop w/automatic, 122836; 4-door sedan w/manual, 108108; 4-door sedan w/automatic, 112852; all other Colt models, 000001.

Example: LL41C3B100001 is a 1973 Dodge Dart 4-Door Sedan, with 225 CID, 2-bbl. 6-cylinder engine, serial number 100001, built in Hamtramck, MI.

For Colt, seventh digit indicates transmission code (5 = 4-speed manual, 9 = automatic).

Powertrains

Engine	Net HP	Engine Code	Transmission Availability[1]		Colt	Dart[4]	Challenger	Charger	Coronet	Polara & Monaco
97.5 CID (1.6L) OHC, 1-bbl., 4-cyl.[2]	85	K	4-speed manual		S	—	—	—	—	—
				MPG:	22.6 (wgn. 22.8)	—	—	—	—	—
			3-speed Automatic		$178	—	—	—	—	—
				MPG:	22.7 (wgn. 21.9)	—	—	—	—	—
122 CID (2.0L) OHC, 2-bbl., 4-cyl.[2]	95	U	4-speed manual		$142	—	—	—	—	—
				MPG:	NA	—	—	—	—	—
			3-speed Automatic		$320	—	—	—	—	—
				MPG:	19.1	—	—	—	—	—
198 CID (3.2L), 1-bbl., 6-cyl.[3]	95	B	3-speed manual		—	S	—	—	—	—
				MPG:	—	NA	—	—	—	—
			3-speed TorqueFlite automatic		—	$178	—	—	—	—
				MPG:	—	16	—	—	—	—
225 CID (3.7L), 2-bbl., 6-cyl.	105	C	3-speed manual		—	$39[5]	—	S	S (ex. wgns.)	—
				MPG:	—	NA	—	11.5	11.5	—
			3-speed TorqueFlite automatic		—	$250	—	$211	$211 (ex. wgns.)	—
				MPG:	—	16.7	—	NA	NA	—
318 CID (5.2L), 2-bbl., V8	150	G	3-speed manual		—	$151	S	$112	S (wgns.)/ $112 (others)	—
				MPG:	—	12.5	12.5	11.4	11.4	—
			3-speed TorqueFlite automatic		—	$362	$211	$333	$211 (wgns.)/ $333 (others)	S (Pol.) & wgn.)
				MPG:	—	NA	NA	11.6	11.6	—
340 CID (5.6L), 4-bbl., V8	240	H	3-speed manual		—	S (340 Sport)	$181	$209 (w/ Rallye pkg.)	—	—
				MPG:	—	NA	11.8	NA	—	—
			3-speed TorqueFlite automatic		—	$211	$392	$420 (w/ Rallye pkg.)	—	—
				MPG:	—	10.9	10.9	NA	—	—
360 CID (5.9L), 2-bbl., V8	170	K	3-speed TorqueFlite automatic		—	—	—	—	—	S (Mon.)/ $35 (Pol.)
				MPG:	—	—	—	—	—	NA
400 CID (6.6L) Magnum, 2-bbl., V8	175/ 185[6]	M	3-speed TorqueFlite automatic		—	—	—	$370	$247 (wgns.)/ $370 (others)	$56 (ex. Wgns.)
				MPG:	—	—	—	NA	NA	7.9

Engine	Net HP	Engine Code	Transmission Availability[1]	Colt	Dart[4]	Challenger	Charger	Coronet	Polara & Monaco
400 CID (6.6L), Magnum 4-bbl., V8	260/ 220[6]	P	3-speed TorqueFlite automatic	—	—	—	—	$287 (wgns.)/ $409 (others)	$ (Wgns. only)
	MPG:			—	—	—	—	NA	NA	NA
440 CID (7.2L) Magnum, 4-bbl., V8	220	U	3-speed TorqueFlite automatic	—	—	—	$444 (Rallye & SE only)	$321 (wgns. only)	$132
	MPG:			—	—	—	NA	NA	NA	NA

[1]*Unless otherwise noted: All 3-speed manual and automatic transmissions are column-shifts, except on Dart 340 Sport and Challenger. All 4-speeds are floor-shift. Floor-shift w/3-speed manual is available on Dart Sport at extra cost, and floor-shift automatic is available on Dart Sport or Charger models at extra cost.* [2]*Mitsubishi built engine.* [3]*Not available in California.* [4]*Dart 340 Sport only available with 340 CID V8 engine.* [5]*Standard for cars sold in California.* [6]*Horsepower ratings for Monaco cars and Polara/Monaco station wagons.*

Major Options

	Colt	Dart	Challenger	Charger	Coronet	Polara	Monaco
Air conditioning[1]	$339	$358	$369	$378	$378	$412	$412
Tilt steering wheel w/"Rim Blow"	S[2]	—	—	—	—	$60	$60
Automatic speed control	—	—	—	—	—	$68	$68
Electric rear window defogger[3]	$	$27	$29	$31	$31	$31	$31
Tinted glass, all windows	$33	$36	$36	$40	$40	$40	$40
Front vent window, 4-dr. only	—	—	—	—	—	$36	$36
Power windows	—	—	—	$126[4]	$126	$126	$126
Power door locks, 2-dr./4-dr.	—	—	—	—	—	$47/$73	$47/$73
Music Master AM radio	$60	$60	$60	$88	$88	$88	$88
AM/FM stereo	—	$125	$192	$211	$211	$211	$211
AM/FM stereo w/8-track tape	—	—	—	$362	$362	$363	$363
Front bucket seats w/console[6]	S	$120[7]	$52	$105	—	$130	—
Front seat center folding armrest	—	—	—	—	$56	$56	—
Vinyl top	—	$61	$81	$115[8]	$115	$108	$108
Sunroof, electric[9]	—	$223	—	$286[10]	—	—	—
Power steering, variable-ratio	—	$93	$104	$114	$114	S	S
Power brakes, w/front disc[11]	—	$130	$65	$65	$65	S	S
Rallye road wheels	—	$58	$53	$58	$58	—	—
White sidewall tires, std. size	$31	$35	$38	$38	$38	$38	$38

Popular Option Groups & Packages

	Colt	Dart	Challenger	Charger	Coronet	Polara	Monaco
Brougham package	—	—	—	—	—	—	$319
Decor package	$	—	—	—	—	—	—
Light package	—	$29	$35	$	$	$50	S[12]
Luxury equipment package	—	—	—	—	—	$[13]	$
Rallye package	—	—	$180	$85	—	—	—
Utility package	—	$85	—	—	—	—	—

— = Not Available; S = Standard equipment. [1]*Requires 225 CID 6-cyl. or V8 engine on Dart, and requires V8 engine on Charger & Coronet.* [2]*Colt does not include "Rim Blow" steering wheel mounted horn.* [3]*Blower type defogger on all except Colt and Dart Sport (available for $49), which use grid style w/filaments embedded on glass. Not available on Colt wagon.* [4]*Not available on Charger coupe.* [5]*AM/FM radio (non-stereo) on Dart.* [6]*Only available on 2-door models, and requires automatic transmission. Bucket seats available on Polara Custom 2-Door Hardtops without a console.* [7]*For Dart 2-door models only. Includes full-floor carpeting.* [8]*Standard on Charger SE.* [9]*Requires vinyl top. Only available on 2-door hardtop models. On Dart series, only available on Sport and Sport 340 models.* [10]*Price shown is w/full vinyl top. With canopy vinyl top, $251. With formal vinyl top, $171.* [11]*Standard on Dart Sport 340 and Coronet station wagons. All but Dart have manual front disc brakes as standard.* [12]*Excludes front fender-mounted turn signal indicators.* [13]*Available only on Polara Custom.*

Paint Colors

Dodge	Code	Dodge	Code	Dodge	Code
Dark Silver metallic	A5	Bright Blue metallic	B5	Pale Green	F1
Light Blue	B1	Dark Blue metallic[2]	B9	Light Green metallic	F3
Super Blue[1]	B3	Bright Red	E5	Dark Green metallic	F8

Dodge	Code	Colt	Code
Bronze metallic[1]	K6	Spice metallic[5,6,7]	016
Parchment	L4	Sea Green metallic[5,6]	017
Aztec Gold	L6	Bright Yellow[8]	021
Turquoise metallic	Q5	Cherry Blossom White[5,7]	024
Medium Tan metallic[3]	T6	Sunburst Yellow[6]	025
Dark Tan metallic[2]	T8	Alpine Silver[8]	028
Eggshell White	W1	Bright Red[6]	055
Black	X9	Sunset Orange[8]	064
Top Banana[2,4]	Y1	Pacific Blue metallic[6]	065
Yellow[2]	Y2		
Light Gold	Y3		
Golden metallic	Y6		
Dark Gold metallic	JY9		

Single tones are coded W1, W1. Two-tones are coded X9, W1 where first two digits are accent or roof color, and second two digits are basic body color. [1]Available only on Dart, Challenger, Coronet and Charger. [2]Available only on Polara and Monaco. [3]Available only on Coronet and Charger. [4]Available at extra cost. [5]Not available on Colt GT. [6]Not available on Colt wagon. [7]Not available on Colt coupe. [8]Available only on Colt GT.

Colt

"Dodge Colt— with everything it takes to be perfect for your first car, and just as perfect as a second, third or fourth car. Depend on it."

Nameplate year of origin: 1971.
Current bodystyle lifespan: 1971 through 1978 (hardtop); 1971 through 1977 (wagon); 1971 through 1976 (coupe and sedan).
Predecessor to this model: None.
Replacement for this model: Colt (1979 to 1983).
Primary competition: AMC Gremlin, Buick Opel, Chevrolet Vega, and Ford Pinto.
Notable changes: New GT model. Minor trim and detail changes to other models.
Major standard equipment: Non-breathable vinyl front bucket seats, recessed door handles, two-spoke steering wheel, tilt steering column, heater, front and rear rubber bumper guards, front disc brakes, hubcaps, and 6.00 × 13

Measurements

	2-doors	Sedan	Wagon
Wheelbase	95.3"	95.3"	95.3"
Length	163.4"	163.4"	164.4"
Width	61.8"	61.4"	61.4"
Height	52.5"	53.6"	55.5"
Legroom — front	42.7"	42.7"	42.7"
Legroom — rear	30.5"	30.5"	30.5"
Headroom — front	36.9"	37.8"	37.8"
Headroom — rear	35.5"	37.0"	37.3"
Cargo capacity (cu. ft.)	8.1	8.1	60.0
Fuel capacity (gals.)	13.0	13.0	11.0

BSW tires. Hardtop, sedan and wagon add: Breathable vinyl front bucket seats, reclining seat backs, open package tray, recessed door locks, vinyl bodyside molding, rocker panel molding, and full wheel covers. Wagon adds: Fold-down rear seat. GT adds: Soft-rim three-spoke sport steering wheel, front floor console w/shifter, GT bodyside tape stripes, GT logo, argent rallye wheel with chrome hubs and lug nuts, and WSW tires.

Models Available

	Model No.	Base MSRP	Change from LY	Shipping Wt. (lbs.)	Model Year Sales	Change from LY
Colt 2-Door Coupe	6L21	$2,264	+8.07%	2010	NA	NA
Colt 2-Door Hardtop	6H23	$2,497	+9.18%	2055	NA	NA
Colt 4-Door Sedan	6H41	$2,437	+9.14%	2045	NA	NA
Colt 4-Door Station Wagon	6H45	$2,675	+9.14%	2150	NA	NA
Colt GT 2-Door Hardtop	6P23	$2,578	NEW	2055	NA	NEW
TOTALS		*Avg. price* $2,490	+9.87%	*Production* 35,520*		+4.30%*

*Total and comparison to LY are based on estimated model year sales.

Dart

"More than one million economy lovers
have bought Dart already. How about you?"

Nameplate year of origin: 1960 (used on entry-level full-size Dodge).
Current bodystyle lifespan: 1967 through 1976.
Predecessor to this model: Dart (1963 to 1966).
Replacement for this model: Aspen (1976 to 1980).
Percentage of division's production: 43.38%.
Corporate siblings: Plymouth Valiant (including Scamp and Duster).
Primary competition: Buick Apollo, Oldsmobile Omega, Mercury Comet, and Pontiac Ventura.
Notable changes: Restyled front end, and minor trim and detail changes.
Major standard equipment: All-vinyl front bench seat (Swinger and base Dart), cloth and vinyl front bench seat (all others), simulated woodgrain I/P cluster appliqué, two-speed electric windshield wipers, front door armrests, cigarette lighter (ex. Dart Sport), heater and defroster, front door window vents (sedans only), wheel opening moldings (Sport only), grille surround and front edge moldings, and 6.95 × 14 BSW tires. Swinger and Custom add: Cut-pile carpeting, rear seat armrests, roof drip-rail molding, bodyside moldings w/painted insert, and dual horns. Dart 340 Sport adds: Bodyside and rear deck lid performance tape stripes, and E70 × 14 BSW tires.

Measurements

	Dart	Dart Sport
Wheelbase	111.0"	108.0"
Length	203.8"	200.0"
Width	69.6"	71.8"
Height	54.1"	53.1"
Legroom — front	41.5"	41.5"
Legroom — rear	35.9"	30.0"
Headroom — front	38.6"	37.5"
Headroom — rear	37.3"	36.5"
Cargo capacity (cu. ft.)	14.3	15.9
Fuel capacity (gals.)	16.0	16.0

Models Available

	Model No.	Base MSRP	Change from LY*	Shipping Wt. (lbs.)	Model Year Production	Change from LY*
Dart Sport 2-Door Coupe	LL29	$2,424	+4.66%	2850	68,113	+70.79%
Dart Swinger Special 2-Dr. Hardtop	LL23	$2,462	+3.75%	2895	17,480	-9.01%
Dart 4-Door Sedan	LL41	$2,504	+3.47%	2910	21,539	-17.22%
Dart Sport 340 2-Door Coupe	LM29	$2,853	+3.41%	3205	11,315	+30.06%
Dart Swinger 2-Door Hardtop	LH23	$2,617	+3.52%	2890	107,619	-10.03%
Dart Custom 4-Door Sedan	LH41	$2,658	+3.26%	2910	62,626	+25.40%
TOTALS	*Avg. price*	$2,586	+3.66%	*Production*	288,692	+9.62%

*Comparisons of Dart Sport models are made to equivalent 1972 Dodge Demon models.

Challenger

"Here's a sporty car that's everything its name implies: Challenger!"

Nameplate year of origin: 1970.
Current bodystyle lifespan: 1970 through 1974.
Predecessor to this model: None.
Replacement for this model: None.
Percentage of division's sales volume: 4.90%.
Corporate siblings: Plymouth Barracuda.
Primary competition: AMC Javelin, Chevrolet Camaro, Ford Mustang, and Pontiac Firebird.
Notable changes: Minor trim and detail changes.
Major standard equipment: All-vinyl bucket seats w/integral head restraints, deep cut-pile carpeting, simulated woodgrain door inserts, dome light, front and rear door/quarter panel armrests and ashtrays, concealed two-speed windshield wipers w/washers, wheel opening and roof drip-rail moldings, grille surround and deck lid moldings, dual body paint stripes, front disc brakes, and 7.35 × 14 BSW tires.

Measurements

Wheelbase	110.0"
Length	198.2"
Width	76.4"
Height	50.9"
Legroom — front	42.3"
Legroom — rear	30.9"
Headroom — front	37.4"
Headroom — rear	35.6"
Cargo capacity (cu. ft.)	8.6
Fuel capacity (gals.)	18.0

Models Available

	Model No.	Base MSRP	Change from LY	Shipping Wt. (lbs.)	Model Year Production	Change from LY
Challenger 2-Door Hardtop	JH23	$3,011	+7.92%	3155	32,596	+75.86%
TOTALS	Avg. price	$3,011	+2.55%	Production	32,596	+22.27%

Charger

"Remember when exciting cars used to be expensive? Forget it."

Nameplate year of origin: 1966.
Current bodystyle lifespan: 1971 through 1974.
Predecessor to this model: Charger (1968 to 1970).
Replacement for this model: Charger SE (1975 to 1978).
Percentage of division's sales volume: 17.93%.
Corporate siblings: Plymouth Satellite Sebring.
Primary competition: AMC Matador, Chevrolet Chevelle and Monte Carlo, Ford Torino, Mercury Montego, and Pontiac LeMans and Grand Prix.
Notable changes: Revised front and rear styling.
Major standard equipment: All-vinyl front bench seat, color-keyed carpeting, simulated woodgrained vinyl trim on door panels (except coupe), dome light w/front door courtesy switch, concealed two-speed windshield wipers w/washers, dual horns, and E78 × 14 BSW tires. SE adds: All-vinyl split-back front bench seat w/center armrest, rallye instrument cluster, formal vinyl roof w/fixed louvered quarter windows, "SE" stand-up hood ornament, and bodyside paint stripe.

Measurements

Wheelbase	115.0"
Length	212.7"
Width	77.0"
Height	52.5"
Legroom — front	41.9"
Legroom — rear	34.1"
Headroom — front	37.3"
Headroom — rear	36.4"
Cargo capacity (cu. ft.)	14.3
Fuel capacity (gals.)	19.5

Models Available

	Model No.	Base MSRP	Change from LY	Shipping Wt. (lbs.)	Model Year Production	Change from LY
Ambassador 2-Door Hardtop	89-7	$4,477	+11.42%	3774	*	*
Charger 2-Door Coupe	WL21	$2,810	+5.96%	3395	11,995	+53.72%
Charger 2-Door Hardtop	WH23	$3,060	+5.05%	3450	45,415	+0.12%
Charger SE 2-Door Hardtop Coupe	WP29	$3,375	+3.88%	3540	61,908	+176.01%
TOTALS	Avg. price	$3,082	+4.89%	Production	119,318	+57.84%

Coronet

"Lots of change for your family dollar,
including the all-new Torsion-Quiet Ride."

Nameplate year of origin: 1950 (as hardtop designation); 1953 (as series).
Current bodystyle lifespan: 1971 through 1978. Renamed Monaco for 1977 to 1978.
Predecessor to this model: Coronet (1968 to 1970).
Replacement for this model: Diplomat (1977 to 1979).
Percentage of division's sales volume: 13.15%.
Corporate siblings: Plymouth Satellite.
Primary competition: AMC Matador, Chevrolet Chevelle, Ford Torino, Mercury Montego, and Pontiac LeMans.
Notable changes: Revised front and rear styling.
Major standard equipment: All-vinyl front bench seat, cigarette lighter

Measurements

	Sedans	Wagons
Wheelbase	118.0"	118.0"
Length	212.9"	217.6"
Width	77.8"	78.8"
Height	54.0"	56.4"
Legroom — front	41.9"	41.9"
Legroom — rear	36.7"	36.7"
Headroom — front	38.5"	39.7"
Headroom — rear	37.3"	38.1"

w/front and rear ashtrays, front and rear door armrests, 3-spoke color-keyed steering wheel, dome light w/front door courtesy switch, concealed two-speed windshield wipers w/washers, and E78 × 14 BSW tires. Custom adds: Pleated cloth-and-vinyl bench seats (sedan only), color-keyed carpeting, simulated woodgrain inserts on I/P, door trim inserts and steering wheel, and drip rail, wheel-lip and bodyside moldings. Wagons add: Power front disc brakes, dual action tailgate w/concealed hinges, and H78 × 14 BSW tires. Crestwood wagon adds: All-vinyl split-back front bench seat w/fold-down center armrest, cargo compartment carpeting and dome light, rear roof air deflector, and exterior simulated woodgrained bodyside overlays.

Measurements (cont.)

	Sedans	Wagons
Cargo capacity (cu. ft.)	16.7	91.3
Fuel capacity (gals.)	19.5	21.0

Models Available

	Model No.	Base MSRP	Change from LY	Shipping Wt. (lbs.)	Model Year Production	Change from LY
Coronet 4-Door Sedan	WL41	$2,867	+5.37%	3440	14,395	+27.47%
Coronet 4-Door, 2-S. Wagon	WL45	$3,314	+3.27%	3955	4,874	-10.60%
Coronet Custom 4-Door Sedan	WH41	$3,017	+4.36%	3430	46,491	+7.79%
Coronet Custom 4-Dr., 2-S. Wagon	WH45	$3,442	+1.77%	3955	13,018	NA**
Coronet Custom 4-Dr., 3-S. Wagon	WH46	$3,560	+2.89%	4000	*	NA**
Coronet Crestwood 4-Dr., 2-S. Wgn.	WP45	$3,671	+1.86%	3970	8,755	+35.30%
Coronet Crestwood 4-Dr., 3-S. Wgn.	WP46	$3,791	+2.93%	4005	*	NA*
TOTALS		Avg. price $3,380	+3.10%		Production 87,533	+31.93%

*Production of 2-seat and 3-seat station wagons was kept as combined total.   **Calculation of change from last year is not available, since 1972 Coronet and Coronet Custom wagon production was kept as combined total.*

Polara

"The big Dodge that makes a lot of sense."

Nameplate year of origin: 1959.
Current bodystyle lifespan: 1969 through 1973.
Predecessor to this model: Polara (1967 to 1968).
Replacement for this model: Monaco (1974 to 1976).
Percentage of division's sales volume: 16.23%.
Corporate siblings: Dodge Monaco, and Plymouth Fury.
Primary competition: AMC Ambassador, Chevrolet Impala, Ford LTD, Oldsmobile Delta 88, and Pontiac Catalina.
Notable changes: Revised front and rear styling.
Major standard equipment: Peyton cloth-and-vinyl front bench seat, color-keyed carpeting, leather-grained black vinyl instrument cluster appliqué, glove box lock, inside hood release, concealed two-speed windshield wipers w/washers, full-length bodyside molding, wheel covers, and

Measurements

	Cars	Wagons
Wheelbase	122.0"	122.0"
Length	226.6"	227.9"
Width	79.6"	79.6"
Height	56.1"	58.3"
Legroom — front	41.8"	41.8"
Legroom — rear	39.1"	39.1"
Headroom — front	38.8"	39.6"
Headroom — rear	38.4"	39.2"
Cargo capacity (cu. ft.)	22.4	104.2
Fuel capacity (gals.)	23.0	23.0

G78 × 15 BSW tires. Custom adds: Custom cloth-and-vinyl front bench seat, simulated woodgrained instrument cluster and lower I/P appliqué, 3-spoke color-keyed steering wheel w/simulated woodgrained inserts, simulated woodgrained door trim insert, and full-length bodyside molding w/vinyl insert. Wagons add: All-vinyl front bench seat, cargo compartment side storage panels, aerodynamic roof air deflector, cargo compartment lock and carpeting (Custom only), Auto-Lock electric tailgate lock system (3-seat wagons only), and J78 × 15 BSW tires (2-seat wagons) or L84 × 15 BSW tires (3-seat wagons).

Models Available

	Model No.	Base MSRP	Change from LY	Shipping Wt. (lbs.)	Model Year Production	Change from LY
Polara 2-Door Hardtop	DL23	$3,752	+3.05%	3835	6,432	-8.40%
Polara 4-Door Sedan	DL41	$3,729	+3.07%	3865	15,015	-40.39%
Polara 4-Door, 2-Seat Wagon	DL45	$4,186	NEW	4420	3,327	NEW

	Model No.	Base MSRP	Change from LY	Shipping Wt. (lbs.)	Model Year Production	Change from LY
Polara Custom 2-Door Hardtop	DM23	$3,928	+2.56%	3835	17,406	+15.74%
Polara Custom 4-Door Sedan	DM41	$3,911	+2.70%	3870	23,939	+21.28%
Polara Custom 4-Door Hardtop	DM43	$4,001	+2.64%	3905	29,341	+30.38%
Polara Custom 4-Dr., 2-S. Wagon	DM45	$4,370	+2.53%	4440	3,702	+5.86%
Polara Custom 4-Dr., 3-S. Wagon	DM46	$4,494	+2.81%	4485	8,839	+15.39%
TOTALS		*Avg. price* $4,046	+3.96%		*Production* 108,001	-0.79%

Monaco

"The big Dodge that's creating a quiet sensation."

Nameplate year of origin: 1965.

Current bodystyle lifespan: 1969 through 1973.

Predecessor to this model: Monaco (1967 to 1968).

Replacement for this model: 1974 through 1977. Royal Monaco was direct replacement for Monaco (1974 to 1976); Monaco series renamed Royal Monaco (1977).

Percentage of division's sales volume: 4.42%.

Corporate siblings: Dodge Polara and Plymouth Fury.

Primary competition: AMC Ambassador Brougham, Chevrolet Caprice, Ford LTD, Mercury Monterey, Oldsmobile Delta 88, and Pontiac Bonneville/Grand Ville.

Notable changes: Revised front and rear styling.

Major standard equipment: Cloth and vinyl split-back front bench seat w/fold-down center armrest, color-keyed carpeting, simulated wood-grained instrument cluster and lower I/P appliqué, 3-spoke color-keyed steering wheel w/simulated woodgrained inserts, simulated woodgrained door trim insert w/carpeted lower panel, door panel assist straps, electric clock, combination dome/map light, light package (less fender-mounted turn signal indicators), concealed two-speed windshield wipers w/washers, concealed head lamps, deluxe wheel covers, and H78 × 15 BSW tires. Wagon adds: All-vinyl split-bench front seat w/fold-down center armrest, cargo compartment side storage panels, aerodynamic roof air deflector, cargo compartment lock and carpeting, Auto-Lock electric tailgate lock system (3-seat wagon only), exterior simulated woodgrained overlay, and J78 × 15 BSW tires (2-seat wagon) or L84 × 15 BSW tires (3-seat wagon).

Measurements

	Cars	Wagons
Wheelbase	122.0"	122.0"
Length	228.7"	230.1"
Width	79.6"	79.6"
Height	56.3"	58.3"
Legroom — front	41.8"	41.8"
Legroom — rear	39.1"	39.1"
Headroom — front	38.8"	39.6"
Headroom — rear	38.4"	39.2"
Cargo capacity (cu. ft.)	22.4	104.2
Fuel capacity (gals.)	23.0	23.0

Models Available

	Model No.	Base MSRP	Change from LY	Shipping Wt. (lbs.)	Model Year Production	Change from LY
Monaco 2-Door Hardtop	DP23	$4,276	+2.96%	3985	6,133	-21.23%
Monaco 4-Door Sedan	DP41	$4,218	+3.00%	4020	6,316	-2.44%
Monaco 4-Door Hardtop	DP43	$4,339	+2.92%	4060	9,031	-39.95%
Monaco 4-Door, 2-Seat Wagon	DP45	$4,730	+2.23%	4470	2,337	-9.03%
Monaco 4-Door, 3-Seat Wagon	DP46	$4,859	+2.17%	4515	5,579	+8.44%
TOTALS		*Avg. price* $4,484	+2.63%		*Production* 29,396	-20.58%

FORD

"Listening better. Building better. That's Ford."

Ford entered the 1973 model year with few changes in styling, model lines, or powertrain choices. Of course, all models received some type of facelift to meet the federal front bumper standards, with the Torino, Thunderbird and full-size Ford line changing the most. The model year would turn out to be less successful than Ford might have hoped for, as about two percent of their market share was lost, mainly to Oldsmobile and Pontiac, despite a production increase of about 100,000 units. Market share would rebound for 1974, mainly on the strength of the new Mustang II, but the current model year's market share of 22.10 percent would be a struggle for Ford to maintain through 1976. After that, because of the rise in the Oldsmobile Cutlass's popularity, followed by General Motors' success with its downsizing efforts, it was a gradual decline until the 1986 model year when Ford rebounded on the success of the Taurus.

The full-size Ford line, consisting of the Custom 500, Galaxie 500, LTD and LTD Brougham, received a styling update on the new-for-1971 bodies. At the front end, a new grille and new box-style bumpers gave the '73 models a more formal "Lincoln-esque" appearance.

On the LTD and LTD Brougham, an egg-crate style center grille, with three-by-three egg-crate inserts, was flanked by similarly sized grille sections on each side which housed the dual headlights and were separated from the center grille by a thin vertical body color strip. The lesser Custom 500 and Galaxie were distinguished by a single full-width grille of horizontal crosshatch design, seven rows high, with a vertical center bar. Turn signal and parking lamps were mounted vertically on the front fender ends of all four models. Bodysides of all models were smoothed out, with the creases over the wheel openings being eliminated, and the openings themselves more rounded. Interiors received modest upgrades to patterns, colors and trim. In the greenhouse area, station wagons adopted the frameless door windows also used on the new pillared hardtop sedans. At the back, a variation of the rectangular Ford taillight theme was set onto the rear panel that slanted rearward from the decklid downward to the bumper. Station wagon rear styling continued similar to the 1972 models. Near the end of the model year, a Country Squire wagon without the traditional woodgrain bodyside appliqués was introduced. (Herein it is not listed as a separate model, and production is included with the regular model.) An interesting option for the full-size Ford station wagons with dual facing rear seats was a "recre-ation table" available for $42 that included magnetized checkers. This option predated a similar activity table option touted as a "new convenience" 35 years later on Chrysler Corporation minivans.

The Mustang pony car was entering its final year as a sporty muscle car. All models added a new grille with vertical rectangular parking lights and a new front bumper formed of color-keyed, high-impact molded urethane, similar to the one used on the 1972 Mustang Mach I. The bumper was repositioned further forward with impact absorbing struts behind it to meet the new federal requirements. Only detail changes were made to the rest of the car, including a new tape stripe treatment for the Mach I on the side and rear end.

The popular Maverick received its first new grille and front bumper change, featuring a flatter, more vertical contour, and horizontally mounted rectangular parking/turn signal lamps mounted on the grille just inside of the headlights. The Pinto added front bumper guards as standard equipment, but would delay the use of energy absorbing bumper struts for another year. Minor interior changes to both cars were limited to trim and upholstery designs.

The mid-size Torino line had been completely redesigned for 1972, so the changes for this year were mainly focused on the front end. The large center "fish-mouth" grille was replaced on the Gran Torino by a more conventional crosshatch grille, three rows high and six columns across with rounded corners with an inset crosshatch pattern, set above a new box-style bumper, and between the dual headlights. The base Torino line used a similar but full-width grille that encompassed the dual headlights. The base models had parking/turn signal lamps set in the fender end caps, while all other models had them placed in the outer center section of the grille. The SportsRoof Gran Torino Sport returned as the sportiest of Ford's mid-size line, although this would be the final year for the SportsRoof design since its introduction in 1968. At the top end a Gran Torino Brougham line was added, acknowledging the growing trend toward mid-size luxury cars.

The luxury trend continued in the Thunderbird, which had also been completely redesigned for 1972, and was more closely related to the Lincoln Continental Mark IV than to any other Ford product. As with other models, the Thunderbird featured revised front end styling with a large, square egg-crate grille design, six rows tall and twelve columns wide, set above a box-style bumper. New headlight surrounds put each lamp in its own chrome bezel, and parking lamps were set into the front fender ends, as on the full-size Ford models. Atop the new header panel and above the grille was a new stand-up, fold-down hood ornament, a Thunderbird first. Newly available this year was the "Sure-Track" brake control system, optional for $189. The system was very similar in concept and operation to modern day anti-lock brake systems. Overall, the new styling and features seemed to work as sales jumped 50 percent over 1972.

Model changes consisted of the full-size LTD convertible being discontinued for 1973, leaving only the Mustang

convertible in the Ford line. By year's end, the Mustang drop top would also disappear. Also gone was the full-size base Custom series, which had been produced mostly for fleet use the past several years. This came at the same time as Chevrolet dropped its base full-size model, the Biscayne, leaving only Plymouth with a bare bones full-size sedan, the Fury I. Powertrain choices remained mostly the same, excepting the discontinuation of the long-running 170 CID and 240 CID 6-cylinder engines that had been introduced for the 1961 and 1965 model years respectively.

Galaxie 500 4-Door Pillared Hardtop

Galaxie 500 Country Sedan Station Wagon
with Custom 500 Ranch Wagon, rear

Galaxie 500 instrument panel

Gran Torino 2-Door Hardtop

Gran Torino 4-Door Pillared Hardtop

Gran Torino 4-Door Station Wagon
with Torino 4-Door Station Wagon, rear

LTD Brougham 2-Door Hardtop
with optional sunroof

Maverick 4-Door Sedan
with Luxury Décor option

Pinto 2-Door Sedan

Mustang 2-Door Convertible

Mustang Mach I 2-Door SportsRoof Hardtop

Pinto 2-Door Station Wagon

Pinto interior with Sports Accent group

Thunderbird 2-Door Hardtop

Model year production: 2,349,367, up 4.55% from 1972.
Domestic market share: 22.10% (2nd place).
Base price range: $2,021 to $6,437.
Ford average base price: $3,462, up 3.92%.
Introduction date: September 22, 1972.
Assembly plants: Atlanta, GA (A); Oakville, Ontario, Canada (B); Mahwah, NJ (E); Dearborn, MI (F); Chicago, IL (G); Lorain, OH (H); Los Angeles, CA (J); Kansas City, MO (K); Norfolk, VA (N); Twin Cities, MN (P); San Jose, CA (R); Allen Park, MI (S —*pilot plant*); Metuchen, NJ (T); Louisville, KY (U); Wayne, MI (W); St. Thomas, Ontario, Canada (X); Wixom, MI (Y); and St. Louis, MO (Z).

Data plate identification (VIN): Eleven digit code read as follows: First digit indicates year (3 = 1973); second digit indicates assembly plant code (see list above); third and fourth digits indicate model number (model number in model charts); fifth digit indicates engine code (see powertrain chart); remaining digits are sequential with beginning numbers of 100001. *Example:* 3F01F100001 is a 1973 Ford Mustang 2-Door hardtop, with 302 CID, 2-bbl. V8 engine, serial number 100001, built in Dearborn, MI.

Powertrains

Engine	Net HP	Engine Code	Transmission Availability[1]		Pinto	Maverick	Mustang	Torino	Full-size	Thunderbird
97.6 CID (1.6L) OHC, 1-bbl., 4-cyl.	54	NA	4-speed manual		S (ex. wgn.)	—	—	—	—	—
				MPG:	NA	—	—	—	—	—
122 CID (2.0L) OHC, 2-bbl., 4-cyl.	85	X	4-speed manual		S (wgn.)/ $49 (others)	—	—	—	—	—
				MPG:	NA	—	—	—	—	—
			3-speed Select-Shift Cruise-O-Matic		$170 (wgn.) / $219 (others)	—	—	—	—	—
				MPG:	NA	—	—	—	—	—
200 CID (3.3L), 1-bbl., 6-cyl.	84	U	3-speed manual		—	S	—	—	—	—
				MPG:	—	NA	—	—	—	—
			3-speed Select-Shift Cruise-O-Matic		—	$177	—	—	—	—
				MPG:	—	NA	—	—	—	—
250 CID (4.1L), 1-bbl., 6-cyl.	88[2]	L	3-speed manual		—	$39	S (ex. Mach I)	S (cars)[3]	—	—
				MPG:	—	NA	NA	14.0	—	—
			3-speed Select-Shift Cruise-O-Matic		—	$217	$204	$211 (cars)[3]	—	—
				MPG:	—	NA	NA	NA	—	—
302 CID (5.0L), 2-bbl., V8	135	F	3-speed manual		—	$122	S (Mach I)/$87 (others)	S (wgns.)/ $91 (cars)[3]	—	—
				MPG:	—	NA	NA	NA	—	—

1973

Engine	Net HP	Engine Code	Transmission Availability[1]		Pinto	Maverick	Mustang	Torino	Full-size	Thunderbird
			3-speed Select-Shift Cruise-O-Matic		—	$299	$204 (Mach I)/ $291 (others)	$211 (wgns.)/ $302 (cars)[3]	—	—
				MPG:	—	NA	NA	NA	—	—
351 CID (5.8L), 2-bbl., V8	160	H	3-speed Select-Shift Cruise-O-Matic		—	—	$245 (Mach I)/ $332 (others)	$255 (wgns.)/ $346 (cars)[3]	S	—
				MPG:	—	—	NA	NA	NA	—
351 CID (5.8L) Cobra Jet, 4-bbl., V8[3]	246[2]	Q	4-speed manual w/ Hurst Shifter		—	—	$300 (Mach I)/ $387 (others)	$327[4] (2-Drs. only)	—	—
				MPG:	—	—	NA	NA	—	—
			3-speed Select-Shift Cruise-O-Matic		—	—	$332 (Mach I)/ $419 (others)	$337 (2-Drs. only)	—	—
				MPG:	—	—	NA	NA	—	—
400 CID (6.6L), 2-bbl., V8	168	S	3-speed Select-Shift Cruise-O-Matic		—	—	—	$298 (wgns.)/ $399 (cars)[3]	$52	—
				MPG:	—	—	—	NA	NA	—
429 CID Thunder Jet (6.9L), 4-bbl., V8	201	K/N[5]	3-speed Select-Shift Cruise-O-Matic		—	—	—	$428 (wgns.)/ $529 (cars)[3]	$178	S
				MPG:	—	—	—	NA	NA	NA
460 CID (7.5L), 4-bbl., V8	200[6]	A	3-speed Select-Shift Cruise-O-Matic		—	—	—	—	$254	$76
				MPG:	—	—	—	—	NA	NA

[1]Unless otherwise noted: All manual transmissions are floor-shifts, except on Maverick. All automatics are column-shift, except on Pinto and Mustang. Floor-shift is available for $24 extra on Maverick with 3-speed manual, and Maverick with automatic (requires bucket seats); and at no cost on Gran Torino or Gran Torino Sport with bucket seats and automatic. [2]Horsepower rating in Mustang is 95 w/250 CID, and 264 w/351 CID 4-bbl. [3]Except Gran Torino Sport, which follows the same powertrain combinations as wagons, plus the 351 CID 4-bbl, available in all 2-doors. [4]Standard on models equipped with Rallye Equipment Group option. [5]Engine code N in Thunderbird. [6]Horsepower rating in Thunderbird is 208.

Major Options

	Pinto	Maverick	Mustang	Torino	Full-size	Thunderbird
SelectAire Air conditioning	$363[1]	$363	$368	$402	$410[2]	$437[2]
Tilt steering wheel	—	—	$41	—	$44	$51
Fingertip speed control	—	—	—	—	$99	$103
Rear window defogger	—	$27	—	—	$30	—
Electric rear window defroster	$43[3]	—	$57	$47	$62	$82
Tinted glass, all windows	$36	$49	$36	$42	$53	$51
Power windows	—	—	$113	$124	$129	$130
Power door locks, 2-dr./4-dr.	—	—	—	$46/$69	$46/$69	$59
Power seat, 6-way w/std. seating	—	—	—	$102	$102	$202
Front bucket seats w/console	—	$98[4]	$68[4]	$205	—	N/C
AM radio	$59	$59	$59	$64	$64	S
AM/FM stereo	$190	$190	$191	$208	$234	$146
AM/FM stereo w/8-track tape	—	—	—	—	$363	$299
Vinyl top, full	$75	$75	$80	$93	$110[5]	$137
Sunroof, power-operated	$117[6]	—	—	—	$496	$505
Power trunk lid release	—	—	—	—	$14	—

	Pinto	Maverick	Mustang	Torino	Full-size	Thunderbird
Power steering	—	$92	$103	$112	S	S
Power brakes, w/front disc	—	—	$62	$68	S	S
Deluxe wheel covers	$23	$25	$23–$79	$87	$62–$87	$62
Forged aluminum wheels	$142	$142	$142	—	—	—
Magnum 500 chrome wheels	—	—	—	$151	—	—
White sidewall tires, std. size[7]	$42	$29	$36	$32	$32	S

Popular Option Groups & Packages[8]

	Pinto	Maverick	Mustang	Torino	Full-size	Thunderbird
Accent group	$65–$87	—	—	$38	—	—
Appearance protection group	—	$25–$31	—	$39–$46	$47–$54	$72
Convenience group	$33	$19	$46	—	$59	—
Décor group	—	—	$51	—	—	—
Deluxe bumper group	$24	$49	$25	$42–$68	$49–$61	$30
Exterior décor group	—	$83	—	—	—	$237
Glamour paint option group	—	—	—	—	—	$162
Instrumentation group	—	—	$71	$118	—	—
Interior décor group	—	$65–$82	—	—	—	—
Light group	—	—	—	—	$25–$32	$44
Luxury décor group	$153–$192	$390	—	—	—	—
Protection group	$60	—	$36	—	—	—
Rallye Equipment group	—	—	—	$443[9]	—	—
Sports accent group	$347	—	—	—	—	—
Sports interior option	—	—	$115	—	—	—
Squire option	$237	—	—	—	—	—
Squire Brougham option	—	—	—	—	$264	—
Turnpike convenience group	—	—	—	—	—	$133
Visibility group	—	—	—	$37	—	—

— = Not Available; S = Standard equipment.   [1]Requires 2.0L 4-cylinder engine on Pinto.   [2]SelectAire air conditioner w/automatic temperature control is available for $487 on full-size Fords, and $506 on Thunderbird.   [3]Not available on Pinto Runabout. Includes tinted rear window.   [4]Bucket seats only on Maverick; console not available. Console only on Mustang; bucket seats standard.   [5]For wagons, $138.   [6]Manually operated.   [7]Price on wagons: Pinto, $28.   [8]Price ranges cover all models available. See appendix for option groups and packages for content details and model availability variations.   [9]$386 on Gran Torino Sport.

Paint Colors

	Code		Code		Code
Light Gray metallic[1]	1A	Dark Green metallic	4Q	Medium Yellow Gold[2]	6C
Black	1C	Light Green	4S	Yellow	6D
Silver Moondust metallic[1]	1D	Emerald Fire metallic[1]	4U	Medium Bright Yellow[2]	6E
Bright Red[2]	2B	Green Diamond[1]	4Y	Gold Glow metallic[2]	6F
Red metallic[2]	2C	Copper Diamond Flare metallic[1]	52	Gold Fire metallic[1]	6G
Burgundy Fire metallic[1]	2G	Light Pewter metallic[2]	5A	Medium Gold metallic	6L
Maroon[1]	2J	Cinnamon Fire metallic[1]	5D	White	9A
Bright Red metallic[2]	2L	Dark Brown metallic	5F	Pearl White	9C
Pastel Blue[1]	3A	Medium Brown (Ginger) metallic[2]	5H		
Light Blue[2]	3B	Ginger Glow metallic[2]	5J		
Medium Blue metallic	3D	Almond Fire metallic[1]	5K		
Dark Blue metallic[1]	3G	Tan	5L		
Blue Glow metallic[2]	3K	Medium Copper metallic[2]	5M		
Silver Blue Fire metallic[1]	3L	Medium Orange metallic[2]	5N		
Silver Blue metallic[2]	3M	Mahogany Fire metallic[1]	5P		
Light Grabber Blue[2]	3N	Dark Brown metallic[1]	5Q		
Light Grabber Blue[2]	3P	Gold metallic[1]	5R		
Pastel Blue[2]	3Q	Medium Beige[1]	5S		
Bright Green Gold metallic[2]	4B	Saddle Bronze metallic[2]	5T		
Ivy Bronze metallic[2]	4C	Orange[2]	5W		
Green Fire metallic[1]	4D	Light Goldenrod (or Light Yellow Gold)	6B		
Medium Aqua[2]	4N				
Medium Green metallic	4P				

In two-tone combinations, first two digits are lower color and second two digits are upper color. Two-tones available on Pinto for $52, Gran Torino Sport for $57, and full-size Fords (except Country Squire) for $30. Fire metallic paints require optional Glamour paint group. Metallic glow paints are $35 extra on Maverick & Mustang, $38 on Torino & full-size Fords. [1]*Available exclusively on Thunderbird.* [2]*Available on all models except Thunderbird.*

Pinto

"Back to Basics."

Nameplate year of origin: 1971.
Current bodystyle lifespan: 1971 through 1980.
Predecessor to this model: None.
Replacement for this model: Escort (1981 to 1985).
Percentage of division's production: 20.62%.
Corporate siblings: None.
Primary competition: AMC Gremlin, Buick Opel, Chevrolet
  Vega, Dodge Colt, and Plymouth Cricket.
Notable changes: Minor trim and detail changes.
Major standard equipment: All-vinyl high-back front
  bucket seats, illuminated I/P controls, enclosed glove box,
  color-keyed rubber floor mat, mini console, front bumper
  guards, rack-and-pinion steering, hubcaps, and 6.00 × 13
  BSW tires. Runabout adds: Color-keyed carpeting and
  fold-down rear seat. Station wagon adds: Passenger and
  cargo compartment carpeting, front disc brakes, bright window and belt moldings, and A78 × 13 BSW tires.

Measurements

	Sedan	Runabout	Wagon
Wheelbase	94.2"	94.2"	94.2"
Length	164.1"	164.1"	173.8"
Width	69.4"	69.4"	69.7"
Height	49.7"	49.6"	51.0"
Legroom — front	41.0"	41.0"	41.0"
Legroom — rear	31.5"	31.5"	31.5"
Headroom — front	37.5"	37.5"	38.3"
Headroom — rear	36.3"	36.3"	39.6"
Cargo capacity (cu. ft.)	5.9	6.1	60.6
Fuel capacity (gals.)	11.0	11.0	12.0

Models Available

	Model No.	Base MSRP	Change from LY	Shipping Wt. (lbs.)	Model Year Production	Change from LY
Pinto 2-Door Sedan	10	$2,021	+3.11%	2115	116,146	-35.83%
Pinto 3-Dr. Runabout (hatchback)	11	$2,144	+3.18%	2145	150,603	-23.91%
Pinto 2-Door Station Wagon	12	$2,343	+3.44%	2386	217,763	+114.58%
TOTALS		*Avg. price* $2,169	+3.25%		*Production* 484,512	+0.85%

Mustang

"There's still nothing like it."

Nameplate year of origin: 1964 (also used on a 1963 show car).
Current bodystyle lifespan: 1971 through 1973.
Predecessor to this model: Mustang (1969 to 1970).
Replacement for this model: Mustang II (1974 to 1978).
Percentage of division's production: 5.74%.
Corporate siblings: Mercury Cougar.
Primary competition: AMC Javelin, Chevrolet Camaro, Dodge Challenger, Ply-
  mouth Barracuda, and Pontiac Firebird.
Notable changes: Minor trim and detail changes.
Major standard equipment: All-vinyl high-back bucket seats, nylon loop color-keyed
  carpeting, two-spoke steering wheel w/woodgrain inserts, courtesy lights, color-

Measurements

Wheelbase	109.0"
Length	193.8"
Width	74.1"
Height	50.7"
Legroom — front	41.7"
Legroom — rear	28.2"
Headroom — front	37.2"
Headroom — rear	36.0"
Cargo capacity (cu. ft.)	9.5
Fuel capacity (gals.)	19.5

keyed racing mirrors, hubcaps, and E78 × 14 BSW tires. Convertible adds: Knitted vinyl bucket seats, power operated top, color-
keyed top boot, tinted rear glass, and power front disc brakes. Grandé adds: Cloth-and-vinyl interior trim, woodgrain I/P trim,
electric clock, vinyl top w/Grandé script on C-pillar, LH remote and RH manual color-keyed racing mirrors, bodyside accent
stripes, trunk mat, and deluxe wheel covers. Mach I adds: Integral sports lamps, Mach I bodyside and decklid decals, black-out
grille, competition suspension, wheel trim rings w/hubcaps, and E70 × 14 W/O tires.

Models Available

	Model No.	Base MSRP	Change from LY	Shipping Wt. (lbs.)	Model Year Production	Change from LY
Mustang 2-Door Hardtop	01	$2,760	+3.02%	2995	51,430	-10.32%
Mustang 2-Door SportsRoof Hardtop	02	$2,820	+3.07%	3008	10,820	-30.74%
Mustang 2-Door Convertible	03	$3,102	+4.62%	3126	11,853	+85.17%
Mustang Grande 2-Door Hardtop	04	$2,946	+2.83%	3003	25,274	+40.06%
Mustang Mach I 2-Door SportsRoof Hardtop	05	$3,088	+2.83%	3115	35,440	+28.06%
TOTALS	*Avg. price*	$2,943	+3.28%	*Production*	134,817	+7.77%

Maverick

"Surprising value in a compact."

Nameplate year of origin: 1970.
Current bodystyle lifespan: 1970 through 1977.
Predecessor to this model: Falcon (1966 to 1969).
Replacement for this model: Fairmont (1978 to 1983).
Percentage of division's production: 12.42%.
Corporate siblings: Mercury Comet.
Primary competition: AMC Hornet, Chevrolet Nova, Plymouth Valiant, and Pontiac Ventura.
Notable changes: Minor trim and detail changes.
Major standard equipment: Cloth-and-vinyl front bench seat, nylon loop pile carpeting, illuminated I/P controls, two-spoke steering wheel, hubcaps, and 6.45 × 14 BSW tires. Grabber adds: "Tooled" all-vinyl upholstery, outside color-keyed dual racing mirrors, Grabber paint and tape stripe treatment, hubcaps w/trim rings, and D70 × 14 R/WL tires.

Measurements

	2-Door	4-Door
Wheelbase	103.0"	109.9"
Length	183.3"	190.2"
Width	70.5"	70.5"
Height	52.9"	52.9"
Legroom — front	40.7"	40.7"
Legroom — rear	31.8"	36.0"
Headroom — front	37.5"	37.8"
Headroom — rear	35.9"	36.5"
Cargo capacity (cu. ft.)	9.5	10.1
Fuel capacity (gals.)	15.0	15.0

Models Available

	Model No.	Base MSRP	Change from LY	Shipping Wt. (lbs.)	Model Year Production	Change from LY
Maverick 2-Door Sedan	91	$2,248	+5.05%	2646	148,943	+2.06%
Maverick 4-Door Sedan	92	$2,305	+5.01%	2759	110,382	+49.80%
Maverick Grabber 2-Door Sedan	93	$2,427	+5.20%	2689	32,350	-8.48%
TOTALS	*Avg. price*	$2,327	+5.09%	*Production*	291,675	+14.40%

Torino

"The solid mid-size car. Smooth. Strong. And Quiet."

Nameplate year of origin: 1968.
Current bodystyle lifespan: 1972 through 1976.
Predecessor to this model: Fairlane and Torino (1970 to 1971).
Replacement for this model: LTD II (1977 to 1979).
Percentage of division's sales volume: 21.14%.
Corporate siblings: Mercury Montego.
Primary competition: AMC Matador, Chevrolet Chevelle, Dodge Coronet and Charger, Plymouth Satellite, and Pontiac LeMans.

Measurements

	2-Doors	4-Doors	Wagons
Wheelbase	114.0"	118.0"	118.0"
Length	208.0"	212.0"	215.6"
Width	79.3"	79.3"	79.0"
Height	52.1"	53.0"	55.0"
Legroom — front	42.5"	42.5"	42.5"
Legroom — rear	33.2"	37.8"	37.3"

Notable changes: Revised front-end styling, and minor trim and detail changes.

Major standard equipment: All-vinyl low-back front bench seat, rubber floor mats, windshield and rear window bright moldings, hubcaps, and F78 × 14 BSW tires. Wagon adds: Three-way tailgate, power front disc brakes, and G78 × 14 BSW tires. Gran Torino adds: Cloth and vinyl front bench seat, nylon loop carpeting, concealed windshield wipers, side window bright moldings, and wheel lip moldings. Gran Torino Brougham adds: Brougham cloth and vinyl "Flight Bench" front seat, electric clock, and deluxe steering wheel. Gran Torino Squire adds: All-vinyl bench seat, simulated woodgrain bodyside paneling, and full wheel covers. Gran Torino Sport adds: Pleated vinyl bench seat, LH remote and RH manual outside color-keyed dual racing mirrors, bright wheel trim rings w/hubcaps, and F70 × 14 R/WL tires.

Measurements (cont.)

	2-Doors	4-Doors	Wagons
Headroom — front	37.9"	38.5"	38.6"
Headroom — rear	36.5"	37.3"	38.6"
Cargo capacity (cu. ft.)	14.8*	14.8	84.9
Fuel capacity (gals.)	22.5	22.5	20.5

SportsRoof is 16.0.

Models Available

	Model No.	Base MSRP	Change from LY	Shipping Wt. (lbs.)	Model Year Production	Change from LY
Torino 2-Door Hardtop	25	$2,732	+2.21%	3503	28,005	-16.48%
Torino 4-Door Pillared Hardtop	27	$2,701	+2.27%	3577	37,524	+12.06%
Torino 4-Door, 6-p. Wagon	40	$3,198	+8.22%	4063	23,982	+8.01%
Gran Torino 2-Door Hardtop	30	$2,921	+1.49%	3540	138,962*	+5.05%
Gran Torino 4-Door Pillared Hardtop	31	$2,890	+1.19%	3631	98,404*	-3.81%
Gran Torino 4-Door, 6-p. Wagon	42	$3,344	+8.01%	4097	60,738	+34.34%
Gran Torino Sport 2-Door Hardtop	38	$3,154	+1.94%	3650	17,090	-45.29%
Gran Torino Sport 2-Door SportsRoof HT	35	$3,154	+1.94%	3664	51,853	-14.71%
Gran Torino Brougham 2-Door Hardtop	30*	$3,071	NEW	3554	*	NEW
Gran Torino Brougham 4-Dr. Pillared HT	31*	$3,051	NEW	3647	*	NEW
Gran Torino Squire 4-Door, 6-p. Wagon	43	$3,559	+2.09%	4129	40,023	+12.44%
TOTALS	Avg. price	$3,070	+3.22%	Production	496,581	-0.01%

Production of Gran Torino Brougham models included with Gran Torino models.

Custom 500, Galaxie 500 and LTD

"Quiet is the sound of a well-made car."

Nameplate year of origin: 1957 (Custom), 1959 (Galaxie), and 1965 (LTD).

Current bodystyle lifespan: 1971 through 1978 (restyled in 1973 and 1975).

Predecessor to this model: Custom/Galaxie/LTD (1969 to 1970).

Replacement for this model: LTD (1979 to 1991).

Percentage of division's sales volume: 36.37%.

Corporate siblings: Mercury Monterey and Marquis.

Primary competition: AMC Ambassador, Chevrolet BelAir/Impala/Caprice, Dodge Polara/Monaco, Plymouth Fury, and Pontiac Catalina.

Notable changes: Revised front and rear styling.

Major standard equipment: Cloth and vinyl front bench seat, nylon loop carpeting, bright front and rear window moldings, power steering, hubcaps, and G78 × 15 BSW tires. Ranch Wagon adds: All-vinyl front bench seat, power tailgate window, and J78 × 15 BSW tires. Galaxie 500 and Country Sedan add: Upgraded cloth and vinyl upholstery (all-vinyl on wagon), front door courtesy light switches, woodgrained I/P trim, and wheel lip moldings. LTD adds: Upgraded cloth and vinyl upholstery, glove box light, electric clock, luggage compartment light, body-

Measurements

	2-Doors	4-Doors	Wagons
Wheelbase	121.0"	121.0"	121.0"
Length	219.5"	219.5"	223.4"
Width	79.5"	79.5"	79.9"
Height	53.6"	55.0"	57.1"
Legroom — front	41.6"	41.7"	41.7"
Legroom — rear	35.7"	38.3"	37.2"
Headroom — front	37.6"	38.5"	39.0"
Headroom — rear	37.5"	37.4"	39.5"
Cargo capacity (cu. ft.)	17.1	17.1	96.2
Fuel capacity (gals.)	22.0	22.0	21.0

side protection moldings w/black vinyl insert, and rocker panel molding. Country Squire adds: Simulated woodgrain exterior paneling, cargo area light, and full wheel covers. LTD Brougham adds: Brougham cloth and vinyl high-back bench seat, front and rear seat center armrests, cut pile nylon carpeting, and full wheel covers.

Models Available

	Model No.	Base MSRP	Change from LY	Shipping Wt. (lbs.)	Model Year Production	Change from LY
Custom 500 4-Door Pillared Hardtop	53	$3,606	+6.78%	4059	42,549	+71.09%
Custom 500 Ranch Wagon 4-Door 6-p.	72	$4,050	+2.77%	4529	22,432	+33.25%
Custom 500 Ranch Wagon 4-Dr. w/DFRS**	72	$4,164	+2.79%*	4579	**	**
Galaxie 500 2-Door Hardtop	58	$3,778	+5.77%	4034	70,808	-12.43%
Galaxie 500 4-Door Pillared Hardtop	54	$3,771	+6.62%	4086	85,654	-17.77%
Galaxie 500 4-Door Hardtop	56	$3,833	+6.35%	4102	25,802	-10.84%
Galaxie 500 Country Sedan 4-Dr. 6-p. Wgn.	74	$4,146	+2.93%	4555	51,290	-7.15%
Galaxie 500 Country Sedan 4-Dr. Wgn. w/DFRS**	74	$4,260	+2.95%*	4605	**	**
LTD 2-Door Hardtop	62	$3,950	+1.75%	4059	120,864	+19.61%
LTD 4-Door Pillared Hardtop	63	$3,958	+1.75%	4107	122,851	+264.09%
LTD 4-Door Hardtop	64	$4,001	+1.94%	4123	28,608	-72.54%
LTD Country Squire 4-Dr. 6-p. Wgn.	76	$4,401	+1.92%	4579	142,933	+17.72%
LTD Country Squire 4-Dr. Wgn. w/DFRS**	76	$4,515	+1.96%*	4629	**	**
LTD Brougham 2-Door Hardtop	68	$4,107	+1.81%	4077	68,901	+36.68%
LTD Brougham 4-Door Pillared Hardtop	66	$4,113	+2.03%	4130	49,553	+34.26%
LTD Brougham 4-Door Hardtop	67	$4,157	+2.04%	4148	22,268	-4.69%
TOTALS		Avg. price $4,084	+4.89%		Production 854,513	+2.67%

*Prices are compared to 1972 models w/optional DFRS (dual-facing rear seats).   **Station wagons w/DFRS became separate models for 1973, instead of an option as in 1972. Production is included with 2-seat, 6-passenger models of same trim level.

Thunderbird

"Still unique in all the World."

Nameplate year of origin: 1955.
Current bodystyle lifespan: 1972 through 1976.
Predecessor to this model: Thunderbird (1967 to 1971; restyled in 1970).
Replacement for this model: Thunderbird (1977 to 1979).
Percentage of division's sales volume: 3.71%.
Corporate siblings: Lincoln Continental Mark IV.
Primary competition: Buick Riviera and Oldsmobile Toronado.
Notable changes: Revised front and rear styling.
Major standard equipment: Cloth and vinyl split bench front seat w/fold-down center armrests, cut pile nylon carpeting, simulated woodgrain I/P and door panel trim, electric clock, power interior ventilation system, power steering, power front disc brakes, full wheel covers, and 230R × 15 WSW radial tires.

Measurements

Wheelbase	120.4"
Length	218.9"
Width	79.7"
Height	53.1"
Legroom — front	42.0"
Legroom — rear	36.4"
Headroom — front	37.7"
Headroom — rear	37.0"
Cargo capacity (cu. ft.)	13.9
Fuel capacity (gals.)	22.5

Models Available

	Model No.	Base MSRP	Change from LY	Shipping Wt. (lbs.)	Model Year Production	Change from LY
Thunderbird 2-Door Hardtop	87	$6,437	+21.61%	4505	87,269	+50.95%
TOTALS		Avg. price $6,437	+21.61%		Production 87,269	+50.95%

LINCOLN

*"The best cars we've ever built. Luxurious near the
point of perfection. Designed to be quiet."*

Although little was new about the 1973 Lincolns, they were selling better than ever, setting model year production records for the marque division as a whole and for the Continental Mark IV in comparison to all of its predecessors in the Mark series. Styling changes for the Lincoln Continental coupe and sedan models were limited to improvements in ride quality and sound dampening, which were high on the priority list as Lincoln strove to win sales from Cadillac. The changes amounted to improved sound insulation, larger radial ply tires, plus some suspension readjustments. Other detail changes for the Continental included a new inside hood latch release, anti-theft spare tire lock, larger and re-located rear-seat radio speakers, standard front bumper guards, and a front bumper energy-absorbing system.

For the Continental Mark IV, a new front bumper and grille design was required to meet the new federal bumper standards. Whereas the new-for-1972 Mark IV used a tall grille that dropped down into the center bumper area, the new standards required an energy-absorbing system that the 1972 design could not meet. Therefore, a more box-like bumper design was implemented with a solid center section and standard front bumper guards. The grille continued to be of a thin vertical strip design with a very "classic car" look. As before, the grille was higher than the hood and front end lines, so the center section of the hood was raised slightly as it met the chrome plated surround of the grille, which had a stand-up hood ornament affixed. The parking/turn signal lamps continued to be vertically mounted wraparound units in the front fender end caps, but were sectioned into an egg-crate design with six prominent lines horizontally wrapped around the fender end. As for other new features, a new inside hood release was added as standard equipment for the Mark IV, as was the anti-theft spare tire lock. Also new for 1973 was the Silver Luxury group, the first in a long series of "color" luxury groups to be offered on the Mark series, often pairing specific exterior and interior colors with other specific options or styling cues. Finally, Lincoln's anti-lock braking system, introduced a few years earlier, continued to be standard on the Mark IV and optional on the Continental coupe and sedan.

Continental 4-Door Sedan with Town Car
package (front) and Continental 2-Door
Hardtop with Town Coupe (rear)

Continental instrument panel

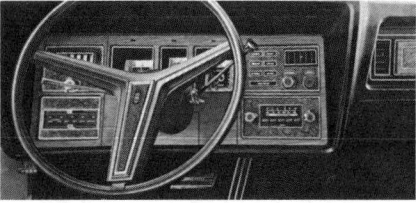

Continental Mark IV instrument panel

Continental Mark IV 2-Door Hardtop

Model year production: 128,073, up 35.44% from 1972.
Domestic market share: 1.20% (12th place).
Base price range: $7,230 to $8,984.
Lincoln average base price: $7,896, up 2.95%.
Introduction date: September 22, 1972.
Assembly plants: Allen Park, MI (S —*pilot plant*); and Wixom, MI (Y).
Data plate identification (VIN): Eleven digit code read as follows: First digit indicates year (3 = 1973); second digit indicates assembly plant code (see list above); third and fourth digits indicate model number (model number in model charts); fifth digit indicates engine code (see powertrain chart); remaining digits are sequential with beginning numbers of 800001. *Example:* 3Y82A800001 is a 1973 Lincoln Continental 4-Door Sedan, with 460 CID, 4-bbl. V8 engine, serial number 800001, built in Wixom, MI.

Powertrains

Engine	Net HP	Engine Code	Transmission Availability		Continental	Mark IV
460 CID (7.5L), 4-bbl., V8	219	A	3-speed SelectShift Automatic		S	—
				MPG:	7.9	—
460 CID (7.5L), 4-bbl., V8	208	A	3-speed SelectShift Automatic		—	S
				MPG:	—	7.9

Major Options

	Continental	Mark IV
Air conditioning, Auto-Temp	S	S
Tilt steering wheel	$70	$70
Automatic speed control	$92	$92
Automatic headlamp dimmer	$50	$50
Electric rear window defroster	$83	$83
Tinted glass, all windows	S	S
Power windows	S	S
Power front vent windows, 4-door	$68	—
Power door locks	$[1]	$[1]
Power seat, 6-way w/std. seating	$90	S
Passenger seat recliner	$61	$61
Leather seating upholstery	$169	$179
RH remote-control mirror, LH std.	$27	$27
Intermittent windshield wipers	$26	$26
AM radio, w/power antenna	S	S
AM/FM stereo	$142	$142
AM/FM stereo w/8-track tape	$269	$269
Vinyl top, full	$152	S
Sunroof, power-operated	$611	$611
Power trunk lid release	$[1]	$[1]
Power steering	S	S
Power brakes, w/front disc	S	—
"Sure-Track" antilock brake system	$192	S
Luxury wheel covers	$58	S
White sidewall tires, std. size	S	S

Popular Option Groups & Packages

	Continental	Mark IV
Appearance protection group	$52	$47
Lock Convenience group	$104	$93
Silver luxury group	—	$400
Town Car package, 4-door only	$399	—
Town Coupe package, 2-door only	$467	—

— = *Not Available;* S = *Standard equipment.* [1]*Included in, and available only with, optional Lock Convenience group.*

Paint Colors

	Code
Light Gray metallic	1A
Black	1C
Silver Moondust metallic[1]	1D
Red Moondust metallic[2]	2G
Maroon	2J
Pastel Blue	3A
Medium Blue metallic	3D
Dark Blue metallic	3G
Silver Blue Moondust metallic[2]	3L
Ivy Moondust metallic[2]	4D
Medium Green metallic	4P
Dark Green metallic	4Q
Light Green	4S
Lime Gold Moondust metallic[2]	4U
Green Diamond	4Y
Copper Diamond Flare metallic	52
Light Ginger Moondust metallic[2]	5D
Dark Brown metallic	5F
Ginger Gold Moondust metallic[2]	5K
Tan	5L
Dark Copper Moondust metallic[2]	5P
Dark Brown metallic	5Q
Medium Beige	5S
Light Yellow Gold	6B
Yellow	6D
Gold Moondust metallic[2]	6G
Medium Gold metallic	6L
White	9A
White Décor	9C

In two-tone combinations, first two digits are lower color, and second two digits are upper color. [1]*Available only on Continental Mark IV with Silver Luxury group.* [2]*Moondust metallic paints available for $128 extra.*

Continental

*"Personal styling ... all the luxury you'd expect ...
and a ride that's smooth and sure."*

Nameplate year of origin: 1940 (1961 as a regular series).
Current bodystyle lifespan: 1970 through 1979 (restyled in 1974).
Predecessor to this model: Continental (1961 to 1969).
Replacement for this model: Town Car (1980 to 1991).
Percentage of division's production: 45.78%.
Corporate siblings: None.
Primary competition: Cadillac deVille and Chrysler Imperial.
Notable changes: Minor trim and detail changes.
Major standard equipment: Choice of Brocade cloth and vinyl, or Westminster knit cloth and vinyl front bench seat w/two-way power adjustment, folding center armrests in front and rear seat, cut-pile carpeting, simulated rosewood appliqués on I/P and steering wheel, electric clock, rim-blow steering wheel, power windows w/lock feature, AM radio w/power antenna, automatic temperature control air conditioning, visor-mounted vanity mirror, LH remote control rearview mirror, tinted glass, interior lighting (ashtrays, courtesy, glove box, luggage compartment, dome/map, and rear seat reading), gray carpeted luggage compartment, dual custom tape stripes, cornering lights, rear wheel opening fender skirts, front bumper guards, deluxe wheel covers, and 230R × 15 WSW tires.

Measurements

	Coupe	Sedan
Wheelbase	127.0"	127.0"
Length	229.9"	229.9"
Width	79.6"	79.6"
Height	54.5"	55.5"
Legroom — front	41.7"	41.7"
Legroom — rear	38.8"	41.7"
Headroom — front	38.4"	38.8"
Headroom — rear	37.5"	38.1"
Cargo capacity (cu. ft.)	18.1	18.1
Fuel capacity (gals.)	22.0	22.0

Models Available

	Model No.	Base MSRP	Change from LY	Shipping Wt. (lbs.)	Model Year Production	Change from LY
Continental 2-Door Hardtop Coupe	81	$7,230	+2.29%	5016	13,348	+28.25%
Continental 4-Door Sedan	82	$7,474	+2.36%	5049	45,288	+27.35%
TOTALS		*Avg. price* $7,352	+2.32%	*Production*	58,636	+27.56%

Continental Mark IV

"Quite simply, the most beautiful automobile in America."

Nameplate year of origin: 1956 (Continental Mark II).
Current bodystyle lifespan: 1972 through 1976.
Predecessor to this model: Continental Mark III (1969 to 1971).
Replacement for this model: Continental Mark V (1977 to 1979).
Percentage of division's production: 54.22%.
Corporate siblings: Ford Thunderbird.
Primary competition: Buick Riviera, Cadillac Eldorado, and Oldsmobile Toronado.
Notable changes: Revised front styling and minor trim and detail changes.
Major standard equipment: Westminster cloth and vinyl "Twin Comfort" lounge seat w/six-way power adjustment, folding center armrests in front and rear seat, simulated burl walnut woodgrain appliqué on I/P and steering wheel, deep cut-pile carpeting, electric Cartier Timepiece, trip odometer, power windows w/lock feature, AM radio w/power antenna, automatic temperature control air conditioning, LH remote control rearview mirror, tinted glass, interior lighting (ashtrays, courtesy, glove box, I/P warning, luggage compartment, engine compartment, dome/map, and C-pillar reading), black carpeted luggage compartment, vinyl roof w/opera window, custom pinstripe, customer monogram on doors, cornering lights, front bumper guards, "Sure Track" anti-lock power brake system, luxury wheel covers, and 230R × 15 WSW tires.

Measurements

Wheelbase	120.4"
Length	223.3"
Width	79.8"
Height	52.4"
Legroom — front	42.0"
Legroom — rear	36.4"
Headroom — front	37.7"
Headroom — rear	37.0"
Cargo capacity (cu. ft.)	13.9
Fuel capacity (gals.)	22.5

Models Available

	Model No.	Base MSRP	Change from LY	Shipping Wt. (lbs.)	Model Year Production	Change from LY
Continental Mark IV 2-Door Hardtop	89	$8,984	+3.98%	4908	69,437	+42.90%
TOTALS	Avg. price	$8,984	+3.98%	Production	69,437	+42.90%

MERCURY

"Built better to ride better."

Mercury for 1973 was all about improvement of driving and ride qualities. Over the past three years, numerous tests for ride comfort and quality had been performed with the results touted in both print and television advertising. The 1973 Mercury deluxe sales brochure even devotes two full pages to a summary of eight of those tests, showing Mercury's superior ride qualities over its direct competition, such as comparisons with "European Limousines" costing up to six times as much as a Mercury Marquis. Some of the most memorable tests involved a tea party in the rear seat of a 1970 Marquis without spilling a drop, a jeweler in a 1971 Marquis splitting a $250,000 diamond, and a 1972 Monterey carrying a highly explosive nitro carbol connected to a sensitive detonator, while driving over rough Texas terrain. The ads seemed to work, as all through this period, sales and production for Mercury continued on a steady increase. Interesting from the marketing point of view was the fact that Mercury buyers were moving upscale to the more luxurious models in greater numbers than ever before, leaving the base lines to drop in sales. This result was in line with the overall U.S. market, as consumers moved away from the sporty cars of Chevrolet, Ford and Plymouth, and into the more luxurious cars of Buick, Dodge, Oldsmobile and Mercury.

The full-size Monterey and Marquis received the bulk of the visual changes in Mercury showrooms for the new season. The lower-priced Monterey series used an egg-crate grille design in a three-piece setup that was similar to the 1973 Ford LTD's, with a main center grille and smaller grille areas to the side with the dual headlamps set in them. A full-width, straight bumper completed the new look. The Marquis continued to use hidden headlights and a full-width egg-crate grille, with a section running across the lower portion of the headlight door. The egg-crate grille design of the 1973s was a finer pattern, more elegant looking than the 1972 models. The front fender end caps seemed less pointed this year and housed vertical parking/turn signal lamps, rather than having them in the bumper with the egg-crate grille design wrapping around the front fender end. Bodysides were flatter and also looked similar to the Ford's, with a lower body feature line running full-length between the bumpers and marking the point where the sheetmetal angled inwards down to the rocker panel. An upper feature line ran from the upper edge of the front parking lights to the upper edge of the taillights. The beltline began off the front fender edges, an inch or two below the glass area, and turned upwards to encompass the rear side or door window, fading away as it reached the top. At the rear horizontal taillamps were used, with an egg-crate grille design between the lamps and backup lights mounted to the inward side, all set above a full-width bumper that looked prepared to meet the federal government's rear bumper standards for 1974.

Inside the new full-size Mercurys had a new instrument panel design that was less modular and more driver oriented. Unlike last year's models, the Marquis and Monterey now shared a common layout, with the Marquis having the entire facing covered in simulated woodgrain, while the Monterey had only the driver's side gauge cluster lined with the fake wood trim. The driver's "pod" housed a horizontal speedometer this year with an air vent and light and wiper controls to the left, and clock, optional radio, and ventilation controls stacked to the right side. Two air vents mounted horizontally near the center, and a third on the far right side of the dash sat above the large glove box door. New upholstery materials and patterns completed the redesigned look. The Monterey and Monterey Custom 4-Door Hardtop models were dropped for the new year, and the full-size station wagon line now provided standard six-passenger seating, with the eight-passenger, dual facing rear seats becoming an option rather than a separate model.

Cougar entered its final season as an upscale pony car and Mustang sibling, with a front end facelift that included a straight-across bumper and a shortened vertical bar grille.

A wide chrome band surrounded the grille, with the Cougar "cat" logo at the center top. Dual headlights remained in the same position set into coves in large bezels with a black vertical bar grille pattern surrounding the lights. Parking/turn signal lamps remained in the front fender ends that jutted forward from the rest of the front end. Four section vertical taillamps, with sequential turn signals, center mounted license plate and backup lights alongside, were housed in the loop style rear bumper. There were no model changes for the Cougar, but the Cougar and Ford Mustang convertibles were the last to remain in the corporate Ford line. For 1974, the Cougar would move up to the mid-size platform to take on the Monte Carlo and Grand Prix in the personal luxury market.

Like the Cougar, the mid-size Montego line received a front end facelift to meet the new federal bumper standards, with a straight bumper that had a slight "V" in the center, and a crosshatch grille of reduced height. Otherwise, styling remained much the same, and no model changes were made for 1973. All Montego two- and four-doors, except the GT Fastback, were introduced at the beginning of the year with the 250 CID 6-cylinder engines; however, by the end of the

model year, all models had the 302 CID V8 engine as standard equipment, with an appropriate adjustment in base price. Station wagons no longer offered a six-cylinder engine as of the start of the 1973 model year. The compact Comet added a box style bumper but was otherwise mostly unchanged.

The imported Capri had revised interior and body trim for 1973. Exterior changes included a new egg-crate style grille, larger taillights and backup lights combined into a single housing, and new front fender Capri insignia emblems. Inside a revised dashboard now had a glove compartment rather than the open style box of the earlier models, and larger gauges to improve readability. New seats with deeper "buckets" were introduced, and a center console with a storage compartment was added as an option. The prior year's 1.6L engine was discontinued, making the 2.0-liter OHC 4-cylinder the new standard engine. This was the same engine used as an option in the 1973 Ford Pinto. The 2.6-liter "Cologne" V6 engine continued as the optional offering. The Italian-built two-seater Pantera, which Ford freely admitted had "highly specialized appeal," continued with virtually no changes.

**Capri 2600 2-Door Sport Coupe
with Décor group**

Pantera 2-Door Sport Coupe

**Comet 4-Door Sedan
with Custom exterior package**

Cougar 2-Door Convertible

Comet 2-Door Sedan with GT package

Marquis Brougham 4-Door Hardtop

Cougar XR-7 2-Door Hardtop

Marquis 2-Door Hardtop

Montego 4-Door Pillared Hardtop

Colony Park 4-Door Station Wagon

Montego GT 2-Door Fastback

Montego MX Villager 4-Door Station Wagon (front) and Montego MX 4-Door Station Wagon (rear)

Monterey Custom 4-Door Pillared Hardtop

Montego MX Brougham interior

Model year production: 486,470, up 10.07% from 1972.
Domestic market share: 4.58% (8th place).
Base price range: $2,432 to $5,206.
Mercury average base price: $3,913, up 6.18%.
Introduction date: September 1972.
Assembly plants: Oakville, Ontario, Canada (B); Dearborn, MI (F); Lorain, OH (H); Kansas City, MO (K); Allen Park, MI (S—*pilot plant*); and St. Louis, MO (Z). Capri assembly plants: Cologne, Germany (A), and Genk, Belgium (B). Pantera assembly plant: Modena, Italy.
Data plate identification (VIN): Eleven digit code read as follows: First digit indicates year (3 = 1973); second digit indicates assembly plant code (see list above); third and fourth digits indicate model number (model number in model charts); fifth digit indicates engine code (see power-

train chart); remaining digits are sequential with beginning numbers of 500001. *Example:* 3K31F500001 is a 1973 Mercury Comet 2-Door sedan, with 302 CID, 2-bbl. V8 engine, serial number 500001, built in Kansas City (Claycomo), MO. 1973 Capri uses eleven digit code read as follows: First digit indicates country of origin (G = Germany); second digit indicates assembly plant code (see list above); third and fourth digits indicate model number (model number in model charts); fifth digit indicates year (N = 1973); sixth digit indicates month; remaining digits are sequential with beginning number of 42151. 1973 Pantera uses eleven digit code read as follows: First through sixth digits indicate 1973 DeTomaso Pantera built in Italy, TH-PNLD; remaining digits are sequential serial number.

Powertrains

Engine	Net HP	Engine Code	Transmission Availability[1]		Capri	Comet	Cougar	Montego	Monterey	Marquis
122 CID (2.0L) OHC, 2-bbl., 4-cyl.	85	X	4-speed manual		S (2000)	—	—	—	—	—
				MPG:	NA	—	—	—	—	—
			3-speed automatic		$182 (2000)	—	—	—	—	—
				MPG:	NA	—	—	—	—	—
160 CID (2.6L), 2-bbl., V6	107	Z	4-speed manual		S (2600)	—	—	—	—	—
				MPG:	NA	—	—	—	—	—
			3-speed automatic		$182 (2600)	—	—	—	—	—
				MPG:	—	—	—	—	—	—
200 CID (3.3L), 1-bbl., 6-cyl.	84	U	3-speed manual		—	S	—	—	—	—
				MPG:	—	NA	—	—	—	—
			3-speed SelectShift Automatic		—	$178	—	—	—	—
				MPG:	—	NA	—	—	—	—
250 CID (4.1L), 1-bbl., 6-cyl.	88[2]	L	3-speed manual		—	—	—	S (cars)[3]	—	—
				MPG:	—	—	—	NA	—	—
			3-speed SelectShift Automatic		—	$216	—	$207 (cars)	—	—
				MPG:	—	NA	—	NA	—	—

Engine	Net HP	Engine Code	Transmission Availability[1]	Capri	Comet	Cougar	Montego	Monterey	Marquis
302 CID (5.0L), 2-bbl., V8	135	F	3-speed manual	—	$122	—	S (GT & wgns.)/$112 (cars)	—	—
			MPG:	—	NA	—	NA	—	—
			3-speed SelectShift Automatic	—	$300	—	$216 (GT & wgns.)/ $328 (cars)	—	—
			MPG:	—	NA	—	NA	—	—
351 CID (5.8L), 2-bbl., V8	160[4]	H	3-speed SelectShift Automatic	—	—	S	$261 (GT & wgns.)/$373 (cars)	S (ex.[5])	—
			MPG:	—	—	NA	NA	NA	—
351 CID (5.8L) CJ, 4-bbl., V8	246[6]	Q	4-speed manual w/ Hurst Shifter ®	—	—	$89	$439 (2-dr. only)[3]	—	—
			MPG:	—	—	NA	NA	—	—
			3-speed SelectShift Automatic	—	—	$75	$455 (2-dr. only)[3]	—	—
			MPG:	—	—	NA	NA	—	—
400 CID (6.6L), 2-bbl., V8	168	S	3-speed SelectShift Automatic	—	—	—	$312 (GT & wgns.)/$424 (cars)	S[5]/$73 (ex.[5])	S[7]
			MPG:	—	—	—	NA	NA	—
429 CID (6.9L), 4-bbl., V8	200	K	3-speed SelectShift Automatic	—	—	—	$417 (GT & wgns.)/ $529 (cars)	$102[5]/ $175 (ex.[5])	S (ex.[7])/ $102[7]
			MPG:	—	—	—	NA	NA	NA
460 CID (7.5L), 4-bbl., V8	200	A	3-speed SelectShift Automatic	—	—	—	—	$178[5]/ $251 (ex.[5])	$76 (ex.[7])/ $178[7]
			MPG:	—	—	—	—	NA	NA

[1]Unless otherwise noted: All manual transmissions are floor-shifts, except on Comet. All automatics are column-shift, except on Capri and Cougar. Floor-shift is available for $13 extra on Comet with 3-speed manual and on Comet with automatic (requires bucket seats), and at no cost on Montego, Montego MX or Montego GT with optional bucket seats, console and automatic transmission. [2]92 in Montego. [3]Available on Montego GT for $327 w/4-speed, and $343 w/automatic. Not available on MX Brougham. [4]168 in Cougar. [5]Monterey Custom and Monterey station wagons. [6]266 in Cougar. [7]Marquis station wagon and Colony Park station wagon.

Major Options

	Capri	Comet	Cougar	Montego	Full-size
Whisper-Aire air conditioning	$[1]	$360	$364	$398	$431[2]
Tilt steering wheel	—	—	$40	—	$44
Automatic speed control	—	—	—	—	$67
Rear window defogger	—	$28	—	—	—
Electric rear window defroster	—	—	$57	$62	$62
Tinted glass, all windows	—	$36	$34	$42	$50
LH remote control mirror[3]	—	$23[3]	$12	$13	$12
Power windows	—	—	$103	$112	$141
Power door locks, 2-dr./4-dr.	—	—	—	$44/$67	$[4]
Power seat, 6-way w/std. seating	—	—	$69[5]	$102	$102
Front bucket seats w/console[6]	—	$98	$68	$188	—
Dual facing rear seats, wagons	—	—	—	$76	$122
AM radio	$59	$59	$59	$64	$64
AM/FM stereo	$[1]	$195	$195	$213	$233
AM/FM stereo w/8-track tape	—	—	—	—	$363
Leather-wrapped steering wheel	—	$23	$23	$25	—
Anti-theft alarm system	—	—	—	—	$79
Vinyl top, full	$63	$75	$80	$97	$116[7]
Sunroof, power-operated	$119[8]	—	$431	—	$496

	Capri	Comet	Cougar	Montego	Full-size
Power trunk lid release	—	—	—	—	$[4]
Power steering	—	$92	$103	$112	S
Power brakes, w/front disc	S	—	S	$68[9]	S
"Sure-Track" anti-lock brakes	—	—	—	—	$189
Rear wheel opening fender skirts	—	—	—	—	$35
Deluxe wheel covers	—	$23	$23	$25	$25
Luxury wheel covers	—	—	—	$43	$58
Wire wheel covers	—	—	$75	—	—
Styled steel wheels	—	—	$52	—	—
Forged aluminum wheels	—	$142	—	—	—
White sidewall tires, std. size	—	$27	$28	$32	$35

Popular Option Groups & Packages[10]

	Capri	Comet	Cougar	Montego	Full-size
Appearance protection group	—	$25–$28	$22	$29	$42
Bumper protection group	—	$31	—	—	$24–$36
Convenience group	—	$28	$43	$48	—
Custom option package	—	$346	—	—	—
Décor group	$152	—	$81	—	$63
Deluxe trim option	—	$66	—	—	—
GT package	—	$184	—	—	—
Instrumentation group	$69	—	—	$100	—
Lock convenience group	—	—	—	—	$83–$96
Luxury interior trim package	—	—	—	—	$184
Visibility group	—	—	—	—	$50
Visibility light group	—	—	—	$25	—

— = Not Available; S = Standard equipment. [1]Available as dealer installed option only. [2]Whisper-Aire air conditioner w/automatic temperature control is available for $508. [3]LH remote and RH manual on Comet. [4]Available only as part of the Lock Convenience group. [5]Four-way power seat, driver's side only on Cougar. [6]Bucket seats only on Comet, and console not available. Console only on Cougar; bucket seats standard. Available only on two-door models, and at no cost on Montego GT. [7]For wagons, $139. [8]Manually operated. [9]Standard on station wagons. [10]Price ranges cover all models available—see Appendix IV for option groups and packages for content details and model availability variations.

Paint Colors

Mercury	Code	Mercury	Code	Capri	Code
Black	1C	Tan	5L	Medium Brown metallic	S
Silver metallic	1G	Medium Copper metallic	5M	Yellow	T
Bright Red	2B	Saddle Bronze metallic	5T		
Red metallic	2C	Light Goldenrod	6B	Pantera	Code
Bright Red metallic	2L	Medium Goldenrod	6C	Red	V108
Light Blue	3B	Yellow	6D	Bronze metallic	V109
Medium Blue metallic	3D	Medium Bright Yellow	6E	White	V204
Blue Glamour metallic[1,2]	3K	Gold Glamour metallic[1,2]	6F	Medium Green	V305
Silver Blue Glamour metallic[2]	3M	Medium Gold metallic	6L	Aqua Green metallic	V306
Light Grabber Blue	3N	White	9A	Lime	V307
Light Grabber Blue	3P	Special White	9C	Medium Blue	V406
Pastel Blue	3Q			Yellow	V502
Green Gold metallic	4B			Beige metallic	V503
Ivy Glamour metallic[1,2]	4C	Capri	Code	Silver metallic	V613
Medium Aqua	4N	Medium Blue metallic	1		
Medium Green metallic	4P	Medium Gray metallic	2	
Dark Green metallic	4Q	Light Green metallic	5	
Light Green	4S	Copper metallic	7	
Light Pewter metallic	5A	Dark Green metallic	8	
Ginger metallic	5H	Red	J	
Ginger Glamour metallic[2]	5J	Silver metallic	O	

In two-tone combinations, first two digits are lower color, and second two digits are upper color. Two-tones available on Comet for $28. [1]Glamour paints available for $35 extra on Comet and Cougar, $38 extra on Montego. [2]Glamour paints available for $38 extra on full-size Mercurys.

Pantera

*"Built in Italy by Alejandro de Tomaso,
and imported for Lincoln-Mercury."*

Nameplate year of origin: 1971 (for U.S. market).
Current bodystyle lifespan: 1969 through 1974.
Predecessor to this model: None.
Replacement for this model: None.
Primary competition: Chevrolet Corvette.
Notable changes: No significant changes.
Major standard equipment: Cloth-and-vinyl high-back front bucket seats, floor car-
peting, central floor console, three-spoke steering wheel, padded door armrest w/in-
tegral assist handles, power windows, air conditioning, windshield wipers w/wash-
ers, rack and pinion steering, four wheel power disc brakes, 351 CID 4-bbl.
"Cleveland" V8 engine w/266 hp rating, fully synchronized 5-speed manual transmission, monocoque body construction, coil
springs and wishbone suspension, styled steel wheels, and 185R/70 × 15 front & 215R/70 × 15 (or GR70 × 15) rear BSW tires.
Option available: Dealer installed AM/FM Stereo.

Measurements

Wheelbase	98.9"
Length	167.7"
Width	71.8"
Height	44.4"
Legroom — front	42.5"
Headroom — front	35.2"
Cargo capacity (cu. ft.)	4.0
Fuel capacity (gals.)	21.0

Models Available

	Model No.	Base MSRP	Change from LY	Shipping Wt. (lbs.)	Model Year Production	Change from LY
Pantera L 2-Door Sport Coupe		$9,995	+11.06%	3000	1,830	+18.00%
TOTALS		*Avg. price* $9,995	+11.06%		*Production* 1,830	+18.00%

Capri

"Capri ... the sexy European."

Nameplate year of origin: 1971 (Originally used on 1952 Lincoln Capri).
Current bodystyle lifespan: 1971 through 1977 (major restyle for 1976).
Predecessor to this model: None.
Replacement for this model: Capri (1979 to 1986).
Primary competition: Buick Opel GT and Dodge Colt GT.
Notable changes: Minor trim and detail changes.
Major standard equipment: All-vinyl front bucket seats, full-loop carpeting, front
armrests, recessed door handles, passenger side assist bar, simulated woodgrain I/P
appliqué, lockable glove compartment, day/night rear view mirror, power front disc
brakes, rack-and-pinion steering, styled wheels, and 165 × 13 BSW tires. 2600 adds:
Instrumentation group and V6 engine.

Measurements

Wheelbase	100.8"
Length	169.1"
Width	64.8"
Height	50.8"
Legroom — front	41.4"
Legroom — rear	30.3"
Headroom — front	37.4"
Headroom — rear	35.9"
Cargo capacity (cu. ft.)	7.2
Fuel capacity (gals.)	12.0

Models Available

	Model No.	Base MSRP	Change from LY	Shipping Wt. (lbs.)	Model Year Sales (est.)	Change from LY
Capri 2000 2-Door Sport Coupe	EC	$2,983	+18.00%	2231	NA	NA
Capri 2600 2-Door Sport Coupe	EC	$3,261	+15.43%	2341	NA	NA
TOTALS		*Avg. price* $3,122	+16.64%		*Production* 113,500	+38.40%

Comet

"Built better to last longer."

Nameplate year of origin: 1960.
Current bodystyle lifespan: 1971 through 1977.
Predecessor to this model: Comet (1964 to 1965).
Replacement for this model: Zephyr (1978 to 1983).
Percentage of division's production: 17.41%.
Corporate siblings: Ford Maverick.
Primary competition: AMC Hornet, Buick Apollo, Dodge Dart, and Oldsmobile Omega.
Notable changes: Minor trim and detail changes.
Major standard equipment: Upbeat stripe cloth-and-vinyl front bench seat, color-keyed carpeting, illuminated I/P controls, "Blend-Air" heater with three-speed blower, front and rear ashtrays w/front lighted, two-speed windshield wipers w/washers, two-spoke steering wheel, LH outside rearview mirror, hubcaps, and 6.45 × 14 BSW tires.

Measurements

	2-Door	4-Door
Wheelbase	103.0"	109.9"
Length	185.5"	192.4"
Width	70.5"	70.5"
Height	52.9"	52.9"
Legroom — front	40.7"	40.7"
Legroom — rear	31.8"	36.0"
Headroom — front	37.5"	37.8"
Headroom — rear	35.9"	36.5"
Cargo capacity (cu. ft.)	9.5	10.1
Fuel capacity (gals.)	15.0	15.0

Models Available

	Model No.	Base MSRP	Change from LY	Shipping Wt. (lbs.)	Model Year Production	Change from LY
Comet 2-Door Sedan	31	$2,432	+11.46%	2813	55,707	+4.58%
Comet 4-Door Sedan	30	$2,489	+11.22%	2904	28,984	-0.37%
TOTALS	*Avg. price*	$2,461	+11.33%	*Production*	84,691	+2.83%

Cougar

"It's not like anybody else's car."

Nameplate year of origin: 1967.
Current bodystyle lifespan: 1971 through 1973.
Predecessor to this model: Cougar (1969 to 1970).
Replacement for this model: Cougar XR-7 (1974 to 1976).
Percentage of division's production: 12.46%.
Corporate siblings: Ford Mustang.
Primary competition: AMC Javelin, Chevrolet Camaro, Dodge Challenger, Plymouth Barracuda, and Pontiac Firebird.
Notable changes: Revised front end and minor trim and detail changes.
Major standard equipment: All-vinyl high-back bucket seats, nylon loop color-keyed carpeting, consolette w/ashtray, two-spoke oval color-keyed steering wheel w/woodgrain inserts, courtesy lights, color-keyed racing mirrors, sequential rear turn signals, power front disc brakes, hubcaps, and E78 × 14 BSW tires. Convertible adds: Woven vinyl bucket seats, décor group interior, deluxe seat belts, power operated top, color-keyed top boot, tinted rear glass, and rocker panel molding. XR-7 adds: Leather and vinyl high-back front bucket seats, simulated cherry woodgrain I/P and steering wheel trim, three-spoke "Rim-Blow" steering wheel, I/P assist handle on passenger side, door pull assist straps, tachometer and full gauges, map light, deluxe seat belts, bright pedal trim, vinyl top, LH remote color-keyed racing mirrors, rocker panel molding, and special XR-7 wheel covers. XR-7 convertible adds base Cougar convertible features.

Measurements

Wheelbase	112.1"
Length	199.5"
Width	75.1"
Height	50.7"
Legroom — front	41.7"
Legroom — rear	28.9"
Headroom — front	37.2"
Headroom — rear	35.9"
Cargo capacity (cu. ft.)	10.4
Fuel capacity (gals.)	19.5

Models Available

	Model No.	Base MSRP	Change from LY	Shipping Wt. (lbs.)	Model Year Production	Change from LY
Cougar 2-Door Hardtop	91	$3,372	+11.80%	3396	21,069	-11.22%

	Model No.	Base MSRP	Change from LY	Shipping Wt. (lbs.)	Model Year Production	Change from LY
Cougar 2-Door Convertible	92	$3,726	+10.56%	3524	1,284	+3.55%
Cougar XR-7 2-Door Hardtop	93	$3,679	+10.71%	3416	35,110	+31.00%
Cougar XR-7 2-Door Convertible	94	$3,903	+10.04%	3530	3,165	+64.07%
TOTALS		*Avg. price* $3,670	+10.74%		*Production* 60,628	+12.90%

Montego

"The personal-size car with the ride of a big car."

Nameplate year of origin: 1968.
Current bodystyle lifespan: 1972 through 1976.
Predecessor to this model: Montego (1970 to 1971).
Replacement for this model: Cougar (1977 to 1979).
Percentage of division's sales volume: 32.23%.
Corporate siblings: Ford Torino.
Primary competition: AMC Matador, Buick Century, Dodge Coronet and Charger, Oldsmobile Cutlass, and Pontiac LeMans.
Notable changes: Revised front-end styling and minor trim and detail changes.
Major standard equipment: Cloth-and-vinyl or all-vinyl low-back front bench seat, rubber floor mats, windshield and rear window bright moldings, drip rail moldings, manual front disc brakes, and F78 × 14 BSW tires. Wagon

Measurements

	2-Doors	4-Doors	Wagons
Wheelbase	114.0"	118.0"	118.0"
Length	211.3"	215.3"	218.5"
Width	78.6"	78.6"	79.6"
Height	52.1"	53.0"	54.9"
Legroom — front	42.5"	42.5"	42.1"
Legroom — rear	33.2"	37.8"	37.1"
Headroom — front	37.9"	38.5"	38.3"
Headroom — rear	36.5"	37.3"	38.6"
Cargo capacity (cu. ft.)	14.8*	14.8	84.9
Fuel capacity (gals.)	22.5	22.5	20.5

*GT is 16.0.

adds: All-vinyl front bench seat, three-way tailgate, power front disc brakes, and G78 × 14 BSW tires. MX adds: Color-keyed deep loop carpeting, simulated Cherry woodgrain I/P trim, concealed windshield wipers, side window bright moldings, wheel lip moldings, front and rear bumper guards, and deluxe sound insulation. MX Brougham adds: Choice of Brougham cloth-and-vinyl or super-soft vinyl "Flight Bench" front seat w/fold-down center armrest, deluxe two-spoke steering wheel w/woodgrain inserts, deluxe sound insulation, and deluxe wheel covers. MX Villager adds to MX Brougham: All-vinyl "Flight Bench" front seat w/fold-down center armrest and simulated woodgrain bodyside and tailgate paneling. GT adds: Choice of all-vinyl bucket seats or vinyl "Flight Bench" front seat w/fold-down center armrest, color-keyed deep loop carpeting, full instrumentation including tachometer, electric clock, sports type three-spoke steering wheel, deluxe sound insulation, color-keyed dual racing mirrors, performance hood w/dual scoops, choice of deluxe wheel covers or bright wheel trim rings w/hubcaps, and F78 × 14 WSW tires.

Models Available

	Model No.	Base MSRP	Change from LY	Shipping Wt. (lbs.)	Model Year Production	Change from LY
Montego 2-Door Hardtop	03	$2,814	+2.02%	3653	7,082	-28.92%
Montego 4-Door Pillared Hardtop	02	$2,804	+1.85%	3719	7,459	-13.85%
Montego MX 2-Door Hardtop	07	$2,929	+1.67%	3683	27,812	+7.79%
Montego MX 4-Door Pillared Hardtop	04	$2,897	+1.26%	3772	25,300	+8.18%
Montego MX 4-Door, 6-p. Wagon	08	$3,417	+7.32%	4124	7,012	+11.87%
Montego MX Brougham 2-Door Hardtop	11	$3,097	+1.31%	3706	40,951	+44.11%
Montego MX Brougham 4-Dr. Pillared HT	10	$3,077	+0.98%	3813	24,329	+38.71%
Montego MX Villager 4-Door, 6-p. Wagon	18	$3,606	+7.71%	4167	12,396	+34.20%
Montego GT 2-Door Fastback	16	$3,413	+2.00%	3662	4,464	-23.30%
TOTALS		*Avg. price* $3,117	+3.01%		*Production* 156,805	+16.07%

Monterey

"Easy handling every mile you drive."

Nameplate year of origin: 1952 (series); 1950 (Mercury coupe designation).
Current bodystyle lifespan: 1971 through 1978 (restyled in 1973 and Monterey nameplate discontinued in 1974).
Predecessor to this model: Monterey (1969 to 1970).
Replacement for this model: None.
Percentage of division's sales volume: 11.34%.
Corporate siblings: Ford Custom 500/Galaxie 500/LTD and Mercury Marquis.
Primary competition: Buick LeSabre, Dodge Monaco, Oldsmobile Delta 88, and Pontiac Bonneville.
Notable changes: Revised front and rear styling.
Major standard equipment: Cloth and vinyl front bench seat, nylon loop carpeting, simulated woodgrain I/P appliqués, bright front and rear window moldings, side window and drip rail moldings, dome light, power steering, power front disc brakes, bright bodyside molding, front bumper guards, hubcaps, and HR78 × 15 BSW tires. Wagon adds: All-vinyl front bench seat, power tailgate window, and JR78 × 15 BSW tires. Monterey Custom adds: Choice of cloth and vinyl or all-vinyl front bench seat w/upgraded upholstery, rocker panel and wheel lip moldings, and deluxe wheel covers.

Measurements

	2-Doors	4-Doors	Wagons
Wheelbase	124.0"	124.0"	121.0"
Length	222.5"	224.7"	220.4"
Width	79.3"	79.3"	79.4"
Height	53.9"	55.3"	57.1"
Legroom — front	41.6"	41.7"	41.7"
Legroom — rear	35.7"	39.9"	37.1"
Headroom — front	37.6"	38.5"	39.0"
Headroom — rear	36.7"	37.5"	39.5"
Cargo capacity (cu. ft.)	18.2	18.2	96.2
Fuel capacity (gals.)	22.0	22.0	21.0

Models Available

	Model No.	Base MSRP	Change from LY	Shipping Wt. (lbs.)	Model Year Production	Change from LY
Monterey 2-Door Hardtop	46	$4,004	+4.49%	4167	6,452	-4.15%
Monterey 4-Door Pillared Hardtop	44	$3,961	+4.43%	4225	16,622	-12.57%
Monterey 4-Door, 6-pass. Station Wagon	72	$4,379	-1.48%	4623	4,275	-7.95%
Monterey Custom 2-Door Hardtop	56	$4,207	+4.26%	4239	6,962	+17.80%
Monterey Custom 4-Door Pillared Hardtop	54	$4,124	+4.25%	4295	20,873	+23.66%
TOTALS	*Avg. price*	$4,196	+4.68%	*Production*	55,184	-1.76%

Marquis

"A smooth ride on most any road."

Nameplate year of origin: 1967.
Current bodystyle lifespan: 1971 through 1978 (restyled in 1973 and 1975).
Predecessor to this model: Marquis (1969 to 1970).
Replacement for this model: Marquis & Grand Marquis (1979 to 1991).
Percentage of division's sales volume: 26.55%.
Corporate siblings: Ford Custom 500/Galaxie 500/LTD and Mercury Monterey.
Primary competition: Buick Centurion/Electra 225 and Estate Wagon, Chrysler Newport and Town & Country, Oldsmobile Ninety-Eight and Custom Cruiser, and Pontiac Grand Ville and Grand Safari.
Notable changes: Revised front and rear styling.
Major standard equipment: Choice of cloth-and-vinyl or all-vinyl front bench seat, nylon loop pile carpeting, simulated woodgrain I/P and steering wheel appliqué, three-spoke steering wheel, electric clock, dome light, deluxe sound insulation package, rocker panel molding, front bumper guards, rear wheel opening fender skirts, deluxe wheel covers, and HR78 × 15 BSW tires.

Measurements

	2-Doors	4-Doors	Wagons
Wheelbase	124.0"	124.0"	121.0"
Length	222.5"	224.8"	220.5"
Width	79.6"	79.3"	79.4"
Height	54.0"	55.3"	57.1"
Legroom — front	41.6"	41.5"	41.5"
Legroom — rear	35.6"	39.9"	37.1"
Headroom — front	37.4"	38.3"	38.8"
Headroom — rear	36.5"	37.3"	39.3"
Cargo capacity (cu. ft.)	18.2	18.2	96.2
Fuel capacity (gals.)	22.0	22.0	21.0

Wagon adds: All-vinyl front bench seat, cargo area light, power tailgate window, and JR78 × 15 BSW tires. Colony Park adds: All vinyl front bench seat w/fold-down center armrest, deluxe two-spoke steering wheel, cargo area light, power tailgate window, cherry woodgrain yacht deck exterior paneling w/planking, and deluxe wheel covers. Marquis Brougham adds: Brougham cloth and vinyl front bench seat w/fold-down center armrest, rear seat center armrests, shag cut pile carpeting, RH visor vanity mirror, courtesy lights, power windows, door pull straps, front and rear door courtesy lights, rear roof pillar reading light, luggage compartment light, and halo vinyl roof.

Models Available

	Model No.	Base MSRP	Change from LY	Shipping Wt. (lbs.)	Model Year Production	Change from LY
Marquis 2-Door Hardtop	66	$4,727	+3.39%	4411	5,973	+8.46%
Marquis 4-Door Pillared Hardtop	63	$4,648	+3.45%	4477	15,250	+7.99%
Marquis 4-Door Hardtop	68	$4,727	+3.13%	4453	2,185	+38.03%
Marquis 4-Door, 6-pass. Wagon	74	$4,608	+3.67%	4685	2,464	+18.18%
Marquis Colony Park 4-Door, 6-pass. Wagon	76	$4,713	+3.58%	4730	23,283	+15.31%
Marquis Brougham 2-Door Hardtop	64	$5,151	+3.66%	4475	22,770	+13.49%
Marquis Brougham 4-Door Pillared Hardtop	62	$5,072	+3.72%	4547	46,624	+21.92%
Marquis Brougham 4-Door Hardtop	67	$5,206	+3.42%	4565	10,613	-17.35%
TOTALS		Avg. price $4,084	+3.50%		Production 129,162	+12.67%

OLDSMOBILE

"What's new from Oldsmobile for 1973? Plenty."

Oldsmobile was on a roll after a surprisingly successful 1972 model year in which it secured a third place spot in overall industry production for the first time since World War II. Plymouth and Pontiac had both slipped as the muscle car era ended, and with consumer interest shifting toward more luxury, Oldsmobile was in the perfect position to give buyers what they wanted. In much the same way that the sixties had been successful for Pontiac with its muscle car image helping it to maintain a third place ranking for about eight years, Oldsmobile would manage to stay in the number three spot for most of the next 15 years. The only two exceptions to Oldsmobile's third place ranking were in the 1974 model year, when Plymouth temporarily came back up to third place on the strength of the compact Valiant during the oil shortage and ensuing recession, and then again for the 1980 model year when Buick had the highly successful introduction of the front-wheel-drive Skylark as well as a newly redesigned mid-size sedan line.

All-new styling was introduced on the mid-size Cutlass series for 1973, in keeping with the newly termed "Colonnade" hardtop styling of the other GM mid-size cars, but maintaining the Oldsmobile bodyside styling cues that had distinguished the full-size models since 1971. Front-end styling was in typical Olds fashion with a twin port grille

separated by a wide body-colored center section with the Oldsmobile "rocket" logo mounted in the center. The two sections of grille itself each consisted of 20 vertical bars that extended below the bumper line and curved under the front pan, all outlined by a chrome surround. The front bumper was a single bar-style affair which followed the contour of the front end, including the slightly pointed grille that protruded past the front fender ends, which housed single round headlamps set into chrome bezels. The parking/turn signal lights were set below the front bumper at the ends and wrapped around the front edge to include the side marker light.

As for the aforementioned bodyside styling, a lower body feature line began under the bottom corner of the front bumper, followed over the round topped front wheel opening, creating a small flare, and then proceeded across the rest of the front fender aft of the wheel opening at the same level at which it began. As the line passed onto the front door it began to turn upward pointing in the general direction of the front door handle, and gradually faded away at mid-body height. At the rear, a similar lower line began at the top edge of the rear bumper, followed the curve of the rear bumper which wrapped under the car, ran forward to pass over the rear wheel opening, creating a slight flare, and then back down to the same level it had been at the rear of the wheel opening. From there it curved upward onto the rear door of sedans and wagons, generally pointing towards the front door handle and fading away at mid-body height, while on the coupes, it also turned upwards, and faded away at a point directly under the door lock cylinder. An upper feature line began from the top front edge of the front fender, and onto the bodyside as it approached the cowl, and faded away at the mid-point across the door on two-door models, and at the rear edge on four-door models. The line picked up again under the rear quarter side window and led onto the top of the rear quarter panel, ending as it curved downward to follow the edge of the taillight.

"Colonnade" hardtop styling, which featured frameless door glass, meant that there were no longer true hardtop models, nor a convertible. Four-door models had a six-window side glass configuration with a fixed glass rear quarter window. Station wagons had a similarly shaped rear quarter vent window available on three-seat models. All models had curved corners where the glass met the center B-pillar. Rooflines varied by model, with the station wagons using a rear liftgate, rather than the previous door-type tailgate that swung open or down. Four-door models had a slight fastback look, as the rear window sloped into a decklid that also sloped, but at a less severe angle. As with the Buick Century, coupes came in two differing rooflines — the Cutlass and Cutlass S models used a near fastback style roofline similar to the sedans, with a triangular fixed rear quarter window, whereas the Cutlass Supreme two-door featured a somewhat more formal roofline with a smaller rear quarter opera window and a V-shaped profile to the sloping backlite. This "special" roofline was shared with the Buick Century Regal and was similar to that of the Chevrolet Monte Carlo and Pontiac Grand Prix.

At the rear, the Cutlass coupes and sedans used vertical taillamps inset into the rear quarter panel with an Olds rocket logo centered in the lens; the light extended into the bumper, which curved under the car, similar to the 1968–1972 Cutlass rear bumpers. The license plate mount was low on the center of the bumper, and backup lights were placed on each side of the license tag mount, but higher on the bumper. Vista-Cruiser station wagons, now built on the same platform as other intermediate GM wagon models, used a straight-across rear bumper with dual upside down, half-moon taillamps recessed into each end of the bumper, and backup lights near the center and flanking the license plate mounting.

Inside, the mid-size Oldsmobile line was equally new. The instrument panel was fully padded with two round dials centered in front of the driver housing the gauges in tunneled pods, and horizontal air vents mounted to each side of the gauges near the top. Below the air vents were light and windshield wiper controls on the left side and radio and ventilation controls on the right, with both having simulated woodgrain

trim appliques. All of this was within a driver's pod that was slightly wrapped around the driver in a cockpit style configuration. On the passenger side of the car were two round air vents along each side of the top opening of the glove box. Door panels consisted of a large formed plastic center section, carpeted lower panel, and a padded vinyl upper section. This basic door panel configuration would be used on most GM A-body and G-body cars for the next 15 years. Seats in the Cutlass line were the most luxurious ever used in the mid-size line, with optional recliners, swivel bucket seats, fold-down center armrests and many other luxury style features being available. Under the hood, the Cutlass series was still powered by a selection of Rocket V8 engines, but with a new EGR (exhaust gas recirculation) system designed to control peak combustion temperatures and minimize the formation of nitrogen oxide. The optional W30 455 CID V8 engine was gone, but there was still a High-Output 455 CID V8 engine available for two-door models.

The Vista-Cruiser station wagon was marketed by Oldsmobile as a separate model again for 1973, but was now considered a part of the Cutlass line in most industry references of the time, as it shared its body and chassis with all intermediate-size GM wagons, rather than having the unique stretched wheelbase and body of years past. Also, the Vista-Cruiser lost its unique raised roof and "Vista" glass panels in the roof, so for the 1973 model year, the Vista-Cruiser had a standard "Vista-Vent" manually operated sunroof as its sole connection to previous Vista-Cruisers. Otherwise most details of the redesigned Cutlass line apply to the Vista-Cruiser. For 1974, the Vista-Cruiser would officially be folded into the Cutlass series. Interestingly, the Cutlass and Vista-Cruiser model year production combined outsold the Chevrolet Chevelle series for the first time ever in 1973. It was just the first taste of huge popularity for the Cutlass, which eventually led to overuse and dilution of the nameplate in the Oldsmobile model lineup. But for now, the Cutlass was "King of the Road" at Oldsmobile.

Model changes for the Cutlass line included the discontinuation of the entry-level F-85 sedan, Cutlass S Sport coupe, Cutlass station wagon, and the Cutlass Supreme convertible. Another Hurst/Olds Cutlass was offered for 1973, with standard FE2 suspension and Hurst's console-mounted Dual/Gate shifter attached to a specially calibrated automatic transmission. Also standard were power front disc brakes and swivel bucket seats. Several Hurst-designed options were available at extra cost. The Hurst/Olds package drew 1,097 orders, the highest sales total to date for a Hurst/Olds. There were also approximately 9,500 Cutlass S coupes and approximately 500 Cutlass coupes (industry records differ) equipped with the optional 4-4-2 package, which by 1973 was down to a trim and decal package.

Omega was the name given to an all-new compact car, which was heavily based on the GM X-body Chevrolet Nova.

The Nova, which was given a restyling this year, shared all of its styling features with the new Omega, except for the front grille and header panel and the rear panel and taillights. Omega wore the expected Oldsmobile front end design, with a vertical bar grille divided into two sections by a body color panel with the Oldsmobile rocket logo mounted in the center. Single round headlamps were mounted in chrome bezels on the fender ends. Taillights, horizontal units with round corners on the bottom, were divided into three sections, with the backup lights being in the center section. The Omega's standard 250 CID six-cylinder engine was a Chevrolet designed engine, and most of the interior features including the instrument panel design were quite similar to the Nova, with only slight trim differences. As with the Nova, the Omega was available in a two-door coupe or hatchback coupe and a four-door sedan.

Full-size Oldsmobiles received only minor changes for the 1973 season. The Delta 88 and Ninety-Eight series returned with few changes, other than the impact absorbing front bumper system and swing-away grille as used on most other Oldsmobiles. For the Ninety-Eight, the base and Luxury sub-series returned in both two-door and four-door hardtop versions. The Ninety-Eight Regency sedan, which was introduced midway through the 1972 model year as a special model to celebrate Oldsmobile's 75th anniversary, also returned, now as a sub-series of the Ninety-Eight. The nameplate would remain through the demise of the Ninety-Eight series in 1996, and would live on for two more seasons as an ultra-luxury version of the renamed Eighty-Eight series, essentially being the replacement for the Ninety-Eight series. The full-size Custom Cruiser wagons came in two versions for 1973, with or without simulated woodgrain vinyl bodyside and tailgate appliqués, and each was offered in 6-passenger, 2-seat or 9-passenger, 3-seat versions, all with unique model numbers. It was the first time for the Custom Cruiser to be offered sans the wood trim.

Finally, the front-wheel-drive Toronado continued with only a minor styling update. To meet the new front bumper standards, the Toronado gained a smaller bumper with a more pronounced impact area which sat slightly lower than on previous models. A full-width air intake slot was added above the bumper, continued below the headlights. The lowering of the impact area also meant that the grille area which was previously fully contained in the outer portions of the lower bumper area, though still in the same location, now sat partly atop the bumper and below the air intake slot. The Toronado also gained a new box style rear bumper, seemingly in preparation for the 1974 rear bumper standards, and thin blade taillights were vertically mounted on the rear quarter panels. The unique high-level stop lamps continued to be mounted under the rear window.

Custom Cruiser 4-Door Station Wagon

Cutlass S interior

Cutlass 2-Door Colonnade Hardtop Coupe

Cutlass S 4-4-2 option stripe and trim detail

Cutlass Supreme 2-Door
Colonnade Hardtop Coupe

Cutlass S 2-Door Colonnade Hardtop Coupe

Cutlass Supreme 2-Door
Colonnade Hardtop Coupe

Cutlass Supreme 4-Door
Colonnade Hardtop Sedan

Delta 88 4-Door Hardtop

Delta 88 Royale 2-Door Hardtop

Ninety-Eight 2-Door Hardtop

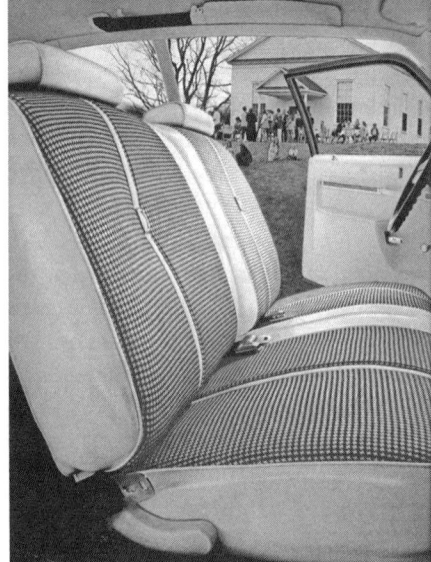

Omega coupe nylon houndstooth interior

Omega 2-Door Hatchback Coupe

Toronado Custom 2-Door Hardtop

Omega line — Hatchback, Coupe, Sedan

Toronado instrument panel

Vista-Cruiser 4-Door Station Wagon

Model year production: 922,758, up 21.07% from 1972.

Domestic market share: 8.68% (3rd place).

Base price range: $2,613 to $5,441.

Oldsmobile average base price: $4,106, up 2.94%.

Introduction date: September 1972.

Assembly plants: Linden, NJ (E); Framingham, MA (G); Van Nuys, CA (L); Lansing, MI (M); Arlington, TX (R); Kansas City — Fairfax, KS (X); and Willow Run, MI (W).

Data plate identification (VIN): Thirteen digit code read as follows: First digit indicates division (3 = Oldsmobile); second through fourth digits indicate series and body style (model number in model charts); fifth digit is engine code (see powertrain chart); sixth digit indicates model year (3 = 1973); seventh digit indicates assembly plant (see list above); remaining digits are sequential with beginning number of 100001, except for Toronado which begins with 700001. *Example:* 3L69K3X100001 is a 1973 Oldsmobile Delta 88 4-Door Town Sedan, with 350 CID, 4-bbl. V8 engine, serial number 100001, built in Kansas City — Fairfax, KS.

Powertrains

Engine	Net HP	Engine Code VIN/GM	Transmission Availability		Omega	Cutlass & Vista-Cruiser	Delta 88	98 & Custom Cruiser	Toronado
250 CID (4.1L), 1-bbl., 6-cyl.	100	D	3-speed manual		S	—	—	—	—
				MPG:	NA	—	—	—	—

Engine	Net HP	Engine Code VIN/GM	Transmission Availability		Omega	Cutlass & Vista-Cruiser	Delta 88	98 & Custom Cruiser	Toronado
			3-speed Turbo		$190	—	—	—	—
			Hydra-matic	MPG:	15.7	—	—	—	—
350 CID (5.7L), 2-bbl., V8	160	H/L34	3-speed Turbo		—	—	S	—	—
			Hydra-matic	MPG:	—	—	NA	—	—
350 CID (5.7L), 4-bbl., V8	180	K/L34[1]	3-speed manual		$164	S	—	—	—
				MPG:	NA	NA	—	—	—
			4-speed manual		—	$190 (2-Drs. only)	—	—	—
				MPG:	—	9.4	—	—	—
			3-speed Turbo		$364	$215	$40	—	—
			Hydra-matic	MPG:	9.5	9.5	NA	—	—
455 CID (7.4L), 4-bbl., V8	225	T/L75	3-speed Turbo		—	—	$169	S	—
			Hydra-matic	MPG:	—	—	8.1	7.6	—
455 CID (7.4L), 4-bbl., V8	250[2]	U/L75	3-speed Turbo		—	$373	$199	$30	S
			Hydra-matic	MPG:	—	7.3	NA	NA	7.6
455 CID (7.4L) H.O., 4-bbl., V8	275[2]	V/L74	4-speed manual		—	$359 (2-Drs. only)	—	—	—
				MPG:	—	NA	—	—	—
			3-speed Turbo		—	$405[3]	—	—	—
			Hydra-matic	MPG:	—	7.3	—	—	—

All Oldsmobile V8 engines are officially known as Rocket V8s. [1]*Engine code "M" with dual exhaust and 200 hp rating available at extra cost, except on Omega.* [2]*Includes dual exhaust.* [3]*Available only with other selected optional equipment.*

Major Options

	Omega	Cutlass	Vista-Cruiser	Delta 88	Custom Cruiser	Ninety-Eight	Toronado
Four-Season air conditioner[1]	$381	$397	$397	$431	$431	$431	$431
Tilt-Away steering wheel	$44	$44	$44	$44	$44	$44	$44
Tilt-and-telescope steering wheel	—	—	—	—	—	$82	$82
Cruise control	—	$62	$62	$66	$66	$66	$66
Electric rear window defroster	$31[2]	$62	$35[2]	$62	$62	$62	$62
Remote control mirror, LH	$12	$12	$12	$12	$12	S	S
Soft Ray tinted glass, all windows	$39	$42	$42	$49	$49	$49	$49
Power windows, 2-dr./4-dr.	—	$75/$113	$113	$129	$129	$129[3]	$129
Power door locks, 2-dr./4-dr.	—	$45/$69	$69	$46/$69	$69	$46/$69	$46
Power front seat, w/std. seat	—	$103	$103	$103	$103	$103[4]	$103
Front bucket seats, w/console	$124	$126	—	—	—	—	—
AM radio	$65	$73	$73	$85	$85	$85	$85
AM/FM stereo	$135[5]	$233	$233	$233	$233	$233	$233
AM/FM stereo w/8-track tape	—	$363	$363	$363	$363	$363	$363
Vinyl top[6]	$82	$99	—	$123	—	$138	$135
Vista Vent sunroof, manual	—	$275[7]	S	—	—	—	—
Power trunk lid release	—	—	—	$14	—	$14	$14
Power steering, "Vari-Ratio"	$113	$113	$113	S	S	S	S[8]
Power brakes, w/front disc	$68	$46	S	S	S	S	S[9]
Deluxe wheel covers	$25	$26	$26	$31	$31	$31	S
Wire wheel covers	—	$82	$82	$82	—	—	—
Super Stock II wheels	—	$72	$72	—	—	—	—
Super Stock III wheels	$64	$72	$72	—	—	—	—
WSW tires, std. size	$28	$30	$30	S	S	S	S

Popular Option Groups & Packages

	Omega	Cutlass	Vista-Cruiser	Delta 88	Custom Cruiser	Ninety-Eight	Toronado
Brougham interior package	—	—	—	—	—	—	$154
Salon package	—	$361	—	—	—	—	—

	Omega	Cutlass	Vista-Cruiser	Delta 88	Custom Cruiser	Ninety-Eight	Toronado
W29 4-4-2 package	—	$120	—	—	—	—	—
W45 Hurst/Olds package	—	$435	—	—	—	—	—

— = Not Available; S = Standard equipment. [1]*V8 engine required for Omega. Power brakes required on Omega and Cutlass. "Comfortron" air conditioner with automatic climate control is available for $76 additional on Delta 88, Custom Cruiser, Ninety-Eight and Toronado.* [2]*Blower type defogger.* [3]*Standard on Ninety-Eight Luxury and Regency models.* [4]*Not available on Ninety-Eight Regency. Available on Ninety-Eight Luxury for $77.* [5]*AM/FM radio, non-stereo, for Omega.* [6]*Padded vinyl top on Ninety-Eight and Toronado.* [7]*Two-door models only. Electrically operated sunroof $50 higher, and requires power windows.* [8]*"Constant-Ratio" steering on Toronado.* [9]*"True-Track" anti-lock braking system available on Toronado for $192.*

Paint Colors

	Code		Code		Code
Cameo White	11	Brewster Green	48	Omega Red[2]	75
Ebony Black[1]	19	Omega Yellow[2]	51	Honey Beige[1]	81
Wedgewood Blue metallic	24	Chamois Gold	56	Omega Orange metallic[2]	97
Zodiac Blue metallic	26	Mayan Gold metallic	60		
Eclipse Blue metallic	29	Silver Taupe metallic	64		
Emerald Green metallic	42	Tanbark metallic[1]	66		
Crystal Green metallic	44	Chestnut metallic	68		
Moss Green Gold metallic	46	Cranberry Red metallic	74		

In two-tone combinations, the first two digits indicate lower color and the next two digits are the upper color. Magic Mirror two-tone available for $36 on Cutlass, $27 on Vista-Cruiser, $31 on Custom Cruiser and $43 on 88, 98 and Toronado. [1]Available on all models except Omega. [2]Available only on Omega.

Omega

"Meet Omega. A whole new kind of Olds."

Nameplate year of origin: 1973.
Current bodystyle lifespan: 1973 through 1974.
Predecessor to this model: None.
Replacement for this model: Omega (1975 to 1979).
Percentage of division's production: 6.54%.
Corporate siblings: Buick Apollo, Chevrolet Nova, and Pontiac Ventura.
Primary competition: Dodge Dart, and Mercury Comet.
Notable changes: All-new model based on GM's X-body platform.
Major standard equipment: Knit vinyl front bench seat, full-floor carpeting, rear quarter/rear door armrests, deluxe steering wheel, door-operated dome lamp, dual speed wipers w/washers, window surround moldings, roof drip moldings, front and rear wheel opening moldings, hubcaps, and E78 × 14 BSW tires. Hatchback model adds: Fold-down rear seat.

Measurements

	Coupe & HBK	Sedan
Wheelbase	111.0"	111.0"
Length	197.5"	197.5"
Width	72.4"	72.4"
Height	52.4"	53.8"
Legroom — front	41.7"	41.7"
Legroom — rear	33.4"	35.3"
Headroom — front	38.0"	39.3"
Headroom — rear	36.9"	37.3"
Cargo capacity (cu. ft.)	13.6*	13.6
Fuel capacity (gals.)	21.5	21.5

Hatchback maximum with rear seat down, 27 cu. ft.

Models Available

	Model No.	Base MSRP	Change from LY	Shipping Wt. (lbs.)	Model Year Production	Change from LY
Omega 2-Door Coupe	B27	$2,613	NEW	3117	26,126	NEW
Omega 2-Door Hatchback	B17	$2,762	NEW	3229	21,433	NEW
Omega 4-Door Town Sedan	B69	$2,641	NEW	3180	12,804	NEW
TOTALS		Avg. price $2,672	NEW		Production 60,363	NEW

Cutlass

"Every year a little better: Not just prettier."

Nameplate year of origin: 1961 as F-85 Deluxe sport coupe designation; 1962 as F-85 sub-series; and 1965 as series designation. Also used on 1955 Oldsmobile show car.

Current bodystyle lifespan: 1973 through 1977.

Predecessor to this model: Cutlass (1968 to 1972).

Replacement for this model: Cutlass (1978 to 1988; restyled in 1981).

Percentage of division's production: 41.30%.

Corporate siblings: Buick Century, Chevrolet Malibu, and Pontiac LeMans.

Primary competition: Dodge Coronet and Mercury Montego.

Notable changes: Completely redesigned.

Major standard equipment: Choice of Lagoon cloth or Morocceen vinyl front bench seat, color-keyed rubber floor

Measurements

	Cutlass Coupe	Supreme Coupe	Cutlass Sedan	Supreme Sedan
Wheelbase	112.0"	112.0"	116.0"	116.0"
Length	207.0"	208.9"	211.0"	212.9"
Width	76.5"	76.5"	76.5"	76.5"
Height	53.3"	53.1"	54.0"	54.0"
Legroom — front	42.1"	42.1"	42.1"	42.1"
Legroom — rear	33.7"	33.7"	38.4"	38.3"
Headroom — front	37.7"	37.7"	38.3"	38.3"
Headroom — rear	37.0"	37.0"	37.5"	37.5"
Cargo capacity (cu. ft.)	16.0	16.4	16.0	16.0
Fuel capacity (gals.)	22.0	22.0	22.0	22.0

mat (coupe), full-floor carpeting (sedan), deluxe armrests front and rear, manual front disc brakes, rocker panel and wheel lip moldings (sedan), bright window surround moldings, wheel covers, and F78 × 14 BSW tires. "S" adds: Full-floor carpeting and rocker panel and wheel lip moldings. Supreme adds: Choice of Lansing cloth or Morocceen vinyl front bench seat w/fold-down center armrest, padded luxury door panels with door pull straps, deluxe steering wheel, cigar lighter, and ribbed louver ornament on lower front fender behind wheel.

Models Available

	Model No.	Base MSRP	Change from LY	Shipping Wt. (lbs.)	Model Year Production	Change from LY
Cutlass 2-Door Colonnade HT Coupe	F37	$3,049	+2.56%	3713	22,022	-41.73%
Cutlass 4-Door Colonnade HT Sedan	G29	$3,137	+2.32%	3786	35,578	-8.52%
Cutlass S 2-Door Colonnade HT Coupe	G37	$3,159	+2.33%	3721	77,558	-1.15%
Cutlass Supreme 2-Door Colonnade HT Coupe	J57	$3,324	+2.03%	3694	219,857	+109.21%
Cutlass Supreme 4-Door Colonnade HT Sedan	J29	$3,395	+1.98%	3808	26,099	+74.52%
TOTALS	*Avg. price*	$3,213	+1.00%	*Production*	381,114	+25.92%

Vista-Cruiser

"The brand new wagon with a window on top."

Nameplate year of origin: 1964.

Current bodystyle lifespan: 1973 (continued through 1977 as part of the Cutlass series).

Predecessor to this model: Vista-Cruiser (1968 to 1972).

Replacement for this model: None.

Percentage of division's production: 2.65%.

Corporate siblings: Buick Century, Chevrolet Malibu, and Pontiac LeMans.

Primary competition: Dodge Coronet and Mercury Montego.

Notable changes: Completely redesigned.

Major standard equipment: Choice of Lansing cloth or Morocceen vinyl front bench seat, color-keyed full-floor carpeting, deluxe armrests front and rear, deluxe steering wheel, rear compartment side vent window (3-seat model), tailgate ajar lamp, Vista-vent roof ventilator, bright rocker panel and wheel lip moldings, bright window surround moldings, woodgrain vinyl body and tailgate panels, remote-control tailgate release, power front disc brakes, wheel covers, and H78 × 14 BSW tires.

Measurements

Wheelbase	116.0"
Length	219.3"
Width	76.8"
Height	55.3"
Legroom — front	42.1"
Legroom — rear	36.8"
Headroom — front	38.8"
Headroom — rear	39.4"
Cargo capacity (cu. ft.)	85.0
Fuel capacity (gals.)	22.0

Models Available

	Model No.	Base MSRP	Change from LY	Shipping Wt. (lbs.)	Model Year Production	Change from LY
Vista-Cruiser 4-Door, 2-Seat Station Wagon	J35	$3,789	+1.47%	4240	10,894	+3.04%
Vista-Cruiser 4-Door, 3-Seat Station Wagon	J45	$3,902	-0.15%	4290	13,531	-36.59%
TOTALS	*Avg. price*	$3,846	+0.64%	*Production*	24,425	-23.46%

Delta 88

"It gives you a lot more than just size."

Nameplate year of origin: 1965 (88 series began in 1949).
Current bodystyle lifespan: 1971 through 1976.
Predecessor to this model: Delta 88 (1969 to 1970).
Replacement for this model: Delta 88 (1977 to 1985).
Percentage of division's production: 24.23%.
Corporate siblings: Buick LeSabre/Centurion, Chevrolet BelAir/Impala/Caprice, and Pontiac Catalina/Bonneville/Grand Ville.
Primary competition: Chrysler Newport and Mercury Monterey.
Notable changes: Minor trim and detail changes.
Major standard equipment: Lansing cloth and Morocceen vinyl bench seat, full-floor carpeting, deluxe steering wheel, front cigar lighter, bright wheel opening moldings, bright rocker panel molding, full wheel covers, and H78 × 15 BSW tires. Royale adds: Bravo cloth with Morocceen trim front bench seat (all except convertible), pleated all–Morocceen front bench seat (convertible), fold-down center armrest (all except Town Sedan), door panel and I/P woodgrain appliqués, front and rear cigar lighters, chrome accented control pedals, bodyside molding w/vinyl inserts, louver style chrome fender trim, and front and rear vinyl bumper impact strips.

Measurements

	Delta 88	Royale
Wheelbase	124.0"	124.0"
Length	225.0"	226.3"
Width	79.5"	79.6"
Height	54.3"	53.6"
Legroom — front	42.4"	42.4"
Legroom — rear	38.5"	38.8"
Headroom — front	38.3"	38.3"
Headroom — rear	38.0"	38.0"
Cargo capacity (cu. ft.)	NA	NA
Fuel capacity (gals.)	NA	NA

Models Available

	Model No.	Base MSRP	Change from LY	Shipping Wt. (lbs.)	Model Year Production	Change from LY
Delta 88 2-Door Hardtop Coupe	L57	$4,047	+1.15%	4192	27,096	-15.42%
Delta 88 4-Door Town Sedan	L69	$3,991	+1.09%	4243	42,476	-7.85%
Delta 88 4-Door Hardtop Sedan	L39	$4,108	+1.18%	4270	27,986	-21.25%
Delta 88 Royale 2-Door Hardtop Coupe	N57	$4,221	+1.01%	4206	27,096	-21.11%
Delta 88 Royale 2-Door Convertible	N67	$4,442	+1.25%	4298	7,088	+81.74%
Delta 88 Royale 4-Door Town Sedan	N69	$4,156	+1.34%	4255	42,672	+24.95%
Delta 88 Royale 4-Door Hardtop Sedan	N39	$4,293	+1.30%	4296	49,145	+15.35%
TOTALS	*Avg. price*	$4,180	+1.19%	*Production*	223,559	-2.23%

Custom Cruiser

"First it's an Oldsmobile. Then it's a station wagon."

Nameplate year of origin: 1971 (1940 as a designation on 90 series cars).
Current bodystyle lifespan: 1971 through 1976.
Predecessor to this model: None.
Replacement for this model: Custom Cruiser (1977 to 1990).
Percentage of division's production: 4.22%.
Corporate siblings: Buick Estate Wagon, Chevrolet BelAir/Impala/Caprice, and Pontiac Catalina Safari/Grand Safari.

Measurements

Wheelbase	127.0"
Length	228.3"
Width	79.5"
Height	57.2"
Legroom — front	42.1"

Primary competition: Chrysler Town & Country and Mercury Colony Park.

Notable changes: Minor trim and detail changes.

Major standard equipment: Oxen-grain Morocceen vinyl bench seat, full-floor carpeting, front and rear deluxe armrests, Glide-Away tailgate, power tailgate window, LH and RH rear view mirrors, rear wheel opening fender skirts, full wheel covers, and L78 × 15 BSW tires. "R" models add: Simulated woodgrain vinyl bodyside and tailgate appliqués.

Measurements (cont.)

Legroom — rear	39.4"
Headroom — front	39.6"
Headroom — rear	39.3"
Cargo capacity (cu. ft.)	106.1
Fuel capacity (gals.)	NA

Models Available

	Model No.	Base MSRP	Change from LY	Shipping Wt. (lbs.)	Model Year Production*	Change from LY*
Custom Cruiser 4-Door, 2-S. Wagon	Q35	$4,630	NEW	4997	12,397	NEW
Custom Cruiser 4-Door, 3-S. Wagon	Q45	$4,769	NEW	5061	26,511	NEW
Custom Cruiser 4-Door, 2-S. Wagon	R35	$4,785	+1.81%	4999	NA	NA
Custom Cruiser 4-Door, 3-S. Wagon	R45	$4,924	+1.45%	5063	NA	NA
TOTALS		*Avg. price* $4,772	+0.10%		*Production* 38,908	+55.67%

*Production of "Q" non-woodgrained, and "R" woodgrained models kept as combined total.

Ninety-Eight

"Drive it and draw your own conclusions."

Nameplate year of origin: 1941.

Current bodystyle lifespan: 1971 through 1976.

Predecessor to this model: Ninety-Eight (1969 to 1970).

Replacement for this model: Ninety-Eight (1977 to 1984).

Percentage of division's production: 15.01%.

Corporate siblings: Buick Electra 225, Cadillac Calais, and Cadillac deVille.

Primary competition: Chrysler New Yorker and Mercury Marquis.

Notable changes: Minor trim and detail changes.

Major standard equipment: Choice of Minuet cloth w/Morocceen vinyl trim or Oxen-grain Morocceen vinyl front bench seat w/fold-down center armrest, full-floor luxury carpeting, carpeted lower door panels, simulated woodgrain appliqués on I/P and door panels, door pull straps, electric clock, deluxe safety belts, remote-control LH rear view mirror, wheel opening moldings, rocker panel molding, rear bumper guards, rear fender skirts, wheel covers, and J78 × 15 BSW tires. Luxury adds: Choice of Bravo cloth w/Morocceen vinyl trim or all-Morocceen vinyl front bench seat w/fold-down center armrest, power controls on door armrest in chrome bezel, two-way power front seat, power windows, and spare tire cover. Regency adds: Textured velour 60/40 front seat with two-way power adjustment for each side, fold-down center armrests front and rear, zippered front seatback pouch pockets, French walnut woodgrain I/P, door panel and seat side shield trim, Tiffany-styled timepiece facing, power windows, door-mounted entry courtesy lights, and fully-lined trunk compartment w/spare tire cover.

Measurements

Wheelbase	127.0"
Length	230.3"
Width	79.6"
Height	54.7"
Legroom — front	42.4"
Legroom — rear	41.1"
Headroom — front	39.3"
Headroom — rear	38.2"
Cargo capacity (cu. ft.)	20.2
Fuel capacity (gals.)	NA

Models Available

	Model No.	Base MSRP	Change from LY	Shipping Wt. (lbs.)	Model Year Production	Change from LY
Ninety-Eight 2-Door Hardtop Coupe	T37	$4,799	+1.07%	4435	7,850	-40.13%
Ninety-Eight 4-Door Hardtop Sedan	T39	$4,860	+1.10%	4522	13,989	-20.39%
Ninety-Eight Luxury Coupe 2-Door HT	V37	$5,071	+1.24%	4471	26,925	+10.11%
Ninety-Eight Luxury Sedan 4-Door HT	V39	$5,164	+1.29%	4560	55,695	-20.34%
Ninety-Eight Regency Sedan 4-Door HT	X39	$5,418	NEW	4594	34,009	NEW
TOTALS		*Avg. price* $5,062	+2.99%		*Production* 138,468	+10.72%

Toronado

"There's nothing common about it."

Nameplate year of origin: 1966.
Current bodystyle lifespan: 1971 through 1978.
Predecessor to this model: Toronado (1966 to 1970).
Replacement for this model: Toronado (1979 to 1985).
Percentage of division's production: 6.06%.
Corporate siblings: Buick Riviera and Cadillac Eldorado.
Primary competition: Ford Thunderbird.
Notable changes: Revised front end and minor trim and detail changes.
Major standard equipment: Choice of Laredo cloth fabric or Morocceen vinyl Custom-Sport front bench seat, full-floor carpeting, cross-brushed metal inlays on I/P and steering wheel, simulated woodgrain appliqué on door panels, deluxe steering wheel, electric clock, color-keyed chrome-accented pedals, deluxe safety belts, LH remote-control rear view mirror, front and rear bumper guards w/vinyl inserts, chrome wheel covers, dual exhaust system, and J78 × 15 BSW tires.

Measurements

Wheelbase	122.0"
Length	226.8"
Width	79.8"
Height	53.2"
Legroom — front	42.4"
Legroom — rear	35.2"
Headroom — front	38.1"
Headroom — rear	37.1"
Cargo capacity (cu. ft.)	NA
Fuel capacity (gals.)	NA

Models Available

	Model No.	Base MSRP	Change from LY	Shipping Wt. (lbs.)	Model Year Production	Change from LY
Toronado Custom 2-Door Hardtop	Y57	$5,441	+1.87%	4654	55,921	+14.36%
TOTALS		*Avg. price* $5,441	+1.87%		*Production* 55,921	+14.36%

PLYMOUTH

"Extra care in engineering makes a difference in Plymouth."

The 1973 Plymouth line was in the same situation as its Dodge and Chrysler counterparts, having no new models for a second year in a row. Most of the line received refreshed front-end styling to accommodate the new bumper standards. But even with that change, only the Fury line appeared significantly different from its 1972 counterparts, as the loop style front bumper was discontinued. Under the hood was a new electronic ignition system on all cars except the Cricket. The new system did away with points and condenser, reducing the need for timing adjustments, which thereby eliminated the major cause of engine misfiring. Also added were an electric assist choke, an exhaust gas recirculation (EGR) system, proportional exhaust gas recirculation (PEGR) system and the orifice spark advance control (OSAC) system.

The compact A-bodied Valiant Group, which included the Valiant 4-door sedan, Scamp 2-door hardtop, and Duster 2-door coupes, received a front-end restyling, and the Duster also had a rear panel update. The front-end restyling began with single round headlamps mounted in a chrome bezel that was slightly pointed on the vertical edges to match the front fender line. Below the new raised center section of the hood was a three-section horizontal grille, with each section being chrome lined, and having a horizontal crosshatch insert three rows high and 14 columns across. Between the main portion of the grille and the headlight bezels was a smaller three-row grille section with a center-mounted rectangular parking/turn signal lamp. Above all of this was a chrome trim piece that was larger over the center portion of the grille and carried the Plymouth name across the facing. A small chrome strip along the bottom completed the look of a fully surrounded grille. At the back end, Valiant and Scamp models continued to use a sloping rear trunk lid and bumper, with taillights set into each end of the bumper. Meanwhile the Duster received a new rear panel with large rectangular taillamps divided into two sections horizontally, as opposed to the prior year's louvered style taillamps.

The mid-size Satellite series entered the new year with few styling changes for sedans and wagons, and only a mild update for the front of the coupe models. All models used an egg-crate grille insert, with the coupes' being four rows high and having a horizontal center divider and the four-door models' being three rows high, angling rearward at the outer ends. The dual headlights of four-door models were set into individual argent colored bezels; two-door models wore their dual headlights in chrome housings that protruded slightly and angled back towards the fender ends. Four-door models used a bumper design similar to the former loop style bumper, having a raised center section and turning up at the ends, but no longer encompassing the grille. Although there were no model changes for the season, the Satellite would see a 50 percent increase in production this year, nearly matching the total production of the full-size Fury. Also, the Road Runner, while never a huge seller, saw its sales triple over the 1972 season. As for the other "hot" Plymouth, the Barracuda, its most significant change was to drop the Slant Six engine as standard equipment, making 1973 the first of only two years in which the Barracuda was available only with V8 engines. The top line 'Cuda was still in the lineup, but lacked some of the muscle of prior years, with the 318 CID V8 as standard equipment and the 340 CID V8 its only optional engine.

The full-size Fury line dispensed with the double-loop front bumper styling in favor of a more typical box-style bumper, and a horizontal bar grille with a chrome surround. Dual headlights were set into individual chrome bezels on each side of the grille, with parking/turn signal lamps being set into lower grille sections within the bumper. A new hood was also added having a raised center section that was the width of the grille and came to a slight point before the hood rolled down over the front edge to meet the grille. The model lineup was pared back as the Fury entered its last year with the new-for-'69 fuselage design. Missing from the 1973 line was the Fury II 2-door hardtop and the similarly trimmed Suburban 3-seat station wagon, the Fury III 2-door Formal hardtop, and the Gran Fury 2-door Formal hardtop. Despite these missing models, Fury sales were only about 2,000 units below 1972's impressive levels. At mid-year, the Fury Special was introduced, a striking trim package that featured dark metallic chestnut paint, a parchment vinyl roof and bodyside moldings, a color-keyed interior with shag carpeting and "tapestry" cloth seat inserts and a requisite standup hood ornament. Also planned was an "Aspen" décor package, featuring a hood ornament, powder-blue paint and interior color, special decals, and a trunk rack, but no proof of production could be found.

Plymouth's captive import model the Cricket was sold into 1973, but the cars were essentially leftover 1972 models. The Cricket was a slightly Americanized version of the Avenger, a small line of cars built and sold in the United Kingdom by the Chrysler subsidiary Hillman. They were a very basic mode of transportation, with few standard features and only five options on the list. Styling was just as basic, and was quite similar to the Japanese-built Dodge Colt and Datsun 510 models. A flat front-end had a relatively small bar-style bumper, with a full-width blacked-out grille carrying dual headlamps. Parking and turn signal lights were set in the pan below the bumper. Around back, sedans used a unique boomerang style taillamp, while wagons had more conventional vertical taillights. Apparently there were a substantial number of unsold Crickets built during 1972, and because the cars were manufactured during that year, Chrysler was able to sell the remainders as 1973 models even though they did not meet the federal requirements for front bumpers. The Cricket did add standard front bumper guards, though, to give the appearance of added protection. Quality issues on the early models imported for 1971 kept consumers away from the beginning, and only about 27,500 were sold in its first year. It was downhill from there, despite the addition of the station wagon in the spring of 1972.

Cricket 4-Door Sedan with Cricket
4-Door Station Wagon, rear

'Cuda 2-Door Hardtop with Barracuda
2-Door Hardtop, rear

Duster 2-Door Coupe

Duster 2-Door Coupe with Twister package

Fury Gran Coupe 2-Door Hardtop

Fury I 4-Door Sedan

Fury Sport Suburban 4-Door Station Wagon

Road Runner 2-Door Coupe

Satellite Custom 4-Door Sedan
with Satellite 4-Door Sedan, rear

Satellite Regent 4-Door Station Wagon

Scamp 2-Door Hardtop
with Valiant 4-Door Sedan, rear

Satellite Sebring-Plus 2-Door Hardtop

Model year production: 882,196, up 15.18% from 1972.
Domestic market share: 8.30% (5th place).
Base price range: $2,376 to $4,599.
Plymouth average base price: $3,541, up 8.09%.
Introduction date: September 26, 1972.
Assembly plants: Lynch Road, Detroit, MI (A); Hamtramck, MI (B); Jefferson Ave., Detroit, MI (C); Belvidere, IL (D); Newark, DE (F); and St. Louis, MO (G). *Cricket:* Ryton-on-Dunsmore, Warwickshire, England (R).

Data plate identification (VIN): Thirteen digit code read as follows: First four digits indicate series and body style (model number in model charts); fifth digit indicates engine code (see powertrain chart); sixth digit indicates year (3 = 1973); seventh digit indicates assembly plant (see list above); remaining digits are sequential with beginning numbers of 100001. *Example:* VL41C3B100001 is a 1973 Plymouth Valiant 4-Door Sedan, with 225 CID, 2-bbl. 6-cylinder engine, serial number 100001, built in Hamtramck, MI.

Powertrains

Engine	Net HP	Engine Code	Transmission Availability[1]		Cricket	Duster & Valiant	Barracuda	Satellite, Sebring & Custom	Satellite Sebring Plus, Road Runner & Wagons	Fury
91.4 CID (1.5L), 1-bbl., 4-cyl.	55	G	4-speed manual		S (Sedan)	—	—	—	—	—
				MPG:	NA	—	—	—	—	—
			3-speed automatic		$178 (Sedan)	—	—	—	—	—
				MPG:	NA	—	—	—	—	—

Engine	Net HP	Engine Code	Transmission Availability[1]	Cricket	Duster & Valiant	Barracuda	Satellite, Sebring & Custom	Satellite Sebring Plus, Road Runner & Wagons	Fury
91.4 CID (1.5L), 2 × 1-bbl., 4-cyl.	70	L	4-speed manual	S (Wagon)/ $ (Sedan)	—	—	—	—	—
			MPG:	NA	—	—	—	—	—
			3-speed automatic	$178 (Wagon)/ $ (Sedan)	—	—	—	—	—
			MPG:	NA	—	—	—	—	—
198 CID (3.2L), 1-bbl., 6-cyl.[2]	95	B	3-speed manual	—	S (ex. Duster 340)[2]	—	—	—	—
			MPG:	—	NA	—	—	—	—
			3-speed Torque-Flite automatic	—	$178 (ex. Duster 340)[2]	—	—	—	—
			MPG:	—	16.0	—	—	—	—
225 CID (3.7L), 1-bbl., 6-cyl.	105	C	3-speed manual	—	$39 (ex. Duster 340)[3]	—	S	—	—
			MPG:	—	NA	—	11.5	—	—
			4-speed manual	—	$234 (ex. Duster 340)	—	—	—	—
			MPG:	—	NA	—	—	—	—
			3-speed Torque-Flite automatic	—	$245 (ex. Duster 340)	—	$210	—	—
			MPG:	—	16.7	—	NA	—	—
318 CID (5.2L), 2-bbl., V8	150	G	3-speed manual	—	$147 (ex. Duster 340)	S	$112	S	—
			MPG:	—	12.5	12.5	11.4	11.4	—
			4-speed manual	—	$342 (ex. Duster 340)	$185	—	$205 (Coupes only)	—
			MPG:	—	NA	NA	—	11.8	—
			3-speed Torque-Flite automatic	—	$353 (ex. Duster 340)	$225	$322	$225	S (ex. wgns.)
			MPG:	—	NA	NA	11.6	11.6	NA
340 CID (5.6L), 4-bbl., V8	180	H	3-speed manual	—	S (Duster 340)	$90	—	—	—
			MPG:	—	NA	NA	—	—	—
			4-speed manual	—	$195 (Duster 340)	$275	—	—	—
			MPG:	—	NA	NA	—	—	—
			3-speed Torque-Flite automatic	—	$208 (Duster 340)	$315	—	—	—
			MPG:	—	NA	NA	—	—	—
360 CID (5.9L), 2-bbl., V8	200	K	3-speed Torque-Flite automatic	—	—	—	—	—	S (wgns.)/ $41 (others)
			MPG:	—	—	—	—	—	NA
400 CID (6.6L), 2-bbl., V8	175/ 185[4]	M	3-speed Torque-Flite automatic	—	—	—	$440	$343 (except Road Runner)	$39 (wgns.)/ $80 (others)
			MPG:	—	—	—	NA	NA	8.8
400 CID (6.6L), 4-bbl., V8	260	P	4-speed manual	—	—	—	—	$390 (Road Runner only)	—
			MPG:	—	—	—	—	9.2	—
			3-speed Torque-Flite automatic	—	—	—	$506	$408	—
			MPG:	—	—	—	NA	NA	—

Engine	Net HP	Engine Code	Transmission Availability[1]		Cricket	Duster & Valiant	Barracuda	Satellite, Sebring & Custom	Satellite Sebring Plus, Road Runner & Wagons	Fury
440 CID (7.2L), 4-bbl., V8	280/ 220[4]	T,U	4-speed manual		—	—	—	—	$460 (Road Runner only)	—
				MPG:	—	—	—	—	NA	—
			3-speed Torque-Flite automatic		—	—	—	—	$480 (Road Runner only)	$115 (wgns.)/ $156 (others)
				MPG:	—	—	—	—	8.6	NA

[1]Unless otherwise noted: All 4-speed manuals are floor-shift. All 3-speed manual and automatic transmissions are column shift, except as follows: Cricket w/automatic is floor-shift; Barracuda with 3-speed manual is floor shift. All transmissions are floor-mounted shift on the following models with bucket seats: Duster 340, Barracuda, 'Cuda, and Road Runner. Floor-shift available on Duster and Scamp models for $27 extra. [2]Not available in California. [3]Required (or standard) in California. [4]Second horsepower ratings are as installed in Fury models.

Major Options

	Cricket	Valiant	Barracuda	Satellite	Fury I, II, III	Gran Fury
Air conditioning[1]	$338	$358	$369	$378	$378	$412
Tilt steering wheel w/"Rim Blow"	—	—	—	—	—	$60
Automatic speed control	—	—	—	—	—	$68
Electric rear window defogger[2]	—	$27	$29	$31	$31	$31
Tinted glass, all windows	—	$36	$36	$40	$50	$50
Front vent window, 4-dr. only	—	—	—	—	—	$36
Power windows	—	—	—	$126	$126	$126
Power door locks, 2-dr./4-dr.	—	—	—	—	—	$47/$73
AM radio	$	$65	$65	$65	$80	$80
AM/FM stereo	—	—	$194	$194	$212	$212
AM/FM stereo w/8-track tape	—	—	—	$353	$363	$363
Front bucket seats w/console	S[3]	$120[4]	$52[4]	$105[3]	—	$103[3]
Vinyl top	—	$76	$81	$100	$108	$108
Sunroof, electric	—	$223[5]	$434	$171[5]	$480[6]	$480[6]
Power steering, variable-ratio	—	$92	$104	$114	$	S
Power brakes, w/front disc[7]	S	$65	$65	$65	$65	S
Premiere wheel covers	—	—	—	$58	$58	$58
Rallye road wheels	—	$58	$53	$58	$58	—
White sidewall tires, std. size	$	$30	$31	$31	$38	$38

Popular Option Groups & Packages

	Cricket	Valiant	Barracuda	Satellite	Fury I, II, III	Gran Fury
Brougham package	—	—	—	—	—	$
Custom Exterior group	—	$[8]	—	—	—	—
Decor package	$	—	—	—	—	—
Gold Duster package	—	$161[9]	—	—	—	—
Light package	—	$29	$29	$	$62	S
Rallye package	—	—	$85	$85	—	—
Spacemaker Pak	—	$85[9]	—	—	—	—
Twister package	—	$[9]	—	—	—	—

—= Not Available; S = Standard equipment. [1]Requires 225 CID 6-cyl. or V8 engine on Valiant, and requires V8 engine on Satellite. Dual air conditioning for Suburban station wagons available for $598. [2]Blower type defogger on all except Duster, which uses grid style filaments embedded on glass (available for $49). [3]Available on Satellite Sebring Plus and Road Runner, and requires automatic transmission. Bucket seats available on Fury Gran Coupe 2-Door Hardtops without a console. Bucket seats only on Cricket. [4]For Duster only, and includes full-floor carpeting. Bucket seats are standard on Barracuda, price shown is for console only. [5]Only available on 2-door models, and is manually operated on Satellite. [6]Requires vinyl top. Not available on station wagons. [7]Standard on Duster 340 and Satellite station wagons. All others have manual front disc brakes as standard, except 6-cylinder Valiant, Scamp and Duster models, which have manual drum brakes. [8]Not available on Scamp. [9]Available on Duster only.

Paint Colors

Plymouth	Code	Plymouth	Code	Cricket	Code
Silver Frost metallic	A5	Chestnut metallic[2]	T8	Carib Blue	154
Blue Sky	B1	Chestnut metallic[2]	T9	Sunfire Yellow	155
Basin Street Blue[1]	B3	Spinnaker White	W1	Sure Fire Red	156
True Blue metallic	B5	Formal Black	X9	Prairie Wind[5]	157
Regal Blue[2]	B9	Lemon Twist[4]	Y1	Golden Glory metallic	161
Rallye Red	E5	Sun Fire Yellow[2]	Y2	Grasshopper Green metallic	162
Mist Green	F1	Honey Gold	Y3		
Amber Sherwood metallic	F3	Golden Haze metallic	Y6		
Forest Green metallic	F8	Tahitian Gold metallic	JY9		
Autumn Bronze metallic[1]	K6				
Sahara Beige	L4	Cricket	Code		
Coral Turquoise metallic[2]	Q5	Polar White	108		
Mojave Tan metallic[3]	T6	Phantom Mist metallic[5]	149		

Single tones are coded W1, W1. Two-tones are coded X9, W1 where first two digits are accent or roof color, and second two digits are basic body color. [1]Available only on Valiant, Barracuda and Satellite. [2]Available only on Fury. [3]Available only on Satellite. [4]Available at extra cost, except on Fury. [5]Available only on Cricket Wagon and sedan with optional Décor package.

Cricket

"Plymouth's little car comes through with big value in two versions."

Nameplate year of origin: 1971.
Current bodystyle lifespan: 1971 through 1973.
Predecessor to this model: None.
Replacement for this model: Arrow (1976 to 1980).
Primary competition: AMC Gremlin, Buick Opel, Chevrolet Vega, and Ford Pinto.
Notable changes: Carry-over from 1972.
Major standard equipment: Vinyl front bucket seats, recessed door handles, three-spoke steering wheel, heater, front and rear rubber bumper guards, rack and pinion steering, power front disc brakes, hubcaps, and 5.60 × 13 BSW tires. Wagon adds: Fold-down rear seat.

Measurements

	Sedan	Wagon
Wheelbase	98.0"	98.0"
Length	166.7"	NA
Width	62.5"	62.5"
Height	54.9"	55.5"
Legroom — front	NA	NA
Legroom — rear	NA	NA
Headroom — front	NA	NA
Headroom — rear	NA	NA
Cargo capacity (cu. ft.)	NA	NA
Fuel capacity (gals.)	10.8	10.8

Models Available

	Model No.	Base MSRP	Change from LY	Shipping Wt. (lbs.)	Model Year Production	Change from LY
Cricket 4-Door Sedan	4B41	$2,017	+0.00%	1958	NA	NA
Cricket 4-Door Station Wagon	4C45	$2,399	+0.00%	NA	NA	NA
TOTALS		*Avg. price* $2,208	+0.00%		*Production* 4,000*	NA

Exact model year sales for 1973 are unknown. Total model year sales would be included in the estimated 14,000 sold for 1972, as the 1973 models were leftover 1972 models.

Valiant

"The 13-year veteran of the compact field and still going strong."

Nameplate year of origin: 1960 (Valiant); 1970 (Duster); 1971 (Scamp).
Current bodystyle lifespan: 1967 through 1976.
Predecessor to this model: Valiant (1963 to 1966).
Replacement for this model: Volaré (1976 to 1980).

Measurements

	Duster	Scamp	Valiant
Wheelbase	108.0"	111.0"	108.0"
Length	195.8"	199.6"	195.8"

Percentage of division's production: 43.14%.
Corporate siblings: Dodge Dart.
Primary competition: AMC Hornet, Chevrolet Nova, and Ford Maverick.
Notable changes: Restyled front end and minor trim and detail changes.
Major standard equipment: All-vinyl front bench seat w/integral headrest (Valiant and Duster), black I/P trim (Valiant and Duster), simulated woodgrain I/P cluster appliqué (Scamp), two-speed electric windshield wipers, front door armrests, heater and defroster, front door window vents (Valiant), hubcaps, and 6.95 × 14 BSW tires. Scamp adds: Pleated vinyl front bench seat, cut-pile carpeting, interior décor package, cigarette lighter, roof drip-rail molding, wheel lip moldings, and dual horns. Duster 340 adds: Accent tape stripes, roof drip rail molding, heavy-duty suspension and shock absorbers, dual exhaust, and E70 × 14 BSW tires.

Measurements (cont.)

	Duster	*Scamp*	*Valiant*
Width	71.8"	71.0"	71.0"
Height	53.1"	54.3"	52.8"
Legroom — front	41.5"	41.5"	41.5"
Legroom — rear	30.0"	35.9"	34.6"
Headroom — front	37.5"	38.6"	38.4"
Headroom — rear	36.5"	37.3"	37.3"
Cargo capacity (cu. ft.)	15.9*	14.3	14.0
Fuel capacity (gals.)	16.0	16.0	16.0

With Spacemaker Pak fold-down rear seat option, 56.0 cu. ft.

Models Available

	Model No.	Base MSRP	Change from LY	Shipping Wt. (lbs.)	Model Year Production	Change from LY
Duster 2-Door Coupe	VL29	$2,376	+3.89%	2830	249,243	+17.40%
Valiant 4-Door Sedan	VL41	$2,447	+3.55%	2865	61,826	+294.27%
Scamp 2-Door Hardtop	VH23	$2,617	+3.52%	2885	53,792	+8.74%
Duster 340 2-Door Coupe	VS29	$2,822	+2.92%	3175	15,731	-70.27%
TOTALS	*Avg. price*	$2,566	+3.45%	*Production*	380,592	+15.20%

Barracuda

"Sporty appearance and sporty performance."

Nameplate year of origin: 1964.
Current bodystyle lifespan: 1970 through 1974.
Predecessor to this model: Barracuda (1967 to 1969).
Replacement for this model: None.
Percentage of division's sales volume: 2.52%.
Corporate siblings: Dodge Challenger.
Primary competition: AMC Javelin, Chevrolet Camaro, and Ford Mustang.
Notable changes: Minor trim and detail changes.
Major standard equipment: All-vinyl bucket seats w/integral head restraints, cut-pile carpeting, color-keyed headlining and armrests, inside day/night rear view mirror, LH rearview mirror, concealed two-speed windshield wipers, color-keyed grille w/horizontal inset bars, front and rear bumper guards, manual front disc brakes, hubcaps, and 7.35 × 14 BSW tires. 'Cuda adds: Chrome wheel opening and rocker panel sill moldings, performance style hood, black-out rear deck panel, heavy-duty suspension, power front disc brakes, and F70 × 14 BSW tires.

Measurements

Wheelbase	108.0"
Length	193.0"
Width	75.6"
Height	50.9"
Legroom — front	42.1"
Legroom — rear	28.9"
Headroom — front	37.4"
Headroom — rear	35.7"
Cargo capacity (cu. ft.)	8.6
Fuel capacity (gals.)	18.0

Models Available

	Model No.	Base MSRP	Change from LY	Shipping Wt. (lbs.)	Model Year Production	Change from LY
Barracuda 2-Door Hardtop	BH23	$2,935	+8.30%	3140	11,587	+9.08%
'Cuda 2-Door Hardtop	BS23	$3,120	+5.66%	3235	10,626	+35.74%
TOTALS	*Avg. price*	$3,028	+6.92%	*Production*	22,213	+20.40%

Satellite

"Built to be seen ... and not heard."

Nameplate year of origin: 1965 (as a Belvedere trim level); 1971 (as series).

Current bodystyle lifespan: 1971 through 1978.

Predecessor to this model: Belvedere/Satellite (1968 to 1970).

Replacement for this model: Fury (1975 to 1978).

Percentage of division's sales volume: 24.73%.

Corporate siblings: Dodge Charger and Coronet.

Primary competition: AMC Matador, Chevrolet Chevelle, and Ford Torino.

Notable changes: Revised front and rear styling.

Major standard equipment: All-vinyl front bench seat, color-keyed rubber floor covering, cigarette lighter (sedan only), dome light, concealed two-speed windshield wipers,

Measurements

	2-Doors	Sedans	Wagons
Wheelbase	115.0"	117.0"	117.0"
Length	210.8"	213.3"	216.1"
Width	79.1"	78.6"	79.2"
Height	52.2"	53.7"	55.0"
Legroom — front	41.9"	41.9"	41.9"
Legroom — rear	34.1"	36.7"	36.7"
Headroom — front	37.3"	38.5"	39.7"
Headroom — rear	36.4"	37.3"	38.1"
Cargo capacity (cu. ft.)	14.3	16.7	91.3
Fuel capacity (gals.)	19.5	19.5	21.0

dual horns (sedan only), rocker panel sill molding (sedan only), hubcaps, and E78 × 14 BSW tires. Road Runner adds (to base Satellite Coupe features): Rallye gauge cluster, bodyside and roof "Strobe" tape stripe, special Road Runner trim and ornamentation, performance hood, front and rear sway bars, heavy-duty springs, dual exhaust w/chrome tips, "Beep-Beep" horn, argent-painted rallye wheels w/chrome hubs, and F70 × 14 W/L tires. Custom and Sebring add: Cloth-and-vinyl front bench seat, color-keyed carpeting, front door and rear side armrests, front and rear door armrests, drip rail moldings, and wheel-lip moldings without sill molding. Sebring Plus adds: Vinyl bucket seats, rallye gauge cluster, premium door trim panels, simulated woodgrain inserts on I/P, door trim inserts and steering wheel, special Sebring-Plus trim and ornamentation, belt moldings, bodyside tape stripes, and deluxe wheel covers. Wagons add: Fold-down rear seatback, power front disc brakes, three-way tailgate, tailgate "auto lock" system (3-seat wagons only), and H78 × 14 BSW tires. Regent wagon adds: All-vinyl split-back front bench seat w/fold-down center armrest, cargo compartment carpeting and dome light, exterior simulated woodgrained bodyside overlays, and reflectorized rear tailgate woodgrain trim.

Models Available

	Model No.	Base MSRP	Change from LY	Shipping Wt. (lbs.)	Model Year Production	Change from LY
Satellite 2-Door Coupe	RL21	$2,755	+5.60%	3375	13,570	+29.15%
Satellite 4-Door Sedan	RL41	$2,824	+5.45%	3450	14,716	+15.02%
Satellite 4-Door, 2-Seat Wagon	RL45	$3,272	+3.81%	3950	6,906	-6.38%
Road Runner 2-Door Coupe	RM21	$3,115	+1.14%	3525	19,056	+149.82%
Satellite Sebring 2-Door Hardtop	RH23	$2,997	+4.39%	3390	51,575	+50.13%
Satellite Custom 4-Door Sedan	RH41	$2,974	+4.42%	3445	46,748	+33.67%
Satellite Custom 4-Dr., 2-S. Wagon	RH45	$3,400	+2.26%	3945	6,733	+22.75%
Satellite Custom 4-Dr., 3-S. Wagon	RH46	$3,518	+3.38%	3990	7,705	+36.69%
Satellite Sebring Plus 2-Dr. Hardtop	RP23	$3,258	+4.69%	3455	43,628	+103.88%
Satellite Regent 4-Dr., 2-S. Wagon	RP45	$3,621	+2.09%	3950	2,781	+46.91%
Satellite Regent 4-Dr., 3-S. Wagon	RP46	$3,740	+3.17%	4010	4,786	+64.64%
TOTALS	*Avg. price*	$3,225	+3.57%	*Production*	218,204	+50.53%

Fury

"The first thing you'll notice is that luxury, comfort and convenience come standard."

Nameplate year of origin: 1956.

Current bodystyle lifespan: 1969 through 1973.

Predecessor to this model: Fury (1967 to 1968).

Replacement for this model: Gran Fury (1974 to 1977).

Measurements

	Cars	Wagons
Wheelbase	120.0"	122.0"

Percentage of division's sales volume: 29.61%.
Corporate siblings: Dodge Monaco and Dodge Polara.
Primary competition: AMC Ambassador, Chevrolet BelAir/Impala/Caprice, and Ford Custom 500/Galaxie 500/LTD.
Notable changes: Revised front-end styling and minor trim and detail changes.
Major standard equipment: All vinyl front bench seat, front and rear armrests, cigarette lighter, dome light, front door courtesy light switches, glove box lock, inside hood release, concealed two-speed windshield wipers w/washers, bright drip rail molding, dual horns, hubcaps, and F78 × 15 BSW tires. Fury II adds: Cloth-and-vinyl front bench seat, loop-pile carpeting, and bright full-length bodyside molding. Fury III adds: Cloth-and-vinyl front bench seat, simulated wood-grained appliqué on I/P cluster and pad, 3-spoke steering wheel w/simulated woodgrained inserts, simulated woodgrained door trim insert, front and rear armrests w/bright base, bright wheel lip moldings, and full-length bodyside molding w/black vinyl insert. Gran Fury adds: All-vinyl split back front bench seat w/fold-down center armrest, door pull straps, carpeted lower door panels, electric clock, rear door dome light courtesy switches, extra quiet insulation, bright belt moldings, bright rocker panel sill molding, full-length bodyside molding w/color-keyed vinyl insert and deluxe wheel covers. Wagons add: All-vinyl front bench seat, color-keyed rubber floor mats (Suburban), color-keyed carpeting (Custom), cargo light (Custom 3-seat), aerodynamic roof air deflector, power tailgate window, power steering, and J78 × 15 BSW tires (2-seat wagons) or L84 × 15 BSW tires (3-seat wagons). Sport Suburban adds: All-vinyl split back front bench seat w/fold-down center armrest, door pull straps, simulated wood-grained appliqué on I/P cluster and pad, 3-spoke steering wheel w/simulated woodgrained inserts, simulated woodgrained door trim insert, carpeted lower door panels, electric clock, rear door dome light courtesy switches, simulated woodgrain bodyside panels, and deluxe wheel covers.

Measurements (cont.)

	Cars	Wagons
Length	223.4"	227.5"
Width	79.8"	79.8"
Height	54.9"	58.3"
Legroom — front	41.8"	41.8"
Legroom — rear	39.1"	39.1"
Headroom — front	38.8"	39.6"
Headroom — rear	38.4"	39.2"
Cargo capacity (cu. ft.)	22.4	104.2
Fuel capacity (gals.)	23.0	23.0

Models Available

	Model No.	Base MSRP	Change from LY	Shipping Wt. (lbs.)	Model Year Production	Change from LY
Fury I 4-Door Sedan	PL41	$3,575	+3.68%	3865	17,365	+23.98%
Fury II 4-Door Sedan	PM41	$3,694	+3.56%	3845	21,646	+7.95%
Fury Suburban 4-Door, 2-S. Wagon	PM45	$4,150	+4.69%	4410	5,206	-3.02%
Fury III 2-Door Hardtop	PH23	$3,883	+3.02%	3815	34,963	+64.89%
Fury III 4-Door Sedan	PH41	$3,866	+3.18%	3860	51,742	+10.77%
Fury III 4-Door Hardtop	PH43	$3,932	+3.12%	3880	51,215	+5.34%
Fury Custom Suburban 4-Dr., 2-S. Wagon	PH45	$4,246	+4.50%	4420	9,888	-10.65%
Fury Custom Suburban 4-Dr., 3-S. Wagon	PH46	$4,354	+5.14%	4465	15,671	+11.61%
Gran Fury Coupe 2-Door Hardtop	PP23	$4,064	+3.54%	3845	18,127	+14.44%
Gran Fury Sedan 4-Door Hardtop	PP43	$4,110	+3.50%	3890	14,852	-15.38%
Fury Sport Suburban 4-Dr., 2-S. Wagon	PP45	$4,497	+3.88%	4435	4,832	-2.80%
Fury Sport Suburban 4-Dr., 3-S. Wagon	PP46	$4,599	+4.38%	4495	15,680	-1.56%
TOTALS	Avg. price	$4,081	+4.35%	Production	261,187	-0.76%

PONTIAC

"The Wide-Track people have a way with cars."

Highlighting a revised model line for 1973 were Pontiac's newly redesigned mid-size cars that included the all-new Grand Am line. Combining the interior luxuries of the Grand Prix with performance attributes of the Trans Am, and placing them in the mid-size LeMans body, Pontiac created a car that rivaled the best European sport sedans in performance and handling, at a much lower price. While the Grand Am and its LeMans running mates arrived later than anticipated, consumers agreed that they were worth the wait, as the mid-size Pontiacs enjoyed a 45 percent production increase over 1972. The rest of the line received significant facelifts, boosting Pontiac to a new model year production record for 1973. But with the entire industry having such a good year, Pontiac was unable to recapture third place in the production rankings, a position it held for most of the 1960s, as it was losing out to a rapidly rising Oldsmobile division, this year by a mere 3,127 units. Pontiac ended the record-breaking year in fourth place, ahead of a faltering Plymouth line. Another notable production milestone took place on November 27, 1972, when the 16 millionth Pontiac, a blue 1973 Catalina 4-Door Sedan, rolled off the line.

Pontiac's perennially popular Grand Prix was the star of the new mid-size line, now being built on the mid-size four-door platform, which it shared with the Chevrolet Monte Carlo, whereas the previous generation had been built on its own unique stretched version of the four-door A-body platform. The prior generation's basic look was retained, including the single round headlamps of the 1971 to 1972 versions, fender end mounted parking/turn signal lights, and a radiator style grille, newly split by a body colored panel wearing the Pontiac "arrow" logo. Each side of the grille held eight vertical bars that extended below the bar-type front bumper into the body-colored front pan. The traditional "coke-bottle" bodyside styling continued in a new form with a dip near the rear of the door sill line marking the contracted middle section of the "coke bottle." The Grand Prix's roofline was shared with the Monte Carlo, having a V-shaped rear window and fixed rear quarter opera windows. Inside it featured an updated version of its driver's cockpit look, with the panel wrapping around the driver and flowing into the center console. Real African crossfire mahogany wood inlays surrounded the gauges, which consisted of four small round dials housing fuel, oil, temperature and ammeter gauges, flanked by two large round dials housing the speedometer and clock. Round air vents were strategically placed to greatly improve interior airflow. Ventilation and radio controls were placed toward the center of the car, yet still inside the driver's cockpit area. Under the hood, the Grand Prix was still powered by the standard 400 CID V8 engine, with the 455 CID V8 engine still being available. The Super Duty version of the 455 CID V8 engine, discussed later with the Firebird details, was available for this year only, and was also offered on the new Grand Am and LeMans, making these extremely potent cars on the road. The "SJ" option continued as an optional package for the Grand Prix, with 20,749 cars having the package.

The mid-size LeMans line was also all-new for 1973, built with the corporate "Colonnade" hardtop styling, and using mostly the same powerplants as last year. With the new bodies, the convertible body style was eliminated, as were the two-door pillared coupe and the four-door hardtop. Three basic trim levels returned with slight variations, such as the LeMans Sport now being a two-door Colonnade hard-

top, rather than a convertible, and the base LeMans coupe being discontinued. Styling of the LeMans was pure Pontiac, with a V-shaped hood line creating a point at the front, which defined the traditional split grille design. Each grille opening housed twenty-three vertical bars on the LeMans and LeMans Sport series, while the Luxury LeMans had each grille opening divided into five sections, with each having six vertical bars. All models had the parking/turn signal lights set in the chrome bumper ends beneath single round headlamps in a square chrome bezel. A horizontal opening ran between the parking lights, below the grille and bumper rub strip area.

Bodysides of the new LeMans were distinctive and controversial to some. Front and rear fender "pontoons" were created, with the rear one ending in a pointed rear design that would last only for this model year, before the federal rear bumper standards necessitated a change. At the front, the "pontoon" was created by an upper feature line that began at the top edge of the front fender and ran onto the fender side as it passed over the wheel opening, ending about midway through the door on coupes, and near the back of the front door on four-door models. At this point, the line turned forward, sweeping down to the mid-level of the rear edge of the front wheel opening and continuing on the front edge back to the top corner of the front bumper. A similar line began at the top edge of the rear bumper, and ran forward following the rise and curve of the trunk lid, leveling off as it came to the rear window line, then curving downward beneath the rear quarter window to fade away near the door handle of coupes, and on the rear door of four-door models. The lower part of the rear line began at the same point, crossing the rear wheel opening at the same level as the front wheel opening, and turning upward to gradually fade as it met the upper rear line. At the rear, the sloping trunk lid met the bumper, and dipped between two horizontally mounted taillights, which were three-section units with the center one housing the backup lights.

All-new interiors were designed for the LeMans, with a new instrument panel similar in appearance to prior years, having a driver's side pod that housed all controls. Two large round gauges were mounted directly in front of the driver housing the speedometer to the right and oil, amp and temperature warning lights to the left surrounding a center mounted clock. A smaller round fuel gauge sat between the two larger gauges. Ventilation and radio controls were placed to the right of the pod, near the center of the car, with light and wiper controls to the left, along with an air vent. Other interior features were typical of the period. New optional features included a manual or power-operated sunroof. The GTO option was still available, this year on either the LeMans or LeMans Sport coupes, with 4,806 GTO option packages being sold.

The most exciting new mid-size Pontiac for enthusiasts

was the Grand Am. Conceptually a replacement for the GTO, the Grand Am added in European-style ride and handling features and took the concept to a whole new level of luxury and performance. Being based on the LeMans, as previously mentioned, its identifying exterior feature was its front-end design. The Grand Am used a body-colored urethane front end that was impact-resistant, much like the type introduced on the 1968 GTO. The Grand Am's real difference was created by its sloping grille with three slots per side, creating a pointed "snout," and extending front fender caps that created a tunneled effect for the headlights. Each of the six grille slots housed six vertical bars. Taillights at the rear were similar to the LeMans units, except that they were divided into two horizontal sections by a body-colored strip. Inside the Grand Am had the appearance of a Grand Prix, because it largely was, with an instrument panel, bucket seats and floor console lifted right out of Pontiac's personal/luxury coupe. Unique Grand Am door panels were used, along with unique upholstery patterns. Both two- and four-door versions were offered, with the former outselling the latter four to one. An interesting body style considered for production was a Grand Am station wagon. One example was built, but the powers that be decided the factory, which built exclusively mid-size GM station wagons at the time, did not have the capacity to add another variation on station wagons.

Full-size Pontiacs were given a slight restyling to accommodate the new front bumper requirements, and along with the new styling, all full-sized models were moved to the Catalina chassis for the first time since the 1953 model year. When the more luxurious and upscale Star Chief line was introduced for 1954, it rode a two-inch longer wheelbase, a tradition that carried on through the sixties, and ended with the 1972 model year. The front ends of the Catalina, Bonneville and Grand Ville were similar, using a full-width grille that wrapped around onto the sides of the front fender ends, a vertical center body-colored panel dividing the grille into two sections, a new front bumper with a protruding bar carrying the optional bumper guards, and a center grille section extending into the lower bumper area. Two different grille inserts were used. The Catalina had a horizontal bar grille, nine rows high above the bumper at the tallest point in the center section. The portion of the grille between the pointed front center area and the wrap-around ends was seven rows high, with dual round headlamps partially set into the outer ends. Each grille half was surrounded by a larger chrome trim bar. The Bonneville and Grand Ville used a horizontal cross-hatch style grille five rows high and four columns across at the center tall section, and four rows high and ten columns across for the remainder. Every opening held two horizontal bars within. At the rear end, Catalina and Bonneville models shared a two-unit taillight set into the body-colored rear panel, with backup lights set into half of the innermost end. The Grand Ville used a larger horizontal unit divided hori-

zontally into three sections, and vertical backup lights were set into the rear fender end caps. While most other body styling remained similar to the prior two years, the Grand Ville coupe and sedan added a more formal rear roofline similar to those of the larger GM C-bodied Oldsmobile Ninety-Eight and Buick Electra 225 models. A revised instrument panel gave more of a "cockpit" style look, with round primary gauges set in square pods. Model changes included the Catalina convertible being dropped due to low sales volume and the Grand Ville series being moved to the Catalina body. Also, the top-of-the-line Grand Safari station wagon was moved from the Bonneville line to the Grand Ville series. At mid-year, Pontiac introduced the RTS system, or Radial Tuned Suspension, designed to make the most of the new radial tires that were becoming more commonplace. A popular car magazine of the era road-tested a Bonneville coupe with the RTS option and commented that it was comparable to the original Chrysler 300 muscle cars in terms of speed and acceleration, and a vast improvement on full-size handling and ride qualities.

The compact Pontiac was now known as simply the Ventura, dropping its "Ventura II" designation used in 1971 and 1972. Although it was not entirely new, a front-end facelift gave the appearance of new styling, with a new variation on the four-section grille set into the body-colored front-end panel. Each grille opening was lined in chrome trim and had about thirty-five vertical bars per section. At the rear, slot-style taillights were horizontally mounted, with two rows per side, the backup lights being in the center section. A new Custom trim level and new hatchback models drew more consumer interest to the line. Interiors were updated to include a restyled instrument panel, new plastic door panels, and revised seat designs. The Sprint option continued to be available on any two-door model, offering a unique "two-nostril" grille with blacked-out wire mesh insert, similar to the Firebird's design. Other Sprint features included exterior body striping and custom interior appointments.

Styling changes for the performance-oriented Firebird line consisted of adding a center vertical bar below the grille and within the lower horizontal opening of the body-colored urethane front end, strengthening the bumper to allow it to meet the new federal bumper requirements. Four models continued to be available, with the Trans Am nearly quadrupling in sales, and the entire line having more than a 50 percent increase in production — only a year after the line was nearly killed because of the 1972 factory strikes and declining sales. Noteworthy for performance enthusiasts is that this would be the last year for the "LS2" Super-Duty 455 CID V8, formerly known as the 455 H.O. engine, as pending emission standards and rising insurance costs were forcing a decline in interest for both consumers and Pontiac. There were two versions of this engine in production during the model year, one early and one late. The early version is the true Ram Air version, new for 1973, which uses a Ram Air IV type camshaft, with a horsepower rating of 310 at 4000 rpm. After March 15, 1973, a regular production type camshaft was used, giving a horsepower rating of 290 at 4000 rpm. Only 50 Firebird Formulas and 252 Trans Ams were built with the SD engine. The engine was also available on Grand Am and Grand Prix models, although production data are not available, and it is not known whether any were ac-

tually produced. On the topic of rarity, there were only 1,370 base Firebirds sold with a six-cylinder engine for 1973. A new option for the year was a hood decal that came to symbolize the Firebird Trans Am. The large stylized bird with flames emitting from the wings, known as the "chicken" in pop culture, was designed by John Schinella, and graced the hoods of most Trans Am models through the second generation's demise in 1981. It carried on in smaller format, and locations other than the hood, on some later Trans Ams.

Bonneville 4-Door Hardtop

Catalina 2-Door Hardtop

Firebird Esprit 2-Door Hardtop Coupe

Firebird Trans Am 2-Door Hardtop Coupe
(top and left) and Firebird Formula
2-Door Hardtop Coupe (right)

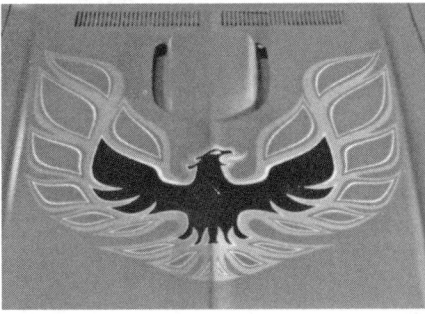

Firebird Trans Am optional hood decal

Grand Am 2-Door Colonnade Hardtop Coupe

Grand Prix 2-Door Hardtop Coupe

Grand Prix 2-Door Hardtop Coupe

Grand Safari 4-Door Station Wagon

Grand Ville 2-Door Convertible

LeMans 2-Door Colonnade
Hardtop Coupe with GTO package

LeMans 4-Door Colonnade Hardtop Sedan

LeMans Safari 4-Door, 3-Seat Station Wagon

LeMans Sport Coupe 2-Door
Colonnade Hardtop

Luxury LeMans 2-Door
Colonnade Hardtop Coupe

Ventura 2-Door Coupe with Sprint option (left)
and Ventura 2-Door Hatchback Coupe (right)

Ventura 4-Door Sedan

Ventura Custom 2-Door Coupe

Model year production: 919,632, up 30.14% from 1972.
Domestic market share: 8.65% (4th place).
Base price range: $2,452 to $4,821.
Pontiac average base price: $3,665, down 1.66%.
Introduction date: September 21, 1972.
Assembly plants: Lakewood, GA (A); Southgate, CA (C); Doraville, GA (D); Framingham, MA (G); Van Nuys, CA (L); Norwood, OH (N); Pontiac, MI (P); Tarrytown, NY (T); Lordstown, OH (U); Kansas City — Fairfax, KS (X); Fremont, CA (Z); and Oshawa, Ontario, Canada (1).
Data plate identification (VIN): Thirteen digit code read as

follows: First digit indicates division (2 = Pontiac); second through fourth digits indicate series and body style (model number in model charts); fifth digit is engine code (see powertrain chart); sixth digit indicates model year (3 = 1973); seventh digit indicates assembly plant (see list above); remaining digits are sequential with beginning number of 100001. *Example:* 2D35M3G100001 is a 1973 Pontiac Le-Mans 4-Door, 2-Seat Safari station wagon, with 350 CID, 2-bbl. V8 engine, serial number 100001, built in Framingham, MA.

Powertrains

Engine	Net HP	Engine Code	Transmission Availability[1]		Ventura	Firebird[2]	LeMans[3]	Grand Am & Grand Prix[4]	Catalina & Bonneville[5]	Grand Ville & Grand Safari[6]
250 CID (4.1L), 1-bbl., 6-cyl.	100	D	3-speed manual		S	S (F)	S (L)	—	—	—
				MPG:	NA	NA	NA	—	—	—
			2-speed automatic		$169	—	—	—	—	—
				MPG:	15.7	—	—	—	—	—
			3-speed Turbo Hydra-matic		—	$205 (F)	$205 (L)	—	—	—
				MPG:	—	NA	NA	—	—	—
350 CID (5.7L), 2-bbl., V8	150	M	3-speed manual		$118	S (FEs)/ $118 (F)	S (LL)/ $118 (L)	—	—	—
				MPG:	NA	NA	NA	—	—	—
			4-speed manual		$318	$200 (FEs)/ $318 (F)	—	—	—	—
				MPG:	NA	NA	—	—	—	—
			3-speed Turbo Hydra-matic		$318	$215 (FEs)/ $333 (F)	$215 (LL)/ $333 (L)	—	S (C)	—
				MPG:	NA	NA	9.9	—	NA	—
350 CID (5.7L), 2-bbl., V8	175[7]	N	3-speed manual		$158	S (FF)	—	—	—	—
				MPG:	NA	NA	—	—	—	—

Engine	Net HP	Engine Code	Transmission Availability[1]		Ventura	Firebird[2]	LeMans[3]	Grand Am & Grand Prix[4]	Catalina & Bonneville[5]	Grand Ville & Grand Safari[6]
			4-speed manual		$358	$200 (FF)	—	—	—	—
				MPG:	NA	NA	—	—	—	—
			3-speed Turbo Hydra-matic		$358	$215 (FF)	—	—	—	—
				MPG:	NA	NA	—	—	—	—
400 CID (6.6L), 2-bbl., V8	170	R	4-speed manual		—	$251 (FEs)	—	—	—	—
				MPG:	—	NA	—	—	—	—
			3-speed Turbo Hydra-matic		—	$287 (FEs)	$287 (LL)/ $405 (L)[8]	S (GA)	S (B & CS)/ $51 (C)	—
				MPG:	—	NA	8.8	8.8	7.8	—
400 CID (6.6L), 2-bbl., V8	185[7]	P	4-speed manual		—	$291 (FEs)	—	—	—	—
				MPG:	—	NA	—	—	—	—
			3-speed Turbo Hydra-matic		—	$327 (FEs)	$327 (LL)/ $445 (L)	$40 (GA)	$40 (B & CS)/ $91 (C)	—
				MPG:	—	NA	NA	NA	NA	—
400 CID (6.6L), 4-bbl., V8	200	S	4-speed manual		—	—	—	—	—	—
				MPG:	—	—	—	—	—	—
			3-speed Turbo Hydra-matic		—	—	$307 (LL)/ $425 (L)	—	$62 (B)/ $46 (CS)/ $103 (C)	S (GS)
				MPG:	—	—	NA	—	9.2	NA
400 CID (6.6L), 4-bbl., V8	250[7]	T	4-speed manual		—	$297 (FF)	S (w/ GTO pkg.)/ $287 (LL)/ $405 (L)	—	—	—
				MPG:	—	8.6	NA	—	—	—
			3-speed Turbo Hydra-matic		—	$333 (FF)	$46 w/ GTO pkg.)/ $333 (LL)/ $451 (L)	S (GP)/ $46 (GA)	$108 (B)/ $92 (CS)/ $149 (C)	—
				MPG:	—	NA	NA	NA	NA	—
455 CID (7.4L), 2-bbl., V8	215	W	3-speed Turbo Hydra-matic		—	—	$57 (w/ GTO pkg.)/ $344 (LL)/ $462 (L)	—	$119 (B)/ $103 (CS)/ $160 (C)/ S (GV)/	$57 (GS)
				MPG:	—	—	NA	—	NA	NA
455 CID (7.4L), 4-bbl., V8	250[7]	Y	4-speed manual		—	S (TA)/ $357 (FF)	$103 (w/ GTO pkg.)/ $390 (LL)/ $508 (L)	$11 (GP)/ $57 (GA)	—	—
				MPG:	—	NA	NA	NA	—	—
			3-speed Turbo Hydra-matic		—	N/C (TA)/ $390 (FF)	$149 (w/ GTO pkg.)/ $436 (LL)/ $554 (L)	$57 (GP)/ $103 (GA)	$176 (B)/ $160 (CS)/ $217 (C)	$57 (GV)/ $114 (GS)
				MPG:	—	NA	7/12	8.4	NA	8.1
455 CID (7.4L), Super Duty 4-bbl., V8	310[7]	X	4-speed manual		—	$521 (TA)/ $878 (FF)	—	—	—	—
				MPG:	—	NA	—	—	—	—
			3-speed Turbo Hydra-matic		—	$521 (TA)/ $901 (FF)	—	$532 (GP)/ $578 (GA)	—	—
				MPG:	—	NA	—	NA	—	—

[1]Unless otherwise noted: All 3-speed manual transmissions are column shift, except on Firebird models. All 4-speed manual transmissions are floor shift, and only available on 2-door models (and Grand Am 4-door), unless specially ordered. All automatic transmissions are column shift, with the following exceptions: Firebird,

Grand Am, and Grand Prix. Floor-shift with 3-speed manual can be ordered on Ventura models for $26 extra, on LeMans models for $82 extra (heavy-duty 3-speed). Column shift automatic may be available on Firebird and Grand Prix models when certain other equipment is ordered. Floor shift w/automatics is available on specific Ventura, LeMans and Grand Prix models in combination w/optional bucket seats. [2]*F = base Firebird, FEs = Firebird Esprit; FF = Firebird Formula; TA = Firebird Trans Am.* [3]*L = LeMans & LeMans Safari; LL = Luxury LeMans.* [4]*GS = Grand Safari; GV = Grand Ville.* [5]*C = Catalina; CS = Safari; B = Bonneville.* [6]*GA = Grand Am; GP = Grand Prix.* [7]*Includes dual exhaust.* [8]*Not available in California.*

Major Options

	Firebird	Ventura	LeMans & Grand Am	Grand Prix	Catalina & Safari	Bonneville	Grand Ville & Grand Safari
Custom air conditioning[1]	$397	$381	$397	$431	$431	$431	$431
Tilt steering wheel	$41	—	$44	$44	$44	$44	$44
Automatic cruise control	—	—	$62	$62	$67	$67	$67
Rear window defroster, electric	$31[2]	$31[2]	$62	$62	$62	$62	$62
Soft-Ray tinted glass, all windows	$37	$37	$39	$49	$49	$49	$49
Power windows, 2-dr./4-dr.	$75[3]	—	$75/$113	$75	$129	$129	$129
Power door locks, 2-dr./4-dr.	$44	—	—	$44	$44/$67	$44/$67	$44/$67
Power front seat, w/std. seat	—	—	$103	$103	$103	$103	$103
Front bucket seats, w/console	$57[4]	$132[4]	$162	$162	—	—	—
AM radio	$65	$65	$65	$85	$85	$85	$85
AM/FM stereo	$233	—	$233	$233	$233	$233	$233
AM/FM stereo w/8-track tape	$363[3]	—	$363	$363	$363	$363	$363
Woodgrain exterior trim, wagons	—	—	$154	—	—	—	$154
Vinyl top, full[5]	$87	$82	$97	$116	$116	$116	$116
Vinyl top, landau	—	—	—	$97	—	—	—
Sunroof, manual[6]	—	$179	$275	$275	—	—	—
Sunroof, power[6]	—	—	$325	$325	—	—	—
Power steering, variable-ratio	$113[7]	$100	$113[7]	S	S	S	S
Power brakes, w/front disc	$46[7]	$68	$46[7]	S	S	S	S
Deluxe wheel covers	$26	—	$26	S	$26	$26	S
Custom Finned covers	—	—	$50	$24	$50	$50	$24
Rally II wheels	$87	$87	$87	$61	$87	$87	—
Honeycomb aluminum wheels	$123	—	$123[8]	$123	—	—	—
WSW tires	$30	$28	$30	$30	$32	$32	$32

Popular Option Groups & Packages

	Firebird	Ventura	LeMans & Grand Am	Grand Prix	Catalina & Safari	Bonneville	Grand Ville & Grand Safari
Custom Trim option group	$77	—	—	—	—	—	—
Custom Safari package	—	—	$317	—	—	—	—
Décor group	—	—	$	—	—	—	—
GTO option package	—	—	$368	—	—	—	—
Lamp group	$10	—	—	—	—	—	—
Rallye gauge cluster package	$46	$46	$100[9]	$51	—	—	—
Firm ride and Handling packages	—	—	$188	—	—	—	—
SJ option package	—	—	—	$379	—	—	—
Sprint option package	—	$176	—	—	—	—	—

— = Not Available; S = Standard equipment. [1]*Not available with 250 CID 6-cylinder engine. Automatic climate control available for $473 on LeMans and Grand Am and for $507 on Grand Prix, Catalina, Bonneville, Grand Ville and Grand Safari.* [2]*Blower type defogger.* [3]*Other optional equipment required at extra cost (i.e., console).* [4]*Rear seat console available for $26 on Firebird. Ventura has front mini-console.* [5]*Vinyl roof available on Catalina Safari and Grand Safari for $138. Not available on LeMans station wagons. Price on Firebird is for base and Formula; price on Esprit is $72.* [6]*Available only on 2-door models.* [7]*Power steering and power brakes standard on Firebird Trans Am and Grand Am. Power brakes standard on LeMans station wagons.* [8]*Available only on Grand Am.* [9]*$51 on Grand Am.*

Paint Colors

	Code		Code		Code
Cameo White[1]	11	Verdant Green metallic	42	Desert Sand	56
Starlight Black[2]	19	State Green metallic	44	Valencia Gold metallic	60
Porcelain Blue metallic	24	Golden Olive metallic	46	Ascot Silver metallic	64
Regatta Blue metallic	26	Brewster Green[1]	48	Burnished Umber metallic[2]	66
Admiralty Blue metallic	29	Sunlight Yellow[3]	51	Burma Brown metallic	68

	Code
Florentine Red metallic	74
Buccaneer Red[1,3]	75
Mesa Tan[2]	81
Navajo Orange metallic[3]	97

In two-tone combinations, the first two digits indicate lower color and the next two digits are the upper color. Two-tones available for $31 on Ventura, $22 on LeMans wagons, and $39 on all other models, except Firebird. Trans Am "Bird" hood decal available for $55 extra. Colors without footnotes are available on all models, except Firebird Trans Am. [1]Only colors available on Firebird Trans Am. Available on all other models, unless otherwise marked. [2]Available only on LeMans, Grand Am, Grand Prix, Catalina, Bonneville and Grand Ville. [3]Available only on Ventura and all Firebird models, except Trans Am.

Firebird

"Pontiac's sports cars."

Measurements

Wheelbase	108.0"
Length	192.1"
Width	73.4"
Height	50.4"
Legroom — front	43.9"
Legroom — rear	28.5"
Headroom — front	37.5"
Headroom — rear	35.9"
Cargo capacity (cu. ft.)	8.8
Fuel capacity (gals.)	18.0

Nameplate year of origin: 1967.
Current bodystyle lifespan: 1970 through 1981.
Predecessor to this model: Firebird (1967 to 1969).
Replacement for this model: Firebird (1982 to 1992).
Percentage of division's production: 5.04%.
Corporate siblings: Chevrolet Camaro.
Primary competition: AMC Javelin, Dodge Challenger, Ford Mustang, and Plymouth Barracuda.
Notable changes: Minor trim and detail changes.
Major standard equipment: All-Morrokide vinyl front bucket seats, nylon loop-pile carpeting, black deluxe two-spoke steering wheel, ashtray light, dual speed wipers w/washers, bright front and rear window moldings, narrow rocker panel moldings, small full-width air dam, moon hubcaps, and E78 × 14 BSW tires. Esprit adds: Choice of Custom trim cloth-and-Morrokide vinyl or Custom trim all-Morrokide vinyl front bucket seats w/deep contour design, distinctive door trim panels, I/P assist grip, Custom Cushion steering wheel, rear quarter ashtray, roof insulator pad, formed rubber trunk mat, dual body-colored mirror w/LH remote, body-colored door handle inserts, bright roof drip rail and belt reveal moldings, bright rear hood edge molding, bright wheel opening and rocker panel moldings, Firebird emblems on fenders and rear deck lid, dual horns and deluxe wheel covers. Formula adds: Custom Cushion steering wheel, blacked-out grille, dual body-colored mirror w/LH remote, Formula (350, 400 or 455) emblems on front fenders, fiberglass hood w/dual forward facing scoops, larger stabilizer bars, firm control shocks, dual exhausts and F70 × 14 BSW tires. Trans Am adds: Formula steering wheel, rally gauge cluster package, aluminum-swirl finish I/P trim plate, dual body-colored mirror w/LH remote, blacked-out grille, full-width rear deck spoiler, wheel opening air deflectors, front fender air extractors, Trans Am decal on front fender and rear spoiler, "455" decal on hood scoop, fast-ratio power steering, power brakes, larger stabilizer bars, high-rate rear springs, Safe-T-Track differential, firm control shocks, performance dual exhausts, Rally II wheels, and F60 × 15 R/WL tires.

Models Available

	Model No.	Base MSRP	Change from LY	Shipping Wt. (lbs.)	Model Year Production	Change from LY
Firebird 2-Door Hardtop Coupe	S87	$2,895	+2.01%	3159	14,096	+17.47%
Firebird Esprit 2-Door Hardtop Coupe	T87	$3,249	+1.72%	3309	17,249	+51.11%
Firebird Formula 2-Door Hardtop Coupe	U87	$3,276	+1.71%	3318	10,166	+93.64%
Firebird Trans Am 2-Door Hardtop Coupe	V87	$4,204	-1.22%	3504	4,802	+273.41%
TOTALS		*Avg. price* $3,406	+0.85%		*Production* 46,313	+54.63%

Ventura

"Pontiac's low priced compact car."

Measurements

	Coupe & HBK	Sedan
Wheelbase	111.0"	111.0"
Length	197.5"	197.5"

Nameplate year of origin: 1960.
Current bodystyle lifespan: 1971 through 1974; restyled in 1973.
Predecessor to this model: None.
Replacement for this model: Ventura (1975 to 1977) and Phoenix (1977 to 1979).
Percentage of division's production: 10.49%.

Corporate siblings: Buick Apollo, Chevrolet Nova, and Oldsmobile Omega.

Primary competition: AMC Hornet, Dodge Dart, Ford Maverick, Mercury Comet, and Plymouth Valiant.

Notable changes: Completely restyled, and new hatchback model.

Major standard equipment: Cloth with Morrokide vinyl trim front bench seat, color-keyed rubber floor covering, woodgrain vinyl door trim w/door pull straps on two-doors, deluxe two-spoke steering wheel, bright front and rear window moldings, moon hubcaps, rear seat armrest ashtrays, and E78 × 14 BSW tires. Hatchback model adds: Fold-down rear seat, cargo area light, and fully trimmed vinyl cargo area sidewalls. Custom adds: Choice of special cloth or Morrokide vinyl front bench seat, bright front-seat side panels, color-keyed carpeting (including Hatchback load floor), Custom Cushion steering wheel, pedal trim plates, glove box light, RH doorjamb switch for dome light, added body and underhood insulation, bright drip rail and rocker panel moldings, Custom identification, and deluxe wheel covers.

Measurements (cont.)

	Coupe & HBK	Sedan
Width	72.4"	72.4"
Height	52.6"	53.9"
Legroom — front	41.7"	41.7"
Legroom — rear	33.4"	35.3"
Headroom — front	38.2"	39.5"
Headroom — rear	36.8"	37.3"
Cargo capacity (cu. ft.)	14.6*	13.7
Fuel capacity (gals.)	21.5	21.5

Hatchback maximum with rear seat down, 27.3 cu. ft.

Models Available

	Model No.	Base MSRP	Change from LY	Shipping Wt. (lbs.)	Model Year Production	Change from LY*
Ventura 2-Door Coupe	Y27	$2,452	+1.07%	3064	49,153	-47.81%
Ventura 2-Door Hatchback	Y17	$2,603	NEW	3170	26,335	NEW
Ventura 4-Door Sedan	Y69	$2,481	+1.10%	3124	21,012	-32.66%
Ventura Custom 2-Door Coupe	Z27	$2,609	NEW	3097	NA*	NEW
Ventura Custom 2-Door Hatchback	Z17	$2,759	NEW	3203	NA*	NEW
Ventura Custom 4-Door Sedan	Z69	$2,638	NEW	3157	NA*	NEW
TOTALS	Avg. price	$2,590	+6.16%	Production	96,500	+32.58%

Production of Custom models kept as combined total with base models. Therefore, comparisons to LY are made on total by body style and not model number.

LeMans

"Pontiac's new mid-size car."

Nameplate year of origin: 1961 (as a Tempest sub-series).

Current bodystyle lifespan: 1973 through 1977.

Predecessor to this model: Tempest/LeMans (1968 to 1972).

Replacement for this model: LeMans (1978 to 1981).

Percentage of division's production: 22.36%.

Corporate siblings: Buick Century, Chevrolet Chevelle, and Oldsmobile Cutlass.

Primary competition: AMC Matador, Dodge Charger and Coronet, Ford Torino, Mercury Montego, and Plymouth Satellite.

Notable changes: Completely redesigned.

Major standard equipment: Cloth-and-vinyl front bench seat, color-keyed loop-pile carpeting, deluxe three-spoke steering wheel, simulated American Walnut woodgrain

Measurements

	Coupes	Sedans	Wagons
Wheelbase	112.0"	116.0"	116.0"
Length	207.4"	211.4"	213.3"
Width	77.7"	77.7"	77.7"
Height	52.9"	54.3"	55.0"
Legroom — front	42.4"	42.4"	42.4"
Legroom — rear	33.7"	38.4"	36.8"
Headroom — front	37.8"	38.5"	38.8"
Headroom — rear	36.9"	37.2"	39.4"
Cargo capacity (cu. ft.)	15.1	15.1	85.1
Fuel capacity (gals.)	21.5	21.5	22.0

vinyl accents on I/P, door panels and steering wheel, bright front and rear window moldings, bright rear quarter window trim, manual front disc brakes, hubcaps, and F78 × 14 BSW tires. Wagon adds: All-Morrokide vinyl front bench seat, vinyl coated metal cargo area sidewalls, textured steel cargo floor w/special vinyl paint, swing up tailgate w/fixed window and remote release, I/P mounted "door ajar" warning light for tailgate, swing-out rear quarter vents (3-seat wagon only), vertical rub strips on tailgate, bright rocker panel molding, power front disc brakes, and H78 × 14 BSW tires. Sport Coupe adds: Choice of cloth-and-vinyl or all-Morrokide vinyl front bench seat w/fold-down center armrest, or all-Morrokide bucket seats, and vertically louvered rear quarter windows. Luxury LeMans adds: Choice of cloth-and-vinyl or all-vinyl notchback bench seat w/fold-down center armrest, special interior trim w/monogram on center armrest, custom cushion steering wheel, door panels w/carpeted lower panels and front door assist straps, glove box and ashtray lights, simulated woodgrain vinyl inlay on glove box door, added body insulation, rear seat armrest ashtrays, bright drip rail and quarter window moldings, bright rear hood edge and rear deck moldings, front wheel opening moldings, full-length lower bodyside molding, rear-wheel fender skirts, and deluxe wheel covers.

Models Available

	Model No.	Base MSRP	Change from LY*	Shipping Wt. (lbs.)	Model Year Production	Change from LY*
LeMans 2-Door Colonnade HT Coupe	D37	$2,920	+2.42%	3579	68,230	-15.12%
LeMans 4-Door Colonnade HT Sedan	D29	$2,918	+3.70%	3605	26,554	+36.43%
LeMans 4-Door, 2-Seat Safari Station Wagon	D35	$3,296	+0.76%	3956	10,446	+25.37%
LeMans 4-Door, 3-Seat Safari Station Wagon	D45	$3,429	+1.51%	3993	6,127	+16.35%
LeMans Sport Coupe 2-Door Colonnade HT	F37	$3,008	NEW	3594	50,999	NEW
Luxury LeMans 2-Door Colonnade HT Coupe	G37	$3,274	+2.44%	3799	33,916	+292.50%
Luxury LeMans 4-Door Colonnade HT Sedan	G29	$3,344	+0.75%	3867	9,377	-75.07%
TOTALS	Avg. price	$3,170	+2.34%	Production	205,649	+20.97%

*Comparisons made to closest 1972 body styles (e.g., 1973 LeMans "D29" 4-Door colonnade hardtop model compared to 1972 LeMans "D69" 4-Door Sedan model).

Grand Am

*"The feel of a Grand Prix ... the response of a GTO ...
the qualities you've admired in the desirable imports."*

Nameplate year of origin: 1973.
Current bodystyle lifespan: 1973 through 1975.
Predecessor to this model: None.
Replacement for this model: Grand Am (1978 to 1980).
Percentage of division's production: 4.69%.
Corporate siblings: Buick Century Regal, Chevrolet Chevelle Laguna, and Oldsmobile Cutlass Salon.
Primary competition: AMC Matador, Dodge Charger and Coronet, Ford Torino, Mercury Montego, and Plymouth Satellite.
Notable changes: All-new model, based on LeMans.
Major standard equipment: Choice of wide-wale corduroy or all-vinyl w/Morrokide front bucket seats w/recliners and adjustable lower back support, color-keyed loop-pile carpeting, pedal trim plates, custom sport three-spoke steering wheel w/padded center, cockpit-style I/P and center floor console w/genuine African crossfire mahogany inlay trim, door pull assist straps, electric clock, trip odometer, ashtray and glove box lights, courtesy lights, fixed rear quarter window w/louvers (coupe only), bright front and rear window moldings, bright side window and drip rail moldings, bright rear hood edge molding, bright wheel opening moldings, black-accented rocker panel moldings, body colored door handle inserts, power steering, power brakes, firm ride package, custom finned wheel covers, and GR70 × 15 BSW tires.

Measurements

	Coupe	Sedan
Wheelbase	112.0"	116.0"
Length	208.6"	212.6"
Width	77.7"	77.7"
Height	52.9"	54.3"
Legroom — front	42.4"	42.4"
Legroom — rear	33.5"	38.6"
Headroom — front	37.8"	38.5"
Headroom — rear	36.9"	37.2"
Cargo capacity (cu. ft.)	15.1	15.1
Fuel capacity (gals.)	25.0	25.0

Models Available

	Model No.	Base MSRP	Change from LY	Shipping Wt. (lbs.)	Model Year Production	Change from LY
Grand Am 2-Door Colonnade HT Coupe	H37	$4,264	NEW	3992	34,445	NEW
Grand Am 4-Door Colonnade HT Sedan	H29	$4,353	NEW	4018	8,691	NEW
TOTALS	Avg. price	$4,309	NEW	Production	43,136	NEW

Grand Prix

"Pontiac's classic luxury sport."

Nameplate year of origin: 1962.
Current bodystyle lifespan: 1973 through 1977.
Predecessor to this model: Grand Prix (1969 to 1972).
Replacement for this model: Grand Prix (1978 to 1987).
Percentage of division's production: 16.73%.
Corporate siblings: Chevrolet Monte Carlo.
Primary competition: Dodge Charger and Plymouth Satellite Sebring.
Notable changes: Completely redesigned.
Major standard equipment: Choice of cloth-and-vinyl or all-vinyl w/Morrokide front notchback bench seat w/fold-down center armrests or front bucket seats w/center floor console, color-keyed loop-pile carpeting, pedal trim plates, custom cushion three-spoke steering wheel, cockpit-style I/P w/genuine African crossfire mahogany inlay trim, genuine African crossfire mahogany inlay trim on door panels and console, electric clock, ashtray light, I/P courtesy lights, trunk compartment light and side panels, fixed rear quarter window w/bright trim, bright front and rear window moldings, bright side window sill and drip rail moldings, bright rear hood edge molding, bright wheel opening moldings, black-accented wide rocker panel moldings, body colored door handle inserts, power steering, power brakes, dual exhausts, deluxe wheel covers, and G78 × 15 BSW tires.

Measurements

Wheelbase	116.0"
Length	216.6"
Width	78.3"
Height	52.9"
Legroom — front	42.4"
Legroom — rear	33.5"
Headroom — front	37.6"
Headroom — rear	37.3"
Cargo capacity (cu. ft.)	14.3
Fuel capacity (gals.)	25.0

Models Available

	Model No.	Base MSRP	Change from LY	Shipping Wt. (lbs.)	Model Year Production	Change from LY
Grand Prix 2-Door Hardtop Coupe	K57	$4,583	+2.48%	4025	153,899	+67.35%
TOTALS		*Avg. price* $4,583	+2.48%	*Production*	153,899	+67.35%

Catalina and Safari

"Pontiac's lowest priced full-sized car."

Nameplate year of origin: 1950 (as hardtop model designation), 1959 (as series).
Current bodystyle lifespan: 1971 through 1976.
Predecessor to this model: Catalina (1969 to 1970).
Replacement for this model: Catalina (1977 to 1981).
Percentage of division's production: 25.78%.
Corporate siblings: Buick LeSabre and Centurion, Chevrolet BelAir/Impala/Caprice, and Oldsmobile Delta 88.
Primary competition: AMC Ambassador, Dodge Polara, Ford Custom 500/Galaxie 500/LTD, and Plymouth Fury.
Notable changes: Revised styling.
Major standard equipment: Cloth-and-Morrokide vinyl bench seat, color-keyed loop-pile carpeting, deluxe two-spoke steering wheel, American walnut woodgrain vinyl I/P accents, dual ashtrays w/LH ashtray light, trunk compartment mat, bright rocker panel molding, bright hood rear edge molding, power steering, power front disc brakes, hubcaps, and G78 × 15 BSW tires. Safari wagon adds: All-Morrokide vinyl front bench seat, glove box lights, RH rear view mirror, Glide-Away tailgate w/power-operated rear window, rear bumper guards, and L78 × 15 BSW tires.

Measurements

	2-door	4-doors	Wagons
Wheelbase	124.0"	124.0"	127.0"
Length	224.8"	224.8"	228.8"
Width	79.6"	79.6"	79.9"
Height	53.5"	54.2"	57.5"
Legroom — front	42.7"	42.7"	42.5"
Legroom — rear	35.8"	38.8"	38.9"
Headroom — front	38.3"	39.1"	39.6"
Headroom — rear	37.0"	37.9"	39.3"
Cargo capacity (cu. ft.)	20.5	20.5	106.4
Fuel capacity (gals.)	25.8	25.8	22.0

Models Available

	Model No.	Base MSRP	Change from LY	Shipping Wt. (lbs.)	Model Year Production	Change from LY
Catalina 2-Door Hardtop Coupe	L57	$3,869	+1.60%	4190	74,394	+23.51%
Catalina 4-Door Sedan	L69	$3,770	+1.54%	4234	100,592	+21.19%
Catalina 4-Door Hardtop	L39	$3,938	+1.65%	4270	31,663	+13.04%
Safari 4-Door, 2-Seat Station Wagon	L35	$4,311	+1.87%	4791	15,762	+8.43%
Safari 4-Door, 3-Seat Station Wagon	L45	$4,457	+1.94%	4873	14,654	+14.79%
TOTALS		Avg. price $4,069	+1.58%		Production 237,065	+3.86%

Bonneville

"Pontiac's original full-sized Wide-Track."

Nameplate year of origin: 1957.
Current bodystyle lifespan: 1971 through 1976.
Predecessor to this model: Bonneville (1969 to 1970).
Replacement for this model: Bonneville (1977 to 1981).
Percentage of division's production: 5.10%.
Corporate siblings: Buick LeSabre and Centurion, Chevrolet BelAir/Impala/Caprice, and Oldsmobile Delta 88.
Primary competition: AMC Ambassador, Dodge Monaco, and Mercury Monterey.
Notable changes: Revised styling.
Major standard equipment: Choice of cloth-and-Morrokide vinyl or all-Morrokide vinyl front bench seat, loop-pile carpeting, lower door panel carpeting, custom cushion steering wheel, simulated American walnut woodgrain vinyl I/P accents, electric clock, pedal trim plates, rear door courtesy light switches (four-doors), luggage compartment mat and side panel trim, luggage compartment light, body-color door handle inserts, bright windshield and rear window moldings, bright hood rear edge molding, wide rocker panel moldings w/rear extensions, bright wheel opening moldings, deluxe wheel covers, and H78 × 15 BSW tires.

Measurements

	2-door	4-doors
Wheelbase	124.0"	124.0"
Length	224.8"	224.8"
Width	79.6"	79.6"
Height	53.5"	54.2"
Legroom — front	42.7"	42.7"
Legroom — rear	35.8"	38.8"
Headroom — front	38.3"	39.1"
Headroom — rear	37.0"	37.9"
Cargo capacity (cu. ft.)	20.5	20.5
Fuel capacity (gals.)	25.8	25.8

Models Available

	Model No.	Base MSRP	Change from LY	Shipping Wt. (lbs.)	Model Year Production	Change from LY
Bonneville 2-Door Hardtop Coupe	N57	$4,225	-0.07%	4292	13,866	+31.21%
Bonneville 4-Door Sedan	N69	$4,163	-0.14%	4333	15,830	+63.13%
Bonneville 4-Door Hardtop Sport Sedan	N39	$4,292	-0.02%	4369	17,202	+8.83%
TOTALS		Avg. price $4,227	-3.90%		Production 46,898	-6.75%

Grand Ville and Grand Safari

"Pontiac's most luxurious full-sized car."

Nameplate year of origin: 1971.
Current bodystyle lifespan: 1971 through 1976.
Predecessor to this model: None.
Replacement for this model: None.
Percentage of division's production: 9.81%.
Corporate siblings: Buick LeSabre and Centurion, Chevrolet BelAir/Impala/Caprice, and Oldsmobile Delta 88.

Measurements

	2-doors	4-door	Wagons
Wheelbase	124.0"	124.0"	127.0"
Length	224.8"	224.8"	226.8"
Width	79.6"	79.6"	79.5"
Height	53.5"	54.2"	58.3"

Primary competition: Chrysler Newport, Dodge Monaco, and Mercury Marquis.

Notable changes: Revised styling.

Major standard equipment: Fluted damask cloth w/Morrokide vinyl trim front bench seat w/fold-down center armrest, color-keyed loop-pile carpeting, custom cushion steering wheel, custom door panels w/pull straps and lower panel carpeting, simulated American walnut woodgrain vinyl trim on I/P and door panels, electric clock, rear door courtesy light switches (four-door), luggage compartment mat and side panel trim, luggage compartment light, body-color door handle inserts, bright windshield and rear window moldings, bright drip rail moldings, bright hood rear edge molding, wide rocker panel moldings w/rear extensions, front wheel opening moldings, rear wheel opening fender skirts, bodyside protective molding, deluxe wheel covers, and H78 × 15 BSW tires. Convertible adds: All-Morrokide vinyl front bench seat w/fold-down center armrest, two rear quarter interior lights, and inward-folding power-operated vinyl convertible top w/glass rear window. Grand Safari wagon adds: All-Morrokide vinyl front bench seat w/fold-down center armrest, carpeted cargo area, RH rear view mirror, rear bumper guards, deletes fender skirts, and L78 × 15 BSW tires.

Measurements (cont.)

	2-doors	4-door	Wagons
Legroom — front	42.7"	42.7"	42.5"
Legroom — rear	35.8"	38.8"	38.9"
Headroom — front	38.3"	39.1"	39.6"
Headroom — rear	37.0"	37.9"	39.3"
Cargo capacity (cu. ft.)	20.5*	20.5	106.4
Fuel capacity (gals.)	25.8	25.8	22.0

Convertible is 14.4 cu. ft.

Models Available

	Model No.	Base MSRP	Change from LY	Shipping Wt. (lbs.)	Model Year Production	Change from LY
Grand Ville 2-Door Hardtop Coupe	P47	$4,524	+1.85%	4321	23,963	+20.71%
Grand Ville 2-Door Convertible	P67	$4,766	+2.72%	4339	4,447	+100.95%
Grand Ville 4-Door Hardtop Sport Sedan	P49	$4,592	+1.89%	4376	44,092	+6.64%
Grand Safari 4-Door, 2-Seat Station Wagon*	P35	$4,674	+2.03%	4823	6,894	+21.48%
Grand Safari 4-Door, 3-Seat Station Wagon*	P45	$4,821	+2.12%	4925	10,776	+26.18%
TOTALS		*Avg. price* $4,675	+3.22%		*Production* 90,172	+42.20%

Comparisons of 1973 Grand Safari "P" series are made to 1972 Grand Safari "N" series.

1974

As the model year began, the oil embargo was in full swing, and fears of fuel shortages and long lines at the gas pumps came true. For the automobile industry, fears of fewer sales came true, as consumers who were buying new cars were opting for smaller cars because of their better fuel economy, and were increasingly turning to imported cars to meet their needs. With an economic recession looming, it became clear that the 1974 model year was not going to be a record breaker. However, it is worth noting that the only domestic four-cylinder cars at the time — the Chevy Vega, the Ford Pinto, and related Mustang II — all had their best model year of the decade. As often happens in times of economic turmoil, the mid-range auto manufacturers suffered the most in 1974. In fact Chrysler, traditionally at the upper mid-price range, found its sales tumbling to nearly half of their prior year total. The lone bright spot in the industry was American Motors, which always seemed to shine in times of economic downturns. Having traditionally been labeled as "the small car specialists," AMC proved once again that they could sell quality small cars, and to make the point the Gremlin series alone outsold the combined total of all Chrysler models.

Adding to the cost of new cars for this year were the seat belt starter interlock system and 5 mph rear bumpers that were required for 1974 cars. The seat belt starter interlock system prevented the car from starting unless all front-seat occupants were belted. A relatively complex electronics package, by 1974 standards, was required to provide the seat switch and belt monitoring, decision making, and warning and starter controls. The interlock system was later repealed by an act of Congress because of public disapproval of the system. The new 5 mph rear bumper standards were met by installing stout box-like, shelf-style bumpers on hydraulic impact shocks on most cars. Both of these systems are detailed in the introduction of this book.

As previously mentioned, American Motors came out the big winner as the only manufacturer to have a sales increase this year. A newly designed Matador coupe was the sole new model in the lineup, and the first all-new design from AMC since the 1971 Javelin. While the Javelin was still in the lineup for one more season, it seems likely that the new Matador coupe's sporty, rounded styling was designed to replace the Javelin and the Matador two-door hardtop with the one model, as it covered the gamut of trim levels with its base Matador coupe, a sporty "X" model, and the luxury Brougham model. With the new coupe's introduction came a restyling for the front end of the Matador and Ambassador sedan and station wagons, both having a unique center front-end extension that made them highly recognizable. The Hornet and Gremlin series continued with only minor styling changes. This would be the last season for the long-running Ambassador series, a nameplate that had been in production for more than 40 years. Although the Javelin name would disappear this year, the AMX name would return for 1977 as an option package for the Hornet. In the American Motors Jeep line, the sporty car-like Commando was gone, and in its place was a lower priced, two-door version of the Wagoneer named Cherokee.

Despite sales and production being down, Ford Motor Company had to be the luckiest manufacturer this year. Having made a decision several years prior to return the Mustang to its original size and concept, after the car had become somewhat oversized and overweight, Ford introduced a smaller and newly named Mustang II just in time for consumers wanting smaller cars and higher fuel mileage. One of only three really new 1974 models, the Mustang II was selected by *Motor Trend* magazine as its "Car of the Year" for multiple reasons including its excellent combination of highway and urban driving capabilities, its reasonable size and economy without being stripped-down, and its timing in the marketplace. The reasons were summed up by *Motor Trend* editors: "in selecting the Mustang II we feel Ford, and perhaps the rest of Detroit will follow, has placed good taste, function and handling/performance before frill, flash and fad."

With the original Mustang platform gone, the final Ford convertibles, the Mustang and the Mercury Cougar, were also gone. This also meant that the Cougar would have to move to another chassis, or be dropped, so Mercury chose to move the Cougar upmarket into the mid-size personal luxury class dominated by the Chevy Monte Carlo and Pontiac Grand Prix. Based on the existing Torino/Montego two-door platform, the new Cougar was offered only in the XR-7 version. It retained prior front-end design themes such as the three-section grille and wrap-around front parking lights. The Cougar XR-7 added features such as opera windows, and it had some Montego styling characteristics. At mid-year, Ford introduced its version of the Cougar, the Gran Torino Elite, better known as just the Elite, and advertised it as a small Thunderbird, finally giving Ford a competitor for the Monte Carlo. The mid-size Ford Torino and Mercury Montego lines, which were completely redesigned for 1972, received some front and rear end updates, along with a general cleanup of bodyside trim, providing for a fresh new look. Lincoln introduced a mildly facelifted Continental line but had few other changes. The rest of the Ford Motor Company offerings received the obligatory grille changes and required rear end changes. Similarly the trucks, which were restyled for 1973, were little changed, other than the Ranchero, which received the Torino's new grille and rear end updates.

Chrysler Corporation would celebrate the 50th anniversary of its founding this year, recognizing the occasion with two special option packages and a completely redesigned line of full-size cars. The St. Regis and Crown Coupe packages marking the anniversary were available for the New Yorker and Imperial two-door models and were really only gold paint treatments with gold padded canopy style vinyl tops and rear quarter windows. The special packages would become regular options for the 1975 models, but in a variety of colors. For most of the rest of the line there were only detail changes; however, Chrysler did make front hydraulic impact-absorption bumper systems, side impact beams, and collapsible steering columns standard on all models for the 1974 season. A larger displacement 360 CID V8 engine replaced the 340 CID V8 engine, but it didn't stop the discontinuation of the Dodge Challenger and Plymouth Barracuda after 1974, signaling the end of Chrysler's muscle car era. Also making its final appearance for 1974 was the Satellite nameplate. For the captive import Dodge Colt line, revised styling was introduced, adding a more "American" appearance, and a new top line Custom wagon was added with standard woodgrain bodyside appliqués. There were not major design changes to the Dodge truck line, but Chrysler did add two Plymouth "truck" models to allow Chrysler-Plymouth dealers to cash in on the recently expanding truck market. The Voyager van was added as a passenger van version of the Dodge B100 Sportsman vans. Also new was the Trail Duster, basically a Dodge Ramcharger with a slightly modified grille.

By 1974, there was much media speculation that General Motors' Wankel engine would be ready for sale as an option in the Vega. This ongoing story kept GM in the news in a good light, but with fuel economy being high on customers' list of priorities, GM probably correctly assumed that no one would pay extra to get poorer fuel mileage, even if it did come with better performance and reliability. More details on the Wankel engine are included in the introduction of this book. While fuel economy had never been a strong selling point for GM, it was an especially weak suit for Buick and Oldsmobile, which had but one six-cylinder model each in their entire fleet. This most likely contributed to a sales decline for the two divisions that surpassed 30 percent. Chevrolet on the other hand had an extremely good year, despite issues surrounding the Vega's engine durability, and would end the year holding more than 26 percent of the total U.S. market share. Chevrolet outsold and outproduced the combined total of its four GM stablemates.

Not having the luck of timing on their side as Ford did, GM introduced restyled full-size models in 1974, to include the Riviera, Toronado and Eldorado. While all were still based on their original 1971 bodies and chassis, significant changes were seen to greenhouse window areas and instrument panels of various models, while all had new front- and rear-end styling. Also having new front end designs of a slanted variety were the Chevrolet Vega and Camaro and the Pontiac Firebird. The new designs provided for better front end protection systems, and in the case of the Firebird, reaffirmed Pontiac's commitment to using body-colored urethane front ends to minimize damage in minor front-end collisions. For performance enthusiasts, it was a sad moment when it was announced that 1974 would be the last year for the once mighty 454 CID V8 engine to be installed in the Corvette. It would also be the last year for the Buick 455 CID V8 engine to be used in Buick's mid-size Century and Regal models.

The rest of the GM line received only the expected new grilles and detail features. Several nameplates were gone this year, including the Buick Centurion, which was replaced by the LeSabre Custom, and the Chevelle DeLuxe, which was replaced by the Malibu, with a newly named Malibu Classic taking over the former Malibu spot. Interestingly with only Malibu and Laguna models remaining in the Chevelle line, Chevrolet clung to the Chevelle name through the end of the body style's lifespan in 1977, with the name still appearing on the cars. The former luxury Chevelle Laguna model was transformed into a sporty Laguna Type S-3 model offered only in a coupe, while Oldsmobile added a Cutlass Supreme Cruiser to the mid-size line to complement the Vista-Cruiser sans the sunroof. With the new rear bumper standards, the Corvette added a body-colored rear end treatment to match last year's new body-colored front bumper design. Together with the Pontiac Firebird, they became the trendsetters for all cars to come. The 1974 season also brought the temporary end of the Camaro Z28, which was not having near the success that the Pontiac Firebird Trans Am was about to achieve. The Z28 would return during the 1977 model year. Also missing this year was Buick's Opel GT sport coupe. GM's truck lines were given only minor updates, having been all-new for 1973, including the car-based Chevrolet ElCamino and GMC Sprint. The Chevy Vega Panel Express did gain the new front end styling of its Kammback wagon running mate.

1974 Overview and Changes from Prior Year

- **Total industry model year production:** 8,642,209, down 18.69%.
- **Total estimated captive import sales:** 187,925, down 13.64%.
- **Market share by corporation:** GM 48.63%; Ford 30.98%; Chrysler 15.41%; AMC 4.98%.

- **Number of models and body types available:** 303, up from 298.
- **Highest production series:** Chevrolet BelAir/Impala/Caprice — 629,847.
- **Lowest production series:** Cadillac Fleetwood 75 — 1,900.
- **Highest individual model production:** Plymouth Duster 2-Door Coupe — 277,409.
- **Lowest individual model production:** Mercury Marquis 4-Door Hardtop — 784.
- **Industry average base price:** $4,092, up 10.30%.
- **Highest individual model base price:** Cadillac Fleetwood 75 Limousine, $13,254.
- **Lowest individual model base price:** Chevrolet Vega 2-Door Notchback Coupe, $2,380.
- **Highest average MPG with base powertrain:** Chevrolet Vega, 24.6 MPG.
- **Lowest average MPG with base powertrain:** Lincoln Continental, 7.9 MPG
- **Indianapolis 500 Pace Car:** Hurst/Olds Cutlass 2-Door Coupe w/Hurst Hatch (T-tops).
- *Motor Trend* magazine "Car of the Year": Ford Mustang II.

AMERICAN MOTORS

"Introducing the 1974 cars. We back them better because we build them better."

As had been the case during prior downturns in the American economy, AMC benefited from its line of economy-minded and typically lower-priced automobiles. The oil embargo and the economic recession that followed during 1974 sent car buyers toward just such vehicles. By the end of 1974 production, American Motors would reach its highest production total since the 1963 model year when it produced 453,554 cars and held 6.36 percent of the domestic market with a seventh place ranking. Unfortunately, things can change quickly in the automotive world. Increasing sales and expanded availability of imported cars would cut into the small, financially struggling company's sales, making this the last season ever that it would exceed 400,000 units of production or hold a ranking above tenth place among the domestic makes.

The first "all-new" model from American Motors in three years hit the road this year in the form of the Matador Coupe. Touted as America's sportiest new car, the coupe of-

fered a sleekly styled fastback roofline and some unique styling features would make a big splash, just as the sporty Javelin and similarly styled fastbacks were fading out in popularity. Highlights of the new Matador coupe's styling included the traditional "pony car proportions" of a long hood and short rear deck. Most evident, though, were the deeply tunneled headlamps, bulging curves, and four oversized round taillights. All of this was a concerted effort to provide the most aerodynamic car possible to the AMC-sponsored NASCAR teams, which were on a winning streak with the soon-to-be-gone Javelin. The effort continued the wins for several years to come. For the general public, a new Matador Coupe equipped with the "401 X" package was one of the fastest cars on the road in its size class. Inside, the coupes could be equipped as luxuriously as the customer wished.

The Matador sedan and wagon were facelifted this year, along with the "full-sized" Ambassador. While the main body was mostly carried over from the 1967 structure, the front and rear styling was completely changed, more in an effort to meet federal safety requirements than for the sake of creating a new look. At the front, a new "coffin nose" grille and bumper theme was apparent with a full-width grille and single headlamps on Matadors and dual headlamps for the Ambassador. The new front-end look, although a "love it or hate it" style, was definitely unique and sold quite well. Around back, a slightly slanted rear end design housed longer horizontal taillamps on sedans, while the wagons used a tall vertical taillamp mounted in the fender end. Interiors were the most opulent ever offered by American Motors, and the Ambassador continued to offer standard features still optional on other comparable cars from the Big Three, such as power front disc brakes, air conditioning, and luxury upholstery.

The rest of the American Motors line was relatively unchanged, with larger fuel tanks on some models and styling tweaks to the front and rear ends to accommodate the federal bumper requirements, including standard bumper guards on all models. The most obvious change was on the Gremlin, which had a new color-keyed, horizontal bar grille. The horizontal bar theme carried onto the lower portion of the headlamp area and around the corner to meet the combination side-marker and turn signal lamp. Hornets maintained their familiar styling and continued to be the most popular of the AMC lines, with the single-model Gremlin not far behind. The Javelin, now in its last year, was mostly unchanged and was so overshadowed by the new Matador coupe that few consumers realized the Javelin was still offered. Although the 401 CID V8 was still available, it required purchasing the "401 Go" package. Also, for the last time, all engines were designed to run on leaded, low-lead, or unleaded fuel. Next year's engines would be designed to burn unleaded fuel only.

While this would be the last year for the Ambassador, its legacy would live on in the Matador Brougham for 1975. The two lines had always shared many features, including almost everything from the cowl back, since the late 1950s, when the "mid-size" car was known as the Rambler, later the Classic, then Rebel, and finally in 1971 the Matador. For 1974, the new coupe helped push Matador sales up more than 60 percent. This was the best performance for the Matador nameplate since its introduction in 1971, and a high point of sales for any mid-size American Motors line since the popular Rambler Classic of the early and mid-sixties.

Ambassador Brougham 4-Door Station Wagon

Ambassador Brougham 4-Door Sedan

Gremlin 2-Door Sedan with X package

Hornet 3-Door Hatchback

Hornet Sportabout 4-Door Wagon
with DL package

Javelin 2-Door Hardtop

Matador 2-Door Coupe

Matador 2-Door Coupe
with Oleg Cassini package

Matador 4-Door Station Wagon
with optional woodgrain

Model year production: 430,151, up 34.09% from 1973.
Domestic market share: 4.98% (8th place).
Base price range: $2,481 to $4,960.
American Motors average base price: $3,305, up 5.66%.
Introduction date: September 15, 1973.
Assembly plants: Kenosha, Wisconsin, and Brampton, Ontario, Canada.
Data plate identification (VIN): Thirteen digit code read as follows: First digit indicates company (A = American Motors); second digit indicates model year (4 = 1974); third digit is transmission code (see powertrain chart); fourth through sixth digits indicate car line/body type/series numbers (three-digit model number in model charts); seventh digit is engine code (see powertrain chart); eighth digit indicates assembly plant (1 through 6 = Kenosha, 7 through 9 = Ontario); remaining digits are sequential with beginning number of 00001. *Example:* A4A167H100001 is a 1974 Matador 2-Door, 304 CID, 2-bbl. V8, with Torque-Command Automatic, serial number 00001, built in Kenosha.

Powertrains

Engine	Net HP	Engine/ Trans. Codes	Transmission Availability[1]		Gremlin[2]	Hornet[3]	Javelin	Matador[4]	Ambassador
232 CID (3.8L), 1-bbl., 6-cyl.	100	E/S	3-speed manual		S	S	S (Javelin)	S (ex. "X" & wgn.)[5]	—
		E/A	Torque-Command 3-sp. Automatic	MPG:	15.6 $200	NA $200	NA $218	NA $224 (ex. "X" & wgn.)[5]	— —
				MPG:	15.9	15.5	NA	NA	—
258 CID (4.2L), 1-bbl., 6-cyl.	110	A/S	3-speed manual		$51	$51	—	S (wgn.)[5]/ $51 (ex. "X" & wgn.)	—
		A/A	Torque-Command 3-sp. Automatic	MPG:	NA $251	11.7 $251	— $261 (Javelin)	NA $224 (wgn.)[5]/ $272 (ex. "X" & wgn.)	— —
				MPG:	13.2	14.3	NA	NA	—
304 CID (5.0L), 2-bbl., V8	150	H/S	3-speed manual		$154	$138	$94 (Javelin)/ S (AMX)	—	—
		H/A	Torque-Command 3-sp. Automatic	MPG:	NA $374	NA $359	NA $344 (Javelin)/ $250 (AMX)	— S ("X")/ $99 (wgn.)[5]/ $349 (others)	S[5]
				MPG:	NA	NA	12.1	12.4	NA
360 CID (5.9L), 2-bbl., V8	175	N/A	Torque-Command 3-sp. Automatic		—	—	$386 (Javelin)/ $278 (AMX)	$51 ("X")/ $150 (wgn.)/ $400 (others)	$51
				MPG:	—	—	11.6	NA	10.8
360 CID (5.9L), 4-bbl., V8	195 (220 w/dual exhaust)[6]	P/F	4-speed manual[7]		—	—	$287 (Javelin)/ $189 (AMX)	—	—
				MPG:	—	—	10.8	—	—
		P/A	Torque-Command 3-sp. Automatic		—	—	$396 (Javelin)/ $298 (AMX)	$71 ("X")/ $170 (wgn.)/ $420 (others)	$71
				MPG:	—	—	NA	10	10.4
401 CID (6.6L), 4-bbl., V8	235[6]	Z/F	4-speed manual[7]		—	—	$360 (Javelin)/ $262 (AMX)	—	—
				MPG:	—	—	NA	—	—
		Z/A	Torque-Command 3-sp. Automatic		—	—	$469 (Javelin)/ $371 (AMX)	$145 ("X")/ $244 (wgn.)/ $494 (others)	$145
				MPG:	—	—	NA	NA	NA

[1]Unless otherwise noted: All manual transmissions are floor-shift, except on Hornet and Matador. All automatics, except AMX, are column-shift. Floor-shift is standard on all AMX models, and available for $20 extra on Gremlin w/automatic, Hornet Hatchback, Javelin w/V8 and automatic, and any Matador Coupe with bucket seats and console. Transmission code: w/Automatic floor shift, "C"; w/3-speed synchronized manual, "E." [2]Optional 3.08 axle ratio required for 6-cyl. Gremlins sold in California. [3]Optional 3.08 axle ratio required for 6-cyl. Hornets sold in California. [4]Optional 3.54 axle ratio required for 6-cyl. Matador coupes and sedans sold

in California. ⁵*Matador wagons and all Ambassadors built for sale in California have the 360 CID V8 code N engine as standard equipment. Prices adjust accordingly.* ⁶*Dual exhaust standard on AMX and all with 401 CID V8. Available on Javelin, Matador and Ambassador with 360 CID 4-bbl. V8, for approximately $30.* ⁷*Not available for cars sold in California.*

Major Options

	Gremlin	Hornet	Javelin	Matador	Ambassador
All-season air conditioning	$400	$400	$400	$400	S
Adjust-O-Tilt steering wheel	$43	$43	$43	$46	$46
Cruise-command speed control (w/V8)	—	—	—	$61	$61
Electric rear window defogger	—	—	$45	$48	$48
Tinted glass, all windows	$37	$40	$40	$42	S
Power windows	—	—	—	$123	$123
Front bucket seats	$131	$131	S	$131¹	—
Third row seat & power tailgate window (wagons)	—	—	—	$108	$108
AM radio	$66	$66	$66	$70	S
AM/FM stereo multiplex w/4 speakers	—	—	$196	$230	$161
Vinyl top (excluding wagon models)	—	$88	$88	$91	$109
Color-keyed woodgrain paneling (wagons)	—	$95	—	$113	S
Power steering	$99	$99	$106	$111	S
Power brakes	$44	$44	—	—	—
Power front disc brakes	$81	$81	$32	$32	S
Custom wheel covers	$50	$50	$50	$23	S
Spoke style wheels	$74	$84	$104	$104	—

Popular Option Groups & Packages

	Gremlin	Hornet	Javelin	Matador	Ambassador
360 "Go" package (AMX only)	—	—	$428	—	—
401 "Go" package (AMX only)	—	—	$476	—	—
Custom trim package	$109	—	—	—	—
Décor group	$37	—	—	—	—
D/L package (Sportabout only)	—	$264	—	—	—
Handling package	—	$25	$30	$30	—
Insulation group	$30	$30	$30	S	S
Interior appointment package	$19	—	—	—	—
Levi's custom trim package	$165²	$150²	—	—	—
Light group	$35	$35	$35	$35	S
"Oleg Cassini" package³	—	—	—	$299	—
Protection group	$35	$35	$35	$35	$35
Rally-Pac instrument package	—	—	$77	—	—
Visibility group	$50	$50	$50	$50	S
"X" package	$314	$207⁴	—	—	—

— = Not Available; S = Standard equipment ¹Two-door coupes only. ²Available on Gremlin and Hornet HBK only. Hornet with "X" package, $101; Gremlin with "X" package, $50. ³Available only on Matador Brougham. ⁴HBK and Sportabout only.

Paint Colors

	Code	Gremlin/Hornet	Javelin	Matador/Ambassador
Snow White	A1	x	x	x¹
Trans-Am Red	D7	x	x	x
Diamond Blue metallic	E1	x	x	—
Fawn Beige	E6	x	x	x
Mellow Yellow	E9	x	x	—
Maxi Blue	F2	x	x	—
Daisy Yellow	F4	—	—	x
Vineyard Burgundy metallic	F5	—	—	x
Medium Blue metallic	F6	—	—	x
Dark Blue metallic	F7	x	x	x
Golden Tan metallic	F8	x	x	x
Copper metallic	F9	x	x	x¹

	Code	Gremlin/Hornet	Javelin	Matador/Ambassador
Silver Green metallic	G1	x	x	x
Medium Green metallic	G2	x	x	x
Dark Green metallic	G3	x	x	x
Plum	G4	x	x	—
Pewter Mist metallic	G5	—	—	x
Sienna Orange	G6	x	x	x
Classic Black	P1	—	—	x[1]

Two-tone paint combinations are available on Hornet, Matador and Ambassador (except Sportabout and wagons) at $30–$37 depending upon model. Special two-tone package available for $69 on wagons. Non-standard model colors are available at extra cost.   [1]*Oleg Cassini package is only available with these colors.*

Gremlin

"Unique and fun-to-drive."

Nameplate year of origin: 1970.

Current bodystyle lifespan: 1970 through 1983; Gremlin (1970 to 1978), restyled and renamed Spirit (1979 to 1982). 4WD added and rebadged Eagle SX/4 (1981 to 1983).

Predecessor to this model: None.

Replacement for this model: Spirit (1979 to 1982) and Eagle SX/4 (1981 to 1983).

Percentage of division's production: 30.66%.

Corporate siblings: None; however many components were shared with the Hornet.

Primary competition: Buick/Opel 1900, Chevrolet Vega, Dodge Colt, and Ford Pinto.

Notable changes: Revised front-end styling and minor interior trim changes.

Major standard equipment: Vinyl bench front seat with foam cushions, front door pockets, fold-down rear seat, rubber floor and trunk mats, interior lights, double bodyside paint stripes, hubcaps, and 6.45 × 14 BSW tires.

Measurements

Wheelbase	96.0"
Length	170.3"
Width	70.6"
Height	52.3"
Legroom — front	40.7"
Legroom — rear	29.2"
Headroom — front	38.0"
Headroom — rear	36.4"
Cargo capacity (cu. ft.)	6.4*
Fuel capacity (gals.)	21.0

*26.8 cu. ft. with rear seat down.

Models Available

	Model No.	Base MSRP	Change from LY	Shipping Wt. (lbs.)	Model Year Production	Change from LY
Gremlin 2-Door Sedan	46-5	$2,481	+18.26%	2649	131,905	+57.73%
TOTALS		*Avg. price* $2,481	+18.26%		*Production* 131,905*	+57.73%

*Production by engine type: 6-cylinder, 119,642; V8, 12,263.

Hornet

"A compact car that's designed to save you money."

Nameplate year of origin: 1951 (previously used on 1951 to 1957 Hudson series).

Current bodystyle lifespan: 1970 through 1987; Hornet (1970 to 1977), restyled and renamed Concord (1978 to 1982); 4WD added and rebadged Eagle (1980 to 1987).

Predecessor to this model: (Rambler) American (1964 to 1969).

Replacement for this model: Concord (1978 to 1982) and Eagle (1980 to 1987).

Percentage of division's production: 33.90%.

Corporate siblings: None; however many components were shared with the Gremlin.

Measurements

	Sedans	Hatchback	Sportabout
Wheelbase	108.0"	108.0"	108.0"
Length	187.0"	187.0"	187.0"
Width	71.0"	71.1"	71.0"
Height	52.2"	52.2"	52.2"
Legroom — front	42.1"	40.7"	40.7"
Legroom — rear	35.5"	32.1"	35.6"
Headroom — front	38.1"	38.1"	38.1"
Headroom — rear	37.0"	36.7"	37.4"

Primary competition: Chevrolet Nova, Dodge Dart, Ford Maverick, Plymouth Valiant, and Pontiac Ventura.

Notable changes: Revised front end styling, and trim and detail changes.

Major standard equipment: "Nassau" fabric-covered front bench seat with foam cushions, full-floor carpeting, instrument panel package tray, custom steering wheel, exterior pinstripes, hubcaps, and 6.95 × 14 BSW tires. Hatchback adds: Flip open rear windows and gas-charged lift-gate supports. Sportabout adds: Spring-type liftgate and hidden rear compartment lock.

Measurements (cont.)

	Sedans	Hatchback	Sportabout
Cargo capacity (cu. ft.)	11.1	30.5*	56.4*
Fuel capacity (gals.)	22.0	22.0	22.0

Maximum with rear seat down, and 3.8 cu. ft. below cargo area on Sportabout.

Models Available

	Model No.	Base MSRP	Change from LY	Shipping Wt. (lbs.)	Model Year Production	Change from LY
Hornet 2-Door Sedan	06-7	$2,774	+20.71%	2767	*	*
Hornet 2-Door Hatchback	03-7	$2,849	+16.33%	2791	*	*
Hornet 4-Door Sedan	05-7	$2,824	+20.53%	2833	*	*
Hornet 4-Door Sportabout Wagon	08-7	$3,049	+13.98%	2900	67,709*	*
TOTALS	Avg. price	$2,874	+17.73%		Production 145,818*	+35.61%

Production by body style is not available except for Sportabout. Production by engine type: 6-cylinder cars, 70,052; 6-cylinder wagon, 57,414; V8 car, 8,057; V8 wagon, 10,295.

Javelin

"Control. Head turning style. Outstanding performance. This is the '74 Javelin."

Nameplate year of origin: 1968.
Current bodystyle lifespan: 1971 through 1974.
Predecessor to this model: Javelin (1968 to 1970).
Replacement for this model: None.
Percentage of division's production: 6.40%.
Corporate siblings: None.
Primary competition: Chevrolet Camaro, Dodge Challenger, Ford Mustang, Plymouth Barracuda, and Pontiac Firebird.
Notable changes: New grille (except AMX) and trim and detail changes.
Major standard equipment: "Hi-back" vinyl front bucket seats with deep-foam cushions, color-keyed carpeting, custom steering wheel, sport hubcaps, and D78 × 14 BSW tires. AMX adds: 304 CID V8, three-spoke sport steering wheel, deck-mounted rear spoiler, specific tape stripe package, front sway bar, slotted 14 × 6 wheels, space saver spare tire, and F70 × 14 RWL tires.

Measurements

Wheelbase	110.0"
Length	192.3"
Width	75.2"
Height	NA
Legroom — front	42.5"
Legroom — rear	NA
Headroom — front	37.5"
Headroom — rear	35.6"
Cargo capacity (cu. ft.)	10.2
Fuel capacity (gals.)	16.0

Models Available

	Model No.	Base MSRP	Change from LY	Shipping Wt. (lbs.)	Model Year Production	Change from LY
Javelin 2-Door Hardtop	79-7	$2,999	+3.81%	2869	22,556	-10.47%
Javelin AMX 2-Door Hardtop	79-8	$3,299	+3.38%	3184	4,980	-12.74%
TOTALS	Avg. price	$3,149	+3.59%		Production 27,536	-10.89%

Matador

"Mid-size cars that give you many big car advantages.
Including the only new mid-size for 1974 ...
the exciting new AMC Matador Coupe."

Nameplate year of origin: 1971.
Current bodystyle lifespan: 1974 through 1978 (Coupe only); 1967 through 1978 (Rebel, 1967–1968; restyled in 1969; restyled and renamed Matador in 1971; and sedan and wagon restyled in 1974).
Predecessor to this model: Matador (1971 to 1973).
Replacement for this model: None.
Percentage of division's production: 23.23%.
Corporate siblings: AMC Ambassador (shared components from the cowl back).
Primary competition: Chevrolet Chevelle, Dodge Coronet, Ford Torino, Plymouth Satellite, and Pontiac LeMans.
Notable changes: All-new coupe; restyled front and rear for sedan and wagon models.
Major standard equipment: Regatta fabric front bench seat with foam cushions, color-keyed carpeting, rear shelf light with door switches (coupe), dome light (sedan and wagon), bodyside scuff moldings with vinyl insert (sedan and wagon), manual front disc brakes, and E78 × 14 BSW tires. Wagon adds: "Tru-Knit" vinyl trim seats, rubber cargo area mat, hidden rear compartment with lock, dual-swing tailgate, and H78 × 14 BSW tires. Brougham adds to base: Custom fabric seat and door panel trim, custom two-spoke steering wheel, woodgrain instrument panel and steering wheel appliqués, rocker panel moldings, hood stripe, décor package contents, Brougham identification behind rear side windows, and wheel covers. "X" adds to base: Vinyl bench seat, three-spoke sports steering wheel, rally side-stripes and rear deck stripes, black-out grille, slot-styled wheels, "X" model identification adjacent to Matador name plate on hood and front fenders, and F70 × 14 RWL tires.

Measurements

	Coupe	Sedan	Wagon
Length	209.3"	216.0"	215.5"
Wheelbase	114.0"	118.0"	118.0"
Width	77.4"	77.3"	77.2"
Height	51.8"	54.7"	56.8"
Legroom — front	43.0"	42.8"	42.8"
Legroom — rear	33.3"	39.6"	39.6"
Headroom — front	37.6"	39.6"	39.9"
Headroom — rear	36.0"	37.5"	38.5"
Cargo capacity (cu. ft.)	14.3	19.1	95.2*
Fuel capacity (gals.)	24.5	24.5	21.0

Includes 8.0 cu.ft. of space below cargo floor.

Models Available

	Model No.	Base MSRP	Change from LY	Shipping Wt. (lbs.)	Model Year Production	Change from LY
Matador 2-Door Coupe	16-7	$3,096	+8.52%*	3437	31,169	**
Matador 4-Door Sedan	15-7	$3,052	+5.72%	3425	27,994	**
Matador 4-Door Station Wagon	18-7	$3,378	+6.06%	3739	9,709	**
Matador Brougham 2-Door Coupe	16-9	$3,249	NEW	3456	21,026	NEW
Matador "X" 2-Door Coupe	16-8	$3,699	NEW	3672	10,074	NEW
TOTALS		*Avg. price* $3,295	+10.82%		*Production* 99,922	+62.20%

*Production by engine type: 6-cylinder cars, 25,826; 6-cylinder wagon, 2,975; V8 car, 64,387; V8 wagon, 6,734. Also included in these figures are 6,165 coupes that were equipped with the Oleg Cassini package, and 700 coupes that were equipped with the 401 CID V8.   *Comparison made to 1973 Matador 2-Door HT.   **Comparison to LY is not available due to production total not being kept by body style in 1973.*

Ambassador

"There's a good chance that everything you'd want
on your new luxury car is standard equipment
on the '74 Ambassador Brougham."

Nameplate year of origin: 1933 (from top-of-the-line Nash).
Current bodystyle lifespan: 1967 through 1974.
Predecessor to this model: Ambassador (1963 to 1966).
Replacement for this model: None.
Percentage of division's production: 5.81%.

Measurements

	Sedan	Wagon
Wheelbase	122.0"	122.0"
Length	220.0"	219.5"

Corporate siblings: AMC Matador (shared components from the cowl back).

Primary competition: Chevrolet BelAir/Impala/Caprice, Ford LTD, and Plymouth Fury.

Notable changes: Restyled front and rear design.

Major standard equipment: "Abbington" fabric-covered front bench seat with foam cushions, custom steering wheel, "All-season" air conditioning, power steering, power front disc brakes, insulation group, light group, visibility group, bodyside scuff moldings with vinyl insert, Ambassador-specific hubcaps, and F78 × 14 WSW tires. Wagon adds: Vinyl upholstery, roof-top luggage rack with tailgate air deflector, simulated wood-grain side and rear panels, cargo area carpeting, locking cargo compartment under rear floor, dual-swing tailgate, and H78 × 14 WSW tires.

Measurements (cont.)

	Sedan	Wagon
Width	77.3"	77.2"
Height	54.7"	56.8"
Legroom — front	42.8"	42.8"
Legroom — rear	39.6"	39.6"
Headroom — front	39.6"	39.9"
Headroom — rear	37.5"	38.5"
Cargo capacity (cu. ft.)	19.1	95.2*
Fuel capacity (gals.)	24.5	21.0

*Includes 8.0 cu.ft. of space below cargo floor.

Models Available

	Model No.	Base MSRP	Change from LY	Shipping Wt. (lbs.)	Model Year Production	Change from LY
Ambassador 4-Door Sedan	85-7	$4,559	+2.20%	3851	17,901	*
Ambassador 4-Door Station Wagon	88-7	$4,960	+2.04%	4125	7,070	*
TOTALS	Avg. price	$4,760	+3.47%		Production 24,971	-32.74%

*Comparison to LY is not available because production total was not kept by body style in 1973.

BUICK

"Wouldn't you really rather have a Buick?"

Although they were arguably among the best looking cars of the mid–1970s, 1974 proved to be a rather uninspiring year for Buick. Across the line, most styling changes were related to updates of styling at the rear of the car, and modest interior updates to accommodate the newly mandated safety requirements. The imported Opel also received minimal changes for the new season, and the 1900 4-door sedan was discontinued. The more significant updates were seen in the full-size Buick line.

The new-for-'73 compact-sized Apollo added a sporty looking GSX option package, but it lacked the looks, performance and appeal of the original Skylark-based GSX models of 1970 and 1971 vintage. Although it seemed to be an action to keep up with Pontiac, which was offering a GTO package on the compact Ventura for 1974, the GSX was purely a visual package, and could be ordered with the 6-cylinder or V8 engines.

In the popular Century mid-size lineup, slightly revised grilles were seen, with the luxury Regal models wearing a vertical bar grille with vertically mounted rectangular parking lamps set between the grille and headlights, while all other Century models used a horizontal bar grille with vertical accent bars, and round parking lamps. Two new models were added, the Regal sedan and the Gran Sport coupe models. The Regal sedan had all of the Regal coupe's features, including the two-inch front-end extension. The Gran Sport carried special styling and performance features to distinguish it from the average Century coupe. All Century base models now carried the Century 350 designation, making the Century 350 option package obsolete.

Full-sized Buicks, including the Riviera, received a new instrument panel design featuring a wraparound cockpit designed to provide easier access to controls and instruments. All controls and instruments were lined with bright chrome accents, with the instrument cluster face featuring a brushed gold appearance. The glove box was also redesigned and located higher on the instrument panel. Outside, the Riviera and LeSabre had new vertical bar grilles, while the Electra had a horizontal theme with vertical bars set behind. Both the LeSabre and Electra 225 used a divided dual-headlamp style that had each lamp set within its own chrome bezel, with a small body-colored strip separating the two units.

At the back end, LeSabre models used a new wrap-around horizontal taillight. The Electra 225's non-wrap-around horizontal taillight was capped at each end by vertical bumper ends running up the rear edge of the quarter panel, and having the backup lights inset near the top. The Riviera traded its infamous "boattail" design for a completely flat rear panel, with horizontal taillights, paired with high-level lamps set under the rear window, as seen on the Oldsmobile Toronado since 1971. The new rear bumper system added about 3 inches in length to the already large full-size Buicks.

The Centurion series and the former base LeSabre "L-model" series were dropped; therefore the 1974 LeSabre directly replaced the 1973 LeSabre Custom, and the newly named LeSabre Luxus series replaced the 1973 Centurion.

Introduced as a new option for the Riviera and most other full-size Buicks, excluding the LeSabre convertible and the Estate Wagon, was the GM Air Cushion Restraint System. Buick neglected to mention this option in its 1974 sales brochure, apparently not sensing its historical significance.

1974

Apollo 2-Door Coupe with GSX package

Apollo 4-Door Sedan

Century Gran Sport 2-Door
Colonnade Hardtop Coupe

Century Regal 2-Door
Colonnade Hardtop Coupe

Electra 225 Limited 4-Door Hardtop Sedan

Electra 225 Custom 2-Door Hardtop Coupe

Estate Wagon with Century Luxus
4-Door Station Wagon, rear

LeSabre 4-Door Hardtop Sedan

LeSabre Luxus 2-Door Convertible

Riviera 2-Door Hardtop Coupe

Riviera optional 40/40 seat with center console

Opel 1900 Sportwagon 2-Door Station Wagon

Opel Manta 2-Door Sport Coupe

Model year production: 495,062, down 39.71% from 1973.
Domestic market share: 5.73% (6th place).
Base price range: $3,037 to $5,921.
Buick average base price: $4,523, up 13.96%.
Introduction date: September 16, 1973; Opel introduced November 29, 1973.
Assembly plants: Baltimore, MD (B); Southgate, CA (C); Doraville, GA (D); Framingham, MA (G); Flint, MI (H); Kansas City/Leeds, MO (K); Van Nuys, CA (L); Tarrytown, NY (T); Kansas City/Fairfax, KS (X); Fremont, CA (Z). *Opel:* Russelsheim, Germany (5); Antwerp, Belgium (9).
Data plate identification (VIN): Thirteen digit code read as follows: First digit indicates division (4 = Buick); second through fourth digits indicate series and body style (model number in model charts); fifth digit is engine code (see powertrain chart); sixth digit indicates model year (4 = 1974); seventh digit indicates assembly plant (see list above); remaining digits are sequential with beginning number of 100001, or 400001, depending upon assembly plant. *Example:* 4N69H4H100001 is a 1974 Buick LeSabre 4-Door Sedan, with 350 CID, 2-bbl. V8 engine, serial number 100001, built in Flint, MI. 1974 Opels use a 13-digit code read as follows: First digit is O for Opel; the next three digits indicate series and body style (Manta=L77, 1900 2-door=L11, 1900 4-door=L69, 1900 Wagon=L15); fifth digit indicates engine code = N; sixth digit indicates year (D = 1974); seventh digit indicates assembly plant (see list above). Remaining digits are sequential with beginning numbers as follows: 1900 Deluxe 2-door sedan NA; 1900 Deluxe 2-door wagon, 018213; Manta coupe, 014780; Manta Rallye coupe, 014785; Manta Luxus coupe, 020693.

Powertrains

Engine	Net HP	Engine Code	Transmission Availability[1]		Opel	Apollo	Century	LeSabre & Centurion	Electra & Estate Wagon	Riviera
116 CID (1.9L), 2-bbl., 4-cyl.	75	N	4-speed manual		S	—	—	—	—	—
				MPG:	19.8	—	—	—	—	—
			3-speed automatic		$230	—	—	—	—	—
				MPG:	18.2	—	—	—	—	—
250 CID (4.1L), 1-bbl., 6-cyl.	100	D	3-speed manual		—	S	—	—	—	—
				MPG:	—	NA	—	—	—	—
			3-speed Turbo Hydra-matic		—	$196	—	—	—	—
				MPG:	—	15.7	—	—	—	—
350 CID (5.7L), 2-bbl., V8	150	H	3-speed manual		—	$118	—	—	—	—
				MPG:	—	NA	—	—	—	—
			3-speed Turbo Hydra-matic		—	$324	S	S	—	—
				MPG:	—	NA	10.1	10	—	—
350 CID (5.7L), 4-bbl., V8	175	J	3-speed manual		—	$164	—	—	—	—
				MPG:	—	NA	—	—	—	—
			3-speed Turbo Hydra-matic		—	$370	$46	$46	—	—
				MPG:	—	9.9	10.4	10.4	—	—
455 CID (7.4L), 2-bbl., V8	175[1]	T	3-speed Turbo Hydra-matic		—	—	NA (Wgns.)/ $184 (others)	$124	—	—
				MPG:	—	—	8.7	8.1	—	—
455 CID (7.4L), 4-bbl., V8	210[1]	U	3-speed Turbo Hydra-matic		—	—	$184 (Wgns.)/ $230 (others)	$170	S	S
				MPG:	—	—	8.4	8.3	8.3	8.3
455 CID (7.4L), GS Stage I, 4-bbl., V8[2]	255	W	3-speed Turbo Hydra-matic		—	—	$609[3]	—	—	—
				MPG:	—	—	8.4	—	—	—
455 CID (7.4L), Riviera Stage I, 4-bbl., V8[2]	245	W	3-speed Turbo Hydra-matic		—	—	—	$343	$173	$216[4]
				MPG:	—	—	—	8.3	8.3	8.3

[1]*Dual exhaust on 455 CID, 2-bbl. V8 adds 15 horsepower, and on 455 CID, 4-bbl. V8 dual exhaust adds 20 horsepower. Available at $30 extra on either engine.* [2]*Includes dual exhaust, power disc brakes (Century GS only), High Energy ignition, positive traction performance rear axle (Riviera and Century GS only), and Gran Sport package (on Century GS only).* [3]*Includes the Gran Sport option package. Available only on Century 350 coupe.* [4]*Available as part of Stage I option group.*

Major Options

	Opel	Apollo	Century	LeSabre	Estate Wagon	Electra 225	Riviera
Air conditioning, manual[1]	$[2]	$381	$397	$431	$431	$431	$431
Tilt-wheel steering	—	—	$44	$44	$44	$44	S
GM Air Cushion Restraint System	—	—	—	$225[3]	—	$225	$225	
Cruise Master speed control	—	—	$65	$65	$65	$65	$65
Electric rear window defogger	$	$33[4]	$64	$64	$64	$64	$64
Tinted glass, all windows	$	$30	$42	$42	$50	$42	$42
Power windows, 2-dr./4-dr.	—	—	$75/$113	$129	$129	$129[5]	$85
Power door locks, 2-dr./4-dr.	—	—	$46/$69	$46/$69	$69	$46/$69[5]	$46
Power front seat, w/bench seat	—	—	$103	$103	$103	$103[5]	$103
Front bucket seats, w/console	S	$155	$180	—	—	—	$61
AM radio	$[2]	$65	$73	$86	$86	$86	$86
AM/FM stereo	—	$233	$233	$233	$233	$233	$233
AM/FM stereo w/8-track tape	—	$363	$363	$363	$363	$363	$363
Vinyl top	$[5]	$82	$99[6]	$123	$138	$138[7]	$125
Sunroof, manual[8]	$104	—	$275	$539	—	$539	$539
Woodgrain exterior panels (wagons)	$	—	$168[9]	—	$177	—	—
Power steering, variable-ratio	—	$113	S	S	S	S	S
Power brakes, w/front disc	S	$68	$46[10]	S	S	S	S
Styled road wheels	—	$66	$95	$118	$118	$118	$118

Popular Option Groups & Packages

	Opel	Apollo	Century	LeSabre	Estate Wagon	Electra 225	Riviera
Accessory group	—	$36	$36	$26	—	—	—
Appearance group	—	$	$	—	—	—	—
Convenience group	—	$20	$27	$27	—	—	—
Firm ride & handling package	—	$15	$15	$15	—	$15	$15
GSX package	—	$96	—	—	—	—	—
Gran Sport package	—	—	$108[11]	—	—	—	$171
Luxus ride & performance pkg.	—	—	—	$423	—	—	—
Stage I option[12]	—	—	$609	—	—	—	$139

—= Not Available; S = Standard equipment. [1]*Power brakes required. Automatic climate control is available for $76 additional on Century Regal, Riviera and full-size Buicks.* [2]*Available as dealer installed option. Vinyl top for Manta only.* [3]*Not available on convertible.* [4]*Blower type defogger.* [5]*Standard on Limited.* [6]*Regal w/Landau top is $310. Not available on station wagons.* [7]*Limited Landau 2-door, $525, and Limited 4-door, $385.* [8]*Two-door models only. Electrically operated sunroof $50 higher.* [9]*Luxus wagon, $136.* [10]*Standard on station wagons.* [11]*Available on Century 350 coupe only.* [12]*See Powertrain table.*

Paint Colors

Buick	Code	Buick	Code	Opel	Code
Arctic White	11	Nugget Gold	55	Strato Blue metallic	L-235
Regal Black	19	Nutmeg metallic	59	Jade Mist metallic	L-303
Medium Blue metallic	24	Silver Cloud metallic	64	Signal Green	L-308
Mediterranean Blue metallic	26	Cinnamon metallic	66	Rallye Gold	L-411
Midnight Blue metallic	29	Dark Brown metallic	69	Antique Bronze metallic	L-412
Crystal Lake Blue metallic	36	Ruby Red	72	Signal Yellow	L-445
Mint Green*	40	Burgundy metallic	74	Polar White	L-452
Ranch Green	44	Apple Red*	75	Burgundy	L-501
Leaf Green metallic	46	Plum metallic	79	Flame Red	L-508
Forest Green metallic	49				
Sand Beige	50	*Opel*	*Code*	
Canary Yellow*	51	Grecian Silver metallic	L-135	
Ginger metallic*	53	Regency Blue metallic	L-204	
Gold Mist metallic	54	Signal Blue	L-224	

*In two-tone combinations, the first two digits indicate lower color, and the next two digits are the upper color. Available on Apollo for $31, Century for $27–$36, and LeSabre (except convertible) for $43.   *Available on Apollo only.*

Opel

"A proven best seller in Germany. Available at more than 2,200 Buick-Opel dealers throughout America."

Nameplate year of origin: Opel 1900, 1971; Manta, 1972.
Current bodystyle lifespan: Opel 1900 (1971–1975); Manta (1971–1975).
Predecessor to this model: Kadett (1966–1972); 1900 Sport Coupe (1971–1972 for Manta). **Replacement for this model:** Opel (1976 to 1980—Isuzu built).
Primary competition: AMC Gremlin, Chevrolet Vega, Dodge Colt, and Ford Pinto.
Notable changes: Minor trim and detail changes.
Major standard equipment: *1900 1.9 Liter Sedan and Sportwagon:* Reclining vinyl front bucket seats with foam cushions, front door pockets, fold-down rear seat, rubber floor mats, interior lights, aluminized exhaust system, exterior pinstripes, hubcaps, and 165 × 13 BSW tires. *Manta:* Reclining vinyl bucket seats, center console, two-spoke steering wheel, woodgrain vinyl I/P gauge cluster appliqué, and 165 × 13 BSW tires. Rallye adds: Tachometer, console mounted gauges (L to R: ampere, clock, and oil pressure), special black paint treatment on hood and bodyside stripes, firm shocks, 3.67 rear axle ratio, and 4-spoke steel wheels. Luxus adds: Corduroy upholstery, color-keyed center console, sound deadening insulation, glove box light, carpeted luggage compartment, and exterior identification badges.

Measurements

	1900	Manta
Wheelbase	95.7"	95.7"
Length	170.2"	176.1"
Width	64.3"	64.3"
Height	55.1"	53.4"
Legroom — front	41.9"	41.9"
Legroom — rear	30.5"	28.5"
Headroom — front	38.2"	37.4"
Headroom — rear	37.3"	36.6"
Cargo capacity (cu. ft.)	10.8*	11.5
Fuel capacity (gals.)	12.0	12.0

Sportwagon, 62.6 cu. ft.

Models Available

	Model No.	Base MSRP	Change from LY	Shipping Wt. (lbs.)	Model Year Production	Change from LY
(1900) 1.9 Liter 2-Door Sedan	51	$2,483	+27.87%	2151	NA	NA
(1900) Sportwagon 2-Door Wagon	54	$2,709	+27.06%	2172	NA	NA
Manta 2-Door Sport Coupe	57	$2,579	+26.99%	2128	NA	NA
Manta Rallye 2-Door Sport Coupe	57R	$2,758	+26.90%	2139	7,959	-4.08%
Manta Luxus 2-Door Sport Coupe	57L	$2,769	+26.83%	2139	14,026	-20.02%
TOTALS		*Avg. price* $2,745	+26.91%		*Production* 55,000*	NA

Total is estimated model year sales.

Apollo

"We decided to give the small-car buyer a car to move up to."

Nameplate year of origin: 1973.
Current bodystyle lifespan: 1973 through 1974.
Predecessor to this model: None.
Replacement for this model: Apollo (1975) and Skylark (1975 to 1979).
Percentage of division's production: 11.45%.
Corporate siblings: Chevrolet Nova, Oldsmobile Omega, and Pontiac Ventura.
Primary competition: Dodge Dart and Mercury Comet.
Notable changes: New grille and trim and detail changes.
Major standard equipment: Glenbrook cloth and Madrid-grain vinyl or Oxen- and Madrid-grain vinyl front bench seat with foam cushions, cut-pile carpeting, rear quarter/rear door armrests, deluxe steering wheel, dual speed wipers w/washers, extra sound deadening insulation, roof drip moldings, front and rear wheel opening moldings, hubcaps, and E78 × 14 BSW tires. Hatchback model adds: Fold-down rear seat and load floor carpeting.

Measurements

	Coupe & HBK	Sedan
Wheelbase	111.0"	111.0"
Length	200.2"	200.2"
Width	72.7"	72.7"
Height	53.7"	54.6"
Legroom — front	41.7"	41.7"
Legroom — rear	33.5"	35.3"
Headroom — front	38.0"	39.3"
Headroom — rear	36.9"	37.3"
Cargo capacity (cu. ft.)	13.6*	13.6
Fuel capacity (gals.)	21.0	21.0

Hatchback maximum with rear seat down, 27 cu. ft.

Models Available

	Model No.	Base MSRP	Change from LY	Shipping Wt. (lbs.)	Model Year Production	Change from LY
Apollo 2-Door Coupe	B27	$3,037	+16.58%	3216	28,286	+95.41%
Apollo 2-Door Hatchback	B17	$3,160	+14.74%	3321	11,644	+18.00%
Apollo 4-Door Sedan	B69	$3,060	+16.44%	3256	16,779	+98.57%
TOTALS		Avg. price $3,086	+15.90%		Production 56,709	+72.93%

Century

"The Buick that's attracting people who never bought Buicks before."

Nameplate year of origin: 1936.
Current bodystyle lifespan: 1973 through 1977.
Predecessor to this model: Skylark (1968 to 1972).
Replacement for this model: Century (1978 to 1981).
Percentage of division's production: 36.35%.
Corporate siblings: Chevrolet Malibu, Oldsmobile Cutlass, and Pontiac LeMans.
Primary competition: Dodge Coronet, and Mercury Montego.
Notable changes: Minor trim and detail changes. New Regal sedan and Gran Sport coupe models.
Major standard equipment: Meridian cloth and Madrid-grain vinyl front bench seat, cut-pile carpeting, deluxe steering wheel, front disc brakes, wheel covers, and G78 × 14 BSW tires. Gran Sport adds: Special blacked-out grille and headlight trim, special stripe on rear deck, Gran Sport ornamentation, and rallye ride and handling suspension w/stabilizer bars front and rear, heavy-duty front and rear springs and shock absorbers. Luxus adds: Gossamer cloth and Madrid-grain vinyl or Oxen- and Madrid-grain expanded vinyl notchback front seat w/center fold-down armrest, ashtray light, under-dash courtesy lights, glove compartment light, "Luxus" badging, wheel opening moldings, and rocker panel molding. Wagons add: Oxen-grain and Madrid-grain vinyl front bench seat (Luxus wagon has same upholstery as coupes and sedans), and H78 × 14 BSW tires. Regal adds: Regatta cloth and Madrid-grain vinyl or Oxen- and Madrid-grain expanded vinyl notchback seat with center armrest.

Measurements

	Century Coupes	Regal Coupes	Century Sedans	Regal Sedans	Century Wagons
Wheelbase	112.0"	112.0"	116.0"	116.0"	116.0"
Length	209.5"	212.0"	213.5"	216.0"	218.2"
Width	79.0"	79.0"	79.0"	79.0"	79.0"
Height	53.5"	53.3"	54.1"	54.1"	55.3"
Legroom — front	42.1"	42.1"	42.1"	42.1"	42.1"
Legroom — rear	32.9"	32.9"	37.0"	37.0"	36.8"
Headroom — front	37.7"*	37.5"	38.3"	38.3"	38.8"
Headroom — rear	37.0"*	37.4"	37.5"	37.5"	39.4"
Cargo capacity (cu. ft.)	15.1	15.1	14.6	14.6	85.1
Fuel capacity (gals.)	NA	NA	NA	NA	22.0

*Luxus coupe dimensions are the same as Regal coupe.

Models Available

	Model No.	Base MSRP	Change from LY*	Shipping Wt. (lbs.)	Model Year Production	Change from LY*
Century 350 2-Door Colonnade HT Coupe	D37	$3,790	+23.98%	3845	30,910	-44.95%
Century 350 4-Door Colonnade HT Sedan	D29	$3,836	+25.48%	3890	22,856	-40.17%
Century 350 4-Door Station Wagon, 2-S.	F35	$4,205	+20.63%	4272	4,860	-37.37%
Century 350 4-Door Station Wagon, 3-S.	F45	$4,320	+19.97%	4305	*	*
Century Gran Sport 2-Dr. Colonnade HT Cpe.	D37	$3,904	NEW	3850	2,256	NEW
Century Luxus 2-Door Colonnade HT Coupe	H57	$4,089	+22.76%	3835	44,930	-37.35%
Century Luxus 4-Door Colonnade HT Sedan	H29	$4,109	+23.54%	3910	11,159	-50.27%
Century Luxus 4-Door Station Wagon, 2-S.	K35	$4,371	+19.69%	4312	6,791	-36.20%

	Model No.	Base MSRP	Change from LY*	Shipping Wt. (lbs.)	Model Year Production	Change from LY*
Century Luxus 4-Door Station Wagon, 3-S.	K45	$4,486	+19.09%	4345	*	*
Century Regal 2-Door Colonnade HT Coupe	J57	$4,201	+21.07%	3900	57,512	-37.18%
Century Regal 4-Door Colonnade HT Sedan	J29	$4,221	NEW	3930	9,333	NEW
TOTALS	Avg. price	$4,163	+21.16%	Production	190,607	-36.14%

*Production of 3-seat wagon models included with 2-seat models.

LeSabre

"The Buick for people who didn't think they could afford one."

Nameplate year of origin: 1959 (also used on 1951 GM show car).
Current bodystyle lifespan: 1971 through 1976.
Predecessor to this model: LeSabre (1969 to 1970).
Replacement for this model: LeSabre (1977 to 1985).
Percentage of division's production: 22.99%.
Corporate siblings: Chevrolet BelAir/Impala/Caprice, Pontiac Catalina/Bonneville/Grand Ville, and Oldsmobile Delta 88.
Primary competition: Chrysler Newport and Mercury Monterey.
Notable changes: Revised greenhouse area for coupes and revised front and rear styling. LeSabre Luxus replaces Centurion series.
Major standard equipment: Gossamer cloth and Madrid-grain vinyl bench seat or Oxen-grain and Madrid-grain vinyl bench seat, full-floor carpeting, woodgrained vinyl trim on door panels, deluxe steering wheel, LH outside rear view mirror, hood-mounted three-section rectangular "ventiport" ornaments, wheel opening moldings, rocker panel molding, wheel covers, and H78 × 15 BSW tires. Luxus adds: Potomac cloth and Madrid-grain vinyl bench seat in 4-door sedan, Potomac cloth and Madrid-grain vinyl or Oxen- and Madrid-grain expanded vinyl notchback bench seat w/fold-down front center armrest in hardtop models, Oxen- and Madrid-grain expanded vinyl notchback seat w/fold-down front center armrest in Convertible, I/P woodgrain appliqués, custom steering wheel, wide rocker panel molding, "Luxus" interior and exterior badging, and deluxe wheel covers.

Measurements

Wheelbase	124.0"
Length	225.9"
Width	79.9"
Height	54.9"
Legroom — front	42.3"
Legroom — rear	38.8"
Headroom — front	38.9"
Headroom — rear	38.0"
Cargo capacity (cu. ft.)	19.7
Fuel capacity (gals.)	NA

Models Available

	Model No.	Base MSRP	Change from LY*	Shipping Wt. (lbs.)	Model Year Production	Change from LY*
LeSabre 2-Door Hardtop Coupe	N57	$4,424	+6.50%	4297	12,522	-69.77%
LeSabre 4-Door Sedan	N69	$4,355	+6.45%	4337	18,572	-56.65%
LeSabre 4-Door Hardtop Sedan	N39	$4,482	+6.28%	4387	11,879	-78.74%
LeSabre Luxus 2-Door Hardtop Coupe	P57	$4,575	+5.51%	4307	27,243	+61.36%
LeSabre Luxus 2-Door Convertible	P67	$4,696	+3.57%	4372	3,627	-36.80%
LeSabre Luxus 4-Door Sedan	P69	$4,466	NEW	4352	16,039	NEW
LeSabre Luxus 4-Door Hardtop Sedan	P39	$4,629	+5.44%	4397	23,910	+6.96%
TOTALS	Avg. price	$4,518	+7.24%	Production	113,792	-53.03%

*Comparisons made are to 1973 LeSabre and Centurions with the same model number.

Estate Wagon

"A Buick wagon is everything a Buick automobile is — but with more room."

Nameplate year of origin: 1940 (as designation for station wagons).
Current bodystyle lifespan: 1971 through 1976.
Predecessor to this model: Estate Wagon (1970).

Measurements

Wheelbase	127.0"
Length	231.1"

Replacement for this model: Estate Wagon (1977 to 1990).
Percentage of division's production: 2.91%.
Corporate siblings: Chevrolet BelAir/Impala/Caprice, Pontiac Catalina Safari/Grand Safari, and Oldsmobile Custom Cruiser.
Primary competition: Chrysler Town & Country and Mercury Colony Park.
Notable changes: Revised front and rear styling.
Major standard equipment: Gossamer cloth and Madrid-grain vinyl (2-seat only) or Oxen-grain and Madrid-grain vinyl (3-seat) with front bench seat, forward facing 3rd seat w/divided 2nd seat on 3-seat wagon, full-floor carpeting, hidden storage compartment, Glide-Away tailgate, power tailgate window, LH and RH rear view mirrors, hood-mounted four-section rectangular "ventiport" ornaments, deluxe wheel covers, and L78 × 15 BSW tires.

Measurements (cont.)

Width	79.9"
Height	57.9"
Legroom — front	42.1"
Legroom — rear	39.4"
Headroom — front	39.6"
Headroom — rear	39.3"
Cargo capacity (cu. ft.)	106.0
Fuel capacity (gals.)	NA

Models Available

	Model No.	Base MSRP	Change from LY	Shipping Wt. (lbs.)	Model Year Production	Change from LY
Estate Wagon 4-Door, 2-S. Wagon	R35	$5,019	+8.05%	5082	4,581	-62.70%
Estate Wagon 4-Door, 3-S. Wagon	R45	$5,163	+7.79%	5182	9,831	-58.19%
TOTALS		*Avg. price* $5,091	+7.92%		*Production* 14,412	-59.74%

Electra 225

"If you are looking for a luxury car, you need look no further — or pay any more — than Buick Electra."

Nameplate year of origin: 1959.
Current bodystyle lifespan: 1971 through 1976.
Predecessor to this model: Electra (1969 to 1970).
Replacement for this model: Electra 225 (1977 to 1984).
Percentage of division's production: 20.08%.
Corporate siblings: Cadillac Calais, Cadillac deVille, and Oldsmobile Ninety-Eight.
Primary competition: Chrysler New Yorker and Mercury Marquis Brougham.
Notable changes: Revised front and rear styling.
Major standard equipment: Oxen-grain and Madrid-grain vinyl or Grandeur cloth and Madrid-grain vinyl bench seat, cut-pile carpeting, simulated woodgrain appliqués on door panels and instrument panel, electric clock, custom steering wheel, custom safety belts, remote-control LH rear view mirror, hood-mounted 4-section rectangular "ventiport" ornaments, bodyside protection molding, wheel opening moldings, full-length rocker panel molding, rear fender skirts, super deluxe wheel covers, and J78 × 15 BSW tires. Custom adds: Oxen- and Madrid-grain expanded vinyl notchback seat with fold-down center armrest, door pull straps, and carpeted lower door panels. Limited adds: Lombardy cloth and Madrid-grain vinyl bench seat w/fold-down center armrest (Sedan), Lombardy cloth and Madrid-grain vinyl 60/40 notchback front seat w/fold-down center armrest (Coupe), two-way power seat adjustment, litter container mounted on kick panel, combination dome and reading lamp, electronic digital quartz clock, and wide rocker panel moldings.

Measurements

Wheelbase	127.0"
Length	229.8"
Width	79.3"
Height	54.9"
Legroom — front	42.6"
Legroom — rear	41.3"
Headroom — front	39.3"
Headroom — rear	38.2"
Cargo capacity (cu. ft.)	NA
Fuel capacity (gals.)	NA

Models Available

	Model No.	Base MSRP	Change from LY	Shipping Wt. (lbs.)	Model Year Production	Change from LY
Electra 225 2-Door Hardtop Coupe	T37	$5,260	+9.24%	4607	3,339	-63.80%
Electra 225 4-Door Hardtop Sedan	T39	$5,373	+9.03%	4682	5,750	-66.55%
Electra 225 Custom 2-Dr. Hdtp. Cpe.	V37	$5,438	+8.91%	4627	15,099	-65.94%
Electra 225 Custom 4-Dr. Hdtp. Sdn.	V39	$5,550	+8.72%	4702	29,089	-72.82%
Electra 225 Limited 2-Dr. Hdtp. Cpe.	X37	$5,886	NEW	4682	16,086	NEW
Electra 225 Limited 4-Dr. Hdtp. Sdn.	X39	$5,921	NEW	4732	30,051	NEW
TOTALS		*Avg. price* $5,571	+12.32%		*Production* 99,414	-44.08%

Riviera

"It may just be the ultimate personal luxury car."

Nameplate year of origin: 1963 (1949 as designation for hardtop models).
Current bodystyle lifespan: 1971 through 1976.
Predecessor to this model: Riviera (1966 to 1970).
Replacement for this model: Riviera (1977 to 1978).
Percentage of division's production: 4.07%.
Corporate siblings: Cadillac Eldorado and Oldsmobile Toronado.
Primary competition: Ford Thunderbird.
Notable changes: Revised front and rear styling.
Major standard equipment: Manchester cloth and Madrid-grain vinyl notchback front seat w/fold-down center armrest, cut-pile carpeting, simulated woodgrain appliqué on door panels and I/P, electronic digital quartz clock, tilt steering wheel, light package (ashtray, courtesy, glove compartment and trunk), LH remote-control rear view mirror, dual exhaust, deluxe wheel covers, and J78 × 15 BSW tires.

Measurements

Wheelbase	122.0"
Length	226.4"
Width	80.0"
Height	53.7"
Legroom — front	42.2"
Legroom — rear	35.4"
Headroom — front	38.1"
Headroom — rear	37.1"
Cargo capacity (cu. ft.)	15.1
Fuel capacity (gals.)	NA

Models Available

	Model No.	Base MSRP	Change from LY	Shipping Wt. (lbs.)	Model Year Production	Change from LY
Riviera 2-Door Hardtop	Y87	$5,678	+8.75%	4572	20,129	-40.94%
TOTALS		*Avg. price* $5,678	+8.75%		*Production* 20,129	-40.94%

CADILLAC

"A legend becomes a lifestyle."

While the entire Cadillac line appeared very similar to the previous season, there were many changes to be found. Partially due to the federal safety requirements, all models received new rear end treatments and front-end design modifications. The Eldorado carried a new fine mesh crosshatch grille and a new header piece mounted above the grille fashioned from brushed aluminum, instantly changing the car's frontal appearance from sporty luxury to classic luxury. All other Cadillac models wore a wider egg-crate style grille flanked by the dual headlamps which were now mounted side-by-side in a chrome bezel with the turn signal/parking lights moved to the outside edges wrapping around the front fenders to include the front cornering lights. Combined with smaller front bumper guards, these changes produced a less cluttered look than in prior years.

Bodysides saw changes to the rear quarter panels on all except the Eldorado. Whereas upper and lower feature lines had previously converged in a point at the center of the rear end the lower line was now eliminated, leaving a remnant of the upper line. The visual effect was to make the already long cars look even longer. At the rear, all models received a similar look this year. Beneath the trunk lid was a pair of slender horizontal taillamps, with backup lights set in the middle. These were placed just above a box-style bumper that met rearward slanting vertical taillamps housed in chrome bezels, which capped the rear quarter panels. It was a well-executed update on the vertical taillamp theme used since 1965, and possibly the best looking of all the new rear bumper systems.

Many changes could be found inside this year's Cadillac line also. All models received a new instrument panel design featuring a flat face covered in simulated woodgrain appliqués and a unique upper level, full-width section set close to the windshield that housed various warning lights, with the Cadillac name in the center. This instrument panel design would become an identifying Cadillac design for the next ten years, even through the downsizing period. Also there were many new upholstery designs, typical of mid-seventies design excess.

Cadillac met safety concerns in a way that few other companies could match this year. Not only did they continue to offer their Track Master electronic skid control system, but they also added an optional airbag restraint system, known as the Air Cushion Restraint System. Developed by General Motors to test public reaction and sales potential, the airbags were one of the first significant attempts to improve passenger safety not otherwise government mandated since Ford Motor Company's 1956 safety campaign.

No changes were made to the model lineup, as could be expected. Cadillac Calais and de Ville 2-door hardtops became 2-door coupes this year with the corporate move toward eliminating the hardtop body style. They were still called two-door hardtops in company sales literature, although they now had a B-pillar that created fixed rear quarter windows. However, the front door glass still remained a frameless design, a precedent set by the 1971 Fleetwood Sixty-Special Brougham and the General Motors 1973 intermediate line. Interestingly, in a year of steep sales decline the Calais 2-door was the only Cadillac model to post a production increase during the 1974 model year, and when combined with Coupe deVille production, they nearly matched 1973 levels. Apparently despite fuel shortages and huge price increases, Cadillac's luxury coupes still maintained a faithful, and wealthy, customer base.

Calais 2-Door Hardtop with
Calais 4-Door Hardtop, rear

Eldorado 2-Door Convertible

Instrument panel

Fleetwood 75 Limousine rear seating area

Sedan deVille 4-Door Hardtop

Fleetwood Sixty-Special Brougham
4-Door Sedan

Model year production: 239,955, down 20.69% from 1973.
Domestic market share: 2.78% (10th place).
Base price range: $7,371 to $13,254.
Cadillac average base price: $9,482, up 19.35%.
Introduction date: September 16, 1973.
Assembly plants: Linden, NJ (E); and Detroit, MI (Q).
  Note: Both plants built the deVille, but all other series were built in Detroit.
Data plate identification (VIN): Thirteen digit code read as follows: First digit indicates division (6 = Cadillac); second through fourth digits indicate series and body style (model number in model charts); fifth digit is engine code (see powertrain chart); sixth digit indicates model year (4 = 1974); seventh digit indicates assembly plant (see list above); remaining digits are sequential with beginning number of 100001 (all but Eldorado); and 400001 (Eldorado). *Example:* 6D49R4Q100001 is a 1974 Cadillac Sedan deVille 4-Door Hardtop, with 472 CID, 4-bbl. V8 engine, serial number 100001, built in Detroit, MI.

Powertrains

Engine	Net HP	Engine Code	Transmission Availability[1]		Calais & deVille	Fleetwood Brougham	Fleetwood Seventy-Five	Eldorado
472 CID (7.8L), 4-bbl., V8	205	R	3-speed Turbo Hydra-matic		S	S	S	—
				MPG:	8.9	8.9	8.7	—

Engine	Net HP	Engine Code	Transmission Availability[1]	Calais & deVille	Fleetwood Brougham	Fleetwood Seventy-Five	Eldorado
500 CID (8.2L), 4-bbl., V8	210	S	3-speed Turbo Hydra-matic	—	—	—	S
			MPG:	—	—	—	10.4

Major Options

	Calais	deVille	Eldorado	Fleetwood Brougham	Fleetwood Seventy-Five
Automatic climate control	$523	$523	$523	$523	S
Electric rear window defogger	$62	$62	$62	$62	S
Controlled cycle windshield wiper	$25	$25	$25	$25	$25
Tilt and telescope steering wheel	$92	$92	$92	$92	$92
GM Air Cushion Restraint System	$225	$225	$225[1]	$225	—
Cruise control	$92	$92	$92	$92	$92
Twilight Sentinel	$49	$49	$49	$49	S
Soft Ray tinted glass	$57	$57	$57	$57	$57
Leather upholstery[2]	—	$169	$179	$169	—
Dual Comfort front seat	—	$103	$103	S	—
Power front seat, 2-way	$26	S	S	S[3]	S
Power front seat, 6-way bench	$115	$89	$89	—	—
Power front seat, 6-way Dual Comfort, driver/passenger	—	$89/$115	$89/$115	$89/$115	—
Lighted vanity mirror[4]	$43	$43	$43	$43	$43
Power door locks	$69	$69	$69	$69	$115
AM/FM stereo, signal seeking	$340	$340	$340	$340	$430[5]
AM/FM stereo w/8-track tape	$426	$426	$426	$426	$426
Remote control trunk release/lock	$56	$56	$56	$56	$56
Padded vinyl top	$152	$152	$157	S	$741
Electric sunroof[6]	$610	$610	$610	$610	—
Lamp monitor system	$48	$48	$48	$48	$48
Special wheel discs	$40	$40	—	$40	$40
Steel-belted radial WSW tires	$156	$156	$156	$156	$162
Airbag restraint system[7]	$225	$225	$225	$225	—
Track Master anti-skid control	$205	$205	$205	$205	$205
Automatic level control	$78	$78	$78	$78	$78

Popular Option Groups & Packages

	Calais	deVille	Eldorado	Fleetwood Brougham	Fleetwood Seventy-Five
Brougham d'Elegance package	—	—	—	$750	$[8]
Custom Cabriolet package, coupe	—	$210	$385	—	—
de Ville d'Elegance package	—	$300[9]	—	—	—
Fleetwood Talisman package	—	—	—	$1,800	—

—= Not Available; S = Standard equipment. All radios include rear seat speaker and power antenna. [1]Not available on convertible. [2]Standard on Eldorado convertible. Available on Calais and Seventy-Five by special order only. [3]Driver side only. [4]Price is for one side (driver or passenger) only. Not available on driver's side of Eldorado convertible. [5]Fleetwood Seventy-Five models include rear seat controls. [6]Requires vinyl top. [7]Not available on Eldorado convertible. [8]Available on special order only. [9]Coupe price listed. Sedan is $355.

Paint Colors

	Code		Code		Code
Cotillion White	11	Jasper Green	44	Regal Blue Firemist metallic*	92
Georgian Silver metallic	13	Pinehurst Green metallic	49	Victorian Amber Firemist metallic*	94
Deauville Gray metallic	18	Promenade Gold metallic	54	Pharaoh Gold Firemist metallic*	95
Sable Black	19	Apollo Yellow	57	Persian Lime Firemist metallic*	96
Antigua Blue metallic	24	Canyon Amber	59	Terra Cotta Firemist metallic*	98
Diplomat Blue metallic	29	Conestoga Tan	63	Cranberry Firemist metallic*	99
Lido Green metallic	30	Chesterfield Brown metallic	69		
Mandarin Orange metallic	34	Andes Copper metallic	71	*Firemist paint available for $128 extra.	
Pueblo Beige metallic	38	Dynasty Red	72		

Calais

"Most attractive values.... The Calais.

Nameplate year of origin: 1965.
Current bodystyle lifespan: 1971 through 1976.
Predecessor to this model: Calais (1969 to 1970).
Replacement for this model: None.
Percentage of division's production: 2.82%.
Corporate siblings: Buick Electra 225, Cadillac deVille, and Oldsmobile 98.
Primary competition: Chrysler New Yorker Brougham and Oldsmobile 98 Regency.
Notable changes: Revised front and rear-end styling and minor trim and detail changes.
Major standard equipment: Mimosa cloth w/vinyl bolsters or expanded vinyl front bench seat w/fold-down center armrest, door pull assist straps, electric clock, cigar lighter (2 in front), power windows, LH remote-control rear view mirror, front cornering lights, rear wheel fender skirts, wheel opening moldings, full wheel covers, and L78 × 15 BSW tires.

Measurements

Wheelbase	130.0"
Length	230.7"
Width	79.8"
Height	55.5"
Legroom — front	42.0"
Legroom — rear	NA
Headroom — front	39.2"
Headroom — rear	38.2"
Cargo capacity (cu. ft.)	19.3
Fuel capacity (gals.)	27.0

Models Available

	Model No.	Base MSRP	Change from LY	Shipping Wt. (lbs.)	Model Year Production	Change from LY
Calais 2-Door Hardtop Coupe	C47	$7,371	+25.66%	4900	4,449	+5.88%
Calais 4-Door Hardtop	C49	$7,545	+24.96%	4979	2,324	-38.81%
TOTALS		Avg. price $7,458	+25.30%		Production 6,773	-15.34%

deVille

"The luxury cars enjoyed by more motorists than any others."

Nameplate year of origin: 1959 (series); 1949 (as Hardtop designation).
Current bodystyle lifespan: 1971 through 1976.
Predecessor to this model: deVille (1969 to 1970).
Replacement for this model: deVille (1977 to 1984).
Percentage of division's production: 71.94%.
Corporate siblings: Buick Electra 225, Cadillac Calais, and Oldsmobile 98.
Primary competition: Chrysler Imperial and Lincoln Continental.
Notable changes: Revised front-end styling, and trim and detail changes.
Major standard equipment: Maharajah cloth w/vinyl bolsters and front seat center armrest, 2-way power front seat adjuster, cut-pile carpeting, door pull assist straps, courtesy lights, courtesy lamp/assist strap combination on B-pillar of 2-doors, electric clock, cigar lighters (2 front & 2 rear), power windows, LH remote-control rear view mirror, front cornering lights, rear wheel fender skirts, wheel opening moldings, rocker panel moldings, full wheel covers, and L78 × 15 BSW tires.

Measurements

Wheelbase	130.0"
Length	230.7"
Width	79.8"
Height	55.5"
Legroom — front	42.0"
Legroom — rear	NA
Headroom — front	39.2"
Headroom — rear	38.2"
Cargo capacity (cu. ft.)	19.3
Fuel capacity (gals.)	27.0

Models Available

	Model No.	Base MSRP	Change from LY	Shipping Wt. (lbs.)	Model Year Production	Change from LY
Coupe deVille 2-Door Hardtop	D47	$7,867	+25.51%	4924	112,201	-0.57%
Sedan deVille 4-Door Hardtop	D49	$8,100	+24.62%	5032	60,419	-41.56%
TOTALS		Avg. price $7,984	+25.05%		Production 172,620	-20.17%

Eldorado

"Our most elegant personal cars.
Including America's only luxury convertible."

Nameplate year of origin: 1953.
Current bodystyle lifespan: 1971 through 1978.
Predecessor to this model: Fleetwood Eldorado (1967 to 1970).
Replacement for this model: Eldorado (1979 to 1985).
Percentage of division's production: 16.84%.
Corporate siblings: Buick Riviera and Oldsmobile Toronado.
Primary competition: Lincoln Continental Mark IV.
Notable changes: New grille and minor trim and detail changes.
Major standard equipment: Mohawk fabric w/Meridian fabric bolster upholstered front bench seat w/fold-down center armrest (hardtop), Sierra grain leather front bench seat w/fold-down center armrest (convertible), 2-way power seat adjuster, cut-pile carpeting, door pull assist straps, courtesy lights, quartz digital clock, cigar lighters (2 front & 2 rear), power windows, LH remote-control rear view mirror, front cornering lights, rear wheel fender skirts, wheel opening moldings, rocker panel moldings, full wheel covers, and L78 × 15 BSW tires.

Measurements

Wheelbase	126.3"
Length	224.1"
Width	79.8"
Height	NA
Legroom — front	43.0"
Legroom — rear	NA
Headroom — front	38.1"
Headroom — rear	37.1"
Cargo capacity (cu. ft.)	NA
Fuel capacity (gals.)	27.0

Models Available

	Model No.	Base MSRP	Change from LY	Shipping Wt. (lbs.)	Model Year Production	Change from LY
Eldorado 2-Door Hardtop	L47	$9,110	+23.78%	4960	32,812	-22.13%
Eldorado 2-Door Convertible	L67	$9,437	+22.86%	5019	7,600	-18.41%
TOTALS		Avg. price $9,274	+23.31%		Production 40,412	-21.46%

Fleetwood Sixty-Special Brougham

"Cadillac in the grand manner."

Nameplate year of origin: 1938.
Current bodystyle lifespan: 1971 through 1976.
Predecessor to this model: Fleetwood Sixty-Special (1969 to 1970).
Replacement for this model: Fleetwood Brougham (1977 to 1984).
Percentage of division's sales volume: 7.61%.
Corporate siblings: None.
Primary competition: None.
Notable changes: Revised front and rear-end styling, and trim and detail changes.
Major standard equipment: Morocco matelasse[1] or Sierra grain leather dual comfort front seat, driver side 2-way power seat adjuster, front and rear seat fold-down center armrests, cut-pile carpeting, rear seat carpeted foot rests, door pull assist straps, front passenger reading light, courtesy lights, quartz digital clock, cigar lighters (2 front & 2 rear), power windows, LH remote-control rear view mirror, padded vinyl roof, front cornering lights, rear wheel fender skirts, wheel opening moldings, rocker panel moldings w/upper ridge, full wheel covers, and L78 × 15 BSW tires.

[1]Matelasse is a French word meaning quilted, padded or cushioned. Usually refers to hand-quilted fabrics.

Measurements

Wheelbase	133.0"
Length	233.7"
Width	79.8"
Height	55.5"
Legroom — front	42.0"
Legroom — rear	NA
Headroom — front	39.3"
Headroom — rear	38.3"
Cargo capacity (cu. ft.)	19.3
Fuel capacity (gals.)	27.0

Models Available

	Model No.	Base MSRP	Change from LY	Shipping Wt. (lbs.)	Model Year Production	Change from LY
Fltwd. Sixty-Special Brougham 4-Dr. Sedan	B69	$9,537	+22.82%	5143	18,250	-26.41%
TOTALS		Avg. price $9,537	+22.82%		Production 18,250	-26.41%

Fleetwood Seventy-Five

"The flagships.... The Seventy-Fives."

Nameplate year of origin: 1927 (models using Fleetwood bodies); 1935 (75 series).
Current bodystyle lifespan: 1971 through 1976.
Predecessor to this model: Fleetwood Seventy-Five (1969 to 1970).
Replacement for this model: Fleetwood Limousine (1977 to 1984).
Percentage of division's sales volume: 0.79%.
Corporate siblings: None.
Primary competition: None.
Notable changes: Revised front and rear-end styling and trim and detail changes.
Major standard equipment: Potomac grey cord fabric upholstery (Medici crushed velour upholstery available), 2-way power front seat adjuster, front and back seat fold-down center armrests, cut-pile carpeting, full-width folding seats (rearward facing for three additional passengers), rear seat carpeted foot rests, door pull assist straps, dual automatic climate control system (front and rear), courtesy lights, electric clock, cigar lighters (2 front & 4 rear), passenger control panel (controls power windows, reading lights, rear automatic climate control system, and the glass partition in the Limousine), automatic level control, LH and RH remote-control rear view mirror, front cornering lights, rear wheel fender skirts, wheel opening moldings, full-length rocker panel moldings, full wheel covers, and L78 × 15 BSW tires.

Measurements

Wheelbase	151.5"
Length	252.2"
Width	80.0"
Height	NA
Legroom — front	NA
Legroom — rear	NA
Headroom — front	NA
Headroom — rear	NA
Cargo capacity (cu. ft.)	NA
Fuel capacity (gals.)	27.0

Models Available

	Model No.	Base MSRP	Change from LY	Shipping Wt. (lbs.)	Model Year Production	Change from LY
Fltwd. Seventy-Five 4-Door Sedan, 9-p.	F23	$13,120	+9.81%	5719	895	-12.00%
Fltwd. Seventy-Five 4-Door Limousine	F33	$13,254	+9.72%	5883	1,005	-3.64%
TOTALS		*Avg. price* $13,187	+9.76%		*Production* 1,900	-7.77%

CHEVROLET

"Building a better way to see the U.S.A."

The 1974 model year found Chevrolet focusing on refinement, on meeting the challenges of new federal safety standards, and on meeting the sudden demand for cars with outstanding fuel economy. Fortunately for Chevy, they had several four- and six-cylinder models that offered better fuel economy than some of their competitors. The Vega's engine problems on earlier models continued to mount but were mostly resolved by the time the new models were introduced, and Vega sales would continue to climb. All models except the Nova had new or revised rear styling to meet the federal rear bumper standards, while the Vega and Camaro had new front end styling to provide better crash protection. Despite the Vega's bad press, the ongoing fuel crisis, and the ensuing economic recession, Chevrolet had an extremely good year with the "value" division of General Motors ending the year

holding more than 26 percent of the U.S. market and out-selling the combined total of its four GM stablemates.

The only major restyling of the Vega during the nameplate's lifetime occurred for the 1974 model year. Since slender blade-type bumpers, used by both the Vega and Camaro last year, were no longer able to meet federal requirements, a new box-style front bumper was employed. A new sloping grille covered the extended area created by the front bumper's energy absorbing struts. The new look included a slotted grille, divided down the middle with four slots per side. At the outer end of the slots was a vertically mounted rectangular parking/turn signal light. To complement the new front, a redesigned rear panel carried round cornered square taillights, with the backup light set in the lower portion, for both notchback coupes and hatchbacks. Wagons continued to have a vertical taillamp, while all three body styles employed a new box style rear bumper. The new bumpers were the industry's first chromed aluminum units, to save weight. Another change for the season was that the LX notchback and Kammback Estate wagon officially became models, rather than option packages, although they did not receive their own model numbers. The GT option was now available on the Estate wagon as well as the hatchback and Kammback wagon. While Vega sales continued to increase, its primary competitor, the Ford Pinto, continued to outsell it.

As already mentioned, the Camaro also received a new front end, for reasons similar to those on the Vega. Camaro models received a sloping front end with a box style bumper, but used a chrome-lined crosshatch grille with a slight point, or "V" shape. The grille, fourteen columns across and eight rows high, carried a red, white and blue ribbon logo at the center. Between the semi-tunneled headlights and the new grille were round parking/turn signal lights. Below the bumper was an additional air inlet opening that was the width of the upper grille, and had chrome trim around the opening. The main portion of the car's body and interior was unchanged, but a new rear fascia included wrap-around taillights and a center-mounted license tag covering the fuel filler. The taillights were mounted in a chrome bezel, and on the LT model a chrome strip ran between the top and bottom edges across the rear panel. The Z28 performance option was discontinued at the end of the model year because of poor gas mileage and falling sales, but it would return after a brief hiatus. In 1974 13,802 Camaros were sold with the Z28 option.

Despite having added two new corporate siblings to compete with for 1973, the Nova continued a sales increase. After the makeover of the 1973 models, there were no significant changes for 1974. The most noticeable change was the new placement of the Chevrolet bowtie emblem; formerly a small appendage after the Nova name on the right side front edge of the hood, it was now a large emblem at the center of the grille. The Nova SS sported new stripes on the hood and decklid, instead of on the bodysides, and oversized "Nova SS" decals on the front fenders behind the wheel opening molding. The sporty package was now offered on all Nova or Nova Custom coupes and hatchbacks.

Mid-size Chevelle models introduced a realigned naming structure. The base Chevelle Deluxe was discontinued, and a newly named Malibu Classic took over the "luxury" spot of the one-year-only Laguna series. But the Laguna name continued on a new sporty model carrying the '73 Laguna urethane-covered front-end design, and adding the suffix "Type S-3," which in theory took the place of the discontinued SS option. With the Chevelle name gone from all models, many people believe that Malibu was now the official name of Chevy's mid-size line, but in fact the Chevelle name

continued to be the identifying name of the line and appeared on the lower front corner of the grille on all models, in script on Malibus and in block letters on the Laguna Type S-3. In fact, the Chevelle name would continue to identify the mid-size line through the current body style's lifespan, which would end in 1977.

All Chevelle models received a front end freshening, while all except station wagons introduced a new rear panel and bumper design. For Malibu models a new grille sans the extensions below the headlights was used, with large chrome trim covering the sides and top of the raised center section of the header panel. The grille itself was divided into six sections with a center vertical bar and three horizontal bars, each of the sections having an intricate egg-crate grille insert. On Malibu models the insert was argent colored, and on Malibu Classic, the insert had chrome edging. For the new Laguna coupe, a grille opening similar to the 1973 Laguna's was used, being rectangular in shape with rounded corners. The grille was an egg-crate design six rows high and twenty-two columns across, with a horizontal chrome center bar, a "Laguna S-3" name badge in the center of the bar, and square parking/turn signal lights mounted near the ends of the bar. Around back, all coupes and sedans had new horizontally mounted rectangular taillights with rounded corners and the backup light contained within the center of the lens, while all wagons had new horizontal rectangular taillights. The rear bumper was flattened out as the license plate mounting moved from the center of the bumper to the center of the body colored rear panel. Interior changes were mostly related to new cloth and vinyl trim designs, and there were no significant powertrain changes.

Chevy's luxury/sport coupe, the Monte Carlo, gained a new grille, rear bumper and taillight design, but few other changes. The Monte's new grille was a larger-opening egg-crate design, three rows high and twenty-two columns across, with an additional single row set in the oval shaped openings of the front bumper, directly below the grille. The Monte Carlo emblem, formerly placed in the middle of the grille, moved to the center of the header panel directly above the grille, and the script Monte Carlo name, which had appeared on the header above the grille, moved down onto the chrome grille surround. At the back end, new taillight lenses had a small chrome paint stripe around the outer edge and a Monte Carlo emblem set into the center, but remained in the same spot with no additional trim. In line with the new rear bumper requirements, the license plate mounting was moved above the bumper, causing the rear panel to be changed and the decklid opening to be raised. Backup lights were also moved out of the bumper, to a place on each side of the license plate opening on the rear panel. The Landau coupe and Monte Carlo S added for 1973 continued to be available, but the Monte Carlo base model was discontinued. The base model was really a de-contented Monte Carlo destined to give the line a lower entry price on the redesigned car and not necessarily a sales leader. Therefore, it no longer had a purpose in the line, as the S was far and away the sales leader, with the Landau not far behind.

Full-size Chevrolets also presented a new face this year, along with revised rear end styling to accommodate new bumpers and new taillamps that still retained the distinguishing two taillights for Bel Airs and three lights for Impala and Caprice models. The front header panel retained the same basic configuration as in 1973, but the grille extended lower by a few inches, necessitating a new front bumper that dipped slightly through the center section. On the newly named Caprice Classic models, the dual headlights were set into their own bezels to the outer edges next to the pointed fender end caps, and vertical parking/turn signal lights were mounted to the inside of the headlights. A small body color strip separated the parking lights and the grille. The Caprice grille had twelve vertical sections across, all being chrome lined, and each housing vertical crosshatch inserts four columns wide and seven rows high. An additional chrome piece ran around the front fender edge from the bodyside molding and underneath the taillights to the grille. A thicker bar above the grille had the Caprice ornament centered at the top. Bel Air and Impala models used a shorter horizontal crosshatch grille, twelve columns wide and eight rows tall, with chrome-lined extensions on each side housing the dual headlights and parking/turn signal lights mounted in a vertical wrap-around lens on the fender end. Around back a box-style bumper was introduced, with a new rear panel carrying the two- or three-section horizontal taillights. Backup lights were placed within the center of the second light from the outside edge. Slightly enlarged rear quarter end caps gave the new rear design a concave look.

Also new on the big Chevrolets was a new greenhouse design for the coupes. The Caprice and Impala Custom used a new upright B-pillar with a large fixed rear quarter window in combination with the large concave rear window of the prior three years. The Impala Sport Coupe did away with the rounded style rear window and roofline, which was still used on the four-door models, and instead had a flat rear window and a roofline angled similarly to the Custom Coupe. It also used the same rear quarter window design as on the 1973 Impala Custom Coupe instead of the rounded version used on the Sport Coupe from 1971 through 1973. One other exterior change was that rear fender skirts were now available as an option on Impala and Bel Air, except station wagons, but were still standard on the Caprice. Also, the inline six-cylinder engine was no longer offered, making 1974 the first year that only V8 engines were offered in full-size Chevys. But it was only a temporary change, as the six-cylinder would return for 1977.

America's only home-built sports car, the Corvette, gained a new urethane rear end treatment, thereby completely eliminating traditional chrome bumpers. The new rear design added a slanting rear panel that placed the taillights in frenched circular pods and came to a point at the level where the chrome bumper would have been on last year's model. Below the point, the rear panel tucked under slightly, and then turned downward to form a flat panel, which housed the license tag in the center. Exhaust outlets exited under the panel. There were not any other significant changes.

Finally, a unique option for 1974 was the "Spirit of America" limited edition coupe models that were introduced to celebrate the United States of America's upcoming bicentennial. Although it was two years early, many companies were jumping on the bandwagon ahead of time, so it was not that unusual for the time. Sporting white exteriors with red and blue trim, the option was available on the Impala Sport Coupe, Nova Custom coupe, and Vega hatchback. Complete details of the package contents are listed in Appendix IV. Production for the Vega and Impala editions are not available, but production totaled 14,463 for the Nova with the limited edition package, which is suspected to have been the most popular of the three models.

Bel Air 4-Door Station Wagon

Camaro 2-Door Coupe with Z28 package

Camaro Type LT 2-Door Coupe

Caprice Classic 2-Door Convertible

Chevelle Laguna Type S-3
2-Door Colonnade Hardtop Coupe

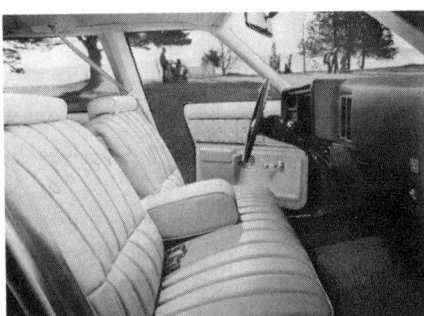

Chevelle Malibu Classic Estate interior

Impala Sport Coupe 2-Door Hardtop
with Spirit of America option

Monte Carlo S 2-Door Hardtop Coupe

Nova 2-Door Coupe with SS package

Caprice Classic 2-Door Convertible

Chevelle Malibu Classic
2-Door Colonnade Hardtop Coupe

Corvette Stingray 2-Door Convertible

Impala 4-Door Sedan

Monte Carlo Landau 2-Door Hardtop Coupe

Nova Custom 4-Door Sedan

Caprice Classic 2-Door Hardtop

Chevelle Malibu Classic Estate
4-Door Station Wagon

Corvette Stingray 2-Door Coupe

Impala Station Wagon
Glide-Away tailgate operation

Nova 2-Door Hatchback Coupe
with Spirit of America option

Vega 2-Door Hatchback Coupe
with Spirit of America option

Vega 2-Door Notchback Coupe

Model year production: 2,305,728, down 10.61% from 1973.
Domestic market share: 26.68% (1st place).
Base price range: $2,380 to $6,002.
Chevrolet average base price: $3,635, up 5.52%.
Introduction date: September 22, 1973.
Assembly plants: Lakewood, GA (A); Baltimore, MD (B); Southgate, CA (C); Doraville, GA (D); Framingham, MA (G); Janesville, WI (J); Kansas City/Leeds, MO (K); Van Nuys, CA (L); Norwood, OH (N); Arlington, TX (R); St. Louis, MO (S); Tarrytown, NY (T); Lordstown, OH (U); Willow Run, MI (W); Wilmington, DE (Y); Fremont, CA (Z); Oshawa, Ontario, Canada (1); and Ste. Therese, Quebec, Canada (2).

Data plate identification (VIN): Thirteen digit code read as follows: First digit indicates division (1 = Chevrolet); second through fourth digits indicate series and body style (model number in model charts); fifth digit is engine code (see powertrain chart); sixth digit indicates model year (4 = 1974); seventh digit indicates assembly plant (see list above); remaining digits are sequential with beginning number of 100001, except Chevelle, Monte Carlo and Corvette which start at 400001. *Example:* 1S87H4N100001 is a 1974 Chevrolet Camaro Type LT 2-Door Sport Coupe, with 350 CID, 2-bbl. V8 engine, serial number 100001, built in Norwood, OH.

Powertrains

Engine	Net HP	Engine Code	Transmission Availability[1]		Vega	Nova	Camaro	Chevelle Malibu[2]	Laguna & Monte Carlo	Full-Size Chevy	Corvette
140 CID (2.3L) OHC, 1-bbl., 4-cyl.	75	A	3-speed manual		S	—	—	—	—	—	—
				MPG:	24.6	—	—	—	—	—	—
			4-speed manual		$51	—	—	—	—	—	—
				MPG:	18.1	—	—	—	—	—	—
			3-speed Turbo Hydra-matic		$193	—	—	—	—	—	—
				MPG:	19.6	—	—	—	—	—	—
140 CID (2.3L) OHC, 2-bbl., 4-cyl.	85	B	3-speed manual		$41	—	—	—	—	—	—
				MPG:	NA	—	—	—	—	—	—
			4-speed manual		$92	—	—	—	—	—	—
				MPG:	19.4	—	—	—	—	—	—
			3-speed Turbo Hydra-matic		$234	—	—	—	—	—	—
				MPG:	19.4	—	—	—	—	—	—
250 CID (4.1L) Turbo-Thrift, 1-bbl., 6-cyl.	100	D	3-speed manual		—	—	S	S (ex. LT)	S (Mcs)	—	—
				MPG:	—	—	NA	NA	NA	—	—
			3-speed Turbo Hydra-matic		—	—	$200	$210 (ex. LT)	S (MCcs)/ $210 (Mcs)	—	—
				MPG:	—	—	15.4	15.2	15.7	—	—
350 CID (5.7L) Turbo-Fire, 2-bbl., V8[3]	145	H	3-speed manual		—	$108	S (LT)/ $112 (ex. LT)	S (Mw)/ $142 (Mcs)	S	—	—
				MPG:	—	NA	NA	NA	NA	—	—
			4-speed manual		—	—	$200 (LT)/ $312 (ex. LT)	—	—	—	—
				MPG:	—	—	NA	—	—	—	—

Engine	Net HP	Engine Code	Transmission Availability[1]		Vega	Nova	Camaro	Chevelle Malibu[2]	Laguna & Monte Carlo	Full-Size Chevy	Corvette
			3-speed Turbo Hydra-matic		—	$308	$210 (LT)/ $322 (ex. LT)	S (MCw)/ $142 (MCcs)/ $210 (Mw)/ $352 (Mcs)	$210	S (ex. Caprice & Wagons)	—
				MPG:	—	9.9	NA	9.9	9.9	10.1	—
350 CID (5.7L) Turbo-Fire, 4-bbl., V8[4]	160	K	3-speed manual		—	$184	$76 (LT)/ $188 (ex. LT)	—	—	—	—
				MPG:	—	NA	NA	—	—	—	—
			4-speed manual		—	$374	$276 (LT)/ $388 (ex. LT)	—	—	—	—
				MPG:	—	8.9	NA	—	—	—	—
			3-speed Turbo Hydra-matic		—	$384	$286 (LT)/ $398 (ex. LT)	—	—	—	—
				MPG:	—	9.9	9.8	—	—	—	—
350 CID (5.7L) Turbo-Fire, 4-bbl., V8[4]	185	L	3-speed manual		—	$184	$76 (LT)/ $188 (ex. LT)	—	—	—	—
				MPG:	—	NA	NA	—	—	—	—
			4-speed manual		—	$374	$276 (LT)/ $388 (ex. LT)	—	—	—	—
				MPG:	—	8.9	NA	—	—	—	—
			3-speed Turbo Hydra-matic		—	$384	$286 (LT)/ $398 (ex. LT)	—	—	—	—
				MPG:	—	9.9	9.8	—	—	—	—
350 CID (5.7L) Turbo-Fire, 4-bbl., V8	195	J	4-speed manual		—	—	—	—	—	—	S
				MPG:	—	—	—	—	—	—	NA
			3-speed Turbo Hydra-matic		—	—	—	—	—	—	NC
				MPG:	—	—	—	—	—	—	NA
350 CID (5.7L) Turbo-Fire Special, 4-bbl., V8	245/ 250[5]	T	4-speed manual		—	—	S[6]	—	—	—	$299
				MPG:	—	—	NA	—	—	—	NA
			4-speed manual, close-ratio		—	—	$200[6]	—	—	—	$299
				MPG:	—	—	NA	—	—	—	13.0
			3-speed Turbo Hydra-matic		—	—	$297[6]	—	—	—	$396
				MPG:	—	—	NA	—	—	—	13.0
400 CID (6.6L) Turbo-Fire, 2-bbl., V8	150	R	3-speed Turbo Hydra-matic		—	—	—	$51 (MCw)/ $193 (MCcs)/ $260 (Mw)/ $403 (Mcs)	$260	S (Caprice)/ $51 (others ex. wgns.)	—
				MPG:	—	—	—	8.8	8.8	8.8	—
400 CID (6.6L) Turbo-Fire, 4-bbl., V8	180	U	3-speed Turbo Hydra-matic		—	—	—	—	—	S (Wagons)	—
				MPG:	—	—	—	—	—	9.6	—
454 CID (7.4L) Turbo-Jet, 4-bbl., V8	235	Y	4-speed manual		—	—	—	$331 (MCc)/ $543 (Mc)	$399	—	—
				MPG:	—	—	—	NA	NA	—	—
			3-speed Turbo Hydra-matic		—	—	—	$231 (MCw)/ $351 (MCcs)/	$440	$134 (wgns.)/ $180	—

Engine	Net HP	Engine Code	Transmission Availability[1]	Vega	Nova	Camaro	Chevelle Malibu[2] $440 (Mw)/ $563 (Mcs)	Laguna & Monte Carlo	Full-Size Chevy (Caprice)/ $231 (others)	Corvette
			MPG:	—	—	—	8.6	8.6	9.6	—
454 CID (7.4L) Turbo-Jet, 4-bbl., V8	270	Z	4-speed manual	—	—	—	—	—	—	$250
			MPG:	—	—	—	—	—	—	NA
			4-speed manual, close-ratio	—	—	—	—	—	—	$250
			MPG:	—	—	—	—	—	—	NA
			3-speed Turbo Hydra-matic	—	—	—	—	—	—	$347
			MPG:	—	—	—	—	—	—	NA

[1]Unless otherwise specified: All 3-speed manuals are column shift. All 4-speed manuals are floor shift. All automatics are column shift, except on Vega, Camaro and Corvette. Floor shift automatic is optional on Nova, Chevelle and Monte Carlo with other specified equipment at extra cost. [2]Mc = Malibu coupe; Mcs = Malibu coupe & sedan; Mw = Malibu wagons; MCc = Malibu Classic coupe; MCcs = Malibu Classic coupe & sedan; MCw = Malibu Classic wagons. [3]Not available in California. [4]Available only in California. [5]Horsepower rating on Corvette. [6]Available only with Z28 option.

Major Options

	Vega	Camaro	Nova	Chevelle	Monte Carlo	Full-size Chevy	Corvette
Four-season air conditioning[1]	$349	$397	$381	$397	$397	$405	$452
Comfortilt steering wheel	—	$44	$44	$44	$44	$44	S
Tilt-and-telescope steering wheel	—	—	—	—	—	—	$82
Cruise-Master speed control	—	—	—	—	$62	$62	—
Rear window defogger[2]	$52	$31	$31	$31	$31	$31	$41
Dual sport mirrors, LH remote	—	$26	—	$26	$26	—	—
Soft-Ray tinted glass, all windows	$36	$39	$39	$42	$45	$49	S
Power windows, 2-dr./4-dr.	—	$75[3]	—	$75/$113[4]	$75	$82/ $124[4]	$83
Power door locks, 2-dr./4-dr.	—	—	—	$45/$69	$45	$45/$69	—
Power front seat, w/std. seat	—	—	—	$103[5]	$103	$103[5]	—
Front bucket seats, w/console[6]	S	$57	$57	$190	$190	—	S
Rear facing third seat, wagons	—	—	—	$133	—	—	—
AM radio	$59	$65	$65	$65	$65	$65	$65
AM/FM stereo	—	$233	$233	$233	$233	$233	$276
AM/FM stereo w/8-track tape	—	—	—	$363	$363	$363	—
Vinyl top, full	$75[7]	$87	$82	$92[7]	$123	$106[8]	$62[9]
Vinyl top, landau[10]	—	—	—	—	$123	—	—
Sky Roof (sunroof), power[11]	—	—	$	$325	$325	—	—
Power steering, variable-ratio	$92	$113[12]	$100	$113[13]	S	S	$113
Power brakes, w/front disc	—	$46	$68	$46[14]	S	S	$46[15]
Custom or Deluxe wheel covers	—	$26	$26	$26	S	S	$60
Wire wheel covers	—	$82	—	$82	$68	$82	—
Rally wheels w/trim rings	$26	$44	$44	$44	$30	—	S
Turbine I wheels	—	$111	—	$111	—	—	—
Turbine II aluminum wheels	—	—	—	—	$98	—	—
WSW tires	$26	$28	$28	$30	$30	$32	$32

Popular Option Groups & Packages

	Vega	Camaro	Nova	Chevelle	Monte Carlo	Full-size Chevy	Corvette
Auxiliary lighting package	—	$18	$18	$24	$21	$17	—
Custom interior package	$125	—	—	—	—	—	$154
Custom exterior package	$77	—	—	—	—	—	—
Décor group	$26	—	—	—	—	—	—
Exterior décor package	—	—	$59	$34	—	—	—
F40/41 Suspension Package[16]	$129	$30	$30	$17	$17	$17	—
GT package	$353	—	—	—	—	—	—
Interior décor/Quiet sound group	—	$35	$87	—	—	$44	—

	Vega	Camaro	Nova	Chevelle	Monte Carlo	Full-size Chevy	Corvette
Off Road package (incl. FE7 Gymkhana pkg., a $7 option)	—	—	—	—	—	—	$400
Special instrumentation package	$62	$82	—	$82	$67	—	S
Spirit of America package	$	—	$399	—	—	$399	—
Sports décor package	$82	—	—	—	—	—	—
SS package	—	—	$136	—	—	—	—
Style trim group	—	$52	—	—	—	—	—
Z28 special equipment package	—	$572[17]	—	—	—	—	—

— = Not Available; S = Standard equipment. [1]Requires V8 engine on Chevelle, Camaro and Nova. Comfortron air conditioning with automatic temperature control is available for $482 on Bel Air, Impala and Caprice. [2]Blower type defogger. "Electro-Clear" wire type on Vega. [3]Other select equipment required. [4]Power windows not available on Bel Air or Malibu. Price for power windows on Impala Sport coupe and Caprice convertible is the same as for four-door models. [5]Power seat not available on Bel Air, Malibu or Laguna. [6]Bucket seats standard on Vega and Camaro, with console being optional on Camaro. Swivel bucket seats available on Chevelle Malibu, Malibu Classic and Monte Carlo. [7]Not available on station wagon. [8]Price is $138 on full-size Chevrolet wagons. [9]Requires optional removable top at $267 extra on Corvette convertible. [10]Standard on Monte Carlo Landau coupe, Malibu Classic Landau coupe, and Vega LX Notchback. [11]Power operated available only on coupe models. Sky Roof pull-back vinyl sunroof opening on Nova two-door models only. [12]Standard with V8. [13]Standard on Laguna Type S-3. [14]Standard on station wagons. [15]Power front and rear disc brakes. [16]F41 on Camaro and Nova. Vega has front/rear stabilizers, A70/13B WL tires, and 13x6" wheels. [17]Z28 package on LT is $502.

Paint Colors

	Code		Code		Code
Classic White[1]	10	Bright Green metallic[3,5]	46	Dark Taupe metallic[2,3,4]	69
Antique White	11	Medium Green metallic[4]	47	Red metallic[6]	74
Silver metallic[1]	13	Dark Green metallic[1]	48	Medium Red[4,5]	75
Corvette Silver Mist metallic[1]	14	Medium Dark Green metallic[3,4,5]	49	Mille Miglia Red[1]	76
Corvette Gray metallic[1]	17	Cream Beige[3,4,5]	50	Corvette Orange metallic[1]	80
Tuxedo Black[2,3]	19	Bright Yellow[4,5]	51	Bright Orange[4]	86
Corvette Medium Blue metallic[1]	22	Light Gold metallic[4,5]	53		
Light Blue metallic[3]	24	Sandstone[3,5]	55	
Medium Blue[4]	25	Corvette Bright Yellow[1]	56	
Bright Blue metallic[3,5]	26	Golden Brown metallic[3,5]	59	
Midnight Blue metallic[3,4,5]	29	Silver metallic	64	
Aqua Blue metallic[3,5]	36	Bronze metallic	66	
Lime Yellow[5]	40	Bright Orange[4]	67	
Medium Green[3]	44	Dark Brown metallic[1]	68	

In two-tone combinations, the first two digits indicate lower color and the next two digits are the upper color. Colors listed with no footnotes are available on all models except Corvette. [1]Available only on Corvette. [2]Available on Laguna Type S-3. [3]Available on Malibu, Malibu Classic, Monte Carlo and full-size Chevrolet models. [4]Available on Vega. [5]Available on Camaro and Nova. [6]Available on all models.

Vega

"The little car that changed the world."

Nameplate year of origin: 1971.

Current bodystyle lifespan: 1971 through 1977 (some models moved to Monza series, continuing through 1979).

Predecessor to this model: Corvair (1965 to 1969).

Replacement for this model: Cavalier (1982 to 1993).

Percentage of division's production: 19.78%.

Corporate siblings: None.

Primary competition: AMC Gremlin, Dodge Colt, and Ford Pinto.

Notable changes: Revised front and rear styling and minor trim and detail changes.

Major standard equipment: Knit vinyl high-back front bucket seats w/foam cushions, sliding seat adjustment for both front seats (driver's side only on Notchback), full-floor carpeting, fold-down rear seat and rear liftgate (Hatchback and Kammback wagon), two-spoke steering wheel, glove box, storage well in driver's door, two-speed wipers w/washers, bright front and rear window moldings, and A78 × 13 BSW tires. Estate Wagon adds: Woodgrain vinyl panels on bodysides and tailgate, and special exterior nameplates. LX adds: Custom Interior trim package, additional sound insulation, bodyside protective moldings, vinyl roof, and full wheel covers.

Measurements

	Coupes	Wagon
Wheelbase	97.0"	97.0"
Length	176.0"	176.0"
Width	65.6"	65.6"
Height	51.9"	52.0"
Legroom — front	42.8"	42.8"
Legroom — rear	28.9"	30.1"
Headroom — front	38.4"	38.5"
Headroom — rear	38.4"	38.3"
Cargo capacity (cu. ft.)	8.7*	50.2
Fuel capacity (gals.)	16.0	16.0

*Hatchback maximum with rear seat down, 27 cu. ft.

Models Available

	Model No.	Base MSRP	Change from LY	Shipping Wt. (lbs.)	Model Year Production	Change from LY
Vega 2-Door Notchback Coupe	V11	$2,380	+14.04%	2369	58,724	+0.51%
Vega LX 2-Door Notchback Coupe	V11	$2,708	NEW	NA	5,996	NEW%
Vega 2-Door Hatchback Coupe	V77	$2,492	+13.69%	2440	276,028	+3.72%
Vega 2-Door Kammback (Wagon)	V15	$2,623	+12.91%	2514	88,248	-14.11%
Vega 2-Door Kammback Estate (Wagon)	V15	$2,851	NEW	NA	27,089	NEW
TOTALS		Avg. price $2,611	+18.64%		Production 456,085	+6.74%

Camaro

"The way it looks is the way it goes. Camaro not only looks quick, sleek and nimble. Camaro is."

Nameplate year of origin: 1967.
Current bodystyle lifespan: 1970 through 1981.
Predecessor to this model: Camaro (1967 to 1969).
Replacement for this model: Camaro (1982 to 1992).
Percentage of division's production: 6.55%.
Corporate siblings: Pontiac Firebird.
Primary competition: AMC Javelin, Dodge Challenger, and Plymouth Barracuda.
Notable changes: Front and rear end restyling and minor trim and detail changes.
Major standard equipment: Choice of mixed-tone cloth-and-vinyl or solid all-vinyl front "Strato" bucket seats, color-keyed cut-pile carpeting, flat black instrument panel facing, four-spoke soft rim sport steering wheel, bright front and rear window moldings, hubcaps, and E78 × 14 BSW tires. Type LT adds: Ribbed cloth or knit vinyl deep contoured front bucket seats, door map pockets, Interior Décor/Quiet Sound group, simulated Meridian walnut woodgrain vinyl accents on I/P cluster, Type LT emblem on steering wheel, special instrumentation package, electric clock, LH remote and RH manual sport mirrors, LT identification on front and rear end panels, bright accent molding on grille, black accented bodyside molding, variable-ratio power steering, and rally wheels.

Measurements

Wheelbase	108.0"
Length	195.4"
Width	74.4"
Height	49.1"
Legroom — front	43.9"
Legroom — rear	29.6"
Headroom — front	37.3"
Headroom — rear	36.0"
Cargo capacity (cu. ft.)	6.7
Fuel capacity (gals.)	18.0

Models Available

	Model No.	Base MSRP	Change from LY	Shipping Wt. (lbs.)	Model Year Production	Change from LY
Camaro 2-Door Sport Coupe	Q87	$2,890	+3.92%	3309	102,045	+58.40%
Camaro Type LT 2-Door Sport Coupe	S87	$3,506	+7.28%	3566	48,963	+51.46%
TOTALS		Avg. price $3,198	+5.74%		Production 151,008	+56.08%

Nova

"Sensibly sized, good looking, low priced, well built. Honesty is the best policy."

Nameplate year of origin: 1962, as top of the line Chevy II model; became series name in 1969.
Current bodystyle lifespan: 1968 through 1974; restyled in 1973.
Predecessor to this model: Chevy II (1966 to 1967).
Replacement for this model: Nova and Concours (1975 to 1979).
Percentage of division's production: 16.94%.
Corporate siblings: Buick Apollo, Oldsmobile Omega, and Pontiac Ventura.

Measurements

	Coupe & HBK	Sedan
Wheelbase	111.0"	111.0"
Length	196.7"	196.7"
Width	72.4"	72.4"
Height	52.5"	53.9"

Primary competition: AMC Hornet, Ford Maverick, and Plymouth Valiant.

Notable changes: Minor trim and detail changes.

Major standard equipment: Choice of patterned cloth-and-vinyl or all-vinyl front bench seat, color-keyed rubber floor covering, vinyl covered door panels, black two-spoke steering wheel and steering column, dual speed wipers w/washers, bright front and rear window moldings, and E78 × 14 BSW tires. Hatchback model adds: Fold-down rear seat. Custom adds: Choice of patterned cloth or all-vinyl front bench seat, color-keyed deep-twist carpeting (includes cargo area on hatchback), 10" wide non-glare rearview mirror, glove compartment light, right front door courtesy light switch, luggage compartment mat, bright roof drip molding, bright parking light and taillight accents, Nova Custom nameplates on front fenders, Interior Décor/Quiet Sound group, front and rear bumper impact strips.

Measurements (cont.)

	Coupe & HBK	Sedan
Legroom — front	41.7"	41.7"
Legroom — rear	33.4"	35.3"
Headroom — front	38.2"	39.5"
Headroom — rear	36.9"	37.3"
Cargo capacity (cu. ft.)	14.6*	13.8
Fuel capacity (gals.)	21.0	21.0

Hatchback maximum with rear seat down, 27.3 cu. ft.

Models Available

	Model No.	Base MSRP	Change from LY	Shipping Wt. (lbs.)	Model Year Production	Change from LY
Nova 2-Door Coupe	X27	$2,646	+11.32%	3150	159,957	+17.77%
Nova 2-Door Hatchback	X17	$2,798	+10.68%	3260	34,349	-23.59%
Nova 4-Door Sedan	X69	$2,677	+11.22%	3192	74,122	+22.96%
Nova Custom 2-Door Coupe	Y27	$2,821	+10.58%	3206	51,027	-12.59%
Nova Custom 2-Door Hatchback	Y17	$2,971	+10.00%	3299	46,284	+0.49%
Nova Custom 4-Door Sedan	Y69	$2,850	+10.47%	3233	24,798	+3.25%
TOTALS		*Avg. price* $2,794	+10.69%		*Production* 390,537	+5.69%

Chevelle

"Welcome to Chevelle, 1974. Our mid-size Chevrolet."

Nameplate year of origin: 1964.

Current bodystyle lifespan: 1973 through 1977.

Predecessor to this model: Chevelle (1968 to 1972).

Replacement for this model: Malibu (1978 to 1983).

Percentage of division's production: 14.25%.

Corporate siblings: Buick Century, Oldsmobile Cutlass, and Pontiac LeMans.

Primary competition: AMC Matador, Ford Torino, and Plymouth Satellite.

Notable changes: New grille, revised rear end, and minor trim and detail changes.

Major standard equipment: Choice of pattern cloth-and-vinyl or all-vinyl front bench seat, color-keyed cut-pile nylon carpeting, black steering wheel and column, bright front and rear window surround moldings, bright rear quarter window molding, hubcaps, and E78 × 14 BSW tires.

Measurements

	Coupes	Sedans	Wagons
Wheelbase	112.0"	116.0"	116.0"
Length	205.3"*	206.9"	216.2"
Width	76.6"	76.6"	76.6"
Height	53.1"	53.8"	55.7"
Legroom — front	42.1"	42.1"	42.1"
Legroom — rear	32.9"	37.0"	36.8"
Headroom — front	37.7"	38.3"	38.8"
Headroom — rear	37.0"	37.5"	39.4"
Cargo capacity (cu. ft.)	15.3	15.3	85.0**
Fuel capacity (gals.)	22.0	22.0	22.0

Overall length of Laguna Type S-3 is 206.9". **Plus 9.8 cu. ft. of hidden storage space on two-seat models.*

Wagon adds: All-vinyl front bench seat, vinyl coated metal cargo area sidewalls, swing up tailgate w/fixed window, I/P mounted "door ajar" warning light for tailgate, power front disc brakes, and H78 × 14 BSW tires. Malibu Classic adds: Choice of luxury cloth or all-vinyl front bench seat w/fold-down center armrest, color-keyed steering wheel and column, simulated woodgrain vinyl accents on I/P, luxury upper door panel trim, glove compartment light, bright roof drip molding, hood rear edge molding, bright rocker panel and wheel opening moldings, and bright accented dual unit taillights. Malibu Classic wagon adds: All-vinyl front bench seat w/fold-down center armrest. Malibu Classic Estate wagon adds: Woodgrain vinyl bodyside and tailgate panels. Laguna Type S-3 adds: All-vinyl front swivel bucket seats, four-spoke sport steering wheel, sports instrumentation, Type S-3 identification on I/P and door panels, dual sport mirrors w/LH remote control, unique Laguna urethane front end styling, color-keyed bumper impact strips, front and rear bumper guards, Laguna Type S-3 nameplates on front fender, grille and rear panel, radial tuned suspension, rally wheels w/trim rings, and GR70 × 14 BSW tires.

Models Available

	Model No.	Base MSRP	Change from LY*	Shipping Wt. (lbs.)	Model Year Production	Change from LY*
Malibu 2-Door Colonnade HT Coupe	C37	$2,878	+4.92%	3573	53,373	+149.67%
Malibu 4-Door Colonnade HT Sedan	C29	$2,973	+5.66%	3638	38,240	+84.24%
Malibu 4-Door, 2-Seat Station Wagon**	C35	$3,364	+8.31%	4191	14,991	+37.03%
Malibu Classic 2-Door Colonnade HT Coupe	D37	$3,131	+8.19%	3609	121,094	-28.26%
Malibu Classic 2-Door Colonnade Landau Coupe	D37	$3,307	NEW	3627	NA***	NEW
Malibu Classic 4-Door Colonnade HT Sedan	D29	$3,128	+8.95%	3695	55,925	-7.83%
Malibu Classic 4-Door, 2-Seat Station Wagon**	D35	$3,781	+14.92%	4283	18,895	-23.04%
Malibu Classic Estate 4-Dr., 2-S. Station Wgn.**	G35	$3,954	+13.78%	4306	10,222	+6.19%
Laguna Type S-3 2-Door Colonnade HT Coupe	E37	$3,816	+19.14%	3951	15,792	-63.22%
TOTALS		*Avg. price* $3,359	+6.72%		*Production* 328,532	-15.05%

*Comparisons made to equivalent 1973 model numbers; i.e., 1974 Malibu "C" models equal 1973 Chevelle Deluxe "C" models and 1974 Malibu Classic "D" models equal 1973 Malibu "D" models. **Production of wagons with third seat option is included above, but breaks out as follows: Malibu, 2,583; Malibu Classic, 4,909; Malibu Classic Estate, 4,742. ***Production of Malibu Classic Landau coupe kept as combined total with Malibu Classic coupe.

Monte Carlo

"Elegance isn't something you add to the Monte Carlo. It's something you find in it."

Nameplate year of origin: 1970.
Current bodystyle lifespan: 1973 through 1977.
Predecessor to this model: Monte Carlo (1970 to 1972).
Replacement for this model: Monte Carlo (1978 to 1987).
Percentage of division's production: 13.54%.
Corporate siblings: Pontiac Grand Prix.
Primary competition: Dodge Charger, Ford Gran Torino Elite, and Plymouth Satellite Sebring.
Notable changes: Revised grille and trim and detail changes.
Major standard equipment: Choice of knit cloth and vinyl or all-vinyl front bench seat, color-keyed cut-pile nylon carpeting, color-keyed instrument cluster, soft-rim steering wheel, simulated wood burl accents on I/P and steering wheel, carpeting on lower edge of rear seat back, door map pockets and pull assist straps, LH outside rear view mirror, black-accented rocker panel moldings w/front and rear extensions, bright wheel opening moldings, full wheel covers, and GR70 × 15 BSW tires. Landau adds: Visor vanity mirror, Landau emblem on door panels, Landau vinyl roof with outline moldings, Landau rear quarter nameplate, dual sport mirrors w/LH remote control, fender peak accent stripes, and cast aluminum Turbine II wheels.

Measurements

Wheelbase	116.0"
Length	212.7"
Width	77.6"
Height	52.7"
Legroom — front	42.1"
Legroom — rear	32.9"
Headroom — front	37.5"
Headroom — rear	37.4"
Cargo capacity (cu. ft.)	14.7
Fuel capacity (gals.)	22.0

Models Available

	Model No.	Base MSRP	Change from LY	Shipping Wt. (lbs.)	Model Year Production	Change from LY
Monte Carlo S 2-Door Hardtop Coupe	H57	$3,781	+6.15%	3926	184,873	+3.88%
Monte Carlo Landau 2-Door Hardtop Coupe	H57	$4,025	+5.75%	3945	127,344	+18.16%
TOTALS		*Avg. price* $3,903	+8.59%		*Production* 312,217	+7.40%

Bel Air, Impala
and Caprice Classic

"A lavish measure of comfort, fine handling and beautiful styling: these are the distinguishing marks of the new Chevrolets."

Nameplate year of origin: 1950 (Bel Air, as hardtop model designation and 1953 as series); 1958 (Impala); and 1966 (Caprice).

Current bodystyle lifespan: 1971 through 1976.

Predecessor to this model: Biscayne/Bel Air/Impala/Caprice (1969 to 1970).

Replacement for this model: Impala and Caprice (1977 to 1990).

Percentage of division's production: 27.32%.

Corporate siblings: Buick LeSabre, Oldsmobile Delta 88, Pontiac Catalina/Bonneville/Grand Ville.

Primary competition: AMC Ambassador, Dodge Monaco, Ford Custom 500/Galaxie 500/LTD, and Plymouth Fury.

Notable changes: Revised front and rear end styling.

Major standard equipment: Choice of patterned cloth-and-vinyl or all-vinyl front bench seat, color-keyed cut-pile nylon carpeting, color-keyed soft-rim steering wheel, color-keyed steering column, LH rear view mirror, dual unit taillights w/silver accents, rocker panel sill moldings, single horn, power steering, power front disc brakes, hubcaps, and G78 × 15 BSW tires. Wagon adds: All-vinyl front bench seat, Glide-Away tailgate w/power-operated rear window, and L78 × 15 BSW tires. Impala adds: Choice of patterned deluxe cloth-and-vinyl or all-vinyl front bench seat (all-vinyl only in wagon), woodgrain vinyl accent trim on I/P and door panels, glove box and luggage compartment lights, triple unit taillights w/silver accents, front and rear wheel opening moldings (Custom Coupe only), and bodyside moldings (w/black vinyl insert on Custom Coupe only). Caprice adds: Choice of velvet-look plush knit cloth and vinyl or all-vinyl front bench seat, fold-down center armrest (four-doors only), electric clock, rear door courtesy light switches (four-doors), wide bodyside molding w/black vinyl insert, specific triple unit taillights, rear wheel opening fender skirts, and full wheel covers. Convertible adds: Expanded vinyl front bench seat, and inward-folding power-operated vinyl convertible top w/glass rear window. Caprice Estate wagon adds: All-vinyl interior w/cargo area color-keyed soft textured vinyl sidewalls, and translucent woodgrain vinyl exterior panels.

Measurements

	2-doors	4-doors	Wagons
Wheelbase	121.5"	121.5"	125.0"
Length	222.7"	222.7"	228.4"
Width	79.5"	79.5"	79.5"
Height	53.8"	54.5"	58.3"
Legroom — front	42.5"	42.5"	42.5"
Legroom — rear	35.8"	38.8"	38.9"
Headroom — front	38.1"	38.9"	39.6"
Headroom — rear	37.1"	38.0"	39.3"
Cargo capacity (cu. ft.)	18.9*	18.9	106.4
Fuel capacity (gals.)	26.0	26.0	22.0

Caprice coupe and Impala Custom coupe is 18.1 cu. ft. Convertible is 14.4 cu. ft.

Models Available

	Model No.	Base MSRP	Change from LY	Shipping Wt. (lbs.)	Model Year Production	Change from LY
Bel Air 4-Door Sedan	K69	$3,695	+13.80%	4148	24,778	-40.77%
Bel Air 4-Door, 2-Seat Station Wagon	K35	$4,195	+4.30%	4829	6,437	-55.76%
Bel Air 4-Door, 3-Seat Station Wagon	K45	$4,309	+4.18%	4884	2,913	-53.92%
Impala 2-Door Hardtop Sport Coupe	L57	$3,897	+3.40%	4167	50,036	+16.42%
Impala 2-Door Hardtop Custom Coupe	L47	$3,964	+3.34%	4169	98,062	-44.54%
Impala 4-Door Sedan	L69	$3,870	+3.14%	4205	133,164	-30.11%
Impala 4-Door Hardtop Sport Sedan	L39	$3,950	+3.35%	4256	76,492	-45.03%
Impala 4-Door, 2-Seat Station Wagon	L35	$4,292	+4.20%	4891	23,455	-50.03%
Impala 4-Door, 3-Seat Station Wagon	L45	$4,406	+4.09%	4936	23,259	-46.73%
Caprice Classic 2-Door Hardtop Coupe	N47	$4,221	+3.41%	4245	59,484	-22.88%
Caprice Classic 2-Door Convertible	N67	$4,483	+3.18%	4308	4,670	-36.37%
Caprice Classic 4-Door Sedan	N69	$4,203	+3.42%	4294	43,367	-25.39%
Caprice Classic 4-Door Hardtop Sedan	N39	$4,272	+5.08%	4344	48,387	-31.03%
Caprice Estate 4-Door, 2-Seat Station Wagon.	N35	$4,531	+3.40%	4960	12,280	-46.54%
Caprice Estate 4-Door, 3-Seat Station Wagon	N45	$4,645	+3.31%	5004	23,063	-41.66%
TOTALS	*Avg. price*	$4,200	+4.25%	*Production*	629,847	-35.60%

Corvette

*"The 1974 Corvette still represents what it set out to be:
A car that combines the road-holding and handling
qualities of a true sports car with the grace
and refinement of a personal luxury car."*

Nameplate year of origin: 1953 (also used on show car of same year).
Current bodystyle lifespan: 1968 through 1982.
Predecessor to this model: Corvette (1963 to 1967).
Replacement for this model: Corvette (1984 to 1996).
Percentage of division's production: 1.63%.
Corporate siblings: None.
Primary competition: Pantera (Imported by Lincoln-Mercury).
Notable changes: Revised rear styling.
Major standard equipment: All-vinyl high-back contoured bucket seats, center floor
console, color-keyed cut-pile carpeting, tilt steering wheel, sports instrumentation
with full gauges including tachometer, electric clock, tinted glass, LH rear view sport mirror, carpeted cargo area with light concealed behind seats, anti-theft audio alarm system, removable roof panels (coupe), hide-away folding top (convertible), domed
hood w/air scoop, four wheel disc brakes, rally wheels w/trim rings, and GR70 × 15 BSW tires.

Measurements

Wheelbase	98.0"
Length	185.5"
Width	69.0"
Height	47.7"
Legroom — front	42.1"
Headroom — front	36.2"
Cargo capacity (cu. ft.)	6.5
Fuel capacity (gals.)	18.0

Models Available

	Model No.	Base MSRP	Change from LY	Shipping Wt. (lbs.)	Model Year Production	Change from LY
Corvette Stingray 2-Door Coupe	Z37	$6,002	+6.51%	3309	32,028	+31.41%
Corvette Stingray 2-Door Convertible	Z67	$5,766	+6.80%	3315	5,474	-10.16%
TOTALS		*Avg. price* $5,884	+6.65%		*Production* 37,502	+23.10%

CHRYSLER

"A totally new expression of an idea that has never changed."

Completely new styling and improved engine control systems marked the 50th anniversary Chrysler models. To celebrate the occasion, two option packages were introduced in March of 1974, the St. Regis package for the New Yorker Brougham coupe and the Crown Coupe package for the Imperial coupe. Engineering features of the new Chrysler models included improved electronics for the Ignition system, the continued use of unibody construction, and torsion-bar front suspension. Exterior styling completely abandoned the 1969–1973 era "fuselage" design, in favor of more angular and formal styling, much in the same vein of its contemporary Buick and Mercury competition. Unfortunately with the onset of fuel shortages and a rapid move by consumers to smaller cars, the large Chrysler models did not sell in the quantities expected, and production dropped by nearly half from the 1973 production total, which had been the highest production year in Chrysler history.

As for the new exterior styling, all models except the Imperial shared a similar front-end appearance, but each series differed in rear end and rear quarter design. At the front, for the Newport, New Yorker and Town & Country was a new take on the 1973 design, with a more substantial front box-style bumper. Dual round headlamps were set in a bright bezel with vertical, wrap-around parking/turn signal lights set into the front fender extensions. A bold new grille also extended outward slightly from the main header panel. The Newport wore an egg-crate grille design three rows high and ten columns across, with a smaller four row by four column egg-crate design inset within each opening. A rectangular emblem with the Newport crest was located at the lower right corner of the grille. A bright chrome strip arched over the grille, and the Chrysler name in block letters sat above the grille on the header panel facing. The New Yorker and Town & Country wagon shared a similar front-end design, but with a different grille than the Newport used. For these upper-end models, a split horizontal design, similar to that on the 1973 models, was divided at the middle and into four sections vertically, each of the eight sections containing thin horizontal bars. The bottom sections dipped slightly towards the center of the car, paralleling the lines of the bumper. A chrome strip ran up the sides of the grille and arched over the top into a huge chrome panel that wrapped over the top of the header panel. The Chrysler name stretched across the chrome facing in block letters, and a stand-up hood ornament was placed on top of the chromed portion of the header panel.

Bodyside panels of all models were relatively simple with a slight flare to the front wheel openings and a lower body feature line running from the side of the front bumper to the bottom of the rear bumper. As it crossed onto the rear quarter panel of two-doors, and near the rear door edge of four-door models, the line angled downward at about a 45-degree angle, before continuing toward the rear bumper. On New Yorkers, this line was highlighted with chrome, and on the Town & Country wagons, it also marked the lower edge of the simulated woodgrain bodyside appliqués. An upper bodyside feature line began at the top edge of the front fenders and gently ran along the side below the side windows, continuing onto the rear quarter panel, disappearing as it approached the rear end caps. Rear wheel opening "fender skirts" were standard on the Town & Country, New Yorker and Imperial, and optional for Newport models. In the greenhouse area, 2- and 4-door hardtop models were still offered, and the 4-door versions had a unique concave curve to the trailing edge of the rear door window. Cars in the Newport and Town & Country series shared many body features from the cowl back with the Dodge Monaco and Plymouth Fury lines, while retaining uniquely Chrysler sheetmetal and trim.

For the rear end design, Newport models used a vertical, rectangular taillamp with rounded edges and split into two sections horizontally by a thin chrome strip. The taillamps dipped slightly into the rear bumper which itself matched the slight rearward slant of the trunk lid. Backup lights were housed within the bumper directly below the taillamps. Wagons used a horizontal, wrap-around design which carried onto the tailgate for about six inches and had a small emblem set in the center, and backup lights were set into the bumper as was the license tag mount. New Yorker models used a full-width horizontal taillamp configuration divided into four sections on each side of the center mounted fuel-filler door. Taillights, brake lights and turn signal lamps were set into the three outer sections, with the backup lamps set into the inner section. The license plate was mounted in the lower center portion of the rear bumper.

Exterior styling of the luxury Imperial models used unique front and rear ends, but the bodysides followed those of the regular Chrysler models. In what would be its final restyling, the Imperial wore a vertical bar, waterfall-style grille that began on top of the header panel and was split down the middle into two sections by a body-color divider, the entire grille slightly pointed towards the center. Twelve bars per side carried into a small open area of the lower bumper facing. Flanking the grille were hidden headlights with body-colored doors and the Imperial name in script on the lower right corner of the driver's side door, with vertical parking/turn signal lamps set into the fender ends. At the top front edge of the header on the body-color divider was a stand-up Imperial eagle ornament. At the rear, Imperials used a vertical taillamp inset into the rearward slanting end cap and continuing into the rear bumper ends. The effect mimicked a small tailfin. Rear reflectors and backup lights were set into the lower portions of the bumper. As with the Newport series, the fuel filler was placed behind the license tag mount, which was in the center, with the top portion in the rear body-colored panel under the trunk opening, and with the lower portion inset in a cove of the rear bumper. Only 57 of the 50th anniversary Imperials were sold, along with an unknown number of New Yorkers.

Powerplants and transmissions returned in much the same form as prior years, with the expected updated electronic and emission controls as all companies struggled to meet federal requirements that were coming for next year. Inside, all models shared similar features with the expected escalation of materials, features and design, as each series was progressively more luxurious. The unique cloth-and-vinyl "Navajo" patterned seat upholstery continued to be available for Newport series cars. The instrument panel was typical Chrysler fare, with a square speedometer pod centered over the steering column, radio and ventilation controls to the right of the driver, and fuel, temperature and alternator gauges, plus windshield wiper, clock and light controls to the left side. Two air vents were mounted to the left of the driver, two in the center of the dashboard, and two to the far right end. Seats were of typical mid-range cloth and vinyl materials for the Newport and Town & Country, while the New Yorker had plush cloths and softer vinyls, and the Imperial offered an available leather interior.

Imperial LeBaron 2-Door Hardtop interior
with optional leather upholstery

Imperial LeBaron 4-Door Hardtop

New Yorker Brougham instrument panel

New Yorker 4-Door Hardtop

Newport 2-Door Hardtop

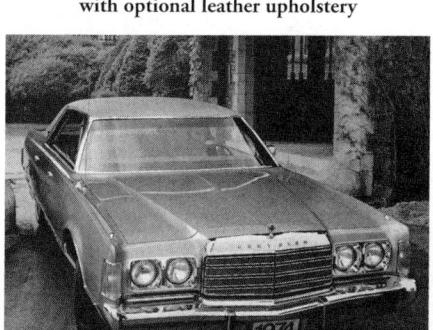

New Yorker Brougham 4-Door Hardtop

Newport optional Navajo interior

Town & Country 4-Door Station Wagon

Newport Custom 4-Door Hardtop

Model year production: 131,799 down 47.48% from 1973.
Domestic market share: 1.53% (11th place).
Base price range: $4,442 to $7,668.
Chrysler average base price: $5,540, up 7.78%.
Introduction date: September 1973.
Assembly plants: Jefferson Ave., Detroit, MI (C); and
  Newark, DE (F).
Data plate identification (VIN): Thirteen digit code read as

follows: First four digits indicate series and body style
(model number in model charts); fifth digit indicates engine
code (see powertrain chart); sixth digit indicates year (4 =
1974); seventh digit indicates assembly plant (see list above);
remaining digits are sequential with beginning numbers of
100001. *Example:* CL43M4C100001 is a 1974 Chrysler Newport 4-Door Hardtop, with 400 CID, 2-bbl. V8 engine, serial number 100001, built in Detroit, MI.

Powertrains

Engine	Net HP	Engine Code	Transmission Availability[1]		Newport	Town & Country	New Yorker	Imperial
400 CID (6.6L), 2-bbl., V8	185	M,N	3-speed Torque Flite automatic		S[1]	—	—	—
				MPG:	8.9	—	—	—
400 CID (6.6L) 4-bbl., V8	205	P	3-speed Torque Flite automatic		$40[2]	—	—	—
				MPG:	8.9	—	—	—

Engine	Net HP	Engine Code	Transmission Availability[1]		Newport	Town & Country	New Yorker	Imperial
440 CID (7.1L), 4-bbl., V8	230	T,U	3-speed Torque Flite automatic	MPG:	$132 9.1	S 8.9	S 9.1	S 9.1

[1]Not available in California.   [2]Required in California.

Major Options

	Newport	Town & Country	New Yorker	Imperial
Air conditioning[1]	$450	$450	$450	S
Tilt and telescope steering wheel	$93	$93	$93	$100
Automatic speed control	$73	$73	$73	$98
Automatic headlamp dimmer	—	—	—	$53
Electric rear window defroster	$33	—	$33	$33
Tinted glass, all windows	$57	$57	$57	S
Manual front vent window, 4-doors	$36	$36	$36	$36
Power front vent window, 4-dr. HT	$141	$141	$141	$141
Power windows	$137	$137	$137[2]	S
Power door locks, 2-dr./4-dr.	$51/$78	$78	$51/$78	$52/$76
Power front bench seat, 6-way	$113	$113	$113	$235
Power 50/50 or bucket seat, 6-way	$204	$204	$204	$235
AM radio	$98	$98	$98	S
AM/FM stereo w/search tuner	$305	$305	$305	$333
AM/FM stereo w/8-track tape	$392	$392	$392	$433
Electronic digital clock	$42	$42	$42[2]	S
Vinyl top	$132	—	$132	S
Remote control trunk release	$17	—	$17	$34
Sunroof, electric[3]	$616	—	$616	$616
Security alarm system	$108	$108	$108	$105
Premier wheel covers	$43	$43	$43	S
Chrome styled road wheels	$101	—	$101	—
White sidewall tires, std. size	$28	$38	$32	$31

Popular Option Groups & Packages

	Newport	Town & Country	New Yorker	Imperial
Accessory package	—	—	—	$54
Basic Group	$720	$768	$619	—
Crown Coupe package	—	—	—	$527
Easy Order package	$1,021	$1,125	$1,111	—
St. Regis package	—	—	$	—
Navajo package	$	—	—	—

—= Not Available; S = Standard equipment.   [1]Auto-Temp air conditioning available for $529.   [2]Standard on New Yorker Brougham.   [3]Requires vinyl top. Only available on 2-door hardtop models.

Paint Colors

	Code		Code		Code
Silver Frost metallic	A5	Sahara Beige	L4	Golden Haze metallic	Y6
Powder Blue	B1	Dark Moonstone metallic	L8	Tahitian Gold metallic	Y9
Lucerne Blue metallic	B5	Sienna metallic	T5		
Starlight Blue metallic	B8	Dark Chestnut metallic	T9	*Single tones are coded W1, W1. Two-tones are available*	
Burnished Red metallic	E7	Spinnaker White	W1	*for $44, and are coded X9, W1 where first two digits*	
Frosty Green metallic	G2	Formal Black	X9	*are accent or roof color and second two digits are basic*	
Deep Sherwood metallic	G8	Sun Fire Yellow	Y2	*body color.*	
Avocado Gold metallic	J6	Golden Fawn	Y4		

Newport

*"Newport has the styling, comfort and convenience that a big car
can offer, but at a price that is affordable to nearly everyone."*

Nameplate year of origin: 1961 (as series); 1950 (as HT model of the T & C).
Current bodystyle lifespan: 1974 through 1978.
Predecessor to this model: Newport (1969 to 1973).
Replacement for this model: Newport (1979 to 1981).
Percentage of division's sales volume: 58.70%.
Corporate siblings: Chrysler New Yorker and Imperial.
Primary competition: Buick LeSabre, Mercury Monterey, and Oldsmobile Delta 88.
Notable changes: Completely redesigned.
Major standard equipment: Cloth-and-vinyl front bench seat, color-keyed loop pile carpeting, trip odometer, lighted LH front ashtray w/two rear seat ashtrays, 12" inside day/night mirror, two-speed electric windshield wipers w/washers, front and rear wheel lip moldings, drip rail molding, bright windshield and rear window moldings, rear hood molding, dual horns, power brakes, power steering, deluxe wheel covers, and H78 × 15 BSW tires. Custom adds: Cloth-and-vinyl 50/50 split back front seat w/fold-down center armrest and (for 4-door models only) passenger side recliner, seat side shields, deck lid molding, upper door frame moldings (sedan only), rocker panel sill molding, and dual bodyside paint stripes.

Measurements

Wheelbase	124.0"
Length	224.7"
Width	79.5"
Height	54.9"
Legroom — front	42.2"
Legroom — rear	39.9"
Headroom — front	37.9"
Headroom — rear	37.7"
Cargo capacity (cu. ft.)	20.2
Fuel capacity (gals.)	26.5

Models Available

	Model No.	Base MSRP	Change from LY	Shipping Wt. (lbs.)	Model Year Production	Change from LY
Newport 2-Door Hardtop	CL23	$4,517	+6.18%	4380	13,784	-49.80%
Newport 4-Door Sedan	CL41	$4,442	+6.24%	4430	26,944	-50.24%
Newport 4-Door Hardtop	CL43	$4,581	+6.14%	4440	8,968	-55.55%
Newport Custom 2-Door Hardtop	CM23	$4,870	+8.61%	4430	7,206	-41.38%
Newport Custom 4-Door Sedan	CM41	$4,803	+8.69%	4480	10,569	-47.40%
Newport Custom 4-Door Hardtop	CM43	$4,955	+8.50%	4500	9,892	-50.66%
TOTALS	*Avg. price*	$4,695	+7.43%	*Production*	77,363	-49.83%

Town & Country

*"Town & Country has luxury, performance,
style and utility written all over it."*

Nameplate year of origin: 1941.
Current bodystyle lifespan: 1974 through 1977.
Predecessor to this model: Town & Country (1969 to 1973).
Replacement for this model: LeBaron Town & Country (1978 to 1978).
Percentage of division's sales volume: 6.22%.
Corporate siblings: Dodge Monaco and Plymouth Fury.
Primary competition: Buick Estate Wagon, Mercury Colony Park, and Oldsmobile Custom Cruiser.
Notable changes: Completely redesigned.
Major standard equipment: All-vinyl 50/50 split front seat w/individual fold-down center armrests and passenger-side recliner, color-keyed loop pile carpeting including cargo area, electric clock, interior lights (cargo, glove box, map/courtesy and ashtray lights), power tailgate window, sound absorbing headliner, trip odometer, front ashtray w/two rear seat ashtrays, 12" inside day/night mirror, three-speed electric windshield wipers w/washers, concealed storage compartments in rear wheelhouse cover, "Power Auto-Lock" tailgate lock (activates when ignition turned on), fender mounted turn signal indicators, bodyside simulated woodgrain appliqués, drip rail molding, rear wheel opening skirts, roof air deflector, dual horns, large diameter front sway bar, deluxe wheel covers, and L78 × 15 BSW tires.

Measurements

Wheelbase	124.0"
Length	224.7"
Width	79.4"
Height	59.1"
Legroom — front	42.2"
Legroom — rear	39.9"
Headroom — front	38.7"
Headroom — rear	38.7"
Cargo capacity (cu. ft.)*	100.8
Fuel capacity (gals.)	24.0

*Plus 6.8 cu. ft. in concealed compartment on
2-seat wagon.*

Models Available

	Model No.	Base MSRP	Change from LY	Shipping Wt. (lbs.)	Model Year Production	Change from LY
Town & Country 4-Door, 2-S. Wagon	CP45	$5,532	+5.55%	4915	2,236	-58.23%
Town & Country 4-Door, 3-S. Wagon	CP46	$5,661	+5.50%	4970	5,958	-59.43%
TOTALS		Avg. price $5,597	+5.52%		Production 8,194	-59.11%

New Yorker

"New Yorkers live up to their Chrysler heritage with rich new styling, new comfort and convenience features, and luxurious new interiors."

Nameplate year of origin: 1939.
Current bodystyle lifespan: 1974 through 1978.
Predecessor to this model: New Yorker (1969 to 1973).
Replacement for this model: New Yorker (1979 to 1981).
Percentage of division's sales volume: 24.14%.
Corporate siblings: Chrysler Newport and Imperial.
Primary competition: Buick Electra 225, Mercury Marquis, and Oldsmobile Ninety-Eight.
Notable changes: Completely redesigned.
Major standard equipment: Cloth-and-vinyl front bench seat w/fold-down center armrest, color-keyed loop-pile carpeting, color-keyed seat belts, trip odometer, electric clock, dual front ashtrays w/two rear seat ashtrays, interior lights (glove box, map/courtesy and ashtray lights), 12" inside day/night mirror, three-speed electric windshield wipers w/washers, carpeted trunk floor, LH remote control mirror, full-length bodyside molding, front wheel lip molding, drip rail molding, bright window moldings, rear taillight periphery moldings, rear wheel opening skirts, fender-mounted turn signal indicators, undercoating, hood insulation pad, unique deluxe wheel covers, and JR78 × 15 BSW tires. Brougham adds: Cloth-and-vinyl 50/50 split bench seat w/individual fold-down center armrest and passenger side recliner on 4-door, rear seat fold-down center armrest, power windows, console-type armrests on all doors, and headlight time-delay switch.

Measurements

Wheelbase	124.0"
Length	224.7"
Width	79.7"
Height	54.9"
Legroom — front	42.2"
Legroom — rear	39.9"
Headroom — front	37.9"
Headroom — rear	37.7"
Cargo capacity (cu. ft.)	20.2
Fuel capacity (gals.)	26.5

Models Available

	Model No.	Base MSRP	Change from LY	Shipping Wt. (lbs.)	Model Year Production	Change from LY
New Yorker 4-Door Sedan	CH41	$5,418	+8.43%	4560	3,072	-61.56%
New Yorker 4-Door Hardtop	CH43	$5,550	+8.29%	4595	3,066	-59.76%
New Yorker Brougham 2-Door Hardtop	CS23	$5,846	+8.00%	4540	7,980	-13.17%
New Yorker Brougham 4-Door Sedan	CS41	$5,795	+8.04%	4640	4,533	-46.93%
New Yorker Brougham 4-Door Hardtop	CS43	$5,927	+7.92%	4540	13,165	-50.57%
TOTALS		Avg. price $5,707	+8.13%		Production 31,816	-46.95%

Imperial

"A beautiful new generation of luxury motor cars."

Nameplate year of origin: 1926 (as series); 1924 (as sedan model designation).
Current bodystyle lifespan: 1974 through 1978 (1974–1975 as Imperial, 1976–1978 as New Yorker Brougham).
Predecessor to this model: Imperial (1969 to 1973).
Replacement for this model: Imperial (1981 to 1983).
Percentage of division's sales volume: 10.95%.

Measurements

Wheelbase	124.0"
Length	231.1"
Width	79.7"
Height	54.7"
Legroom — front	42.3"

Corporate siblings: Chrysler New Yorker and Newport.
Primary competition: Cadillac Calais and DeVille and Lincoln Continental.
Notable changes: Completely redesigned.
Major standard equipment: All-vinyl 50/50 split bench seat w/individual fold-down
center armrest and passenger side recliner, color-keyed loop-pile carpeting, color-keyed seat belts, rear seat passenger assist straps and C-pillar pillows, trip odometer, air conditioning, electronic digital clock, power windows, tinted glass, dual front ashtrays w/two rear seat ashtrays, interior lights (glove box, map/courtesy and ashtray lights), 12" inside day/night mirror, three-speed electric windshield wipers w/washers, carpeted trunk floor and spare tire cover, LH remote control mirror, full vinyl top with frenched rear window, full-length rocker panel molding, front wheel lip molding, rear wheel opening skirts, drip rail molding, bright window moldings, rear bumper periphery molding, fender-mounted turn signal indicators, undercoating, hood insulation pad, deluxe wheel covers, and LR78 × 15 BSW tires.

Measurements (cont.)

Legroom — rear	39.5"
Headroom — front	38.1"
Headroom — rear	37.0"
Cargo capacity (cu. ft.)	20.2
Fuel capacity (gals.)	26.5

1974

Models Available

	Model No.	Base MSRP	Change from LY	Shipping Wt. (lbs.)	Model Year Production	Change from LY
Imperial 2-Door Hardtop	YM23	$7,537	+10.37%	4825	3,850	+50.21%
Imperial 4-Door Hardtop	YM43	$7,668	+8.66%	4965	10,576	-25.34%
TOTALS		*Avg. price* $7,603	+9.50%		*Production* 14,426	-13.77%

DODGE

"Extra care in engineering makes a difference in Dodge ... Depend on it."

Dodge entered its 60th anniversary year with high expectations after the great sales year of 1973. An all-new full-size Dodge Monaco was introduced that did away forever with the fuselage design introduced in 1969. However, with the ongoing fuel crisis and economic woes, big cars were not selling, and only the restyled, imported Colt would show a sales increase at the end of the model year. Even Dodge's highly popular compact Dart series suffered a small drop in sales and production.

The new Monaco was what could be expected from Dodge, as it had to follow the new-for-1971 GM and Ford full-size models, but on a budget. Even more than in previous years, the Dodge Monaco shared major components with its lesser Plymouth Fury stablemate, including chassis, upper sheetmetal, glass and other major components. In fact, in base form, from a distance, it was difficult to distinguish a Dodge Monaco from a Plymouth Fury. The greenhouse area came off looking very much like the 1971 through 1973 GM full-size cars, with slender A-pillars, round-cornered, slightly curved rear windows, a straight beltline surrounding the front and sides, and a kick-up to the rear side window as it met the C-pillar. Front fenders and rear quarter panels seemed to copy the restyled 1973 Ford line, with more angular lines.

The bodysides carried three feature lines with the upper one beginning at the upper front edge of the front door and gradually tapering downward just above the door handles, to end mid-height near the end of the rear quarter panel. The mid-level feature line was straight and ran the entire length of the car just above the wheel openings. The lower feature line created a crease in the lower body that ran between the wheel openings, and also from the forward edge of the front wheel opening to meet the front bumper. Overall it was a pleasing design, if not original in concept.

At the front end, a more integrated design was featured with a horizontal style grille composed of four medium sized bars, with several more slender bars between each row. Dual headlights sat at each end in large chrome bezels, rising higher than the grille. Capping the entire setup was a chrome strip that was wider across the header panel above the grille. The box-style bumper continued the grille theme in the center, with parking/turn signal lamps set in the outer grille area of the bumper. At the rear, larger rectangular taillamps were set in the rear panel, dipping into the bumper. The quarter panel caps had a small, tailfin-like ridge, which helped to distinguish the Monaco from the Fury. Station wagons used a vertical two-section taillamp and, as in the past, shared all features of their body with the Chrysler Town & Country and Plymouth Fury Suburban models.

Inside, a new flat faced instrument panel with a slightly overhanging top pad created a more driver friendly environment by doing away with the tightly packed pod of previous models. An elongated speedometer proved to be easier to read than the prior square design, while more horizontal space was given for the other gauges, as well as radio and climate controls, making better placement for all of them. An additional new feature was a soft blue backlighting and side-lighting technique that created a glare-free illumination of all gauges. A new center-mounted glove box with coin holder placed it within easy reach of both driver and passengers. Eight air outlets increased airflow to the passenger compartment by 65 percent. As had become a trend in Chrysler products, most optional seating choices used high front seatbacks providing built-in headrests. With these optional seats having fold-down center armrests, the seatbacks looked very much like bucket seatbacks, and quite possibly could have been, at least internally, to save on production costs. New materials and upholstery designs added a luxurious look and feel.

The mid-size Coronet line received an all-new front end, abandoning the loop-style front bumper for a design that was similar to the new Monaco front end in appearance. The new grille used three horizontal bars and was capped on each end by dual headlamps, with each set into its own bezel, and a small outer extension of the grille. A chrome piece surrounded the entire grille, with a fine textured egg-crate grille inset horizontally between the grille bars and front end sur-

round. The center section of the grille dropped slightly at the header on top, and into the bumper at the bottom. Parking and turn signal lamps were set into the new box-style bumper. Around back, a larger bumper, with larger horizontal taillamps on sedans, completed the new look, while the remainder of the car was the same as the past three seasons.

The remainder of the Dodge line was mostly unchanged. Under the hood, the 360 CID V8 engine replaced the 340 CID V8 in all applications, and the 198 CID 6-cylinder entered its last season as the base powerplant in the compact Dart. The Charger was entering its last year as a mid-size sports model within the Dodge line, as mid-size sporting cars with luxury features were quickly gaining in popularity. The Charger was the last Dodge model to retain Chrysler's loop-style front bumper. The sporty Challenger was entering its final year, as the muscle-car era had all but dried up in the past few years. With the Dart being the most popular Dodge by a landslide, there was not much need to change the styling, although a rearward slanting rear panel containing horizontal taillights above a new box style bumper was added to meet the new rear safety standards. A new top-of-the-line Dart S.E., a.k.a. Special Edition, model was added at mid-year to meet new upscale competition from the Oldsmobile Omega and Buick Apollo, as well as the upcoming Ford Granada and Mercury Monarch. Features mainly included more luxurious interior appointments and vinyl tops.

Challenger 2-Door Hardtop with Rallye package

Charger 2-Door Hardtop

Colt GT 2-Door Hardtop

Coronet Custom 4-Door Sedan

Dart Sport 2-Door Coupe

Dart Swinger 2-Door Hardtop with Dart Custom 4-Door Sedan, rear

Monaco Brougham 4-Door Station Wagon

Monaco Custom 2-Door Hardtop

Model year production: 442,072, down 33.58% from 1973.
Domestic market share: 5.12% (7th place).
Base price range: $2,878 to $5,477.
Dodge average base price: $3,840, up 8.43%.
Introduction date: September 25, 1973.
Assembly plants: Lynch Road, Detroit, MI (A); Hamtramck, MI (B); Jefferson Ave., Detroit, MI (C); Belvidere, IL (D); Newark, DE (F); and St. Louis, MO (G). *Colt manufacturer:* Mitsubishi Heavy Industries, Tokyo, Japan.
Data plate identification (VIN): Thirteen digit code read as follows: First four digits indicate series and body style (model number in model charts); fifth digit indicates engine code (see powertrain chart); sixth digit indicates year (4 = 1974); seventh digit indicates assembly plant for all except Colt (see list above); for Colt seventh digit indicates transmission code [5 = 4-speed manual, 9 = automatic]; remaining digits are sequential with beginning numbers of 100001 for all Dodge models except Colt. Colt sequential numbers are currently unknown. *Example:* LL41C4B100001 is a 1974 Dodge Dart 4-Door Sedan, with 225 CID, 2-bbl. 6-cylinder engine, serial number 100001, built in Hamtramck, MI.

Powertrains

Engine	Net HP	Engine Code	Transmission Availability[1]		Colt	Dart[4]	Challenger	Charger	Coronet	Monaco
97.5 CID (1.6L) OHC, 1-bbl., 4-cyl.	85	K	4-speed manual		S	—	—	—	—	—
				MPG:	22.6 (wgn. 22.8)	—	—	—	—	—
			3-sp. automatic		$	—	—	—	—	—
				MPG:	22.7 (wgn. 21.9)	—	—	—	—	—
122 CID (2.0L) OHC, 2-bbl., 4-cyl.	95	U	4-speed manual		$142	—	—	—	—	—
				MPG:	NA	—	—	—	—	—
			3-sp. automatic		$	—	—	—	—	—
				MPG:	19.1	—	—	—	—	—
198 CID (3.2L), 1-bbl., 6-cyl.[2]	95	B	3-speed manual		—	S (ex. SE)	—	—	—	—
				MPG:	—	NA	—	—	—	—
			3-sp. Torque Flite automatic		—	$199 (ex. SE)	—	—	—	—
				MPG:	—	16.0	—	—	—	—
225 CID (3.7L), 2-bbl., 6-cyl.	105	C	3-speed manual		—	$40 (ex. SE)	—	S (ex. SE)	S (cars)	—
				MPG:	—	NA	—	NA	NA	—
			3-sp. Torque Flite automatic		—	S (SE)/ $239 (others)	—	$210 (ex. SE)	$210 (cars)	—
				MPG:	—	16.7	—	11.5	11.5	—
318 CID (5.2L), 2-bbl., V8	150	G	3-speed manual		—	$151 (ex. SE)	S	S (SE)/ $111 (others)	S (wgns.)/ $111 (cars)	—
				MPG:	—	12.5	12.5	11.4	11.4	—
			4-speed manual[3]		—	$331 (ex. SE)	$180	$180 (SE)/$291 (others)	—	—
				MPG:	—	11.8	11.8	11.8	—	—

Engine	Net HP	Engine Code	Transmission Availability[1]		Colt	Dart[4]	Challenger	Charger	Coronet	Monaco
			3-sp. Torque Flite automatic		—	$350 $111 (SE)/ (others)	$199	$210 (SE)/$321 (others)	$210 (wgns.)/ $321 (cars)	—
				MPG:	—	11.6	11.6	11.6	11.6	—
360 CID (5.9L), 2-bbl., V8[4]	180	K	3-speed manual		—	—	—	$162 (SE)/$291 (others)	$162 (wgns.)/ $291 (cars)	—
				MPG:	—	—	—	9.6	9.6	—
			3-sp. Torque Flite automatic		—	—	—	$400 (SE)/$510 (others)	$400 (wgns.)/ $510 (cars)	S[5]
				MPG:	—	—	—	9.6	9.6	10.4
360 CID (5.9L), 4-bbl., V8[4]	200	J	3-speed manual		—	S (360 Sport)	$219	$222 (SE)/$331 (others)	$222 (wgns.)/ $331 (cars)	—
				MPG:	—	11.8	11.8	11.8	11.8	—
			4-speed manual		—	$180 (360 Sport)	$399	$409 (SE)/$520 (others)	—	—
				MPG:	—	NA	NA	NA	—	—
			3-sp. TorqueFlite automatic		—	$199 (360 Sport)	$430	$440 (SE)/$550 (others)	$440 (wgns.)/ $550 (cars)	$35[5]
				MPG:	—	10.9	10.9	NA	NA	9.9
360 CID (5.9L), 4-bbl., V8[4]	245	L	3-speed manual		—	—	$259	$259 (SE)/$370 (others)	$259 (wgns.)/ $370 (cars)	—
				MPG:	—	—	9.6	11.8	11.8	—
			4-speed manual		—	—	$439	$449 (SE)/$560 (others)	—	—
				MPG:	—	—	NA	9.1	—	—
			3-sp. Torque Flite automatic		—	—	$470	$481 (SE)/$592 (others)	$481 (wgns.)/ $592 (cars)	—
				MPG:	—	—	8.5	10.2	10.2	—
400 CID (6.6L), 2-bbl., V8[4]	205/ 185[6]	M	3-sp. Torque Flite automatic		—	—	—	—	—	$40[5]
				MPG:	—	—	—	—	—	7.9
400 CID (6.6L), 4-bbl., V8[4]	250/ 240[6]	P	4-speed manual		—	—	—	$378 (SE)[2]/$489 (ex. SE)[2]	—	—
				MPG:	—	—	—	9.2	—	—
			3-sp. Torque Flite automatic		—	—	—	$410 (SE)[2]/$522 (ex. SE)[2]	$410 (wgns.)2/ $522 (cars)2	S[7]/$45 (others)
				MPG:	—	—	—	NA	NA	8.2
440 CID (7.2L), 4-bbl., V8[4]	275/ 230[6]	U	4-speed manual		—	—	—	$468 (SE)/$579 (ex. SE)[3]	—	—
				MPG:	—	—	—	NA	—	—
			3-sp. Torque Flite automatic		—	—	—	$500 (SE)/$669 (ex. SE)	—	$90[7]/ $130 (others)
				MPG:	—	—	—	8.5	—	8.9

[1]Unless otherwise noted: All manual transmissions are column-shift, except on Colt, Dart Sport 360 and Challenger. All automatics are column-shift, except on Colt which is floor-shift. Floor-shift is available for $28 extra on any Dart w/manual transmission and Dart Sport w/automatic, or at no charge on Challenger w/automatic. [2]Not available in California. [3]Available only with Rallye package. [4]Prices for 360 CID, 400 CID and 440 CID V8 engines are estimates based upon

multiple references, as price increases throughout the year make it difficult to determine the correct prices at the time of introduction. [5]Except Monaco Brougham and Monaco wagons. [6]Lower horsepower ratings are for Monaco. [7]Monaco Brougham and Monaco wagons.

Major Options

	Colt	Dart	Challenger	Charger	Coronet	Monaco
Air conditioning[1]	$391	$395	$384	$378	$378	$412
Tilt steering wheel w/"Rim Blow"	S[2]	—	—	—	—	$60
Automatic speed control	—	—	—	$64	$64	$64
Electric rear window defogger[3]	$	$49	$28	$62	$62	$31
Tinted glass, all windows	$	$36	$36	$40	$40	$40
Front vent window, 4-dr. only	—	—	—	—	—	$38
Power windows	—	—	—	$135[4]	$135	$135
Power door locks, 2-dr./4-dr.	—	—	—	—	—	$49/$75
Music Master AM radio	$	$75	$75	$90	$90	$92
AM/FM stereo	—	—	$205	$230	$230	$254
AM/FM stereo w/8-track tape	—	—	—	$360	$360	$397
Front bucket seats w/console[5]	S	$146	$52	$162	—	—
Front seat center folding armrest[6]	—	—	—	—	$56	—
Vinyl top[7]	$	$87	$84	$133	$101	$115
Sunroof, manual[8]	—	$151	$261	$261[9]	—	$513
Power steering, variable-ratio	—	$92	$104	$114	$114	S
Power brakes, w/front disc[10]	—	$130	$65	$65	$65	S
Chrome road wheels	—	—	$82	$90	$90	$102
Rallye road wheels	—	$58	$53	$58	$58	—
White sidewall tires, std. size	$	$35	$38	$38	$38	$38

Popular Option Groups & Packages

	Colt	Dart	Challenger	Charger	Coronet	Monaco
Brougham package	—	—	—	$112	$112	
Custom package	—	$72	—	—	—	
Decor package	$	—	—	—	—	—
Light package	—	$29	$35	$37	$40	S
Luxury Equipment package	—	—	—	$1,427	$1,427	$1,447
Rallye package	—	$497	$182	$119		
Utility package	—	$85	—	—	—	—

— = Not Available; S = Standard equipment. [1]Requires 225 CID 6-cyl. or V8 engine on Dart, and V8 engine on Charger & Coronet. [2]Colt does not include "Rim Blow" steering wheel mounted horn. [3]Heated style that uses filaments embedded on glass. Blower style on Challenger and Monaco. Not available on wagons. [4]Not available on Charger coupe. [5]Only available on 2-door models, and requires automatic transmission. Available at no cost on Charger SE. Includes full-floor carpeting on Dart. [6]Standard on Charger SE, and Monaco Brougham. [7]Standard on Charger SE. Available only on Colt 2-door models. [8]Requires vinyl top. Manual sunroof on Dart coupes, Challenger and Charger. Power sunroof on Monaco series, except wagons. [9]Price shown is w/canopy vinyl top. With full vinyl top, $275. With formal vinyl top, $171. [10]Standard on Dart Sport 360 and Coronet station wagons. All but Dart have manual front disc brakes as standard.

Paint Colors

Dodge	Code	Dodge	Code	Colt	Code
Yellow[1]	DY2	Dark Moonstone metallic	KL8	Pacific Blue metallic[8,10,12]	065
Eggshell White	EW1	Sienna metallic	KT5	Sapporo White[8,12]	067
Bright Red	FE5	Dark Chestnut metallic[1]	KT9		
Burnished Red metallic[2]	GE7	Golden Fawn	KY4	*Single tones are coded W1, W1. Two-tones are coded*	
Parchment	HL4	Yellow Blaze[5]	KY5	*X9, W1 where first two digits are accent or roof color,*	
Dark Silver metallic[3]	JA5	Black	TX9	*and second two digits are basic body color.* [1]*Available*	
Aztec Gold[4]	JL6			*only on Monaco.* [2]*Available only on Dart and Chal-*	
Gold metallic	JY6			*lenger.* [3]*Not available on Dart and Challenger.*	
Dark Gold metallic	JY9	Colt	Code	[4]*Available only on Chargers.* [5]*Available only on*	
Powder Blue	KB1	Bright Yellow[6,7]	003	*Dart, Challenger, Coronet and Charger.* [6]*Available*	
Lucerne Blue metallic	KB5	Spice metallic[8,9]	016	*only on Colt GT.* [7]*Available only on Colt coupe.*	
Starlight Blue metallic[1]	KB8	Sea Green metallic[8]	017	[8]*Not available on Colt GT.* [9]*Not available on Colt*	
Frosty Green metallic	KG2	Silver metallic[6]	028	*hardtop.* [10]*Not available on Colt Custom wagon.*	
Dark Sherwood metallic	KG8	Red[10,11]	055	[11]*Not available on 4-door sedan.* [12]*Not available on*	
Avocado Gold metallic	KJ6	Sunset Orange[6]	064	*Colt coupe.*	

Colt

"From Japan to America C/O Dodge."

Nameplate year of origin: 1971.
Current bodystyle lifespan: 1971 through 1978 (hardtop and wagon); 1971 through 1976 (coupe and sedan).
Predecessor to this model: None.
Replacement for this model: Colt (1979 to 1983).
Primary competition: AMC Gremlin, Buick Opel, Chevrolet Vega, and Ford Pinto.
Notable changes: New front and rear styling.
Major standard equipment: Vinyl front bucket seats, recessed door handles, two-spoke steering wheel, tilt steering column, heater, front and rear rubber bumper guards, front disc brakes, hubcaps, and 6.00 × 13 BSW tires. Hardtop, sedan and wagon add: Breathable vinyl front bucket seats, reclining seat backs, three-spoke steering wheel, recessed door locks, bright sill, belt, drip and wheel opening moldings, rocker panel molding, and full wheel covers. Wagon adds: Fold-down rear seat. Custom wagon adds: Carpeted cargo area w/skid strips, vinyl cargo side trim including pillars, wheel house covers, simulated woodgrain side and tailgate trim, and WSW tires. GT adds: Soft-rim three-spoke GT steering wheel, front floor console w/shifter, GT bodyside tape stripes, GT logo, argent rallye road wheels with chrome hubs and lug nuts, and BR70 × 13 WSW tires.

Measurements

	2-doors	Sedan	Wagon
Wheelbase	95.3"	95.3"	95.3"
Length	172.2"	171.3"	172.0"
Width	63.6"	63.6"	62.9"
Height	52.5"	53.6"	55.5"
Legroom — front	42.7"	42.7"	42.7"
Legroom — rear	30.5"	30.5"	30.5"
Headroom — front	36.9"	37.8"	37.8"
Headroom — rear	35.5"	36.7"	37.3"
Cargo capacity (cu. ft.)	8.1	8.1	58.5
Fuel capacity (gals.)	13.5	13.5	11.0

Models Available

	Model No.	Base MSRP	Change from LY	Shipping Wt. (lbs.)	Model Year Production	Change from LY
Colt 2-Door Coupe	6L21	$2,585	+14.18%	2101	NA	NA
Colt 2-Door Hardtop	6H23	$2,830	+13.34%	2101	NA	NA
Colt 4-Door Sedan	6H41	$2,816	+15.55%	2145	NA	NA
Colt 4-Door Station Wagon	6H45	$3,096	+15.74%	2256	NA	NA
Colt GT 2-Door Hardtop	6P23	$3,015	+16.95%	2123	NA	NA
Colt Custom 4-Door Station Wagon	6P45	$3,271	NEW	2289	NA	NEW
TOTALS	*Avg. price*	$2,936	+17.88%	*Production*	42,925*	+20.84%*

Total and comparison to LY is based on estimated model year sales.

Dart

"Satisfied Dart owners? We've got over a million of 'em."

Nameplate year of origin: 1960 (used on entry-level full-size Dodge).
Current bodystyle lifespan: 1967 through 1976.
Predecessor to this model: Dart (1963 to 1966).
Replacement for this model: Aspen (1976 to 1980).
Percentage of division's production: 58.72%.
Corporate siblings: Plymouth Valiant (including Scamp and Duster).
Primary competition: Buick Apollo, Oldsmobile Omega, Mercury Comet, and Pontiac Ventura.
Notable changes: Minor trim and detail changes.
Major standard equipment: All-vinyl front bench seat (Swinger and base Dart), cloth and vinyl front bench seat (all others), simulated woodgrain I/P cluster appliqué, two-speed electric windshield wipers, foot-operated windshield washers, front door armrests, cigarette lighter (except Dart Sport), heater and defroster, front door window vents (sedans only),

Measurements

	Dart	Dart Sport
Wheelbase	111.0"	108.0"
Length	201.7"	198.2"
Width	69.6"	71.8"
Height	54.1"	53.1"
Legroom — front	41.7"	41.7"
Legroom — rear	35.8"	29.9"
Headroom — front	37.3"	37.2"
Headroom — rear	36.9"	36.4"
Cargo capacity (cu. ft.)	15.4	19.8*
Fuel capacity (gals.)	16.0	16.0

With fold-down rear seat option, 56.0 cu. ft.

wheel opening moldings (Sport only), grille surround and front edge moldings, hubcaps, and 6.95 × 14 BSW tires. Sport, Swinger and Custom add: Cut-pile carpeting, rear seat armrests (except Sport), simulated woodgrain vinyl appliqué door panel trim (except Sport), roof drip-rail molding, and bodyside moldings w/painted insert (except Sport). Dart 360 Sport adds: Bodyside and rear deck lid performance tape stripes, special suspension, dual exhausts and E70 × 14 BSW tires. Special Edition adds: Crushed velour cloth and vinyl front bucket seats w/freestanding center armrest or low back front bench seat, door pull assist straps, color-keyed cut-pile carpeting, premium steering wheel, bright pedal dress-up, trunk carpeting, dual horns, deluxe insulation package, light package, three-speed electric windshield wipers and washers, LH remote control mirror, full vinyl roof, bodyside tape stripes, upper door frame moldings (sedan), stand-up SE hood ornament, power steering, front sway bar, and color-keyed wheel covers.

Models Available

	Model No.	Base MSRP	Change from LY*	Shipping Wt. (lbs.)	Model Year Production	Change from LY*
Dart Sport 2-Door Coupe	LL29	$2,802	+15.59%	2990	59,567	-12.55%
Dart Swinger Special 2-Dr. Hardtop	LL23	$2,842	+15.43%	3035	16,155	-7.58%
Dart 4-Door Sedan	LL41	$2,885	+15.22%	3055	*	NA*
Dart Sport 360 2-Door Coupe	LM29	$3,244	+13.70%	3330	3,951	-65.08%
Dart Swinger 2-Door Hardtop	LH23	$3,001	+14.67%	3030	89,242	-17.08%
Dart Custom 4-Door Sedan	LH41	$3,043	+14.48%	3055	78,216*	NA*
Dart Special Edition 2-Door Hardtop	LP23	$3,718	NEW	3200**	12,385***	NEW
Dart Special Edition 4-Door Sedan	LP41	$3,761	NEW	3215**	***	NEW
TOTALS		Avg. price $3,162	+22.26%		Production 259,516	-10.11%

*Base and Custom sedan production kept combined; therefore comparison to LY is not possible.   **Estimated curb weights of 3599 (2-door) and 3641 (4-door) are reported in multiple sources, but probably inaccurate.   ***Special Edition production not available by body style.

Challenger

"Challenger '74. Turn it on … it'll do the same for you!"

Nameplate year of origin: 1970.
Current bodystyle lifespan: 1970 through 1974.
Predecessor to this model: None.
Replacement for this model: None.
Percentage of division's sales volume: 3.72%.
Corporate siblings: Plymouth Barracuda.
Primary competition: AMC Javelin, Chevrolet Camaro, and Pontiac Firebird.
Notable changes: Minor trim and detail changes.
Major standard equipment: All-vinyl bucket seats w/integral head restraints, deep loop pile carpeting, simulated woodgrain door inserts, dome light, front and rear door/quarter panel armrests and ashtrays, concealed two-speed windshield wipers w/washers, wheel opening and roof drip-rail moldings, grille surround and deck lid moldings, dual body paint stripes, front disc brakes, and 7.35 × 14 BSW tires.

Measurements

Wheelbase	110.0"
Length	198.6"
Width	77.4"
Height	50.9"
Legroom — front	42.1"
Legroom — rear	30.8"
Headroom — front	37.4"
Headroom — rear	35.6"
Cargo capacity (cu. ft.)	9.6
Fuel capacity (gals.)	18.0

Models Available

	Model No.	Base MSRP	Change from LY	Shipping Wt. (lbs.)	Model Year Production	Change from LY
Challenger 2-Door Hardtop	JH23	$3,143	+4.38%	3225	16,437	-49.57%
TOTALS		Avg. price $3,143	+4.38%		Production 16,437	-49.57%

Charger

"How to assert yourself beautifully."

Nameplate year of origin: 1966.
Current bodystyle lifespan: 1971 through 1974.
Predecessor to this model: Charger (1968 to 1970).
Replacement for this model: Charger SE (1975 to 1978).
Percentage of division's sales volume: 8.11%.
Corporate siblings: Plymouth Satellite Sebring.
Primary competition: AMC Matador, Chevrolet Chevelle and Monte Carlo, Ford Torino, Mercury Montego, and Pontiac LeMans and Grand Prix.
Notable changes: Minor trim and detail changes.
Major standard equipment: All-vinyl front bench seat, color-keyed carpeting, simulated woodgrained vinyl trim on I/P and door panels (except coupe), dome light w/front door courtesy switch, concealed two-speed windshield wipers w/washers, dual horns, hubcaps, and E78 × 14 BSW tires (coupe). Hardtop adds: All-vinyl or cloth-and-vinyl front bench seat and F78 × 14 BSW tires. SE adds: All-vinyl split-back front bench seat w/center armrest, rallye instrument cluster, formal vinyl roof w/fixed louvered quarter windows, "SE" stand-up hood ornament, belt and hood moldings, front hood and decklid moldings, and bodyside paint stripe, deluxe wheel covers, and F78 × 14 BSW tires.

Measurements

Wheelbase	115.0"
Length	214.0"
Width	77.0"
Height	52.2"
Legroom — front	41.9"
Legroom — rear	34.1"
Headroom — front	37.1"
Headroom — rear	36.4"
Cargo capacity (cu. ft.)	16.7
Fuel capacity (gals.)	19.5

Models Available

	Model No.	Base MSRP	Change from LY	Shipping Wt. (lbs.)	Model Year Production	Change from LY
Charger 2-Door Coupe	WL21	$3,111	+10.71%	3470	4,908*	NA*
Charger 2-Door Hardtop	WH23	$3,311	+8.20%	3490	*	NA*
Charger SE 2-Door Hardtop Coupe	WP29	$3,641	+7.88%	3625	30,957	-50.00%
TOTALS		*Avg. price* $3,354	+8.85%		*Production* 35,865	-69.94%

Charger coupe and hardtop and Coronet sedan production kept as combined total, and above figure is estimated based on production split between 1973 Charger and Coronet. Therefore comparison to LY is not possible.

Coronet

"Lots of room, comfort, and style make Coronet the happy medium."

Nameplate year of origin: 1950 (as hardtop designation); 1953 (as series).
Current bodystyle lifespan: 1971 through 1978. Renamed Monaco for 1977 to 1978.
Predecessor to this model: Coronet (1968 to 1970).
Replacement for this model: Diplomat (1977 to 1979).
Percentage of division's sales volume: 12.85%.
Corporate siblings: Plymouth Satellite.
Primary competition: AMC Matador, Chevrolet Chevelle, Ford Torino, Mercury Montego, and Pontiac LeMans.
Notable changes: New front end styling and trim and detail changes.
Major standard equipment: All-vinyl front bench seat, cigarette lighter w/front and rear ashtrays, front and rear door armrests, 3-spoke color-keyed steering wheel, dome light w/front door courtesy switch, concealed two-speed windshield wipers w/washers, and E78 × 14 BSW tires. Custom adds: Cloth-and-vinyl bench seats (sedan only), color-keyed carpeting, simulated woodgrain inserts on I/P, door trim inserts and steering wheel, and drip rail, wheel-lip and bodyside moldings. Wagons add: Power front disc brakes, dual action tailgate w/concealed hinges, and H78 × 14 BSW tires. Crestwood wagon adds: All-vinyl split-back front bench seat w/fold-down center armrest, cargo compartment carpeting and dome light, rear roof air deflector, and exterior simulated woodgrained bodyside overlays.

Measurements

	Sedans	Wagons
Wheelbase	118.0"	118.0"
Length	212.4"	220.7"
Width	77.8"	78.8"
Height	53.6"	56.4"
Legroom — front	41.9"	41.9"
Legroom — rear	36.7"	36.7"
Headroom — front	38.3"	39.7"
Headroom — rear	37.3"	38.1"
Cargo capacity (cu. ft.)	19.1	86.8
Fuel capacity (gals.)	19.5	21.0

Models Available

	Model No.	Base MSRP	Change from LY	Shipping Wt. (lbs.)	Model Year Production	Change from LY
Coronet 4-Door Sedan	WL41	$3,170	+10.57%	3510	1,205*	NA*
Coronet 4-Door, 2-S. Wagon	WL45	$3,598	+2.23%	4085	*	NA*
Coronet Custom 4-Door Sedan	WH41	$3,273	+8.49%	3500	55,559**	NA**
Coronet Custom 4-Dr., 2-S. Wagon	WH45	$3,781	+9.85%	4090	**	NA**
Coronet Custom 4-Dr., 3-S. Wagon	WH46	$4,095	+15.03%	4130	**	NA**
Coronet Crestwood 4-Dr., 2-S. Wgn.	WP45	$4,016	+9.40%	4100	**	NA**
Coronet Crestwood 4-Dr., 3-S. Wgn.	WP46	$4,332	+14.27%	4135	**	NA**
TOTALS		Avg. price $3,722	+10.11%		Production 56,804	-35.11%

*Coronet base production was kept combined with base Charger, and above figure is estimated based on production split between 1973 Charger and Coronet; therefore comparison to LY is not possible.   **Production of Coronet Custom and Crestwood models were kept as combined total; therefore comparison to LY is not possible.

Monaco

"Affordable luxury is a part of Dodge's grand design for 1974."

Nameplate year of origin: 1965.
Current bodystyle lifespan: 1974 through 1977. Renamed Royal Monaco for 1977.
Predecessor to this model: Polara and Monaco (1969 to 1973).
Replacement for this model: St. Regis (1979 to 1981).
Percentage of division's sales volume: 16.62%.
Corporate siblings: Plymouth Fury.
Primary competition: AMC Ambassador Brougham, Chevrolet Caprice, Ford LTD, Mercury Monterey, Oldsmobile Delta 88, and Pontiac Bonneville/Grand Ville.
Notable changes: Completely redesigned.
Major standard equipment: Cloth and vinyl front bench seat, color-keyed carpeting, simulated woodgrained I/P appliqué, 3-spoke color-keyed steering wheel w/simulated woodgrained inserts, driver door storage compartment, day/night inside rear view mirror, LH outside rear view mirror, concealed two-speed windshield wipers w/electric washers, drip rail and beltline moldings, bright bodyside molding, rubber trunk mat, power steering, hubcaps, and G78 × 15 BSW tires. Custom adds: Desmond cloth and vinyl front bench seat, simulated woodgrained door trim insert w/carpeted lower panel, glove box light, wheel lip moldings, vinyl insert bodyside moldings, and trunk light. Brougham adds: Iraq cloth and vinyl 50/50 split front seat w/individual fold-down center armrest, door panel assist straps, electric clock, rear door dome light switch, map light, cigarette lighter light, dual horns, bodyside tape stripes, deluxe wheel covers, and HR78 × 15 BSW tires. Wagon adds: All-vinyl upholstery (w/seating configurations and other trim matching trim levels above), cargo compartment side storage panels, roof air deflector, and J78 × 15 BSW tires. Three-seat wagon adds: L78 × 15 BSW tires. Brougham wagon adds: Cargo compartment carpeting, cargo side panel lock, cargo area light, exterior woodgrained vinyl appliqué w/bright surround molding, and JR78 × 15 BSW tires (2-seat wagon) or LR78 × 15 BSW tires (3-seat wagon).

Measurements

	Cars	Wagons
Wheelbase	122.0"	124.0"
Length	220.5"	223.6"
Width	79.3"	79.4"
Height	54.8"	58.5"
Legroom — front	42.2"	42.2"
Legroom — rear	38.2"	39.1"
Headroom — front	38.7"	39.7"
Headroom — rear	37.8"	39.3"
Cargo capacity (cu. ft.)	20.4	100.8
Fuel capacity (gals.)	25.0	24.0

Models Available

	Model No.	Base MSRP	Change from LY*	Shipping Wt. (lbs.)	Model Year Production**	Change from LY*
Monaco 2-Door Hardtop	DM23	$4,048	+3.05%	4150	20,810	-75.00%**
Monaco 4-Door Sedan	DM41	$4,024	+2.89%	4170	NA	NA**
Monaco 4-Door, 2-Seat Wagon	DM45	$4,471	+2.31%	4760	NA	NA**
Monaco Custom 2-Door Hardtop	DH23	$4,112	NEW	4155	34,414	NEW
Monaco Custom 4-Door Sedan	DH41	$4,095	NEW	4175	NA	NEW
Monaco Custom 4-Door Hardtop	DH43	$4,185	NEW	4205	NA	NEW
Monaco Custom 4-Door, 2-Seat Wagon	DH45	$4,477	NEW	4770	NA	NEW
Monaco Custom 4-Door, 3-Seat Wagon	DH46	$4,591	NEW	4815	NA	NEW
Monaco Brougham 2-Door Hardtop	DP23	$4,682	+9.49%	4370	18,226	-38.00%**

	Model No.	Base MSRP	Change from LY*	Shipping Wt. (lbs.)	Model Year Production**	Change from LY*
Monaco Brougham 4-Door Sedan	DP41	$4,624	+9.63%	4410	NA	NA**
Monaco Brougham 4-Door Hardtop	DP43	$4,729	+8.99%	4445	NA	NA**
Monaco Brougham 4-Door, 2-Seat Wagon	DP45	$5,080	+7.40%	4860	NA	NA**
Monaco Brougham 4-Door, 3-Seat Wagon	DP46	$5,193	+6.87%	4905	NA	NA**
TOTALS	*Avg. price* $4,485		+4.01%		*Production* 73,450**	-34.78%**

*Comparisons made as follows: 1974 Monaco to 1973 Polara Custom, and 1974 Monaco Brougham to 1973 Monaco. 1974 Monaco Custom considered new model as there is no equivalent 1973 model.   **Production kept by sub-series only; therefore model to model comparisons are not possible. Total comparisons are 1973 Polara Custom and Monaco to 1974 Monaco series.

FORD

"The closer you look, the better we look."

For Ford, 1974 began as an exciting year and ended with the company gaining the most market share in the industry. The all-new, downsized Mustang II created all of the excitement in the showroom. Introduced just short of 10 years after the original Mustang, the new Mustang II was slightly smaller than the original and brought back much of the original "pony car" concept of a sporty, compact car with youthful styling, in a package that could be equipped to any taste, from a basic coupe to the sporty Mach I hatchback or a luxury Ghia model. Many comparisons could be made between the Mustang II and the 1964 Mustang, with the most interesting being that both were based on an existing Ford model, using some of its major components. The original was based on the Falcon, while the new Mustang II shared many components with the Pinto. It seems an unlikely choice, but the end result was successful. And it was impressive enough to be named the 1974 "Car of the Year" by *Motor Trend* magazine editors. By the end of the model year, production of the new Mustang II was nearly triple that of the 1973 Mustang.

The Mustang II's styling was an evolution of Mustangs past. Up front, a protruding trapezoidal egg-crate grille with rounded corners, parking/turn-signal lights set within each end of the grille, and single headlamps on the fender ends maintained a familiar Mustang look. A bodyside crease beginning near the top edge of the front fenders ran onto the door, fading out just below the side mirror. Another crease began just aft of the door's midpoint, a few inches lower, and arced slightly as it ran to a point mid-level at the end of the rear quarter panel. It then ran across the rear of the car to the other side, intersecting the large triple-lens taillamps that slanted forward over the line. Along each side was also a variation of the first generation Mustang's bodyside feature

line. Beginning midway through the door below the bodyside crease, a line ran backwards to a point just ahead of the rear wheel opening, then slanted down and forward about ten inches, and then ran forward, fading away near the front fender. Offering the Mustang II in what were actually two-door coupe and three-door hatchback models, Ford went to great lengths to call the coupe a 2-door hardtop and the hatchback a 3-door fastback, trying to maintain the connection to earlier Mustangs.

Inside the Mustang II, more luxurious accommodations could be found, with all gauges and controls set into a large driver's side pod. Within this pod were two large round dials containing the speedometer and standard tachometer, with warning lights for various systems to the right, and three smaller round dials to the lower right containing fuel, temperature and oil gauges. Other interior appointments included front bucket seats, color-keyed carpeting, and European style door armrests.

Unfortunately for traditional enthusiasts, the performance part of the Mustang II equation was missing. Powertrain choices consisted of a new 2.3L 4-cylinder, the first all-metric powerplant built in the United States, and a new, German-designed 2.8L V6 engine. Improved engine design meant that the horsepower rating of the 2.3L engine actually equaled that of the 1973 Mustang with the standard 6-cylinder, and the 2.8L V6 closely matched the output of the 302 CID V8 engine in the 1973 Mustang. With the new Mustang II being smaller and lighter than the 1973 model it replaced, performance with these engines was respectable. However, there is no question that the Mustang II was not a tire smoking performance machine like the 1971 Mustang Boss 351 with a 330-horsepower rating. On the positive side, the Mustang II offered better handling and nearly twice the gas mileage of its predecessor. It arrived in showrooms just in time to take advantage of the first oil crisis in America.

The mid-size Torino was given new front and rear styling treatments, along with more powerful engines and computer-selected coil springs to improve ride quality. The base Torino line continued to use a front-end design similar to the previous year's, with a large, full-width crosshatch grille and wrap-around parking/turn signal lamps. For Gran Torino models, styling changes at the front end centered on a more formal grille design consisting of eight sections divided by vertical bars, the outermost sections being filled by the parking/turn signal lights. Restyled quarter panels for both Torinos and Gran Torinos were more rounded at the back and housed the enlarged, wrap-around horizontal taillights that sat directly above the new box style, energy-absorbing bumper. For station wagons, the rear design was similar to 1973, with an upgrade to the bumper system. New rear fender skirts were available, except on station wagons, the base Torino line, and with certain wheel options. Also new was an optional opera window positioned behind the rear side window, available on any two-door Torino and standard on the Gran Torino Brougham. The 2-door models' rear side windows were now of a fixed position design. Interior styling received the requisite color and trim updates.

Soon after the introduction of the 1974 Torino, a new top-of-the-line model was added, the Gran Torino Elite 2-Door Hardtop, featuring its own look to compete in the mid-size, entry-level, personal/luxury market dominated by the Chevrolet Monte Carlo. Combining the sportiness of a Gran Torino Sport with the luxury of a Thunderbird, the Elite became the best selling Torino model for 1974, and would become its own series for 1975. The Elite was not totally new, as Ford described it, but it did have a number of special design features. The Elite wore unique front-end sheetmetal inspired by the Thunderbird, featuring single headlamps set in chrome bezels, and parking lamps on the tips of the pointed front fenders. The Elite egg-crate grille was also similar in design to the Thunderbird's. The rear quarter panels and doors were shared with the Mercury Cougar, and the Elite did not have the same body line as other Torinos. The rear panel also featured larger taillights that ran the full width of the car, wrapping around the quarter panel ends, with the center portion being reflective only. The Elite came standard with a 351 CID, 2-bbl. V8 engine and automatic transmission. It also featured standard luxury items such as a vinyl roof, opera windows, split bench seat, "Westminster" cloth upholstery, woodgrain trim, and complete instrumentation.

The popular Pinto added the previously optional 2.0L 4-cylinder engine as standard equipment, along with an improved version of the standard 4-speed manual transmission. Newly designed front disc brakes were standard this year for all models, and both front and rear suspensions were upgraded. The Pinto was so popular in this, its best sales year ever, that if it had been its own division of Ford, it would have ranked 6th in industry production, outselling AMC, Buick, Dodge, Mercury, and all of the luxury makes, with only three models.

Styling changes to the compact Maverick were limited to those necessary to accommodate the new rear bumper, but new features were added to the sporty Grabber model including dual color-keyed outside mirrors, a new lower bodyside paint treatment, and wide oval tires with raised white letters. Despite receiving few visual changes, both cars added nearly five inches in length and over 100 pounds of weight.

The full-size LTD models and the personal luxury Thunderbird were given some minor refinements and the required changes to accommodate the new rear bumper standards.

Galaxie 500 4-Door Hardtop

Gran Torino 4-Door Pillared Hardtop

Gran Torino Brougham 2-Door Hardtop

Gran Torino Elite 2-Door Hardtop

Gran Torino Elite 2-Door Hardtop

Gran Torino instrument panel

Gran Torino Sport 2-Door Hardtop

LTD 2-Door Hardtop

LTD Country Squire 4-Door Station Wagon

Maverick 2-Door Sedan

Maverick Grabber 2-Door Sedan

Mustang II 2-Door Hardtop Coupe

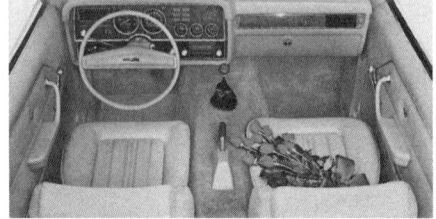

Mustang II Ghia interior

Mustang II Mach I 3-Door Hatchback

Pinto 3-Door Runabout Hatchback

Pinto Squire 2-Door Station Wagon

Thunderbird 2-Door Hardtop

Thunderbird 2-Door Hardtop

Model year production: 2,179,791, down 7.22% from 1973.
Domestic market share: 25.22% (2nd place).
Base price range: $2,527 to $7,330.
Ford average base price: $4,022, up 16.19%.
Introduction date: September 1973.
Assembly plants: Atlanta, GA (A); Oakville, Ontario, Canada (B); Mahwah, NJ (E); Dearborn, MI (F); Chicago, IL (G); Lorain, OH (H); Los Angeles, CA (J); Kansas City, MO (K); Norfolk, VA (N); Twin Cities, MN (P); San Jose, CA (R); Allen Park, MI (S —*pilot plant*); Metuchen, NJ (T); Louisville, KY (U); Wayne, MI (W); St. Thomas, Ontario, Canada (X); Wixom, MI (Y); and St. Louis, MO (Z).

Data plate identification (VIN): Eleven digit code read as follows: First digit indicates year (4 = 1974); second digit indicates assembly plant code (see list above); third and fourth digits indicate model number (model number in model charts); fifth digit indicates engine code (see powertrain chart); remaining digits are sequential with beginning numbers of 100001. *Example:* 4F02Z100001 is a 1974 Ford Mustang II 2-Door Coupe, with 170.8 CID, 2-bbl. V6 engine, serial number 100001, built in Dearborn, MI.

Powertrains

Engine	Net HP	Engine Code	Transmission Availability[1]		Pinto	Mustang II	Maverick	Torino[2]	Full-size[2]	Thunderbird[2]
122 CID (2.0L) OHC, 2-bbl., 4-cyl.	86	X	4-speed manual		S	—	—	—	—	—
				MPG:	22.8	—	—	—	—	—
			3-speed Select-Shift Cruise-O-Matic		$170	—	—	—	—	—
				MPG:	16.9	—	—	—	—	—
140 CID (2.3L) OHC, 2-bbl., 4-cyl.	82/88[3]	Y	4-speed manual		$48	S (others)/ $229 (credit on Mach I)	—	—	—	—
				MPG:	21	16.6	—	—	—	—
			3-speed Select-Shift Cruise-O-Matic		$218	$204 (ex. Mach I)	—	—	—	—
				MPG:	16.7	16.9	—	—	—	—
170.8 CID (2.8L), 2-bbl., V6	105	Z	4-speed manual		—	S (Mach I)/ $229 (others)	—	—	—	—
				MPG:	—	17.3	—	—	—	—
			3-speed Select-Shift Cruise-O-Matic		—	$204 (Mach I)/ $433 (others)	—	—	—	—
				MPG:	—	15	—	—	—	—
200 CID (3.3L), 1-bbl., 6-cyl.	84	T	3-speed manual		—	—	S	—	—	—
				MPG:	—	—	NA	—	—	—
			3-speed Select-Shift Cruise-O-Matic		—	—	$177	—	—	—
				MPG:	—	—	15	—	—	—
250 CID (4.1L), 1-bbl., 6-cyl.	91	L	3-speed manual		—	—	$39	—	—	—
				MPG:	—	—	16.7	—	—	—
			3-speed Select-Shift Cruise-O-Matic		—	—	$217	—	—	—
				MPG:	—	—	15.6	—	—	—
302 CID (5.0L), 2-bbl., V8	140	F	3-speed manual		—	—	$122	S (cars)[4]	—	—
				MPG:	—	—	NA	11	—	—
			3-speed Select-Shift Cruise-O-Matic		—	—	$299	S (wgns.)[4]/ $211 (others)	—	—
				MPG:	—	—	12.1	11.8	—	—
351 CID (5.8L), 2-bbl., V8	162	H	3-speed Select-Shift Cruise-O-Matic		—	—	—	$44 (wgns.)/ $255 (others)	S (cars)	—
				MPG:	—	—	—	10.8	10.7	—
351 CID (5.8L), 4-bbl., V8	180	Q	3-speed Select-Shift Cruise-O-Matic		—	—	—	$338 (2-Drs. only)[4,5]	—	—
				MPG:	—	—	—	9.9	—	—
400 CID (6.6L), 2-bbl., V8	170	S	3-speed Select-Shift Cruise-O-Matic		—	—	—	$135 (wgns.)/ $346 (others)[4]	S (wgns.)/ $90 (others)	—
				MPG:	—	—	—	8.8	10	—
460 CID (7.5L), 4-bbl., V8	220	A	3-speed Select-Shift Cruise-O-Matic		—	—	—	$274 (wgns.)/ $505 (others)[4]	$202 (wgns.)/ $292 (others)	S
				MPG:	—	—	—	7.5	9.1	8.1

[1]*Unless otherwise noted: All manual transmissions are floor-shifts, except on Maverick. All automatics are column-shift, except on Pinto and Mustang II. Floor-shift is available for $24 extra on Maverick with 3-speed manual, and Maverick with automatic (requires bucket seats or Luxury Décor option).* [2]*Optional axle ratio required on Torino, Thunderbird and full-size Fords with V8 sold in California.* [3]*Horsepower rating in Mustang II.* [4]*Not available in California.* [5]*The 351 CID 4-bbl. V8 is standard on Gran Torino Elite. The 400 CID engine is optional for $10, and the 460 CID V8 engine is optional for $167.*

Major Options

	Pinto	Maverick	Mustang II	Torino	Full-size	Thunderbird
SelectAire Air conditioning	$363[1]	$363	$368	$402	$410[2]	$437[2]
Tilt steering wheel	—	—	—	—	$44	$51
Fingertip speed control	—	—	—	—	$99	$103
Rear window defogger[3]	$28	$27	—	—	$30	—
Electric rear window defroster[3]	$43	—	$57	$47	$62	$82
Tinted glass, all windows	$36	$49	$36	$42	$53	$51
Power windows	—	—	—	$124	$129	$130
Power door locks, 2-dr./4-dr.	—	—	—	$46/$69	$46/$69	$59
Power seat, 6-way w/std. seating	—	—	—	$102	$102	$202
Front bucket seats w/console	—	$98[4]	S[4]	$205	—	N/C
AM radio	$59	$59	$59	$64	$64	S
AM/FM stereo	$190	$190	$213	$208	$234	$146
AM/FM stereo w/8-track tape	—	—	$333	—	$363	$299
Vinyl top, full	$75	$75	$80	$93	$110[5]	$137
Sunroof, power-operated	$117[6]	—	$143[6]	—	$496	$505
Power trunk lid release	—	—	—	—	$14	—
Power steering	—	$92	$102	$112	S	S
Power brakes, w/front disc	—	—	$43	$68	S	S
Deluxe wheel covers	—	—	—	$87	$62–$87	$62
Forged aluminum wheels	$142	$142	$99–$141	—	—	—
Magnum 500 chrome wheels	—	—	$42[7]	$151	—	—
White sidewall tires, std. size[8]	$42	$29	$29	$32	$32	S

Popular Option Groups & Packages[9]

	Pinto	Maverick	Mustang II	Torino	Full-size	Thunderbird
Accent group	$65–$87	—	—	$38	—	—
Appearance protection group	—	—	—	$39–$46	$47–$54	$72
Convenience group	—	$22–$33	$41	—	$59	—
Décor group	—	—	—	—	—	—
Deluxe bumper group	$36	$49	—	$42–$68	$49–$61	$30
Exterior décor group	—	$76	—	—	—	$237
Glamour paint option group	—	—	—	—	—	$162
Instrumentation group	—	—	—	$118	—	—
Interior décor group	—	$65–$82	—	—	—	—
Light group	$24	—	$42	—	$25–$32	$44
Luxury décor group	$153–$192	$401	$96	—	—	—
Maintenance group	—	—	$42	—	—	—
Mirror group	$42	—	—	—	—	—
Protection group	$51	$36–$42	$39–$45	—	—	—
Rallye package	—	—	$144–$315	—	—	—
Sports accent group	$395	—	—	—	—	—
Sports interior option	—	—	—	—	—	—
Squire option	$237	—	—	—	—	—
Squire Brougham option	—	—	—	—	$264	—
Turnpike convenience group	—	—	—	—	—	$133
Visibility group	—	—	—	$37	—	—

—= Not Available; S = Standard equipment. [1]*Requires 2.3L 4-cylinder engine and A78 × 13 tires on Pinto.* [2]*SelectAire air conditioner w/automatic temperature control is available for $487 on full-size Fords and $506 on Thunderbird.* [3]*Defogger available only on Pinto Sedan and Maverick and is required in New York state. Defroster available on any Pinto and required on all Fords in New York state, except above models. Price includes tinted rear window with defroster on Pinto.* [4]*Bucket seats only on Maverick and Mustang II; console not available.* [5]*For wagons, $138.* [6]*Manually operated sunroof. Not available on Mustang II 2+2 or Mach I models.* [7]*Styled steel wheels on Mustang II.* [8]*Price on wagons: Pinto, $28.* [9]*Price ranges cover all models available. See Appendix IV for content details and model availability variations.*

Paint Colors

	Code	Pinto	Mustang II	Maverick	Torino	Full-size	Thunderbird
Black	1C		x			x	x
Silver Cloud metallic	1E						x
Silver Metallic	1G	x	x	x			
Bright Red	2B	x	x	x	x		
Red	2E		x			x	
Burgundy Fire metallic[1]	2G						x
Dark Red	2M		x				
Platinum	3A						x
Light Blue	3B	x	x	x		x	
Medium Blue metallic	3D		x		x	x	x
Bright Blue metallic	3E	x	x	x			
Dark Blue metallic	3G		x		x	x	x
Silver Blue Fire metallic[1]	3L						x
Silver Blue Glow metallic	3M		x	x	x		
Light Grabber Blue	3N	x		x			
Silver Blue Starfire metallic[1]	3P						x
Pastel Blue	3Q		x		x		
Pastel Lime	4A		x		x	x	x
Bright Green Gold metallic[2]	4B	x	x		x		
Dark Green metallic	4Q		x		x	x	
Green Glow metallic	4T	x	x	x	x	x	
Lime Gold Moondust metallic	4U						x
Dark Yellow Green metallic	4V	x	x	x			
Medium Lime metallic	4W	x	x	x			
Green Starfire metallic[1]	4Y						x
Cinnamon Starfire metallic[1]	51						x
Mahogany Starfire metallic[1]	52						x
Medium Brown metallic	5H	x	x	x		x	
Ginger Glow metallic[2]	5J	x	x	x	x	x	
Medium Copper metallic	5M		x		x	x	
Dark Brown metallic	5Q						x
Autumn Fire metallic[1]	5R						x
Medium Beige	5S						x
Saddle Bronze metallic	5T	x	x	x	x	x	
Tan Glow metallic	5U	x	x	x	x	x	
Buff	5V						x
Orange	5W	x	x	x			
Medium Yellow Goldenrod	6C	x	x	x			
Yellow Gold Glow metallic[2]	6F		x		x	x	
Gold Fire metallic[1]	6G						x
Medium Gold metallic	6L						x
Dark Olive Gold metallic	6M		x		x		x
Medium Ivy Yellow	6N		x		x	x	x
Wimbledon White	9A				x	x	
Pearl White	9C	x	x				x
Polar White	9D			x			

In two-tone combinations, first two digits are lower color and second two digits are upper color. Two-tones available full-size Fords (except Country Squire) for $30.
[1]*Fire/Starfire metallic paints require purchase of Glamour paint option group.* [2]*Metallic glow paints are $35 extra on Maverick & Mustang II, $38 on Torino & full-size Fords.*

Pinto

"Built to be a basic, dependable, economical little car.
And this year we've improved the basics."

Nameplate year of origin: 1971.
Current bodystyle lifespan: 1971 through 1980.
Predecessor to this model: None.
Replacement for this model: Escort (1981 to 1985).
Percentage of division's production: 24.97%.
Corporate siblings: None.
Primary competition: AMC Gremlin, Buick Opel, Chevrolet Vega, and Dodge Colt.
Notable changes: Minor trim and detail changes.
Major standard equipment: All-vinyl high-back front bucket seats, variable intensity illuminated I/P controls, mini-front console, color-keyed rubber floor mat, bright front and rear window moldings, rack-and-pinion steering, manual front disc brakes, hubcaps, and 6.00 × 13 BSW tires. Runabout adds: Color-keyed carpeting in passenger compartment and load floor, and fold-down rear seat. Station wagon adds: Flip-out rear quarter windows and A78 × 13 BSW tires.

Measurements

	Sedan	Runabout	Wagon
Wheelbase	94.2"	94.2"	94.2"
Length	169.0"	169.0"	178.8"
Width	69.4"	69.4"	69.7"
Height	50.3"	50.3"	51.9"
Legroom — front	40.8"	40.8"	40.8"
Legroom — rear	30.7"	30.7"	30.7"
Headroom — front	37.3"	37.3"	37.9"
Headroom — rear	36.2"	36.2"	39.3"
Cargo capacity (cu. ft.)	5.0	6.1*	60.6
Fuel capacity (gals.)	13.0	13.0	12.0

With rear seat folded down, 41.3 cu. ft.

Models Available

	Model No.	Base MSRP	Change from LY	Shipping Wt. (lbs.)	Model Year Production	Change from LY
Pinto 2-Door Sedan	10	$2,527	+25.04%	2372	132,061	+13.70%
Pinto 3-Dr. Runabout (hatchback)	11	$2,676	+24.81%	2406	174,754	+16.04%
Pinto 2-Door Station Wagon	12	$2,771	+18.27%	2576	237.394	+9.01%
TOTALS		Avg. price $2,658	+22.53%		Production 544,209	+12.32%

Mustang II

"The right car at the right time."

Nameplate year of origin: 1964 (also used on a 1963 show car).
Current bodystyle lifespan: 1974 through 1978.
Predecessor to this model: Mustang (1971 to 1973).
Replacement for this model: Mustang (1979 to 1993).
Percentage of division's production: 17.71%.
Corporate siblings: None.
Primary competition: Buick Opel Manta and Mercury Capri.
Notable changes: Completely redesigned.
Major standard equipment: Low-back vinyl bucket seats, color-keyed cut-pile carpeting, two-spoke steering wheel, courtesy lights, tachometer, dual outside color-keyed mirrors, and B78 × 13 BSW tires. 2+2 adds: Fold-down rear seat and styled steel wheels. Ghia adds (to 2-door): Luxury interior group, deluxe color-keyed seat belts, digital clock, dual remote control outside color-keyed mirrors, vinyl insert bodyside molding, bodyside pinstripes, super sound package, vinyl roof, styled steel wheels, and BR78 × 13 WSW tires. Mach I adds (to 2+2): Dual remote control outside color-keyed mirrors, specific Mach I paint stripes and identification, wheel trim rings, and BR70 × 13 B/WL tires.

Measurements

	Coupe	3-Door
Wheelbase	96.2"	96.2"
Length	175.0"	175.0"
Width	70.2"	70.2"
Height	49.9"	49.6"
Legroom — front	37.2"	37.2"
Legroom — rear	27.7"	27.7"
Headroom — front	37.2"	37.2"
Headroom — rear	35.9"	34.1"
Cargo capacity (cu. ft.)	6.7	28.1*
Fuel capacity (gals.)	13.0	13.0

With rear seat folded down.

Models Available

	Model No.	Base MSRP	Change from LY*	Shipping Wt. (lbs.)	Model Year Production	Change from LY*
Mustang II 2-Door Hardtop Coupe	02	$3,134	+13.55%	2620	177,671	+245.46%
Mustang II 2+2 3-Door (hatchback)	03	$3,328	+18.01%	2699	74,799	+591.30%
Mustang II Ghia 2-Door Hardtop Coupe	04	$3,480	+18.13%	2686	89,477	+254.03%
Mustang II Mach I 3-Door (hatchback)	05	$3,674	+18.98%	2778	44,046	+24.28%
TOTALS		Avg. price $3,404	+15.66%		Production 385,993	+186.31%

Comparisons of 2+2 made to 1973 Mustang SportsRoof, and Ghia to 1973 Mustang Grande. Use model numbers as guide to comparisons.

Maverick

"The economical car we build for families."

Nameplate year of origin: 1970.
Current bodystyle lifespan: 1970 through 1977.
Predecessor to this model: Falcon (1966 to 1969).
Replacement for this model: Fairmont (1978 to 1983).
Percentage of division's production: 13.81%.
Corporate siblings: Mercury Comet.
Primary competition: AMC Hornet, Chevrolet Nova, and Plymouth Valiant.
Notable changes: Minor trim and detail changes.
Major standard equipment: Cloth-and-vinyl front bench seat, nylon loop pile carpeting, illuminated I/P controls, two-spoke steering wheel, hubcaps, and 6.45 × 14 BSW tires. Sedan adds: C78 × 14 BSW tires. Grabber adds: All-vinyl upholstery, LH remote and RH manual outside color-keyed mirrors, Grabber tape stripes, hubcaps w/trim rings, and D70 × 14 WO RWL tires.

Measurements

	2-Door	4-Door
Wheelbase	103.0"	109.9"
Length	187.0"	193.9"
Width	70.5"	70.5"
Height	53.0"	52.8"
Legroom — front	40.7"	40.7"
Legroom — rear	32.0"	36.2"
Headroom — front	37.5"	37.8"
Headroom — rear	36.0"	36.7"
Cargo capacity (cu. ft.)	11.3	13.1
Fuel capacity (gals.)	15.0	15.0

Models Available

	Model No.	Base MSRP	Change from LY	Shipping Wt. (lbs.)	Model Year Production	Change from LY
Maverick 2-Door Sedan	91	$2,790	+24.11%	2739	139,818	-6.13%
Maverick 4-Door Sedan	92	$2,824	+22.52%	2851	137,728	+24.77%
Maverick Grabber 2-Door Sedan	93	$2,923	+20.44%	2787	23,502	-27.53%
TOTALS		Avg. price $2,846	+22.31%		Production 301,048	+3.21%

Torino

"The mid-size Torino proves that solid can be beautiful."

Nameplate year of origin: 1968.
Current bodystyle lifespan: 1972 through 1976.
Predecessor to this model: Fairlane and Torino (1970 to 1971).
Replacement for this model: LTD II (1977 to 1979).
Percentage of division's sales volume: 19.66%.
Corporate siblings: Mercury Montego.
Primary competition: AMC Matador, Chevrolet Chevelle, Dodge Coronet and Charger, Plymouth Satellite, and Pontiac LeMans.

Measurements

	2-Doors	Elite	4-Doors	Wagons
Wheelbase	114.0"	114.0"	118.0"	118.0"
Length	213.6"*	215.5"	217.6"*	222.6"*
Width	79.3"	78.5"	79.3"	79.0"
Height	52.8"	53.0"	53.5"	54.9"
Legroom — front	42.5"	42.1"	42.5"	42.5"
Legroom — rear	33.2"	32.2"	37.8"	37.3"

Notable changes: Revised front- and rear-end styling.

Major standard equipment: All-vinyl low-back front bench seat, loop-pile carpeting, windshield and rear window bright moldings, bright drip rail molding, manual front disc brakes, hubcaps, and G78 × 14 BSW tires. Wagon adds: Three-way tailgate, bright rear quarter window moldings, power front disc brakes, and H78 × 14 BSW tires. Gran Torino adds: Cloth and vinyl front bench seat, nylon loop carpeting, concealed windshield wipers, side window bright moldings, and wheel lip moldings. Gran Torino Brougham adds: Brougham cloth and vinyl "Flight Bench" split front seat, electric clock, deluxe steering wheel, vinyl top, opera window on 2-doors, and HR78 × 14 WSW tires. Gran Torino Squire adds: All-vinyl bench seat, simulated woodgrain bodyside paneling, full wheel covers, and HR78 × 14 WSW tires. Gran Torino Sport adds: Pleated vinyl bench seat, LH remote and RH manual outside color-keyed dual racing mirrors, and bright wheel trim rings w/hubcaps. Gran Torino Elite adds: Westminster cloth "Flight Bench" split front seat, simulated woodgrain I/P and door trim, complete instrumentation, vinyl roof w/opera windows, and specific front end treatment w/single headlamps and fender endcap mounted parking/turn signal lights.

Measurements (cont.)

	2-Doors	Elite	4-Doors	Wagons
Headroom — front	37.6"	37.4"	38.3"	38.4"
Headroom — rear	36.2"	36.3"	37.0"	38.5"
Cargo capacity (cu. ft.)	16.5	16.5	16.5	84.9
Fuel capacity (gals.)	26.5	26.5	26.5	21.2

Overall length of base Torino models is 2.2" less than listed, due to different front end. See 1974 Ford introduction.

Models Available

	Model No.	Base MSRP	Change from LY	Shipping Wt. (lbs.)	Model Year Production	Change from LY
Torino 2-Door Hardtop	25	$3,236	+18.45%	3709	22,738	-18.81%
Torino 4-Door Pillared Hardtop	27	$3,239	+19.92%	3793	31,161	-16.96%
Torino 4-Door, 2-S., 6-p. Wagon	40	$3,818	+19.39%	4175	15,393	-35.81%
Gran Torino 2-Door Hardtop	30	$3,411	+16.78%	3742	76,290	*
Gran Torino 4-Door Pillared Hardtop	31	$3,454	+19.52%	3847	72,728	*
Gran Torino 4-Door, 2-S., 6-p. Wagon	42	$4,017	+20.13%	4209	29,866	-50.83%
Gran Torino Sport 2-Door Hardtop	38	$3,824	+21.24%	3771	23,142	+35.41%
Gran Torino Brougham 2-Door Hardtop	32	$3,975	+29.44%	3794	26,402	*
Gran Torino Brougham 4-Dr. Pillared HT	33	$3,966	+29.99%	3887	11,464	*
Gran Torino Squire 4-Dr., 2-S., 6-p. Wgn.	43	$4,300	+20.82%	4250	22,837	-42.94%
Gran Torino Elite 2-Door Hardtop	21	$4,437	NEW	3960	96,604	NEW
TOTALS		Avg. price $3,789	+23.40%		Production 428,625	-13.68%

Comparison not possible due to production of 1973 Gran Torino Brougham models being included with Gran Torino models.

Custom 500, Galaxie 500 and LTD

"The closer you look, the better we look."

Nameplate year of origin: 1957 (Custom), 1959 (Galaxie), and 1965 (LTD).

Current bodystyle lifespan: 1971 through 1978 (restyled in 1973 and 1975).

Predecessor to this model: Custom/Galaxie/LTD (1969 to 1970).

Replacement for this model: LTD (1979 to 1991).

Percentage of division's sales volume: 21.17%.

Corporate siblings: Mercury Monterey and Marquis.

Primary competition: AMC Ambassador, Chevrolet BelAir/Impala/Caprice, Dodge Monaco, Plymouth Fury, and Pontiac Catalina.

Notable changes: Revised rear styling and minor trim and detail changes.

Measurements

	2-Doors	4-Doors	Wagons
Wheelbase	121.0"	121.0"	121.0"
Length	222.5"	222.5"	225.2"
Width	79.5"	79.5"	79.9"
Height	53.5"	54.9"	57.1"
Legroom — front	41.5"	41.5"	41.7"
Legroom — rear	35.5"	38.3"	37.1"
Headroom — front	37.3"	38.3"	38.7"
Headroom — rear	37.3"	37.3"	39.1"
Cargo capacity (cu. ft.)	19.9	19.9	94.6
Fuel capacity (gals.)	22.0	22.0	21.0

Major standard equipment: Cloth and vinyl front bench seat, color-keyed nylon loop pile carpeting, black camera case I/P instrument cluster appliqué w/woodtone appliqué on passenger side, bright moldings (front and rear window, drip rail and grille), power steering, power front disc brakes, chrome hubcaps, and G78 × 15 BSW tires. Ranch Wagon adds: All-vinyl front bench seat, power tailgate window, and J78 × 15 BSW tires. Galaxie 500 and Country Sedan adds: Karmel cloth and vinyl upholstery (all-vinyl on wagon), front door courtesy light switches, woodgrained I/P trim, and wheel lip moldings. LTD adds: Tailored cloth and vinyl upholstery, glove box light, electric clock, deluxe two-spoke steering wheel, luggage compartment light, bodyside protection moldings w/black vinyl insert, and rocker panel molding. LTD wagon adds: Cargo area light, and full wheel covers. Country Squire adds: Simulated woodgrain exterior paneling. LTD Brougham adds: Brougham cloth and vinyl "Flight Bench" seat w/fold-down front and rear seat center armrests, Brougham door panel trim w/simulated woodgrain appliqués, cut-pile nylon carpeting, electric clock, bright seat side shields, full simulated woodgrain I/P appliqué, vinyl roof, bright chrome grille surround moldings, and full wheel covers.

Models Available

	Model No.	Base MSRP	Change from LY	Shipping Wt. (lbs.)	Model Year Production	Change from LY
Custom 500 4-Door Pillared Hardtop	53	$3,982	+10.43%	4180	28,941	-31.98%
Custom 500 Ranch Wagon 4-Door 6-p.	72	$4,488	+10.81%	4654	12,104	-46.04%
Custom 500 Ranch Wagon 4-Door w/DFRS*	72	$4,608	+10.66%	4687	*	*
Galaxie 500 2-Door Hardtop	58	$4,211	+11.46%	4157	34,214	-51.68%
Galaxie 500 4-Door Pillared Hardtop	54	$4,164	+10.42%	4196	49,661	-42.02%
Galaxie 500 4-Door Hardtop	56	$4,237	+10.54%	4212	11,526	-55.33%
Galaxie 500 Country Sedan 4-Door 6-p. Wgn.	74	$4,584	+10.56%	4690	22,400	-56.33%
Galaxie 500 Country Sedan 4-Dr. Wgn. w/DFRS*	74	$4,704	+10.42%	4723	*	*
LTD 2-Door Hardtop	62	$4,389	+11.11%	4215	73,296	-39.36%
LTD 4-Door Pillared Hardtop	63	$4,370	+10.41%	4262	72,251	-41.19%
LTD 4-Door Hardtop	64	$4,438	+10.92%	4277	12,375	-56.74%
LTD 4-Door, 6-p. Wagon**	76	$4,752	+10.61%	4737	39,084	-72.66%
LTD 4-Door Wagon w/DFRS**	76	$4,872	+10.48%	4770	**	**
LTD Country Squire 4-Door 6-p. Wagon**	76	$4,898	+11.29%	4752	**	**
LTD Country Squire 4-Door Wagon w/DFRS**	76	$5,018	+11.14%	4785	**	**
LTD Brougham 2-Door Hardtop	68	$4,669	+13.68%	4247	30,203	-56.16%
LTD Brougham 4-Door Pillared Hardtop	66	$4,647	+12.98%	4292	11,371	-77.05%
LTD Brougham 4-Door Hardtop	67	$4,717	+13.47%	4310	64,047	+187.62%
TOTALS	Avg. price	$4,542	+11.20%	Production	461,473	-46.00%

*Production is included with 2-seat, 6-passenger models of same series.   **Production of woodgrain and non-woodgrain Country Squire models, as well as 2-Seat, 6-passenger, and 8-passenger with Dual Facing Rear Seats were kept as a single total.

Thunderbird

"Make a little Thunder of your own."

Nameplate year of origin: 1955.
Current bodystyle lifespan: 1972 through 1976.
Predecessor to this model: Thunderbird (1967 to 1971; restyled in 1970).
Replacement for this model: Thunderbird (1977 to 1979).
Percentage of division's sales volume: 2.68%.
Corporate siblings: Lincoln Continental Mark IV.
Primary competition: Buick Riviera and Oldsmobile Toronado.
Notable changes: Minor trim and detail changes.
Major standard equipment: Aurora cloth and vinyl individually adjustable split bench front seat w/fold-down center armrests and automatic seatback release, deluxe seat belts, courtesy lighting (dome, door, under dash, glove box and ashtray), cut pile nylon carpeting, simulated woodgrain I/P and door panel trim, electric clock, AM radio, power windows, power interior ventilation system, Odense grain vinyl roof w/opera windows, fully lined luggage compartment w/light, unique Thunder-

Measurements

Wheelbase	120.4"
Length	224.8"
Width	79.7"
Height	53.0"
Legroom — front	42.0"
Legroom — rear	36.4"
Headroom — front	37.5"
Headroom — rear	36.8"
Cargo capacity (cu. ft.)	13.4
Fuel capacity (gals.)	26.5

bird hood ornament, bright moldings (rear hood edge, beltline ,drip rails and wheel openings), bodyside molding w/protective vinyl insert, power steering, power front disc brakes, full wheel covers, and 230R × 15 WSW radial tires.

Models Available

	Model No.	Base MSRP	Change from LY	Shipping Wt. (lbs.)	Model Year Production	Change from LY
Thunderbird 2-Door Hardtop	87	$7,330	+13.87%	4825	58,443	-33.03%
TOTALS		Avg. price $7,330	+13.87%	Production	58,443	-33.03%

LINCOLN

"A standard for judging luxury cars."

The 1974 model year was not kind to any of the American manufacturers, an those companies trying to sell big luxury cars seem to take the biggest hit. Lincoln, however, seem to fare much better than Cadillac or the Chrysler Imperial, as sales dropped only to about the 1972 model year levels, and production ranked among Lincoln's top three model years. Lincoln's strategy of stressing its superior ride quality as compared to its competition seemed to be the right marketing path.

For the new model year, all three Lincoln models received updated rear bumpers and styling changes to meet the federal rear bumper standards. Lincoln also took the opportunity to freshen the front end of the Continental coupe and sedan, eliminating such things as the ornamentation on the hidden headlight doors, and adding a vertical bar grille that brought the more classic look of the Mark IV to the line. On the Continentals, the raised center section was part of the body colored front header panel and bore the Lincoln name in widely spaced block letters above the grille. The Continental vertical bar grille opening was therefore shorter than on the Mark IV, but also wider. The Continental name in script on the left headlight door was the only other decoration on the front of the car, aside from the stand-up ornament atop the header panel.

At the rear, the 1974 Continentals continued to use a horizontal taillamp theme, this year set above the rear bumper, only a few inches high, surrounded by chrome trim, with a small section that wrapped around the rear quarter panel end, doubling as a side marker light. The Mark IV also had a new rear bumper and rear end look, which continued to feature the "Continental" spare tire look in the trunk lid, extending into the rear bumper as a slight protrusion. Taillights on the Continental Mark IV were also wrap-around

vertical units, but ended just short of the "Continental" spare tire hump, with backup lights set to the inside of the lens. The name "Continental" continued to arch around the curve of the spare tire hump, with the Lincoln emblem placed low in the center as a cover for the trunklid keyhole. No styling changes were made to the front of the Continental Mark IV.

Under the hood, the big Ford 460 CID V8 engine mated to the Select-Shift three-speed automatic transmission continued to be standard fare. The new year brought the addition of a solid-state ignition system for improved control of emissions. However, the fuel crisis of the period highlighted the need for Lincoln to make improvements in fuel economy, as its estimated eight miles per gallon was among the worst ratings for all automobiles.

Lincoln introduced a new option this year that would eventually make its way to other Ford products, the "Quick Defrost" defroster system. In this unique system, a heating element of gold-plated Mylar was fashioned as an integral part of both the windshield and the rear window, eliminating grid lines and offering a faster defrosting time. The Mylar gave the windows a gold tint from the outside. Also newly available was a gold tinted glass panel moonroof that joined the silver tinted version introduced after the start of the 1973 model year on any Mark IV with the Silver luxury group. Other new features in comfort and convenience included an automatic light system, called "Autolamp," which automatically turned the headlamps on and off according to outdoor light conditions and could be adjusted to stay on for up to 90 seconds after leaving the car before automatically shutting off. Also new this year, the optional vanity mirrors were moved from the glove box to the sun visor, and were illuminated.

Continental interior

Continental 4-Door Sedan
with Town Car option

Continental Mark IV interior
with Gold Luxury group

Continental Mark IV 2-Door Hardtop
with Gold Luxury group

Model year production: 93,985, down 26.62% from 1973.
Domestic market share: 1.09% (12th place).
Base price range: $7,931 to $10,049.
Lincoln average base price: $8,699, up 10.17%.
Introduction date: September 1973.
Assembly plants: Allen Park, MI (S—*pilot plant*); and Wixom, MI (Y).
Data plate identification (VIN): Eleven digit code read as follows: First digit indicates year (4 = 1974); second digit indicates assembly plant code (see list above); third and fourth digits indicate model number (model number in model charts); fifth digit indicates engine code (see power-train chart); remaining digits are sequential with beginning numbers of 800001. *Example:* 4Y82A800001 is a 1974 Lincoln Continental 4-Door Sedan, with 460 CID, 4-bbl. V8 engine, serial number 800001, built in Wixom, MI.

Powertrains*

Engine	Net HP	Engine Code	Transmission Availability		Continental	Mark IV
460 CID (7.5L), 4-bbl., V8	215	A	3-speed SelectShift Automatic		S	—
				MPG:	7.9	—
460 CID (7.5L), 4-bbl., V8	220	A	3-speed SelectShift Automatic		—	S
				MPG:	—	7.9

*Optional 3.00:1 axle ratio required on cars sold in California. Cost is $27.

Major Options

	Continental	Mark IV		Continental	Mark IV
Air conditioning, Auto-Temp	S	S	Anti-theft alarm system	$77	$77
Tilt steering wheel	$70	$70	AM radio, w/power antenna	S	—
Automatic speed control	$92	$92	AM/FM stereo	$142	S
Electric rear window defroster	$83	$83	AM/FM stereo w/8-track tape	$269	$127
Quick Defrost, front/rear windows	—	$307	Vinyl top, full	$152	S
Tinted glass, all windows	S	S	Moonroof, power-operated & tinted	—	$777
Power windows	S	S	Sunroof, power-operated	$611	$611
Power front vent windows[1]	$68	$68	Power trunk lid release	$[1]	$[1]
Power door locks, 2-dr./4-dr.	$[2]	$[2]	Power steering	S	S
Power seat, 6-way w/pass. recliner	$59	S	Power brakes, w/front disc	S	—
Leather seating upholstery	$169	$179	"Sure-Track" antilock brake system	$192	S
Illuminated dual visor vanity mirrors	$87	$87	Luxury wheel covers	$76	S
RH remote-control mirror, LH std.	$27	$27	White sidewall tires, std. size	S	S
Intermittent windshield wipers	$26	$26			

Popular Option Groups & Packages

	Continental	Mark IV
Appearance protection group	$59	$35
Gold luxury group	—	$439
Headlamp convenience group	$89	$89
Lock convenience group, 2-dr./4-dr.	$79/$104	$93
Silver luxury group	—	$400
Town Car package, 4-door only	$636	—
Town Coupe package, 2-door only	$567	—

— = Not Available; S = Standard equipment. [1]On Continentals, only available for 4-door sedans. [2]Included in, and available only with, optional Lock Convenience group.

Paint Colors

	Code
Black	1C
Silver Moondust metallic[1]	1D
Light Silver Cloud metallic	1E
Red Moondust metallic[1]	2G
Platinum	3A
Medium Blue metallic	3D
Dark Blue metallic	3G
Silver Blue Moondust metallic[1]	3L
Silver Blue Diamond Fire metallic[2]	3P
Pastel Lime	4A
Bright Lime Gold Moondust metallic[1]	4U
Green Diamond Fire metallic[2]	4Y
Ginger Diamond Fire metallic[2]	51
Copper Diamond Fire metallic[2]	52
Unique Gold Diamond Fire metallic[3]	54
Dark Brown metallic	5Q
Bright Gold Bronze metallic	5R
Medium Beige	5S
Buff	5V
Gold metallic	5Z
Yellow Gold Moondust metallic[1]	6G
Medium Gold metallic	6L
Medium Dark Gold metallic	6M
Maize Yellow	6N
White Décor	9C
White	9D

In two-tone combinations, first two digits are lower color, and second two digits are upper color. [1]Moondust metallic paints available for $128 extra. [2]Diamond Fire metallic paints available for $167 extra. [3]Available only on Continental Mark IV with Silver Luxury group.

Continental

"One of the automotive industry's most luxurious rides."

Nameplate year of origin: 1940 (1961 as a regular series).
Current bodystyle lifespan: 1970 through 1979 (restyled in 1974).
Predecessor to this model: Continental (1961 to 1969).
Replacement for this model: Town Car (1980 to 1991).
Percentage of division's production: 39.02%.
Corporate siblings: None.
Primary competition: Cadillac deVille and Chrysler Imperial.
Notable changes: Restyled front and rear and minor trim and detail changes.
Major standard equipment: Westminster knit cloth and vinyl front bench seat w/two-way power adjustment, folding center armrests in front and rear seat, 18 oz. cut-pile carpeting, simulated rosewood appliqués on I/P and steering wheel, electric clock, rim-blow steering wheel, power windows w/lock feature, AM radio w/power antenna, automatic temperature control air conditioning, visor–mounted vanity mirror, LH remote control rearview mirror, tinted glass, interior lighting (ashtrays, courtesy, glove box, luggage compartment, dome/map, and rear seat reading), gray carpeted luggage compartment, dual custom tape stripes, cornering lights, rear wheel opening fender skirts, front bumper guards, deluxe wheel covers, and 235R15 WSW tires.

Measurements

	Coupe	Sedan
Wheelbase	127.2"	127.2"
Length	232.6"	232.6"
Width	80.0"	80.0"
Height	54.9"	55.4"
Legroom — front	41.7"	41.7"
Legroom — rear	38.8"	41.7"
Headroom — front	38.3"	38.7"
Headroom — rear	37.4"	38.0"
Cargo capacity (cu. ft.)	20.5	20.5
Fuel capacity (gals.)	22.0	22.0

Models Available

	Model No.	Base MSRP	Change from LY	Shipping Wt. (lbs.)	Model Year Production	Change from LY
Continental 2-Door Hardtop Coupe	81	$7,931	+9.70%	5366	7,318	-45.18%
Continental 4-Door Sedan	82	$8,116	+8.59%	5361	29,351	-35.19%
TOTALS		*Avg. price* $8,024	+9.13%		*Production* 36,669	-37.46%

Continental Mark IV

"The car that has become a legend in its own time."

Nameplate year of origin: 1956 (Continental Mark II).
Current bodystyle lifespan: 1972 through 1976.
Predecessor to this model: Continental Mark III (1969 to 1971).
Replacement for this model: Continental Mark V (1977 to 1979).
Percentage of division's production: 60.98%.
Corporate siblings: Ford Thunderbird.
Primary competition: Buick Riviera, Cadillac Eldorado, and Oldsmobile Toronado.
Notable changes: Revised rear styling, and minor trim and detail changes.
Major standard equipment: Westminster knit cloth and vinyl "Twin Comfort"
  lounge seat w/six-way power adjustment, folding center armrests in front and rear
  seat, simulated burl walnut woodgrain appliqué on I/P and steering wheel, 25 oz.
  cut-pile carpeting, electric Cartier Timepiece, trip odometer, power windows
  w/lock feature, AM/FM stereo w/power antenna, automatic temperature control air conditioning, LH remote control rearview
  mirror, tinted glass, interior lighting (ashtrays, courtesy, glove box, I/P warning, luggage compartment, engine compartment,
  dome/map, and C-pillar reading), black carpeted luggage compartment, vinyl roof w/opera window, custom pinstripe, customer
  monogram on doors, cornering lights, front bumper guards, "Sure Track" anti-lock power brake system, luxury wheel covers, and
  235R15 WSW tires.

Measurements

Wheelbase	120.4"
Length	228.4"
Width	79.8"
Height	53.3"
Legroom — front	42.0"
Legroom — rear	36.4"
Headroom — front	37.5"
Headroom — rear	36.8"
Cargo capacity (cu. ft.)	14.8
Fuel capacity (gals.)	26.5

Models Available

	Model No.	Base MSRP	Change from LY	Shipping Wt. (lbs.)	Model Year Production	Change from LY
Continental Mark IV 2-Door Hardtop	89	$10,049	+11.85%	5362	57,316	-17.46%
TOTALS	Avg. price	$10,049	+11.85%	Production	57,316	-17.46%

MERCURY

"Test your car's ride against our ride. At the sign of the cat."

Mercury production for the year fell, as did the rest of the industry, with the full-size models plummeting to half of their 1973 levels. Still, with the new Cougar XR-7 and the compact Comet lines doubling in sales, Mercury managed to increase market share while posting a less severe decline than the industry average. Unfortunately for Mercury, as had historically been the case, when a recession or higher fuel prices came about, American Motors (or its Nash and Rambler predecessors) benefited most, and 1974 was no exception, causing Mercury to drop to a ninth place standing in industry production for the model year, a position it would not return to anytime in the near future.

With the Cougar XR-7's former next of kin, the Mustang, downsized to a compact this year, Mercury seized the opportunity to move the sporty/luxury car upscale to com-

pete more directly with the popular personal luxury cars of the day like the Chevrolet Monte Carlo and Pontiac Grand Prix. This move would take the Cougar out of the pony car arena, which was withering away by 1974, and put it into a market it was well suited to take on, as proven by its 50 percent increase in production. Sharing a body and chassis with the Montego, the two-door Cougar XR-7 had a modified greenhouse area along with its own unique front-end styling. The base Cougar and convertible models were no longer in production. Seeing the popularity of the Cougar prompted Ford to introduce an equivalent Ford Elite model at mid-year.

From the front, the new Cougar used most of the Montego's general design, including the front bumper, but used a vertical bar center grille section with a large chrome surround.

The dual headlights were set in chrome surrounds within outer grille sections, which also used vertical bars, looking much like the 1973 Cougar design. A round chrome hood ornament, featuring an acrylic insert with the Cougar cat emblem, was placed above the grille on the header panel. Parking and turn signal lamps were wrap-around units mounted in the front fender end caps. Vinyl insert bodyside protective moldings followed the lower body feature line from bumper to bumper, with partial wheel lip moldings connecting the vinyl strips. A chrome trim piece followed the top edge of the front fender onto the door, and then continued up and over the roof, with the chrome marking the front edge of the standard landau vinyl top. A rectangular opera window containing the Cougar emblem and stationary rear quarter windows were other new Cougar XR-7 features. At the rear, Cougar XR-7 shared a rear bumper with the Montego, which met the new federal government standards. This also meant the Cougar had similar horizontal taillamps divided into three sections with a rear panel appliqué between the lights.

Under the hood, the 351 CID V8 was still standard equipment, and the 400 CID and 460CID engines were available for the first time in Cougars. Befitting its new "luxury" status, an automatic was standard, even with the 351 CID V8 "CJ" engine that was still available. Inside the Cougar XR-7 shared its instrument panel and most of its interior trim with the Montego, but had exclusive rights to the sporty bucket seats and console with floor shifter, which were standard on the Cougar. Also, instead of using simulated woodgrain appliqués on the instrument panel, and door panels, the Cougar opted for a more monochromatic look, using padded, sculpted door panels with pull assist straps, and gauge surround inserts that matched the interior upholstery color.

The Montego had a revised grille that was shorter and wider, with a revised crosshatch design. At the back end, the loop-style bumper was gone, replaced by a box-style bumper as required to meet the new safety standards. Horizontal taillamps, which wrapped around the rear quarter ends, were divided into three sections, with the center section containing the backup lights. The Montego also gained more luxury options including tilt steering wheel, cruise control, an anti-theft alarm system, and an available eight-track tape player. The Montego GT was dropped as the muscle car era ended, but the look was still available with the Sports Appearance Group option that included dual hood scoops and black-out trim.

The compact Comet became a lifesaver for Mercury this year, as the oil embargo and recession pushed Comet production to more than 125,000 cars in 1974. New front and rear box-style bumpers were the biggest visual changes to the Comet. A new Custom option was added, which Mercury advertised as having "a little Cougar luxury."

Also having few changes for the new model year was the imported Pantera L high-performance sport coupe. Changes for the 1974 models include a new bumper system, larger standard tires, and a slightly redesigned interior. Technically this would be the last model year that the Pantera was imported, although it is rumored that some leftover cars were sold and titled as 1975 models. In either case, it was yet another chapter closed on Ford's performance empire of the past fifteen years.

Styling for the full-size Mercurys was freshened after the much more extensive restyling done for 1973. Montereys had a revised grille that gave a more elegant look, with a large opening crosshatch grille in a three row by sixteen column configuration, with each of the openings having an egg-crate style insert three rows high and two columns wide. After several years of declining sales, the Monterey would be discontinued after 1974. The upscale Marquis used a new vertical style grille that consisted of twelve rectangles across, with each rectangle having three vertical bar inserts. The headlight doors lost the grille-like inserts of the 1973 models but they still wore the chrome trim that had surrounded the inserts. Any resemblance to Lincoln was purely intentional. The big Mercury station wagons offered two unique options for American made wagons of the period. A rear window washer, available for $38, was a first on U.S. cars, though the idea was not new, as some of the 1940s fastback GM models offered a rear window wiper system. They also offered a recreation table for $42 on models equipped with the optional dual facing rear seats, an option the full-size Ford wagons also offered. A luxurious new Grand Marquis option was intended to help the Marquis better compete with the Buick Electra, Chrysler New Yorker, and Oldsmobile Ninety-Eight.

Finally, the German-built Capri entered the new model year with new, plastic covered bumpers and a new 2.8 liter "Cologne" V6 engine which was essentially a "punched out" version of last year's 2600cc V6 engine with numerous design improvements. The most significant changes were the exhaust emission control devices added in the form of the "Thermactor" air pump system and the Exhaust Gas Recirculation (EGR) system. The "Thermactor" air pump injected air into the exhaust manifold to burn off any fuel vapors remaining in the exhaust. The intent of this was to reduce combustion temperatures, and therefore the production of oxides of nitrogen. Other changes included factory installed air conditioning being available as a factory option for the first time, having previously been available only as a dealer installed option.

Capri 2-Door Sport Coupe with Décor option

Pantera L 2-Door Sport Coupe

Comet 2-Door Sedan with Custom option

Comet 4-Door Sedan

Cougar XR-7 2-Door Hardtop

Marquis 2-Door Hardtop

Marquis 4-Door Pillared Hardtop

Marquis 4-Door Station Wagon

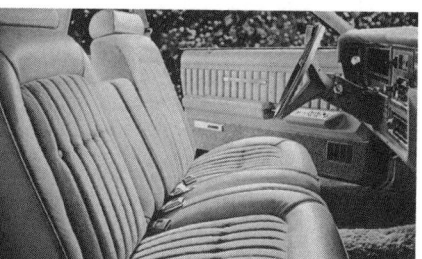

Marquis Brougham interior
with Grand Marquis trim option

Colony Park 4-Door Station Wagon

Montego 2-Door Hardtop
with Sports Appearance group

Montego 4-Door Pillared Hardtop

Monterey Custom 4-Door Pillared Hardtop

Model year production: 403,977, down 16.96% from 1973.

Domestic market share: 4.67% (9th place).

Base price range: $2,957 to $5,435.

Mercury average base price: $4,276, up 10.98%.

Introduction date: September 1973. Capri introduced August 1973.

Assembly plants: Oakville, Ontario, Canada (B); Lorain, OH (H); Kansas City, MO (K); Allen Park, MI (S—*pilot plant*); and St. Louis, MO (Z). Capri assembly plants: Cologne, Germany (A); and Genk, Belgium (B). Pantera assembly plant: Modena, Italy.

Data plate identification (VIN): Eleven digit code read as follows: First digit indicates year (4 = 1974); second digit indicates assembly plant code (see list above); third and fourth digits indicate model number (model number in model charts); fifth digit indicates engine code (see powertrain chart); remaining digits are sequential with beginning numbers of 500001. *Example:* 4K31F500001 is a 1974 Mercury Comet 2-Door sedan, with 302 CID, 2-bbl. V8 engine, serial number 500001, built in Kansas City (Claycomo), MO. 1974 Capri uses eleven digit code read as follows: First digit indicates country of origin (G = Germany); second digit indicates assembly plant code (see list above); third and fourth digits indicate model number (model number in model charts); fifth digit indicates year (P = 1974); sixth digit indicates month; remaining digits are sequential with beginning number of 00001. 1974 Pantera uses eleven digit code read as follows: First through sixth digits indicate 1974 DeTomaso Pantera built in Italy, THPNLD; remaining digits are sequential serial number.

Powertrains*

Engine	Net HP	Engine Code	Transmission Availability[1]		Capri	Comet	Montego	Cougar	Monterey & Full-size wagons	Marquis
122 CID (2.0L) OHC, 2-bbl., 4-cyl.	85	X	4-speed manual		S (2000)	—	—	—	—	—
			MPG:	18.8	—	—	—	—	—	—
			3-speed automatic		$182 (2000)	—	—	—	—	—
			MPG:	16.9	—	—	—	—	—	—
170.8 CID (2.8L), 2-bbl., V6	105	Z	4-speed manual		S (2800)	—	—	—	—	—
			MPG:	18.7	—	—	—	—	—	—
			3-speed automatic		$182 (2600)	—	—	—	—	—
			MPG:	15.8	—	—	—	—	—	—
200 CID (3.3L), 1-bbl., 6-cyl.	84	U	3-speed manual		—	S	—	—	—	—
			MPG:		—	18.9	—	—	—	—
			3-speed Select Shift Automatic		—	$178	—	—	—	—
			MPG:		—	15.6	—	—	—	—
250 CID (4.1L), 1-bbl., 6-cyl.	91	L	3-speed manual		—	$38	—	—	—	—
			MPG:		—	17.2	—	—	—	—
			3-speed Select Shift Automatic		—	$216	—	—	—	—
			MPG:		—	15.6	—	—	—	—
302 CID (5.0L), 2-bbl., V8	140	F	3-speed manual		—	$123	S[2]	—	—	—
			MPG:		—	NA	11.9	—	—	—
			3-speed Select Shift Automatic		—	$301	$216[2]	—	—	—
			MPG:		—	12.1	11.4	—	—	—
351 CID (5.8L), 2-bbl., V8	162	H	3-speed Select Shift Automatic		—	—	$261[3]	S	—	—
			MPG:		—	—	9.1	9.5	—	—
351 CID (5.8L) CJ, 4-bbl., V8	180	Q	3-speed Select Shift Automatic		—	—	$343 (2-Drs. Ex. Brghm.)[2]	$82[2]	—	—
			MPG:		—	—	9.5	9.3	—	—
400 CID (6.6L), 2-bbl., V8	170	S	3-speed Select Shift Automatic		—	—	$370	$112	S	—
			MPG:		—	—	8.8	8.8	9.1	—
460 CID (7.5L), 4-bbl., V8	195[4]	A	3-speed Select Shift Automatic		—	—	$502	$244	$178	S
			MPG:		—	—	7.2	8.6	8.1	8.1

*Optional 3.00:1 axle ratio required on Cougar, Montego and full-size Mercurys with V8 sold in California. [1]Unless otherwise noted: All manual transmissions are column shift, except on Capri. All automatics are column-shift, except on Capri and Cougar. Floor-shift is available for $13 extra on Comet with 3-speed manual and Comet with automatic (requires bucket seats, GT and Custom option). [2]Not available in California. [3]Required as standard in California. [4]Horsepower rating in Cougar: 220 w/460 CID 4-bbl.

Major Options

	Capri	Comet	Montego	Cougar	Full-size
Whisper-Aire air conditioning[1]	$364[2]	$360	$398	$398	$431
Tilt steering wheel	—	—	$49	$44	$44
Automatic speed control	—	—	$99	$99	$67
Rear window defogger	—	$28	$30	$30	$30
Electric rear window defroster	—	—	$47	$62	$62
Tinted glass, all windows	—	$36	$42	$37	$50
Dual remote control mirrors	—	$23[3]	$38	$38	$13[4]
Power windows, 2-dr./4-dr.	—	—	$86/$112	$86	$141
Power front vent windows, 4-door	—	—	—	—	$64
Power door locks, 2-dr./4-dr.	—	—	$44/$67	$45	$[5]
Power seat, 6-way w/std. seating	—	—	$102	$91	$102
Front bucket seats w/console	—	$117[6]	—	S	—
Dual facing rear seats, wagons	—	—	$76	—	$122

	Capri	Comet	Montego	Cougar	Full-size
AM radio	$53	$59	$64	$64	$64
AM/FM stereo (non-stereo, Capri)	$101	$195	$213	$213	$233
AM/FM stereo w/8-track tape	—	—	$363	$363	$363
Anti-theft alarm system	—	—	$79	$79	$79
Vinyl top, full	$63	$75	$97	$38	$116[7]
Sunroof, power-operated	$120[8]	—	—	$471	$496
Power trunk lid release	—	—	—	—	$5[5]
Power steering	—	$92	$112	S	S
Power brakes, w/front disc	S	—	$68[9]	S	S
"Sure-Track" anti-lock brakes	—	—	—	—	$189
Rear wheel opening fender skirts	—	—	—	—	$35
Deluxe wheel covers	—	$23	$33	—	$25
Luxury wheel covers	—	—	$43	—	$58
Sport style wheel covers	—	—	—	$62	—
Styled steel wheels	—	—	$117	$79	—
Forged aluminum wheels	—	$142	—	—	—
White sidewall tires, std. size	—	$27	$32	$32	$35

Popular Option Groups & Packages

	Capri	Comet	Montego	Cougar	Full-size
Appearance protection group	—	$36	$38	$33	$47
Bumper protection group	—	$31	$36	$36	$36
Convenience group	—	$43	$51	$50	—
Custom option package	—	$378	—	—	—
Custom trim group	—	—	$316[10]	—	—
Décor group	$153	—	—	—	$63
Deluxe trim option	—	$84	—	—	—
Grand Marquis luxury trim group[11]	—	—	—	—	$319
GT package	—	$225	—	—	—
Lock convenience group	—	—	—	—	$88–$96
Sports Appearance group	—	—	$310	—	—
Visibility light group	—	—	$29	$29	$57

—= Not Available; S = Standard equipment. [1]Whisper-Aire air conditioner w/automatic temperature control is available for $475 on Montego and Cougar, and for $508 on Monterey and Marquis. [2]Available as dealer installed option only. [3]LH remote and RH manual on Comet. [4]LH only on full-size Mercurys. [5]Available only as part of the Lock Convenience group. [6]Available only on Comet 2-door, and without console. [7]Vinyl roof available on station wagons for $139. [8]Manually operated. [9]Standard on station wagons. [10]Custom trim available on Montego MX Villager wagon for $124. [11]Available on Marquis wagon for $384, and Colony Park wagon for $184.

Paint Colors

Mercury	Code	Mercury	Code	Capri	Code
Black	1C	Ginger Glamour metallic[1]	5J	Light Beige	C
Silver metallic	1G	Medium Chestnut metallic	5M	Red	N
Medium Slate Blue metallic	1H	Saddle Bronze metallic	5T	Medium Brown metallic	S
Bright Red	2B	Tan metallic	5U	Yellow	T
Red	2E	Orange	5W		
Light Blue	3B	Dark Copper metallic	5Y	Pantera	Code
Medium Blue metallic	3D	Medium Goldenrod	6C	White #2	NA
Bright Blue metallic	3E	Gold Glamour metallic[1]	6F	Silver metallic #2	NA
Dark Blue metallic	3G	Medium Dark Gold metallic	6M	Blue	NA
Silver Blue Glamour metallic[1]	3M	Maize Yellow	6N	Green	NA
Light Grabber Blue	3N	White	9A	Red #2	NA
Pastel Blue	3Q	White Décor	9C	Orange	NA
Pastel Lime	4A	White	9D	Yellow	NA
Green Gold metallic	4B				
Dark Green metallic	4Q	Capri	Code		
Medium Ivy Bronze metallic	4T	Medium Blue metallic	1	In two-tone combinations, first two digits are lower color, and second two digits are upper color. Two-tones available on Comet for $28. [1]Glamour paints available for $35 extra on Comet, and $38 extra on Montego, Cougar, and full-size Mercurys.	
Dark Yellow Green metallic	4V	Silver metallic	3		
Medium Lime Yellow	4W	Medium Green	5		
Ginger metallic	5H	Copper metallic	7		

Pantera

"Luxury in a Truly Exciting Road Machine."

Nameplate year of origin: 1971 (for U.S. market).
Current bodystyle lifespan: 1969 through 1974.
Predecessor to this model: None.
Replacement for this model: None.
Primary competition: Chevrolet Corvette.
Notable changes: Minor changes.
Major standard equipment: Cloth-and-vinyl high-back front bucket seats, floor carpeting, central floor console, three-spoke steering wheel, padded door armrest w/integral assist handles, power windows, air conditioning, windshield wipers w/washers, rack and pinion steering, four wheel power disc brakes, 351 CID 4-bbl. "Cleveland" V8 engine w/266 hp rating, fully synchronized 5-speed manual transmission, monocoque body construction, coil springs and wishbone suspension, styled steel wheels, and C60 × 15 front & H60 × 15 rear BSW Goodyear Arriva tires. Option available: Dealer installed AM/FM Stereo.

Measurements

Wheelbase	98.4"
Length	175.3"
Width	71.3"
Height	44.1"
Legroom — front	42.5"
Headroom — front	35.2"
Cargo capacity (cu. ft.)	4.0
Fuel capacity (gals.)	20.5

Models Available

	Model No.	Base MSRP	Change from LY	Shipping Wt. (lbs.)	Model Year Sales (est.)	Change from LY
Pantera L 2-Door Sport Coupe		$11,061	+10.67%	3150	1,230	-32.79%
TOTALS	Avg. price	$11,061	+10.67%	Production	1,230	-32.79%

Capri

"Capri ... the Sexy Subcompact You Can Afford."

Nameplate year of origin: 1971 (originally used on 1952 Lincoln Capri).
Current bodystyle lifespan: 1971 through 1977 (major restyle for 1976).
Predecessor to this model: None.
Replacement for this model: Capri (1979 to 1986).
Primary competition: Dodge Colt GT and Ford Mustang II 2+2.
Notable changes: Minor trim and detail changes.
Major standard equipment: All-vinyl front bucket seats, full-loop carpeting, front armrests, recessed door handles, passenger side assist bar, simulated woodgrain I/P appliqué, lockable glove compartment, day/night rear view mirror, power front disc brakes, rack-and-pinion steering, styled wheels, and 165 × 13 BSW tires. 2800 adds: Instrumentation group and V6 engine.

Measurements

Wheelbase	100.8"
Length	177.0"
Width	64.8"
Height	50.9"
Legroom — front	41.4"
Legroom — rear	31.1"
Headroom — front	37.4"
Headroom — rear	35.9"
Cargo capacity (cu. ft.)	7.2
Fuel capacity (gals.)	12.7

Models Available

	Model No.	Base MSRP	Change from LY	Shipping Wt. (lbs.)	Model Year Sales (est.)	Change from LY
Capri 2000 2-Door Sport Coupe	EC	$3,566	+19.54%	2301	NA	NA
Capri 2800 2-Door Sport Coupe	EC	$3,807	+16.74%	2411	NA	NA
TOTALS	Avg. price	$3,687	+18.08%	Production	90,000	-20.70%

Comet

"The tough little car that built a name for durability."

Nameplate year of origin: 1960.
Current bodystyle lifespan: 1971 through 1977.
Predecessor to this model: Comet (1964 to 1965).
Replacement for this model: Zephyr (1978 to 1983).
Percentage of division's production: 31.11%.
Corporate siblings: Ford Maverick.
Primary competition: AMC Hornet, Buick Apollo, Dodge Dart, and
 Oldsmobile Omega.
Notable changes: Minor trim and detail changes.
Major standard equipment: Striped cloth-and-vinyl front bench seat,
 color-keyed cut-pile carpeting, "Blend-Air" heater with three-speed
 blower, front and rear ashtrays w/front lighted, two-speed windshield
 wipers w/washers, deluxe two-spoke steering wheel, front bumper guards,
 hubcaps, and 6.45 × 14 BSW tires.

Measurements

	2-Door	4-Door
Wheelbase	103.0"	109.9"
Length	190.0"	196.9"
Width	70.5"	70.5"
Height	53.0"	52.8"
Legroom — front	40.7"	40.7"
Legroom — rear	31.8"	36.0"
Headroom — front	37.5"	37.8"
Headroom — rear	35.9"	36.5"
Cargo capacity (cu. ft.)	11.3	12.8
Fuel capacity (gals.)	15.0	15.0

Models Available

	Model No.	Base MSRP	Change from LY	Shipping Wt. (lbs.)	Model Year Production	Change from LY
Comet 2-Door Sedan	31	$2,957	+21.59%	2861	64,751	+16.23%
Comet 4-Door Sedan	30	$2,991	+20.17%	2969	60,944	+110.27%
TOTALS		Avg. price $2,974	+20.87%		Production 125,695	+48.42%

Montego

*"A smooth, quiet and luxurious ride, with the ease
and handling of a more personal-size car."*

Nameplate year of origin: 1968.
Current bodystyle lifespan: 1972 through 1976.
Predecessor to this model: Montego (1970 to 1971).
Replacement for this model: Cougar (1977 to 1979).
Percentage of division's sales volume: 24.26%.
Corporate siblings: Ford Torino.
Primary competition: AMC Matador, Buick Century,
 Dodge Coronet and Charger, Oldsmobile Cutlass, and
 Pontiac LeMans.
Notable changes: New grille and minor trim and detail
 changes.
Major standard equipment: Choice of cloth-and-vinyl or
 all-vinyl low-back front bench seat, color-keyed deep loop
 carpeting, black I/P trim, windshield and rear window
 bright moldings, drip rail moldings, front bumper guards,
manual front disc brakes, hubcaps, and G78 × 14 BSW tires. MX adds: Simulated woodgrain I/P trim, side window bright moldings, wheel lip moldings, rocker panel moldings, and deluxe sound insulation. Wagon adds: All-vinyl front bench seat, three-way
tailgate, front and rear bumper guards, power front disc brakes, and H78 × 14 BSW tires. MX Brougham adds: Choice of
Brougham cloth-and-vinyl or super-soft vinyl "Flight Bench" front seat w/fold-down center armrest, deluxe two-spoke steering
wheel w/woodgrain inserts, and deluxe wheel covers. MX Villager adds: All-vinyl bench "Flight Bench" front seat w/fold-down
center armrest, power tailgate window, simulated woodgrain bodyside and tailgate paneling w/bright moldings, and HR78 × 14
BSW tires.

Measurements

	2-Doors	4-Doors	Wagons
Wheelbase	114.0"	118.0"	118.0"
Length	215.5"	219.5"	223.1"
Width	78.6"	78.6"	79.6"
Height	52.9"	53.6"	55.0"
Legroom — front	42.5"	42.5"	42.1"
Legroom — rear	33.2"	37.8"	37.1"
Headroom — front	37.9"	38.5"	38.3"
Headroom — rear	36.5"	37.3"	38.6"
Cargo capacity (cu. ft.)	16.5	16.5	93.0*
Fuel capacity (gals.)	26.5	26.5	21.0

Includes 8.1 cu. ft. of hidden cargo space.

Models Available

	Model No.	Base MSRP	Change from LY	Shipping Wt. (lbs.)	Model Year Production	Change from LY
Montego 2-Door Hardtop	03	$3,262	+15.92%	3977	7,645	+7.95%
Montego 4-Door Pillared Hardtop	02	$3,295	+17.51%	4062	5,674	-23.93%
Montego MX 2-Door Hardtop	07	$3,378	+15.33%	3990	20,957	-24.65%
Montego MX 4-Door Pillared Hardtop	04	$3,413	+17.81%	4092	19,446	-23.14%
Montego MX 4-Door, 6-p. Wagon	08	$4,018	+17.59%	4426	4,085	-41.74%
Montego MX Brougham 2-Door Hardtop	11	$3,581	+15.63%	4010	20,511	-49.91%
Montego MX Brougham 4-Dr. Pillared HT	10	$3,615	+17.48%	4143	13,467	-44.65%
Montego MX Villager 4-Door, 6-p. Wagon	18	$4,242	+17.64%	4426	6,234	-49.71%
TOTALS	Avg. price	$3,601	+15.51%	Production	98,019	-37.49%

Cougar XR-7

"Cougar for '74 — totally new and totally unlike any Cougar anybody's ever seen before!"

Nameplate year of origin: 1967.
Current bodystyle lifespan: 1974 through 1976.
Predecessor to this model: Cougar (1971 to 1973).
Replacement for this model: Cougar XR-7 (1977 to 1979).
Percentage of division's production: 22.69%.
Corporate siblings: Ford Gran Torino Elite.
Primary competition: Chevrolet Monte Carlo and Pontiac Grand Prix.
Notable changes: Completely redesigned.
Major standard equipment: Choice of all-vinyl "Twin Comfort" Lounge front seat or all-vinyl bucket seats w/center console, luxury-weight cut-pile carpeting, performance instrument panel, luxury two-spoke color-keyed steering wheel w/wood-grain inserts, courtesy lights, color-keyed racing mirrors, power steering, power front disc brakes, specially tuned suspension system, luxury wheel covers, and HR78 × 14 BSW tires.

Measurements

Wheelbase	114.0"
Length	215.5"
Width	78.5"
Height	52.7"
Legroom — front	42.1"
Legroom — rear	32.2"
Headroom — front	37.4"
Headroom — rear	36.3"
Cargo capacity (cu. ft.)	16.5
Fuel capacity (gals.)	26.5

Models Available

	Model No.	Base MSRP	Change from LY	Shipping Wt. (lbs.)	Model Year Production	Change from LY
Cougar XR-7 2-Door Hardtop	93	$4,631	+25.88%	4255	91,670	+161.09%
TOTALS	Avg. price	$4,631	+26.19%	Production	91,670	+51.20%

Monterey

"The luxury is built in, solidly, to last and to give you years of quality and satisfaction."

Nameplate year of origin: 1952 (series); 1950 (Mercury coupe designation).
Current bodystyle lifespan: 1971 through 1978 (restyled in 1973 and discontinued in 1974).
Predecessor to this model: Monterey (1969 to 1970).
Replacement for this model: None.
Percentage of division's sales volume: 6.80%.

Measurements

	2-Doors	4-Doors	Wagons
Wheelbase	124.0"	124.0"	121.0"
Length	226.8"	226.8"	225.7"
Width	79.6"	79.6"	79.8"
Height	53.9"	55.3"	57.1"

Corporate siblings: Ford Custom 500/Galaxie 500/LTD and Mercury Marquis.

Primary competition: Buick LeSabre, Dodge Monaco, Oldsmobile Delta 88, and Pontiac Bonneville.

Notable changes: Minor trim and detail changes.

Major standard equipment: Cloth and vinyl front bench seat, nylon loop carpeting, simulated woodgrain I/P appliqués, bright front and rear window moldings, side window and drip rail moldings, dome light, power steering, power front disc brakes, bright bodyside molding, front bumper guards, hubcaps, and HR78 × 15 BSW tires.

Measurements (cont.)

	2-Doors	4-Doors	Wagons
Legroom — front	41.6"	41.7"	41.7"
Legroom — rear	35.7"	39.9"	37.1"
Headroom — front	37.6"	38.5"	39.0"
Headroom — rear	36.7"	37.5"	39.5"
Cargo capacity (cu. ft.)	20.5	20.5	103.7*
Fuel capacity (gals.)	22.0	22.0	21.0

*Includes 9.1 cu. ft. of hidden cargo space.

1974

Wagon adds: All-vinyl front bench seat, power tailgate window, and JR78 × 15 BSW tires. Monterey Custom adds: Choice of cloth-and-vinyl or all-vinyl front bench seat, deluxe steering wheel, rocker panel and wheel lip moldings, "Custom" series script on C-pillar, and deluxe wheel covers.

Models Available

	Model No.	Base MSRP	Change from LY	Shipping Wt. (lbs.)	Model Year Production	Change from LY
Monterey 2-Door Hardtop	46	$4,326	+8.04%	4506	2,003	-68.96%
Monterey 4-Door Pillared Hardtop	44	$4,283	+8.13%	4559	6,185	-62.79%
Monterey 4-Door, 6-pass. Station Wagon	72	$4,647	+6.12%	4916	1,669	-60.96%
Monterey Custom 2-Door Hardtop	56	$4,439	+5.51%	4504	4,510	-35.22%
Monterey Custom 4-Door Pillared Hardtop	54	$4,396	+6.60%	4561	13,113	-37.18%
TOTALS	Avg. price	$4,418	+5.30%		Production 27,480	-50.20%

Marquis

"Our most elegant Mercury was built to be more than beautiful. It was built to give you a smooth, steady, quiet ride with a feeling of solid comfort."

Nameplate year of origin: 1967.

Current bodystyle lifespan: 1971 through 1978 (restyled in 1973 and 1975).

Predecessor to this model: Marquis (1969 to 1970).

Replacement for this model: Marquis & Grand Marquis (1979 to 1991).

Percentage of division's sales volume: 15.13%.

Corporate siblings: Ford Custom 500/Galaxie 500/LTD and Mercury Monterey.

Primary competition: Buick Electra 225 and Estate Wagon, Chrysler Newport and Town & Country, Oldsmobile Ninety-Eight and Custom Cruiser, and Pontiac Grand Ville and Grand Safari.

Notable changes: Revised front-end styling and minor trim and detail changes.

Measurements

	2-Doors	4-Doors	Wagons
Wheelbase	124.0"	124.0"	121.0"
Length	226.8"	226.8"	225.7"
Width	79.6"	79.6"	79.8"
Height	53.9"	55.3"	57.1"
Legroom — front	41.6"	41.7"	41.7"
Legroom — rear	35.7"	39.9"	37.1"
Headroom — front	37.6"	38.5"	39.0"
Headroom — rear	36.7"	37.5"	39.5"
Cargo capacity (cu. ft.)	20.5	20.5	103.7*
Fuel capacity (gals.)	22.0	22.0	21.0

*Includes 9.1 cu. ft. of hidden cargo space.

Major standard equipment: Choice of cloth-and-vinyl or all-vinyl front bench seat, nylon loop pile carpeting, simulated woodgrain I/P and steering wheel appliqué, three-spoke steering wheel, electric clock, dome light, deluxe sound insulation package, rocker panel molding, front bumper guards, rear wheel opening fender skirts, deluxe wheel covers, and HR78 × 15 BSW tires. Wagon adds: All-vinyl front bench seat, bright seat side shields, cargo area light, power tailgate window, and JR78 × 15 BSW tires. Colony Park adds: All-vinyl front bench seat w/fold-down center armrest, deluxe two-spoke steering wheel, cargo area light, power tailgate window, simulated woodgrain yacht deck exterior paneling on bodysides and tailgate, and deluxe wheel covers. Marquis Brougham adds: Brougham cloth and vinyl front bench seat w/fold-down center armrest, rear seat center armrests, shag cut pile carpeting, RH visor vanity mirror, courtesy lights, power windows, door pull straps, front and rear door courtesy lights, rear roof pillar reading light, luggage compartment light, and halo vinyl roof.

Models Available

	Model No.	Base MSRP	Change from LY	Shipping Wt. (lbs.)	Model Year Production	Change from LY
Marquis 2-Door Hardtop	66	$4,996	+5.69%	4698	2,633	-55.92%
Marquis 4-Door Pillared Hardtop	63	$4,996	+7.49%	4757	6,910	-54.69%
Marquis 4-Door Hardtop	68	$4,996	+4.48%	4753	784	-64.12%
Marquis 4-Door, 6-pass. Wagon	74	$4,876	+5.82%	4916	1,111	-54.91%
Marquis Colony Park 4-Door, 6-pass. Wagon	76	$4,982	+5.71%	4973	10,802	-53.61%
Marquis Brougham 2-Door Hardtop	64	$5,435	+5.51%	4762	10,207	-55.17%
Marquis Brougham 4-Door Pillared Hardtop	62	$5,435	+7.16%	4833	24,477	-47.50%
Marquis Brougham 4-Door Hardtop	67	$5,435	+4.40%	4853	4,189	-60.53%
TOTALS	*Avg. price*	$5,144	+5.77%	*Production*	61,113	-52.69%

OLDSMOBILE

"Looks like a great year to step into an Olds!"

Oldsmobile introduced two new models for 1974, the Cutlass Supreme Cruiser in two- and three-seat configurations, and a Ninety-Eight Regency 2-Door Hardtop. The new Cutlass Supreme Cruiser was basically the Vista-Cruiser without the woodgrain exterior paneling and the "Vista-Vent" sunroof. Having all the luxury features of its four-door running mate, the Ninety-Eight Regency 2-Door Hardtop replaced the slow-selling Ninety-Eight 2-Door Hardtop base model. For the new season, all series except the Toronado had new grilles that slanted back to wrap slightly over the top edge of the front header panel, and larger, box-style front bumpers which eliminated the body colored front pan. Also new for all models were the federally mandated rear bumpers and the new seat belt system with starter interlock.

The Cutlass series, which by year end would account for half of Oldsmobile's production and sales, now had two different front end designs. All models had a new front bumper which was more of a box styled design and did away with the body-color pan below the bumper, and also included openings below the bumper impact strip that carried grille inserts in the opening. Base Cutlass models had parking/turn signal lights mounted in the bumper directly below the headlights and a new crosshatch grille pattern which emphasized the horizontal bars by putting the vertical bars towards the rear. The Cutlass S, Supreme and new Cruiser station wagons used a taller, vertical bar grille with about twenty-four bars, surrounded by a chrome strip. Unique to these models was a square parking/turn signal light placed into the body-colored area between the headlight and grille on each side. On all Cutlasses the grille continued into the lower bumper openings. With the required new rear bumper system, taillights on the new models were vertical units in a chrome bezel, mounted on the V-shaped end of the new rear quarter panel cap, ending at the bumper. Cutlass Supreme and Salon taillights were divided into two narrow vertical lenses; Cutlass and S models had a single lens with a chrome Oldsmobile logo in the center. With the curved-under bumper design gone, the decklid no long met the rear bumper, so a new filler panel was introduced, which on Supreme models had a brushed aluminum strip directly below the decklid opening, with a red reflector at each end and the backup light set next to the reflector. Station wagon "Cruiser" models used a new horizontal lamp about a foot in length, with a small backup light centered within each. Finally, new vertical three-slot side marker lights were implemented at both front and rear.

Other changes in the mid-size Oldsmobile line included the Vista-Crusier station wagon series being officially moved into the Cutlass line. The wood-paneled mid-size wagon also gained a stablemate, the Cutlass Supreme Cruiser, which, as noted above, dispensed with the faux wood paneling and "Vista-Vent" sunroof. Cutlass engine choices stayed the same, apart from a slight change in the torque specifications of the 350, and a 20 horsepower rating cut to the 455 CID V8 engines. Manual transmissions were no longer offered for the Cutlass line, leaving the Turbo Hydra-matic as the sole transmission choice. Power steering also became standard on all models.

Last year's popular Salon package was extended to the Cutlass Supreme coupe for 1974, and an optional vinyl landau "half-roof" joined the options list for the upmarket Cutlass two-doors. The landau top would become one of the most popular exterior options across all makes of American cars. Other specialty models included the return of the Cutlass coupe Hurst/Olds option. A coupe with aftermarket removable roof panels served as the pace car for the 1974 Indianapolis 500 race, with former race winner Jim Rathmann selected as the pace car driver. A Cutlass S coupe with Hurst/ Olds option could also be ordered with a pace car replica option that mimicked the look of the real Indy pace car, albeit with a fixed roof. Buyers of the pace car replica had their choice between an H/O with the 230-horsepower 455 CID V8 engine (option package W30) or the 200-horsepower 350 CID V8 engine (option package W25), which was required in California. Records show that 1,800 Hurst/Olds packages were produced for 1974, although it is not known how many of those also had the pace car replica package. Additional production figures for option packages include 6,766 Supreme sedans and 31,207 Supreme coupes equipped with the Salon option package. Finally, there were 7,204 Cutlass and Cutlass S coupes equipped with the 4-4-2 option package, but the breakdown between the two models is not currently known.

Full-size Oldsmobile Delta 88, Custom Cruiser and Ninety-Eight models all added a new instrument panel design with a message center housing a column of warning lights on each side of the speedometer. Also, they all offered a new optional pulse-wiper system that allowed for selecting a slower than low speed wiping action to clear light rain or mist from the windshield. All three of the series also had updated front-end styling and revised rear-end styling to accommodate the impact absorbing bumpers.

A new option for the Toronado and all other full-size Oldsmobiles except the Delta 88 convertible and Custom Cruiser was the GM Air Cushion Restraint System featuring airbags for the driver and front seat passenger. In a small description near the end of the 1974 sales brochure, Oldsmobile billed the system as a highly sophisticated new protective feature. Few customers purchased it, and the option disappeared after 1976.

Delta 88 models came with a taller new wrap-over grille that extended into the lower bumper area, and parking/turn signal lights that were now mounted in the bumper ends below the headlights. At the rear were new vertically stacked rectangular, wrap-around taillamps in the rear fender ends, divided by a horizontal strip into two sections. As with the Cutlass, the new rear bumper design resulted in the trunk lid no longer meeting the rear bumper, so a brushed aluminum strip was mounted on a plastic filler panel with backup lights placed in each end, and the Oldsmobile name in block letters stretched across the center section. The fuel filler cap, which was previously behind the license tag in the bumper, was now behind a door in the center section of the

rear filler panel and aluminum trim piece, while the license plate mounting moved below the rear bumper impact strip. In the greenhouse area, Delta 88 two-door hardtop models were still true hardtops having an opening, but small, rear quarter window, and adding a triangular fixed rear quarter window between the newly created B-pillar and the C-pillar. The look was somewhat similar to the Colonnade hardtop design of the Cutlass two-doors.

The Custom Cruiser, which shared most of its body styling with the luxurious Ninety-Eight models, also received a new grille that wrapped over slightly onto the header panel, and contained a grille pattern in the front bumper openings below the impact strip. The grille on both models was divided into five sections by thicker vertical bars, and within each section was an egg-crate grille pattern two columns wide and ten rows high above the bumper, and three rows high within the bumper. The Oldsmobile "rocket" emblem was placed in the center of the body-colored fascia between the two grille sections on the Custom Cruiser, while the Ninety-Eight used the "rocket" emblem as a stand-up hood ornament. Both models carried the Oldsmobile name in script on the lower driver's side grille area, and had parking/turn signal lights mounted in the bumper ends directly below the headlights. Around back, the Custom Cruiser taillights were still a vertical unit with a slightly arched top, sitting beneath a small tailfin on the rear quarter panel, and having backup lights placed low on the rear panel between the taillights and the Glide-Away tailgate. The Ninety-Eight had what appeared to be the same taillight this year, and like most other Oldsmobiles used a rear filler panel between the trunk lid and the bumper, covered with a stainless steel trim panel housing horizontal backup lights in each end.

The new-for-1973 Omega had a revised grille and front bumper. The grille was still of a split design, with each side having twelve seemingly free floating vertical rectangles, which wrapped up onto the top corner of the front header panel slightly, but still gave the appearance of a vertical bar grille as in the first year model. The front bumper implemented enlarged air openings that were now as wide as the grille above, but the parking/turn signal lights were moved from the bumper ends to the outward ends of the new bumper openings. Few other changes were seen, but there were two new options of interest. The S package was similar in spirit to Buick's GSX option on the Apollo. While it was intended to provide a sporty coupe to compete with the equally new Pontiac Ventura GTO option, it was truly all show and not much go, as it could be ordered on any Omega two-door, whether it be a six-cylinder or a V8 model. The other option, which was also offered on the other GM X-body cars, was the camper conversion tent available on the Hatchback. The tent used the hatchback liftgate as a roof, and had covered sides with screen windows. A fabric extension created an awning for sitting behind the car to eat, cook or chat, and the awning could be closed and zipped shut to create a sleeping area within the cargo compartment of the car, of course with the rear seat folded down. It was one of the interesting "oddball" options GM created that would reappear on the Pontiac Aztek sport utility vehicle from 2001 through 2005.

The front-wheel-drive Toronado received a minor facelift, with a new front end that finally gave the second generation car a traditional grille. Although small, a chrome edged, three-slot, horizontal grille appeared with the Toronado name in small block letters above it. The front bumper was redesigned, having a rather large top shelf, and rectangular openings that provided additional air inlets and were set in the bumper ends directly below the headlamps. Parking and turn signal lights continued to be mounted vertically in the fender cap ends.

Custom Cruiser Station Wagon

Cutlass 2-Door Colonnade Hardtop Coupe with 4-4-2 package

Cutlass 4-Door Colonnade Hardtop Sedan

Cutlass S 2-Door Colonnade Hardtop Coupe

Cutlass Supreme Cruiser 4-Door Station Wagon

Delta 88 Royale 2-Door Convertible

Cutlass Salon 4-Door Colonnade Hardtop Sedan

Ninety-Eight Regency 2-Door Hardtop

Omega 2-Door Hatchback

Delta 88 Royale 2-Door Hardtop

Toronado Custom 2-Door Hardtop

Vista-Cruiser 4-Door, 2-Seat Station Wagon

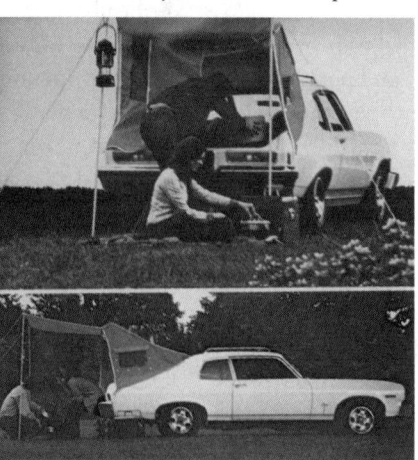

Omega 2-Door Hatchback with dealer-installed camper conversion and roof rack

Model year production: 581,195, down 37.02% from 1973.
Domestic market share: 6.73% (4th place).
Base price range: $2,883 to $5,760.
Oldsmobile average base price: $4,397, up 7.09%.
Introduction date: September 1973.
Assembly plants: Doraville, GA (D); Linden, NJ (E); Framingham, MA (G); Van Nuys, CA (L); Lansing, MI (M); Arlington, TX (R); Kansas City/Fairfax, KS (X); and Willow Run, MI (W).
Data plate identification (VIN): Thirteen digit code read as follows: First digit indicates division (3 = Oldsmobile); second through fourth digits indicate series and body style (model number in model charts); fifth digit is engine code (see powertrain chart); sixth digit indicates model year (4 = 1974); seventh digit indicates assembly plant (see list above); remaining digits are sequential with beginning number of 100001, except for Toronado which begins with 700001. *Example:* 3L69K4X100001 is a 1974 Oldsmobile Delta 88 4-Door Town Sedan with 350 CID, 4-bbl. V8 engine, serial number 100001, built in Kansas City/Fairfax, KS.

Powertrains

Engine*	Net HP	Engine Code	Transmission Availability		Omega	Cutlass & Vista-Cruiser	Delta 88	98 & Custom Cruiser	Toronado
250 CID (4.1L), 1-bbl., 6-cyl.	100	D	3-speed manual		S	—	—	—	—
				MPG:	NA	—	—	—	—
			3-speed Turbo Hydra-matic		$190	—	—	—	—
				MPG:	15.7	—	—	—	—
350 CID (5.7L), 4-bbl., V8	180	K	3-speed Turbo Hydra-matic		$364	S	S	—	—
				MPG:	9.5	9.5	9.0	—	—
350 CID (5.7L), 4-bbl., V8	200	M[1]	3-speed Turbo Hydra-matic		$394	$30	$30	—	—
				MPG:	9.5	9.5	9.0	—	—
455 CID (7.4L), 4-bbl., V8	210	T	3-speed Turbo Hydra-matic		—	—	$123	S	—
				MPG:	—	—	8.1	7.6	—
455 CID (7.4L), 4-bbl., V8	220	U[1]	3-speed Turbo Hydra-matic		—	—	$153	$30	—
				MPG:	—	—	8.1	7.6	—
455 CID (7.4L) H.O., 4-bbl., V8	230	W[1]	3-speed Turbo Hydra-matic		—	$137[2]	—	—	S
				MPG:	—	7.3	—	8.3	

*All Oldsmobile V8 engines are officially known as Rocket V8s. [1]Includes dual exhaust. [2]Available only on coupes and with other selected optional equipment.

Major Options

	Omega	Cutlass	Vista-Cruiser	Delta 88	Custom Cruiser	Ninety-Eight	Toronado
Four-Season air conditioner[1]	$381	$397	$397	$431	$431	$431	$431
Tilt-Away steering wheel	$44	$44	$44	$44	$44	$44	$44
Tilt-and-Telescope steering wheel	—	—	—	—	—	$82	$82
Cruise control	—	$67	$67	$67	$67	$67	$67
Electric rear window defroster	$31[2]	$62	—	$62	$62	$62	$62
Remote control mirror, LH	$12	$12	$12	$12	$12	$12	$12
Soft Ray tinted glass, all windows	$39	$42	$42	$49	$49	S	S
Power windows, 2-dr./4-dr.	—	$75/$113	$113	$129	$129	$129[3]	$129[4]
Power door locks, 2-dr./4-dr.	—	$46/$69	$69	$46/$69	$69	$46/$69	$46
Power front seat, 6-way w/std. seat	—	$103	$103	$103	$103	$103[5]	$103
Front bucket seats, w/console	$124	$126	—	—	—	—	—
AM radio	$65	$73	$73	$85	$85	$85	$85
AM/FM stereo	$233	$233	$233	$233	$233	$233	$233
AM/FM stereo w/8-track tape	—	$363	$363	$363	$363	$363	$363
Vinyl top[6]	$82	$99[7]	—	$123	—	$138	$135[8]
Vista Vent sunroof, manual	$95	$95	S	—	—	—	—
Sunroof, power operated[9]	—	$325	—	—	—	—	$589

	Omega	Cutlass	Vista-Cruiser	Delta 88	Custom Cruiser	Ninety-Eight	Toronado
Power trunk lid release	—	$14	—	$14	—	$14	$14
Power steering, "Vari-Ratio"	$113	S	S	S	S	S	S[10]
Power brakes, w/front disc	$68	$46[11]	S	S	S	S	S[12]
Deluxe wheel covers	$26	$26	$26	$31	$31	$31	$31
Wire wheel covers	—	$98	$98	$82	—	—	—
Super Stock II wheels	$72	$72	$72	—	—	—	—
WSW tires, std. size	$28	$30	$35	S	S	S	S
GM Air Cushion Restraint System	—	—	—	$225[13]	—	$225	$225

Popular Option Groups & Packages

	Omega	Cutlass	Vista-Cruiser	Delta 88	Custom Cruiser	Ninety-Eight	Toronado
Brougham interior package	—	—	—	—	—	—	$154
Convenience Group	—	$26	$27	—	—	—	—
FE2/F41 Suspension[14]	$15	$18/21	$21	$21	$21	$21	$21
"S" package	$161	—	—	—	—	—	—
Salon package	—	$361	—	—	—	—	—
W29 4-4-2 package	—	$121	—	—	—	—	—
W45 Hurst/Olds package	—	$	—	—	—	—	—

—= Not Available; S = Standard equipment. [1]V8 engine and power steering required for Omega. Power brakes required on Cutlass. "Tempmatic" air conditioner with automatic climate control is available for $30 additional on Delta 88, Custom Cruiser, Ninety-Eight and Toronado. [2]Blower type defogger. [3]Standard on Ninety-Eight Luxury and Regency models. [4]Available for $85 with optional opera roof. [5]Available on Ninety-Eight Luxury and Regency for $77. [6]Padded vinyl top on Delta 88, Ninety-Eight and Toronado. [7]Landau roof available on Cutlass Supreme coupe for $106. [8]Opera roof available on Toronado for $363. [9]Two-door models only. [10]"Constant-Ratio" steering on Toronado. [11]Standard on Cutlass Cruiser station wagon. [12]"True-Track" anti-lock braking system available on Toronado for $192. [13]Not available on convertible. [14]FE2 available on Omega and Cutlass. F41 on Cutlass requires heavy-duty wheels, except on wagons. FE2 is included with 4-4-2 package.

Paint Colors

	Code		Code		Code
Cameo White	11	Cypress Green metallic	46	Cinnamon metallic	66
Ebony Black[1]	19	Balsam Green metallic	49	Clove Brown metallic[1]	69
Wedgewood Blue metallic[1]	24	Colonial Cream	50	Cranberry metallic	74
Zodiac Blue metallic	26	Omega Maize[2]	51	Omega Red[2]	75
Eclipse Blue metallic	29	Omega Gold metallic[2]	53		
Reef Turquoise metallic	36	Colonial Gold	55		
Omega Lime[2]	40	Citation Bronze metallic	59		
Sage Green[1]	44	Silver Taupe metallic	64		

In two-tone combinations, the first two digits indicate lower color, and the next two digits are the upper color. [1]Available on all models except Omega. [2]Available only on Omega.

Omega

"It's a lot of little Oldsmobile."

Nameplate year of origin: 1973.
Current bodystyle lifespan: 1973 through 1974.
Predecessor to this model: None.
Replacement for this model: Omega (1975 to 1979).
Percentage of division's production: 8.65%.
Corporate siblings: Buick Apollo, Chevrolet Nova, and Pontiac Ventura.
Primary competition: Dodge Dart and Mercury Comet.
Notable changes: New grille and minor trim and detail changes.
Major standard equipment: Choice of black-and-white houndstooth checked vinyl or ribbed-knit vinyl front bench seat, cut-pile carpeting, simulated woodgrain I/P and door appliqués, rear quarter/rear door arm-

Measurements

	Coupe & HBK	Sedan
Wheelbase	111.0"	111.0"
Length	200.3"	200.3"
Width	72.4"	72.4"
Height	52.5"	53.8"
Legroom — front	41.7"	41.7"
Legroom — rear	33.4"	35.3"
Headroom — front	38.0"	39.3"
Headroom — rear	36.9"	37.3"

rests, deluxe steering wheel, door-operated dome lamp, dual speed wipers w/washers, chrome window surround moldings, roof drip moldings, chrome front and rear wheel opening moldings, hubcaps, and E78 × 14 BSW tires. Hatchback model adds: Fold-down rear seat.

Measurements (cont.)

	Coupe & HBK	Sedan
Cargo capacity (cu. ft.)	13.6*	13.6
Fuel capacity (gals.)	NA	NA

Hatchback maximum with rear seat down, 27 cu. ft.

1974

Models Available

	Model No.	Base MSRP	Change from LY	Shipping Wt. (lbs.)	Model Year Production	Change from LY
Omega 2-Door Coupe	B27	$2,883	+10.33%	3224	27,075	+3.63%
Omega 2-Door Hatchback	B17	$3,032	+9.78%	3328	12,449	-41.92%
Omega 4-Door Town Sedan	B69	$2,911	+10.22%	3272	10,756	-16.00%
TOTALS	Avg. price	$2,942	+10.10%	Production	50,280	-16.70%

Cutlass

"For people who didn't think they could afford an Olds."

Nameplate year of origin: 1961 (as F-85 Deluxe sport coupe designation; 1962 as F-85 sub-series; and 1965 as series designation. Also used on 1955 Oldsmobile show car).

Current bodystyle lifespan: 1973 through 1977.

Predecessor to this model: Cutlass (1968 to 1972).

Replacement for this model: Cutlass (1978 to 1988; restyled in 1981).

Percentage of division's production: 50.80%.

Corporate siblings: Buick Century, Chevrolet Malibu, and Pontiac LeMans.

Primary competition: Dodge Coronet and Mercury Montego.

Notable changes: Restyled front and rear end and minor trim and detail changes.

Major standard equipment: Choice of Lansing nylon or Morocceen vinyl front bench seat, color-keyed rubber floor mat (coupe), full-floor carpeting (sedan), soft grip steering wheel, simulated woodgrain I/P and door panel appliqués, deluxe armrests front and rear, rocker panel and wheel lip moldings (sedan), bright window surround moldings, power steering, manual front disc brakes, wheel covers, and F78 × 14 BSW tires. "S" adds: Logan cloth front bench seat, cut-pile carpeting, chrome rocker panel and wheel lip moldings, and chrome hood molding. Supreme adds: Choice of Bravado and Laurel nylon cloth or Morocceen vinyl front bench seat w/fold-down center armrest and embossed vinyl inserts on all seatbacks, padded luxury door panels with door pull straps, deluxe steering wheel, and ribbed louver ornament on lower front fender behind wheel, and G78 × 14 BSW tires (4-door only). Supreme Cruiser adds: Morocceen vinyl front bench seat w/fold-down center armrest and embossed vinyl inserts on all seatbacks, remote-control tailgate release (in glove compartment), rear vent window (3-seat model only), and H78 × 14 BSW tires. Vista-Cruiser adds: Vista-vent roof and woodgrain paneling on sides and tailgate.

Measurements

	Cutlass Coupe	Supreme Coupe	Cutlass Sedan	Supreme Sedan	Wagons
Wheelbase	112.0"	112.0"	116.0"	116.0"	116.0"
Length	211.5"	211.5"	214.6"	215.5"	220.0"
Width	76.5"	76.5"	76.5"	76.5"	76.8"
Height	53.4"	53.2"	56.1"	56.1"	55.3"
Legroom — front	42.1"	42.1"	42.1"	42.1"	42.1"
Legroom — rear	33.7"	33.7"	38.4"	38.3"	36.8"
Headroom — front	37.7"	37.7"	38.3"	38.3"	38.8"
Headroom — rear	37.0"	37.0"	37.5"	37.5"	39.4"
Cargo capacity (cu. ft.)	16.0	16.4	16.0	16.0	85.1
Fuel capacity (gals.)	22.0	22.0	22.0	22.0	22.0

Models Available

	Model No.	Base MSRP	Change from LY	Shipping Wt. (lbs.)	Model Year Production	Change from LY
Cutlass 2-Door Colonnade HT Coupe	F37	$3,558	+16.69%	3868	16,063	-27.06%
Cutlass 4-Door Colonnade HT Sedan	G29	$3,633	+15.81%	3924	25,718	-27.71%
Cutlass S 2-Door Colonnade HT Coupe	G37	$3,655	+15.70%	3883	50,860	-34.42%
Cutlass Supreme 2-Door Colonnade HT Coupe	J57	$3,850	+15.82%	3872	172,360	-21.60%
Cutlass Supreme 4-Door Colonnade HT Sedan	J29	$3,921	+15.49%	3969	12,525	-52.01%
Cutlass Supreme Cruiser 4-Dr., 2-S. Wagon	H35	$4,055	NEW	4369	3,437	NEW
Cutlass Supreme Cruiser 4-Dr., 3-S. Wagon	H45	$4,168	NEW	4406	3,101	NEW
Vista-Cruiser 4-Door, 2-Seat Station Wagon	J35	$4,265	+12.56%	4380	4,191	-61.53%
Vista-Cruiser 4-Door, 3-Seat Station Wagon	J45	$4,378	+12.20%	4417	7,013	-48.17%
TOTALS	Avg. price	$3,943	+16.18%	Production	295,268	-27.19%

Delta 88

"Beautiful to see, even more beautiful to own."

Nameplate year of origin: 1965 (88 series began in 1949).
Current bodystyle lifespan: 1971 through 1976.
Predecessor to this model: Delta 88 (1969 to 1970).
Replacement for this model: Delta 88 (1977 to 1985).
Percentage of division's production: 20.92%.
Corporate siblings: Buick LeSabre, Chevrolet BelAir/Impala/Caprice, and Pontiac Catalina/Bonneville/Grand Ville.
Primary competition: Chrysler Newport and Mercury Monterey.
Notable changes: Restyled front and rear end and minor trim and detail changes.
Major standard equipment: Nylon and Madrid-grain Morocceen vinyl bench seat, cut-pile carpeting, instrument panel message center, door panel and I/P woodgrain appliqués, front and rear bumper vinyl impact strips, bright rocker panel molding, full wheel covers, and H78 × 15 BSW tires. Royale adds: Regatta nylon with Morocceen trim front bench seat (Town Sedan only), Regatta nylon with Morocceen trim Custom Sport front bench seat w/fold down center armrest (all except Town Sedan), Royale ornamentation, cut-pile carpeting on cowl side panels and lower door panels, deluxe steering wheel, courtesy and glove box lights, map light, bright metal accented floor pedals, color-coordinated bodyside molding w/vinyl inserts, and bright window moldings.

Measurements

Wheelbase	124.0"
Length	226.9"
Width	79.5"
Height	54.3"
Legroom — front	42.4"
Legroom — rear	38.5"
Headroom — front	38.3"
Headroom — rear	38.0"
Cargo capacity (cu. ft.)	NA
Fuel capacity (gals.)	NA

Models Available

	Model No.	Base MSRP	Change from LY	Shipping Wt. (lbs.)	Model Year Production	Change from LY
Delta 88 2-Door Hardtop Coupe	L57	$4,220	+4.27%	4375	11,615	-57.13%
Delta 88 4-Door Town Sedan	L69	$4,164	+4.33%	4396	17,939	-57.77%
Delta 88 4-Door Hardtop Sedan	L39	$4,281	+4.21%	4428	11,941	-57.33%
Delta 88 Royale 2-Door Hardtop Coupe	N57	$4,375	+3.65%	4397	27,515	+1.55%
Delta 88 Royale 2-Door Convertible	N67	$4,590	+3.33%	4454	3,716	-47.57%
Delta 88 Royale 4-Door Town Sedan	N69	$4,304	+3.56%	4414	22,504	-47.26%
Delta 88 Royale 4-Door Hardtop Sedan	N39	$4,441	+3.45%	4462	26,363	-46.36%
TOTALS	Avg. price	$4,339	+3.82%	Production	121,593	-45.61%

Custom Cruiser

*"Start with the luxuries of a big Olds sedan, translate them into
an elegant station wagon—that's Oldsmobile's Custom Cruiser."*

Nameplate year of origin: 1971 (1940 as a designation on 90 series cars).
Current bodystyle lifespan: 1971 through 1976.
Predecessor to this model: None.
Replacement for this model: Custom Cruiser (1977 to 1990).
Percentage of division's production: 2.74%.
Corporate siblings: Buick Estate Wagon, Chevrolet BelAir/Impala/Caprice, and Pontiac Catalina Safari/Grand Safari.
Primary competition: Chrysler Town & Country and Mercury Colony Park.
Notable changes: New grille, and minor trim and detail changes.
Major standard equipment: Choice of Logan-pattern nylon or Madrid-grain Morocceen vinyl front bench seat w/fold-down center armrest, cut-pile carpeting, instrument panel message center, Glide-Away tailgate, power tailgate window, LH and RH rear view mirrors, vinyl bumper impact strips, rear wheel opening fender skirts, full wheel covers, and L78 × 15 BSW tires. "R" models add: Simulated woodgrain vinyl bodyside and tailgate appliqués w/chrome trim surround.

Measurements

Wheelbase	127.0"
Length	231.2"
Width	79.5"
Height	57.2"
Legroom — front	42.1"
Legroom — rear	39.4"
Headroom — front	39.6"
Headroom — rear	39.3"
Cargo capacity (cu. ft.)	106.1
Fuel capacity (gals.)	NA

Models Available

	Model No.	Base MSRP	Change from LY	Shipping Wt. (lbs.)	Model Year Production	Change from LY*
Custom Cruiser 4-Door, 2-S. Wagon	Q35	$4,821	+0.75%	5120	4,441	-64.18%
Custom Cruiser 4-Door, 3-S. Wagon	Q45	$4,960	+1.11%	5182	11,475	-56.72%
Custom Cruiser 4-Door, 2-S. Wagon	R35	$4,976	+7.47%	5123	NA	NA
Custom Cruiser 4-Door, 3-S. Wagon	R45	$5,115	+7.26%	5184	NA	NA
TOTALS		Avg. price $4,968	+4.11%		Production 15,916	-59.09%

Production of "Q" non-woodgrained and "R" woodgrained models kept as combined total.

Ninety-Eight

"Oldsmobile's easy step into the luxury car field."

Nameplate year of origin: 1941.
Current bodystyle lifespan: 1971 through 1976.
Predecessor to this model: Ninety-Eight (1969 to 1970).
Replacement for this model: Ninety-Eight (1977 to 1984).
Percentage of division's production: 15.01%.
Corporate siblings: Buick Electra 225, Cadillac Calais, and Cadillac deVille.
Primary competition: Chrysler New Yorker and Mercury Marquis.
Notable changes: Revised front and rear end styling, and minor trim and detail changes.
Major standard equipment: Choice of textured nylon w/Morocceen vinyl trim or Oxen-grain Morocceen vinyl front bench seat w/fold-down center armrest, cut-pile carpeting, carpeted lower door panels, simulated woodgrain appliqués on I/P, door pull straps, electric clock, deluxe safety belts, remote-control LH rear view mirror, wheel opening moldings, rocker panel molding, front and rear bumper guards, rear fender skirts, wheel covers, and J78 × 15 BSW tires. Luxury adds: Choice of textured Bravado nylon or Oxen-grain Morocceen vinyl front bench seat w/fold-down center armrest, power controls on door armrest in chrome bezel, two-way power front seat, power windows, and spare tire cover. Regency adds: Choice of Nylon velour or Laredo textured nylon 60/40 front seat deeply tufted w/"loose" cushion look, two-way power adjustment for each side, fold-down center armrests front and rear, zippered front seatback pouch pockets, French walnut woodgrain I/P, door panel and seat side shield trim, Tiffany-styled digital quartz-crystal clock, power windows, door-mounted entry courtesy lights, stand-up Oldsmobile "Rocket" hood ornament, and fully-lined trunk compartment w/spare tire cover.

Measurements

Wheelbase	127.0"
Length	232.4"
Width	79.8"
Height	54.2"
Legroom — front	42.4"
Legroom — rear	41.1"
Headroom — front	39.3"
Headroom — rear	38.2"
Cargo capacity (cu. ft.)	20.2
Fuel capacity (gals.)	NA

1974

Models Available

	Model No.	Base MSRP	Change from LY	Shipping Wt. (lbs.)	Model Year Production	Change from LY
Ninety-Eight 4-Door Hardtop Sedan	T39	$5,130	+5.56%	4690	4,395	-68.58%
Ninety-Eight Luxury Coupe 2-Door HT	V37	$5,341	+5.32%	4638	9,236	-65.70%
Ninety-Eight Luxury Sedan 4-Door HT	V39	$5,434	+5.23%	4730	21,896	-60.69%
Ninety-Eight Regency Coupe 2-Door HT	X37	$5,603	NEW	4664	10,719	NEW
Ninety-Eight Regency Sedan 4-Door HT	X39	$5,696	+5.13%	4759	24,310	-28.52%
TOTALS		Avg. price $5,441	+7.47%		Production 70,556	-49.05%

Toronado

"One of the world's most distinguished motorcars, designed and built in the belief that engineering can be beautiful."

Nameplate year of origin: 1966.
Current bodystyle lifespan: 1971 through 1978.
Predecessor to this model: Toronado (1966 to 1970).
Replacement for this model: Toronado (1979 to 1985).
Percentage of division's production: 4.75%.
Corporate siblings: Buick Riviera and Cadillac Eldorado.
Primary competition: Ford Thunderbird.
Notable changes: Revised front end and minor trim and detail changes.
Major standard equipment: Choice of Bravado nylon or Morocceen vinyl Custom-Sport front bench seat, cut-pile carpeting, simulated woodgrain appliqué on I/P and steering wheel, two-spoke steering wheel, digital clock w/quartz-crystal movement, color-keyed chrome-accented pedals, deluxe safety belts, LH remote-control rear view mirror, front and rear bumper guards w/vinyl inserts, color-keyed bumper impact strips, dual exhaust, chrome wheel covers, and J78 × 15 BSW tires.

Measurements

Wheelbase	122.0"
Length	228.0"
Width	79.5"
Height	53.2"
Legroom — front	42.4"
Legroom — rear	35.2"
Headroom — front	38.1"
Headroom — rear	37.1"
Cargo capacity (cu. ft.)	17.0
Fuel capacity (gals.)	26.0

Models Available

	Model No.	Base MSRP	Change from LY	Shipping Wt. (lbs.)	Model Year Production	Change from LY
Toronado Custom 2-Door Hardtop	Y57	$5,760	+5.86%	4698	27,528	-50.68%
TOTALS		Avg. price $5,760	+5.86%		Production 27,528	-50.68%

PLYMOUTH

"Extra care in engineering makes a difference in Plymouth ... coming through for you."

Historically ranking third in the annual sales and production rankings up through the 1950s, and fourth behind Pontiac during their peak in the 1960s, Plymouth had recently begun to slip. After the brand attained third place again as recently as 1971, Oldsmobile overtook it in 1972, and Pontiac in 1973. For the 1974 model year Plymouth would again finish in third place behind Ford and Chevrolet in total model year production, in large part due to the economical Valiant series which garnered nearly two-thirds of all Plymouth sales during the fuel crisis of the period. In fact, the four model lineup of the Valiant group, to include the Scamp and Duster models, had higher production totals than the entire lines of Dodge, Mercury, and American Motors, and outsold the combined total of Chrysler, Cadillac and Lincoln for the 1974 model year. If the Valiant had been its own brand, it would have finished in seventh place between Buick and Dodge. Unfortunately it would be the last time for a third place finish by Plymouth, as its cars had become too similar to Dodge models in styling and price, and a recovery from the impending downturn in sales would never be attained. Interestingly, the entire Plymouth line would see a production total higher than the 1974 Valiant production total output only one more time before its demise in 2001, that being in 1977.

As if to accentuate the aforementioned similarities between Dodge and Plymouth models, the Valiant sedan was moved to the 111-inch wheelbase used by the Dart sedan, and already shared by the Scamp and Dart hardtops. The Valiant and Scamp also shared a restyled rear panel and bumper design with the Dart. The new panel was rearward slanting and housed horizontal taillights above a new box style bumper that was added to meet the new rear safety standards. It was one of the more attractive rear end designs for the 1974 season. Two new Brougham models were added to give the compact line a little more luxury. More luxurious looking interiors and more standard features copied the similarly new Dart Special Edition. Available in both 2-door hardtop and 4-door sedan body styles, the Valiant Brougham 2-door hardtop was the first of that body style to bear the Valiant name since 1966.

The full-size Plymouth was completely redesigned for 1974, dispensing with the last vestiges of the fuselage style bodies. Even more than in previous years, the Fury shared major components with its Dodge Monaco stablemate, including chassis, upper sheetmetal, glass and other major components. In fact, in base form, from a distance, it was difficult to distinguish a Dodge Monaco from a Plymouth Fury. The greenhouse area had slender A-pillars and round-cornered, slightly curved rear windows, and a straight beltline surrounding the front and sides, with a kick-up to the rear side window as it met the C-pillar. Front fenders and rear quarter panels had more angular lines. The bodysides carried two feature lines with the upper one beginning at the upper front edge of the headlight bezel and running straight along the entire length of the car to a point on the rear end cap near

the top corner of the taillights. The lower feature line created a nearly invisible crease in the lower body that ran between the wheel openings, extending from the wheel openings to meet the bumpers.

At the front end, a more basic design was featured with a horizontal grille composed of multiple thin bars, with a small section of grille in the lower bumper area. Dual headlights sat at each end in large, divided chrome bezels. Capping the entire setup was a chrome strip that was wider across the header panel above the grille. The box-style bumper housed the parking/turn signal lamps in its outer grille area. At the back end, three-section horizontal taillamps were set in the rear panel, dipping slightly into the bumper. The quarter panel caps had a small, tailfin-like ridge on top. Station wagons used a vertical single lens tail lamp and, as in the past, shared all features of their body with the Chrysler Town & Country and Dodge Monaco models.

Inside, a new instrument panel, with a slightly overhanging top pad created a more driver friendly environment by doing away with the tightly packed pod of previous models. The traditional square speedometer used by Plymouth for many years had fuel and temperature gauges at the bottom, light and wiper controls as well as air vents to the left side, and radio and climate controls to the right side. As had become a trend in Chrysler products, many of the optional seating choices used high front seat backs providing built-in head rests. With these optional seats having fold-down center armrests, the seat backs looked very much like bucket seat backs, and quite possibly could have been, at least internally, to save on production costs. The new interior design and layout gave even the most basic Fury I a greatly improved appearance.

The mid-size Satellite sedans and wagons had a new grille design split into two horizontal sections with thin horizontal bars between each. Otherwise there were few changes to the line. The sporty Barracuda entered its final year of production with virtually no changes, as the muscle-car era had ended, and sales had eroded to a fraction of their peak. And, speaking of muscle, the 340 CID V8 engine was replaced by a more powerful and efficient 360 CID V8 engine, which was available in at least one model of each of the four Plymouth series.

'Cuda 2-Door Hardtop
with Barracuda 2-Door Hardtop, rear

Duster 2-Door Coupe
with Duster 360 2-Door Coupe, rear

Fury Gran Sedan 4-Door Hardtop

Fury Sport Suburban 4-Door Station Wagon
with Fury Custom Suburban wagon, rear

Road Runner 2-Door Coupe

Road Runner interior with optional
Wimbledon cloth-and-vinyl bucket seats

Satellite Custom 4-Door Sedan
with Satellite 2-Door Coupe, rear

Satellite Regent 4-Door Station Wagon
with Satellite Custom wagon, rear

Valiant 4-Door Sedan

Model year production: 757,808, down 14.10% from 1973.
Domestic market share: 8.77% (3rd place).
Base price range: $2,753 to $4,895.
Plymouth average base price: $3,787, up 8.99%.
Introduction date: September 25, 1973.
Assembly plants: Lynch Road — Detroit, MI (A); Hamtramck, MI (B); Jefferson Ave. — Detroit, MI (C); Belvidere, IL (D); Newark, DE (F); St. Louis, MO (G); and Windsor, Ontario, Canada (R).

Data plate identification (VIN): Thirteen digit code read as follows: First four digits indicate series and body style (model number in model charts); fifth digit indicates engine code (see powertrain chart); sixth digit indicates year (4 = 1974); seventh digit indicates assembly plant (see list above); remaining digits are sequential with beginning numbers of 100001. *Example:* VL41C4B100001 is a 1974 Plymouth Valiant 4-Door Sedan, with 225 CID, 2-bbl. 6-cylinder engine, serial number 100001, built in Hamtramck, MI.

Powertrains

Engine	Net HP	Engine Code	Transmission Availability[1]		Duster & Valiant	Barracuda	Satellite, Sebring & Custom	Satellite Sebring Plus, Road Runner & Wagons	Fury I, II and III	Fury Gran & Wagons
198 CID (3.2L), 1-bbl., 6-cyl.[2]	95	B	3-speed manual		S (ex. Brghm. & Duster 360)[2]	—	—	—	—	—
				MPG:	NA	—	—	—	—	—
			3-speed Torque Flite automatic		$195 (ex. Brghm. & Duster 360)[2]	—	—	—	—	—
				MPG:	16.0	—	—	—	—	—
225 CID (3.7L), 1-bbl., 6-cyl.	105	C	3-speed manual		$39 (ex. Brghm. & Duster 360)[3]	—	S[2]	—	—	—
				MPG:	NA	—	11.5	—	—	—
			4-speed manual		$234 (ex.	—	—	—	—	—

1974

Engine	Net HP	Engine Code	Transmission Availability[1]		Duster & Valiant	Barracuda	Satellite, Sebring & Custom	Satellite Sebring Plus, Road Runner & Wagons	Fury I, II and III	Fury Gran & Wagons
					Brghm. & Duster 360)					
				MPG:	NA	—	—	—	—	—
			3-speed Torque Flite automatic		S (Brghm.)/ $244 (ex. Brghm. & Duster 360)[3]	—	$215[2]	—	—	—
				MPG:	16.7	—	NA	—	—	—
318 CID (5.2L), 2-bbl., V8	150	G	3-speed manual		$147 (ex. Brghm. & Duster 360)	S	$116[3]	S	—	—
				MPG:	12.5	12.5	11.4	11.4	—	—
			4-speed manual		$342 (ex. Brghm. & Duster 360)	$195	—	$205 (Coupes only)	—	—
				MPG:	NA	NA	—	11.8	—	—
			3-speed Torque Flite automatic		$83 (Brghm.)/ $362 (ex. Brghm. & Duster 360)	$225	$331	$225	—	—
				MPG:	NA	NA	11.6	11.6	—	—
360 CID (5.9L), 2-bbl., V8	200/ 170[4]	K	3-speed Torque Flite automatic		—	—	—	—	S[2]	—
				MPG:	—	—	—	—	10.4	—
360 CID (5.9L), 4-bbl., V8	245	J,L	3-speed manual		S (Duster 360)	$90	—	—	—	—
				MPG:	11.8	11.8	—	—	—	—
			4-speed manual		$195 (Duster 360)	$285	—	$232 (Road Runner only)	—	—
				MPG:	11.8	11.8	—	9.1	—	—
			3-speed Torque Flite automatic		$208 (Duster 360)	$315	$376[5]	$250[5]	$39[3]	—
				MPG:	10.9	10.9	10.2	10.2	9.9	—
400 CID (6.6L), 2-bbl., V8	205	M	3-speed Torque Flite automatic		—	—	—	—	—	S[2]
				MPG:	—	—	—	—	—	8.9
400 CID (6.6L), 4-bbl., V8	250/ 240[4]	N,P	4-speed manual		—	—	—	$414 (Road Runner only)	—	—
				MPG:	—	—	—	9.2	—	—
			3-speed Torque Flite automatic		—	—	$548[2]	$432	$80	$39
				MPG:	—	—	8.8	8.8	8.9	8.9
440 CID (7.2L), 4-bbl., V8	275/ 250[4]	T,U	4-speed manual		—	—	—	$474 (Road Runner only)	—	—
				MPG:	—	—	—	NA	—	—
			3-speed Torque Flite automatic		—	—	—	$494 (Road Runner only)	$156	$115
				MPG:	—	—	—	8.6	9.1	9.1

[1]Unless otherwise noted: All 4-speed manuals are floor-shift. All 3-speed manual and automatic transmissions are column shift, except as follows: Barracuda with 3-speed manual is floor shift. All transmissions are floor-mounted shift on the following models with bucket seats: Duster 360, Barracuda, 'Cuda, and Road Runner. Floor-shift available on Duster and Scamp models for $27 extra.   [2]Not available in California.   [3]Required (or standard) in California.   [4]Second horsepower ratings are as installed in Fury models.   [5]Only available in California, except in Road Runner where it is available in all 50 states.

Major Options

	Valiant	Barracuda	Satellite	Fury I, II, III	Fury Gran
Air conditioning[1]	$395	$384	$398	$406	$406
Tilt & telescoping steering wheel	—	—	—	—	$92
"Auto-Speed" control	—	—	$67	$67	$67
Electric rear window defroster	$49	$28[2]	$62	$31[2]	$31
Tinted glass, all windows	$37	$37	$45	$52	$52
Front vent window, 4-dr. only	—	—	—	$35	$35
Dual remote control mirrors	—	—	—	$40	$40
Remote control trunk release	—	—	—	$16	$16
Power windows	—	—	$125	$131	$131
Power door locks, 2-dr./4-dr.	—	—	—	$49/$75	$49/$75
Electric clock	—	$17	$19	$18	$18
AM radio	$73	$73	$88	$88	$88
AM/FM stereo	—	$187	$226	$226	$226
AM/FM stereo w/8-track tape	—	—	$391	$391	$391
Front bucket seats w/console	$181[3]	$54[4]	$155[5]	—	$96[5]
Full floor carpeting, color-keyed[7]	$18	S	$20	$20	S
Vinyl top	$87	$84	$99	$112	$112
Sunroof, electric	$151[8]	$182	$182[8]	$513[9]	$513[9]
Power steering, variable-ratio	$92	$104	$115	S	S
Power brakes, w/front disc[10]	$66	S	$46	S	S
Deluxe wheel covers	$26	$26	$28	$28	S
Premiere wheel covers	—	—	$51	$61	$33
Rallye road wheels	$56	$56	$56	—	—
Styled road wheels, chrome	$78	$78	$82	$82	$82
White sidewall tires, std. size	$35	$38	$38	$38	$38

Popular Option Groups & Packages

	Valiant	Barracuda	Satellite	Fury I, II, III	Fury Gran
Basic group	$114	$196	—	—	—
Brougham package	—	—	—	—	$193[11]
Easy Order package	—	—	$717	$400	$404
Gold Duster package	$187[12]	—	—	—	—
Luxury equipment package	—	—	$1,480	$1,418	$1,392
Rallye I/P group	—	$79	$80	—	—
Salon package	—	—	—	$235[13]	—
Space Duster Package	$85[12]	—	—	—	—
Sports décor group	—	$71	—	—	—
Twister package	$124[12]	—	—	—	—

—= Not Available; S = Standard equipment. [1]Automatic air conditioning available on Fury for $484. [2]Blower type defogger. [3]For Duster only, and includes full-floor carpeting. [4]Bucket seats are standard on Barracuda, and price shown is for console only. [5]Available on Satellite Sebring Plus and Road Runner, and requires automatic transmission. Bucket seats are standard on Road Runner. [6]Available on Fury Gran models with a center cushion instead of a console. [7]Carpeting is standard on all except Duster, Valiant, Satellite (base), Road Runner, and Fury I. [8]Only available on 2-door models, and is manually operated. [9]Requires vinyl top. Not available on station wagons. [10]Standard on Duster 360 and Satellite station wagons. All others have manual front disc brakes as standard, except 6-cylinder Valiant, Scamp and Duster models which have manual drum brakes. [11]Available on Custom Suburban and Sport Suburban for $155. [12]Available on Duster only. Gold Duster and Twister package combination is $235. [13]Available only on Fury III 4-doors, and Custom Suburban wagon. Price is estimated.

Paint Colors

	Code		Code		Code
Silver Frost metallic[1]	A5	Sahara Beige	L4	Yellow Blaze[4]	Y5
Powder Blue	B1	Aztec Gold metallic	L6	Golden Haze metallic	Y6
Lucerne Blue metallic	B5	Dark Moonstone metallic	L8	Tahitian Gold metallic	Y9
Starlight Blue metallic[2]	B8	Sienna metallic	T5		
Rallye Red	E5	Dark Chestnut metallic[2]	T9	
Burnished Red metallic[3]	E7	Spinnaker White	W1	
Frosty Green metallic	G2	Formal Black	X9	
Deep Sherwood metallic	G8	Sunfire Yellow[2]	Y2	
Avocado Gold metallic	J6	Classic White[1]	10	
Classic White[1]	10	Golden Fawn	Y4	

Single tones are coded W1, W1. Two-tones are coded X9, W1 where first two digits are accent or roof color, and second two digits are basic body color. [1]Available only on Fury and Satellite. [2]Available only on Fury. [3]Available only on Valiant, Barracuda and Satellite. [4]Not available on Fury.

Valiant

"Compare our compacts.... They're a lot of car for the money."

Nameplate year of origin: 1960 (Valiant); 1970 (Duster); 1971 (Scamp).
Current bodystyle lifespan: 1967 through 1976.
Predecessor to this model: Valiant (1963 to 1966).
Replacement for this model: Volaré (1976 to 1980).
Percentage of division's production: 62.92%.
Corporate siblings: Dodge Dart.
Primary competition: AMC Hornet, Chevrolet Nova, and Ford Maverick.
Notable changes: Restyled rear end for Scamp and Valiant, and minor trim and detail changes.
Major standard equipment: All-vinyl front bench seat w/integral headrest (Valiant and Duster), black I/P trim (Valiant and Duster), simulated woodgrain I/P cluster appliqué (Scamp), two-speed electric windshield wipers, front door

Measurements

	Duster	Scamp	Valiant
Wheelbase	108.0"	111.0"	111.0"
Length	194.1"	197.6"	197.6"
Width	71.8"	71.0"	71.0"
Height	53.1"	52.8"	54.3"
Legroom — front	41.7"	41.7"	41.7"
Legroom — rear	29.9"	31.9"	35.8"
Headroom — front	37.2"	37.3"	38.4"
Headroom — rear	36.4"	36.6"	37.2"
Cargo capacity (cu. ft.)	19.8*	15.4	15.4
Fuel capacity (gals.)	16.0	16.0	16.0

With Space Duster package fold-down rear seat option, 56.0 cu. ft.

armrests, heater and defroster, front door window vents (Valiant), hubcaps, and 6.95 × 14 BSW tires. Scamp adds: Pleated vinyl front bench seat, cut-pile carpeting, interior décor package, cigarette lighter, roof drip-rail molding, wheel lip moldings, and dual horns. Duster 360 adds: Accent tape stripes, roof drip rail molding, heavy-duty suspension and shock absorbers, dual exhaust, and E70 × 14 BSW tires. Brougham adds: Velour cloth and vinyl front bucket seats w/fold-down center armrest or low back front bench seat, door pull assist straps, color-keyed cut-pile carpeting, premium steering wheel, bright pedal dress-up, trunk carpeting, dual horns, deluxe insulation package, light package, three-speed electric windshield wipers and washers, LH remote control mirror, full vinyl roof, bodyside tape stripes, upper door frame moldings (sedan), stand-up hood ornament, power steering, front sway bar, and color-keyed wheel covers.

Models Available

	Model No.	Base MSRP	Change from LY	Shipping Wt. (lbs.)	Model Year Production	Change from LY
Duster 2-Door Coupe	VL29	$2,753	+15.87%	2975	277,409	+11.30%
Valiant 4-Door Sedan	VL41	$2,866	+17.12%	3035	127,430	+106.11%
Scamp 2-Door Hardtop	VH23	$3,001	+14.67%	3010	51,699	-3.89%
Valiant Brougham 2-Door Hardtop	VP23	$3,718	NEW	3180	13,766	NEW
Valiant Brougham 4-Door Sedan	VP41	$3,743	NEW	3195	2,545	NEW
Duster 360 2-Door Coupe	VS29	$3,212	+13.82%	3315	3,969	-74.77%
TOTALS	*Avg. price*	$3,216	+25.34%		*Production* 476,818	+25.28%

Barracuda

"For the sporting life."

Nameplate year of origin: 1964.
Current bodystyle lifespan: 1970 through 1974.
Predecessor to this model: Barracuda (1967-1969).
Replacement for this model: None.
Percentage of division's sales volume: 1.55%.
Corporate siblings: Dodge Challenger.
Primary competition: AMC Javelin and Chevrolet Camaro.
Notable changes: Minor trim and detail changes.
Major standard equipment: All-vinyl bucket seats w/integral head restraints, cut-pile carpeting, color-keyed headlining and armrests, inside day/night rear view mirror, LH rearview mirror, concealed two-speed windshield wipers, color-keyed grille

Measurements

Wheelbase	108.0"
Length	195.6"
Width	75.6"
Height	50.9"
Legroom — front	42.1"
Legroom — rear	28.9"
Headroom — front	37.4"
Headroom — rear	35.7"
Cargo capacity (cu. ft.)	8.6
Fuel capacity (gals.)	18.0

w/horizontal inset bars, front and rear bumper guards, manual front disc brakes, hubcaps, and 7.35 × 14 BSW tires. 'Cuda adds: Chrome wheel opening and rocker panel sill moldings, performance style hood, black-out rear deck panel, heavy-duty suspension, power front disc brakes, and F70 × 14 BSW tires.

Models Available

	Model No.	Base MSRP	Change from LY	Shipping Wt. (lbs.)	Model Year Production	Change from LY
Barracuda 2-Door Hardtop	BH23	$3,067	+4.50%	3210	6,745	-41.79%
'Cuda 2-Door Hardtop	BS23	$3,252	+4.23%	3300	4,989	-53.05%
TOTALS		Avg. price $3,160	+4.36%		Production 11,734	-47.18%

Satellite

"Out to win you over with mid-size value and family size room."

Nameplate year of origin: 1965 (as a Belvedere trim level); 1971 (as series).
Current bodystyle lifespan: 1971 through 1978.
Predecessor to this model: Belvedere/Satellite (1968 to 1970).
Replacement for this model: Fury (1975 to 1978).
Percentage of division's sales volume: 19.92%.
Corporate siblings: Dodge Charger and Coronet.
Primary competition: AMC Matador, Chevrolet Chevelle, and Ford Torino.
Notable changes: Revised front and rear styling.
Major standard equipment: All-vinyl front bench seat, color-keyed rubber floor covering, cigarette lighter (sedan only), dome light, concealed two-speed windshield wipers, dual horns (sedan only), rocker panel sill molding (sedan only),

Measurements

	2-Doors	Sedans	Wagons
Wheelbase	115.0"	117.0"	117.0"
Length	208.9"	212.4"	217.1"
Width	79.1"	78.6"	79.2"
Height	52.2"	53.7"	56.4"
Legroom — front	41.9"	41.9"	41.9"
Legroom — rear	34.1"	36.7"	36.7"
Headroom — front	37.3"	38.5"	39.7"
Headroom — rear	36.4"	37.3"	38.1"
Cargo capacity (cu. ft.)	14.3	16.7	91.3
Fuel capacity (gals.)	19.5	19.5	21.0

hubcaps, and E78 × 14 BSW tires. Road Runner adds (to base Satellite Coupe features): Rallye gauge cluster, bodyside and roof "Strobe" tape stripe, special Road Runner trim and ornamentation, performance hood, front and rear sway bars, heavy-duty springs, dual exhaust w/chrome tips, "Beep-Beep" horn, argent-painted rallye wheels w/chrome hubs, and G70 × 14 W/L tires. Custom and Sebring add: Cloth-and-vinyl front bench seat, color-keyed carpeting, front door and rear side armrests, front and rear door armrests, drip rail moldings, and wheel-lip moldings without sill molding. Sebring Plus adds: Vinyl bucket seats, rallye gauge cluster, premium door trim panels, simulated woodgrain inserts on I/P, door trim inserts and steering wheel, special Sebring Plus trim and ornamentation, belt moldings, bodyside tape stripes, and deluxe wheel covers. Wagons add: Fold-down rear seatback, power front disc brakes, three-way tailgate, tailgate "auto lock" system (3-seat wagons only), and H78 × 14 BSW tires. Regent wagon adds: All-vinyl split-back front bench seat w/fold-down center armrest, cargo compartment carpeting and dome light, exterior simulated woodgrained bodyside overlays, and reflectorized rear tailgate woodgrain trim.

Models Available

	Model No.	Base MSRP	Change from LY	Shipping Wt. (lbs.)	Model Year Production	Change from LY
Satellite 2-Door Coupe	RL21	$3,054	+10.85%	3435	10,634	-21.64%
Satellite 4-Door Sedan	RL41	$3,125	+10.66%	3520	12,726	-13.52%
Satellite 4-Door, 2-Seat Wagon	RL45	$3,554	+8.62%	4065	4,622	-33.07%
Road Runner 2-Door Coupe	RM21	$3,444	+10.56%	3615	11,555	-39.36%
Satellite Sebring 2-Door Hardtop	RH23	$3,252	+8.51%	3455	31,980	-37.99%
Satellite Custom 4-Door Sedan	RH41	$3,228	+8.54%	3515	45,863	-1.89%
Satellite Custom 4-Dr., 2-S. Wagon	RH45	$3,738	+9.94%	4065	4,354	-35.33%
Satellite Custom 4-Dr., 3-S. Wagon	RH46	$4,051	+15.15%	4110	5,591	-27.44%
Satellite Sebring Plus 2-Dr. Hardtop	RP23	$3,955	+8.04%	3555	18,480	-57.64%
Satellite Regent 4-Dr., 2-S. Wagon	RP45	$3,965	+9.50%	4065	2,026	-27.15%
Satellite Regent 4-Dr., 3-S. Wagon	RP46	$4,280	+14.71%	4130	3,132	-34.56%
TOTALS		Avg. price $3,566	+10.56%		Production 150,963	-30.82%

Fury

"Beautifully restyled from front to rear. Plymouth tough is beautiful."

Nameplate year of origin: 1956.

Current bodystyle lifespan: 1974 through 1977 (renamed Gran Fury for 1975 to 1977).

Predecessor to this model: Fury (1969 to 1973).

Replacement for this model: Gran Fury (1980 to 1981).

Percentage of division's sales volume: 15.61%.

Corporate siblings: Dodge Monaco.

Primary competition: AMC Ambassador, Chevrolet BelAir/Impala/Caprice, and Ford Custom 500/Galaxie 500/LTD.

Notable changes: Completely redesigned.

Major standard equipment: All vinyl front bench seat, front and rear armrests, nylon loop-pile carpeting, cigarette lighter, dome light, front door courtesy light switches, glove box lock, inside hood release, concealed two-speed windshield wipers w/washers, bright drip rail molding, dual

Measurements

	Cars	Wagons
Wheelbase	120.0"	122.0"
Length	223.4"	227.5"
Width	79.8"	79.8"
Height	54.9"	58.3"
Legroom — front	41.8"	41.8"
Legroom — rear	39.1"	39.1"
Headroom — front	38.8"	39.6"
Headroom — rear	38.4"	39.2"
Cargo capacity (cu. ft.)	22.4	104.2
Fuel capacity (gals.)	23.0	23.0

horns, hubcaps, and G78 × 15 BSW tires. Fury II adds: Cloth-and-vinyl front bench seat, and bright ¾-length bodyside molding. Fury III adds: Cloth-and-vinyl front bench seat, simulated woodgrained appliqué on I/P cluster and pad, 3-spoke steering wheel w/simulated woodgrained inserts, simulated woodgrained door trim insert, front and rear armrests w/bright base, glove box light, bright wheel lip moldings, and full-length bodyside molding. Fury Gran adds: Cloth-and-vinyl split back front bench seat w/fold-down center armrest, door pull straps, carpeted lower door panels, electric clock, rear door dome light courtesy switches, extra quiet insulation, bright belt moldings, bright rocker panel sill molding, full-length bodyside paint stripe, deluxe wheel covers, and H78 × 15 BSW tires. Wagons add: All-vinyl front bench seat, color-keyed rubber floor mats (Suburban), color-keyed carpeting (Custom), cargo light (Custom 3-seat), aerodynamic roof air deflector, power tailgate window, power steering, and J78 × 15 BSW tires (2-seat wagons) or L78 × 15 BSW tires (3-seat wagons). Sport Suburban adds: All-vinyl split back front bench seat w/fold-down center armrest, door pull straps, simulated woodgrained appliqué on I/P cluster and pad, 3-spoke steering wheel w/simulated woodgrained inserts, simulated woodgrained door trim insert, carpeted lower door panels, electric clock, rear door dome light courtesy switches, simulated woodgrain bodyside panels, and deluxe wheel covers.

Models Available

	Model No.	Base MSRP	Change from LY	Shipping Wt. (lbs.)	Model Year Production	Change from LY
Fury I 4-Door Sedan	PL41	$3,866	+8.14%	4185	8,162	-53.00%
Fury II 4-Door Sedan	PM41	$3,988	+7.96%	4165	11,649	-46.18%
Fury Suburban 4-Door, 2-S. Wagon	PM45	$4,434	+6.84%	4745	2,490	-52.17%
Fury III 2-Door Hardtop	PH23	$4,183	+7.73%	4125	14,167	-59.48%
Fury III 4-Door Sedan	PH41	$4,165	+7.73%	4180	27,965	-45.95%
Fury III 4-Door Hardtop	PH43	$4,233	+7.66%	4205	18,778	-63.33%
Fury Custom Suburban 4-Dr., 2-S. Wagon	PH45	$4,532	+6.74%	4755	3,887	-60.69%
Fury Custom Suburban 4-Dr., 3-S. Wagon	PH46	$4,643	+6.64%	4800	5,628	-64.09%
Fury Gran Coupe 2-Door Hardtop	PP23	$4,392	+8.07%	4300	9,617	-46.95%
Fury Gran Sedan 4-Door Hardtop	PP43	$4,440	+8.03%	4370	8,191	-44.85%
Fury Sport Suburban 4-Dr., 2-S. Wagon	PP45	$4,790	+6.52%	4795	1,712	-64.57%
Fury Sport Suburban 4-Dr., 3-S. Wagon	PP46	$4,895	+6.44%	4850	6,047	-61.43%
TOTALS	*Avg. price* $4,380		+7.33%	*Production*	118,293	-54.71%

PONTIAC

"The Wide-Track people have a way with cars."

In times of economic turmoil, the mid-range auto manufacturers usually suffer the most. This held true for 1974; in fact, as the fuel crisis and ensuing recession took hold, Pontiac suffered more than most others in its price class. One might suspect the reason had something to do with the Pontiac performance car image, but it is interesting that the only series in the Pontiac lineup to see a sales and production increase was the Firebird. In fact, the most powerful Firebird, the Trans Am, would end the year with its second consecutive season of triple digit sales increases. And oddly, the division's lone compact series, the Ventura, declined in sales at a time when most other compacts were increasing. Of course, at the time, enthusiasts also thought it was an "odd" that Pontiac chose to move the famed GTO option to the compact Ventura. If this action seemed to dilute the character of the GTO name, it at least gave the well-recognized name one more year of production before it was put out to pasture for the next thirty years. It was an interesting season for GM's performance division, and one that likely had a huge bearing on its future.

Firebird models received their first major restyling since their introduction as a mid-year 1970 model. A new sloping front end was added, with the expected Pontiac split grille design having two grille openings as used on past models, and each grille housing eighteen vertical bars. Firebird logo decals were placed on the point of the body-colored nose between the grille sections, as well as on the rear deck panel. A more traditional front bumper design, again fashioned out of flexible body-colored urethane, carried a wide black rub strip, which defined the main portion of the bumper. In the lower portion of the body-colored front-end were parking lights at the outer ends beneath the headlights, and two air intake openings to the outside of each black bumper guard, with a license plate mounting in between. At the rear, redesigned slot-type taillights were used, being three rows high, and having the backup lights set to the inward side, alongside the center mounted license plate. The body-colored urethane rear bumper also had black rub strips and bumper guards, like the front. All of the big V8 engine options continued to be available, clear up to the 455 CID Super Duty V8 engine, which was installed in 943 Firebird Trans Ams.

The compact Ventura received a facelift for the new season, adopting the twin-opening grille used on the 1973 Ventura Sprint option. All Ventura models had an argent-colored honeycomb grille insert, placed deep into the two chrome trimmed grille openings. On Ventura two-doors equipped with the optional Sprint or GTO package, the grille was blacked out. In a change that did not meet with overwhelming enthusiasm, the GTO option was moved to the compact Ventura line, in a bid to revive the performance nameplate's sagging sales. Offering a 350 CID V8 as its only engine choice, the Ventura-based GTO was definitely not the muscle car the name once stood for. In fact, aside from its dual exhaust, heavy-duty transmission, and Trans Am style "shaker" hood scoop, it was mainly a trim and decal package, not totally unlike its immediate predecessor. However, there was enough interest in the car to sell 7,058 Ventura coupes and hatchbacks with the GTO option, exceeding the 1973 LeMans based total by more than 2,000 units.

The restyled-for-1973 LeMans models received updated rear end styling to better conform to new rear bumper impact standards, and also received new grille designs up front. The LeMans and LeMans Sport Coupe used a twin port grille divided into three horizontal sections by two chrome bars, with each section having dark argent crosshatch style inserts. The Luxury LeMans had a twin port grille divided into five sections by vertical chrome bars, each section having nine horizontal bars deeply inset. For all three trim levels, the bottom of the grille was aligned with the bottom of the headlight bezel, and the top of the grille was about an inch shorter than the top of the headlight bezel. At the rear, the line of the trunk lid was raised slightly, new vertical waterfall-style taillamps running off the top of the rear quarter panel down towards the bumper were added, and a new, more typical, box style bumper was introduced, all of which went a long ways towards eliminating the pointed look of the 1973 models, even though the bodyside styling was unchanged. The new taillight lenses were divided by thin chrome strips into four sections. The base LeMans wagons added the 350 CID V8 engine as standard equipment, accounting for a rather large increase in both price and weight. A new model addition was the Luxury Lemans Safari wagon, which had all of the Luxury Lemans sedan features plus the woodgrain vinyl exterior trim as standard equipment. Although the GTO option package was moved to the Ventura series, a GT option was available on either the LeMans coupe or LeMans Sport Coupe, and quickly became known as a "GTO without the go."

The sporty Grand Am line continued to use a body-colored urethane front end, this year with six vertical grille openings per side on the sloping front fascia. Each of the narrow vertical openings was chrome lined and contained nine horizontal bars. At the rear, waterfall style taillamps similar to those of the Lemans were used, but on the Grand Am they were two vertical "slot" type lights separated by a body color strip. New features such as the raised deck lid were shared by the LeMans and Grand Am. On the inside the real African crossfire mahogany wood trim was still used on the console, but the inserts on the instrument panel were now simulated vinyl trim due to issues with the wood splintering on the 1973 models. The same change was made to the Grand Prix instrument panel. A special "All-American Grand Am painted in white with red and blue striping was shown at car shows, but production versions cannot be verified.

The Grand Prix received new box-style bumpers, which were V-shaped in the middle to follow the body contours, at both front and rear. The radiator grille theme continued for 1974, this year consisting of nine vertical openings per side, with the center point grille split continuing to be body-colored with the red Pontiac "arrow" attached. At the rear, the taillights slightly wrapped over the top of the rear quarter panel, and were divided into three vertical strips, with the middle lens being the backup light. Otherwise there were few changes to be found on the Grand Prix. The SJ option was installed on 13,841 cars this year.

Bonneville and Catalina two-door hardtops received a new roofline, in conformance with their GM running mates, including the Buick LeSabre coupes, Chevrolet Impala Sport Coupe, and Oldsmobile Delta 88 coupes. A smaller vertical rear seat window was used, with a larger triangular-shaped fixed rear quarter window placed behind it. The new configu-ration did away with the curved rear window, providing a larger flat window and resulting in better rearward vision for the driver. All full-size Pontiacs reverted to a chrome radiator style grille with large top and side chrome trim and a vertical center bar providing Pontiac's traditional split grille theme. On Catalinas, each side of the split contained five horizontal chrome bars, with horizontal crosshatch inserts behind the bars. The Bonneville, Grand Safari and Grand Ville shared a grille consisting of an egg-crate chrome bar pattern, with horizontal crosshatch inserts behind the bars. All models had horizontally mounted parking/turn signal lights directly below the headlights. The Grand Ville and Grand Safari added a chrome extension to each end of the parking/turn signal lights, with the inner one ending at the grille, and the outer one wrapping around the edge of the front fender. All three of the car lines had boxier rear bumpers, with the Catalina and Bonneville using taillights similar to the 1973 versions. Grand Ville models had larger new horizontal tail-lamps running fully across the rear end to the center mounted license plate housing. The lamps were divided into six vertical sections, with the innermost housing the backup lights, and then further split by a large horizontal chrome strip. It was an intricate looking design befitting the Grand Ville's luxury car image. There were no model changes, although the full-size Safari station wagon was officially renamed as the Cata-lina Safari wagon, as that was the series it was aligned with since its 1971 introduction. Finally, full-size Pontiacs added an interesting new option for 1974; adjustable accelerator and brake pedals were available for $52 on all Catalinas and for $47 on all Bonneville, Grand Ville and Grand Safari mod-els.

Bonneville 4-Door Sedan interior

Firebird Esprit 2-Door Hardtop Coupe

Catalina 2-Door Hardtop

Firebird Formula 2-Door Hardtop Coupe (left)
and Firebird Trans Am 2-Door Hardtop Coupe

Firebird 2-Door Hardtop Coupe

Firebird instrument panel with
Formula steering wheel and rally gauges

Grand Am 4-Door Colonnade Hardtop Sedan

Grand Prix 2-Door Hardtop Coupe

Grand Safari 4-Door Station Wagon

Grand Ville 2-Door Convertible

Grand Ville 4-Door Hardtop

LeMans 2-Door Colonnade
Hardtop Coupe with GT package

Luxury LeMans 2-Door Colonnade
Hardtop Coupe

Luxury LeMans instrument panel

Luxury LeMans Safari 4-Door Station Wagon

Ventura 2-Door Coupe with GTO package

Ventura 2-Door Hatchback Coupe

Ventura 2-Door Hatchback Coupe
with Sprint package

Ventura Custom 4-Door Sedan

Model year production: 580,635, down 36.86% from 1973.
Domestic market share: 6.72% (5th place).
Base price range: $2,722 to $5,071.
Pontiac average base price: $3,894, up 6.22%.
Introduction date: September 22, 1973.
Assembly plants: Lakewood, GA (A); Southgate, CA (C); Framingham, MA (G); Van Nuys, CA (L); Norwood, OH (N); Pontiac, MI (P); Tarrytown, NY (T); Lordstown, OH (U); Willow Run, MI (W); Kansas City — Fairfax, KS (X); Fremont, CA (Z); and Oshawa, Ontario, Canada (1).
Data plate identification (VIN): Thirteen digit code read as follows: First digit indicates division (2 = Pontiac); second through fourth digits indicate series and body style (model number in model charts); fifth digit is engine code (see powertrain chart); sixth digit indicates model year (4 = 1974); seventh digit indicates assembly plant (see list above); remaining digits are sequential with beginning number of 100001, except LeMans models built in Oshawa, Canada, which start at 500001. *Example:* 2D35M4G100001 is a 1974 Pontiac LeMans 4-Door, 2-Seat Safari station wagon, with 350 CID, 2-bbl. V8 engine, serial number 100001, built in Framingham, MA.

Powertrains

Engine	Net HP	Engine Code	Transmission Availability[1]		Ventura	Firebird[2]	LeMans[3]	Grand Am & Grand Prix[3]	Catalina & Bonneville[4]	Grand Ville & Grand Safari
250 CID (4.1L), 1-bbl., 6-cyl.	100	D	3-speed manual		S	S (F)	S (L)	—	—	—
				MPG:	NA	NA	NA	—	—	—
			3-speed Turbo Hydra-matic		$200	$205 (F)	$205 (L)	—	—	—
				MPG:	15.7	NA	NA	—	—	—
350 CID (5.7L), 2-bbl., V8	155/ 170[5]	M/N[5]	3-speed manual		$118	S (FF & FEs)/ $118 (F)	S (LL)/ $118 (L)	—	—	—
				MPG:	NA	NA	NA	—	—	—
			4-speed manual		$318	$200 (FF & FEs)/ $318 (F)	$190 (LL)/ $308 (L)	—	—	—
				MPG:	NA	NA	8.4	—	—	—
			3-speed Turbo Hydra-matic		$318	$215 (FF & FEs)/ $333 (F)	$215 (LL)/ $333 (L)	—	—	—
				MPG:	NA	9.9	9.6	—	—	—
350 CID (5.7L), 4-bbl., V8	170/ 200[5]	J[6]/K[5]	3-speed manual		$164	—	—	—	—	—
				MPG:	NA	—	—	—	—	—
			4-speed manual		$364	—	$354 (L)	—	—	—
				MPG:	8.9	—	9.4	—	—	—
			3-speed Turbo Hydra-matic		$364	—	$261 (LL)/ $379 (L)	—	—	—
				MPG:	9.9	—	9.2	—	—	—
400 CID (6.6L), 2-bbl., V8	175/ 190[5]	R/P[5]	4-speed manual		—	$251 (FF & FEs)	$241 (LL)/ $359 (L)	-$46 (GA, credit)	—	—
				MPG:	—	NA	NA	NA	—	—
			3-speed Turbo Hydra-matic		—	$287 (FF & FEs)	$287 (LL)/ $405 (L)	S (GA)	S	—
				MPG:	—	NA	8.8	8.8	9.2	—
400 CID (6.6L), 4-bbl., V8	200	S	4-speed manual		—	—	—	N/C (GA)	—	—
				MPG:	—	—	—	NA	—	—
			3-speed Turbo Hydra-matic		—	—	$333 (LL)/ $451 (L)	S (GP)/ $46 (GA)	$62 (B & C)	—
				MPG:	—	—	NA	NA	7.8	—
400 CID (6.6L), 4-bbl., V8	225[5]	T	4-speed manual		—	S (TA)/ $297 (FF)	$327 (LL)/ $446 (L)	—	—	—
				MPG:	—	8.6	NA	—	—	—
			3-speed Turbo Hydra-matic		—	N/C (TA)/ $318 (FF)	$373 (LL)/ $491 (L)	$40 (GP)/ $86 (GA)	$102 (B & C)	—
				MPG	—	NA	NA	NA	NA	—
455 CID (7.4L), 2-bbl., V8	215	W	3-speed Turbo Hydra-matic		—	—	$430 (wgns. only)	—	$119 (B & C)/ $103 (CS)	S
				MPG	—	—	NA	—	NA	8.4
455 CID (7.4L), 4-bbl., V8	250[5]	Y	4-speed manual		—	$57 (TA)/ $354 (FF)	$424 (LL)/ $542 (L)	$108 (GA)	—	—
				MPG:	—	NA	NA	NA	—	—

Engine	Net HP	Engine Code	Transmission Availability[1]	Ventura	Firebird[2]	LeMans[3]	Grand Am & Grand Prix[3]	Catalina & Bonneville[4]	Grand Ville & Grand Safari
			3-speed Turbo Hydra-matic	—	$57 (TA)/ $375 (FF)	$470 (LL)/ $588 (L)	$57 (GP)/ $154 (GA)	$159 (B & C)/ $143 (CS)	$40
			MPG:	—	NA	NA	8.4	NA	8.1
455 CID (7.4L), Super Duty 4-bbl., V8	290[5]	X	4-speed manual	—	$578 (TA)/ $875 (FF)	—	—	—	—
			MPG:	—	NA	—	—	—	—
			3-speed Turbo Hydra-matic	—	$578 (TA)/ $911 (FF)	—	—	—	—
			MPG:	—	NA	—	—	—	—

[1]Unless otherwise noted: All 3-speed manual transmissions are column shift, except on Firebird models. All 4-speed manual transmissions are floor shift, and only available on 2-door models, unless specially ordered. All automatic transmissions are column shift, with the following exceptions: Firebird, Grand Am, and Grand Prix. Floor-shift with 3-speed manual can be ordered on Ventura models for $26 extra, on LeMans models for $82 extra (heavy-duty 3-speed). Column shift automatic is available on Grand Prix models when certain equipment selections are made. Floor shift w/automatics is available on specific Ventura, LeMans and Grand Prix models in combination w/optional bucket seats. [2]F = base Firebird, FEs = Firebird Esprit; FF = Firebird Formula; TA = Firebird Trans Am. [3]L = LeMans; LL = Luxury LeMans and all LeMans Safari; GA = Grand Am; GP = Grand Prix. [4]C = Catalina; CS = Catalina Safari; B = Bonneville. [5]Not available in California. [6]Includes dual exhaust.

Major Options

	Firebird	Ventura	LeMans & Grand Am	Grand Prix	Catalina	Bonneville	Grand Ville & Grand Safari
Custom air conditioning[1]	$397	$381	$397	$431	$431	$431	$431
Tilt steering wheel	$44	$44	$44	$44	$44	$44	$44
Automatic cruise control	—	—	$62	$67	$67	$67	$67
Rear window defogger, blower	$31	$31	$31	—	$31	$31	$31
Electric rear window defroster	$62	—	$62	$62	$62	$62	$62
Dual sport mirrors, LH remote	$26	$26	$26	$26	$26	$26	$26
Soft-Ray tinted glass, all windows	$37	$39	$42	$49	$49	$49	$49
Power windows, 2-dr./4-dr.	$75[2]	—	$75/$113	$75	$129	$129	$129
Power door locks, 2-dr./4-dr.	$44	—	$44/67	$44	$44/$67	$44/$67	$44/$67
Power front seat, w/std. seat	—	—	$103	$103	$103	$103	$103
Front bucket seats, w/console	$58[3]	$190	$138[4]	S	—	—	—
AM radio	$65	$65	$65	$85	$85	$85	$85
AM/FM stereo	$233	$233	$233	$233	$233	$233	$233
AM/FM stereo w/8-track tape	$363[2]	—	$363	$363	$363	$363	$363
Woodgrain exterior trim (wagons)	—	—	$154	—	$154	—	$154
Vinyl top, full[5]	$87	$82	$97	$116	$116	$116	$116
Vinyl top, landau	—	—	$97	$116	—	—	—
Sunroof, manual[4]	—	—	$275	$275	—	—	—
Sunroof, power[4]	—	—	$325	$325	—	—	—
Power steering, variable-ratio	S	$100	$113[6]	S	S	S	S
Power brakes, w/front disc	$46[7]	$68	$46[8]	S	S	S	S
Deluxe wheel covers	$26	$28	—	—	$26	S	S
Custom finned wheel covers	$50	—	$50	S	$50	$24	$24
Rally II wheels	$87	$75	$87	$87	$87	$61	$61
Honeycomb aluminum wheels	$123	—	$54[9]	$54	—	—	—
WSW tires	$44	$38	$46	$32	$32	$35	$35

Popular Option Groups & Packages

	Firebird	Ventura	LeMans & Grand Am	Grand Prix	Catalina	Bonneville	Grand Ville & Grand Safari
Custom trim group	—	—	$77	—	—	—	$90
GT option package	—	—	$246	—	—	—	—
GTO option package	—	$461[10]	—	—	—	—	—
Lamp group	$10	—	—	—	—	—	—

	Firebird	Ventura	LeMans & Grand Am	Grand Prix	Catalina	Bonneville	Grand Ville & Grand Safari
Rallye gauge cluster package	$49	$100	S[8]	$90	—	—	—
RTS package	$155	$170	$165	$139	$172	$155	$155
SJ option package	—	—	—	$385	—	—	—
Sprint option package	—	$168	—	—	—	—	—

— = Not Available; S = Standard equipment.   [1]*Not available with 250 CID 6-cylinder engine. Automatic climate control available for $507 on Grand Prix, Catalina, Bonneville, Grand Ville and Grand Safari, and for $473 on Grand Am.*   [2]*Other optional equipment required at extra cost, i.e. console.*   [3]*Rear seat console available for $26.*   [4]*Vinyl roof available on Catalina Safari and Grand Safari for $138. Not available on LeMans station wagons. Price on Firebird is for base and Formula; price on Esprit is $72.*   [5]*Standard on Grand Am.*   [6]*Available only on 2-door models.*   [7]*Standard on Trans Am.*   [8]*Standard on Grand Am and LeMans station wagons.*   [9]*Available only on Grand Am.*   [10]*Price given is for coupe. Price on Hatchback is $440.*

Paint Colors

	Code		Code		Code
Cameo White	11	Pinemist Green metallic	49	Honduras Maroon metallic	74
Tuxedo Black	19	Carmel Beige	50	Buccaneer Red	75
Porcelain Blue metallic	24	Sunstorm Yellow	51		
Regatta Blue metallic	26	Denver Gold metallic	53		
Admiralty Blue metallic	29	Colonial Gold	55		
Gulfmist Aqua metallic	36	Crestwood Brown metallic	59		
Fernmist metallic	40	Ascot Silver metallic	64		
Lakemist Green	44	Fire Coral Bronze metallic	66		
Limefire Green metallic	46	Shadowmist Brown metallic	69		

In two-tone combinations, the first two digits indicate lower color and the next two digits are the upper color. Two-tone available at $138 on Ventura; $152 on Le-Mans cars; $134 on LeMans wagons; $152 on full-size. Trans Am "Bird" hood decal available for $55 extra. Color availability by series is not available.

Firebird

"Pontiac's sports cars."

Nameplate year of origin: 1967.
Current bodystyle lifespan: 1970 through 1981.
Predecessor to this model: Firebird (1967 to 1969).
Replacement for this model: Firebird (1982 to 1992).
Percentage of division's production: 12.70%.
Corporate siblings: Chevrolet Camaro.
Primary competition: AMC Javelin, Dodge Challenger, and Plymouth Barracuda.
Notable changes: Revised front end and minor trim and detail changes.
Major standard equipment: All-Morrokide vinyl front bucket seats, nylon loop-pile carpeting, black deluxe two-spoke steering wheel, ashtray light, dual speed wipers w/washers, Firebird emblems on fenders and rear deck lid, bright front and rear window moldings, narrow rocker panel moldings, Endura front and rear bumpers w/integral bumper guards, moon hubcaps, and E78 × 14 BSW tires. Esprit adds: Choice of Custom trim cloth-and-Morrokide vinyl or perforated all-Morrokide vinyl front bucket seats w/deep contour design, distinctive door trim panels, door and I/P assist straps, Custom Cushion steering wheel, pedal trim plates, rear quarter ashtray, formed rubber trunk mat, dual body-colored mirror w/LH remote, body-colored door handle inserts, bright roof drip rail and belt reveal moldings, bright rear hood edge molding, bright wheel opening and rocker panel moldings, dual horns and deluxe wheel covers. Formula adds: Custom Cushion steering wheel, blacked-out grille, dual body-colored mirror w/LH remote, Formula (350, 400 or 455) emblems on front fenders, fiberglass hood w/dual forward facing simulated scoops, front and rear stabilizer bars, firm control shocks, performance dual exhausts and F70 × 14 BSW tires. Trans Am adds: Formula steering wheel, rally gauge cluster package, aluminum-swirl finish I/P trim plate, dual body-colored mirror w/LH remote, blacked-out grille, full-width rear deck spoiler, wheel opening air deflectors, front fender air extractors, Trans Am decal on front fender and rear spoiler, "455" decal on hood scoop, fast-ratio power steering, power brakes, larger stabilizer bars, high-rate rear springs, Safe-T-Track differential, firm control shocks, performance dual exhausts, Rally II wheels w/trim rings, and F60 × 15 R/WL tires.

Measurements

Wheelbase	108.0"
Length	196.0"
Width	73.2"
Height	50.4"
Legroom — front	43.9"
Legroom — rear	29.6"
Headroom — front	37.5"
Headroom — rear	35.9"
Cargo capacity (cu. ft.)	8.8
Fuel capacity (gals.)	20.2

Models Available

	Model No.	Base MSRP	Change from LY	Shipping Wt. (lbs.)	Model Year Production	Change from LY
Firebird 2-Door Hardtop Coupe	S87	$3,175	+9.67%	3283	26,372	+87.09%
Firebird Esprit 2-Door Hardtop Coupe	T87	$3,527	+8.56%	3540	22,583	+30.92%
Firebird Formula 2-Door Hardtop Coupe	U87	$3,614	+10.32%	3548	14,519	+42.82%
Firebird Trans Am 2-Door Hardtop Coupe	V87	$4,401	+4.69%	3655	10,255	+113.56%
TOTALS		Avg. price $3,679	+8.02%		Production 73,729	+59.20%

Ventura

"Pontiac's low priced compact car."

Nameplate year of origin: 1960.
Current bodystyle lifespan: 1971 through 1974; restyled in 1973.
Predecessor to this model: None.
Replacement for this model: Ventura (1975 to 1977) and Phoenix (1977 to 1979).
Percentage of division's production: 14.09%.
Corporate siblings: Buick Apollo, Chevrolet Nova, and Oldsmobile Omega.
Primary competition: AMC Hornet, Dodge Dart, Ford Maverick, Mercury Comet, and Plymouth Valiant.
Notable changes: New grille and minor trim and detail changes.
Major standard equipment: Cloth with Morrokide vinyl trim front bench seat, color-keyed vinyl-coated rubber floor covering, woodgrain vinyl door trim w/door pull straps on two-doors, black deluxe two-spoke steering wheel, bright front and rear window moldings, moon hubcaps, rear seat armrest ashtrays, and E78 × 14 BSW tires. Hatchback model adds: Fold-down rear seat, cargo area light, and fully trimmed vinyl cargo area sidewalls. Custom adds: Choice of custom cloth or all-Morrokide vinyl front bench seat, bright front-seat side panels, color-keyed carpeting (including Hatchback load floor), Custom Cushion steering wheel, pedal trim plates, glove box light, RH doorjamb switch for dome light, added body and underhood insulation, bright drip rail and rocker panel moldings, Custom identification, and deluxe wheel covers.

Measurements

	Coupe & HBK	Sedan
Wheelbase	111.0"	111.0"
Length	199.4"	199.4"
Width	72.5"	72.5"
Height	52.6"	53.9"
Legroom — front	41.7"	41.7"
Legroom — rear	33.4"	35.3"
Headroom — front	38.2"	39.5"
Headroom — rear	36.8"	37.3"
Cargo capacity (cu. ft.)	14.6*	13.7
Fuel capacity (gals.)	20.5	20.5

Hatchback maximum with rear seat down, 27.3 cu. ft.

Models Available

	Model No.	Base MSRP	Change from LY	Shipping Wt. (lbs.)	Model Year Production	Change from LY*
Ventura 2-Door Coupe	Y27	$2,722	+11.01%	3147	47,782	-2.79%
Ventura 2-Door Hatchback	Y17	$2,873	+10.37%	3257	16,694	-36.61%
Ventura 4-Door Sedan	Y69	$2,751	+10.88%	3169	17,323	-17.56%
Ventura Custom 2-Door Coupe	Z27	$2,881	+10.43%	3184	NA*	NA*
Ventura Custom 2-Door Hatchback	Z17	$3,031	+9.86%	3262	NA*	NA*
Ventura Custom 4-Door Sedan	Z69	$2,910	+10.31%	3208	NA*	NA*
TOTALS		Avg. price $2,861	+10.46%		Production 81,799	-15.23%

Production of Custom models kept as combined total with base models. Therefore, comparisons to LY are made on total by body style and not model number.

LeMans

"Pontiac's mid-size car."

Nameplate year of origin: 1961 (as a Tempest sub-series).
Current bodystyle lifespan: 1973 through 1977.
Predecessor to this model: Tempest/LeMans (1968 to 1972).
Replacement for this model: LeMans (1978 to 1981).
Percentage of division's production: 22.83%.
Corporate siblings: Buick Century, Chevrolet Chevelle, and Oldsmobile Cutlass.
Primary competition: AMC Matador, Dodge Charger and Coronet, Ford Torino, Mercury Montego, and Plymouth Satellite.
Notable changes: Revised rear end and minor trim and detail changes.
Major standard equipment: Cloth-and-vinyl front bench seat, color-keyed loop-pile carpeting, deluxe three-spoke

Measurements

	Coupes	Sedans	Wagons
Wheelbase	112.0"	116.0"	116.0"
Length	208.8"	212.8"	216.0"
Width	77.9"	77.9"	78.0"
Height	52.9"	54.3"	55.0"
Legroom — front	42.4"	42.4"	42.4"
Legroom — rear	32.9"	37.0"	36.8"
Headroom — front	37.9"	38.6"	38.8"
Headroom — rear	36.8"	37.2"	39.4"
Cargo capacity (cu. ft.)	15.1	15.1	85.1
Fuel capacity (gals.)	21.8	21.8	22.0

steering wheel, simulated dark flame chestnut woodgrain vinyl accents on I/P, door panels and steering wheel, bright front and rear window moldings, bright rear quarter window trim, manual front disc brakes, hubcaps, and F78 × 14 BSW tires. Wagon adds: All-Morrokide vinyl front bench seat, vinyl coated metal cargo area sidewalls, textured steel cargo floor w/special vinyl paint, swing up tailgate w/fixed window and remote release, I/P mounted "door ajar" warning light for tailgate, swing-out rear quarter vents (3-seat wagon), vertical rub strips on tailgate, bright rocker panel molding, power front disc brakes, and H78 × 14 BSW tires. Sport Coupe adds: Choice of all-Morrokide vinyl front bench seat w/fold-down center armrest, or all-Morrokide bucket seats, simulated dark flame chestnut woodgrain vinyl accents on glove box door, vertically louvered rear quarter windows and Sport Coupe identification. Luxury LeMans adds: Choice of cloth-and-vinyl or all-vinyl notchback bench seat w/fold-down center armrest, or all-Morrokide bucket seats (coupe), special interior trim w/monogram on center armrest, custom cushion steering wheel, door panels w/carpeted lower panels and front door assist straps, glove box and ashtray lights, simulated dark flame chestnut woodgrain vinyl accents on I/P and glove box door, added body insulation, rear seat armrest ashtrays, formal rear quarter opera window (coupe), bright drip rail and quarter window moldings, bright rear hood edge and rear deck moldings, front wheel opening moldings, full-length lower bodyside molding, rear-wheel fender skirts, deluxe wheel covers, and F78 × 14 BSW tires on coupes, and G78 × 14 BSW tires on sedans.

Models Available

	Model No.	Base MSRP	Change from LY	Shipping Wt. (lbs.)	Model Year Production	Change from LY
LeMans 2-Door Colonnade HT Coupe	D37	$3,047	+4.35%	3552	37,061	-45.68%
LeMans 4-Door Colonnade HT Sedan	D29	$3,067	+5.11%	3628	17,266	-34.98%
LeMans 4-Door, 2-Seat Safari Station Wagon	D35	$3,761	+14.11%	4333	3,004	-71.24%
LeMans 4-Door, 3-Seat Safari Station Wagon	D45	$3,894	+13.56%	4371	4,743	-22.59%
LeMans Sport Coupe 2-Door Colonnade HT	F37	$3,131	+4.09%	3580	37,955	-25.58%
Luxury LeMans 2-Door Colonnade HT Coupe	G37	$3,410	+4.15%	3808	25,882	-23.69%
Luxury LeMans 4-Door Colonnade HT Sedan	G29	$3,480	+4.07%	3904	4,513	-51.87%
Luxury LeMans 4-Door, 2-Seat Safari Wagon	G35	$3,761	NEW	4363	952	NEW
Luxury LeMans 4-Door, 3-Seat Safari Wagon	G45	$3,894	NEW	4401	1,178	NEW
TOTALS	*Avg. price*	$3,494	+10.22%	*Production*	132,554	-35.54%

Grand Am

"The mid-size Pontiac with foreign intrigue ... American ingenuity."

Nameplate year of origin: 1973.
Current bodystyle lifespan: 1973 through 1975.
Predecessor to this model: None.
Replacement for this model: Grand Am (1978 to 1980).
Percentage of division's production: 2.94%.

Measurements

	Coupe	Sedan
Wheelbase	112.0"	116.0"
Length	210.9"	214.9"

Corporate siblings: Buick Century Regal, Chevrolet Chevelle Laguna, and Oldsmobile Cutlass Salon.
Primary competition: AMC Matador X, Dodge Charger, and Mercury Montego.
Notable changes: Minor trim and detail changes.
Major standard equipment: Choice of wide-wale Corduroy or all-vinyl w/Morrokide front bucket seats w/recliners and adjustable lower back support, color-keyed loop-pile carpeting, pedal trim plates, custom sport three-spoke steering wheel w/padded center, cockpit-style I/P w/simulated African crossfire mahogany inlay trim, center floor console w/genuine African crossfire mahogany inlay trim, door pull assist straps, electric clock, trip odometer, ashtray and glove box lights, courtesy lights, fixed rear quarter window w/louvers (coupe), bright front and rear window moldings, bright side window and drip rail moldings, bright rear hood edge molding, bright wheel opening moldings, black-accented rocker panel moldings, body colored door handle inserts, power steering, power brakes, firm ride package, custom finned wheel covers, and GR70 × 15 BSW tires.

Measurements (cont.)

	Coupe	Sedan
Width	77.7"	77.7"
Height	52.9"	54.3"
Legroom — front	42.4"	42.4"
Legroom — rear	33.5"	38.6"
Headroom — front	37.9"	38.6"
Headroom — rear	36.8"	37.2"
Cargo capacity (cu. ft.)	15.1	15.1
Fuel capacity (gals.)	25.0	25.0

Models Available

	Model No.	Base MSRP	Change from LY	Shipping Wt. (lbs.)	Model Year Production	Change from LY
Grand Am 2-Door Colonnade HT Coupe	H37	$4,496	+5.44%	3992	13,961	-59.47%
Grand Am 4-Door Colonnade HT Sedan	H29	$4,585	+5.33%	4073	3,122	-64.08%
TOTALS		Avg. price $4,541	+5.38%		Production 17,083	-60.40%

Grand Prix

"Pontiac's classic luxury sport."

Nameplate year of origin: 1962.
Current bodystyle lifespan: 1973 through 1977.
Predecessor to this model: Grand Prix (1969 to 1972).
Replacement for this model: Grand Prix (1978 to 1987).
Percentage of division's production: 17.19%.
Corporate siblings: Chevrolet Monte Carlo.
Primary competition: Ford Gran Torino Elite and Mercury Cougar XR-7.
Notable changes: New front end and minor trim and detail changes.
Major standard equipment: Choice of cloth-and-vinyl or all-vinyl w/Morrokide front notchback bench seat w/fold-down center armrests or front bucket seats w/center floor console, color-keyed cut-pile carpeting, pedal trim plates, color-keyed Custom Cushion three-spoke steering wheel, cockpit-style I/P, simulated African crossfire mahogany inlay trim on I/P and door panels, I/P courtesy lights, genuine African crossfire mahogany inlay trim on console, electric clock, ashtray light, monogrammed fixed rear quarter window w/bright trim, bright front and rear window moldings, bright side window sill and drip rail moldings, bright rear hood edge molding, bright wheel opening moldings, black-accented wide rocker panel moldings, body colored door handle inserts, trunk compartment light and side panels, power steering, power brakes, dual exhausts, deluxe wheel covers, and G78 × 15 BSW tires.

Measurements

Wheelbase	116.0"
Length	217.5"
Width	77.9"
Height	52.9"
Legroom — front	42.4"
Legroom — rear	33.5"
Headroom — front	37.7"
Headroom — rear	37.2"
Cargo capacity (cu. ft.)	14.3
Fuel capacity (gals.)	25.0

Models Available

	Model No.	Base MSRP	Change from LY	Shipping Wt. (lbs.)	Model Year Production	Change from LY
Grand Prix 2-Door Hardtop Coupe	K57	$4,784	+4.39%	4096	99,817	-35.14%
TOTALS		Avg. price $4,784	+4.39%		Production 99,817	-35.14%

Catalina

"Pontiac's lowest priced full-sized car."

Nameplate year of origin: 1950 (as hardtop model designation), 1959 (as series).
Current bodystyle lifespan: 1971 through 1976.
Predecessor to this model: Catalina (1969 to 1970).
Replacement for this model: Catalina (1977 to 1981).
Percentage of division's production: 19.05%.
Corporate siblings: Buick LeSabre, Chevrolet BelAir/Impala/Caprice, and Oldsmobile Delta 88.
Primary competition: AMC Ambassador, Dodge Monaco, Ford LTD, and Plymouth Fury.
Notable changes: Revised front and rear styling, new two-door roofline, and minor trim and detail changes.
Major standard equipment: Cloth-and-Morrokide vinyl bench seat, color-keyed loop-pile carpeting, deluxe two-spoke steering wheel, dark flame chestnut woodgrain vinyl I/P accents, dual ashtrays w/LH ashtray light, trunk mat, bright rocker panel molding, bright hood rear edge molding, power steering, power front disc brakes, hubcaps, and G78 × 15 BSW tires. Safari wagon adds: All-Morrokide vinyl front bench seat, glove box lights, RH rear view mirror, Glide-Away tailgate w/power-operated rear window, rear bumper guards, and L78 × 15 BSW tires.

Measurements

	2-door	4-doors	Wagons
Wheelbase	124.0"	124.0"	127.0"
Length	226.0"	226.0"	231.3"
Width	79.6"	79.6"	79.6"
Height	53.5"	54.2"	57.5"
Legroom — front	42.7"	42.7"	42.5"
Legroom — rear	35.8"	38.8"	38.9"
Headroom — front	38.3"	39.1"	39.6"
Headroom — rear	37.4"	37.9"	39.3"
Cargo capacity (cu. ft.)	20.5	20.5	106.4
Fuel capacity (gals.)	25.8	25.8	22.0

Models Available

	Model No.	Base MSRP	Change from LY	Shipping Wt. (lbs.)	Model Year Production	Change from LY
Catalina 2-Door Hardtop Coupe	L57	$4,096	+5.87%	4279	40,657	-45.35%
Catalina 4-Door Sedan	L69	$4,008	+6.31%	4294	46,025	-54.25%
Catalina 4-Door Hardtop	L39	$4,165	+5.76%	4352	11,769	-62.83%
Catalina Safari 4-Door, 2-Seat Station Wagon	L35	$4,507	+4.55%	4973	5,662	-64.08%
Catalina Safari 4-Door, 3-Seat Station Wagon	L45	$4,653	+4.40%	5037	6,486	-55.74%
TOTALS	Avg. price	$4,286	+5.33%		Production 110,599	-53.35%

Bonneville

"Pontiac's original full-sized Wide-Track."

Nameplate year of origin: 1957.
Current bodystyle lifespan: 1971 through 1976.
Predecessor to this model: Bonneville (1969 to 1970).
Replacement for this model: Bonneville (1977 to 1981).
Percentage of division's production: 3.54%.
Corporate siblings: Buick LeSabre, Chevrolet BelAir/Impala/Caprice, and Oldsmobile Delta 88.
Primary competition: AMC Ambassador, Dodge Monaco, and Mercury Monterey.
Notable changes: Revised front and rear styling, new two-door roofline, and minor trim and detail changes.
Major standard equipment: Choice of cloth-and-Morrokide vinyl or all-Morrokide vinyl front bench seat, loop-pile carpeting, lower door panel carpeting, custom cushion steering wheel, simulated dark flame chestnut woodgrain vinyl I/P accents, electric clock, pedal trim plates, rear door courtesy light switches (four-doors), luggage compartment mat and side panel trim, luggage compartment light, body-color door handle inserts, bright windshield and rear window moldings, bright hood rear edge molding, wide rocker panel moldings w/rear extensions, bright wheel opening moldings, deluxe wheel covers, and H78 × 15 BSW tires.

Measurements

	2-door	4-doors
Wheelbase	124.0"	124.0"
Length	226.0"	226.0"
Width	79.6"	79.6"
Height	53.5"	54.2"
Legroom — front	42.7"	42.7"
Legroom — rear	35.8"	38.8"
Headroom — front	38.3"	39.1"
Headroom — rear	37.4"	37.9"
Cargo capacity (cu. ft.)	20.5	20.5
Fuel capacity (gals.)	25.8	25.8

Models Available

	Model No.	Base MSRP	Change from LY	Shipping Wt. (lbs.)	Model Year Production	Change from LY
Bonneville 2-Door Hardtop Coupe	N57	$4,407	+4.31%	4356	7,639	-44.91%
Bonneville 4-Door Sedan	N69	$4,345	+4.37%	4384	6,770	-57.23%
Bonneville 4-Door Hardtop Sport Sedan	N39	$4,474	+4.24%	4444	6,151	-64.24%
TOTALS	*Avg. price*	$4,409	+4.31%		*Production* 20,560	-56.16%

Grand Ville and Grand Safari

"Pontiac's most luxurious full-sized car."

Nameplate year of origin: 1971.

Current bodystyle lifespan: 1971 through 1976.

Predecessor to this model: None.

Replacement for this model: None.

Percentage of division's production: 7.66%.

Corporate siblings: Buick LeSabre, Chevrolet BelAir/Impala/Caprice, and Oldsmobile Delta 88.

Primary competition: Chrysler Newport, Dodge Monaco, and Mercury Marquis.

Notable changes: Revised front-end styling and minor trim and detail changes.

Major standard equipment: Cloth w/Morrokide vinyl trim front notchback seat w/fold-down center armrest, color-keyed loop-pile carpeting, Custom Cushion steering wheel, custom door panels w/pull straps and lower panel carpet-

Measurements

	2-doors	4-door	Wagons
Wheelbase	124.0"	124.0"	127.0"
Length	226.0"	226.0"	231.3"
Width	79.6"	79.6"	79.6"
Height	53.5"	54.2"	58.3"
Legroom — front	42.7"	42.7"	42.5"
Legroom — rear	35.8"	38.8"	38.9"
Headroom — front	38.9"	39.1"	39.6"
Headroom — rear	37.6"	37.6"	39.3"
Cargo capacity (cu. ft.)	20.5*	20.5	106.4
Fuel capacity (gals.)	25.8	25.8	22.0

Convertible is 14.4 cu. ft.

ing, simulated dark flame chestnut woodgrain vinyl trim on I/P and door panels, electric clock, rear door courtesy light switches (four-door), luggage compartment mat and side panel trim, luggage compartment light, body-color door handle inserts, bright windshield and rear window moldings, bright drip rail moldings, bright hood rear edge molding, wide rocker panel moldings w/rear extensions, front wheel opening moldings, rear wheel opening fender skirts, bodyside protective molding, deluxe wheel covers, and H78 × 15 BSW tires. Convertible adds: All-Morrokide vinyl front bench seat w/fold-down center armrest, two rear quarter interior lights, and inward-folding power-operated vinyl convertible top w/glass rear window. Grand Safari wagon adds: All-Morrokide vinyl front bench seat w/fold-down center armrest, carpeted cargo area, RH rear view mirror, rear bumper guards, deletes fender skirts, and L78 × 15 BSW tires.

Models Available

	Model No.	Base MSRP	Change from LY	Shipping Wt. (lbs.)	Model Year Production	Change from LY
Grand Ville 2-Door Hardtop Coupe	P47	$4,706	+4.02%	4432	11,631	-51.46%
Grand Ville 2-Door Convertible	P67	$4,948	+3.82%	4476	3,000	-32.54%
Grand Ville 4-Door Hardtop Sport Sedan	P49	$4,774	+3.96%	4515	21,714	-50.75%
Grand Safari 4-Door, 2-Seat Station Wagon	P35	$4,924	+5.35%	5011	2,894	-58.02%
Grand Safari 4-Door, 3-Seat Station Wagon	P45	$5,071	+5.19%	5112	5,255	-51.23%
TOTALS	*Avg. price*	$4,885	+4.47%		*Production* 44,494	-50.66%

[1]*Matelasse is a French word meaning quilted, padded or cushioned. Usually refers to hand-quilted fabrics.*

1975

With the fuel crisis still a fresh memory and the American economy still stuck in a quagmire, the auto industry's hope to maintain at least 1974's rate of production proved out of reach. By year's end, the medium to upper-priced cars gained sales as the greater portion of the industry continued to drop, losing almost 20 percent from the prior year. This seemed to contradict the typical sales trend during a recession, as usually the lower-priced models would be expected to gain in sales. However, this year would prove any existing theories to be wrong, as the luxury lines of Cadillac, Chrysler and Lincoln all posted sales gains, and the mid-price lines of Buick, Mercury and Oldsmobile advanced as well. Apparently Ford, Chevrolet, AMC and Plymouth had performed so well with their compact and smaller lines during 1974 that the demand for those cars was reduced for this season. Or possibly the lingering recession meant that fewer people shopping in the lower-priced market could afford to buy a new car. Whatever the reason may have been, it was obvious that consumers had abandoned the muscle car and wanted more luxury in their cars, and this trend would eventually lead to more standard features and more luxurious offerings in the lower-priced field.

With most of the government mandated safety features under their belt, it was now time to concentrate on the pollution controls. But not before GM introduced the first air cushion restraint system to be available on American cars. Late in the 1974 season, GM announced that it would offer optional airbags for $300 as a passive restraint system in its full-sized Buick, Oldsmobile and Cadillac closed models. The new system was not very popular with consumers, but GM can take credit for trying to improve safety per the government's mandates. To meet the pollution control requirements for 1975, manufacturers would either use a combination of electronics and fuel mixture changes, or adopt the catalytic converter system. The catalytic converter system, as detailed in the introduction to this book, was the more popular approach, especially with V8 engines, and an effec-

tive choice in combination with the engines currently offered by Detroit. Although consumers complained of the added expense and slightly decreased engine performance, catalytic converters did help to decrease pollutants, and with careful engine tuning, improved fuel economy could be offered.

A unique phenomenon through most of the 1973 to 1980 period was the great variety of interior prints and colors available. Several of these reached a peak in popularity around 1975. Among the more popular offerings were all-white interiors with generally bright colored trim and accent features. This theme was seen most often on GM compact and mid-size cars around the 1975 and 1976 time frame, and also on some other brands and models. The accent colors — typically bright hues of blue, green or red, and occasionally black, dark blue, or dark green — were used on all interior trim, including carpeting, instrument panel, steering wheel, steering column, front kick panels, seat belts, console (if ordered), and rear window filler panel. Although prices and details for every year and model are not included in this book, an example of colors and price is included in the 1975 Oldsmobile section. GM divisions called them by different names, with Chevy simply offering white seats with accent colors, while Oldsmobile named its package the Compati-color interior. Lincoln was offering luxury "color groups," some of them having white upholstery with bright contrasting trim colors such as lipstick red or blue diamond. Also reaching a peak in popularity this year, but seen throughout many of the other years covered by this book, were patterned upholsteries. Unique patterns included the new AMC Pacer's basket weave upholstery, and checkered pattern materials used on various Chrysler models. Chrysler also had offered woven Native American patterns in their Navajo interior trim for the Newport. The distinctive colors and patterns added character and color to what could have otherwise been some rather mundane cars.

Chrysler Corporation, which made-over its full-size line last year, turned to the mid-size line for a makeover this year. Two new two-door models appeared on the existing mid-size 115-inch wheelbase platform, the first of which was the Dodge Charger replacement. Returning as the Charger SE, the formerly sports-type muscle car was suddenly a personal luxury car squarely targeted towards Monte Carlo and Grand Prix territory. The second car was a near twin to the Charger SE, named the Chrysler Cordoba. Originally while under development, the Cordoba was to be a top of the line Plymouth model, giving Plymouth a direct competitor to the Chevrolet Monte Carlo. However, closer to production time, the corporate bean counters decided that more profits could be made by having it be a Chrysler model with a higher price tag, and with Chrysler in dire need of cash, the Chrysler Cordoba was born. As for the rest of the mid-size lines, front-end restyling was seen across the board, and it became more difficult to tell the differences between the Dodges and Plymouths this year, with the grille detail being the main identifying trait. The Plymouth was renamed the Fury, and the full-size Fury line became the Gran Fury. As an interesting side note, this would be the only year that a Fury model named Road Runner was ever built. On the Dodge side, all mid-size models became Coronets, including the two-doors that were formerly base Chargers.

The compact Dart and Valiant lines continued to sell well, while the Barracuda and Challenger both vanished. As previously mentioned, Plymouth's full-size line was renamed Gran Fury, with the top-of-the-line Brougham being given a distinctive front-end styling. Similarly with the Dodge Monaco, a top end Royal Monaco Brougham was added with its own unique frontal styling. In the full-size Chrysler line, styling was refreshed throughout the series, but it was down to the final season for the venerable Imperial, which had been just holding its own since being placed back under the Chrysler nameplate for 1971, and was never able to break 17,000 units of production since that time. Otherwise there were few changes in the captive-import Dodge Colt line, or within the Dodge truck lines.

American Motors had the most interesting new car introduction for 1975, with the new compact Pacer hatchback. Billed as the "first wide small car," the Pacer was definitely unique in its styling. AMC had designed the car around the Wankel rotary engine that General Motors was designing, but when that project was cancelled, AMC was left having to cram its inline six-cylinder engine under the hood. Unfortunately it left the Pacer overweight and underpowered, but still it was a distinctive car to look at, very roomy on the inside, and easy to drive with its large rounded windows that provided outstanding visibility. Missing from the option list this year was AMC's 401 CID V8 engine, which was discontinued along with the Javelin and Ambassador.

New quad rectangular headlights were approved for use in 1974 by NHTSA for the 1975 model year and immediately began appearing on some GM models. New sporty compact

hatchbacks, based on the Vega platform, were among the first to appear with the new lights. These were the new Chevrolet Monza 2+2, the Oldsmobile Starfire, and the Buick Skyhawk. All three used dual rectangular lights. A formal roofline Towne Coupe, which used traditional round headlights, joined the new Monza at mid-year, and then for 1976 the Pontiac Sunbird Coupe joined the trio, using the rectangular headlights. Other models in the GM line using the new rectangular headlights included the entire Cadillac line, the Buick Electra and Riviera, and the Oldsmobile 98 and Toronado, as well as the Pontiac Grand Ville and Grand Safari models.

All four of GM's compact lines were restyled, featuring a more modern appearance that cleverly disguised their 1968 lineage. The newly designed X-body models returned with the Buick Apollo gaining a new "old" name for its two-door model, now known as the Skylark. Being a better-known name than Apollo, the Skylark would become the series name for both two-door and four-door models in 1976. All four of the GM compacts also added low-priced, stripped down two-door coupes at mid-year to help stimulate sales. These were named the Buick Skylark S, Chevrolet Nova S, Oldsmobile Omega F-85, and Pontiac Ventura S. Changes for GM's other small car lines were minimal, with the Camaro and Firebird adding new wrap-around rear windows to improve visibility, and a new Pontiac Astre model being added, which was essentially a little snazzier version of the Chevrolet Vega. In GM's mid-size lines, Oldsmobile expanded its popular Cutlass line by making the former Salon option package an actual model in two-door and four-door varieties. Pontiac changed the name of its Luxury LeMans line to Grand LeMans, which was more in keeping with other model names such as Grand Prix, Grand Ville and Grand Am, but it would the last season for the Grand Ville and Grand Am names. The Grand Am would be back again, two more times, though in very different forms. Other GM models that were entering their final model year were all but one of the convertibles. This meant the final season for the Chevrolet Caprice Classic, Pontiac Grand Ville, Oldsmobile Delta 88 Royale, and Buick LeSabre Custom full-sized convertibles, as well as the Corvette convertible. Also, this was the final year for the German-built Opels. As rising exchange rates made prices on German-built cars extremely high, GM would turn to its Japanese partner, Isuzu, for its new generation of Opel models.

Powering some GM cars this year was a new Buick-built 231 CID V6 engine, which in itself was not completely new, as it could trace its roots back to the 1962 Buick Special. After several years of use in Buicks, the design was sold several times, with one of its uses being in Kaiser Corporation's Jeep models, and eventually the design was bought back by GM and improved for use in the new Buick Skyhawk, among several other GM models. This year also marked the last time the large 454 CID V8 engine was available in Chevrolet's mid-size Chevelle and Monte Carlo lines. In the GM truck lines, updates were minor, and the Chevy El Camino and GMC Sprint followed the changes of the Chevelle car lines. This would be the final season for the Vega Panel Express due to declining sales and rising interest in the regular van line.

Across town in Dearborn, Ford had two all-new compacts ready for the streets this year. Named the Ford Granada and Mercury Monarch, these virtual twins were built upon the existing Maverick and Comet four-door chassis and powertrains, but were otherwise entirely new. Although they were originally intended to replace the older models, the Comet and especially the Maverick had sold so well last year that Ford was not inclined to drop them. So the Maverick and Comet continued a few more years as lower priced alternatives to the Granada and Monarch, allowing the latter to be positioned as more upscale models. The new cars' styling and design were so well done that Ford often compared them to expensive European models such as Mercedes-Benz in their advertising. Another new model in the Ford corporate lineup was the Mercury Bobcat, a near twin to the Ford Pinto, with a slightly higher level of standard features. The Bobcat compared to the Pinto as the Pontiac Astre did to the Chevrolet Vega.

Ford's full-size lineup was given another restyling this time affecting the front and rear styling of the Fords, Lincolns and Mercurys, as well as the rooflines of all, particularly in the two-door models. It should also be noted that two long-time nameplates were gone this year with the Mercury Monterey quietly disappearing at the end of the 1974 season, and the Ford Custom 500 and related Ranch Wagons being offered only as fleet models for mainly taxi and law enforcement use. In the mid-size lines, last year's personal luxury mid-year entrant, the Gran Torino Elite, was broken out into its own model as the Elite. Although it sold only half as many as its main competitor, the Chevy Monte Carlo, it did quite well considering it also had new competition in the Dodge Charger SE.

Across the line, Ford made few powertrain changes, though the Mustang II did receive a new and larger V6

engine option. Other Ford models received few changes for the new model year. The truck lines returned with minor changes, although Ford did introduce new E-series Econoline and Club Wagon vans. The Club Wagons were passenger type vans, while the Econoline was the workhorse van.

1975 Overview and Changes from Prior Year

- **Total industry model year production:** 7,050,307, down 18.42%.
- **Total estimated captive import sales:** 105,356, down 43.94%.
- **Market share by corporation:** GM 52.28%; Ford 29.69%; Chrysler 14.61%; AMC 3.43%.
- **Number of models and body types available:** 319, up from 303.
- **Highest production series:** Chevrolet BelAir/Impala/ Caprice — 421,684.
- **Lowest production series:** Cadillac Fleetwood 75 — 1,671.
- **Highest individual model production:** Oldsmobile Cutlass Supreme 2-Door Colonnade HT —150,874.
- **Lowest individual model production:** Cadillac Fleetwood 75 Limousine —795.
- **Industry average base price:** $4,592, up 12.21%.
- **Highest individual model base price:** Cadillac Fleetwood 75 Limousine, $14,557.
- **Lowest individual model base price:** Ford Pinto 2-Door Sedan, $2,769.
- **Highest highway MPG with base powertrain:** Chevrolet Vega, 28 MPG.
- **Lowest highway MPG with base powertrain:** Ford LTD and Mercury Marquis wagons, and Cadillac Fleetwood 75, 14 MPG.
- **Indianapolis 500 Pace Car:** Buick Century Custom "Free Spirit" 2-Door Coupe w/Hurst Hatch (T-tops).
- *Motor Trend* magazine "Car of the Year": Chevrolet Monza 2+2.

AMERICAN MOTORS

"Introducing the new Pacer and the 1975 passenger cars.
We back them better because we build them better."

The second "all-new" model from American Motors Corporation in as many years hit dealer showrooms at mid-season this model year, amid much anticipation, in the form of the Pacer. Touted as America's first wide small car, the little round coupe offered unique styling features and a lot of interior space in a small package. However, the rest of the AMC line received only minor updates, with the only styling update given to the Hornet. As in the rest of the industry, prices continued to rise, while sales continued to fall. Unfortunately, comparing production numbers, it seems likely that most of Pacer's success came at the expense of the Gremlin and Hornet. Without losing faith, American Motors spent heavily promoting their unusual new car.

The unique features of the Pacer were plentiful. Its relatively short wheelbase and length made it very easy to maneuver and park. The wide stance, or track, of the Pacer was touted as wider than that of the Granada, Duster or Maverick, giving Pacer a road feel that was more like larger, heavier cars. Its unitized body design utilized built-in roll bar type center pillars to add body rigidity and strength. Inside, offering more interior room than most intermediate-sized cars, the Pacer was roomy and offered great visibility over the short, sloping hood, and to the sides and rear with the large expanses of glass. One very unusual Pacer feature was that its passenger side door was nearly four inches longer than the driver's door for easier rear seat entry and exit. As stated in the introductory sales literature, "You can walk right into the rear compartment!"

Outside, the Pacer truly showed off its unique character. Aside from the aforementioned characteristics, the Pacer's front-end styling had a horizontal grille design with about ten closely spaced slats set directly above the front bumper. The headlights were single, round units set at each end of the grille, rising above the hood. The result was a tunnel-like effect similar to the Matador coupe, except where the Matador had a round tunnel, the Pacer's was square with rounded edges. Next to the outside of each headlamp bezel was a horizontal parking lamp/turn signal light that wrapped around into the front fender. On the bodyside, a feature line began at the center of the parking lamp/turn signal light and continued horizontally after the front wheel opening, back to a point just below the door handle, where it curved upwards and over the roof to the other side, where it ran up to the front. Another crease began at the upper front corner of

the rear quarter window, running across the roof to the other side. The effect was to create a basket handle look. It also provided a breaking point for vinyl top options and two-tone paint options. At the back, horizontal taillights wrapped around the rear quarters, mimicking the front parking lights, and in between was a chrome appliqué with the AMC name and logo on the left, and a Pacer nameplate on the right. The license tag was mounted at the center of the chrome strip.

The unique roofline and window configuration is what gave Pacer its true character, with everything rounded. Windshield glass was rounded at the top corners. The rear quarter windows curved downwards to follow the rear hatch opening, as well as wrapping around from side to rear, to meet the hatch. Also, the bottom corners of the rear quarter glass and the top corners of the hatchback glass were rounded, completing the "egg on wheels" look. The Pacer was the first AMC product to offer a rear window washer/wiper option, and only the second model to use concealed windshield wipers, the first being the 1974 Matador coupe.

If there was a shortcoming to the Pacer, it was in its powertrain. The car had originally been designed to utilize a rotary Wankel engine being developed by General Motors as its primary powertrain offering. Therefore, American Motors regrettably directed all of its efforts into the Pacer around the assumption that the rotary engine would be its powerplant. When GM suddenly dropped the development of the rotary engine in 1974 due to high costs and low fuel economy, AMC had to come up with a quick fix. While no one would deny that American Motors engines were well-built, long-lasting and dependable, their inline six-cylinder engines were the only engines available that would fit into the Pacer's engine bay, and the design of the car was already approved for production. Engineers had to make last minute changes to the Pacer to accommodate the six-cylinder engines, thereby delaying the Pacer's introduction by nearly five months. When the new car arrived, it was several hundred pounds over its original weight target due to the engine change, and suffered from sluggish performance. However, if a consumer wanted a well equipped and unique looking urban runabout, the Pacer fit the bill.

Missing from the 1975 AMC lineup were the Javelin and Ambassador. Obviously, with the pony car and muscle car market dried up, the Javelin no longer made sense to continue producing in such low quantity. Unfortunately, the Ambassador was just too similar to the Matador to justify its continued existence, ending a nameplate that had been around for more than 40 years. The Matador 4-door sedan and station wagons were, however, spiritual successors to the discontinued Ambassador; for 1975 they assumed the model numbers of the equivalent 1974 Ambassadors.

The rest of the American Motors line received minimal changes. Under the hood, all of the 1975 AMC engines were designed to burn unleaded fuel only. Externally, the Hornet received a front-end facelift but continued with its familiar styling elsewhere. It continued to be one of the most popular

series of the American Motors line, with only the new Pacer outselling it for 1975. The Hornet's new grille was made up of six square sections, with the two ends containing rectangular turn signal/parking lights. These were capped by headlamps within black surrounds, and the whole grille and headlamp area was outlined with a thin edge painted silver. Each of the six sections came to a slight point at its midsection, which matched the point of the fender end, and each section contained ten vertical bars trimmed in silver. Finally, model changes included the 1974 Matador Brougham and "X" coupes being dropped, and instead becoming option packages for 1975.

Gremlin 2-Door Sedan with Levi's option

Hornet 3-Door Hatchback

Hornet 4-Door Sedan

Pacer 2-Door Sedan

Matador Brougham 4-Door Sedan

Matador X 2-Door Coupe

Pacer 2-Door Sedan with D/L package

Pacer interior with optional individual reclining seats and Basketry fabric upholstery

---

Model year production: 241,701, down 43.81% from 1974.
Domestic market share: 3.43% (11th place).
Base price range: $2,798 to $3,844.
American Motors average base price: $3,287, down 0.53%.
Introduction date: November 15, 1974. Pacer introduced February 28, 1975.
Assembly plants: Kenosha, Wisconsin, and Brampton, Ontario, Canada.
Data plate identification (VIN): Thirteen digit code read as follows: First digit indicates company (A = American Mo-

tors); second digit indicates model year (5 = 1975); third digit is transmission code (see powertrain chart); fourth through sixth digits indicate car line–body type–series numbers (three-digit model number in model charts); seventh digit is engine code (see powertrain chart); eighth digit indicates assembly plant (1 through 6 = Kenosha, 7 through 9 = Ontario); remaining digits are sequential with beginning number of 00001. *Example:* A5A167H100001 is a 1975 Matador 2-Door, 304 CID, 2-bbl. V8, with Torque-Command Automatic, serial number 00001, built in Kenosha.

Powertrains[1]

Engine	Net HP	Engine/ Trans. Codes[2]	Transmission Availability[2]		Gremlin	Pacer	Hornet	Matador[3]
232 CID (3.8L), 1-bbl., 6-cyl.	90	E/S E/A	3-speed manual[4] Torque-Command 3-sp. Automatic		S $252	S $252	S $252	— — —
				MPG: Calif.	19/24 17/23	18/24 15/19	18/24 15/19	
258 CID (4.2L), 1-bbl., 6-cyl.	95	A/S A/A	3-speed manual[4] Torque-Command 3-sp. Automatic		$59 $311	$59 $311	$59 $311	S (ex. wgn.[5]) S (wgn.[5])/ $262 (others)
				MPG: Calif.	21/30 14/20	17/25 14/22	17/25 14/22	15/21
304 CID (5.0L), 2-bbl., V8	120	H/S H/A	3-speed manual Torque-Command 3-sp. Automatic		$154 $404	— —	$138 $390	— $99 (wgn.)/ $361 (others)
				MPG: Calif.	14/19 13/21	— —	14/19 13/21	13/17 13/18
360 CID (5.9L), 2-bbl., V8	140	N/A	Torque-Command 3-sp. Automatic		—	—	—	$158 (wgn.)/ $420 (others)
				MPG: Calif.	— —	— —	— —	13/15 12/16
360 CID (5.9L), 4-bbl., V8 w/ Power Package[6]	180	P/A	Torque-Command 3-sp. Automatic		—	—	—	$268 (wgn.)/ $530 (others)
				MPG: Calif.	— —	— —	— —	12/16 11/16

[1]Optional axle ratio required on cars sold in California: Gremlin 6-cylinders, 3.08:1; Gremlin V8, 3.15:1; Pacer, 3.08:1; Hornet 6-cylinders, 3.08:1. Also note that some AMC Matadors were built with the 401 CID V8 engine; however it was only available for special order or law enforcement applications that would be coded P. [2]Unless otherwise noted: All manual transmissions are column-shift, except Gremlin, Pacer w/X package, and Hornet Hatchback. All automatics are column-shift as standard. Add $21 for floor-shifter on Gremlin automatics, Hornet Hatchback or Sportabout with 258 CID 6 or 304 CID V8 and automatic transmission, Pacer with bucket or individual reclining seats, and Matador Coupe with bucket seats and console. Transmission code with automatic floor shift is C; 3-speed synchronized manual is E. [3]All Matadors built for sale in California have the 304 CID V8 engine as standard equipment. Prices adjust accordingly. [4]3-speed manual with overdrive available for $157, except on Matador. Transmission code O. [5]3-speed manual became standard on Matador wagons after the start of production. [6]Dual exhaust standard on Matador with 360 CID 4-bbl. V8.

Major Options

	Gremlin	Pacer	Hornet	Matador
All-season air conditioning	$400	$400	$400	$450
Adjust-O-Tilt steering wheel[1]	$43	$49	$43	$46
Cruise-command speed control[1]	—	$65	—	$65
Electric rear window defogger	—	$60	—	$60
Tinted glass, all windows	$45	$49	$49	$50
Power windows	—	—	—	$
Front bucket seats	$99	$99	$99	$140[2]
Third row seat & power tailgate window, wagons	—	—	—	$121
AM radio	$69	$69	$69	$70
AM/FM stereo multiplex w/4 speakers	$179	$179	$179	$230
AM/FM stereo w/8-track tape player	—	$299	—	$300
Vinyl top (excluding wagon models)	$74	$100	$100	$115
Woodgrain paneling, wagons only	—	—	$99	$118
Power steering	$119	$119	$119	$130
Power front disc brakes	$79	$79	$79	$90[3]
Custom wheel covers	—	$30	$30	$30
Styled road wheels	$115	$115	$115	$121
Aluminum styled wheels	—	$200	—	—
White sidewall tires, standard size	$34	$34	$36	$38

Popular Option Groups & Packages

	Gremlin	Pacer	Hornet	Matador
Brougham package	—	—	—	$105[4]
Custom trim package	$135	—	—	—
Décor group	—	$49	—	—
D/L package	—	$289	$299[5]	—
Handling package	—	$30	$25	$30
Insulation group	$30	$30	$30	S
Interior appointment package	$20	—	—	—
LEVI'S ® custom trim package	$220[6]	—	$125[6]	—
Light group	$35	$35	$35	$35
"Oleg Cassini" package[7]	—	—	—	$299
Protection group	$35	$35	$35	$35
Rallye option package	$133	$135	$125	—
Visibility group	$50	$50	$50	$50
"X" package	$201	$339	$227[8]	$199[2]

— = Not Available; S = Standard equipment. [1]Requires automatic transmission. [2]Two-door coupes only. [3]Standard on Matador station wagon. [4]Price given for coupe and sedan. Available on wagons for $145. [5]Price given is for Sedans. Available on Sportabout for $293. Not available on Hornet hatchback. [6]Available on Gremlin and Hornet HBK only. [7]Available only on Matador with Brougham package. [8]Price given is for hatchback. Available on Sportabout for $139.

Paint Colors

	Code	Gremlin & Hornet	Pacer	Matador
Red	D7	x	x	x
Fawn Beige	E6	x	x	x
Mellow Yellow	E9	x	x	x
Copper metallic	F9	—	—	x[1]
Dark Green metallic	G3	x	x	x
Sienna Orange	G6	x	—	x[1]
Alpine White	G7	x	x	x[1]
Pastel Blue	G8	x	x	—
Medium Blue metallic	G9	x	x	x
Deep Blue metallic	H1	x	—	x
Dark Cocoa metallic	H4	x	x	x
Green Apple	H5	x	—	—
Golden Jade metallic	H6	—	x	—
Aztec Copper metallic	H7	—	x	—
Autumn Red metallic	H8	—	x	x
Silver Dawn metallic	H9	x	x	x
Brandywine metallic	J2	—	x	—
Ivory Green	J7	x	x	x
Caramel Tan	J8	x	x	x
Classic Black	P1	x	—	x[1]

Non-standard model colors are available at extra cost. [1]The "Oleg Cassini" package is only available in these colors.

Gremlin

"The small car that makes it fun to be economical."

Nameplate year of origin: 1970.
Current bodystyle lifespan: 1970 through 1983; Gremlin (1970 to 1978), restyled and renamed Spirit (1979 to 1982). 4WD added and re-badged Eagle SX/4 (1981 to 1983).
Predecessor to this model: None.
Replacement for this model: Spirit (1979 to 1982) and Eagle SX/4 (1981 to 1983).
Percentage of division's production: 18.97%.
Corporate siblings: None, however many components were shared with the Hornet.

Measurements

Wheelbase	96.0"
Length	170.3"
Width	70.6"
Height	52.3"
Legroom — front	40.7"
Legroom — rear	29.2"
Headroom — front	38.0"

Primary competition: Buick/Opel 1900, Chevrolet Vega, Dodge Colt, and Ford Pinto.

Notable changes: Minor trim and detail changes.

Major standard equipment: Vinyl bench front seat with foam cushions, front door armrests, fold-down rear seat, color-keyed rubber floor covering, dome light, front and rear bumper guards, aluminum hubcaps, and 6.45 × 14 BSW tires.

Measurements (cont.)

Headroom — rear	36.4"
Cargo capacity (cu. ft.)	6.4*
Fuel capacity (gals.)	21.0

26.8 cu. ft. with rear seat down.

Models Available

	Model No.	Base MSRP	Change from LY	Shipping Wt. (lbs.)	Model Year Production	Change from LY
Gremlin 2-Door Sedan	46-5	$2,798	+12.78%	2694	45,848	-65.24%
TOTALS		Avg. price $2,798	+12.78%		Production 45,848*	-65.24%

Production by engine type (compared to LY): 6-cylinder, 42,630 (-64.37%); V8, 3,218 (-73.76%).

Pacer

"The all new Pacer. The first wide small car!"

Nameplate year of origin: 1975 (Previously used by Ford Motor Company on 1958 Edsel series).

Current bodystyle lifespan: 1975 through 1980.

Predecessor to this model: None.

Replacement for this model: None.

Percentage of division's production: 29.85%.

Corporate siblings: None.

Primary competition: Chevrolet Monza and Mercury Bobcat.

Notable changes: All-new model.

Major standard equipment: Diamant fabric front bench seat with foam cushions, color-keyed carpeting, fold-down rear seat, custom steering wheel, courtesy dome light, ashtray and cigarette lighter, glove box w/lock, integrated front door armrests, concealed two-speed electric wipers w/washers, large rear lift gate w/built-in assist struts, color-keyed rubber cargo area mat, bodyside scuff moldings, rack-and-pinion steering, aluminum hubcaps, and 6.95 × 14 BSW tires.

Measurements

Wheelbase	100.0"
Length	171.5"
Width	77.0"
Height	53.6"
Legroom — front	42.0"
Legroom — rear	34.8"
Headroom — front	38.3"
Headroom — rear	37.4"
Cargo capacity (cu. ft.)	29.6*
Fuel capacity (gals.)	22.0

With rear seat folded down.

Models Available

	Model No.	Base MSRP	Change from LY	Shipping Wt. (lbs.)	Model Year Production	Change from LY
Pacer 2-Door Sedan (hatchback)	66-7	$3,299	NEW	2995	72,158	NEW
TOTALS		Avg. price $3,299	NEW		Production 72,158	NEW

Hornet

"The compact car that is economical to buy, own and operate."

Nameplate year of origin: 1951 (Previously used on 1951 to 1957 Hudson series).

Current bodystyle lifespan: 1970 through 1987; Hornet (1970 to 1977), restyled and renamed Concord (1978 to 1982); 4WD added and re-badged Eagle (1980 to 1987).

Predecessor to this model: (Rambler) American (1964 to 1969).

Measurements

	Sedans	Hatchback	Sportabout
Wheelbase	108.0"	108.0"	108.0"
Length	187.0"	187.0"	187.0"
Width	71.0"	71.1"	71.0"

Replacement for this model: Concord (1978 to 1982) and Eagle (1980 to 1987).

Percentage of division's production: 26.53%.

Corporate siblings: None; however, many components were shared with the Gremlin.

Primary competition: Chevrolet Nova, Dodge Dart, Ford Maverick, Plymouth Valiant, and Pontiac Ventura.

Notable changes: New front end styling and trim and detail changes.

Major standard equipment: Fabric-covered front bench seat with foam cushions, color-keyed carpeting, instrument panel package tray, dome light, front and rear bumper guards, aluminum hubcaps, and 6.95 × 14 BSW tires. Hatchback adds: Folding second seat, flip open rear quarter windows, carpeted cargo mats, and gas-charged lift-gate supports. Sportabout adds: Folding second seat, gas-charged lift-gate supports, carpeted cargo mats, and hidden rear compartment lock.

Measurements (cont.)

	Sedans	Hatchback	Sportabout
Height	51.7"	52.2"	52.2"
Legroom — front	42.1"	40.7"	40.7"
Legroom — rear	35.5"	32.1"	35.6"
Headroom — front	38.1"	38.1"	38.1"
Headroom — rear	37.0"	36.7"	37.4"
Cargo capacity (cu. ft.)	11.1	30.5*	56.4*
Fuel capacity (gals.)	22.0	22.0	22.0

Maximum with rear seat down, and 3.8 cu. ft. below cargo floor on Sportabout.

1975

Models Available

	Model No.	Base MSRP	Change from LY	Shipping Wt. (lbs.)	Model Year Production	Change from LY
Hornet 2-Door Sedan	06-7	$3,074	+10.81%	2815	*	*
Hornet 2-Door Hatchback	03-7	$3,174	+11.41%	2839	*	*
Hornet 4-Door Sedan	05-7	$3,124	+10.62%	2881	*	*
Hornet 4-Door Sportabout Wagon	08-7	$3,374	+10.66%	2948	7,239*	-89.31%*
TOTALS		Avg. price $3,187	+10.87%		Production 64,113*	-56.03%

Production by body style is not available except for Sportabout. Production by engine type (compared to LY): 6-cylinder cars, 36,305 (-48.17%); 6-cylinder wagon, 3,016 (-94.75%); V8 car, 20,569 (+155.29%); V8 wagon, 4,223 (-58.98%).

Matador

"The mid-size car that stands out in style and economy."

Nameplate year of origin: 1971.

Current bodystyle lifespan: 1974 through 1978 (Coupe only); 1967 through 1978 (Rebel, 1967–1968; restyled in 1969; restyled and renamed Matador in 1971; and sedan and wagon restyled in 1974).

Predecessor to this model: Matador (1971 to 1973).

Replacement for this model: None.

Percentage of division's production: 24.65%.

Corporate siblings: None.

Primary competition: Chevrolet Chevelle Malibu, Dodge Coronet, Ford Torino, Plymouth Fury, and Pontiac LeMans.

Notable changes: Minor trim and detail changes.

Major standard equipment: Fabric front bench seat with foam cushions, color-keyed carpeting, day/night rearview mirror, dome light activated by door switches, rear shelf light (coupe only), Extra Quiet insulation package, bodyside scuff moldings with vinyl insert (sedan and wagon), front sway bar, manual front disc brakes, and ER78 × 14 BSW tires (coupe) or FR78 × 14 BSW tires (sedan). Wagon adds: All-vinyl upholstery, cargo area carpet, hidden rear compartment with lock, dual-swing tailgate, power front disc brakes, and HR78 × 14 BSW tires.

Measurements

	Coupe	Sedan	Wagon
Wheelbase	114.0"	118.0"	118.0"
Length	209.3"	216.0"	215.5"
Width	77.4"	77.3"	77.2"
Height	51.8"	54.7"	56.8"
Legroom — front	43.0"	42.8"	42.8"
Legroom — rear	33.3"	39.6"	39.6"
Headroom — front	37.6"	39.6"	39.9"
Headroom — rear	36.0"	37.5"	38.5"
Cargo capacity (cu. ft.)	14.3	19.1	95.2*
Fuel capacity (gals.)	24.5	24.5	21.0

Includes 8.0 cu.ft. of space below cargo floor.

Models Available

	Model No.	Base MSRP	Change from LY	Shipping Wt. (lbs.)	Model Year Production	Change from LY
Matador 2-Door Coupe	16-7	$3,446	+11.30%	3562	22,368	-28.24%

	Model No.	Base MSRP	Change from LY	Shipping Wt. (lbs.)	Model Year Production	Change from LY
Matador 4-Door Sedan	85-7	$3,452	+13.11%	3586	27,522	-1.69%
Matador 4-Door Station Wagon	88-7	$3,844	+13.80%	3878	9,692	-0.18%
TOTALS		Avg. price $3,581	+8.68%		Production 59,582	-40.40%

Production by engine type (compared to LY): 6-cylinder cars, 9,390 (-63.64%); 6-cylinder wagon, 1,575 (-47.06%); V8 car, 40,500 (-37.10%); V8 wagon, 8,117 (+20.54%). Also included in these figures are 1,817 coupes equipped with the Oleg Cassini package and 4 coupes with the 401 CID V8 engine.

BUICK

"Dedicated to the free spirit in just about everyone."

Patriotism was reaching new heights as the United States of America's bicentennial approached. Many companies became involved in the celebration and used it as a marketing opportunity, with some getting an earlier start than others. Buick began with the 1975 model year, changing their long running "Wouldn't you really rather have a Buick?" advertising campaign to a new "free spirit" campaign to create a new image. The introduction page of the 1975 Buick sales brochure provided a prelude to some new ideas from Buick, including the new V6 engine and new, more elegant interiors, plus offering a full range of cars, from small to big: "A fresh, new spirit is emerging in America. A spirit of honesty. A spirit of integrity. A spirit of freedom. A free spirit. One that embraces new thoughts, new ideas, new concepts. We at Buick recognize this free spirit ... we believe it is reflected most clearly in our 1975 products." At the end of the ad campaign's three-year run in 1977, Buick proved the "Free Spirit" was truly alive, as sales increases greatly exceeded the industry average, nearly matching the sales increases being made by the even more popular Oldsmobile line.

The "new" V6 engine was really an old engine, modernized and brought back to life. Originally used in the "senior compact" 1961–1963 Buick Special, it was one of the first domestic V-type 6-cylinder engines produced in mass quantities. As the size of the Special grew from a compact to an intermediate, and sales of 6-cylinder engines fell, the tooling and castings for the 225 CID V6 engine were sold to Kaiser-Willys Corporation, which used the engine as an option in the CJ "Universal" series and the Commando series from 1966 through 1970. During 1970, Kaiser-Willys sold the Jeep and related entities to American Motors, which continued to use the engine through the 1971 model year. A couple of years later, the tooling was sold back to General Motors. Back in Buick's hands, the engine was given major updates and enlarged slightly to become the 3.8-liter, 231

CID V6 engine. Buick became a huge promoter of the V6 engine, adding turbocharging by the end of the decade and proving that a V6 could be as powerful as a V8 engine, while getting better fuel mileage. History would bear out the V6 engine to be one of the most important engine developments for General Motors in the second half of the 20th century, right after the small-block Chevrolet V8, with the reincarnated 3.8-liter V6 engine being used in various versions for the next 33 years. The "new" V6 also shared many parts with the new-for-1975 260 CID V8 engine, and would later be the basis for spin-offs such as the 3.1-liter V6 engine.

In terms of new product, Buick introduced the all-new Skyhawk based on GM's new H-body, which was an offshoot of the Chevrolet Vega platform. A small, sporty car seemed very uncharacteristic for a Buick, but with ever-increasing prices for the imported Opel line due to currency exchange rates, the Skyhawk made a good replacement on the showroom floor for the Manta coupes, or even the Opel GT that was last imported for the 1973 model year. The Skyhawk was nicely equipped, and with the V6 engine was more powerful than a Vega could ever hope to be. The H-body cars were stylistically similar, as described in the introduction for 1975, with the Skyhawk having a small, blacked-out crosshatch style grille, and the Buick logo mounted above on the front fascia. Chrome lined black bumpers and black window trim accented with chrome completed the Skyhawk's exterior distinguishing features. Interiors with more luxurious appointments than other GM H-bodies marked the Skyhawk and gave it a more European feel. The Skyhawk, Electra and Riviera were the first Buick models to adopt the dual rectangular headlights appearing for the first time on the American market in 1975.

The redesigned compact Apollo line was given a completely new appearance and higher level of luxury. Capping off the makeover was the return of the popular Skylark nameplate, which was applied to all of the 2-door models, leaving the lesser-known Apollo name for the 4-doors. Apollo and Skylark's new styling again was based on the Chevrolet Nova, adding more squared off lines with an upright front end. The Apollo wore a grille split by a single horizontal bar with many thin vertical bars in between. Single round headlamps were still used, with large wrap-around turn signal/parking lamps that matched the grille theme on the fender ends, giving the appearance of a full-width grille. Around back was a pair of wrap-around horizontal taillamps, purposely designed to simulate the LeSabre lights. Three rectangular ventiports on the front fenders completed the Buick look outside, and inside nicer fabrics, woodgrain trim, and luxury touches such as carpeted lower door panels and map pockets gave the Skylark a more luxurious look than the Nova. A top-of-the-line S/R (Sport Rallye) trim level was added, to give a luxury sport character to the new models, in keeping with the Century Regal luxury sport theme.

The Century line still contained the Regal models, although marketing was making a move to clearly distinguish the Regal from the Century. A freshened front end appearance gave the Regal an all vertical bar grille split into two sections giving a formal appearance, while other Century models carried a horizontally split grille divided by 10 vertical bars, and four smaller horizontal bars with each of the squares created. Century had vertical rectangular turn signal/parking lamps set on the ends of the grille, while the Regal's smaller grille allowed for placing them between the headlight and grille. The new V6 engines were employed as standard equipment on all Century coupe and sedan models, which dropped the weight of each model by more than 150 pounds and helped increase fuel efficiency. Price increases were kept to a minimum of about two percent for the V6-powered cars, but reached nearly 10 percent for V8-equipped models. Apparently the effects of the fuel shortages were wearing out because sales increases were greatest on the V8-equipped cars. There were not model changes, but the Custom designation replaced the short-lived Luxus trim level on both Century and LeSabre lines.

A Buick Century Custom with the "Free Spirit" package was selected as the Indianapolis 500 race pace car, the first Buick since 1959, and only the second time since 1947 that a convertible had not been used for pace car duties. It was also one of the first uses of what became known as the "T-top," featuring removable lift-out roof panels above the driver and front seat passenger to create the feel of driving a convertible while retaining structural rigidity. The T-top in the pace car, manufactured by the Hurst Corporation, known for manufacturing speed equipment, was not offered for production cars in 1975, although a few "prototypes" may have been built. But they would be added to the option list in 1976. Approximately 400 replica pace cars were built.

Full-sized Buicks, including the Riviera, added all-new front end styling that featured Buick's first use of dual rec-

tangular headlights on the Electra and Riviera. The Riviera had a vertical bar grille similar to the Century Regal's new grille, and side-by-side rectangular headlamps. Square-ish turn signal/parking lamps similar to those of the past few years were also used. Like all full-sized Buicks, the Riviera also received a restyled instrument panel divided into upper and lower sections. All gauges were mounted in the upper portion in front of the driver while the lower section held such items as the radio and light switch. Front-end styling of the Electra included a full-width crosshatch grille with highlighted vertical bars and bounded on each end by a thicker vertical bar where the feature line of the hood jutted out from the fenders slightly. To the outside of this bar, the side-by-side rectangular headlamps were mounted, above grille extensions that used only vertical bars. The lower portion of the front bumper contained two slotted openings for better airflow to the engine and housed turn signal/parking lights that wrapped around each end. LeSabres had a similar grille, only with horizontal bars being highlighted, and dual round headlamps were used.

All Electra models and LeSabre four-door models gained a new greenhouse area. Electra two-doors now had a large fixed rear quarter window, in a similar fashion to the Colonnade hardtop styling used on Century two-door models. All LeSabre four-door sedans introduced a fixed "vent window" design on the rear doors, and four-door hardtop models in both LeSabre and Electra introduced a C-pillar rear quarter window. The Electra "225" designation was used only on the lower-level Electra, which this year replaced the previous Electra 225 Custom, and the former Electra 225 Limited was now officially called Electra Limited. An even more opulent option for the Electra Limited was the Park Avenue package, which added many interior luxury items. The Park Avenue name had been used previously by Cadillac on its 1962 and 1963 Sedan deVille short-decklid models. And for the ultimate in luxury a Deluxe Park Avenue package that included every option available on an Electra was available for $1,675, but only sold 37 copies. Apparently it was a little too pricey for even Buick's traditional buyers. For those who noticed such things, the 1975 Estate Wagon wore three ventiports per side, as opposed to the four ventiports in 1974.

Shortly after the start of the model year, lower-priced "S" models were added to the Skyhawk 2+2 coupe and Skylark coupe with reduced standard features and accompanying lower prices, $3,860 and $3,234 respectively. These were a complement to the low-priced Century Special coupe introduced at the beginning of the model year. Finally, the imported German-built Opel models entered their last year of sales in the United States. The addition of fuel-injected engines was the only change, other than the 4-door sedan no longer being imported. Foreign exchange rates made German Opels so expensive to import that GM decided to turn to Japan for the next Opel.

Apollo 4-Door Sedan

Century Regal 2-Door
Colonnade Hardtop Coupe

Century Regal 4-Door
Colonnade Hardtop Sedan

Century Special 2-Door
Colonnade Hardtop Coupe

Electra 225 Limited 2-Door Hardtop Coupe

Estate Wagon with Century Custom
4-Door Station Wagon, rear

LeSabre 4-Door Sedan

LeSabre Custom 2-Door Convertible

Riviera 2-Door Hardtop Coupe
with padded landau top

Skyhawk 2-Door Hatchback Coupe

Skylark 2-Door Coupe

Skylark S/R interior

Opel 1900 2-Door Sedan

Opel 1900 Sportwagon 2-Door Wagon

Opel Manta 2-Door Coupe

Opel Manta Rallye 2-Door Coupe

Model year production: 511,215, up 3.26% from 1974.
Domestic market share: 7.25% (5th place).
Base price range: $3,234 to $6,420.
Buick average base price: $4,681, up 3.47%.
Introduction date: September 27, 1974; Opel introduced May 1975.
Assembly plants: Baltimore, MD (B); Southgate, CA (C); Doraville, GA (D); Framingham, MA (G); Flint, MI (H); Kansas City/Leeds, MO (K); Van Nuys, CA (L); Tarrytown, NY (T); Kansas City/Fairfax, KS (X); Fremont, CA (Z); St. Therese, Quebec, Canada (2). Opel assembly plants: Russelsheim, Germany (5).
Data plate identification (VIN): Thirteen digit code read as follows: First digit indicates division (4 = Buick); second through fourth digits indicate series and body style (model number in model charts); fifth digit is engine code (see powertrain chart); sixth digit indicates model year (5 = 1975); seventh digit indicates assembly plant (see list above); remaining digits are sequential with beginning number of 100001, or 400001, depending upon assembly plant. *Example:* 4N69J5H100001 is a 1975 Buick LeSabre 4-Door Sedan, with 350 CID, 4-bbl. V8 engine, serial number 100001, built in Flint, MI. 1975 Opels use a 13-digit code read as follows: First digit is O for Opel; next three digits indicate series and body style (Manta=L77, 1900 2-door= L11, 1900 Wagon=L15); fifth digit indicates engine code (N); sixth digit indicates year (D = 1975); seventh digit indicates assembly plant (see list above); remaining digits are sequential with beginning numbers as follows: 1900 Deluxe 2-door sedan—057575; 1900 Deluxe 2-door wagon—057665; Manta coupe—058366.

Powertrains

Engine	Net HP	Engine Code	Transmission Availability		Opel	Skyhawk	Apollo & Skylark	Century & Regal	LeSabre	Electra & Estate Wagon	Riviera
116 CID (1.9L), FI, 4-cyl.	75	N	4-speed manual		S	—	—	—	—	—	—
			3-speed automatic		$254	—	—	—	—	—	—
				MPG:	19/27	—	—	—	—	—	—
				Calif.	18/26	—	—	—	—	—	—
231 CID (3.8L), 2-bbl., V6	110	C	3-speed manual		—	—	S (Skylark only)	S (ex. wgns.)	—	—	—
			4-speed manual		—	S	—	—	—	—	—
			3-speed Turbo Hydra-matic		—	$237	$237 (Skylark only)	$237 (ex. wgns.)	—	—	—
				MPG:	—	19/25	16/24	16/24	—	—	—
				Calif.	—	17/23	15/21	14/19	—	—	—
250 CID (4.1L), 1-bbl., 6-cyl.	105	D	3-speed manual		—	—	S (Apollo only)	—	—	—	—
			3-speed Turbo Hydra-matic		—	—	$237 (Apollo only)	—	—	—	—
				MPG:	—	—	16/21	—	—	—	—
				Calif.	—	—	15/20	—	—	—	—
260 CID (4.3L), 2-bbl., V8	110	F	3-speed Turbo Hydra-matic		—	—	$315 (Apollo)/ $263 (Skylark)	—	—	—	—
				MPG:	—	—	15/19	—	—	—	—
				Calif.	—	—	13/17	—	—	—	—
350 CID (5.7L), 2-bbl., V8	145	H	3-speed Turbo Hydra-matic		—	—	$367 (Apollo)/ $315 (Skylark)	$315 (ex. wgns.)		—	—
				MPG:	—	—	14/19	12/19		—	—
350 CID (5.7L), 4-bbl., V8	165	J	3-speed Turbo Hydra-matic		—	—	$418 (Apollo)/ $366 (Skylark)	S (wgns.)/ $366 (others)	S	—	—
				MPG:	—	—	14/18	13/20[1]	12/16	—	—

Engine	Net HP	Engine Code	Transmission Availability		Opel	Skyhawk	Apollo & Skylark	Century & Regal	LeSabre	Electra & Estate Wagon	Riviera
400 CID (6.6L), 4-bbl., V8	185	S	3-speed Turbo Hydra-matic		—	—	—	—	$72	— (Credit option)	$63 —
				MPG:	—	—	—	—	12/15	11/15	—
455 CID (7.5L), 4-bbl., V8	205	T, U, V, W[2]	3-speed Turbo Hydra-matic		—	—	—	—	$135	S	S
				MPG:	—	—	—	—	12/15	11/15	12/15
				Calif.	—	—	—	—	11/16	10/14	10/13

[1]For wagons, MPG = 12/16.   [2]Some GM sources suggest that a Pontiac engine may have been used in some Buicks; therefore all possible engine codes are listed.

Major Options

	Opel	Skyhawk	Apollo & Skylark	Century	LeSabre	Estate Wagon	Electra 225	Riviera
Climate Control air conditioning[1]	$[2]	$398	$435	$453	$487	$487	$487	$487
Tilt-wheel steering	—	$45	$45	$45	$45	$45	$45	S
Tilt and telescoping steering column	—	—	—	—	$85	$85	$85	$40
GM Air Cushion Restraint System (ex. convertible)	—	—	—	—	$300	—	$300	$300
Cruise Master speed control	—	—	$65	$65	$65	$65	$65	$65
Electric rear window defogger	$35	$60	$35[3]	$60	$60	$60	$73	$60
Tinted glass, all windows	$28	$35	$38	$45	$45	$50	$45	$45
Power windows, 2-dr./4-dr.	—	—	$91/$132	$91/$132	$149	$149	S	S
Power door locks, 2-dr./4-dr.[4]	—	—	$90	$90	$90	$90	$90	$90
Power front seat, 6-way, w/bench seat	—	—	—	$117	$117	$117	$117[5]	$117
Front bucket seats, w/console	S	S	$155[6]	$180[6]	—	—	—	$61
AM radio	$[2]	$63	$69	$73	$86	$86	$86	$86
AM/FM stereo	—	$214	$233	$233	$233	$233	$233	$233
AM/FM stereo w/8-track tape	—	—	$363	$363	$363	$363	$363	$363
Vinyl top	$88[2]	—	$92[7]	$108[7]	$132	$142	$154[8]	$132
Sunroof, electric[9]	$125[2]	—	—	$275	—	—	$539	$539
Woodgrain exterior panels (wagons)	—	—	—	$173[10]	—	$182	—	—
Power steering, variable-ratio	—	$111	$129	S	S	S	S	S
Power brakes, w/front disc	S	S	$55	$55[11]	S	S	S	S
Full wheel covers	—	$30	$30	$32[12]	$32[12]	S	S	S
Styled road wheels	—	$84	$89	$89	$89	$89	$89	$89
WSW tires, standard size	—	$26	$28	$28	$40	$40	$40	$40

Popular Option Groups & Packages

	Opel	Skyhawk	Apollo & Skylark	Century	LeSabre	Estate Wagon	Electra 225	Riviera
Accessory group	—	—	$36	$36	$26	—	—	—
Appearance group	—	—	$31	$31	—	—	—	—
Convenience group	—	—	$29	$29	$29	—	—	—
Firm ride & handling package	—	—	$15	$15	$15	$15	$15	$15
Gran Sport package	—	—	—	$110	—	—	—	—
GS ride & handling package	—	—	—	—	—	—	—	$73
Indianapolis 500 pace car replica package	—	—	—	$	—	—	—	—
Park Avenue package	—	—	—	—	—	—	$495[13]	—

— = Not Available; S = Standard equipment.   [1]Manual controlled. Power brakes required. Automatic climate control is available for $81 additional on Century Regal, Riviera and full-size Buicks.   [2]Radio and air conditioning available as dealer installed option. Vinyl top in black, and sunroof available for Manta only.   [3]Blower type defogger.   [4]Includes automatic seatback release on two-door models.   [5]Two-way seat standard on Limited.   [6]Standard on Apollo S/R and Skylark S/R. Not available on Regal models.   [7]Price is $5 less on Apollo/Skylark S/R models, and on Regal. Regal w/Landau top, $389. Not available on Century station wagons.   [8]Electra 4-Doors are $142. Landau padded vinyl top for coupes, $389.   [9]Available on two-door models only.   [10]Custom wagon, $141.   [11]Standard on station wagons.   [12]Standard on Regal and LeSabre Custom models.   [13]Also available is a Park Avenue DeLuxe package for $1,675 extra.

Paint Colors

Buick	Code	Buick	Code	Opel	Code
Arctic White	11	Ginger metallic	53	Regency Blue metallic	L-204
Silver Mist metallic	13	Sandstone	55	Signal Blue	L-224
Dove Gray	15	Honey Gold metallic	57*	Strato Blue metallic	L-235
Pewter metallic	16	Almond Mist metallic	58	Jade Mist metallic	L-303
Antique Silver metallic	18*	Walnut Mist metallic	59	Signal Green	L-308
Regal Black	19	Golden Tan metallic	63	Rallye Gold	L-411
Horizon Blue metallic	21	Bittersweet metallic	64	Antique Bronze metallic	L-412
Glacier Blue	24	Ruby Red	72	Signal Yellow	L-445
Majestic Blue metallic	26	Burgundy metallic	74	Polar White	L-452
Blue Haze metallic	28*	Apple Red	75	Burgundy	L-501
Indigo metallic	29	Rhone Red metallic	79	Flame Red	L-508
Ranch Green	44	Pumpkin metallic	80	Fire Glow	L-529
Verde Mist metallic	49				
Sand Beige	50	*Opel*	*Code*		
Canary Yellow	51	Grecian Silver metallic	L-135		

In two-tone combinations, the first two digits indicate lower color; the next two digits are the upper color.
*Available on Riviera only.

Opel

"For 1975, the fuel-injected Opels."

Nameplate year of origin: Opel 1900, 1971; Manta, 1972.
Current bodystyle lifespan: Opel 1900 (1971–1975); Manta (1971–1975).
Predecessor to this model: Kadett (1966–1972); 1900 Sport Coupe (1971–1972 for Manta).
Replacement for this model: Opel (1976 to 1980—Isuzu built).
Primary competition: AMC Gremlin, Chevrolet Vega, Dodge Colt, Ford Pinto, Mercury Bobcat, and Pontiac Astre.
Notable changes: New fuel-injected engines and minor trim and detail changes.
Major standard equipment: *1900 1.9 Liter Sedan and Sportwagon:* Reclining vinyl front bucket seats with foam cushions, front door pockets, fold-down rear seat, rubber floor mats, interior lights, aluminized exhaust system, exterior pinstripes, hubcaps, and 165 × 13 BSW tires. *Manta:* Reclining vinyl bucket seats, center console, two-spoke steering wheel, woodgrain vinyl I/P gauge cluster appliqué, and 165 × 13 BSW tires.

Measurements

	1900	Manta
Wheelbase	95.7"	95.7"
Length	170.2"	176.1"
Width	64.3"	64.3"
Height	55.1"	53.4"
Legroom — front	41.9"	41.9"
Legroom — rear	30.5"	28.5"
Headroom — front	38.2"	37.4"
Headroom — rear	37.3"	36.6"
Cargo capacity (cu. ft.)	10.8*	11.5
Fuel capacity (gals.)	12.0	12.0

*Sportwagon, 62.6 cu. ft.

Models Available

	Model No.	Base MSRP	Change from LY	Shipping Wt. (lbs.)	Model Year Sales*	Change from LY
(1900) 1.9 Liter 2-Door Sedan	51	$3,645	+14.80%	2128	NA	NA
(1900) Sportwagon 2-Door Wagon	54	$3,962	+15.11%	2201	NA	NA
Manta 2-Door Sport Coupe	57	$3,745	+14.35%	2156	NA	NA
TOTALS		*Avg. price* $3,784	+11.93%		*Production* 15,000*	-72.73%

*Model year sales are unknown for the shortened 1975 model year, and because GM withdrew the German-built Opels from the market before the end of the model year. It is also presumed that some models built in 1974 were sold as 1975 models. The figures above are estimated based upon the average of estimates from various sources.

Skyhawk

"The smallest Buick in 60 years. And the sportiest."

Nameplate year of origin: 1975.
Current bodystyle lifespan: 1975 through 1980.
Predecessor to this model: None.
Replacement for this model: Skyhawk (1982 to 1989).
Percentage of division's production: 5.76%.
Corporate siblings: Chevrolet Monza and Oldsmobile Starfire (closely related to Chevrolet Vega and Pontiac Astre).
Primary competition: AMC Pacer, Ford Mustang II and "Lincoln-Mercury" Capri.
Notable changes: All-new model.
Major standard equipment: Choice of cloth or vinyl front bucket seats with foam cushions, full-length center console, fold-down rear seat, cut-pile carpeting including cargo area, simulated woodgrain I/P and console trim, gauges including tachometer, rallye steering wheel, dual speed wipers w/washers, functional B-pillar vent louvers, extra sound deadening insulation, bright window surround moldings, front and rear wheel opening moldings, dual bodyside pinstripes, blackout grille, Buick tri-shield front and rear panel emblems, hubcaps, and BR78 × 13 BSW tires.

Measurements

Wheelbase	97.0"
Length	179.3"
Width	65.4"
Height	50.2"
Legroom — front	42.9"
Legroom — rear	29.9"
Headroom — front	37.7"
Headroom — rear	35.3"
Cargo capacity (cu. ft.)	28.1*
Fuel capacity (gals.)	18.5

With rear seat folded down.

Models Available

	Model No.	Base MSRP	Change from LY	Shipping Wt. (lbs.)	Model Year Production	Change from LY
Skyhawk 2+2 2-Door Hatchback	S07	$4,186	NEW	2891	29,448	NEW
TOTALS		Avg. price $4,186	NEW		Production 29,448	NEW

Skylark/Apollo

"Sporty coupes and sedans with a European influence."

Nameplate year of origin: Apollo, 1973; Skylark, 1953.
Current bodystyle lifespan: 1975 through 1979.
Predecessor to this model: Apollo (1973 to 1974).
Replacement for this model: Skylark (1980 to 1985).
Percentage of division's production: 11.45%.
Corporate siblings: Chevrolet Nova, Oldsmobile Omega, and Pontiac Ventura.
Primary competition: Dodge Dart and Mercury Monarch.
Notable changes: Completely redesigned. Two-door models renamed Skylark.
Major standard equipment: "S" model (Skylark only): Front vinyl bench seat without pattern, front door armrest, cut-pile carpeting, functional ventilation louvers (B-pillar), and E78 × 14 BSW tires. Skylark adds: Choice of cloth or vinyl front bench seat with foam cushions, cut-pile carpeting including hatchback load floor, fold-down rear seat (hatchback only), front door operated courtesy lights, front and rear ashtrays, rear quarter/rear door armrests, deluxe steering wheel, functional ventilation louvers (B-pillar on two-doors, C-pillar on sedans), dual speed wipers w/4-jet washers, roof drip moldings, front and rear wheel opening moldings, hubcaps, and FR78 × 14 BSW tires. S/R adds: Choice of Prado cloth or vinyl front bucket seats w/passenger recliner, carpeted door trim w/map pocket and reflector, Sports shifting console, combination turn signal and high/low beam headlight control stalk, and stand-up hood ornament.

Measurements

	Coupe & HBK	Sedan
Wheelbase	111.0"	111.0"
Length	200.3"	200.3"
Width	69.9"	69.9"
Height	53.2"	54.2"
Legroom — front	41.7"	41.7"
Legroom — rear	33.4"	35.3"
Headroom — front	38.3"	39.3"
Headroom — rear	36.6"	36.6"
Cargo capacity (cu. ft.)	14.6*	13.8
Fuel capacity (gals.)	21.0	21.0

Hatchback maximum with rear seat down, 28.4 cu. ft.

Models Available

	Model No.	Base MSRP	Change from LY*	Shipping Wt. (lbs.)	Model Year Production	Change from LY*
Skylark "S" 2-Door Coupe	W27	$3,234	NEW	3309	**	NEW
Skylark 2-Door Coupe	B27	$3,463	+14.03%	3341	27,869	-2.11%
Skylark 2-Door Hatchback	B17	$3,586	+13.48%	3438	6,814	-41.48%
Apollo 4-Door Sedan	B69	$3,436	+12.29%	3366	21,138	+25.98%
Skylark S/R 2-Door Coupe	C27	$4,136	NEW	3349	3,746	NEW
Skylark S/R 2-Door Hatchback	·C17	$4,253	NEW	3441	1,505	NEW
Apollo S/R 4-Door Sedan	C69	$4,092	NEW	3388	2,241	NEW
TOTALS		Avg. price $3,743	+21.30%		Production 63,133	+11.33%

*Compared to equivalent 1974 Apollo models.   **Production of "S" coupe was kept with Skylark base coupe production.

Century

*"A measure of any fine car is its ability to make a statement.
The 1975 Buick Century is such a car."*

Nameplate year of origin: 1936.
Current bodystyle lifespan: 1973 through 1977.
Predecessor to this model: Skylark (1968 to 1972).
Replacement for this model: Century (1978 to 1981).
Percentage of divisions' production: 35.89%.
Corporate siblings: Chevrolet Malibu, Oldsmobile Cutlass, and Pontiac LeMans.
Primary competition: Dodge Coronet, and Mercury Montego.
Notable changes: New grille and trim and detail changes. New Century Special added.
Major standard equipment: Century Special: Choice of vinyl or cloth front bench seat, rubber floor covering, 4-jet windshield washer, front disc brakes, variable ratio power steering, and GR78 × 15 BSW tires. Century (base) adds: Cut-pile carpeting, deluxe steering wheel, bumper protective strips w/white accents front and rear, and wheel covers. Custom adds: Choice of cloth or expanded vinyl notchback front seat w/center fold-down armrest, ashtray light, under-dash courtesy lights, glove compartment light, "Custom" badging, wheel opening moldings, and rocker panel molding. Wagons add: Vinyl front bench seat (Century base only; Custom wagon has same upholstery choices as coupes and sedans), and HR78 × 15 BSW tires. Regal adds: Choice of luxury cloth or expanded vinyl notchback seat with center armrest, and door pull assist straps.

Measurements

	Century Coupes	Regal Coupes	Century Sedans	Regal Sedans	Century Wagons
Wheelbase	112.0"	112.0"	116.0"	116.0"	116.0"
Length	209.5"	212.0"	213.5"	216.0"	218.2"
Width	79.0"	79.0"	79.0"	79.0"	79.0"
Height	53.5"*	53.3"	54.1"	54.1"	55.3"
Legroom — front	42.4"	42.4"	42.4"	42.4"	42.3"
Legroom — rear	32.9"	32.9"	37.0"	37.0"	36.8"
Headroom — front	37.7"*	37.5"	38.3"	38.3"	38.8"
Headroom — rear	37.0"*	37.4"	37.5"	37.5"	39.4"
Cargo capacity (cu. ft.)	15.1	15.1	14.6	14.6	85.1
Fuel capacity (gals.)	NA	NA	NA	NA	NA

*Custom coupe dimensions are the same as Regal coupe.

Models Available

	Model No.	Base MSRP	Change from LY*	Shipping Wt. (lbs.)	Model Year Production	Change from LY*
Century Special 2-Dr. Colonnade HT Coupe	E37	$3,815	NEW	3613	**	NEW
Century 2-Door Colonnade HT Coupe	D37	$3,894	+2.74%	3674	39,556	+27.97%
Century 4-Door Colonnade HT Sedan	D29	$3,944	+2.82%	3730	22,075	-3.42%

	Model No.	Base MSRP	Change from LY*	Shipping Wt. (lbs.)	Model Year Production	Change from LY*
Century 4-Door Station Wagon, 2-S.	F35	$4,636	+10.25%	4320	4,416	-9.14%
Century 4-Door Station Wagon, 3-S.	F45	$4,751	+9.98%	4370	***	***
Century Custom 2-Door Colonnade HT Coupe	H57	$4,154	+1.59%	3671	32,966	-26.63%
Century Custom 4-Door Colonnade HT Sedan	H29	$4,211	+2.48%	3763	9,995	-10.43%
Century Custom 4-Door Station Wagon, 2-S.	K35	$4,802	+9.86%	4350	7,078	+4.23%
Century Custom 4-Door Station Wagon, 3-S.	K45	$4,917	+9.61%	4400	***	***
Century Regal 2-Door Colonnade HT Coupe	J57	$4,257	+1.33%	3733	56,646	-1.51%
Century Regal 4-Door Colonnade HT Sedan	J29	$4,311	+2.13%	3800	10,726	+14.93%
TOTALS	Avg. price	$4,336	+4.74%	Production	183,458	-3.75%

*Comparisons of Custom models are made to the 1974 Luxus models. **Production of Century Special, E37, kept as combined total with Century 2-Door coupe, D37. ***Production of 3-seat wagon models included with 2-seat models.

LeSabre

"Its ride, its design, the comfort of its interior and its affordability make it an outstanding value."

Nameplate year of origin: 1959 (also used on 1951 GM show car).
Current bodystyle lifespan: 1971 through 1976.
Predecessor to this model: LeSabre (1969 to 1970).
Replacement for this model: LeSabre (1977 to 1985).
Percentage of division's production: 21.36%.
Corporate siblings: Chevrolet BelAir/Impala/Caprice, Pontiac Catalina/Bonneville/Grand Ville, and Oldsmobile Delta 88.
Primary competition: Chrysler Newport and Mercury Marquis.
Notable changes: Revised greenhouse area for sedans, revised front and rear styling.
Major standard equipment: Choice of cloth or vinyl front bench seat, full-floor carpeting, woodgrained vinyl trim on door panels, deluxe steering wheel, I/P woodgrain appliqués, LH outside rear view mirror, front fender-mounted three-section rectangular "ventiport" ornaments, bumper protective strips w/white accent stripes front and rear, wheel opening moldings, rocker panel molding between wheel openings, wheel covers, and HR78 × 15 BSW tires. Custom adds: Choice of cloth or vinyl notchback front bench seat w/fold-down front center armrest, custom steering wheel, full-length rocker panel molding, "Custom" interior and exterior badging, and deluxe wheel covers.

Measurements

Wheelbase	124.0"
Length	226.9"
Width	79.9"
Height	54.6"
Legroom — front	42.1"
Legroom — rear	38.8"
Headroom — front	38.9"
Headroom — rear	38.0"
Cargo capacity (cu. ft.)	19.7*
Fuel capacity (gals.)	NA

*Custom Coupe, 17.5; Convertible, 14.0; Custom sedans, 16.8.

Models Available

	Model No.	Base MSRP	Change from LY*	Shipping Wt. (lbs.)	Model Year Production	Change from LY*
LeSabre 2-Door Hardtop Coupe	N57	$4,840	+9.40%	4294	8,647	-30.95%
LeSabre 4-Door Sedan	N69	$4,771	+9.55%	4355	14,088	-24.14%
LeSabre 4-Door Hardtop Sedan	N39	$4,898	+9.28%	4411	9,119	-23.23%
LeSabre Custom 2-Door Hardtop Coupe	P57	$5,007	+9.44%	4316	25,016	-8.17%
LeSabre Custom 2-Door Convertible	P67	$5,133	+9.31%	4392	5,300	+46.13%
LeSabre Custom 4-Door Sedan	P69	$4,936	+10.52%	4388	17,026	+6.15%
LeSabre Custom 4-Door Hardtop Sedan	P39	$5,061	+9.33%	4439	30,005	+25.49%
TOTALS	Avg. price	$4,949	+9.55%	Production	109,201	-4.03%

*Comparisons of Custom models are made to the 1974 Luxus models.

Estate Wagon

"The comforts of a full-size Buick, with the utility of a wagon."

Nameplate year of origin: 1940 (as designation for station wagons).
Current bodystyle lifespan: 1971 through 1976.
Predecessor to this model: Estate Wagon (1970).
Replacement for this model: Estate Wagon (1977 to 1990).
Percentage of division's production: 2.69%.
Corporate siblings: Chevrolet BelAir/Impala/Caprice, Pontiac Catalina Safari/Grand Safari, and Oldsmobile Custom Cruiser.
Primary competition: Chrysler Town & Country and Mercury Marquis Colony Park.
Notable changes: Revised front and rear styling.
Major standard equipment: Vinyl front bench seat, forward facing 3rd seat w/divided 2nd seat on 3-seat wagon, full-floor carpeting, hidden storage compartment, Glide-Away tailgate, power tailgate window, LH and RH rear view mirrors, fendermounted three-section rectangular "ventiport" ornaments, deluxe wheel covers, and LR78 × 15 BSW tires.

Measurements

Wheelbase	127.0"
Length	231.8"
Width	79.9"
Height	58.4"
Legroom — front	42.1"
Legroom — rear	39.4"
Headroom — front	39.6"
Headroom — rear	39.3"
Cargo capacity (cu. ft.)	105.7
Fuel capacity (gals.)	NA

1975

Models Available

	Model No.	Base MSRP	Change from LY	Shipping Wt. (lbs.)	Model Year Production	Change from LY
Estate Wagon 4-Door, 2-S. Wagon	R35	$5,447	+8.53%	5055	4,128	-9.89%
Estate Wagon 4-Door, 3-S. Wagon	R45	$5,591	+8.29%	5135	9,612	-2.23%
TOTALS		*Avg. price* $5,519	+8.41%		*Production* 13,740	-4.66%

Electra

"A luxury car of the fine quality you expect from Buick."

Nameplate year of origin: 1959.
Current bodystyle lifespan: 1971 through 1976.
Predecessor to this model: Electra (1969 to 1970).
Replacement for this model: Electra 225 (1977 to 1984).
Percentage of division's production: 18.57%.
Corporate siblings: Cadillac Calais, Cadillac deVille, and Oldsmobile Ninety-Eight.
Primary competition: Chrysler New Yorker and Mercury Grand Marquis.
Notable changes: New greenhouse area and revised front and rear styling.
Major standard equipment: Cloth front bench seat (sedan) and cloth notchback front bench seat (coupe), fold-down front seat armrest, cut-pile carpeting, simulated woodgrain appliqués on door panels and instrument panel, door pull straps, carpeted lower door panels, power windows, electronic digital quartz clock, custom steering wheel, custom safety belts, remote-control LH rear view mirror, fender-mounted 4-section rectangular "ventiport" ornaments, bodyside protection molding, wheel opening moldings, full-length rocker panel molding, rear fender skirts, super deluxe wheel covers, and JR78 × 15 BSW tires. Limited adds: Limited cloth 60/40 notchback front seat w/fold-down center armrest, two-way power seat adjustment, combination dome and reading lamp (sedan), and wider rocker panel moldings.

Measurements

Wheelbase	127.0"
Length	233.4"
Width	79.9"
Height	55.1"
Legroom — front	42.2"
Legroom — rear	40.8"
Headroom — front	39.3"
Headroom — rear	38.2"
Cargo capacity (cu. ft.)	20.3
Fuel capacity (gals.)	NA

Models Available

	Model No.	Base MSRP	Change from LY	Shipping Wt. (lbs.)	Model Year Production	Change from LY
Electra 225 2-Dr. Hardtop Coupe	V37	$6,041	+11.09%	4582	16,145	+6.93%
Electra 225 4-Dr. Hardtop Sedan	V39	$6,201	+11.73%	4706	27,357	-5.95%

	Model No.	Base MSRP	Change from LY	Shipping Wt. (lbs.)	Model Year Production	Change from LY
Electra Limited 2-Dr. Hdtp. Cpe.	X37	$6,352	+7.92%	4633	17,650	+9.72%
Electra Limited 4-Dr. Hdtp. Sdn.	X39	$6,516	+10.05%	4762	33,778	+12.40%
TOTALS		Avg. price $6,278	+12.68%		Production 94,930	-4.51%

Riviera

"A luxury car of a most personal nature."

Nameplate year of origin: 1963 (1949 as designation for hardtop models).
Current bodystyle lifespan: 1971 through 1976.
Predecessor to this model: Riviera (1966 to 1970).
Replacement for this model: Riviera (1977 to 1978).
Percentage of division's production: 3.39%.
Corporate siblings: Cadillac Eldorado and Oldsmobile Toronado.
Primary competition: Ford Thunderbird.
Notable changes: Revised front end styling and trim and detail changes.
Major standard equipment: Cloth notchback front seat w/fold-down center armrest, cut-pile carpeting, simulated woodgrain appliqué on door panels and I/P, door pull handle, power windows, electronic digital quartz clock, custom steering wheel, tilt steering wheel, light package (ashtray, courtesy, glove compartment and trunk), LH remote-control rear view mirror, dual exhaust, front bumper guards, deluxe wheel covers, and JR78 × 15 BSW tires.

Measurements

Wheelbase	122.0"
Length	223.0"
Width	80.0"
Height	53.7"
Legroom — front	42.2"
Legroom — rear	35.4"
Headroom — front	38.1"
Headroom — rear	37.1"
Cargo capacity (cu. ft.)	15.1
Fuel capacity (gals.)	NA

Models Available

	Model No.	Base MSRP	Change from LY	Shipping Wt. (lbs.)	Model Year Production	Change from LY
Riviera 2-Door Hardtop	Z87	$6,420	+13.07%	4539	17,306	-14.02%
TOTALS		Avg. price $6,420	+13.07%		Production 17,306	-14.02%

CADILLAC

"1975 Cadillac ... a standard for the World in American-built cars."

For the third year in a row, Cadillacs were given significant updates in both styling and standard equipment. Of course in the mid–1970s environment of inflation, prices also reached new heights for post-war Cadillac models, surpassing those of the ultra-luxury 1957–1960 Eldorado Broughams. Still, Cadillac sales increased as did those of other luxury brands, and Cadillac production surpassed that of American Motors, a position that AMC would never reclaim.

The front end styling of all Cadillacs was completely new, utilizing an egg-crate design that recurred within the bumper. Above the bumper, a wide band of chrome ran across the top and down the sides of the grille and, on all but the Eldorado, continued along the top edge of the bumper, beneath the headlights, and around the front fender corner to the front wheel opening. Also common to all Cadillacs was the introduction of dual rectangular headlights. On the Eldorado, parking/turn signal lamps were mounted into the lower bumper area in alignment with the headlights, as well as a set mounted in the upper portion of the vertical front fender fins, while the bumper itself fitted under the lamps on the pointed fender end. The rest of the line used more conventional rectangular shaped parking/turn signal lamps which wrapped around the squared off front fenders and also housed the cornering lights on the fender side. At the back end, all models used lamps set into the vertical pseudo-tailfin that capped the rear quarter panels, and also horizontally mounted brake lights between the decklid and rear bumper.

New window treatments graced most models, with the Calais coupe and Coupe deVille getting large rear quarter windows, and the Calais sedan and Sedan deVille using a nearly triangular rear quarter window, which mimicked the appearance of the early 1960s Cadillac 6-window sedans and hardtops. Eldorado coupes were given a rear quarter window design that was rectangular in shape, except across the bottom from the rear edge of the door where it ran upwards, paralleling the bodyside kick-up line. The bodysides of all Cadillacs this year were devoid of chrome, other than rocker panel and wheel opening trim and the requisite vinyl bodyside molding to guard against door dings in parking lots. Arguably they were the best looking of General Motors' trio of C-body cars for this year.

Interiors were given new door panel designs and many new upholstery choices ranging from the Morgan plaid upholstery used in the entry-level Calais models, to the delicate looking Maharajah upholstery in deVilles, and the softer, more supple leathers available in all models. Instrument panels continued the new theme introduced for 1974, with a central point around the steering column for gauges, radio and climate controls near the center of the dash, and an upper-level warning lamp system that extended across the width of the car. All cars had rear seat fold-down center armrests for more traveling comfort. Added standard features this year included the 500 CID V8 engine previously used only in the Eldorado, automatically controlled air conditioning and climate control as well as AM/FM radio, power door locks, steel-belted radial tires, and light monitors for all Cadillac models. A final note, the Sixty-Special and Seventy-Five series designations were officially dropped from the Fleetwood Brougham sedan and the Fleetwood Limousine and nine-passenger sedan models after more than 35 years for the former, and 40 years for the latter, in the Cadillac line.

Calais 2-Door Hardtop Coupe

Coupe deVille 2-Door Hardtop Coupe

Eldorado 2-Door Convertible

Fleetwood Brougham 4-Door Sedan

Fleetwood Limousine

Eldorado 2-Door Hardtop Coupe interior with Mosaic check cloth upholstery

Model year production: 263,403, up 9.77% from 1974.
Domestic market share: 3.50% (10th place).
Base price range: $8,184 to $14,557.
Cadillac average base price: $10,592, up 11.70%.
Introduction date: September 19, 1974.
Assembly plants: Linden, NJ (E); and Detroit, MI (Q).
Data plate identification (VIN): Thirteen digit code read as follows: First digit indicates division (6 = Cadillac); second through fourth digits indicate series and body style (model number in model charts); fifth digit is engine code (see powertrain chart); sixth digit indicates model year (5 = 1975); seventh digit indicates assembly plant (see list above); remaining digits are sequential with beginning number of 100001. *Example:* 6D49S5Q100001 is a 1975 Cadillac Sedan deVille 4-Door Hardtop, with 500 CID, 4-bbl. (or EFI) V8 engine, serial number 100001, built in Detroit, MI.

Powertrains

Engine	Net HP	Engine Code	Transmission Availability[1]		Calais & DeVille	Fleetwood 75 (Sdn. & Limo.)	Eldorado
500 CID (8.2L), 4-bbl., V8	190	S	3-speed Turbo Hydra-matic		S	S	S
				MPG:	11/16	11/14	11/16
				Calif.	11/14	10/13	11/14
500 CID (8.2L), EFI, V8	215	S	3-speed Turbo Hydra-matic		$600	$600	$600
				MPG:	11/16	11/14	11/16

Major Options

	Calais	deVille	Eldorado	Fleetwood Brougham	Fleetwood Seventy-Five
Automatic climate control	S	S	S	S	S
Electric rear window defogger	$73	$73	$73	$73	S
Controlled cycle windshield wiper	$27	$27	$27	$27	$27
Tilt and telescope steering wheel	$98	$98	$98	$98	$98
Cruise control	$100	$100	$100	$100	$100
Twilight Sentinel	$48	$48	$48	$48	S
Soft Ray tinted glass	S	S	S	S	S
Leather upholstery[1]	—	$200	$212	$212	—
Dual Comfort front seat	—	$103	$103	S	—
Power front seat, 6-way bench	$125	S	S	—	$93[2]
Power front seat, 6-way Dual Comfort, driver/passenger	—	$125	$125	S	—
Lighted vanity mirror[3]	$45	$45	$45	$45	$45
Illuminated entry system	$50	$50	$50	$50	$50
AM/FM stereo, signal seeking	$147	$147	S	S	$275[4]
AM/FM stereo w/8-track tape	$239	$239	$93	$93	$239
Remote control trunk release/lock	$62	$62	$62	$62	$62
Padded vinyl top[5]	$156	$156	$162	S	$745
Electric sunroof[5, 6]	$668	$668	$668	$668	—
Theft-Deterrent system	$108	$108	$108	$108	$108
Lamp monitor system	S	S	S	S	S
Fuel monitor system	$25	$25	$25	$25	$25
Air Cushion restraint system	$300	$300	$300[5]	$300	—
Track Master anti-skid control	$250	$250	$250	$250	$250
Automatic level control	$84	$84	$84	$84	S
Special turbine style wheel discs	$45	$45	—	$45	$45
Steel-belted radial WSW tires	S	S	S	S	S

Popular Option Groups & Packages

	Calais	deVille	Eldorado	Fleetwood Brougham	Fleetwood Seventy-Five
Brougham d'Elegance package	—	—	—	$784	—
Custom Cabriolet package, coupe	—	$236	$413	—	—
de Ville d'Elegance package	—	$350	—	—	—
Fleetwood Talisman package	—	—	—	$1,788	—

—= Not Available; S = Standard equipment. All radios include rear seat speaker and power antenna. [1]Standard on Eldorado convertible. Available on Calais and Seventy-Five by special order only. [2]Not available on Limousine. [3]Price is for one side (driver or passenger) only. Not available on driver's side of Eldorado convertible. [4]Fleetwood Seventy-Five models include rear seat controls. [5]Not available on Eldorado convertible. [6]Electric glass Astroroof available on the same models for $843. Available for Fleetwood Seventy-Five models on special order.

Paint Colors

	Code		Code		Code
Cotillion White	11	Jennifer Blue	24	Mandarin Orange metallic	34
Georgian Silver metallic	13	Commodore Blue metallic	29	Firethorn metallic	36
Vapor Gray	15	Lido Green metallic	30	Pueblo Beige metallic	38
Sable Black	19	Dunbarton Green	32	Jasper Green	44

	Code		Code		Code
Inveraray Green metallic	49	Roxena Red	77	Emberust Firemist metallic*	98
Bombay Yellow	52	Rosewood metallic	78	Cerise Firemist metallic*	99
Tarragon Gold metallic	54	Gossamer Blue Firemist metallic*	92		
Knickerbocker Tan	65	Galloway Green Firemist metallic*	94	*Firemist paint available for $138 extra.	
Roan Brown metallic	69	Cameo Rosewood Firemist metallic*	97		

1975

Calais

"New flair for a most attractive value."

Nameplate year of origin: 1965.
Current bodystyle lifespan: 1971 through 1976.
Predecessor to this model: Calais (1969 to 1970).
Replacement for this model: None.
Percentage of division's production: 3.15%.
Corporate siblings: Buick Electra 225, Cadillac deVille, and Oldsmobile 98.
Primary competition: Chrysler New Yorker Brougham.
Notable changes: Revised front-end and greenhouse area and minor trim changes.
Major standard equipment: Morgan plaid cloth w/vinyl bolsters or all vinyl front bench seat w/fold-down center armrest, door pull assist straps, electric clock, power windows, power door locks, automatic climate control, LH remote-control rear view mirror, front cornering lights, rear wheel fender skirts, wheel opening moldings, full wheel covers, and LR78 × 15 WSW tires.

Measurements

Wheelbase	130.0"
Length	230.7"
Width	79.8"
Height	55.5"
Legroom — front	42.0"
Legroom — rear	NA
Headroom — front	39.2"
Headroom — rear	38.2"
Cargo capacity (cu. ft.)	19.3
Fuel capacity (gals.)	27.0

Models Available

	Model No.	Base MSRP	Change from LY	Shipping Wt. (lbs.)	Model Year Production	Change from LY
Calais 2-Door Hardtop Coupe	C47	$8,148	+11.03%	5003	5,800	+30.37%
Calais 4-Door Hardtop	C49	$8,377	+11.03%	5087	2,500	+7.57%
TOTALS		*Avg. price* $8,281	+11.03%		*Production* 8,300	+22.55%

deVille

"The new version of the most popular luxury car in America."

Nameplate year of origin: 1959 (series); 1949 (as Hardtop designation).
Current bodystyle lifespan: 1971 through 1976.
Predecessor to this model: deVille (1969 to 1970).
Replacement for this model: deVille (1977 to 1984).
Percentage of division's production: 65.90%.
Corporate siblings: Buick Electra 225, Cadillac Calais, and Oldsmobile 98.
Primary competition: Chrysler Imperial and Lincoln Continental.
Notable changes: Revised front-end and greenhouse area and minor trim changes.
Major standard equipment: Maharajah cloth or Manhattan velour w/vinyl bolsters and front and rear seat center armrests, 6-way power front seat adjuster, cut-pile carpeting, hinged door pull assist handles, courtesy lights, courtesy lamp/assist strap combination on B-pillar of 2-doors, electric clock, power windows, power door locks, automatic climate control, LH remote-control rear view mirror, front cornering lights, rear wheel fender skirts, wheel opening moldings, rocker panel moldings, full wheel covers, and LR78 × 15 WSW tires.

Measurements

Wheelbase	130.0"
Length	230.7"
Width	79.8"
Height	55.5"
Legroom — front	42.0"
Legroom — rear	NA
Headroom — front	39.2"
Headroom — rear	38.2"
Cargo capacity (cu. ft.)	19.3
Fuel capacity (gals.)	27.0

Models Available

	Model No.	Base MSRP	Change from LY	Shipping Wt. (lbs.)	Model Year Production	Change from LY
Coupe deVille 2-Door Hardtop	D47	$8,600	+9.32%	5049	110,218	-1.77%
Sedan deVille 4-Door Hardtop	D49	$8,801	+8.65%	5146	63,352	+4.85%
TOTALS		Avg. price $8,701	+8.98%		Production 173,570	+0.55%

Eldorado

"One of the world's most exciting cars.
Including the one of a kind Eldorado convertible."

Nameplate year of origin: 1953.
Current bodystyle lifespan: 1971 through 1978.
Predecessor to this model: Fleetwood Eldorado (1967 to 1970).
Replacement for this model: Eldorado (1979 to 1985).
Percentage of division's production: 16.99%.
Corporate siblings: Buick Riviera and Oldsmobile Toronado.
Primary competition: Lincoln Continental Mark IV.
Notable changes: Revised front and rear end, revised greenhouse area, and minor trim changes.
Major standard equipment: Choice of Metamora plaid fabric, Mosaic check fabric or Monticello velour w/vinyl bolsters front bench seat w/fold-down center armrest (hardtop), Sierra grain leather front bench seat w/fold-down center armrest (convertible), 6-way power seat adjuster, cut-pile carpeting, hinged door pull assist handles, courtesy lights, quartz digital clock, power windows, power door locks, automatic climate control, LH remote-control rear view mirror, front cornering lights, wheel opening moldings, rocker panel moldings, full wheel covers, and LR78 × 15 BSW tires.

Measurements

Wheelbase	126.3"
Length	224.1"
Width	79.8"
Height	NA
Legroom — front	43.0"
Legroom — rear	NA
Headroom — front	38.1"
Headroom — rear	37.1"
Cargo capacity (cu. ft.)	NA
Fuel capacity (gals.)	27.0

Models Available

	Model No.	Base MSRP	Change from LY	Shipping Wt. (lbs.)	Model Year Production	Change from LY
Eldorado 2-Door Hardtop	L47	$9,935	+9.06%	5108	35,802	+9.11%
Eldorado 2-Door Convertible	L67	$10,354	+9.72%	5167	8,950	+17.76%
TOTALS		Avg. price $10,145	+9.39%		Production 44,752	+10.74%

Fleetwood Brougham

"One of the world's great sedans ... gets even better."

Nameplate year of origin: 1966.
Current bodystyle lifespan: 1971 through 1976.
Predecessor to this model: Fleetwood Sixty-Special (1969 to 1970).
Replacement for this model: Fleetwood Brougham (1977 to 1984).
Percentage of division's sales volume: 7.61%.
Corporate siblings: None.
Primary competition: None.
Notable changes: Revised front-end and greenhouse area and minor trim changes.
Major standard equipment: Choice of Moselle knit fabric, Monticello velour or soft leather Dual Comfort front seat, driver side 2-way power seat adjuster, front and rear seat fold-down center armrests, cut-pile carpeting, rear seat carpeted foot rests, hinged door pull assist handles, front passenger reading light, courtesy lights, quartz

Measurements

Wheelbase	133.0"
Length	233.7"
Width	79.8"
Height	55.5"
Legroom — front	42.0"
Legroom — rear	NA
Headroom — front	39.3"
Headroom — rear	38.3"
Cargo capacity (cu. ft.)	19.3
Fuel capacity (gals.)	27.0

digital clock, power windows, power door locks, automatic climate control, LH remote-control rear view mirror, padded vinyl roof, front cornering lights, rear wheel fender skirts, wheel opening moldings, rocker panel moldings w/upper ridge, full wheel covers, and LR78 × 15 WSW tires.

Models Available

	Model No.	Base MSRP	Change from LY	Shipping Wt. (lbs.)	Model Year Production	Change from LY
Fleetwood Brougham 4-Door Sedan	B69	$10,414	+9.20%	5242	18,755	+2.77%
TOTALS		Avg. price $10,414	+9.20%		Production 18,755	+2.77%

1975

Fleetwood
"The flagships."

Nameplate year of origin: 1927 (models using Fleetwood bodies); 1935 (Fleetwood series).
Current bodystyle lifespan: 1971 through 1976.
Predecessor to this model: Fleetwood Seventy-Five (1969 to 1970).
Replacement for this model: Fleetwood Limousine (1977 to 1984).
Percentage of division's sales volume: 0.63%.
Corporate siblings: None.
Primary competition: None.
Notable changes: Revised front-end and minor trim changes.
Major standard equipment: Choice of Potomac cloth in graystone, Medici crushed velour in dark blue, or Moselle knit cloth in black, 2-way power front seat adjuster, front and back seat fold-down center armrests, cut-pile carpeting, full-width folding seats (rearward facing for three additional passengers), rear seat carpeted foot rests, hinged door pull assist handles, power windows, power door locks, dual automatic climate control system (front and rear), courtesy lights, electric clock, passenger control panel (controls power windows, reading lights, automatic climate control, and the glass partition in the Limousine), automatic level control, LH and RH remote-control rear view mirror, front cornering lights, rear wheel fender skirts, wheel opening moldings, full-length rocker panel moldings, full wheel covers, and LR78 × 15 BSW tires.

Measurements

Wheelbase	151.5"
Length	252.2"
Width	80.0"
Height	NA
Legroom — front	NA
Legroom — rear	NA
Headroom — front	NA
Headroom — rear	NA
Cargo capacity (cu. ft.)	NA
Fuel capacity (gals.)	27.0

Models Available

	Model No.	Base MSRP	Change from LY	Shipping Wt. (lbs.)	Model Year Production	Change from LY
Fleetwood 4-Door Nine-passenger Sdn.	F23	$14,218	+8.37%	5720	876	-2.12%
Fleetwood 4-Door Limousine	F33	$14,557	+9.83%	5862	795	-20.90%
TOTALS		Avg. price $14,388	+9.10%		Production 1,671	-12.05%

CHEVROLET
"Chevrolet makes sense for America."

Nearly half of Chevy's 1975 model lineup had a noticeable styling change of some type. In addition there was a new series named Monza. Borrowing its nameplate from the sporty Corvair model of 1960 through 1969, the Monza was based on the Vega's H-body platform and came in two distinct models. Introduced at the beginning of the model year was a Monza 2+2 Hatchback with sports car styling and sleek hatchback profile; then, in the spring of 1975, a Monza Towne Coupe appeared with a more formal appearance, having a notchback body design, an upright front end and upright roofline. The Monza looked to be a head-to-head competitor for Ford's Mustang II, introduced in 1974, but by year's end, sales and production would prove it to be less popular. One bright spot was that the Monza 2+2 was selected as the "1975 Car of the Year" by *Motor Trend* magazine for its overall combination of ride, handling ease, performance, economy and styling. The coveted award meant a lot of comparisons in the media with the 1974 winner, the Ford Mustang II. Overall for Chevrolet, it would be another year of big production declines, as the once popular full-size models of Chevy, Ford and Plymouth all had big declines, but the largest General Motors division would retain its number one spot in industry sales and production for another season.

First to arrive in the new Monza series, the sporty 2+2 Hatchback coupe came with a standard Vega four-cylinder engine or an optional new 4.3 litre V8 that was the smallest Chevrolet V8 engine ever. Both engines were relatively lightweight and in keeping with the sporty feel of the 2+2. Styling of the 2+2, and the similar S hatchback coupe added at mid-year, was sleek from front to rear. Front styling used a sloped, body-color urethane panel with dual rectangular headlights set in the outer ends, and a body-color slot-style grille in between. The grille used two rows divided into four sections above the bumper, and below the bumper were four additional slots, as well as parking/turn signal lights set below the headlights. Bumpers were aluminum with black impact strips, and added small bumper guards below the bumper. Bodysides were smooth with a feature line midway up running between the wheel openings, and encompassing the rear of the car just above the rear bumper. At the back were horizontal taillights that wrapped around the rear quarter end, and ended in a point on the side. Gas charged struts supported the liftgate that housed a large rear window. In the greenhouse area, the doors opened slightly into the roof, and used hidden drip rails for improved aerodynamics, while the fixed rear quarter windows tapered to a point. Like its corporate relations, the Buick Skyhawk and Oldsmobile Starfire, the Monza used a louvered B-pillar that was part of the power ventilation system, which helped circulate interior air when the windows were closed.

The new Towne Coupe that debuted at mid-year had completely different styling from the S and 2+2 models. The coupe was intentionally designed to having "flowing and uncluttered" lines, and have a "cleanness and neatness of line that make it distinctive in this size of sensibly priced car," according to Chevrolet promotional materials. The upright front end was in stark contrast to the hatchback's sleek and sporty design. Using single round headlamps set in an over-

sized chrome bezel on each front fender end, with a horizontal crosshatch grille that was four rows high and eight columns across with parking/turn signal lights set in the outer section of each end, the look was far from the typical "econobox." Bodysides were somewhat similar to the hatchbacks, but using an entirely different greenhouse area of course, as the coupe had a formal roofline with large opera windows, and a standard vinyl top. Also the coupe used traditional doors with drip rails running above the window. At the rear of the coupe were large, somewhat square taillights with the outer edge slanted to follow the slope of the bodyside, and having vertical backup lights on the inner end. The flat black rear panel housed the license tag mount in the center, and sat above a simple box style bumper.

Inside the two body styles of the Monza series differed as well, with each having its own unique instrument panel. The coupe used a small driver's pod behind the steering wheel housing the gauges, and then a secondary "cove" set into the middle or the instrument panel housing ventilation controls, and vertical rectangular air vents. Below the entire area was a lower panel angled up towards the driver with light and wiper controls to the left of the steering column, and cigar lighter and radio to the right. The hatchbacks had a large driver's pod housing the full set of gauges, and the lower angled panel housed the ventilation and radio controls to the right of the steering column, with other controls to the left. Air vents near the center of the car were horizontal units and placed outside of the driver's pod. Otherwise, the entire Monza line shared similar upholstery and trim designs.

The popular compact Nova was again restyled, this time with a more dramatic effect than the rather minor restyling of 1973. While still built on the 111-inch wheelbase introduced for 1968, and still basically the same size as the 1974 version, both inside and out, the new Nova looked completely different. Most apparent were the smoother bodysides and flowing lines, particularly on the two-door models, as they retained a semi-fastback roofline. The sedans received a more formal and angular roofline, providing a more modern appearance. Up front was a slight curve to the new front end, with single round headlamps set in each end, their bezels rising slightly above a full-width grille in between. The grille was in six sections, divided in the center by a vertical chrome bar, and sectioned horizontally by two chrome bars, with the entire grille surrounded by a chrome strip. Within each of the six sections were egg-crate inserts. At each end of the grille, just inboard of the headlights, were vertical parking/turn signal lights. At the rear was a panel that slanted slightly from the decklid opening to the rear bumper, holding dual unit taillights side by side in each end. Each unit was divided into three horizontal sections, with the center of the inner light housing the backup lights. A new top-line LN model was introduced, with more luxurious appointments than the Nova Custom and available only in the coupe and sedan model. Also new at mid-year, for one year only, was a stripped-down basic Nova coupe named the Nova S, with rubber floor mats, all black interiors and no exterior chrome except on the front window. Full details of the standard equipment for both models are included in the Nova section that follows.

Mid-size Chevelle Malibu models wore a new vertical bar grille with ten columns across, each column containing an egg-crate insert design nine rows high and four columns across. Around back all coupes and sedans had wider but shorter rectangular taillights set further to the outside of a new rear panel, with backup lights set to the inside of the lens. A new trunk lid was straight across at the rear end, rather than having a raised area at each end to accommodate the taillights as used on the past two years. The sporty Laguna Type S-3 added a sportier, slanting style grille urethane front header panel, creating a look that followed the slant of the new Monza 2+2, and the Camaro's sporty look. For the Laguna, a four-section grille, two high and two per side, carried an egg-crate insert within each section that was five rows high and fourteen columns across. Parking lights were set behind the outer ends of the upper sections, and the Laguna Type S-3 name badge was on the lower section on the driver's side. Otherwise the mid-size line was mostly unchanged. This would be the last year for the 454 CID V8 in mid-size Chevys.

Similar changes were seen with the Monte Carlo, which had a new vertical crosshatch grille design, having seven columns across and two rows high, with each section housing three vertical bars. Another row continued into the oval openings in the bumper on each side of the center license plate mount. At the back, a new taillight design was still positioned vertically, but was more angular and now wrapped over slightly onto the rear quarter panel end. The lights were divided into four sections by horizontal body-colored strips.

The full-size Chevrolet line underwent a revamping, with all four-door hardtop models adding a triangular rear quarter window and sedans adding a fixed quarter window in the rear door. Both the Impala and Caprice Classic lines gained a Landau coupe, which added a padded vinyl landau top to the fixed rear quarter window roofline, also used by the Impala Custom and Caprice Classic coupes. All models used different front ends with the Impala and Bel Air models utilizing the basic 1974 Caprice front end with a different grille insert in a horizontal crosshatch pattern eight columns across and twelve rows high. At the back, seemingly larger taillights were used, although still three units on the Impala and two units on the Bel Air. Station wagons still used essentially the same rear end design with vertically divided lenses. Caprice Classic models adopted a completely different front-end design that brought the dual round headlights, housed in divided chrome bezels, back closer to the fender on the ends, and had the grille protruding farther, creating a gently curved front end as seen from above. The grille itself was again outlined with chrome on the sides and top, and had a vertical crosshatch pattern being three rows high and thirty columns across. At the back three-section horizontal taillamps were still used, but this year they wrapped around the rear quarter panel edge, and each section was individually chrome outlined with a body color strip dividing them, and a horizontal chrome strip across the center of each. Interiors and powertrains for all cars were mostly carried over.

The subcompact Vega, known for making changes only as needed, followed the same formula again, with styling looking exactly the same as in 1974. Vega ads still touted more than 250 changes for the year; most were to meet emission or safety requirements, but some were useful new options like a tilt steering wheel and AM/FM stereo radio. However, a long-awaited newcomer to the Vega line, the Cosworth Vega, appeared for 1975 after an 18-month delay that was mainly due to an EPA testing failure. The Cosworth boasted a high-performance two-litre, four-cylinder aluminum engine with an electronic fuel injection system, dual overhead camshafts, and stainless steel exhaust header, putting out as much horsepower as Chevy's new small V8 engine. Special suspension components were developed, and other exterior features such as black paint with gold trim and exclusive cast aluminum wheels made the Cosworth easily identifiable. A list of Cosworth equipment is included within the Vega details.

Having few styling changes this year were the Camaro and Corvette. A 1975 Camaro could be identified most easily by its new wrap-around rear window, and from the front, the Camaro logo was moved from the grille to the header panel, directly above the center of the grille, but otherwise changes amounted to the required equipment to meet emissions standards, plus the addition of radial tires, front disc brakes and a new 21 gallon gas tank as standard equipment.

Corvette changes visually amounted to standard front and rear bumper guards. However, a big disappointment to performance enthusiasts was the discontinuation of the big 454 CID V8 engine in the Corvette, a necessary move to meet the tougher emission standards and to improve fuel economy. This would be the "final" year for Corvette convertible production, after a 23-year model run, but unbeknownst to Corvette faithful at the time, the convertible would be back for the 1986 model year.

Bel Air 4-Door Sedan

Caprice Classic 2-Door Convertible

Chevelle Malibu 4-Door Station Wagon

Corvette Stingray 2-Door Coupe
with Corvette Stingray convertible, rear

Impala 4-Door Station Wagon

Camaro 2-Door Coupe with Rally Sport package

Caprice Classic 4-Door Hardtop Sport Sedan

Chevelle Malibu Classic 4-Door
Colonnade Hardtop Sedan

Corvette coupe interior with
optional leather upholstery

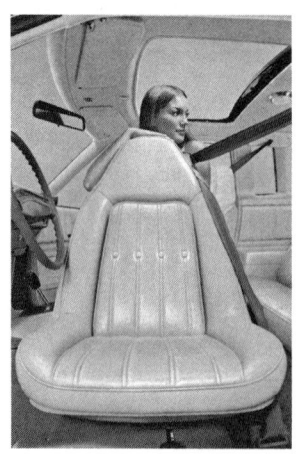

Monte Carlo interior with optional swivel bucket
seats and Sky Roof

Camaro Type LT 2-Door Coupe

Chevelle Laguna Type S-3 2-Door
Colonnade Hardtop Coupe

Chevelle Malibu Classic Landau
2-Door Colonnade Hardtop Coupe

Impala Custom Coupe 2-Door Hardtop

Monte Carlo Landau 2-Door Hardtop Coupe

Monza 2+2 2-Door Hatchback Coupe

Monza 2+2 interior

Monza 2-Door Towne Coupe

Monza 2-Door Towne Coupe

Monza S 2-Door Hatchback Coupe

Nova 2-Door Hatchback Coupe

Nova 2-Door Hatchback Coupe with SS package

Nova LN 4-Door Sedan

Nova LN interior

Vega 2-Door Kammback Wagon
with GT package

Vega 2-Door Notchback Coupe

Vega Cosworth 2-Door Hatchback Coupe

Vega Cosworth 2-Door Hatchback Coupe

Model year production: 1,763,561, down 23.84% from 1974.
Domestic market share: 25.01% (1st place).
Base price range: $2,786 to $6,797.
Chevrolet average base price: $4,229, up 16.35%.
Introduction date: September 1974. Laguna Type S-3 introduced December 1974; Cosworth Vega introduced April 17, 1975; and Monza Towne Coupe introduced April 1975.
Assembly plants: Lakewood, GA (A); Baltimore, MD (B); Southgate, CA (C); Doraville, GA (D); Framingham, MA (G); Janesville, WI (J); Kansas City/Leeds, MO (K); Van Nuys, CA (L); Norwood, OH (N); Arlington, TX (R); St. Louis, MO (S); Tarrytown, NY (T); Lordstown, OH (U); Willow Run, MI (W); Wilmington, DE (Y); Fremont, CA (Z); Oshawa, Ontario, Canada (1); and Ste. Therese, Quebec, Canada (2).

Data plate identification (VIN): Thirteen digit code read as follows: first digit indicates division (1 = Chevrolet); second through fourth digits indicate series and body style (model number in model charts); fifth digit is engine code (see powertrain chart); sixth digit indicates model year (5 = 1975); seventh digit indicates assembly plant (see list above); remaining digits are sequential with beginning number of 100001, except Chevelle, Monte Carlo and Corvette which start at 400001, and Camaro which starts at 500001. *Example:* 1S87H5N500001 is a 1975 Chevrolet Camaro Type LT 2-Door Sport Coupe, with 350 CID, 2-bbl. V8 engine, serial number 500001, built in Norwood, OH.

Powertrains

Engine	Net HP	Engine Code	Transmission Availability[1]		Vega	Monza	Camaro	Nova	Chevelle[2]	Monte Carlo & Laguna Type S-3	Full-Size Chevy	Corvette
122 CID (2.0L) DOHC, EFI, 4-cyl.	110	E	4-speed manual		S (Cosworth only)	—	—	—	—	—	—	—
				MPG:	16/29	—	—	—	—	—	—	—
			5-speed manual		$244 (Cosworth only)	—	—	—	—	—	—	—
				MPG:	NA	—	—	—	—	—	—	—
140 CID (2.3L) OHC, 1-bbl., 4-cyl.	78	A	3-speed manual		S	S[3,4]	—	—	—	—	—	—
			4-speed manual		$56	$56[3,4]	—	—	—	—	—	—
			3-speed Turbo Hydra-matic		$235	$235[3,4]	—	—	—	—	—	—
				MPG:	19/28	19/28	—	—	—	—	—	—
140 CID (2.3L) OHC, 2-bbl., 4-cyl.	87	B	3-speed manual		$50	S	—	—	—	—	—	—
			4-speed manual		$106	$56	—	—	—	—	—	—
			3-speed Turbo Hydra-matic		$285	$235	—	—	—	—	—	—
				MPG:	22/29	21/29	—	—	—	—	—	—
				Calif.	19/28	18/28	—	—	—	—	—	—
250 CID (4.1L), 1-bbl., 6-cyl.	105	D	3-speed manual		—	—	—	S (Spt. Cpe.)	S	S (Mcs, MCcs)	—	—
			3-speed Turbo Hydra-matic		—	—	—	$235 (Spt. Cpe.)	$235	$235 (Mcs, MCcs)	—	—
				MPG:	—	—	16/21	16/21	16/21	—	—	—
				Calif.	—	—	15/20	15/20	15/20	—	—	—
262 CID (4.3L), 2-bbl., V8	110	G	3-speed manual		—	—	—	$75	—	—	—	—
			4-speed manual		—	$198[3]	—	—	—	—	—	—
			3-speed Turbo Hydra-matic		—	$433[3]	—	$310	—	—	—	—
				MPG:	—	15/23	—	14/18	—	—	—	—
350 CID (5.7L), 2-bbl., V8	125		3-speed Turbo Hydra-matic		—	$[5]	—	—	—	—	—	—
				Calif.	—	15/20	—	—	—	—	—	—
350 CID (5.7L), 2-bbl., V8	145	V	3-speed manual		—	—	S (LT)/ $145 (Spt. Cpe.)	$125	$250 (Mcs, MCcs)[3]	S[3]	—	—

1975

Engine	Net HP	Engine Code	Transmission Availability[1]	Vega	Monza	Camaro	Nova	Chevelle[2]	Monte Carlo & Laguna Type S-3	Full-Size Chevy	Corvette
			3-speed Turbo Hydra-matic	—	—	$235 (LT)/$380 (Spt. Cpe.)	$360	S (Mw)/$485 (Mcs, MCcs)[3]	$235[3]	S (ex. wgns.)	—
			MPG:	—	—	14/19	14/19	13/18	13/18	12/18	—
350 CID (5.7L), 4-bbl., V8	155/165[6]	L	3-speed manual	—	—	$54 (LT)/$199 (Spt. Cpe.)	$179	$250 (Mcs, MCcs)[5]	S[5]	—	—
			4-speed manual	—	—	$275 (LT)/$418 (Spt. Cpe.)	$398	—	—	—	S
			3-speed Turbo Hydra-matic	—	—	$289 (LT)/$434 (Spt. Cpe.)	$414	S (Mw)/$485 (Mcs, MCcs)[5]	$235[5]	—	N/C
			MPG:	—	—	13/20	13/20	13/18	13/18	—	13/20
			Calif.	—	—	13/18	13/18	12/16	12/16	11/16	13/18
350 CID (5.7L), 4-bbl., V8	205	J	4-speed manual	—	—	—	—	—	—	—	$336
			4-speed manual, close-ratio	—	—	—	—	—	—	—	$456
			3-speed Turbo Hydra-matic *MPG:*	—	—	—	—	—	—	—	$456 / NA
400 CID (6.6L), 4-bbl., V8	175	U	3-speed Turbo Hydra-matic	—	—	—	—	$113 (Mw)/$598 (Mcs, MCcs)	$368	S (wgns.)/$113 (others)	—
			MPG:	—	—	—	—	13/17[7]	13/17	11/17[7]	—
454 CID (7.4L), 4-bbl., V8	215	Y	3-speed Turbo Hydra-matic	—	—	—	—	$285 (Mw)/$825 (Mcs, MCcs)[8]	$595[8]	$172 (wgns.)/$315 (others)[9]	—
			MPG:	—	—	—	—	11/16[7]	11/16	11/15[7]	—

[1]Unless otherwise specified: All 3-speed manuals are column shift. All 4- and 5-speed manuals are floor shift. All automatics are column shift, except on Vega, Monza, Camaro and Corvette. Floor shift automatic is optional on Nova, Chevelle and Monte Carlo with other specified equipment at extra cost. [2]Mcs = Malibu coupe & sedan; Mw = All Malibu wagons; MCcs = Malibu Classic coupe and sedan. [3]Not available in California. [4]Available only on Monza S. [5]Available only in California. [6]Horsepower rating on Corvette. [7]Estimated mileage ratings for station wagons are one mpg lower for both city and highway. [8]Price includes power brakes with front discs on all models. [9]$291 for all Caprice models, except Wagons.

Major Options

	Vega	Monza	Camaro	Nova	Chevelle	Monte Carlo	Full-size Chevy	Corvette
Four-season air conditioning[1]	$398	$398	$435	$435	$450	$450	$458	$490
Comfortilt steering wheel	$45	$45	$49	$49	$49	$49	$49	S
Tilt-and-telescope steering wheel	—	—	—	—	—	—	—	$82
Cruise-Master speed control	—	—	—	—	$69	$72	$72	—
Rear window defogger[2]	—	—	$41	$41	$41	$41	$42	$46
Electro-Clear rear window defogger	$60	$60	—	—	—	—	—	—
Dual sport mirrors, LH remote	$25	$25	$27	$27	$27	—	—	—

	Vega	Monza	Camaro	Nova	Chevelle	Monte Carlo	Full-size Chevy	Corvette
Soft-Ray tinted glass, all windows	$43	$43	$45	$45	$48	$51	$51	S
Power windows, 2-dr./4-dr.	—	—	$91	$91/$132	$91/$132	$91	$99/$149[3]	$93
Power door locks, 2-dr./4-dr.	—	—	$56	$36/$82	$56/$90	$56	$56/$90	—
Power front seat, w/std. seat	—	—	—	—	$113	$113	$113	—
Front bucket seats, w/console[4]	$	S	$68	$155	$180	$180	—	S
Leather upholstery	—	$196	—	—	—	—	—	—
Rear facing third seat, wagons	—	—	—	—	$145	—	—	—
AM radio	$63	$63	$69	$69	$69	$69	$69	—
AM/FM stereo	$213	$213	$233	$233	$233	$233	$233	$284
AM/FM stereo w/8-track tape	—	—	$363	—	$363	$363	$363	—
Vinyl top, full[5]	$79	S	$87	$87	$96	$123	$109	$83
Vinyl top, landau[6]	—	—	—	—	$106	$106	—	—
Sky Roof (sunroof), power[7]	—	—	—	—	$350	$350	—	—
Power steering, variable-ratio	$111	$111	S	$129	$129[8]	S	S	$129
Power brakes, w/front disc	$51	$51	$55	$55	$55[9]	S	S	$55[10]
Wire wheel covers	—	—	$89	—	$89	$75	$89	—
Rally wheels w/trim rings	$30	—	$46	$46	$46	$46	—	S
Forged aluminum wheels	—	$153	—	—	—	—	—	—
Turbine I wheels	—	—	$111	$110	$111	—	—	—
Turbine II aluminum wheels	—	—	—	—	—	$115	—	—
WSW tires	$32	$32	$33	$33	$34	$34	$35	$35

Popular Option Groups & Packages

	Vega	Monza	Camaro	Nova	Chevelle	Monte Carlo	Full-size Chevy	Corvette
Auxiliary lighting package	—	$12	$23	$22	$28	$26	$22	—
Custom interior package	$134	—	—	—	—	—	—	$154
Custom exterior package	$82	—	—	—	—	—	—	—
Décor group	$32	—	—	—	—	—	—	—
Exterior décor package	—	—	—	$73	$49	—	—	—
GT package	$425	—	—	—	—	—	—	—
Gymkhana suspension package	—	—	$112	—	—	—	—	$7
Interior décor/Quiet sound group	—	—	$35	$39	—	—	$44	—
Off Road package	—	—	—	—	—	—	—	$403
Rally Sport package	—	—	$238	—	—	—	—	—
Special Custom interior package	—	—	—	—	—	—	—	—
Special instrumentation package	$67	—	$88	—	$88	$71	—	S
Sports décor package	—	—	$42	—	—	—	—	—
SS package	—	—	—	$178	—	—	—	—
Style trim group	—	—	$55	—	—	—	—	—

—= Not Available; S = Standard equipment. [1]Requires optional power steering and power brakes on Chevelle, which may be standard on some models. Comfortron air conditioning with automatic temperature control is available for $535 on Bel Air, Impala and Caprice. [2]Blower type defogger. [3]Power windows not available on Bel Air. Price for power windows on Impala Sport coupe and Caprice convertible is the same as for four-door models. [4]Bucket seats standard on Vega, Monza and Camaro, with console being optional except on Monza Towne Coupe. Available only on Nova coupes or hatchbacks. Swivel bucket seats available only on Chevelle coupes and Monte Carlo. Vega console is a "mini" console. [5]Requires optional removable top on Corvette convertible for $267. Price is $138 on full-size Chevrolet wagons. Not available on Chevelle station wagons or Monza 2+2. Standard on Vega LX coupe and Monza Towne Coupe. [6]Standard on Monte Carlo Landau coupe, Malibu Classic Landau coupe, and Vega LX Notchback. Available on Malibu coupes and Monte Carlo. [7]Sky Roof pull-back vinyl sunroof opening on Nova two-door models only. Power operated available only on coupe models. [8]Power steering is standard on V8-equipped Malibu models and on Laguna Type S-3. [9]Standard on station wagons. [10]Power front and rear disc brakes.

Paint Colors*

	Code		Code		Code
Classic White[1]	10	Silver Blue metallic[4]	21	Firethorn metallic[3]	36
Antique White	11	Corvette Bright Blue metallic[1]	22	Mahogany metallic[3]	37
Metallic Silver[3,5,6,7]	13	Medium Blue[5,7]	24	Medium Green[5,7,8]	44
Corvette Silver Mist metallic[1]	13	Bright Blue metallic[8]	26	Light Green metallic[2,3]	45
Light Gray[5,7]	15	Corvette Steel Blue metallic[1]	27	Corvette Bright Green metallic[1]	42
Medium Gray metallic[4]	16	Midnight Blue metallic[5,7]	29	Dark Green metallic[2,3,4,5,7]	49
Tuxedo Black[6,7]	19	Dark Blue metallic[3]	35	Cream Beige[2,3,4,5,7]	50

	Code		Code
Bright Yellow[2,3,4,5,8]	51	Corvette Orange Flame metallic[1]	70
Sandstone[2,5,7]	55	Medium Red[7]	72
Corvette Bright Yellow[1]	56	Dark Red metallic[1,2,5,6,7]	74
Dark Sandstone metallic[5]	58	Light Red[2,3,4,5,8]	75
Dark Brown metallic[7]	59	Mille Miglia Red[1]	76
Light Saddle metallic[5,7,8]	63	Burgundy metallic[4]	79
Medium Orange metallic[5,6,7,8]	64	Orange metallic[2,3,4]	80
Bronze metallic[2,3]	66		
Corvette Medium Saddle metallic[1]	67		

In two-tone combinations, the first two digits indicate lower color; the next two digits are the upper color.

Two-tone available at extra cost on Nova, $31; Malibu cars, $31; full-size $31. *Colors listed with no footnotes are available on all models except Corvette. [1]Available on Corvette. [2]Available on Vega. [3]Available on Monza Towne Coupe. [4]Available on Monza 2+2 Hatchback. [5]Available on Camaro and Nova. Code 26 Bright Blue metallic not available on Camaro. [6]Available on Laguna Type S-3. [7]Available on all Chevelle Malibu, Monte Carlo and full-size Chevrolet models. [8]Not available on Nova LN models.*

Vega

"Vega. Economy plus, plus, plus."

Nameplate year of origin: 1971.
Current bodystyle lifespan: 1971 through 1977 (some models moved to Monza series, continuing through 1979).
Predecessor to this model: Corvair (1965 to 1969).
Replacement for this model: Cavalier (1982 to 1993).
Percentage of division's production: 11.74%.
Corporate siblings: Pontiac Astre.
Primary competition: AMC Gremlin, Dodge Colt, and Ford Pinto.
Notable changes: Minor trim and detail changes.
Major standard equipment: Knit vinyl high-back front bucket seats, sliding seat adjustment for both front seats (driver's side only on Notchback), cut-pile carpeting, fold-down rear seat and rear liftgate (Hatchback and Kammback wagon), two-spoke steering wheel, glove box, map pocket in driver's door, two-speed wipers w/washers, bright front and rear window moldings, manual front disc brakes, and A78 × 13 BSW tires. Estate

Measurements

	Coupes	Wagon
Wheelbase	97.0"	97.0"
Length	175.4"	175.4"
Width	65.4"	65.4"
Height	51.9"	51.6"
Legroom — front	42.8"	42.8"
Legroom — rear	28.9"	30.1"
Headroom — front	38.4"	38.5"
Headroom — rear	38.4"	38.3"
Cargo capacity (cu. ft.)	8.7*	50.2
Fuel capacity (gals.)	16.0	16.0

Hatchback maximum with rear seat down, 18.9 cu. ft.

Wagon adds: Woodgrain vinyl panels on bodysides and tailgate, and special exterior nameplates. LX adds: Choice of custom cloth-and-vinyl or all-vinyl interior trim, sport steering wheel, electric clock, additional sound insulation, bodyside protective moldings, vinyl roof, wheel opening moldings, and full wheel covers. Cosworth adds: Custom interior w/choice of black or white perforated vinyl, or black cloth front bucket seats, black carpeting, gold color bezeled instrument cluster, special gauge cluster w/8000 rpm tachometer, sport steering wheel, consecutive vehicle number plate on I/P, added sound insulation, black exterior paint w/gold stripe and "COSWORTH TWIN CAM" lettering on front fender, HD clutch, special front and rear stabilizer bars, quick ratio steering, cast aluminum alloy wheels, and BR70 × 13 BSW tires.

Models Available

	Model No.	Base MSRP	Change from LY	Shipping Wt. (lbs.)	Model Year Production	Change from LY
Vega 2-Door Notchback Coupe	V11	$2,786	+17.06%	2415	33,878	-42.31%
Vega LX 2-Door Notchback Coupe	V11	$3,119	+15.18%	NA	1,255	-79.07%
Vega 2-Door Hatchback Coupe	V77	$2,899	+16.33%	2478	112,912	-59.09%
Vega Cosworth 2-Door Hatchback Coupe	V77	$5,916	NEW	2480*	2,061	NEW
Vega 2-Door Kammback (Wagon)	V15	$3,016	+14.98%	2531	47,474	-46.20%
Vega 2-Door Kammback Estate (Wagon)	V15	$3,244	+13.78%	NA	8,659	-68.03%
TOTALS		*Avg. price* $3,497	+33.93%		*Production* 206,239	-54.78%

*Curb weight.

Monza

"The small car of tomorrow will be a little more everything.
The 1975 Monza is all this today."

Measurements

	Coupe	Hatchback
Wheelbase	97.0"	97.0"
Length	177.8"	179.3"
Width	65.4"	65.4"
Height	49.8"	50.2"
Legroom — front	43.0"	43.0"
Legroom — rear	28.2"	29.5"
Headroom — front	37.6"	37.7"
Headroom — rear	37.2"	35.3"
Cargo capacity (cu. ft.)	6.6	23.4*
Fuel capacity (gals.)	18.5	18.5

*Capacity with rear seat down.

Nameplate year of origin: 1975 (1960 as Corvair sub-series).
Current bodystyle lifespan: 1975 through 1980.
Predecessor to this model: Corvair Monza (1965 to 1969).
Replacement for this model: Cavalier (1982 to 1993).
Percentage of division's production: 7.76%.
Corporate siblings: Buick Skyhawk and Oldsmobile Starfire.
Primary competition: AMC Pacer, Dodge Colt, and Ford Mustang II.
Notable changes: All-new model.
Major standard equipment: Choice of patterned cloth or all-vinyl front bucket seats, cut-pile carpeting, fold-down rear seat and rear liftgate (hatchbacks), two-spoke steering wheel, door map pockets, simulated Bird's-eye Maple woodgrain I/P trim, full instrumentation including tachometer, electric clock, bright front and rear window moldings, bright side window moldings, full wheel covers, and A78 × 13 BSW tires. 2+2 adds: High-rise center shift console, day/night rear view mirror, four-spoke steering wheel, bright wheel openings, sport suspension, and BR78 × 13 BSW tires. Towne Coupe adds: Choice of patterned cloth or all-vinyl front bucket and rear bucket-style seating, full vinyl roof, special sound insulation package, and full wheel covers.

Models Available

	Model No.	Base MSRP	Change from LY	Shipping Wt. (lbs.)	Model Year Production	Change from LY
Monza 2-Door Towne Coupe	M27	$3,570	NEW	2675	69,238	NEW
Monza S 2-Door Hatchback Coupe	R07	$3,648	NEW	2685	9,795	NEW
Monza 2+2 2-Door Hatchback Coupe	R07	$3,953	NEW	2753	57,170	NEW
TOTALS		*Avg. price* $3,724	NEW		*Production* 136,203	NEW

Camaro

"Our sensibly sporty small car."

Measurements

Wheelbase	108.0"
Length	195.4"
Width	74.4"
Height	49.1"
Legroom — front	43.9"
Legroom — rear	29.6"
Headroom — front	37.3"
Headroom — rear	36.0"
Cargo capacity (cu. ft.)	6.4
Fuel capacity (gals.)	21.0

Nameplate year of origin: 1967.
Current bodystyle lifespan: 1970 through 1981.
Predecessor to this model: Camaro (1967 to 1969).
Replacement for this model: Camaro (1982 to 1992).
Percentage of division's production: 8.30%.
Corporate siblings: Pontiac Firebird.
Primary competition: None.
Notable changes: New rear window and minor trim and detail changes.
Major standard equipment: Choice of mixed-tone cloth-and-vinyl or solid all-vinyl front "Strato" bucket seats, color-keyed cut-pile carpeting, flat black instrument panel facing, four-spoke soft rim sport steering wheel, bright front and rear window moldings, hubcaps, and FR78 × 14 BSW tires. Type LT adds: Ribbed cloth or knit vinyl deep contoured front bucket seats, door map pockets, Interior Décor/Quiet Sound group, simulated Meridian walnut woodgrain vinyl accents on I/P cluster, Type LT emblem on steering wheel, special instrumentation package, electric clock, LH remote and RH manual sport mirrors, LT identification on front and rear end panels, bright accent molding on grille, black accented bodyside molding, variable-ratio power steering, and rally wheels.

Models Available

	Model No.	Base MSRP	Change from LY	Shipping Wt. (lbs.)	Model Year Production	Change from LY
Camaro 2-Door Sport Coupe	Q87	$3,540	+22.49%	3421	105,927	+3.80%
Camaro Type LT 2-Door Sport Coupe	S87	$4,057	+15.72%	3616	39,843	-18.63%
TOTALS		Avg. price $3,799	+18.78%		Production 145,770	-3.47%

Nova

"The ever-sensible Nova. Emphatically refined for 1975."

Nameplate year of origin: 1962, as top of the line Chevy II model; became series name in 1969.

Current bodystyle lifespan: 1975 through 1979.

Predecessor to this model: Nova (1968 to 1974; restyled in 1973).

Replacement for this model: Citation (1980 to 1985).

Percentage of division's production: 15.55%.

Corporate siblings: Buick Apollo/Skylark, Oldsmobile Omega, and Pontiac Ventura.

Primary competition: AMC Hornet, Ford Maverick and Granada, and Plymouth Valiant.

Notable changes: Completely redesigned.

Major standard equipment: All-vinyl front bench seat, color-keyed cut-pile carpeting, front door armrests w/integral pull bars, black two-spoke steering wheel and steering column, bright front and rear window moldings, and FR78 × 14 BSW tires. Hatchback model adds: Fold-down rear seat.

Measurements

	Coupe & HBK	Sedan
Wheelbase	111.0"	111.0"
Length	196.7"	196.7"
Width	72.2"	72.2"
Height	54.3"	54.3"
Legroom — front	41.7"	41.7"
Legroom — rear	33.4"	35.3"
Headroom — front	38.5"	39.5"
Headroom — rear	36.3"	36.5"
Cargo capacity (cu. ft.)	14.2*	13.0
Fuel capacity (gals.)	21.0	21.0

Hatchback maximum with rear seat down, 28.4 cu. ft.

Custom adds: Choice of cloth-and-vinyl or perforated all-vinyl front bench seat, simulated teakwood inserts w/bright accents on I/P, glove compartment light, Custom nameplates on front door panels, bright roof drip and belt moldings, bright parking light and taillight accents, Nova Custom nameplates on front fenders, grille and rear panel, Interior Décor/Quiet Sound group, rocker panel molding, front and rear bumper impact strips, and front and rear bumper guards. LN adds: Brushed knit and sewn shadow striped cloth individual wide-back reclining front seats w/adjustable backrests, center floor console, matching door panels w/carpeted lower panels and map pockets in front doors, color-keyed steering wheel and steering column, electric clock, auxiliary lighting package, full-width luggage compartment mat, white LN emblem on rear side window glass, bright side window and B-pillar moldings, bright rear end panel surround w/LN emblem, LN emblem on hood and front fenders, metric engine displacement decals on front fenders (above side marker light), and full wheel covers w/body-colored accent and LN emblem.

Models Available

	Model No.	Base MSRP	Change from LY	Shipping Wt. (lbs.)	Model Year Production	Change from LY
Nova S 2-Door Coupe	X27	$3,099	NEW	NA	21,725	NEW
Nova 2-Door Coupe	X27	$3,205	+21.13%	3276	82,024	-48.72%
Nova 2-Door Hatchback	X17	$3,347	+19.62%	3391	16,373	-52.33%
Nova 4-Door Sedan	X69	$3,209	+19.87%	3306	66,347	-10.49%
Nova Custom 2-Door Coupe	Y27	$3,402	+20.60%	3335	26,288	-48.48%
Nova Custom 2-Door Hatchback	Y17	$3,541	+19.19%	3421	15,250	-67.05%
Nova Custom 4-Door Sedan	Y69	$3,415	+19.82%	3415	22,180	-10.56%
Nova LN 2-Door Coupe	Y27	$3,782	NEW	NA	12,533	NEW
Nova LN 4-Door Sedan	Y69	$3,795	NEW	NA	10,262	NEW
TOTALS		Avg. price $3,422	+22.47%		Production 272,982	-30.10%

Chevelle

"This may be the most satisfying new car you ever brought home."

Nameplate year of origin: 1964.
Current bodystyle lifespan: 1973 through 1977.
Predecessor to this model: Chevelle (1968 to 1972).
Replacement for this model: Malibu (1978 to 1983).
Percentage of division's production: 16.13%.
Corporate siblings: Buick Century, Oldsmobile Cutlass, and Pontiac LeMans.
Primary competition: AMC Matador, Ford Torino, and Plymouth Fury.
Notable changes: New grille and minor trim and detail changes.
Major standard equipment: Choice of pattern cloth-and-vinyl or all-vinyl front bench seat, color-keyed cut-pile nylon carpeting, black steering wheel and column, bright front and rear window surround moldings, bright rear quarter window molding, hubcaps, and FR78 × 15 BSW tires.

Measurements

	Coupes	Sedans	Wagons
Wheelbase	112.0"	116.0"	116.0"
Length	205.3"*	206.9"	215.2"
Width	76.6"	76.6"	76.6"
Height	53.1"	53.8"	55.7"
Legroom — front	42.4"	42.4"	42.1"
Legroom — rear	32.9"	37.0"	36.8"
Headroom — front	37.7"	38.3"	38.8"
Headroom — rear	37.0"	37.5"	39.4"
Cargo capacity (cu. ft.)	15.3	15.3	85.0**
Fuel capacity (gals.)	22.0	22.0	22.0

*Overall length of Laguna Type S-3 is 207.3."   **Plus 9.8 cu. ft. of hidden storage space on two-seat models.*

Wagon adds: All-vinyl front bench seat, vinyl coated metal cargo area sidewalls, swing up tailgate w/fixed window, I/P mounted "door ajar" warning light for tailgate, power front disc brakes, and HR78 × 15 BSW tires. Malibu Classic adds: Choice of ribbed cloth or all-vinyl front bench seat w/fold-down center armrest, color-keyed steering wheel and column, simulated woodgrain vinyl accents on I/P, luxury upper door panel trim, glove compartment light, bright roof drip molding, hood rear edge molding, bright rocker panel and wheel opening moldings, and bright accented dual unit taillights w/brushed chrome between taillights. Malibu Classic wagon adds: All-vinyl front bench seat w/fold-down center armrest. Malibu Classic Estate wagon adds: Wood-grain vinyl bodyside and tailgate panels. Laguna Type S-3 adds: Choice of sport cloth or all-vinyl front bench seat, round dial instrumentation w/simulated woodgrain on I/P, Type S-3 identification on I/P and door panels, dual sport mirrors w/LH remote control, unique Laguna urethane front end styling, bumper impact strips, Laguna Type S-3 nameplates on front fender, grille and rear panel, radial tuned suspension, rally wheels w/trim rings, and GR78 × 15 BSW tires.

Models Available

	Model No.	Base MSRP	Change from LY	Shipping Wt. (lbs.)	Model Year Production	Change from LY
Malibu 2-Door Colonnade HT Coupe	C37	$3,407	+18.38%	3642	37,000	-30.68%
Malibu 4-Door Colonnade HT Sedan	C29	$3,402	+18.41%	3713	37,862	-0.99%
Malibu 4-Door, 2-Seat Station Wagon*	C35	$4,318	+28.36%	4207	13,977	-6.76%
Malibu Classic 2-Door Colonnade HT Coupe	D37	$3,698	+18.11%	3681	80,937	-33.16%
Malibu Classic 2-Door Colonnade Landau Coupe	D37	$3,930	+18.84%	3710	23,069	NA**
Malibu Classic 4-Door Colonnade HT Sedan	D29	$3,695	+18.13%	3778	51,071	-8.68%
Malibu Classic 4-Door, 2-Seat Station Wagon*	D35	$4,556	+20.50%	4275	22,368	+18.38%
Malibu Classic Estate 4-Dr., 2-S. Station Wgn.*	G35	$4,748	+20.08%	4301	9,237	-9.64%
Laguna Type S-3 2-Door Colonnade HT Coupe	E37	$4,113	+7.78%	3908	7,788	-50.68%
TOTALS	*Avg. price*	$3,985	+18.64%	*Production*	283,309	-13.77%

Production of wagons with third seat option is included above, but breaks out as follows: Malibu, 2,377; Malibu Classic, 6,394; Malibu Classic Estate, 4,600.
**Production of 1974 Malibu Classic Landau coupe kept as combined total with Malibu Classic coupe; therefore comparison to LY is not possible.*

Monte Carlo

"Monte Carlo from Chevrolet. A car this impressive wouldn't have to be sensible. But it is."

Nameplate year of origin: 1970.
Current bodystyle lifespan: 1973 through 1977.

Measurements

Wheelbase	116.0"

Predecessor to this model: Monte Carlo (1970 to 1972).
Replacement for this model: Monte Carlo (1978 to 1987).
Percentage of division's production: 14.74%.
Corporate siblings: Pontiac Grand Prix.
Primary competition: Dodge Charger SE and Ford Elite.
Notable changes: Revised grille and trim and detail changes.
Major standard equipment: Choice of tailored knit cloth and vinyl or all-vinyl front bench seat, color-keyed cut-pile nylon carpeting, color-keyed instrument cluster, soft-rim steering wheel, simulated wood burl accents on I/P and steering wheel, door pull assist straps, glove compartment light, electric clock, LH outside rear view mirror, bright roof drip and window surround moldings, bright rocker panel moldings w/front and rear extensions, bright wheel opening moldings, full wheel covers, and GR70 × 15 BSW tires. Landau adds: Visor vanity mirror, Landau emblem on door panels, Landau vinyl roof w/rear quarter nameplate, dual sport mirrors w/LH remote control, fender peak accent stripes, and cast aluminum Turbine II wheels.

Measurements (cont.)

Length	213.3"
Width	77.6"
Height	52.7"
Legroom — front	42.1"
Legroom — rear	32.9"
Headroom — front	37.5"
Headroom — rear	37.4"
Cargo capacity (cu. ft.)	14.7
Fuel capacity (gals.)	22.0

1975

Models Available

	Model No.	Base MSRP	Change from LY	Shipping Wt. (lbs.)	Model Year Production	Change from LY
Monte Carlo 2-Door Hardtop Coupe	H57	$4,249	+12.38%	3927	148,529	-19.66%
Monte Carlo Landau 2-Door Hardtop Coupe	H57	$4,519	+12.27%	3946	110,380	-13.32%
TOTALS		*Avg. price* $4,384	+12.32%	*Production*	258,909	-17.07%

Bel Air, Impala and Caprice Classic

"If the room, ride and comfort of a full-size car make sense
for you, discover how nicely the 1975 Chevrolets meet your needs."

Nameplate year of origin: 1950 (Bel Air, as hardtop model designation and 1953 as series); 1958 (Impala); and 1966 (Caprice).
Current bodystyle lifespan: 1971 through 1976.
Predecessor to this model: Biscayne/Bel Air/Impala/Caprice (1969 to 1970).
Replacement for this model: Impala and Caprice (1977 to 1990).
Percentage of division's production: 24.01%.
Corporate siblings: Buick LeSabre, Oldsmobile Delta 88, and Pontiac Catalina/Bonneville/Grand Ville.
Primary competition: Dodge Monaco, Ford LTD, and Plymouth Gran Fury.
Notable changes: Revised front and rear end styling.
Major standard equipment: Choice of patterned cloth-and-vinyl or all-vinyl front bench seat, color-keyed cut-pile nylon carpeting, black I/P trim, black steering wheel and column, LH rear view mirror, dual unit taillights w/silver accents,

Measurements

	2-doors	4-doors	Wagons
Wheelbase	121.5"	121.5"	125.0"
Length*	222.7"	222.7"	228.4"
Width	79.5"	79.5"	79.5"
Height	53.7"	54.5"	58.3"
Legroom — front	42.5"	42.5"	42.5"
Legroom — rear	35.8"	38.8"	38.9"
Headroom — front	38.1"	38.9"	39.6"
Headroom — rear	37.1"	38.0"	39.3"
Cargo capacity (cu. ft.)	18.9**	18.9	106.4
Fuel capacity (gals.)	26.0	26.0	22.0

*Caprice is 0.1" longer.   **Caprice coupe and Impala Custom coupe: 18.1 cu. ft.
Convertible: 15.9 cu. ft.

rocker panel sill moldings, single horn, power steering, power front disc brakes, hubcaps, and HR78 × 15 BSW tires. Wagon adds: All-vinyl front bench seat, Glide-Away tailgate w/power-operated rear window, and LR78 × 15 BSW tires. Impala adds: Choice of patterned deluxe cloth-and-vinyl or all-vinyl front bench seat (all-vinyl only in wagon), color-keyed soft-rim steering wheel, color-keyed steering column, woodgrain vinyl accent trim on I/P and door panels, glove box and luggage compartment lights, luggage compartment mat, triple unit taillights w/silver accents, front and rear wheel opening moldings (Custom Coupe only), and bodyside protective moldings. Caprice adds: Choice of velvet-look knit cloth and vinyl or all-vinyl front bench seat, fold-down center armrest (four-doors only), electric clock, rear door courtesy light switches (four-doors), color-keyed bodyside molding, specific triple unit taillights, rear wheel opening fender skirts, and full wheel covers. Landau coupe models add: Elk-grain padded vinyl roof, bodyside pinstriping, dual remote-control sport mirrors, front and rear bumper impact strips, Landau name on rear quarter window glass, and wheel covers w/Landau crest and body-color paint. Convertible adds: Expanded vinyl front bench seat, and inward-folding power-operated vinyl convertible top w/glass rear window. Caprice Estate wagon adds: All-vinyl interior w/cargo area color-keyed soft textured vinyl sidewalls, and translucent woodgrain vinyl exterior panels.

Models Available

	Model No.	Base MSRP	Change from LY	Shipping Wt. (lbs.)	Model Year Production	Change from LY
Bel Air 4-Door Sedan	K69	$4,345	+17.59%	4179	15,871	-35.95%
Bel Air 4-Door, 2-Seat Station Wagon	K35	$4,878	+16.28%	4856	4,032	-37.36%
Bel Air 4-Door, 3-Seat Station Wagon	K45	$4,998	+15.99%	4913	2,386	-18.09%
Impala 2-Door Hardtop Sport Coupe	L57	$4,575	+17.40%	4207	21,333	-57.36%
Impala 2-Door Hardtop Custom Coupe	L47	$4,626	+16.70%	4190	49,455	-49.57%
Impala 2-Door Landau Custom Coupe	L47	$4,901	NEW	NA	2,465	NEW
Impala 4-Door Sedan	L69	$4,548	+17.52%	4218	91,330	-31.42%
Impala 4-Door Hardtop Sport Sedan	L39	$4,631	+17.24%	4265	47,125	-38.39%
Impala 4-Door, 2-Seat Station Wagon	L35	$5,001	+16.52%	4910	17,998	-23.27%
Impala 4-Door, 3-Seat Station Wagon	L45	$5,121	+16.23%	4959	19,445	-16.40%
Caprice Classic 2-Door Hardtop Coupe	N47	$4,837	+14.59%	4275	36,041	-39.41%
Caprice Classic 2-Door Landau Coupe	N47	$5,075	NEW	NA	3,752	NEW
Caprice Classic 2-Door Convertible	N67	$5,113	+14.05%	4342	8,349	+78.78%
Caprice Classic 4-Door Sedan	N69	$4,819	+14.66%	4311	33,715	-22.26%
Caprice Classic 4-Door Hardtop Sedan	N39	$4,891	+12.59%	4360	40,482	-16.34%
Caprice Estate 4-Door, 2-Seat Station Wagon.	N35	$5,231	+15.45%	4978	9,047	-26.33%
Caprice Estate 4-Door, 3-Seat Station Wagon	N45	$5,351	+15.20%	5036	18,858	-18.23%
TOTALS		*Avg. price* $4,879	+16.15%		*Production* 421,684	-33.05%

Corvette

"How are you at building a dream?"

Nameplate year of origin: 1953 (also used on show car of same year).
Current bodystyle lifespan: 1968 through 1982.
Predecessor to this model: Corvette (1963 to 1967).
Replacement for this model: Corvette (1984 to 1996).
Percentage of division's production: 2.19%.
Corporate siblings: None.
Primary competition: None.
Notable changes: Minor trim and detail changes.
Major standard equipment: All-vinyl high-back contoured bucket seats, center floor console, color-keyed cut-pile carpeting, tilt steering wheel, sports instrumentation with full gauges including tachometer, electric clock, tinted glass, LH rear view sport mirror, carpeted cargo area with light concealed behind seats, anti-theft audio alarm system, removable roof panels (coupe), hide-away folding top (convertible), domed hood w/air scoop, four wheel disc brakes, rally wheels w/trim rings, and GR70 × 15 BSW tires.

Measurements

Wheelbase	98.0"
Length	185.2"
Width	69.0"
Height	47.9"
Legroom — front	42.1"
Headroom — front	36.2"
Cargo capacity (cu. ft.)	6.5
Fuel capacity (gals.)	18.0

Models Available

	Model No.	Base MSRP	Change from LY	Shipping Wt. (lbs.)	Model Year Production	Change from LY
Corvette Stingray 2-Door Coupe	Z37	$6,797	+13.25%	3433	33,836	+5.65%
Corvette Stingray 2-Door Convertible	Z67	$6,537	+13.37%	3446	4,629	-15.44%
TOTALS		*Avg. price* $6,667	+13.31%		*Production* 38,465	+2.57%

CHRYSLER

"The exciting new Chryslers for 1975. Excellence in three sizes."

Indeed 1975 was exciting for Chrysler. By the end of the 1975 model year, Chrysler defied the entire automotive industry trend of the 1974 to 1975 period with a nearly 100 percent increase in production and sales, and more than doubled its production ranking. Chrysler would set a model year production record and leapfrog past American Motors and Cadillac, ending up only slightly behind Dodge in its total model year production. And most remarkably, this was all accomplished with only one new model introduction, one that outsold the entire 1974 Chrysler line-up. That model was the all-new Cordoba.

The new Cordoba definitely carried the expected styling for a mid-size personal/luxury car from the outside, with a long hood, short deck design. Being quite similar to the Dodge Charger SE in styling, the Cordoba also seemed to carry styling features lifted from other companies' designs. At the front, the Cordoba carried single round headlamps housed in round bezels that marked the end of a tunneled styled hood and front fender line, the look of which was very similar to that used on the 1973–1975 Chevrolet Monte Carlo and 1974–1978 AMC Matador coupe. As with the Charger SE, round parking lights were placed between the headlights and grille in a similar, but smaller tunnel, making for a rolling hood surface for the outer front portions of the hood. Chrysler described Cordoba styling as "restrained, refined and taut good looks." For a Chrysler, that was a fitting definition, as previous Chrysler models were among the largest, and sometimes most cumbersome looking, cars on the road.

The Cordoba grille, set slightly forward from the lights, had a vertical crosshatch design three rows high and sixteen columns across. In keeping with other Chrysler models, a heavier bar ran up each side of the grille, and a larger panel of chrome sat above the grille on the front header with the Chrysler name in block letters across the front. The hood had a chrome windsplit molding, with a unique Cordoba hood ornament set at the front edge of the header panel above the grille. The front bumper carried a single section of the grille design in the lower center portion, and otherwise conformed to the contours of the front end.

The main body section of the Cordoba was derived from the new greenhouse and rear quarter areas developed for the new Coronet and Fury 2-Door hardtops. While the sheetmetal was different, all of the basic underpinnings were the same. For the Cordoba, bodyside sheetmetal was identical to the Charger SE, and included a subtle bulge over the wheel

openings, marked by a slight horizontal crease running from the front fender edge to the front portion of the door, and a second similar crease from the rear edge of the door to the rear quarter panel end. Fixed opera windows were used for the rear side windows, as was typical of nearly all personal luxury cars of the period. The rear of the car was squared off and upright, following the pattern set by the upright roofline. Taillights were of a vertical rectangular design split into two sections by a narrow vertical bar and recessed into an area created between the trunk lid and the rear quarter panel ends. Backup lights were set into the bumper within an area that mirrored the design of the trunk lid arch above it.

Luxury was what defined Cordoba on the inside, a key to Chrysler's strategy to set it apart from the Charger SE. There were several choices in cloth, velour, vinyl, and leather trim, all of which looked clearly more luxurious than the Charger's upholstery choices. The instrument panel design was shared with all of the Chrysler corporate mid-size cars, with the Cordoba using black-faced instruments and simulated walnut appliqués, surrounded by filigree metal edging to give a more elegant effect. The use of the walnut and filigree metal trim extended to the door panels, and floor console, which could be ordered with the optional bucket seats.

Cordoba powertrains were traditional Chrysler V8 engines, but as a smaller car, the Cordoba had the 360 CID V8 engine as standard equipment. This engine was also available in the Newport for the first time this year. Economy minded buyers could opt for the even smaller but very dependable 318 CID V8 engine, or for more performance, a 400 CID V8 engine could be selected. By year's end, the Cordoba proved itself to be the right car at the right time, becoming Chrysler Corporation's most successful new car for 1975. At the same time, it could be said that the Cordoba stole sales from Dodge, as it outsold the Charger SE five to one.

The full-size Chrysler line, to include the Imperial, received only minor styling changes and those updates required to meet federal emission standards, including catalytic converters, Phase II electronic ignitions, and the required use of unleaded fuel. Newport models received a new horizontal crosshatch grille design that was divided into eight rows high, and ten columns across, with two bars per section used horizontally. With the base New Yorker being discontinued this year, the remaining New Yorker Brougham series similarly received few changes. Again this year, as in most previous years, the Town & Country wagon shared its grille with the New Yorker Brougham. The new grille for these cars consisted of a fine horizontal crosshatch pattern set into equally divided sections with three on each side. For all of these models, oval openings were added in the lower bumper area alongside the front license plate mounting area for improved cooling and air induction. New Yorker Brougham models also received an extra-wide rocker panel sill molding and a redesigned taillamp configuration that was full-width and split into two sections by a small horizontal chrome molding. Backup lights were set near the center next to the fuel filler door, which had a red reflector and the Chrysler gryphon emblem on it. Powertrains and interiors were mostly unchanged.

Imperial models were essentially unchanged as they entered their final season in the Chrysler lineup after nearly 50 years as the traditionally largest and most luxurious series in the Chrysler corporate line. After a two year absence the LeBaron name returned as a sub-series, featuring LeBaron script on the rear sail panel. The Imperial name would make a return on a highly made-over version of the Cordoba for the 1981 through 1983 model years, and again on a mildly reworked front-wheel-drive version of the New Yorker Fifth Avenue for the 1990 to 1993 seasons. Neither of these met with much success in terms of sales, but they did help encourage the luxury image Chrysler was striving to maintain as it switched to a lineup of mostly front-wheel-drive cars that were smaller and more fuel-efficient.

Cordoba 2-Door Hardtop Coupe

Cordoba 2-Door Hardtop Coupe

Cordoba interior

Imperial LeBaron 4-Door Hardtop

Imperial LeBaron 4-Door Hardtop
with optional Corinthian leather interior

Imperial LeBaron 2-Door Hardtop

New Yorker Brougham 4-Door Hardtop

Newport 4-Door Sedan

New Yorker Brougham 2-Door Hardtop
with St. Regis package

Newport Custom 2-Door Hardtop

Town & Country 4-Door Station Wagon

Model year production: 260,379 up 97.56% from 1974.
Domestic market share: 3.69% (9th place).
Base price range: $4,854 to $8,844.
Chrysler average base price: $6,057, up 9.33%.
Introduction date: October 1, 1974.
Assembly plants: Jefferson Ave., Detroit, MI (C); Newark, DE (F); and Windsor, Ontario, Canada (R).
Data plate identification (VIN): Thirteen digit code read as follows: First four digits indicate series and body style (model number in model charts); fifth digit indicates engine code (see powertrain chart); sixth digit indicates year (5 = 1975); seventh digit indicates assembly plant (see list above); remaining digits are sequential with beginning numbers of 100001.
Example: CL43M5C100001 is a 1975 Chrysler Newport 4-Door Hardtop, with 400 CID, 2-bbl. V8 engine, serial number 100001, built in Detroit, MI.

1975

Powertrains

Engine	Net HP	Engine Code	Transmission Availability[1]		Cordoba	Newport	Town & Country	New Yorker Brougham	Imperial
318 CID (5.2L), 2-bbl., V8	150	G	3-speed Torque Flite automatic		−$47 (credit option)	—	—	—	—
				MPG:	13/17	—	—	—	—
				Calif.	11/14	—	—	—	—
360 CID (5.9L), 2-bbl., V8	180	K	3-speed Torque Flite automatic		S	−$33 (credit option)	—	—	—
				MPG:	13/22	11/18	—	—	—
400 CID (6.6L), 2-bbl., V8	165/ 175	M,N	3-speed Torque Flite automatic		$33	S	−$165 (credit option)	−$165 (credit option)	—
				MPG:	13/16	11/15	10/15	10/15	—
400 CID (6.6L), 4-bbl., V8	235	P	3-speed Torque Flite automatic		$73	$40	—	—	—
				MPG:	11/17	NA	—	—	—
				Calif.	12/17	10/15	—	—	—
440 CID (7.2L), 2-bbl., V8	215	T	3-speed Torque Flite automatic	MPG:	—	$165 10/16	S 10/16	S 10/16	S 10/16
440 CID (7.2L), 4-bbl., V8	260	U	3-speed Torque Flite automatic		—	—	$40	$40	$40
				MPG:	—	—	NA	NA	NA

Major Options

	Cordoba	Newport	Town & Country	New Yorker Brougham	Imperial
Air conditioning[1]	$437	$475	$475	$475	S
Tilt and telescope steering wheel	—	$93	$93	$93	$100
Automatic speed control	$67	$73	$73	$73	$98
Automatic headlamp dimmer	—	—	—	—	$53
Electric rear window defogger	$73	$73	—	$73	$73
Tinted glass, all windows	$51	$57	$57	$57	S
Manual front vent window, 4-doors	—	$36	$36	$36	—
Power front vent window, 4-dr. HT	—	$141	$141	$141	—
Power windows	$97	$139	$137	$137	S
Power door locks, 2-dr./4-dr.	$60	$61/$88	$88	$61/$88	$52/$76
Power front bench seat, 6-way	$117	$113	$113	$113	$235
Power 50/50 or bucket seat, 6-way	$243	$204	$204	$204	$235
AM radio	$99	$98	$98	$98	S
AM/FM stereo w/search tuner	$254	$305	$305	$305	$333
AM/FM stereo w/8-track tape	$397	$392	$392	$392	$433
Electronic digital clock	S	$42	$42	$42	S
Vinyl top	$109	$132	—	$132	S
Remote control trunk release	$18	$19	—	$19	S

	Cordoba	Newport	Town & Country	New Yorker Brougham	Imperial
Sunroof, electric[2]	$296	$616	—	$616	$616
Security alarm system	—	$108	$108	$108	$105
Wire wheel covers	$58	$43	$43	$43	S
Urethane cast road wheels	$109	—	—	—	—
Chrome styled road wheels	—	$105	$105	$105	—
White sidewall tires, std. size	S	$40	$40	S	S

Popular Option Groups & Packages

	Cordoba	Newport	Town & Country	New Yorker Brougham	Imperial
Basic group	—	$820	$875	$661	—
Crown Coupe package	—	—	—	—	$569
Easy Order package	$760	$1,140	$1,275	$1,267	—
St. Regis package	—	—	—	$569	—

— = Not Available; S = Standard equipment.   [1]Auto-Temp air conditioning is standard on Imperial, and available for $552 on Newport, Town & Country and New Yorker Brougham.   [2]Requires vinyl top. Only available on 2-door hardtop models. Manually operated on Cordoba.

Paint Colors

	Code		Code		Code
Silver Cloud metallic	A2	Platinum metallic	J2	Formal Black	X9
Powder Blue	B1	Avocado Gold metallic	J6	Golden Fawn	Y4
Astral Blue metallic	B2	Bittersweet metallic	K3	Yellow Blaze[1]	Y5
Lucerne Blue metallic[1]	B5	Sahara Beige	L4	Inca Gold metallic	Y6
Starlight Blue metallic	B8	Moondust metallic	L5	Spanish Gold metallic	Y9
Rallye Red[1]	E5	Cinnamon metallic[1]	T4		
Vintage Red metallic	E9	Sienna metallic	T5		
Frosty Green metallic	G2	Dark Chestnut metallic	T9		
Deep Sherwood metallic	G8	Spinnaker White	W1		

Single tones are coded WI, WI. Two-tones are available for $44, and are coded X9, WI where first two digits are accent or roof color, and second two digits are basic body color.   [1]Available only on Cordoba.

Cordoba

"The new small Chrysler."

Nameplate year of origin: 1975 (Also used on special-order 1970 Newport hardtops).

Current bodystyle lifespan: 1975 through 1979.

Predecessor to this model: None.

Replacement for this model: Cordoba (1980 to 1983).

Percentage of division's sales volume: 57.65%.

Corporate siblings: Dodge Charger SE.

Primary competition: Buick Regal, Mercury Cougar XR-7, and Oldsmobile Cutlass Supreme.

Notable changes: All-new model.

Major standard equipment: Choice of cloth-and-vinyl or velour cloth-and-vinyl front bench seat w/fold-down center armrest, color-keyed 24-oz. deep-pile shag carpeting, simulated woodgrained vinyl trim on I/P and door panels, color-keyed three-spoke steering wheel, bright pedal dress-up, glove box and ashtray light, electronic digital clock, AM radio, premium steering wheel, molded cloth headliner, trunk light, carpeted trunk and spare tire cover, LH rear view mirror, rear quarter opera window and opera lamp, belt and drip rail moldings, wheel lip moldings, rocker panel sill molding, bodyside and deck lid dual paint stripes, stand-up hood ornament, power front disc brakes, power steering, premium wheel covers, and GR78 × 15 WSW tires.

Measurements

Wheelbase	115.0"
Length	215.3"
Width	76.3"
Height	52.6"
Legroom — front	41.9"
Legroom — rear	33.9"
Headroom — front	37.7"
Headroom — rear	36.6"
Cargo capacity (cu. ft.)	14.5
Fuel capacity (gals.)	25.5

Models Available

	Model No.	Base MSRP	Change from LY	Shipping Wt. (lbs.)	Model Year Production	Change from LY
Cordoba 2-Door Hardtop Coupe	SS29	$5,072	NEW	3975	150,105	NEW
TOTALS	Avg. price	$5,072	NEW	Production	150,105	NEW

Newport

"Comfort reigns supreme."

Nameplate year of origin: 1961 (as series); 1950 (as HT model of the T & C).
Current bodystyle lifespan: 1974 through 1978.
Predecessor to this model: Newport (1969 to 1973).
Replacement for this model: Newport (1979 to 1981).
Percentage of division's sales volume: 26.40%.
Corporate siblings: Chrysler New Yorker and Imperial.
Primary competition: Buick LeSabre, Mercury Marquis, and Oldsmobile Delta 88.
Notable changes: Minor trim and detail changes.
Major standard equipment: Cloth-and-vinyl front bench seat, color-keyed loop pile carpeting, trip odometer, lighted front ashtray w/two rear seat ashtrays, 12" inside day/night mirror, two-speed electric windshield wipers w/washers, front and rear wheel lip moldings, drip rail and belt moldings, bright windshield and rear window moldings, rear hood molding, dual horns, deluxe wheel covers, and HR78 × 15 BSW tires. Custom adds: Cloth-and-vinyl 50/50 split back front seat w/fold-down center armrest and (for 4-door models only) passenger side recliner, seat side shields, deck lid molding, upper door frame moldings (sedan only), rocker panel sill molding, and dual bodyside paint stripes.

Measurements

Wheelbase	124.0"
Length	224.7"
Width	79.5"
Height	55.3"
Legroom — front	41.6"
Legroom — rear	39.7"
Headroom — front	37.9"
Headroom — rear	37.0"
Cargo capacity (cu. ft.)	20.2
Fuel capacity (gals.)	26.5

Models Available

	Model No.	Base MSRP	Change from LY	Shipping Wt. (lbs.)	Model Year Production	Change from LY
Newport 2-Door Hardtop	CL23	$4,937	+9.30%	4395	10,485	-23.93%
Newport 4-Door Sedan	CL41	$4,854	+9.28%	4440	24,339	-9.67%
Newport 4-Door Hardtop	CL43	$5,008	+9.32%	4475	6,846	-23.66%
Newport Custom 2-Door Hardtop	CM23	$5,329	+9.43%	4450	5,831	-19.08%
Newport Custom 4-Door Sedan	CM41	$5,254	+9.39%	4500	9,623	-8.95%
Newport Custom 4-Door Hardtop	CM43	$5,423	+9.45%	4520	11,626	+17.53%
TOTALS	Avg. price	$5,134	+9.36%	Production	68,750	-11.13%

Town & Country

"The most versatile luxury car of all."

Nameplate year of origin: 1941.
Current bodystyle lifespan: 1974 through 1977.
Predecessor to this model: Town & Country (1969 to 1973).
Replacement for this model: LeBaron Town & Country (1978 to 1978).
Percentage of division's sales volume: 2.56%.
Corporate siblings: Dodge Monaco and Plymouth Gran Fury.
Primary competition: Buick Estate Wagon, Mercury Colony Park, and Oldsmobile Custom Cruiser.
Notable changes: Minor trim and detail changes.
Major standard equipment: All-vinyl 50/50 split front seat w/individual fold-down

Measurements

Wheelbase	124.0"
Length	227.2"
Width	79.4"
Height	58.9"
Legroom — front	41.6"
Legroom — rear	39.7"
Headroom — front	38.7"
Headroom — rear	38.9"
Cargo capacity (cu. ft.)*	100.8

center armrests and passenger-side recliner, color-keyed loop pile carpeting including cargo area, electric clock, interior lights (cargo, glove box, map/courtesy and ashtray), power tailgate window, sound absorbing headliner, trip odometer, front ashtray w/two rear seat ashtrays, 12" inside day/night mirror, three-speed electric windshield wipers w/washers, concealed storage compartments in rear wheelhouse cover, "Power Auto-Lock" tailgate lock (activates when ignition turned on), fender mounted turn signal indicators, bodyside simulated woodgrain appliqués, drip rail molding, rear wheel opening skirts, roof air deflector, dual horns, large diameter front sway bar, deluxe wheel covers, and L78 × 15 BSW tires.

Measurements (cont.)

Fuel capacity (gals.)	24.0

Plus 6.8 cu. ft. in concealed compartment on 2-seat wagon.

Models Available

	Model No.	Base MSRP	Change from LY	Shipping Wt. (lbs.)	Model Year Production	Change from LY
Town & Country 4-Door, 2-S. Wagon	CP45	$6,099	+10.25%	5015	1,891	-15.43%
Town & Country 4-Door, 3-S. Wagon	CP46	$6,244	+10.30%	5050	4,764	-20.04%
TOTALS		*Avg. price* $6,172	+10.27%	*Production*	6,655	-18.78%

New Yorker Brougham

"Impressively luxurious."

Nameplate year of origin: 1939.
Current bodystyle lifespan: 1974 through 1978.
Predecessor to this model: New Yorker (1969 to 1973).
Replacement for this model: New Yorker (1979 to 1981).
Percentage of division's sales volume: 10.00%.
Corporate siblings: Chrysler Newport and Imperial.
Primary competition: Buick Electra 225, Mercury Marquis, and Oldsmobile Ninety-Eight.
Notable changes: Minor trim and detail changes.
Major standard equipment: Cloth-and-vinyl 50/50 split bench seat w/individual fold-down center armrest and passenger side recliner on 4-doors, rear seat fold-down center armrest, color-keyed loop-pile carpeting, color-keyed seat belts, trip odometer, electric clock, dual front ashtrays w/two rear seat ashtrays, interior lights (glove box, map/courtesy and ashtray), 12" inside day/night mirror, three-speed electric windshield wipers w/washers, power windows, console-type armrests on all doors, headlight time-delay switch, carpeted trunk floor, LH remote control mirror, full-length bodyside molding, front wheel lip molding, drip rail molding, bright window moldings, rear taillight periphery moldings, rear wheel opening skirts, fender-mounted turn signal indicators, undercoating, hood insulation pad, unique deluxe wheel covers, and JR78 × 15 WSW tires.

Measurements

Wheelbase	124.0"
Length	224.7"
Width	79.7"
Height	54.9"
Legroom — front	41.6"
Legroom — rear	39.7"
Headroom — front	37.9"
Headroom — rear	37.0"
Cargo capacity (cu. ft.)	20.2
Fuel capacity (gals.)	26.5

Models Available

	Model No.	Base MSRP	Change from LY	Shipping Wt. (lbs.)	Model Year Production	Change from LY
New Yorker Brougham 2-Door Hardtop	CS23	$6,334	+8.35%	4650	7,567	-5.18%
New Yorker Brougham 4-Door Sedan	CS41	$6,277	+8.32%	4630	5,698	+25.70%
New Yorker Brougham 4-Door Hardtop	CS43	$6,424	+8.39%	4690	12,774	-2.97%
TOTALS		*Avg. price* $6,345	+11.18%	*Production*	26,039	-18.16%

Imperial

"Committed to every comfort. Confident of every comparison."

Nameplate year of origin: 1926 (as series); 1924 (as sedan model designation).
Current bodystyle lifespan: 1974 through 1978 (1974 to 1975 as Imperial, and 1976 to 1978 as New Yorker Brougham).
Predecessor to this model: Imperial (1969 to 1973).
Replacement for this model: Imperial (1981 to 1983).
Percentage of division's sales volume: 3.39%.
Corporate siblings: Chrysler New Yorker and Newport.
Primary competition: Cadillac Calais and DeVille and Lincoln Continental.
Notable changes: Minor trim and detail changes.
Major standard equipment: Velour and vinyl 50/50 split bench seat w/individual fold-down center armrest and passenger side recliner, plush pile carpeting, color-keyed seat belts, Lavaliere rear seat passenger assist straps (4-door only), C-pillar pillows and reading lamps, simulated Brazilian rosewood I/P and door appliqués, trip odometer, air conditioning w/automatic temperature control, electronic digital clock, power windows, tinted glass, dual front ashtrays w/two rear seat ashtrays, interior lights (glove box, map/courtesy and ashtray), 12" inside day/night mirror, three-speed electric windshield wipers w/washers, carpeted trunk floor and spare tire cover, LH remote control mirror, full vinyl top with frenched rear window, full-length rocker panel molding, front wheel lip molding, rear wheel opening skirts, drip rail molding, bright window moldings, rear bumper and taillamp periphery moldings, fender-mounted turn signal indicators, undercoating, hood insulation pad, deluxe wheel covers, and LR78 × 15 WSW tires.

Measurements

Wheelbase	124.0"
Length	232.7"
Width	79.7"
Height	54.5"
Legroom — front	42.1"
Legroom — rear	39.5"
Headroom — front	38.1"
Headroom — rear	37.0"
Cargo capacity (cu. ft.)	20.2
Fuel capacity (gals.)	26.5

Models Available

	Model No.	Base MSRP	Change from LY	Shipping Wt. (lbs.)	Model Year Production	Change from LY
Imperial LeBaron 2-Door Hardtop	YM23	$8,698	+15.40%	4965	2,728*	-29.14%
Imperial LeBaron 4-Door Hardtop	YM43	$8,844	+15.34%	5065	6,102	-42.30%
TOTALS		*Avg. price* $8,771	+15.37%		*Production* 8,830	-38.79%

*There were 1,641 Imperial LeBaron 2-door hardtops built with the Crown Coupe package.

DODGE

"This is the day you discover a new way to go. Dodge for 1975."

A new Charger and renovated Coronet and Monaco lines highlighted the 1975 Dodge lineup. The all-new Charger SE introduced for 1975 would place Dodge in head-on competition with the Chevrolet Monte Carlo, Ford Elite and Pontiac Grand Prix. The former Charger base models were moved back to a restyled Coronet line for the first time since 1970, when Dodge moved its 1971 mid-size two-door hardtop models to the Charger series. Dodge's high volume line, the Dart, continued to pull in over half of Dodge sales, and the imported subcompact Colt continued to increase in sales as the market continued to shift toward smaller cars. Overall for Dodge, sales and production slid by over 30 per-cent for the second year in a row, as lingering oil shortage and recession fears seemed to affect Dodge and Plymouth more than other manufacturers. Of course a lack of signifi-cant new product in its smaller car lines probably had a lot to do with this situation.

The new Charger SE looked the part of a luxury car from the outside but showed no hint of its formerly sporty lines, other than continuing a long hood, short deck design. Like the nearly identical Chrysler Cordoba, Charger SE also seemed to carry styling features lifted from other companies' designs, much as had been the case with the new-for-1974 Monaco. At the front, the Charger SE carried single round headlamps housed in round bezels that marked the end of a tunneled styled hood and front fender line, the look of which was very similar to that used on the 1973–1975 Chevrolet Monte Carlo and 1974–1978 AMC Matador coupe. Dodge took the idea a step further and placed round parking lights between the headlights and grille in a similar but smaller tunnel, making for a rolling hood surface for the front portions of the hood. This addition gave the Charger SE the look of a contemporary Jaguar sedan, or as Dodge described it, "crafted in the grand tradition of European elegance." The grille itself, set slightly forward from the lights, had an overall crosshatch design four rows high and six rows across, with small vertical bars embedded within each opening. A red Dodge nameplate was affixed in the lower driver's side corner of the grille. The front bumper carried a single section of the grille design in the center, and otherwise conformed to the contours of the front end.

The main body section of the Charger SE, like that of the Chrysler Cordoba, was derived from the new greenhouse and rear quarter areas developed for the new Coronet and Fury two-door hardtops. While the sheetmetal was different, all of the basic underpinnings were the same. For the Charger SE, bodyside sheetmetal included a subtle bulge over the wheel openings, marked by a slight horizontal crease running from the front fender edge to the front portion of the door, and a second similar crease from the rear edge of the door to the rear quarter panel end. Opera windows replaced the roll-down rear quarter window of old, putting Dodge in line stylistically with its main competitors. The rear of the car was squared off and upright, taking a cue from the upright roofline. Taillights were of a semi-square configuration split into two sections by a horizontal strip, and set into a depressed area created between the trunk lid and the rear quarter panel ends, where they then wrapped around the end of the rear quarter panel as it protruded into a small fin-like design. The wraparound taillights were perhaps the most visible feature distinguishing the Charger SE from the Cordoba. Backup lights were set into the bumper that conformed to the sheetmetal design above it, much like the front bumper did. Chrysler Corporation can take credit for having one of 1975's most stylish and well-integrated steel bumper designs on the Charger SE and Cordoba.

Inside the new Charger SE was all about luxury with plenty of choices in cloth, velour and vinyl. The new instrument panel, also shared with the Coronet, was slathered in simulated woodgrain vinyl appliqués, which were also applied to the door panels. Bucket seats were available, but a floor shifter and console were not, as least not initially. Also missing were sporty option packages, and not even a tachometer was offered; instead buyers were offered the Brougham package with crushed velour seats and trunk carpeting. Under the hood were V8 powertrain offerings that mirrored those offered previously, but with the car's weight having increased

nearly 400 pounds, performance did not even meet the less than enthusiastic performance of Chargers of the past three years. In the end, sales of the new Charger SE dropped from the already low 1974 levels. The problem was that the Charger name was synonymous with sporty cars, and this sudden diversion to luxury left many potential customers looking for something else. As if to prove the point, another issue faced by the new Charger SE came from within Chrysler Corporation, in the form of the Chrysler Cordoba. Better equipped than the Charger SE and similarly styled, the Cordoba racked up nearly five times the sales of the new Charger SE model.

The Coronet line received a new front-end treatment using single round headlamps set into pointed chrome bezels, and sharing most front end sheetmetal with the newly designated Plymouth Fury, known formerly as the Satellite line. The Coronet grille was a two-piece affair split by a thin body colored divider, with each grille of a crosshatch configuration four rows high and fifteen rows across, and the Dodge name on a red emblem set into the lower driver's side of the grille. For sedans and wagons, the rest of the car was the same as in 1974 with some minor trim changes. The new 2-door models, as mentioned previously, shared a formal roofline with the new Charger SE, but were still true two-door hardtops with roll-down rear quarter windows, a feature becoming unique outside of Chrysler Corporation, especially among newly designed two-door models. Inside, all Coronet models shared a mildly redesigned instrument panel with the new Charger SE, and also shared powertrains with the exception of the 225 CID 6-cylinder that was the standard powerplant on all Coronet and Coronet Custom models, except station wagons.

The full-size Monaco series was remade with new names and new faces for the top two sub-series. The base Monaco model added a new grille with a horizontal crosshatch design that was three rows high and fourteen columns across, and otherwise looked much like the 1974 version. However, the 1974 Monaco Custom and Monaco Brougham were re-christened Royal Monaco and Royal Monaco Brougham respectively. With the new names came a new front end design that included hidden headlights, a feature most recently used by Dodge on the 1973 Monaco Brougham. The two Royal Monaco series used a much more formal looking egg-crate grille design, topped by a wider chrome bar carrying the Dodge name in block letters. For Brougham two-door models a new Landau vinyl top with fixed rear quarter opera window, combined with the new front end appearance, gave the big two-door a far more luxurious look. It would be the last season for 4-door hardtop models.

The compact Dart series soldiered on with the same model lineup, with a new horizontal strip grille that had the parking/turn signal lamp area recessed. New options included the sporty looking "Hang 10" package for the Dart Sport coupe. The new Dart Special Edition, introduced midway through the 1974 model year, moved the popular compact toward a more luxury-oriented market. For the imported Colt line, the Colt coupe had a model number change from 6L to 6M which reflected the higher degree of standard equipment added for 1975. Similarly, the Colt 2-Door hardtop added more distinctive features and was renamed the

Colt Carousel to denote its new status, so its model number changed from 6H to 6S. Carousel was also the name used in Japan for Mitsubishi's two-door hardtop equivalent. Finally, the Colt Custom wagon was discontinued, but all of its extra features, including the simulated woodgrain exterior panels, were put into a new Estate package for the Colt wagon.

Charger SE 2-Door Hardtop Coupe

Colt Carousel 2-Door Hardtop

Coronet Crestwood 4-Door Station Wagon

Coronet Custom 2-Door Hardtop

Dart Custom 4-Door Sedan

Dart Sport 2-Door Coupe

Royal Monaco 4-Door Hardtop

Royal Monaco Brougham 2-Door Hardtop Coupe

Model year production: 307,631, down 30.41% from 1974.
Domestic market share: 4.36% (8th place).
Base price range: $3,269 to $5,905.
Dodge average base price: $4,498, up 17.15%.
Introduction date: October 1, 1974.
Assembly plants: Lynch Road, Detroit, MI (A); Hamtramck, MI (B); Jefferson Ave., Detroit, MI (C); Belvidere, IL (D); Newark, DE (F); St. Louis, MO (G); and Windsor, Ontario, Canada (R). Colt manufacturer: Mitsubishi Heavy Industries, Tokyo, Japan.
Data plate identification (VIN): Thirteen digit code read as follows: First four digits indicate series and body style

(model number in model charts); fifth digit indicates engine code (see powertrain chart); sixth digit indicates year (5 = 1975); seventh digit indicates assembly plant for all except Colt (see list above) and for Colt seventh digit indicates transmission code (5 = 4-speed manual, NA = 5-speed manual, 9 = automatic); remaining digits are sequential with beginning numbers of 100001 for all Dodge models except Colt. Colt sequential numbers are currently unknown. *Example:* LL41C5A100001 is a 1975 Dodge Dart 4-Door Sedan, with 225 CID, 2-bbl. 6-cylinder engine, serial number 100001, built in Detroit, MI.

Powertrains

Engine	Net HP	Engine Code	Transmission Availability[1]		Colt	Dart	Coronet & Coronet Custom	Coronet Brougham & Wagons	Charger SE	Monaco & Royal Monaco	Royal Monaco Brougham & Wagons
97.5 CID (1.6L) OHC, 1-bbl., 4-cyl.	85	K	4-speed manual		S (ex. GT)	—	—	—	—	—	—
			3-speed Torque Flite automatic		$250 (ex. GT)	—	—	—	—	—	—
				MPG:	21/31	—					
122 CID (2.0L) OHC, 2-bbl., 4-cyl.	95	U	4-speed manual		$142 (ex. GT)	—	—	—	—	—	—
			5-speed manual		S (GT)/ $93 (ex. GT)	—	—	—	—	—	—
			3-speed Torque Flite automatic		$157 (GT)/ $392 (ex. GT)	—	—	—	—	—	—
				MPG:	19/28	—	—	—	—	—	—
				Calif.	17/27	—	—	—	—	—	—
225 CID (3.7L), 2-bbl., 6-cyl.	95	C	3-speed manual		—	S (ex. SE & Sport 360)	S	—	—	—	—
			3-speed Torque Flite automatic		—	S (SE)/ $200 (ex. SE & Sport 360)	$210	—	—	—	—
				MPG:	—	17/23	14/22	—	—	—	—
				Calif.	—	15/19	14/22	—	—	—	—
318 CID (5.2L), 2-bbl., V8	145	G	3-speed manual		—	$151 (ex. SE & Sport 360)	—	—	—	—	—
			3-speed Torque Flite automatic		—	$151 (SE)/ $351 (ex. SE & Sport 360)	$338	S	-$89 (credit option)	—	—
				MPG:	—	13/20	13/17	13/17	13/17	—	—
				Calif.	—	12/16	11/14	11/14	11/14	—	—
360 CID (5.9L), 2-bbl., V8	180	K	3-speed Torque Flite automatic		—	—	$427	$89	S	S	—
				MPG:	—	—	13/22	13/22	13/22	11/18	—
360 CID (5.9L), 4-bbl., V8[2]	230	L	3-speed Torque Flite automatic		—	S (Sport 360)	$540	$242	$153	—	—
				MPG:	—	13/19	12/19	12/19	12/19	—	—
				Calif.	—	11/17	11/19	11/19	11/19	—	—
400 CID (6.6L), 2-bbl., V8[3]	175	M,N	3-speed Torque Flite automatic		—	—	—	—	—	$40[3]	—
				MPG:	—	—	—	—	—	10/14	
400 CID (6.6L), 4-bbl., V8	190	P	3-speed Torque Flite automatic		—	—	$460	$162	$73	$73	S
				MPG:	—	—	11/17	11/17	11/17	11/16	11/16
				Calif.	—	—	12/17	12/17	12/17	11/16	11/16
440 CID (7.2L), 4-bbl., V8	215	T,U	3-speed Torque Flite automatic		—	—	—	—	$149	$149	$76
				MPG:	—	—	—	—	10/15	10/15	10/15
				Calif.	—	—	—	—	9/13	9/13	9/13

[1]Unless otherwise noted: All transmissions are column-shift, except on Colt. Floor-shift is available for $30 extra on any Dart w/manual transmission and Dart Sport w/automatic. [2]Not available in California. [3]Available only in California.

Major Options

	Colt	Dart	Coronet	Charger SE	Monaco
Air conditioning[1]	$412	$407	$415	$415	$425
Tilt steering wheel w/"Rim Blow"	S[2]	—	—	—	$16
Automatic speed control	—	—	$55	$55	$55
Electric rear window defogger	$	$39	$73	$73	$73
Tinted glass, all windows	S	$44	$50	$50	$56
Front vent window, 4-dr. only	—	—	—	—	$38
Power windows	—	—	$139	$97	$135
Power door locks	—	—	—	—	$58/$85
Power front seat	—	—	$117	$117	$117
Music Master AM radio	$	$66	$72	$72	$72
AM/FM stereo	—	—	$254	$254	$254
AM/FM stereo w/8-track tape	—	—	$397	$397	$397
Front bucket seats[3]	S	$133[3]	—	S	—
Vinyl top[4]	$	$88	$109	$109	$117
Sunroof, manual[5]	—	$178	$296	$296[6]	$634
Power steering, variable-ratio	—	$92[7]	$114	S	S
Power brakes, w/front disc[8]	$	$65	$65	S	S
Chrome road wheels	—	—	$109	$109	$138
Rallye road wheels	—	$66	$82	$82	—
White sidewall tires, std. size	$	$38	$40	$40	$40

Popular Option Groups & Packages

	Colt	Dart	Coronet	Charger SE	Monaco
Basic group	—	$273	—	—	—
Brougham package	—	—	$230[9]	—	—
Estate package	$185	—	—	—	—
E-Z order package	—	—	$812	$812	$435[10]
"Hang 10" package	—	$254	—	—	—
Luxury Equipment package	—	—	$1,669	—	$1,612
Rallye package	—	$594	$225	—	—

— = Not Available; S = Standard equipment.   [1]Requires 225 CID 6-cyl. or V8 engine on Dart, and requires V8 engine on Charger & Coronet.   [2]Colt does not include "Rim Blow" steering wheel mounted horn.   [3]Requires automatic transmission. Available only on 2-door models, and includes full-floor carpeting.   [4]Standard on Dart SE and Royal Monaco Brougham coupe. Available only on Colt 2-door models.   [5]Requires vinyl top. Manual sunroof on Dart coupes and Charger. Power sunroof on Monaco series, except wagons.   [6]Price shown is w/canopy vinyl top. Prices slightly higher with other top options.   [7]Standard on Dart SE.   [8]Standard on Dart Sport 360 and Coronet Crestwood station wagons. All others have manual front disc brakes as standard.   [9]Available on Coronet Custom sedan only.   [10]Price given for Royal Monaco. Price on Monaco station wagons is $460.

Paint Colors

Dodge	Code	Dodge	Code	Colt[8]	Code
Silver Cloud metallic	A2	Claret Red	R6	Bright Yellow	063
Silver Frost metallic	A5	Cinnamon metallic[7]	T4	Sunset Orange	064
Powder Blue[1]	B1	Sienna metallic	T5	White	067
Astral Blue metallic[2]	B2	Dark Chestnut metallic[2]	T9	Yellow	090
Lucerne Blue metallic[3]	B5	Eggshell White	W1	Green metallic	091
Starlight Blue metallic[4]	B8	Black	X9	Orange	092
Bright Red[3]	E5	Golden Fawn	Y4		
Vintage Red metallic	E9	Yellow Blaze[3]	Y5		
Frosty Green metallic	G2	Inca Gold metallic	Y6		
Deep Sherwood metallic	G8	Dark Gold metallic	Y9		
Platinum metallic[4]	J2				
Avocado Gold metallic[5]	J6	Colt[8]	Code		
Bittersweet metallic[5]	K3	Spice metallic	016		
Parchment	L4	Sea Green metallic	017		
Moondust metallic[5]	L5	Silver metallic	030		
Aztec Gold metallic[6]	L6	Brite Red	055		

Single tones are coded W1, W1. Two-tones are coded X9, W1 where first two digits are accent or roof color, and second two digits are basic body color.   [1]Not available on Charger SE.   [2]Available only on Monaco.   [3]Available only on Dart, Coronet and Charger SE.   [4]Available on Charger SE and Monaco only.   [5]Not available on Dart.   [6]Available on Coronet only.   [7]Available on Dart and Charger SE only.   [8]Availability by model is not currently known for Colt models.

Colt

"Of all the small cars that cross the oceans, Dodge Colt is unique."

Nameplate year of origin: 1971.
Current bodystyle lifespan: 1971 through 1978 (hardtop); 1971 through 1977 (wagon); 1971 through 1976 (coupe and sedan).
Predecessor to this model: None.
Replacement for this model: Colt (1979 to 1983).
Primary competition: AMC Gremlin, Buick Opel, Chevrolet Vega, and Ford Pinto.
Notable changes: Minor trim and detail changes.
Major standard equipment: Vinyl front bucket seats w/reclining seat backs, full-floor carpeting, recessed door handles, two-spoke steering wheel, tilt steering column, tinted glass, deluxe sound insulation, beltline, drip rail, windshield, and rear window moldings, front and rear rubber bumper guards, locking fuel filler door, manual front disc brakes, wheel covers, and A78 × 13 BSW tires. Sedan and wagon add: Fold-down rear seat (wagon only), three-spoke steering wheel, wheel opening moldings, and rocker panel molding. Carousel hardtop adds: Cloth and vinyl bucket seat w/reclining seat backs, floor console, blue denim instrument panel, shag carpeting, AM/FM radio, multi-colored side and rear stripes, wheel lip moldings, and road wheels. GT adds: Soft-rim three-spoke sports steering wheel, front floor console w/shifter, rallye gauge cluster w/tachometer, GT bodyside tape stripes, GT logo, argent rallye road wheels with chrome hubs and lug nuts, and BR70 × 13 WSW tires.

Measurements

	2-doors	Sedan	Wagon
Wheelbase	95.3"	95.3"	95.3"
Length	171.1"	171.1"	172.0"
Width	63.6"	63.6"	62.8"
Height	53.1"	53.7"	54.1"
Legroom — front	42.7"	42.7"	42.7"
Legroom — rear	30.5"	30.5"	30.5"
Headroom — front	36.9"	37.8"	38.2"
Headroom — rear	35.5"	37.0"	37.3"
Cargo capacity (cu. ft.)	12.0	12.0	58.3
Fuel capacity (gals.)	13.5	13.5	11.0

Models Available

	Model No.	Base MSRP	Change from LY	Shipping Wt. (lbs.)	Model Year Sales	Change from LY
Colt 2-Door Coupe	6M21	$2,945	+13.93%	2155	NA	NA
Colt 4-Door Sedan	6H41	$3,101	+10.12%	2155	NA	NA
Colt 4-Door Station Wagon	6H45	$3,394	+9.63%	2330	NA	NA
Colt Carousel 2-Door Hardtop	6S23	$3,405	+20.32%	2200	NA	NA
Colt GT 2-Door Hardtop	6P23	$3,628	+20.33%	2330	NA	NA
TOTALS		*Avg. price* $3,295	+12.23%	*Production* 60,356*		+40.61%*

Total and comparison to LY is based on estimated model year sales.

Dart

"Our best sellers — a real success story."

Nameplate year of origin: 1960 (used on entry-level full-size Dodge).
Current bodystyle lifespan: 1967 through 1976.
Predecessor to this model: Dart (1963 to 1966).
Replacement for this model: Aspen (1976 to 1980).
Percentage of division's production: 55.62%.
Corporate siblings: Plymouth Valiant (including Scamp and Duster).
Primary competition: Buick Apollo/Skylark, Oldsmobile Omega, Mercury Comet, and Pontiac Ventura.
Notable changes: Minor trim and detail changes.
Major standard equipment: All-vinyl front bench seat (sedan and Swinger), cloth and vinyl front bench seat (Sport, Swinger Special and Custom sedan), front door armrests, rear seat armrests (except Sport and Swinger Special), rubber color-keyed floor mats, simulated woodgrain I/P cluster appliqué, two-speed electric windshield wipers and washers, front ashtray and cigarette lighter (except Dart Sport), front door window vents (sedans

Measurements

	Dart	Dart Sport
Wheelbase	111.0"	108.0"
Length	203.2"	200.3"
Width	69.6"	71.8"
Height	54.0"	53.2"
Legroom — front	41.6"	41.6"
Legroom — rear	35.6"	29.9"
Headroom — front	38.3"	37.2"
Headroom — rear	37.2"	36.4"
Cargo capacity (cu. ft.)	17.7*	19.8
Fuel capacity (gals.)	16.0	16.0

Sedans, 16.0.

only), grille surround and front edge moldings, hubcaps, and 6.95 × 14 BSW tires. Sport, Swinger and Custom add: Color-keyed carpeting, simulated woodgrain vinyl appliqué door panel trim (except Sport), roof drip rail molding, wheel opening moldings, lower deck panel appliqué, and bodyside moldings w/painted insert (except Sport). Dart 360 Sport adds: Bodyside performance tape stripes, rear deck panel appliqué, heavy-duty suspension, front sway bar, power front disc brakes, dual exhausts and E70 × 14 BSW tires. Special Edition adds: Crushed velour cloth and vinyl front bucket seats w/freestanding center armrest or low back front bench seat, door pull assist straps, color-keyed cut-pile carpeting, premium steering wheel, bright pedal dress-up, trunk carpeting, dual horns, deluxe insulation package, light package, three-speed electric windshield wipers and washers, LH remote control mirror, full vinyl roof, bodyside tape stripes, upper door frame moldings (sedan), stand-up SE hood ornament, power steering, front sway bar, color-keyed wheel covers, and E78 × 14 WSW tires.

Models Available

	Model No.	Base MSRP	Change from LY	Shipping Wt. (lbs.)	Model Year Production	Change from LY
Dart Sport 2-Door Coupe	LL29	$3,297	+17.67%	2980	37,192*	NA*
Dart Swinger Special 2-Dr. Hardtop	LL23	$3,341	+17.56%	3045	7,028	-56.50%
Dart 4-Door Sedan	LL41	$3,269	+13.31%	3060	19,349	NA*
Dart Sport 360 2-Door Coupe	LM29	$4,014	+23.74%	3335	NA*	NA*
Dart Swinger 2-Door Hardtop	LH23	$3,518	+17.23%	3035	93,557*	NA*
Dart Custom 4-Door Sedan	LH41	$3,444	+13.18%	3060	NA*	NA*
Dart Special Edition 2-Door Hardtop	LP23	$4,232	+13.82%	3260	13,971*	NA*
Dart Special Edition 4-Door Sedan	LP41	$4,159	+10.58%	3280	NA*	NA*
TOTALS		*Avg. price* $3,659	+15.73%		*Production* 171,097	-34.07%

Dart Sport and Sport 360 production kept as combined total. Dart Swinger and Custom production kept as combined total. Dart Special Edition hardtop and sedan production kept as combined total. Therefore, change from LY cannot be calculated on these models.

Coronet

"The new mid-size value."

Nameplate year of origin: 1950 (as hardtop designation); 1953 (as series).
Current bodystyle lifespan: 1971 through 1978. Renamed Monaco for 1977 to 1978.
Predecessor to this model: Coronet (1968 to 1970).
Replacement for this model: Diplomat (1977 to 1979).
Percentage of division's sales volume: 13.49%.
Corporate siblings: Plymouth Fury.
Primary competition: AMC Matador, Chevrolet Chevelle, Ford Torino, Mercury Montego, and Pontiac LeMans.
Notable changes: New front end styling and trim and detail changes. New 2-door models.
Major standard equipment: All-vinyl front bench seat, rubber color-keyed floor mat (sedan and wagon), color-keyed carpeting (hardtop), 3-spoke color-keyed steering wheel, dome light w/front door courtesy switch, concealed two-speed windshield wipers w/washers, bumper guards, and F78 × 14 BSW tires. Custom adds: Cloth-and-vinyl bench seats (sedan), all-vinyl front bench seat (wagon), color-keyed carpeting, deluxe steering wheel, drip rail and belt moldings, and wheel-lip and bodyside moldings. Brougham adds: All-vinyl split-back front bucket seats w/center armrest, simulated woodgrain inserts on I/P, door trim inserts and steering wheel, color-keyed shag carpeting, vinyl bodyside protection molding, stand-up hood ornament, and deluxe wheel covers. Wagons add: Dual action tailgate w/concealed hinges, power front disc brakes, and H78 × 14 BSW tires. Crestwood wagon adds: All-vinyl split-back front bench seat w/fold-down center armrest, cargo compartment carpeting and dome light, rear roof air deflector, and exterior simulated woodgrained bodyside overlays.

Measurements

	Hardtops	Sedans	Wagons
Wheelbase	115.0"	117.5"	117.5"
Length	213.8"	212.4"	220.7"
Width	77.4"	78.6"	79.2"
Height	52.6"	53.9"	56.5"
Legroom — front	41.9"	41.9"	41.9"
Legroom — rear	33.9"	36.7"	36.3"
Headroom — front	37.7"	38.6"	39.7"
Headroom — rear	36.6"	37.4"	39.9"
Cargo capacity (cu. ft.)	14.5	19.4	86.8
Fuel capacity (gals.)	25.5	25.5	21.0

Models Available

	Model No.	Base MSRP	Change from LY	Shipping Wt. (lbs.)	Model Year Production	Change from LY**
Coronet 2-Door Hardtop	WL21	$3,591	+8.46%*	3565	11,608**	NEW
Coronet 4-Door Sedan	WL41	$3,641	+14.86%	3595	NA**	NA**
Coronet 4-Door, 2-Seat Wagon	WL45	$4,358	+28.63%	4185	8,019**	NA**
Coronet Custom 2-Door Hardtop	WH21	$3,777	NEW	3645	11,893**	NEW
Coronet Custom 4-Door Sedan	WH41	$3,754	+14.70%	3635	NA**	NA**
Coronet Custom 4-Dr., 2-S. Wagon	WH45	$4,560	+20.60%	4240	NA**	NA**
Coronet Custom 4-Dr., 3-S. Wagon	WH46	$4,674	+14.14%	4290	NA**	NA**
Coronet Brougham 2-Door Hardtop	WP23	$4,154	NEW	3800	9,975	NEW
Coronet Crestwood 4-Dr., 2-S. Wgn.	WP45	$4,826	+20.17%	4230	NA**	NA**
Coronet Crestwood 4-Dr., 3-S. Wgn.	WP46	$4,918	+13.53%	4290	NA**	NA**
TOTALS		Avg. price $4,225	+13.52%		Production 41,495	-26.95%

*Comparison made to 1974 Charger 2-door hardtop which used the same model number. **Comparison of production to LY is not possible as 1975 totals were kept differently from 1974. 1975 totals are estimated and combined for base Coronet 2- and 4-doors; combined for Coronet Custom 2- and 4-doors; and combined for all station wagons.

Charger SE

*"Introducing a very Special Edition Charger.
An all-new expression of personal luxury."*

Nameplate year of origin: 1966.
Current bodystyle lifespan: 1975 through 1978.
Predecessor to this model: Charger (1971 to 1974).
Replacement for this model: Magnum XE (1978 to 1979), Mirada (1980 to 1983).
Percentage of division's sales volume: 9.75%.
Corporate siblings: Chrysler Cordoba.
Primary competition: AMC Matador, Chevrolet Monte Carlo, Ford Elite, Mercury Cougar XR-7, and Pontiac Grand Prix.
Notable changes: Completely redesigned.
Major standard equipment: All-vinyl front bucket seats w/center armrest, color-keyed shag carpeting, simulated woodgrained vinyl trim on I/P and door panels, bright pedal dress-up, electronic digital clock, premium steering wheel, belt and drip rail moldings, textured vinyl bodyside and partial wheel lip moldings, stand-up SE hood ornament, power front disc brakes, power steering, premium wheel covers, and GR78 × 15 WSW tires.

Measurements

Wheelbase	115.0"
Length	215.3"
Width	76.3"
Height	52.6"
Legroom — front	41.9"
Legroom — rear	33.9"
Headroom — front	37.7"
Headroom — rear	36.6"
Cargo capacity (cu. ft.)	14.5
Fuel capacity (gals.)	25.5

Models Available

	Model No.	Base MSRP	Change from LY	Shipping Wt. (lbs.)	Model Year Production	Change from LY
Charger SE 2-Door Hardtop Coupe	XS29	$4,903	+34.66%	3950	30,000	-3.09%
TOTALS		Avg. price $4,903	+46.17%		Production 30,000	-16.35%

*Estimated production based on model year sales of 30,812, due to production being kept combined within Coronet hardtop figures.

Monaco

"The affordable full-sized experience."

Nameplate year of origin: 1965.
Current bodystyle lifespan: 1974 through 1977; renamed Royal Monaco for 1977.
Predecessor to this model: Polara and Monaco (1969 to 1973).

Measurements

	Cars	Wagons
Wheelbase	121.5"	124.0"

Replacement for this model: St. Regis (1979 to 1981).
Percentage of division's sales volume: 13.49%.
Corporate siblings: Plymouth Gran Fury.
Primary competition: Chevrolet Caprice, Ford LTD, Mercury Marquis, Oldsmobile Delta 88, and Pontiac Bonneville/Grand Ville.
Notable changes: Trim and detail changes. New front-end design for Brougham.
Major standard equipment: Cloth and vinyl front bench seat, color-keyed carpeting, simulated woodgrained I/P appliqué, three-spoke color-keyed steering wheel w/simulated woodgrained inserts, driver's door storage compartment, day/night inside rear view mirror, LH outside rear view mirror, drip rail and beltline moldings, bright bodyside molding, rubber trunk mat, power steering, hubcaps, and GR78 × 15 BSW tires. Royal Monaco adds: Dorchester and Oxford cloth and vinyl front bench seat, simulated woodgrained door trim insert, glove box light, wheel lip moldings, upper door frame moldings (sedan), vinyl insert bodyside moldings, trunk light, and hidden headlights. Royal Monaco Brougham adds: Cloth and vinyl 50/50 split front seat w/individual fold-down center armrest and passenger recliner on 4-door models, door panel pull assist straps, electric clock, map lights, deluxe steering wheel, dual horns, hood and bodyside tape stripes, full vinyl roof w/fixed opera windows (2-door), front sway bar, deluxe wheel covers, and HR78 × 15 BSW tires. Wagons add: All-vinyl upholstery (w/seating configurations and other trim matching trim levels above), cargo area light, cargo compartment side storage panels, power tailgate window, tailgate ajar warning light, roof air deflector, and LR78 × 15 BSW tires. Brougham wagon adds: Cargo compartment carpeting, cargo side panel lock, and exterior woodgrained vinyl appliqué w/bright surround molding on bodyside and tailgate.

Measurements (cont.)

	Cars	Wagons
Length*	223.4"	226.8"
Width	79.3"	79.4"
Height	55.4"	58.9"
Legroom — front	41.6"	41.6"
Legroom — rear	38.2"	38.3"
Headroom — front	38.7"	38.7"
Headroom — rear	37.8"	40.5"
Cargo capacity (cu. ft.)	20.4	100.8
Fuel capacity (gals.)	26.5	24.0

Royal Monaco and Royal Monaco Brougham models are 2.2" longer.

1975

Models Available

	Model No.	Base MSRP	Change from LY	Shipping Wt. (lbs.)	Model Year Production	Change from LY*
Monaco 2-Door Hardtop	DM23	$4,631	+14.40%	4225	NA	NA
Monaco 4-Door Sedan	DM41	$4,605	+14.44%	4280	NA	NA
Monaco 4-Door, 2-Seat Wagon	DM45	$5,109	+14.27%	4885	8,019	NA
Royal Monaco 2-Door Hardtop	DH23	$4,868	+18.39%	4240	34,802	NA
Royal Monaco 4-Door Sedan	DH41	$4,848	+18.39%	4285	NA	NA
Royal Monaco 4-Door Hardtop	DH43	$4,951	+18.30%	4310	NA	NA
Royal Monaco 4-Door, 2-Seat Wagon	DH45	$5,292	+18.20%	4905	NA	NA
Royal Monaco 4-Door, 3-Seat Wagon	DH46	$5,415	+17.95%	4945	NA	NA
Royal Monaco Brougham 2-Door Hardtop	DP29	$5,460	+16.62%	4370	22,218	NA
Royal Monaco Brougham 4-Door Sedan	DP41	$5,262	+13.80%	4455	NA	NA
Royal Monaco Brougham 4-Door Hardtop	DP43	$5,382	+13.81%	4485	NA	NA
Royal Monaco Brougham 4-Dr., 2-S. Wgn.	DP45	$5,779	+13.76%	4980	NA	NA
Royal Monaco Brougham 4-Dr., 3-S. Wgn.	DP46	$5,905	+13.71%	5025	NA	NA
TOTALS		Avg. price $5,193	+15.77%		Production 65,039*	-11.45%*

Comparison of production to LY is not possible as 1975 totals were kept differently from 1974. 1975 totals are combined for Monaco and Royal Monaco cars, combined for Royal Monaco Brougham cars, and combined for all station wagons.

FORD

"The closer you look, the better we look."

The debut of an all-new compact car, restyled full-size Fords, and a new mid-size personal luxury coupe highlighted the 1975 Ford line. The new Granada compact and its Mer-cury twin, the Monarch, came along just in time to face off with the newly redesigned line of General Motors compacts, and just a scant twelve months before the arrival of Chrysler's new Dodge Aspen and Plymouth Volaré twins. The Elite was a new mid-size personal luxury coupe designed to compete head-to-head with the Chevrolet Monte Carlo, but it came along just as sales of the Oldsmobile Cutlass Supreme and the Pontiac Grand Prix were heading upwards. Finally, the newly restyled full-size LTD was introduced as news was beginning to come out about General Motors downsizing its full-size models. While it would be a good year for Ford in terms of model year production, the Granada seemed to steal sales from the Maverick, and the Pinto and Mustang II both suffered from GM's introduction of sporty new compact hatchbacks like the Chevrolet Monza and Buick Skyhawk. It appeared that 1975 was the beginning of a drop in market share that would not fully correct itself until the mid–1980s.

The new Granada was built on the Maverick 4-door platform but showed no hint of its rather mundane underpinnings. In fact nothing visible to consumers even gave a clue that it might be related to the Maverick. Other than chassis, drivetrains and some other unseen components, everything else about the Granada was new. The exterior styling of the new compact leaned more to the luxury side rather than sporty, with a traditional Ford front end look using a larger horizontal crosshatch style grille consisting of six columns across and five rows high, with similar two-by-two sections inset within each opening. A chrome strip surrounded the grille with a larger top section that wrapped onto the top of the header panel and had the Ford name in block letters widely spaced across the top. The hood added a slightly raised center section to meet the raised front grille line. Single round headlamps sat in square chrome bezels, which continued a small section of the grille design on each side. Parking and turn signal lamps were vertically mounted on pointed fender ends, and the entire front-end look was much like those of the new LTD and Elite, adding to a luxurious appearance.

Bodyside styling for the Granada was relatively basic with an upper feature line running from the top of the parking light bezel straight back to the top of the rear taillight bezel. A lower line ran from the mid-section of the bumper to the same position on the rear bumper, rising at the round-topped wheel openings to create flares. The greenhouse area followed the expected mid–1970s design, with 2-door models having a fixed rear quarter opera window rather than opening windows, and the 4-door models having a rear door fixed quarter window. The windshield and rear window seemed to use an equal rake. At the rear, large wraparound horizontal lamps featured red lenses at the outer ends with horizontal chrome paint appliqués dividing them into two sections, a vertical rectangular backup lamp next to it, and a square amber turn signal lens repeating the chrome paint appliqués at the inner end of the lamp. A body color panel with center-mounted fuel filler stretched between the taillamps, and when the exterior décor group was ordered a chrome bor-

dered appliqué with vinyl trim color-coordinated to the interior or vinyl top covered that panel. Powertrains included the basic 200 and 250 CID 6-cylinder engines and optional 302 and 351 CID V8 engines, with transmission choices of 3-speed manual shift or 3-speed SelectShift Cruise-O-Matic automatic transmission.

Inside the Granada was one of the most luxurious looking interiors ever used in an American car of this size and price. Pleated seats, individual front seat recliners, and burled walnut trim appliqués were included even on the base Granada models. The instrument panel had a hooded top pad and a driver's side "cockpit" type design that was made popular by the Pontiac Grand Prix since 1969. All gauges were contained in chrome-edged, black painted square or rectangular pods, with the aforementioned burled walnut trim on the face of the panel. On the passenger side the lower part molded to resemble pleated vinyl, housed the ashtray near the center and glove box to the right. Above was another section of burled walnut trim appliqué, within which the optional electronic digital clock was embedded. All of these features combined to make the Granada appear very luxurious, and Ford was not shy about touting this fact. In one of its biggest and most infamous advertising campaigns, Ford unabashedly compared the Granada to the Mercedes-Benz 280 sedans. While the ads made interesting comparisons, it was the fact that the Granada was one-third the price of the nearly $13,000 Mercedes that sold the Granada. (By 1977 an ad would compare the Granada to a "$20,000 Mercedes" 450SE.)

The popular Mustang II models continued with minor styling changes that included a new header panel that was not quite as deep as the 1974 model's, and a new grille that continued the same basic design, but carried only five horizontal bars instead of the seven used in 1974. In the spring of 1975, the base 4-cylinder cars were renamed to Mustang II MPG, to emphasize the higher fuel economy offered. Oddly, the 302 CID V8 engine was also added as an option around the same time, in an effort to restore the Mustang's former performance image, and probably just as likely because GM's new H-body lines were offering a 305 CID V8 engine. Around the same time, the Ghia coupe was given restyled standard hubcaps, the stand-up hood ornament was eliminated, and some other features were no longer standard. These measures were taken in an effort to hold down prices.

The full-size Ford line was now technically named the Ford LTD line, as the long running Custom 500 and Galaxie 500 nameplates were dropped, along with their related Ranch Wagon and Country Sedan station wagon designations. Though officially the Custom 500 and Ranch Wagon were gone, in reality their names were applied to stripped down versions of the LTD 4-Door Pillared Hardtop and Wagon, sold only as fleet vehicles or on special order. The remaining LTD models were not really "bumped down" a notch in trim level to fill the gaps left by the Custom and Galaxie series, but rather the LTD nameplate was moving the full-size Ford up-market, and to that end a newly fashioned LTD Landau was introduced carrying more standard features than any full-size Ford to come before it. All true hardtops were gone with the restyling, both 2-door and 4-door, leaving a new 2-door pillared hardtop and the continuing 4-door pillared hardtop styles.

Styling of the new LTDs built on the theme begun in 1973 with a large rectangular center grille, three-section parking/turn signal lamps vertically mounted on the end of pointed front fenders, and dual round headlamps set in between. Base LTD and Brougham models used headlamps mounted in a large chrome pod, separated by a thin vertical rendition of the LTD emblem. The new LTD Landau models used dual round hidden headlights, a feature not seen on a full-size Ford since 1970. The headlight doors were body-colored and had a horizontally styled LTD emblem affixed, while the edges of the door opening were chrome-lined. At the rear of the car, all but the station wagons used a slanting, vertically mounted three-section taillamp on a pointed rear fender end, which copied the front-end design. On the rear panel between the taillamps was a large, full-width appliqué of red reflectorized plastic surrounding a center body colored section that had the LTD name in the center and backup lights at each end. This rear panel area of LTD Landau models was similar but used a patterned chrome inlay where the body color section was on other models.

Bodyside styling, powertrain choices, and interior design of the LTD continued mostly unchanged, although upholstery materials were upgraded with more luxurious looking patterns gracing the LTD Landau. A new exterior option was rear wheel opening fender skirts for all but station wagon models. All LTD 2-door models were still named 2-door hardtops, as they had frameless door windows, but they were really pillared hardtops, as they used fixed quarter windows. These rear side windows were a unique design consisting of a narrow fixed window immediately next to the door opening, and then a large fixed rear quarter window that was somewhat triangular in shape filing out the C-pillar area, and greatly improving rearward visibility as compared to prior 2-door Ford models. Station wagons were down to a newly named LTD wagon, which was essentially the prior Country Sedan wagon, and the LTD Country Squire, which adopted the new front end styling of the LTD and LTD Landau respectively. Otherwise these models were mostly the same as in 1974 from the cowl back. The unique recreation table with magnetized checkers was still available on any full-size Ford wagon with dual facing rear seats for $49 extra,

and dual facing rear seats (DFRS) were again optional instead of part of the regular model line.

The new Elite, a spin-off of the Torino series, was originally introduced midway through the 1974 model year as competition for the highly popular Chevrolet Monte Carlo. Advertised as being in the "Thunderbird tradition," the Elite actually shared its chassis with the Torino 2-door hardtops, and many of its body panels with the Mercury Cougar. Differences from the Torino and Cougar were most evident at the front, where the Elite used single round headlamps in square chrome bezels, set in a tunneled area extending partially into the hood. It was the same type of design used on the Monte Carlo, the AMC Matador coupe, and the new Dodge Charger SE and Chrysler Cordoba twins, but more angular on the Elite. The Elite grille was a pointed, heavily chromed affair, eight columns across, two rows high, and with each section carrying an argent colored three-by-three egg-crate style insert. Parking and turn signal lamps of the new Elite were vertically mounted on pointed fender ends much like those of its larger cousin, the Thunderbird. Doors and rear quarters were shared with the Cougar, and unique twin opera windows that were rectangular in shape and slanted forward at the top were used. Inside, the Elite interior was taken straight from the Gran Torino Brougham.

Base Torino models were given the same front-end treatment as the Gran Torino models for this season. The grille of all Torino models was slightly revised from the 1974 models, using the same eight vertical sections across, but for 1975 the insert sections were of a small egg-crate design. One factor in a steep Torino sales decline may have been that its competition was offering standard 6-cylinder engines in base and mid-level models, while Ford stayed with their larger 351 CID V8 engines as standard equipment. The other likely factor was internal competition from the Granada. Also, note that for this season a third-row rear seat in Torino station wagons became optional equipment whereas previously the three-seat wagons were stand-alone models.

The compact Maverick returned for 1975 with very few changes, as the new Granada was expected to take at least a few potential Maverick customers. The Pinto used the 140 CID 4-cylinder engine as standard equipment this year, and added the Mustang II's 170.8 CID V6 engine as optional equipment in combination with an automatic transmission only. Otherwise the Pinto had no significant changes. Finally, the luxurious Thunderbird entered its 20th anniversary year with virtually no changes. None of these lines had any model changes for the 1975 model year.

Elite 2-Door Hardtop

Granada 2-Door Sedan

LTD Country Squire 4-Door Station Wagon

Maverick Grabber 2-Door Sedan

Pinto 2-Door Sedan

Elite 2-Door Hardtop

Granada 4-Door Sedan

LTD Landau 4-Door Pillared Hardtop

Mustang II 2-Door Hardtop Coupe

Pinto 2-Door Station Wagon with Squire option

Gran Torino Brougham 2-Door Hardtop
with Gran Torino Brougham
4-Door Pillared Hardtop, rear

Granada Ghia 4-Door Sedan interior

Maverick 4-Door Sedan

Mustang II Mach I 3-Door Hatchback

Thunderbird 2-Door Hardtop

Model year production: 1,586,764, down 27.21% from 1974.
Domestic market share: 22.51% (2nd place).
Base price range: $2,769 to $7,701.
Ford average base price: $4,375, up 8.79%.
Introduction date: September 27, 1974.
Assembly plants: Atlanta, GA (A); Oakville, Ontario, Canada (B); Mahwah, NJ (E); Dearborn, MI (F); Chicago, IL (G); Lorain, OH (H); Los Angeles, CA (J); Kansas City, MO (K); Twin Cities, MN (P); San Jose, CA (R); Allen Park, MI (S—*pilot plant*); Metuchen, NJ (T); Louisville, KY (U); Wayne, MI (W); St. Thomas, Ontario, Canada (X); and Wixom, MI (Y).

Data plate identification (VIN): Eleven digit code read as follows: First digit indicates year (5 = 1975); second digit indicates assembly plant code (see list above); third and fourth digits indicate model number (model number in model charts); fifth digit indicates engine code (see powertrain chart); remaining digits are sequential with beginning numbers of 100001. *Example:* 5F02Z100001 is a 1975 Ford Mustang II 2-Door Coupe, with 170.8 CID, 2-bbl. V6 engine, serial number 100001, built in Dearborn, MI.

1975

Powertrains[1]

Engine	Net HP	Engine Code	Transmission Availability[2]		Pinto	Mustang II	Maverick	Granada	Torino & Elite	LTD	T-Bird
140 CID (2.3L) OHC, 2-bbl., 4-cyl.	82	Y	4-speed manual		S	-$272 (credit on Mach I)/ S (others)	—	—	—	—	—
			3-speed Select-Shift Cruise-O-Matic		$202	$239 (ex. Mach I)	—	—	—	—	—
				MPG:	18/26	18/26	—	—	—	—	—
				Calif.	17/25	17/25	—	—	—	—	—
170.8 CID (2.8L), 2-bbl., V6	105	Z	4-speed manual		—	S (Mach I)/$272 (others)	—	—	—	—	—
				MPG:	—	15/22	—	—	—	—	—
			3-speed Select-Shift Cruise-O-Matic		$484[3]	—	—	—	—	—	—
				MPG:	16/22	—	—	—	—	—	—
				Calif.	14/21	—	—	—	—	—	—
200 CID (3.3L), 1-bbl., 6-cyl.	84	T	3-speed manual		—	—	S	S (base)[4]	—	—	—
			3-speed Select-Shift Cruise-O-Matic	MPG:	—	—	$239 17/24	$239 (base)[4] 17/24	—	—	—
250 CID (4.1L), 1-bbl., 6-cyl.	91	L	3-speed manual		—	—	$42	S (Ghia)/ $42 (base)	—	—	—
			3-speed Select-Shift Cruise-O-Matic		—	—	$281	$239 (Ghia)/ $281 (base)	—	—	—
				MPG:	—	—	16/21	15/20	—	—	—
				Calif.	—	—	15/21	15/20	—	—	—
302 CID (5.0L), 2-bbl., V8	140	F	3-speed manual[4]		—	—	$122	$86 (Ghia)/ $128 (base)	—	—	—
			3-speed Select-Shift Cruise-O-Matic		—	$203 (Mach I)/ $456 (others)	$361	$325 (Ghia)/ $367 (base)	—	—	—
				MPG:	—	10/18	13/18	12/16	—	—	—
				Calif.	—	12/16	13/18	10/14	—	—	—
351 CID (5.8L), 2-bbl., V8	162	H	3-speed Select-Shift Cruise-O-Matic		—	—	—	$373 (Ghia)/ $415 (base)	S	S (ex. wgns.)	—
				MPG:	—	—	—	12/16	11/16	11/15	—
				Calif.	—	—	—	9/13	10/16	10/16	—
400 CID (6.6L), 2-bbl., V8	170	S	3-speed Select-Shift Cruise-O-Matic		—	—	—	—	$87	S (wgns.)/ $87 (others)	—
				MPG:	—	—	—	—	10/14	10/14	—
				Calif.	—	—	—	—	9/14	9/14	—

Engine	Net HP	Engine Code	Transmission Availability[2]	Pinto	Mustang II	Maverick	Granada	Torino & Elite	LTD	T-Bird
460 CID (7.5L), 4-bbl., V8	220	A	3-speed Select-Shift Cruise-O-Matic	—	—	—	—	$292	$236 (wgns.)/ $322 (others)	S
MPG:				—	—	—	—	10/16	10/16	10/15
Calif.				—	—	—	—	11/13	10/13	9/13

[1]Optional axle ratio required on Torino, Thunderbird and full-size Fords with V8 sold in California: 3.00:1.   [2]Unless otherwise noted: All manual transmissions are floor-shift, except on Maverick and Granada. All automatics are column-shift, except on Pinto and Mustang II. Floor-shift is available for $26 extra on Maverick with 3-speed manual, and Maverick with automatic (requires bucket seats or a Luxury Décor option), and for $29 extra on Granada (required with 302 CID V8 and 3-speed manual).   [3]Not available on Pinto 2-Door Sedan.   [4]Not available in California.

Major Options

	Pinto	Maverick	Mustang II	Granada	Torino	Elite	Full-size	T-Bird
SelectAire Air conditioning	$416	$417	$417	$430	$470[1]	$470[1]	$478[1]	S[1]
Tilt steering wheel	—	—	—	—	$56	$56	$56	$66
Fingertip speed control	—	—	—	—	$108	$108	$108	$113
Rear window defogger	$35[2]	$38	—	$40	—	—	$44	—
Electric rear window defroster	$60[2]	—	$63	$68	$73	$73	$68	$91[2]
Tinted glass, all windows	$42	$57	$41	$43	$48	S	S	S
Dual remote-control mirrors	—	—	$39	$42	$42	$3	S	
Power windows, 2-dr./4-dr.	—	—	—	$91/$129	$99/$144	$99	$104/$154	$130
Power door locks, 2-dr./4-dr.	—	—	—		$59/$85	$59	$59/$85	$4
Power seat, 6-way w/std. seat	—	—	—	$110[5]	$120	$120	$120	$124
Front bucket seats w/console[6]	S	$129	$63	—	$68	—	—	—
Third row seat/DFRS (wagons)	—	—	—	—	$88	—	$125	—
AM radio	$65	$65	$65	$65	$72	$72	$72	—
AM/FM stereo	$225	$225	$225	$225	$230	$230	$246	S
AM/FM stereo w/8-track tape	—	—	$347	$347	$376	$376	$379	$175
Vinyl top, full	$83	$83	$83[7]	$92	$100	S	$110[8]	S
Sunroof, power-operated	$210[9]	—	$210[9]	$517	$525	$525	$564	$611
Moonroof, power-operated	—	—	$454[9]	$786	—	$859	—	$859
Power trunk lid release	—	—	—	—	—	—	$15	$4
Power steering	—	$124	$117	$134	S	S	S	S
Power brakes, w/front disc	—	$76	$55	$55[10]	S	S	S	S
Fender skirts	—	—	—	—	$41	—	$38	—
Deluxe wheel covers	$30	—	—	—	$39	S	$36	$67
Wire wheel covers	—	—	—	—	—	$93	—	$88
Styled Steel wheels w/trim ring	$113	$113	$45	—	—	—	—	—
Forged/cast aluminum wheel[11]	$166	$166	$158	—	—	$220	—	$220
Magnum 500 chrome wheels[12]	—	—	$158	$166	$169	—	$37	$32	S
White sidewall tires, std. size	$30	$22	$31	$33	$36	$37	$32	S

Popular Option Groups & Packages

	Pinto	Maverick	Mustang II	Granada	Torino	Elite	Full-size	T-Bird
Accent group	$51	—	—	—	$33	—	—	—
Convenience group	$70	$42	$70	$66	$72	$95	$95	$55
Décor group	—	—	—	—	—	—	—	—
Deluxe bumper group	$58	$58	—	$59	$65	$48	$50	—
Exterior accent group	—	—	$162	—	—	—	—	—
Exterior décor group	$127	$90	—	$128	—	—	—	—
Ghia luxury group	—	—	$162	—	—	—	—	—
Interior décor group	—	$96	—	$233	—	$384	—	—
Landau luxury group	—	—	—	—	—	—	$472[13]	—
Light group	$33	$30	$35	$35	—	$44	$77	$111
Luxury décor group	$228	$462	—	—	—	—	—	$13
Luxury décor interior group	—	$205	$106	—	—	—	—	—

	Pinto	Maverick	Mustang II	Granada	Torino	Elite	Full-size	T-Bird
Maintenance group	—	—	$48	—	—	—	—	—
Protection group	$32	$37	$29	$37	—	$32	$54	$81
Rallye package	—	—	$282	—	—	—	—	—
Sports accent group	$501	—	—	—	—	—	—	—
Squire option	$241	—	—	—	—	—	—	—
Squire Brougham option	—	—	—	—	$184	—	$266	—
Turnpike convenience group	—	—	—	—	—	—	—	$156
Wagon Brougham option	—	—	—	—	—	—	$378	—

—= Not Available; S = Standard equipment. [1]SelectAire air conditioner w/automatic temperature control is available for $547 on Torino, $555 on full-size Fords, and $99 on Thunderbird. [2]Defogger is available only on Pinto Sedan. Defroster is available on any Pinto. Price includes tinted rear window with defroster on Pinto. Thunderbird also offers a combination electric windshield and rear window defroster for $337. [3]Available only through the Convenience Group. [4]Available only in Power Lock group consisting of power door locks and power trunk lid release for $74. [5]4-way power seat on Granada. [6]Bucket seats only on Pinto and Maverick; console not available. Bucket seats standard on Mustang II; price shown is for console. Bucket seats available only on Gran Torino Sport at no cost, with price shown for console. [7]Half (landau) vinyl roof on Mustang II Ghia coupe is available for no charge. [8]Available on wagons for $138. [9]Manually operated. Not available on Mustang II 2+2 or Mach I models. [10]Four-wheel power disc brakes on Granada available for $210. [11]Forged aluminum wheels are deep-dish design on Elite and Thunderbird. [12]Magnum 500 wheels are four-spoke cast aluminum on Mustang II, and five-spoke on Granada and Torino. [13]Available on Country Squire wagon for $683. Thunderbird offers the following luxury groups priced with velour trim/leather trim: Copper, $651/$724; Jade, $566/$638; Silver, $542/$615.

Paint Colors

	Code	Thunderbird	Others		Code	Thunderbird	Others
Black	1C	x	x	Ginger Glow metallic[2]	5J		x
Silver metallic	1G		x	Medium Copper metallic	5M		x
Medium Slate Blue metallic	1H		x	Dark Brown metallic	5Q	x	x
Silver Starfire metallic[1]	1J	x		Saddle Bronze metallic	5T		x
Bright Red	2B		x	Tan Glow metallic[2]	5U		x
Red	2E		x	Orange	5W		x
Burgundy Fire metallic[1]	2G	x		Dark Copper metallic	5Y		x
Dark Red	2M	x	x	Yellow	6D		x
Maroon metallic	2Q		x	Bright Yellow	6E		x
Medium Bright Blue metallic	3E		x	Gold Fire metallic[1]	6G	x	
Dark Blue metallic	3G	x	x	Medium Gold metallic	6L		x
Silver Blue Glow metallic[2]	3M		x	Medium Ivy Yellow	6N	x	x
Blue Starfire metallic[1]	3P	x		Cream	6P	x	
Pastel Blue	3Q	x	x	Dark Gold metallic	6Q	x	
Silver Blue Starfire metallic[1]	3R	x		Medium Jade Diamond Fire metallic[1]	7F	x	
Bright Lime Starfire metallic[1]	41	x		Medium Gold metallic	8C		x
Light Green	47		x	Wimbledon White	9A		x
Green Glow metallic[2]	4T		x	Pearl White	9C		x
Lime Gold Moondust metallic	4U	x		White	9D	x	x
Dark Yellow Green metallic	4V	x	x				
Light Gold metallic	4Z	x	x				
Ginger Bronze Starfire metallic[1]	51	x					
Copper Starfire metallic[1]	52	x					
Unique Gold Starfire metallic[1]	54	x					

In two-tone combinations, first two digits are lower color and second two digits are upper color. [1]Fire/Starfire metallic paints are $185 extra. [2]Metallic glow paints are $49 extra on Pinto, Maverick, Mustang II, and Granada; $54 extra on Torino, Elite, full-size Fords and Thunderbird.

Pinto

"Our basic little economy car."

Nameplate year of origin: 1971.
Current bodystyle lifespan: 1971 through 1980.
Predecessor to this model: None.
Replacement for this model: Escort (1981 to 1985).
Percentage of division's production: 14.10%.
Corporate siblings: Mercury Bobcat.
Primary competition: AMC Gremlin, Chevrolet Vega, and Dodge Colt.

Measurements

	Sedan	Runabout	Wagon
Wheelbase	94.4"	94.4"	94.7"
Length	169.0"	169.0"	178.8"
Width	69.4"	69.4"	69.7"
Height	50.3"	50.3"	52.0"
Legroom — front	40.8"	40.8"	40.8"

Notable changes: Minor trim and detail changes.

Major standard equipment: All-vinyl high-back front bucket seats, mini-front console, color-keyed rubber floor mat, bright front and rear window moldings, rack-and-pinion steering, manual front disc brakes, hubcaps, and B78 × 13 BSW tires. Runabout adds: Color-keyed carpeting in passenger compartment and load floor, and fold-down rear seat. Station wagon adds: Flip-out rear quarter windows and bright window and belt moldings.

Measurements (cont.)

	Sedan	Runabout	Wagon
Legroom — rear	30.7"	30.7"	30.7"
Headroom — front	37.3"	37.3"	37.9"
Headroom — rear	36.2"	36.2"	39.3"
Cargo capacity (cu. ft.)	6.3	6.1*	57.6
Fuel capacity (gals.)	13.0	13.0	14.0

*With rear seat folded down, 29.0 cu. ft.

Models Available

	Model No.	Base MSRP	Change from LY	Shipping Wt. (lbs.)	Model Year Production	Change from LY
Pinto 2-Door Sedan	10	$2,769	+9.58%	2495	64,081	-51.48%
Pinto 3-Dr. Runabout (hatchback)	11	$2,984	+11.51%	2528	68,919	-60.56%
Pinto 2-Door Station Wagon	12	$3,153	+13.79%	2692	90,763	-61.77%
TOTALS		Avg. price $2,969	+11.69%		Production 223,763	-58.88%

Mustang II

"Our small, sporty personal car."

Nameplate year of origin: 1964 (also used on a 1963 show car).
Current bodystyle lifespan: 1974 through 1978.
Predecessor to this model: Mustang (1971 to 1973).
Replacement for this model: Mustang (1979 to 1993).
Percentage of division's production: 11.88%.
Corporate siblings: None.
Primary competition: Buick Opel Manta and Mercury Capri.
Notable changes: Minor trim and detail changes.

Major standard equipment: Low-back vinyl bucket seats, color-keyed cut-pile carpeting, soft vinyl and carpet door trim panels, European-type armrests, woodtone I/P appliqués, two-spoke steering wheel, courtesy lights, tachometer, bright windshield and rear window molding, bright drip rail, belt and center pillar molding, color-keyed urethane coated bumpers, full wheel covers, and BR78 × 13 BSW tires. 2+2 adds: Fold-down rear seat, liftgate w/hydraulic struts, and styled steel wheels. Ghia adds (to 2-door): Choice of Westminster cloth or super-soft vinyl low-back bucket seats, shag carpeting, deluxe color-keyed seat belts, soft-vinyl headlining, quartz crystal digital clock, dual remote control outside color-keyed mirrors, vinyl insert bodyside molding, vinyl roof, Ghia identification, and spoke style wheel covers. Mach I adds (to 2+2): Dual remote control outside color-keyed mirrors, specific Mach I lower bodyside and liftgate paint stripes and identification, styled steel wheels w/wheel trim rings, and BR70 × 13 B/WL tires.

Measurements

	Coupe	3-Door
Wheelbase	96.2"	96.2"
Length	175.0"	175.0"
Width	70.2"	70.2"
Height	50.0"	49.7"
Legroom — front	37.2"	37.2"
Legroom — rear	27.7"	27.7"
Headroom — front	37.2"	37.2"
Headroom — rear	35.9"	34.1"
Cargo capacity (cu. ft.)	6.7	28.1*
Fuel capacity (gals.)	13.0	13.0

*With rear seat folded down.

Models Available

	Model No.	Base MSRP	Change from LY	Shipping Wt. (lbs.)	Model Year Production	Change from LY
Mustang II 2-Door Hardtop Coupe	02	$3,529	+12.60%	2660	85,155	-52.07%
Mustang II 2+2 3-Door (hatchback)	03	$3,818	+14.72%	2697	30,038	-59.84%
Mustang II Ghia 2-Door Hardtop Coupe	04	$3,938	+13.16%	2704	52,320	-41.53%
Mustang II Mach I 3-Door (hatchback)	05	$4,188	+13.99%	2879	21,062	-52.18%
TOTALS		Avg. price $3,868	+13.64%		Production 188,575	-51.15%

Maverick

"The proven family compact."

Nameplate year of origin: 1970.
Current bodystyle lifespan: 1970 through 1977.
Predecessor to this model: Falcon (1966 to 1969).
Replacement for this model: Fairmont (1978 to 1983).
Percentage of division's production: 10.25%.
Corporate siblings: Mercury Comet.
Primary competition: AMC Hornet, Chevrolet Nova, and Plymouth
   Valiant.
Notable changes: Minor trim and detail changes.
Major standard equipment: Random stripe cloth-and-vinyl front bench
   seat, nylon loop pile carpeting, illuminated I/P controls, two-spoke color-
   keyed steering wheel and column, flipper rear quarter window (2-door),
   bright drip rail and wheel opening moldings, bright hubcaps, and BR78 ×
   14 BSW tires. Sedan adds: CR78 × 14 BSW tires. Grabber adds: All-vinyl
upholstery, leather wrapped steering wheel, dual color-keyed mirrors w/LH remote control, bright window and belt moldings,
Grabber decal on hood and fenders, special paint/tape treatment on bodyside and lower back panel, styled steel wheels w/trim
rings, and DR70 × 14 RWL tires.

Measurements

	2-Door	4-Door
Wheelbase	103.0"	109.9"
Length	187.0"	193.9"
Width	70.5"	70.5"
Height	52.9"	52.9"
Legroom — front	40.7"	40.7"
Legroom — rear	32.0"	36.2"
Headroom — front	37.5"	37.8"
Headroom — rear	36.0"	36.7"
Cargo capacity (cu. ft.)	11.3	13.1
Fuel capacity (gals.)	16.0	16.0

Models Available

	Model No.	Base MSRP	Change from LY	Shipping Wt. (lbs.)	Model Year Production	Change from LY
Maverick 2-Door Sedan	91	$3,025	+8.42%	2820	63,404	-54.65%
Maverick 4-Door Sedan	92	$3,061	+8.39%	2943	90,695	-34.15%
Maverick Grabber 2-Door Sedan	93	$3,282	+12.28%	2827	8,473	-63.95%
TOTALS		*Avg. price* $3,123	+9.73%	*Production*	162,572	-46.00%

Granada

"Elegance in a new, efficient size."

Nameplate year of origin: 1975.
Current bodystyle lifespan: 1975 through 1980.
Predecessor to this model: None.
Replacement for this model: Granada (1981 to 1982).
Percentage of division's production: 19.07%.
Corporate siblings: Mercury Monarch.
Primary competition: Chevrolet Nova LN, Dodge Dart SE, Plymouth Valiant
   Brougham, and Pontiac Ventura SJ.
Notable changes: All-new model.
Major standard equipment: Vinyl front 40/40 seat w/individual recliners, 12-oz. cut-
   pile carpeting, burled walnut I/P appliqués, two rear seat ashtrays, luggage compartment mat, sound and ride package, mitered corner door frame moldings (4-door),
   bright front and rear window moldings, bright belt and rocker panel moldings,
   bright drip rail and wheel opening moldings, opera window w/bright moldings (2-
door), hood ornament, full wheel covers, and DR78 × 14 BSW tires. Ghia adds: Super-soft vinyl "floating pillow" seats w/indi-
vidual recliners, 22-oz. cut-pile carpeting, deluxe door trim, luxury steering wheel, digital clock, Ghia interior ornamentation,
day/night rearview mirror, deluxe color-keyed seat belts, rear door courtesy light switches (4-door), LH remote control mirror,
opera window Ghia crests (2-door), center pillar appliqué w/Ghia crest (4-door), vinyl insert bodyside and wheel lip moldings,
vinyl roof, vinyl lower rear panel appliqué w/decklid tape stripes, hood and bodyside tape stripes, luggage compartment carpeting
w/side linings and spare tire cover, deluxe sound and ride package, unique Ghia wheel covers, and WSW tires; deletes rocker
panel molding (coupe).

Measurements

Wheelbase	109.9"
Length	197.7"
Width	73.6"
Height	53.4"
Legroom — front	41.1"
Legroom — rear	36.0"
Headroom — front	38.5"
Headroom — rear	37.6"
Cargo capacity (cu. ft.)	14.6*
Fuel capacity (gals.)	19.2

*Sedan has 14.8 cu. ft. Ghia models have 1.6
cu. ft. less.

Models Available

	Model No.	Base MSRP	Change from LY	Shipping Wt. (lbs.)	Model Year Production	Change from LY
Granada 2-Door Sedan	81	$3,698	NEW	3153	100,810	NEW
Granada 4-Door Sedan	82	$3,756	NEW	3203	118,168	NEW
Granada Ghia 2-Door Sedan	83	$4,225	NEW	3311	40,028	NEW
Granada Ghia 4-Door Sedan	84	$4,283	NEW	3361	43,652	NEW
TOTALS	Avg. price	$3,991	NEW	Production	302,658	NEW

Torino

"The solid mid-size."

Nameplate year of origin: 1968.
Current bodystyle lifespan: 1972 through 1976.
Predecessor to this model: Fairlane and Torino (1970 to 1971).
Replacement for this model: LTD II (1977 to 1979).
Percentage of division's sales volume: 12.30%.
Corporate siblings: Mercury Montego.
Primary competition: AMC Matador, Chevrolet Chevelle, Dodge Coronet, Plymouth Fury, and Pontiac LeMans.
Notable changes: Revised front-end styling for base Torino. Minor trim and detail changes.
Major standard equipment: Tooled all-vinyl front bench seat, 12-oz. color-keyed cut-pile carpeting, windshield and rear window bright moldings, quarter window moldings, bright drip rail and belt moldings, power front disc brakes, power steering, hubcaps, and HR78 × 14 BSW tires. Wagon adds:

Measurements

	2-Doors	4-Doors	Wagons
Wheelbase	114.0"	118.0"	118.0"
Length	213.6"	217.6"	222.6"
Width	79.3"	79.3"	79.0"*
Height	52.5"	53.2"	54.8"
Legroom — front	42.5"	42.5"	42.5"
Legroom — rear	33.2"	37.8"	37.3"
Headroom — front	37.6"	38.3"	38.4"
Headroom — rear	36.2"	37.0"	38.5"
Cargo capacity (cu. ft.)	16.5	16.5	84.9
Fuel capacity (gals.)	26.5	26.5	21.2

Squire is 79.9".

Three-way tailgate, fold-down second seat, removable cargo floor carpeting, and bright tailgate window molding. Gran Torino adds: Cloth and vinyl front bench seat, distinctive Gran Torino ornamentation, bright rocker panel and rear extension moldings, wheel lip moldings, and paint filled lower back panel molding. Gran Torino wagon adds: Pleated all-vinyl bench seat and interior trim. Gran Torino Sport adds: Choice of super-soft all-vinyl bucket seats or Flight Bench seat w/fold-down center armrest, unique door trim, unique 8-pod I/P w/tachometer, trip odometer, oil, ampere, temperature and fuel gauges, deluxe color-keyed seat belts, wide bright belt moldings, dual remote control color-keyed mirrors, dual paint stripes, front and rear fender rocker extension moldings, unique Sport ornamentation on grille, fuel door and roof quarter, unique turbine wheel covers, and WSW tires. Gran Torino Brougham adds: Westminster cloth or super-soft all-vinyl split front seat w/dual fold-down center armrests, 22-oz. cut-pile carpeting, unique door trim, bright pedal trim, woodtone I/P and door panel appliqués, vinyl roof, opera window (2-door), front and rear panel rocker extension moldings, unique red lens appliqué on lower back panel, hood ornament, exterior Brougham identification, deluxe wheel covers, and WSW tires. Gran Torino Squire adds: Power tailgate window, simulated woodgrain bodyside paneling, and full wheel covers.

Models Available

	Model No.	Base MSRP	Change from LY	Shipping Wt. (lbs.)	Model Year Production	Change from LY
Torino 2-Door Formal Hardtop	25	$3,954	+22.19%	3981	13,394	-41.09%
Torino 4-Door Pillared Hardtop	27	$3,957	+22.17%	4053	22,928	-26.42%
Torino 4-Door, 2-S., 6-p. Wagon	40	$4,336	+13.57%	4406	13,291	-13.66%
Gran Torino 2-Door Formal Hardtop	30	$4,314	+26.47%	3992	35,324	-53.70%
Gran Torino 4-Door Pillared Hardtop	31	$4,338	+25.59%	4084	53,161	-26.90%
Gran Torino 4-Door, 2-S., 6-p. Wagon	42	$4,673	+16.33%	4450	23,951	-19.81%
Gran Torino Sport 2-Door Formal Hardtop	38	$4,790	+25.26%	4038	5,126	-77.85%
Gran Torino Brougham 2-Door Formal HT	32	$4,805	+20.88%	4081	4,849	-81.63%
Gran Torino Brougham 4-Door Pillared HT	33	$4,837	+21.96%	4157	5,929	-48.28%
Gran Torino Squire 4-Dr., 2-S., 6-p. Wgn.	43	$4,952	+15.16%	4490	17,157	-24.87%
TOTALS	Avg. price	$4,496	+18.65%	Production	195,110	-54.48%

Elite

"A mid-size car in the Thunderbird tradition."

Nameplate year of origin: 1974.
Current bodystyle lifespan: 1974 through 1976.
Predecessor to this model: None.
Replacement for this model: None.
Percentage of division's sales volume: 7.78%.
Corporate siblings: Mercury Cougar XR-7.
Primary competition: AMC Matador coupe, Chevrolet Monte Carlo, Dodge Charger SE, and Pontiac Grand Prix.
Notable changes: Separated from Torino line. Minor trim and detail changes.
Major standard equipment: Westminster cloth-and-vinyl front bench seat, plush color-keyed cut-pile carpeting on floor and lower door panels, deluxe color-keyed seat belts, deluxe steering wheel, five-pod I/P, simulated walnut woodgrain appliqués on I/P, door and steering wheel, tinted glass, full vinyl roof, unique twin opera windows, bright windshield and rear window moldings, quarter window moldings, bright drip rail and belt moldings, wide bodyside protective moldings w/vinyl insert color-keyed to roof, wide wheel lip moldings, distinctive Elite ornamentation, front bumper guards, power front disc brakes, power steering, full wheel covers, and HR78 × 15 BSW tires.

Measurements

Wheelbase	114.0"
Length	216.1"
Width	78.5"
Height	53.0"
Legroom — front	42.1"
Legroom — rear	32.2"
Headroom — front	37.4"
Headroom — rear	36.3"
Cargo capacity (cu. ft.)	16.5
Fuel capacity (gals.)	26.5

1975

Models Available

	Model No.	Base MSRP	Change from LY*	Shipping Wt. (lbs.)	Model Year Production	Change from LY*
Elite 2-Door Hardtop	21	$4,767	+7.44%	4154	123,372	+27.71%
TOTALS	*Avg. price*	$4,767	+7.44%	*Production*	123,372	+27.71%

Comparisons made to the equivalent 1974 Gran Torino Elite model.

LTD

"New, luxurious standard-size cars."

Nameplate year of origin: 1965.
Current bodystyle lifespan: 1971 through 1978 (restyled in 1973 and 1975).
Predecessor to this model: Custom/Galaxie/LTD (1969 to 1970).
Replacement for this model: LTD (1979 to 1991).
Percentage of division's sales volume: 21.93%.
Corporate siblings: Mercury Marquis.
Primary competition: Chevrolet Impala/Caprice, Dodge Monaco, Plymouth Gran Fury, and Pontiac Catalina/Bonneville.
Notable changes: Restyled.
Major standard equipment*: Summit Brocade cloth and vinyl front bench seat, color-keyed nylon loop pile carpeting, woodtone I/P and door appliqués, deluxe steering wheel, interior courtesy lighting, bright moldings (front and rear window, belt, drip rail, rear hood edge, and wheel lip), vinyl insert bodyside moldings, textured lower rear appliqué w/bright Reflex surround molding, rocker panel molding, C-pillar LTD crest (4-door), hood ornament, front bumper guards, chrome hubcaps, and HR78 × 15 BSW tires. Wagon adds: Load floor carpeting, power tailgate window, sound insulation package, and JR78 × 15 BSW tires. Brougham adds: Westminster knit cloth and vinyl front bench seat w/fold-down center armrest, bright seat side shields, electric clock, luggage compartment light, rear door courtesy light switch, full vinyl roof, dual accent paint stripes, rocker panel front and rear extension moldings, and full wheel covers. Landau adds: Niles knit cloth and vinyl "Flight Bench" seat

Measurements

	2-Doors	4-Doors	Wagons
Wheelbase	121.0"	121.0"	121.0"
Length	223.9"	223.9"	225.6"
Width	79.5"	79.5"	79.9"
Height	53.7"	54.3"	56.7"
Legroom — front	41.5"	41.5"	41.7"
Legroom — rear	35.5"	38.3"	37.1"
Headroom — front	37.3"	38.3"	38.7"
Headroom — rear	37.3"	37.3"	39.1"
Cargo capacity (cu. ft.)	20.0	20.0	94.6*
Fuel capacity (gals.)	24.2	24.2	21.0

Additional 9.1 cu. ft. of below deck storage on 2-seat wagons, and 5.4 cu. ft. on wagons w/DFRS.

w/fold-down center armrests, front seatback assist straps, 22-oz. shag carpeting, digital clock, luxury steering wheel, luxury door trim panels, burled walnut I/P and door trim appliqués, bright chrome windsplit and fender peak moldings, wide vinyl insert bodyside moldings, hidden headlights, and full Landau wheel covers. Country Squire adds: Simulated woodgrain exterior bodyside and tailgate paneling, cargo area light, Landau series hood ornament and hidden headlights, bright hood windsplit molding, and full wheel covers.

Custom 500 and Ranch Wagon features not available.

Models Available

	Model No.	Base MSRP	Change from LY	Shipping Wt. (lbs.)	Model Year Production	Change from LY
Custom 500 4-Door Pillared Hardtop	53	$4,300	+7.99%	4377	31,043	+7.26%
Ranch Wagon 4-Door, 2-S., 6-p. Station Wagon	72	$4,850	+8.07%	4787	6,930	-42.75%
LTD 2-Door Pillared Hardtop	62	$4,753	+8.29%	4359	82,382	+14.02%
LTD 4-Door Pillared Hardtop	63	$4,712	+7.83%	4408	82,382	+14.02%
LTD 4-Door, 2-Seat, 6-p. Station Wagon	74	$5,158	+8.54%*	4803	22,935	+2.39%*
LTD Brougham 2-Door Pillared Hardtop	68	$5,133	+9.94%	4391	32,327	+7.03%
LTD Brougham 4-Door Pillared Hardtop	66	$5,099	+9.73%	4419	41,550	-35.13%
LTD Country Squire 4-Door, 2-seat, 6-p. Wagon	76	$5,440	+11.07%	4845	24,005	-38.58%
LTD Landau 2-Door Pillared Hardtop	65	$5,484	NEW	4419	26,919	NEW
LTD Landau 4-Door Pillared Hardtop	64	$5,453	NEW	4446	32,506	NEW
TOTALS	Avg. price	$5,038	+10.94%		Production 348,029	-24.58%

LTD wagon comparisons made to 1974 Country Sedan.

Thunderbird

"The 20th Anniversary Thunderbird.
Could it be the best luxury car buy in America?"

Nameplate year of origin: 1955.
Current bodystyle lifespan: 1972 through 1976.
Predecessor to this model: Thunderbird (1967 to 1971; restyled in 1970).
Replacement for this model: Thunderbird (1977 to 1979).
Percentage of division's sales volume: 2.69%.
Corporate siblings: Lincoln Continental Mark IV.
Primary competition: Buick Riviera and Oldsmobile Toronado.
Notable changes: Minor trim and detail changes.
Major standard equipment: Aurora nylon cloth and vinyl individually adjustable split bench front seat w/fold-down center armrests and automatic seatback release, deluxe seat belts, courtesy lighting (dome, door, under dash, glove box and ashtray), 24 oz. cut pile carpeting, simulated woodgrain I/P and door panel trim, electric clock, AM/FM stereo radio, power windows, power interior ventilation system, Odense grain vinyl roof w/opera windows, fully lined luggage compartment w/light, unique Thunderbird hood ornament, bright moldings (rear hood edge, beltline, drip rails), bodyside and partial wheel lip moldings w/protective vinyl insert, sound insulation package, power steering, power front disc brakes, full wheel covers, and LR78 × 15 WSW tires.

Measurements

Wheelbase	120.4"
Length	225.6"
Width	79.7"
Height	53.0"
Legroom — front	42.0"
Legroom — rear	36.4"
Headroom — front	37.5"
Headroom — rear	36.8"
Cargo capacity (cu. ft.)	13.5
Fuel capacity (gals.)	26.5

Models Available

	Model No.	Base MSRP	Change from LY	Shipping Wt. (lbs.)	Model Year Production	Change from LY
Thunderbird 2-Door Hardtop	87	$7,701	+5.06%	4893	42,685	-26.96%
TOTALS	Avg. price	$7,701	+5.06%		Production 42,685	-26.96%

LINCOLN

*"The 1975 Continentals. They have been
redesigned to surpass even our previous standard."*

Following in the path of the prior three years, Lincoln, along with the full-size Fords and Mercurys, was touting its cars' superior ride and handling qualities as determined by consumers in road tests. These tests usually asked owners of specific makes to compare the new Lincoln's ride and handling to their car. Over the years Cadillac was most frequently the competitor compared against, but Mercedes-Benz was also a popular target. To further improve the perceived advantage, all 1975 Lincoln models received an upgrade to the steering gear and a new Hydro-boost braking system to improve handling and braking. Aside from these changes, the Lincoln Continental coupe and sedan received a restyling for the 1975 model year, while the Continental Mark IV now had five optional luxury groups.

At first glance the 1975 Continental coupe and sedan looked quite similar to 1974, which was purely intentional, as Lincoln sales since their 1970 redesign were the highest they had ever been. A closer look revealed the changes made to the rear quarters and greenhouse area of both models. And as could be expected, a new grille design gave the restyled cars a freshened look. The new rear quarter panel design kept the prior lower body feature line, but the upper feature line which had previously bumped up slightly below the rear quarter side window was now flat and ran in a straight line from the front fender to the end or the rear quarter panel, ending at the top edge of the new, taller taillamps. The new grille consisted of vertical chrome bars dividing the grille into six sections, with each section containing six thinner vertical bars.

Rear end styling changed substantially for 1975, with new vertical wraparound taillamps replacing last year's wide horizontal units. A full-width red reflective panel with an inset strip containing the backup lamps stretched between the taillamps, filling the area between the trunk lid and bumper.

For the greenhouse area, Lincoln chose to follow General Motors' lead with "Colonnade" type door openings. This design used center B-pillars, fixed rear quarter windows for the coupe, and frameless glass in the doors, much like a true hardtop model would use. While similar to Ford's "pillarless hardtop" models in this respect, the difference was in the design of the B-pillar where the Lincoln, and similar GM "Colonnade" style, brought the roofline downward between the doors, rather than a post that came up from between the doors to the roof. The design gave the new Lincolns an even more formal luxury appearance. New on coupes was a more upright rear window that provided more rear seat headroom and more closely followed the sedan's roofline. Continental sedans added an oval opera window in the wide C-pillar, improving visibility for rear seat passengers. Inside the Continentals received some new trim designs and a new "floating" pillow upholstery design for the Town Car and Town Coupe option packages.

The personal luxury Continental Mark IV coupe received the previously mentioned handling upgrades, but was otherwise unchanged. Four new optional luxury groups expanded on the theme begun in 1972 with the Silver Luxury group, and the Gold Luxury group added for 1974. This year's offerings included these two plus a Blue Diamond, Versailles, Saddle/White, and a popular Lipstick/White luxury group. No other significant changes were made to either car, including the powertrain teams, as the 460 CID V8 engine and SelectShift automatic transmission continued to be standard equipment.

Continental 2-Door Hardtop Coupe

Continental 4-Door Sedan
with Town Car option

Continental Mark IV 2-Door Hardtop
with Lipstick and White luxury group

Model year production: 101,843, up 8.36% from 1974.
Domestic market share: 1.45% (12th place).
Base price range: $9,214 to $11,082.
Lincoln average base price: $9,984, up 14.78%.
Introduction date: September 1974.
Assembly plants: Allen Park, MI (S —*pilot plant*); and Wixom, MI (Y).
Data plate identification (VIN): Eleven digit code read as follows: First digit indicates year (5 = 1975); second digit indicates assembly plant code (see list above); third and fourth digits indicate model number (model number in model charts); fifth digit indicates engine code (see powertrain chart); remaining digits are sequential with beginning numbers of 800001. *Example:* 5Y82A800001 is a 1975 Lincoln Continental 4-Door Sedan, with 460 CID, 4-bbl. V8 engine, serial number 800001, built in Wixom, MI.

Powertrains*

Engine	Net HP	Engine Code	Transmission Availability		Continental	Mark IV
460 CID (7.5L), 4-bbl., V8	194	A	3-speed Select-Shift Automatic		—	S
				MPG:	—	10/15
				Calif.	—	9/13
460 CID (7.5L), 4-bbl., V8	206	A	3-speed Select-Shift Automatic		S	—
				MPG:	10/15	—
				Calif.	9/13	—

Optional 3.00:1 axle ratio required on cars sold in California, at $31 extra.

Major Options

	Continental	Mark IV		Continental	Mark IV
Air conditioning, Auto-Temp	S	S	Intermittent windshield wipers	$27	$27
Tilt steering wheel	S	S	Anti-theft alarm system	$108	$108
Automatic speed control	$104	S	AM/FM stereo, w/power antenna	S	S
Electric rear window defroster	$87	$87	AM/FM stereo w/8-track tape	$139	$139
Quick Defrost, front/rear windows	—	$344	AM/FM stereo w/automatic search	—	$139
Tinted glass, all windows	S	S	Vinyl top, landau (coupe)	$164	$500[1]
Power windows	S	S	Moonroof, power-operated & tinted	$843	$843
Power front vent windows	$76	$76	Sunroof, power-operated	$668	$668
Power door locks	S	S	Power brakes, four wheel disc	$172	S
Power seat, 6-way w/pass. recliner	$69	$69	"Sure-Track" antilock brake system	$249	$200
Leather seating upholstery	$200	$212	Extended range fuel tank, 32 gals.	$95	—
Illuminated dual visor vanity mirrors	$100	$100	Luxury wheel covers	$83	S
RH remote-control mirror, LH std.	$29	$29	Forged aluminum wheels	—	$287

Popular Option Groups & Packages

	Continental	Mark IV		Continental	Mark IV
Blue Diamond luxury group	—	$516	Silver luxury group	—	$516
Gold luxury group	—	$516	Town Coupe/Town Car package	$532	—
Headlamp Convenience group	$95	$95	Versailles luxury group	—	$995
Lipstick/White luxury group	—	$465[2]			
Saddle/White luxury group	—	$465[2]			
Security Lock group	$13	$13			

—= *Not Available; S = Standard equipment.* [1]*Includes unique wide chrome beltline and roof moldings, full padding w/French seams, and a frenched rear window.* [2]*Price is $516 when ordered with Moondust or Diamond Fire paint.*

Paint Colors

	Code		Code
Black	1C	Blue Diamond Fire metallic[1]	3P
Silver Diamond Fire metallic[1]	1J	Medium Pastel Blue	3Q
Red Moondust metallic[2]	2G	Silver Blue Diamond Fire metallic[1]	3R
Dark Red	2M	Bright Lime Gold Diamond Fire metallic[1]	41
Medium Taupe Diamond Fire metallic[1,3]	2P	Aqua Blue Diamond Fire metallic[1,4]	45
Dark Blue metallic	3G	Dark Jade metallic[3]	46

	Code		Code
Light Green	47	Medium Ivy metallic	6N
Lime Gold Moondust metallic[2]	4U	Cream	6P
Dark Yellow Green metallic	4V	Dark Gold metallic	6Q
Light Gold metallic	4Z	Medium Jade Diamond Fire metallic[1]	7F
Ginger Bronze Diamond Fire metallic[1]	51	White	9D
Copper Diamond Fire metallic[1]	52		
Unique Gold Diamond Fire metallic[1]	54		
Dark Brown metallic	5Q		
Yellow Gold Moondust metallic[2]	6G		

In two-tone combinations, first two digits are lower color, and second two digits are upper color. [1]Diamond Fire metallic paints available for $193 extra. [2]Moondust metallic paints available for $141 extra. [3]Available only on Continental. [4]Available only on Continental Mark IV.

Continental

*"The new 1975 Continentals are built
to continue their winning record."*

Nameplate year of origin: 1940 (1961 as a regular series).
Current bodystyle lifespan: 1970 through 1979 (restyled in 1974).
Predecessor to this model: Continental (1961 to 1969).
Replacement for this model: Town Car (1980 to 1991).
Percentage of division's production: 53.71%.
Corporate siblings: None.
Primary competition: Cadillac deVille and Chrysler Imperial.
Notable changes: Restyled.
Major standard equipment: Luxury cloth front bench seat w/six-way power adjustment, folding center armrests in front and rear seat, cut-pile carpeting, simulated wood appliqués on I/P and steering wheel, Cartier-signed digital clock, tilt steering wheel, power windows, power door locks, AM/FM stereo w/power antenna, automatic temperature control air conditioning, visor-mounted vanity mirror, LH remote control rearview mirror, tinted glass, power deck lid release, interior lighting (ashtrays, courtesy, glove box, luggage compartment, dome/map, and rear seat reading), gray carpeted luggage compartment, Normande grain full vinyl roof, dual custom tape stripes, premium bodyside moldings, cornering lights, rear wheel opening fender skirts, front bumper guards, full wheel covers, and 230R15 WSW tires.

Measurements

	Coupe	Sedan
Wheelbase	127.2"	127.2"
Length	232.9"	232.9"
Width	80.0"	80.0"
Height	55.3"	55.6"
Legroom — front	41.9"	41.9"
Legroom — rear	41.1"	41.7"
Headroom — front	38.4"	38.5"
Headroom — rear	38.1"	38.6"
Cargo capacity (cu. ft.)	19.3	19.3
Fuel capacity (gals.)	24.2	24.2

Models Available

	Model No.	Base MSRP	Change from LY	Shipping Wt. (lbs.)	Model Year Production	Change from LY
Continental 2-Door Hardtop Coupe	81	$9,214	+16.18%	5219	21,185	+189.49%
Continental 4-Door Sedan	82	$9,656	+18.97%	5229	33,513	+14.18%
TOTALS	Avg. price	$9,435	+17.59%	Production	54,698	+49.17%

Continental Mark IV

*"A legend in its own lifetime and one of the world's
most admired, most desired motorcars."*

Nameplate year of origin: 1956 (Continental Mark II).
Current bodystyle lifespan: 1972 through 1976.
Predecessor to this model: Continental Mark III (1969 to 1971).
Replacement for this model: Continental Mark V (1977 to 1979).
Percentage of division's production: 46.29%.

Measurements

Wheelbase	120.4"
Length	228.1"
Width	79.8"
Height	53.5"

Corporate siblings: Ford Thunderbird.
Primary competition: Buick Riviera, Cadillac Eldorado, and Oldsmobile Toronado.
Notable changes: Minor trim and detail changes.
Major standard equipment: Luxury cloth "Twin Comfort" lounge seats w/six-way power adjustment, folding center armrests in front and rear seat, simulated burl walnut woodgrain appliqué on I/P and steering wheel, color-keyed cut-pile carpeting, electric Cartier Timepiece, trip odometer, automatic speed control, tilt steering wheel, power windows, power door locks, AM/FM stereo w/power antenna, automatic temperature control air conditioning, LH remote control rearview mirror, tinted glass, interior lighting (ashtrays, courtesy, glove box, I/P warning, luggage compartment, engine compartment, dome/map, and C-pillar reading), power decklid release, black carpeted luggage compartment, Normande grain full vinyl roof w/opera window, dual custom pinstripe, customer monogram on doors, cornering lights, bumper guards, "Sure Track" power brake system, luxury wheel covers, and 230R15 WSW tires.

Measurements (cont.)	
Legroom — front	42.0"
Legroom — rear	35.9"
Headroom — front	37.5"
Headroom — rear	36.6"
Cargo capacity (cu. ft.)	14.4
Fuel capacity (gals.)	26.5

Models Available

	Model No.	Base MSRP	Change from LY	Shipping Wt. (lbs.)	Model Year Production	Change from LY
Continental Mark IV 2-Door Hardtop	89	$11,082	+10.28%	5142	47,145	-17.75%
TOTALS	*Avg. price* $11,082		+10.28%	*Production*	47,145	-17.75%

MERCURY

"Get your new Mercury at the sign of the cat."

After surviving the 1974 model year in better shape than expected, Mercury entered the 1975 model year with high expectations for its two new models, the compact Monarch and the subcompact Bobcat. The Monarch and its twin the Ford Granada were conceived as a replacement for the Comet and Maverick. But with the Maverick selling so well, Ford was reluctant to discontinue it or the Comet, and they remained in the lineup. The Bobcat was a "badge-engineered" Ford Pinto twin, and was intended to draw economy-minded consumers to Lincoln-Mercury showrooms. The all-new Monarch and Bobcat models were Ford Motor Company's second wave of "badge-engineered" models, following the Ford Maverick and Mercury Comet twins. By year's end, the strategy of adding smaller cars paid off, and Mercury was one of the few nameplates to increase production for the model year.

Styling of the new Bobcat was a near exact copy of the Pinto with a taller, narrower Mercury style vertical bar grille, broader taillights, and a higher level of standard interior features. The grille featured more than sixty bars across, with the center bar being slightly wider, and with a chrome surround across the top and down each side. Square parking/turn signal lights sat between the grille and the single round headlights housed in a chrome bezel. The name "Mercury"

in block letters was spelled out across the front of the hood on the sloping face of a raised center section necessary to accommodate the taller grille. At the rear, the Bobcat Villager wagon used Pinto taillights, while the 3-door Runabout carried what looked to be the standard Pinto taillight lenses and backup light, with an additional Pinto taillight lens from the opposite side of the car attached on the inward side, all surrounded by a chrome bezel. Inside the Bobcat was laid out like the Pinto, but used more woodgrain trim and more expensive looking upholstery trim and designs. Powering the Bobcat, which Mercury described as the "Sporty little cousin of the Big Cat," was the standard 140 CID four-cylinder Pinto engine with a four-speed manual transmission. Although the Bobcat attained only about 15 percent of the sales that the lower-priced Pinto would achieve, it is interesting to note that production of Bobcat hatchbacks was about 50 percent greater than that of the two-door Villager wagon, while Pinto results were historically the opposite with the wagon outselling the hatchback by a roughly similar margin.

The new "precision-sized" Monarch was built on the Comet 4-door platform, but gave no hint to its heritage. Marketed as an in-between compact and mid-size car, the new Monarch was within an inch of the Comet on the outside, but much larger inside. Aside from the drivetrains and a few suspension components, everything else about the Monarch was new. The exterior styling followed in the Mercury theme of luxury, with a vertical multi-bar grille with a wide chrome band across the top and down each side. The Mercury name in block letters sat above the grille on the front header, as did the stand-up "M" Monarch logo hood ornament. The hood added a slightly raised center section to meet the raised front grille line. Single round headlamps sat in a square body-colored bezel with chrome edging. Parking and turn signal lamps were vertically mounted with a chrome-ribbed bezel, on pointed fender ends. The front bumper used elongated oval openings in the center area.

Bodyside styling for the Monarch followed that of its Ford Granada twin, with an upper feature line running from the top of the parking light bezel straight back to near the top of the rear taillight bezel. A lower line began at the top corner of the front bumper, running to the same position on the rear bumper, and creating flares over the round-topped wheel openings as the line arced over them. The greenhouse area was typical mid–1970s Mercury design, with 2-door models having a fixed rear quarter opera window rather than opening windows, and the 4-door models having a rear door fixed quarter window. The windshield and rear window seemed to use an equal rake. At the rear, wraparound horizontal lamps featured red lenses at the outer ends, a square amber turn signal lens next to it, and a square backup light at the inner end. A chrome paint appliqué followed the chrome taillight bezel around the lens about a half-inch from the outer edge. A body color panel with center-mounted fuel filler door and chrome surround trim stretched between the taillamps; on Ghia models, a chrome surrounded appliqué with vinyl trim color-coordinated to the interior or vinyl top covered this panel. Powertrains for the Monarch included the 200 CID six-cylinder, standard on the base model, and 250 CID 6-cylinder, standard on the Ghia model, and optionally the 302 and 351 CID V8 engines, with transmission choices of standard 3-speed manual shift or optional 3-speed SelectShift Cruise-O-Matic automatic transmission.

Inside the Monarch was probably the most luxurious looking interior ever seen in an American car of this size and price up to this model year. Smooth vinyl bucket seats with individual front seat recliners, and woodgrain trim appliqués were standard. The instrument panel had a hooded top pad and a driver's side "cockpit" type design. All gauges were contained in chrome-edged, square or rectangular pods with woodgrain trim on the face of the panel. On the passenger side the lower part, molded to resemble pleated vinyl, housed the center-mounted ashtray and a large glove box to the right. Above was another section of burled walnut trim appliqué, with two vertical air vents at the left end near the center of the car, the optional electronic digital clock above the glove box, and a single vertical air vent to the far right end.

The full-size Mercury line received a facelift this year, with new grilles and revised rear end styling. The entry-level Monterey was discontinued for this year. The base Marquis took its place, but with only a minimal loss of features, placing it approximately at the level of the prior Monterey Custom line. However, Mercury did move the prior season's Grand Marquis option package to full-fledged model status for 1975. With all full-sized Mercurys now being in the Marquis family, they all shared a common front-end styling theme, something not seen on full-size Mercurys in nearly a decade. The Marquis signature hidden headlights continued this year with a vinyl padded center section containing the Marquis logo and outlined in chrome. A new grille pattern was introduced being divided into six sections, with each containing five vertical bars, and the entire grille divided in the center by a thicker chrome bar. The grille was encapsulated in a chrome surround. A vertical Lincoln-style stand-up hood ornament sat atop the front header panel. Taller turn signal/parking lamps with four chrome ribs wrapped around the pointed fender ends. A sloping rear end design continued, but used revised wraparound horizontal taillamps, with four horizontal ribs on the lenses. A body-colored center section, with backup lights at each end, continued in a location similar to last year. Discontinued along with the Monterey were all of the four-door hardtop models. While sales of the Marquis seemed to jump up by nearly 40 percent, when the loss of the Monterey series is taken into account, full-sized Mercury sales were down about 5 percent, or roughly 4,000 units.

The remainder of the Mercury line was mostly unchanged for the 1975 model year. The mid-size Cougar and Montego series added elongated oval openings in the lower center area of the front bumper to add cooling airflow to the radiator and engine, but otherwise had only a few mechanical upgrades, such as those necessary to install the new emissions equipment including a catalytic converter, and interior trim and detail changes. The Montego also added power steering and power front disc brakes as standard equipment on all models. The Comet received very few changes, as the Monarch became the focus of Mercury in the compact arena.

Although there was technically not a 1975 Capri model, it was covered both in the full-line 1975 Lincoln-Mercury sales brochure and in Ford corporate information. The reason for not having a 1975 was a delay in introduction of the soon to be released Capri II, so when it finally made it to the United States, it was marketed as the 1976 Capri II, being introduced in March 1975. Since a 1975 Capri was marketed, it is included in an abbreviated format with all information contained within the model listing. Also, the imported deTomaso Pantera was dropped, although records indicate that several hundred left-over 1974 models were most likely retitled and sold as 1975 models.

Bobcat 3-Door Runabout hatchback

Comet 2-Door Sedan with Custom option

Marquis Brougham 2-Door Hardtop

Monarch Ghia 2-Door Coupe

Montego MX Brougham 2-Door Hardtop
with Custom Trim option

Bobcat Runabout interior with Polyknit fabric

Cougar XR-7 2-Door Hardtop

Colony Park 4-Door Station Wagon

Monarch Ghia coupe interior
with optional leather upholstery

Bobcat Villager 2-Door Station Wagon

Grand Marquis 4-Door Pillared Hardtop

Monarch 4-Door Sedan

Montego 4-Door Pillared Hardtop

Model year production: 404,650, up 0.17% from 1974.
Domestic market share: 5.74% (7th place).
Base price range: $3,189 to $6,469.
Mercury average base price: $4,671, up 9.23%.
Introduction date: September 1974. Bobcat introduced March 1975.
Assembly plants: Atlanta, GA (A); Oakville, Ontario, Canada (B); Mahwah, NJ (E); Lorain, OH (H); Kansas City, MO (K); San Jose, CA (R); Allen Park, MI (S—*pilot plant*); Metuchen, NJ (T); Wayne, MI (W); and St. Louis, MO (Z).

Data plate identification (VIN): Eleven digit code read as follows: First digit indicates year (5 = 1975); second digit indicates assembly plant code (see list above); third and fourth digits indicate model number (model number in model charts); fifth digit indicates engine code (see power-train chart); remaining digits are sequential with beginning numbers of 500001. *Example:* 5K31F500001 is a 1975 Mercury Comet 2-Door sedan, with 302 CID, 2-bbl. V8 engine, serial number 500001, built in Kansas City (Claycomo), MO.

Powertrains

Engine	Net HP	Engine Code	Transmission Availability[1]		Bobcat	Comet	Monarch	Cougar & Montego[2]	Marquis & Wagons[2]	Marquis Brougham & Grand Marquis[2]
140 CID (2.3L) OHC, 2-bbl., 4-cyl.	82	Y	4-speed manual 3-speed Select-Shift Cruise-O-Matic	MPG: Calif.	S $202 18/26 17/25	— — — —	— — — —	— — — —	— — — —	— — — —
170.8 CID (2.8L), 2-bbl., V6	105	Z	3-speed Select-Shift Cruise-O-Matic	MPG: Calif.	$484 15/22 14/21	— — —	— — —	— — —	— — —	— — —
200 CID (3.3L), 1-bbl., 6-cyl.	84	T	3-speed manual 3-speed Select-Shift Cruise-O-Matic	MPG:	— — 17/24	S[3] $241 17/24	S (base)[3] $239 (base)[3]	— — —	— — —	— — —
250 CID (4.1L), 1-bbl., 6-cyl.	91	L	3-speed manual		—	$42[4]	S (Ghia)[4]/ $42 (base)	—	—	—
			3-speed Select-Shift Cruise-O-Matic		—	$283	$239 (Ghia)/ $281 (base)	—	—	—
				MPG: Calif.	— —	16/21 15/21	15/20 15/20	— —	— —	— —
302 CID (5.0L), 2-bbl., V8	140	F	3-speed manual[3]		—	$123	$86 (Ghia)/ $128 (base)	—	—	—
			3-speed Select-Shift Cruise-O-Matic		—	$364	$325 (Ghia)/ $367 (base)	—	—	—
				MPG: Calif.	— —	13/18 12/16	12/16 10/14	— —	— —	— —
351 CID (5.8L), 2-bbl., V8	162	H	3-speed Select-Shift Cruise-O-Matic		—	—	$373 (Ghia)/ $415 (base)	S	—	—
				MPG: Calif.	— —	— —	12/16 9/13	11/16 10/16	— —	— —
400 CID (6.6L), 2-bbl., V8	170	S	3-speed Select-Shift Cruise-O-Matic		—	—	—	$86	S	—
				MPG: Calif.	— —	— —	— —	10/14 9/14	10/14 9/14	— —
460 CID (7.5L), 4-bbl., V8	220	A	3-speed Select-Shift Cruise-O-Matic	MPG: Calif.	— — —	— — —	— — —	$247 10/16 10/13	$196 10/15 9/13	S 10/15 9/13

[1]Unless otherwise noted: All manual transmissions are floor-shift, except on Comet and Monarch. All automatics are column-shift, except on Bobcat, Capri and Cougar w/standard bucket seats. Floor-shift is available for $25 extra on Comet with 3-speed manual, and Comet with automatic (requires bucket seats or a Luxury Décor option), and for $29 extra on Monarch (required with 302 CID V8 and 3-speed manual).   [2]Optional 3.00:1 axle ratio required on Cougars, Montegos and full-size Mercurys sold in California.   [3]Not available in California.   [4]Standard on all models in California.

Major Options

	Bobcat	Comet	Monarch	Montego	Cougar	Marquis
Air conditioning[1]	$416	$416	$430	$467	$467	$504
Tilt steering wheel	—	—	—	$55	$55	$55

	Bobcat	Comet	Monarch	Montego	Cougar	Marquis
Automatic speed control	—	—	—	$103	$103	$103
Rear window defogger	$35	$37	$40	—	—	—
Electric rear window defroster	$60[2]	—	$68	$70	$70	$70
Tinted glass, all windows	$42	$41	$43	$47	$49	S
Dual remote control mirrors	—	$25[3]	$36	$49	$49	$4[4]
Power windows, 2-dr./4-dr.	—	—	$90/$129	$100/$138	$100	$154
Power front vent windows, 4-door	—	—	—	—	—	$72
Power door locks, 2-dr./4-dr.	—	—	—	$59/$84	$59	$5[5]
Power seat, 6-way w/std. seating	—	—	$104[6]	$124	$124	$124
Front bucket seats w/console[7]	S	$	$160	—	S	—
Dual facing rear seats (wagons)	—	—	—	$86	—	$127
AM radio	$65	$65	$65	$74	$74	$74
AM/FM stereo	$225	$218	$225	$238	$238	$249
AM/FM stereo w/8-track tape	—	—	$347	$383	$383	$383
Anti-theft alarm system	—	—	$76	$90	$90	$90
Vinyl top, full	$83	$88	$92	$103	$41	$124[8]
Moonroof, power-operated glass	—	—	$762	—	$832	—
Sunroof, power-operated metal	$210[9]	—	$517	—	$525	$637
Power trunk lid release	—	—	—	—	—	$5[5]
Power steering	—	$124	$124	S	S	S
Power brakes, w/front disc[10]	—	$74	$54	S	S	S
"Sure-Track" anti-lock brakes	—	—	$181	—	—	$197
Rear wheel opening fender skirts	—	—	—	—	—	$47
Deluxe wheel covers	$30	$30	S	$37	—	S
Luxury wheel covers	—	—	—	$69	S	$69
Styled steel wheels	—	$104	—	$130	$61	—
Cast aluminum sport wheels	—	—	$165	—	—	—
Forged aluminum wheels	$166	$186	—	—	—	—
White sidewall tires, std. size	$30	$33	$33	$40	$40	$40

Popular Option Groups & Packages

	Bobcat	Comet	Monarch	Montego	Cougar	Marquis
Appearance protection group	$32	$35	$36	$38	$34	$50
Bumper protection group	$58	$59	$59	$47	$47	$47
Convenience group	$70	$51	—	$45	$45	—
Custom interior option	—	$183	—	—	—	—
Custom option package	—	$456	—	—	—	—
Custom trim group	—	—	—	$384[11]	—	—
Grand Marquis luxury trim group[12]	—	—	—	—	—	$278
GT package	—	$354	—	—	—	—
Interior décor group	—	—	$234	—	—	—
Light group	$33	—	—	—	—	$91
Lock convenience group	—	—	—	—	—	$66–$91
Security Lock group	—	$12	$16	$17	$17	$17
Special Value package	—	$253	—	—	—	—
Sports Accent/Appearance group	$501	—	—	$279	—	—
Visibility light group	—	—	—	$70	$70	—
Visibility/Convenience group	—	—	$101	—	—	—

—= Not Available; S = Standard equipment. [1]Air conditioner w/automatic temperature control is available for $507 on Montego and Cougar, and for $541 on Marquis. [2]Price includes tinted rear window on Runabout. [3]LH remote and RH manual on Comet. [4]LH only standard on full-size Mercurys. [5]Available only as part of the Lock Convenience group. [6]Power four-way seat on Monarch. [7]Bucket seats only on Bobcat; console not available. Available on Comet 2-door, and without console. For Monarch, available only on Ghia, and leather upholstery w/o console. [8]Vinyl roof available on station wagons for $147. [9]Manually operated. [10]Power four wheel disc brakes available for $210 on Monarch, and $170 on Marquis. [11]Custom trim available on Montego MX Villager wagon for $138. [12]Available on Marquis Colony Park wagon only. Standard on Grand Marquis.

Paint Colors

Mercury	Code	Mercury	Code	Mercury	Code
Black	1C	Light Green	47	Yellow	6D
Silver metallic	1G	Ivy Bronze Glamour metallic[1]	4T	Bright Yellow	6E
Medium Slate Blue metallic	1H	Dark Yellow Green metallic	4V	Medium Gold metallic	8C
Bright Red	2B	Light Green Gold metallic	4Z	White	9D
Red	2E	Ginger Glamour metallic[1]	5J		
Dark Red	2M	Medium Copper metallic	5M		
Maroon metallic	2Q	Dark Brown metallic	5Q		
Dark Blue metallic	3G	Saddle Bronze metallic	5T		
Bright Blue Glamour metallic[1]	3K	Tan Glamour metallic[1]	5U		
Silver Blue Glamour metallic[1]	3M	Orange	5W		
Medium Pastel Blue	3Q	Dark Copper metallic	5Y		

In two-tone combinations, first two digits are lower color, and second two digits are upper color. Two-tones available on Comet for $33. [1]Glamour paints available for $35 extra on Comet, $49 on Monarch, $51 on Montego, Cougar, and full-size Mercury's.

1975

Bobcat

"Small cars you can live with for a long time."

Nameplate year of origin: 1975.
Current bodystyle lifespan: 1975 through 1980.
Predecessor to this model: None.
Replacement for this model: Lynx (1981 to 1985).
Percentage of division's production: 8.46%.
Corporate siblings: Ford Pinto.
Primary competition: AMC Gremlin, Dodge Colt, and Pontiac Astre.
Notable changes: All-new model.
Major standard equipment: All-vinyl low-back front bucket seats, color-keyed cut-pile carpeting, carpeted cargo area, fold-down rear seat, I/P mini console, simulated woodgrain parking brake lever handle and I/P appliqué, deluxe two-spoke steering wheel, deluxe safety belts, bright window moldings, protective bodyside molding w/vinyl insert, wide wheel lip moldings, rocker panel moldings, rack-and-pinion steering, manual front disc brakes, styled steel wheels w/center ornament, and B78 × 13 BSW tires. Villager adds: Flip-out rear quarter windows, deluxe sound insulation, "Liftgate Ajar" warning system, standard size wheel lip moldings, and simulated rosewood paneling on bodysides and rear tailgate panel.

Measurements

	Runabout	Wagon
Wheelbase	94.5"	94.8"
Length	169.0"	178.8"
Width	69.4"	69.7"
Height	50.5"	52.0"
Legroom — front	40.8"	40.8"
Legroom — rear	30.4"	30.4"
Headroom — front	37.3"	37.9"
Headroom — rear	35.8"	38.9"
Cargo capacity (cu. ft.)	6.1*	57.6
Fuel capacity (gals.)	13.0	14.0

*With rear seat folded down, 29.0 cu. ft.

Models Available

	Model No.	Base MSRP	Change from LY	Shipping Wt. (lbs.)	Model Year Production	Change from LY
Bobcat 3-Door Runabout (HBK)	20	$3,189	NEW	NA	20,561	NEW
Bobcat 2-Door Villager Wagon	22	$3,481	NEW	NA	13,583	NEW
TOTALS		*Avg. price* $3,335	NEW		*Production* 34,243	NEW

Capri

"Capri ... the Sexy European."

Nameplate year of origin: 1971 (originally used on 1952 Lincoln Capri).
Current bodystyle lifespan: 1971 through 1977 (major restyle for 1976).
Predecessor to this model: None.
Replacement for this model: Capri (1979 to 1986).

Measurements

Wheelbase	100.8"
Length	177.0"

Primary competition: Buick Skylark, Chevrolet Cosworth Vega, and Ford Mustang II 2+2.

Notable changes: No changes.

Major standard equipment: All-vinyl front bucket seats, full-loop carpeting, front armrests, recessed door handles, passenger side assist bar, simulated woodgrain I/P appliqué, lockable glove compartment, day/night rear view mirror, electric rear window defroster, power front disc brakes, rack-and-pinion steering, styled wheels, and 165 × 13 BSW tires. 2800 adds: Instrumentation group and V6 engine. Options available: Automatic transmission, $256; air conditioning, $364; Décor group, $178; AM radio, $65; AM/FM radio, $119; manual sunroof, $141, tinted windshield, $23; and vinyl roof, $83.

Measurements (cont.)

Width	64.8"
Height	50.9"
Legroom — front	41.4"
Legroom — rear	31.1"
Headroom — front	37.4"
Headroom — rear	35.9"
Cargo capacity (cu. ft.)	7.2
Fuel capacity (gals.)	12.7

Models Available

	Model No.	Base MSRP	Change from LY	Shipping Wt. (lbs.)	Model Year Sales (est.)	Change from LY
Capri 2000 2-Door Sport Coupe	EC	$3,566	0.00%	2301	NA	NA
Capri 2800 2-Door Sport Coupe	EC	$3,807	0.00%	2411	NA	NA
TOTALS	*Avg. price*	$3,687	0.00%	*Production*	NA	NA

Comet

"Designed with big-car ideas and big-car soundness."

Nameplate year of origin: 1960.
Current bodystyle lifespan: 1971 through 1977.
Predecessor to this model: Comet (1964 to 1965).
Replacement for this model: Zephyr (1978 to 1983).
Percentage of division's production: 13.31%.
Corporate siblings: Ford Maverick.
Primary competition: AMC Hornet and Dodge Dart.
Notable changes: Minor trim and detail changes.
Major standard equipment: Cloth-and-vinyl front bench seat, color-keyed 12-oz. cut-pile carpeting, front and rear ashtrays w/front lighted, two-speed windshield wipers w/washers, deluxe two-spoke steering wheel, deluxe sound package, hubcaps, and BR78 × 14 BSW tires.

Measurements

	2-Door	4-Door
Wheelbase	103.0"	109.9"
Length	189.4"	196.6"
Width	70.5"	70.5"
Height	52.9"	52.9"
Legroom — front	40.7"	40.7"
Legroom — rear	31.8"	36.0"
Headroom — front	37.5"	37.8"
Headroom — rear	35.9"	36.5"
Cargo capacity (cu. ft.)	11.3	12.8
Fuel capacity (gals.)	16.0	16.0

Models Available

	Model No.	Base MSRP	Change from LY	Shipping Wt. (lbs.)	Model Year Production	Change from LY
Comet 2-Door Sedan	31	$3,236	+9.44%	3070	22,768	-64.84%
Comet 4-Door Sedan	30	$3,270	+9.33%	3193	31,080	-49.00%
TOTALS	*Avg. price*	$3,253	+9.38%	*Production*	53,648	-57.16%

Monarch

"America's newest fine car in a new precision size."

Nameplate year of origin: 1975 (used on Canadian Ford brand from 1946 to 1961).
Current bodystyle lifespan: 1975 through 1980.
Predecessor to this model: None.

Measurements

Wheelbase	109.9"

Replacement for this model: Cougar (1981 to 1982).
Percentage of division's production: 25.69%.
Corporate siblings: Ford Granada.
Primary competition: Buick Skylark and Oldsmobile Omega.
Notable changes: All-new model.
Major standard equipment: All-vinyl front bucket seats w/recliners, 18-oz. cut-pile carpeting, simulated high-gloss woodgrain I/P appliqué, locking glove box, bright window moldings, full-length bodyside molding, stand-up hood ornament, manual front disc brakes, wheel covers, and DR78 × 14 BSW tires. Ghia adds: Super-soft all-vinyl front bucket seats w/recliners, 22-oz. cut-pile shag carpeting, deluxe color-keyed seat belts, luxury steering wheel, digital clock, day/night rearview mirror, LH remote control outside mirror, carpeted luggage compartment, deluxe sound and ride package, Odense grain vinyl roof, chrome lower bodyside moldings w/Odense grain vinyl inserts, wheel lip moldings, unique Ghia wheel covers, and DR78 × 14 WSW tires. Grand Ghia adds: Choice of velour or soft grain leather front bucket seats w/recliners, front floor console, deep cut-pile carpeting, dome/dual map reading light, power windows, Normande grain vinyl roof, power steering, power four wheel disc brakes, and cast aluminum spoke wheels.

Measurements (cont.)

Length	197.7"
Width	74.0"
Height	53.4"
Legroom — front	41.1"
Legroom — rear	36.0"
Headroom — front	38.5"
Headroom — rear	37.6"
Cargo capacity (cu. ft.)	14.4
Fuel capacity (gals.)	19.2

1975

Models Available

	Model No.	Base MSRP	Change from LY	Shipping Wt. (lbs.)	Model Year Production	Change from LY
Monarch 2-Door Sedan	35	$3,764	NEW	3234	29,151	NEW
Monarch 4-Door Sedan	34	$3,822	NEW	3284	34,307	NEW
Monarch Ghia 2-Door Sedan	38	$4,291	NEW	3302	17,755	NEW
Monarch Ghia 4-Door Sedan	37	$4,349	NEW	3352	22,723	NEW
Monarch Grand Ghia 4-Door Sedan	37	$5,375	NEW	3441	*	NEW
TOTALS		*Avg. price* $4,320	NEW		*Production* 103,936	NEW

Monarch Grand Ghia was a mid-year introduction, and production was kept as combined with Ghia 4-door as model number was identical.

Montego

"The mid-size Montego makes eminent good sense for the family facing today's rising costs."

Nameplate year of origin: 1968.
Current bodystyle lifespan: 1972 through 1976.
Predecessor to this model: Montego (1970 to 1971).
Replacement for this model: Cougar (1977 to 1979).
Percentage of division's sales volume: 16.11%.
Corporate siblings: Ford Torino.
Primary competition: AMC Matador, Buick Century, Dodge Coronet, Oldsmobile Cutlass, and Pontiac LeMans.
Notable changes: Minor trim and detail changes.
Major standard equipment: Choice of cloth-and-vinyl or all-vinyl low-back front bench seat, color-keyed carpeting, black I/P trim, windshield and rear window bright moldings, drip rail moldings, front bumper guards, power steering, power front disc brakes, hubcaps, and HR78 × 14 BSW tires. MX adds: Simulated woodgrain I/P trim, side window bright moldings, wheel lip moldings, rocker panel moldings, upper bodyside tape stripes, and deluxe sound insulation. MX wagon adds: All-vinyl front bench seat, three-way tailgate, carpeted load floor, and front and rear bumper guards. MX Brougham adds: Choice of Brougham cloth-and-vinyl or super-soft vinyl "Flight Bench" front seat w/fold-down center armrest, deluxe two-spoke steering wheel w/woodgrain inserts, Brougham door panels w/lower carpeting, and deluxe wheel covers. MX Villager adds: All-vinyl bench "Flight Bench" front seat w/fold-down center armrest, power tailgate window, and simulated woodgrain bodyside and tailgate paneling w/bright surround moldings.

Measurements

	2-Doors	4-Doors	Wagons
Wheelbase	114.0"	118.0"	118.0"
Length	215.5"	219.5"	224.4"
Width	78.6"	78.6"	79.6"
Height	52.6"	53.3"	54.9"
Legroom — front	42.5"	42.5"	42.1"
Legroom — rear	33.2"	37.8"	37.1"
Headroom — front	37.9"	38.5"	38.3"
Headroom — rear	36.5"	37.3"	38.6"
Cargo capacity (cu. ft.)	16.5	16.5	93.0*
Fuel capacity (gals.)	26.5	26.5	21.0

Includes 8.1 cu. ft. of hidden cargo space.

Models Available

	Model No.	Base MSRP	Change from LY	Shipping Wt. (lbs.)	Model Year Production	Change from LY
Montego 2-Door Hardtop	03	$4,092	+25.44%	4003	4,051	-47.01%
Montego 4-Door Pillared Hardtop	02	$4,128	+25.28%	4066	4,142	-27.00%
Montego MX 2-Door Hardtop	07	$4,304	+27.41%	4030	13,666	-34.79%
Montego MX 4-Door Pillared Hardtop	04	$4,328	+26.81%	4111	16,033	-17.55%
Montego MX 4-Door, 6-p. Wagon	08	$4,674	+16.33%	4464	4,508	+10.35%
Montego MX Brougham 2-Door Hardtop	11	$4,453	+24.35%	4054	8,791	-57.41%
Montego MX Brougham 4-Dr. Pillared HT	10	$4,498	+24.43%	4130	8,235	-38.85%
Montego MX Villager 4-Door, 6-p. Wagon	18	$4,909	+15.72%	4522	5,754	-7.70%
TOTALS	Avg. price	$4,423	+22.85%	Production	65,180	-33.50%

Cougar XR-7

"Cougar invites you to enter the world of sleek elegance and bold glamour."

Nameplate year of origin: 1967.
Current bodystyle lifespan: 1974 through 1976.
Predecessor to this model: Cougar (1971 to 1973).
Replacement for this model: Cougar XR-7 (1977 to 1979).
Percentage of division's production: 15.57%.
Corporate siblings: Ford Elite.
Primary competition: Buick Regal, Dodge Charger SE, Oldsmobile Cutlass Supreme, and Pontiac Grand Prix.
Notable changes: Minor trim and detail changes.
Major standard equipment: Choice of super soft all-vinyl "Twin Comfort" Lounge front seat or all-vinyl bucket seats w/console, deep 22-oz. cut-pile carpeting, performance instrument panel, luxury two-spoke color-keyed steering wheel w/woodgrain inserts, courtesy lights, tinted glass, landau vinyl roof w/opera windows, power steering, power front disc brakes, specially tuned suspension system, luxury wheel covers, and HR78 × 14 BSW tires.

Measurements

Wheelbase	114.0"
Length	215.5"
Width	78.5"
Height	52.7"
Legroom — front	42.1"
Legroom — rear	32.2"
Headroom — front	37.4"
Headroom — rear	36.3"
Cargo capacity (cu. ft.)	16.5
Fuel capacity (gals.)	26.5

Models Available

	Model No.	Base MSRP	Change from LY	Shipping Wt. (lbs.)	Model Year Production	Change from LY
Cougar XR-7 2-Door Hardtop	93	$5,218	+12.68%	4108	62,987	-31.29%
TOTALS	Avg. price	$5,218	+12.68%	Production	62,987	-31.29%

Marquis

"One of the world's finest riding cars, engineered to give you satisfaction and confidence in every critical area."

Nameplate year of origin: 1967.
Current bodystyle lifespan: 1971 through 1978 (restyled in 1973 and 1975).
Predecessor to this model: Marquis (1969 to 1970).
Replacement for this model: Marquis & Grand Marquis (1979 to 1991).

Measurements

	2-Doors	4-Doors	Wagons
Wheelbase	124.0"	124.0"	121.0"
Length	229.0"	229.0"	225.7"
Width	79.6"	79.6"	79.8"

Percentage of division's sales volume: 20.87%.
Corporate siblings: Ford LTD.
Primary competition: Buick Electra 225 and Estate Wagon, Chrysler Newport and Town & Country, Oldsmobile Ninety-Eight and Custom Cruiser, and Pontiac Grand Ville and Grand Safari.
Notable changes: Minor trim and detail changes.
Major standard equipment: Cloth-and-vinyl front bench seat w/fold-down center armrest, deep cut-pile carpeting, simulated woodgrain I/P and steering wheel appliqué, deluxe two-spoke steering wheel, electric clock, dome light, LH remote control mirror, tinted glass, sound insulation package, bright window moldings, rocker panel molding, front

Measurements (cont.)

	2-Doors	4-Doors	Wagons
Height	53.8"	54.7"	57.1"
Legroom — front	41.6"	41.7"	41.7"
Legroom — rear	35.7"	39.9"	37.1"
Headroom — front	37.6"	38.5"	39.0"
Headroom — rear	36.7"	37.5"	39.5"
Cargo capacity (cu. ft.)	22.7	22.7	103.7*
Fuel capacity (gals.)**	24.2	24.2	21.0

*Includes 9.1 cu. ft. of hidden cargo space. **Extended range fuel tank, available for $94, adds 10 gallons to wagons, and 8 gallons to others.

bumper guards, deluxe wheel covers, and HR78 × 15 BSW tires. Wagon adds: All-vinyl front bench seat w/fold-down center armrest, bright seat side shields, cargo area light, three-way tailgate w/power tailgate window, and JR78 × 15 BSW tires. Marquis Brougham adds: Brougham cloth and vinyl front bench seat w/fold-down center armrest, rear seat center armrests, 22-oz. cut-pile carpeting, Brougham door panels w/lower carpeted panel and door pull assist strap, RH visor vanity mirror, courtesy lights, power windows, front and rear door courtesy lights, luggage compartment light, vinyl roof, full-length fender peak molding, rear wheel opening fender skirts, and Brougham wheel covers. Colony Park adds: All vinyl "Flight Bench" front seat w/fold-down center armrest, cargo area light, three-way tailgate w/power tailgate window, and simulated rosewood exterior paneling on bodysides and tailgate. Grand Marquis adds: Choice of leather-and-velour or leather-with-vinyl individually adjustable Twin Comfort Lounge seats, digital clock, carpeted luggage compartment, dome/dual map reading light, full-length bodyside protective molding w/color-keyed vinyl insert, hood and deck lid paint stripes, specific Grand Marquis nameplates and ornamentation, and JR78 × 15 BSW tires.

Models Available

	Model No.	Base MSRP	Change from LY	Shipping Wt. (lbs.)	Model Year Production	Change from LY
Marquis 2-Door Hardtop	66	$5,049	+1.06%	4470	6,807	+158.53%
Marquis 4-Door Pillared Hardtop	63	$5,115	+2.38%	4513	20,058	+190.27%
Marquis 4-Door, 6-pass. Station Wagon	74	$5,411	+10.97%	4880	1,904	+71.38%
Marquis Colony Park 4-Door, 6-pass. Wagon	76	$5,598	+12.36%	4953	11,652	+7.87%
Marquis Brougham 2-Door Hardtop	64	$5,972	+9.88%	4747	7,125	-30.19%
Marquis Brougham 4-Door Pillared Hardtop	62	$6,037	+11.08%	4799	19,667	-19.65%
Grand Marquis 2-Door Hardtop	61	$6,403	NEW	4762	4,945	NEW
Grand Marquis 4-Door Pillared Hardtop	60	$6,469	NEW	4815	12,307	NEW
TOTALS	Avg. price	$5,757	+11.91%	Production	84,465	+38.21%

OLDSMOBILE

"It's a good feeling to have an Olds around you."

Every car in the Oldsmobile lineup had at least a slightly revised appearance this season. The line also boasted the all-new Starfire subcompact, the smallest Oldsmobile since the runabouts of Oldsmobile's early years more than 70 years prior, and a completely redesigned compact Omega. After the highly successful 1974 season for the mid-size Cutlass line, it seemed Oldsmobile could do no wrong, and by the end of the 1975 model year, the Cutlass line again would account for over half of the division's sales and production. To add to the fuel efficiency, a new 260 CID V8 engine was introduced as standard on the mid-size Cruiser station wagons and as optional equipment on all other Cutlass models, as well as the compact Omega. The successful results would move Oldsmobile back into the third spot for industry production, a position it would relinquish only once over the next dozen seasons.

The all-new Starfire hatchback was a spinoff of the similarly new Buick Skyhawk and Chevrolet Monza 2+2, all of which were based on Chevrolet Vega H-body underpinnings. For the Starfire, aside from styling, that's about as far as the connection to Chevrolet would go. Power under the hood came from Buick's "new" V6 engine,* while differing suspension gave the Starfire a sportier feel. Sometime after the start of the year, a "Sport Hatchback" model was added, which became known as the SX for the 1976 model year. See details of this model's equipment under the 1976 Oldsmobile section.

Styling of the Starfire was very similar to the other GM H-body cars with a rakish windshield and sloping fastback profile. At the front, the Starfire carried a smaller version of an Oldsmobile grille consisting of two rectangular, horizontal air inlets that were chrome lined with black egg-crate style grille inserts, divided by a body-color panel. A red Starfire emblem was placed near the middle above the grille, where the swept-back header and sloping hood dipped between dual rectangular headlamps, creating a tunneled effect. The body-colored front bumper assembly had chrome trim on top, a black bumper impact strip, and twin air inlets set directly below the grille. Parking and turn signal lights were mounted in the lower bumper ends directly under the headlights. Along the bodysides was a mid-level feature line running end to end, beginning a few inches above the front bumper and ending slightly above the rear bumper. The Starfire also offered a bright-edged paint stripe that ran along the bodysides between the front and rear bumper rub strips. The rear of the door glass frame and the B-pillar carried a ribbed vent design, and was actually a functional vent for the flow-through ventilation system. Around back were horizontal wraparound taillights set between the hatchback lid opening and the rear bumper. Backup lights were set at the inner end of the taillights, and a brushed aluminum trim piece was in between, with the Starfire emblem centered on the trim.

Inside the Starfire had a very nice appearance, with an instrument pod centered in front of the driver carrying a full set of gauges, including a tachometer.* Below the pod was a horizontal strip that started to the left of the steering column holding light and wiper controls, and continued to the right side with ventilation and miscellaneous controls, and on to the center of the instrument panel for the radio controls. All of these areas were lined with simulated woodgrain appliqués, and gauges had bright surrounds lining their round openings. Door panels were of color-keyed vinyl, plastics and carpeting, but looked very luxurious. Bucket seats with a center floor console, housing the gear shifter and parking brake, were

standard, and actually offered leather upholstery as an option. A fold-down rear bench seat allowed the subcompact Starfire to carry quite a load.

Compact Omega models received a major redesign for the new model year, and were among the better-looking compacts available. Nearly all body panels and the greenhouse area were shared with the other GM X-body cars, meaning a fixed rear quarter window on two-doors, and four-door models with a fixed quarter window in the rear door. GM's flow-through ventilation system exited through C-pillar vents on sedans and through the B-pillar vent style moldings on coupes and hatchbacks. This would be a one-year only design, as GM would move the vents to the door opening near the latch where it could not be seen from the outside, and eliminate the chance for water leaks. At the front was a new take on the wrapover front header panel. Single round headlamps and a body-color center panel with the Oldsmobile "rocket" logo continued, but the grille was of a crosshatch design consisting of two chrome lined grilles per side, each having a vertical crosshatch grille insert of three rows high and ten columns across. The uppermost row angled rearward at about a 45-degree angle. The two outermost grille sections held a rectangular parking/turn signal light that was inset, as it was partially set into the angled top row of the grille. This was all above a shelf style front bumper with an oblong rectangular opening in the center.

Two-door Omega models tended to have a nearly fastback profile, while the four-door sedans were more upright and formal in appearance, though not having a vertical rear window by any means. At the rear, the Omega had a gently sloping rear panel with wraparound taillights, inward mounted backup lights, and a centered license plate housing. Body color panels sat between the license plate mount and the backup lights. Inside, the Omega shared its instrument panel layout with its corporate siblings, but with some changes to the gauge cluster. Vertical ventilation controls were found on the right side of the driver's pod, and a vertical air vent was located on the far left side. In between, a horizontal speedometer set in a long, thin rectangular opening was flanked by round fuel and temperature gauges, set into an aluminum style bezel. At the bottom of the driver's pod were the optional radio to the right and light and wiper controls to the left. Seating was surprisingly comfortable and well trimmed for a car in Omega's price range. The reclining individual front seats in the Omega Salon were a one-of-a-kind feature in a car of this size and price.

All three Omega models returned for 1975, coupe, hatchback and sedan, and were joined by a sport/luxury Salon model, inspired by the success of the Cutlass Salon option of 1973 and 1974. The Salon featured standard reclining bucket seats, front floor sports console, and a specific suspension tuning for better response. The F-85 name returned to the Oldsmobile line after a two-year absence, this time being used on the compact Omega series as an entry-level coupe, instead of in the mid-size Cutlass series as an entry-level sedan. It was a stripped-down version of the base Omega coupe, which Oldsmobile hoped would keep economy-minded buyers in the Oldsmobile showroom.

The popular Cutlass Supreme coupes adopted swiveling bucket seats as an option, formerly seen as an option for the Cutlass S only—but now with a unique twist. For the Supreme, reversible inserts allowed owners to switch between vinyl and fabric upholstery, a gimmick that lasted only for this one model year. As with the Omega Salon, reclining individual lounge seats with center floor console were a standard feature inside the Cutlass Salon, which now held full model status, rather than being an option package on the Cutlass Supreme as it had been for the past two seasons. Outside, all Cutlass models shared the same general styling makeover with a differing grille pattern and taillight configuration for the Cutlass Salon. All models now wore a wider split grille that housed vertical rectangular parking/turn signal lights at the outer ends, and continued their use of round headlamps set into the front fender ends. Each grille on all but the Salon was divided into eight vertical sections with used dark inserts. The Salon used a fine textured insert surrounded by chrome trim, with the insert being of a horizontal crosshatch design, four rows high and about thirty columns across. Base and S models used an Oldsmobile rocket emblem in the center of the nose, while the Supreme and Salon used the rocket stand-up hoood ornament. At the rear, Supreme and Salon models used a vertical taillamp, divided by a vertical chrome strip with the Oldsmobile logo on it, while the Cutlass S and base models used two stacked square taillight lenses, divided by a body color strip. The station wagon models continued to use horizontal lamps about a foot in length, set into the bumper, with a small backup light centered within each.

The Cutlass Hurst/Olds coupe option was again available, and still with a choice of 350 CID or 455 CID V8 engines. As a sign of the times, the 350 V8 actually edged out the 455 V8 in sales. This year, the option package was only available on the Cutlass Supreme coupe and it featured standard "Hurst/Hatch" removable roof panels. The option would be available on specific models in 1976, and by 1977 would begin to see more widespread popularity. The 2,536 1975 Hurst/Oldsmobiles built would be the last until the 1979 model year. Also, the 4-4-2 option package was still available with 212 base Cutlass coupes and 6,015 Cutlass S coupes produced with the package.

Delta 88 models again had a change in the greenhouse area, this year for the four-door models. The Town Sedan added a fixed rear door mounted quarter window, while the four-door hardtop added a triangular fixed quarter window within the C-pillar. This quarter window greatly improved rearward visibility. Along with this change the rear window was now flatter and more formal in appearance. Similar changes were made to the Ninety-Eight four-door hardtops, while the two-door models were given a fixed rear quarter window, making them into a hardtop coupe, since they now had a fixed B-pillar and no longer had an opening rear quarter window, although the front door glass was still frameless. The Delta 88 Royale convertible was in its last season, and would see sales quadruple as buyers flocked to buy the last of a quickly vanishing body style. The grille on Delta 88s was split into two sections per side this year, with a rocket emblem on the body color center panel divider, and each of the four sections being chrome lined, with a vertical crosshatch insert of five rows high and twelve columns across. Around back, a larger single square taillight lens wrapped around the rear panel edge to double as the side marker light. Note that several sources, including the EPA, list a 400 CID V8 engine being available on Delta 88, Custom Cruiser, and Ninety-Eight models, but Oldsmobile literature does not show this option. It is possible a Pontiac 400 CID V8 engine may have been supplied for use in high-altitude counties, in California, or even to meet high demand, but this could not be confirmed.

The Ninety-Eight and the Toronado were the first full-size Oldsmobile models to make use of dual rectangular headlights. For the Ninety-Eight, the top edge of the headlight bezel was level with the grille. Fender end caps were still slightly pointed, and this meant that the bezel was divided into two sections. The new grille was still split by a body color header panel, and consisted of three chrome lined sections, with each section carrying eight vertical rectangles stacked two rows high and four columns across. At the rear, the Ninety-Eight series used a new, taller taillight in a larger chrome housing, the shape of which resembled a cathedral window. For the Toronado, rectangular headlights replaced the round ones on an otherwise unchanged front end, but around back a new bumper included vertical ends on the rear quarter panel, looking quite similar to current Cadillac design. Taillights were mounted vertically under the decklid opening, and were still supplemented by the "eye-level" signal lamps placed directly under the rear window. The Custom Cruiser used what appeared to be the same grille design as the Ninety-Eight this year, but it did have a different header panel than the Ninety-Eight since it still used round headlamps. Otherwise there were few other changes to be found.

Custom Cruiser 4-Door Station Wagon

Cutlass 4-Door Colonnade Hardtop Sedan

Cutlass S 2-Door Colonnade Hardtop Coupe

Cutlass S 2-Door Colonnade
Hardtop Coupe with 4-4-2 package

Cutlass S coupe interior with swivel bucket seats

Cutlass Salon 2-Door
Colonnade Hardtop Coupe

Cutlass Supreme 2-Door
Colonnade Hardtop Coupe

Delta 88 2-Door Hardtop

Delta 88 Royale 4-Door Hardtop

Ninety-Eight LS Luxury Coupe 2-Door Hardtop

Ninety-Eight Regency 4-Door Hardtop

Omega 4-Door Sedan

Omega Salon 2-Door Coupe

Starfire 2-Door Hatchback Coupe

Starfire instrument panel

Toronado Brougham interior

Toronado Brougham 2-Door Hardtop Coupe

Vista-Cruiser 4-Door Station Wagon

Starfire interior

1975

Model year production: 631,995, up 8.74% from 1974.
Domestic market share: 8.96% (3rd place).
Base price range: $3,203 to $6,753.
Oldsmobile average base price: $4,679, up 6.41%.
Introduction date: September 27, 1974.
Assembly plants: Doraville, GA (D); Linden, NJ (E); Framingham, MA (G); Van Nuys, CA (L); Lansing, MI (M); Arlington, TX (R); Kansas City/Fairfax, KS (X); Willow Run, MI (W); Fremont, CA (Z); and St. Therese, Quebec, Canada (2).
Data plate identification (VIN): Thirteen digit code read as

follows: First digit indicates division (3 = Oldsmobile); second through fourth digits indicate series and body style (model number in model charts); fifth digit is engine code (see powertrain chart); sixth digit indicates model year (5 = 1975); seventh digit indicates assembly plant (see list above); remaining digits are sequential with beginning number of 100001, except for Toronado which begins with 700001. *Example:* 3L69K5X100001 is a 1975 Oldsmobile Delta 88 4-Door Town Sedan, with 350 CID, 4-bbl. V8 engine, serial number 100001, built in Kansas City/Fairfax, KS.

Powertrains

Engine	Net HP	Engine Code	Transmission Availability[1]		Starfire	Omega	Cutlass & Vista-Cruiser	Delta 88	98 & Custom Cruiser	Toronado
231 CID (3.8L), 2-bbl., V6[2]	110	C	4-speed manual		S	—	—	—	—	—
			3-speed Turbo Hydra-matic		$235	—	—	—	—	—
				MPG:	19/25	—	—	—	—	—
				Calif.	17/23	—	—	—	—	—
250 CID (4.1L), 1-bbl., 6-cyl.	105	D	3-speed manual		—	S (base)	S[3]	—	—	—
			3-speed Turbo Hydra-matic		—	S (Salon)/ $237 (Base)	$237[3]	—	—	—
				MPG:	—	16/21	16/21	—	—	—
				Calif.	—	15/20	16/21	—	—	—
260 CID (4.3L), 2-bbl., V8	110	F	3-speed manual		—	$78 (Base)	$78[3]	—	—	—
			3-speed Turbo Hydra-matic		—	$78 (Salon)/ $315 (Base)	S[4]/$315[3]	—	—	—
				MPG:	—	15/19	15/19	—	—	—
				Calif.	—	13/17	15/19	—	—	—
350 CID (5.7L), 2-bbl., V8	155	H, J	3-speed Turbo Hydra-matic		—	$130 (Salon)/ $367 (Base)	—	—	—	—
				MPG:	—	14/19	—	—	—	—
350 CID (5.7L), 4-bbl., V8	170[5]	K	3-speed Turbo Hydra-matic		—	$180 (Salon)/ $315 (Base)	S[6]/$102[4]/ $315[3]	S	—	—

Engine	Net HP	Engine Code	Transmission Availability[1]		Starfire	Omega	Cutlass & Vista-Cruiser	Delta 88	98 & Custom Cruiser	Toronado
				MPG:	—	14/18	15/20	14/18	—	—
				Calif.	—	14/18	13/19	12/16	—	—
400 CID (6.6L), 2-bbl., V8[7]	175	R	3-speed Turbo Hydra-matic		—	—	—	$6	—	—
				MPG:	—	—	—	12/17	—	—
400 CID (6.6L), 4-bbl., V8[7]	185	S	3-speed Turbo Hydra-matic		—	—	—	—	-$62 (Credit option)	—
				MPG:	—	—	—	—	11/15	—
455 CID (7.4L), 4-bbl., V8	190	T	3-speed Turbo Hydra-matic		—	—	$119[5]/ $220[4]/ $535[3]	$135	S	—
				MPG:	—	—	13/19	13/18	12/16	—
				Calif.	—	—	11/19	11/16	10/15	—
455 CID (7.4L) H.O., 4-bbl., V8	215	W	3-speed Turbo Hydra-matic		—	—	—	—	—	S
				MPG:	—	—	—	—	—	11/16
				Calif.	—	—	—	—	—	10/15

All Oldsmobile V8 engines are officially known as Rocket V8s. [1]*Unless otherwise specified: All 3-speed manuals are column shift. All 4-speed manuals are floor shift. All automatics are column shift, except on Starfire. Floor shift automatic is optional on Omega and Cutlass with other specified equipment at extra cost.* [2]*Engine built by Buick.* [3]*Excluding Salon, Cruiser and Vista-Cruiser.* [4]*Cutlass Salon.* [5]*Horsepower rating for Omega is 165.* [6]*Cutlass Cruiser and Vista-Cruiser wagons.* [7]*400 CID V8 engines built by Pontiac. See introductory text for more information.*

Major Options

	Starfire	Omega	Cutlass	Delta 88	Custom Cruiser	Ninety-Eight	Toronado
Four-Season air conditioner[1]	$398	$435	$453	$487	$487	$487	$487
Tilt-Away steering wheel	$45	$45	$45	$45	$45	$45	$45
Tilt-and-Telescope steering wheel	—	—	—	—	—	$89	$89
Cruise control	—	$65	$65	$65	$65	$65	$65
Electric rear window defroster	$60	$35[2]	$60	$60	$60	$72	$60
Remote control mirror, LH	$25	$13	$13	$13	$13	$45	$45
Tinted glass, all windows	$35	$38	$45	$45	$50	S	S
Power windows, 2-dr./4-dr.	—	$91/$132	$91/$132	$149	$149[3]	$56/$90	$56
Power door locks, 2-dr./4-dr.	—	$56/$90	$56/$90	$56/$90	$90	$56/$90	$56
Power front seat, 6-way w/std. seat	—	—	$117	$117	$117	$90[4]	$117[5]
Front bucket seats, w/console	S	$155[6]	$180[7]	—	—	—	—
Leather upholstery	$198	—	—	$300[8]	—	$300	$300
Air cushion restraint system	—	—	—		—		
AM radio	$63	$69	$73	$85	$85	$85	$85
AM/FM stereo	$214	$233	$233	$233	$233	$233	$233
AM/FM stereo w/8-track tape	—	$363	$363	$363	$363	$363	$363
Vinyl top, full[9]	—	$87	$103	$127	—	$142[10]	$142
Vista Vent sunroof, manual	—	—	$99[11]	—	—	$16	$16
Power trunk lid release	—	$16	$16	$16	—	S	S[12]
Power steering, "Vari-Ratio"	$111	$129	S	S	S	S	S[14]
Power brakes, w/front disc	S	$55	$55[13]	S	S	S	S
Deluxe wheel covers	—	$30	$32	S	S	S	S
Super Stock II wheels	$72	$79	$79	—	—	S	S
WSW tires, std. size	$26	$28	$28	$40	$40	$300	$300
GM Air Cushion Restraint System	—	—	—	$300[15]	—	$300	$300

Popular Option Groups & Packages

	Starfire	Omega	Cutlass	Delta 88	Custom Cruiser	Ninety-Eight	Toronado
Compaticolor option package	$	$	—	—	—	—	—
"S" package	—	$178	—	—	—	—	—
W29 4-4-2 package	—	—	$128	—	—	—	—
W45 Hurst/Olds package	—	—	$1,095	—	—	—	—

—= *Not Available; S = Standard equipment.* [1]*Power steering required on Omega with V8 engines. Power brakes required on Cutlass. "Tempmatic" air conditioner with automatic climate control is available for $37 additional on Cutlass, Delta 88, Custom Cruiser, Ninety-Eight and Toronado.* [2]*Blower type defogger.* [3]*Optional remote-control mirror required.* [4]*Standard on Ninety-Eight Regency.* [5]*Standard on Toronado Brougham.* [6]*Standard on Omega Salon.* [7]*Standard on Cutlass Salon. Swivel bucket seats optional on Cutlass S and Cutlass Supreme coupes only.* [8]*Not available on Delta 88 Royale convertible.* [9]*Landau roof available on Cutlass Salon and Supreme coupes for $106, and on Ninety-Eight Luxury coupe or Toronado for $363.* [10]*Two-door models, $154.* [11]*Available on two-door models and Cutlass Supreme Cruiser only. Standard on Vista-Cruiser station wagon.* [12]*"Constant-Ratio" steering on Toronado.* [13]*Standard on Cutlass Cruiser and Vista Cruiser station wagons.* [14]*"True-Track" anti-lock braking system available on Toronado for $192.* [15]*Not available on convertible.*

Paint Colors

	Code		Code		Code
Cameo White	11	Forest Green metallic	49	Rallye Red[4]	75
Inca Silver metallic[1]	13	Colonial Cream	50	Burgundy metallic[2]	79
Dove Gray[1]	15	Sebring Yellow[4]	51	Sunfire Orange metallic[2]	80
Shadow Gray metallic[2]	16	Sandstone[1]	55		
Ebony Black[3]	19	Omega Bronze metallic[5]	58		
Glacier Blue metallic	21	Sable Brown metallic[3]	59		
Horizon Blue[1]	24	Canyon Copper metallic[1]	63		
Spectre Blue metallic	26	Persimmon metallic[1]	64		
Midnight Blue metallic[1]	29	Crimson Red[3]	72		
Sage Green[1]	44	Cranberry metallic[1]	74		

In two-tone combinations, the first two digits indicate lower color, and the next two digits are the upper color. Two-tone paint available for $38 extra on Omega, Delta 88 and Custom Cruiser. [1]*Not available on Starfire.* [2]*Available only on Starfire.* [3]*Available on all models except Starfire and Omega.* [4]*Available only on Starfire and Omega.* [5]*Available only on Omega.*

Starfire

"The sporty little 4-seater from Oldsmobile."

Nameplate year of origin: 1954 (as designation for 98 convertible); 1961 (as series).
Current bodystyle lifespan: 1975 through 1980.
Predecessor to this model: None.
Replacement for this model: Firenza (1982 to 1988).
Percentage of division's production: 4.92%.
Corporate siblings: Buick Skyhawk and Chevrolet Monza (closely related to Chevrolet Vega and Pontiac Astre).
Primary competition: AMC Pacer, Ford Mustang II and "Lincoln-Mercury" Capri.
Notable changes: All-new model.
Major standard equipment: High-backed bucket seats in grained vinyl with choice of velour or perforated-vinyl inserts, center floor console w/gear shifter and parking brake, folding rear seatback, plush-pile carpeting on all floor surfaces and rear seatback, door panel map pockets, simulated woodgrain I/P appliqué, I/P gauges including tachometer, deluxe sport steering wheel w/steel spokes and padded softgrip rim, dual speed wipers w/washers, functional B-pillar vent louvers, chrome window surround moldings, chrome front and rear wheel lip moldings, power front disc brakes, hubcaps, and BR78 × 13 BSW tires.

Measurements

Wheelbase	151.5"
Wheelbase	97.0"
Length	179.3"
Width	65.4"
Height	50.0"
Legroom — front	42.9"
Legroom — rear	35.6"
Headroom — front	37.7"
Headroom — rear	36.3"
Cargo capacity (cu. ft.)	28.1*
Fuel capacity (gals.)	18.5

With rear seat folded down.

Models Available

	Model No.	Base MSRP	Change from LY	Shipping Wt. (lbs.)	Model Year Production	Change from LY
Starfire 2-Door Hatchback Coupe	T07	$3,873	NEW	2889	31,081	NEW
TOTALS		*Avg. price* $3,873	NEW	*Production*	31,081	NEW

1975

Omega

"It's a lot of little Olds. Still at a compact price."

Nameplate year of origin: 1973.
Current bodystyle lifespan: 1975 through 1979.
Predecessor to this model: Omega (1973 to 1974).
Replacement for this model: Omega (1980 to 1984).
Percentage of division's production: 6.62%.
Corporate siblings: Buick Apollo/Skylark, Chevrolet Nova, and Pontiac Ventura.
Primary competition: Dodge Dart and Mercury Monarch.
Notable changes: Completely restyled.
Major standard equipment: F85: Racine fabric front bench seat, black rubber floor mat, functional ventilation louvers (B-pillar), hubcaps, and E78 × 14 BSW tires. Omega adds: Breathable knit vinyl front bench seat, cut-pile carpeting, simulated woodgrain I/P appliqués, door-operated dome lamps, dual speed wipers w/washers, functional ventilation louvers (B-pillar on two-doors, C-pillar on sedans), chrome window surround moldings, roof drip moldings, chrome front and rear wheel opening moldings, and FR78 × 14 BSW tires. Hatchback model adds: Fold-down rear seat. Salon adds: Choice of LaPorte cloth or Tetra vinyl front bucket seats w/recliner, sports console with shifter, deluxe steering wheel, map pockets in doors, vinyl roof, vinyl insert bodyside moldings, and specially tuned suspension.

Measurements

	Coupe & HBK	Sedan
Wheelbase	111.0"	111.0"
Length	199.6"	199.6"
Width	69.9"	69.9"
Height	53.2"	54.2"
Legroom — front	41.7"	41.7"
Legroom — rear	33.4"	35.3"
Headroom — front	38.3"	39.3"
Headroom — rear	36.6"	36.6"
Cargo capacity (cu. ft.)	14.2*	13.8
Fuel capacity (gals.)	21.0	21.0

Hatchback maximum with rear seat down, 28.4 cu. ft.

Models Available

	Model No.	Base MSRP	Change from LY	Shipping Wt. (lbs.)	Model Year Production	Change from LY
Omega F-85 2-Door Coupe	S27	$3,203	NEW	3276	NA	NEW
Omega 2-Door Coupe	B27	$3,422	+18.70%	3315	15,979	-40.98%
Omega 2-Door Hatchback	B17	$3,546	+16.95%	3408	6,287	-49.50%
Omega 4-Door Sedan	B69	$3,450	+18.52%	3361	13,971	+29.89%
Omega Salon 2-Door Coupe	C27	$4,181	NEW	3402	2,176	NEW
Omega Salon 2-Door Hatchback	C17	$4,298	NEW	3491	1,694	NEW
Omega Salon 4-Door Sedan	C69	$4,192	NEW	3451	1,758	NEW
TOTALS	*Avg. price*	$2,942	+27.67%	*Production*	41,865	-16.74%

Cutlass

"No wonder Cutlass has become the most popular Olds in history."

Nameplate year of origin: 1961 (as F-85 Deluxe sport coupe designation; 1962 as F-85 sub-series; and 1965 as series designation; also used on 1955 Oldsmobile show car).
Current bodystyle lifespan: 1973 through 1977.
Predecessor to this model: Cutlass (1968 to 1972).
Replacement for this model: Cutlass (1978 to 1988; restyled in 1981).
Percentage of division's production: 51.06%.
Corporate siblings: Buick Century, Chevrolet Malibu, and Pontiac LeMans.
Primary competition: Dodge Coronet and Mercury Montego.
Notable changes: Restyled front and rear end and minor trim and detail changes.
Major standard equipment: Choice of Laredo w/vinyl trim or all-vinyl front bench seat, color-keyed rubber floor mat

Measurements

	Coupes	Sedans	Wagons
Wheelbase	112.0"	116.0"	116.0"
Length	211.7"	215.7"	220.4"
Width	76.5"	76.5"	76.8"
Height	53.4"	56.1"	55.3"
Legroom — front	42.1"	42.1"	42.1"
Legroom — rear	33.7"	38.4"	36.8"
Headroom — front	37.7"	38.3"	38.8"
Headroom — rear	37.0"	37.5"	39.4"
Cargo capacity (cu. ft.)	16.0	16.0	85.1
Fuel capacity (gals.)	22.0	22.0	22.0

(coupe), full-floor carpeting (sedan), soft grip steering wheel, simulated French walnut woodgrain I/P and door panel appliqués, deluxe armrests front and rear, rocker panel and wheel lip moldings (sedan), bright window surround moldings, power steering, manual front disc brakes, wheel covers, and FR78 × 15 BSW tires. "S" adds: Cut-pile carpeting, deluxe steering wheel, and chrome rocker panel and wheel lip moldings. Supreme adds: Choice of cloth-and-vinyl or all-vinyl front Custom Sport seat w/fold-down center armrest, luxury door panels with door pull straps, deluxe steering wheel, ribbed louver ornament on lower front fender behind wheel, and stand-up "rocket" hood ornament. Supreme Cruiser adds: All-vinyl front Custom sport seat w/fold-down center armrest, cut-pile carpeting on passenger and cargo floors, remote-control tailgate release (in glove compartment), rear vent window (3-seat model only), power front disc brakes, and HR78 × 15 BSW tires. Vista-Cruiser adds: Vista-vent roof and woodgrain paneling on sides and tailgate. Salon adds: Choice of LaPorte velour w/vinyl trim or all-vinyl individual reclining lounge seats, center floor sports console w/shifter and map case lamp, map pockets in door, stand-up Salon-specific hood ornament, and GR78 × 15 BSW tires.

Models Available

	Model No.	Base MSRP	Change from LY	Shipping Wt. (lbs.)	Model Year Production	Change from LY
Cutlass 2-Door Colonnade HT Coupe	F37	$3,742	+5.17%	3657	12,797	-20.33%
Cutlass 4-Door Colonnade HT Sedan	G29	$3,818	+5.09%	3729	30,144	+17.21%
Cutlass S 2-Door Colonnade HT Coupe	G37	$3,840	+5.06%	3663	42,921	-15.61%
Cutlass Supreme 2-Door Colonnade HT Coupe	J57	$4,035	+4.81%	3677	150,874	-12.47%
Cutlass Supreme 4-Door Colonnade HT Sedan	J29	$4,092	+4.36%	3775	15,517	+23.89%
Cutlass Supreme Cruiser 4-Door, 2-S. Wagon	H35	$4,665	+15.04%	4376	8,329	+142.33%
Cutlass Supreme Cruiser 4-Door, 3-S. Wagon	H45	$4,778	+14.64%	4413	3,096	-0.16%
Vista-Cruiser 4-Door, 2-Seat Station Wagon	J35	$4,875	+14.30%	4380	7,089	+69.15%
Vista-Cruiser 4-Door, 3-Seat Station Wagon	J45	$4,988	+13.93%	4417	7,101	+1.25%
Cutlass Salon 2-Door Colonnade HT Coupe	K57	$4,641	NEW	3915	39,050	NEW
Cutlass Salon 4-Door Colonnade HT Sedan	K29	$4,713	NEW	4008	5,810	NEW
TOTALS	Avg. price	$4,381	+16.18%	Production	322,728	+9.30%

Delta 88

"It's really put together. Beautifully."

Nameplate year of origin: 1965 (88 series began in 1949).
Current bodystyle lifespan: 1971 through 1976.
Predecessor to this model: Delta 88 (1969 to 1970).
Replacement for this model: Delta 88 (1977 to 1985).
Percentage of division's production: 18.68%.
Corporate siblings: Buick LeSabre, Chevrolet BelAir/Impala/Caprice, and Pontiac Catalina/Bonneville/Grand Ville.
Primary competition: Chrysler Newport and Mercury Marquis.
Notable changes: Restyled front end and greenhouse and minor trim and detail changes.
Major standard equipment: Choice of Legato knit nylon or all-vinyl front bench seat, cut-pile carpeting, instrument panel message center, deluxe steering wheel, door panel and I/P French walnut woodgrain appliqués, front and rear bumper vinyl impact strips, bright window moldings, bright rocker panel molding, full wheel covers, and HR78 × 15 BSW tires. Royale adds: Choice of Lombardy velour or Doeskin vinyl Custom Sport front seat w/fold-down center armrest (vinyl seat standard on convertible), Royale ornamentation, cut-pile carpeting on cowl side panels and lower door panels, brushed aluminum door panel trim, courtesy and glove box lights, map light, bright metal accented floor pedals, color-coordinated bodyside molding w/vinyl inserts, and Royale specific wheel covers.

Measurements

Wheelbase	124.0"
Length	226.9"
Width	79.5"
Height	54.3"
Legroom — front	42.4"
Legroom — rear	38.5"
Headroom — front	38.3"
Headroom — rear	38.0"
Cargo capacity (cu. ft.)	NA
Fuel capacity (gals.)	NA

Models Available

	Model No.	Base MSRP	Change from LY	Shipping Wt. (lbs.)	Model Year Production	Change from LY
Delta 88 2-Door Hardtop Coupe	L57	$4,830	+14.45%	4343	8,522	-26.63%

	Model No.	Base MSRP	Change from LY	Shipping Wt. (lbs.)	Model Year Production	Change from LY
Delta 88 4-Door Town Sedan	L69	$4,774	+14.65%	4356	16,112	-10.18%
Delta 88 4-Door Hardtop Sedan	L39	$4,991	+14.25%	4404	9,283	-22.26%
Delta 88 Royale 2-Door Hardtop Coupe	N57	$4,985	+13.94%	4386	23,465	-14.72%
Delta 88 Royale 2-Door Convertible	N67	$5,200	+13.29%	4455	21,038	+466.15%
Delta 88 Royale 4-Door Town Sedan	N69	$4,914	+14.17%	4385	7,181	-68.09%
Delta 88 Royale 4-Door Hardtop Sedan	N39	$5,051	+13.74%	4454	32,481	+23.21%
TOTALS	*Avg. price*	$4,949	+14.06%	*Production*	118,082	-2.89%

Custom Cruiser

*"Custom Cruiser isn't just a station wagon.
It's a luxury wagon — but with built-in Olds toughness."*

Nameplate year of origin: 1971 (1940 as a designation on 90 series cars).
Current bodystyle lifespan: 1971 through 1976.
Predecessor to this model: None.
Replacement for this model: Custom Cruiser (1977 to 1990).
Percentage of division's production: 2.55%.
Corporate siblings: Buick Estate Wagon, Chevrolet BelAir/Impala/Caprice, and Pontiac Catalina Safari/Grand Safari.
Primary competition: Chrysler Town & Country and Mercury Colony Park.
Notable changes: New grille and minor trim and detail changes.
Major standard equipment: Tetra vinyl w/Madrid vinyl trim front bench seat w/fold-down center armrest, cut-pile carpeting on floors and cargo compartment floor, instrument panel message center, Glide-Away tailgate, power tailgate window, LH and RH rear view mirrors, vinyl bumper impact strips, rear wheel opening fender skirts, full wheel covers, and LR78 × 15 BSW tires. "R" models add: Semi-transparent simulated woodgrain vinyl bodyside and tailgate appliqués w/chrome trim surround.

Measurements

Wheelbase	127.0"
Length	231.2"
Width	79.5"
Height	57.2"
Legroom — front	42.1"
Legroom — rear	39.4"
Headroom — front	39.6"
Headroom — rear	39.3"
Cargo capacity (cu. ft.)	106.1
Fuel capacity (gals.)	NA

Models Available

	Model No.	Base MSRP	Change from LY	Shipping Wt. (lbs.)	Model Year Production	Change from LY*
Custom Cruiser 4-Door, 2-S. Wagon	Q35	$5,413	+8.78%	5095	6,008	+35.28%
Custom Cruiser 4-Door, 3-S. Wagon	Q45	$5,552	+8.54%	5146	10,080	-12.16%
Custom Cruiser 4-Door, 2-S. Wagon	R35	$5,568	+15.49%	5107	NA	NA
Custom Cruiser 4-Door, 3-S. Wagon	R45	$5,707	+15.06%	5161	NA	NA
TOTALS	*Avg. price*	$5,560	+11.92%	*Production*	16,088	+1.08%

Production of "Q" non-woodgrained and "R" woodgrained models kept as combined total.

Ninety-Eight

*"Ninety-Eight offers an exceptional opportunity
to attain your first luxury car."*

Nameplate year of origin: 1941.
Current bodystyle lifespan: 1971 through 1976.
Predecessor to this model: Ninety-Eight (1969 to 1970).
Replacement for this model: Ninety-Eight (1977 to 1984).
Percentage of division's production: 12.48%.
Corporate siblings: Buick Electra 225, Cadillac Calais, and Cadillac deVille.

Measurements

Wheelbase	127.0"
Length	232.4"
Width	79.8"
Height	54.2"

Primary competition: Chrysler New Yorker and Mercury Grand Marquis.

Notable changes: Revised front and rear end styling and minor trim and detail changes.

Major standard equipment: Pleated Repose cloth w/Doeskin vinyl trim Custom Sport front bench seat w/fold-down center armrest, cut-pile carpeting, carpeted lower door panels, power controls on door armrest in chrome bezel, two-way power front seat, power windows, French walnut woodgrain I/P trim, door pull straps, electric clock, deluxe safety belts, remote-control LH rear view mirror, wheel opening moldings, rocker panel molding, stand-up Oldsmobile "Rocket" hood ornament, front and rear bumper guards, rear fender skirts, wheel covers, and JR78 × 15 BSW tires. Regency adds: Nylon velour 60/40 front seat deeply tufted w/"loose" cushion look, two-way power adjustment for driver's side, fold-down center armrests front and rear, zippered front seatback pouch pockets, French walnut woodgrain door panel and seat side shield trim, digital quartz-crystal clock, door-mounted entry courtesy lights, and fully-lined trunk compartment w/spare tire cover.

Measurements (cont.)

Legroom — front	42.4"
Legroom — rear	41.1"
Headroom — front	39.3"
Headroom — rear	38.2"
Cargo capacity (cu. ft.)	20.2
Fuel capacity (gals.)	NA

1975

Models Available

	Model No.	Base MSRP	Change from LY	Shipping Wt. (lbs.)	Model Year Production	Change from LY
Ninety-Eight (LS) Luxury Coupe 2-Door HT	V37	$5,950	+11.40%	4591	8,798	-4.74%
Ninety-Eight (LS) Luxury Sedan 4-Door HT	V39	$6,091	+12.09%	4743	18,091	-17.38%
Ninety-Eight Regency Coupe 2-Door HT	X37	$6,212	+10.87%	4621	16,697	+55.77%
Ninety-Eight Regency Sedan 4-Door HT	X39	$6,353	+11.53%	4755	35,264	+45.06%
TOTALS		*Avg. price* $6,152	+13.06%		*Production* 78,850	+11.76%

Toronado

*"It's a good feeling—and a great experience—
to have a Toronado around you."*

Nameplate year of origin: 1966.

Current bodystyle lifespan: 1971 through 1978.

Predecessor to this model: Toronado (1966 to 1970).

Replacement for this model: Toronado (1979 to 1985).

Percentage of division's production: 3.69%.

Corporate siblings: Buick Riviera and Cadillac Eldorado.

Primary competition: Ford Thunderbird.

Notable changes: Revised front end and minor trim and detail changes.

Major standard equipment: Pleated nylon cloth w/Doeskin vinyl trim Custom-Sport front bench seat w/fold-down center armrest, cut-pile carpeting, simulated woodgrain appliqué on I/P, two-spoke steering wheel, digital clock w/quartz-crystal movement, chrome-accented floor pedals, deluxe safety belts, LH remote-control rear view mirror, front and rear bumper guards w/vinyl inserts, chrome wheel covers, and JR78 × 15 BSW tires. Brougham adds: Doeskin vinyl 60/40 divided front seat and six-way power adjustment for driver and passenger.

Measurements

Wheelbase	122.0"
Length	227.6"
Width	79.5"
Height	53.2"
Legroom — front	42.4"
Legroom — rear	35.2"
Headroom — front	38.1"
Headroom — rear	37.1"
Cargo capacity (cu. ft.)	17.0
Fuel capacity (gals.)	26.0

Models Available

	Model No.	Base MSRP	Change from LY	Shipping Wt. (lbs.)	Model Year Production	Change from LY
Toronado Custom 2-Door Hardtop	Y57	$6,523	+13.25%	4647	4,419	-83.98%
Toronado Brougham 2-Door Hardtop	Z57	$6,753	NEW	4691	18,882	NEW
TOTALS		*Avg. price* $6,638	+15.24%		*Production* 23,301	-15.52%

PLYMOUTH

"Introducing the 1975 Plymouths."

The highlight of the 1975 Plymouth line was the newly renamed mid-size Fury series. The former Satellite line returned, including the Road Runner, under the Fury name and received new front end styling, while the semi-fastback styling of the former Sebring coupes and hardtops was replaced with more formal rooflines on the new Fury hardtops. The new front-end design featured single round headlamps set in square chrome bezels, with a slight v-shape to the bezel as it matched the pointed shape of the header panel. A round cornered horizontal grille carried twelve vertical sections, with a horizontal crosshatch pattern of three rows high and four columns across set within each section. The outer section of each side also housed the parking/turn signal lights. A stand-up hood ornament sat atop the header panel on most models, while all carried a front bumper contoured to match the header panel. Bodyside panels remained mostly unchanged, but with the new front end, the cars ended up about four inches longer, and slightly narrower, than the equivalent 1974 Satellite model.

For the new Fury two-door models, a new greenhouse area was introduced that was quite similar to that of the new Chrysler Cordoba and Dodge Charger SE, utilizing a more upright rear window and a gently sloping decklid design. Rear quarter side windows were still opening windows, at a time when fixed rear quarter windows were becoming more common and the true hardtop was disappearing, leaving Plymouth with at least one unique feature in the mid-size market. At the rear, the decklid carried a slightly raised center section that seemed to simulate the Lincoln Continental Mark IV's style of faux spare tire carrier, though here it was angular and less pronounced. Vertical taillights sat in the rear fender ends with backup lights in the lower section of the lens. Reflectors were set into the lower section of the bumper. Sedans and wagons continued with essentially the old Satellite rear design, with sedans having three-section bumper mounted taillights, and wagons using vertical two-section wraparound taillights set in the rear quarter panel end. The new Fury models were virtual twins of the Dodge Coronet models in all respects, which seemed to be a contributing factor toward the slide in Plymouth sales.

Full-size Fury models, which had been newly redesigned for 1974, received some front end styling changes, and the line was renamed the Gran Fury, to distinguish it from the newly named Fury mid-size series. With the name change, the bare bones Fury I four-door sedan was dropped, and the Fury II became the Gran Fury, the Fury III became the Gran Fury Custom, and the top-line Gran Fury Brougham replaced the former Fury Gran Coupe and Gran Sedan models. The Suburban station wagon lineup remained intact. Styling of the newly named Gran Fury line was mostly unchanged from its 1974 Fury counterparts. The base Gran Fury and Gran Fury Custom had a grille update that added a horizontal center bar and a center mounted vertical Plymouth emblem. The Gran Fury Brougham, however, received a completely new grille with an equally new single headlamp setup with vertical parking/turn signal lamps set inboard of the headlights in a divided rectangular chrome bezel. The new grille was of a horizontal crosshatch design consisting of twelve sections across and four rows high, with small horizontal bars inset within each section. Openings in the lower section of the bumper carried some of the grille sections on each side of the license plate mount, while on the Gran Fury and Gran Fury Custom, this area was used for the parking and turn signal lights.

Valiant, Duster and Scamp models saw no significant styling or powertrain changes, except for a revised horizontal crosshatch style grille with a center mounted Valiant insignia. In this most popular of Plymouth series, the number of models was expanded to include a new Custom mid-level trim for the Duster two-door coupe and Valiant four-door sedan. Custom models added features that were standard on the Scamp two-door hardtop, as they were all in the "VH" line, which meant adding full-floor carpeting, deluxe steering wheel, and exterior drip rail moldings to name a few. The top of the line Valiant Brougham added the TorqueFlite automatic transmission to its standard equipment list, making the Valiant unique among its competition. Also two new upholstery choices were offered for the Duster, one being a striped tan and brown colored Caravan cloth option ($49), and the other being a Decorator Special option package that featured white vinyl bucket seats with a plaid cloth insert, surrounded by red vinyl trim. The Decorator Special option package also included a white floor console with woodgrain trim, plus red carpeting on the floor and the back of the fold-down rear seat. Other Plymouth models offered similarly colorful interior options including a variegated blue color Boca Raton cloth-and-vinyl bench seat for the Fury Sport (a no cost option) and a brown striped Holiday cloth-and-vinyl split-back bench seat for the Gran Fury Sport Suburban, available for $53.

Duster 2-Door Coupe with Gold Duster package

Duster interior with Decorator Special package

Fury Custom 4-Door Sedan

Fury Sport 2-Door Hardtop

Fury Sport interior with Boca Raton trim

Gran Fury Brougham 2-Door Formal Hardtop

Gran Fury Custom 4-Door Hardtop

Gran Fury Custom Suburban and
Sport Suburban 4-Door Station Wagons

Road Runner 2-Door Hardtop Coupe

Valiant Brougham 2-Door Hardtop

Valiant Custom 4-Door Sedan

Model year production: 461,788, down 39.06% from 1974.
Domestic market share: 6.55% (6th place).
Base price range: $3,243 to $5,537.
Plymouth average base price: $4,355, up 14.99%.
Introduction date: October 1, 1974.
Assembly plants: Lynch Road, Detroit, MI (A); Hamtramck, MI (B); Jefferson Ave., Detroit, MI (C); Belvidere, IL (D); Newark, DE (F); St. Louis, MO (G); and Windsor, Ontario, Canada (R).

Data plate identification (VIN): Thirteen digit code read as follows: First four digits indicate series and body style (model number in model charts); fifth digit indicates engine code (see powertrain chart); sixth digit indicates year (5 = 1975); seventh digit indicates assembly plant (see list above); remaining digits are sequential with beginning numbers of 100001. *Example:* VL41C5B100001 is a 1975 Plymouth Valiant 4-Door Sedan, with 225 CID, 2-bbl. 6-cylinder engine, serial number 100001, built in Hamtramck, MI.

Powertrains

Engine	Net HP	Engine Code	Transmission Availability[1]		Valiant	Duster	Fury & Fury Custom	Fury Sport, Road Runner & Wagons	Gran Fury & Gran Fury Custom	Gran Fury Brougham & Wagons
225 CID (3.7L), 1-bbl., 6-cyl.	95	C	3-speed manual		S (ex. Brghm.)	S (ex. Duster 360)	S[2]	—	—	—
			3-speed Torque Flite automatic		S (Brghm.)/ $205 (others)	$205 (ex. Duster 360)	$225[2]	—	—	—
				MPG:	18/23	18/23	14/22	—	—	—
				Calif.	15/20	15/20	—	—	—	—
318 CID (5.2L), 2-bbl., V8	145/ 150[3]	G	3-speed manual		$120 (ex. Brghm.)	$120 (ex. Duster 360)	$116[4]	S (ex. wgns.)	—	—
			3-speed Torque Flite automatic		$96 (Brghm.)/ $325 (others)	$325 (ex. Duster 360)	$341	S (wgns.)/ $235 (others)	—	—
				MPG:	13/20	13/20	12/17	12/17	—	—
				Calif.	12/16	12/16	11/14	11/14	—	—
360 CID (5.9L), 2-bbl., V8	180	K	3-speed Torque Flite automatic		—	—	—	$47 (wgns.)/ $280 (others)	S[2]	—
				MPG:	—	—	—	13/22	11/18	—
360 CID (5.9L), 4-bbl., V8	230/ 190[3]	J, L	3-speed Torque Flite automatic		—	S (Duster 360)	$386[5]	$86 (wgns.)/ $321 (others)[5]	$39[4]	—
				MPG:	—	13/19	11/18	11/18	NA	—
				Calif.	—	11/17	11/19	11/19	11/15	—
400 CID (6.6L), 2-bbl., V8	175/ 190[3]	M	3-speed Torque Flite automatic		—	—	—	$97 (wgns.)/ $332 (others)	$44	S[2]
				MPG:	—	—	—	13/16	11/15	11/15
400 CID (6.6L), 4-bbl., V8	195/ 235[3]	N, P	4-speed manual		—	—	—	$327 (Road Runner only)	—	—
			3-speed Torque Flite automatic		—	—	$468[2]	$117 (wgns.)/ $352 (others)	$84	$40
				MPG:	—	—	10/17	10/17	11/16	11/16
				Calif.	—	—	12/17	12/17	10/15	10/15
440 CID (7.2L), 4-bbl., V8	215	T, U	3-speed Torque Flite automatic		—	—	—	—	$156	$116
				MPG:	—	—	—	—	10/15	10/15
				Calif.	—	—	—	—	9/14	9/14

[1]Unless otherwise noted: All 4-speed manuals are floor-shift. All 3-speed manual and automatic transmissions are floor-mounted shift on the following models with bucket seats: Duster 360, and Road Runner. Floor-shift available on Duster and Scamp models for $27 extra. [2]Not available in California. [3]Second horsepower ratings are as installed in Fury models. For 318 V8, the second rating is also as installed in Gran Fury models. [4]Required (or standard) in California. [5]Available only in California, except in Road Runner where it is available in all 50 states.

Major Options

	Valiant	Fury & Fury Custom	Fury Sport, Road Runner & Wagons	Gran Fury & Gran Fury Custom	Gran Fury Brougham & Wagons
Air conditioning[1]	$407	$407	$407	$407	$407
Tilt & telescoping steering wheel	—	—	—	—	$99
"Auto-Speed" control	—	$75	$75	$75	$75
Electric rear window defroster	$67	$73	$73	$73	$73
Tinted glass, all windows	$44	$52	$52	$59	$59
Front vent window, 4-dr. only	—	—	—	$35	$35
Remote control trunk release	—	—	—	$19	$19
Power windows	—	$138	$138	$138	$138
Power door locks, 2-dr./4-dr.	—	—	—	$58/$85	$58/$85
Power seat, bench	$117	$117	$117	$117	
Electric clock	—	$15	$15	$15	$15
AM radio	$73	$80	$80	$88	$88
AM/FM stereo	—	$254	$254	$254	$254
AM/FM stereo w/8-track tape	—	$397	$397	$397	$397
Front bucket seats w/console	$137[2]	—	$155[3]	—	—
Full floor carpeting, color-keyed[4]	S	$20	$20	S	S
Vinyl top	$88	$117	$117	$117	$117
Sunroof, electric	$178[5]	$296[5]	$296[5]	$634[6]	$634[6]
Performance hood treatment	—	—	$26	—	—
Power steering, variable-ratio	$103	$103	$103	S	S
Power brakes, w/front disc[7]	$66	$58	$58	S	S
Deluxe wheel covers	$26	$28	—	$32	S
Premiere wheel covers	—	$56	$24	$66	$34
Rallye road wheels	$66	$72	$72	—	—
Styled road wheels, chrome	—	$117	$117	$138	$106
Styled road wheels, urethane	—	—	$138	—	—
White sidewall tires, std. size	$38	$40	$40	$40	$40

Popular Option Groups & Packages

	Valiant	Fury & Fury Custom	Fury Sport, Road Runner & Wagons	Gran Fury & Gran Fury Custom	Gran Fury Brougham & Wagons
Basic group	$125	$	—	—	—
Decorator special package	$272[8]	—	—	—	—
Easy Order package[9]	$580	$815	$765	$435	$436
Exterior décor package	—	$116			
Gold Duster package	$181[8]	—	—	—	—
Light package	$31				
Luxury equipment package[10]	—	$1,688	$1,599	$1,610	$1,552
Rallye I/P group	—	$	$	—	—
Salon package	—	$230	—	—	—
Space Duster Package	$89[8]	—	—	—	—

— = Not Available; S = Standard equipment. [1]Automatic air conditioning available on Gran Fury for $484. [2]For Duster only, and includes full-floor carpeting. Bucket seats without console are available on Scamp for $83. [3]Bucket seats are standard on Fury Sport and Road Runner, and console is optional. Not available on wagons. [4]Carpeting is standard on all except Fury (base) and Road Runner. [5]Available only on 2-door models, and is manually operated on Valiant/Duster models. [6]Requires vinyl top. Not available on station wagons. [7]Standard on Duster 360 and Fury station wagons. All others have manual front disc brakes as standard, except 6-cylinder Valiant, Scamp and Duster models, which have manual drum brakes. [8]Available on Duster only. [9]Merchandising package on Valiant; includes Light pkg., Basic group, Protection group, power steering, deluxe wheel covers, and a variety of interior and exterior trim upgrades. Easy Order package not available on base Fury RL models or Road Runner. $484 on Fury Wagon. [10]Available only on Fury Custom and Fury Sport.

Paint Colors

	Code		Code		Code
Silver Cloud metallic	A2	Astral Blue metallic	B2	Starlight Blue metallic[2]	B8
Powder Blue	B1	Lucerne Blue metallic[1]	B5	Rallye Red[1]	E5

	Code		Code		Code
Vintage Red metallic	E9	Aztec Gold metallic[5]	L6	Inca Gold metallic	Y6
Frosty Green metallic	G2	Cinnamon metallic	T4	Spanish Gold metallic	Y9
Deep Sherwood metallic	G8	Sienna metallic	T5		
Platinum metallic[2]	J2	Dark Chestnut metallic	T9		
Avocado Gold metallic[3]	J6	Spinnaker White	W1		
Bittersweet metallic[3]	K3	Formal Black	X9		
Sahara Beige[4]	L4	Golden Fawn	Y4		
Moondust metallic[3]	L5	Yellow Blaze[1]	Y5		

Single tones are coded W1, W1. Two-tones are coded X9, W1 where first two digits are accent or roof color, and second two digits are basic body color. [1]Not available on Gran Fury. [2]Not available on Valiant and Fury. [3]Not available on Valiant. [4]Not available on Fury. [5]Available only on Fury.

Valiant

"Proves a compact needn't look like one."

Nameplate year of origin: 1960 (Valiant); 1970 (Duster); 1971 (Scamp).

Current bodystyle lifespan: 1967 through 1976.

Predecessor to this model: Valiant (1963 to 1966).

Replacement for this model: Volaré (1976 to 1980).

Percentage of division's production: 58.04%.

Corporate siblings: Dodge Dart.

Primary competition: AMC Hornet, Chevrolet Nova, and Ford Maverick.

Notable changes: Minor trim and detail changes.

Major standard equipment: All-vinyl front bench seat (Valiant), Cloth-and-vinyl front bench seat (Duster), black I/P trim (Valiant and Duster), simulated woodgrain I/P cluster appliqué (Scamp), two-speed electric windshield wipers, front and rear door armrests, heater and defroster, front door window vents (Valiant), hubcaps, 6.95 × 14 BSW tires (Duster), and D78 × 14 BSW tires (Valiant and Scamp). Scamp and Custom models add: Pleated vinyl front bench seat, cut-pile carpeting, interior décor package, cigarette lighter, roof drip-rail molding, wheel lip moldings, and dual horns. Duster 360 adds: Performance tape stripes, roof drip rail molding, heavy-duty suspension and shock absorbers, dual exhaust, and E70 × 14 BSW tires. Brougham adds: Velour cloth and vinyl front bucket seats w/fold-down center armrest or low back front bench seat, door pull assist straps, color-keyed cut-pile carpeting, premium steering wheel, bright pedal dress-up, trunk carpeting, dual horns, deluxe insulation package, light package, three-speed electric windshield wipers and washers, LH remote control mirror, full vinyl roof, bodyside tape stripes, upper door frame moldings (sedan), stand-up hood ornament, automatic transmission, power steering, front sway bar, and luxury wheel covers.

Measurements

	Duster	Scamp	Valiant
Wheelbase	108.0"	111.0"	111.0"
Length	196.1"	199.0"	199.0"
Width	71.0"	69.6"	71.0"
Height	53.2"	52.7"	54.1"
Legroom — front	41.6"	41.6"	41.6"
Legroom — rear	29.8"	31.7"	35.6"
Headroom — front	37.2"	37.3"	38.3"
Headroom — rear	36.4"	36.6"	37.2"
Cargo capacity (cu. ft.)	19.8*	15.4	15.4
Fuel capacity (gals.)	16.0	16.0	16.0

With Space Duster package fold-down rear seat option, 56.0 cu. ft.

Models Available

	Model No.	Base MSRP	Change from LY	Shipping Wt. (lbs.)	Model Year Production	Change from LY
Duster 2-Door Coupe	VL29	$3,243	+17.80%	2970	79,884	−71.20%
Valiant 4-Door Sedan	VL41	$3,247	+13.29%	3040	44,471	−65.10%
Duster Custom 2-Door Coupe	VH29	$3,418	NEW	2970	38,826	NEW
Scamp 2-Door Hardtop	VH23	$3,518	+17.23%	3020	23,581	−54.39%
Valiant Custom 4-Door Sedan	VH41	$3,422	NEW	3040	56,258	NEW
Valiant Brougham 2-Door Hardtop	VP23	$4,232	+13.82%	3240	5,781	−58.01%
Valiant Brougham 4-Door Sedan	VP41	$4,139	+10.58%	3250	17,803	+599.53%
Duster 360 2-Door Coupe	VS29	$3,979	+23.88%	3315	1,421	−64.20%
TOTALS		*Avg. price* $3,650	+13.50%		*Production* 268,025	−43.79%

Fury

"The small Fury from Plymouth. Excitement.
Luxury. And a fresh new point of view."

Nameplate year of origin: 1956. Applied to mid-size platform for 1975.
Current bodystyle lifespan: 1971 through 1978.
Predecessor to this model: Satellite (1971 to 1974).
Replacement for this model: Caravelle (1985 to 1988).
Percentage of division's sales volume: 26.19%.
Corporate siblings: Dodge Coronet.
Primary competition: AMC Matador, Chevrolet Chevelle, and Ford Torino.
Notable changes: Revised front and rear styling.
Major standard equipment: All-vinyl front bench seat, color-keyed rubber floor covering, cigarette lighter (sedan only), dome light, concealed two-speed windshield wipers, dual horns (sedan only), rocker panel sill molding (sedan only),

Measurements

	2-Doors	Sedans	Wagons
Wheelbase	115.0"	117.5"	117.5"
Length	213.8"	217.9"	225.6"
Width	77.4"	77.7"	79.2"
Height	52.6"	53.9"	56.5"
Legroom — front	41.9"	41.9"	41.9"
Legroom — rear	33.9"	36.7"	36.7"
Headroom — front	37.7"	38.6"	39.7"
Headroom — rear	36.6"	37.4"	38.1"
Cargo capacity (cu. ft.)	14.3	16.7	91.3
Fuel capacity (gals.)	19.5	19.5	21.0

hubcaps, and E78 × 14 BSW tires. Road Runner adds (to base Fury Coupe features): Bodyside and roof tape stripes, deck lid tape stripe, special Road Runner interior trim and ornamentation, performance hood, front and rear sway bars, heavy-duty springs, low-restriction dual exhaust w/chrome tips, "Beep-Beep" horn, argent-painted rallye wheels w/chrome hubs, and G70 × 14 W/L tires. Fury Custom adds: Cloth-and-vinyl front bench seat, color-keyed carpeting, front door and rear side armrests, front and rear door armrests, drip rail moldings, and wheel-lip moldings without sill molding. Fury Sport adds: Vinyl bucket seats, rallye gauge cluster, premium door trim panels, simulated woodgrain inserts on I/P, door trim inserts and steering wheel, special Sport trim and ornamentation, belt moldings, bodyside tape stripes, and deluxe wheel covers. Wagons add: Fold-down rear seatback, power front disc brakes, three-way tailgate, tailgate "auto lock" system (3-seat wagons only), and H78 × 14 BSW tires. Sport Suburban wagon adds: All-vinyl split-back front bench seat w/fold-down center armrest, cargo compartment carpeting and dome light, exterior simulated woodgrained bodyside overlays, and reflectorized rear tailgate woodgrain trim.

Models Available

	Model No.	Base MSRP	Change from LY	Shipping Wt. (lbs.)	Model Year Production	Change from LY
Fury 2-Door Hardtop	RL21	$3,542	+15.98%	3555	8,398	-21.30%
Fury 4-Door Sedan	RL41	$3,591	+14.91%	3585	11,432	-10.17%
Fury Suburban 4-Door, 2-S. Wagon	RL45	$4,309	+21.24%	4180	4,468	-3.33%
Road Runner 2-Door Coupe	RM21	$3,973	+15.36%	3760	7,183	-37.84%
Fury Custom 2-Door Hardtop	RH23	$3,711	+14.11%	3635	27,486	-14.05%
Fury Custom 4-Door Sedan	RH41	$3,704	+14.75%	3635	31,080	-32.23%
Fury Custom Suburban 4-Dr., 2-S. Wagon	RH45	$4,512	+20.71%	4230	3,890	-10.66%
Fury Custom Suburban 4-Dr., 3-S. Wagon	RH46	$4,632	+14.34%	4286	4,285	-23.36%
Fury Sport 2-Dr. Hardtop	RP23	$4,105	+16.62%	3790	17,782	-3.78%
Fury Sport Suburban 4-Door, 2-S. Wagon	RP45	$4,770	+20.30%	4230	1,851	-8.64%
Fury Sport Suburban 4-Door, 3-S. Wagon	RP46	$4,867	+13.45%	4295	3,107	-0.80%
TOTALS	*Avg. price*	$4,156	+16.56%	*Production*	120,962	-19.87%

Gran Fury

"You'll wonder how so much luxury can be priced so reasonably."

Nameplate year of origin: 1956.
Current bodystyle lifespan: 1974 through 1977 (renamed Gran Fury for 1975 to 1977).
Predecessor to this model: Fury (1969 to 1973).
Replacement for this model: Gran Fury (1980 to 1981).

Measurements

	Cars	Wagons
Wheelbase	121.5"	124.0"
Length	219.9"	225.9"

Percentage of division's sales volume: 15.77%.

Corporate siblings: Dodge Monaco.

Primary competition: Chevrolet Impala/Caprice and Ford LTD.

Notable changes: New grille for Brougham and minor trim and detail changes.

Major standard equipment: Cloth-and-vinyl front bench seat, color-keyed front and rear armrests, nylon loop-pile carpeting, cigarette lighter, dome light, front door courtesy light switches, glove box lock, inside hood release, concealed two-speed windshield wipers w/washers, bright drip rail molding, bright 3/4-length bodyside molding, dual horns, hubcaps, and GR78 × 15 BSW tires. Gran Fury Custom adds: Cloth-and-vinyl front bench seat, simulated woodgrained appliqué on I/P cluster and pad, 3-spoke steering wheel w/simulated woodgrained inserts, simulated woodgrained door trim insert, bright base armrests, glove box light, bright wheel lip moldings, and full-length bodyside molding. Gran Fury Brougham adds: Cloth-and-vinyl split back front bench seat w/fold-down center armrest, door pull straps, carpeted lower door panels, electric clock, rear door dome light courtesy switches, extra quiet insulation, bright belt moldings, bright rocker panel sill molding, full-length bodyside paint stripe, deluxe wheel covers, and HR78 × 15 BSW tires. Wagons add: All-vinyl front bench seat, color-keyed carpeting, simulated woodgrain inserts on steering wheel and door trim (Custom), cargo light (Custom 3-seat), aerodynamic roof air deflector, power tailgate window, power steering, and LR78 × 15 BSW tires. Sport Suburban adds: All-vinyl split back front bench seat w/fold-down center armrest, door pull straps, simulated woodgrained appliqué on I/P cluster and pad, 3-spoke steering wheel w/simulated woodgrained inserts, simulated woodgrained door trim insert, carpeted lower door panels, electric clock, rear door dome light courtesy switches, simulated woodgrain bodyside panels, dual horns, and deluxe wheel covers.

Measurements (cont.)

	Cars	Wagons
Width	79.9"	79.4"
Height	54.2"	58.9"
Legroom — front	41.6"	41.6"
Legroom — rear	38.2"	39.0"
Headroom — front	38.0"	38.7"
Headroom — rear	37.0"	38.7"
Cargo capacity (cu. ft.)	22.4	100.8
Fuel capacity (gals.)	23.0	23.0

Models Available

	Model No.	Base MSRP	Change from LY	Shipping Wt. (lbs.)	Model Year Production	Change from LY
Gran Fury 4-Door Sedan	PM41	$4,565	+14.47%	4260	8,185	-29.74%
Gran Fury Suburban 4-Door, 2-S. Wagon	PM45	$5,067	+14.28%	4855	2,295	-7.83%
Gran Fury Custom 2-Door Hardtop	PH23	$4,781	+14.30%	4205	6,041	-57.36%
Gran Fury Custom 4-Door Sedan	PH41	$4,761	+14.31%	4260	19,043	-31.90%
Gran Fury Custom 4-Door Hardtop	PH43	$4,837	+14.27%	4290	11,292	-39.87%
Gran Fury Custom Suburban 4-Dr., 2-S. Wgn.	PH45	$5,176	+14.21%	4870	3,155	-18.83%
Gran Fury Custom Suburban 4-Dr., 3-S. Wgn.	PH46	$5,294	+14.02%	4915	4,500	-20.04%
Gran Fury Brougham Formal 2-Door Hardtop	PP23	$5,146	+17.17%	4310	6,521	-32.19%
Gran Fury Brougham 4-Door Hardtop	PP43	$5,067	+14.12%	4400	5,521	-32.60%
Gran Fury Sport Suburban 4-Dr., 2-S. Wagon	PP45	$5,455	+13.88%	4885	1,508	-11.92%
Gran Fury Sport Suburban 4-Dr., 3-S. Wagon	PP46	$5,573	+13.85%	4930	4,740	-21.61%
TOTALS	Avg. price	$5,066	+15.65%	Production	72,801	-38.46%

PONTIAC

"Pontiac strikes again."

The 1975 model year brought Pontiac into the subcompact arena with the new Astre — uncharted territory for the nearly 49-year-old division. However, there were numerous other new subcompacts entering the market at the same time, including GM's own line of H-bodied, Vega-based cars, the Buick Skyhawk, Chevrolet Monza, and Oldsmobile Starfire, and most of these new models were more modern designs.

This gave Pontiac some difficulties in selling the Astre right from the start. Fortunately there was some promise in the completely restyled Ventura, and freshened front-end styling for nearly all of the other models, giving dealers some hope that this year would improve over the past season. In the end, only the Firebird series had a production increase, with the Trans Am gaining most among the four models and becoming the best selling Firebird model for the first time ever. And despite a second year of sales and production decline, Pontiac would end the year moving back into fourth place in industry production for 1975 as Plymouth continued to falter. It was a position that Pontiac would retain through the end of the seventies.

For the most part, the Astre was one of General Motors' most obvious badge engineering attempts to date. A Pontiac-style split grille using a horizontal opening with egg-crate style inserts and square parking/turn signal lights set into the outer ends created the Astre's frontal appearance. Around back, slot-style taillights, in two horizontal sections per side, were another Pontiac identifier, and upgraded interior upholstery combined to define the main differences from the Vega. A few interesting options included the GT package for the hatchback and wagon, and a little known factory sponsored package called the "Li'l Wide Track" package available on the Astre hatchback. The Li'l Wide Track package, for $402, added a front air dam, rear spoiler, quarter window louvers, striping (on the hood, lower body, spoiler, door handles and wheel centers), a chrome exhaust extension and cast aluminum wheels. The package was designed by BORT (British Overseas Racing Team) and produced by Motortown Corporation, based in Detroit, Michigan. The parts were then sent to be installed at the Vega/Astre Lordstown Assembly plant in Ohio. It is unknown how many were actually produced, but the number is estimated around 200 copies.

Power for the Astre came from the Vega's infamous 140 CID 4-cylinder engine. If it were not for the Firebird-like front end appearance with split grille styling, it would be hard to tell that the Astre was anything other than a new look for the Vega. The Astre had been sold successfully in Canada since 1973, so it was hoped it could add some traffic to American showrooms. Management soon recognized that there were so many new cars competing in the same market this year that the new Astre had to be lower priced if it was to succeed. So, at mid-year the Astre S was added, which included the two-door notchback coupe, the lowest priced Vega body style, as well as the hatchback and wagon. The idea was to lower the price by deleting some of the standard features that made the Astre unique, and essentially giving it the same base trim as the Vega. Whether it was successful in its mission is doubtful, because Astre production would fall from an already weak level during the next two seasons of its short lifespan.

A completely restyled Ventura brought some much needed improvement to the compact Pontiac's appearance. It was still basically the same size as the 1974 version, both inside and out, but its visual appeal was greatly improved. Under the hood could be found the same base 250 CID 6-cylinder engine and optional 350 CID V8 engine, but a new 260 CID V8 engine was added to the option list. Outside,

smoother bodysides were introduced, particularly on the two-door models, which retained a "semi"-fastback roofline and gained wide louvered B-pillars that included functional ventilation. Also on the coupes were fixed rear quarter windows, but a swing-out window option was available. The sedans received a more formal and upright roofline, providing a more modern appearance than their predecessors. Up front, the Ventura grille consisted of four square openings in a body colored front fascia, with a slightly pointed center bearing the Pontiac arrow logo to give it the required Pontiac identity. Each of the four grille areas held six horizontal bars, and the outer openings had a square parking/turn signal light mounted in the center, much like the lights used on this year's Firebird. On the new SJ models and the optional Sprint package, the parking lights were called "Road-style" lights as they had a crosshairs style chrome overlay. Around back, horizontal taillights with a slotted look were used, with each side having three slender rows of lenses separated by black trim. The lenses themselves were unique in that they had five distinct colored areas, with red light and brake light lenses to the outer and inner ends, a white backup light in the center, and small amber turn signal lights between the backup light and the red portions of the lens. Inside were new fabrics and patterns that gave the Ventura a more upscale appearance. At mid-year, a Ventura "S" coupe was introduced with fewer standard features and a lower price tag.

At first glance, the Firebird line appeared not to have any changes, but there were several to be found. Most important to many was that the 455 CID V8 engine was no longer available on any Firebird model. This left the 400 CID V8 engine as the top powerplant choice for the Formula, and it was standard fare on the Trans Am. New features included the RTS package (Radial Tuned Suspension) becoming standard equipment, as it was on all other Pontiacs for 1975, and new 15-inch wheels and tires. Also, because the new models used a catalytic converter, the Formula and Trans Am no longer came with dual exhausts. Visually a new grille insert pattern had six horizontal bars per side, and the parking/turn signal lights were new square units placed within the grille at the outer ends. The lens itself had a crosshairs design on it, and was named by Pontiac as a "Road-style" light. At the rear, all Firebirds added a new wraparound rear window that greatly improved rearward visibility.

The personal luxury Grand Prix received an updated grille pattern with four vertical openings per side, and a large pattern crosshatch insert set behind. New taillamp lenses divided into four sections by chrome trim, with backup lights across the bottom of the lens, completed the identifying features of the 1975 version from the outside. A new LJ luxury option package featured distinctive two-tone paint, padded Landau roof, and velour interior upholstery plus many popular options such as power windows, and power door locks. Package pricing ranged from $577 with a solid exterior color if desired, to $699 with the special two-tone exterior color treatment. There were 14,855 Grand Prix's sold with the package, and another 7,146 having the less expensive SJ sport option package. Perhaps because of its price and less fuel-efficient engine (the 455 CID four-barrel engine was standard), Grand Prix SJ production dropped to just 7,146 units. But another 5,094 455 CID V8 engines were installed in base and LJ models, while the 400 two-barrel was installed in just 1,701 of them, so a more likely reason for the slide was the popularity of the Chevrolet Monte Carlo and Oldsmobile Cutlass Supreme, and the new Ford Elite, Dodge Charger SE and Chrysler Cordoba, all competing for the same slice of the pie.

The mid-size Pontiac lines all received updated grilles and revised taillights and rear panel trim, but were otherwise not greatly changed. Changing the name of the Luxury LeMans to Grand LeMans was an obvious attempt to bolster LeMans series sales by taking part of the successful Grand Prix's name. To make the connection mean more, the Grand Prix cockpit-style instrument panel was standard on the newly named car. Along with the Grand LeMans name change, the luxury mid-size model changed from a standard V8 engine to a standard six-cylinder to help improve the fuel economy image. LeMans and LeMans Sport Coupes had a new grid pattern grille, two rows high and five columns across. Within each of the ten openings per side were four horizontal bars. Parking and turn signal lights were set into the ends of the dual rectangular openings in the front bumper directly below the grille. The Grand LeMans had three rectangular openings per side, each housing seven vertical bars, and wrapping slightly onto the top of the front header panel. The parking/turn signal lights were of the "Road style" design and placed in the center of the outer grille section, with a new stand-up hood ornament atop the center of the header panel. Most other exterior details of the LeMans series were unchanged from 1974. The mid-size European-style Grand Am offered an available formal opera window for the coupe, but was otherwise mostly unchanged. The 455 CID V8 engine was still offered, but the 4-speed manual transmission was no longer available, making the Turbo Hydra-matic the standard transmission. Unfortunately, sales had never been spectacular, and had fallen ever since its introduction in 1973, resulting in the Grand Am being temporarily discontinued. The name would return in a less "enthusiastic" version for 1978.

Pontiac's full-size lineup received new front-end styling and a new roofline for four-door models. The Bonneville and newly named Grand Ville Brougham received dual side-by-side rectangular headlamps, Pontiac's first use of the newly approved lights. A new four-section crosshair style grille appeared, with a slight point, and thicker vertical center bar carrying the Pontiac arrow logo, to define Pontiac's traditional split grille theme. Each of the four grille sections had a horizontal crosshatch insert, seven rows high and ten columns across. The overall effect was to give a wider and lower appearance while allowing the new hood to be lower on the outer front edges. The lower-priced Catalina series stayed with dual round headlights, but had new twin-unit wraparound parking/turn signal lights on the fender ends, and a new horizontal bar grille. The new grille used a body-colored vertical center bar, with three horizontal grille sections stacked along each side of the center. Each chrome lined section carried five horizontal bar inserts. Around back the Bonneville shared taillights with the Grand Ville Brougham; these were of a horizontal design six columns across and two rows high, with the outer sections wrapping around the rear quarter end panels to serve as side marker lights. The Catalina used a flat taillight configuration similar to that on the 1974 models, this year being divided into three stacked horizontal sections rather than two. Catalina Safari and Grand Safari wagons continued to use a small rectangular wraparound taillight with backup lights in the bottom portion of the lens. Bonneville and Grand Ville Brougham four-door hardtops received a new six-window design with a fixed rear quarter window in the C-pillar. Along with the hardtop change, the Catalina four-door hardtop was discontinued, and a new design for the four-door sedan was introduced. The new sedan had a fixed quarter window within the rear door and a flatter style rear window, as opposed to last year's curved window. Other changes included the Bonneville becoming a "P" series model, and the Grand Ville Brougham reclassified as a new "R" series model. Also, the Grand Safari remained in the "P" series, thereby becoming a Bonneville related model, but it was the same code as the 1974 Grand Ville had been, which possibly explains why the Grand Safari for 1975 used Grand Ville level upholstery trim. Finally, it was the last year for the Grand Ville name, which added the Brougham suffix for its final season, and also the last year for the full-size Pontiac convertible. It would be eight years before a convertible returned to the Pontiac line.

Astre 2-Door Hatchback Coupe
with L'il Wide Track package

Astre 2-Door Hatchback Coupe
with GT package

Astre Safari 2-Door Station Wagon

Astre SJ 2-Door Hatchback Coupe

Bonneville 2-Door Hardtop Coupe

Catalina 4-Door Sedan

Firebird Esprit 2-Door Hardtop Coupe

Firebird Formula 2-Door Hardtop Coupe (left)
with Firebird Trans Am 2-Door Hardtop Coupe

Grand Am 2-Door Colonnade Hardtop Coupe

Grand Am interior

Grand LeMans 2-Door Colonnade
Hardtop Coupe with Lemans
4-Door Colonnade Hardtop Sedan, rear

Grand Prix 2-Door Hardtop Coupe

Grand Ville Brougham 2-Door Convertible

Grand Prix 2-Door Hardtop Coupe

Grand Safari 4-Door Station Wagon

LeMans Safari 4-Door, 3-Seat Station Wagon

Ventura 2-Door Hatchback Coupe
with Sprint package

Ventura Custom 4-Door Sedan

Ventura SJ 2-Door Coupe

Model year production: 531,732, down 8.42% from 1974.
Domestic market share: 7.54% (4th place).
Base price range: $3,162 to $5,896.
Pontiac average base price: $4,232, up 8.69%.
Introduction date: September 27, 1974.
Assembly plants: Lakewood, GA (A); Southgate, CA (C); Framingham, MA (G); Van Nuys, CA (L); Norwood, OH (N); Pontiac, MI (P); Tarrytown, NY (T); Lordstown, OH (U); Willow Run, MI (W); Kansas City/Fairfax, KS (X); and Oshawa, Ontario, Canada (1).
Data plate identification (VIN): Thirteen digit code read as follows: First digit indicates division (2 = Pontiac); second through fourth digits indicate series and body style (model number in model charts); fifth digit is engine code (see powertrain chart); sixth digit indicates model year (5 = 1975); seventh digit indicates assembly plant (see list above); remaining digits are sequential with beginning number of 100001. *Example:* 2D35M5G100001 is a 1975 Pontiac Le-Mans 4-Door, 2-Seat Safari station wagon, with 350 CID, 2-bbl. V8 engine, serial number 100001, built in Framingham, MA.

Powertrains

Engine	Net HP	Engine Code	Transmission Availability[1]		Astre	Ventura	Firebird[2]	LeMans[3]	Grand Am & Grand Prix[4]	Catalina & Bonneville[5]	Grand Ville & Grand Safari[6]
140 CID (2.3L) OHC, 1-bbl., 4-cyl.	78	A	3-speed manual		S (base)	—	—	—	—	—	—
			4-speed manual		$56 (base)	—	—	—	—	—	—
			3-speed Turbo Hydra-matic		$235 (base)	—	—	—	—	—	—
				MPG:	19/28	—	—	—	—	—	—
140 CID (2.3L) OHC, 2-bbl., 4-cyl.	87	B	3-speed manual		$50 (base)	—	—	—	—	—	—
			4-speed manual		S (SJ)/ $106 (base)						
			3-speed Turbo Hydra-matic		$179 (SJ)/ $229 (base)						
				MPG:	22/29	—	—	—	—	—	—
				Calif.	18/28	—	—	—	—	—	—
250 CID (4.1L), 1-bbl., 6-cyl.	100	D	3-speed manual		—	S	S (F & FEs)	S (L)	—	—	—
			3-speed Turbo Hydra-matic		—	$237	$237 (F & FEs)	S (GL)/ $237 (L)	—	—	—
				MPG:	—	16/21	16/21	16/21	—	—	—
				Calif.	—	15/20	15/20	15/20	—	—	—
260 CID (4.3L), 2-bbl., V8	110	F	3-speed manual		—	$78	—	—	—	—	—
			3-speed Turbo Hydra-matic		—	$315	—	—	—	—	—
				MPG:	—	15/19	—	—	—	—	—
				Calif.	—	13/17	—	—	—	—	—
350 CID (5.7L), 2-bbl., V8	155	M	3-speed manual		—	$130	$130 (F & FEs)	$130 (L)	—	—	—
			4-speed manual		—	—	$349 (F & FEs)	—	—	—	—
			3-speed Turbo Hydra-matic		—	$367	$367 (F & FEs)	$130 (GL)/ $367 (L)	—	—	—
				MPG:	—	14/19	13/18	12/18	—	—	—

Engine	Net HP	Engine Code	Transmission Availability[1]	Astre	Ventura	Firebird[2]	LeMans[3]	Am & Grand Prix[4]	Grand Catalina & Bonneville[5]	Grand Ville & Grand Safari[6]
350 CID (5.7L), 4-bbl., V8	175	J	4-speed manual	—	—	S (FF)/ $399 (F & FEs)	—	—	—	—
			3-speed Turbo Hydra-matic	—	$417	N/C (FF)/ $417 (F & FEs)	$180 (GL)/ $417 (L)	—	—	—
			MPG:	—	14/18	12/18	13/17	—	—	—
			Calif.	—	14/18	11/15	10/13	—	—	—
400 CID (6.6L), 2-bbl., V8	170	R[7]	3-speed Turbo Hydra-matic	—	—	—	—	S (GA)/ -$50 (GP, credit)	S	-$66 (GV, credit)
			MPG:	—	—	—	—	12/17	12/17	12/17
400 CID (6.6L), 4-bbl., V8	185	S	4-speed manual	—	—	S (TA)/ $56 (FF)	—	—	—	—
			3-speed Turbo Hydra-matic	—	—	N/C (TA)/ $56 (FF)	$236 (GL)/ $473 (L)	S (GP)/ $50 (GA)	S (CS)/ $66 (B & C)	S
			MPG:	—	—	13/18	13/18	13/18	12/15	12/15
			Calif.	—	—	11/15	11/15	11/15	11/15	11/15
455 CID (7.4L), 4-bbl., V8	200	Y	3-speed Turbo Hydra-matic	—	—	—	—	$62 (GP)/ $112 (GA)	$62 (CS)/ $128 (B & C)	$62
			MPG:	—	—	—	—	12/17	11/18	11/18
			Calif.	—	—	—	—	10/14	10/14	10/14

[1]*Unless otherwise noted: All 3-speed manual transmissions are column shift, except on Astre and Firebird models. All 4-speed manual transmissions are floor shift, and available only on 2-door models, unless specially ordered. All automatic transmissions are column shift, with the following exceptions: Astre, Firebird, Grand Am, and Grand Prix. Floor-shift with 3-speed manual can be ordered on Ventura models for $26 extra and on LeMans models for $82 extra (heavy-duty 3-speed). Column shift automatic is available on Grand Prix models when certain equipment selections are made. Floor shift w/automatics is available on specific Ventura, LeMans and Grand Prix models in combination w/optional bucket seats.* [2]*F = base Firebird; FEs = Firebird Esprit; FF = Firebird Formula; TA = Firebird Trans Am.* [3]*L = LeMans & LeMans Sport coupe; GL = Grand LeMans; LS = all LeMans Safaris.* [4]*GA = Grand Am; GP = Grand Prix.* [5]*C = Catalina; CS = Catalina Safari; B = Bonneville.* [6]*GV = Grand Ville Brougham.* [7]*Not available in California.*

Major Options

	Astre	Firebird	Ventura	LeMans & Grand Am	Grand Prix	Catalina & Bonneville	Grand Ville Brougham
Custom air conditioning[1]	$398	$435	$435	$450	$487	$487	$487
Tilt steering wheel	$45	$45	$45	$45	$45	$45	$45
Automatic cruise control	—	—	$65	$65	$65	$65	—
Rear window defroster, electric	$60	$35[2]	$35[2]	$60	$60	$60	$60
Soft-Ray tinted glass, all windows	$35	$40	$38	$45	$45	$45	$45
Power windows, 2-dr./4-dr.	—	$91[3]	$91/$132	$91/$132	$91	$91/$149	S
Power door locks, 2-dr./4-dr.	—	$56	—	$56/$90	$56	$56/$90	$56/$90
Power front seat, w/std. seat	—	—	—	$117	$117	$117	$117
Front bucket seats, w/console	—	$60[4]	$140	$145[5]	S	—	—
AM radio	$63	$69	$69	$69	$85	$85	$85
AM/FM stereo	$213	$233	$233	$233	$233	$233	$233
AM/FM stereo w/8-track tape	—	$363[3]	—	$363	$363	$363	$363
Woodgrain exterior trim, wagons	—	—	—	$150	—	$150	—
Vinyl top, full[6]	$79	$99	$87	$99	$119	$141	S
Vinyl top, landau	—	—	—	$99	$99	—	—
Sunroof, manual[5]	—	—	—	$300	$300	—	—
Sunroof, power[5]	—	—	—	$350	$350	—	—
Power steering, variable-ratio	$111	S	$129	$129[7]	S	S	S
Power brakes, w/front disc	$51	$55[7]	$55	$55[7]	S	S	S
Deluxe wheel covers	S	$30	$30	—	—	$31	—

	Astre	Firebird	Ventura	LeMans & Grand Am	Grand Prix	Catalina & Bonneville	Grand Ville Brougham
Custom finned wheel covers	—	$54	$54	$54	S	$55	S
Rally II wheels[8]	$75	$91	$91	$79	$25	$92	—
Honeycomb wheels	—	$127	—	$108[9]	—	—	—
WSW tires	$26	$28	$28	$28	$28	$40	$40

Popular Option Groups & Packages

	Astre	Firebird	Ventura	LeMans & Grand Am	Grand Prix	Catalina & Bonneville	Grand Ville Brougham
Custom trim group	—	$75	—	$80	$120	$95	—
GT option package	$434	—	—	$257	—	—	—
LJ option package	—	—	—	—	$699	—	—
Rallye gauge cluster package	—	$99	$99	$96[10]	$96	—	—
SJ option package	—	—	—	—	$277	—	—
Sprint option package	—	—	$207	—	—	—	—

—= Not Available; S = Standard equipment. [1]Not available with 250 CID 6-cylinder engine. Automatic climate control is available for $524 on Grand Prix, Catalina, Bonneville, Grand Ville Brougham and Grand Safari, and for $487 on LeMans and Grand Am. [2]Blower type defroster. [3]Other optional equipment required at extra cost, i.e. console. [4]Rear seat console available for $26. [5]Available only on 2-door models. [6]Vinyl roof available on Catalina Safari and Grand Safari for $141. Price on Bonneville four-door is $119. Available only on base Firebird and Esprit. Not available on LeMans station wagons. [7]Power steering and power brakes standard on LeMans station wagons and Grand Am, and Firebird Formula and Trans Am. [8]Rally or Rally III wheels on Astre. [9]Available only on coupes. [10]Available only on LeMans Sport Coupe or Grand LeMans. Standard on Grand Am.

Paint Colors

	Code		Code		Code
Cameo White	11	Augusta Green metallic	45	Roman Red	72
Sterling Silver metallic	13	Alpine Green metallic	49	Honduras Maroon metallic	74
Graystone	15	Carmel Beige	50	Buccaneer Red	75
Starlight Black	19	Sunstorm Yellow	51	Tampico Orange metallic	80
Arctic Blue	24	Sandstone	55		
Bimini Blue metallic	26	Ginger Brown metallic	58		
Stellar Blue metallic	29	Oxford Brown metallic	59		
Gray metallic	31	Copper Mist metallic	63		
Burgundy metallic	39	Persimmon metallic	64		
Lakemist Green	44	Fire Coral Bronze metallic	66		

In two-tone combinations, the first two digits indicate lower color and the next two digits are the upper color. Trans Am "Bird" hood decal available for $55 extra. Color availability by series is not available.

Astre

"Pontiac's new subcompacts."

Nameplate year of origin: 1975.
Current bodystyle lifespan: 1975 through 1977 (some models moved to Sunbird series, continuing through 1979).
Predecessor to this model: None.
Replacement for this model: J2000/Sunbird (1982 to 1993).
Percentage of division's production: 12.12%.
Corporate siblings: Chevrolet Vega.
Primary competition: AMC Gremlin, Dodge Colt, and Mercury Bobcat.
Notable changes: All-new model.
Major standard equipment: Choice of cloth and Morrokide vinyl or all-Morrokide vinyl front bucket seats, color-keyed cut-pile carpeting, simulated African crossfire mahogany woodgrain vinyl inserts on I/P, fold-down rear seat and rear liftgate (hatchback and wagon), deluxe two-spoke steering wheel, glove box, map pocket in driver's door, bright front and rear window moldings, bright side window moldings, bright drip rail

Measurements

	Coupes	Wagon
Wheelbase	97.0"	97.0"
Length	175.4"	175.4"
Width	65.4"	65.4"
Height	51.9"	51.6"
Legroom — front	43.5"	43.5"
Legroom — rear	29.6"	30.2"
Headroom — front	37.1"	38.9"
Headroom — rear	35.3"	38.3"
Cargo capacity (cu. ft.)	8.7*	46.6
Fuel capacity (gals.)	16.0	16.0

Hatchback maximum with rear seat down, 18.9 cu. ft.

moldings, manual front disc brakes, hubcaps, and A78 × 13 BSW tires. "S" model deletes and replaces: Black cut-pile carpeting, black two-spoke steering wheel and column, black I/P trim, side window moldings, and drip rail moldings. SJ adds: Special cloth and Morrokide vinyl upholstery and interior trim, custom cushion steering wheel, Rally gauge cluster package, dual body colored sport mirrors w/LH remote-control, body color door handle inserts, wheel opening and rocker panel moldings, rubber bumper strips, RTS suspension package, Rally III wheels, and BR78 × 13 BSW tires.

Models Available

	Model No.	Base MSRP	Change from LY	Shipping Wt. (lbs.)	Model Year Production*	Change from LY
Astre S 2-Door Notchback Coupe	C11	$2,841	NEW	2416	8,339	NEW
Astre S 2-Door Hatchback Coupe	C77	$2,954	NEW	2487	40,809	NEW
Astre S 2-Door Station Wagon	C15	$3,071	NEW	2539	15,322	NEW
Astre 2-Door Hatchback Coupe	V77	$3,079	NEW	2499	NA*	NEW
Astre 2-Door Station Wagon	V15	$3,175	NEW	2545	NA*	NEW
Astre SJ 2-Door Hatchback Coupe	X77	$3,610	NEW	2558	NA*	NEW
Astre SJ 2-Door Station Wagon	X15	$3,686	NEW	2602	NA*	NEW
TOTALS	Avg. price	$3,202	NEW	Production	64,470	NEW

Production kept only by body style and not by model number.

Firebird

"Pontiac's sports cars."

Nameplate year of origin: 1967.
Current bodystyle lifespan: 1970 through 1981.
Predecessor to this model: Firebird (1967 to 1969).
Replacement for this model: Firebird (1982 to 1992).
Percentage of division's production: 15.81%.
Corporate siblings: Chevrolet Camaro.
Primary competition: None.
Notable changes: New rear window and minor trim and detail changes.
Major standard equipment: All-Morrokide vinyl front bucket seats, cut-pile carpeting, deluxe two-spoke steering wheel, ashtray light, Firebird emblems on grille panel and rear deck lid, bright front and rear window moldings, narrow rocker panel moldings, Endura front and rear bumpers w/integral bumper guards, RTS suspension package, variable-ratio power steering, moon hubcaps, and FR78 × 15

Measurements

Wheelbase	151.5"
Wheelbase	108.1"
Length	196.0"
Width	73.0"
Height	50.4"
Legroom — front	44.1"
Legroom — rear	29.6"
Headroom — front	37.5"
Headroom — rear	35.9"
Cargo capacity (cu. ft.)	8.8
Fuel capacity (gals.)	20.2

BSW tires. Esprit adds: Custom trim all-Morrokide vinyl front bucket seats w/deep contour design, distinctive door trim panels, door and I/P assist straps, custom cushion steering wheel, pedal trim plates, rear quarter ashtray, rubber trunk mat, added acoustical insulation, dual body-colored mirror w/LH remote, body-colored door handle inserts, bright roof drip rail and belt reveal moldings, bright rear hood edge molding, bright wheel opening and rocker panel moldings, dual horns and deluxe wheel covers. Formula adds: Custom Cushion steering wheel, blacked-out grille, dual body-colored mirror w/LH remote, Formula (350 or 400) emblems on front fenders, fiberglass hood w/dual forward facing simulated scoops, and dual chrome tailpipe extensions. Trans Am adds: Formula steering wheel, rally gauge cluster package, aluminum-swirl finish I/P trim plate, dual body-colored mirror w/LH remote, blacked-out grille, full-width rear deck spoiler, wheel opening air deflectors, front fender air extractors, Trans Am decal on front fender and rear spoiler, shaker hood scoop, power brakes, power flex fan, Safe-T-Track differential, firm control shocks, dual chrome tailpipe extensions, Rally II wheels w/trim rings, and GR70 × 15 BSW tires.

Models Available

	Model No.	Base MSRP	Change from LY	Shipping Wt. (lbs.)	Model Year Production	Change from LY
Firebird 2-Door Hardtop Coupe	S87	$3,713	+16.94%	3386	22,293	-15.47%
Firebird Esprit 2-Door Hardtop Coupe	T87	$3,958	+12.22%	3431	20,826	-7.78%
Firebird Formula 2-Door Hardtop Coupe	U87	$4,349	+20.34%	3631	13,670	-5.85%
Firebird Trans Am 2-Door Hardtop Coupe	V87	$4,740	+7.70%	3716	27,274	+165.96%
TOTALS	Avg. price	$4,190	+13.88%	Production	84,063	+14.02%

Ventura

"Pontiac's complete lineup of compact cars."

Nameplate year of origin: 1960.
Current bodystyle lifespan: 1975 through 1979 (Ventura 1975 to 1977; Phoenix 1977 to 1979).
Predecessor to this model: Ventura/Ventura II (1971 to 1974; restyled in 1973).
Replacement for this model: Phoenix (1980 to 1984).
Percentage of division's production: 14.09%.
Corporate siblings: Buick Apollo/Skylark, Chevrolet Nova, and Oldsmobile Omega.
Primary competition: AMC Hornet, Dodge Dart, Ford Granada, and Mercury Monarch.
Notable changes: Completely redesigned.
Major standard equipment: Choice of cloth w/Morrokide vinyl trim or all-knit vinyl w/Morrokide vinyl trim front bench seat, cut-pile carpeting, color-keyed deluxe two-spoke steering wheel, simulated gunstock walnut

Measurements

	Coupe & HBK	Sedan
Wheelbase	111.1"	111.1"
Length	199.6"	199.6"
Width	72.4"	72.4"
Height	52.7"	53.8"
Legroom — front	41.7"	41.7"
Legroom — rear	33.4"	35.3"
Headroom — front	38.5"	39.5"
Headroom — rear	36.3"	36.5"
Cargo capacity (cu. ft.)	14.2*	13.8
Fuel capacity (gals.)	20.5	20.5

Hatchback maximum with rear seat down, 28.4 cu. ft.

I/P trim, front door dome light switches, rear seat armrest ashtrays, bright front and rear window moldings, bright drip rail moldings, manual front disc brakes, RTS package, moon hubcaps, and FR78 × 14 BSW tires. S Coupe deletes and replaces: Knit cloth front bench seat, black I/P and steering wheel, delete front door dome light switches and rear seat ashtray, and black rubber floor mat. Hatchback model adds: Fold-down rear seat, painted metal load floor, cargo area light, and fully trimmed cargo area sidewalls. Custom adds: Choice of custom cloth or all-Morrokide vinyl front bench seat, color-keyed carpeting on hatchback load floor, custom cushion steering wheel, pedal trim plates, glove box light, side window reveal moldings, rocker panel moldings, Custom identification, and deluxe wheel covers. SJ adds: Choice of cloth and Morrokide vinyl or all-Morrokide vinyl deep contour front bucket seats, front seat floor console w/floor-mounted shifter, simulated dark flame chestnut on I/P and console, column-mounted headlight dimmer switch, dome light switches on all doors, I/P courtesy lights, trunk mat and sidewall panels, road-style parking/turn signal lamps, side window reveal moldings, bright wheel opening moldings, rocker panel moldings w/front and rear extensions and argent or charcoal paint above the rocker moldings, bodyside accent stripes, and SJ identification.

Models Available

	Model No.	Base MSRP	Change from LY	Shipping Wt. (lbs.)	Model Year Production	Change from LY*
Ventura S 2-Door Coupe	E27	$3,162	NEW	3276	NA*	NEW
Ventura 2-Door Coupe	Y27	$3,293	+20.98%	3299	34,023	-28.80%
Ventura 2-Door Hatchback	Y17	$3,432	+19.46%	3383	10,463	-37.32%
Ventura 4-Door Sedan	Y69	$3,304	+20.10%	3335	22,068	+27.39%
Ventura Custom 2-Door Coupe	Z27	$3,449	+19.72%	3338	NA*	NA*
Ventura Custom 2-Door Hatchback	Z17	$3,593	+18.54%	3398	NA*	NA*
Ventura Custom 4-Door Sedan	Z69	$3,464	+19.04%	3378	NA*	NA*
Ventura SJ 2-Door Coupe	B27	$3,829	NEW	3340	NA*	NEW
Ventura SJ 2-Door Hatchback	B17	$3,961	NEW	3400	NA*	NEW
Ventura SJ 4-Door Sedan	B69	$3,846	NEW	3370	NA*	NEW
TOTALS	*Avg. price* $3,533		+23.48%		*Production* 66,554	-18.64%

Production of S, Custom and SJ models kept as combined total with base models. Therefore, comparisons to LY are made on total by body style and not model number.

LeMans

"Pontiac's new lineup of mid-size cars."

Nameplate year of origin: 1961 (as a Tempest sub-series).
Current bodystyle lifespan: 1973 through 1977.
Predecessor to this model: Tempest/LeMans (1968 to 1972).
Replacement for this model: LeMans (1978 to 1981).

Measurements

	Coupes	Sedans	Wagons
Wheelbase	112.0"	116.0"	116.0"

Percentage of division's production: 17.47%.

Corporate siblings: Buick Century, Chevrolet Chevelle, and Oldsmobile Cutlass.

Primary competition: AMC Matador, Dodge Coronet, Ford Torino, and Mercury Montego.

Notable changes: New grille and minor trim and detail changes.

Major standard equipment: Cloth-and-vinyl front bench seat, color-keyed cut-pile carpeting, deluxe three-spoke steering wheel, simulated dark flame chestnut woodgrain vinyl accents on I/P, door panels and steering wheel, trunk mat, bright front and rear window moldings, bright roof drip rail and rear quarter window trim, bright rocker panel molding, manual front disc brakes, RTS package, hubcaps, and FR78 × 15 BSW tires. Wagon adds: All-Morrokide vinyl front bench seat, vinyl coated metal cargo area sidewalls, textured steel cargo floor w/special vinyl paint, swing up tailgate w/fixed window and remote release, I/P mounted "door ajar" warning light for tailgate, swing-out rear quarter vents (3-seat wagon only), vertical rub strips on tailgate, power front disc brakes, and HR78 × 15 BSW tires. Sport Coupe adds: Choice of all-Morrokide vinyl front bench seat w/fold-down center armrest or all-Morrokide bucket seats, simulated dark flame chestnut woodgrain vinyl accents on glove box door, vertically louvered rear quarter windows and LeMans Sport Coupe identification. Grand LeMans adds: Choice of cloth-and-vinyl or all-vinyl notchback bench seat w/fold-down center armrest, or all-Morrokide bucket seats, cockpit style instrument panel design, custom cushion steering wheel, door panels w/carpeted lower panels (only on models built after October), front door assist straps, glove box and ashtray lights, simulated dark flame chestnut woodgrain vinyl accents on I/P and glove box door, added body insulation, rear seat armrest ashtrays, formal rear quarter opera window (coupe only), bright drip rail and quarter window moldings, bright rear hood edge and rear deck moldings, front wheel opening moldings, body color door handle inserts, full-length rocker panel molding w/front and rear extensions, rear-wheel fender skirts (except on Safari), hood ornament, and deluxe wheel covers.

Measurements (cont.)

	Coupes	Sedans	Wagons
Length	208.0"	212.0"	215.4"
Width	77.4"	77.4"	77.4"
Height	52.9"	54.3"	55.0"
Legroom — front	42.5"	42.5"	42.5"
Legroom — rear	32.9"	37.0"	36.8"
Headroom — front	37.7"	38.3"	38.9"
Headroom — rear	37.0"	37.5"	39.4"
Cargo capacity (cu. ft.)	15.1	15.1	82.9
Fuel capacity (gals.)	22.0	22.0	22.0

1975

Models Available

	Model No.	Base MSRP	Change from LY*	Shipping Wt. (lbs.)	Model Year Production	Change from LY*
LeMans 2-Door Colonnade HT Coupe	D37	$3,590	+17.82%	3656	20,636	-44.32%
LeMans 4-Door Colonnade HT Sedan	D29	$3,612	+17.77%	3729	15,065	-12.75%
LeMans 4-Door, 2-Seat Safari Station Wagon	D35	$4,555	+21.11%	4401	3,898	+29.76%
LeMans 4-Door, 3-Seat Safari Station Wagon	D45	$4,688	+20.39%	4439	2,393	-49.55%
LeMans Sport Coupe 2-Door Colonnade HT	F37	$3,708	+18.43%	3688	23,817	-37.25%
Grand LeMans 2-Door Colonnade HT Coupe	G37	$4,101	+20.26%	3723	19,310	-25.39%
Grand LeMans 4-Door Colonnade HT Sedan	G29	$4,157	+19.45%	3786	4,906	+8.71%
Grand LeMans 4-Door, 2-Seat Safari Wagon	G35	$4,749	+26.27%	4462	1,393	+46.32%
Grand LeMans 4-Door, 3-Seat Safari Wagon	G45	$4,882	+25.37%	4500	1,501	+27.42%
TOTALS	Avg. price	$4,227	+20.98%	Production	92,919	-29.90%

*Comparisons to LY for Grand LeMans made to 1974 Luxury LeMans of same model number.

Grand Am

"Pontiac's great American road car."

Nameplate year of origin: 1973.

Current bodystyle lifespan: 1973 through 1975.

Predecessor to this model: None.

Replacement for this model: Grand Am (1978 to 1980).

Percentage of division's production: 2.01%.

Corporate siblings: Buick Century Regal, Chevrolet Chevelle Laguna, and Oldsmobile Cutlass Salon.

Primary competition: Dodge Charger SE and Mercury Cougar XR-7.

Notable changes: Minor trim and detail changes.

Measurements

	Coupe	Sedan
Wheelbase	112.0"	116.0"
Length	211.0"	215.0"
Width	77.0"	77.0"
Height	52.9"	54.3"
Legroom — front	42.5"	42.5"
Legroom — rear	33.5"	38.6"

Major standard equipment: Choice of cloth-and-vinyl or all-vinyl w/Morrokide front bucket seats w/RH recliner, color-keyed loop-pile carpeting, pedal trim plates, custom sport three-spoke steering wheel w/padded center, cockpit-style I/P and center console w/simulated African crossfire mahogany inlay trim, door pull assist straps, electric clock, trip odometer, ashtray and glove box lights, courtesy lights, fixed rear quarter window w/louvers (coupe only), bright front and rear window moldings, bright side window and drip rail moldings, bright rear hood edge molding, bright wheel opening moldings, rocker panel moldings, body colored door handle inserts, color-keyed body striping, power steering, power front disc brakes, RTS package, custom finned wheel covers, and GR70 × 15 BSW tires.

Measurements

	Coupe	Sedan
Headroom — front	37.7"	38.3"
Headroom — rear	37.0"	37.5"
Cargo capacity (cu. ft.)	15.1	15.1
Fuel capacity (gals.)	25.0	25.0

Models Available

	Model No.	Base MSRP	Change from LY	Shipping Wt. (lbs.)	Model Year Production	Change from LY
Grand Am 2-Door Colonnade HT Coupe	H37	$4,887	+8.70%	4008	8,786	-37.07%
Grand Am 4-Door Colonnade HT Sedan	H29	$4,976	+8.53%	4055	1,893	-39.37%
TOTALS		Avg. price $4,932	+8.61%	Production	10,679	-37.49%

Grand Prix

"Pontiac's classic personal car."

Nameplate year of origin: 1962.
Current bodystyle lifespan: 1973 through 1977.
Predecessor to this model: Grand Prix (1969 to 1972).
Replacement for this model: Grand Prix (1978 to 1987).
Percentage of division's production: 16.28%.
Corporate siblings: Chevrolet Monte Carlo.
Primary competition: Dodge Charger SE, Ford Elite, and Mercury Cougar XR-7.
Notable changes: Minor trim and detail changes.
Major standard equipment: Choice of cloth-and-vinyl or all-vinyl w/Morrokide front notchback bench seat w/fold-down center armrests or front bucket seats w/center floor console, color-keyed cut-pile carpeting, pedal trim plates, custom cushion three-spoke steering wheel, cockpit-style I/P, simulated African crossfire mahogany inlay trim on I/P, console and door panels, I/P courtesy lights, electric clock, ashtray light, monogrammed fixed rear quarter window w/bright trim, bright front and rear window moldings, bright side window sill and drip rail moldings, bright rear hood edge molding, bright wheel opening moldings, black-accented wide rocker panel moldings, body colored door handle inserts, trunk compartment light and side panels, rear bumper guards, front and rear bumper rub strips, power steering, power brakes, RTS package, deluxe wheel covers, and GR78 × 15 BSW tires.

Measurements

Wheelbase	116.0"
Length	212.7"
Width	77.8"
Height	52.9"
Legroom — front	42.5"
Legroom — rear	33.5"
Headroom — front	37.5"
Headroom — rear	37.4"
Cargo capacity (cu. ft.)	14.3
Fuel capacity (gals.)	25.0

Models Available

	Model No.	Base MSRP	Change from LY	Shipping Wt. (lbs.)	Model Year Production	Change from LY
Grand Prix 2-Door Hardtop Coupe	K57	$5,296	+10.70%	4032	86,582	-13.26%
TOTALS		Avg. price $5,296	+10.70%	Production	86,582	-13.26%

Catalina

"Pontiac's lowest priced full-sized car."

Nameplate year of origin: 1950 (as hardtop model designation), 1959 (as series).
Current bodystyle lifespan: 1971 through 1976.
Predecessor to this model: Catalina (1969 to 1970).
Replacement for this model: Catalina (1977 to 1981).
Percentage of division's production: 13.35%.
Corporate siblings: Buick LeSabre, Chevrolet BelAir/Impala/Caprice, and Oldsmobile Delta 88.
Primary competition: Dodge Monaco, Ford LTD, and Plymouth Gran Fury.
Notable changes: Revised front-end styling, new four-door sedan roofline, and minor trim and detail changes.
Major standard equipment: Cloth-and-Morrokide vinyl bench seat, thick cut-pile carpeting, deluxe three-spoke steering wheel, dark flame chestnut woodgrain vinyl I/P accents, dual ashtrays w/LH ashtray light, glove box light, trunk mat, bright rocker panel molding, bright hood rear edge molding, RTS package, front and rear bumper rub strips, hubcaps, and HR78 × 15 BSW tires. Safari wagon adds: All-Morrokide vinyl front bench seat, glove box lights, RH rear view mirror, Glide-Away tailgate w/power-operated rear window, rear bumper guards, and LR78 × 15 BSW tires.

Measurements

	2-door	4-door	Wagon
Wheelbase	124.0"	124.0"	127.0"
Length	226.0"	226.0"	231.3"
Width	79.6"	79.6"	79.6"
Height	53.5"	54.2"	57.5"
Legroom — front	42.7"	42.7"	42.5"
Legroom — rear	35.8"	38.8"	38.9"
Headroom — front	38.3"	39.1"	39.6"
Headroom — rear	37.4"	37.9"	39.3"
Cargo capacity (cu. ft.)	20.5	20.5	105.7
Fuel capacity (gals.)	25.8	25.8	22.0

Models Available

	Model No.	Base MSRP	Change from LY	Shipping Wt. (lbs.)	Model Year Production	Change from LY
Catalina 2-Door Hardtop Coupe	L57	$4,700	+14.75%	4334	21,644	-46.76%
Catalina 4-Door Sedan	L69	$4,612	+15.07%	4347	40,398	-12.23%
Catalina Safari 4-Door, 2-Seat Station Wagon	L35	$5,149	+14.24%	4933	3,964	-29.99%
Catalina Safari 4-Door, 3-Seat Station Wagon	L45	$5,295	+13.80%	5000	4,992	-23.03%
TOTALS	Avg. price	$4,939	+15.24%		Production 70,998	-35.81%

Bonneville and Grand Safari

"Pontiac's original full-sized Wide-Track."

Nameplate year of origin: 1957.
Current bodystyle lifespan: 1971 through 1976.
Predecessor to this model: Bonneville (1969 to 1970).
Replacement for this model: Bonneville (1977 to 1981).
Percentage of division's production: 5.23%.
Corporate siblings: Buick LeSabre, Chevrolet BelAir/Impala/Caprice, and Oldsmobile Delta 88.
Primary competition: Dodge Royal Monaco and Mercury Marquis.
Notable changes: Revised front and rear styling, new two-door roofline, and minor trim and detail changes.
Major standard equipment: Choice of cloth-and-Morrokide vinyl or all-Morrokide vinyl front bench seat w/fold-down center armrest, cut-pile carpeting, lower door panel carpeting, door pull straps, custom cushion steering wheel, simulated dark flame chestnut woodgrain vinyl I/P accents, electric clock, pedal trim plates, courtesy light switches on all doors, luggage compartment mat and side panel trim, luggage compartment light, body-color door handle inserts, bright windshield and rear window moldings, bright hood rear edge molding, fixed rear quarter window, wide rocker panel moldings w/rear extensions, bright wheel opening moldings, rear fender skirts, RTS package, deluxe

Measurements

	2-door	4-door	Wagons
Wheelbase	124.0"	124.0"	127.0"
Length	226.0"	226.0"	231.3"
Width	79.6"	79.6"	79.6"
Height	53.5"	54.2"	58.3"
Legroom — front	42.7"	42.7"	42.5"
Legroom — rear	38.8"	38.8"	38.9"
Headroom — front	38.9"	39.1"	39.6"
Headroom — rear	37.6"	37.9"	39.3"
Cargo capacity (cu. ft.)	20.5	20.5	105.7
Fuel capacity (gals.)	25.8	25.8	22.0

wheel covers, and HR78 × 15 BSW tires. Grand Safari wagon adds: Choice of cloth and Morrokide vinyl or all-Morrokide vinyl front bench seat w/fold-down center armrest in Grand Ville Brougham trim, glove box lights, RH rear view mirror, Glide-Away tailgate w/power-operated rear window, delete rear fender skirts, rear bumper guards, and LR78 × 15 BSW tires.

Models Available

	Model No.	Base MSRP	Change from LY	Shipping Wt. (lbs.)	Model Year Production	Change from LY
Bonneville 2-Door Hardtop Coupe	P47	$5,085	+15.38%	4370	7,854	+2.81%
Bonneville 4-Door Hardtop Sedan	P49	$5,153	+15.18%	4503	12,641	
+105.51%						
Grand Safari 4-Door, 2-Seat Station Wagon	P35	$5,433	+10.34%	5035	2,568	-11.26%
Grand Safari 4-Door, 3-Seat Station Wagon	P45	$5,580	+10.04%	5090	4,752	-9.57%
TOTALS	Avg. price	$5,313	+20.51%	Production	27,815	+35.29%

Grand Ville Brougham

"Pontiac's most luxurious full-sized car."

Nameplate year of origin: 1971.
Current bodystyle lifespan: 1971 through 1976.
Predecessor to this model: None.
Replacement for this model: None.
Percentage of division's production: 5.20%.
Corporate siblings: Buick LeSabre, Chevrolet BelAir/Impala/Caprice, and Oldsmobile Delta 88.
Primary competition: Chrysler Newport, Dodge Royal Monaco Brougham, and Mercury Marquis Brougham.
Notable changes: Revised front-end styling and minor trim and detail changes.
Major standard equipment: Choice of velour or all-Morrokide vinyl trim front notchback seat w/fold-down center armrest, cut-pile carpeting, custom cushion steering wheel, custom door panels w/pull straps and lower panel carpeting, simulated dark flame chestnut woodgrain vinyl trim on

Measurements

	2-doors	4-door
Wheelbase	124.0"	124.0"
Length	226.0"	226.0"
Width	79.6"	79.6"
Height	53.5"	54.2"
Legroom — front	42.7"	42.7"
Legroom — rear	35.8"	38.8"
Headroom — front	38.9"	38.6"
Headroom — rear	37.6"	37.6"
Cargo capacity (cu. ft.)	20.5*	20.5
Fuel capacity (gals.)	25.8	25.8

Convertible is 14.4 cu. ft.

I/P and door panels, electric clock, courtesy light switches on all doors, Cordova vinyl top, velour luggage compartment trim, luggage compartment light, body-color door handle inserts, bright windshield and rear window moldings, bright window sill and drip rail moldings, bright hood rear edge molding, wide rocker panel moldings w/rear extensions, front wheel opening moldings, front and rear bumper rub strips, rear wheel opening fender skirts, special accent stripes, RTS suspension, deluxe wheel covers, and HR78 × 15 BSW tires. Convertible adds: All-Morrokide vinyl front bench seat w/fold-down center armrest, two rear quarter interior lights, and inward-folding power-operated vinyl convertible top w/glass rear window.

Models Available

	Model No.	Base MSRP	Change from LY	Shipping Wt. (lbs.)	Model Year Production	Change from LY
Grand Ville Brougham 2-Door Hardtop Coupe	R47	$5,729	+21.74%	4404	7,447	-35.97%
Grand Ville Brougham 2-Door Convertible	R67	$5,858	+18.39%	4520	4,519	+50.63%
Grand Ville Brougham 4-Door Hardtop Sedan	R49	$5,896	+23.50%	4558	15,686	-27.76%
TOTALS	Avg. price	$5,828	+19.31%	Production	27,652	-37.85%

See the 1975 Buick introduction for further information on the 231 CID V6 engine history.

1976

The United States Bicentennial celebration was in full swing by the start of the 1976 model year, with recognitions of the event having started back in 1974. That included the automobile industry, with Chevrolet introducing a trio of "Spirit of America" special editions. For 1976, the occasion would be marked by a car that was significant for more than one reason, that being the production of the final 200 Cadillac Eldorado convertibles. Finished in white with white leather interior and red accents, the "Bicentennial Cadillacs," as they were often referred to, were significant in being the "last" production built American convertibles. Demand and prices soared, then quickly deflated, but they will be remembered more as the last of the large American convertibles, as the body style returned to production just over five years later.

For most manufacturers, the new year brought a slight break from the constant implementation of new government regulations, giving the auto companies a chance to regroup and spend some money on sprucing up their cars. However, significant new model introductions were made this year. The Chevrolet Chevette was the smallest American-built mass-produced new car introduced since Crosley left the market in 1952. It was also the first serious attempt to introduce the "global car" concept to U.S. consumers. The Chevette was based on GM's T-body, which was also the basis for the Opel Isuzu, built in Japan, and a variety of other similar models sold in Brazil and in Europe. While sharing most of their architecture, the T-body cars were not universally the same, making the 1981 Ford Escort the car that would truly be able to carry the title of the first "world car." Also new from General Motors was the groundbreaking "smaller Cadillac," named Seville. Originally planned to be called the LaSalle, in honor of the 1930s era low-priced Cadillac, the Seville was a fully loaded compact to mid-size car that was anything but cheap. Introduced in May of 1975 as an early 1976 model, the Seville used a classic formal roofline and bodylines, with a relatively long hood and short deck, yet it was built with many existing components from other GM

car lines, most notably, the Chevrolet Nova chassis components and a fuel-injected 350 CID Oldsmobile engine. This was the first time Cadillac had ever used an engine that was not its own, since the early years of its history. Finally, the new Dodge Aspen and Plymouth Volaré twins bowed this year to much fanfare, as the frequently cash-strapped Chrysler was finally able to produce a replacement for the Dart and Valiant lines which were last "completely" redesigned for the 1967 model year.

Chrysler spent much effort in maintaining for the Aspen and Volaré various qualities that were successful in the old Dart and Valiant, such as the size, the powerplants, and their relative ease of maintenance. Though less spartan in the basic trim levels and totally new in looks, the new twins were not so far different that a similarity, or lineage, could not be seen. In fact, to make sure the new cars got off to a good start, the Dart and Valiant were kept in production for most of the 1976 model year, so the old and the new sat side-by-side on the showroom floor. The new models were deemed good enough in testing for *Motor Trend* magazine to name the new compact duo their "Car of the Year" for 1976. It wasn't long, though, before electrical problems and then rust issues came to light, and within a few years, the new Chrysler F-body cars would become the most recalled cars in history. Another new model in Plymouth showrooms, which did not get a lot of attention initially, was the Arrow, a subcompact "captive import" built by Chrysler's Japanese partner, Mitsubishi. A version of the Colt that was sold in Japan, the Arrow was sold through Plymouth rather than Dodge dealers in America. It sold quite well, if not spectacularly, and certainly added traffic to dealer lots.

The Chrysler Corporation lineup featured little new styling but more name juggling. Dodge went back to its early '70s practice of applying the Coronet name to four-door models, while the two-door models were now known as Chargers. Note however that the Charger two-doors were still of the new hardtop coupe design introduced with the

1975 Coronet two-doors, and that the Charger SE was still of a differing body design. It was also the final year for the Coronet nameplate. With the Imperial gone from the Chrysler lineup, the New Yorker Brougham assumed its former styling and position in the lineup, while the 1976 Newport and Newport Custom took on the body styling of the 1975 Newport Custom and New Yorker Brougham respectively. At Plymouth not much else changed, other than the Road Runner package moving from the mid-size line to the new compact Volaré platform. Dodge and Plymouth truck, van and off-road vehicles were given minor trim changes.

In what seemed like collaboration between two of Detroit's automakers, two full-sized models were available this year with new option packages that utilized a stainless steel wrap-over roof bar and a landau vinyl top. One came from Chrysler with its Dodge Royal Monaco Brougham two-door hardtop offering the Diplomat package, and the other was from General Motors with the Oldsmobile Delta 88 Royale and its Crown Landau package. Though it's unlikely that any collaboration occurred, it seems odd for a similar design to come from two different companies in the same year. Maybe there was leftover stainless steel in Detroit, as so much of the exterior trim was now plastic, or maybe there was a desperate stainless steel salesperson, making good deals!

At General Motors, the new Chevette captured most of the attention in the marketplace, and it immediately became the most fuel-efficient American-built car available, and very nearly the most fuel-efficient of any car available in the United States. At the other monetary extreme was the all-new Cadillac Seville, which generated a fair amount of publicity for being not only the smallest Cadillac in ages, but also GM's most expensive car, aside from the Cadillac Fleetwood 75 series sedan and limousine. The expense was not such a bad thing for luxury car buyers, though, as the Seville compared favorably in media reviews with the best of the European models that often cost thousands more. The one additional new model in the GM lineup didn't make much of a splash as it was not completely new, that being Pontiac's version of the H-body subcompact line, known as the Sunbird. Based on the Chevy Monza Towne Coupe, the Sunbird offered sporty features like a Firebird style front end and standard bucket seats and floor shifter, all in a two-door coupe package. Pontiac would not add the 2+2 hatchback coupe to the line until the 1978 model year. The 1976 model year also marked Pontiac's 50th anniversary year, and while nothing official was published to mark the event, two special models were produced. They were the Grand Prix SJ with the LJ and Golden Anniversary options, painted in gold metallic, and the Special Edition Firebird Trans Am package, the first in a series of black painted Trans Ams with gold accent striping. Otherwise, the General had few truly new offerings, as it was busy readying itself and its dealers for the first round of downsizing to come out of Detroit for 1977.

All of the GM mid-size cars featured the new rectangular headlights introduced for 1975, except for the base Chevy Malibu series and the sporty Chevy Chevelle Laguna Type S-3. The Buick Century and Regal sedans and the Chevy Malibu Classic and Monte Carlo series all used stacked headlights, while the Buick Century and Regal coupes, Pontiac LeMans and Grand Prix series, and all Oldsmobile Cutlass models used side-by-side units. Also adding side-by-side rectangular headlights were the full-sized Buick LeSabre, Chevrolet Caprice, Oldsmobile Delta 88, and Pontiac Bonneville, whose Brougham line replaced last year's Grand Ville Brougham series. The rectangular headlights were also available on the Pontiac Catalina when the Custom package was purchased. GM's truck and van lines received minor styling revisions, and the car-based Chevy El Camino and GMC Sprint pickups also gained stacked rectangular headlights in higher trim levels.

At American Motors, after a highly successful launch for the new Pacer, 1976 would become even better with more than a 50 percent increase in sales. Meanwhile, the Gremlin and Hornet sales perked up some after the big drop last season from their record 1974 levels. The Matador continued with few changes, with the sedans and wagons becoming the oldest body styles still in production among American cars after the Dodge Dart and Plymouth Valiant lines were shut down. The Matador four-door bodies dated from the new-for-1967 Rebel and Ambassador series. AMC's Jeep truck line added a new CJ-7 Jeep that was ten inches longer than the original CJ-5, and it would become an instant success.

Ford Motor Company's recently launched Granada and Monarch were both exceedingly popular, and for 1976 the Granada would become the best-selling and highest production nameplate for the model year, ousting the full-size Chevrolet from its traditional spot. An economy-minded "MPG" sub-series was introduced for the Ford Pinto and Mercury Bobcat lines this year, but it was really nothing more than an added decal logo for those models equipped with the standard powertrain. The Mustang II added a performance minded Cobra II package for the Mach I hatchback model, and the newly restyled and renamed (à la Mustang II), German-built Capri II added a sportier "S" model. All Ford models received some minor styling changes, but no drastic changes were seen in the domestic line. Powertrains continued with few changes, although this would be the last year for the big 460 CID V8 engine to be standard equipment in any of the Ford models. The 1976 model year would be the last for the once popular Torino and Montego nameplates, and also the last for the relatively new Elite model that was often compared to the Thunderbird by Ford. For 1977, the Thunderbird would actually replace the Elite in both size and market positioning as a Chevrolet Monte Carlo, Dodge Charger SE and Pontiac Grand Prix rival. The Ford truck line continued into the new season with few changes.

1976 Overview and Changes from Prior Year

- **Total industry model year production:** 8,651,399, up 22.71%.
- **Total estimated captive import sales:** 178,152, up 69.10%.
- **Market share by corporation:** GM 55.55%; Ford 29.26%; Chrysler 11.92%; AMC 3.27%.
- **Number of models and body types available:** 297, down from 319.
- **Highest production series:** Ford Granada — 548,784.
- **Lowest production series:** Cadillac Fleetwood 75 — 1,815.
- **Highest individual model production:** Ford Granada 4-Door Sedan — 287,923.
- **Lowest individual model production:** Dodge Monaco Custom 4-Door, 2-seat wagon — 547.
- **Industry average base price:** $4,756, up 3.57%.
- **Highest individual model base price:** Cadillac Fleetwood 75 Limousine, $15,239.
- **Lowest individual model base price:** AMC Gremlin 2-Door Sedan, $2,889.
- **Highest combined MPG with base powertrain:** Chevrolet Chevette, 32 MPG.
- **Lowest combined MPG with base powertrain:** Cadillac Fleetwood 75, 12 MPG.
- **Indianapolis 500 Pace Car:** Buick Century 2-Door Coupe with Turbo-charged V6 engine.
- *Motor Trend* **magazine "Car of the Year":** Dodge Aspen and Plymouth Volaré.

1976

AMERICAN MOTORS

"The 1976 AMC passenger cars. Built with you in mind."

American Motors benefited from the improving economic situation and the lingering worries of gas shortages and long lines at the pump. It seemed plenty of consumers were concerned enough about saving fuel to provide economy-minded American Motors with a huge increase in sales of 6-cylinder models while V8 powered car sales dropped drastically, following a trend that AMC had seen for the past three years. As AMC struggled to compete with the Big Three in Detroit, the latest recession cut into its ability to continue developing new product, so there were not any big changes in the lineup for 1976. Still, the model year ended with AMC looking toward a brighter future. Unfortunately, in reality this would be AMC's last year to hold more than a 3 percent share of U.S. production.

The Gremlin series expanded to two models this year, with a "new" base Gremlin, and the existing Gremlin being renamed the Gremlin Custom. The base Gremlin for 1976 carried a new model number of 46-3, while the "new" Gremlin Custom model was model number 46-5, which had been used on 4-passenger Gremlin models since the line's introduction in 1970. The base Gremlin still carried all the same standard features as the 1975 Gremlin, while the Gremlin Custom added some of the more popular extra-cost features such as carpeting and exterior bright trim. Also, some of the most popular option packages, such as the "X" package and Levi's package, were available only on the Custom.

The Pacer had few changes for the 1976 model year as it had only been on the market about six months when the new model year introductions rolled around. Moving bumper guards from the standard equipment to the optional equipment list was the most obvious external change. On the inside there were virtually no changes to be found. A couple of interesting points on the Pacer interiors, which also apply to the 1975 models, include the unique fabric offerings and the interesting door panel design. Optional individual reclining seats with a choice of Basketry Print fabric with vinyl bolsters or Hyde Park fabric were available when ordered with the "D/L" package.* The Basketry Print fabric was very unusual, continuing the AMC tradition of custom interiors over the past few years including the unique Levi's package and the Gucci package.

Door panels in the Pacer were unique in two respects,

Basketry Print fabric is available for $63, and Hyde Park fabric available for $84, only on Pacer. This unique interior was available on Pacer Sedans from 1975 to 1977. See photo of Basketry Print fabric following the 1975 AMC introduction.

the most obvious being a large oblong section on the rear two-thirds of the door, which housed the armrests, door pull straps, door locks and door handle, as well as outside mirror controls when ordered. Only the window controls were outside of this area towards the front of the door. The second unique feature was a raised section created by the aforementioned oblong section extending above the door beltline by a few inches. This top section proved to be an annoyance for those who liked to drive with their arm resting out the window, as it was not flat on top.

As for the other AMC products, the Hornet and Matador, there were very few changes to be found. The 304 CID V8 engine was now the standard Matador wagon engine, as the 6-cylinder engines were slow sellers and no longer provided adequate power, given the added emissions equipment and heavier weight of the wagon. AMC began to turn its attention to making the Hornet appeal to buyers seeking more luxury. This was an industrywide trend of the past five years, and the solution for the Hornet was to add more features to the D/L option package and offer a new Touring interior package, to give the six-year-old compact a new look on the inside. In retrospect, it may have been a plan to prepare consumers for the upcoming Hornet replacement.

Gremlin 2-Door Sedan

Gremlin 2-Door Sedan with X package

Hornet 2-Door Sedan

Hornet 3-Door Hatchback with X package

Hornet 4-Door Sedan

Hornet Sportabout 4-Door wagon
with D/L package

Matador 2-Door Coupe with Brougham package

Matador 4-Door Station Wagon
with Brougham package

Matador Coupe interior with Barcelona package

Pacer 2-Door Sedan with D/L package

Pacer 2-Door Sedan with X package
and two-tone paint

Model year production: 283,275, up 17.20% from 1975.
Domestic market share: 3.27% (10th place).
Base price range: $2,889 to $4,373.
American Motors average base price: $3,415, up 3.90%.
Introduction date: September 24, 1975.
Assembly plants: Kenosha, Wisconsin, and Brampton, Ontario, Canada.
Data plate identification (VIN): Thirteen digit code read as follows: First digit indicates company (A = American Motors); second digit indicates model year (6 = 1976); third digit is transmission code (see powertrain chart); fourth through sixth digits indicate car line/body type/series numbers (three-digit model number in model charts); seventh digit is engine code (see powertrain chart); eighth digit indicates assembly plant (1 through 6 = Kenosha, 7 through 9 = Ontario); Remaining digits are sequential with beginning number of 00001. *Example:* A6A167H100001 is a 1976 Matador 2-Door, 304 CID, 2-bbl. V8, with Torque-Command Automatic, serial number 00001, built in Kenosha.

Powertrains[1]

Engine	Net HP	Engine/ Trans. Code[2]	Transmission Availability[2]		Gremlin	Pacer	Hornet	Matador[3]
232 CID (3.8L), 1-bbl., 6-cyl.	90	E/S	3-speed manual[4]		S	S	S	—
				MPG:	17/30/21	17/25/20	17/25/20	—
				Calif.	16/26/20	16/26/20	16/26/20	—
		E/A	Torque-Command 3-sp. Automatic		$252	$252	$252	—
				MPG:	19/25/21	17/23/19	17/23/19	—
				Calif.	15/19/16	15/19/16	15/19/16	—
258 CID (4.2L), 1-bbl., 6-cyl.	95	A/S	3-speed manual[4]		$59	$59	$59 (ex. Wgn.)	S (ex. Wgn.)
				MPG:	20/31/23	20/31/23	20/31/23	15/19/17
				Calif.	15/24/18	15/24/18	15/24/18	—
		A/A	Torque-Command 3-sp. Automatic		$311	$311	$311	$262 (ex. Wgn.)
				MPG:	18/25/21	17/22/19	17/22/19	16/19/17
				Calif.	14/20/16	14/20/16	14/20/16	—
258 CID (4.2L), 2-bbl., 6-cyl.	105	C/S	Torque-Command 3-sp. Automatic		—	$351	—	—
				MPG:	—	17/22/19	—	—
304 CID (5.0L), 2-bbl., V8	120	H/S	3-speed manual		$162	—	$145 (ex. Wgn.)	—
				MPG:	16/22/18	—	16/22/18	—
				Calif.	13/16/14	—	13/16/14	—
		H/A	Torque-Command 3-sp. Automatic		$424	—	$407	S (Wgn.)/ $372 (others)
				MPG:	13/19/16	—	13/18/15	13/16/14
				Calif.	12/20/15	—	12/20/15	11/15/12
360 CID (5.9L), 2-bbl., V8	140	N/A	Torque-Command 3-sp. Automatic		—	—	—	$59 (Wgn.)/ $431 (others)
				MPG:	—	—	—	12/16/14
				Calif.	—	—	—	11/16/12
360 CID (5.9L), 4-bbl., V8[5]	180	P/A	Torque-Command 3-sp. Automatic		—	—	—	$175 (Wgn.)/ $547 (others)
				MPG:	—	—	—	12/16/13
				Calif.	—	—	—	11/16/13

[1]*Optional axle ratio required on cars sold in California: Gremlin 6-cylinders, 3.08:1; Pacer, 3.08:1; Hornet 6-cylinders, 3.08:1; Matador 6-cylinder coupes and sedans, 3.54:1; all Matador V8s, 3.15:1.* [2]*Unless otherwise noted: All manual transmissions are column-shifts, except Gremlin, Pacer w/"X" package and Hornet Hatchback. All automatics are column-shift as standard. Add $21 for floor-shifter on Gremlin automatics, Hornet Hatchback or Sportabout w/258 CID 6 or 304 CID V8 and automatic transmission, and Pacer w/bucket or individual reclining seats. Add $62 on Matador Coupe with V8, bucket seats and console. Transmission code: w/Automatic floor shift is C, w/3-speed synchronized manual is E.* [3]*Matador coupes and sedans built for sale in California follow the same standard and optional availability as station wagons. Prices adjust accordingly.* [4]*3-speed manual with overdrive available for $157, except on Matador (transmission code O).* [5]*Dual exhaust standard on Matador with 360 CID 4-bbl. V8.*

Major Options

	Gremlin	Pacer	Hornet	Matador
All-season air conditioning	$425	$425	$425	$473
Adjust-O-Tilt steering wheel[1]	$52	$52	$52	$54
Cruise-command speed control[1]	$69	$69	$69	$72
Electric rear window defogger	$63	$63	$63[2]	$73[2]
Tinted glass, all windows	$44	$52	$47	$51
Power windows, 4-doors	—	—	—	$138
Front bucket seats, vinyl upholstered	$50	$104	$52[3]	$96[3]
Front floor consol (requires bucket seats)	$25	$25	$25	$
Third row seat & power tailgate window — wagons	—	—	—	$127
AM radio	$73	$73	$75	$76
AM/FM stereo multiplex w/4 speakers	$199	$199	$199	$199
AM/FM stereo w/8-track tape player	—	$299	—	$299
Vinyl top (excluding wagon models)	$74	$105	$93	$105
Woodgrain paneling (wagons only)	—	—	$99	$118
Power steering	$125	$125	$119	$130
Power front disc brakes	$84	$84	$84	$60[4]
Wheel covers	$32	$32	$30	$30
Styled road wheels	$121	$121	$121	$121
Aluminum styled wheels	$210	$210	—	—
White sidewall tires, standard size	$36	$36	$36	$38

Popular Option Groups & Packages

	Gremlin	Pacer	Hornet	Matador
Barcelona package[5]	—	—	—	$149
Brougham package	—	—	—	$179[6]
Convenience group	$49	$49	$49	$52
Custom trim package	$29[7]	—	—	—
Décor group	$45	$89	—	$59
D/L package	—	$199	$169[8]	—
Extra Quiet insulation package	$32	$35	$30	S
Interior appointment package	$21	—	—	—
Interior décor group	$50[7]	—	—	—
LEVI'S custom trim package	$89[7]	—	$49[7]	—
Opera window-roof package (coupe only)	—	—	—	$524
Protection group	$59	$37	$59	$31
Rallye option package	—	$139	—	—
Rear visibility group	—	$105	—	—
Touring interior package	—	—	$169	—
Visibility group	$45	$55	$50	$50
"X" package	$189[7]	$339	$179[9]	$249[10]

— = Not Available; S = Standard equipment.   [1]Requires automatic transmission.   [2]Available only on Hornet hatchback and Sportabout, and Matador coupe and sedan. Blower type defroster available on Hornet sedans for $41.   [3]Hornet hatchback and Matador coupe only.   [4]Standard on Matador station wagon.   [5]Available only with Brougham package on coupe.   [6]Price given for sedan. Available on coupe for $249 and wagon for $199.   [7]Available only on Gremlin Custom. Levi's trim only on Hornet Hatchback.   [8]Price given is for Sedans w/"Kasmir Knit" fabric interior. Available on Sportabout w/"Potomac" stripe fabric for $350; w/vinyl for $309; or w/Touring interior for $214. Not available on Hornet hatchback.   [9]Price given is for hatchback. Available on Sportabout for $139.   [10]Matador coupe only.

Paint Colors

	Code	Gremlin & Hornet	Pacer	Matador		Code	Gremlin & Hornet	Pacer	Matador
Sienna Orange	G6	x	x	x	Brandywine metallic	J2	x	x	—
Alpine White	G7	x	x	x	Marine Aqua metallic	6A	x	x	x
Medium Blue metallic	G9	x	x	x	Seaspray Green	6B	x	—	x
Dark Cocoa metallic	H4	—	—	x[1]	Evergreen metallic	6C	x	x	x
Golden Jade metallic	H6	x	x	x	Sand Tan	6D	x	—	—
Aztec Copper metallic	H7	x	—	x[1]	Burnished Bronze metallic	6E	—	x	—
Autumn Red metallic	H8	x	x	x[1]	Silver Frost metallic	6J	—	x	—

	Code	Gremlin & Hornet	Pacer	Matador			Code	Gremlin & Hornet	Pacer	Matador
Limefire metallic	6K	—	x	x		Classic Black	P1	x	—	x[1]
Firecracker Red	6P	x	x	x
Brilliant Blue	6R	—	x	—
Nautical Blue metallic	6T	x	x	x
Sunshine Yellow	6V	x	x	x

Non-standard model colors are available at $21 extra cost. Two-tone paint combinations available on Pacer for $52; Hornet (except Sportabout) for $36; Matador coupe and sedan for $42; and Matador wagon for $79. [1]The "Oleg Cassini" package is available only in these colors.

Gremlin

"The small car that makes it fun to be economical."

Nameplate year of origin: 1970.
Current bodystyle lifespan: 1970 through 1983; Gremlin (1970 to 1978), restyled and renamed Spirit (1979 to 1982). 4WD added and rebadged Eagle SX/4 (1981 to 1983).
Predecessor to this model: None.
Replacement for this model: Spirit (1979 to 1982) and Eagle SX/4 (1981 to 1983).
Percentage of division's production: 18.66%.
Corporate siblings: None; however many components were shared with the Hornet.
Primary competition: Buick/Opel Isuzu, Chevrolet Vega, Dodge Colt, Ford Pinto, and Plymouth Arrow.
Notable changes: New grille and trim and detail changes. New base model, with former base model renamed Gremlin Custom.
Major standard equipment: Vinyl bench front seat with foam cushions, fold-down rear seat, color-keyed rubber floor covering, dome light, front bumper nerfing strips, rear bumper guards, aluminum hubcaps, and 6.45 × 14 BSW tires. Custom adds: "Fairway" pleated vinyl custom bench seat, front and rear carpeting, custom steering wheel and door trim panels, bright drip rail and rocker panel moldings, dual body-side paint stripes, spare tire cover, and specific Gremlin Custom grille.

Measurements

Wheelbase	151.5"
Wheelbase	96.0"
Length	169.4"
Width	70.6"
Height	52.3"
Legroom — front	40.7"
Legroom — rear	29.2"
Headroom — front	38.0"
Headroom — rear	36.4"
Cargo capacity (cu. ft.)	6.4*
Fuel capacity (gals.)	21.0

*26.9 cu. ft. with rear seat down.

Models Available

	Model No.	Base MSRP	Change from LY	Shipping Wt. (lbs.)	Model Year Production	Change from LY
Gremlin 2-Door Sedan	46–3	$2,889	NEW	2771	*	NEW
Gremlin Custom 2-Door Sedan	46–5	$2,998	+7.15%	2774	*	*
TOTALS		*Avg. price* $2,944	+5.20%		*Production* 52,941*	+15.47%

*Production records kept only by engine type (compared to LY): 6-cylinder, 52,115 (+22.25%); V8, 826 (-74.33%).

Pacer

"The first wide small car, has more of everything for everybody! That's a big order, but Pacer fills it beautifully."

Nameplate year of origin: 1975 (previously used by Ford Motor Company on 1958 Edsel series).
Current bodystyle lifespan: 1975 through 1980.
Predecessor to this model: None.
Replacement for this model: None.
Percentage of division's production: 41.32%.
Corporate siblings: None.
Primary competition: Chevrolet Monza and Mercury Bobcat.
Notable changes: Minor trim and detail changes.

Measurements

Wheelbase	100.0"
Length	170.0"
Width	77.0"
Height	52.7"
Legroom — front	40.7"
Legroom — rear	34.9"
Headroom — front	38.3"
Headroom — rear	37.4"

Major standard equipment: Fabric front bench seat with foam cushions, color-keyed carpeting, fold-down rear seat, courtesy dome light, ashtray and cigarette lighter, integrated front door armrests, concealed two-speed electric wipers and washers, large rear lift gate w/built-in assist struts, color-keyed rubber cargo area mat, body-side scuff moldings, aluminum hubcaps, and 6.95 × 14 BSW tires.

Measurements (cont.)

Cargo capacity (cu. ft.)	29.5*
Fuel capacity (gals.)	22.0

With rear seat folded down.

Models Available

	Model No.	Base MSRP	Change from LY	Shipping Wt. (lbs.)	Model Year Production	Change from LY
Pacer 2-Door Sedan (hatchback)	66-7	$3,499	+6.06%	3114	117,244	+62.48%
TOTALS	Avg. price	$3,499	+6.06%	Production	117,244	+62.48%

Hornet

"Hornet is a solid choice with value-minded buyers everywhere."

Nameplate year of origin: 1951 (previously used on 1951 to 1957 Hudson series).

Current bodystyle lifespan: 1970 through 1987; Hornet (1970 to 1977), restyled and renamed Concord (1978 to 1982); 4WD added and rebadged Eagle (1980 to 1987).

Predecessor to this model: (Rambler) American (1964 to 1969).

Replacement for this model: Concord (1978 to 1982) and Eagle (1980 to 1987).

Percentage of division's production: 25.27%.

Corporate siblings: None; however many components were shared with the Gremlin.

Primary competition: Chevrolet Nova, Dodge Aspen, Dodge Dart, Ford Maverick, Plymouth Valiant, Plymouth Volaré, and Pontiac Ventura.

Notable changes: Minor trim and detail changes.

Major standard equipment: Fabric-covered front bench seat with foam cushions, color-keyed carpeting, instrument panel package tray, dome light, parking brake warning light, front bumper corner nerfing strips, rear bumper guards, aluminum hubcaps, and 6.95 × 14 BSW tires. Hatchback adds: Folding second seat with foam cushions, flip open rear quarter windows, carpeted cargo mats, and gas-charged lift-gate supports. Sportabout adds: Folding second seat, gas-charged lift-gate supports, carpeted cargo mats, hidden rear compartment lock, and D78 × 14 BSW tires.

Measurements

	Sedans	Hatchback	Sportabout
Wheelbase	108.0"	108.0"	108.0"
Length	186.0"	186.0"	186.0"
Width	71.0"	71.1"	71.0"
Height	51.7"	52.2"	52.2"
Legroom — front	42.1"	40.7"	40.7"
Legroom — rear	35.5"	32.1"	35.6"
Headroom — front	38.1"	38.1"	38.1"
Headroom — rear	37.0"	36.7"	37.4"
Cargo capacity (cu. ft.)	11.1	30.5*	56.4*
Fuel capacity (gals.)	22.0	22.0	22.0

Maximum with rear seat down, and 3.8 cu. ft. below cargo floor on Sportabout.

Models Available

	Model No.	Base MSRP	Change from LY	Shipping Wt. (lbs.)	Model Year Production	Change from LY
Hornet 2-Door Sedan	06-7	$3,199	+4.07%	2909	*	*
Hornet 2-Door Hatchback	03-7	$3,199	+0.79%	2920	*	*
Hornet 4-Door Sedan	05-7	$3,199	+2.40%	2971	*	*
Hornet 4-Door Sportabout Wagon	08-7	$3,549	+5.19%	3040	29,763*	+311.15%
TOTALS	Avg. price	$3,287	+3.14%	Production	71,577*	+11.64%

Production by body style is not available except for Sportabout. Production by engine type (compared to LY): 6-cylinder cars, 41,025 (+13.00%); 6-cylinder wagon, 26,787 (+788.16%); V8 car, 789 (-96.16%); V8 wagon, 2,976 (-29.53%).

Matador

"The economy car that lets you move up all the way in style."

Nameplate year of origin: 1971.

Current bodystyle lifespan: 1974 through 1978 (Coupe only); 1967 through 1978 (Rebel, 1967–1968; restyled in 1969; restyled and renamed Matador in 1971; and sedan and wagon restyled in 1974).

Predecessor to this model: Matador (1971 to 1973).

Replacement for this model: None.

Percentage of division's production: 14.65%.

Corporate siblings: None.

Primary competition: Chevrolet Malibu, Dodge Charger, Dodge Coronet, Ford Torino, Plymouth Fury, and Pontiac LeMans.

Notable changes: Minor trim and detail changes.

Major standard equipment: Fabric front bench seat with foam cushions, color-keyed carpeting, day/night rearview mirror, courtesy dome light activated by door switches, custom steering wheel, Extra Quiet insulation package, bodyside scuff moldings with vinyl insert (sedan and wagon), front and rear bumper guards, front sway bar, manual front disc brakes, and ER78 × 14 BSW tires (coupe) or FR78 × 14 BSW tires (sedan). Wagon adds: All-vinyl upholstery, cargo area carpet, courtesy dome light activated by door and tailgate switches, hidden rear compartment with lock, dual-swing tailgate, front bumper guards, power front disc brakes, and HR78 × 14 BSW tires.

Measurements

	Coupe	Sedan	Wagon
Wheelbase	114.0"	118.0"	118.0"
Length	209.4"	216.0"	215.5"
Width	77.4"	75.7"	75.7"
Height	51.8"	54.7"	56.8"
Legroom — front	43.0"	42.8"	42.8"
Legroom — rear	33.3"	39.6"	39.6"
Headroom — front	37.6"	39.6"	39.9"
Headroom — rear	36.0"	37.5"	38.5"
Cargo capacity (cu. ft.)	14.3	19.1	95.2*
Fuel capacity (gals.)	24.5	24.5	21.0

Includes 8.0 cu.ft. of space below cargo floor.

Models Available

	Model No.	Base MSRP	Change from LY	Shipping Wt. (lbs.)	Model Year Production	Change from LY
Matador 2-Door Coupe	16-7	$3,621	+5.08%	3562	*	*
Matador 4-Door Sedan	85-7	$3,627	+5.07%	3589	*	*
Matador 4-Door Station Wagon	88-7	$4,373	+13.76%	4015	11,049	+14.00%
TOTALS		*Avg. price* $3,874	+8.18%		*Production* 41,513*	-30.33%

*Production by body style is not available. Production by engine type (compared to LY): 6-cylinder cars, 4,993 (-46.83%); V8 car, 25,471 (-37.11%). Also, the wagon has a standard V8 for 1976, therefore a greater price increase than other Matador models.   **Comparison to LY is not available due to production total not being recorded by body style this year.*

BUICK

"Dedicated to the Free Spirit in just about everyone."

Buick entered the 1976 model year introducing several new styling themes for its most popular mid-size Century line, while losing several once-significant names and models. Although actual Gran Sport models had disappeared a few years back, the GS option packages were now also lost to history, if only temporarily. Also gone were the LeSabre convertible and the German-built Opel 1900 and Opel Manta, longtime staples of the Buick line. Buick was embracing change, and the "free spirit" marketing campaign was working.

All Century models received a facelift, but it took three different forms depending upon the model. The 4-door sedans and wagons were among the first American cars to utilize dual rectangular headlights that were stacked. In between, all used a grille and turn signal/parking light arrangement similar to last year's Regal models, with the grille now being of a crosshatch design outlined in chrome. The Century and Century Custom used a Buick nameplate on the lower driver's side of the grille, and the Regal sedan used a

Regal script nameplate mid-level on the right side. Bodyside, rear end and interior styling continued with few changes.

Century coupes received two different front-end designs with side-by-side rectangular headlamps, and a new rear end look, all of which were completely different from the four-door models. The Century Special, Century and Century Custom all sported a canted front nose, which was slightly pointed in the center. The only chrome used on the front end was in the light bezels, bumper and the crosshatch design grille inserts. The actual grille consisted of three equally spaced horizontal openings on each side, surrounded by a body color front fascia. The front side marker light was set at the height of the turn signal on each fender end, seen from the side. The upscale Regal received a formal, upright front end design with a wider grille than the sedans, set slightly forward of the headlights and having a finer texture cross-hatch pattern highlighted by three slightly larger horizontal bars and an even larger chrome grille surround. The headlight bezels wrapped slightly around to the sides, housing a thin vertical side reflector. These touches gave the Century Regal coupe the more formal look it deserved.

The Century Special and Century coupes continued with the "fastback" roofline of the 1973–1975 models with a flatter rear window, while the Century Custom and Regal coupes used the more formal Regal roofline of 1973–1975 with opera windows and curved rear window. At the rear, all coupes used a new rear end design with slender taillights running up the trailing edge of the rear quarter, and horizontal units set under the decklid, with the license plate housing in the middle. A Buick Century was selected as the Indianapolis 500 race pace car for the second consecutive year. This year's pace car again utilized the optional "T-top," but the real news was under the hood, where a modified turbocharged version of Buick's V6 engine resided. Built by Rajay Industries, the turbocharger more than doubled the power of the stock V6 engine. It was an exciting glimpse into Buick's future, though the turbocharger was not yet offered on production cars. There were 1,290 pace car replicas built for 1976 by way of adding the Free Spirit package to a Century Custom coupe, with or without optional T-tops.

The base LeSabre, after the start of the model year, became the first full-size Buick to offer the V6 engine. LeSabre Customs offered only V8 power. Both LeSabre and Estate Wagon took a hint from the Electra 225 and adopted dual rectangular headlights with turn signal/parking lamps directly beneath. The new grille — no longer full-width, but set inboard of the headlights so that a body-color strip now ran below and beside the headlight bezels — was of a crosshatch design, surrounded by chrome, with a large chrome header carrying the Buick name in widely-spaced block lettering. Similarly, the Electra adopted the turn signal/parking lamp move from in the bumper to under the headlights. A variation of last year's vertical bar "waterfall" look grille followed the LeSabre's narrower design with the headlight bezels now surrounded by a body-color strip. Finally the Riviera added a new crosshatch design grille, but kept its other styling cues. Most other features for all of the above series continued as they were last year, as this would be their final year before being downsized.

The subcompact Skyhawk continued into 1976 with very few changes. The mid-year 1975 de-contented S model was successful enough to be carried on, but after an initial boom, sales quickly dropped, ending at nearly half of the first year's level. A mid-year 1976 addition, the Free Spirit package, built on the theme of the Century Custom Indy 500 pace car replica, added similar black, orange and red striping, with a Buick "eagle" logo, with silver paint only. Only 918 were sold. The Apollo name that had been used since the introduction of the new compact Buicks in 1973 and on last year's restyled four-door models was dropped, making all compact Buicks part of the Skylark family. Otherwise the 1976 Skylark was distinguished by a new crosshatch grille in a strongly horizontal pattern.

New Buick Opel models came from GM's Japanese partner Isuzu, a company of which GM had purchased a 34.2 percent share in 1971. The new Isuzu-built car had its roots in Germany as one of General Motors' first "global" platforms, the development of which began in 1970. Known as the "T-car," the new Opel started life on the road in Germany for the 1973 model year as the third-generation Opel Kadett, which was not imported to North America. The "T-car" spawned many cars around the world, to include the Opel Isuzu (a.k.a. Buick Opel) and the Chevrolet Chevette, both introduced for the 1976 model year in the United States.

The new Opel Isuzu, as it was named for 1976, included a base and a deluxe 2-door coupe. Initial advertising focused on making sure consumers knew the correct name as in this example from a magazine advertisement: "*Introducing Opel Isuzu. (pronounce it 'ee-'soo-zoo').*" Exterior styling at the front had a look very similar to the German-built 1900 series of prior years, and featured a grille made up of seven chrome-lined squares, with horizontal rectangular turn signal/parking lamps at each end, and a thicker chrome bar running across the top of the area. Single round headlamps were set in the fender ends. The rest of the body seemed to combine a little of the Manta with the 1900 series styling, creating a semi-fastback look. At the rear were rectangular, horizontally mounted tail lamps with amber turn signals, a feature that was becoming more common in the American market. Interior accommodations seemed more Japanese in design with three round gauges set in a trapezoidal pod in front of the driver, and radio and air conditioning controls mounted near the center. Woodgrain appliqués on the instrument panel, console and door panels gave the new Opel a Buick feel and appearance.

Century Custom 4-Door
Colonnade Hardtop Sedan

Century Custom 4-Door, 3-Seat Station Wagon

Century Regal 2-Door
Colonnade Hardtop Coupe

Century Special 2-Door
Colonnade Hardtop Coupe

Electra 225 Limited 4-Door
Hardtop with Park Avenue package

Estate Wagon

LeSabre Custom 2-Door Hardtop

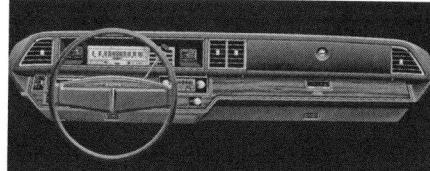

LeSabre Custom instrument panel

Riviera 2-Door Hardtop Coupe
with S/R package

Skyhawk 2-Door Hatchback Coupe

Skyhawk 2-Door Hatchback Coupe
with Astro roof and roof crown molding

Skyhawk interior

Skylark S/R 2-Door Hatchback Coupe

Opel Isuzu 2-Door Coupe

Model year production: 737,502, up 44.26% from 1975.
Domestic market share: 8.50% (5th place).
Base price range: $3,453 to $6,852.
Buick average base price: $4,838, up 3.36%.
Introduction date: September 25, 1975; Opel introduced April 29, 1976.
Assembly plants: Baltimore, MD (B); Southgate, CA (C); Doraville, GA (D); Framingham, MA (G); Flint, MI (H); Kansas City/Leeds, MO (K); Van Nuys, CA (L); Tarrytown, NY (T); Kansas City/Fairfax, KS (X); Fremont, CA (Z); St. Therese, Quebec, Canada (2). Opel assembly plant: Fujisawa, Japan (8).
Data plate identification (VIN): Thirteen digit code read as follows: First digit indicates division (4 = Buick); second through fourth digits indicate series and body style (model number in model charts); fifth digit is engine code (see powertrain chart); sixth digit indicates model year (6 = 1976); seventh digit indicates assembly plant (see list above); remaining digits are sequential with beginning number of 100001, or 400001, depending upon assembly plant. *Example:* 4N69J6H100001 is a 1976 Buick LeSabre 4-Door Sedan, with 350 CID, 4-bbl. V8 engine, serial number 100001, built in Flint, MI. 1976 Opels use a 13-digit code read the same as other 1976 Buicks except that the final six digits are sequential with beginning number of 700001.

Powertrains

Engine	Net HP	Engine Code	Transmission Availability		Opel	Skyhawk	Skylark	Century & Regal	LeSabre	Electra & Estate Wagon	Riviera
110.8 CID (1.8L) OHC, 2-bbl., 4-cyl.	80	B	4-speed manual		S	—	—	—	—	—	—
				MPG:	23/36/27	—	—	—	—	—	—
				Calif.	22/32/26	—	—	—	—	—	—
			3-speed Turbo Hydra-matic		$250	—	—	—	—	—	—
				MPG:	23/31/26	—	—	—	—	—	—
				Calif.	22/29/25	—	—	—	—	—	—
231 CID (3.8L), 2-bbl., V6	105	C	3-speed manual			—	—	S (ex. S/R)	S (ex. Regal Sdn. & wgns.)	—	—	—
				MPG:	—	—	16/25/19	16/25/19	—	—	—
			4-speed manual		—	S	—	—	—	—	—
				MPG:	—	18/30/22	—	—	—	—	—
				Calif.	—	17/26/20	—	—	—	—	—
			5-speed manual		—	$244	—	—	—	—	—
				MPG:	—	19/30/22	—	—	—	—	—
			3-speed Turbo Hydra-matic		—	$244	S (S/R)/ $262 (others)	$262 (ex. Regal Sdn. & wgns.)	S (LeSabre)	—	—
				MPG:	—	18/26/21	17/25/20	17/25/20	16/20/17	—	—
				Calif.	—	18/24/20	16/22/19	16/22/19	—	—	—
260 CID (4.3L), 2-bbl., V8	110	F	3-speed Turbo Hydra-matic		—	—	$35 (S/R)/ $297 (others)	—	—	—	—
				MPG:	—	—	16/23/19	—	—	—	—
				Calif.	—	—	14/20/16	—	—	—	—

Engine	Net HP	Engine Code	Transmission Availability	Opel	Skyhawk	Skylark	Century & Regal	LeSabre	Electra & Estate Wagon	Riviera
350 CID (5.7L), 2-bbl., V8[1]	140	H	3-speed Turbo Hydra-matic	—	—	$85 (S/R)/ $347 (others)	S (Regal Sdn.)/ $347 (ex. Regal Sdn. & wgns.)	—	—	—
			MPG:	—	—	14/20/ 17	14/21/ 16	—	—	—
350 CID (5.7L), 4-bbl., V8[1]	155	J	3-speed Turbo Hydra-matic	—	—	$140 (S/R)/ $402 (others)	S (Wgns.)/ $55 (Regal Sdn.)/ $402 (ex. Regal Sdn. & wgns.)	S (LeSabre Custom)	-$159 (credit on Electra only)	—
			MPG:	—	—	14/22/ 17	15/21/ 17[2]	14/18/ 15	14/18/ 15	—
			Calif.	—	—	14/20/ 16	14/20/ 16[2]	12/18/ 14	12/18/ 14	—
455 CID (7.4L), 4-bbl., V8	205	T	3-speed Turbo Hydra-matic	—	—	—	—	$159 (LeSabre Custom)	S	S
			MPG:	—	—	—	—	12/18/ 14	12/18/ 14[2]	12/18/ 14
			Calif.	—	—	—	—	11/16/ 13	11/16/ 13[2]	11/16/ 13

[1]Not available on Century Special.   [2]On Century wagons, MPG is 14/18/15; on Estate Wagon, 11/16/13.

Major Options

	Opel	Skyhawk	Skylark	Century	LeSabre	Estate Wagon	Electra 225	Riviera
Climate-Control air conditioning[1]	$	$424	$452	$476	$512	$512	$512	$512
Tilt-wheel steering[2]	—	$48	$52	$52	$53	$53	$53	S
Tilt and telescoping steering column	—	—	—	—	$95	$95	$95	$42
GM Air Cushion Restraint System	—	—	—	—	$315	—	$315	$262
Cruise control	—	—	$73	$73	$79	$79	$79	$79
Electric rear window defogger	$35	$66	$43[3]	$77	$78	$78	$78	$78
Tinted glass, all windows	S	$44	$46	$50	$64	$64	$64	$64
Power windows, 2-dr./4-dr.	—	—	$89/$140	$89/$140	$159	$159	S	S
Power door locks, 2-dr./4-dr.	—	—	$62/$89	$62/$89	$90	$90	$90	$90
Power front seat, 6-way, w/bench seat	—	—	—	$124	$126	$126	$126	$126
Front bucket seats, w/console	S[4]	S[4]	$150[5]	$203[5]	—	—	—	$72
AM radio	—	$71	$75	$79	$92	$92	$92	$92
AM/FM stereo	$210	$219	$233	$233	$236	$236	$236	$236
AM/FM stereo w/8-track tape	—	—	$337	$337	$341	$341	$341	$341
Vinyl top	—	—	$96[6]	$111[6]	$139[7]	—	$139[7]	$152[7]
Sunroof, electric[8]	—	—	—	$370	—	—	$725	$725
Astroroof, sliding glass[8]	—	$550[8]	—	—	—	—	$891	$891
Hurst hatch-roof, T-tops[8]	—	—	—	$550	—	—	—	—
Woodgrain panels (wagons)	—	—	—	$146	—	$193	—	—
Power steering	—	$120	$136	S	S	S	S	S
Power brakes, w/front disc	S	S	$55	$55[9]	S	S	S	S
Full wheel covers	—	$39	$31	$32[10]	$32[10]	S	S	S
Styled road wheels	—	$84	$89	$89	$151	$151	S	S
WSW tires, standard size	—	$26	$28	$30	$41	$47	$47	$47

Popular Option Groups & Packages

	Opel	Skyhawk	Skylark	Century	LeSabre	Estate Wagon	Electra 225	Riviera
Accessory group	—	$11	$11	—	—	—	—	—
Appearance group	—	$31	$31	—	—	—	—	—
Convenience group	—	$20	$29	$29	$29	—	—	—
Firm ride & handling pkg.	—	$15	$15	$15	$15	$15	$15	$15
Indianapolis 500 pace car replica package	—	—	—	$876	—	—	—	—
Free Spirit package	—	$148	—	$	—	—	—	—
Park Avenue package	—	—	—	—	—	—	$419	—
S/R coupe package	—	—	—	$379[11]	—	—	—	$276

—= Not Available; S = Standard equipment. [1]Manually controlled. Power brakes required, except on Skyhawk. Semi-automatic climate control is available for $37 additional on Century Regal, LeSabre and Estate Wagon. Automatic climate control is available for $82 additional on Electra and Riviera. [2]Requires power steering on Skyhawk; requires automatic transmission on Skylark and Century. Not available with Air Cushion Restraint System. [3]Blower type defogger. [4]Opel Deluxe and Skyhawk models only. Opel base and Skyhawk S have bucket seats w/o console. [5]Standard on Skylark S/R. Available for $79 extra on Century Custom and Regal models. [6]Price is $5 less on Skylark S/R models and Century 2-doors. Century Custom or Regal coupes w/Landau top, $110. Not available on Century station wagons. [7]A variety of vinyl top configurations available, ranging in price from $62 to $549. Prices shown are for full, non-padded, vinyl top on two-door models. [8]Available on two-door models only. Skyhawk Astroroof is fixed and includes roof crown molding. [9]Standard on Century Regal and Century station wagons. [10]Standard on Century Regal and LeSabre Custom models. [11]Available only on Century Regal coupe.

Paint Colors

Buick	Code	Buick	Code	Opel Isuzu	Code
Liberty White	11	Mt. Vernon Cream	50	Pacific Blue	B
Pewter Gray metallic	13	Colonial Yellow	51	Leaf Green	G
Medium Gray metallic	16	Cream Gold	57	Sunrise Red	R
Regal Black	19	Buckskin	65	Earth Tan	T
Potomac Blue metallic	28	Musket Brown metallic	67	Cloud White	W
Continental Blue metallic	35	Red	72	Moon Yellow	Y
Boston Red metallic	36	Firecracker Orange	78		
Independence Red metallic	37				
Concord Green metallic	40	In two-tone combinations, the first two digits indicate			
Dark Green metallic	49	lower color, and the next two digits are the upper color.			

Opel Isuzu

"Introducing Opel Isuzu. Designed in Germany, built in Japan, and sold and serviced through your local Buick dealer."

Nameplate year of origin: 1976.

Current bodystyle lifespan: 1976 through 1979.

Predecessor to this model: Opel 1900 (1971–1975); Manta (1971–1975).

Replacement for this model: None. (The same car was sold after 1980 as the Isuzu I-Mark.)

Primary competition: AMC Gremlin, Chevrolet Vega, Dodge Colt, Ford Pinto, Mercury Bobcat, and Pontiac Astre.

Notable changes: Completely redesigned; based on new-for-1973 German Opel Kadett.

Major standard equipment: Reclining vinyl front bucket seats, rubber floor mats, interior lights, column-mounted headlight dimmer switch, and 6.15 × 13 BSW tires. Deluxe adds: Full-floor carpeting, center console w/gauges and clock, tachometer, woodgrain vinyl trim on I/P gauge cluster, console and doors, trunk mat, side window moldings, bodyside protective moldings, rocker panel molding, front and rear bumper guards, and wheel trim rings.

Measurements

Wheelbase	151.5"
Wheelbase	94.3"
Length	168.0"*
Width	61.8"
Height	50.8"
Legroom — front	40.6"
Legroom — rear	30.9"
Headroom — front	37.0"
Headroom — rear	35.1"
Cargo capacity (cu. ft.)	9.9
Fuel capacity (gals.)	NA

*Deluxe and models for sale in California, 170.5".

Models Available

	Model No.	Base MSRP	Change from LY	Shipping Wt. (lbs.)	Model Year Production	Change from LY**
Opel Isuzu 2-Door Coupe	T77	$3,282	-9.96%*	2061	NA	NA
Opel Isuzu Deluxe 2-Door Coupe	T77	$3,595	NEW	2081	NA	NEW
TOTALS	*Avg. price*	$3,439	-9.13%**		*Production* 25,000**	+66.67%

*Comparisons to LY made to 1975 Opel 1900 2-Door Sedan.   **Model year sales are estimated based upon dealer sales reporting, and change from LY is compared to the entire 1975 Opel line.

Skyhawk

"The epitome of the new small Buicks."

Nameplate year of origin: 1975.
Current bodystyle lifespan: 1975 through 1980.
   Predecessor to this model: None.
Replacement for this model: Skyhawk (1982 to 1989).
Percentage of division's production: 2.14%.
Corporate siblings: Chevrolet Monza and Oldsmobile Starfire (closely related to Chevrolet Vega and Pontiac Astre).
Primary competition: AMC Pacer, Ford Mustang II and "Lincoln-Mercury" Capri II.
Notable changes: Minor trim and detail changes.
Major standard equipment: Choice of cloth and vinyl or all-vinyl front bucket seats with foam cushions, fold-down rear seat, cut-pile carpeting including cargo area, simulated woodgrain I/P, gauges including tachometer, rallye steering wheel, functional B-pillar vent louvers, dual speed wipers w/washers, bright window surround moldings, front and rear wheel opening moldings, blackout grille, hubcaps, and B78 × 13 BSW tires. Skyhawk adds: Full instrumentation, full-length floor console, LH remote control outside rear view sport mirror, and BR78 × 13 BSW tires.

Measurements

Wheelbase	97.0"
Length	179.3"
Width	65.4"
Height	50.1"
Legroom — front	42.8"
Legroom — rear	29.6"
Headroom — front	37.7"
Headroom — rear	35.3"
Cargo capacity (cu. ft.)	27.8*
Fuel capacity (gals.)	18.5

*With rear seat folded down.

Models Available

	Model No.	Base MSRP	Change from LY	Shipping Wt. (lbs.)	Model Year Production*	Change from LY
Skyhawk S 2-Door Hatchback	T07	$3,903	+1.11%	2857	NA	NA
Skyhawk 2-Door Hatchback	S07	$4,216	+1.03%	2889	NA	NA
TOTALS	*Avg. price*	$4,060	+1.07%		*Production* 15,769	-46.45%

*Production and comparisons by model not available as they were kept as combined total.

Skylark

"The only V6-powered compact made in America comes from Buick."

Nameplate year of origin: 1953.
Current bodystyle lifespan: 1975 through 1979.
Predecessor to this model: Apollo (1973 to 1974).
Replacement for this model: Skylark (1980 to 1985).
Percentage of division's production: 15.52%.
Corporate siblings: Chevrolet Nova, Oldsmobile Omega, and Pontiac Ventura.
Primary competition: Dodge Aspen and Mercury Monarch.
Notable changes: Apollo name discontinued; four-doors renamed Skylark; trim and detail changes.

Measurements

	Coupe & HBK	Sedan
Wheelbase	111.0"	111.0"
Length	200.3"	200.3"
Width	72.7"	72.7"
Height	52.1"	53.1"
Legroom — front	41.7"	41.7"
Legroom — rear	33.4"	35.3"

Major standard equipment: S model: Front vinyl bench seat, front door armrest, cut-pile carpeting, and E78 × 14 BSW tires. Skylark adds: Choice of patterned cloth or vinyl front bench seat with foam cushions, cut-pile carpeting including hatchback load floor, fold-down rear seat (hatchback only), front door operated courtesy lights, front and rear ashtrays, rear quarter/rear door armrests, deluxe steering wheel, dual speed wipers w/4-jet washers, roof drip moldings, front and rear wheel opening moldings, and hubcaps. S/R adds: Cloth front bucket seats w/passenger recliner, carpeted door trim w/map pocket and reflector, sports shifting console, combination turn signal and high/low beam headlight control stalk, stand-up hood ornament, and FR78 × 14 BSW tires.

Measurements (cont.)

	Coupe & HBK	Sedan
Headroom — front	38.3"	39.3"
Headroom — rear	36.6"	36.6"
Cargo capacity (cu. ft.)	14.2*	13.6
Fuel capacity (gals.)	21.0	21.0

*Hatchback maximum with rear seat down, 28.4 cu. ft.

Models Available

	Model No.	Base MSRP	Change from LY	Shipping Wt. (lbs.)	Model Year Production	Change from LY
Skylark S 2-Door Coupe	W27	$3,435	+6.22%	3316	**	NEW
Skylark 2-Door Coupe	B27	$3,549	+2.48%	3327	51,260	+85.13%
Skylark 2-Door Hatchback	B17	$3,687	+2.82%	3396	6,730	-1.63%
Skylark 4-Door Sedan	B69	$3,609	+5.03%*	3283	48,157	+127.82%*
Skylark S/R 2-Door Coupe	C27	$4,281	+3.51%	3319	3,880	+3.58%
Skylark S/R 2-Door Hatchback	C17	$4,398	+3.41%	3338	1,248	-17.08%
Skylark S/R 4-Door Sedan	C69	$4,324	+5.67%*	3312	3,243	+44.71%*
TOTALS	Avg. price	$3,898	+4.13%	Production	114,491	+81.35%

*Change from LY compared to equivalent 1975 Apollo models.   **Production of S coupe was kept with Skylark base coupe production.

Century

"A leaner, smaller breed of Buick, that also happens to be the only American mid-size car powered by a V6 engine. A rather special distinction."

Nameplate year of origin: 1936.
Current bodystyle lifespan: 1973 through 1977.
Predecessor to this model: Skylark (1968 to 1972).
Replacement for this model: Century (1978 to 1981).
Percentage of division's production: 41.37%.
Corporate siblings: Chevrolet Malibu, Oldsmobile Cutlass, and Pontiac LeMans.
Primary competition: Dodge Charger and Coronet and Mercury Montego.
Notable changes: All-new front end styling and new rear styling for coupes.
Major standard equipment: (Century Special) Choice of cloth or vinyl front bench seat, rubber floor covering, 4-jet windshield washer, front disc brakes, variable ratio power steering, and FR78 × 15 BSW tires. Century (base) adds: Cut-pile carpeting, deluxe steering wheel, bumper protective strips w/white accents front and rear, wheel covers, and GR78 × 15 BSW tires (coupe only). Custom adds: Choice of cloth or expanded vinyl notchback front seat w/center fold-down armrest, ashtray light, under-dash courtesy lights, glove compartment light, "Custom" badging, wheel opening moldings, rocker panel molding, and power front disc brakes. Wagons add: Vinyl front bench seat (Century base only; Custom wagon has same upholstery choices as coupes and sedans), and HR78 × 15 BSW tires. Regal adds: Choice of luxury cloth or expanded vinyl notchback seat with center armrest, door pull assist straps, and GR78 × 15 BSW tires.

Measurements

	Coupes	Sedans	Wagons
Wheelbase	112.0"	116.0"	116.0"
Length	209.7"	213.5"	218.2"
Width	77.0"	79.0"	79.0"
Height	52.8"*	53.6"	55.3"
Legroom — front	42.4"	42.4"	42.3"
Legroom — rear	32.9"	37.1"	36.8"
Headroom — front	37.2"*	37.9"	38.8"
Headroom — rear	36.7"*	37.3"	39.4"
Cargo capacity (cu. ft.)	14.7	15.6	85.1
Fuel capacity (gals.)	NA	NA	NA

*Custom coupe and Regal coupe: Height, 52.6"; front headroom, 37.0"; rear headroom, 37.1".

Models Available

	Model No.	Base MSRP	Change from LY	Shipping Wt. (lbs.)	Model Year Production	Change from LY
Century Special 2-Dr. Colonnade HT Coupe	E37	$3,935	+3.15%	3508	*	NA
Century 2-Door Colonnade HT Coupe	D37	$4,070	+4.52%	3652	59,484	+50.38%
Century 4-Door Colonnade HT Sedan	D29	$4,105	+4.08%	3741	33,632	+52.35%
Century Custom 2-Door Colonnade HT Coupe	H57	$4,346	+4.62%	3609	34,036	+3.25%
Century Custom 4-Door Colonnade HT Sedan	H29	$4,424	+5.06%	3721	19,728	+97.83%
Century Custom 4-Door Station Wagon, 2-S.	K35	$4,987	+3.85%	4363	16,625	+134.88%
Century Custom 4-Door Station Wagon, 3-S.	K45	$5,099	+3.70%	4413	**	**
Century Regal 2-Door Colonnade HT Coupe	J57	$4,465	+4.89%	3710	124,498	+119.78%
Century Regal 4-Door Colonnade HT Sedan	J29	$4,825	+11.92%	4104	17,118	+59.59%
TOTALS	Avg. price	$4,473	+3.17%	Production	305,121	+66.32%

*Production of Century Special, E37, kept as combined total with Century 2-Door coupe, D37. **Production of 3-seat wagon models included with 2-seat models.

LeSabre

"For comfortably whisking off on all manner of escapes."

Nameplate year of origin: 1959 (also used on 1951 GM show car).
Current bodystyle lifespan: 1971 through 1976.
Predecessor to this model: LeSabre (1969 to 1970).
Replacement for this model: LeSabre (1977 to 1985).
Percentage of division's production: 18.59%.
Corporate siblings: Chevrolet Impala and Caprice, Pontiac Catalina and Bonneville, and Oldsmobile Delta 88.
Primary competition: Chrysler Newport and Mercury Marquis.
Notable changes: New grille and trim and detail changes.
Major standard equipment: Choice of cloth and vinyl or all-vinyl notchback front bench seat w/fold-down center armrest, full-floor carpeting, woodgrained vinyl trim on door panels, custom steering wheel, I/P woodgrain appliqués, LH outside rear view mirror, front fender-mounted three-section rectangular "ventiport" ornaments, bumper protective strips w/white accent stripes front and rear, wheel opening moldings, full-length rocker panel molding, deluxe wheel covers, and GR78 × 15 BSW tires. Custom adds: HR78 × 15 BSW tires.

Measurements

Wheelbase	124.0"
Length	226.8"
Width	79.9"
Height	54.0"
Legroom — front	42.1"
Legroom — rear	38.8"
Headroom — front	38.9"
Headroom — rear	38.0"
Cargo capacity (cu. ft.)	16.8*
Fuel capacity (gals.)	NA

*Coupe: rear legroom, 35.8"; rear headroom, 36.5"; cargo capacity, 17.5.

Models Available

	Model No.	Base MSRP	Change from LY	Shipping Wt. (lbs.)	Model Year Production	Change from LY
LeSabre 2-Door Hardtop Coupe	N57	$4,815	-0.52%	4129	3,861	-55.35%
LeSabre 4-Door Sedan	N69	$4,747	-0.50%	4170	4,315	-69.37%
LeSabre 4-Door Hardtop Sedan	N39	$4,871	-0.55%	4259	2,312	-74.65%
LeSabre Custom 2-Door Hardtop Coupe	P57	$5,114	+2.14%	4275	45,669	+82.56%
LeSabre Custom 4-Door Sedan	P69	$5,046	+2.23%	4328	34,841	+104.63%
LeSabre Custom 4-Door Hardtop Sedan	P39	$5,166	+2.07%	4386	46,109	+53.67%
TOTALS	Avg. price	$4,960	+0.21%	Production	137,107	+25.55%

Estate Wagon

"It's more than just a full-size wagon, it's a full-size Buick."

Nameplate year of origin: 1940 (as designation for station wagons).
Current bodystyle lifespan: 1971 through 1976.
Predecessor to this model: Estate Wagon (1970).
Replacement for this model: Estate Wagon (1977 to 1990).
Percentage of division's production: 2.76%.
Corporate siblings: Chevrolet Impala and Caprice, Pontiac Catalina Safari and Grand Safari, and Oldsmobile Custom Cruiser.
Primary competition: Chrysler Town & Country and Mercury Marquis Colony Park.
Notable changes: New grille and trim and detail changes.
Major standard equipment: Vinyl front bench seat, forward facing 3rd seat w/divided 2nd seat on 3-seat wagon, full-floor carpeting, hidden storage compartment, Glide-Away tailgate, power tailgate window, LH and RH rear view mirrors, fender-mounted three-section rectangular "ventiport" ornaments, deluxe wheel covers, and LR78 × 15 BSW tires.

Measurements

Wheelbase	127.0"
Length	231.8"
Width	79.9"
Height	57.8"
Legroom — front	42.1"
Legroom — rear	39.4"
Headroom — front	39.6"
Headroom — rear	39.3"
Cargo capacity (cu. ft.)	105.7
Fuel capacity (gals.)	NA

Models Available

	Model No.	Base MSRP	Change from LY	Shipping Wt. (lbs.)	Model Year Production	Change from LY
Estate Wagon 4-Door, 2-S. Wagon	R35	$5,591	+2.64%	5013	5,990	+45.11%
Estate Wagon 4-Door, 3-S. Wagon	R45	$5,731	+2.50%	5139	14,384	+49.65%
TOTALS		Avg. price $5,661	+2.57%		Production 20,374	+48.28%

Electra 225

"Luxury cars of a most satisfying nature."

Nameplate year of origin: 1959.
Current bodystyle lifespan: 1971 through 1976.
Predecessor to this model: Electra (1969 to 1970).
Replacement for this model: Electra 225 (1977 to 1984).
Percentage of division's production: 16.89%.
Corporate siblings: Cadillac Calais, Cadillac deVille, and Oldsmobile Ninety-Eight.
Primary competition: Chrysler New Yorker Brougham and Mercury Grand Marquis.
Notable changes: New grille and trim and detail changes.
Major standard equipment: Cloth and vinyl front bench seat (sedan only) or choice of cloth and vinyl or all-vinyl notchback front bench seat w/fold-down center armrest, cut-pile carpeting, simulated woodgrain appliqués on door panels and instrument panel, door pull straps, carpeted lower door panels, power windows, electronic digital quartz clock, custom steering wheel, custom safety belts, remote-control LH rear view mirror, fender-mounted 4-section rectangular "ventiport" ornaments, bodyside protection molding, wheel opening moldings, full-length rocker panel molding, rear fender skirts, super deluxe wheel covers, and JR78 × 15 BSW tires. Limited adds: Custom cloth 60/40 notchback front seat w/fold-down center armrest, two-way power seat adjustment, combination dome and reading lamp (sedan), and wider rocker panel moldings.

Measurements

Wheelbase	127.0"
Length	233.3"
Width	79.9"
Height	54.5"
Legroom — front	42.2"
Legroom — rear	40.8"
Headroom — front	39.3"
Headroom — rear	38.2"
Cargo capacity (cu. ft.)	20.3
Fuel capacity (gals.)	NA

Models Available

	Model No.	Base MSRP	Change from LY	Shipping Wt. (lbs.)	Model Year Production	Change from LY
Electra 225 2-Dr. Hardtop Coupe	V37	$6,367	+5.40%	4502	18,442	+14.23%

	Model No.	Base MSRP	Change from LY	Shipping Wt. (lbs.)	Model Year Production	Change from LY
Electra 225 4-Dr. Hardtop Sedan	V39	$6,527	+5.26%	4641	26,655	-2.57%
Electra 225 Limited 2-Dr. Hdtp. Cpe.	X37	$6,689	+5.31%	4521	28,395	+60.88%
Electra 225 Limited 4-Dr. Hdtp. Sdn.	X39	$6,852	+5.16%	4709	51,067	+51.18%
TOTALS	Avg. price	$6,609	+5.28%		Production 124,559	+31.21%

Riviera

"A road car; a luxury car. It's two of the nicest cars you've ever wanted."

Nameplate year of origin: 1963 (1949 as designation for hardtop models).
Current bodystyle lifespan: 1971 through 1976.
Predecessor to this model: Riviera (1966 to 1970).
Replacement for this model: Riviera (1977 to 1978).
Percentage of division's production: 2.72%.
Corporate siblings: Cadillac Eldorado and Oldsmobile Toronado.
Primary competition: Ford Thunderbird.
Notable changes: Minor trim and detail changes.
Major standard equipment: Cloth notchback front seat w/fold-down center armrest, cut-pile carpeting, simulated woodgrain appliqué on door panels and I/P, door pull handle, power windows, electronic digital quartz clock, custom steering wheel, tilt steering wheel, light package (ashtray, courtesy, glove compartment and trunk), LH remote-control rear view mirror, dual exhaust, front bumper guards, deluxe wheel covers, and JR78 × 15 BSW tires.

Measurements

Wheelbase	122.0"
Length	218.6"
Width	79.9"
Height	53.0"
Legroom — front	42.2"
Legroom — rear	35.4"
Headroom — front	38.1"
Headroom — rear	37.1"
Cargo capacity (cu. ft.)	15.1
Fuel capacity (gals.)	NA

Models Available

	Model No.	Base MSRP	Change from LY	Shipping Wt. (lbs.)	Model Year Production	Change from LY
Riviera 2-Door Hardtop	Z87	$6,798	+5.89%	4531	20,082	+16.04%
TOTALS	Avg. price	$6,798	+5.89%		Production 20,082	+16.04%

CADILLAC

"An American tradition of excellence since 1902."

Cadillac was fortunate enough to be in the spotlight twice this season. The first time was for the all-new Seville, which was introduced in May 1975 as a 1976 model. The second model making news was when Cadillac announced production of the "last" American-built convertible, as the final 1976 Eldorado convertible rolled off the line at Cadillac's Clark Avenue plant in Detroit on April 21, 1976. Both pro-vided Cadillac a lot of publicity, as the Seville was billed as being "among the most fully equipped cars in the world," not to mention the most expensive American built sedan for 1976,* and the Eldorado convertible was touted as the "Last of a magnificent breed." The Seville alone sold so well that it would push Cadillac to another record setting model year production total, surpassing the recently achieved 1973 high

1976 Cadillac Fleetwood Limousine and nine-passenger sedan are higher priced, but not considered traditional production sedans.

point. But it would not take long for the Seville to gain rivals, and not much longer for convertibles to make a comeback, eventually even an Eldorado convertible.

The new Seville had been in the works for several years, and the new smaller Cadillac, which many thought would be named the LaSalle after the 1930s era smaller Cadillac that sold so well during the depression, could not have come to market at a better time. Making it to market just months after the OPEC oil embargo crisis had ended, a smaller, fuel-efficient luxury car was just what many consumers were wanting. Competitors of the Seville's size and price were limited to the BMW 3-series, Jaguar XJ6 and Mercedes-Benz 280 series cars, with no domestic competition in sight. Choosing to target Mercedes as the car to beat, Cadillac went for a design that was larger than most compact cars of the day, but slightly smaller than most mid-size cars. After many different concept designs, the final version was based on a new platform, designated the K-body, which was essentially a stretched version of the GM X-body that was the foundation of the Chevrolet Nova, Buick Skylark, Oldsmobile Omega and Pontiac Ventura. However, there was enough design change with the roughly 3-inch stretch that few would have guessed where the Seville's real roots lay.

Exterior styling would set the trend for GM car design, revealing a glimpse of the upcoming GM downsized cars, with a squared-off look across the entire car and an upright rear window and accompanying formal roofline that would become popular on nearly all domestic four-door sedans for the next 10 years. At the front was the now familiar Cadillac egg-crate grille framed with dual side-by-side headlamps set above slender rectangular turn signal/parking lights that met large, square side marker and cornering lights on the front corner of the fender, with all of the lights housed in chrome bezels and set above a heavy looking bumper. A single, full-length bodyside feature line that began off the front fender edge was barely perceptible until the rear quarter panel where a slight concave area was created between it and the line of the rear deck until they met at the end of the quarter panel. Square taillamps wrapped around to the quarter panel to complete the clean lines of the car, which was relatively unadorned other than rocker panel and wheel opening moldings, a vinyl bodyside protective strip, and the Seville nameplate.

Under the hood, Seville carried General Motors' most technically advanced engine yet. The engine's basis was an Oldsmobile 350 CID V8 fitted with Cadillac's relatively new electronic fuel injection system that utilized port injection. The engine was mated to the same "400 series" Turbo Hydramatic transmission that was used in all other Cadillacs. Suspension features included traditional front coil and rear leaf springs, combined with unequal length upper and lower suspension arms to improve handling, and automatic level control, all combining to make the Seville the best driving Cadillac in many years.

The Seville interior was pure Cadillac, with an instrument panel design matching that of all other Cadillacs, including the upper "information band" that grouped the fuel gauge, digital clock and warning lights together on the upper panel in front of the driver. Everything in the interior was intentionally designed to show its Cadillac heritage, while keeping in mind its intentions of competing with international brands such as Mercedes-Benz. The result was a fully equipped car that was smaller, lighter and more luxurious than anything to precede it from an American manufacturer. Although touted as being "fully equipped," in typical mid-'70s American fashion the Seville still offered around 25 options, allowing buyers to personalize their new car.

The remainder of the Cadillac line was mostly a carry-over from the 1975 line. As previously mentioned, this was to be the last year for the Eldorado convertible, although the big front-wheel-drive coupe would continue for another two model years in its present form. A final run of 200 all-white Eldorado convertibles led up to the final Cadillac convertible built on April 21, 1976. All 200 convertibles had wire wheel covers, white tops, white interiors with red piping, red dash, and red carpeting, and came to be known as "Bicentennial" convertibles due to the color scheme.

The Calais line was also entering its last season. While the Calais never attained the popularity of the higher priced and usually better equipped deVilles, it had filled its intended purpose over the past eleven seasons as an entry-level Cadillac for those who aspired to own a large American luxury car at a more affordable price. Finally, this was also the last season for the remainder of the Cadillac line in its present form, as the deVille, Fleetwood Brougham and Fleetwood limousine and nine-passenger sedan would all be downsized next year.

Calais 2-Door Hardtop Coupe

Coupe deVille 2-Door Hardtop Coupe

Eldorado 2-Door Convertible

1976

Eldorado 2-Door Hardtop Coupe

Fleetwood Brougham 4-Door Sedan

Fleetwood Brougham interior

Fleetwood Limousine

Sedan deVille 4-Door Hardtop

Seville 4-Door Sedan

Seville 4-Door Sedan

Seville instrument panel

Model year production: 323,985, up 31.44% from 1975.
Domestic market share: 3.74% (9th place).
Base price range: $8,629 to $15,239.
Cadillac average base price: $11,096, up 4.76%.
Introduction date: September 12, 1975.
Assembly plants: Linden, NJ (E), and Detroit, MI (Q).
Data plate identification (VIN): Thirteen digit code read as
  follows: First digit indicates division (6 = Cadillac); second
  through fourth digits indicate series and body style (model

number in model charts); fifth digit is engine code (see
powertrain chart); sixth digit indicates model year (6 =
1976); seventh digit indicates assembly plant (see list above);
remaining digits are sequential with beginning number of
100001, except Seville which begins with 450001. *Example:*
6D49S6Q100001 is a 1976 Cadillac Sedan deVille 4-Door
Hardtop, with 500 CID, 4-bbl. (or EFI) V8 engine, serial
number 100001, built in Detroit, MI.

Powertrains

Engine	Net HP	Engine Code	Transmission Availability[1]		Seville	Eldorado	DeVille & Fleetwood	Limousines
350 CID (5.7L), EFI, V8	180	R	Turbo Hydra-matic 3-sp. Automatic		S	—	—	—
				MPG:	15/21/17	—	—	—
				Calif.	13/19/15	—	—	—

Engine	Net HP	Engine Code	Transmission Availability[1]		Seville	Eldorado	DeVille & Fleetwood	Limousines
500 CID (8.2L), 4-bbl., V8	190	S	Turbo Hydra-matic 3-sp. Automatic		—	S	S	S
				MPG:	—	12/16/13	12/16/13	11/14/12
				Calif.	—	11/15/12	11/15/12	10/14/11
500 CID (8.2L), EFI, V8	215	S	Turbo Hydra-matic 3-sp. Automatic		—	$647	$647	—
				MPG:	—	11/15/12	11/15/12	—
				Calif.	—	10/15/12	10/15/12	—

Major Options

	Seville	Calais	deVille	Eldorado	Fleetwood Brougham	Fleetwood
Automatic climate control	S	S	S	S	S	S
Electric rear window defogger	$77	$77	$77	$77	$77	$77[2]
Controlled cycle windshield wiper	S	$28	$28	$28	$28	$28
Tilt and telescope steering wheel	S	$102	$102	$102	$102	$102
Cruise control	$104	$104	$104	$104	$104	$104
Twilight Sentinel	$47	$47	$47	$47	$47	$47
Soft Ray tinted glass	S	S	S	S	S	S
Leather upholstery[1]	$235	—	$220	$235	$235	—
Dual Comfort 50/50 front seat	S	—	$185	$185	S[2]	—
Power front seat, 6-way bench	$125	$125	S	S	—	$93[3]
Power front seat, 6-way Dual Comfort, driver/passenger	—	—	$125	$125	S	—
Lighted vanity mirror, passenger	$44	$44	$44	$44	$44	$60
Illuminated entry system	$52	$52	$52	$52	$52	$52
AM/FM stereo, signal seeking	S	$209	$209	$61	$61	$275[4]
AM/FM stereo w/8-track tape	$97	$245	$245	$158	$158	$372[4]
Automatic door locks	$100	$100	$100	$100	$100	$100
Remote trunk release w/electric pulldown	—	$68	$68	$68	$68	$68
Padded vinyl top[5]	S	$163	$163	$170	S	$819
Sunroof[5, 6]	$701	$701	$701	$701	$701	—
Astroroof[5, 6]	$885	$885	$885	$885	$885	—
Theft-Deterrent system	$114	$114	$114	$114	$114	$114
Lamp monitor system	S	S	S	S	S	S
Fuel monitor system	S	$26	$26	$26	$26	$26
Air Cushion Restraint System	—	$315	$315	$315[5]	$315	—
Track Master anti-skid control	—	$263	$263	—	$263	$263
Automatic level control	S	$92	$92	$92	$92	S
Special turbine style wheel discs	—	$45	$45	—	$45	$45
Wire spoke wheel covers	$167	$167	$167	—	$167	$167
Steel-belted radial WSW tires	S	S	S	S	S	S

Popular Option Groups & Packages

	Seville	Calais	deVille	Eldorado	Fleetwood Brougham	Fleetwood
Brougham d'Elegance package	—	—	—	—	$885	—
Custom Cabriolet package, coupe	—	—	$329	$432	—	—
de Ville d'Elegance package	—	—	$650	—	—	—
Fleetwood Talisman package	—	—	—	—	$1,813	—

—= Not Available; S = Standard equipment. All radios include rear seat speaker and power antenna. [1]Standard on Eldorado convertible. Available on Fleetwood by special order only. [2]Dual Comfort 60/40 seat is standard on Fleetwood Brougham, available on Deville for $123. [3]Not available on Limousine. [4]Fleetwood Limousine and Nine-passenger sedan models include rear seat controls. [5]Not available on Eldorado convertible. [6]Price given is with full vinyl roof. Available on all models, except Seville, with painted roofs for $99 additional cost. Available for Fleetwood models only on special order.

Paint Colors

	Code		Code		Code
Cotillion White	11	Academy Gray metallic	16	Innsbruck Blue metallic	28
Georgian Silver metallic	13	Sable Black	19	Commodore Blue metallic	29

	Code		Code		Code
Dunbarton Green	32	Phoenician Ivory	52	Galloway Green Firemist metallic*	94
Firethorn metallic	36	Brentwood Brown metallic	67	Florentine Gold Firemist metallic*	95
Claret metallic	37	Chesterfield Brown metallic	69	Emberglow Firemist metallic*	96
Pueblo Beige metallic	38	Crystal Blue Firemist metallic*	90	*Firemist paint available for $146 extra.	
Kingswood Green metallic	39	Amberlite Firemist metallic*	91		
Calumet Cream	50	Greenbrier Firemist metallic*	93		

Seville

"International style luxury."

Nameplate year of origin: 1976; 1956 (as a designation on Eldorado 2-Door Hard-tops).

Current bodystyle lifespan: 1976 through 1979.

Predecessor to this model: None.

Replacement for this model: Seville (1980 to 1985).

Percentage of division's production: 19.55%.

Corporate siblings: None.

Primary competition: None.

Notable changes: All-new model.

Major standard equipment: Mansion knit cloth 50/50 split front seat w/individual fold-down center armrests, six-way driver and two-way passenger power seat adjustment, one-piece deep pile carpeting, seatback and overhead entry assist straps, hinged door pull handles, individual rear seat reading lamps, electric clock, power windows, power door locks, tilt and telescoping steering wheel, controlled wiper cycle system, automatic climate control, AM/FM signal-seeking stereo radio w/automatic power antenna, dual remote-control rear view mirrors, padded vinyl roof, remote trunk release, trunk carpeting including deck lid, fuel monitor system, lamp monitors, front cornering lights, wheel opening moldings, stand-up wreath and crest hood-ornament, automatic level control, automatic parking brake release, bodyside and decklid accent striping, full wheel covers, and GR78 × 15 wide WSW tires.

Measurements

Wheelbase	114.3"
Length	204.0"
Width	71.8"
Height	54.7"
Legroom — front	41.7"
Legroom — rear	38.2"
Headroom — front	38.6"
Headroom — rear	36.8"
Cargo capacity (cu. ft.)	12.8
Fuel capacity (gals.)	21.0

Models Available

	Model No.	Base MSRP	Change from LY	Shipping Wt. (lbs.)	Model Year Production*	Change from LY
Seville 4-Door Sedan	S69	$12,479	NEW	4232	60,127	NEW
TOTALS	*Avg. price*	$12,479	NEW	*Production*	60,127	NEW

*Included in total are approximately 16,000 Sevilles produced as mid-year 1975 models prior to the official September 12, 1975, introduction of 1976 model year Cadillacs.

Calais

"Cadillac value in action."

Nameplate year of origin: 1965.

Current bodystyle lifespan: 1971 through 1976.

Predecessor to this model: Calais (1969 to 1970).

Replacement for this model: None.

Percentage of division's production: 2.02%.

Corporate siblings: Buick Electra 225, Cadillac deVille, and Oldsmobile 98.

Primary competition: Chrysler New Yorker Brougham.

Notable changes: Minor trim and detail changes.

Major standard equipment: Morgan plaid cloth w/vinyl bolsters or expanded vinyl

Measurements

Wheelbase	130.0"
Length	230.7"
Width	79.8"
Height	54.3"
Legroom — front	42.0"
Legroom — rear	NA
Headroom — front	39.2"
Headroom — rear	38.2"

front bench seat w/fold-down center armrest, door pull assist straps, electric clock, power windows, power door locks, automatic climate control, AM/FM radio w/automatic power antenna, LH remote-control rear view mirror, front cornering lights, rear wheel fender skirts, wheel opening moldings, full wheel covers, and LR78 × 15 wide WSW tires.

Measurements (cont.)

Cargo capacity (cu. ft.)	19.3
Fuel capacity (gals.)	27.0

Models Available

	Model No.	Base MSRP	Change from LY	Shipping Wt. (lbs.)	Model Year Production	Change from LY
Calais 2-Door Hardtop Coupe	C47	$8,629	+5.44%	4989	4,500	-22.41%
Calais 4-Door Hardtop	C49	$8,825	+5.35%	5083	1,700	-32.00%
TOTALS		*Avg. price* $8,727	+5.39%		*Production* 6,200	-25.30%

deVille

"America's favorite luxury car."

Nameplate year of origin: 1959 (series); 1949 (as Hardtop designation).
Current bodystyle lifespan: 1971 through 1976.
Predecessor to this model: deVille (1969 to 1970).
Replacement for this model: deVille (1977 to 1984).
Percentage of division's production: 59.21%.
Corporate siblings: Buick Electra 225, Cadillac Calais, and Oldsmobile 98.
Primary competition: Lincoln Continental.
Notable changes: Minor trim and detail changes.
Major standard equipment: Choice of Merlin plaid cloth, Magnan ribbed fabric or Manhattan velour w/vinyl bolsters and front and rear seat center armrests, 6-way power front seat adjuster, cut-pile carpeting, hinged door pull assist handles, visor vanity mirror, driver and passenger reading lights, courtesy lights, courtesy lamp/assist strap combination on B-pillar of 2-doors, electric clock, power windows, power door locks, automatic climate control, AM/FM radio w/automatic power antenna, LH remote-control rear view mirror, front cornering lights, rear wheel fender skirts, wheel opening moldings, rocker panel moldings, full wheel covers, and LR78 × 15 wide WSW tires.

Measurements

Wheelbase	130.0"
Length	230.7"
Width	79.8"
Height	54.3"
Legroom — front	42.0"
Legroom — rear	NA
Headroom — front	39.2"
Headroom — rear	38.2"
Cargo capacity (cu. ft.)	19.3
Fuel capacity (gals.)	27.0

Models Available

	Model No.	Base MSRP	Change from LY	Shipping Wt. (lbs.)	Model Year Production	Change from LY
Coupe deVille 2-Door Hardtop	D47	$9,067	+5.43%	5025	114,482	+3.87%
Sedan deVille 4-Door Hardtop	D49	$9,285	+5.27%	5127	67,677	+6.83%
TOTALS		*Avg. price* $9,166	+5.35%		*Production* 182,159	+4.95%

Eldorado

"Personal size luxury."

Nameplate year of origin: 1953.
Current bodystyle lifespan: 1971 through 1978.
Predecessor to this model: Fleetwood Eldorado (1967 to 1970).
Replacement for this model: Eldorado (1979 to 1985).
Percentage of division's production: 15.99%.
Corporate siblings: Buick Riviera and Oldsmobile Toronado.

Measurements

Wheelbase	126.3"
Length	224.1"
Width	79.8"
Height	54.1"
Legroom — front	43.0"

Primary competition: Lincoln Continental Mark IV.

Notable changes: Minor trim and detail changes.

Major standard equipment: Choice of Merlin plaid fabric or Mansion knit fabric front seat w/individual fold-down center armrest (coupe), Sierra grain leather front bench seat w/individual fold-down center armrest (convertible), 6-way power seat adjuster, cut-pile carpeting, hinged door pull assist handles, visor vanity mirror, driver and passenger reading lights, courtesy lights, electric clock, power windows, power door locks, automatic climate control, AM/FM signal-seeking stereo radio w/automatic power antenna, LH remote-control rear view mirror, front cornering lights, wheel opening moldings, rocker panel moldings, automatic level control, full wheel covers, and LR78 × 15 wide WSW tires.

Measurements (cont.)

Legroom — rear	NA
Headroom — front	38.1"
Headroom — rear	37.1"
Cargo capacity (cu. ft.)	NA
Fuel capacity (gals.)	27.0

Models Available

	Model No.	Base MSRP	Change from LY	Shipping Wt. (lbs.)	Model Year Production	Change from LY
Eldorado 2-Door Coupe	L47	$10,586	+6.55%	5085	35,184	-1.73%
Eldorado 2-Door Convertible	L67	$11,049	+6.71%	5153	14,000	+56.42%
TOTALS		*Avg. price* $10,818	+6.63%		*Production* 49,184	+9.90%

1976

Fleetwood Brougham

"Executive size luxury."

Nameplate year of origin: 1966.

Current bodystyle lifespan: 1971 through 1976.

Predecessor to this model: Fleetwood Sixty-Special (1969 to 1970).

Replacement for this model: Fleetwood Brougham (1977 to 1984).

Percentage of division's sales volume: 7.96%.

Corporate siblings: None.

Primary competition: None.

Notable changes: Minor trim and detail changes.

Major standard equipment: Choice of Mansion knit fabric or Minoa ribbed velour dual comfort 60/40 front seat, driver's side 2-way power seat adjuster, front and rear seat fold-down center armrests, cut-pile carpeting, rear seat carpeted foot rests, hinged door pull assist handles, front passenger reading light, courtesy lights, quartz digital clock, power windows, power door locks, automatic climate control, AM/FM signal-seeking stereo radio w/automatic power antenna, LH remote-control rear view mirror, padded vinyl roof, front cornering lights, rear wheel fender skirts, wheel opening moldings, rocker panel moldings w/upper ridge, automatic level control, full wheel covers, and LR78 × 15 WSW tires.

Measurements

Wheelbase	133.0"
Length	233.7"
Width	79.8"
Height	55.3"
Legroom — front	NA
Legroom — rear	NA
Headroom — front	NA
Headroom — rear	NA
Cargo capacity (cu. ft.)	19.3
Fuel capacity (gals.)	27.0

Models Available

	Model No.	Base MSRP	Change from LY	Shipping Wt. (lbs.)	Model Year Production	Change from LY
Fleetwood Brougham 4-Door Sedan	B69	$10,935	+5.00%	5213	24,500	+30.63%
TOTALS		*Avg. price* $10,935	+5.00%		*Production* 24,500	+30.63%

Fleetwood

"Flagships of the Cadillac line."

Nameplate year of origin: 1927 (models using Fleetwood bodies); 1935 (Fleetwood series).

Measurements

Wheelbase	151.5"

Current bodystyle lifespan: 1971 through 1976.
Predecessor to this model: Fleetwood Seventy-Five (1969 to 1970).
Replacement for this model: Fleetwood Limousine (1977 to 1984).
Percentage of division's sales volume: 0.59%.
Corporate siblings: None.
Primary competition: None.
Notable changes: Minor trim and detail changes.
Major standard equipment: Choice of light gray Magnan knit interior or Medici crushed velour in dark blue or black, 2-way power front seat adjuster, front and back seat fold-down center armrests, cut-pile carpeting, full-width folding seats (rearward facing for three additional passengers), rear seat carpeted foot rests, hinged door pull assist handles, power windows, power door locks, dual automatic climate control system (front and rear), courtesy lights, electric clock, AM/FM radio w/automatic power antenna, passenger control panel (controls power windows, reading lights, radio, automatic climate control, and the glass partition in the Limousine), automatic level control, LH and RH remote-control rear view mirror, front cornering lights, rear wheel fender skirts, wheel opening moldings, full-length rocker panel moldings, full wheel covers, and LR78 × 15 WSW tires.

Measurements (cont.)

Length	252.2"
Width	80.0"
Height	57.2"
Legroom — front	NA
Legroom — rear	NA
Headroom — front	NA
Headroom — rear	NA
Cargo capacity (cu. ft.)	NA
Fuel capacity (gals.)	27.0

Models Available

	Model No.	Base MSRP	Change from LY	Shipping Wt. (lbs.)	Model Year Production	Change from LY
Fleetwood 4-Door Nine-passenger Sdn.	F23	$14,889	+4.72%	5746	981	+11.99%
Fleetwood 4-Door Limousine	F33	$15,239	+4.69%	5889	834	+4.91%
TOTALS	*Avg. price*	$15,064	+4.70%	*Production*	1,815	+8.62%

CHEVROLET

"Chevrolet offers America's largest family of small cars."

Chevrolet had been touting America's Bicentennial for the past two years. For the actual 1976 celebration year, the division combined the celebration with its sponsorship of the Olympic games for 1976. To commemorate the Olympics, Chevrolet introduced a special Nova Medalist option. It was hard to miss the advertising, whether on billboards, radio or television, or in magazines and newspapers. The Chevrolet name was everywhere, and the exposure no doubt contributed to a nearly 20 percent increase in model year production. The big product news from GM's largest division was the all-new Chevette subcompact, the first of a new kind of American car. The Chevette, clearly aimed at competing with the rising tide of import cars, was a worthy competitor, having a modern and competent powertrain, but lacking the more innovative front-wheel drive configuration that was becoming the standard for this class of car. The remainder of the Chevrolet line was mostly carried over from 1975, with the expected annual updates to front or rear styling.

Chevette was the name given to General Motors' first "world car," otherwise known as the T-car. The T-car was first introduced in Brazil as the Chevette two-door sedan, eventually adding four-door, hatchback and station wagon models. Over its lifetime the T-car was sold in fifteen countries under numerous names, including the Buick/Opel Isuzu in the United States, and later the Pontiac T1000 and 1000. By the end of its lifetime it would be the last surviving rear-wheel-drive subcompact offered in the United States. Styling was minimalist and looked economical while having an American car look, so as not to copy imported cars. Up front was a slightly sloped front end with a basic horizontal four-slot grille, two per side, lined with argent colored trim on the entry-level Scooter two-seat model, or with chrome outlined argent trim on the regular Chevette model. The grille was actually part of the hood, allowing easier access to the engine compartment when open. Single round headlamps were set on each side of the grille in squarish bezels, with parking and turn signal lights set directly below in the bumper. Bodysides were smooth with a slight curve, and a lower body feature line between the wheel openings. At the rear gas-charged struts held the large hatch open for loading access. A flat rear panel sat below the hatch opening with a center license plate mounting and tri-colored, rectangular chrome-rimmed taillights on each end. The outer lens was red for brake and taillights, the center was amber for the turn signal, and the inner lamp was red with the backup light in the center.

Under the hood was a standard 1.4 liter, 4-cylinder overhead cam engine, with a 1.6 liter engine being an optional choice. Being a world car, it was international in design and conformed to the international metric standard of measurement, and was GM's first "metric" car. Inside, the Chevette looked the role it was intended to play, basic and economical. The Scooter was the most spartan in appearance, having only two front bucket seats, an open glove box, a strap attached to the rather plain door panel, and no rear seat. It was marketed mainly towards those wanting a delivery vehicle, or anyone wanting just a little runabout type car without any frills. All Chevettes were rather basic looking inside, in the sense that the upper parts of the door panels were body-colored metal, and all of the instrument panel, steering wheel and steering column were done in black. The Custom Interior option added color-keyed instrument panel with woodgrain trim, and more stylish door panels with woodgrain trim.

Chevrolet's other compact car offerings, the Vega and Monza, continued with few visual changes, although under the hood could be found a great deal of improvement to the 140 CID four-cylinder engine. Now known as the "Dura-Built" engine, it had new hydraulic lifters, improved oil passages and crankcase ventilation, a revised cooling system, and many other changes that allowed GM to offer an industry first 5-year, 60,000 mile limited engine warranty. This was all done to combat the negative publicity caused by problems with the engine in the first few years of production. On the outside, the Vega gained a new grille design consisting of three horizontal slots that ran full-width between the headlights, with the parking and turn signal lights placed behind the grille. Taillights were now taller on the hatchback and coupe models, and divided into three sections with the center section being amber for turn signals and the lower section carrying the backup lights. Two new models options were introduced, including a Vega coupe with Cabriolet equipment featuring a special padded vinyl landau roof, opera windows and other trim, keeping the Vega in tune with the times. Also new was the option to add the GT package to the Vega Estate wagon, making it a very sporty looking "woody" wagon. The subcompact "hot rod," the Cosworth Vega, was offered again this year with the Vega's styling updates, but no other significant changes. The Monza line was mostly unchanged, with a lowered center floor hump being introduced. At mid-year a sliding sunroof option was added, as was a "Spyder" appearance package option for either the Towne coupe or the 2+2 hatchback coupe. Details of the

package are contained in Appendix IV. Although it was mostly an appearance option package, the Spyder option did require the optional 2-barrel version of the "Dura-Built" four-cylinder engine, and it could easily be made into a performance-type car with the selection of appropriate options. A total of 2,339 were built for the 1976 model year.

At the opposite end of the size and weight spectrum was the full-size Chevy line consisting of the Impala and Caprice Classic. While the Bel Air name was discontinued, it lived on in the form of a new Impala S 4-Door Sedan. Echoing what happened in 1975, the Impala for 1976 took on the front-end appearance of the 1975 Caprice Classic line, having the rounded type front end. A new grille insert of a horizontal crosshatch design was introduced, consisting of four rows high and sixteen columns across, with a gold bowtie emblem in the center. Dual round headlamps and all other styling features returned as on their immediate predecessors, except that the Impala Sport Coupe was no longer offered, making the 1975 version the last true Impala two-door hardtop. The 1976 Impala Sport Sedan would be the last Impala four-door hardtop model. The uppermost Caprice Classic line retained the basic styling of the prior year, but added dual rectangular headlights to distinguish it from the Impala. Also a new egg-crate pattern grille was introduced that was three rows high and sixteen columns across. The Caprice emblem was moved to the front header panel above the large chrome grille surround. Other Caprice styling features remained the same, although the full-size Chevrolet convertible was gone forever. This would be the last year for the big 454 CID V8 engine in Chevrolet cars.

The sporty Corvette and Camaro continued into the new year with few changes. The rear end of the Corvette was slightly modified to incorporate new bumper guards, and the convertible was no longer available. The Camaro added power brakes to the standard equipment list, a new vinyl sport roof was introduced, and there were detail changes to the interior. The Type LT also received a new brushed rear panel, redesigned seats, and a tan, leather-look trim appliqué around the instruments.

The compact Nova line, which had been restyled for the previous season, returned with a revised model lineup and minor styling changes. Most attention was focused on the new Concours line, which simultaneously replaced the Nova Custom and Nova LN models. Technically a part of the Nova line, but marketed as a separate model to better compete with the new Ford Granada's upper line Ghia models, the Concours was pure Nova, with most features found on the prior LN as standard. Identifying features of the new Concours included a unique grille insert, two rows high and twelve columns across, in an egg-crate fashion with smaller three by three egg-crate design inserts. A small "Nova" name badge was set into the lower driver's side corner. The entire front end had a large strip of chrome on the ends, wrapping over the headlights and widening as it ran across the top of the grille. Atop the header panel was a three-dimensional Concours hood ornament. The basic Nova was unchanged from 1975, and the SS package continued to be available on both the coupe and hatchback with 7,416 SS cars rolling off the line. Another special Nova, the "Medalist" package, was produced to commemorate the 1976 Olympic games. While pricing for the package is not currently available, there were 5,489 produced with no breakdown by model available. Although the Nova and Concours were marketed as two separate lines, both were contained in the same sales brochure, and they will be treated as a single series herein.

Both the Chevelle and Monte Carlo mid-size lines received new front end styling featuring stacked dual rectangular headlights and new grilles for the Malibu Classic and the Monte Carlo, while the Malibu had an updated grille and continued to use single round headlamps, with only minor detail changes to the rest of the car. The Chevelle Malibu's new vertical crosshatch grille was twelve rows high and eight columns across with a center chrome divider and a blue bowtie emblem in the center. The Malibu Classic introduced a unique diamond pattern grille surrounded by a large chrome trim piece, and having a center divider bar. A stand-up hood ornament was placed on top of the header panel. The Laguna Type S-3 continued into its final season with virtually no changes, other than new two-section taillights with a red outer lens and white backup light lens to the inside, which was used on all Chevelle models except station wagons. A final, mostly unnoticed change was that the name Chevelle no longer physically appeared on the cars, only in the official name in advertising and sales literature. The Monte Carlo line had a three-opening horizontal grille, with each opening having an insert two rows high and fourteen columns across. The Monte Carlo emblem was placed in the center. Around back, taillights were again changed, this year continuing the wraparound design but losing the body-color trim and becoming a solid red lens, with backup lights at the bottom. A new option that became quite popular was the "Fashion-Tone" two-tone option. This option added a complementary paint color in the area created by the Monte Carlo's uniquely curved front fender feature line.

Camaro 2-Door Sport Coupe

Caprice Classic Landau 2-Door Hardtop Coupe

Chevelle Malibu Classic
2-Door Colonnade Hardtop Coupe

Camaro 2-Door Sport Coupe
with Rally Sport package

Chevelle Laguna Type S-3 2-Door
Colonnade Hardtop Coupe

Chevette 2-Door Hatchback Coupe

Chevette interior

Caprice Classic 4-Door Hardtop Sport Sedan

Chevelle Malibu 4-Door
Colonnade Hardtop Sedan

Chevette 2-Door Hatchback Coupe,
front, and Chevette 2-Door Hatchback
Coupe with woody option, rear

Corvette Stingray 2-Door Coupe

Corvette interior

Impala 4-Door Hardtop Sport Sedan

Impala 4-Door Station Wagon

Monte Carlo 2-Door Hardtop Coupe

Monte Carlo Landau 2-Door Hardtop Coupe

Monte Carlo 2-Door Hardtop Coupe
with Fashion-Tone styling package

Monza 2-Door Towne Coupe

Nova 2-Door Coupe with SS package

Monza 2+2 2-Door Hatchback Coupe

Nova 2-Door Hatchback Coupe (right) and
Nova 4-Door Sedan with Medalist package

Nova Concours 4-Door Sedan

Vega 2-Door Hatchback Coupe with GT package

Vega 2-Door Kammback Wagon
with Estate package and GT package

Vega 2-Door Notchback Coupe
with Cabriolet package

Vega Cosworth 2-Door Hatchback Coupe

Model year production: 2,103,862, up 19.30% from 1975.
Domestic market share: 24.32% (1st place).
Base price range: $2,899 to $7,605.
Chevrolet average base price: $4,355, up 2.98%.
Introduction date: October 2, 1975.
Assembly plants: Baltimore, MD (B); Southgate, CA (C); Doraville, GA (D); Janesville, WI (J); Kansas City/Leeds, MO (K); Van Nuys, CA (L); Norwood, OH (N); Arlington, TX (R); St. Louis, MO (S); Tarrytown, NY (T); Lordstown, OH (U); Willow Run, MI (W); Wilmington, DE (Y); Fremont, CA (Z); Oshawa, Ontario, Canada (1); and Ste. Therese, Quebec, Canada (2).

Data plate identification (VIN): Thirteen digit code read as follows: First digit indicates division (1 = Chevrolet); second through fourth digits indicate series and body style (model number in model charts); fifth digit is engine code (see powertrain chart); sixth digit indicates model year (6 = 1976); seventh digit indicates assembly plant (see list above); remaining digits are sequential with beginning number of 100001, except Chevelle, Monte Carlo and Corvette which start at 400001, and Camaro which starts at 500001. *Example:* 1S87H6N500001 is a 1976 Chevrolet Camaro Type LT 2-Door Sport Coupe, with 350 CID, 2-bbl. V8 engine, serial number 500001, built in Norwood, OH.

Powertrains

Engine	Net HP	Engine Code	Transmission Availability[1]		Chevette	Vega & Monza	Nova	Camaro	Chevelle Malibu[2]	Monte Carlo & Laguna	Full-Size Chevy	Corvette
85 CID (1.4L) OHC, 1-bbl., 4-cyl.	52	1	4-speed manual		S	—	—	—	—	—	—	—
				MPG:	27/29/32	—	—	—	—	—	—	—
				Calif.	22/33/26	—	—	—	—	—	—	—
			3-speed Turbo Hydra-matic		$244 (ex. Scooter)	—	—	—	—	—	—	—
				MPG:	24/31/26	—	—	—	—	—	—	—
				Calif.	23/26/24	—	—	—	—	—	—	—
98 CID (1.6L) OHC, 1-bbl., 4-cyl.	60	E	4-speed manual		$51	—	—	—	—	—	—	—
				MPG:	30/39/33	—	—	—	—	—	—	—
				Calif.	24/34/28	—	—	—	—	—	—	—
			3-speed Turbo Hydra-matic		$295 (ex. Scooter	—	—	—	—	—	—	—
				MPG:	26/33/29	—	—	—	—	—	—	—
				Calif.	23/29/26	—	—	—	—	—	—	—
122 CID (2.0L) DOHC, EFI, 4-cyl.	110	O	4-speed manual		—	S (Cosworth only)	—	—	—	—	—	—
				MPG:	—	16/29/20	—	—	—	—	—	—
			5-speed manual		—	$244 (Cosworth only)	—	—	—	—	—	—
				MPG:	—	NA	—	—	—	—	—	—
140 CID (2.3L) OHC, 1-bbl., 4-cyl.	70	A	3-speed manual		—	S	—	—	—	—	—	—
				MPG:	—	24/35/28	—	—	—	—	—	—
			4-speed manual		—	$60[3]	—	—	—	—	—	—
				MPG:	—	21/33/25	—	—	—	—	—	—
			3-speed Turbo Hydra-matic	MPG:	—	$244[3] 19/28/22	—	—	—	—	—	—
140 CID (2.3L) OHC, 2-bbl., 4-cyl.	84	B	3-speed manual		—	$56[3]	—	—	—	—	—	—
				MPG:	—	22/35/27	—	—	—	—	—	—
				Calif.	—	19/30/23	—	—	—	—	—	—
			4-speed manual		—	$116[3]	—	—	—	—	—	—
				MPG:	—	NA	—	—	—	—	—	—
			5-speed manual		—	$300[3]	—	—	—	—	—	—
				MPG:	—	NA	—	—	—	—	—	—
			3-speed Turbo Hydra-matic	MPG:	—	$300[3] 20/28/23	—	—	—	—	—	—
				Calif.	—	19/27/22	—	—	—	—	—	—

Engine	Net HP	Engine Code	Transmission Availability[1]	Chevette	Vega & Monza	Nova	Camaro	Chevelle Malibu[2]	Monte Carlo & Laguna	Full-Size Chevy	Corvette
250 CID (4.1L), 1-bbl., 6-cyl.	105	D	3-speed manual	—	—	S	S (Spt. Cpe.)	S (Mcs, MCc)	—	—	—
			MPG:	—	—	18/25/21	17/25/20	17/25/20	—	—	—
			3-speed Turbo Hydra-matic	—	—	$260	$260 (Spt. Cpe.)	S (MCs)/ $260 (Mcs, MCc)	—	—	—
			MPG:	—	—	18/24/20	17/23/20	17/22/19	—	—	—
			Calif.	—	—	15/21/17	15/21/17	15/21/17	—	—	—
262 CID (4.3L), 2-bbl., V8	110	G	3-speed manual	—	$224 (Monza only)[4]	—	—	—	—	—	—
			MPG:	—	15/22/17	—	—	—	—	—	—
			4-speed manual	—	$284 (Monza only)[4]	—	—	—	—	—	—
			MPG:	—	NA	—	—	—	—	—	—
			5-speed manual	—	$468 (Monza only)[4]	—	—	—	—	—	—
			MPG:	—	NA	—	—	—	—	—	—
			3-speed Turbo Hydra-matic	—	$468 (Monza only)[4]	—	—	—	—	—	—
			MPG:	—	15/21/18	—	—	—	—	—	—
			Calif.	—	14/18/16	—	—	—	—	—	—
305 CID (5.0L), 2-bbl., V8	140	Q	3-speed manual	—	—	$165 ($162 on HBK)	S (LT)/ $165 (Spt. Cpe.)	—	—	—	—
			MPG:	—	—	15/21/17	15/21/17	—	—	—	—
			4-speed manual	—	—	—	—	—	—	—	—
			MPG:	—	—	—	—	—	—	—	—
			3-speed Turbo Hydra-matic	—	$468 (Monza only)[4,5]	$425 ($422 on HBK)	$260 (LT)/ $425 (Spt. Cpe.)	$294 (MCs)/ $530 (Mcs, MCc)	S	—	—
			MPG:	—	16/23/18	15/21/17	15/21/17	14/20/17	14/20/17	—	—
			Calif.	—	15/20/17	13/18/15	13/18/15	—	—	—	—
350 CID (5.7L), 2-bbl., V8	145	V	3-speed Turbo Hydra-matic	—	—	—	—	S (Mw)/ $324 (MCs)/ $560 (Mcs, MCc)	$30	S (ex. Wgns.)	—
			MPG:	—	—	—	—	14/18/15	14/18/15	—	—

Engine	Net HP	Engine Code	Transmission Availability[1]	Chevette	Vega & Monza	Nova	Camaro	Chevelle Malibu[2]	Monte Carlo & Laguna	Full-Size Chevy	Corvette
350 CID (5.7L), 4-bbl., V8	165	L	3-speed manual	—	—	$250 ($247 on HBK)	$85 (LT)/ $250 (Spt. Cpe.)	—	—	—	—
			MPG:	—	—	13/19/ 15	13/19/ 15	—	—	—	—
			Calif.	—	—	13/18/ 15	13/18/ 15	—	—	—	—
			4-speed manual	—	—	$492 ($489 on HBK)	$327 (LT)/ $492 (Spt. Cpe.)	—	—	—	—
			MPG:	—	—	NA	NA	—	—	—	—
			3-speed Turbo Hydra-matic	—	—	$510 ($507 on HBK)	$345 (LT)/ $510 (Spt. Cpe.)	—	—	$56 (ex. Wgns.)	—
			MPG:	—	—	14/19/ 16	14/19/ 16	—	—	—	—
			Calif.	—	—	13/16/ 14	13/16/ 14	13/18/ 15	13/18/ 15	11/16/ 13	—
350 CID (5.7L), 4-bbl., V8	180	L	4-speed manual	—	—	—	—	—	—	—	S
			MPG:	—	—	—	—	—	—	—	13/19/ 15
			3-speed Turbo Hydra-matic	—	—	—	—	—	—	—	N/C
			MPG:	—	—	—	—	—	—	—	14/19/ 16
			Calif.	—	—	—	—	—	—	—	13/16/ 14
350 CID (5.7L), 4-bbl., V8	210	X	4-speed manual	—	—	—	—	—	—	—	$481
			MPG:	—	—	—	—	—	—	—	NA
			3-speed Turbo Hydra-matic	—	—	—	—	—	—	—	$615
			MPG:	—	—	—	—	—	—	—	NA
400 CID (6.6L), 4-bbl., V8	175	U	3-speed Turbo Hydra-matic	—	—	—	—	$118 (Mw)/ $444 (MCs)/ $678 (Mcs, MCc)	$148	S (Wgns.)/ $176 (others)	—
			MPG:	—	—	—	—	13/19/ 15	13/19/ 15	11/17/ 14[6]	—
			Calif.	—	—	—	—	12/15/ 13	12/15/ 13	11/15/ 13	—
454 CID (7.4L), 4-bbl., V8	225	S	3-speed Turbo Hydra-matic	—	—	—	—	—	—	$223 (Wgns.)/ $375 (others)[7]	—
			MPG:	—	—	—	—	—	—	11/15/ 13[6]	—

[1]Unless otherwise specified: All 3-speed manuals are column shift. All 4- and 5-speed manuals are floor shift. All automatics are column shift, except on Chevette, Vega, Monza, Camaro and Corvette. Floor shift automatic is optional on Nova, Chevelle and Monte Carlo with other specified equipment at extra cost. [2]Mcs = Malibu coupe & sedan; Mw = All Malibu wagons; MCc = Malibu Classic coupes; MCs = Malibu Classic sedan. [3]Not available on Vega Cosworth. [4]When ordered on

Monza Towne Coupe, requires Cabriolet or Sport equipment options. [5]*Available after the start of the model year.* [6]*Estimated mileage ratings for station wagons are one MPG lower for both city and highway.* [7]*$350 for all Caprice Classic models.*

Major Options

	Chevette	Vega	Monza	Camaro	Nova	Chevelle	Monte Carlo	Full-size Chevy	Corvette
Four-season air conditioning[1]	$424	$424	$424	$479	$479	$471	$471	$485	$523
Comfortilt steering wheel	—	$48	$48	$52	$52	$52	$52	$53	S
Cruise-Master speed control	—	—	—	—	$73	$73	$73	$74	—
Rear window defogger[2]	—	—	—	$43	$43	$43	$43	$44	$78
Electro-Clear rear window defogger	$66	$66	$66	—	—	—	$77	—	—
Dual sport mirrors, remote	$43	$25[3]	$25[3]	$27[3]	$46	$46	$46	$47	—
Soft-Ray tinted glass, all windows	$44	$44	$44	$46	$46	$49	$53	$63	S
Power windows, 2-dr./4-dr.	—	—	—	$99	$99/$140	$99/$140	$99	$105/$159	$107
Power door locks, 2-dr./4-dr.	—	—	—	$62	$62/$89	$62/$89	$62	$63/$90	—
Power front seat, w/std. seat	—	—	—	—	—	$124	$124	$126	—
Front bucket seats, w/console[4]	$16	S	$73	$71	$326	$211	$211	—	S
Rear facing third seat (wagons)	—	—	—	—	—	$143	—	—	—
AM radio	$70	$70	$70	$75	$75	$75	$75	$76	—
AM/FM stereo	—	$212	$212	$226	$226	$226	$226	$229	$281
AM/FM stereo w/8-track tape	—	—	—	$324	$324	$324	$324	$328	—
Vinyl top, full[5]	$90	—	—	$96	$96	$109	$129	$125	—
Vinyl top, landau[6]	—	—	$	—	$150	—	—	—	—
Sky Roof (sunroof), power	—	—	—	—	—	—	$370	—	—
Power steering, variable-ratio	—	$120	$120	S	$136	$136[7]	S	S	$151
Power brakes, w/front disc	$55	$55	$55	$58[7]	$58[7]	$58[7]	S	S	$59[8]
Full wheel covers	$36	$28	—	$30	$30	S	S	$31	—
Wire wheel covers	—	—	—	—	—	$89	$79	$100	—
Rally wheels w/trim rings	S	$97	$97	$60	$60	$60	$46	—	S
Forged aluminum wheels	—	—	$204	—	—	—	—	—	$299
WSW tires	$32	$32	$32	$33	$35	$30	$30	$37	$37

Popular Option Groups & Packages

	Chevette	Vega	Monza	Camaro	Nova	Chevelle	Monte Carlo	Full-size Chevy	Corvette
Auxiliary lighting package	—	$29	$15	$21	$21	$41	$41	$37	—
Cabriolet package	—	$	$256	—	—	—	—	—	—
Custom appearance group	—	—	—	—	$75[9]	—	—	—	—
Custom interior package	$164	—	—	—	—	—	—	—	$194
Custom exterior package	$82	$88	—	—	—	—	—	—	—
Exterior décor package	—	—	—	—	$73	$51	—	—	—
GT package	—	$457	—	—	—	—	—	—	—
Gymkhana suspension package	—	—	—	—	—	—	—	—	$35
Quiet sound group	$39	$43	—	—	—	—	—	$45	—
Rally equipment package	$251	—	—	—	—	—	—	—	—
Rally Sport package	—	—	—	$260[10]	—	—	—	—	—
Special instrumentation package	$56	$72	$72	$92	$160	—	—	—	S
Sport equipment package	—	—	$118	—	—	—	—	—	—
Sports décor package	$77	—	—	—	—	—	—	—	—
Spyder equipment group	—	—	$342	—	—	—	—	—	—
SS package	—	—	—	—	$187	—	—	—	—
Woody package	$306	—	—	—	—	—	—	—	—

—= Not Available; S = Standard equipment. [1]*Not available on Chevette Scooter or Cosworth Vega. Requires optional power steering and power brakes on Chevelle with 6-cylinder engine. Price is $452 on Camaro and Nova with V8 engine. Comfortron air conditioning with automatic temperature control is available for $567 on Impala and Caprice.* [2]*Blower type defogger.* [3]*Dual sport mirror with LH remote only.* [4]*Bucket seats standard on Chevette, Vega, Monza and Camaro, with console being optional except on Vega. Available on Nova coupes or hatchbacks. Swivel bucket seats available only on Chevelle coupes and Monte Carlo.* [5]*Price is $150 on full-size Chevrolet wagons. Not available on Chevelle station wagons.* [6]*Standard on Monte Carlo Landau coupe, and Malibu Classic Landau coupe. Available on Monza Towne Coupe (as part of Cabriolet package) and Nova coupes.* [7]*Standard on all models when equipped with V8 engine.* [8]*Power front and rear disc brakes.* [9]*Available on Nova Concours only.* [10]*Price given is for base Camaro. Available on Camaro LT for $173.*

Paint Colors

	Code		Code
Classic White[1]	10	Dark Green metallic[2]	49
Antique White	11	Cream[8]	50
Silver metallic[1,2,3,4,5,6]	13	Bright Yellow[2,4,6]	51
Medium Gray metallic		Gold metallic[9]	53
(two-tone only)	16	Corvette Bright Yellow[1,3]	56
Tuxedo Black[2,3,4,5]	19	Cream Gold metallic[5,8]	57
Light Blue[7]	21	Corvette Buckskin metallic[1]	64
Corvette Blue metallic[1]	22	Buckskin[2,3,4,5,8]	65
Light Blue metallic[3,4,5,6,8]	28	Burnt Orange[6]	66
Corvette Dark Green metallic[1,3,4,5,8]	33	Medium Saddle metallic[2,3,4,5,8]	67
Dark Blue metallic	35	Corvette Dark Brown metallic[1]	69
Firethorn metallic[2,3,4,5]	36	Corvette Orange Flame[1]	70
Mahogany metallic[1,2,3,4,5]	37	Red[1,5,8]	72
Lime Green metallic[2,3,4,5]	40	Light Red[6,7]	75
Lime Green[7]	45	Medium Orange[2,3,4,6]	78

In two-tone combinations, the first two digits indicate lower color and the next two digits are the upper color. Two-tone paint available for $40 on Nova and Chevelle. Fashion Tone paint for Monte Carlo is $104–$233 depending upon other equipment. Colors listed with no footnotes are available on all models, except Corvette, and those marked with footnote 8. [1]Available on Corvette. [2]Available on Vega. [3]Available on Monza. [4]Available on Camaro and Nova. [5]Available on all Chevelle Malibu, Monte Carlo and full-size Chevrolet models. [6]Available on Chevette, except Scooter. [7]Available on Chevette Scooter. [8]Not available on Laguna Type S-3. [9]Available only with the Nova Medalist package.

Chevette

"A new kind of American car."

Nameplate year of origin: 1976.
Current bodystyle lifespan: 1976 through 1987.
Predecessor to this model: None.
Replacement for this model: None (captive imports Sprint and Spectrum introduced in 1985 as supplementary models).
Percentage of division's production: 8.93%.
Corporate siblings: None.
Primary competition: Plymouth Arrow.
Notable changes: All-new model.
Major standard equipment: Scooter: Choice of cloth-and-vinyl or all-vinyl front bucket seats, rear seat deleted, black floor carpeting, door pull strap, armrests deleted, open compartment glove box, black two-spoke steering wheel and column, cargo compartment under floor storage, argent colored headlight bezels and grille trim, polished aluminum bumpers (not chromed), and 155/80 × 13 BSW tires.
Chevette adds: Fold-down rear seat, color-keyed carpeting, door armrests, glove box w/latch type door, bright front and rear window trim, dark argent headlamp bezel inserts, chrome trimmed headlight bezel and grille trim, deluxe chrome bumpers, and hubcaps.

Measurements

Wheelbase	94.3"
Length	158.7"
Width	61.8"
Height	52.3"
Legroom — front	41.5"
Legroom — rear	28.7"
Headroom — front	38.1"
Headroom — rear	37.3"
Cargo capacity (cu. ft.)	26.1*
Fuel capacity (gals.)	16.0

Maximum with rear seat folded down, or in Chevette Scooter.

Models Available

	Model No.	Base MSRP	Change from LY	Shipping Wt. (lbs.)	Model Year Production	Change from LY
Chevette Scooter 2-Door Hatchback	J08	$2,899	NEW	1870	9,810	NEW
Chevette 2-Door Hatchback	B08	$3,098	NEW	1924	178,007	NEW
TOTALS	*Avg. price*	$2,999	NEW	*Production*	187,817	NEW

Vega

"Built to take it."

Nameplate year of origin: 1971.
Current bodystyle lifespan: 1971 through 1977 (some models moved to Monza series, continuing through 1979).
Predecessor to this model: Corvair (1965 to 1969).
Replacement for this model: Cavalier (1982 to 1993).
Percentage of division's production: 7.63%.
Corporate siblings: Pontiac Astre.
Primary competition: AMC Gremlin, Dodge Colt, and Ford Pinto.
Notable changes: Minor trim and detail changes.
Major standard equipment: Cloth-and-vinyl high-back front bucket seats, sliding seat adjustment for both front seats, cut-pile carpeting, fold-down rear seat and rear liftgate (Hatchback and Kammback wagon), two-spoke steering wheel, glove box, map pocket in driver's door, two-speed wipers w/washers, bright front and rear window moldings, manual front disc brakes, and A78 × 13 BSW tires. Estate Wagon adds: Woodgrain vinyl panels on bodysides and tailgate, and special exterior nameplates. Cosworth adds: Custom interior w/choice of black or white perforated vinyl or black cloth front bucket seats, black carpeting, gold color bezeled instrument cluster, special gauge cluster w/8000 rpm tachometer, sport steering wheel, consecutive vehicle number plate on I/P, added sound insulation, black exterior paint w/gold stripe and "COSWORTH TWIN CAM" lettering on front fender, HD clutch, special front and rear stabilizer bars, quick ratio steering, cast aluminum alloy wheels, and BR70 × 13 BSW tires.

Measurements

	Coupes	Wagon
Wheelbase	97.0"	97.0"
Length	175.4"	175.4"
Width	65.4"	65.4"
Height	51.8"	51.8"
Legroom — front	42.8"	42.8"
Legroom — rear	28.9"	30.1"
Headroom — front	37.0"	38.5"
Headroom — rear	37.1"	38.3"
Cargo capacity (cu. ft.)	8.7*	24.8**
Fuel capacity (gals.)	16.0	16.0

*Hatchback maximum with rear seat down, 18.9 cu. ft.
**Wagon maximum with rear seat down, 46.6 cu. ft.

1976

Models Available

	Model No.	Base MSRP	Change from LY	Shipping Wt. (lbs.)	Model Year Production	Change from LY
Vega 2-Door Notchback Coupe	V11	$2,984	+7.11%	2443	27,619	-18.48%
Vega 2-Door Hatchback Coupe	V77	$3,099	+6.90%	2534	77,409	-31.44%
Vega Cosworth 2-Door Hatchback Coupe	V77	$6,066	+2.54%	NA	1,447	-29.79%
Vega 2-Door Kammback (Wagon)	V15	$3,227	+7.00%	2578	46,114	-2.86%
Vega 2-Door Kammback Estate (Wagon)	V15	$3,450	+6.35%	NA	7,935	-8.36%
TOTALS		Avg. price $3,765	+7.68%		Production 160,524	-22.17%

Monza

"Put on your driving gloves and meet the family."

Nameplate year of origin: 1975 (1960 as Corvair sub-series).
Current bodystyle lifespan: 1975 through 1980.
Predecessor to this model: Corvair Monza (1965 to 1969).
Replacement for this model: Cavalier (1982 to 1993).
Percentage of division's production: 3.85%.
Corporate siblings: Buick Skyhawk, Oldsmobile Starfire, and Pontiac Sunbird.
Primary competition: AMC Pacer, Dodge Colt, and Ford Mustang II.
Notable changes: Minor trim and detail changes.
Major standard equipment: Choice of patterned cloth or all-vinyl front bucket seats, cut-pile carpeting, fold-down rear seat and rear liftgate (hatchbacks), two-spoke steering wheel, door map pockets, simulated woodgrain I/P trim, bright front and rear window moldings, bright side window moldings, and A78 × 13 BSW tires. Towne Coupe adds: Sport cloth front bucket seats and full wheel covers. 2+2 adds: Stitched instru-

Measurements

	Coupe	Hatchback
Wheelbase	97.0"	97.0"
Length	177.8"	179.3"
Width	65.4"	65.4"
Height	49.8"	50.2"
Legroom — front	42.8"	42.8"
Legroom — rear	28.2"	29.6"
Headroom — front	37.5"	37.7"
Headroom — rear	37.2"	35.3"
Cargo capacity (cu. ft.)	6.6	23.4*
Fuel capacity (gals.)	18.5	18.5

*Capacity with rear seat down.

ment panel pad, Quiet sound group package, special two-spoke steering wheel, and finned wheel covers w/GT-type center hub and bright wheel nuts.

Models Available

	Model No.	Base MSRP	Change from LY	Shipping Wt. (lbs.)	Model Year Production	Change from LY
Monza 2-Door Towne Coupe	M27	$3,359	-5.91%	2625	46,735	-32.50%
Monza 2+2 2-Door Hatchback Coupe	R07	$3,727	-5.72%	2668	34,170	-40.23%
TOTALS		*Avg. price* $3,543	-4.85%		*Production* 80,905	-40.60%

Camaro

"Welcome to the 1976 Camaro."

Nameplate year of origin: 1967.
Current bodystyle lifespan: 1970 through 1981.
Predecessor to this model: Camaro (1967 to 1969).
Replacement for this model: Camaro (1982 to 1992).
Percentage of division's production: 8.70%.
Corporate siblings: Pontiac Firebird.
Primary competition: None.
Notable changes: Minor trim and detail changes.
Major standard equipment: Choice of sport cloth-and-vinyl or solid all-vinyl front bucket seats, color-keyed cut-pile carpeting, black instrument panel, black four-spoke soft rim sport steering wheel w/black column, bright front and rear window moldings, narrow rocker panel molding, hubcaps, and FR78 × 14 BSW tires. Type LT adds: Cloth-and-vinyl or knit vinyl deep contoured front bucket seats, tan leather-look accents on I/P cluster, color-keyed steering wheel and column, color-keyed lower instrument panel, special door panels w/door map pockets, special instrumentation package, electric clock, Interior Décor/Quiet Sound group, LH remote and RH manual sport mirrors, LT identification on front and rear end panels, bright accent molding on grille, brushed rear panel accent molding, variable-ratio power steering, and rally wheels.

Measurements

Wheelbase	108.0"
Length	195.4"
Width	74.4"
Height	49.1"
Legroom — front	43.9"
Legroom — rear	29.6"
Headroom — front	37.3"
Headroom — rear	36.0"
Cargo capacity (cu. ft.)	6.4
Fuel capacity (gals.)	21.0

Models Available

	Model No.	Base MSRP	Change from LY	Shipping Wt. (lbs.)	Model Year Production	Change from LY
Camaro 2-Door Sport Coupe	Q87	$3,762	+6.27%	3421	130,538	+23.23%
Camaro Type LT 2-Door Sport Coupe	S87	$4,320	+6.48%	3576	52,421	+31.57%
TOTALS		*Avg. price* $4,041	+6.38%		*Production* 182,959	+25.51%

Nova

"Dedicated to the three million Novas before it."

Concours

"Introducing the 1976 Concours. A luxurious Chevy compact with a plain Chevy price."

Nameplate year of origin: Nova: 1962, as top of the line Chevy II model; became series name in 1969. Concours: 1976.
Current bodystyle lifespan: 1975 through 1979.
Predecessor to this model: Nova (1968 to 1974; restyled in 1973).

Measurements

	Coupe & HBK	Sedan
Wheelbase	111.0"	111.0"

Replacement for this model: Citation (1980 to 1985).
Percentage of division's production: 15.91%.
Corporate siblings: Buick Skylark, Oldsmobile Omega, and Pontiac Ventura.
Primary competition: AMC Hornet, Ford Maverick and Granada, and Plymouth Valiant and Volaré.
Notable changes: New Concours sub-series. Minor trim and detail changes.
Major standard equipment: All-vinyl front bench seat, color-keyed cut-pile carpeting, front door armrests w/integral pull bars, black two-spoke steering wheel and steering column, bright front and rear window moldings, hubcaps, and E78 × 14 BSW tires. Hatchback model adds: All-vinyl front bench seat, and fold-down rear seat. Concours adds: Knit cloth-and-vinyl front bench seat w/fold-down center armrest, door panels w/carpeted lower panels and map pockets in front doors, rear door armrests, color-keyed steering wheel and steering column, electric clock, instrument cluster w/woodgrain vinyl accents, smoked lenses, and additional bright trim, full-width luggage compartment mat, dark argent-accented bodyside louvers (coupes only), bright side window and roof drip moldings, bright wheel opening, fender and rocker panel moldings, high level acoustic package, deluxe bumpers w/black bumper impact strips, front and rear bumper guards, full wheel covers, and FR78 × 14 BSW tires.

Measurements (cont.)

	Coupe & HBK	Sedan
Length*	196.7"	196.7"
Width	72.2"	72.2"
Height	54.3"	54.3"
Legroom — front	41.7"	41.7"
Legroom — rear	33.4"	35.3"
Headroom — front	38.5"	39.5"
Headroom — rear	36.3"	36.5"
Cargo capacity (cu. ft.)	14.2**	13.0
Fuel capacity (gals.)	21.0	21.0

*Length of Concours is 1" longer. **Hatchback maximum with rear seat down, 28.4 cu. ft.*

Models Available

	Model No.	Base MSRP	Change from LY*	Shipping Wt. (lbs.)	Model Year Production	Change from LY*
Nova 2-Door Coupe	X27	$3,248	+1.34%	3188	131,859	+60.76%
Nova 2-Door Hatchback	X17	$3,417	+2.09%	3391	18,719	+14.33%
Nova 4-Door Sedan	X69	$3,283	+2.31%	3221	123,767	+86.54%
Concours 2-Door Coupe	Y27	$3,795	+11.55%	3324	22,298	-15.18%
Concours 2-Door Hatchback	Y17	$3,972	+12.17%	3401	7,574	-50.33%
Concours 4-Door Sedan	Y69	$3,830	+12.15%	3367	30,511	+37.56%
TOTALS	*Avg. price*	$3,591	+4.94%		Production 334,728	+22.62%

Comparisons to LY for Concours are made to 1975 Nova Custom models with same model number.

Chevelle

"The 1976 Chevelle. It's a size whose time has come."

Nameplate year of origin: 1964.
Current bodystyle lifespan: 1973 through 1977.
Predecessor to this model: Chevelle (1968 to 1972).
Replacement for this model: Malibu (1978 to 1983).
Percentage of division's production: 15.84%.
Corporate siblings: Buick Century, Oldsmobile Cutlass, and Pontiac LeMans.
Primary competition: AMC Matador, Ford Torino, and Plymouth Fury.
Notable changes: New grille and minor trim and detail changes.
Major standard equipment: Choice of sport cloth-and-vinyl or all-vinyl front bench seat, color-keyed cut-pile nylon carpeting, black steering wheel and column, bright front and rear window surround moldings, bright rear quarter window molding, hood rear edge molding, hubcaps, and FR78 × 15 BSW tires. Wagon adds: All-vinyl front bench seat, vinyl coated metal cargo area sidewalls, swing up tailgate w/fixed window, I/P mounted "door ajar" warning light for tailgate, power steering, power front disc brakes, and HR78 × 15 BSW tires. Malibu Classic adds: Choice of knit cloth-and-vinyl or all-vinyl front bench seat w/fold-down center armrest, color-keyed steering wheel and

Measurements

	Coupes	Sedans	Wagons
Wheelbase	112.0"	116.0"	116.0"
Length	205.3"*	209.3"	215.2"
Width	76.6"	76.6"	76.8"
Height	53.1"	53.8"	55.7"
Legroom — front	42.1"	42.1"	42.1"
Legroom — rear	32.9"	37.0"	36.8"
Headroom — front	37.7"	38.3"	38.8"
Headroom — rear	37.0"	37.5"	39.4"
Cargo capacity (cu. ft.)	15.3	15.3	85.0**
Fuel capacity (gals.)	22.0	22.0	22.0

*Overall length of Laguna Type S-3 is 207.3". **Plus 9.8 cu. ft. of hidden storage space on two-seat models.*

column, simulated woodgrain vinyl accents on I/P, glove compartment light, bright roof drip and sill moldings, bright rocker panel and wheel opening moldings, and stand-up hood ornament. Malibu Classic wagon adds: All-vinyl front bench seat w/fold-down center armrest. Malibu Classic Estate wagon adds: Woodgrain vinyl bodyside and tailgate panels. Laguna Type S-3 adds: Choice of sport cloth-and-vinyl or all-vinyl front bench seat, round dial instrumentation w/simulated woodgrain on I/P, Type S-3 identification on I/P and door panels, dual sport mirrors w/LH remote control, unique Laguna urethane front end styling, louvered rear quarter windows, color-keyed bumper impact strips, Laguna Type S-3 nameplates on front fender, grille and rear panel, radial tuned suspension, rally wheels w/trim rings, and GR78 × 15 BSW tires.

Models Available

	Model No.	Base MSRP	Change from LY	Shipping Wt. (lbs.)	Model Year Production	Change from LY
Malibu 2-Door Colonnade HT Coupe	C37	$3,636	+6.72%	3650	30,592	-17.32%
Malibu 4-Door Colonnade HT Sedan	C29	$3,671	+7.91%	3729	38,469	+1.60%
Malibu 4-Door, 2-Seat Station Wagon*	C35	$4,543	+5.21%	4238	16,565	+18.52%
Malibu Classic 2-Door Colonnade HT Coupe	D37	$3,926	+6.17%	3688	82,634	+2.10%
Malibu Classic 2-Door Colonnade Landau Coupe	D37	$4,124	+4.94%	3717	30,167	+30.77%
Malibu Classic 4-Door Colonnade HT Sedan	D29	$4,196	+13.56%	3827	77,560	+51.87%
Malibu Classic 4-Door, 2-Seat Station Wagon*	D35	$4,776	+4.83%	4300	36,252	+62.07%
Malibu Classic Estate 4-Dr., 2-S. Station Wgn.*	G35	$4,971	+12.35%	4326	11,904	+28.87%
Laguna Type S-3 2-Door Colonnade HT Coupe	E37	$4,621	+4.70%	3978	9,100	+16.85%
TOTALS	Avg. price	$4,274	+7.24%	Production	333,243	+17.63%

*Production of wagons with third seat option is included above, but breaks out as follows: Malibu, 2,984; Malibu Classic, 11,617; Malibu Classic Estate, 6,386.

Monte Carlo

"When a car makes you feel good about its looks, that's styling. When it makes you feel good about yourself, that's character. Monte Carlo has both."

Nameplate year of origin: 1970.
Current bodystyle lifespan: 1973 through 1977.
Predecessor to this model: Monte Carlo (1970 to 1972).
Replacement for this model: Monte Carlo (1978 to 1987).
Percentage of division's production: 16.79%.
Corporate siblings: Pontiac Grand Prix.
Primary competition: Dodge Charger SE and Ford Elite.
Notable changes: Revised grille and trim and detail changes.
Major standard equipment: Choice of tailored knit cloth and vinyl or all-vinyl front bench seat, color-keyed cut-pile nylon carpeting, color-keyed instrument cluster, soft-rim steering wheel, simulated wood burl accents on I/P and steering wheel, door pull assist straps, glove compartment light, electric clock, LH outside rear view

Measurements

Wheelbase	116.0"
Length	212.7"
Width	77.6"
Height	52.7"
Legroom — front	42.1"
Legroom — rear	32.9"
Headroom — front	37.5"
Headroom — rear	37.4"
Cargo capacity (cu. ft.)	14.7
Fuel capacity (gals.)	22.0

mirror, bright roof drip and window surround moldings, bright rocker panel moldings w/front and rear extensions, bright wheel opening moldings, full wheel covers, and GR70 × 15 BSW tires. Landau adds: Visor vanity mirror, Landau emblem on door panels, Landau vinyl roof w/rear quarter nameplate, dual sport mirrors w/LH remote control, fender peak accent stripes, and cast aluminum Turbine II wheels.

Models Available

	Model No.	Base MSRP	Change from LY	Shipping Wt. (lbs.)	Model Year Production	Change from LY
Monte Carlo 2-Door Hardtop Coupe	H57	$4,673	+9.98%	3907	191,370	+28.84%
Monte Carlo Landau 2-Door Hardtop Coupe	H57	$4,966	+9.89%	3926	161,902	+46.68%
TOTALS	Avg. price	$4,820	+9.93%	Production	353,272	+36.45%

Impala and Caprice Classic

"A tradition that keeps getting better and better."

Nameplate year of origin: 1958 (Impala) and 1966 (Caprice).
Current bodystyle lifespan: 1971 through 1976.
Predecessor to this model: Biscayne/Bel Air/Impala/Caprice (1969 to 1970).
Replacement for this model: Impala and Caprice (1977 to 1990).
Percentage of division's production: 24.01%.
Corporate siblings: Buick LeSabre, Oldsmobile Delta 88, and Pontiac Catalina and Bonneville.
Primary competition: Dodge Monaco, Ford LTD, and Plymouth Gran Fury.
Notable changes: Revised front and rear end styling.
Major standard equipment: Choice of patterned knit cloth-and-vinyl or all-vinyl front bench seat (all-vinyl only in

Measurements

	2-doors	4-doors	Wagons
Wheelbase	121.5"	121.5"	125.0"
Length	222.9"	222.9"	228.6"
Width	79.5"	79.5"	79.5"
Height	53.7"	54.4"	58.1"
Legroom — front	42.5"	42.5"	42.5"
Legroom — rear	35.8"	38.8"	38.9"
Headroom — front	38.1"	38.9"	39.6"
Headroom — rear	37.1"	38.0"	39.3"
Cargo capacity (cu. ft.)	18.1	18.9	106.4
Fuel capacity (gals.)	26.0	26.0	22.0

1976

wagon), color-keyed soft-rim steering wheel, color-keyed steering column, color-keyed cut-pile nylon carpeting, woodgrain vinyl accent trim on I/P and door panels, glove box and luggage compartment lights, luggage compartment mat, triple unit taillights w/silver accents, rocker panel moldings, front and rear wheel opening moldings (Custom Coupe only), bodyside protective moldings, hubcaps, and HR78 × 15 BSW tires. Impala S deletes: Some acoustical insulation, bodyside moldings, door window trim moldings, and luggage compartment mat and light, and has H78 × 15 BSW tires. Wagon adds: All-vinyl front bench seat, Glide-Away tailgate w/power-operated rear window, and LR78 × 15 BSW tires. Caprice adds: Choice of velvet-look knit cloth and vinyl or all-vinyl front bench seat, fold-down center armrest (four-doors only), electric clock, rear door courtesy light switches (four-doors), color-keyed bodyside molding, specific triple unit taillights, rear wheel opening fender skirts, and full wheel covers. Landau coupe models add: Elk-grain padded vinyl roof, bodyside pinstriping, dual remote-control sport mirrors, front and rear bumper impact strips, Landau name on rear quarter window glass, and wheel covers w/Landau crest and body-color paint. Caprice Estate wagon adds: All-vinyl interior w/cargo area color-keyed soft textured vinyl sidewalls, and translucent woodgrain vinyl exterior panels.

Models Available

	Model No.	Base MSRP	Change from LY	Shipping Wt. (lbs.)	Model Year Production	Change from LY
Impala S 4-Door Sedan	L69	$4,507	+3.73%*	NA	18,265	+15.08%*
Impala 2-Door Hardtop Custom Coupe	L47	$4,763	+2.96%	4175	43,219	-12.61%
Impala 2-Door Landau Custom Coupe	L47	$5,058	+3.20%	NA	10,841	+339.80%
Impala 4-Door Sedan	L69	$4,706	+3.47%	4222	86,057	-5.77%
Impala 4-Door Hardtop Sport Sedan	L39	$4,798	+3.61%	4245	39,849	-15.44%
Impala 4-Door, 2-Seat Station Wagon	L35	$5,166	+3.30%	4912	19,657	+9.22%
Impala 4-Door, 3-Seat Station Wagon	L45	$5,283	+3.16%	4972	21,329	+9.69%
Caprice Classic 2-Door Hardtop Coupe	N47	$5,043	+4.26%	4244	28,161	-21.86%
Caprice Classic 2-Door Landau Coupe	N47	$5,284	+4.12%	NA	21,926	+484.38%
Caprice Classic 4-Door Sedan	N69	$5,013	+4.03%	4285	47,411	+40.62%
Caprice Classic 4-Door Hardtop Sedan	N39	$5,078	+3.82%	4314	55,308	+36.62%
Caprice Estate 4-Door, 2-Seat Station Wagon.	N35	$5,429	+3.79%	4948	10,029	+10.85%
Caprice Estate 4-Door, 3-Seat Station Wagon	N45	$5,546	+3.64%	5007	21,804	+15.62%
TOTALS	*Avg. price*	$5,052	+3.55%	*Production*	423,856	+0.52%

*Comparison of Impala S made to similarly equipped 1975 Bel Air sedan.

Corvette

"Only a Corvette. America's only true production sports car."

Nameplate year of origin: 1953 (also used on show car of same year).
Current bodystyle lifespan: 1968 through 1982.
Predecessor to this model: Corvette (1963 to 1967).
Replacement for this model: Corvette (1984 to 1996).
Percentage of division's production: 2.21%.
Corporate siblings: None.
Primary competition: None.
Notable changes: Minor trim and detail changes.
Major standard equipment: All-vinyl high-back contoured bucket seats, center floor console, color-keyed cut-pile carpeting, tilt steering wheel, sports instrumentation with full gauges including tachometer, electric clock, tinted glass, LH rear view sport mirror, carpeted cargo area with light concealed behind seats, anti-theft audio alarm system, removable roof panels, domed hood w/air scoop, four wheel disc brakes, rally wheels w/trim rings, and GR70 × 15 BSW tires.

Measurements

Wheelbase	98.0"
Length	185.2"
Width	69.0"
Height	48.0"
Legroom — front	42.1"
Headroom — front	36.2"
Cargo capacity (cu. ft.)	6.5
Fuel capacity (gals.)	18.0

Models Available

	Model No.	Base MSRP	Change from LY	Shipping Wt. (lbs.)	Model Year Production	Change from LY
Corvette Stingray 2-Door Coupe	Z37	$7,605	+11.89%	3445	46,558	+37.60%
TOTALS	*Avg. price*	$7,605	+14.07%	*Production*	46,558	+21.04%

CHRYSLER

"A line of automobiles that offer you affordable luxury, including the luxury of choice."

After the highly successful introduction of the personal luxury mid-size Chrysler, or the "small" Chrysler as the advertising department liked to call it, there were high hopes that the momentum would continue for 1976. This was the year that Chrysler ramped up its use of Hollywood celebrities to market their cars. Although he began advertising with Chrysler in 1975, shortly after the Cordoba's introduction, actor Ricardo Montalbán, with his famous Spanish accent, made the phrase "rich Corinthian leather" one of the most common catchphrases of the mid-to-late 1970s. The sales and attention created by the advertising resulted in an expansion for 1976. Similarly, Jack Jones, an American jazz and pop singer, hawked New Yorker Broughams in print and on television with the "It's the talk of the town" theme. For the Cordoba, sales and production would finish higher than its initial season for the model year, and the newly re-packaged New Yorker Brougham would hold its own, managing to maintain a level consistent with the departed Imperial production, plus last year's New Yorker Brougham production.

However, the rest of the Chrysler line took another hit as sales of all full-size cars were faltering, even with memories of the recent fuel crisis fading, and improving gas mileage for all cars.

Chrysler's most popular model entered 1976 with refinements that gave the Cordoba an even more luxurious flair. A new vertical bar grille added the touch of elegance Chrysler needed to further increase Cordoba sales. In fact, in the highly popular mid-size personal luxury car market, the Cordoba had finished second to the Chevrolet Monte Carlo in sales for 1975, and Chrysler wanted to keep it that way. By the end of the model year, however, lower pricing for the Pontiac Grand Prix and increasing popularity for the Oldsmobile Cutlass Supreme relegated the Cordoba to fourth place in that market segment, despite a sales increase. Other changes for the Cordoba included the 400 CID V8 engine becoming standard equipment, and the smaller 318 and 360 CID V8s being available at no cost. This year also saw the introduction of a 4-barrel intake on the 360 CID V8 engine, which was available on the Cordoba or Newport series at no cost.

With the luxurious top-line Imperial gone, Chrysler juggled series names to make full use of all the existing bodies and trim without changing the model numbers. The CS series, bearing the New Yorker Brougham name, was applied to the body and trim used for the YM series 1975 Imperial LeBaron series. Similarly, the CM series bearing the Newport Custom name was applied to the body and trim used for the CS series 1975 New Yorker Brougham series. Equipment and feature levels of both the Newport Custom and New Yorker Brougham were maintained close to 1975 levels, to keep the price levels in check with their traditional marketing levels. As an example, the rear wheel opening fender skirts that were standard on the 1975 New Yorker Brougham were optional on the 1976 Newport Custom. Also, the New Yorker Brougham series no longer had a 4-door sedan model.

The CL base series Newport and the CP series Town & Country wagon returned for 1976 exactly the same as in 1975, even using the same grille and trim. All of this meant that the Newport and its sub-series Newport Custom actually had differing front and rear-end styling treatments. Also the St. Regis vinyl top and trim option introduced on the 1975 New Yorker Brougham 2-door was now available on both the Newport Custom and New Yorker Brougham 2-door models. An interesting historical tidbit was that 1976 was the first time since 1968 that the Town & Country did not use the New Yorker grille, even though all the while it was technically a sub-series of the Newport.

Cordoba 2-Door Hardtop Coupe

New Yorker Brougham 2-Door Hardtop
with St. Regis package

New Yorker Brougham 4-Door Hardtop

Newport 4-Door Sedan

Newport Custom 2-Door Hardtop

Newport Custom 4-Door Hardtop

Newport Custom interior with
Highlander plaid trim option

Town & Country 4-Door Station Wagon

Model year production: 244,938 down 5.93% from 1975.
Domestic market share: 2.82% (11th place).
Base price range: $4,993 to $6,737.
Chrysler average base price: $5,707, down 5.78%.
Introduction date: October 16, 1975.
Assembly plants: Jefferson Ave., Detroit, MI (C); Newark, DE (F); and Windsor, Ontario, Canada (R).
Data plate identification (VIN): Thirteen digit code read as

follows: First four digits indicate series and body style (model number in model charts); fifth digit indicates engine code (see powertrain chart); sixth digit indicates year (6 = 1976); seventh digit indicates assembly plant (see list above); remaining digits are sequential with beginning numbers of 100001. *Example:* CL43M6C100001 is a 1976 Chrysler Newport 4-Door Hardtop, with 400 CID, 2-bbl. V8 engine, serial number 100001, built in Detroit, MI.

Powertrains

Engine	Net HP	Engine Code	Transmission Availability[1]		Cordoba	Newport	Town & Country	New Yorker Brougham
318 CID (5.2L), 2-bbl., V8	150	G	3-speed Torque Flite automatic		N/C	—	—	—
				MPG:	13/18/15	—	—	—
				Calif.	12/16/14	—	—	—
360 CID (5.9L), 2-bbl., V8	170	K	3-speed Torque Flite automatic		N/C	N/C	—	—
				MPG:	12/19/14	13/17/14	—	—
360 CID (5.9L), 4-bbl., V8			3-speed Torque Flite automatic		N/C[1]	N/C[1]	—	—
				MPG:	NA	NA	—	—
				Calif.	12/18/14	11/17/13	—	—
400 CID (6.6L), 2-bbl., V8	165/175	M	3-speed Torque Flite automatic		S[1]	S	N/C	N/C
				MPG:	11/16/13	12/18/14	11/17/13	12/18/14
400 CID (6.6L), 4-bbl., V8	210[2]/240	N[2]/P	3-speed Torque Flite automatic		$45[3]	$45[3]	N/C	N/C
				MPG:	10/16/12	9/17/12	9/15/11	9/17/12
				Calif.	11/15/12	10/16/12	10/14/11	10/16/12
440 CID (7.2L), 4-bbl., V8	205	T	3-speed Torque Flite automatic		—	$184	S	S
				MPG:	—	11/16/13	11/16/12	11/16/12
				Calif.	—	9/13/11	9/13/11	9/13/11

[1]*Not available in California.*   [2]*When equipped with electronic "Lean Burn" system. Not available in California.*   [3]*Required, or standard, in California.*

Major Options

	Cordoba	Newport	Town & Country	New Yorker Brougham
Air conditioning[1]	$490	$533	$533	$533
Tilt steering wheel	$59	$59	$59	S
Tilt and telescope steering wheel	—	$100	$100	$41
Automatic speed control	$77	$83	$83	$83
Electric rear window defroster	$81	$82	—	$82
Tinted glass, all windows	$52	$66	$66	$66
Manual front vent window (4-doors)	—	$40	$40	$40
Power windows	$104	$167	$167	S
Power door locks, 2-dr./4-dr.	$65	$66/$95	$95	$66/$95
Power front bench seat, 6-way	$130	$132	$132	$132
Power 60/40 or bucket seat, 6-way	$130	$132	$132	$132
Front bucket seats w/floor console	$214	—	—	—
AM radio	$79	$99	$99	$99
AM/FM stereo w/search tuner	$314	$318	$318	$318
AM/FM stereo w/8-track tape	$357	$375	$375	$375
Electronic digital clock	S	$45	$24	$24
Vinyl top, full[2]	$115	$143	—	$143
Dual remote control mirrors	$45	$45	$45	$30
Remote control trunk release	$19	$19	—	$19
Sunroof, electric	$311[3]	$897	—	$897
Wire wheel covers	$62	$43	$43	$43
Urethane cast road wheels	$113	—	—	—
Chrome styled road wheels	—	$147	$147	$147
White sidewall tires, std. size	S	$43	$43	S

Popular Option Groups & Packages

	Cordoba	Newport	Town & Country	New Yorker Brougham
Basic package	—	$894	$950	$698
Deluxe wiper/washer package	—	$16	—	—
Easy order package	$856	$1,268	$1,370	$1,327
Light package	—	$75	$37	S
St. Regis option group[4]	—	$598[4]	—	$598
Town & Country package	—	—	$122	—

— = Not Available; S = Standard equipment.   [1]Auto-Temp air conditioning is available for $618 on Newport, Town & Country and New Yorker Brougham.   [2]Landau vinyl roof available on Cordoba for $100.   [3]Requires vinyl top. Only available on 2-door hardtop models. Manually operated on Cordoba.   [4]Newport Custom and New Yorker Brougham 2-door hardtops only.

Paint Colors

	Code		Code		Code
Silver Cloud metallic	A2	Tropic Green metallic[1]	J5	Golden Fawn	Y4
Powder Blue[1]	B1	Bittersweet metallic	K3	Yellow Blaze[2]	Y5
Astral Blue metallic	B2	Sahara Beige[1]	L4	Inca Gold metallic	Y6
Jamaican Blue metallic[2]	B5	Moondust metallic[1]	L5	Spanish Gold metallic	Y9
Starlight Blue metallic	B8	Dark Chestnut metallic[1]	T9		
Rallye Red[2]	E5	Saddle Tan	U2	
Vintage Red metallic	E9	Carmel Tan metallic[2]	U3	
Jade Green metallic	F2	Light Chestnut metallic[2]	U6	
Deep Sherwood metallic	G8	Spinnaker White	W1	
Platinum metallic	J2	Formal Black	X9	

Single tones are coded W1, W1. Two-tones are coded X9, W1 where first two digits are accent or roof color and second two digits are basic body color.   [1]Not available on Cordoba.   [2]Available only on Cordoba.

Cordoba

"The small Chrysler."

Nameplate year of origin: 1975 (also used on special-order 1970 Newport hardtops).
Current bodystyle lifespan: 1975 through 1979.
Predecessor to this model: None.
Replacement for this model: Cordoba (1980 to 1983).
Percentage of division's sales volume: 68.43%.
Corporate siblings: Dodge Charger SE.
Primary competition: Buick Regal, Mercury Cougar XR-7, and Oldsmobile Cutlass
   Supreme.
Notable changes: Minor trim and detail changes.
Major standard equipment: Choice of cloth-and-vinyl or velour cloth-and-vinyl
   front bench seat w/fold-down center armrest, color-keyed 24-oz. deep-pile shag
   carpeting, simulated woodgrained vinyl trim on I/P and door panels, color-keyed
three-spoke steering wheel, bright pedal dress-up, glove box and ashtray light, electronic digital clock, premium steering wheel, molded cloth headliner, trunk light, carpeted trunk and spare tire cover, LH rear view mirror, rear quarter opera window and opera lamp, belt and drip rail moldings, wheel lip moldings, rocker panel sill molding, bodyside and deck lid paint stripes, stand-up hood ornament, power front disc brakes, power steering, premium wheel covers, and GR78 × 15 WSW tires.

Measurements

Wheelbase	115.0"
Length	215.3"
Width	76.3"
Height	52.6"
Legroom — front	41.9"
Legroom — rear	33.9"
Headroom — front	37.7"
Headroom — rear	36.6"
Cargo capacity (cu. ft.)	14.5
Fuel capacity (gals.)	25.5

Models Available

	Model No.	Base MSRP	Change from LY	Shipping Wt. (lbs.)	Model Year Production	Change from LY
Cordoba 2-Door Hardtop Coupe	SS29	$5,392	+6.31%	4130	167,618	+11.67%
TOTALS	*Avg. price*	$5,392	+6.31%	*Production*	167,618	+11.67%

Newport

"Luxury with a fine sense of value."

Nameplate year of origin: 1961 (as series); 1950 (as HT model of the T & C).
Current bodystyle lifespan: 1974 through 1978.
Predecessor to this model: Newport (1969 to 1973).
Replacement for this model: Newport (1979 to 1981).

Measurements

Wheelbase	124.0"
Length	226.6"
Width	79.5"

Percentage of division's sales volume: 15.96%.

Corporate siblings: Chrysler New Yorker Brougham.

Primary competition: Buick LeSabre, Mercury Marquis, and Oldsmobile Delta 88.

Notable changes: Minor trim and detail changes for Newport. Newport Custom name was the replacement for the 1975 New Yorker Brougham, and used the same body styling and exterior trim.

Major standard equipment: Cloth-and-vinyl front bench seat w/fold-down center armrest, color-keyed loop pile carpeting, trip odometer, lighted front ashtray w/two rear seat ashtrays, 12" inside day/night mirror, two-speed electric windshield wipers w/washers, front and rear wheel lip moldings, drip rail and belt moldings, bright windshield and rear window moldings, rear hood molding, dual horns, front bumper guards, deluxe wheel covers, and HR78 × 15 BSW tires. Custom adds: Cloth-and-vinyl 50/50 split back front seat w/individual fold-down center armrest, passenger side recliner (for 4-door models), seat side shields, deck lid molding, upper door frame moldings (sedan only), rocker panel sill molding, dual bodyside paint stripes, rear bumper guards, unique grille, and unique rear bumper and taillights.

Measurements (cont.)

Height	54.4"
Legroom — front	42.1"
Legroom — rear	39.5"
Headroom — front	38.7"
Headroom — rear	37.0"
Cargo capacity (cu. ft.)	20.2
Fuel capacity (gals.)	26.5

Models Available

	Model No.	Base MSRP	Change from LY	Shipping Wt. (lbs.)	Model Year Production	Change from LY
Newport 2-Door Hardtop	CL23	$5,076	+2.82%	4455	2,916	-72.19%
Newport 4-Door Sedan	CL41	$4,993	+2.86%	4490	12,926	-46.89%
Newport 4-Door Hardtop	CL43	$5,147	+2.78%	4525	3,448	-49.63%
Newport Custom 2-Door Hardtop	CM23	$5,479	+2.81%	4530	3,855	-33.89%
Newport Custom 4-Door Sedan	CM41	$5,407	+2.91%	4565	9,448	-1.82%
Newport Custom 4-Door Hardtop	CM43	$5,576	+2.82%	4585	6,497	-44.12%
TOTALS	*Avg. price*	$5,280	+2.83%	*Production*	39,090	-43.14%

Town & Country

"There's so much more to this wagon than space."

Nameplate year of origin: 1941.

Current bodystyle lifespan: 1974 through 1977.

Predecessor to this model: Town & Country (1969 to 1973).

Replacement for this model: LeBaron Town & Country (1978 to 1978).

Percentage of division's sales volume: 1.84%.

Corporate siblings: Dodge Royal Monaco and Plymouth Gran Fury.

Primary competition: Buick Estate Wagon, Mercury Colony Park, and Oldsmobile Custom Cruiser.

Notable changes: Minor trim and detail changes.

Major standard equipment: All-vinyl 50/50 split front seat w/individual fold-down center armrests and passenger-side recliner, color-keyed loop pile carpeting including cargo area, electric clock, interior lights (cargo, glove box, map/courtesy and ashtray), power tailgate window, sound absorbing headliner, trip odometer, front ashtray w/two rear seat ashtrays, 12" inside day/night mirror, three-speed electric windshield wipers w/washers, concealed storage compartments in rear wheelhouse cover, "Power Auto-Lock" tailgate lock (activates when ignition turned on), fender mounted turn signal indicators, bodyside simulated woodgrain appliqués, drip rail molding, rear wheel opening skirts, roof air deflector, dual horns, large diameter front sway bar, deluxe wheel covers, and L78 × 15 BSW tires.

Measurements

Wheelbase	124.0"
Length	227.7"
Width	79.5"
Height	57.6"
Legroom — front	42.1"
Legroom — rear	39.7"
Headroom — front	38.9"
Headroom — rear	38.9"
Cargo capacity (cu. ft.)*	100.8
Fuel capacity (gals.)	24.0

Plus 6.8 cu. ft. in concealed compartment on 2-seat wagon.

Models Available

	Model No.	Base MSRP	Change from LY	Shipping Wt. (lbs.)	Model Year Production	Change from LY
Town & Country 4-Door, 2-S. Wagon	CP45	$6,084	-0.25%	5045	1,271	-32.79%
Town & Country 4-Door, 3-S. Wagon	CP46	$6,244	0.00%	5075	3,227	-32.26%
TOTALS	*Avg. price*	$6,172	-0.12%	*Production*	4,498	-32.41%

New Yorker Brougham

"It's the talk of the town."

Nameplate year of origin: 1939.
Current bodystyle lifespan: 1974 through 1978.
Predecessor to this model: New Yorker (1969 to 1973).
Replacement for this model: New Yorker (1979 to 1981).
Percentage of division's sales volume: 13.77%.
Corporate siblings: Chrysler Newport.
Primary competition: Buick Electra 225, Mercury Grand Marquis, and Oldsmobile Ninety-Eight.
Notable changes: Minor trim and detail changes. New Yorker Brougham name was the replacement for the 1975 Imperial, and used the same body styling and exterior trim.
Major standard equipment: Velour-and-vinyl 50/50 split bench seat w/individual fold-down center armrest, passenger side recliner on 4-doors, rear seat fold-down center armrest, color-keyed loop-pile carpeting, color-keyed seat belts, Lavaliere straps on inside rear roof pillars (4-door), vinyl covered rear pillar pillows, trip odometer, electric clock, dual front ashtrays w/two rear seat ashtrays, interior lights (glove box, map/courtesy and ashtray), 12" inside day/night mirror, luxury three-spoke steering wheel, three-speed electric windshield wipers w/washers, power windows, console-type armrests on all doors, headlight time-delay switch, carpeted trunk floor, LH remote control mirror, full-length bodyside molding, front wheel lip molding, drip rail molding, bright window moldings, rear taillight periphery moldings, rear wheel opening skirts, fender-mounted turn signal indicators, concealed headlamps, undercoating, hood insulation pad, unique deluxe wheel covers, and JR78 × 15 WSW tires.

Measurements

Wheelbase	124.0"
Length	232.7"
Width	79.7"
Height	54.5"
Legroom — front	42.1"
Legroom — rear	39.5"
Headroom — front	37.9"
Headroom — rear	37.0"
Cargo capacity (cu. ft.)	20.2
Fuel capacity (gals.)	26.5

1976

Models Available

	Model No.	Base MSRP	Change from LY	Shipping Wt. (lbs.)	Model Year Production	Change from LY
New Yorker Brougham 2-Door Hardtop	CS23	$6,641	+4.85%	4865	9,748	+28.82%
New Yorker Brougham 4-Door Hardtop	CS43	$6,737	+4.87%	4950	23,984	+87.76%
TOTALS	*Avg. price*	$6,689	+5.42%	*Production*	33,732	+29.54%

DODGE

"Dodge for 1976."

The all-new Aspen debuted for the 1976 model year. Chrysler spent large sums of money to promote the new car and its virtual twin the Plymouth Volaré, which often shared the spotlight in a single advertisement. A lot was at stake since they were replacing the most popular cars in the company's line. Before the end of the model year, the Dart was gone. However, by the end of the year the combined total of Dart and Aspen sales exceeded that of the 1975 Dart, at a time when the rest of the Dodge line was faltering in sales.

To maintain a resemblance to the popular Dart, the Aspen adopted certain front-end styling cues from the Dart, yet presented a fresh look. The Aspen used a horizontal bar grille with indented areas between the main center section and the single round headlamps. A similar box-style bumper was also used, only the Aspen had the parking/turn signal lights mounted below each headlamp in the bumper, rather than in the grille. The Aspen also had its headlights mounted in chrome bezels, while the Dart headlights were in the grille, but in both cases, the entire front end was surrounded by chrome trim. The main central section of the hood was also raised slightly near the front edge as it met the extended center section of the grille, and was capped by a large chrome section with the Dodge name in block letters across it.

Bodysides of the new Aspen featured a lower bodyside

crease running from bumper to bumper, and arching over the wheel openings about an inch from the edge. Two-door coupe models added a slight "Coke-bottle" design flare-out as the bodyside crease crossed the rear quarter panel. Rooflines seemed to follow a fastback line for the coupes and a more upright design for sedans that was much like that of the Dart sedan, including a rear door fixed quarter window. At the back, horizontal taillamps of varying designs were used depending upon trim level, with all wagons using a vertical lamp. All coupe and sedan models had a rectangular, two-level lamp, set to the outer edges of the rear panel, with the upper portion being for taillight and stop lights, and the lower portion housing backup and amber turn signal lights. On base Aspens, an additional red reflector extended from the top level of the taillamp towards the center of the car, resembling a hockey stick shape, and each side was outlined in chrome trim. On Aspen Custom and Special Edition models, a full-width reflector ran between the upper light portions, while a full-width chrome trim piece ran below the lower sections, and the combined unit was outlined in chrome trim.

Under the hood were the predictable basic Chrysler powerplants, with the old "Slant Six" serving as the base engine and the 318 CID and 360 CID V8 engines as optional equipment. Inside, the Aspen used contemporary Chrysler design elements for the instrument panel with a hooded area in front of, and slightly curving around, the driver housing all the essential gauges and controls. A square speedometer sat in the middle with rectangular pods to the left housing an air vent, wiper and light controls, and rectangular pods to the right housing radio and climate controls. The Aspen interior, especially in the Special Edition trim level, looked much more upscale than the Dart could have ever hoped to be. Not only were plush upholstery and carpet materials used, but also equipment such as power windows, power door locks and power seats was available. As could be expected, the new Aspen sedans were the top sellers in the line, but unexpectedly, the station wagons were the second best sellers, proving that there was a demand for smaller station wagons, something AMC knew all along with its Hornet Sportabout. While much of the advertising emphasis was centered on Aspen luxury features, an available "R/T" package garnered a lot of attention. The package added spoilers and special tape stripes to the Aspen coupe, making for a very sporty looking package. Approximately 6,254 "R/T" equipped Aspens were sold for 1976, with another 1,824 having the Super Pak package.

The Dodge Dart line continued to soldier on for a final run, even though the Aspen was in full production. For its final season, few changes were made except that the 360 CID V8 engine was no longer offered, so the Dart Sport 360 was dropped, and the prior year's Special Edition models were made an option package for the Dart sedan or Swinger hardtops. A note of special interest is that the 1976 Dodge Dart Swinger, and its Plymouth Valiant Scamp equivalent, were the last American built compact-sized, two-door hardtop models, and had been since 1970, although no one seemed to notice. True hardtops of any type were a quickly vanishing breed.

After a single year of having Coronet 2-Door Hardtops, the mid-size "W" series 2-door models were moved back under the Charger nameplate, where they had been from 1971 through 1974. With the move, no significant changes of any type were apparent. Standard equipment was cut back on the new-for-1975 Charger SE, in an effort to make the car more affordable, and likely to lessen comparisons to its Chrysler Cordoba twin. Aside from some minor trim changes and the move of the two-door models, there were few significant updates to either the Coronet or the Charger models. An interesting new option for the Charger SE was the Daytona trim package, essentially a paint and tape stripe treatment meant to stir up images of performance cars of the past. Unfortunately there was not a performance package to back up the appearance.

For the full-size Monaco line only trim and detail changes were made, but the base Monaco two-door hardtop and all Monaco 4-door hardtop models were discontinued, as sales had bottomed out over recent years. Also gone was the Royal Monaco Brougham 2-seat station wagon, as most buyers of the top-of-the-line Dodge wagon were opting for the 3-seat version. Introduced after the start of the model year was a new Diplomat option package for the top line Royal Monaco Brougham 2-Door hardtop which featured a rectangular opera window, formal landau vinyl top and stainless steel strap wrapping over the top at the leading edge of the vinyl roof.

The imported Dodge Colt suffered its first downturn since being brought to the U.S. for the 1971 model year, with year-to-year sales down more than 20 percent. Several factors played into this downturn, not the least of which was a new Mitsubishi-built hatchback sold through Plymouth dealerships as the Arrow. Also sure to be stealing sales were the new Chevrolet Chevette and Buick's new Opel Isuzu captive import, now built in Japan. Other newer imported models were also introduced in the past two years, such as the new front-wheel-drive Volkswagen Rabbit and the recently restyled Toyota Corolla, which were both gaining in popularity.

Aspen 2-Door Coupe with R/T package

Aspen SE 4-Door Sedan

Aspen SE 4-Door Station Wagon

Charger 2-Door Hardtop Coupe

Charger SE 2-Door Hardtop Coupe

Colt 4-Door Station Wagon cargo area

Coronet Brougham 4-Door Sedan

Colt 4-Door Sedan interior
and instrument panel

Royal Monaco Brougham 2-Door Hardtop
Coupe with Diplomat package

Dart Swinger 2-Door Hardtop

Dart 4-Door Sedan

Model year production: 352,915, up 14.72% from 1975.
Domestic market share: 4.07% (8th place).
Base price range: $3,258 to $5,869.
Dodge average base price: $4,318, down 4.01%.
Introduction date: October 16, 1975.
Assembly plants: Lynch Road, Detroit, MI (A); Hamtramck, MI (B); Jefferson Ave., Detroit, MI (C); Belvidere, IL (D); Newark, DE (F); St. Louis, MO (G); and Windsor, Ontario, Canada (R). Colt manufacturer: Mitsubishi Heavy Industries, Tokyo, Japan (code 1 through 9).
Data plate identification (VIN): Thirteen digit code read as follows: First four digits indicate series and body style

(model number in model charts); fifth digit indicates engine code (see powertrain chart); sixth digit indicates year (6 = 1976); seventh digit indicates assembly plant for all except Colt (see list above; for Colt seventh digit indicates transmission code [5 = 4-speed manual, NA = 5-speed manual, 9 = automatic]); remaining digits are sequential with beginning numbers of 100001 for all Dodge models except Colt. Colt sequential numbers are currently unknown. *Example:* NL41C6B100001 is a 1976 Dodge Aspen 4-Door Sedan, with 225 CID, 2-bbl. 6-cylinder engine, serial number 100001, built in Hamtramck, MI.

Powertrains

Engine	Net HP	Engine Code	Transmission Availability[1]		Colt	Dart	Aspen	Coronet	Charger	Monaco & Royal Monaco	Royal Monaco Brougham & Wagons
97.5 CID (1.6L) OHC, 1-bbl., 4-cyl.	83	K	4-speed manual		S (ex. GT)	—	—	—	—	—	—
				MPG:	24/37/29	—	—	—	—	—	—
				Calif.	22/32/26	—	—	—	—	—	—
			3-speed Torque Flite automatic		$250 (ex. GT)	—	—	—	—	—	—
				MPG:	24/30/26	—	—	—	—	—	—
				Calif.	21/29/24	—	—	—	—	—	—
122 CID (2.0L) OHC, 2-bbl., 4-cyl.	96	U	4-speed manual		$232 (ex. GT)	—	—	—	—	—	—
				MPG:	20/33/24	—	—	—	—	—	—
				Calif.	18/31/22	—	—	—	—	—	—
			5-speed manual		S (GT)/ $325 (ex. GT)	—	—	—	—	—	—
				MPG:	NA	—	—	—	—	—	—
			3-speed Torque Flite automatic		$157 (GT)/ $482 (ex. GT)	—	—	—	—	—	—
				MPG:	20/28/23	—	—	—	—	—	—
				Calif.	19/24/21	—	—	—	—	—	—
225 CID (3.7L), 2-bbl., 6-cyl.	100	C	3-speed manual		—	S	S[2]	S (Sdns.)	S (ex. SE)	—	—
				MPG:	—	19/26/22	18/27/22	18/30/22	18/30/22	—	—
				Calif.	—	16/23/18	17/24/20	—	—	—	—
			"Overdrive4" 4-speed manual		—	$127	$127[2]	—	—	—	—
				MPG:	—	NA	NA	—	—	—	—
			3-speed Torque Flite automatic		—	$250	$250	$273 (Sdns.)	$273 (ex. SE)	—	—

Engine	Net HP	Engine Code	Transmission Availability[1]		Colt	Dart	Aspen	Coronet	Charger	Monaco & Royal Monaco	Royal Monaco Brougham & Wagons
				MPG:	—	18/24/21	18/23/20	16/23/19	16/23/19	—	—
				Calif.	—	15/20/17	13/17/15	—	—	—	—
318 CID (5.2L), 2-bbl., V8	150	G	3-speed manual[3]		—	$137	$165	$238 (Sdns.)	$238 (ex. SE)	—	—
				MPG:	—	14/22/17	14/22/17	15/21/17	15/21/17	—	—
			"Overdrive4" 4-speed manual[3]		—	$264	$312	—	—	—	—
				MPG:	—	NA	NA	—	—	—	—
			3-speed Torque Flite automatic		—	$387	$415	$511 (Sdns.)	S (SE)/$511 (others)	S (ex. RM)	—
				MPG:	—	16/21/18	16/21/18	13/18/15	13/18/15	13/18/15	—
				Calif.	—	12/15/13	12/17/14	12/16/14	12/16/14	—	—
360 CID (5.9L), 2-bbl., V8[3]	170	K	3-speed Torque Flite automatic		—	—	$465	S (Wgns.)/$565 (Sdns.)	$54 (SE)/$565 (others)	S (RM)/$55 (others)	—
				MPG:	—	—	13/19/15	12/19/14	12/19/14	13/17/14	—
360 CID (5.9L), 4-bbl., V8	175[4]/220	J[4],L	3-speed Torque Flite automatic		—	$626	—	$45 (Wgns.)/$610 (Sdns.)	$99 (SE)/$610 (others)	$45 (RM)/$100 (others)	—
				MPG:	—	13/19/15	—	13/17/14	13/17/14	NA	—
				Calif.	—	12/16/13	—	12/18/14	12/18/14	11/17/13	—
400 CID (6.6L), 2-bbl., V8[3]	175	M	3-speed Torque Flite automatic		—	—	—	$48 (Wgns.)/$613 (Sdns.)	$102 (SE)/$613 (others)	$49 (RM)/$104 (others)	S
				MPG:	—	—	—	11/16/13	11/16/13	12/18/14	12/18/14
400 CID (6.6L), 4-bbl., V8	185[4]/210	N[4],P	3-speed Torque Flite automatic		—	—	—	$93 (Wgns.)/$658 (Sdns.)	$147 (SE)/$658 (others)	$94 (RM)/$149 (others)	$45
				MPG:	—	—	—	10/16/12	10/16/12	9/17/12	9/7/12
				Calif.	—	—	—	11/15/12	11/15/12	10/16/12	10/16/12
440 CID (7.2L), 4-bbl., V8	205	T	3-speed Torque Flite automatic		—	—	—	—	—	$218 (RM)/$273 (others)	$169
				MPG:	—	—	—	—	—	11/15/13	11/16/12
				Calif.	—	—	—	—	—	9/14/11	9/14/11

[1]Unless otherwise noted: All transmissions are column-shifts, except on Colt or any model w/4-speed manual. Floor-shift is available for $28 extra on any Dart or Aspen w/3-speed manual transmission and Aspen Coupes w/automatic; and Charger Sport w/bucket seats, console and automatic transmission. Floor-shift automatic is standard on Charger SE.   [2]Not available in California on wagons.   [3]Not available in California.   [4]Available only in California.

Major Options

	Colt	Dart	Aspen	Coronet	Charger	Monaco
Air conditioning	$412	$431	$431	$490	$490	$504[1]
Tilt steering wheel	S	—	$54	$59	$59	$83[2]
Automatic speed control	—	—	$70	$77	$77	$78
Electric rear window defogger	$70	$74	$74	$81	$81	$82
Tinted glass, all windows	S	$44	$44	$52	$52	$66
Power windows[3]	—	—	$135	$147	$104	$167
Power door locks[3]	—	—	$86	$94	$65	$95
Power front seat	—	—	$119	$130	$130	$132
Music Master AM radio	$70	$72	$72	$79	$79	$80
AM/FM stereo	—	—	$233	$254	$254	$257
AM/FM stereo w/8-track tape	—	—	—	$357	$357	$362
Front bucket seats	S	$128[4]	$187[4]	—	$296[4]	—
Vinyl top[5]	$	$92	$92	$115	$115	$131
Sunroof, manual[6]	—	$186	$186	$311	$311	$627
Power steering, standard w/V8s	—	$131	$131	$143	$143	S
Power brakes, w/front disc[7]	$	$81	$56	$61	S	S
Premier wheel covers	—	—	$54	—	—	$70
Wire wheel covers	—	—	$86	$94	$94	—
Rallye road wheels	—	$66	$66	$75	$75	$147
White sidewall tires, std. size	$30	$32	$32	$39	$39	$39

Popular Option Groups & Packages

	Colt	Dart	Aspen	Coronet	Charger	Monaco
Brougham package	—	—	—	—	$303	—
Custom package	—	$218	—	—	—	—
Daytona package	—	—	—	—	$345[8]	—
Decorator trim package	—	$178	—	—	—	—
Deluxe insulation package	S	$51	$51	$55	$55	$41
Diplomat package	—	—	—	—	—	$834
Estate package	$185	—	—	—	—	—
Exterior décor group[9]	—	$84	—	$175	$175	—
E-Z order package	—	$740	$758	$870	$870/$1,027[8]	$547[10]
Interior décor group	—	$92[9]	—	—	—	—
Sport "Lite" package	—	$68	—	—	—	—
Luxury equipment package	—	—	—	$1,739	$1,739[11]	$1,836
R/T décor package	—	—	$95	—	—	—
R/T package	—	—	$196	—	—	—
Special Edition package	—	$438	—	—	—	—
Super Pak package	—	—	$	—	—	—

—= Not Available; S = Standard equipment. [1]"Auto-Temp" automatic air conditioning is available on Monaco for $590, and for Monaco w/Luxury equipment package for $85. [2]Tilt and telescope steering wheel is available on Monaco for $100. [3]Prices given for 4-Door models. On 2-door models price for power windows on Aspen is $95, and Monaco is $110. Price for power door locks on Aspen is $60, and Monaco is $64. [4]Available only on 2-door models. On Dart requires automatic transmission. Price on Dart Sport is $68. Dart hardtops are not available with console. Charger SE w/standard bucket seats has console only available for $90. [5]Standard on Dart SE and Royal Monaco Brougham coupe. Aspen Landau top on 2-door models is $137. For Colt, available only on 2-door models. Not available on station wagons. [6]Manual sunroof on Dart and Aspen coupes and Charger models. Power sunroof on Monaco series coupes, and requires vinyl top. Available on Monaco sedans for $758. [7]Standard on Aspen w/V8 engine, Coronet Crestwood station wagons, and Charger SE. All others, except Dart, have manual front disc brakes standard. Dart has manual drum brakes. [8]On Charger SE. [9]Sport only. [10]Price given for base Monaco. Price on Monaco station wagons is $471. [11]Excluding Charger SE.

Paint Colors

Dodge	Code	Dodge	Code	Dodge	Code
Silver Cloud metallic[1]	A2	Starlight Blue metallic[6]	B8	Deep Sherwood Sunfire metallic[1]	G9
Silver Frost metallic[2]	A5	Bright Red[3,4,5]	E5	Platinum metallic[6]	J2
Powder Blue[3,4,5,6]	B1	Vintage Red Sunfire metallic[3,4,5,6]	E8	Tropic Green metallic[4,5,6,7]	J5
Astral Blue metallic[6]	B2	Vintage Red metallic[3,4,5,6]	E9	Bittersweet metallic[4,6]	K3
Big Sky Blue[7]	B4	Jade Green metallic[1]	F2	Parchment[3,6,7]	L4
Jamaican Blue metallic[3,4,5,7]	B5	Deep Sherwood metallic[1]	G8	Moondust metallic[4,5,6]	L5

Dodge	Code	Dodge	Code	Colt[8]	Code
Claret Red[7]	R6	Inca Gold metallic[3,4,5,6]	Y6	Orange	092
Cinnamon metallic[3,4,5,7]	T4	Spanish Gold metallic[1]	Y9		
Dark Chestnut metallic[6]	T9				
Saddle Tan[6,7]	U2	Colt[8]	Code		
Carmel Tan metallic[3,4,5,7]	U3	Maroon	020		
Light Chestnut metallic[4]	U6	Bright Blue metallic	022		
Spitfire Orange[7]	V1	Bright Gold metallic	023		
Eggshell White[1]	W1	Silver metallic	030		
Black[1]	X9	Sapporo White	067		
Harvest Gold[7]	Y3	Bright Yellow	090		
Golden Fawn[3,4,5,6]	Y4	April Green metallic	091		
Yellow Blaze[3,4,5]	Y5				

Single tones are coded W1, W1. Two-tones are coded X9, W1 where first two digits are accent or roof color and second two digits are basic body color. Two-tone paint package available on Aspen Custom Coupe for $158 extra. Sunfire metallic paints available at extra cost on specified models. [1]Available on all models. [2]Available only in two-tone combinations. [3]Available on Dart. [4]Available on Coronet. [5]Available on Charger. [6]Available on Monaco. [7]Available on Aspen. [8]Availability by model is not currently known for Colt models.

1976

Colt

"How did Dodge Colt put so much in such a little car?"

Nameplate year of origin: 1971.
Current bodystyle lifespan: 1971 through 1978 (hardtop); 1971 through 1977 (wagon); 1971 through 1976 (coupe and sedan).
Predecessor to this model: None.
Replacement for this model: Colt (1979 to 1983).
Primary competition: AMC Gremlin, Buick Opel, Chevrolet Vega, Ford Pinto, and Plymouth Arrow.
Notable changes: Minor trim and detail changes.
Major standard equipment: Vinyl front bucket seats w/reclining seat backs, full-floor carpeting, recessed door handles, two-spoke steering wheel, tilt steering column, tinted glass, deluxe sound insulation, beltline, drip rail, windshield, and rear window moldings, front and rear rubber bumper guards, locking fuel filler door, manual front disc brakes, wheel cov-

Measurements

	2-doors	Sedan	Wagon
Wheelbase	95.3"	95.3"	95.3"
Length	171.1"	171.1"	172.0"
Width	63.6"	63.6"	62.8"
Height	53.1"	53.7"	54.1"
Legroom — front	42.7"	42.7"	42.7"
Legroom — rear	30.5"	30.5"	30.5"
Headroom — front	36.9"	37.8"	38.2"
Headroom — rear	35.5"	37.0"	37.3"
Cargo capacity (cu. ft.)	12.0	12.0	58.3
Fuel capacity (gals.)	13.5	13.5	11.0

ers, and A78 × 13 BSW tires. Sedan and wagon add: Fold-down rear seat (wagon only), three-spoke steering wheel, wheel opening moldings, and rocker panel molding. Carousel hardtop adds: Cloth and vinyl bucket seat w/reclining seat backs, floor console, blue denim instrument panel, shag carpeting, AM/FM radio, multi-colored side and rear stripes, wheel lip moldings, and road wheels. GT adds: Soft-rim three-spoke sports steering wheel, front floor console w/shifter, rallye gauge cluster w/tachometer, GT bodyside tape stripes, GT logo, argent rallye road wheels with chrome hubs and lug nuts, and BR70 × 13 WSW tires.

Models Available

	Model No.	Base MSRP	Change from LY	Shipping Wt. (lbs.)	Model Year Sales	Change from LY
Colt 2-Door Coupe	6M21	$3,175	+7.81%	2185	NA	NA
Colt 4-Door Sedan	6H41	$3,341	+7.74%	2185	NA	NA
Colt 4-Door Station Wagon	6H45	$3,646	+7.42%	2325	NA	NA
Colt Carousel 2-Door Hardtop	6S23	$3,748	+10.07%	2230	NA	NA
Colt GT 2-Door Hardtop	6P23	$3,748	+3.31%	2295	NA	NA
TOTALS	*Avg. price*	$3,532	+7.19%	*Production*	47,383*	-21.49%*

*Total and comparison to LY are based on estimated model year sales.

Dart

"The value car is more than ever a Dodge success story."

Nameplate year of origin: 1960 (used on entry-level full-size Dodge).
Current bodystyle lifespan: 1967 through 1976.
Predecessor to this model: Dart (1963 to 1966).
Replacement for this model: Aspen (1976 to 1980).
Percentage of division's production: 15.15%.
Corporate siblings: Plymouth Valiant (including Scamp and Duster).
Primary competition: Buick Skylark, Oldsmobile Omega, Mercury Comet, and Pontiac Ventura.
Notable changes: Minor detail changes.
Major standard equipment: All-vinyl front bench seat (sedan and Swinger), cloth and vinyl front bench seat (Sport, Swinger Special and Custom sedan), front door armrests, rear seat armrests (except Sport and Swinger Special), rubber color-keyed floor mats, simulated woodgrain I/P cluster appliqué, two-speed electric windshield wipers and washers, front ashtray and cigarette lighter (ex. Dart Sport), front door window vents (sedans only), grille surround and front edge moldings, hubcaps, and 6.95 × 14 BSW tires. Sport, Swinger and Custom add: Color-keyed carpeting, simulated woodgrain vinyl appliqué door panel trim (except Sport), roof drip rail molding, wheel opening moldings, lower deck panel appliqué, and bodyside moldings w/painted insert (except Sport).

Measurements

	Dart	Dart Sport
Wheelbase	111.0"	108.0"
Length	203.4"	200.9"
Width	69.8"	71.7"
Height	54.0"	53.4"
Legroom — front	41.9"	41.9"
Legroom — rear	35.2"	29.4"
Headroom — front	38.3"	37.2"
Headroom — rear	37.2"	36.4"
Cargo capacity (cu. ft.)	17.7*	20.1
Fuel capacity (gals.)	16.0	16.0

Sedans, 16.0.

Models Available

	Model No.	Base MSRP	Change from LY	Shipping Wt. (lbs.)	Model Year Production	Change from LY
Dart Sport 2-Door Coupe	LL29	$3,258	-1.18%	2990	13,642	NA*
Dart Swinger Special 2-Dr. Hardtop	LL23	$3,337	-0.12%	3050	3,036	-56.80%
Dart 4-Door Sedan	LL41	$3,295	+0.80%	3070	27,849	NA*
Dart Swinger 2-Door Hardtop	LH23	$3,510	-0.23%	3035	8,937	NA*
TOTALS	*Avg. price*	$3,350	-8.45%	*Production*	53,464	-68.75%

Change from LY cannot be calculated due to 1975 model production being combined with other models.

Aspen

"For a small car, it's unbelievable."

Nameplate year of origin: 1976.
Current bodystyle lifespan: 1976 through 1980.
Predecessor to this model: Dart (1967 to 1976).
Replacement for this model: Aries (1981 to 1989).
Percentage of division's production: 53.81%.
Corporate siblings: Plymouth Volaré.
Primary competition: AMC Hornet, Buick Skylark, Chevrolet Nova, Ford Granada, Mercury Monarch, Oldsmobile Omega, and Pontiac Ventura.
Notable changes: All-new model.
Major standard equipment: All-vinyl front bench seat (sedan and wagon), cloth and vinyl front bench seat (coupe), color-keyed carpeting, three-spoke steering wheel, two-speed electric windshield wipers and washers, front ashtray, color-keyed bumper filler, roof drip rail molding, windshield and backlight moldings, and D78 × 14 BSW tires. Wagon adds: Rear liftgate, power front disc brakes, heavy-duty suspension, and F78 × 14 BSW tires. Custom adds: Vinyl bench seat (coupe), cloth and vinyl bench seat (sedan), cigarette lighter, rear armrests w/ashtrays, simulated woodgrain I/P appliqué, belt moldings, wide body-

Measurements

	Coupe	Sedan	Wagon
Wheelbase	108.5"	112.5"	112.5"
Length	197.5"	201.5"	201.5"
Width	72.8"	72.8"	72.8"
Height	53.1"	54.8"	54.8"
Legroom — front	42.2"	42.3"	42.3"
Legroom — rear	30.7"	36.6"	36.6"
Headroom — front	37.5"	39.2"	39.2"
Headroom — rear	36.1"	37.5"	38.7"
Cargo capacity (cu. ft.)	14.5	14.2	71.9
Fuel capacity (gals.)	18.0	18.0	18.0

side chrome moldings w/black painted insert, and rear deck appliqué. SE adds: Vinyl 60/40 split front bench seat w/individual recliners, luxury door trim panels w/lower carpeting, simulated woodgrain overlay on glove box door w/glove box lock, luxury steering wheel, landau vinyl roof (coupe), full vinyl roof (sedan), color-keyed wide vinyl bodyside molding, full wheel lip molding, hood ornament and windsplit molding, deluxe insulation package, day/night rear view mirror, undercoating w/hood silencer pad, power steering and automatic transmission, dual horns, and premium wheel covers. SE wagon adds: All vinyl bench seat, cigarette lighter and rear seat ashtray, cargo compartment carpet and storage bins w/locking doors, woodgrain side panel and liftgate appliqué, and belt moldings.

Models Available

	Model No.	Base MSRP	Change from LY	Shipping Wt. (lbs.)	Model Year Production	Change from LY
Aspen 2-Door Sport Coupe	NL29	$3,336	NEW	3160	22,249	NEW
Aspen 4-Door Sedan	NL41	$3,371	NEW	3190	13,981	NEW
Aspen 4-Door Station Wagon	NL45	$3,658	NEW	3560	33,265	NEW
Aspen Custom 2-Door Sport Coupe	NH29	$3,518	NEW	3170	21,064	NEW
Aspen Custom 4-Door Sedan	NH41	$3,553	NEW	3200	28,632	NEW
Aspen SE 2-Door Sport Coupe	NP29	$4,413	NEW	3375	18,604	NEW
Aspen SE 4-Door Sedan	NP41	$4,400	NEW	3410	21,323	NEW
Aspen SE 4-Door Station Wagon	NP45	$3,988	NEW	3565	30,782	NEW
TOTALS		*Avg. price* $3,780	NEW		*Production* 189,900	NEW

Coronet

"A great family car because Dodge planned it that way."

Nameplate year of origin: 1950 (as hardtop designation); 1953 (as series).

Current bodystyle lifespan: 1971 through 1978. Renamed Monaco for 1977 to 1978.

Predecessor to this model: Coronet (1968 to 1970).

Replacement for this model: Diplomat (1977 to 1979).

Percentage of division's sales volume: 9.01%.

Corporate siblings: Plymouth Fury.

Primary competition: AMC Matador, Chevrolet Chevelle, Ford Torino, Mercury Montego, and Pontiac LeMans.

Notable changes: Minor trim and detail changes. Two-door models moved to Charger line.

Major standard equipment: Cloth-and-vinyl front bench seat, color-keyed carpeting, simulated woodgrain inserts on I/P, deluxe steering wheel, full-length bodyside molding, drip rail and belt moldings, deck lid and rear quarter moldings, upper door frame moldings, two-speed windshield wipers w/washers, rear bumper guards, single horn, front disc brakes, hubcaps, and F78 × 14 BSW tires. Brougham adds: Velour cloth-and-vinyl front bench seat w/fold-down center armrest, deluxe padded door trim, color-keyed shag carpeting, color-keyed vinyl bodyside protection molding, Brougham nameplate and medallion on rear roof pillars, stand-up hood ornament, and deluxe wheel covers. Wagons add: All-vinyl front bench seat, cargo compartment carpeting on 3-seat wagons, dual action tailgate w/concealed hinges, simulated woodgrained appliqué on tailgate door, power front disc brakes, and H78 × 14 BSW tires. Crestwood wagon adds: All-vinyl split-back front bench seat w/fold-down center armrest, cargo compartment carpeting and dome light, rear roof air deflector, tan vinyl insert bodyside protective molding, and exterior simulated woodgrained bodyside overlays.

Measurements

	Sedans	Wagons
Wheelbase	117.5"	117.5"
Length	212.4"	220.7"
Width	78.6"	79.2"
Height	53.9"	56.5"
Legroom — front	41.9"	41.9"
Legroom — rear	36.7"	36.3"
Headroom — front	38.6"	39.7"
Headroom — rear	37.4"	39.9"
Cargo capacity (cu. ft.)	19.4	86.8
Fuel capacity (gals.)	25.5	20.0

Models Available

	Model No.	Base MSRP	Change from LY	Shipping Wt. (lbs.)	Model Year Production	Change from LY*
Coronet 4-Door Sedan	WL41	$3,770	+3.54%	3625	10,853*	NA*
Coronet 4-Door, 2-Seat Wagon	WL45	$4,634	+6.33%	4285	1,840*	NA*
Coronet 4-Door, 3-Seat Wagon	WL46	$4,776	NEW	4350	3,039	NEW

	Model No.	Base MSRP	Change from LY	Shipping Wt. (lbs.)	Model Year Production	Change from LY*
Coronet Brougham 4-Door Sedan	WP41	$4,059	NEW	3875	12,831	NEW
Coronet Crestwood 4-Dr., 2-S. Wgn.	WP45	$5,023	+4.08%	4285	1,092*	NA*
Coronet Crestwood 4-Dr., 3-S. Wgn.	WP46	$5,165	+5.02%	4360	2,154*	NA*
TOTALS		Avg. price $4,571	+8.19%		Production 31,809	-23.34%

*Comparison of production to LY is not possible as 1975 totals were kept combined for base Coronet 2- and 4-doors, and combined for all station wagons.

Charger

"The sporty styling only hints at the comfort and agility."

Nameplate year of origin: 1966.
Current bodystyle lifespan: 1975 through 1978.
Predecessor to this model: Charger (1971 to 1974).
Replacement for this model: Magnum XE (1978 to 1979), Mirada (1980 to 1983). Monaco coupes replace Charger and Charger Sport (1977 to 1978).
Percentage of division's sales volume: 14.95%.
Corporate siblings: Chrysler Cordoba and Plymouth Fury coupes.
Primary competition: AMC Matador, Chevrolet Monte Carlo, Ford Elite, Mercury Cougar XR-7, and Pontiac Grand Prix.
Notable changes: Minor trim and detail changes.
Major standard equipment: Choice of all-vinyl or cloth-and-vinyl front bench seat, color-keyed carpeting, simulated woodgrained vinyl trim on I/P, deluxe steering wheel, inside day/night rearview mirror, two-speed windshield wipers w/washers, bright trim moldings (windshield, backlight, hood rear edge, deck lid, taillamp surround, belt, drip rail, bodyside and partial wheel opening), hubcaps and F78 × 14 BSW tires. Sport adds: Choice of velour cloth-and-vinyl front bench seat w/fold-down center armrest or all-vinyl bucket seat w/center cushion and folding armrest, 24 oz. color-keyed shag carpeting, dual horns, color-keyed vinyl insert bodyside molding, Sport nameplate and medallion on rear roof pillar, and deluxe wheel covers. SE adds: All-vinyl front bucket seats, 24 oz. color-keyed shag carpeting, simulated woodgrained vinyl trim on I/P, deluxe door trim panels, deluxe steering wheel, belt and drip rail moldings, LH outside rear view mirror, bright moldings (windshield, backlight, rear hood edge, belt, drip and wheel lip), stand-up SE hood ornament, deluxe sound package, power front disc brakes, power steering, premium wheel covers, and G78 × 15 BSW tires.

Measurements

	Charger & Sport	Charger SE
Wheelbase	115.0"	115.0"
Length	213.7"	215.3"
Width	77.7"	77.1"
Height	52.6"	52.6"
Legroom — front	42.3"	42.4"
Legroom — rear	32.4"	32.3"
Headroom — front	37.6"	37.6"
Headroom — rear	37.6"	36.6"
Cargo capacity (cu. ft.)	14.7	14.7
Fuel capacity (gals.)	25.5	25.5

Models Available

	Model No.	Base MSRP	Change from LY	Shipping Wt. (lbs.)	Model Year Production	Change from LY**
Charger 2-Door Hardtop	WL23	$3,736	+4.04%*	3595	6,613	NA**
Charger Sport 2-Door Hardtop	WH23	$4,025	NEW	3600	10,811	NEW
Charger SE 2-Door Hardtop Coupe	XS22	$4,763	-2.86%	3945	35,337	+17.79%**
TOTALS		Avg. price $4,175	-14.85%		Production 52,761	+75.87%**

*Comparison made to equivalent 1975 Dodge Coronet 2-door hardtop model.   **Comparisons of SE and total are made with 1975 estimates, due to 1975 production being kept combined within Coronet hardtop figures.

Monaco

"Uncommon luxury and comfort in full-sized cars."

Nameplate year of origin: 1965.
Current bodystyle lifespan: 1974 through 1977. Renamed Royal Monaco for 1977.
Predecessor to this model: Polara and Monaco (1969 to 1973).

Measurements

	Cars	Wagons
Wheelbase	121.5"	124.0"

Replacement for this model: St. Regis (1979 to 1981).
Percentage of division's sales volume: 7.08%.
Corporate siblings: Plymouth Gran Fury.
Primary competition: Chevrolet Caprice, Ford LTD, Mercury Marquis, Oldsmobile Delta 88, and Pontiac Bonneville.
Notable changes: Trim and detail changes. New front-end design for base Monaco.
Major standard equipment: Cloth and vinyl front bench seat, color-keyed carpeting, padded door trim panels, color-keyed deluxe steering wheel, day/night inside rear view mirror, LH outside rear view mirror, drip rail and beltline moldings, bright bodyside molding, rubber trunk mat, hidden headlights, front sway bar, hubcaps, and G78 × 15 BSW tires. Royal Monaco adds: Princeton cloth and vinyl front bench seat, simulated woodgrained I/P appliqué and door panel trim, glove box light, wheel lip moldings, upper door frame moldings (sedan), vinyl insert bodyside moldings, trunk light, and GR78 × 15 BSW tires. Royal Monaco Brougham adds: Cloth and vinyl 50/50 split front seat w/fold-down center armrest and passenger recliner on 4-door models, luxury door panels w/pull assist straps, electric clock, map lights, deluxe steering wheel, rear door dome light switch, dual horns, hood and bodyside tape stripes, canopy vinyl roof w/fixed opera windows (2-door), and deluxe wheel covers. Wagons add: All-vinyl upholstery (w/seating configurations and other trim matching trim levels above), cargo compartment side storage panels, power tailgate window, tailgate ajar warning light, and L78 × 15 BSW tires. Royal Monaco wagon adds: Cargo area light, roof air deflector, and LR78 × 15 BSW tires. Brougham wagon adds: Cargo compartment carpeting, cargo side panel lock, and exterior woodgrained vinyl appliqué w/bright surround molding on bodyside and tailgate.

Measurements (cont.)

	Cars	Wagons
Length*	223.4"	226.8"
Width	79.3"	79.4"
Height	55.4"	58.9"
Legroom — front	41.6"	41.6"
Legroom — rear	38.2"	38.3"
Headroom — front	38.7"	38.7"
Headroom — rear	37.8"	40.5"
Cargo capacity (cu. ft.)	20.4	100.8
Fuel capacity (gals.)**	26.5	24.0

*Royal Monaco and Royal Monaco Brougham models are 2.2" longer.   **Fuel capacity is 20.5 gallons on cars equipped with 318 CID V8 engine.*

1976

Models Available

	Model No.	Base MSRP	Change from LY	Shipping Wt. (lbs.)	Model Year Production	Change from LY*
Monaco 4-Door Sedan	DM41	$4,388	-4.71%	4160	3,686	NA
Monaco 4-Door, 2-Seat Wagon	DM45	$4,948	-3.15%	4910	597	NA
Royal Monaco 2-Door Hardtop	DH23	$4,778	-1.85%	4280	1,591	NA
Royal Monaco 4-Door Sedan	DH41	$4,763	-1.75%	4325	9,049	NA
Royal Monaco 4-Door, 2-Seat Wagon	DH45	$5,241	-0.96%	4915	547	NA
Royal Monaco 4-Door, 3-Seat Wagon	DH46	$5,364	-0.94%	4950	1,006	NA
Royal Monaco Brougham 2-Door Hardtop	DP29	$5,382	-1.43%	4430	2,742	NA
Royal Monaco Brougham 4-Door Sedan	DP41	$5,211	-0.97%	4520	3,890	NA
Royal Monaco Brougham 4-Dr., 3-S. Wgn.	DP46	$5,869	-0.61%	4995	1,873	NA
TOTALS						
	Avg. price	$5,105	-1.69%	Production	24,981*	-61.59%*

Comparison of production to LY is not possible, as 1975 totals were kept combined for Monaco and Royal Monaco cars, for Royal Monaco Brougham cars, and for all station wagons.

FORD

"The closer you look, the better we look."

The new model year brought few visible changes to the 1976 Ford line. Most of the updates were mechanical changes to promote fuel efficiency by reducing weight, lowering axle ratios, and introducing catalytic converters on most models, which helped reduce exhaust emissions. Material changes to reduce weight included an expanded use of plastic for grilles and trim. To further emphasize fuel efficiency, all cars carrying a 4-cylinder engine were officially given the added name suffix of "MPG," although they were still the same model number when equipped with an optional 6-cylinder or V8 engine, and only the Pinto and Mustang II could be had with a 4-cylinder. Two changes of interest included the addition of two new Pinto models and a new Stallion option for the Pinto, Maverick and Mustang II, both of which are detailed below. Otherwise, only slight trim revisions and modified grilles on some lines would distinguish the 1976 models from their predecessors.

The subcompact Pinto and compact Maverick received the most obvious changes. The Pinto used a new horizontal crosshatch grille design containing rectangular parking/turn signal lamps mounted near each end. Inside, the Pinto added new choices in upholstery materials, including a plaid cloth interior. A new, very basic Pinto Pony "MPG" 2-door sedan deleted some of the standard Pinto trim and was available with fewer equipment choices, allowing Ford to keep its base price under $2,900 and advertise it as an "import fighter." An interesting one-year-only option was a new Squire option for the Pinto hatchbacks consisting of the same bodyside paneling as the Squire option on the Pinto station wagon. Before the model year began, reports were surfacing about "exploding Pintos." The reference was to the higher than typical rate of fires in Pintos in rear-end collisions as a result of punctured fuel tanks. More details on this can be found in the introduction of this book. Despite the problems, Pinto production was up 30 percent.

The Maverick, which originally was slated to be discontinued this year, soldiered on as lingering fears of another fuel crisis kept sales at a sustainable level, even though the Granada had stolen many potential Maverick customers. The Maverick had sold well over a million units with three basic models since its introduction in 1970, and was undoubtedly one of Ford's many success stories of the period. Changes for 1976 mostly centered on its revised front-end appearance. A new horizontal bar grille that appeared to be slightly V-shaped, and canted forward at the top, was divided vertically at the center and trimmed with chrome accents on a black background. The use of black included the headlight surrounds, which were lined in chrome around the outer edges. Finally, with the introduction of the Stallion (detailed in following paragraph), the Grabber coupe was discontinued.

Mustang II models continued in basically the same form as when introduced for the 1974 model year. A new option for 1976 was the Cobra II package, which sounded like a high-performance option, but in reality was little more than a trim and handling package, as it was available on any 2+2 hatchback model, and could be ordered with the MPG 4-cylinder engine. Another new option package was the Stallion, which was also offered on the Pinto and Maverick. Available on Pinto hatchbacks, the Maverick coupe and Mustang II coupe or 2+2, the Stallion package was essentially an exterior appearance package with blackout grille, a larger front fender "Stallion" decal, and, most obviously, a distinctive two-tone paint job. Lower bodysides and lower bumper areas were painted in black, with selected colors used on the rest of the car. Most cars produced seemed to be bright

red, bright yellow or white, although other choices were available. Ordering the "Tu-Tone" option with the Stallion package added black paint to the upper body panels, including the roof (except on Pinto), fender tops, trunk (on Maverick and Mustang II coupe), and hood.

The Granada entered its second year with no significant changes but was the new sales leader of the Ford lineup, capturing nearly 30 percent of Ford's 1976 model year production. The highly popular 4-door sedans were the sales leaders, and the remarkable 80 percent increase in production came as Chrysler Corporation's new Dodge Aspen and Plymouth Volaré twins were being introduced. It was a remarkable feat that could only be compared to the success of the Falcon and Maverick that preceded the Granada, proving once again that Ford could successfully sell cars in this size class.

The mid-size Torino line entered its final model year with virtually no changes, except that the Gran Torino Sport hardtop was discontinued. Torino sales and production held steady even though it came with a standard 351 CID V8 engine at a time when most of its direct competition came with standard six-cylinder engines that may have been less powerful, but provided much better gas mileage. Adding some punch to the line was the popularity of ABC-TV's *Starsky & Hutch* prime time television show featuring a custom Gran Torino. Ford offered approximately 1,000 replica Gran Torino 2-doors for sale in the spring of 1976, but as shown by the tripling of base Torino 2-door sales, there were most likely many "do-it-yourself" aftermarket paint jobs. The Elite personal luxury sport coupe also continued mostly unchanged, and likely picked up any sales lost by the Gran Torino Sport being dropped, as sales increased by almost 20 percent. As the short-lived Elite was also entering its final model year, it is interesting in retrospect to speculate as to whether the Elite may have been a marketing test to see if a smaller and lower priced Thunderbird would sell better, as the 1977 model year would see a new downsized Thunderbird introduced, based on the former Torino/Elite chassis.

The full-size Ford LTD line, having been restyled for 1975, entered the new model year with few changes. Base LTD, LTD Brougham and LTD Landau trim levels continued to be offered, as were their LTD wagon and LTD Country Squire wagon counterparts. Although no longer available for special order by the public, the Custom 500 4-door pillared hardtop and the related Ranch Wagon were still available for fleet buyers. Ford marketed the LTD Landau as a smaller, lighter and more maneuverable alternative to larger luxury cars at a much lower price. The large Fords also continued the marketing strategy of the last decade in selling the LTD's "fine car, quiet ride" qualities.

Finally, the Thunderbird entered its final season as a full-size personal luxury car. Originally producing a two-seat model at the T-Bird's 1955 model year introduction, Ford had wisely forecast more future potential in the upscale, personal car market, and for the 1958 season, the company brought out a new four-passenger Thunderbird that was built alongside Lincoln models, and shared many of their luxury features. Since that time, the Thunderbird continued as a large personal luxury car, even adding four-door models from 1967 through 1971. Since 1972 it had shared most of its equipment and design features with the Lincoln Continental Mark IV. As previously mentioned, this would all change for 1977 as the Thunderbird would reinvent itself once again on the mid-size Ford platform.

Elite 2-Door Hardtop

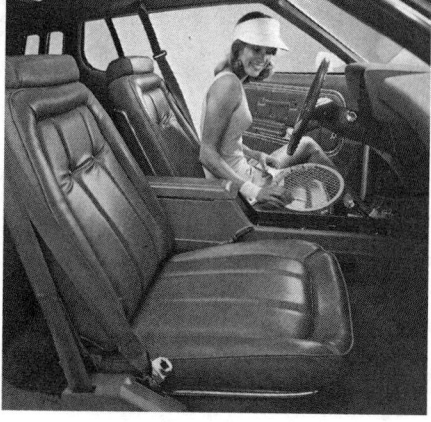

Elite interior with optional bucket seats and console

Gran Torino 4-Door Pillared Hardtop

LTD Country Squire 4-Door Station Wagon

Gran Torino Squire 4-Door Station Wagon

Granada Ghia 4-Door Sedan

Maverick 2-Door Sedan with Luxury décor group

LTD Landau 2-Door Hardtop Coupe

LTD Landau 4-Door Pillared Hardtop

Mustang II 2+2 3-Door Hatchback

Maverick 4-Door Sedan

Mustang II 2-Door Hardtop Coupe with Stallion package

Pinto 3-Door Runabout with Squire option

Mustang II 2+2 3-Door Hatchback with Stallion package and Tu-Tone paint

1976

**Thunderbird 2-Door Hardtop
with Crème and Gold luxury group**

Pinto Pony MPG 2-Door Sedan

Model year production: 1,926,420, up 21.41% from 1975.
Domestic market share: 22.27% (2nd place).
Base price range: $2,895 to $7,790.
Ford average base price: $4,438, up 1.42%.
Introduction date: October 3, 1975.
Assembly plants: Atlanta, GA (A); Oakville, Ontario, Canada (B); Mahwah, NJ (E); Dearborn, MI (F); Chicago, IL (G); Lorain, OH (H); Los Angeles, CA (J); Kansas City, MO (K); Twin Cities, MN (P); San Jose, CA (R); Allen Park, MI (S —pilot plant); Metuchen, NJ (T); Louisville, KY (U); Wayne, MI (W); St. Thomas, Ontario, Canada (X); and Wixom, MI (Y).

Data plate identification (VIN): Eleven digit code read as follows: First digit indicates year (6 = 1976); second digit indicates assembly plant code (see list above); third and fourth digits indicate model number (model number in model charts); fifth digit indicates engine code (see powertrain chart); remaining digits are sequential with beginning numbers of 100001. *Example:* 6F02Z100001 is a 1976 Ford Mustang II 2-Door Coupe, with 170.8 CID, 2-bbl. V6 engine, serial number 100001, built in Dearborn, MI.

Powertrains[1]

Engine	Net HP	Engine Code	Transmission Availability[2]		Pinto	Mustang II	Maverick	Granada	Torino & Elite	LTD	T-Bird
140 CID (2.3L) OHC, 2-bbl., 4-cyl.	92	Y	4-speed manual		S	-$272 (credit on Mach I)/ S (others)	—	—	—	—	—
				MPG:	24/35/ 28	24/34/ 27	—	—	—	—	—
				Calif.	20/31/ 24	24/34/ 27	—	—	—	—	—
			3-speed Select-Shift Cruise-O-Matic		$186	$239 (ex. Mach I)	—	—	—	—	—
				MPG:	22/32/ 26	22/31/ 26	—	—	—	—	—
				Calif.	21/32/ 25	22/31/ 26	—	—	—	—	—
170.8 CID (2.8L), 2-bbl., V6	103	Z	4-speed manual		—	S (Mach I)[3]/$266 (others)[3]	—	—	—	—	—
				MPG:	—	17/25/19	—	—	—	—	—
			3-speed Select-Shift Cruise-O-Matic		$447[4]	$239 (Mach I)/ $505 (others)	—	—	—	—	—
				MPG:	18/25/ 21	17/23/ 19	—	—	—	—	—
				Calif.	17/23/ 19	15/20/ 17	—	—	—	—	—
200 CID (3.3L), 1-bbl., 6-cyl.	81	T	3-speed manual		—	—	S	S (base)[3]	—	—	—
				MPG:	—	—	22/30/ 25	22/30/ 25	—	—	—

Engine	Net HP	Engine Code	Transmission Availability[2]	Pinto	Mustang II	Maverick	Granada	Torino & Elite	LTD	T-Bird
			3-speed Select-Shift Cruise-O-Matic	—	—	$245	$245 (base)[3]	—	—	—
			MPG:	—	—	18/23/20	18/23/20	—	—	—
250 CID (4.1L), 1-bbl., 6-cyl.	90	L	3-speed manual	—	—	$96[5]	S (Ghia)/ $96 (base)[5]	—	—	—
			MPG:	—	—	18/23/20	18/24/21	—	—	—
			Calif.	—	—	16/23/19	15/20/17	—	—	—
			3-speed Select-Shift Cruise-O-Matic	—	—	$341	$245 (Ghia)/ $341 (base)	—	—	—
			MPG:	—	—	17/21/19	16/21/18	—	—	—
			Calif.	—	—	15/21/18	15/21/17	—	—	—
302 CID (5.0L), 2-bbl., V8	134	F	3-speed manual[3]	—	—	$148	$88 (Ghia)/ $154 (base)	—	—	—
			MPG:	—	—	16/22/18	15/22/17	—	—	—
			4-speed manual[3]	—	-$18 (credit on Mach I)/ $248 (Others)	—	—	—	—	—
			MPG:	—	15/21/17			—	—	—
			3-speed Select-Shift Cruise-O-Matic	—	$184 (Mach I)/$450 (Others)	$393	$333 (Ghia)/ $399 (base)	—	—	—
			MPG:	—	16/19/17	14/20/16	15/21/17	—	—	—
			Calif.	—	12/18/14	14/19/16	12/18/14	—	—	—
351 CID (5.8L), 2-bbl., V8	152	H	3-speed Select-Shift Cruise-O-Matic	—	—	—	$378 (Ghia)/ $445 (base)	S	S (ex. Wgns.)	—
			MPG:	—	—	—	14/18/16	13/19/15	13/19/15	—
			Calif.	—	—	—	13/17/14	12/17/14	12/17/14	—
400 CID (6.6L), 2-bbl., V8	180	S	3-speed Select-Shift Cruise-O-Matic	—	—	—	—	$100	S (Wgns.)/ $100 (others)	—
			MPG:	—	—	—	—	13/18/15	13/17/14	—
			Calif.	—	—	—	—	11/16/13	11/16/13	—
460 CID (7.5L), 4-bbl., V8	202	A	3-speed Select-Shift Cruise-O-Matic	—	—	—	—	$292	$251 (Wgns.)/ $353 (others)	S

Engine	Net HP	Engine Code	Transmission Availability[2]	Pinto	Mustang II	Maverick	Granada	Torino & Elite	LTD	T-Bird
MPG:				—	—	—	—	12/16/13	12/16/13	12/16/13
Calif.				—	—	—	—	11/15/12	11/15/12	11/15/12

[1]Optional axle ratio required on cars sold in California: Pinto Pony MPG w/automatic, 3.18:1; Mustang II with V8 and automatic, 2.79:1.   [2]Unless otherwise noted: All manual transmissions are floor-shifts, except on Maverick and Granada. All automatics are column-shift, except on Pinto and Mustang II. Floor-shift is available for $27 extra on Maverick with 3-speed manual and Maverick with automatic (requires bucket seats or a Luxury Décor option), and for $29 extra on Granada (required with 302 CID V8 and 3-speed manual). Floor-shift also available for $146 in combination w/bucket seats and console on Gran Torino 2-Door and Elite.   [3]Not available in California.   [4]$500 on Pinto wagon. Not available on Pinto Pony MPG. For all other models, price includes power front disc brakes.   [5]Standard in California.

Major Options

	Pinto	Maverick	Mustang II	Granada	Torino	Elite	LTD	T-Bird
SelectAire Air conditioning	$420	$420	$420	$437	$478[1]	$478[1]	$486[1]	S[1]
Tilt steering wheel	—	—	—	$54	$59	$59	$59	$68
Fingertip speed control	—	—	—	$96	$105	$105	$107	$120
Rear window defogger	—	$40	—	$43	—	—	$43	—
Electric rear window defroster	$70[2]	—	$70	$76	$83	$83	$83	$99[2]
Tinted glass, all windows	$46	$59	$46	$47	$51	$55	$64	$66
Dual remote-control mirrors	$42	—	$42	$42	$46	$46	$43[3]	$[3]
Power windows, 2-dr./4-dr.	—	—	—	$95/$133	$104/$145	$104	$108/$161	S
Power door locks, 2-dr./4-dr.	—	—	—	$63/$88	$68/$96	$68	$68/$96	S
Power seat, 6-way w/std. seat	—	—	—	$119[5]	$130	$130	$132	$132
Front bucket seats w/console[6]	S	$147	$71	$152	$146	$146	—	—
Third row seat/DFRS (wagons)	—	—	—	—	$104	—	$126	—
AM radio	$71	$71	$71	$71	$78	$78	$78	S
AM/FM stereo	$173	$210	$173	$210	$229	$229	$229	$145
AM/FM stereo w/8-track tape	—	$299	$299	$299	$326	$326	$326	$249
Vinyl top, full (Pinto, Elite: ½)	$125	$94	$86[7]	$102	$112	S	$126[8]	S
Sunroof, power-operated	$230[9]	—	$230[9]	$517	$545	$545	$632	$716
Moonroof, power-operated	—	—	$470[9]	$786	—	$859	—	$879
Power trunk lid release	—	—	—	—	—	$17	$[4]	$[4]
Power steering	$117	$124	$117	$124	S	S	S	S
Power brakes, w/front disc	$54	$53	$54	$57[10]	S	S	S	S
Fender skirts	—	—	—	—	$41	—	$42	—
Deluxe wheel covers	$28	—	—	—	$37	S	$93	$67
Luxury/color-key wheel covers	—	—	—	—	$95	$61	$93	$
Styled Steel wheels w/trim ring	$119	$89	$51	$95	—	—	—	—
Forged/cast aluminum wheel[11]	$172	$187	$182	$207	—	$226	—	$251
Magnum 500 chrome wheels	—	—	—	—	$178	—	—	—
White sidewall tires, std. size	$33	$30	$33	$36	$39	$39	$41	S

Popular Option Groups & Packages

	Pinto	Maverick	Mustang II	Granada	Torino	Elite	LTD	T-Bird
Accent group	—	—	—	—	$45	—	—	—
Cobra II package	—	—	$325	—	—	—	—	—
Convenience group	—	$64	$35	$75	$84	$57	$104	$84
Convenience/Light group	$102	—	—	—	—	—	—	—
Deluxe bumper group	—	—	—	$61	$67	$50	$59	—
Exterior accent group	—	—	$169	—	—	—	—	—
Exterior décor group	—	$99	—	$128	—	—	—	—
Ghia luxury group	—	—	$177	—	—	—	—	—
Harmony Color group	—	—	—	—	—	—	$99	—
Interior décor group	—	$106	—	$181	—	$384	—	—
Landau luxury group	—	—	—	—	—	—	$472[12]	—
Light group	—	$34	$41	$37	$43	$41	$79	$164
Luxury décor group	$271	$508	—	$576	—	—	—	$[12]
Luxury décor interior group	—	$217	$117	—	—	—	—	—

	Pinto	Maverick	Mustang II	Granada	Torino	Elite	LTD	T-Bird
Protection group	$134	$39	$43	$39	$42	$34	$55	$87
Rallye package	—	—	$237	—	—	—	—	—
Sports Coupe package	—	—	—	$482	—	—	—	—
Stallion group	$283	$329	$72	—	—	—	—	—
Squire option	$305	—	—	—	—	—	—	—
Squire Brougham option	—	—	—	—	$184	—	$266	—
Turnpike convenience group	—	—	—	—	—	—	—	$172
Visibility group	—	—	—	$47	—	—	—	—
Wagon Brougham option	—	—	—	—	—	—	$396	—

—= Not Available; S = Standard equipment. [1]SelectAire air conditioner w/automatic temperature control is available for $520 on Torino and Elite, $566 on full-size Fords, and $88 on Thunderbird. [2]Price includes tinted rear window on Pinto. Thunderbird also offers a combination electric windshield and rear window for $355. [3]Standard on LTD Landau. On Thunderbird, LH is standard; RH available in Convenience group. [4]Available only in Convenience group on LTD and LTD Brougham (standard on Landau), or in Power Lock group on Thunderbird, consisting of power door locks and power trunk lid release for $86. [5]4-way power seat on Granada. [6]Bucket seats only on Pinto and Maverick, console not available. Bucket seats standard on Mustang II, price shown is for console. Bucket seats available only on Gran Torino Sport at no cost, with price shown for console. [7]Half (landau) vinyl roof on Mustang II Ghia coupe is available for no charge. [8]Available on wagons for $151. N/C on LTD Brougham and Landau 2-doors. [9]Manually operated. Not available on Mustang II 2+2 or Mach I models. [10]Four-wheel power disc brakes on Granada available for $210. [11]Forged aluminum wheels are deep-dish design on Elite and Thunderbird. Granada has lacy aluminum spoke wheels. [12]Available on Country Squire wagon for $708. Thunderbird offers the following luxury groups priced with velour (vinyl on Lipstick) trim/leather trim: Lipstick, $337/$546; Bordeaux, $624/$700; Crème and gold, $717/$793.

Paint Colors

	Code	Thunderbird	Others		Code	Thunderbird	Others
Black	1C	x	x	Dark Brown metallic	5Q	x	x
Silver metallic	1G		x	Saddle Bronze metallic	5T		x
Medium Slate Blue metallic	1H		x	Tan Glow metallic[2]	5U		x
Silver Starfire metallic[1]	1J	x		Orange	61		x
Dove Gray	1N	x	x	Bright Yellow	6E		x
Coral	2A		x	Cream	6P	x	x
Bright Red	2B		x	Tan	6U	x	x
Burgundy Fire metallic[1]	2G	x		Medium Gold metallic	6V		x
Dark Red	2M	x	x	Light Gold	6W		x
Bright Red	2R		x	Bright Yellow Gold Starfire			
Dark Red metallic	2S	x		metallic[1]	6Y	x	
Medium Bright Blue metallic	3E		x	Light Jade	7A	x	
Bright Dark Blue metallic	3G	x	x	Medium Jade Diamond Flare			
Silver Blue Glow metallic[2]	3M		x	metallic[1]	7F	x	
Blue Starfire metallic[1]	3P	x		Light Aqua metallic	7Q		x
Light Blue	3S	x	x	Chartreuse	7R		x
Dark Jade metallic	46	x	x	White	9D	x	x
Light Green	47		x				
Medium Ivy Bronze metallic	4T		x				
Dark Yellow Green metallic	4V		x				
Ginger Bronze Starfire metallic[1]	51	x					

In two-tone combinations, first two digits are lower color, and second two digits are upper color. [1]Starfire metallic paints are $204 extra. [2]Metallic glow paints are $54 extra on Pinto, Maverick, Mustang II, and Granada; $59 extra on Torino, Elite, LTD and Thunderbird.

Pinto

"The tough, small economy car that's fun to drive."

Nameplate year of origin: 1971.
Current bodystyle lifespan: 1971 through 1980.
Predecessor to this model: None.
Replacement for this model: Escort (1981 to 1985).
Percentage of division's production: 15.06%.
Corporate siblings: Mercury Bobcat.
Primary competition: AMC Gremlin, Chevrolet Vega, and Dodge Colt.
Notable changes: New grille and minor trim and detail changes.

Measurements

	Sedan	Runabout	Wagon
Wheelbase	94.5"	94.5"	94.5"
Length	169.0"	169.0"	178.8"
Width	69.4"	69.4"	69.7"
Height	50.6"	50.6"	52.0"
Legroom — front	40.8"	40.8"	40.8"
Legroom — rear	30.7"	30.7"	30.7"

Major standard equipment: All-vinyl high-back front bucket seats, mini-front console, color-keyed carpeting, bright front and rear window moldings, bright belt molding, rack-and-pinion steering, manual front disc brakes, hubcaps, and A78 × 13 BSW tires. Pony deletes: Mini-console and bright belt molding, and replaces carpeting w/rubber floor mat. Runabout adds: Color-keyed load floor carpeting, fold-down rear seat, and rear liftgate. Station wagon adds: Flip-out rear quarter windows, and B78 × 13 BSW tires.

Measurements (cont.)

	Sedan	Runabout	Wagon
Headroom — front	37.3"	37.3"	37.9"
Headroom — rear	36.2"	36.2"	39.3"
Cargo capacity (cu. ft.)	6.3	6.1*	31.3*
Fuel capacity (gals.)	13.0	13.0	14.0

*With rear seat folded down, Runabout, 29.0 cu. ft.; Wagon, 57.2 cu. ft.

Models Available

	Model No.	Base MSRP	Change from LY	Shipping Wt. (lbs.)	Model Year Production	Change from LY
Pinto Pony 2-Door Sedan	10	$2,895	NEW	2450	NA*	NEW
Pinto 2-Door Sedan	10	$3,025	+9.25%	2452	92,264	+43.98%
Pinto 3-Dr. Runabout (hatchback)	11	$3,200	+7.24%	2482	92,540	+34.27%
Pinto 2-Door Station Wagon	12	$3,365	+6.72%	2635	105,328	+16.05%
TOTALS	Avg. price	$3,121	+5.14%	Production	290,132	+29.66%

*Production kept as combined total with Pinto 2-door sedan.

Mustang II

"Our small, sporty personal car."

Nameplate year of origin: 1964 (also used on a 1963 show car).
Current bodystyle lifespan: 1974 through 1978.
Predecessor to this model: Mustang (1971 to 1973).
Replacement for this model: Mustang (1979 to 1993).
Percentage of division's production: 9.74%.
Corporate siblings: None.
Primary competition: Chevrolet Monza, Mercury Capri, and Pontiac Sunbird.
Notable changes: Minor trim and detail changes.
Major standard equipment: Low-back vinyl bucket seats, color-keyed cut-pile carpeting, soft vinyl and carpet door trim panels, European-type armrests, woodtone I/P appliqués, two-spoke steering wheel, courtesy lights, gauges (including tachometer, fuel, ammeter and temperature), bright windshield and rear window molding, bright drip rail, belt and center pillar molding, color-keyed urethane coated bumpers, full wheel covers, and BR78 × 13 BSW tires. 2+2 adds: Fold-down rear seat, liftgate w/hydraulic struts, and styled steel wheels. Ghia adds (to 2-door): Choice of Westminster cloth or super-soft vinyl low-back bucket seats, shag carpeting, deluxe color-keyed seat belts, soft-vinyl headlining, quartz crystal digital clock, dual remote control outside color-keyed mirrors, vinyl insert bodyside molding, vinyl roof, Ghia identification, and spoke style wheel covers. Mach I adds (to 2+2): Dual remote control outside color-keyed mirrors, specific Mach I lower bodyside and liftgate paint stripes and identification, styled steel wheels w/wheel trim rings, and BR70 × 13 B/WL tires.

Measurements

	Coupe	3-Door
Wheelbase	96.2"	96.2"
Length	175.0"	175.0"
Width	70.2"	70.2"
Height	50.0"	49.7"
Legroom — front	37.2"	37.2"
Legroom — rear	27.7"	27.7"
Headroom — front	37.2"	37.2"
Headroom — rear	35.9"	34.1"
Cargo capacity (cu. ft.)	6.7	22.8*
Fuel capacity (gals.)**	13.0	13.0

*With rear seat folded down. **16.5 gallons with optional V8 engine.

Models Available

	Model No.	Base MSRP	Change from LY	Shipping Wt. (lbs.)	Model Year Production	Change from LY
Mustang II 2-Door Hardtop Coupe	02	$3,525	-0.11%	2678	78,508	-7.81%
Mustang II 2+2 3-Door (hatchback)	03	$3,781	-0.97%	2706	62,312	+107.44%
Mustang II Ghia 2-Door Hardtop Coupe	04	$3,859	-2.01%	2729	37,515	-28.30%
Mustang II Mach I 3-Door (hatchback)	05	$4,209	+0.50%	2822	9,232	-56.17%
TOTALS	Avg. price	$3,844	-0.64%	Production	187,567	-0.53%

Maverick

"The proven family compact."

Nameplate year of origin: 1970.
Current bodystyle lifespan: 1970 through 1977.
Predecessor to this model: Falcon (1966 to 1969).
Replacement for this model: Fairmont (1978 to 1983).
Percentage of division's production: 7.25%.
Corporate siblings: Mercury Comet.
Primary competition: AMC Hornet, Chevrolet Nova, and Plymouth Valiant.
Notable changes: New grille and minor trim and detail changes.
Major standard equipment: Random stripe cloth-and-vinyl front bench seat, nylon loop pile carpeting, illuminated I/P controls, two-spoke color-keyed steering wheel and column, flipper rear quarter window (2-door), bright drip rail and wheel opening moldings, bright hubcaps, and C78 × 14 BSW tires.

Measurements

	2-Door	4-Door
Wheelbase	103.0"	109.9"
Length	187.0"	193.9"
Width	70.5"	70.5"
Height	52.9"	52.9"
Legroom — front	40.7"	40.7"
Legroom — rear	32.0"	36.2"
Headroom — front	37.5"	37.8"
Headroom — rear	36.0"	36.7"
Cargo capacity (cu. ft.)	11.3	13.1
Fuel capacity (gals.)	16.0	16.0

1976

Models Available

	Model No.	Base MSRP	Change from LY	Shipping Wt. (lbs.)	Model Year Production	Change from LY
Maverick 2-Door Sedan	91	$3,117	+3.04%	2873	60,611	-4.41%
Maverick 4-Door Sedan	92	$3,189	+4.18%	2763	79,076	-12.81%
TOTALS		*Avg. price* $3,153	+0.97%		*Production* 139,687	-14.08%

Granada

"America's success car."

Nameplate year of origin: 1975.
Current bodystyle lifespan: 1975 through 1980.
Predecessor to this model: None.
Replacement for this model: Granada (1981 to 1982).
Percentage of division's production: 28.49%.
Corporate siblings: Mercury Monarch.
Primary competition: Chevrolet Nova, Dodge Aspen, Plymouth Volaré, and Pontiac Ventura.
Notable changes: Minor trim and detail changes.
Major standard equipment: Vinyl front bench seat, 12-oz. cut-pile carpeting, burled walnut I/P appliqués, two rear seat ashtrays, luggage compartment mat, mitered corner door frame moldings (4-door), bright front and rear window moldings, bright beltline molding, bright drip rail and wheel opening moldings, opera window w/bright moldings (2-door), hood ornament, full wheel covers, and DR78 × 14

Measurements

Wheelbase	109.9"
Length	197.7"
Width	74.0"
Height	53.4"
Legroom — front	41.1"
Legroom — rear	36.0"
Headroom — front	38.5"
Headroom — rear	37.6"
Cargo capacity (cu. ft.)	14.4*
Fuel capacity (gals.)	19.2

*Sedan has 14.1 cu. ft. Ghia models have 0.4 cu. ft. less.

BSW tires. Ghia adds: Kasman cloth "Flight Bench" front seat, 18-oz. cut-pile carpeting, deluxe door trim, luxury steering wheel, digital clock, Ghia interior ornamentation, day/night rearview mirror, deluxe color-keyed seat belts, rear door courtesy light switches (4-door), LH remote control mirror, opera window Ghia crests (2-door), center pillar appliqué w/Ghia crest (4-door), vinyl insert bodyside and wheel lip moldings, vinyl lower rear panel appliqué w/decklid tape stripes, hood and bodyside tape stripes, luggage compartment carpeting w/side linings and spare tire cover, deluxe sound and ride package, unique Ghia wheel covers, and WSW tires.

Models Available

	Model No.	Base MSRP	Change from LY	Shipping Wt. (lbs.)	Model Year Production	Change from LY
Granada 2-Door Sedan	81	$3,707	+0.24%	3119	161,618	+60.32%
Granada 4-Door Sedan	82	$3,798	+1.12%	3168	287,923	+143.66%
Granada Ghia 2-Door Sedan	83	$4,265	+0.95%	3280	46,786	+16.88%
Granada Ghia 4-Door Sedan	84	$4,355	+1.68%	3339	52,457	+20.17%
TOTALS	*Avg. price*	$4,031	+1.02%	*Production*	548,784	+81.32%

Torino

"Full-size value in a mid-size car."

Nameplate year of origin: 1968.
Current bodystyle lifespan: 1972 through 1976.
Predecessor to this model: Fairlane and Torino (1970 to 1971).
Replacement for this model: LTD II (1977 to 1979).
Percentage of division's production: 10.02%.
Corporate siblings: Mercury Montego.
Primary competition: AMC Matador, Chevrolet Chevelle, Dodge Charger/Coronet, Plymouth Fury, and Pontiac Le-Mans.
Notable changes: Minor trim and detail changes.
Major standard equipment: Cloth-and-vinyl front bench seat, color-keyed cut-pile carpeting, windshield and rear window bright moldings, quarter window moldings, bright drip rail and belt moldings, power front disc brakes, power steering, hubcaps, and HR78 × 14 BSW tires. Wagon adds: Three-way tailgate, fold-down second seat, removable cargo floor carpeting, and bright tailgate window molding. Gran Torino adds: Cloth and vinyl front bench seat, distinctive Gran Torino ornamentation, bright rocker panel and rear extension moldings, wheel lip moldings, and paint filled lower back panel molding. Gran Torino wagon adds: Pleated all-vinyl bench seat and interior trim. Gran Torino Brougham adds: Westminster cloth or super-soft all-vinyl split front seat w/dual fold-down center armrests, luxury cut-pile carpeting, unique door trim, bright pedal trim, woodtone I/P and door panel appliqués, vinyl roof, opera window (2-door), front and rear panel rocker extension moldings, unique red lens appliqué on lower back panel, hood ornament, exterior Brougham identification, deluxe wheel covers, and WSW tires. Gran Torino Squire adds: Power tailgate window, simulated woodgrain bodyside paneling, and full wheel covers.

Measurements

	2-Doors	4-Doors	Wagons
Wheelbase	114.0"	118.0"	118.0"
Length	214.4"	218.4"	223.2"
Width	79.3"	79.3"	79.0"*
Height	52.6"	53.3"	54.9"
Legroom — front	42.5"	42.5"	42.5"
Legroom — rear	33.2"	37.8"	37.3"
Headroom — front	37.6"	38.3"	38.4"
Headroom — rear	36.2"	37.0"	38.5"
Cargo capacity (cu. ft.)	16.5	16.5	84.9
Fuel capacity (gals.)	26.5	26.5	21.2

*Squire is 79.9."

Models Available

	Model No.	Base MSRP	Change from LY	Shipping Wt. (lbs.)	Model Year Production	Change from LY
Torino 2-Door Formal Hardtop	25	$4,172	+5.51%	3976	34,518	+157.71%
Torino 4-Door Pillared Hardtop	27	$4,206	+6.29%	4061	17,394	-24.14%
Torino 4-Door, 2-S., 6-p. Wagon	40	$4,521	+4.27%	4409	17,281	+30.02%
Gran Torino 2-Door Formal Hardtop	30	$4,461	+3.41%	3999	23,939	-32.23%
Gran Torino 4-Door Pillared Hardtop	31	$4,495	+3.62%	4081	40,568	-23.69%
Gran Torino 4-Door, 2-S., 6-p. Wagon	42	$4,769	+2.05%	4428	30,596	+27.74%
Gran Torino Brougham 2-Door Formal HT	32	$4,883	+1.62%	4063	3,183	-34.36%
Gran Torino Brougham 4-Door Pillared HT	33	$4,915	+1.61%	4144	4,473	-24.56%
Gran Torino Squire 4-Dr., 2-S., 6-p. Wgn.	43	$5,083	+2.65%	4454	21,144	-24.87%
TOTALS	*Avg. price*	$4,612	+2.58%	*Production*	193,096	-1.03%

Elite

"Fine car styling, road car spirit, mid-size price."

Nameplate year of origin: 1974.
Current bodystyle lifespan: 1974 through 1976.
Predecessor to this model: None.
Replacement for this model: None.
Percentage of division's production: 7.60%.
Corporate siblings: Mercury Cougar XR-7.
Primary competition: AMC Matador coupe, Chevrolet Monte Carlo, Dodge Charger SE, and Pontiac Grand Prix.
Notable changes: Minor trim and detail changes.
Major standard equipment: Westminster cloth-and-vinyl front bench seat, color-keyed cut-pile carpeting on floor and lower door panels, deluxe color-keyed seat belts, deluxe steering wheel, five-pod I/P, simulated walnut woodgrain appliqués on I/P, door and steering wheel, tinted glass, full vinyl roof, unique twin opera windows, bright windshield and rear window moldings, quarter window moldings, bright drip rail and belt moldings, wide bodyside protective moldings w/vinyl insert color-keyed to roof, wide wheel lip moldings, distinctive Elite ornamentation, front bumper guards, power front disc brakes, power steering, full wheel covers, and HR78 × 15 BSW tires.

Measurements

Wheelbase	114.0"
Length	216.4"
Width	78.5"
Height	53.0"
Legroom — front	42.1"
Legroom — rear	32.2"
Headroom — front	37.4"
Headroom — rear	36.3"
Cargo capacity (cu. ft.)	16.5
Fuel capacity (gals.)	26.5

1976

Models Available

	Model No.	Base MSRP	Change from LY	Shipping Wt. (lbs.)	Model Year Production	Change from LY
Elite 2-Door Hardtop	21	$4,879	+2.35%	4169	146,475	+18.73%
TOTALS	*Avg. price*	$4,879	+2.35%	*Production*	146,475	+18.73%

LTD

"New, luxurious standard-size cars."

Nameplate year of origin: 1965.
Current bodystyle lifespan: 1971 through 1978 (restyled in 1973 and 1975).
Predecessor to this model: Custom/Galaxie/LTD (1969 to 1970).
Replacement for this model: LTD (1979 to 1991).
Percentage of division's production: 19.09%.
Corporate siblings: Mercury Marquis.
Primary competition: Chevrolet Impala/Caprice, Dodge Monaco, Plymouth Gran Fury, and Pontiac Catalina.
Notable changes: Minor trim and detail changes.
Major standard equipment: Cloth and vinyl front bench seat, color-keyed nylon loop pile carpeting, woodtone I/P and door appliqués, deluxe steering wheel, interior courtesy lighting, bright moldings (front and rear window, belt, drip rail, rear hood edge, and wheel lip), vinyl insert bodyside

Measurements

	2-Doors	4-Doors	Wagons
Wheelbase	121.0"	121.0"	121.0"
Length	223.9"	223.9"	225.6"
Width	79.5"	79.5"	79.9"
Height	53.7"	54.7"	56.7"
Legroom — front	41.5"	41.5"	41.7"
Legroom — rear	35.5"	38.3"	37.1"
Headroom — front	37.3"	38.3"	38.7"
Headroom — rear	37.3"	37.3"	39.1"
Cargo capacity (cu. ft.)	21.9	21.9	94.6*
Fuel capacity (gals.)	24.2	24.2	21.0

Additional 9.1 cu. ft. of below deck storage on 2-seat wagons, and 5.4 cu. ft. on wagons w/DFRS.

moldings, textured lower rear appliqué w/bright Reflex surround molding, rocker panel molding, C-pillar LTD crest (4-door), hood ornament, front bumper guards, chrome hubcaps, and HR78 × 15 BSW tires. Wagon adds: Load floor carpeting, power tailgate window, sound insulation package, and JR78 × 15 BSW tires. Brougham adds: Westminster knit cloth and vinyl front bench seat w/fold-down center armrest, bright seat side shields, electric clock, luggage compartment light, rear door courtesy light switch, half-vinyl roof (2-door), full vinyl roof (4-door), dual accent paint stripes, rocker panel front and rear extension moldings, and full wheel covers. Landau adds: Niles knit cloth and vinyl "Flight Bench" seat w/fold-down center armrests, front seatback assist straps, 22-oz. shag carpeting, digital clock, luxury steering wheel, luxury door trim panels, burled walnut I/P and door trim appliqués, bright chrome windsplit and fender peak moldings, wide vinyl insert bodyside moldings, hidden headlights, and full Landau wheel covers. Country Squire adds: Simulated woodgrain exterior bodyside and tailgate paneling, cargo area light, Landau series hood ornament and hidden headlights, bright hood windsplit molding, and full wheel covers.

Models Available

	Model No.	Base MSRP	Change from LY	Shipping Wt. (lbs.)	Model Year Production	Change from LY
LTD 2-Door Pillared Hardtop	62	$4,780	+0.57%	4257	62,844	+32.49%
LTD 4-Door Pillared Hardtop	63	$4,752	+0.85%	4303	108,168	+31.30%
LTD 4-Door, 2-Seat, 6-p. Station Wagon	74	$5,207	+0.95%	4752	30,237	+31.84%
LTD Brougham 2-Door Pillared Hardtop	68	$5,299	+3.23%	4299	20,863	-35.46%
LTD Brougham 4-Door Pillared Hardtop	66	$5,245	+2.86%	4332	32,917	-20.78%
LTD Country Squire 4-Door, 2-seat, 6-p. Wagon	76	$5,523	+1.53%	4809	47,379	+97.37%
LTD Landau 2-Door Pillared Hardtop	65	$5,613	+2.35%	4346	29,673	+10.23%
LTD Landau 4-Door Pillared Hardtop	64	$5,560	+1.96%	4394	35,663	+9.71%
TOTALS	*Avg. price*	$5,247	+4.15%	*Production*	367,744	+5.66%

Thunderbird

"Possibly the best luxury car buy in the world today."

Nameplate year of origin: 1955.
Current bodystyle lifespan: 1972 through 1976.
Predecessor to this model: Thunderbird (1967 to 1971; restyled in 1970).
Replacement for this model: Thunderbird (1977 to 1979).
Percentage of division's production: 2.75%.
Corporate siblings: Lincoln Continental Mark IV.
Primary competition: Buick Riviera and Oldsmobile Toronado.
Notable changes: Minor trim and detail changes.
Major standard equipment: Aurora nylon cloth and vinyl individually adjustable split bench front seat w/fold-down center armrests and automatic seatback release, deluxe seat belts, courtesy lighting (dome, door, under dash, glove box and ashtray), 24 oz. cut pile carpeting, simulated woodgrain I/P and door panel trim, door panel assist straps, electric clock, AM/FM stereo radio, power windows, power interior ventilation system, Odense grain vinyl roof w/opera windows, fully lined luggage compartment w/light, unique Thunderbird hood ornament, bright moldings (rear hood edge, beltline, drip rails), bodyside and partial wheel lip moldings w/protective vinyl insert, sound insulation package, power steering, power front disc brakes, full wheel covers, and JR78 × 15 WSW tires.

Measurements

Wheelbase	120.4"
Length	225.7"
Width	79.7"
Height	52.8"
Legroom — front	42.0"
Legroom — rear	36.4"
Headroom — front	37.5"
Headroom — rear	36.8"
Cargo capacity (cu. ft.)	13.5
Fuel capacity (gals.)	26.5

Models Available

	Model No.	Base MSRP	Change from LY	Shipping Wt. (lbs.)	Model Year Production	Change from LY
Thunderbird 2-Door Hardtop	87	$7,790	+1.16%	4808	52,935	+24.01%
TOTALS	*Avg. price*	$7,790	+1.16%	*Production*	52,935	+24.01%

LINCOLN

"Designed to justify your high expectations of riding comfort, style and luxury."

With the past few years of record high production, Lincoln began its 56th season with few changes, but high expectations. Most of the changes for the new model year involved making some previously standard equipment optional, thereby allowing Lincoln to reduce prices slightly while its main rival raised prices about 5 percent. In essence, features added as new standard items for 1975 were removed, taking the standard equipment list back to 1974 levels. The strategy was successful as production increased more than 20 percent above the 1975 total.

The expansion of the color luxury groups and the new Designer series was part of a marketing plan to allow consumers to individualize their Mark IV. It began with the popular Silver luxury group, and expanded from there. This year brought four new color luxury groups and an even more exclusive Designer Series based on the special upholstery and color selections of four of the world's top designers — Cartier, Bill Blass, Emilio Pucci and Hubert de Givenchy. Each edition also had the designer's signature, placed next to the Lincoln emblem, etched in gold on the opera window, and on an instrument panel plate.

During the previous three years, significant improvements had been made to the fuel and emissions systems, such as continual upgrades of Ford's solid-state ignition system, and the introduction of catalytic converters for 1975. Other changes such as lighter weight materials and lower rolling-resistance radial tires contributed to lower weight and higher fuel economy. Since 1974, estimated fuel economy for Lincoln sedans had improved 50 percent, proving to consumers that luxury cars could get better gas mileage.

The 1976 model year would be the last for Lincoln to sell only traditional full-size cars. While downsizing of the Continental and Mark series would not happen until 1980, a third model based on the much smaller Granada would be introduced partway through the 1977 model year. This new model would give Lincoln the opportunity to offer its buyers improved fuel economy in a smaller package as an alternative to the Cadillac Seville.

Continental 2-Door Hardtop Coupe

Continental 4-Door Sedan with
Town Car package and Coach roof

Continental Mark IV 2-Door Hardtop

Continental Mark IV 2-Door Hardtop

Model year production: 124,756, up 22.50% from 1975.
Domestic market share: 1.44% (12th place).
Base price range: $9,142 to $11,060.
Lincoln average base price: $9,832, down 1.53%.
Introduction date: October 3, 1975.
Assembly plants: Allen Park, MI (S—*pilot plant*); and Wixom, MI (Y).
Data plate identification (VIN): Eleven digit code read as follows: First digit indicates year (6 = 1976); second digit indicates assembly plant code (see list above); third and fourth digits indicate model number (model number in model charts); fifth digit indicates engine code (see powertrain chart); remaining digits are sequential with beginning numbers of 800001. *Example:* 6Y82A800001 is a 1976 Lincoln Continental 4-Door Sedan, with 460 CID, 4-bbl. V8 engine, serial number 800001, built in Wixom, MI.

Powertrains

Engine	Net HP	Engine Code	Transmission Availability[1]	Continental	Mark IV
460 CID (7.5L), 4-bbl., V8	202	A	3-speed Select-Shift Automatic	S	S
			MPG:	12/16/13	12/16/13
			Calif.	11/15/12	11/15/12

Major Options

	Continental	Mark IV		Continental	Mark IV
Air conditioning, Auto-Temp	S	S	Intermittent windshield wipers	$28	$28
Tilt steering wheel	$69	$69	Anti-theft alarm system	$115	$115
Automatic speed control	$117	$117	AM/FM stereo, w/power antenna	$148	$148
Electric rear window defroster	$81	$81	AM/FM stereo w/8-track tape	$288	—
Quick Defrost, front/rear windows	—	$360	AM/FM stereo w/automatic search	$300	$300
Tinted glass, all windows	S	S	Vinyl top, full[2]	$168	S
Power windows	S	S	Moonroof, power-operated & tinted	$885	$885
Power front vent windows	$80	$80	Sunroof, power-operated	$701	$701
Power door locks	$[1]	$[1]	Power brakes, four wheel disc	$172	S
Power seat, 6-way w/pass. recliner	$76	$76	"Sure-Track" antilock brake system	$263	$263
Leather seating upholstery	$220	$235	Extended range fuel tank, 32 gals.	$100	—
Illuminated dual visor vanity mirrors	$100	$100	Luxury wheel covers	$83	S
RH remote-control mirror, LH std.	$31	$31	Forged aluminum wheels	$300	$300

Popular Option Groups & Packages

	Continental	Mark IV		Continental	Mark IV
Appearance protection group	$61	$53	Red/Rose luxury group	—	$552
Bill Blass designer series	—	$1,500[3]	Saddle/White luxury group	—	$477
Blue Diamond luxury group	—	$477[4]	Security Lock group	$17	$17
Cartier designer series	—	$1,500[3]	Town Coupe/Town Car package	$731	—
Dark Jade/Light Jade luxury group	—	$477[4]	Versailles luxury group	—	$1,033
Emilio Pucci designer series	—	$1,500[3]			
Givenchy designer series	—	$1,500			
Gold/Cream luxury group	—	$477[4]			
Headlamp Convenience group	$101	—			
Jade/White luxury group	—	$477[4]			
Lipstick/White luxury group	—	$477			
Power Lock convenience group	$113[1]	$87			

— = *Not Available; S = Standard equipment.* [1]*Power door locks require optional Power Lock convenience group. Price on coupe is $87.* [2]*Landau vinyl roof on Continental coupe for $341, and on Continental Mark IV for $512. A coach vinyl roof is available on Continental w/Town Car or Town Coupe option for $333. Coach vinyl roof includes unique wide chrome beltline and roof bow moldings, custom half-vinyl roof w/full padding, and a frenched rear window.* [3]*With Versailles cloth interior, price is $2,000.* [4]*Price is $552 when ordered with moondust or diamond fire paint.*

Paint Colors

	Code		Code		Code
Black	1C	Dark Red	2M	Lipstick Red[4]	2U
Silver Diamond Fire metallic[1]	1J	Medium Taupe Diamond Fire		Dark Blue metallic	3G
Black Diamond Fire metallic[1]	1L	metallic[1,3]	2P	Blue Diamond Fire metallic[1]	3P
Dove Gray	1N	Dark Red metallic	2S	Light Blue	3S
Red Moondust metallic[2]	2G	Rose Crystal metallic[4]	2T	Aqua Blue Diamond Fire metallic[1,4]	45

	Code		Code
Dark Jade metallic	46	Cream	6P
Ginger Bronze Diamond Fire		Tan	6U
metallic[1]	51	Bright Yellow Gold Diamond Fire	
Unique Gold Diamond Fire		metallic[1]	6Y
metallic[1,3]	54	Light Jade	7A
Medium Chestnut Diamond Fire		Light Jade Crystal metallic[4]	7B
metallic[1]	59	Light Apricot Crystal metallic[4]	8A
Dark Brown metallic	5Q	White	9D

In two-tone combinations, first two digits are lower color, and second two digits are upper color. [1]*Diamond Fire metallic paints available for $193 extra.* [2]*Moondust metallic paints available for $147 extra.* [3]*Available only on Continental.* [4]*Available only on Continental Mark IV.*

Continental

"For 1976 Continental owners, this is a year in which the luxury car becomes even more personal."

Nameplate year of origin: 1940 (1961 as a regular series).
Current bodystyle lifespan: 1970 through 1979 (restyled in 1974).
Predecessor to this model: Continental (1961 to 1969).
Replacement for this model: Town Car (1980 to 1991).
Percentage of division's production: 55.02%.
Corporate siblings: None.
Primary competition: Cadillac deVille.
Notable changes: Minor trim and detail changes.
Major standard equipment: Luxury cloth front bench seat w/six-way power adjustment, folding center armrests in front and rear seat, cut-pile carpeting, simulated wood appliqués on I/P and steering wheel, Cartier-signed digital clock, tilt steering wheel, power windows, AM radio w/power antenna, automatic temperature control air conditioning, visor–mounted vanity mirror, LH remote control rearview mirror, tinted glass, power deck lid release, interior lighting (ashtrays, courtesy, glove box, luggage compartment, dome/map, and rear seat reading), gray carpeted luggage compartment, full vinyl roof, cornering lights, rear wheel opening fender skirts, front bumper guards, full wheel covers, and KR78 × 15 WSW tires.

Measurements

	Coupe	Sedan
Wheelbase	127.2"	127.2"
Length	232.9"	232.9"
Width	80.0"	80.0"
Height	55.3"	55.5"
Legroom — front	42.0"	42.0"
Legroom — rear	40.8"	41.6"
Headroom — front	38.4"	38.5"
Headroom — rear	38.1"	38.6"
Cargo capacity (cu. ft.)	20.2	20.2
Fuel capacity (gals.)	24.2	24.2

Models Available

	Model No.	Base MSRP	Change from LY	Shipping Wt. (lbs.)	Model Year Production	Change from LY
Continental 2-Door Hardtop Coupe	81	$9,142	-0.78%	5035	24,663	+16.42%
Continental 4-Door Sedan	82	$9,293	-3.76%	5083	43,983	+31.24%
TOTALS		*Avg. price* $9,218	-2.31%		*Production* 68,646	+25.50%

Continental Mark IV

"A legend in its own lifetime and one of the world's most admired, most desired motorcars."

Nameplate year of origin: 1956 (Continental Mark II).
Current bodystyle lifespan: 1972 through 1976.
Predecessor to this model: Continental Mark III (1969 to 1971).
Replacement for this model: Continental Mark V (1977 to 1979).
Percentage of division's production: 44.98%.
Corporate siblings: Ford Thunderbird.
Primary competition: Buick Riviera, Cadillac Eldorado, and Oldsmobile Toronado.

Measurements

Wheelbase	120.4"
Length	228.1"
Width	79.8"
Height	53.5"
Legroom — front	42.2"
Legroom — rear	34.2"

1976

Notable changes: Minor trim and detail changes.

Major standard equipment: Luxury cloth "Twin Comfort" lounge seats w/six-way power adjustment, folding center armrests in front and rear seat, simulated burl walnut woodgrain appliqué on I/P and steering wheel, color-keyed cut-pile carpeting, electric Cartier Timepiece, trip odometer, power windows, AM radio w/power antenna, automatic temperature control air conditioning, LH remote control rearview mirror, tinted glass, interior lighting (ashtrays, courtesy, glove box, I/P warning, luggage compartment, engine compartment, dome/map, and C-pillar reading), power decklid release, black carpeted luggage compartment, full vinyl roof w/opera window, dual custom pinstripe, customer monogram on doors, cornering lights, bumper guards, luxury wheel covers, and KR78 × 15 WSW tires.

Measurements (cont.)

Headroom — front	37.5"
Headroom — rear	36.6"
Cargo capacity (cu. ft.)	14.9
Fuel capacity (gals.)	26.5

Models Available

	Model No.	Base MSRP	Change from LY	Shipping Wt. (lbs.)	Model Year Production	Change from LY
Continental Mark IV 2-Door Hardtop	89	$11,060	-0.20%	5051	56,110	+19.02%
TOTALS	*Avg. price*	$11,060	-0.20%	*Production*	56,110	+19.02%

MERCURY

"Test any car against our car ... at the sign of the cat."

After a steady flow of new and restyled models in the last few years, the 1976 model year was relatively quiet for Mercury. The Capri name returned on a car that looked very similar to the previous version but, on closer inspection, proved to have modest styling updates and a new hatchback body. A new Capri II moniker emphasized the changes. The domestic part of the Mercury lineup received only minor changes for what would be a good but not spectacular year. Production was up significantly, but still fell short of the industry average increase, and as a result, Mercury's share of the market shrank slightly. However, by the end of the model year, Mercury landed in sixth place in overall production, moving ahead of an ailing Plymouth line for the first time in history.

The Comet received a minor front-end styling update, using the same grille as before, but with the vertical bars blacked out, giving the grille a horizontal bar appearance. New parking/turn signal lights with clear lenses, and without the crosshair ornamentation seen the prior year, went with the revised look. Also, the headlamp bezel surround was painted black this year rather than argent as in the past. Another change, unnoticeable to most consumers, was the addition of a larger gas tank, to extend the driving range.

The remainder of the domestic Mercury line continued with few changes. In fact, sales literature and advertising for the Montego, Cougar and Marquis lines use the exact same

pictures between 1975 and 1976 models, as there were no visual differences. This would mark the final season for the mid-size Montego, although its name would return nearly three decades later on a far different Mercury. Also, some previously standard equipment was made optional on the Cougar and Marquis to help minimize price increases.

The new-for-1975 Bobcat and Monarch received very few changes as they entered their second year. Bobcat models equipped with the standard 140 CID four-cylinder engine were officially known as the Bobcat MPG for 1976, but unlike their Pinto cousins, Bobcats did not bear the MPG nameplate on the car. The Monarch, which Mercury liked to compare to the Mercedes-Benz 280 for ride and handling performance, remained the top-selling Mercury series for a second year in a row.

As noted above, the Capri returned for the 1976 model year with a slightly revised name and a mostly new body. Where the previous model had been a coupe, the Capri II was a hatchback. Bodyside styling was also changed with elimination of the "hockey stick" crease and faux air intakes in front of the rear wheels of the original Capri. The hood line was lowered slightly at the front, and the rear quarter windows were enlarged. Returning mostly unchanged were the long hood, short deck profile, the quadruple headlight arrangement, and interior design. Split folding rear seats were available as an option with the new hatchback, giving the new Capri II more cargo room. Several small changes were made to the chassis and powertrain including moving the fuel tank to a location under the spare tire well, and a new one-piece drive shaft, replacing the original's two-piece shaft. The Capri II came in base and Ghia models, with optional Décor and "S" trim packages. The "S" trim package came in three special editions, the "Black Cat" (black with gold stripes and gold wheels), the rare "White Cat" and the even rarer "Crimson Cat." On all three editions, most of the chrome trim was either blacked out or replaced with gold trim, and the seat upholstery was black vinyl with gold cloth inserts.

1976

Capri II 3-Door Hatchback with Décor group

Bobcat 3-Door Runabout
with woodgrain option

Bobcat Villager 2-Door Station Wagon

Comet 2-Door Sedan with Sports Accent group

Comet 4-Door Sedan

Cougar XR-7 2-Door Hardtop

Grand Marquis 2-Door Hardtop
with Tu-Tone group

Grand Monarch Ghia 4-Door Sedan

Marquis 4-Door Pillared Hardtop

Monarch 2-Door Sedan

Cougar XR-7 interior

Montego MX 2-Door Hardtop

Montego MX Brougham
4-Door Pillared Hardtop

Montego MX Villager 4-Door Station Wagon

Model year production: 480,361, up 18.71% from 1975.
Domestic market share: 5.55% (6th place).
Base price range: $3,338 to $6,528.
Mercury average base price: $4,761, up 1.94%.
Introduction date: October 3, 1975. Capri II introduced March 1975.
Assembly plants: Atlanta, GA (A); Oakville, Ontario, Canada (B); Mahwah, NJ (E); Lorain, OH (H); Kansas City, MO (K); San Jose, CA (R); Metuchen, NJ (T); Wayne, MI (W); and St. Louis, MO (Z). Capri assembly plant: Cologne, Germany (A).
Data plate identification (VIN): Eleven digit code read as follows: First digit indicates year (6 = 1976); second digit indicates assembly plant code (see list above); third and fourth digits indicate model number (model number in model charts); fifth digit indicates engine code (see power-train chart); Remaining digits are sequential with beginning numbers of 500001. *Example:* 6K31F500001 is a 1976 Mercury Comet 2-Door sedan, with 302 CID, 2-bbl. V8 engine, serial number 500001, built in Kansas City (Claycomo), MO. 1976 Capri II uses eleven digit code read as follows: First digit indicates country of origin (G = Germany); second digit indicates assembly plant code (see list above); third and fourth digits indicate model number (model number in model charts); fifth digit indicates year (R = 1976); sixth digit indicates month; remaining digits are sequential with beginning number of 00001.

Powertrains[1]

Engine	Net HP	Engine Code	Transmission Availability[2]		Bobcat	Capri II	Comet	Monarch	Cougar XR-7 & Montego	Marquis
140 CID (2.3L) OHC, 2-bbl., 4-cyl.	82	Y	4-speed manual		S	S	—	—	—	—
				MPG:	24/34/27	24/34/27	—	—	—	—
				Calif.	20/31/25	20/31/25	—	—	—	—
			3-speed Select-Shift Cruise-O-Matic[3]		$186	$276	—	—	—	—
				MPG:	22/31/26	22/31/26	—	—	—	—
				Calif.	21/32/26	21/32/26	—	—	—	—
170.8 CID (2.8L), 2-bbl., V6	105	Z	4-speed manual		—	$272	—	—	—	—
				MPG:	—	18/28/21	—	—	—	—
				Calif.	—	16/27/20	—	—	—	—
			3-speed Select-Shift Cruise-O-Matic[3]		$450[4]	$548	—	—	—	—
				MPG:	17/25/20	18/25/21	—	—	—	—
				Calif.	17/23/20	17/23/20	—	—	—	—
200 CID (3.3L), 1-bbl., 6-cyl.	84	T	3-speed manual		—	—	S[5]	S (base)[5]	—	—
				MPG:	—	—	22/30/25	22/30/25	—	—
			3-speed Select-Shift Cruise-O-Matic		—	—	$245	$245 (base)[5]	—	—
				MPG:	—	—	18/23/20	18/23/20	—	—
250 CID (4.1L), 1-bbl., 6-cyl.	91	L	3-speed manual		—	—	$96[6]	S (Ghia)[6]/ $96 (base)	—	—
				MPG:	—	—	18/23/20	18/24/21	—	—
				Calif.	—	—	16/23/19	15/20/17	—	—
			3-speed Select-Shift Cruise-O-Matic		—	—	$341	$245 (Ghia)/ $341 (base)	—	—
				MPG:	—	—	17/21/19	16/21/18	—	—

Engine	Net HP	Engine Code	Transmission Availability[2]		Bobcat	Capri II	Comet	Monarch	Cougar XR-7 & Montego	Marquis
				Calif.	—	—	15/21/18	16/21/18	—	—
302 CID (5.0L), 2-bbl., V8	140	F	3-speed manual[5]		—	—	$148	$88 (Ghia)/$154 (base)	—	—
				MPG:	—	—	16/22/18	15/22/17	—	—
			3-speed Select-Shift Cruise-O-Matic		—	—	$393	$333 (Ghia)/$399 (base)	—	—
				MPG:	—	—	14/20/16	15/21/17	—	—
				Calif.	—	—	14/19/16	12/18/14	—	—
351 CID (5.8L), 2-bbl., V8	162	H	3-speed Select-Shift Cruise-O-Matic		—	—	—	$379 (Ghia)/$445 (base)	S	—
				MPG:	—	—	—	14/18/16	13/19/15	—
				Calif.	—	—	—	13/17/14	12/17/14	—
400 CID (6.6L), 2-bbl., V8	170	S	3-speed Select-Shift Cruise-O-Matic		—	—	—	—	$93	S
				MPG:	—	—	—	—	13/17/14	13/17/14
				Calif.	—	—	—	—	11/16/13	11/16/13
460 CID (7.5L), 4-bbl., V8	220	A	3-speed Select-Shift Cruise-O-Matic		—	—	—	—	$292	$212
				MPG:	—	—	—	—	12/16/13	12/16/13
				Calif.	—	—	—	—	11/15/12	11/15/12

[1]Optional axle ratio required on Capri II w/140 CID 4-cyl. and 4-speed manual sold in California: 3.22:1. [2]Unless otherwise noted: All manual transmissions are floor-shift, except on Comet and Monarch. All automatics are column-shift, except on Bobcat, Capri II and Cougar XR-7 w/standard bucket seats. Floor-shift is available for $27 extra on Comet with 3-speed manual and Comet with automatic (requires bucket seats or a Custom option), and for $27 extra on Monarch (requires bucket seats, and is required with 302 CID V8 and 3-speed manual). [3]Three-speed (German-built) automatic transmission on Capri II. [4]$500 on Villager wagon. For all models, price includes power front disc brakes. [5]Not available in California. [6]Standard on all models in California.

Major Options

	Bobcat	Capri II	Comet	Monarch	Montego	Cougar	Marquis
Air conditioning[1]	$420	$429	$420	$437	$483	$483	$512
Tilt steering wheel	—	—	—	$54	$59	$59	$59
Automatic speed control	—	—	—	$93	$101	$101	$101
Rear window defogger	—	—	$43	$43	—	—	—
Electric rear window defroster	$67	$69	—	$73	$80	$80	$80
Tinted glass, all windows	$46	$47	$45	$47	$53	$53	$66
Dual remote control mirrors	$13[2]	$12[2]	$27[2]	$42	$50	$50	$14[2]
Power windows, 2-dr./4-dr.	—	—	—	$95/$133	$104/$145	$104	$109/$162
Power front vent windows, 4-door	—	—	—	—	—	—	$79
Power door locks, 2-dr./4-dr.	—	—	—	$63/$88	$68/$96	$68	$[3]
Power seat, 6-way w/std. seating	—	—	—	$119[4]	$130	$130	$132
Front bucket seats w/console[5]	S	S	$119	$125	—	$143	—
Leather interior trim	—	—	—	$181	—	—	—
Dual facing rear seats (wagons)	—	—	—	—	$108	—	$126
AM radio	$71	$71	$71	$71	$78	$78	$78
AM/FM stereo (non-stereo, Capri)	$173	$136	$216	$210	$236	$236	$236

1976

	Bobcat	Capri II	Comet	Monarch	Montego	Cougar	Marquis
AM/FM stereo w/8-track tape	$192	—	$299	$299	$339	$339	$339
Anti-theft alarm system	—	—	—	—	—	—	$100
Vinyl top, full	$86	$95	$89	$102	$112	$41	$126[6]
Moonroof, power-operated	—	—	—	$786	—	$859	—
Sunroof, power-operated	$230[7]	$181[7]	—	$517	—	$545	$632
Power trunk lid release	—	—	—	—	$17	$17	$3[3]
Power steering	$117	$129	$124	$124	S	S	S
Power brakes, w/front disc	$54	S	$53	$57[8]	S	S	S[8]
"Sure-Track" anti-lock brakes	—	—	—	—	—	—	$217
Rear wheel opening fender skirts	—	—	—	—	—	—	$41
Deluxe wheel covers	—	—	$29	S	$32	—	$26
Luxury wheel covers	—	—	—	—	$68	S	$76
Styled steel wheels w/trim rings	$48	—	$89	$89	$97	$93	—
Cast aluminum sport wheels	—	$113	—	$201	—	$199	—
Forged aluminum wheels	$136	—	$192	—	—	—	$237
White sidewall tires, std. size	$33	—	$30	$36	$38	$39	$41

Popular Option Groups & Packages

	Bobcat	Capri II	Comet	Monarch	Montego	Cougar	Marquis
Appearance protection group	$35	—	$39	$39	$42	$34	$55
Bumper protection group	$64	—	$64	$64	$53	$53	$53
Convenience group	—	—	—	$75	$66	$57	—
Custom interior option	—	—	$222	—	—	—	—
Custom option package	—	—	$496	—	—	—	—
Décor group	—	$217	—	$181	—	—	—
Grand Marquis luxury trim group[9]	—	—	—	—	—	—	$305
Light/Convenience group	$92	—	—	—	—	—	—
Lock convenience group	—	—	—	—	—	—	$86–$112
Runabout woodgrain group	$214	—	—	—	—	—	—
"S" option group	$96	$241	—	$482	—	—	—
Security Lock group	—	—	$16	$17	$18	—	$18
Sports Accent group/trim option	$269	—	$235	—	—	—	—
Visibility light group	—	—	—	—	$82	$82	$118
Visibility/Convenience group[10]	—	—	$51	$122	—	—	—

—= Not Available; S = Standard equipment. [1]Air conditioner w/automatic temperature control is available for $520 on Montego and Cougar, and for $549 on Marquis. [2]LH remote only on Bobcat and Capri II. LH remote and RH manual on Comet. LH only on Marquis. [3]Available only as part of the Lock Convenience group. [4]Power four-way seat on Monarch. [5]Bucket seats only on Bobcat, console not available. Available on Comet 2-door, and without console. For Monarch, available only on Ghia, or with Décor group. [6]Vinyl roof available on station wagons for $151. [7]Manually operated. [8]Power four wheel disc brakes available for $210 on Monarch, and for $170 on Marquis. [9]Available only on Colony Park wagon. Standard on Grand Marquis. [10]For Monarch, Convenience and Visibility groups are separate options. Price given is for both.

Paint Colors

Mercury	Code	Mercury	Code	Capri	Code
Black	1C	Dark Brown metallic	5Q	Bronze metallic	45
Silver metallic	1G	Saddle Bronze metallic	5T	Light Green metallic	56
Medium Slate Blue metallic	1H	Tan Glamour metallic[1]	5U	White	B6
Bright Red	2B	Bright Yellow	6E	Orange	D5
Dark Red	2M	Cream	6P	Dark Red	06
Bright Red	2R	Medium Dark Gold Glamour		Yellow	T6
Bright Blue metallic	3E	metallic[1]	6T	Matte Black	NA
Bright Dark Blue metallic	3G	Tan	6U		
Silver Blue Glamour metallic[1]	3M	Medium Gold Glamour metallic[1]	6V	
Light Blue	3S	Light Gold	6W	
Dark Jade metallic	46	White	9D	
Light Green	47			
Medium Ivy Bronze Glamour				
metallic[1]	4T	Capri	Code	
Dark Yellow Green metallic	4V	Medium Blue metallic	16	
Medium Chestnut metallic	5M	Silver metallic	35	

In two-tone combinations, first two digits are lower color, and second two digits are upper color. Two-tones available on Comet (roof two-tone for $33, and lower-body for $55), Marquis Brougham for $145, and Grand Marquis for $59. [1]Glamour paints available for $54 extra on Bobcat, Comet, and Monarch, $59 on Montego, Cougar, and Marquis.

Bobcat

*"Spirited, sporty styling with plenty of room — Mercury Bobcat
is a small car you can be proud to call your own!"*

Nameplate year of origin: 1975.
Current bodystyle lifespan: 1975 through 1980.
Predecessor to this model: None.
Replacement for this model: Lynx (1981 to 1985).
Percentage of division's production: 9.92%.
Corporate siblings: Ford Pinto.
Primary competition: AMC Gremlin, Dodge Colt, and Pontiac Astre.
Notable changes: Minor trim and detail changes.
Major standard equipment: All-vinyl low-back front bucket seats, color-keyed cut-pile carpeting, carpeted cargo area, fold-down rear seat, I/P mini console, simulated woodgrain parking brake lever handle and I/P appliqué, deluxe two-spoke steering wheel, deluxe safety belts, bright window and belt moldings, B-pillar bright molding, protective bodyside molding w/vinyl insert, wide wheel lip moldings, rocker panel moldings, rack-and-pinion steering, manual front disc brakes, Styled steel wheels w/center ornament, and B78 × 13 BSW tires. Villager adds: Flip-out rear quarter windows, deluxe sound insulation, "Liftgate Ajar" warning system, standard size wheel lip moldings, and simulated rosewood paneling on bodysides and rear tailgate panel.

Measurements

	Runabout	Wagon
Wheelbase	94.5"	94.8"
Length	169.0"	178.8"
Width	69.4"	69.7"
Height	50.6"	52.0"
Legroom — front	40.8"	40.8"
Legroom — rear	30.4"	30.4"
Headroom — front	37.3"	37.9"
Headroom — rear	35.8"	38.9"
Cargo capacity (cu. ft.)	6.1*	57.6
Fuel capacity (gals.)	13.0	14.0

With rear seat folded down, 25.4 cu. ft.

1976

Models Available

	Model No.	Base MSRP	Change from LY	Shipping Wt. (lbs.)	Model Year Production	Change from LY
Bobcat 3-Door Runabout (HBK)	20	$3,338	+4.67%	2535	28,905	+39.97%
Bobcat 2-Door Villager Wagon	22	$3,643	+4.65%	2668	18,731	+37.90%
TOTALS		*Avg. price* $3,335	+4.66%		*Production* 47,636	+39.15%

Capri II

"A great road machine admirably suited to today's driving."

Nameplate year of origin: 1971 (Originally used on 1952 Lincoln Capri).
Current bodystyle lifespan: 1971 through 1977 (major restyle for 1976).
Predecessor to this model: None.
Replacement for this model: Capri (1979 to 1986).
Primary competition: Buick Skyhawk, Chevrolet Cosworth Vega, and Ford Mustang II 2+2.
Notable changes: New hatchback body configuration and new sheetmetal.
Major standard equipment: All-vinyl front bucket seats w/recliners, full-loop carpeting, front armrests, recessed door handles, fold-down rear seats, day/night rear view mirror, power front disc brakes, rack-and-pinion steering, styled steel wheels, and 165SR × 13 BSW tires. Ghia adds: Embossed vinyl front bucket seats, individually folding rear seats, front floor console, simulated woodgrain I/P appliqué, opening rear quarter window, assist handles front and rear on headliner, and upgraded sound insulation package.

Measurements

Wheelbase	100.9"
Length	174.8"
Width	66.9"
Height	51.0"
Legroom — front	41.4"
Legroom — rear	31.1"
Headroom — front	37.4"
Headroom — rear	35.9"
Cargo capacity (cu. ft.)	7.4*
Fuel capacity (gals.)	12.7

With rear seat folded down, 22.6 cu. ft.

Models Available

	Model No.	Base MSRP	Change from LY	Shipping Wt. (lbs.)	Model Year Sales (est.)	Change from LY
Capri II 3-Door Sport Coupe	EC	$4,117	+15.45%	2513	NA	NA

	Model No.	Base MSRP	Change from LY	Shipping Wt. (lbs.)	Model Year Sales (est.)	Change from LY
Capri II Ghia 3-Door Sport Coupe	EC	$4,740	NEW	2562	NA	NEW
TOTALS	*Avg. price* $4,429		+20.13%		*Production* 85,000	NA

Comet

"Big-car soundness and small car practicality!"

Nameplate year of origin: 1960.
Current bodystyle lifespan: 1971 through 1977.
Predecessor to this model: Comet (1964 to 1965).
Replacement for this model: Zephyr (1978 to 1983).
Percentage of division's production: 7.51%.
Corporate siblings: Ford Maverick.
Primary competition: AMC Hornet and Dodge Dart.
Notable changes: Minor trim and detail changes.
Major standard equipment: Cloth-and-vinyl front bench seat, color-keyed 12-oz. cut-pile carpeting, front and rear ashtrays w/front lighted, two-speed windshield wipers w/washers, deluxe two-spoke steering wheel, bright window moldings, deluxe sound insulation package, hubcaps, and C78 × 14 BSW tires.

Measurements

	2-Door	4-Door
Wheelbase	103.0"	109.9"
Length	189.5"	196.4"
Width	70.5"	70.5"
Height	52.9"	52.9"
Legroom — front	40.7"	40.7"
Legroom — rear	31.8"	36.0"
Headroom — front	37.5"	37.8"
Headroom — rear	35.9"	36.5"
Cargo capacity (cu. ft.)	11.3	12.8
Fuel capacity (gals.)	19.2	19.2

Models Available

	Model No.	Base MSRP	Change from LY	Shipping Wt. (lbs.)	Model Year Production	Change from LY
Comet 2-Door Sedan	31	$3,398	+5.01%	2952	15,068	-33.82%
Comet 4-Door Sedan	30	$3,465	+5.96%	3058	21,006	-32.41%
TOTALS		*Avg. price* $3,432	+5.49%		*Production* 36,074	-33.01%

Monarch

"Precision packaging and advanced engineering provide for Monarch's ease of handling."

Nameplate year of origin: 1975 (used on Canadian Ford brand from 1946 to 1961).
Current bodystyle lifespan: 1975 through 1980.
Predecessor to this model: None.
Replacement for this model: Cougar (1981 to 1982).
Percentage of division's production: 30.36%.
Corporate siblings: Ford Granada.
Primary competition: Buick Skylark, Dodge Aspen, and Oldsmobile Omega.
Notable changes: Minor trim and detail changes.
Major standard equipment: All-vinyl front bucket seats w/recliners, 18-oz. cut-pile carpeting, simulated high-gloss woodgrain I/P appliqué, locking glove box, bright window moldings, full-length bodyside molding, stand-up hood ornament, manual front disc brakes, wheel covers, and DR78 × 14 BSW tires. Ghia adds: Super-soft all-vinyl front bucket seats w/recliners, 22-oz. cut-pile shag carpeting, deluxe color-keyed seat belts, luxury steering wheel, digital clock, day/night rearview mirror, LH remote control outside mirror, carpeted luggage compartment, deluxe sound and ride package, Odense grain vinyl roof, chrome lower bodyside moldings w/Odense grain vinyl inserts, wheel lip moldings, unique Ghia wheel covers, and DR78 × 14 WSW tires. Grand Ghia adds: Choice of velour or soft grain leather front bucket seats w/recliners, front floor console, deep cut-pile carpeting, dome/dual map reading light, power windows, Normande grain vinyl roof, power steering, power four wheel disc brakes, and cast aluminum spoke wheels.

Measurements

Wheelbase	109.9"
Length	197.7"
Width	74.1"
Height	53.4"
Legroom — front	41.1"
Legroom — rear	36.0"
Headroom — front	38.5"
Headroom — rear	37.6"
Cargo capacity (cu. ft.)	14.1
Fuel capacity (gals.)	19.2

Models Available

	Model No.	Base MSRP	Change from LY	Shipping Wt. (lbs.)	Model Year Production	Change from LY
Monarch 2-Door Sedan	35	$3,773	+0.24%	3111	47,466	+62.83%
Monarch 4-Door Sedan	34	$3,864	+1.10%	3164	56,351	+64.26%
Monarch Ghia 2-Door Sedan	38	$4,331	+0.93%	3200	14,950	-15.80%
Monarch Ghia 4-Door Sedan	37	$4,422	+1.68%	3250	27,056	+19.07%
Monarch Grand Ghia 4-Door Sedan	37	$5,740	+6.79%	3401	*	NA
TOTALS	Avg. price	$4,426	+2.45%		Production 145,823	+40.30%

Monarch Grand Ghia production was kept as combined with Ghia 4-door due to being the same model number.

Montego

"Our stylish, roomy mid-size Mercury."

Nameplate year of origin: 1968.
Current bodystyle lifespan: 1972 through 1976.
Predecessor to this model: Montego (1970 to 1971).
Replacement for this model: Cougar (1977 to 1979).
Percentage of division's sales volume: 10.64%.
Corporate siblings: Ford Torino.
Primary competition: AMC Matador, Buick Century, Dodge Coronet and Charger, Oldsmobile Cutlass, and Pontiac Le-Mans.
Notable changes: No significant changes.
Major standard equipment: Choice of cloth-and-vinyl or all-vinyl low-back front bench seat, color-keyed carpeting, black I/P trim, windshield and rear window bright moldings, drip rail moldings, front bumper guards, power steering, power front disc brakes, hubcaps, and HR78 × 14 BSW tires. MX adds: Simulated woodgrain I/P trim, side window bright moldings, wheel lip moldings, rocker panel moldings, upper bodyside tape stripes, and deluxe sound insulation. MX wagon adds: All-vinyl front bench seat, three-way tailgate, carpeted load floor, and front and rear bumper guards. MX Brougham adds: Choice of Brougham cloth-and-vinyl or super-soft vinyl "Flight Bench" front seat w/fold-down center armrest, deluxe two-spoke steering wheel w/woodgrain inserts, Brougham door panels w/lower carpeting, and deluxe wheel covers. MX Villager adds: All-vinyl bench "Flight Bench" front seat w/fold-down center armrest, power tailgate window, and simulated woodgrain bodyside and tailgate paneling w/bright surround moldings.

Measurements

	2-Doors	4-Doors	Wagons
Wheelbase	114.0"	118.0"	118.0"
Length	215.7"	219.0"	223.2"
Width	78.6"	78.6"	79.6"
Height	52.6"	53.3"	54.9"
Legroom — front	42.5"	42.5"	42.1"
Legroom — rear	33.2"	37.8"	37.1"
Headroom — front	37.9"	38.5"	38.3"
Headroom — rear	36.5"	37.3"	38.6"
Cargo capacity (cu. ft.)	16.5	16.5	93.0*
Fuel capacity (gals.)	26.5	26.5	21.0

Includes 8.1 cu. ft. of hidden cargo space.

Models Available

	Model No.	Base MSRP	Change from LY	Shipping Wt. (lbs.)	Model Year Production	Change from LY
Montego 2-Door Hardtop	03	$4,299	+5.06%	4057	2,287	-43.54%
Montego 4-Door Pillared Hardtop	02	$4,343	+5.21%	4130	3,403	-17.84%
Montego MX 2-Door Hardtop	07	$4,465	+3.74%	4085	12,367	-9.51%
Montego MX 4-Door Pillared Hardtop	04	$4,498	+3.93%	4133	12,666	-21.00%
Montego MX 4-Door, 6-p. Wagon	08	$4,778	+2.23%	4478	5,012	+11.18%
Montego MX Brougham 2-Door Hardtop	11	$4,621	+3.77%	4097	3,905	-55.58%
Montego MX Brougham 4-Dr. Pillared HT	10	$4,670	+3.82%	4150	5,043	-38.76%
Montego MX Villager 4-Door, 6-p. Wagon	18	$5,065	+3.18%	4478	6,412	+11.44%
TOTALS	Avg. price	$4,592	+3.82%		Production 51,095	-21.61%

Cougar XR-7

"Elegant, sophisticated Cougar XR-7 is a unique breed of cat—
the luxurious personal-size car that puts you way out in front of the rest!"

Nameplate year of origin: 1967.
Current bodystyle lifespan: 1974 through 1976.
Predecessor to this model: Cougar (1971 to 1973).
Replacement for this model: Cougar XR-7 (1977 to 1979).
Percentage of division's production: 17.44%.
Corporate siblings: Ford Elite.
Primary competition: Buick Regal, Dodge Charger SE, Oldsmobile Cutlass Supreme, and Pontiac Grand Prix.
Notable changes: Minor trim and detail changes.
Major standard equipment: Choice of super soft all-vinyl "Twin Comfort" Lounge front seat or all-vinyl bucket seats w/console, deep cut-pile carpeting, performance instrument panel, deluxe steering wheel, courtesy lights, landau vinyl roof w/opera windows, power steering, power front disc brakes, specially tuned suspension system, luxury wheel covers, and HR78 × 14 BSW tires.

Measurements

Wheelbase	114.0"
Length	214.5"
Width	78.5"
Height	52.6"
Legroom — front	42.1"
Legroom — rear	32.2"
Headroom — front	37.4"
Headroom — rear	36.3"
Cargo capacity (cu. ft.)	16.5
Fuel capacity (gals.)	26.5

Models Available

	Model No.	Base MSRP	Change from LY	Shipping Wt. (lbs.)	Model Year Production	Change from LY
Cougar XR-7 2-Door Hardtop	93	$5,125	-1.78%	4168	83,765	+32.99%
TOTALS	*Avg. price*	$5,125	-1.78%	*Production*	83,765	+32.99%

Marquis

"Beautiful in styling, rich in appointments
and innovative in engineering."

Nameplate year of origin: 1967.
Current bodystyle lifespan: 1971 through 1978 (restyled in 1973 and 1975).
Predecessor to this model: Marquis (1969 to 1970).
Replacement for this model: Marquis & Grand Marquis (1979 to 1991).
Percentage of division's sales volume: 24.14%.
Corporate siblings: Ford LTD.
Primary competition: Buick Electra 225 and Estate Wagon, Chrysler Newport and Town & Country, Oldsmobile Ninety-Eight and Custom Cruiser, and Pontiac Bonneville and Grand Safari.
Notable changes: Minor trim and detail changes.
Major standard equipment: Cloth-and-vinyl front bench seat w/fold-down center armrest, deep cut-pile carpeting, simulated woodgrain I/P and steering wheel appliqué, deluxe

Measurements

	2-Doors	4-Doors	Wagons
Wheelbase	124.0"	124.0"	121.0"
Length	229.0"	229.0"	225.7"
Width	79.6"	79.6"	79.8"
Height	53.8"	54.7"	57.1"
Legroom — front	41.6"	41.7"	41.7"
Legroom — rear	35.7"	39.9"	37.1"
Headroom — front	37.6"	38.5"	39.0"
Headroom — rear	36.7"	37.5"	39.5"
Cargo capacity (cu. ft.)	22.7	22.7	103.7*
Fuel capacity (gals.)**	24.2	24.2	21.0

*Includes 9.1 cu. ft. of hidden cargo space.   **Extended range fuel tank, available for $94, adds 10 gallons to wagons and 8 gallons to others.

two-spoke steering wheel, dome light, sound insulation package, bright window moldings, rocker panel molding, front bumper guards, hubcaps, and HR78 × 15 BSW tires. Wagon adds: All-vinyl front bench seat w/fold-down center armrest, bright seat side shields, cargo area light, three-way tailgate w/power tailgate window, and JR78 × 15 BSW tires. Brougham adds: Brougham cloth and vinyl front bench seat w/fold-down center armrest, rear seat center armrests, 22-oz. cut-pile carpeting, Brougham door panels w/lower carpeted panel and door pull assist strap, electric clock, RH visor vanity mirror, LH remote control mirror, courtesy lights, power windows, front and rear door courtesy lights, luggage compartment light, vinyl roof, full-length fender peak molding, rear wheel opening fender skirts, and Brougham wheel covers. Colony Park adds: All vinyl "Flight Bench" front seat w/fold-down center armrest, cargo area light, three-way tailgate w/power tailgate window, and simulated rosewood exterior paneling on bodysides and tailgate. Grand Marquis adds: Choice of leather-and-velour or leather-with-vinyl individually adjustable Twin Comfort Lounge seats, digital clock, carpeted luggage compartment, dome/dual map reading light, tinted glass, full-length body-side protective molding w/color-keyed vinyl insert, hood and deck lid paint stripes, specific Grand Marquis nameplates and orna-mentation, and JR78 × 15 BSW tires.

Models Available

	Model No.	Base MSRP	Change from LY	Shipping Wt. (lbs.)	Model Year Production	Change from LY
Marquis 2-Door Hardtop	66	$5,063	+0.28%	4436	10,450	+53.52%
Marquis 4-Door Pillared Hardtop	63	$5,063	-1.02%	4460	28,212	+40.65%
Marquis 4-Door, 6-pass. Station Wagon	74	$5,275	-2.51%	4796	2,493	+30.93%
Marquis Colony Park 4-Door, 6-pass. Wagon	76	$5,590	-0.14%	4878	15,114	+29.71%
Marquis Brougham 2-Door Hardtop	64	$5,955	-0.28%	4652	10,431	+46.40%
Marquis Brougham 4-Door Pillared Hardtop	62	$6,035	-0.03%	4693	22,411	+13.95%
Grand Marquis 2-Door Hardtop	61	$6,439	+0.56%	4679	9,207	+86.19%
Grand Marquis 4-Door Pillared Hardtop	60	$6,528	+0.91%	4723	17,650	+43.41%
TOTALS	*Avg. price*	$5,744	-0.23%	*Production*	115,968	+37.30%

1976

OLDSMOBILE

"Can we build one for you?"

Oldsmobile entered the 1976 model year anticipating an even better year than 1975 had been. The GM mid-luxury level division seemed to be at the right place at the right time, as American consumers turned from sporty muscle cars to more luxury with a dash of sport. Confidence in their product was so high that the inside front cover of Oldsmobile sales literature this year proudly proclaimed that "Over a half-million Americans will buy a '76 Olds...." A seemingly bold statement if it had come from other manufacturers, it was believable since many years had passed since Oldsmobile sold fewer than a half million cars. In fact, Oldsmobile's success this year was entirely due to the overwhelming popularity of the mid-size Cutlass series, which itself sold over a half million cars and ousted the full-size Chevrolet from the top selling series spot it had held for most of the past two decades. To further emphasize the extent of the Cutlass "craze," this single series would outsell the entire lines of Mercury, Ply-mouth, Dodge, Chrysler, American Motors, and the com-bined totals of Cadillac and Lincoln.

New frontal styling again appeared on the Cutlass line, with the most significant change being the adoption of dual rectangular headlights. Also significant was new bodyside styling for the coupes. Most importantly, a third "opera-win-dow" coupe, the Cutlass Supreme Brougham, joined the line and was an immediate success, ending the year as the second

best selling Cutlass, right behind the Supreme coupe. Price-wise, the new Supreme Brougham was slotted between the Supreme and the Salon, with an emphasis on interior luxury. Standard features included pillow-like "loose cushion" seating surfaces in velour and knit fabric with a 60/40 divided front seat, and deep-pile carpeting covering the floors. Interest-ingly, this expansion on the Cutlass name would eventually lead to its overuse in the Oldsmobile line.

Cutlass front-end styling differed between the Cutlass S series and the rest of the line, much as it had in prior years. From the top edge of the new rectangular headlights to the bottom, the entire front end of the Cutlass S sloped down-ward at about a 45 degree angle, leaving the headlights in a scoop-like bezel. Parking/turn signal lights were horizontal units placed directly below the headlights, and were shared with other Cutlass models. A body-color fascia and the tra-ditional two-piece grille continued this year with each side having nine chrome-lined vertical slots on the Cutlass S. The remainder of the Cutlass line used an upright, flat-face, wa-terfall style grille divided by a body colored center panel. The grille itself consisted of two sections per side, each car-rying ten vertical bars, with a thin body colored strip between the two sections. The grille began on top of the header panel just inches from the hood opening. It ran forward several inches before dropping straight down over the front of the car to the bumper. As previously mentioned, side-by-side rectangular headlamps above horizontal parking/turn signal lights completed the new look.

Bodyside styling for all two-door Cutlass models was smoothed out this year, doing away with the lower body "pontoons" used on the larger Oldsmobiles since 1971, and the Cutlass since 1973. While four-door models still used the styling feature, the coupes now had a feature line running straight along the lower bodyside at the level of the bumper impact strips, which was also at the point where the body began to roll under to the rocker panels. An upper feature line began immediately behind the front door at door handle level, ran straight up to the belt line area, and sharply turned ninety degrees and ran to the rear of the car where it eventually created the top edge of the rear quarter panel, ending as it angled downward to meet the taillights. Otherwise, styling features of the 1976 models followed those of the prior models in most respects. One exception was that the Vista-Cruiser no longer had a standard "Vista-vent" window, making the wagon known for years as the "wagon with a view" just another station wagon. The name would be discontinued after the 1977 model year.

The 1975 Cutlass powertrain lineup was carried over into 1976, although a five-speed manual transmission, with 5th gear overdrive, was a newly available option with the 260 CID V8 engine. This sporting combination was fitted to 964 Cutlass S coupes and 862 Cutlass Supreme coupes. Power-assisted front disc brakes, previously standard only on station wagons, were now added as standard equipment to all Cutlass Salons, Supreme Broughams, and Supreme four-door sedans. The slow-selling fastback style base Cutlass coupe was dropped, and its companion sedan was rechristened as a Cutlass S sedan, leaving the Cutlass S coupe as the only fastback style two-door in the Cutlass series. The 4–4–2 package lost the louvered hood and the racing stripes on the hood and decklid. The lower bodyside stripes were much larger, however, and included the 4–4–2 identification as a graphic element. Other features of the package were unchanged, and 9,576 Cutlass S coupes were sold with the $134 option package. A new $550 option for Supreme, Supreme Brougham, and Salon coupes was a "T-top" hatch roof with removable tinted-glass panels. Two other models dropped for 1976 in-

cluded the Cutlass Supreme Cruiser and wood-panelled Vista-Cruiser wagons with third row seating, which became an option for this season.

While styling for the Toronado and relatively new Starfire was mostly unchanged this year, all other Oldsmobiles received a facelift. The Omega traded its waterfall style grille for a full chrome grille, replacing the traditional Olds body-colored center section with a narrower center chrome section. To each side were two grille sections having about 15 vertical bars apiece, and to the outer ends were vertical parking/turn signal lamps. The new design went a long way toward giving the Chevrolet Nova-based Omega an identity that compared with the popular Cutlass and the larger Delta 88 models.

The Delta 88, Custom Cruiser wagons, and the luxurious Ninety-Eight all received a new "flat-front" look, with all models carrying dual rectangular headlights mounted above horizontal parking/turn signal lamps. All models also continued to use a wide body-colored center panel, with grille inserts on each side. The Delta 88 continued to use two grille sections per side, with each section being square and holding thirteen vertical bars. The Custom Cruiser went back to sharing its front end with the Ninety-Eight series, and this year the two biggest cars in the Oldsmobile lineup used an egg-crate grille pattern being six rows high and fourteen columns across, and only one grille on each side of the center panel. The Custom Cruiser had the Olds rocket logo on the body-colored center panel, while the Ninety-Eight models had the logo on a stand-up hood ornament.

There were several model changes besides those mentioned for the Cutlass series. The Starfire had a new SX model, which had actually been introduced late in the 1975 season. SX Starfires included upgraded interiors, exterior striping and standard radial tires. In the full-sized models, the only model change was the discontinuation of the Delta 88 convertible, which coincided with the loss of all full-size GM convertibles except the Cadillac Eldorado. Lastly, there was a unique one-year-only option added for the Delta 88 Royale two-door hardtop, called the Crown Landau package. The package, which sold 4,360 units, used a stainless steel roof band with a padded landau vinyl roof that did away with the stationary rear quarter window.

Custom Cruiser 4-Door Station Wagon

Cutlass S 2-Door Colonnade Hardtop Coupe

Cutlass S 2-Door Colonnade
Hardtop Coupe with 4-4-2 package

Cutlass S 4-Door Colonnade Hardtop Sedan

Cutlass Supreme Brougham
2-Door Colonnade Hardtop Coupe

Cutlass Supreme Cruiser
4-Door, 3-Seat Station Wagon

Delta 88 instrument panel
with message center inset

Delta 88 Royale 2-Door Hardtop with Crown
Landau package

Delta 88 Royale 4-Door Town Sedan

Delta 88 Royale 4-Door Hardtop

Omega 2-Door Hatchback with SX package

Ninety-Eight Regency 2-Door Hardtop Coupe

Ninety-Eight Regency 4-Door Hardtop

Omega 4-Door Sedan

Omega F-85 2-Door Coupe

Starfire 2-Door Hatchback
Coupe with GT package

Starfire SX interior

Toronado Brougham 2-Door Hardtop Coupe

Model year production: 891,368, up 41.04% from 1975.
Domestic market share: 10.30% (3rd place).
Base price range: $3,390 to $7,137.
Oldsmobile average base price: $4,925, up 2.42%.
Introduction date: September 25, 1975.
Assembly plants: Southgate, CA (C); Doraville, GA (D); Linden, NJ (E); Framingham, MA (G); Van Nuys, CA (L); Lansing, MI (M); Arlington, TX (R); Kansas City/Fairfax, KS (X); Willow Run, MI (W); and St. Therese, Quebec, Canada (2).
Data plate identification (VIN): Thirteen digit code read as

follows: First digit indicates division (3 = Oldsmobile); second through fourth digits indicate series and body style (model number in model charts); fifth digit is engine code (see powertrain chart); sixth digit indicates model year (6 = 1976); seventh digit indicates assembly plant (see list above); remaining digits are sequential with beginning number of 100001, except for Toronado which begins with 700001. *Example:* 3L69J6X100001 is a 1976 Oldsmobile Delta 88 4-Door Town Sedan, with 350 CID, 4-bbl. V8 engine, serial number 100001, built in Kansas City/Fairfax, KS.

Powertrains

Engine	Net HP	Engine Code	Transmission Availability[1]		Starfire	Omega	Cutlass	Delta 88	98 & Custom Cruiser	Toronado
231 CID (3.8L), 2-bbl., V6[2]	105	C	4-speed manual		S	—	—	—	—	—
				MPG:	22/35/26	—	—	—	—	—
				Calif.	17/26/20	—	—	—	—	—
			5-speed manual		$244	—	—	—	—	—
				MPG:	NA	—	—	—	—	—
			3-speed Turbo Hydra-matic		$244	—	—	—	—	—
				MPG:	20/28/23	—	—	—	—	—
				Calif.	18/24/20	—	—	—	—	—
250 CID (4.0L), 1-bbl., 6-cyl.	105	D	3-speed manual		—	S	S[3]	—	—	—
				MPG:	—	17/25/20	17/25/20	—	—	—
			3-speed Turbo Hydra-matic		—	$262	$262[3]	—	—	—
				MPG:	—	18/23/20	17/22/19	—	—	—
				Calif.	—	15/21/17	15/21/17	—	—	—
260 CID (4.3L), 2-bbl., V8	110	F	3-speed manual		—	$90	$90[3]	—	—	—
				MPG:	—	16/25/19	16/26/19	—	—	—
				Calif.	—	14/21/17	14/21/16	—	—	—
			5-speed manual (ex. F85 & base 4-dr.)		—	$352	N/C[4]/$352[3]	—	—	—
				MPG:	—	NA	NA	—	—	—
			3-speed Turbo Hydra-matic		—	$352	S[4]/$352[3]	—	—	—
				MPG:	—	16/23/19	16/22/18	—	—	—
				Calif.	—	14/20/16	14/21/16	—	—	—
350 CID (5.7L), 2-bbl., 6-cyl.	145	X	3-speed Turbo Hydra-matic		—	$402[5]	—	—	—	—
				MPG:	—	14/20/17	—	—	—	—
350 CID (5.7L), 4-bbl., V8	155[6]/170	H, J or R	3-speed Turbo Hydra-matic		—	$460	S[7]/$112[4]/$460[3]	S	—	—
				MPG:	—	14/22/17	15/21/17	14/17/15	—	—
				Calif.	—	14/20/16	13/19/15	12/16/14	—	—
455 CID (7.4L), 4-bbl., V8	190/215[8]	S/T[8]	3-speed Turbo Hydra-matic		—	$126[7]/$238[4]/$583[3]	$147	S	S	—
				MPG:	—	—	13/19/15	13/18/15	13/17/14	12/17/14
				Calif.	—	—	11/19/14	11/16/13	10/15/12	10/15/12

[1]Unless otherwise specified: All 3-speed manuals are column shift. All 4- and 5-speed manuals are floor shift. All automatics are column shift, except on Starfire. Floor shift automatic is optional on Omega and Cutlass with other specified equipment at extra cost.   [2]See the 1976 Buick powertrain section for notes on the 231 (3.8L) V6 engine and availability.   [3]Except Salon, Cruiser and Vista-Cruiser.   [4]Cutlass Salon.   [5]Not available in California.   [6]Horsepower rating for Omega is 155.   [7]Cutlass Cruiser and Vista-Cruiser wagons.   [8]Horsepower rating for Toronado is 215.

Major Options

	Starfire	Omega	Cutlass	Delta 88	Custom Cruiser	Ninety-Eight	Toronado
Four-Season air conditioner[1]	$424	$452	$476	$512	$512	$512	$512
Tilt-Away steering wheel	$48	$52	$52	$53	$53	$53	$53
Tilt-and-telescope steering wheel	—	—	—	—	—	$95	$95
Cruise control	—	$73	$73	$79	$79	$79	$79
Electric rear window defroster	$66	$43[2]	$77	$78	$78	$78	$78
Dual rearview mirrors, LH remote	$27	$26	$26	$26	$26	S	S
Tinted glass, all windows	$44	$46	$50	$64	$64	$64	$64
Power windows, 2-dr./4-dr.	—	$99/$140	$99/$140	$159	$159[3]	S	S
Power door locks, 2-dr./4-dr.	—	$62/$89	$62/$89	$63/$90	$90	$63/$90	$63
Power front seat, 6-way w/std. seat	—	—	$124	$126	$126	$98[4]	$126[4]
Front bucket seats, w/console	$73[5]	$150[6]	$150[6]	—	—	—	—
Third row seat (wagons)	—	—	$133	—	—	—	—

	Starfire	Omega	Cutlass	Delta 88	Custom Cruiser	Ninety-Eight	Toronado
Air Cushion Restraint System	—	—	—	$315	—	$315	$315
AM radio	$71	$75	$79	$92	$92	$92	$92
AM/FM stereo	$219	$233	$233	$236	$236	$236	$236
AM/FM stereo w/8-track tape	$316	$337	$337	$341	$341	$341	$341
Vinyl top, full[7]	—	$91	$109	$136	—	$150[8]	$150
Hatch roof (T-top)	—	—	$550[9]	—	—	—	—
Power trunk lid release	—	—	$17	$17	—	$17	$17
Power steering, "Vari-Ratio"	$120	$136	S	S	S	S	S
Power brakes, w/front disc	$55	$58	$58[10]	S	S	S	S
Deluxe wheel covers	—	$32	$32	S	S	S	S
Wire wheel covers	—	$111	$120	$104	—	—	—
Super Stock II wheels	—	—	$64	—	—	—	—
Super Stock III wheels	$84	$89	$89	—	—	—	—
WSW tires, std. size		$38	$38	$41	$41	S	S

Popular Option Groups & Packages

	Starfire	Omega	Cutlass	Delta 88	Custom Cruiser	Ninety-Eight	Toronado
Convenience light package	—	$28	$31	—	—	—	—
Crown Landau package	—	—	—	$598	—	—	—
GT package	$391	—	—	—	—	—	—
SX package	—	$171	—	—	—	—	—
W29 4-4-2 package	—	—	$134	—	—	—	—

—= Not Available; S = Standard equipment. [1]Power steering required on Omega with V8 engines. Power brakes required on Cutlass. "Tempmatic" air conditioner with automatic climate control is available for $37 additional on Cutlass, Delta 88, Custom Cruiser, Ninety-Eight and Toronado. [2]Blower type defogger. [3]Optional remote-control mirror required. [4]Standard on Ninety-Eight Regency and Toronado Brougham. [5]Bucket seats are standard on Starfire. [6]Standard on Cutlass Salon. Swivel bucket seats included on Cutlass S, Cutlass Supreme and Cutlass Supreme coupes only. Not available on Omega sedans. [7]Landau roof available on Cutlass Salon and Supreme coupes for $109, and on Omega coupes or Ninety-Eight Luxury coupe for $150. [8]Two-door models, $162. [9]Available on Supreme, Supreme Brougham and Salon coupes only. [10]Standard on Supreme sedan, Supreme Brougham, Salon, Supreme Cruiser and Vista Cruiser.

Paint Colors

	Code		Code		Code
White	11	Lime metallic	40	Red-Orange[1]	78
Silver metallic	13	Dark Green metallic	49		
Medium Gray metallic	16	Cream	50		
Ebony Black	19	Bright Yellow[1]	51		
Light Blue metallic	28	Yellow[2]	57		
Dark Blue metallic	35	Buckskin	65		
Red metallic	36	Saddle metallic	67		
Mahogany metallic	37	Red[2]	72		

In two-tone combinations, the first two digits indicate lower color and the next two digits are the upper color. Two-tone paint available for $35 extra on Omega and Delta 88, $40 extra on Cutlass, and $48 on Custom Cruiser. [1]Available only on Starfire and Omega. [2]Available on all models except Starfire and Omega.

Starfire

"It's not just a ride — it's an experience!"

Nameplate year of origin: 1954 (as designation for 98 convertible); 1961 (as series).
Current bodystyle lifespan: 1975 through 1980
Predecessor to this model: None.
Replacement for this model: Firenza (1982 to 1988).
Percentage of division's production: 3.27%.
Corporate siblings: Buick Skyhawk and Chevrolet Monza (closely related to Chevrolet Vega and Pontiac Astre).
Primary competition: AMC Pacer, Ford Mustang II and "Lincoln-Mercury" Capri.
Notable changes: Minor trim and detail changes. New SX model added.
Major standard equipment: High-backed bucket seats in grained vinyl with choice of velour or perforated-vinyl inserts, folding rear seatback, plush-pile carpeting on all floor surfaces and rear seatback, deluxe steering wheel, door panel map pockets,

Measurements

Wheelbase	97.0"
Length	179.3"
Width	65.4"
Height	50.0"
Legroom — front	42.9"
Legroom — rear	35.6"
Headroom — front	37.7"
Headroom — rear	36.3"
Cargo capacity (cu. ft.)	28.1*
Fuel capacity (gals.)	18.5

*With rear seat folded down.

simulated woodgrain I/P appliqué, I/P gauges including tachometer, dual speed wipers w/washers, functional B-pillar vent louvers, chrome window surround moldings, chrome front and rear wheel lip moldings, manual front disc brakes, hubcaps, and B78 × 13 BSW tires. SX adds: Choice of Prado velour w/Dover brushed knit or soft Wallaby vinyl high-back bucket seats, deluxe sport steering wheel w/brushed metal spokes and padded softgrip rim, bodyside striping, and BR78 × 13 BSW tires.

Models Available

	Model No.	Base MSRP	Change from LY	Shipping Wt. (lbs.)	Model Year Production	Change from LY
Starfire 2-Door Hatchback Coupe	T07	$3,882	+0.23%	2857	8,305	-73.28%
Starfire SX 2-Door Hatchback Coupe	D07	$4,062	NEW	2864	20,854	NEW
TOTALS	Avg. price	$3,972	+2.56%		Production 29,159	-6.18%

Omega

"Omega is more than a lot of compact. It's a lot of little Oldsmobile—still at a compact price!"

Nameplate year of origin: 1973.
Current bodystyle lifespan: 1975 through 1979.
Predecessor to this model: Omega (1973 to 1974).
Replacement for this model: Omega (1980 to 1984).
Percentage of division's production: 6.53%.
Corporate siblings: Buick Skylark, Chevrolet Nova, and Pontiac Ventura.
Primary competition: Dodge Aspen and Mercury Monarch.
Notable changes: Revised front-end styling and minor trim and detail changes.
Major standard equipment: F85: Racine fabric front bench seat, rubber floor mat, hubcaps, and E78 × 14 BSW tires. Omega adds: Choice of Nero knit vinyl or brushed knit fabric front bench seat, cut-pile carpeting, simulated woodgrain I/P appliqués, door-operated dome lamps, dual speed wipers w/washers, chrome window surround moldings, roof drip moldings, chrome front and rear wheel opening moldings, and F78 × 14 BSW tires. Hatchback model adds: Fold-down rear seat. Brougham adds: Choice of brushed knit Dover cloth or Wallaby vinyl front bench seat, deluxe steering wheel, map pockets in doors, vinyl insert bodyside moldings, bright rocker panel molding, and stand-up hood ornament.

Measurements

	Coupe & HBK	Sedan
Wheelbase	111.0"	111.0"
Length	199.6"	199.6"
Width	69.9"	69.9"
Height	53.2"	54.2"
Legroom — front	41.7"	41.7"
Legroom — rear	33.4"	35.3"
Headroom — front	38.3"	39.3"
Headroom — rear	36.6"	36.6"
Cargo capacity (cu. ft.)	14.2*	13.8
Fuel capacity (gals.)	21.0	21.0

Hatchback maximum with rear seat down, 28.4 cu. ft.

Models Available

	Model No.	Base MSRP	Change from LY	Shipping Wt. (lbs.)	Model Year Production	Change from LY
Omega F-85 2-Door Coupe	S27	$3,390	+5.84%	3171	3,918	NA*
Omega 2-Door Coupe	B27	$3,485	+1.84%	3174	15,347	-3.96%
Omega 2-Door Hatchback	B17	$3,627	+2.28%	3248	4,497	-28.47%
Omega 4-Door Sedan	B69	$3,514	+1.86%	3196	20,221	+44.74%
Omega Brougham 2-Door Coupe	E27	$3,675	NEW	3178	5,363	NEW
Omega Brougham 2-Door Hatchback	E17	$3,817	NEW	3258	1,235	NEW
Omega Brougham 4-Door Sedan	E69	$3,704	NEW	3212	7,587	NEW
TOTALS	Avg. price	$3,602	-4.11%		Production 58,168	+38.94%

Production kept as combined total with Omega Coupe in 1975; therefore comparison is not possible.

Cutlass

"And you thought people bought Cutlass just for its good looks."

Nameplate year of origin: 1961 (as F-85 Deluxe sport coupe designation); 1962 (as F-85 sub-series); and 1965 (as series designation). Also used on 1955 Oldsmobile show car.

Current bodystyle lifespan: 1973 through 1977.

Predecessor to this model: Cutlass (1968 to 1972).

Replacement for this model: Cutlass (1978 to 1988; restyled in 1981).

Percentage of division's production: 56.11%.

Corporate siblings: Buick Century, Chevrolet Malibu, and Pontiac LeMans.

Primary competition: Dodge Charger/Coronet and Mercury Montego.

Notable changes: Restyled front end and coupe bodysides, and minor trim and detail changes.

Measurements

	Coupes	Sedans	Wagons
Wheelbase	112.0"	116.0"	116.0"
Length	209.6"	215.2"	220.4"
Width	76.5"	76.5"	76.8"
Height	53.4"	56.1"	55.3"
Legroom — front	42.1"	42.1"	42.1"
Legroom — rear	33.7"	38.4"	36.8"
Headroom — front	37.7"	38.3"	38.8"
Headroom — rear	37.0"	37.5"	39.4"
Cargo capacity (cu. ft.)	16.0	16.0	85.1
Fuel capacity (gals.)	22.0	22.0	22.0

1976

Major standard equipment: Osborne plaid cloth front bench seat, cut-pile carpeting, deluxe steering wheel, simulated woodgrain I/P and door panel appliqués, deluxe armrests front and rear, door pull strap (coupe), wheel lip moldings, bright window surround moldings, power steering, manual front disc brakes, wheel covers, and FR78 × 15 BSW tires. Supreme adds: Choice of cloth-and-vinyl or all-vinyl front Custom Sport seat w/fold-down center armrest, luxury door panels with door pull straps, stand-up "rocket" hood ornament, and power front disc brakes (sedan only). Supreme Brougham adds: Lamancha velour and Dover knit 60/40 divided front seat w/fold down center armrest, deep-pile carpeting, rocker panel moldings, and deluxe wheel covers. Supreme Cruiser adds: All-vinyl front custom sport seat w/fold-down center armrest, cut-pile carpeting on passenger and cargo floors, remote-control tailgate release (in glove compartment), rear vent window (3-seat model only), power front disc brakes, and HR78 × 15 BSW tires. Vista-Cruiser adds: Woodgrain paneling on sides and tailgate. Salon adds: Choice of velour w/vinyl trim or all-vinyl individual reclining lounge seats, stand-up Salon-specific hood ornament, FE2 suspension package, and GR78 × 15 BSW tires.

Models Available

	Model No.	Base MSRP	Change from LY	Shipping Wt. (lbs.)	Model Year Production	Change from LY
Cutlass S 2-Door Colonnade HT Coupe	G37	$3,999	+4.14%	3608	59,179	+37.88%
Cutlass S 4-Door Colonnade HT Sedan	G29	$4,033	+5.63%*	3690	34,994	+16.09%*
Cutlass Supreme 2-Door Colonnade HT Coupe	J57	$4,291	+6.34%	3637	186,647	+23.71%
Cutlass Supreme 4-Door Colonnade HT Sedan	J29	$4,415	+7.89%	3730	37,112	+139.17%
Cutlass Supreme Cruiser 4-Door, 2-S. Wagon	H35	$4,923	+5.53%	4298	13,964	+67.66%**
Vista-Cruiser 4-Door, 2-Seat Station Wagon	J35	$5,041	+3.41%	4304	20,560	+190.03%**
Cutlass Supreme Brougham 2-Dr. Colonnade HT	M57	$4,580	NEW	3668	91,312	NEW
Cutlass Salon 2-Door Colonnade HT Coupe	K57	$4,890	+5.37%	3829	48,440	+24.05%
Cutlass Salon 4-Door Colonnade HT Sedan	K29	$4,965	+5.35%	3949	7,921	+36.33%
TOTALS	*Avg. price*	$4,571	+4.34%	*Production*	500,129	+54.97%

*Comparison made to 1975 Cutlass 4-Door Colonnade HT Sedan with same G29 model number. models. For 1976, the third seat was an option.   **Change from LY calculation for wagons includes 1975 3-seat

Delta 88

"The kind of full-sized value car buyers are looking for these days—and one beautiful driving car."

Nameplate year of origin: 1965 (88 series began in 1949).

Current bodystyle lifespan: 1971 through 1976.

Predecessor to this model: Delta 88 (1969 to 1970).

Measurements

Wheelbase	124.0"
Length	226.9"

Replacement for this model: Delta 88 (1977 to 1985).
Percentage of division's production: 17.14%.
Corporate siblings: Buick LeSabre, Chevrolet Impala and Caprice, and Pontiac Catalina and Bonneville.
Primary competition: Chrysler Newport and Mercury Marquis.
Notable changes: Restyled front-end, and minor trim and detail changes.
Major standard equipment: Choice of Ogden nylon knit or Doeskin vinyl front bench seat, cut-pile carpeting, instrument panel message center, simulated I/P woodgrain appliqué, front and rear bumper vinyl impact strips, bright drip rail and window moldings, bright wheel opening and rocker panel moldings, full wheel covers, and HR78 × 15 BSW tires. Royale adds: Pleated crush velour front bench seat w/fold-down center armrest, Royale ornamentation, cut-pile carpeting on cowl side panels and lower door panels, deluxe steering wheel, door panel simulated woodgrain trim, courtesy and glove box lights, bright metal accented floor pedals, and color-coordinated bodyside molding w/vinyl inserts.

Measurements (cont.)

Width	79.5"
Height	54.3"
Legroom — front	42.4"
Legroom — rear	38.5"
Headroom — front	38.3"
Headroom — rear	38.0"
Cargo capacity (cu. ft.)	20.8
Fuel capacity (gals.)	NA

Models Available

	Model No.	Base MSRP	Change from LY	Shipping Wt. (lbs.)	Model Year Production	Change from LY
Delta 88 2-Door Hardtop Coupe	L57	$4,975	+3.00%	4243	7,204	-15.47%
Delta 88 4-Door Town Sedan	L69	$4,918	+3.02%	4279	17,115	+6.23%
Delta 88 4-Door Hardtop Sedan	L39	$5,038	+3.01%	4336	9,759	+5.13%
Delta 88 Royale 2-Door Hardtop Coupe	N57	$5,146	+3.23%	4263	33,364	+42.19%
Delta 88 Royale 4-Door Town Sedan	N69	$5,078	+3.34%	4294	33,268	+363.28%
Delta 88 Royale 4-Door Hardtop Sedan	N39	$5,217	+3.29%	4368	52,103	+60.41%
TOTALS		Avg. price $5,062	+2.28%		Production 152,813	+29.41%

Custom Cruiser

"In station-wagon circles, the Olds Custom Cruiser is one wagon to look up to."

Nameplate year of origin: 1971 (1940 as a designation on 90 series cars).
Current bodystyle lifespan: 1971 through 1976.
Predecessor to this model: None.
Replacement for this model: Custom Cruiser (1977 to 1990).
Percentage of division's production: 2.50%.
Corporate siblings: Buick Estate Wagon, Chevrolet Impala and Caprice, and Pontiac Catalina Safari and Grand Safari.
Primary competition: Chrysler Town & Country and Mercury Colony Park.
Notable changes: New grille, and minor trim and detail changes.
Major standard equipment: Ventilated vinyl cushions w/Doeskin vinyl trim front bench seat w/fold-down center armrest, cut-pile carpeting on floors and cargo compartment floor, lower door panel carpeting, instrument panel message center, Glide-Away tailgate, power tailgate window, LH and RH rear view mirrors, vinyl bumper impact strips, rear wheel opening fender skirts, full wheel covers, and LR78 × 15 BSW tires. "R" models add: Simulated woodgrain vinyl bodyside and tailgate appliqués w/chrome trim surround.

Measurements

Wheelbase	127.0"
Length	231.0"
Width	79.5"
Height	57.2"
Legroom — front	42.1"
Legroom — rear	39.4"
Headroom — front	39.6"
Headroom — rear	39.3"
Cargo capacity (cu. ft.)	106.1
Fuel capacity (gals.)	NA

Models Available

	Model No.	Base MSRP	Change from LY	Shipping Wt. (lbs.)	Model Year Production	Change from LY*
Custom Cruiser 4-Door, 2-S. Wagon	Q35	$5,563	+2.77%	4987	2,572	NA
Custom Cruiser 4-Door, 3-S. Wagon	Q45	$5,705	+2.76%	5060	3,626	NA
Custom Cruiser 4-Door, 2-S. Wagon	R35	$5,719	+2.71%	5009	3,849	NA
Custom Cruiser 4-Door, 3-S. Wagon	R45	$5,861	+2.70%	5071	12,269	NA
TOTALS		Avg. price $5,712	+2.73%		Production 22,316	+38.71%

*Comparison to LY not possible due to production of 1975 "Q" non-woodgrained and "R" woodgrained models being kept as combined total.

Ninety-Eight

*"Few cars in the world can approach the luxury
car qualities of an Oldsmobile 98. Fewer luxury cars
still can make these qualities so easy to own."*

Nameplate year of origin: 1941.
Current bodystyle lifespan: 1971 through 1976.
Predecessor to this model: Ninety-Eight (1969 to 1970).
Replacement for this model: Ninety-Eight (1977 to 1984).
Percentage of division's production: 11.72%.
Corporate siblings: Buick Electra 225, Cadillac Calais, and Cadillac deVille.
Primary competition: Chrysler New Yorker and Mercury Grand Marquis.
Notable changes: Revised front-end styling and minor trim and detail changes.
Major standard equipment: Choice of Ogden nylon knit fabric or Doeskin vinyl
front bench seat w/fold-down center armrest, cut-pile carpeting, carpeted lower
door panels, door pull straps, power controls on door armrest in chrome bezel, two-
way power front seat, power windows, simulated woodgrain I/P trim, deluxe steer-
ing wheel, electric clock, remote-control LH rear view mirror, bright bodyside protective molding, wheel opening moldings,
rocker panel molding, stand-up Oldsmobile "rocket" hood ornament, front and rear bumper guards, rear fender skirts, wheel
covers, and JR78 × 15 BSW tires. Regency adds: Choice of velour or Doeskin vinyl 60/40 front seat deeply tufted w/"loose"
cushion look, six-way power adjustment for driver's side, fold-down center armrests front and rear, zippered front seatback pouch
pockets, French walnut woodgrain door panel and seat side shield trim, digital quartz-crystal clock, door-mounted entry courtesy
lights, and fully-lined trunk compartment w/spare tire cover.

Measurements

Wheelbase	127.0"
Length	232.2"
Width	79.8"
Height	54.2"
Legroom — front	42.4"
Legroom — rear	41.1"
Headroom — front	39.3"
Headroom — rear	38.2"
Cargo capacity (cu. ft.)	22.2
Fuel capacity (gals.)	NA

1976

Models Available

	Model No.	Base MSRP	Change from LY	Shipping Wt. (lbs.)	Model Year Production	Change from LY
Ninety-Eight (LS) Luxury Coupe 2-Door HT	V37	$6,271	+5.39%	4501	6,056	-31.17%
Ninety-Eight (LS) Luxury Sedan 4-Door HT	V39	$6,419	+5.38%	4633	16,802	-7.13%
Ninety-Eight Regency Coupe 2-Door HT	X37	$6,544	+5.34%	4535	26,282	+57.41%
Ninety-Eight Regency Sedan 4-Door HT	X39	$6,691	+5.32%	4673	55,339	+56.93%
TOTALS	*Avg. price*	$6,481	+5.36%	*Production*	104,479	+32.50%

Toronado

"Proud classic among luxury cars. A rare experience on the road."

Nameplate year of origin: 1966.
Current bodystyle lifespan: 1971 through 1978.
Predecessor to this model: Toronado (1966 to 1970).
Replacement for this model: Toronado (1979 to 1985).
Percentage of division's production: 2.73%.
Corporate siblings: Buick Riviera and Cadillac Eldorado.
Primary competition: Ford Thunderbird.
Notable changes: Minor trim and detail changes.
Major standard equipment: Choice of nylon knit or all-vinyl front bench seat
w/fold-down center armrest, cut-pile carpeting, simulated woodgrain appliqué on
I/P, two-spoke steering wheel, digital clock w/quartz-crystal movement, chrome-ac-
cented floor pedals, LH remote-control rear view mirror, rocker panel and wheel lip
moldings, front bumper guards, chrome wheel covers, and JR78 × 15 BSW tires.
Brougham adds: Choice of geometric-weave velour or Doeskin vinyl 60/40 divided
front seat, fold-down center armrest front and rear, and six-way power adjustment
for driver and passenger.

Measurements

Wheelbase	122.0"
Length	227.6"
Width	79.5"
Height	53.2"
Legroom — front	42.4"
Legroom — rear	35.2"
Headroom — front	38.1"
Headroom — rear	37.1"
Cargo capacity (cu. ft.)	17.0
Fuel capacity (gals.)	26.0

Models Available

	Model No.	Base MSRP	Change from LY	Shipping Wt. (lbs.)	Model Year Production	Change from LY
Toronado Custom 2-Door Hardtop	Y57	$6,891	+5.64%	4694	2,555	-42.18%
Toronado Brougham 2-Door Hardtop	Z57	$7,137	+5.69%	4729	21,749	+15.18%
TOTALS		*Avg. price* $7,014	+5.66%		*Production* 24,304	+4.30%

PLYMOUTH

"Introducing the 1976 Plymouth line, featuring the all-new Volaré."

With the passing of the Cricket early in the 1973 model year and the Barracuda during the 1974 model year, Plymouth had entered 1975 with only three basic model lines — the compact Valiant group, the mid-size Fury group, and the full-size Gran Fury series. For 1976, two new series joined the ranks: the Mitsubishi-built subcompact Arrow import and the highly anticipated compact Volaré. The Volaré was intended as a replacement for the Valiant, Scamp and Duster models, but since as a group they made up more than half of Plymouth sales during the past two years, Plymouth could not just drop them until the Volaré proved itself. Fortunately the Volaré did just that, taking nearly 60 percent of Plymouth production and sales in its first season.

The Volaré was a virtual twin to the Dodge Aspen in all aspects, down to the base prices being only $12 less on Plymouth versions and styling differences being limited to the grille and taillight designs. The Volaré used an egg-crate style grille, divided into six equally sized horizontal sections, three on each side, and had small square parking/turn signal lamps set in indented areas between the grille and single round headlamps set in a chrome bezel. The box-style bumper was similar to the Valiant's. The center section of the hood was slightly raised and turned downward to meet the top of the grille. Top-of-the line Premier models used a stand-up Plymouth logo hood ornament, and all models had the Plymouth nameplate on the center driver's side section of the grille.

Volaré styling featured a lower bodyside crease running from bumper to bumper and arching over the round wheel openings about an inch from the edge. Two-door models added a slight "coke-bottle" design flare-out as the bodyside crease crossed the rear quarter panel. Rooflines were of a semi-fastback design for the coupes and a more upright style for sedans that were much like that of the Valiant sedan, including a rear door fixed quarter window. At the back, rec-tangular taillamps divided into two horizontal sections were used on coupes and sedans, with all wagons using a vertical lamp. Backup lights were on the inward side of taillamps, except on station wagons, where they were at the bottom of the taillights. On Volaré Custom and Premier models, a chrome panel ran between the taillights and was divided into two sections, matching the taillamp design.

Powering the new Volaré line were the basic Chrysler powerplants, with the proven, but aging, 225 CID "Slant Six" serving as the base engine, and the 318 CID and 360 CID V8 engines as optional equipment. Inside, the Volaré used contemporary Chrysler design elements for the instrument panel with a hooded area in front of, and slightly curving around, the driver housing all the essential gauges and controls. A square speedometer sat in the middle with rectangular pods to the left housing an air vent, wiper and light controls, and rectangular pods to the right housing radio and climate controls. The Volaré interior was more upscale than the Valiant ever was, except in the recent Brougham trim. Adding to the more luxurious feel was optional equipment such as power windows, power door locks and power seats.

As could be expected, Volaré sedans were the top sellers in the line, but surprisingly, the two station wagon models nearly outsold the three sedan models available, being only 343 units behind in production, proving that there was a demand for smaller station wagons, something AMC had known all along with its popular Hornet Sportabout. The Road Runner, which was always a mid-size car since its introduction, was moved to the Volaré series as an option package and an optional décor package on the base coupe, consisting mostly of tape stripes and sporty road wheels. Approximately 5,500 were produced with the Road Runner package, and an additional estimated 1,500 with the late season Super Pak wheel flare and spoilers option. While a 360 CID V8 engine was available, it was still a far cry from the high-powered Road Runner muscle cars of just five years prior.

The Arrow, imported from Japan and built by Mitsubishi, was Plymouth's second attempt at selling a captive import in the United States. The first attempt with the Cricket, a British-built Hillman model, was a resounding failure in its run from 1971 through early 1973. The Arrow was a slightly smaller version of the soon-to-be-released 1977 Dodge Colt, which was itself a revision of the 1971–1976 Colt. With a rakish fastback roofline, the Arrow was to be direct competition for the highly popular Datsun B210 hatchback coupes and the newly introduced Chevrolet Chevette. A Mitsubishi-built 1.6L 4-cylinder engine powered the Arrow, and the new "Silent Shaft" 2.0 L engine was available on all but the base Arrow 160. The "Silent Shaft" utilized two counter-balancing shafts located at different heights on opposite sides of the crankshaft, and rotating in opposite directions, to eliminate vibrations caused by piston travel and crankshaft rotation, making the Mitsubishi engine one of the quietest 4-cylinder cars on the road. Front-end styling used single round headlamps, a three-row horizontal slot-type grille, and parking/turn signal lamps mounted inboard of the headlights on the filler pan between the grille and front bumper. The rear panel was flat, with large rectangular taillamps divided into three sections horizontally. A single body-side feature line ran the full length of the car beginning and ending about an inch above the bumpers. The rear side window was unique in that the bottom edge curved upward to meet the top as it followed the slope of the roof downward, and a small rear quarter window to the rear of this had a three-slot cover to aid rearward visibility.

The Fury and Gran Fury lines returned for the new model year with few styling or feature changes, but with several model changes. For the mid-size Fury, the Road Runner was gone, having become an option package for the new Volaré 2-Door Coupe as previously mentioned. The former Custom series, including the Custom Suburban, was also gone, replaced by the Fury Salon 4-door and the Fury Sport 2-door, which was taken down a notch as it moved from the premium RP series to the high-level RH series. Also, all base model Furys now included standard color-keyed carpeting. In the full-size Gran Fury series, the 4-door hardtop body style was discontinued, and in the Gran Fury Brougham line a 4-door sedan took its place. Also missing was the Gran Fury Sport Suburban 2-seat station wagon. All Gran Furys adopted the single headlight styling introduced on the 1975 Gran Fury Brougham line.

After this, its seventeenth model year, the Valiant name would fade away, as the Volaré took its place as the compact Plymouth. No significant changes were made to styling or powertrain offerings. Model changes included the Duster 360 being dropped, and the prior Custom and Brougham trim levels becoming option packages. As if to emphasize the supposedly higher trim level and placement of the new Volaré line, a lower-priced Scamp Special 2-door hardtop was introduced that sold for nearly $200 less than the regular Scamp hardtop, and carried the standard features of the Valiant sedan. Other prices were adjusted only slightly with coupes being slightly lower, and the sedan being slightly higher.

Arrow GT 2-Door Hatchback Coupe

Duster 2-Door Coupe
with Silver Duster package

Fury Sport 2-Door Hardtop Coupe

Fury Sport Suburban 4-Door Station Wagon

Gran Fury Brougham 2-Door Hardtop Coupe

Gran Fury Custom 4-Door Sedan (left)
and Gran Fury Custom 2-Door Hardtop (right)

Scamp 2-Door Hardtop

Valiant 4-Door Sedan with Brougham package

Volaré 2-Door Coupe interior with
Premium bucket seat and console interior

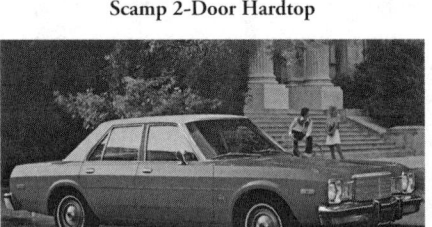

Volaré 4-Door Sedan

Volaré Premier 2-Door Coupe

Volaré Premier 4-Door Station Wagon

Volaré Premier instrument panel

Model year production: 453,944, down 1.70% from 1975.
Domestic market share: 5.23% (7th place).
Base price range: $3,241 to $5,761.
Plymouth average base price: $4,271, down 1.91%.
Introduction date: October 16, 1975. Arrow introduced January 1976.
Assembly plants: Lynch Road, Detroit, MI (A); Hamtramck, MI (B); Jefferson Ave., Detroit, MI (C); Belvidere, IL (D); Newark, DE (F); and St. Louis, MO (G). Arrow manufacturer: Mitsubishi Heavy Industries, Tokyo, Japan (code 1 through 9).

Data plate identification (VIN): Thirteen digit code read as follows: First four digits indicate series and body style (model number in model charts); fifth digit indicates engine code (see powertrain chart); sixth digit indicates year (6 = 1976); seventh digit indicates assembly plant (see list above); remaining digits are sequential with beginning numbers of 100001. *Example:* VL41C6B100001 is a 1976 Plymouth Valiant 4-Door Sedan, with 225 CID, 2-bbl. 6-cylinder engine, serial number 100001, built in Hamtramck, MI.

Powertrains

Engine	Net HP	Engine Code	Transmission Availability[1]		Arrow	Valiant, Duster & Scamp	Volaré	Fury	Gran Fury & Gran Fury Custom[2]	Gran Fury Brougham & Wagons
97.5 CID (1.6L) OHC, 1-bbl., 4-cyl.	83	K	4-speed manual		S (base & GS)	—	—	—	—	—
				MPG:	25/37/29	—	—	—	—	—
				Calif.	22/34/27	—	—	—	—	—
			5-speed manual		S (GT)	—	—	—	—	—
				MPG:	NA	—	—	—	—	—
			3-speed Automatic		$250 (base & GS)	—	—	—	—	—
				MPG:	26/34/29	—	—	—	—	—
				Calif.	24/32/27	—	—	—	—	—
122 CID (2.0L) OHC, 2-bbl., 4-cyl.	96	U	5-speed manual		$332 (GS)/ $232 (GT)	—	—	—	—	—
				MPG:	20/33/24	—	—	—	—	—
				Calif.	18/31/22	—	—	—	—	—

Engine	Net HP	Engine Code	Transmission Availability[1]	Arrow	Valiant, Duster & Scamp	Volaré	Fury	Gran Fury & Gran Fury Custom[2]	Gran Fury Brougham & Wagons
			3-speed Automatic	$582 (GS)/ $482 (GT)	—	—	—	—	—
			MPG:	20/28/23	—	—	—	—	—
			Calif.	19/24/21	—	—	—	—	—
225 CID (3.7L), 2-bbl., 6-cyl.	100	C	3-speed manual	—	—	S	S[3]	S (ex. wgns.)	—	—
			MPG:	—	19/26/21	18/27/22	18/30/22	—	—
			Calif.	—	16/23/18	17/24/20	—	—	—
			"Overdrive4" 4-speed manual	—	—	$127	$127[3]	—	—	—
			MPG:	—	NA	NA	—	—	—
			3-speed TorqueFlite automatic	—	$250	$250	$273 (ex. wgns.)	—	—
			MPG:	—	18/24/21	18/23/20	16/23/19	—	—
			Calif.	—	15/20/17	13/17/15	—	—	—
318 CID (5.2L), 2-bbl., V8	150	G	3-speed manual[4]	—	$112	$165	$238 (ex. wgns.)	—	—
			MPG:	—	14/22/17	14/22/17	15/21/17	—	—
			"Overdrive4" 4-speed manual[4]	—	$239	$312	—	—	—
			MPG:	—	NA	NA	—	—	—
			3-speed TorqueFlite automatic	—	$362	$415	$511 (ex. wgns.)	S (ex. GFC)	—
			MPG:	—	16/21/18	16/21/18	13/18/15	13/18/15	—
			Calif.	—	12/15/13	12/17/14	12/16/14	—	—
360 CID (5.9L), 2-bbl., V8[4]	170	K	3-speed Torque Flite automatic	—	—	$465	S (Wgns.)/ $565 (others)	S (GFC)/ $55 (others)	—
			MPG:	—	—	13/19/15	12/19/14	13/17/14	—
360 CID (5.9L), 4-bbl., V8	175[5]/ 220	J[5],L	3-speed Torque Flite automatic	—	—	—	$45 (Wgns.)/ $610 (others)	$45 (GFC)/ $100 (others)	—
			MPG:	—	—	—	NA	NA	—
			Calif.	—	—	—	12/18/14	11/17/13	—
400 CID (6.6L), 2-bbl., V8[4]	175	M	3-speed Torque Flite automatic	—	—	—	$48 (Wgns.)/ $613 (others)	$49 (GFC)/ $104 (others)	S
			MPG:	—	—	—	11/16/13	12/18/14	12/18/14
400 CID (6.6L), 4-bbl., V8	185[5]/ 210	N[5],P	3-speed Torque Flite automatic	—	—	—	$93 (Wgns.)/ $658 (others)	$94 (GFC)/ $149 (others)	$45
			MPG:	—	—	—	11/15/12	9/17/12	9/17/12
			Calif.	—	—	—	11/15/12	10/16/12	10/16/12
440 CID (7.2L), 4-bbl., V8	205	T	3-speed Torque Flite automatic	—	—	—	—	$218 (GFC)/ $273 (others)	$169
			MPG:	—	—	—	—	11/15/13	11/15/12
			Calif.	—	—	—	9/14/11	9/14/11	9/14/11

[1]*Unless otherwise noted: All transmissions are column-shift, except on Arrow, or any model w/4-speed manual. Floor-shift is available for $28 extra on any Scamp, Duster or Volaré w/3-speed manual transmission; Volaré coupes w/automatic; and Fury Sport w/bucket seats, console and automatic transmission.* [2]*GFC = Gran Fury Custom.* [3]*Not available in California on wagons.* [4]*Not available in California.* [5]*Available only in California.*

Major Options

	Arrow	Valiant	Volaré	Fury	Gran Fury
Air conditioning[1]	$412	$431	$430	$490	$504
Tilt & telescoping steering wheel	—	—	—	—	$99
"Auto-Speed" control	—	—	$70	$77	$78
Electric rear window defroster	$79	$74	$74	$81	$81
Tinted glass, all windows	S	$44	$44	$59	$59
Front vent window, 4-dr. only	—	—	—	—	$35
Power windows, 2-dr./4-dr.	—	—	$95/$135	$147	$167
Power door locks, 2-dr./4-dr.	—	—	$60/$86	$65/$94	$64/$110
Power seat, bench	—	—	$120	$130	$132
AM radio	$	$73	$72	$79	$80
AM/FM stereo	$	—	$233	$254	$257
AM/FM stereo w/8-track tape	—	—	—	$357	$362
Front bucket seats w/console	—	$128[2]	$187[3]	$295[3]	—
Vinyl top, full[4]	$92	$92	$92	$115	$131
Sunroof, electric	—	$186[5]	$186[5]	$311[5]	$627[5]
Power steering, standard w/V8s	—	$131	$131	$143	S
Power brakes, w/front disc[6]	—	$56	$56	S	S
Deluxe wheel covers	—	$32	$32	$36	S
Premiere wheel covers	—	—	$54	—	$70
Wire wheel covers	—	—	$86	$94	—
Rallye road wheels	—	$66	$66	—	—
White sidewall tires, std. size	$	$32	$32	$40	$40

Popular Option Groups & Packages

	Arrow	Valiant	Volaré	Fury	Gran Fury
Brougham package	—	$438	—	—	—
Custom package	—	$176	—	—	—
Exterior decor package	—	—	—	$155	—
Deluxe Insulation package	—	$51	$51	$55	—
Easy Order package	—	$745	$754	$870	$479
Interior décor package	—	$92	—	—	—
Feather Duster package	—	$51[7]	—	—	—
Light package	—	$33	$33	$45	$74
Luxury equipment package[8]	—	—	—	$1,688	$1,811
Protection group	—	$27	$27	—	—
Road Runner package	—	—	$205	—	—
Road Runner décor group	—	—	$95	—	—
Silver Duster package	—	$179[7]	—	—	—
Spacemaker package	—	$104[7]	$104	—	—
Super Pak package	—	—	$312	—	—
Two-tone decor package	—	—	$158	—	—

— = Not Available; S = Standard equipment.   [1]Automatic air conditioning available on Gran Fury for $590.   [2]For Duster only, and includes full-floor carpeting. Bucket seats without console are available on Scamp for $82.   [3]Available on 2-door models only.   [4]Standard on Gran Fury Brougham coupe. Volaré Landau top on 2-door models is $137. Canopy vinyl roof on Fury 2-doors at same price. Not available on station wagons.   [5]Available only on 2-door models. Manually operated on Duster and Volaré. Requires vinyl top. Not available on station wagons.   [6]Standard on Duster 360 and Fury station wagons. All others have manual front disc brakes as standard, except 6-cylinder Valiant, Scamp and Duster models, which have manual drum brakes.   [7]Duster only.   [8]Available only on Fury Sport, Fury Sport Suburban, Fury Salon Gran Fury Custom and Custom Suburban, Gran Fury Brougham and Sport Suburban.

Paint Colors

Plymouth	Code	Plymouth	Code	Plymouth	Code
Silver Cloud metallic	A2	Vintage Red metallic[1]	E9	Claret Red[4]	R6
Powder Blue[1]	B1	Deep Sherwood metallic	G8	Cinnamon metallic[5]	T4
Astral Blue metallic[1,2,3]	B2	Platinum metallic[1,2,3]	J2	Dark Chestnut metallic[5]	T9
Big Sky Blue[4]	B4	Tropic Green metallic[2]	J5	Saddle Tan[1,3]	U2
Jamaican Blue metallic[5]	B5	Bittersweet metallic[1,2]	K3	Carmel Tan metallic[5]	U3
Starlight Blue metallic[1,2,3]	B8	Sahara Beige[3]	L4	Spitfire Orange[4]	V1
Rallye Red[1,5]	E5	Moondust metallic[1,2]	L5	Spinnaker White	W1

Plymouth	Code		Arrow	Code
Formal Black	X9		Copper	004
Harvest Gold[4]	Y3		Bright Blue metallic	022
Golden Fawn[1]	Y4		Bright Gold metallic	023
Yellow Blaze[1,5]	Y5		Bright Red	055
Inca Gold metallic[1]	Y6		Bright Yellow	090
Spanish Gold metallic	Y9		Green metallic[6]	091
			Orange	092

Single tones are coded W1, W1. Two-tones are coded X9, W1 where first two digits are accent or roof color, and second two digits are basic body color. [1]Not available on Volaré. [2]Not available on Valiant. [3]Not available on Fury. [4]Available only on Volaré. [5]Not available on Gran Fury. [6]Some sources show this color as a late year addition.

Arrow

*"Plymouth's sporty little hatchback ... 1976 Arrow.
What more can a little car give?"*

Nameplate year of origin: 1976.
Current bodystyle lifespan: 1976 through 1980.
Predecessor to this model: None.
Replacement for this model: Champ (1979 to 1983).
Primary competition: AMC Gremlin and Chevrolet Chevette.
Notable changes: All-new model.
Major standard equipment: All-vinyl front bucket seats w/reclining seatbacks, folding rear seat, black I/P trim, tilt steering column, two-speed electric windshield wipers, cigarette lighter, heater and defroster, tinted glass, argent painted bumpers, front and rear window moldings, drip rail moldings, power front disc brakes, and 6.00 × 13 BSW tires. GS adds: Richmond vinyl front bucket seats w/accent trim, woodtone I/P trim, full-floor carpeting including cargo area, ashtray light, right roof rail assist grip, flipper rear quarter windows, rear panel trim molding, rocker panel sill moldings, wheel lip molding, chrome plated bumpers, and styled road wheels. GT adds: Black or white all-vinyl bucket seats w/vertical stripe in opposite color, floor console w/ammeter, oil pressure gauge and coin holder, rally gauge cluster w/tachometer, overhead console for dome and map lights and warning lights, soft-rim sports style steering wheel, dual black sport mirrors, GT up-and-over tape stripe, and 165SR × 13 WSW tires.

Measurements

Wheelbase	92.1"
Length	167.3"
Width	63.4"
Height	52.5"
Legroom — front	41.7"
Legroom — rear	28.0"
Headroom — front	36.8"
Headroom — rear	34.4"
Cargo capacity (cu. ft.)	17.3
Fuel capacity (gals.)	11.9

Models Available

	Model No.	Base MSRP	Change from LY	Shipping Wt. (lbs.)	Model Year Sales*	Change from LY
Arrow 160 2-Door Hatchback Cpe.	7L24	$3,175	NEW	2110	NA	NEW
Arrow GS 2-Door Hatchback Cpe.	7H24	$3,407	NEW	2115	NA	NEW
Arrow GT 2-Door Hatchback Cpe.	7P24	$3,748	NEW	2290	NA	NEW
TOTALS	*Avg. price*	$3,443	NEW	*Production*	20,769	NEW

*Model year sales by trim level is not available.

Valiant

*"A remarkably smart, comfortable, well-equipped
and well-engineered compact from Plymouth."*

Nameplate year of origin: 1960 (Valiant); 1970 (Duster); 1971 (Scamp).
Current bodystyle lifespan: 1967 through 1976.
Predecessor to this model: Valiant (1963 to 1966).
Replacement for this model: Volaré (1976 to 1980).
Percentage of division's production: 15.71%.

Measurements

	Duster	Scamp	Valiant
Wheelbase	108.0"	111.0"	111.0"
Length	197.0"	199.6"	199.6"
Width	71.7"	71.0"	71.0"

1976

Corporate siblings: Dodge Dart.

Primary competition: AMC Hornet, Chevrolet Nova, and Ford Maverick.

Notable changes: Minor trim and detail changes.

Major standard equipment: All-vinyl front bench seat (Valiant and Scamp Special), cloth-and-vinyl front bench seat (Duster), black I/P trim, two-speed electric windshield wipers w/washers, front door window vents (Valiant), swing-out rear quarter windows (Duster), hubcaps, 6.95 × 14 BSW tires. Scamp adds: Pleated vinyl front bench seat, cut-pile carpeting, interior décor package, simulated woodgrain I/P cluster appliqué, cigarette lighter, roof drip-rail molding, wheel lip moldings, and dual horns.

	Duster	Scamp	Valiant
Height	53.4"	53.0"	54.0"
Legroom — front	41.9"	41.9"	41.9"
Legroom — rear	29.4"	31.3"	35.2"
Headroom — front	37.2"	37.3"	38.3"
Headroom — rear	36.4"	36.6"	37.2"
Cargo capacity (cu. ft.)	20.1*	17.7	16.6
Fuel capacity (gals.)	16.0	16.0	16.0

*With Space Duster package fold-down rear seat option, 56.0 cu. ft.

Models Available

	Model No.	Base MSRP	Change from LY	Shipping Wt. (lbs.)	Model Year Production	Change from LY
Duster 2-Door Coupe	VL29	$3,241	-0.06%	2975	26,688	-66.59%
Scamp Special 2-Door Hardtop	VL23	$3,337	NEW	3020	3,308	NEW
Valiant 4-Door Sedan	VL41	$3,276	+0.89%	3050	32,901	-26.02%
Scamp 2-Door Hardtop	VH23	$3,510	-0.23%	3020	5,147	-78.17%
TOTALS	*Avg. price*	$3,341	-8.46%	*Production*	68,044	-74.61%

Volaré

"The new small car with the accent on comfort."

Nameplate year of origin: 1976.

Current bodystyle lifespan: 1976 through 1980.

Predecessor to this model: Valiant (1967 to 1976).

Replacement for this model: Reliant (1981 to 1989).

Percentage of division's production: 58.87%.

Corporate siblings: Dodge Aspen.

Primary competition: AMC Hornet, Chevrolet Nova, and Ford Granada.

Notable changes: All-new model.

Major standard equipment: All-vinyl front bench seat (sedan and wagon), cloth and vinyl front bench seat (coupe), color-keyed carpeting, three-spoke steering wheel, two-speed electric windshield wipers and washers, front ashtray, color-keyed bumper filler, roof drip rail molding, quarter window

Measurements

	Coupe	Sedan	Wagon
Wheelbase	108.5"	112.5"	112.5"
Length	197.5"	201.5"	201.5"
Width	72.8"	72.8"	72.8"
Height	53.1"	54.8"	54.8"
Legroom — front	42.2"	42.3"	42.3"
Legroom — rear	30.7"	36.6"	36.6"
Headroom — front	37.5"	39.2"	39.2"
Headroom — rear	36.1"	37.5"	38.7"
Cargo capacity (cu. ft.)	14.5	14.2	71.9
Fuel capacity (gals.)	18.0	18.0	18.0

reveal moldings, windshield and backlight moldings, and D78 × 14 BSW tires. Wagon adds: Rear liftgate, power front disc brakes, heavy-duty suspension, and F78 × 14 BSW tires. Custom adds: Vinyl bench seat (coupe), cloth and vinyl bench seat (sedan), cigarette lighter, rear armrests w/ashtrays, simulated woodgrain I/P appliqué, belt moldings, wide bodyside chrome moldings w/black insert, and rear deck lower appliqué. Premier adds: Vinyl 60/40 split front bench seat w/individual recliners and fold-down center armrest, luxury door trim panels w/lower carpeting, door pull handles, glove box lock, luxury 3-spoke steering wheel (w/automatic transmission only), day/night rear view mirror, landau vinyl roof (coupe), full vinyl roof (sedan), upper door frame moldings (sedan), color-keyed wide vinyl bodyside molding, full wheel lip molding, hood ornament and wind-split molding, deluxe insulation package, undercoating w/hood silencer pad, power steering and automatic transmission, dual horns, and premium wheel covers. Premier wagon adds: All vinyl bench seat, cigarette lighter and rear seat ashtray, cargo compartment carpet and storage bins w/locking doors, upper door frame molding, woodgrain bodyside panel and liftgate appliqué, and belt moldings.

Models Available

	Model No.	Base MSRP	Change from LY	Shipping Wt. (lbs.)	Model Year Production	Change from LY
Volaré 2-Door Sport Coupe	HL29	$3,324	NEW	3160	30,191	NEW
Volaré 4-Door Sedan	HL41	$3,359	NEW	3190	19,186	NEW
Volaré 4-Door Station Wagon	HL45	$3,612	NEW	3560	40,497	NEW
Volaré Custom 2-Door Sport Coupe	HH29	$3,506	NEW	3170	27,656	NEW
Volaré Custom 4-Door Sedan	HH41	$3,541	NEW	3200	32,765	NEW
Volaré Premier 2-Door Sport Coupe	HP29	$4,402	NEW	3375	27,442	NEW
Volaré Premier 4-Door Sedan	HP41	$4,389	NEW	3410	33,080	NEW
Volaré Premier 4-Door Station Wagon	HP45	$3,976	NEW	3565	44,191	NEW
TOTALS		Avg. price $3,768	NEW		Production 255,008	NEW

Fury

"Luxurious styling that's outstanding at the price."

Nameplate year of origin: 1956. Applied to mid-size platform for 1975.
Current bodystyle lifespan: 1971 through 1978.
Predecessor to this model: Satellite (1971 to 1974).
Replacement for this model: Caravelle (1985 to 1988).
Percentage of division's sales volume: 18.86%.
Corporate siblings: Dodge Charger and Coronet.
Primary competition: AMC Matador, Chevrolet Chevelle, and Ford Torino.
Notable changes: Minor trim and detail changes.
Major standard equipment: All-vinyl front bench seat, color-keyed carpeting, cigarette lighter, dome light, lockable glove box, upper door frame molding, concealed two-speed windshield wipers w/washers, rocker panel sill molding, hubcaps, and F78 × 14 BSW tires. Fury Sport and Salon add: Velour-and-vinyl front bench seat w/fold-down center armrest, shag carpeting, premium door trim panels w/pull handles, simulated woodgrain inserts on I/P, door trim inserts and steering wheel, Sport ornamentation on C-pillar of coupe, Salon ornamentation on decklid and C-pillar of sedan, belt moldings, bodyside tape stripes (Sport only), hood ornament, hood rear edge molding, dual horns, and deluxe wheel covers. Suburban wagon adds: Fold-down rear seatback, power front disc brakes, three-way tailgate, and H78 × 14 BSW tires. Sport Suburban wagon adds: All-vinyl split-back front bench seat w/fold-down center armrest, cargo compartment carpeting and dome light, exterior simulated woodgrained bodyside overlays and tailgate trim, and deluxe wheel covers.

Measurements

	2-Doors	4-Doors	Wagons
Wheelbase	115.0"	117.5"	117.5"
Length	213.7"	218.4"	224.2"
Width	77.7"	77.7"	78.8"
Height	52.6"	53.9"	56.5"
Legroom — front	42.3"	42.3"	42.3"
Legroom — rear	32.4"	35.2"	35.2"
Headroom — front	37.6"	38.6"	39.7"
Headroom — rear	37.6"	37.3"	38.1"
Cargo capacity (cu. ft.)	14.5	19.4	86.8*
Fuel capacity (gals.)	19.5	19.5	21.0

Plus 8.3 cu.ft. of concealed space on 2-seat station wagons.

Models Available

	Model No.	Base MSRP	Change from LY	Shipping Wt. (lbs.)	Model Year Production	Change from LY
Fury 2-Door Hardtop	RL23	$3,699	+4.43%	3590	11,341	+35.04%
Fury 4-Door Sedan	RL41	$3,733	+3.95%	3625	18,006	+57.51%
Fury Suburban 4-Door, 2-S. Wagon	RL45	$4,597	+6.68%	4285	3,765	-15.73%
Fury Suburban 4-Door, 3-S. Wagon	RL46	$4,739	NEW	4350	3,810	NEW
Fury Sport 2-Dr. Hardtop	RH23	$3,988	-2.85%	3595	23,312	+31.10%
Fury Salon 4-Door Sedan	RH41	$4,022	NEW	3645	16,768	NEW
Fury Sport Suburban 4-Door, 2-S. Wagon	RH45	$4,986	+4.53%	4285	1,567	-15.34%
Fury Sport Suburban 4-Door, 3-S. Wagon	RH46	$5,128	+5.36%	4360	3,143	+1.16%
TOTALS		Avg. price $4,362	+4.94%		Production 81,712	-32.45%

Gran Fury

"Value can be beautiful."

Nameplate year of origin: 1956.

Current bodystyle lifespan: 1974 through 1977 (renamed Gran Fury for 1975 to 1977).

Predecessor to this model: Fury (1969 to 1973).

Replacement for this model: Gran Fury (1980 to 1981).

Percentage of division's sales volume: 6.56%.

Corporate siblings: Dodge Monaco.

Primary competition: Chevrolet Impala/Caprice and Ford LTD.

Notable changes: New front end for base and Custom, and minor trim and detail changes.

Major standard equipment: Cloth-and-vinyl front bench seat, color-keyed front and rear armrests, nylon loop-pile carpeting, cigarette lighter, dome light, front door courtesy light switches, glove box lock, inside hood release, concealed two-speed windshield wipers w/washers, bright drip rail molding,

Measurements

	2-Doors	4-Doors	Wagons
Wheelbase	121.5"	121.5"	124.0"
Length	222.4"	222.4"	226.4"
Width	79.8"	79.8"	79.4"
Height	54.1"	54.8"	57.6"
Legroom — front	42.1"	42.1"	42.1"
Legroom — rear	34.3"	36.9"	37.9"
Headroom — front	38.0"	38.7"	38.9"
Headroom — rear	37.7"	37.8"	38.7"
Cargo capacity (cu. ft.)	20.4	20.4	100.8*
Fuel capacity (gals.)	26.5	26.5**	24.0

*Plus 6.8 cu. ft. of concealed space on 2-seat station wagons.   **20.5 gallons on 4-door sedans with 318 CID V8 engine.*

dual horns, hubcaps, and GR78 × 15 BSW tires. Gran Fury Custom adds: Princeton cloth-and-vinyl front bench seat w/fold-down center armrest, simulated woodgrained appliqué on I/P cluster and pad, 3-spoke steering wheel w/simulated woodgrained inserts, simulated woodgrained door trim insert, bright base armrests, glove box light, bright wheel lip moldings, and full-length bodyside molding w/black insert. Gran Fury Brougham adds: Brocade-like cloth-and-vinyl 50/50 split front bench seat w/individual fold-down center armrest, door pull straps, carpeted lower door panels, electric clock, rear door dome light courtesy switches, extra quiet insulation, bright belt moldings, bright rocker panel sill molding, full-length bodyside paint stripe, deluxe wheel covers, and HR78 × 15 BSW tires. Wagons add: All-vinyl front bench seat, color-keyed carpeting, simulated woodgrain inserts on steering wheel and door trim (Custom), cargo light, aerodynamic roof air deflector, power tailgate window, power steering, and LR78 × 15 BSW tires. Sport Suburban adds: All-vinyl split back front bench seat w/fold-down center armrest, door pull straps, simulated woodgrained appliqué on I/P cluster and pad, 3-spoke steering wheel w/simulated woodgrained inserts, simulated woodgrained door trim insert, carpeted lower door panels, electric clock, rear door dome light courtesy switches, simulated woodgrain bodyside panels, dual horns, and deluxe wheel covers.

Models Available

	Model No.	Base MSRP	Change from LY	Shipping Wt. (lbs.)	Model Year Production	Change from LY
Gran Fury 4-Door Sedan	PM41	$4,349	-4.73%	4140	5,560	-32.07%
Gran Fury Suburban 4-Door, 2-S. Wagon	PM45	$4,909	-3.12%	4880	1,046	-54.42%
Gran Fury Custom 2-Door Hardtop	PH23	$4,730	-1.07%	4265	1,513	-74.95%
Gran Fury Custom 4-Door Sedan	PH41	$4,715	-0.97%	4305	12,088	-36.52%
Gran Fury Custom Suburban 4-Dr., 2-S. Wgn.	PH45	$5,193	+0.33%	4895	1,018	-67.73%
Gran Fury Custom Suburban 4-Dr., 3-S. Wgn.	PH46	$5,316	+0.42%	4940	1,700	-62.22%
Gran Fury Brougham Formal 2-Door Hardtop	PP29	$5,334	+3.65%	4400	1,823	-72.04%
Gran Fury Brougham 4-Door Sedan	PP41	$5,162	NEW	4435	1,869	NEW
Gran Fury Sport Suburban 4-Dr., 3-S. Wagon	PP46	$5,761	+3.37%	4975	1,794	-62.15%
TOTALS	*Avg. price*	$5,052	-0.27%	*Production*	28,411	-60.97%

PONTIAC

"The Mark of Great Cars."

Fifty years after the "Chief of the Sixes" entered the automobile market as a lower-priced companion car to the mid-range eight-cylinder Oakland, there was little fanfare to mark Pontiac's anniversary. In fact, no acknowledgment of the achievement appeared in print until the 1977 sales brochures came out. Two models commemorated the event, a Golden Anniversary Grand Prix and a Special Edition Trans Am, but neither was widely advertised. Instead Pontiac's focus for 1976 was to improve sales in two market segments that had become very popular, but in which Pontiac's line had grown weak—all while holding the line on prices. The most successful moves were the introduction of a new subcompact coupe named Sunbird and the revamping of the Grand Prix lineup to add a new-lower priced base model, while the former base Grand Prix took on the SJ name and the features of the former option package. Along with the restructured Grand Prix line, the mid-size LeMans was given a facelift and the slow-selling Grand Am was discontinued. The Firebirds continued to climb the sales charts, while the remainder of the line was consolidated to fewer models to improve focus on the various nameplates. For example, the full-size line jettisoned the Grand Ville name and shifted its remaining models into the Bonneville line as the new Bonneville Brougham. And in the Ventura series, the entry-level "S" coupe was discontinued, and the Ventura SJ trim level replaced the former mid-level Ventura Custom, which was now gone, leaving only the base Ventura and Ventura SJ. By year's end, the mission paid off with a sales and production increase of more than 40 percent.

Sunbird was the name given to the corporate H-body car from Pontiac. Arriving a year later than its three siblings, the Sunbird initially came in only a two-door coupe model, based on the Chevrolet Monza Towne Coupe introduced as a mid-year 1975 model. This meant a formal rear roofline, large rear quarter side windows with a louvered B-pillar, and rather plain body styling. However, the Sunbird received its own unique Pontiac treatment, including the expected split grille and slotted look taillights that had become a regular feature on Pontiac's smaller car lines. The front end of the Sunbird used dual rectangular headlights set next to vertical parking/turn signal lights, which in turn were set to the outer ends of a sloping front-end treatment that was lined in chrome. The grille had a horizontal crosshatch pattern, seven rows high and eight columns across. The outer two columns of the grille overlaid the parking/turn signal lights. Chromed

aluminum bumpers with black rub strips were used both front and rear. At the back, rectangular taillights divided into three horizontal sections had an outer red brake and taillight lens, an inner white backup light lens, and in between an amber turn signal lens. The basics of the Sunbird interior were shared with its H-body siblings, but a Pontiac touch was evident. Standard bucket seats were contoured and door panels were padded and carpeted to give a luxury feel. Under the hood was a standard 140 CID 4-cylinder engine, straight from the Chevrolet Vega. Fortunately, the 231 CID V6 Buick-built engine was available as an option with a choice of 3-, 4-, or 5-speed manual transmissions, or the dependable Turbo Hydra-matic automatic transmission, and many Sunbirds were sold with this larger engine.

The Grand Prix line received a facelift, with a split, vertical bar waterfall type grille that began on top of the front header panel on each side of the "V" point of the header panel. Each side of the grille carried 15 vertical bars. As in other years of this generation Grand Prix, the pointed hood began at the outer edges of the hood where it met the A-pillar, angling forward to a point. New dual rectangular headlight styling allowed for the hood to be flattened above the lights. Parking and turn signal lights were again placed on the fender ends, this year in a bezel with four horizontal bars across the lens. At the rear, a new taillight bezel divided the lens into five horizontal sections, with the backup light in the bottom section. The LJ option, introduced last year, was still available with 29,045 base Grand Prix's having the option ordered. Soon after the start of the model year, a special Golden Anniversary Grand Prix commemorating Pontiac's 50th anniversary of vehicle production was introduced. Built as a Grand Prix SJ with LJ appointments, the Golden Anniversary Grand Prix received its own specific exterior color, Anniversary Gold, and was trimmed in white with a buckskin color interior. Each vehicle also received a new feature, removable "T-top" glass roof panels known as the "Hurst Hatch," since they were produced by the Hurst Corporation, known for creating the Hurst/Oldsmobiles and special Hurst shifters of the period. In all, 4,807 of these special models were produced, with each being shipped to Hurst for the "hatch roof" conversion before being sent to their final destinations. Although the Hurst Hatch was initially scheduled as optional equipment in all 1976 Grand Prix models from the start of production, conversion issues delayed the availability of the option on non-anniversary models until mid–January 1976. As a result, only 10,016 Grand Prix's were built with Hurst Hatches this year, including the 4,807 Golden Anniversary models.

Mid-size LeMans models received another front end styling update and a revised rear end look for 1976. Side-by-side dual rectangular headlamps were introduced with side marker and turn signal lamps set on the fender side of the bezel. Parking and turn signal lights were moved into the rectangular bumper openings beneath the grille. The new grille for all models was the same height as the headlight bezels, using the requisite two-port openings with a body-colored pointed center section, and the lower height of the rectangular headlights meant that the hood could be flattened out above them. All of this combined to make the cars look much lower and wider than in the previous three years. The grille pattern for the LeMans and LeMans Sport Coupe was divided into two sections horizontally on each side, and each of the four sections held a deeply recessed horizontal cross-hatch insert, five rows high and four columns across. The top-of-the-line Grand LeMans had its own grille with three square side-by-side sections per side, with each of the six openings having five vertical bars inset. A stand-up hood ornament sat on top of the front header panel. At the back, new horizontal taillamps were introduced with an outer rectangular shaped unit, divided into two sections horizontally, and wrapping around the rear quarter end to include the side marker light. LeMans Sport Coupe and Grand LeMans models added a second square unit, also divided into two sections horizontally, extending the taillights onto the rear panel directly below the trunk lid opening. On Grand LeMans, a chrome finish panel extended from the taillights to the license place recess and a small band continued above the recess. Backup lights were still located on each side of the center mounted license plate on the rear panel. On Grand LeMans models, a brushed chrome trim piece covered the area between the taillights and the license plate mounting. Station wagons still used the same rear styling with horizontal taillights placed near the ends of the bumper. For coupe models, Pontiac completely abandoned the large triangular rear quarter window this year, offering only formal "opera window" style or louvered, near rectangular rear quarter windows. Powertrains were mostly the same with the only change being the 260 CID V8 engine added as the smallest V8 engine option for cars sold in California, while Federal-equipped cars still used the 350 CID 2-barrel V8 engine as the base V8.

The 455 CID V8 engine was once again available in the Firebird Trans Am, albeit with nearly 50 fewer horsepower than before. A new front end for all Firebird models kept a two-port grille similar to that of 1974 and 1975, but fully integrated the front bumper into the design and eliminated the black rub strip, giving a much smoother look to the front. At the rear the body-colored urethane bumper was similarly molded into the rear panel for a cleaner look. The Formula had redesigned hood scoops built into a slightly raised section of the hood near the center, and the Trans Am continued to rise in popularity. At mid-year, a Special Edition black Trans Am was announced with the following features: Starlight Black exterior with gold accent striping, black or buckskin interior trim with gold accents (available in either standard or custom trim), gold-lettered GR70x15 tires, and Hurst Hatch roof. Roof drip rail and side window sill moldings were eliminated. Prior to production the gold-lettered tires were dropped in favor of less costly black sidewall tires or optional white-letter tires. The pre-production announcement stated that production would be limited to just 2,400 units, and was scheduled to begin on April 1, 1976.

The compact Ventura received a new two-port grille with three horizontal sections on base models (two on SJ models), and each section carrying an egg-crate insert two rows high, with turn signals set into the outer ends. The inner end of each grille port angled to create a "V" shape that accentuated the point of the nose. Most other styling and powertrain features remained unchanged. The optional Sprint package was dropped, but the Sprint paint and tape treatment was available as the Special Appearance group. Finally, the Ventura SJ was moved down a notch in trim to take the place of the 1975 Ventura Custom, while the Ventura S coupe was eliminated.

From the front end, the only visible change to the 1976 Astre was that the Pontiac name on the driver's side grille insert was moved down to the bottom of the grille, adjacent to the parking/turn signal lamp. The mid-year 1975 Astre S, series C, introduced as a lower priced alternative to the better equipped Astre and Astre SJ versions, was renamed as simply Astre for 1976. It gained a few of the 1975 Astre, series V, standard features and became the only Astre as the Astre SJ was eliminated. Custom interior and exterior packages were available, however, that had basically the same content as the former SJ model.

Finally, the full-size Pontiacs entered their last year of production in their current form, as they were scheduled for downsizing for the 1977 model year. The base Catalina received a new grille pattern with six stacked horizontal openings per side. A new Custom option featured additional interior and exterior trim, but was easily identified from the outside by its rectangular headlights lifted from the Bonneville. The Bonneville line, in addition to sporting a new grille with a center vertical divider and a horizontal crosshatch pattern in four columns per side, gained a two-door coupe and four-door hardtop in a new Bonneville Brougham subseries. In fact, these were not really new models, merely replacements for the discontinued Grand Ville nameplate. Along with the Grand Ville name, the last surviving Pontiac convertible model was also gone. With the changes, full-size Pontiac sales were up for the first time since 1973.

Astre 2-Door Hatchback Coupe

Astre 2-Door Notchback Coupe

Astre Safari 2-Door Station
Wagon with GT package

Bonneville 2-Door Hardtop Coupe

Bonneville Brougham 4-Door Hardtop
(front) and Catalina 2-Door Hardtop
Coupe with Custom package (rear)

Catalina 4-Door Sedan

Catalina Safari 4-Door Station Wagon

Firebird Esprit 2-Door Hardtop Coupe

Firebird Formula 2-Door Hardtop Coupe

Firebird Trans Am 2-Door Hardtop Coupe

Firebird Trans Am 2-Door Hardtop
Coupe with Special Edition package

Grand LeMans 2-Door Colonnade
Hardtop Coupe (front) and LeMans
4-Door Colonnade Hardtop Sedan (rear)

Grand Prix SJ 2-Door Hardtop Coupe

Grand Prix SJ 2-Door Hardtop Coupe
with Golden Anniversary package
next to 1926 Pontiac coupe

Grand Safari 4-Door Station Wagon

LeMans 4-Door Colonnade Hardtop Sedan

LeMans Safari 4-Door Station Wagon

Sunbird 2-Door Coupe

Ventura 2-Door Hatchback Coupe

Ventura SJ 2-Door Coupe

Sunbird interior

Model year production: 748,842, up 40.83% from 1975.
Domestic market share: 8.66% (4th place).
Base price range: $3,064 to $5,906.
Pontiac average base price: $4,453, up 5.22%.
Introduction date: September 25, 1975.
Assembly plants: Lakewood, GA (A); Southgate, CA (C); Framingham, MA (G); Van Nuys, CA (L); Norwood, OH (N); Pontiac, MI (P); Tarrytown, NY (T); Lordstown, OH (U); Willow Run, MI (W); Kansas City/Fairfax, KS (X); Oshawa, Ontario, Canada (1); and Ste. Therese, Quebec, Canada (2).

Data plate identification (VIN): Thirteen digit code read as follows: First digit indicates division (2 = Pontiac); second through fourth digits indicate series and body style (model number in model charts); fifth digit is engine code (see powertrain chart); sixth digit indicates model year (6 = 1976); seventh digit indicates assembly plant (see list above); remaining digits are sequential with beginning number of 100001. *Example:* 2D35M6G100001 is a 1976 Pontiac LeMans 4-Door, 2-Seat Safari station wagon, with 350 CID, 2-bbl. V8 engine, serial number 100001, built in Framingham, MA.

Powertrains

Engine	Net HP	Engine Code	Transmission Availability[1]		Astre & Sunbird	Ventura	Firebird[2]	LeMans[3]	Grand Prix	Catalina & Bonneville[4]	Catalina Safari & Grand Safari
140 CID (2.3L) OHC, 1-bbl., 4-cyl.	70	A	3-speed manual		S	—	—	—	—	—	—
				MPG:	21/34/26	—	—	—	—	—	—
			4-speed manual		$60	—	—	—	—	—	—
				MPG:	NA	—	—	—	—	—	—
			3-speed Turbo Hydra-matic		$244	—	—	—	—	—	—
				MPG:	19/28/22	—	—	—	—	—	—
140 CID (2.3L) OHC, 2-bbl., 4-cyl.	84	B	3-speed manual		$56	—	—	—	—	—	—
				MPG:	22/35/26	—	—	—	—	—	—
				Calif.	19/30/23	—	—	—	—	—	—
			4-speed manual		$116	—	—	—	—	—	—
				MPG:	NA	—	—	—	—	—	—
			5-speed manual		$300	—	—	—	—	—	—
				MPG:	NA	—	—	—	—	—	—
			3-speed Turbo Hydra-matic		$300	—	—	—	—	—	—
				MPG:	20/28/23	—	—	—	—	—	—
				Calif.	19/27/22	—	—	—	—	—	—
231 CID (3.8L), 2-bbl., V6	105	C	3-speed manual		$189 (Sunbird)	—	—	—	—	—	—
				MPG:	18/30/22	—	—	—	—	—	—
				Calif.	17/26/20	—	—	—	—	—	—
			4-speed manual		$249 (Sunbird)	—	—	—	—	—	—
				MPG:	NA	—	—	—	—	—	—
			5-speed manual		$433	—	—	—	—	—	—

1976

Engine	Net HP	Engine Code	Transmission Availability[1]		Astre & Sunbird	Ventura	Firebird[2]	LeMans[3]	Grand Prix	Catalina & Bonneville[4]	Catalina Safari & Grand Safari
				MPG:	(Sunbird) NA	—	—	—	—	—	—
			3-speed Turbo Hydra-matic		$433	—	—	—	—	—	—
				MPG:	(Sunbird) 18/26/21	—	—	—	—	—	—
				Calif.	18/24/20	—	—	—	—	—	—
250 CID (4.0L), 1-bbl., 6-cyl.	110	D	3-speed manual		—	S	S (F & FEs)	S (L & LSC)	—	—	—
				MPG:	—	17/25/20	17/25/20	17/25/20	—	—	—
			3-speed Turbo Hydra-matic		—	$262	$262 (F & FEs)	S (GL)/ $262 (L & LSC)	—	—	—
				MPG:	—	18/23/20	17/23/20	17/22/19	—	—	—
				Calif.	—	15/21/17	15/21/17	15/21/17	—	—	—
260 CID (4.3L), 2-bbl., V8	110	F	3-speed manual		—	$90	—	$90 (L & LSC)	—	—	—
				MPG:	—	16/25/19	—	16/26/19	—	—	—
				Calif.	—	14/21/17	—	14/21/16	—	—	—
			5-speed manual		—	$352	—	$352 (LSC)	—	—	—
				MPG:	—	NA	—	NA	—	—	—
			3-speed Turbo Hydra-matic		—	$352	—	$90 (GL)/ $352 (L & LSC)	—	—	—
				MPG:	—	16/23/19	—	16/22/18	—	—	—
				Calif.	—	14/20/16	—	13/18/15	—	—	—
350 CID (5.7L), 2-bbl., V8	160[5]	M	3-speed Turbo Hydra-matic		—	$367	S (FF)/ $402 (F & FEs)	$140 (GL)/ $402 (L & LSC)	S (base)	—	—
				MPG:	—	14/20/17	16/21/18	14/19/16	14/19/16	—	—
350 CID (5.7L), 4-bbl., V8	165	J	3-speed Turbo Hydra-matic		—	$417	$55 (FF)[6]/ $458 (F & FEs)[6]	$180 (GL)[6]/ $417 (L)[6]	$55 (base)	—	—
				MPG:	—	14/22/17	14/22/17	14/21/16	14/20/16	—	—
				Calif.	—	14/20/16	13/18/15	13/18/15	13/18/15	—	—
400 CID (6.6L), 2-bbl., V8	170	R[7]	3-speed Turbo Hydra-matic		—	—	—	S (LS)/ $203 (GL)/ $440 (L)	-$55 (SJ credit option)/ $63 (base)	-$73 (BB credit option)/ S (CB)	—
				MPG:	—	—	—	14/19/16	14/19/16	13/19/15	—
400 CID (6.6L), 4-bbl., V8	185	S	4-speed manual		—	—	S (TA)/ $118 (FF)/ $500 (F & Fes)	—	—	—	—
				MPG:	—	—	12/17/14	—	—	—	—
			3-speed Turbo Hydra-matic		—	—	N/C (TA)/	$55 (LS)/ $118	S (SJ)/ $118	S (BB)/ $73	—

Engine	Net HP	Engine Code	Transmission Availability[1]	Astre & Sunbird	Ventura	Firebird[2]	LeMans[3]	Grand Prix	Catalina & Bonneville[4]	Catalina Safari & Grand Safari
						$118 (FF)/ $520 (F & FEs)	$258 (GL)/ $495 (L)	(base)	(CB)	
			MPG:	—	—	15/22/18	15/20/17	15/20/17	13/17/15	—
			Calif.	—	—	15/19/16	13/18/15	13/18/15	13/17/14	—
455 CID (7.4L), 4-bbl., V8	200	Y	3-speed Turbo Hydra-matic	—	—	$125 (TA)	$118 (LS)/ $321 (GL)/ $558 (L)	$63 (SJ)/ $181 (base)	$64 (BB)/ $137 (CB)	S
			MPG:	—	—	12/17/14	14/20/16	14/20/16	13/18/15	13/17/14
			Calif.	—	—	—	12/18/15	13/19/15	12/17/13	11/16/13

[1]Unless otherwise noted: All 3-speed manual transmissions are floor shift, except on Ventura. All 4-speed and 5-speed manual transmissions are floor shift. All automatic transmissions are column shift, with the following exceptions: Astre, Sunbird, and Firebird. Floor-shift with 3-speed manual can be ordered on Ventura models for $30 extra. Floor shift w/automatics is available on specific Ventura, LeMans and Grand Prix models in combination w/optional bucket seats and console. [2]F = base Firebird; FEs = Firebird Esprit; FF = Firebird Formula; TA = Firebird Trans Am. [3]L = LeMans; LSC = LeMans Sport coupe; GL = Grand LeMans; LS = all LeMans Safaris. [4]CB = Catalina and Bonneville; BB = Bonneville Brougham. [5]Horsepower rating on Ventura is 145. [6]Available only in California. [7]Not available in California.

Major Options

	Astre	Sunbird	Firebird	Ventura	LeMans	Grand Prix	Catalina & Bonneville
Custom air conditioning[1]	$424	$424	$452	$452	$476	$505	$512
Tilt steering wheel	$48	$48	$52	$52	$52	$52	$53
Automatic cruise control	—	—	$73	$73	$73	$73	$73
Rear window defroster, electric	$65	$66	$43[2]	$43[2]	$77	$77	$44[2]
Soft-Ray tinted glass, all windows	$44	$44	$46	$46	$50	$50	$64
Power windows, 2-dr./4-dr.	—	—	$99[3]	$99/$140	$99/$140	$99	$105/$159[4]
Power door locks, 2-dr./4-dr.	—	—	$62	—	$62/$89	$62	$65/$95
Power front seat, 6-way w/std. seat	—	—	—	—	$124	$124	$126
Front bucket seats, w/console	S	S	S	$218	$231[5]	$231	—
AM radio	$70	$70	$75	$75	$75	$75	$92
AM/FM stereo	$212	$212	$233	$233	$233	$233	$236
AM/FM stereo w/8-track tape	—	—	$337[3]	$337	$337	$337	$341
Woodgrain exterior trim, wagons	—	—	—	—	$154	—	$156
Vinyl top, full[6]	—	$81	$96	$91	$109	$119	$125
Vinyl top, landau[5]	—	$132	—	$150	$119	$119	$125
Sunroof, removable[5]	—	$149	—	—	—	—	—
Sunroof, power[5]	—	—	—	—	$370	$370	—
Hurst Hatch roof, T-tops[5]	—	—	$	—	—	$	—
Power steering, variable-ratio	$120	$120	S	$136	$136[7]	S	S
Power brakes, w/front disc	$55	$55	$58[7]	$58	$58[7]	S	S
Custom/finned wheel covers	$46	S	$57	$57	$57	$57	S
Rally II wheels[8]	$101	$55	$97	$97	$97	$97	$66
Honeycomb wheels	—	—	$135	—	—	$135	—
WSW tires	$32	$32	—	$33	$35	$40	$40

Popular Option Groups & Packages

	Astre	Sunbird	Firebird	Ventura	LeMans	Grand Prix	Catalina & Bonneville
Catalina Custom package	—	—	—	—	—	—	$228
Custom exterior group	$88	—	—	—	—	—	—

	Astre	Sunbird	Firebird	Ventura	LeMans	Grand Prix	Catalina & Bonneville
Custom interior group	$148	—	—	—	—	—	—
Custom trim group	—	—	$81	—	$88[9]	—	—
Formula appearance package	—	—	$100	—	—	—	—
GT option package	$465	—	—	—	—	—	—
LJ luxury appointment package	—	—	—	—	—	$336	—
Luxury appointment package	$104	$139	—	—	—	—	—
Special appearance group	—	—	—	$92	—	—	—
Special Edition Trans Am package	—	—	$1,100	—	—	—	—
SJ golden anniversary package	—	—	—	—	—	$550	—

—= Not Available; S = Standard equipment. [1]Automatic climate control is available for $513 on LeMans, for $542 on Grand Prix, and for $549 on Catalina, Bonneville, and Grand Safari. [2]Blower type defroster. [3]Other optional equipment required at extra cost; i.e. console. [4]Standard on Bonneville Brougham. [5]Available only on 2-door models. [6]Canopy style vinyl roof on Firebird, Esprit and Formula. Vinyl roof available on Catalina Safari and Grand Safari for $150. Price on Bonneville two-door is $147. Not available on LeMans station wagons. [7]Power steering and power brakes standard on all LeMans station wagons, Firebird Formula and Firebird Trans Am. Power brakes standard on Grand LeMans 4-Door. [8]Rally III wheels on Astre and Sunbird. [9]Available only on LeMans 4-door.

Paint Colors

	Code		Code
Cameo White[1,2]	11	Bavarian Cream[2]	50
Sterling Silver metallic[1,2]	13	Goldenrod Yellow[1,2,3]	51
Medium Gray metallic[2]	16	Anniversary Gold metallic	55
Starlight Black[2]	19	Cream Gold[4]	57
Athena Blue metallic[2]	28	Buckskin Tan[5]	65
Polaris Blue metallic[2]	35	Durango Bronze metallic[2]	67
Firethorn Red metallic[1,2]	36	Roman Red[4]	72
Cordovan Maroon metallic[2]	37	Carousel Red[1,2,3]	78
Metalime Green metallic[2]	40		
Alpine Green metallic	49		

In two-tone combinations, the first two digits indicate lower color and the next two digits are the upper color.

Two-tones available only on Ventura, LeMans, Catalina, Bonneville, and Grand Prix w/luxury appointment package. Trans Am "Bird" hood decal available at $60 extra cost. [1]Only colors available on Trans Am. [2]Available in two-tone combinations. [3]Available only on Astre, Sunbird, Firebird and Ventura models. [4]Available only on LeMans, Grand Prix, Catalina and Bonneville models. [5]Available only on Grand Prix with LJ luxury appointment package and in two-tone combination as an upper color with either Durango Bronze or Bavarian Cream lower color.

Astre

"Pontiac's subcompact cars."

Nameplate year of origin: 1975.
Current bodystyle lifespan: 1975 through 1977 (some models moved to Sunbird series, continuing through 1979).
Predecessor to this model: None.
Replacement for this model: J2000/Sunbird (1982 to 1993).
Percentage of division's production: 6.73%.
Corporate siblings: Chevrolet Vega.
Primary competition: AMC Gremlin, Dodge Colt, and Mercury Bobcat.
Notable changes: Minor trim and detail changes.
Major standard equipment: Choice of cloth and Morrokide vinyl or all-Morrokide vinyl front bucket seats, color-keyed cut-pile carpeting, simulated rosewood vinyl inserts on I/P, fold-down rear seat and rear liftgate (hatchback and wagon), deluxe two-spoke steering wheel, glove box, map pocket in drivers door, bright front and rear window moldings, bright side window moldings, bright drip rail moldings, front and rear bumper rub strips, manual front disc brakes, hubcaps, and A78 × 13 BSW tires.

Measurements

	Coupes	Wagon
Wheelbase	97.0"	97.0"
Length	177.6"	177.6"
Width	65.4"	65.4"
Height	51.9"	51.6"
Legroom — front	42.8"	42.8"
Legroom — rear	28.9"	30.0"
Headroom — front	38.6"	38.6"
Headroom — rear	38.4"	40.3"
Cargo capacity (cu. ft.)	8.7*	46.6
Fuel capacity (gals.)	16.0	16.0

*Hatchback maximum with rear seat down, 18.9 cu. ft.

Models Available

	Model No.	Base MSRP	Change from LY	Shipping Wt. (lbs.)	Model Year Production	Change from LY*
Astre 2-Door Notchback Coupe	C11	$3,064	+7.85%	2439	18,143	+117.57%

	Model No.	Base MSRP	Change from LY	Shipping Wt. (lbs.)	Model Year Production	Change from LY*
Astre 2-Door Hatchback Coupe	C77	$3,179	+7.62%	2505	19,116	-53.16%
Astre 2-Door Station Wagon	C15	$3,306	+7.65%	2545	13,125	-14.34%
TOTALS	*Avg. price*	$3,183	-0.60%	*Production*	50,384	-21.85%

Comparisons made to total 1975 body style production, as 1975 production was not kept by model number.

Sunbird

"A great small car from the Wide-Track people."

Nameplate year of origin: 1976.
Current bodystyle lifespan: 1976 through 1980.
Predecessor to this model: None.
Replacement for this model: J2000/Sunbird (1982 to 1993).
Percentage of division's production: 6.95%.
Corporate siblings: Chevrolet Monza Towne Coupe.
Primary competition: Ford Mustang II.
Notable changes: All-new model.
Major standard equipment: All-Morrokide vinyl front bucket seats, cut-pile carpeting, floor shifter and floor-mounted parking brake w/mini-console, deluxe two-spoke steering wheel, simulated rosewood appliqués on I/P, bright window moldings on all windows, roof drip rail moldings, wheel opening moldings, manual front disc brakes, custom wheel covers, and A78 × 13 BSW tires.

Measurements

Wheelbase	97.0"
Length	177.8"
Width	65.4"
Height	49.8"
Legroom — front	42.8"
Legroom — rear	28.2"
Headroom — front	37.7"
Headroom — rear	36.9"
Cargo capacity (cu. ft.)	6.6
Fuel capacity (gals.)	18.5

Models Available

	Model No.	Base MSRP	Change from LY	Shipping Wt. (lbs.)	Model Year Production	Change from LY
Sunbird 2-Door Coupe	M27	$3,431	NEW	2653	52,031	NEW
TOTALS	*Avg. price*	$3,431	NEW	*Production*	52,031	NEW

Firebird

"Pontiac's sports cars."

Nameplate year of origin: 1967.
Current bodystyle lifespan: 1970 through 1981.
Predecessor to this model: Firebird (1967 to 1969).
Replacement for this model: Firebird (1982 to 1992).
Percentage of division's production: 14.79%.
Corporate siblings: Chevrolet Camaro.
Primary competition: None.
Notable changes: New front-end styling and bumpers and minor trim and detail changes.
Major standard equipment: All-Morrokide vinyl front bucket seats, cut-pile carpeting, deluxe two-spoke steering wheel, ashtray light, Firebird emblems on grille panel, sail panel and rear deck lid, bright front and rear window moldings, bright grille moldings, Endura front and rear bumpers w/integral bumper guards, trunk floor mat, variable-ratio power steering, manual front disc brakes, hubcaps, and FR78 × 15 BSW tires. Esprit adds: Custom all-Morrokide vinyl front bucket seats w/deep contour design, distinctive door trim panels, door and I/P assist straps, custom cushion steering wheel, pedal trim plates, rear quarter ashtray, added acoustical insulation, dual body-colored mirror w/LH remote, body-colored door handle inserts, bright roof drip rail and belt reveal moldings, bright rear hood edge molding, bright wheel opening and rocker panel moldings, and deluxe wheel covers.

Measurements

Wheelbase	108.1"
Length	196.8"
Width	73.0"
Height	50.4"
Legroom — front	44.1"
Legroom — rear	29.6"
Headroom — front	37.5"
Headroom — rear	35.9"
Cargo capacity (cu. ft.)	8.8
Fuel capacity (gals.)	20.2

Formula adds: Custom Cushion steering wheel, full-length floor console, blacked-out grille, dual body-colored mirror w/LH remote, Formula identification, steel hood w/dual simulated hood scoops, dual chrome splitter tailpipe extensions, and front and rear stabilizer bars. Trans Am adds: Formula steering wheel, rally gauge cluster package, aluminum-swirl finish I/P trim plate, dual body-colored mirror w/LH remote, blacked-out grille, wraparound rear deck spoiler, wheel opening air deflectors, front fender air extractors, Trans Am decal on front fender and rear spoiler, shaker hood scoop, power brakes, power flex fan, Safe-T-Track differential, firm control shocks, dual chrome splitter tailpipe extensions, Rally II wheels w/trim rings, and GR70 × 15 BSW tires.

Models Available

	Model No.	Base MSRP	Change from LY	Shipping Wt. (lbs.)	Model Year Production	Change from LY
Firebird 2-Door Hardtop Coupe	S87	$3,906	+5.20%	3383	21,209	-4.86%
Firebird Esprit 2-Door Hardtop Coupe	T87	$4,162	+5.15%	3431	22,252	+6.85%
Firebird Formula 2-Door Hardtop Coupe	U87	$4,566	+4.99%	3625	20,613	+50.79%
Firebird Trans Am 2-Door Hardtop Coupe	W87	$4,987	+5.21%	3640	46,701	+71.23%
TOTALS		*Avg. price* $4,405	+5.14%		*Production* 110,775	+31.78%

Ventura

"Pontiac's compact cars."

Nameplate year of origin: 1960.
Current bodystyle lifespan: 1975 through 1979 (Ventura 1975 to 1977; Phoenix 1977 to 1979).
Predecessor to this model: Ventura/Ventura II (1971 to 1974; restyled in 1973).
Replacement for this model: Phoenix (1980 to 1984).
Percentage of division's production: 9.90%.
Corporate siblings: Buick Skylark, Chevrolet Nova/Concours, and Oldsmobile Omega.
Primary competition: AMC Hornet, Dodge Aspen, Ford Granada, and Mercury Monarch.
Notable changes: New grille and minor trim and detail changes.
Major standard equipment: Cloth w/Morrokide vinyl trim front bench seat, cut-pile carpeting, color-keyed deluxe two-spoke steering wheel, simulated rosewood I/P trim, front door dome light switches, rear seat armrest ashtrays, bright front and rear window moldings, bright drip rail moldings, manual front disc brakes, hubcaps, and E78 × 14 BSW tires. Hatchback model adds: Fold-down rear seat, painted metal load floor, cargo area light, and fully trimmed cargo area sidewalls. SJ adds: Choice of cloth and Morrokide vinyl or all-Morrokide vinyl front bench seat, simulated rosewood on I/P and console, custom cushion steering wheel, dome light switches on all doors, I/P courtesy lights, trunk mat and sidewall panels, side window reveal moldings, bright wheel opening moldings, rocker panel moldings, bright rear end panel, SJ identification, stand-up hood ornament, and custom finned wheel covers.

Measurements

	Coupe & HBK	Sedan
Wheelbase	111.1"	111.1"
Length	199.6"	199.6"
Width	72.4"	72.4"
Height	52.7"	53.8"
Legroom — front	41.7"	41.7"
Legroom — rear	33.2"	34.9"
Headroom — front	38.5"	39.5"
Headroom — rear	36.3"	36.5"
Cargo capacity (cu. ft.)	14.2*	13.8
Fuel capacity (gals.)	20.5	20.5

Hatchback maximum with rear seat down, 28.4 cu. ft.

Models Available

	Model No.	Base MSRP	Change from LY*	Shipping Wt. (lbs.)	Model Year Production	Change from LY**
Ventura 2-Door Coupe	Y27	$3,326	+1.00%	3234	28,473	-2.16%**
Ventura 2-Door Hatchback	Y17	$3,503	+2.07%	3348	6,428	-21.14%**
Ventura 4-Door Sedan	Y69	$3,361	+1.73%	3271	27,773	+47.62%**
Ventura SJ 2-Door Coupe	Z27	$3,612	+4.73%	3290	4,815	NA**
Ventura SJ 2-Door Hatchback	Z17	$3,775	+5.07%	3380	1,823	NA**
Ventura SJ 4-Door Sedan	Z69	$3,637	+4.99%	3326	4,804	NA**
TOTALS		*Avg. price* $3,536	+0.07%		*Production* 74,116	+11.36%

*1976 Ventura SJ model prices compared to 1975 Ventura Custom models of same model number. **Production of 1975 S, Custom and SJ models were kept as combined total by body style and not model; therefore comparisons to LY are shown by bodystyle under base Ventura models.*

LeMans

"Pontiac's complete lineup of mid-size cars."

Nameplate year of origin: 1961 (as a Tempest subseries).
Current bodystyle lifespan: 1973 through 1977.
Predecessor to this model: Tempest/LeMans (1968 to 1972).
Replacement for this model: LeMans (1978 to 1981).
Percentage of division's production: 17.47%.
Corporate siblings: Buick Century, Chevrolet Chevelle, and Oldsmobile Cutlass.
Primary competition: AMC Matador, Dodge Coronet, Ford Torino, and Mercury Montego.
Notable changes: New grille and minor trim and detail changes.
Major standard equipment: Cloth-and-vinyl front bench seat, color-keyed cut-pile carpeting, deluxe three-spoke steering wheel, simulated rosewood vinyl accents on I/P, door panels

Measurements

	Coupes	Sedans	Wagons
Wheelbase	112.0"	116.0"	116.0"
Length	208.0"	212.0"	215.4"
Width	77.4"	77.4"	77.4"
Height	52.9"	54.3"	55.0"
Legroom — front	42.5"	42.5"	42.5"
Legroom — rear	32.9"	37.0"	36.8"
Headroom — front	37.4"	38.0"	38.7"
Headroom — rear	36.5"	36.9"	39.0"
Cargo capacity (cu. ft.)	15.1	15.1	82.9
Fuel capacity (gals.)	21.8	21.8	22.0

and steering wheel, bright front and rear window moldings, bright roof drip rail and rear quarter window trim, bright rocker panel molding, trunk mat, manual front disc brakes, hubcaps, and FR78 × 15 BSW tires. Wagon adds: All-Morrokide vinyl front bench seat, vinyl coated metal cargo area sidewalls, load floor carpeting, swing-up tailgate w/fixed window and remote release, I/P mounted "door ajar" warning light for tailgate, swing-out rear quarter vents (3-seat wagon only), vertical rub strips on tailgate, power front disc brakes, and HR78 × 15 BSW tires. Sport Coupe adds: Choice of all-Morrokide vinyl front bench seat w/fold-down center armrest or all-Morrokide bucket seats, simulated rosewood vinyl accents on glove box door, choice of vertically louvered rear quarter windows or rear quarter opera window, and LeMans Sport Coupe identification. Grand LeMans adds: Choice of cloth-and-vinyl or all-vinyl notchback bench seat w/fold-down center armrest or all-Morrokide bucket seats, cockpit style instrument panel design, custom cushion steering wheel, door panels w/carpeted lower panels and upper padded panel, front door assist straps, glove box and ashtray lights, simulated rosewood vinyl accents on I/P and glove box door, added body insulation, rear seat armrest ashtrays, formal rear quarter opera window (coupe only), bright drip rail and quarter window moldings, bright rear hood edge and rear deck moldings, front wheel opening moldings, body color door handle inserts, full-length rocker panel molding w/front and rear extensions, rear-wheel fender skirts (except on Safari), stand-up hood ornament, and deluxe wheel covers.

Models Available

	Model No.	Base MSRP	Change from LY	Shipping Wt. (lbs.)	Model Year Production	Change from LY*
LeMans 2-Door Colonnade HT Coupe	D37	$3,768	+4.96%	3651	21,130	+2.39%
LeMans 4-Door Colonnade HT Sedan	D29	$3,813	+5.56%	3760	22,199	+47.35%
LeMans 4-Door, 2-Seat Safari Station Wagon	D35	$4,687	+2.90%	4336	8,249	+111.62%
LeMans 4-Door, 3-Seat Safari Station Wagon	D45	$4,820	+2.82%	4374	5,901	+146.59%
LeMans Sport Coupe 2-Door Colonnade HT	F37	$3,916	+5.61%	3668	15,582	-34.58%
Grand LeMans 2-Door Colonnade HT Coupe	G37	$4,330	+5.58%	3747	14,757	-23.58%
Grand LeMans 4-Door Colonnade HT Sedan	G29	$4,433	+6.64%	3860	8,411	+71.44%
Grand LeMans 4-Door, 2-Seat Safari Wagon	G35	$4,928	+3.77%	4389	NA*	NA*
Grand LeMans 4-Door, 3-Seat Safari Wagon	G45	$5,061	+3.67%	4427	NA*	NA*
TOTALS	*Avg. price*	$4,417	+4.51%	*Production*	96,229	+3.56%

*Production and comparisons to LY for Grand LeMans Safari wagons are not possible due to production total being kept as combined total with LeMans Safari wagons.

Grand Prix

"Pontiac's classic personal car."

Nameplate year of origin: 1962.
Current bodystyle lifespan: 1973 through 1977.
Predecessor to this model: Grand Prix (1969 to 1972).
Replacement for this model: Grand Prix (1978 to 1987).
Percentage of division's production: 30.46%.
Corporate siblings: Chevrolet Monte Carlo.
Primary competition: Dodge Charger SE, Ford Elite, and Mercury Cougar XR-7.
Notable changes: New front end and minor trim and detail changes.
Major standard equipment: Choice of cloth-and-vinyl or all-vinyl w/Morrokide front notchback bench seat w/fold-down center armrests, color-keyed cut-pile carpeting, custom cushion three-spoke steering wheel, cockpit-style I/P, simulated rosewood inlay trim on I/P, console and door panels, I/P courtesy lights, electric clock, ashtray light, monogrammed fixed rear quarter window w/bright trim, bright front and rear window moldings, bright side window sill and drip rail moldings, bright rear hood edge molding, bright wheel opening moldings, rocker panel moldings, trunk map, rear bumper guards, front and rear bumper rub strips, power steering, power brakes, RTS package, deluxe wheel covers, and GR78 × 15 BSW tires. SJ adds: All Morrokide-vinyl front bucket seats w/center floor console, rally gauge cluster, pedal trim plates, dual body-colored sport mirrors w/LH remote control, wide rocker panel moldings, body colored door handle inserts, trunk compartment light and side panels, bodyside tape stripes, rear stabilizer bar, and custom finned wheel covers.

Measurements

Wheelbase	116.0"
Length	212.7"
Width	77.8"
Height	52.9"
Legroom — front	42.5"
Legroom — rear	33.5"
Headroom — front	37.5"
Headroom — rear	37.4"
Cargo capacity (cu. ft.)	14.3
Fuel capacity (gals.)	25.0

1976

Models Available

	Model No.	Base MSRP	Change from LY	Shipping Wt. (lbs.)	Model Year Production	Change from LY
Grand Prix 2-Door Hardtop Coupe	J57	$4,798	NEW	4048	139,859	NEW
Grand Prix SJ 2-Door Hardtop Coupe	K57	$5,223	-9.40%*	4052	88,232	+61.53%*
TOTALS	*Avg. price*	$5,011	-5.39%	*Production*	228,091	+163.44%

*Comparison of 1976 Grand Prix SJ, model K57, to 1975 Grand Prix, model K57.

Catalina

"Pontiac's lowest priced full-sized car."

Nameplate year of origin: 1950 (as hardtop model designation), 1959 (as series).
Current bodystyle lifespan: 1971 through 1976.
Predecessor to this model: Catalina (1969 to 1970).
Replacement for this model: Catalina (1977 to 1981).
Percentage of division's production: 9.71%.
Corporate siblings: Buick LeSabre, Chevrolet Impala/Caprice, and Oldsmobile Delta 88.
Primary competition: Dodge Monaco, Ford LTD, and Plymouth Gran Fury.
Notable changes: Minor trim and detail changes.
Major standard equipment: Cloth-and-Morrokide vinyl bench seat, thick cut-pile carpeting, deluxe three-spoke steering wheel, rosewood vinyl I/P accents, dual ashtrays w/LH ashtray light, glove box light, trunk mat, bright rocker panel molding, bright hood rear edge molding, bright quarter window and roof drip rail moldings, RTS package, front and rear bumper rub strips, hubcaps, and HR78 × 15 BSW tires. Safari wagon adds: All-Morrokide vinyl front bench seat, glove box lights, RH rear view mirror, Glide-Away tailgate w/power-operated rear window, rear bumper guards, and LR78 × 15 BSW tires.

Measurements

	2-door	4-door	Wagon
Wheelbase	123.4"	123.4"	127.0"
Length	226.0"	226.0"	231.3"
Width	79.6"	79.6"	79.6"
Height	53.5"	54.2"	57.5"
Legroom — front	42.6"	42.7"	42.6"
Legroom — rear	35.8"	38.5"	38.7"
Headroom — front	37.9"	38.8"	39.3"
Headroom — rear	37.0"	37.6"	39.0"
Cargo capacity (cu. ft.)	20.5	20.5	105.7
Fuel capacity (gals.)	25.8	25.8	22.0

Models Available

	Model No.	Base MSRP	Change from LY	Shipping Wt. (lbs.)	Model Year Production	Change from LY
Catalina 2-Door Hardtop Coupe	L57	$4,844	+3.06%	4256	15,262	-29.49%
Catalina 4-Door Sedan	L69	$4,767	+3.36%	4276	47,235	+16.92%
Catalina Safari 4-Door, 2-Seat Station Wagon	L35	$5,324	+3.40%	4944	4,735	+19.45%
Catalina Safari 4-Door, 3-Seat Station Wagon	L45	$5,473	+3.36%	5000	5,513	+10.44%
TOTALS	Avg. price	$5,102	+3.30%	Production	72,745	+2.46%

Bonneville and Grand Safari

"The latest edition of the original Wide-Track."

Nameplate year of origin: 1957.

Current bodystyle lifespan: 1971 through 1976.

Predecessor to this model: Bonneville (1969 to 1970).

Replacement for this model: Bonneville (1977 to 1981).

Percentage of division's production: 8.61%.

Corporate siblings: Buick LeSabre, Chevrolet Impala/Caprice, and Oldsmobile Delta 88.

Primary competition: Dodge Royal Monaco and Mercury Marquis.

Notable changes: Minor trim and detail changes.

Major standard equipment: Choice of cloth-and-Morrokide vinyl or all-Morrokide vinyl front bench seat w/fold-down center armrest, cut-pile carpeting, lower door panel carpeting, door pull straps, custom cushion steering wheel, simu-

Measurements

	2-door	4-door	Wagons
Wheelbase	123.4"	123.4"	127.0"
Length	226.0"	226.0"	231.3"
Width	79.6"	79.6"	79.6"
Height	53.5"	54.2"	57.5"
Legroom — front	42.6"	42.7"	42.6"
Legroom — rear	35.8"	38.5"	38.7"
Headroom — front	37.9"	38.8"	39.3"
Headroom — rear	37.0"	37.6"	39.0"
Cargo capacity (cu. ft.)	20.5	20.5	105.7
Fuel capacity (gals.)	25.8	25.8	22.0

lated rosewood woodgrain vinyl I/P accents, electric clock, pedal trim plates, courtesy light switches on all doors, luggage compartment mat and side panel trim, luggage compartment light, body-color door handle inserts, bright windshield and rear window moldings, bright hood rear edge molding, fixed rear quarter window, wide rocker panel moldings w/rear extensions, bright wheel opening moldings, rear fender skirts, RTS package, deluxe wheel covers, and HR78 × 15 BSW tires. Grand Safari wagon adds: All-Morrokide vinyl front bench seat w/fold-down center armrest, glove box lights, RH rear view mirror, Glide-Away tailgate w/power-operated rear window, delete rear fender skirts, rear bumper guards, and LR78 × 15 BSW tires. Brougham adds: Choice of velour or all-Morrokide vinyl trim front notchback seat w/fold-down center armrest, 24 oz. cut-pile carpeting, custom door panels w/pull straps and lower panel carpeting, electric clock, power windows, added acoustical insulation, Cordova vinyl top, velour luggage compartment trim, special accent stripes, and stand-up hood ornament.

Models Available

	Model No.	Base MSRP	Change from LY	Shipping Wt. (lbs.)	Model Year Production	Change from LY
Bonneville 2-Door Hardtop Coupe	P47	$5,246	+3.17%	4308	9,189	+17.00%
Bonneville 4-Door Hardtop Sedan	P49	$5,312	+3.09%	4460	14,942	+18.20%
Grand Safari 4-Door, 2-Seat Station Wagon	P35	$5,746	+5.76%	5035	3,462	+34.81%
Grand Safari 4-Door, 3-Seat Station Wagon	P45	$5,895	+5.65%	5091	6,176	+29.97%
Bonneville Brougham 2-Door Hardtop Coupe*	R47	$5,734	+0.17%	4341	10,466	+40.54%
Bonneville Brougham 4-Door Hardtop Sedan*	R49	$5,906	+0.09%	4514	20,236	+29.01%
TOTALS	Avg. price	$5,640	+6.16%	Production	64,471	+131.79%

Comparisons made to 1975 Grand Ville Brougham models of same model number.

1977

As the nation wrapped up its celebratory Bicentennial year, the economy had greatly improved, and the oil embargoes and fuel crisis seemed distant memories. Now the auto manufacturers and dealerships hoped that the country was ready to get back to the business of buying new cars. By the end of the 1977 model year, proof of good times' return was found in a production total second only to the record-breaking 1973 model year, and a total never to be reached again. More proof of a better economy could be found in the details of the high production as all of the medium and luxury priced brands increased their production total from their 1973 level, while the lower-priced brands decreased from their 1973 levels. Increasing brands included Chrysler, Lincoln, Mercury, Buick, Cadillac and Oldsmobile. Brands having a decrease from 1973 included Ford, Chevrolet, Dodge, Plymouth and American Motors. Pontiac was virtually flat, falling 7,500 units short of the 1973 mark.

Efforts continued throughout the industry to improve fuel economy, as all four of the major manufacturers were actively trying to increase their Corporate Average Fuel Economy numbers. At General Motors, the first round of aerodynamically designed and downsized models entered the marketplace in the form of the new full-size Chevrolet, Pontiac, Oldsmobile, Buick and Cadillac lines. GM was quick to point out that with these new cars, and fuel efficiency improvements across the line, they had reached a 1977 average of 18.4 miles per gallon, which exceeded the 1978 standard a year early. The company also touted its 10 percent fuel economy improvement over 1976 models, and an astounding 53 percent improvement over the efficiency of their 1974 models.

The auto manufacturers were also recognizing other issues that affected customer satisfaction and therefore sales. After the rust-through problems in some of the early and mid–1970s cars from all manufacturers, by 1977, all were expanding their use of pre-coated steel and electro-coat primers in their painting processes to help reduce corrosion. Ford Motor Company began a quality improvement program that this year included body, powertrain and chassis improvements as well as longer periods between required maintenance. For example, features standard on all 1977 Ford Motor Company cars this year included improved paint and anti-corrosion processes, new DuraSpark high-voltage solid-state ignition, self-adjusting front disc brakes, and double wrapped and aluminized mufflers for longer life. Maintenance schedule improvements included 50,000 miles before required spark plug, fuel filter and air cleaner checks or replacements, and recommended oil change intervals of 10,000 miles for 4-cylinder and V6 engines, and 7,500 mile intervals for inline 6-cylinder and V8 engines. American Motors, always trying to prove its quality as a unique selling point against its "Big Three" competitors, introduced the "Buyers Protection Plan II," doubling the original plan's term to 24 months or 24,000 miles of coverage on all major drivetrain components. Chrysler Corporation, which had in years past offered some of the first extended warranties, was offering a 12-month/ 12,000 mile on the entire car, except for tires. And after years of problems with the 140 CID 4-cylinder Vega engine, GM introduced a 5-year/60,000 mile engine guarantee to show its confidence in the engine's quality.

General Motors' new full-size cars were about a foot shorter, 800 pounds lighter, more aerodynamically efficient and as a result more fuel-efficient than last year's models. Styling of the new models shared an angular "three-box" theme, although the cars did endure wind tunnel testing during their development to improve efficiency and reduce interior wind noise. The only real downside to the new cars was that they began to lose their individuality of styling between makes, especially when viewed in profile, though designers did do a good job to make the front and rear designs as identifiable as possible for each make. Also, interior designs and trim levels were distinct and fitting to their respective price levels. Another important change was the use of smaller engines, with the big 454 and 455 CID V8 engines being gone this year. In fact the largest engine available in any Chevrolet model was the 350 CID V8.

Along with the newly downsized GM full-size models, the Buick Riviera was also downsized, from its former E-body platform shared with the Oldsmobile Toronado and Cadillac Eldorado, to the B-body chassis of the Buick LeSabre and related models. The Riviera's two-year stint on the B-body would make these cars rather ordinary compared to their prior status in the Buick lineup. The only new series introduction from GM occurred at mid-year with Pontiac's introduction of the luxury compact Phoenix, which was based on the Ventura, and would next year replace the nameplate. The Phoenix was the first American car to make use of the rectangular two-lamp headlight system approved by NHTSA in 1976. Also at mid-year, Chevrolet returned the Z/28 model to the Camaro lineup, and Pontiac added a Sport Hatch to the sub-compact Sunbird line, based on the Chevrolet Monza 2+2 hatchback. There were not many other changes except for a restyled front end on the popular Firebird line, probably to avoid overshadowing the introduction of the full-size lineup. The GMC and Chevrolet truck lines were not greatly changed for 1977 either. The Oldsmobile Cutlass line continued to grow in popularity, so much so that it set a record high for model year production of the mid-size line this year, a height it would not achieve again. Remarkably the Cutlass Supreme coupe and Cutlass Supreme Brougham coupes alone sold 367,586 units, outselling the entire lines of American Motors, Cadillac, Chrysler and Lincoln. The Cutlass line as a whole outsold these four makes as well as Dodge, Mercury and Plymouth. It was quite an achievement from the oldest manufacturer of American cars.

Chrysler offered up two new model introductions at mid-year with the Dodge Diplomat and Chrysler LeBaron series. Built on the new-for-1976 Dodge Aspen and Plymouth Volaré four-door platform, the Diplomat and LeBaron came in coupe and sedan form, wearing the new side-by-side rectangular headlamps. The new models were billed as mid-size but were not termed "downsized" since the traditional mid-size cars remained in the line. The existing mid-size models were the newly named Dodge Monaco and Plymouth Fury, both of which received a facelift featuring stacked rectangular headlights. There were few other significant styling changes for the car or light-duty truck lines, though it would be the last year for the 440 CID V8 engine to be in the car lineup.

Ford Motor Company introduced a completely restyled line of mid-size cars and moved the Thunderbird down-market to compete head-to-head with the Dodge Charger SE and the popular GM personal luxury Monte Carlo and Grand Prix coupes. The Thunderbird, which technically replaced the Elite, would succeed in its new mission with a record-breaking production year, and the base Thunderbird model chalking up the highest individual model production total in the industry. The other mid-size lines were redesigned with stacked rectangular headlights on the new LTD II (replacing the Torino) and side-by-side headlights on the Cougar (which picked up four-door and wagon models and replaced the Montego). Ford and Mercury hoped the popular LTD and Cougar names would improve the image and sales of their aging mid-size models; the LTD II nameplate also allowed Ford to give the impression that it was a newly downsized LTD model, to help meet the competition of GM's smaller Chevrolet Impala and Caprice. The Cougar XR-7 was also included in the redesign, now sharing features with the Thunderbird, and was aimed at the higher priced Chrysler Cordoba, Oldsmobile Cutlass Supreme and Buick Regal coupes.

With the Thunderbird no longer sharing the Lincoln Continental Mark series platform, the model was restyled and renamed the Mark V, retaining its former size, but with more modern and angular lines, giving it at an advantage over its only direct competitor, the Cadillac Eldorado, which last had a styling update for 1975. Lincoln also got into the mid-year new model act with GM and Chrysler, by introducing the new Lincoln Versailles. Heavily based on the Ford Granada and Mercury Monarch, the Versailles was intended to compete directly with the Cadillac Seville, but its relation to its lower priced running mates was too obvious, and sales did not reach the level Lincoln had hoped. In Ford's truck lines, there was not a lot of new styling to be found, except for the Ranchero, which adopted the new look of the LTD II models. For Bronco enthusiasts, this would be the final year of that model in its original "compact" form.

American Motors continued facing financial problems, but would rise to the occasion as it always seemed to, by introducing the Pacer station wagon. The new wagon greatly improved the original Pacer's proportions, and came along just in time to retain some Pacer sales, as the hatchback model sales plunged by more than 80 percent this year. The 1977 model year also marked the return of the AMX nameplate — not as a model, but as a trim and decal package for the Hornet hatchback. For 1978, the AMX name would become its own series. In the AMC Jeep lineup, the Cherokee lineup added a four-door version, and the Wagoneer began moving up in terms of luxury, as AMC was doing with its car lines. This would eventually put Wagoneer in position to be the luxury leader of the yet to be created sport utility market.

The 1977 model year will most likely go down in history as one of the last really good seasons for the American automotive industry in terms of sales and production. The year also marked the end of the line for some of the most popular cars of the seventies: the Ford Maverick and its twin, the Mercury Comet; AMC's Hornet; the Chevrolet Vega and Pontiac Astre; the Pontiac Ventura; and the Chevrolet Chevelle nameplate. The Chevelle name was really last used by the press and public for the 1973 model line when the Chevelle Deluxe was still in the lineup. Once the Deluxe disappeared for the 1974 year, leaving the Malibu and Laguna names, they were popularly referred to by those subseries names, even though the Chevelle name still appeared on the cars and in most of the division's advertising and marketing materials. Finally, it was the last year for the traditional full-sized models from Dodge and Plymouth, the Royal Monaco and Gran Fury respectively, though the Gran Fury name would return for 1980 on a smaller full-size Plymouth. With those full-sized models leaving, the full-sized station wagon would be gone also, spelling the end for the long-running Chrysler Town & Country as a Chrysler series. The name would return as the designation for the new 1978 Chrysler LeBaron station wagon. It was a sign of the times for the venerable nameplate.

1977 Overview and Changes from Prior Year

- **Total industry model year production:** 9,597,754, up 10.94%.
- **Market share by corporation:** GM 58.30%; Ford 26.59%; Chrysler 12.89%; AMC 2.22%.
- **Number of models and body types available:** 271, down from 297.

- **Highest production series:** Oldsmobile Cutlass — 673,397.
- **Lowest production series:** Cadillac Fleetwood 75 — 2,614.
- **Highest individual model production:** Ford Thunderbird 2-Door Hardtop — 318,140.
- **Lowest individual model production:** Dodge Royal Monaco Brougham 4-Door, 2-seat wagon — 906.
- **Industry average base price:** $4,855, up 2.09%.
- **Highest individual model base price:** Cadillac Fleetwood 75 Limousine, $18,858.
- **Lowest individual model base price:** AMC Gremlin 2-Door Sedan, $2,995.
- **Highest combined MPG with base powertrain:** Chevrolet Chevette, 33 MPG.
- **Lowest combined MPG with base powertrain:** Cadillac Eldorado and Chrysler Newport/New Yorker, 14 MPG.
- **Indianapolis 500 Pace Car:** Oldsmobile Delta 88 2-Door Coupe.
- *Motor Trend* magazine "Car of the Year": Chevrolet Caprice.

1977

AMERICAN MOTORS

"There's more to an AMC!"

Having just completed a decent sales year and increased production with only minor product changes, American Motors came up with several new products for 1977. These included a two-door station wagon being added to the Pacer line, a return of the legendary "AMX" nameplate, and a "first" ever 4-cylinder engine for the Gremlin. In fact, the four-cylinder engine was the first for an AMC product or preceding company, excluding Jeeps, since the 1924 Nash. In what would turn out to be a good year for the auto industry as a whole, with production up nearly 11 percent, AMC would not enjoy such fortunes. For AMC, production would end up down by nearly 25 percent. Fortunately there were still a few "good years" to come.

The two-year-old Pacer series added a new station wagon model whose lengthened roofline gave the car a more conventional look. It immediately became popular, and while the sedan's sales tumbled by 80 percent, the wagon handily

outsold the sedan nearly two-to-one, so that Pacer sales overall fell by half. It is also worth noting that its only real competitors in the two-door compact wagon market were the Ford Pinto and the Chevrolet Vega, both smaller cars that saw their 1977 sales slide 25 percent and 45 percent respectively. Seemingly, the new Pacer wagon was able to accomplish something few others could, taking GM and Ford by surprise. Inside, the wagon had nearly 20 cubic feet more cargo space than the sedan while adding only four inches to the overall length of the car.

The aging Gremlin managed to celebrate several firsts this year. The series received completely new front and rear styling, its first major design update; then, at mid-year, Gremlin got its first four-cylinder engine. Gremlin's new face consisted of a slightly angled-back front panel, with a rectangular shaped egg-crate grille, four rows tall and fourteen columns across, with the bottom corners rounded. Horizontally mounted, rectangular turn signal/parking lamps were set in the grille ends, and a Gremlin nameplate was attached to the leading edge of the driver's side of the hood. The single round headlamps were set into slightly tunneled bezels, mildly resembling the Pacer's look. The raised portions above the headlights created a feature line on the hood running to the cowl. At the back end, a new, all-glass liftgate was larger in size, and sat above enlarged taillights that mimicked the headlights in size and shape.

The Gremlin's new four-cylinder engine was a Volkswagen/Audi design that American Motors purchased and assembled in a former VW plant in Pennsylvania which AMC had purchased a year earlier. As part of the agreement with VW/Audi, American Motors was not to use the VW or Audi names when referring to the engine. The AMC version of the engine had different tolerances and AMC defined specs. Parts were manufactured in Europe and shipped to the U.S. where they were assembled. The original deal was for AMC to buy the engine design and eventually move manufacturing to the plant in the United States. Unfortunately, they never

sold enough of the engines to begin actual manufacturing in Kenosha. All of the 2.0 liter engines were assembled in the U.S. plant from major castings supplied by VW. The VW/Audi versions were different in many aspects, including being fuel-injected, whereas the AMC version was carbureted. The VW/Audi engine had been used in the Audi A100, VW van, and Porsche 924. The four-cylinder Gremlin became a distinct model, known as the Gremlin 2.0L, and was given the 46-4 model designation. This gave the Gremlin three models for the first time ever. For the second time in as many years, the Gremlin Custom model 46-5 became the base Gremlin, whose model number 46-3 was now eliminated, and a new model 46-7 became the Gremlin Custom.

Once again the remaining AMC products, the Hornet and Matador, received very few styling changes. The most interesting development was the return of the AMX name. Now an option package on the Hornet hatchback, the AMX was truly nothing more than a decal and performance appearance package, and offered little to continue the true performance image the original AMX had created.

Gremlin 2-Door Sedan

Hornet Sportabout 4-Door Wagon
with X package

Hornet 3-Door Hatchback with AMX package

Matador 2-Door Coupe

Pacer 2-Door Sedan with D/L package

Matador 4-Door Station Wagon

Hornet 4-Door Sedan with D/L package

Matador 4-Door Sedan

Pacer 2-Door Station Wagon with D/L package

Model year production: 213,125, down 24.26% from 1976.
Domestic market share: 2.22% (11th place).
Base price range: $2,995 to $4,899.
American Motors average base price: $3,744, up 9.63%.
Introduction date: October 5, 1976; Gremlin 2.0L introduced January 1977.
Assembly plants: Kenosha, Wisconsin, and Brampton, Ontario, Canada.
Data plate identification (VIN): Thirteen digit code read as follows: First digit indicates company (A = American Motors); second digit indicates model year (7 = 1977); third digit is transmission code (see powertrain chart); fourth through sixth digits indicate car line–body type–series numbers (three-digit model number in model charts); seventh digit is engine code (see powertrain chart); eighth digit indicates assembly plant (1 through 6 = Kenosha, 7 through 9 = Ontario); remaining digits are sequential with beginning number of 00001. *Example:* A7A167H100001 is a 1977 Matador 2-Door, 304 CID, 2-bbl. V8, with Torque-Command Automatic, serial number 00001, built in Kenosha.

Powertrains[1]

Engine	Net HP	Engine/Trans. Codes[2]	Transmission Availability[2]		Gremlin	Pacer	Hornet	Matador[3]
121 CID (2.0L) OHC, 2-bbl., 4-cyl.[4]	80	G/S	3-speed manual		$253	—	—	—
				MPG:		—	—	—
		G/F	4-speed manual		$358	—	—	—
				MPG:	22/34/26	—	—	—
		G/A	Torque-Command 3-sp. Automatic		$520	—	—	—
				MPG:	20/29/24	—	—	—
232 CID (3.8L), 1-bbl., 6-cyl.	88	E/S	3-speed manual		S	S	S	—
				MPG:	20/27/23	18/23/20	18/23/20	—
				Calif.	15/22/18	—	15/22/18	—
		E/F	4-speed manual		$105	$105	$105[5]	—
				MPG:	NA	18/23/20	18/23/20	—
		E/A	Torque-Command 3-sp. Automatic		$267	$267	$267	—
				MPG:	18/24/20	18/23/20	18/23/20	—
				Calif.	14/18/16	14/18/16	14/18/16	—
258 CID (4.2L), 1-bbl., 6-cyl.	98	A/A	Torque-Command 3-sp. Automatic		—	—	—	S (ex. Wgn.)
				MPG:	—	—	—	15/21/17
				Calif.	14/17/15	14/17/15	14/17/15	—
258 CID (4.2L), 2-bbl., 6-cyl.	114	C/S	3-speed manual		$79	$79	$79	—
				MPG:	17/26/20	17/24/19	17/24/19	—
		C/F	4-speed manual		$184	$184	$184[5]	—
				MPG:	17/26/20	17/24/19	17/24/19	—
		C/A	Torque-Command 3-sp. Automatic		$346	$346	$346	—
				MPG:	17/23/19	17/23/19	17/23/19	—
				Calif.	15/21/17	15/21/17	15/21/17	—
304 CID (5.0L), 2-bbl., V8	129	H/A	Torque-Command 3-sp. Automatic		—	—	$407	S (Wgn)/ $120 (others)
				MPG:	—	—	NA	13/17/15
				Calif.	—	—	—	12/16/13
360 CID (5.9L), 2-bbl., V8	140	N/A	Torque-Command 3-sp. Automatic		—	—	—	$60 (Wgn)/

Engine	Net HP	Engine/ Trans. Codes[2]	Transmission Availability[2]	Gremlin	Pacer	Hornet	Matador[3]
							$180 (others)
			MPG:	—	—	—	13/16/14
			Calif.	—	—	—	10/16/12

[1]Optional axle ratio required on cars sold in California: Gremlin 6-cylinders (except w/4-speed manual), 3.08:1; Pacer, 3.08:1; Hornet 6-cylinders, 3.08:1; Matador V8s, 3.15:1. [2]Unless otherwise noted: All manual transmissions are column-shift, except Gremlin, Pacer w/X package, and Hornet Hatchback. All automatics are column-shift as standard. Add $21 for floor-shifter on Gremlin automatics, Hornet Hatchback or Sportabout. [3]Matador coupes and sedans built for sale in California follow the same standard and optional availability as station wagons. Prices adjust accordingly. [4]Available on base Gremlin only in 49 states. Not available for cars sold in California. [5]Four-speed manual available only on Hatchback.

Major Options

	Gremlin	Pacer	Hornet	Matador
All-season air conditioning	$451	$451	$451	$502
Adjust-O-Tilt steering wheel[1]	—	$55	$55	$57
Cruise-command speed control[1]	—	$73	$60	$77
Electric rear window defogger	$67	$67	$67[2]	$78[2]
Tinted glass, all windows	$47	$50	$50	$55
Power windows	—	—	—	$146[3]
Front bucket seats, vinyl upholstered	$49	$69	S[4]	$102[4]
Front floor console, requires bucket seats	$27	$27	$27[4]	$
Third row seat & power tailgate window (wagons)	—	—	—	$135
AM radio	$80	$80	$80	$81
AM/FM stereo multiplex w/4 speakers	$211	$211	$211	$211
AM/FM stereo w/8-track tape player	—	$317	—	$317
Vinyl top (excluding wagon models)	$74	$111	$99	$111
Woodgrain paneling (wagons only)	—	$105	$105	$118
Power steering	$133	$133	$133	S
Power front disc brakes	$60	$60	$60	S
Wheel covers	$34	$34	$34	S
Styled road wheels	$121	$128	$121	$121
Aluminum styled wheels	$198	$223	$198	$198
White sidewall tires, standard size	$38	$38	$38	$40

Popular Option Groups & Packages

	Gremlin	Pacer	Hornet	Matador
AMX package	—	—	$799[5]	—
Barcelona package[6]	—	—	—	$158
D/L package	—	$449	$299	—
Extra Quiet insulation package	$34	$37	$34	S
Interior décor/convenience group	$65	$82	$71	$86
Levi's custom trim package	$99[7]	$99	$49[5]	—
Light group	$28	$30	$30	S
Performance package	$259	$349	$239[5]	—
Protection group	$62	$56	$62	—
Visibility group	$67	$67	$67	$76
"X" package	$299[7]	$379[8]	$199	—

— = Not Available; S = Standard equipment. [1]Requires automatic transmission. [2]Available only on Hornet hatchback and Sportabout, and Matador coupe and sedan. Blower type defroster available on Hornet sedans for $44. [3]Price on station wagon including tailgate window is $190. Power tailgate window only is $44. [4]Hornet hatchback and Matador coupe only. [5]Available only on Hornet hatchback. [6]Available only on coupe. [7]Available only on Gremlin Custom. [8]Available only on Pacer sedan.

Paint Colors

	Code		Code		Code
Sand Tan[1]	6D	Firecracker Red	6P	Sunshine Yellow	6V
Silver Frost metallic	6J	Brilliant Blue	6R	Misty Jade metallic	7A

	Code		Code
Mocha Brown metallic	7B	Captain Blue metallic	7W
Autumn Red metallic	7C	Tawny Orange	7Y
Powder Blue	7D	Sun Orange	7Z
Midnight Blue metallic	7K	Alpine White	G7
Loden Green metallic	7L	Brandywine metallic	J2
Golden Ginger metallic[1]	7M	Classic Black	P1
Lime Green	7P		

Non-standard model colors are available at $23 extra cost. Two-tone paint combinations available on Pacer sedan for $55; Hornet (except Sportabout) for $38; Matador coupe and sedan for $45; and Matador wagon for $84. [1]The Barcelona package is only available in these colors.

Gremlin

"For 1977, we've given Gremlin a fresh new look that's bound to make it even more appealing."

Nameplate year of origin: 1970.
Current bodystyle lifespan: 1970 through 1983; Gremlin (1970 to 1978), restyled and renamed Spirit (1979 to 1982); 4WD added and rebadged Eagle SX/4 (1981 to 1983).
Predecessor to this model: None.
Replacement for this model: Spirit (1979 to 1982) and Eagle SX/4 (1981 to 1983).
Percentage of division's production: 21.66%.
Corporate siblings: None; however many components were shared with the Hornet.
Primary competition: Buick/Opel Isuzu, Chevrolet Vega, Dodge Colt, Ford Pinto, and Plymouth Arrow.
Notable changes: New front and rear styling and trim updates.
Major standard equipment: Rallye Perforated vinyl bench front seat with foam cushions, fold-down rear seat, color-keyed carpeting, dome light, carpeted cargo area, rear bumper guards, aluminum hubcaps, and 6.45 × 14 BSW tires. Custom adds: "Fairway" pleated vinyl custom bench seat, custom steering wheel and door trim panels, bright drip rail and rocker panel moldings, dual bodyside paint stripes, and spare tire cover.

Measurements

Wheelbase	96.0"
Length	166.4"
Width	70.6"
Height	52.3"
Legroom — front	40.7"
Legroom — rear	29.2"
Headroom — front	38.0"
Headroom — rear	36.4"
Cargo capacity (cu. ft.)	6.4*
Fuel capacity (gals.)	21.0**

*26.9 cu. ft. with rear seat down. **13.0 gallons on Custom 2-Liter model.

Models Available

	Model No.	Base MSRP	Change from LY	Shipping Wt. (lbs.)	Model Year Production	Change from LY
Gremlin 2-Liter 2-Door Sedan	46-4	$3,248	NEW	2564	7,558	NEW
Gremlin 2-Door Sedan	46-5	$2,995	-0.10%	2811	38,613*	-25.91%*
Gremlin Custom 2-Door Sedan	46-7	$3,248	+12.43%	2824	*	*
TOTALS	Avg. price	$3,164	+7.48%	Production	46,171*	-12.79%

*Production records kept only by engine type.

Pacer

"Now there are two great Pacer models to choose from!"

Nameplate year of origin: 1975 (previously used by Ford Motor Company on 1958 Edsel series).
Current bodystyle lifespan: 1975 through 1980.
Predecessor to this model: None.
Replacement for this model: None.
Percentage of division's production: 27.34%.
Corporate siblings: None.
Primary competition: Chevrolet Monza and Mercury Bobcat.

Measurements

	Sedan	Wagon
Wheelbase	100.0"	100.0"
Length	170.0"	174.0"
Width	77.0"	77.0"
Height	52.7"	53.0"
Legroom — front	42.0"	42.0"

Notable changes: Minor trim and detail changes. New station wagon model.

Major standard equipment: Basketry print fabric front bench seat with foam cushions, color-keyed carpeting, fold-down rear seat, courtesy dome light, ashtray and cigarette lighter, integrated front door armrests, concealed two-speed electric wipers and washers, large rear lift gate w/built-in assist struts, color-keyed rubber cargo area mat, bodyside scuff moldings, aluminum hubcaps, and 6.95 × 14 BSW tires. Wagon adds: Rallye perforated vinyl upholstery, rear quarter window vents, locking stowage compartment in rear quarter panel, and D78 × 14 BSW tires.

Measurements (cont.)

	Sedan	Wagon
Legroom — rear	34.9"	34.9"
Headroom — front	38.3"	38.4"
Headroom — rear	37.0"	38.1"
Cargo capacity (cu. ft.)	29.5*	47.8*
Fuel capacity (gals.)	22.0	22.0

With rear seat folded down.

Models Available

	Model No.	Base MSRP	Change from LY	Shipping Wt. (lbs.)	Model Year Production	Change from LY
Pacer 2-Door Sedan (hatchback)	66-7	$3,649	+4.29%	3156	20,265	-82.72%
Pacer 2-Door Station Wagon	68-7	$3,799	NEW	3202	37,999	NEW
TOTALS		*Avg. price* $3,724	+6.43%		*Production* 58,264	-50.31%

Hornet

"If you're among those who are value-minded, the Hornet is the one to look at."

Nameplate year of origin: 1951 (previously used on 1951–1957 Hudson series).

Current bodystyle lifespan: 1970 through 1987; Hornet (1970 to 1977), restyled and renamed Concord (1978 to 1982); 4WD added and re-badged Eagle (1980 to 1987).

Predecessor to this model: (Rambler) American (1964 to 1969).

Replacement for this model: Concord (1978 to 1982) and Eagle (1980 to 1987).

Percentage of division's production: 36.52%.

Corporate siblings: None; however many components were shared with the Gremlin.

Primary competition: Chevrolet Nova, Dodge Aspen, Ford Maverick, Plymouth Volaré, and Pontiac Ventura.

Notable changes: Minor trim and detail changes.

Major standard equipment: Veracruz fabric-covered front bench seat, color-keyed carpeting, instrument panel package tray, dome light, parking brake warning light, front bumper corner rub strips, rear bumper guards, aluminum hubcaps, and 6.95 × 14 BSW tires. Hatchback adds: Rallye perforated vinyl bucket seats, folding second seat, sports steering wheel, flip-open rear quarter windows, carpeted cargo mats, and gas-charged liftgate supports. Sportabout adds: Rallye perforated vinyl front bench seat, folding second seat, gas-charged liftgate supports, carpeted cargo mats, and hidden rear compartment lock.

Measurements

	Sedans	Hatchback	Sportabout
Wheelbase	108.0"	108.0"	108.0"
Length	186.0"	186.0"	186.0"
Width	71.0"	71.0"	71.0"
Height	52.7"	52.2"	52.7"
Legroom — front	42.1"	40.7"	40.7"
Legroom — rear	35.5"	32.1"	35.6"
Headroom — front	38.1"	38.1"	38.1"
Headroom — rear	37.0"	36.7"	37.4"
Cargo capacity (cu. ft.)	11.1	30.5*	62.8*
Fuel capacity (gals.)	22.0	22.0	22.0

Maximum with rear seat down, and 3.8 cu. ft. below cargo floor on Sportabout.

Models Available

	Model No.	Base MSRP	Change from LY	Shipping Wt. (lbs.)	Model Year Production	Change from LY
Hornet 2-Door Sedan	06-7	$3,399	+6.25%	2971	6,076	*
Hornet 2-Door Hatchback	03-7	$3,499	+9.38%	3012	11,545	*
Hornet 4-Door Sedan	05-7	$3,449	+7.81%	3035	31,331	*
Hornet 4-Door Sportabout Wagon	08-7	$3,699	+4.23%	3100	28,891	-2.93%
TOTALS		*Avg. price* $3,512	+6.85%		*Production* 77,843	+8.75%

Comparison to 1976 not available as production by body style was not kept. Production by engine type (compared to LY): 6-cylinder, 73,252 (+8.76%); V8, 4,091 (-39.32%).

Matador

"Matador, the popular intermediate, packs big-car comfort,
style and luxury and a smooth quiet ride into
a trim mid-size car at a moderate price."

Nameplate year of origin: 1971.
Current bodystyle lifespan: 1974 through 1978 (Coupe only);
  1967 through 1978 (Rebel, 1967–1968; restyled in 1969;
  restyled and renamed Matador in 1971; and sedan and wagon
  restyled in 1974).
Predecessor to this model: Matador (1971 to 1973).
Replacement for this model: None.
Percentage of division's production: 14.47%.
Corporate siblings: None.
Primary competition: Chevrolet Malibu, Dodge Monaco,
  Ford LTD II, Plymouth Fury, and Pontiac LeMans.
Notable changes: Minor trim and detail changes.
Major standard equipment: Brampton plaid fabric individual
  reclining front seats, color-keyed carpeting, custom steering
  wheel, Extra Quiet insulation package, bodyside scuff mold-
ings, front and rear bumper guards, front sway bar, power steering, power front disc brakes, full wheel covers, and F78 × 14 BSW
tires. Wagon adds: Crush-grain vinyl individual reclining front seats, cargo area carpet, courtesy dome light activated by door and
tailgate switches, hidden rear compartment with lock, dual-swing tailgate, front bumper guards, and H78 × 14 BSW tires.

Measurements

	Coupe	Sedan	Wagon
Wheelbase	114.0"	118.0"	118.0"
Length	209.4"	216.0"	215.5"
Width	77.4"	77.3"	77.2"
Height	51.8"	54.8"	56.8"
Legroom — front	43.0"	42.8"	42.8"
Legroom — rear	33.3"	39.6"	39.6"
Headroom — front	37.6"	39.6"	39.9"
Headroom — rear	36.0"	37.5"	38.5"
Cargo capacity (cu. ft.)	14.3	19.1	95.2*
Fuel capacity (gals.)	24.5	24.5	21.0

Includes 8.0 cu.ft. of space below cargo floor.

1977

Models Available

	Model No.	Base MSRP	Change from LY	Shipping Wt. (lbs.)	Model Year Production	Change from LY
Matador 2-Door Coupe	16-7	$4,499	+24.25%	3704	6,825	*
Matador 4-Door Sedan	85-7	$4,549	+25.42%	3713	12,944	*
Matador 4-Door Station Wagon	88-7	$4,899	+12.03%	4104	11,078	+0.26%
TOTALS		Avg. price $4,649	+20.02%		Production 30,847	-25.69%

*Comparison to 1976 not available as production by body style was not kept. Production by engine type for coupe and sedan (compared to LY): 6-cylinder, 2,447
(-51.99%); V8, 17,322 (-31.99%).*

BUICK

"Dedicated to the Free Spirit in just about everyone."

As GM's all-new downsized line of full-size cars hit
showrooms, Buick found itself sharing more with its sister
divisions than it ever had before. Any differentiation between
a LeSabre and a Chevy Impala, a Pontiac Catalina, or an
Oldsmobile Delta 88 now had to depend upon styling and
luxury features to get the consumer's attention. Like the other
GM full-sized models, the LeSabre, Estate Wagon, Electra
and Riviera all dropped 800 pounds on average, becoming
lighter than the "mid-size" Century models, while still being
slightly larger cars.

The angular styling of the new full-size Buicks lost any
remaining hint of a bodyside "sweep" line, with a lower bodyside line between the wheel openings and a beltline crease,
both being very straight. The LeSabre and Estate Wagon
now featured full rear wheel openings, whereas the Electra's
were somewhat flattened at the top, with a pronounced flare.
Electras added a bodyside molding that began just behind
the front wheel opening, just below the height of its peak,
and ran to the rear of the car, terminating several inches
ahead of the rear fender tip.

The front end of all full-size models, except the Riviera, had a rather flat grille with the LeSabre and Estate Wagon using thin vertical bars, broken into eight sections by equally thin horizontal bars. The Electra used a more formal twelve-section crosshatch grille, with each section containing a crosshatch insert. All grilles had a chrome surround, with the Electra's appearing slightly thicker. Outside of the vertical grille area, the front panel angled back above the long, horizontal turn signal/parking lamps, which wrapped around the fender edge and had a built-in side marker light. They appeared to be a continuation of the lower part of the grille on LeSabre and Estate Wagon models. Dual rectangular headlamps were set directly above in a chrome bezel that canted rearwards from bottom to top, following the front fender edge. Rectangular "portholes" were the only remaining traditional Buick styling cue on the outside.

Rear-end styling differed markedly among the full-size Buick models. LeSabres used a large, horizontal taillight divided into upper and lower sections, which wrapped around the rear corner. LeSabre Custom and the new Sport Coupe used amber turn signals mounted in the upper portion of the taillight. The Estate Wagon used a rectangular wraparound taillight divided into two sections by a large horizontal chrome strip which housed the backup lights. Electra featured something like a small tailfin, rising slightly above the trunk lid and extending rearward to form a point. Horizontal taillights were divided into upper and lower sections by a thin chrome strip, but they did not wrap around to the bodyside; rather a separate side marker light ran vertically up the rear fender extension.

The newly designed Riviera was a rather odd car in the scheme of things. Breaking from its ten-year history of sharing certain body and chassis features of the corporate E-body platform with the front-wheel-drive Cadillac Eldorado and Oldsmobile Toronado, the Riviera continued its unique position as General Motors' only full-size, rear-wheel-drive, personal luxury car. But sales had been languishing, so Buick decided to save costs by having the Riviera share its new body and chassis features with more mundane cars like Chevrolet's Impala and Buick's own LeSabre. To keep the Riviera somewhat unique, it received its own front-end treatment and unique rear quarters. Up front was a very flat front end, with a classic Buick "waterfall" style grille consisting of 18 vertical openings each lined with chrome trim, which curved forward at the bottom to nearly meet the top of the front bumper. Chrome trim outlined the grille with a larger bar across the top carrying the Buick name. A stand-up hood ornament with the Riviera "R" logo topped the front fascia. Dual rectangular headlamps mounted above combination turn signal/parking lamps flanked the grille layout. The Riviera's bodysides had the same lower crease as the LeSabre, but on the Riviera it wore a chrome molding, with the Riviera name on the front fender portion. The beltline crease was unique

in that it had a slight "kick-up" just behind the door, creating a uniquely shaped opera window that added a resemblance to the 1963 Riviera, and kept it from being confused with any other GM full-size coupe. Around back the Riviera had flat horizontal taillights with the Riviera logo positioned in the center, these also being reminiscent of the original Riviera.

Inside, the full-size Buicks all shared a similar design. A flat-topped, flat-faced instrument panel was divided into three sections. The left side housed all the important driver controls, with gauges housed in round, silver-faced pods with black lettering, and controls for wipers and lights to the left side. The right side was of similar size and housed the round-dial quartz clock on models so equipped to the left, and an air vent to the right, with the glove box below it. In the center was a section that dropped down lower than the side sections, housing radio and climate controls, as well as additional air vents. Under the overhang area of the instrument panel top were miniature floodlights, a uniquely Buick feature, that lit the entire face of the instrument panel at night. Across the top of the dashboard, near the windshield base, was a small car-width strip divided into small sections, with the area directly in front of the driver housing the warning lights for fuel level, temperature, and more. This was a feature initially seen on the 1976 Cadillac Seville. Seating configurations followed those of recent full-size Buicks, except that the Riviera no longer offered a bucket seat and floor console option. Additionally, in a small change across the board for GM this year, the third seat in station wagons became optional equipment on two-seat wagons, rather than being a stand-alone model.

Mid-size Buick Centurys were mostly carry-over with minor trim changes. Regal coupes had a grille divided into six sections (three stacked on each side), each containing many vertical bars, while the Regal sedan had a grille divided into four sections by a center vertical bar and a horizontal bar, each containing five sections of horizontal bars. The rest of the Century line had detail changes to the grilles, but were otherwise not greatly different from 1976 models. If not for the exceptionally popular Regal models, the mid-size Century line would have seen a sharp drop in sales, as only the Regal and station wagons increased in sales for 1977.

Skylark models gained a new vertical bar, "waterfall" style grille, with more chrome across the front end. The instrument panel was restyled to added larger round gauges that were more visible. In a curious side note, the 1977 Buick brochure mentions the Skylark Custom in the details of available equipment, although the Custom was not introduced until 1978 when it replaced the S/R. There must have been some thought to renaming the S/R to Custom in 1977, which would have put its naming of trim levels in line with the rest of the Buick line, but apparently there was a last minute change to keep the S/R nomenclature after the printing of sales literature. The compact Skyhawk received a new body-colored two-row grille divided into eight square openings across each row. Other changes were minimal, but a new "Free Spirit" decal package was new on the option list. Also, despite relatively low popularity, the Skyhawk-exclusive fixed Astroroof option with brushed aluminum targa band remained available. New this year was a manually operated sliding sunroof that could be ordered with the targa band.

Opels for 1977 became known as Buick/Opels by Isuzu,

with the "by Isuzu" de-emphasized and relegated to a very small portion of the front fender Opel badge, as the former "Buick Opel Isuzu" badging, carrying three different company names, seemed overly confusing. A new Deluxe 4-Door Sedan was added, but otherwise there were not significant changes. By 1977, Opels were sold in only about 700 Buick dealers across the country, down from a high of over 2,000 in the early years of the decade.

Century Custom 2-Door Colonnade
Hardtop Coupe with T-top roof

Century Custom 2-Door Colonnade
Hardtop Coupe with T-top roof detail

Century Custom 4-Door Station Wagon

Century Regal 4-Door
Colonnade Hardtop Sedan

Century Regal 2-Door
Colonnade Hardtop Coupe

Electra 225 Limited 4-Door Sedan
with Park Avenue package

Estate Wagon

Electra 225 2-Door Coupe

LeSabre Sport Coupe 2-Door

Riviera 2-Door Coupe

LeSabre 4-Door Sedan

Skyhawk 2-Door Hatchback Coupe with Astroroof and roof crown molding

Skylark 4-Door Sedan

Skylark S/R 2-Door Coupe

Opel Isuzu 2-Door Coupe (front) with Opel Isuzu 4-Door Sedan (rear)

Model year production: 869,277, up 17.87% from 1976.

Domestic market share: 9.01% (5th place).

Base price range: $3,642 to $7,358.

Buick average base price: $5,082, up 5.05%.

Introduction date: September 30, 1976.

Assembly plants: Baltimore, MD (B); Southgate, CA (C); Linden, NJ (E); Framingham, MA (G); Flint, MI (H); Van Nuys, CA (L); Tarrytown, NY (T); Kansas City/Fairfax, KS (X); Fremont, CA (Z); St. Therese, Quebec, Canada (2). Opel assembly plant: Fujisawa, Japan (8).

Data plate identification (VIN): Thirteen digit code read as follows: First digit indicates division (4 = Buick); second through fourth digits indicate series and body style (model number in model charts); fifth digit is engine code (see powertrain chart); sixth digit indicates model year (7 = 1977); seventh digit indicates assembly plant (see list above); remaining digits are sequential with beginning number of 100001. *Example:* 4N69J7H100001 is a 1977 Buick LeSabre 4-Door Sedan, with 350 CID, 2-bbl. V8 engine, serial number 100001, built in Flint, MI. 1977 Opels use a 13-digit code read the same as other 1977 Buicks except that the final six digits are sequential with beginning number of 400017 for sedans, and 700016 for coupes.

Powertrains[1]

Engine	Net HP	Engine Code: VIN/GM	Transmission Availability		Opel	Skyhawk	Skylark	Century & Regal[2]	LeSabre	Electra, Riviera & Estate Wagon
110.8 CID (1.8L) OHC, 2-bbl., 4-cyl.	80	B	4-speed manual		S	—	—	—	—	—
				MPG:	23/36/27	—	—	—	—	—
				Calif.	22/33/26	—	—	—	—	—
			5-speed manual		$110	—	—	—	—	—
				MPG:	25/38/28	—	—	—	—	—
			3-speed automatic		$250	—	—	—	—	—
				MPG:	24/30/26	—	—	—	—	—
				Calif.	24/29/26	—	—	—	—	—
231 CID (3.8L), 2-bbl., V6[3]	105	C/ LD5	3-speed manual		—	—	S (ex. S/R)	—	—	—
				MPG:	—	—	16/26/19	—	—	—
				Calif.	—	—	12/24/15	—	—	—
			4-speed manual		—	S	—	—	—	—
				MPG:	—	18/29/21	—	—	—	—
				Calif.	—	13/26/17	—	—	—	—
			5-speed manual		—	$248	—	—	—	—
				MPG:	—	19/34/25	—	—	—	—
			Turbo Hydra-matic 3-sp. Automatic		—	$248[4]	S (S/R)/ $282 (others)	—	S (ex. Spt. Cpe.)[4]	—
				MPG:	—	19/27/22	18/26/21	—	17/25/20	—
				Calif.	—	14/19/16	16/21/18	—	16/21/18	—
231 CID (3.8L), 2-bbl., V6[3]	105	C/ LD7	3-speed manual		—	—	S (ex. S/R)	S (ex. Regal Sdn. & Wgns.)	—	—
				MPG:	—	—	16/26/19	18/26/21	—	—
				Calif.	—	—	12/24/15	12/24/15	—	—
			4-speed manual		—	S	—	—	—	—

Engine	Net HP	Engine Code: VIN/GM	Transmission Availability		Opel	Skyhawk	Skylark	Century & Regal[2]	LeSabre	Electra, Riviera & Estate Wagon
				MPG:	—	17/27/21	—	—	—	—
				Calif.	—	16/27/20	—	—	—	—
			5-speed manual		—	$248	—	—	—	—
				MPG:	—	19/34/25	—	—	—	—
			Turbo Hydra-matic 3-sp. Automatic		—	$248	S (S/R)/ $282 (others)	$282 (ex. Regal Sdn. & Wgns.)	S (ex. Spt. Cpe.)[5]	—
				MPG:	—	19/27/22	18/26/21	17/25/20	17/25/20	—
				Calif.	—	16/23/18	16/21/18	16/21/18	16/21/18	—
301 CID (4.9L), 2-bbl., V8[6]	135	Y/ L27	Turbo Hydra-matic 3-sp. Automatic		—	—	$65 (S/R)/ $347 (others)	—	S (Spt. Cpe.)/ $110 (others)	—
				MPG:	—	—	17/23/19	—	17/23/19	—
305 CID (5.0L), 2-bbl., V8[6]	145	U/ LG3	Turbo Hydra-matic 3-sp. Automatic		—	—	$65 (S/R)/ $347 (others)[4]	—	S (Spt. Cpe.)/ $110 (others)[4]	—
				MPG:	—	—	16/22/19	—	17/23/19	—
350 CID (5.7L), 2-bbl., V8	140	H/ L32	Turbo Hydra-matic 3-sp. Automatic		—	—	—	S (Regal Sdn.)/ $449 (ex. Wgns.)[4]	$35 (Spt. Cpe.)/ $180 (others)[4]	—
				MPG:	—	—	—	15/20/17	15/21/17	—
350 CID (5.7L), 4-bbl., V8	155	J/ L77	Turbo Hydra-matic 3-sp. Automatic		—	—	—	S (Wgns.)[2]/ $55 (Regal Sdn.)/$504 (others)[4]	$80 (Spt. Cpe.)/ $235 (others)[4]	S (Electra & Riviera)[4,7]
				MPG:	—	—	—	15/22/18[8]	15/22/18	15/22/18
				Calif.	—	—	—	—	14/20/16	14/20/16
350 CID (5.7L), 4-bbl., V8	170	L/ LM1	Turbo Hydra-matic 3-sp. Automatic		—	—	$155 (S/R) $437 (others)[5]	$55 (Regal Sdn.)/$504 (others)	—	—
				MPG:	—	—	15/20/17	14/19/16[8]	—	—
				Calif.	—	—	15/21/17	14/20/16	—	—
350 CID (5.7L), 4-bbl., V8	170	R/ L34	Turbo Hydra-matic 3-sp. Automatic		—	—	—	$55 (Regal Sdn.)/$504 (ex. Wgns.)[5]	$80 (Spt. Cpe.)/$235 (others)	S (Estate Wagon)[7]
				MPG:	—	—	—	16/21/18	16/22/18	15/21/17
403 CID (6.6L), 4-bbl., V8	185	K/ L80	Turbo Hydra-matic 3-sp. Automatic		—	—	—	$65 (wgns. only)[2]	$173 (Spt. Cpe.)/ $322 (others)	$65[7]
				MPG:	—	—	—	13/19/15	15/21/17	15/21/17
				Calif.	—	—	—	—	13/19/15	13/19/15

[1]Optional axle ratio required on cars sold in California: Skyhawk, 2.93:1; Skylark V6, 3.23:1. [2]Century Special Coupe available only with LD7 engine. High-altitude Century Wagons use LM1 or L80 engine. [3]The LD5 even-firing engine replaced the LD7 engine as follows: For cars built in Flint (MI), on approximately March 21, 1977; for cars built in Fairfax (KS), Lordstown (OH), St. Therese (Canada), and Southgate (MI), on approximately May 1, 1977. [4]Not available in California or high-altitude counties. [5]Only available in California, or high-altitude counties. [6]According to Buick sales literature and EPA gas mileage guides, some early production Federal cars and all cars built for sale in California were built with the 301 CID V8 (L27) engine. [7]L80 engine is standard for high-altitude Estate Wagons and California and high-altitude Electras and Rivieras. [8]EPA estimate for Century Wagons: with L77, 14/19/16; with LM1, 13/17/15.

Major Options

	Opel	Skyhawk	Skylark	Century	LeSabre	Estate Wagon	Electra 225	Riviera
Air conditioning[1]	$424	$442	$478	$499	$539	$539	$539	$539
Tilt-wheel steering[2]	—	$50	$57	$57	$58	$58	$58	$58
Cruise-Master speed control	—	—	$80	$80	$84	$84	$84	$84
Electric rear window defogger	$55	$71	$48[3]	$82	$83	$83	$83	$83
Tinted glass, all windows	S	$48	$50	$54	$69	$69	$69	$69
Power windows, 2-dr./4-dr.	—	—	$108/$151	$108/$151	$114/$171	$171	S	S
Power door locks, 2-dr./4-dr.	—	—	$68/$96	$68/$96	$70/$98	$70/$98	$70/$98	$70/$98
Power front seat, 6-way, w/bench seat	—	—	—	$137	$139	$139	$139	$139
Front bucket seats, w/console	S[4]	S[4]	$159[5]	$218[5]	—	—	—	—
Third row seating (wagons)	—	—	—	$152	—	$145	—	—
AM radio	—	$71	$75	$79	$92	$92	$92	$92
AM/FM stereo[6]	$136	$219	$233	$233	$236	$236	$236	$236
AM/FM stereo w/8-track tape	—	$316	$337	$337	$341	$341	$341	$341
Vinyl top[7]	—	—	$98[8]	$111[8]	$153[8]	—	$196	$196
Sunroof, electric	—	$210[9]	—	$394[9]	$734	—	$734	$734
Astroroof, sliding glass	—	$591[9]	—	—	$898	—	$898	$898
Hurst hatch-roof, T-tops[9]	—	—	—	$587[9]	—	—	—	—
Woodgrain exterior panels (wagons)	—	—	—	$185	—	$198	—	—
Power steering	—	$130	$147	S	S	S	S	S
Power brakes, w/front disc	S	$58	$61	$61[10]	S	S	S	S
Full wheel covers	—	$42	$33	$34[11]	$34[11]	S	S	S
Wire wheel covers[12]	—	—	$121	$133[11]	$102[11]	$68	$68	—
Styled wheels	—	$90	$94	$94[11]	$92	—	$92	—
Chrome plated road wheel	—	—	$132	$161[11]	$163	$163	$163	$64
WSW tires, standard size	—	$38	$39	$41	$45	$43	$43	$43

Popular Option Groups & Packages

	Opel	Skyhawk	Skylark	Century	LeSabre	Estate Wagon	Electra 225	Riviera
Accessory group	—	—	$12	—	$48	—	—	—
Acoustical package	S	$36	$36	—	—	—	—	—
Appearance group	—	$67	$33	—	—	—	—	—
Convenience group	—	$21	$31	$31	—	—	—	—
F40 firm ride handling package	—	—	$22	$18	$18	$18	$18	$18
FE2 Rallye ride/handling package	—	—	$42	$36	—	—	—	$18
Free Spirit package	—	$148	—	—	—	—	—	—
Limited package	—	—	—	—	—	$1,442	—	—
Park Avenue package	—	—	—	—	—	—	$385[13]	—
S/R coupe package	—	—	—	$499[13]	—	—	—	—

— = Not Available; S = Standard equipment. [1]Manually controlled. Semi-automatic climate control is available for $397 additional on Century Regal, LeSabre and Estate Wagon. Automatic climate control is available for $82 additional on Electra and Riviera. [2]Tilt and telescoping steering column available on LeSabre, Estate Wagon, Electra and Riviera at $50 additional cost. [3]Blower type defogger. [4]Opel Deluxe and Skyhawk models only. Opel base and Skyhawk S have bucket seats w/o console. Console for Skyhawk S is $77 extra. [5]Standard on Skylark S/R. Available for $79 extra on Century Custom and Regal models. [6]Non-stereo on Opel. CB radio available on Skylark and Century for $195 extra; available on all full-size Buicks for $197 extra. [7]A variety of vinyl top configurations available, ranging in price from $135 to $417. Prices shown are for full, non-padded, vinyl top on two-door models. [8]Price is $5 less on Skylark S/R models, and $18 less on LeSabre Custom. Century Custom or Regal coupes w/Landau top, $120. Not available on Century station wagons. [9]Available on two-door models only. Skyhawk Astroroof is fixed and includes roof crown molding, and sunroof option is manually operated. Hurst-Hatch available only on Century Custom and Regal coupes. [10]Standard on Century Custom Sedan and wagons, and Century Regal. [11]Standard on Century Custom and Regal and LeSabre Custom models. Deduct price of wheel covers from price of other optional wheels and wheel covers on these models. [12]Wire wheels available on full-size Buicks for $101–$135 depending upon model. Custom wire wheels available on Riviera at no extra cost. [13]S/R available only on Century Regal coupe, and Park Avenue only on Electra Limited sedan.

Paint Colors

Buick	Code	Buick	Code	Buick	Code
White	11	Medium Gray metallic*	16	Dark Blue metallic	29
Silver metallic	13	Black	19	Firethorn metallic	36
Gray metallic*	15	Light Blue metallic	22	Dark Aqua metallic	38

Buick	Code	Buick	Code	Opel Isuzu	Code
Medium Green metallic	44	Orange metallic	78	Crimson Red	R
Dark Green metallic	48	Medium Blue metallic*	85	New Westway Tan	T
Cream Gold	50	Blue Firemist metallic	91	Magnolia White	W
Yellow	51	Amber Firemist metallic	92	Jasmine Yellow	Y
Buckskin	61	Red Firemist metallic	93		
Gold metallic	63				
Brown metallic	69	*Opel Isuzu*	*Code*		
Red	72	Horizon Blue	B		
Bright Red	75	New Palm Green	G		

*In two-tone combinations, the first two digits indicate lower color; the next two digits are the upper color. Two-tone combinations are $60 extra for LeSabre and Electra. Firemist paints available only on Riviera at $152 extra.   *Used in two-tone combinations only.*

Opel

"The new Buick Opels by Isuzu."

Nameplate year of origin: 1976.
Current bodystyle lifespan: 1976 through 1979.
Predecessor to this model: Opel 1900 (1971–1975); Manta (1971–1975).
Replacement for this model: None. (The same car was sold after 1980 as the Isuzu I-Mark).
Primary competition: AMC Gremlin, Chevrolet Vega, Dodge Colt, Ford Pinto, Mercury Bobcat, and Pontiac Astre.
Notable changes: Four-door sedan added; otherwise minor trim and detail changes.
Major standard equipment: Reclining vinyl front bucket seats, rubber floor mats, interior lights, column-mounted headlight dimmer switch, and 6.15 × 13 BSW tires. *Deluxe adds:* Full-floor carpeting, center console w/gauges and clock, tachometer, woodgrain vinyl trim on I/P gauge cluster, console and doors, trunk mat, side window moldings, rocker panel molding, front and rear bumper guards, and wheel trim rings.

Measurements

Wheelbase	94.3"
Length	168.0"*
Width	61.8"
Height	53.5"
Legroom — front	40.6"
Legroom — rear	30.9"
Headroom — front	37.0"
Headroom — rear	35.1"
Cargo capacity (cu. ft.)	9.9
Fuel capacity (gals.)	13.7

*Deluxe models, 170.5".

Models Available

	Model No.	Base MSRP	Change from LY	Shipping Wt. (lbs.)	Model Year Sales	Change from LY*
Opel 2-Door Coupe	T77	$3,297	+0.46%	2068	NA	NA
Opel Deluxe 2-Door Coupe	Y77	$3,559	-1.00%	2083	NA	NA
Opel Deluxe 4-Door Sedan	Y69	$3,603	NEW	2138	NA	NEW
TOTALS	*Avg. price*	$3,486	+1.39%	*Production*	29,065*	+16.27%

*Model year sales are estimated based upon dealer sales reporting, and change from LY is compared to the entire 1976 Opel line.

Skyhawk

"More than mere transportation. Skyhawk is built to the principle that driving can be not only fun, but downright adventurous."

Nameplate year of origin: 1975.
Current bodystyle lifespan: 1975 through 1980.
Predecessor to this model: None.
Replacement for this model: Skyhawk (1982 to 1989).
Percentage of division's production: 2.77%.
Corporate siblings: Chevrolet Monza, Oldsmobile Starfire and Pontiac Sunbird (closely related to Chevrolet Vega and Pontiac Astre).
Primary competition: AMC Pacer, Ford Mustang II and "Lincoln-Mercury" Capri II.

Measurements

Wheelbase	97.0"
Length	179.3"
Width	65.4"
Height	50.2"
Legroom — front	42.8"
Legroom — rear	29.6"
Headroom — front	37.7"

Notable changes: Minor trim and detail changes.

Major standard equipment: Choice of cloth and vinyl or all-vinyl front bucket seats with foam cushions, fold-down rear seat, cut-pile carpeting including cargo area, simulated woodgrain I/P, dual speed wipers w/washers, functional B-pillar vent louvers, bright window surround moldings, front and rear wheel opening moldings, hubcaps, and B78 × 13 BSW tires. Skyhawk adds: Full instrumentation including tachometer, full-length floor console, rallye steering wheel, electric clock, LH remote control outside rear view sport mirror, bodyside accent stripes, and BR78 × 13 BSW tires.

Measurements (cont.)

Headroom — rear	35.3"
Cargo capacity (cu. ft.)	27.8*
Fuel capacity (gals.)	18.5

*With rear seat folded down.

Models Available

	Model No.	Base MSRP	Change from LY	Shipping Wt. (lbs.)	Model Year Production*	Change from LY
Skyhawk S 2-Door Hatchback	T07	$3,981	+2.00%	2805	NA	NA
Skyhawk 2-Door Hatchback	S07	$4,294	+1.85%	2817	NA	NA
TOTALS		*Avg. price* $4,138	+1.92%		*Production* 24,004	+52.48%

*Production and comparisons by model not available as they were kept as combined total.

Skylark

"Anything but an average small car."

Nameplate year of origin: 1953.
Current bodystyle lifespan: 1975 through 1979.
Predecessor to this model: Apollo (1973 to 1974).
Replacement for this model: Skylark (1980 to 1985).
Percentage of division's production: 13.05%.
Corporate siblings: Chevrolet Nova, Oldsmobile Omega, and Pontiac Ventura.
Primary competition: Dodge Aspen and Mercury Monarch.
Notable changes: New grille and minor trim and detail changes.
Major standard equipment: S model: Front vinyl bench seat, front door armrest, cut-pile carpeting, and E78 × 14 BSW tires. Skylark adds: Choice of patterned cloth or vinyl front bench seat with foam cushions, cut-pile carpeting including hatchback load floor, fold-down rear seat (hatchback only), front door operated courtesy lights, cigar lighter w/front and rear ashtrays, rear quarter/rear door armrests, day/night inside rearview mirror,

Measurements

	Coupe & HBK	Sedan
Wheelbase	111.0"	111.0"
Length	200.2"	200.2"
Width	72.7"	72.7"
Height	52.2"	53.1"
Legroom — front	41.7"	41.7"
Legroom — rear	33.2"	34.9"
Headroom — front	38.2"	39.1"
Headroom — rear	36.7"	37.1"
Cargo capacity (cu. ft.)	14.3*	13.2
Fuel capacity (gals.)	21.0	21.0

*Hatchback maximum with rear seat down, 28.4 cu. ft.

deluxe steering wheel, dual speed wipers w/4-jet washers, front and rear wheel opening moldings, and hubcaps. S/R adds: Cloth front bucket seats w/passenger recliner, carpeted door trim w/map pocket and reflector, sports shifting console, combination turn signal and high/low beam headlight control stalk, roof drip moldings, stand-up hood ornament, and ER78 × 14 BSW tires.

Models Available

	Model No.	Base MSRP	Change from LY	Shipping Wt. (lbs.)	Model Year Production	Change from LY
Skylark S 2-Door Coupe	W27	$3,642	+6.03%	3258	*	NA
Skylark 2-Door Coupe	B27	$3,765	+6.09%	3257	49,858	-2.74%
Skylark 2-Door Hatchback	B17	$3,942	+6.92%	3379	5,316	-20.69%
Skylark 4-Door Sedan	B69	$3,825	+5.99%	3296	48,121	-0.07%
Skylark S/R 2-Door Coupe	C27	$4,527	+5.75%	3277	5,023	+29.46%
Skylark S/R 2-Door Hatchback	C17	$4,695	+6.75%	3304	1,154	-7.53%
Skylark S/R 4-Door Sedan	C69	$4,587	+6.08%	3271	4,000	+23.34%
TOTALS		*Avg. price* $4,140	+6.23%		*Production* 113,472	-0.89%

*Production of S coupe was kept with Skylark base coupe production.

Century

*"A notable exception to what the term
'mid-size' car has traditionally implied."*

Nameplate year of origin: 1936.
Current bodystyle lifespan: 1973 through 1977.
Predecessor to this model: Skylark (1968 to 1972).
Replacement for this model: Century (1978 to 1981).
Percentage of division's production: 37.76%.
Corporate siblings: Chevrolet Malibu, Oldsmobile Cutlass, and Pontiac LeMans.
Primary competition: Dodge Monaco and Mercury Cougar.
Notable changes: Minor trim and detail changes.
Major standard equipment: (Century Special) Choice of cloth or vinyl front bench seat, rubber floor covering, 4-jet windshield washer, front disc brakes, variable ratio power steering, and FR78 × 15 BSW tires. Century (base) adds: Cut-pile carpeting, deluxe steering wheel, bumper protective strips w/white accents front and rear, wheel covers, and GR78 × 15 BSW tires (coupe only). Custom adds: Choice of cloth or vinyl notchback front seat w/center fold-down armrest, ashtray light, under-dash courtesy lights, glove compartment light, "Custom" badging, wheel opening moldings, rocker panel molding, and power front disc brakes. Wagons add: Vinyl notchback front bench seat, and HR78 × 15 BSW tires. Regal adds: Choice of luxury cloth or vinyl notchback seat with center armrest, door pull assist straps, and GR78 × 15 BSW tires (sedan only).

Measurements

	Coupes	Sedans	Wagons
Wheelbase	112.0"	116.0"	116.0"
Length	209.8"	213.6"	218.3"
Width	76.5"	79.0"	79.0"
Height	52.7"	53.6"	55.3"
Legroom — front	42.4"	42.4"	42.3"
Legroom — rear	32.9"	37.1"	36.8"
Headroom — front	37.2"*	37.9"	38.5"
Headroom — rear	36.7"*	37.3"	39.4"
Cargo capacity (cu. ft.)	14.7**	15.6	85.1
Fuel capacity (gals.)	NA	NA	NA

Custom coupe and Regal coupe: front headroom, 37.0"; rear headroom, 37.1".
**Century Special cargo capacity, 16.7.*

Models Available

	Model No.	Base MSRP	Change from LY	Shipping Wt. (lbs.)	Model Year Production	Change from LY
Century Special 2-Dr. Colonnade HT Coupe	E37	$4,170	+5.97%	3590	*	NA
Century 2-Door Colonnade HT Coupe	D37	$4,304	+5.75%	3520	52,864	-11.13%
Century 4-Door Colonnade HT Sedan	D29	$4,364	+6.31%	3692	29,065	-13.58%
Century Custom 2-Door Colonnade HT Coupe	H57	$4,628	+6.49%	3549	20,834	-38.79%
Century Custom 4-Door Colonnade HT Sedan	H29	$4,688	+5.97%	3688	13,645	-30.83%
Century Custom 4-Door Station Wagon, 2-S.	K35	$5,219	+4.65%	4260	19,282	+15.98%
Century Regal 2-Door Colonnade HT Coupe	J57	$4,713	+5.55%	3550	174,560	+40.21%
Century Regal 4-Door Colonnade HT Sedan	J29	$5,244	+8.68%	3928	17,946	+4.84%
TOTALS	*Avg. price*	$4,666	+4.32%	*Production*	328,196	+7.56%

Production of Century Special, E37, kept as combined total with Century 2-Door coupe, D37.

LeSabre

"For comfortably whisking off on all manner of escapes."

Nameplate year of origin: 1959 (also used on 1951 GM show car).
Current bodystyle lifespan: 1977 through 1985.
Predecessor to this model: LeSabre (1971 to 1976).
Replacement for this model: LeSabre (1986 to 1991).
Percentage of division's production: 21.94%.
Corporate siblings: Chevrolet Impala and Caprice, Pontiac Catalina and Bonneville, and Oldsmobile Delta 88.
Primary competition: Chrysler Newport and Mercury Marquis.
Notable changes: Completely redesigned.
Major standard equipment: Choice of cloth or vinyl front bench seat, cut-

Measurements

	Coupe	Sedan
Wheelbase	115.9"	115.9"
Length	218.2"	218.2"
Width	77.2"	77.2"
Height	54.6"	55.3"
Legroom — front	42.2"	42.2"
Legroom — rear	38.7"	39.5"
Headroom — front	38.4"	39.1"

pile carpeting, woodgrained vinyl trim on door panels, courtesy and dome light, I/P woodgrain appliqués, LH outside rear view mirror, front fender-mounted three-section rectangular "ventiport" ornaments, bumper protective strips front and rear, and FR78 × 15 BSW tires. Custom adds: Cloth or vinyl notchback front seat w/fold-down center armrest, wheel opening moldings, full-length rocker panel molding, rear panel molding, and deluxe wheel covers. Sport coupe adds: Custom cloth or vinyl notchback front seat w/fold-down center armrest, rallye steering wheel, specific suspension and steering, amber turn signal lights, black accents around chrome moldings, exclusive V8 engine, chrome road wheels, and FR78 × 15 WSW tires.

Measurements (cont.)

	Coupe	Sedan
Headroom — rear	38.2"	38.0"
Cargo capacity (cu. ft.)	21.2	21.2
Fuel capacity (gals.)	21.0	21.0

Models Available

	Model No.	Base MSRP	Change from LY	Shipping Wt. (lbs.)	Model Year Production	Change from LY
LeSabre 2-Door Coupe	N37	$5,033	+4.53%	3466	8,455	+118.98%
LeSabre 4-Door Sedan	N69	$5,093	+7.29%	3504	19,827	+359.49%
LeSabre Custom 2-Door Coupe	P37	$5,322	+4.07%	3474	58,589*	+28.29%
LeSabre Custom 4-Door Sedan	P69	$5,382	+6.66%	3516	103,855	+198.08%
LeSabre Sport 2-Door Coupe	F37	$5,819	NEW	3634	*	NEW
TOTALS	Avg. price	$5,330	+7.46%	Production	190,726	+39.11%

*Production of LeSabre Sport Coupe, F37, kept as combined total with LeSabre Custom 2-Door coupe, P37.

Estate Wagon

*"A car of remarkable capabilities.
As multi-talented as your lifestyle is multi-faceted."*

Nameplate year of origin: 1940 (as designation for station wagons).
Current bodystyle lifespan: 1977 through 1990.
Predecessor to this model: Estate Wagon (1971 to 1976).
Replacement for this model: Roadmaster Estate Wagon (1991 to 1996).
Percentage of division's production: 2.88%.
Corporate siblings: Chevrolet Impala and Caprice, Pontiac Catalina Safari and Grand Safari, and Oldsmobile Custom Cruiser.
Primary competition: Chrysler Town & Country and Mercury Marquis.
Notable changes: Completely redesigned.
Major standard equipment: Vinyl front bench seat, cut-pile carpeting including load floor, glove box light, I/P flood lights, front-door operated dome light, lockable hidden storage compartments, three-way tailgate, power tailgate window w/reveal moldings, LH and RH rear view mirrors, fender-mounted three-section rectangular "ventiport" ornaments, rocker panel moldings, deluxe wheel covers, and HR78 × 15 BSW tires.

Measurements

Wheelbase	115.9"
Length	216.7"
Width	77.2"
Height	57.0"
Legroom — front	42.2"
Legroom — rear	38.4"
Headroom — front	39.2"
Headroom — rear	39.2"
Cargo capacity (cu. ft.)	87.3
Fuel capacity (gals.)	22.0

Models Available

	Model No.	Base MSRP	Change from LY	Shipping Wt. (lbs.)	Model Year Production	Change from LY
Estate Wagon 4-Door, 2-S. Wagon	R35	$5,903	+5.58%	4015	25,075	+23.07%
TOTALS	Avg. price	$5,903	+4.27%	Production	25,075	+23.07%

Electra

"A beautiful reflection of a sophisticated day and age."

Nameplate year of origin: 1959.
Current bodystyle lifespan: 1977 through 1984.
Predecessor to this model: Electra 225 (1971 to 1976).
Replacement for this model: Electra (1985 to 1990).
Percentage of division's production: 18.59%.
Corporate siblings: Cadillac deVille, Cadillac Fleetwood Brougham, and Oldsmobile Ninety-Eight.
Primary competition: Chrysler New Yorker Brougham and Mercury Grand Marquis.
Notable changes: Completely redesigned.
Major standard equipment: Choice of cloth or vinyl notchback front bench seat w/fold-down center armrest, cut-pile carpeting, simulated woodgrain appliqués on door panels and instrument panel, door pull straps, carpeted lower door panels, power windows, quartz round-dial clock, custom steering wheel and safety belts, remote-control LH rear view mirror, fender-mounted 4-section rectangular "ventiport" ornaments, wheel opening moldings, rocker panel molding, deluxe wheel covers, and GR78 × 15 BSW tires. Limited adds: Custom cloth or vinyl 60/40 notchback front seat w/fold-down center armrest, two-way power driver's seat adjustment, front seatback map pockets, door pull handle, litter pocket, light group, and wider rocker panel moldings.

Measurements

Wheelbase	118.9"
Length	222.1"
Width	77.2"
Height	55.7"
Legroom — front	42.2"
Legroom — rear	40.9"
Headroom — front	39.1"
Headroom — rear	38.0"
Cargo capacity (cu. ft.)	20.4
Fuel capacity (gals.)	21.0

1977

Models Available

	Model No.	Base MSRP	Change from LY	Shipping Wt. (lbs.)	Model Year Production	Change from LY
Electra 225 2-Door Coupe	V37	$6,673	+4.81%	3761	15,762	-14.53%
Electra 225 4-Door Sedan	V69	$6,866	+5.19%	3814	25,633	-3.83%
Electra Limited 2-Door Coupe	X37	$7,033	+5.14%	3785	37,871	+33.37%
Electra Limited 4-Door Sedan	X69	$7,226	+5.46%	3839	82,361	+61.28%
TOTALS	*Avg. price*	$6,950	+5.16%	*Production*	161,627	+29.76%

Riviera

*"The 1977 Riviera, like the first Riviera built in 1963,
is designed to be a personal luxury car of great distinction."*

Nameplate year of origin: 1963 (1949 as designation for hardtop models).
Current bodystyle lifespan: 1977 through 1978.
Predecessor to this model: Riviera (1971 to 1976).
Replacement for this model: Riviera (1979 to 1985).
Percentage of division's production: 3.01%.
Corporate siblings: Buick LeSabre, Chevrolet Impala/Caprice, Oldsmobile Delta 88, and Pontiac Catalina/Bonneville.
Primary competition: Ford Thunderbird Town Landau.
Notable changes: Completely redesigned.
Major standard equipment: Choice of cloth or vinyl 50/50 front seat w/individual fold-down center armrests, inertia front seatback locks, cut-pile carpeting, simulated woodgrain appliqué on door panels and I/P, door pull handle, power windows, choice of quartz digital clock or quartz round-dial clock, custom steering wheel, light group, LH remote-control rear view mirror, deluxe wheel covers, and GR78 × 15 BSW tires.

Measurements

Wheelbase	115.9"
Length	218.2"
Width	77.2"
Height	54.6"
Legroom — front	42.2"
Legroom — rear	38.7"
Headroom — front	38.1"
Headroom — rear	38.0"
Cargo capacity (cu. ft.)	19.8
Fuel capacity (gals.)	21.0

Models Available

	Model No.	Base MSRP	Change from LY	Shipping Wt. (lbs.)	Model Year Production	Change from LY
Riviera 2-Door Coupe	Z37	$7,358	+8.24%	3784	26,138	+30.16%
TOTALS	Avg. price	$7,358	+8.24%	Production	26,138	+30.16%

CADILLAC

"The next generation of the luxury car."

As Cadillac entered its 75th anniversary year, executives must have been holding their breath as the new downsized Cadillac deVille and Fleetwood models were introduced. Although the new cars retained nearly all of the traditional Cadillac features and style, the competition was still offering larger Lincoln Continentals at slightly lower prices, so there was a lot of nervousness all through GM as to how consumers would react, especially to the Cadillac. But the new designs were well accepted, and sales increased for all of the newly downsized models over the previous model year.

All of the regular-size Cadillac line was downsized, dropping nearly 1,000 pounds on average, and nearly a foot in length, while maintaining the traditional Cadillac spaciousness and comfort. A portion of the weight savings could be attributed to the all-new powerplant developed for the smaller Cadillac. A new 7.0 liter, 425 cubic inch V8 engine, developed from the basic design of the 472 CID and 500 CID V8 engines that preceded it, was more than 100 pounds lighter. The new engine used a smaller bore and the same stroke to maintain a 180 horsepower rating and a very good torque rating of 320 lb. ft. at only 2000 rpm. The new engine was mated to a refined Turbo Hydra-matic 400 automatic transmission.

The new bodies were styled in the same vein as their predecessors, but in a smaller scale. Bodysides retained the square looking wheel openings, but lost the rear fender skirts. The line that formerly ran from the top of the front fender, tapering down along the body and fading away just short of the rear bumper, now faded away on the front door, and a second line beginning at the raised portion of the hood followed the beltline under the side windows, and then tapered slightly downward along the rear quarter panel.

The similarities continued with the front and rear styling, with dual rectangular headlights set on each side of a horizontal crosshatch grille that continued with a small grille section inset in the bumper. One small difference was

in placement of the turn signal/parking lamp, which now sat between the headlights and grille, but the side marker and cornering lights were still placed on the front fender edge connected to the headlight bezel. Around back, the rear bumper was capped by vertical fins at each end, creating the appearance of a small tailfin, much like its predecessors. On the new cars, however, all of the lights were placed in a single lens that sat in the top half of the fin, and the trunk lid opening extended down to the bumper for better access.

Inside, the new Cadillacs had all of the familiar features of their predecessors, with a new take on the dual-level instrument panel. It still used the upper control band with warning lights and fuel gauge, and the face of the panel was still divided into three sections, and the outer sections were still covered in simulated woodgrain appliqués. What was different was the slightly odd upside-down triangular section around the steering column was gone, and the center section housing radio and climate controls was pushed outward slightly to make them more accessible. Upholstery and trim also continued in a similar style, with woodgrain trim topping the door panels, and a return to door pull straps, rather than the hinged type door pulls used on the prior models.

The popular Seville continued to sell quite well, despite the apparent 23 percent production decline seen below that results from comparing a 12-month period with a 17-month period. The Seville adopted a finer vertical tiered crosshatch grille and newly designed wire wheel covers to match those on the new deVille, and could be purchased with or without a vinyl top this year for no extra cost. Otherwise, the successful formula was not tampered with.

The Eldorado line was back to a single model line for the first time since 1970. With the convertible gone, at least temporarily, and a new Eldorado expected with the next year or two, only a minor facelift was given to the Eldorado. A new grille much like that of the Seville was applied, with a thick chrome header. New taillights were adopted that put the brake and taillights fully into the vertical bumper ends, creating the need for a rear quarter panel side marker light, which carried the Eldorado name.

Coupe deVille 2-Door Coupe

Eldorado 2-Door Hardtop Coupe

Fleetwood Brougham 4-Door Sedan

Fleetwood Limousine

Sedan deVille 4-Door Sedan

Seville 4-Door Sedan

Model year production: 358,341, up 10.60% from 1976.
Domestic market share: 3.71% (9th place).
Base price range: $9,654 to $18,858.
Cadillac average base price: $13,237, up 19.29%.
Introduction date: September 23, 1976.
Assembly plants: Linden, NJ (E); and Detroit, MI (Q).
Data plate identification (VIN): Thirteen digit code read as follows: First digit indicates division (6 = Cadillac); second through fourth digits indicate series and body style (model number in model charts); fifth digit is engine code (see powertrain chart); sixth digit indicates model year (7 = 1977); seventh digit indicates assembly plant (see list above); remaining digits are sequential with beginning number of 100001. *Example:* 6D69T7Q100001 is a 1977 Cadillac Sedan deVille 4-Door Sedan, with 425 CID, EFI V8 engine, serial number 100001, built in Detroit, MI.

Powertrains

Engine	Net HP	Engine Code: VIN/GM Code	Transmission Availability[2]		Seville	Eldorado	deVille & Fleetwood Brougham	Fleetwood Limousine
350 CID (5.7L), EFI, V8	180	R	Turbo Hydra-matic 3-sp. Automatic		S	—	—	—
				MPG:	14/19/16	—	—	—
				Calif.	12/17/14	—	—	—
425 CID (7.0L), 4-bbl., V8	180	S/L33	Turbo Hydra-matic 3-sp. Automatic		—	S	S	S
				MPG:	—	11/18/14	14/18/16	12/18/14
				Calif.	—	11/16/13	12/16/14	11/16/13
425 CID (7.0L), EFI, V8	195	T/L35	Turbo Hydra-matic 3-sp. Automatic		—	$702	$702	—
				MPG:	—	11/17/13	12/18/14	—
				Calif.	—	NA	11/17/13	—

Major Options

	Seville	deVille	Eldorado	Fleetwood Brougham	Fleetwood Limousine
Automatic Climate Control	S	S	S	S	S
Electric rear window defogger	$83	$83	$83	$83	$83
Controlled cycle windshield wiper	S	$30	$30	$30	$30
Tilt and telescope steering wheel	S	$109	$109	$109	$109

	Seville	deVille	Eldorado	Fleetwood Brougham	Fleetwood Limousine
Cruise Control	$111	$111	$111	$111	$111
Twilight Sentinel	$51	$51	$51	$51	$51
Guidematic headlamp control	$58	$58	$58	$58	$58
Leather upholstery	$235	$252	$252	$252	—[1]
Dual Comfort 50/50 front seat	S	$187	$187	S	—
Power front seat, 6-way bench	$107	S	S	—	$99
Power front seat, 6-way Dual Comfort, driver/passenger	$248	$197	$197	S	—
Lighted vanity mirror, passenger	$47	$47	$47	$47	$47
Illuminated entry system	$56	$56	$56	$56	$56
AM/FM stereo, signal seeking	S	$156	S	S	$326[2]
AM/FM stereo w/8-track tape	$100	$254	$100	$100	$254
Automatic door locks	$101	$101	$101	$101	$101
Remote trunk release w/electric pulldown	$61	$73	$73	$73	$73
Padded vinyl top	S	$179	$186	S	S
Sunroof[3]	$742	$742	$742	$742	—[1]
Astroroof[3]	$938	$938	$938	$938	—[1]
Theft-Deterrent system	$123	$123	$123	$123	$123
Fuel monitor system	S	$28	$28	$28	$28
Automatic level control	S	$100	S	S	S
Special turbine style wheel discs	—	$49	—	$49	$49
Wire spoke wheel covers	$176	$176	—	$129	$176
Steel-belted radial WSW tires	S	S	S	S	S

Popular Option Groups & Packages

	Seville	deVille	Eldorado	Fleetwood Brougham	Fleetwood Limousine
Brougham d'Elegance package	—	—	—	$885	—
Custom Cabriolet package, coupe	—	$348	$457	—	—
de Ville d'Elegance package	—	$650	—	—	—
Custom Biarritz package	—	—	$1,760	—	—

— = Not Available; S = Standard equipment. [1]Available by special order only. [2]Fleetwood models include rear seat controls. [3]Price given is with full padded vinyl roof. Available on all models with painted roofs for $105 additional cost.

Paint Colors

	Code		Code		Code
Cotillion White	11	Sovereign Gold metallic	54	Buckskin Firemist metallic**	95
Georgian Silver metallic	13	Sonora Tan	61	Frost Orange Firemist metallic**	96
Academy Gray metallic*	15	Saffron metallic	67	Damson Plum Firemist metallic**	98
Sable Black	19	Demitasse Brown metallic	69	Desert Rose Firemist metallic**	99
Jennifer Blue	24	Bimini Beige	74		
Hudson Bay Blue metallic	29	Crimson	77	*In two-tone combinations, the first two digits indicate*	
Seamist Green	40	Maderia Maroon	79	*lower color; the next two digits are the upper color.*	
Edinburgh Green metallic	49	Cerulean Blue Firemist metallic**	90	**Used for two-tones only. **Firemist paint available*	
Naples Yellow	50	Thyme Green Firemist metallic**	94	*for $153 extra.*	

Seville

"Seville is a unique American luxury car. International in size. Timeless in styling. Engineered to be one of the finest production cars built anywhere in the world."

Nameplate year of origin: 1976; 1956 (as a designation on Eldorado 2-Door Hard-tops).
Current bodystyle lifespan: 1976 through 1979.

Measurements

Wheelbase	114.3"
Length	204.0"

Predecessor to this model: None.
Replacement for this model: Seville (1980 to 1985).
Percentage of division's production: 12.90%.
Corporate siblings: None.
Primary competition: Lincoln Versailles.
Notable changes: New grille and trim and detail changes.
Major standard equipment: Mansion knit cloth 50/50 split front seat w/individual fold-down center armrests, six-way driver and two-way passenger power seat adjustment, one-piece deep pile carpeting, seatback and overhead entry assist straps, hinged door pull handles, individual rear seat reading lamps, electric clock, power windows, power door locks, tilt and telescoping steering wheel, controlled wiper cycle system, automatic climate control, AM/FM signal-seeking stereo radio w/automatic power antenna, dual remote-control rear view mirrors, padded vinyl roof, remote trunk release, trunk carpeting including deck lid, fuel monitor system, lamp monitors, front cornering lights, wheel opening moldings, stand-up wreath and crest hood-ornament, automatic level control, automatic parking brake release, bodyside and decklid accent striping, full wheel covers, and GR78 × 15 wide WSW tires.

Measurements (cont.)

Width	71.8"
Height	54.6"
Legroom — front	41.7"
Legroom — rear	38.2"
Headroom — front	38.6"
Headroom — rear	36.8"
Cargo capacity (cu. ft.)	12.8
Fuel capacity (gals.)	21.0

Models Available

	Model No.	Base MSRP	Change from LY	Shipping Wt. (lbs.)	Model Year Sales	Change from LY
Seville 4-Door Sedan	S69	$13,359	+7.05%	4192	46,212	-23.14%
TOTALS	Avg. price	$13,359	+7.05%	Production	46,212	-23.14%

deVille

"The next generation of America's favorite luxury car."

Nameplate year of origin: 1959 (series); 1949 (as hardtop designation).
Current bodystyle lifespan: 1977 through 1984.
Predecessor to this model: deVille (1971 to 1976).
Replacement for this model: deVille (1985 to 1993).
Percentage of division's production: 65.35%.
Corporate siblings: Buick Electra, Cadillac Fleetwood Brougham and Oldsmobile 98.
Primary competition: Lincoln Continental.
Notable changes: Completely redesigned.
Major standard equipment: Choice of Merlin plaid cloth, Magnan ribbed fabric or Manhattan velour w/vinyl bolsters and front and rear seat center armrests, 6-way power front seat adjuster, cut-pile carpeting, hinged door pull assist handles, visor vanity mirror, driver and passenger reading lights, courtesy lights, courtesy lamp/assist strap combination on B-pillar of 2-doors, electric clock, power windows, power door locks, automatic climate control, AM/FM radio w/automatic power antenna, LH remote-control rear view mirror, front cornering lights, wheel opening moldings, rocker panel moldings, full wheel covers, and GR78 × 15 WSW tires.

Measurements

Wheelbase	121.5"
Length	221.2"
Width	76.4"
Height	55.3"
Legroom — front	42.1"
Legroom — rear	39.7"
Headroom — front	38.0"
Headroom — rear	37.9"
Cargo capacity (cu. ft.)	25.0
Fuel capacity (gals.)	24.0

Models Available

	Model No.	Base MSRP	Change from LY	Shipping Wt. (lbs.)	Model Year Production	Change from LY
Coupe deVille 2-Door Coupe	D47	$9,654	+6.47%	4186	138,750	+21.20%
Sedan deVille 4-Door Sedan	D69	$9,864	+6.47%	4222	95,421	+40.99%
TOTALS	Avg. price	$9,759	+6.47%	Production	234,171	+28.55%

Eldorado

"The legend lives for 1977."

Nameplate year of origin: 1953.
Current bodystyle lifespan: 1971 through 1978.
Predecessor to this model: Fleetwood Eldorado (1967 to 1970).
Replacement for this model: Eldorado (1979 to 1985).
Percentage of division's production: 13.21%.
Corporate siblings: Oldsmobile Toronado.
Primary competition: Lincoln Continental Mark V.
Notable changes: Minor trim and detail changes.
Major standard equipment: Choice of Merlin plaid fabric or Mansion knit fabric front seat w/individual fold-down center armrest, 6-way power seat adjuster, cut-pile carpeting, hinged door pull assist handles, visor vanity mirror, driver and passenger reading lights, courtesy lights, electric clock, power windows, power door locks, automatic climate control, AM/FM signal-seeking stereo radio w/automatic power antenna, LH remote-control rear view mirror, front cornering lights, wheel opening moldings, rocker panel moldings, stand-up wreath and crest hood-ornament, automatic level control, full wheel covers, and LR78 × 15 wide WSW tires.

Measurements

Wheelbase	126.3"
Length	224.0"
Width	79.8"
Height	54.2"
Legroom — front	42.2"
Legroom — rear	35.2"
Headroom — front	37.7"
Headroom — rear	36.7"
Cargo capacity (cu. ft.)	NA
Fuel capacity (gals.)	27.0

Models Available

	Model No.	Base MSRP	Change from LY	Shipping Wt. (lbs.)	Model Year Production	Change from LY
Eldorado 2-Door Coupe	L47	$11,187	+5.68%	4955	47,344	+34.56%
TOTALS	*Avg. price*	$11,187	+3.42%	*Production*	47,344	-3.74%

Fleetwood Brougham

"A very special kind of Cadillac ... for very special people."

Nameplate year of origin: 1966.
Current bodystyle lifespan: 1977 through 1992.
Predecessor to this model: Fleetwood Sixty-Special and Fleetwood Brougham (1971 to 1976).
Replacement for this model: Fleetwood Brougham (1993 to 1996).
Percentage of division's sales volume: 7.81%.
Corporate siblings: Buick Electra, Cadillac deVille and Oldsmobile 98.
Primary competition: Lincoln Continental w/Town Car package.
Notable changes: Completely redesigned.
Major standard equipment: Choice of Mansion knit fabric or Minoa ribbed velour dual comfort 60/40 front seat, driver side 2-way power seat adjuster, front and rear seat fold-down center armrests, cut-pile carpeting, hinged door pull assist handles, front passenger reading light, courtesy lights, quartz digital clock, power windows, power door locks, automatic climate control, AM/FM signal-seeking stereo radio w/automatic power antenna, LH remote-control rear view mirror, padded vinyl roof, front cornering lights, wheel opening moldings, rocker panel moldings w/upper ridge, automatic level control, full wheel covers, and GR78 × 15 WSW tires.

Measurements

Wheelbase	121.5"
Length	221.2"
Width	76.4"
Height	56.7"
Legroom — front	42.1"
Legroom — rear	39.7"
Headroom — front	38.0"
Headroom — rear	37.9"
Cargo capacity (cu. ft.)	25.0
Fuel capacity (gals.)	24.0

Models Available

	Model No.	Base MSRP	Change from LY	Shipping Wt. (lbs.)	Model Year Production	Change from LY
Fleetwood Brougham 4-Door Sedan	B69	$11,546	+5.59%	4340	28,000	+14.29%
TOTALS	*Avg. price*	$11,546	+5.59%	*Production*	28,000	+14.29%

Fleetwood Limousine

"The new Flagships of the fleet ... the next generation of the Limousine."

Nameplate year of origin: 1927 (models using Fleetwood bodies); 1935 (Fleetwood series).
Current bodystyle lifespan: 1977 through 1984.
Predecessor to this model: Fleetwood Seventy-Five (1971 to 1976).
Replacement for this model: Fleetwood 75 Limousine (1985 to 1987).
Percentage of division's sales volume: 0.73%.
Corporate siblings: None.
Primary competition: None.
Notable changes: Completely redesigned.
Major standard equipment: Choice of light gray Magnan knit interior or Medici crushed velour in dark blue or black, 2-way power front seat adjuster, front and back seat fold-down center armrests, cut-pile carpeting, full-width folding seats (rearward facing for three additional passengers), rear seat carpeted foot rests, hinged door pull assist handles, power windows, power door locks, dual automatic climate control system (front and rear), courtesy lights, electric clock, AM/FM radio w/automatic power antenna, passenger control panel (controls power windows, reading lights, radio, automatic climate control, and the glass partition in the Limousine), automatic level control, LH and RH remote-control rear view mirror, front cornering lights, wheel opening moldings, full-length rocker panel moldings, full wheel covers, and HR78 × 15 WSW tires.

Measurements

Wheelbase	144.5"
Length	244.2"
Width	79.8"
Height	56.9"
Legroom — front	NA
Legroom — rear	NA
Headroom — front	NA
Headroom — rear	NA
Cargo capacity (cu. ft.)	NA
Fuel capacity (gals.)	24.0

1977

Models Available

	Model No.	Base MSRP	Change from LY	Shipping Wt. (lbs.)	Model Year Production	Change from LY
Fleetwood 4-Door Limousine	F23	$18,193	+22.19%	4738	1,582	+61.26%
Fleetwood 4-Door Formal Limousine	F33	$18,858	+23.75%	4806	1,032	+23.74%
TOTALS	*Avg. price*	$18,526	+22.98%	*Production*	2,614	+44.02%

CHEVROLET

"The 1977 Chevrolets."

Despite the year's dull advertising slogan, there was plenty of excitement in Chevrolet's 1977 model line. Most important were the all-new, downsized Impala and Caprice full-size models. Having been the country's most popular line of cars for many years, and most recently for the 1975 model year, these models had a lot riding on their public acceptance. In the end Chevrolet had a success on its hands, as the new line of Impala and Caprice models garnered a sales increase of more than 50 percent over last year, and narrowly edged out the 1976 production leader, the Oldsmobile Cutlass, to reclaim the top spot in production and sales. Also, in a remarkable comeback of the "pony car," the Camaro saw production increase to its highest level since the first generation 1969 models. The increasing sales of the Camaro and

its corporate sibling, the Pontiac Firebird, prompted Chevrolet to bring back the Z28, giving enthusiasts hope that the popular muscle car would regain its former position of performance domination.

The new Impala and Caprice Classic models were the most significant model introductions since the new mid-size Chevelle line in 1973. Nearly 700 pounds lighter, and about a foot shorter than last year's models, the full-size Chevy line was also pared back to six basic models, with a coupe, sedan and wagon in each line, and all hardtop models completely gone. The weight loss, modern design, and improved overall comfort and driveability prompted *Motor Trend* magazine to select the Caprice Classic as its "Car of the Year" for 1977. At mid-year, the Landau coupe would return as an option package, and later become a full-fledged model for the 1978 season. Also, for the first time, the third row seats for full-size wagons were now an option, rather than a separate model with unique model number. Styling for the new cars followed the pattern of all the new GM full-size models, with an angular "three-box" style, although they did endure wind tunnel testing during their development to improve efficiency and reduce interior wind noise.

At the front end, the Impala and Caprice used completely different designs. For the Impala, dual rectangular headlights sat above horizontal dual unit parking and turn signal lights, all set within a single bezel. Between the lights and below a slightly raised center hood section was a full-width grille in a large opening egg-crate design, three rows high and eight columns across, with each opening having an inset of three vertical bars. A gold Chevrolet emblem rested in the center of the grille. Horizontal openings in the front bumper carried an additional grille row set beneath the three outer columns. A thin chrome strip surrounded all grille areas. On the fancier Caprice Classic, dual rectangular headlights were set near the fender ends, with wrap-around parking/turn signal lights within the fender end cap. Additional parking and turn signal lights were housed in the bumper below the headlights. The Caprice grille was an intricate design composed of thirty vertical columns across, and each column consisting of seven square openings. Above the top of the grille and surrounding the headlights was a large chrome trim piece, and the Chevrolet name in block letters was placed at mid-height on the driver's side of the grille. A Caprice logo hood ornament sat atop the front header panel. Horizontal openings in the bumper on each side of the front license plate mounting housed additional grille inserts consisting of eleven vertical columns with three rows of squares.

The rest of the exterior was common between the two models for the most part. Two bodyside feature lines appeared on all models, with an upper line running full length from near the top of the front fender to a point near the top of the rear quarter panel. On station wagons, the upper line ran to a point above the wraparound taillights, but was less prominent than on the sedans as it ran across the rear quarter panels. A lower feature line ran from the middle of the front bumper to the middle of the rear bumper, and was also used on wagons. Round-topped full wheel openings were slightly flared as the line ran over them. The greenhouse area of sedans and wagons was rather formal and upright, with both models using fixed rear door quarter windows. Rear door windows went down only partway as a result of the inner door construction and lack of space for the windows to retract fully.

Coupes had a very unusual greenhouse area. A fixed rear quarter window was somewhat rectangular in shape, with the rear edge slanting slightly rearward from top to bottom, and paralleling the angle of the roofline. The bottom of the window, about three-fourths of the way back, angled upwards to meet the rear edge. What was unique was the resulting rear window design. A "folded" type wraparound rear window gave the look of a sporty coupe with a more rakish slope than the relatively upright C-pillar, which it met by wrapping around creased corners. Similar glass was also seen on this year's Oldsmobile Toronado coupe with the XS option, and was a modern, angular take on the rounded wraparound rear windows of the 1971–1973 Impala sport coupes.

At the rear of the cars, two variations of a square, triple-unit taillight were used, placed on either side of the license plate opening. On the Impala, the center lens housed the backup light. For the Caprice, a Caprice emblem was mounted in the middle of the center lens, and vertical backup lights were placed between the taillights and the license plate housing. Taillights for both wagon models were square, wraparound units, divided into three sections horizontally, with the middle section housing the backup lights, and the license plate being mounted in the center of the rear bumper.

Smaller powerplants came with the smaller bodies, and 250 CID inline six-cylinder engines powered the new Chevrolets for the first time since 1972 for the Impala, and for the first time ever in a Caprice. Station wagons came with a standard 305 CID V8 engine, which was optional in coupes and sedans, and the largest engine available was now the 350 CID V8. Inside, the new models had a totally new instrument panel design that looked like it could have been lifted out of a Cadillac. The upper pad appeared to act as a hood, shielding the gauges from glare, while the panel below angled back and away from the driver and passengers, creating a roomier feel and adding leg and knee space for front seat passengers. On the driver's side, gauges were set in a rectangular pod with a horizontal speedometer, and round dials on each side housing fuel, temperature and oil pressure to the left, and warning lights to the right. In the center of the panel, horizontal air vents capped a centrally located electric clock, when equipped, and a large pod below housing the ventilation controls and optional radio. Seats used the expected materials with knit cloths and soft vinyls, but front seats featured a new "shell" design that created a thinner seatback, creating more rear passenger leg room.

The mid-size Chevelle line, which was suddenly not much smaller than the new full-size Chevrolet models, was in line for its own downsizing next year. Therefore, not much effort was put into annual updating. Despite the similar size to the big Chevy models and the ever-growing popularity of the mid-size Oldsmobile Cutlass line, the Chevelle line lost only about 5,000 units from last year's pace — roughly half of the production of the Laguna Type S-3 coupe, which was discontinued for 1977. The Malibu Classic line received a new grille insert with 45 vertical bars, the center one being slightly wider, and all surrounded with a thick chrome piece as with last year's model. The Chevelle Malibu line was mostly unchanged; however, new taillights were adopted for all Malibu and Classic coupe and sedan models. The new lenses were divided into six square units arranged horizontally, with the inner three housing the backup lights. On base Malibus they were set into a body color rear panel, while on the Malibu Classic, they were set within a full width brushed finish panel broken only by the license plate mount. In another change for 1977, the Malibu Classic Estate wagon became an option package, even as mid-size station wagon sales increased.

The Monte Carlo's three-row grille, introduced last year, continued for '77, adding new inserts that gave a freshened look. Within each row were chrome-line sections across, each containing a two-by-two egg-crate style, argent-colored insert. Around back the vertical taillight mounted on the rear quarter end cap was divided into four sections horizontally, with the bottom section housing the backup lights. It was visually shortened from prior years, by having what would have been a fifth section at the top replaced with an extension of the body color rear end cap.

The compact Camaro and Nova did not receive any big changes for the year. However, there were two big newsmakers for the Camaro, with the most exciting for enthusiasts being the return of the Z28, this time as an actual model and not an option package. Disappointingly it was not nearly as powerful as the originals, but at least it was powered by the same 350 CID V8 engine available in the Corvette, so that was some consolation. Also, as sales continued to rise, Camaro made history by outselling its longtime rival, the Ford Mustang, for the first time ever this year, although it was a somewhat hollow victory as the Mustang II was an economy car compared to the Camaro at this point. The Nova adopted the 1976 grille of its more luxurious running mate, the Concours, while the 1977 Concours had a new vertical crosshatch grille. The new Concours grille pattern had 23 chrome faced vertical bars per side, separated by a wider center bar, and placed at the forefront, with three horizontal bars behind, with a thin chrome outline, giving a very elegant look to the Nova-based car. A thick chrome strip ran across the raised center section of the header panel with the Chevrolet name etched in script on the driver's side. Also chrome lined square headlight bezels were introduced for the Concours, while around back, the Concours added three-unit taillights to distinguish it from the lesser two-unit Nova taillights. This was a mark first used on full-size Chevrolet models in 1958, and then ever since 1961, to denote whether a series was a lower or an upper trim level. Most other features remained unchanged.

In the subcompact line of cars, the popular Chevette continued into the new year with few changes. The "Woody" option, which had not been popular, was replaced by a new Sandpiper option that was strictly an appearance package. Sales fell in its second year as easing fuel economy concerns sent buyers towards larger cars. Vega production fell below 100,000 units for the first time in history, and it also became the last year for the once popular compact, as the reputation it had developed for quality problems had finally caught up to it, despite GM's best efforts to reassure consumers that the problems were resolved. The 2.3 litre, 140 CID 4-cylinder engine that had been the main problem was also dropped with the Vega name. The Vega Kammback wagon would continue on under the Monza nameplate beginning in 1978. Also, after two years of lower than expected sales, the Cosworth Vega was dropped for 1977.

Among few changes for the Monza was the newly optional Sport Front End appearance package for the Towne Coupe, which featured the body-colored urethane front end from the sporty 2+2 hatchback, giving the coupe a much sportier look than its standard "luxury" style nose. The Spyder Appearance and Equipment packages gained more attention through increased advertising exposure. Once again the performance equipment package was available for both coupe and hatchback, while the appearance package was solely for the hatchback. An interesting mid-year model appeared as a factory-supported aftermarket model, named the Mirage. Produced by Michigan Auto Techniques, the Mirage package added flared body panels and a large air dam and rear spoilers, all painted white with full-length red and blue striping on the lower bodysides and on the top of the hood, roof and hatch lid. Specific wheels, blackout trim and Mirage decals were also used. Approximately 4,100 were produced during its short six-month lifespan.

Finally, the Corvette had several small changes this season, noticeable only on close inspection. Foremost was that the Stingray name was dropped from the front fender of the car. This is significant as the Stingray name had been associated with this generation of Corvette since its beginnings in 1968, and was the name of the concept car the production Corvette was based on. Other exterior changes included new black windshield posts to give a "thin pillar" look. Interior changes included a choice of leather seating or cloth and leather upholstery as standard equipment, and easier luggage compartment access. Also new was the headlight "hi-lo" beam switch and wiper controls being moved to the turn signal stalk on the steering column, a feature added to most other GM models over the past few years.

1977

Camaro Type LT 2-Door Sport Coupe

Caprice Classic 4-Door Sedan

Chevelle Malibu 4-Door Station Wagon

Chevette 2-Door Hatchback
with Sandpiper package

Impala interior

Camaro Z28 2-Door Sport Coupe

Caprice Classic 4-Door Station Wagon

Chevelle Malibu Classic 2-Door
Colonnade Hardtop Coupe

Corvette 2-Door Coupe

Monte Carlo Landau 2-Door Hardtop Coupe

Monza 2-Door Towne Coupe
with Sport Front End Appearance package

Caprice Classic 2-Door Coupe

Caprice Classic instrument panel

Chevette 2-Door Hatchback with Rally package

Impala 4-Door Sedan

Monza 2+2 2-Door Hatchback Coupe
with Spyder Appearance package

Nova 2-Door Coupe

Nova 2-Door Coupe with Rally package

Nova Concours 2-Door Coupe
with Cabriolet roof

Nova Concours 4-Door Sedan

Vega 2-Door Hatchback Coupe with GT package

Vega 2-Door Kammback Wagon with Estate
package

1977

Model year production: 2,319,464, up 10.25% from 1976.
Domestic market share: 24.17% (1st place).
Base price range: $2,999 to $8,648.
Chevrolet average base price: $4,386, up 0.70%.
Introduction date: September 30, 1976. Camaro Z28 introduced February 1977.
Assembly plants: Baltimore, MD (B); Southgate, CA (C); Doraville, GA (D); Janesville, WI (J); Kansas City/Leeds, MO (K); Van Nuys, CA (L); Norwood, OH (N); Arlington, TX (R); St. Louis, MO (S); Tarrytown, NY (T); Lordstown, OH (U); Willow Run, MI (W); Wilmington, DE (Y); Fremont, CA (Z); Oshawa, Ontario, Canada (1); and Ste. Therese, Quebec, Canada (2).

Data plate identification (VIN): Thirteen digit code read as follows: First digit indicates division (1 = Chevrolet); second through fourth digits indicate series and body style (model number in model charts); fifth digit is engine code (see powertrain chart); sixth digit indicates model year (7 = 1977); seventh digit indicates assembly plant (see list above); remaining digits are sequential with beginning number of 100001. *Example:* 1S87L7N100001 is a 1977 Chevrolet Camaro Type LT 2-Door Sport Coupe, with 350 CID, 4-bbl. V8 engine, serial number 100001, built in Norwood, OH.

Powertrains

Engine	Net HP	Engine Code	Transmission Availability[1]		Chevette	Vega & Monza	Camaro	Nova & Concours	Chevelle Malibu[2]	Monte Carlo	Full-Size Chevy	Corvette
85 CID (1.4L) OHC, 1-bbl., 4-cyl.	57	1	4-speed manual		S	—	—	—	—	—	—	—
				MPG:	28/42/33	—	—	—	—	—	—	—
			3-speed Turbo Hydra-matic		$248	—	—	—	—	—	—	—
				MPG:	25/35/29	—	—	—	—	—	—	—
98 CID (1.6L) OHC, 1-bbl., 4-cyl.	63	E	4-speed manual		$55	—	—	—	—	—	—	—
				MPG:	31/43/36	—	—	—	—	—	—	—
				Calif.	28/39/32	—	—	—	—	—	—	—
			3-speed Turbo Hydra-matic		$303	—	—	—	—	—	—	—
				MPG:	26/36/30	—	—	—	—	—	—	—
				Calif.	25/32/28	—	—	—	—	—	—	—
140 CID (2.3L) OHC,	84	B	4-speed manual		—	S	—	—	—	—	—	—
				MPG:	—	24/33/28	—	—	—	—	—	—

Engine	Net HP	Engine Code	Transmission Availability[1]		Chevette	Vega & Monza	Camaro	Nova & Concours	Chevelle Malibu[2]	Monte Carlo	Full-Size Chevy	Corvette
2-bbl., 4-cyl.				Calif.	—	23/33/27	—	—	—	—	—	—
			5-speed manual		—	$248	—	—	—	—	—	—
				MPG:	—	NA	—	—	—	—	—	—
			3-speed Turbo Hydra-matic		—	$248	—	—	—	—	—	—
				MPG:	—	21/28/24	—	—	—	—	—	—
				Calif.	—	21/30/24	—	—	—	—	—	—
250 CID (4.1L), 1-bbl., 6-cyl.	110	D	3-speed manual[3]		—	—	S[4]	S	S (Mcs, MCc)	—	—	—
				MPG:	—	—	18/25/20	19/27/22	18/25/20	—	—	—
			4-speed manual[3]		—	—	$252[4]	$252	—	—	—	—
				MPG:	—	—	NA	NA	—	—	—	—
			3-speed Turbo Hydra-matic		—	—	$282[4]	$282	S (MCs)/$282 (Mcs, MCc)	—	S (ex. Wgns.)	—
				MPG:	—	—	17/22/19	18/23/20	17/22/19	—	17/22/19	—
				Calif.	—	—	15/19/16	15/21/17	15/19/16	—	15/19/16	—
305 CID (5.0L), 2-bbl., V8	145	U	3-speed manual[3]		—	—	$120[4]	$120	—	—	—	—
				MPG:	—	—	16/22/19	16/22/19	—	—	—	—
			4-speed manual[3]		—	$205 (Monza only)	$372[4]	$372	—	—	—	—
				MPG:	—	16/22/18	NA	NA	—	—	—	—
			3-speed Turbo Hydra-matic		—	$453 (Monza only)	$402[4]	$402	S (Mw)/$120 (MCs)/$402 (Mcs, MCc)	S	S (Wgns.)[3]/$120 (others)[3]	—
				MPG:	—	17/25/20	15/21/18	16/21/18	16/21/17	16/20/17	16/21/18[5]	—
				Calif.	—	14/20/17	14/19/16	14/19/16	—	—	14/19/16	—
350 CID (5.7L), 4-bbl., V8	170/180[6]	L	3-speed manual[3]		—	—	$210[4]	$210	—	—	—	—
				MPG:	—	—	14/18/15	14/18/15	—	—	—	—
			4-speed manual[3]		—	—	$462[4]	$462	—	—	—	S
				MPG:	—	—	NA	NA	—	—	—	14/18/15
			3-speed Turbo Hydra-matic		—	—	$494[4]	$494	S (MCw)/$90 (Mw)/$210 (MCs)/$492 (Mcs, MCc)	$90	$90 (Wgns.)/$210 (others)	N/C
				MPG:	—	—	15/20/17	15/20/17	14/19/16	14/19/16	15/20/17[5]	15/20/17
				Calif.	—	—	14/18/15	14/18/15	13/17/15	13/17/15	14/18/15	14/18/15

Engine	Net HP	Engine Code	Transmission Availability[1]	Chevette	Vega & Monza	Camaro	Nova & Concours	Chevelle Malibu[2]	Monte Carlo	Full-Size Chevy	Corvette
350 CID (5.7L), 4-bbl., V8	195/ 210[6]	L/X (L82)[6]	4-speed manual[3]	—	—	S (Z28 only)	—	—	—	—	$495
			MPG:	—	—	NA	—	—	—	—	NA
			3-speed Turbo Hydra-matic	—	—	$282 (Z28 only)	—	—	—	—	$641
			MPG:	—	—	NA	—	—	—	—	NA

[1]Unless otherwise specified: All 3-speed manuals are column shift. All 4- and 5-speed manuals are floor shift. All automatics are column shift, except on Chevette, Vega, Monza, Camaro and Corvette. Floor shift automatic is optional on Nova, Chevelle and Monte Carlo with other specified equipment at extra cost. [2]Mcs = Malibu coupe & sedan; Mw = All Malibu wagons; MCc = Malibu Classic coupes; MCs = Malibu Classic sedan; MCw = Malibu Classic wagon. [3]Not available in California or high altitude areas. [4]Not available on Camaro Z28. [5]Estimated mileage ratings for station wagons are one mpg lower for city, highway and combined. [6]Special engines (and HP ratings) for Camaro Z28/Corvette.

Major Options

	Chevette	Vega	Monza	Camaro	Nova	Chevelle	Monte Carlo	Full-size Chevy	Corvette
Four-season air conditioning[1]	$442	$442	$442	$507	$507	$499	$499	$527	$553
Comfortilt steering wheel	—	$50	$50	$57	$57	$57	$57	$58	S[2]
Cruise-Master speed control	—	—	—	$80	$80	$80	$80	$84	$88
Rear window defogger[3]	—	—	—	$48	$48	$48	$48	$48	—
Electro-Clear rear window defogger	$71	$71	$71	—	—	—	$82	$83	$84
Dual sport mirrors, remote	$46	$28[4]	$28[4]	$30[4]	$30[4]	$51	$51	$51	$36[4]
Soft-Ray tinted glass, all windows	$48	$48	$48	$50	$50	$54	$58	$69	S
Power windows, 2-dr./4-dr.	—	—	—	$108	$108/$151	$108/$151	$108	$114/$171	$116
Power door locks, 2-dr./4-dr.	—	—	—	$68	$68/$96	$68/$96	$68	$70/$98	—
Power front seat, w/std. seat	—	—	—	—	—	$137	$137	$139	—
Front bucket seats, w/console[5]	$17	$77	$77	$75	$347	$204	$244	—	S
Rear facing third seat (wagons)	—	—	—	—	—	$143	—	$117	—
AM radio	$67	$67	$67	$72	$72	$72	$72	$73	—
AM/FM stereo	—	$212	$212	$226	$226	$226	$226	$229	—
AM/FM stereo w/8-track tape	—	$304	$304	$324	$324	$324	$324	$328	$281
Vinyl top, full[6]	—	—	—	—	$96	$111	$131	$135	$414
Vinyl top, landau[7]	—	—	$145	$96	$96	—	—	—	—
Sky Roof (sunroof), power[8]	—	$210	$210	—	—	—	$394	—	—
Power steering, variable-ratio	—	$129	$129	S	$146	$146[9]	S	S	S
Power brakes, w/front disc	$58	$58	$58	$61	$61	$61[9]	S	S	S[10]
Full wheel covers	$30	$30	$33	$33	$33	$33	S	$36	—
Wire wheel covers	—	—	—	—	$108	—	—	—	—
Rally wheels w/trim rings	S	$104	S	$65	$65	$65	$50	—	S
Forged aluminum wheels	—	—	$209	—	—	—	—	—	$321
WSW tires	$38	$38	$38	$43	$39	$45	$45	$41	—

Popular Option Groups & Packages

	Chevette	Vega	Monza	Camaro	Nova	Chevelle	Monte Carlo	Full-size Chevy	Corvette
Auxiliary lighting package	$38	$31	$20	—	—	—	—	$38	—
Custom appearance group	—	—	—	—	$81	—	—	—	—
Custom interior package	$199	$188	—	—	—	—	—	—	—
Estate wagon package	—	—	—	—	—	$185	—	$210	—
Exterior décor package	—	—	—	$61[11]	$78	$54	—	—	—
GT package	—	$401	—	—	—	—	—	—	—
Gymkhana suspension package	—	—	—	—	—	—	—	—	$38
Interior décor/Quiet sound group	$42	$46	—	$57	—	—	—	$41	—
Rally equipment package	$321	—	—	—	$186	—	—	—	—
Rally Sport package	—	—	—	$281[12]	—	—	—	—	—
Sand Piper package	$199	—	—	—	—	—	—	—	—

	Chevette	Vega	Monza	Camaro	Nova	Chevelle	Monte Carlo	Full-size Chevy	Corvette
Special instrumentation package	$60	$77	$77	$99	$99	—	—	—	S
Sport equipment package	—	—	$134	—	—	—	—	—	—
Sport front-end appearance	—	—	$118	—	—	—	—	—	—
Spyder appearance package	—	—	$199	—	—	—	—	—	—
Spyder equipment group	—	—	$274	—	—	—	—	—	—

— = Not Available; S = Standard equipment. [1]Requires optional power steering and power brakes on Chevelle with 6-cylinder engine. Price is $478 on Camaro and Nova with V8 engine. Comfortron air conditioning with automatic temperature control is available for $607 on Impala and Caprice. [2]Tilt/Telescope leather-wrapped sport steering wheel available on Corvette for $165. [3]Blower type defogger. [4]Dual sport mirror with LH remote only. [5]Bucket seats standard on Chevette, Vega, Monza and Camaro, with console being optional. Available on Nova coupes or hatchbacks. Swivel bucket seats available only on Chevelle coupes and wagons, and Monte Carlo. [6]Not available on station wagons. [7]Standard on Monte Carlo Landau coupe and Malibu Classic Landau coupe. Available on Monza Towne Coupe, Malibu coupes, and Monte Carlo. Camaro has vinyl sport roof (front part o roof). [8]Manually operated on Vega and Monza. [9]Standard on station wagons. [10]Power front and rear disc brakes. [11]Exterior style trim group for Camaro. [12]Price given is for base Camaro. Available on Camaro LT for $186.

Paint Colors

	Code		Code
Classic White[1]	10	Cream Gold[5]	50
Antique White	11	Bright Yellow[2,3,4,7,8]	51
Silver metallic[1,2,3,4,5,6,7]	13	Corvette Bright Yellow[1]	56
Medium Gray metallic (two-tone)	15	Light Buckskin[2,3,4,5,8]	61
Black[1,2,3,4,5,7,8]	19	Buckskin metallic[3,4,5]	63
Light Blue[2,8]	21	Bright Orange[2,8]	64
Light Blue metallic[3,4,5]	22	Orange[1]	66
Light Blue metallic[1]	26	Brown metallic[2,3,4,5,7,8]	69
Dark Blue[1]	28	Medium Red[1,5]	72
Dark Blue metallic[2,3,4,5,8]	29	Light Red[2,3,4,6,7]	75
Light Lime[2,6]	32	Orange metallic[2,3,4,5,7,8]	78
Firethorn metallic	36	Tan Buckskin[1]	80
Aqua metallic[2,3,4,8]	37	Dark Red[1]	83
Medium Green metallic[3,4,5]	44	Medium Blue metallic (two-tone	
Dark Blue Green metallic[5]	48	only)	85

In two-tone combinations, the first two digits indicate lower color, and the next two digits are the upper color. Two-tone paint available for $43 on Nova and Chevelle and $44 on Impala and Caprice. Fashion Tone paint for Monte Carlo is $112 but varies depending upon other equipment. Colors listed with no footnotes are available on all models except Corvette. [1]Available on Corvette. [2]Available on Vega. [3]Available on Monza. [4]Available on Camaro, Nova and Concours. See footnote 7 for Camaro Z28 availability. [5]Available on all Chevelle Malibu, Monte Carlo and full-size Chevrolet models. [6]Available on all Chevette models. [7]Marked colors are the only ones available for Camaro Z28. [8]Available on Chevette, except Scooter.

Chevette

"What are friends for if not to tell each other about a car like Chevette."

Nameplate year of origin: 1976.
Current bodystyle lifespan: 1976 through 1987.
Predecessor to this model: None.
Replacement for this model: None (captive imports Sprint and Spectrum introduced in 1985 as supplementary models).
Percentage of division's production: 5.75%.
Corporate siblings: None.
Primary competition: Plymouth Arrow.
Notable changes: Minor trim and detail changes.
Major standard equipment: Choice of plaid cloth-and-vinyl or all-vinyl front bucket seats, fold-down rear seat (can be deleted on Scooter for $65 credit), black floor carpeting, door pull strap, armrests deleted, open compartment glove box, black two-spoke steering wheel and column, cargo compartment under floor storage, argent colored headlight bezels and grille trim, polished aluminum bumpers (not chromed), and 155/80 × 13 BSW tires. Chevette adds: Color-keyed carpeting, door armrests, glove box w/latch type door, bright front and rear window trim, dark argent headlamp bezel inserts, chrome trimmed headlight bezel and grille trim, deluxe chrome bumpers, and hubcaps.

Measurements

Wheelbase	94.3"
Length	158.7"
Width	61.8"
Height	52.3"
Legroom — front	41.5"
Legroom — rear	28.1"
Headroom — front	38.1"
Headroom — rear	37.3"
Cargo capacity (cu. ft.)	26.3*
Fuel capacity (gals.)	13.0

*Maximum with rear seat folded down.

Models Available

	Model No.	Base MSRP	Change from LY	Shipping Wt. (lbs.)	Model Year Production	Change from LY
Chevette Scooter 2-Door Hatchback	J08	$2,999	+3.45%	1898	13,191	+34.46%
Chevette 2-Door Hatchback	B08	$3,225	+4.10%	1958	120,278	-32.43%
TOTALS	Avg. price	$3,112	+3.79%	Production	133,469	-28.94%

Vega

"Tough ... for the fun of it."

Nameplate year of origin: 1971.
Current bodystyle lifespan: 1971 through 1977 (some models moved to Monza series, continuing through 1979).
Predecessor to this model: Corvair (1965 to 1969).
Replacement for this model: Cavalier (1982 to 1993).
Percentage of division's production: 3.38%.
Corporate siblings: Pontiac Astre.
Primary competition: AMC Gremlin, Dodge Colt, and Ford Pinto.
Notable changes: Minor trim and detail changes.
Major standard equipment: Cloth-and-vinyl high-back front bucket seats, sliding seat adjustment for both front seats, cut-pile carpeting, fold-down rear seat and rear liftgate (Hatchback and Kammback wagon), two-spoke steering wheel, glove box, map pocket in driver's door, two-speed wipers w/washers, bright front and rear window moldings, manual front disc brakes, and A78 × 13 BSW tires. Estate Wagon adds: Woodgrain vinyl panels on bodysides and tailgate, and special exterior nameplates.

Measurements

	Coupes	Wagon
Wheelbase	97.0"	97.0"
Length	175.4"	175.4"
Width	65.4"	65.4"
Height	51.8"	51.8"
Legroom — front	42.9"	42.9"
Legroom — rear	29.1"	30.2"
Headroom — front	37.0"	38.5"
Headroom — rear	37.1"	40.1"
Cargo capacity (cu. ft.)	9.3*	24.8**
Fuel capacity (gals.)	16.0	16.0

*Hatchback maximum with rear seat down, 26.5 cu. ft.
**Wagon maximum with rear seat down, 46.6 cu. ft.

Models Available

	Model No.	Base MSRP	Change from LY	Shipping Wt. (lbs.)	Model Year Production	Change from LY
Vega 2-Door Notchback Coupe	V11	$3,249	+8.88%	2459	12,365	-55.23%
Vega 2-Door Hatchback Coupe	V77	$3,359	+8.39%	2522	37,395	-51.69%
Vega 2-Door Kammback (Wagon)	V15	$3,572	+9.14%	2571	25,181	-45.39%
Vega 2-Door Kammback Estate (Wagon)	V15	$3,745	+8.55%	NA	3,461	-56.38%
TOTALS	Avg. price	$3,469	-7.87%	Production	78,402	-51.16%

Monza

"MMMonza. It puts the driving back in driving."

Nameplate year of origin: 1975 (1960 as Corvair subseries).
Current bodystyle lifespan: 1975 through 1980.
Predecessor to this model: Corvair Monza (1965 to 1969).
Replacement for this model: Cavalier (1982 to 1993).
Percentage of division's production: 3.16%.
Corporate siblings: Buick Skyhawk, Oldsmobile Starfire, and Pontiac Sunbird.
Primary competition: AMC Pacer, Dodge Colt, and Ford Mustang II.
Notable changes: Minor trim and detail changes.

Measurements

	Coupe	Hatchback
Wheelbase	97.0"	97.0"
Length	177.8"	179.3"
Width	65.4"	65.4"
Height	49.8"	50.2"
Legroom — front	42.8"	42.8"
Legroom — rear	28.2"	29.6"

1977

Major standard equipment: Choice of patterned cloth or all-vinyl front bucket seats, cut-pile carpeting, fold-down rear seat and rear liftgate (hatchbacks), two-spoke steering wheel, soft molded door panels w/map pockets, simulated woodgrain I/P trim, bright front and rear window moldings, bright side window surround moldings, and A78 × 13 BSW tires. Towne Coupe adds: Herringbone cloth-and-vinyl front bucket seats, bright chrome bumpers, and full wheel covers. 2+2 adds: Special two-spoke steering wheel, Quiet Sound group package, body-color urethane front end fascia w/black bumper rub strips, bright chrome rear bumper, front and rear bumper guards, and finned wheel covers w/GT-type center hub and bright wheel nuts.

Measurements (cont.)

Headroom — front	37.5"	37.7"
Headroom — rear	37.2"	35.3"
Cargo capacity (cu. ft.)	6.6	30.2*
Fuel capacity (gals.)	18.5	18.5

Capacity with rear seat down.

Models Available

	Model No.	Base MSRP	Change from LY	Shipping Wt. (lbs.)	Model Year Production	Change from LY
Monza 2-Door Towne Coupe	M27	$3,560	+5.98%	2580	34,133	-26.96%
Monza 2+2 2-Door Hatchback Coupe	R07	$3,840	+3.03%	2671	39,215	+14.76%
TOTALS	*Avg. price*	$3,700	+4.43%	*Production*	73,348	-9.34%

Camaro

"Great road-hugging shape. Pure driving pleasure."

Nameplate year of origin: 1967.
Current bodystyle lifespan: 1970 through 1981.
Predecessor to this model: Camaro (1967 to 1969).
Replacement for this model: Camaro (1982 to 1992).
Percentage of division's production: 9.44%.
Corporate siblings: Pontiac Firebird.
Primary competition: None.
Notable changes: Minor trim and detail changes.
Major standard equipment: Choice of sport cloth-and-vinyl or solid all-vinyl front bucket seats, color-keyed cut-pile carpeting, black instrument panel, black four-spoke soft rim sport steering wheel w/black column, bright front and rear window moldings, narrow rocker panel molding, hubcaps, and FR78 × 14 BSW tires. Type LT adds: Cloth-and-vinyl or knit vinyl deep contoured front bucket seats, tan leather-look accents on I/P cluster, color-keyed steering wheel and column, color-keyed lower instrument panel, special door panels w/door map pockets, special instrumentation package, electric clock, Interior Décor/Quiet Sound group, LH remote and RH manual sport mirrors, LT identification on front and rear end panels, bright accent molding on grille, brushed rear panel accent molding, variable-ratio power steering, and rally wheels. Z28 adds: All-vinyl front bucket seats, special instrumentation package, front and rear spoilers, specific Z28 decals (hood, front fenders, front and rear spoilers, over wheel openings and along rocker panels, and door handle inserts), black anodized window trim and headlight/taillight bezels, black painted parking light recesses, black painted rocker panels and rear trunk panel, body colored bumpers, and Space-Saver spare tire.

Measurements

Wheelbase	108.0"
Length	195.4"
Width	74.4"
Height	49.2"
Legroom — front	44.1"
Legroom — rear	29.6"
Headroom — front	37.3"
Headroom — rear	36.0"
Cargo capacity (cu. ft.)	6.4
Fuel capacity (gals.)	21.0

Models Available

	Model No.	Base MSRP	Change from LY	Shipping Wt. (lbs.)	Model Year Production	Change from LY
Camaro 2-Door Sport Coupe	Q87	$4,113	+9.33%	3369	131,717	+0.90%
Camaro Type LT 2-Door Sport Coupe	S87	$4,478	+3.66%	3422	72,787	+38.85%
Camaro Z28 2-Door Sport Coupe	Q87	$5,170	NEW	NA	14,349	NEW
TOTALS	*Avg. price*	$4,587	+13.51%	*Production*	218,853	+19.62%

Nova

"It even looks like a good buy to the competition."

Concours

"It looks luxurious. It works beautifully."

Nameplate year of origin: Nova: 1962, as top-of-the-line Chevy II model; became series name in 1969. Concours: 1976.

Current bodystyle lifespan: 1975 through 1979.

Predecessor to this model: Nova (1968 to 1974; restyled in 1973).

Replacement for this model: Citation (1980 to 1985).

Percentage of division's production: 15.75%.

Corporate siblings: Buick Skylark, Oldsmobile Omega, and Pontiac Ventura.

Primary competition: AMC Hornet, Ford Maverick and Granada, and Plymouth Volaré.

Notable changes: Minor trim and detail changes.

Major standard equipment: Choice of plaid cloth-and-vinyl or all-vinyl front bench seat, color-keyed cut-pile carpeting, front door armrests w/integral pull handle, black two-spoke steering wheel and steering column, bright front and rear window moldings, hubcaps, and E78 × 14 BSW tires. Hatchback model adds: All-vinyl front bench seat, load floor carpeting, and fold-down rear seat. Concours adds: All-vinyl front bench seat w/fold-down center armrest, door panels w/carpeted lower panels and map pockets in front doors, door panel woodgrain trim inserts, rear door armrests, color-keyed steering wheel and steering column, electric clock, instrument cluster w/woodgrain vinyl accents, smoked lenses, and additional bright trim, full-width luggage compartment mat, dark argent-accented bodyside louvers (coupes only), bright side window and roof drip moldings, bright wide wheel opening moldings, bright rocker panel moldings, high level acoustic package, deluxe bumpers w/black bumper impact strips, front and rear bumper guards, full wheel covers, and F78 × 14 BSW tires.

Measurements

	Coupe & HBK	Sedan
Wheelbase	111.0"	111.0"
Length*	196.7"	196.7"
Width	72.2"	72.2"
Height	54.3"	54.3"
Legroom — front	41.7"	41.7"
Legroom — rear	33.1"	35.1"
Headroom — front	38.5"	39.5"
Headroom — rear	36.6"	36.6"
Cargo capacity (cu. ft.)	13.4**	13.0
Fuel capacity (gals.)	21.0	21.0

*Concours is 1" longer. **Hatchback maximum with rear seat down, 28.4 cu. ft.

Models Available

	Model No.	Base MSRP	Change from LY	Shipping Wt. (lbs.)	Model Year Production	Change from LY
Nova 2-Door Coupe	X27	$3,248	+1.34%	3188	131,859	+60.76%
Nova 2-Door Hatchback	X17	$3,417	+2.09%	3391	18,719	+14.33%
Nova 4-Door Sedan	X69	$3,283	+2.31%	3221	123,767	+86.54%
Concours 2-Door Coupe	Y27	$3,795	+11.55%	3324	22,298	-15.18%
Concours 2-Door Hatchback	Y17	$3,972	+12.17%	3401	7,574	-50.33%
Concours 4-Door Sedan	Y69	$3,830	+12.15%	3367	30,511	+37.56%
TOTALS	*Avg. price*	$3,591	+4.94%	*Production*	334,728	+22.62%

Chevelle

"America's smart money car."

Nameplate year of origin: 1964.

Current bodystyle lifespan: 1973 through 1977.

Predecessor to this model: Chevelle (1968 to 1972).

Replacement for this model: Malibu (1978 to 1983).

Percentage of division's production: 14.15%.

Corporate siblings: Buick Century, Oldsmobile Cutlass, and Pontiac LeMans.

Measurements

	Coupes	Sedans	Wagons
Wheelbase	112.0"	116.0"	116.0"
Length	205.7"	209.7"	215.4"
Width	76.9"	76.9"	76.8"
Height	53.3"	54.0"	55.7"

Primary competition: AMC Matador, Ford LTD II, and Plymouth Fury.

Notable changes: Minor trim and detail changes.

Major standard equipment: Choice of sport cloth-and-vinyl or all-vinyl front bench seat, color-keyed cut-pile nylon carpeting, black steering wheel and column, bright front and rear window surround moldings, bright rear quarter window molding, hood rear edge molding, hubcaps, and FR78 × 15 BSW tires. Wagon adds: All-vinyl front bench seat, vinyl coated metal cargo area sidewalls, swing-up tailgate w/fixed window, I/P mounted "door ajar" warning light for tailgate, power steering, power front disc brakes, and HR78 × 15 BSW tires. Malibu Classic adds: Choice of knit cloth-and-vinyl or all-vinyl front bench seat w/fold-down center armrest, color-keyed steering wheel and column, simulated woodgrain vinyl accents on I/P, glove compartment light, bright roof drip and sill moldings, bright rocker panel and wheel opening moldings, and stand-up hood ornament. Malibu Classic wagon adds: All-vinyl front bench seat w/fold-down center armrest.

Measurements (cont.)

	Coupes	Sedans	Wagons
Legroom — front	42.1"	42.1"	42.1"
Legroom — rear	32.9"	36.9"	33.3"
Headroom — front	37.2"	37.9"	38.5"
Headroom — rear	36.7"	37.3"	39.2"
Cargo capacity (cu. ft.)	15.3	15.3	85.0*
Fuel capacity (gals.)	22.0	22.0	22.0

Plus 9.8 cu. ft. of hidden storage space on two-seat models.

Models Available

	Model No.	Base MSRP	Change from LY	Shipping Wt. (lbs.)	Model Year Production	Change from LY
Malibu 2-Door Colonnade HT Coupe	C37	$3,885	+6.85%	3551	28,793	-5.88%
Malibu 4-Door Colonnade HT Sedan	C29	$3,935	+7.19%	3628	39,064	+1.55%
Malibu 4-Door, 2-Seat Station Wagon*	C35	$4,734	+4.20%	4139	22,037	+33.03%
Malibu Classic 2-Door Colonnade HT Coupe	D37	$4,125	+5.07%	3599	73,739	-10.76%
Malibu Classic 2-Door Colonnade Landau Coupe	D37	$4,353	+5.55%	3623	37,215	+23.36%
Malibu Classic 4-Door Colonnade HT Sedan	D29	$4,475	+6.65%	3725	76,776	-1.01%
Malibu Classic 4-Door, 2-Seat Station Wagon*	D35	$5,065	+6.05%	4233	50,592	+39.56%
TOTALS	Avg. price	$4,367	+2.19%	Production	328,216	-1.51%

Production of wagons with third seat option is included above, but breaks out as follows: Malibu, 4,014; Malibu Classic, 19,053.

Monte Carlo

"Like you, it's an original."

Nameplate year of origin: 1970.
Current bodystyle lifespan: 1973 through 1977.
Predecessor to this model: Monte Carlo (1970 to 1972).
Replacement for this model: Monte Carlo (1978 to 1987).
Percentage of division's production: 17.72%.
Corporate siblings: Pontiac Grand Prix.
Primary competition: Dodge Charger SE and Ford Thunderbird.
Notable changes: Revised grille and trim and detail changes.
Major standard equipment: Choice of tailored knit cloth and vinyl or all-vinyl front bench seat, color-keyed cut-pile nylon carpeting, color-keyed instrument cluster, soft-rim steering wheel, simulated wood burl accents on I/P and steering wheel, door pull assist straps, glove compartment light, electric clock, LH outside rear view mirror, bright roof drip and window surround moldings, bright rocker panel moldings w/front and rear extensions, bright wheel opening moldings, full wheel covers, and GR70 × 15 BSW tires. Landau adds: Visor vanity mirror, Landau emblem on door panels, Landau vinyl roof w/rear quarter nameplate, dual sport mirrors w/LH remote control, front fender peak accent stripes, and cast aluminum Turbine II wheels.

Measurements

Wheelbase	116.0"
Length	213.3"
Width	77.6"
Height	52.8"
Legroom — front	42.4"
Legroom — rear	32.9"
Headroom — front	37.0"
Headroom — rear	37.1"
Cargo capacity (cu. ft.)	14.7
Fuel capacity (gals.)	22.0

Models Available

	Model No.	Base MSRP	Change from LY	Shipping Wt. (lbs.)	Model Year Production	Change from LY
Monte Carlo 2-Door Hardtop Coupe	H57	$4,968	+6.31%	3852	224,327	+17.22%

	Model No.	Base MSRP	Change from LY	Shipping Wt. (lbs.)	Model Year Production	Change from LY
Monte Carlo Landau 2-Door Hardtop Coupe	H57	$5,298	+6.69%	3871	186,711	+15.32%
TOTALS	Avg. price	$5,133	+6.50%	Production	411,038	+16.35%

Impala and Caprice Classic

"The New Chevrolet. A whole new car, a whole new ball game. Now that's more like it."

Nameplate year of origin: 1958 (Impala); and 1966 (Caprice).

Current bodystyle lifespan: 1977 through 1990.

Predecessor to this model: Biscayne/Bel Air/Impala/Caprice (1971 to 1977).

Replacement for this model: Caprice and Impala SS (1991 to 1996).

Percentage of division's production: 28.53%.

Corporate siblings: Buick LeSabre, Oldsmobile Delta 88, and Pontiac Catalina and Bonneville.

Primary competition: Dodge Royal Monaco, Ford LTD, and Plymouth Gran Fury.

Notable changes: Completely redesigned.

Major standard equipment: Choice of knit cloth-and-vinyl or all-vinyl front bench seat, color-keyed steering wheel and

Measurements

	2-doors	4-doors	Wagons
Wheelbase	116.0"	116.0"	116.0"
Length	212.1"	212.1"	214.3"
Width	75.5"	75.5"	79.1"
Height	56.0"	56.0"	58.0"
Legroom — front	42.2"	42.4"	42.2"
Legroom — rear	38.8"	39.0"	38.2"
Headroom — front	39.4"	39.4"	39.2"
Headroom — rear	38.2"	38.2"	39.4"
Cargo capacity (cu. ft.)	19.8	20.2	87.7
Fuel capacity (gals.)	21.0	21.0	22.0

steering column, color-keyed cut-pile nylon carpeting, woodgrain vinyl accent trim on I/P and door panels, glove box light, bright front and rear window moldings, bright side window and body sill/door moldings, hubcaps, and FR78 × 15 BSW tires. Wagon adds: All-vinyl front bench seat, three-way tailgate w/power-operated rear window, tailgate-ajar warning light, vinyl coated textured metal sidewalls, and HR78 × 15 BSW tires. Caprice adds: Choice of velvet-look knit cloth-and-vinyl or all-vinyl front bench seat, fold-down center armrest (four-doors only), front door pull straps and lower door panel carpeting, electric clock, courtesy lights, added acoustical insulation, specific triple unit taillights, bright roof drip moldings, bright wheel opening moldings, stand-up hood ornament, and full wheel covers. Caprice wagon adds: All-vinyl front bench seat w/specific design, three-way tailgate w/power-operated rear window, tailgate window moldings, tailgate-ajar warning light, vinyl coated textured metal sidewalls, and HR78 × 15 BSW tires.

Models Available

	Model No.	Base MSRP	Change from LY	Shipping Wt. (lbs.)	Model Year Production	Change from LY
Impala 2-Door Hardtop Custom Coupe	L47	$4,876	+2.37%	3533	58,092***	+34.41%
Impala 4-Door Sedan	L69	$4,901	+4.14%	3564	196,824	+128.71%
Impala 4-Door, 2-Seat Station Wagon	L35	$5,289	+2.38%	4042	65,363**	+232.52%
Caprice Classic 2-Door Hardtop Coupe	N47	$5,187	+2.86%	3571	71,973***	+155.58%
Caprice Classic 4-Door Sedan	N69	$5,237	+4.47%	3606	212,840	+348.93%
Caprice Classic 4-Door, 2-Seat Station Wagon*	N35	$5,617	+3.46%	4088	56,569**	+464.05%
TOTALS	Avg. price	$5,185	+2.63%	Production	661,661	+56.11%

*Comparisons of Caprice Classic wagon made to 1976 Caprice Classic Estate wagon. **Production of wagons with third seat option is included above, but breaks out as follows: Impala, 28,255; Caprice Classic, 33,639. ***Production of coupes with Landau option is included above, but breaks out as follows: Impala, 2,745; Caprice Classic, 9,607.

Corvette

"The only one."

Nameplate year of origin: 1953 (also used on show car of same year).
Current bodystyle lifespan: 1968 through 1982.
Predecessor to this model: Corvette (1963 to 1967).
Replacement for this model: Corvette (1984 to 1996).
Percentage of division's production: 2.12%.
Corporate siblings: None.
Primary competition: None.
Notable changes: Minor trim and detail changes.
Major standard equipment: Choice of all-leather or cloth-and-leather high-back contoured bucket seats, center floor console, color-keyed cut-pile carpeting, tilt steering wheel, sports instrumentation with full gauges including tachometer, electric clock, tinted glass, LH rear view sport mirror, carpeted cargo area with light concealed behind seats, anti-theft audio alarm system, removable roof panels, domed hood w/air scoop, four wheel disc brakes, rally wheels w/trim rings, and GR70 × 15 BSW tires.

Measurements

Wheelbase	98.0"
Length	185.2"
Width	69.0"
Height	48.0"
Legroom — front	42.1"
Headroom — front	36.2"
Cargo capacity (cu. ft.)	7.8
Fuel capacity (gals.)	18.0

Models Available

	Model No.	Base MSRP	Change from LY	Shipping Wt. (lbs.)	Model Year Production	Change from LY
Corvette 2-Door Coupe	Z37	$8,648	+13.71%	3448	49,213	+5.70%
TOTALS		*Avg. price* $8,648	+13.71%	*Production*	49,213	+5.70%

CHRYSLER

"A line of automobiles that offer you affordable luxury, including the luxury of choice."

Chrysler began the 1977 model year with a carryover line of cars that had very few changes from the prior two years. All of that changed in May 1977, when Chrysler took the next major step to introduce a car smaller than Cordoba, the LeBaron. This was a fundamental shift in the way Chrysler was trying to position itself in the marketplace, now aiming more clearly for all Buick, Oldsmobile and Mercury customers, rather than as in the past trying to position itself with the higher end of these makes, and just below the Cadillac and Lincoln customers. Chrysler's year-end results would prove that the right choice had been made, with production surpassing that of American Motors, and resulting in the third record-setting model year total for Chrysler during the 1970s. Aiding in the record-breaking production was a large increase in the traditional full-size Chrysler models. Apparently after seeing the newly downsized Buicks and Cadillacs, some consumers were opting to buy a large car while they could still get one. Also contributing to the increase was the fact that the new LeBaron and Cordoba would outsell the similar yet lower-priced Dodge Diplomat and Charger SE, proving the market trend toward more luxury was appealing to consumers in the smaller car markets.

The new "mid-size" LeBaron series was comparable, in nearly all aspects, to the new Dodge Diplomat, with differing front and rear styling. The front end of the LeBaron was the most unusual of any recent Chrysler with parking and turn signal lights being placed above the dual rectangular headlights. This would become a unique Chrysler styling and identification feature on the mid-size, M-body Chrysler brand models through the end of their lifespan in 1989. Just above the bumper, the headlights were set on each side of a twelve-section crosshatch grille, three rows high and four columns across, with each section having four horizontal bars recessed within.

LeBaron bodyside features all appeared to be taken straight from the F-bodied Dodge Aspen and Plymouth Volaré twins, with one notable exception. The rear quarter panels of LeBaron coupes had a "kick-up" feature line just behind the door, which ran upwards several inches, and then quickly turned rearward to meet the top edge of the wraparound taillamps. The coupes also used a unique rear roof design that was more formal than that of the F-body cars — not bolt upright, but not the near-fastback look of the Aspen and Volaré coupes. Another exclusive feature was a V-shaped rear window that was similar to that of GM's mid-size specialty coupes such as the Chevrolet Monte Carlo and Buick Regal. At the rear, the trunk lid gently sloped downward between the horizontally mounted taillamps on coupes, and ended above the taillamps on sedans where they had a body-colored center panel. The rear end of coupes was slightly pointed, following the rear window shape, while on the sedans it was flat. For both body styles, the Chrysler name in block letters adorned the area between the taillamps. Taillamps were horizontal rectangular units, with a LeBaron eagle logo painted in the center, and wrapped around the rear quarter panel end to provide the rear side marker light. Backup lights were mounted within the lower portion of the rear bumper at each end.

Padded door panels with assist straps, carpeted lower door panels and courtesy lights on doors and in rear pillars all combined to add to the luxury feel of the new LeBaron. The top line Medallion models offered optional velour and leathers in keeping with the Cordoba and full-size Chrysler traditions. A full list of available options included nearly everything that could be found on the New Yorker Brougham, making it possible to equip the LeBaron similarly to a Cadillac Seville. A 318 CID 2-barrel V8 engine mated to a TorqueFlite automatic transmission powered the LeBaron for its first few months, with other choices appearing by the start of the 1978 model year.

The highly popular Cordoba added a new lower-priced "S" model after the start of the model year. The new "S" differed only slightly in interior trim and a few of the standard features, such as interior courtesy lights. A revised grille was introduced with a vertical crosshatch design. Elsewhere on the car, more rectangular opera windows were seen, and the taillamps appeared to be more recessed into the bezel. Inside, new "Checkmate" black-and-white cloth upholstery and Corinthian leather seats were available.

Once again, the full-size Chrysler lineup played a juggling game with the series names. The base Newport CL series took over the styling and trim characteristics of the departed Newport Custom CM series. The Town & Country station wagons picked up the former Newport Custom's grille, which was also now found on the Newport. Following through the changes of the past two seasons, the resulting 1977 Newport series was identical in looks to the 1975 New Yorker Brougham series, barring some trim pieces, yet the 1977 Newport still carried mostly the same trim and equipment levels as its 1975 counterpart. In the end it was a clever marketing decision to move the Newport series upscale in appearance, without having to spend any money. Last season's New Yorker Brougham line returned with virtually no changes. This year would be the final one for the full-size Town & Country station wagons. The Dodge Royal Monaco and Plymouth Gran Fury station wagons were in their last season also, but for Chrysler the Town & Country name would move to a smaller platform under the LeBaron series for 1978.

Cordoba 2-Door Hardtop Coupe

Cordoba 2-Door Hardtop Coupe

LeBaron Medallion 2-Door Coupe

LeBaron Medallion 4-Door Sedan

New Yorker Brougham 4-Door Hardtop

Newport 2-Door Hardtop

Newport 4-Door Sedan

Town & Country 4-Door Station Wagon

Model year production: 336,520 up 37.39% from 1976.
Domestic market share: 3.49% (10th place).
Base price range: $5,066 to $7,215.
Chrysler average base price: $5,816, up 1.91%.
Introduction date: October 1, 1976. LeBaron introduced in May 1977.
Assembly plants: Jefferson Ave., Detroit, MI (C); Newark, DE (F); St. Louis, MO (G); and Windsor, Ontario, Canada (R).

Data plate identification (VIN): Thirteen digit code read as follows: First four digits indicate series and body style (model number in model charts); fifth digit indicates engine code (see powertrain chart); sixth digit indicates year (7 = 1977); seventh digit indicates assembly plant (see list above); remaining digits are sequential with beginning numbers of 100001. *Example:* CL43N7C100001 is a 1977 Chrysler Newport 4-Door Hardtop, with 400 CID, 4-bbl. V8 engine, serial number 100001, built in Detroit, MI.

Powertrains

Engine	Net HP	Engine Code	Transmission Availability		LeBaron	Cordoba	Newport	Town & Country	New Yorker Brougham
318 CID (5.2L), 2-bbl., V8[1]	145	G	3-speed Torque Flite automatic	*MPG:* *Calif.*	S 15/22/18 11/15/13	N/C 13/18/15 11/16/13	— — —	— — —	— — —
360 CID (5.9L), 2-bbl., V8[1]	155	K	3-speed Torque Flite automatic	*MPG:*	— —	N/C 14/20/16	N/C 12/18/14	— —	— —
360 CID (5.9L), 4-bbl., V8[2]	170	K	3-speed Torque Flite automatic	*Calif.*	— —	N/C[2] 11/16/14	N/C[2] 11/18/13	— —	— —
400 CID (6.6L), 4-bbl., V8[1]	190	N	3-speed Torque Flite automatic	*MPG:*	— —	S 11/19/14	S 11/18/13	N/C 10/16/12	N/C 11/18/13
440 CID (7.2L), 4-bbl., V8[3]	205	T	3-speed Torque Flite automatic	*MPG:* *Calif.*	— — —	— — —	$196 10/16/12 9/14/11	S 10/16/12 9/14/11	S 10/16/12 9/14/11

[1]Includes electronic "Lean Burn" system, except in California. [2]Available only in California and designated high altitude areas. [3]Includes electronic "Lean Burn" system.

Major Options

	LeBaron	Cordoba	Newport	Town & Country	New Yorker Brougham
Air conditioning[1]	$563	$518	$560	$560	$560
Tilt steering wheel	$59	$59	—	—	—
Tilt and telescope steering wheel	—	—	$106	$106	$106
Automatic speed control	$84	$84	$95	$95	$95
Electric rear window defroster	$86	$86	$87	—	$87
Tinted glass, all windows	$57	$57	$72	$72	$72
Manual front vent window, 4-doors	—	—	$43	$43	$43
Power windows, 2-dr./4-dr.	$129/$179	$113	$187	$187	S
Power door locks, 2-dr./4-dr.	$83/$116	$71	$72/$102	$102	$72/$102
Power front bench seat, 6-way	$143	$143	$152	$152	—
Power seat 50/50 or bucket, 6-way[2]	$143	$143	$304	$304	$145
Front bucket seats w/floor console	$128	$128	—	—	$223
Leather interior trim	$208	$208	—	—	—
AM radio	$76	$76	$99	$99	$99
AM/FM stereo w/search tuner	$314	$314	$318	$318	$318

	LeBaron	Cordoba	Newport	Town & Country	New Yorker Brougham
AM/FM stereo w/8-track tape	$332	$332	$349	$349	$349
Vinyl top, full[3]	$132	$116	$145	—	$145
Dual remote control mirrors	$47	$47	$48	$32	S
Remote control trunk release	$24	$21	$21	—	$21
Metal sunroof, electric	$626	$330[4]	$764	—	$764
Glass sunroof, electric	$788	—	$908	—	$908
T-Bar roof	—	$605	—	—	—
Wire wheel covers	$73	$73	—	—	—
Urethane cast road wheels	—	$120	—	—	—
Chrome styled road wheels	$140	$120	$132	$132	$132
Forged aluminum road wheels	$196	$120	$132	$132	$132
White sidewall tires, std. size	$43	$43	$48	$48	S

Popular Option Groups & Packages

	LeBaron	Cordoba	Newport	Town & Country	New Yorker Brougham
Basic accessory package	—	—	$939	$999	$730
Crown roof package	—	$733	—	—	—
Easy order package	$	$1,110	$1,305	$1,429	$1,384
Light package	$75	$26	$80	$39	S
St. Regis option group[5]	—	—	$600[5]	—	$600
Town & Country package	—	—	—	$128	—

—= Not Available; S = Standard equipment.   [1]Auto-Temp air conditioning is available for $645 on Newport, Town & Country and New Yorker Brougham.   [2]Left and right power adjustment on Newport, New Yorker Brougham and Town & Country.   [3]Landau vinyl roof available on Cordoba for $112.   [4]Requires vinyl top. Only available on 2-door hardtop models. Manually operated on Cordoba.   [5]Newport Custom and New Yorker Brougham 2-door hardtops only.

Paint Colors

	Code		Code		Code
Burnished Silver metallic[1]	A1	Russet Sunfire metallic[2,3]	R8	Spinnaker White	W1
Silver Cloud metallic[2,3]	A2	Dove Gray[4]	RA1	Formal Black Sunfire metallic	X8
Wedgewood Blue[3]	B2	Pewter Gray metallic[4]	RA2	Jasmine Yellow[2,3]	Y1
Cadet Blue metallic	B3	Charcoal Gray Sunfire metallic[4]	RA9	Golden Fawn[2,3]	Y4
Starlight Blue Sunfire metallic	B9	Mint Green metallic[4]	RF3	Inca Gold metallic[2,3]	Y6
Vintage Red Sunfire metallic[2,3]	E8	Augusta Green Sunfire metallic[4]	RF9	Spanish Gold metallic[2,3]	Y9
Jade Green metallic[2,3]	F2	Tapestry Red Sunfire metallic[4]	RR7		
Forest Green Sunfire metallic[2,3]	F7	Sable Tan Sunfire metallic[4]	RT9		
Burnished Copper metallic[2,3]	K6	Classic Cream[4]	RY3		
Mojave Beige[3]	L3	Coffee Sunfire metallic[2,3]	T7		
Moondust metallic[3]	L5	Caramel Tan metallic[2,4]	U3		
Claret Red[2]	R6	Light Chestnut metallic[2]	U6		

Single tones are coded W1, W1. Two-tones are coded X9, W1 where first two digits are accent or roof color, and second two digits are basic body color.   [1]Available with St. Regis option package only.   [2]Available only on Cordoba.   [3]Available only on full-size Chryslers.   [4]Available only on LeBaron.

LeBaron

"Introducing Chrysler LeBaron. The beginning of a totally new class of automobiles."

Nameplate year of origin: 1957, as subseries name for Imperial (also used on LeBaron custom bodied Chryslers beginning in 1930).
Current bodystyle lifespan: 1977½ through 1979.
Predecessor to this model: None.
Replacement for this model: LeBaron (1980 to 1981).
Percentage of division's production: 13.70%.
Corporate siblings: Dodge Diplomat.
Primary competition: Buick Regal, Mercury Cougar, and Oldsmobile Cutlass Supreme.

Measurements

	Coupe	Sedan
Wheelbase	112.7"	112.7"
Length	204.0"	206.1"
Width	73.5"	72.8"
Height	53.3"	55.3"
Legroom — front	42.5"	42.5"
Legroom — rear	34.1"	36.6"

1977

Notable changes: All-new model, based on Dodge Aspen/Plymouth Volaré 4-door platform.

Major standard equipment: Cortez cloth and vinyl front bench seat, door pull straps, color-keyed carpeting, one-piece cloth headliner, windshield header mounted reading lamps (coupe only), simulated woodgrain I/P cluster and glove box door appliqué, rocker panel sill moldings w/front and rear extensions, bright roof drip rail and quarter window moldings (coupes), bright upper door frame moldings (sedan), opera lamps (coupe), full vinyl padded top (sedan), bright belt molding, rear bumper guards, lower deck panel stripe (sedan), stand-up hood ornament, power steering, power brakes, deluxe wheel covers, and FR78 × 15 BSW tires. Medallion adds: Verdi velour 60/40 front split-bench seat w/fold-down center armrests and dual recliners, shag carpeting, fold-down rear seat armrest (sedan), bright pedal trim, map reading lamp, door mounted courtesy lights, three upper assist handles (sedan), B-pillar assist straps (coupe), rear pillar vanity lamps and mirrors (sedan), trunk dress-up package, LH remote control outside rearview mirror, quarter window glass accents and medallion (coupe), bodyside accent tape stripes coordinated w/body color on coupes and vinyl top color on sedans, deluxe sound insulation package (w/o undercoating and hood pad), and premiere wheel covers.

Measurements (cont.)

	Coupe	Sedan
Headroom — front	37.4"	39.2"
Headroom — rear	36.2"	37.5"
Cargo capacity (cu. ft.)	16.3	16.6
Fuel capacity (gals.)	19.5	19.5

Models Available

	Model No.	Base MSRP	Change from LY	Shipping Wt. (lbs.)	Model Year Production	Change from LY
LeBaron 2-Door Coupe	FH22	$5,066	NEW	3510	7,280	NEW
LeBaron 4-Door Sedan	FH41	$5,224	NEW	3560	12,600	NEW
LeBaron Medallion 2-Door Coupe	FP22	$5,436	NEW	3615	14,444	NEW
LeBaron Medallion 4-Door Sedan	FP41	$5,594	NEW	3675	11,776	NEW
TOTALS	Avg. price	$5,330	NEW	Production	46,100	NEW

Cordoba

"A personal automobile of marked distinction and character."

Nameplate year of origin: 1975 (also used on special-order 1970 Newport hardtops).
Current bodystyle lifespan: 1975 through 1979.
Predecessor to this model: None.
Replacement for this model: Cordoba (1980 to 1983).
Percentage of division's sales volume: 48.48%.
Corporate siblings: Dodge Charger SE.
Primary competition: Buick Regal, Mercury Cougar XR-7, and Oldsmobile Cutlass Supreme.
Notable changes: Minor trim and detail changes.
Major standard equipment: Velour cloth-and-vinyl front bench seat w/fold-down center armrest, color-keyed 22-oz. deep-pile carpeting, simulated woodgrained vinyl trim on I/P and door panels, luxury three-spoke steering wheel, luxury padded door trim w/carpeted lower panels and seat backs, bright pedal dress-up, glove box and ashtray lights, electronic digital clock, premium steering wheel, molded cloth headliner, trunk light, carpeted trunk and spare tire cover, LH rear view mirror, rear quarter formal opera window and opera lamp, drip rail moldings, wheel lip moldings, rocker panel sill molding, bodyside and deck lid paint stripes, stand-up hood ornament, front and rear bumper guards, power steering, power brakes, premiere wheel covers, and GR78 × 15 BSW tires.

Measurements

Wheelbase	115.0"
Length	215.3"
Width	76.3"
Height	52.6"
Legroom — front	41.9"
Legroom — rear	33.9"
Headroom — front	37.7"
Headroom — rear	36.6"
Cargo capacity (cu. ft.)	14.5
Fuel capacity (gals.)	25.5

Models Available

	Model No.	Base MSRP	Change from LY	Shipping Wt. (lbs.)	Model Year Production	Change from LY*
Cordoba S 2-Door Hardtop Coupe	SP29	$5,368	NEW	4045	NA	NEW
Cordoba 2-Door Hardtop Coupe	SS29	$5,418	+0.48%	4045	163,138	NA
TOTALS	Avg. price	$5,393	+0.02%	Production	163,138	-2.67%

*Change from LY not available due to production of Cordoba S being included with Cordoba.

Newport

"It's a lot of Chrysler for the money."

Nameplate year of origin: 1961 (as series); 1950 (as HT model of the T & C).
Current bodystyle lifespan: 1974 through 1978.
Predecessor to this model: Newport (1969 to 1973).
Replacement for this model: Newport (1979 to 1981).
Percentage of division's sales volume: 17.20%.
Corporate siblings: Chrysler New Yorker Brougham.
Primary competition: Buick LeSabre, Mercury Marquis, and Oldsmobile Delta 88.
Notable changes: Minor trim and detail changes. Newport was the replacement for
   the 1976 Newport Custom, and used the same body styling and exterior trim.
Major standard equipment: Cloth-and-vinyl split back front bench seat w/fold-
   down center armrest, color-keyed loop pile carpeting, trip odometer, lighted front
   ashtray w/two rear seat ashtrays, 12" inside day/night mirror, two-speed electric
   windshield wipers w/washers, front and rear wheel lip moldings, drip rail and belt moldings, bright windshield and rear window
   moldings, rear hood molding, decklid molding, dual horns, front and rear bumper guards, rear taillight periphery molding,
   deluxe wheel covers, and HR78 × 15 BSW tires.

Measurements

Wheelbase	124.0"
Length	226.6"
Width	79.5"
Height	55.1"
Legroom — front	42.1"
Legroom — rear	38.3"
Headroom — front	38.7"
Headroom — rear	37.8"
Cargo capacity (cu. ft.)	20.2
Fuel capacity (gals.)	26.5

Models Available

	Model No.	Base MSRP	Change from LY	Shipping Wt. (lbs.)	Model Year Production	Change from LY
Newport 2-Door Hardtop	CL23	$5,374	+5.87%	4400	10,566	+262.35%
Newport 4-Door Sedan	CL41	$5,280	+5.75%	4455	32,506	+151.48%
Newport 4-Door Hardtop	CL43	$5,433	+5.56%	4485	14,808	+329.47%
TOTALS	*Avg. price*	$5,362	+1.57%	*Production*	57,880	+48.07%

Town & Country

"The utility you want— and the luxury you love."

Nameplate year of origin: 1941.
Current bodystyle lifespan: 1974 through 1977.
Predecessor to this model: Town & Country (1969 to 1973).
Replacement for this model: LeBaron Town & Country (1978 to 1978).
Percentage of division's sales volume: 2.16%.
Corporate siblings: Dodge Royal Monaco and Plymouth Gran Fury.
Primary competition: Buick Estate Wagon, Mercury Colony Park, and Oldsmobile
   Custom Cruiser.
Notable changes: Minor trim and detail changes.
Major standard equipment: All-vinyl 50/50 split front seat w/individual fold-down
   center armrests and passenger-side recliner, color-keyed loop pile carpeting including cargo area, electric clock, interior lights (cargo, glove box, map/courtesy and
   ashtray), power tailgate window, sound absorbing headliner, trip odometer, front
   ashtray w/two rear seat ashtrays, 12" inside day/night mirror, three-speed electric
   windshield wipers w/washers, concealed storage compartments in rear wheelhouse cover, "Power Auto-Lock" tailgate lock (activates when ignition turned on), fender mounted turn signal indicators, bodyside simulated woodgrain appliqués, drip rail molding, rear wheel opening skirts, roof air deflector, dual horns, large diameter front sway bar, deluxe wheel covers, and L78 × 15
   BSW tires.

Measurements

Wheelbase	124.0"
Length	227.7"
Width	79.4"
Height	57.0"
Legroom — front	42.2"
Legroom — rear	39.7"
Headroom — front	38.9"
Headroom — rear	38.9"
Cargo capacity (cu. ft.)*	102.4
Fuel capacity (gals.)	24.0

Plus 4.3 cu. ft. in concealed compartment on 2-seat wagon.

Models Available

	Model No.	Base MSRP	Change from LY	Shipping Wt. (lbs.)	Model Year Production	Change from LY
Town & Country 4-Door, 2-S. Wagon	CP45	$6,461	+6.20%	5025	1,930	+51.85%
Town & Country 4-Door, 3-S. Wagon	CP46	$6,647	+6.45%	5060	5,345	+65.63%
TOTALS	*Avg. price*	$6,554	+6.33%	*Production*	7,275	+61.74%

New Yorker Brougham

"What a beautiful New Yorker! It's the talk of the town."

Nameplate year of origin: 1939.
Current bodystyle lifespan: 1974 through 1978.
Predecessor to this model: New Yorker (1969 to 1973).
Replacement for this model: New Yorker (1979 to 1981).
Percentage of division's sales volume: 18.46%.
Corporate siblings: Chrysler Newport.
Primary competition: Buick Electra 225, Mercury Grand Marquis, and Oldsmobile Ninety-Eight.
Notable changes: Minor trim and detail changes.
Major standard equipment: Velour-and-vinyl 50/50 split bench seat w/individual fold-down center armrest, passenger side recliner on 4-door, rear seat fold-down center armrest, color-keyed loop-pile carpeting, color-keyed seat belts, Lavaliere straps on inside rear roof pillars (4-door), vinyl covered rear pillar pillows, trip odometer, electric clock, dual front ashtrays w/two rear seat ashtrays, interior lights (glove box, map/courtesy and ashtray), 12" inside day/night mirror, luxury three-spoke steering wheel, three-speed electric windshield wipers w/washers, power windows, console-type armrests on all doors, headlight time-delay switch, carpeted trunk floor, LH remote control mirror, full-length bodyside molding, front wheel lip molding, drip rail molding, bright window moldings, rear taillight periphery moldings, rear wheel opening skirts, fender-mounted turn signal indicators, concealed headlamps, undercoating, hood insulation pad, unique deluxe wheel covers, and JR78 × 15 WSW tires.

Measurements

Wheelbase	124.0"
Length	231.0"
Width	79.7"
Height	54.5"
Legroom — front	42.1"
Legroom — rear	39.5"
Headroom — front	37.9"
Headroom — rear	37.0"
Cargo capacity (cu. ft.)	20.2
Fuel capacity (gals.)	26.5

Models Available

	Model No.	Base MSRP	Change from LY	Shipping Wt. (lbs.)	Model Year Production	Change from LY
New Yorker Brougham 2-Door Hardtop	CS23	$7,090	+6.76%	4685	16,875	+73.11%
New Yorker Brougham 4-Door Hardtop	CS43	$7,215	+7.10%	4770	45,252	+88.68%
TOTALS	*Avg. price*	$7,153	+6.93%	*Production*	62,127	+84.18%

DODGE

"1977 Dodge."

Dodge began the 1977 model year with four series of cars, the new-for-'76 Aspen, the Charger, a realigned and newly named mid-size Monaco, and the full-size Royal Monaco, in addition to the imported Colt. A little more than halfway through the selling season, a fifth line would be added, the Diplomat, a twin of the new Chrysler LeBaron. With all of the new and repositioned product on showroom floors, Dodge was anticipating a good year. In the end, Dodge achieved its highest production year since 1974 and its best market share since 1973, although the mid-range Chrysler division still finished eighth in overall industry production rankings.

Based heavily on the new-for-1976 "compact" Aspen, the Diplomat used the longer chassis of the Aspen 4-door models and was termed a new "mid-size" model. This close relationship is most evident under the hood and in the green-house area of the sedans. But with all-new exterior styling, and clever marketing, the Diplomat would be advertised as a luxury car, and immediately capture consumer attention. The new Diplomat could be construed as Chrysler Corporation's first attempt at downsizing, as it was the intended replacement for the mid-size Monaco. Styling of the Diplomat's front end created a luxury look using a chromed four-section grille, with each section consisting of a finely textured egg-crate design, and the entire grille topped by a thick header bar across the top. To each side of the grille were side-by-side rectangular headlamps, set back slightly from the grille and mounted atop horizontal parking lamp and turn signal lamp units. Side marker lights and turn signal lights also wrapped around the front fender edge.

Bodyside features all appeared to be taken straight from the Aspen with one notable exception. The rear quarter panels of Diplomat coupes had a "kick-up" just behind the door, which ran upwards several inches, and then quickly turned rearward to meet the top edge of the wraparound tail-lamps. The coupes also used a unique rear roof design that was more formal than that of the Aspen — not bolt upright, but not the near-fastback look of the Aspen coupe. Another exclusive feature was a V-shaped rear window that was similar to that of GM's mid-size specialty coupes such as the Chevrolet Monte Carlo and Buick Regal. At the rear, the trunk lid gently sloped downward between the horizontally mounted taillamps on coupes, and ended above the taillamps on sedans where they had a body-colored center panel. In both cases the Dodge name in block letters adorned the area between the taillamps. Taillamps on both models were divided into six sections with the outermost wrapping around the rear quarter panel end to serve as the rear side marker light. Backup lights were mounted within the lower portion of the rear bumper at each end.

Diplomat's luxury continued inside, with materials and features that matched those of the Royal Monaco series. The top line Medallion models offered optional velour and leather upholsteries that were not available on any other Dodge line. Padded door panels with assist straps, carpeted lower door panels and courtesy lights on doors and in rear pillars all added to the luxury feel. Under the hood, the workaday 318 CID 2-barrel V8 engine mated to a TorqueFlite automatic transmission was the only choice for the Diplomat's rather short first season.

The Aspen quickly proved it could fill the huge vacancy left by the highly popular Dart, as it would end the 1977 model year with more than 50 percent of all Dodge car sales,

just as the Dart did consistently. Few changes were made, mostly amounting to detail improvements and new optional features, such as a T-Bar roof for the coupe models. In a seemingly odd move, the Aspen Special Edition wagon was given a new model number in the NH Custom series, rather than the NP Special Edition series where it began life. In retrospect this move was probably looking ahead to the 1978 season, when a wagon would be added to the new Diplomat series, and the Aspen Special Edition series would become an option package. Regardless of the move, Aspen wagons became the sales leader of the line, outselling the sedan by almost 30 percent. The optional sporty packages continued to be available as well with the R/T package finding its way onto 4,465 Aspen coupes, and the Super Pak package on 2,284.

The Monaco line was reorganized and marketed as "A grand new car in two sizes," a move to stave off loss of sales as General Motors' new downsized cars rolled out. In reality, the "new" mid-size Monaco was a mild facelift for the former Coronet series. The "new" full-size Monaco was a rehash of the 1976 Monaco line, sans the base Monaco, leaving the Royal Monaco and Royal Monaco Brougham models. Along with the realignment, the Royal Monaco took the place of the 1976 Monaco series, and the Royal Monaco Brougham replaced last year's Royal Monaco in series stature, as confirmed by the model number changes in the charts that follow, and the standard equipment lists. Royal Monaco coupes and sedans had a new taillight design with three vertical sections flanking the backup light on each side, replacing the formerly horizontal three-section design. Little else changed for what would be the last season for traditional "full-size" Dodge cars.

The "new" mid-size Monaco directly replaced the Coronet, which had been slowly fading in popularity. The Charger and Charger Sport two-door models moved back into the Monaco lineup, as they had been in 1975, and were now named the Monaco and Monaco Brougham hardtops. The facelift mentioned previously featured dual rectangular headlamps in a stacked configuration and new grille insert patterns for the grille, which continued to be of a two-piece design split by a thin vertical body-colored strip. At the rear, coupes used slightly larger taillamps which wrapped around the rear quarter filler panel ends and were split horizontally into three sections, while sedans continued to use taillamps set into the rear bumper with a new lens design that was split into three sections both horizontally and vertically. Other changes mostly included upgrades of trim and standard equipment to befit the image of the once top-of-the-line Monaco status. A mid-year Monaco Special coupe model was introduced as a sporty variant with standard bucket seats with center cushion and armrest and specific exterior tape striping.

The Colt series introduced redesigned base coupe, sedan, and new Custom coupe models labeled as M/M models, for Mileage-Maker, signifying cars that get high gas mileage, much as Ford had done with its MPG moniker. The trio of new, more fuel-efficient cars were about 200 pounds lighter and nearly nine inches shorter than the 1976 models they replaced. Styling of the new M/M series cars used single round headlamps set in chrome bezels, with an egg-crate grille with three horizontal bars between them, and rectangular parking/turn signal lamps set into a slightly recessed grille area next to the headlights. At the rear, large horizontal taillamps wrapped around the rear quarter panel ends, and were nearly full-width, being interrupted only by the license tag housing. Overall body styling, while mostly changed, still looked quite similar to the original 1971 design. The new Custom M/M coupe was equipped at the same level as the

M/M sedan that carried more standard features this year than in 1976. The hardtop and station wagons models did not shift to the smaller chassis but returned with some styling changes, such as a new horizontal grille design made up of small horizontally rectangular openings. Round single headlamp units and round parking/turn signal lamps mounted next to the headlights provided a look similar to the Charger SE design. The Carousel hardtop, last year offered in white with a blue denim top, this year came only in a deeper blue color with a blue denim top. All Colt models now offered as standard equipment power front disc brakes and an electric rear window defroster, items not found as standard equipment on any American-built subcompact cars of the period.

Aspen Custom 4-Door Sedan

Aspen SE 2-Door Coupe with T-top
and landau roof options

Charger SE 2-Door Hardtop Coupe
with Daytona package

Aspen SE 4-Door Station Wagon
with Hillcrest plaid interior option

Colt 4-Door Station Wagon
with Estate wagon package

Diplomat 4-Door Sedan

Colt M/M 2-Door Coupe

Diplomat Medallion 2-Door Coupe

Monaco Brougham 4-Door Sedan

Monaco Brougham 2-Door Hardtop Coupe

Royal Monaco 2-Door Hardtop

Royal Monaco Brougham Velcord velour
interior with Diplomat package

Royal Monaco Brougham 4-Door Sedan

1977

Model year production: 441,947, up 25.23% from 1976.
Domestic market share: 4.58% (8th place).
Base price range: $3,582 to $5,730.
Dodge average base price: $4,628, up 7.19%.
Introduction date: October 1, 1976. Diplomat introduced in late April 1977.
Assembly plants*: Lynch Road, Detroit, MI (A); Hamtramck, MI (B); Jefferson Ave., Detroit, MI (C); Belvidere, IL (D); Newark, DE (F); St. Louis, MO (G); and Windsor, Ontario, Canada (R). Colt manufacturer: Mitsubishi Heavy Industries, Tokyo, Japan (code 1 through 9).
Data plate identification (VIN): Thirteen digit code read as follows: First four digits indicate series and body style (model number in model charts); fifth digit indicates engine code (see powertrain chart); sixth digit indicates year (7 = 1977); seventh digit indicates assembly plant for all except

Colt (see list above), and for Colt seventh digit indicates transmission code (5 = 4-speed manual, 5-speed manual code unknown, 9 = automatic); remaining digits are sequential with beginning numbers of 100001 for all Dodge models except Colt. Colt sequential numbers are currently unknown. *Example:* NL41C7C100001 is a 1977 Dodge Aspen 4-Door Sedan, with 225 CID, 2-bbl. 6-cylinder engine, serial number 100001, built in Jefferson Ave. plant, Detroit, MI.

**Sources differ on which of the three Michigan based assembly plants were in production of 1977 model year Dodge cars. Auto industry references from the early 1980s show only the Jefferson Avenue plant as active in 1977, while other contemporary sources show only the Lynch Road and Hamtramck plants as active. Most likely both are correct, as one or more may have been down to convert to production of the mid-year Diplomat or the upcoming 1978 Dodge Omni. In either case, note that all were in production of some type of Chrysler, Dodge or Plymouth vehicles for 1977.*

Powertrains

Engine	Net HP	Engine Code	Transmission Availability[1]		Colt	Aspen	Diplomat	Monaco	Charger SE	Royal Monaco[2]
97.5 CID (1.6L) OHC, 1-bbl., 4-cyl.	83	K	4-speed manual		S (Cpe/ Sdn)	—	—	—	—	—
				MPG:	29/45/35	—	—	—	—	—
				Calif.	21/34/25	—	—	—	—	—
			3-speed Automatic		$270 (Cpe/ Sdn)	—	—	—	—	—
				MPG:	26/35/30	—	—	—	—	—
				Calif.	21/32/25	—	—	—	—	—
97.5 CID (1.6L) OHC "Silent Shaft," 1-bbl., 4-cyl.	83	K	5-speed manual overdrive		S (HTs)	—	—	—	—	—
				MPG:	29/45/35	—	—	—	—	—
			3-speed Automatic		$452 (Sdn. Only)[3]	—	—	—	—	—
				MPG:	26/35/30	—	—	—	—	—
122 CID (2.0L) OHC, 2-bbl., 4-cyl.	96	U	5-speed manual overdrive		S (Wgn.)/ $182 (HTs)	—	—	—	—	—
				MPG:	20/33/24	—	—	—	—	—
				Calif.	15/27/19	—	—	—	—	—
			3-speed Automatic		$277 (Wgn.)/ $452 (HTs)	—	—	—	—	—
				MPG:	21/28/24	—	—	—	—	—
				Calif.	18/29/22	—	—	—	—	—

Engine	Net HP	Engine Code	Transmission Availability[1]		Colt	Aspen	Diplomat	Monaco	Charger SE	Royal Monaco[2]
225 CID (3.7L), 1-bbl., 6-cyl.	100	C	3-speed manual		—	S	—	—	—	—
				MPG:	—	20/29/23	—	—	—	—
				Calif.	—	16/23/18	—	—	—	—
			"Overdrive4"		—	$134[4]	—	—	—	—
			4-speed manual	MPG:	—	NA	—	—	—	—
			3-speed Torque		—	$270	—	—	—	—
			Flite automatic	MPG:	—	18/24/20	—	—	—	—
				Calif.	—	16/19/17	—	—	—	—
225 CID (3.7L) Super Six, 2-bbl., 6-cyl.[5]	110	D	3-speed manual		—	$38	—	S (Cars)	—	—
				MPG:	—	17/24/20	—	17/22/19	—	—
			3-speed Torque		—	$308	—	$295 (Cars)	—	—
			Flite automatic	MPG:	—	16/21/18	—	16/21/18	—	—
318 CID (5.2L), 2-bbl., V8	145	G	3-speed manual[5]		—	$170	—	$261 (Cars)	—	—
				MPG:	—	15/25/19	—	14/23/17	—	—
			"Overdrive4"		—	$304	—	—	—	—
			4-speed manual[5]	MPG:	—	NA	—	—	—	—
			3-speed Torque		—	$440	S	$556 (Cars)[6]	S	S (RM)
			Flite automatic	MPG:	—	15/20/17	15/20/17	13/18/15	13/18/15	13/18/15
				Calif.	—	11/15/13	11/15/13	11/16/13	11/16/13	—
360 CID (5.9L), 2-bbl., V8[5]	170	K	3-speed Torque Flite automatic		—	$490	—	S (Wgns.)/ $613 (Cars)	$57	S (RMB)/ $58 (RM)
				MPG:	—	14/19/16	—	14/20/16	14/20/16	12/18/14
360 CID (5.9L), 4-bbl., V8[7]	175	L	3-speed Torque Flite automatic		—	$549[8]	—	$47 (Wgns.)/ $661 (Cars)	$105[9]	$48 (RMB)/ $106 (RM)[6,9]
				MPG:	—	11/17/13	—	11/16/12	11/16/12	NA
				Calif.	—	12/17/14	—	11/18/14	11/18/14	11/18/13
400 CID (6.6L), 4-bbl., V8[5,7]	190	N	3-speed Torque Flite automatic		—	—	—	$98 (Wgns.)/ $712 (Cars)	$156	S (Wgns.)/ $99 (RMB)/ $158 (RM)
				MPG:	—	—	—	11/19/14	11/19/14	11/18/13
440 CID (7.2L), 4-bbl., V8[5,7]	195	T	3-speed Torque Flite automatic		—	—	—	—	—	$132 (Wgns.)[6]/ $231 (RMB)/ $289 (RM)
				MPG:	—	—	—	—	—	9/17/11
				Calif.	—	—	—	—	—	9/14/11

[1]Unless otherwise noted: All transmissions are column-shift, except on Colt or any model w/4-speed manual. Floor-shift is available for $30 extra on any Aspen w/3-speed manual transmission. Aspen Coupes and Wagons w/automatic, Monaco Brougham 2-door and Charger SE w/bucket seats, console and automatic transmission are all available w/floor-shift in combination with other required equipment.   [2]RM = Royal Monaco coupes and sedans; RMB = Royal Monaco Brougham coupes and sedans.   [3]Price for GT and Carousel Hardtops is $95.   [4]Not available on wagons.   [5]Not available in California or designated high altitude areas.   [6]Required as standard equipment in California and designated high altitude areas, with appropriate adjustment in price.   [7]Includes electronic "Lean Burn" system on Aspen w/360 CID V8, and all with 400 and 440 CID V8s.   [8]Available on coupes only.   [9]Available only in California or designated high altitude areas.

Major Options

	Colt	Aspen	Diplomat	Monaco	Charger SE	Royal Monaco
Air conditioning[1]	$395	$454	$518	$518	$518	$546[1]
Tilt steering wheel	S	$54	$59	$59	$59	$88[2]
Automatic speed control	—	$77	$84	$84	$84	$88
Electric rear window defogger	S	$79	$86	$86	$86	$87
Tinted glass, all windows	S	$48	$57	$57	$57	$72
Power windows[3]	—	$145	$158	$158	$113	$179
Power door locks[4]	—	$92	$101	$101	$71	$102
Power front seat	—	$131	$143	$143	$143	$145
Music Master AM radio	$69	$69	$76	$76	$76	$77
AM/FM stereo	—	$215	$234	$234	$234	$237
AM/FM stereo w/8-track tape	—	$304	$332	$332	$332	$337

	Colt	Aspen	Diplomat	Monaco	Charger SE	Royal Monaco
Front bucket seats w/console	S	$198[5]	$198[5]	$18[5]	$94[5]	—
Vinyl top, full[6]	$92	$92	$116	$116	$116	$141
Landau vinyl top, 2-doors	—	$148	$116	$116	$112	$141
Sunroof, manual[7]	—	$198	$626[7]	$330	$330	$626[7]
T-Bar roof, w/glass panels	—	$554	—	—	$605	—
Power steering, standard w/V8s	—	$140	$153	$153	S	S
Power brakes, w/front disc[8]	S	$59	S	S	S	S
Premium wheel covers	—	$57	$57	—	—	$74
Wire wheel covers	—	$99	$99	$108	$73	—
Rallye road wheels	—	$68	$[9]	$80	$45	—
Chrome rally wheels	—	$119	—	—	—	$156
Styled wheels	—	—	—	$154	$120	—
White sidewall tires, std. size	$48	$42	$42	$43	$43	$45

Popular Option Groups & Packages

	Colt	Aspen	Diplomat	Monaco	Charger SE	Royal Monaco
Daytona package	—	—	—	—	$166	—
Deluxe insulation package	S	$65	$	$62	$55	$43
Diplomat package	—	—	—	—	—	$834
Estate package	$260	—	—	—	—	—
E-Z order package	—	$801	$	$872	$987	$581[10]
Freeway Cruise package	$361	—	—	—	—	—
Fold-down rear seat package[11]	—	$110	—	—	—	—
Light package	—	$35	$	$48	$26	$82
Luxury equipment package	—	—	—	$1,792	—	$1,969
Red & White Special package	$177	—	—	—	—	—
R/T décor package	—	$101	—	—	—	—
R/T package	—	$207	—	—	—	—
R/T "Super Pak" package	—	$318	—	—	—	—
Special Edition package	—	—	—	—	—	—

—= Not Available; S = Standard equipment. [1]"Auto-Temp" automatic air conditioning is available on Royal Monaco for $630, and for Royal Monaco w/Luxury equipment package for $83. [2]Tilt and telescope steering wheel is available on Royal Monaco for $106. [3]Prices given for 4-Door models. On 2-door models price for power windows on Aspen is $104, Diplomat is $117, Monaco is $113, and Royal Monaco is $119. [4]Prices given for 4-door models. Prices for 2-door models: Aspen $65, Diplomat $74, Monaco $81, and Royal Monaco $72. [5]Available on Aspen coupes, Diplomat coupes, and Monaco Brougham Hardtop only. Charger SE price w/standard bucket seats has console available for $18. [6]Standard on Royal Monaco Brougham sedan. Aspen Landau top on 2-door models is $137. Landau top also available on Diplomat 2-doors. For Colt, available only on 2-door models. Not available on station wagons. [7]Manual sunroof on Aspen coupes, Monaco coupes, and Charger SE. Power sunroof on Diplomat and Royal Monaco series coupes, and requires vinyl top. Available on Royal Monaco sedans for $768. [8]Standard on Aspen w/V8 engine. Colt has manual front disc brakes standard. [9]New design forged aluminum road wheel on Diplomat. [10]Price given for base Royal Monaco. Price on Royal Monaco station wagons is $67. [11]Coupes only.

Paint Colors

Dodge	Code	Dodge	Code	Dodge	Code
Silver Cloud metallic[1,2,3,4]	A2	Coffee Sunfire metallic[2,3,4]	T7	Sunrise Orange[6]	RK2
Silver Frost metallic[5]	A5	Carmel Tan metallic[1,3,6]	U3	Brite Canyon Red[6]	RR4
Wedgewood Blue[2,4]	B2	Little Chestnut metallic[3]	U6	Tapestry Red Sunfire metallic[6]	RR7
Cadet Blue metallic[2,3,4,6]	B3	Spitfire Orange[1]	V1	Crimson Red Sunfire metallic[6]	RR9
French Racing Blue[1]	B5	Eggshell White[7]	W1	Sable Tan Sunfire metallic[6]	RT9
Regatta Blue metallic[1]	B6	Black Sunfire metallic[7]	X8	Classic Cream[6]	RY3
Starlight Blue Sunfire metallic[7]	B9	Jasmine Yellow[2,3,4]	Y1	Black[6]	TX9
Bright Red[2]	E5	Harvest Gold[5]	Y3		
Vintage Red Sunfire metallic[1,2,3,4]	E8	Golden Fawn[2,3,4]	Y4	Colt	Code
Jade Green metallic[1,2,3,4]	F2	Yellow Blaze[1]	Y5	Maroon metallic	020
Forest Green Sunfire metallic[1,2,3,4]	F7	Inca Gold metallic[3,4]	Y6	Bright Blue metallic	022
Deep Sherwood Sunfire metallic	G9	Spanish Gold metallic[1,2,3,4]	Y9	Silver metallic	030
Burnished Copper metallic[2,3,4]	K6	Dove Gray[6]	RA1	Bright Red	055
Mojave Beige[1,2,4]	L3	Pewter Gray metallic[6]	RA2	Warm White	061
Moondust metallic[2,4]	L5	Charcoal Gray Sunfire metallic[6]	RA9	Tan metallic	063
Claret Red[3]	R6	Mint Green metallic[6]	RF3	April Green metallic	064
Russet Sunfire metallic[1,2,3,4]	R8	Augusta Green Sunfire metallic[6]	RF9	Bright Yellow	090
Mocha Tan[1,2,4]	T2	Citron metallic[6]	RJ3	Orange	092

Single tones are coded W1,W1. Two-tones are coded X9,W1 where first two digits are accent or roof color, and second two digits are basic body color. Two-tone paint package available on Aspen Custom Coupe for $158 extra. [1]Available on Aspen. [2]Available on Monaco. [3]Available on Charger SE. [4]Available on Royal Monaco. [5]Available only in two-tone combinations. [6]Available on Diplomat. Paint codes with three digits are 1978 paint codes that were used on some mid-year 1977 Diplomats. [7]Available on all models.

Colt

"Giving you more of what you buy a small car for."

Nameplate year of origin: 1971.
Current bodystyle lifespan: 1971 through 1978 (hardtop); 1971 through 1977 (wagon); 1977 through 1979 (M/M).
Predecessor to this model: None.
Replacement for this model: Colt (1979 to 1983).
Primary competition: AMC Gremlin, Buick Opel, Chevrolet Vega, and Ford Pinto.
Notable changes: Redesign of coupes and sedan, and minor trim and detail changes for other models.
Major standard equipment: Vinyl front bucket seats w/reclining seat backs, full-floor carpeting, recessed door handles, two-spoke steering wheel, tilt steering column, trip odometer, tinted glass, flipper rear quarter windows (coupes), rear window defroster, deluxe sound insulation, bright drip rail,

Measurements

	M/M models	Hardtops	Wagon
Wheelbase	92.1"	95.3"	95.3"
Length	162.6"	171.1"	172.1"
Width	60.4"	63.6"	62.8"
Height	53.5"	54.4"	55.7"
Legroom — front	40.0"	42.7"	42.7"
Legroom — rear	30.5"	30.5"	30.5"
Headroom — front	36.8"	36.9"	38.2"
Headroom — rear	36.8"	35.5"	37.3"
Cargo capacity (cu. ft.)	6.0	12.0	58.3
Fuel capacity (gals.)	13.1	13.5	11.0

sill, windshield, and rear window moldings, front and rear rubber bumper guards, locking fuel filler door, power front disc brakes, wheel covers, and A78 × 13 WSW tires. Custom coupe, sedan and wagon add: Floor console (ex. wagon), fold-down rear seat (wagon only), sports steering wheel (ex. wagon), bright beltline and wheel opening moldings, argent rallye road wheels, and 165SR × 13 WSW tires. Carousel hardtop adds: Cloth and vinyl bucket seat w/reclining seat backs, floor console, blue denim instrument panel, shag carpeting, AM/FM radio, and multi-colored side and rear stripes. GT adds: Soft-rim three-spoke sports steering wheel, front floor console w/shifter, rallye gauge cluster w/tachometer, GT bodyside tape stripes, and GT logo.

Models Available

	Model No.	Base MSRP	Change from LY	Shipping Wt. (lbs.)	Model Year Sales	Change from LY
Colt M/M 2-Door Coupe	6M21	$2,999	-5.54%	1980	NA	NA
Colt Custom M/M 2-Door Coupe	6H21	$3,341	NEW	2000	NA	NEW
Colt M/M 4-Door Sedan	6H41	$3,422	+2.42%	2065	NA	NA
Colt 4-Door Station Wagon	6H45	$3,981	+9.19%	2285	NA	NA
Colt Carousel 2-Door Hardtop	6S23	$4,041	+7.82%	2185	NA	NA
Colt GT 2-Door Hardtop	6P23	$3,988	+6.40%	2185	NA	NA
TOTALS	*Avg. price*	$3,629	+2.75%	*Production*	69,963*	+47.65%*

*Total and comparison to LY based on estimated model year sales.

Aspen

"The unbelievable Aspen—The small car at a small price."

Nameplate year of origin: 1976.
Current bodystyle lifespan: 1976 through 1980.
Predecessor to this model: Dart (1967 to 1976).
Replacement for this model: Aries (1981 to 1989).
Percentage of division's production: 60.19%.
Corporate siblings: Plymouth Volaré.
Primary competition: AMC Hornet, Buick Skylark, Chevrolet Nova, Ford Granada, Oldsmobile Omega, and Pontiac Ventura.

Measurements

	Coupe	Sedan	Wagon
Wheelbase	108.7"	112.7"	112.7"
Length	197.5"	201.1"	201.1"
Width	72.8"	72.8"	72.8"
Height	53.3"	55.0"	55.2"
Legroom — front	42.2"	42.3"	42.3"

Notable changes: Minor trim and detail changes.

Major standard equipment: All-vinyl front bench seat (sedan and wagon), cloth and vinyl front bench seat (coupe), front door armrests, color-keyed carpeting, three-spoke steering wheel, two-speed electric windshield wipers and washers, front ashtray, color-keyed bumper filler, roof drip rail molding, quarter window moldings (coupe and wagon), windshield and backlight moldings, and D78 × 14 BSW tires. **Wagon adds:** Rear liftgate w/"open" warning light, power front disc brakes, heavy-duty suspension, and F78 × 14 BSW tires. **Custom adds:** Vinyl bench seat (coupe), Revere cloth and vinyl bench seat (sedan), cigarette lighter, rear armrests w/ashtrays, simulated woodgrain I/P appliqué, belt moldings, wide bodyside chrome moldings w/black painted insert, and rear deck appliqué. **SE adds:** Soft vinyl 60/40 split front bench seat w/individual recliners, luxury door trim panels w/lower carpeting, simulated woodgrain overlay on glove box door w/glove box lock, luxury steering wheel, landau vinyl roof (coupe), full vinyl roof (sedan), color-keyed wide vinyl bodyside molding, full wheel lip molding, hood ornament and windsplit molding, deluxe insulation package, day/night rear view mirror, undercoating w/hood silencer pad, power steering and automatic transmission, dual horns, premium wheel covers, and DR78 × 14 BSW tires. **SE wagon adds:** Deluxe vinyl bench seat, cigarette lighter and rear seat ashtray, cargo compartment carpet and storage bins w/locking doors, woodgrain side panel and liftgate appliqué, and belt moldings.

Measurements (cont.)

	Coupe	Sedan	Wagon
Legroom — rear	31.6"	36.6"	36.6"
Headroom — front	37.4"	39.2"	39.2"
Headroom — rear	35.9"	37.5"	38.7"
Cargo capacity (cu. ft.)	14.5	14.5	72.8
Fuel capacity (gals.)*	18.0	18.0	20.0

Fuel capacity on all V8 equipped models is 20.0 gallons.

Models Available

	Model No.	Base MSRP	Change from LY	Shipping Wt. (lbs.)	Model Year Production	Change from LY
Aspen 2-Door Sport Coupe	NL29	$3,582	+7.73%	3180	24,378*	+9.57%
Aspen 4-Door Sedan	NL41	$3,631	+7.71%	3235	25,838	+84.81%
Aspen 4-Door Station Wagon	NL45	$3,953	+8.06%	3445	59,458	+78.74%
Aspen Custom 2-Door Sport Coupe	NH29	$3,764	+6.99%	3185	26,389	+25.28%
Aspen Custom 4-Door Sedan	NH41	$3,813	+7.32%	3240	40,455	+41.29%
Aspen SE 2-Door Sport Coupe	NP29	$4,317	-2.18%	3375	15,908	-14.49%
Aspen SE 4-Door Sedan	NP41	$4,366	-0.77%	3440	21,522	+0.93%
Aspen SE 4-Door Station Wagon	NH45	$4,283	+7.40%	3450	52,064	+69.14%
TOTALS	*Avg. price*	$3,964	+4.87%		*Production* 266,012	+40.08%

Diplomat

"New Diplomat from Dodge. It's going to make you reexamine your idea of what luxury cars are all about."

Nameplate year of origin: 1977 (previously used as designation on Dodge Coronet 2-door hardtops, 1950–1953, and as an option package on Royal Monaco Brougham 2-door hardtops, 1976–1977).

Current bodystyle lifespan: 1977½ through 1979.

Predecessor to this model: Coronet (1971 to 1976); Monaco (1977–1978).

Replacement for this model: Diplomat (1980 to 1989).

Percentage of division's production: 7.74%.

Corporate siblings: Chrysler LeBaron.

Primary competition: Buick Regal, Mercury Cougar, and Oldsmobile Cutlass Supreme.

Notable changes: All-new model, based upon Aspen 4-door platform.

Major standard equipment: Cloth and vinyl front bench seat, door pull straps, color-keyed carpeting, one-piece cloth headliner, windshield header mounted reading lamps and sculptured cavities to store sunvisors (coupe only), simulated woodgrain I/P cluster and glove box door appliqué, wide body rocker panel sill moldings w/front and rear extensions, bright roof drip rail and quarter window moldings (coupes), bright upper door frame moldings (sedan), full vinyl padded top (sedan), bright belt molding, rear bumper guards, lower deck panel stripe (sedan), stand-up hood ornament, power steering, power brakes, deluxe wheel covers, and FR78 × 15 BSW tires. **Medallion adds:** Cloth 60/40 front split-bench seat

Measurements

	Coupe	Sedan
Wheelbase	112.7"	112.7"
Length	204.1"	206.1"
Width	73.5"	72.8"
Height	53.3"	55.3"
Legroom — front	42.5"	42.5"
Legroom — rear	34.1"	36.6"
Headroom — front	37.4"	39.2"
Headroom — rear	36.2"	37.5"
Cargo capacity (cu. ft.)	16.3	16.6
Fuel capacity (gals.)	19.5	19.5

w/fold-down center armrests and dual recliners, fold-down rear seat armrest, bright pedal trim, map reading lamp, courtesy lights, upper assist handles (sedan), B-pillar assist straps (coupe), rear pillar vanity lamps and mirrors (sedan), trunk dress-up package, LH remote control outside rearview mirror, dual chrome quarter window stripes (coupe), bodyside accent tape stripes coordinated w/body color on coupes and vinyl top color on sedans, deluxe sound insulation package (w/o undercoating and hood pad), and premium wheel covers.

Models Available

	Model No.	Base MSRP	Change from LY	Shipping Wt. (lbs.)	Model Year Production	Change from LY
Diplomat 2-Door Coupe	GH22	$4,943	NEW	3510	12,335	NEW
Diplomat 4-Door Sedan	GH41	$5,101	NEW	3560	8,092	NEW
Diplomat Medallion 2-Door Coupe	GP22	$5,313	NEW	3615	9,156	NEW
Diplomat Medallion 4-Door Sedan	GP41	$5,471	NEW	3675	4,631	NEW
TOTALS	Avg. price	$5,207	NEW	Production	34,214	NEW

Monaco

"Picture yourself in this new mid-size Monaco."

Nameplate year of origin: 1965.
Current bodystyle lifespan: 1971 through 1978. Previously named Coronet (1971 to 1976).
Predecessor to this model: Coronet (1968 to 1970).
Replacement for this model: Diplomat (1977½ to 1979).
Percentage of division's sales volume: 14.41%.
Corporate siblings: Plymouth Fury.
Primary competition: AMC Matador, Chevrolet Chevelle, Ford LTD II, Mercury Cougar, and Pontiac LeMans.
Notable changes: Minor trim and detail changes. Two-door models moved back from Charger line.
Major standard equipment: Cloth-and-vinyl front bench seat, color-keyed carpeting, simulated woodgrain inserts on I/P, deluxe steering wheel, two-speed windshield wipers w/wash-

Measurements

	Coupes	Sedans	Wagons
Wheelbase	115.0"	117.5"	117.5"
Length	213.7"	212.4"	220.7"
Width	77.7"	78.6"	79.2"
Height	52.6"	53.9"	56.5"
Legroom — front	42.3"	41.9"	41.9"
Legroom — rear	32.4"	36.7"	36.3"
Headroom — front	37.6"	38.6"	39.7"
Headroom — rear	37.6"	37.4"	39.9"
Cargo capacity (cu. ft.)	14.7	19.4	86.8
Fuel capacity (gals.)	25.5	25.5	20.0

ers, drip rail and wheel lip moldings, deck lid and rear quarter moldings, front and rear bumper guards, single horn, power front disc brakes, hubcaps, and F78 × 15 BSW tires. Brougham adds: Velour cloth-and-vinyl front bench seat w/fold-down center armrest, deluxe padded door trim, color-keyed vinyl bodyside protection molding, Brougham nameplate and medallion on rear roof pillars, upper door frame moldings, stand-up hood ornament w/hood windsplit molding, and deluxe wheel covers. Wagons add: All-vinyl front bench seat, cargo compartment, dual action tailgate w/concealed hinges, simulated woodgrained appliqué on tailgate door, power front disc brakes, and H78 × 15 BSW tires. Crestwood wagon adds: All-vinyl split-back front bench seat w/ fold-down center armrest, cargo compartment light, rear roof air deflector, tan vinyl insert bodyside protective molding, upper door frame moldings, stand-up hood ornament w/hood windsplit molding, and exterior simulated woodgrained bodyside overlays.

Models Available

	Model No.	Base MSRP	Change from LY*	Shipping Wt. (lbs.)	Model Year Production	Change from LY*
Monaco 2-Door Hardtop	WL23	$3,911	+4.68%	3630	10,368	+56.78%**
Monaco 4-Door Sedan	WL41	$3,988	+5.78%	3655	15,433	+42.20%
Monaco 4-Door, 2-Seat Wagon	WL45	$4,724	+1.94%	4335	3,037	+65.05%
Monaco 4-Door, 3-Seat Wagon	WL46	$4,867	+1.91%	4395	4,297	+41.40%
Monaco Special 2-Door Hardtop	WS23	$3,995	NEW	NA	**	NEW**
Monaco Brougham 2-Door HT Coupe	WH23	$4,146	+3.01%	3635	11,405	+5.49%
Monaco Brougham 4-Door Sedan	WH41	$4,217	+3.89%	3665	14,908	+16.19%
Monaco Crestwood 4-Dr., 2-S. Wgn.	WH45	$5,224	+4.00%	4330	1,341	+22.80%

	Model No.	Base MSRP	Change from LY*	Shipping Wt. (lbs.)	Model Year Production	Change from LY*
Monaco Crestwood 4-Dr., 3-S. Wgn.	WH46	$5,367	+3.91%	4405	2,895	+34.40%
TOTALS		*Avg. price* $4,493	-1.71%		*Production* 63,684	+29.35%

*Comparisons to LY are made to equivalent models in 1976 Coronet and Charger series.   ***Production of mid-year Monaco Special included in base Monaco hardtop production.*

Charger SE

"The night belongs to Charger."

Nameplate year of origin: 1966.
Current bodystyle lifespan: 1975 through 1978.
Predecessor to this model: Charger (1971 to 1974).
Replacement for this model: Magnum XE (1978 to 1979), Mirada (1980 to 1983).
Percentage of division's sales volume: 8.19%.
Corporate siblings: Chrysler Cordoba.
Primary competition: AMC Matador, Chevrolet Monte Carlo, Ford Thunderbird, Mercury Cougar XR-7, and Pontiac Grand Prix.
Notable changes: New grille and minor trim and detail changes.
Major standard equipment: All-vinyl front bucket seats, color-keyed carpeting, simulated woodgrained vinyl trim on I/P, deluxe door trim panels, deluxe steering wheel, inside day/night rearview mirror, two-speed windshield wipers w/washers, bright trim moldings (windshield, backlight, hood rear edge, deck lid, belt, drip rail, bodyside and partial wheel opening), stand-up SE hood ornament, deluxe sound package, power front disc brakes, power steering, unique premium wheel covers, and GR78 × 15 BSW tires.

Measurements

Wheelbase	115.0"
Length	215.3"
Width	77.1"
Height	52.6"
Legroom — front	42.4"
Legroom — rear	32.3"
Headroom — front	37.6"
Headroom — rear	36.6"
Cargo capacity (cu. ft.)	16.3
Fuel capacity (gals.)	25.5

Models Available

	Model No.	Base MSRP	Change from LY	Shipping Wt. (lbs.)	Model Year Production	Change from LY
Charger SE 2-Door Hardtop Coupe	XS22	$5,098	+7.03%	3895	36,204	+2.45%
TOTALS		*Avg. price* $5,098	+22.12%*		*Production* 36,204	-31.38%*

*Comparisons to LY include the 1976 Charger and Charger Sport that were moved to the Monaco series for 1977.

Royal Monaco

"Traditionally sized for full-sized room and comfort, all seven Royal Monaco models offer unusual luxury."

Nameplate year of origin: 1975 (Royal Monaco; 1965 for Monaco name).
Current bodystyle lifespan: 1974 through 1977. Renamed Royal Monaco for 1977.
Predecessor to this model: Polara and Monaco (1969 to 1973).
Replacement for this model: St. Regis (1979 to 1981).
Percentage of division's sales volume: 9.47%.
Corporate siblings: Plymouth Gran Fury.
Primary competition: Chevrolet Caprice, Ford LTD, Mercury Marquis, Oldsmobile Delta 88, and Pontiac Bonneville.
Notable changes: Minor trim and detail changes.
Major standard equipment: Pompeii cloth and vinyl front bench seat, simulated woodgrained I/P appliqué and door panel trim, color-keyed carpeting, padded door trim panels, color-keyed deluxe steering wheel, glove box light, day/night inside rear view mirror, LH outside rear view mirror,

Measurements

	Cars	Wagons
Wheelbase	121.5"	124.0"
Length	225.6"	226.8"
Width	79.3"	79.4"
Height	55.4"	58.9"
Legroom — front	41.6"	41.6"
Legroom — rear	38.2"	38.3"
Headroom — front	38.7"	38.7"
Headroom — rear	37.8"	40.5"
Cargo capacity (cu. ft.)	20.4	100.8
Fuel capacity (gals.)*	26.5	24.0

*Fuel capacity is 20.5 gallons on cars equipped with 318 CID V8 engine.

door frame and wheel lip moldings, rubber trunk mat, trunk light, hubcaps, and GR78 × 15 BSW tires. Brougham adds: Bancroft all-vinyl 50/50 split front seat w/fold-down center armrest, luxury door trim panels w/pull assist straps, electric clock, I/P lighting, dual horns, hood and bodyside accent tape stripes, upper door frame moldings (4-doors), and deluxe wheel covers. Wagons add: All-vinyl upholstery (w/seating configurations and other trim matching trim levels above), cargo compartment carpeting, cargo compartment side storage panels, cargo compartment light, power tailgate window, tailgate ajar warning light, and H78 × 15 BSW tires. Brougham wagon adds: Exterior woodgrained vinyl appliqué w/bright surround molding on bodyside and tailgate, and roof air deflector.

Models Available

	Model No.	Base MSRP	Change from LY*	Shipping Wt. (lbs.)	Model Year Production	Change from LY*
Royal Monaco 2-Door Hardtop	DM23	$4,711	NEW	4050	1,901	NEW
Royal Monaco 4-Door Sedan	DM41	$4,716	+7.47%	4125	9,491	+157.49%
Royal Monaco 4-Door, 2-Seat Wagon	DM45	$5,353	+8.19%	4905	1,333	+123.28%
Royal Monaco Brougham 2-Door Hardtop	DH29	$5,011	+4.88%	4205	6,348	+298.99%
Royal Monaco Brougham 4-Door Sedan	DH41	$4,996	+4.89%	4270	18,361	+102.91%
Royal Monaco Brougham 4-Dr., 2-S. Wgn.	DH46	$5,607	+6.98%	4900	906	+65.63%
Royal Monaco Brougham 4-Dr., 3-S. Wgn.	DH46	$5,730	+6.82%	4935	3,493	+247.22%
TOTALS	*Avg. price*	$5,163	+1.15%	*Production*	41,833	+67.46%

Comparison to LY is made by model number.

FORD

"When America needs a better idea, Ford puts it on wheels."

In a year when its main competitor, Chevrolet, was introducing all-new, smaller full-size models, Ford banked on consumer demand for its big, full-size models while unveiling two important debuts of its own: a newly restyled and renamed mid-size line, the LTD II, and a completely new, smaller, lower-priced generation of the Thunderbird. The subcompact Pinto received a mild facelift, but the rest of the Ford line remained mostly unchanged. By the end of the year, it was clear that 1977 was basically a holding pattern while Ford waited for the next big introduction to come in 1978.

The Thunderbird entered a completely different market segment than it had ever occupied since its introduction in 1955. For 1977, after 19 years as a full-sized sporty luxury car, the Thunderbird became a mid-size personal luxury car, competing with the likes of the Chevrolet Monte Carlo, Pontiac Grand Prix, and Dodge Charger SE. With the downsizing, Thunderbird now shared a body and chassis with the newly restyled and renamed LTD II models, as well as the Mercury Cougar. The Thunderbird was also no longer built at the Wixom, Michigan, plant alongside Lincolns as it had been since 1958, when it became a four-passenger luxury car. Nearly all Thunderbird bodyside sheetmetal was shared with

the LTD II, with the Thunderbird using six vertical louvers on the front fenders. Powertrain options and instrument panel styling followed that of the LTD II as well. However, nearly everything else was different. Four-section vertical parking/turn signal lamps were mounted in pointed front fender ends paired with hidden headlights, and a large-opening egg-crate style grille, six rows high and twelve columns across, with a slight point in the center, sat above a slightly pointed front bumper. The traditional long hood, short deck styling returned with the hood having a slightly raised V-shaped center section flowing back from the grille, and a slightly indented section on the decklid that led into a separation of the taillamps at the rear. Taillamps were of a full-width design, with a low center reflective section connecting the two larger portions. Brake and taillights had a Thunderbird emblem in the center, and backup lights occupied a thin strip across the top of these lights.

The most distinctive part of the Thunderbird's exterior styling was its greenhouse design. A broad B-pillar housing a small vertical opera window wrapped over the roof, edged in chrome trim. Large rear quarter windows behind the B-pillar and met with a slender C-pillar, leading into a very wide and flat rear window. The wrapover section was body colored, with a pinstripe running off the rear quarter panel, turning up the B-pillar and over to the opposite side. The opera window had an etched Thunderbird emblem near the bottom, and the pinstripe was continued in the opera window as a line etching as it crossed through from top to bottom. As previously mentioned the instrument panel was mostly carried over from the former Torino and Elite, but upholstery materials and trim were more upscale, befitting the Thunderbird's image. At mid-year a Town Landau model was introduced as a higher trim level Thunderbird, and included identifying features such as brushed aluminum wrap-over roof ornamentation, unique tape stripes, contrasting accent paint on the front fender louvers, and turbine cast aluminum wheels.

The purpose of the restyling and renaming of the mid-size Ford line was twofold: first, to give new life to Ford's entry in a vastly expanding mid-size market, currently led by the Oldsmobile Cutlass line; and second, to offer an alternative for those buyers who would consider a smaller full-size car, hence the "LTD II" name replacing Torino. Presumably Ford hoped the new name would lead some to believe this was the new downsized LTD. This tactic would be used again in 1983, when the Granada was phased out and the LTD name was applied to its replacement, while the real full-size models took on the LTD Crown Victoria name. Obviously the LTD name carried a lot of value and recognition with Ford buyers.

Billed as combining "LTD's traditional high level of workmanship with Mustang II's sporty spirit," the new LTD II used new sheetmetal and interior design on the former Torino platform. Front end styling was seemingly an update on the former Elite coupe's theme, with pointed front fender extensions carrying vertical three-section parking/turn signal lamps, an egg-crate design grille with a slightly raised center hood section, and stacked dual rectangular headlights (a configuration that would never appear on another Ford model). Bodysides and greenhouse areas were more angular and lost the curvaceous styling that the Torino had been known for, with the LTD II having only a lower body feature line which ran between the top edges of the bumpers. There was also a barely noticeable upper body feature line that extended off the top of the front fenders to the back end of the rear side windows.

In the greenhouse area all windows had squared off corners, including the C-pillar opera windows used on all two-doors and four-doors, except the base LTD II S models. At the rear, trunklid and fender end caps slanted rearward to meet the box style rear bumper. Pointed fender end caps carried vertical wraparound taillamps. A body colored panel between the trunk lid opening and bumper had a raised center section which housed backup lights on the outer ends, with red lenses adjacent to the inside, and the Ford name in block letters spaced across the center. LTD II and LTD II Brougham models had a chrome piece encompassing and filling in the areas around the backup lights and Ford name. On LTD II station wagons, from the cowl rearward, new sheetmetal was applied to the doors and rear quarter panel in line with the other LTD II models, the greenhouse and rear end styling were carried over from the Torino. Inside, the LTD II carried a slightly updated version of the Torino's instrument panel with flush mounted gauges rather than the Torino's tunneled style gauges. The LTD II continued to keep the headlight and heater/air conditioning controls to the left of the steering column, with radio and windshield wiper controls to the right. Interior upholstery and seating options were updated, but not greatly changed. Powertrain changes included making the 302 CID V8 engine standard equipment on hardtops, and the 351 CID V8 standard on station wagons, while the 460 CID V8 engine was no longer offered in the mid-size lineup.

For the rest of the Ford lineup, there were not many significant changes. The Pinto received a mild facelift that featured a sloping body-colored front end with tunneled style single round headlamps, two-section parking/turn signal lights, and a horizontal crosshatch grille that was six rows high and ten across. At the rear, enlarged taillamps were seen, and a new all-glass rear hatch was an available option on the 3-door Runabout. An outgrowth of the expanding Ford specialty programs for 1977 was the Pinto Cruising Wagon, which became a new option package. There was actually a small series of "Cruising" option packages available that included the Pinto Wagon and the Econoline van. The popular Granada continued with very few changes, but added more luxury options such as an automatic climate control system and leather upholstery. The compact Maverick was in its final year, and the sporty Mustang II and full-size LTD were nearing the end of their lifespan, and therefore saw only minor changes with improved engine and emission systems, a few new options, and a few new interior color and trim choices, along with new exterior color choices. A few noteworthy model changes included the discontinuation of the LTD Brougham series and the designation of the Pinto Squire station wagon as its own model rather than an option package, although it still carried the same model number as the basic Pinto wagon.

Granada 2-Door Sedan

Granada Ghia 4-Door Sedan

LTD 4-Door Pillared Hardtop

LTD Country Squire 4-Door Station Wagon

LTD II 4-Door Station Wagon

LTD II Brougham 2-Door Hardtop Coupe

LTD II S 4-Door Pillared Hardtop

LTD Landau 2-Door Pillared Hardtop

Maverick 2-Door Sedan
with Exterior Décor group

Maverick 4-Door Sedan
with Exterior Décor group

Mustang II 2+2 3-Door Hatchback
with Cobra II package

Mustang II Ghia 2-Door Coupe
with Ghia Sports group

Pinto 2-Door Station Wagon with Cruising
Wagon package and optional graphics

Pinto 3-Door Runabout Hatchback
with optional glass third door

Thunderbird 2-Door Hardtop Coupe
with Exterior Décor group

Thunderbird 2-Door Hardtop Coupe
with Tu-Tone paint

Thunderbird interior with optional
Interior Luxury group

Model year production: 1,829,300, down 5.04% from 1976.
Domestic market share: 19.06% (2nd place).
Base price range: $3,099 to $7,990.
Ford average base price: $4,606, up 3.80%.
Introduction date: October 1, 1976.
Assembly plants: Atlanta, GA (A); Oakville, Ontario, Canada (B); Mahwah, NJ (E); Dearborn, MI (F); Chicago, IL (G); Lorain, OH (H); Los Angeles, CA (J); Kansas City, MO (K); Twin Cities, MN (P); San Jose, CA (R); Allen Park, MI (S—*pilot plant*); Metuchen, NJ (T); Louisville, KY (U); Wayne, MI (W); and St. Thomas, Ontario, Canada (X).
Data plate identification (VIN): Eleven digit code read as

follows: First digit indicates year (7 = 1977); second digit indicates assembly plant code (see list above); third and fourth digits indicate model number (model number in model charts); fifth digit indicates engine code (see powertrain chart); remaining digits are sequential with beginning numbers of 100001. *Example:* 7F02Z100001 is a 1977 Ford Mustang II 2-Door Coupe, with 170.8 CID, 2-bbl. V6 engine, serial number 100001, built in Dearborn, MI. *Note: Some 1977 Pinto and Mustang models were produced with 8 as the first digit. The affected cars have two "f" scripts preceding and following the VIN on the ID plate (usual is one "f" script), and have serial numbers between 400001 and 499999.*

Powertrains*

Engine	Net HP	Engine Code	Transmission Availability[1]		Pinto	Mustang II	Maverick	Granada	LTD II & Thunderbird	LTD
140 CID (2.3L) OHC, 2-bbl., 4-cyl.	89	Y	4-speed manual		S	-$282 (credit on Mach I)/ S (Others)	—	—	—	—
				MPG:	26/37/30	23/33/26	—	—	—	—
				Calif.	24/34/28	22/34/26	—	—	—	—
			3-speed Select-Shift Cruise-O-Matic		$248	$248 (ex. Mach I)	—	—	—	—
				MPG:	23/32/26	21/29/24	—	—	—	—
				Calif.	22/30/25	19/25/22	—	—	—	—
170.8 CID (2.8L), 2-bbl., V6	93	Z	4-speed manual		—	S (Mach I)[2]/$282 (others)[2]	—	—	—	—
				MPG:	—	20/27/23	—	—	—	—
				Calif.	—	NA	—	—	—	—
			3-speed Select-Shift Cruise-O-Matic		$530[3]	$248 (Mach I)/ $530 (others)	—	—	—	—
				MPG:	18/23/20	17/23/19	—	—	—	—
				Calif.	17/20/18	16/22/18	—	—	—	—

Engine	Net HP	Engine Code	Transmission Availability[1]		Pinto	Mustang II	Maverick	Granada	LTD II & Thunderbird	LTD
200 CID (3.3L), 1-bbl., 6-cyl.	96	T	3-speed manual		—	—	S[2]	—	—	—
				MPG:	—	—	21/28/24	—	—	—
			4-speed manual w/overdrive		—	—	—	S[2]	—	—
				MPG:	—	—	—	21/28/24	—	—
			3-speed Select-Shift Cruise-O-Matic		—	—	$258[2]	$186[2]	—	—
				MPG:	—	—	18/24/20	—	—	—
250 CID (4.1L), 1-bbl., 6-cyl.	98	L	3-speed manual		—	—	$96[2]	—	—	—
				MPG:	—	—	NA	—	—	—
			4-speed manual w/overdrive		—	—	—	$96[2]	—	—
				MPG:	—	—	—	21/28/24	—	—
			3-speed Select-Shift Cruise-O-Matic		—	—	$354[4]	$282[4]	—	—
				MPG:	—	—	17/22/19	18/23/20	—	—
				Calif:	—	—	18/23/20	16/20/18	—	—
302 CID (5.0L), 2-bbl., V8	137	F	3-speed manual		—	—	$148	—	—	—
				MPG:	—	—	16/22/18	—	—	—
				Calif:	—	—	NA	—	—	—
			4-speed manual[5,6]		—	-$48 (credit on Mach I)/ $234 (others)	—	$187	—	—
				MPG:	—	15/21/17	—	16/24/18	—	—
				Calif:	—	NA	—	NA	—	—
			3-speed Select-Shift Cruise-O-Matic		—	$200 (Mach I)/ $482 (others)	$419	$373	S (ex. Wgns.)[2]	-$66 (credit on all ex. Wgns.)[2]
				MPG:	—	16/19/17	17/22/19	16/22/18	15/19/17	15/19/17
				Calif:	—	13/18/14	13/18/14	13/20/16	—	—
351 CID (5.8L), 2-bbl., V8	149	H	3-speed Select-Shift Cruise-O-Matic		—	—	—	$433	S (Wgns.)[2]/ $66 (ex. Wgns. & Brghm 4-dr.)[4]	S (ex. Wgns.)[2]
				MPG:	—	—	—	NA	14/20/16	13/19/15
				Calif:	—	—	—	NA	12/18/14	—
400 CID (6.6L), 2-bbl., V8	173	S	3-speed Select-Shift Cruise-O-Matic		—	—	—	—	$100 (Wgns.)[4]/ $155 (others)	S (Wgns.)/ $100 (others)[4]
				MPG:	—	—	—	—	13/18/15	13/18/15
				Calif:	—	—	—	—	10/16/12	10/16/12
460 CID (7.5L), 4-bbl., V8	197	A	3-speed Select-Shift Cruise-O-Matic		—	—	—	—	—	$132 (Wgns.)[2]/ $232 (others)[2]
				MPG:	—	—	—	—	—	11/16/13

*Optional axle ratios required on some cars sold in California; however there are too many variations to include within this section. [1]Unless otherwise noted: All manual transmissions are floor-shift, except on Maverick. All automatics are column-shift, except on Pinto and Mustang II. Floor-shift is available for $29 extra on Granada w/optional bucket seats and automatic, and standard w/Sports Coupe option. Floor-shift w/bucket seats and console is also available for $158 on LTD II and LTD II Brougham 2-doors, and Thunderbird. Included on Thunderbird w/optional Interior Decor group. [2]Not available in California. [3]Not available on Pinto Pony. Station wagons require power front disc brakes at extra cost. [4]Required (or standard) in California. [5]4-speed manual w/overdrive on Granada. [6]Sports Performance package is required w/4-speed manual on Mustang II.

Major Options

	Pinto	Maverick	Mustang II	Granada	LTD II	Thunderbird	LTD
Air conditioning[1]	$437	$443	$437	$461	$505	$505	$526
Tilt steering wheel	—	—	—	$58	$63	$63	$64

	Pinto	Maverick	Mustang II	Granada	LTD II	Thunderbird	LTD
Fingertip speed control	—	—	—	$105	$114	$114	$114
Rear window defogger	—	$43	—	$43	—	—	$47
Electric rear window defroster	$70[2]	—	$70	$80	$87	$87	$87
Tinted glass, all windows	$49	$64	$49	$51	$57	$61	$71
Dual remote-control mirrors	$47	—	$47	$47	$51	$51	$[3]
Power trunk lid release	—	—	—	$17	—	$[4]	$[4]
Power windows, 2-dr./4-dr.	—	—	—	$105/$145	$114/$158	$114	$120/$175
Power door locks, 2-dr./4-dr.[4]	—	—	—	$66/$93	$92/$121	$[4]	$75/$139
Power seat, 6-way w/std. seat	—	—	—	$131[5]	$143	$143	$143
Front bucket seats w/console[6]	S	$99	$75	$168	$158	$158	—
Leather upholstery	—	—	—	$192	—	$241	$241[7]
Third row seat/DFRS, wagons	—	—	—	—	$100	—	$126
AM radio	$65	$66	$65	$66	$72	S	$72
AM/FM stereo	$161	$176	$161	$176	$192	$120	$192
AM/FM stereo w/8-track tape	—	$243	$229	$243	$266	$193	$266
Vinyl top, full (Pinto, half)	$125	$88[8]	$88[8]	$101	$162	$132[9]	$116[9]
Sunroof, power-operated	$237[10]	—	$237[10]	—	—	—	—
Moonroof, power-operated	—	—	—	$812	—	$888	$888
Power steering	$125	$134	$125	$137	S	S	S
Power brakes, w/front disc	$57	$57	$57	$58[11]	S	S	S[11]
Fender skirts	—	—	—	—	—	—	$43
Deluxe wheel covers	$29	—	—	$24	$36	—	$93
Wire wheel covers	$112	$112	$82	$90	$134	$99	$134
Styled steel wheels w/trim ring	$107	$127	$78	$101	—	S	—
Forged/Cast aluminum wheel[12]	$233	—	$204	—	$270	$234	$270
Cast aluminum lacy wheels	—	$243	$204[12]	$213	—	—	—
White sidewall tires, std. size	$37	$36	$37	$37	$45	$45	$42

Popular Option Groups & Packages

	Pinto	Maverick	Mustang II	Granada	LTD II	Thunderbird	LTD
Accent group	—	—	—	—	$58	—	—
Appearance décor package	—	—	$151	—	—	—	—
Cobra II package	—	—	$514	—	—	—	—
Convenience group	—	$67	$65	$81	$132	$96	$133
Convenience/Light group	$128	—	—	—	—	—	—
Cruising Wagon package[13]	$357	—	—	—	—	—	—
Deluxe bumper group	$65	$63	—	$66	$72	$72	$66
Deluxe equipment group	—	—	$172	—	—	—	—
Exterior accent group	—	—	$211	—	—	—	—
Exterior décor group	$128	$114	—	—	$276	$368	—
Ghia sports group	—	—	$398	—	—	—	—
Interior décor group	$181	$113	—	$192	—	$299	—
Landau luxury group	—	—	—	—	—	—	$474[14]
Light group	—	$36	$42	$35	$49	$46	$38
Luxury décor group	—	—	—	$618	—	—	—
Luxury interior group	—	—	$147	—	—	$724	—
Protection group	$139	$54	$34	$36	$46	$43	$46
Rallye package	—	—	$101	—	—	—	—
Sport Coupe package	—	—	—	$511	—	—	—
Sports Instrumentation group	—	—	—	—	$130	$111	—
Sports Rallye package	$84	—	—	—	—	—	—
Sports Performance package	—	—	$51–$491	—	—	—	—
Squire Brougham option	—	—	—	—	$203	—	$266
Visibility group	—	—	—	$58	—	—	—
Wagon Brougham option	—	—	—	—	—	—	$396

—= Not Available; S = Standard equipment. ¹Air conditioner w/automatic temperature control is available for $500 on Granada, $546 on Thunderbird and LTD II, and $599 on LTD. ²Includes tinted rear window. ³LH only and standard on LTD Landau. Requires Convenience group on other models. ⁴Available only in Power lock group (Thunderbird, $92) consisting of power door locks and power trunk lid release, or Convenience group (LTD). ⁵4-way power seat on Granada. ⁶Bucket seats only on Pinto and Maverick, console not available. Bucket seats standard on Mustang II, price shown is for console. Bucket seats w/console available on LTD II Brougham at no cost. ⁷Available only with Landau luxury group. ⁸Half (landau) vinyl roof on Mustang II Ghia coupe is available for no charge. Maverick

2-door has ¾ vinyl roof, and 4-door has halo vinyl roof. [9]*Not available on wagons. N/C on LTD Landau 2-door, and standard on LTD Landau 4-door. Thunderbird uses two-piece vinyl roof, in front of and behind center pillar wrap-over.* [10]*Manually operated. Not available on Mustang II 2+2 or Mach I models. Flip-up open air roof also available on Mustang II 2-doors for $145.* [11]*Four-wheel power disc brakes available on Granada for $246; on LTD for $184.* [12]*Cast turbine style wheels on LTD II and Thunderbird. Granada has lacy aluminum spoke wheels. While cast aluminum lacy spoke wheels on Mustang II, $252.* [13]*Special paint/tape treatment including all-around 3-color paint/tape treatment and luggage rack is available for $54, or delete the standard stripe/panel appliqués for $55 credit.* [14]*Available on LTD Landau models only. Available on Country Squire wagon for $451, and on LTD wagon for $538. Thunderbird offers the following luxury groups priced with velour (vinyl on Lipstick) trim/leather trim: Lipstick, $337/$546; Bordeaux, $624/$700; Crème and gold, $717/$793.*

Paint Colors

	Code		Code		Code
Black	1C	Dark Brown metallic	5Q	Tan	8H
Silver metallic	1G	Orange	61	Medium Tan metallic	8J
Dove Gray	1N	Bright Yellow	6E	Bright Saddle metallic	8K
Coral	2A	Cream	6P	Chamois metallic	8W
Dark Red	2M	Tan	6U	Champagne metallic	8Y
Bright Red	2R	Medium Gold metallic	6V	White	9D
Lipstick Red	2U	Bright Aqua metallic glow[2]	7H		
Rose metallic[1]	2Y	Light Jade metallic	7L		
Bright Dark Blue metallic	3G	Light Aqua metallic[2]	7Q		
Light Blue	3U	Chartreuse	7R		
Bright Blue metallic glow	3V	Dark Emerald metallic[2]	7S		
Dark Jade metallic	46	Medium Emerald metallic glow[2]	7T		
Light Green	47	Pastel Beige	86		
Dark Yellow Green metallic	4V	Vista Orange	8G		

In two-tone combinations, first two digits are lower color, and second two digits are upper color. Metallic glow paints are $57 extra on Pinto, Maverick, Mustang II and Granada, and $62 extra on LTD II, Thunderbird and LTD. "Tu-Tone" paint/tape treatment available for $51 on Pinto, $94 on Maverick, $88 on LTD II, and $49 on Thunderbird. [1]*Thunderbird color only.* [2]*Mustang II color only.*

Pinto

"New style and sporty performance."

Nameplate year of origin: 1971.
Current bodystyle lifespan: 1971 through 1980.
Predecessor to this model: None.
Replacement for this model: Escort (1981 to 1985).
Percentage of division's production: 11.07%.
Corporate siblings: Mercury Bobcat.
Primary competition: AMC Gremlin, Chevrolet Vega, and Dodge Colt.
Notable changes: New front and rear styling treatment and minor trim and detail changes.
Major standard equipment: Choice of Kersten cloth-and-vinyl or Colton all-vinyl high-back front bucket seats, color-keyed carpeting, bright front and rear window moldings, bright drip and belt moldings, rack-and-pinion steering, manual front disc brakes, hubcaps, and A78 × 13 BSW tires.

Measurements

	Sedan	Runabout	Wagon
Wheelbase	94.5"	94.5"	94.5"
Length	169.3"	169.3"	179.1"
Width	69.4"	69.4"	69.7"
Height	50.6"	50.6"	52.0"
Legroom — front	40.8"	40.8"	40.8"
Legroom — rear	30.7"	30.7"	30.7"
Headroom — front	37.3"	37.3"	37.9"
Headroom — rear	36.2"	36.2"	39.3"
Cargo capacity (cu. ft.)	6.3	6.1*	31.3*
Fuel capacity (gals.)	13.0	13.0	14.0

With rear seat folded down, Runabout, 29.0 cu. ft.; Wagon, 57.2 cu. ft.

Pony deletes: Color-keyed I/P and steering wheel, bright drip and rear window moldings, and bright belt molding. Runabout adds: Black rubber load floor mat, fold-down rear seat, and rear liftgate. Station wagon adds: Flip-out rear quarter windows, and liftgate "open" warning light. Squire adds: Choice of Alpine cloth-and-vinyl or Ruffino all-vinyl low back front bucket seats, load floor carpeting, Squire script on rear gate, simulated woodgrain vinyl paneling, and full wheel covers.

Models Available

	Model No.	Base MSRP	Change from LY	Shipping Wt. (lbs.)	Model Year Production	Change from LY
Pinto Pony 2-Door Sedan	10	$3,099	+7.05%	2313	NA*	NA*
Pinto 2-Door Sedan	10	$3,237	+7.01%	2315	48,863	-47.04%
Pinto 3-Dr. Runabout (hatchback)	11	$3,353	+4.78%	2351	74,237	-19.78%
Pinto 2-Door Station Wagon	12	$3,548	+5.44%	2515	79,449	-24.57%

	Model No.	Base MSRP	Change from LY	Shipping Wt. (lbs.)	Model Year Production	Change from LY
Pinto Squire 2-Dr. Station Wagon	12	$3,891	NEW	2552	NA*	NEW
TOTALS		Avg. price $3,426	+5.14%		Production 202,549	-30.19%

*Production kept as combined totals for 2-door sedan and 2-door station wagons.

Mustang II

"Sweet handling."

Nameplate year of origin: 1964 (also used on a 1963 show car).
Current bodystyle lifespan: 1974 through 1978.
Predecessor to this model: Mustang (1971 to 1973).
Replacement for this model: Mustang (1979 to 1993).
Percentage of division's production: 8.37%.
Corporate siblings: None.
Primary competition: Chevrolet Monza, Mercury Capri, and Pontiac Sunbird.
Notable changes: Minor trim and detail changes.
Major standard equipment: Low-back Corinthian vinyl bucket seats, color-keyed cut-pile carpeting, soft vinyl and carpet door trim panels, European-type armrests, woodtone I/P appliqués, two-spoke steering wheel, courtesy lights, gauges (including tachometer, fuel, ammeter and temperature), bright windshield and rear window molding, bright drip rail, belt and center pillar molding, color-keyed urethane coated bumpers, full wheel covers, and B78 × 13 BSW tires. 2+2 adds: Brushed aluminum I/P appliqués, fold-down rear seat, liftgate w/hydraulic struts, styled steel wheels, and B78 B/WL tires. Ghia adds (to 2-door): Choice of Stirling plaid cloth-and-vinyl or Luxury all-vinyl low-back bucket seats, luxury décor trim panels, deluxe color-keyed seat belts, soft-vinyl headlining, quartz crystal digital clock, dual remote control outside color-keyed mirrors, vinyl insert bodyside molding, pinstripes, half vinyl roof, opera windows, Ghia identification, deluxe wheel covers, and BR78 × 13 BSW tires. Mach I adds (to 2+2): Dual remote control outside color-keyed mirrors, black Mach I lower bodysides and liftgate paint stripes and identification, styled steel wheels w/wheel trim rings, and BR70 × 13 B/WL tires.

Measurements

	Coupe	3-Door
Wheelbase	96.2"	96.2"
Length	175.0"	175.0"
Width	70.2"	70.2"
Height	50.3"	50.0"
Legroom — front	37.2"	37.2"
Legroom — rear	27.7"	27.7"
Headroom — front	37.2"	37.2"
Headroom — rear	35.9"	34.1"
Cargo capacity (cu. ft.)	6.7	22.8*
Fuel capacity (gals.)**	13.0	13.0

*With rear seat folded down.   **16.5 gallons with optional V8 engine.

Models Available

	Model No.	Base MSRP	Change from LY	Shipping Wt. (lbs.)	Model Year Production	Change from LY
Mustang II 2-Door Hardtop Coupe	02	$3,702	+5.02%	2627	67,783	-13.66%
Mustang II 2+2 3-Door (hatchback)	03	$3,901	+3.17%	2672	49,161	-21.11%
Mustang II Ghia 2-Door Hardtop Coupe	04	$4,119	+6.74%	2667	29,510	-21.34%
Mustang II Mach I 3-Door (hatchback)	05	$4,332	+2.92%	2785	6,719	-27.22%
TOTALS		Avg. price $4,014	+4.42%		Production 153,173	-18.34%

Maverick

"Dependable family compact."

Nameplate year of origin: 1970.
Current bodystyle lifespan: 1970 through 1977.
Predecessor to this model: Falcon (1966 to 1969).
Replacement for this model: Fairmont (1978 to 1983).
Percentage of division's production: 5.38%.
Corporate siblings: Mercury Comet.

Measurements

	2-Door	4-Door
Wheelbase	103.0"	109.9"
Length	187.0"	193.9"
Width	70.5"	70.5"

Primary competition: AMC Hornet, Chevrolet Nova, and Plymouth Volaré.

Notable changes: Minor trim and detail changes.

Major standard equipment: Random stripe cloth-and-vinyl front bench seat, nylon loop pile carpeting, integral door armrests w/door pull assist handle, two-spoke color-keyed steering wheel and column, flipper rear quarter window (2-door), bright drip rail and wheel opening moldings, bright hubcaps w/black-out center, and C78 × 14 BSW tires.

Measurements (cont.)

	2-Door	4-Door
Height	53.5"	53.4"
Legroom — front	40.7"	40.7"
Legroom — rear	32.0"	36.2"
Headroom — front	37.5"	37.8"
Headroom — rear	36.0"	36.7"
Cargo capacity (cu. ft.)	11.3	13.1
Fuel capacity (gals.)	19.2	19.2

Models Available

	Model No.	Base MSRP	Change from LY	Shipping Wt. (lbs.)	Model Year Production	Change from LY
Maverick 2-Door Sedan	91	$3,322	+6.58%	2782	40,086	-33.86%
Maverick 4-Door Sedan	92	$3,395	+6.46%	2887	58,420	-26.12%
TOTALS	Avg. price	$3,359	+6.52%		Production 98,506	-29.48%

Granada

"Designed to give you efficient use of space, fuel and money."

Nameplate year of origin: 1975.

Current bodystyle lifespan: 1975 through 1980.

Predecessor to this model: None.

Replacement for this model: Granada (1981 to 1982).

Percentage of division's production: 21.35%.

Corporate siblings: Mercury Monarch.

Primary competition: Chevrolet Nova, Dodge Aspen, Plymouth Volaré, and Pontiac Ventura.

Notable changes: Minor trim and detail changes.

Major standard equipment: Corinthian vinyl front bench seat, 12-oz. cut-pile carpeting, burled walnut I/P appliqués, two rear seat ashtrays, luggage compartment mat, mitered corner door frame moldings (4-door), bright front and rear window moldings, bright belt moldings, bright drip rail and wheel opening moldings, opera window w/bright moldings (2-door), hood ornament, full wheel covers, and DR78 × 14 BSW tires. Ghia adds: Kasman cloth "Flight Bench" front seat, 14-oz. cut-pile carpeting, deluxe door trim, luxury steering wheel, digital clock, Ghia interior ornamentation, day/night rearview mirror, deluxe color-keyed seat belts, rear door courtesy light switches (4-door), LH remote control mirror, opera window Ghia crests (2-door), C-pillar appliqué w/Ghia crest (4-door), wide vinyl insert bodyside and wheel lip moldings, vinyl lower rear panel appliqué w/decklid tape stripes, hood, bodyside and decklid tape stripes, luggage compartment carpeting, deluxe sound and ride package, unique Ghia wheel covers, and WSW tires.

Measurements

Wheelbase	109.9"
Length	197.7"
Width	74.0"
Height	53.3"
Legroom — front	41.1"
Legroom — rear	36.0"
Headroom — front	38.5"
Headroom — rear	37.6"
Cargo capacity (cu. ft.)	14.8*
Fuel capacity (gals.)	19.2

Ghia models have 1.7 cu. ft. less.

Models Available

	Model No.	Base MSRP	Change from LY	Shipping Wt. (lbs.)	Model Year Production	Change from LY
Granada 2-Door Sedan	81	$4,022	+8.50%	3124	157,612	-2.48%
Granada 4-Door Sedan	82	$4,118	+8.43%	3174	163,071	-43.36%
Granada Ghia 2-Door Sedan	83	$4,452	+4.38%	3229	34,166	-26.97%
Granada Ghia 4-Door Sedan	84	$4,548	+4.43%	3229	35,730	-31.89%
TOTALS	Avg. price	$4,285	+6.29%		Production 390,579	-28.83%

LTD II

"A sporty, new, trim-size line in the LTD tradition."

Nameplate year of origin: 1977.
Current bodystyle lifespan: 1977 through 1979.
Predecessor to this model: Torino (1972 to 1976).
Replacement for this model: None.
Percentage of division's production: 12.70%.
Corporate siblings: Mercury Cougar.
Primary competition: AMC Matador, Chevrolet Chevelle, Dodge Monaco, Plymouth Fury, and Pontiac LeMans.
Notable changes: Completely restyled and renamed.
Major standard equipment: Kirsten cloth-and-vinyl front bench seat, color-keyed cut-pile carpeting, windshield and rear window bright moldings, bright drip rail moldings, bright hubcaps, and HR78 × 14 BSW tires. Wagon adds: Colton all-vinyl bench seat, three-way tailgate, fold-down second seat, removable cargo floor carpeting, and bright tail-

Measurements

	2-Doors	4-Doors	Wagons
Wheelbase	114.0"	118.0"	118.0"
Length	215.5"	219.5"	223.1"
Width	78.0"	78.0"	79.0"
Height	52.6"	53.3"	54.9"
Legroom — front	42.5"	42.5"	42.5"
Legroom — rear	33.2"	37.8"	37.3"
Headroom — front	37.6"	38.3"	38.4"
Headroom — rear	36.2"	37.0"	38.5"
Cargo capacity (cu. ft.)	15.1	15.1	84.9*
Fuel capacity (gals.)	26.0	26.0	21.3

Plus 8.1 cu. ft. of lockable below-deck storage.

gate window molding. LTD II adds: Ardmore and Kasman cloth-and-vinyl front bench seat, woodtone I/P appliqués, deluxe door trim, bright rear panel appliqué, bright side window and wheel lip moldings, opera window (2-door), and bright rocker panel molding. LTD II wagon adds: Mateo all-vinyl bench seat and interior trim. LTD II Brougham adds: Doral cloth or super-soft all-vinyl split front seat w/dual fold-down center armrests, 14 oz. cut-pile carpeting, luxury door trim w/carpeted lower panels, wide bodyside moldings w/vinyl inserts and integral wheel lip moldings, hood ornament, unique Brougham identification, luxury sound package, deluxe wheel covers, and WSW tires. LTD II Squire adds: Power tailgate window, 10 oz. load floor carpeting, simulated woodgrain bodyside paneling, and full wheel covers.

Models Available

	Model No.	Base MSRP	Change from LY*	Shipping Wt. (lbs.)	Model Year Production	Change from LY*
LTD II S 2-Door Hardtop	25	$4,528	+8.53%	3789	9,531	-72.39%
LTD II S 4-Door Pillared Hardtop	27	$4,579	+8.87%	3894	18,775	+7.94%
LTD II S 4-Door, 2-Seat, 6-pass. Wagon	40	$4,806	+6.30%	4393	9,636	-44.24%
LTD II 2-Door Hardtop	30	$4,785	+7.26%	3789	57,449	+139.98%
LTD II 4-Door Pillared Hardtop	31	$4,870	+8.34%	3904	56,704	+39.78%
LTD II 4-Door, 2-Seat, 6-pass. Wagon	42	$5,064	+6.19%	4404	23,237	-24.05%
LTD II Brougham 2-Door Hardtop	32	$5,121	+4.87%	3898	20,979	+559.10%
LTD II Brougham 4-Door Pillared Hardtop	33	$5,206	+5.92%	3930	18,851	+321.44%
LTD II Squire 4-Door, 2-Seat, 6-p. Wagon	43	$5,335	+4.96%	4430	17,162	-18.83%
TOTALS	*Avg. price*	$4,983	+6.72%	*Production*	232,324	+20.32%

All comparisons made to equivalent 1976 Torino models.

Thunderbird

"A new kind of thunder."

Nameplate year of origin: 1955.
Current bodystyle lifespan: 1977 through 1979.
Predecessor to this model: Thunderbird (1972 to 1976).
Replacement for this model: Thunderbird (1980 to 1982).
Percentage of division's production: 17.39%.
Corporate siblings: Mercury Cougar XR-7.
Primary competition: Chevrolet Monte Carlo and Pontiac Grand Prix.
Notable changes: Completely redesigned.

Measurements

Wheelbase	114.0"
Length	215.5"
Width	78.5"
Height	53.0"
Legroom — front	42.5"
Legroom — rear	33.2"
Headroom — front	37.6"

Major standard equipment: Willshire cloth and vinyl front bench seat w/automatic seatback release, cut pile carpeting, simulated burled walnut woodgrain I/P and door panel trim, electric clock, AM radio, power ventilation system, Thunderbird hood ornament and nameplates, bright moldings (rear hood edge, beltline, drip rails), rocker panel and wheel lip moldings, opera windows, roof wrap-over moldings, front fender louvers, full wheel covers, and HR78 × 15 BSW tires. Town Landau adds: Luxury interior group, 22K gold Town Landau plaque on RH side of I/P with owner's name engraved, dual remote-control sport mirrors, brushed aluminum wrap-over roof molding, unique tape stripes (bodyside, hood, header panel, decklid, hidden headlamp doors), hood ornament w/color-coordinated acrylic logo insert, Town Landau script on opera windows, accent paint on front fender louvers, front cornering lights, and body-color accent painted turbine spoke cast aluminum wheels.

Measurements (cont.)

Headroom — rear	36.2"
Cargo capacity (cu. ft.)	14.2
Fuel capacity (gals.)	26.0

Models Available

	Model No.	Base MSRP	Change from LY	Shipping Wt. (lbs.)	Model Year Production	Change from LY
Thunderbird 2-Door Hardtop	87	$5,063	-35.01%	3907	318,140	+501.00%
Thunderbird Town Landau 2-Dr. HT	87	$7,990	NEW	4104	NA*	NEW
TOTALS	*Avg. price*	$6,527	-16.22%	*Production*	318,140	+501.00%

Town Landau production is included with base Thunderbird.

LTD

"The full-size car that kept its size."

Nameplate year of origin: 1965.
Current bodystyle lifespan: 1971 through 1978 (restyled in 1973 and 1975).
Predecessor to this model: Custom/Galaxie/LTD (1969 to 1970).
Replacement for this model: LTD (1979 to 1991).
Percentage of division's production: 23.73%.
Corporate siblings: Mercury Marquis.
Primary competition: Chevrolet Impala/Caprice, Dodge Royal Monaco, Plymouth Gran Fury, and Pontiac Catalina.
Notable changes: Minor trim and detail changes.
Major standard equipment: Redondo cloth and vinyl front bench seat, color-keyed nylon loop pile carpeting, woodtone I/P and door appliqués, deluxe steering wheel, interior courtesy lighting, bright moldings (front and rear window, belt, drip rail, rear hood edge, and wheel lip), vinyl insert bodyside moldings, textured lower rear appliqué w/bright Reflex surround molding, rocker panel molding, C-pillar LTD crest (4-door), hood ornament, front bumper guards, chrome hubcaps, and HR78 × 15 BSW tires. Wagon adds: Ruffino all vinyl bench seat, fold-down rear seat, power tailgate window, sound insulation package, and JR78 × 15 BSW tires. Landau adds: Ardmore cloth and vinyl "Flight Bench" seat w/fold-down center armrests, front seatback assist straps, 22-oz. shag carpeting, electric clock, luxury steering wheel, luxury door trim panels, burled walnut I/P and door trim appliqués, rear door courtesy light switch, electric clock, luggage compartment light, half-vinyl roof (2-door), full vinyl roof (4-door), dual accent paint stripes, wide vinyl insert bodyside moldings, hidden headlights, and full wheel covers. Country Squire adds: Simulated woodgrain exterior bodyside and tailgate paneling, cargo area light, hidden headlights, and full wheel covers.

Measurements

	2-Doors	4-Doors	Wagons
Wheelbase	121.0"	121.0"	121.0"
Length	224.1"	224.1"	225.6"
Width	79.5"	79.5"	79.9"
Height	53.7"	54.8"	56.7"
Legroom — front	41.5"	41.5"	41.7"
Legroom — rear	35.5"	38.3"	37.1"
Headroom — front	37.3"	38.3"	38.7"
Headroom — rear	37.3"	37.3"	39.1"
Cargo capacity (cu. ft.)	21.9	21.9	94.6*
Fuel capacity (gals.)	24.2	24.2	21.0

Additional 9.1 cu. ft. of below deck storage on 2-seat wagons, and 5.4 cu. ft. on wagons w/DFRS.

Models Available

	Model No.	Base MSRP	Change from LY	Shipping Wt. (lbs.)	Model Year Production	Change from LY
LTD 2-Door Pillared Hardtop	62	$5,128	+0.57%	4190	73,637	+17.17%
LTD 4-Door Pillared Hardtop	63	$5,152	+0.85%	4240	160,255	+48.15%

	Model No.	Base MSRP	Change from LY	Shipping Wt. (lbs.)	Model Year Production	Change from LY
LTD 4-Door, 2-Seat, 6-p. Station Wagon	74	$5,415	+0.95%	4635	90,711*	NA*
LTD Landau 2-Door Pillared Hardtop	65	$5,717	+2.35%	4270	44,396	+49.62%
LTD Landau 4-Door Pillared Hardtop	64	$5,742	+1.96%	4319	65,030	+82.35%
LTD Country Squire 4-Door, 2-seat, 6-p. Wagon	74	$5,866	+1.53%	4674	NA*	NA*
TOTALS	Avg. price	$5,503	+4.15%	Production	434,029	+18.02%

*Production of 1977 Country Squire combined with base LTD wagon, so comparison to 1976 is not possible.

LINCOLN

"Designed to justify your high expectations of riding comfort, style and luxury."

1977

The 1977 model year was a successful one for Lincoln. An all-new smaller Lincoln, the Versailles, was the marque's first attempt to sell a smaller Lincoln since the Zephyr was introduced in the mid–1930s. Arriving at mid-year, the Versailles appeared to be a worthy competitor for the Cadillac Seville, but consumers would quickly tell Lincoln otherwise. Also, a newly redesigned and redesignated Continental Mark V was introduced. Noteworthy for 1977 was the fact that this was Lincoln's first year for the traditional full-size Continentals to compete against the newly downsized Cadillac models. While the Cadillac deVille saw sales rise more than 20 percent, the Lincoln Continental coupe and sedan had a nearly 40 percent increase, albeit at a volume less than half of Cadillac's. Still it was a good showing for Lincoln, which achieved a record model year production of 191,355, and the best production and sales volumes for the regular Lincoln Continental coupe and sedan line since the introduction of the first all-new post–World War II Lincolns in 1949.

Versailles was Lincoln's attempt to improve the corporate average fuel economy for the upcoming implementation of an average 18 miles per gallon requirement for the 1978 model year. It was also intended as a direct competitor to the highly successful Cadillac Seville. To that end, Lincoln based its new car on the popular Ford Granada and Mercury Monarch twins introduced for the 1975 model year. Everything about the Versailles' chassis and powertrain setup, as well as its exterior design, was shared with these two cars, with only a few exceptions: the front end and hood design, the bumpers, the rear decklid, and trim — both inside and out. One of the Versaille's most notable features was probably unknown to most consumers. That was the U.S. auto industry's first application of base coat/clear coat paint. First developed in Europe, the process used basecoats of highly pigmented enamel paint, followed by additional coats of clear acrylic enamel, resulting in a smooth and lustrous finish. Within thirty years, nearly every new car sold would use this type of paint process. Additionally, Lincoln developed a quality control measure for the paint process by using a "Distinctness of Image" (or DI) meter, which used a beam of light to measure the reflectivity of the paint to a calibrated standard, to provide a consistent finish with maximum gloss for each Versailles.

The Versailles front end presented a vertical bar grille in keeping with Lincoln tradition. Narrower than the Granada's, it required a more pointed and raised center hood section. The grille itself consisted of five chrome-lined vertical sections per side, with each section having three less prominent argent colored vertical bars within, and a small gap down the center between the two sides. The entire grille was surround in chrome. A Lincoln logo stand-up hood ornament sat above the grille atop the chrome surround, while a Versailles insignia was placed above the center of the grille on the face of the chrome surround. Pointed fender end caps seemingly extended forward farther than the Granada and Monarch, and housed vertical wrap-around parking/turn signal and side marker lamps. Between the grille and fender caps were Lincoln's first dual rectangular headlights, set above horizontal parking/turn signal lamps.

Taillights were of a horizontal design in basically the same format as those of the Granada and Monarch, but having a forward slanting end as they wrapped around on the rear quarter panel. The taillights had a silver outlined center section inset within the lens that housed the small backup lights at the inner ends. The rear decklid was similar, yet completely different from the Ford and Mercury twins, as it used the "Continental" spare tire hump made famous by the Continental Mark series. A door at the lower center portion of the decklid gave access to the fuel filler cap. Bodysides and greenhouse design were all taken straight from the Granada and Monarch, but using upper bodyside moldings which ran from the top of the front side marker/parking lights, straight to the top edge of the taillights, whereas the Granada and Monarch used lower bodyside moldings.

Under the hood, the Versailles was powered by Ford's long-running 351 CID, 2-barrel V8 engine, except in California and high-altitude areas where the newer 302 CID V8 was standard equipment. Both engines were mated to a standard Select-shift automatic transmission. Inside the Versailles, the resemblance to its siblings was also apparent, with the upholstery and trim being the only hints that this was a more luxurious car. The instrument panel was modified to use square, brushed aluminum gauges and simulated walnut wood trim appliqués in keeping with the current Continental's design. Also to keep up with the bigger Continental's look inside, the same steering wheels, similar upholstery materials, and the same application of insulation and other materials were used to provide the quietest of rides.

Although Lincoln took the same approach that Cadillac did, by using components of existing models to create a new "smaller" sedan, Lincoln underestimated the power of styling and design. Whereas the Seville's shared components with the Chevrolet Nova were entirely unseen by consumers with the Seville's unique extended chassis, body panels, roofline and interior, the Versailles was very obviously built from the Ford Granada and Mercury Monarch body, sharing many body panels and interior components, as well as most of the chassis features. In fact, a fully equipped 1976 Mercury Grand Monarch Ghia sedan would have been very much like the Versailles, aside from the front and rear-end appearance. More than 15,000 Versailles sedans were built in its first six months of production, but because consumers justifiably perceived the Versailles as nothing more than a gussied up Mercury Monarch at more than twice the price, not nearly that many were sold, and dealers still had some of the first year's models well into the 1978 model year.

In brighter Lincoln news, the Continental Mark V debuted with a more modern, angular look, while maintaining much of the look and feel of the Mark IV, and riding on essentially the same chassis and body structure. The use of lighter weight materials allowed the Mark V to lose nearly 400 pounds of weight, and with the smaller 400 CID V8 engine as standard equipment, it also gained, however slightly, in fuel economy. The new Mark V vertical bar grille was identical in appearance to the Versailles grille as described previously. Also similar was the use of vertical wraparound parking/turn signal lights in the fender end caps, though the Mark V used clear lenses. The tradition of hidden headlights that began with the Mark III continued on the Mark V.

Along the bodysides and in the greenhouse area, the roundness of the Mark IV was gone, and in its place were straight, flat planes and angular corners. An upper bodyside feature line ran straight back from the upper front fender corner to near the top of the taillamp bezel, where it angled downward to follow the slope of the rear end, ending at the rear bumper. This was also the line that the pinstriping followed on cars so equipped. The lower feature line ran between the bumpers, passing over the wheel openings to create a flare, just as the Mark IV had used. Three functional fender louvers were added on the front fenders to aid in cooling of the engine compartment. The rear end now used tall vertical taillamps divided into five sections by the chrome bezel. Backup lights were mounted in the bumper below the "Continental" spare tire design on the deck lid, and next to the design above the bumper, between it and the taillights were horizontal taillights and reflectors. The greenhouse area bore the most prominent changes, with a triangular fixed rear quarter window and a more angular roof edge leading down into the rear window. The look was quite similar to the newly redesigned and downsized Ford Thunderbird, which had been the Mark IV's corporate twin through 1976.

Finally, the Continental coupe and sedan entered 1977 with a new vertical bar grille that was narrower and appeared taller. Unlike the Versailles and Mark V, the Continental grille contained about 40 vertical bars, with no segmentation, but it kept a similar large chrome surround. The Continental continued to have a stand-up Lincoln hood ornament, as well as the Lincoln Continental nameplate on the driver's side headlamp door. Another change was that the Continental began the year with the 460 CID V8 engine as standard equipment, except in California, but sometime shortly after the start of the year, the 400 CID V8 engine became standard equipment for all Continentals, except in designated high altitude counties. There was one new interesting option for 1977, a fixed moonroof. Basically a new take on the 1954–1956 Ford Crown Victoria and Mercury Sun Valley's tinted glass roof over the forward passenger compartment, the Lincoln moonroof included a sliding sunshade and ended at the B-pillar, so it was slightly larger on the coupes than on sedans because of the longer doors on coupes.

Continental 4-Door Sedan
with Town Car package

Continental fixed moonroof, left
and sliding moonroof option, right

Versailles 4-Door Sedan

Continental Mark V brochure introduction:
from front, 1940 Continental, 1956 Mark II,
1968 Mark III, 1972 Mark IV

Continental Mark V 2-Door Hardtop Coupe

Versailles interior

Versailles 4-Door Sedan

1977

Model year production: 191,355, up 53.38% from 1976.
Domestic market share: 1.99% (12th place).
Base price range: $9,474 to $11,500.
Lincoln average base price: $10,502, up 6.81%.
Introduction date: October 1, 1976; Versailles introduced March 28, 1977.
Assembly plants: Allen Park, MI (S—*pilot plant*); Wayne, MI (W), and Wixom, MI (Y).
Data plate identification (VIN): Eleven digit code read as

follows: First digit indicates year (7 = 1977); second digit indicates assembly plant code (see list above); third and fourth digits indicate model number (model number in model charts); fifth digit indicates engine code (see power-train chart); remaining digits are sequential with beginning numbers of 800001. *Example:* 7Y82A800001 is a 1977 Lincoln Continental 4-Door Sedan, with 460 CID, 4-bbl. V8 engine, serial number 800001, built in Wixom, MI.

Powertrains

Engine	Net HP	Engine. Code	Transmission Availability		Versailles	Continental	Continental Mark V
302 CID (5.0L), 2-bbl., V8	161	H	3-speed Select-Shift automatic[1]		S[2]	—	—
				MPG:			
				Calif.	NA	—	—
351 CID (5.8L), 2-bbl., V8	161	H	3-speed Select-Shift automatic[1]		S	—	—
				MPG:	NA	—	—
				Calif.	NA	—	—
400 CID (6.6L), 2-bbl., V8	179	S	3-speed Select-Shift automatic		—	S[2]	S
				MPG:	—	13/18/15	13/18/15
				Calif.	—	NA	NA

Engine	Net HP	Engine. Code	Transmission Availability	Versailles	Continental	Continental Mark V
460 CID (7.5L), 4-bbl., V8[3]	208	A	3-speed Select-Shift automatic	— MPG: —	S[2] 11/16/13	$133 11/16/13

[1]Floor shift available on Versailles for $33 with optional Reclining Bucket Seat group.   [2]400 CID V8 required as standard in California, and not available in 49 states. After start of year became standard equipment in all areas, with the 460 CID V8 engine being $133 extra, except in California.   [3]Not available in California. Required in high-altitude areas.

Major Options

	Versailles	Continental	Mark V
Air conditioning, Auto-Temp	S	S	S
Tilt steering wheel	$73	$73	$73
Automatic speed control	$117	$117	$117
Electric rear window defroster	$83	$83	$83
Quick Defrost, front/rear windows	—	—	$
Tinted glass, all windows	S	S	S
Power windows	S	S	S
Power front vent windows	—	$84	$
Power door locks	$[1]	$[1]	$[1]
Illuminated entry system	S	$56	$56
Power seat, 6-way w/pass. recliner	S[2]	$225	$223
Leather seating upholstery	$	$235	$252
RH remote-control mirror, LH std.	S	$32	$32
Intermittent windshield wipers	S	$31	$31
AM/FM stereo, w/power antenna[3]	—	$144	$144
AM/FM stereo w/8-track tape	($84)	$373	$373
AM/FM stereo w/automatic search	S	$287	$287
Vinyl top, full[4]	S	$179	$187
Fixed glass moonroof w/sun shade	—	$960	—
Moonroof, power-operated & tinted	$960	$960	$960
Power brakes, four wheel disc	S	—	S
"Sure-Track" antilock brake system	—	$463	$280
Luxury wheel covers	—	$88	S
Cast aluminum turbine-style wheels	—	$333	$267
Forged aluminum wheels	S	$333	$267

Popular Option Groups & Packages

	Versailles	Continental	Mark V
Appearance protection group	$55	$67	$63
Bill Blass designer series	—	—	$1,600
Cartier designer series	—	—	$2,100[5]
Cordovan luxury group	—	—	$640
Dark Jade/Light Jade luxury group	—	—	$640[6]
Defroster group	—	$107	$107
Emilio Pucci designer series	—	—	$1,600
Givenchy designer series	—	—	$2,100[5]
Gold/Cream luxury group	—	—	$640[6]
Headlamp Convenience group	—	$109	$109
Interior light group	—	$120	$120
Majestic velour luxury group	—	—	$1,300
Power Lock convenience group	$123[1]	$123[1]	$95[1]
Reclining Bucket seat group	$450	—	—
Red/Rose luxury group	—	—	$640[6]
Midnight Blue/Cream luxury group	—	—	$640
Town Coupe/Town Car package	—	$925	—
Williamsburg Limited Edition	—	$1,413[5]	—

— = Not Available; S = Standard equipment.   [1]Power door locks require optional Power Lock convenience group. Price on coupe is $95.   [2]Four-way power seat on Versailles.   [3]Citizen Band (CB) radio available for $269, and includes power antenna in right rear quarter panel.   [4]Landau vinyl roof w/frenched seams and rear window available on Continental Mark V for $457. Fully padded coach vinyl roof is available on Continental w/Town Car or Town Coupe option for $279. Coach *vinyl roof includes wide vinyl padded roof bow molding and fully padded custom half-vinyl roof w/frenched rear window and side quarter windows.   [5]Price with leather seats is $1,600.   [6]Price is $725 when ordered with Diamond Fire paint.*

Paint Colors

	Code[1]		Code[1]
Black	1C	Cinnamon Gold moondust metallic[3,4,5]	5K
Silver Diamond Fire metallic[2]	*1J*	Midnight Cordovan[3,4]	5L
Black Diamond Fire metallic[2]	1L	Cordovan metallic[4]	5R
Dove Gray	1N	Cream	6P
Medium Gray metallic (two-tone only)	1P	Tan	6U
Medium Silver metallic[3]	1S	Bright Yellow Gold Diamond Fire metallic	6Y
Light Silver metallic[4]	1T	Light Jade Crystal metallic	7B
Light Silver metallic	1Y	Light Jade metallic	7Y
Red Moondust metallic[5]	2G	Light Apricot Crystal metallic	8A
Dark Diamond Fire Red metallic[2]	2S	Cordovan metallic	8N
Rose Crystal metallic	2T	Light Cordovan	8P
Midnight Blue[4]	31	Medium Ember Diamond Fire metallic[2]	8V
Medium Blue Diamond Fire metallic[2]	32	Medium Nectar Diamond Fire metallic[2]	8Z
Midnight Blue metallic[3]	35	White	9D
Wedgewood Blue[4]	36	White[4]	9F
Medium Blue metallic	37		
Bright Dark Blue metallic	3G		
Light Blue	3U		
Dark Jade metallic	46		
Light Chamois[4]	5G		

In two-tone combinations, first two digits are lower color, and second two digits are upper color. [1]Versailles two-tone combinations: 31/36, 5K/5G, 5L/8N, and 1S/1Y. [2]Diamond Fire metallic paints available for $205 extra. [3]On Versailles, available as lower body two-tone paint only. [4]Only colors available on Versailles. [5]Moondust metallic paints available for $153 extra.

Versailles

"An investment in engineering."

Nameplate year of origin: 1977½ (1975 as a Continental option package).
Current bodystyle lifespan: 1977½ through 1980.
Predecessor to this model: None.
Replacement for this model: Continental (1982 to 1987).
Percentage of division's production: 8.07%.
Corporate siblings: Ford Granada and Mercury Monarch.
Primary competition: Cadillac Seville.
Notable changes: All-new model.
Major standard equipment: Luxury all nylon "Flight Bench" front seat w/four-way power adjustment, folding center armrests in front and rear seat, deep-pile carpeting, simulated wood appliqués on I/P, steering wheel and doors, leather steering wheel and I/P pad, rear passenger and front passenger side roof rail assist straps, package shelf w/Kasman fabric, Cartier-signed digital clock, power windows, AM/FM Multiplex radio w/power antenna, automatic temperature control air conditioning, LH and RH illuminated visor vanity mirrors, LH and RH remote control rearview mirror, tinted glass, power deck lid release, interior lighting (ashtrays, courtesy, glove box, luggage compartment, dome/map, and rear seat reading), 18-oz. color-keyed carpeted luggage compartment floor w/14oz. carpeted decklid liner, full vinyl roof, coach lamps, illuminated entry system, cornering lights, high luster bodyside molding w/vinyl insert, bumper protection group, forged aluminum wheels, and FR78 × 14 wide WSW tires.

Measurements

Wheelbase	109.9"
Length	200.9"
Width	75.1"
Height	54.1"
Legroom — front	40.7"
Legroom — rear	35.6"
Headroom — front	38.2"
Headroom — rear	37.6"
Cargo capacity (cu. ft.)	14.1
Fuel capacity (gals.)	19.2

Models Available

	Model No.	Base MSRP	Change from LY	Shipping Wt. (lbs.)	Model Year Production	Change from LY
Versailles 4-Door Sedan	84	$11,500	NEW	3759	15,434	NEW
TOTALS	*Avg. price*	$11,500	NEW	*Production*	15,434	NEW

Continental

"A standard by which luxury cars are judged."

Nameplate year of origin: 1940 (1961 as a regular series).
Current bodystyle lifespan: 1970 through 1979 (restyled in 1974).
Predecessor to this model: Continental (1961 to 1969).
Replacement for this model: Town Car (1980 to 1991).
Percentage of division's production: 49.96%.
Corporate siblings: None.
Primary competition: Cadillac deVille.
Notable changes: Restyled grille and minor trim and detail changes.
Major standard equipment: Luxury cloth front bench seat w/six-way power adjustment, folding center armrests in front and rear seat, cut-pile carpeting, simulated wood appliqués on I/P and steering wheel, Cartier-signed digital clock, power windows, AM/FM radio w/power antenna, automatic temperature control air conditioning, visor-mounted vanity mirror, LH remote control rearview mirror, tinted glass, power deck lid release, interior lighting (ashtrays, courtesy, glove box, luggage compartment, dome/map, and rear seat reading), fully lined and carpeted luggage compartment w/tire cover, full vinyl roof, cornering lights, bright rocker panel moldings w/rear extensions, rear wheel opening fender skirts, front and rear bumper guards w/pad and rub strips, deluxe wheel covers, and KR78 × 15 WSW Michelin tires.

Measurements

	Coupe	Sedan
Wheelbase	127.2"	127.2"
Length	233.0"	233.0"
Width	80.0"	80.0"
Height	55.3"	55.2"
Legroom — front	42.0"	42.0"
Legroom — rear	41.3"	42.0"
Headroom — front	38.0"	38.1"
Headroom — rear	38.1"	38.6"
Cargo capacity (cu. ft.)	20.2	20.2
Fuel capacity (gals.)	24.2	24.2

Models Available

	Model No.	Base MSRP	Change from LY	Shipping Wt. (lbs.)	Model Year Production	Change from LY
Continental 2-Door Hardtop Coupe	81	$9,474	+3.63%	4836	27,440	+11.26%
Continental 4-Door Sedan	82	$9,636	+3.69%	4880	68,160	+54.97%
TOTALS		*Avg. price* $9,555	+3.66%		*Production* 95,600	+43.15%

Continental Mark V

"In the tradition of the first Continentals."

Nameplate year of origin: 1956 (Continental Mark II).
Current bodystyle lifespan: 1977 through 1979.
Predecessor to this model: Continental Mark IV (1972 to 1976).
Replacement for this model: Continental Mark VI (1980 to 1983).
Percentage of division's production: 41.97%.
Corporate siblings: None.
Primary competition: Buick Riviera, Cadillac Eldorado, and Oldsmobile Toronado.
Notable changes: Completely restyled and renamed.
Major standard equipment: Velour "Twin Comfort" lounge seats w/six-way power adjustment, folding center armrests in front and rear seat, walnut woodgrain appliqué on I/P and steering wheel, color-keyed cut-pile carpeting, visor vanity mirror, electric Cartier Timepiece, trip odometer, power windows, AM/FM radio w/power antenna, automatic temperature control air conditioning, LH remote control rearview mirror, tinted glass, door panel courtesy lights, power decklid release, fully lined luggage compartment, full vinyl roof w/opera window, dual custom pinstripe, customer monogram on doors, functional fender louvers, cornering lights, front and rear bumper guards w/pads and rub strips, luxury wheel covers, and JR78 × 15 WSW Michelin tires.

Measurements

Wheelbase	120.4"
Length	230.3"
Width	79.8"
Height	53.0"
Legroom — front	42.3"
Legroom — rear	34.0"
Headroom — front	37.5"
Headroom — rear	37.1"
Cargo capacity (cu. ft.)	18.1
Fuel capacity (gals.)	26.0

Models Available

	Model No.	Base MSRP	Change from LY	Shipping Wt. (lbs.)	Model Year Production	Change from LY
Continental Mark V 2-Door Hardtop	89	$11,396	+3.04%	4652	80,321	+43.15%
TOTALS	*Avg. price*	$11,396	+3.04%	*Production*	80,321	+43.15%

MERCURY

"Who says they don't build them like they used to?
Prove it for yourself … at the sign of the cat."

Mercury's line of cars for 1977 featured redesigned mid-size models renamed with the popular Cougar nameplate, while the rest of the line was mostly carried over. The new Cougar line was a restyled continuation of the Montego that was retired at the end of the 1976 model year. A full line of two-doors, four-doors, and even a Cougar station wagon was offered. The top-line Cougar XR-7 differed slightly in appearance, and was marketed within the rest of the Cougar line, but was more directly related to the downsized Ford Thunderbird, a connection the XR-7 would keep through the end of its use as a nameplate in 1997. Other landmarks for the year included introduction of a new "DuraSpark" solid-state ignition system, the final season of production for the Comet, and the final season for the European Ford Capri to be imported.

In revamping the former Montego line, Mercury hoped to capitalize on the popularity of the Cougar name. Sales did increase, but mostly in the entry-level coupe and sedan models, and after a single model year the high-end Brougham series and the station wagons would be gone. With the Cougar XR-7 more closely related to the Ford Thunderbird, it carried all of the same general styling features of the Cougar line as described here, but the XR-7 will continue to be presented in the model listings as a separate line, as Mercury promoted the whole line as a new car only for this model year, and for 1978 and beyond, they would again become separated.

The new Cougar, like its twin the Ford LTD II, adopted the angular styling that was becoming commonplace on cars of the period, with mostly straight and unadorned bodysides, straight beltlines, and angular window and rooflines. Up front, all Cougars shared new dual rectangular side-by-side headlamps, with a Lincoln-style vertical bar chrome grille consisting of six vertical sections with each having three vertical bars inset. Leading front fender edges were pointed and extended forward, housing the parking/turn signal lamps in the ends, leaving the headlights set back between the grille and the fenders. Along the bodysides, a feature line ran between the top edges of the front and rear bumpers, creating a flare over the wheel openings. Another extended the line of the front fender under the side windows. At the rear, the coupes and sedans used a vertical, wraparound taillamp divided into two sections by a horizontal bar. In a body-color panel below the trunklid, a nearly full-width strip held a taillight and backup light at each end and a reflective section in the center carrying the Cougar name in block letters, with the entire area in a chrome bezel. The XR-7 boasted its own unique rear-end styling with horizontal, wraparound taillights divided into six sections, with the second from the inside housing the backup light. The taillights ended at a pronounced center section of the decklid that extended to bumper level, intentionally mimicking a Continental Mark V spare tire design, though in more angular form.

In the greenhouse area, the Cougar wagons differed from the other models in essentially continuing the design of the Montego wagons since 1973. This was the most obvious connection to prior cars of any of the Cougar models. Regular Cougar coupes had a vertical rectangular fixed rear quarter window, which slanted forward slightly. Brougham models added a quasi-rectangular opera window. Cougar sedans had similarly angled rear door windows, and the Brougham sedan added a more triangular shaped opera window. The Cougar XR-7 used a roofline similar to Cougar coupes, but had a unique opera window in a similar shape with three vertical louvers on the leading edge, and a Cougar cat emblem affixed to the B-pillar. The XR-7's quarter window was narrower than that of Cougar coupes and leaned forward more at its leading edge, forming a parallelogram shape. Interiors of all Cougars were similar in basic layout, but used new materials and stitch designs to give a more luxurious appearance over the Montego.

Powering the Cougar line was Mercury's first use of the 302 CID V8 engine in its mid-size lineup. The smaller engine and somewhat lighter cars provided higher fuel economy for all models. Standard on station wagons was the 351 CID V8 engine, which was also available on the other models, and the 400 CID V8 engine was optional for all Cougars. The 460 CID V8 engine was offered only on the Marquis for 1977. By the end of the year, the Cougar XR-7 alone would have the highest production total since the Cougar introductory year of 1967.

The subcompact Bobcat continued with few changes, unlike its Ford Pinto twin, which added new front-end styling. The wood paneled Villager Wagon technically became an option package for this year, as the Bobcat wagon without woodgrain became available for the first time; however, in most references, including Ford Motor Company documents, it is listed as a separate model, despite sharing the same model number with the base, non-woodgrain station wagon. Other changes for the Bobcat included anodized aluminum front and rear bumpers to save weight, Mercury's new "DuraSpark" ignition system, and a few new options like an all-glass third door, and a flip-up/removable glass moonroof.

Comet, Monarch and Marquis series all had very few changes for the new year; in fact the Comet had virtually no changes for its final year. The Monarch line dropped the luxurious Grand Monarch Ghia, mostly as a move to make room for the mid-year Lincoln Versailles, which was based on the Ford Granada and Mercury Monarch platform. The new-for-1975 Monarch continued to be a popular Mercury offering, although with the downsizing of GM's full-size models, the Marquis became the top-selling Mercury for 1977. The

biggest change in the full-size Mercury line was to make the Colony Park an option package after nearly 20 years as a successful Mercury model. Other Marquis models had some new trim choices and a few new colors, but were otherwise mostly carry-over models.

The imported Capri had few changes for the 1977 model year, and although the "II" was officially dropped from the Capri name, the 1977 Capri was still usually referred to as a "Capri II." This year also saw Ford of Europe introduce its "triple stalk controls" for the lights, wipers and washers, and the "High Energy" ignition system, both of which made their way into the Capri. Under the hood, one noteworthy change was the introduction of the Motorcraft variable-venturi carburetor, which was used on all 2.8 liter V6 equipped Capris sold California. The new carburetor offered a combination of low exhaust emissions with better drivability and improved fuel economy, but unfortunately it proved too complex and troublesome, and caused Capri owners, and Ford, a lot of headaches. Two option packages were featured for 1977, the all-new "Rally Cat" featuring twin white racing stripes front to rear, with a rear deck spoiler, and the "Le Cat" Black Capri S that was basically the same as the "Black Cat" of 1976, featuring a choice of black or white exterior with gold striping, dual racing mirrors, heavy-duty suspension, gold luxury cloth seating with black trim and instrument panel, and a console. Officially, 1977 was the last year for the European Capri built to U.S. specifications to be imported. However, it continued to be sold well into the 1978 model year until inventory was exhausted. In some areas of the country, 1977 models were modified with dealer installed trim kits, and registered and sold as 1978 models.

Capri II 2-Door Hatchback Coupe
with Le Cat Black package

Bobcat Villager 2-Door Station Wagon

Capri II 2-Door Hatchback Coupe
with Rally Cat package

Comet 4-Door Sedan with Custom trim (front)
and Comet 2-Door Sedan (rear)

Bobcat 3-Door Runabout Hatchback
with optional glass rear door

Cougar 2-Door Hardtop Coupe

Cougar Brougham 2-Door Hardtop
Coupe (front) and Cougar Villager
4-Door Station Wagon (rear)

Cougar Brougham 4-Door Pillared Hardtop

Cougar Villager 4-Door Station Wagon

Cougar XR-7 2-Door Hardtop Coupe

Grand Marquis 4-Door Pillared Hardtop

Marquis 4-Door Station Wagon
with Colony Park option

Marquis Brougham 2-Door Hardtop

Monarch Ghia 2-Door Sedan interior with
leather bucket seat option

Monarch 2-Door Sedan with S option (left)
and Monarch 4-Door Sedan

1977

Model year production: 531,549, up 10.66% from 1976.
Domestic market share: 5.54% (6th place).
Base price range: $3,438 to $6,975.
Mercury average base price: $4,962, up 4.21%.
Introduction date: October 1, 1976.
Assembly plants: Atlanta, GA (A); Lorain, OH (H); Kansas City, MO (K); San Jose, CA (R); Metuchen, NJ (T); Wayne, MI (W); St. Thomas, Ontario, Canada (X); and St. Louis, MO (Z). Capri assembly plant: Cologne, Germany (A).
Data plate identification (VIN): Eleven digit code read as follows: First digit indicates year (7 = 1977); second digit indicates assembly plant code (see list above); third and fourth digits indicate model number (model number in model charts); fifth digit indicates engine code (see powertrain chart); remaining digits are sequential with beginning numbers of 500001. *Example:* 7K31F500001 is a 1977 Mercury Comet 2-Door sedan, with 302 CID, 2-bbl. V8 engine, serial number 500001, built in Kansas City (Claycomo), MO. 1977 Capri uses eleven digit code read as follows: First digit indicates country of origin (G = Germany); second digit indicates assembly plant code (see list above); third and fourth digits indicate model number (model number in model charts); fifth digit indicates year (T = 1977); sixth digit indicates month; remaining digits are sequential with beginning number of 00001.

Powertrains*

Engine	Net HP	Engine Code	Transmission Availability[1]		Bobcat	Capri	Comet	Monarch	Cougar	Marquis & Marquis Brougham	Grand Marquis
140 CID (2.3L) OHC, 2-bbl., 4-cyl.	89	Y	4-speed manual		S	S	—	—	—	—	—
				MPG:	26/37/ 30	25/36/ 30	—	—	—	—	—

Engine	Net HP	Engine Code	Transmission Availability[1]		Bobcat	Capri	Comet	Monarch	Cougar	Marquis & Marquis Brougham	Grand Marquis
				Calif.	24/34/28	NA	—	—	—	—	—
			3-speed Select-Shift automatic		$248	$276	—	—	—	—	—
				MPG:	23/32/26	23/32/26	—	—	—	—	—
				Calif.	22/30/25	22/30/25	—	—	—	—	—
170.8 CID (2.8L), 2-bbl., V6	93	Z	4-speed manual		—	$272	—	—	—	—	—
				MPG:	—	18/28/21	—	—	—	—	—
				Calif.	—	NA	—	—	—	—	—
			3-speed Select-Shift automatic		$530[2]	$548	—	—	—	—	—
				MPG:	18/23/20	18/25/21	—	—	—	—	—
				Calif.	17/20/18	17/22/19	—	—	—	—	—
200 CID (3.3L), 1-bbl., 6-cyl.	96	T	3-speed manual		—	—	S[3]	—	—	—	—
				MPG:	—	—	21/28/24	—	—	—	—
			4-speed manual w/overdrive		—	—	—	S (ex. Ghia)[3]	—	—	—
				MPG:	—	—	—	21/28/24	—	—	—
			3-speed Select-Shift automatic		—	—	$258[3]	$186 (ex. Ghia)[3]	—	—	—
				MPG:	—	—	18/24/20	18/24/20	—	—	—
250 CID (4.1L), 1-bbl., 6-cyl.	98	L	3-speed manual		—	—	$96[3]	—	—	—	—
				MPG:	—	—	16/25/19	—	—	—	—
			4-speed manual w/overdrive		—	—	—	S (Ghia)[3]/ $96 (others)[3]	—	—	—
				MPG:	—	—	—	21/28/24	—	—	—
			3-speed Select-Shift automatic		—	—	$354[4]	$186 (Ghia)[4]/ $282 (others)[4]	—	—	—
				MPG:	—	—	17/22/19	18/23/20	—	—	—
				Calif.	—	—	18/23/20	16/20/18	—	—	—
302 CID (5.0L), 2-bbl., V8	137	F	4-speed manual w/overdrive		—	—	—	$90 (Ghia)/ $187 (others)	—	—	—
				MPG:	—	—	—	16/24/18	—	—	—
				Calif.	—	—	—	NA	—	—	—
			3-speed Select-Shift automatic		—	—	$410	$276 (Ghia)/ $372 (others)	S (ex. Wgns.)[3]	—	—
				MPG:	—	—	17/22/19	16/22/18	15/19/17	—	—
				Calif.	—	—	13/18/14	13/20/16	—	—	—

Engine	Net HP	Engine Code	Transmission Availability[1]	Bobcat	Capri	Comet	Monarch	Cougar	Marquis & Marquis Brougham	Grand Marquis
351 CID (5.8L), 2-bbl., V8	161	H	3-speed Select-Shift automatic	—	—	—	$337 (Ghia)/ $433 (others)	S (Wgns.)[3]/ $66 (others)[4]	—	—
			MPG:	—	—	—	NA	14/20/ 16	—	—
			Calif.	—	—	—	NA	12/18/ 14	—	—
400 CID (6.6L), 2-bbl., V8	173	S	3-speed Select-Shift automatic	—	—	—	—	$66 (Wgns.)[4]/ $132 (others)	S	S[4]
			MPG:	—	—	—	—	13/18/ 15	13/18/ 15	—
			Calif.	—	—	—	—	10/16/ 12	10/16/ 12	10/16/ 12
460 CID (7.5L), 4-bbl., V8	197	A	3-speed Select-Shift automatic MPG:	— —	— —	— —	— —	— —	$132[3] 11/16/ 13	S[3] 11/16/ 13

Optional axle ratio required on some cars sold in California. Due to numerous variations they are not included within this section. [1]Unless otherwise noted: All manual transmissions are floor-shift, except on Comet. All automatics are column-shift, except on Bobcat and Capri II. Floor-shift is available for $30 extra on Monarch with optional bucket seats and automatic, and standard with "S" option group. Floor-shift w/bucket seats and console is also available for $247 on Cougar 2-door, and for $175 on Cougar 2-door with Brougham option and Cougar XR-7. [2]Station wagons require power front disc brakes at extra cost. [3]Not available in California. [4]Standard in California.

Major Options

	Bobcat	Capri	Comet	Monarch	Cougar	Marquis
Air conditioning[1]	$437	$429	$437	$461	$505	$539
Tilt steering wheel	—	—	—	$58	$63	$64
Automatic speed control	—	—	—	$89	$97	$108
Rear window defogger	—	—	$43	$43	—	—
Electric rear window defroster	$70	$69	—	$75	$82	$82
Tinted glass, all windows	$47	$47	$46	$51	$57	$68
Dual remote control mirrors	—	$12[2]	$29[2]	$47	$51	$14[2]
Power windows, 2-dr./4-dr.	—	—	—	$105/$145	$114/$158	$134/$189
Power front vent windows, 4-door	—	—	—	—	—	$83
Power door locks, 2-dr./4-dr.	—	—	—	$66/$93	$[3]	$[3]
Power seat, 6-way w/std. seating	—	—	—	$131[4]	$143	$143
Front bucket seats w/console[5]	S	S	$[5]	$139	$207	—
Leather interior trim	—	—	—	$204	$241	—
Dual facing rear seats (wagons)[6]	—	—	—	—	$113	$163
AM radio	$72	$71	$72	$72	$79	$79
AM/FM stereo	$161	$216	$176	$176	$192	$192
AM/FM stereo w/8-track tape	—	—	$243	$243	$266	$266
Vinyl top, full	$133	$95	$86	$101	$161	$136[7]
Moonroof, power-operated	$147[8]	—	—	$855	$934	$934
Sunroof, power-operated	$245[8]	$181[8]	—	—	—	—
Power trunk lid release	—	—	—	$17	$[3]	$[3]
Power steering	$133	$129	$134	$127	S	S
Power brakes, w/front disc	$57	S	$55	$58[9]	S	S[9]
Rear wheel opening fender skirts	—	—	—	—	—	$43
Deluxe wheel covers	—	—	$27	$27	$29	—
Luxury wheel covers	—	—	—	—	$61	$80
Wire wheel covers	$92	—	$116	$92	$129	$100
Styled steel wheels w/trim rings	$88	—	$98	$90	$101	—
Cast aluminum sport wheels	—	$113	$234	$213	$239	—
Forged aluminum wheels	$159	—	—	—	—	$237
White sidewall tires, std. size	$37	—	$36	$37	$41	$45

Popular Option Groups & Packages

	Bobcat	Capri	Comet	Monarch	Cougar	Marquis
Appearance protection group	$37	—	$41	$41	$50	—
Bumper protection group	$61	—	$61	$63	$68	$55
Brougham décor group	—	—	—	—	$164	—
Colony Park option package	—	—	—	—	—	$351
Convenience group	—	—	—	$45	$97	—
Convenience/Visibility group	—	—	$96	—	—	—
Custom interior option	—	—	$312	—	—	—
Custom option package	—	—	$627	—	—	—
Décor group	—	$217	—	$192	—	—
Grand Marquis decor group[10]	—	—	—	—	—	$526
Light group	—	—	—	$43	$53	—
Light/Convenience group	$131	—	—	—	—	—
Lock Convenience group, 2-dr./4-dr.	—	—	—	—	—	$108/$136
Power lock group, 2-dr./4-dr.	—	—	—	—	$92/$121	—
"S" option group	$131	$241	—	$512	—	—
Sports Accent group/trim option	$308	—	$249	—	—	—
Sports Instrumentation group	—	—	—	—	$151	—
Sports Instrumentation/Handling group	$89	—	—	—	—	—
Visibility group	—	—	—	$52	—	$91
XR-7 décor group	—	—	—	—	$395	—

— = Not Available; S = Standard equipment. [1]Air conditioner w/automatic temperature control is available for $505 on Monarch, for $551 on Cougar, and for $578 on Marquis. [2]LH remote only on Capri. LH remote and RH manual on Comet. LH only on Marquis. [3]Available only as part of the Power Lock group (Cougar), or Lock Convenience group (Marquis). [4]Power four-way seat on Monarch. [5]Bucket seats only on Bobcat; console not available. Available on Comet 2-door, only with Custom Interior option, and does not include console. For Monarch, available only on Ghia, or with Décor group. For Cougar, available only on 2-doors. [6]Third row rear-facing seat in Cougar station wagon. [7]Vinyl roof available on station wagons for $151. [8]Manually operated. [9]Power four wheel disc brakes available for $273 on Monarch, and for $180 on Marquis. [10]Available only on Marquis station wagon, and requires Colony Park option package, for $351.

Paint Colors

Mercury	Code	Mercury	Code
Black	1C	Bright Saddle metallic	8K
Silver metallic	1G	Chamois metallic	8W
Dove Gray	1N	Champagne metallic	8Y
Medium Gray metallic (two-tone only)	1P	White	9D
Dark Red	2M		
Bright Red	2R	Capri	Code
Lipstick Red	2U		
Bright Dark Blue metallic	3G	Green metallic	27
Light Blue	3U	Blue metallic	67
Bright Blue Glamour metallic[1,2]	3V	Yellow	97
Dark Jade metallic	46	White	B7
Light Green	47	Orange	H7
Dark Yellow Green metallic	4V	Gold metallic	N7
Dark Brown metallic	5Q	Bright Red	R7
Bright Yellow	6E	Silver metallic	V7
Cream	6P		
Light Tan	6U	
Cinnamon Gold Glamour metallic[1,3]	6W	
Medium Gold metallic[1,4]	6V	
Light Jade Glamour metallic[1,5]	7L	
Vista Orange	8G	
Tan	8H	
Medium Tan metallic	8J	

In two-tone combinations, first two digits are lower color, and second two digits are upper color. Two-tones available on Comet for $41; Cougar (except wagons) for $104; Marquis Brougham 2-door for $197; Grand Marquis for $66. [1]Glamour paints available for $58 extra on Bobcat, Comet, and Monarch, and $63 on Cougar and Marquis. [2]Available only on Bobcat, Comet, Monarch, Cougar and Marquis. [3]Available only on Comet, Monarch and Cougar. [4]Available only on Comet, Monarch and Marquis. [5]Available only on Comet, Monarch, Cougar and Marquis.

Bobcat

"No wonder everybody loves that Bobcat ... it's such a good sport!"

Nameplate year of origin: 1975.
Current bodystyle lifespan: 1975 through 1980.
Predecessor to this model: None.
Replacement for this model: Lynx (1981 to 1985).
Percentage of division's production: 5.92%.
Corporate siblings: Ford Pinto.
Primary competition: AMC Gremlin, Dodge Colt, and Pontiac Astre.
Notable changes: Minor trim and detail changes.
Major standard equipment: All-vinyl low-back front bucket seats, color-keyed cut-pile carpeting, carpeted cargo area, fold-down rear seat, simulated woodgrain parking brake lever handle, shift knob, and I/P appliqué, deluxe two-spoke steering wheel, deluxe safety belts, bright window and belt moldings, B-pillar bright molding, wide wheel lip moldings, rocker panel moldings, rack-and-pinion steering, manual front disc brakes, deluxe wheel covers, and A78 × 13 BSW tires. Villager adds: Flip-out rear quarter windows, deluxe sound insulation, "Liftgate Ajar" warning system, standard size wheel lip moldings, and simulated rosewood paneling on bodysides and rear tailgate panel.

Measurements

	Runabout	Wagon
Wheelbase	94.5"	94.8"
Length	169.0"	178.8"
Width	69.4"	69.7"
Height	50.6"	52.0"
Legroom — front	40.8"	40.8"
Legroom — rear	30.4"	30.4"
Headroom — front	37.3"	37.9"
Headroom — rear	35.8"	38.9"
Cargo capacity (cu. ft.)	6.1*	57.7
Fuel capacity (gals.)	13.0	14.0

With rear seat folded down, 25.4 cu. ft.

Models Available

	Model No.	Base MSRP	Change from LY	Shipping Wt. (lbs.)	Model Year Production	Change from LY
Bobcat 3-Door Runabout (HBK)	20	$3,438	+3.00%	2369	18,405	-36.33%
Bobcat 2-Door Station Wagon	22	$3,629	NEW	2505	NA*	NEW*
Bobcat 2-Door Villager Wagon	22	$3,771	+3.51%	NA	13,047	-30.35%
TOTALS	Avg. price	$3,335	+3.50%	Production	31,452	-33.97%

Production of Bobcat wagon and Bobcat Villager wagon kept as combined total since both are the same model number.

Capri

*"A sexy European at a price surprisingly modest
for such an exciting piece or road machinery."*

Nameplate year of origin: 1971 (originally used on 1952 Lincoln Capri).
Current bodystyle lifespan: 1971 through 1977 (major restyle for 1976).
Predecessor to this model: None.
Replacement for this model: Capri (1979 to 1986).
Primary competition: Buick Skyhawk, Ford Mustang II 2+2, and Oldsmobile Starfire SX.
Notable changes: Minor trim and detail changes.
Major standard equipment: All-vinyl front bucket seats w/recliners, full-loop carpeting, front armrests, recessed door handles, fold-down rear seats, day/night rear view mirror, power front disc brakes, rack-and-pinion steering, styled steel wheels, and 165SR × 13 BSW tires. Ghia adds: Embossed vinyl front bucket seats, individually folding rear seats, front floor console, simulated woodgrain I/P appliqué, opening rear quarter window, assist handles front and rear on headliner, and upgraded sound insulation package.

Measurements

Wheelbase	100.9"
Length	174.8"
Width	66.9"
Height	51.0"
Legroom — front	41.4"
Legroom — rear	31.1"
Headroom — front	37.4"
Headroom — rear	35.9"
Cargo capacity (cu. ft.)	7.4*
Fuel capacity (gals.)	11.9

With rear seat folded down, 22.6 cu. ft.

Models Available

	Model No.	Base MSRP	Change from LY	Shipping Wt. (lbs.)	Model Year Sales (est.)	Change from LY
Capri 3-Door Sport Coupe	EC	$4,373	+6.22%	2513	NA	NA
Capri Ghia 3-Door Sport Coupe	EC	$4,585	-3.27%	2571	NA	NEW
TOTALS		*Avg. price* $4,479	+1.14%	*Production*	60,000	-29.41%

Comet

"Practical and stylish but one tough little car."

Nameplate year of origin: 1960.
Current bodystyle lifespan: 1971 through 1977.
Predecessor to this model: Comet (1964 to 1965).
Replacement for this model: Zephyr (1978 to 1983).
Percentage of division's production: 4.05%.
Corporate siblings: Ford Maverick.
Primary competition: AMC Hornet.
Notable changes: Minor trim and detail changes.
Major standard equipment: Cloth-and-vinyl front bench seat, color-keyed 12-oz. cut-pile carpeting, front and rear ashtrays w/front lighted, two-speed windshield wipers w/washers, deluxe two-spoke steering wheel, bright window moldings, deluxe sound insulation package, hubcaps, and C78 × 14 BSW tires.

Measurements

	2-Door	4-Door
Wheelbase	103.0"	109.9"
Length	189.4"	196.3"
Width	70.5"	70.5"
Height	53.5"	53.8"
Legroom — front	40.7"	40.7"
Legroom — rear	31.8"	36.0"
Headroom — front	37.5"	37.8"
Headroom — rear	35.9"	36.5"
Cargo capacity (cu. ft.)	11.3	12.8
Fuel capacity (gals.)	19.2	19.2

Models Available

	Model No.	Base MSRP	Change from LY	Shipping Wt. (lbs.)	Model Year Production	Change from LY
Comet 2-Door Sedan	31	$3,544	+4.30%	2960	9,109	-39.55%
Comet 4-Door Sedan	30	$3,617	+4.39%	3065	12,436	-40.80%
TOTALS		*Avg. price* $3,581	+4.34%	*Production*	21,545	-40.28%

Monarch

"The precision size car with a touch of class.
Ride-Engineered by Lincoln-Mercury."

Nameplate year of origin: 1975 (used on Canadian Ford brand from 1946 to 1961).
Current bodystyle lifespan: 1975 through 1980.
Predecessor to this model: None.
Replacement for this model: Cougar (1981 to 1982).
Percentage of division's production: 24.02%.
Corporate siblings: Ford Granada and Lincoln Versailles.
Primary competition: Buick Skylark, Dodge Aspen, and Oldsmobile Omega.
Notable changes: Minor trim and detail changes.
Major standard equipment: All-vinyl front bucket seats w/recliners, 18-oz. cut-pile carpeting, simulated high-gloss woodgrain I/P appliqué, locking glove box, bright window moldings, full-length bodyside molding, stand-up hood ornament, manual front disc brakes, wheel covers, and DR78 ×

Measurements

	2-door	4-door
Wheelbase	109.9"	109.9"
Length	197.7"	197.7"
Width	74.0"	74.0"
Height	53.4"	53.4"
Legroom — front	40.3"	40.3"
Legroom — rear	34.4"	36.1"
Headroom — front	38.0"	38.2"
Headroom — rear	36.5"	37.6"
Cargo capacity (cu. ft.)	14.8	14.8
Fuel capacity (gals.)	19.2	19.2

14 BSW tires. Ghia adds: Super-soft all-vinyl front bucket seats w/recliners, 22-oz. cut-pile shag carpeting, deluxe color-keyed seat belts, luxury steering wheel, digital clock, day/night rearview mirror, LH remote control outside mirror, carpeted luggage compartment, deluxe sound and ride package, Odense grain vinyl roof, chrome lower bodyside moldings w/Odense grain vinyl inserts, wheel lip moldings, unique Ghia wheel covers, and DR78 × 14 WSW tires.

Models Available

	Model No.	Base MSRP	Change from LY	Shipping Wt. (lbs.)	Model Year Production	Change from LY
Monarch 2-Door Sedan	35	$4,076	+8.03%	3123	44,509	-6.23%
Monarch 4-Door Sedan	34	$4,154	+7.51%	3173	55,592	-1.35%
Monarch Ghia 2-Door Sedan	38	$4,643	+7.20%	3244	11,051	-26.08%
Monarch Ghia 4-Door Sedan	37	$4,722	+6.78%	3305	16,545	-38.85%
TOTALS	Avg. price	$4,399	-0.62%	Production	127,697	-12.43%

Cougar

"A beautiful idea for families who would like to enter the exciting world of the Cat Set without a setback in their budget."

Nameplate year of origin: 1968.
Current bodystyle lifespan: 1977 through 1979.
Predecessor to this model: Montego (1972 to 1976).
Replacement for this model: Cougar (1981 to 1982).
Percentage of division's sales volume: 13.17%.
Corporate siblings: Ford LTD II.
Primary competition: AMC Matador, Buick Century, Dodge Monaco, Oldsmobile Cutlass, and Pontiac LeMans.
Notable changes: Completely restyled and renamed.
Major standard equipment: Cloth-and-vinyl front bench seat, color-keyed carpeting, simulated rosewood I/P trim, cut-pile color-keyed carpeting, two-spoke color-keyed steering wheel, deluxe sound package, windshield and rear window bright moldings, drip rail moldings, power steering, power front disc brakes, hubcaps, and HR78 × 14 BSW tires.

Measurements

	2-Doors	4-Doors	Wagons
Wheelbase	114.0"	118.0"	118.0"
Length	215.5"	219.5"	223.1"
Width	78.6"	78.6"	79.6"
Height	52.6"	53.3"	54.9"
Legroom — front	42.3"	42.3"	42.1"
Legroom — rear	32.8"	36.2"	37.1"
Headroom — front	37.3"	38.0"	38.3"
Headroom — rear	36.3"	37.0"	38.6"
Cargo capacity (cu. ft.)	14.7	14.7	93.0*
Fuel capacity (gals.)	26.0	26.0	21.3

*Includes 8.1 cu. ft. of hidden cargo space.

Wagon adds: All-vinyl front bench seat, three-way tailgate, power tailgate window, and carpeted load floor. Brougham adds: Cloth-and-vinyl "Flight Bench" front seat w/fold-down center armrest, deluxe two-spoke steering wheel w/woodgrain inserts, electric clock, day/night rearview mirror, Brougham door panels w/lower carpeting, full-length bodyside molding w/vinyl insert, and deluxe wheel covers. Villager adds: All-vinyl bench "Flight Bench" front seat w/fold-down center armrest, and simulated woodgrain bodyside and tailgate paneling w/bright surround moldings.

Models Available

	Model No.	Base MSRP	Change from LY*	Shipping Wt. (lbs.)	Model Year Production	Change from LY*
Cougar 2-Door Hardtop	91	$4,700	+5.26%	3811	15,910	+28.65%
Cougar 4-Door Pillared Hardtop	90	$4,832	+7.43%	3893	15,256	+20.45%
Cougar 4-Door, 6-pass. Station Wagon	92	$5,104	+6.82%	4434	4,951	-1.22%
Cougar Brougham 2-Door Hardtop	95	$4,990	+7.99%	3852	8,392	+114.90%
Cougar Brougham 4-Door Pillared HT	94	$5,230	+11.99%	3946	16,946	+236.03%
Cougar Villager 4-Door, 6-pass. Wagon	96	$5,363	+5.88%	4482	8,569	+33.64%
TOTALS	Avg. price	$5,037	+9.67%	Production	70,024	+37.05%

*Comparisons made to equivalent 1976 Montego MX and MX Brougham models.

Cougar XR-7

"A car like nobody else's car. Again!"

Nameplate year of origin: 1967.
Current bodystyle lifespan: 1977 through 1979.
Predecessor to this model: Cougar XR-7 (1974 to 1976).
Replacement for this model: Cougar XR-7 (1980 to 1983).
Percentage of division's production: 23.48%.
Corporate siblings: Ford Thunderbird.
Primary competition: Buick Regal, Dodge Charger SE, Oldsmobile Cutlass Supreme, and Pontiac Grand Prix.
Notable changes: Completely restyled.
Major standard equipment: All-vinyl "Flight Bench" front seat w/fold-down center armrest, cut-pile carpeting, simulated walnut I/P appliqués, electric clock, deluxe steering wheel, courtesy lights, landau vinyl roof w/louvered opera windows, body-side paint stripes, XR-7 sound package, power steering, power front disc brakes, specially tuned suspension system, XR-7 wheel covers, and HR78 × 15 BSW tires.

Measurements

Wheelbase	114.0"
Length	215.5"
Width	78.6"
Height	52.6"
Legroom — front	42.3"
Legroom — rear	32.8"
Headroom — front	37.3"
Headroom — rear	36.3"
Cargo capacity (cu. ft.)	14.7
Fuel capacity (gals.)	26.0

Models Available

	Model No.	Base MSRP	Change from LY	Shipping Wt. (lbs.)	Model Year Production	Change from LY
Cougar XR-7 2-Door Hardtop	93	$5,274	+2.91%	3909	124,799	+48.99%
TOTALS	Avg. price	$5,274	+2.91%	Production	124,799	+48.99%

Marquis

"Marquis renews its commitment to full-size six-passenger comfort and worthwhile improvement."

Nameplate year of origin: 1967.
Current bodystyle lifespan: 1971 through 1978 (restyled in 1973 and 1975).
Predecessor to this model: Marquis (1969 to 1970).
Replacement for this model: Marquis & Grand Marquis (1979 to 1991).
Percentage of division's sales volume: 29.35%.
Corporate siblings: Ford LTD.
Primary competition: Buick Electra 225 and Estate Wagon, Chrysler Newport and Town & Country, Oldsmobile Ninety-Eight and Custom Cruiser, and Pontiac Bonneville and Grand Safari.
Notable changes: Minor trim and detail changes.
Major standard equipment: Cloth-and-vinyl front bench seat w/fold-down center armrest, deep cut-pile carpeting, simu-

Measurements

	2-Doors	4-Doors	Wagons
Wheelbase	124.0"	124.0"	121.0"
Length	229.0"	229.0"	228.3"
Width	79.6"	79.6"	79.9"
Height	53.8"	54.7"	56.9"
Legroom — front	41.8"	41.9"	41.7"
Legroom — rear	35.2"	39.4"	37.1"
Headroom — front	37.3"	37.8"	39.0"
Headroom — rear	35.8"	36.9"	39.5"
Cargo capacity (cu. ft.)	22.7	22.7	103.7*
Fuel capacity (gals.)	24.2	24.2	21.0

Includes 9.1 cu. ft. of hidden cargo space.

lated woodgrain I/P and steering wheel appliqué, deluxe two-spoke steering wheel, dome light, sound insulation package, bright window moldings, rocker panel molding, front bumper guards, hubcaps, and HR78 × 15 BSW tires. Wagon adds: All-vinyl front bench seat w/fold-down center armrest, bright seat side shields, cargo area light, three-way tailgate w/power tailgate window, and JR78 × 15 BSW tires. Brougham adds: Brougham cloth and vinyl front bench seat w/fold-down center armrest, rear seat center armrests, 22-oz. cut-pile carpeting, Brougham door panels w/lower carpeted panel and door pull assist strap, electric clock, RH visor vanity mirror, LH remote control mirror, courtesy lights, power windows, front and rear door courtesy lights, luggage compartment light, vinyl roof, full-length fender peak molding, rear wheel opening fender skirts, and Brougham wheel covers. Grand Marquis adds: Choice of leather-and-velour or leather-with-vinyl individually adjustable Twin Comfort Lounge seats, digital clock, carpeted luggage compartment, dome/dual map reading light, tinted glass, full-length bodyside protective molding w/color-keyed vinyl insert, hood and deck lid paint stripes, specific Grand Marquis nameplates and ornamentation, and JR78 × 15 BSW tires.

Models Available

	Model No.	Base MSRP	Change from LY	Shipping Wt. (lbs.)	Model Year Production	Change from LY
Marquis 2-Door Hardtop	66	$5,496	+8.55%	4293	13,242	+26.72%
Marquis 4-Door Pillared Hardtop	63	$5,496	+8.55%	4326	36,103	+27.97%
Marquis 4-Door, 6-pass. Station Wagon	74	$5,631	+6.75%	4628	20,363	+716.81%
Marquis Brougham 2-Door Hardtop	64	$6,229	+4.60%	4350	12,237	+17.31%
Marquis Brougham 4-Door Pillared Hardtop	62	$6,324	+4.79%	4408	29,411	+31.23%
Grand Marquis 2-Door Hardtop	61	$6,880	+6.85%	4516	13,445	+46.03%
Grand Marquis 4-Door Pillared Hardtop	60	$6,975	+6.85%	4572	31,231	+76.95%
TOTALS	*Avg. price*	$6,147	+7.03%	*Production*	156,032	+34.55%

OLDSMOBILE

"In man's search for excellence ... 1977 Oldsmobile. Can we build one for you?"

For 1977, Oldsmobile became only the third American manufacturer, after Ford and Chevrolet, to break the one million mark in model year production. It would be the first of several million-plus years for Oldsmobile over the next ten model years. Nearly all of this success was built upon the sales of the high-flying Cutlass, which seemed unstoppable, having doubled its sales since the 1974 model year. But another factor this year was the successful introduction of GM's all-new downsized full-size line, which for Oldsmobile included the Delta 88, Custom Cruiser, and Ninety-Eight models. Production of these three series was up about 40 percent over the previous year. It all added up to one remarkable year for America's oldest automobile manufacturer.

The new full-size models shared the "three box" look of other GM full-sized models, with the most obvious sharing seen in the four-door models, both sedan and wagons, while two-door models used differing rear quarter window and roof designs for each division. Oldsmobile was best able to translate the front-end look of its 1976 models onto smaller bodies, using a relatively flat and upright front fascia, and maintaining the twin grilles split by a wide body-colored panel on the Delta 88 and Custom Cruiser, and a center panel covered in chrome for the Ninety-Eight to give a more elegant appearance. Dual rectangular headlights set above horizontal parking and turn signal lights were used on all models. The Delta 88 and Custom Cruiser wagon shared a grille design that was divided into two sections per side, with each section holding fourteen horizontal bars. The Ninety-Eight grille had one section per side with a wide band of chrome across the top and down the side, with an intricate egg-crate grille texture insert. The Oldsmobile crest was in an emblem on the center panel of all models, and an Oldsmobile "rocket" hood ornament stood atop the front header panel.

Bodysides of the new full-size Oldsmobiles had an upper feature line beginning at the top front edge of the front fender, running straight back to meet the line of the back edge of the rear quarter window on two-doors, and the back edge of the rear door on four-doors. This line on station wagons ran straight through to the back of the car, around to the tailgate, and back up the other side. A lower feature line ran straight down the bodyside between the top corners of the bumpers, and created a slight flare to the wheel openings as it passed through. Wheel openings were flat across the top, and the Ninety-Eight and Custom Cruiser no longer had rear wheel opening fender skirts. (They would return on the Ninety-Eight when it underwent a slight styling update for the 1980 model year.)

The Ninety-Eight sedans took on a very formal roofline with little slope to the rear glass, whereas the Delta 88 kept somewhat more slope. Both featured fixed quarter windows in the rear doors. Coupes' rooflines were more similar, but with distinct window designs: a large, essentially triangular rear side window for the Ninety-Eight, but a smaller, rectangular window for the Delta 88, having a vertical rear edge so that the C-pillar had a very broad base.

At the rear, the Delta 88 used horizontal taillamps set

in the rear panel between the deck lid opening and the rear bumper. Backup lights were mounted in the slightly extended rear fender caps, and a side marker light was set on the fender side, giving the effect of a wraparound taillamp design. The license plate mounting was provided between the two tail-lamps. Custom Cruisers shared the same square, wraparound taillamp used by all GM full-size wagons with an Oldsmobile touch by mounting the backup lights squarely in the center of the taillight lens. Ninety-Eights continued to carry a vertical taillamp mounted on the rear fender cap end, though this year they were of a rectangular design with a vertical chrome strip down the center and a logo in the center of the lens. Long horizontal backup lights were housed in the rear panel between the deck lid opening and rear bumper, and were surrounded by a red reflective strip.

Interiors of the new models compared closely to their immediate predecessors in terms of look and size, but with a completely different instrument panel design. The new panel used a large central control area that extended to the passenger side of the car, leaving only the glove box on the right side of the car. Included in the woodgrained gauge and control cluster were light controls and a square air vent to the far left, a horizontal speedometer above the steering column with fuel and temperature gauges below, then an electronic message center with warning lights to the immediate right, and ventilation controls and optional radio stacked below the warning lights. To the right of this, in the center of the car at the top, was an air vent, and to the right of that a square air vent with other optional controls below such as the fuel economy meter, or clock.

With the weight drop created by the downsizing, the powerful Olds Rocket 455 CID V8 engine was discontinued. In its place was a new 403 CID V8 engine derived from the Oldsmobile 350 CID V8 engine first introduced in 1968. The 403 CID engine also became the standard powerplant for the still huge Toronado, resulting in these models feeling underpowered; however, the new engine did have "MISAR" (Microprocessed Sensing/Automatic Regulation), an electronic spark-timing device that helped improve fuel mileage. Also, the newly downsized models added a diagnostic connector for the engine electrical system allowing faster diagnosis of engine electrical problems.

The 61st annual Indianapolis 500 race on May 29, 1977, was led by a Delta 88 2-Door Coupe in specially prepared pace car trim. This was Oldsmobile's sixth time to serve as pace car, and the fourth time since 1970. Special features of the pace car included the new 403 CID V8 engine modified to fulfill its duties, and a unique roof created by removing the entire section above the doors and quarter windows, creating a targa top appearance. Oldsmobile also released a Delta 88 Royale coupe replica available through dealers with specific two-tone silver paint and many other features including the 403 CID V8 engine. (See Appendix IV for full details of the pace car replica's contents.) Approximately 2,400 of the replicas were produced.

The wildly popular Cutlass line entered its final year of production before being downsized with some modest changes. The entry-level Cutlass S line was given the same squared-off front-end look of the Salon and Supreme models, but it used the vertical slot type grille design from last year's model, with eight chrome-lined slots per side that wrapped over the top of the header panel. The grille of the other Cutlass models was refined to include five vertical bar sections per side, with each section holding four slender bars. The optional 4-4-2 package utilized the angled front-end design of the 1976 Cutlass S, but modified with fourteen horizontal bars placed in two sections per side, and divided by a large body colored center section. Oddly, in its final year before downsizing, the Cutlass line received a new instrument panel design. Still using familiar elements, such as the dual round gauge pods set in front of the driver, it was now more of a cockpit design, with the entire driver's side, including radio and ventilation controls, curving around the driver. The lower portion of the panel was now more swept back to provide the illusion of more interior space.

Specific model details included the Salon sedan being dropped, but the highly popular Supreme Brougham coupe was given a sedan running mate, resulting in more than twice as many Brougham sedans being sold as compared to the Salon sedan. The remaining Salon coupe still carried a standard V8 engine, as did the Vista-Cruiser, while all other Cutlass models had a standard V6 engine. The Vista-Cruiser nameplate made its final appearance as the mid-size Cutlass series station wagon, and going forward the name Cutlass Cruiser would be used. The 4-4-2 option package, available only on the Cutlass S coupe, included, in addition to its unique front end design, a lower bodyside stripe kit, the FE2 handling package, and a solid black rub strip on the chrome bumpers, without the white stripe that was used on other Cutlass models. There were 11,649 4-4-2 optioned Cutlass S coupes produced in 1977, second only to 1970's total.

In the compact Oldsmobile lines, the Omega integrated a new grille insert with an egg-crate pattern into an otherwise unchanged front-end appearance. The new grille design gave the Omega a similar design to the Ninety-Eight series. At the back, larger backup lights were set in the center of longer taillight housings. An inner taillight was added where there used to be a body color panel on F-85 models and a brushed aluminum panel on all other Omegas. And, not that anyone noticed, but this was the final season for the F-85 nameplate. The sporty Starfire hatchback added a new grille that slanted rearward and used ten vertical slots per side, resembling the 1976 Cutlass S front end. Under the hood, a standard 140 CID 4-cylinder engine was added to help Oldsmobile meet the upcoming EPA mileage standards; however the 231 CID V6 was still a popular option.

The Toronado line, as previously mentioned, adopted the new 6.6L 403 CID V8 engine as standard equipment and also added "Four Season" air conditioning to its basic equipment list. A new horizontal crosshatch style grille was introduced, four rows high and ten columns across. The single model Toronado Brougham added a unique model, the XSR, and a similarly unique option package, the XS, this year as an attempt to bring some attention and added sales to the ailing Toronado line. While the XS was listed by Oldsmobile as an option package, the XSR was given its own model number, W57. Both the XS and XSR featured a uniquely engineered wraparound rear window that had square corners so that the glass literally looked as if it folded around the corners. This type of window treatment, which

had shown up in many design drawings and mock-ups from General Motors throughout the 1970s, also appeared this year in a similar form on the new Chevrolet Impala and Caprice coupes. The main difference between the XS and XSR was in their roof openings. The XS option used a traditional glass sunroof, or "Astroroof" as Oldsmobile called it, while the XSR used two power-operated, inward sliding glass panels that stacked on top of each other in the center "T" bar section of the roof. Problems in assembly and operation, combined with higher than expected costs for the sliding panels, resulted in only one XSR being produced, despite its appearing in the Oldsmobile dealer and showroom literature for 1977. Meanwhile the XS option package sold 2,712 units.

1977

Custom Cruiser 4-Door Station Wagon

Cutlass S 2-Door Colonnade Hardtop Coupe

Cutlass S 2-Door Colonnade Hardtop Coupe with 4-4-2 option

Cutlass Supreme 2-Door Colonnade Hardtop Coupe

Cutlass Supreme Brougham 4-Door Colonnade Hardtop Sedan

Delta 88 Royale 2-Door Coupe

Delta 88 Royale 4-Door Sedan

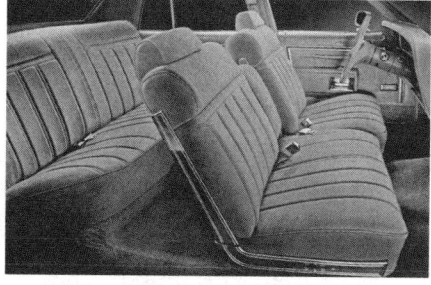

Delta 88 Royale 4-Door Sedan interior

Ninety-Eight LS 4-Door Sedan

Ninety-Eight Regency 2-Door Coupe

Omega 2-Door Hatchback Coupe with SX package

Omega 4-Door Sedan

Omega F-85 2-Door Coupe

Toronado Brougham 2-Door Hardtop Coupe
with XS package

Omega 2-Door Hatchback with V6 Sports Pack

Starfire SX 2-Door Hatchback Coupe

Toronado XSR 2-Door Hardtop Coupe

Toronado Brougham 2-Door Hardtop Coupe

Vista-Cruiser 4-Door, 3-Seat Station Wagon

Model year production: 1,135,732, up 27.41% from 1976.
Domestic market share: 11.83% (3rd place).
Base price range: $3,653 to $11,132.
Oldsmobile average base price: $5,263, up 6.86%.
Introduction date: September 30, 1976.
Assembly plants: Southgate, CA (C); Doraville, GA (D); Linden, NJ (E); Framingham, MA (G); Van Nuys, CA (L); Lansing, MI (M); Arlington, TX (R); Kansas City/Fairfax, KS (X); Willow Run, MI (W); and St. Therese, Quebec, Canada (2).
Data plate identification (VIN): Thirteen digit code read as follows: First digit indicates division (3 = Oldsmobile); second through fourth digits indicate series and body style (model number in model charts); fifth digit is engine code (see powertrain chart); sixth digit indicates model year (7 = 1977); seventh digit indicates assembly plant (see list above); remaining digits are sequential with beginning number of 100001. *Example:* 3L69J7X100001 is a 1977 Oldsmobile Delta 88 4-Door Town Sedan, with 350 CID, 4-bbl. V8 engine, serial number 100001, built in Kansas City/Fairfax, KS.

Powertrains

Engine	Net HP	Engine Code VIN/GM	Transmission Availability[1]		Starfire	Omega	Cutlass	Delta 88	98 & Custom Cruiser	Toronado
140 CID (2.3L) OHC, 2-bbl., 4-cyl.	84	B/L11	4-speed manual		S	—	—	—	—	—
				MPG:	24/33/28	—	—	—	—	—
				Calif.	23/33/27	—	—	—	—	—
			5-speed manual		$248	—	—	—	—	—
				MPG:	NA	—	—	—	—	—
			3-speed Turbo Hydra-matic		$248	—	—	—	—	—
				MPG:	21/28/24	—	—	—	—	—
				Calif.	21/30/24	—	—	—	—	—
231 CID (3.8L), 2-bbl., V6[2]	105	C/LD5	3-speed manual		—	S	S[3]	—	—	—
				MPG:	—	16/27/20	16/26/19	—	—	—
				Calif.	—	12/24/15	12/24/15	—	—	—
			4-speed manual		$140	—	—	—	—	—
				MPG:	18/29/21	—	—	—	—	—
				Calif.	13/26/17	—	—	—	—	—
			5-speed manual		$388	—	$282[3]	—	—	—
				MPG:	NA	—	NA	—	—	—
			3-speed Turbo Hydra-matic		$388[4]	$282	$282[3]	S	—	—
				MPG:	19/26/21	19/26/21	17/25/20	17/25/20	—	—
				Calif.	14/19/16	15/20/17	16/21/18	16/21/18	—	—

Engine	Net HP	Engine Code VIN/GM	Transmission Availability[1]		Starfire	Omega	Cutlass	Delta 88	98 & Custom Cruiser	Toronado
231 CID (3.8L), 2-bbl., V6[2]	105	C/LD7	3-speed manual		—	S	S[3]	—	—	—
				MPG:	—	16/27/20	16/26/19	—	—	—
				Calif.	—	12/24/15	12/24/15	—	—	—
			4-speed manual		$140					
				MPG:	18/29/21	—	—	—		
				Calif.	13/26/17	—	—	—		
			5-speed manual		$388	—	$282[3]	—	—	—
				MPG:	NA	—	NA	—		
			3-speed Turbo Hydra-matic		$388	$282	$282[3]	S		
				MPG:	19/26/21	19/26/21	17/25/20	17/25/20	—	—
				Calif.	14/19/16	15/20/17	16/21/18	16/21/18	—	—
260 CID (4.3L), 2-bbl., V8	110	F/LV8	5-speed manual		—	—	N/C[5]/$327[3]	—	—	—
				MPG:			17/26/20	—		
			3-speed Turbo Hydra-matic			—	S[5]/$327[3]	$45		
				MPG:		—	16/21/18	17/23/19	—	—
301 CID (4.9L), 2-bbl., V8[4]	135	Y/L27	3-speed Turbo Hydra-matic		—	$65	—	$66	—	—
				MPG:	—	17/23/19	—	17/23/19	—	—
305 CID (5.0L), 2-bbl., V8[6]	145	U/LG3	3-speed manual		—	$65	—	—	—	—
				MPG:	—	16/22/19	—	—		
			3-speed Turbo Hydra-matic		—	$347	—	—	—	—
				MPG:	—	16/21/18	—	—		
350 CID (5.7L), 4-bbl., V8	170	R/L34	3-speed Turbo Hydra-matic		—	$437[7]	S[8]/$110[5]/$437[3]	$155	S	—
				MPG:	—	—	16/21/18	16/22/18	16/21/18	—
				Calif.	—	15/21/17	14/20/16	15/21/17	14/20/16	—
403 CID (6.6L), 4-bbl., V8	185[9]	K/L80	3-speed Turbo Hydra-matic		—	—	$65[8]/$502[3]	$175[5]/$220	$65	S
				MPG:	—	—	15/21/18	15/21/18	15/21/18	13/19/15
				Calif.	—	—	13/19/15	13/19/15	13/19/15	12/18/14

[1]Unless otherwise specified: All 3-speed manuals are column shift. All 4- and 5-speed manuals are floor shift. All automatics are column shift, except on Starfire. Floor shift automatic is optional on Omega, Cutlass and Delta 88 2-doors with other required equipment at extra cost. [2]The LD5 even-firing engine replaced the LD7 engine as follows: For cars built in Flint (MI), on approximately March 21, 1977; for cars built in Fairfax (KS), Lordstown (OH), St. Therese (Canada), and Southgate (MI), on approximately May 1, 1977. [3]Except Cutlass Salon and Vista-Cruiser. [4]Not available in California. [5]Cutlass Salon. [6]Engine available on cars built after October 1, 1976. [7]Available only in California or with high altitude emission equipment. [8]Vista-Cruiser wagons. [9]Horsepower rating for Toronado is 200.

Major Options

	Starfire	Omega	Cutlass	Delta 88	Custom Cruiser	Ninety-Eight	Toronado
Four-Season air conditioner[1]	$442	$478	$499	$539	$539	$539	S
Tilt-Away steering wheel	$50	$57	$57	$58	$58	$58	$58
Tilt-and-Telescope steering wheel	—	—	—	—	—	$101	$101
Cruise control	—	$80	$80	$84	$84	$84	$84
Electric rear window defroster	$71	$48[2]	$82	$83	$83	$83	$83
Dual rearview mirrors, LH remote	$29	$43	$43	$43	$38	S	S
Tinted glass, all windows	$48	$50	$54	$69	$69	$69	$69
Power windows, 2-dr./4-dr.	—	$108/$151	$108/$151	$114/$171	$114	S	S
Power door locks, 2-dr./4-dr.	—	$68/$96	$68/$96	$70/$98	$131[3]	$70/$98	$70
Power front seat, 6-way w/std. seat	—	—	$137	$139	$139	$109[4]	S
Front bucket seats, w/console	$77[5]	$159[6]	$159[6]	—	—	—	—
Third row seat, wagons	—	—	$152	—	$175	—	—
AM radio	$71	$75	$79	$92	$92	$92	—
AM/FM stereo[7]	$219	$233	$233	$236	$236	$236	$236
AM/FM stereo w/8-track tape[7]	$316	$337	$337	$341	$341	$341	$341
Woodgrain exterior panels (wagons)	—	—	$134	—	$172	—	—
Vinyl top, full	—	$93	$111	$138	—	$179[8]	$155
Vinyl top, landau (coupes only)	—	$162	$111	$166	—	$179	$258[9]

	Starfire	Omega	Cutlass	Delta 88	Custom Cruiser	Ninety-Eight	Toronado
Hatch roof (T-top)	—	—	$587[10]	—	—	—	—
Sunroof, power operated, metal	—	—	—	—	—	$734	—
Astroroof, power operated, glass	—	—	—	—	—	$898	$898
Power trunk lid release	—	—	$18	$18	—	$18	$18
Power steering, "Vari-Ratio"	$127	$144	S	S	S	S	S
Power brakes, w/front disc	$58	$61	S	S	S	S	S
Deluxe wheel covers	$41	$34	$34	$39	$39	S	S
Wire wheel covers	—	—	$120	$104	$104	$104	—
Chrome road wheels	—	—	—	$117	$117	$100	—
Chrome sport wheels	$84	$89	$89	$117	—	—	—
WSW tires, std. size	—	$39	$41	$41	$41	$43	$50

Popular Option Groups & Packages

	Starfire	Omega	Cutlass	Delta 88	Custom Cruiser	Ninety-Eight	Toronado
4-4-2 package	—	—	$169	—	—	—	—
Appearance package	—	—	—	—	—	—	$300
Convenience group	—	$29	$34	$35	$35	$10	$10
Indy 500 pace car replica package	—	—	—	$914	—	—	—
GT package	$567	—	—	—	—	—	—
SX package	—	$187	—	—	—	—	—
V6 Sports pack	—	$320	—	—	—	—	—
XS custom package	—	—	—	—	—	—	$2,998

—= Not Available; S = Standard equipment. [1]Power steering required on Omega with V8 engines. "Tempmatic" air conditioner with automatic climate control is available for $39 additional on Cutlass, Delta 88, Custom Cruiser, Ninety-Eight and Toronado. [2]Blower type defogger. [3]Includes power tailgate lock. [4]Standard on Ninety-Eight Regency. [5]Bucket seats are standard on Starfire. [6]Standard on Cutlass Salon. Swivel bucket seats available on Cutlass S. Bucket seats available at no cost on Cutlass Supreme and Cutlass Supreme Brougham coupes only, with console $75 extra. [7]CB radio available on all models with AM/FM stereo (with or without tape player), except on Starfire and Omega, at $118 additional. [8]Two-door models, $162. [9]Landau roof available on Toronado XS and XSR, standard on Brougham. [10]Available on Supreme, Supreme Brougham and Salon coupes only.

Paint Colors

	Code		Code		Code
White	11	Medium Green metallic	44	Mandarin Orange metallic	78
Silver metallic	13	Dark Green metallic[2]	48	Medium Blue metallic (two-tone	
Medium Gray metallic (two-tone		Yellow[2]	50	only)	85
only)	16	Bright Yellow[1]	51		
Ebony Black	19	Light Buckskin	61	
Light Blue metallic	22	Buckskin metallic	63	
Dark Blue metallic	29	Brown metallic	69	
Firethorn Red metallic	36	Red[2]	72	
Dark Aqua metallic[1]	38	Bright Red[1]	75	

In two-tone combinations, the first two digits indicate lower color, and the next two digits are the upper color. Two-tone paint available for $42 extra on Omega and Cutlass, and $51 extra on Delta 88 coupe. [1]Available only on Starfire and Omega. [2]Available on all models except Starfire and Omega.

Starfire

"Who says you can't have style, luxury and practicality—in the same sporty package?"

Nameplate year of origin: 1954 (as designation for 98 convertible); 1961 (as series).
Current bodystyle lifespan: 1975 through 1980
Predecessor to this model: None.
Replacement for this model: Firenza (1982 to 1988).
Percentage of division's production: 1.68%.
Corporate siblings: Buick Skyhawk, Chevrolet Monza, and Pontiac Sunbird (closely related to Chevrolet Vega and Pontiac Astre).
Primary competition: AMC Pacer, Ford Mustang II and "Lincoln-Mercury" Capri.
Notable changes: New grille and minor trim and detail changes.
Major standard equipment: High-backed bucket seats in grained vinyl, folding rear

Measurements

Wheelbase	97.0"
Length	179.0"
Width	65.4"
Height	50.0"
Legroom—front	42.8"
Legroom—rear	29.6"
Headroom—front	37.7"
Headroom—rear	35.3"
Cargo capacity (cu. ft.)	23.4*

seatback, plush-pile carpeting on all floor surfaces and rear seatback, deluxe steering wheel, door panel map pockets, simulated woodgrain I/P appliqué, I/P gauges including tachometer, dual speed wipers w/washers, chrome window surround and belt molding, manual front disc brakes, hubcaps, and B78 × 13 BSW tires. SX adds: Choice of velour brushed knit or soft vinyl high-back bucket seats, deluxe sport steering wheel w/brushed metal spokes and padded softgrip rim, chrome front and rear wheel lip moldings, bodyside striping, and BR78 × 13 BSW tires.

Measurements (cont.)

Fuel capacity (gals.)	18.5

*With rear seat folded down.

Models Available

	Model No.	Base MSRP	Change from LY	Shipping Wt. (lbs.)	Model Year Production	Change from LY
Starfire 2-Door Hatchback Coupe	T07	$3,802	-2.06%	2672	4,910	-40.88%
Starfire SX 2-Door Hatchback Coupe	D07	$4,000	-1.53%	2700	14,181	-32.00%
TOTALS		Avg. price $3,901	-1.79%		Production 19,091	-34.53%

Omega

"There are a lot of compact cars in the running. But Omega's room, ride and value make it the people's choice."

Nameplate year of origin: 1973.
Current bodystyle lifespan: 1975 through 1979.
Predecessor to this model: Omega (1973 to 1974).
Replacement for this model: Omega (1980 to 1984).
Percentage of division's production: 5.63%.
Corporate siblings: Buick Skylark, Chevrolet Nova, and Pontiac Ventura.
Primary competition: Dodge Aspen and Mercury Monarch.
Notable changes: Minor trim and detail changes.
Major standard equipment: F85: Nylon knit cloth front bench seat, rubber floor mat, chrome windshield and backlight moldings, hubcaps, and E78 × 14 BSW tires. Omega adds: Choice of all-vinyl or soft knit fabric front bench seat, cut-pile carpeting, simulated woodgrain I/P appliqués, door-operated dome lamps, dual speed wipers w/washers, chrome window surround moldings, chrome front and rear wheel opening moldings, full wheel covers, and F78 × 14 BSW tires. Hatchback model adds: Fold-down rear seat. Brougham adds: Choice of tailored brushed knit cloth or Wallaby vinyl front bench seat, deluxe steering wheel, vinyl insert bodyside moldings, bright rocker panel molding, and stand-up hood ornament.

Measurements

	Coupe & HBK	Sedan
Wheelbase	111.0"	111.0"
Length	199.6"	199.6"
Width	69.9"	69.9"
Height	53.2"	54.2"
Legroom — front	41.7"	41.7"
Legroom — rear	32.4"	35.2"
Headroom — front	38.2"	39.1"
Headroom — rear	36.7"	37.1"
Cargo capacity (cu. ft.)	14.2*	13.8
Fuel capacity (gals.)	21.0	21.0

*Hatchback maximum, 12.9 cu. ft.; with rear seat down, 30.2 cu. ft.

Models Available

	Model No.	Base MSRP	Change from LY	Shipping Wt. (lbs.)	Model Year Production	Change from LY
Omega F-85 2-Door Coupe	S27	$3,653	+7.76%	3109	2,241	-42.80%
Omega 2-Door Coupe	B27	$3,740	+7.32%	3127	18,611	+21.27%
Omega 2-Door Hatchback	B17	$3,905	+7.66%	3196	4,739	+5.38%
Omega 4-Door Sedan	B69	$3,797	+8.05%	3162	21,723	+7.43%
Omega Brougham 2-Door Coupe	E27	$3,934	+7.05%	3151	6,478	+20.79%
Omega Brougham 2-Door Hatchback	E17	$4,105	+7.55%	3228	1,189	-3.72%
Omega Brougham 4-Door Sedan	E69	$3,994	+7.83%	3188	9,003	+18.66%
TOTALS		Avg. price $3,875	+7.60%		Production 63,984	+10.00%

Cutlass

"America's best selling mid-size car line."

Nameplate year of origin: 1961 (as F-85 Deluxe sport coupe designation); 1962 (as F-85 sub-series); and 1965 (as series designation). Also used on 1955 Oldsmobile show car.

Current bodystyle lifespan: 1973 through 1977.

Predecessor to this model: Cutlass (1968 to 1972).

Replacement for this model: Cutlass (1978 to 1988; restyled in 1981).

Percentage of division's production: 55.71%.

Corporate siblings: Buick Century, Chevrolet Malibu, and Pontiac LeMans.

Primary competition: Dodge Monaco and Mercury Cougar.

Notable changes: New front end for S models and minor trim and detail changes.

Measurements

	Coupes	Sedans	Wagons
Wheelbase	112.0"	116.0"	116.0"
Length	209.6"	215.2"	220.4"
Width	76.5"	76.5"	76.8"
Height	53.4"	56.1"	55.3"
Legroom — front	42.4"	42.4"	42.4"
Legroom — rear	32.9"	36.9"	36.8"
Headroom — front	37.2"	37.9"	38.4"
Headroom — rear	36.7"	37.3"	39.0"
Cargo capacity (cu. ft.)	16.3	15.9	85.1
Fuel capacity (gals.)	22.0	22.0	22.0

Major standard equipment: Nylon knit cloth front bench seat, cut-pile carpeting, deluxe steering wheel, simulated woodgrain I/P and door panel appliqués, deluxe armrests front and rear, wheel lip moldings, bright window surround moldings, power steering, power front disc brakes, wheel covers, and FR78 × 15 BSW tires. Supreme adds: Choice of cloth-and-vinyl or all-vinyl front bench seat w/fold-down center armrest, luxury door panels with door pull straps, and stand-up "rocket" hood ornament. Supreme Brougham adds: "Loose cushion" look velour with vinyl bolster 60/40 divided front seat w/fold down center armrest, deep-pile carpeting, rocker panel moldings, and deluxe wheel covers. Vista-Cruiser adds: All-vinyl front bench seat w/fold-down center armrest, cut-pile carpeting on passenger and cargo floors, remote-control tailgate release (in glove compartment), rear vent window (3-seat model only), and HR78 × 15 BSW tires. Salon adds: Choice of brushed velour w/vinyl trim or soft all-vinyl individual reclining lounge seats, front floor console, stand-up Salon-specific hood ornament, FE2 suspension package, and GR78 × 15 BSW tires.

Models Available

	Model No.	Base MSRP	Change from LY	Shipping Wt. (lbs.)	Model Year Production	Change from LY
Cutlass S 2-Door Colonnade HT Coupe	G37	$4,351	+8.80%	3535	70,155	+18.55%
Cutlass S 4-Door Colonnade HT Sedan	G29	$4,387	+8.78%	3618	42,923	+22.66%
Cutlass Supreme 2-Door Colonnade HT Coupe	J57	$4,670	+8.83%	3565	242,874	+30.12%
Cutlass Supreme 4-Door Colonnade HT Sedan	J29	$4,734	+7.23%	3666	37,929	+2.20%
Vista-Cruiser 4-Door, 2-Seat Station Wagon	H35*	$5,243	+4.01%	4218	40,654	+25.56%
Cutlass Supreme Brougham 2-Dr. Colonnade HT Coupe	M57	$4,969	+8.49%	3584	124,712	+36.58%
Cutlass Supreme Brougham 4-Door Colonnade HT Sedan	K29	$5,033	NEW	3692	16,738	NEW
Cutlass Salon 2-Door Colonnade HT Coupe	K57	$5,269	+7.75%	3787	56,757	+17.17%
TOTALS	*Avg. price*	$4,832	+5.72%	*Production*	632,742	+26.52%

Model number of Vista-Cruiser was changed from J35 to H35 for 1977. For 1976 and prior models, the H35 model number was assigned to the Cutlass Supreme Cruiser.

Delta 88

"Olds has just raised its standards for what you can expect in a down-to-earth American family car."

Nameplate year of origin: 1965 (88 series began in 1949).

Current bodystyle lifespan: 1977 through 1985.

Predecessor to this model: Delta 88 (1971 to 1976).

Replacement for this model: Delta 88 (1986 to 1991).

Measurements

Wheelbase	151.5"
Wheelbase	116.0"
Length	217.5"

Percentage of division's production: 18.81%.
Corporate siblings: Buick LeSabre, Chevrolet Impala and Caprice, and Pontiac Catalina and Bonneville.
Primary competition: Chrysler Newport and Mercury Marquis.
Notable changes: Completely redesigned.
Major standard equipment: Choice of nylon knit or all-vinyl front bench seat, cut-pile carpeting, cut-pile carpeting on lower door panels, simulated I/P woodgrain appliqué, electronic message center in I/P, courtesy and glove box lights, bright drip rail and window moldings, bright wheel opening and rocker panel moldings, full wheel covers, and FR78 × 15 BSW tires. Royale adds: Pleated velour Custom sport bench front seat w/fold-down center armrest, Royale ornamentation inside and on exterior C-pillar, door pull straps, deluxe steering wheel, door panel simulated woodgrain trim, bright metal accented floor pedals, front and rear bumper vinyl impact strips, and color-coordinated bodyside protective moldings.

Measurements (cont.)

Width	76.8"
Height	55.7"
Legroom — front	42.2"
Legroom — rear	39.5"
Headroom — front	39.1"
Headroom — rear	38.2"
Cargo capacity (cu. ft.)	20.2
Fuel capacity (gals.)	21.0

Models Available

	Model No.	Base MSRP	Change from LY	Shipping Wt. (lbs.)	Model Year Production	Change from LY
Delta 88 2-Door Coupe	L37	$5,145	+3.42%	3431	8,788	+21.99%
Delta 88 4-Door Town Sedan	L69	$5,205	+5.84%	3472	26,084	+52.40%
Delta 88 Royale 2-Door Coupe	N37	$5,363	+4.22%	3440	61,138	+83.25%
Delta 88 Royale 4-Door Town Sedan	N69	$5,433	+6.99%	3496	117,571	+253.41%
TOTALS	*Avg. price*	$5,287	+4.44%	*Production*	213,581	+39.77%

Custom Cruiser

"To top our best in luxury, comfort, ride — and space efficiency — we created a new kind of wagon."

Nameplate year of origin: 1971 (1940 as a designation on 90 series cars).
Current bodystyle lifespan: 1977 through 1990.
Predecessor to this model: Custom Cruiser (1971 to 1976).
Replacement for this model: Custom Cruiser (1991 to 1992).
Percentage of division's production: 2.89%.
Corporate siblings: Buick Estate Wagon, Chevrolet Impala and Caprice, and Pontiac Catalina Safari and Grand Safari.
Primary competition: Chrysler Town & Country and Mercury Colony Park.
Notable changes: Completely redesigned.
Major standard equipment: Choice of velour or all-vinyl front bench seat w/fold-down center armrest, cut-pile carpeting on floors and cargo compartment floor, lower door panel carpeting, simulated I/P woodgrain appliqué, electronic message center in I/P, courtesy and glove box lights, cargo area light, bright drip rail and window moldings, bright wheel opening and rocker panel moldings, three-way tailgate, full wheel covers, and HR78 × 15 BSW tires.

Measurements

Wheelbase	116.0"
Length	216.7"
Width	77.2"
Height	57.0"
Legroom — front	42.2"
Legroom — rear	38.4"
Headroom — front	39.1"
Headroom — rear	39.2"
Cargo capacity (cu. ft.)	87.3
Fuel capacity (gals.)	22.0

Models Available

	Model No.	Base MSRP	Change from LY	Shipping Wt. (lbs.)	Model Year Production	Change from LY*
Custom Cruiser 4-Door, 2-S. Wagon	Q35	$5,923	+3.57%	4064	32,827	NA*
TOTALS	*Avg. price*	$5,923	+3.69%	*Production*	32,827	+47.10%

Comparison to LY is made to combined production of 1976 "Q" non-woodgrained, and "R" woodgrained models, and "45" three-seat models, as woodgrain trim and third row seat is now an option for the 1977 model year.

Ninety-Eight

"The traditional luxury you expect— plus the
unexpected luxury of good gas mileage."

Nameplate year of origin: 1941.
Current bodystyle lifespan: 1977 through 1984.
Predecessor to this model: Ninety-Eight (1971 to 1976).
Replacement for this model: Ninety-Eight (1985 to 1990).
Percentage of division's production: 12.28%.
Corporate siblings: Buick Electra 225, Cadillac deVille, and Cadillac Fleetwood
   Brougham.
Primary competition: Chrysler New Yorker and Mercury Grand Marquis.
Notable changes: Completely redesigned.
Major standard equipment: Choice of Ogden nylon knit fabric or Doeskin vinyl
   front bench seat w/fold-down front and rear center armrests, cut-pile carpeting, car-
   peted lower door panels, door pull straps, power controls on door armrest in chrome
   bezel, two-way power front seat, power windows, simulated woodgrain I/P trim, deluxe steering wheel, electronic message center
   in I/P, electric clock, remote-control LH rear view mirror, bright bodyside protective molding, wheel opening moldings, rocker
   panel molding, stand-up Oldsmobile crest hood ornament, bumper impact strips, wheel covers, and GR78 × 15 BSW tires. Regency
   adds: Choice of velour or white vinyl 60/40 front seat button-tufted w/"loose" cushion look, front seatback pouches, six-way power
   adjustment for driver's side, digital quartz-crystal clock, door-mounted entry courtesy lights, and fully lined trunk compartment.

Measurements

Wheelbase	119.0"
Length	220.4"
Width	76.8"
Height	56.6"
Legroom — front	42.2"
Legroom — rear	40.9"
Headroom — front	39.1"
Headroom — rear	38.0"
Cargo capacity (cu. ft.)	20.2
Fuel capacity (gals.)	24.5

Models Available

	Model No.	Base MSRP	Change from LY	Shipping Wt. (lbs.)	Model Year Production	Change from LY*
Ninety-Eight LS 2-Door Coupe	V37	$6,609	+5.39%	3753	5,058	-16.48%
Ninety-Eight LS 4-Door Sedan	V69	$6,786	+5.72%	3807	14,323	-14.75%
Ninety-Eight Regency 2-Door Coupe	X37	$6,949	+6.19%	3767	32,072	+22.03%
Ninety-Eight Regency 4-Door Sedan	X69	$7,133	+6.61%	3840	87,970	+58.97%
TOTALS	*Avg. price*	$6,869	+5.99%	*Production*	139,423	+33.45%

Comparisons of 4-door sedans made to 1976 4-door hardtop models.

Toronado

"Front-wheel drive and the inner world
of Toronado — a rare driving pleasure."

Nameplate year of origin: 1966.
Current bodystyle lifespan: 1971 through 1978.
Predecessor to this model: Toronado (1966 to 1970).
Replacement for this model: Toronado (1979 to 1985).
Percentage of division's production: 3.00%.
Corporate siblings: Cadillac Eldorado.
Primary competition: Lincoln Continental Mark V.
Notable changes: New grille and minor trim and detail changes.
Major standard equipment: Choice of ribbed velour or white all-vinyl front bench
   seat w/fold-down center armrest and "loose-cushion" look interior, rear seat fold-
   down center armrest, cut-pile carpeting, simulated woodgrain appliqué on I/P, two-
   spoke steering wheel, digital clock w/quartz-crystal movement, chrome-accented
   floor pedals, Four-season air conditioning, LH remote-control rear view mirror, bright window opening moldings, bright rocker
   panel and wheel lip moldings, front bumper guards, front and rear bumper rub strips, chrome wheel covers, and JR78 × 15 BSW
   tires. XSR adds: Tinted heat-reflective power-operated sliding glass roof panels, wraparound rear window, and specific "XSR"
   nameplate on interior and exterior of B-pillar.

Measurements

Wheelbase	122.0"
Length	227.5"
Width	79.7"
Height	53.2"
Legroom — front	42.2"
Legroom — rear	35.2"
Headroom — front	37.7"
Headroom — rear	36.7"
Cargo capacity (cu. ft.)	17.0
Fuel capacity (gals.)	26.0

Models Available

	Model No.	Base MSRP	Change from LY	Shipping Wt. (lbs.)	Model Year Production	Change from LY
Toronado Brougham 2-Door Hardtop	Z57	$8,134	+13.97%	4634	34,083	+56.71%
Toronado XSR 2-Door Hardtop	W57	$11,132	NEW	4688	1	NEW
TOTALS	*Avg. price*	$9,633	+37.34%	*Production*	34,084	+40.24%

PLYMOUTH

"Building cars for this big traveling country."

A rather uneventful year for Plymouth, 1977 nonetheless brought a modest improvement in sales and production by the end of the model year. Facing competition from the newly downsized Chevrolet full-size models and the wildly popular mid-size Oldsmobile Cutlass, the struggling full-size Gran Fury and mid-size Plymouth Fury lines both managed sales increases, albeit from severely depressed levels over the past two model years. The imported Arrow and the new-for-1976 Volaré also saw sales and production increases, which, in combination with the Fury's upswing, resulted in the first year-to-year production increase for Plymouth since 1973 — and its last until 1981. Despite a small decrease in market share, this was still a great accomplishment considering that the line was missing its perennial favorites, the Valiant and Duster series, and that the Volaré was beginning to compile the worst recall record of any car from the time period.

The mid-size Fury models were the only Plymouths to have any styling changes this year, and the brand's first to use rectangular headlights, in this case vertically stacked units. A new vertical crosshatch grille, two rows high and about three dozen columns across, was surrounded by a wide swath of chrome with the Plymouth name in block letters widely spaced across the top bar. Parking and turn signal lights were moved into the bumper ends. All of these changes gave the Fury a more luxurious front-end appearance. Around back, the coupes had a slightly revised Fury emblem and painted inset stripe, while sedans had a new three-section lens with red tail and brake lamps to the outside, amber turn signals to the inside, and backup lights with a black surround in between. Other changes were minor, consisting of such things as a wider bodyside protective molding on Fury Salons, and larger 15-inch wheels as standard equipment.

The Volaré line carried into the new year unchanged, but added some new sporty option packages. The Super Pak spoiler and wheel flare package from last season was combined with some elements of the Road Runner package to make the new "Front Runner" Super Pak. Advertised as the "Sun Runners," this was not truly an option package, but was the name given by the advertising department for any Volaré coupe that had the optional T-Bar roof or a sunroof. Together the "Sun Runners" and "Front Runners" were advertised as the Plymouth "Fun Runners." While virtually all other features remained the same as in their 1976 introductory year, the model number of the Volaré Premier station wagon was changed to the HH series that more closely matched its Custom interior trim level; however, it was still considered part of the top model Premier series.

The Mitsubishi-built captive import, the Arrow, offered up few changes, but continued to be a solid seller, offering inexpensive but dependable transportation. One significant change was to add the exclusive "Silent Shaft" engine design features introduced on the 1976 2.0L engine to the 1.6L, 1600cc 4-cylinder engine. With this change the Silent Shaft version of the 1.6L engine was now standard in the GT model, which had used the larger 2.0L "Silent Shaft" 4-cylinder engine as standard for 1976. The Arrow 160 and GS models still used the regular design 1.6L engine. The GT version also used a 5-speed manual transmission exclusively with the smaller engine.

The only model changes for 1977 were in the full-size Gran Fury series that was entering its final year of production in its current form. A base Gran Fury 2-door hardtop was added, and the mid-range PH series Gran Fury Custom and Custom Suburban names were replaced by the Brougham and Sport Suburban names. This meant the high-end PP series no longer existed. No other significant changes were made to the Gran Fury line although they would be the last Plymouths to offer the big 440 CID V8 engine.

Arrow 2-Door Hatchback

Fury 4-Door Sedan, front, and Plymouth Fury
2-Door Hardtop Coupe, rear

Fury Sport Suburban 4-Door Station Wagon

Gran Fury 4-Door Sedan

Gran Fury Brougham 2-Door Hardtop

Gran Fury Sport Suburban
4-Door Station Wagon

Volaré 2-Door Coupe with Road Runner package
and Super Pak package

Volaré 4-Door Station Wagon

Volaré Custom 2-Door Coupe
with two-tone paint

Volaré Custom 4-Door Sedan

Volaré Premier interior with Hillcrest trim
option

Model year production: 458,717, up 5.90% from 1976.
Domestic market share: 4.78% (7th place).
Base price range: $3,570 to $5,681.
Plymouth average base price: $4,506, up 5.50%.
Introduction date: October 1, 1976. Arrow introduced November 1976.
Assembly plants: Lynch Road, Detroit, MI (A); Hamtramck, MI (B); Jefferson Ave., Detroit, MI (C); Belvidere, IL (D); Newark, DE (F); and St. Louis, MO (G). Arrow manufacturer: Mitsubishi Heavy Industries, Tokyo, Japan (code 1 through 9).

Data plate identification (VIN): Thirteen digit code read as follows: First four digits indicate series and body style (model number in model charts); fifth digit indicates engine code (see powertrain chart); sixth digit indicates year (7 = 1977); seventh digit indicates assembly plant (see list above); remaining digits are sequential with beginning numbers of 100001. *Example:* HL41C7G100001 is a 1977 Plymouth Volaré 4-Door Sedan, with 225 CID, 1-bbl. 6-cylinder engine, serial number 100001, built in St. Louis, MO.

Powertrains

Engine	Net HP	Engine Code	Transmission Availability[1]		Arrow	Volaré	Fury	Gran Fury	Gran Fury Brougham & Gran Fury Wagons
97.5 CID (1.6L) OHC, 1-bbl., 4-cyl.	83	K	4-speed manual		S (ex. GT)	—	—	—	—
				MPG:	26/39/31	—	—	—	—
			5-speed manual		S (GT)	—	—	—	—
				MPG:	NA	—	—	—	—
				Calif.	20/35/24	—	—	—	—
			3-speed Automatic		$	—	—	—	—
				MPG:	26/35/30	—	—	—	—
				Calif.	21/32/25	—	—	—	—
122 CID (2.0L) OHC, 2-bbl., 4-cyl.	96	U	5-speed manual		$300 (GS & GT)	—	—	—	—
				MPG:	20/33/24	—	—	—	—
				Calif.	15/27/19	—	—	—	—
			3-speed Automatic		$ (GS & GT)	—	—	—	—
				MPG:	21/28/24	—	—	—	—
				Calif.	18/29/22	—	—	—	—
225 CID (3.7L), 1-bbl., 6-cyl.	100	C	3-speed manual		—	S	—	—	—
				MPG:	—	20/29/23	—	—	—
				Calif.	—	16/23/18	—	—	—
			"Overdrive4" 4-speed manual		—	$134[2]	—	—	—
				MPG:	—	NA	—	—	—
			3-speed Torque Flite automatic		—	$270	—	—	—
				MPG:	—	18/24/20	—	—	—
				Calif.	—	16/19/17	—	—	—
225 CID (3.7L) Super Six, 2-bbl., 6-cyl.[3]	110	D	3-speed manual		—	$38	S (cars)	—	—
				MPG:	—	17/24/20	17/22/19	—	—
			3-speed Torque Flite automatic		—	$308	$295 (cars)	—	—
				MPG:	—	16/21/18	16/21/18	—	—
318 CID (5.2L), 2-bbl., V8	145	G	3-speed manual[3]		—	$170	$258 (cars)	—	—
				MPG:	—	15/25/19	14/23/17	—	—
			"Overdrive4" 4-speed manual[3]		—	$304	—	—	—
				MPG:	—	NA	—	—	—
			3-speed Torque Flite automatic		—	$440	$547 (cars)	S	—
				MPG:	—	15/20/17	13/18/15	13/18/15	—
				Calif.	—	11/15/13	11/16/13	—	—
360 CID (5.9L), 2-bbl., V8[3]	155	K	3-speed Torque Flite automatic		—	$493	S (wgns.)/ $604 (cars)	$58	S (cars)
				MPG:	—	14/19/16	14/20/16	12/18/14	12/18/14
360 CID (5.9L), 4-bbl., V8[4]	175	L	3-speed Torque Flite automatic		—	$550[5]	$47 (wgns.)[6,7]/ $652 (cars)	$106	$48 (cars)
				MPG:	—	11/17/13	11/16/12	12/18/14	12/18/14
				Calif.	—	12/17/14	11/18/14	11/18/13	11/18/13
400 CID (6.6L), 4-bbl., V8[4]	190	N	3-speed Torque Flite automatic		—	—	$98 (wgns.)[3]/ $703 (cars)	$158	S (wgns.)/ $99 (cars)
				MPG:	—	—	11/19/14	11/18/13	11/18/14
40 CID (7.2L), 4-bbl., V8[4]	195	T	3-speed Torque Flite automatic		—	—	—	$289	$132 (wgns.)/ $231 (cars)
				MPG:	—	—	—	9/17/11	9/17/11
				Calif.	—	—	—	9/14/11	9/14/11

[1]*Unless otherwise noted: All transmissions are column-shift, except on Arrow, or any model w/4-speed manual. Floor-shift is available for $30 extra on any Volaré w/3-speed manual transmission. Also available on Volaré coupes w/automatic; and Fury Sport w/bucket seats, console and automatic transmission in combination with other required equipment.* [2]*Not available on wagons.* [3]*Not available in California or designated high altitude areas.* [4]*Includes electronic "Lean Burn" system on Volaré w/360 CID V8, and all with 400 and 440 CID V8s.* [5]*Available on coupes only with other required equipment.* [6]*Available only in California or designated high altitude areas.* [7]*Required as standard equipment in California and designated high altitude areas, with appropriate adjustment in price.*

Major Options

	Arrow	Volaré	Fury	Gran Fury
Air conditioning[1]	$395	$454	$518	$546
Tilt steering wheel[2]	S	$54	$59	$106
Automatic speed control	—	$77	$84	$88
Electric rear window defroster	$79[3]	$79	$86	$87
Tinted glass, all windows	S	$48	$57	$72
Front vent window, 4-dr. only	—	—	—	$43
Dual remote control sport mirrors		$50	$55	$48[4]
Power windows, 2-dr./4-dr.	—	$104/$145	$113/$158	$186
Power door locks, 2-dr./4-dr.	—	$65/$92	$71/$101	$72/$102
Power seat, bench	—	$131	$143	$145
Remote-control trunklid release	—	—	—	$21
AM radio	$3	$69	$76	$77
AM/FM stereo	$3	$215	$234	$237
AM/FM stereo w/8-track tape	—	$304	$332	$337
Front bucket seats w/console	S[5]	$198[5]	$50[5]	—
Vinyl top, full[6]	$92	$92	$116	$141
Sunroof, electric[7]	—	$198	$330	$768
T-Bar roof	—	$554	—	—
Power steering (standard w/V8)	—	$140	$153	S
Power brakes, w/front disc	S	$59[8]	S	S
Deluxe wheel covers	—	$32	$35	$35
Premium wheel covers	—	$57	—	$74
Wire wheel covers	—	$99	$108	—
Rallye road wheels	—	$68	$80	—
Chrome styled road wheels	—	$119	$154	$156
White sidewall tires, std. size	$	$37	$43	$40

Popular Option Groups & Packages

	Arrow	Volaré	Fury	Gran Fury
Deluxe Insulation package	—	$65	$62	$43
Easy Order package	—	$801	$872	$530
"Front Runner" Super Pak	—	$318	—	—
Light package	—	$35	$48	$79
Luxury equipment package[9]	—	—	$1,837	$1,922
Protection group	—	$28	—	—
Road Runner package	—	$216	—	—
Road Runner décor group	—	$101	—	—
Spacemaker package	—	$110	—	—
Two-tone decor package	—	$177	—	—

— = Not Available; S = Standard equipment. [1]*Automatic air conditioning available on Gran Fury for $630.* [2]*Tilt and telescoping steering wheel on Gran Fury.* [3]*Electric rear window defroster is standard on GS and GT. AM radio not available on GT, and AM/FM radio (non-stereo) is only available on GT.* [4]*Regular chrome non-sport mirrors on Gran Fury.* [5]*Available on Volaré 2-door models and Fury Sport only. Standard on Arrow GT. Bucket seats only are standard on Arrow 160 and GS models without a console.* [6]*Standard on Gran Fury Brougham coupe. Volaré Landau top on 2-door models is $148. Canopy vinyl roof on Fury 2-doors at same price. Not available on station wagons.* [7]*Only available on 2-door models, and is manually operated on Volaré and Fury. Requires vinyl top on Gran Fury.* [8]*Standard on Volaré Premier. All others have manual front disc brakes as standard.* [9]*Available only on Fury Sport, Fury Sport Suburban, Fury Salon Gran Fury Custom and Custom Suburban, Gran Fury Brougham and Sport Suburban.*

Paint Colors

Plymouth	Code	Plymouth	Code	Plymouth	Code
Silver Cloud metallic	A2	French Racing Blue[2]	B5	Rallye Red[4]	E5
Wedgewood Blue[1]	B2	Regatta Blue metallic[3]	B6	Vintage Red Sunfire metallic	E8
Cadet Blue metallic[1]	B3	Starlight Blue Sunfire metallic	B9	Jade Green metallic	F2

Plymouth	Code	Plymouth	Code	Arrow	Code
Forest Green Sunfire metallic	F7	Formal Black Sunfire metallic	X8	Silver metallic	030
Burnished Copper metallic[1]	K6	Jasmine Yellow[1]	Y1	Bright Yellow	090
Mojave Beige[3,5]	L3	Golden Fawn[1]	Y4	Orange	092
Moondust metallic[1]	L5	Yellow Blaze[2]	Y5		
Russet Sunfire metallic	R8	Inca Gold metallic[1]	Y6		
Light Mocha Tan[3]	T2	Spanish Gold metallic	Y9		
Coffee Sunfire metallic[1]	T7				
Caramel Tan metallic[3]	U3	Arrow	Code		
Spitfire Orange[2]	V1	Copper metallic	004		
Spinnaker White	W1	Bright Blue metallic	022		

Single tones are coded W1, W1. Two-tones are coded X9, W1 where first two digits are accent or roof color, and second two digits are basic body color. [1]Not available on Volaré. [2]High-impact color designed primarily for use on Volaré Coupes. [3]Available only on Volaré. [4]Available only on Fury. [5]Available only on Gran Fury.

Arrow

"What more can a little car give?"

Nameplate year of origin: 1976.
Current bodystyle lifespan: 1976 through 1980.
Predecessor to this model: None.
Replacement for this model: Champ (1979 to 1983).
Primary competition: AMC Gremlin and Chevrolet Chevette.
Notable changes: Minor trim and detail changes.
Major standard equipment: All-vinyl front bucket seats w/reclining seatbacks, folding rear seat, black I/P trim, tilt steering column, two-speed electric windshield wipers, cigarette lighter, heater and defroster, tinted glass, argent painted grille and bumpers, front and rear window moldings, drip rail moldings, power front disc brakes, and 6.00 × 13 BSW tires. GS adds: Richmond vinyl front bucket seats w/accent trim, woodtone I/P trim, full-floor carpeting including cargo area, ashtray light, right roof rail assist grip, flipper rear quarter windows, rear panel trim molding, rocker panel sill moldings, wheel lip molding, chrome plated bumpers, and styled road wheels. GT adds: Blue or white all-vinyl buckets seats w/vertical stripe in opposite color, floor console w/ammeter, oil pressure gauge and coin holder, rally gauge cluster w/tachometer, overhead console for dome and map lights, and warning lights, soft-rim sports style steering wheel, dual black sport mirrors, GT up-and-over tape stripe, and 165SR × 13 WSW tires.

Measurements

Wheelbase	92.1"
Length	167.3"
Width	63.4"
Height	52.2"
Legroom — front	41.7"
Legroom — rear	28.0"
Headroom — front	36.8"
Headroom — rear	34.4"
Cargo capacity (cu. ft.)	17.3
Fuel capacity (gals.)	13.2

Models Available

	Model No.	Base MSRP	Change from LY	Shipping Wt. (lbs.)	Model Year Sales*	Change from LY
Arrow 160 2-Door Hatchback Cpe.	7L24	$3,379	+6.43%	2110	NA	NA
Arrow 160 GS 2-Door Hatchback Cpe.	7H24	$3,654	+7.25%	2110	NA	NA
Arrow 160 GT 2-Door Hatchback Cpe.	7P24	$4,098	+9.34%	2090	NA	NA
TOTALS	*Avg. price*	$3,710	+7.75%	*Production*	51,849	+149.65%

Model year sales by trim level not available.

Volaré

"The accent is on comfort and styling!"

Nameplate year of origin: 1976.
Current bodystyle lifespan: 1976 through 1980.
Predecessor to this model: Valiant (1967 to 1976).
Replacement for this model: Reliant (1981 to 1989).
Percentage of division's production: 71.45%.

Measurements

	Coupe	Sedan	Wagon
Wheelbase	108.5"	112.5"	112.5"
Length	197.5"	201.5"	201.5"

Corporate siblings: Dodge Aspen.

Primary competition: AMC Hornet, Chevrolet Nova, and Ford Granada.

Notable changes: Minor trim and detail changes.

Major standard equipment: All-vinyl front bench seat (sedan and wagon), cloth and vinyl front bench seat (coupe), color-keyed carpeting, three-spoke steering wheel, two-speed electric windshield wipers and washers, front ashtray, bright grille surround molding, roof drip rail molding, quarter window reveal moldings, windshield and backlight moldings, and D78 × 14 BSW tires. Wagon adds: Rear liftgate, power front disc brakes, heavy-duty suspension, and F78 × 14 BSW tires. Custom adds: Custom pleated vinyl bench seat (coupe), cloth and vinyl bench seat (sedan), custom door trim panels, cigarette lighter, rear armrests w/ashtrays, simulated woodgrain I/P appliqué, belt moldings, wide bodyside chrome moldings w/black insert, and rear deck lower appliqué. Premier adds: Vinyl 60/40 split front bench seat w/individual recliners and fold-down center armrest, shag carpeting, luxury door trim panels w/lower carpeting, door pull handles, glove box lock, luxury 3-spoke steering wheel (w/automatic transmission only), day/night rear view mirror, landau vinyl roof (coupe), full vinyl roof (sedan), upper door frame moldings (sedan), color-keyed wide vinyl bodyside molding, full wheel lip molding, hood ornament and windsplit molding, deluxe insulation package, undercoating w/hood silencer pad, power front disc brakes, power steering, dual horns, premium wheel covers, and DR78 × 14 BSW tires. Premier wagon adds: Deluxe pleated vinyl bench seat, cigarette lighter and rear seat ashtray, cargo compartment carpet and storage bins w/locking doors, upper door frame molding, woodgrain bodyside panel and liftgate appliqué, and belt moldings.

Measurements (cont.)

	Coupe	Sedan	Wagon
Width	72.8"	72.8"	72.8"
Height	53.1"	54.8"	54.8"
Legroom — front	42.2"	42.3"	42.3"
Legroom — rear	30.7"	37.4"	37.4"
Headroom — front	37.5"	39.2"	39.2"
Headroom — rear	36.1"	38.7"	38.7"
Cargo capacity (cu. ft.)	14.5*	14.4	72.8
Fuel capacity (gals.)	18.0	18.0	20.0

*Premier coupe is 13.6 cu. ft.

Models Available

	Model No.	Base MSRP	Change from LY	Shipping Wt. (lbs.)	Model Year Production	Change from LY
Volaré 2-Door Sport Coupe	HL29	$3,570	+7.40%	3180	32,264	+6.87%
Volaré 4-Door Sedan	HL41	$3,619	+7.74%	3235	36,688	+91.22%
Volaré 4-Door Station Wagon	HL45	$3,941	+8.09%	3445	70,913	+75.11%
Volaré Custom 2-Door Sport Coupe	HH29	$3,752	+7.02%	3185	30,230	+9.31%
Volaré Custom 4-Door Sedan	HH41	$3,801	+7.34%	3240	45,130	+37.74%
Volaré Premier 2-Door Sport Coupe	HP29	$4,305	-2.20%	3375	17,852	-34.95%
Volaré Premier 4-Door Sedan	HP41	$4,354	-0.80%	3440	26,050	-21.25%
Volaré Premier 4-Door Station Wagon	HH45	$4,271	+7.42%	3450	68,612	+55.26%
TOTALS	Avg. price	$3,952	+4.88%	Production	327,739	+28.52%

Fury

"Fury does great things with mid-size motoring—and does it with style!"

Nameplate year of origin: 1956. Applied to mid-size platform for 1975.

Current bodystyle lifespan: 1971 through 1978.

Predecessor to this model: Satellite (1971 to 1974).

Replacement for this model: Caravelle (1985 to 1988).

Percentage of division's sales volume: 20.67%.

Corporate siblings: Dodge Monaco.

Primary competition: AMC Matador, Chevrolet Chevelle, and Ford LTD II.

Notable changes: New front-end design and minor trim and detail changes.

Major standard equipment: Regency cloth-and-vinyl front bench seat, color-keyed carpeting, cigarette lighter, dome light, lockable glove box, concealed two-speed windshield

Measurements

	2-Doors	4-Doors	Wagons
Wheelbase	115.0"	117.4"	117.5"
Length	213.7"	218.4"	225.6"
Width	77.7"	77.7"	78.8"
Height	52.6"	54.0"	55.8"
Legroom — front	42.6"	42.6"	42.6"
Legroom — rear	32.0"	34.8"	35.2"
Headroom — front	37.7"	38.7"	39.6"
Headroom — rear	36.6"	37.3"	38.1"
Cargo capacity (cu. ft.)	14.7	19.7	84.7*
Fuel capacity (gals.)	25.5	25.5	20.0

*Plus 5.2 cu.ft. of concealed space on 2-seat station wagons.

wipers w/washers, rocker panel sill molding, decklid lower molding (coupe), bumper guards, hubcaps, and F78 × 15 BSW tires. Fury Sport and Salon adds: Velour-and-vinyl front bench seat w/fold-down center armrest, shag carpeting, premium door trim panels w/pull handles, simulated woodgrain inserts on I/P, door trim inserts and steering wheel, Sport ornamentation on C-pillar of coupe, Salon ornamentation on decklid and C-pillar of sedan, belt moldings, upper door frame molding (Salon only), bodyside tape stripes (Sport only), hood ornament, hood rear edge molding, and dual horns. Suburban wagon adds: Fold-down rear seatback, power front disc brakes, three-way tailgate, and H78 × 15 BSW tires. Sport Suburban wagon adds: All-vinyl split-back front bench seat w/fold-down center armrest, cargo compartment carpeting and dome light, and exterior simulated woodgrained bodyside overlays and tailgate trim.

Models Available

	Model No.	Base MSRP	Change from LY	Shipping Wt. (lbs.)	Model Year Production	Change from LY
Fury 2-Door Hardtop	RL23	$3,893	+5.24%	3625	11,909	+5.01%
Fury 4-Door Sedan	RL41	$3,944	+5.65%	3655	20,103	+11.65%
Fury Suburban 4-Door, 2-S. Wagon	RL45	$4,687	+1.96%	4335	5,626	+49.43%
Fury Suburban 4-Door, 3-S. Wagon	RL46	$4,830	+1.92%	4390	5,141	+34.93%
Fury Sport 2-Dr. Hardtop	RH23	$4,132	+3.61%	3630	24,385	+4.60%
Fury Salon 4-Door Sedan	RH41	$4,185	+4.05%	3665	22,188	+32.32%
Fury Sport Suburban 4-Door, 2-S. Wagon	RH45	$5,192	+4.13%	4330	1,827	+16.59%
Fury Sport Suburban 4-Door, 3-S. Wagon	RH46	$5,335	+4.04%	4400	3,634	+15.62%
TOTALS	*Avg. price*	$4,525	+3.74%	*Production*	94,813	+16.03%

Gran Fury

"It puts a new value on fine motoring."

Nameplate year of origin: 1956.
Current bodystyle lifespan: 1974 through 1977 (renamed Gran Fury for 1975 to 1977).
Predecessor to this model: Fury (1969 to 1973).
Replacement for this model: Gran Fury (1980 to 1981).
Percentage of division's sales volume: 7.88%.
Corporate siblings: Dodge Royal Monaco.
Primary competition: Chevrolet Impala/Caprice and Ford LTD.
Notable changes: New front end for base and Custom, and minor trim and detail changes.
Major standard equipment: Textured cloth-and-vinyl front bench seat, color-keyed front and rear armrests, nylon loop-pile carpeting, simulated woodgrained appliqué on I/P cluster, cigarette lighter, dome light, front door courtesy light switches, glove box lock, inside hood release, concealed two-

Measurements

	2-Doors	4-Doors	Wagons
Wheelbase	121.4"	121.4"	124.0"
Length	222.4"	222.4"	226.4"
Width	79.8"	79.8"	79.4"
Height	54.1"	54.8"	56.9"
Legroom — front	42.1"	42.1"	42.1"
Legroom — rear	34.2"	36.8"	37.3"
Headroom — front	38.0"	38.7"	38.9"
Headroom — rear	37.7"	37.8"	40.5"
Cargo capacity (cu. ft.)	20.4	20.4	102.4*
Fuel capacity (gals.)	26.5	26.5**	20.0

*Plus 4.3 cu. ft. of concealed space on 2-seat station wagons. **20.5 gallons on 4-door sedans with 318 CID V8 engine.*

speed windshield wipers w/washers, bright belt and drip rail molding, dual horns, hubcaps, and GR78 × 15 BSW tires. Brougham adds: Princeton brocade-like cloth-and-vinyl front bench seat w/fold-down center armrest, door pull straps, carpeted lower door panels, simulated woodgrained appliqué on I/P, rear door dome light courtesy switches, extra quiet insulation, bright belt moldings, and bright rocker panel sill molding. Wagons add: All-vinyl front bench seat, color-keyed carpeting, simulated woodgrain inserts on steering wheel, cargo light, aerodynamic roof air deflector, power tailgate window, power steering, and LR78 × 15 BSW tires. Sport Suburban adds: All-vinyl split back front bench seat w/fold-down center armrest, door pull straps, simulated woodgrained appliqué on I/P cluster and pad, 3-spoke steering wheel w/simulated woodgrained inserts, simulated woodgrained door trim insert, carpeted lower door panels, electric clock, rear door dome light courtesy switches, simulated woodgrain bodyside panels, dual horns, and deluxe wheel covers.

Models Available

	Model No.	Base MSRP	Change from LY*	Shipping Wt. (lbs.)	Model Year Production	Change from LY*
Gran Fury 2-Door Hardtop	PM23	$4,692	NEW	4070	1,504	NEW
Gran Fury 4-Door Sedan	PM41	$4,677	+7.54%	4145	10,162	+82.77%
Gran Fury Suburban 4-Door, 2-S. Wagon	PM45	$5,315	+8.27%	4880	1,442	+37.86%
Gran Fury Brougham 2-Door Hardtop	PH23	$4,963	+4.93%	4190	3,242	+114.28%
Gran Fury Brougham 4-Door Sedan	PH41	$4,948	+4.94%	4250	15,021	+24.26%
Gran Fury Sport Suburban 4-Dr., 2-S. Wagon	PH45	$5,558	+7.03%	4880	1,194	+17.29%
Gran Fury Sport Suburban 4-Dr., 3-S. Wagon	PH46	$5,681	+6.87%	4925	3,600	+111.76%
TOTALS	Avg. price	$5,119	+1.33%	Production	36,165	+27.29%

*Comparisons to LY are made to the equivalent 1976 model numbers: i.e., 1977 PH model Broughams and Sport Suburbans compared to 1976 PH model Customs and Custom Suburbans.

PONTIAC

"The Mark of Great Cars."

The 1977 model year was significant for Pontiac in many respects, from the new downsized Catalina and Bonneville full-size models, to the increasingly popular Grand Prix and Firebird models, to the two new engines it would introduce, including a 4-cylinder engine that would be important to GM's future ability to compete with the accelerating popularity of import cars. The new year also brought an official printed documentation of Pontiac's 50th anniversary year in its sales brochures for the year, complete with infamous historical errors regarding the Grand Prix (such as the statement that it was introduced in 1963). Pontiac was again on a roll, with large sales increases for the all-new full-size models, the Firebird and Grand Prix lines, and a new mid-year compact, named Phoenix, being added to the line. At year's end, production had risen more than 20 percent, and Pontiac was able to maintain its fourth place ranking.

Just as significant to Pontiac as the new models was the introduction of two new engines. A special brochure to introduce the new engines opened with the following statement: "Coincident with the celebration of Pontiac's Golden Anniversary year and part and parcel of the most dramatic model resizing in recent automotive history, it is appropriate that two complementary new engines debut in 1977 — the 2.5-litre (151 cu. in.) L-4 and the 5-litre (301 cu. in.) V8." Initially referred to as the 5.0 Litre Pontiac V8 engine, the 301 CID engine was soon redesignated 4.9 Litre to avoid confusion with the Chevrolet and Oldsmobile 5.0 Litre engines of 305 and 307 cubic inch displacement, respectively. Pontiac's two new engines employed identical bore and stroke specifications allowing for shared components such as pistons,

rings and connecting rods. At the time, no one could have foreseen that these would be the last Pontiac engines designed, and that all of Pontiac's own V8 engines, including the new 301 CID V8, would be gone by the end of the 1981 model year. Fortunately for Pontiac, the new four-cylinder engine would be used in a wide variety of upcoming GM models, being adapted for front-wheel drive applications, and it would serve the company well for many years to come. Also noteworthy in the powertrain department was that all inline six-cylinder engines were gone, being replaced by V6 engines from Buick.

All-new Bonneville and Catalina models brought new life to the full-sized Pontiacs, which had been struggling for the past few years. With the downsizing, all hardtop models were gone, and in their place were three basic models — coupe, sedan and station wagon. All three shared the "three box" look of other GM full-size models, though the coupes received their own unique rooflines. All four-doors had a rear door glass design with a roll-down rear window and a fixed upright rectangular quarter window. For Pontiac, the coupes used a large, nearly triangular fixed rear quarter window, and a gently sloped flat rear window. At the front, there was no doubt that these were Pontiacs, with their requisite split grille styling and center mounted Pontiac logo. The Catalina had almost a crosshair grille design, with two horizontal chrome-lined openings per side, and a chrome vertical center bar. Within each of the four openings were six horizontal bars. Bonneville and Grand Safari models used a cross-hatch grille pattern, with a similar center bar, and the grille pattern was extended to the rectangular openings of the front bumper below the rub strip. Each side of the grille had a four by four horizontal crosshatch design, with each opening housing a small three rows by four column insert. All models had parking/turn signal lights mounted near the bumper ends and a side marker light on the fender side edge of the headlight bezel. At the rear, large wraparound taillights were set in a convex shaped rear panel, with the license plate mounted in the center. For Catalinas, the taillights were divided into two sections horizontally by a piece of body-colored trim. On Bonnevilles, the lights extended nearly to the license plate recess and were divided into three sections horizontally by chrome trim, with five slimmer vertical chrome strips.

Bodysides of the new full-size Pontiacs used an upper feature line beginning at the top edge of the front fender, running straight back to meet the line of the back edge of the rear quarter window on coupe, and the back edge of the rear door on sedans. This line on the Safari wagons ran straight through to the back of the car, across the tailgate, and back up the other side. A lower feature line ran straight along the bodyside between the midpoints of the bumper ends, creating a minuscule flare over the rounded front wheel opening. On Catalinas there was no flare on the rear wheel opening, while on Bonneville models, the feature line passed through the bottom edge of the rear wheel opening fender skirts. The Bonneville was the lone model to use them among GM's newly downsized full-size cars. Interiors were more luxurious looking by virtue of using stitching and "pillow" effects both on seats and door panels. A new striped velour pattern called "Valencia" was popular among Bonneville Brougham customers. The Catalina coupe and sedan came with standard Buick V6 engines, while the Bonneville had as standard the new Pontiac-built 301 CID V8 engine. The 350 CID and 400 CID V8 engine remained as optional choices, although the big 455 CID V8 engine was discontinued.

The sporty Firebird line wore a new nose with dual rectangular headlights set into the outer ends of lower and more elongated grille recesses with new honeycomb inserts. The inner ends of the grilles were now angled, producing a tapered body-color split at the center. Along with the rectangular headlights came a flatter hood, as it no longer required an upward bump at the sides to clear the headlights. The popular black Special Edition Trans Am package this year was exclusively available with the new Hatch Roof T-Top option. With the 455 CID V8 engine being dropped, the Pontiac 400 CID V8 became the top Firebird engine choice, and was standard equipment on the Trans Am, where it was tweaked to have 20 more horsepower, and was known as the "T/A 6.6" engine. The black SE Trans Am, 15,567 units of which were produced, was immortalized in the 1977 movie *Smokey and the Bandit*, starring Burt Reynolds and Sally Field, resulting in the popular Trans Am being forever known as the "Bandit" Trans Am.

Grand Prix added new front-end styling and new taillights for 1977. The new front-end styling foreshadowed the upcoming downsized 1978 models, with dual rectangular headlights now separated by a vertical rectangular parking/turn signal light. The grille itself was still of a vertical design, this year not wrapping up onto the header as far as the 1976 models did, and having five sections per side. Each section had two inset vertical bars, and the grille continued into the lower portion of the bumper, reminiscent of the classic 1971–1972 Grand Prix design. At the rear, new taillight lenses carried only a center mounted Grand Prix logo and were set in a chrome-trimmed bezel. The former LJ option package officially became a Grand Prix model for 1977, but with the new model came another round of model number juggling. What was originally known as the model K57 Grand Prix base model had become the Grand Prix SJ for 1976 and was now the new Grand Prix LJ. The J57 model number, applied to the base Grand Prix for 1976, continued unchanged, but the SJ was given a new H57 designation. The comparisons in the model charts that follow are based on the name, and not the model number.

New grille inserts were the most apparent change to the 1977 LeMans line. The LeMans and LeMans Sport Coupe lines featured a vertically slotted grille with six openings per side, while the Grand LeMans models had five slots with a horizontal center dividing line, creating ten square openings per side. Some of the other changes for the year included adding the woodgrain vinyl appliqués as standard equipment to the Grand LeMans Safari and making the previously standard rear wheel fender skirts an option for the Grand LeMans line. Two new option packages appeared for the final season of this generation of mid-size Pontiacs. One was the return of the GT package after a one-year absence, this time featuring over-the-roof striping, rather than full-length bodyside striping.

The other new package, exclusively for the LeMans Sport Coupe, was named the Can Am. Originally proposed by Pontiac management as a new GTO, to capitalize on the revived interest in performance cars, as borne out by the return of the Chevrolet Camaro Z28 and the success of Pontiac's own Trans Am, the idea was panned by GM executives, so Pontiac designers busily found a way around the decision to determine another way to build the product they wanted. The result was reminiscent of how the original GTO came into being, this time with Pontiac out-sourcing some of the final component finishing to Motortown, Inc. When the Can Am program was announced to dealers, they quickly collected more than 5,000 orders. As production began, the process was to send Cameo White LeMans Sport Coupes fitted with the optional T/A 400 CID V8 engine, or 403 CID V8 for cars destined for California, to Motortown, Inc., near Detroit, where they would add the decals and striping, shaker hood and rear decklid spoiler. Full details of the package content can be found in Appendix IV.

1977

As the story goes, several months after production commenced, the mold used to produce the Can Am's rear spoiler was damaged beyond repair. Apparently, Motortown had not created a backup mold, and General Motors executives were not interested in spending more money on a model that was in its final year of production, so the Can Am's production run was halted at 1,133 units. At this point, the story takes an interesting turn, as there were several hundred LeMans Sport Coupes already built with the Trans Am engine installed. These were sent out to dealers as regular models, and sold without the additional Can Am shaker hood and markings. Some estimates place Can Am production as high as 1,337 units, but it is quite possible that this number comes from how many were sold with the T/A engine, and not necessarily with the additional Can Am equipment. No matter what the total production was, the Can Am was a bargain priced performance car that lived up to its GTO heritage. Unfortunately, it will never be known whether, had the full 5,000 units been produced, the concept might have survived into the new downsized 1978 LeMans models. A prototype 1978 Grand Am C/A was built, and is featured in Appendix VIII.

The compact Ventura line returned with a new rectangular front grille pattern and square headlight bezels that combined to give the front end a flatter appearance, though it still had a traditional Pontiac split grille and still sloped. The new grille was made up of six rectangular pods per side, stacked two high and three across, each having five vertical slots within. The outer two pods held the parking/turn signal lights behind the grille. The square headlight bezel had a combination side marker and turn signal light mounted on the fender side. SJ models received new taillamps extending fully to the license plate recess, and rimmed in chrome with a horizontal chrome center strip. Little else changed for the 1977 Ventura, a name that would once again fade away into history after this year, at it had several times over the past seventeen years. The reason was that at mid-year a more luxurious car based on the Ventura was introduced, named the Phoenix. While sharing most features of the Ventura SJ from the cowl back, the Phoenix boasted unique front-end styling with a square themed design. Single square headlamps in square bezels flanked five vertical grille sections per side, each containing four vertical slots, with the parking/turn signal lights set behind the outer grille section. In the center, instead of a pointed body-colored nose typical of many prior Pontiac

models, the Phoenix had a slightly pointed square-shaped body-colored nose, with a matching square body-colored center bumper pad. Gray rub strips and outer bumper pads also dressed up the bumper in lieu of traditional bumper guards. The Phoenix shared the SJ taillamps. Powertrain choices remained similar to those of the Ventura SJ, except that the 231 CID V6 engine was standard, while the 151 CID 4-cylinder was available as a delete credit option. Differing interior upholstery patterns and trim with a front-seat folddown center armrest was standard Phoenix fare, while the rest of the interior was basically the same as the Ventura SJ.

The action of adding the Phoenix as a second compact line was similar to what Chevrolet had done with the Nova in adding a top-line Concours model for the 1976 and 1977 model years. Quite possibly the addition of the Phoenix was intended to make the lower-priced GM makes more competitive with Ford and Mercury, which had both the Maverick/Comet and the Granada/Monarch from 1975 through 1977, as well as Plymouth and Dodge, which had the Valiant/Dart plus the Volaré/Aspen in 1976, and now had the Diplomat for 1977. However, it is also speculated that the Phoenix served another purpose, to introduce publicly a front-end treatment similar to what the mid-size LeMans would carry when it would be downsized in the fall, and a new name that would be recognizable when the downsized compact line, the front-wheel-drive X-cars, were introduced in the spring of 1979. The second theory seems to be proven, as the mid-year sales brochure proclaimed, "...we made Phoenix the only American car today with single rectangular headlamps. And set them inside a distinctive new split grille."

The Astre and Sunbird subcompacts carried revised styling, and both offered available Formula appearance packages, even on the Astre Safari. The new Astre grille insert consisted of four vertical rectangle sections per side, with the outer section housing the parking/turn signal lights, and the three inner sections carrying six vertical bars per section. For the Sunbird, a new honeycomb pattern grille insert was introduced. Shortly after the start of the model year, a Sunbird Sport Hatch was introduced that carried the Sunbird front-end styling with the hatchback body of the existing GM H-body hatchbacks. Horizontal rectangular taillamps with outer red lens, center amber turn signal, and white backup lights to the inside were divided into three horizontal strips by chrome trim. Most other features were the same as the Sunbird coupe.

Astre Safari 2-Door Station Wagon (left)
and Astre 2-Door Notchback Coupe

Bonneville 2-Door Coupe

Catalina 4-Door Sedan

Astre 2-Door Hatchback Coupe with Formula package

Bonneville 2-Door Coupe with two-tone paint

Bonneville interior with
Valencia striped velour trim

Catalina Safari 4-Door Station Wagon

Firebird Formula 2-Door Hardtop Coupe

Firebird Trans Am 2-Door Hardtop Coupe
with Special Edition package and T-tops

Grand LeMans 2-Door Colonnade Hardtop
Coupe (top) and LeMans Sport Coupe
2-Dr Colonnade Hardtop Coupe

Grand LeMans 4-Door
Colonnade Hardtop Sedan

Firebird Trans Am
2-Door Hardtop
Coupe with
Special Edition
package and T-
tops, stripe detail

1977

Grand Prix 2-Door Hardtop Coupe

LeMans Safari 4-Door Station Wagon

Phoenix 2-Door Coupe

Sunbird 2-Door Coupe

Ventura SJ 4-Door Sedan

Grand Prix SJ 2-Door Hardtop Coupe

Grand Safari 4-Door Station Wagon

LeMans Sport 2-Door Colonnade Hardtop Coupe with Can Am package

Sunbird 2-Door Coupe with Formula package

Ventura 2-Door Coupe

Model year production: 912,427, up 21.85% from 1976.

Domestic market share: 9.51% (4th place).

Base price range: $3,305 to $5,992.

Pontiac average base price: $4,591, up 3.10%.

Introduction date: September 30, 1976. Phoenix introduced February 1977.

Assembly plants: Lakewood, GA (A); Southgate, CA (C); Framingham, MA (G); Van Nuys, CA (L); Norwood, OH (N); Pontiac, MI (P); Tarrytown, NY (T); Lordstown, OH (U); Willow Run, MI (W); Kansas City/Fairfax, KS (X); Oshawa, Ontario, Canada (1); and Ste. Therese, Quebec, Canada (2).

Data plate identification (VIN): Thirteen digit code read as follows: First digit indicates division (2 = Pontiac); second through fourth digits indicate series and body style (model number in model charts); fifth digit is engine code (see powertrain chart); sixth digit indicates model year (7 = 1977); seventh digit indicates assembly plant (see list above); remaining digits are sequential with beginning number of 100001. *Example:* 2D35L7G100001 is a 1977 Pontiac LeMans 4-Door, 2-Seat Safari station wagon, with 350 CID, 4-bbl. V8 engine, serial number 100001, built in Framingham, MA.

Powertrains

Engine	Net HP	Engine Code: VIN/GM	Transmission Availability[1]		Astre & Sunbird	Ventura & Phoenix	Firebird[2]	LeMans[3]	Grand Prix	Catalina	Bonneville & Safaris
140 CID (2.3L) OHC, 2-bbl., 4-cyl.	84	B/L11	4-speed manual		S (Astre Cpe.)	—	—	—	—	—	—
				MPG:	24/33/28	—	—	—	—	—	—
				Calif.	23/33/27	—	—	—	—	—	—
			5-speed manual		$248 (Astre Cpe.)	—	—	—	—	—	—
				MPG:	NA	—	—	—	—	—	—
			3-speed Turbo Hydra-matic		$248 (Astre Cpe.)	—	—	—	—	—	—
				MPG:	21/28/24	—	—	—	—	—	—
				Calif.	21/30/24	—	—	—	—	—	—
151 CID (2.5L), 2-bbl., 4-cyl.	90	V/LS6	4-speed manual		$20 (Astre Cpe.)/S (others)	-$120 (credit option Cpe. & Sdn. only)	—	—	—	—	—
				MPG:	26/37/30	22/34/26	—	—	—	—	—
			5-speed manual		$268 (Astre Cpe.)/$248 (others)	$162 (Cpe. & Sdn. only)	—	—	—	—	—
				MPG:	NA	NA	—	—	—	—	—
			3-speed Turbo Hydra-matic		$268 (Astre Cpe.)/$248 (others)	$162 (Cpe. & Sdn. only)	—	—	—	—	—
				MPG:	24/32/27	21/29/24	—	—	—	—	—
				Calif.	19/25/21	—	—	—	—	—	—
231 CID (3.8L), 2-bbl., V6[4]	105	C/LD7	3-speed manual		—	S	S (F & FEs)	S (L)	—	—	—
				MPG:	—	17/27/20	16/26/19	16/26/19	—	—	—
			4-speed manual		$120 (Sunbird)	$257	$257 (F & FEs)	—	—	—	—
				MPG:	18/29/21	NA	NA	—	—	—	—
				Calif.	13/26/17	12/25/16	12/24/15	—	—	—	—
			5-speed manual		$368 (Sunbird)	$282 (2-drs. only)	—	—	—	—	—
				MPG:	NA	NA	—	—	—	—	—
			3-speed Turbo		$368	$282	$282	S (GL)/	—	S	—

1977

Engine	Net HP	Engine Code: VIN/GM	Transmission Availability[1]		Astre & Sunbird	Ventura & Phoenix	Firebird[2]	LeMans[3]	Grand Prix	Catalina	Bonneville & Safaris
			Hydra-matic		(Sunbird)		(F & FEs)	$282 (L)			
				MPG:	19/26/ 21	18/26/ 21	17/25/ 20	17/25/ 20	—	17/25/ 20	—
				Calif.	14/19/ 16	15/20/ 17	16/21/ 18	16/21/ 18	—	16/21/ 18	—
301 CID (4.9L), 2-bbl., V8	135	Y/L27	3-speed manual		—	$65	S (FF)/ $65 (F & FEs)	$65 (L)	—	—	—
				MPG:	—	15/23/ 18	15/23/ 18	NA	—	—	—
			4-speed manual		—	$322	$257 (FF)/ $317 (F & FEs)	—	—	—	—
				MPG:	—	NA	NA	—	—	—	—
			3-speed Turbo Hydra-matic		—	$347	$282 (FF)/ $342 (F & FEs)	S (LS)/ $65 (GL)/ $347 (L)	S	$66	S
				MPG:	—	17/23/ 19	17/23/ 19	16/23/ 19	16/23/ 19	17/23/ 19	17/23/ 19
305 CID (5.0L), 2-bbl., V8	150[5]	U/LG3	3-speed Turbo Hydra-matic		—	$347	$282 (FF)/ $342 (F & FEs)	—	—	—	—
				MPG:	—	16/22/ 18	NA	—	—	—	—
350 CID (5.7L), 4-bbl., V8	170	L/LM1	3-speed Turbo Hydra-matic		—	$435[6]	$372 (FF)	$90 (LS)[6]	$90	$157	$91
				MPG:	—	NA	16/22/ 18	14/21/ 17	14/21/ 17	16/22/ 18	16/22/ 18
				Calif.	—	15/21/ 17	15/21/ 17	15/21/ 17	14/20/ 16	14/20/ 16	14/21/ 17
350 CID (5.7L), 4-bbl., V8	170	P	3-speed Turbo Hydra-matic		—	$435[6]	$372 (FF)	$90 (LS)[6]	$90	$157	$91
				MPG:	—	NA	16/22/ 18	14/21/ 17	14/21/ 17	16/22/ 18	16/22/ 18
				Calif.	—	15/21/ 17	15/21/ 17	14/20/ 16	14/20/ 16	14/21/ 17	14/21/ 17
350 CID (5.7L), 4-bbl., V8	170	R/L34	3-speed Turbo Hydra-matic		—	$435[6]	$372 (FF)	$90 (LS)[6]	$90	$157	$91
				MPG:	—	NA	16/22/ 18	14/21/ 17	14/21/ 17	16/22/ 18	16/22/ 18
				Calif.	—	15/21/ 17	15/21/ 17	—	—	15/21/ 18	15/21/ 18
400 CID (6.6L), 4-bbl., V8[7]	180	Z	4-speed manual		—	—	S (TA)/ $412 (FF)/ $477 (F & FEs)	—	—	—	—
				MPG:	—	—	12/19/ 15	—	—	—	—

Engine	Net HP	Engine Code: VIN/GM	Transmission Availability[1]	Astre & Sunbird	Ventura & Phoenix	Firebird[2]	LeMans[3]	Grand Prix	Catalina	Bonneville & Safaris
			3-speed Turbo Hydra-matic	—	—	$282 (TA)/ $437 (FF)/ $502 (F & FEs)	$155 (LS)/ $220 (GL)/ $502 (L)	$155	—	—
			MPG:	—	—	15/20/ 17	14/21/ 17	14/21/ 17		
400 CID (6.6L) T/A, 4-bbl., V8	200	Z	3-speed Turbo Hydra-matic	—	—	$332 (TA)/ $487 (FF)	—	—	—	—
			MPG:	—	—	NA	—	—	—	—
403 CID (6.6L), 4-bbl., V8	185	K/L80	4-speed manual	—	—	S (TA)/ $412 (FF)/ $477 (F & FEs)				
			MPG:	—	—	12/19/ 15	—	—	—	—
			3-speed Turbo Hydra-matic	—	—	$282 (TA)/ $437 (FF)/ $502 (F & FEs)	$155 (LS)/ $220 (GL)/ $502 (L)	$155	$223	$157
			MPG:	—	—	15/20/ 17	14/21/ 17	14/21/ 17	15/21/ 18	15/21/ 18
			Calif.	—	—	14/20/ 16	13/19/ 15	13/19/ 15	13/19/ 15	13/19/ 15

[1]Unless otherwise noted: All 3-speed manual transmissions are floor shift, except on Ventura. All 4-speed and 5-speed manual transmissions are floor shift. All automatic transmissions are column shift, with the following exceptions: Astre, Sunbird, and Firebird. Floor-shift with 3-speed manual can be ordered on Ventura models for $31 extra. Floor shift w/automatic is available on specific Ventura, LeMans and Grand Prix models in combination w/optional bucket seats and console. [2]F = base Firebird, FEs = Firebird Esprit; FF = Firebird Formula; TA = Firebird Trans Am. [3]L = LeMans and LeMans Sport coupe; GL = Grand LeMans; LS = all LeMans Safaris. [4]The LD5 even-firing engine replaced the LD7 engine as follows: for cars built in Flint (MI), on approximately March 21, 1977; for cars built in Fairfax (KS), Lordstown (OH), St. Therese (Canada), and Southgate (MI), on approximately May 1, 1977. [5]Horsepower rating on Ventura is 145. [6]Requires California or high altitude emission equipment. [7]Not available in California.

Major Options

	Astre	Sunbird	Firebird	Ventura & Phoenix	LeMans	Grand Prix	Catalina & Bonneville
Custom air conditioning[1]	$442	$442	$478	$478	$499	$513	$540
Tilt steering wheel	$50	$50	$57	$57	$57	$57	$58
Automatic cruise control	—	—	$80	$80	$80	$84	$84
Intermittent windshield wipers	$28	$28	—	$30	$30	$30	$30
Rear window defroster, electric	$71	$71	$82	$48[2]	$82	$82	$83
Soft-Ray tinted glass, all windows	$48	$48	$50	$50	$54	$58	$69
Power windows, 2-dr./4-dr.	—	—	$108[3]	$108/$151	$108/$151	$108	$114/$171
Power door locks, 2-dr./4-dr.	—	—	$68	—	$68/$103	$68	$68/$103
Power front seat, 6-way w/std. seat	—	—	—	—	$137	$137	$139
Front bucket seats, w/console[4]	S	S	S	$347	$204[5]	$204	—
Third row seating (wagons)	—	—	—	—	$152	—	$165
AM radio	$74	$74	$79	$79	$79	$79	$92
AM/FM stereo	$212	$212	$233	$233	$233	$233	$236

	Astre	Sunbird	Firebird	Ventura & Phoenix	LeMans	Grand Prix	Catalina & Bonneville
AM/FM stereo w/8-track tape	$304	$304	$337[3]	$337	$337	$337	$341
AM/FM stereo w/CB radio	—	—	—	—	$453	$453	$459
Woodgrain exterior trim (wagons)	$160	—	—	—	—	—	—
Vinyl top, full[6]	—	$83	$105	$93	$111	$121	$140[7]
Vinyl top, padded landau[8]	—	$144	—	$162	$180	$180	$282
Sunroof, removable[8]	—	$162	—	—	—	—	—
Sunroof, power steel[8]	—	—	—	—	$394	$394	$735
Sunroof, power glass[8]	—	—	—	—	$625	$625	$898
Hatch roof, glass panel T-tops	—	—	$587[9]	—	—	$587	—
Power steering, variable-ratio	$129	$129	S	$146	$146[10]	S	S
Power brakes, w/front disc	$58	$58	$61	$61	$61[10]	S	S
Custom wheel covers	—	S	—	$	—	—	$
Wire wheel covers	—	—	$102	$102	$102	$102	$102
Rally II wheels[11]	$92	$44	$106	$106	$106	$106	$106
Cast aluminum "snowflake" wheels	$173	$124	$189	$189	$189	$189	$189
WSW tires	$38	$38	$43	$39	$45	$45	$45

Popular Option Groups & Packages

	Astre	Sunbird	Firebird	Ventura & Phoenix	LeMans	Grand Prix	Catalina & Bonneville
Can Am appearance package	—	—	—	—	$375	—	—
Can Am option package	—	—	—	—	$1,214	—	—
Custom exterior group	$94	—	—	—	—	—	—
Custom interior group	$183	—	—	—	—	—	—
Custom trim group	—	—	$118	—	$208	—	—
Formula appearance package	$558	$543	$127	—	—	—	—
GT option package	—	—	—	—	$463	—	—
Luxury appointment package	$147	$147	—	—	—	—	—
Luxury trim group	—	$144	—	—	—	—	—
Sky Bird appearance package	—	—	$342	—	—	—	—
Special appearance group	$34	$82	—	$	—	—	$140/$135
Special Edition Trans Am package	—	—	$556[9]	—	—	—	—

— = Not Available; S = Standard equipment. [1]Automatic climate control is available for $539 on LeMans, for $552 on Grand Prix, and for $579 on Catalina, Bonneville, and Grand Safari. [2]Blower type defroster. [3]Other optional equipment required at extra cost; i.e., console. [4]Front bucket seats and mini-console standard on Astre and Sunbird. Front bucket seats standard on Firebird, with console available on base and Esprit. Console standard on Firebird Formula and Trans Am. [5]Available only on LeMans Sport Coupe and Grand LeMans 2-door coupe models. [6]Canopy style vinyl roof on Firebird, Esprit and Formula. Vinyl roof available on Catalina Safari and Grand Safari for $150. Price on Bonneville two-door is $147. Not available on LeMans station wagons. Not available on Sunbird hatchback models. [7]Price is $135 on Bonneville. Standard on Bonneville Brougham. [8]Available on 2-door coupe models only. [9]Hatch roof, or T-tops, available with Special Edition Trans Am package only. [10]Power steering and power brakes standard on all LeMans Safari station wagons. Power brakes standard on Grand LeMans 4-Door. [11]Rally II wheels standard on Firebird Trans Am and Grand Prix SJ. Body-colored Rally II wheels also available at same price.

Paint Colors

	Code		Code
Cameo White	11	Bahia Green metallic[3]	44
Sterling Silver metallic	13	Berkshire Green[1]	48
Dark Charcoal (lower two-tone only)[1]	15	Cream Gold[1]	50
		Goldenrod Yellow[7]	51
Starlight Black	19	Gold metallic[5]	55
Lombard Blue[2]	21	Blue[5]	58
Glacier Blue metallic[3]	22	Mojave Tan[4]	61
Nautilus Blue metallic[4]	29	Buckskin metallic[4]	63
Royal Lime[2]	32	Fiesta Orange[2]	64
Firethorn Red metallic[4]	36	Brentwood Brown metallic	69
Cordovan Maroon metallic (two-tone only)[1]	37	Roman Red[1]	72
		Buccaneer Red[7]	75
Aquamarine metallic[6,7]	38	Mandarin Orange[4]	78

In two-tone combinations, the first two digits indicate lower color; the next two digits are the upper color. Colors without footnotes are available on all models. Two-tone colors available only on Ventura, Grand Prix (LJ or SJ only), and Catalina/Bonneville (coupes and sedans only). Trans Am "Bird" hood decal available at $66 extra cost. [1]Available only on LeMans, Grand Prix, Catalina and Bonneville models. [2]Available only on Astre. [3]Available on all models except Astre and Firebird Trans Am. [4]Available on all models except Firebird Trans Am. [5]Used as accent colors on Firebird. [6]Not available on Firebird Trans Am. [7]Available only on Astre, Sunbird, Firebird and Ventura models.

Astre

"New sizzle for Astre."

Nameplate year of origin: 1975.
Current bodystyle lifespan: 1975 through 1977 (some models moved to Sunbird series, continuing through 1979).
Predecessor to this model: None.
Replacement for this model: J2000/Sunbird (1982 to 1993).
Percentage of division's production: 3.59%.
Corporate siblings: Chevrolet Vega.
Primary competition: AMC Gremlin, Dodge Colt, and Mercury Bobcat.
Notable changes: Minor trim and detail changes.
Major standard equipment: Choice of cloth and Morrokide vinyl or all-Morrokide vinyl front bucket seats, color-keyed cut-pile carpeting (includes load floor carpeting on Safari), simulated rosewood vinyl inserts on I/P, deluxe three-spoke steering wheel, fold-down rear seat and rear liftgate (hatchback and wagon), bright front and rear window moldings, bright side window moldings, bright drip rail moldings, front and rear bumper rub strips, manual front disc brakes, hubcaps, and A78 × 13 BSW tires.

Measurements

	Coupes	Wagon
Wheelbase	97.0"	97.0"
Length	177.6"	177.6"
Width	65.4"	65.4"
Height	51.9"	51.6"
Legroom — front	42.8"	42.8"
Legroom — rear	28.9"	30.0"
Headroom — front	38.6"	38.6"
Headroom — rear	39.4"	40.3"
Cargo capacity (cu. ft.)	8.9*	46.6
Fuel capacity (gals.)	16.0	16.0

Hatchback maximum with rear seat down, 28.6 cu. ft.

1977

Models Available

	Model No.	Base MSRP	Change from LY	Shipping Wt. (lbs.)	Model Year Production	Change from LY
Astre 2-Door Notchback Coupe	C11	$3,305	+7.87%	2480	10,327	-43.08%
Astre 2-Door Hatchback Coupe	C77	$3,430	+7.90%	2573	12,120	-36.60%
Astre 2-Door Station Wagon	C15	$3,595	+8.74%	2608	10,341	-21.21%
TOTALS		*Avg. price* $3,443	+8.18%		*Production* 32,788	-34.92%

Sunbird

"It's no coincidence that America's hot new sport coupe is a Pontiac."

Nameplate year of origin: 1976.
Current bodystyle lifespan: 1976 through 1980.
Predecessor to this model: None.
Replacement for this model: J2000/Sunbird (1982 to 1993).
Percentage of division's production: 6.95%.
Corporate siblings: Buick Skyhawk, Chevrolet Monza, and Oldsmobile Starfire.
Primary competition: Ford Mustang II.
Notable changes: New Sport-Hatch model, and minor trim and detail changes.
Major standard equipment: Choice of cloth or all-Morrokide vinyl front bucket seats, cut-pile carpeting, floor shifter and floor-mounted parking brake w/mini-console, deluxe cushion three-spoke steering wheel, simulated rosewood appliqués on I/P, bright window moldings on all windows, roof drip rail moldings, wheel opening moldings, manual front disc brakes, custom wheel covers, and A78 × 13 BSW tires. Hatchback adds: Fold-down rear seat, and load-floor carpeting.

Measurements

	Coupe	Hatchback
Wheelbase	97.0"	97.0"
Length	177.8"	179.3"
Width	65.4"	65.4"
Height	49.8"	50.2"
Legroom — front	42.8"	42.8"
Legroom — rear	28.2"	29.6"
Headroom — front	37.7"	37.7"
Headroom — rear	36.9"	35.3"
Cargo capacity (cu. ft.)	6.6	30.2*
Fuel capacity (gals.)	18.5	18.5

Capacity with rear seat down.

Models Available

	Model No.	Base MSRP	Change from LY	Shipping Wt. (lbs.)	Model Year Production	Change from LY
Sunbird 2-Door Coupe	M27	$3,659	+6.65%	2662	41,708	-19.84%
Sunbird Sport Hatch 2-Door Hatchback Coupe	M07	$3,784	NEW	2693	13,690	NEW
TOTALS	*Avg. price*	$3,722	+8.47%	*Production*	55,398	+6.47%

Firebird

"The magnificent Firebirds. Four of America's great sport legends."

Nameplate year of origin: 1967.
Current bodystyle lifespan: 1970 through 1981.
Predecessor to this model: Firebird (1967 to 1969).
Replacement for this model: Firebird (1982 to 1992).
Percentage of division's production: 17.07%.
Corporate siblings: Chevrolet Camaro.
Primary competition: None.
Notable changes: New front-end styling and bumpers and minor trim and detail changes.
Major standard equipment: All-Morrokide vinyl front bucket seats, cut-pile carpeting, deluxe cushion three-spoke steering wheel, simulated rosewood I/P appliqué, ashtray light, bright front and rear window moldings, bright grille moldings, Firebird emblems on sail panel and trunk lid, Endura front and rear bumpers, trunk floor mat, variable-ratio power steering, manual front disc brakes, RTS package, hubcaps, and FR78 × 15 BSW tires. Esprit adds: Custom all-Morrokide vinyl front bucket seats w/deep contour design, distinctive door trim panels, door and I/P assist straps, luxury cushion steering wheel, pedal trim plates, rear quarter ashtray, added acoustical insulation, dual body-colored mirror w/LH remote, body-colored door handle inserts, bright roof drip rail and belt reveal moldings, bright rear hood edge molding, bright wheel opening and rocker panel moldings, and deluxe wheel covers. Formula adds: Luxury custom cushion steering wheel, full-length floor console, blacked-out grille, dual body-colored mirror w/LH remote, Formula identification, steel hood w/dual simulated hood scoops, dual chrome splitter tailpipe extensions, and front and rear stabilizer bars. Trans Am adds: Formula steering wheel, rally gauge cluster package w/electric clock, machine-turned I/P trim plate, dual body-colored mirror w/LH remote, blacked-out grille, wraparound rear deck spoiler, wheel opening air deflectors, front fender air extractors, Trans Am decal on front fender and rear spoiler, shaker hood scoop, power brakes, power flex fan, Safe-T-Track differential, firm control shocks, dual chrome splitter tailpipe extensions, Rally II wheels w/trim rings, and GR70 × 15 BSW tires.

Measurements

Wheelbase	108.1"
Length	196.8"
Width	73.0"
Height	50.4"
Legroom — front	44.1"
Legroom — rear	29.6"
Headroom — front	37.5"
Headroom — rear	35.9"
Cargo capacity (cu. ft.)	8.8
Fuel capacity (gals.)	20.2

Models Available

	Model No.	Base MSRP	Change from LY	Shipping Wt. (lbs.)	Model Year Production	Change from LY
Firebird 2-Door Hardtop Coupe	S87	$4,270	+9.32%	3264	30,642	+44.48%
Firebird Esprit 2-Door Hardtop Coupe	T87	$4,551	+9.35%	3312	34,548	+55.26%
Firebird Formula 2-Door Hardtop Coupe	U87	$4,977	+9.00%	3411	21,801	+5.76%
Firebird Trans Am 2-Door Hardtop Coupe	W87	$5,456	+9.40%	3525	68,745	+47.20%
TOTALS	*Avg. price*	$4,814	+9.27%	*Production*	155,736	+40.59%

Ventura

"The only true compact with the punch of a Pontiac."

Nameplate year of origin: 1960.
Current bodystyle lifespan: 1975 through 1979 (Ventura 1975 to 1977; Phoenix 1977 to 1979).
Predecessor to this model: Ventura/Ventura II (1971 to 1974; restyled in 1973).

Measurements

	Coupe & HBK	Sedan
Wheelbase	111.1"	111.1"

Replacement for this model: Phoenix (1980 to 1984).

Percentage of division's production: 7.30%.

Corporate siblings: Buick Skylark, Chevrolet Nova/Concours, and Oldsmobile Omega.

Primary competition: AMC Hornet, Dodge Aspen, Ford Granada, and Mercury Monarch.

Notable changes: New grille and minor trim and detail changes.

Major standard equipment: Cloth w/Morrokide vinyl trim front bench seat, cut-pile carpeting, deluxe cushion three-spoke steering wheel, cockpit-style instrument cluster w/simulated rosewood I/P trim, front door dome light switches, rear seat armrest ashtrays, bright front and rear window moldings, bright drip rail moldings, manual front disc brakes, hubcaps, and E78 × 14 BSW tires. Hatchback model adds: Fold-down rear seat, painted metal load floor, cargo area light, and fully trimmed cargo area sidewalls. SJ adds: Choice of cloth and Morrokide vinyl or all–Morrokide vinyl diamond-pattern front bench seat, padded door trim w/map pockets, simulated rosewood on I/P, luxury cushion steering wheel, I/P assist strap, carpeting on load floor (hatchback only), dome light switches on all doors, I/P courtesy lights, trunk mat and sidewall panels, side window reveal moldings, bright wheel opening moldings, extra-wide rocker panel moldings ribbed w/front and rear extensions, bright rear end panel, SJ identification, stand-up hood ornament w/hood windsplit molding, and deluxe wheel covers.

Measurements (cont.)

	Coupe & HBK	Sedan
Length	199.6"	199.6"
Width	72.4"	72.4"
Height	52.7"	53.8"
Legroom — front	41.7"	41.7"
Legroom — rear	33.2"	34.9"
Headroom — front	38.5"	39.5"
Headroom — rear	36.3"	36.5"
Cargo capacity (cu. ft.)	14.2*	13.8
Fuel capacity (gals.)	20.5	20.5

Hatchback maximum with rear seat down, 28.4 cu. ft.

1977

Models Available

	Model No.	Base MSRP	Change from LY	Shipping Wt. (lbs.)	Model Year Production	Change from LY
Ventura 2-Door Coupe	Y27	$3,596	+8.12%	3127	26,675	-6.31%
Ventura 2-Door Hatchback	Y17	$3,792	+8.25%	3249	4,015	-37.54%
Ventura 4-Door Sedan	Y69	$3,650	+8.60%	3167	27,089	-2.46%
Ventura SJ 2-Door Coupe	Z27	$3,985	+10.33%	3206	3,418	-29.01%
Ventura SJ 2-Door Hatchback	Z17	$4,165	+10.33%	3293	1,100	-39.66%
Ventura SJ 4-Door Sedan	Z69	$4,012	+10.31%	3236	4,339	-9.68%
TOTALS	*Avg. price*	$3,867	+9.36%	*Production*	66,636	+10.09%

Phoenix

"This is the first Pontiac Phoenix. Our new luxury compact."

Nameplate year of origin: 1977.

Current bodystyle lifespan: 1975 through 1979 (Ventura 1975 to 1977; Phoenix 1977 to 1979).

Predecessor to this model: Ventura/Ventura II (1971 to 1974; restyled in 1973).

Replacement for this model: Phoenix (1980 to 1984).

Percentage of division's production: 22.64%.

Corporate siblings: Buick Skylark, Chevrolet Nova/Concours, and Oldsmobile Omega.

Primary competition: AMC Hornet, Dodge Aspen, Ford Granada, and Mercury Monarch.

Notable changes: New model based on Ventura.

Major standard equipment: Cloth front bench seat w/fold-down center armrest, cut-pile carpeting, padded door trim w/map pockets, custom cushion three-spoke steering wheel, cockpit-style instrument cluster w/simulated rosewood I/P trim, I/P assist strap, I/P courtesy lights, trunk mat and sidewall panels, bright front and rear window moldings, side window reveal moldings, bright drip rail moldings, bright wheel opening moldings, extra-wide ribbed rocker panel moldings w/front and rear extensions, bright rear end panel, stand-up hood ornament w/hood windsplit molding, center body colored bumper pad, front and rear gray bumper outer pads, gray front and rear bumper rub strips, decklid lock cover, manual front disc brakes, deluxe wheel covers, and E78 × 14 BSW tires.

Measurements

	Coupe	Sedan
Wheelbase	111.1"	111.1"
Length	203.4"	203.4"
Width	72.4"	72.4"
Height	52.7"	53.8"
Legroom — front	41.7"	41.7"
Legroom — rear	32.4"	35.2"
Headroom — front	38.2"	39.1"
Headroom — rear	36.7"	37.1"
Cargo capacity (cu. ft.)	14.2	13.8
Fuel capacity (gals.)	21.0	21.0

Models Available

	Model No.	Base MSRP	Change from LY	Shipping Wt. (lbs.)	Model Year Production	Change from LY
Phoenix 2-Door Coupe	X27	$4,075	NEW	3227	10,489	NEW
Phoenix 4-Door Sedan	X69	$4,122	NEW	3275	13,639	NEW
TOTALS		*Avg. price* $4,099	NEW		*Production* 24,128	NEW

LeMans

"Pontiac's had 16 years of experience building mid-size cars. And it shows."

Nameplate year of origin: 1961 (as a Tempest subseries).
Current bodystyle lifespan: 1973 through 1977.
Predecessor to this model: Tempest/LeMans (1968 to 1972).
Replacement for this model: LeMans (1978 to 1981).
Percentage of division's production: 8.92%.
Corporate siblings: Buick Century, Chevrolet Chevelle, and Oldsmobile Cutlass.
Primary competition: AMC Matador, Dodge Monaco, Ford LTD II, and Mercury Cougar.
Notable changes: Minor trim and detail changes.
Major standard equipment: Cloth-and-vinyl front bench seat w/vertical piping pattern, color-keyed cut-pile carpeting, deluxe-cushion three-spoke steering wheel, simulated rosewood vinyl accents on I/P, door panels and steering wheel,

Measurements

	Coupes	Sedans	Wagons
Wheelbase	112.0"	116.0"	116.0"
Length	208.0"	212.0"	215.4"
Width	77.4"	77.4"	77.4"
Height	52.9"	54.3"	55.0"
Legroom — front	42.5"	42.5"	42.5"
Legroom — rear	32.9"	37.0"	36.8"
Headroom — front	37.4"	38.1"	38.7"
Headroom — rear	36.5"	36.9"	39.0"
Cargo capacity (cu. ft.)	15.1	15.1	85.1
Fuel capacity (gals.)	21.8	21.8	22.0

formal rear quarter window (coupe), bright front and rear window moldings, bright roof drip rail and rear quarter window trim, trunk mat, manual front disc brakes, hubcaps, and FR78 × 15 BSW tires. Wagon adds: All-Morrokide vinyl front bench seat, vinyl coated metal cargo area sidewalls, load floor carpeting, swing-up tailgate w/fixed window and remote release, I/P mounted "door ajar" warning light for tailgate, swing-out rear quarter vents (3-seat wagon only), vertical rub strips on tailgate, power front disc brakes, and HR78 × 15 BSW tires. Sport Coupe adds: Choice of all-Morrokide or cloth-and-Morrokide vinyl front bench seat w/fold-down center armrest, or all-Morrokide bucket seats, simulated rosewood vinyl accents on glove box door, choice of vertically louvered rear quarter windows or rear quarter opera window, wider taillight design, bright rocker panel molding, bright wheel opening and hood rear edge moldings, body-colored door handle inserts, and LeMans Sport Coupe identification. Grand LeMans adds: Choice of cloth-and-vinyl or all-vinyl diamond pattern notchback bench seat w/fold-down center armrest, or all-Morrokide bucket seats, Grand Prix cockpit style instrument panel design, luxury cushion steering wheel, padded upper door panels w/pull straps and carpeted lower panels, electric clock, simulated rosewood vinyl accents on I/P and glove box door, added body insulation, door lamp switches on all doors, formal rear quarter opera window (coupe only), bright rear hood edge and rear deck moldings, bright wheel opening moldings, body color door handle inserts, full-length rocker panel molding w/front and rear extensions, stand-up hood ornament w/hood windsplit molding, and deluxe wheel covers. Grand LeMans Safari adds: Woodgrain exterior vinyl appliqué panels w/woodtone trim.

Models Available

	Model No.	Base MSRP	Change from LY	Shipping Wt. (lbs.)	Model Year Production	Change from LY*
LeMans 2-Door Colonnade HT Coupe	D37	$4,057	+7.67%	3550	16,038	-24.10%
LeMans 4-Door Colonnade HT Sedan	D29	$4,105	+7.66%	3638	23,060	+3.88%
LeMans 4-Door, 2-Seat Safari Station Wagon	D35	$4,889	+4.31%	4135	10,081	NA*
LeMans Sport Coupe 2-Door Colonnade HT	F37	$4,216	+7.66%	3558	13,654	-12.37%
Grand LeMans 2-Door Colonnade HT Coupe	G37	$4,614	+6.56%	3587	7,581	-48.63%
Grand LeMans 4-Door Colonnade HT Sedan	G29	$4,742	+6.97%	3740	5,584	-33.61%
Grand LeMans 4-Door, 2-Seat Safari Wagon	G35	$5,144	+4.38%	4179	5,393	NA*
TOTALS		*Avg. price* $4,538	+2.73%		*Production* 81,391	-15.42%

*Comparison to LY for Safari wagons is not possible due to 1976 production being kept as combined total.

Grand Prix

"Pontiac's classic personal car."

Nameplate year of origin: 1962.
Current bodystyle lifespan: 1973 through 1977.
Predecessor to this model: Grand Prix (1969 to 1972).
Replacement for this model: Grand Prix (1978 to 1987).
Percentage of division's production: 31.61%.
Corporate siblings: Chevrolet Monte Carlo.
Primary competition: Dodge Charger SE, Ford Thunderbird, and Mercury Cougar XR-7.
Notable changes: New front end and minor trim and detail changes.
Major standard equipment: Choice of cloth-and-vinyl or all-vinyl w/Morrokide front notchback bench seat w/fold-down center armrests, color-keyed cut-pile carpeting, luxury cushion three-spoke steering wheel, cockpit-style I/P, simulated rosewood inlay trim on I/P and door panels, door pull straps, I/P courtesy lights, electric clock, ashtray light, monogrammed fixed rear quarter window w/bright trim, bright front and rear window moldings, bright side window sill and drip rail moldings, bright rear hood edge molding, bright wheel opening moldings, rocker panel moldings, trunk mat, front and rear bumper rub strips, power steering, power brakes, deluxe wheel covers, and GR78 × 15 BSW tires. LJ adds: Velour bucket seats w/center floor console, pedal trim plates, velour door panel inserts, dual body-colored sport mirrors w/LH remote control, wide rocker panel moldings, and deluxe wheel covers. SJ adds: All Morrokide-vinyl front bucket seats w/center floor console, rally gauge cluster w/trip odometer, dual body-colored sport mirrors w/LH remote control, wide rocker panel moldings, body colored door handle inserts, trunk compartment light and side panels, bodyside tape stripes, added acoustical insulation, Rally RTS package, Rally II wheels w/trim rings, and GR70 × 15 BSW tires.

Measurements

Wheelbase	116.0"
Length	212.7"
Width	77.8"
Height	52.9"
Legroom — front	42.5"
Legroom — rear	33.5"
Headroom — front	37.2"
Headroom — rear	36.9"
Cargo capacity (cu. ft.)	15.1
Fuel capacity (gals.)	25.0

1977

Models Available

	Model No.	Base MSRP	Change from LY*	Shipping Wt. (lbs.)	Model Year Production	Change from LY*
Grand Prix 2-Door Hardtop Coupe	J57	$5,120	+6.71%	3804	168,247	+20.30%
Grand Prix LJ 2-Door Hardtop Coupe	K57	$5,483	NEW	3815	66,741	NEW
Grand Prix SJ 2-Door Hardtop Coupe	H57	$5,753	+10.15%	3976	53,442	-39.43%
TOTALS	*Avg. price*	$5,452	+8.81%	*Production*	288,430	+26.45%

Comparisons based on model name, rather than model numbers as they were realigned again this year.

Catalina

"Years from now they'll still be talking about its value."

Nameplate year of origin: 1950 (as hardtop model designation), 1959 (as series).
Current bodystyle lifespan: 1977 through 1981.
Predecessor to this model: Catalina (1971 to 1976).
Replacement for this model: Parisienne (1983 to 1986) and Safari (1987 to 1989).
Percentage of division's production: 8.19%.
Corporate siblings: Buick LeSabre, Chevrolet Impala/Caprice, and Oldsmobile Delta 88.
Primary competition: Dodge Royal Monaco, Ford LTD, and Plymouth Gran Fury.
Notable changes: Completely redesigned.
Major standard equipment: Cloth-and-Morrokide vinyl bench seat, thick cut-pile carpeting, deluxe custom cushion steering wheel, rosewood vinyl I/P accents, ashtray w/light,

Measurements

	2-door	4-door	Wagon
Wheelbase	115.9"	115.9"	115.9"
Length	213.8"	213.8"	214.7"
Width	75.4"	75.4"	75.4"
Height	54.5"	54.9"	58.0"
Legroom — front	42.2"	42.2"	42.6"
Legroom — rear	38.9"	39.5"	38.7"
Headroom — front	38.5"	39.2"	39.3"
Headroom — rear	38.0"	38.0"	39.0"
Cargo capacity (cu. ft.)	20.3	20.3	87.3
Fuel capacity (gals.)	20.0	20.0	22.5

glove box light, trunk mat, bright windshield and rear window moldings, bright quarter window and roof drip rail moldings, bright rocker panel molding, bright hood rear edge molding, front and rear bumper rub strips, RTS package, hubcaps, and FR78 × 15 BSW tires. Safari wagon adds: All-Morrokide vinyl front bench seat, three-way tailgate w/power-operated rear window, rear bumper guards, and HR78 × 15 BSW tires.

Models Available

	Model No.	Base MSRP	Change from LY	Shipping Wt. (lbs.)	Model Year Production	Change from LY
Catalina 2-Door Coupe	L37	$5,053	+4.31%	3473	14,752	-3.34%
Catalina 4-Door Sedan	L69	$5,050	+5.94%	3501	46,926	-0.65%
Catalina Safari 4-Door, 2-Seat Station Wagon	L35	$5,492	+3.16%	4024	13,058	+27.42%*
TOTALS	Avg. price	$5,198	+1.89%	Production	74,736	+2.74%

*Comparison to LY made to combined total of 1976 Catalina Safari 2- and 3-seat wagons.

Bonneville and Grand Safari

"This will be the model for great American road cars to come."

Nameplate year of origin: 1957.
Current bodystyle lifespan: 1977 through 1981.
Predecessor to this model: Bonneville (1971 to 1976).
Replacement for this model: Bonneville "Model G" (1982 to 1986).
Percentage of division's production: 14.60%.
Corporate siblings: Buick LeSabre, Chevrolet Impala/Caprice, and Oldsmobile Delta 88.
Primary competition: Dodge Royal Monaco and Mercury Marquis.
Notable changes: Completely redesigned.
Major standard equipment: Choice of velour cloth or all-Morrokide vinyl front bench seat w/fold-down center armrest, cut-pile carpeting, lower door panel carpeting, door

Measurements

	2-door	4-door	Wagon
Wheelbase	115.9"	115.9"	115.9"
Length	213.8"	213.8"	214.7"
Width	75.4"	75.4"	75.4"
Height	54.5"	54.9"	58.0"
Legroom — front	42.2"	42.2"	42.6"
Legroom — rear	38.9"	39.5"	38.7"
Headroom — front	38.5"	39.2"	39.3"
Headroom — rear	38.0"	38.0"	39.0"
Cargo capacity (cu. ft.)	20.3	20.3	87.3
Fuel capacity (gals.)	20.0	20.0	22.5

pull straps, luxury custom cushion steering wheel, simulated rosewood woodgrain vinyl I/P accents, pedal trim plates, courtesy light switches on all doors, luggage compartment mat and light, bright windshield and rear window moldings, bright hood rear edge molding, fixed rear quarter window, wide rocker panel moldings w/rear extensions, bright wheel opening moldings, stand-up hood ornament w/hood windsplit molding, rear fender skirts, RTS package, deluxe wheel covers, and FR78 × 15 BSW tires. Grand Safari wagon adds: All-Morrokide vinyl front bench seat, door pull straps, electric clock, three-way tailgate w/power-operated rear window, delete rear fender skirts, simulated woodgrain bodyside and tailgate appliqués, and HR78 × 15 BSW tires. Brougham adds: Choice of velour or all-Morrokide vinyl trim front 60/40 split seat w/fold-down center armrest, custom door panels w/pull straps and lower panel carpeting, RH visor vanity mirror, electric clock, power windows, custom pedal trim plates, chrome LH remote-control mirror, added acoustical insulation, bright window sill molding, and velour luggage compartment trim.

Models Available

	Model No.	Base MSRP	Change from LY	Shipping Wt. (lbs.)	Model Year Production	Change from LY
Bonneville 2-Door Coupe	N37	$5,411	+3.15%	3579	37,817	+311.55%
Bonneville 4-Door Sedan	N69	$5,457	+2.73%	3616	13,697	-8.33%
Grand Safari 4-Door, 2-Seat Station Wagon	N35	$5,772	+0.45%	4066	18,304	+89.91%*
Bonneville Brougham 2-Door Coupe	Q37	$5,897	+2.84%	3617	15,901	+51.93%
Bonneville Brougham 4-Door Sedan	Q69	$5,992	+1.46%	3680	47,465	+134.56%
TOTALS	Avg. price	$5,706	+1.17%	Production	133,184	+106.58%

*Comparison to LY made to combined total of 1976 Grand Safari 2- and 3-seat wagons.

1978

After a successful 1977 model year, all four American manufacturers rolled out a variety of new models this year — some entirely new, some newly downsized, others highly restyled or with new body styles, and a few new nameplates thrown in for good measure. The industry enjoyed another great year, with production ultimately missing the exceptional 1977 pace by less than 2 percent, or about 170,000 cars. "Captive import" models remained in four of the twelve brands' showrooms, and sales were still running at near their 1973 levels, even as the regular imported car brands such as Honda, Toyota and Datsun (Nissan) were making yearly advances, with climbing sales and expanding model lines. Unfortunately Detroit seemed to take little notice, satisfied with their new smaller car introductions, improving fuel economy and the current environment of a good economy and brisk sales.

This was the first year of the government Corporate Average Fuel Economy requirements that required a sales weighted average of 18 miles per gallon for each corporation. All manufacturers would meet the requirement, but not without behind the scenes complaints. However, no amount of crying foul was going to change the situation or the law. One new feature that all manufacturers began using to shed weight for better fuel economy was space saving spare tires, or "doughnuts" as they were known in contemporary culture, as standard equipment. However, with much of the buying public unwilling to give up their conventional full-size spare tire, most companies offered regular spare tires as an option, usually at little or no cost. In addition to saving weight, a smaller spare added trunk space — a real advantage in the downsized cars. It is not documented in the standard feature listings of this book whether a space saving spare was standard or optional because it was so common for buyers to be given the choice at no cost. The actual model year of the switch for a given model can usually be seen in the differences in cargo capacity between years when there were otherwise no major styling changes made to a given model. Space saver

spare tires usually became standard equipment the same year a new model was introduced, after 1977, or the year a given model was downsized. The difference is generally about 1.5 cubic feet of space between a space saver tire and a conventional spare tire. Note that some cars offered space saving spares prior to this time period. For example, the 1967 Chevrolet Camaro and Pontiac Firebird, to maximize their rather small cargo space, offered a "Space Saver" spare tire that inflated with a can of Freon gas included with the tire.

A very competitive three-way fight developed in the 1978 *Motor Trend* "Car of the Year" competition, with Chrysler Corporation being the winner against Ford's new compacts and GM's new mid-size cars. There were actually two winners, the new front-wheel-drive subcompact four-door hatchbacks named the Dodge Omni and Plymouth Horizon. The near identical models, often referred to in the media as twins, or the "Omnirizon," were selected for their front-drive technology, roominess and overall economy. Chrysler of Europe, created by a merger of Simca and the Rootes Group in 1967, designed the Omni/Horizon twins, while their four-cylinder engines were based on a design Chrysler purchased from Volkswagen. The Omni and Horizon were the first North American mass-produced cars with a transverse mounted engine, and the first front-drive subcompact four-door hatchbacks made in America. They were also the first front-wheel-drive American-built cars from Chrysler, and the first to use a semi-independent rear suspension, with trailing arms and coil springs.

Another new model in the line was the Dodge Magnum XE. Based heavily on the ailing Dodge Charger SE, the Magnum's purpose was to bring some excitement back to the Dodge lineup of cars. Styled with a sloped front end and clear covered headlights, it had the right looks, and in its first year on the market outsold the Dodge Charger SE's first three years of production. The Magnum's success would spell the end of the line for the mid-size Charger, though the name would return. Other Chrysler products returned with only minor changes, and the full-size Dodge Royal Monaco, Plymouth Gran Fury, and Chrysler Town & Country station wagons were gone. By the end of this model year the Fury and Monaco names would be dropped, with both returning during the 1980s. Also gone by year's end would be the remaining Chrysler Newport and New Yorker models, marking the end of an era for Chrysler's traditional full-size line. This also made the big Chryslers the last of the true pillarless hardtop models with opening front and rear windows. Once the most popular of body styles, hardtops had declined in sales and production, not so much because consumers lost interest as because of the extra weight and expense required to retain body strength and rigidity, which in turn affected fuel economy. Insurance companies and safety advocates were also voicing growing concerns over rollover protection — the same factor that led to convertibles being taken out of production. Dollars and cents surely influenced the shift, too, as the growing more profitable luxury coupes and sedans increasingly stole sales from the sportier hardtop styles.

Though it was never mentioned or officially celebrated in sales literature, 1978 was Plymouth's 50th anniversary year. Two unique, one-year-only models appeared in the form of the racing-inspired Dodge Aspen and Plymouth Volaré Super Coupe twins (detailed further under their respective model listings). The Volaré Super Coupe was available only in Crimson Sunfire Metallic and the Aspen Super Coupe only in Sable Tan Sunfire Metallic. These were rare cars, even in 1978, with Chrysler producing only 494 Volaré Super Coupes and 531 Aspen Super Coupes. New in the captive import lines were a pair of well-equipped sport coupes built by Mitsubishi, named the Dodge Challenger and Plymouth Sapporo. Built on the Colt rear-wheel-drive platform, the coupes were true hardtops and carried a lot of standard features, along with a higher than typical price for an imported car. Dodge's truck line boasted unique models in the "Li'l Red Express" and "Midnight Express" trucks. Both were stepside models featuring exhaust stacks, gold pinstriping, decal packages, and red and black paint respectively. Otherwise there were few changes for the Dodge or Plymouth truck lines.

American Motors probably presented the most remarkable feat of the year, by introducing a new compact named Concord that was based heavily on the old Hornet body, but revised so cleverly that many buyers were unaware of the connection. Financial restraints had always made it difficult for AMC to create entirely new models, but the new Concord looked the part, at least in coupe and sedan form. Only the four-door wagon gave obvious clues to its Hornet Sportabout heritage. The Concord used the front fenders of the restyled 1977 Gremlin and added new square headlights, new vinyl top treatments including landau tops for two-doors, and luxurious interiors bringing it into a more competitive position in the marketplace. The results proved the change was right, with Concord sales up more than 50 percent above last year's

Hornet, which had been on a sales climb for the past two model years. Two changes were found under the hood this year, one being AMC's first full year of usage for the four-cylinder engine that AMC purchased in "knock-down" form from Volkswagen. Introduced in February 1977 for the Gremlin, it was available this year in the Concord, making Concord AMC's first and only car to be available with a 4-, 6-, or 8-cylinder engine. The other new offering was for the Pacer, whose sales had dropped off dramatically since introduction. The 304 CID V8 engine was added to the option list for improved performance in the bulky compact. To accommodate the physically larger engine and the radiator it required, AMC revised the hood with a new raised center section, accompanied by a taller grille. The AMX nameplate, which had returned as an option package on the 1977 Hornet Hatchback, regained full model status for 1978, though it remained mostly a trim and decal package for looks, rather than the performance car it once was. The Matador series returned for one final season with virtually no changes. This would also be the last year for the Gremlin nameplate.

Ford Motor Company celebrated its 75th anniversary this year with fully loaded special editions of their most popular personal/luxury cars, the Ford Thunderbird and Lincoln Continental Mark V Diamond Jubilee Editions. New compact models, the Ford Fairmont and Mercury Zephyr, replaced the venerable Maverick and Comet. Based on an entirely new "Fox" chassis platform, the new compact twins were so far advanced from their predecessors that they immediately became Ford's most successful new car introductions ever, selling more than 610,000 between the two lines in the 1978 model year. They were both offered in two- and four-door sedan models, as well as a four-door station wagon that was Ford's first compact wagon since the 1970 Falcon station wagon. At mid-year sporty two-door coupe models joined the lines under the special names of Fairmont Futura and Zephyr Z-7. The Ford compacts were the second line of cars in the company, after the Mustang II, to be offered with the full range of 4-, 6-, and 8-cylinder engines. Ford's popular Granada and related Mercury Monarch were given a facelift, adding the industry's new square headlights. With the introduction of the new compact station wagons, the mid-size LTD II and Cougar station wagons were dropped from the lineup after just one year. Entering their final seasons in their current form were the full-size Ford LTD and Mercury Marquis, which would be downsized for the 1979 season. The smallest Ford of the decade was introduced this year with the new captive import, the Fiesta, a subcompact front-wheel-drive two-door hatchback model that was quite popular in Europe. Ford hoped to continue the trend in the United States, and would succeed in that mission. Ford's truck lines added new grilles and square headlights, but otherwise continued with relatively minor changes.

General Motors introduced downsized mid-size car

lines this year, following last year's successful introduction of full-size models. Coupes, sedans and wagons all shared a wheelbase of 108.1 inches (down from 112 or 116 inches depending on model), total length dropped by 13–23 inches, and curb weights fell by 500–1100 pounds. Wagons got the greatest cuts, with their lengths now about the same as sedans, and their weights much closer to sedans. GM's mid-size Century, Malibu, Cutlass and LeMans were now smaller and lighter than the "compact" Skylark, Nova, Omega and Phoenix. While the basic designs were solid, the unfortunate use of a fastback style body for the Buick Century and Oldsmobile Cutlass coupes and sedans meant that their sales declined. The more conventional notchback bodies of the Chevrolet Malibu and Pontiac LeMans both saw sales increases. The A-specialty bodied coupes, which had been top sellers for GM during the past few years, were included in the redesign, and retained as much of their individuality as GM could manage, given the smaller bodies and the fact that they were now built on the same chassis as all other mid-size coupes. While the Chevrolet Monte Carlo, Pontiac Grand Prix, and Oldsmobile Cutlass Supreme experienced minor declines in sales, the Buick Regal actually saw an increase for 1978. Pontiac also marked the return of the Grand Am nameplate, though it was mostly a trim package with a unique front end appearance, and lacked the European sports sedan image that the original Grand Am projected.

Other news from the various GM divisions this year included Buick celebrating its 75th anniversary. In commemoration of the event a special Riviera "LXXV" package offered a leather interior and special paint and trim details. The 1978 model year was also the first year for Buick's turbocharged V6 engine, which became available in the Regal and LeSabre Sport coupe models. After the engine debuted in the 1976 Buick Century Indianapolis 500 pace car, so much interest was shown by GM management, the press and the public that it was decided to take it into production. Cadillac models remained basically unchanged, though the Seville added the new Oldsmobile diesel V8 engine to its option list this year. The Oldsmobile diesel V8 was also available on all full-size Oldsmobiles this year, and enjoyed initial success as it could boost fuel economy by nearly 50 percent in some models. Meanwhile the Oldsmobile Toronado and its corporate cousin, the Cadillac Eldorado, were in their final year of production as GM's last traditional large cars.

Chevrolet's sporty Corvette marked its 25th anniversary with a special two-tone model and a restyling that included a large wraparound rear window, reminiscent of the look first seen on the 1963–1967 Corvette Sting Ray fastback models. Another special edition was introduced when the Corvette was selected as the official pace car for the Indianapolis 500 race held May 28, 1978. Pace car replicas became an immediate hit; having originally planned only 300, Chevrolet eventually produced 6,502, or enough for approximately one per

Chevrolet dealer. Other changes in the Chevy line included a facelift for the Camaro that now used body-colored front and rear bumpers and fascias, giving the line a sportier look. With the Vega gone, its notchback coupe and Kammback wagon were moved into the Monza lineup. The Monza and the related Oldsmobile Starfire and Pontiac Sunbird lines would join the growing trend of offering the full range of 4-, 6- and 8-cylinder power plants, as would the recently introduced Pontiac Phoenix compact. (The Buick Skyhawk stuck with V6 power only.) With the Ventura gone from the lineup, the Phoenix line was expanded to pick up the lower priced Ventura models, effectively making the Phoenix line a model for model replacement of the Ventura. Other changes in the Pontiac lineup included the discontinued Astre's station wagon being moved to the Sunbird line as the Sunbird Sport Safari. The Chevrolet and GMC truck lines had new Chevy ElCamino and newly named GMC Caballero car-based pickups this year, which became very popular. Other GM truck lines were given revisions and upgrades.

1978 Overview and Changes from Prior Year

- **Total industry model year production:** 9,424,455, down 1.81%.
- **Total estimated captive import sales:** 204,679, down 2.94%.
- **Market share by corporation:** GM 57.75%; Ford 28.95%; Chrysler 11.44%; AMC 1.86%.
- **Number of models and body types available:** 253, down from 271.
- **Highest production series:** Chevrolet Impala/Caprice — 612,397.
- **Lowest production series:** Cadillac Fleetwood 75 —1,530.
- **Highest individual model production:** Ford Thunderbird 2-Door Hardtop — 333,757.
- **Lowest individual model production:** Dodge Monaco Crestwood 4-Door, 2-seat wagon — 668.
- **Industry average base price:** $5,231, up 7.74%.
- **Highest individual model base price:** Cadillac Fleetwood 75 Limousine, $20,363.
- **Lowest individual model base price:** Chevette Scooter 2-Door Hatchback Coupe, $2,999.
- **Highest combined MPG with base powertrain:** Chevrolet Chevette, 34 MPG (30 Calif.).
- **Lowest combined MPG with base powertrain:** Cadillac Eldorado and Fleetwood 75, 11 MPG (Eldorado, 11 Calif.)
- **Indianapolis 500 Pace Car:** Chevrolet Corvette 2-Door Coupe.
- *Motor Trend* **magazine "Car of the Year":** Dodge Omni and Plymouth Horizon.

AMERICAN MOTORS

"The quality Americans want ... the size America needs."

While American Motors was continuing to have great success with its Jeep operations, the car side of the business was in a slide that required some desperate actions. With little cash to work with, the company tried to breathe new life into what were once the company's two best-selling lines, the Gremlin and the Hornet. An all-new car was out of the question, as that would require millions of dollars more than the company could afford. So, as had historically been the case with AMC, and the earlier companies that had combined to make up the current American Motors Corporation, they had to make do with the major components they already had. For 1978, the Hornet was replaced with the Concord.

The Concord shared front fenders with the Gremlin, as had the Hornet in the early years through the 1972 model year. Since the two cars were built off of a similar platform, this was not an unusual practice within the industry, especially in times of belt tightening, such as AMC was experiencing. Therefore the Concord front end was a similar sloping type with curved corners, and on two-door models, doors were shared with the Gremlin. However, the purpose of the new Concord was to help move AMC cars upscale with a theme of luxury and economy, rather than the strictly economy look and feel of the Hornet. So the Concord was given a luxurious theme with a six-section grille with egg-crate inserts five rows by five columns across, each surrounded by chrome, with turn signal/parking lamps set into the outer sections, and the entire grille surrounded by more chrome. AMC's first square single unit headlamps were set in chrome bezels, and the entire front end was encapsulated in a band of chrome, which on the top side ran across the leading edge of the hood. Topping off the new front end was a round stand-up hood ornament.

At the back end, the Hornet's wraparound rectangular taillamps were gone, and a new slightly concave rear end cap held new round-edged rectangular units with tri-colored lenses, matching the gently rounded front-end styling. The new lenses consisted of amber turn signals on the outside edge, taillight and brake lights in the larger center section, and the backup lights towards the middle in a smaller section. A large license plate housing was set in the center, again with the rounded corner theme.

The former Sportabout, now simply called the Concord station wagon, and the hatchback models continued to have the old Hornet look for the rest of the body, including the greenhouse area. It was the sedans that were made to look completely different, especially with the D/L trim, which would make up most of this year's production. While the former Hornet's roofline remained, the D/L package added half-vinyl roofs that completely changed the look, especially on the two-door sedans which used the vinyl top to create an enlarged B-pillar and faux opera window. Both sedans had the vinyl roof completely surrounded with chrome trim, with a slightly wider band running behind the door and over the roof. Rear window surrounds used body color trim, and the new opera window created on the two-door models was surrounded with a thin strip of chrome and painted trim. One last touch was a thin chrome strip on the trailing edge of the roof above the rear window that imitated the look of a convertible top bow, giving the look of a cabriolet top — a popular option, or aftermarket item, on American luxury cars of the period.

Inside the new Concords were as plush as the Matadors with Brougham options had ever been. Padded door panels, plush looking velveteen seating material, and soft feel vinyls that imitated the look and feel of leather made the interior as posh as any luxury car. The instrument panel was also given a makeover to upgrade the look. But there was still a lot of the Hornet look that couldn't be covered up, especially in the hatchback and wagon models. One thing that the Hornet never had, besides the aforementioned luxury, was a 4-cylinder engine, which AMC had introduced in mid–1977 on the Gremlin and now offered in the new compact Concord. The Concord was the first American Motors product to be offered with a choice of 4-cylinder, 6-cylinder or V8 power within a single model line.

Since a sporty car image was not befitting of the luxury theme created for the Concord, the AMX, formerly an option package offered on the 1977 Hornet, became its own series. It was even separated from the Concord by the Gremlin and Pacer in the 1978 AMC sales literature to emphasize that this was not another Concord model. The new AMX carried most of the 1977 option package features but added the Concord front and rear ends, albeit with a different grille and mostly blacked-out trim. The new blackout mesh grille used round amber turn signal/parking lamps, and only the grille and headlight bezels were lined with a thin strip of chrome. A targa top band of brushed aluminum at the B-pillar and a rear-window louver in black also distinguished the new model. The AMX also had an optional rallye stripe, for Classic Black cars only, that ran along bodysides near the top edge back across the door, then turned up over the roof to meet the other side. An available AMX decal package placed a spear and flame motif on the hood and hatchback decklid.

After a successful introductory year for the Pacer station wagon, a new V8 engine option was added to the Pacer option list to help overcome the public's perceived desire for better performance. This was a result of the original Pacer design's being overweight, after the sudden decision of GM to stop its development of the lightweight rotary engine AMC intended to use in the Pacer, and the decision to use the heavy 6-cylinder engine in its place. Unfortunately the V8 was heavier yet, and fuel economy suffered even more, and the Pacer's sales slipped even further for 1978. Installation of a V8 engine necessitated a restyling of the front end to raise the hood to accommodate the taller engine. The taller hood required a raised center section of the grille, which now adopted a new egg-crate design. These changes substantially altered the Pacer's formerly smooth front-end styling and diminished the rounded "egg" shape it had become known for. Nonetheless, the Pacer's 1978 production total plummeted 80 percent from its 1976 high point.

The Matador, AMC's largest model, and the Gremlin,

AMC's smallest model, were entering their final season. No major changes were made for Matadors, although the Barcelona package had been revamped and expanded to include sedans when it was introduced at mid-year in 1977, and was commonly referred to as the Barcelona II package. There were 396 Matador coupes produced with the Barcelona package in this final year, and an unknown number of sedans. Similarly, the Gremlin saw few changes, other than the addition of a 4-cylinder engine, the dropping of the V8 engine option, and a revised "X" package that incorporated the Levi's interior, formerly its own option package. The Gremlin would live on in the restyled and renamed Spirit series for 1979.

Finally, it should be mentioned that during this model year, AMC entered into an agreement with French auto maker Renault to market its cars in AMC's U.S. showrooms. The first Renault to appear was the mini-compact LeCar. Part of this agreement was also to allow Renault dealers to market Jeep models outside of the United States. It was the beginning of a relationship that would last through the sale of AMC to Chrysler Corporation in 1987.

1978

AMX 2-Door Hatchback Coupe

Concord 2-Door Hatchback with Sport package

Concord 2-Door Sedan with D/L package

Concord 4-Door Sedan with D/L package

Gremlin Custom 2-Door Sedan with GT package

Gremlin Custom 2-litre
2-Door Sedan with X package

Matador 2-Door Coupe with Barcelona package

Matador 4-Door Sedan

Matador 4-Door Station Wagon

Pacer 2-Door Sedan with Sport package

Pacer 2-Door Station Wagon with D/L package

Model year production: 175,204, down 17.79% from 1977.
Domestic market share: 1.86% (11th place).
Base price range: $3,539 to $5,299.
American Motors average base price: $4,188, up 11.86%.
Introduction date: September 9, 1977. Concord introduced October 1977.
Assembly plants: Kenosha, Wisconsin, and Brampton, Ontario, Canada.
Data plate identification (VIN): Thirteen digit code read as follows: First digit indicates company (A = American Motors); second digit indicates model year (8 = 1978); third digit is transmission code (see powertrain chart); fourth through sixth digits indicate car line–body type–series numbers (three-digit model number in model charts); seventh digit is engine code (see powertrain chart); eighth digit indicates assembly plant (1 through 6 = Kenosha, 7 through 9 = Ontario); Remaining digits are sequential with beginning number of 00001. *Example:* A8A167H100001 is a 1978 Matador 2-Door, 304 CID, 2-bbl. V8, with Torque-Command Automatic, serial number 00001, built in Kenosha.

Powertrains[1]

Engine	Net HP	Engine/Trans. Codes	Transmission Availability[2]		Gremlin	Pacer	Concord	AMX	Matador[3]
121 CID (2.0L) OHC, 2-bbl., 4-cyl.	80	G/F	4-speed manual[4]		S[5]	—	N/C	—	—
				MPG:	22/34/26	—	21/33/25	—	—
		G/A	Torque-Command 3-sp. Automatic		$270[5]	—	$320[6]	—	—
				MPG:	20/29/24	—	20/29/24	—	—
				Calif.	19/27/22	—	19/27/22	—	—
232 CID (3.8L), 1-bbl., 6-cyl.	90	E/S	3-speed manual		S (base[4]/Custom[7])	S	S	—	—
				MPG:	20/28/23	19/26/22	19/26/22	—	—
		E/F	4-speed manual		S (Custom)[4]	$111	$111	—	—
				MPG:	20/28/23	19/26/22	19/26/22	—	—
		E/A	Torque-Command 3-sp. Automatic		$296 (base[4])	296	296	—	—
				MPG:	18/25/21	18/23/20	18/23/20	—	—
258 CID (4.2L), 2-bbl., 6-cyl.	120	C/F	4-speed manual		S (base — Calif.)/$231 (Custom — 49 states)	$231	$231	S	—
				MPG:	16/25/19	16/25/19	16/25/19	16/25/19	—
				Calif.	13/21/16	13/21/16	13/21/16	13/21/16	—
		C/A	Torque-Command 3-sp. Automatic		$270[7]/$390[4]	$390	$390	$320[6]	S (ex. Wgn.)
				MPG:	16/21/18	16/21/18	16/21/18	16/21/18	15/21/17
				Calif.	13/17/14	13/17/14	13/17/14	13/17/14	—
304 CID (5.0L), 2-bbl., V8	130	H/A	Torque-Command 3-sp. Automatic		—	$528	$528	$553[6]	—
				MPG:	—	14/19/16	14/19/16	14/19/16	—
360 CID (5.9L), 2-bbl., V8	140	N/A	Torque-Command 3-sp. Automatic		—	—	—	—	S(Wgn)/$190 (others)
				MPG:	—	—	—	—	12/17/14
				Calif.	—	—	—	—	10/16/12

[1]Optional axle ratio required on cars sold in California: Gremlin 6-cylinders (except w/4-speed manual), 3.08:1; Pacer, 3.08:1; Concord 6-cylinders, 3.08:1; Matador V8s, 3.15:1.   [2]Unless otherwise noted: Add $24 for floor-shifter on Gremlin automatics, Concord automatics except when equipped with 4-cylinder engine, Pacer 6-cylinders w/bucket or individual reclining seats, and add $70 on Matador Coupe with 360 CID V8, bucket seats and console. Floor shift is standard on AMX. Transmission code with automatic floor shift is C.   [3]Coupes and sedans built for sale in California follow the same standard and optional availability as station wagons.

Prices adjust accordingly. ⁴Not available in California. ⁵Only powertrain offered on Gremlin Custom 2-Liter model. ⁶Requires floor shift, which is included in price. Transmission code is C. ⁷Available only in California.

Major Options

	Gremlin	Pacer	Concord	AMX	Matador
All-season air conditioning	$478	$478	$478	$478	$590
Adjust-O-Tilt steering wheel[1]	—	$64	$64	$64	$67
Electronic Cruise Command speed control[1]	—	$99	$99	$99	$99
Electric rear window defogger	$81	$81	$81	$81	$88
Tinted glass, all windows	$52	$58	$52	$52	$64
Power windows, 4-doors	—	—	—	—	$155
Power door locks	—	$72	—	—	—
Front bucket seats, vinyl upholstered	$49	N/C	$69[2]	S	N/C[2]
Front floor console (requires bucket seats)	$29	$29	$29	S	$
Third row seat & power tailgate window (wagons)	—	—	—	—	$143
AM radio	$80	$80	$80	$80	$81
AM/FM stereo multiplex w/4 speakers	$224	$224	$224	$224	$224
AM/FM stereo w/cassette tape player	—	$336	$336	$336	$336
AM/FM stereo w/Citizens Band radio (CB)[3]	—	$299	$299	$299	$299
Vinyl top (excluding wagon models)	—	$118	$105	—	$118
Woodgrain paneling (wagons only)	—	$111	$75	—	$133
Power steering	$141	$147	$147	$147	S
Power front disc brakes	$64	$64	$64	$64	S
Wheel covers	$36	S	S	—	S
Styled road wheels	$71	$136	$71	S	$71
Aluminum styled wheels	$236	$236	$236	$171	$236
White sidewall tires, standard size	S	S	$18	$60	S

Popular Option Groups & Packages

	Gremlin	Pacer	Concord	AMX	Matador
AMX decal package	—	—	—	$49	—
Barcelona package[4]	—	—	—	—	$849
D/L package	—	S	$299	—	—
Extra Quiet insulation package	$45	S	$45	$45	S
Gauge package	$75[5]	$99	$99	S	—
GT package	$649	—	—	—	—
Interior décor/convenience group	$69	$59	$79	$59	$59
Levi's custom trim package	—	—	—	$49	—
Light Group	—	S	—	—	S
Sport package	—	$165[6]	$289[7]	—	—
Protection group	$42	—	$27	—	—
Visibility group	$71	$61	$71	$71	$81
"X" package	$249[5]	—	—	—	—

— = Not Available; S = Standard equipment. [1]Requires automatic transmission. [2]Hornet hatchback and Matador coupe only. [3]AM/CB radio available on Gremlin for $119, and on all other models for $199. [4]Price given is for coupe. Available on sedan for $699. [5]Available only on Gremlin Custom. [6]Not available on wagon. Requires 258 CID 6-cylinder or 304 CID V8 engine. [7]Price given is for hatchbacks. Available on sedans and wagon for $379.

Paint Colors

	Code	AMX		Code	AMX
Alpine White	G7	x	Sun Orange	7Z	—
Sand Tan	6D	—	Khaki	8A	—
Firecracker Red	6P	x	British Bronze metallic	8B	—
Sunshine Yellow	6V	x	Quicksilver metallic	8C	x
Mocha Brown metallic	7B	—	Claret metallic	8D	—
Autumn Red metallic	7C	—	Classic Black	P1	x
Powder Blue	7D	—			
Midnight Blue metallic	7K	—	
Loden Green metallic	7L	—	
Golden Ginger metallic	7M	—	
Captain Blue metallic	7W	—	

Not all colors were standard on all models. Breakdown by model is currently unavailable. Only AMX color offerings are known at this time. Non-standard model colors are available at $24 extra cost. Two-tone paint combinations available on Pacer sedan for $55, Concord D/L for $75, Matador coupe and sedan for $43, and Matador wagon for $84.

Gremlin

"The fun Americans want ... the size America needs."

Nameplate year of origin: 1970.

Current bodystyle lifespan: 1970 through 1983; Gremlin (1970 to 1978), restyled and renamed Spirit (1979 to 1982). 4WD added and rebadged Eagle SX/4 (1981 to 1983).

Predecessor to this model: None.

Replacement for this model: Spirit (1979 to 1982) and Eagle SX/4 (1981 to 1983).

Percentage of division's production: 10.37%.

Corporate siblings: None; however many components were shared with the Concord.

Primary competition: Buick/Opel Isuzu, Chevrolet Monza, Dodge Colt, Ford Pinto, and Plymouth Arrow.

Notable changes: Minor trim and detail changes.

Major standard equipment: Crush grain vinyl bench front seat, fold-down rear seat, color-keyed carpeting, dome light, custom steering wheel, carpeted cargo area, spare tire cover, bodyside scuff moldings, rear bumper guards, rocker panel moldings, wheel covers, and B78 × 14 WSW tires. Custom adds: Soft-feel vinyl bucket seats, woodgrain I/P overlays, and bright drip rail and wheel lip moldings.

Measurements

Wheelbase	96.0"
Length	166.4"
Width	70.6"
Height	52.3"
Legroom — front	40.7"
Legroom — rear	29.2"
Headroom — front	38.0"
Headroom — rear	36.4"
Cargo capacity (cu. ft.)	6.4*
Fuel capacity (gals.)	21.0**

*26.9 cu. ft. with rear seat down.   **3.0 gallons on Custom 2-Liter model.*

Models Available

	Model No.	Base MSRP	Change from LY	Shipping Wt. (lbs.)	Model Year Production	Change from LY
Gremlin Custom 2-Liter 2-Door Sedan	46-4	$3,789	+16.66%	2556	6,349	-16.00%
Gremlin 2-Door Sedan	46-5	$3,539	+18.16%	2834	15,755*	-59.20%*
Gremlin Custom 2-Door Sedan	46-7	$3,789	+16.66%	2822	*	*
TOTALS		Avg. price $3,706	+17.13%	Production	22,104*	-52.13%

Production records kept only by engine type.

Pacer

"The room and ride Americans want ... the size America needs."

Nameplate year of origin: 1975 (previously used by Ford Motor Company on 1958 Edsel series).

Current bodystyle lifespan: 1975 through 1980.

Predecessor to this model: None.

Replacement for this model: None.

Percentage of division's production: 9.96%.

Corporate siblings: None.

Primary competition: Chevrolet Monza, Mercury Bobcat, and Pontiac Sunbird.

Notable changes: New grille and trim and detail changes.

Major standard equipment: D/L features including velveteen crush fabric individual reclining front seats, custom door trim panels w/assist straps, woodgrain I/P and steering wheel overlays, color-keyed carpeting, fold-down rear seat, Light Group, day/night mirror, Extra Quiet insulation package, concealed two-speed electric wipers and washers, large rear liftgate w/built-in assist struts, wide rocker panel moldings, color-keyed bodyside scuff moldings, bumper nerfing strips, color-keyed wheel covers, and D78 × 14 WSW tires. Wagon adds: Soft-feel vinyl individual reclining front seats, cargo area skid strips, rear quarter window vents, and locking stowage compartment in rear quarter panel.

Measurements

	Sedan	Wagon
Wheelbase	100.0"	100.0"
Length	170.0"	174.0"
Width	77.0"	77.0"
Height	52.7"	53.0"
Legroom — front	42.0"	42.0"
Legroom — rear	34.9"	34.9"
Headroom — front	38.3"	38.4"
Headroom — rear	37.0"	38.1"
Cargo capacity (cu. ft.)	29.5*	47.8*
Fuel capacity (gals.)	22.0	22.0

With rear seat folded down.

Models Available

	Model No.	Base MSRP	Change from LY	Shipping Wt. (lbs.)	Model Year Production	Change from LY
Pacer 2-Door Sedan (hatchback)	66-7	$4,048	+10.93%	3197	7,411	-63.43%
Pacer 2-Door Station Wagon	68-7	$4,193	+10.37%	3245	13,820	-63.63%
TOTALS		*Avg. price* $4,121	+10.65%		*Production* 21,231	-63.56%

Concord

"Introducing AMC's new Concord. The convenience and luxury Americans want ... the size America needs."

Nameplate year of origin: 1978 (previously used by Chrysler Corporation on 1951–1952 Plymouth series).

Current bodystyle lifespan: 1970 through 1987; Hornet (1970–1977), restyled and renamed Concord (1978 to 1982); 4WD added and rebadged Eagle (1980 to 1987).

Predecessor to this model: Hornet (1970 to 1977).

Replacement for this model: Eagle (1980 to 1987).

Percentage of division's production: 55.72%.

Corporate siblings: None; however, many components were shared with the Gremlin.

Primary competition: Chevrolet Nova, Dodge Aspen, Ford Fairmont, Plymouth Volaré, and Pontiac Phoenix.

Notable changes: Restyled and renamed Concord.

Major standard equipment: Velveteen fabric front bench seat, color-keyed carpeting, padded custom door trim panels, woodgrain I/P overlay on center section, instrument panel package tray, custom steering wheel, dual bodyside pinstripes, color-keyed bodyside scuff moldings, rocker panel, wheel lip and drip rail moldings, hood front edge moldings, hood ornament and windsplit molding, rear bumper guards, front sway bar, front disc brakes, wheel covers, and C78 × 14 BSW tires. Hatchback adds: Soft-feel vinyl bucket seats, folding second seat, sport steering wheel, flip-open rear quarter windows, carpeted cargo area, and gas-charged liftgate supports. Sportabout adds: Soft-feel vinyl front bench seat, folding second seat, gas-charged liftgate supports, carpeted cargo area, and hidden locking rear compartment.

Measurements

	Sedans	Hatchback	Wagon
Wheelbase	108.0"	108.0"	108.0"
Length	186.0"	186.0"	186.0"
Width	71.0"	71.0"	71.0"
Height	51.6"	51.6"	51.3"
Legroom — front	40.8"	40.8"	40.8"
Legroom — rear	35.7"	36.1"	31.1"
Headroom — front	38.1"	38.1"	38.1"
Headroom — rear	37.5"	36.7"	37.9"
Cargo capacity (cu. ft.)	10.8	32.0*	59.2*
Fuel capacity (gals.)	22.0	22.0	22.0

Maximum with rear seat down, and 2.2 cu. ft. below cargo floor on wagon.

Models Available

	Model No.	Base MSRP	Change from LY*	Shipping Wt. (lbs.)	Model Year Production	Change from LY*
Concord 2-Door Sedan	06-7	$3,749	+10.30%	3029	50,482	+730.84%
Concord 2-Door Hatchback	03-7	$3,849	+10.00%	3051	2,572	-77.72%
Concord 4-Door Sedan	05-7	$3,849	+11.60%	3099	42,126	+34.45%
Concord 4-Door Station Wagon	08-7	$4,049	+9.46%	3133	23,573	-18.41%
TOTALS		*Avg. price* $3,874	+10.32%		*Production* 118,753	+52.55%

Comparisons made to 1977 Hornet. Production by engine type (compared to LY): 4-cylinder, 3,780 (new); 6-cylinder, 110,972 (+50.46%); V8, 6,541 (+59.89%).

AMX

"An exciting sporty car that makes driving
come alive at an affordable price."

Nameplate year of origin: 1968.
Current bodystyle lifespan: 1978 (previously option package on 1977 Hornet hatchback).
Predecessor to this model: Javelin AMX (1971 to 1974).
Replacement for this model: AMX (1979 to 1980).
Percentage of division's production: 0.59%.
Corporate siblings: Concord hatchback, and many components shared with the Gremlin.
Primary competition: Chevrolet Nova w/Rallye package, Dodge Aspen w/R/T package, and Plymouth Volaré w/Road Runner package.
Notable changes: All-new model, based on 1977 Hornet hatchback w/AMX package.
Major standard equipment: Soft-feel vinyl front bucket seats, color-keyed carpeting, console, custom door trim panels w/map pockets, brushed aluminum I/P overlays, rally instrumentation and tachometer, I/P package tray, soft-feel sports steering wheel, folding second seat, flip-open rear quarter windows, carpeted cargo mats, gas-charged liftgate supports, "AMX" bodyside and interior graphics, front and rear painted bumpers, black front air dam, black front and rear fender flares, black rear window louvers, LH remote and RH manual flat black mirrors, other blacked out features (including unique grille, headlight bezels, rear window molding, door and quarter frames, lower back panel, license plate depression and wiper arms), brushed aluminum roof band w/special insignia, front sway bar, slot style wheels, and DR78 × 14 BSW tires.

Measurements

Wheelbase	108.0"
Length	186.0"
Width	71.0"
Height	51.6"
Legroom — front	40.8"
Legroom — rear	36.1"
Headroom — front	38.1"
Headroom — rear	36.7"
Cargo capacity (cu. ft.)	32.0*
Fuel capacity (gals.)	22.0

Maximum with rear seat down.

Models Available

	Model No.	Base MSRP	Change from LY	Shipping Wt. (lbs.)	Model Year Production	Change from LY
AMX 2-Door Hatchback	03-9	$4,649	NEW	3159	2,540	NEW
TOTALS	*Avg. price*	$4,649	NEW	*Production*	2,540	NEW

Matador

"A remarkable buy with the remarkable security
of AMC's exclusive Buyer Protection Plan."

Nameplate year of origin: 1971.
Current bodystyle lifespan: 1974 through 1978 (Coupe only); 1967 through 1978 (Rebel, 1967–1968; restyled in 1969; restyled and renamed Matador in 1971; and sedan and wagon restyled in 1974).
Predecessor to this model: Matador (1971 to 1973).
Replacement for this model: None.
Percentage of division's production: 4.96%.
Corporate siblings: None.
Primary competition: Chevrolet Impala, Dodge Monaco, Ford LTD II, and Plymouth Fury.
Notable changes: Minor trim and detail changes.
Major standard equipment: Velveteen crush fabric individual reclining front seats, color-keyed carpeting, custom steering wheel, Extra Quiet insulation package, Light group, bodyside scuff moldings, front and rear bumper guards, front sway bar, power steering, power front disc brakes, full wheel covers, and F78 × 14 WSW tires. Wagon adds: Crush-grain vinyl individual reclining front seats, cargo area carpet, courtesy dome light activated by door and tailgate switches, hidden rear compartment with lock, dual-swing tailgate, and H78 × 14 BSW tires.

Measurements

	Coupe	Sedan	Wagon
Wheelbase	114.0"	118.0"	118.0"
Length	209.4"	216.0"	215.5"
Width	77.4"	77.3"	77.2"
Height	51.8"	54.8"	56.8"
Legroom — front	43.0"	42.8"	42.8"
Legroom — rear	33.3"	39.6"	39.6"
Headroom — front	37.6"	39.6"	39.9"
Headroom — rear	36.0"	37.5"	38.5"
Cargo capacity (cu. ft.)	14.3	19.1	95.2*
Fuel capacity (gals.)	24.5	24.5	21.0

Includes 8.0 cu.ft. of space below cargo floor.

Models Available

	Model No.	Base MSRP	Change from LY	Shipping Wt. (lbs.)	Model Year Production	Change from LY
Matador 2-Door Coupe	16-7	$4,799	+6.67%	3709	2,006	-70.61%
Matador 4-Door Sedan	85-7	$4,849	+6.59%	3718	4,824	-62.73%
Matador 4-Door Station Wagon	88-7	$5,299	+8.16%	4146	3,746	-66.19%
TOTALS	Avg. price	$4,982	+7.17%	Production	10,576	-65.71%

Production by engine type for coupe and sedan (compared to LY): 6-cylinder, 23 (-99.10%); V8, 10,553 (-39.08%).

BUICK

"A Little Science. A Little Magic."

Buick entered its 75th anniversary year riding high after three straight years of significant sales increases, with 1977 representing the highest model year production in history. The Buick theme was "75 Years of Greatness," but advertising featured the "Science and Magic" theme shown above. The sales literature featured early Buicks making use of "science" to help create such things as 2- and 4-cylinder engines that won races in the 1900s and 1910s, and hydraulic shock absorbers for 1928, and their legendary "Straight Eight" engine introduced in 1931. It then compared these features to the new 1978 models with the "magic" of downsizing and the development of turbocharged engines. In the end, despite an all-new mid-size line, the ad campaign proved to be weak, and sales and production for the model year fell nearly 8 percent in a market that was only slightly down from the prior year.

Buick's mid-size line took its turn at downsizing this year, and in the process the Regal was officially separated from the Century line. The Regal became Buick's version of GM's mid-size two-door A-specialty coupes, which all carried the same angular design theme, with formal rooflines and styling characteristics that differentiated each of them from regular A-body cars. The Regal had a uniquely Buick front and rear design highlighted by a waterfall grille and horizontal taillamps. The Century utilized the more unusual fastback styled A-body, which it shared with the Oldsmobile Cutlass. The design was relatively well received on the coupes, and the new wagons did very well, but the sedans did not fare as well.

The new Regal, even in its most basic form, appeared to be an expensive car. A classic looking vertical bar waterfall grille, which appeared to be lifted straight from the Riviera, was set between the new style single rectangular headlamps. The chrome headlamp bezel and accompanying turn signal/

parking light combination leaned back, making the upright grille stand out even more. Bodysides were relatively plain, with only one feature line, and distinctive creases over each of the wheel openings. The gentle crease on the wheel openings was far enough from the opening edge that it created a slightly "flared fender" appearance while fading away at each end, and it seemed to sweep back slightly on the rearward side, creating a resemblance to the 1953 Buick Skylark's "open" wheel opening design. A feature line ran forward about ten inches across the base of a broad, upright C-pillar. Around back a flat decklid angled downward to meet horizontal taillamps that were positioned above the bumper. A slim, vertical side marker light followed the slant of the rear panel. The roofline was formal with an upright rear window and an almost perfectly rectangular rear quarter window.

Centurys on the other hand took on an aerodynamic looking fastback roofline while retaining the interior space and generous trunk capacity of a regular sedan. At the front the headlamps and turn signal/parking light units sloped back very slightly, flanking a crosshatch style grille defined by chrome cross bars dividing it into three rows and eight columns. Within each opening were four horizontal bars, and the Buick name was affixed to the driver's side. The entire front end was lined in chrome and appeared to be a single unit. The only bodyside feature lines were low on the body, running between the bumper midpoints and arching around the wheel openings. They were very similar to the Regal's, if not exactly the same on the front fender. Station wagons were of a traditional box style rear quarter area with horizontal taillamps set into the bumper, but the coupes and sedans featured a sloping rear roof and trunk lid design that began just above the top of the rear seatback cushion, sloping downward with a large rear window set above rear vents used as part of the GM flow-through ventilation system. The slope continued with the trunk lid, and then turned more sharply downward about a foot above the rear bumper. Rectangular taillamps wrapped around the edge onto the rear quarter, and were divided into three sections, with taillamps and brake light in the upper two sections and the lower one housing a square backup light to the inside and an amber turn signal lens across the rest of the section.

Like all of the new GM mid-size cars, the Regal and Century were unusual in that all rear door windows were of a fixed design on four-doors, and all rear quarter windows were fixed on two-doors. Four-door sedans did receive manually operated, triangular rear quarter vent windows behind the doors, while station wagons used a vertical vent window in the back door. The supposed purpose of the fixed rear window was to allow more hip room in the rear seat for carrying three passengers, as the doors could be thinner since they did not require space for the mechanisms to raise and lower the window. The exterior styling of the Century might have been better suited to an economy or sporty car from Chevrolet or Pontiac, as the look was not entirely befitting the more formal and traditional Buick style. Dismal sales and production totals resulted for the Century. One unique option for the new Century and Regal, as well as LeSabre and Riviera, was the new Designer Accent paint option. For most models, the colors were limited to blues and tan colors, and consisted of darker toned paint on the bodyside area below the beltline and above the rocker panel area, running most of the length of the car, surrounded by the lighter tone on the remainder of the body. The two-tone option proved to be popular and would extend to other Buick lines over the next few years.

Inside, the new Regal and Century used materials that were commonly shared across all four of the GM mid-size lines. For example, patterns for the upholstery and seat designs may have been different, but the fabrics were shared. Instrument panel designs appeared different also, but they were all laid out in the same format. For Buick, the instruments were set in a large pod in front of the driver, with three square brushed aluminum faced gauges directly over the steering column, vertical air conditioning vents set at the outer edges, and other controls near the bottom of the pod. In the center of the dashboard, set lower, was a smaller pod containing heating and air conditioning controls on top, with the radio below. The passenger side contained the bin-style glove box below a digital clock, if so equipped. Door panels were also standard GM fare with built-in armrests and pull straps, the design of which was different for each of the trim levels.

The other Buick models underwent relatively little change. The downsized full-size cars from 1977 continued with new grille designs and new taillamps for the Electra series that now wrapped around the faux tailfin created by a revised filler panel on the rear quarter panel. The Electra's new grille was of an egg-crate design split horizontally into two sections. The LeSabre's grille was divided into three horizontal sections per side with a horizontal crosshatch pattern within each. The bottom sections' strips carried across to the turn signal/parking lamp and around the front fender edge to the attached side marker light. The former Park Avenue option for the Electra was moved up to full-fledged model status and was now also offered in a two-door coupe model. The Riviera saw only minor trim changes; however, it was the only Buick model to represent the division's 75th anniversary with the Riviera LXXV option package. Details of the package can be found in Appendix IV.

In the small car range, the Opels built by Isuzu continued with a new horizontal bar grille and a new S/C Sport Coupe model, but were otherwise unchanged. The Skylark also received a new grille consisting of four horizontal bars creating three areas filled with small vertical bars, and a large chrome piece affixed to the header panel, giving it an upscale appearance. A new option package for the year was the Sport package that added a full blackout appearance to any Skylark model except hatchbacks, as well as several suspension and handling upgrades. Finally, the Skyhawk soldiered on for another year with minimal changes.

Century 4-Door Station Wagon
with Sport Wagon package

Century 4-Door Station Wagon

Century Custom 4-Door Sedan (front)
and Century Special 4-Door Sedan (rear)

Century Special 2-Door Coupe
with Designers' Accent paint

Estate Wagon with Limited option

Regal Sport Coupe 2-Door

Skyhawk 2-Door Hatchback Coupe
with roof crown molding

Opel Isuzu Deluxe 2-Door Coupe

Century Sport Coupe 2-Door

LeSabre 2-Door Coupe (front)
and LeSabre 4-Door Sedan

Riviera 2-Door Coupe

Skylark 2-Door Coupe with Sport package

Electra 225 4-Door Sedan

LeSabre Custom instrument panel

Riviera 2-Door Coupe
with LXXV anniversary package

Skylark Custom 4-Door Sedan

1978

Model year production: 803,186, down 7.60% from 1977.
Domestic market share: 8.52% (5th place).
Base price range: $3,872 to $8,082.
Buick average base price: $5,458, up 7.40%.
Introduction date: October 6, 1977. Regal introduced August 1977.
Assembly plants: Southgate, CA (C); Linden, NJ (E); Framingham, MA (G); Flint, MI (H); Van Nuys, CA (L); Tarrytown, NY (T); Lordstown, OH (U); Willow Run, MI (W); Kansas City/Fairfax, KS (X); Fremont, CA (Z); St. Therese, Quebec, Canada (2). *Opel assembly plant:* Fujisawa, Japan (8).
Data plate identification (VIN): Thirteen digit code read as follows: First digit indicates division (4 = Buick); second through fourth digits indicate series and body style (model number in model charts); fifth digit is engine code (see powertrain chart); sixth digit indicates model year (8 = 1978); seventh digit indicates assembly plant (see list above); remaining digits are sequential with beginning number of 100001. *Example:* 4N69X8H100001 is a 1978 Buick LeSabre 4-Door Sedan, with 350 CID, 4-bbl. V8 engine, serial number 100001, built in Flint, MI. 1978 Opels use a 13-digit code read the same as other 1978 Buicks except that the final six digits are sequential with beginning number of 400001 for sedans, and 700001 for coupes.

Powertrains[1]

Engine	Net HP	Engine Code: VIN/GM	Transmission Availability		Opel	Skyhawk	Skylark	Century	Regal	LeSabre	Electra, Riviera & Estate Wagon
110.8 CID (1.8L) OHC, 2-bbl., 4-cyl.	80	B	4-speed manual		S	—	—	—	—	—	—
				MPG:	24/34/27	—	—	—	—	—	—
				Calif.	22/32/26	—	—	—	—	—	—
			5-speed manual		$119	—	—	—	—	—	—
				MPG:	25/38/30	—	—	—	—	—	—
				Calif.	24/38/28	—	—	—	—	—	—
			Turbo Hydra-matic 3-sp. Automatic		$316	—	—	—	—	—	—
				MPG:	24/31/27	—	—	—	—	—	—
				Calif.	24/29/26	—	—	—	—	—	—
196 CID (3.2L), 2-bbl., V6[2]	90	C/LC9	3-speed manual		—	—	—	S (ex. Wgns.)	S	—	—
				MPG:	—	—	—	19/33/23	19/33/23	—	—
			Turbo Hydra-matic 3-sp. Automatic		—	—	—	$307 (ex. Wgns.)	$307 (ex. Sport Cpe.)	—	—
				MPG:	—	—	—	18/26/21	18/26/21	—	—
231 CID (3.8L), 2-bbl., V6[3]	105	A/LD5 or 2/LC6	3-speed manual		—	—	S[2]	$40 (ex. Wgns.)	$40 (ex. Sport Cpe.)	—	—
				MPG:	—	—	16/26/19	16/28/19	16/28/19	—	—
			4-speed manual		—	S	—	$165 (ex. Wgns.)	$165 (ex. Sport Cpe.)	—	—
				MPG:	—	16/28/19	—	NA	NA	—	—
				Calif.	—	16/27/20	—	NA	NA	—	—
			5-speed manual		—	$175	—	—	—	—	—
				MPG:	—	19/34/25	—	—	—	—	—
			Turbo Hydra-matic 3-sp. Automatic		—	$270	$307	S (Wgns.)/ $282	$282 (ex.	S (ex. Spt.	—

Engine	Net HP	Engine Code: VIN/GM	Transmission Availability	Opel	Skyhawk	Skylark	Century (others)[4]	Regal Sport Cpe.)[4]	LeSabre Cpe.)	Electra, Riviera & Estate Wagon
MPG:				—	19/27/22	18/26/21	19/27/22	19/27/22	17/25/20	—
Calif.				—	16/23/18	15/22/18	16/23/18	16/23/18	15/21/17	—
231 CID (3.8L), Turbo-charged, 2-bbl., V6	150	G/ LC5	Turbo Hydra-matic 3-sp. Automatic	—	—	—	—	S (Sport Cpe. only)[2]	—	—
MPG:				—	—	—	—	19/26/21	—	—
231 CID (3.8L), Turbo-charged, 4-bbl., V6	165	3/ LC8	Turbo Hydra-matic 3-sp. Automatic	—	—	—	—	$50 (Sport Cpe. only)[5]	S (Sport Cpe. only)[2]	—
MPG:				—	—	—	—	17/25/20	16/22/19	—
Calif.				—	—	—	—	NA	NA	
301 CID (4.9L), 2-bbl., V8	140	Y/ L27	Turbo Hydra-matic 3-sp. Automatic	—	—	—	—	—	$208 (ex. Sport Cpe.)[2]	—
MPG:				—	—	—	—	—	17/24/20	—
305 CID (5.0L), 2-bbl., V8	145	U/ LG3	Turbo Hydra-matic 3-sp. Automatic	—	—	$467[2]	$120 (Wgns.)[6]/ $507 (others)	$497 (ex. Sport Cpe.)	$208 (ex. Sport Cpe.)[7]	—
MPG:				—	—	15/22/18	16/22/19 (Wgn) 17/25/20 (others)	17/25/20	—	—
Calif.				—	—	—	13/19/15 (Wgn) 14/21/17 (others)	14/21/17	13/19/15	—
305 CID (5.0L), 4-bbl., V8	160	H/ LG4	Turbo Hydra-matic 3-sp. Automatic	—	—	—	$170 (Wgns.)/ $557 (others)[2]	$449 (ex. Sport Cpe.)[2]	—	—
MPG:				—	—	—	16/23/18 (Wgn) 18/26/21 (others)	16/21/18	—	—
350 CID (5.7L), 4-bbl., V8	155	X/ L77	Turbo Hydra-matic 3-sp. Automatic	—	—	—	—	—	$313 (ex. Sport Cpe.)[1]	S[2,8]
MPG:				—	—	—	—	—	15/22/18	15/22/18
350 CID (5.7L), 4-bbl., V8	170	L/ LM1	Turbo Hydra-matic 3-sp. Automatic	—	—	$572[2]	$265 (Wgns.)[6]	—	—	—
MPG:				—	—	16/22/19	16/21/18	—	—	—

Engine	Net HP	Engine Code: VIN/GM	Transmission Availability	Opel	Skyhawk	Skylark	Century	Regal	LeSabre	Electra, Riviera & Estate Wagon
350 CID (5.7L), 4-bbl., V8	170	R/ L34	Turbo Hydra-matic 3-sp. Automatic	—	—	$572[7]	—	—	$313 (ex. Sport Cpe.)[7]	S[8]
			Calif.	—	—	13/18/15	—	—	14/21/17	14/21/17
403 CID (6.6L), 4-bbl., V8	185	K/ L80	Turbo Hydra-matic 3-sp. Automatic	—	—	—	—	—	$403 (ex. Sport Cpe.)	$90
			MPG:	—	—	—	—	—	14/20/17	14/20/16
			Calif.	—	—	—	—	13/19/16	13/19/16	—

[1]Optional axle ratio required on cars sold in high-altitude counties: Skyhawk, 2.93:1; Skylark V6, 3.23:1; LeSabre, Estate Wagon, Electra and Riviera w/403 V8, 2.73:1. [2]Not available in California or high-altitude counties. Skylark with LD5/LC6 requires optional automatic transmission in California. [3]The LC6 231 CID V6 engine available only in California. [4]Standard on Regal and Century Coupes and Century Sedans in California. [5]Available as standard equipment on Regal Sport Coupes sold in California and high-altitude counties after January 1, 1978. [6]Century Custom Wagon and Century Sport Wagon for sale in high-altitude counties have LM1 engine standard, and in California have LG3 engine standard. [7]Only available in California or designated high-altitude counties. [8]L34 engine is standard in California and high-altitude counties on Estate Wagons, Electra and Riviera's. LM1 optional for high-altitude counties only on Century Wagons.

Major Options

	Opel	Skyhawk	Skylark	Century	Regal	LeSabre	Estate Wagon	Electra 225	Riviera
Air conditioning[1]	$460	$470	$508	$544	$544	$581	$581	$581	$581
Tilt-wheel steering[2]	—	$62	$69	$69	$69	$70	$70	$70	$70
Cruise-Master speed control	—	—	$90	$90	$90	$95	$95	$95	$95
Electric rear window defogger	$59	$79	$51[3]	$92	$92	$94	$94	$94	$94
Tinted glass, all windows	S	$54	$56	$62	$62	$76	$76	$76	$76
Power windows, 2-dr./4-dr.	—	—	$118/$163	$124/$169	$124	$130/$190	$190	S	S
Power door locks, 2-dr./4-dr.	—	—	$74/$106	$80/$112	$80	$82/$114	$114	$82/$114	$82
Power front seat, 6-way, driver's side	—	—	—	$151	$151	$151	$151	$120	$120
Front bucket seats, w/console	S[4]	S[4]	$169[5]	$130[5]	$130	—	—	—	—
Third row seating (wagons)	—	—	—	—	—	—	$186	—	—
AM radio	$77	$74	$79	$83	$83	$96	$96	$96	—
AM/FM stereo[6]	$148	$222	$236	$236	$236	$239	$239	$239	S
AM/FM stereo w/tape player[6]	—	$320	$341	$341	$341	$355	$355	$355	$116
Vinyl top[7]	—	—	$102[8]	$116[8]	$116[8]	$142	—	$196	$196
Sunroof, electric	—	$215[9]	—	$499[9]	$499	$778	—	$778	$778
Astroroof, sliding glass	—	$615[9]	—	$699[9]	$699	$978	—	$978	$978
Hatch-roof, T-tops	—	—	—	—	$625	—	—	—	—
Woodgrain exterior panels (wagons)	—	—	—	$256	—	—	$235	—	—
Power steering	—	$134	$152	$152[10]	$152[10]	S	S	S	S
Power brakes, w/front disc	S	$99	$69	$69[10]	$69[10]	S	S	S	S
Full wheel covers	—	$42	$38	$38[11]	$38[11]	$38[11]	S	S	—
Wire wheel covers[12]	—	—	$150	$150[11]	$112	$113[11]	$75	$75	S
Styled wheel covers	—	—	$101	$101	$63	$65	$65	$65	—
Designers wheels	—	—	—	$117	$99	—	—	—	$62
Chrome plated road wheel	—	—	$130	$159	$141	$161	$161	$161	$62
WSW tires, standard size	—	$43	$44	$39	$39	$46	$39	$39	$39

Popular Option Groups & Packages

	Opel	Skyhawk	Skylark	Century	Regal	LeSabre	Estate Wagon	Electra 225	Riviera
75th anniversary package	—	—	—	—	—	—	—	—	$586

	Opel	Skyhawk	Skylark	Century	Regal	LeSabre	Estate Wagon	Electra 225	Riviera
Appearance group	—	$73	—	—	—	—	—	—	—
Convenience group	—	$23	$34	$44	$18	$92	—	—	—
F40 firm ride handling package	—	—	$24	$20	$20	$20	$20	$20	$20
FE2 Rallye ride/handling package	—	—	$46	$36	$36	—	—	—	$20
Limited package	—	—	—	—	—	—	$1,568	—	—
Sport coupe/sedan package	—	—	$200	—	—	—	—	—	—
Sport wagon package	—	—	—	$430	—	—	—	—	—

—= Not Available; S = Standard equipment. [1]Manually controlled. Automatic climate control is available for $88 additional on Century, Regal, LeSabre, Estate Wagon, Electra and Riviera. [2]Tilt and telescoping steering column available on LeSabre, Estate Wagon, Electra and Riviera at $50 additional cost. [3]Blower type defogger. [4]Opel Deluxe and Skyhawk models only. Opel base and Skyhawk S have bucket seats w/o console. Console for Skyhawk S is $77 extra. [5]Standard on Skylark Custom. Available only on Century Custom models. [6]Non-stereo on Opel. Tape player can be 8-track or cassette tape. CB radio available on Skylark and Century for $333 extra; available on all full-size Buicks for $338 extra. [7]A variety of vinyl top configurations available, ranging in price from $151 to $405. Prices shown are for full, non-padded vinyl top on two-door models. [8]Price is $5 less on Skylark Custom models. Regal coupe w/Landau top, $155. Not available on Century station wagons. [9]Available on two-door models only. Skyhawk Astroroof is fixed and includes roof crown molding, and sunroof option is manually operated. [10]Standard on Regal Sport coupe. Power brakes standard on station wagons, and required when V8 engine and A/C are ordered on coupes and sedans. [11]Standard on Century Custom, Regal Limited, and LeSabre Custom models. Deduct price of wheel covers from price on other optional wheels and wheel covers on these models. [12]Wire wheels available on full-size Buicks for $101–$135 depending upon model. Custom wire wheels available on Riviera at no extra cost.

Paint Colors

Buick	Code	Buick	Code	Opel	Code
White	11	Gold metallic*	56	Horizon Blue	B
Silver metallic	15	Tan	61	New Palm Green	G
Gray metallic*	16	Dark Gold metallic	63	Crimson Red	R
Black	19	Saffron metallic	67	New Westway Tan	T
Pastel Blue	21	Brown	69	Magnolia White	W
Medium Blue metallic	22	Bright Red	75	Jasmine Yellow	Y
Ultramarine Blue metallic	24	Red	77		
Dark Blue metallic	29	Dark Red	79		
Light Green metallic	44	Blue Firemist metallic	91		
Medium Green metallic	45	Amber Firemist metallic	92		
Dark Green metallic	48	Red Firemist metallic	93		
Yellow	51				

*In two-tone combinations, the first two digits indicate lower color, and the next two digits are the upper color. Two-tone combinations are $60 extra for LeSabre and Electra. Firemist paints available only on Riviera at $165 extra. *Used in two-tone combinations only.*

Opel

"One of them might be just right for you."

Nameplate year of origin: 1976.
Current bodystyle lifespan: 1976 through 1979.
Predecessor to this model: Opel 1900 (1971–1975); Manta (1971–1975).
Replacement for this model: None (the same car was sold after 1980 as the Isuzu I-Mark).
Primary competition: AMC Gremlin, Chevrolet Monza, Dodge Colt, Dodge Omni, Ford Pinto, Mercury Bobcat, Plymouth Horizon, and Pontiac Sunbird.
Notable changes: Sport coupe model added, new grille, and minor trim and detail changes.
Major standard equipment: Reclining vinyl front bucket seats, full-floor carpeting, interior lights, column-mounted headlight dimmer switch, tinted glass, trunk mat, and 6.15 × 13 BSW tires. *Deluxe adds:* Center console w/clock, woodgrain vinyl trim on I/P gauge cluster, console and doors, side window moldings, rocker panel molding, front and rear bumper guards, and wheel trim rings. *Sport Coupe adds:* Bumpers w/black filler panels, front air dam, blacked-out trim (grille, headlamp bezels, window moldings, sport mirrors, door handles, C-pillar vent louvers, and tail lamp trim), black stripes on spoiler and lower bodysides, "SC" identification on the lower front fender, specially tuned suspension and shock absorbers, and sport wheels.

Measurements

	Coupe	Sedan
Wheelbase	94.3"	94.3"
Length	168.0"*	170.5"
Width	61.8"	61.8"
Height	50.6"	51.3"
Legroom — front	40.7"	40.7"
Legroom — rear	30.2"	30.9"
Headroom — front	37.0"	37.9"
Headroom — rear	35.0"	36.6"
Cargo capacity (cu. ft.)	9.9	9.9
Fuel capacity (gals.)	13.7	13.7

Sport Coupe, 168.3"; Deluxe coupe, 170.5".

1978

Models Available

	Model No.	Base MSRP	Change from LY	Shipping Wt. (lbs.)	Model Year Sales	Change from LY*
Opel 2-Door Coupe	T77	$3,507	+6.40%	2075	NA	NA
Opel Deluxe 2-Door Coupe	Y77	$3,722	+4.61%	2090	NA	NA
Opel Deluxe 4-Door Sedan	Y69	$3,824	+6.16%	2145	NA	NA
Opel 2-Door Sport Coupe	W77	$3,878	NEW	2086	NA	NEW
TOTALS	*Avg. price*	$3,733	+7.10%	*Production*	18,800*	-35.32%

Model year sales are estimated based upon dealer sales reporting, and change from LY is compared to the entire 1977 Opel line.

Skyhawk

"Introduced in 1975, it remains a bold, graceful, alert automobile three years later. A car fairly brimming with individuality."

Nameplate year of origin: 1975.
Current bodystyle lifespan: 1975 through 1980.
Predecessor to this model: None.
Replacement for this model: Skyhawk (1982 to 1989).
Percentage of division's production: 3.06%.
Corporate siblings: Chevrolet Monza, Oldsmobile Starfire and Pontiac Sunbird.
Primary competition: AMC Pacer and Ford Mustang II.
Notable changes: Minor trim and detail changes.
Major standard equipment: Vinyl front bucket seats with foam cushions, fold-down rear seat, cut-pile carpeting including cargo area, simulated woodgrain I/P, dual speed wipers w/washers, functional B-pillar vent louvers, bright window surround moldings, front and rear wheel opening moldings, hubcaps, and B78 × 13 BSW tires. Skyhawk adds: Choice of cloth or vinyl front bucket seats, full instrumentation including tachometer, full-length floor console, rallye steering wheel, electric clock, LH remote control outside rear view sport mirror, bodyside accent stripes, wheel opening moldings, and BR78 × 13 BSW tires.

Measurements

Wheelbase	97.0"
Length	179.3"
Width	65.4"
Height	50.2"
Legroom — front	43.0"
Legroom — rear	29.6"
Headroom — front	37.7"
Headroom — rear	35.3"
Cargo capacity (cu. ft.)	27.8*
Fuel capacity (gals.)	18.5

With rear seat folded down.

Models Available

	Model No.	Base MSRP	Change from LY	Shipping Wt. (lbs.)	Model Year Production*	Change from LY
Skyhawk 'S' 2-Door Hatchback	T07	$4,103	+3.06%	2678	NA	NA
Skyhawk 2-Door Hatchback	S07	$4,367	+1.70%	2707	NA	NA
TOTALS	*Avg. price*	$4,235	+2.36%	*Production*	24,589	+2.27%

Production and comparisons by model not available as they were kept as combined total.

Skylark

"Small enough, yet large enough."

Nameplate year of origin: 1953.
Current bodystyle lifespan: 1975 through 1979.
Predecessor to this model: Apollo (1973 to 1974).
Replacement for this model: Skylark (1980 to 1985).
Percentage of division's production: 14.22%.
Corporate siblings: Chevrolet Nova, Oldsmobile Omega, and Pontiac Phoenix.

Measurements

	Coupe & HBK	Sedan
Wheelbase	111.0"	111.0"
Length	200.2"	200.2"

Primary competition: Dodge Aspen and Mercury Monarch.

Notable changes: New grille and minor trim and detail changes.

Major standard equipment: S model: Front vinyl bench seat, front door armrest, cut-pile carpeting, and E78 × 14 BSW tires. Skylark adds: Choice of patterned cloth or vinyl front bench seat with foam cushions, cut-pile carpeting including hatchback load floor, fold-down rear seat and rear cargo area light (hatchback only), cigar lighter w/front and rear ashtrays, rear quarter/rear door armrests, day/night inside rearview mirror, deluxe steering wheel, dual speed wipers w/4-jet washers, front and rear wheel opening moldings, and hubcaps. Custom adds: Choice of custom cloth or custom vinyl front bench seat w/passenger side recliner, carpeted door trim w/map pocket and reflector, front door operated courtesy lights, combination turn signal and high/low beam headlight control stalk, roof drip moldings, stand-up hood ornament, deluxe wheel covers, and ER78 × 14 BSW tires.

Measurements (cont.)

	Coupe & HBK	Sedan
Width	72.7"	72.7"
Height	52.2"	53.1"
Legroom — front	41.7"	41.7"
Legroom — rear	33.3"	35.2"
Headroom — front	38.2"	39.1"
Headroom — rear	36.7"	37.1"
Cargo capacity (cu. ft.)	14.3*	13.2
Fuel capacity (gals.)	21.0	21.0

*Hatchback maximum with rear seat down, 29.2 cu. ft.

Models Available

	Model No.	Base MSRP	Change from LY	Shipping Wt. (lbs.)	Model Year Production	Change from LY
Skylark 'S' 2-Door Coupe	W27	$3,872	+6.32%	3201	9,050	NA*
Skylark 2-Door Coupe	B27	$3,999	+6.22%	3203	33,037	-33.74%
Skylark 2-Door Hatchback	B17	$4,181	+6.06%	3313	2,642	-50.30%
Skylark 4-Door Sedan	B69	$4,074	+6.51%	3234	40,951	-14.90%
Skylark Custom 2-Door Coupe	C27	$4,242	-6.30%	3186	12,740	+153.63%
Skylark Custom 2-Door Hatchback	C17	$4,424	-5.77%	3285	1,277	+10.66%
Skylark Custom 4-Door Sedan	C69	$4,317	-5.89%	3219	14,523	+263.08%
TOTALS	Avg. price	$4,158	+0.43%	Production	114,220	+0.66%

*Comparison from LY for S coupe is not available as 1977 production was kept with Skylark base coupe production, so change of combined models is entered under base coupe.

Century

"An aerodynamic, European look with special accent on function."

Nameplate year of origin: 1936.

Current bodystyle lifespan: 1978 through 1984 (Coupe to 1980; Wagon as Regal model 1982 to 1983; and Sedan as Regal model 1982 to 1984).

Predecessor to this model: Skylark (1973 to 1977).

Replacement for this model: Century (1982 to 1996).

Percentage of division's sales volume: 10.92%.

Corporate siblings: Chevrolet Malibu, Oldsmobile Cutlass, and Pontiac LeMans.

Primary competition: Chrysler LeBaron, Dodge Diplomat, Dodge Monaco, and Mercury Cougar.

Notable changes: Completely redesigned.

Major standard equipment: Choice of cloth or vinyl front bench seat (wagon: vinyl only), cut-pile carpeting, front door operated dome lights, door pull straps, adjustable rear vent windows (2-doors), fixed rear seat window w/swing-out rear quarter vent windows (4-door models), stand-up hood ornament, front disc brakes, bumper protective strips w/white stripe front and rear, wheel covers, and P185/75R × 14 BSW tires. Custom adds: Choice of cloth or vinyl notchback front seat w/center fold-down armrest (wagon: vinyl only) or vinyl bucket seats (available at no extra charge), front ashtray light, under-dash courtesy lights, glove compartment light, "Custom" badging, stand-up hood ornament w/hood windsplit molding, wheel opening moldings, and rocker panel moldings. Wagons add: Power brakes and P195/75R × 14 BSW tires. Sport coupe adds: Choice of cloth or vinyl notchback front seat w/center fold-down armrest or vinyl bucket seats (available at no extra charge), front ashtray light, under-dash courtesy lights, glove compartment light, FE2 rallye ride and handling package, specific paint treatment, Designer's

Measurements

	Coupes	Sedans	Wagons
Wheelbase	108.1"	108.1"	108.1"
Length	195.6"	195.6"	194.9"
Width	72.2"	72.2"	72.2"
Height	53.3"	54.2"	54.5"
Legroom — front	42.6"	42.6"	42.6"
Legroom — rear	35.2"	38.0"	35.9"
Headroom — front	37.2"	37.9"	38.5"
Headroom — rear	37.9"	38.7"	38.8"
Cargo capacity (cu. ft.)	16.4	16.4	71.8
Fuel capacity (gals.)	17.5	17.5	17.7

1978

sport wheels, and P205/75R × 14 W/O BSW tires. Limited adds: Choice of cloth or vinyl 55/45 notchback front bench seat w/fold-down center armrest, front ashtray light, under-dash courtesy lights, glove compartment light, "Limited" badging, stand-up hood ornament w/hood windsplit molding, wheel opening moldings, and rocker panel moldings.

Models Available

	Model No.	Base MSRP	Change from LY	Shipping Wt. (lbs.)	Model Year Production	Change from LY
Century Special 2-Door Coupe	E87	$4,389	+1.97%	3003	10,818	NA*
Century Special 4-Door Sedan	E09	$4,486	NEW	3014	12,533	NEW
Century Special 4-Door Station Wagon, 2-S.	E35	$4,976	NEW	3148	9,586	NEW
Century Custom 2-Door Coupe	H87	$4,633	+0.11%	3011	12,434	-40.32%
Century Custom 4-Door Sedan	H09	$4,733	+0.96%	3038	18,361	+34.56%
Century Custom 4-Door Station Wagon, 2-S.	H35	$5,276	+1.09%	3181	24,014	+24.54%
Century Sport 2-Door Coupe	G87	$5,019	NEW	3051	**	NEW
Century Limited 2-Door Coupe	L87	$4,991	NEW	3048	**	NEW
Century Limited 4-Door Sedan	L09	$5,091	NEW	3075	**	NEW
TOTALS	Avg. price	$4,844	+6.17%	Production	87,746	-35.53%

*Comparison to LY is not available, as 1977 Century Special production was kept combined with Century coupe production.   **Production for Sport and Limited models is included within the Special and Custom figures.

Regal

"We've lavished it with science to improve its roadability. And we've touched it with magic to make it luxurious and fun to drive."

Nameplate year of origin: 1973 (as Century subseries).
Current bodystyle lifespan: 1978 through 1987.
Predecessor to this model: Century Regal (1973 to 1977).
Replacement for this model: Regal (1988 to 1997).
Percentage of division's sales volume: 29.46%.
Corporate siblings: Chevrolet Monte Carlo, Oldsmobile Cutlass Calais and Cutlass Supreme, and Pontiac Grand Prix.
Primary competition: Chrysler Cordoba, Dodge Charger SE, Dodge Magnum XE, Ford Thunderbird and Mercury Cougar.
Notable changes: Completely redesigned.
Major standard equipment: Choice of cloth or vinyl notchback front seat w/center fold-down armrest or vinyl front bucket seats, front door operated dome light, door pull straps, simulated woodgrain appliqués on I/P and door panels, ashtray light, under-dash courtesy lights, glove compartment light, wheel opening moldings, rocker panel molding, bumper protective strips w/white accents front and rear, front disc brakes, wheel covers, and P195/75R × 14 BSW tires. Sport adds: Distinctive domed hood, fast-ratio power steering, power front disc brakes, turbocharged engine, FE2 rallye ride and handling package, and P205/70R × 14 BSW tires. Limited adds: Choice of cloth or vinyl 55/45 notchback seat w/fold-down center armrest, door pull assist straps, and wide rocker panel, belt reveal and pillar appliqué moldings.

Measurements

Wheelbase	108.1"
Length	199.6"
Width	72.2"
Height	53.4"
Legroom — front	42.6"
Legroom — rear	36.4"
Headroom — front	37.9"
Headroom — rear	38.1"
Cargo capacity (cu. ft.)	16.5
Fuel capacity (gals.)	17.5

Models Available

	Model No.	Base MSRP	Change from LY	Shipping Wt. (lbs.)	Model Year Production	Change from LY
Regal 2-Door Coupe	J47	$4,852	+2.95%	2992	236,652	+35.57%
Regal Sport 2-Door Coupe	K47	$5,853	NEW	3153	*	NEW
Regal Limited 2-Door Coupe	M47	$5,233	NEW	3041	*	NEW
TOTALS		Avg. price	$5,313	+13.85%	Production	236,652	+22.93%

*Production of Regal Sport and Limited kept as combined total with Regal 2-Door coupe.

LeSabre

*"LeSabre has always been a full-size family car
with a hearty aptitude for comfort and convenience."*

Nameplate year of origin: 1959 (also used on 1951 GM show car).
Current bodystyle lifespan: 1977 through 1985.
Predecessor to this model: LeSabre (1971 to 1976).
Replacement for this model: LeSabre (1986 to 1991).
Percentage of division's sales volume: 21.41%.
Corporate siblings: Chevrolet Impala and Caprice, Pontiac Catalina and
Bonneville, and Oldsmobile Delta 88.
Primary competition: Chrysler Newport and Mercury Marquis.
Notable changes: New grille and minor trim and detail changes.
Major standard equipment: Choice of cloth or vinyl front bench seat, cut-
pile carpeting, woodgrained vinyl trim on door panels, front door oper-
ated dome light, I/P woodgrain appliqués, LH outside rear view mirror,
front fender-mounted three-section rectangular "ventiport" ornaments,
bumper protective strips front and rear, and FR78 × 15 BSW tires. Cus-

Measurements

	Coupe	Sedan
Wheelbase	115.9"	115.9"
Length	218.2"	218.2"
Width	77.2"	77.2"
Height	55.0"	55.7"
Legroom — front	42.2"	42.2"
Legroom — rear	38.7"	39.5"
Headroom — front	38.4"	39.1"
Headroom — rear	38.2"	39.5"
Cargo capacity (cu. ft.)	21.2	21.2
Fuel capacity (gals.)	21.0	21.0

tom adds: Cloth or vinyl notchback front seat w/fold-down center armrest, front ashtray and glove compartment light, wheel
opening moldings, full-length rocker panel molding, rear panel molding, and deluxe wheel covers. Sport Coupe adds: Front ashtray and glove compartment light, rallye steering wheel, specific suspension and steering, "Turbo 3.8 Liter" badge and chrome
louvers replacing ventiports, black accents around chrome moldings, grille and taillights, black B-pillar molding w/special sport
coupe emblem, turbocharged engine, and chrome road wheels.

Models Available

	Model No.	Base MSRP	Change from LY	Shipping Wt. (lbs.)	Model Year Production	Change from LY
LeSabre 2-Door Coupe	N37	$5,384	+6.97%	3446	8,265*	-2.25%*
LeSabre 4-Door Sedan	N69	$5,459	+7.19%	3489	23,354	+17.79%
LeSabre Custom 2-Door Coupe	P37	$5,657	+6.29%	3413	53,675	-8.39%
LeSabre Custom 4-Door Sedan	P69	$5,757	+6.97%	3450	86,638	-16.58%
LeSabre Sport 2-Door Coupe	F37	$6,213	+6.77%	3559	*	*
TOTALS	*Avg. price*	$5,694	+6.83%	*Production*	171,932	-9.85%

Production of LeSabre Sport Coupe, F37, kept as combined total with LeSabre 2-Door coupe, N37.

Estate Wagon

*"If you want a lot of hard work and a lot of luxury
from the same car, you've come to the right place."*

Nameplate year of origin: 1940 (as designation for station wagons).
Current bodystyle lifespan: 1977 through 1990.
Predecessor to this model: Estate Wagon (1971 to 1976).
Replacement for this model: Roadmaster Estate Wagon (1991 to 1996).
Percentage of division's sales volume: 3.23%.
Corporate siblings: Chevrolet Impala and Caprice, Pontiac Catalina Safari and Grand
Safari, and Oldsmobile Custom Cruiser.
Primary competition: Mercury Marquis.
Notable changes: New grille and minor trim and detail changes.
Major standard equipment: Vinyl front bench seat, cut-pile carpeting including load
floor, glove box light, I/P flood lights, front-door operated dome light, lockable
hidden storage compartments, three-way tailgate, power tailgate window w/reveal

Measurements

Wheelbase	151.5"
Wheelbase	115.9"
Length	216.7"
Width	79.9"
Height	56.5"
Legroom — front	42.2"
Legroom — rear	38.2"
Headroom — front	39.3"
Headroom — rear	39.4"
Cargo capacity (cu. ft.)	87.7
Fuel capacity (gals.)	22.0

1978

moldings, LH and RH rear view mirrors, fender-mounted three-section rectangular "ventiport" ornaments, rocker panel moldings, deluxe wheel covers, and HR78 × 15 BSW tires.

Models Available

	Model No.	Base MSRP	Change from LY	Shipping Wt. (lbs.)	Model Year Production	Change from LY
Estate Wagon 4-Door, 2-S. Wagon	R35	$6,301	+6.74%	4063	25,964	+3.55%
TOTALS	Avg. price	$6,301	+6.74%	Production	25,964	+3.55%

Electra

"There is an Electra for whatever your taste may dictate."

Nameplate year of origin: 1959.
Current bodystyle lifespan: 1977 through 1984.
Predecessor to this model: Electra 225 (1971 to 1976).
Replacement for this model: Electra (1985 to 1990).
Percentage of division's sales volume: 15.13%.
Corporate siblings: Cadillac deVille, Cadillac Fleetwood Brougham, and Oldsmobile Ninety-Eight.
Primary competition: Chrysler New Yorker Brougham and Mercury Grand Marquis.
Notable changes: New grille and minor trim and detail changes.
Major standard equipment: Choice of cloth or vinyl notchback front bench seat w/fold-down center armrest, cut-pile carpeting, simulated woodgrain appliqués on door panels and I/P, door pull straps, carpeted lower door panels, power windows, quartz round-dial clock, custom steer-

Measurements

	Coupe	Sedan
Wheelbase	118.9"	118.9"
Length	222.1"	222.1"
Width	77.2"	77.2"
Height	55.0"	55.9"
Legroom — front	42.2"	42.2"
Legroom — rear	39.9"	40.9"
Headroom — front	38.2"	39.1"
Headroom — rear	38.0"	38.0"
Cargo capacity (cu. ft.)	20.4	20.4
Fuel capacity (gals.)	21.0	21.0

ing wheel and safety belts, remote-control LH rear view mirror, fender-mounted 4-section rectangular "ventiport" ornaments, wheel opening moldings, rocker panel molding, deluxe wheel covers, and GR78 × 15 BSW tires. Limited adds: Custom cloth or textured vinyl 55/45 notchback front seat w/fold-down center armrest, two-way power driver's seat adjustment, front seatback map pockets, door pull handle, litter pocket, dome reading light, and front and rear fender rocker panel moldings. Park Avenue adds: Button-tufted crushed velour cloth 50/50 split seats w/individual fold-down center armrests, door courtesy and warning lights, and C-pillar mounted coach side lights.

Models Available

	Model No.	Base MSRP	Change from LY	Shipping Wt. (lbs.)	Model Year Production	Change from LY
Electra 225 2-Door Coupe	V37	$7,144	+7.06%	3682	8,259	-47.60%
Electra 225 4-Door Sedan	V69	$7,319	+6.60%	3730	14,590	-43.08%
Electra Limited 2-Door Coupe	X37	$7,526	+7.01%	3710	33,365*	-11.90%**
Electra Limited 4-Door Sedan	X69	$7,701	+6.57%	3757	63,335*	-20.67%**
Electra Park Avenue 2-Door Coupe	U37	$7,837	NEW	3730	*	NEW**
Electra Park Avenue 4-Door Sedan	U69	$8,088	NEW	3777	*	NEW**
TOTALS	Avg. price	$7,603	+9.40%	Production	121,549	-24.80%

*Production of Park Avenue models kept as combined total with Limited models. **Comparisons to LY include 1978 Limited and Park Avenue models compared to 1977 Limited models, which offered the Park Avenue option package.*

Riviera

"More than mere transportation. To drive a Riviera is to experience a real sense of communication with the road."

Nameplate year of origin: 1963 (1949 as designation for hardtop models).
Current bodystyle lifespan: 1977 through 1978.
Predecessor to this model: Riviera (1971 to 1976).
Replacement for this model: Riviera (1979 to 1985).
Percentage of division's sales volume: 2.56%.
Corporate siblings: Buick LeSabre, Chevrolet Impala/Caprice, Oldsmobile Delta 88, and Pontiac Catalina/Bonneville.
Primary competition: Ford Thunderbird Town Landau.
Notable changes: Minor trim and detail changes.
Major standard equipment: Choice of bolstered crushed velour cloth or textured vinyl 50/50 front seat w/individual fold-down center armrests, two-way power driver's seat, thick cut-pile carpeting, simulated woodgrain appliqué on door panels and I/P, door pull handle, power windows, choice of quartz digital clock or quartz round-dial clock, AM/FM stereo radio, padded rallye steering wheel, light group, LH remote-control rear view sport mirror, custom wire wheel covers, and GR78 × 15 BSW tires.

Measurements

Wheelbase	115.9"
Length	218.2"
Width	77.2"
Height	55.0"
Legroom — front	42.2"
Legroom — rear	38.7"
Headroom — front	38.1"
Headroom — rear	38.0"
Cargo capacity (cu. ft.)	19.8
Fuel capacity (gals.)	21.0

Models Available

	Model No.	Base MSRP	Change from LY	Shipping Wt. (lbs.)	Model Year Production	Change from LY
Riviera 2-Door Coupe	Z37	$8,082	+9.84%	3701	20,535	-21.44%
TOTALS	*Avg. price*	$8,082	+9.84%	*Production*	20,535	-21.44%

CADILLAC

"Behind the great name ... great cars."

Nineteen-seventy-eight brought a brief lull for Cadillac with only minor changes this year. Consistent with the overall market, Cadillac sales and production maintained the 1977 levels. A rise in sales of the Seville and Fleetwood Brougham was offset by a slight decline in sales of the deVille and the soon to be replaced Eldorado. Sales of the Fleetwood Limousines fell sharply, but it was a one-year anomaly that had little effect on the luxury division's overall sales and production. This successful season was Cadillac's first with every model having a base price above $10,000.

The one-year-old C- and D-bodied Cadillacs were given a new egg-crate grille design that was three rows high and twenty columns across. Also new, as on all Cadillac models this year, were amber front turn signal/parking light lenses. Around back, the DeVille and Fleetwood models had a new taillight arrangement with vertical lamps inset within new bumper ends, and a rear side marker light set on the outside vertical bumper end. Interiors had new upholstery materials and small detail changes such as the relocation of the power seat adjuster control from the seat to the front door armrest on the driver's side and the addition of new seatback pockets, except on the Limousines. Also, an AM/FM signal-seeking stereo with an automatic power antenna was added to the constantly growing standard equipment list. A not so obvious change this year was the use of an aluminum hood to save weight on Fleetwood Brougham, fuel-injected deVilles and all cars built for sale in California.

An egg-crate grille design was also new on the Eldorado, but in this application it was four rows high and twenty-six columns across. Otherwise the Eldorado was mostly unchanged as it entered its final season as one of America's largest first front-wheel-drive automobiles. Next year would bring an all-new Eldorado.

The Seville was mostly unchanged on the outside, aside

from new engraved taillight emblems. What was new in the Seville probably went undetected by most consumers, as items such as four-wheel disc brakes and electronic level con-trol were added to the standard equipment list. Despite the lack of significantly new cars or styling changes, the model year could be called successful for GM's luxury car division.

Coupe deVille 2-Door Coupe

Eldorado 2-Door Hardtop Coupe
with Custom Biarritz Classic package

Eldorado 2-Door Hardtop Coupe

Fleetwood Brougham 4-Door Sedan

Eldorado interior with
Custom Biarritz Classic package

Sedan deVille 4-Door Sedan

Seville 4-Door Sedan

Model year production: 348,832, down 2.65% from 1977.
Domestic market share: 3.66% (9th place).
Base price range: $10,444 to $20,363.
Cadillac average base price: $14,228, up 7.49%.
Introduction date: September 29, 1977.
Assembly plants: Linden, NJ (E); and Detroit, MI (Q).
Data plate identification (VIN): Thirteen digit code read as follows: First digit indicates division (6 = Cadillac); second through fourth digits indicate series and body style (model number in model charts); fifth digit is engine code (see powertrain chart); sixth digit indicates model year (8 = 1978); seventh digit indicates assembly plant (see list above); remaining digits are sequential with beginning number of 100001. *Example:* 6D69T8Q100001 is a 1978 Cadillac Sedan deVille 4-Door Sedan, with 425 CID, EFI V8 engine, serial number 100001, built in Detroit, MI.

Powertrains

Engine	Net HP	Engine code: VIN/GM	Transmission Availability		Seville	Eldorado	DeVille & Fleetwood	Fleetwood Limousine
350 CID (5.7L), EFI, V8	170	B/L49	Turbo Hydra-matic 3-sp. Automatic		S	—	—	—
				MPG:	14/20/16	—	—	—
				Calif.	12/19/14	—	—	—
350 CID (5.7L), Diesel, V8	120	N/LF9	Turbo Hydra-matic					

Engine	Net HP	Engine code: VIN/GM	Transmission Availability		Seville	Eldorado	DeVille & Fleetwood	Fleetwood Limousine
			3-sp. Automatic		$287	—	—	—
				MPG:	21/30/24	—	—	—
				Calif.	21/30/24	—	—	—
425 CID (7.0L), 4-bbl., V8	180	S/L33	Turbo Hydra-matic 3-sp. Automatic		—	S	S	S
				MPG:	—	10/15/11	13/19/15	10/15/11
				Calif.	—	10/15/11	11/16/13	10/15/12
425 CID (7.0L), EFI, V8	195	T/L35	Turbo Hydra-matic 3-sp. Automatic		—	—	$744	—
				MPG:	—	—	12/18/14	—
				Calif.	—	—	12/18/14	—

Major Options

	Seville	deVille	Eldorado	Fleetwood Brougham	Fleetwood Limousine
Automatic Climate Control	S	S	S	S	S
Electric rear window defogger	$94	$94	$94	$94	$94
Controlled cycle windshield wiper	S	$32	$32	$32	$32
Tilt and Telescope steering wheel	S	$121	$121	$121	$121
Cruise Control	$122	$122	$122	$122	$122
Twilight Sentinel	$54	$54	$54	$54	$54
Guidematic headlamp control	$62	$62	$62	$62	$62
Leather upholstery	$315	$295	$315	$315	—[2]
Power front passenger seat, 6-way	$118	$150	$150	S	—
Power 50/50 front seat recliners	$116	$116	$116	$116	—
Lighted vanity mirror, passenger	$50	$50	$50	$50	$50
Illuminated entry system	$59	$59	$59	$59	$59
AM/FM stereo, w/digital display	$106	$106	$106	$106	$203[1]
AM/FM stereo w/tape & seek/scan	$225	$225	$225	$225	—
Automatic door locks	$114	$114	$114	$114	$114
Remote trunk release w/electric pulldown	$67	$80	$80	$80	$80
Padded vinyl top	N/C	$215	$222	S	S
Sunroof[2]	$795	$795	$795	$795	—[3]
Astroroof[2]	$995	$995	$995	$995	—[3]
Theft-Deterrent system	$130	$130	$130	$130	$130
Fuel monitor system	S	$29	$29	$29	$29
Electronic level control	S	$140	S	S	S
Special turbine style wheel discs	—	$54	—	$54	$54
Wire spoke wheel covers	$179	$233	—	$179	$179
Chrome plated wire wheels	$541	—	—	—	—

Popular Option Groups & Packages

	Seville	deVille	Eldorado	Fleetwood Brougham	Fleetwood Limousine
Brougham d'Elegance package	—	—	—	$938	—
DeVille d'Elegance package	—	$689	—	—	—
Custom Cabriolet package, coupe	—	$369	$484	—	—
Custom Biarritz package	—	—	$1,865	—	—
Custom Biarritz Classic package	—	—	$2,466	—	—
Elegante package	$2,600	—	—	—	—
Phaeton package	—	$1,929	—	—	—

—= Not Available; S = Standard equipment. [1]Fleetwood models include rear seat controls. [2]Price given is with full padded vinyl roof. Available on all models with painted roofs for $111 additional cost. [3]Available by special order only.

Paint Colors

	Code		Code		Code
Cotillion White	11	Colonial Yellow	54	Aztec Gold Firemist metallic*	95
Platinum metallic	15	Arizona Beige	62	Western Saddle Firemist metallic*	96
Pewter metallic	16	Demitasse Brown metallic	64	Autumn Haze Firemist metallic*	98
Sable Black	19	Ruidoso Brown metallic	69	Canyon Copper Firemist metallic*	99
Columbia Blue	21	Mulberry metallic	74		
Sterling Blue metallic	22	Carmine Red	80		
Commodore Blue metallic	28	Mediterranean Blue Firemist			
Seamist Green	40	metallic*	90		
Blackwatch Green metallic	49	Basil Green Firemist metallic*	94		

*In two-tone combinations, the first two digits indicate lower color, and the next two digits are the upper color.
Firemist paint available for $163 extra.

Seville

"It stands alone among the world's great cars."

Nameplate year of origin: 1976; 1956 (as a designation on Eldorado 2-Door Hardtops).
Current bodystyle lifespan: 1976 through 1979.
Predecessor to this model: None.
Replacement for this model: Seville (1980 to 1985).
Percentage of division's production: 16.34%.
Corporate siblings: None.
Primary competition: Lincoln Versailles.
Notable changes: Minor trim and detail changes.
Major standard equipment: Dover cloth Dual Comfort 50/50 split front seat w/individual fold-down center armrests, six-way driver and two-way passenger power seat adjustment, one-piece deep pile carpeting, seatback and overhead entry assist straps, hinged door pull handles, individual rear seat reading lamps, electric clock, power windows, power door locks, tilt and telescoping steering wheel, controlled wiper cycle system, automatic climate control, AM/FM signal-seeking stereo radio w/automatic power antenna, dual remote-control rear view mirrors, padded vinyl roof (no cost option), remote trunk release, trunk carpeting including deck lid, fuel monitor system, lamp monitors, front cornering lights, wheel opening moldings, stand-up wreath and crest hood-ornament, electronic level control, automatic parking brake release, bodyside and decklid accent striping, full wheel covers, four-wheel disc brakes, and GR78 × 15 wide WSW tires.

Measurements

Wheelbase	114.3"
Length	204.0"
Width	71.8"
Height	54.6"
Legroom — front	41.7"
Legroom — rear	38.2"
Headroom — front	38.6"
Headroom — rear	36.8"
Cargo capacity (cu. ft.)	12.8
Fuel capacity (gals.)	21.0

Models Available

	Model No.	Base MSRP	Change from LY	Shipping Wt. (lbs.)	Model Year Production	Change from LY
Seville 4-Door Sedan	S69	$14,267	+6.80%	4179	56,985	+23.31%
TOTALS	*Avg. price*	$14,267	+6.80%	*Production*	56,985	+23.31%

deVille

"A luxury car that's right for the times."

Nameplate year of origin: 1959 (series); 1949 (as Hardtop designation).
Current bodystyle lifespan: 1977 through 1984.
Predecessor to this model: deVille (1971 to 1976).
Replacement for this model: deVille (1985 to 1993).
Percentage of division's production: 59.26%.
Corporate siblings: Buick Electra, Cadillac Fleetwood Brougham and Oldsmobile 98.

Measurements

Wheelbase	121.5"
Length	221.2"
Width	76.4"
Height	55.3"
Legroom — front	42.1"

Primary competition: Lincoln Continental.
Notable changes: Minor trim and detail changes.
Major standard equipment: Front bench seat w/choice of Hampton woven cloth or Random velour w/vinyl bolsters and front and rear seat center armrests, 6-way power front seat adjuster, cut-pile carpeting, hinged door pull assist handles, visor vanity mirror, driver and passenger reading lights, courtesy lights, courtesy lamp/assist strap combination on B-pillar of 2-doors, electric clock, power windows, power door locks, automatic climate control, AM/FM radio w/seek and scan and automatic power antenna, LH remote-control rear view mirror, front cornering lights, wheel opening moldings, rocker panel moldings, full wheel covers, and GR78 × 15 WSW tires.

Measurements (cont.)

Legroom — rear	39.7"
Headroom — front	38.0"
Headroom — rear	37.9"
Cargo capacity (cu. ft.)	25.0
Fuel capacity (gals.)	25.3

Models Available

	Model No.	Base MSRP	Change from LY	Shipping Wt. (lbs.)	Model Year Production	Change from LY
Coupe deVille 2-Door Coupe	D47	$10,444	+8.18%	4163	117,750	-15.14%
Sedan deVille 4-Door Sedan	D69	$10,668	+8.15%	4236	88,951	-6.78%
TOTALS		*Avg. price* $10,556	+8.17%		*Production* 206,701	-11.73%

Eldorado

"Front-Wheel Drive and a flair all its own."

Nameplate year of origin: 1953.
Current bodystyle lifespan: 1971 through 1978.
Predecessor to this model: Fleetwood Eldorado (1967 to 1970).
Replacement for this model: Eldorado (1979 to 1985).
Percentage of division's production: 13.42%.
Corporate siblings: Oldsmobile Toronado.
Primary competition: Lincoln Continental Mark V.
Notable changes: Minor trim and detail changes.
Major standard equipment: Choice of Halifax knit cloth or Random velour front seat w/individual fold-down center armrest, 6-way power seat adjuster, cut-pile carpeting, hinged door pull assist handles, visor vanity mirror, driver and passenger reading lights, courtesy lights, electric clock, power windows, power door locks, automatic climate control, AM/FM signal-seeking stereo radio w/automatic power antenna, LH remote-control rear view mirror, front cornering lights, wheel opening moldings, rocker panel moldings, stand-up wreath and crest hood-ornament, automatic level control, full wheel covers, and LR78 × 15 wide WSW tires.

Measurements

Wheelbase	126.3"
Length	224.0"
Width	79.8"
Height	54.2"
Legroom — front	42.2"
Legroom — rear	35.2"
Headroom — front	37.7"
Headroom — rear	36.7"
Cargo capacity (cu. ft.)	NA
Fuel capacity (gals.)	27.0

Models Available

	Model No.	Base MSRP	Change from LY	Shipping Wt. (lbs.)	Model Year Production	Change from LY
Eldorado 2-Door Coupe	L47	$11,921	+6.56%	4906	46,816	-1.12%
TOTALS		*Avg. price* $11,921	+6.56%		*Production* 46,816	-1.12%

Fleetwood Brougham

"A special kind of Cadillac."

Nameplate year of origin: 1966.
Current bodystyle lifespan: 1977 through 1992.
Predecessor to this model: Fleetwood Sixty-Special and Fleetwood Brougham (1971 to 1976).

Measurements

Wheelbase	121.5"
Length	221.2"

Replacement for this model: Fleetwood Brougham (1993 to 1996).
Percentage of division's sales volume: 10.55%.
Corporate siblings: Buick Electra, Cadillac deVille and Oldsmobile 98.
Primary competition: Lincoln Continental w/Town Car package.
Notable changes: Minor trim and detail changes.
Major standard equipment: Florentine velour Dual Comfort 50/50 front seat w/6-way driver side and 2-way passenger side power seat adjuster, front and rear seat fold-down center armrests, cut-pile carpeting, hinged door pull assist handles, front passenger reading light, courtesy lights, quartz digital clock, power windows, power door locks, automatic climate control, AM/FM signal-seeking stereo radio w/automatic power antenna, LH remote-control rear view mirror, padded vinyl roof, front cornering lights, wheel opening moldings, rocker panel moldings, automatic level control, full wheel covers, and HR78 × 15 WSW tires.

Measurements (cont.)

Width	76.4"
Height	56.7"
Legroom — front	42.1"
Legroom — rear	39.7"
Headroom — front	38.0"
Headroom — rear	37.9"
Cargo capacity (cu. ft.)	25.0
Fuel capacity (gals.)	25.3

Models Available

	Model No.	Base MSRP	Change from LY	Shipping Wt. (lbs.)	Model Year Production	Change from LY
Fleetwood Brougham 4-Door Sedan	B69	$12,292	+6.46%	4314	36,800	+31.43%
TOTALS	Avg. price	$12,292	+6.46%	Production	36,800	+31.43%

Fleetwood Limousine

"Flagships of the Cadillac fleet."

Nameplate year of origin: 1927 (models using Fleetwood bodies); 1935 (Fleetwood series).
Current bodystyle lifespan: 1977 through 1984.
Predecessor to this model: Fleetwood Seventy-Five (1971 to 1976).
Replacement for this model: Fleetwood 75 Limousine (1985 to 1987).
Percentage of division's sales volume: 0.44%.
Corporate siblings: None.
Primary competition: None.
Notable changes: Minor trim and detail changes.
Major standard equipment: Florentine velour w/2-way power front seat adjuster, front and rear seat fold-down center armrests, cut-pile carpeting, two fold-down seats (rearward facing for two additional passengers), hinged door pull assist handles, power windows, power door locks, dual automatic climate control system (front and rear), courtesy lights, electric clock, AM/FM radio w/automatic power antenna, passenger control panel (controls power windows, reading lights, radio [optional], automatic climate control, and the glass partition in the Formal Limousine), automatic level control, LH and RH remote-control rear view mirror, front cornering lights, wheel opening moldings, full-length rocker panel moldings, full wheel covers, and HR78 × 15 WSW tires. Formal Limousine adds: Black leather 45/45 front seat, and sliding glass partition separating driver and passenger compartment.

Measurements

Wheelbase	144.5"
Length	244.2"
Width	79.8"
Height	56.9"
Legroom — front	NA
Legroom — rear	NA
Headroom — front	NA
Headroom — rear	NA
Cargo capacity (cu. ft.)	NA
Fuel capacity (gals.)	25.3

Models Available

	Model No.	Base MSRP	Change from LY	Shipping Wt. (lbs.)	Model Year Production	Change from LY
Fleetwood 4-Door Limousine	F23	$19,642	+7.96%	4772	848	-46.40%
Fleetwood 4-Door Formal Limousine	F33	$20,363	+7.98%	4858	682	-33.91%
TOTALS	Avg. price	$20,003	+7.97%	Production	1,530	-41.47%

CHEVROLET

"See what's new today in a Chevrolet."

The only major change to the 1968–1982 generation of Corvettes occurred this year to mark the 25th anniversary of America's only true sports car. Unfortunately, the press coverage and enthusiast excitement surrounding the event drew attention away from the introduction of the all-new mid-size Malibu and Monte Carlo lines. The best efforts of the advertising department helped sales and production of the Malibu to rise slightly, but the Monte Carlo slipped, most likely hurt by the success of its corporate cousin, the Oldsmobile Cutlass. By year's end, the uptick in Malibu sales was wiped out by the Monte Carlo's downturn. When all was said and done, the Chevrolet division still was able to end the year with total production up slightly over 1977, in an overall market that was down slightly from the prior year. All of the strength for the division this year ended up being in the Chevette, with its new four-door version, and the Camaro, as the sporty "pony car" was in the middle of a sales resurgence.

The Corvette received a third facelift since the bodystyle was introduced in 1968; however, this time it could be more accurately described as a "rear-end" lift. Nearly all of the Corvette styling themes since 1974 were retained, but a new wraparound rear window added a fastback look to the car, echoing the 1963 through 1967 coupe designs (sans the 1963 split-window feature). The design would prove to be so aerodynamically superior that it would continue well into the 21st century. Adding the large rear window actually allowed for increased luggage space and room for storage of the removable roof panels in that space, as well as a roll-up shade to screen the compartment from view. Other new features included upgraded transmissions, a larger fuel tank, and a restyled instrument panel with round instruments and a large glove box. For the 25th anniversary year, a special paint package (RPO B2Z) was introduced to commemorate the occasion, with the main identifying feature being a silver metallic upper body over charcoal silver lower body. A total of 15,283 Corvettes left the factory with the anniversary paint scheme. Details of the package can be found in Appendix IV. Early in 1978, the Corvette was selected as the official pace car for the 62nd Indianapolis 500 race on May 28, 1978. When a Pace Car replica package was shown at the New York auto show in February, it was an immediate hit. Chevrolet announced a limited edition pace car replica version for a list price of $13,653. Limited availability and huge demand meant that many were quickly marked up by dealerships or

resold by the original owners for a profit. But when the 2,500 units originally planned for production sold out, a decision was made to increase production, which ended up being 6,502 units, one for every Chevrolet dealer across the country. As had happened with the "last" 1976 Cadillac Eldorado convertibles, many speculators lost money on the Limited Edition Corvette.

While the Malibu name had been around since the very first Chevelle was introduced in 1964, the popular mid-size subseries had always been preceded by the Chevelle name, even after the 1973 Chevelle Deluxe was discontinued. An appropriate time to make Malibu the official name of the series finally arrived with the completely redesigned, and downsized, 1978 mid-size line. With the redesign, more traditional coupe and sedan body styles were introduced, leaving the Colonnade hardtop styling behind. The new Malibu coupes and sedans were nearly 600 pounds lighter and more than a foot shorter; wagons were nearly two feet shorter and 1,000 pounds lighter. As mentioned the boxy new models were of a more traditional design with a slanting rear roofline, but not the near "fastback" style of the prior models. Two-door models had large fixed rear quarter windows, while four-doors used fixed rear door windows with swing-out rear quarter windows to provide ventilation, giving the sedans a six-window design. Station wagons had the fixed rear door window, but included a small opening vent window within the door. At the rear of station wagons, the "Hatchgate" was introduced, combining a drop-down tailgate and lift-up full-glass window supported by hydraulic struts.

Malibu front-end styling included new single square headlights with an outer wraparound side marker/turn signal light, and an inner mounted vertical parking/turn signal light. The bezel housing the three lights was canted forward, giving the headlights a hooded appearance. An intricate looking horizontal crosshatch grille used wide bars, in a pattern six rows high and sixteen columns across, creating the illusion of individual small rectangles. A chrome grille surround completed the new look. Around back, new wraparound triple-unit horizontal taillights were used on coupes and sedans, with the innermost lenses housing the backup lights, and the wraparound portion angling with its forwardmost point at the bottom, opposing the slant of the front lights. Wagons wore slim horizontal taillamps in the rear bumper. License plate housings were in the rear panel of coupes and sedans and within the tailgate of station wagons. Bodysides were relatively smooth, with a lower feature line running between the bumpers, and creating a flat-topped wheel opening flare as the line passed over them. The lower line was used as placement for the bodyside molding on the Malibu Classic line. A faint upper feature line began on the front fender, falling off to the side about an inch as it ran across the fender, passing under the door glass and continuing to the rear quarter panel end. The upper line was the demarcation line for cars with two-tone paint packages. The two lines also marked the boundaries of the woodgrain trim on the Malibu Classic wagon with the Estate Wagon option package.

Powering the smaller Malibu line was a new, Chevrolet-designed 3.3-liter, 200 CID V6 engine, standard in all models except in California, where a more powerful Buick-built 3.8-liter, 231 CID V6 engine was standard. The optional 305 CID V8 engine added 40 horsepower, increasing the power available by more than 40 percent over the 200 CID V6 engine, and was well worth the investment, despite its slightly lower fuel economy. The 350 CID V8 engine was still available in Malibu station wagons, except in California.

Inside, the new Malibu adopted a dual pod instrument panel. The main pod, set in front of the driver, held a horizontal speedometer with a fuel gauge to the left and warning lights for other functions to the right side (an optional instrumentation package replaced this arrangement with six round gauges), and a separated section along the bottom with light and wiper controls to the left and other optional controls, such as rear window defroster, to the right. A pod in the center, located lower on the convex style instrument panel, housed the ventilation and optional radio controls. An ashtray and cigarette lighter were mounted below this center pod. Door panels on all models had an armrest built in, and an extended area forward of the armrest held optional power window, door lock and remote mirror controls. Interior upholstery and patterns were not greatly different from prior years, but a new one-piece hardboard molded headliner with foam covering, and was similar to those used on the new-for-1977 full-size Chevrolets, helped in noise reduction.

The mid-size personal luxury Monte Carlo was also completely redesigned, retaining some exterior styling features reminiscent of the 1973–1977 models. The Monte Carlo's identifying fender "swoosh" lines continued with the front line beginning with the forward canting headlight bezel, which was similar to the Malibu's and housed single square headlights with an outer wraparound side marker/turn signal light and an inner mounted vertical parking/turn signal light. The line continued off the top of the front fender onto the bodyside, fading away just over halfway through the door, at a level below that of the door handle. The rear quarter line began just inches behind the door opening, running up and somewhat forward, then curving sharply back to run under the rear quarter window and C-pillar, then running a few inches below the rear quarter panel top edge that was at trunk lid level, to end just above the rear side marker light. A large squarish fixed rear quarter window combined with a slim chrome lined B-pillar and frameless door windows to give the appearance of true hardtop styling. The rear roofline of the Monte Carlo was nearly upright and seemed appropriate to the personal luxury car image. Back to the front end of the Monte Carlo, the vertical grille jutted forward several inches from the forward-leaning headlight bezels, and was outlined in chrome with an egg-crate style insert, seven rows high and about thirty-two columns across. A stand-up hood ornament was placed on the front header panel. At the back end a body-color slanting rear panel carried horizontal taillamps divided into five sections, with the innermost housing the backup lights. On the side of the rear panel cap was a vertical side marker light that was mounted so closely, it appeared to be part of a wraparound taillight. Body-colored bumpers, front and rear, wore chrome colored vinyl rub strips. The standard powertrain for the Monte Carlo was a 231 CID V6 engine paired with a 3-speed manual transmission. A 305 CID V8 engine was available, and a four-speed manual or Turbo Hydra-matic transmission was available with both engines, except in California, where the Turbo Hydra-matic was required. Interior design followed that of the Malibu, to which the Monte Carlo was more closely related now.

Full-size Chevrolets, which were newly downsized for 1977, entered this model year with new grille designs, and the Landau coupes became actual models, instead of an option as they were last year. The new Caprice grille consisted of an egg-crate pattern five rows high and fourteen columns across. Impala models used a new horizontal crosshatch grille with four prominent horizontal bars set in front of five vertical bars, creating a pattern four rows high and six columns across. The Landau coupes both were essentially defined by appearance details, adding front-half vinyl roofs, often referred to as canopy roofs by some manufacturers, sport mirrors, pinstriping and wire wheel covers.

The Camaro, which was in the midst of a dramatic resurgence, was given a facelift that dispensed with the traditional chrome bumpers and introduced body colored urethane front and rear fascias. At the front, a sloping grille design continued, and headlights and parking/turn signal lights were mounted in the same positions, with headlight bezels being similar to the old style. The parking/turn signal lights were now square instead of round, and the grille insert was a horizontal crosshatch grid pattern four rows high and ten columns across, with the Camaro logo mounted in the center. Within the body colored bumper were additional air intakes with a grille insert two rows high and ten columns across. At the rear, wraparound taillights were now larger tri-colored units with the outermost lens being brake and taillights, the center amber turn signal lights, and the innermost the backup lights. In between the two was either a black or body-colored panel, depending upon the model. Interior trim was vastly improved for the new year, with several distinct patterns, again depending upon model or options selected. Joining the sport coupe and LT coupe this year was the Z28, entering its first full model year as a Camaro model, rather than an option package. The Rally Sport package continued to be available for both the Camaro Sport Coupe and Type LT. Powering the Camaro models were the same engine and transmission combinations as last year.

The Nova was nearing the end of its lifespan, and there were no major changes to the popular compact for this season. The most noticeable change was that the Concours name was gone, and the Nova Custom name took its place, assuming the Concours' styling features and once again being the top-line Nova as it had been prior to 1975. With the name change, the hatchback coupe was dropped from the Nova Custom line. The Rally package continued to be available, offering a unique argent colored, diamond pattern grille with horizontal rectangular parking and turn signal lights inset, along with unique badging and tape stripes. The package was offered on any two-door Nova or Nova Custom.

With the Vega gone, the Monza line took on the former Kammback wagon and added a lower-priced Monza S hatchback to take the place of the former Vega hatchback. As a result of the combining of the two series into one, the Monza now came in base Monza and Monza S forms, all sharing a new, gently sloped front end similar to the Vega's, but with a differing grille, a chrome-lined "crosshair" type grille, with the vertical and horizontal bar having a gold Chevrolet bowtie emblem in the center. The grille insert consisted of four dark argent horizontal bars per section, and vertical parking/turn signal lights were placed behind the bars at the outer ends of the grille. Square chrome bezels surrounded single round headlamps. Models in the base series included a Monza S and Monza 2+2 hatchback and a Monza two-door coupe, with the 2+2 hatchback and coupe using last year's Monza body from the cowl back, while the Monza S hatchback and Monza and Monza Estate two-door wagons used the old Vega body from the cowl back.

The sporty body-colored urethane front-end now distinguished the Monza Sport models in 2+2 hatchback and two-door coupe configurations. The 1978 version of the urethane front end had a full-width slotted opening running below the headlights and above the bumper, with a thin chrome surround, a thin chrome horizontal center bar, and the name Monza in chrome block letters set on the center

chrome bar. The bodies of the coupes and 2+2 hatchbacks were mostly unchanged otherwise, with all models having a vertically ribbed B-pillar and the same wrap-around taillights on the hatchbacks, vertical taillights on the wagons, and new tri-color units for coupes in the same shape as before, but with the center lens being amber for the turn signals, and the innermost lens housing the backup lights. Interiors for the coupe and 2+2 hatchback continued to be the Monza design, while the Monza S hatchback and wagons used the Vega interior with appropriate Monza upgrades, including an optional center console. Under the hood, all Monzas had the new Pontiac-built 151 CID "Iron Duke" four-cylinder engine as standard equipment. Chevy's new 3.2 liter V6 engine was optional equipment in all but California, the 3.8 liter Buick-built V6 engine was added as an option, and the 5.0 liter V8 engine remained the top powerplant choice in all but the wagons. After combining the two series, sales dropped slightly from 1977's depressed levels, possibly as a result of buyer confusion over what the new Monza line was supposed to represent. The Spyder equipment and appearance packages continued to be offered on the Monza Sport 2+2 hatchback.

Chevette added a four-door hatchback model to the lineup, just in time to compete against the new front-wheel-drive Dodge Omni and Plymouth Horizon. The four-door Chevette was so popular that despite all the publicity surrounding the new Chrysler twins, it exceeded their combined model year production by 961 units. Riding on a wheelbase extended by three inches, the new four-door had slightly more rear legroom. Styling changes included a new grille with two openings per side, split by a body colored center, and each grille side having a "large-opening" grid pattern, two rows high by three columns across. And around back, new tri-color taillight lenses were introduced with a center amber lens for turn signals, and an inner lens housing the backup lights. Beneath the hood, the underwhelming 1.4 liter 4-cylinder engine was dropped, and replaced by the formerly optional 1.6 liter 4-cylinder engine as standard equipment. A "High-Output" 1.6 liter engine was new for the year, and added a two-barrel carburetor, an underhood insulator (apparently to control the extra noise created), and a whopping five horsepower increase to its output. Also missing this year were the Rally and Sandpiper option packages, as the Chevette went for a more upscale look, offering only upgraded Custom interior and Custom exterior option packages. As a side note, this would be the last year for the Chevette to use single round headlamps.

1978

Camaro 2-Door Sport Coupe

Caprice Classic 4-Door Sedan

Corvette 2-Door Coupe
with Silver Anniversary package

Malibu Classic 4-Door Station Wagon

Monte Carlo instrument panel

Camaro Z28 2-Door Sport Coupe

Chevette 2-Door Hatchback
Coupe with Sky Roof

Impala 2-Door Coupe with Power Sky Roof

Malibu Classic Landau 2-Door Coupe

Monza 2+2 2-Door Hatchback Coupe

Monza S 2-Door Hatchback Coupe

Caprice Classic 4-Door Station Wagon
with Estate Package (front) and
Impala 4-Door Station Wagon (rear)

Chevette 4-Door Hatchback Sedan

Malibu 4-Door Sedan

Monte Carlo 2-Door Hardtop Coupe

Monza Estate 2-Door Station Wagon

Monza Sport 2-Door Coupe

Nova 4-Door Sedan

Nova Custom 2-Door Coupe

Nova Custom 2-Door Coupe
with Rally Equipment package

Model year production: 2,374,545, up 2.37% from 1977.
Domestic market share: 25.20% (1st place).
Base price range: $2,999 to $9,645.
Chevrolet average base price: $4,633, up 5.64%.
Introduction date: October 6, 1977. Monza S and Monza wagons introduced December 1, 1977.
Assembly plants: Baltimore, MD (B); Southgate, CA (C); Doraville, GA (D); Janesville, WI (J); Kansas City/Leeds, MO (K); Van Nuys, CA (L); Norwood, OH (N); Arlington, TX (R); St. Louis, MO (S); Tarrytown, NY (T); Lordstown, OH (U); Willow Run, MI (W); Wilmington, DE (Y); Fremont, CA (Z); Oshawa, Ontario, Canada (1); and Ste. Therese, Quebec, Canada (2).

Data plate identification (VIN): Thirteen digit code read as follows: First digit indicates division (1 = Chevrolet); second through fourth digits indicate series and body style (model number in model charts); fifth digit is engine code (see powertrain chart); sixth digit indicates model year (8 = 1978); seventh digit indicates assembly plant (see list above); remaining digits are sequential with beginning number of 100001. *Example:* 1S87L8N100001 is a 1978 Chevrolet Camaro Type LT 2-Door Sport Coupe, with 350 CID, 4-bbl. V8 engine, serial number 100001, built in Norwood, OH.

1978

Powertrains

Engine	Net HP	Engine Code: VIN/ GM	Transmission Availability[1]		Chevette	Monza	Camaro	Nova	Malibu	Monte Carlo	Full-Size Chevy	Corvette
98 CID (1.6L) OHC, 1-bbl., 4-cyl.	63	E/LY5	4-speed manual		S	—	—	—	—	—	—	—
				MPG:	30/40/ 34	—	—	—	—	—	—	—
				Calif.	27/36/ 30	—	—	—	—	—	—	—
			3-speed Turbo Hydra-matic		$270	—	—	—	—	—	—	—
				MPG:	25/33/ 28	—	—	—	—	—	—	—
				Calif.	22/29/ 24	—	—	—	—	—	—	—
98 CID (1.6L) OHC, 2-bbl., "High-Output" 4-cyl.[2]	68	J/LW5	4-speed manual		$55	—	—	—	—	—	—	—
				MPG:	30/40/ 34	—	—	—	—	—	—	—
			3-speed Turbo Hydra-matic		$325	—	—	—	—	—	—	—
				MPG:	25/33/ 28	—	—	—	—	—	—	—
151 CID (2.5L), 2-bbl., 4-cyl.	85	V/LX6	4-speed manual		—	S	—	—	—	—	—	—
				MPG:	—	24/34/28	—	—	—	—	—	—
				Calif.	—	21/31/24	—	—	—	—	—	—
			5-speed manual		—	$175	—	—	—	—	—	—
				MPG:	—	NA	—	—	—	—	—	—
			3-speed Turbo Hydra-matic		—	$270[3]	—	—	—	—	—	—
				MPG:	—	23/31/26	—	—	—	—	—	—
				Calif.	—	23/31/26	—	—	—	—	—	—
196 CID (3.2L),	90	C/ LC9	4-speed manual		—	$130	—	—	—	—	—	—
				MPG:	—	19/33/23	—	—	—	—	—	—

Engine	Net HP	Engine Code: VIN/GM	Transmission Availability[1]	Chevette	Monza	Camaro	Nova	Malibu	Monte Carlo	Full-Size Chevy	Corvette
2-bbl., V6[2]			5-speed manual	—	$305	—	—	—	—	—	—
			MPG:	—	NA	—	—	—	—	—	—
			3-speed Turbo Hydra-matic	—	$400	—	—	—	—	—	—
			MPG:	—	18/26/21	—	—	—	—	—	—
200 CID (3.3L), 2-bbl., V6[2]	95	M/ L26	3-speed manual	—	—	—	—	S[2]	—	—	—
			MPG:	—	—	—	—	21/29/24	—	—	—
			3-speed Turbo Hydra-matic	—	—	—	—	$307[2]	—	—	—
			MPG:	—	—	—	—	19/25/21	—	—	—
231 CID (3.8L), 2-bbl., V6	105	A/ LD5	3-speed manual	—	—	—	—	—	S (Cpe.)[2]	—	—
			MPG:	—	—	—	—	—	16/28/19	—	—
			4-speed manual	—	$130	—	—	—	$125 (Cpe.)[2]	—	—
			MPG: *Calif.*	15/28/19 16/27/20	—	—	—	—	—	—	—
			5-speed manual	—	$305[2]	—	—	—	—	—	—
			MPG:	—	NA	—	—	—	—	—	—
			3-speed Turbo Hydra-matic	—	$400	—	—	$307[4,5]	S (Landau)/ $307 (Cpe.)[4]	—	—
			MPG: *Calif.*	—	18/26/21 16/23/18	—	—	16/23/18	19/27/22 16/23/18	—	—
250 CID (4.1L), 1-bbl., 6-cyl.	110/ 90[6]	D/ L22	3-speed manual	—	—	S[2,7]	S[2]	—	—	—	—
			MPG:	—	—	18/27/ 21	19/26/ 21	—	—	—	—
			3-speed Turbo Hydra-matic	—	—	$307[4,7]	$307[4]	—	—	S (ex. Wgns.)	—
			MPG:	—	—	17/24/ 19	18/24/ 20	—	—	17/24/19	—
			Calif.	—	—	15/20/ 17	15/20/ 17	—	—	15/20/17	—
305 CID (5.0L), 2-bbl., V8	145/ 135[6]	U/ LG3	4-speed manual	—	$320 (Cpe./ 2+2 only)	$310[2,7]	$310[2]	$315[2]	$275 (Cpe.)[2]	—	—
			MPG:	—	16/22/ 18	15/21/ 17	15/21/ 17	16/22/ 18	16/22/ 18	—	—
			3-speed Turbo Hydra-matic	—	$590 (Cpe./ 2+2 only)[4]	$492[4,7]	$492[4]	$497[3,4]	$150 (Landau)/ $457 (Cpe.)[4]	S (Wgns.)/ $185 (others)[3]	—
			MPG:	—	17/25/ 20	16/22/ 19	16/22/ 19	17/25/ 20	17/25/ 20	16/22/ 19	—
			Calif.	—	14/21/ 17	13/19/ 15	13/19/ 15	14/21/ 17	14/21/ 17	13/19/ 15	—
350 CID (5.7L), 4-bbl., V8	170/ 160[6]	L/ LM1	4-speed manual	—	—	$425[2,7]	—	—	—	—	—
			MPG:	—	—	14/19/16	—	—	—	—	—
			3-speed Turbo Hydra-matic	—	—	$607[4,7]	$607[3]	$612 (Wgns. only)[3,6]	—	$115 (Wgns.)/ $300 (others)[3]	—
			MPG:	—	—	15/21/ 17	15/21/ 17	16/22/19	—	15/21/17	—
			Calif.	—	—	13/18/ 15	13/18/ 15	13/19/15	—	13/18/15	—
350 CID (5.7L),	185/ 175[6]	L/ L48	4-speed manual	—	—	S (Z28)[2]	—	—	—	—	S
			MPG:	—	—	14/19/16	—	—	—	—	14/19/

Engine	Net HP	Engine Code: VIN/GM	Transmission Availability[1]		Chevette	Monza	Camaro	Nova	Malibu	Monte Carlo	Full-Size Chevy	Corvette
4-bbl., V8			3-speed Turbo Hydra-matic		—	—	$45 (Z28)	—	—	—	—	16 N/C
				MPG:	—	—	15/21/17	—	—	—	—	15/21/17
				Calif.	—	—	13/18/15	—	—	—	—	13/18/15
350 CID (5.7L), 4-bbl., V8[8]	220	H/ L82	4-speed manual, heavy-duty		—	—	—	—	—	—	—	$525
				MPG:	—	—	—	—	—	—	—	14/19/16
			3-speed Turbo Hydra-matic		—	—	—	—	—	—	—	$525
				MPG:	—	—	—	—	—	—	—	15/21/17

[1]Unless otherwise specified: All 3-speed manuals are column shift. All 4- and 5-speed manuals are floor shift. All automatics are column shift, except on Chevette, Monza, Camaro and Corvette. Floor shift automatic is optional on Nova, Malibu and Monte Carlo with other specified equipment at extra cost.   [2]Not available in California or high altitude areas.   [3]Estimated mileage ratings for station wagons are one to two mpg lower for city, highway and combined.   [4]Required for cars sold in California, with smallest engine size marked being standard, and larger engines optional at proportionally higher cost.   [5]Only available in California or high altitude areas.   [6]Rating in high-altitude areas. For Malibu and Impala/Caprice this powertrain combination is required on wagons sold in high-altitude areas.   [7]Not available on Camaro Z28.   [8]L82 engine not available in California, Florida, Maryland, Oregon, Washington, and cities of Boston, MA, Chicago, IL (and Cook county area), and Grand Rapids, MI.

Major Options

	Chevette	Monza	Camaro	Nova	Malibu	Monte Carlo	Impala & Caprice	Corvette
Four-season air conditioning[1]	$470	$470	$539	$539	$544	$544	$569	$605
Comfortilt steering wheel	—	$62	$69	$69	$69	$69	$70	S[2]
Cruise-Master speed control	—	—	$90	$90	$90	$90	$95	$99
Rear window defogger[3]	—	—	$51	$51	$51	$51	$51	—
Electro-Clear rear window defogger	$82	$97	—	—	$92	$92	$94	$98
Dual sport mirrors, remote	$49	$31[4]	$33[4]	$33[4]	$57	$57	$57	$40[4]
Soft-Ray tinted glass, all windows	$54	$54	$56	$56	$62	$62	$76	S
Power windows, 2-dr./4-dr.	—	—	$124	$118/$164	$124/$172	$124	$130/$190	$130
Power door locks, 2-dr./4-dr.	—	—	$80	$74/$112	$80/$112	$80	$82/$114	$120
Power front seat, w/std. seat	—	—	—	—	$151	$151	$151	—
Front bucket seats, w/console[5]	S	$77	$80	$190	$190	$190	—	S
Rear facing third seat (wagons)	—	—	—	—	—	—	$127	—
AM radio	S[6]	$71	$79	$77	$79	$79	$80	—
AM/FM stereo	—	$215	$229	$229	$229	$229	$229	$286
AM/FM stereo w/tape player[7]	—	$308	$328	$328	$328	$328	$332	$419
Vinyl top, full[8]	—	—	—	$97	$116	$131	$142	—
Vinyl top, landau[9]	—	$153	$102	$179	S	S	S	—
Sky Roof (sunroof), power[10]	$215	$215	—	—	$499	$499	$595	—
Removable glass roof panels (T-Tops)	—	—	$625	—	—	$625	—	$349
Power steering, variable-ratio	—	$134	S	$152	$152	$152[11]	S	S
Power brakes, w/front disc	$66	$66	$69[12]	$69	$69[12]	$69[12]	S	S[13]
Full wheel covers	$42	$37	$37	$37	$37	S	$38	—
Wire wheel covers	—	—	—	$120	$146	$109	—	—
Rally wheels w/trim rings	S	$80	$85	$69	$78	$41	—	S
Forged aluminum wheels	—	$258	$265	—	—	—	—	$345
Custom styled wheels	—	—	$133	—	—	—	—	—
WSW tires	S[6]	$19	$46	$44	$37	$42	$46	—

Popular Option Groups & Packages

	Chevette	Monza	Camaro	Nova	Malibu	Monte Carlo	Impala & Caprice	Corvette
25th Silver Anniversary paint package	—	—	—	—	—	—	—	$399
Auxiliary lighting package	$35	$33	—	—	—	—	$35	—
Custom exterior package	$99	—	—	—	—	—	—	—
Estate wagon package	—	—	—	—	$235	—	$235	—
Gymkhana suspension package	—	—	—	—	—	—	—	$89
Indianapolis 500 pace car replica package	—	—	—	—	—	—	—	$4,008
Interior décor and/or Quiet sound group	$45	$34	$61	—	$46	—	$51	—
Rally equipment package	—	—	—	$199	—	—	—	—
Rally Sport package	—	—	$370[14]	—	—	—	—	—
Special instrumentation package	—	$82	$106	$106	$118	$97	—	S
Spyder appearance package	—	$216	—	—	—	—	—	—
Spyder equipment group	—	$252	—	—	—	—	—	—

— = Not Available; S = Standard equipment. [1]Price is $508 on Camaro and Nova with V8 engine. Comfortron air conditioning with automatic temperature control is available for $655 on Impala and Caprice. [2]Tilt/Telescope w/leather-wrapped sport steering wheel available on Corvette for $175. [3]Blower type defogger. [4]Dual sport mirror with LH remote only. [5]Bucket seats standard on Chevette, Monza and Camaro, with console being optional on Monza and Camaro. Mini-console standard on Chevette. Bucket seats and console available on Nova coupes or hatchbacks, Malibu Classic coupes and Monte Carlo. [6]Available on Chevette Scooter: AM radio for $71; WSW tires for $43. [7]Tape player is choice of cassette or 8-track. [8]Not available on station wagons. [9]Standard on all Landau coupe models: Malibu Classic, Monte Carlo, Impala and Caprice. Cabriolet roof available on Monza Towne Coupe and Nova coupes. Camaro has vinyl sport roof (front part of roof). [10]Manually operated on Chevette and Monza. [11]Standard on Monte Carlo Landau coupe. [12]Standard on Camaro Z28 and on Malibu station wagons. [13]Power front and rear disc brakes. [14]Price is $251 on Camaro Type LT.

Paint Colors

	Code		Code		Code
Dark Gray metallic[1]	07	Frost Blue[1]	26	Camel metallic	63
Classic White[1]	10	Dark Blue metallic[2]	29	Saffron metallic	67
Antique White	11	Orange[2]	34	Dark Camel metallic[2,3,4]	69
Silver metallic[1]	13	Light Green metallic[2,3,6]	44	Red[1]	72
Silver metallic	15	Medium Green metallic[2]	45	Light Red[3,4,6]	75
Gray metallic (two-tone)[2]	16	Dark Blue-Green metallic[3,4]	48	Carmine metallic[2,3,4]	77
Black[1,2,3,4]	19	Bright Yellow[3,4,6]	51	Dark Carmine metallic[2]	79
Dull Black (low gloss black)[5]	19	Yellow[1]	52	Mahogany metallic[1]	82
Pastel Blue[2,6]	21	Gold metallic (two-tone only)[2]	56	Dark Blue metallic[1]	83
Light Blue metallic	22	Frost Beige[1]	59	Brown metallic[1]	89
Ultramarine Blue metallic[3,4]	24	Light Camel[2,3,6]	61		

In two-tone combinations, the first two digits indicate lower color and the next two digits are the upper color. Two-tone paint available for $46 on Nova, $62 on Malibu coupe and sedan, $110 on Malibu wagon, and $47 on Impala and Caprice. Colors listed with no footnotes are available on all models, except Corvette. [1]Available on Corvette. Dark Gray metallic is for Corvette 25th anniversary paint package only. [2]Available on all Chevelle Malibu, Monte Carlo and full-size Chevrolet models. [3]Available on Monza. [4]Available on Camaro and Nova. [5]Low gloss black is for Camaro Rally Sport only. [6]Available on Chevette.

Chevette

"It'll drive you happy."

Nameplate year of origin: 1976.

Current bodystyle lifespan: 1976 through 1987.

Predecessor to this model: None.

Replacement for this model: None (captive imports Sprint and Spectrum introduced in 1985 as supplementary models).

Percentage of division's production: 12.59%.

Corporate siblings: None.

Primary competition: Dodge Colt and Omni, Ford Fiesta, and Plymouth Arrow and Horizon.

Notable changes: Four-door hatchback added, new grille, and minor trim and detail changes.

Major standard equipment: Choice of sport cloth-and-vinyl or all-vinyl front bucket seats, fold-down rear seat (can be deleted for credit), color-keyed cut-pile carpeting, door pull strap, armrests deleted, open

Measurements

	2-Door	4-Door
Wheelbase	94.3"	97.3"
Length	158.8"	161.7"
Width	61.8"	61.8"
Height	52.3"	53.3"
Legroom — front	41.5"	41.5"
Legroom — rear	30.5"	34.1"
Headroom — front	38.1"	38.1"
Headroom — rear	37.3"	37.4"
Cargo capacity (cu. ft.)	26.3*	27.8*
Fuel capacity (gals.)	13.0	13.0

*Maximum with rear seat folded down.

compartment glove box, black two-spoke steering wheel and column, cargo compartment under-floor storage, argent colored headlight bezels and grille trim, polished aluminum bumpers (not chromed), and P155/80 × 13 BSW tires. Chevette adds: Choice of all-vinyl or cloth-and-vinyl front bucket seats, mini-console, door armrests, cigarette lighter, glove box w/latch type door, swing-out rear window (coupe), AM radio, bright front and rear window trim, chrome headlamp bezel inserts, chrome grille trim, deluxe chrome bumpers w/rub strips, bright wheel trim rings, and P155/80 × 13 WSW tires.

Models Available

	Model No.	Base MSRP	Change from LY	Shipping Wt. (lbs.)	Model Year Production	Change from LY
Chevette Scooter 2-Door Hatchback Coupe	J08	$2,999	0.00%	1932	12,829	-2.74%
Chevette 2-Door Hatchback Coupe	B08	$3,354	+4.00%	1965	118,375	-1.58%
Chevette 4-Door Hatchback Sedan	B68	$3,464	NEW	2035	167,769	NEW
TOTALS	*Avg. price*	$3,272	+5.15%	*Production*	298,973	+124.00%

Monza

"Take the wheel, have some fun."

Nameplate year of origin: 1975 (1960 as Corvair subseries).
Current bodystyle lifespan: 1975 through 1980.
Predecessor to this model: Corvair Monza (1965 to 1969); Vega Kammback wagon (1971 to 1977).
Replacement for this model: Cavalier (1982 to 1993).
Percentage of division's production: 5.85%.
Corporate siblings: Buick Skyhawk, Oldsmobile Starfire, and Pontiac Sunbird.
Primary competition: Dodge Challenger, Ford Mustang II, and Plymouth Sapporo.
Notable changes: New wagon model, new front-end styling. and detail changes.
Major standard equipment: Choice of patterned cloth or all-vinyl front bucket seats, cut-pile carpeting, color-keyed instrument panel, fold-down rear seat and rear liftgate (hatchbacks and wagons), two-spoke steering wheel, soft molded door panels w/map pockets, simulated woodgrain I/P trim, bright front and rear window moldings, bright side window surround moldings, aluminum front and rear bumpers (S and wagons), chrome front and rear bumpers (coupe and 2+2), bumper rub strips, full wheel covers (hubcaps on S), and A78 × 13 WSW tires. Estate wagon adds: Bodyside simulated woodgrain vinyl appliqués w/tan colored surround trim. Sport adds: Custom interior w/choice of Sport cloth-and-vinyl or all-vinyl front bucket seats, brushed metal accents on I/P, body-color urethane front end fascia w/body-color bumper and bumper guards, chrome rear bumper w/black rub strip, and finned wheel covers w/GT-type center hub and bright wheel nuts. 2+2 adds to Sport: Chrome rear bumper w/body-color (or contrasting color) rub strip, and front and rear bumper guards color-matched to bumper guards.

Measurements

	S HBK	Coupe	2+2 HBK	Wagon	Sport Coupe	Sport 2+2 HBK
Wheelbase	97.0"	97.0"	97.0"	97.0"	97.0"	97.0"
Length	177.4"	178.6"	178.6"	177.4"	178.7"	179.3"
Width	65.4"	65.4"	65.4"	65.4"	65.4"	65.4"
Height	50.2"	49.8"	50.2"	51.8"	49.8"	50.2"
Legroom — front	42.8"	42.8"	42.8"	42.9"	42.8"	42.8"
Legroom — rear	30.1"	28.2"	29.6"	30.2"	28.2"	29.6"
Headroom — front	37.0"	37.6"	37.7"	38.5"	37.6"	37.7"
Headroom — rear	37.1"	37.2"	35.3"	40.1"	37.2"	35.3"
Cargo capacity (cu. ft.)	26.5*	6.6	10.1**	46.6	6.6	10.1**
Fuel capacity (gals.)	16.0	18.5	18.5	15.0	18.5	18.5

*Capacity with rear seat folded down.   **Capacity with rear seat down is 30.2 cu. ft.*

Models Available

	Model No.	Base MSRP	Change from LY	Shipping Wt. (lbs.)	Model Year Production	Change from LY
Monza S 2-Door Hatchback Coupe*	M77	$3,697	+10.06%	2643	2,326	-93.78%
Monza 2-Door Coupe	M27	$3,462	+2.75%	2688	37,878	+10.97%
Monza 2+2 2-Door Hatchback Coupe	M07	$3,609	NEW	2732	36,227	NEW
Monza 2-Door Station Wagon*	M15	$3,698	+5.00%	2723	24,255	-3.68%
Monza Estate 2-Door Station Wagon*	M15	$3,932	+4.99%	NA	2,478	-28.40%
Monza Sport 2-Door Coupe	R27	$3,930	NEW	2730	6,823	NEW
Monza Sport 2+2 2-Door Hatchback Coupe	R07	$4,077	+6.17%	2777	28,845	-26.44%
TOTALS	Avg. price	$3,772	+1.95%	Production	138,832	+89.28%

Comparisons are made to equivalent 1977 Vega models.

Camaro

"Unique, responsive, fun to drive."

Nameplate year of origin: 1967.
Current bodystyle lifespan: 1970 through 1981.
Predecessor to this model: Camaro (1967 to 1969).
Replacement for this model: Camaro (1982 to 1992).
Percentage of division's production: 11.48%.
Corporate siblings: Pontiac Firebird.
Primary competition: None.
Notable changes: Revised front and rear styling.
Major standard equipment: Choice of solid all-vinyl front bucket seats or vinyl two-tone interior with white front bucket seats and colored I/P, carpet and other trim, color-keyed cut-pile carpeting, color-keyed four-spoke soft rim sport steering wheel w/color-keyed column, bright front and rear window moldings, hubcaps, and FR78 × 14 BSW tires. Type LT adds: Choice of custom cloth-and-vinyl or custom all-vinyl deep contoured front bucket seats, special door panels, special instrumentation package, electric clock, Interior Décor/Quiet Sound group, LH remote and RH manual sport mirrors, LT identification on B-pillars, argent colored grille, black rear panel accent molding, bright rocker panel molding on black rocker panel, and body-colored rally wheels w/bright center caps and trim rings. Z28 adds: All-vinyl front bucket seats, special instrumentation package, specific Z28 logos and decals (hood, front fenders, grille, over wheel openings and along rocker panels), black anodized window surround trim and headlight/taillight bezels, black painted grille and parking light recesses, black painted rocker panels and rear trunk panel, front fender louvers, rear spoiler, dual resonator and tailpipes, sport suspension, body color special rally wheels, space saver spare tire, and GR70 × 15 R/WL tires.

Measurements

Wheelbase	108.0"
Length	197.6"
Width	74.5"
Height	49.2"
Legroom — front	43.9"
Legroom — rear	28.4"
Headroom — front	37.2"
Headroom — rear	36.0"
Cargo capacity (cu. ft.)	6.4
Fuel capacity (gals.)	21.0

Models Available

	Model No.	Base MSRP	Change from LY	Shipping Wt. (lbs.)	Model Year Production	Change from LY
Camaro 2-Door Sport Coupe*	Q87	$4,414	+7.32%	3300	146,393	+11.14%
Camaro Type LT 2-Door Sport Coupe*	S87	$4,814	+7.50%	3352	71,331	-2.00%
Camaro Z28 2-Door Sport Coupe	Q87	$5,604	+8.39%	NA	54,907	+282.65%
TOTALS	Avg. price	$4,944	+7.78%	Production	272,631	+24.57%

Production of Camaros with Rally Sport package is included above, but breaks out as follows: Camaro Sport Coupe, 11,902; Camaro Type LT, 5,696.

Nova

"Wanted for all its worth."

Nameplate year of origin: Nova: 1962, as top of the line Chevy II model; became series name in 1969.

Current bodystyle lifespan: 1975 through 1979.

Predecessor to this model: Nova (1968 to 1974; restyled in 1973).

Replacement for this model: Citation (1980 to 1985).

Percentage of division's production: 12.13%.

Corporate siblings: Buick Skylark, Oldsmobile Omega, and Pontiac Phoenix.

Primary competition: AMC Concord, Ford Granada, and Plymouth Volaré.

Notable changes: Minor trim and detail changes.

Major standard equipment: All-vinyl front bench seat, color-keyed cut-pile carpeting, front door armrests w/integral pull handle, color-keyed two-spoke steering wheel and steering column, bright front and rear window moldings, full-width luggage compartment mat, hubcaps, and E78 × 14 BSW tires. Hatchback model adds: Load floor carpeting, and fold-down rear seat. Custom adds: All-vinyl front bench seat w/fold-down center armrest, door panels w/carpeted lower panels and map pockets in front doors, door panel woodgrain trim inserts, rear door armrests, color-keyed steering wheel and steering column, simulated woodgrain trim on instrument cluster w/bright accents, bright side window and roof drip moldings, bright rocker panel moldings, high level acoustic insulation package, deluxe bumpers w/black bumper impact strips, front and rear bumper guards, full wheel covers, and F78 × 14 BSW tires.

Measurements

	Coupe & HBK	Sedan
Wheelbase	111.0"	111.0"
Length	196.7"	196.7"
Width	72.2"	72.2"
Height	52.7"	53.6"
Legroom — front	41.7"	41.7"
Legroom — rear	32.4"	35.2"
Headroom — front	38.2"	39.1"
Headroom — rear	36.7"	37.1"
Cargo capacity (cu. ft.)	13.4*	13.0
Fuel capacity (gals.)	21.0	21.0

Hatchback maximum with rear seat down, 29.2 cu. ft.

Models Available

	Model No.	Base MSRP	Change from LY	Shipping Wt. (lbs.)	Model Year Production	Change from LY
Nova 2-Door Coupe	X27	$3,702	+6.32%	3132	101,858	-23.32%
Nova 2-Door Hatchback	X17	$3,866	+6.03%	3258	12,665	-29.83%
Nova 4-Door Sedan	X69	$3,777	+6.94%	3173	123,158	-12.67%
Nova Custom 2-Door Coupe*	Y27	$3,960	-0.78%	3261	23,953	-16.25%
Nova Custom 4-Door Sedan*	Y69	$4,035	-0.76%	3298	26,475	-32.59%
TOTALS	*Avg. price*	$3,868	+1.47%	*Production*	288,109	+21.12%

Comparisons to LY for Nova Custom are made to 1977 Concours models with same model number.

Malibu

"The new-size Malibu. Now that's good news."

Nameplate year of origin: 1964.

Current bodystyle lifespan: 1978 through 1983.

Predecessor to this model: Chevelle (1973 to 1977).

Replacement for this model: Celebrity (1982 to 1990).

Percentage of division's production: 15.10%.

Corporate siblings: Buick Century, Oldsmobile Cutlass, and Pontiac LeMans.

Primary competition: AMC Matador, Dodge Diplomat and Ford LTD II.

Notable changes: Completely redesigned.

Major standard equipment: Cloth-and-vinyl front bench seat, color-keyed cut-pile nylon carpeting, color-coordinated delta-spoke steering wheel, color-keyed I/P and steering column, black instrument cluster trim, bright front and rear

Measurements

	Coupes	Sedans	Wagons
Wheelbase	108.1"	108.1"	108.1"
Length	192.7"	192.7"	193.4"
Width	71.5"	71.5"	71.2"
Height	53.3"	54.2"	54.5"
Legroom — front	42.8"	42.8"	42.8"
Legroom — rear	35.1"	38.0"	35.9"
Headroom — front	37.9"	38.7"	38.8"
Headroom — rear	37.8"	37.7"	38.8"
Cargo capacity (cu. ft.)	16.1	16.1	72.4
Fuel capacity (gals.)	17.5	17.5	18.2

1978

window surround moldings, bright roof drip rail molding, hubcaps, and P185/75R14 BSW tires. Wagon adds: All-vinyl front bench seat, vinyl coated metal cargo area sidewalls, bright rear quarter window molding, swing-up tailgate window and drop-down tailgate door, and P195/75R14 BSW tires. Malibu Classic adds: Choice of knit cloth-and-vinyl or all-vinyl front bench seat, glove compartment light, bright window frame moldings, lower bodyside protective molding, bright wheel opening moldings, and full wheel covers.

Models Available

	Model No.	Base MSRP	Change from LY*	Shipping Wt. (lbs.)	Model Year Production	Change from LY*
Malibu 2-Door Coupe	T27	$4,204	+8.21%	3001	27,089	-5.92%
Malibu 4-Door Sedan	T19	$4,279	+8.74%	3006	44,426	+13.73%
Malibu 4-Door, 2-Seat Station Wagon	T35	$4,516	-4.60%	3169	30,850	+39.99%
Malibu Classic 2-Door Sport Coupe	W27	$4,461	+8.15%	3031	60,992	-17.29%
Malibu Classic 2-Door Landau Coupe	W27	$4,684	+7.60%	NA	29,160	-21.64%
Malibu Classic 4-Door Sedan	W19	$4,561	+1.92%	3039	102,967	+34.11%
Malibu Classic 4-Door, 2-Seat Station Wagon	W35	$4,714	-6.93%	3196	63,152	+24.83%
TOTALS	Avg. price	$4,488	+2.77%	Production	358,636	+9.27%

*All comparisons made to 1977 Chevelle models of similar name. Model number prefix comparisons are as follows: 1977 "C" = 1978 "T"; 1977 "D" = 1978 "W."

Monte Carlo

"The third generation Monte Carlo. There's no other car quite like it."

Nameplate year of origin: 1970.
Current bodystyle lifespan: 1978 through 1987.
Predecessor to this model: Monte Carlo (1973 to 1977).
Replacement for this model: Lumina (1990 to 1994).
Percentage of division's production: 15.08%.
Corporate siblings: Buick Regal, Oldsmobile Cutlass Supreme and Cutlass Calais, and Pontiac Grand Prix.
Primary competition: Dodge Magnum XE and Ford Thunderbird.
Notable changes: Completely redesigned.
Major standard equipment: Choice of woven cloth or all-vinyl front bench seat, color-keyed cut-pile nylon carpeting, color-keyed instrument cluster, soft-rim delta-spoke steering wheel, black I/P facing w/bright trim, door pull assist straps, glove compartment light, I/P courtesy lights, electric clock, bright roof drip and window surround moldings, bright rocker panel moldings w/front and rear extensions, bright wheel opening moldings, full wheel covers, and P205/70R14 BSW tires. Landau adds: Special Landau identification, Landau elk-grain vinyl roof w/rear quarter nameplate, special white-metalized rear quarter window, dual sport mirrors, specific wide rocker panel molding, bodyside pinstriping, power steering, power brakes, and deluxe wheel covers.

Measurements

Wheelbase	108.1"
Length	200.4"
Width	71.5"
Height	53.9"
Legroom — front	42.8"
Legroom — rear	36.3"
Headroom — front	37.6"
Headroom — rear	37.8"
Cargo capacity (cu. ft.)	16.1
Fuel capacity (gals.)	17.5

Models Available

	Model No.	Base MSRP	Change from LY	Shipping Wt. (lbs.)	Model Year Production	Change from LY
Monte Carlo 2-Door Hardtop Coupe	Z37	$4,785	-3.68%	3040	216,730	-3.39%
Monte Carlo Landau 2-Door Hardtop Coupe	Z37	$5,678	+7.17%	NA	141,461	-24.24%
TOTALS	Avg. price	$5,232	+1.92%	Production	358,191	-12.86%

Impala and Caprice Classic

"The New Chevrolet. America's favorite car."

Nameplate year of origin: 1958 (Impala); and 1966 (Caprice).
Current bodystyle lifespan: 1977 through 1990.
Predecessor to this model: Biscayne/Bel Air/Impala/Caprice (1971 to 1977).
Replacement for this model: Caprice and Impala SS (1991 to 1996).
Percentage of division's production: 25.79%.
Corporate siblings: Buick LeSabre, Oldsmobile Delta 88, and Pontiac Catalina and Bonneville.
Primary competition: Dodge Monaco, Ford LTD, and Plymouth Fury.
Notable changes: New grille and minor trim and detail changes.

Measurements

	2-doors	4-doors	Wagons
Wheelbase	116.0"	116.0"	116.0"
Length	212.1"	212.1"	214.3"
Width	75.5"	75.5"	79.1"
Height	56.0"	56.0"	58.0"
Legroom — front	42.2"	42.4"	42.2"
Legroom — rear	38.8"	39.0"	38.2"
Headroom — front	39.4"	39.4"	39.2"
Headroom — rear	38.2"	38.2"	39.4"
Cargo capacity (cu. ft.)	19.8	20.2	87.7
Fuel capacity (gals.)	21.0	21.0	22.0

Major standard equipment: Choice of knit cloth-and-vinyl or all-vinyl front bench seat, color-keyed steering wheel and steering column, color-keyed cut-pile nylon carpeting, woodgrain vinyl accent trim on I/P and door panels, glove box light, bright front and rear window moldings, bright side window and body sill/door moldings, hubcaps, and FR78 × 15 BSW tires. Landau adds: Elk-grain vinyl top on forward portion of roof, dual sport mirrors, accent striping, distinctive Landau nameplates, and wire wheel covers. Wagon adds: All-vinyl front bench seat, three-way tailgate w/power-operated rear window, tailgate-ajar warning light, vinyl coated textured metal sidewalls, and HR78 × 15 BSW tires. Caprice adds: Choice of velvet-look knit cloth-and-vinyl or all-vinyl front bench seat, fold-down center armrest (four-doors only), front door pull straps and lower door panel carpeting, electric clock, courtesy lights, added acoustical insulation, specific triple unit taillights, bright roof drip moldings, bright wheel opening moldings, stand-up hood ornament, and full wheel covers. Caprice wagon adds: All-vinyl front bench seat w/specific upholstery design, three-way tailgate w/power-operated rear window, tailgate window moldings, tailgate-ajar warning light, vinyl coated textured metal sidewalls, and HR78 × 15 BSW tires.

Models Available

	Model No.	Base MSRP	Change from LY	Shipping Wt. (lbs.)	Model Year Production	Change from LY
Impala 2-Door Sport Coupe	L47	$5,208	+6.81%	3511	33,990	-41.49%
Impala 2-Door Landau Coupe	L47	$5,598	NEW	NA	4,652	NEW
Impala 4-Door Sedan	L69	$5,283	+7.79%	3530	183,161	-6.94%
Impala 4-Door, 2-Seat Station Wagon*	L35	$5,777	+9.23%	4037	68,941	+5.47%
Caprice Classic 2-Door Coupe	N47	$5,526	+6.54%	3548	37,301	-48.17%
Caprice Classic 2-Door Landau Coupe	N47	$5,830	NEW	NA	22,771	NEW
Caprice Classic 4-Door Sedan	N69	$5,626	+7.43%	3578	203,837	-4.23%
Caprice Classic 4-Door, 2-Seat Station Wagon*	N35	$6,012	+7.03%	4079	57,744	+2.08%
TOTALS	*Avg. price*	$5,608	+8.16%	*Production*	612,397	-7.45%

Production of wagons with third seat option is included above, but breaks out as follows: Impala, 28,518; Caprice Classic, 32,952.

Corvette

"1953–1978. Chevrolet presents the Silver Anniversary Corvette."

Nameplate year of origin: 1953 (also used on show car of same year).
Current bodystyle lifespan: 1968 through 1982.
Predecessor to this model: Corvette (1963 to 1967).
Replacement for this model: Corvette (1984 to 1996).
Percentage of division's production: 1.97%.
Corporate siblings: None.
Primary competition: None.

Measurements

Wheelbase	98.0"
Length	185.2"
Width	69.0"
Height	48.0"
Legroom — front	42.1"
Headroom — front	36.2"

Notable changes: New fastback rear window styling and minor trim and detail changes.

Major standard equipment: Choice of all-leather or cloth-and-leather high-back contoured bucket seats, center floor console, color-keyed cut-pile carpeting, tilt steering wheel, sports instrumentation with full gauges including tachometer, electric clock, tinted glass, LH rear view sport mirror, carpeted cargo area with light concealed behind seats, anti-theft audio alarm system, removable roof panels, Silver Anniversary emblems on front header panel, and rear deck, domed hood w/air scoop, four wheel disc brakes, rally wheels w/trim rings, and P225/70R15 BSW tires.

Measurements (cont.)

Cargo capacity (cu. ft.)	7.8
Fuel capacity (gals.)	24.0

Models Available

	Model No.	Base MSRP	Change from LY	Shipping Wt. (lbs.)	Model Year Production	Change from LY
Corvette 2-Door Coupe	Z87	$9,645	+11.53%	3401	46,776	-4.95%
TOTALS	*Avg. price*	$9,645	+11.53%	*Production*	46,776	-4.95%

CHRYSLER

"A line of automobiles that offer you affordable luxury, including the luxury of choice."

Like some of its competitors, Chrysler for 1978 took the marketing approach of offering more for less. This strategy obviously took aim at the newly downsized full-size cars from General Motors, and to a lesser extent their new intermediate line for this model year. Chrysler was in a position to offer traditional, larger cars with more equipment and at pricing similar to or lower than their GM counterparts, and they made full use of the situation in their marketing for as long as they could. However, before the model year ended, the large Newport and New Yorker would go the way of the Town & Country station wagon before them, and be replaced by Chrysler's first real effort at downsized models for 1979.

As for changes to the Newport and New Yorker, one would expect nothing significant, and that would be a correct supposition. In fact, it is surprising Chrysler changed anything so soon before dropping these cars, but minor details did change for 1978. Changes to the New Yorker Brougham amounted to a new brightwork detailing of the taillamps, a new rear deck tape stripe, and a new optional wheel cover with brushed finish center. New on the Newport was an electronic vacuum fluorescent digital clock. Both series used smaller standard tire sizes, dropped by one size, which helped to lighten the car slightly. Finally, the Newport 4-Door Sedan was dropped, leaving only a 2-Door Hardtop and a 4-Door Hardtop in both the Newport and New Yorker Brougham lines. This made the 1978 Chryslers the last American true pillarless hardtop models, with frameless door glass and fully opening windows both front and rear.

Similar to what happened with the Cordoba after its introduction in 1975, the LeBaron, in its first full year of production, nearly matched the entire 1974 Chrysler production total. The corporate namesake division was definitely finding the right customer even as its showroom partner Plymouth continued to struggle to attract buyers. For 1978, the LeBaron line remained unchanged in both its interior and exterior styling, but was expanded by adding lower priced "S" models and a new station wagon model appropriately named the Town & Country. The LeBaron was also fitted with the 225 CID "Slant Six" engine as its new standard powerplant, which helped to minimize the price increase while boosting fuel economy. The 318 CID V8 was still offered, as was the larger 360 CID V8, which was particularly useful when the new Town & Country was equipped with one of several optional trailer-towing packages offered by Chrysler.

The new smaller, but technically not downsized, LeBaron station wagon looked far more opulent than its rather mundane, but much larger predecessor. The front end was the same as its LeBaron coupe and sedan counterparts, and at the rear it wore horizontal wraparound taillamps, much like those of its immediate predecessor. But on the bodysides and tailgate was the element giving the new wagon its real character. As the sales brochure aptly described, "It's a striking new wagon.... With a style that sets it apart from any wagon on the road — body panels which simulate the rich look of handcrafted wood. You've got to go all the way back to the 1940's and 50's to find a car with such distinctive styling elegance." Indeed the new wagon's simulated wood panels were carefully designed to mimic those found on the original wood-bodied Town & Country convertible and sedan models. Inside was equally luxurious with available leather seating for the first time in many years in a Chrysler station wagon.

The new "S" models were very similar to the base LeBaron line only with slightly fewer standard features, which brought the base price of a coupe below $5,000, keeping it within reach of potential Plymouth customers. Unfortunately there are very few specific details as to the standard features of the lower-priced models, as they were not included in the regular annual sales literature offered, and were mainly marketed at the local dealer level, as a lower priced alternative. As can be seen in the production totals that follow, they were not extremely successful.

The Cordoba, which continued its similar "S" model from 1977, received all new front-end styling. To keep pace with current trends, new stacked rectangular headlights took the place of the unique combination of round headlights and smaller round parking lights that had defined the Cordoba's face. The parking/turn signal lamps were now vertically mounted units that wrapped around the pointed front fender caps. A new egg-crate grille insert was also implemented, but unfortunately the original Cordoba's look and appeal were lost in the translation, and the new configuration looked very similar to the 1977 Ford LTD II grille design. Other changes for the Cordoba included more angular opera windows and redesigned taillamps that appeared to be larger, by having less trim around the perimeter.

In the powertrain department, a new 4-speed manual with overdrive, dubbed "Overdrive4," was available on the LeBaron coupe or sedans with the Slant Six or 318 CID V8 engines. Overdrive meant that the engine would turn fewer RPM at a given speed, thereby increasing fuel economy. Also new was a lock-up torque converter added to the rugged TorqueFlite automatic transmission, which also helped to improve fuel economy at steady highway speeds. In practice this feature improved gas mileage more in combination with the 318 and 360 V8s than it did on the 400 V8, and it really did nothing to help the mighty 440 V8. Ultimately it did not matter, as the 400 CID V8 and the 440 CID V8 would go the way of the big Chryslers, and the top end engine for 1979 cars would be the 360 CID V8.

1978

Cordoba 2-Door Hardtop Coupe with T-Top

LeBaron Medallion 4-Door Sedan

Newport 2-Door Hardtop

Cordoba 2-Door Hardtop Coupe
with spokesman Ricardo Montalban

LeBaron Town & Country
4-Door Station Wagon

LeBaron 2-Door Coupe

New Yorker Brougham 4-Door Hardtop

Newport 2-Door Hardtop

Model year production: 303,019 down 9.96% from 1977.
Domestic market share: 3.18% (10th place).
Base price range: $4,894 to $7,831.
Chrysler average base price: $5,846, up 0.52%.
Introduction date: October 7, 1977.
Assembly plants: Jefferson Ave., Detroit, MI (C); St. Louis, MO (G); and Windsor, Ontario, Canada (R).
Data plate identification (VIN): Thirteen digit code read as follows: First four digits indicate series and body style (model number in model charts); fifth digit indicates engine code (see powertrain chart); sixth digit indicates year (8 = 1978); seventh digit indicates assembly plant (see list above); remaining digits are sequential with beginning numbers of 100001. *Example:* CL43N8C100001 is a 1978 Chrysler Newport 4-Door Hardtop, with 400 CID, 4-bbl. V8 engine, serial number 100001, built in Detroit, MI.

Powertrains

Engine	Net HP	Engine Code	Transmission Availability		LeBaron	LeBaron Town & Country	Cordoba	Newport	New Yorker Brougham
225 CID (3.7L), 1-bbl., 6-cyl.[1]	100	C	3-speed Torque Flite automatic	*Calif.*	$165 14/19/16	$165 14/19/16	—	—	—
225 CID (3.7L) Super Six, 2-bbl., 6-cyl.[2]	110	D	"Overdrive4" 4-speed manual	*MPG:*	S 17/25/20	S 17/25/20	—	—	—
			3-speed Torque Flite automatic	*MPG:*	$165 17/22/19	$165 17/22/19	—	—	—
318 CID (5.2L), 2-bbl., V8[3]	140	G	"Overdrive4" 4-speed manual[2]	*MPG:*	$176 15/25/18	—	—	—	—
			3-speed Torque Flite automatic	*MPG:*	$341 15/22/18	$341 15/22/18	N/C 14/21/16	—	—
318 CID (5.2L), 4-bbl., V8[1,3]	155	H	3-speed Torque Flite automatic	*Calif.*	$386 14/22/16	$386 14/22/16	N/C 13/21/16	—	—
360 CID (5.9L), 2-bbl., V8[2]	155	K	3-speed Torque Flite automatic	*MPG:*	$450 14/22/17	$450 14/22/17	N/C 14/22/17	N/C 13/20/15	—
360 CID (5.9L), 4-bbl., V8[1]	170	J,L	3-speed Torque Flite automatic	*Calif.*	$435 12/19/14	$435 12/19/14	N/C 12/19/14	N/C 12/19/14	—
400 CID (6.6L), 4-bbl., V8[2,3]	190	N	3-speed Torque Flite automatic	*MPG:*	—	—	S 13/20/15	S 11/18/14	S 11/18/14
440 CID (7.2L), 4-bbl., V8[3]	195	T	3-speed Torque Flite automatic	*MPG:*	—	—	—	$207 10/16/12	$207 10/16/12

[1]Available only in California and designated high altitude areas. [2]Not available in California. [3]Includes electronic "Lean Burn" system.

Major Options

	LeBaron	Cordoba	Newport	New Yorker Brougham
Air conditioning[1]	$563	$563	$602	$602
Tilt steering wheel	$74	$74	—	—
Tilt and telescope steering wheel	—	—	$122	$103
Automatic speed control	$99	$99	$104	$104
Electric rear window defroster	$94	$94	$101	$101
Tinted glass, all windows	$65	$65	$79	$79
Manual front vent window, 4-doors	—	—	$46	$46
Power windows, 2-dr./4-dr.	$129/$179	$133	$203	S
Power door locks, 2-dr./4-dr.	$83/$116	$86	$84/$118	$84/$118
Power front bench seat, 6-way	$155	$160	$162	S
Power seat 50/50 or bucket, 6-way[2]	$160	$160	$324	$324
Front bucket seats w/floor console	$128	$128	—	—
Leather interior trim	$410	$270	$274	$274
AM radio	$81	$81	$103	$103
AM/FM stereo	$237	$237	$369[3]	$369[3]
AM/FM stereo w/8-track tape	$336	$336	$353	$353
Vinyl top, full[4]	$137	$121	$149	$149
Dual remote control mirrors	$56	$50	$51	$33[5]

	LeBaron	Cordoba	Newport	New Yorker Brougham
Remote control trunk release	$22	$24	$24	$24
Metal sunroof, electric	$626	$516	—	—
Glass sunroof, electric	$788	—	$912[6]	$912[6]
T-Bar roof[7]	$643	$643	—	—
Rear wheel opening skirts	—	—	$49	$49
Premiere wheel covers	$41	$41	$50	$50
Wire wheel covers	$99	$99	—	—
Chrome styled road wheels	—	—	$145	$145
Forged aluminum road wheels	$248	$253	—	—
White sidewall tires, std. size	$48	$48	$25	S

Popular Option Groups & Packages

	LeBaron	Cordoba	Newport	New Yorker Brougham
Basic group	$1,219	$1,053	$1,222	$1,084
Crown Landau package	—	$785	—	—
Deluxe insulation package	$80	S	$46	S
Deluxe wiper/washer package	$41	S	S	S
Light package	$80	$28	$85	S
St. Regis option group[8]	—	—	$643	$643
Salon package[9]	—	—	—	$639

—= Not Available; S = Standard equipment. [1]Auto-Temp air conditioning is available for $693 on Newport and New Yorker Brougham. [2]Left power adjustment only on LeBaron and Cordoba. Left and right power adjustment on Newport and New Yorker Brougham. [3]Includes electronic search tuner. [4]Landau vinyl roof available on Cordoba for $117. [5]LH remote is standard. [6]Nedwport and New Yorker require vinyl top. [7]T-Bar roof only available on 2-door models. [8]Available only on 2-door models. Requires Basic Group. [9]New Yorker Brougham 4-door hardtop only.

Paint Colors

	Code		Code		Code
Spinnaker White	EW1	Pewter Gray metallic	RA2	Formal Black[2]	TX9
Golden Fawn	KY4	Wedgewood Gray metallic	RA3		
Spanish Gold metallic[1]	LY9	Charcoal Gray Sunfire metallic	RA9	Single tones are coded EW1,EW1. Two-tones are coded
Caramel Tan metallic	MU3	Mint Green metallic	RF3	on body ID plate as TX9,EW1 where three digits on
Cadet Blue metallic	PB3	Augusta Green Sunfire metallic	RF9	line 2 are lower body color, and three digits on line 3
Starlight Blue Sunfire metallic[2]	PB9	Tapestry Red Sunfire metallic	RR7	are upper body color or two-tone color. [1]Available
Jasmine Yellow[1]	PY1	Sable Tan Sunfire metallic[3]	RT9	only on full-size Chryslers. [2]Not available on
Dove Gray	RA1	Classic Cream[3]	RY3	LeBaron Town & Country wagon. [3]Available only
				on LeBaron and Cordoba.	

LeBaron

"It's the new symbol of leadership."

Nameplate year of origin: 1957, as subseries name for Imperial (also used on LeBaron custom bodied Chryslers beginning in 1930).

Current bodystyle lifespan: 1977½ through 1979.

Predecessor to this model: None.

Replacement for this model: LeBaron (1980 to 1981).

Percentage of division's production: 42.37%.

Corporate siblings: Dodge Diplomat.

Primary competition: Buick Century and Regal, Mercury Cougar, and Oldsmobile Cutlass Salon and Supreme.

Notable changes: Minor trim and detail changes. New lower-priced "S" series and wagon added.

Major standard equipment: Cortez ribbed velour cloth and vinyl front bench seat, door pull straps, color-keyed carpet-

Measurements

	Coupe	Sedan	Wagon
Wheelbase	112.7"	112.7"	112.7"
Length	204.1"	206.1"	202.8"
Width	73.5"	73.3"	73.3"
Height	53.3"	55.3"	55.7"
Legroom — front	42.5"	42.5"	42.5"
Legroom — rear	34.1"	36.6"	36.6"
Headroom — front	37.4"	39.2"	39.2"
Headroom — rear	36.2"	37.5"	38.7"
Cargo capacity (cu. ft.)	16.1	16.2	72.7
Fuel capacity (gals.)	19.5	19.5	19.5

1978

ing, one-piece cloth headliner, windshield header mounted reading lamps (coupe only), simulated woodgrain I/P cluster and glove box door appliqué, two-speed windshield wipers, LH manual mirror, rocker panel sill moldings w/front and rear extensions, bright roof drip rail moldings, quarter window moldings (coupes), bright upper door frame moldings (sedan), opera lamps (coupe), full vinyl padded top (sedan), bright belt molding, rear bumper guards, lower deck panel stripe (sedan), stand-up hood ornament, power steering, power brakes, deluxe wheel covers, and FR78 × 15 BSW tires. "S" deletes: Door pull straps, rocker panel sill molding extensions, drip rail moldings, and deluxe wheel covers; upholstery replaced with cloth and vinyl front bench seat. Medallion adds: Verdi velour 60/40 front split-bench seat w/fold-down center armrests and passenger recliner, shag carpeting, fold-down rear seat armrest (sedan), bright pedal trim, map reading lamp, door mounted courtesy lights, three upper assist handles (sedan), B-pillar assist straps (coupe), rear pillar vanity lamps and mirrors (sedan), trunk dress-up package, LH remote control outside rearview mirror, quarter window glass accents and medallion (coupe), bodyside accent tape stripes coordinated w/body color on coupes and vinyl top color on sedans, deluxe sound insulation package (w/o undercoating and hood pad), and premium wheel covers. Town & Country adds: Box calf vinyl bench seat w/fold-down center armrest, gas hydraulic liftgate struts, carpeted cargo area w/stainless steel skid strips on floor and rear seat back, carpeted lockable stowage bines, liftgate-open warning light, and simulated wood bodyside and liftgate with surround moldings.

Models Available

	Model No.	Base MSRP	Change from LY	Shipping Wt. (lbs.)	Model Year Production	Change from LY
LeBaron "S" 2-Door Coupe	FM22	$4,894	NEW	3335	2,101*	NEW
LeBaron "S" 4-Door Sedan	FM41	$5,060	NEW	3400	2,101*	NEW
LeBaron 2-Door Coupe	FH22	$5,144	+1.54%	3420	15,999	+119.77%
LeBaron 4-Door Sedan	FH41	$5,310	+1.65%	3465	22,215	+76.31%
LeBaron Town & Country 4-Dr. Wagon	FH45	$5,724	NEW	3600	21,504	NEW
LeBaron Medallion 2-Door Coupe	FP22	$5,526	+1.64%	3495	29,213	+102.25%
LeBaron Medallion 4-Door Sedan	FP41	$5,692	+1.75%	3550	35,259	+199.41%
TOTALS	*Avg. price*	$5,336	+0.10%	*Production*	128,392	+178.51%

These are actual production numbers according to James M. Flammang and Ron Kowalke, Standard Catalog of American Cars, 1976–1999 *(Iola, WI: Krause Publications, 1999) p. 325. However, production breakdown between coupe and sedan could not be verified from industry or corporate records, nor other sources.*

Cordoba

"Very personal. Very formal. The very picture of style."

Nameplate year of origin: 1975 (also used on special-order 1970 Newport hardtops).
Current bodystyle lifespan: 1975 through 1979.
Predecessor to this model: None.
Replacement for this model: Cordoba (1980 to 1983).
Percentage of division's production: 35.66%.
Corporate siblings: Dodge Charger SE and Magnum XE.
Primary competition: Buick Regal, Mercury Cougar XR-7, and Oldsmobile Cutlass Supreme.
Notable changes: New front-end treatment and minor trim and detail changes.
Major standard equipment: Cortez ribbed velour cloth and Whittier cloth front bench seat w/fold-down center armrest, color-keyed shag pile carpeting, simulated woodgrained vinyl trim on I/P and door panels, luxury three-spoke steering wheel,

Measurements

Wheelbase	114.9"
Length	215.8"
Width	77.1"
Height	53.1"
Legroom — front	42.6"
Legroom — rear	32.1"
Headroom — front	37.7"
Headroom — rear	36.6"
Cargo capacity (cu. ft.)	16.3
Fuel capacity (gals.)	25.5

luxury padded door trim w/carpeted lower panels and seat backs, bright pedal dress-up, glove box and ashtray light, electronic digital clock, premium steering wheel, molded cloth headliner, trunk light, carpeted trunk and spare tire cover, LH rear view mirror, rear quarter formal opera window and opera lamp, drip rail moldings, wheel lip moldings, rocker panel sill molding, bodyside and deck lid paint stripes, stand-up hood ornament, front and rear bumper guards, power steering, power brakes, luxury wheel covers, and GR78 × 15 BSW tires. See comments in 1978 Chrysler introduction regarding "S" model features.

Models Available

	Model No.	Base MSRP	Change from LY	Shipping Wt. (lbs.)	Model Year Production*	Change from LY*
Cordoba "S" 2-Door Hardtop Coupe	SS29	$5,611	+7.25%	4020	NA	NA
Cordoba 2-Door Hardtop Coupe	SS29	$5,811	+4.53%	4020	108,054	NA
TOTALS	*Avg. price*	$5,711	+5.90%	*Production*	108,054	-33.77%

*Change from LY not available due to production of Cordoba "S" being included with Cordoba, and both the Cordoba and Cordoba "S" using the same model number for 1978.

Newport

"Full-size elegance, performance, ride and comfort ...
all comfortably priced! That's Newport for '78."

Nameplate year of origin: 1961 (as series); 1950 (as HT model of the Town and Country).
Current bodystyle lifespan: 1974 through 1978.
Predecessor to this model: Newport (1969 to 1973).
Replacement for this model: Newport (1979 to 1981).
Percentage of division's production: 9.93%.
Corporate siblings: Chrysler New Yorker Brougham.
Primary competition: Buick LeSabre, Mercury Marquis, and Oldsmobile Delta 88.
Notable changes: Minor trim and detail changes.
Major standard equipment: Cambridge cloth-and-vinyl split back front bench seat w/fold-down center armrest, color-keyed loop pile carpeting, trip odometer, lighted front ashtray w/two rear seat ashtrays, 12" inside day/night mirror, two-speed electric windshield wipers w/washers, front and rear wheel lip moldings, drip rail and belt moldings, bright windshield and rear window moldings, rear hood molding, decklid molding, dual horns, front and rear bumper guards, rear taillight periphery molding, deluxe wheel covers, and GR78 × 15 BSW tires.

Measurements

Wheelbase	123.9"
Length	227.1"
Width	79.7"
Height	54.7"
Legroom — front	42.1"
Legroom — rear	38.3"
Headroom — front	37.9"
Headroom — rear	37.0"
Cargo capacity (cu. ft.)	22.2
Fuel capacity (gals.)	26.5

Models Available

	Model No.	Base MSRP	Change from LY	Shipping Wt. (lbs.)	Model Year Production	Change from LY
Newport 2-Door Hardtop	CL23	$5,804	+8.00%	4395	5,987	-43.34%
Newport 4-Door Hardtop	CL43	$5,888	+8.37%	4460	24,089	+62.68%
TOTALS	*Avg. price*	$5,846	+9.02%	*Production*	30,076	-48.04%

New Yorker Brougham

"In the luxury class, an automobile unique
in its blending of quality and affordability."

Nameplate year of origin: 1939.
Current bodystyle lifespan: 1974 through 1978.
Predecessor to this model: New Yorker (1969 to 1973).
Replacement for this model: New Yorker (1979 to 1981).
Percentage of division's production: 12.04%.
Corporate siblings: Chrysler Newport.
Primary competition: Buick Electra 225, Mercury Grand Marquis, and Oldsmobile Ninety-Eight.
Notable changes: Minor trim and detail changes.

Measurements

Wheelbase	123.9"
Length	231.0"
Width	79.7"
Height	54.7"
Legroom — front	42.2"
Legroom — rear	38.0"
Headroom — front	38.1"

1978

Major standard equipment: Crushed velour 50/50 split bench seat w/individual fold-down center armrest, passenger side recliner on 4-door, rear seat fold-down center armrest, color-keyed loop-pile carpeting, color-keyed seat belts, Lavaliere straps on inside rear roof pillars (4-door), vinyl covered rear pillar pillows, trip odometer, electric clock, dual front ashtrays w/two rear seat ashtrays, interior lights (glove box, map/courtesy and ashtray), 12" inside day/night mirror, luxury three-spoke steering wheel, three-speed electric windshield wipers w/washers, power windows, console-type armrests on all doors, headlight time-delay switch, carpeted trunk floor, LH remote control mirror, full-length bodyside molding, front wheel lip molding, drip rail molding, bright window moldings, rear taillight periphery moldings, fender-mounted turn signal indicators, concealed headlamps, undercoating, hood insulation pad, deluxe wheel covers, and HR78 × 15 WSW tires.

Measurements (cont.)

Headroom — rear	37.0"
Cargo capacity (cu. ft.)	22.2
Fuel capacity (gals.)	26.5

Models Available

	Model No.	Base MSRP	Change from LY	Shipping Wt. (lbs.)	Model Year Production	Change from LY
New Yorker Brougham 2-Door Hardtop	CS23	$7,702	+8.63%	4620	9,624	-42.97%
New Yorker Brougham 4-Door Hardtop	CS43	$7,831	+8.54%	4670	26,873	-40.61%
TOTALS	Avg. price	$7,767	+8.58%	Production	36,497	-41.25%

DODGE

"Designed for the open road."

Dodge began the 1978 model year with an optimistic outlook. The Aspen continued to be the brand's bestseller, and the recently introduced Diplomat was selling well from the start. Newly offered with all V8s and some 6-cylinder cars with the TorqueFlite automatic transmission was a direct-drive lock-up torque converter clutch that helped improve fuel economy. And with the all-new subcompact Omni joining the lineup, it seemed Dodge was on track to continue sales and production increases for the fourth year in a row. On the contrary, though, Dodge sales followed the industry trend with a slight downturn for 1978, starting an extended downhill slide for Dodge that would eventually end in 1984.

The new subcompact Omni 4-door hatchback and its virtual twin the Plymouth Horizon took the car buying public by surprise. The new "L-body" cars were the first high production front-wheel-drive cars with transverse-mounted engines ever assembled in America. They were also Chrysler's first "metric" cars, with most fasteners being in metric sizes. A lot of the design features of the Omni seemed to be copied from its main competitor, the Volkswagen Rabbit. In fact, the foundation of the Omni engine was a short block 1.7 liter 4-cylinder engine purchased from Volkswagen and modified to Chrysler specifications to include exhaust manifolds and engine mounts to fit the Omni, as well as the addition of Chrysler's own Electronic Lean Burn fuel system. The engine was mated to either the standard 4-speed manual or the optional A404 automatic transmission, a new Chrysler automatic designed for front-wheel-drive applications. In either configuration, the Omni was the highest gas mileage car in Dodge history.

The exterior design of the Omni was indeed much in the same vein as the popular VW Rabbit. Square and boxy best described the overall look, with a nearly invisible lower body feature line between the wheel openings and a full-length indentation that began at the top of the parking lamp/turn signal bezel, running straight to the top of the taillight bezel. This indentation served as the location of a trim strip on Omnis that had two-tone paint or the optional Premium package, with or without the simulated woodgrain bodyside appliqués; the strip marked the top edge of the bodyside paint color or the woodgrain appliqué on cars so equipped. Up front a six bar horizontal bar grille sat between single square headlamps. At the rear of a broad C-pillar, the hatchback slanted downwards, parallel to the edge of the back door, until it met the bodyside indentation, where it turned downwards to meet the vertical rear panel. The rear panel housed the license tag in an indentation between the square wraparound taillamps, which were divided horizontally into three sections, with the lower section carrying the backup lights to the inside and amber turn signal lights to the outside.

Inside, the Omni appeared roomy for a car of such small stature. Comfortable looking front bucket seats and a fold-down rear bench seat were standard fare. The instrument panel was a simple, straightforward affair, with a pod directly in front of the driver housing essential gauges and a strip across the lower panel housing the light switch to the left and radio and ventilation controls in the middle. The turn signal stalk also controlled the wipers and headlight dimmer. The basic Omni looked very plain inside, with flat panel upholstery and nondescript door panels. The Custom package added stitched patterns to the seats and some padded features to the upper door panel. Moving up to the Premium package added lower door panel carpeting and upper padding to the door panel, full-width simulated woodgrain appliqués on the dash, and embossed vinyl or suedelike cloth seats with reclining seatbacks. The choices made the Omni a versatile car, from basic transportation to a car for a small family wanting a little luxury look. Such available features as a roof rack and woodgrain bodyside appliqués, usually seen only on station wagons, added to the real and perceived versatility.

The five-month-old Diplomat line had few changes to appearance or content, but did gain a new station wagon model in its mid-range trim level. From the cowl back it was basically an Aspen wagon with differing rear fascia and liftgate, allowing the Diplomat wagon to use wraparound taillamps that were similar to those used on the coupe and sedan, without the forward slant. During the first part of the 1978 calendar year, a more basic "S" series was added, which deleted some of the luxury features that were standard on the Diplomat to make the advertised Diplomat price of entry more attractive, and to bridge a price gap created with the Aspen pared back to a single base line of coupe, sedan and wagon. The previous year's Aspen Custom and Special Edition models were replaced with Custom and Special Edition option packages.

Aside from the model changes, the Aspen received a new seven-bar horizontal chrome grille that sat directly below the extended area created by the raised center section of the hood. Single round headlamps remained, with new square parking/turn signal lights divided into three sections placed between the headlights and grille. The front bumper was now solid, without the old openings that had housed those lights. At the rear, new horizontally mounted rectangular taillamps were enlarged to replace the L-shaped 1976–1977 units. Occupying nearly one-third of the rear panel, each taillight was divided into three stacked horizontal strips with backup lamps at the inside. The Special Edition package added a chrome section between the taillights also divided into three sections, with the Dodge name across the center section.

Few other changes were seen, but for 1978 Chrysler tried to recapture some of its prior performance heritage. The Aspen coupe was the basis for some special sporty coupes, advertised as "The Street Fleet from Dodge." There were four basic variations, beginning with the existing R/T package and its related R/T décor package. Next up the price ladder was the R/T Super Pak package, and then a "Street Kit" package that paid homage to NASCAR driver Richard Petty, who famously drove many Dodge and Plymouth models to victory lane during the past 15 years, and finally a "Super Coupe" package. Combined production amounted to less than 5 percent of the total for Aspen Coupes, with 1,546 units having the R/T package, 628 with the R/T Sport Pak package, 531 with the Super Coupe package, and 145 with the Street Kit package. Details of the contents of each are included in Appendix IV.

The mid-size Monaco series had to fill the vacancy left by the discontinued full-size Royal Monaco, while at the same time competing with GM's new downsized intermediate line of cars. No changes were made for the 1978 season, which would be the last for the eight-year-old mid-size body; next year the Diplomat would fill the role of the "mid-size" Dodge. The Charger SE, also entering its final season, added a new running mate, the Magnum XE. Built from the same components as the Charger SE and Chrysler Cordoba, the Magnum XE was designed to bring a sporty mid-size car back to the Dodge line, since the Charger SE had taken up the role of a luxury sport coupe. The main differences for the Magnum XE were its unique front-end styling and its bodyside panels. The front-end design foretold of Dodge front-end styling for many of its car lines of the next 10 years, using a three-bar horizontal body-colored grille with chrome accent strips. To each side were dual rectangular headlamps with swing-down transparent covers that retracted when the headlights were switched on. A similar design would be used on next year's Monaco replacement. New bodyside sheet-metal for the Magnum XE bulged to the rear of the front wheel opening in an area extending midway onto the door; a second raised area ran forward from the rear wheel opening slightly onto the door, ending at the back edge of the door handle. These bulges represented the same general area highlighted in the two-tone paint scheme of the optional Daytona package for the 1976 and 1977 Charger SE. At the rear, the Magnum XE had taillights similar to the Charger SE's rectangular three-section units, with an additional silver accent stripe within each section. An optional Gran Touring or "GT" package was introduced with mostly handling upgrades, attracting 861 buyers.

The imported Dodge line offered a new pillarless hardtop sport coupe named Challenger, sister to Plymouth's new Sapporo and sharing its platform with a restyled Colt station wagon. Both the Challenger and the Colt wagon carried angular lines, though the two bore no real resemblance to each other, and the wagon's overall appearance set it apart from other Colt models. The wagon's new horizontal grille, which was canted slightly forward, sat between new dual round headlights, and amber parking/turn signal lamps wrapped around the ends onto the front fender. An upright C- and D-pillar design added a small amount of additional cargo space in the back. The Colt coupes and sedans would be replaced late in the 1978 model year by a smaller, front-wheel-drive, hatchback Colt line. The 2-door hardtop Colt Carousel and GT hardtops were discontinued, being replaced by the new Challenger. The Challenger's styling was typical of Japanese design of the period, with similarities to its main imported rival the Toyota Celica. A full-width horizontal grille, divided into two sections by a thin vertical body-color break, had dual rectangular headlights at each end. Bodylines and feature lines were quite angular in contrast to the large wraparound rear window. The Challenger, in contrast to the Sapporo, also used a partially louvered rear quarter window. At the rear, rectangular wraparound taillights with a horizontal dividing strip were connected by a full-width red reflective panel. Inside, the Challenger had a Japanese take on the American "driver's cockpit" design used extensively on American sports cars of the period, with a standard center console and small overhead console. Under the hood were Mitsubishi-built Silent Shaft 4-cylinder engines, in 1.6 and 2.6 liter sizes, with standard 5-speed manual or optional TorqueFlite automatic transmission.

Aspen 2-Door Coupe with Super Coupe package

Charger SE 2-Door Hardtop Coupe

Diplomat 4-Door Station Wagon

Magnum XE 2-Door Hardtop
Coupe with GT package

Aspen 4-Door Station Wagon with Special
Edition Wagon woodgrain group

Colt 4-Door Station Wagon with Estate package

Diplomat Medallion 2-Door Coupe

Magnum XE interior with bucket seats and T-Top

Challenger 2-Door Hardtop

Colt Custom M/M 2-Door Coupe

Magnum XE 2-Door Hardtop Coupe

Monaco 2-Door Hardtop with SS package

Monaco Brougham 2-Door Hardtop

Monaco Crestwood 4-Door Station Wagon

Omni 4-Door Hatchback with Premium
woodgrain package (left)
and Premium package (right)

Omni instrument panel

Aspen 2-Door Coupe with R/T package

1978

Model year production: 391,223, down 11.48% from 1977.
Domestic market share: 4.10% (8th place).
Base price range: $3,783 to $5,692.
Dodge average base price: $4,856, up 4.92%.
Introduction date: October 7, 1977. Omni introduced in January 1978.
Assembly plants*: Lynch Road, Detroit, MI (A); Hamtramck, MI (B); Jefferson Ave., Detroit, MI (C); Belvidere, IL (D); Newark, DE (F); St. Louis, MO (G); and Windsor, Ontario, Canada (R). *Imports:* Colt — Kurashiki, Okayama, Japan (code 1 through 9); Challenger — Okazaki, Aichi, Japan (code 1 through 9).
Data plate identification (VIN): Thirteen digit code read as follows: First four digits indicate series and body style

(model number in model charts); fifth digit indicates engine code (see powertrain chart); sixth digit indicates year (8 = 1978); seventh digit indicates assembly plant (see list above); remaining digits are sequential with beginning numbers of 100001. *Example:* NL41D8A100001 is a 1978 Dodge Aspen 4-Door Sedan, with 225 CID, 2-bbl. 6-cylinder engine, serial number 100001, built in the Lynch Road plant, Detroit, MI.

*Again for 1978, sources differ on which of the three Michigan assembly plants were in production of 1978 model year Dodge cars. Auto industry references from the early 1980s show only the Lynch Road plant as active in 1978, while other contemporary sources show the Jefferson Avenue plant was also active. All sources agreed that the Hamtramck plant was shut down by or during the 1978 model year, but they do not agree on when. The Hamtramck plant was officially closed January 4, 1980, and demolished a year later.

Powertrains

Engine	Net HP	Engine Code	Transmission Availability[1]		Colt	Challenger	Omni	Aspen	Diplomat	Charger SE & Magnum XE	Monaco[2]
97.5 CID (1.6L) OHC, 1-bbl., 4-cyl.	83	K	4-speed manual		S	S	—	—	—	—	—
				MPG:	34/45/38	29/40/33	—	—	—	—	—
				Calif.	31/41/35	26/35/30	—	—	—	—	—
			3-speed Torque Flite automatic		$	$	—	—	—	—	—
				MPG:	29/38/32	27/35/30	—	—	—	—	—
				Calif.	28/36/31	25/32/28	—	—	—	—	—
104.7 CID (1.7L) OHC, 2-bbl., 4-cyl.	75	A	4-speed manual		—	—	S	—	—	—	—
				MPG:	—	—	25/38/29	—	—	—	—
				Calif.	—	—	24/35/28	—	—	—	—
			3-speed Torque Flite automatic		—	—	$303	—	—	—	—
				MPG:	—	—	23/31/26	—	—	—	—
				Calif.	—	—	22/28/24	—	—	—	—
158.6 CID (2.6L) OHC, 2-bbl., 4-cyl.	96	F	5-speed manual		$176 (wgn. only)	$176	—	—	—	—	—

Engine	Net HP	Engine Code	Transmission Availability[1]		Colt	Challenger	Omni	Aspen	Diplomat	Charger SE & Magnum XE	Monaco[2]
				MPG:	24/35/28	24/35/28	—	—	—	—	—
				Calif.	22/33/26	22/33/26	—	—	—	—	—
			3-speed Torque Flite automatic		$ (wgn. only)	$	—	—	—	—	—
				MPG:	22/28/24	22/28/24	—	—	—	—	—
				Calif.	21/26/23	21/26/23	—	—	—	—	—
225 CID (3.7L), 1-bbl., 6-cyl.	100	C	3-speed manual		—	—	—	S (cars)	—	—	—
				MPG:	—	—	—	20/28/23	—	—	—
			"Overdrive4" 4-speed manual		—	—	—	$142 (cars)[3]	—	—	—
				MPG:	—	—	—	NA	—	—	—
			3-speed Torque Flite automatic		—	—	—	$293 (cars)	S[4]	—	—
				MPG:	—	—	—	20/27/23	—	—	—
				Calif.	—	—	—	14/19/18	14/19/16	—	—
225 CID (3.7L) Super Six, 2-bbl., 6-cyl.[5]	110	D	3-speed manual		—	—	—	S (wgns.)/$41 (cars)	—	—	S (cars)
				MPG:	—	—	—	18/28/21	—	—	18/25/20
			"Overdrive4" 4-speed manual		—	—	—	$183 (cars)[3]	S	—	—
				MPG:	—	—	—	18/25/20	17/25/20	—	—
			3-speed Torque Flite automatic		—	—	—	$293 (wgns.)/$334 (cars)	$165	—	$320 (cars)
				MPG:	—	—	—	18/25/21	17/22/19	—	17/22/19
318 CID (5.2L), 2-bbl., V8[6]	140	G	3-speed manual[5]		—	—	—	$129 (wgns.)/$170 (cars)	—	—	$176 (cars)
				MPG:	—	—	—	15/25/18	—	—	NA
			"Overdrive4" 4-speed manual[5]		—	—	—	$312 (cars)[3]	$176	—	—
				MPG:	—	—	—	15/25/18	15/25/18	—	—
			3-speed Torque Flite automatic		—	—	—	$426 (wgns.)/$463 (cars)	$341	S	$496 (cars)
				MPG:	—	—	—	15/22/18	15/22/18	14/21/16	14/21/16
318 CID (5.2L), 4-bbl., V8[7]	155	H	3-speed Torque Flite automatic		—	—	—	$399 (wgns.)/$439 (cars)	$386	—	S[4]
				Calif.	—	—	—	14/22/16	14/22/16	13/21/16	13/21/18
360 CID (5.9L), 2-bbl., V8[5]	170	K	3-speed Torque Flite automatic		—	—	—	$490	$450	$109	S (wgns.)/$605 (cars)
				MPG:	—	—	—	15/22/17	14/22/17	14/22/17	14/22/17
360 CID (5.9L), 4-bbl., V8[6]	175	J,L	3-speed Torque Flite automatic		—	—	—	$549[8]	$495[7]	$154[7]	$45 (wgns.)/$650 (cars)
				MPG:	—	—	—	10/17/13	—	—	10/17/13
				Calif.	—	—	—	12/15/13	12/19/14	12/19/14	12/19/14
400 CID (6.6L), 4-bbl., V8[5,6]	190	N	3-speed Torque Flite automatic		—	—	—	—	—	$203	$94 (Wgns.)/$699

Engine	Net HP	Engine Code	Transmission Availability[1]	Colt	Challenger	Omni	Aspen	Diplomat	Charger SE & Magnum XE	Monaco[2]
			MPG:	—	—	—	—	—	13/20/15	(Cars) 13/20/15
400 CID (6.6L) High-Output, 4-bbl., V8[5]	NA	P	3-speed Torque Flite automatic	—	—	—	—	—	$330	$222 (Wgns.)/ $827 (Cars)
			MPG:	—	—	—	—	—	—	10/14/11

[1]*Unless otherwise noted: All transmissions are column-shift, except on Colt, Challenger, Omni, and any model w/4-speed manual. Floor-shift is available for $30 extra on any Aspen w/3-speed manual transmission. Aspen w/automatic, Diplomat coupe, Charger SE, Magnum XE, and Monaco 2-door w/bucket seats, console and automatic transmission are all available w/floor-shift in combination with specified equipment or packages.* [2]*440 CID V8 engines were still available for order in special applications for Monaco models.* [3]*Not available on wagons.* [4]*Required as standard equipment in California and designated high altitude areas, with appropriate adjustment in price.* [5]*Not available in California or designated high altitude areas.* [6]*Includes electronic "Lean Burn" system on marked V8s. Not included for Aspen in California with 360 CID 4-bbl. V8.* [7]*Available only in California or designated high altitude areas.* [8]*Available on coupes only.*

Major Options

	Colt	Challenger	Omni	Aspen	Diplomat	Monaco	Charger SE	Magnum XE
Air conditioning	$493	$471	$493	$484	$563	$563	$563	$563
Tilt steering wheel	S	S	—	$65	$71	$71	$71	$71
Automatic speed control	—	$102	—	$86	$94	$94	$94	$94
Electric rear window defogger	S	S	—	$83	$91	$91	$91	$91
Tinted glass, all windows	S	S	$56	$53	$65	$65	$65	$65
Power windows[1]	—	—	—	$157	$179	$179	$129	$129
Power door locks[1]	—	—	—	$98	$116	$116	$83	$83
Power front seat	—	—	—	$142	$155	$155	$155	$155
AM radio	$69	—	—	$74	$81	$81	$81	$81
AM/FM stereo	—	$164	$143	$217	$237	$237	$237	$237
AM/FM stereo w/8-track tape	—	—	—	$308	$336	$336	$336	$336
Front bucket seats w/console	S	S	$42	$157[2]	$165[2]	$58[2]	$277	$58[2]
Vinyl top, full[3]	$92	—	$93	$93	S	$121	$121	$121
Landau vinyl top, 2-doors	—	—	—	$164	$137	$121	$117	$117
Sunroof, power metal[4]	—	—	—	$	$626[4]	—	$516	$516
T-Bar roof, w/glass panels	—	—	—	$572	$642	—	$642	$642
Dual remote control mirrors	—	S	$46	$46	$50	$50	$50	$50
Power steering, std. w/V8	$176	—	—	$145	S	$159	S	S
Power brakes, w/front disc[5]	S	S	—	$66	S	S	S	S
Premium wheel covers	—	—	—	$71	$41	$39	S	S
Wire wheel covers	—	—	—	$127	$99	$138	$99	$99
Rallye road wheels	—	—	$73	$72	—	—	—	—
Forged aluminum wheels	—	S	—	—	$248	—	$248	$248
Styled wheels	—	—	—	$127	—	$126	—	$87
White sidewall tires, std. size	$48	—	$16	$42	$48	$48	$48	$48

Popular Option Groups & Packages

	Colt	Challenger	Omni	Aspen	Diplomat	Monaco	Charger SE	Magnum XE
Basic group	—	$591	—	$644	$1,219	—	$1,029	$984
Custom exterior package	—	—	$71	$73	—	—	—	—
Custom interior package	—	—	$82	$118	—	—	—	—
Deluxe insulation package	—	S	—	$47	$80	$68	$55	$55
Estate package	$341	—	—	—	—	—	—	—
Gran Touring "GT" package	—	—	—	—	—	—	—	$497
Light package	—	—	$44	$44	$80	$51	$28	$28
Popular equipment group	—	—	$250	—	—	—	—	—
Premium exterior package	—	—	$167	—	—	—	—	—
Premium interior package	—	—	$242	—	—	—	—	—

1978

	Colt	Challenger	Omni	Aspen	Diplomat	Monaco	Charger SE	Magnum XE
Premium package	—	$486	—	—	—	—	—	—
Premium woodgrain package	—	—	$312	—	—	—	—	—
Red & White Special pkg.	$195	—	—	—	—	—	—	—
R/T décor package	—	—	—	$51	—	—	—	—
R/T package	—	—	—	$289	—	—	—	—
R/T "Sport Pak" package	—	—	—	$499	—	—	—	—
Special Edition exterior pkg.[6]	—	—	—	$157	—	—	—	—
Special Edition interior pkg.	—	—	—	$483	—	—	—	—
SS package	—	—	—	—	—	$225	—	—
Street Kit Car package	—	—	—	$1,085	—	—	—	—
Sunrise package[7]	—	—	—	$77	—	—	—	—
Super Coupe package	—	—	—	$1,420	—	—	—	—

—= Not Available; S = Standard equipment. [1]Prices given for 4-door models. On 2-door models, price for power windows on Aspen is $113, Diplomat is $129, and Monaco is $134. Price for power door locks on Aspen is $71, Diplomat is $86, and Monaco is $83. [2]Available on Aspen coupes and Diplomat coupes only. Monaco Brougham price w/standard bucket seats has console available for $58. Magnum XE has standard bucket seats. [3]Not available on station wagons. [4]Manual sunroof on Aspen coupes, Monaco coupes, and Charger SE. Glass sunroof, $788 on Diplomat. T-Bar roof for 2-doors only. [5]Standard on Aspen wagons. Colt has manual front disc brakes standard. [6]Special Edition woodgrain group for station wagon is $221. [7]Sunrise décor package is also available for $186.

Paint Colors

Dodge	Code	Dodge	Code	Colt and Challenger	Code
Low Luster Black (accent color)[1,2]	DX9	Charcoal Gray Sunfire metallic[6,7]	RA9	Spitfire Orange	073
Eggshell White[3]	EW1	Mint Green metallic[3]	RF3	Bright Yellow[8]	090
Silver Frost metallic[2]	JA5	Augusta Green Sunfire metallic[3]	RF9	Bright Silver metallic[8]	093
Golden Fawn[4]	KY4	Citron metallic[1,5]	RJ3	Canyon Red metallic[8]	094
Yellow Blaze[1]	KY5	Sunrise Orange[1]	RK2	Ballast Sand metallic[8]	095
Spanish Gold metallic[4]	LY9	Bright Canyon Red[4,5,7]	RR4	Charcoal Gray metallic[2]	096
Caramel Tan metallic[1,5,6,7]	MU3	Tapestry Red Sunfire metallic[3]	RR7	Light Silver metallic[2]	097
Spitfire Orange[1,5]	MV1	Sable Tan Sunfire metallic[6,7]	RT9		
Wedgewood Blue[4]	PB2	Classic Cream[5,6,7]	RY3		
Cadet Blue metallic[4,5,6,7]	PB3	Black[3]	TX9		
Regatta Blue metallic[1]	PB6				
Starlight Blue Sunfire metallic[3]	PB9	Colt and Challenger	Code		
Light Mocha Tan[1,5]	PT2	Tan metallic[8]	003		
Jasmine Yellow[4]	PY1	Green[8]	006		
Dove Gray[6]	RA1	Bright Blue metallic	022		
Pewter Gray metallic[3]	RA2	Warm White[8]	061		

Single tones are coded W1, W1. Two-tones are coded on body ID plate as TX9, EW1, where three digits on line 2 are lower body color, and three digits on line 3 are upper body color or two-tone color. Two-tone paint package available on Aspen Coupe for $188 extra. [1]Available on Omni. [2]Available only in two-tone combinations. [3]Available on all models. [4]Available on Monaco. [5]Available on Aspen. [6]Available on Diplomat. [7]Available on Charger SE and Magnum XE, except Canyon Red is only on Magnum XE. [8]Not available on Challenger.

Colt

"A little Dodge goes a long way."

Nameplate year of origin: 1971.
Current bodystyle lifespan: 1971 through 1978 (hardtop); 1978 through 1981 (wagon); 1977 through 1979 (coupe and sedan).
Predecessor to this model: None.
Replacement for this model: Colt (1979 to 1983).
Primary competition: AMC Gremlin, Buick Opel, Chevrolet Monza, and Ford Pinto.
Notable changes: Complete redesign of station wagon, and minor trim and detail changes for other models.
Major standard equipment: Vinyl front bucket seats w/reclining seat backs, full-floor carpeting, two-spoke steering wheel, tilt steering column, trip odometer, tinted glass, flipper rear quarter windows (coupes), rear window defroster, deluxe sound insulation, bright drip rail, sill, windshield, and rear window moldings, front and rear rubber bumper guards, locking

Measurements

	M/M models	Wagon
Wheelbase	92.1"	99.0"
Length	162.6"	179.3"
Width	60.4"	65.2"
Height	52.8"	52.4"
Legroom — front	40.0"	40.6"
Legroom — rear	30.5"	33.5"
Headroom — front	36.8"	36.6"
Headroom — rear	36.8"	36.2"
Cargo capacity (cu. ft.)	6.0	59.0
Fuel capacity (gals.)	13.1	13.1

fuel filler door, power front disc brakes, wheel covers, and 6.00 × 13 WSW tires. Sedan and Custom coupe adds: Floor console, sports steering wheel, bright beltline and wheel opening moldings, styled steel road wheels, and 165SR × 13 WSW tires. Wagon adds: Fold-down rear seat, sports steering wheel, belt line and drip rail moldings, and 165SR × 14 WSW tires.

Models Available

	Model No.	Base MSRP	Change from LY	Shipping Wt. (lbs.)	Model Year Sales	Change from LY
Colt M/M 2-Door Coupe	6M21	$3,764	+25.51%	2050	NA	NA
Colt Custom M/M 2-Door Coupe	6H21	$4,257	+27.42%	2065	NA	NA
Colt M/M 4-Door Sedan	6H41	$4,158	+21.51%	2110	NA	NA
Colt 4-Door Station Wagon	6H45	$5,231	+31.40%	2460	NA	NA
TOTALS	*Avg. price*	$4,353	+19.95%	*Production*	47,931*	-31.49%*

Total and comparison to LY based on estimated model year sales.

Challenger

"Presenting an exciting international event: The New Challenger By Dodge."

Nameplate year of origin: 1970.
Current bodystyle lifespan: 1978 through 1983.
Predecessor to this model: None.
Replacement for this model: Dodge Conquest (1984 to 1989; sold under Chrysler name, 1987–1989).
Primary competition: Buick Skyhawk, Ford Mustang II, Mercury Capri II, and Oldsmobile Starfire.
Notable changes: All-new model. Sold also as the Plymouth Sapporo.
Major standard equipment: Plaid cloth and vinyl front bucket seats w/reclining seat backs, color-keyed carpeting, two-spoke sports steering wheel, tilt steering column, sports car instrumentation, trip odometer, tinted glass, rear window defroster, remote deck lid release, overhead console w/reading light, digital clock and 3-way dome light, deluxe sound insulation package, dual power remote control mirrors, bright drip rail, windshield, and rear window moldings, body-colored quarter window louvers, front and rear rubber bumper guards, dual horns, locking fuel filler door, power front disc brakes, cast aluminum road wheels, and 195/70HR × 14 BSW tires.

Measurements

Wheelbase	99.0"
Length	183.1"
Width	66.9"
Height	51.8"
Legroom — front	40.6"
Legroom — rear	32.8"
Headroom — front	36.4"
Headroom — rear	36.0"
Cargo capacity (cu. ft.)	10.4
Fuel capacity (gals.)	15.9

Models Available

	Model No.	Base MSRP	Change from LY	Shipping Wt. (lbs.)	Model Year Sales	Change from LY
Challenger 2-Door Hardtop	2H29	$6,051	NEW	2435	14,196	NEW
TOTALS	*Avg. price*	$6,051	NEW	*Production*	14,196	NEW

Omni

"The versatile new Omni. It does it all."

Nameplate year of origin: 1978.
Current bodystyle lifespan: 1978 through 1990.
Predecessor to this model: None.
Replacement for this model: None.
Percentage of division's sales volume: 18.14%.

Measurements

Wheelbase	99.2"
Length	163.2"
Width	66.2"
Height	53.4"

Corporate siblings: Plymouth Horizon.
Primary competition: Chevrolet Chevette and Ford Fiesta.
Notable changes: All-new model.
Major standard equipment: Vinyl front bucket seats, color-keyed perforated hard-board headlining, color-keyed carpeting, door armrests, three-spoke steering wheel, door armrests, fold-down rear seat, folding rear shelf security panel, AM radio, day/night inside rear view mirror, bright liftgate window accents, bright aluminum front and rear bumper face bars w/rub strips, manual front disc brakes, and P155/80R × 13 WSW tires.

Measurements (cont.)

Legroom — front	41.8"
Legroom — rear	33.0"
Headroom — front	38.3"
Headroom — rear	37.4"
Cargo capacity (cu. ft.)	10.2*
Fuel capacity (gals.)	13.0

With rear seat folded down, 35.8.

Models Available

	Model No.	Base MSRP	Change from LY	Shipping Wt. (lbs.)	Model Year Production	Change from LY
Omni 4-Door Hatchback	ZL44	$3,976	NEW	2145	70,971	NEW
TOTALS	*Avg. price*	$3,976	NEW	*Production*	70,971	NEW

Aspen

"The right size, the right price, and the most popular Dodge in history."

Nameplate year of origin: 1976.
Current bodystyle lifespan: 1976 through 1980.
Predecessor to this model: Dart (1967 to 1976).
Replacement for this model: Aries (1981 to 1989).
Percentage of division's production: 42.54%.
Corporate siblings: Plymouth Volaré.
Primary competition: AMC Concord, Buick Skylark, Chevrolet Nova, Ford Fairmont, Mercury Zephyr, Oldsmobile Omega, and Pontiac Phoenix.
Notable changes: Trim and detail changes.
Major standard equipment: All-vinyl front bench seat (sedan and wagon), cloth and vinyl front bench seat (coupe), front door armrests, color-keyed carpeting, two-spoke steering wheel, two-speed electric windshield wipers and washers, front ashtray, color-keyed bumper filler, roof drip rail molding, quarter window moldings (coupe and wagon), windshield and backlight moldings, hubcaps, and D78 × 14 BSW tires. Wagon adds: Rear liftgate, fold-down second seat, power front disc brakes, and F78 × 14 BSW tires.

Measurements

	Coupe	Sedan	Wagon
Wheelbase	108.7"	112.7"	112.7"
Length	197.2"	201.2"	201.2"
Width	73.3"	73.3"	73.3"
Height	53.3"	55.3"	55.7"
Legroom — front	42.5"	42.5"	42.5"
Legroom — rear	31.7"	36.6"	36.6"
Headroom — front	37.4"	39.2"	39.2"
Headroom — rear	35.9"	37.5"	38.7"
Cargo capacity (cu. ft.)	14.8	14.8	73.1
Fuel capacity (gals.)*	18.0	18.0	19.5

Fuel capacity on all V8 equipped models is 19.5 gallons.

Models Available

	Model No.	Base MSRP	Change from LY	Shipping Wt. (lbs.)	Model Year Production	Change from LY
Aspen 2-Door Sport Coupe	NL29	$3,783	+5.61%	3135	48,311	+98.17%
Aspen 4-Door Sedan	NL41	$3,911	+7.71%	3175	64,320	+148.94%
Aspen 4-Door Station Wagon	NL45	$4,253	+7.59%	3405	53,788	-9.54%
TOTALS	*Avg. price*	$3,982	+0.47%	*Production*	166,419	-37.44%

Diplomat

"It measures up to most luxury cars in everything but price."

Nameplate year of origin: 1977 (previously used as designation on Dodge Coronet 2-door hardtops, 1950–1953, and as an option package on Royal Monaco Brougham 2-door hardtops, 1976–1977).

Current bodystyle lifespan: 1977½ through 1979.

Predecessor to this model: Coronet (1971 to 1976); Monaco (1977–1978).

Replacement for this model: Diplomat (1980 to 1989).

Percentage of division's production: 15.67%.

Corporate siblings: Chrysler LeBaron.

Primary competition: Buick Regal, Mercury Cougar, and Oldsmobile Cutlass Supreme.

Notable changes: Minor trim and detail changes. New wagon model added. Base "S" series added mid-year.

Measurements

	Coupe	Sedan	Wagon
Wheelbase	112.7"	112.7"	112.7"
Length	204.1"	206.1"	202.8"
Width	73.5"	73.3"	73.3"
Height	53.3"	55.3"	55.7"
Legroom — front	42.5"	42.5"	42.5"
Legroom — rear	34.0"	36.6"	36.6"
Headroom — front	37.5"	39.2"	39.2"
Headroom — rear	36.2"	37.5"	38.7"
Cargo capacity (cu. ft.)	14.2	14.4	72.7
Fuel capacity (gals.)	19.5	19.5	19.5

Major standard equipment: Cloth and vinyl front bench seat, door pull straps, color-keyed carpeting, one-piece cloth headliner, windshield header mounted reading lamps and sculptured cavities to store sunvisors (coupe only), simulated woodgrain I/P cluster and glove box door appliqué, stand-up hood ornament, power steering, power brakes, wheel covers, and FR78 × 15 BSW tires. Diplomat adds: Wide body rocker panel sill moldings w/front and rear extensions, bright roof drip rail and quarter window moldings (coupes), bright upper door frame moldings (sedan), full vinyl padded top (sedan), bright belt molding, rear bumper guards, lower deck panel stripe (sedan), and deluxe wheel covers. Medallion adds: Cloth 60/40 front split-bench seat w/fold-down center armrests and dual recliners, fold-down rear seat armrest, bright pedal trim, map reading lamp, courtesy lights, upper assist handles (sedan), B-pillar assist straps (coupe), rear pillar vanity lamps and mirrors (sedan), trunk dress up package, LH remote control outside rearview mirror, dual chrome quarter window stripes (coupe), bodyside accent tape stripes coordinated w/body color on coupes and vinyl top color on sedans, deluxe sound insulation package (w/o undercoating and hood pad), and premium wheel covers.

Models Available

	Model No.	Base MSRP	Change from LY	Shipping Wt. (lbs.)	Model Year Production	Change from LY
Diplomat "S" 2-Door Coupe	GM22	$4,771	NEW	3315	1,665	NEW
Diplomat "S" 4-Door Sedan	GM41	$4,937	NEW	3395	1,667	NEW
Diplomat 2-Door Coupe	GH22	$5,021	+1.58%	3510	11,294	-8.44%
Diplomat 4-Door Sedan	GH41	$5,187	+1.69%	3560	12,951	+60.05%
Diplomat 4-Door Station Wagon	GH45	$5,538	NEW	3560	10,906	NEW
Diplomat Medallion 2-Door Coupe	GP22	$5,403	+1.69%	3615	11,986	+30.91%
Diplomat Medallion 4-Door Sedan	GP41	$5,569	+1.79%	3675	10,841	+134.10%
TOTALS	*Avg. price*	$5,204	-0.06%	*Production*	61,300	+79.17%

Charger SE

"Elegance and road car manners make it a rare one."

Nameplate year of origin: 1966.

Current bodystyle lifespan: 1975 through 1978.

Predecessor to this model: Charger (1971 to 1974).

Replacement for this model: Magnum XE (1978 to 1979), Mirada (1980 to 1983).

Percentage of division's sales volume: 0.70%.

Corporate siblings: Chrysler Cordoba and Dodge Magnum XE.

Primary competition: AMC Matador, Chevrolet Monte Carlo, Ford Thunderbird, Mercury Cougar XR-7, and Pontiac Grand Prix.

Measurements

Wheelbase	114.9"
Length	215.8"
Width	77.1"
Height	53.1"
Legroom — front	42.4"
Legroom — rear	32.4"
Headroom — front	37.7"

Notable changes: Minor trim and detail changes.
Major standard equipment: Regency cloth-and-vinyl front bucket seats, color-keyed shag carpeting, simulated woodgrained vinyl trim on I/P, deluxe door trim panels, deluxe steering wheel, inside day/night rearview mirror, two-speed windshield wipers w/washers, bright trim moldings (windshield, backlight, hood rear edge, deck lid, belt, drip rail, bodyside and partial wheel opening), bodyside protective molding, stand-up SE hood ornament, fender mounted turn signal indicators, deluxe sound package, trunk mat, power front disc brakes, power steering, deluxe wheel covers, and FR78 × 15 BSW tires.

Measurements (cont.)

Headroom — rear	36.6"
Cargo capacity (cu. ft.)	16.3
Fuel capacity (gals.)	25.5

Models Available

	Model No.	Base MSRP	Change from LY*	Shipping Wt. (lbs.)	Model Year Production	Change from LY*
Charger SE 2-Door Hardtop Coupe	XP22	$5,368	+5.30%	3895	2,735	-92.45%
TOTALS	Avg. price	$5,368	+5.30%	Production	2,735	-92.45%

Comparisons to LY are made to the 1977 Charger SE model number XS22. For the 1978 model year, the model number XS22 was assigned to the Magnum XE.

Magnum XE

"Magnum XE ... the totally personal approach to driving excitement."

Nameplate year of origin: 1978.
Current bodystyle lifespan: 1978 through 1979 (1975 to 1978 as Charger SE).
Predecessor to this model: Charger (1971 to 1974).
Replacement for this model: Mirada (1980 to 1983).
Percentage of division's sales volume: 12.22%.
Corporate siblings: Chrysler Cordoba and Dodge Charger SE.
Primary competition: AMC Matador, Chevrolet Monte Carlo, Ford Thunderbird, Mercury Cougar XR-7, and Pontiac Grand Prix.
Notable changes: All-new model.
Major standard equipment: All vinyl low-back front bucket seats, color-keyed shag carpeting, simulated woodgrain trim on I/P, deluxe door trim panels, deluxe two-spoke steering wheel, inside day/night rearview mirror, two-speed windshield wipers w/washers, bright trim moldings (windshield, backlight, hood rear edge, deck lid, belt, drip rail, bodyside and wheel opening), trunk mat, power front disc brakes, power steering, deluxe wheel covers w/XE emblem, and FR78 × 15 BSW tires.

Measurements

Wheelbase	114.9"
Length	215.3"
Width	77.1"
Height	52.9"
Legroom — front	42.6"
Legroom — rear	32.1"
Headroom — front	37.7"
Headroom — rear	36.6"
Cargo capacity (cu. ft.)	16.3
Fuel capacity (gals.)	25.5

Models Available

	Model No.	Base MSRP	Change from LY	Shipping Wt. (lbs.)	Model Year Production	Change from LY
Magnum XE 2-Door Hardtop Coupe	XS22	$5,509	NEW	3895	47,827	NEW
TOTALS	Avg. price	$5,509	NEW	Production	47,827	NEW

Monaco

"Other mid-size cars seem to come up short."

Nameplate year of origin: 1965.
Current bodystyle lifespan: 1971 through 1978. Previously named Coronet (1971 to 1976).
Predecessor to this model: Coronet (1968 to 1970).

Measurements

	Coupes	Sedans	Wagons
Wheelbase	114.9"	117.4"	117.5"

Replacement for this model: Diplomat (1977½ to 1979).
Percentage of division's sales volume: 10.73%.
Corporate siblings: Plymouth Fury.
Primary competition: AMC Matador, Chevrolet Malibu, Ford LTD II, Mercury Cougar, and Pontiac LeMans.
Notable changes: Minor trim and detail changes.
Major standard equipment: Cloth-and-vinyl front bench seat, color-keyed carpeting, simulated woodgrain inserts on I/P, deluxe steering wheel, two-speed windshield wipers w/washers, drip rail and wheel lip moldings, deck lid and rear quarter moldings, front and rear bumper guards, single horn, power front disc brakes, hubcaps, and F78 × 15 BSW tires. Brougham adds: Velour cloth-and-vinyl front bench seat w/fold-down center armrest, deluxe padded door trim,

Measurements (cont.)

	Coupes	Sedans	Wagons
Length	213.2"	218.0"	225.1"
Width	77.7"	77.7"	78.8"
Height	52.9"	54.3"	56.9"
Legroom — front	42.6"	42.6"	42.6"
Legroom — rear	32.1"	34.9"	34.4"
Headroom — front	37.7"	38.7"	39.6"
Headroom — rear	36.6"	37.3"	39.7"
Cargo capacity (cu. ft.)	14.7	19.7	85.5
Fuel capacity (gals.)*	20.5	20.5	20.0

Coupes and sedans with V8 engine, 25.5.

color-keyed vinyl bodyside protection molding, Brougham nameplate and medallion on rear roof pillars, upper door frame moldings, stand-up hood ornament w/hood windsplit molding, and deluxe wheel covers. Wagons add: All-vinyl front bench seat, cargo compartment, dual action tailgate w/concealed hinges, simulated woodgrained appliqué on tailgate door, power front disc brakes, and H78 × 15 BSW tires. Crestwood wagon adds: All-vinyl split-back front bench seat w/fold-down center armrest, cargo compartment light, rear roof air deflector, tan vinyl insert bodyside protective molding, upper door frame moldings, stand-up hood ornament w/hood windsplit molding, and exterior simulated woodgrained bodyside overlays.

Models Available

	Model No.	Base MSRP	Change from LY	Shipping Wt. (lbs.)	Model Year Production	Change from LY
Monaco 2-Door Hardtop	WL23	$4,254	+8.77%	3610	7,509	-27.58%*
Monaco 4-Door Sedan	WL41	$4,344	+8.93%	3635	16,333	+5.83%
Monaco 4-Door, 2-Seat Wagon	WL45	$5,103	+8.02%	4310	1,665	-45.18%
Monaco 4-Door, 3-Seat Wagon	WL46	$5,246	+7.79%	4375	2,544	-40.80%
Monaco Brougham 2-Door HT Coupe	WH23	$4,507	+8.71%	3615	4,727	-58.55%
Monaco Brougham 4-Door Sedan	WH41	$4,568	+8.32%	3650	6,937	-53.47%
Monaco Crestwood 4-Dr., 2-S. Wgn.	WH45	$5,549	+6.22%	4305	668	-50.19%
Monaco Crestwood 4-Dr., 3-S. Wgn.	WH46	$5,692	+6.06%	4380	1,588	-45.15%
TOTALS	Avg. price	$4.845	+7.84%	Production	41,971	-34.09%

An estimated 1,540 Monaco 2-door hardtops were equipped with the optional SS package.

FORD

"When America needs a better idea, Ford puts it on wheels."

Ford celebrated its 75th anniversary for 1978, both as a marque and as a corporation, and recognized the occasion with a special edition Thunderbird. More significant were two new models that would become top sellers, the compact Fairmont and the imported minicompact the Fiesta, built by Ford in Germany. The Fairmont, offered in a full range of models, would set a new full model year production record. The previous Ford record for first full model year production was set by the Mustang in 1965 (not including the early 1964 models), closely followed by the Falcon in 1960, which was Maverick's predecessor.

Replacing the popular and long running Maverick, the all-new Fairmont had big shoes to fill. It was a task made easier by offering four different body styles — 2- and 4-door sedans, sport coupe and station wagon — as compared to the Maverick's two sedan body styles. Part of Fairmont's success can be contributed to its modern yet no-nonsense styling. The compact Fairmont employed a design philosophy based on optimizing space, fuel efficiency and cost efficiency, while offering a wide variety of powertrains, interior décor options, and convenience features. Though built as a replacement for the aging Maverick, in retrospect it could be considered

Ford's first attempt at downsizing of its mid-size cars, as the "Fox" platform it was built on would, by 1983, provide the platform for the "mid-size" LTD. The Fox platform would spawn numerous future Ford models including the 1979 Mustang, 1981 Granada, and 1980 Thunderbird, as well as their Mercury counterparts.

Fairmont styling was angular and in tune with the look of the newly downsized General Motors mid-size cars. The front end featured single square headlights, with vertical parking/turn signal lights to the inside, with a horizontally themed grille, and the entire front surrounded by chrome trim. The grille itself was split into two sections down the middle, with two chrome-lined horizontal bars dividing it into six sections, and each section carrying an argent-colored egg-crate insert two rows high and twelve columns across. Bumpers, front and rear, were of a lightweight aluminum construction. The hood was relatively flat, with a modestly raised section down the center, above the grille. Bodysides had two feature lines with the upper line beginning at the upper edge of the front fender, running straight back through the door handles, to a point several inches below the upper edge of the rear quarter panel. Where this line ended marked the point for the wagon's liftgate to angle forward up to the roof, and on sedans marked the point where the quarter panel and trunk lid angled about thirty degrees forward to meet the flat upper panel of the trunk lid. The lower feature line was indented, and ran full-length between the top corners of the bumpers, with a slight flare to the flat-topped wheel openings created as the feature line passed through.

Other styling features included large, horizontally mounted, non-wraparound taillamps filling the rear panel on each side of the license tag mounting, using lenses divided into seven vertical rectangular sections with the inner one being the backup light. The wagon had a vertical wraparound taillamp divided into three tiers, with the backup lights and license plate mounting centered on the liftgate below the rear window.

After the start of the model year, a sporty Futura coupe model was introduced. Its most distinguishing features were in its exterior design with a distinctive front end, wrap-over roof design, and sloping rear panel. The front end used dual rectangular units set above two-section parking/turn signal lamps. The Futura grille was made up of six squares in two rows on each side, lined with bright trim, and each square containing dark argent colored five by five egg-crate style inserts. This basic front-end design would carry through all of the Fairmont lifespan. The wrap-over roof design was copied from the Thunderbird, sans the opera window, and utilizing a slightly smaller rear quarter window and a horizontal faux vent at the base of the broad B-pillar. The rear panel slanted forward, paralleling the rear window slant, with a center mounted license plate, flanked by vertical backup lamps, and a horizontal taillamp filling out the rest of the panel. The

taillamps were composed of eight vertical sections with the outermost wrapping around the rear fender ends.

The Fairmont's greenhouse area was angular and upright with a moderate slant to the rear window (slightly more on the Futura). Four-door sedans had a narrow quarter window behind the rear door; two-door sedans had either a large, fixed rear passenger window or a smaller version when ordered with functional rear window louvers which replaced the rearmost portion. Inside, the Fairmont was much more modern in appearance than the Maverick ever was, with luxurious looking upholstery and trim options. Even in basic form, the layout of the instrument panel and seating arrangements far surpassed the Maverick's. Two large round dials, housing the speedometer to the right, and fuel, oil and temperature gauges to the left, sat directly in front of the driver, with ventilation controls to the center of the car, all set in a large hooded pod, similar to the design used in the LTD II and Thunderbird. The radio was in a smaller pod at the center, set low. Eight different upholstery and seating combinations were available.

Powering the Fairmont were three of Ford's most popular and fuel-efficient engines, the 140 CID (2.3 liter) 4-cylinder engine from the Pinto and Mustang II; the 200 CID (3.3 liter) 6-cylinder, a long-running Ford staple; and the 302 (5.0 liter) CID V8 engine, used in nearly every Ford model that offered a V8 engine at some point in time. Initially not available in the station wagon, the 4-cylinder engine left the Fairmont feeling underpowered under hard acceleration, but provided the best fuel economy ratings of any car in its class. The 4-cylinder met with some sales success, pointing the way for other manufacturers to offer such an engine, as well as 6- and 8-cylinders, in a car larger than a subcompact.

Granada was the only existing Ford line to receive any significant changes from the prior season. A new front end gave a more modern look with the introduction of single rectangular headlamps set over a horizontal rectangular parking/turn signal light. Whereas the previous three years had the headlights set into a section of the grille, the new design was set directly in the body colored header panel. A new grille was composed of three horizontal sections inset with an egg-crate pattern three rows high and twenty-two columns across. The entire grille was wrapped in a large chrome surround and carried the Ford name on the lower driver's side corner. At the back, new horizontally ribbed taillamp lenses had a wraparound red taillight and brake lens, an amber center portion for turn signals, and a white for the backup light at the inner end. Amber rear turn signal lenses were becoming more popular, especially on cars aimed at the popular European sedans. This was exactly the market Granada was meant to compete in, and to further stress the point, a new ESS line was added. The ESS added blackout grille and trim moldings to de-emphasize chrome, which was considered an American styling identifier. Bucket seats and a standard 4-speed manual overdrive transmission also promoted the "European Sport Sedan" theme. The original Granada's comparisons to a Mercedes sedan were made more apparent visually in the ESS, as body colored wheel covers that virtually copied the Mercedes design were part of the package.

Returning for the 1978 model year with few visual changes were the Pinto, LTD II and Thunderbird. The all-glass hatch introduced for 1977 remained a popular $25 option for the Pinto Runabout. The Pinto Squire station wagon went back officially to being an option package, after a one-year listing as a standard model yet using the base station wagon's model number. As discussed elsewhere, lawsuits against Ford over fatal fires involving Pintos in rear end crashes hit sales hard last year, and for 1978 would put model year production at its lowest point ever. In the mid-size range, the LTD II wagons were discontinued with the introduction of the Fairmont station wagon. Thanks to the Fairmont's design efficiencies, it actually had nearly as much passenger space as 1977 LTD II wagon, and only 9.5 cubic feet less cargo space, while being 1650 pounds lighter and 30 inches shorter in overall length. The "large" mid-size Fords were no match for the newly downsized GM intermediates, and sales quickly dropped. The personal luxury Thunderbird line offered a new, top-of-the-line Diamond Jubilee edition to mark Ford's 75th anniversary. The new model, loaded with standard features, was the first Ford model to top the $10,000 base price mark. At mid-year, a "T-Bar" roof option was added for Thunderbird models. Also appearing in many Ford models were new audio equipment options, with the relatively new cassette tape decks being offered, usually at the same price as the existing 8-track tape options, and a new CB radio option on some models to satisfy the latest craze to sweep the nation.

The smallest Ford to be sold in the United States since World War II came ashore from Germany in the form of the Fiesta hatchback. Billed as Europe's most successful new car in history, the Fiesta was only slightly modified to suit Americans' driving style and meet federal safety requirements. Available only with a 1.6 liter (97.6 CID) four-cylinder engine and 4-speed manual transmission, and only in a two-door hatchback body style, it was also the first front-wheel-drive Ford, and paved the way for new Ford models to come.

Styling of the Fiesta up front was simple and devoid of chrome except for the Ford name on the grille, and the straight, box-style bumper which used black rubber endcaps and held the turn signal/parking lights near each end. Single round headlamps were set into each fender end with black trim, and a black five-bar horizontal grille set between them. An integral front spoiler completed the short-overhang front end. Overall exterior styling consisted of straight lines and was very angular from almost any angle. Round topped wheel openings added virtually the only curves to the bodyside. A mid-level feature line provided a break to the otherwise plain bodysides. Thin roof pillars and large windows all around gave the car a light and airy look. Around back, a hatchback liftgate that opened from the bumper level provided easy access to the cargo area. The bumper was similar, if not identical, to the front bumper in design, and had backup lights mounted on the outer ends. The rear panel, formed by the lower portion of the liftgate, was upright and about a foot tall, holding the license plate in the center, and flanked by vertical taillights. From the top of the rear panel the hatch angled up and forward to join the roof above the rear wheel. The interior was every bit that of an economy car, with bucket seats, manual floor shifter and basic gauges, yet somewhat roomier than most cars in its class. As it turned out, the Fiesta would not be as popular as it was in Europe, but it did not seem to cut into Pinto sales, and did compare favorably with other import competitors of the day, such as the Honda Civic and Volkswagen Rabbit.

Finally, two cars were entering their final season in their current form. The popular Mustang II continued with few changes other than a new "T-Bar convertible" roof option available on the Mustang II 2+2 and Mach I models. Only in this final model year did Mustang II production increase over the prior year, notching up a 25 percent gain. More than 1.1 million Mustang IIs were built over its short five-year lifespan. The full-size Ford LTDs were also in their final year before being downsized and were therefore changed very little. Rear fender skirts would be available for the last time ever, exclusively on the 1978 LTD Landau models, as a $50 option. By 1978, production was barely one-third of what it had been just five years earlier, and only about half that of the downsized Chevrolet Impala and Caprice line, its main competitor.

Fairmont 2-Door Sedan
with Exterior Accent group

Fairmont 4-Door Sedan
with Exterior Décor group

Fairmont 4-Door Station Wagon
with Squire Wagon option

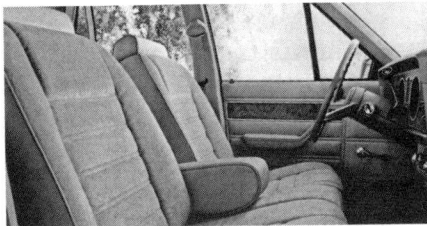

Fairmont interior with optional
Interior Décor group

Granada Ghia 2-Door Sedan

LTD II Brougham 4-Door Pillared Hardtop
with optional opera windows

Mustang II 2-Door Hardtop
with Fashion Accessory package

Pinto 2-Door Sedan
with Rallye Appearance package

Fiesta 3-Door Hatchback

LTD 2-Door Pillared Hardtop

LTD II S 2-Door Hardtop
with Sports Appearance package

Mustang II 3-Door 2+2 Hatchback with King
Cobra package and T-roof convertible option

Pinto 2-Door Station Wagon with Cruising
Wagon package and standard graphics

Granada ESS 4-Door Sedan

LTD 4-Door Station Wagon

LTD Landau 4-Door Pillared Hardtop

Mustang II Mach I 3-Door 2+2 Hatchback

Thunderbird 2-Door Hardtop Coupe
with Sports Décor package

**Thunderbird Diamond Jubilee Edition
2-Door Hardtop Coupe**

Model year production: 1,923,655, up 5.16% from 1977.
Domestic market share: 20.41% (2nd place).
Base price range: $3,139 to $10,106.
Ford average base price: $5,001, up 8.57%.
Introduction date: October 7, 1977; Fairmont Futura introduced December 2, 1977.
Assembly plants: Atlanta, GA (A); Oakville, Ontario, Canada (B); Dearborn, MI (F); Chicago, IL (G); Lorain, OH (H); Kansas City, MO (K); San Jose, CA (R); Metuchen, NJ (T); Louisville, KY (U); Wayne, MI (W); and St. Thomas, Ontario, Canada (X). *Fiesta:* Cologne, Saarlouie, Germany (C).
Data plate identification (VIN): Eleven digit code read as follows: First digit indicates year (8 = 1978); second digit indicates assembly plant code (see list above); third and fourth digits indicate model number (model number in model charts); fifth digit indicates engine code (see powertrain chart); remaining digits are sequential with beginning numbers of 100001. *Example:* 8F02Z100001 is a 1978 Ford Mustang II 2-Door Coupe, with 170.8 CID, 2-bbl. V6 engine, serial number 100001, built in Dearborn, MI. 1978 Fiesta uses a twelve digit code read as follows: First digit indicates country of origin (G = Germany); second digit indicates assembly plant code (see list above); third and fourth digits indicate model number (model number in model charts); fifth digit indicates production year code (T = 1978); sixth digit indicates production month code; remaining digits are sequential with beginning numbers of G00001.

Powertrains

Engine	Net HP	Engine Code	Transmission Availability[1]		Fiesta	Pinto	Mustang II	Fairmont	Granada	LTD II & T-Bird	LTD
97.6 CID (1.6L) OHC, 2-bbl., 4-cyl.	66	W	4-speed manual		S	—	—	—	—	—	—
				MPG:	34/46/38	—	—	—	—	—	—
				Calif.	30/43/35	—	—	—	—	—	—
140 CID (2.3L) OHC, 2-bbl., 4-cyl.	88	Y	4-speed manual		—	S	-$213 (credit on Mach I)/S (others)	S	—	—	—
				MPG:	—	25/35/29	23/33/26	23/33/26	—	—	—
				Calif.	—	25/34/29	20/30/24	20/30/24	—	—	—
			3-speed Select-Shift Cruise-O-Matic		—	$281	$281 (ex. Mach I)	$368 (ex. Wgn.)[2]	—	—	—
				MPG:	—	21/29/24	22/31/25	22/33/26	—	—	—
				Calif.	—	21/29/24	19/26/22	—	—	—	—
170.8 CID (2.8L), 2-bbl., V6	90	Z	4-speed manual		—	—	S (Mach I)[2]/$213 (others)[2]	—	—	—	—
				MPG:	—	—	20/26/22	—	—	—	—
			3-speed Select-Shift Cruise-O-Matic		—	$554[3]	$281 (Mach I)[4]/ $494 (others)[4]	—	—	—	—

Engine	Net HP	Engine Code	Transmission Availability[1]		Fiesta	Pinto	Mustang II	Fairmont	Granada	LTD II & T-Bird	LTD
				MPG:	—	18/22/20	16/20/18	—	—	—	—
				Calif.	—	17/22/19	16/23/18	—	—	—	—
200 CID (3.3L), 1-bbl., 6-cyl.	96	T	3-speed manual		—	—	—	$120[2]	—	—	—
				MPG:	—	—	—	21/29/24	—	—	—
			3-speed Select-Shift Cruise-O-Matic		—	—	—	$401 (Wgn.)[2]/ $488 (others)[4]	—	—	—
				MPG:	—	—	—	19/26/22	—	—	—
				Calif.	—	—	—	18/23/20	—	—	—
250 CID (4.1L), 1-bbl., 6-cyl.	98	L	4-speed manual w/overdrive		—	—	—	—	S[2]	—	—
				MPG:	—	—	—	—	21/28/24	—	—
			3-speed Select-Shift Cruise-O-Matic		—	—	—	—	$193[4]	—	—
				MPG:	—	—	—	—	18/26/21	—	—
				Calif.	—	—	—	—	16/24/19	—	—
302 CID (5.0L), 2-bbl., V8	139	F	4-speed manual[5,6]		—	—	$148 (Mach I)[2]/ $361 (others)[2]	—	$181[2]	—	—
				MPG:	—	—	16/23/19	—	16/25/19	—	—
			3-speed Select-Shift Cruise-O-Matic		—	—	$200 (Mach I)[4]/ $482 (others)[4]	$600 (Wgn.)/ $687 (Sdns.)	$374[4]	S[7]	S (ex. Wgns.)[2]
				MPG:	—	—	16/23/19	16/23/19	16/23/19	15/22/17	15/22/17
				Calif.	—	—	16/21/18	16/21/18	15/23/18	NA	—
351 CID (5.8L), 2-bbl., V8	149	H	3-speed Select-Shift Cruise-O-Matic		—	—	—	—	—	$157	S (Wgns.)[2]/ $157 (others)[2]
				MPG:	—	—	—	—	—	14/20/18	13/21/16
				Calif.	—	—	—	—	—	12/18/14	—
400 CID (6.6L), 2-bbl., V8	173	S	3-speed Select-Shift Cruise-O-Matic		—	—	—	—	—	$283	$126 (Wgns.)[4]/ $283 (others)[4]
				MPG:	—	—	—	—	—	13/17/15	13/20/15
				Calif.	—	—	—	—	—	12/18/14	11/18/14
460 CID (7.5L), 4-bbl., V8	197	A	3-speed Select-Shift Cruise-O-Matic		—	—	—	—	—	—	$271 (Wgns.)[2]/ $428 (others)[2]
				MPG:	—	—	—	—	—	—	12/17/14

[1]Unless otherwise noted: All manual transmissions are floor-shift. All automatics are column-shift, except on Pinto and Mustang II. Floor-shift is available for $30 extra on Fairmont w/automatic (ex. w/2.3L engine), and Granada with optional bucket seats and automatic. Floor-shift w/bucket seats and console is also available for $211 on LTD II 2-Door and Thunderbird, and for $37 on LTD II Brougham 2-Door and Thunderbird with optional Interior Decor group. [2]Not available in California. [3]Not available on Pinto Pony. Station wagons require power front disc brakes at extra cost. [4]Required (or standard) in California. [5]4-speed manual w/overdrive on Granada. [6]Requires optional power front disc brakes, power rack and pinion steering, and 195R70 radial ply WSW tires on Mustang II. Requires optional power front disc brakes on Granada. [7]Not available for Thunderbird in California. 5.8L or 6.6L engine required.

Major Options

	Fiesta	Pinto	Mustang II	Fairmont	Granada	LTD II	Thunderbird	LTD
Air conditioning[1]	$459	$459	$459	$465	$494	$543	$543	$562
Tilt steering wheel	—	—	—	—	$58	$70	$70	$70
Fingertip speed control	—	—	—	—	$102	$117	$117	$117
Rear window defogger	—	—	—	$47	$47	—	—	$50
Electric rear window defroster	$77	S[2]	$77	$84	$84	$93	$93	$93
Tinted glass, all windows	$48	S[2]	$53	$52	$54	$62	$66	$75
Dual remote-control mirrors	—	$49	$49	$36	$53	$58	$58	$[3]
Power trunk lid release	—	—	—	—	$19	$[4]	$[4]	$[4]
Power windows, 2-dr./4-dr.	—	—	—	—	$116/$160	$126/$175	$126	$129/$188
Power door locks, 2-dr./4-dr.[4]	—	—	—	—	$76/$104	$[4]	$[4]	$82/$113
Power seat, 6-way w/std. seat	—	—	—	—	$90[5]	$149	$149	$149
Front bucket seats w/console[6]	—	S	$75	$72	$75	$211	$211	—
Leather upholstery	—	—	—	—	$271	—	$296	$296[7]
AM radio	$65	S[2]	$72	$72	$72	$79	S	$79
AM/FM stereo	—	$89	$161	$176	$176	$192	$113	$192
AM/FM stereo w/tape player[8]	—	—	$229	$243	$243	$266	$187	$266
Vinyl top, full (Pinto, half)	—	$125	$99[9]	$89[10]	$102[10]	$112	$138[10]	$141[10]
Moonroof, power-operated	$167[11]	$167[11]	$167[11]	—	$820	—	$691	$896
T-Roof convertible	—	—	$629	—	—	—	$747	—
Power steering	—	$131	$131	$140	$148	S	S	S
Power brakes, w/front disc	$64	$64	$64	$63	$63[12]	S	S	S[12]
Deluxe wheel covers	—	—	—	$34	$37	$38	—	$99
Wire wheel covers	—	$90	$90	$114	$96	$143	$105	$137
Styled Steel wheels w/trim ring	—	$78	$78	—	$96	—	$146	—
Forged/cast aluminum wheel[13]	—	$252	$252	$276	—	$301	$264	$301
Cast aluminum lacy wheels	—	—	$252[13]	—	$242[13]	—	—	—
White sidewall tires, std. size	$65	$42	$42	$42	$42	$46	$46	$46

Popular Option Groups & Packages[14]

	Pinto	Mustang II	Fairmont	Granada	LTD II	Thunderbird	LTD
Appearance décor package	—	$167	—	—	—	—	—
Cobra II package	—	$677	—	—	—	—	—
Convenience group	—	$81	$60	$89	$139	$103	$146
Convenience/Light group	$128	—	—	—	—	—	—
Cruising Wagon package[15]	$401	—	—	—	—	—	—
Deluxe bumper group	$70	—	$70	$70	$76	$76	$72
ES option	—	—	$300	—	—	—	—
Exterior accent group	—	$245	$96	—	—	—	—
Exterior décor group	$40	—	$214	—	—	$382	—
Fashion accessory group	—	$207	—	—	—	—	—
Ghia sports group	—	$361	—	—	—	—	—
Interior accent group	$40	—	$89	—	—	—	—
Interior décor group	$181	—	$301	$211	—	$316	—
King Cobra package	—	$1,253	—	—	—	—	—
Landau luxury group	—	—	—	—	—	—	$457[16]
Light group	—	$52	$40	$39	$54	$49	$38
Luxury interior group	—	$155	—	$476	—	$783	—
Protection group	$96	$33	$43	$43	$58	$46	$49
Rallye appearance package	$201	$163	—	—	—	—	—
Sports appearance package	—	—	—	—	$363	—	—
Sports décor group	—	—	—	—	—	$446	—
Sports Instrumentation group	—	—	—	—	$138	$118	—
Sports Rallye package	$96	—	—	—	—	—	—
Sports Touring package	—	—	—	—	$434	—	—
Squire wagon option	$315	—	$365	—	—	—	—
Visibility group	—	—	—	$58	—	—	—

— = Not Available; S = Standard equipment. [1]Air conditioner w/automatic temperature control is available for $535 on Granada, $588 on Thunderbird and LTD II, and $607 on LTD. [2]Standard on all except Pinto Pony. Defroster includes tinted rear window. Pinto Pony prices: defroster, $77; tinted glass, $53; AM radio,

$65; AM/FM Stereo, $161. ³LH only standard on LTD Landau. Requires Convenience Group on other models. ⁴Available only in Power Lock Group (LTD II and Thunderbird, $100; 4-doors, $132) consisting of power door locks and power trunk lid release, or Convenience Group (LTD). ⁵4-way power seat on Granada. ⁶Bucket seats only on Pinto and Fairmont; console not available. Bucket seats standard on Mustang II; price shown is for console. Requires individual reclining seats (no cost) and interior décor group on Granada. Bucket seats w/console available on LTD II 2-door only, and on LTD II Brougham 2-door for $37. ⁷Available only with Landau luxury group. ⁸Citizens Band (CB) 40-channel radio available for $270 on Granada, $295 on LTD II and Thunderbird. Signal-searching AM/FM stereo available for $319 on Granada, for $270 on Thunderbird, and for $349 on LTD II, and LTD. ⁹Half (landau) vinyl roof on Mustang II Ghia coupe is standard. ¹⁰Not available on wagons. Half-vinyl roof for Granada 2-doors w/o moonroof is $102; LTD II 2-doors front or rear half is $112. N/C on LTD Landau 2-door, and standard on LTD Landau 4-door. Thunderbird uses two-piece vinyl roof, broken by center pillar wrap-over. ¹¹Manually operated flip-up open-air sunroof on Fiesta, Pinto, and Mustang II 2-door coupe. ¹²Four-wheel power disc brakes on Granada available for $300; available on LTD for $197. ¹³Cast turbine style wheels on LTD II and Thunderbird. Granada has lacy aluminum spoke wheels. White cast aluminum lacy spoke wheels on Mustang II, $265; Granada, $255. White forged aluminum on Pinto and Mustang II, $265. ¹⁴Fiesta option packages: Décor Group, $362; Ghia Group, $701; Sport Group, $529. ¹⁵Special paint/tape treatment including all-around 3-color paint/tape treatment and luggage rack is available for $59, or delete the standard stripe/panel appliqués for $55 credit. ¹⁶Available on LTD Landau models only. Available on Country Squire wagon for $391, and on LTD wagon for $580.

Paint Colors

All except Fiesta	Code	All except Fiesta	Code	Fiesta	Code
Black	1C	Bright Yellow	6E	Black	A
Silver metallic	1G	Cream	6P	White	B
Dove Gray	1N	Gold	6W	Gold metallic	C
Medium Gray metallic ("tu-tone" only)	1P	Bright Aqua metallic	7H	Orange	D
		Medium Jade metallic	7L	Mid Beige	G
Red	21	Light Aqua metallic	7Q	Orange	H
Bright Red	2B	Medium Jade	7W	Green	K
Dark Red	2M	Light Green Emerald	7Z	Red	R
Bright Red	2R	Russet metallic	81	Silver metallic	V
Lipstick Red	2U	Light Chamois	83	Midnight Blue	X
Medium Blue	34	Tangerine	85	Dark Red ClearCoat metallic	3
Dark Midnight Blue	3A	Pastel Beige	86	Blue	6
Diamond Blue metallic	3E	Medium Tan metallic	8J	Beige	8
Bright Dark Blue metallic	3G	Dark Cordovan metallic	8N	Yellow	9
Light Blue	3U	Chamois metallic	8W		
Bright Blue metallic	3V	Champagne metallic	8Y		
Dark Jade metallic	46	White	9D		
Medium Chestnut metallic	5M	White (special)	9E		
Dark Brown metallic	5Q				
Ember metallic	5Y				
Antique Cream	62				

In two-tone combinations, first two digits are lower color, and second two digits are upper color. Metallic glow paints are $40 extra on Pinto and Mustang II, $46 extra on Fairmont and Granada, and $62 extra on LTD II, Thunderbird and LTD. "Tu-Tone" paint/tape treatment available for $49 on Pinto, $42 on Fairmont w/ES option, $53 on LTD II and Thunderbird, and $59 on LTD Landau.

Fiesta

"Introducing Ford Fiesta. Europe's most successful new car in history comes to America."

Nameplate year of origin: 1978 (U.S.; 1976 in Europe).
Current bodystyle lifespan: 1978 through 1980 (1976 to 1983 globally).
Predecessor to this model: None.
Replacement for this model: Escort (1981 to 1985).
Primary competition: None.
Notable changes: All-new model.
Major standard equipment: All-vinyl high-back front bucket seats, color-keyed passenger compartment carpeting, brushed aluminum I/P appliqué, two-spoke steering wheel, open glove box, fold-down rear seat, overhead courtesy light w/door switches, concealed storage compartment under load floor, black window moldings, painted drip rails, rack-and-pinion steering, manual front disc brakes, argent road wheels, and 145SR × 12 BSW tires.

Measurements

Wheelbase	90.0"
Length	147.1"
Width	61.7"
Height	52.3"
Legroom — front	40.1"
Legroom — rear	34.3"
Headroom — front	37.6"
Headroom — rear	36.8"
Cargo capacity (cu. ft.)	6.8*
Fuel capacity (gals.)	10.0

With rear seat folded down, 29.0 cu. ft, plus 0.6 cu. ft. under floor storage.

Models Available

	Model No.	Base MSRP	Change from LY	Shipping Wt. (lbs.)	Model Year Production	Change from LY
Fiesta 3-Door Hatchback	FB	$4,141	NEW	1684	81,273	NEW
TOTALS	Avg. price	$4,141	NEW	Production	81,273	NEW

Pinto

"America's traditional best selling better idea subcompact."

Nameplate year of origin: 1971.
Current bodystyle lifespan: 1971 through 1980.
Predecessor to this model: None.
Replacement for this model: Escort (1981 to 1985).
Percentage of division's production: 9.82%.
Corporate siblings: Mercury Bobcat.
Primary competition: AMC Gremlin, Chevrolet Chevette, and Dodge Colt.
Notable changes: Minor trim and detail changes.
Major standard equipment: Choice of Kersten cloth-and-vinyl or Colton all-vinyl high-back front bucket seats, color-keyed carpeting, AM radio, tinted glass, electric rear window defroster, bright front and rear window moldings, bright drip and belt moldings, rack-and-pinion steering, manual front disc brakes, hubcaps, and A78 × 13 BSW tires. Pony deletes: Color-keyed I/P and steering wheel, AM radio, tinted glass, electric rear window defroster, bright drip and rear window moldings, and bright belt molding. Runabout adds: Black rubber load floor mat, fold-down rear seat, and rear liftgate. Station wagon adds: Flip-out rear quarter windows and liftgate "open" warning light.

Measurements

	Sedan	Runabout	Wagon
Wheelbase	94.5"	94.5"	94.5"
Length	169.3"	169.3"	179.1"
Width	69.4"	69.4"	69.7"
Height	50.6"	50.6"	52.1"
Legroom — front	40.8"	40.8"	40.8"
Legroom — rear	30.7"	30.7"	30.7"
Headroom — front	37.3"	37.3"	37.9"
Headroom — rear	36.2"	36.2"	39.3"
Cargo capacity (cu. ft.)	6.3	6.1*	31.3*
Fuel capacity (gals.)	13.0	13.0	14.0

With rear seat folded down, Runabout, 29.0 cu. ft.; Wagon, 57.2 cu. ft.

Models Available

	Model No.	Base MSRP	Change from LY	Shipping Wt. (lbs.)	Model Year Production	Change from LY
Pinto Pony 2-Door Sedan	10	$3,139	+1.29%	2321	NA*	NA*
Pinto 2-Door Sedan	10	$3,629	+12.11%	2337	62,317	+27.53%
Pinto 3-Dr. Runabout (hatchback)	11	$3,744	+11.66%	2381	74,313	+0.10%
Pinto 2-Door Station Wagon	12	$4,028	+13.53%	2521	52,269	-34.21%
TOTALS	Avg. price	$3,635	+6.11%	Production	188,899	-6.74%

Production kept as combined totals for Pony and 2-door sedan.

Mustang II

"...takes you away from an ordinary day!"

Nameplate year of origin: 1964 (also used on a 1963 show car).
Current bodystyle lifespan: 1974 through 1978.
Predecessor to this model: Mustang (1971 to 1973).
Replacement for this model: Mustang (1979 to 1993).
Percentage of division's production: 10.00%.
Corporate siblings: None.
Primary competition: Chevrolet Monza, Plymouth Sapporo, and Pontiac Sunbird.

Measurements

	Coupe	3-Door
Wheelbase	96.2"	96.2"
Length	175.0"	175.0"
Width	70.2"	70.2"
Height	50.3"	50.0"
Legroom — front	37.2"	37.2"

Notable changes: Minor trim and detail changes.

Major standard equipment: All-vinyl low-back bucket seats, color-keyed cut-pile carpeting, soft vinyl and carpet door trim panels, European-type armrests, woodtone I/P appliqués, two-spoke steering wheel, courtesy lights, gauges (including tachometer, fuel, ammeter and temperature), bright windshield and rear window molding, bright drip rail, belt and center pillar molding, color-keyed urethane coated bumpers, full wheel covers, and B78 × 13 BSW tires. 2+2 adds: Brushed aluminum I/P appliqués, fold-down rear seat, liftgate w/hydraulic struts, styled steel wheels, and B78 B/WL tires (WSW — N/C). Ghia adds (to 2-door): Choice of Stirling plaid cloth-and-vinyl or Luxury all-vinyl low-back bucket seats, luxury décor trim panels, deluxe color-keyed seat belts, soft-vinyl headlining, quartz crystal digital clock, dual remote control outside color-keyed mirrors, vinyl insert bodyside molding, pinstripes, half vinyl roof, opera windows, Ghia identification, deluxe wheel covers, and BR78 × 13 BSW tires. Mach I adds (to 2+2): Dual remote control outside color-keyed mirrors, black Mach I lower bodysides and liftgate paint stripes and identification, styled steel wheels w/wheel trim rings, and BR70 × 13 B/WL tires.

Measurements (cont.)

	Coupe	3-Door
Legroom — rear	27.7"	27.7"
Headroom — front	37.2"	37.2"
Headroom — rear	35.9"	34.1"
Cargo capacity (cu. ft.)	8.2	22.8*
Fuel capacity (gals.)**	13.0	13.0

*With rear seat folded down.   **16.5 gallons with optional V8 engine.

Models Available

	Model No.	Base MSRP	Change from LY	Shipping Wt. (lbs.)	Model Year Production	Change from LY
Mustang II 2-Door Hardtop Coupe	02	$3,824	+3.30%	2608	81,304	+19.95%
Mustang II 2+2 3-Door (hatchback)	03	$4,068	+4.28%	2654	68,408	+39.15%
Mustang II Ghia 2-Door Hardtop Coupe	04	$4,242	+2.99%	2646	34,730	+17.69%
Mustang II Mach I 3-Door (hatchback)	05	$4,523	+4.41%	2733	7,968	+18.59%
TOTALS	Avg. price	$4,164	+3.76%	Production	192,410	+25.62%

Fairmont

"The Ford in your future."

Nameplate year of origin: 1978.
Current bodystyle lifespan: 1978 through 1983.
Predecessor to this model: Maverick (1970 to 1977).
Replacement for this model: Tempo (1984 to 1994).
Percentage of division's production: 23.96%.
Corporate siblings: Mercury Zephyr.
Primary competition: AMC Concord, Chevrolet Nova, and Plymouth Volaré.
Notable changes: All-new model.
Major standard equipment: All vinyl low-back front bucket seats, color-keyed cut-pile carpeting, integral door armrests w/door pull assist handle, two-spoke color-keyed steering wheel, simulated woodgrain appliqué around instrument cluster, bright windshield and rear window moldings,

Measurements

	2-Door	Futura	4-Door	Wagon
Wheelbase	105.5"	105.5"	105.5"	105.5"
Length	193.8"	195.8"	193.8"	193.8"
Width	71.0"	71.0"	71.0"	71.0"
Height	53.5"	52.2"	53.5"	54.8"
Legroom — front	41.8"	41.8"	41.8"	41.8"
Legroom — rear	35.4"	36.1"	37.7"	35.4"
Headroom — front	38.5"	37.1"	38.5"	39.0"
Headroom — rear	37.7"	36.1"	37.7"	39.0"
Cargo capacity (cu. ft.)	16.8	16.1	16.8	79.5
Fuel capacity (gals.)	16.0	16.0	16.0	16.0

bright drip rail moldings, front bumper guards, manual front disc brakes, modified strut front suspension, hubcaps, and B78 × 14 BSW tires. Futura coupe adds: Deluxe seat trim, luxury door trim panels, color-keyed safety belts, high gloss simulated woodgrain appliqué on I/P, inside hood release, bright LH manual mirror, wrap-over roof design w/accent paint stripes, bright door window frames and belt moldings, bright wheel lip opening moldings, lower bodyside protection molding w/vinyl insert, deluxe sound insulation package, unique front and rear end appearance, and deluxe wheel covers. Wagon adds: Fold-down rear seat, carpet on load floor and rear seat back, cargo area light, bright quarter window and liftgate moldings, "liftgate-open" warning light, and CR78 × 14 BSW tires.

Models Available

	Model No.	Base MSRP	Change from LY*	Shipping Wt. (lbs.)	Model Year Production	Change from LY*
Fairmont 2-Door Sedan	91	$3,624	+9.09%	2568	78,776	+96.52%
Fairmont 4-Door Sedan	92	$3,710	+9.28%	2610	136,849	+134.25%
Fairmont 4-Door, 5-p. Station Wagon	94	$4,063	NEW	2718	128,390	NEW
Fairmont Futura 2-Door Coupe	93	$4,103	NEW	2605	116,966	NEW
TOTALS	Avg. price	$3,875	+15.38%	Production	460,981	+367.97%

*Comparisons of total production and of Fairmont 2- and 4-door sedans are made to 1977 Maverick 2- and 4-door sedans of same model number.

Granada

"Compare it to cars costing thousands more."

Nameplate year of origin: 1975.
Current bodystyle lifespan: 1975 through 1980.
Predecessor to this model: None.
Replacement for this model: Granada (1981 to 1982).
Percentage of division's production: 12.98%.
Corporate siblings: Mercury Monarch.
Primary competition: AMC Concord, Chevrolet Nova, Dodge Aspen, Plymouth Volaré, and Pontiac Ventura.
Notable changes: New front end and minor trim and detail changes.
Major standard equipment: Corinthian all-vinyl "Flight Bench" front seat, 10-oz. cut-pile carpeting, burled walnut I/P appliqués w/Granada script, two rear seat ashtrays, luggage compartment mat, bright front and rear window moldings, bright belt moldings, bright drip rail and wheel opening moldings, opera window w/bright moldings (2-door), hood ornament, manual front disc brakes, full wheel covers, and DR78 × 14 BSW tires. Ghia adds: Ghia Corinthian all-vinyl "Flight Bench" front seat, 18-oz. cut-pile carpeting, deluxe door trim, luxury steering wheel, digital clock, Ghia interior ornamentation, day/night rearview mirror, deluxe color-keyed seat belts, rear door courtesy light switches (4-door), LH remote control mirror, opera window Ghia interior and exterior ornamentation, wide vinyl insert bodyside and wheel lip moldings, vinyl lower rear panel appliqué w/decklid tape stripes, bodyside tape stripes, luggage compartment carpeting, deluxe sound and ride package, color-keyed wheel covers, and ER78 × 14 BSW tires. ESS adds: Chainmail vinyl front bucket seats w/European style headrests, 18-oz. cut-pile carpeting, leather wrapped steering wheel, deluxe door trim w/woodtone appliqués, day/night rearview mirror, deluxe color-keyed seat belts, rear door courtesy light switches (4-door), dual color-keyed remote control mirrors, louvered opera window appliqués (2-door), black trim (window frames, wipers, grille, back panel appliqué and rocker panels), black bodyside moldings w/bright inserts, luggage compartment trim, sound package, deluxe bumper group, ESS ornamentation on front fenders, hood and decklid paint stripes, heavy-duty suspension, color-keyed wheel covers, and FR78 × 14 BSW tires.

Measurements

Wheelbase	109.9"
Length	197.7"
Width	74.0"
Height	53.3"
Legroom — front	41.1"
Legroom — rear	36.0"
Headroom — front	38.5"
Headroom — rear	37.6"
Cargo capacity (cu. ft.)	14.8*
Fuel capacity (gals.)	18.0

*Ghia and ESS models have 1.7 cu. ft. less.

Models Available

	Model No.	Base MSRP	Change from LY	Shipping Wt. (lbs.)	Model Year Production*	Change from LY*
Granada 2-Door Sedan	81	$4,300	+6.91%	3087	110,481	-29.90%
Granada 4-Door Sedan	82	$4,390	+6.61%	3122	139,305	-14.57%
Granada Ghia 2-Door Sedan	81	$4,685	+5.23%	3147	NA*	NA*
Granada Ghia 4-Door Sedan	82	$4,776	+5.01%	3230	NA*	NA*
Granada ESS 2-Door Sedan	81	$4,872	+4.38%	3145	NA*	NA*
Granada ESS 4-Door Sedan	82	$4,962	+4.43%	3180	NA*	NA*
TOTALS	Avg. price	$4,664	+6.29%	Production	249,786	-36.05%

*Model year production and change from LY are not available due to production totals being kept by body style and model number, and not by trim level.

LTD II

"The trim, sporty mid-size."

Nameplate year of origin: 1977.
Current bodystyle lifespan: 1977 through 1979.
Predecessor to this model: Torino (1972 to 1976).
Replacement for this model: None.
Percentage of division's production: 8.87%.
Corporate siblings: Mercury Cougar.
Primary competition: Chevrolet Malibu, Dodge Monaco, Plymouth Fury, and Pontiac LeMans.
Notable changes: Minor trim and detail changes.
Major standard equipment: Kirsten cloth-and-vinyl front bench seat, 10 oz. color-keyed cut-pile carpeting, black I/P appliqué w/five-pod instrument cluster, windshield and rear window bright moldings, bright drip rail and side window moldings, bright hubcaps, and HR78 × 14 BSW tires. LTD II adds: Rossano pleated cloth-and-vinyl front "Flight Bench" seat, high level door trim panels w/woodtone accents, woodtone I/P cluster appliqués and RH panel, deluxe door trim, bright rear panel appliqué, bright side window and wheel lip moldings, opera window (2-door), deluxe sound package, stand-up hood ornament, aluminum lower back panel appliqué, and bright rocker panel and wheel lip moldings. LTD II Brougham adds: Doral cloth-and-vinyl split front seat w/dual fold-down center armrests, 18 oz. cut-pile carpeting, luxury door trim w/carpeted lower panels, wide bodyside moldings w/vinyl inserts and integral wheel lip moldings, dual accent paint stripes, hood ornament, unique Brougham identification, luxury sound package, deluxe wheel covers, and WSW tires.

Measurements

	2-Doors	4-Doors
Wheelbase	114.0"	118.0"
Length	215.5"	219.5"
Width	78.6"	78.6"
Height	52.6"	53.3"
Legroom — front	42.5"	42.5"
Legroom — rear	33.2"	37.8"
Headroom — front	37.6"	38.3"
Headroom — rear	36.2"	37.0"
Cargo capacity (cu. ft.)	15.9	15.9
Fuel capacity (gals.)	21.0	21.0

Models Available

	Model No.	Base MSRP	Change from LY	Shipping Wt. (lbs.)	Model Year Production	Change from LY
LTD II S 2-Door Hardtop	25	$4,850	+7.11%	3746	9,004	-5.53%
LTD II S 4-Door Pillared Hardtop	27	$4,935	+7.77%	3836	21,122	+12.50%
LTD II 2-Door Hardtop	30	$5,112	+6.83%	3773	76,285*	-2.73%*
LTD II 4-Door Pillared Hardtop	31	$5,222	+7.23%	3872	64,133*	-15.12%*
LTD II Brougham 2-Door Hardtop	30	$5,448	+6.39%	3791	NA*	NA*
LTD II Brougham 4-Door Pillared Hardtop	31	$5,558	+6.76%	3901	NA*	NA*
TOTALS	*Avg. price*	$5,188	+5.40%	*Production*	170,544	-26.59%

*Model year production and change from LY for Brougham models were kept with mid-level LTD II models, and given the same model numbers. Therefore change from LY for LTD II includes 1977 LTD II Brougham production.

Thunderbird

"An achievement in the Thunderbird tradition."

Nameplate year of origin: 1955.
Current bodystyle lifespan: 1977 through 1979.
Predecessor to this model: Thunderbird (1972 to 1976).
Replacement for this model: Thunderbird (1980 to 1982).
Percentage of division's production: 18.34%.
Corporate siblings: Mercury Cougar XR-7.
Primary competition: Chevrolet Monte Carlo and Pontiac Grand Prix.
Notable changes: Minor trim and detail changes.
Major standard equipment: Cloth and vinyl front bench seat w/automatic seatback release, 10 oz. cut pile carpeting, simulated burled walnut woodgrain I/P and door panel trim, full-length door armrest, electric clock, AM radio, bright moldings (rear hood edge, beltline, drip rails), rocker panel and wheel lip moldings, opera windows,

Measurements

Wheelbase	114.0"
Length	215.5"
Width	78.0"
Height	53.0"
Legroom — front	42.5"
Legroom — rear	33.2"
Headroom — front	37.6"
Headroom — rear	36.2"
Cargo capacity (cu. ft.)	15.6
Fuel capacity (gals.)	21.0

roof wrap over moldings, front fender louvers, full wheel covers, and GR78 × 15 BSW tires. Town Landau adds: Crushed velour split front bench seat w/individual fold-down center armrests and passenger side recliner, six-way power driver's seat, illuminated visor vanity mirror, 22K gold Town Landau plaque on RH side of I/P with owner's name engraved, AM/FM stereo w/search radio, tilt steering wheel, power windows, power lock group, interior luxury décor group, convenience group, light group, tinted glass, dual remote-control sport mirrors, brushed aluminum wrap-over roof molding, unique tape stripes (bodyside, hood, header panel, decklid, hidden headlamp doors), hood ornament w/color-coordinated acrylic logo insert, Town Landau script on opera windows, accent paint on front fender louvers, front cornering lights, and body-color accent painted turbine spoke cast aluminum wheels, and HR78 × 15 WSW tires. Diamond Jubilee edition adds to Town Landau features: Biscuit patterned luxury cloth split front bench seats w/individual fold-down center armrests, door and front seatback assist straps, 36 oz. cut-pile carpeting, ebony woodtone appliqués on I/P, door/quarter trim panels and steering wheel, fingertip speed control, leather-wrapped steering wheel, leather-covered I/P pad, power radio antenna, bright pedal trim accents, 18 oz. color-keyed trunk carpeting and molded deck lid liner, Diamond Jubilee opera window insignia, padded vinyl roof w/covered rear quarter window, owner's initials on front door, color-keyed grille and bumper rub strips, and color-keyed cast aluminum wheels.

Models Available

	Model No.	Base MSRP	Change from LY	Shipping Wt. (lbs.)	Model Year Production	Change from LY
Thunderbird 2-Door Hardtop	87	$5,498	+8.59%	3907	333,757	+4.91%
Thunderbird Town Landau 2-Dr. HT	87	$8,533	+6.80%	4104	NA*	NA*
Thunderbird Diamond Jubilee 2-Dr. HT	87	$10,106	NEW	NA	18,994	NEW
TOTALS	*Avg. price*	$8,046	+23.28%	*Production*	352,751	+10.88%

Town Landau production is included with base Thunderbird.

1978

LTD

"The luxury you want, the roominess you need."

Nameplate year of origin: 1965.
Current bodystyle lifespan: 1971 through 1978 (restyled in 1973 and 1975).
Predecessor to this model: Custom/Galaxie/LTD (1969 to 1970).
Replacement for this model: LTD (1979 to 1991).
Percentage of division's production: 16.03%.
Corporate siblings: Mercury Marquis.
Primary competition: Chevrolet Impala/Caprice and Pontiac Catalina.
Notable changes: Minor trim and detail changes.
Major standard equipment: Athea cloth-and-vinyl front bench seat, color-keyed cut-pile carpeting, woodtone I/P and door appliqués, deluxe steering wheel, interior courtesy lighting, bright moldings (front and rear window, belt, drip rail, rear hood edge, and wheel lip), vinyl insert bodyside

Measurements

	2-Doors	4-Doors	Wagons
Wheelbase	121.0"	121.0"	121.0"
Length	224.1"	224.1"	225.7"
Width	79.5"	79.5"	79.7"
Height	53.7"	54.8"	56.7"
Legroom — front	41.5"	41.5"	41.7"
Legroom — rear	35.5"	38.3"	37.1"
Headroom — front	37.3"	38.3"	38.7"
Headroom — rear	37.3"	37.3"	39.1"
Cargo capacity (cu. ft.)	22.1	22.1	94.6*
Fuel capacity (gals.)	24.2	24.2	21.0

Additional 9.1 cu. ft. of below-deck storage on 2-seat wagons, and 5.0 cu. ft. on wagons w/DFRS.

moldings, textured lower rear appliqué w/bright Reflex surround molding, rocker panel molding, C-pillar LTD crest (4-door), hood ornament, front bumper guards, chrome hubcaps, and HR78 × 15 BSW tires. Wagon adds: Ruffino all vinyl bench seat, fold-down rear seat, load floor carpeting, power tailgate window, sound insulation package, and JR78 × 15 BSW tires. Landau adds: Ardmore cloth and vinyl "Flight Bench" seat w/fold-down center armrests, front seatback assist straps, electric clock, luxury steering wheel, luxury door trim panels, burled walnut I/P and door trim appliqués, rear door courtesy light switch, electric clock, luggage compartment light, LH remote control mirror, half-vinyl roof (2-door), full vinyl roof (4-door), dual accent paint stripes, wide vinyl insert bodyside moldings, hidden headlights, and full wheel covers. Country Squire adds: Simulated woodgrain exterior bodyside and tailgate paneling, cargo area light, hidden headlights, and full wheel covers.

Models Available

	Model No.	Base MSRP	Change from LY	Shipping Wt. (lbs.)	Model Year Production	Change from LY
LTD 2-Door Pillared Hardtop	62	$5,398	+4.43%	3972	57,466	-21.96%
LTD 4-Door Pillared Hardtop	63	$5,483	+5.45%	4032	112,392	-29.87%
LTD 4-Door, 2-Seat, 6-p. Station Wagon*	74	$5,885	+8.68%	4532	71,285**	-21.42%*
LTD Landau 2-Door Pillared Hardtop	65	$5,970	+5.27%	4029	27,305	-38.50%
LTD Landau 4-Door Pillared Hardtop	64	$6,055	+6.42%	4081	39,836	-38.74%
LTD Country Squire 4-Door, 2-s., 6-p. Wagon*	74	$6,304	+7.47%	4576	NA**	NA*
TOTALS	Avg. price	$5,849	+6.28%	Production	308,284	-28.97%

*Wagons available w/removable DFRS (dual facing rear seats) for $143 extra.   **Production of Country Squire wagon combined with base LTD wagon, so comparison is made to combined 1977 total.*

LINCOLN

"A standard by which luxury cars are judged."

To commemorate the 75th anniversary of Ford Motor Company, the corporation's luxury division pulled out all the stops for a fully equipped, ultra-luxurious Continental Mark V named the Diamond Jubilee edition. Much like the lower-priced, and less well equipped, Ford Thunderbird Diamond Jubilee edition, the Mark V was meant to showcase all of the technology, styling and engineering excellence that Ford had in its current arsenal. With automotive production holding fairly steady through 1978, with only a slight decline, Ford Motor Company as a whole increased its market share by more than 2.5 percent to end the year with a 28.95 percent share. Unfortunately it was all done on the strength of the new Ford Fairmont and Mercury Zephyr, as Lincoln dropped more than 20 percent in sales and lost a bit of market share. Fortunately, the media began reporting the traditional full-size Lincoln's imminent demise, spurring sales to pick up by the end of the model year.

The Continental Mark V grille was changed to match the Continental coupe and sedan, using a vertical bar design without sections. Other changes were mainly limited to the new color luxury groups added. Lincoln advertising went to great lengths in comparing the Mark V to the Cadillac Eldorado, touting the Mark's distinctive styling, more comfortable and convenient interior features, and the more "pleasant" instrument panel design, with beveled lenses and instruments set in high-gloss walnut-tone inlays, whereas the Eldorado's most prominent feature was the air vents. As previously mentioned the Mark V Diamond Jubilee edition was a fully loaded car with added features such as the latest in electronic technology including a "Miles to Empty" fuel gauge, a garage door opener mounted in the sun visor, an AM/FM stereo with Quadrasonic 8-track tape player, and then all of the luxury features such as 36-ounce carpeting, leather instrument panel pad, leather padded console, and exterior coach lamps. Needless to say it was a lavish and expensive car — in fact the package cost an astonishing $8,000, more than a new Mercury Grand Marquis. Details of the Mark V Diamond Jubilee edition content are included in Appendix IV.

The mid-year 1977 introduction of the smaller Lincoln, the Versailles, appeared successful at first, and Lincoln ramped up production to ensure adequate dealer inventory for the expected buyers. But luxury car buyers saw through the dressed up Granada façade and stayed away in droves, leaving Lincoln with a lot of leftover 1977 models to sell, and in turn causing 1978 model year production to drop nearly in half. Changes for the 1978 edition included the addition of a new electronic engine control system and variable venturi carburetor to its list of standard features. The Versailles was the first Ford vehicle with the EEC system, and the only one so equipped in 1978.

The Continental coupe and sedan were carried over with little change from the prior year. For both the Continental and Mark V, the 400 CID V8 engine was standard and the optional 460 CID V8 was in its final year of production, owing to the poor fuel mileage of the big block engine. Also, the Continental dispensed with rear wheel opening fender skirts for this year, a feature that had begun with the introduction of the current bodystyle in 1970. Next year would be better for Lincoln as it would have the traditional full-size car market all to itself.

Continental 2-Door Coupe
with Town Coupe package

Continental 2-Door Sedan
with Town Car package

Continental Mark V 2-Door Hardtop Coupe

Continental Mark V 2-Door Hardtop Coupe

Versailles 4-Door Sedan with moonroof

Versailles 4-Door Sedan

Continental Mark V Diamond Jubilee Edition
interior

1978

Model year production: 169,620, down 11.36% from 1977.
Domestic market share: 1.80% (12th place).
Base price range: $10,196 to $12,529.
Lincoln average base price: $11,360, up 8.17%.
Introduction date: October 7, 1977.
Assembly plants: Wayne, MI (W), and Wixom, MI (Y).
Data plate identification (VIN): Eleven digit code read as
follows: First digit indicates year (8 = 1978); second digit

indicates assembly plant code (see list above); third and
fourth digits indicate model number (model number in
model charts); fifth digit indicates engine code (see powertrain chart); remaining digits are sequential with beginning
numbers of 800001. *Example:* 8Y82A800001 is a 1978 Lincoln Continental 4-Door Sedan, with 460 CID, 4-bbl. V8
engine, serial number 800001, built in Wixom, MI.

Powertrains

Engine	Net HP	Engine Code	Transmission Availability		Versailles	Continental & Mark V
302 CID (5.0L), variable venturi, V8	137	F	3-speed Select-Shift automatic[1]		S	—
				MPG:	16/23/18	—
				Calif.	15/22/18	—
400 CID (6.6L), 2-bbl., V8	179	S	3-speed Select-Shift automatic		—	S
				MPG:	—	13/20/15
				Calif.	—	11/18/14
460 CID (7.5L), 4-bbl., V8	208	A	3-speed Select-Shift automatic		—	$187[2]
				MPG:	—	11/17/13

[1]*Floor shift available with reclining bucket seat group for $33.*   [2]*Not available in California.*

Major Options

	Versailles	Continental	Mark V
Air conditioning, Auto-Temp	S	S	S
Tilt steering wheel	$77	$77	$77
Automatic speed control	S	$127	$127
Electric rear window defroster	$95	$95	$95
Tinted glass, all windows	S	S	S
Power windows	S	S	S

	Versailles	Continental	Mark V
Power front vent windows	—	$89	$89
Power door locks	$[1]	$[1]	$[1]
Illuminated entry system	S	$63	$63
Power seat, 6-way w/pass. recliner	S[2]	$236	$236
Leather seating upholstery	$295	$295	$315
RH remote-control mirror, LH std.	S	$37	$37
Intermittent windshield wipers	S	$35	$35
AM/FM stereo, w/power antenna[3]	—	$144	$144
AM/FM stereo w/8-track tape	($84)	$203	$203
AM/FM stereo w/automatic search	S	$287	$287
Vinyl top, full[4]	S	$215	$223
Fixed glass moonroof w/sun shade	—	$1,027	—
Moonroof, power-operated & tinted	$1,027	$1,027	$1,027
Power brakes, four wheel disc	S	—	S
"Sure-Track" antilock brake system	—	$496	$296
Wire wheel covers	N/C	$233	$233
Cast aluminum turbine-style wheels	—	$333	$333
Forged aluminum wheels	S	$333	$333

Popular Option Groups & Packages

	Versailles	Continental	Mark V
Appearance protection group	$57	$76	$69
Bill Blass designer series	—	—	$1,533[5]
Cartier designer series	—	—	$1,800
Color luxury group[6]	—	—	$680[6]
Defroster group	$115	$115	$115
Diamond Jubilee Edition	—	—	$8,000
Emilio Pucci designer series	—	—	$1,800
Givenchy designer series	—	—	$1,800
Headlamp convenience group	—	$133	$133
Interior light group	—	$127	$127
Power lock group	$147[1]	$147[1]	$115[1]
Reclining bucket seat group	$467	—	—
Town Coupe/Town Car package	—	$1,440	—
Williamsburg Limited Edition	—	$1,525[5]	—

—= Not Available; S = Standard equipment. [1]Power door locks require optional Power Lock convenience group. Price on coupe is $115. [2]Four-way power seat on Versailles. [3]Citizen Band (CB) radio available for $321, and includes power antenna in right rear quarter panel. [4]Landau vinyl roof w/frenched seams and rear window available on Continental Mark V for $484; Carriage roof (simulated convertible top) available for $1,133. Fully padded coach vinyl roof is available on Continental w/Town Car or Town Coupe option for $269; with Williamsburg Limited Edition for $332; and with Continental coupe or sedan for $547. Coach vinyl roof includes wide vinyl padded roof bow molding, and fully padded custom half-vinyl roof w/frenched rear window and side quarter windows. [5]Price with leather seats is $1,800. [6]Color luxury groups available: Chamois, Champagne, Cordovan, Dove Grey, Gold/Cream, Jade/Light Jade, Red/Rose, and Wedgewood Blue. Price is $775 when ordered with moondust paint.

Paint Colors

	Code		Code		Code
Black	1C	Light Champagne	52	Midnight Jade[1]	7V
Medium Silver metallic[1]	1S	Dark Champagne metallic[1]	5A	Light Jade metallic[1]	7Y
Black[1]	1W	Champagne moondust metallic[1,2]	5C	Light Chamois	83
Light Silver moondust metallic[1,2]	1Y	Light Champagne[1]	5D	Midnight Cordovan	84
Dark Red moondust metallic[1,2]	23	Light Chamois[1]	5G	Crystal Apricot moondust metallic[1,2]	88
Medium Red metallic	2G	Medium Chamois[1]	5K	White	9D
Midnight Blue	31	Midnight Cordovan[1]	5L	White[1]	9F
Diamond Blue metallic[3]	32	Dark Cordovan metallic[1]	5R		
Medium Blue	34	Jubilee Gold metallic[3]	66	*In two-tone combinations, first two digits are lower*	
Midnight Blue metallic[1]	35	Gold metallic[1]	67	*color, and second two digits are upper color.* [1]*Clear*	
Wedgewood Blue[1]	36	Cream[1]	68	*coat paint colors.* [2]*Moondust metallic paints avail-*	
Medium Blue metallic[1]	37	Cream	6P	*able for $189 extra. Not available on Versailles.*	
Diamond Blue moondust metallic[1,2]	38	Midnight Jade	72	[3]*Available only on the Continental Mark V Diamond Jubilee Edition.*	

Versailles

"A new Lincoln, a new concept. An investment in engineering."

Nameplate year of origin: 1977½ (1975 as a Continental option package).
Current bodystyle lifespan: 1977½ through 1980.
Predecessor to this model: None.
Replacement for this model: Continental (1982 to 1987).
Percentage of division's production: 5.27%.
Corporate siblings: Ford Granada and Mercury Monarch.
Primary competition: Cadillac Seville.
Notable changes: All-new model at mid-year 1977.
Major standard equipment: Luxury all nylon "Flight Bench" front w/four-way power adjustment, folding center armrests in front and rear seat, deep-pile carpeting, simulated wood appliqués on I/P, steering wheel and doors, leather steering wheel and I/P pad, rear passenger and front passenger side roof rail assist straps, package shelf w/Kasman fabric, Cartier-signed digital clock, power windows, automatic speed control, AM/FM Multiplex radio w/power antenna, automatic temperature control air conditioning, LH and RH illuminated visor vanity mirrors, LH and RH remote control rearview mirror, tinted glass, power deck lid release, interior lighting (ashtrays, courtesy, glove box, luggage compartment, dome/map, and rear seat reading), 18-oz. color-keyed carpeted luggage compartment floor w/14oz. carpeted decklid liner, full vinyl roof, coach lamps, illuminated entry system, cornering lights, high luster bodyside molding w/vinyl insert, bumper protection group, forged aluminum wheels, and FR78 × 14 wide WSW tires.

Measurements

Wheelbase	109.9"
Length	200.9"
Width	75.1"
Height	54.1"
Legroom — front	40.7"
Legroom — rear	35.6"
Headroom — front	38.2"
Headroom — rear	37.6"
Cargo capacity (cu. ft.)	14.1
Fuel capacity (gals.)	19.2

Models Available

	Model No.	Base MSRP	Change from LY	Shipping Wt. (lbs.)	Model Year Production	Change from LY
Versailles 4-Door Sedan	84	$12,529	+8.95%	3759	8,931	-42.13%
TOTALS	Avg. price	$12,529	+8.95%	Production	8,931	-42.13%

Continental

*"Lincoln Continental ... a luxury car with
the look of luxury ... inside and out."*

Nameplate year of origin: 1940 (1961 as a regular series).
Current bodystyle lifespan: 1970 through 1979 (restyled in 1974).
Predecessor to this model: Continental (1961 to 1969).
Replacement for this model: Town Car (1980 to 1991).
Percentage of division's production: 51.93%.
Corporate siblings: None.
Primary competition: Cadillac deVille.
Notable changes: Minor trim and detail changes.
Major standard equipment: Luxury cloth front bench seat w/six-way power adjustment, folding center armrests in front and rear seat, cut-pile carpeting, simulated wood appliqués on I/P and steering wheel, Cartier-signed digital clock, power windows, AM/FM radio w/power antenna, automatic temperature control air conditioning, visor-mounted vanity mirror, LH remote control rearview mirror, tinted glass, power deck lid release, interior lighting (ashtrays, courtesy, glove box, luggage compartment, dome/map, and rear seat reading), fully lined and carpeted luggage compartment w/tire cover, full vinyl roof, cornering lights, bright rocker panel moldings w/rear extensions, front and rear bumper guards w/pad and rub strips, deluxe wheel covers, and 225 × 15 WSW tires.

Measurements

	Coupe	Sedan
Wheelbase	127.2"	127.2"
Length	233.0"	233.0"
Width	80.0"	80.0"
Height	55.3"	55.2"
Legroom — front	42.0"	42.0"
Legroom — rear	41.3"	42.0"
Headroom — front	38.0"	38.1"
Headroom — rear	38.1"	38.6"
Cargo capacity (cu. ft.)	20.2	20.2
Fuel capacity (gals.)	24.2	24.2

1978

Models Available

	Model No.	Base MSRP	Change from LY	Shipping Wt. (lbs.)	Model Year Production	Change from LY
Continental 2-Door Hardtop Coupe	81	$10,196	+7.62%	4659	20,997	-23.55%
Continental 4-Door Sedan	82	$10,396	+7.89%	4660	67,110	-1.54%
TOTALS	*Avg. price*	$10,296	+7.76%	*Production*	88,087	-7.86%

Continental Mark V

"The Mark of Continental tradition."

Nameplate year of origin: 1956 (Continental Mark II).
Current bodystyle lifespan: 1977 through 1979.
Predecessor to this model: Continental Mark IV (1972 to 1976).
Replacement for this model: Continental Mark VI (1980 to 1983).
Percentage of division's production: 42.80%.
Corporate siblings: None.
Primary competition: Buick Riviera, Cadillac Eldorado, and Oldsmobile Toronado.
Notable changes: Revised grille and minor trim and detail changes.
Major standard equipment: Velour "Twin Comfort" lounge seats w/six-way power adjustment, folding center armrests in front and rear seat, walnut woodgrain appliqué on I/P and steering wheel, color-keyed cut-pile carpeting, visor vanity mirror, electric Cartier Timepiece, trip odometer, power windows, AM/FM radio w/power antenna, automatic temperature control air conditioning, LH remote control rearview mirror, tinted glass, door panel courtesy lights, power decklid release, fully lined luggage compartment, full vinyl roof w/opera window, dual custom pinstripe, customer monogram on doors, functional fender louvers, cornering lights, front and rear bumper guards w/pads and rub strips, luxury wheel covers, and 225 × 15 WSW tires.

Measurements

Wheelbase	120.4"
Length	230.3"
Width	79.8"
Height	53.0"
Legroom — front	42.3"
Legroom — rear	34.0"
Headroom — front	37.5"
Headroom — rear	37.1"
Cargo capacity (cu. ft.)	18.1
Fuel capacity (gals.)	26.0

Models Available

	Model No.	Base MSRP	Change from LY	Shipping Wt. (lbs.)	Model Year Production	Change from LY
Continental Mark V 2-Door Hardtop	89	$12,318	+8.09%	4567	72,602	-9.61%
TOTALS	*Avg. price*	$12,318	+8.09%	*Production*	72,602	-9.61%

MERCURY

"With 18 different models, one of them is right for you … at the sign of the cat."

As Ford Motor Company entered its 75th anniversary year, Mercury was embarking on its own 40th year in business. As pointed out in Mercury sales literature for 1978, "Ford Motor Company was in its 35th year when the first Mercury automobile was introduced on November 4, 1938," and the 1939 Mercury was "the first Ford-produced car styled entirely within the company and the first built up from a clay model by Ford stylists." The catalog copy went on to proclaim that the Lincoln-Mercury Division was proud of its contributions to Ford's history, and to be part of its heritage. In retrospect, it seems like a story of contradictions, as the original Mercury was based on the Ford design, and all of its 1978 model products were based on Ford division models, but it makes for a good story. Regardless of how they presented the history to consumers, Mercury had a banner year for 1978, with sales and production making large gains in the face of a slight decline for the industry as a whole. The sales increase was sustained largely on the strength of the overwhelmingly successful Comet replacement, the Zephyr, which increased sales by six times over the Comet's 1977 level. Continued growth in popularity of the Cougar XR-7 and sustained sales of the traditional full-size Marquis, now in its final season, added to the strong showing. The gain allowed Mercury to move ever closer to its target of ousting Buick from fifth place in industry production.

The most important product introduction for Mercury since the 1975 model year was the all-new Zephyr. Named after the legendary Lincoln-Zephyr, created for the depression era luxury market, the new Mercury Zephyr and its fraternal twin, the Ford Fairmont, made the biggest and most upbeat impression on the media and the public since the introduction of the Ford Mustang in 1964. The compact Mercury Comet replacement was designed to compete with any of the current compact or mid-size market offerings whether domestic or imported, and it succeeded in that mission. Available in four body styles, two- and four-door sedans, two-door sport coupe, and a four-door station wagon (the first compact Mercury wagon since the early 1960s), the Zephyr and its Ford twin employed a design philosophy based on optimizing space, fuel efficiency and cost efficiencies, while offering a wide variety of powertrains, décor options, and convenience features.

Zephyr design was modern and in tune with styling of the period, with simple, angular lines. Front-end styling consisted of dual rectangular headlights set above horizontal parking/turn signal lights, all within a chrome bezel, and set on each end of a vertical bar grille, with the entire front surrounded by a strip of chrome trim. The grille looked expensive as it consisted of multiple thin vertical bars, and carried the Mercury name in block letters on the lower driver's side. The Zephyr used aluminum front and rear bumpers, as was becoming the industry norm to save weight and increase fuel efficiency. The hood was relatively flat, with a wide and slightly raised section down the center, above the grille. Bodysides had two feature lines with the upper line beginning at the upper edge of the front fender, running straight back through the door handles, to a point several inches below the upper edge of the rear quarter panel. Where this line ended marked the point for the wagon's liftgate to angle forward to the roof, and on sedans marked the point where the quarter panel and trunk lid angled about thirty degrees forward to meet the flat upper panel of the trunk lid. The lower feature line, a more prominent indentation, ran full-length between the top corners of the bumpers, creating a slight flare to the flat-topped wheel openings as the feature line passed over them.

Zephyr's other exterior design features included two vertical fake front fender louvers and large, horizontal, rectangular taillamps filling most of the rear panel on each side of the license tag mounting. Whereas the Fairmont's taillamp lenses were vertically ribbed, the Zephyr's were divided into four horizontal sections with a vertical backup light at the inside. The wagon had a vertically mounted wraparound taillamp divided into three sections, with the backup lights flanking the license plate mount at the center of the liftgate below the rear window. After the start of the model year, a sporty "Z-7" coupe model was introduced. Its most distinguishing features were in its exterior design with a distinctive wrap-over roof design and a slanting rear panel. The wrap-over roof design resembled that of the Ford Thunderbird, sans the opera window, and used a similar style rear quarter window. The rear panel slanted forward, paralleling the rear window slant, with a center mounted license plate, flanked by vertical backup lamps, and horizontal taillamps filling out the rest of the panel. The taillamps were composed of five horizontal sections with the outer ends wrapping around the rear fender ends.

The sides of the greenhouse area were angular and upright with a moderate slant to the rear window on sedans and a more sloping rear window on the Z-7, more nearly matching the slope of the windshield. Four-door sedans had a narrow quarter window behind the rear door; two-door sedans had either a large, fixed rear passenger window or a smaller version when fitted with optional functional louvers that replaced the rear portion. Inside, the Zephyr had a more modern instrument panel, upholstery and trim appearance than anything offered by the Comet, except perhaps in Custom trim. Even in basic form, the layout of the Zephyr instrument panel and seating arrangements far surpassed that of its predecessor. Two large round dials, housing the speedometer to the right and fuel, oil and temperature gauges to the left, sat directly in front of the driver, with ventilation controls to the center of the car, all set in a large hooded pod, similar to the design used in the Cougar. A smaller pod, set lower at the center, held the radio. Besides the interior option packages mentioned later, there were multiple accessory trim options available such as Corinthian vinyl, Kirsten cloth, and Logan cloth.

Powering the Zephyr were Ford Motor Company's most popular and fuel-efficient engines, the 140 CID 4-cylinder engine from the Bobcat; the 200 CID 6-cylinder, a long-running Ford staple; and the 302 CID V8, used in nearly every Ford and most Mercury models that offered a V8 engine at some point in time. Initially not available in the station wagon, the 4-cylinder engine left the Zephyr feeling underpowered under hard acceleration, but provided the best fuel economy ratings of any car in its class.

The only existing Mercury model to receive significant visual changes was the Monarch. A new front-end design brought a more modern look with the introduction of single rectangular headlamps set over horizontal rectangular parking/turn signal lights. A larger grille still used vertical bars, but was taller with a larger top grille bar on the front header panel, and the Mercury name in script near the lower corner on the driver's side. The former Ghia series became an option group for 1978, and a new ESS option package added black-out grille and trim moldings to de-emphasize chrome, which was considered an American styling identifier, to create a European look. The use of bucket seats, a standard 4-speed manual overdrive transmission and heavy duty suspension seemed to enhance the "European Sport Sedan" theme. With the Monarch and Ford Granada twin having been compared in ads to a Mercedes-Benz sedan ever since their introductions, they were made more visually comparable with the ESS option, as body colored wheel covers that virtually copied the Mercedes design were part of the package.

Mostly carried over from the 1977 model year were the Bobcat, Cougar and Marquis series. The Bobcat added variable-ratio power steering to its option list, but was otherwise unchanged for the fourth season in a row. The Cougar line was also mostly unchanged in appearance and features, although a new Midnight/Chamois décor group was available that gave the Cougar XR-7 the look of a small Lincoln Continental Mark V. The former Cougar Brougham models were dropped and replaced by a Brougham option package, and the Cougar station wagons were gone, though they would return for another one-year stint during the 1982 model year in a very different Cougar line. The traditional, full-size Mercury Marquis was in its final season and had what Mercury described as "refinements," though any changes were hard to find. The Colony Park wagon was again an option package rather than a full-fledged model as it had once been. New audio options for various Mercury models included automatic electronic signal searching radios, cassette tape players and Citizens Band, or CB, radios.

Finally the German-built Capri was no longer imported for sale in the United States. However, there were apparently many leftover 1977 models, with an estimated 20,000 of which were sold during the 1978 model year, some as 1977 models, and some updated by dealers and retitled as 1978 models. Whatever the reason for the excess supply, there were enough available that the 1977 Capri was included in the 1978 Lincoln-Mercury sales literature. Since the Lincoln-Mercury division itself sold them as 1977 models, they will not be included for the 1978 model year, so refer to the 1977 Mercury listing for further details.

Bobcat 2-Door Station Wagons with Villager option shown in front

Bobcat 3-Door Runabout Hatchbacks with Sports Package option shown in front

Cougar 4-Door Pillared Hardtop with Brougham option

Cougar XR-7 interior with Midnight and Chamois package

Cougar XR-7 2-Door Hardtop Coupe with Midnight and Chamois package

Grand Marquis 2-Door Hardtop with Tu-Tone paint option

Monarch 2-Door Sedan

Left: Marquis 4-Door Station Wagon with Colony Park option

Left: Marquis Brougham 4-Door Pillared Hardtop

Monarch 4-Door Sedan with ESS package

Zephyr 2-Door Sedan

Zephyr 4-Door Sedan with
Luxury Exterior Décor package

Zephyr 4-Door Station Wagon
with Villager option

Zephyr interior with Flight Bench seat option

Right: Zephyr Z-7 2-Door Sports Coupe

Model year production: 635,051, up 19.47% from 1977.
Domestic market share: 6.74% (6th place).
Base price range: $3,777 to $7,399.
Mercury average base price: $5,199, up 4.78%.
Introduction date: October 7, 1977.
Assembly plants: Atlanta, GA (A); Lorain, OH (H); Kansas City, MO (K); San Jose, CA (R); Metuchen, NJ (T); Wayne, MI (W); St. Thomas, Ontario, Canada (X); and St. Louis, MO (Z).
Data plate identification (VIN): Eleven digit code read as

follows: First digit indicates year (8 = 1978); second digit indicates assembly plant code (see list above); third and fourth digits indicate model number (model number in model charts); fifth digit indicates engine code (see powertrain chart); remaining digits are sequential with beginning numbers of 500001. *Example:* 8K31F500001 is a 1978 Mercury Zephyr 2-Door sedan, with 302 CID, 2-bbl. V8 engine, serial number 500001, built in Kansas City (Claycomo), MO.

Powertrains

Engine	Net HP	Engine Code	Transmission Availability[1]		Bobcat	Zephyr	Monarch	Cougar	Marquis
140 CID (2.3L) OHC, 2-bbl., 4-cyl.	89	Y	4-speed manual		S	S	—	—	—
				MPG:	25/35/29	23/33/26	—	—	—
				Calif.	25/34/29	20/30/24	—	—	—
			3-speed Select-Shift automatic		$281	$368 (ex. Wgn.)[2]	—	—	—
				MPG:	21/29/24	22/33/26	—	—	—
				Calif.	21/29/24	—	—	—	—
170.8 CID (2.8L), 2-bbl., V6	93	Z	3-speed Select-Shift automatic		$554	—	—	—	—
				MPG:	18/22/20	—	—	—	—
				Calif.	17/22/19	—	—	—	—
200 CID (3.3L), 1-bbl., 6-cyl.	96	T	3-speed manual		—	$120[2]	—	—	—
				MPG:	—	21/29/24	—	—	—
			3-speed Select-Shift automatic		—	$401[3]	—	—	—
				MPG:	—	19/26/22	—	—	—
				Calif.	—	18/23/20	—	—	—
250 CID (4.1L), 1-bbl., 6-cyl.	98	L	4-speed manual w/overdrive		—	—	S[2]	—	—
				MPG:	—	—	21/28/24	—	—
			3-speed Select-Shift automatic		—	—	$193[3]	—	—
				MPG:	—	—	18/26/21	—	—
				Calif.	—	—	16/24/19	—	—
302 CID (5.0L), 2-bbl., V8	137	F	4-speed manual		—	—	$181[2]	—	—
				MPG:	—	—	16/25/19	—	—

Engine	Net HP	Engine Code	Transmission Availability[1]		Bobcat	Zephyr	Monarch	Cougar	Marquis
			3-speed Select-Shift automatic		—	$600[4]	$374[3]	S[2]	—
				MPG:	—	16/23/19	16/23/19	15/22/17	—
				Calif.	—	16/21/18	15/23/18	—	—
351 CID (5.8L), 2-bbl., V8	161	H	3-speed Select-Shift automatic		—	—	—	$157[3]	S[2]
				MPG:	—	—	—	14/20/16	13/21/16
				Calif.	—	—	—	12/18/14	—
400 CID (6.6L), 2-bbl., V8	173	S	3-speed Select-Shift automatic		—	—	—	$283	$126[3]
				MPG:	—	—	—	13/17/15	13/20/15
				Calif.	—	—	—	12/18/14	11/18/14
460 CID (7.5L), 4-bbl., V8	197	A	3-speed Select-Shift automatic		—	—	—	—	$271[2]
				MPG:	—	—	—	—	12/17/14

[1]Unless otherwise noted: All manual transmissions are floor-shifts. All automatics are column-shift, except on Bobcat. Floor-shift is available for $30 extra on Zephyr and Monarch with optional bucket seats and automatic. Floor-shift w/bucket seats and console is also available for $247 on Cougar 2-door, and for $141 on Cougar Brougham 2-door and XR-7.   [2]Not available in California.   [3]Required (or standard) in California.   [4]Requires optional power steering, and power front disc brakes.

Major Options

	Bobcat	Zephyr	Monarch	Cougar	Cougar XR-7	Marquis
Air conditioning[1]	$459	$465	$494	$543	$543	$583
Tilt steering wheel	—	—	$58	$70	$70	$72
Automatic speed control	—	—	$102	$117	$117	$120
Rear window defogger	—	$47	$47	—	—	—
Electric rear window defroster	$77	$84	$84	$93	$93	$93
Tinted glass, all windows	S	$52	$54	$66	$66	$75
Dual remote control mirrors	—	$30[2]	$53	$58	$58	$16[2]
Manual front door vent windows	—	$54[3]	—	—	—	—
Power windows, 2-dr./4-dr.	—	—	$116/$160	$126/$175	$126	$129/$188
Power door locks, 2-dr./4-dr.	—	—	$76/$104	$4	$4	$4
Power seat, 6-way w/std. seating	—	—	$90[5]	$149	$149	$149
Front bucket seats w/console[6]	S	S	$195	$247	$175	—
Leather interior trim	—	—	$271	—	$296	—
Dual facing rear seats (wagons)	—	—	—	—	—	$186
AM radio	$72	$72	$72	$79	$79	$79
AM/FM stereo	$161	$176	$176	$192	$192	$192
AM/FM stereo w/tape[7]	—	$243	$243	$266	$266	$266
AM/FM stereo w/auto-search	—	—	$319	$349	$349	$349
Vinyl top, full[8]	$145	$89	$102	$163	—	$141
Moonroof, power-operated[9]	$167[9]	—	$820	$789[9]	$789	$896
Power trunk lid release	—	—	$19	$4	$4	$4
Power steering	$131	$140	$148	S	S	S
Power brakes, w/front disc	S	$63	$63[10]	S	S	S[10]
Rear wheel opening fender skirts	—	—	—	—	—	$50
Deluxe wheel covers	N/C	S	$37	$38	—	S
Luxury wheel covers	—	—	—	$68	—	$84
Wire wheel covers	$20	$81	$96	$143	$105	$109
Styled steel wheels w/trim rings	S	N/C	$96	$143	$146[11]	—
Cast aluminum sport wheels	—	$242	$242[11]	$303	$264	—
Forged aluminum wheels	$128[11]	—	—	—	—	$264
White sidewall tires, std. size	$42	$42	$42	$46	$46	$50

Popular Option Groups & Packages

	Bobcat	Zephyr	Monarch	Cougar	Cougar XR-7	Marquis
Appearance protection group	$40	$43	$43	$53	$45	$58
Bumper protection group	$70	$70	$70	$76	$76	$59
Brougham décor group	—	—	—	$211	—	—
Brougham option, 2-dr./4-dr.	—	—	—	$271/$383	—	—

	Bobcat	Zephyr	Monarch	Cougar	Cougar XR-7	Marquis
Colony Park option package	—	—	—	—	—	$547
Convenience group	—	$47	$60	$139	$139	—
Décor group	—	—	$211	—	—	—
ES option package	—	$180	—	—	—	—
ESS option group	—	—	$524	—	—	—
Ghia option group	—	—	$426	—	—	—
Grand Marquis decor group[12]	—	—	—	—	—	$559
Interior Accent group	$40	$72	—	—	—	—
Light group	—	$40	$43	$51	$51	—
Light/Convenience group	$137	—	—	—	—	—
Lock Convenience group, 2-dr./ 4-dr.	—	—	—	—	—	$122/$149
Luxury exterior décor group	—	$96	—	—	—	—
Luxury interior package	—	$289	—	—	—	—
Midnight/Chamois décor group	—	—	—	—	$592	—
Power lock group, 2-dr./4-dr.	—	—	—	$100/$132	$100	—
Sports Accent group/trim option	$235	—	—	—	—	—
Sports Instrumentation group	—	—	—	$138	$118	—
Sports Package option	$108	—	—	—	—	—
Villager option package	—	$169	—	—	—	—
Visibility group	—	—	$58	—	—	$96
XR-7 décor group	—	—	—	—	$461	—

—= Not Available; S = Standard equipment. [1]Air conditioner w/automatic temperature control is available for $535 on Monarch, for $588 on Cougar/XR-7, and for $628 on Marquis. [2]LH remote and RH manual on Zephyr. LH only on Marquis. [3]Available on any model except the Zephyr Z-7. [4]Available only as part of the Power Lock group (Cougar), or Lock Convenience group (Marquis). [5]Power four-way seat on Monarch. [6]Bucket seats only on Bobcat; console not available. Zephyr is not available with console, and bucket seats are a $72 option on 6-cyl. or V8 equipped coupe and sedan models without the Luxury Interior Option. For Monarch, bucket seats included with Ghia and ESS options. For Cougar, available only on 2-doors. [7]Price for choice of eight-track tape or cassette tape. Citizens Band (CB) radio available on Monarch for $270 extra and on Cougar/XR-7 for $295 extra. [8]Not available on station wagons. Landau ¾ vinyl roof standard on Cougar XR-7. [9]Manually operated, flip-up/removable type on Bobcat. Available on Cougar 2-doors only. [10]Power four wheel disc brakes available for $300 on Monarch, and for $197 on Marquis. [11]White cast or white forged aluminum wheels available for $13 more on Bobcat and Monarch. Cougar XR-7 price is for styled road wheels. [12]Available only on Marquis station wagon, and requires Colony Park options, for $351.

Paint Colors

	Code		Code		Code
Black	1C	Bright Blue Glamour metallic[1,2]	3V	Tangerine	85
Silver metallic	1G	Dark Jade metallic	46	Medium Tan Glamour metallic[1,5]	8J
Dove Gray	1N	Medium Chestnut metallic	5M	Dark Cordovan metallic	8N
Medium Gray metallic (two-tone only)	1P	Dark Brown metallic	5Q	Champagne metallic	8Y
Red	21	Antique Cream	62	White	9D
Dark Red	2M	Bright Yellow	6E		
Bright Red	2R	Medium Jade Glamour metallic[1,3]	6L		
Lipstick Red	2U	Cream	6P		
Medium Blue	34	Cinnamon Gold Glamour metallic[1,4]	6W		
Dark Midnight Blue	3A	Medium Jade	7W		
Bright Dark Blue metallic	3G	Russet metallic	81		
Light Blue	3U	Light Chamois	83		

In two-tone combinations, first two digits are lower color, and second two digits are upper color. Two-tones available on Zephyr for $42, and Cougar for $95. [1]Glamour paints available for $40 extra on Bobcat, $46 on Zephyr and Monarch, and $62 on Cougar and Marquis. [2]Available only on Monarch, Cougar, and Marquis. [3]Available only on Zephyr, Monarch, Cougar, and Marquis. [4]Available only on Bobcat and Cougar. [5]Available only on Monarch and Marquis.

Bobcat

"A fun-to-drive car."

Nameplate year of origin: 1975.
Current bodystyle lifespan: 1975 through 1980.
Predecessor to this model: None.
Replacement for this model: Lynx (1981 to 1985).
Percentage of division's production: 5.08%.

Measurements

	Runabout	Wagon
Wheelbase	94.5"	94.8"
Length	169.3"	179.1"

1978

Corporate siblings: Ford Pinto.
Primary competition: AMC Gremlin, Dodge Colt, and Pontiac Sunbird.
Notable changes: Minor trim and detail changes.
Major standard equipment: All-vinyl low-back front bucket seats, color-keyed cut-pile carpeting, carpeted cargo area, fold-down rear seat, simulated woodgrain parking brake lever handle, shift knob, and I/P appliqué, deluxe two-spoke steering wheel, deluxe safety belts, tinted glass, bright window and belt moldings, B-pillar bright molding, wide wheel lip moldings, rocker panel moldings, rack-and-pinion steering, power front disc brakes, styled steel wheels w/trim rings, and BR78 × 13 BSW tires. Villager adds: Flip-out rear quarter windows, deluxe sound insulation, "Liftgate Ajar" warning system, standard size wheel lip moldings, and simulated rosewood paneling on bodysides and rear tailgate panel.

Measurements (cont.)

	Runabout	Wagon
Width	69.4"	69.7"
Height	50.6"	52.1"
Legroom — front	40.2"	40.2"
Legroom — rear	29.6"	29.6"
Headroom — front	37.3"	37.9"
Headroom — rear	35.8"	38.9"
Cargo capacity (cu. ft.)	6.1*	57.2
Fuel capacity (gals.)	13.0	14.0

*With rear seat folded down, 29.0 cu. ft.

Models Available

	Model No.	Base MSRP	Change from LY	Shipping Wt. (lbs.)	Model Year Production	Change from LY
Bobcat 3-Door Runabout (HBK)	20	$3,830	+11.40%	2389	23,428	+27.29%
Bobcat 2-Door Station Wagon	22	$4,112	+13.31%	2532	NA*	NEW*
Bobcat 2-Door Villager Wagon	22	$4,244	+12.54%	NA	8,840	-32.24%
TOTALS	Avg. price	$4,062	+12.44%	Production	32,268	+2.59%

*Production of Bobcat wagon and Bobcat Villager wagon kept as combined total since both are the same model number.

Zephyr

"Energy engineered for mileage and space."

Nameplate year of origin: 1978 (previously used on 1936–1942 Lincoln Zephyr series).
Current bodystyle lifespan: 1978 through 1983.
Predecessor to this model: Comet (1971 to 1977).
Replacement for this model: Topaz (1984 to 1994).
Percentage of division's production: 23.96%.
Corporate siblings: Ford Fairmont.
Primary competition: AMC Concord, Dodge Aspen, and Pontiac Phoenix.
Notable changes: All-new model.
Major standard equipment: All-vinyl low-back front bucket seats, cut-pile carpeting, integral door armrests w/door pull assist handle, two-spoke color-keyed steering wheel, simulated woodgrain appliqué around instrument cluster, upper bodyside dual paint stripes, bright windshield and rear window moldings, bright drip rail moldings, bright rocker panel and wheel lip moldings, manual front disc brakes, modified strut front suspension, deluxe wheel covers, and B78 × 14 BSW tires. Wagon adds: Carpeted load floor area, cargo area light, liftgate "open" warning light, and BR78 × 14 BSW tires. Z-7 sport coupe adds: Deluxe seat trim, luxury door trim panels, color-keyed safety belts, high gloss simulated woodgrain appliqué on I/P, inside hood release, bright LH manual mirror, wrap-over roof design w/accent paint stripes, bright door window frames and belt moldings, lower bodyside protection molding w/vinyl insert, and deluxe sound insulation package,

Measurements

	Sedans	Z-7	Wagon
Wheelbase	105.5"	105.5"	105.5"
Length	193.8"	195.8"	193.8"
Width	71.0"	71.0"	71.0"
Height	53.5"	52.2"	54.8"
Legroom — front	41.8"	41.8"	41.8"
Legroom — rear	35.4"	32.7"	35.4"
Headroom — front	38.3"	37.1"	39.0"
Headroom — rear	37.5"	36.1"	39.0"
Cargo capacity (cu. ft.)	16.8	16.1	79.7
Fuel capacity (gals.)	16.0	16.0	16.0

Models Available

	Model No.	Base MSRP	Change from LY*	Shipping Wt. (lbs.)	Model Year Production	Change from LY*
Zephyr 2-Door Sedan	31	$3,777	+6.57%	2572	27,673	+203.80%
Zephyr 4-Door Sedan	32	$3,863	+6.80%	2614	47,334	+280.62%

	Model No.	Base MSRP	Change from LY*	Shipping Wt. (lbs.)	Model Year Production	Change from LY*
Zephyr 4-Door Station Wagon	36	$4,216	NEW	2722	32,596	NEW
Zephyr Z-7 2-Door Sport Coupe	35	$4,154	NEW	2609	44,569	NEW
TOTALS	*Avg. price*	$4,003	+11.79%	*Production*	152,172	+606.30%

*Comparisons of total production, and of Zephyr 2- and 4-door sedans, are made to 1977 Comet 2- and 4-door sedans.

Monarch

"A precision-size car for American drivers."

Nameplate year of origin: 1975 (used on Canadian Ford brand from 1946 to 1961).

Current bodystyle lifespan: 1975 through 1980.

Predecessor to this model: None.

Replacement for this model: Cougar (1981 to 1982).

Percentage of division's production: 14.44%.

Corporate siblings: Ford Granada and Lincoln Versailles.

Primary competition: Buick Skylark, Dodge Diplomat, and Oldsmobile Omega.

Notable changes: Revised front end and minor trim and detail changes.

Major standard equipment: All-vinyl "Flight Bench" front seats w/fold-down center armrest, cut-pile carpeting, simulated burled walnut I/P appliqué, locking glove box, cigar lighter, bright window moldings, full-length upper bodyside molding, stand-up hood ornament, manual front disc brakes, hubcaps, and DR78 × 14 BSW tires.

Measurements

	2-door	4-door
Wheelbase	109.9"	109.9"
Length	197.7"	197.7"
Width	74.0"	74.0"
Height	53.4"	53.4"
Legroom — front	40.3"	40.3"
Legroom — rear	34.4"	36.1"
Headroom — front	38.0"	38.2"
Headroom — rear	36.5"	37.6"
Cargo capacity (cu. ft.)	14.8	14.8
Fuel capacity (gals.)	19.2	19.2

Models Available

	Model No.	Base MSRP	Change from LY	Shipping Wt. (lbs.)	Model Year Production	Change from LY
Monarch 2-Door Sedan	33	$4,366	+7.11%	3058	38,939	-12.51%
Monarch 4-Door Sedan	34	$4,457	+7.29%	3102	52,775	-5.07%
TOTALS	*Avg. price*	$4,412	+0.29%	*Production*	91,714	-28.18%

Cougar

"Bold road car. Smart personal car."

Nameplate year of origin: 1968.

Current bodystyle lifespan: 1977 through 1979.

Predecessor to this model: Montego (1972 to 1976).

Replacement for this model: Cougar (1981 to 1982).

Percentage of division's sales volume: 7.36%.

Corporate siblings: Ford LTD II.

Primary competition: AMC Matador, Buick Century, Dodge Monaco, Oldsmobile Cutlass, and Pontiac LeMans.

Notable changes: Minor trim and detail changes.

Major standard equipment: Cloth-and-vinyl front bench seat, color-keyed carpeting, simulated rosewood I/P appliqués, 10-oz. cut-pile color-keyed carpeting, two-spoke color-keyed steering wheel, deluxe sound package, windshield and rear window bright moldings, drip rail moldings, full wheel lip moldings, stand-up Cougar hood ornament, power steering, power front disc brakes, hubcaps, and HR78 × 14 BSW tires.

Measurements

	2-Doors	4-Doors
Wheelbase	114.0"	118.0"
Length	215.5"	219.5"
Width	78.6"	78.6"
Height	52.6"	53.3"
Legroom — front	42.3"	42.3"
Legroom — rear	32.8"	37.2"
Headroom — front	37.3"	38.0"
Headroom — rear	36.3"	37.0"
Cargo capacity (cu. ft.)	15.9	15.9
Fuel capacity (gals.)	21.0	21.0

1978

Models Available

	Model No.	Base MSRP	Change from LY	Shipping Wt. (lbs.)	Model Year Production	Change from LY
Cougar 2-Door Hardtop	91	$5,052	+7.49%	3761	21,398	+34.49%
Cougar 4-Door Pillared Hardtop	92	$5,179	+7.18%	3848	25,364	+66.26%
TOTALS	*Avg. price*	$5,116	+1.57%	*Production*	46,762	-33.22%

Cougar XR-7

"The embodiment of personal luxury and comfort in a true intermediate size automobile."

Nameplate year of origin: 1967.
Current bodystyle lifespan: 1977 through 1979.
Predecessor to this model: Cougar XR-7 (1974 to 1976).
Replacement for this model: Cougar XR-7 (1980 to 1983).
Percentage of division's production: 26.22%.
Corporate siblings: Ford Thunderbird.
Primary competition: Buick Regal, Dodge Charger SE and Magnum XE, Oldsmobile Cutlass Supreme, and Pontiac Grand Prix.
Notable changes: Minor trim and detail changes.
Major standard equipment: All-vinyl "Flight Bench" front seat w/fold-down center armrest, cut-pile carpeting, simulated baby burl walnut I/P appliqués, electric clock, deluxe steering wheel, courtesy lights, landau vinyl roof w/louvered opera windows, bodyside paint stripes, Cougar stand-up hood ornament, XR-7 sound package, power steering, power front disc brakes, specially tuned suspension system, XR-7 wheel covers, and HR78 × 15 BSW tires.

Measurements

Wheelbase	114.0"
Length	215.5"
Width	78.6"
Height	52.6"
Legroom — front	42.3"
Legroom — rear	32.8"
Headroom — front	37.3"
Headroom — rear	36.3"
Cargo capacity (cu. ft.)	15.9
Fuel capacity (gals.)	21.0

Models Available

	Model No.	Base MSRP	Change from LY	Shipping Wt. (lbs.)	Model Year Production	Change from LY
Cougar XR-7 2-Door Hardtop	93	$5,720	+8.46%	3865	166,508	+33.42%
TOTALS	*Avg. price*	$5,720	+8.46%	*Production*	166,508	+33.42%

Marquis

"Six-passenger room. Elegance."

Nameplate year of origin: 1967.
Current bodystyle lifespan: 1971 through 1978 (restyled in 1973 and 1975).
Predecessor to this model: Marquis (1969 to 1970).
Replacement for this model: Marquis & Grand Marquis (1979 to 1991).
Percentage of division's sales volume: 22.93%.
Corporate siblings: Ford LTD.
Primary competition: Buick Electra 225 and Estate Wagon, Chrysler Newport, Oldsmobile Ninety-Eight and Custom Cruiser, and Pontiac Bonneville and Grand Safari.
Notable changes: Minor trim and detail changes.
Major standard equipment: Athea cloth-and-vinyl front bench seat w/fold-down center armrest, cut-pile carpeting,

Measurements

	2-Doors	4-Doors	Wagons
Wheelbase	124.0"	124.0"	121.0"
Length	229.0"	229.0"	228.3"
Width	79.6"	79.6"	79.9"
Height	53.8"	54.7"	56.9"
Legroom — front	41.8"	41.9"	41.7"
Legroom — rear	35.2"	39.4"	37.1"
Headroom — front	37.3"	37.9"	39.0"
Headroom — rear	35.8"	36.9"	39.5"
Cargo capacity (cu. ft.)	22.7	22.7	103.7*
Fuel capacity (gals.)	24.2	24.2	21.0

Includes 9.1 cu. ft. of hidden cargo space.

simulated woodgrain I/P and steering wheel appliqué, deluxe two-spoke steering wheel, dome light, sound insulation package, bright window moldings, rocker panel molding, front bumper guards, hubcaps, and HR78 × 15 BSW tires. Wagon adds: All-vinyl front bench seat w/fold-down center armrest, bright seat side shields, cargo area light, three-way tailgate w/power tailgate window, and JR78 × 15 BSW tires. Brougham adds: Willshire cloth and vinyl "Flight Bench" front bench seat w/fold-down center armrest, rear seat center armrests, 18-oz. Tiffany carpeting, Brougham door panels w/lower carpeted panel and door pull assist strap, electric clock, RH visor vanity mirror, LH remote control mirror, courtesy lights, power windows, front and rear door courtesy lights, luggage compartment light, vinyl roof, full-length fender peak molding, rear wheel opening fender skirts, and Brougham wheel covers. Grand Marquis adds: Media velour or leather-with-vinyl individually adjustable Twin Comfort Lounge seats, digital clock, carpeted luggage compartment, dome/dual map reading light, tinted glass, full-length bodyside protective molding w/color-keyed vinyl insert, hood and deck lid paint stripes, specific Grand Marquis nameplates and ornamentation, and JR78 × 15 BSW tires.

Models Available

	Model No.	Base MSRP	Change from LY	Shipping Wt. (lbs.)	Model Year Production	Change from LY
Marquis 2-Door Hardtop	61	$5,897	+8.55%	4296	11,176	-15.60%
Marquis 4-Door Pillared Hardtop	62	$5,949	+8.55%	4328	27,793	-23.02%
Marquis 4-Door, 6-pass. Station Wagon	74	$6,106	+6.75%	4578	16,883	-17.09%
Marquis Brougham 2-Door Hardtop	63	$6,525	+4.60%	4317	10,368	-15.27%
Marquis Brougham 4-Door Pillared Hardtop	64	$6,638	+4.79%	4346	26,030	-11.50%
Grand Marquis 2-Door Hardtop	65	$7,290	+6.85%	4342	15,624	+16.21%
Grand Marquis 4-Door Pillared Hardtop	66	$7,399	+6.85%	4414	37,753	+20.88%
TOTALS	Avg. price	$6,543	+7.03%	Production	145,627	-6.67%

1978

OLDSMOBILE

*"In man's search for a new measure of excellence ...
1978 Oldsmobile. Can we build one for you?"*

As the new model year arrived with a new line of downsized Cutlass models, it had to be a nail-biter for Oldsmobile executives. The most popular car in their line, the Cutlass, had sold over a half million cars for the past two years and propelled the Olds division to over a million units of production for 1977. Everyone knew that the new cars had to maintain the successful formula of price, features, design, ride and performance found in the former models. Would they succeed? By model year-end, the production totals showed a mixed picture. While Cutlass series production dropped more than 15 percent, it still remained over half a million, and with the Delta 88 finding more acceptance after its downsizing in 1977, Oldsmobile still squeaked out just over a million cars for 1978.

The new Cutlass line came in four basic body styles within six different subseries. Using General Motors' new A-body fastback styling were the new base Salon and Salon Brougham models, sharing their main body styling with the Buick Century. Then there was the newly named Cutlass

Cruiser using the new two-seat, four-door station wagon body used by all GM mid-size cars. Three new coupe models were built on what was known as the A-body "specialty" platform, which was shared with the Chevrolet Monte Carlo, Pontiac Grand Prix and Buick Regal. All of these models shared a basic platform with a 108.1-inch wheelbase as well as a central body structure, including rooflines and doors on most models. Of all the new GM mid-size models, it was the popular Cutlass coupes with the A-specialty body that received styling most closely resembling their predecessors.

At the front Cutlass Supreme, Supreme Brougham and Calais models carried the Oldsmobile split grille with a wide center body-colored panel between vertically themed wrapover grilles. On both Supreme models, the grille had three sections per side, each with about eight vertical bars per section. The new Calais had a single grille on each side consisting of eleven vertical slots, much like the 1977 Cutlass S, but with two horizontal bars running behind the grille. All three coupe models carried single square headlamps and inboard vertical, rectangular parking/turn signal lamps in a chrome bezel, a chrome hood windsplit molding, and a stand-up hood ornament. They also shared a formal roofline with an upright rear window and a nearly rectangular rear quarter side window, having a curved corner on the lower rear side. Bodysides had a slight curve, with no lower body feature line, but a slight flare to the wheel openings. The main identifying feature in profile that was kept from the past was the rear quarter panel upper feature line. Running forward just about an inch below the top edge of the rear quarter panel, it extended forward over the broad C-pillar to a point a few inches shy of the rear quarter window, where it sharply turned downward, then faded away before reaching mid-level on the bodyside. Around back a flat decklid with a fading crease above the inner edge of the taillamps angled downward to meet the bumper across the center. Vertical rectangular taillamps, divided by a vertical bar into two sections, were set in a chrome bezel. The trunk lid opening went around the license plate mount placed in the center of the rear end, which doubled as the access door to the fuel tank filler cap.

Cutlass Salon models featured an aerodynamic looking fastback roofline while retaining the interior space and generous trunk capacity of a regular sedan. At the front, a flat front end surface had square headlamps and inward mounted turn signal/parking lights set into an outer bezel, flanking a traditional Olds split style grille with center body-colored panel. The grille of the base Cutlass Salon contained two square ports per side, with each having an egg-crate grille insert set back about an inch from the leading edge. Salon Brougham models had four vertical sections per side, with each section having a vertical crosshatch insert four rows high and six columns across. Neither grille design wrapped over into the header like that of the Calais and Supreme. On the lower bodyside a faint feature line ran between the lower edge of the bumper impact strips and created a slight flare over the wheel openings as it passed through. The lower line was the breaking point for the two-tone paint on coupes having the 4-4-2 option package. A barely perceptible upper body feature line ran from the top corner of the front fascia to the rear of the car at the height of the top corner of the taillight bezel. This upper line was where optional pinstripes were placed, and also marked the upper demarcation line on two-toned cars.

At the rear, the Cutlass Cruiser wagon used a traditional box style rear quarter area, with a split tailgate having a lift-up window and drop-down tailgate but the Salon coupes and sedans having the sloping rear roof and trunk lid designs were less than traditional. The roof began to slope just above the top of the rear seatback cushion, angling downward with a large rear window set above rear vents used as part of the GM flow-through ventilation system. The slope continued through the trunk lid, then turned more sharply downward about a foot above the rear bumper. Flat, rectangular taillamps divided into multiple sections were placed in the outer

extremes of the rear end. As with the Supreme and Calais coupes, the decklid met the bumper, and was cut out around the center-mounted license plate housing, which doubled as the fuel filler door.

As with all of the new GM mid-size cars, the greenhouse areas of the Cutlass fastbacks were unique in that all rear door windows were of a fixed design on four-doors, and all rear quarter windows were fixed on two-doors. Four-door sedans did receive triangular rear quarter pop-out vent windows behind the rear doors, while station wagons used a vertical rear quarter vent window in the back door. The supposed purpose of the fixed rear window was to allow more hip room in the rear seat for carrying three passengers, as the doors were thinner since they did not have to accommodate a mechanism to raise and lower the window. The exterior styling of the fastback looked quite appropriate with the sporty 4-4-2 option, but otherwise seemed an odd choice for the popular family type cars.

Instrument panel design for the Cutlass was a modern pod design, with a horizontal pod running in front of the driver and over to the center dashboard area. Vertical air vents were at each end, with wiper and light controls to the left side of the speedometer housing, and warning lights, another air vent and optional clock to the right side. The speedometer housing consisted of a horizontal, black background speedometer with fuel, temperature and gear selector below. Supreme speedometer housings were in a brushed aluminum style background, and optional full gauges were on a black background. A secondary square pod was mounted below the horizontal pod in the center of the car housing the optional radio and ventilation controls, with an ashtray and lighter below. To the right side of the instrument panel were two horizontal air vents mounted above the glove box. Seats were in basic styles and patterns similar to those used on larger Oldsmobiles, with cushions being thinner in design this year to help maximize space efficiency. An exclusive mid-year "Tahoe" interior option, available only on the Cutlass Salon Brougham and the Cutlass Cruiser wagon, offered bold geometric patterns in deep brown, tan and rust colors. Refraining from saying the upholstery was inspired by Native American blankets, Oldsmobile took the politically correct route stating they were "Inspired by America's original designers."

The Cutlass series names were realigned for the new models as mentioned earlier. There had not been a base Cutlass model for two seasons, and the former base "S" level cars were dropped with this redesign. The new entry-level Cutlass was now named the Cutlass Salon, which was formerly the "European" sport/luxury model. The former Cutlass Supreme models were now called Cutlass Salon Brougham. All of the Salon models were in the fastback line of two-door coupes and four-door sedans. The new notchback styled models consisted of a line of three coupes, two of which directly replaced 1977 models. The Cutlass Supreme two-door coupe was technically a new model in the sub-series "R" models, even though in 1977 there was a "J" model coupe named Cutlass Supreme, but as previously mentioned it was now a Cutlass Salon Brougham coupe. The Cutlass Supreme Brougham coupe was a direct replacement for the 1977 model, and a newly named Cutlass Calais coupe was the sport/luxury model that replaced the 1977 Cutlass Salon coupe. Lastly, a newly named Cutlass Cruiser wagon replaced the popular Vista-Cruiser wagons and was the only Cutlass model to have a production increase, with about 4,000 additional units. The 4-4-2 appearance option was still available, this year on the Cutlass Salon coupe, and could be ordered with any of the available Salon engines, including the standard 231 CID V6. (Production figures for the 4-4-2 option package are not currently available.) In the end, the popular coupe models lost only about 25,000 units of production, but the new fastback bodied Cutlass line turned out to be the big loser, shedding about 75,000 units from last year's sales. A more significant drop at Buick sent a clear signal to GM that consumers did not want fastback styled family cars, and this design would be gone by the 1980 model year.

Oldsmobile's other major news for 1978 was the introduction of its new Diesel V8 engine. Based on an Oldsmobile 350 CID gasoline V8, the Diesel engines were successful in their first year, with more than 30,000 cars being equipped with the fuel-saving engine. Diesel equipped cars were noisier, requiring more sound insulation in the cowl area, and they also put out more visible exhaust, but consumers interested in this engine were looking for the 50 percent increase in

fuel mileage that was possible according to EPA estimates. Also new this year was the replacement of the old 140 CID 4-cylinder engine, originally designed for the Chevrolet Vega and used in the Starfire for 1977, with the 151 CID "Iron Duke" 4-cylinder engine built by Pontiac. The new engine was essentially half of the division's new-for-1977 301 CID V8 engine.

While the Starfire did not have any other significant changes, the compact Omega, which was actually now bigger than the Cutlass, boasted a redesigned grille with three rectangular sections holding ten horizontal bars per side this year, but otherwise only minor detail changes. The base Omega F-85 two-door coupe model was discontinued, as was the perennially slow-selling Omega Brougham two-door hatchback. Full-size Oldsmobiles received new grille configurations with few other styling updates. The Delta 88 received a three row horizontal grille, still split in the center by a wide body color panel, with each of the three rows containing an egg-crate insert four rows high and sixteen columns across. The new grille design was shared with the Custom Cruiser. The Ninety-Eight series grille was again an egg-crate design but with larger openings, now being nine rows high and nine columns across, and divided by a chrome center panel with the Oldsmobile crest set in a red emblem. The Toronado, entering its final season as a massive front-wheel drive coupe, wore a new vertical bar grille having 22 openings which were body colored and outlined with chrome trim. The XS option package featuring the large wraparound rear window and sunroof was offered again this year, with 2,415 Toronados having the package.

1978

Cutlass Calais 2-Door Coupe

**Cutlass Cruiser 4-Door Station Wagon
with woodgrain option**

Top, left: **Custom Cruiser 4-Door Station Wagon
with rear-facing third seat option**

Cutlass Salon 2-Door Coupe with 4-4-2 package

Cutlass Salon 4-Door Sedan

Cutlass Salon interior with Tahoe trim

Cutlass Salon Brougham 2-Door Coupe

Oldsmobile Cutlass Supreme 2-Door Coupe

Cutlass Supreme 2-Door Coupe interior

Cutlass Supreme Brougham 2-Door Coupe

Delta 88 2-Door Coupe

Ninety-Eight Regency 2-Door Coupe

Omega 2-Door Hatchback Coupe
with SX package

Delta 88 Royale 4-Door Sedan

Omega Brougham 4-Door Sedan
with LS package

Starfire SX 2-Door Hatchback Coupe

Toronado Brougham 2-Door Hardtop Coupe

Model year production: 1,015,805, down 10.56% from 1977.
Domestic market share: 10.78% (3rd place).
Base price range: $4,009 to $9,412.
Oldsmobile average base price: $5,388, up 2.36%.
Introduction date: October 6, 1977.
Assembly plants: Southgate, CA (C); Doraville, GA (D); Linden, NJ (E); Framingham, MA (G); Lansing, MI (M); Arlington, TX (R); Lordstown, OH (U); Kansas City/Fairfax, KS (X); Willow Run, MI (W); and St. Therese, Quebec, Canada (2).
Data plate identification (VIN): Thirteen digit code read as

follows: First digit indicates division (3 = Oldsmobile); second through fourth digits indicate series and body style (model number in model charts); fifth digit is engine code (see powertrain chart); sixth digit indicates model year (8 = 1978); seventh digit indicates assembly plant (see list above); remaining digits are sequential with beginning number of 100001. *Example:* 3L69R8X100001 is a 1978 Oldsmobile Delta 88 4-Door Town Sedan, with 350 CID, 4-bbl. V8 engine, serial number 100001, built in Kansas City — Fairfax, KS.

Powertrains

Engine	Net HP	Engine Code: VIN/GM	Transmission Availability[1]	Starfire	Omega	Cutlass	Delta 88	98 & Custom Cruiser	Toronado
151 CID (2.5L),	85	V/LX8[2]	4-speed manual	S	—	—	—	—	—

Engine	Net HP	Engine Code: VIN/GM	Transmission Availability[1]		Starfire	Omega	Cutlass	Delta 88	98 & Custom Cruiser	Toronado
2-bbl., 4-cyl.				MPG:	24/34/28	—	—	—	—	—
				Calif.	21/31/24	—	—	—	—	—
			5-speed manual		$175	—	—	—	—	—
				MPG:	NA	—	—	—	—	—
				Calif.	NA	—	—	—	—	—
			3-speed Turbo Hydra-matic		$270	—	—	—	—	—
				MPG:	23/31/26	—	—	—	—	—
				Calif.	23/31/26	—	—	—	—	—
231 CID (3.8L), 2-bbl., 6-cyl.	105	A/LD5	3-speed manual[3]		—	S	S[4]	—	—	—
				MPG:	—	16/28/19	16/28/19	—	—	—
			4-speed manual		$170	$125[3]	—	—	—	—
				MPG:	16/28/19	NA	—	—	—	—
				Calif.	16/27/20	—	—	—	—	—
			5-speed manual		$345	$300[3]	$300[4]	—	—	—
				MPG:	NA	NA	NA	—	—	—
				Calif.	NA	—	—	—	—	—
			3-speed Turbo Hydra-matic		$440	$307	S[5]/$307[4]	S	—	—
				MPG:	19/27/22	18/26/21	19/27/22	17/25/20	—	—
				Calif.	16/23/18	15/21/17	16/23/18	15/21/17	—	—
260 CID (4.3L), 2-bbl., V8	110	F/LV8	3-speed manual[3]		—	—	$100[4]	—	—	—
				MPG:	—	—	20/29/23	—	—	—
			5-speed manual[3]		—	—	$400[4]	—	—	—
				MPG:	—	—	NA	—	—	—
			3-speed Turbo		—	—	$100[5]/$407[4]	$100[3]	—	—
			Hydra-matic	MPG:	—	—	19/27/22	17/23/19	—	—
				Calif.	—	—	17/25/20	—	—	—
305 CID (5.0L), 2-bbl., V8	145	U/LG3	3-speed manual		—	$150[3]	—	—	—	—
				MPG:	—	15/21/17	—	—	—	—
			4-speed manual		$320	$275[3]	$275[3,4]	—	—	—
				MPG:	16/22/18	NA	16/18/22	—	—	—
			3-speed Turbo Hydra-matic		$590	$457[3]	$150[5,6]/$457[4,6]	—	—	—
				MPG:	17/25/20	16/22/19	—	—	—	—
				Calif.	14/21/17	—	14/21/17	—	—	—
305 CID (5.0L), 4-bbl., V8[3]	160	H/LG4	3-speed Turbo		—	—	$200[5]/$50[4]	—	—	—
			Hydra-matic	MPG:	—	—	18/26/21	—	—	—
350 CID (5.7L), Diesel-FI, V8	120	L/LF9	3-speed Turbo Hydra-matic		—	—	—	$850	$740	—
				MPG:	—	—	—	21/30/24	21/30/24	—
				Calif.	—	—	—	21/30/24	21/30/24	—
350 CID (5.7L), 4-bbl., V8[6]	160	L/LM1	3-speed Turbo Hydra-matic		—	$572	$265[5]	—	—	—
				Calif.	—	13/18/15	13/18/15	—	—	—
350 CID (5.7L), 4-bbl., V8	170	R/L34	3-speed Turbo Hydra-matic		—	—	—	$265	S	—
				MPG:	—	—	—	16/23/19	15/22/17	—
				Calif.	—	—	—	15/22/17	14/20/16	—
403 CID (6.6L), 4-bbl., V8	185[7]	K/L80	3-speed Turbo Hydra-matic		—	—	—	$330	$65	S
				MPG:	—	—	—	14/20/16	14/20/16	13/19/15
				Calif.	—	—	—	13/19/16	13/19/16	12/17/14

[1]Unless otherwise specified: All 3-speed manuals are column shift. All 4- and 5-speed manuals are floor shift. All automatics are column shift, except on Starfire. Floor shift automatic is optional on Omega, Cutlass and Delta 88 2-doors with other required equipment at extra cost. [2]Engine code for California is I/LS6. [3]Not available in California. [4]Except Cutlass Cruiser wagon. [5]Cutlass Cruiser wagon only. [6]Available only in California or with high altitude emission equipment. [7]Horsepower rating for Toronado is 200.

1978

Major Options

	Starfire	Omega	Cutlass	Delta 88	Custom Cruiser	Ninety-Eight	Toronado
Four-Season air conditioner[1]	$470	$508	$544	$581	$581	$581	S
Tilt-Away steering wheel	$62	$69	$69	$70	$70	$70	$70
Tilt-and-Telescope steering wheel	—	—	—	$117	$117	$117	$117
Cruise control	—	$90	$90	$95	$95	$95	$95
Electric rear window defroster	$79	$53[2]	$95	$97	$97	$97	$97
Tinted glass, all windows	$48	$50	$55	$70	$70	$70	$70
Power windows, 2-dr./4-dr.	—	$118/$156	$124/$172	$130/$190	$190	S	S
Power door locks, 2-dr./4-dr.	—	$74/$106	$80/$112	$82/$114	$149[3]	$82/$114	$82
Power front seat, 6-way w/std. seat	—	—	$151	$151	$151	$120[4]	S
Leather upholstery	—	—	—	$350	—	$255	$255
Front bucket seats, w/console[5]	$78	$87	$87	$87	—	—	—
Third row seat (wagons)	—	—	—	—	$186	—	—
AM radio	$74	$79	$83	$96	$96	$96	—
AM/FM stereo[6]	$222	$236	$236	$239	$239	$239	S
AM/FM stereo w/tape[6]	$320	$341	$341	$345	$345	$345	$106
Woodgrain exterior panels (wagons)	—	—	$235	—	$235	—	—
Vinyl top, full	—	$97	$116[7]	$142	—	$161	$161
Vinyl top, landau (coupes only)	—	$179	$190	$220	—	$268	$268[8]
Hatch roof (T-top)	—	—	$625[9]	—	—	—	—
Sunroof, power operated, metal	—	—	$499	$695	—	$778	$778
Astroroof, power operated, glass	$215[10]	—	$699	$895	—	$978	$978
Power trunk lid release	—	—	$18	$18	—	$18	$18
Power steering, "Vari-Ratio"	$134	$152	$152	S	S	S	S
Power brakes, w/front disc	$66	$69	$69	S	S	S	S
Deluxe wheel covers	$41	$34	$39	$39	$39	S	S
Wire wheel covers	—	$135	$135	$110	$110	$110	—
Chrome road wheels	—	—	—	$120	$120	$79	—
Chrome sport (Super Stock III) wheels	$79	$84	$84	$89	—	—	—
WSW tires, std. size	—	$39	$41	$43	$43	$43	$50

Popular Option Groups & Packages

	Starfire	Omega	Cutlass	Delta 88	Custom Cruiser	Ninety-Eight	Toronado
4-4-2 package	—	—	$260[11]	—	—	—	—
Appearance package	—	—	—	—	—	—	$293
GT package	$627	—	—	—	—	—	—
LS package	—	$1,943	—	—	—	—	—
SX package	—	$203	—	—	—	—	—
XS custom package	—	—	—	—	—	—	$2,700

— = Not Available; S = Standard equipment. [1]"Tempmatic" air conditioner with automatic climate control is available for $40 additional on Cutlass, and $45 additional on Delta 88, Custom Cruiser, Ninety-Eight and Toronado. [2]Blower type defogger. [3]Includes power tailgate lock. [4]Standard on Ninety-Eight Regency. [5]Bucket seats are standard on Starfire and Cutlass Calais. Bucket seats are available on Omega coupes and hatchback, on any Cutlass model, and on Delta 88 coupes. Console is available for $75 with bucket seats. [6]Tape player is choice of cassette or 8-track. CB radio available on all models with AM/FM stereo (with or without tape player), except on Starfire and Omega, at $230 additional. [7]Not available on Cutlass Cruiser. [8]Landau roof available on Toronado XS, standard on Brougham. [9]Available on Supreme, Supreme Brougham and Calais coupes only. [10]Manual removable glass roof. [11]Available on Coupes only. Price on Salon Brougham is $111.

Paint Colors

	Code		Code		Code
White	11	Bright Blue metallic[2]	24	Medium Green metallic[1]	45
Silver metallic	15	Dark Blue metallic[1]	29	Dark Green metallic[2]	48
Gray metallic (two-tone only)	16	Dark Carmel Firemist metallic[1]	32	Bright Yellow[2]	51
Ebony Black	19	Light Golden Carmel Firemist metallic[1]	33	Medium Gold metallic (two-tone only)	56
Pastel Blue[1]	21	Light Green metallic	44	Light Camel Beige	61
Light Blue metallic	22				

	Code		Code
Medium Camel metallic	63	Carmine Red metallic	77
Russet metallic	67	Dark Carmine Red metallic[1]	79
Dark Camel metallic	69		
Bright Red[2]	75		

In two-tone combinations, the first two digits indicate lower color and the next two digits are the upper color.

Two-tone paint available for $42 extra on Omega and Cutlass, and $51 extra on Delta 88. Firemist paints available for $165 extra. [1]Available on all models except Starfire and Omega. [2]Available only on Starfire and Omega.

Starfire

"The Starfire experience: Moving the body. And the mind."

Nameplate year of origin: 1954 (as designation for 98 convertible); 1961 (as series).
Current bodystyle lifespan: 1975 through 1980
Predecessor to this model: None.
Replacement for this model: Firenza (1982 to 1988).
Percentage of division's production: 1.71%.
Corporate siblings: Buick Skyhawk, Chevrolet Monza, and Pontiac Sunbird.
Primary competition: AMC Pacer and Ford Mustang II.
Notable changes: Minor trim and detail changes.
Major standard equipment: High-backed bucket seats in grained vinyl, folding rear seatback, plush-pile carpeting on all floor surfaces and rear seatback, deluxe steering wheel, door panel map pockets, simulated woodgrain I/P appliqué, I/P gauges including tachometer, dual speed wipers w/washers, chrome window surround and belt molding, manual front disc brakes, hubcaps, and B78 × 13 BSW tires. SX adds: Choice of velour brushed knit or soft vinyl high-back bucket seats, deluxe sport steering wheel w/brushed metal spokes and padded softgrip rim, chrome front and rear wheel lip moldings, bodyside striping, and BR78 × 13 BSW tires.

Measurements

Wheelbase	97.0"
Length	179.3"
Width	65.4"
Height	50.0"
Legroom — front	43.0"
Legroom — rear	29.6"
Headroom — front	37.7"
Headroom — rear	35.3"
Cargo capacity (cu. ft.)	23.4*
Fuel capacity (gals.)	18.5

With rear seat folded down.

Models Available

	Model No.	Base MSRP	Change from LY	Shipping Wt. (lbs.)	Model Year Production	Change from LY
Starfire 2-Door Hatchback Coupe	T07	$3,925	+3.24%	2786	9,265	+88.70%
Starfire SX 2-Door Hatchback Coupe	D07	$4,131	+3.28%	2790	8,056	-43.19%
TOTALS	*Avg. price*	$4,028	+3.26%		*Production* 17,321	-9.27%

Omega

"Let it be your declaration of independence."

Nameplate year of origin: 1973.
Current bodystyle lifespan: 1975 through 1979.
Predecessor to this model: Omega (1973 to 1974).
Replacement for this model: Omega (1980 to 1984).
Percentage of division's production: 4.93%.
Corporate siblings: Buick Skylark, Chevrolet Nova, and Pontiac Phoenix.
Primary competition: Dodge Aspen and Mercury Monarch.
Notable changes: Minor trim and detail changes.
Major standard equipment: Choice of all-vinyl or soft knit fabric front bench seat, cut-pile carpeting, simulated woodgrain I/P appliqués, door-operated dome lamps, dual speed wipers w/washers, chrome window surround moldings, chrome front and rear wheel opening moldings, full wheel covers, and E78 × 14 BSW tires. Hatchback model adds: Fold-down rear seat. Brougham adds: Choice of tailored brushed knit cloth or

Measurements

	Coupe & HBK	Sedan
Wheelbase	111.0"	111.0"
Length	199.6"	199.6"
Width	69.9"	69.9"
Height	53.2"	54.2"
Legroom — front	41.7"	41.7"
Legroom — rear	32.4"	35.2"
Headroom — front	38.2"	39.1"
Headroom — rear	36.7"	37.1"
Cargo capacity (cu. ft.)	14.2*	13.8
Fuel capacity (gals.)	21.0	21.0

Hatchback maximum, 12.9 cu. ft.; with rear seat down, 30.2 cu. ft.

patterned all-vinyl front bench seat, deluxe steering wheel, vinyl insert bodyside moldings, bright rocker panel molding, and stand-up hood ornament.

Models Available

	Model No.	Base MSRP	Change from LY	Shipping Wt. (lbs.)	Model Year Production	Change from LY
Omega 2-Door Coupe	B27	$3,973	+6.23%	3105	15,632	-16.01%
Omega 2-Door Hatchback	B17	$4,138	+5.97%	3171	4,084	-13.82%
Omega 4-Door Sedan	B69	$4,048	+6.61%	3143	19,478	-10.33%
Omega Brougham 2-Door Coupe	E27	$4,179	+6.23%	3126	3,798	-41.37%
Omega Brougham 4-Door Sedan	E69	$4,254	+6.51%	3167	7,125	-20.86%
TOTALS	Avg. price	$4,118	+6.27%		Production 50,117	-21.67%

Cutlass

"The beautiful new styling says a lot about your good taste. So does its practicality and value."

Nameplate year of origin: 1961 (as F-85 Deluxe sport coupe designation); 1962 (as F-85 sub-series); and 1965 (as series designation). Also used on 1955 Oldsmobile show car.

Current bodystyle lifespan: 1978 through 1988 (restyled in 1981).

Predecessor to this model: Cutlass (1973 to 1977).

Replacement for this model: Cutlass (1988 to 1997).

Percentage of division's production: 51.94%.

Corporate siblings: Buick Century/Regal, Chevrolet Malibu/Monte Carlo, and Pontiac LeMans/Grand Am/Grand Prix.

Primary competition: Dodge Diplomat and Mercury Cougar.

Notable changes: Completely redesigned.

Major standard equipment: Knit cloth front bench seat, cut-pile carpeting, two-spoke steering wheel, bright window surround moldings, adjustable rear vent windows (2-doors), fixed rear seat window w/swing-out rear quarter vent windows (4-door models), wheel lip moldings, rocker panel molding, wheel covers, and P185/75R14 BSW tires. Salon Brougham and Supreme add: Choice of cloth-and-vinyl or all-vinyl custom sport front bench seat w/fold-down center armrest, simulated woodgrain I/P appliqués, luxury door panels with door pull straps, fixed rear quarter window (Supreme), and stand-up hood ornament. Supreme Brougham adds: "Loose cushion" look velour with vinyl bolster 55/45 divided front seat w/fold down center armrest, deep-pile carpeting, wide rocker panel moldings, and deluxe wheel covers. Calais adds: Choice of brushed velour w/vinyl trim or soft all-vinyl reclining bucket seats, custom sport steering wheel, full gauge instrumentation including tachometer, specific front and rear stabilizer bars, and special-ratio steering gear. Cutlass Cruiser adds: All-vinyl front bench seat, cut-pile carpeting on passenger and cargo floors, fold-down rear seat, door pull straps, rear door fixed window w/opening quarter vent window, rear window liftgate w/drop-down tailgate, and P195/75R14 BSW tires.

Measurements

	Salon Coupes	Salon Sedans	Supreme & Calais	Wagon
Wheelbase	108.1"	108.1"	108.1"	108.1"
Length	197.7"	197.7"	200.1"	197.0"
Width	72.2"	72.2"	72.2"	72.2"
Height	53.3"	53.3"	54.2"	54.5"
Legroom — front	42.8"	42.8"	42.8"	42.8"
Legroom — rear	35.1"	38.0"	36.4"	36.2"
Headroom — front	37.9"	38.7"	37.9"	38.5"
Headroom — rear	38.2"	37.7"	38.1"	38.8"
Cargo capacity (cu. ft.)	16.1	16.1	16.1	71.8
Fuel capacity (gals.)	18.1	18.1	18.1	17.9

Models Available

	Model No.*	Base MSRP	Change from LY	Shipping Wt. (lbs.)	Model Year Production	Change from LY
Cutlass Salon 2-Door Coupe	G87	$4,408	+1.31%	3056	21,198	-69.78%
Cutlass Salon 4-Door Sedan	G09	$4,508	+2.76%	3070	29,509	-31.25%
Cutlass Salon Brougham 2-Door Coupe	J87	$4,696	+0.56%	3107	10,741	-95.58%

	Model No.*	Base MSRP	Change from LY	Shipping Wt. (lbs.)	Model Year Production	Change from LY
Cutlass Salon Brougham 4-Door Sedan	J09	$4,796	+1.31%	3121	21,902	-42.26%
Cutlass Cruiser 4-Door, 2-Seat Station Wagon	H35	$5,242	-0.02%	3213	44,617	+9.75%
Cutlass Supreme 2-Door Coupe	R47	$4,842	+3.68%	3161	240,917	-0.81%
Cutlass Supreme Brougham 2-Door Coupe	M47	$5,247	+5.59%	3138	117,880	-5.48%
Cutlass Calais 2-Door Coupe	K47	$5,196	-1.39%	3146	40,842	-28.04%
TOTALS		Avg. price $4,867	+0.72%		Production 527,606	-16.62%

*Model numbers were reassigned to new nameplates. See 1978 Oldsmobile introduction for details. Comparisons are made based on these changes.

Delta 88

*"If you're looking for a low-priced full-size car,
you're closer to Olds than you think."*

Nameplate year of origin: 1965 (88 series began in 1949).
Current bodystyle lifespan: 1977 through 1985.
Predecessor to this model: Delta 88 (1971 to 1976).
Replacement for this model: Delta 88 (1986 to 1991).
Percentage of division's production: 23.89%.
Corporate siblings: Buick LeSabre, Chevrolet Impala and Caprice, and Pontiac Catalina and Bonneville.
Primary competition: Chrysler Newport and Mercury Marquis.
Notable changes: Minor trim and detail changes.
Major standard equipment: Choice of nylon knit or all-vinyl front bench seat, cut-pile carpeting, cut-pile carpeting on lower door panels, deluxe steering wheel, simulated I/P woodgrain appliqué, electronic message center in I/P, courtesy and glove box lights, bright drip rail and window moldings, bright wheel opening and rocker panel moldings, front and rear bumper vinyl impact strips, stand-up hood ornament, full wheel covers, and FR78 × 15 BSW tires. Royale adds: Pleated velour Custom sport bench front seat w/fold-down center armrest, door pull straps, simulated woodgrain trim on door panels, glove box light, bright metal accented floor pedals, Royale ornamentation on C-pillar, and bodyside protective moldings.

Measurements

Wheelbase	116.0"
Length	217.5"
Width	76.8"
Height	55.7"
Legroom — front	42.4"
Legroom — rear	39.0"
Headroom — front	39.5"
Headroom — rear	38.2"
Cargo capacity (cu. ft.)	20.3
Fuel capacity (gals.)	21.0

1978

Models Available

	Model No.	Base MSRP	Change from LY	Shipping Wt. (lbs.)	Model Year Production	Change from LY
Delta 88 2-Door Coupe	L37	$5,483	+6.57%	3404	17,469	+98.78%
Delta 88 4-Door Town Sedan	L69	$5,559	+6.80%	3449	25,322	-2.92%
Delta 88 Royale 2-Door Coupe	N37	$5,707	+6.41%	3415	68,469	+11.99%
Delta 88 Royale 4-Door Town Sedan	N69	$5,807	+6.88%	3477	131,430	+11.79%
TOTALS		Avg. price $5,639	+6.67%		Production 242,690	+13.63%

Custom Cruiser

*"The full-size wagon that feels too luxurious,
too quiet, too easy to drive to be a wagon."*

Nameplate year of origin: 1971 (1940 as a designation on 90 series cars).
Current bodystyle lifespan: 1977 through 1990.
Predecessor to this model: Custom Cruiser (1971 to 1976).
Replacement for this model: Custom Cruiser (1991 to 1992).
Percentage of division's production: 3.40%.

Measurements

Wheelbase	116.0"
Length	216.7"
Width	77.2"
Height	57.0"

Corporate siblings: Buick Estate Wagon, Chevrolet Impala and Caprice, and Pontiac Catalina Safari and Grand Safari.

Primary competition: Mercury Marquis Colony Park.

Notable changes: Minor trim and detail changes.

Major standard equipment: Choice of velour or all-vinyl front bench seat w/fold-down center armrest, cut-pile carpeting on floors and cargo compartment floor, lower door panel carpeting, simulated I/P woodgrain appliqué, electronic message center in I/P, courtesy and glove box lights, cargo area light, bright drip rail and window moldings, bright wheel opening and rocker panel moldings, three-way tailgate, full wheel covers, and GR78 × 15 BSW tires.

Measurements (cont.)

Legroom — front	42.2"
Legroom — rear	38.4"
Headroom — front	39.1"
Headroom — rear	39.2"
Cargo capacity (cu. ft.)	87.0
Fuel capacity (gals.)	22.0

Models Available

	Model No.	Base MSRP	Change from LY	Shipping Wt. (lbs.)	Model Year Production	Change from LY
Custom Cruiser 4-Door, 2-S. Wagon	Q35	$6,324	+6.77%	4045	34,491	+5.07%
TOTALS	*Avg. price*	$6,324	+6.77%	*Production*	34,491	+5.07%

Ninety-Eight

"The thinking man's luxury car: Compare it to luxury cars costing thousands more — you'll readily see why."

Nameplate year of origin: 1941.

Current bodystyle lifespan: 1977 through 1984.

Predecessor to this model: Ninety-Eight (1971 to 1976).

Replacement for this model: Ninety-Eight (1985 to 1990).

Percentage of division's production: 11.69%.

Corporate siblings: Buick Electra 225, Cadillac deVille, and Cadillac Fleetwood Brougham.

Primary competition: Chrysler New Yorker and Mercury Grand Marquis.

Notable changes: Minor trim and detail changes.

Major standard equipment: Choice of Ogden nylon knit fabric or Doeskin vinyl front bench seat w/fold-down front and rear center armrests, cut-pile carpeting, carpeted lower door panels, door pull straps, driver's door armrest console, two-way power front seat, power windows, simulated woodgrain I/P trim, deluxe steering wheel, electronic message center in I/P, electric clock, wheel opening moldings, rocker panel molding, stand-up Oldsmobile crest hood ornament, bumper impact strips, wheel covers, and FR78 × 15 BSW tires. Regency adds: Velour 60/40 front seat button-tufted w/"loose" cushion look, front seatback pouches, six-way power adjustment for driver's side, digital clock, door-mounted entry courtesy lights, and fully-lined trunk compartment.

Measurements

Wheelbase	119.0"
Length	220.4"
Width	76.8"
Height	56.6"
Legroom — front	42.4"
Legroom — rear	40.1"
Headroom — front	39.5"
Headroom — rear	37.6"
Cargo capacity (cu. ft.)	20.3
Fuel capacity (gals.)	24.5

Models Available

	Model No.	Base MSRP	Change from LY	Shipping Wt. (lbs.)	Model Year Production	Change from LY
Ninety-Eight LS 2-Door Coupe	V37	$7,064	+6.88%	3753	2,956	-41.56%
Ninety-Eight LS 4-Door Sedan	V69	$7,241	+6.70%	3805	9,136	-36.21%
Ninety-Eight Regency 2-Door Coupe	X37	$7,427	+6.88%	3767	28,573	-10.91%
Ninety-Eight Regency 4-Door Sedan	X69	$7,611	+6.70%	3836	78,100	-11.22%
TOTALS	*Avg. price*	$7,336	+6.79%	*Production*	118,765	-14.82%

Toronado

*"Neither snow nor rain nor gloom of night intrudes
on the serene inner world of Toronado."*

Nameplate year of origin: 1966.
Current bodystyle lifespan: 1971 through 1978.
Predecessor to this model: Toronado (1966 to 1970).
Replacement for this model: Toronado (1979 to 1985).
Percentage of division's production: 2.44%.
Corporate siblings: Cadillac Eldorado.
Primary competition: Lincoln Continental Mark V.
Notable changes: Minor trim and detail changes.
Major standard equipment: Velour "loose-cushion" look 50/50 split front seat
  w/fold-down center armrest, rear seat fold-down center armrest, cut-pile carpeting,
  simulated woodgrain appliqué on I/P, two-spoke steering wheel, digital clock,
  chrome-accented floor pedals, Four-season air conditioning, LH remote-control rear
  view mirror, bright window opening moldings, bright rocker panel and wheel lip moldings, front bumper guards, front and rear
  bumper rub strips, color-coordinated bodyside protective moldings, chrome wheel covers, and JR78 × 15 BSW tires.

Measurements

Wheelbase	122.0"
Length	227.5"
Width	79.7"
Height	53.2"
Legroom — front	42.2"
Legroom — rear	35.2"
Headroom — front	37.7"
Headroom — rear	36.7"
Cargo capacity (cu. ft.)	17.0
Fuel capacity (gals.)	26.0

Models Available

	Model No.	Base MSRP	Change from LY	Shipping Wt. (lbs.)	Model Year Production	Change from LY
Toronado Brougham 2-Door Hardtop	Z57	$8,899	+9.40%	4624	24,815	-27.19%
TOTALS	*Avg. price*	$8,899	-7.62%	*Production*	24,815	-27.19%

PLYMOUTH

"Building cars for this big traveling country."

Plymouth entered the 1978 model year in an unusual position. Debuts of the all-new front-wheel-drive Horizon subcompact and a new captive import sports model, the Sapporo, named for the city in Japan where the 1972 Olympic winter games had been held, were bright spots. However, missing from the line was the full-size Gran Fury, leaving the aged mid-size Fury to carry the banner of top-of-the line Plymouth. To make matters worse, styling changes to the Volaré were minimal, and the rust-through issues of the 1976 and 1977 models had become such a huge problem that all of the first two years' cars were recalled, making consumers wary of the Volaré. To top it all off, every model remaining in the Plymouth line, save the imported Arrow, was duplicated model for model, at nearly the same pricing, in the Dodge lineup. The end result was that every line dropped 25 percent or more in production, though the new Horizon's contribution of about 95,000 additional units helped keep the overall drop in model year sales down to about 15 percent. It is worth noting that the Horizon outsold the Dodge Omni by almost 25,000 cars for its initial season, proving that Plymouth could still sell cars.

The new subcompact Horizon and its virtual twin the Dodge Omni took the car buying public by surprise. The new "L-body" cars, sometimes referred to jointly as the "Omnirizon," were the first high production front-wheel-drive cars with transverse-mounted 4-cylinder engines ever assembled in America. They were also Chrysler Corporation's first "metric" cars, with most fasteners being in metric sizes. Available initially only as a 4-door hatchback, the Horizon seemed to copy a lot of the design features of its main competitor, the Volkswagen Rabbit. In fact, the foundation of the Horizon engine was a short block 1.7 liter 4-cylinder engine purchased from Volkswagen and modified to Chrysler specifications. Modifications included different exhaust manifolds and engine mounts to fit the Horizon, as well as the addition of Chrysler's own Electronic Lean Burn fuel system. The engine was mated to either the standard 4-speed manual or the optional A404 automatic transmission, a new Chrysler automatic designed for front-wheel-drive applications, and resulted in the highest gas mileage car in Plymouth history.

The Horizon exterior design was quite similar to the popular VW Rabbit. "Boxy looking" best described the overall look. A nearly invisible lower body feature line ran between the wheel openings, and a full-length indentation began at the top of the parking lamp/turn signal bezel, running straight to the top of the taillight bezel. This indentation served as the location of trim to defining the top edge of the bodyside color on Horizons that had two-tone paint; the trim strip also appeared on cars with the optional Premium package, with or without the simulated woodgrain bodyside appliqués. Positioned between single square headlamps was an egg-crate grille divided into two sections horizontally and carrying a Plymouth logo in the center. Parking and turn signal lamps were mounted at each end and wrapped around the front fender edge to serve as side marker lights. At the rear of a broad C-pillar, the rear hatchback slanted downwards, parallel to the rear edge of the back door, until it met the bodyside indentation, where it turned downwards to meet the vertical rear panel. The rear panel housed the license tag in an indentation between the square wraparound taillamps which were divided into three sections, with the larger outer section being the red taillight and stoplights, and a smaller horizontally divided section to the inside carrying the backup lights on bottom, and amber turn signal light on top.

The Horizon interior was quite roomy for a subcompact car. Front bucket seats and a fold-down rear bench seat were standard features. The instrument panel was of a simple design, with a pod directly in front of the driver housing essential gauges and a strip across the lower panel housing the light switch to the left and radio and ventilation controls in the middle. The turn signal stalk also controlled the wipers and headlight dimmer. The basic Horizon looked very plain inside, with flat panel upholstery and relatively plain door panels. The Custom package added stitched patterns to the seats and some padded features to the upper door panel. Moving up to the Premium package added lower door panel carpeting and upper padding to the door panel, full-width simulated woodgrain appliqués on the dash, and embossed vinyl or suedelike cloth seats with reclining seatbacks. One could equip the Horizon to any degree of economy or convenience desired.

Volaré received a new oversized egg-crate grille design and a new undecorated parking/turn signal light lens. At the rear of all but wagon models were new, slightly enlarged horizontally mounted rectangular taillamps. Each taillight was broken vertically into three sections, with the backup lamp toward the inside, the center portion split into an amber turn signal and a red taillight/brake light lens, and the outermost portion being a red reflector. Trim on the taillight unit varied with option packages selected. The model lineup was simplified this year, with the former Custom and Premier models becoming option packages. The Custom package added chrome trim around the turn signal and brake light, making them appear smaller. The Premier package added a wide stainless trim molding to the rear panel area between the taillight bezels, with the Plymouth name in block letters.

Chrysler this year attempted to recapture its prior performance heritage, using the Volaré coupe as the basis for some very special sporty coupes collectively advertised as "The Fun Runners." There were five basic variations, beginning with the Funrunner package and Funrunner décor package. Next was the Road Runner package and its related Road Runner décor package, both of which existed in prior years. Next up the price ladder was the Road Runner "Front Runner" Sport Pak package, then the "Street Kit" package that paid homage to NASCAR driver Richard Petty, who famously drove many Dodge and Plymouth models to victory lane during the past 15 years, and finally a "Super Coupe" package that came only in a dark russet color with black hood and trim, along with wheel flares and spoilers. Production of each package amounted to less than 5 percent of Volaré Coupe production with 1,357 units having the Road Runner package, 617 with the Road Runner Sport Pak package, 494 with the Super Coupe package, and 247 with the Street Kit package. A detail of package contents for each is included in Appendix IV. Also technically a part of the "Fun Runner" advertising theme was the "Sun Runner" duo that was basically any Volaré coupe with the optional sunroof or T-Bar roof.

The mid-size Fury series took the position of Plymouth's full-size car line with the Gran Fury series having been discontinued at the end of the 1977 model year. This essentially meant the Fury would have to compete with GM's downsized line of full-size cars, while the Volaré competed with both GM's compact and newly downsized mid-size models in what would be a losing battle. No styling changes were made for the Fury's 1978 season, which would be the last for the eight-year-old mid-size body. Under the hood a revised TorqueFlite automatic transmission with a direct-drive lock-up torque converter clutch helped improve fuel economy and was standard with all V8s, as well as most 6-cylinder Fury and Volaré models.

The imported Plymouth line boasted a new sport coupe named Sapporo. Sharing its platform with the Dodge Challenger and Dodge Colt station wagon, the Sapporo was a well-equipped, sporty pillarless hardtop with the highest price of any Plymouth for 1978. Exterior styling featured a horizontal bar grille with dual rectangular headlights at each end, while at the back three-section taillights were set in a wraparound band of simulated chrome. Bodylines and feature lines were quite angular in contrast to the large wraparound rear window. A targa style chrome band with opera lights was used behind the rear quarter windows that retracted in true hardtop fashion, and a canopy style vinyl roof was standard equipment. Inside, the Sapporo had a Japanese take on the American "driver's cockpit" design with all gauges in round tunneled portals. Under the hood was either of two Mitsubishi-built Silent Shaft 4-cylinder engines, a standard 1.6 liter or optional 2.6 liter, with 5-speed manual or optional TorqueFlite automatic transmission. The Arrow hatchback coupe continued to be available, and offered up few changes except for new color choices, new bodyside tape graphics for the Arrow GT, and a new "Arrow Jet" decal and paint package.

Arrow 2-Door Hatchback

**Arrow GT 2-Door Hatchback
with Arrow Jet package**

**Fury 2-Door Hardtop (front)
and Fury 4-Door Sedan (rear)**

Fury Sport Suburban 4-Door Station Wagon

Fury Sport 2-Door Hardtop Coupe

**Horizon 4-Door Hatchback
with Custom Exterior package**

**Horizon 4-Door Hatchback
with Premium woodgrain package**

Sapporo 2-Door Hardtop

**Volaré 2-Door Coupe with Super Coupe package
(front) and Road Runner package (rear)**

**Volaré 4-Door Sedan
with Premier Exterior package**

Sapporo interior

1978

Volaré 4-Door Station Wagon
with Premier Exterior woodgrain package

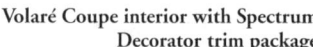

Volaré Coupe interior with Spectrum
Decorator trim package

Model year production: 383,935, down 16.30% from 1977.

Domestic market share: 4.04% (8th place).

Base price range: $3,771 to $5,688.

Plymouth average base price: $4,587, up 1.79%.

Introduction date: October 7, 1977. Horizon introduced January 1978.

Assembly plants: Lynch Road, Detroit, MI (A); Hamtramck, MI (B); Belvidere, IL (D); Newark, DE (F). *Arrow:* Kurashiki, Okayama, Japan (code 1 through 9). *Sapporo:* Okazaki, Aichi, Japan (code 1 through 9).

Data plate identification (VIN): Thirteen digit code read as follows: First four digits indicate series and body style (model number in model charts); fifth digit indicates engine code (see powertrain chart); sixth digit indicates year (8 = 1978); seventh digit indicates assembly plant (see list above); remaining digits are sequential with beginning numbers of 100001. *Example:* HL41C8A100001 is a 1978 Plymouth Volaré 4-Door Sedan, with 225 CID, 1-bbl. 6-cylinder engine, serial number 100001, built in Detroit, MI.

Powertrains

Engine	Net HP	Engine Code	Transmission Availability[1]		Arrow	Sapporo	Horizon	Volaré	Fury[2]
97.5 CID (1.6L) OHC, 2-bbl., 4-cyl.	83	K	5-speed manual		S	S	—	—	—
				MPG:	29/39/33	29/40/33	—	—	—
				Calif.	27/38/31	26/35/30	—	—	—
			3-speed Automatic		$323	$323	—	—	—
				MPG:	29/38/32	27/35/30	—	—	—
				Calif.	28/36/31	25/32/28	—	—	—
104.7 CID (1.7L) OHC, 2-bbl., 4-cyl.	75	A	4-speed manual		—	—	S	—	—
				MPG:	—	—	25/38/29	—	—
				Calif.	—	—	24/35/28	—	—
			3-speed Torque Flite automatic		—	—	$303	—	—
				MPG:	—	—	23/31/26	—	—
				Calif.	—	—	22/28/24	—	—
122 CID (2.0L) OHC, 2-bbl., 4-cyl.	96	U	5-speed manual		$60	—	—	—	—
				MPG:	27/36/31	—	—	—	—
				Calif.	25/36/29	—	—	—	—
			3-speed Automatic		$383	—	—	—	—
				MPG:	24/31/27	—	—	—	—
				Calif.	25/31/28	—	—	—	—
158.6 CID (2.6L) OHC, 2-bbl., 4-cyl.	96	F	5-speed manual		—	$419	—	—	—
				MPG:	—	24/35/28	—	—	—
				Calif.	—	22/33/26	—	—	—
			3-speed Automatic		—	$419	—	—	—
				MPG:	—	22/28/24	—	—	—
				Calif.	—	21/26/23	—	—	—
225 CID (3.7L), 1-bbl., 6-cyl.	100	C	3-speed manual[3]		—	—	—	S (cars)	—
				MPG:	—	—	—	20/29/23	—

Engine	Net HP	Engine Code	Transmission Availability[1]	Arrow	Sapporo	Horizon	Volaré	Fury[2]
			"Overdrive4" 4-speed manual	—	—	—	$142[4]	—
			MPG:	—	—	—	NA	—
			3-speed Torque Flite automatic	—	—	—	$293 (cars)	—
			MPG:	—	—	—	20/27/23	—
			Calif.	—	—	—	14/19/16	—
225 CID (3.7L) Super Six, 2-bbl., 6-cyl.[3]	110	D	3-speed manual[3]	—	—	—	S (wgns.)/$41 (cars)	S (cars)
			MPG:	—	—	—	18/28/21	18/25/20
			3-speed Torque Flite automatic	—	—	—	$293 (wgns.)/$334 (cars)	$320 (cars)
			MPG:	—	—	—	18/25/21	17/22/19
			Calif.	—	—	—	14/19/16	—
318 CID (5.2L), 2-bbl., V8[3]	140	G	3-speed manual[3]	—	—	—	$129 (wgns.)/$170 (cars)	$176 (cars)
			MPG:	—	—	—	15/25/18	NA
			"Overdrive4" 4-speed manual[3]	—	—	—	$312[4]	—
			MPG:	—	—	—	NA	—
			3-speed Torque Flite automatic	—	—	—	$426 (wgns.)/$467 (cars)	$496 (cars)
			MPG:	—	—	—	15/22/18	14/21/16
318 CID (5.2L), 4-bbl., V8[5]	155	H	3-speed Torque Flite automatic	—	—	—	$469 (wgns.)/$510 (cars)	$541 (cars)[6]
			Calif.	—	—	—	14/22/16	13/21/16
360 CID (5.9L), 2-bbl., V8[3]	155	K	3-speed Torque Flite automatic	—	—	—	$536 (wgns.)/$572[7]	S (wgns.)/$605 (cars)
			MPG:	—	—	—	15/22/17	14/22/17
360 CID (5.9L), 4-bbl., V8[8]	175	J,L	3-speed Torque Flite automatic	—	—	—	$760[4]	$45 (wgns.)[5,6]/$775 (cars)[5]
			MPG:	—	—	—	10/17/13	10/17/13
			Calif.	—	—	—	12/15/13	12/19/14
400 CID (6.6L), 4-bbl., V8[8]	190	N	3-speed Torque Flite automatic	—	—	—	—	$94 (wgns.)/$829 (cars)
			MPG:	—	—	—	—	13/20/15
			Calif.	—	—	—	—	11/19/14

[1]Unless otherwise noted: All transmissions are column-shifts, except on Arrow, Sapporo, Horizon, or any model w/4-speed manual. Floor-shift is available on any Volaré Coupe or Fury Sport hardtop in combination with other required equipment.   [2]Although not listed, the 440 CID V8 engines were still available for order in special applications on Fury models.   [3]Not available in California or designated high altitude areas.   [4]Available on coupes only with other required equipment.   [5]Available only in California or designated high altitude areas.   [6]Required as standard equipment in California and designated high altitude areas, with appropriate adjustment in price.   [7]Available on sedans only.   [8]Includes electronic "Lean Burn" system on Volaré w/360 CID V8, and all with 400 CID V8s.

Major Options

	Arrow	Sapporo	Horizon	Volaré	Fury
Air conditioning	$493	$471	$493	$484	$563
Tilt steering wheel	S	S	—	$65	$74

	Arrow	Sapporo	Horizon	Volaré	Fury
Automatic speed control	—	—	—	$86	$99
Electric rear window defroster	$94[1]	S	$80	$83	$94
Tinted glass, all windows	S	S	$56	$53	$65
Dual remote control sport mirrors	—	S	$46	$46	$58
Power windows, 2-dr./4-dr.	—	$[2]	—	$113/$157	$129/$179
Power door locks, 2-dr./4-dr.	—	—	—	$71/$98	$83/$116
Power seat, bench	—	—	—	$147	$160
AM radio	$[3]	—	S	$74	$81
AM/FM stereo	$[3]	$	$143	$217	$237
AM/FM stereo w/8-track tape	—	—	—	$308	$336
Front bucket seats w/console	S[4]	S	S[4]	$157[4]	$58[4]
Vinyl top, full[5]	$92	S	$93	$93	$121
T-Bar roof	—	—	—	$572	—
Power steering, standard w/V8s	—	S	$148	$145	$159
Power brakes, w/front disc	S	S	$68	$66	S
Deluxe wheel covers	—	—	—	$36	$39
Premium wheel covers	—	S	—	$71	—
Wire wheel covers	—	—	—	$127	$138
Rallye road wheels	$	—	$73	$72	—
Chrome-styled road wheels	—	—	—	$127	$126[6]
White sidewall tires, std. size	$	S	$16	$42	$48

Popular Option Groups & Packages

	Arrow	Sapporo	Horizon	Volaré	Fury
Arrow Jet package	$240	—	—	—	—
Basic group	—	—	—	$655	$739
Basic package	—	$591	—	—	—
Custom exterior package	—	—	$71	$86	—
Custom interior package	—	—	$82	$224	—
Deluxe Insulation package	—	—	—	$38	$66
Funrunner package	—	—	—	$77	—
Funrunner décor package	—	—	—	$180	—
Light package	—	—	$44	$44	$51
Popular equipment group	—	—	$250	—	—
Premier exterior package	—	—	—	$138	—
Premier interior package	—	—	—	$483	—
Premium exterior package	—	—	$167	—	—
Premium interior package	—	—	$242	—	—
Premium woodgrain exterior pkg.	—	—	$312	$221[7]	—
Premium package	—	$486	—	—	—
Protection group	—	—	—	$35	—
Road Runner décor group	—	—	—	$51	—
Road Runner Sport Pak[8]	—	—	—	$499	—
Road Runner package	—	—	—	$294	—
Spectrum decorator trim package	—	—	—	$160	—
Street Kit package	—	—	—	$1,085	—
Super Coupe package	—	—	—	$1,417	—
Two-tone decor package	—	—	$107	$62	—

— = Not Available; S = Standard equipment. [1]Electric rear window defroster is standard on GS and GT. [2]Available only as part of the Premium package. [3]AM radio not available on GT, and AM/FM radio (non-stereo) is available only on GT. [4]Available on Volaré coupe and Fury Sport only. Bucket seats only are standard on Horizon with price shown for console only. Bucket seats and console are standard on Arrow GT, and on Arrow and Arrow GS models they are standard, but without an available console. [5]Canopy vinyl roof on Sapporo. Volaré Landau top on 2-door models is $164. Canopy vinyl roof on Fury 2-Doors is $100. Not available on Arrow GT or station wagons. [6]Aluminum fascia road wheels on Fury. [7]Called Premier exterior woodgrain package and available only on Volaré wagon. [8]Requires Road Runner package and dual remote-control racing mirrors.

Paint Colors

Plymouth	Code	Plymouth	Code	Plymouth	Code
Spinnaker White	EW1	Yellow Blaze[2]	KY5	Caramel Tan metallic[2,3]	MU3
Golden Fawn[1]	KY4	Spanish Gold metallic[1]	LY9	Spitfire Orange[2,4]	MV1

Plymouth	Code	Plymouth	Code	Plymouth	Code
Wedgewood Blue[1]	PB2	Classic Cream[3]	RY3	Medium Gray metallic[8]	096
Cadet Blue metallic[1,3]	PB3	Formal Black	TX9		
Regatta Blue metallic[2]	PB6				
Starlight Blue Sunfire metallic[4]	PB9	*Arrow & Sapporo*	Code		
Light Mocha Tan[2,3]	PT2	Green	006		
Jasmine Yellow[1]	PY1	Black	015		
Pewter Gray metallic	RA2	Bright Blue metallic	022		
Charcoal Gray Sunfire metallic[5]	RA9	Warm White	061		
Mint Green metallic	RF3	Caramel Tan metallic	063		
Augusta Green Sunfire metallic	RF9	Spitfire Orange	073		
Citron metallic[2,3,6]	RJ3	Flat Black[7]	074		
Sunrise Orange[2]	RK2	Bright Yellow	090		
Brite Canyon Red[1,3]	RR4	Bright Silver metallic	093		
Tapestry Red Sunfire metallic	RR7	Canyon Red metallic[8]	094		
Crimson Red Sunfire metallic[5]	RR9	Ballast Sand metallic[9]	095		
Sable Tan Sunfire metallic[5]	RT9				

Single tones are coded EW1, EW1. Two-tones are coded on body ID plate as TX9, EW1 where three digits on line 2 are lower body color, and three digits on line 3 are upper body color or two-tone color. [1]Available only on Fury. [2]Available only on Horizon. [3]Available only on Volaré. [4]High-impact color designed primarily for use on Volaré Coupes. [5]For two-tone combinations on Horizon and Volaré only—Charcoal Gray (a.k.a. Dark Silver Metallic) with Pewter Gray, and Crimson Red with Tapestry Red. Sable Tan with Caramel Tan is for Horizon only. [6]Not available on Volaré wagon. [7]Available only as accent color with Arrow Jet package. [8]Available only on Sapporo. [9]Available on both Arrow and Sapporo.

Arrow

"Me and my Arrow."

Nameplate year of origin: 1976.
Current bodystyle lifespan: 1976 through 1980.
Predecessor to this model: None.
Replacement for this model: Champ (1979 to 1983).
Primary competition: AMC Gremlin and Chevrolet Chevette.
Notable changes: Minor trim and detail changes.
Major standard equipment: All-vinyl front bucket seats w/reclining seatbacks, folding rear seat, black I/P trim, tilt steering column, two-speed electric windshield wipers, cigarette lighter, heater and defroster, tinted glass, black painted grille, argent painted bumpers, front and rear window moldings, drip rail moldings, power front disc brakes, and 6.00 × 13 BSW tires. GS adds: All-vinyl front bucket seats w/reclining seatbacks, woodtone I/P trim, full-floor carpeting including cargo area, ashtray light, trip odometer, right roof rail assist grip, flipper rear quarter windows, rear panel trim molding, rocker panel sill moldings, wheel lip molding, chrome plated bumpers, GS bodyside tape stripes, and styled road wheels. GT adds: Black and white checkmate cloth buckets seats w/reclining seatbacks, floor console w/ammeter, oil pressure gauge and coin holder, rally gauge cluster w/tachometer, overhead console for dome and map lights, and warning lights, soft-rim sports style steering wheel, dual body-color sport mirrors, GT lower body tape stripes, and 165SR × 13 R/WL tires.

Measurements

Wheelbase	92.1"
Length	167.3"
Width	63.4"
Height	51.0"
Legroom — front	41.7"
Legroom — rear	28.0"
Headroom — front	36.8"
Headroom — rear	34.4"
Cargo capacity (cu. ft.)	17.3
Fuel capacity (gals.)	13.2

Models Available

	Model No.	Base MSRP	Change from LY	Shipping Wt. (lbs.)	Model Year Sales*	Change from LY
Arrow 2-Door Hatchback Coupe	7L24	$4,206	+24.47%	2175	NA	NA
Arrow GS 2-Door Hatchback Coupe	7H24	$4,541	+24.27%	2180	NA	NA
Arrow GT 2-Door Hatchback Coupe	7P24	$5,199	+26.87%	2175	NA	NA
TOTALS	*Avg. price*	$4,649	+25.29%	*Production*	28,296	-45.43%

*Model year sales by trim level is not available.

Sapporo

"The new sophisticated car from Plymouth."

Nameplate year of origin: 1978.
Current bodystyle lifespan: 1978 through 1983.
Predecessor to this model: None.
Replacement for this model: Conquest (1984 to 1989 — sold under Chrysler name, 1987–1989).
Primary competition: Chevrolet Monza, Ford Mustang II, and Pontiac Sunbird.
Notable changes: All-new model. Sold also as the Dodge Challenger.
Major standard equipment: Pleated cloth front bucket seats w/reclining seatbacks and lumbar support, easy entrance passenger seat w/memory, loop pile carpeting, center floor console, door trim panels w/knit inserts, door armrests w/integral door pull, assist grips, dome and interior spot lamps, overhead console w/digital clock and warning lights, vanity mirror, two-spoke sport steering wheel, tilt steering column, I/P cluster w/trip odometer, tachometer, temperature, fuel, oil, and electrical gauges, tinted glass, rear window defogger, dual power color-keyed racing mirrors, canopy vinyl roof w/wrap-over stainless targa band, rear sail panel opera lamps, drip rail and belt moldings, front and rear window moldings, decklid moldings, vinyl bodyside moldings, front and rear bumper guards, premium wheel covers, and 195HR × 14 WSW tires.

Measurements

Wheelbase	99.0"
Length	183.1"
Width	66.7"
Height	51.8"
Legroom — front	40.6"
Legroom — rear	32.5"
Headroom — front	36.4"
Headroom — rear	35.0"
Cargo capacity (cu. ft.)	10.4
Fuel capacity (gals.)	15.2

Models Available

	Model No.	Base MSRP	Change from LY	Shipping Wt. (lbs.)	Model Year Sales*	Change from LY
Sapporo 2-Door Luxury Hardtop	3H29	$6,087	NEW	2455	14,183	NEW
TOTALS	*Avg. price*	$6,087	NEW	*Production*	14,183	NEW

*Model year production is not available.

Horizon

"New confidence. New comfort. A new kind of car for America. Discover a new Horizon."

Nameplate year of origin: 1978.
Current bodystyle lifespan: 1978 through 1990.
Predecessor to this model: None.
Replacement for this model: None.
Percentage of division's sales volume: 24.96%.
Corporate siblings: Dodge Omni.
Primary competition: Chevrolet Chevette and Ford Fiesta.
Notable changes: All-new model.
Major standard equipment: Vinyl front high-back bucket seats, molded color-keyed headlining, color-keyed cut-pile carpeting, door trim panels w/front and rear armrests, three-spoke steering wheel, fold-down rear seat, folding rear shelf security panel, AM radio, day/night inside rear view mirror, bright windshield and liftgate window accents, bright grille, headlight and taillight accents, bright aluminum front and rear bumper face bars w/rub strips, manual front disc brakes, argent colored styled sport road wheels, and P155/80R × 13 WSW tires.

Measurements

Wheelbase	99.2"
Length	163.2"
Width	66.2"
Height	53.4"
Legroom — front	41.8"
Legroom — rear	33.0"
Headroom — front	38.3"
Headroom — rear	37.4"
Cargo capacity (cu. ft.)	10.2*
Fuel capacity (gals.)	13.0

*With rear seat folded down, 35.8.

Models Available

	Model No.	Base MSRP	Change from LY	Shipping Wt. (lbs.)	Model Year Production	Change from LY
Horizon 4-Door Hatchback	ML44	$3,976	NEW	2145	95,817	NEW
TOTALS	Avg. price	$3,976	NEW	Production	95,817	NEW

Volaré

"The accent is on comfort and styling!"

Nameplate year of origin: 1976.
Current bodystyle lifespan: 1976 through 1980.
Predecessor to this model: Valiant (1967 to 1976).
Replacement for this model: Reliant (1981 to 1989).
Percentage of division's production: 56.73%.
Corporate siblings: Dodge Aspen.
Primary competition: AMC Concord, Chevrolet Nova, and Ford Granada.
Notable changes: Minor trim and detail changes.
Major standard equipment: All-vinyl low-back front bench seat, color-keyed carpeting, three-spoke steering wheel, two-speed electric windshield wipers and washers, front ashtray, bright grille surround molding, roof drip rail molding, quarter window reveal moldings, windshield and backlight moldings, front sway bar, and D78 × 14 BSW tires. Wagon adds: Rear liftgate, cargo area stowage bins, power front disc brakes, heavy-duty suspension, and F78 × 14 BSW tires.

Measurements

	Coupe	Sedan	Wagon
Wheelbase	108.7"	112.7"	112.7"
Length	197.2"	201.2"	201.2"
Width	73.3"	73.3"	73.3"
Height	53.3"	55.3"	55.7"
Legroom — front	42.5"	42.5"	42.5"
Legroom — rear	31.7"	36.6"	36.6"
Headroom — front	37.4"	39.2"	39.2"
Headroom — rear	35.9"	37.5"	38.7"
Cargo capacity (cu. ft.)	14.8	14.8	73.1
Fuel capacity (gals.)	18.0	18.0	19.5

1978

Models Available

	Model No.	Base MSRP	Change from LY	Shipping Wt. (lbs.)	Model Year Production	Change from LY
Volaré 2-Door Sport Coupe	HL29	$3,771	+5.63%	3140	61,702	+91.24%
Volaré 4-Door Sedan	HL41	$3,899	+7.74%	3175	85,365	+132.68%
Volaré 4-Door Station Wagon	HL45	$4,241	+7.61%	3405	70,728	-0.26%
TOTALS	Avg. price	$3,970	+0.47%	Production	217,795	-33.55%

Fury

"Fury is a tomorrow car with comfort and engineering features for today. It's a big car at a small price."

Nameplate year of origin: 1956. Applied to mid-size platform for 1975.
Current bodystyle lifespan: 1971 through 1978.
Predecessor to this model: Satellite (1971 to 1974).
Replacement for this model: Caravelle (1985 to 1988).
Percentage of division's sales volume: 18.32%.
Corporate siblings: Dodge Monaco.
Primary competition: AMC Matador, Chevrolet Malibu, and Ford LTD II.
Notable changes: Minor trim and detail changes.

Measurements

	2-Doors	4-Doors	Wagons
Wheelbase	114.9"	117.4"	117.5"
Length	213.2"	218.0"	225.1"
Width	77.7"	77.7"	78.8"
Height	52.9"	54.3"	56.9"
Legroom — front	42.6"	42.6"	42.6"
Legroom — rear	32.1"	34.9"	34.4"
Headroom — front	37.7"	38.7"	39.6"

Major standard equipment: Regency cloth-and-vinyl front bench seat, color-keyed carpeting, cigarette lighter, dome light, lockable glove box, concealed two-speed windshield wipers w/washers, rocker panel sill molding, decklid lower molding (coupe), bumper guards, hubcaps, and F78 × 15 BSW tires. Fury Sport and Salon add: Velour-and-vinyl front bench seat w/fold-down center armrest, shag carpeting, premium door trim panels w/pull handles, simulated wood-grain inserts on I/P, door trim inserts and steering wheel,

Measurements

	2-Doors	4-Doors	Wagons
Headroom — rear	36.6"	37.3"	39.7"
Cargo capacity (cu. ft.)	14.7	19.7	85.5*
Fuel capacity (gals.)**	20.5	20.5	20.0

*Plus 5.2 cu.ft. of concealed space on 2-seat station wagons.   **25.5 gallon fuel capacity on cars equipped with a V8 engine.*

Sport ornamentation on C-pillar of coupe, Salon ornamentation on decklid and C-pillar of sedan, belt moldings, upper door frame molding (Salon only), bodyside tape stripes (Sport only), hood ornament, hood rear edge molding, and dual horns. Suburban wagon adds: Fold-down rear seatback, power front disc brakes, three-way tailgate, and H78 × 15 BSW tires. Sport Suburban wagon adds: All-vinyl split-back front bench seat w/fold-down center armrest, cargo compartment carpeting and dome light, and exterior simulated woodgrained bodyside overlays and tailgate trim.

Models Available

	Model No.	Base MSRP	Change from LY	Shipping Wt. (lbs.)	Model Year Production	Change from LY
Fury 2-Door Hardtop	RL23	$4,236	+8.81%	3600	9,473	-20.46%
Fury 4-Door Sedan	RL41	$4,326	+9.69%	3635	28,245	+40.50%
Fury Suburban 4-Door, 2-S. Wagon	RL45	$5,084	+8.47%	4310	3,328	-40.85%
Fury Suburban 4-Door, 3-S. Wagon	RL46	$5,227	+8.22%	4370	3,342	-34.99%
Fury Sport 2-Dr. Hardtop	RH23	$4,483	+8.49%	3610	9,736	-60.07%
Fury Salon 4-Door Sedan	RH41	$4,568	+9.15%	3645	12,976	-41.52%
Fury Sport Suburban 4-Door, 2-S. Wagon	RH45	$5,545	+6.80%	4300	1,106	-39.46%
Fury Sport Suburban 4-Door, 3-S. Wagon	RH46	$5,688	+6.62%	4375	2,117	-41.74%
TOTALS	*Avg. price*	$4,895	+8.17%	*Production*	70,323	-25.83%

PONTIAC

"The Best Year Yet."

Pontiac's "best year yet" theme was meant to capture the excitement generated by last year's new full-size models and the sales increases achieved by the hot-selling Grand Prix and Trans Am models, in hopes of maintaining the success with the introduction of an all-new mid-size lineup, now smaller, lighter, better handling, and more fuel efficient. For the most part the mission was successful, with sales of the LeMans line up more than 30 percent over last year. For whatever reason, the Firebird line, led by the increasingly popular Trans Am, recorded another solid gain for the year. However, the newly downsized Grand Prix's production was down, and the reborn Grand Am performed at a lower than expected level. No doubt some of the downturn was due to the new models having less power and more angular styling than their more successful predecessors, but at least the Grand Prix was still maintaining production of more than 200,000 units, which meant the 1978 version would still be in the top

three best selling years ever for the personal/luxury coupe. And overall, Pontiac would end the model year with a production total easily within its top five ever.

The newly downsized LeMans models shared their conventional notchback coupe and sedan body design with the Chevrolet Malibu, rather than using the fastback Buick and Oldsmobile design. The former Colonnade hardtop styling was gone, and lighter engines were employed, allowing the new models to be around 600 pounds lighter than their predecessors, and more than a foot shorter in overall length. The styling of the greenhouse area on the new models was of a fairly traditional design with a gently slanting rear roofline, but not the near "fastback" style of the prior models. Two-door models used a large fixed rear quarter window, while four-doors used fixed rear door windows with pivoting rear quarter windows to provide ventilation, creating a six-window sedan appearance not totally unlike their immediate predecessors. Station wagons also used a fixed rear door window, but included a small opening vent window within the rear portion of the door window. The LeMans Safari station wagons employed a "new" tailgate design featuring a drop-down tailgate and lift-up full-glass window supported by hydraulic struts. It could not be considered a completely new idea, as it was the same tailgate design as used on Pontiac station wagons up through the 1958 model year. The prior generation's bodyside "pontoon" styling was gone replaced by flatter and more basic lines. An upper body feature line began on the front fenders, and ran straight back along the beltline to the bottom rear corner of the side quarter window, where it turned back to angle up along the rear edge of the window, fading away by the time it reached the top. The lower bodyside line ran straight along the body from the top edge of the front bumper to the top edge of the rear bumper, creating a flare as it passed over the rounded wheel openings. On the Grand LeMans, the lower line also served as the location of the lower body stainless trim which connected to the chrome colored vinyl bumper rub strips, creating a chrome trim line that encompassed the car. This line served as the lower trim line for the Grand LeMans Safari with woodgrain trim, and the breaking point for accent two-tone paint on Grand Am models.

The new LeMans models featured a wide, pointed body-colored center panel up front that created the traditional Pontiac split grille theme. All LeMans and Grand Am models used a one-piece body-colored urethane front bumper and header panel, and all but the station wagons used body-colored urethane rear bumpers, with the previously mentioned chrome colored vinyl rub strips used on the body-colored bumpers. Station wagons had a traditional chrome box-type rear bumper with a black rub strip. Overall the front-end design was bolt upright with only the center "point" breaking the otherwise flat appearance, not totally unlike the 1976–1977 LeMans front end. The split grille of all models consisted of a three by three horizontal crosshatch pattern per side, with each opening housing five vertical bars, and the parking/turn signal light placed behind the center row of the outer column and adjacent to the new single square headlights. Side marker and turn signal lights were housed on the fender side of the headlight bezel with two horizontal chrome trim strips across the lens. At the rear, full-width wraparound taillights, separated by the center mounted license plate, were divided into three sections horizontally by chrome trim strips, and had an inward mounted backup light, with a red brake light next to that, a centrally located amber turn signal lens, then an outer combination brake light and taillight red lens that wrapped around the rear quarter panel end to include the side marker light. Taillights on station wagons were similar to those used on the other mid-size GM station wagons, with horizontal taillights mounted within the outer ends of the rear bumper.

Grand Am coupes and sedans returned to the mid-size line after a two-year absence. Hoping to bring back the touring car appeal created by the original model, Pontiac greatly missed the mark by making this generation of Grand Am too similar in design and content to not only the Grand Prix, but also the LeMans. In other words, there was nothing unique about this Grand Am other than its front-end design and two-tone accent paint. As for its front end design, the Grand Am featured a sloping body-colored urethane fascia with integrated bumper and a pointed center feature carrying the Pontiac "arrow" or dart emblem. The grille consisted of five vertical openings per side, divided by body-colored strips, with each opening housing twelve horizontal bars. Single square headlamps were set into chrome bezels, with horizontal parking/turn signal lights placed below the headlights, and side marker and turn signal lights mounted vertically on the fender side of the headlight bezel.

The new Grand Prix incorporated elements of last year's styling into an angular and formal looking design. The prior car's pointed hood and decklid design were gone, as were the dip in the door and the kick-up feature line below the rear quarter window. The new front end featured a classic Grand Prix radiator grille and chrome bumper harking back to the popular 1971 and 1972 design, and protruding in a "V" at the center. The grille consisted of five vertical openings per side, with a thick center bar and thick chrome bars across the top and down the sides. The grille pattern extended into the lower portion of the chrome front bumper. Dual rub strips were a distinctive feature of the Grand Prix bumpers, both front and rear, with side marker lights mounted on the outer ends of the bumpers between the rub strips. At the back, taillights were square units divided into six horizontal sections, with backup lights mounted directly below in the bumper. The trunk lid extended down to the bumper level with cutouts for the license plate mount and taillights, creating easier access to the large trunk. The Grand Prix's bodysides were smooth without a noticeable feature line to mar the clean appearance, and only slight fender flares on the round wheel openings. The greenhouse area included a formal upright roofline, and slender B-pillars created the illusion of true hardtop styling, despite having a fixed rear quarter window.

Interior design was basically the same for all three of the new mid-size models, utilizing an instrument panel similar to the 1977 Grand Prix's, with a cockpit-style driver's side panel. All gauges were mounted in round pods, with two large pods directly in front of the driver housing the speedometer and optional tachometer or clock, depending upon options selected. A small round gauge placed high between the two large pods housed warning lights. To the right of the driver were four additional small round pods housing the fuel and ammeter gauges along with other optional gauges. There were eight small round air outlets, two stacked

1978

vertically at each end of the panel, and four mounted in a square pattern in the center. Interior upholstery choices differed among the models, with a wide variety offered including "loose-pillow" look seats available on Grand Prix LJ and Grand LeMans models, and new leather-upholstered "Viscount" bucket seats with built-in loop-style headrests available exclusively on the Grand Prix. Traditional bucket seats and floor console were optional on any of the new mid-size Pontiacs, including the station wagons.

Powering most of the new line of cars was the Buick-built 231 CID V6 engine. Those models with sportier intentions, such as the Grand Am and Grand Prix LJ and SJ models, were powered by Pontiac's own 301 CID V8 engine. This engine was not available in California, so the Chevy-built 305 CID V8 engine was standard for those cars. These were the only engines offered, except on the LeMans Safari wagons, where the 350 CID V8 engine was still offered. A missed opportunity was not having the 350 CID V8 available in all of the mid-size models, as it was offered in mid-size Oldsmobile models and could have improved sales for GM's performance division. As an historical note, a Grand Am CA show car appeared at some auto shows, adding spoilers, a rear-opening shaker hood-scoop and wheel flares to a Grand Am coupe, and creating what could have been the continuation of the short-lived 1977 LeMans Can Am coupe. The show car also featured T-tops, something that was never offered in production on the LeMans and Grand Am coupes.

The departed Astre's station wagon was moved to the sportier Sunbird line, and a lower-priced base Sunbird coupe was added. The two existing Sunbird models were renamed Sunbird Sport. Styling for all models consisted of mostly detail changes, with the new Sunbird Sport Safari adding Sunbird nameplates, and amber parking/turn signal lenses up front replacing the white lenses of the prior year. Otherwise it looked very much like the 1977 Astre Safari wagon. The Sunbird coupe and hatchback models received a new grille insert consisting of three and a half vertical sections per side, with each section having three vertical openings. The outermost housed the parking/turn signal lights with an amber lens, and the inner section was the "half" section as it

was angled to accommodate the "V" and point of the body-colored nose.

The performance minded Firebird underwent few changes for the new model year, but continued with the "Sky Bird" option on the Esprit and the very popular black Special Edition Trans Am packages. At mid-year another special "color" edition was added, replacing the "Sky Bird" with the "Red Bird" option for the Esprit. Similar in content to the blue "Sky Bird," the "Red Bird" was also a color-coordinated appearance package. The black and gold Special Edition had been so popular that Pontiac decided to reverse the colors and added a gold Special Edition Trans Am with brown and gold stripes and decals and Solar Gold metallic paint. Also added to the package was the T-top, which had been an additional option on the prior versions of the special editions. At mid-year, the "Hurst Hatch" type roof panels, identified by a metal band around the top cut-out, were replaced by a GM Fisher Body–produced version that had no band and a larger opening. Production of the two SE T/A's totaled 3,643 for the black version and 8,676 for the gold version. The most important change was felt under the right foot, and not visually apparent. After years of horsepower ratings spiraling downward, Pontiac raised the compression ratio of the T/A 400 CID V8 engine and added different cylinder heads, which contributed to a 10 percent increase in horsepower. It marked the beginnings of a revival of interest in performance cars. A slightly revised grille insert was more of a diamond pattern, rather than the previous honeycomb pattern. Other changes included black taillight surrounds replacing the former body-colored surrounds, more rounded Trans Am logo decals, and a metal Pontiac nameplate placed on the grille, replacing the former header mounted decal.

The Phoenix line replaced the former Ventura and Ventura SJ models with new Phoenix and Phoenix LJ names, model for model. The LJ featured a small styling distinction in the form of wraparound taillights divided into eight lenses by thin chrome strips. The mid-year 1977 Phoenix "X" series models were discontinued with the new year, and the Ventura SJ hatchback did not appear in the Phoenix LJ line for this season. The base Phoenix did not have the gray outer pads on the front bumper this year.

Bonneville Brougham 4-Door Sedan

Catalina 2-Door Coupe

Firebird Esprit 2-Door Hardtop Coupe
with Sky Bird package

Firebird Formula 2-Door Hardtop Coupe

Firebird Trans Am 2-Door Hardtop Coupe
with Special Edition package

Firebird Trans Am interior

Grand Am 2-Door Coupe

Grand Am 4-Door Sedan

Grand LeMans 2-Door Coupe

Grand LeMans 4-Door Sedan

Grand Prix 2-Door Coupe

Grand Prix 2-Door Coupe

Grand Prix instrument panel

Grand Prix interior with optional
leather Viscount bucket seats

LeMans 2-Door Coupe

LeMans Safari 4-Door Station Wagon

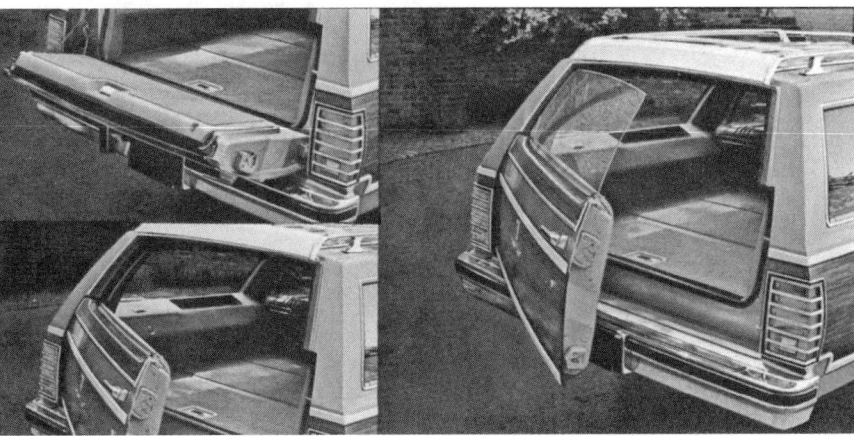

Grand Safari 3-way tailgate operation detail

1978

Phoenix 2-Door Hatchback Coupe

Phoenix LJ 2-Door Coupe

Phoenix LJ 4-Door Sedan

Sunbird 2-Door Coupe

Sunbird Safari 2-Door Station Wagon

Sunbird Sport Hatch 2-Door Hatchback

Model year production: 900,380, down 1.32% from 1977.
Domestic market share: 9.55% (4th place).
Base price range: $3,590 to $6,784.
Pontiac average base price: $5,076, up 10.58%.
Introduction date: October 6, 1977.
Assembly plants: Lakewood, GA (A); Baltimore, MD (B); Van Nuys, CA (L); Norwood, OH (N); Pontiac, MI (P); Tarrytown, NY (T); Lordstown, OH (U); Willow Run, MI (W); Kansas City/Fairfax, KS (X); Oshawa, Ontario, Canada (1); and Ste. Therese, Quebec, Canada (2).
Data plate identification (VIN): Thirteen digit code read as follows: First digit indicates division (2 = Pontiac); second through fourth digits indicate series and body style (model number in model charts); fifth digit is engine code (see powertrain chart); sixth digit indicates model year (8 = 1978); seventh digit indicates assembly plant (see list above); remaining digits are sequential with beginning number of 100001. *Example:* 2D35U8B100001 is a 1978 Pontiac Le-Mans 4-Door Safari station wagon, with 305 CID, 4-bbl. V8 engine, serial number 100001, built in Baltimore, Maryland.

Powertrains

Engine	Net HP	Engine Code: VIN/GM	Transmission Availability[1]		Sunbird	Phoenix	Firebird[2]	LeMans[3]	Grand Am	Grand Prix	Catalina[3]	Bonneville & Safaris
151 CID (2.5L), 2-bbl., 4-cyl.	90	V/ LX6	4-speed manual[4]		S	—	—	—	—	—	—	—
				MPG:	24/34/ 28	—	—	—	—	—	—	—
			5-speed manual[4]		$175	—	—	—	—	—	—	—
				MPG:	NA	—	—	—	—	—	—	—
			3-speed Turbo Hydra-matic		$270	$[4]	—	—	—	—	—	—
				MPG:	23/31/ 26	21/37/ 23	—	—	—	—	—	—
				Calif.	23/31/ 26	—	—	—	—	—	—	—
231 CID (3.8L), 2-bbl., V6	105	A/ LD5	3-speed manual[4]		—	S	S (F & FEs)	S (cs)	—	S (GP)	—	—
				MPG:	—	16/28/ 19	16/25/ 19	16/28/ 19	—	16/28/ 19	—	—
			4-speed manual		$170	—	—	—	—	—	—	—
				MPG:	16/28/ 19	—	—	—	—	—	—	—
				Calif.	16/27/ 20	—	—	—	—	—	—	—

Engine	Net HP	Engine Code: VIN/GM	Transmission Availability[1]		Sunbird	Phoenix	Firebird[2]	LeMans[3]	Grand Am	Grand Prix	Catalina[3]	Bonneville & Safaris
			5-speed manual		$345	—	—	—	—	—	—	—
				MPG:	NA	—	—	—	—	—	—	—
				Calif.	NA	—	—	—	—	—	—	—
			3-speed Turbo Hydra-matic		$440	$307	$307 (F & FEs)	S (s)/$307 (cs)	—	$307 (GP)	S (cs)	—
				MPG:	19/27/22	18/26/20	17/25/20	19/27/22	—	19/27/22	17/25/20	—
				Calif.	16/23/18	15/27/17	15/21/17	16/23/18	—	16/23/18	15/21/17	—
301 CID (4.9L), 2-bbl., V8[4]	140	Y/L27	3-speed Turbo Hydra-matic		—	—	—	$150 (s)/$457 (cs)	S	S (LJ)/$457 (GP)	S (s)/$150 (cs)	S
				MPG:	—	—	—	18/25/20	18/25/20	18/25/20	17/24/20	17/24/20
301 CID (4.9L), 4-bbl., V8[4]	150	W/L37	4-speed manual		—	—	—	—	$125	—	—	—
				MPG:	—	—	—	—	NA	—	—	—
			3-speed Turbo Hydra-matic		—	—	—	$507 (cs)	$50	S (SJ)/$50 (LJ)/$507 (GP)	—	—
				MPG:	—	—	—	17/24/20	17/24/20	17/24/20	—	—
305 CID (5.0L), 4-bbl., V8	145	U/LG3	4-speed manual		—	$275[4]	S (FF)/$275 (F & FEs)	—	—	—	—	—
				MPG:	—	15/21/17	15/21/17 (FF)	—	—	—	—	—
			3-speed Turbo Hydra-matic		—$457	N/C	(FF)/$457 (F & FEs)	$200 (s)/$507 (cs)[5]	$50[5]	S (SJ)[5]/$50 (LJ)[5]/$507 (GP)[5]	—	—
				MPG:	—	16/22/19	16/22/19	16/21/19	—	—	—	—
				Calif.	—	13/19/15	13/19/15	14/21/17	14/21/17	14/21/17	—	—
350 CID (5.7L), 4-bbl., V8	155	X/L77	3-speed Turbo Hydra-matic		—	—	$115 (FF)/$572 (F & FEs)	—	—	—	$115 (s)[4]/$265 (cs)[4]	$115[2]
				MPG:	—	—	15/21/17	—	—	—	15/22/18	16/22/18
				Calif.	—	—	13/18/15	—	—	—	—	—
350 CID (5.7L), 4-bbl., V8[5]	170	L/LM1	3-speed Turbo Hydra-matic	*Calif.*	—	$265 / 13/18/15	—	$265 (s) / NA	—	—	—	—
350 CID (5.7L), 4-bbl., V8	170	R/L34	3-speed Turbo Hydra-matic	*Calif.*	—	—	—	—	—	—	$165 (s)[5]/$315(cs)[5] / 15/21/18	S[5] / 15/21/18
400 CID (6.6L), 4-bbl.,	180	Z/L78	4-speed manual		—	—	S (TA)/$205 (FF)	—	—	—	—	—
				MPG:	—	—	12/16/14	—	—	—	—	—

1978

Engine	Net HP	Engine Code: VIN/GM	Transmission Availability[1]	Sunbird	Phoenix	Firebird[2]	LeMans[3]	Grand Am	Grand Prix	Catalina[3]	Bonneville & Safaris
V8[4]			3-speed Turbo Hydra-matic	—	—	N/C (TA)/ $562 (FF)	—	—	—	$190 (s)/ $330 (cs)	$190
			MPG:	—	—	14/19/16	—	—	—	14/19/16	14/19/16
400 CID T/A (6.6L), 4-bbl., V8[4]	220	Z/L78	4-speed manual	—	—	$75 (TA)/ $280 (FF)	—	—	—	—	—
			MPG:	—	—	12/16/14	—	—	—	—	—
			3-speed Turbo Hydra-matic	—	—	$75 (TA)/ $637 (FF)	—	—	—	—	—
			MPG:	—	—	14/19/16	—	—	—	—	—
403 CID (6.6L), 4-bbl., V8[5]	185	K/L80	3-speed Turbo Hydra-matic	—	—	N/C (TA)/ $562 (FF)	—	—	—	$190 (s)/ $330 (cs)	$190
			Calif.	—	—	14/19/16	—	—	—	13/19/16	13/19/16

[1]Unless otherwise noted: All 3-speed manual transmissions are floor shift, except on Phoenix. All 4-speed and 5-speed manual transmissions are floor shift. All automatic transmissions are column shift, except Sunbird and Firebird. Floor-shift with 3-speed manual can be ordered on Phoenix models for $33 extra. Floor shift w/automatics is available on specific Phoenix, LeMans and Grand Prix models in combination w/optional bucket seats and console. [2]F = base Firebird; FEs = Firebird Esprit; FF = Firebird Formula; TA = Firebird Trans Am. [3]cs = Coupes and Sedans; s = Safaris. [4]Not available in California. [5]Available only in California or designated high altitude areas.

Major Options

	Sunbird	Firebird	Phoenix	LeMans & Grand Am	Grand Prix	Catalina & Bonneville
Custom air conditioning[1]	$470	$508	$508	$544	$544	$581
Tilt steering wheel	$62	$69	$69	$69	$69	$70
Automatic cruise control	—	$90	$90	$90	$90	$95
Intermittent windshield wipers	$35	$38	$38	$38	$38	$39
Rear window defroster, electric	$82	$90	$50[2]	$90	$90	$92
Dual sport mirrors, remote-control	—	$43	$70	$70	$70	$71
Soft-Ray tinted glass, all windows	$64	$64	$64	$75	$75	$84
Power windows, 2-dr./4-dr.	—	$118[3]	$124/$169	$124/$169	$124	$130/$190[4]
Power door locks, 2-dr./4-dr.	—	$74	$80/$115	$80/$115	$80	$82/$120[5]
Power front seat, 6-way w/std. seat	—	—	—	$151	$151	$151
Front bucket seats, w/console[6]	$77	S	$275	$235[7]	$235	—
Third row seating (wagons)	—	—	—	—	—	$165
AM radio	$74	$83	$79	$83	$83	$96
AM/FM stereo	$215	$236	$236	$236	$236	$239
AM/FM stereo w/8-track tape	$308	$329[3]	$329	$329	$329	$330
AM/FM stereo w/CB radio	—	$518	—	$571	$571	$577
Woodgrain exterior trim (wagons)	$149	—	—	—	—	—
Vinyl top, full[8]	—	$111	$97	$116	$121	$142
Vinyl top, padded landau[7]	$153	—	$179	$239	$239	$294
Sunroof, removable[7]	$172	—	—	—	—	—
Sunroof, power steel[7]	—	—	—	$499	$499	$695
Sunroof, power glass[7]	—	—	—	$699	$699	$895
Hatch roof, glass panel T-tops	—	$625[9]	—	—	$625	—
Power steering, variable-ratio	$134	S	$152	$152[10]	$152[10]	S
Power brakes, w/front disc	$66	$69	$69	$69[10]	$69[10]	S
Custom wheel covers	S	—	$	—	—	$
Wire wheel covers	—	$150	$150	$150	$150	$150
Rally II wheels[11]	$	$106	$106	$106	$106	$
Cast aluminum "snowflake" wheels	$124	$	$	$	$	$
WSW tires	$38	$43	$39	$45	$45	$45

Popular Option Groups & Packages

	Sunbird	Firebird	Phoenix	LeMans & Grand Am	Grand Prix	Catalina & Bonneville
Custom exterior group	—	—	—	$75	—	—
Exterior appearance package	—	—	—	$159	$165	$159
Custom trim group	—	—	—	$247	—	—
Formula appearance package	$621	$137	—	—	—	—
Red Bird appearance package	—	$461	—	—	—	—
Sky Bird appearance package	—	$461	—	—	—	—
Special appearance group	$87	—	$73	—	—	—
Special Edition Trans Am package	—	$1,259	—	—	—	—
WS6 Trans Am performance package	—	$324	—	—	—	—

—= Not Available; S = Standard equipment. [1]Automatic climate control is available for $584 on LeMans, Grand Am, and Grand Prix, and for $626 on Catalina, Bonneville, and Grand Safari. [2]Blower type defroster. [3]Other optional equipment required at extra cost; i.e., console. [4]Standard on Bonneville Brougham. [5]Price on Catalina Safari and Grand Safari wagons is $146 and includes power tailgate lock. [6]Front bucket seats standard on Sunbird and Firebird, with console available on both. Bucket seats and console standard on Grand Am, Firebird Formula and Trans Am. [7]Available only on 2-door coupe models. [8]Canopy style vinyl roof on Firebird, and Esprit. Vinyl roof is not available on any Safari wagon model. Not available on Sunbird hatchback models. [9]Included in Special Edition Trans Am package. [10]Power brakes standard on all LeMans Safari station wagons. Power steering and power brakes standard on Grand Am, and Grand Prix LJ and SJ. [11]Body-colored Rally II wheels also available.

Paint Colors

	Code		Code
Antique White	11	Sundance Yellow[3,7]	51
Platinum metallic	15	Burnished Gold metallic[9]	56
Dark Charcoal (two-tone only w/15)	16	Blue[4]	58
Starlight Black	19	Desert Sand[6]	61
Dresden Blue[1]	21	Laredo Brown metallic[2]	63
Glacier Blue metallic[2]	22	Ember Mist metallic[2]	67
Martinique Blue metallic[3]	24	Chesterfield Brown metallic	69
Nautilus Blue metallic[1]	29	Roman Red[10]	72
Lombard Blue[4]	30	Mayan Red[3]	75
Redbird Red[5]	42	Carmine metallic[2]	77
Seafoam Green metallic[6]	44	Claret metallic[1]	79
Mayfair Green metallic[1]	45		
Berkshire Green[3,7]	48		
Solar Gold metallic[8]	50		

In two-tone combinations, the first two digits indicate lower color and the next two digits are the upper color. Colors without footnotes are available on all models.

Two-tone colors available only on LeMans, Grand Prix, Catalina, and Bonneville (coupes and sedans only). Two-tone lower body accent paint available on Grand Am. Trans Am "Bird" hood decal available at $66 extra cost. [1]Available only on LeMans, Grand Prix, Catalina, Bonneville and Grand Safari models. [2]Available on all models except Grand Am and Firebird Trans Am. [3]Available only on Sunbird, Firebird and Phoenix models. [4]Used only on Firebird w/Skybird option package. [5]Used only on Firebird w/Redbird option package. [6]Available on all models except Firebird. [7]Not available on Firebird Trans Am. [8]Firebird Trans Am w/Special Edition package only. [9]Used only as two-tone color, or as accent colors on Firebird. [10]Available only on Grand Am.

Sunbird

"Built for the way America loves to drive."

Nameplate year of origin: 1976.
Current bodystyle lifespan: 1976 through 1980.
Predecessor to this model: None.
Replacement for this model: J2000/Sunbird (1982 to 1993).
Percentage of division's production: 9.64%.
Corporate siblings: Buick Skyhawk, Chevrolet Monza, and Oldsmobile Starfire.
Primary competition: Ford Mustang II.
Notable changes: New wagon model and minor trim and detail changes.
Major standard equipment: All vinyl front bucket seats, cut-pile carpeting, floor shifter and floor-mounted parking brake w/mini-console, deluxe cushion three-spoke steering wheel, simulated rosewood appliqués on I/P, distinctive door and quarter panel trim, bright front and rear window moldings,

Measurements

	Coupe	Hatchback	Wagon
Wheelbase	97.0"	97.0"	97.0"
Length	177.8"	178.3"	177.6"
Width	65.4"	65.4"	65.4"
Height	49.8"	50.2"	49.8"
Legroom — front	43.0"	43.0"	43.0"
Legroom — rear	28.2"	29.6"	30.2"
Headroom — front	37.5"	37.7"	38.5"
Headroom — rear	37.2"	35.3"	40.1"
Cargo capacity (cu. ft.)	6.6	30.2*	46.6
Fuel capacity (gals.)	18.5	18.5	16.0

*Capacity with rear seat down.

roof drip rail moldings, LH outside mirror, Sunbird exterior identification, argent colored grille, manual front disc brakes, hubcaps, and A78 × 13 BSW tires. Sport models add: Custom all-vinyl bucket seats, padded door trim, body-colored door handle inserts, bright windowsill moldings, bright wheel opening moldings, bright rocker panel moldings, bright rear end panel trim, chrome grille trim, and custom wheel covers. Hatchback adds: Fold-down rear seat, load-floor and rear seat back carpeting, and belt line molding. Sport Safari adds: Instrument panel assist straps, carpeted load floor, hubcaps, and B78 × 13 BSW tires.

Models Available

	Model No.	Base MSRP	Change from LY	Shipping Wt. (lbs.)	Model Year Production	Change from LY
Sunbird 2-Door Coupe	E27	$3,590	NEW	2662	20,413	NEW
Sunbird Sport 2-Door Coupe*	M27	$3,823	+4.48%	2662	32,572	-21.90%
Sunbird Sport Hatch 2-Door Hatchback Coupe	M07	$3,962	+4.70%	2694	25,380	+85.39%
Sunbird Sport Safari 2-Door Station Wagon**	M15	$3,741	+4.06%	2610	8,424	-18.54%
TOTALS	Avg. price	$3,779	+1.55%	Production	86,789	+56.66%

*Comparisons of Sport Coupe made to 1977 Sunbird coupe of same model number. **Comparisons of Sport Safari made to 1977 Astre station wagon.

Firebird

"Pontiac's sports machines."

Nameplate year of origin: 1967.
Current bodystyle lifespan: 1970 through 1981.
Predecessor to this model: Firebird (1967 to 1969).
Replacement for this model: Firebird (1982 to 1992).
Percentage of division's production: 20.80%.
Corporate siblings: Chevrolet Camaro.
Primary competition: None.
Notable changes: Minor trim and detail changes.
Major standard equipment: All-Morrokide vinyl front bucket seats, cut-pile carpeting, deluxe cushion three-spoke steering wheel, simulated rosewood I/P appliqué, ashtray light, bright front and rear window moldings, bright grille moldings, Firebird emblems on sail panel and trunk lid, Endura front and rear bumpers, trunk

Measurements

Wheelbase	108.1"
Length	196.8"
Width	73.4"
Height	50.4"
Legroom — front	43.9"
Legroom — rear	28.4"
Headroom — front	37.2"
Headroom — rear	36.0"
Cargo capacity (cu. ft.)	8.8
Fuel capacity (gals.)	21.0

floor mat, variable-ratio power steering, manual front disc brakes, RTS package, hubcaps, and FR78 × 15 BSW tires. Esprit adds: Custom all-Morrokide vinyl front bucket seats, distinctive door trim panels, door and I/P assist straps, luxury cushion steering wheel, pedal trim plates, rear quarter ashtray, added acoustical insulation, dual body-colored mirror w/LH remote, body-colored door handle inserts, bright roof drip rail and belt reveal moldings, bright rear hood edge molding, bright wheel opening and rocker panel moldings, and deluxe wheel covers. Formula adds: Luxury cushion steering wheel, full-length front console, blacked-out grille, dual body-colored mirror w/LH remote, Formula identification, steel hood w/dual simulated hood scoops, power brakes, Trans Am front and rear stabilizer bars, Rally II wheels, and GR70 × 15 BSW tires. Trans Am adds: Formula steering wheel, rally gauge cluster package w/electric clock, aluminum machine-turned I/P trim plate, dual body-colored mirror w/LH remote, blacked-out grille, front center airdam, wraparound rear deck spoiler, wheel opening air deflectors, front fender air extractors, Trans Am decal on front fender and rear spoiler, shaker hood scoop, power brakes, power flex fan, Safe-T-Track differential, firm control shocks, dual chrome splitter tailpipe extensions, Rally II wheels w/trim rings, and GR70 × 15 BSW tires.

Models Available

	Model No.	Base MSRP	Change from LY	Shipping Wt. (lbs.)	Model Year Production	Change from LY
Firebird 2-Door Hardtop Coupe	S87	$4,593	+7.56%	3254	32,672	+6.62%
Firebird Esprit 2-Door Hardtop Coupe	T87	$4,897	+7.60%	3285	36,926	+6.88%
Firebird Formula 2-Door Hardtop Coupe	U87	$5,533	+11.17%	3452	24,346	+11.67%
Firebird Trans Am 2-Door Hardtop Coupe	W87	$5,889	+7.94%	3511	93,341	+35.78%
TOTALS	Avg. price	$5,228	+8.61%	Production	187,285	+20.26%

Phoenix

"A very special luxury compact."

Nameplate year of origin: 1977.

Current bodystyle lifespan: 1975 through 1979 (Ventura 1975 to 1977; Phoenix 1977 to 1979).

Predecessor to this model: Ventura/Ventura II (1971 to 1974; restyled in 1973).

Replacement for this model: Phoenix (1980 to 1984).

Percentage of division's production: 8.50%.

Corporate siblings: Buick Skylark, Chevrolet Nova, and Oldsmobile Omega.

Primary competition: AMC Concord, Dodge Aspen, Ford Granada, and Mercury Monarch.

Notable changes: Minor trim and detail changes.

Major standard equipment: Cloth-and-vinyl front bench seat, cut-pile carpeting, deluxe cushion three-spoke steering wheel, cockpit-style instrument cluster w/simulated rosewood I/P trim, bright front and rear window moldings, side window reveal moldings, bright drip rail moldings, bright wheel opening moldings, bright rear end panel, center body colored bumper pad, gray front and rear bumper rub strips, decklid lock cover, manual front disc brakes, hubcaps, and E78 × 14 BSW tires. Hatchback adds: Fold-down rear seat, and load floor carpeting. LJ adds: Cloth front bench seat w/fold-down center armrest, padded door trim w/map pockets, I/P assist strap, added acoustical insulation, extra-wide ribbed rocker panel moldings w/front and rear extensions, front and rear gray bumper outer pads, stand-up hood ornament w/hood windsplit molding, wraparound taillamps, and deluxe wheel covers.

Measurements

	Coupe & HBK	Sedan
Wheelbase	111.1"	111.1"
Length	203.4"	203.4"
Width	72.4"	72.4"
Height	52.7"	53.8"
Legroom — front	41.7"	41.7"
Legroom — rear	32.4"	35.2"
Headroom — front	38.2"	39.1"
Headroom — rear	36.7"	37.1"
Cargo capacity (cu. ft.)	14.2*	13.8
Fuel capacity (gals.)	21.0	21.0

Cargo capacity for hatchback with rear seat folded down is 29.5 cu. ft.

Models Available

	Model No.	Base MSRP	Change from LY*	Shipping Wt. (lbs.)	Model Year Production	Change from LY*
Phoenix 2-Door Coupe	Y27	$3,907	+8.65%	3119	26,143	-1.99%
Phoenix 2-Door Hatchback	Y17	$4,103	+8.20%	3202	3,252	-19.00%
Phoenix 4-Door Sedan	Y69	$3,992	+9.37%	3169	32,529	+20.08%
Phoenix LJ 2-Door Coupe	Z27	$4,399	+10.39%	3228	6,210	+81.69%
Phoenix LJ 4-Door Sedan	Z69	$4,484	+11.76%	3277	8,393	+93.43%
TOTALS	Avg. price	$4,177	+4.88%	Production	76,527	-15.69%

Comparisons made to 1977 Ventura models of same model number.

LeMans

"Pontiac's dramatically redesigned mid-size cars. It's hard to imagine a better mid-size buy."

Nameplate year of origin: 1961 (As a Tempest subseries).

Current bodystyle lifespan: 1978 through 1981.

Predecessor to this model: LeMans (1973 to 1977).

Replacement for this model: 6000 (1982 to 1991).

Percentage of division's production: 12.20%.

Corporate siblings: Buick Century, Chevrolet Malibu, and Oldsmobile Cutlass.

Primary competition: Dodge Diplomat and Monaco, Ford LTD II, and Mercury Cougar.

Notable changes: Completely redesigned.

Major standard equipment: Cloth-and-vinyl front bench seat, cut-pile carpeting, deluxe cushion steering wheel, cockpit

Measurements

	Coupes	Sedans	Wagons
Wheelbase	108.1"	108.1"	108.1"
Length	199.2"	198.5"	197.8"
Width	72.4"	72.4"	72.6"
Height	53.5"	54.1"	54.5"
Legroom — front	42.8"	42.8"	42.8"
Legroom — rear	35.1"	38.0"	35.9"
Headroom — front	37.9"	38.7"	39.0"
Headroom — rear	37.8"	37.7"	39.1"
Cargo capacity (cu. ft.)	16.4	16.4	72.4
Fuel capacity (gals.)	17.5	17.5	18.3

1978

style instrument panel design, simulated regal walnut vinyl accents on I/P, door panels and steering wheel, bin-type glove box, bright front and rear window moldings, bright roof drip rail and rear quarter window trim, wheel opening moldings, trunk mat, RTS suspension package, manual front disc brakes, hubcaps, and P185/75R14 BSW tires. Wagon adds: All-Morrokide vinyl front bench seat, textured steel cargo floor painted w/vinyl paint, swing-up tailgate window and drop-down tailgate, stationary rear door glass w/swing-out rear quarter vents, power front disc brakes, and P195/75R14 BSW tires. Grand LeMans adds: Choice of all-vinyl or velour loose-pillow design notchback bench seat w/fold-down center armrest, luxury cushion steering wheel, padded upper door panels w/pull straps and carpeted lower panels, door lamp switches on all doors, bright rear hood edge molding, bright wheel opening and rocker panel moldings, bright window sill moldings, body color door handle inserts, lower bodyside protective molding, stand-up hood ornament w/hood windsplit molding, and deluxe wheel covers. Grand LeMans Safari adds: All-Morrokide vinyl front bench seat, Grand LeMans interior door and I/P trim, plank-like woodgrain exterior vinyl appliqué panels w/woodtone trim, and simulated woodgrain inserts in outside door handles.

Models Available

	Model No.	Base MSRP	Change from LY*	Shipping Wt. (lbs.)	Model Year Production	Change from LY*
LeMans 2-Door Coupe	D27	$4,427	+9.12%	3038	20,581	+28.33%
LeMans 4-Door Sedan	D19	$4,512	+9.91%	3047	22,728	-1.44%
LeMans 4-Door, 2-Seat Safari Station Wagon	D35	$4,980	+1.86%	3225	15,714	+55.88%
Grand LeMans 2-Door Coupe	F27	$4,801	+4.05%	3070	18,433	+143.15%
Grand LeMans 4-Door Sedan	F19	$4,915	+3.65%	3098	21,252	+280.59%
Grand LeMans 4-Door, 2-Seat Safari Wagon	F35	$5,310	+3.23%	3242	11,125	+106.29%
TOTALS	*Avg. price*	$4,824	+6.30%	*Production*	109,833	+34.94%

Comparison to LY made to models of same series name and similar body style.

Grand Am

"For a few glorious years in the early seventies, one car came blazing on the scene to establish itself as an impressive American grand touring car. Well, now it's back."

Nameplate year of origin: 1973.
Current bodystyle lifespan: 1978 through 1980.
Predecessor to this model: Grand Am (1973 to 1975).
Replacement for this model: 6000 STE (1983 to 1989).
Percentage of division's production: 1.18%.
Corporate siblings: Buick Century, Chevrolet Malibu, and Oldsmobile Cutlass.
Primary competition: Ford Granada ESS and Mercury Monarch ESS.
Notable changes: Completely redesigned.
Major standard equipment: Choice of cloth-and-vinyl or all-vinyl notchback front bench seat w/fold-down center armrest, cut-pile carpeting, deluxe cushion steering wheel, padded upper door panels w/pull straps and carpeted lower panels, cockpit-style instrument cluster w/simulated regal walnut I/P trim, door lamp switches on all doors, bright front and rear window moldings, bright drip rail moldings, body color door handle inserts, lower bodyside protective molding, distinctive two-tone lower body and bumper paint treatment, power steering, power front disc brakes, rally RTS suspension with front and rear stabilizer bars, hubcaps, and 205/70R14 BSW tires.

Measurements

	Coupe	Sedan
Wheelbase	108.1"	108.1"
Length	199.2"	198.5"
Width	72.4"	72.4"
Height	53.5"	54.1"
Legroom — front	42.8"	42.8"
Legroom — rear	35.1"	38.0"
Headroom — front	37.9"	38.7"
Headroom — rear	37.8"	37.7"
Cargo capacity (cu. ft.)	16.4	16.4
Fuel capacity (gals.)	17.5	17.5

Models Available

	Model No.	Base MSRP	Change from LY	Shipping Wt. (lbs.)	Model Year Production	Change from LY
Grand Am 2-Door Coupe	G27	$5,520	NEW	3209	7,767	NEW
Grand Am 4-Door Sedan	G19	$5,634	NEW	3239	2,841	NEW
TOTALS	*Avg. price*	$5,557	NEW	*Production*	10,608	NEW

Grand Prix

*"Pontiac can give a car no higher praise
than the name Grand Prix."*

Nameplate year of origin: 1962.
Current bodystyle lifespan: 1978 through 1987.
Predecessor to this model: Grand Prix (1973 to 1977).
Replacement for this model: Grand Prix (1988 to 1996).
Percentage of division's production: 25.37%.
Corporate siblings: Buick Regal, Chevrolet Monte Carlo, and Oldsmobile Cutlass Supreme/Calais.
Primary competition: Dodge Charger SE/Magnum XE, Ford Thunderbird, and Mercury Cougar XR-7.
Notable changes: Completely redesigned.
Major standard equipment: Choice of cloth-and-vinyl or all-vinyl front notchback bench seat w/fold-down center armrest, cut-pile carpeting, deluxe cushion steering wheel, simulated regal walnut inlay trim on I/P, padded upper door panels w/lower panel carpeting and door pull straps, I/P courtesy lights, electric clock, bright front and rear window moldings, bright side window sill and drip rail moldings, bright rear hood edge molding, bright wheel opening moldings, wide rocker panel moldings, trunk mat, front and rear bumper rub strips, manual front disc brakes, RTS package, deluxe wheel covers, and 195/75R14 BSW tires. LJ adds: Velour "loose-pillow" look notchback front bench seat w/fold-down center armrest, custom stitched instrument panel, luxury cushion steering wheel, pedal trim plates, velour door panel inserts, dual body-colored sport mirrors w/LH remote control, LJ identification, wide rocker panel moldings, power steering, power front disc brakes, and deluxe wheel covers. SJ adds: All-vinyl front bucket seats w/center floor console, custom color-keyed seat belts, custom stitched instrument panel, custom sport leather-wrapped steering wheel, pedal trim plates, rally gauge cluster w/trip odometer, electric clock, added acoustical insulation, dual body-colored sport mirrors w/LH remote control, wide rocker panel moldings w/extensions, bodyside accent tape stripes, RTS package, power steering, power front disc brakes, and cast aluminum wheels.

Measurements

Wheelbase	108.1"
Length	201.2"
Width	72.8"
Height	53.3"
Legroom — front	42.8"
Legroom — rear	36.3"
Headroom — front	37.6"
Headroom — rear	37.8"
Cargo capacity (cu. ft.)	16.1
Fuel capacity (gals.)	15.0

1978

Models Available

	Model No.	Base MSRP	Change from LY	Shipping Wt. (lbs.)	Model Year Production	Change from LY
Grand Prix 2-Door Hardtop Coupe	J37	$4,880	-4.69%	3101	127,253	-24.37%
Grand Prix LJ 2-Door Hardtop Coupe	K37	$5,815	+6.06%	3216	65,122	-2.43%
Grand Prix SJ 2-Door Hardtop Coupe	H37	$6,088	+5.82%	3229	36,069	-32.51%
TOTALS	*Avg. price*	$5,594	+2.61%	*Production*	228,444	-20.80%

Catalina

"Pontiac's lowest priced full-size car."

Nameplate year of origin: 1950 (as hardtop model designation), 1959 (as series).
Current bodystyle lifespan: 1977 through 1981.
Predecessor to this model: Catalina (1971 to 1976).
Replacement for this model: Parisienne (1983 to 1986) and Safari (1987 to 1989).
Percentage of division's production: 6.86%.
Corporate siblings: Buick LeSabre, Chevrolet Impala/Caprice, and Oldsmobile Delta 88.
Primary competition: Ford LTD.
Notable changes: Minor trim and detail changes.
Major standard equipment: Cloth-and-vinyl front bench seat, cut-pile carpeting, deluxe cushion steering wheel, simulated

Measurements

	2-door	4-door	Wagon
Wheelbase	115.9"	115.9"	115.9"
Length	214.3"	214.3"	215.1"
Width	78.0"	78.0"	80.0"
Height	54.5"	54.9"	58.0"
Legroom — front	42.2"	42.2"	42.2"
Legroom — rear	38.7"	39.5"	38.2"
Headroom — front	38.1"	38.8"	38.8"
Headroom — rear	38.0"	38.0"	38.8"
Cargo capacity (cu. ft.)	20.3	20.3	87.1
Fuel capacity (gals.)	21.0	21.0	22.0

regal walnut vinyl I/P accents, ashtray w/light, glove box light, trunk mat, brushed aluminum B-pillar appliqué (coupe), bright windshield and rear window moldings, bright quarter window and roof drip rail moldings, bright rocker panel molding, bright hood rear edge molding, front and rear bumper rub strips, stand-up hood ornament w/hood windsplit molding, RTS package, hubcaps, and FR78 × 15 BSW tires. Safari wagon adds: All-Morrokide vinyl front bench seat, three-way tailgate w/power-operated rear window, rear bumper guards, and HR78 × 15 BSW tires.

Models Available

	Model No.	Base MSRP	Change from LY	Shipping Wt. (lbs.)	Model Year Production	Change from LY
Catalina 2-Door Coupe	L37	$5,439	+7.64%	3438	9,224	-37.47%
Catalina 4-Door Sedan	L69	$5,484	+8.59%	3470	39,707	-15.38%
Catalina Safari 4-Door, 2-Seat Station Wagon	L35	$6,011	+9.45%	3976	12,819	-1.83%
TOTALS	Avg. price	$5,645	+8.59%	Production	61,750	-17.38%

Bonneville and Grand Safari

*"You don't tamper with a car as successful
as last year's Bonneville. You refine it."*

Nameplate year of origin: 1957.
Current bodystyle lifespan: 1977 through 1981.
Predecessor to this model: Bonneville (1971 to 1976).
Replacement for this model: Bonneville "Model G" (1982 to 1986).
Percentage of division's production: 15.45%.
Corporate siblings: Buick LeSabre, Chevrolet Impala/Caprice, and Oldsmobile Delta 88.
Primary competition: Mercury Marquis.
Notable changes: Minor trim and detail changes.
Major standard equipment: Choice of special pattern velour cloth or all-vinyl notchback front seat w/fold-down center armrest, cut-pile carpeting, lower door panel carpeting, door pull straps, luxury custom cushion steering wheel, simulated

Measurements

	2-door	4-door	Wagon
Wheelbase	115.9"	115.9"	115.9"
Length	214.3"	214.3"	215.1"
Width	78.0"	78.0"	80.0"
Height	54.5"	54.9"	58.0"
Legroom — front	42.2"	42.2"	42.2"
Legroom — rear	38.7"	39.5"	38.2"
Headroom — front	38.1"	38.8"	38.8"
Headroom — rear	38.0"	38.0"	38.8"
Cargo capacity (cu. ft.)	20.3	20.3	87.1
Fuel capacity (gals.)	21.0	21.0	22.0

regal walnut vinyl I/P accents, pedal trim plates, courtesy light switches on all doors, ashtray w/light, glove box light, brushed aluminum B-pillar appliqué (coupe), luggage compartment mat and light, bright windshield and rear window moldings, bright hood rear edge molding, fixed rear quarter window, wide rocker panel moldings w/rear extensions, bright wheel opening moldings, stand-up hood ornament w/hood windsplit molding, rear fender skirts, RTS package, deluxe wheel covers, and FR78 × 15 BSW tires. Grand Safari wagon adds: All-Morrokide vinyl front bench seat, door pull straps, electric clock, three-way tailgate w/power-operated rear window, delete rear fender skirts, simulated woodgrain Safari siding and tailgate appliqués, and HR78 × 15 BSW tires. Brougham adds: Velour "loose-pillow" look luxury trim 60/40 split front seat w/fold-down center armrest, custom door panels w/pull straps and lower panel carpeting, RH visor vanity mirror, electric clock, power windows, rear quarter courtesy lights, custom pedal trim plates, chrome LH remote-control mirror, added acoustical insulation, bright window sill molding, and velour luggage compartment trim.

Models Available

	Model No.	Base MSRP	Change from LY	Shipping Wt. (lbs.)	Model Year Production	Change from LY
Bonneville 2-Door Coupe	N37	$5,913	+9.28%	3579	22,510	-40.48%
Bonneville 4-Door Sedan	N69	$6,023	+10.37%	3616	48,647	+255.17%
Grand Safari 4-Door, 2-Seat Station Wagon	N35	$6,319	+9.48%	4066	13,847	-24.35%
Bonneville Brougham 2-Door Coupe	Q37	$6,674	+13.18%	3617	36,192	+126.61%
Bonneville Brougham 4-Door Sedan	Q69	$6,784	+13.22%	3680	17,948	-62.19%
TOTALS	Avg. price	$6,343	+11.16%	Production	139,144	+4.48%

1979

Pushing for a third successful year in a row, the auto industry introduced a large number of new and restyled models for 1979. Ford and Chrysler joined the downsizing trend for full-sized cars, introducing the new Ford LTD, Mercury Marquis, Dodge St. Regis, and the Chrysler Newport and New Yorker lines. General Motors continued its downsizing efforts, moving the last of its traditional big cars, the Cadillac Eldorado and Oldsmobile Toronado, to a smaller and much more modern front-wheel-drive platform. Rejoining these two models after two years on GM's full-size B-body platform was the Buick Riviera. Although the model year production would top the nine million mark for the third year in a row, a second fuel shortage triggered another economic recession, making sales suffer for the last few months of the season.

The 1979 Buick Riviera represented the first time for the personal luxury car, or any Buick for that matter, to use front-wheel drive, even though for years it shared some basic chassis design with the Eldorado and Toronado, which had used front-wheel-drive since the 1960s. This season also marked Riviera's first use of a 6-cylinder engine in the new S-Type model, but that was acceptable for buyers, as the engine was Buick's turbocharged V6 engine, which was just as powerful as the available V8 engine yet performed better on a gallon of gas. Of the new trio of cars the Toronado ended up most closely resembling its immediate predecessor, with the Eldorado looking similar also. But it would be the Riviera S-Type that would win the affections of *Motor Trend* magazine's editors to earn the coveted "Car of the Year" award, mostly on the strength of its powerful V6 engine which gave the Riviera better performance, as well as for its ride and handling characteristics.

Most of the rest of the GM line entered the final year of the 1970s with the expected new grilles and trim. Only the popular Pontiac Firebird would receive a significant makeover, and it would come in time for the 10th anniversary of Firebird's most popular model since 1975, the Trans Am.

To celebrate the occasion a special 10th Anniversary edition debuted with special two-tone silver and charcoal paint, specific decals, red instrument panel lighting, and a silver leather interior among many other features. It was also the most expensive Pontiac model ever sold up to that time. Also given a minor update was the Chevrolet Corvette, which adopted the spoiler of the 1978 25th anniversary edition for all cars this year. The Chevy Chevette, one of the few remaining GM cars with round headlamps, gained new square units for 1979. GM's other small car lines were mostly unchanged as the X-body cars were beginning their final year as rear-wheel-drive cars. Assembly lines would be shut down after just a few months of production to change over plants to build the new 1980 front-wheel-drive X-cars. When the plants shut down, the longtime Nova nameplate would be gone for good, at least on a rear-wheel-drive car. Finally, this would be the end of the line for Buick's captive import, the Isuzu Opel. After moving to the Japanese-built model, the Opel line never seemed to match its former success as a German-built car, so GM pulled the plug in the summer of 1979. The same car would return for 1980 under the Isuzu nameplate as the Japanese manufacturer began to set up a dealership organization in the United States.

As mentioned at the beginning, Ford Motor Company introduced all-new full-size Ford LTD and Mercury Marquis models for 1979. Unlike General Motors, which also downsized the standard engines, Ford passed on using six-cylinder engines in its big cars, retaining the popular 302 CID V8 engine as standard on the LTD and introducing it in place of the 351 CID V8 engine as standard equipment in the Mercury Marquis. Ford emulated GM's successful formula with formal rooflines and angular body designs, offering two- and four-door sedans as well as the expected station wagon, as Ford continued to market itself as the "Wagonmaster." The traditional-sized Lincoln Continental and Continental Mark V were making their final appearance for 1979 in their current form, and special Collector's Series models were produced to commemorate the occasion. They would both be downsized for the coming season.

Ford's other big news was the rollout of an all-new Mustang and its new Mercury counterpart named the Capri, both of which were based on Ford's "Fox" platform that was new for the Fairmont and Zephyr last year. The Mustang was returned to its better-known performance image, while still having an economical four-cylinder engine standard, but lost its traditional styling cues, including the round-ended grille with pony emblem and distinctive bodyside cove. For performance, the new Mustang and Capri offered V6 and V8 engines as well as a special new turbocharged four-cylinder. At mid-year, the new Mustang was selected to be the official pace car for the Indianapolis 500 race, and as had been done in 1964 when the original Mustang served as pace car, Ford built replicas of the pace car for the general public. Offered with a choice of the new turbo four or the 302 CID V8 engine, the pace car replica sold 10,471 copies, the highest number ever sold up to that time.

In an attempt to make the Lincoln Versailles more competitive with the Cadillac Seville, a new formal roofline was fashioned which squared off the roofline and rear door quarter windows, making the luxury compact sedan appear lower, longer and more luxurious.

The Ford Pinto and Mercury Bobcat, which had outlived their original Vega and Gremlin competitors, were given new square headlights as part of a makeover to modernize their looks until a replacement model was ready. The new year marked the final season for Ford's current mid-size models, the LTD II and Cougar, leaving the Granada and Monarch to take the position as Ford's mid-size cars next year. The Thunderbird and Cougar XR-7 models, which were built on the same mid-size chassis, would move to the new "Fox" platform for 1980. With the mid-size line being dropped, 1979 also meant the end of the line for the once popular Ranchero pickup. Other Ford truck models had few changes for the year.

Chrysler joined in the downsized big car market with its new R-bodied Dodge St. Regis and Chrysler Newport and New Yorker sedans. Offered only as four-door models, they were technically pillared hardtops, using frameless front door glass and a thin B-pillar, setting them apart from the GM and Ford big cars. Because of Chrysler's current financial situation, though, the cars were not really "all-new" but rather a modernized version of the intermediate B-body platform introduced in 1971 for the Dodge Charger and Coronet and the Plymouth Satellite (most recently named the Charger SE, Magnum XE, Monaco and Fury). However, all of the visual components looked completely new, and sales improved for the Chrysler models, though the Dodge just couldn't get moving out of the showroom. While the Dodge Magnum XE and Chrysler Cordoba continued to be available, there were not significant changes for this year. It was the same with the Dodge Aspen and Diplomat, Plymouth Volaré and Chrysler LeBaron.

The Dodge Omni and Plymouth Horizon added new two-door running mates for 1979. The new two-door hatchbacks, named the Omni 024 and Horizon TC3, were built on a 2.5-inch shorter wheelbase but were nearly 8 inches longer overall, with a longer hood and sporty fastback rooflines not unlike the early Dodge Chargers. The new two-door models shared powertrains and basic interior design features with their respective four-door models. The Dodge Colt captive imports added a small new front-wheel drive hatchback coupe, and Plymouth gained the identical model under the Champ nameplate. In the truck and van lines, not much changed, except for the introduction of two new Mitsubishi-built small trucks. The Arrow pickup truck was added to the expanding Plymouth truck line, which already consisted of the Voyager vans and Trail Duster sport utility truck. Front-end styling was similar to that of the Arrow hatchback and nearly identical to the Dodge D50 truck that was also introduced. The Arrow pickup came in a base and a Sport model.

May 1, 1979, marked 25 years since the formation of American Motors Corporation out of the remaining products of the former Hudson and Nash motorcar companies. To commemorate the merger, a special 25th anniversary edition of the Concord was created. Unfortunately, this year also marked the beginning of the end for the lone surviving independent American manufacturer. Talks began this year with Renault which eventually led to the French automaker taking a $200 million stake in American Motors. Part of the plan was to build Renault cars in the Kenosha, Wisconsin, plant as well as to sell Renault cars in AMC showrooms. The latter happened almost immediately, with the mini-compact LeCar, the compact 18i, and the sporty Fuego coupe joining AMC products in the showroom. While the plan to build cars did not materialize as soon as expected, it did eventually lead to the introduction of the jointly designed AMC Alliance, and later Encore, being built and sold in the United States.

New from AMC this year was the Spirit compact, created on the chassis of the prior Gremlin, and offered in two versions, liftback and sedan. The sedan used the same basic body design of the Gremlin with enlarged side windows and new front and rear styling. The liftback, however, had a new roofline, creating a sporty-looking hatchback model that would also serve as the basis for this year's AMX model. The Pacer continued to struggle even as AMC did its best to continue to add luxury features, making it one of the most luxurious compact cars currently available. With the mid-size Matador gone from the lineup, the American Motors line now consisted entirely of compact sized cars, taking it full circle back to its small car roots of 25 years prior. In the AMC Jeep line, the Wagoneer Limited was introduced, officially marking the move of the four-door wagon, as it was then called, into the luxury arena. Priced at $12,485, it was the first AMC product to break the $10,000 price barrier, and would go on to define the luxury SUV (sport utility vehicle) market in the United States. The era of the SUV would not truly begin until around 1982, when other manufacturers took notice that consumers would buy large four-door wagon type vehicles, and also about the time that smaller types of these vehicles with car-like features began showing up in the form of the Chevy S-10 Blazer and Ford Bronco II.

1979 Overview and Changes from Prior Year

- **Total industry model year production:** 9,186,473, down 2.53%.
- **Total estimated captive import sales:** 234,041, up 14.35%.
- **Market share by corporation:** GM 58.46%; Ford 29.22%; Chrysler 10.47%; AMC 1.84%.
- **Number of models and body types available:** 245, down from 253.

- **Highest production series:** Chevrolet Impala/Caprice — 588,638.
- **Lowest production series:** Cadillac Fleetwood 75 — 2,025.
- **Highest individual model production:** Ford Thunderbird 2-Door Hardtop — 284,141.
- **Lowest individual model production:** Buick Skylark 2-Door Hatchback Coupe — 608.
- **Industry average base price:** $5,737, up 9.67%.
- **Highest individual model base price:** Cadillac Fleetwood 75 Limousine, $21,735.
- **Lowest individual model base price:** Chevette Scooter 2-Door Hatchback Coupe, $3,299.
- **Highest estimated MPG with base powertrain:** Chevrolet Chevette, 29 MPG.
- **Lowest estimated MPG with base powertrain:** Lincoln Continental and Continental Mark V, 12 MPG.
- **Indianapolis 500 Pace Car:** Ford Mustang 2-Door Hatchback w/T-tops.
- *Motor Trend* magazine "Car of the Year": Buick Riviera S-Type 2-Door Coupe.

AMERICAN MOTORS

"The only new cars backed by the Buyer Protection Plan."

The 1979 model year was an important one for American Motors in several ways, some of which would ultimately determine its future as an automotive concern. To kick off the new model year, the replacement for the Gremlin was introduced, under the name Spirit. As had been done in 1978 for the new Concord when it replaced the Hornet series, the new Spirit was intended to take the old Gremlin to new heights, while adding a sportier image to the AMC lineup. At mid-year, a Silver Anniversary Concord DL Limited Edition model was introduced to commemorate 25 years since the merger of Hudson and Nash that formed American Motors Corporation. The limited edition model came in two- or four-door sedans and featured two-tone silver paint treatment, special wire wheel covers, black or russet corduroy interior, and Silver Anniversary nameplates inside and out. This would be the last model year for V8 engines at American Motors, as the emphasis on fuel economy and the government's regulations introduced for 1978 made the discontinuation necessary. Sales of the V8 engines had dropped steadily since 1976 for AMC.

Styling for the new Spirit made use of the old Gremlin's fenders, hood and doors, but completely new rear quarters. Built on the former Gremlin platform, the new Liftback model, or Coupe as it was often called, had a fastback style rear design with a large liftgate window, and dispensed with the cut-off rear-end look of the Gremlin. The rear end's relatively flat panel housed nearly full-width tail lamps, interrupted only by the license plate housing. Large round side marker lamps on the rear quarters gave the Spirit a unique look. The new Liftback coupe had better overall proportions than the stubby-looking Gremlin. However, to help retain Gremlin loyalists, within weeks after the Liftback coupe's introduction, the new "Sedan" hit showroom floors. The Sedan had all the distinguishing traits of the Gremlin, including the cut-off slant-back roofline and the 1977–1978 Gremlin's oversized squarish taillamps and large rear window liftgate. A larger rear quarter window on the Spirit sedan, with a flat lower edge extending to a traditional C-pillar, eliminated the upward and reverse cant of the Gremlin's window that hindered rearward visibility. Overall, it was a welcome addition for traditional Gremlin buyers, giving the old car a new look.

At the front end, the new Spirit models shared an all-new look that would soon be on all AMC models. Dual rectangular headlights were mounted above two-section parking and turn signal lights. In between was a five bar horizontal grille with black mesh set behind. In the center was a round medallion with the AMC logo in the center. Under the hood could be found all the familiar Gremlin engine choices; the new Liftback model also offered the 304 CID V8, which gave the new car a performance image, especially in combination with the optional GT package. Inside the new Spirit received updated trim and designs that rivaled the Concord in luxurious appointments, including redesigned instrument panels with woodgrain appliqués, full-length front floor consoles, and rich looking upholstery and materials. It all added up to the most luxurious compact car American Motors had ever produced.

To further raise the ante for performance-minded drivers, the AMX model was all new this year being based on the Spirit Liftback, rather than the former Concord Hatchback model. The AMX had all of the Spirit Liftback styling features, along with most of the prior year's add-on features, such as fender flares, front and rear spoilers, and blackout paint treatments on most areas of brightwork. Powering the AMX could be a standard 258 CID 6-cylinder engine or the optional 304 CID V8 engine. Interior features expanded on the Spirit's generous appointments, with brushed aluminum accents, leather appointments, and a full array of gauges. Always ahead of their time, AMC had unknowingly created one of the first "pocket rockets," as they would come to be known.

The 1978 Concord had paved the way for AMC to move "upmarket," and this year continued the trend with a new front-end appearance and interior styling tweaks. The new front end used the same new dual rectangular headlight configuration as the new Spirit, with similar turn signal/parking lights in a single unit. The Concord, however, had its own new waterfall style grille, divided into six sections by slightly larger vertical chrome bars. The grille overlapped what was once the chrome surrounding the entire front end,

and was capped by a larger chrome piece on the leading edge of the hood, with Concord script engraved in the upper driver's side. Above it all was a new vertical, rectangular hood ornament. Hatchbacks could be ordered with a half-vinyl roof that included a brushed aluminum "targa-roof" band arching over the roof. With the Matador gone from the lineup, the Pacer languished on with very few changes, adding a door pull grip to the top front end of the raised door panel area. It was the only AMC model remaining that had not received major styling updates recently, excepting of the course the addition of the station wagon in 1977 and the new hood and grille for 1978.

As part of American Motors' attempt at moving up-market, the Spirit and Concord tripled the size of their model lineups: the previously optional D/L package became separate models, the Pacer base series was eliminated with a new D/L taking its place, and an even more luxurious Limited model was added to all but the Concord Hatchback. The new Limited series featured previously optional equipment such as leather upholstery, AM radio, power door locks, tilt steering wheel, and option groups including e.g., the light and visibility groups. Full details of standard equipment are in the model listings that follow. Also note that these new trim levels did not carry different model numbers, so the production figures in the model listings are by body style, with all trim levels included within the total.

Finally, there were several newsworthy events for the company as a whole this year. First was the fact that American Motors recorded record-breaking profits for 1979. This came largely on the strength of the new Spirit and AMX lines, and the continued popularity of the Concord. Secondly, to back up the company's long-standing Buyer's Protection Program and their full 12-month/12,000 mile warranty, AMC added a three-year corrosion warranty for the new 1979 models. Also during 1979, American Motors strengthened the relationship with Renault begun last year, with the French company paying for a $200 million dollar interest in AMC. With Renault becoming a major stockholder in the company, plans began for developing a joint venture car to be assembled in Kenosha, Wisconsin, with Renault supplied drivetrains.

AMX 2-Door Liftback

AMX 2-Door Liftback

Concord D/L 2-Door Hatchback

Concord D/L 2-Door Sedan
with 25th Anniversary package

Concord D/L 4-Door Sedan

Concord D/L 4-Door Station Wagon

Pacer D/L 2-Door Station Wagon

Pacer Limited 2-Door Hatchback Coupe

Spirit D/L 2-Door Liftback

Spirit D/L 2-Door Sedan

Model year production: 169,439, down 3.29% from 1978.
Domestic market share: 1.84% (12th place).
Base price range: $3,853 to $6,189.
American Motors average base price: $4,971, up 18.67%.
Introduction date: September 19, 1978.
Assembly plants: Kenosha, Wisconsin, and Brampton, Ontario, Canada.
Data plate identification (VIN): Thirteen digit code read as follows: First digit indicates company (A = American Motors); second digit indicates model year (9 = 1979); third digit is transmission code (see powertrain chart); fourth through sixth digits indicate car line–body type–series numbers (three-digit model number in model charts); seventh digit is engine code (see powertrain chart); eighth digit indicates assembly plant (1 through 6 = Kenosha, 7 through 9 = Ontario); remaining digits are sequential with beginning number of 00001. *Example:* A9A067H100001 is a 1979 Concord 2-Door Sedan, 304 CID, 2-bbl. V8, with Torque-Command Automatic, serial number 00001, built in Kenosha.

Powertrains[1]

Engine	Net HP	Engine/ Trans. Codes[2]	Transmission Availability[2]		Spirit	AMX	Pacer	Concord
121 CID (2.0L) OHC, 2-bbl., 4-cyl.	80	G/F	4-speed manual[3]		S[3]	—	—	NC[3,4]
				MPG:	22/33	—	—	2233
		G/A	Torque-Command 3-sp. Automatic		S (Calif.)[5]/ $296 (49 states)	—	—	NC[4] (Calif.)/ $323[4] (49 states)
				MPG:	20	—	—	20
				Calif.	19	—	—	19
232 CID (3.8L), 1-bbl., 6-cyl.[3]	90	E/S	3-speed manual		$20	—	—	—
				MPG:	20	—	—	—
		E/F	4-speed manual		$50	—	—	S
				MPG:	18	—	—	18

Engine	Net HP	Engine/ Trans. Codes[2]	Transmission Availability[2]		Spirit	AMX	Pacer	Concord
		E/A	Torque-Command 3-sp. Automatic		$346	—	—	$323
				MPG:	19	—	—	18
258 CID (4.2L), 2-bbl., 6-cyl.	100	C/F	4-speed manual[3]		$180[3]	S[3]	S[3]	$130[3]
				MPG:	17	17	17	17
		C/A	Torque-Command 3-sp. Automatic		$270 (Calif.)[5]/ $476 (49 states)	S (Calif.)[5]/ $296 (49 states)[6]	S (Calif.)[5]/ $323 (49 states)	S (Calif.)[5]/ $426 (49 states)
				MPG:	17	17	17	17
				Calif.	15	15	15	15
304 CID (5.0L), 2-bbl., V8[3]	125	H/F	4-speed manual		$250 (Liftback only)	$250	—	—
				MPG:	13	13	—	—
		H/A	Torque-Command 3-sp. Automatic		$546 (Liftback only)	$546	$573	$573
				MPG:	15	15	14	15

[1]Optional axle ratio required on cars sold in California: Spirit 6-cylinder automatic, 3.08:1; Pacer 6-cylinder, 3.08:1; Concord 6-cylinders, 3.08:1. [2]Unless otherwise noted: Add $25 for floor-shifter on Spirit automatics and on Pacer 6-cylinders w/bucket or individual reclining seats. Floor-shift is standard on AMX and Pacer V8s. Transmission code with automatic floor shift is C. [3]Not available in California. [4]Not available on Concord Wagons. [5]Standard for cars sold in California. Base prices adjust accordingly; i.e., add $296 for Spirit or AMX, and $323 for Pacer or Concord. [6]Requires floor shift which is included in price. Transmission code is C.

Major Options

	Spirit[1]	AMX	Pacer[1]	Concord[1]
Air conditioning	$513	$513	$513	$513
Tilt steering wheel	$72	$72	$72	$72
Cruise control[2]	$104	$104	$104	$104
Electric rear window defogger	$89	$89	$89	$89
Tinted glass, all windows	$57	$57	$63	$60
Power windows and door locks	—	—	$194	—
Power door locks	$72	$72	$72	$72[3]
Front bucket seats, vinyl upholstered	S	S	—	—
Front floor console (requires bucket seats)	$75	S	—	—
AM radio	$84	$84	$84	$84
AM/FM stereo multiplex w/4 speakers	$236	$236	$236	$236
AM/FM stereo w/cassette tape player	—	—	$353	$353
AM/FM stereo w/Citizens Band radio (CB)[4]	$314	$314	$314	$314
Vinyl top (excluding wagon models)	—	—	$124[5]	—
Pop-up moonroof	$178[5]	$178	$178[5]	$178[5]
Woodgrain paneling (wagons only)	—	—	$117	$75
Power steering[6]	$152	$152	$158	$158
Power front disc brakes	$70	$70	$70	$70
Color-keyed wheel covers	$	—	S	S
Spoke style wheels	$145	—	$145	$145
Turbo cast II aluminum wheels	$300	S	$300	$300
White sidewall tires, standard size	$48	—	S	$48

Popular Option Groups & Packages

	Spirit[1]	AMX	Pacer[1]	Concord[1]
Convenience group	$75	$75	$75	$75
Extra Quiet insulation package	$48	S	S	$48
Gauge package	$104	S	$129	—
GT package	$450[7]	—	—	—
GT rally-tuned suspension, w/GT package only	$99	—	—	—

	Spirit[1]	AMX	Pacer[1]	Concord[1]
Light Group	$45	$35	$39	$49
Protection group	$42	—	—	$87
Visibility group	$50	—	$50	$62

— = Not Available; S = Standard equipment.   [1]Note that many of these features may be included as standard in the D/L or Limited trim levels. Therefore prices may also vary by trim levels. Consult the major standard equipment section in the model listings that follow to confirm standard equipment.   [2]Not available with 4-cylinder engine or manual transmission.   [3]Price given is for 2-door models. Available on 4-door sedan and wagon for $104.   [4]CB radio is 40-channel version.   [5]Not available with roof rack or on wagon models.   [6]Required with V8 engine and air conditioning.   [7]Price given is with D/L trim. Available with Limited trim level for $200.

Paint Colors

	Code	AMX		Code	AMX
Firecracker Red	6P	x	Saxon Yellow	9L	x
Khaki	8A	—	Starboard Blue metallic	9M	—
British Bronze metallic	8B	—	Morocco Buff	9N	x
Quick Silver metallic	8C	—	Bordeaux metallic	9P	—
Alpaca Brown metallic	9A	—	Misty Beige metallic — clearcoat*	9Z*	—
Olympic White	9B	x	Classic Black	P1	x
Russet metallic	9C	—			
Wedgewood Blue	9E	x	*Non-standard model colors are available at $26 extra cost, except on AMX. Two-tone paint combinations available on Spirit and Pacer for $65; and Concord for $100. *Available only on Pacer for $60 extra cost.*		
Cumberland Green metallic	9H	—			
Sable Brown metallic	9K	—			

Spirit

*"Introducing a lively new means of
American transportation—AMC Spirit."*

Nameplate year of origin: 1979.
Current bodystyle lifespan: 1970 through 1983; Gremlin (1970 to 1978), restyled and renamed Spirit (1979 to 1982). 4WD added and rebadged Eagle SX/4 (1981 to 1983).
Predecessor to this model: Gremlin (1970 to 1978).
Replacement for this model: Eagle SX/4 (1981 to 1983).
Percentage of division's production: 24.73%.
Corporate siblings: None; however many components were shared with the Concord.
Primary competition: Buick/Opel Isuzu, Chevrolet Monza, Dodge Colt, Dodge Omni 024, Ford Pinto, Plymouth Arrow, and Plymouth Horizon TC3.
Notable changes: Completely restyled and renamed Spirit.
Major standard equipment: Sport vinyl bucket seats, fold-down rear seat, color-keyed carpeting and seat belts, custom steering wheel, carpeted cargo area, spare tire cover, dual bodyside pinstripes, bright moldings

Measurements

	Liftback	Sedan
Wheelbase	96.0"	96.0"
Length	168.5"	166.8"
Width	71.1"	71.1"
Height	51.6"	51.7"
Legroom — front	40.8"	40.8"
Legroom — rear	27.7"	27.8"
Headroom — front	37.8"	38.1"
Headroom — rear	33.5"	36.4"
Cargo capacity (cu. ft.)	24.8*	28.6*
Fuel capacity (gals.)	21.0	21.0**

*With rear seat folded down. **13.0 gallons on 4-cylinder models.

(drip rail, wheel lip and windshield surround), chrome-plated aluminum bumpers with black end caps, rear bumper guards, full wheel covers, and C78 × 14 BSW tires. D/L adds: Choice of caberfae corduroy or sport vinyl bucket seats, folding split rear seat back, custom door trim panels, custom headliner and sunvisors, luxury woodgrain steering wheel, walnut burl woodgrain I/P overlays, I/P package shelf, electronic quartz digital clock, day/night mirror, courtesy lights, front bumper guards, color-keyed full wheel covers, and C78 × 14 WSW tires. Limited adds: Genuine leather bucket seats, full-length console w/center armrest, 18oz. color-keyed carpeting, AM radio, power door locks, power liftback release (Liftback only), dual remote control mirrors, tilt steering wheel, light group, visibility group, convenience group, protection group, and P195/75R14 WSW tires.

Models Available

	Model No.	Base MSRP	Change from LY*	Shipping Wt. (lbs.)	Model Year Production	Change from LY*
Spirit 2-Door Sedan	46-7	$3,853	+1.69%**	2489	*	-16.00%**

	Model No.	Base MSRP	Change from LY*	Shipping Wt. (lbs.)	Model Year Production	Change from LY*
Spirit 2-Door Liftback	43-7	$3,953	NEW	2545	*	NEW
Spirit D/L 2-Door Sedan	46-7	$4,090	NEW	2579	*	NEW
Spirit D/L 2-Door Liftback	43-7	$4,190	NEW	2635	*	NEW
Spirit Limited 2-Door Sedan	46-7	$5,090	NEW	2676	*	NEW
Spirit Limited 2-Door Liftback	43-7	$5,190	NEW	2732	*	NEW
TOTALS	Avg. price	$4,394	+18.58%	Production	52,714	+138.48%

*Production records by model or body style were not kept, only by engine installation. Production by engine type (compared to 1978 Gremlin): 4-cylinder, 16,237 (+155.74%); 6-cylinder, 36,241 (+130.03%); V8, 3,893 (new). These numbers include 3,657 AMX models, which did not offer a 4-cylinder engine, and with most presumably having the V8 engine. **Comparison made to 1978 Gremlin Custom.

AMX

"The styling says sizzle. The performance is nothing short of inspiring. Meet AMX for 1979."

Nameplate year of origin: 1968.
Current bodystyle lifespan: 1979 through 1980.
Predecessor to this model: AMX (1978).
Replacement for this model: None.
Percentage of division's production: 0.85%.
Corporate siblings: Spirit liftback; many components shared with the Concord.
Primary competition: Buick Skyhawk w/Road Hawk package, Chevrolet Monza w/Spyder package, Dodge Challenger, Ford Mustang, Mercury Capri, Oldsmobile Starfire w/Firenza package, Plymouth Sapporo, and Pontiac Sunbird w/Formula package.
Notable changes: Now based on newly redesigned Spirit liftback coupe.
Major standard equipment: Caberfae or sport vinyl custom front bucket seats, 12 oz. color-keyed carpeting, full-length console w/integral center armrest, custom door trim panels w/brushed aluminum accents, brushed aluminum I/P overlays, gauge package, intermittent windshield wipers, I/P package tray, color-keyed leather wrapped sports steering wheel, custom headliner and sun visors, folding split rear seat back, power liftgate release, Extra Quiet insulation package, dual black remote control mirrors, "AMX" graphics w/"AMX" flame decal on hood, black bumpers w/bumper guards and nerfing strips (front and rear), color-keyed front air dam and rear deck spoiler w/accent stripes, color-keyed front and rear fender flares w/accent stripes, unique black grille insert and black headlight bezels, front sway bar, Turbocast II aluminum wheels w/black accents, and ER60 × 14 OWL tires.

Measurements

Wheelbase	96.0"
Length	168.5"
Width	71.1"
Height	51.6"
Legroom — front	40.8"
Legroom — rear	27.7"
Headroom — front	37.8"
Headroom — rear	33.5"
Cargo capacity (cu. ft.)	24.8*
Fuel capacity (gals.)	21.0

*Maximum with rear seat down.

Models Available

	Model No.	Base MSRP	Change from LY	Shipping Wt. (lbs.)	Model Year Production	Change from LY
AMX 2-Door Liftback	43-9	$6,090	+31.00%	2899	3,657	+43.98%
TOTALS	Avg. price	$6,090	+31.00%	Production	3,657	+43.98%

Pacer

"An exceptional blend of big car room, ride and comfort. A unique, distinctive car for the discriminating buyer."

Nameplate year of origin: 1975 (previously used by Ford Motor Company on 1958 Edsel series).
Current bodystyle lifespan: 1975 through 1980.
Predecessor to this model: None.

Measurements

	Sedan	Wagon
Wheelbase	100.0"	100.0"

Replacement for this model: None.
Percentage of division's production: 4.79%.
Corporate siblings: None.
Primary competition: Buick Skyhawk and Mercury Bobcat.
Notable changes: Minor trim and detail changes.
Major standard equipment: Choice of Caberfae corduroy or sport individual reclining front seats or front bucket seats, fold-down rear seat, 12 oz. color-keyed carpeting and color-keyed seat belts, custom door trim panels, custom headliner and sunvisors, custom steering wheel w/woodgrain overlays, walnut burl woodgrain I/P overlays, carpeted cargo area w/skid strips, electric clock, day/night mirror, courtesy lights, Extra Quiet insulation package, bright moldings (wheel lip and windshield surround), hood ornament and hood windsplit molding, front and rear bumper guards, front sway bar, color-keyed full wheel covers, and P195/75R14 WSW tires.
Limited adds: Genuine leather individual reclining seats w/beige corduroy accents, folding center armrest, 18oz. color-keyed carpeting, luxury woodgrain steering wheel, AM radio, power windows, power door locks, dual remote control mirrors, tilt steering wheel, light group, visibility group, convenience group, protection group, and color-keyed styled wheel covers.

Measurements (cont.)

	Sedan	Wagon
Length	172.7"	177.7"
Width	77.0"	77.0"
Height	52.8"	53.1"
Legroom — front	40.7"	40.7"
Legroom — rear	35.0"	35.0"
Headroom — front	38.4"	38.5"
Headroom — rear	36.9"	38.0"
Cargo capacity (cu. ft.)	32.2*	52.5*
Fuel capacity (gals.)	21.0	21.0

*With rear seat folded down.

Models Available

	Model No.	Base MSRP	Change from LY*	Shipping Wt. (lbs.)	Model Year Production*	Change from LY*
Pacer D/L 2-Door Sedan	66-7	$5,039	NEW	3197	2,863	-61.37%
Pacer D/L 2-Door Station Wagon	68-7	$5,189	NEW	3245	7,352	-46.80%
Pacer Limited 2-Door Sedan	66-7	$6,039	NEW	3197	*	
Pacer Limited 2-Dr. Station Wgn.	68-7	$6,189	NEW	3245	*	NEW
TOTALS		Avg. price $5,614	+36.25%		Production 10,215	-51.89%

*D/L and Limited series are combined, and compared with base series of 1978 Pacer models. Price comparison by models is not possible as 1978 Pacer came only in a base model.

Concord

"Elegant comfort and an excellent value."

Nameplate year of origin: 1978 (previously used by Chrysler Corporation on 1951–1952 Plymouth series).
Current bodystyle lifespan: 1970 through 1987; Hornet (1970–1977), restyled and renamed Concord (1978 to 1982); 4WD added and rebadged Eagle (1980 to 1987).
Predecessor to this model: Hornet (1970 to 1977).
Replacement for this model: Eagle (1980 to 1987).
Percentage of division's production: 48.26%.
Corporate siblings: None; however, many components were shared with the Spirit.
Primary competition: Buick Skylark, Dodge Diplomat, Mercury Monarch, Oldsmobile Omega, and Pontiac Phoenix.
Notable changes: New grille and headlight treatment and minor trim and detail changes.
Major standard equipment: Sport vinyl notched bench front seat, fold-down rear seat (hatchback and wagon), 12 oz. color-keyed carpeting and color-keyed seat belts, custom steering wheel, carpeted cargo area, lighted ashtray, dual bodyside pinstripes, bright moldings (drip rail, wheel lip, hood front edge, and windshield surround), chrome-plated aluminum bumpers with black end caps, rear bumper guards, front sway bar, full wheel covers, and D78 × 14 BSW tires. D/L adds: Velveteen Crush fabric or sport vinyl individual reclining front seats, custom door trim panels, custom headliner and sunvisors, custom steering wheel w/woodgrain overlays, walnut burl woodgrain I/P overlays, I/P package shelf, electronic quartz digital clock, day/night mirror, courtesy lights, front bumper guards, color-keyed wide bodyside scuff moldings, engine compartment light, and color-keyed full wheel covers. Limited adds: Genuine leather individual reclining front

Measurements

	Sedans	Hatchback	Wagon
Wheelbase	108.0"	108.0"	108.0"
Length	186.0"	186.0"	186.0"
Width	71.0"	71.0"	71.0"
Height	51.6"	51.6"	51.3"
Legroom — front	40.8"	40.8"	40.8"
Legroom — rear	35.7"	36.1"	36.1"
Headroom — front	38.1"	38.1"	38.1"
Headroom — rear	37.5"	36.7"	37.9"
Cargo capacity (cu. ft.)	10.8	32.0*	59.2*
Fuel capacity (gals.)	22.0	22.0	22.0

*Maximum with rear seat down, and 2.2 cu. ft. below cargo floor on wagon.

seats w/beige corduroy accents, 18 oz. color-keyed carpeting, AM radio, power door locks, dual remote control mirrors, tilt steering wheel, luxury woodgrain steering wheel, light group, visibility group, convenience group, protection group, color-keyed styled wheel covers, and P195/75R14 WSW tires.

Models Available

	Model No.	Base MSRP	Change from LY*	Shipping Wt. (lbs.)	Model Year Production	Change from LY*
Concord 2-Door Sedan	06-7	$4,389	+17.07%	2873	40,110	-20.55%
Concord 2-Door Hatchback	03-7	$4,324	+12.34%	2888	2,331	-9.37%
Concord 4-Door Sedan	05-7	$4,489	+16.63%	2939	40,134	-4.73%
Concord 4-Door Station Wagon	08-7	$4,689	+15.81%	2977	20,278	-13.98%
Concord D/L 2-Door Sedan	06-7	$4,688	NEW	2982	*	NEW
Concord D/L 2-Door Hatchback	03-7	$4,623	NEW	3003	*	NEW
Concord D/L 4-Door Sedan	05-7	$4,788	NEW	3040	*	NEW
Concord D/L 4-Door Station Wagon	08-7	$4,988	NEW	3072	*	NEW
Concord Limited 2-Door Sedan	06-7	$5,688	NEW	3090	*	NEW
Concord Limited 4-Door Sedan	05-7	$5,788	NEW	3146	*	NEW
Concord Limited 4-Door Station Wagon	08-7	$5,988	NEW	3177	*	NEW
TOTALS	*Avg. price*	$4,949	+27.76%	*Production*	102,853	-13.39%

*Production of base, D/L and Limited series was kept combined, and comparison is made with base series of 1978 Concord models. Production by engine type (compared to LY): 4-cylinder, 6,355 (+68.12%); 6-cylinder, 91,842 (-17.24%); V8, 4,656 (-28.82%).

BUICK

"After all, life is to enjoy."

A little science and magic did not seem to help Buick during the 1978 model year, but a new model to begin the 1979 season and a second following at mid-year promised an upbeat end to a roller coaster decade. Excitement built early on for dealers and consumers as the Riviera was downsized. For the first time ever it was sharing a front-wheel-drive platform and powertrain with its sister E-body cars, the Cadillac Eldorado and Oldsmobile Toronado. The new car, the fifth Buick to be downsized since 1977, brought back some of the excitement that surrounded the original 1963 Riviera. Buyers flocked to the Riviera, driving sales up to more than two-and-half times the 1978 total, with production outpacing the combined 1977–1978 B-body Riviera's by more than 5,000 units. The only factors holding Buick back from a production increase this model year, aside from the brief fuel shortage and recession scare, were the failure of the fastback-styled Century models to catch on with the public, and the Skylark's being discontinued three months into the selling season to make way for the all-new X-body Skylark to be introduced in the spring as a 1980 model. And although Buick sales slid more than most, it was not the fault of any of the full-size Buicks, the all-new Riviera, or the Regal.

The new Riviera was so far advanced from its immediate predecessor that it was destined to become an instant success. The new front-wheel-drive format used four-wheel independent suspension to improve ride and handling, while a choice of a V8 or turbocharged V6 engine ensured brisk performance. On the outside, a formal roofline with an all-new, aerodynamic flush-mounted windshield and a gently curved bodyside feature line provided a modern take on the original 1963 Riviera. Fully rounded wheel openings added a sporting touch. At the front a classic Buick "waterfall" style grille divided into eight sections graced the front end, dropping slightly into the top center of the front bumper. Black bumper strips with a white pinstripe ran near the top of the bumper from the grille outwards and around the corner, adding a divided front bumper look as seen on many early 1930s model luxury cars. Dual rectangular headlamps above the turn signal/parking lamps were set in chrome bezels, with a thin chrome section dividing them and continuing the waterfall grill theme. Around back the sloping trunk lid led into chrome-rimmed horizontal rectangular tail light housings, with the Riviera logo placed in the middle of each and serving double duty as the backup lights.

The Riviera was just as new inside, boasting as much interior room as both its immediate predecessor and the 1971 through 1976 Rivieras — this despite an exterior a foot shorter than the '77–'78 models, and a two-inch shorter wheelbase. Some of the space came from the switch to front-wheel drive eliminating the transmission tunnel; at the same time a small amount of luggage space was lost in the transition. Within the all-new interior the instrument panel drew the most attention. A flat, full-width top surface joined a tall, flat, full-width instrument panel slathered in simulated woodgrain trim. All driver controls were set in rectangular pods directly above the steering column, while radio, climate controls, and the newly available computer-controlled Trip Monitor option were stacked in the center section. A massive glove box completed the instrument panel. The new Trip Monitor, an $850 option introduced early in 1979, was an onboard computer with touch button features to calculate everything from the number of hours to reach a destination, to the estimated time of arrival, number of miles left before needing to refuel, and miles remaining to destination. Also included in the option were a digital speedometer and trip odometer, digital engine temperature display, and digital clock. Apparently Buick didn't feel the technology had yet proven itself enough for a digital odometer, as a traditional odometer was set below the digital speedometer.

Nearly all of the other 1979 Buicks received new front-end styling or new grilles. The compact Skyhawk added a new front end with single square headlamps on each side of a new body-colored grille that was six columns wide and two rows high, with a horizontal crosshatch design inset. A chrome hawk logo was placed on the header panel above the grille. Along the bodysides, new vertical louvers covered the rear portion of the rear quarter side window and an additional vertical bar widened the door pillar, giving the rear quarter window a smaller and more formal appearance, although the full window was still in place beneath. It definitely set the Skyhawk apart from its corporate kin. A new option package called the Road Hawk added a front air dam and rear spoiler as well as many blackout features, making it the sportiest looking Skyhawk to date; special interior trim, a silver and gray paint scheme, and a Rallye ride-and-handling package rounded out the Road Hawk features.

Skylark entered its final year as a body-on-frame, rear-wheel drive compact car with a facelift that included a new egg-crate grille design divided in half vertically and horizontally. The front turn signal/parking lamps now had fully amber lenses broken by a single horizontal strip. The Custom hatchback model was dropped, as the hatchbacks had always been a slower selling body style. Soon after production of the 1979 models commenced, the announcement was made that all-new front-wheel-drive replacements for the aging X-

cars would be introduced in the spring of 1979, so by December production was shut down for the factories to retool. As a result, production for the 1979 model year was down nearly 75 percent.

The mid-size Regal and Century models received new grilles, with the Regal's waterfall design using slightly thicker chrome bars and the Century wearing a new crosshatch grille design consisting of vertical segments three rows high and twenty rows across. New for the Century was a Turbo Coupe package combining the 231 c.i.d. turbo V6 engine with blackout exterior trim, turbine-style wheels, a "turbo hood" with raised center hump, large "Turbo Coupe" rear decal and other sporty cosmetic touches. Otherwise, only detail trim changes were seen. Production of the Regal rose again this year, while the Century tumbled by more than 30 percent, wiping out the Regal's gains and showing Buick that the public was not taking to the fastback body design. A similar situation was occurring with the Oldsmobile Cutlass line, but fortunately the situation would be corrected for the four-door models next year. One sign of the situation was the elimination of the Century Limited 2-Door coupe from the line for 1979.

Full-size Buicks also received new grilles, and in the case of the Electra, a new header panel. For the LeSabre and Estate Wagon, two cross bars divided the grille into three sections filled with many thin chrome vertical bars, making for a more luxurious looking grille. The Electra added a new front fascia panel that extended the top point of the front fender further out, and slanting down to the bumper, as opposed to the prior version which was like the LeSabre's and sloped forward along the headlight area only. The Electra's new upright grille was divided into sections three rows high and six sections across, each section being filled with an egg-crate pattern. The new side marker lights were now separated from the turn signal/parking lamp combination. The Estate Wagon continued to offer the Limited package, which added the Electra front-end styling to the luxury wagon.

Finally, Buick's imported Opels added square headlights and wore a slightly updated horizontal theme grille, with slightly larger parking lamps. Otherwise few changes were made. Sharply rising dollar to yen currency exchange rates caused price increases of well over 20 percent. This factor combined with continually declining sales, and Isuzu's desire to enter the U.S. market with its own sales and marketing, prompted General Motors to discontinue selling the Opel in Buick showrooms. After this decision was made, some Buick dealerships picked up the Isuzu franchise, and beginning in 1981, continued selling the Isuzu I-Mark which was the replacement for the Buick Opel/Isuzu, along with the rest of the Isuzu line.

1979

Century Limited 4-Door Sedan
with Designers' Accent paint

Electra Park Avenue 4-Door Sedan

Regal instrument panel

Skyhawk 2-Door Hatchback Coupe

Skylark 4-Door Sedan

Century Special 2-Door Coupe (top)
and Century Custom 4-Door Sedan

Estate Wagon

Regal Sport Coupe 2-Door

Skyhawk 2-Door Hatchback Coupe
with Road Hawk package

Century Turbo Coupe 2-Door (top)
and Century Sport Coupe 2-Door

LeSabre Sport Coupe 2-Door

Riviera S Type 2-Door Coupe

Skylark 2-Door Coupe

Opel Isuzu Deluxe 2-Door Coupe

Model year production: 727,274, down 9.45% from 1978.
Domestic market share: 7.92% (5th place).
Base price range: $4,082 to $10,388.
Buick average base price: $6,009, up 10.10%.
Introduction date: September 28, 1978.
Assembly plants: Linden, NJ (E); Framingham, MA (G); Flint, MI (H); Tarrytown, NY (T); Lordstown, OH (7); Willow Run, MI (W); Kansas City/Fairfax, KS (X); Fremont, CA (Z); St. Therese, Quebec, Canada (2). *Opel assembly plant:* Fujisawa, Japan (8).
Data plate identification (VIN): Thirteen digit code read as follows: First digit indicates division (4 = Buick); second through fourth digits indicate series and body style (model number in model charts); fifth digit is engine code (see powertrain chart); sixth digit indicates model year (9 = 1979); seventh digit indicates assembly plant (see list above); remaining digits are sequential with beginning number of 100001 with the following exceptions — all cars built at Lordstown, OH, series N, F, P, X, J, and W built at Flint, MI, and series Y and Z built at Linden, NJ, have beginning serial number of 400001. *Example:* 4N69X9H400001 is a 1979 Buick LeSabre 4-Door Sedan, with 350 CID, 4-bbl. V8 engine, serial number 400001, built in Flint, MI. 1979 Opels use a 13-digit code read the same as other 1979 Buicks except that the final six digits are sequential with beginning number of 700001.

Powertrains[1]

Engine	Net HP	Engine Code: VIN/GM	Transmission Availability		Opel	Skyhawk	Skylark	Century & Regal[2]	LeSabre[2]	Electra & Estate Wagon	Riviera
110.8 CID (1.8L) OHC, 2-bbl., 4-cyl.	80	B	4-speed manual		S	—	—	—	—	—	—
				MPG:	26	—	—	—	—	—	—
				Calif.	24	—	—	—	—	—	—
			5-speed manual		$138	—	—	—	—	—	—
				MPG:	26	—	—	—	—	—	—
				Calif.	24	—	—	—	—	—	—
			Turbo Hydra-matic 3-sp. Automatic		$345	—	—	—	—	—	—
				MPG:	25	—	—	—	—	—	—
				Calif.	23	—	—	—	—	—	—
196 CID (3.2L), 2-bbl., V6[3]	105	C/LC9	3-speed manual		—	—	—	S (ex. W & SC)	—	—	—
				MPG:	—	—	—	18	—	—	—
			4-speed manual		—	—	—	$135 (ex. W & SC)	—	—	—
				MPG:	—	—	—	16	—	—	—
			Turbo Hydra-matic 3-sp. Automatic		—	—	—	$335 (ex. W & SC)	—	—	—
				MPG:	—	—	—	20	—	—	—
231 CID (3.8L), 2-bbl., V6[4]	115	A/LD5 *or* 2/LC6	3-speed manual		—	—	S[3]	—	—	—	—
				MPG:	—	—	18	—	—	—	—
			4-speed manual		—	S	—	$175 (ex. W & SC)	—	—	—
				MPG:	—	16	—	16	—	—	—
				Calif.	—	14	—	—	—	—	—
			5-speed manual		—	$175	—	—	—	—	—
				MPG:	—	18	—	—	—	—	—
				Calif.	—	16	—	—	—	—	—
			Turbo Hydra-matic 3-sp. Automatic		—	$295	$335	S (W)/ $375 (ex. W & SC)[5]	S (ex. SC)	—	—
				MPG:	—	19	19	19	18/27	—	—
				Calif.	—	16	16	16	16	—	—
231 CID (3.8L), Turbocharged, 2-bbl., V6	150	G/LC5	Turbo Hydra-matic 3-sp. Automatic		—	—	—	S (Regal Turbo SC)[3]	—	—	—
				MPG:	—	—	—	—	—	—	—
231 CID (3.8L), Turbocharged, 4-bbl., V6	170	3/LC8	Turbo Hydra-matic 3-sp. Automatic		—	—	—	$50 (Regal Turbo SC)/ $470 (ex. W & SC)	S (SC only)[3]	—	S (Riviera S)[6]

Engine	Net HP	Engine Code: VIN/GM	Transmission Availability		Opel	Skyhawk	Skylark	Century & Regal[2]	LeSabre[2]	Electra & Estate Wagon	Riviera
				MPG:	—	—	—	17	16	—	16
				Calif.	—	—	—	16	15	—	15
301 CID (4.9L), 2-bbl., V8	140	Y/L27	Turbo Hydra-matic 3-sp. Automatic		—	—	—	$195 (W)/$235 (Regal SC)/$590 (ex. W & SC)[3]	$246 (ex. SC)[3]	—	—
				MPG:	—	—	—	18	17	—	—
301 CID (4.9L), 4-bbl., V8	150	W/L37	Turbo Hydra-matic 3-sp. Automatic		—	—	—	$245 (W)/$285 (Regal SC)/$640 (ex. W & SC)[3]	—	—	—
				MPG:	—	—	—	17	—	—	—
305 CID (5.0L), 2-bbl., V8	130	U/LG3	Turbo Hydra-matic 3-sp. Automatic		—	—	$530[3]	—	$246 (ex. SC)[7]	—	—
				MPG:	—	—	16	—	16	—	—
305 CID (5.0L), 4-bbl., V8	155	H/LG4	Turbo Hydra-matic 3-sp. Automatic		—	—	—	$320 (W)/$656 (ex. W & SC)[7]	—	—	—
				MPG:	—	—	—	16	—	—	—
350 CID (5.7L), 4-bbl., V8	155	X/L77	Turbo Hydra-matic 3-sp. Automatic		—	—	—	—	$371 (ex. SC)[3]	S[3,8]	S (Riviera)[3,8]/ -$110 (credit on Riviera S)
				MPG:	—	—	—	—	15	15	16
350 CID (5.7L), 4-bbl., V8	165	L/LM1	Turbo Hydra-matic 3-sp. Automatic		—	—	$655[3]	$320 (W)[9]	—	—	—
				MPG:	—	—	16	16	—	—	—
				Calif.	—	—	13	—	—	—	—
350 CID (5.7L), 4-bbl., V8	160	R/L34	Turbo Hydra-matic 3-sp. Automatic		—	—	$655[7]	—	$371 (ex. SC)[7]	S[8]	S (Riviera)[8]/ -$110 (credit on Riviera S)
				MPG:	—	—	15	—	14	14	16
				Calif.	—	—	—	—	14	14	14
403 CID (6.6L), 4-bbl., V8	175	K/L80	Turbo Hydra-matic 3-sp. Automatic		—	—	—	—	$441 (ex. SC)	$70	—
				MPG:	—	—	—	—	14	14	—
				Calif.	—	—	—	—	—	13	—

[1]Optional axle ratio required on cars sold in high-altitude counties: Skyhawk, 2.93:1; Skylark V6, 3.23:1. [2]SC = Sport Coupe; W = wagon. [3]Not available in California or high-altitude counties. Skylarks with LD5/LC6 requires optional automatic transmission in California. [4]LC6 231 CID V6 engine available only in California. [5]Standard on Regal and Century Coupes and Century Sedans in California. Prices adjust accordingly. [6]Riviera S rated at 175hp. [7]Available only in California or designated high-altitude counties. [8]L34 engine is standard in California and high-altitude counties on Estate Wagons, Electra and Riviera. [9]Century Wagons for sale in high-altitude counties are suggested to be equipped with LM1 engine.

Major Options

	Opel	Skyhawk	Skylark	Century	Regal	LeSabre	Estate Wagon	Electra 225	Riviera
Air conditioning[1]	$532	$496	$529	$562	$562	$605	$605	$605	S
Tilt-wheel steering[2]	—	$68	$75	$75	$75	$77	$77	$77	$77
Cruise-Master speed control	—	—	$103	$103	$103	$108	$108	$108	$108
Electric rear window defogger	$82	$87	$55[3]	$99	$99	$94	$94	$94	$101
Dual rearview mirrors, LH remote & RH manual	—	S	$45	$45	$40	$19	$19	S	S
Tinted glass, all windows	S	$60	$64	$70	$70	$84	$84	S	S

	Opel	Skyhawk	Skylark	Century	Regal	LeSabre	Estate Wagon	Electra 225	Riviera
Power windows, 2-dr./4-dr.	—	—	$126/$178	$132/$187	$132	$138/$205	$205	S	S
Power door locks, 2-dr./4-dr.	—	—	$80/$111	$86/$120	$86	$88/$122	$122	$88/$122	S
Power front seat, 6-way, driver's side	—	—	—	$163	$163	$166	$166	$166	S
Front bucket seats, w/console	S[4]	S	$170[5]	$135[5]	$135	$94[5]	—	—	S[5]
AM radio	$90	S	$82	$86	$86	$99	$99	$99	—
AM/FM stereo[6]	$171	$148	$236	$236	$236	$239	$239	$239	S
AM/FM stereo w/tape player[6]	—	$250	$345	$345	$345	$355	$355	$355	$116
Woodgrain exterior panels (wagons)	—	—	—	$289	—	—	$293	—	—
Vinyl top[7]	—	—	$104[8]	$116[8]	$116[8]	$145	—	$164	$285
Sunroof, electric	—	$180[9]	—	$529	$529	$725	—	$798	$798
Astroroof, sliding glass	—	$641[9]	—	$729[9]	$729	$925	—	$998	$998
Hatch-roof, T-tops	—	—	—	—	$655	—	—	—	—
Third row seating (wagons)	—	—	—	—	—	—	$194	—	—
Designers' accent paint	—	$175[10]	$161	$183	$182	$209	$240	—	$193
Power steering	—	$146	$163	$163[11]	$163[11]	S	S	S	S
Power brakes, w/front disc	S	$71	$76	$76[11]	$76[11]	S	S	S	S
Wire wheel covers	—	—	$160	$150	$118	$161	$119	$119	$120
Deluxe wheel covers	—	—	$42	$42	S	$42[12]	S	S	S[13]
Designers' sport wheels	—	$58[13]	—	$125	$106	—	—	—	S[13]
Special wheels, other[14]	—	$230	$99	—	$106	$667	$625	$625	—
Chrome plated road wheel	—	—	$139	$169	$150	$171	$152	$152	—
WSW tires, standard size	—	$45	$46	$40	$40	$48	$48	$48	S

Popular Option Groups & Packages

	Opel	Skyhawk	Skylark	Century	Regal	LeSabre	Estate Wagon	Electra 225	Riviera
Acoustical package	—	$25	$42	—	—	—	—	—	—
Convenience group	—	$24	$43	$47	$19	$99	$68	—	—
Decor package	—	—	—	—	$473	—	—	—	—
F40 firm ride handling package	—	—	$25	$21	$21	$21	$21	$21	—
FE2 Rallye ride/handling package	—	—	$48	$38	$38	—	—	—	$21
Limited package	—	—	—	—	—	—	$1,853	—	—
Road Hawk package	—	$696	—	—	—	—	—	—	—
Sport coupe/sedan package	—	—	$221	—	—	—	—	—	—
Sport package	—	—	—	—	—	$254	—	—	—
Sport wagon package	—	—	—	$473	—	—	—	—	—
Turbo Coupe package	—	—	—	$40	—	—	—	—	—

—= Not Available; S = Standard equipment. [1]Manually controlled. Automatic climate control is available for $88 additional on Century, Regal, LeSabre, Estate Wagon, Electra and Riviera. [2]Tilt and telescoping steering column available on LeSabre, Estate Wagon, Electra and Riviera at $50 additional cost. [3]Blower type defogger. [4]Opel Deluxe and SC models only. Opel base model has bucket seats standard and console is $20 extra. [5]Standard on Skylark Custom and Riviera S-Type. Available only on Century Custom and LeSabre coupe models. LeSabre models require Sport package. [6]Non-stereo on Opel. Tape player is 8-track or for $5 additional cassette tape. CB radio available on Skylark and Century for $338 extra; available on all full-size Buicks for $342 extra. [7]A variety of vinyl top configurations available, ranging in price from $145 to $200. Prices shown are for full, non-padded, vinyl top on two-door models. [8]Price is $5 less on Skylark Custom models. Regal coupe w/Landau top, $155. Not available on Century station wagons. [9]Available on two-door models only. Skyhawk Astroroof is fixed and includes roof crown molding, and Vista-vent sunroof option is manually operated. [10]For Skyhawk, Designer Paint was an option package. See appendix for details. [11]Standard on Regal Sport Coupe. Power brakes standard on station wagons, and required when V8 engine and A/C are ordered on coupes and sedans. [12]Standard on LeSabre Limited. [13]Custom sport wheels on Skyhawk. Deluxe wheel covers standard on Riviera and Designer sport wheel covers standard on Riviera S-Type. [14]Styled aluminum wheels on Skyhawk and Skylark, Turbine wheels on Regal, and chrome wire wheels on LeSabre, Estate Wagon and Electra.

Paint Colors

Buick	Code	Buick	Code	Buick	Code
White	11	Light Blue metallic	22	Pastel Green	40
Silver metallic	15	Bright Blue metallic	24	Medium Green metallic	44
Gray metallic*	16	Dark Blue metallic	29	Bright Yellow	51
Black	19	Caramel Firemist metallic	33	Light Yellow	54
Pastel Blue	21	Beige metallic	38	Gold metallic*	55

Buick	Code	Buick	Code	Opel	Code
Medium Beige	61	Saffron Firemist metallic	99	Cream	NA
Camel metallic	63			Blue	NA
Dark Brown metallic	69				
Red	75	*Opel*	*Code*		
Carmine metallic	77	Mat Black**	NA		
Dark Carmine metallic	79	Matterhorn Silver	NA		
Yellow Beige*	84	Magnolia White	NA		
Medium Blue metallic*	85	Crimson Red	NA		
Charcoal Firemist metallic	98	Brown metallic	NA		

*In two-tone combinations, the first two digits indicate lower color and the next two digits are the upper color. Two-tone combinations are $48 extra on Skylark, and $58 extra for LeSabre. Firemist paints available only on Electra and Riviera at $172 extra. See major option list for prices of Designers' accent paints. *Used in Designers' Accent two-tone combinations only. **Used on Sport Coupe only.*

Opel

"If you're looking for a great Japanese car, look for a great American name. Buick."

Nameplate year of origin: 1976.
Current bodystyle lifespan: 1976 through 1979.
Predecessor to this model: Opel 1900 (1971–1975); Manta (1971–1975).
Replacement for this model: None. (The same car was sold after 1980 as the Isuzu I-Mark.)
Primary competition: AMC Spirit, Chevrolet Monza, Dodge Colt, Dodge Omni, Ford Pinto, Mercury Bobcat, Plymouth Horizon, and Pontiac Sunbird.
Notable changes: Trim and detail changes.
Major standard equipment: Reclining vinyl front bucket seats, full-floor carpeting, interior lights, column-mounted headlight dimmer switch, tinted glass, trunk mat, and 6.15 × 13 BSW tires. *Deluxe adds:* Center console w/clock, woodgrain vinyl trim on I/P gauge cluster, console and doors, side window moldings, rocker panel molding, front and rear bumper guards, and wheel trim rings. *Sport Coupe adds:* Bumpers w/black filler panels, front air dam, blacked-out trim (grille, headlamp bezels, window moldings, sport mirrors, door handles, C-pillar vent louvers, and taillamp trim), black stripes on spoiler and lower bodysides, "SC" identification on the lower front fender, specially tuned suspension and shock absorbers, and sport wheels.

Measurements

	Coupe	Sedan
Wheelbase	94.3"	94.3"
Length	168.0"*	170.5"
Width	61.8"	61.8"
Height	50.6"	51.3"
Legroom — front	40.7"	40.7"
Legroom — rear	30.2"	30.9"
Headroom — front	37.0"	37.9"
Headroom — rear	35.0"	36.6"
Cargo capacity (cu. ft.)	9.9	9.9
Fuel capacity (gals.)	13.7	13.7

Sport Coupe, 168.3"; Deluxe coupe, 170.5".

Models Available

	Model No.	Base MSRP	Change from LY	Shipping Wt. (lbs.)	Model Year Sales	Change from LY*
Opel 2-Door Coupe	T77	$4,335	+23.57%	2083	NA	NA
Opel Deluxe 2-Door Coupe	Y77	$4,645	+24.76%	2101	NA	NA
Opel Deluxe 4-Door Sedan	Y69	$4,726	+23.56%	2152	NA	NA
Opel 2-Door Sport Coupe	W77	$4,779	+23.20%	2097	NA	NA
TOTALS	*Avg. price*	$4,621	+23.77%	*Production*	17,560*	-6.60%

Model year sales are estimated based upon dealer sales reporting, and change from LY is compared to the entire 1978 Opel line.

Skyhawk

"Introduced in 1975, the Buick Skyhawk was an exciting new arrival.
Five model years later, we are happy to report, it is still exciting."

Nameplate year of origin: 1975.
Current bodystyle lifespan: 1975 through 1980.
Predecessor to this model: None.
Replacement for this model: Skyhawk (1982 to 1989).
Percentage of division's production: 3.18%.
Corporate siblings: Chevrolet Monza, Oldsmobile Starfire and Pontiac Sunbird.
Primary competition: AMC AMX, AMC Pacer, and Dodge Omni 024.
Notable changes: New front end and minor trim and detail changes.
Major standard equipment: Vinyl front bucket seats with foam cushions, fold-down rear seat, cut-pile carpeting including cargo area, full-length floor console, simulated woodgrain I/P and console trim, sport steering wheel, LH remote control and RH manual outside rear view sport mirrors, dual speed wipers w/washers, functional B-pillar vent louvers, bright window surround moldings, front and rear wheel opening moldings, hubcaps, and B78 × 13 BSW tires. Skyhawk adds: Choice of cloth or vinyl front bucket seats, appearance group, and BR78 × 13 BSW tires.

Measurements

Wheelbase	97.0"
Length	179.3"
Width	65.4"
Height	50.2"
Legroom — front	43.0"
Legroom — rear	29.6"
Headroom — front	37.7"
Headroom — rear	35.3"
Cargo capacity (cu. ft.)	27.8*
Fuel capacity (gals.)	18.5

With rear seat folded down.

Models Available

	Model No.	Base MSRP	Change from LY	Shipping Wt. (lbs.)	Model Year Production	Change from LY
Skyhawk 'S' 2-Door Hatchback	T07	$4,380	+6.75%	2724	4,766	NA
Skyhawk 2-Door Hatchback	S07	$4,598	+5.29%	2740	18,373	NA
TOTALS	*Avg. price*	$4,489	+6.00%	*Production*	23,139	-5.90%

Production and comparisons by model not available as they were kept as combined total for 1978.

Skylark

"Proof that a car doesn't have to be big to be roomy
and comfortable. All it has to be is a Buick."

Nameplate year of origin: 1953.
Current bodystyle lifespan: 1975 through 1979.
Predecessor to this model: Apollo (1973 to 1974).
Replacement for this model: Skylark (1980 to 1985).
Percentage of division's production: 3.99%.
Corporate siblings: Chevrolet Nova, Oldsmobile Omega, and Pontiac Phoenix.
Primary competition: Dodge Aspen and Mercury Monarch.
Notable changes: New grille and minor trim and detail changes.
Major standard equipment: S model: Front vinyl bench seat, front door armrest, cut-pile carpeting, and E78 × 14 BSW tires. Skylark adds: Choice of patterned cloth or vinyl front bench seat with foam cushions, cut-pile carpeting including hatchback load floor, fold-down rear seat and rear cargo area light (hatchback only), accessory package, deluxe steering wheel, roof drip rail moldings, front and rear wheel opening moldings, and hubcaps. Custom adds: Choice of custom cloth or custom vinyl front bench seat w/passenger side recliner, carpeted door trim w/map pocket and reflector, convenience package, combination turn signal and high/low beam headlight control stalk, roof drip moldings, stand-up hood ornament, and deluxe wheel covers.

Measurements

	Coupe & HBK	Sedan
Wheelbase	111.0"	111.0"
Length	200.2"	200.2"
Width	72.7"	72.7"
Height	52.2"	53.1"
Legroom — front	41.7"	41.7"
Legroom — rear	33.3"	35.2"
Headroom — front	38.2"	39.1"
Headroom — rear	36.7"	37.1"
Cargo capacity (cu. ft.)	14.3*	13.2
Fuel capacity (gals.)	21.0	21.0

Hatchback maximum with rear seat down, 29.2 cu. ft.

1979

Models Available

	Model No.	Base MSRP	Change from LY	Shipping Wt. (lbs.)	Model Year Production	Change from LY
Skylark 'S' 2-Door Coupe	W27	$4,082	+4.37%	3105	1,605	-82.27%
Skylark 2-Door Coupe	B27	$4,208	+4.29%	3114	8,596	-73.98%
Skylark 2-Door Hatchback	B17	$4,357	+3.32%	3195	608	-76.99%
Skylark 4-Door Sedan	B69	$4,308	+4.56%	3158	10,849	-73.51%
Skylark Custom 2-Door Coupe	C27	$4,462	+4.20%	3123	3,546	-72.17%
Skylark Custom 4-Door Sedan	C69	$4,562	+4.47%	3176	3,822	-73.68%
TOTALS	*Avg. price*	$4,330	+3.11%	*Production*	29,026	-74.59%

Century

"Function in an excitingly different form."

Nameplate year of origin: 1936.

Current bodystyle lifespan: 1978 through 1984 (Coupe to 1980; Wagon as Regal model 1982 to 1983; and Sedan as Regal model 1982 to 1984).

Predecessor to this model: Skylark (1973 to 1977).

Replacement for this model: Century (1982 to 1996).

Percentage of division's production: 7.68%.

Corporate siblings: Chevrolet Malibu, Oldsmobile Cutlass, and Pontiac LeMans.

Primary competition: Chrysler LeBaron, Dodge Diplomat, and Mercury Cougar.

Notable changes: Minor trim and detail changes.

Major standard equipment: Choice of cloth or vinyl front bench seat (wagon, vinyl only), cut-pile carpeting, front-door operated dome lights, door pull straps, fixed rear seat window w/swing out rear quarter vent windows (4-door models), stand-up hood ornament, front disc brakes, bumper protective strips w/white stripe front and rear, wheel covers, and P185/75R × 14 BSW tires. Custom adds: Choice of cloth or vinyl notchback front seat w/center fold-down armrest (wagon, cloth front and vinyl rear), front- and rear-door operated dome lights, front ashtray light, under-dash courtesy lights, glove compartment light, "Custom" badging, stand-up hood ornament w/hood windsplit molding, wheel opening moldings, and rocker panel moldings. Wagons add: Power brakes, and P195/75R × 14 BSW tires. Sport Coupe adds: Choice of cloth or vinyl notchback front seat w/center fold-down armrest or vinyl bucket seats (available at no extra charge), front ashtray light, under-dash courtesy lights, glove compartment light, LH remote and RH manual outside rear view sport mirrors, FE2 rallye ride and handling package, specific paint treatment, Designers' sport wheels, and P205/75R × 14 W/O BSW tires. Limited adds: Choice of cloth or vinyl 55/45 notchback front bench seat w/fold-down center armrest, convenience group, custom steering wheel, "Limited" badging, stand-up hood ornament w/hood windsplit molding, wheel opening moldings, and rocker panel moldings.

Measurements

	Coupes	Sedans	Wagons
Wheelbase	108.1"	108.1"	108.1"
Length	196.0"	196.0"	196.0"
Width	72.2"	72.2"	72.2"
Height	54.1"	55.0"	55.7"
Legroom — front	42.6"	42.6"	42.6"
Legroom — rear	35.1"	38.0"	35.9"
Headroom — front	37.9"	38.7"	38.8"
Headroom — rear	38.2"	37.7"	38.8"
Cargo capacity (cu. ft.)	16.1	16.1	71.8
Fuel capacity (gals.)	17.5	17.5	17.7

Models Available

	Model No.	Base MSRP	Change from LY	Shipping Wt. (lbs.)	Model Year Production	Change from LY
Century Special 2-Door Coupe	E87	$4,599	+4.78%	3038	3,152	NA*
Century Special 4-Door Sedan	E09	$4,699	+4.75%	3053	7,364	-41.24%
Century Special 4-Door Station Wagon, 2-S.	E35	$5,247	+5.45%	3158	10,413	+8.63%
Century Custom 2-Door Coupe	H87	$4,843	+4.53%	3051	2,474	-80.10%
Century Custom 4-Door Sedan	H09	$4,968	+4.97%	3071	6,987	NA*
Century Custom 4-Door Station Wagon, 2-S.	H35	$5,561	+5.40%	3194	21,100	-12.13%
Century Sport 2-Door Coupe	G87	$5,151	+2.63%	3047	1,653	NA*
Century Limited 4-Door Sedan	L09	$5,336	+4.81%	3104	2,694	NA*
TOTALS	*Avg. price*	$5,051	+4.27%	*Production*	55,837	-36.37%

*Comparison to LY is not available, as 1978 Century Sport production was kept combined with Century Special coupe production and 1978 Century Limited was kept combined with Century Custom production.

Regal

"It doesn't just look sophisticated. It is."

Nameplate year of origin: 1973 (as Century subseries).
Current bodystyle lifespan: 1978 through 1987.
Predecessor to this model: Century Regal (1973 to 1977).
Replacement for this model: Regal (1988 to 1997).
Percentage of division's production: 37.59%.
Corporate siblings: Chevrolet Monte Carlo, Oldsmobile Cutlass Calais and Cutlass Supreme, and Pontiac Grand Prix.
Primary competition: Chrysler Cordoba, Dodge Magnum XE, Ford Thunderbird and Mercury Cougar.
Notable changes: Minor trim and detail changes.
Major standard equipment: Choice of cloth or vinyl notchback front seat w/center fold-down armrest or vinyl front bucket seats, front door operated dome light, door pull straps, simulated woodgrain appliqués on I/P and door panels, ashtray light, under-dash courtesy lights, glove compartment light, wheel opening moldings, rocker panel molding, bumper protective strips w/white accents front and rear, front disc brakes, deluxe wheel covers, and P195/75R × 14 BSW tires. Sport adds: Distinctive domed hood, fast-ratio power steering, power front disc brakes, turbocharged engine, FE2 rallye ride and handling package, and P205/70R × 14 BSW tires. Limited adds: Choice of cloth or vinyl 55/45 notchback seat w/fold-down center armrest, and wide rocker panel moldings w/front and rear extension, belt reveal and pillar appliqué moldings.

Measurements

Wheelbase	108.1"
Length	200.0"
Width	72.2"
Height	53.4"
Legroom — front	42.6"
Legroom — rear	36.3"
Headroom — front	37.9"
Headroom — rear	38.1"
Cargo capacity (cu. ft.)	16.3
Fuel capacity (gals.)	17.5

Models Available

	Model No.	Base MSRP	Change from LY	Shipping Wt. (lbs.)	Model Year Production	Change from LY
Regal 2-Door Coupe	J47	$5,080	+4.70%	3029	157,228	NA*
Regal Sport 2-Door Coupe	K47	$6,227	+6.39%	3190	21,389	NA*
Regal Limited 2-Door Coupe	M47	$5,477	+4.66%	3071	94,748	NA*
TOTALS	*Avg. price*	$5,595	+5.31%		*Production* 273,365	+15.51%

Comparison to 1978 is not possible since production of Regal Sport and Limited was kept as combined total with Regal 2-Door coupe.

LeSabre

"LeSabre is first, last and always, a car designed for the family, with a respect for individuality."

Nameplate year of origin: 1959 (also used on 1951 GM show car).
Current bodystyle lifespan: 1977 through 1985.
Predecessor to this model: LeSabre (1971 to 1976).
Replacement for this model: LeSabre (1986 to 1991).
Percentage of division's production: 20.73%.
Corporate siblings: Chevrolet Impala and Caprice, Pontiac Catalina and Bonneville, and Oldsmobile Delta 88.
Primary competition: Chrysler Newport and Mercury Marquis.
Notable changes: Revised grille and minor trim and detail changes.
Major standard equipment: Choice of cloth or vinyl front bench seat, cut-pile carpeting, woodgrained vinyl trim on door panels, front door operated dome light, I/P woodgrain appliqués, LH outside rear view mirror, front fender-mounted three-section rectangular "ventiport" ornaments, bumper protective strips front and rear, and FR78 × 15 BSW tires. Limited adds: Choice of cloth or vinyl notchback front seat w/fold-down center armrest, front ashtray and glove compartment light, front- and rear-door operated dome light, wheel opening moldings, full-length rocker panel molding, rear panel molding, and deluxe wheel covers. Sport Coupe adds: Front ashtray and glove compartment light, sport steering wheel, specific suspension and

Measurements

	Coupe	Sedan
Wheelbase	115.9"	115.9"
Length	218.2"	218.2"
Width	77.2"	77.2"
Height	55.0"	55.7"
Legroom — front	42.4"	42.4"
Legroom — rear	38.1"	39.0"
Headroom — front	38.8"	39.4"
Headroom — rear	38.2"	38.2"
Cargo capacity (cu. ft.)	21.2	21.2
Fuel capacity (gals.)	21.0	21.0

steering, "Turbo 3.8 Litre" badge with three-section chrome rectangular ventiports, black accents around chrome moldings, grille and taillights, black B-pillar molding w/special sport coupe emblem, turbocharged engine, and chrome road wheels.

Models Available

	Model No.	Base MSRP	Change from LY	Shipping Wt. (lbs.)	Model Year Production	Change from LY
LeSabre 2-Door Coupe	N37	$5,680	+5.50%	3428	7,542	NA*
LeSabre 4-Door Sedan	N69	$5,780	+5.88%	3459	25,431	+8.89%
LeSabre Limited 2-Door Coupe**	P37	$6,124	+8.26%	3454	38,290	-28.66%
LeSabre Limited 4-Door Sedan**	P69	$6,249	+8.55%	3503	75,939	-12.35%
LeSabre Sport 2-Door Coupe	F37	$6,621	+9.57%	3545	3,582	NA*
TOTALS	Avg. price	$6,091	+6.97%	Production	150,784	-12.30%

*Comparison to 1978 is not possible since production of LeSabre Sport Coupe was kept as combined total with LeSabre 2-Door coupe. **Comparison of 1979 LeSabre Limited models is made to 1978 LeSabre Custom models since they carry the same model numbers.*

Estate Wagon

"Just maybe it's right for you."

Nameplate year of origin: 1940 (as designation for station wagons).
Current bodystyle lifespan: 1977 through 1990.
Predecessor to this model: Estate Wagon (1971 to 1976).
Replacement for this model: Roadmaster Estate Wagon (1991 to 1996).
Percentage of division's production: 2.93%.
Corporate siblings: Chevrolet Impala and Caprice, Pontiac Catalina Safari and Grand Safari, and Oldsmobile Custom Cruiser.
Primary competition: Mercury Marquis.
Notable changes: Revised grille and minor trim and detail changes.
Major standard equipment: Vinyl front bench seat, cut-pile carpeting including load floor, glove box light, I/P flood lights, front-door operated dome light, lockable hidden storage compartments, three-way tailgate, power tailgate window w/reveal moldings, LH and RH rear view mirrors, fender-mounted three-section rectangular "ventiport" ornaments, rocker panel moldings, deluxe wheel covers, and HR78 × 15 BSW tires.

Measurements

Wheelbase	115.9"
Length	216.7"
Width	79.9"
Height	56.5"
Legroom — front	42.4"
Legroom — rear	37.7"
Headroom — front	39.6"
Headroom — rear	39.4"
Cargo capacity (cu. ft.)	88.6
Fuel capacity (gals.)	22.0

Models Available

	Model No.	Base MSRP	Change from LY	Shipping Wt. (lbs.)	Model Year Production	Change from LY
Estate Wagon 4-Door, 2-S. Wagon	R35	$6,714	+6.55%	4021	21,312	-17.92%
TOTALS	Avg. price	$6,714	+6.55%	Production	21,312	-17.92%

Electra

"There are wools, and then there's Scottish cashmere.
There are full-size automobiles and then there's Buick Electra."

Nameplate year of origin: 1959.
Current bodystyle lifespan: 1977 through 1984.
Predecessor to this model: Electra 225 (1971 to 1976).
Replacement for this model: Electra (1985 to 1990).
Percentage of division's production: 16.72%.

Measurements

	Coupe	Sedan
Wheelbase	118.9"	118.9"
Length	222.1"	222.1"

Corporate siblings: Cadillac deVille, Cadillac Fleetwood Brougham, and
  Oldsmobile Ninety-Eight.
Primary competition: Chrysler New Yorker and Mercury Grand Marquis.
Notable changes: New grille and minor trim and detail changes.
Major standard equipment: Choice of cloth or vinyl notchback front
  bench seat w/fold-down center armrest, cut-pile carpeting, simulated
  woodgrain appliqués on door panels and I/P, door pull straps, carpeted
  lower door panels, tinted glass, power windows, quartz round-dial clock,
  custom color-coordinated steering wheel and safety belts, remote-control
  LH rear view mirror, fender-mounted 4-section rectangular "ventiport"
  ornaments, wheel opening moldings, rocker panel molding, deluxe wheel
  covers, and GR78 × 15 BSW tires. Limited adds: Custom cloth or tex-
tured vinyl 55/45 notchback front seat w/fold-down center armrest, two-way power driver's seat adjustment, front seat-back map
pockets, door pull handle, litter pocket, dome reading light, and front and rear fender rocker panel moldings. Park Avenue adds:
Button-tufted crushed velour cloth 50/50 split seats w/individual fold-down center armrests, door courtesy and warning lights,
and C-pillar mounted coach side lights.

Measurements (cont.)

	Coupe	Sedan
Width	77.2"	77.2"
Height	55.0"	55.9"
Legroom — front	42.4"	42.4"
Legroom — rear	39.2"	40.1"
Headroom — front	38.5"	39.4"
Headroom — rear	38.0"	37.6"
Cargo capacity (cu. ft.)	20.4	20.4
Fuel capacity (gals.)	21.0	21.0

Models Available

	Model No.	Base MSRP	Change from LY	Shipping Wt. (lbs.)	Model Year Production	Change from LY
Electra 225 2-Door Coupe	V37	$7,581	+6.12%	3767	5,358	-35.13%
Electra 225 4-Door Sedan	V69	$7,756	+5.97%	3831	11,055	-24.23%
Electra Limited 2-Door Coupe	X37	$7,981	+6.05%	3789	28,878*	-13.45%*
Electra Limited 4-Door Sedan	X69	$8,156	+5.91%	3853	76,340*	+16.84%*
Electra Park Avenue 2-Door Coupe	U37	$8,423	+7.48%	3794	*	*
Electra Park Avenue 4-Door Sedan	U69	$8,598	+6.31%	3860	*	*
TOTALS		*Avg. price* $8,083	+6.31%		*Production* 121,631	+0.07%

Production of Park Avenue models kept as combined total with Limited models; therefore comparisons to LY include both Limited and Park Avenue models.

1979

Riviera

"Like its predecessors, it suggests the future."

Nameplate year of origin: 1963 (1949 as designation for hardtop models).
Current bodystyle lifespan: 1979 through 1985.
Predecessor to this model: Riviera (1977 to 1978).
Replacement for this model: Riviera (1986 to 1993).
Percentage of division's production: 7.17%.
Corporate siblings: Cadillac Eldorado and Oldsmobile Toronado.
Primary competition: Ford Thunderbird Heritage.
Notable changes: Completely redesigned.
Major standard equipment: Choice of crushed velour cloth or vinyl 45/55 front seat
  w/individual fold-down center armrests, six-way power driver's seat, thick cut-pile
  carpeting, door courtesy and warning lights, simulated woodgrain appliqué on door
  panels and I/P, deluxe steering wheel, door pull strap, tinted glass, power windows,
  quartz crystal digital clock, AM/FM stereo radio w/automatic power antenna, power
door locks, air conditioning, light group, dual remote-control rear view chrome mirrors, cornering lights, automatic level control,
super deluxe wheel covers, and P205/75R × 15 WSW tires. S-Type adds: Choice of cloth or vinyl front bucket seats, storage console, sport steering wheel, black I/P trim, dual remote-control rear view sport mirrors, black moldings and outside trim, amber
front park and turn signal lenses, FE2 rallye ride-and-handling package, turbocharged engine, Designers' sport wheel covers, and
GR70 × 15 W/O narrow-white-stripe tires.

Measurements

Wheelbase	151.5"
Wheelbase	114.0"
Length	206.6"
Width	70.4"
Height	54.3"
Legroom — front	42.8"
Legroom — rear	39.4"
Headroom — front	37.9"
Headroom — rear	37.9"
Cargo capacity (cu. ft.)	17.0
Fuel capacity (gals.)	20.0

Models Available

	Model No.	Base MSRP	Change from LY	Shipping Wt. (lbs.)	Model Year Production	Change from LY
Riviera 2-Door Coupe	Z57	$10,112	+25.12%	3759	37,881	+84.47%
Riviera S-Type 2-Door Coupe	Y57	$10,388	NEW	3774	14,300	NEW
TOTALS	*Avg. price*	$10,250	+26.83%		*Production* 52,181	+151.11%

CADILLAC

"More than ever ... an American standard for the world."

An all-new Eldorado topped Cadillac's 1979 model line. Along with its introduction came an array of electronics that were just being developed, keeping Cadillac at the forefront of automotive electronics. One of the big ones getting attention was Cadillac's Trip Computer. The computer required entry of the number of miles to be traveled at the beginning of a trip, and based on that would instantly calculate any of several possible questions, such as average trip speed, miles to travel before needing gas, miles to destination, length of time spent traveling, and estimated arrival time. It also served as an electronic tachometer, voltmeter, engine temperature gauge, and clock, and could calculate fuel consumption. It would be the first of what many consumers considered gadgets at the time, but are now a part of many automobiles on the market.

From the outside the Eldorado looked totally different from its immediate predecessor — smaller, more angular, and very modern looking. But there were enough hints of the original Eldorado, combined with the expected Cadillac styling cues, to identify this car as a Cadillac Eldorado. Under the hood was a newly available 5.7 Liter, 350 cubic inch V8 engine with electronic fuel injection as used in the Seville. A diesel version was also available. Other chassis features included a newly designed four-wheel independent suspension, four-wheel disc brakes, and electronic level control.

Dipping into the center section of the front bumper, a slightly pointed egg-crate grille with a large chrome header bar sat between dual rectangular headlamps, all between traditional pointed front fender ends, a styling cue that every Eldorado to date had maintained. A large, horizontal side marker and cornering lamp was set into the front fender a few inches back from the tip, just above bumper height. Bodysides were devoid of feature lines, bearing only a lower body protective molding to detract from the clean lines. A wide chrome rocker panel molding made the car appear longer than it really was. The rear quarter window was a rectangular fixed window, and a very wide C-pillar led to the upright rear window, all of which created a very formal roofline. The only body feature line to be found began where the roof met the rear quarter panel, and created the top edge of the panel, ending in slender, vertical taillights that formed a pointed, slightly slanted rear fender tip. Backup lamps flanked the license plate mount, which dipped slightly into the center of the bumper. A new feature applied for the first time on the Eldorado, and its corporate siblings, was a flush-mounted windshield that reduced wind noise and made the car more aerodynamic. Other noise eliminating features included nearly flush side windows and an aerodynamic cowl with a narrower opening where the windshield wipers were located.

Inside, a new instrument panel design eliminated the upper gauge and warning light bar. The panel face itself was flat and covered in simulated burled wood, and was laid out much like the 1978 version, with all gauges and driver controls directly in front of the driver, a center section housing radio and climate controls, and a huge glove box on the passenger side. New upholstery materials and designs, along with increased headroom and legroom, both front and rear, plus more usable trunk space than the 1978 Eldorado — all in a car 20 inches shorter and 1100 pounds lighter — made for a comfortable interior environment. Additional new features inside included front side window defoggers mounted on the instrument panel ends, new electronic digital radios and the Cadillac exclusive Trip Computer that was also available on Seville.

The rest of the line was mostly unchanged, but all added Cadillac's new electronic radio as standard equipment with a digital display and electronic seek-and-scan tuning. The Seville also added a convex remote-control right-hand mirror providing a wider viewing angle, a power trunk lid pulldown, and Cadillac's new Trip Computer option. Fleetwoods and deVilles had a new egg-crate grille design that was five rows high and thirty columns across with a larger chrome header panel above it all. A thin chrome strip ran above the headlights and the grille bar, giving the front end a taller look. Also new this year for the big Cadillacs were a retuned suspension and new body mounts for a smoother, quieter

ride. In what was otherwise a slightly depressed market, Cadillac sales and production rose for 1979 mainly on the strength of the new Eldorado, with Cadillac surpassing all of Chrysler Corporation's struggling divisions to capture seventh place in industry production standings for the model year.

Coupe deVille (front) and Sedan deVille with Phaeton package

Eldorado instrument panel

Seville 4-Door Sedan

Coupe deVille 2-Door Coupe

Fleetwood Brougham 4-Door Sedan

Eldorado 2-Door Coupe

Fleetwood Limousine

1979

Model year production: 380,249, up 9.01% from 1978.
Domestic market share: 4.14% (7th place).
Base price range: $11,139 to $21,735.
Cadillac average base price: $15,527, up 9.13%.
Introduction date: September 28, 1978.
Assembly plants: Southgate, CA (C); Linden, NJ (E); and Detroit, MI (Q).
Data plate identification (VIN): Thirteen digit code read as follows: First digit indicates division (6 = Cadillac); second

through fourth digits indicate series and body style (model number in model charts); fifth digit is engine code (see powertrain chart); sixth digit indicates model year (9 = 1979); seventh digit indicates assembly plant (see list above); remaining digits are sequential with beginning number of 100001. *Example:* 6D69T9Q100001 is a 1979 Cadillac Sedan deVille 4-Door Sedan, with 425 CID, EFI V8 engine, serial number 100001, built in Detroit, MI.

Powertrains

Engine	Net HP	Engine/Code: VIN/GM	Transmission Availability		Seville	Eldorado	DeVille & Fleetwood	Fleetwood Limousines
350 CID (5.7L), EFI, V8	170	B/L49	Turbo Hydra-matic 3-sp. Automatic		S	S	—	—
				MPG:	14	14	—	—
				Calif.	13	13	—	—
350 CID (5.7L), Diesel, V8	125	N/LF9	Turbo Hydra-matic 3-sp. Automatic		$287	$287	$849	—
				MPG:	21	21	20	—
425 CID (7.0L), 4-bbl., V8	180	S/L33	Turbo Hydra-matic 3-sp. Automatic		—	—	S	S
				MPG:	—	—	14	10
				Calif.	—	—	13	10

Engine	Net HP	Engine/ Code: VIN/GM	Transmission Availability		Seville	Eldorado	DeVille & Fleetwood	Fleetwood Limousines
425 CID (7.0L), EFI, V8	195	T/L35	Turbo Hydra-matic 3-sp. Automatic	MPG:	— —	— —	$783[1] 12	— —

[1]Standard on cars equipped for sale in California.

Major Options

	Seville	deVille	Eldorado	Fleetwood Brougham	Fleetwood Limousine
Automatic climate control	S	S	S	S	S
Electric rear window defogger	$101	$101	$101	$101	$101
Controlled cycle windshield wiper	S	$38	S	S	$38
Tilt and telescope steering wheel	S	$130	$130	$130	$130[1]
Cruise control	$137	$137	$137	$137	$137
Twilight Sentinel	S	$56	S	S	$56
Guidematic headlamp control	$91	$91	$91	$91	$91
Leather upholstery	$330	$350	$350	$350	—[2]
Power front passenger seat, 6-way	$125	$160	$160	S	—
Power 50/50 front seat recliners	$122	$122	$122	$122	—
Lighted vanity mirror, passenger	$52	$52	$52	$52	$52
Illuminated entry system	S	$62	S	S	$62
AM/FM stereo, w/digital display	$195	$195	$195	$195	$398[3]
AM/FM stereo w/tape & seek/scan	$225	$225	$225	$225	—
Cadillac trip computer	$920	—	$920	—	—
Automatic door locks	$121	$121	$121	$121	$121
Remote trunk release w/electric pulldown	S	$85	S	S	$85
Padded vinyl top	N/C	$225	—	S	S
Sunroof[4]	$798	$798	$953	$798	—[2]
Astroroof[4]	$998	$998	$1,163	$998	—[2]
Theft-deterrent system	$137	$137	$137	$137	$137
Fuel monitor system	S	$31	$31	$31	$31
Electronic level control	S	$160	S	S	S
Special turbine style wheel discs	—	$59	—	$59	$59
Wire spoke wheel covers	$189	$292	—	$292	$292
Cast aluminum wheels	—	—	$350	—	—
Chrome plated wire wheels	$569	$628	—	$628	—

Popular Option Groups & Packages

	Seville	deVille	Eldorado	Fleetwood Brougham	Fleetwood Limousine
Brougham d'Elegance package	—	—	—	$987	—
DeVille d'Elegance package	—	$725	—	—	—
Custom Cabriolet package, coupe	—	$384	$350	—	—
Custom Biarritz package	—	—	$2,250	—	—
Elegante package	$2,735	—	—	—	—
Phaeton package	—	$2,029	—	—	—

—= Not Available; S = Standard equipment. [1]Standard on Formal Limousine. [2]Available by special order only. [3]Fleetwood models include rear seat controls. [4]Price given is with full padded vinyl roof. Available on all models with painted roofs for $165 additional cost.

Paint Colors

	Code		Code		Code
Cotillion white	11	Light Yellow	54	Slate Firemist metallic*	90
Silver metallic	15	Pastel Beige	62	Light Gold Firemist metallic*	91
Sable black	19	Dark Gold metallic	68	Biscayne Aqua Firemist metallic*	92
Light Blue metallic	22	Dark Brown metallic	69	Light Cedar Firemist metallic*	93
Crater Lake Blue metallic	29	Dark Cedar metallic	76	Medium Green Firemist metallic*	94
Atlantis Aqua metallic	41	Saxony red	78	Light Blue Firemist metallic*	95
Blackwatch Green metallic	49	Light Gray	89	Western Saddle Firemist metallic*	96

	Code
Charcoal Firemist metallic*	98
Saffron Firemist metallic*	99

*In two-tone combinations, the first two digits indicate lower color and the next two digits are the upper color.
Firemist paint available for $171 extra.

Seville

"Again for 1979 ... Seville stands alone among the world's great cars."

Nameplate year of origin: 1976; 1956 (as a designation on Eldorado 2-Door Hard-tops).
Current bodystyle lifespan: 1976 through 1979.
Predecessor to this model: None.
Replacement for this model: Seville (1980 to 1985).
Percentage of division's production: 14.07%.
Corporate siblings: None.
Primary competition: Lincoln Versailles.
Notable changes: Minor trim and detail changes.
Major standard equipment: Choice of Dante and Roma cloth dual comfort 50/50 split front seat w/individual fold-down center armrests, six-way driver and two-way passenger power seat adjustment, one-piece deep pile carpeting, seatback and overhead entry assist straps, hinged door pull handles, individual rear seat reading lamps, electric clock, power windows, power door locks, tilt and telescoping steering wheel, controlled wiper cycle system, automatic climate control, AM/FM Signal-seeking stereo radio w/automatic power antenna and digital tuner and digital display, dual remote-control rear view mirrors, padded vinyl roof (no cost option), remote trunk release with power trunk lid pull-down, trunk carpeting including deck lid, fuel monitor system, lamp monitors, front cornering lights, wheel opening moldings, stand-up wreath and crest hood-ornament, electronic level control, automatic parking brake release, bodyside and decklid accent striping, full wheel covers, four-wheel disc brakes, and GR78 × 15 WSW tires.

Measurements

Wheelbase	151.5"
Wheelbase	114.3"
Length	204.0"
Width	71.8"
Height	54.6"
Legroom — front	41.7"
Legroom — rear	38.2"
Headroom — front	38.6"
Headroom — rear	36.8"
Cargo capacity (cu. ft.)	12.8
Fuel capacity (gals.)	19.6

1979

Models Available

	Model No.	Base MSRP	Change from LY	Shipping Wt. (lbs.)	Model Year Production	Change from LY
Seville 4-Door Sedan	S69	$15,646	+9.67%	4180	53,487	-6.14%
TOTALS	*Avg. price*	$15,646	+9.67%	*Production*	53,487	-6.14%

deVille

"America's favorite luxury car combines contemporary styling and traditional Cadillac comfort."

Nameplate year of origin: 1959 (series); 1949 (as Hardtop designation).
Current bodystyle lifespan: 1977 through 1984.
Predecessor to this model: deVille (1971 to 1976).
Replacement for this model: deVille (1985 to 1993).
Percentage of division's production: 56.57%.
Corporate siblings: Buick Electra, Cadillac Fleetwood Brougham and Oldsmobile 98.
Primary competition: Lincoln Continental.
Notable changes: Minor trim and detail changes.
Major standard equipment: Durand knit cloth front bench seat with front and rear seat center armrests, 6-way power front seat adjuster, cut-pile carpeting, hinged door pull assist handles, passenger side visor vanity mirror, dome light w/dual spot map lamps, courtesy lights, courtesy lamp/assist strap combination on B-pillar of 2-doors, electric clock, power windows, power door locks, automatic climate control,

Measurements

Wheelbase	121.5"
Length	221.2"
Width	76.4"
Height	55.3"
Legroom — front	42.1"
Legroom — rear	39.7"
Headroom — front	38.0"
Headroom — rear	37.9"
Cargo capacity (cu. ft.)	25.0
Fuel capacity (gals.)	25.0

digital display AM/FM electronically tuned stereo radio w/seek and scan and automatic power antenna, LH remote-control rear view mirror, lamp monitors, front cornering lights, wheel opening moldings, rocker panel moldings, full wheel covers, and GR78 × 15 WSW tires.

Models Available

	Model No.	Base MSRP	Change from LY	Shipping Wt. (lbs.)	Model Year Production	Change from LY
Coupe deVille 2-Door Coupe	D47	$11,139	+6.65%	4143	121,890	+3.52%
Sedan deVille 4-Door Sedan	D69	$11,493	+7.73%	4212	93,211	+4.79%
TOTALS		*Avg. price* $11,316	+7.20%	*Production*	215,101	+4.06%

Eldorado

"The new breed of Eldorado. World-class in engineering. Cadillac in luxury."

Nameplate year of origin: 1953.
Current bodystyle lifespan: 1979 through 1985.
Predecessor to this model: Fleetwood Eldorado (1971 to 1978).
Replacement for this model: Eldorado (1986 to 1991).
Percentage of division's production: 17.73%.
Corporate siblings: Buick Riviera and Oldsmobile Toronado.
Primary competition: Lincoln Continental Mark V.
Notable changes: Completely redesigned.
Major standard equipment: Dante knit cloth 50/45 dual comfort front seat w/individual fold-down center armrest, 6-way power driver seat adjuster, plush cut-pile carpeting, door pull assist straps, carpeted rear shelf panel, trunk carpeting, dome light w/dual spot map lights, illuminated entry system, power windows, power door locks, automatic climate control, digital display AM/FM electronically tuned stereo radio w/seek and scan and automatic power antenna, LH and RH remote-control rear view mirrors, front cornering lights, wheel opening moldings, rocker panel moldings, stand-up wreath and crest hood-ornament, lamp monitors, automatic level control, four wheel disc brakes, full wheel covers, and P205/75R × 15 wide WSW tires.

Measurements

Wheelbase	114.0"
Length	204.0"
Width	72.0"
Height	54.2"
Legroom — front	42.8"
Legroom — rear	39.4"
Headroom — front	37.9"
Headroom — rear	37.9"
Cargo capacity (cu. ft.)	19.6
Fuel capacity (gals.)	19.6

Models Available

	Model No.	Base MSRP	Change from LY	Shipping Wt. (lbs.)	Model Year Production	Change from LY
Eldorado 2-Door Coupe	L57	$14,240	+19.45%	3792	67,436	+44.04%
TOTALS		*Avg. price* $14,240	+19.45%	*Production*	67,436	+44.04%

Fleetwood Brougham

"One of the world's great sedans."

Nameplate year of origin: 1966.
Current bodystyle lifespan: 1977 through 1992.
Predecessor to this model: Fleetwood Sixty-Special and Fleetwood Brougham (1971 to 1976).
Replacement for this model: Fleetwood Brougham (1993 to 1996).
Percentage of division's sales volume: 11.10%.
Corporate siblings: Buick Electra, Cadillac deVille and Oldsmobile 98.
Primary competition: Lincoln Continental w/Town Car package.

Measurements

Wheelbase	121.5"
Length	221.2"
Width	76.4"
Height	56.7"
Legroom — front	42.1"
Legroom — rear	39.7"

Notable changes: Minor trim and detail changes.

Major standard equipment: Dante knit cloth dual comfort 45/55 front seat w/ 6-way driver side and 2-way passenger side power seat adjuster, front and rear seat fold-down center armrests, cut-pile carpeting, hinged door pull assist handles, dome light w/dual spot map lamps, quartz digital clock, power windows, power door locks, automatic climate control, digital display AM/FM electronically tuned stereo radio w/seek and scan and automatic power antenna, LH and RH remote-control rear view mirrors, lamp monitors, rear quarter opera lamps, front cornering lights, wheel opening moldings, rocker panel moldings, electronic level control, four wheel disc brakes, full wheel covers, and HR78 × 15 wide WSW tires.

Measurements (cont.)

Headroom — front	38.0"
Headroom — rear	37.9"
Cargo capacity (cu. ft.)	25.0
Fuel capacity (gals.)	25.0

Models Available

	Model No.	Base MSRP	Change from LY	Shipping Wt. (lbs.)	Model Year Production	Change from LY
Fleetwood Brougham 4-Door Sedan	B69	$13,446	+9.39%	4250	42,200	+14.67%
TOTALS	*Avg. price*	$13,446	+9.39%	*Production*	42,200	+14.67%

Fleetwood Limousine

"Flagships of the Cadillac fleet."

Nameplate year of origin: 1927 (models using Fleetwood bodies); 1935 (Fleetwood series).

Current bodystyle lifespan: 1977 through 1984.

Predecessor to this model: Fleetwood Seventy-Five (1971 to 1976).

Replacement for this model: Fleetwood 75 Limousine (1985 to 1987).

Percentage of division's sales volume: 0.53%.

Corporate siblings: None.

Primary competition: None.

Notable changes: Minor trim and detail changes.

Major standard equipment: Dante cloth w/2-way power front seat adjuster, front and rear seat fold-down center armrests, cut-pile carpeting, two fold-down seats (rearward facing for two additional passengers), hinged door pull assist handles, power windows, power door locks, dual automatic climate control system (front and rear), courtesy lights, electric clock, AM/FM radio w/automatic power antenna, passenger control panel (controls power windows, reading lights, radio (optional), automatic climate control, and the glass partition in the Formal Limousine), automatic level control, LH and RH remote-control rear view mirror, front cornering lights, wheel opening moldings, full-length rocker panel moldings, full wheel covers, and HR78 × 15 wide WSW tires. Formal Limousine adds: Black leather 45/45 front seat and sliding glass partition separating driver and passenger compartment.

Measurements

Wheelbase	144.5"
Length	244.2"
Width	79.8"
Height	56.9"
Legroom — front	NA
Legroom — rear	NA
Headroom — front	NA
Headroom — rear	NA
Cargo capacity (cu. ft.)	NA
Fuel capacity (gals.)	25.3

Models Available

	Model No.	Base MSRP	Change from LY	Shipping Wt. (lbs.)	Model Year Production*	Change from LY*
Fleetwood 4-Door Limousine	F23	$20,987	+6.85%	4782	2,025	NA
Fleetwood 4-Door Formal Limousine	F33	$21,735	+6.74%	4866	NA	NA
TOTALS	*Avg. price*	$21,361	+6.79%	*Production*	2,025	+32.35%

*Change from LY not available, as 1979 Limousine production was kept combined as one total.

1979

CHEVROLET

"The 1979 Chevrolets."

Nineteen-seventy-nine was one of those rare years when there was not much new in the Chevrolet line. Aside from various changes related to improvement of fuel economy and emission controls, plenty of new grilles and some front end styling revisions, new Camaro Berlinetta and Rally Sport models (both being replacements of previous models and options), and new standard features for the Corvette, it just didn't seem a very eventful year for Chevrolet. That is until April of 1979, when the highly anticipated front-wheel-drive "X"-car was introduced. For Chevy, it came in the form of the Citation, which took the place of the perennially popular Nova. It was a big gamble that occurred just as a second fuel crisis hit the United States early in 1979. Because it was sold as a 1980 model, the Citation is covered in the 1980 Chevrolet section.

Chevette models had the greatest production increase of all 1979 Chevy models, and the popular mini-compact was on its way to becoming the best-selling Chevrolet model by 1981. For the new year Chevettes were given new square headlights and a full-width grille. As the grille had previously been built into the hood, a new hood was part of the facelift, now ending above the grille. The new grille was a horizontal crosshatch design, seven rows high and sixteen columns across, with a chrome surround and the Chevy bowtie emblem placed in the center. A new option, available for $50 extra, was an optional automatic shoulder belt system in which the shoulder belt was attached to the front door frame, rather than the B-pillar post, so that front-seat passengers merely had to sit in the seat and close the door to have the shoulder belt in place, although the lap belt still needed to be manually buckled. Otherwise the Chevette offered few changes. Chevette was one of the industry's few bright spots with nearly a 25 percent sales increase, in a year when sales for most models declined.

Still being advertised as "The New Chevrolet," the full-sized Impala and Caprice Classic continued into their third season in their smaller form. Both models received new grilles and general front-end appearance, and all but the station wagons used new taillight configurations. For the Caprice Classic line, a new grille with a vertical theme was introduced. The new grille pattern consisted of ten chrome-lined vertical sections, with each carrying an egg-crate insert two columns wide and nine rows high. The four outer sections carried into the rectangular bumper openings below with three more rows of egg-crate pattern. The amber side marker lights mounted within the wrap-around headlight bezel were divided horizontally into three sections. Around back, the Caprice Classic had slimmer three-unit taillamps in a hooded chrome bezel, with a horizontal backup light mounted separately below the center unit on each side. For the Impala, a new horizontal crosshatch grille design was six columns across and eight rows high. As with the Caprice, the grille pattern continued into the bumper opening. Also new for the Impala was the parking/turn signal lights being moved into the bumper, just like the Caprice used, rather than horizontally below the dual rectangular headlights. At the back of the Impala, hooded, chrome-outlined taillights similar to the Caprice's were used, but the backup light on Impalas was placed in the center of the center taillight unit.

Mid-size Malibu models, which were newly downsized for 1978, featured a new grille and taillight design for 1979. A modified version of last year's egg-crate design, the new grille had four rows lined in chrome, each with two rows of egg-crate style inserts within, a total of twenty-two columns across. At the back, three-unit horizontal taillights continued to be used on cars, with the backup light moving to the center section. On station wagons, the backup light moved to the innermost end of the horizontal taillights set in the bumper ends. Also in the mid-size range, the Monte Carlo received a slightly revised grille insert that was less like an egg-crate pattern, and more towards a horizontal crosshatch design, with wider columns than last year. New four-section taillights now wrapped around the quarter panel end. Each lens was further split horizontally, with each of the eight sections created per side being lined by chrome trim. Interiors remained mostly unchanged on both the Malibu and Monte Carlo, and there were no model changes.

The compact Nova entered its final season, to be replaced in the spring of 1979 with the front-wheel-drive Citation. Oddly, Chevrolet saw fit to give the Nova a restyled front end for its final three months of production, featuring new square headlights and a horizontal bar grille with ten bars, the top and bottom bars being thicker. The grille was topped by a heavy chrome piece on the leading edge of the hood, with the Chevrolet name in script on the driver's side. The Rally Nova continued to be offered for 1979, sans the unique grille it formerly had, and 2,299 were built before Nova production ended on December 22, 1978.

The Camaro line carried into the new year with the same styling and powertrains. A combination of sport and luxury that was previously found in the Camaro Type LT was now found in the newly named Camaro Berlinetta. Effectively having the same features, the Berlinetta accounted for about the same proportion of total Camaro sales as the Type LT. The two-toned Rally Sport became its own model this year, having formerly been an option package that was available on either the Sport Coupe or Type LT.

As "America's only true production sports car," the Corvette entered 1979 with many unseen improvements, but continued with the popular fastback style rear window introduced for its 25th anniversary year. Changes included a new dual snorkel air intake for the air cleaner, a larger diameter exhaust system with new open flow mufflers to improve power output, and new gearing in the automatic transmission to make better use of the power. Portions of the 1978

Indianapolis 500 pace car replica package were retained as part of the 1979 Corvette's standard features, including the enlarged wheel flares, which created a psuedo spoiler look at the front. It was all part of the Corvette philosophy of continual evolution for America's only sports car.

Finally, the subcompact Monza had no significant styling or powertrain changes for 1979. As it was nearing the end of its lifespan, certain slow-selling models were cut. The one-year-only, Vega-bodied Monza S hatchback was the first to go, followed by the woodgrained Estate wagon and the Monza Sport 2-door coupe. The Spyder appearance and equipment packages were still available, with new green and blue color combinations available. There were 9,679 Monzas built with the Spyder equipment package, and 8,670 produced with the Spyder appearance package.

Camaro Berlinetta 2-Door Sport Coupe
with removable glass roof panels

Camaro Z28 2-Door Sport Coupe

Caprice Classic 4-Door Sedan

Corvette 2-Door Coupe

Chevette Scooter 2-Door Hatchback Coupe

Chevette 4-Door Hatchback Sedan

Malibu 2-Door Coupe

Malibu 4-Door Station Wagon (left)
and Malibu Classic 4-Door Station Wagon
with Estate package (right)

Impala 2-Door Sport Coupe

Malibu Classic instrument panel

Malibu Classic 4-Door Sedan

Monte Carlo 2-Door Coupe
with removable glass roof panels

1979

Monte Carlo Landau 2-Door Coupe

Monza Sport 2+2 Hatchback Coupe
with Spyder Appearance package

Monza 2-Door Coupe

Monza 2-Door Station Wagon

Nova 2-Door Coupe
with Rally Equipment package

Nova Custom 2-Door Coupe

Model year production: 2,284,749, down 3.78% from 1978.
Domestic market share: 24.87% (1st place).
Base price range: $3,299 to $10,245.
Chevrolet average base price: $5,008, up 8.10%.
Introduction date: September 28, 1978.
Assembly plants: Lakewood, GA (A); Baltimore, MD (B); Southgate, CA (C); Doraville, GA (D); Janesville, WI (J); Kansas City/Leeds, MO (K); Van Nuys, CA (L); Norwood, OH (N); Arlington, TX (R); St. Louis, MO (S); Tarrytown, NY (T); Lordstown, OH (U); Willow Run, MI (W); Wilmington, DE (Y); Fremont, CA (Z); and Oshawa, Ontario, Canada (1).
Data plate identification (VIN): Thirteen digit code read as follows: First digit indicates division (1 = Chevrolet); second through fourth digits indicate series and body style (model number in model charts); fifth digit is engine code (see powertrain chart); sixth digit indicates model year (9 = 1979); seventh digit indicates assembly plant (see list above); remaining digits are sequential with beginning number of 100001, except the following: Malibu, Monte Carlo and Corvette begin with 400001, and Camaro begins with 500001. *Example:* 1S87L9N500001 is a 1979 Chevrolet Camaro Berlinetta 2-Door Sport Coupe, with 350 CID, 4-bbl. V8 engine, serial number 500001, built in Norwood, OH.

Powertrains

Engine	Net HP	Engine Code VIN/ GM	Transmission Availability[1]		Chevette	Monza	Nova	Camaro	Malibu	Monte Carlo	Full-Size Chevy	Corvette
98 CID (1.6L) OHC, 2-bbl., 4-cyl.	63	0/L17	4-speed manual		S	—	—	—	—	—	—	—
				MPG:	29	—	—	—	—	—	—	—
				Calif.	27	—	—	—	—	—	—	—
			3-speed Turbo Hydra-matic		$295	—	—	—	—	—	—	—
				MPG:	25	—	—	—	—	—	—	—
98 CID (1.6L) OHC, 2-bbl., "High-Output" 4-cyl.	68	9/L18	4-speed manual		$60	—	—	—	—	—	—	—
				MPG:	NA	—	—	—	—	—	—	—
			3-speed Turbo Hydra-matic		$355	—	—	—	—	—	—	—
				MPG:	NA	—	—	—	—	—	—	—
151 CID (2.5L), 2-bbl., 4-cyl.	85	V/ LX8[2]	4-speed manual		—	S	—	—	—	—	—	—
				MPG:	—	24	—	—	—	—	—	—
				Calif.	—	20	—	—	—	—	—	—
			5-speed manual		—	$175[3]	—	—	—	—	—	—
				MPG:	—	22	—	—	—	—	—	—
			3-speed Turbo		—	$295[4]	—	—	—	—	—	—

Engine	Net HP	Engine Code VIN/GM	Transmission Availability[1]		Chevette	Monza	Nova	Camaro	Malibu	Monte Carlo	Full-Size Chevy	Corvette
			Hydra-matic	MPG:	—	22	—	—	—	—	—	—
				Calif.	—	20	—	—	—	—	—	—
196 CID (3.2L), 2-bbl., V6[3]	90	C/ LC9	4-speed manual		—	$160	—	—	—	—	—	—
				MPG:	—	17	—	—	—	—	—	—
			5-speed manual		—	$335	—	—	—	—	—	—
				MPG:	—	17	—	—	—	—	—	—
			3-speed Turbo Hydra-matic		—	$455	—	—	—	—	—	—
				MPG:	—	20	—	—	—	—	—	—
200 CID (3.3L), 2-bbl., V6[3]	95	M/ L26	3-speed manual		—	—	—	—	S	S	—	—
				MPG:	—	—	—	—	22	22	—	—
			3-speed Turbo Hydra-matic		—	—	—	—	$307	$307	—	—
				MPG:	—	—	—	—	18	19	—	—
231 CID (3.8L), 2-bbl., V6	105	A/ LD5	4-speed manual		—	$200[5]	—	—	—	—	—	—
				Calif.	—	14	—	—	—	—	—	—
			5-speed manual		—	$375[5]	—	—	—	—	—	—
				Calif.	—	16	—	—	—	—	—	—
			3-speed Turbo Hydra-matic		—	$495[5]	—	—	$400[5,6]	$400[5,6]	—	—
				Calif.	—	16	—	—	16	16	—	—
250 CID (4.1L), 1-bbl., 6-cyl.	110	D/ L22	3-speed manual		—	—	S	S[7]	—	—	—	—
				MPG:	—	—	19	18	—	—	—	—
			3-speed Turbo Hydra-matic		—	—	$335[4]	$335[4,7]	—	—	S (ex. Wgns.)	—
				MPG:	—	—	16	16	—	—	15	—
				Calif.	—	—	15	15	—	—	15	—
267 CID (4.4L), 2-bbl., V8[3]	145	J/ L39	4-speed manual		—	—	—	—	$135	—	—	—
				MPG:	—	—	—	—	17	—	—	—
			3-speed Turbo Hydra-matic		—	—	—	—	$335[6]	$335	—	—
				MPG:	—	—	—	—	18	18	—	—
305 CID (5.0L), 4-bbl., V8	145	U/ LG4	4-speed manual[3]		—	$395 (NA Wgn.)	$370	$370[7]	$430	—	—	—
				MPG:	—	15	15	15	15	—	—	—
			3-speed Turbo Hydra-matic		—	$690 (NA Wgn.)[6]	$570[4]	$570[4,7]	$630[4,6]	$630	S (Wgns.)/ $235 (others)[6]	—
				MPG:	—	18	16	16	17	17	16	—
				Calif.	—	14	13	13	16	16	13	—
350 CID (5.7L), 4-bbl., V8	170	L/ LM1	3-speed manual		—	—	—	$360[7]	—	—	—	—
				MPG:	—	—	—	NA	—	—	—	—
			4-speed manual		—	—	—	$495[7]	—	—	—	—
				MPG:	—	—	—	13	—	—	—	—
			3-speed Turbo Hydra-matic		—	—	$695[4]	$695[4,7]	$695 (Wgns. only)[8]	—	$125 (Wgns.)/ $360 (others)[6]	—
				MPG:	—	—	16	16	16	—	16	—
				Calif.	—	—	13	13	13	—	13	—
350 CID (5.7L), 4-bbl., V8	185	4/ LM1	4-speed manual		—	—	—	S (Z28 only)	—	—	—	—
				MPG:	—	—	—	13	—	—	—	—
			3-speed Turbo Hydra-matic		—	—	—	$59 (Z28 only)[4]	—	—	—	—
				MPG:	—	—	—	16	—	—	—	—
				Calif.	—	—	—	13	—	—	—	—

1979

Engine	Net HP	Code VIN/ GM	Engine Transmission Availability[1]		Chevette	Monza	Nova	Camaro	Malibu	Monte Carlo	Full-Size Chevy	Corvette
350 CID (5.7L), 4-bbl., V8	195	6/ L48	4-speed manual		—	—	—	—	—	—	—	S
				MPG:	—	—	—	—	—	—	—	13
			3-speed Turbo Hydra-matic		—	—	—	—	—	—	—	N/C
				MPG:	—	—	—	—	—	—	—	16
				Calif.	—	—	—	—	—	—	—	13
350 CID (5.7L), 4-bbl., V8[3]	225	8/ L82	4-speed manual		—	—	—	—	—	—	—	$565
				MPG:	—	—	—	—	—	—	—	13
			3-speed Turbo Hydra-matic		—	—	—	—	—	—	—	$565
				MPG:	—	—	—	—	—	—	—	16

[1]Unless otherwise specified: All 3-speed manuals are column shift. All 4- and 5-speed manuals are floor shift. All automatics are column shift, except on Chevette, Monza, Camaro and Corvette. Floor shift automatic is optional on Nova, Malibu and Monte Carlo with other specified equipment at extra cost.   [2]Code for engines in California equipped cars is LS6 until January 1979, and LS8 after January 1979.   [3]Not available in California or high-altitude areas.   [4]Required for cars sold in California, with smallest engine size marked being standard, and larger engines optional at proportionally higher cost.   [5]Only available in California or high altitude areas.   [6]Estimated mileage ratings for station wagons are one to two mpg lower for both city, highway and combined.   [7]Not available on Camaro Z28.   [8]Available in all states but California. Required in high-altitude areas.

Major Options

	Chevette	Monza	Camaro	Nova	Malibu	Monte Carlo	Impala & Caprice	Corvette
Air conditioning[1]	$496	$496	$562	$562	$562	$562	$605	$635
Comfortilt steering wheel	$68	$68	$75	$75	$75	$75	$77	S[2]
Cruise-Master speed control	—	—	$103	$103	$103	$103	$108	$113
Rear window defogger[3]	—	—	—	$55	$55	—	$57	—
Electro-Clear rear window defogger	$87	$87	$99	—	$99	$99	$101	$102
Dual sport mirrors, remote	$40[4]	$40[4]	$43[4]	$43[4]	$68	$68	$69	$45[4]
Soft-Ray tinted glass, all windows	$60	$60	$64	$64	$70	$70	$84	S
Power windows, 2-dr./4-dr.	—	—	$132	$126/$178	$132/$187	$132	$138/$205	$141
Power door locks, 2-dr./4-dr.	—	—	$86	$80/$111	$86/$120	$86	$88/$122	$272[5]
Power front seat, w/std. seat	—	—	—	—	$163	$163	$166	—
Front bucket seats, w/console[6]	S	$75	$80	$165	$165	$165	—	S
Rear facing third seat (wagons)	—	—	—	—	—	—	$139	—
AM radio	S[7]	S	$85	$82	$85	$85	$87	—
AM/FM stereo	$148	$148	$232	$232	$232	$232	$236	$90
AM/FM stereo w/tape player[8]	—	$242	$335	$335	$335	$335	$340	$228
AM/FM stereo w/CB radio[8]	—	—	$570	—	$570	$570	$578	$439
Vinyl top, full[9]	—	—	—	$99	$116	$131	$145	—
Vinyl top, landau[10]	—	$156	$112	$190	S	S	S	—
Sky Roof (sunroof), power[11]	—	$180	—	—	$529	$529	$625	—
Removable glass roof panels (T-Tops)	—	—	$655	—	—	$655	—	$365
Power steering, variable-ratio	—	$146	S	$163	$163	$163[12]	S	S
Power brakes, w/front disc	$71	$71	$76[13]	$76	$76[13]	$76[12]	S	S[14]
Full wheel covers	$45	$43	$43	$43	$43	S	$44	—
Wire wheel covers	—	—	—	$130	$160	$117	$120	—
Rally wheels w/trim rings	S	$88	$93	$88	$90	$47	—	S
Forged aluminum wheels	—	—	—	—	—	—	—	$380
Custom styled wheels	—	—	$143	—	—	—	—	—
WSW tires	S[7]	$16	$49	$47	$40	$44	$49	—

Popular Option Groups & Packages

	Chevette	Monza	Camaro	Nova	Malibu	Monte Carlo	Impala & Caprice	Corvette
Auxiliary lighting package	$37	$30	$37	$43	$50	$31	$38	—
Custom interior package	$181	—	—	—	—	—	—	—
Deluxe appointment group	$137	—	—	—	—	—	—	—

	Chevette	Monza	Camaro	Nova	Malibu	Monte Carlo	Impala & Caprice	Corvette
Deluxe exterior package	$104	—	—	—	—	—	—	—
Estate wagon package	—	—	—	—	$258	—	$262	—
Exterior Décor package	—	$231	—	—	—	—	—	—
Gymkhana suspension package	—	—	—	—	—	—	—	$49
Interior Décor and/or Quiet sound group	$47	$39	$64	—	$51	—	$56	—
Rally equipment package	—	—	—	$211	—	—	—	—
Special instrumentation package	$67	$88	$112	$112	$125	$102	—	S
Spyder appearance package	—	$231	—	—	—	—	—	—
Spyder equipment group	—	$164	—	—	—	—	—	—
Style trim group	—	—	$73	—	—	—	—	—

—= Not Available; S = Standard equipment. [1]Price is $529 on Camaro and Nova with V8 engine. Comfortron air conditioning with automatic temperature control is available for $688 on Impala and Caprice. [2]Tilt/Telescope w/leather-wrapped sport steering wheel available on Corvette for $190. [3]Blower type defogger. [4]Dual sport mirror with LH remote only. [5]Price includes power windows, which are required to purchase power door locks. [6]Bucket seats standard on Chevette, Monza and Camaro, with console being optional on Monza and Camaro. Mini-console standard on Chevette. Bucket seats and console available on Nova coupes or hatchbacks, Malibu Classic coupes and Monte Carlo. [7]Available on Chevette Scooter: AM radio for $74; WSW tires for $37. [8]Tape player is choice of cassette or 8-track. AM/FM stereo w/Citizens Band (CB) radio includes power antenna. [9]Not available on station wagons. [10]Standard on all Landau coupe models: Malibu Classic, Monte Carlo, Impala and Caprice. Cabriolet roof available on Monza Towne Coupe and Nova coupes. Camaro has vinyl sport roof (front part of roof). [11]Manually operated on Chevette and Monza. [12]Standard on Monte Carlo Landau coupe. [13]Standard on Camaro Z28 and Malibu station wagons. [14]Power front and rear disc brakes.

Paint Colors

	Code		Code		Code
Classic White[1]	10	Oyster White (two-tone only)[1]	39	Red[2]	75
White[2,3]	11	Light Green[2,3]	40	Carmine metallic[2,3]	77
Silver metallic[1]	13	Medium Green metallic[2,3]	44	Dark Carmine metallic[3]	79
Silver metallic[2,3]	15	Indy Silver metallic[1]	47	Brown metallic[1]	82
Gray metallic (two-tone only)[3]	16	Bright Yellow[2]	51	Dark Blue metallic[1]	83
Black	19	Yellow[1]	52	Medium Blue metallic (two-tone only)[3]	85
Pastel Blue[3]	21	Light Yellow[3]	54		
Light Blue metallic[2,3]	22	Dark Green metallic[1]	58		
Bright Blue metallic[2]	24	Frost Beige[1]	59		
Frost Blue[1]	28	Beige[2,3]	61		
Dark Blue metallic[2,3]	29	Camel metallic[2,3]	63		
Dark Red (two-tone only)[1]	35	Dark Brown metallic[1]	67		
Medium Blue (two-tone only)[1]	36	Dark Brown metallic[2,3]	69		
Medium Beige[1]	37	Red[1]	72		

In two-tone combinations, the first two digits indicate lower color and the next two digits are the upper color. Two-tone paint available for $55 on Nova, $115 on Malibu, $116 on Monte Carlo, and $56 on Impala and Caprice. Black is available on all models. [1]Available on Corvette. [2]Available on Chevette, Monza, Camaro and Nova. [3]Available on Malibu, Monte Carlo, Impala and Caprice.

Chevette

"A lot of car for your money."

Nameplate year of origin: 1976.
Current bodystyle lifespan: 1976 through 1987.
Predecessor to this model: None.
Replacement for this model: None (captive imports Sprint and Spectrum introduced in 1985 as supplementary models).
Percentage of division's production: 16.16%.
Corporate siblings: None.
Primary competition: Dodge Colt and Omni, Ford Fiesta, and Plymouth Arrow and Horizon.
Notable changes: New front-end styling and minor trim and detail changes.
Major standard equipment: Vinyl front bucket seats, fold-down rear seat (can be deleted for credit), color-keyed cut-pile carpeting, door armrests, dome courtesy light, open compartment glove box, black two-spoke steering wheel and column, cargo compartment under-floor storage, argent

Measurements

	2-Door	4-Door
Wheelbase	94.3"	97.3"
Length	158.8"	161.7"
Width	61.8"	61.8"
Height	52.3"	53.3"
Legroom — front	41.5"	41.5"
Legroom — rear	30.5"	34.1"
Headroom — front	38.1"	38.1"
Headroom — rear	37.3"	37.4"
Cargo capacity (cu. ft.)	26.3*	27.8*
Fuel capacity (gals.)	13.0	13.0

*Maximum with rear seat folded down.

colored headlight bezels and grille trim, polished aluminum bumpers (not chromed), and 155/80R13 BSW tires. Chevette adds: Choice of all-vinyl or cloth-and-vinyl front bucket seats, center console, color-keyed I/P w/brushed aluminum trim, sport steering wheel, cigarette lighter, glove box w/latch type door and lock, swing-out rear window (coupe), AM radio, bright front and rear window trim, chrome headlamp bezel inserts, deluxe grille trim, deluxe chrome bumpers w/rub strips, bright wheel trim rings, and 155/80R13 WSW tires.

Models Available

	Model No.	Base MSRP	Change from LY	Shipping Wt. (lbs.)	Model Year Production	Change from LY
Chevette Scooter 2-Door Hatchback Coupe	J08	$3,299	+10.00%	1929	24,099	+87.85%
Chevette 2-Door Hatchback Coupe	B08	$3,794	+13.12%	1978	136,145	+15.01%
Chevette 4-Door Hatchback Sedan	B68	$3,914	+12.99%	2057	208,865	+24.50%
TOTALS	*Avg. price*	$3,669	+12.12%	*Production*	369,109	+23.46%

Monza

"More car, more kicks, less money."

Nameplate year of origin: 1975 (1960 as Corvair subseries).
Current bodystyle lifespan: 1975 through 1980.
Predecessor to this model: Corvair Monza (1965 to 1969); Vega Kammback wagon (1971 to 1977).
Replacement for this model: Cavalier (1982 to 1993).
Percentage of division's production: 7.17%.
Corporate siblings: Buick Skyhawk, Oldsmobile Starfire, and Pontiac Sunbird.
Primary competition: Dodge Omni 024, Ford Pinto, and Plymouth Horizon TC3.
Notable changes: Minor trim and detail changes.
Major standard equipment: Choice of patterned cloth or all-vinyl front bucket seats, cut-pile carpeting, color-keyed instrument panel, fold-down rear seat and rear liftgate (hatchbacks and wagons), two-spoke steering wheel, soft molded door panels w/ map pockets, simulated woodgrain I/P trim, bright front and rear window moldings, bright side window surround moldings, aluminum front and rear bumpers (wagons), chrome front and rear bumpers (coupe and 2+2), bumper rub strips, full wheel covers, and A78 × 13 WSW tires. Wagons add: B78 × 13 WSW tires. Sport adds: Custom interior w/choice of Sport cloth-and-vinyl or all-vinyl front bucket seats, brushed metal accents on I/P, body-color urethane front end fascia w/body-color bumper and bumper guards, chrome rear bumper w/ body-color (or contrasting color), front and rear bumper guards color-matched to bumper and finned wheel covers w/GT-type center hub and bright wheel nuts.

Measurements

	Coupe	2+2 HBK	Sport 2+2 HBK	Wagon
Wheelbase	97.0"	97.0"	97.0"	97.0"
Length	179.2"	179.2"	179.3"	178.1"
Width	65.4"	65.4"	65.4"	65.4"
Height	49.8"	50.2"	50.2"	51.8"
Legroom — front	43.0"	43.0"	43.0"	43.0"
Legroom — rear	28.2"	29.6"	29.6"	30.2"
Headroom — front	37.6"	37.7"	37.7"	38.5"
Headroom — rear	37.2"	35.3"	35.3"	40.1"
Cargo capacity (cu. ft.)	6.6	10.1*	10.1*	46.6
Fuel capacity (gals.)	18.5	18.5	18.5	15.0

Capacity with rear seat folded down is 27.8 cu. ft.

Models Available

	Model No.	Base MSRP	Change from LY	Shipping Wt. (lbs.)	Model Year Production	Change from LY
Monza 2-Door Coupe	M27	$3,617	+4.48%	2577	61,110	+61.33%
Monza 2+2 2-Door Hatchback Coupe	M07	$3,844	+6.51%	2630	56,871	+56.99%
Monza 2-Door Station Wagon	M15	$3,974	+7.46%	2631	15,190	-37.37%
Monza Sport 2+2 2-Door Hatchback Coupe	R07	$4,291	+5.25%	2676	30,662	+6.30%
TOTALS	*Avg. price*	$3,932	+5.89%	*Production*	163,833	+18.01%

Camaro

"The Hugger."

Nameplate year of origin: 1967.
Current bodystyle lifespan: 1970 through 1981.
Predecessor to this model: Camaro (1967 to 1969).
Replacement for this model: Camaro (1982 to 1992).
Percentage of division's production: 12.37%.
Corporate siblings: Pontiac Firebird.
Primary competition: Dodge Challenger, Ford Mustang and Plymouth Sapporo.
Notable changes: New Berlinetta model and minor trim and detail changes.
Major standard equipment: All-vinyl front bucket seats, color-keyed cut-pile carpeting, color-keyed four-spoke soft rim sport steering wheel w/color-keyed column, bright front and rear window moldings, hubcaps, and FR78 × 14 BSW tires. Rally Sport adds: Black rocker panel, black dual sport mirrors, hood and forward portion of roof painted black w/tri-color stripes separating from body color, front stabilizer bar, special shock absorbers, power steering, and color-keyed Rally wheels. Berlinetta adds: Custom all-vinyl front bucket seats, special door panels, special instrumentation package, electric clock, Interior Décor/Quiet Sound group, LH remote and RH manual sport mirrors, Berlinetta nameplate on B-pillars, bright grille, brushed rear panel accent molding, black painted rocker panels, dual pinstriping, custom styled wheels, and FR78 × 14 WSW tires. Z28 adds: All-vinyl front bucket seats, large rim steering wheel, special instrumentation package, specific Z28 logos and decals (hood, front spoiler and fenders, doors, and front and rear panels), black anodized window surround trim and headlight/taillight bezels, black painted grille and parking light recesses, black painted rocker panels and rear trunk panel, front fender louvers, front and rear spoiler, dual resonator and tailpipes, sport suspension, body color special rally wheels, space saver spare tire, and GR70 × 15 R/WL tires.

Measurements

Wheelbase	108.0"
Length	197.6"
Width	74.5"
Height	49.2"
Legroom — front	43.9"
Legroom — rear	28.4"
Headroom — front	37.2"
Headroom — rear	36.0"
Cargo capacity (cu. ft.)	6.4
Fuel capacity (gals.)	21.0

Models Available

	Model No.	Base MSRP	Change from LY	Shipping Wt. (lbs.)	Model Year Production	Change from LY
Camaro 2-Door Sport Coupe	Q87	$4,677	+5.96%	3305	111,357	-23.93%
Camaro Rally Sport 2-Door Sport Coupe	Q87	$5,073	NEW	3305	19,101	NEW%
Camaro Berlinetta 2-Door Sport Coupe	S87	$5,396	+12.09%	3358	67,236	-5.74%
Camaro Z28 2-Door Sport Coupe	Q87	$6,115	+9.12%	NA	84,877	+54.58%
TOTALS	*Avg. price*	$5,315	+7.51%	*Production*	282,571	+3.65%

Nova

"Wanted for all its worth."

Nameplate year of origin: Nova: 1962, as top of the line Chevy II model; became series name in 1969.
Current bodystyle lifespan: 1975 through 1979.
Predecessor to this model: Nova (1968 to 1974; restyled in 1973).
Replacement for this model: Citation (1980 to 1985).
Percentage of division's production: 4.28%.
Corporate siblings: Buick Skylark, Oldsmobile Omega, and Pontiac Phoenix.
Primary competition: AMC Concord, Ford Granada, and Plymouth Volaré.
Notable changes: Minor trim and detail changes.
Major standard equipment: All-vinyl front bench seat, color-keyed cut-pile carpeting, front door armrests w/integral pull handle, color-keyed two-spoke steering wheel and steering column, bright front and rear window moldings, full-width luggage compartment mat, hubcaps, and E78 × 14 BSW tires. Hatchback model adds: Load floor carpeting and fold-down

Measurements

	Coupe & HBK	Sedan
Wheelbase	111.0"	111.0"
Length	196.7"	196.7"
Width	72.2"	72.2"
Height	52.7"	53.6"
Legroom — front	41.7"	41.7"
Legroom — rear	32.4"	35.2"
Headroom — front	38.2"	39.1"
Headroom — rear	36.7"	37.1"
Cargo capacity (cu. ft.)	13.4*	13.0
Fuel capacity (gals.)	21.0	21.0

Hatchback maximum with rear seat down, 29.2 cu. ft.

1979

rear seat. Custom adds: Custom vinyl front bench seat, door panels w/carpeted lower panels, door panel woodgrain trim inserts, rear door armrests, color-keyed steering wheel and steering column, simulated woodgrain trim on instrument cluster w/bright accents, bright side window and roof drip moldings, bright rocker panel moldings, high level acoustic insulation package, full wheel covers, and F78 × 14 BSW tires.

Models Available

	Model No.	Base MSRP	Change from LY	Shipping Wt. (lbs.)	Model Year Production	Change from LY
Nova 2-Door Coupe	X27	$3,955	+6.83%	3135	36,800	-63.87%
Nova 2-Door Hatchback	X17	$4,118	+6.52%	3264	4,819	-61.95%
Nova 4-Door Sedan	X69	$4,055	+7.36%	3179	40,883	-66.80%
Nova Custom 2-Door Coupe	Y27	$4,164	+5.15%	3194	7,529	-68.57%
Nova Custom 4-Door Sedan	Y69	$4,264	+5.68%	3228	7,690	-70.95%
TOTALS	*Avg. price*	$4,111	+6.29%	*Production*	97,721	-66.08%

Malibu

"A fresh new slice of apple pie."

Nameplate year of origin: 1964.
Current bodystyle lifespan: 1978 through 1983.
Predecessor to this model: Chevelle (1973 to 1977).
Replacement for this model: Celebrity (1982 to 1990).
Percentage of division's production: 18.04%.
Corporate siblings: Buick Century, Oldsmobile Cutlass, and Pontiac LeMans.
Primary competition: Dodge Diplomat and Ford LTD II.
Notable changes: New grille and minor trim and detail changes.
Major standard equipment: Cloth-and-vinyl front bench seat, color-keyed cut-pile nylon carpeting, color-coordinated delta-spoke steering wheel, color-keyed I/P and steering column, black instrument cluster trim, bright front and rear window surround moldings, bright roof drip rail molding, hubcaps, and P185/75R14 BSW tires. Wagon adds: All-vinyl front bench seat, vinyl coated metal cargo area sidewalls, bright rear quarter window molding, swing-up tailgate window and drop-down tailgate door, and P195/75R14 BSW tires. Malibu Classic adds: Choice of knit cloth-and-vinyl or all-vinyl front bench seat, glove compartment light, bright window frame moldings, lower bodyside protective molding, bright wheel opening moldings, and full wheel covers.

Measurements

	Coupes	Sedans	Wagons
Wheelbase	108.1"	108.1"	108.1"
Length	192.7"	192.7"	193.4"
Width	71.5"	71.5"	71.2"
Height	53.3"	54.2"	54.5"
Legroom — front	42.8"	42.8"	42.8"
Legroom — rear	35.1"	38.0"	35.9"
Headroom — front	37.9"	38.7"	38.8"
Headroom — rear	37.8"	37.7"	38.8"
Cargo capacity (cu. ft.)	16.6	16.6	72.4
Fuel capacity (gals.)	17.5	17.5	18.2

Models Available

	Model No.	Base MSRP	Change from LY*	Shipping Wt. (lbs.)	Model Year Production	Change from LY*
Malibu 2-Door Coupe	T27	$4,398	+4.61%	2983	41,848	+54.48%
Malibu 4-Door Sedan	T19	$4,498	+5.12%	2988	59,674	+34.32%
Malibu 4-Door, 2-Seat Station Wagon	T35	$4,745	+5.07%	3155	50,344	+63.19%
Malibu Classic 2-Door Sport Coupe	W27	$4,676	+4.82%	3017	60,751	-0.40%
Malibu Classic 2-Door Landau Coupe	W27	$4,915	+4.93%	NA	25,213	-13.54%
Malibu Classic 4-Door Sedan	W19	$4,801	+5.26%	3024	104,222	+1.22%
Malibu Classic 4-Door, 2-Seat Station Wagon	W35	$4,955	+5.11%	3183	70,095	+10.99%
TOTALS	*Avg. price*	$4,713	+4.99%	*Production*	412,147	+14.92%

Monte Carlo

"Imagine yourself in a 1979 Monte Carlo."

Nameplate year of origin: 1970.
Current bodystyle lifespan: 1978 through 1987.
Predecessor to this model: Monte Carlo (1973 to 1977).
Replacement for this model: Lumina (1990 to 1994).
Percentage of division's production: 13.87%.
Corporate siblings: Buick Regal, Oldsmobile Cutlass Supreme and Cutlass Calais, and Pontiac Grand Prix.
Primary competition: Dodge Magnum XE and Ford Thunderbird.
Notable changes: Minor trim and detail changes.
Major standard equipment: Cloth front bench seat, color-keyed cut-pile carpeting, color-keyed instrument panel w/black instrument trim panels, soft-rim two-spoke steering wheel, door pull assist straps, glove compartment light, I/P courtesy lights, electric clock, bright roof drip and window surround moldings, bright rocker panel moldings w/front and rear extensions, bright wheel opening moldings, full wheel covers, and P205/70R14 BSW tires. Landau adds: RH visor vanity mirror, specific Landau identification, Landau elk-grain vinyl roof w/rear quarter nameplate, dual sport mirrors w/LH remote, bright rocker panel molding, bodyside pinstriping, power steering, power brakes, and deluxe wheel covers.

Measurements

Wheelbase	108.1"
Length	200.4"
Width	71.5"
Height	53.9"
Legroom — front	42.8"
Legroom — rear	36.3"
Headroom — front	37.6"
Headroom — rear	37.8"
Cargo capacity (cu. ft.)	16.1
Fuel capacity (gals.)	17.5

Models Available

	Model No.	Base MSRP	Change from LY	Shipping Wt. (lbs.)	Model Year Production	Change from LY
Monte Carlo 2-Door Hardtop Coupe	Z37	$4,995	+4.39%	3039	225,073	+3.85%
Monte Carlo Landau 2-Door Hardtop Coupe	Z37	$5,907	+4.03%	NA	91,850	-35.07%
TOTALS	*Avg. price*	$5,451	+4.20%	*Production*	316,923	-11.52%

Impala and Caprice Classic

"The New Chevrolet. America has driven it to the top."

Nameplate year of origin: 1958 (Impala) and 1966 (Caprice).
Current bodystyle lifespan: 1977 through 1990.
Predecessor to this model: Biscayne/Bel Air/Impala/Caprice (1971 to 1976).
Replacement for this model: Caprice and Impala SS (1991 to 1996).
Percentage of division's production: 25.76%.
Corporate siblings: Buick LeSabre, Oldsmobile Delta 88, and Pontiac Catalina and Bonneville.
Primary competition: Dodge St. Regis and Ford LTD.
Notable changes: New grille and minor trim and detail changes.
Major standard equipment: Choice of knit cloth or all-vinyl front bench seat, color-keyed steering wheel and steering column, color-keyed cut-pile nylon carpeting, woodgrain vinyl accent trim on I/P and door panels, glove box light, bright front and rear window moldings, bright side window and body sill/door moldings, hubcaps, and FR78 × 15 BSW tires. Landau adds: Elk-grain vinyl top on forward portion of roof, dual sport mirrors, accent striping, distinctive Landau nameplates, and wire wheel covers. Wagon adds: All-vinyl front bench seat, three-way tailgate w/power-operated rear window, tailgate-ajar warning light, vinyl coated textured metal sidewalls, and HR78 × 15 BSW tires. Caprice adds: Choice of velvet-look knit cloth or all-vinyl front bench seat, fold-down center armrest (four-doors only), front door pull straps and lower door panel carpeting, electric clock, courtesy lights, added acoustical insulation, specific triple unit taillights, bright roof drip moldings, bright wheel opening moldings, stand-up hood ornament, and full wheel covers. Caprice wagon adds: All-vinyl front bench seat w/fold-down center armrest, three-way tailgate w/power-operated rear window, tailgate window moldings, tailgate-ajar warning light, vinyl coated textured metal sidewalls, and HR78 × 15 BSW tires.

Measurements

	2-doors	4-doors	Wagons
Wheelbase	116.0"	116.0"	116.0"
Length	212.5"	212.5"	214.7"
Width	75.5"	75.5"	79.1"
Height	56.0"	56.0"	58.0"
Legroom — front	42.2"	42.4"	42.4"
Legroom — rear	38.8"	39.0"	37.7"
Headroom — front	39.4"	39.4"	39.6"
Headroom — rear	38.2"	38.2"	39.4"
Cargo capacity (cu. ft.)	19.8	20.2	88.6
Fuel capacity (gals.)	21.0	21.0	22.0

1979

Models Available

	Model No.	Base MSRP	Change from LY	Shipping Wt. (lbs.)	Model Year Production	Change from LY
Impala 2-Door Sport Coupe	L47	$5,497	+5.55%	3495	26,589	-21.77%
Impala 2-Door Landau Coupe	L47	$5,961	+6.48%	NA	3,247	-30.20%
Impala 4-Door Sedan	L69	$5,597	+5.94%	3513	172,717	-5.70%
Impala 4-Door, 2-Seat Station Wagon*	L35	$6,109	+5.75%	4013	68,354	-0.85%
Caprice Classic 2-Door Coupe	N47	$5,837	+5.63%	3538	36,629	-1.80%
Caprice Classic 2-Door Landau Coupe	N47	$6,234	+6.93%	NA	21,824	-4.16%
Caprice Classic 4-Door Sedan	N69	$5,962	+5.97%	3564	203,017	-0.40%
Caprice Classic 4-Door, 2-Seat Station Wagon*	N35	$6,389	+6.27%	4056	56,261	-2.57%
TOTALS	*Avg. price*	$5,948	+6.08%	*Production*	588,638	-3.88%

Production of wagons with third seat option is included above, but breaks out as follows: Impala, 28,710; Caprice Classic, 32,693.

Corvette

"The one and only."

Nameplate year of origin: 1953 (also used on show car of same year).
Current bodystyle lifespan: 1968 through 1982.
Predecessor to this model: Corvette (1963 to 1967).
Replacement for this model: Corvette (1984 to 1996).
Percentage of division's production: 2.36%.
Corporate siblings: None.
Primary competition: None.
Notable changes: Minor trim and detail changes.
Major standard equipment: Choice of all-leather or cloth-and-leather high-back contoured bucket seats, center floor console, color-keyed cut-pile carpeting, tilt steering wheel w/four-spoke sport steering wheel, sports instrumentation with full gauges including tachometer, AM/FM radio, electric clock, tinted glass, LH rear view sport mirror, carpeted cargo area with light concealed behind seats, luggage space roll shade, anti-theft audio alarm system, removable roof panels, domed hood w/air scoop, front and rear bumper guards, power steering, power four wheel disc brakes, rally wheels w/trim rings, and P225/70R15 BSW tires.

Measurements

Wheelbase	98.0"
Length	185.2"
Width	69.0"
Height	48.0"
Legroom — front	42.1"
Headroom — front	36.8"
Cargo capacity (cu. ft.)	8.4
Fuel capacity (gals.)	24.0

Models Available

	Model No.	Base MSRP	Change from LY	Shipping Wt. (lbs.)	Model Year Production	Change from LY
Corvette 2-Door Coupe	Z87	$10,245	+6.22%	3372	53,807	+15.03%
TOTALS	*Avg. price*	$10,245	+6.22%	*Production*	53,807	+15.03%

CHRYSLER

"Why pay the price of a Chrysler and not get one?"

Downsized Newport and New Yorker models were the stars of the 1979 Chrysler lineup. Available in only two models, a lone 4-door pillared hardtop in each series, the cars gained more than 35 percent in combined production over 1978. Unfortunately these gains were offset by a large drop in Cordoba output and a slight dip for the popular LeBaron series, leaving Chrysler as a whole down only a few points, which was in line with the industry average. As a second recession and fears of another oil shortage loomed, Chrysler struggled to position its cars at the forefront of the near-luxury field, while attempting to make them more fuel efficient.

The Newport and New Yorker shared all-new exterior and interior styling on a "new" 118.5-inch wheelbase, making them the first truly downsized Chrysler models. Most features including many body panels were shared with the equally new Dodge St. Regis. Both Chrysler models shared basic bodyside styling and interior design, differing in their front and rear styling treatments and the level of trim applied to the interior. All three were available only in a new for Chrysler 4-door pillared hardtop design, meaning that there was a center roof pillar but no upper door frame, as a sedan would have. In general the greenhouse area was formal and upright in appearance, and both series used a stationary rear quarter window in the rear doors.

Newport and New Yorker models, now known as R-body Chryslers, may have looked new, but in reality they represented a very clever redesign of the B-body mid-size sedan platform of 1971–1978, most recently known as the Dodge Monaco and Plymouth Fury. Technically per Chrysler records, the former B-body Charger SE, Magnum XE, and Chrysler Cordoba were now known as R-body cars also, even though nothing of note changed for the cars. This was apparently a way to make these cars the two-door counterparts of the new four-door Chrysler Newport and New Yorker and Dodge St. Regis models.

For the bodysides, styling was now very angular in keeping with the trends of the time. Front fender end caps were thin and angled forward as they sloped down to meet the bumper. An upper bodyside feature line began at the top edge of the front fender and ran along the beltline, continuing to the rear of the car in virtually a straight line. A mid-level feature line began on the side of the front fender cap just a few inches from the top and front edges and ran straight back to the top of the taillights, just above the slightly flared front and rear wheel openings. A lower feature line ran straight along the bodyside at the same level as the bumper rub strips. About the only curve to any of the sheetmetal was the arch of the full wheel openings. Also, rear wheel fender skirts were a thing of the past for Chrysler.

At the front end, the Newport had an egg-crate patterned grille, four rows high and eight columns across, with each opening filled with egg-crate inserts in a three by three configuration. A chrome trim piece surrounded the entire grille being thinner on the bottom, then sharply curving up the sides, widening near the top, where a large top portion carried the Chrysler name in block letters across the face. A standup hood ornament sat atop the upper bar on the front header panel. Dual rectangular headlamps were set above a

large rectangular parking/turn signal light, and recessed slightly in the area between the grille and front fender end caps. The New Yorker used a grille of vertical design with sixteen larger vertical bars and three smaller bars in the spaces between them. Atop the smaller bars were two horizontal bars dividing the grille into three vertical sections. A large unadorned chrome trim piece covered the area above the grille and extended back to the edge of the hood, with a stand-up hood ornament atop this chrome panel. New Yorkers used hidden headlights, as in the recent past, with parking/turn signal lights mounted below in the bumper. The Chrysler name was on the driver's side headlight cover. Newports had horizontal side marker lights; New Yorkers had vertical ones. Front and rear bumper facings were made 50 to 60 pounds lighter on both cars via the use of chrome-plated, high-strength aluminum alloy units. The Newport and New Yorker both used black bumper guard and rub strip facings, while cars with the new "Fifth Avenue Edition" package used body-colored facings.

The rear styling of each car was also different. Newports used a wraparound horizontal taillight split into two horizontal sections with chrome trim, and a large license plate housing with vertical backup lights on each side sat between the taillights. New Yorkers used a full-width multi-section tail lamp divided into three sections beneath the raised center portion of the trunk lid, and a slightly recessed lamp extending to the outer ends. The center section was actually a reflective lens. Backup lights were mounted in the rear bumper ends, and the license plate was housed in the center of the bumper. Because the New Yorker taillight did not wrap around, a side marker light nearly square in shape was mounted in the rear quarter panel end cap area.

Another distinction lay in the greenhouse area, where the New Yorker's standard vinyl landau top extended onto the rear door to surround, and slightly encroach on, the quarter window (termed an opera window in Chrysler's promotional materials). Also a vertical light was added on the thin pillar ahead of the opera window.

Inside, the Newport and New Yorker shared a new instrument panel design that slanted away from the driver and passengers as it went downward. It was divided into three sections, the largest of which, in front of the driver, contained round recessed gauges, with two large ones centered over the steering column for the speedometer and odometer, four smaller gauges to the left, and two instruments to the right housing fuel, ammeter, temperature, and oil pressure gauges along with various other warning lights. To the outer edges of this area were vertical rectangular air vents, and below that other controls for things such as headlights and rear window defroster. The smaller center section housed the radio, heater/air conditioning controls, and an ashtray/cigarette lighter drawer at the bottom. On the passenger side was a horizontal air vent next to the electronic digital clock (if so equipped), above a large glove box. An additional air vent was set at the far right end. These three areas used a black facing on the Newport, a medium dark simulated woodgrain on the New Yorker, and a light simulated driftwood panel for New Yorkers with the optional "Fifth Avenue Edition" package. Upholstery and door panel designs were up to the traditional levels of Chrysler luxury with Newports using cloths and vinyls and New Yorkers using mainly velours or leather upholstery. Door panels for all had carpeted lower areas and door pull straps in addition to a door-mounted armrest. The aforementioned "Fifth Avenue Edition" package was basically a luxury décor option that included leather upholstery, padded vinyl top, and front fender louvers among many other items that are listed in Appendix IV. In all, there were 16,113 Fifth Avenue packages sold — 37 percent of all 1979 New Yorkers — making it one of Chrysler's most popular décor packages ever.

The Cordoba series received another minor refreshing with a new vertical bar grille pattern that had 23 bars in total, with a finely textured egg-crate grille insert between the bars. Around back, taillamps were enlarged and appeared nearly flat with a dual ridge dividing the lens vertically, and a Cordoba medallion placed in the center. The front corner lamps adopted clear lenses but for a thin, vertical amber reflector. Two different types of two-tone options added a distinctive style to those Cordobas so equipped. In the first option, the Special Appearance package, the two-tone dividing line followed the raised center section of the hood to a point several inches from the rear edge, where it curved outward, and ran just an inch below the beltline, curving up behind the door glass and arching over the roof to the other side. As it was offered only with Black or Dark Blue lower body and Dove Gray upper hood and roof, these cars made quite a statement.

The second option was a regular two-tone option wherein the entire hood, front fascia panel, and fender tops were included in the upper color; the strip below the beltline and curving up and over the roof was the same as with the Special Appearance package. An interesting late season option was the "300" package, offering a modern take on the long-running, high performance name. Unfortunately the Cordoba had the show but not the go; still it managed to find 3,811 buyers in the short time it was offered. Available only in Spinnaker White paint with a red leather interior, the package was most identifiable by traditional "300" crosshair bars on a blacked-out grille.

The year-and-a-half-old LeBaron series received a new grille design and revised taillamps to distinguish them for the new year. The grille was now divided into six sections, three rows horizontally on each side of the center, and was filled with a multitude of small vertical bars, giving the grille inserts a fine texture. Taillights were the same shape, but were now vertically divided into three roughly equal sections, with a LeBaron crest emblem in the center section. Otherwise most other features remained similar to the original design. A new Salon trim level replaced the former base LeBaron model, and the base LeBaron replaced the mid-year 1978 LeBaron S model. A new 4-speed overdrive manual floor shift transmission was standard equipment on all models with the standard 225 CID "Slant Six" 6-cylinder engine for this season only, except in California where an automatic was required. It was intended to improve fuel economy, but it turned out consumers were not eager for a manual transmission in their luxury car, so for 1980 all Chrysler models would have the TorqueFlite automatic transmission as standard equipment.

Cordoba 2-Door Hardtop Coupe

LeBaron Medallion 2-Door Coupe

LeBaron Medallion 4-Door Sedan with sunroof

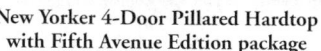

**New Yorker 4-Door Pillared Hardtop
with Fifth Avenue Edition package**

Newport 4-Door Pillared Hardtop

Model year production: 291,598 down 3.77% from 1978.
Domestic market share: 3.17% (10th place).
Base price range: $5,381 to $10,026.
Chrysler average base price: $6,370, up 8.96%.
Introduction date: October 5, 1978.
Assembly plants: Lynch Road, Detroit, MI (A); Newark, NJ (F); St. Louis, MO (G); and Windsor, Ontario, Canada (R).
Data plate identification (VIN): Thirteen digit code read as follows: First four digits indicate series and body style (model number in model charts); fifth digit indicates engine code (see powertrain chart); sixth digit indicates year (9 = 1979); seventh digit indicates assembly plant (see list above); remaining digits are sequential with beginning numbers of 100001. *Example:* TH42H9F100001 is a 1979 Chrysler Newport 4-Door Pillared Hardtop, with 318 CID, 4-bbl. V8 engine, serial number 100001, built in Newark, NJ.

1979

Powertrains

Engine	Net HP	Engine Code	Transmission Availability		LeBaron	LeBaron Town & Country	Cordoba	Newport	New Yorker
225 CID (3.7L), 1-bbl., 6-cyl.	100	C	4-speed manual w/overdrive[1]		S	S	—	—	—
				MPG:	18/28	18/28	—	—	—
			3-speed Torque Flite automatic[2]		S	S	—	—	—
				Calif.	NA	NA	—	—	—
225 CID (3.7L) Super Six, 2-bbl., 6-cyl.[1]	110	D	3-speed Torque Flite automatic		$193	$193	—	S	—
				MPG:	17/23	17/23	—	17/23	—
318 CID (5.2L), 2-bbl., V8[1]	135	G	3-speed Torque Flite automatic		$236	$236	S	$239	N/C
				MPG:	16/23	16/23	16/23	16/23	16/23
318 CID (5.2L), 4-bbl., V8[2]	145	H	3-speed Torque Flite automatic		$296	$296	$61[3]	$300[3]	—
				MPG:	—	—	13	—	—
				Calif.	14	13	13	13	—
360 CID (5.9L), 2-bbl., V8[1]	150	K	3-speed Torque Flite automatic		$426	$426	$191	$432	S
				MPG:	14/22	14/22	14/22	14/22	14/22
360 CID (5.9L), 4-bbl., V8[2,4]	195	J/L[4]	3-speed Torque Flite automatic		$487	$487	$251	$493	$60[3]
				MPG:	13	12	13	12	12
				Calif.	12	12	12	12	12

[1]*Not available in California.* [2]*Available only in California and designated high altitude areas.* [3]*Required as standard equipment in California and designated high altitude areas, with appropriate adjustment in price.* [4]*Available with federal emissions only in combination with heavy-duty package.*

Major Options

	LeBaron	Cordoba	Newport	New Yorker
Air conditioning	$584	$584	$628	$628
Air conditioning, w/Auto-Temp control	—	$628	$673	$673
Tilt steering wheel	$77	$77	$79	$60
Leather covered steering wheel	$60	$40	$60	$41
Automatic speed control	$107	$107	$112	$112
Electric rear window defroster	$96	$98	$105	$105
Tinted glass, all windows	$73	$73	S	S
Power windows, 2-dr./4-dr.	$137/$194	$137	$212	S
Power door locks, 2-dr./4-dr.	$89/$124	$89	$126	$126
Power front bench seat, 6-way	$167	$167	$170	$170
Power seat 50/50 or bucket, 6-way[1]	$167	$167	$170	$170
Front bucket seats w/floor console	$110[2]	$170	—	—
Leather interior trim	$283[3]	$283	—	$287
AM radio	$87	$87	$106	$106
AM/FM stereo	$240	$240	$253	$253
AM/FM stereo w/8-track tape	$343	$343	$360	$360
AM/FM stereo w/CB transceiver	$527	$527	$543	$543
Vinyl top[4]	$165	$132	$152	S
Dual remote control mirrors, chrome	$54	$54	$44	$24[5]
Remote control trunk release	$25	$26	$35	$35
Metal sunroof, electric	—	$546	—	—
Glass sunroof, electric	$627	—	$993	$993
T-Bar roof[6]	$675	$675	—	—
Premiere wheel covers	$90	$45	$54	$54
Wire wheel covers	$300	$255	$259	$259
Chrome styled road wheels	—	$213	$216	$216
Aluminum fascia road wheels	—	$164	$175	$175
Forged aluminum road wheels	$305	$260	—	—
White sidewall tires, std. size	$50	$50	$51	$51

Popular Option Groups & Packages

	LeBaron	Cordoba	Newport	New Yorker
"300" option package	—	$2,040	—	—
Basic group	$1,385	$1,089	$1,176	$1,098
Crown Roof package	—	$823	—	—
Crown Roof two-tone package	—	$971	—	—
Deluxe insulation package	$93	S	S	S
Deluxe wiper/washer package	$47	S	$41	S
"Fifth Avenue Edition" package	—	—	—	$1,500
Light package	$84	$291	$96	$91
Special Appearance package	—	$527	—	—
Sport Appearance package	$219	—	—	—

— = Not Available; S = Standard equipment.   [1]Left side power adjustment only.   [2]Available only on LeBaron Salon. Console is not available.   [3]Leather interior with 60/40 split front bench seat for Town & Country wagon is $430.   [4]Landau vinyl top on LeBaron coupe, Cordoba and New Yorker. Full vinyl roof on LeBaron sedan and Newport. LeBaron coupe with landau vinyl top is $148.   [5]LH remote is standard.   [6]T-Bar roof only available on 2-door models. Newport and New Yorker require vinyl top.

Paint Colors

	Code		Code		Code
Spinnaker White	EW1	Frost Blue metallic[3,4,5]	SC2	Designers Beige (two-tone only)[6]	SL2
Cadet Blue metallic[1,2]	PB3	Nightwatch Blue[3,4,5]	SC9	Chianti Red[1,2,3]	SR5
Dove Gray[1]	RA1	Teal Frost metallic[1]	SG4	Regent Red Sunfire metallic	SR8
Sable Tan Sunfire metallic	RT9	Teal Green Sunfire metallic	SG8	Pearl Gray (two-tone only)[3]	SS1
Ensign Blue metallic[1,2]	SB7	Designers Cream (two-tone only)[6]	SL1	Light Cashmere[2,3,4]	ST1

	Code
Medium Cashmere metallic[4,5,7]	ST5
Linen Cream (two-tone only)[3]	SY1
Formal Black	TX9

Single tones are coded EW1,EW1. Two-tones are coded on body ID plate as TX9,EW1 where three digits on line 2 are lower body color, and three digits on line 3 are upper body color or two-tone color. [1]Not available on LeBaron Town & Country wagon. [2]Available on LeBaron. [3]Available on Cordoba. [4]Available on Newport. [5]Available on New Yorker. [6]Available only on New Yorker with Fifth Avenue package. [7]Available on LeBaron Town & Country wagon.

LeBaron

"The personal car with the pleasing price."

Nameplate year of origin: 1957, as subseries name for Imperial. Also used on LeBaron custom bodied Chryslers beginning in 1930.

Current bodystyle lifespan: 1977½ through 1979.

Predecessor to this model: None.

Replacement for this model: LeBaron (1980 to 1981).

Percentage of division's production: 39.05%.

Corporate siblings: Dodge Diplomat.

Primary competition: Buick Century and Regal, Mercury Cougar, and Oldsmobile Cutlass Salon and Supreme.

Notable changes: New grille and minor trim and detail changes.

Major standard equipment: Whittier cloth-and-vinyl front bench seat, color-keyed carpeting, one-piece cloth headliner, simulated woodgrain I/P cluster and glove box door appliqué, two-speed windshield wipers, LH manual mirror, rocker panel sill moldings w/rear extensions, bright roof drip rail moldings, quarter window moldings (coupes), bright upper door frame moldings (sedan), opera lamps (coupe), full vinyl padded top (sedan), bright belt molding, rear bumper guards, lower deck panel stripe (sedan), stand-up hood ornament, power steering, power brakes, hubcaps, and FR78 × 15 BSW tires. Salon adds: Cloth-and-vinyl front bench seat w/fold-down center armrest, door pull straps, windshield header mounted reading lamps (coupe only), deluxe shelf panel, dual horns, bright center pillar moldings, color-coordinated bodyside accent stripes, front fender sill molding extensions, and deluxe wheel covers. Medallion adds: Verdi velour 60/40 front split-bench seat w/ fold-down center armrests and passenger recliner, shag carpeting, fold-down rear seat armrest (sedan), bright pedal trim, map reading lamp, door mounted courtesy lights, three upper assist handles (sedan), B-pillar assist straps (coupe), rear pillar vanity lamps and mirrors (sedan), trunk dress-up package, LH remote control outside rearview mirror, quarter window glass accents and medallion (coupe), bodyside accent tape stripes coordinated w/body color on coupes and vinyl top color on sedans, deluxe sound insulation package (w/o undercoating and hood pad), and premium wheel covers. Town & Country adds: All vinyl bench seat w/fold-down center armrest, gas hydraulic liftgate struts, carpeted cargo area w/stainless steel skid strips on floor and rear seat back, carpeted lockable stowage bins, liftgate-open warning light, and simulated wood bodyside and liftgate appliqués with surround moldings.

Measurements

	Coupe	Sedan	Wagon
Wheelbase	112.7"	112.7"	112.7"
Length	204.1"	206.1"	202.8"
Width	73.5"	72.8"	72.8"
Height	53.0"	55.3"	55.7"
Legroom — front	42.5"	42.5"	42.5"
Legroom — rear	34.0"	36.6"	36.6"
Headroom — front	37.5"	39.2"	39.2"
Headroom — rear	36.2"	37.5"	38.7"
Cargo capacity (cu. ft.)	16.0	16.6	72.3
Fuel capacity (gals.)	19.5	19.5	19.5

Models Available

	Model No.	Base MSRP	Change from LY	Shipping Wt. (lbs.)	Model Year Production	Change from LY
LeBaron 2-Door Coupe	FM22	$5,381	+9.95%	3270	25,019	NA*
LeBaron 4-Door Sedan	FM41	$5,479	+8.28%	3330	NA*	NA*
LeBaron Salon 2-Door Coupe	FH22	$5,623	+9.31%	3285	35,096	NA*
LeBaron Salon 4-Door Sedan	FH41	$5,851	+10.19%	3350	NA*	NA*
LeBaron Town & Country 4-Dr. Wagon	FH45	$6,331	+10.60%	3585	17,463	-18.79%
LeBaron Medallion 2-Door Coupe	FP22	$6,017	+8.90%	3345	35,475	NA*
LeBaron Medallion 4-Door Sedan	FP41	$6,245	+9.72%	3425	NA*	NA*
TOTALS	*Avg. price*	$5,847	+9.58%	*Production*	113,863	-11.32%

*Totals and comparisons to LY are not possible due to production of coupes and sedans being kept as combined total for 1979.

Cordoba

"The contemporary classic."

Nameplate year of origin: 1975 (also used on special-order 1970 Newport hardtops).
Current bodystyle lifespan: 1975 through 1979.
Predecessor to this model: None.
Replacement for this model: Cordoba (1980 to 1983).
Percentage of division's sales volume: 25.10%.
Corporate siblings: Dodge Magnum XE.
Primary competition: Buick Regal, Mercury Cougar XR-7, and Oldsmobile Cutlass Supreme.
Notable changes: Minor trim and detail changes.
Major standard equipment: Cloth split-back front bench seat w/fold-down center armrest, color-keyed long pile carpeting, simulated woodgrained vinyl trim on I/P and door panels, luxury three-spoke steering wheel, luxury padded door trim w/carpeted lower panels and seat backs, bright pedal dress-up, glove box and ashtray light, electronic digital clock, premium steering wheel, molded cloth headliner, trunk light, carpeted trunk and spare tire cover, LH rear view mirror, rear quarter formal opera window and opera lamp, drip rail moldings, wheel lip moldings, rocker panel sill molding, bodyside and deck lid paint stripes, stand-up hood ornament, front and rear bumper guards, power steering, power brakes, luxury wheel covers, and FR78 × 15 BSW tires.

Measurements

Wheelbase	114.9"
Length	215.8"
Width	77.1"
Height	53.1"
Legroom — front	42.6"
Legroom — rear	32.1"
Headroom — front	37.7"
Headroom — rear	36.6"
Cargo capacity (cu. ft.)	16.3
Fuel capacity (gals.)	21.0

Models Available

	Model No.	Base MSRP	Change from LY	Shipping Wt. (lbs.)	Model Year Production	Change from LY
Cordoba 2-Door Hardtop Coupe	SS29	$6,337	+9.05%	3680	73,195	NA*
TOTALS	*Avg. price*	$6,337	+10.96%	*Production*	73,195	-32.26%

*Change from LY not available due to production of 1978 Cordoba S being included with Cordoba, and both the Cordoba and Cordoba S using the same model number for 1978.

Newport

"Now you can have it all ... Now."

Nameplate year of origin: 1961 (as series); 1950 (as HT model of the T & C).
Current bodystyle lifespan: 1979 through 1981.
Predecessor to this model: Newport (1974 to 1978).
Replacement for this model: E Class (1983 to 1984).
Percentage of division's sales volume: 20.89%.
Corporate siblings: Chrysler New Yorker and Dodge St. Regis.
Primary competition: Buick LeSabre, Mercury Marquis, and Oldsmobile Delta 88.
Notable changes: Completely redesigned.
Major standard equipment: Cloth-and-vinyl split back front bench seat w/fold-down center armrest, color-keyed long pile carpeting, trip odometer, I/P courtesy lights, two-spoke steering wheel w/woodtone trim, front and rear ashtrays, inside day/night mirror, two-speed electric windshield wipers w/washers, dual outside rear view mirrors, front and rear wheel lip moldings, drip rail and belt moldings, bright windshield and rear window moldings, rear hood molding, dual horns, front and rear bumper guards, rear license plate periphery molding, deluxe wheel covers, and P/195 × 75R15 BSW tires.

Measurements

Wheelbase	118.5"
Length	220.2"
Width	77.1"
Height	54.5"
Legroom — front	42.3"
Legroom — rear	38.3"
Headroom — front	38.2"
Headroom — rear	37.4"
Cargo capacity (cu. ft.)	21.3
Fuel capacity (gals.)	21.0

Models Available

	Model No.	Base MSRP	Change from LY	Shipping Wt. (lbs.)	Model Year Production	Change from LY
Newport 4-Door Pillared Hardtop	TH42	$6,405	+8.78%*	3530	60,904	+152.83%*
TOTALS	Avg. price	$6,405	+9.56%	Production	60,904	+102.50%

*Comparison made to 1978 Newport 4-Door Hardtop.

New Yorker

"The most fabulous New Yorker of them all."

Nameplate year of origin: 1939.
Current bodystyle lifespan: 1979 through 1981.
Predecessor to this model: New Yorker (1974 to 1978).
Replacement for this model: New Yorker/Fifth Avenue (New Yorker, 1982; New Yorker Fifth Avenue, 1983; Fifth Avenue 1984 to 1989).
Percentage of division's sales volume: 14.96%.
Corporate siblings: Chrysler Newport and Dodge St. Regis.
Primary competition: Buick Electra, Mercury Grand Marquis, and Oldsmobile Ninety-Eight.
Notable changes: Completely redesigned.
Major standard equipment: Crushed velour 60/40 split bench seats w/individual adjustment and fold-down center armrest, passenger side recliner, rear seat fold-down center armrest, color-keyed long-pile carpeting, color-keyed seat belts, carpeted rear shelf panel, trip odometer, digital clock, interior lights (glove box, map/courtesy and ashtray), luxury three-spoke steering wheel w/soft center pad and woodtone rim insert, two-speed electric windshield wipers w/washers, tinted glass, power windows, black carpeted trunk floor and spare tire cover, LH remote control and RH manual mirrors, front wheel lip molding, drip rail molding, bright front windshield molding, rear taillight periphery moldings, bodyside and hood accent stripes, color-keyed door handle inserts, fender-mounted turn signal indicators, concealed headlamps, undercoating, hood insulation pad, unique New Yorker wheel covers, and P205/75R15 BSW tires.

Measurements

Wheelbase	118.5"
Length	221.5"
Width	77.1"
Height	54.5"
Legroom — front	42.3"
Legroom — rear	38.2"
Headroom — front	38.6"
Headroom — rear	37.4"
Cargo capacity (cu. ft.)	21.3
Fuel capacity (gals.)	21.0

Models Available

	Model No.	Base MSRP	Change from LY	Shipping Wt. (lbs.)	Model Year Production	Change from LY
New Yorker 4-Door Pillared Hardtop	TP42	$10,026	+28.03%*	3800	43,636	+62.38%*
TOTALS	Avg. price	$10,026	+29.09%	Production	43,636	+19.56%

*Comparisons made to 1978 Chrysler New Yorker Brougham 4-Door Hardtop.

DODGE

"Hey that's my Dodge!"

After nearly 15 years in the Dodge lineup, the long familiar Monaco and Charger names were missing from dealer showrooms as the 1979 model year began. In concept, the all-new St. Regis and new-for-1978 Magnum XE had replaced the popular nameplates. Interestingly, within a short four-year period, all of the well-known series names that began as much as 25 years earlier had been replaced. The Challenger name remained, albeit on an imported car far different from its namesake. Possibly these changes had something to do with the sales declines that Dodge was facing. By the end of the 1979 model year, Cadillac would surpass production totals of both Dodge and Plymouth. Dodge sales for the calendar year bested Plymouth, but this was mainly due to the fact that Plymouth's largest car was now the compact Volaré. It is tempting to wonder what might have been if the Dart, Coronet, Charger and Monaco nameplates had survived into the new decade, but at least the Charger and Monaco would resurface again, albeit on much different cars than their predecessors. Also absent this year were the 400 CID and 440 CID V8 engines for the general public, though they were still available in trucks and special purpose applications. Despite what turned out to be a less than spectacular year, Dodge had several new models for 1979, including the full-size St. Regis, a new Omni model known as the Omni 024, and a new mini-compact, front-wheel-drive Colt import.

The Omni 024 name was derived from its series name of "O"mni and its model number of 24, designating a 2-Door Hatchback, resulting in 024. From the beginning, the 024 was marketed separately from the Omni 4-Door in sales literature and advertising, as they were built with differing chassis and body panels, but they remained linked in the Dodge lineup due to the common name, series and model identifiers. (Beginning in 1982, the Charger name was reincarnated for the 2.2-liter performance version of the 024. The seemingly successful Charger name revival transitioned to be the series name of the line for 1983, and marked the official separation of the Omni 2-door and 4-door models.) The new 024 rode on a slightly shorter wheelbase than the 4-door but was 10 inches longer overall and much more aerodynamic looking in design, combining a long sloping hood with a slanted front fascia and a long sloping hatchback, much like GM's H-body cars (Chevrolet Monza 2+2 and related cars). The 024's body-color front end, devoid of chrome other than the small Dodge nameplate on the driver's side of the sloping front fascia, sported single square headlights in a tunneled housing, with a six-slot, body-color grille. The integrated body-color front bumper housed a lower open grille area and parking/turn signal lamps in a recessed pod directly below the headlights. At the rear, horizontal wraparound taillamps with tri-color lenses were divided into three sections horizontally and were nearly full-width, with only a recessed license plate housing interrupting the clean sweep.

Bodyside lines of the 024 were straight and full-length with the upper line running at a level just below the door handle, and the lower running between the top edges of the bumpers. The greenhouse area used a narrow, nearly rectangular window for the rear seat passengers, an angled C-pillar with three louvers on the leading edge (on all but the base trim level), and a triangular window between the C-pillar

and the slope of the hatchback. Inside, the interior was similar to that of its 4-door relative, with a small pod directly in front of the driver carrying round-dial instrumentation, and ventilation and radio controls in the center of the lower instrument panel area. A variety of option packages allowed the 024 to be outfitted toward economy, sporty or luxury. As for the Omni 4-door, few changes were made to the successful subcompact.

The new St. Regis was the Dodge version of Chrysler's corporate R-body, the "new," downsized, full-size models. They looked new but in reality shared a platform modified from the B-body Dodge Coronet/Charger design introduced in 1971. Similar or shared components included the torsion-bar front suspension, lower body structure, and powertrain components. But the St. Regis looked totally different from its Coronet or Charger cousins. At the front end, dual rectangular headlamps with clear retractable covers, a design lifted from the Magnum XE, sat beside a horizontal cross-hatch grille, six columns wide and seven rows high, with the bottom row visually extended by a trim piece that stretched under the headlamps and around to the bodyside, ending at the same point as the side marker light. The grille was nearly upright and protruded past the more sloping outer area housing the headlamps. The unusual front treatment gave the St. Regis a uniquely sporty and luxurious look.

The rest of the body was shared with the Chrysler Newport and New Yorker. Two bodyside feature lines ran the length of the car, with the upper beginning at the top of the wraparound combination turn signal/side marker light and ending at the top corner of the wraparound horizontal taillamps. The lower feature line extended from bumper to bumper, about an inch below the top surface of each. Tail-lamps were of horizontal design with lenses having an egg-crate stamping pattern three rows high. Backup lights sat in the rear panel alongside the license plate housing and between the taillamps.

A nearly upright rear window and rear doors with fixed quarter windows combined to give the roofline a very formal look. The St. Regis doors used frameless windows, creating what was known as the pillared hardtop style, something Ford had used from 1971 through 1978 and abandoned for their 1979 downsized cars. General Motors had introduced the same concept in 1971 on the Cadillac Sixty-Special, and more popularly on their 1973 mid-size line where the pillared hardtop style was named the Colonnade hardtop.

Inside the St. Regis were Dodge's most luxurious interiors to date. Plush cloth and soft leather upholsteries combined with a wide array of seating options were available that would have been fit for an Imperial when it was still in the corporate line. An all-new flattop instrument panel design slanted away from the occupant from the top down, making the front seat passenger area feel enormous. The face of the panel was divided into the typical three-section affair with gauges surrounding the driver, glove box and clock to the right, and ventilation and radio controls in the center. The gauges were all set into round tunneled housings with vertical air vents on each side, and a black facing. The glove box door itself was padded in trim the same color as the rest of the interior, but had an inverted U-shaped area around it finished in black and housing horizontal air vents and the electronic digital clock. The heater, air conditioner and radio controls, and ashtray and cigarette lighter were all placed in the center section also done in black, and outlined by the instrument panel trim color.

Aspen, Diplomat and Magnum XE models returned with mostly grille and taillight changes, and only minor powertrain changes were seen across the line. The compact Aspen, which remained the most popular Dodge series, added Sunrise coupe and Sport wagon packages, and deleted the "Street Kit" and "Super Coupe" packages, and was otherwise unchanged. The mid-size Diplomat gained an intricate egg-crate grille design three rows high and eight columns across, and having a four by four egg-crate design within each of the larger sections. At the back end, the wraparound taillamps were now split into two sections vertically by a small chrome divider, and then further divided horizontally into two sections that were sectioned yet again into two levels. Last year's Diplomat S line became the Diplomat, and the mid-level Diplomat became the Diplomat Salon. The top-level Medallion remained. The only noticeable change for the Magnum

XE, as it entered its final season, was a new taillight lens now split into two horizontal sections, rather than three.

The imported Colts added a new front-wheel-drive, two-door hatchback model to the lineup which Dodge often referred to as Colt FWD, since the rear-wheel drive Colt coupes and sedan were still available for the '79 model year as carry-over models (they would be gone for the 1980 model year). The small, four-seat hatchback's design was rather uninteresting, with a black horizontal crosshatch grille set between single rectangular headlamps, and nary a feature line to be found other than the faint bodyside line near the tops of the wheel openings, and a line on each side of the hood running in the same plane as the inner headlight edge. Horizontal wraparound taillamps, below the lip of the hatch, had tricolor lenses. Inside the Colt FWD offered a well-thought-out instrument panel design and some interesting interior fabric choices with checks and plaids. The engine was typical Mitsubishi design with the MCA-Jet system and a hemi-head overhead cam. The transmission was an interesting, "Twin-Stick" four-speed manual — actually a regular 4-speed transmission with a second stick that allowed the driver to choose power or economy modes to suit the driver's needs. The new Colt FWD hatchback was basic transportation at its technological best, for 1979, and was a virtual twin to the new Plymouth Champ. The oldest Colt model, the hardtop, was discontinued for 1979. The Challenger returned without any significant updates.

Aspen 4-Door Sedan
with Special Edition package

Aspen 4-Door Station Wagon
with Sport package (front) and Aspen
2-Door Coupe with R/T package (rear)

Challenger 2-Door Hardtop

Challenger instrument panel

Colt 4-Door Sedan

Colt Custom 2-Door Hatchback
with Sport package

Diplomat Medallion 2-Door Coupe

Magnum XE 2-Door Hardtop Coupe
with GT package

St. Regis 4-Door Pillared Hardtop

Omni 4-Door Hatchback with Custom package

St. Regis interior

Omni 024 2-Door Hatchback
with Sport Two-Tone package

Model year production: 351,177, down 10.24% from 1978.
Domestic market share: 3.82% (9th place).
Base price range: $4,399 to $6,532.
Dodge average base price: $5,408, up 11.37%.
Introduction date: October 5, 1978.
Assembly plants: Lynch Road, Detroit, MI (A); Belvidere, IL (D); Newark, DE (F); St. Louis, MO (G); and Windsor, Ontario, Canada (R). *Imports:* Colt — Kurashiki, Okayama, Japan (code 1 through 9); Challenger — Okazaki, Aichi, Japan (code 1 through 9).

Data plate identification (VIN): Thirteen digit code read as follows: First four digits indicate series and body style (model number in model charts); fifth digit indicates engine code (see powertrain chart); sixth digit indicates year (9 = 1979); seventh digit indicates assembly plant (see list above); remaining digits are sequential with beginning numbers of 100001. *Example:* NL41D9A100001 is a 1979 Dodge Aspen 4-Door Sedan, with 225 CID, 2-bbl. 6-cylinder engine, serial number 100001, built in Lynch Road plant, Detroit, MI.

Powertrains[1]

Engine	Net HP	Engine Code	Transmission Availability[2]		Colt FWD[3]	Colt WD & Challenger	Omni	Aspen	Diplomat	Magnum XE	St. Regis
86 CID (1.4L) OHC, 2-bbl., 4-cyl.	70	J	"Twin-stick" 4-speed manual		S (base)	—	—	—	—	—	—
				MPG:	37	—	—	—	—	—	—
				Calif.	32	—	—	—	—	—	—
97.5 CID (1.6L) OHC, 2-bbl., 4-cyl.	77	K	"Twin-stick" 4-speed manual		S (Custom)	S (Colt)	—	—	—	—	—
				MPG:	32/44	30/40	—	—	—	—	—
				Calif.	30	28	—	—	—	—	—
			5-speed manual		—	S (Challenger)	—	—	—	—	—
				MPG:	—	26/35	—	—	—	—	—
				Calif.	—	27	—	—	—	—	—
			3-speed Torque Flite automatic		—	$358 (Colt ex. wgn.)	—	—	—	—	—
				MPG:	—	26/37	—	—	—	—	—

Engine	Net HP	Engine Code	Transmission Availability[2]		Colt FWD[3]	Colt WD & Challenger	Omni	Aspen	Diplomat	Magnum XE	St. Regis
104.7 CID (1.7L) OHC, 2-bbl., 4-cyl.	70	A	4-speed manual		—	—	S	—	—	—	—
				MPG:	—	—	25/38	—	—	—	—
				Calif.	—	—	24	—	—	—	—
			3-speed Torque Flite automatic		—	—	$319	—	—	—	—
				MPG:	—	—	24/37	—	—	—	—
				Calif.	—	—	21	—	—	—	—
155.9 CID (2.6L) OHC, 2-bbl., 4-cyl.	77	F	5-speed manual		—	$377 (Challenger)/ $477 (Colt wgn.)	—	—	—	—	—
				MPG:	—	21	—	—	—	—	—
			3-speed Torque Flite automatic		—	$578 (Challenger)/ $776 (Colt wgn.)	—	—	—	—	—
				MPG:	—	21	—	—	—	—	—
225 CID (3.7L), 1-bbl., 6-cyl.	100	C	3-speed manual		—	—	—	S[4]	—	—	—
				MPG:	—	—	—	18/26	—	—	—
			4-speed manual w/overdrive		—	—	—	$149[4]	S[4]	—	—
				MPG:	—	—	—	18/28	18/28	—	—
			3-speed Torque Flite automatic		—	—	—	$319 (ex. wgns.)[5]	S[5]/ $193[6]	—	—
				MPG:	—	—	—	18	18	—	—
				Calif.	—	—	—	16	16	—	—
225 CID (3.7L) Super Six, 2-bbl., 6-cyl.[4]	110	D	3-speed Torque Flite automatic		—	—	—	$362	N/C	—	S
				MPG:	—	—	—	18	17	—	17/23
318 CID (5.2L), 2-bbl., V8[4]	135	G	3-speed Torque Flite automatic		—	—	—	$535	$429	S	$239
				MPG:	—	—	—	16/23	16/23	16/23	16
318 CID (5.2L), 4-bbl., V8	145	H	3-speed Torque Flite automatic	—	—	—	$590	$489	$61[5]	S[5]/$300[6]	
				Calif.	—	—	—	14	14	13	13
360 CID (5.9L), 2-bbl., V8[4]	150	K	3-speed Torque Flite automatic		—	—	—	—	$619	$191	$432
				MPG:	—	—	—	—	14	14	14
360 CID (5.9L), 4-bbl., V8[7]	195	L	3-speed Torque Flite automatic		—	—	—	$894	$690	$251	$493
				MPG:	—	—	—	13	13	12	12
				Calif.	—	—	—	13	14	13	13

[1]Optional axle ratios may be required on cars sold in California or high-altitude counties. [2]Unless otherwise noted: All transmissions are column-shift, except on Colt, Challenger, Omni, and any model w/4-speed manual. Floor-shift is available for $35 extra on any Aspen w/3-speed manual transmission. Aspens w/automatic, Diplomat coupes, and Magnum XE are all available w/floor-shift in combination with specified equipment or packages. [3]All Colt front-wheel-drive hatchback models shipped within the first 60 days of introduction have the 1.4L and 4-speed manual transmission as standard equipment, with a price adjustment credited to the price of the car. [4]Not available in California or designated high altitude areas. [5]Required as standard equipment in California and designated high altitude areas, with appropriate adjustment in price. [6]Except in California and high-altitude areas. [7]Available w/federal emissions only in combination w/heavy duty package, or GT package on Magnum XE.

Major Options

	Colt	Challenger	Omni	Aspen	Diplomat	Magnum XE	St. Regis
Air conditioning	$471	$494	$507	$507	$584	$584	$628
Tilt steering wheel	S	S	—	$71	$77	$77	$79
Automatic speed control	—	$107	—	$98	$107	$107	$112
Electric rear window defogger	S	S	—	$90	$98	$98	$105
Tinted glass, all windows	S	S	$61	$61	$73	$73	S
Power windows[1]	—	—	—	$169	$194	$137	$212

	Colt	Challenger	Omni	Aspen	Diplomat	Magnum XE	St. Regis
Power door locks[1]	—	—	—	$106	$124	$89	$126
Power front seat	—	—	—	$153	$167	$167	$170
AM radio	$78	—	S[2]	$79	$87	$87	$106
AM/FM stereo	$153	$164	$141[2]	$220	$240	$240	$253
AM/FM stereo w/8-track tape	—	—	—	$314	$343	$343	$360
Front bucket seats[3]	S	S	S	$107	$164	S	—
Vinyl top, full[4]	$102	$107	$93	$95	$165	—	$152
Landau vinyl top, 2-doors	—	—	—	$174	$148	$132	—
Sunroof, power glass[5]	—	—	$176	—	$827	—	$993
Sunroof, power metal[5]	—	—	—	—	—	$546	—
T-Bar roof, w/glass panels[6]	—	—	—	$600	$675	$675	—
Dual remote mirrors, chrome	—	—	$49	$49	$54	$54	$44
Dual remote mirrors, sport	—	S	$61	$61	$67	$67	—
Power steering, std. w/V8	$163	—	$156	$156	S	S	S
Power brakes, w/front disc[7]	S	S	$72	$72	S	S	S
Premium wheel covers	—	—	—	$79	$90	$45	$54
Wire wheel covers	—	—	—	$136	$300	—	$259
Styled road wheels, w/trim	—	—	$73	$136	—	$213	$216
Forged/cast aluminum wheels	—	S	$246	$280	$305	$260	—
White sidewall tires, std. size	S	—	$34	$45	$50	$50	$51

Popular Option Groups & Packages

	Colt	Challenger	Omni	Aspen	Diplomat	Magnum XE	St. Regis
Basic group	—	$650	—	$712	$1,238	$1,018	$1,176
Custom exterior package	—	—	$74	$75	—	—	—
Custom interior package	—	—	$101	$162	—	—	—
Deluxe insulation package	—	S	—	—	$93	—	—
Estate package	$314	—	—	—	—	—	—
Gran Touring "GT" package	—	—	—	—	—	$601	—
Light package	—	—	$46	$46	$84	$29	$96
024 sport package	—	—	$340	—	—	—	—
Popular equipment group	—	—	$279	—	—	—	—
Premium exterior package	—	—	$178	—	—	—	—
Premium interior package	—	—	$270	—	—	—	—
Premium package	—	$486	—	—	—	—	—
Premium woodgrain package	—	—	—	$331	—	—	—
Rallye package	—	—	$340	—	—	—	—
Red & White Special pkg.	$195	—	—	—	—	—	—
R/T handling performance package	—	—	—	$216	—	—	—
R/T package	—	—	—	$651	—	—	—
Special Edition exterior pkg.[8]	—	—	—	$134	—	—	—
Special Edition interior pkg.	—	—	—	$402	—	—	—
Sport appearance package	$[9]	—	—	—	$219	—	—
Sport Wagon package	—	—	—	$630	—	—	—
Sunrise package[10]	—	—	—	$60	—	—	—

— = Not Available; S = Standard equipment.   Note that many of the Omni option group and package prices are lower on the 024 models, which have more standard equipment than the Omni 4-door models.   [1]Prices given for 4-door models. On 2-door models price for power windows on Aspen is $120, and Diplomat is $137. Price for power door locks on Aspen is $76, and Diplomat is $89.   [2]For Omni 024 AM/FM radio is standard. AM/FM stereo is $67 extra.   [3]Available on Aspen and Diplomat coupes, and standard in certain option packages. Omni has standard bucket seats with optional shift console for $32 and front storage console for $22. Console for Aspen, $51; Magnum XE, $103. All Colts have standard bucket seats and Colt 4-door has standard console.   [4]Not available on station wagons. Canopy style on Challenger.   [5]Removable sunroof on Omni.   [6]For 2-door models only.   [7]Standard on Aspen wagons. Colt has manual front disc brakes standard.   [8]Special Edition woodgrain group for station wagon is $232.   [9]Sport package available for Colt Custom hatchback only.   [10]Sunrise décor package is also available for $90.

Paint Colors

Dodge Domestic Models	Code	Dodge Domestic Models	Code	Dodge Domestic Models	Code
Eggshell White[1]	EW1	Sable Tan Sunfire metallic[3,4,5,6]	RT9	Nightwatch Blue[2,5,6]	SC9
Cadet Blue metallic[2,3,4]	PB3	Oxford Grey[6,7]	SA6	Teal Frost metallic[1,4]	SG4
Dove Grey[4,5,6]	RA1	Ensign Blue metallic[2,3,4]	SB7	Teal Green Sunfire metallic[1]	SG8
Pewter Grey metallic[2,3,5]	RA2	Frost Blue metallic[5,6]	SC2	Turquoise metallic[2]	SQ6

Dodge Domestic Models	Code
Chianti Red[2,3,4,5]	SR5
Regent Red Sunfire metallic[3,4,5,6]	SR8
Garnet Red Sunfire metallic[6,7]	SR9
Light Cashmere[1]	ST1
Medium Cashmere metallic[2,3,4,6]	ST5
Flame Orange[2]	SV3
Light Yellow[3]	SY2
Bright Yellow[2]	SY4
Black[1]	TX9

Colt and Challenger	Code
Spitfire Orange[8]	073
Bright Blue metallic[8]	B22

Colt and Challenger	Code
Caramel Tan and Ballast Sand metallic[9]	C59
Green metallic[8]	G80
Bright Silver metallic and Charcoal[9]	H03
Bright Silver metallic[8]	H29
Caramel Tan metallic[8]	K19
Light Tan[8]	S37
Warm White[8]	W61
Black and Light Tan[9]	X86
Yellow[8]	Y90
Canyon Red metallic[8]	NA
Bright Blue metallic and White[9]	NA

Colt and Challenger	Code
Spitfire Orange and Bright Silver metallic[9]	NA

Single tones are coded W1, W1. Two-tones are coded on body ID plate as TX9, EW1 where three digits on line 2 are lower body color and three digits on line 3 are upper body color or two-tone color. Two-tone paint packages available: Omni 024 Sport, $164; Omni 4-door Classic, $114; Aspen, $142; Magnum XE, $221; St. Regis, $160. [1]Available on all models. [2]Available on Omni. Bright Yellow is only available on 024 models. [3]Available on Aspen. Light Yellow is only available on coupes. [4]Available on Diplomat. Dove Gray, Cadet Blue, Ensign Blue and Teal Frost are not available on station wagon. [5]Available on Magnum XE. [6]Available on St. Regis. [7]Available only in two-tone combinations. [8]Not available on Challenger. [9]Challenger two-tone combination.

Colt

"The all-purpose imports from Dodge."

Nameplate year of origin: 1971.
Current bodystyle lifespan: 1979 through 1983 (hatchback); 1978 through 1981 (wagon); 1977 through 1979 (coupe and sedan).
Predecessor to this model: None.
Replacement for this model: Colt (1984 to 1988).
Primary competition: AMC Spirit, Buick Opel, Chevrolet Chevette, Chevrolet Monza, Ford Fiesta, and Ford Pinto.
Notable changes: All-new front-wheel-drive hatchback, and minor trim and detail changes for other models.
Major standard equipment: Vinyl front bucket seats w/reclining seat backs, full-floor carpeting, fold-down rear seat (HBK), two-spoke steering wheel, tilt steering column (except HBK), trip odometer, tinted glass, flipper rear quarter windows (HBK and coupes), rear window defroster, deluxe sound insulation (except HBK), bright drip rail, sill, windshield, and rear window moldings (except HBK), door and quarter window reveal moldings (HBK), front and rear rubber bumper guards, locking fuel filler door, power front disc brakes, wheel covers (except HBK), 6.15 × 13 WSW tires (HBK), and 6.00 × 13 WSW tires (Coupe). Custom hatchback adds: Cloth-and-vinyl bucket seats w/reclining seat backs, floor console, rear shelf security panel, sports steering wheel, remote hatchback release, custom tape stripes, and 155SR × 13 WSW tires. Coupe and sedan add: Floor console (sedan only), simulated woodgrain I/P appliqué, sports steering wheel (sedan only), bright beltline, drip rail and wheel opening moldings (sedan only), bright windshield and backlight molding, bright sill molding, styled steel road wheels (sedan only), and 165SR × 13 WSW tires (sedan only). Wagon adds: Fold-down rear seat, clock, sports steering wheel, belt line and drip rail moldings, and 165SR × 14 WSW tires.

Measurements

	FWD HBK	Coupe & Sedan	Wagon
Wheelbase	90.6"	92.1"	99.0"
Length	156.9"	162.6"	179.3"
Width	62.4"	60.4"	65.2"
Height	50.6"	52.8"	52.4"
Legroom — front	40.6"	40.0"	40.6"
Legroom — rear	29.7"	30.5"	33.5"
Headroom — front	36.8"	36.8"	36.6"
Headroom — rear	36.0"	36.8"	36.2"
Cargo capacity (cu. ft.)	6.5*	6.5	59.0
Fuel capacity (gals.)	10.5	13.2	13.2

With rear seat down, 27.4 cu. ft.

Models Available

	Model No.	Base MSRP	Change from LY	Shipping Wt. (lbs.)	Model Year Sales	Change from LY
Colt 2-Door Hatchback	4M24	$4,425	NEW	1730	NA	NEW
Colt Custom 2-Door Hatchback	4H24	$4,743	NEW	1775	NA	NEW
Colt 2-Door Coupe	6M21	$3,984	+5.84%	1945	NA	NA
Colt 4-Door Sedan	6H41	$4,490	+7.98%	2020	NA	NA
Colt 4-Door Station Wagon	6H45	$5,591	+6.88%	2445	NA	NA
TOTALS		*Avg. price* $4,647	+6.76%		*Production* 60,646*	+26.53%*

Total and comparison to LY based on estimated model year sales.

Challenger

"A stirring means of going the distance."

Nameplate year of origin: 1970.
Current bodystyle lifespan: 1978 through 1983.
Predecessor to this model: None.
Replacement for this model: Dodge Conquest (1984 to 1986).
Primary competition: Buick Skyhawk, Ford Mustang, Mercury Capri, and Oldsmobile Starfire.
Notable changes: Minor trim and detail changes.
Major standard equipment: Plaid cloth and vinyl front bucket seats w/reclining seat backs, color-keyed carpeting, two-spoke sports steering wheel, tilt steering column, sports car instrumentation, trip odometer, tinted glass, rear window defroster, remote deck lid release, overhead console w/reading light, digital clock and 3-way dome light, deluxe sound insulation package, dual power remote control mirrors, bright drip rail, windshield, and rear window moldings, body-colored quarter window louvers, front and rear rubber bumper guards, dual horns, locking fuel filler door, power front disc brakes, cast aluminum road wheels, and 195/70HR × 14 BSW tires.

Measurements

Wheelbase	99.0"
Length	183.1"
Width	65.9"
Height	51.8"
Legroom — front	40.6"
Legroom — rear	32.5"
Headroom — front	36.4"
Headroom — rear	35.0"
Cargo capacity (cu. ft.)	10.8
Fuel capacity (gals.)	15.9

Models Available

	Model No.	Base MSRP	Change from LY	Shipping Wt. (lbs.)	Model Year Sales	Change from LY
Challenger 2-Door Hardtop	2H29	$6,487	+7.21%	2410	16,920	+19.19%
TOTALS	*Avg. price*	$6,487	+7.21%	*Production*	16,920	+19.19%

Omni

"Omni does it all."

Nameplate year of origin: 1978.
Current bodystyle lifespan: 1978 through 1990.
Predecessor to this model: None.
Replacement for this model: None.
Percentage of division's sales volume: 33.70%.
Corporate siblings: Plymouth Horizon.
Primary competition: Chevrolet Chevette and Ford Fiesta.
Notable changes: All-new 2-door 024 model. Minor trim and detail changes for the 4-door.
Major standard equipment: Vinyl front bucket seats, color-keyed molded headlining, color-keyed carpeting, door armrests, three-spoke steering wheel, door armrests, fold-down rear seat, folding rear shelf security panel, electric rear window defroster, AM radio, day/night inside rear view mirror, bright liftgate window accents, bright aluminum front and rear bumper face bars w/rub strips, manual front disc brakes, and P155/80R × 13 WSW tires. 024 adds: Cloth upholstered headliner, simulated woodgrain I/P inserts, four-spoke sport steering wheel, AM/FM radio, remote hatchback release, bright sill and wheel lip moldings, wheel trim rings, and P165/75R × 13 WSW tires; deletes electric rear window defroster.

Measurements

	2+2 HBK	4-door HBK
Wheelbase	96.7"	99.2"
Length	173.3"	163.2"
Width	66.0"	66.2"
Height	51.4"	53.4"
Legroom — front	42.5"	41.8"
Legroom — rear	28.5"	33.0"
Headroom — front	37.5"	38.3"
Headroom — rear	34.7"	37.4"
Cargo capacity (cu. ft.)	10.7*	10.5*
Fuel capacity (gals.)	13.0	13.0

With rear seat folded down, 2+2 HBK is 33.8; 4-door HBK is 36.1.

Models Available

	Model No.	Base MSRP	Change from LY	Shipping Wt. (lbs.)	Model Year Production	Change from LY
Omni 024 2+2 2-Door Hatchback	ZL24	$4,864	NEW	2195	46,781	NEW
Omni 4-Door Hatchback	ZL44	$4,469	+12.40%	2135	71,556	+0.82%
TOTALS		*Avg. price* $4,667	+17.37%		*Production* 118,337	+66.74%

Aspen

"The practical, affordable answer."

Nameplate year of origin: 1976.
Current bodystyle lifespan: 1976½ through 1980.
Predecessor to this model: Dart (1967 to 1976).
Replacement for this model: Aries (1981 to 1989).
Percentage of division's production: 34.56%.
Corporate siblings: Plymouth Volaré.
Primary competition: AMC Concord, Buick Skylark, Chevrolet Nova, Ford Fairmont, Mercury Zephyr, Oldsmobile Omega, and Pontiac Phoenix.
Notable changes: Minor trim and detail changes.
Major standard equipment: All-vinyl front bench seat (sedan and wagon), cloth and vinyl front bench seat (coupe), front door armrests, color-keyed carpeting, two-spoke steering wheel, two-speed electric windshield wipers and washers, front ashtray, color-keyed bumper filler, roof drip rail molding, quarter window moldings (coupe and wagon), windshield and backlight moldings, hubcaps, and D78 × 14 BSW tires.
Wagon adds: Rear liftgate, fold-down second seat, front disc brakes, and ER78 × 14 BSW tires.

Measurements

	Coupe	Sedan	Wagon
Wheelbase	108.7"	112.7"	112.7"
Length	197.2"	201.2"	201.2"
Width	72.8"	72.8"	72.8"
Height	53.3"	55.3"	55.7"
Legroom — front	42.7"	42.7"	42.7"
Legroom — rear	32.6"	37.8"	36.6"
Headroom — front	37.6"	39.3"	39.2"
Headroom — rear	36.2"	37.7"	38.7"
Cargo capacity (cu. ft.)	16.2	16.2	73.1
Fuel capacity (gals.)*	18.0	18.0	19.5

Fuel capacity on all V8 equipped models is 19.5 gallons.

Models Available

	Model No.	Base MSRP	Change from LY	Shipping Wt. (lbs.)	Model Year Production	Change from LY*
Aspen 2-Door Sport Coupe	NL29	$4,399	+16.28%	3050	88,268*	NA*
Aspen 4-Door Sedan	NL41	$4,516	+15.47%	3115	NA*	NA*
Aspen 4-Door Station Wagon	NL45	$4,838	+13.75%	3325	33,086	-38.49%
TOTALS		*Avg. price* $4,584	+15.12%		*Production* 121,354	-27.08%

Comparison to LY is not possible due to production of coupes and sedans being kept combined for 1979.

Diplomat

"Sensibly yours."

Nameplate year of origin: 1977 (previously used as designation on Dodge Coronet 2-door hardtops, 1950–1953, and as an option package on Royal Monaco Brougham 2-door hardtops, 1976–1977).
Current bodystyle lifespan: 1977½ through 1979.
Predecessor to this model: Coronet (1971 to 1976); Monaco (1977–1978).
Replacement for this model: Diplomat (1980 to 1989).
Percentage of division's production: 14.72%.

Measurements

	Coupe	Sedan	Wagon
Wheelbase	112.7"	112.7"	112.7"
Length	204.1"	206.1"	202.8"
Width	73.5"	73.3"	73.3"
Height	53.3"	55.3"	55.7"
Legroom — front	42.5"	42.5"	42.5"
Legroom — rear	34.0"	36.6"	36.6"

Corporate siblings: Chrysler LeBaron.
Primary competition: Buick Regal, Mercury Cougar, and Oldsmobile Cutlass Supreme.
Notable changes: Minor trim and detail changes.
Major standard equipment: Cloth and vinyl front bench seat, door pull straps, color-keyed carpeting, one-piece cloth headliner, windshield header mounted reading lamps and sculptured cavities to store sunvisors (coupe only), simulated

Measurements (cont.)

	Coupe	Sedan	Wagon
Headroom — front	37.5"	39.2"	39.2"
Headroom — rear	36.2"	37.5"	38.7"
Cargo capacity (cu. ft.)	14.2	14.4	72.7
Fuel capacity (gals.)	19.5	19.5	19.5

woodgrain I/P cluster and glove box door appliqué, stand-up hood ornament, power steering, power brakes, wheel covers, and FR78 × 15 BSW tires. Salon adds: Wide body rocker panel sill moldings w/front and rear extensions, bright roof drip rail and quarter window moldings (coupes), bright upper door frame moldings (sedan), full vinyl padded top (sedan), bright belt molding, rear bumper guards, lower deck panel stripe (sedan), and deluxe wheel covers. Medallion adds: Cloth 60/40 front split-bench seat w/ fold-down center armrests and dual recliners, fold-down rear seat armrest, bright pedal trim, map reading lamp, courtesy lights, upper assist handles (sedan), B-pillar assist straps (coupe), rear pillar vanity lamps and mirrors (sedan), trunk dress up package, LH remote control outside rearview mirror, dual chrome quarter window stripes (coupe), bodyside accent tape stripes coordinated w/body color on coupes and vinyl top color on sedans, deluxe sound insulation package (w/o undercoating and hood pad), and premium wheel covers.

Models Available

	Model No.	Base MSRP	Change from LY*	Shipping Wt. (lbs.)	Model Year Production	Change from LY**
Diplomat 2-Door Coupe	GM22	$5,234	+9.70%	3270	13,929**	NA**
Diplomat 4-Door Sedan	GM41	$5,336	+8.08%	3330	NA**	NA**
Diplomat Salon 2-Door Coupe	GH22	$5,482	+9.18%	3285	17,577**	NA**
Diplomat Salon 4-Door Sedan	GH41	$5,714	+10.16%	3350	NA**	NA**
Diplomat 4-Door Station Wagon	GH45	$6,127	+10.64%	3545	7,785	-28.62%
Diplomat Medallion 2-Door Coupe	GP22	$5,966	+10.42%	3345	12,394**	NA**
Diplomat Medallion 4-Door Sedan	GP41	$6,198	+11.29%	3425	NA**	NA**
TOTALS	*Avg. price*	$5,722	+9.97%	*Production*	51,685	-15.69%

*Comparisons made to equivalent model numbers for 1978. ***Comparison to LY is not possible due to production of coupes and sedans being kept combined for 1979.*

Magnum XE

"The total driving experience."

Nameplate year of origin: 1978.
Current bodystyle lifespan: 1978 through 1979 (1975 to 1978 as Charger SE).
Predecessor to this model: Charger (1971 to 1974).
Replacement for this model: Mirada (1980 to 1983).
Percentage of division's sales volume: 7.22%.
Corporate siblings: Chrysler Cordoba.
Primary competition: Chevrolet Monte Carlo, Ford Thunderbird, Mercury Cougar XR-7, and Pontiac Grand Prix.
Notable changes: Minor trim and detail changes.
Major standard equipment: All vinyl low-back front bucket seats, color-keyed shag carpeting, simulated woodgrain trim on I/P, deluxe door trim panels, deluxe two-spoke steering wheel, inside day/night rearview mirror, two-speed windshield wipers w/washers, bright trim moldings (windshield, backlight, hood rear edge, deck lid, belt, drip rail, bodyside and wheel opening), trunk mat, power front disc brakes, power steering, deluxe wheel covers w/XE emblem, and FR78 × 15 BSW tires.

Measurements

Wheelbase	114.9"
Length	215.8"
Width	77.1"
Height	53.1"
Legroom — front	42.4"
Legroom — rear	32.4"
Headroom — front	37.7"
Headroom — rear	36.6"
Cargo capacity (cu. ft.)	16.3
Fuel capacity (gals.)	21.0

Models Available

	Model No.	Base MSRP	Change from LY	Shipping Wt. (lbs.)	Model Year Production	Change from LY
Magnum XE 2-Door Hardtop Coupe	XS22	$6,039	+9.62%	3675	25,367	-46.96%
TOTALS	Avg. price	$6,039	+9.62%	Production	25,367	-46.96%

St. Regis

"The new Dodge St. Regis. Luxury you can measure."

Nameplate year of origin: 1979 (also used on 1955 Chrysler New Yorker DeLuxe 2-door hardtop).
Current bodystyle lifespan: 1979 through 1981.
Predecessor to this model: Monaco (1974 to 1976) and Royal Monaco (1977).
Replacement for this model: None.
Percentage of division's sales volume: 9.81%.
Corporate siblings: Chrysler Newport and New Yorker.
Primary competition: Chevrolet Impala/Caprice, Ford LTD, and Pontiac Catalina/Bonneville.
Notable changes: All-new model.
Major standard equipment: Saxony and Whittier cloth 60/40 split front seat w/fold-down center armrest and passenger side recliner, color-keyed long-pile carpeting, molded color-keyed headliner, two-spoke steering wheel w/woodtone trim, gauges (oil, fuel, temperature and alternator), tinted glass, LH and RH manual outside mirrors, two-speed windshield wipers w/washers, drip rail, belt line and wheel lip moldings, front and rear bumper rub strips, dual horns, power front disc brakes, power steering, deluxe wheel covers, and P195 × 75R15 BSW tires.

Measurements

Wheelbase	118.5"
Length	220.2"
Width	77.1"
Height	54.5"
Legroom — front	42.3"
Legroom — rear	38.2"
Headroom — front	38.6"
Headroom — rear	37.4"
Cargo capacity (cu. ft.)	21.3
Fuel capacity (gals.)	21.0

1979

Models Available

	Model No.	Base MSRP	Change from LY	Shipping Wt. (lbs.)	Model Year Production	Change from LY
St. Regis 4-Door Pillared Hardtop	EH42	$6,532	NEW	3565	34,434	NEW
TOTALS	Avg. price	$6,532	NEW	Production	34,434	NEW

FORD

"When America needs a better idea, Ford puts it on wheels."

Ford's 1979 model year brought the introduction of all-new versions of two of its most popular lines of the last twenty years, the sporty Mustang and the full-size LTD. It also brought a new face for its oldest model, while the traditional mid-size Ford was entering its final season. It would be an interesting year for Ford as it struggled to meet the EPA's CAFE requirements, and rumors began to spread of a replacement for the Pinto, code-named "Erika," a highly anticipated front-wheel-drive "world car." However, it would be two more years before the new Escort arrived. Little did anyone know the brewing recession would make 1979 the best of the next six seasons.

The all-new downsized LTD was, in the corporate mindset, Ford's most important new car. Since the beginning of the decade, Ford's full-size cars had sold at about 80 to 85 percent of the volume of Chevrolet full-size cars. Both lines had slid since the fuel crisis of 1974 as smaller, more fuel-efficient cars became more popular, but by 1978, Ford's LTD line was selling at half the rate of the smaller Chevrolet Impala and Caprice lines. In fact in 1978 the Thunderbird even outsold the larger LTD. It was hoped the new LTD would bring buyers of full-size cars back to the showrooms, but as fate would have it, Chrysler also debuted newly down-sized full-size cars, and a second fuel crisis along with a recession began, and the new LTD managed only a slight increase to sell at about 60 percent of the rate of new Impalas and Caprices. Still Ford proved that they got the design right, as the car lasted in its basic form through the 1991 model year.

The new LTD had all the design features of most other downsized cars of the day, with boxy lines, tall upright greenhouse areas, minimal bodyside sculpting, lighter weight and smaller engines for more fuel efficiency, while maintaining both the interior passenger space and cargo space of their much larger predecessors. The LTD continued the tradition of two differing front-end designs that began in 1975, this time with the base LTD using a single square headlamp design while the upper LTD Landau series and related Country Squire wagon got a more elegant dual rectangular headlamp configuration with a heavily chromed egg-crate grille with a center division bar. Another difference was that the LTD had parking lights inset in each side of the grille with turn signals mounted in vertical fender end caps. Both grilles were repeated in dual bumper openings. The LTD Landau used horizontal parking/turn signal lights below the headlights and wrapping around the front fender edge. At the rear, large vertical rectangular taillights were a throwback to the late 1960s full-size Fords. Beneath the taillights were thin horizontal backup lights, and on Landau models a chrome strip ran across the lip of the decklid between the backup lights. Wagon models used yet another variation of their traditional vertical taillamps set in the rear fender end panel, albeit larger than any previous lights. Two feature lines visually stretched the bodysides: an upper one running straight back from the top of the front turn signal, a few inches above the flat-topped wheel openings, and a lower one at the height of the bumper rub strips, defining the top edge of an indented lower body section.

The 4-door greenhouse resembled that of the new Chrysler Newport and Dodge St. Regis, with a fairly formal roofline and a fixed quarter window in the rear door. Two-doors had a forward-leaning B-pillar and fairly narrow rear passenger window.

Inside the new LTD was all about comfort and luxury, with all but the base LTD offering fold-down center armrests and with woodgrain instrument panel and door panel trim on most models. The horizontally themed instrument cluster was much like that used by Cadillacs of the period, and also the aforementioned late 1960s Fords. Ventilation and audio controls were in a center stack below the upper horizontal area. Powering the new full-size models was the highly regarded 302 CID V8 engine, with the long-running 351 CID V8 engine being optional. The large 400 CID and 460 CID V8 engines were no longer available in Ford passenger cars, in the interest of meeting EPA standards.

While the LTD may not have met corporate expectations, the newly redesigned Mustang met and exceeded consumer expectations, becoming Ford's second highest selling line for 1979, right behind the highly popular Fairmont. The new Mustang was built on the "Fox" platform shared with the Fairmont, and it shared most of its engine and transmission choices, with the exceptions of a new 5-speed manual that was available only on the Mustang with the 4-cylinder engine, and a 2.8 liter V6 engine option in place of the Fairmont's inline six. (However, halfway through the model year, a shortage of 2.8L V6 engines supplied by Ford's German subsidiary forced Ford to install the 200 C.I.D., 3.3L inline 6-cylinder engine in many 1979 Mustangs.) The 5.0 liter (302 C.I.D.) V8 was also available, along with a variety of options to suit any owner's taste from sport to luxury. It all added up to the exact same formula that had made the original Mustang a success.

The design of the Mustang was intended to bring a sporty look and feel back, yet it carried none of the traditional Mustang styling cues, such as the oblong grille with running pony in the center or the bodyside cove indentation behind the doors. Rather, the Mustang relied on a swept-back grille and fender line at the front to provide a sporty look. The sloping black grille in a body-color fascia consisted of a five row by ten column egg-crate pattern, with dual rectangular headlamps set at each end. Parking and turn signal lights were set below the outer headlight in the front bumper rub strip area, while side marker lamps slanted with the front fender line and were set on the side of the fender end cap. Bodysides followed the latest trends with only two straight-line feature lines. The upper line began at the top of the front bumper following the leading edge of the side marker light up, then bending to run straight to the top edge of the wrap-around taillamps, passing just above the door handle. The lower line followed the top edge of the bodyside molding and bumper rub strips encircling the car, and creating a slight flare as it passed over the wheel openings. Sharing a platform with the Fairmont meant similar cowl, windshield and door configurations giving the Mustang a rather upright roofline in two-door sedan configuration, but the overall look was still very sporty.

As in years past, the Mustang was available in more than one bodystyle. A "3-door" (hatchback) version offered a more rakish roofline, bending at the base of the rear glass to slope gently over the last foot or so and meet a rear panel nearly identical to that of the 2-door. Both had horizontal wrap-around taillamps in six vertical sections, the innermost being the backup light. Both bodystyles utilized faux louvers (three for the 2-door, four for the 3-door) behind the rear passenger window, which itself was effectively triangular on the 3-door but less so on the 2-door.

Inside the Mustang updated the well-designed Mustang II layout with a hooded driver's side area and a recessed passenger side area housing the glove box and air vents. The driver's pod used round dial gauges: two large ones for the speedometer and tach and two smaller ones flanking the larger ones on each side housing the fuel, temperature, oil pressure and alternator gauges. Air vents and assorted warning lights were placed to the far left, while another air vent and the ventilation controls were to the far right. The optional radio was mounted between the upper pod area and the optional floor shifter console. Various steering wheels were used including a sport three-spoke slot style and a luxury four-spoke style that was required with options such as fingertip cruise control which had the buttons mounted on the upper two spokes of the steering wheel.

Many different option packages were offered for Mustang, including the high-performance "COBRA" package that featured the new 2.3 litre turbocharged engine as standard equipment. Turbocharging of engines was a relatively new outgrowth of the desire to improve performance and the need to increase fuel economy. While GM opted to use the technology to boost the performance of its six-cylinder engines, Ford was the first to do it with a four-cylinder engine. Mustangs equipped with the turbo engine also were the first U.S. built cars to use metric wheels and Michelin TRX metric sized tires.

One of the more widely recognized option packages was the Indianapolis 500 pace car replica package offered after the announcement that the new Mustang would be the official pace car of the race. Available on the 3-door hatchback model only, or as Ford officially called it, the 3-door sedan, the replica option was nearly $4,000 and 10,478 replicas were built, making them the highest production pace car replica ever sold to date. Exterior features included specific paint and tape stripe treatment, a special front fascia and hood scoop, and Cobra-style black lower bodyside treatment and black greenhouse moldings. Inside were Recaro seats, a Cobra-style instrument panel, and AM/FM stereo. While the real pace car used a T-Bar roof, the replicas used a flip-up sunroof. The "T-Bar convertible" roof option would not be available on the new Mustang until 1981, as the new car's structure required more modification to meet federal safety standards. While the real pace car used a modified 302 CID V8 engine, the replicas were available with the turbocharged four-cylinder standard or the 302 CID V8. A full list of features is found in Appendix IV.

After eight years on the market, Pinto received a third facelift, with new square headlights set next to vertical parking/turn signal lamps in a sloping front end, and capping a new three bar horizontal grille containing egg-crate style inserts. Around back, larger taillamp lenses without surrounding chrome trim were introduced. They were in the same general configuration as the prior year's with the backup light to the inside of the lens. Pinto Pony added a new station wagon, and shared the use of blackout trim on the grille and headlight surrounds with the Pinto Pony runabout. A new ESS option mimicked the Granada's more substantive package of the same name, with extensive blackout trim.

Other lines had only minor changes, most notably with the Thunderbird adding a new large opening grille. The grille consisted of a heavily chromed four by four opening, with argent colored inserts set to the back. A new taillight design placed the backup lights in the center, and left the outer taillights as slightly larger, filling the upper space previously taken by the backup lights. Otherwise, the Thunderbird, Fiesta, Fairmont and Granada were mostly unchanged from 1978. The LTD II base S models were dropped for public consumption and only sold as fleet models, with 834 2-doors and 9,649 4-doors built. But as sales continued to decline and with the new LTD being so similar in size, the LTD II was quietly discontinued in January 1979, likely to prevent it from stealing sales from the new LTD.

Fairmont 2-Door Sedan
with Exterior Accent group

Fairmont 4-Door Sedan

Fairmont 4-Door Station Wagon
with Squire Wagon option

1979

Fairmont Futura 2-Door Coupe

Granada 2-Door Sedan

LTD II 2-Door Hardtop Coupe
with Sports Touring package

Mustang 2-Door Sedan with Sport option

Mustang Ghia interior

Fairmont Futura interior

Granada Ghia 4-Door Sedan

LTD II Brougham 4-Door Pillared Hardtop
with opera window option

Mustang 3-Door Sedan with Cobra package
and hood graphics, and turbocharged engine

Pinto 2-Door Sedan with Exterior Décor group

Fiesta 3-Door Hatchback
with Sport Group option

LTD 4-Door Station Wagon

LTD Landau 4-Door Sedan

Mustang Ghia 3-Door Sedan

Pinto 2-Door Station Wagon with Cruising
Wagon and Rallye packages

Pinto 3-Door Runabout with Rallye package

Thunderbird 2-Door Hardtop Coupe
with T-Bar roof

Thunderbird Heritage Edition
2-Door Hardtop Coupe

Model year production: 1,825,454, down 5.10% from 1978.
Domestic market share: 19.87% (2nd place).
Base price range: $3,434 to $11,060.
Ford average base price: $5,532, up 10.60%.
Introduction date: October 6, 1978.
Assembly plants: Atlanta, GA (A); Oakville, Ontario, Canada (B); Mahwah, NJ (E); Dearborn, MI (F); Chicago, IL (G); Lorain, OH (H); Kansas City, MO (K); San Jose, CA (R); Metuchen, NJ (T); Louisville, KY (U); Wayne, MI (W); and St. Thomas, Ontario, Canada (X). *Fiesta:* Cologne, Saarlouie, Germany (C).
Data plate identification (VIN): Eleven digit code read as follows: first digit indicates year (9 = 1979); second digit indicates assembly plant code (see list above); third and fourth digits indicate model number (model number in model charts); fifth digit indicates engine code (see powertrain chart); remaining digits are sequential with beginning numbers of 100001. *Example:* 9F02Z100001 is a 1979 Ford Mustang 2-Door Sedan, with 170.8 CID, 2-bbl. V6 engine, serial number 100001, built in Dearborn, MI. 1979 Fiesta uses an eleven digit code read as follows: First digit indicates country of origin (G = Germany); second digit indicates assembly plant code (see list above); third and fourth digits indicate model number (model number in model charts); fifth digit indicates production year code (W = 1979); sixth digit indicates production month code; remaining digits are sequential with beginning numbers of 00001.

1979

Powertrains

Engine	Net HP	Engine Code	Transmission Availability[1]		Fiesta	Pinto	Mustang	Fairmont	Granada	LTD II & Thunderbird	LTD
97.6 CID (1.6L) OHC, 2-bbl., 4-cyl.	66	W	4-speed manual w/overdrive		S	—	—	—	—	—	—
				MPG:	28/39	—	—	—	—	—	—
				Calif.	26/40	—	—	—	—	—	—
140 CID (2.3L) OHC, 2-bbl., 4-cyl.	88	Y	4-speed manual		—	S	S	S	—	—	—
				MPG:	—	22/32	21/31	20/31	—	—	—
				Calif.	—	22/32	17/27	17/27	—	—	—
			3-speed Select-Shift Cruise-O-Matic		—	$307[2]	$307	$401 (Cars)[3]	—	—	—
				MPG:	—	21	21	20	—	—	—
				Calif.	—	20	—	18	—	—	—
140 CID (2.3L) OHC, 2-bbl., Turbo 4-cyl.	150	A	4-speed manual		—	—	$542	—	—	—	—
				MPG:	—	—	18	—	—	—	—
				Calif.	—	—	17	—	—	—	—
170.8 CID (2.8L), 2-bbl., V6	109	Z	4-speed manual		—	—	$273[3]	—	—	—	—
				MPG:	—	—	20	—	—	—	—
			3-speed Select-Shift Cruise-O-Matic[4]		—	$580[2]	$580	—	—	—	—
				MPG:	—	18	18	—	—	—	—
				Calif.	—	NA	16	—	—	—	—
200 CID (3.3L), 1-bbl., 6-cyl.	96	T,B	4-speed manual w/overdrive		—	—	—	$241[3]	—	—	—
				MPG:	—	—	—	19	—	—	—
			3-speed Select-Shift Cruise-O-Matic		—	—	—	$548 (Wgn.)[3]/ $642 (Cars)[4]	—	—	—
				MPG:	—	—	—	18	—	—	—
				Calif.	—	—	—	16	—	—	—

Engine	Net HP	Engine Code	Transmission Availability[1]		Fiesta	Pinto	Mustang	Fairmont	Granada	LTD II & Thunderbird	LTD
250 CID (4.1L), 1-bbl., 6-cyl.	98	L	4-speed manual w/overdrive		—	—	—	—	S[3]	—	—
				MPG:	—	—	—	—	18/25	—	—
			3-speed Select-Shift		—	—	—	—	$307[4]	—	—
			Cruise-O-Matic	MPG:	—	—	—	—	17/24	—	—
				Calif.	—	—	—	—	16/21	—	—
302 CID (5.0L), 2-bbl., V8	140	F	4-speed manual[5,6]		—	—	$514[3]	—	$283[3]	—	—
				MPG:	—	—	15	—	15	—	—
			3-speed Select-Shift Cruise-O-Matic[4]		—	—	$821	$831 (Wgn.)/ $925 (Cars)	$590	S[3]	S[7]
				MPG:	—	—	16	16	16/22	14/20	15
				Calif.	—	—	15	15	14	—	14
351 CID (5.8L), 2-bbl., V8	149	H	3-speed Select-Shift Cruise-O-Matic		—	—	—	—	—	$263[4]	$263[8]
				MPG:	—	—	—	—	—	—	—
				Calif.	—	—	—	—	—	11/17	14

[1]Unless otherwise noted: All manual transmissions are floor-shifts. All automatics are column-shift, except on Pinto and Mustang. Floor-shift is available for $31 extra on Fairmont w/automatic (ex. w/2.3L engine), and Granada with optional bucket seats and automatic. Floor-shift w/bucket seats and console is also available for $211 on LTD II 2-Door and Thunderbird, and for $37 on LTD II Brougham 2-Door and Thunderbird with optional Interior Decor group. [2]Not available on Pinto Pony except in California. With V6 engine, power front disc brakes are required at extra cost. [3]Not available in California. [4]Required at extra cost in California. [5]4-speed manual w/overdrive on Granada. [6]Requires optional power front disc brakes, power rack and pinion steering, and C78 × 14 tires on Mustang. Requires optional power steering and power brakes on Fairmont. Requires optional power front disc brakes on Granada. [7]Not available on wagons in California. [8]Required at extra cost on wagons in California.

Major Options

	Pinto	Mustang	Fairmont	Granada	LTD II	Thunderbird	LTD
Air conditioning[1]	$484	$484	$484	$514	$562	$562	$597
Tilt steering wheel	—	$81	$81	$69	$75	$75	$76
Fingertip speed control	—	$116	$116	$116	$126	$126	$126
Rear window defogger	—	—	$51	$51	—	—	$57
Electric rear window defroster	S[2]	$84	$90	$90	$99	$99	$100
Tinted glass, all windows	S[2]	$59	$59	$64	$70	$70	$83
Dual remote-control mirrors	$52	$52	$43[3]	$63	$68	$68	$55[3]
Power trunk lid release	—	$[4]	$22	$22	$[4]	$[4]	$[4]
Power windows, 2-dr./4-dr.	—	—	$116/$163	$120/$171	$132/$187	$132	$137/$203
Power door locks, 2-dr./4-dr.[4]	—	$[4]	$73/$101	$78/$110	$[4]	$[4]	$[4]
Power seat, 6-way w/std. seat	—	—	$94[5]	$94[5]	$163	$163	$164
Front bucket seats w/console[6]	S	$140	S	$99	$211	$211	—
Leather upholstery	—	$282	—	$271	—	$309	—
AM radio	S[2]	$72	$72	$72	$79	S	$79
AM/FM stereo[7]	$89	$176	$176	$176	$192	$113	$192
AM/FM stereo w/8-track tape	—	$243	$243	$243	$266	$187	$266
AM/FM stereo w/cassette tape	$157	$243	$243	$243	$266	$187	$266
Vinyl top, full	—	$102	$90[8]	$106[8]	$116[8]	$132[8]	$143[8]
Moonroof, power-operated	$199[9]	$199[9]	$199[9]	$899	—	$691	—
T-Roof convertible	—	—	—	—	—	$747	—
Power steering	$141	$141	$149	$155	S	S	S
Power brakes, w/front disc	$70	$70	$70	$70	S	S	S
Deluxe wheel covers	—	—	$37	$41	$45	—	S
Wire wheel covers	$99	$99	$127	$108	$161	$118	$145
Styled Steel wheels w/trim ring	$54	$94	$116	$124	—	$166	—
Forged/Cast aluminum wheel[10]	$289	$289	$327	—	$361	$316	—
Cast aluminum lacy wheels	$289	—	—	$289[10]	—	—	—
White sidewall tires, std. size	$43	$43	$43	$43	$47	$47	$47

Popular Option Groups & Packages[11]

	Pinto	Mustang	Fairmont	Granada	LTD II	Thunderbird	LTD
Appearance protection group	$33	$33	$43	—	—	—	—
Cobra package[12]	—	$1,173	—	—	—	—	—
Convenience group	$108	—	$65	$94	$155	$117	$84
Cruising Wagon package[13]	$566	—	—	—	—	—	—
Deluxe bumper group	S	—	$57	$78	$63	—	—
ES option	—	—	$329	—	—	—	—
ESS option	$236	—	—	—	—	—	—
Exterior accent group	—	$72	$82	—	—	—	$66
Exterior décor group	$40	—	$223	—	—	$405	—
Futura Sports group	—	—	$102	—	—	—	—
Ghia option	—	—	$498	—	—	—	—
Indy 500 pace car replica pkg.	—	$4,000[14]	—	—	—	—	—
Interior accent group	$40	$120	$84	—	—	—	—
Interior décor group	$175	—	$311	$211	—	$322	—
Landau luxury group	—	—	—	—	—	—	$705[15]
Light group	$37	$37	$43	$46	$57	$51	$41
Luxury interior group	—	—	—	—	—	$816	—
Power Lock group, 2-dr./4-dr.	—	$99	—	—	$111/$143	$111	$112/$146
Protection group	—	—	—	$47	$61	$49	$55
Sport option	—	$175	—	—	—	—	—
Sports appearance package	—	—	—	—	$301	—	—
Sports Instrumentation group	—	—	—	—	$151	$129	—
Sports décor group	—	—	—	—	—	$518	—
Sports package	$110	—	—	—	—	—	—
Sports Touring package	—	—	—	—	$379	—	—
Squire wagon option	$315	—	$399	—	—	—	—

—= Not Available; S = Standard equipment. [1]Air conditioner w/automatic temperature control is available for $555 on Granada, $607 on Thunderbird and LTD II, and $642 on LTD. [2]Standard on all except Pinto Pony. Defroster includes tinted rear window. Pinto Pony prices: Defroster, $84; Tinted glass, $59; AM radio, $65; AM/FM Stereo, $161. [3]LH remote/RH manual on Fairmont. LH remote is standard on LTD Landau w/RH being $37. [4]Available only in Power lock group. [5]4-way power seat on Fairmont and Granada. [6]Bucket seats only on Pinto and Fairmont; console not available. Bucket seats standard on Mustang; price shown is for console. Requires interior décor group on Granada. Bucket seats w/console available on LTD II 2-door only, and on LTD II Brougham 2-door for $37. [7]Citizens Band (CB) 40-channel radio available for $270 on Granada, $295 on LTD II, Thunderbird, and LTD. Signal-searching AM/FM stereo available for $319 on Granada, for $349 on LTD II, and for $270 on Thunderbird. Signal-searching AM/FM stereo w/8-track available for $432 on LTD. [8]Not available on wagons. Half-vinyl roof for Fairmont Futura w/flip-up open air roof is $90; half-vinyl roof for Granada 2-doors w/o moonroof is $106; LTD II 2-doors front or rear half is $116. N/C on LTD Landau 2-door, and standard on LTD Landau 4-door. Thunderbird uses two-piece vinyl roof, in front of and behind center pillar wrap-over. [9]Manually operated flip-up sunroof on Fiesta, Pinto, Mustang, and Fairmont. [10]Granada has cast lacy aluminum spoke wheels. White forged aluminum on Pinto, $307. Mustang offers Forged Metric Aluminum wheels for $298 and requires TRX tires at extra cost. [11]Fiesta option packages: Décor group, $390; Ghia group, $722; Sport group, $556. [12]Cobra hood graphics available for $78 with Cobra package. [13] Available on Pinto runabout for $367. Delete option of the standard stripe/panel appliqués on wagon for $55 credit. [14]Estimated price with 2.3L Turbo engine. [15]Available on LTD Landau models only. Available on Country Squire wagon for $758.

Paint Colors

All except Fiesta	Code	All except Fiesta	Code	Fiesta	Code
Black	1C	Pastel Chamois	5P	Light Blue metallic	1
Pewter metallic[1]	1E	Dark Brown metallic	5Q	Jupiter Red metallic	3
Silver metallic	1G	Medium Vaquero glow metallic	5W	Cosmos Blue metallic	5
Dove Gray	1N	Antique Cream	62	Signal Yellow	9
Medium Gray metallic	1P	Bright Yellow	64	Diamond White	B
Bright Red	2B	Cream	6P	Oyster Gold metallic	C
Red glow metallic	2H	Light Gold	6W	Green	K
Maroon	2J	Medium Pine metallic	75	Orange	O
Dark Red	2M	Light Medium Pine	76	Light Beige	P
Bright Red	2P	Medium Jade metallic	7L	Venetian Red	R
Light Medium Blue	3F	Light Chamois	83	Light Blue	T
Blue glow metallic	3H	Tangerine	85	Strato Silver metallic	V
Bright Blue	3J	Camel glow metallic	8J	Midnight Blue	X
Midnight Blue metallic	3L	Dark Cordovan metallic	8N		
Dark Jade metallic	46	Chamois metallic[2]	8W	

In two-tone combinations, first two digits are lower color, and second two digits are upper color. Metallic glow paints are $41 extra on Pinto and Mustang, $48 extra on Fairmont and Granada, and $64 extra on LTD II, Thunderbird and LTD. "Tu-Tone" paint/ |
Dark Pine metallic	4D	Champagne metallic	8Y	
Medium Chestnut metallic	5M	Polar White	9D	
Burnt Orange glow metallic	5N	Special White	9E	

1979

tape treatment available for $76 on Pinto, $51 on Fairmont w/ES option, $163 on Granada, and $118 on LTD. A lower body "Tu-Tone," in black only, for Mustangs is available for $78; on LTD II and Thunderbird in a variety of colors, and with other trim for $82; and on Fairmont sedans, including other trim and color-keyed turbine wheel covers, for $207. ¹Used only on 1979½ Mustang Indy 500 Pace car replicas. ²Available on Thunderbird only.

Fiesta

"Wundercar!"

Nameplate year of origin: 1978 (U.S.; 1976 in Europe).
Current bodystyle lifespan: 1978 through 1980 (1976 to 1983 globally).
Predecessor to this model: None.
Replacement for this model: Escort (1981 to 1985).
Primary competition: Dodge Colt and Plymouth Champ.
Notable changes: Minor trim and detail changes.
Major standard equipment: All-vinyl high-back front bucket seats, color-keyed passenger compartment carpeting, brushed aluminum I/P appliqué, two-spoke steering wheel, open glove box, fold-down rear seat, overhead courtesy light w/door switches, concealed under load floor storage compartment, black window moldings, painted drip rails, rack-and-pinion steering, manual front disc brakes, argent road wheels, and 145SR × 12 BSW tires.

Measurements

Wheelbase	90.0"
Length	147.1"
Width	61.7"
Height	52.3"
Legroom — front	40.1"
Legroom — rear	34.3"
Headroom — front	37.6"
Headroom — rear	36.8"
Cargo capacity (cu. ft.)	6.8*
Fuel capacity (gals.)	10.0

With rear seat folded down, 29.0 cu. ft, plus 0.6 cu. ft. under-floor storage.

Models Available

	Model No.	Base MSRP	Change from LY	Shipping Wt. (lbs.)	Model Year Sales	Change from LY
Fiesta 3-Door Hatchback	FB	$4,493	+8.50%	1693	77,733	-4.36%
TOTALS	*Avg. price*	$4,493	+8.50%	*Production*	77,733	-4.36%

Pinto

"New design for '79."

Nameplate year of origin: 1971.
Current bodystyle lifespan: 1971 through 1980.
Predecessor to this model: None.
Replacement for this model: Escort (1981 to 1985).
Percentage of division's production: 10.84%.
Corporate siblings: Mercury Bobcat.
Primary competition: AMC Spirit, Chevrolet Chevette, Dodge Colt, and Plymouth Champ.
Notable changes: New front-end design and minor trim and detail changes.
Major standard equipment: Choice of Diamond pattern cloth-and-vinyl or Wicker weave all-vinyl high-back front bucket seats, color-keyed carpeting, AM radio, tinted glass, electric rear window defroster, bright front and rear window moldings, bright drip and belt moldings, deluxe bumper group, rack-and-pinion steering, manual front disc brakes, hubcaps, and A78 × 13 BSW tires. Runabout adds: Black rubber load floor mat, fold-down rear seat, and rear liftgate. Station wagon adds: Pivoting rear quarter windows, bright window moldings, counterbalanced liftgate, and liftgate "open" warning light. Pony deletes: Color-keyed I/P and steering wheel, AM radio, tinted glass, electric rear window defroster, deluxe bumper group, bright drip and rear window moldings, and bright belt molding.

Measurements

	Sedan	Runabout	Wagon
Wheelbase	94.5"	94.5"	94.8"
Length	170.8"	170.8"	180.6"
Width	69.4"	69.4"	69.7"
Height	50.6"	50.6"	52.1"
Legroom — front	40.8"	40.8"	40.8"
Legroom — rear	30.7"	30.7"	30.7"
Headroom — front	37.3"	37.3"	37.9"
Headroom — rear	36.2"	36.2"	39.3"
Cargo capacity (cu. ft.)	8.2	6.1*	31.3*
Fuel capacity (gals.)	13.0	13.0	14.0

With rear seat folded down, Runabout, 29.0 cu. ft.; Wagon, 57.2 cu. ft.

Models Available

	Model No.	Base MSRP	Change from LY	Shipping Wt. (lbs.)	Model Year Production	Change from LY
Pinto Pony 2-Door Sedan	10	$3,434	+9.40%	2329	NA*	NA*
Pinto Pony 2-Door Station Wagon	12	$3,899	NEW	2515	NA*	NEW
Pinto 2-Door Sedan	10	$3,939	+8.54%	2346	75,789	+21.62%
Pinto 3-Dr. Runabout (hatchback)	11	$4,055	+8.31%	2392	69,383	-6.63%
Pinto 2-Door Station Wagon	12	$4,338	+7.70%	2532	53,846	+3.02%
TOTALS	Avg. price	$3,933	+8.20%		Production 199,018	+5.36%

Production kept as combined totals for Pinto Pony models and Pinto models.

Mustang

"A whole new breed."

Nameplate year of origin: 1964 (also used on a 1963 show car).
Current bodystyle lifespan: 1979 through 1993.
Predecessor to this model: Mustang (1974 to 1978).
Replacement for this model: Mustang (1994 to 2004).
Percentage of division's production: 20.15%.
Corporate siblings: Mercury Capri.
Primary competition: Chevrolet Camaro, Dodge Challenger, Plymouth Sapporo, and Pontiac Firebird.
Notable changes: Completely redesigned.
Major standard equipment: All-vinyl high-back bucket seats, deluxe cut-pile carpeting, door panels w/padded upper panel and bright moldings and carpeted lower panels, full-width woodtone I/P appliqués, deluxe steering wheel, courtesy lights, gauges (including tachometer, trip odometer, fuel, oil pressure, ammeter and temperature), black LH rearview mirror, bright windshield and rear window molding, bright drip rail and side window moldings, color-keyed louvers behind rear quarter window, color-keyed door and window frames w/bright molding, soft color-keyed urethane covered front and rear ends w/black rub strips on bumpers, full wheel covers, and B78 × 13 BSW tires. 3-door adds: Sport steering wheel, fold-down rear seat, liftgate, black louvers behind rear quarter window, black painted door and window frames, black belt and rocker panel moldings, full wrap-around wide black bodyside moldings w/dual accent stripe inserts and 13-inch sport wheels. Ghia adds: Crinkle-grain vinyl low-back bucket seats, color-keyed deluxe seat belts, luxury pile carpeting, Ghia door trim w/badge, soft inserts, map pockets and carpeted lower panels, sport steering wheel, roof-mounted assist grips, light group, RH visor vanity mirror, Ghia sound package, carpeted luggage compartment (2-door), Ghia insignia on decklid/liftgate, color-keyed window frames and louvers, dual remote control color-keyed mirrors, bright belt and rocker panel moldings, pinstripes, full wraparound wide black bodyside moldings w/dual accent stripe inserts, Turbine wheel covers, and BR78 × 14 BSW tires.

Measurements

Wheelbase	100.4"
Length	179.1"
Width	69.1"
Height	51.5"
Legroom — front	40.9"
Legroom — rear	29.8"
Headroom — front	37.2"
Headroom — rear	36.3"
Cargo capacity (cu. ft.)	10.0*
Fuel capacity (gals.)**	11.5**

*3-door, 32.4 cu. ft. w/rear seat folded down.
**12.5 gallons with air conditioning or optional engines.*

1979

Models Available

	Model No.	Base MSRP	Change from LY	Shipping Wt. (lbs.)	Model Year Production	Change from LY
Mustang 2-Door Sedan	02	$4,494	+17.52%	2431	156,666	+92.69%
Mustang 3-Door (hatchback)	03	$4,828	+18.68%	2451	120,535	+76.20%
Mustang Ghia 2-Door Sedan	04	$5,064	+19.38%	2539	56,351	+62.25%
Mustang Ghia 3-Door (hatchback)	05	$5,216	NEW	2548	36,384	NEW
TOTALS	Avg. price	$4,901	+17.68%		Production 369,936	+92.26%

Fairmont

"The best-selling new car ever introduced."

Nameplate year of origin: 1978.
Current bodystyle lifespan: 1978 through 1983.
Predecessor to this model: Maverick (1970 to 1977).
Replacement for this model: Tempo (1984 to 1994).
Percentage of division's production: 21.53%.
Corporate siblings: Mercury Zephyr.
Primary competition: AMC Concord, Chevrolet Nova, and Plymouth Volaré.
Notable changes: Minor trim and detail changes.
Major standard equipment: Wicker weave all-vinyl low-back front bucket seats, color-keyed cut-pile carpeting, integral door armrests w/door pull assist handle, two-spoke color-keyed steering wheel, simulated woodgrain appliqué around instrument cluster, bright windshield and rear window moldings, bright drip rail moldings, front bumper guards, manual front disc brakes, modified strut front suspension, hubcaps, and B78 × 14 BSW tires. Futura coupe adds: Medium grain vinyl front bucket seats, luxury door trim panels, color-keyed safety belts, high gloss simulated woodgrain appliqué on I/P, inside hood release, bright LH manual mirror, wrap-over roof design w/accent paint stripes, bright door window frames and belt moldings, bright wheel lip opening moldings, lower bodyside protection molding w/vinyl insert, deluxe sound insulation package, unique front and rear end appearance, and deluxe wheel covers. Wagon adds: Fold-down rear seat, carpet on load floor and rear seat back, cargo area light, bright quarter window and liftgate moldings, "liftgate-open" warning light, and CR78 × 14 BSW tires.

Measurements

	2-Door	Futura	4-Door	Wagon
Wheelbase	105.5"	105.5"	105.5"	105.5"
Length	194.9"	195.8"	194.9"	194.9"
Width	71.0"	71.0"	71.0"	71.0"
Height	53.6"	52.3"	53.6"	54.4"
Legroom — front	41.8"	NA	41.8"	NA
Legroom — rear	35.4"	NA	37.7"	NA
Headroom — front	38.5"	NA	38.5"	NA
Headroom — rear	37.7"	NA	37.7"	NA
Cargo capacity (cu. ft.)	16.8	16.1	16.8	79.1
Fuel capacity (gals.)	16.0	16.0	16.0	16.0

Models Available

	Model No.	Base MSRP	Change from LY	Shipping Wt. (lbs.)	Model Year Production	Change from LY
Fairmont 2-Door Sedan	91	$4,102	+13.19%	2491	54,798	-30.44%
Fairmont 4-Door Sedan	92	$4,220	+13.75%	2544	133,813	-2.22%
Fairmont 4-Door, 5-p. Station Wagon	94	$4,497	+10.68%	2674	100,691	-21.57%
Fairmont Futura 2-Door Coupe	93	$4,463	+8.77%	2546	106,065	-9.32%
TOTALS	*Avg. price*	$4,321	+11.50%	*Production*	395,367	-14.23%

Granada

"An American Classic."

Nameplate year of origin: 1975.
Current bodystyle lifespan: 1975 through 1980.
Predecessor to this model: None.
Replacement for this model: Granada (1981 to 1982).
Percentage of division's production: 9.93%.
Corporate siblings: Mercury Monarch.
Primary competition: AMC Concord, Chevrolet Nova, Dodge Aspen, Plymouth Volaré, and Pontiac Ventura.
Notable changes: Minor trim and detail changes.
Major standard equipment: Box-weave all-vinyl "Flight Bench" front seat w/fold-down center armrest, 10-oz. cut-pile carpeting, burled walnut I/P appliqués w/Granada script, two rear seat ashtrays, luggage compartment mat, bright front and rear window moldings, bright belt moldings, bright drip rail and wheel opening moldings, opera window w/bright moldings (2-door), hood ornament, manual front disc brakes, full wheel covers, and DR78 × 14 BSW tires. Ghia adds: Smooth-grain

Measurements

Wheelbase	109.9"
Length	197.8"
Width	74.0"
Height	53.3"
Legroom — front	41.1"
Legroom — rear	36.0"
Headroom — front	38.5"
Headroom — rear	37.6"
Cargo capacity (cu. ft.)	15.4*
Fuel capacity (gals.)	18.0

Ghia models have 1.6 cu. ft. less capacity, and ESS models have 0.9 cu. ft. less capacity.

all-vinyl "Flight Bench" front seat w/fold-down center armrest, 18-oz. cut-pile carpeting, deluxe door trim, deluxe steering wheel, digital clock, Ghia interior ornamentation, day/night rearview mirror, deluxe color-keyed seat belts, rear door courtesy light switches (4-door), LH remote control mirror, opera window Ghia interior and exterior ornamentation, wide vinyl insert bodyside and wheel lip moldings, vinyl lower rear panel appliqué w/decklid tape stripes, bodyside tape stripes, luggage compartment carpeting, deluxe sound and ride package, color-keyed wheel covers, and ER78 × 14 BSW tires. ESS adds: Chainmail vinyl front bucket seats w/European style headrests, 18-oz. cut-pile carpeting, leather wrapped steering wheel, deluxe door trim w/woodtone appliqués, day/night rearview mirror, deluxe color-keyed seat belts, rear door courtesy light switches (4-door), dual color-keyed remote control mirrors, louvered opera windows appliqué (2-door), black trim (window frames, wipers, grille, back panel appliqué and rocker panels), black bodyside moldings w/bright inserts, luggage compartment trim, sound package, deluxe bumper group, ESS ornamentation on front fenders, hood and decklid paint stripes, heavy-duty suspension, color-keyed wheel covers, and FR78 × 14 BSW tires.

Models Available

	Model No.	Base MSRP	Change from LY	Shipping Wt. (lbs.)	Model Year Production	Change from LY*
Granada 2-Door Sedan	81	$4,676	+8.74%	3053	76,850	-30.44%
Granada 4-Door Sedan	82	$4,782	+8.93%	3098	105,526	-24.25%
Granada Ghia 2-Door Sedan	81	$5,051	+7.81%	3089	NA*	NA*
Granada Ghia 4-Door Sedan	82	$5,157	+7.98%	3132	NA*	NA*
Granada ESS 2-Door Sedan	81	$5,211	+6.96%	3105	NA*	NA*
Granada ESS 4-Door Sedan	82	$5,317	+7.15%	3155	NA*	NA*
TOTALS	Avg. price	$5,032	+7.89%	Production	182,376	-26.99%

*Model year production and change from LY is not available due to production totals being kept by body style and model number, and not by trim level.

LTD II

"Traditional style and value."

Nameplate year of origin: 1977.
Current bodystyle lifespan: 1977 through 1979.
Predecessor to this model: Torino (1972 to 1976).
Replacement for this model: None.
Percentage of division's production: 2.65%.
Corporate siblings: Mercury Cougar.
Primary competition: Chevrolet Malibu, Dodge Diplomat, and Pontiac LeMans.
Notable changes: Minor trim and detail changes.
Major standard equipment: Cloth-and-vinyl front "Flight Bench" seat, 10 oz. color-keyed cut-pile carpeting, high level door trim panels w/woodtone accents, woodtone I/P cluster appliqués and RH panel, opera window (2-door), windshield and rear window bright moldings, bright drip rail and side window moldings, bright rocker panel and wheel lip mold-

Measurements

	2-Doors	4-Doors
Wheelbase	114.0"	118.0"
Length	217.2"	221.2"
Width	78.6"	78.6"
Height	52.6"	53.3"
Legroom — front	42.5"	42.5"
Legroom — rear	33.2"	37.8"
Headroom — front	37.6"	38.3"
Headroom — rear	36.2"	37.0"
Cargo capacity (cu. ft.)	15.9	15.9
Fuel capacity (gals.)	21.0	21.0

ings, aluminum rear panel appliqué, deluxe sound package, stand-up hood ornament, bright hubcaps, and HR78 × 14 BSW tires. LTD II Brougham adds: Knit cloth-and-vinyl split front seat w/dual fold-down center armrests, 18 oz. cut-pile carpeting, luxury door trim w/carpeted lower panels, deluxe two-spoke steering wheel, electric clock, color-keyed deluxe seat belts, wide bodyside moldings w/vinyl inserts and integral wheel lip moldings, dual accent paint stripes, Brougham identification, luxury sound package, and deluxe wheel covers.

Models Available

	Model No.	Base MSRP	Change from LY	Shipping Wt. (lbs.)	Model Year Production	Change from LY
LTD II 2-Door Hardtop	30	$5,799	+13.44%	3797	18,300*	-76.01%*
LTD II 4-Door Pillared Hardtop	31	$5,924	+13.44%	3860	19,781*	-69.16%*
LTD II Brougham 2-Door Hardtop	30	$6,135	+12.61%	3815	NA*	NA*

	Model No.	Base MSRP	Change from LY	Shipping Wt. (lbs.)	Model Year Production	Change from LY
LTD II Brougham 4-Door Pillared Hardtop	31	$6,259	+12.61%	3889	NA*	NA*
TOTALS	Avg. price	$6,029	+16.23%	Production	38,081	-77.67%

Model year production for Brougham models was kept combined with LTD II models, and given the same model numbers. Therefore change from LY for LTD II includes 1978 LTD II Brougham production.

Thunderbird

"Come fly with me."

Nameplate year of origin: 1955.
Current bodystyle lifespan: 1977 through 1979.
Predecessor to this model: Thunderbird (1972 to 1976).
Replacement for this model: Thunderbird (1980 to 1982).
Percentage of division's production: 15.48%.
Corporate siblings: Mercury Cougar XR-7.
Primary competition: Chevrolet Monte Carlo and Pontiac Grand Prix.
Notable changes: New grille and minor trim and detail changes.

Measurements

Wheelbase	114.0"
Length	217.2"
Width	78.5"
Height	52.8"
Legroom — front	42.5"
Legroom — rear	33.2"
Headroom — front	37.6"
Headroom — rear	36.2"
Cargo capacity (cu. ft.)	15.6
Fuel capacity (gals.)	21.0

Major standard equipment: Cloth and vinyl front bench seat w/automatic seatback release, 10 oz. cut pile carpeting, simulated burled walnut woodgrain I/P and door panel trim, full-length door armrest, electric clock, AM radio, bright moldings (rear hood edge, beltline, drip rails), rocker panel and wheel lip moldings, opera windows, roof wrap-over moldings, front fender louvers, full wheel covers, and GR78 × 15 BSW tires. Town Landau adds: Crushed velour split front bench seat w/individual fold-down center armrests and passenger side recliner, six-way power driver's seat, illuminated visor vanity mirror, 22K gold Town Landau plaque on RH side of I/P with owner's name engraved, AM/FM stereo w/search radio, tilt steering wheel, power windows, power lock group, interior luxury décor group, convenience group, light group, tinted glass, dual remote-control sport mirrors, brushed aluminum wrap-over roof molding, unique tape stripes (bodyside, hood, header panel, decklid, hidden headlamp doors), hood ornament w/color-coordinated acrylic logo insert, Town Landau script on opera windows, accent paint on front fender louvers, front cornering lights, and body-color accent painted turbine spoke cast aluminum wheels, and HR78 × 15 WSW tires. Heritage edition adds to Town Landau features: Biscuit patterned luxury cloth split front bench seats w/individual fold-down center armrests, door and front seatback assist straps, 36 oz. cut-pile carpeting, ebony woodtone appliqués on I/P, door/quarter trim panels and steering wheel, leather covered I/P pad, leather-wrapped steering wheel, LH and RH visor vanity mirrors, fingertip speed control, power radio antenna, bright pedal trim accents, 18 oz. color-keyed trunk carpeting and molded deck lid liner, exclusive monochromatic color scheme in Maroon or Light Medium Blue, padded vinyl roof w/covered rear quarter window and Heritage script, owner's initials on front door plaques, color-keyed grille and bumper rub strips, and color-keyed cast aluminum wheels.

Models Available

	Model No.	Base MSRP	Change from LY	Shipping Wt. (lbs.)	Model Year Production	Change from LY
Thunderbird 2-Door Hardtop	87	$6,328	+15.10%	3893	284,141	NA*
Thunderbird Town Landau 2-Door HT	87	$9,239	+8.27%	4284	NA*	NA*
Thunderbird Heritage 2-Door Hardtop	87	$11,060	+9.44%	4178	NA*	NA*
TOTALS	Avg. price	$8,876	+10.32%	Production	284,141	-19.45%

Town Landau and Heritage production is included with base Thunderbird. Therefore comparisons are not available. Heritage is compared to 1978 Diamond Jubilee edition.

LTD

"A new American road car."

Nameplate year of origin: 1965.

Current bodystyle lifespan: 1979 through 1991.

Predecessor to this model: Custom/Galaxie/LTD (1971 to 1978).

Replacement for this model: Crown Victoria (1992 to 2007, continuing to 2011 for fleet sales).

Percentage of division's production: 19.42%.

Corporate siblings: Mercury Marquis.

Primary competition: Chevrolet Impala/Caprice and Pontiac Catalina.

Notable changes: Completely redesigned.

Major standard equipment: Dual-tone striped cloth-and-vinyl front bench seat, color-keyed cut-pile carpeting, wood-tone I/P and door appliqués, deluxe four-spoke soft-rim steering wheel, interior courtesy lighting, bright moldings (front and rear window, belt, drip rail, rear hood edge, and rocker panel), front bumper guards, deluxe wheel covers, and FR78 × 14 BSW tires. Wagon adds: All vinyl bench seat, fold down rear seat, color-keyed load floor carpeting, power tailgate window, and GR78 × 14 BSW tires. Landau adds: Triple line knit cloth-and-vinyl front bench seat w/fold-down center armrest, electric clock, luxury steering wheel, deluxe door trim panels, rear door courtesy light switch, luggage compartment light, LH remote control mirror, half-vinyl roof (2-door), full vinyl roof (4-door), rear pillar coach lamps (illuminate w/parking lights), dual accent paint stripes on hood, bodysides and decklid, wide rocker panel moldings w/rear extensions, brushed aluminum accent panel on lower decklid, hood ornament, specific Landau front-end styling, and full wheel covers. Country Squire adds: Simulated woodgrain exterior bodyside and tailgate paneling, electric clock, cargo area light, Landau style front-end styling.

Measurements

	2-Doors	4-Doors	Wagons
Wheelbase	114.4"	114.4"	114.4"
Length	209.1"	209.1"	214.7"
Width	77.5"	77.5"	79.3"
Height	54.5"	54.5"	56.8"
Legroom — front	NA	42.0"	NA
Legroom — rear	NA	40.5"	NA
Headroom — front	NA	38.0"	NA
Headroom — rear	NA	37.4"	NA
Cargo capacity (cu. ft.)	23.4	23.4	91.7*
Fuel capacity (gals.)	19.0	19.0	20.0

Additional 9.9 cu. ft. of below deck storage on 2-seat wagons, and 5.7 cu. ft. on wagons w/DFRS.

Models Available

	Model No.	Base MSRP	Change from LY	Shipping Wt. (lbs.)	Model Year Production	Change from LY
LTD 2-Door Sedan	62	$6,184	+14.56%	3421	54,005	-6.02%
LTD 4-Door Sedan	63	$6,284	+14.61%	3463	117,730	+4.75%
LTD 4-Door, 2-Seat, 6-p. Station Wagon**	74	$6,550	+11.30%	3678	37,955	NA*
LTD Landau 2-Door Sedan	64	$6,686	+11.99%	3472	42,314	+54.97%
LTD Landau 4-Door Sedan	65	$6,811	+12.49%	3527	74,599	+87.27%
LTD Country Squire 4-Door, 2-S., 6-p. Wagon**	76	$7,006	+11.14%	3719	29,932	NA*
TOTALS	Avg. price	$6,587	+12.61%	Production	356,535	+15.65%

*Comparison of wagons is not possible due to 1978 production being combined with base LTD and Country Squire wagon.   **Wagons available w/ removable DFRS (dual facing rear seats) for $149 extra.*

LINCOLN

"A standard by which other luxury cars are judged."

The final year of the 1970s brought the last model year for the traditional full-size, American-built car, in the form of the 1979 Lincoln Continental and Continental Mark V.

Both models were basically the last of a line of cars whose basic design work began in the 1960s, making them among the oldest car designs in the marketplace. With the knowledge that next year's models would be downsized, consumers snapped up these last "land yachts" in large numbers despite the economic recession and fuel shortage that was underway. Lincoln recognized the significance of their passing with a special, limited edition Collector's Series Continental sedan and Mark V coupe, both finished in Midnight Blue Metallic with distinctive gold-tone grille, along with many other special features.

Few changes were to be found on the Continentals for their final season. The 400 CID V8 engine that became the standard powerplant for 1978 would see its final year of service in Ford Motor Company passenger cars for 1979, as the standard engine for the Continentals. There were a few new luxury groups added for the Continental Mark V with the Crystal Blue, Turquoise, and White colors, while the Chamois and Jade/Light Jade were dropped.

The Versailles had the only visual changes for 1979. Most significant was its new formal roofline. Recognizing that consumers saw the Versailles as too closely related visually to the Ford Granada and Mercury Monarch, Lincoln took corrective action. A new rear door window and frame with a more rectangular quarter window was implemented and the rear roofline was reconfigured with a more upright rear window to complement the revised rear door design. To add to the new look, the bodyside moldings were removed, giving the Versailles a cleaner appearance in keeping with the larger Lincoln models. The molding was still available as an option, and required when "Dual Shade" (two-tone) paint was ordered.

Over the course of the model year Lincoln sales improved, as American Motors sales continued to fall, allowing Lincoln to move up to 11th place in industry production for the 1979 model year, finally bringing it out of last place. Lincoln had held the 12th place position since 1965, the year before Studebaker went out of business, and stayed there, just above Imperial, before the Chrysler luxury make was moved back into the Chrysler line during 1971. That transition put Lincoln in the bottom spot of the twelve remaining American manufacturers. Unfortunately for Lincoln their sales would tumble in 1980, putting them back into the bottom spot until 1985, when AMC was on its last legs and fading fast, allowing Lincoln to move back up a position.

Continental 2-Door Coupe

Continental 4-Door Sedan
with Collectors Series option

Continental Mark V 2-Door Hardtop Coupe

Continental Mark V 2-Door Hardtop Coupe
with Bill Blass Designer Series option

Continental Mark V 2-Door Hardtop Coupe
with Collectors Series option

Continental Mark V interior features
with Collectors Series option —
note Tom Selleck prior to television fame

Versailles 4-Door Sedan

Versailles 4-Door Sedan

Model year production: 189,546, up 11.75% from 1978.
Domestic market share: 2.06% (11th place).
Base price range: $11,868 to $13,771.
Lincoln average base price: $12,874, up 13.33%.
Introduction date: October 6, 1978.
Assembly plants: Wayne, MI (W), and Wixom, MI (Y).
Data plate identification (VIN): Eleven digit code read as follows: First digit indicates year (9 = 1979); second digit indicates assembly plant code (see list above); third and fourth digits indicate model number (model number in model charts); fifth digit indicates engine code (see powertrain chart); remaining digits are sequential with beginning numbers of 600001. *Example:* 9Y82S600001 is a 1979 Lincoln Continental 4-Door Sedan, with 400 CID, 2-bbl. V8 engine, serial number 600001, built in Wixom, MI.

Powertrains

Engine	Net HP	Engine Code	Transmission Availability		Versailles	Continental & Mark V
302 CID (5.0L), variable venturi, V8	137	F	3-speed Select-Shift automatic		S	—
				MPG:	14	—
400 CID (6.6L), 2-bbl., V8	179	S	3-speed Select-Shift automatic		—	S
				MPG:	—	12
				Calif.	—	10

Major Options

	Versailles	Continental	Mark V
Air conditioning, Auto-Temp	S	S	S
Tilt steering wheel	$81	$81	$81
Automatic speed control	S	$140	$140
Electric rear window defroster	$101	$101	$101
Tinted glass, all windows	S	S	S
Power windows	S	S	S
Power front vent windows	—	$95	$95
Power door locks	$[1]	$[1]	$[1]
Illuminated entry system	S	$65	$65
Power seat, 6-way w/pass. recliner	S[2]	$251	$159
Leather seating upholstery	$312	$312	$333
RH remote-control mirror, LH std.	S	$39	$39
Intermittent windshield wipers	S	$39	$39
AM/FM stereo, w/power antenna[3]	—	$144	$144
AM/FM stereo w/8-track tape	($168)	$203	$203
AM/FM stereo w/cassette tape	($168)	$203	$203
AM/FM electronic stereo, w/search and 8-track tape	S	$407	$407
Vinyl top, full[4]	N/C	$228	$236
Fixed glass moonroof w/sun shade	—	$1,088	—
Moonroof, power-operated & tinted	$1,088	$1,088	$1,088
Power brakes, four wheel disc	S	—	S
"Sure-Track" antilock brake system	—	$525	$313
Wire wheel covers	N/C	$247	$247
Cast aluminum turbine-style wheels	—	$373	$373
Forged aluminum wheels	S	$373	$373

Popular Option Groups & Packages

	Versailles	Continental	Mark V
Appearance protection group	$87	$87	$80
Bill Blass designer series	—	—	$1,809[5]
Cartier designer series	—	—	$1,945
Collector's Series[6]	—	$3,209	$7,859
Color luxury group[7]	—	—	$743[7]
Defroster group	$121	$121	$121
Emilio Pucci designer series	—	—	$1,525
Givenchy designer series	—	—	$2,145

1979

	Versailles	Continental	Mark V
Headlamp convenience group	—	$140	$140
Interior light group	—	$135	$135
Power lock group	$155[1]	$155[1]	$120[1]
Reclining bucket seat group	$491	—	—
Town Coupe/Town Car package	—	$1,527	—
Williamsburg Limited Edition	—	$1,617[8]	—

— = Not Available; S = Standard equipment.   [1]Power door locks require optional Power Lock convenience group. Price on coupe is $120.   [2]Four-way power seat on Versailles.   [3]Citizen Band (CB) radio available for $321, and includes multi-band power antenna.   [4]Landau vinyl roof w/frenched seams and rear window available on Continental Mark V for $513; Carriage roof (simulated convertible top) available for $1,201. Fully padded coach vinyl roof is available on Continental w/Town Car or Town Coupe option for $285; with Williamsburg Limited edition for $352; and with Continental coupe or sedan for $580. Coach vinyl roof includes wide vinyl padded roof bow molding and fully padded custom half-vinyl roof w/ frenched rear window and side quarter windows.   [5]Price given is with full vinyl roof; price with carriage roof is $2,775.   [6]Available on Continental sedan w/Town Car option, or on Mark V coupe. Price on Continental w/leather interior trim is $3,421. Price on Mark V w/bucket seats is $8,259.   [7]Color luxury groups available: Champagne, Cordovan, Crystal Blue, Dove Grey, Gold/Cream, Red/Rose, Turquoise, Wedgewood Blue and White. Price is $843 when ordered with moondust paint (moondust not available with Crystal Blue luxury group).   [8]Price with leather seats is $1,829.

Paint Colors

	Code		Code
Black	1C	Light Champagne	52
Silver metallic[1,2]	1G	Dark Champagne metallic	5A
Dove Grey	1N	Light Champagne moondust metallic[3]	5C
Medium Grey metallic[1]	1S	Dark Cordovan metallic	5R
Light Silver moondust metallic[3]	1Y	Jubilee Gold moondust metallic[3]	66
Dark Red moondust metallic[3]	23	Cream[2]	6P
Light Red moondust metallic[2,3]	2D	Crystal Apricot moondust metallic[3]	88
Dark Red	2M	White	9D
Rose metallic	2W		
Wedgewood Blue	34	
Diamond Blue moondust metallic[3]	38	
Midnight Blue moondust metallic[3]	3Q	
Dark Turquoise metallic	4B	
Medium Turquoise moondust metallic[3]	4C	

In two-tone combinations, first two digits are lower color, and second two digits are upper color. "Dual shade" two-tone paint available only on Versailles for $63 extra, plus required bodyside molding for an additional $77.   [1]Not available on Continental.   [2]Not available on Mark V.   [3]Moondust metallic paints available for $201 extra. Not available on Versailles.

Versailles

"The world of Lincoln Versailles is a very special world."

Nameplate year of origin: 1977½ (1975 as a Continental option package).
Current bodystyle lifespan: 1977½ through 1980.
Predecessor to this model: None.
Replacement for this model: Continental (1982 to 1987).
Percentage of division's production: 11.08%.
Corporate siblings: Ford Granada and Mercury Monarch.
Primary competition: Cadillac Seville.
Notable changes: New formal roofline and minor trim and detail changes.
Major standard equipment: Luxury all cloth "Flight Bench" front w/four-way power adjustment, folding center armrests in front and rear seat, deep-pile carpeting, simulated wood appliqués on I/P, steering wheel and doors, leather steering wheel and I/P pad, rear passenger and front passenger side roof rail assist straps, package shelf w/Kasman fabric, Cartier-signed digital clock, power windows, automatic speed control, electronic AM/FM stereo w/choice of cassette tape or 8-track tape player and w/power antenna, automatic temperature control air conditioning, LH and RH illuminated visor vanity mirrors, LH and RH remote control rearview mirror, tinted glass, power deck lid release, interior lighting (ashtrays, courtesy, glove box, luggage compartment, dome/map, and rear seat reading), 18-oz. color-keyed carpeted luggage compartment floor w/14-oz. carpeted decklid liner, full vinyl roof, coach lamps, illuminated entry system, cornering lights, high luster bodyside molding w/vinyl insert, bumper protection group, forged aluminum wheels, and FR78 × 14 wide WSW tires.

Measurements

Wheelbase	109.9"
Length	201.0"
Width	74.5"
Height	54.1"
Legroom — front	40.7"
Legroom — rear	35.6"
Headroom — front	38.2"
Headroom — rear	37.6"
Cargo capacity (cu. ft.)	14.6
Fuel capacity (gals.)	19.2

Models Available

	Model No.	Base MSRP	Change from LY	Shipping Wt. (lbs.)	Model Year Production	Change from LY
Versailles 4-Door Sedan	84	$13,763	+9.85%	3684	21,007	+135.21%
TOTALS	Avg. price	$13,763	+9.85%	Production	21,007	+135.21%

Continental

"Designed to satisfy fully even the most discriminating owner in terms of styling, solidity and quality."

Nameplate year of origin: 1940 (1961 as a regular series).
Current bodystyle lifespan: 1970 through 1979 (restyled in 1974).
Predecessor to this model: Continental (1961 to 1969).
Replacement for this model: Town Car (1980 to 1991).
Percentage of division's production: 48.85%.
Corporate siblings: None.
Primary competition: Cadillac deVille.
Notable changes: Minor trim and detail changes.
Major standard equipment: Luxury cloth front bench seat w/six-way power adjustment, folding center armrests in front and rear seat, cut-pile carpeting, simulated wood appliqués on I/P and steering wheel, Cartier-signed digital clock, power windows, AM/FM radio w/power antenna, automatic temperature control air conditioning, visor-mounted vanity mirror, LH remote control rearview mirror, tinted glass, power deck lid release, interior lighting (ashtrays, courtesy, glove box, luggage compartment, dome/map, and rear seat reading), fully lined and carpeted luggage compartment w/tire cover, full vinyl roof, cornering lights, bright rocker panel moldings w/rear extensions, front and rear bumper guards w/pad and rub strips, deluxe wheel covers, and LR78 × 15 WSW tires.

Measurements

	Coupe	Sedan
Wheelbase	127.2"	127.2"
Length	233.0"	233.0"
Width	79.6"	79.6"
Height	55.2"	55.4"
Legroom — front	42.0"	42.0"
Legroom — rear	41.3"	42.0"
Headroom — front	38.0"	38.1"
Headroom — rear	38.1"	38.6"
Cargo capacity (cu. ft.)	21.2	21.2
Fuel capacity (gals.)	24.2	24.2

1979

Models Available

	Model No.	Base MSRP	Change from LY	Shipping Wt. (lbs.)	Model Year Production	Change from LY
Continental 2-Door Hardtop Coupe	81	$11,868	+16.40%	4639	16,142	-23.05%
Continental 4-Door Sedan	82	$12,093	+16.32%	4649	76,458	+13.93%
TOTALS	Avg. price	$11,981	+16.36%	Production	92,600	+5.12%

Continental Mark V

"Perhaps it's something you owe yourself."

Nameplate year of origin: 1956 (Continental Mark II).
Current bodystyle lifespan: 1977 through 1979.
Predecessor to this model: Continental Mark IV (1972 to 1976).
Replacement for this model: Continental Mark VI (1980 to 1983).
Percentage of division's production: 40.06%.
Corporate siblings: None.
Primary competition: Buick Riviera, Cadillac Eldorado, and Oldsmobile Toronado.
Notable changes: Minor trim and detail changes.
Major standard equipment: "Ultravelour" "Twin Comfort" lounge seats w/six-way power adjustment, folding center armrests in front and rear seat, walnut woodgrain appliqué on I/P and steering wheel, color-keyed cut-pile carpeting, visor vanity

Measurements

Wheelbase	120.3"
Length	230.3"
Width	79.7"
Height	53.1"
Legroom — front	42.3"
Legroom — rear	34.0"
Headroom — front	37.5"
Headroom — rear	37.1"
Cargo capacity (cu. ft.)	18.1
Fuel capacity (gals.)	25.0

mirror, electric Cartier Timepiece, trip odometer, power windows, AM/FM radio w/power antenna, automatic temperature control air conditioning, LH remote control rearview mirror, tinted glass, door panel courtesy lights, power decklid release, fully lined luggage compartment, full vinyl roof w/opera window, dual custom pinstripe, customer monogram on doors, functional fender louvers (three per side), cornering lights, front and rear bumper guards w/pads and rub strips, luxury wheel covers, and LR78 × 15 dual wide band WSW tires.

Models Available

	Model No.	Base MSRP	Change from LY	Shipping Wt. (lbs.)	Model Year Production	Change from LY
Continental Mark V 2-Door Hardtop	89	$13,771	+11.08%	4589	75,939	+4.60%
TOTALS	*Avg. price*	$13,771	+11.08%	*Production*	75,939	+4.60%

MERCURY

"Presenting the 1979 Mercury fine car collection."

As Mercury entered its 40th anniversary year, it introduced two all-new models just as the second fuel crisis began and a mild recession was taking hold. The freshly downsized full-size Marquis and the American-built Capri both appeared in showrooms for this model year.

Luck seemed to be with Mercury, though, as it had been for the past several years. While the new Marquis could be considered a success, it was a little less popular than might have been hoped for, as consumers turned toward smaller cars again. But the Capri was an immediate hit, and picked up any slack in Marquis sales. Gaining momentum this season was the Bobcat with its first facelift, and the always popular Cougar XR-7 held its own. Zephyr and Monarch models were still popular and only suffered an average decline given the market conditions, while the regular Cougar line was barely on the charts, and would be discontinued before the end of the model year. By the end of the year, Mercury would join a short list of makes to enjoy production increases for the 1979 model year, and would get about as close as it ever would get to topping the production total and market share of one of its chief rivals, Buick.

For the first time, there was an American-built Capri for 1979. While not the slim and trim, tight handling car of the European Capri, the new Capri had other qualities that made it a desirable sporty car in its own right. Based on the new "Fox" chassis and sharing most components with the Ford Mustang, the new Capri used slightly different fenders, a different grille, and different taillights to help distinguish it from its corporate twin. These changes gave the car an appearance that was somewhat reminiscent of the Capri II from the front. Another difference between the Mustang and Capri

was that the Capri was available only as a hatchback, while its Mustang sibling was also available as a two-door coupe. Exterior design included a slightly curved horizontal slat grille in body color on base Capris, blacked-out on optional RS versions, with dual rectangular headlights placed side by side at each end, and sitting within an ever so slightly raised bezel, which led to comparisons to the former European Capri's front-end. Parking and turn signal lights were placed within the bumper rub strip area centered below the dual headlamps. The Capri's fascia was squared off in contrast to the Mustang's sloping nose.

The Capri featured bodysides following the latest trends with only two feature lines. The upper line began high on the front fender near the top of the grille, then ran straight to the back to the top edge of the wraparound taillamps, passing just above the door handle. Above the front and rear wheel openings this feature line became more prominent, flaring into a distinct "blister." The lower line followed the top edge of the bodyside molding and bumper rub strips encircling the car, creating a small lip over the wheel openings as it passed over them. Black rear quarter window louvers, broken horizontally into three sections, were another identifying feature of the Capri exterior. Taillights were of a nearly full-width design, with a black bezel dividing each unit into six horizontal sections, with the center mounted license tag breaking the flow. Backup lights were placed near the center of the lens.

Sharing a platform with the Fairmont meant similar cowl, windshield and door configurations, but the unique rear quarters added a sporty, fastback style profile. Inside, the Capri shared nearly all of its features with the Mustang, with trim changes to distinguish them. The instrument panel featured a hooded driver's side area and a recessed passenger side area housing the glove box and air vents. The driver's pod used round dial gauges with speedometer and tachometer in large pods centered over the steering wheel. Two smaller pods flanked the larger ones on each side housing the fuel, temperature, oil pressure and alternator gauges. Air vents and assorted warning lights were placed to the far left, while another air vent and ventilation controls were to the right. The optional radio was mounted between the upper pod area and the optional floor shifter console. Various steering wheels were used including a sport three-spoke slot style and a luxury four-spoke style, which was required with options such as fingertip cruise control and had the buttons mounted on the upper two spokes.

Engine choices for the 1979 Capri consisted of the 2.3 liter 4 cylinder engine, in naturally aspirated or, new for Mercury, turbocharged form; the 2.8-liter German-built V6 engine; or the ever-popular 302 cubic inch V8, fitted with a 2-barrel carburetor. Transmission options for all versions were 4-speed manual or 3-speed automatic. The V6 engine was initially available only with an automatic transmission, but evidently Ford recognized the need for a manual transmission, and introduced it partway through the 1979 model year. The turbocharged 4-cylinder engine was available on any Capri, at least initially. A sporty RS package or a Turbo RS option, including the turbocharged engine, could be added to the base Capri. A more luxurious interior was part of the Capri Ghia model.

Mercury's new Marquis had all the design features of most other downsized cars of the day, with boxy lines, tall upright greenhouse areas, minimal bodyside sculpting, less bulk and weight, and smaller, more fuel efficient engines, while maintaining both the interior passenger space and cargo space of their much larger predecessors. The 1979 Marquis simultaneously had its first ever exposed headlights and its first use of dual rectangular headlights. Parking and turn signal lights were in large lenses wrapping around the pointed front fender cap edge. In between was a grille looking quite similar to those used on the Marquis of the past few years, with a vertical bar theme divided by a thick center bar, and three rectangular sections on each side, each housing five vertical bars. Two sections were repeated in bumper openings. A stand-up hood ornament sat atop the front header panel. At the rear, large wraparound horizontal taillights were divided into three rows by horizontal chrome paint lines. Between the taillights was a small square body colored panel, then the backup lights, which flanked the license plate hous-

ing. Wagon models used a smaller wraparound rectangular version of the same design, with a small portion extending onto the tailgate door a few inches as a reflector. Along the bodysides were two parallel feature lines, with the upper running between the top edge of the parking/turn signal bezel and the top corner of the taillight bezel. The lower feature line was at the level of the bumper rub strips, and created a slight flare on the fenders as it passed over the wheel openings. Two vertical front fender louvers were quite similar to those on the Zephyr.

The Marquis interior was all about comfort and luxury, with all front seating choices offering fold-down center armrests, woodgrain instrument panel and door panel trim on all models, and a horizontal theme to the instrument cluster, much like that used by Cadillacs of the period. Square, chrome-lined gauges with white facings and black lettering were a unique Mercury touch, giving the Marquis a touch of class last seen in the 1930s. Ventilation and audio controls were in a center stack below the upper horizontal area. Model choices were basically the same, although two- and four-door sedans took the place of the former two-door hardtops and four-door pillared hardtops. Also, the Colony Park returned to model status after two years as an option package. Powering all of the new Marquis models was the highly regarded 302 CID V8 engine, with the long-running 351 CID V8 engine being optional. The large 400 CID and 460 CID V8 engines were no longer available in Ford passenger cars, as it was determined to be too difficult to tune them to meet EPA standards.

The sporty subcompact, the Bobcat, received a new front-end styling treatment as did its virtual twin, the Ford Pinto. A sloping front end design had recessed single rectangular headlamps with vertical parking/turn signal lamps set to the inward side in a chrome lined bezel, placed on each side of a vertical bar chrome grille. At the rear, the Bobcat shared taillights with the Pinto, using a new larger single lens taillight with the backup light mounted to the inside, but devoid of a chrome bezel, except on station wagons, which did not get an updated taillight. Finally, the Bobcat wagon's exterior woodgrain package, the Villager, was again an option package for 1979.

The remainder of the Mercury line was essentially unchanged. As previously mentioned the Cougar 2- and 4-door model line would disappear prior to the end of the model year, and the Cougar XR-7 would be downsized for 1980 and built from the "Fox" platform. The Zephyr and Monarch each added a few new options, such as tilt steering wheel for the Zephyr and new two-tone options for the Monarch.

Bobcat 2-Door Station Wagons
with Villager option shown in front

Bobcat 3-Door Hatchback with Sports package

Capri 2-Door Hatchback

Capri 2-Door Hatchback with RS package

Capri Turbo RS interior

Cougar 2-Door Hardtop Coupe

Cougar 4-Door Pillared Hardtop
with Brougham Décor Group option

Cougar XR-7 2-Door Hardtop Coupe
with Chamois Décor Group option

Grand Marquis 2-Door Sedan

Marquis 4-Door Sedan

Marquis Colony Park 4-Door Station Wagon

Monarch 2-Door Sedan

Monarch 4-Door Sedan with Ghia option

Zephyr 2-Door Sedan

Zephyr interior with Interior Accent group
and Brodie cloth trim

Zephyr 4-Door Sedan with Ghia option

Zephyr 4-Door Station Wagons
with Villager option shown in front

Zephyr Z-7 2-Door Sports Coupe

Model year production: 669,138, up 5.37% from 1978.
Domestic market share: 7.28% (6th place).
Base price range: $4,104 to $7,909.
Mercury average base price: $5,713, up 9.89%.
Introduction date: October 6, 1978.
Assembly plants: Atlanta, GA (A); Lorain, OH (H); Kansas City, MO (K); San Jose, CA (R); Metuchen, NJ (T); Wayne, MI (W); St. Thomas, Ontario, Canada (X); and St. Louis, MO (Z).
Data plate identification (VIN): Eleven digit code read as follows: First digit indicates year (9 = 1979); second digit indicates assembly plant code (see list above); third and fourth digits indicate model number (model number in model charts); fifth digit indicates engine code (see powertrain chart); remaining digits are sequential with beginning numbers of 600001. *Example:* 9K31F600001 is a 1979 Mercury Zephyr 2-Door sedan, with 302 CID, 2-bbl. V8 engine, serial number 600001, built in Kansas City (Claycomo), MO.

Powertrains

Engine	Net HP	Engine Code	Transmission Availability[1]		Bobcat	Capri	Zephyr	Monarch	Cougar	Marquis
140 CID (2.3L) OHC, 2-bbl., 4-cyl.	89	Y	4-speed manual		S	S	S	—	—	—
				MPG:	22	20	20/31	—	—	—
				Calif.	22	17	17/27	—	—	—
			3-speed Select-Shift automatic		$307	$307	$398 (Wgns.)[2]	—	—	—
				MPG:	21	20	20	—	—	—
				Calif.	20	18	18	—	—	—
140 CID (2.3L) OHC, 2-bbl., Turbo 4-cyl.	NA	W,A	4-speed manual		—	$542	—	—	—	—
				MPG:	—	18/30	—	—	—	—
				Calif.	—	17	—	—	—	—
170.8 CID (2.8L), 2-bbl., V6	93	Z	4-speed manual		—	$273[3]	—	—	—	—
				MPG:	—	20	—	—	—	—
				Calif.	—	NA	—	—	—	—
			3-speed Select-Shift automatic		$580[3]	$580[3]	—	—	—	—
				MPG:	19	18	—	—	—	—
				Calif.	NA	16	—	—	—	—
200 CID (3.3L), 1-bbl., 6-cyl.	96	T,B	4-speed manual w/overdrive		—	—	$241[2]	—	—	—
				MPG:	—	—	19	—	—	—
			3-speed Select-Shift automatic		—	—	$548 (Wgn.)[2]/ $639 (Cars)[4]	—	—	—
				MPG:	—	—	18	—	—	—
				Calif.	—	—	16	—	—	—
250 CID (4.1L), 1-bbl., 6-cyl.	98	L	4-speed manual w/overdrive		—	—	—	S[2]	—	—
				MPG:	—	—	—	18	—	—
			3-speed Select-Shift automatic		—	—	—	$307[4]	—	—
				MPG:	—	—	—	17	—	—
				Calif.	—	—	—	16	—	—
302 CID (5.0L), 2-bbl., V8	137	F	4-speed manual		—	$514[3]	$524[2,3]	$283[2,3]	—	—
				MPG:	—	15	15	15	—	—

Engine	Net HP	Engine Code	Transmission Availability[1]	Bobcat	Capri	Zephyr	Monarch	Cougar	Marquis
			3-speed Select-Shift automatic[4]	—	$821[3]	$831 (Wgn.)/ $922 (Cars)	$590[4]	S[2]	S (Wgns.)[2]/ S (Sdns.)
			MPG:	—	16	16	16	14	15
			Calif.	—	15	15	14	—	14
351 CID (5.8L), 2-bbl., V8	161	H	3-speed Select-Shift automatic	—	—	—	—	$263[4]	$263 (Wgns.)[4]/ $263 (Sdns.)
			MPG:	—	—	—	—	13	15
			Calif.	—	—	—	—	11	13

[1]Unless otherwise noted: All manual transmissions are floor-shift. All automatics are column-shift, except on Bobcat and Capri. Floor-shift is available for $37 extra on Zephyr and Monarch with optional bucket seats and automatic. Floor-shift w/bucket seats and console is also available for $259 on any Cougar 2-door, and for $184 on Cougar w/Brougham option and XR-7. [2]Not available in California. [3]Requires optional power brakes on Bobcat and Monarch. Requires optional power steering and power brakes on Capri and Zephyr. [4]Required (or standard) in California.

Major Options

	Bobcat	Capri	Zephyr	Monarch	Cougar	Cougar XR-7	Marquis
Air conditioning[1]	$484	$484	$484	$514	$562	$562	$597
Tilt steering wheel	—	$69	$69	$69	$75	$75	$76
Automatic speed control	—	$104	$104	$104	$125	$125	$130
Rear window defogger	—	—	$51	$51	—	—	—
Electric rear window defroster	S	$84	$90	$90	$99	$99	$100
Tinted glass, all windows	S	$59	$59	$64	$70	$70	$83
Dual remote control mirrors	$52	$30[2]	$35[2]	$59	$64	$64	$56
Manual front door vent windows	—	—	$41[3]	—	—	—	—
Power windows, 2-dr./4-dr.	—	—	$116/$163	$116/$163	$132/$187	$132	$137/$203
Power door locks, 2-dr./4-dr.	—	$4	$78/$107	$78/$107	$4	$4	$4
Power seat, 6-way w/std. seating	—	—	$94[5]	$94[5]	$163	$163	$164
Front bucket seats w/console[6]	S	$127	S	$84	$259	$184	—
Leather interior trim	—	$283	—	$283	—	$309	—
Dual facing rear seats (wagons)	—	—	—	—	—	—	$193
AM radio	S	$72	$72	$72	$79	$79	$79
AM/FM stereo	$89	$176	$176	$176	$192	$192	$192
AM/FM stereo w/tape[7]	$157	$243	$243	$243	$266	$266	$266
AM/FM stereo w/auto-search	—	—	—	$319	$349	$349	$432[1]
Vinyl top, full[8]	—	—	$90	$106	$170[8]	—	$143
Moonroof, power-operated[9]	$199[9]	$199[9]	$199[9]	$849	—	$789	—
Power trunk lid release	—	—	$22	$22	$4	$4	$4
Power steering, variable-ratio	$141	$141	$149	$149	S	S	S
Power brakes, w/front disc	$70	$70	$70	$70	S	S	S[10]
Deluxe wheel covers	N/C	—	S	$40	$43	—	S
Sport or Luxury wheel covers[11]	—	N/C	$41	—	$78	—	$93
Wire wheel covers	$33	$64	$93	$108	$162	$118	$118
Styled steel wheels w/trim rings	S	$65	$95	$114	$163	$166[11]	—
Cast aluminum sport wheels	$164	$240	$278	$278	$345	$301	—
Forged aluminum wheels	$164[11]	$240[11]	—	—	—	—	—
White sidewall tires, std. size	$43	$43	$43	$43	$47	$47	$47

Popular Option Groups & Packages

	Bobcat	Capri	Zephyr	Monarch	Cougar	Cougar XR-7	Marquis
Appearance protection group	$46	$41	$51	$51	$72	$66	$67
Bumper protection group	S	—	$58	$78	$63	$63	—
Brougham décor group	—	—	—	—	$221	—	—
Brougham option, 2-dr./4-dr.	—	—	—	—	$266/$278	—	—
Chamois décor group	—	—	—	—	—	$625	—

	Bobcat	Capri	Zephyr	Monarch	Cougar	Cougar XR-7	Marquis
Convenience group, 2-dr./4-dr.	$96	—	$51	$57	$147/$116	$147	$84
Décor group	—	—	—	$211	—	—	—
ES option package	—	—	$237	—	—	—	—
ESS option group	—	—	—	$524	—	—	—
Ghia option group	—	—	$428	$425	—	—	—
Grand Marquis decor group[12]	—	—	—	—	—	—	$586
Interior Accent group	$42	—	$72	—	—	—	—
Light group	$33	$28	$41	$46	$54	$54	—
Luxury exterior décor group	—	—	$102	—	—	—	—
Luxury interior package	—	—	$323	—	—	—	—
Power lock group, 2-dr./4-dr.	—	$99	—	—	$111/$143	$111	$116/$145
RS option package	—	$249	—	—	—	—	—
Sports Accent group/trim option	$247	—	—	—	—	—	—
Sports Instrumentation group	$94	—	$78	—	$149	$125	—
Sports Package option	$72	—	—	—	—	—	—
Turbo RS option package	—	$1,186	—	—	—	—	—
Villager option package	$111	—	$195	—	—	—	—
Visibility or Visibility/Light group	—	—	—	$64	—	—	$47
XR-7 décor group	—	—	—	—	—	$487	—

—= Not Available; S = Standard equipment. [1]Air conditioner w/automatic temperature control is available for $555 on Monarch, for $607 on Cougar/XR-7, and for $642 on Marquis. [2]LH remote standard on Capri. LH remote and RH manual on Zephyr. [3]Available on any model except the Zephyr Z-7. [4]Available only as part of the Power Lock group. [5]Power four-way seat on Zephyr and Monarch. [6]Bucket seats only on Bobcat; console not available. Capri has bucket seats standard; price is for console only. Zephyr is not available with console, and bucket seats are a $72 option on 6-cyl. or V8 equipped coupe and sedan models without the Luxury Interior package. For Monarch, bucket seats require décor, Ghia, or ESS option. For Cougar, available only on 2-doors. [7]Price for choice of eight-track tape or cassette tape. Citizens Band (CB) radio available on Monarch for $270 extra, and Cougar/XR-7 for $295 extra. Price for auto-search radio on Marquis includes eight-track tape. [8]Not available on station wagons. Full vinyl roof only available on Cougar 4-door sedan. [9]Manually operated, flip-up/removable type on Bobcat, Capri and Zephyr. [10]Power four wheel disc brakes available for $197 on Marquis. [11]Sport covers for Capri and Zephyr, Luxury covers for Cougar and Marquis. White forged aluminum wheels available on Bobcat at same price. Forged TRX type only for Capri. Cougar XR-7 price is for Styled road wheels. [12]Available only on Marquis Colony Park station wagon.

Paint Colors

	Code		Code
Black	1C	Pastel Chamois[1,2,7]	5P
Silver metallic	1G	Dark Brown metallic[8]	5Q
Dove Gray[1,2]	1N	Medium Vaquero Glamour	
Medium Gray metallic[3]	1P	metallic[3,4,6]	5W
Medium Red Glamour metallic[4,5,6]	2H	Antique Cream[2]	62
Dark Maroon[7]	2J	Bright Yellow[3,6]	64
Dark Red[1,2]	2M	Cream[8]	6P
Bright Red[3,8]	2P	Medium Pine Glamour metallic[4,7]	75
Light Medium Blue[3,6]	3F	Light Medium Pine[7]	76
Medium Blue Glamour metallic[4,6]	3H	Medium Jade Glamour metallic[1,4]	7L
Bright Blue[3]	3J	Light Chamois[2,3,6,8]	83
Dark Blue metallic[1,2,7,8]	3L	Tangerine[3]	85
Dark Jade metallic[1,2,3]	46	Medium Tan Glamour metallic[2,4]	8J
Dark Pine metallic[7,8]	4D	Dark Cordovan metallic[1,2,7]	8N
Medium Dark Orange Glamour		White	9C/9D
metallic[2,4,8]	5N		

In two-tone combinations, first two digits are lower color and second two digits are upper color. Two-tones available on Capri for $42, Zephyr sedans for $81, Zephyr Z-7 for $96, Monarch for $123, Cougar for $128, and Marquis for $129. Specific details for Bobcat colors are currently unavailable. [1]Available on Monarch. [2]Available on Cougar. [3]Available on Capri. [4]Glamour paints available for $41 extra on Bobcat and Capri, $48 on Zephyr and Monarch, and $64 on Cougar and Marquis. [5]Available on all except Monarch and base Cougar. [6]Not available on Capri RS or Turbo RS. [7]Available on Marquis. [8]Available on Zephyr.

Bobcat

"A fun-to-drive car."

Nameplate year of origin: 1975.
Current bodystyle lifespan: 1975 through 1980.
Predecessor to this model: None.
Replacement for this model: Lynx (1981 to 1985).

Measurements

	Runabout	Wagon
Wheelbase	94.5"	94.8"

Percentage of division's production: 6.69%.
Corporate siblings: Ford Pinto.
Primary competition: AMC Spirit, Dodge Omni 024, and Pontiac Sunbird.
Notable changes: Minor trim and detail changes.
Major standard equipment: All-vinyl low-back front bucket seats, color-keyed cut-pile carpeting, carpeted cargo area, fold-down rear seat, simulated woodgrain parking brake lever handle, shift knob, and I/P appliqué, deluxe two-spoke steering wheel, deluxe safety belts, AM radio, tinted glass, electric rear window defogger, bright window and belt moldings, B-pillar bright molding, rack-and-pinion steering, power front disc brakes, bumper protection group, styled steel wheels w/trim rings, and BR78 × 13 BSW tires. Wagon adds: Flip-out rear quarter windows, "Liftgate Ajar" warning system, and cargo area lamp.

Measurements (cont.)

	Runabout	Wagon
Length	169.3"	179.1"
Width	69.4"	69.7"
Height	50.6"	52.1"
Legroom — front	40.2"	40.2"
Legroom — rear	29.6"	29.6"
Headroom — front	37.3"	37.9"
Headroom — rear	35.8"	38.9"
Cargo capacity (cu. ft.)	6.1*	57.2
Fuel capacity (gals.)	13.0	14.0

*With rear seat folded down, 29.0 cu. ft.

Models Available

	Model No.	Base MSRP	Change from LY	Shipping Wt. (lbs.)	Model Year Production	Change from LY
Bobcat 3-Door Runabout (HBK)	20	$4,104	+6.57%	2424	35,667	+52.24%
Bobcat 2-Door Station Wagon	22	$4,410	+7.25%	2565	9,119	+3.16%
TOTALS	*Avg. price*	$4,257	+4.80%	*Production*	44,786	+38.79%

Capri

"The all-new '79 Capri. Created in the tradition of the original sexy European ... and built in America."

Nameplate year of origin: 1971 (originally used on 1952 Lincoln Capri).
Current bodystyle lifespan: 1979 through 1986.
Predecessor to this model: Capri (1971 to 1977, imported from Ford Europe).
Replacement for this model: Capri (1991 to 1994, imported from Ford Australia).
Percentage of division's production: 16.46%.
Corporate siblings: Ford Mustang.
Primary competition: AMC AMX, Chevrolet Camaro, Dodge Challenger, Plymouth Sapporo, and Pontiac Firebird.
Notable changes: All-new model.
Major standard equipment: Corinthian vinyl high-back bucket seats, fold-down rear seat, 10-oz. cut-pile carpeting, carpeted luggage area, soft vinyl door panels w/lower panel carpeting, color-keyed garnish moldings, woodtone I/P appliqués, full instrumentation including tachometer and warning lights, sport steering wheel, LH remote control mirror, dual paint stripes, bright windshield and side window moldings, black wraparound wide bodyside moldings w/dual color-keyed center stripes, black cowl grille, rack-and-pinion steering, manual front disc brakes, semi-styled wheels w/trim rings, and B78 × 13 BSW tires. Ghia adds: Edinboro cloth low-back bucket seats w/European-style headrests, deluxe color-keyed seat belts, passenger assist handle on roof rail, passenger visor vanity mirror, Light group, dual remote control rearview mirrors, deluxe sound insulation package, sport wheel covers, and BR78 × 14 BSW tires.

Measurements

Wheelbase	100.4"
Length	179.1"
Width	69.1"
Height	51.5"
Legroom — front	40.9"
Legroom — rear	29.8"
Headroom — front	37.2"
Headroom — rear	35.9"
Cargo capacity (cu. ft.)	10.0*
Fuel capacity (gals.)**	11.5**

*32.4 cu. ft. w/rear seat folded down. **12.5 gallons with air conditioning or optional engines.

Models Available

	Model No.	Base MSRP	Change from LY	Shipping Wt. (lbs.)	Model Year Production	Change from LY
Capri 3-Door Hatchback	14	$4,872	NEW	2424	92,432	NEW
Capri Ghia 3-Door Hatchback	16	$5,237	NEW	2565	17,712	NEW
TOTALS	*Avg. price*	$5,055	NEW	*Production*	110,144	NEW

Zephyr

"Ride-engineered. Sized for today."

Nameplate year of origin: 1978 (previously used on 1936–1942 Lincoln-Zephyr series).
Current bodystyle lifespan: 1978 through 1983.
Predecessor to this model: Comet (1971 to 1977).
Replacement for this model: Topaz (1984 to 1994).
Percentage of division's production: 18.74%.
Corporate siblings: Ford Fairmont.
Primary competition: AMC Concord, Dodge Aspen, and Pontiac Phoenix.
Notable changes: Minor trim and detail changes.
Major standard equipment: All-vinyl low back front bucket seats, cut-pile carpeting, integral door armrests w/door pull assist handle, two-spoke color-keyed steering wheel, simulated woodgrain appliqué around instrument cluster, upper

Measurements

	Sedans	Z-7	Wagon
Wheelbase	105.5"	105.5"	105.5"
Length	193.8"	195.8"	193.8"
Width	71.0"	71.0"	71.0"
Height	53.5"	52.2"	54.8"
Legroom — front	41.8"	41.8"	41.8"
Legroom — rear	35.4"	32.7"	35.4"
Headroom — front	38.3"	37.1"	39.0"
Headroom — rear	37.5"	36.1"	39.0"
Cargo capacity (cu. ft.)	16.8	16.1	79.7
Fuel capacity (gals.)	16.0	16.0	16.0

bodyside dual paint stripes, bright windshield and rear window moldings, bright drip rail moldings, bright rocker panel and wheel lip moldings, manual front disc brakes, modified strut front suspension, deluxe wheel covers, and B78 × 14 BSW tires. Wagon adds: Carpeted load floor area, cargo area light, liftgate "open" warning light, and BR78 × 14 BSW tires. Z-7 sport coupe adds: Deluxe seat trim, luxury door trim panels, color-keyed safety belts, high gloss simulated woodgrain appliqué on I/P, inside hood release, bright LH manual mirror, wrap-over roof design w/accent paint stripes, bright door window frames and belt moldings, lower bodyside protection molding w/vinyl insert, and deluxe sound insulation package,

Models Available

	Model No.	Base MSRP	Change from LY	Shipping Wt. (lbs.)	Model Year Production	Change from LY
Zephyr 2-Door Sedan	31	$4,253	+12.60%	2516	15,920	-42.47%
Zephyr 4-Door Sedan	32	$4,370	+13.12%	2580	41,316	-12.71%
Zephyr 4-Door Station Wagon	36	$4,647	+8.43%	2681	25,218	-22.63%
Zephyr Z-7 2-Door Sport Coupe	35	$4,504	+10.22%	2551	42,923	-3.69%
TOTALS	*Avg. price*	$4,444	+11.02%	*Production*	125,377	-17.61%

Monarch

"Sized right for the times with five passenger roominess."

Nameplate year of origin: 1975 (used on Canadian Ford brand from 1946 to 1961).
Current bodystyle lifespan: 1975 through 1980.
Predecessor to this model: None.
Replacement for this model: Cougar (1981 to 1982).
Percentage of division's production: 11.34%.
Corporate siblings: Ford Granada and Lincoln Versailles.
Primary competition: Buick Skylark, Dodge Diplomat, and Oldsmobile Omega.
Notable changes: Minor trim and detail changes.
Major standard equipment: Corinthian vinyl "Flight Bench" front seats w/fold-down center armrest, cut-pile carpeting, simulated burled walnut I/P appliqué, locking glove box, cigar lighter, luxury sound insulation package, bright window moldings, full-length upper bodyside molding, stand-up hood ornament, manual front disc brakes, full wheel covers, and DR78 × 14 BSW tires.

Measurements

	2-door	4-door
Wheelbase	109.9"	109.9"
Length	197.8"	197.8"
Width	74.0"	74.0"
Height	53.4"	53.4"
Legroom — front	40.6"	40.6"
Legroom — rear	33.9"	35.6"
Headroom — front	38.0"	38.2"
Headroom — rear	36.5"	37.6"
Cargo capacity (cu. ft.)	16.2	16.2
Fuel capacity (gals.)	19.2	19.2

Models Available

	Model No.	Base MSRP	Change from LY	Shipping Wt. (lbs.)	Model Year Production	Change from LY
Monarch 2-Door Sedan	33	$4,735	+8.45%	3070	28,285	-27.36%
Monarch 4-Door Sedan	34	$4,841	+8.62%	3111	47,594	-9.82%
TOTALS		Avg. price $4,788	+8.53%		Production 75,879	-17.27%

Cougar

"Stylish and affordable."

Nameplate year of origin: 1968.
Current bodystyle lifespan: 1977 through 1979.
Predecessor to this model: Montego (1972 to 1976).
Replacement for this model: Cougar (1981 to 1982).
Percentage of division's sales volume: 1.26%.
Corporate siblings: Ford LTD II.
Primary competition: Buick Century, Dodge Diplomat, Oldsmobile Cutlass, and Pontiac LeMans.
Notable changes: Minor trim and detail changes.
Major standard equipment: Cloth-and-vinyl front bench seat, color-keyed carpeting, simulated rosewood I/P appliqués, cut-pile color-keyed carpeting, two-spoke color-keyed steering wheel, deluxe sound package, windshield and rear window bright moldings, drip rail moldings, full wheel lip moldings, stand-up Cougar hood ornament, power steering, power front disc brakes, hubcaps, and HR78 × 14 BSW tires.

Measurements

	2-Doors	4-Doors
Wheelbase	114.0"	118.0"
Length	217.2"	221.2"
Width	78.6"	78.6"
Height	52.6"	53.3"
Legroom — front	42.1"	42.1"
Legroom — rear	32.8"	37.1"
Headroom — front	37.3"	38.0"
Headroom — rear	36.3"	37.0"
Cargo capacity (cu. ft.)	15.9	15.9
Fuel capacity (gals.)	21.0	21.0

Models Available

	Model No.	Base MSRP	Change from LY	Shipping Wt. (lbs.)	Model Year Production	Change from LY
Cougar 2-Door Hardtop	91	$5,379	+6.47%	3792	2,831	-86.77%
Cougar 4-Door Pillared Hardtop	92	$5,524	+6.66%	3843	5,605	-77.90%
TOTALS		Avg. price $5,452	+6.57%		Production 8,436	-81.96%

Cougar XR-7

"A unique personal car."

Nameplate year of origin: 1967.
Current bodystyle lifespan: 1977 through 1979.
Predecessor to this model: Cougar XR-7 (1974 to 1976).
Replacement for this model: Cougar XR-7 (1980 to 1983).
Percentage of division's production: 24.47%.
Corporate siblings: Ford Thunderbird.
Primary competition: Buick Regal, Dodge Magnum XE, Oldsmobile Cutlass Supreme, and Pontiac Grand Prix.
Notable changes: Minor trim and detail changes.
Major standard equipment: All-vinyl "Flight Bench" front seat w/fold-down center armrest, cut-pile carpeting, simulated baby burl walnut I/P appliqués, electric clock, deluxe steering wheel, courtesy lights, landau vinyl roof w/louvered opera windows, bodyside paint stripes, Cougar stand-up hood ornament, XR-7 sound package, power steering, power front disc brakes, specially tuned suspension system, XR-7 wheel covers, and GR78 × 15 BSW tires.

Measurements

Wheelbase	114.0"
Length	217.2"
Width	78.6"
Height	52.6"
Legroom — front	42.2"
Legroom — rear	32.7"
Headroom — front	37.3"
Headroom — rear	36.1"
Cargo capacity (cu. ft.)	15.7
Fuel capacity (gals.)	21.0

Models Available

	Model No.	Base MSRP	Change from LY	Shipping Wt. (lbs.)	Model Year Production	Change from LY
Cougar XR-7 2-Door Hardtop	93	$6,430	+12.41%	3883	163,716	-1.68%
TOTALS		Avg. price $6,430	+12.41%	Production	163,716	-1.68%

Marquis

"The most scientifically designed Marquis in history."

Nameplate year of origin: 1967.
Current bodystyle lifespan: 1979 through 1991.
Predecessor to this model: Marquis (1971 to 1978).
Replacement for this model: Grand Marquis (1992 to 2010).
Percentage of division's sales volume: 21.04%.
Corporate siblings: Ford LTD.
Primary competition: Buick Electra 225 and Estate Wagon, Chrysler Newport, Oldsmobile Ninety-Eight and Custom Cruiser, and Pontiac Bonneville and Grand Safari.
Notable changes: Completely redesigned.
Major standard equipment: Choice of Dynasty poly-knit cloth or Ruffino vinyl "Flight Bench" front seat w/fold-down center armrest, cut-pile carpeting, simulated woodgrain I/P and steering wheel appliqué, color-keyed four-spoke steering wheel, dome light, LH manual rear view mirror, sound insu-

Measurements

	2-Doors	4-Doors	Wagons
Wheelbase	114.3"	114.3"	114.3"
Length	212.0"	212.0"	217.7"
Width	77.5"	77.5"	79.3"
Height	54.5"	54.5"	56.8"
Legroom — front	42.0"	42.0"	42.0"
Legroom — rear	40.5"	40.5"	39.4"
Headroom — front	38.0"	38.0"	38.7"
Headroom — rear	37.3"	37.3"	39.2"
Cargo capacity (cu. ft.)	23.4	23.4	101.8*
Fuel capacity (gals.)	19.0	19.0	20.0

Includes 9.9 cu. ft. of hidden cargo space.

lation package, bright window moldings, rocker panel molding, front bumper guards, full wheel covers, and FR78 × 14 BSW tires. Wagon adds: Removable load floor carpet, cargo area light, lockable stowage compartment, three-way tailgate w/power tailgate window, rear bumper step pad, and GR78 × 14 BSW tires. Brougham adds: Ardmore cloth "Flight Bench" front bench seat w/fold-down center armrest, seatback side shields, 18-oz. Tiffany carpeting, luxury door panels w/lower carpeted panel and door pull assist strap, electric analog clock, LH remote control mirror, courtesy lights, power windows, luggage compartment light, vinyl roof (landau on two-door, and full on four-door), and hood and deck lid paint stripes. Grand Marquis adds: Cloth velour individually adjustable Twin Comfort Lounge seats w/individual fold-down center armrests, rear seat center armrests, digital clock, luxury steering wheel, visor vanity mirror, carpeted luggage compartment, dome/dual map reading light, tinted glass, bodyside, hood and deck lid paint stripes, B-pillar mounted coach lamps, and deluxe wheel covers. Colony Park adds to wagon: Brougham level carpeting and door panel trim, electric clock, power windows, door gate courtesy light switch and cargo area light, LH remote-control mirror, simulated rosewood appliqué on bodysides and door gate w/simulated woodtone/bright surround rails, and deluxe wheel covers.

Models Available

	Model No.	Base MSRP	Change from LY	Shipping Wt. (lbs.)	Model Year Production	Change from LY
Marquis 2-Door Hardtop	61	$6,292	+6.70%	3507	10,035	-10.21%
Marquis 4-Door Pillared Hardtop	62	$6,387	+7.36%	3557	32,289	+16.18%
Marquis 4-Door, 6-pass. Station Wagon	74	$6,701	+9.74%	3775	5,994	-64.50%
Marquis Brougham 2-Door Hardtop	63	$6,986	+7.07%	3540	10,627	+2.50%
Marquis Brougham 4-Door Pillared Hardtop	64	$7,176	+8.10%	3605	24,682	-5.18%
Marquis Colony Park 4-Dr., 6-p. Station Wagon	76	$7,495	NEW	3800	13,758	NEW
Grand Marquis 2-Door Hardtop	65	$7,721	+5.91%	3592	11,066	-29.17%
Grand Marquis 4-Door Pillared Hardtop	66	$7,909	+6.89%	3659	32,349	-14.31%
TOTALS		Avg. price $7,083	+8.25%	Production	140,800	-3.31%

OLDSMOBILE

"In man's search for a new measure of excellence ...
1979 Oldsmobile. Discover that great Olds feeling!"

Oldsmobile's big introduction for 1979 was the downsized version of its personal luxury coupe, the Toronado, which received its first major redesign since 1971, and was remade into a smaller, more sophisticated and fuel efficient coupe. Sales of the new Toronado would rise drastically, and the all-new car became the best-selling Toronado since the industry boom year of 1973. The 350 CID Diesel V8 engine, introduced last year, was available on the Toronado, and had become so popular that a diesel version of the smaller 260 CID V8 engine was introduced for the mid-size Cutlass line. The 4.3-liter diesel engine proved less popular than the 350, despite sales of around 38,000 diesel equipped Cutlass models, and would be canceled by year-end. In a year that brought a second gas crisis and the beginnings of a recession, more value and better gas mileage were high on consumers' list of important features, and Oldsmobile remarkably defied the industry trend for the lower and mid-range price segments, ending the year with a production increase over 1978.

The new Toronado was state of the art in design and engineering, both fortes of Oldsmobile. Having pioneered the modern day use of front-wheel drive in 1966, the Toronado not surprisingly assumed its most refined and well-equipped form to date for 1979. Styling was a fresh and modern take on the 1971–1978 design, with the front end looking very much like the 1978 model on a body nearly two feet shorter overall. Frontal styling continued the use of dual rectangular headlights set above horizontal parking and turn signal lamps, between a pointed front fender end cap and the grille, both of which jutted out slightly. The grille, which had a slight "V" shape when viewed from above, consisted of a horizontal crosshatch design five rows high and four columns across, set in the body-color front fascia, with each opening having a chrome lining. The name Toronado was in block letters across the header panel above the grille. Bodysides were smooth and slightly rounded, in the current GM design fashion, with a lower body feature line running between the tops of the front and rear bumpers, creating a flare over the round wheel openings. Like its corporate siblings, the Buick Riviera and Cadillac Eldorado, the Toronado took on a formal, upright roofline with angular edges, the rounded lower rear edge of the rear quarter window being the only curve to be found. This was accompanied by a flat rear window, leading into a high and relatively flat decklid that bent sharply down towards the bumper at the rear of the car.

Under the hood, Toronado was powered by the Oldsmobile 350 CID V8 engine, with the popular diesel version as an option. These were the smallest displacement engines ever used in the Toronado, but they were more than capable in a car that had lost nearly 900 pounds. Interiors were equally new, with a flat topped and flat faced instrument panel greeting front seat passengers. The new design was divided into two sections by a tall, vertical air conditioner vent in the center. Each side had a upper horizontal section outlined in chrome, housing air vents at each outer end, with a second vent on the left end of the passenger side, and the digital clock centered in a black trim panel. On the driver's side a square speedometer and other gauges were placed in the middle above the steering column, with warning lights to the left end and ventilation controls to the right. The lower portions of the instrument panel were covered in large expanses of simulated woodgrain, with the radio positioned below the ventilation controls, and a huge glove box on the passenger side. Add to that the "loose cushion" look seats and plush carpet, and it was a very luxurious looking interior — and more spacious than the much larger outgoing car. Standard features included air conditioning, AM/FM stereo radio with a power antenna, power windows, power door locks, and many others, yet surprisingly all of these new features and engineering came at a price increase only slightly above the industry average increase.

America's most popular car line, the Cutlass, received updated grilles and a few other detail changes, including the new 260 CID V8 diesel engine option, but were otherwise not greatly changed for the second season. The base Cutlass Salon grille carried three sections per side for 1979 with vertical bar inserts, while the Salon Brougham and Cutlass Cruiser introduced a vertical six slot design with horizontal bar inserts. The Supreme and Supreme Brougham still used the vertical bar theme that wrapped onto the top of the header panel, but this year it was divided into two sections per side with a thicker bar, and then each was further split into two sections by a slightly thicker center bar. The Calais had the most noticeable change, dispensing with the wrapover vertical bar theme in favor of a sporty new egg-crate opening five rows high and four columns across per side. One new model was added with the Cutlass Cruiser Brougham name being revived. The Cruiser Brougham took the place of the Cruiser wagon of last year, model H35, both of which were equivalent in trim level to the Salon Brougham. The Cutlass Cruiser name was moved to a new model number, G35, with features more closely related to the Salon trim level. The new Cutlass Cruiser was adverstised as a "new low-priced way to get a great Olds wagon."

The 4-4-2 appearance and handling package continued to be available on the Cutlass Salon coupe, and a special-edition Hurst/Olds option was offered for the first time since 1975. Based on the notchback Cutlass Calais coupe, the Hurst/Olds option featured the 350 CID, 4-barrel V8 engine used in the larger Delta 88 and Ninety-Eight models and was offered exclusively with the Hurst Dual-Gate shifter automatic transmission. The 2,499 units produced were available only in gold metallic over a choice of white or black paint, with gold cloth or vinyl upholstered bucket seats. There was not a possibility of building more of the H/O models, as the car had not been certified by the EPA, whose regulations stated that as long as an engine/transmission combination had been certified in any production model for that year, the same combination could be used in any other model that the factory desired, so long as fewer than 2,500 were produced. This regulation was also the reason for a 4-speed manual transmission not being offered.

Full-size Oldsmobiles all received front end updates that included revised grilles and, on the Delta 88 and Ninety-Eight, headlight bezels that allowed the headlights and parking lights to be set more nearly flush with the front panel surface. The Delta 88's new grille was of a horizontal cross-hatch configuration with four columns and twelve horizontal bars per side. The Custom Cruiser had an egg-crate pattern divided by the body-color center panel into two sections per side, each section being seven rows tall and six columns across. The largest Oldsmobiles continued to use a chrome covered center panel, with seven vertical openings per side, and each opening having a patterned insert eight rows high and two columns wide. There were no other significant changes, except that the 403 CID V8 engine was no longer offered in the Delta 88 series. Amazingly, the four-model lineup of Delta 88s accounted for nearly 25 percent of Oldsmobile's sales and production, about half of what the nine-model Cutlass series was achieving. Even more remarkable is that the Delta 88 Royale 4-Door Sedan actually outsold the highly popular Cutlass Supreme Brougham 2-Door Coupe in both 1978 and 1979, would continue to do so through the 1980s, and beginning in 1982, would even outsell the most popular Cutlass Supreme 2-Door Coupe — and hardly anyone noticed.

Starfire coupes received a new look with front and rear fascias being all new for their next to the last year. The new sloping nose housed single square headlamps and a taller new vertical bar grille that had two sections per side with the "rocket" logo in the center of the trademark Oldsmobile body colored panel. Each grille section had seven vertical bars, with the outer sections having a rectangular parking/turn signal lamp vertically mounted to the outer edge. A new hood conformed to the raised areas created by the new headlights and the more subtle dip of the center section. A domed section on the hood was outlined with a tape stripe on the Starfire with the GT option, and was blacked out with a tape stripe outline on the Firenza Sport option. The new rear panel was flat and vertical and carried two large non-wrap-around taillamp sections, with vertical backup lights set towards the center along each side of the license plate mounting. The rest of the Starfire features were much the same as they had been since its 1975 introduction, but Oldsmobile did add many commonly ordered features, such as AM radio, floor console, dual sport mirrors, and sport steering wheel, to the standard equipment list, adding value in what had become a competitive market for subcompact cars.

Finally, it was the last season for the rear-wheel-drive version of the compact Omega. With new GM X-cars due in the spring of 1979 as 1980 models, it is somewhat surprising that Oldsmobile made an effort to update anything on the Omega, but they did give it a new grille. While not a major change, the new grille had four sections per side, with four vertical bars per section. With the short four-month production year, sales and production tumbled, but any loss would be recovered quickly with the new front-wheel-drive 1980 Omega line.

Custom Cruiser 4-Door Station Wagon
with woodgrain trim option

Cutlass Calais 2-Door Coupe

Cutlass Cruiser 4-Door Station Wagon
with woodgrain trim option

Cutlass Salon 2-Door Coupe with 4-4-2 package

Cutlass Supreme Brougham 2-Door Coupe

Delta 88 4-Door Sedan

Omega Brougham 4-Door Sedan (front) and
Omega Brougham 2-Door Coupe (rear)

Toronado 2-Door Hardtop Coupe

Cutlass Salon Brougham 4-Door Sedan
(front) with 2-Door Coupe (rear)

Delta 88 interior with Holiday Coupe option

Ninety-Eight LS 4-Door Sedan

Starfire 2-Door Hatchback Coupe

Cutlass Supreme 2-Door Coupe

Delta 88 2-Door Coupe
with Holiday Coupe option

Ninety-Eight Regency 2-Door Coupe

Starfire 2-Door Hatchback line
with Firenza package (front),
GT package (center), and base (rear)

Toronado interior with leather upholstery

Model year production: 1,071,155, up 5.45% from 1978.
Domestic market share: 11.66% (3rd place).
Base price range: $4,095 to $10,112.
Oldsmobile average base price: $5,681, up 5.43%.
Introduction date: September 28, 1978.
Assembly plants: Southgate, CA (C); Doraville, GA (D); Linden, NJ (E); Framingham, MA (G); Van Nuys, CA (L); Lansing, MI (M); Arlington, TX (R); Kansas City/Fairfax, KS (X); Willow Run, MI (W); Fremont, CA (Z); St. Therese, Quebec, Canada (2) and Lordstown, OH (7).
Data plate identification (VIN): Thirteen digit code read as

follows: First digit indicates division (3 = Oldsmobile); second through fourth digits indicate series and body style (model number in model charts); fifth digit is engine code (see powertrain chart); sixth digit indicates model year (9 = 1979); seventh digit indicates assembly plant (see list above); remaining digits are sequential with beginning number of 100001. *Example:* 3L69R9X100001 is a 1979 Oldsmobile Delta 88 4-Door Town Sedan, with 350 CID, 4-bbl. V8 engine, serial number 100001, built in Kansas City/Fairfax, KS.

Powertrains

Engine	Net HP	Engine Code: VIN/GM	Transmission Availability[1]		Starfire	Omega	Cutlass	Delta 88	98 & Custom Cruiser	Toronado
151 CID (2.5L), 2-bbl., 4-cyl.	90	V/LX6[2]	4-speed manual		S	—	—	—	—	—
				MPG:	24/37	—	—	—	—	—
				Calif.	20	—	—	—	—	—
			5-speed manual[3]		$175	—	—	—	—	—
				MPG:	22/32	—	—	—	—	—
			3-speed Turbo Hydra-matic		$295	—	—	—	—	—
				MPG:	22/30	—	—	—	—	—
				Calif.	20	—	—	—	—	—
231 CID (3.8L), 2-bbl., 6-cyl.	115	A/LD5	3-speed manual[3]		—	S	S	—	—	—
				MPG:	—	18/26	18/26	—	—	—
			4-speed manual		$200	—	$135	—	—	—
				MPG:	16/23	—	16/23	—	—	—
				Calif.	14	—	—	—	—	—
			5-speed manual		$375	—	—	—	—	—
				MPG:	17/25	—	—	—	—	—
				Calif.	16/22	—	—	—	—	—
			3-speed Turbo Hydra-matic		$495	$335	$335	S	—	—
				MPG:	19/25	19/25	19/25	18/24	—	—
				Calif.	16/22	16/22	16/22	16/22	—	—
260 CID (4.3L), 2-bbl., V8	105	F/LV8	5-speed manual[3]		—	—	$450[4]	—	—	—
				MPG:	—	—	17/24	—	—	—
			3-speed Turbo Hydra-matic		—	—	$475	$140[3]	—	—
				MPG:	—	—	19/25	17/24	—	—
				Calif.	—	—	16	—	—	—
260 CID (4.3L), Diesel-FI, V8	90	P/LF7	5-speed manual		—	—	$1,045[4]	—	—	—
				MPG:	—	—	25	—	—	—
				Calif.	—	—	25	—	—	—
			3-speed Turbo Hydra-matic		—	—	$1,070[4]	—	—	—
				MPG:	—	—	24/32	—	—	—
				Calif.	—	—	24	—	—	—
301 CID (4.9L), 2-bbl., V8	135	Y/L27	3-speed Turbo Hydra-matic		—	—	—	$195[3]	—	—
				MPG:	—	—	—	17/24	—	—
305 CID (5.0L), 2-bbl., V8	130	G/LG3	4-speed manual		$395	$230[3]	—	—	—	—
				MPG:	15/22	15/22	—	—	—	—
			3-speed Turbo Hydra-matic		$690	$655[3]	—	—	—	—
				MPG:	18/24	16/22	—	—	—	—
				Calif.	14/21	—	—	—	—	—
305 CID (5.0L), 4-bbl., V8	160	H/LG4	4-speed manual[3]		—	—	$390[4]	—	—	—
				MPG:	—	—	15/23	—	—	—
			3-speed Turbo Hydra-matic		—	—	$590	—	—	—
				MPG:	—	—	17/24	—	—	—
				Calif.	—	—	15/21	—	—	—

Engine	Net HP	Code: VIN/GM	Engine Transmission Availability[1]		Starfire	Omega	Cutlass	Delta 88	98 & Custom Cruiser	Toronado
350 CID (5.7L), 4-bbl., V8[5]	165	L/LM1	3-speed Turbo Hydra-matic		—	$655	$655[6]	—	—	—
				Calif.	—	13	13	—	—	—
350 CID (5.7L), 4-bbl., V8	160[7]	R/L34	3-speed Turbo Hydra-matic		—	—	—	$320	S	S
				MPG:	—	—	—	16/22	15/22	16/22
				Calif.	—	—	—	14	14	14
350 CID (5.7L), Diesel-FI, V8	125	N/LF9	3-speed Turbo Hydra-matic		—	—	$1,230[6]	$895	$785	$785
				MPG:	—	—	22/30	21/29	20/28	21/29
				Calif.	—	—	21/29	21/29	21/29	21/29
403 CID (6.6L), 4-bbl., V8	175	K/L80	3-speed Turbo Hydra-matic		—	—	—	—	$70	—
				MPG:	—	—	—	—	14/20	—
				Calif.	—	—	—	—	13	—

[1]Unless otherwise specified: All 3-speed manuals are column-shift. All 4- and 5-speed manuals are floor shift. All automatics are column shift, except on Starfire. Floor shift automatic is optional on Omega, Cutlass and Delta 88 2-doors with other required equipment at extra cost. [2]Engine code for California is I/LS6. [3]Not available in California. [4]Except Cutlass Cruiser. [5]Available only in California or with high altitude emission equipment. [6]Available on Cutlass Cruiser only. [7]Horsepower rating for Toronado is 165.

Major Options

	Starfire	Omega	Cutlass	Delta 88	Custom Cruiser	Ninety-Eight	Toronado
Four-Season air conditioner[1]	$496	$529	$562	$605	$605	$605	S
Tilt-Away steering wheel	$68	$75	$75	$77	$77	$77	$77
Tilt-and-Telescope steering wheel	—	—	—	$121	$121	$121	$121
Cruise control	—	$103	$103	$108	$108	$108	$108
Electric rear window defroster	$87	$55[2]	$99	$101	$101	$101	$101
Tinted glass, all windows	$60	$64	$70	$84	$84	$84	S
Power windows, 2-dr./4-dr.	—	$126/$178	$132/$187	$138/$205	$205	S	S
Power door locks, 2-dr./4-dr.	—	$80/$111	$86/$120	$88/$122	$159[3]	$88/$122	S
Power front seat, 6-way w/std. seat	—	—	$163	$166	$166	$135[4]	S
Leather upholstery	—	—	$264[5]	$287	—	$264	$264
Front bucket seats, w/console[6]	S	$170	$165	$	—	—	—
Third row seat (wagons)	—	—	—	—	$193	—	—
AM radio	S	$82	$86	$99	$99	$99	—
AM/FM stereo	$148	$236	$236	$239	$239	$239	S
AM/FM stereo w/tape[7]	$250	$345	$345	$349	$349	$349	$110
AM/FM stereo w/CB radio[7]	—	—	$574	$581	$581	$581	$294
Dual remote control mirrors	—	—	$70	$70	$70	$97	$58
Woodgrain exterior panels (wagons)	—	—	$261	—	$243	—	—
Vinyl top, full	—	$99	$116[8]	$145	—	$164	—
Vinyl top, landau (coupes only)	—	$190	$194	$185	—	$200	$200
Hatch roof (T-top)	—	—	$655[9]	—	—	—	—
Sunroof, power operated, metal	—	—	$529	$725	—	$798	$798
Astroroof, power operated, glass	$180[10]	—	$729[10]	$925	—	$998	$998
Power trunk lid release	—	$24	$24	$25	—	$25	$25
Power steering, variable ratio	$146	$163	$163	S	S	S	S
Power brakes, w/front disc	$71	$76	$76[11]	S	S	S	S[12]
Deluxe wheel covers	—	$31	$41	$47	$47	S	S
Wire wheel covers	—	$140	$140	$120	$120	$120	$120
Chrome road wheels	—	—	—	$133	—	$133	—
Super Stock III (Rallye) wheels	S	$100	$88	$90	—	—	—
WSW tires, std. size	$36	$37	$40	$40	$40	$40	S

Popular Option Groups & Packages

	Starfire	Omega	Cutlass	Delta 88	Custom Cruiser	Ninety-Eight	Toronado
4-4-2 package	—	—	$276[13]	—	—	—	—

	Starfire	Omega	Cutlass	Delta 88	Custom Cruiser	Ninety-Eight	Toronado
Convenience group	—	$31	$49	$34	$23	$14	$14
Firenza Sport package	$375	—	—	—	—	—	—
GT package	$577	—	—	—	—	—	—
Holiday Coupe package	—	—	—	$288	—	—	—
LS package	—	$2,078	—	—	—	—	—
Regency LX package	—	—	—	—	—	$	—
SX package	—	$231	—	—	—	—	—
W30 H/O package	—	—	$2,054	—	—	—	—

—= Not Available; S = Standard equipment. [1]"Tempmatic" air conditioner with automatic climate control is available for $40 additional on Cutlass and $45 additional on Delta 88, Custom Cruiser, Ninety-Eight and Toronado. [2]Blower type defogger. [3]Includes power tailgate lock. [4]Standard on Ninety-Eight Regency. [5]Available on Cutlass Supreme Brougham only. [6]Bucket seats are standard on Cutlass Calais. Console is available for $80 on Cutlass Calais. Bucket seats are available on Omega coupes and hatchback, and on any Cutlass model except Brougham models. Available on Delta 88 coupes with Holiday package only. [7]Tape player is choice of 8-track or cassette, with cassette player priced $6 higher. Includes power antenna with CB radio. [8]Not available on Cutlass Cruiser. [9]Available on Supreme, Supreme Brougham and Calais coupes only. [10]Manual removable glass roof on Starfire. Available on Cutlass coupes only. [11]Standard on Cutlass Cruiser. [12]Power four-wheel disc brakes available for $205. [13]Price given is on Salon Coupe. Price on Salon Brougham is $122.

Paint Colors

	Code		Code
White[1]	11	Pastel Yellow[2]	54
Silver metallic	15	Gold metallic[1]	55
Gray metallic (two-tone only)	16	Medium Beige	61
Black[1]	19	Camel metallic	63
Pastel Blue[2]	21	Russet Firemist metallic[4]	67
Light Blue metallic	22	Dark Brown metallic	69
Bright Blue metallic[3]	24	Bright Red[3]	75
Dark Blue metallic	29	Carmine metallic	77
Gold Firemist metallic[4]	33	Dark Carmine metallic[2]	79
Pastel Green	40	Medium Blue metallic (two-tone only)	85
Medium Green metallic	44		
Bright Yellow[3]	51	Charcoal Firemist metallic[4]	98

In two-tone combinations, the first two digits indicate lower color and the next two digits are the upper color. Specific two-tone paint schemes available for $181 extra on Omega four-doors, Cutlass Salon and Salon Broughams, Delta 88, Ninety-Eight and Toronado. Firemist paints available for $165 extra. [1]White/Gold metallic and Black/Gold metallic paint combinations used on Hurst/Olds special edition. [2]Available on all models except Starfire and Omega. [3]Available only on Starfire and Omega. [4]Available only on Toronado.

Starfire

"Now all Starfires come with the sporty features you'd pay extra for in many other cars. What a value!"

Nameplate year of origin: 1954 (as designation for 98 convertible); 1961 (as series).
Current bodystyle lifespan: 1975 through 1980
Predecessor to this model: None.
Replacement for this model: Firenza (1982 to 1988).
Percentage of division's production: 1.90%.
Corporate siblings: Buick Skyhawk, Chevrolet Monza, and Pontiac Sunbird.
Primary competition: AMC Pacer and Mercury Capri.
Notable changes: Revised front and rear styling.
Major standard equipment: High-backed vinyl bucket seats, folding rear seatback, plush-pile carpeting on all floor surfaces and rear seatback, floor console with shifter, sport steering wheel, door panel map pockets, simulated woodgrain I/P and door appliqués, I/P gauges including tachometer, AM radio, chrome window surround and belt molding, rear stabilizer bar, manual front disc brakes, rallye wheels, and A78 × 13 BSW tires. SX adds: Choice of velour brushed knit or soft vinyl high-back bucket seats, chrome front and rear wheel lip moldings, bodyside striping, and BR78 × 13 BSW tires.

Measurements

Wheelbase	97.0"
Length	179.3"
Width	65.4"
Height	50.0"
Legroom — front	43.0"
Legroom — rear	29.6"
Headroom — front	37.7"
Headroom — rear	35.3"
Cargo capacity (cu. ft.)	27.8*
Fuel capacity (gals.)	18.5

With rear seat folded down.

1979

Models Available

	Model No.	Base MSRP	Change from LY	Shipping Wt. (lbs.)	Model Year Production	Change from LY
Starfire 2-Door Hatchback Coupe	T07	$4,095	+4.33%	2690	13,144	+41.87%
Starfire SX 2-Door Hatchback Coupe	D07	$4,295	+3.97%	2703	7,155	-11.18%
TOTALS	*Avg. price*	$4,195	+4.15%	*Production*	20,299	+17.19%

Omega

"Oldsmobile elegance. Practical size. Affordable price."

Nameplate year of origin: 1973.
Current bodystyle lifespan: 1975 through 1979.
Predecessor to this model: Omega (1973 to 1974).
Replacement for this model: Omega (1980 to 1984).
Percentage of division's production: 1.38%.
Corporate siblings: Buick Skylark, Chevrolet Nova, and Pontiac Phoenix.
Primary competition: Dodge Aspen and Mercury Monarch.
Notable changes: Minor trim and detail changes.
Major standard equipment: Choice of all-vinyl or soft knit fabric front bench seat, cut-pile carpeting, simulated woodgrain I/P appliqués, door-operated dome lamps, dual speed wipers w/washers, chrome window surround moldings, chrome front and rear wheel opening moldings, full wheel covers, and E78 × 14 BSW tires. Hatchback model adds: Fold-down rear seat. Brougham adds: Choice of tailored brushed knit cloth or patterned all-vinyl front bench seat, deluxe steering wheel, vinyl insert bodyside moldings, bright rocker panel molding, and stand-up hood ornament.

Measurements

	Coupe & HBK	Sedan
Wheelbase	111.0"	111.0"
Length	199.6"	199.6"
Width	69.9"	69.9"
Height	53.2"	54.2"
Legroom — front	41.7"	41.7"
Legroom — rear	32.4"	35.2"
Headroom — front	38.2"	39.1"
Headroom — rear	36.7"	37.1"
Cargo capacity (cu. ft.)	14.0*	12.6
Fuel capacity (gals.)	21.0	21.0

Hatchback maximum, 12.9 cu. ft.; with rear seat down, 30.2 cu. ft.

Models Available

	Model No.	Base MSRP	Change from LY	Shipping Wt. (lbs.)	Model Year Production	Change from LY
Omega 2-Door Coupe	B27	$4,181	+5.24%	3080	4,806	-69.26%
Omega 2-Door Hatchback	B17	$4,345	+5.00%	3157	956	-76.59%
Omega 4-Door Sedan	B69	$4,281	+5.76%	3118	5,826	-70.09%
Omega Brougham 2-Door Coupe	E27	$4,387	+4.98%	3091	1,078	-71.62%
Omega Brougham 4-Door Sedan	E69	$4,487	+5.48%	3149	2,145	-69.89%
TOTALS	*Avg. price*	$4,336	+5.29%	*Production*	14,811	-70.45%

Cutlass

"Millions of satisfied owners know there's something very special about a Cutlass."

Nameplate year of origin: 1961 (as F-85 Deluxe sport coupe designation); 1962 (as F-85 sub-series); and 1965 (as series designation); also used on 1955 Oldsmobile show car.
Current bodystyle lifespan: 1978 through 1988 (restyled in 1981).
Predecessor to this model: Cutlass (1973 to 1977).
Replacement for this model: Cutlass (1988 to 1997).

Measurements

	Salon Coupes	Salon Sedans	Supreme & Calais	Wagons
Wheelbase	108.1"	108.1"	108.1"	108.1"
Length	197.7"	197.7"	200.1"	197.0"
Width	72.2"	72.2"	72.2"	72.2"

Percentage of division's production: 52.63%.

Corporate siblings: Buick Century/Regal, Chevrolet Malibu/Monte Carlo, and Pontiac LeMans/Grand Am/Grand Prix.

Primary competition: Dodge Diplomat and Mercury Cougar.

Notable changes: New grille and minor trim and detail changes.

Major standard equipment: Brushed woven knit front bench seat, cut-pile carpeting, two-spoke steering wheel, bright window surround moldings, adjustable rear vent windows (2-doors), fixed rear seat window w/swing out

Measurements (cont.)

	Salon Coupes	Salon Sedans	Supreme & Calais	Wagons
Height	53.3"	53.3"	54.2"	54.5"
Legroom — front	42.8"	42.8"	42.8"	42.8"
Legroom — rear	35.1"	38.0"	36.3"	36.2"
Headroom — front	37.9"	38.7"	37.9"	38.5"
Headroom — rear	38.2"	37.7"	38.1"	38.8"
Cargo capacity (cu. ft.)	16.1	16.1	16.1	71.8
Fuel capacity (gals.)	18.1	18.1	18.1	18.2

rear quarter vent windows (4-door models), wheel lip moldings, rocker panel molding, wheel covers, and P185/75R14 BSW tires. Cutlass Cruiser adds: All-vinyl front bench seat, cut-pile carpeting on passenger and cargo floors, fold-down rear seat, rear door fixed window w/opening quarter vent window, and rear window liftgate w/drop-down tailgate. Salon Brougham and Supreme add: Choice of cloth-and-vinyl or all-vinyl custom sport front bench seat w/fold-down center armrest, simulated woodgrain I/P appliqués, luxury door panels with door pull straps, fixed rear quarter window (Supreme), and stand-up hood ornament. Cutlass Cruiser Brougham adds: All-vinyl front bench seat w/fold-down center armrest, cut-pile carpeting on passenger and cargo floors, fold-down rear seat, door pull straps, rear door fixed window w/opening quarter vent window, and rear window liftgate w/drop-down tailgate. Supreme Brougham adds: "Loose cushion" look velour with vinyl bolster 55/45 divided front seat w/fold down center armrest, deep-pile carpeting, wide rocker panel moldings, and deluxe wheel covers. Calais adds: Choice of brushed velour w/vinyl trim or soft all-vinyl reclining bucket seats, custom sport steering wheel, full gauge instrumentation including tachometer, specific front and rear stabilizer bars, special-ratio steering gear, and P195/75R14 BSW tires.

Models Available

	Model No.	Base MSRP	Change from LY	Shipping Wt. (lbs.)	Model Year Production	Change from LY
Cutlass Salon 2-Door Coupe	G87	$4,623	+4.88%	3060	8,399	-60.38%
Cutlass Salon 4-Door Sedan	G09	$4,723	+4.77%	3080	20,266	-7.47%
Cutlass Cruiser 4-Door, 2-Seat Station Wagon	G35*	$4,980	NEW	3201	10,755	NEW
Cutlass Salon Brougham 2-Door Coupe	J87	$4,907	+4.49%	3100	3,617	-66.33%
Cutlass Salon Brougham 4-Door Sedan	J09	$5,032	+4.92%	3127	18,714	-14.56%
Cutlass Cruiser Brougham 4-Dr., 2-S. St. Wgn.	H35*	$5,517	+4.88%	3245	42,953	-3.73%
Cutlass Supreme 2-Door Coupe	R47	$5,063	+4.56%	3091	277,944	+15.37%
Cutlass Supreme Brougham 2-Door Coupe	M47	$5,492	+4.67%	3116	137,323	+16.49%
Cutlass Calais 2-Door Coupe	K47	$5,491	+5.68%	3122	43,780	+7.19%
TOTALS	Avg. price	$5,092	+4.63%	Production	563,751	+6.85%

*Model numbers of Cutlass Cruisers were reassigned with new nameplates. See 1979 Oldsmobile introduction for details. Comparisons are made to the same model number.

Delta 88

"Space. Comfort. Fuel efficiency. Nice surprises for families who didn't think they could afford a full-size Oldsmobile."

Nameplate year of origin: 1965 (88 series began in 1949).

Current bodystyle lifespan: 1977 through 1985.

Predecessor to this model: Delta 88 (1971 to 1976).

Replacement for this model: Delta 88 (1986 to 1991).

Percentage of division's production: 23.80%.

Corporate siblings: Buick LeSabre, Chevrolet Impala and Caprice, and Pontiac Catalina and Bonneville.

Primary competition: Chrysler Newport and Mercury Marquis.

Notable changes: Revised grille and minor trim and detail changes.

Major standard equipment: Choice of nylon knit or all-vinyl front bench seat, cut-pile carpeting, cut-pile carpeting on lower door panels, deluxe steering wheel, simu-

Measurements

Wheelbase	116.0"
Length	217.5"
Width	76.8"
Height	55.2"
Legroom — front	42.4"
Legroom — rear	39.0"
Headroom — front	39.4"
Headroom — rear	38.2"
Cargo capacity (cu. ft.)	20.3
Fuel capacity (gals.)	25.0

1979

lated I/P woodgrain appliqué, electronic message center in I/P, courtesy and glove box lights, bright drip rail and window moldings, bright wheel opening and rocker panel moldings, front and rear bumper vinyl impact strips, stand-up hood ornament, full wheel covers, and FR78 × 15 BSW tires. Royale adds: Velour front bench seat w/fold-down center armrest, door pull straps, simulated woodgrain trim on door panels, glove box light, bright metal accented floor pedals, Royale ornamentation on C-pillar, and bodyside protective moldings.

Models Available

	Model No.	Base MSRP	Change from LY	Shipping Wt. (lbs.)	Model Year Production	Change from LY
Delta 88 2-Door Coupe	L37	$5,782	+5.45%	3462	16,202	-7.25%
Delta 88 4-Door Town Sedan	L69	$5,882	+5.81%	3488	25,424	+0.40%
Delta 88 Royale 2-Door Coupe	N37	$6,029	+5.64%	3471	60,687	-11.37%
Delta 88 Royale 4-Door Town Sedan	N69	$6,154	+5.98%	3513	152,626	+16.13%
TOTALS	Avg. price	$5,962	+5.72%	Production	254,939	+5.05%

Custom Cruiser

*"A working wagon with the elegance,
comfort and ride you expect from Oldsmobile."*

Nameplate year of origin: 1971 (1940 as a designation on 90 series cars).
Current bodystyle lifespan: 1977 through 1990.
Predecessor to this model: Custom Cruiser (1971 to 1976).
Replacement for this model: Custom Cruiser (1991 to 1992).
Percentage of division's production: 3.42%.
Corporate siblings: Buick Estate Wagon, Chevrolet Impala and Caprice, and Pontiac Catalina Safari and Bonneville Safari.
Primary competition: Mercury Marquis Colony Park.
Notable changes: Revised grille and minor trim and detail changes.
Major standard equipment: Choice of velour or all-vinyl front bench seat w/fold-down center armrest, cut-pile carpeting on floors and cargo compartment floor, lower door panel carpeting, simulated I/P woodgrain appliqué, electronic message center in I/P, courtesy and glove box lights, cargo area light, bright drip rail and window moldings, bright wheel opening and rocker panel moldings, three-way tailgate, full wheel covers, and HR78 × 15 BSW tires.

Measurements

Wheelbase	116.0"
Length	216.7"
Width	77.2"
Height	57.0"
Legroom — front	42.2"
Legroom — rear	38.4"
Headroom — front	39.1"
Headroom — rear	39.2"
Cargo capacity (cu. ft.)	87.0
Fuel capacity (gals.)	22.0

Models Available

	Model No.	Base MSRP	Change from LY	Shipping Wt. (lbs.)	Model Year Production	Change from LY
Custom Cruiser 4-Door, 2-S. Wagon	Q35	$6,742	+6.61%	4042	36,648	+6.25%
TOTALS	Avg. price	$6,742	+6.61%	Production	36,648	+6.25%

Ninety-Eight

"The thinking man's luxury car: Quiet comfort. Tasteful elegance."

Nameplate year of origin: 1941.
Current bodystyle lifespan: 1977 through 1984.
Predecessor to this model: Ninety-Eight (1971 to 1976).
Replacement for this model: Ninety-Eight (1985 to 1990).

Measurements

Wheelbase	119.0"
Length	220.4"
Width	76.8"

Percentage of division's production: 12.20%.

Corporate siblings: Buick Electra 225, Cadillac deVille, and Cadillac Fleetwood Brougham.

Primary competition: Chrysler New Yorker and Mercury Grand Marquis.

Notable changes: Revised grille and minor trim and detail changes.

Major standard equipment: Velour knit fabric w/vinyl trim front bench seat w/fold-down front and rear center armrests, cut-pile carpeting, carpeted lower door panels, door pull straps, driver's door armrest console, two-way power front seat, power windows, simulated woodgrain I/P trim, deluxe steering wheel, electronic message center in I/P, electric clock, wheel opening moldings, rocker panel molding, stand-up Oldsmobile crest hood ornament, bumper impact strips, wheel covers, and FR78 × 15 BSW tires. Regency adds: Velour 60/40 front seat button-tufted w/"loose" cushion look, front seatback pouches, six-way power adjustment for driver's side, digital clock, door-mounted entry courtesy lights, and fully lined trunk compartment.

Measurements (cont.)

Height	55.5"
Legroom — front	42.4"
Legroom — rear	40.1"
Headroom — front	39.4"
Headroom — rear	37.6"
Cargo capacity (cu. ft.)	20.3
Fuel capacity (gals.)	25.0

Models Available

	Model No.	Base MSRP	Change from LY	Shipping Wt. (lbs.)	Model Year Production	Change from LY
Ninety-Eight LS 2-Door Coupe	V37	$7,492	+6.06%	3806	2,104	-28.82%
Ninety-Eight LS 4-Door Sedan	V69	$7,673	+5.97%	3850	6,720	-26.44%
Ninety-Eight Regency 2-Door Coupe	X37	$7,875	+6.03%	3810	29,965	+4.87%
Ninety-Eight Regency 4-Door Sedan	X69	$8,063	+5.94%	3885	91,862	+17.62%
TOTALS	Avg. price	$7,776	+6.00%	Production	130,651	+10.01%

Toronado

"The all-new Toronado. A new level of engineering excellence."

Nameplate year of origin: 1966.

Current bodystyle lifespan: 1979 through 1985.

Predecessor to this model: Toronado (1971 to 1978).

Replacement for this model: Toronado (1986 to 1992, restyled in 1990).

Percentage of division's production: 4.67%.

Corporate siblings: Buick Riviera and Cadillac Eldorado.

Primary competition: Lincoln Continental Mark V.

Notable changes: Completely redesigned.

Major standard equipment: Velour "loose-cushion" look 50/50 split front seat w/fold-down center armrest and 6-way power driver's seat, rear seat fold-down center armrest, cut-pile carpeting, simulated woodgrain appliqué on I/P, power windows, power door locks, two-spoke steering wheel, digital clock, AM/FM stereo radio w/power antenna, chrome-accented floor pedals, Four-season air conditioning w/side window defroster system, LH remote-control rear view mirror, upholstered trunk and spare tire cover, bright window opening surround moldings, bright rocker panel and wheel lip moldings, front bumper guards, front and rear bumper rub strips, automatic ride level control, chrome wheel covers, and P205/75R15 WSW tires.

Measurements

Wheelbase	114.0"
Length	205.6"
Width	71.4"
Height	54.2"
Legroom — front	42.8"
Legroom — rear	39.4"
Headroom — front	37.9"
Headroom — rear	37.9"
Cargo capacity (cu. ft.)	16.5
Fuel capacity (gals.)	20.0

Models Available

	Model No.	Base MSRP	Change from LY	Shipping Wt. (lbs.)	Model Year Production	Change from LY
Toronado 2-Door Hardtop Coupe	Z57	$10,112	+13.63%	3731	50,056	+101.72%
TOTALS	Avg. price	$10,112	+13.63%	Production	50,056	+101.72%

PLYMOUTH

"That's imagination. That's Plymouth."

With the Fury no longer in the model lineup, the Volaré was the largest Plymouth model available. Originally deemed a compact model, it still was rated in that size class by EPA calculations; however, Plymouth tended to promote it as a mid-size car as it closely matched the downsized GM mid-size line in most exterior dimensions. New in Plymouth showrooms was a sporty 2-door version of the popular Horizon, named the TC3, and an imported Champ hatchback was added to the Japanese import line of Plymouth-badged cars. For this year only, there were more Japanese-built Plymouth models and series offered than there were American-built Plymouths. The duplication of every model except the Arrow in the Dodge lineup further suppressed Plymouth sales and production. Although Plymouth's imported cars nearly doubled their sales total for 1979, the Horizon and Volaré production total was down more than 15 percent for the model year.

Paralleling the Dodge Omni and Omni 024, the Horizon TC3 was marketed alongside its 4-door stablemate for the first few seasons before separated for the 1981 model year. Although built with differing chassis and body panels, they remained linked in the Plymouth lineup due to the common powertrains, series and model identifiers. Beginning in 1982, the Turismo name was introduced as a performance coupe using the Chrysler designed and built 2.2-liter 4-cylinder engine. For 1983, the Turismo name was applied to the entire 2-door line, marking the official separation of the Horizon 2-door and 4-door models.

The new TC3 rode on a slightly shorter wheelbase than the Horizon 4-door, but was 8 inches longer overall and much more aerodynamic looking in design. Its long sloping hood, slanted front fascia, and long sloping hatchback bore a similarity to GM's H-body cars, the Chevrolet Monza 2+2 and related corporate cars. The TC3 front end was devoid of chrome other than the small Plymouth nameplate on the driver's side of the front fascia, and sported single square headlights in a tunneled housing, with a horizontal five-slot, body-colored grille. The body-colored front bumper housed a lower open grille area and parking/turn signal lamps in a recessed pod directly below the headlights. At the rear, broad horizontal taillamps were divided into three sections with a large wraparound outer section containing the brake light and taillights, and a small inner section with an amber turn signal on top and backup lights below. A recessed license plate housing was set between the rear lights and below the rear hatch.

Bodyside lines of the TC3 were straight and full-length with the upper line running at a level just below the door handle, and the lower running between the top edges of the bumpers. The greenhouse area used a fairly narrow, nearly rectangular window for the rear seat passengers (with the trailing edge covered by nonfunctional louvers on all but the base trim level), an angled C-pillar, and a triangular window between the C-pillar and the slope of the hatchback. Inside, the interior was similar to that of the 4-door Horizon, with a small pod directly in front of the driver carrying round-dial instrumentation, and ventilation and radio controls in the center of the lower instrument panel area. A variety of option packages allowed the TC3 to be outfitted toward economy car, sport, or luxury. As for the Horizon 4-door, few changes were made to the successful subcompact.

Styling and trim on the 1979 Volaré basically followed the prior year's look and feel. For the Volaré coupes, most of the former "high-performance" options were gone, with only the Road Runner package surviving intact. A new Duster package carried some of the features of the prior year's Funrunner package. There was also a new Sport package for the coupe and station wagon that added mainly wheel flares and spoilers along with specific tape striping and exterior paint colors, and a performance-handling package. While the body features looked sporty, it was definitely more an appearance package than an actual performance upgrade.

Champ was the name given to the all-new imported four-seat hatchback built by Mitsubishi for sale in the United States, and also sold in identical form as the Dodge Colt. The Champ was rather mundane in terms of styling and design, with a black horizontal crosshatch grille set between single rectangular headlamps in a sloping front fascia, with turn signal/parking lamps set into the bumper ends. A faint bodyside feature line ran near the tops of the wheel openings, and a line on each side of the hood ran back from the inner headlight edge. Inside the Champ looked nicer, with a well thought out instrument panel design and some interesting interior fabric choices, including a red-and-white checked pattern in the optional Premium package. The engine was a typical Mitsubishi design in 1.4 or 1.6 liter displacement, with the MCA-Jet system and a hemi-head overhead cam. The transmission was an interesting "Twin-Stick" four-speed manual with a second stick that allowed the driver to choose power or economy modes. The Champ hatchback was basic transportation at its technological best, for 1979, and was a virtual twin to the new Dodge Colt FWD.

Rectangular headlights became standard for 1979 on all Arrow models, along with a new horizontal bar grille; otherwise the car had few changes. Released as a mid-year model was the "Fire Arrow" option package on the GT, which would become a regular model by the 1980 model year, replacing the Arrow GT. In addition to standard Arrow features, the sporty looking Fire Arrow featured a Warm White exterior with red accented, black tape striping and hood graphics, black and white checkmate cloth-and-vinyl reclining front bucket seats, dual racing mirrors, and cast aluminum road wheels, as well as a standard 2.6 liter "Silent-Shaft" engine with five-speed manual transmission. The luxury style Sapporo returned with no significant updates except the deletion of the standard chrome targa roof bar and canopy vinyl roof, which gave the sporty hardtop a more pleasant appearance.

Arrow 2-Door Hatchback
with Fire Arrow package

Arrow 2-Door Hatchback
with Fire Arrow package

Champ Custom 2-Door Hatchback

Champ instrument panel

Horizon 4-Door Hatchback

Horizon TC3 2-Door Hatchback

Horizon TC3 2-Door Hatchback
with Sport Appearance package

Horizon TC3 instrument panel

Sapporo 2-Door Hardtop

Volaré 2-Door Coupe with two-tone paint
and décor packages

Volaré 2-Door Coupe with Duster package

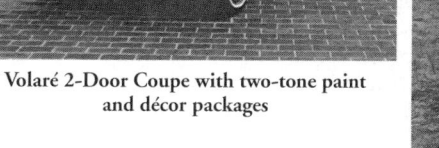

Volaré 4-Door Sedans

1979

Volaré 4-Door Station Wagon with Sport Wagon package (front) and Volaré 2-Door Coupe with Road Runner package (rear)

Model year production: 319,282, down 16.84% from 1978.
Domestic market share: 3.48% (9th place).
Base price range: $4,387 to $4,864.
Plymouth average base price: $4,610, up 0.50%.
Introduction date: October 5, 1978.
Assembly plants: Lynch Road, Detroit, MI (A); Belvidere, IL (D); Newark, DE (F). *Imports:* Arrow and Champ — Kurashiki, Okayama, Japan (code 1 through 9); Sapporo — Okazaki, Aichi, Japan (code 1 through 9).

Data plate identification (VIN): Thirteen digit code read as follows: First four digits indicate series and body style (model number in model charts); fifth digit indicates engine code (see powertrain chart); sixth digit indicates year (9 = 1979); seventh digit indicates assembly plant (see list above); remaining digits are sequential with beginning numbers of 100001. *Example:* HL41C9F100001 is a 1979 Plymouth Volaré 4-door sedan, with 225 CID, 1-bbl. 6-cylinder engine, serial number 100001, built in Newark, DE.

Powertrains[1]

Engine	Net HP	Engine Code	Transmission Availability[2]		Champ[3]	Arrow	Sapporo	Horizon	Volaré
86 CID (1.4L) OHC, 2-bbl., 4-cyl.	70	J	4-speed manual		S (base)	—	—	—	—
				MPG:	37	—	—	—	—
				Calif.	32	—	—	—	—
			"Twin-stick" 4-speed manual		S (base)	—	—	—	—
				MPG:	35	—	—	—	—
				Calif.	32	—	—	—	—
97.5 CID (1.6L) OHC, 2-bbl., 4-cyl.	77	K	4-speed manual		—	S	—	—	—
				MPG:	—	28	—	—	—
				Calif.	—	27	—	—	—
			"Twin-stick" 4-speed manual		S (Custom)	—	—	—	—
				MPG:	33	—	—	—	—
				Calif.	30	—	—	—	—
			5-speed manual		—	$101	S	—	—
				MPG:	—	26	27/36	—	—
			3-speed Automatic		—	$323	—	—	—
				MPG:	—	26	—	—	—
104.7 CID (1.7L) OHC, 2-bbl., 4-cyl.	70	A	4-speed manual		—	—	—	S	—
				MPG:	—	—	—	25/38	—
			3-speed Torque Flite automatic		—	—	—	$319	—
				MPG:	—	—	24		
155.9 CID (2.6L) OHC, 2-bbl., 4-cyl.	77	F	5-speed manual		—	$520	$419	—	—
				MPG:	—	22/35	22/34	—	—
				Calif.	—	22/35	21	—	—
			3-speed Automatic		—	$843	$742	—	—
				MPG:	—	21	21	—	—
225 CID (3.7L), 1-bbl., 6-cyl.	100	C	3-speed manual[4]		—	—	—	—	S[4]
				MPG:	—	—	—	—	18
			4-speed manual w/overdrive		—	—	—	—	$149[4]
				MPG:	—	—	—	—	18
			3-speed Torque Flite automatic		—	—	—	—	$319 (ex. wgns.)[5]
				MPG:	—	—	—	—	18
				Calif.	—	—	—	—	16

Engine	Net HP	Engine Code	Transmission Availability[2]		Champ[3]	Arrow	Sapporo	Horizon	Volaré
225 CID (3.7L) Super Six, 2-bbl., 6-cyl.[4]	110	D	3-speed Torque Flite automatic	MPG:	— —	— —	— —	— —	$362 18
318 CID (5.2L), 2-bbl., V8[4]	135	G	3-speed Torque Flite automatic	MPG:	— —	— —	— —	— —	$535 16
318 CID (5.2L), 4-bbl., V8	145	H	3-speed Torque Flite automatic	Calif.	— —	— —	— —	— —	$590 14
360 CID (5.9L), 4-bbl., V8[6]	195	L	3-speed Torque Flite automatic	MPG:	— —	— —	— —	— —	$894 13

[1]Optional axle ratios may be required on cars sold in California or high-altitude counties. [2]Unless otherwise noted: All transmissions are floor-shift, except on Volaré w/3-speed manual or automatic. Floor-shift is available for $35 extra on any Volaré w/3-speed manual transmission, or Volaré w/automatic transmission in combination with specific equipment or packages. [3]All Champ models shipped within the first 60 days of introduction have the 1.4L and 4-speed manual transmission as standard equipment, with a price adjustment credited to the price of the car. [4]Not available in California or designated high altitude areas. [5]Required as standard equipment in California and designated high altitude areas, with appropriate adjustment in price. [6]Available with federal emissions only in combination w/heavy duty package.

Major Options

	Champ	Arrow	Sapporo	Horizon	Volaré
Air conditioning	$517	$517	$517	$507	$507
Tilt steering wheel	S	S	S	—	$71
Automatic speed control	—	—	$107	—	$98
Electric rear window defroster[1]	S	$94[1]	S	S	$90
Tinted glass, all windows	S	S	S	$61	$61
Dual remote control sport mirrors	—	—	S	$61	$61
Power windows, 2-dr./4-dr.	—	—	$[2]	—	$120/$169
Power door locks, 2-dr./4-dr.	—	—	—	—	$76/$106
Power seat, bench	—	—	—	—	$153
AM radio	$84	$84[3]	—	S	$79
AM/FM stereo	$164[3]	$164[3]	$80	$141	$220
AM/FM stereo w/8-track tape	—	—	—	—	$314
Front bucket seats w/console	S[4]	S[4]	S	$32[4]	$202[4]
Vinyl top, full[5]	—	$107	—	—	$95
Sunroof, removable	$177	—	—	$176	—
T-Bar roof	—	—	—	—	$600
Power steering, standard w/V8s	$156	$177	S	$156	$156
Power brakes, w/front disc	S	S	S	$72	$72
Deluxe wheel covers	—	—	—	$41	$41
Premium wheel covers	—	—	—	—	$79
Wire wheel covers	—	—	—	—	$136
Rallye road wheels	—	—	—	$80	—
Chrome-styled road wheels	—	—	—	—	$136
Cast aluminum road wheels	$240	$240	S	$246	$280
White sidewall tires, std. size	S	$18	S	S	$45

Popular Option Groups & Packages

	Champ	Arrow	Sapporo	Horizon	Volaré
Arrow Jet package	—	$256	—	—	—
Basic group	—	—	—	—	$712
Basic package	—	—	$591	—	—
Custom exterior package	—	—	—	$74	$89
Custom interior package	—	—	—	$101	$191
Deluxe Insulation package	—	—	—	—	$50
Duster Coupe package	—	—	—	—	$60
Duster décor package	—	—	—	—	$90
Light package	—	—	—	$46	$46
Popular equipment group	—	—	—	$279	—

1979

	Champ	Arrow	Sapporo	Horizon	Volaré
Premier exterior package	—	—	—	—	$112
Premier interior package	—	—	—	—	$375
Premium exterior package	—	—	—	$199	—
Premium interior package	—	—	—	$270	—
Premium woodgrain exterior pkg.	—	—	—	$331	$232[6]
Premium package	$487	—	$486	—	—
Protection group	—	—	—	—	$38
Rallye equipment package	—	—	—	$352	—
Road Runner package	—	—	—	—	$594
Sport package	—	—	—	$340	—
Sport Wagon package	—	—	—	—	$630
Two-tone décor package	—	—	—	—	$96
Two-tone paint package	—	—	—	$164[7]	$142

— = Not Available; S = Standard equipment. [1]Electric rear window defroster is standard on GS and GT. [2]Available only as part of the Premium package. [3]AM radio not available on Arrow GT, and AM/FM radio is non-stereo. [4]Available on Volaré coupe. Bucket seats only are standard on Horizon with price above being for floor-shift console only. Bucket seats and console are standard on Champ Custom, Arrow GT, and on Champ, Arrow 160 and Arrow GS models bucket seats are standard, but without an available console. [5]Volaré Landau top on 2-door models is $174. Not available on Arrow GT or station wagons. [6]Called Premier exterior woodgrain package and available only on Volaré wagon. [7]Price is for Classic two-tone package on Horizon 4-door. Sport two-tone package on TC3 is $114.

Paint Colors

Domestic Plymouth Models	Code	Domestic Plymouth Models	Code	Champ, Arrow & Sapporo	Code
Spinnaker White	EW1	Flame Orange[3]	SV3	Ballast Sand metallic — All	C95
Cadet Blue metallic	PB3	Light Yellow[4]	SY2	Bright Silver metallic — All	H93
Pewter Gray metallic	RA2	Bright Yellow[5]	SY4	Charcoal metallic — Arrow	H96
Sable Tan Sunfire metallic[1,2]	RT9	Formal Black	TX9	Champagne metallic — Sapporo	K35
Smoke Gray metallic[2]	SA5			Canyon Red metallic — All	R94
Ensign Blue metallic	SB7	Champ, Arrow & Sapporo	Code	Light Tan — Champ, Arrow	S44
Nightwatch Blue metallic[3]	SC9	Green — Champ, Arrow	006	Black — Champ, Arrow	X15
Teal Frost metallic	SG4	Bright Blue metallic — Champ,		Dull Black — Fire Arrow only	X21
Teal Green Sunfire metallic	SG8	Arrow	022		
Turquoise metallic[3]	SQ6	Warm White — Champ, Arrow	061		
Chianti Red	SR5	Camel Tan metallic — Arrow	063		
Regent Red Sunfire metallic[1]	SR8	Spitfire Orange — Arrow	073		
Garnet Red Sunfire metallic[2]	SR9	Yellow — Arrow	090		
Light Cashmere	ST1	Light Blue metallic — Sapporo	B39		
Medium Cashmere metallic	ST5				

Single tones are coded EW1, EW1. Two-tones are coded on body ID plate as TX9, EW1 where three digits on line 2 are lower body color, and three digits on line 3 are upper body color or two-tone color. Import model two-tone options are not listed. [1]Available only on Volaré. [2]For use in two-tone combinations on Horizon. [3]Available only on Horizon and TC3. [4]Available only on Volaré Coupes. [5]Available only on TC3.

Champ

"Our new front-wheel drive import."

Nameplate year of origin: 1979.
Current bodystyle lifespan: 1979 through 1983.
Predecessor to this model: None.
Replacement for this model: Colt (1984 to 1988).
Primary competition: Chevrolet Chevette and Ford Fiesta.
Notable changes: All-new model.
Major standard equipment: Vinyl front bucket seats w/reclining seat backs, full-floor carpeting, fold-down rear seat, two-spoke steering wheel, trip odometer, tinted glass, flipper rear quarter windows, electric rear window defroster, front and rear window moldings, door and quarter window reveal moldings, front and rear rubber bumper guards, locking fuel filler door, power front disc brakes, and 6.15 × 13 WSW tires. Custom hatchback adds: Cloth-and-vinyl bucket seats w/reclining seat backs, floor console, rear shelf security panel, sports steering wheel, remote hatchback release, custom tape stripes, and 155SR × 13 WSW tires.

Measurements

Wheelbase	90.6"
Length	156.9"
Width	62.4"
Height	50.6"
Legroom — front	40.6"
Legroom — rear	29.7"
Headroom — front	36.8"
Headroom — rear	36.0"
Cargo capacity (cu. ft.)	6.5*
Fuel capacity (gals.)	10.0

*With rear seat down, 27.4 cu. ft.

Models Available

	Model No.	Base MSRP	Change from LY	Shipping Wt. (lbs.)	Model Year Sales*	Change from LY
Champ 2-Door Hatchback	1M24	$4,425	NEW	1730	NA	NEW
Champ Custom 2-Door Hatchback	1H24	$4,743	NEW	1775	NA	NEW
TOTALS	*Avg. price*	$4,647	NEW	*Production*	27,031	NEW

Model year sales by trim level not available.

Arrow

"Keeps you going ... easily."

Nameplate year of origin: 1976.
Current bodystyle lifespan: 1976 through 1980.
Predecessor to this model: None.
Replacement for this model: Champ (1979 to 1983).
Primary competition: AMC Spirit and Chevrolet Chevette.
Notable changes: Minor trim and detail changes.
Major standard equipment: All-vinyl front bucket seats w/reclining seatbacks, folding rear seat, black I/P trim, tilt steering column, two-speed electric windshield wipers, cigarette lighter, heater and defroster, tinted glass, black painted grille, argent painted bumpers, front and rear window moldings, drip rail moldings, power front disc brakes, and 6.00 × 13 BSW tires. GS adds: All-vinyl front bucket seats w/reclining seatbacks, woodtone I/P trim, full-floor carpeting including cargo area, ashtray light, trip odometer, right roof rail assist grip, flipper rear quarter windows, rear panel trim molding, rocker panel sill moldings, wheel lip molding, chrome plated bumpers, GS bodyside tape stripes, and styled road wheels. GT adds: Black and white checkmate cloth buckets seats w/reclining seatbacks, floor console w/ammeter, oil pressure gauge and coin holder, rally gauge cluster w/tachometer, overhead console for dome and map lights, and warning lights, soft-rim sports style steering wheel, dual body-color sport mirrors, GT lower body tape stripes, and 165SR × 13 R/WL tires.

Measurements

Wheelbase	92.1"
Length	167.3"
Width	63.4"
Height	51.0"
Legroom — front	41.7"
Legroom — rear	28.0"
Headroom — front	36.8"
Headroom — rear	34.4"
Cargo capacity (cu. ft.)	17.3
Fuel capacity (gals.)	13.2

1979

Models Available

	Model No.	Base MSRP	Change from LY	Shipping Wt. (lbs.)	Model Year Sales*	Change from LY
Arrow 2-Door Hatchback Coupe	7L24	$4,647	+10.49%	2100	NA	NA
Arrow GS 2-Door Hatchback Coupe	7H24	$5,005	+10.22%	2105	NA	NA
Arrow GT 2-Door Hatchback Coupe	7P24	$5,696	+9.56%	2140	NA	NA
TOTALS	*Avg. price*	$5,116	+10.05%	*Production*	21,829	-22.85%

Model year sales by trim level not available.

Sapporo

"The sports car with sophisticated ideas."

Nameplate year of origin: 1978.
Current bodystyle lifespan: 1978 through 1983.
Predecessor to this model: None.
Replacement for this model: Conquest (1984 to 1989 — sold under Chrysler name, 1987–1989).
Primary competition: Chevrolet Monza, Ford Mustang, Mercury Capri, and Pontiac Sunbird.
Notable changes: Minor trim and detail changes. Sold also as the Dodge Challenger.

Measurements

Wheelbase	99.0"
Length	183.1"
Width	66.5"
Height	51.8"
Legroom — front	40.6"
Legroom — rear	32.5"
Headroom — front	36.4"

Major standard equipment: Choice of velour cloth or all-vinyl front bucket seats
w/reclining seatbacks and lumbar support, easy entrance passenger seat w/memory,
loop pile carpeting, center floor console, door armrests w/integral door pull, assist
grips, dome and interior spot lamps, overhead console w/ digital clock and warning
lights, vanity mirror, two-spoke sport steering wheel, tilt steering column, I/P clus-
ter w/trip odometer, tachometer, temperature, fuel, oil, and electrical gauges, tinted glass, rear window defogger, dual power
color-keyed racing mirrors, drip rail and belt moldings, front and rear window moldings, decklid moldings, vinyl bodyside moldings, front and rear bumper guards, cast aluminum road wheels, and 195/70HR × 14 BSW tires.

Measurements (cont.)

Headroom — rear	35.0"
Cargo capacity (cu. ft.)	10.8
Fuel capacity (gals.)	15.9

Models Available

	Model No.	Base MSRP	Change from LY	Shipping Wt. (lbs.)	Model Year Sales*	Change from LY
Sapporo 2-Door Hardtop	3H29	$6,486	+6.55%	2410	12,322	-13.12%
TOTALS	Avg. price	$6,486	+6.55%	Production	12,322	-13.12%

*Model year production is not available.

Horizon

"Now there's even more confidence on the horizon."

Nameplate year of origin: 1978.
Current bodystyle lifespan: 1978 through 1990.
Predecessor to this model: None.
Replacement for this model: None.
Percentage of division's sales volume: 43.99%.
Corporate siblings: Dodge Omni.
Primary competition: Chevrolet Chevette and Ford Fiesta.
Notable changes: All-new 2-door hatchback model. Minor trim and detail
changes for 4-door.
Major standard equipment: Vinyl front bucket seats, color-keyed molded
headlining, color-keyed carpeting, door armrests, three-spoke steering
wheel, door armrests, fold-down rear seat, folding rear shelf security
panel, electric rear window defroster, AM radio, day/night inside rear
view mirror, bright liftgate window accents, bright aluminum front and
rear bumper face bars w/rub strips, manual front disc brakes, and
P155/80R × 13 WSW tires. TC3 adds: Cloth upholstered headliner, simu-
lated woodgrain I/P inserts, four-spoke sport steering wheel, deletes electric rear window defroster, AM/FM radio, remote hatchback release, bright sill and wheel lip moldings, wheel trim rings, and P165/75R × 13 WSW tires.

Measurements

	2-Door	4-Door
Wheelbase	96.7"	99.2"
Length	172.7"	164.8"
Width	66.0"	66.2"
Height	51.4"	53.7"
Legroom — front	42.5"	42.0"
Legroom — rear	28.6"	33.0"
Headroom — front	37.5"	38.3"
Headroom — rear	34.7"	37.4"
Cargo capacity (cu. ft.)	10.7*	10.5*
Fuel capacity (gals.)	13.0	13.0

*With rear seat folded down, 2+2 HBK is 33.8; 4-door HBK
is 36.1.

Models Available

	Model No.	Base MSRP	Change from LY	Shipping Wt. (lbs.)	Model Year Production	Change from LY
Horizon TC3 2-Door Hatchback	ML24	$4,864	NEW	2195	54,249	NEW
Horizon 4-Door Hatchback	ML44	$4,425	+12.40%	2135	86,214	-10.02%
TOTALS	Avg. price	$4,667	+17.37%	Production	140,463	+46.60%

Volaré

"Room, ride and comfort for less than you imagine."

Nameplate year of origin: 1976.
Current bodystyle lifespan: 1976 through 1980.
Predecessor to this model: Valiant (1967 to 1976).
Replacement for this model: Reliant (1981 to 1989).
Percentage of division's production: 56.01%.
Corporate siblings: Dodge Aspen.
Primary competition: AMC Concord, Chevrolet Nova, and Ford Granada.
Notable changes: Minor trim and detail changes.
Major standard equipment: All-vinyl low-back front bench seat, color-keyed carpeting, three-spoke steering wheel, two-speed electric windshield wipers and washers, front ashtray, bright grille surround molding, roof drip rail molding, quarter window reveal moldings, windshield and backlight moldings, front sway bar, and D78 × 14 BSW tires. Wagon adds: Rear liftgate, cargo area stowage bins, power front disc brakes, heavy-duty suspension, and ER78 × 14 BSW tires.

Measurements

	Coupe	Sedan	Wagon
Wheelbase	108.7"	112.7"	112.7"
Length	197.2"	201.2"	201.2"
Width	72.8"	72.8"	72.8"
Height	53.3"	55.3"	55.7"
Legroom — front	42.5"	42.5"	42.5"
Legroom — rear	31.7"	36.6"	36.6"
Headroom — front	37.4"	39.2"	39.2"
Headroom — rear	35.9"	37.5"	38.7"
Cargo capacity (cu. ft.)	16.2	16.2	73.1*
Fuel capacity (gals.)	18.0	18.0	19.5

An additional 0.6 cu. ft. in rear quarter panel bin storage.

Models Available

	Model No.	Base MSRP	Change from LY	Shipping Wt. (lbs.)	Model Year Production*	Change from LY*
Volaré 2-Door Sport Coupe	HL29	$4,387	+16.34%	3050	134,734	NA
Volaré 4-Door Sedan	HL41	$4,504	+15.52%	3115	NA	NA
Volaré 4-Door Station Wagon	HL45	$4,826	+13.79%	3325	44,085	-37.67%
TOTALS	Avg. price	$4,572	+15.16%	Production	178,819	-17.90%

Comparison to LY is not possible due to production of coupes and sedans being kept combined for 1979.

1979

PONTIAC

"Our Best Get Better."

The 1979 model year for the Pontiac line was one of refinement. The sporty Firebird line, now entering its ninth full model year with the second-generation body style, received a front-end facelift. The compact Phoenix line had a brief final season as a rear-wheel drive model, with production halted by December 1978. The new front-wheel-drive Phoenix would appear in showrooms by April 1979 and be sold as a 1980 model. The rest of the Pontiac line received new grilles, and some had new taillight designs, but mostly the year brought only refinements. Production held relatively steady for the year with a minuscule increase, highlighted by significant increases for the Sunbird, Firebird, LeMans, and Bonneville series.

Full-size Pontiac models received new grilles and taillight treatments, and no longer offered the 400/403 CID V8 engine option, except in California and high-altitude applications, making the 350 CID V8 engine the largest available in the 49-state configuration. The 350 CID V8 engine was Buick-built, leaving the 301 CID V8 engine as the only Pontiac-built engine available in the full-size line. The Catalina's new grille used a horizontal theme with three prominent horizontal bars forming four openings per side, and each opening having five short vertical bars. The center grille split continued to be chrome with the Pontiac arrow logo, and the combination side marker and turn signal lights now were divided into four sections, as on the 1978 Bonneville. Catalina's new taillights were still of the wraparound design, but now divided into only three sections horizontally with a vertical backup light on the inward end which was no longer divided by chrome trim into sections as in prior years. The Bonneville again used a vertically themed grille with five sections per side, but each opening now held fifteen horizontal bars, with additional sections in the oval bumper openings below. The Bonneville combination side-marker and turn signal light had a wide chrome strip dividing the lens into two sections horizontally, matching the design of this year's wraparound taillights. For station wagons, the Grand Safari name was replaced by the newly named Bonneville Safari, the first to bear that name since 1970. Grille designs for the wagons matched their respective series, while no changes were made to the taillight design. Catalina sales continued to slide as the Bonneville line expanded, catering to a variety of preferences, whether a Bonneville Brougham for buyers wanting pillow-soft velour seating and luxury amenities, or a Bonneville coupe for sports-minded drivers wanting newly available bucket seats and console with floor shifter, or the cargo-hauling Bonneville Safari mentioned above.

Nearly one in four new 1979 Pontiacs came from the Firebird series, and the Trans Am specifically broke an all-time sales and production record for the top performance model, with 117,108 being produced. A new front-end design distinguished this year's model; while still identifiably Pontiac, it was not the traditional look enthusiasts were used to, as the grilles were moved to a position within the body-colored urethane front bumper. Dual rectangular headlights were set into the sloping upper portion of the fascia with each unit placed in its own rectangular recess. Directly below, within a projecting bumper area were two horizontal pods housing a horizontal bar grille pattern creating five slot-type openings, and an outer parking/turn signal light. Around back, new full-width, horizontal slotted taillamps had black trim on most models, and body-colored trim on some of the specialty models. New interior upholstery improved interior comfort and appeal, while horsepower continued to rebound, with the 400 CID V8 engine for the 49-state setup reaching 220 horsepower.

While Trans Am's Special Edition package in black was still offered, with 11,554 being sold, the T-tops returned to optional status this year. A very special Limited Edition 10th Anniversary Trans Am was immediately recognizable, as its platinum silver metallic paint dominated the bodysides, trunk and forward portion of the hood, and wrapping over the roof, while dark charcoal paint covered the forward area of the roof, most of the hood, a small portion of the door beltline, and the front and rear bumper accents. On the hood was the biggest bird decal, or "screaming eagle" as Pontiac generally referred to it, that had ever appeared on the Trans Am. The decal was so large that each of the upper wing tips was a separate decal fitted to the fenders. The hood bird,

hood scoop engine call-outs, and various other Trans Am decals followed the general color theme of the car being finished in multiple hues of silver, charcoal, red, and black. To aid in the visual distinction between the anniversary model and standard Trans Ams, a new "turbine" style smooth, brightly polished, dished aluminum wheel was specific to the anniversary edition. A silver interior complete with silver carpeting and embroidered Firebird logo on the seats completed the unique look. The model was given its own unique model number of X87, with "X" usually reserved for special models, and was loaded with standard equipment as detailed in the Firebird model section that follows. The "RedBird" package, introduced at mid-year during the 1978 season, returned for a full season for 1979, with 4,248 Esprits being so equipped. The color series, which began in 1977 with the light blue "SkyBird," was targeted towards female buyers, since by 1979 women made up approximately 40 percent of Firebird sales. The success of the color series of "Birds" was so largely driven by women that they would eventually come to be known as the "Ladybirds."

Mid-size LeMans models received new grilles, each side in a four row by six column egg-crate pattern, with each square opening housing three vertical slots. Parking and turn signal lights were mounted behind the outer two columns of the grille. The fender side combination turn signal and side marker light was divided by chrome trim into four horizontal sections, with the base LeMans using an amber lens and the Grand LeMans series using a white lens with a thin vertical side marker light toward the rear edge. Similarly, taillights of coupes and sedans varied by trim level, with those of the base LeMans being divided into seven horizontal sections by chrome trim, and the Grand LeMans having two chrome strips, dividing the lens into three horizontal sections, and adding multiple vertical dividers creating small squares across the length of the lens, with three sections wrapping onto the side as the side marker light. Powertrains and interior details were mostly unchanged.

The sporty mid-size Grand Am continued to be available, but its performance, both on the road and in the showroom, was nowhere near the level of the original Grand Am. Styling was mostly unchanged on the outside, but inside brushed aluminum instrument panel trim with black gauge faces identified the new 1979 models. In an attempt to improve fuel economy and lower the base price, the Buick-built 231 CID V6 engine became standard equipment, which further diluted the sporting image that the Grand Am name was supposed to represent, and as a result sales and production dropped by nearly half from the prior season's already depressed level.

Always a popular model, the Grand Prix entered the new season with a new grille, new taillights, and new options that added a distinctive look. The new grille changed from a classic vertical theme to a sporty horizontal crosshatch appearance, having three columns and seven horizontal rows per side, with three sections extended into the front bumper openings. At the rear, the taillight lenses were divided by chrome trim strips into four vertical sections. Most other styling and standard features remained the same, although content of the LJ and base models was scaled back slightly. Two new options for the year allowed buyers to add a distinctive touch to their Grand Prix. Most obvious of the two was the new "double two-tone" paint treatment that featured a complementary second bodyside color. The second color was lined by tape stripes, top and bottom, with the upper line being about an inch below the fender tops and door windowsills as it ran the length of the car. The lower line was placed about two inches above the rocker panel molding and wheel opening moldings. This treatment was offered in seven color combinations, the most widely advertised combination being the Willow Mist green upper and lower body color with darker Jadestone green bodysides, typically shown with

the optional landau top. This car was also usually advertised with the new option of real wire wheels, the first such factory offering on Pontiacs since the early 1930s.

For the smaller Pontiac lines, only subtle differences could be found for the new year. Sunbird models received a new horizontally themed chrome grille with seven bars across, the middle of which was thicker. All models also had vertical rectangular parking/turn signal lights set behind the outer grille end, except on the Sport Safari where the grille ended at the lights. Again this year, all Sunbirds except the Sport Safari carried dual rectangular headlamps, while the wagon still carried the single round headlamps of its Astre predecessor. There were no significant changes for the Phoenix, other than the 151 CID 4-cylinder engine credit option being discontinued. Model year production of the Phoenix ended in December 1978, and start-up for production of the new front-wheel-drive Phoenix began in February 1979, for introduction in April as 1980 models.

Bonneville 2-Door Coupe

Bonneville Brougham 4-Door Sedan

Bonneville Safari 4-Door Station Wagon

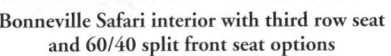

Bonneville Safari interior with third row seat
and 60/40 split front seat options

Catalina 4-Door Sedan

Firebird Esprit 2-Door Hardtop Coupe
with Red Bird package

Firebird Formula 2-Door Hardtop Coupe

Firebird Trans Am 2-Door Hardtop Coupe

Firebird Trans Am 2-Door
Hardtop Coupe with 10th
Anniversary package details

1979

Grand Am 2-Door Coupe

Grand Am 2-Door Coupe interior

Grand LeMans 4-Door Sedan

Grand LeMans Safari 4-Door Station Wagon

Grand Prix LJ 2-Door Hardtop Coupe

Grand Prix SJ 2-Door Hardtop Coupe

LeMans 2-Door Coupe

Phoenix 2-Door Coupe

Sunbird 2-Door Coupe

Sunbird Sport Safari 2-Door Station Wagon

Model year production: 907,412, up 0.78% from 1978.
Domestic market share: 9.88% (4th place).
Base price range: $4,016 to $10,620.
Pontiac average base price: $5,836, up 14.97%.
Introduction date: September 28, 1978.
Assembly plants: Lakewood, GA (A); Baltimore, MD (B); Van Nuys, CA (L); Norwood, OH (N); Pontiac, MI (P); Tarrytown, NY (T); Lordstown, OH (U); Willow Run, MI (W); Kansas City/Fairfax, KS (X); Oshawa, Ontario, Canada (1); and Ste. Therese, Quebec, Canada (2).
Data plate identification (VIN): Thirteen digit code read as follows: First digit indicates division (2 = Pontiac); second through fourth digits indicate series and body style (model number in model charts); fifth digit is engine code (see powertrain chart); sixth digit indicates model year (9 = 1979); seventh digit indicates assembly plant (see list above); remaining digits are sequential with beginning number of 100001. *Example:* 2D35U9B100001 is a 1979 Pontiac LeMans 4-Door Safari station wagon, with 305 CID, 4-bbl. V8 engine, serial number 100001, built in Baltimore, Maryland.

Powertrains

Engine	Net HP	Engine Code: VIN/GM	Transmission Availability[1]		Sunbird	Phoenix	Firebird[2]	LeMans & Grand Am[3]	Grand Prix	Catalina	Bonneville & Safaris
151 CID (2.5L), 2-bbl., 4-cyl.[4]	85	V/LX8	4-speed manual		S	—	—	—	—	—	—
				MPG:	24	—	—	—	—	—	—
			5-speed manual		$175	—	—	—	—	—	—
				MPG:	22	—	—	—	—	—	—
			3-speed Turbo Hydra-matic		$295	—	—	—	—	—	—
				MPG:	22	—	—	—	—	—	—
151 CID (2.5L), 2-bbl., 4-cyl.[5]	85	V/LS6	4-speed manual		S	—	—	—	—	—	—
				Calif.	20	—	—	—	—	—	—
			3-speed Turbo Hydra-matic		$295	—	—	—	—	—	—
				Calif.	20	—	—	—	—	—	—
231 CID (3.8L), 2-bbl., V6	105	A/LD5	3-speed manual[4]		—	S	S (F & FEs)	S (cs)	S (GP/LJ)	—	—
				MPG:	—	17	16	18	18	—	—
			4-speed manual		$200	—	—	$135 (cs)[4]	—	—	—
				MPG:	16	—	—	16	—	—	—
				Calif.	14	—	—	—	—	—	—
			5-speed manual		$375	—	—	—	—	—	—
				MPG:	17	—	—	—	—	—	—
				Calif.	16	—	—	—	—	—	—
			3-speed Turbo Hydra-matic		$495	$335	$335 (F & FEs)	S[6] (s)/ $335 (cs)	$335 (GP/LJ)	S	—
				MPG:	20	19	18	19/25	19/25	18/27	—
				Calif.	16	16	16	16	16	16	—
301 CID (4.9L), 2-bbl., V8[4]	140	Y/L27	3-speed Turbo Hydra-matic		—	—	S (FF)/ $530 (F & FEs)	$195 (s)/$530 (cs)	$530 (GP/LJ)	$195	S
				MPG:	—	—	17	18	18	17	17
301 CID (4.9L), 4-bbl., V8[4]	150	W/L37	4-speed manual		—	—	-$165 (credit-TA)/ N/C (FF)/ $450 (F & FEs)	$450 (cs)	$450 (cs)	—	—
				MPG:	—	—	15	16	16	—	—
			3-speed Turbo Hydra-matic		—	—	-$165 (credit-TA)/ N/C (FF)/ $635 (F & FEs)	$255 (s)/ $590 (cs)	S (SJ)/ $590 (GP/LJ)	$255	$60
				MPG:	—	—	16	17	17	16	16
305 CID (5.0L), 4-bbl., V8[7]	145	U/LG3	4-speed manual[4]		$395	$330	—	—	—	—	—
				MPG:	15	15	—	—	—	—	—
			3-speed Turbo Hydra-matic		$690	$530	S (FF)/ $635 (F & FEs)[5]	$255 (s)/ $590 (cs)[5]	S (SJ)/ $590 (GP/LJ)[5]	—	—
				MPG:	18	16	—	—	—	—	—
				Calif.	14	13	13	16	16	—	—
350 CID (5.7L), 4-bbl., V8	155	X/L77	3-speed Turbo Hydra-matic		—	—	—	—	—	$320[4]	$125[4]
				MPG:	—	—	—	—	—	15	15
350 CID (5.7L), 4-bbl., V8[5]	170	L/LM1	3-speed Turbo Hydra-matic		—	$565	$125 (FF)/ $565 (F & FEs)	$320 (s)	—	—	—
				Calif.	—	13	16	16	—	—	—

Engine	Net HP	Engine Code: VIN/GM	Transmission Availability[1]		Sunbird	Phoenix	Firebird[2]	LeMans & Grand Am[3]	Grand Prix	Catalina	Bonneville & Safaris
350 CID (5.7L), 4-bbl., V8[5]	170	R/L34	3-speed Turbo Hydra-matic		—	—	—	—	—	$320	$125
				Calif.	—	—	—	—	—	14	14
400 CID T/A (6.6L), 4-bbl., V8[4]	220	Z/L78	4-speed manual		—	—	S (TA)/ $340 (FF)	—	—	—	—
				MPG:	—	—	12	—	—	—	—
403 CID (6.6L), 4-bbl., V8[5]	185	K/L80	3-speed Turbo Hydra-matic		—	—	S (TA)/ $250 (FF)	—	—	—	$195
				Calif.	—	—	13	—	—	—	13

[1]Unless otherwise noted: All 3-speed manual transmissions are floor shift, except on Phoenix. All 4-speed and 5-speed manual transmissions are floor shift. All automatic transmissions are column shift, with the following exceptions: Sunbird and Firebird. Floor shift w/automatic is available on specific Phoenix, LeMans, Grand Prix and Bonneville models in combination w/optional bucket seats and console. [2]F = base Firebird, FEs = Firebird Esprit; FF = Firebird Formula; TA = Firebird Trans Am. [3]cs = Coupes and Sedans; s = Safaris. [4]Not available in California. [5]Available only in California or designated high altitude areas. [6]Standard on LeMans coupe and sedan in California. [7]Not available on Sunbird Safari wagon.

Major Options

	Sunbird	Firebird	Phoenix	LeMans & Grand Am	Grand Prix	Catalina & Bonneville
Custom air conditioning[1]	$496	$529	$529	$562	$562	$605
Tilt steering wheel	$68	$75	$75	$75	$75	$77
Automatic cruise control	—	$103	$103	$103	$103	$108
Intermittent windshield wipers	$35	$38	$38	$38	$38	$39
Rear window defroster, electric	$87	$99	$99[2]	$99	$99	$101
Dual sport mirrors, remote-control	$40	$43	$70	$70	$70	$71
Soft-Ray tinted glass, all windows	S	$64	$64	$70	$75	$84
Power windows, 2-dr./4-dr.	—	$132[3]	$126/$178	$132/$187	$132	$138/$205[4]
Power door locks, 2-dr./4-dr.	—	$86	$80/$111	$86/$120	$86	$88/$122[5]
Power front seat, 6-way w/std. seat	—	—	—	$163	$163	$166
Front bucket seats, w/console[6]	$77	$80	$275	$253	$155	$157
Third row seating (wagons)	—	—	—	—	—	$183
AM radio	S	$86	$82	$86	$86	$99
AM/FM stereo	$148	$236	$236	$236	$236	$239
AM/FM stereo w/8-track tape	$242	$345[3]	—	$345	$345	$349
AM/FM stereo w/cassette tape	$242	$351[3]	—	$351	$351	$355
AM/FM stereo w/CB radio	—	$674	—	$574	$574	$581
Remote trunk release	—	$24	—	$24	$24	$25
Vinyl top, full[7]	—	$116	$99	$116	$116	$145
Vinyl top, padded landau[8]	$156	—	$190	$236	$239	$298
Sunroof, removable[8]	$180	—	—	—	—	—
Sunroof, power steel[8]	—	—	—	$529	$529	$725
Sunroof, power glass[8]	—	—	—	$729	$729	$925
Hatch roof, glass panel T-tops	—	$655	—	—	$655	—
Power steering, variable-ratio	$146	S	$163	$163[9]	$163[9]	S
Power brakes, w/front disc	$71	$76[9]	$76	$76[9]	$76[9]	S
Custom finned wheel covers	—	—	$74	$74	$74	$75
Wire wheel covers	$71	$157	$157	$157	$157	$159
Rally II wheels[10]	$64	$146	$146	—	—	$147
Rally IV wheels	—	—	—	$126	$126	—
Cast aluminum "snowflake" wheels	$194	$310	—	$310	$310	$313
Wire wheels	—	—	—	$499[11]	$499	—
WSW tires	$35	$48	$46	$39	$59	$48

Popular Option Groups & Packages

	Sunbird	Firebird	Phoenix	LeMans & Grand Am	Grand Prix	Catalina & Bonneville
Custom exterior group	—	—	$97	$98	—	—
Custom trim group	—	$150	—	$157	—	—
Exterior appearance package	$91	—	—	—	—	$166
Lamp group	$18	$19	$29	$29	$23	$21
Luxury trim group	$190	—	—	$148	—	—
Rally RTS handling package	$149	S	$214	$133	$72	$180
Red Bird appearance package	—	$491	—	—	—	—
Special Edition Trans Am package	—	$674	—	—	—	—
W50 Formula appearance package	—	$92	—	—	—	—
W66 Formula appearance package	$466	—	—	—	—	—
WS6 Special performance package	—	$434	—	—	—	—

—= Not Available; S = Standard equipment. [1]Automatic climate control is available for $653 on LeMans, Grand Am, and Grand Prix, and for $688 on Catalina and Bonneville. [2]Blower type defroster available for $55. [3]Other optional equipment required at extra cost; i.e. console. [4]Standard on Bonneville Brougham. [5]Price on Catalina Safari and Bonneville Safari wagons is $156 and includes power tailgate lock. [6]Front bucket seats standard on Sunbird and Firebird, with console available on both. Bucket seats and console standard on Firebird Formula and Trans Am. Available on any Grand LeMans model, but not available on LeMans. On full-size models, available only on Bonneville coupe. Leather Viscount bucket seats are available on Grand Prix LJ for $349, and on SJ for $319. [7]Canopy style vinyl roof on Firebird, Esprit, and Formula. Vinyl roof is not available on any Safari wagon model, or on Sunbird hatchback models. [8]Available only on 2-door coupe models. [9]Power brakes standard on all Firebird Formula, Trans Am, and LeMans Safari station wagons. Power steering and power brakes standard on Grand Am and on Grand Prix LJ and SJ. Power 4-wheel disc brakes available on Firebird Formula and Trans Am for $150 extra. [10]Body-colored Rally II wheels also available. For Sunbird, Rally wheels are available. [11]Available only on Grand Am.

Paint Colors

	Code		Code
Cameo White	11	Montego Cream[1]	54
Platinum Silver metallic	15	Burnished Gold metallic (two-tone)[6]	56
Dark Charcoal metallic (two-tone)	16	Mission Beige[2]	61
Starlight Black	19	Sierra Copper metallic[7]	63
Sky Mist Blue[1]	21	Heritage Brown metallic[8]	69
Glacier Blue metallic[2]	22	Mayan Red[3]	75
Atlantis Blue metallic[3]	24	Carmine metallic[8]	77
Nocturne Blue metallic	29	Claret metallic[1]	79
Willow Mist Green[2]	40	Redbird Red (two-tone w/75 only)[9]	80
Jadestone Green metallic[4]	44	Blue metallic (two-tone)	85
Solar Gold metallic[5]	50		
Sundance Yellow[3]	51		

In two-tone combinations, the first two digits indicate lower color and the next two digits are the upper color. Colors without footnotes are available on all models. Two-tone colors available only on LeMans, Grand Prix, Catalina, and Bonneville (coupes and sedans only). Two-tone lower body accent paint available on Grand Am. Trans Am "Bird" hood decal available at $95 extra cost. [1]Available only on LeMans, Grand Am, Grand Prix, Catalina, and Bonneville models. [2]Available on all models except Grand Am and Firebird. [3]Available only on Sunbird, Firebird and Phoenix models. [4]Available on all models except Firebird. [5]Available on Firebird models only. [6]Available only on Grand Am. [7]Not available on Firebird Trans Am. [8]Available on all models except Grand Am and Firebird Formula. [9]Used only on Firebird w/Redbird option package.

Sunbird

"For the good times."

Nameplate year of origin: 1976.
Current bodystyle lifespan: 1976 through 1980.
Predecessor to this model: None.
Replacement for this model: J2000/Sunbird (1982 to 1993).
Percentage of division's production: 10.77%.
Corporate siblings: Buick Skyhawk, Chevrolet Monza, and Oldsmobile Starfire.
Primary competition: AMC AMX, Dodge Omni 024 and Plymouth Horizon TC3.
Notable changes: Minor trim and detail changes.
Major standard equipment: All vinyl front bucket seats, cut-pile carpeting, floor shifter and floor-mounted parking brake w/mini-console, deluxe cushion three-spoke steering wheel, simulated rosewood appliqués on I/P, distinctive door and

Measurements

	Coupe	Hatchback	Wagon
Wheelbase	97.0"	97.0"	97.0"
Length	179.2"	179.2"	178.0"
Width	65.4"	65.4"	65.4"
Height	49.8"	50.2"	49.8"
Legroom — front	43.0"	43.0"	43.0"
Legroom — rear	28.2"	29.6"	30.2"
Headroom — front	37.6"	37.7"	38.5"
Headroom — rear	37.2"	35.3"	40.1"
Cargo capacity (cu. ft.)	6.6	27.8*	46.6
Fuel capacity (gals.)	18.5	18.5	16.0

*Capacity with rear seat down.

1979

quarter panel trim, AM radio, tinted glass, bright front and rear window moldings, roof drip rail moldings, LH outside mirror, Sunbird exterior identification, argent colored grille, manual front disc brakes, hubcaps, and A78 × 13 BSW tires. Sport models add: Custom all-vinyl bucket seats, padded door trim, body-colored door handle inserts, dual body-colored sport mirrors w/LH remote, acoustical insulation package, bright windowsill moldings, bright wheel opening moldings, bright rocker panel moldings, bright rear end panel trim, chrome grille trim, and custom wheel covers. Hatchback adds: Fold-down rear seat, load-floor and rear seat back carpeting, and belt line molding. Sport Safari adds: Instrument panel assist straps, carpeted load floor, hubcaps, and B78 × 13 WSW tires.

Models Available

	Model No.	Base MSRP	Change from LY	Shipping Wt. (lbs.)	Model Year Production	Change from LY
Sunbird 2-Door Coupe	E27	$4,016	+11.87%	2593	40,560	+98.70%
Sunbird Sport 2-Door Coupe	M27	$4,274	+11.80%	2593	30,087	-7.63%
Sunbird Sport Hatch 2-Door Hatchback Coupe	M07	$4,379	+10.52%	2642	24,221	-4.57%
Sunbird Sport Safari 2-Door Station Wagon	M15	$4,321	+15.50%	2651	2,920	-65.55%
TOTALS	Avg. price	$4,248	+12.40%	Production	97,770	+12.65%

Firebird

"Announcing the birth of a bold new breed of wow! The 1979 Firebirds."

Nameplate year of origin: 1967.
Current bodystyle lifespan: 1970 through 1981.
Predecessor to this model: Firebird (1967 to 1969).
Replacement for this model: Firebird (1982 to 1992).
Percentage of division's production: 23.30%.
Corporate siblings: Chevrolet Camaro.
Primary competition: Ford Mustang and Mercury Capri.
Notable changes: Minor trim and detail changes.
Major standard equipment: All-vinyl front bucket seats, cut-pile carpeting, deluxe cushion steering wheel, simulated rosewood I/P appliqué, ashtray light, bright front and rear window moldings, Endura front and rear bumpers, trunk floor mat, variable-ratio power steering, manual front disc brakes, RTS package, hubcaps, and

Measurements

Wheelbase	108.2"
Length	198.1"
Width	73.0"
Height	50.4"
Legroom — front	43.8"
Legroom — rear	28.4"
Headroom — front	37.2"
Headroom — rear	36.0"
Cargo capacity (cu. ft.)	7.1
Fuel capacity (gals.)	21.0

FR78 × 15 BSW tires. Esprit adds: Custom all- vinyl front bucket seats, distinctive door trim panels, door and I/P assist straps, luxury cushion steering wheel, pedal trim plates, rear quarter ashtray, added acoustical insulation, dual body-colored mirror w/LH remote, body-colored door handle inserts, bright roof drip rail and belt reveal moldings, bright rear hood edge molding, bright wheel opening and rocker panel moldings, and deluxe wheel covers. Formula adds: Luxury cushion steering wheel, full-length front console, blacked-out grille, dual body-colored mirror w/LH remote, Formula identification, steel hood w/dual simulated hood scoops, power brakes, Trans Am front and rear stabilizer bars, Rally RTS package, Rally II wheels w/trim rings, and 225/70R15 BSW tires. Trans Am adds: Formula steering wheel, rally gauge cluster package w/electric clock, aluminum machine-turned I/P trim plate, dual body-colored mirror w/LH remote, blacked-out grille, front center air dam, wraparound rear deck spoiler, wheel opening air deflectors, front fender air extractors, Trans Am decal on front fender and rear spoiler, shaker hood scoop, power brakes, power flex fan, Safe-T-Track differential, firm control shocks, dual chrome splitter tailpipe extensions, Rally RTS package, Rally II wheels w/trim rings, and 225/70R15 BSW tires. Tenth Anniversary Trans Am features include: Silver leather specifically designed bucket seats w/vinyl bolsters and seatbacks, six-color screaming eagle bird embroidered on seatbacks, thick silver plush carpeting, silver color formula steering wheel w/black spokes and silver horn button, power windows, power door locks, electric trunk opener, additional sound insulation, mirrored T-tops, silver lower body and charcoal upper body two-tone exterior paint, red-silver-charcoal accent striping and "screaming eagle" hood decal, oversized Firebird B-pillar decals, turbine-style polished aluminum wheels, and WS6 Special Performance Package.

Models Available

	Model No.	Base MSRP	Change from LY	Shipping Wt. (lbs.)	Model Year Production	Change from LY
Firebird 2-Door Hardtop Coupe	S87	$5,260	+14.52%	3257	38,642	+18.27%
Firebird Esprit 2-Door Hardtop Coupe	T87	$5,638	+15.13%	3287	30,853	-16.45%
Firebird Formula 2-Door Hardtop Coupe	U87	$6,564	+18.63%	3460	24,851	+2.07%
Firebird Trans Am 2-Door Hardtop Coupe	W87	$6,883	+16.88%	3551	109,608	+17.43%
Firebird Trans Am 10th Anniversary 2-Dr. Coupe	X87	$10,620	NEW	3551	7,500	NEW
TOTALS	*Avg. price*	$6,993	+33.76%	*Production*	211,454	+12.90%

Phoenix

"Far from a common compact."

Nameplate year of origin: 1977.

Current bodystyle lifespan: 1975 through 1979 (Ventura 1975 to 1977; Phoenix 1977 to 1979).

Predecessor to this model: Ventura/Ventura II (1971 to 1974; restyled in 1973).

Replacement for this model: Phoenix (1980 to 1984).

Percentage of division's production: 2.74%.

Corporate siblings: Buick Skylark, Chevrolet Nova, and Oldsmobile Omega.

Primary competition: AMC Concord, Dodge Aspen, Ford Granada, and Mercury Monarch.

Notable changes: No significant changes.

Major standard equipment: Cloth-and-vinyl front bench seat, cut-pile carpeting, deluxe cushion three-spoke steering wheel, cockpit-style instrument cluster w/simulated rosewood I/P trim, bright front and rear window moldings, side window reveal moldings, bright drip rail moldings, bright wheel opening moldings, bright rear end panel, center body colored bumper pad, gray front and rear bumper rub strips, decklid lock cover, manual front disc brakes, hubcaps, and E78 × 14 BSW tires. Hatchback adds: Fold-down rear seat and load floor carpeting. LJ adds: Cloth front bench seat w/fold-down center armrest, padded door trim w/map pockets, I/P assist strap, added acoustical insulation, extra-wide ribbed rocker panel moldings w/front and rear extensions, front and rear gray bumper outer pads, stand-up hood ornament w/hood windsplit molding, and deluxe wheel covers.

Measurements

	Coupe & HBK	Sedan
Wheelbase	111.1"	111.1"
Length	203.4"	203.4"
Width	72.4"	72.4"
Height	52.7"	53.8"
Legroom — front	41.7"	41.7"
Legroom — rear	32.4"	35.2"
Headroom — front	38.2"	39.1"
Headroom — rear	36.7"	37.1"
Cargo capacity (cu. ft.)	13.9*	13.2
Fuel capacity (gals.)	21.0	21.0

Cargo capacity for hatchback with rear seat folded down is 29.2 cu. ft.

Models Available

	Model No.	Base MSRP	Change from LY	Shipping Wt. (lbs.)	Model Year Production	Change from LY
Phoenix 2-Door Coupe	Y27	$4,089	+4.66%	3127	9,233	-64.68%
Phoenix 2-Door Hatchback	Y17	$4,239	+3.31%	3200	923	-71.62%
Phoenix 4-Door Sedan	Y69	$4,189	+4.93%	3177	10,565	-67.52%
Phoenix LJ 2-Door Coupe	Z27	$4,589	+4.32%	3236	1,826	-70.60%
Phoenix LJ 4-Door Sedan	Z69	$4,689	+4.57%	3285	2,353	-71.96%
TOTALS	*Avg. price*	$4,359	+4.36%	*Production*	24,900	-67.46%

LeMans

*"It seems that everything about LeMans
is more than ample. Except its price."*

Nameplate year of origin: 1961 (as a Tempest subseries).
Current bodystyle lifespan: 1978 through 1981.
Predecessor to this model: LeMans (1973 to 1977).
Replacement for this model: 6000 (1982 to 1991).
Percentage of division's production: 14.44%.
Corporate siblings: Buick Century, Chevrolet Malibu, and
  Oldsmobile Cutlass.
Primary competition: Dodge Diplomat, Ford LTD II, and
  Mercury Cougar.
Notable changes: New grille and minor trim and detail
  changes.
Major standard equipment: Dover II cloth-and-vinyl front
  bench seat, cut-pile carpeting, deluxe cushion steering
  wheel, cockpit style instrument panel design, simulated regal

Measurements

	Coupes	Sedans	Wagons
Wheelbase	108.1"	108.1"	108.1"
Length	198.6"	198.6"	197.8"
Width	72.4"	72.4"	72.6"
Height	53.5"	54.1"	54.5"
Legroom — front	42.8"	42.8"	42.8"
Legroom — rear	35.1"	38.0"	35.9"
Headroom — front	37.9"	38.7"	38.8"
Headroom — rear	37.8"	37.7"	38.8"
Cargo capacity (cu. ft.)	16.6	16.6	72.4
Fuel capacity (gals.)	17.5	17.5	18.3

walnut vinyl accents on I/P, door panels and steering wheel, bin-type glove box, bright front and rear window moldings, bright roof drip rail and rear quarter window trim, wheel opening moldings, trunk mat, RTS suspension package, manual front disc brakes, hubcaps, and P185/75R14 BSW tires. Wagon adds: All-Morrokide vinyl front bench seat, textured steel cargo floor painted w/vinyl paint, swing up tailgate window and drop-down tailgate, stationary rear door glass w/swing-out rear quarter vents, power front disc brakes, and P195/75R14 BSW tires. Grand LeMans adds: Choice of all-vinyl or cloth-and-vinyl notch-back bench seat w/fold-down center armrest, luxury cushion steering wheel, padded upper door panels w/pull straps and carpeted lower panels, door lamp switches on all doors, bright rear hood edge molding, bright wheel opening moldings, black rocker panels, bright window sill moldings, body color door handle inserts, lower bodyside protective molding, and stand-up hood ornament w/hood windsplit molding. Grand LeMans Safari adds: All-Morrokide vinyl front bench seat, Grand LeMans interior door and I/P trim, plank-like woodgrain exterior vinyl appliqué panels w/woodtone trim, and simulated woodgrain inserts in outside door handles.

Models Available

	Model No.	Base MSRP	Change from LY	Shipping Wt. (lbs.)	Model Year Production	Change from LY
LeMans 2-Door Coupe	D27	$5,031	+13.64%	3036	14,197	-31.02%
LeMans 4-Door Sedan	D19	$5,134	+13.79%	3042	26,958	+18.61%
LeMans 4-Door, 2-Seat Safari Station Wagon	D35	$5,587	+12.19%	3200	27,517	+75.11%
Grand LeMans 2-Door Coupe	F27	$5,302	+10.44%	3058	13,020	-29.37%
Grand LeMans 4-Door Sedan	F19	$5,430	+10.48%	3087	28,577	+34.47%
Grand LeMans 4-Door, 2-Seat Safari Wagon	F35	$5,931	+11.69%	3234	20,783	+86.81%
TOTALS	*Avg. price*	$5,403	+11.99%	*Production*	131,052	+19.32%

Grand Am

*"The exhilarating '79 Grand Am.
It'll wind you up every time you drive it."*

Nameplate year of origin: 1973.
Current bodystyle lifespan: 1978 through 1980.
Predecessor to this model: Grand Am (1973 to 1975).
Replacement for this model: 6000 STE (1983 to 1989).
Percentage of division's production: 0.65%.
Corporate siblings: Buick Century, Chevrolet Malibu, and Oldsmobile
  Cutlass.

Measurements

	Coupe	Sedan
Wheelbase	108.1"	108.1"
Length	198.6"	198.6"
Width	72.4"	72.4"
Height	53.5"	54.1"

Primary competition: Ford Granada ESS and Mercury Monarch ESS.
Notable changes: Minor trim and detail changes.
Major standard equipment: Choice of Dover II cloth-and-vinyl or all-vinyl notchback front bench seat w/fold-down center armrest, cut-pile carpeting, deluxe cushion steering wheel, padded upper door panels w/pull straps and carpeted lower panels, cockpit-style instrument cluster w/brushed aluminum I/P trim, door lamp switches on all doors, bright front and rear window moldings, bright drip rail moldings, body color door handle inserts, lower bodyside protective molding, distinctive two-tone lower body and bumper paint treatment, power steering, manual front disc brakes, rally RTS suspension with front and rear stabilizer bars, hubcaps, and 205/70R14 BSW tires.

Measurements (cont.)

	Coupe	Sedan
Legroom — front	42.8"	42.8"
Legroom — rear	35.1"	38.0"
Headroom — front	37.9"	38.7"
Headroom — rear	37.8"	37.7"
Cargo capacity (cu. ft.)	16.6	16.6
Fuel capacity (gals.)	17.5	17.5

Models Available

	Model No.	Base MSRP	Change from LY	Shipping Wt. (lbs.)	Model Year Production	Change from LY
Grand Am 2-Door Coupe	G27	$5,530	+0.18%	3080	4,021	-48.23%
Grand Am 4-Door Sedan	G19	$5,529	-1.86%	3084	1,865	-34.35%
TOTALS	Avg. price	$5,530	-0.85%		Production 5,886	-44.51%

Grand Prix

"The most Grand Prix of all."

Nameplate year of origin: 1962.
Current bodystyle lifespan: 1978 through 1987.
Predecessor to this model: Grand Prix (1973 to 1977).
Replacement for this model: Grand Prix (1988 to 1996).
Percentage of division's production: 23.15%.
Corporate siblings: Buick Regal, Chevrolet Monte Carlo, and Oldsmobile Cutlass Supreme/Calais.
Primary competition: Dodge Magnum XE, Ford Thunderbird, and Mercury Cougar XR-7.
Notable changes: New grille and minor trim and detail changes.
Major standard equipment: Choice of cloth-and-vinyl or all-vinyl front notchback bench seat w/fold-down center armrest, cut-pile carpeting, deluxe cushion steering wheel, simulated regal walnut inlay trim on I/P, padded upper door panels w/lower panel carpeting and door pull straps, I/P courtesy lights, electric clock, bright front and rear window moldings, bright side window sill and drip rail moldings, bright rear hood edge molding, stand-up hood ornament w/bright hood windsplit molding, bright wheel opening moldings, wide rocker panel moldings, trunk mat, front and rear bumper rub strips, manual front disc brakes, RTS package, hubcaps, and 195/75R14 BSW tires. LJ adds: Velour "loose-pillow" look notchback front bench seat w/fold-down center armrest, custom stitched instrument panel, luxury cushion steering wheel, luxury carpet, pedal trim plates, velour door panel inserts, dual body-colored sport mirrors w/LH remote control, LJ identification, wide rocker panel moldings w/extensions, power steering, power front disc brakes, and deluxe wheel covers. SJ adds: All-vinyl front bucket seats w/center floor console, custom color-keyed seat belts, custom stitched instrument panel, custom sport leather-wrapped steering wheel, brushed aluminum I/P trim, pedal trim plates, rally gauge cluster w/trip odometer, electric clock, added acoustical insulation, dual body-colored sport mirrors w/LH remote control, wide rocker panel moldings w/extensions, bodyside accent tape stripes, RTS package, power steering, power front disc brakes, and custom finned wheel covers.

Measurements

Wheelbase	108.1"
Length	201.4"
Width	72.7"
Height	53.3"
Legroom — front	42.8"
Legroom — rear	36.3"
Headroom — front	37.6"
Headroom — rear	37.8"
Cargo capacity (cu. ft.)	16.1
Fuel capacity (gals.)	15.0

Models Available

	Model No.	Base MSRP	Change from LY	Shipping Wt. (lbs.)	Model Year Production	Change from LY
Grand Prix 2-Door Hardtop Coupe	J37	$5,454	+11.76%	3126	124,815	-1.92%
Grand Prix LJ 2-Door Hardtop Coupe	K37	$6,555	+12.73%	3285	61,175	-6.06%

	Model No.	Base MSRP	Change from LY	Shipping Wt. (lbs.)	Model Year Production	Change from LY
Grand Prix SJ 2-Door Hardtop Coupe	H37	$6,814	+11.93%	3349	24,060	-33.29%
TOTALS	*Avg. price*	$6,274	+12.16%	*Production*	210,050	-8.05%

Catalina

"Catalina is our most affordable full-size car."

Nameplate year of origin: 1950 (as hardtop model designation), 1959 (as series).
Current bodystyle lifespan: 1977 through 1981.
Predecessor to this model: Catalina (1971 to 1976).
Replacement for this model: Parisienne (1983 to 1986) and Safari (1987 to 1989).
Percentage of division's production: 5.17%.
Corporate siblings: Buick LeSabre, Chevrolet Impala/Caprice, and Oldsmobile Delta 88.
Primary competition: Dodge St. Regis and Ford LTD.
Notable changes: New grille and minor trim and detail changes.
Major standard equipment: Cloth-and-vinyl front bench seat, cut-pile carpeting, deluxe cushion steering wheel, simulated regal walnut I/P accent trim, ashtray w/light, glove box light, trunk mat, brushed aluminum B-pillar appliqué (coupe), bright windshield and rear window moldings, bright quarter window and roof drip rail moldings, bright rocker panel molding, bright hood rear edge molding, front and rear bumper rub strips, stand-up hood ornament w/hood windsplit molding, RTS package, hubcaps, and FR78 × 15 BSW tires. Safari wagon adds: All-Morrokide vinyl front bench seat, three-way tailgate w/power-operated rear window, rear bumper guards, and HR78 × 15 BSW tires.

Measurements

	2-door	4-door	Wagon
Wheelbase	116.0"	116.0"	116.0"
Length	214.3"	214.3"	215.9"
Width	76.4"	76.4"	80.0"
Height	54.5"	54.9"	58.0"
Legroom — front	42.4"	42.4"	42.2"
Legroom — rear	38.1"	39.0"	37.7"
Headroom — front	38.8"	39.4"	39.6"
Headroom — rear	38.2"	38.2"	38.4"
Cargo capacity (cu. ft.)	20.3	20.3	88.7
Fuel capacity (gals.)	21.0	21.0	22.0

Models Available

	Model No.	Base MSRP	Change from LY	Shipping Wt. (lbs.)	Model Year Production	Change from LY
Catalina 2-Door Coupe	L37	$6,020	+10.68%	3476	5,410	-41.35%
Catalina 4-Door Sedan	L69	$6,076	+10.80%	3508	28,121	-29.18%
Catalina Safari 4-Door, 2-Seat Station Wagon	L35	$6,681	+11.15%	3997	13,353	+4.17%
TOTALS	*Avg. price*	$6,259	+10.88%	*Production*	46,884	-24.07%

Bonneville

"This year Bonneville's going to put some distance between itself and the rest of the full-size pack."

Nameplate year of origin: 1957.
Current bodystyle lifespan: 1977 through 1981.
Predecessor to this model: Bonneville (1971 to 1976).
Replacement for this model: Bonneville "Model G" (1982 to 1986).
Percentage of division's production: 19.77%.
Corporate siblings: Buick LeSabre, Chevrolet Impala/Caprice, and Oldsmobile Delta 88.
Primary competition: Chrysler Newport and Mercury Marquis.

Measurements

	2-door	4-door	Wagon
Wheelbase	116.0"	116.0"	116.0"
Length	214.3"	214.3"	215.9"
Width	76.4"	76.4"	80.0"
Height	54.5"	54.9"	58.0"
Legroom — front	42.4"	42.4"	42.2"
Legroom — rear	38.1"	39.0"	37.7"
Headroom — front	38.8"	39.4"	39.6"

Notable changes: New grille and minor trim and detail changes.

Major standard equipment: Choice of special pattern velour cloth or all-vinyl notchback front seat w/fold-down center armrest, cut-pile carpeting, luxury door panels w/lower door panel carpeting, door pull straps, deluxe cushion steering wheel, simulated walnut vinyl I/P accents, courtesy light

Measurements (cont.)

	2-door	4-door	Wagon
Headroom — rear	38.2"	38.2"	38.4"
Cargo capacity (cu. ft.)	20.3	20.3	88.7
Fuel capacity (gals.)	21.0	21.0	22.0

switches on all doors, ashtray w/light, glove box light, sunburst medallion on B-pillar appliqué (coupe) or C-pillar (sedan), luggage compartment mat and light, bright windshield and rear window moldings, bright hood rear edge molding, fixed rear quarter window, wide rocker panel moldings w/rear extensions, bright wheel opening moldings, stand-up hood ornament w/hood windsplit molding, rear fender skirts, RTS package, deluxe wheel covers, and FR78 × 15 BSW tires. Safari wagon adds: All-Morrokide vinyl front bench seat, door pull straps, three-way tailgate w/power-operated rear window, delete rear fender skirts, simulated woodgrain Safari siding and tailgate appliqués, and HR78 × 15 BSW tires. Brougham adds: Velour "loose-pillow" look luxury trim 60/40 split front seat w/fold-down center armrest, custom door panels w/pull straps and lower panel carpeting, luxury cushion steering wheel, RH visor vanity mirror, electric clock, power windows, rear quarter courtesy lights, custom pedal trim plates, chrome LH remote-control mirror, added acoustical insulation, bright window sill moldings, and velour luggage compartment trim w/spare tire cover.

Models Available

	Model No.	Base MSRP	Change from LY	Shipping Wt. (lbs.)	Model Year Production	Change from LY
Bonneville 2-Door Coupe	N37	$6,593	+11.50%	3616	34,127	+51.61%
Bonneville 4-Door Sedan	N69	$6,718	+11.54%	3672	71,906	+47.81%
Bonneville Safari 4-Door, 2-Seat Station Wagon	N35	$7,050	+11.57%	4022	16,925	+22.23%
Bonneville Brougham 2-Door Coupe	Q37	$7,395	+10.80%	3659	39,094	+8.02%
Bonneville Brougham 4-Door Sedan	Q69	$7,584	+11.79%	3726	17,364	-3.25%
TOTALS	*Avg. price*	$7,068	+11.44%	*Production*	179,416	+28.94%

1979

1980

Before the 1980 model year was in full swing, several events occurred that would define the year. The most important was a second fuel shortage that caused an increase in gasoline prices to nearly double their level a year earlier, pushing them across the $1 per gallon mark in most places. Second, a recession began around the same time period, and rising energy costs pushed the economy further downwards, to what would become the worst recession since World War II. Finally, the industry was in its third year of the fuel economy requirements introduced for the 1978 model year. For 1980, the new CAFE requirement was 20 miles per gallon. The 1980 EPA estimates were usually advertised this year as ⑲/26, with the circled number being the EPA mileage estimate and the second number being the manufacturer's highway estimate. (In this book, however, mileage estimates are reported in the format of city mpg/highway mpg, when the information is available; otherwise it is the single EPA estimate.) It had become clear to the manufacturers that to continue meeting the higher requirements to come, they would have to invest more time and money in their power-trains and in designing more aerodynamically efficient cars. With computer technology becoming less expensive, at least by 1980 standards, it became clear that computers could be used to aid in meeting their goals.

General Motors would have the most remarkable year of the four major manufacturers, selling two out of three new 1980 model year cars on the road. In fact, GM was down only about 3 percent from 1979, while the rest of the industry was running about 20 percent lower on average. It should be noted here that GM's new X-cars had the benefit of a 16-month model year, instead of the traditional 12-month, but even on an adjusted basis, General Motors still carried 63 percent of the market. Another industry bright spot was American Motors, whose redesigned and newly named Spirit model, combined with the innovative new Eagle four-wheel-drive car line, led the fourth largest manufacturer to an 18 percent production increase over the 1979 model year.

Fully 18 percent of 1980 model year cars were one of the four new GM X-body cars, introduced in April of 1979: the Chevrolet Citation, Pontiac Phoenix, Oldsmobile Omega or Buick Skylark. Almost unbelievably, fully one in ten new 1980 cars sold was a Chevy Citation. The remarkable season for GM in the midst of a worsening recession can be attributed to the luck of their timing. A fuel shortage was the perfect time to introduce new compact cars with better fuel mileage than any of their competition. General Motors also brought out a more aerodynamically styled line of full-size cars in the fall, improving upon the original downsized cars' fuel efficiency, and introduced restyling for some of the mid-size models, all of which combined to keep traffic in the showrooms. The new compact car line came in four different basic body styles of two- and four-door hatchbacks and notchback coupes and sedans, though not all four were available from every division. All four divisions also made a point to offer a sporty version of the X-car, either as a separate model or as an option package: the Citation X11, Phoenix SJ, Omega SX and Skylark Sport. Price hikes of up to 35 percent may have held back some of the GM X-cars from having even better sales, but in fact GM had been holding back on the 1978 and 1979 price hikes to better compete with the newer Dodge Aspen/Plymouth Volaré and Ford Granada/Mercury Monarch models. GM also opened a new plant in Oklahoma City, Oklahoma, specifically to build the new X-body cars. The plant was soon joined by others including Willow Run, Michigan, which had built X-body cars for many years.

Another completely redesigned car was the popular Cadillac Seville. Now built on the front-wheel-drive platform of the Cadillac Eldorado, the radically styled Seville was a unique modern take on the "bustle-back" sedans of the 1930s. It was a love it or hate it design, and sales, though not horrible, were never as good as the original Seville's through the six years the new design was sold. The previously downsized full-size GM cars were given an aerodynamic makeover this year as well as being lightened by a hundred pounds on average, adopting new high-pressure, lower rolling resistance radial tires, and getting power from a resized range of engines. The main visual features were lowered front-end lines and higher rear deck lids to improve airflow over the cars.

GM introduced a new sedan body design for the Buick Century and Oldsmobile Cutlass four-doors, both of which sorely needed the improvement. Having experienced poor sales with the four-door fastback design introduced with the 1978 downsizing of the mid-size line, GM wisely switched to a formal roofline, notchback sedan for these two models. The result looked much like the original Seville's roofline, and sales soared for these four-door models. The new roofline would be added to the Chevrolet Malibu and Pontiac LeMans lines for 1981. Other GM models were mostly unchanged, with some expected annual updates and some juggling of powertrain combinations for more fuel efficiency. Models entering their final year were the H-bodied Chevrolet Monza, Oldsmobile Starfire, Buick Skyhawk, and Pontiac Sunbird. Production of the Monza and Sunbird extended into December 1980, making way for their new J-car replacements as early 1982 models: the Chevy Cavalier, Pontiac J2000, Oldsmobile Firenza and Buick Skyhawk. The extended production time prompts some sources to speculate that there were Monzas and Sunbirds sold as 1981 models, though no marketing material was found to support this possibility. The J-cars would be a full line of two- and four-door models, including station wagons. Also in its final season was the Pontiac Grand Am, which had not lived up to the original model's Euro-sedan intentions. The concept would reappear in 1983 as the Pontiac 6000 STE and meet with more success. The Grand Am name itself would reappear in 1985 with much more success as the replacement for the compact Pontiac Phoenix. GMC and Chevrolet truck models were given small updates, with the ElCamino and Caballero changes following those of the Chevy Malibu. The full-size truck lines would get a makeover of the 1973–1980 bodystyle for the 1981 model year.

American Motors had come out of the 1979 season with record profits, but was still lacking the cash it needed to develop new models and sustain long-term profitability. As always their engineers' innovative spirit came through, with the announcement of a new four-wheel-drive line of cars named the Eagle. Advertised as the American Eagle, the new car was developed using the Concord body placed on a chassis that used sophisticated 4WD technology gained from the Jeep division. With the Concord's available luxury features, a buyer could have all the capabilities of an off-road vehicle with car-like comfort and convenience. The Eagle was an immediate hit, selling best in cold weather climates, where its traction and higher stance made it ideal for navigating snow covered roads. The remainder of the line returned mostly unchanged except for the Spirit and Concord now

having the Pontiac-built 151 CID 4-cylinder engine as standard equipment. During December 1979, American Motors announced that the Pacer would be discontinued due to declining sales, and by the end of the model year the AMX would also be dropped. An interesting bit of trivia was that the 1980 model year had two nameplates in production that repeated one-year-only series names from the 1958 Edsel model line, itself a short-lived, three-model-year division of Ford Motor Company. Both of these current models were in production for only six model years each. Those nameplates were the AMC Pacer, which was in its last year of production after a relatively successful start in 1975, and the Chevrolet Citation, which began with an undeniably successful 1980 model year, but would be gone from the Chevrolet lineup by the end of the 1985 model year. No significant changes were made to the Jeep lineup, although the Wagoneer did come standard with a six-cylinder engine for 1980, after years of being strictly V8 powered.

After several years in business with Renault, American Motors car business continued to struggle with profitability. By 1986, AMC's falling sales and production resulted in layoffs at its Kenosha plant, and in an effort to save the plant, AMC reached an agreement with Chrysler to build its Gran Fury, Diplomat and Fifth Avenue models there. This relationship paved the way for Chrysler to acquire AMC in 1987, mainly for its strong performing Jeep line. As part of the agreement with Renault, Chrysler would sell the new Renault-designed Premiere as the Eagle Premiere for 1988, with a virtual twin, the Dodge Monaco, introduced for 1990. Chrysler's Eagle division would also take on the recently introduced Renault Medallion, rebadging it as Eagle Medallion.

In 1980, however, Chrysler was in no position to be buying other manufacturers. In fact, this would be probably the worst year to date in Chrysler's 56-year history. Chrysler was proceeding with its downsizing program to improve fuel economy and remain competitive. Three weeks before official introduction of the 1980 models, on September 7, 1979, the Chrysler Corporation petitioned the United States government for $1.5 billion in loan guarantees to avoid bankruptcy. This was only months after former Ford Division president Lee Iacocca was brought in as CEO of Chrysler. He proved to be a capable public spokesman, and with support and prodding from the assembly line workers and the dealership network, he somehow got a reluctant Congress to pass the "Chrysler Corporation Loan Guarantee Act of 1979" on December 20, 1979. The act was signed into law by President Jimmy Carter on January 7, 1980. Shortly thereafter, the military bought thousands of Dodge pickup trucks which entered military service as the Commercial Utility Cargo Vehicle M-880 Series. With such help and new, innovative cars in the pipeline such as the K-car, to be introduced for the 1981 model year, Chrysler sold its Defense unit that built military systems in 1982, avoided bankruptcy and slowly began recovering. By 1983, the government loans were fully repaid, and the stage was set for more success when the new K-car based minivans were introduced for the 1984 model year.

As for Chrysler's 1980 product line, the once popular Chrysler Cordoba was redesigned and downsized, now being built on the platform of the four-door LeBaron. The Cordoba was joined in the remake with a newly named Dodge Mirada, which replaced the Magnum XE and its former running mate, the Dodge Charger SE. The new models used square headlamps, sloping front-end designs, and generally sportier lines to help boost interest. Unfortunately, the smaller mid-size cars did not sell as well as hoped, most likely due to buyers' fears concerning the current Chrysler financial situation. The Cordoba fell 30 percent in sales from the prior year, while the Mirada recorded a slight increase from the depressed level set by the 1979 Magnum XE. The two models would remain in production through 1983 while continuing to decline in production totals from their 1980 peak season.

Chrysler Corporation's other mid-size lines had freshly restyled Chrysler LeBaron and Dodge Diplomat models that were repositioned to have the two-door models built on the 108.7" wheelbase of the Dodge Aspen and Plymouth Volaré coupe, while the four-door models remained on the longer 112.7" wheelbase. The Aspen and Volaré were discontinued before the end of the 1980 model year to make way for the new compact K-cars, the Dodge Aries K and Plymouth Reliant K. The newly downsized full-size lines had few changes for 1980, but Plymouth marked the return of the Gran Fury as a full-size model based heavily on the Chrysler Newport, yet with less standard equipment to enable a lower base price for the Plymouth. The small Omni and Horizon models continued in their original form, adding new features for 1980 such as a DeTomaso sport package for the Omni 024 two-door hatchback. The "captive import" Dodge Colt and Challenger and Plymouth Champ and Sapporo models returned with just a few styling and design changes, but the rear-wheel-drive Colt models were dropped for the 1980 model year, except for the station wagon, which soldiered on for a few more years. A styling update was given to the Dodge D-series truck lines, adding new sheetmetal and square headlights in a new grille design, as well as a new name, the Dodge Ram. The Dodge Ramcharger and Plymouth Trail Duster received similar styling updates, while the rest of the truck and van models were mostly unchanged.

Ford Motor Company completed its downsizing of full-size cars with the introduction of the new Lincoln Continental and next generation Lincoln Continental Mark VI. Both were built on the same stretched version of the platform used by the Ford LTD and Mercury Marquis. Some resultant similarities were seen in the powertrains and the bodies, most visibly in the doors. The Mark VI added a first-ever four-door sedan model, but it would only last through the 1983 season, when the Mark series would return to a coupe model only. Though similarities could be found with the lesser Ford and Mercury models, stylists did an outstanding job of retaining the traditional Lincoln identifying features. With the LTD II and Cougar lines gone, Ford did away with that platform and introduced new Thunderbird and Cougar XR-7 models that were built on a larger version of the "Fox" platform, which was also found now on the Mustang and Capri, plus its original compact Fairmont and Zephyr versions. While the two models retained certain styling cues such as hidden headlights on the Thunderbird, these two models did not live up to the heritage of their predecessors, and sold poorly from the start. The Thunderbird and Cougar XR-7 would decline an average of 45 percent in production for each of the three years of this version, being replaced in 1983 by all-new models that returned the cars to their former heights of success.

The existing Ford Granada and Mercury Monarch became the newly designated mid-size models for the company despite being unchanged from their form previously considered compact. The rest of the Ford lineup received few changes for the 1980 model year, which would be the final season for the slow-selling Lincoln Versailles and the subcompact Ford Pinto and Mercury Bobcat. The latter two series would be replaced for 1981 with Ford's first "World Cars," the Ford Escort and the Mercury Lynx — Ford's next success story. Ford's F-series trucks received a redesign this year, with more aerodynamic looking front ends, but retaining the familiar look of recent Ford trucks. The imported Courier and the Econoline van returned with minor updates, but the Ranchero was gone. One aftermarket company would fashion a "new" Ranchero from the Fairmont Futura sport coupe, named the Fairmont Durango, but Ford would not officially sanction these conversions.

1980 Overview and Changes from Prior Year

- **Total industry model year production:** 7,643,487, down 16.80%.
- **Total estimated captive import sales:** 201,998, down 13.69%.
- **Market share by corporation:** General Motors 68.20%; Ford 20.80%; Chrysler 8.38%; AMC 2.62%.
- **Number of models and body types available:** 252, up from 245.
- **Highest production series:** Chevrolet Citation — 811,540.
- **Lowest production series:** AMC AMX — 865.
- **Highest individual model production:** Chevrolet Citation 4-Door Hatchback — 458,033.

Lowest individual model production: AMC Pacer 2-Door Hatchback — 405.

Industry average base price: $6,769, up 17.99%.

Highest individual model base price: Cadillac Fleetwood 75 Limousine, $23,388.

Lowest individual model base price: Chevette Scooter 2-Door Hatchback Coupe, $3,782.

Highest estimated MPG with base powertrain: Chevrolet Chevette, 26 MPG.

Lowest estimated MPG with base powertrain: Cadillac Eldorado and Seville and Chevrolet Corvette, 14 MPG.

Indianapolis 500 Pace Car: Pontiac Firebird Trans Am 2-Door Coupe w/T-Tops and Turbo V8 engine.

Motor Trend magazine **"Car of the Year":** Chevrolet Citation.

AMERICAN MOTORS

"Built for today. Built to last for tomorrow."

American Motors' advertising emphasis for 1980 shifted to renewing its commitment to build automobiles that last, and rebuilding consumer confidence that AMC was a viable and healthy company — a challenge as sales fell, consumer perceptions fell, and word of the connection to Renault spread. The first two pages of the 1980 sales brochure were devoted completely to the company's commitment to quality. As explained in the opening comments, "The commitment began when American Motors became the first to build economical small cars." This began in 1950 when the compact Nash Rambler was introduced. "It continued with the introduction of the Buyer Protection Plan. Another first." The Buyer Protection Plan was introduced in 1972, at a time when some automakers still offered only 6-month warranties, and it offered extras like free loaner cars for repairs that take more than a day, and free trip interruption protection. "And for 1980, the American Motors commitment continues to grow, with two more firsts: Ziebart® Factory Rust Protection, and a 5-year Full No-Rust-Thru™ Warranty." The latter effort seemed to be a reflection upon the entire industry, as several car lines, mainly from other manufacturers during the mid-seventies, had been prone to rust prematurely.

However, the added attention to quality did not mean a dearth of new product. In fact, AMC brought out one of the most successful innovations in the last decade this year. The 4-wheel-drive (4WD) Eagle line became the first American made passenger cars with the system. Designed in England and built by Chrysler Corporation, the new Eagle was in a class by itself. Considered a light truck for fuel economy ratings, and a multi-purpose vehicle for safety standards, it would be known 25 years later as the grandfather of the crossover utility vehicle. Having only one competitor in 1980, the Subaru station wagon that was introduced in 1975 and the new-for-1980 Subaru 3-door hatchback, AMC was confident they had found a niche market in which to succeed. It

was also a perfect companion on showroom floors for the highly popular Jeep 4WD models.

Eagle was the first mass-produced four-wheel-drive vehicle with independent front suspension, which provided a better ride and improved stability. A viscous coupling provided the necessary slippage to allow the system to distribute power automatically to the wheels front and rear, exactly when needed, while also absorbing unwanted vibrations. Styling was strictly based on the Concord with the addition of injection molded rocker panel extensions and fender flares to minimize the large wheel openings and taller ride height created by adding four-wheel-drive. The Eagle used a blacked-out version of the Concord grille, with the Eagle nameplate on the upper driver's side of the grille.

The Concord's new grille consisted of thin horizontal strips, with a Concord nameplate affixed to the upper driver's side of the grille, and it again met a large chrome molding on the leading edge of the hood which now bore the AMC name and logo on the passenger side. The four-door Concord added a rear quarter window in the C-pillar, vastly improving rearward visibility in the traditional blind-spot areas. Two-doors had a greenhouse change, too, moving to an opera-style rear passenger window within a square chrome frame that enclosed the vertical rectangular window and a set of faux louvers behind it. Both were raised above the beltline, with the vinyl top now extending beneath the window frame. Concord wagons added a black plastic surround panel on the rear side windows. The Concord's rear end styling changed with the adoption of full-width wraparound taillights with license plate housing at the center. The wraparound portion of the new units was reminiscent of what the Hornet had used at one time, but these wider lamps, with amber turn signal lenses at the center and backup lights at the inner end, were outlined in a prominent chrome frame and divided by two thin horizontal chrome strips. All of these features also appeared on the new Eagle series. The slow-selling Concord hatchback was discontinued this year, after a successful beginning as the Hornet hatchback. About the only changes made to the successful Spirit line were to juggle some equipment from the standard to the optional list, and vice versa.

The 258 CID 6-cylinder engine remained as the only American Motors designed and built powerplant available for 1980. This year's new 2.5 liter, 151 CID 4-cylinder engines were procured from General Motors' Pontiac division. The new engines weighed less, were less costly for AMC, and created slightly more horsepower at a lower rpm than the previous Volkswagen/Audi designed engine, while keeping gas mileage essentially unchanged.

Production for the year rose solely on the strength of the new Eagle and the new-for-1979 Spirit compact. The AMX and Concord both struggled, as General Motor's new front-wheel-drive compacts stole a lot of sales from other manufacturers' small car lines. During December 1979, American Motors announced that the slow-selling Pacer would be dropped, to allow for Eagle production to be increased. The Pacer did not receive any changes from the 1979 model year, and in fact some historians believe that the 1980 models sold were leftover 1979 Pacers titled as 1980 models.

AMX 2-Door Liftback

Concord D/L 2-Door Sedan

Concord D/L 4-Door Sedan

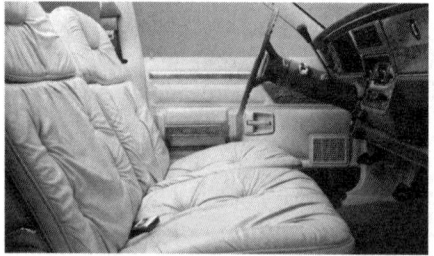

Concord Limited 4-Door Sedan
Chelsea leather interior

Eagle 2-Door Sedan

Eagle 4-Door Station Wagon

Pacer 2-Door Hatchback Coupe

Pacer D/L 2-Door Station Wagon

Spirit 2-Door Sedan

Spirit D/L 2-Door Liftback

Model year production: 200,478, up 18.32% from 1979.
Domestic market share: 2.62% (10th place).
Base price range: $4,505 to $8,115.
American Motors average base price: $5,976, up 20.23%.
Introduction date: October 11, 1979. Eagle introduced September 27, 1979.
Assembly plants: Kenosha, Wisconsin, and Brampton, Ontario, Canada.
Data plate identification (VIN): Thirteen digit code read as follows: First digit indicates company (A = American Motors); second digit indicates model year (0 = 1980); third digit is transmission code (see powertrain chart); fourth through sixth digits indicate car line–body type–series numbers (three-digit model number in model charts); seventh digit is engine code (see powertrain chart); eighth digit indicates assembly plant (1 through 6 = Kenosha, 7 through 9 = Ontario); remaining digits are sequential with beginning number of 00001. *Example:* A0A067C100001 is a 1979 Concord Limited 2-Door Sedan with 258 CID, 2-bbl. 6-cylinder and Torque-Command Automatic, serial number 00001, built in Kenosha.

Powertrains[1]

Engine	Net HP	Engine/ Trans. Codes[2]	Transmission Availability[2]		Spirit	AMX	Pacer	Concord	Eagle
151 CID (2.5L) OHC, 2-bbl., 4-cyl.	82	B/F	4-speed manual		S	—	—	S	—
				MPG:	22/30	—	—	22/30	—
				Calif.	23	—	—	23	—
		B/A	Torque-Command 3-sp. Automatic		$305	—	—	$333	—
				MPG:	20	—	—	20	—
				Calif.	20	—	—	20	—
258 CID (4.2L), 2-bbl., 6-cyl.	100	C/F	4-speed manual		$129	S	S	$129	—
				MPG:	18	18	17	17	—
				Calif.	17	17	16	16	—
		C/A	Torque-Command 3-sp. Automatic		$434	$305	$333	$434	S
				MPG:	18	18	18	18	16
				Calif.	18	17	16	16	14

[1]Optional axle ratio required on all 6-cylinder automatic cars sold in high altitude counties: 2.73:1. [2]Unless otherwise noted: Add $26 for floor-shifter on Spirit automatics and Pacer automatics w/bucket or individual reclining seats. Floor-shift is standard on AMX. Transmission code with automatic floor shift is C.

Major Options[1]

	Spirit	AMX	Pacer	Concord	Eagle
Air conditioning	$529	$529	$529	$529	$529
Tilt steering wheel	$75	$75	$78	$78	$78
Cruise control[2]	$108	$108	$108	$108	$108
Electric rear window defogger	$93	$93	$93	$93	$93
Tinted glass, all windows	$59	$59	$68	$65	$65
Power windows and door locks[3]	—	—	$199	$199	$199
Power door locks	$75	$75	$75	$75[4]	$75[4]
Front bucket seats, vinyl upholstered	S	S	—	—	—
Front floor console, requires bucket seats	$78	$78	—	—	—
AM radio	$89	$89	$89	$89	$89
AM/FM stereo multiplex w/4 speakers	$219	$219	$219	$219	$219
AM/FM stereo w/cassette tape player	$335	$335	$335	$335	$335
AM/FM stereo w/Citizens Band radio (CB)[5]	$475	$475	$475	$475	$475
Pop-up moonroof	$195[6]	$195	$195[6]	$195[6]	$195[6]
Woodgrain paneling, wagons only	—	—	$121	$75	—
Power steering	$164	$164	$164	$164	S
Power front disc brakes	$74	$74	$74	$74	S
Wire wheel covers	$135	—	$100	$135	—
Spoke style wheels	$150	S	$115	$150	—
Turbine forged aluminum wheels	$310	$160	$275	$310	—
Turbo cast II aluminum wheels	$350	$200	—	—	—
White sidewall tires, standard size	S	—	S	$49	$91

1980

Popular Option Groups & Packages[1]

	Spirit	AMX	Pacer	Concord	Eagle
AMX custom interior package	—	$149	—	—	—
Convenience group	$63	$63	$63	$63	$63
Eagle sport package	—	—	—	—	$299
Extra Quiet insulation package	$50	S	S	$50	$50
Gauge package	$129	$75	$129	—	—
GT package	$249[7]	—	—	—	—
GT rally-tuned suspension, w/GT package only	$109	—	—	—	—
Light Group	$45	$35	$39	$49	$49
Protection group	$111	$31	$70	$114	$70
Visibility group	$64	$64	$52	$64	$52

— = Not Available; S = Standard equipment. [1]Note that many of these features may be included as standard in the D/L or Limited trim levels of all but AMX. Therefore prices may also vary by trim levels. Consult the Major standard equipment section in the model listings that follow to confirm standard equipment. [2]Available only with automatic transmission. [3]Power windows must be ordered with power door locks. Price given is for 2-door models. Available on 4-door sedan and wagon for $289. [4]Price given is for 2-door models. Available on 4-door sedan and wagon for $108. [5]CB radio is 40-channel version. [6]Not available with roof rack, or on wagon models. [7]Price given is with base or D/L trim. Not available with Limited trim.

Paint Colors

	Code	Spirit	AMX	Pacer	Concord	Eagle
Quick Silver metallic	8C	x	—	x	x	x
Olympic White	9B	x	x	x	x	x
Russet metallic	9C	x	—	x	x	x
Saxon Yellow	9L	x	x	x	x	x
Bordeaux metallic	9P	x	—	x	x	x
Misty Beige Clearcoat metallic*	9Z	—	—	x	—	—
Smoke Gray metallic	0B	x	—	x	x	x
Cameo Blue	0C	x	x	x	x	x
Medium Blue metallic	0D	x	—	x	x	x
Dark Green metallic	0E	—	—	—	x	x
Navy Blue	0H	x	x	x	x	x
Cameo Tan	0K	x	x	x	x	x
Medium Brown metallic	0L	x	x	x	x	x
Dark Brown metallic	0M	x	—	x	x	x
Cardinal Red	0P	x	x	x	x	x
Caramel	0R	x	—	x	—	—
Classic Black	P1	x	x	x	x	x

*Non-standard model colors are available at $30 extra cost, except on AMX and Eagle Limited. Two-tone paint combinations available on Spirit GT for $84, Pacer for $67, and Concord D/L or Limited for $103. *Available only on Pacer for $90 extra cost.*

Spirit

"There's more to Spirit than meets the eye."

Nameplate year of origin: 1979.

Current bodystyle lifespan: 1970 through 1983; Gremlin (1970 to 1978), restyled and renamed Spirit (1979 to 1982). 4WD added and rebadged Eagle SX/4 (1981 to 1983).

Predecessor to this model: Gremlin (1970 to 1978).

Replacement for this model: Eagle SX/4 (1981 to 1983).

Percentage of division's production: 33.33%.

Corporate siblings: None; however many components were shared with the Concord.

Primary competition: Chevrolet Monza, Dodge Omni 024, Ford Pinto, and Plymouth Horizon TC3.

Notable changes: Minor trim and detail changes.

Measurements

	Liftback	Sedan
Wheelbase	96.0"	96.0"
Length	167.2"	167.0"
Width	71.9"	72.0"
Height	51.5"	51.6"
Legroom — front	40.8"	40.8"
Legroom — rear	27.8"	27.8"
Headroom — front	38.1"	38.1"
Headroom — rear	35.6"	37.7"
Cargo capacity (cu. ft.)	25.5*	27.3*

Major standard equipment: Sport vinyl bucket seats, fold-down rear seat, color-keyed carpeting and seat belts, custom steering wheel, carpeted cargo area, spare tire cover, dual bodyside pinstripes, bright moldings (drip rail, wheel lip and windshield surround), chrome-plated aluminum bumpers with black end caps, rear bumper guards, and C78 × 14 WSW tires. **D/L adds:** Choice of caberfae corduroy or sport vinyl reclining bucket seats, folding split rear seat back, custom door trim panels w/lower carpeted area and integral map pockets, cloth headliner and sunvisors, luxury woodgrain steering wheel, woodgrain I/P overlays, I/P package shelf, electronic quartz digital clock, AM radio, day/night mirror, courtesy lights, front bumper guards, and styled wheel covers. **Limited adds:** Chelsea leather bucket seats, full-length console w/center armrest, 18 oz. color-keyed carpeting, woodgrain armrest overlays, power door locks, power liftback release (Liftback only), dual remote control mirrors, tilt steering wheel, light group, visibility group, convenience group, door edge guards, power steering, and P195/75R14 WSW tires.

Measurements (cont.)

	Liftback	Sedan
Fuel capacity (gals.)	21.0	21.0

With rear seat folded down.

Models Available

	Model No.	Base MSRP	Change from LY	Shipping Wt. (lbs.)	Model Year Production	Change from LY*
Spirit 2-Door Sedan	46-0	$4,505	+16.92%	2512	*	*
Spirit 2-Door Liftback	43-0	$4,605	+16.49%	2556	*	*
Spirit D/L 2-Door Sedan	46-5	$4,904	+19.90%	2611	*	*
Spirit D/L 2-Door Liftback	43-5	$5,004	+19.43%	2656	*	*
Spirit Limited 2-Door Sedan	46-7	$5,351	+5.13%	2630	*	*
Spirit Limited 2-Door Liftback	43-7	$5,451	+5.03%	2675	*	*
TOTALS	*Avg. price*	$4,970	+13.10%	*Production*	71,032	+34.75%

Production records by model or body style were not kept, only by engine installation. Production by engine type (compared to LY): 4-cylinder, 37,799 (+132.80%); 6-cylinder, 33,233 (-8.30%).

AMX

"For car enthusiasts only."

Nameplate year of origin: 1968.
Current bodystyle lifespan: 1979 through 1980.
Predecessor to this model: AMX (1978).
Replacement for this model: None.
Percentage of division's production: 0.20%.
Corporate siblings: Spirit liftback, and many components shared with the Concord.
Primary competition: Buick Skyhawk w/Road Hawk package, Chevrolet Monza w/Spyder package, Dodge Challenger, Ford Mustang, Mercury Capri, Oldsmobile Starfire w/Firenza package, Plymouth Sapporo, and Pontiac Sunbird w/Formula package.
Notable changes: Minor trim and detail changes.
Major standard equipment: Sport vinyl front bucket seats, 12 oz. color-keyed carpeting, full-length console w/integral center armrest, custom door trim panels, gauge package w/tachometer, color-keyed leather wrapped sports steering wheel, fiberglass headliner and vinyl sun visors, folding split rear seat back, power liftgate release, Extra Quiet insulation package, black LH remote control and RH manual mirrors, "AMX" graphics on doors w/nameplate on grille and rear spoiler, black bumpers w/bumper guards and nerfing strips (front and rear), black front air dam, color-keyed rear deck spoiler w/accent stripes, black front and rear fender flares w/accent stripes, black B-pillar and rear panel area, unique black grille insert and black headlight bezels, GT Rally-tuned suspension package, spoke style wheels, and DR70 × 14 OWL tires.

Measurements

Wheelbase	96.0"
Length	167.2"
Width	71.9"
Height	51.5"
Legroom — front	40.8"
Legroom — rear	27.8"
Headroom — front	38.1"
Headroom — rear	35.6"
Cargo capacity (cu. ft.)	25.5*
Fuel capacity (gals.)	21.0

Maximum with rear seat down.

Models Available

	Model No.	Base MSRP	Change from LY	Shipping Wt. (lbs.)	Model Year Production	Change from LY
AMX 2-Door Liftback	43-9	$5,653	-7.18%	2901	865	-76.35%
TOTALS	*Avg. price*	$5,653	-7.18%	*Production*	865	-76.35%

1980

Pacer

"Big in value and comfort and extremely practical."

Nameplate year of origin: 1975 (previously used by Ford Motor Company on 1958 Edsel series).

Current bodystyle lifespan: 1975 through 1980.

Predecessor to this model: None.

Replacement for this model: None.

Percentage of division's production: 0.82%.

Corporate siblings: None.

Primary competition: Buick Skyhawk and Mercury Bobcat.

Notable changes: None.

Major standard equipment: Sport individual reclining front seats, fold-down rear seat, 12 oz. color-keyed carpeting and color-keyed seat belts, custom door trim panels w/woodgrain accents and lower carpet area, custom headliner and sunvisors, custom steering wheel w/woodgrain overlays, Walnut Burl woodgrain I/P overlays, carpeted cargo area w/skid strips in wagon, electric clock, day/night mirror, courtesy lights, Extra Quiet insulation package, bright moldings (wheel lip, rear hood edge, lower grille, and windshield and rear window surround), hood ornament and hood windsplit molding, blackout grille insert, front and rear bumper guards, front sway bar, wide rocker panel moldings, color-keyed wide bodyside scuff moldings, styled wheel covers, and P195/75R14 WSW tires. Limited adds: Chelsea leather individual reclining seats, vinyl folding center armrest, 18 oz. color-keyed carpeting, luxury woodgrain steering wheel, AM radio, power windows and power door locks, dual remote control mirrors, tilt steering wheel, light group, and wire wheel covers.

Measurements

	Sedan	Wagon
Wheelbase	100.0"	100.0"
Length	173.9"	178.8"
Width	77.0"	77.0"
Height	52.7"	53.1"
Legroom — front	40.7"	40.7"
Legroom — rear	35.0"	35.0"
Headroom — front	38.3"	38.5"
Headroom — rear	36.9"	38.0"
Cargo capacity (cu. ft.)	32.2*	52.5*
Fuel capacity (gals.)	21.0	21.0

With rear seat folded down.

Models Available

	Model No.	Base MSRP	Change from LY*	Shipping Wt. (lbs.)	Model Year Production*	Change from LY*
Pacer D/L 2-Door Sedan	66-5	$5,407	+7.30%	3147	405	-85.85%
Pacer D/L 2-Door Station Wagon	68-5	$5,558	+7.11%	3195	1,341	-81.76%
Pacer Limited 2-Door Sedan	66-7	$6,031	-0.13%	3172	*	*
Pacer Limited 2-Dr. Station Wgn.	68-7	$6,182	-0.11%	3220	*	*
TOTALS		Avg. price $5,795	+3.22%		Production 1,746	-82.91%

Production of D/L and Limited series was kept combined. Comparison is made to total of 1979 Pacer models.

Concord

"Concord is the compact that combines good sense and good taste."

Nameplate year of origin: 1978 (previously used by Chrysler Corporation on 1951–1952 Plymouth series).

Current bodystyle lifespan: 1970 through 1987; Hornet (1970–1977), restyled and renamed Concord (1978 to 1982); 4WD added and rebadged Eagle (1980 to 1987).

Predecessor to this model: Hornet (1970 to 1977).

Replacement for this model: Eagle (1980 to 1987).

Percentage of division's production: 37.75%.

Corporate siblings: None; however, many components were shared with the Spirit.

Primary competition: Buick Skylark, Dodge Diplomat, Mercury Monarch, Oldsmobile Omega, and Pontiac Phoenix.

Notable changes: Minor trim and detail changes.

Major standard equipment: Sport vinyl or Stripe Knit fabric bench front

Measurements

	Sedans	Wagon
Wheelbase	108.0"	108.0"
Length	185.0"	185.0"
Width	71.0"	71.0"
Height	51.3"	52.6"
Legroom — front	40.8"	40.8"
Legroom — rear	36.1"	36.1"
Headroom — front	38.1"	38.1"
Headroom — rear	37.5"	37.9"
Cargo capacity (cu. ft.)	11.4	60.8*
Fuel capacity (gals.)	22.0	22.0

Maximum with rear seat down, and 3.8 cu. ft. below cargo floor on wagon.

seat, fold-down rear seat (wagon), 12 oz. color-keyed carpeting and color-keyed seat belts, custom steering wheel, fiberglass head-liner, vinyl sun visors, carpeted cargo area, lighted ashtray, dual bodyside pinstripes, narrow black side scuff moldings, bright moldings (drip rail, narrow wheel lip, narrow rocker panel, hood front edge, rear window surround, and windshield surround), chrome-plated aluminum bumpers with black end caps, hood windsplit molding w/hood ornament, front stabilizer bar, full wheel covers, and D78 × 14 BSW tires. D/L adds: Sport vinyl individual reclining front seats, custom door trim panels, custom headliner and sunvisors, custom steering wheel w/woodgrain overlays, Walnut Burl woodgrain I/P overlays, electronic quartz digital clock, day/night mirror, courtesy lights, Extra Quiet insulation package, front and rear bumper guards, color-keyed wide bodyside scuff moldings (sedans only), Landau vinyl roof (2-door), full vinyl roof w/B-pillar pinstripes (4-door), opera windows, color-keyed rear window surround molding and opera window overlay moldings (sedan), belt moldings (4-door and wagon), woodgrain bodyside panels w/liftgate pinstripes (wagon), styled wheel covers, and D78 × 14 WSW tires. Limited adds: Choice of Chelsea leather or St. Lauren deep plush fabric individual reclining front seats, 18 oz. color-keyed carpeting, custom door trim panels w/woodgrain front armrest overlays, AM radio, power door locks, dual remote control mirrors, tilt steering wheel, luxury woodgrain steering wheel, I/P package shelf, light group, visibility group, convenience group, protection group, engine compart-ment light, power steering, wire wheel covers, and P195/75R14 WSW tires.

Models Available

	Model No.	Base MSRP	Change from LY*	Shipping Wt. (lbs.)	Model Year Production	Change from LY*
Concord 2-Door Sedan	06-0	$5,094	+16.06%	2646	27,845	-30.58%
Concord 4-Door Sedan	05-0	$5,219	+16.26%	2712	35,198	-12.30%
Concord 4-Door Station Wagon	08-0	$5,419	+15.57%	2741	17,413	-14.13%
Concord D/L 2-Door Sedan	06-5	$5,493	+17.17%	2764	*	*
Concord D/L 4-Door Sedan	05-5	$5,618	+17.34%	2834	*	*
Concord D/L 4-Door Station Wagon	08-5	$5,818	+16.64%	2855	*	*
Concord Limited 2-Door Sedan	06-7	$5,940	+4.43%	2789	*	*
Concord Limited 4-Door Sedan	05-7	$6,065	+4.79%	2859	*	*
Concord Limited 4-Door Station Wagon	08-7	$6,265	+4.63%	2886	*	*
TOTALS	*Avg. price*	$5,659	+14.34%	*Production*	80,456	-21.78%

*Production of base, D/L and Limited series was kept combined, and comparison is made with base series of 1979 Concord models. Production by engine type (compared to LY): 4-cylinder, 9,949 (+56.55%); 6-cylinder, 70,507 (-23.23%).

Eagle

"Introducing the beautiful breakthrough that gets you through in comfort. The Eagle has landed ... on all fours!"

Nameplate year of origin: 1980 (previously used by Willys Motors on 1952–1954 Willys Aero subseries).

Current bodystyle lifespan: 1970 through 1987; Hornet (1970–1977), restyled and renamed Concord (1978 to 1982); 4WD added and rebadged Eagle (1980 to 1987).

Predecessor to this model: Hornet (1970 to 1977) and Concord (1978–1982).

Replacement for this model: None.

Percentage of division's production: 21.76%.

Corporate siblings: None; however many components were shared with the Spirit.

Primary competition: None.

Notable changes: All-new model created from Concord by adding four-wheel drive.

Major standard equipment: Durham plaid fabric and vinyl bench front seat, fold-down rear seat (wagon), 12 oz. color-keyed carpeting and color-keyed seat belts, custom steering wheel, electric clock, lighted ashtray, lan-dau vinyl top (2-doors), full vinyl top (4-doors), bright moldings (drip rail, wheel lip, hood front edge, and windshield surround), Krayton injec-tion-molded plastic rocker sill strips and 3" wide fender flares, lower body

Measurements

	Sedans	Wagon
Wheelbase	109.3"	109.3"
Length	186.2"	186.2"
Width	72.0"	72.0"
Height	55.0"	55.8"
Legroom — front	40.8"	40.8"
Legroom — rear	35.7"	31.1"
Headroom — front	38.1"	38.1"
Headroom — rear	37.5"	37.9"
Cargo capacity (cu. ft.)	10.8	59.2*
Fuel capacity (gals.)	22.0	22.0

*Maximum with rear seat down, and 3.8 cu. ft. below cargo floor on wagon.

1980

accent paint w/thin chrome separation strip, stone/gravel deflector under front bumper, chrome-plated aluminum bumpers with black end caps, front and rear bumper guards, power steering, power front disc brakes, argent styled wheel covers, and P195/75R15B WSW tires. Limited adds: Individual reclining front seats, 18 oz. color-keyed carpeting, I/P package shelf, premium door trim, power windows, luxury woodgrain steering wheel, light group, and visibility group.

Models Available

	Model No.	Base MSRP	Change from LY	Shipping Wt. (lbs.)	Model Year Production	Change from LY
Eagle 2-Door Sedan	36-5	$7,168	NEW	3382	10,616*	NEW
Eagle 4-Door Sedan	35-5	$7,418	NEW	3450	9,956*	NEW
Eagle 4-Door Station Wagon	38-5	$7,718	NEW	3470	25,807*	NEW
Eagle Limited 2-Door Sedan	36-7	$7,565	NEW	3397	*	NEW
Eagle Limited 4-Door Sedan	35-7	$7,815	NEW	3465	*	NEW
Eagle Limited 4-Door Station Wagon	38-7	$8,115	NEW	3491	*	NEW
TOTALS	Avg. price	$7,633	NEW	Production	46,379	NEW

*Production of base and Limited series was kept combined.

BUICK

"After all, life is to enjoy."

In a single year, Buick leapfrogged over its corporate rivals Oldsmobile and Pontiac to attain third place in model year production. Of course, a mild economic recession and another brief gas crisis helped smaller cars and hurt performance and large cars more than other models. All of Buick's gain came from the all-new Skylark and restyled Century four-door models. But the unexpected sales drop in Oldsmobile's mid-size Cutlass line and Pontiac's huge drop in Firebird sales, both of which had been recent top sellers, also helped Buick. In the end, Buick was enjoying the long-awaited return to the top three in automobile production, and celebrating the undeniable success of the new Skylark.

Production of the new X-body front-wheel-drive Skylarks increased eightfold over the 1979 model it replaced. On the surface that seems huge; however, the '79 models had only a 3-month production run, while the '80 models enjoyed a 16-month run, so in month to month comparisons, the increase was closer to triple the 1979 models — still an outstanding performance, especially when compared to the underwhelming performance of Buick's recently downsized intermediate lines. Nineteen inches shorter and about 700 pounds lighter than their predecessors, the new Skylarks were 100 percent new, while retaining contemporary Buick styling. At the front, Skylark and Skylark Limited models wore a new crosshatch grille five rows high and eight columns across, lined in chrome. Parking/turn signal lights were mounted to the outside of single rectangular headlights set in chrome bezels that angled back slightly, in contrast to the upright grille. Skylark Sport models had a slot-style grille with three stacked horizontal openings per side. Amber parking/turn signal lights were mounted the same as the others, but set into black trimmed bezels. Around back, horizontal taillamps were nearly full-width, being interrupted by the center-mounted license plate opening. Backup lights sat next to the license plate, while amber turn signals wrapped around the corner of the rear quarter panel. A thin horizontal chrome strip divided the lamps into upper and lower halves.

Bodysides were clean, with the main feature line running between the front and rear bumper rub strips. The top edge of the rear quarter panel extended into a small crease across the C-pillar, which wore a round Buick emblem near its forward edge. Rooflines were of a more formal, notchback design.

Inside, the new Skylarks were much more luxurious looking than their predecessors. It started with the nicely designed instrument panel that had a large rectangular area in front of the driver housing all controls. Within this area were two large round dials with Buick's typical brushed aluminum faces (except on the Sport Coupe and Sport Sedan models, which had black gauge faces), and a small round gauge set between the two housing warning lights. Light and windshield wiper controls were to the left, and radio and air conditioning controls to the right. Only an ashtray, glove box, optional clock and air conditioning vents were found on the passenger side. Door panels also appeared with built-in armrests and door pulls, and upholstered to match the seat fabrics and design. Visually it was a big change from the former models.

For mid-size Buicks the two-door Century with fastback roofline remained in the line for a final season, while the introduction of a formal notchback roofline on four-door Century models created an immediate doubling of the midsize line's sales. Taking a cue from the popularity of the 1976–1979 Cadillac Seville's formal stand-up rear window styling, Buick advertised the new Century sedans as the "Little Limousine." At the front of all Century models was an upright and very intricate new egg-crate grille four rows high and eight columns across, with each section containing an eggcrate insert three rows high and four rows across. The grille now stood out slightly from the rearward slanting headlight bezel, as on the Regal and other Buicks. Parking lights moved to inside of the single square headlamps, while the turn signal/side marker light remained on the outer front edge of the fender. Around back, other than the notchback rear quarters for the new sedan styling, taillights and bumpers remained the same as the past two years. Similarly interiors were mildly updated, with even more opulent upholstery and trim for Limited models.

Regal coupes received a new front-end design, employing dual rectangular headlights set side-by-side, with parking/turn signal lights moved to the bumper below the rub strips. A new egg-crate grille design kicked out slightly at the bottom to meet the bumper, and was nine rows high with nine columns per side with a thick chrome trim piece across the top, and the Buick name set in block letters at the middle. The turbocharged sport coupe continued in the line, although in slightly smaller numbers as production of the turbocharged Monte Carlo began this year, stealing some of the Regal's thunder. Buick would get its revenge a few years down the road with the Regal Grand National.

Full-size Buick models were given the corporate makeover that included more aerodynamic styling with lower front ends and higher deck lids, as well as a smoothing out and tucking in of the bodysides. Thanks to these changes, a new, smaller V8 engine, high-pressure, low rolling resistance tires, and generally improved electronics, the new Buicks were the most fuel efficient to date. All of this was set upon what was still the basic underpinnings of the downsized 1977 models. The LeSabre used a horizontal crosshatch grille design with horizontal bars inset to each opening, with a section extending below the headlights, similar to the 1977 models. Parking/turn signal units were moved to the bumper on all of the new full-sized Buicks. For the Electra, a new grille similar to the Riviera's was introduced, having more of a waterfall style. Around back, both LeSabre and Electra used larger, horizontal taillamps that wrapped around the rear fascia end cap. With the new styling, Electra largely lost the small tailfin look of the 1977 to 1979 models.

The Electra series dropped the "225" designation, used for the past 20 years, and they were the only remaining Buicks to carry ventiports, otherwise known as portholes. The Estate Wagon series, which had been its own separate series from its reintroduction in 1970 through 1979, was moved to the LeSabre line, and the formerly optional Estate Wagon Limited package was added to the Electra line as the Electra Estate Wagon, each carrying the front-end styling of its respective series. Other model changes in the Buick line included the Century Special being dropped and the Century Custom being designated the Century. Both the Century Sport Coupe and Century Sport Wagon option would enter the 1980 model year for their last season. Finally, the subcompact Buick Skyhawk, never a big seller for Buick, would silently disappear early in the season, with no changes. Its disappearance allowed for continuing sales of the Chevrolet Monza and Pontiac Sunbird while GM revamped other factories for the highly anticipated introduction of the new J-car family of subcompacts.

Century 2-Door Coupe

Century 4-Door Sedan

Century Estate 4-Door Station Wagon

1980

Electra Park Avenue 4-Door Sedan

Electra Park Avenue Coupe interior

LeSabre 4-Door Sedan

LeSabre Limited 2-Door Coupe

Regal Limited 2-Door Coupe
with Somerset Limited Edition package

Riviera 2-Door Coupe

Skyhawk 2-Door Hatchback Coupe

Skylark Sport Coupe 2-Door

Skylark Limited 4-Door Sedan

Model year production: 1,010,610, up 38.96% from 1979.

Domestic market share: 12.99% (3rd place).

Base price range: $4,993 to $11,823.

Buick average base price: $7,165, up 19.23%.

Introduction date: October 11, 1979. Skylark introduced April 19, 1979.

Assembly plants: Linden, NJ (E); Framingham, MA (G); Flint, MI (H); Tarrytown, NY (T); Lordstown, OH (7); Willow Run, MI (W); Kansas City/Fairfax, KS (X); Fremont, CA (Z).

Data plate identification (VIN): Thirteen digit code read as follows: First digit indicates division (4 = Buick); second through fourth digits indicate series and body style (model number in model charts); fifth digit is engine code (see powertrain chart); sixth digit indicates model year (A = 1980); seventh digit indicates assembly plant (see list above); remaining digits are sequential with beginning number of 100001 except all cars built at Lordstown, OH; N, F, P, X, J, and W series built at Flint, MI; and Y and Z series built at Linden, NJ, all of which have beginning serial number of 400001. *Example:* 4N69XAH400001 is a 1980 Buick LeSabre 4-Door Sedan, with 350 CID, 4-bbl. V8 engine, serial number 400001, built in Flint, MI.

Powertrains[1]

Engine	Net HP	Engine Code: VIN/GM	Transmission Availability		Skyhawk	Skylark	Century & Regal[2]	LeSabre[2]	Electra[2]	Riviera
151 CID (2.5L), 2-bbl., 4-cyl.	90	5/LW9	4-speed manual		—	S	—	—	—	—
				MPG:	—	24/38	—	—	—	—
			Turbo Hydra-matic		—	$337	—	—	—	—
			3-sp. Automatic	MPG:	—	21/33	—	—	—	—
				Calif.	—	22	—	—	—	—

Engine	Net HP	Engine Code: VIN/GM	Transmission Availability		Skyhawk	Skylark	Century & Regal[2]	LeSabre[2]	Electra[2]	Riviera
173 CID (2.8L), 2-bbl., V6	115	7/LE2	4-speed manual		—	$225	—	—	—	—
				MPG:	—	20/28	—	—	—	—
			Turbo Hydra-matic 3-sp. Automatic		—	$562	—	—	—	—
				MPG:	—	20/27	—	—	—	—
				Calif.	—	18	—	—	—	—
231 CID (3.8L), 2-bbl., V6	110	A/LD5	4-speed manual		S	—	S (ex. W & Regal SC)[3]	—	—	—
				MPG:	20/27	—	20/27	—	—	—
				Calif.	16	—	—	—	—	—
			Turbo Hydra-matic 3-sp. Automatic		$320	—	S (W)/$358 (ex. W & Regal SC)	S (ex. SC & W)	—	—
				MPG:	19/26	—	19/26	18/24	—	—
				Calif.	19	—	19	19	—	—
231 CID (3.8L), Turbo-charged, 4-bbl., V6	170[4]	3/LC8	Turbo Hydra-matic 3-sp. Automatic		—	—	S (Regal SC)/ $500 (Century ex. W)	S (SC only)	—	S (Riviera S-Type)/ $160 (Riviera)
				MPG:	—	—	18/25	16/23	—	16/23
				Calif.	—	—	18	16	—	16
252 CID (4.1L), 4-bbl., V6	125	4/LC4	Turbo Hydra-matic 3-sp. Automatic		—	—	—	$90 (ex. SC & W)	S (ex. W)	—
				MPG:	—	—	—	17/23	17/23	—
260 CID (4.3L), 2-bbl., V8	120	S/LS5	Turbo Hydra-matic 3-sp. Automatic		—	—	$180 (W)/ $205 (ex. W & Regal SC)[5]	$180 (ex. SC & W)	—	—
				MPG:	—	—	18/24	17/23	—	—
301 CID (4.9L), 4-bbl., V8	140	W/L37	Turbo Hydra-matic 3-sp. Automatic		—	—	$295 (W)/ $320 (ex. W & Regal SC)[5]	S (W)/ $295 (ex. SC & W)[6]	S (W)[6]	—
				MPG:	—	—	17/25	16/23	16/23	—
305 CID (5.0L), 4-bbl., V8	155	H/LG4	Turbo Hydra-matic 3-sp. Automatic		—	—	$295 (W)/ $320 (ex. W & Regal SC)[7]	—	—	—
				MPG:	—	—	16/23[6]	—	—	—
				Calif.	—	—	15/22[4]	—	—	—
350 CID (5.7L), 4-bbl., V8[5]	155	X/L77	Turbo Hydra-matic 3-sp. Automatic		—	—	—	$130 (W)/ $425 (ex. SC & W)	$130 (W)/ $335 (ex. W)	S (Riviera)/ -$160 (credit on Riviera S)
				MPG:	—	—	—	15/22	15/22	15/22
				Calif.	—	—	—	15	15	15
350 CID (5.7L), 4-bbl., V8	160	R/L34	Turbo Hydra-matic 3-sp. Automatic		—	—	—	$130 (W)/ $425 (ex. SC & W)[7]	$130 (W)/ $335 (ex. W)[7]	S (Riviera)[7]/ -$160 (credit on Riviera S)
				MPG:	—	—	—	14/21	14/21	14/21
350 CID (5.7L), FI Diesel, V8[8]	105	N/LF9	Turbo Hydra-matic 3-sp. Automatic		—	—	—	$860 (W)	$860 (W)/ $930 (ex. W)	—

Engine	Net HP	Engine Code: VIN/GM	Transmission Availability	Skyhawk	Skylark	Century & Regal[2]	LeSabre[2]	Electra[2]	Riviera
			MPG:	—	—	—	22/34	22/34	—
			Calif.	—	—	—	22	21	—

[1]Optional axle ratio may be required on cars sold in high-altitude counties. [2]SC = Sport Coupes; W = wagons. [3]A 3-speed manual transmission was officially listed as the standard transmission, but it had to be specifically ordered. [4]Riviera rated at 185-hp. [5]Not available in California. [6]Wagons in California rated at 14/21 MPG. [7]Available only in California, or designated high-altitude counties. [8]Diesel engine not available until after start of model year. [9]L34 engine is required and only available in California and high-altitude counties on LeSabre, Electra and Riviera.

Major Options

	Skyhawk	Skylark	Century	Regal	LeSabre	Electra	Riviera
Air conditioning[1]	$531	$564	$601	$601	$647	S	S
Tilt-wheel steering[2]	$68	$75	$81	$81	$83	$83	$83
Cruise-Master speed control	—	$105	$112	$112	$118	$118	$118
Electric rear window defogger	$95	$101	$107	$107	$109	$109	$109
Tinted glass, all windows	$65	$70	$75	$75	$90	S	S
Dual rearview mirrors, LH remote & RH manual	S	$71	$76	$76	$35	S	S
Power windows, 2-dr./4-dr.	—	$133/$189	$132/$187	$132	$133/$205	S	S
Power door locks, 2-dr./4-dr.	—	$84/$123	$93/$132	$93	$95/$135	$82/$122	S
Power front seat, 6-way, driver's side	—	$165	$175	$175	$155	$148	—
Front bucket seats, w/console	S	$48[3]	$145[4]	$145	$102[4]	—	S[4]
Third row seating (wagons)	—	—	—	—	$193	$193	—
AM radio	S	S	$97	$97	$99	—	S
AM/FM stereo	$101	$101	$192	$192	$195	$195	S
AM/FM stereo w/cassette tape player	$188	$491	$285	$285	$302	$302	$302
Vinyl top[5]	—	$116[6]	$124[6]	$124[6]	$155	$174	$305
Sunroof, electric	$193[7]	$240[7]	$561	$561	—	—	$848
Astroroof, sliding glass	$693[7]	—	$773[7]	$773	$981	$1,058	$1,058
Hatch-roof, T-tops	—	—	—	$695	—	—	—
Woodgrain exterior panels (wagons)	—	—	$316	—	$279	S	—
Designers' accent paint	$189[8]	$174	$174[9]	$174[9]	$197	—	$209
Power steering	$158	$164	$174	$163[10]	S	S	S
Power brakes, w/front disc	$76	$76	S	S	S	S	S
Wire wheel covers	—	$194	$208	$164	$164	$130	$166
Deluxe wheel covers	—	$43	$43	S	$43[11]	S	S[12]
Designers' sport wheels	$63[12]	$101	$135	$116	—	—	S[12]
Special wheels, other[13]	$249	—	—	$116	—	—	—
Chrome plated road wheel	—	$141	$163	$48	$188	$154	$130
WSW tires, standard size	$42	$41	$46	$46	$50	$53	S

Popular Option Groups & Packages

	Skyhawk	Skylark	Century	Regal	LeSabre	Electra	Riviera
Decor package	—	—	—	$511	—	—	—
Road Hawk package	$696	—	—	—	—	—	—
Somerset package	—	—	—	$695	—	—	—
Sport package	—	—	—	—	$126	—	—
Sport wagon package	—	—	$511	—	—	—	—
Limited package	—	—	—	—	—	—	—
Turbo Coupe package	—	—	$43	—	—	—	—
F40 firm ride handling package	—	$22	$21	$21	$22	$22	—
F41 Rallye ride/handling package	—	$129	—	—	—	—	—
FE2 Rallye ride/handling package	—	—	$41	$41	—	—	$22
Acoustical package	$27	$43	—	—	—	—	—
Light/Convenience group	$22	$50	—	—	$66	—	—

— = Not Available; S = Standard equipment. [1]Manually controlled. Automatic climate control is available for $99 additional on Century and Regal, $91 on LeSabre, Electra and Riviera. [2]Tilt and telescoping steering column available on LeSabre, Estate Wagon, Electra and Riviera at $48 additional cost. [3]Bucket seats only. [4]Standard on Riviera S-Type. Available only on Century Wagon and LeSabre coupe models. LeSabre models require Sport package. [5]A variety of vinyl top configurations available, ranging in price from $175 to $305. Prices shown are for full, non-padded vinyl top on two-door models. [6]Regal coupe w/Landau top, $175. Not available on Century station wagons. [7]Available on two-door models only. Skyhawk Astroroof is fixed and includes roof crown molding. Skyhawk and Skylark Vista-vent sunroof option is manually operated. [8]For Skyhawk, Designer Paint was an option package. See appendix for details. [9]Available on coupes and wagons only. Regal offers an alternative paint scheme for $230. [10]Standard on Regal Sport coupe. [11]Standard on LeSabre Limited. [12]Custom sport wheels on Skyhawk. Deluxe wheel covers standard on Riviera and Designer sport wheel covers standard on Riviera S-Type. [13]Styled aluminum wheels on Skyhawk, and Turbine wheels on Regal.

Paint Colors

	Code		Code
White	11	Tan metallic	63
Silver metallic	15	Medium Brown metallic[2]	69
Gray metallic[1]	16	Bright Red[4]	72
Black[2]	19	Red metallic	75
Light Blue metallic[2]	21	Dark Red metallic[2]	76
Medium Blue metallic[1]	22	Cinnabar	77
Dark Blue metallic[2]	29	Light Gray[2]	85
Somerset Tan[3]	38	Medium Brown Firemist metallic	97
Dark Green metallic[2]	44	Charcoal Firemist metallic	98
Medium Yellow	50	Dark Brown Firemist metallic	99
Beige[2]	59		

In two-tone combinations, the first two digits indicate lower color and the next two digits are the upper color. Special color paints are available for $166. Firemist paints available only on Electra and Riviera at $186 extra. See major options for pricing of Designers' accent paint. [1]Gray metallic and blue metallic were used with two-tone Designer Accent combinations only. [2]Not available on Century Sport Coupe or Century Wagon w/Sport Wagon option. [3]Available only with Regal Somerset option package in combination with Dark Blue Metallic. [4]Available only on Skyhawk and Skylark.

Skyhawk

"Skyhawk is built with the idea of packing in lots of fun."

Nameplate year of origin: 1975.
Current bodystyle lifespan: 1975 through 1980.
Predecessor to this model: None.
Replacement for this model: Skyhawk (1982 to 1989).
Percentage of division's production: 0.82%.
Corporate siblings: Chevrolet Monza, Oldsmobile Starfire and Pontiac Sunbird.
Primary competition: AMC AMX, AMC Pacer, and Dodge Omni 024.
Notable changes: No changes.
Major standard equipment: Vinyl front bucket seats with foam cushions, fold-down rear seat, cut-pile carpeting including cargo area, full-length floor console, simulated woodgrain I/P and console trim, sport steering wheel, LH remote control and RH manual outside rear view sport mirrors, dual speed wipers w/washers, functional B-pillar vent louvers, bright window surround moldings, front and rear wheel opening moldings, hubcaps, and B78 × 13 BSW tires. Skyhawk adds: Choice of cloth or vinyl front bucket seats, appearance group, and BR78 × 13 BSW tires.

Measurements

Wheelbase	97.0"
Length	179.3"
Width	65.4"
Height	50.2"
Legroom — front	43.0"
Legroom — rear	29.6"
Headroom — front	37.7"
Headroom — rear	35.3"
Cargo capacity (cu. ft.)	27.8*
Fuel capacity (gals.)	18.5

With rear seat folded down.

1980

Models Available

	Model No.	Base MSRP	Change from LY	Shipping Wt. (lbs.)	Model Year Production*	Change from LY*
Skyhawk 'S' 2-Door Hatchback	T07	$4,993	+9.50%	2754	8,322	NA
Skyhawk 2-Door Hatchback	S07	$5,211	+9.06%	2754	NA*	NA
TOTALS	Avg. price	$5,102	+9.27%	Production	8,322	-64.03%

Production and comparisons by model not available as they were kept as combined total for 1980.

Skylark

"Skylark is a car to delight the driver in you."

Nameplate year of origin: 1953.
Current bodystyle lifespan: 1980 through 1985.
Predecessor to this model: Apollo (1975 to 1979).
Replacement for this model: Somerset (1985 to 1987) and Skylark (1986 to 1991).

Measurements

	Coupe	Sedan
Wheelbase	104.9"	104.9"

Percentage of division's production: 26.29%.

Corporate siblings: Chevrolet Citation, Oldsmobile Omega, and Pontiac Phoenix.

Primary competition: Dodge Aspen and Mercury Zephyr.

Notable changes: Completely redesigned.

Major standard equipment: Choice of houndstooth cloth or vinyl notch-back front bench seat w/respective cloth or vinyl door panel inserts, cut-pile carpeting, deluxe steering wheel, front door operated dome light, AM radio w/dual front speakers and windshield antenna, belt reveal moldings, rear end panel molding, bright door and window frame moldings, roof drip rail moldings, narrow rocker panel molding, and P185/80R × 13 BSW tires. Sport adds: Passenger assist straps, black instrument panel, sport steering wheel, gauges (voltmeter, temperature, and trip odometer), dual outside manual sport mirrors, black windshield, door and window frame moldings, front and rear wheel openings, smoked taillight lenses, F41 rallye ride-and-handling package, and P205/70R × 13 BSW tires. Limited adds: Choice of Limited level brushed woven cloth or vinyl front notchback seat w/fold-down center armrest, carpeted door trim rear window package shelf, light package, acoustical insulation package, stand-up hood ornament w/windsplit molding, front and rear wheel opening moldings, wide rocker panel molding w/front and rear extensions, and deluxe wheel covers.

Measurements (cont.)

	Coupe	Sedan
Length	181.1"	181.1"
Width	67.4"	67.4"
Height	53.5"	53.5"
Legroom — front	42.2"	42.2"
Legroom — rear	34.4"	35.5"
Headroom — front	38.1"	38.1"
Headroom — rear	37.4"	37.4"
Cargo capacity (cu. ft.)	14.3	14.3
Fuel capacity (gals.)	14.0	14.0

Models Available

	Model No.	Base MSRP	Change from LY	Shipping Wt. (lbs.)	Model Year Production	Change from LY
Skylark 2-Door Coupe	B37	$5,160	+22.62%	2430	55,114	+541.16%
Skylark 4-Door Sedan	B69	$5,306	+23.17%	2438	80,940	+646.06%
Skylark Limited 2-Door Coupe*	C37	$5,579	+25.03%	2438	42,652**	**
Skylark Limited 4-Door Sedan*	C69	$5,726	+25.52%	2478	86,948**	**
Skylark Sport 2-Door Coupe	D37	$5,774	NEW	2443	**	NEW
Skylark Sport 4-Door Sedan	D69	$5,920	NEW	2471	**	NEW
TOTALS	Avg. price	$5,578	+28.82%	Production	265,654	+815.23%

*Limited models compared to equivalent 1979 Custom models. **Production by body style was kept as combined total for Limited and Sport models. However, it is known that of the total 129,600 built, 100,396 were model C (Limited) series, and 29,204 were model D (Sport) series.

Century

"If you want a mid-size car with the qualities Buick stands for at a budget-pleasing figure, you may have come to the right place."

Nameplate year of origin: 1936.

Current bodystyle lifespan: 1978 through 1984 (Coupe to 1980; Wagon as Regal model 1982 to 1983; and Sedan as Regal model 1982 to 1984).

Predecessor to this model: Skylark (1973 to 1977).

Replacement for this model: Century (1982 to 1996).

Percentage of division's production: 14.69%.

Corporate siblings: Chevrolet Malibu, Oldsmobile Cutlass, and Pontiac LeMans.

Primary competition: Chrysler LeBaron, Dodge Diplomat, and Mercury Cougar.

Notable changes: New front-end treatments and minor trim and detail changes. Notchback sedans replaced fastback-style sedans.

Major standard equipment: Choice of cloth or vinyl notchback front bench seat (wagon, vinyl only on rear seat), cut-pile carpeting, simulated woodgrain I/P trim, front and rear-door operated dome lights, door pull straps, fixed rear door window w/swing out vent windows (4-door models), stand-up hood ornament and windsplit molding, roof drip moldings, power front disc brakes, bumper protective strips front and rear, wheel covers, and P185/75R × 14 BSW tires. Wagon adds: Choice of cloth or

Measurements

	Coupes	Sedans	Wagons
Wheelbase	108.1"	108.1"	108.0"
Length	196.0"	196.0"	200.0"
Width	72.2"	72.2"	72.2"
Height	54.1"	55.0"	55.7"
Legroom — front	42.6"	42.6"	42.6"
Legroom — rear	35.1"	38.0"	35.9"
Headroom — front	37.9"	38.7"	38.8"
Headroom — rear	38.2"	37.7"	38.8"
Cargo capacity (cu. ft.)	16.1	15.9	71.8
Fuel capacity (gals.)	17.5	17.5	17.7

vinyl notchback front bench seat w/vinyl rear seat, P195/75R × 14 BSW tires. Sport coupe adds: Black-trimmed I/P, LH remote and RH manual outside rear view sport mirrors, front and rear wheel opening moldings, FE2 rallye ride and handling package, specific paint treatment, Designers' sport wheels, and P205/75R × 14 W/O BSW tires. Limited adds: Choice of cloth or vinyl 55/45 notchback front seat w/center fold-down armrest, door courtesy and warning lights, front ashtray light, under-dash courtesy lights, glove compartment light, "Limited" badging, stand-up hood ornament w/hood windsplit molding, belt reveal moldings, front and rear wheel opening moldings, and wide rocker panel moldings w/front and rear extensions. Estate Wagon adds (to Wagon): Notchback front seat w/choice of all-cloth, all-vinyl, or cloth front/vinyl rear upholstery, load floor carpeting, front ashtray light, under-dash courtesy lights, glove compartment light, "Estate Wagon" badging, stand-up hood ornament w/hood windsplit molding, front and rear wheel opening moldings, and custom rocker panel moldings.

Models Available

	Model No.	Base MSRP	Change from LY	Shipping Wt. (lbs.)	Model Year Production**	Change from LY**
Century 2-Door Coupe	H87	$5,546	+20.59%	3086	1,074	NA
Century 4-Door Sedan	H69	$5,646	+20.15%	3106	129,740	NA
Century 4-Door Station Wagon, 2-S.	E35	$5,922	+12.86%*	3236	6,493	-37.65%*
Century Sport 2-Door Coupe	G87	$6,063	+17.71%	3150	NA	NA
Century Limited 4-Door Sedan	L69	$6,132	+23.43%	3150	NA	NA
Century Estate Wagon 4-Door, 2-S.	H35	$6,220	+12.86%*	3247	11,122	-47.29%*
TOTALS	*Avg. price*	$5,922	+17.25%	*Production*	148,429	+165.83%

*Comparison of wagons made to 1979 Century Special, model E35, and Century Custom, model H35.   **Comparison to LY not available except on station wagons, as all coupe and sedan model production was kept combined.*

Regal

"It's what all the rest of the mid-size personal luxury cars are trying to be—a Buick."

Nameplate year of origin: 1973 (as Century subseries).
Current bodystyle lifespan: 1978 through 1987.
Predecessor to this model: Century Regal (1973 to 1977).
Replacement for this model: Regal (1988 to 1997).
Percentage of division's production: 23.92%.
Corporate siblings: Chevrolet Monte Carlo, Oldsmobile Cutlass Calais, Cutlass Salon and Cutlass Supreme, and Pontiac Grand Prix.
Primary competition: Chrysler Cordoba, Dodge Mirada, Ford Thunderbird and Mercury Cougar.
Notable changes: Redesigned front end and trim and detail changes.
Major standard equipment: Choice of cloth or vinyl notchback front seat w/center fold-down armrest, door operated dome light, door pull straps, simulated wood-grain appliqués on I/P and door panels, ashtray light, under-dash courtesy lights, glove compartment light, wheel opening moldings, rocker panel molding, bumper protective strips front and rear, power front disc brakes, power steering, wheel covers, and P195/75R × 14 BSW tires. Sport adds: Distinctive domed hood, tungsten halogen high beam headlights, fast-ratio power steering, turbocharged engine, FE2 rallye ride and handling package, and P205/70R × 14 BSW tires. Limited adds: Choice of crushed velour cloth or vinyl 55/45 notchback seat w/fold-down center armrest, and wide rocker panel molding with front and rear extensions, belt reveal and B-pillar appliqué moldings.

Measurements

Wheelbase	108.1"
Length	200.0"
Width	72.2"
Height	54.1"
Legroom — front	42.6"
Legroom — rear	36.3"
Headroom — front	37.9"
Headroom — rear	38.1"
Cargo capacity (cu. ft.)	16.3
Fuel capacity (gals.)	17.5

Models Available

	Model No.	Base MSRP	Change from LY	Shipping Wt. (lbs.)	Model Year Production	Change from LY
Regal 2-Door Coupe	J47	$6,305	+24.11%	3115	NA*	NA*
Regal Sport 2-Door Coupe	K47	$6,952	+11.64%	3194	NA*	NA*
Regal Limited 2-Door Coupe	M47	$6,724	+22.77%	3142	NA*	NA*
TOTALS	*Avg. price*	$6,660	+19.05%	*Production*	241,735	-11.57%

Comparison to 1979 is not possible as production of all Regal models was kept combined.

LeSabre

"Dedicated to the proposition that the buyer of a full-size car should get a comfortable, substantial, well-equipped automobile."

Nameplate year of origin: 1959 (also used on 1951 GM show car).

Current bodystyle lifespan: 1977 through 1985.

Predecessor to this model: LeSabre (1971 to 1976).

Replacement for this model: LeSabre (1986 to 1991).

Percentage of division's production: 9.87%.

Corporate siblings: Chevrolet Impala and Caprice, Pontiac Catalina and Bonneville, and Oldsmobile Delta 88 and Oldsmobile Custom Cruiser.

Primary competition: Chrysler Newport and Mercury Marquis.

Notable changes: Restyled exterior, with some interior trim and detail changes.

Major standard equipment: Choice of cloth or vinyl notchback front bench seat w/fold-down center armrest, cut-pile carpeting, woodgrained vinyl trim on door panels, front door operated dome light, I/P woodgrain appliqués, LH outside rear view mirror, bumper protective strips front and rear, front and rear wheel opening moldings, deluxe wheel covers, and P205/75R × 15 BSW tires. Wagon adds: Choice of cloth or vinyl notchback front bench seat w/vinyl rear seat, cut-pile carpeting including load floor, lockable hidden storage compartments, three-way tailgate, power tailgate window, LH and RH chrome rear view mirrors, and P225/75R × 15 BSW tires. Limited adds: Choice of crushed velour cloth or vinyl notchback front seat w/fold-down center armrest, full-length rocker panel molding, and black pillar moldings. Sport coupe adds: Sport steering wheel, fast-ratio power steering, turbocharged engine, FE2 rallye ride and handling package, "Turbo 3.8 Liter" badge, black accents around chrome moldings, grille and taillights, black B-pillar molding w/special sport coupe emblem, turbocharged engine, chrome road wheels and P225/70R × 15 W/O BSW tires.

Measurements

	Coupe	Sedan	Estate Wagon
Wheelbase	116.0"	116.0"	115.9"
Length	216.6"	216.6"	218.8"
Width	74.6"	74.6"	75.4"
Height	52.7"	55.2"	57.1"
Legroom — front	42.2"	42.2"	42.2"
Legroom — rear	38.3"	39.0"	37.7"
Headroom — front	38.9"	39.5"	39.7"
Headroom — rear	38.4"	38.2"	39.4"
Cargo capacity (cu. ft.)	20.8	20.8	86.8
Fuel capacity (gals.)	21.0	21.0	22.0

Models Available

	Model No.	Base MSRP	Change from LY	Shipping Wt. (lbs.)	Model Year Production	Change from LY
LeSabre 2-Door Coupe	N37	$6,674	+17.50%	3320	8,342	NA**
LeSabre 4-Door Sedan	N69	$6,769	+17.11%	3369	23,873	-6.13%
LeSabre Estate Wagon 4-Door, 2-Seat	R35	$7,673	+14.28%*	3898	9,318*	-56.28%*
LeSabre Limited 2-Door Coupe	P37	$6,929	+13.15%	3327	20,561	-46.30%
LeSabre Limited 4-Door Sedan	P69	$7,071	+13.15%	3375	37,676	-50.39%
LeSabre Sport 2-Door Coupe	F37	$7,782	+17.54%	3430	NA**	NA**
TOTALS	*Avg. price*	$7,150	+15.42%	*Production*	99,770	-33.83%

*Comparison is made to 1979 Estate Wagon, model R35. 1980 production includes the new Electra Estate Wagon, as production was kept combined.   **Comparison to 1979 is not possible as production of LeSabre Sport Coupe for 1980 was kept as combined total with LeSabre 2-Door coupe.*

Electra

"It's the kind of car worth working very hard to own."

Nameplate year of origin: 1959.

Current bodystyle lifespan: 1977 through 1984.

Predecessor to this model: Electra 225 (1971 to 1976).

Replacement for this model: Electra (1985 to 1990).

Percentage of division's production: 6.78%.

Measurements

	Coupe	Sedan	Estate Wagon
Wheelbase	118.9"	118.9"	115.9"
Length	220.9"	220.9"	218.8"

Corporate siblings: Cadillac deVille, Cadillac Fleetwood Brougham, and Oldsmobile Ninety-Eight.

Primary competition: Chrysler New Yorker and Mercury Grand Marquis.

Notable changes: Restyled exterior, with some interior trim and detail changes.

Major standard equipment: Choice of cloth or vinyl 55/45 front bench seat w/fold-down center armrest and two-way drivers side power adjustment, cut-pile carpeting, simulated woodgrain appliqués on door panels and I/P, quartz crystal digital clock, door pull straps, carpeted lower door panels, manual air conditioning w/tinted glass, power windows, custom color-coordinated steering wheel and safety belts, re-

Measurements (cont.)

	Coupe	Sedan	Estate Wagon
Width	74.7"	74.7"	75.4"
Height	55.0"	55.6"	57.1"
Legroom — front	42.2"	42.2"	42.2"
Legroom — rear	41.4"	42.0"	37.7"
Headroom — front	38.6"	39.4"	39.7"
Headroom — rear	37.9"	38.0"	39.4"
Cargo capacity (cu. ft.)	20.8	20.8	86.8
Fuel capacity (gals.)	21.0	21.0	22.0

mote-control LH and manual RH chrome rear view mirrors, acoustic insulation package, fender-mounted 4-section rectangular "ventiport" ornaments, wheel opening moldings, rocker panel molding, deluxe wheel covers, and P215/75R × 15 BSW tires. Wagon adds: Front 55/45 notchback seat w/choice of all-cloth, all-vinyl, or cloth front/vinyl rear upholstery, cut-pile carpeting including load floor, tilt steering wheel, light package, power door locks, door courtesy and warning lights, lockable hidden storage compartments, three-way tailgate w/remote control lock, power tailgate window, simulated woodgrain vinyl exterior appliqué, roof luggage rack, LH and RH chrome rear view mirrors, and P225/75R × 15 BSW tires. Park Avenue adds: Knit velour cloth 50/50 split seats w/individual fold-down center armrests, dual seat belt retractors, door courtesy and warning lights, AM/FM stereo radio, B-pillar mounted electroluminescent coach lights, wide bodyside molding w/front fender ventiports, and custom color-coordinated wheel covers.

Models Available

	Model No.	Base MSRP	Change from LY	Shipping Wt. (lbs.)	Model Year Production	Change from LY
Electra Limited 2-Door Coupe	X37	$9,132	+14.42%	3571	14,058*	-51.32%*
Electra Limited 4-Door Sedan	X69	$9,287	+13.87%	3578	54,422*	-28.71%*
Electra Estate Wagon 4-Door, 2-S.	V35	$10,513	NEW	4105	NA**	NEW**
Electra Park Avenue 2-Door Coupe	W37	$10,244	+21.62%	3600	*	*
Electra Park Avenue 4-Door Sedan	W69	$10,383	+20.76%	3607	*	*
TOTALS		*Avg. price* $10,205	+22.63%	*Production*	68,480	-43.70%

*Production of Park Avenue models kept as combined total with Limited models for both 1979 and 1980; therefore comparisons to LY include both Limited and Park Avenue models.   **Comparisons to LY are not available, as Electra Estate Wagon production was kept combined with the LeSabre Estate Wagon.*

1980

Riviera

"Riviera truly represents an American luxury car with impressive road manners."

Nameplate year of origin: 1963 (1949 as designation for hardtop models).

Current bodystyle lifespan: 1979 through 1985.

Predecessor to this model: Riviera (1977 to 1978).

Replacement for this model: Riviera (1986 to 1993).

Percentage of division's production: 4.81%.

Corporate siblings: Cadillac Eldorado and Oldsmobile Toronado.

Primary competition: Ford Thunderbird Town Landau.

Notable changes: Minor trim and detail changes.

Major standard equipment: Velour cloth 45/55 notchback front seat w/individual fold-down center armrests and six-way power driver's seat, thick cut-pile carpeting, custom color-coordinated steering wheel and safety belts, door courtesy and warning lights, simulated woodgrain appliqué on door panels and I/P, quartz crystal digital clock, deluxe steering wheel, door pull strap, manual air conditioning w/tinted glass, power windows, AM/FM stereo radio w/automatic power antenna, power door locks, light group, dual remote-control chrome rear view mirrors, cornering lights, automatic level control, deluxe wheel covers, and P205/75R × 15 WSW tires.

Measurements

Wheelbase	114.0"
Length	206.6"
Width	70.4"
Height	54.3"
Legroom — front	42.8"
Legroom — rear	39.4"
Headroom — front	37.9"
Headroom — rear	37.9"
Cargo capacity (cu. ft.)	15.8
Fuel capacity (gals.)	20.0

S-Type adds: Cloth front bucket seats w/center floor console, sport steering wheel, black I/P trim, dual remote-control rear view sport mirrors, black moldings and outside trim, amber front park and turn signal lenses, FE2 rallye ride-and-handling package, turbocharged engine, Designers' sport wheel covers, and GR70 × 15 W/O narrow white stripe tires.

Models Available

	Model No.	Base MSRP	Change from LY	Shipping Wt. (lbs.)	Model Year Production	Change from LY
Riviera 2-Door Coupe	Z57	$11,492	+13.65%	3633	41,404	+9.30%
Riviera S-Type 2-Door Coupe	Y57	$11,823	+13.81%	3734	7,217	-49.53%
TOTALS	*Avg. price*	$11,658	+13.73%	*Production*	48,621	-6.82%

CADILLAC

"An American standard for the world."

A completely redesigned Seville and modestly restyled, more aerodynamic full-size models marked Cadillac's entrance into the 1980s. The new ultra-luxury Seville 4-door now shared a front-wheel-drive undercarriage with the Eldorado coupe and its E-body sisters, the Buick Riviera and Oldsmobile Toronado; however the Seville retained its own K-body designation. With its very unusual 1930s era slopeback styling, the Seville did not receive the accolades the original design had. The standard diesel engine was something American consumers shied away from in droves, and production would end the year at about three-fourths the total from 1979. The rest of the Cadillac line fared no better, and sales of the full line dropped by nearly 40 percent.

Seville styling was unmistakably distinctive, and a guaranteed conversation starter. While its new front-end styling maintained much of the original Seville look and was quite similar to the new DeVille and Fleetwood design, the profile and rear end styling were strange enough to stir up the press. A slanting rear window led into a shortened and taller decklid, giving the impression of a fastback look, and having an air of a 1930s bustle-back styling elegance, combined with 1950s Rolls-Royce formality. The roofline itself continued as a straight feature line sweeping down to the rear bumper. The decklid had about a one-foot horizontal portion immediately behind the rear window, then slanted downward to meet the bumper. In profile, the rear door beltline curved slightly downward at the back, and in parallel with it was a bodyside feature line that came to a sharp corner just behind the rear door, angling up the C-pillar. In some trim configurations, a chrome molding extended the horizontal feature line to curve downward to end at the rear bumper, where it met with the roof and decklid endpoints. The molding also served as the color break line on two-tone cars. Thin horizontal taillamps with the license plate mount set in the middle were of a flat, non-wraparound design. It was definitely a love it or hate it design. If imitation is truly the sincerest form of flattery, then the Seville earned what ads said was the "Beauty of being first." Over the next two years the competition would copy the "bustle-back" design, first with the 1981 Chrysler Imperial, then the 1982 Lincoln Continental.

Up front, the Seville carried a grille with vertical bars and a heavier chrome bar across the top, much like that of the restyled deVilles. The grille now dipped into the bumper, as did all Cadillac grilles this year. Dual rectangular headlights set above horizontal parking/turn signal lights, much like those of the first generation, returned. The greenhouse area utilized the Eldorado's flush windshield and nearly flush side window designs, adding potential fuel mileage gains. Inside, the Seville was more spacious due to its new design, and added new luxurious upholstery choices and an ever expanding list of standard equipment. A new instrument panel maintained the Cadillac theme of prior years, with a flat facing covered in simulated teak and butterfly walnut. Horizontal rectangular pods held gauges and controls, with square air vents at each end, and vertical rectangular air vents in the center. Each end of the flat upper dash pad slanted downwards and contained air outlets for side window defoggers. The new body design allowed for a larger trunk, lined with color-coordinated carpeting.

Powering the newly styled Seville was a standard 350 CID V8 diesel engine, a first for Cadillac, or any luxury car for that matter. Designed and built by Oldsmobile, the engine seemed like a good idea to decrease fuel consumption, but the buying public was reluctant to spend large sums of money on unproven technologies that had a stigma of noise and belching black smoke. Knowing some buyers would be turned off by the diesel engine, Cadillac made a new 368 CID V8 engine available as a credit option on the Seville. Standard equipment on all other Cadillac models, the 368 CID V8 was yet another downsizing of the 500 CID V8 engine that had been cut down to 425 cubic inches from 1977 through 1979. It was available with a 4-barrel carburetor intake as standard equipment in the deVille and Fleetwood, or a new digitally controlled electronic fuel-injection system, standard on the Eldorado and optional on Seville. The fuel-injected system also added a new on-board diagnostic system that allowed servicing the car by plugging it into a computer for diagnosis. On the road, the DEFI system, as it was known, was intended to increase power while also improving gas mileage. In reality, the EPA rated the two engines similarly, and the fuel-injected engine actually produced lower horsepower ratings. However, this would quickly change as microprocessor technology was rapidly progressing, and by next year further advances would be developed.

DeVille and Fleetwood models all received a mild redesign to make them more aerodynamic, by tapering the hood line, raising the rear deck lines, and introducing more vertical rear windows, all of which combined to reduce the aerodynamic drag coefficient. Other measures to help improve fuel efficiency included lower rolling-resistance tires, and the aforementioned new engines. Overall styling still looked similar to the 1977–1979 design, but it was obvious the entire front end was sleeker and different. The grille area

was enlarged with a narrow vertical bar texture, and extended slightly into the bumper area, with a large chrome panel across the top of the grille. On each side of the grille were dual headlights set above the parking/turn signal lights, and around the corners capping the fender ends were the side marker, cornering and turn signal lights. The unit as a whole seemed flush and tight, with few gaps to be found, thereby improving the aerodynamics. The bumper was a standard box style bumper, which dipped slightly in the center to accommodate the enlarged grille.

Around back, the taillights continued to be inset in vertical chrome bumper ends which created a small tailfin of sorts, and the redesigned rear roofline and raised decklid increased luggage space. As mentioned previously, the rooflines were more formal and upright. Interiors continued to grow slightly more luxurious with each passing year, and this year was no exception. A new model introduction is a rarity for Cadillac, but in early spring of 1980 a Fleetwood Brougham 2-Door Coupe was added. This was the first time a two-door model had been in the Fleetwood Brougham series.

The new-for-1979 Eldorado returned for the '80s with a more refined grille that continued to be of an egg-crate design, with the vertical bars more strongly emphasized, while the horizontal bars were to the background. New two-tone paint offerings were also introduced. As with the other Cadillac models, new engine offerings rounded out the changes. While disappointing production numbers were a minor setback, Cadillac would rise again by the mid–1980s and break the 1979 sales record by the end of the 1985 model year.

1980

Coupe deVille 2-Door Coupe

Eldorado 2-Door Hardtop Coupe

Fleetwood Brougham 4-Door Sedan

Sedan deVille 4-Door Sedan

Seville 4-Door Sedan with Elegante package

Model year production: 230,276, down 39.44% from 1979.
Domestic market share: 3.01% (9th place).
Base price range: $12,401 to $23,388.
Cadillac average base price: $17,069, up 9.93%.
Introduction date: October 11, 1979. Fleetwood Brougham coupe introduced in February 1980.
Assembly plants: Southgate, CA (C); Linden, NJ (E); and Detroit, MI (9).
Data plate identification (VIN): Thirteen digit code read as follows: First digit indicates division (6 = Cadillac); second through fourth digits indicate series and body style (model number in model charts); fifth digit is engine code (see powertrain chart); sixth digit indicates model year (A = 1980); seventh digit indicates assembly plant (see list above); remaining digits are sequential with beginning number of 100001. *Example:* 6D699A9100001 is a 1980 Cadillac Sedan deVille 4-Door Sedan, with 368 CID, DEFI V8 engine, serial number 100001, built in Detroit, MI.

Powertrains

Engine	Net HP	Engine Code	Transmission Availability		Seville	Eldorado	DeVille & Fleetwood Brougham	Fleetwood Limousines
350 CID (5.7L), EFI, V8	180	8	Turbo Hydra-matic 3-sp. Automatic		—	S[1]	—	—
				Calif.	14/21	14/21	—	—
350 CID (5.7L), Diesel FI, V8	105	N	Turbo Hydra-matic 3-sp. Automatic		S	$266	$924	—
				MPG	21/31	21/31	20/30	—
				Calif.	21	21	21	—
368 CID (6.0L), 4-bbl., V8	150	6	Turbo Hydra-matic 3-sp. Automatic		—	—	S	S
				MPG:	14/22	14/22	15/23	12/17
				Calif.	—	—	14	12
368 CID (6.0L), DEFI, V8	145	9	Turbo Hydra-matic 3-sp. Automatic		-$266 (credit option)	S	—	—
				MPG:	14/22	14/22	15/23	12/17

[1]*Standard on cars equipped for sale in California.*

Major Options

	Seville	deVille	Eldorado	Fleetwood Brougham	Fleetwood Limousine
Automatic Climate Control	S	S	S	S	S
Electric rear window defogger	$170	$170	$170	$170	$170
Controlled cycle windshield wiper	S	$43	S	S	$43
Tilt and telescope steering wheel	S	$142	$142	S	$142[1]
Cruise control	S	$147	$147	$147	$147
Twilight Sentinel	S	$62	S	S	$62
Guidematic headlamp control	$72	$72	$72	$72	$72
Leather upholstery	$595	$435	$466	$466	—[2]
Power front passenger seat, 6-way	S	$395	$171	S	—
Power 50/50 front seat recliners	$71	$130	$130	$71	—
Lighted vanity mirror, dual	$112	$112	$112	$112	$112
Illuminated entry system	S	$67	S	S	$67
AM/FM stereo w/tape & seek/scan	$225	$225	$225	$225	$398[3]
Cadillac trip computer	$920	—	$920	—	—
Automatic door locks	$129	$129	$129	$129	$129
Remote trunk release w/electric pull-down	*S*	$92	S	S	S
Padded vinyl top	—	$240	—	S	S
Astroroof	$1,058	$1,058	$1,058	$1,058	—[2]
Theft-Deterrent system	$153	$153	$153	$153	$153
Fuel monitor system	S	$35	$35	$35	$35
Electronic level control	S	$169	S	$169	S
Special turbine style wheel discs	—	$63	—	S	S
Wire spoke wheel covers	N/C	$320	—	$262	$262
Cast aluminum wheels	N/C	—	$376	—	—
Chrome plated wire wheels	—	$755	—	$755	—

Popular Option Groups & Packages

	Seville	deVille	Eldorado	Fleetwood Brougham	Fleetwood Limousine
Biarritz package	—	—	$2,494	—	—
Brougham d'Elegance package	—	—	—	$1,062	—
DeVille d'Elegance package	—	$1,005	—	—	—
Eleganté package	$2,934	—	—	—	—
Phaeton package	—	$2,029	—	—	—

—= Not Available; S = Standard equipment.   ¹Standard on Formal Limousine.   ²Available by special order only.   ³Fleetwood models include rear seat controls.

Paint Colors

		TWO-TONE COMBINATIONS	
	Code	Eleganté	DeVille & Eldorado*
White	11	—	—
Silver metallic	15	—	—
Black	19	low	low
Light Blue metallic	21	—	up
Medium Blue metallic	22	low	low
Dark Blue metallic	29	—	up
Medium Beige metallic	36	low	low
Pastel Green	41	—	—
Blackwatch Green metallic	49	—	—
Light Yellow	54	—	—
Beige	59	—	—
Tan	61	low	low
Dark Brown metallic	67	—	up
Dark Claret metallic	76	—	up
Carmine	78	—	—
Light Gray	89	up	—
Light Blue Firemist metallic**	90	low	low
Tan Firemist metallic**	91	up or low	up or low
Claret Firemist metallic**	92	low	low
Medium Silver Gray Firemist metallic**	94	up or low	low
Saddle Firemist metallic**	96	low	low
Charcoal Firemist metallic**	98	—	—
Dark Brown Firemist metallic**	99	—	—

In two-tone combinations, the first two digits indicate lower (low) color, the next two digits are the upper (up) color.   *Except Biarritz.   **Firemist paint available for $201 extra.

Seville

"Introducing Seville for the 80's ... quite possibly the most distinctive car in the world ... and the most advanced."

Nameplate year of origin: 1976; 1956 (as a designation on Eldorado 2-Door Hardtops).

Current bodystyle lifespan: 1980 through 1985.

Predecessor to this model: Seville (1976 to 1979).

Replacement for this model: Seville (1986 to 1991).

Percentage of division's production: 17.09%.

Corporate siblings: Buick Riviera, Cadillac Eldorado and Oldsmobile Toronado.

Primary competition: Lincoln Versailles.

Notable changes: Completely redesigned.

Major standard equipment: Plush Heather cloth dual comfort 50/45 split front seat w/individual fold-down center armrests, six-way power adjustment and passenger seat recliner, high pile carpeting, cloth trimmed rear compartment shelf, seatback

Measurements

Wheelbase	114.0"
Length	204.8"
Width	NA
Height	54.3"
Legroom — front	NA
Legroom — rear	NA
Headroom — front	NA
Headroom — rear	NA
Cargo capacity (cu. ft.)	14.5
Fuel capacity (gals.)	23.0

1980

and overhead entry assist straps, door pull straps, individual rear seat reading lamps, illuminated visor vanity mirrors, power windows, power door locks, tilt and telescoping steering wheel, controlled wiper cycle system, electronic climate control system, electronically tuned AM/FM signal-seeking stereo radio w/automatic power antenna and digital display, Twilight Sentinel, dual remote-control electronically heated rear view mirrors w/outside drivers side thermometer, remote trunk release with power trunk lid pull-down, trunk carpeting including spare tire cover and deck lid, fuel monitor system, lamp monitors, front cornering lights, wheel opening moldings, stand-up wreath and crest hood-ornament, electronic level control, automatic parking brake release, bodyside and decklid accent striping, power four-wheel disc brakes, cast aluminum wheels, and P205/75R15 wide WSW tires.

Models Available

	Model No.	Base MSRP	Change from LY	Shipping Wt. (lbs.)	Model Year Production	Change from LY
Seville 4-Door Sedan	S69	$19,662	+25.67%	3911	39,344	-26.44%
TOTALS	Avg. price	$19,662	+25.67%	Production	39,344	-26.44%

deVille

"Destined to be America's favorite luxury car ... again."

Nameplate year of origin: 1959 (series); 1949 (as hardtop designation).
Current bodystyle lifespan: 1977 through 1984.
Predecessor to this model: deVille (1971 to 1976).
Replacement for this model: deVille (1985 to 1993).
Percentage of division's production: 45.46%.
Corporate siblings: Buick Electra, Cadillac Fleetwood Brougham and Oldsmobile 98.
Primary competition: Lincoln Continental.
Notable changes: Restyled exterior, with some interior trim and detail changes.
Major standard equipment: Durand knit w/Renaissance velour cloth front bench seat with front and rear seat center armrests, 6-way power front driver's seat adjuster, front seatback map pockets, cut-pile carpeting, door pull assist straps, passenger side visor vanity mirror, dome light w/dual spot map lamps, courtesy lights, courtesy lamp/assist strap combination on B-pillar of 2-doors, electric clock, power windows, power door locks, automatic climate control, digital display AM/FM electronically tuned stereo radio w/seek and scan and automatic power antenna, LH remote-control rear view mirror, lamp monitors, front cornering lights, wheel opening moldings, rocker panel moldings, full wheel covers, and P215/75R15 wide WSW tires.

Measurements

Wheelbase	121.4"
Length	221.0"
Width	76.4"
Height	55.6"
Legroom — front	NA
Legroom — rear	NA
Headroom — front	NA
Headroom — rear	NA
Cargo capacity (cu. ft.)	NA
Fuel capacity (gals.)	20.6

Models Available

	Model No.	Base MSRP	Change from LY	Shipping Wt. (lbs.)	Model Year Production	Change from LY
Coupe deVille 2-Door Coupe	D47	$12,401	+11.33%	4048	55,490	-54.48%
Sedan deVille 4-Door Sedan	D69	$12,770	+11.11%	4084	49,188	-47.23%
TOTALS	Avg. price	$12,586	+11.22%	Production	104,678	-51.34%

Eldorado

*"World class in engineering. Cadillac in luxury.
A legend on the road."*

Nameplate year of origin: 1953.
Current bodystyle lifespan: 1979 through 1985.
Predecessor to this model: Fleetwood Eldorado (1971 to 1978).

Measurements

Wheelbase	114.0"
Length	204.5"

Replacement for this model: Eldorado (1986 to 1991).
Percentage of division's production: 22.88%.
Corporate siblings: Buick Riviera, Cadillac Seville and Oldsmobile Toronado.
Primary competition: Lincoln Continental Mark VI.
Notable changes: Minor trim and detail changes.
Major standard equipment: Heather knit cloth 50/45 dual comfort front seat w/individual fold-down center armrest, 6-way power driver seat adjuster, plush cut-pile carpeting, door pull assist straps, carpeted rear shelf panel, trunk carpeting, dome light w/dual spot map lights, illuminated entry system, power windows, power door locks, automatic climate control, digital display AM/FM electronically tuned stereo radio w/seek and scan and automatic power antenna, LH and RH remote-control rear view mirrors, front cornering lights, wheel opening moldings, rocker panel moldings, stand-up wreath and crest hood-ornament, lamp monitors, automatic level control, four wheel disc brakes, full wheel covers, and P205/75R × 15 wide WSW tires.

Measurements (cont.)

Width	72.0"
Height	54.2"
Legroom — front	42.8"
Legroom — rear	39.4"
Headroom — front	37.9"
Headroom — rear	37.9"
Cargo capacity (cu. ft.)	19.6
Fuel capacity (gals.)	20.6

Models Available

	Model No.	Base MSRP	Change from LY	Shipping Wt. (lbs.)	Model Year Production	Change from LY
Eldorado 2-Door Coupe	L57	$15,509	+8.91%	3806	52,683	-21.88%
TOTALS	Avg. price	$15,509	+8.91%	Production	52,683	-21.88%

Fleetwood Brougham

"In the proud Fleetwood tradition ... 'The Cadillac of Cadillacs.'"

Nameplate year of origin: 1966.
Current bodystyle lifespan: 1977 through 1992.
Predecessor to this model: Fleetwood Sixty-Special and Fleetwood Brougham (1971 to 1976).
Replacement for this model: Fleetwood Brougham (1993 to 1996).
Percentage of division's sales volume: 13.88%.
Corporate siblings: Buick Electra, Cadillac deVille and Oldsmobile 98.
Primary competition: Lincoln Continental w/Town Car package.
Notable changes: Restyled exterior, with some interior trim and detail changes.
Major standard equipment: Heather knit w/Raphael cloth insert dual comfort 45/55 front seat w/6-way driver side and passenger side power seat adjuster, front and rear seat fold-down center armrests, front seat back map pockets, cut-pile carpeting, hinged door pull assist handles, dome light w/dual spot map lamps, quartz digital clock, power windows, power door locks, automatic climate control, digital display AM/FM electronically tuned stereo radio w/seek and scan and automatic power antenna, LH and RH remote-control rear view mirrors, lamp monitors, rear quarter opera lamps, front cornering lights, wheel opening moldings, rocker panel moldings, electronic level control, four wheel disc brakes, full wheel covers, and P215/75R15 wide WSW tires.

Measurements

Wheelbase	121.4"
Length	221.0"
Width	76.4"
Height	56.7"
Legroom — front	NA
Legroom — rear	NA
Headroom — front	NA
Headroom — rear	NA
Cargo capacity (cu. ft.)	NA
Fuel capacity (gals.)	20.6

Models Available

	Model No.	Base MSRP	Change from LY	Shipping Wt. (lbs.)	Model Year Production	Change from LY
Fleetwood Brougham 2-Door Coupe	B47	$15,307*	NEW	NA	2,300	NEW
Fleetwood Brougham 4-Door Sedan	B69	$14,927	+11.01%	4092	29,659	-29.72%
TOTALS	Avg. price	$15,117	+12.43%	Production	31,959	-24.27%

*Due to several mid-year price increases the coupe's introductory price is higher than the sedan was at the beginning of the model year.

1980

Fleetwood Limousine

"Flagships of the Fleet."

Nameplate year of origin: 1927 (models using Fleetwood bodies); 1935 (Fleetwood series).
Current bodystyle lifespan: 1977 through 1984.
Predecessor to this model: Fleetwood Seventy-Five (1971 to 1976).
Replacement for this model: Fleetwood 75 Limousine (1985 to 1987).
Percentage of division's sales volume: 0.70%.
Corporate siblings: None.
Primary competition: None.
Notable changes: Restyled exterior, with some interior trim and detail changes.
Major standard equipment: Dante cloth front bench seat w/2-way power front seat adjuster, front and rear seat fold-down center armrests, cut-pile carpeting, two fold-down seats (rearward facing for two additional passengers), hinged door pull assist handles, power windows, power door locks, dual automatic climate control system (front and rear), courtesy lights, electric clock, AM/FM radio w/automatic power antenna, passenger control panel (controls power windows, reading lights, radio [optional], automatic climate control, and glass partition in Formal Limousine), automatic level control, LH and RH remote-control rear view mirror, front cornering lights, wheel opening moldings, full-length rocker panel moldings, full wheel covers, and HR78 × 15 wide WSW tires. Formal Limousine adds: Black leather 40/40 front seat and sliding glass partition separating driver and passenger compartments.

Measurements

Wheelbase	144.5"
Length	244.1"
Width	79.8"
Height	56.9"
Legroom — front	NA
Legroom — rear	NA
Headroom — front	NA
Headroom — rear	NA
Cargo capacity (cu. ft.)	NA
Fuel capacity (gals.)	25.0

Models Available

	Model No.	Base MSRP	Change from LY	Shipping Wt. (lbs.)	Model Year Production*	Change from LY*
Fleetwood 4-Door Limousine	F23	$22,586	+7.62%	4629	1,612	NA
Fleetwood 4-Door Formal Limousine	F33	$23,388	+7.61%	4718	NA	NA
TOTALS	*Avg. price*	$22,987	+7.61%	*Production*	1,612	-20.40%

*Change from LY not available, as production was kept combined as one total for 1979 and 1980.

CHEVROLET

"The 1980 Chevrolets."

Chevrolet's model year began April 19, 1979, with the introduction of the highly anticipated front-wheel-drive X-body Nova replacement, the Citation, and model year introductions would continue through the end of October 1979 when a revised Corvette was introduced. Besides the new Citation, the new decade brought a restyle for the full-size cars, facelifts for the mid-size range and the Chevette, and more modest changes to the rest of the line. While Chevy again held onto the first place position in sales and model year production, it was the early introduction of the Citation that would skew the numbers to make it appear on the surface that Chevy outsold its number two rival, Ford, by nearly two to one. When adjusted to a calendar year basis,

Chevy still outsold and outproduced Ford by nearly 50 percent, with all of the increase coming from the new Citation and the highly popular Chevette. It was a promising start to the new decade, but a success that would soon fade as an economic recession took hold and quality issues began to appear in the Citation line.

Powering the new Citation was a standard transverse mounted 151 CID four-cylinder, Pontiac-built engine, mated to a four-speed overdrive manual transmission and utilizing a newly designed front-wheel-drive system, the combination of which gave a 38 mile-per-gallon highway fuel economy rating. As a side note, the transmission was called a "transaxle" when combined with a transverse mounted engine and front-wheel-drive. Exterior styling was aerodynamically efficient, having undergone extensive wind tunnel testing, and the hatchback coupe achieved a .417 drag coefficient, which was low for that time. With smaller exterior dimensions and larger interior volume, which was classified by the EPA measurement index as "mid-size" car proportions, the Citation was an engineering and technical success unlike any car produced in the United States prior to 1980. An optional Chevrolet-built 173 CID V6 engine was the most efficient and powerful Chevy V6 engine to date, and gave the lightweight Citation an impressive 25 additional horsepower, allowing the Citation to perform as well as a V8 equipped 1979 Nova.

Styling for the Citation was aerodynamic, as previously mentioned, with a low front hood line, rakish windshield, and on hatchbacks, a long slanting rear roofline and hatch that helped the car easily move through the air. The hatchbacks came in both two-door and four-door configurations. Two more traditional notchback coupes were also offered, both having a sloping rear window that was similar in profile to the former Nova coupes. The new Club Coupe was equipped the same as the two hatchback models, while the Citation base coupe was a lower-priced, stripped-down version that did away with many extra features that were standard on Citations, but had always been optional on the Nova. One of the main criticisms of the Citation from the media was its price, and the base coupe was designed to answer those critics.

Front-end styling featured a full-width egg-crate grille pattern, with single square headlamps at each end and side marker and turn signal lights on the fender side edge of the wraparound bezel. The grille insert consisted of eighteen columns across and seven openings high, with a gold Chevy bowtie emblem placed in the center. Vertical parking and turn signal lights were inset within the two outer columns. A body colored air dam was placed below the chrome bumper, aiding in the aerodynamic efficiency. Bodysides used a single feature line running between the bottom corners of the front and rear side marker light bezels, creating a small flare as it passed over the wheel opening moldings. The greenhouse area of the hatchbacks was similar to the unsuccessful design used on the larger Buick Century and Oldsmobile Cutlass "fastback" style two-door coupes and four-door sedans of 1978 to 1980 vintage, with the four-door hatchback using a six-window design, and the hatchback coupe having a large triangular rear quarter window. Coupe and Club coupe models used more traditional large rear quarter windows. All rear quarter windows were fixed, but could be ordered with a remote control "swing-out" style quarter window. Also, unlike on the mid-size Malibu sedans, the rear door windows on the four-door hatchback partially retracted, a welcome feature for rear seat passengers. At the back end, all models used a three-unit horizontal rectangular taillight with an inner

backup light lens, an amber center lens for the turn signal light, and the outer end red lens wrapping around the quarter panel end, doubling as the side marker light. A center-mounted cove housed the license plate mounting.

Citation interiors were spacious and inviting, with eye-pleasing materials and patterns on seats and door panels, and used new easy-to-service instrument cluster pods, which were easily removable from the passenger compartment. The instrument panel itself had a three-section cluster in front of the driver, with the center carrying a horizontal speedometer, with square fuel, clock and other gauges mounted below it, or five round dials with the optional Gage Package. To the left were an air vent and light controls, and to the right were ventilation controls and a vertically turned radio. In the center were two rectangular air vents, with ashtray and cigarette lighter below, and to the far right side, a single vent with a large bin-type glove box below. Upholstery materials rivaled the Caprice for their overall appearance and materials, and as previously mentioned the cabin was much roomier than the Nova's had been.

After gaining a new front-end design with square headlights for 1979, the popular Chevette received a revised rear end and rear quarter panels for 1980, with new wraparound taillights, using three-unit lenses with the inner being the backup light. A fourth section on the rear side held the side-marker light, and the formerly square fuel filler door on the left side of the car was now a round door. The rear hatch was also revised, adding a slightly larger rear window and a small ridge below the window, before turning downward to meet the rear panel. Rear quarter windows for both two- and four-door models had a more angular point at the rear end, as opposed to the rounded corner used on earlier models. New designs and patterns improved the interior appearance. A new optional feature, which began as an optional automatic shoulder belt system in the 1979 models, was an automatic seat and shoulder belt system, available for $65 extra. It was Chevrolet's, and General Motors', first completely passive seat and shoulder belt system, and had both belts attached to the front door. The driver or front-seat passenger simply had to sit in the car and close the door to be buckled in. The system was not particular popular in the Chevette, but would lead to an innovative motorized version of the system in some Ford Motor Company models several years later.

The mid-size line received mild styling updates, with the Malibu gaining a classy looking vertical bar grille, and the Monte Carlo getting new dual rectangular headlights and a new grille. The Monte Carlo used side-by-side headlights with the parking/turn signal lights placed horizontally beneath the headlight bezel. The new grille was a four row by sixteen-column egg-crate design, with heavy chrome trim and surround moldings. Body-colored front header panel and bumper assemblies with dual chrome rub strips continued to be used. Also new on the Monte Carlo was a

1980

standard 3.8-liter, 229 CID V6 engine built by Chevrolet, and a newly available 3.8-liter, 231 CID turbocharged V6 engine built by Buick as an option. The vertical bar grille on Malibus was elongated to eliminate the body-colored space between the grille and the headlight bezel; it consisted of forty vertical bars, with a thicker center bar, two horizontal bars set behind, and a chrome surround. With the former standard 3.3-liter, 200 CID V6 engine being dropped, the 3.8-liter, 229 CID V6 engine became the standard powerplant for the Malibu also. The rest of the styling was mostly the same on both cars, with unique new two-tone combinations being available on all models.

The full-size Chevrolets were still touted as "The New Chevrolet," and at least this year there was some truth to the statement, as the Impala and Caprice Classic lines received an aerodynamic exterior makeover. While still utilizing the same chassis, similar interior appearance and designs, and mostly the same powerplants, virtually all of the exterior sheetmetal was new, while still carrying the same basic appearance. The front fenders and hood were lowered at the front, trunk lids and rear quarter panels were raised, bodysides were smoother, and rooflines were more formal, all in an effort to decrease air drag and improve fuel efficiency. Along with the restyling, the cars lost between 100 and 150 pounds, depending upon model. As mentioned earlier, front-end styling was similar to the prior three seasons in general appearance. On all models, new front bumpers dropped slightly below the grille and eliminated the bumper opening air intakes, while parking/turn signal lights were still mounted toward the outer ends of the bumper. The grille insert for the Impala had a similar look to last year's Caprice grille, being eight vertical sections wide with each section having egg-crate style inserts seven rows high and four columns wide, with the Chevy bowtie emblem in the center. A separate side marker light on the fender side of the header panel, vertical and rectangular in shape, was set back an inch or so from the fender tip. For the Caprice, a new large-opening egg-crate style chrome grille was four rows high and twenty columns across. A heavy chrome bar ran across the entire front-end panel and onto the header panel fender sides atop the side marker and turn signal light, which was mounted within the wraparound headlight bezel.

Formal rooflines on full-size models were new to both coupes and sedans, eliminating the angular wraparound rear window of the 1977 through 1979 coupes. Station wagons remained mostly the same from the cowl back, with only a slight revision to sheetmetal on the doors and quarter panels. The coupe and sedan rooflines met raised deck lids that ended in a sharp angle to meet a flat and vertical rear end panel, not completely unlike the prior model's, just a little taller. Slightly larger three-unit taillights continued on both cars, with the Impala again having the backup lights within

the center unit, and the Caprice having separate vertical backup lights mounted between the taillights and the license plate mounting. Interiors featured new upholstery and door panels, but the general layout of the instrument panel and other details were much the same as the prior three years. Powerplants changed completely, with all of last year's choices gone. The new offerings included a standard 3.8-liter V6 engine for coupes and sedans (the 229 CID Chevy engine for the 49 states, and the 231 CID Buick engine for California), and a new standard 4.4-liter V8 engine, built by Chevrolet, in station wagons and available in cars. The 305 CID V8 engine now had with a four-barrel carburetor, and Oldsmobile's 350 CID Diesel V8 engine became available exclusively in station wagons.

The Camaro, which had been gaining in sales as performance cars resurged over the past few years, again fell on hard times, as effects of the 1979 fuel crisis and resulting recession took hold. While the Camaros were not greatly changed from their 1979 counterparts, the Z28 did gain a unique, body-colored four bar horizontal grille insert and a single bar in the under-bumper opening. The horizontal bars were backed by several black vertical bars, and a large color-coordinated Z28 emblem was placed on the driver's side of the grille. Also new were a functional solenoid-operated air-intake hood scoop and functional fender exhaust ports to improve air circulation under the hood.

For the "only true American production sports car," the Corvette, 1980 brought improvements centered on refinements to the body aerodynamics, as well as many new standard features, all of which resulted in a nearly 30 percent price increase. The new body features included a more aerodynamic front bumper cover with an integral air dam, and a deeply recessed horizontal bar grille and parking lights. Functional front fender air exhaust louvers, in black, were added, as was a lower profile hood. At the back end a new rear bumper cover incorporated an integral rear spoiler, with new round taillights and Corvette flag emblems. A long list of new standard features included air conditioning, "Tilt-Telescopic" steering wheel, power windows, dual remote-control mirrors, new ribbed-pattern cloth interior, front cornering lights, and a convenience group featuring time-delay headlights and intermittent wipers among other items.

Finally, the subcompact Monza was entering its final season and received virtually no changes. The sporty looking Spyder equipment package for 1980 combined the former Spyder appearance and Spyder equipment packages into a single package. There were 7,589 Monza 2+2 Sport hatchbacks equipped with the Spyder package for the 1980 model year. Other changes included discontinuation of the optional 305 CID V8 engine and the Vega-based station wagon model. Essentially, the Monza was back to the model lineup it had in 1975 when it was introduced.

Camaro Rally Sport 2-Door Coupe

Camaro Z28 2-Door Sport Coupe

Camaro Z28 2-Door Sport Coupe

Caprice Classic 4-Door Sedan

Caprice Classic 4-Door Station Wagon
with Estate package

Chevette 2-Door Hatchback Coupe

Chevette 4-Door Hatchback Sedan

Citation 2-Door Club Coupe

Chevette interior with Custom trim
and automatic seat-shoulder belt system

Citation 2-Door Hatchback Coupe
with X11 Sport Equipment package

Citation 4-Door Hatchback Sedan

Impala 2-Door Sport Coupe

Citation instrument panel

Corvette 2-Door Coupe

Malibu 2-Door Coupe

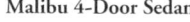

Malibu 4-Door Sedan

1980

Malibu Classic 4-Door Sedan

Malibu Classic 4-Door Station Wagon
with Estate package

Monte Carlo 2-Door Coupe with Turbo V6
and removable glass roof panels

Monza 2-Door Coupe with Cabriolet roof

Monza Sport 2+2 2-Door Hatchback
with Spyder Equipment package

Model year production: 2,286,745, up 0.09% from 1979.
Domestic market share: 29.92% (1st place).
Base price range: $3,782 to $13,140.
Chevrolet average base price: $5,838, up 16.57%.
Introduction date: October 11, 1979. Citation introduced April 19, 1979. Corvette introduced October 25, 1979.
Assembly plants: Lakewood, GA (A); Baltimore, MD (B); Southgate, CA (C); Doraville, GA (D); Janesville, WI (J); Kansas City/Leeds, MO (K); Van Nuys, CA (L); Norwood, OH (N); Arlington, TX (R); St. Louis, MO (S); Tarrytown, NY (T); Lordstown, OH (U); Willow Run, MI (W); Wilmington, DE (Y); Fremont, CA (Z); Oshawa, Ontario, Canada (1); and Oklahoma City, OK (6).

Data plate identification (VIN): Thirteen digit code read as follows: First digit indicates division (1 = Chevrolet); second through fourth digits indicate series and body style (model number in model charts); fifth digit is engine code (see powertrain chart); sixth digit indicates model year (A = 1980); seventh digit indicates assembly plant (see list above); remaining digits are sequential with beginning number of 100001. *Example:* 1S87LAN100001 is a 1980 Chevrolet Camaro Berlinetta 2-Door Sport Coupe, with 350 CID, 4-bbl. V8 engine, serial number 100001, built in Norwood, OH.

Powertrains

Engine	Net HP	Engine Code: VIN/GM	Transmission Availability[1]		Chevette	Monza	Citation	Camaro	Malibu[2]	Monte Carlo	Full-Size Chevy	Corvette
98 CID (1.6L) OHC, 2-bbl., 4-cyl.	63	0/L17	4-speed manual		S	—	—	—	—	—	—	—
				MPG:	26/36	—	—	—	—	—	—	—
				Calif.	26	—	—	—	—	—	—	—
			3-speed Turbo Hydra-matic		$320	—	—	—	—	—	—	—
				MPG:	25	—	—	—	—	—	—	—
				Calif.	25	—	—	—	—	—	—	—
98 CID (1.6L) OHC, 2-bbl., "High-Output" 4-cyl.[2]	68	9/L18	4-speed manual		$60	—	—	—	—	—	—	—
				MPG:	NA	—	—	—	—	—	—	—
				Calif.	NA	—	—	—	—	—	—	—
			3-speed Turbo Hydra-matic		$380	—	—	—	—	—	—	—
				MPG:	NA	—	—	—	—	—	—	—
				Calif.	NA	—	—	—	—	—	—	—
151 CID (2.5L),	85/ 90[3]	V/LX8[3]	4-speed manual		—	S	S	—	—	—	—	—
				MPG:	—	22/35	24/38	—	—	—	—	—

Engine	Net HP	Engine Code: VIN/GM	Transmission Availability[1]		Chevette	Monza	Citation	Camaro	Malibu[2]	Monte Carlo	Full-Size Chevy	Corvette
2-bbl., 4-cyl.				Calif.	—	21/34	24	—	—	—	—	—
			3-speed Turbo		—	$320	$337	—	—	—	—	—
			Hydra-matic	MPG:	—	24/32	22/35	—	—	—	—	—
				Calif.	—	22	22/33	—	—	—	—	—
173 CID (2.8L), 2-bbl., V6	115	7/LE2	4-speed manual		—	—	$225	—	—	—	—	—
				MPG:	—	—	20	—	—	—	—	—
			3-speed Turbo		—	—	$562	—	—	—	—	—
			Hydra-matic	MPG:	—	—	20	—	—	—	—	—
				Calif.	—	—	18	—	—	—	—	—
196 CID (3.2L), 2-bbl., V6[2]	90	C/LC9	4-speed manual		—	$225	—	—	—	—	—	—
				MPG:	—	19/33	—	—	—	—	—	—
			3-speed Turbo		—	$545	—	—	—	—	—	—
			Hydra-matic	MPG:	—	NA	—	—	—	—	—	—
229 CID (3.8L), 2-bbl., V6	95	K/LC3	3-speed manual		—	—	—	S (ex. Z28)	S[2]	—	—	—
				MPG:	—	—	—	20	20/26	—	—	—
			3-speed Turbo		—	—	—	$358 (ex. Z28)	$358[2]	S[2]	S (ex. Wgns.)	—
			Hydra-matic	MPG:	—	—	—	19/26	19/26	19/26	18	—
231 CID (3.8L), 2-bbl., V6[4]	105	2/LD5	4-speed manual		—	$225	—	—	—	—	—	—
				Calif.	—	16	—	—	—	—	—	—
			3-speed Turbo		—	$545	—	$358[5]	$358[5]	S[5]	—	—
			Hydra-matic	Calif.	—	20	—	19/26	19/26	19/26	19	—
231 CID (3.8L), Turbo-charged V6		3/LC8	3-speed Turbo		—	—	—	—	—	$500	—	—
			Hydra-matic	MPG:	—	—	—	—	—	18/25	—	—
				Calif.	—	—	—	—	—	18	—	—
267 CID (4.4L), 2-bbl., V8	145	J/L39	3-speed Turbo Hydra-matic		—	—	—	$538 (ex. Z28)	$538	$180	S (Wgns.)/ $180 (Others)[2]	—
				MPG:	—	—	—	NA	17	17	17	—
305 CID (5.0L), 4-bbl., V8	145	U/LG4	4-speed manual[2]		—	—	—	$439 (ex. Z28)	$439	—	—	—
				MPG:	—	—	—	NA	16	—	—	—
			3-speed Turbo Hydra-matic		—	—	—	$653 (ex. Z28)	$653	$295	$115 (Wgns.)/ $295 (others)	($50 credit)
				MPG:	—	—	—	17	17	17	17	NA
				Calif.	—	—	—	14	15	15	NA	13
350 CID (5.7L), Diesel, V8[2]	170	N/LF9	3-speed Turbo Hydra-matic		—	—	—	—	—	—	$915 (Wgns.)	—
				MPG:	—	—	—	—	—	—	21/31	—
350 CID (5.7L), 4-bbl., V8	170	L/LM1	4-speed manual[2]		—	—	—	S (Z28)	—	—	—	—
				MPG:	—	—	—	NA	—	—	—	—
			3-speed Turbo		—	—	—	$63 (Z28)	—	—	—	—
			Hydra-matic	MPG:	—	—	—	14	—	—	—	—
				Calif.	—	—	—	NA	—	—	—	—
350 CID (5.7L), 4-bbl., V8	185	6/L48	4-speed manual		—	—	—	—	—	—	—	S
				MPG:	—	—	—	—	—	—	—	NA
			3-speed Turbo		—	—	—	—	—	—	—	N/C
			Hydra-matic	MPG:	—	—	—	—	—	—	—	14

1980

Engine	Net HP	Engine Code: VIN/GM	Transmission Availability[1]	Chevette	Monza	Citation	Camaro	Malibu[2]	Monte Carlo	Full-Size Chevy	Corvette
350 CID (5.7L), 4-bbl., V8[2]	225	8/L82	4-speed manual	—	—	—	—	—	—	—	$595
			MPG:	—	—	—	—	—	—	—	14
			3-speed Turbo Hydra-matic	—	—	—	—	—	—	—	$595
			MPG:	—	—	—	—	—	—	—	14

[1]Unless otherwise specified: All manual transmissions are floor shift. All automatics are column shift, except on Chevette, Monza, Camaro and Corvette. Floor shift automatic is optional on Citation, Monte Carlo and Malibu with other specified equipment at extra cost. [2]Not available in California. [3]Code LW9 in Citation (front-wheel drive applications). VIN codes are either 1 or 5. [4]Only available in California or high altitude areas. [5]Required for cars sold in California, with smallest engine size marked being standard, and larger engines optional at proportionally higher cost.

Major Options

	Chevette	Monza	Citation	Camaro	Malibu	Monte Carlo	Impala & Caprice	Corvette
Air conditioning[1]	$531	$531	$564	$566	$601	$601	$647	S
Comfortilt steering wheel	$73	$73	$75	$81	$81	$81	$83	S[2]
Cruise-Master speed control	—	—	$105	$112	$112	$112	$118	$123
Electro-Clear rear window defogger	$95	$95	$101	$107	$107	$107	$109	$109
Dual sport mirrors, remote	$43[3]	$43[3]	$43[3]	$46[3]	$73	$73	$74	S
Soft-Ray tinted glass, all windows	$64	S	$70	$68	$75	$75	$90	S
Power windows, 2-dr./4-dr.	—	—	$133/$189[4]	$143	$143/$202	$143	$149/$221	S
Power door locks, 2-dr./4-dr.	—	—	$87/$123	$93	$93/$132	$93	$95/$135	$140
Power front seat, w/std. seat	—	—	—	—	—	$175	$179	—
Front bucket seats, w/console[5]	S	$80	$80	S	$177	$177	—	S
Rear facing third seat (wagons)	—	—	—	—	—	—	$215[6]	—
AM radio	S[7]	S	S[8]	$97	$97	$97	$99	—
AM/FM stereo	$101[7]	$101	$101[8]	$192	$192	$192	$195	$46
AM/FM stereo w/tape player[9]	—	$176	$176[8]	$272	$272	$272	$276	$155
AM/FM stereo w/CB radio[9]	—	—	$413[8]	$525	$525	$525	$533	$391
Vinyl top, full[10]	—	—	—	—	$124	$140	$155	—
Vinyl top, landau[11]	—	$165	—	—	S	S	S	—
Sky Roof (sunroof), power[12]	—	$193	$240	—	—	$561	$670	—
Removable glass roof panels, (T-Tops)	—	—	—	$695	—	$695	—	$391
Power steering, variable-ratio	—	$158	$164	S	$174	S	S	S
Power brakes, w/front disc	$76	$76	$76	$81[13]	S	S	S	S[14]
Full wheel covers	$48	$46	$43	$46	$46	S	$47	—
Wire wheel covers	—	—	$156	—	$171	$125	$128	—
Rally wheels w/trim rings	S	$94	$78	$100	$96	$50	—	S
Forged aluminum wheels	—	—	—	$337	—	—	—	$407
WSW tires	S[7]	$18	$45	$51	$45	$51	$51	—

Popular Option Groups & Packages

	Chevette	Monza	Citation	Camaro	Malibu	Monte Carlo	Impala & Caprice	Corvette
Auxiliary lighting package	$41	$27	$41	$40	$60	$33	$54	—
Deluxe exterior package	$119	—	$144	—	—	—	—	—
Estate wagon package	—	—	—	—	$276	—	$280	—
Exterior Décor package	—	$154	—	—	—	—	—	—
Gymkhana suspension package	—	—	—	—	—	—	—	$55
Interior Décor and/or Quiet sound group	$50	$42	$72	$68	$55	—	$60	—
Special instrumentation package	—	$94	$109	$120	$134	$109	—	S
Spyder equipment group	—	$521	—	—	—	—	—	—
Style trim group	—	—	—	$78	—	—	—	—
X11 sport equipment package	—	—	$501	—	—	—	—	—

—= Not Available; S = Standard equipment. [1]Comfortron air conditioning with automatic temperature control is available for $738 on Impala and Caprice. [2]Tilt/Telescope w/leather-wrapped sport steering wheel on Corvette. [3]Dual sport mirror with LH remote only. [4]Power remote control swing out rear quarter windows available for $91 on Citation. [5]Bucket seats standard on Chevette, Monza and Camaro, with console being optional on Monza and Camaro. Mini-console standard on Chevette. Bucket seats and console available on Malibu coupes and sedans, and Monte Carlo. [6]Third row seating on Caprice Classic is $167. [7]Available on Chevette Scooter, standard on all other Chevette models: AM radio for $79; WSW tires for $43. [8]Prices for Citation coupe: AM radio for $79; prices for other radios on coupe: AM/FM Stereo for $180; AM/FM stereo w/8-track for $255; AM/FM stereo w/CB radio, $492. [9]Tape player is 8-track with cassette tape being $12 higher. AM/FM stereo w/Citizens Band (CB) radio includes power antenna. [10]Not available on station wagons. [11]Standard on all Landau coupe models: Malibu Classic, Monte Carlo, and Caprice. Cabriolet roof available on Monza coupe. [12]Manually operated on Monza and Citation. [13]Standard on Camaro Z28. [14]Power front and rear disc brakes.

Paint Colors

	Code		Code		Code
Classic White[1]	10	Bright Yellow[2,3]	51	Brown metallic[1]	82
White[2,3,4,5]	11	Yellow[1]	52	Red[1]	83
Silver metallic[1]	13	Yellow[5]	56	Charcoal metallic[3]	84
Silver metallic[2,3,4,5]	15	Gold metallic[3]	57	Gray[2,4,5]	85
Gray metallic (two-tone)	16	Dark Green metallic[1,2,5]	58		
Black	19	Beige[1,2,4,5]	59		
Light Blue metallic[2,4,5]	21	Light Camel metallic[2,4,5]	63		
Medium Blue metallic	22	Dark Brown metallic[3]	67		
Bright Blue metallic[2,3]	24	Medium Camel metallic[4,5]	69		
Dark Blue metallic[1]	28	Red[2,3,4]	72		
Dark Blue metallic[2,3,4,5]	29	Claret metallic[5]	75		
Lime Green metallic[3]	40	Dark Claret metallic	76		
Dark Green metallic[4]	44	Cinnabar[4,5]	77		
Dark Brown metallic[1]	47	Red Orange[2,3]	79		
Yellow[4]	50	Bronze metallic[3]	80		

In two-tone combinations, the first two digits indicate lower color and the next two digits are the upper color. Custom two-tone paint available for $110 on Chevette, $148 on Citation, $123 on Malibu, $171 on Monte Carlo, and $128 on Impala and Caprice. Standard two-tone on Impala for $60. Colors without footnote marks are available on all models. [1]Available on Corvette. [2]Available on Chevette. [3]Available on Camaro. [4]Available on Monza and Citation. [5]Available on Malibu, Monte Carlo, Impala and Caprice.

Chevette

"A lot of car for the money."

Nameplate year of origin: 1976.
Current bodystyle lifespan: 1976 through 1987.
Predecessor to this model: None.
Replacement for this model: None (captive imports Sprint and Spectrum introduced in 1985 as supplementary models).
Percentage of division's production: 19.64%.
Corporate siblings: None.
Primary competition: Dodge Colt and Omni, Ford Fiesta, and Plymouth Arrow and Horizon.
Notable changes: Minor trim and detail changes.
Major standard equipment: Vinyl front bucket seats, fold-down rear seat (can be deleted for credit), color-keyed cut-pile carpeting, door armrests, dome courtesy light, open compartment glove box, black two-spoke steering wheel and column, cargo compartment under floor storage, argent colored headlight bezels and grille trim, polished aluminum bumpers (not chromed), front and rear bumper guards, and 155/80R13 BSW tires.

Measurements

	2-Door	4-Door
Wheelbase	94.3"	97.3"
Length	161.9"	164.9"
Width	61.8"	61.8"
Height	52.3"	52.3"
Legroom — front	41.5"	41.5"
Legroom — rear	30.6"	33.5"
Headroom — front	38.1"	38.3"
Headroom — rear	37.3"	37.4"
Cargo capacity (cu. ft.)	9.8*	9.8*
Fuel capacity (gals.)	13.0	13.0

*Maximum with rear seat folded down on coupe, 27.0 cu. ft.; on sedan, 28.6 cu. ft.

Chevette adds: Choice of all-vinyl or cloth-and-vinyl reclining front bucket seats, center console, color-keyed I/P w/brushed aluminum trim, sport steering wheel, cigarette lighter, glove box w/latch type door and lock, swing-out rear window (coupe), AM radio, bright front and rear window trim, chrome headlamp bezel inserts, deluxe grille trim, deluxe chrome bumpers w/rub strips, hubcaps w/bright wheel trim rings, and 155/80R13 WSW tires.

Models Available

	Model No.	Base MSRP	Change from LY	Shipping Wt. (lbs.)	Model Year Production	Change from LY
Chevette Scooter 2-Door Hatchback Coupe	J08	$3,782	+14.64%	1935	40,998	+70.12%

1980

	Model No.	Base MSRP	Change from LY	Shipping Wt. (lbs.)	Model Year Production	Change from LY
Chevette 2-Door Hatchback Coupe	B08	$4,289	+13.05%	1989	146,686	+7.74%
Chevette 4-Door Hatchback Sedan	B68	$4,418	+12.88%	2048	261,477	+25.19%
TOTALS	*Avg. price*	$4,163	+13.46%	*Production*	449,161	+21.69%

Monza

"Your kind of features. Your kind of fun."

Nameplate year of origin: 1975 (1960 as Corvair subseries).

Current bodystyle lifespan: 1975 through 1980.

Predecessor to this model: Corvair Monza (1965 to 1969); Vega Kammback wagon (1971 to 1977).

Replacement for this model: Cavalier (1982 to 1993).

Percentage of division's production: 7.41%.

Corporate siblings: Buick Skyhawk, Oldsmobile Starfire, and Pontiac Sunbird.

Primary competition: Dodge Omni 024, Ford Pinto, and Plymouth Horizon TC3.

Notable changes: Minor trim and detail changes.

Major standard equipment: Choice of patterned cloth or all-vinyl front bucket seats, cut-pile carpeting, color-keyed instrument panel, fold-down rear seat and rear liftgate (hatchbacks and wagons), two-spoke steering wheel, soft molded door panels w/ map pockets, simulated woodgrain I/P trim, bright front and rear window moldings, bright side window surround moldings, aluminum front and rear bumpers (wagons), chrome front and rear bumpers (coupe and 2+2), bumper rub strips, full wheel covers, and A78 × 13 WSW tires. Wagons adds: B78 × 13 WSW tires. Sport adds: Custom interior w/choice of Sport cloth-and-vinyl or all-vinyl front bucket seats, brushed metal accents on I/P, body-color urethane front end fascia w/body-color bumper and bumper guards, chrome rear bumper w/ body-color (or contrasting color), front and rear bumper guards color-matched to bumper and finned wheel covers w/GT-type center hub and bright wheel nuts.

Measurements

	Coupe	2+2 HBK	Sport 2+2 HBK	Wagon
Wheelbase	97.0"	97.0"	97.0"	97.0"
Length	179.2"	179.2"	179.3"	178.1"
Width	65.4"	65.4"	65.4"	65.4"
Height	49.8"	50.2"	50.2"	51.8"
Legroom — front	43.0"	43.0"	43.0"	43.0"
Legroom — rear	28.2"	29.6"	29.6"	30.2"
Headroom — front	37.6"	37.7"	37.7"	38.5"
Headroom — rear	37.2"	35.3"	35.3"	40.1"
Cargo capacity (cu. ft.)	6.6	10.1*	10.1*	46.6
Fuel capacity (gals.)	18.5	18.5	18.5	15.0

Capacity with rear seat folded down is 27.8 cu. ft.

Models Available

	Model No.	Base MSRP	Change from LY	Shipping Wt. (lbs.)	Model Year Production	Change from LY
Monza 2-Door Coupe	M27	$4,184	+15.68%	2617	95,469	+56.22%
Monza 2+2 2-Door Hatchback Coupe	M07	$4,497	+16.99%	2672	53,415	-6.08%
Monza Sport 2+2 2-Door Hatchback Coupe	R07	$4,921	+14.68%	2729	20,534	-33.03%
TOTALS	*Avg. price*	$4,534	+15.32%	*Production*	169,418	+3.41%

Citation

"The first Chevy of the '80s. A whole new kind of compact car."

Nameplate year of origin: 1980 (previously used by Ford Motor Company on 1958 Edsel series).

Current bodystyle lifespan: 1980 through 1985 (renamed Citation II in 1984).

Predecessor to this model: Nova (1975 to 1979).

Replacement for this model: Beretta and Corsica (1987 to 1996).

Measurements

	Coupe & Club Coupe	2-Door Hatchback	4-Door Hatchback
Wheelbase	104.9"	104.9"	104.9"
Length	176.7"	176.7"	176.7"
Width	68.3"	68.3"	68.3"

Percentage of division's production: 35.49%.

Corporate siblings: Buick Skylark, Oldsmobile Omega, and Pontiac Phoenix.

Primary competition: AMC Concord, Ford Granada, and Plymouth Volaré.

Notable changes: Completely redesigned replacement for Chevrolet Nova.

Major standard equipment: All-vinyl high-back front bench seat, color-keyed cut-pile carpeting, color-keyed two-spoke steering wheel and steering column, AM radio w/windshield mounted antenna,*bright I/P trim plate,*cigarette lighter,*lockable glove box,*dome light, RH door dome light switch,*removable luggage compartment cover (hatchbacks only), bright front and rear window moldings, bright roof drip moldings,*bright wheel opening and rocker panel moldings,*styled steel wheels w/color-accented hubcaps, and P185/80R13 BSW tires.

*Deleted from Citation 2-Door Coupe, model H11.

Measurements (cont.)

	Coupe & Club Coupe	2-Door Hatchback	4-Door Hatchback
Height	53.1"	53.1"	53.1"
Legroom — front	42.0"	42.0"	42.0"
Legroom — rear	34.6"	34.6"	35.5"
Headroom — front	38.2"	38.2"	38.2"
Headroom — rear	37.3"	37.5"	37.5"
Cargo capacity (cu. ft.)	12.5	20.1*	20.1*
Fuel capacity (gals.)	14.0	14.0	14.0

*Hatchback maximum with rear seat down, 41.1 cu. ft.

Models Available

	Model No.	Base MSRP	Change from LY*	Shipping Wt. (lbs.)	Model Year Production	Change from LY*
Citation 2-Door Coupe	H11	$4,491	NEW	2391	42,909	NEW
Citation 2-Door Club Coupe	X11	$4,905	+24.02%	2397	100,340	+172.66%
Citation 2-Door Hatchback Coupe	X08	$5,032	+22.20%	2417	210,258	+4263.10%
Citation 4-Door Hatchback Sedan	X68	$5,153	+27.08%	2437	458,033	+1020.35%
TOTALS	Avg. price	$4,895	+19.07%	Production	811,540	+730.47%

*Comparisons to LY made from equivalent 1980 Citation replacements for 1979 Nova body styles: Citation Club coupe to Nova 2-door coupe, Citation 2-door hatchback to Nova 2-door hatchback, and Citation 4-door hatchback sedan to Nova 4-door sedan.

Camaro

"The Hugger."

Nameplate year of origin: 1967.

Current bodystyle lifespan: 1970 through 1981.

Predecessor to this model: Camaro (1967 to 1969).

Replacement for this model: Camaro (1982 to 1992).

Percentage of division's production: 6.65%.

Corporate siblings: Pontiac Firebird.

Primary competition: Dodge Challenger, Ford Mustang and Plymouth Sapporo.

Notable changes: Minor trim and detail changes.

Major standard equipment: All-vinyl front bucket seats, full-length floor console, color-keyed cut-pile carpeting, color-keyed four-spoke soft rim sport steering wheel w/color-keyed column, bright front and rear window moldings, bright rocker panel molding, hubcaps, and FR78 × 14 BSW tires. Rally Sport adds: Black rocker panel, black dual sport mirrors, hood and forward portion of roof painted black w/tri-color stripes separating from body color, blackout grille trim, front stabilizer bar, special shock absorbers, power steering, and color-keyed Rally wheels. Berlinetta adds: Custom all-vinyl front bucket seats, special door panels, special instrumentation package, electric clock, Interior Décor/Quiet Sound group, LH remote and RH manual sport mirrors, Berlinetta nameplate on B-pillars, bright grille, black taillight surround with chrome trim, black painted rocker panels, dual pinstriping, custom styled wheels, and FR78 × 14 WSW tires. Z28 adds: All-vinyl front bucket seats, large rim steering wheel, special instrumentation package, specific Z28 logos and decals (hood, front spoiler and fenders, doors, and front and rear panels), black anodized window surround trim and headlight/taillight bezels, unique body-color grille, body-color parking light recesses, black painted rocker panels and rear trunk panel, front fender louvers, front and rear spoiler, dual resonator and tailpipes, sport suspension, body color special rally wheels, space saver spare tire, and GR70 × 15 R/WL tires.

Measurements

Wheelbase	108.0"
Length	197.6"
Width	74.5"
Height	49.2"
Legroom — front	43.9"
Legroom — rear	28.4"
Headroom — front	37.2"
Headroom — rear	36.0"
Cargo capacity (cu. ft.)	7.1
Fuel capacity (gals.)	21.0

1980

Models Available

	Model No.	Base MSRP	Change from LY	Shipping Wt. (lbs.)	Model Year Production	Change from LY
Camaro 2-Door Sport Coupe	P87	$5,499	+17.58%	3218	68,174	-38.78%
Camaro Rally Sport 2-Door Sport Coupe	P87	$5,916	+16.62%	NA	12,105	-37.10%
Camaro Berlinetta 2-Door Sport Coupe	S87	$6,262	+16.05%	3253	26,679	-60.32%
Camaro Z28 2-Door Sport Coupe	P87	$7,121	+16.45%	NA	45,137	-46.82%
TOTALS	*Avg. price*	$6,200	+16.64%	*Production*	152,005	-46.21%

Malibu

"It's got everything."

Nameplate year of origin: 1964.
Current bodystyle lifespan: 1978 through 1983.
Predecessor to this model: Chevelle (1973 to 1977).
Replacement for this model: Celebrity (1982 to 1990).
Percentage of division's production: 12.17%.
Corporate siblings: Buick Century, Oldsmobile Cutlass, and Pontiac LeMans.
Primary competition: Dodge Diplomat and Ford Granada.
Notable changes: New grille and minor trim and detail changes.
Major standard equipment: Cloth-and-vinyl front bench seat, color-keyed cut-pile nylon carpeting, color-coordinated delta-spoke steering wheel, color-keyed I/P and steering column, black instrument cluster trim, bright front and rear window surround moldings, bright roof drip rail molding, hubcaps, and P185/75R14 BSW tires. Wagon adds: All-vinyl front bench seat, vinyl coated metal cargo area sidewalls, bright rear quarter window molding, swing-up tailgate window and drop-down tailgate door, full wheel covers, and P195/75R14 BSW tires. Malibu Classic adds: Choice of knit cloth-and-vinyl or all-vinyl front bench seat, glove compartment light, bright window frame moldings, lower bodyside protective molding, bright wheel opening moldings, and full wheel covers.

Measurements

	Coupes	Sedans	Wagons
Wheelbase	108.1"	108.1"	108.1"
Length	192.7"	192.7"	193.4"
Width	71.5"	71.5"	71.2"
Height	53.3"	54.2"	54.5"
Legroom — front	42.8"	42.8"	42.8"
Legroom — rear	35.1"	38.0"	35.9"
Headroom — front	37.9"	38.7"	38.8"
Headroom — rear	37.8"	37.7"	38.8"
Cargo capacity (cu. ft.)	16.6	16.6	72.4
Fuel capacity (gals.)	18.1	18.1	18.2

Models Available

	Model No.	Base MSRP	Change from LY*	Shipping Wt. (lbs.)	Model Year Production	Change from LY*
Malibu 2-Door Sport Coupe	T27	$5,133	+16.71%	2996	28,425	-32.08%
Malibu 4-Door Sedan	T19	$5,246	+16.63%	3001	67,696	+13.44%
Malibu 4-Door, 2-Seat Station Wagon	T35	$5,402	+13.85%	3141	30,794	-38.83%
Malibu Classic 2-Door Sport Coupe	W27	$5,439	+16.32%	3027	28,425	-53.21%
Malibu Classic 2-Door Landau Coupe	W27	$5,688	+15.73%	NA	9,342	-62.95%
Malibu Classic 4-Door Sedan	W19	$5,567	+15.96%	3031	77,938	-25.22%
Malibu Classic 4-Door, 2-Seat Station Wagon	W35	$5,654	+14.11%	3167	35,730	-49.03%
TOTALS	*Avg. price*	$5,447	+15.58%	*Production*	278,350	-32.46%

Monte Carlo

"No other car looks quite like the Chevrolet Monte Carlo."

Nameplate year of origin: 1970.
Current bodystyle lifespan: 1978 through 1987.

Measurements

Wheelbase	108.1"

Predecessor to this model: Monte Carlo (1973 to 1977).

Replacement for this model: Lumina (1990 to 1994).

Percentage of division's production: 6.51%.

Corporate siblings: Buick Regal, Oldsmobile Cutlass Supreme and Cutlass Calais, and Pontiac Grand Prix.

Primary competition: Dodge Mirada and Ford Thunderbird.

Notable changes: New front end styling and minor trim and detail changes.

Major standard equipment: Knit corduroy cloth front bench seat, color-keyed cut-pile carpeting, color-keyed instrument panel w/simulated Carpathian Elm burl woodgrain instrument trim panels, soft-rim two-spoke steering wheel, door panels w/lower panel carpeting, and door pull assist straps, glove compartment light, I/P courtesy lights, electric clock, bright roof drip and window surround moldings, bright rocker panel moldings w/front and rear extensions, bright wheel opening moldings, full wheel covers, and P205/70R14 BSW tires. Landau adds: RH visor vanity mirror, specific Landau identification, Landau elk-grain vinyl roof w/rear quarter nameplate, dual sport mirrors w/LH remote, bright rocker panel molding, bodyside pinstriping, power steering, power brakes, and deluxe wheel covers.

Measurements (cont.)

Length	200.4"
Width	71.5"
Height	53.9"
Legroom — front	42.8"
Legroom — rear	36.3"
Headroom — front	37.6"
Headroom — rear	37.8"
Cargo capacity (cu. ft.)	16.1
Fuel capacity (gals.)	18.1

Models Available

	Model No.	Base MSRP	Change from LY	Shipping Wt. (lbs.)	Model Year Production	Change from LY
Monte Carlo 2-Door Hardtop Coupe	Z37	$6,163	+23.38%	3104	116,580	-48.20%
Monte Carlo Landau 2-Door Hardtop Coupe	Z37	$6,411	+8.53%	NA	32,262	-64.88%
TOTALS	*Avg. price*	$6,287	+15.34%	*Production*	148,842	-53.04%

Impala and Caprice Classic

"The New Chevrolet. We made it right for the '80s."

Nameplate year of origin: 1958 (Impala) and 1966 (Caprice).

Current bodystyle lifespan: 1977 through 1990.

Predecessor to this model: Biscayne/Bel Air/Impala/Caprice (1971 to 1977).

Replacement for this model: Caprice and Impala SS (1991 to 1996).

Percentage of division's production: 25.76%.

Corporate siblings: Buick LeSabre, Oldsmobile Delta 88, and Pontiac Catalina and Bonneville.

Primary competition: Dodge St. Regis and Ford LTD.

Notable changes: Restyled exterior, with some interior trim and detail changes.

Major standard equipment: Choice of knit cloth or all-vinyl front bench seat, color-keyed steering wheel and steering column, color-keyed cut-pile nylon carpeting, woodgrain vinyl accent trim on I/P and door panels, glove box light, bright front and rear window moldings, bright side window and body sill/door moldings, hubcaps, and P205/75R15 BSW tires. Wagon adds: All-vinyl front bench seat, three-way tailgate w/power-operated rear window, tailgate-ajar warning light, vinyl coated textured metal sidewalls, and P225/75R15 BSW tires. Caprice adds: Choice of velvet-look knit cloth or all-vinyl front bench seat, fold-down center armrest (four-doors only), front door pull straps and lower door panel carpeting, electric clock, courtesy lights, added acoustical insulation, specific triple unit taillights, bright roof drip moldings, bright wheel opening moldings, stand-up hood ornament, and full wheel covers. Landau adds: Elk-grain vinyl top on forward portion of roof, dual sport mirrors, accent striping, distinctive Landau nameplates, and wire wheel covers. Caprice wagon adds: All-vinyl front bench seat w/fold-down center armrest, three-way tailgate w/power-operated rear window, tailgate window moldings, tailgate-ajar warning light, vinyl coated textured metal sidewalls, and HR78 × 15 BSW tires.

Measurements

	2-doors	4-doors	Wagons
Wheelbase	116.0"	116.0"	116.0"
Length	212.9"	212.9"	215.1"
Width	75.5"	75.5"	79.1"
Height	56.0"	56.0"	58.0"
Legroom — front	42.4"	42.4"	42.4"
Legroom — rear	37.3"	39.0"	37.7"
Headroom — front	38.8"	39.4"	39.6"
Headroom — rear	38.0"	38.2"	39.4"
Cargo capacity (cu. ft.)	20.9	20.9	88.6
Fuel capacity (gals.)	25.0	25.0	22.0

Models Available

	Model No.	Base MSRP	Change from LY	Shipping Wt. (lbs.)	Model Year Production	Change from LY
Impala 2-Door Sport Coupe	L47	$6,180	+12.42%	3344	10,756	-59.55%
Impala 4-Door Sedan	L69	$6,289	+12.36%	3360	70,801	-59.01%
Impala 4-Door, 2-Seat Station Wagon*	L35	$6,780	+10.98%	4892	17,970	-73.71%
Caprice Classic 2-Door Coupe	N47	$6,579	+12.71%	3376	13,919	-62.00%
Caprice Classic 2-Door Landau Coupe	N47	$7,029	+12.75%	NA	8,857	-59.42%
Caprice Classic 4-Door Sedan	N69	$6,710	+12.55%	3400	91,208	-55.07%
Caprice Classic 4-Door, 2-Seat Station Wagon*	N35	$7,099	+11.11%	3930	23,304	-58.58%
TOTALS	Avg. price	$6,667	+12.08%	Production	236,815	-59.77%

*Production of wagons with third seat option is included above, but breaks out as follows: Impala, 6,767; Caprice Classic, 13,431.

Corvette

"The legend lives on."

Nameplate year of origin: 1953 (also used on show car of same year).
Current bodystyle lifespan: 1968 through 1982.
Predecessor to this model: Corvette (1963 to 1967).
Replacement for this model: Corvette (1984 to 1996).
Percentage of division's production: 1.78%.
Corporate siblings: None.
Primary competition: None.
Notable changes: Revised front and rear styling and minor trim and detail changes.
Major standard equipment: Choice of ribbed cloth-and-leather or all-leather high-back contoured bucket seats, center floor console, color-keyed cut-pile carpeting, "Tilt-Telescopic" steering wheel w/four-spoke sport steering wheel, sports instrumentation with full gauges including tachometer, air conditioning, power windows, AM/FM radio, electric clock, tinted glass, convenience group, dual remote-control sport mirrors, carpeted cargo area with light concealed behind seats, luggage space roll shade, anti-theft audio alarm system, removable roof panels, front cornering lights, functional front fender louvers, domed hood w/air scoop, power steering, power four wheel disc brakes, rally wheels w/trim rings, and P225/70R15 BSW tires.

Measurements

Wheelbase	151.5"
Wheelbase	98.0"
Length	185.3"
Width	69.0"
Height	48.0"
Legroom — front	42.1"
Headroom — front	36.2"
Cargo capacity (cu. ft.)	8.4
Fuel capacity (gals.)	24.0

Models Available

	Model No.	Base MSRP	Change from LY	Shipping Wt. (lbs.)	Model Year Production	Change from LY
Corvette 2-Door Coupe	Z87	$13,140	+6.22%	3206	40,614	-24.52%
TOTALS	Avg. price	$13,140	+6.22%	Production	40,614	-24.52%

CHRYSLER

"Chrysler engineers quality, luxury and value into every car."

The 1980 Chrysler model line featured a highly redesigned mid-size LeBaron line and an all-new rendition of the Cordoba personal luxury car. The Newport and New Yorker full-size Chryslers continued into the new decade mostly unchanged. It was not a good year for Chrysler, as news of the company's government bailout loans continued to make headlines and the second fuel crisis and recession in the past seven years took hold. The luxury Chrysler line seemed to be hit harder than its smaller and lower-priced counterparts, Dodge and Plymouth. Over the 1980 model year, Chrysler production and sales fell by more than half from the 1979 total, and the 1981 numbers would drop by nearly half again. The future would look brighter after the K-car based Chrysler models were introduced for the 1982 model year.

The completely redesigned Cordoba was, like its new Dodge Mirada counterpart, a very well done styling disguise on the 1979 LeBaron coupe platform. Angular bodylines and a sloping front end were identifying features and a complete departure from the original Cordoba design. In fact, Ricardo Montalbán still did some advertising for Chrysler, and for the new 1980s, the pitch was "Look what they've done to my car," after which he would describe all the new styling features. At the front, a sloping, body-colored fascia between squared-off fender ends had single unit square headlights with parking/turn signal lamps set inboard behind vented style grilles. An upright chrome grille consisted of all vertical bars, divided into eight sections by larger vertical bars. The top of the grille stood forward from the sloping fascia. Atop it was a unique "Franklin minted" eagle hood ornament. Bumpers, front and rear, were flush mounted to the fender end cap fillers, and were made of chrome-plated aluminum to save weight.

Bodysides were very angular, with the only curves in sight being the wheel openings. Of three full-length bodyside feature lines, the upper two were indented creases. The top one began as a crease at the top corner edge of the front bumper, rose vertically to a point just below the fender top, then turned and ran straight back to the rear of the car just below the beltline, turning down just ahead of the end of the rear quarter panel. A mid-level crease began at the same spot on the front bumper, arching over the wheel openings about an inch to create slightly flared openings, and ended at the top corner of the rear bumper. The lower feature line nearly paralleled the mid-level crease running between the bottom corners of the front and rear bumper rub strip moldings. The greenhouse area was also angular in design, with a nearly triangular fixed rear quarter window and a slanting opera window to complete the look. An optional cabriolet top dispensed with the opera window, and consequently reduced rearward visibility, but was a popular choice with buyers. Rear styling was square and flat, with a slight rearward slant top to bottom. Taillights consisted of a stack of three horizontal strips per side, with the backup lights mounted on each side of the center panel license tag housing.

Under the hood, the Cordoba came standard with the "Slant Six" 6-cylinder engine or optional 318 CID V8. This was the first year Cordoba had anything less than a V8 engine as standard equipment, and its original 400 CID V8 was no longer offered in any Chrysler model, as a necessity to meet mandated fuel economy requirements. Inside, the Cordoba was as luxurious as in the past, and adopted the full-sized Chryslers' instrument panel design, which sloped away from the driver and passenger as it went from the top to bottom. A full range of upholstery and seating choices were offered, so that the Cordoba could be made as sporty or as luxurious as the buyer wished.

With the Cordoba now based on the same platform as the LeBaron, Chrysler redesigned the mid-size LeBaron line and moved the coupes to the same platform as the Dodge Aspen and Plymouth Volaré. In fact, for 1980 the LeBaron line shared not only powertrains and underpinnings with its lower priced corporate siblings, but also front fenders, hoods and doors, all in an effort to save money for the cash-strapped company. Up front, LeBarons were equipped with dual rectangular halogen headlamps, with the parking/turn signal lamps mounted above them, and this year the upper lights' lenses actually wrapped over slightly onto the top of the header panel, although they were coated on the inside to prevent light from shining upwards. The new vertical bar grille similarly wrapped over the top of the front header panel, and was distinguished by a chrome surround and a large vertical center bar. A stand-up hood ornament sat atop the center of the upper grille panel.

The greenhouse area shared the Aspen and Volaré windshield and front door area, but with new styling for the rear quarters that introduced a formal and nearly upright rear window, with a wrap-over B-pillar and opera window on coupes. A slightly raised and very flat trunk lid turned downward sharply and met new horizontal taillamps, which were large rectangular units alongside the center mounted license plate housing. The outer ends of the taillights were aligned with the trunk lid opening, and a unique rear quarter end cap carried a vertical light split into two sections, with the backup light on the bottom and a red reflective lens on the top half. Other than the front end changes, the LeBaron wagons, including a new non-wood trimmed version, looked very much like their predecessors, except that the taillight lenses were divided into three sections by black painted trim. Interior trim and design was updated, but continued in much the same fashion as when introduced in 1977. Finally, a lower-priced LeBaron Special 4-Door Sedan, introduced after the start of the year, offered less luxurious upholstery and trim and fewer standard features such as wheel covers and courtesy lights. Details of its exact features are not available, and are not presented in the LeBaron standard equipment details that follow. At the other end of the LeBaron range, a Fifth Avenue package added various luxury features, most visibly including a very formal roofline with padded vinyl carriage roof and covered rear quarter windows.

Newport and New Yorker models, which were new for 1979, were not greatly changed for the new season.

1980

Most of Chrysler's efforts were spent on further weight reductions for all of its cars, especially the larger cars, to help increase fuel economy. As a sample of the weight saving measures taken: A new heater core with aluminum cooling fins for the Newport, New Yorker and Cordoba saved one pound per car; changes to the engine block for the 3.7-liter (225 CID) "Slant Six" engine saved four pounds per car; and a new one-piece plastic evaporator housing for the optional air conditioner on Cordoba and LeBaron saved three-and-a-half pounds per car. Many other mechanical components had similar weight savings. Inside the car were even more changes, which consumers would likely never notice: A revised rear-seat fold-down center armrest pivot for Newport, New Yorker and LeBaron 4-door models saved 2.5 pounds per car; optional carpeted floor mats were redesigned to be about five pounds lighter than in 1979 models; and a high-strength steel cargo compartment floor for LeBaron station wagons saved four pounds. There were many more weight saving changes, and when combined with prior years' changes, some 1980 Chrysler models were around a half-ton lighter than their 1975 counterparts.

As the decade ended and a new one began, Chrysler was still expanding its use of option packages, to offer buyers a choice to add more luxury to their cars. Details of most of these are contained in Appendix IV. It is noteworthy that the model year production totals of most of these were quite small, with a notable exception of the New Yorker Fifth Avenue package that continued to be popular, selling 3,608 units for 1980. Production of other packages included 654 LeBaron sedans with the Fifth Avenue package, 386 New Yorker sedans with the Fifth Avenue Special Edition package, 305 Cordoba Crown models with a Special Edition package, and 2,069 Cordoba Crown coupes with the Corinthian edition option.

Cordoba 2-Door Hardtop Coupe
with Cabriolet roof package

LeBaron 4-Door Station Wagon

Cordoba 2-Door Hardtop Coupe

LeBaron Salon 2-Door Coupe

LeBaron Salon interior

LeBaron Salon 2-Door Coupe
with LS Limited package

Newport interior with Verdi II trim

New Yorker 4-Door Pillared Hardtop
with Fifth Avenue Edition package

Model year production: 130,923 down 55.10% from 1979.
Domestic market share: 1.68% (11th place).
Base price range: $5,995 to $10,872.
Chrysler average base price: $7,151, up 12.27%.
Introduction date: October 1, 1979.
Assembly plants: Lynch Road, Detroit, MI (A); St. Louis, MO (G); and Windsor, Ontario, Canada (R).
Data plate identification (VIN): Thirteen digit code read as follows: First four digits indicate series and body style (model number in model charts); fifth digit indicates engine code (see powertrain chart); sixth digit indicates year (A = 1980); seventh digit indicates assembly plant (see list above); remaining digits are sequential with beginning numbers of 100001. *Example:* TH42HAA100001 is a 1980 Chrysler Newport 4-Door Pillared Hardtop, with 318 CID, 4-bbl. V8 engine, serial number 100001, built in Lynch Road plant, Detroit MI.

Powertrains

Engine	Net HP	Engine Code	Transmission Availability		LeBaron	Cordoba	Newport	New Yorker
225 CID (3.7L), 1-bbl., 6-cyl.	90	C	3-speed TorqueFlite automatic[1]		S	S	S	—
				MPG:	17/25	17/25	16/24	—
				Calif.	16	—	—	—
318 CID (5.2L), 2-bbl., V8[2]	120	G	3-speed TorqueFlite automatic		$230	$230	$233	S
				MPG:	15	15	15/23	15/23
318 CID (5.2L), 4-bbl., V8[1]	155	H	3-speed TorqueFlite automatic		$291	$291	$295	N/C[2]
				Calif.	16	16	16	16
360 CID (5.9L), 2-bbl., V8[3]	130	K	3-speed TorqueFlite automatic		—	—	$457	N/C
				MPG:	—	—	14	14
360 CID (5.9L), 4-bbl., V8[1,4]	185	L	3-speed TorqueFlite automatic		—	$545[4]	—	—
				MPG:	—	13	—	—
				Calif.	—	NA	—	—

[1]*Available only in California and designated high altitude areas.*   [2]*Required as standard equipment in California and designated high altitude areas, with appropriate adjustment in price.*   [3]*Not available in California.*   [4]*Available with federal emissions only in combination with heavy-duty package.*

Major Options

	LeBaron	Cordoba	Newport	New Yorker
Air conditioning	$623	$623	$670	$670
Air conditioning, w/Auto-Temp control	$673	$675	$720	$720
Tilt steering wheel	$83	$83	$85	$65
Leather covered steering wheel	$61	$61	$62	$42
Automatic speed control	$116	$116	$122	$122
Electric rear window defroster	$106	$106	$113	$113
Tinted glass, all windows	$78	S	S	S
Power windows, 2-dr./4-dr.	$148/$209	$148	$228	S
Power door locks, 2-dr./4-dr.	$96/$136	$96	$139	$139
Power front bench seat, 6-way	$179	$179	$183	$183
Power seat 50/50 or bucket, 6-way[1]	$179	$179	$183	$183
Front bucket seats w/floor console	$212[2]	$175	—	—
Leather interior trim	$619	$455	—	$432
AM radio	$99	S	$106	S
AM/FM stereo	$200	$101	$209	$103
AM/FM stereo w/8-track tape	$280	$181	$287	$181
AM/FM stereo w/cassette tape	$339	$240	$347	$241
AM/FM stereo w/CB transceiver	$482	$383	$495	$389
Vinyl top[3]	$129	$141	$162	S
Dual remote control mirrors, chrome	$61	$77	$52	$31[4]
Remote control trunk release	$27	$44	$46	$46
Glass sunroof, electric	$871	$787	$1,053	$1,053
T-Bar roof[5]	$715	$715	—	—
Premiere wheel covers	$93	$46	$44	S
Premium wheel covers	$138	$92	$91	$47
Wire wheel covers	$308	$262	$266	$222
Chrome styled road wheels	$194	—	—	—

1980

	LeBaron	Cordoba	Newport	New Yorker
Forged aluminum road wheels	$380	$334	$336	—
White sidewall tires, std. size	$22	$22	$92	$87

Popular Option Groups & Packages

	LeBaron	Cordoba	Newport	New Yorker
"300" option package	—	$2,040	—	—
Basic group	$	$1,082	$1,203	$242
Cabriolet roof package	—	$950	—	—
Cabriolet roof two-tone package	—	$1,071	—	—
Corinthian Edition package	—	$1,818	—	—
Deluxe insulation package	$110	S	S	S
"Fifth Avenue Edition" package	—	—	—	$1,300
"Fifth Avenue Edition" Special Edition	—	—	—	$2,092
Fifth Avenue package	$2,000	—	—	—
Light package	$	$104	$87	$81
LS Coupe package[6]	$421	—	—	—
LS Limited Coupe package[6]	$974	—	—	—
Sport Appearance package	$290	$191	—	—
Sport/Open Road Handling package	—	$192	$269	$177

—= Not Available; S = Standard equipment.   [1]Left side power adjustment only.   [2]Available only on LeBaron Salon. Console is not available.   [3]Landau vinyl top on LeBaron coupe, Cordoba and New Yorker. Full vinyl roof on LeBaron sedan and Newport.   [4]LH remote is standard.   [5]T-Bar roof only available on 2-door models. Newport and New Yorker require vinyl top.   [6]Available only on Salon coupe.

Paint Colors

	Code		Code	
Spinnaker White[1,2]	EW1	Teal Tropic Green metallic[1,2,4]	TG6	Single tones are coded EW1,EW1. Two-tones are coded on body ID plate as TX9,EW1 where three digits on line 2 are lower body color and three digits on line 3 are upper body color or two-tone color. Two-tone paint package available on Newport and New Yorker for $168. [1]Available on LeBaron. [2]Available on Newport and New Yorker. [3]Not available on LeBaron wagon models. [4]Not available with LS package on LeBaron Salon coupe. [5]Available only on New Yorker with Fifth Avenue package and Cordoba with Corinthian package. [6]Not available on New Yorker. [7]Available on Cordoba.
Frost Blue metallic[3]	SC2	Crimson Red metallic	TM7	
Nightwatch Blue	SC9	Baron Red[1,2]	TM9	
Teal Frost metallic[1,2,3,4]	SG4	Graphic Red	TR4	
Designers Cream[5]	SL1	Natural Suede Tan	TT4	
Designers Beige[5]	SL2	Black Walnut metallic[5]	TT7	
Light Cashmere[6]	ST1	Mocha Brown metallic	TT8	
Burnished Silver metallic[1,7]	TA3	Bravo White[7]	TW2	
Light Heather Gray[3]	TD2	Black	TX9	
Light Heather Gray metallic[3]	TD3	Dark Auburn metallic	VH9	
Dark Heather Brown	TD6			

LeBaron

"Quality and Value in a Mid-Size Car."

Nameplate year of origin: 1957, as subseries name for Imperial (also used on LeBaron custom bodied Chryslers beginning in 1930).

Current bodystyle lifespan: 1980 through 1989 (renamed New Yorker, 1982; New Yorker Fifth Avenue, 1983; Fifth Avenue, 1984–1989).

Predecessor to this model: LeBaron (1977½ to 1979).

Replacement for this model: LeBaron (sedan 1982–1985, 2-door 1982–1986, wagon 1982–1988).

Percentage of division's production: 48.49%.

Corporate siblings: Dodge Aspen, Dodge Diplomat, and Plymouth Volaré.

Primary competition: Buick Century and Regal, Mercury Cougar, and Oldsmobile Cutlass Salon and Supreme.

Measurements

	Coupe	Sedan	Wagon
Wheelbase	108.7"	112.7"	112.7"
Length	201.2"	205.2"	205.5"
Width	74.2"	74.2"	74.2"
Height	53.4"	55.3"	55.5"
Legroom — front	42.7"	42.5"	42.5"
Legroom — rear	32.6"	36.6"	36.6"
Headroom — front	37.6"	39.2"	39.2"
Headroom — rear	36.2"	37.5"	38.7"
Cargo capacity (cu. ft.)	14.8	15.6	71.8
Fuel capacity (gals.)	18.0	18.0	18.0

Notable changes: Restyled.

Major standard equipment: Cloth-and-vinyl front bench seat, color-keyed carpeting, one-piece cloth headliner, simulated wood-grain I/P cluster and glove box door appliqué, two-speed windshield wipers, LH manual mirror, rocker panel sill moldings, bright roof drip rail moldings, quarter window moldings (coupes), bright upper door frame moldings (sedan), bright belt molding, front bumper guards, stand-up hood ornament, power steering, power brakes, hubcaps, and P195/75R15 BSW tires. Wagon adds: Oxford vinyl front bench seat, gas hydraulic liftgate struts, and carpeted cargo area w/stainless steel skid strips on floor and rear seat back. Salon adds: Cloth-and-vinyl split-back front bench seat w/fold-down center armrest, door pull straps, windshield header mounted reading lamps (coupe only), deluxe shelf panel, dual horns, bright center pillar moldings, color-coordinated bodyside accent stripes, front fender sill molding extensions, and deluxe wheel covers. Medallion adds: Velour 60/40 front split-bench seat w/ fold-down center armrests and passenger recliner, long-pile carpeting, fold-down rear seat armrest (sedan), bright pedal trim, map reading lamp, door mounted courtesy lights, three upper assist handles (sedan), B-pillar assist straps (coupe), rear pillar vanity lamps and mirrors (sedan), trunk dress up package, LH remote control outside rearview mirror, quarter window glass accents and medallion (coupe), bodyside accent tape stripes coordinated w/body color on coupes and vinyl top color on sedans, deluxe sound insulation package (w/o undercoating and hood pad), and premium wheel covers. Town & Country adds: Oxford vinyl front bench seat w/fold-down center armrest, carpeted lockable stowage bins, liftgate-open warning light, and simulated wood bodyside and liftgate appliqués with surround moldings.

Models Available

	Model No.	Base MSRP	Change from LY	Shipping Wt. (lbs.)	Model Year Production	Change from LY
LeBaron Special 4-Door Sedan	FL41	$5,995	NEW	3330	3,139	NEW
LeBaron 2-Door Coupe	FM22	$6,362	+18.23%	3270	8,000	NA*
LeBaron 4-Door Sedan	FM41	$6,518	+18.96%	3330	8,391	NA*
LeBaron 4-Door Wagon	FM45	$6,723	NEW	3585	1,865	NEW
LeBaron Salon 2-Door Coupe	FH22	$6,643	+18.14%	3285	10,575	NA*
LeBaron Salon 4-Door Sedan	FH41	$6,764	+15.60%	3350	10,980	NA*
LeBaron Town & Country 4-Dr. Wagon	FH45	$7,324	+15.68%	3585	6,074	-65.22%
LeBaron Medallion 2-Door Coupe	FP22	$7,185	+19.41%	3345	5,955	NA*
LeBaron Medallion 4-Door Sedan	FP41	$7,329	+17.36%	3425	8,500	NA*
TOTALS	*Avg. price*	$6,760	+15.63%	*Production*	63,479	-44.25%

Totals and comparisons to LY are not possible due to production of coupes and sedans being kept as combined total for 1979.

1980

Cordoba

"A car whose striking new, resized form strides into the new decade with poise and assurance befitting its proud tradition."

Nameplate year of origin: 1975 (also used on special-order 1970 Newport hardtops).
Current bodystyle lifespan: 1980 through 1983.
Predecessor to this model: Cordoba (1975 to 1979).
Replacement for this model: Laser XE (1984 to 1986).
Percentage of division's sales volume: 35.45%.
Corporate siblings: Dodge Mirada.
Primary competition: Buick Regal, Mercury Cougar XR-7, and Oldsmobile Cutlass Supreme.
Notable changes: Completely redesigned.
Major standard equipment: Cloth-and-vinyl split-back front bench seat w/fold-down center armrest, color-keyed long pile carpeting, simulated woodgrained vinyl trim on I/P and door panels, two-spoke steering wheel, luxury padded door trim w/carpeted lower panels and seat backs, bright pedal dress-up, glove box and ashtray light, electronic digital clock, premium steering wheel, molded cloth headliner, trunk light, carpeted trunk and spare tire cover, LH rear view mirror, rear quarter opera window, drip rail moldings, wheel lip moldings, rocker panel sill molding, bodyside and deck lid paint stripes, stand-up hood ornament, front and rear bumper guards, wheel covers, and P195/75R15 WSW tires. LS deletes and replaces the following features: Cloth and vinyl front bench seat, color-keyed cut-pile carpeting, deletes sill molding and carpeted trunk and spare tire cover, and P195/75R15 BSW tires. Crown adds: Cloth-and-vinyl 60/40 individually adjustable seats w/fold-down center armrest, passenger-side reclining seatback, padded landau vinyl roof, brushed finish up-and-over roof molding,

Measurements

Wheelbase	112.7"
Length	209.8"
Width	72.7"
Height	53.3"
Legroom — front	NA
Legroom — rear	NA
Headroom — front	NA
Headroom — rear	NA
Cargo capacity (cu. ft.)	16.7
Fuel capacity (gals.)	18.0

color-keyed vinyl roof termination and opera window moldings plus opera lamps, "Frenched" rear window, wide sill molding w/rear extensions, and premier wheel covers.

Models Available

	Model No.	Base MSRP	Change from LY	Shipping Wt. (lbs.)	Model Year Production	Change from LY
Cordoba LS 2-Door Hardtop Coupe	SS29	$6,745	+10.12%	3270	3,252	-95.56%*
Cordoba 2-Door Hardtop Coupe	SH29	$6,978	NEW	3270	26,333	NEW
Cordoba Crown 2-Dr. Hardtop Coupe	SP29	$7,428	NEW	3320	16,821	NEW
TOTALS	Avg. price	$7,050	+11.26%	Production	46,406	-36.60%

*Comparison is made to 1979 Cordoba Coupe, model number SS29.

Newport

"Friend of the family."

Nameplate year of origin: 1961 (as series); 1950 (as HT model of the T & C).
Current bodystyle lifespan: 1979 through 1981.
Predecessor to this model: Newport (1974 to 1978).
Replacement for this model: E Class (1983 to 1984).
Percentage of division's sales volume: 8.30%.
Corporate siblings: Chrysler New Yorker, Dodge St. Regis, and Plymouth Gran Fury.
Primary competition: Buick LeSabre, Mercury Marquis, and Oldsmobile Delta 88.
Notable changes: Minor trim and detail changes.
Major standard equipment: Cloth-and-vinyl split back front bench seat w/fold-down center armrest, color-keyed long pile carpeting, trip odometer, I/P courtesy lights, two-spoke steering wheel w/woodtone trim, front and rear ashtrays, inside day/night mirror, two-speed electric windshield wipers w/washers, dual outside rear view mirrors, front and rear wheel lip moldings, drip rail and belt moldings, bright windshield and rear window moldings, rear hood molding, dual horns, front and rear bumper guards, rear license plate periphery molding, deluxe wheel covers, and P195/75R15 WSW tires.

Measurements

Wheelbase	118.5"
Length	220.2"
Width	77.6"
Height	54.5"
Legroom — front	42.3"
Legroom — rear	38.3"
Headroom — front	38.2"
Headroom — rear	37.4"
Cargo capacity (cu. ft.)	21.3
Fuel capacity (gals.)	21.0

Models Available

	Model No.	Base MSRP	Change from LY	Shipping Wt. (lbs.)	Model Year Production	Change from LY
Newport 4-Door Pillared Hardtop	TH42	$7,247	+13.15%	3545	10,872	-82.15%
TOTALS	Avg. price	$7,247	+13.15%	Production	10,872	-82.15%

New Yorker

"It stands out above the rest. The incomparable New Yorker."

Nameplate year of origin: 1939.
Current bodystyle lifespan: 1979 through 1981.
Predecessor to this model: New Yorker (1974 to 1978).
Replacement for this model: New Yorker/Fifth Avenue (New Yorker, 1982; New Yorker Fifth Avenue, 1983; Fifth Avenue 1984 to 1989).
Percentage of division's sales volume: 7.76%.
Corporate siblings: Chrysler Newport, Dodge St. Regis and Plymouth Gran Fury.
Primary competition: Buick Electra, Mercury Grand Marquis, and Oldsmobile Ninety-Eight.

Measurements

Wheelbase	118.5"
Length	221.5"
Width	77.6"
Height	54.5"
Legroom — front	42.3"
Legroom — rear	38.2"
Headroom — front	38.6"

Notable changes: Minor trim and detail changes.

Major standard equipment: Cloth-and-vinyl 60/40 split bench seats w/individual adjustment and fold-down center armrest, passenger side seat-back recliner, rear seat fold-down center armrest, color-keyed long-pile carpeting, color-keyed seat belts, carpeted rear shelf panel, trip odometer, digital clock, interior lights (glove box, map/courtesy and ashtray), luxury three-spoke steering wheel w/soft center pad and woodtone rim insert, two-speed electric windshield wipers w/washers, tinted glass, power windows, black carpeted trunk floor and spare tire cover, LH remote control and RH manual mirrors, front wheel lip molding, drip rail molding, bright front windshield molding, rear taillight periphery moldings, bodyside and hood accent stripes, color-keyed door handle inserts, fender-mounted turn signal indicators, concealed headlamps, undercoating, hood insulation pad, premiere wheel covers, and P205/75R15 wide WSW tires.

Measurements (cont.)

Headroom — rear	37.4"
Cargo capacity (cu. ft.)	21.3
Fuel capacity (gals.)	21.0

Models Available

	Model No.	Base MSRP	Change from LY	Shipping Wt. (lbs.)	Model Year Production	Change from LY
New Yorker 4-Door Pillared Hardtop	TP42	$10,872	+8.44%	3810	10,166	-76.70%
TOTALS	*Avg. price*	$10,872	+8.44%	*Production*	10,166	-76.70%

DODGE

"Drive total performance."

1980

Besides the all-new Mirada sport coupe, which was the Charger's spiritual successor, one of the few bright spots for Dodge in 1980 would turn out to be the continued success of the Omni line. In its third season, sales continued to hold steady while the rest of the industry was facing nearly a 20 percent drop due to the mild recession that began in 1979. The two Omni models would account for nearly half of total Dodge production, a feat equaled most recently by the Aspen, and before that, the Dart. This would turn out to be the last year that Plymouth outsold and outproduced Dodge. This was partly due to Chrysler Corporation's weakened financial condition which required the Plymouth line to be limited to selling smaller, economical cars, while Chrysler sold only the larger and more luxurious cars. Dodge continued to have a full-line showroom that included the increasingly popular truck line that was bringing in additional customers. Plymouth's plight also had something to do with the fact that every car sold in a Plymouth showroom could be had in a Dodge showroom for virtually the same price, with the same or better features and nearly identical looks. Fortunately, hope for a better future was just around the corner with the new front-wheel drive K-cars due for 1981.

The all-new Mirada was another example of what had become business as usual for money-starved Chrysler: a near-miraculous creation of a sporty two-door coupe that used all-new interior and sheetmetal design to cover the 1979 LeBaron coupe platform and its aging but dependable powertrain. The result was the very sporty looking Mirada, which carried the job of replacing the once popular Charger nameplate and the powerful looking Magnum XE. Angular bodylines and a sloping front end with integrated body-colored bumper with chrome rub strip and a five bar horizontal grille were identifying features of the new coupe. Chrome strips outlined each of the grille bars. Single square headlamps, paired with rectangular parking/turn signal lights beside them within the same chrome bezel, were recessed in a tunnel-like opening created by the slant of the front end. Bodysides were very angular, with the only curves in sight being the wheel openings. Of three full-length bodyside feature lines, the upper two were indented creases. The top one began as a crease at the top corner edge of the front bumper, rose following the slope of the front end, and then ran straight back, just below the beltline, to the rear of the car, where it angled down parallel to the rear panel. A mid-level crease began at the same spot on the front bumper, arching over the wheel openings about an inch to create slightly flared openings, and ended at the top corner of the rear bumper. The lower feature line nearly paralleled the mid-level crease running between the bottom corners of the front and rear bumpers.

Another unique design was the angular greenhouse area. A triangular, fixed rear quarter window determined the angle for the rest of the roofline. Three thin chrome strips marked the sloped trailing edge, where it met a few inches of metal creating a B-pillar, and then there was a slanting window in nearly a parallelogram shape leading into the C-pillar. With the optional CMX package the three chrome strips extended up and over the roof to the opposite side, and the strips and the rearmost window were deleted when the Cabriolet package was ordered. Around back were large rectangular taillamps divided into four sections horizontally, and set into the rear panel below the trunk lid opening, and a chrome faced bumper with body color rub strip and end caps.

Inside the Mirada could be outfitted for luxury or sports car appearance. The instrument panel design was similar to that of the St. Regis, as it sloped away from the passengers from top to bottom. All gauges were held in individual recessed circular pods and segmented into a large area for driver controls, a center section for radio, clock, and ventilation controls, both of which used brushed aluminum accents, and a large glove box to the passenger side. Upholstery choices included cloth, vinyl and leather. Powertrain choices included the standard "Slant Six" engine and the two remaining Dodge V8 options, the 318 or the 360. There would be a total of 5,384 Miradas built with the optional CMX package, which added mostly sporty exterior trim, and 936 built with the Cabriolet package, which added a simulated convertible roof. In the end, the Mirada was not successful in its mission to restore Dodge's performance reputation, as it sold only slightly more than 52,000 units over its four-year lifespan.

The once popular Aspen saw its production total drop in half in its final season, despite a freshly styled front-end treatment that would be the only restyling done through the Aspen's short life span. The new front-end design shared fenders and hood with the similarly restyled Diplomat line. For the Aspen, fender ends were more pointed, and the raised center section of the hood was slightly lower on the 1980 models than in previous years. The grille was a horizontal design split into four sections, with each section carrying a horizontal crosshatch insert. The bars dividing the grille into four sections extended to the rectangular parking/turn signal lights set at each end, and these were flanked by single square headlamps, the only year the Aspen featured non-round lamps. Side marker and turn signal lamps were mounted on the side of the front fender end caps and connected to the headlight bezel. The rest of the car appeared much the same as in 1979, and surprisingly the R/T and Sport wagon packages were still offered, despite rather low sales figures. Apparently there were a lot of parts already produced and needing to be used before the Aspen was discontinued. Two new models added were the Special coupe and sedan. These two models were priced at a low base price with standard features such as automatic transmission and power steering, but were not available with all of the usual trim options, therefore keeping the price low.

As noted above, the Diplomat was also restyled, and

shared front fenders and hood with the closely related Aspen series. However, the Diplomat was also given a new rear roofline and rear end styling, and the coupes were moved to the shorter 108.7-inch Aspen coupe platform, with their own new rear quarter styling. The new styling included a formal and upright rear window and a slightly raised and very flat trunk lid, which turned downward sharply and met new horizontal taillamps, which were nearly full-width, broken only by the license plate housing. The taillamps were also much thinner in design than in previous years. Rear quarter panels of sedans were smoother compared to 1979 models, and for 1980 the coupe carried similar contours. The main difference on coupes, besides a shorter rear overhang, was in the rear quarter windows, which combined with a wrap-over B-pillar to create a targa top look when the optional Landau vinyl roof was ordered. At the front end, a vertically divided grille with eight main columns extended under the dual rectangular headlamps, creating eight short columns on each side. Vertical crosshatch inserts were set into all the columns, with parking/turn signal lamps set into five columns under the headlights, and two more wrapping onto the fender end cap housed turn signal and side marker lights. The car's entire design would set the tone for Diplomat styling through the end of its production in 1989. Models added to the line included a new low-price Special sport coupe, similar to the Aspen Sport models, and a Diplomat Salon station wagon with standard woodgrain exterior trim. Also, a new "S-Type" sport coupe package was offered that combined sporty appearance options like bucket seats, brushed aluminum instrument panel trim, and color-keyed styled road wheels. There were 2,188 Diplomat coupes ordered with this package.

The Omni and St. Regis lines, at opposite ends of the size and price spectrum, shared two things this year. One was that they received very few changes this year to either styling or powertrains. The other was that each added special option packages for 1980. The Omni 024 2-door hatchback added a European style "DeTomaso" option package with unique paint and spoilers, a brushed metal roof band, rear quarter louvers, and a lot of blackout trim pieces, and the package found 1,333 buyers. The St. Regis added a luxurious Touring Edition package, which included leather seating areas, a formal design backlight, full vinyl top, wide whitewall tires, and ten spoke color-keyed road wheels, among many other niceties, and was ordered on 438 St. Regis sedans. Both were designed to bring some uniqueness to Dodge, distinguishing these models from the nearly identical Plymouth Horizon TC3 and Gran Fury models.

The new-for-1979 Colt hatchbacks returned with few changes, other than adding a sporty RS package. Colt coupe and sedan models were discontinued midway through the 1979 model year leaving the Colt station wagon as the only larger Colt model, and it continued in the lineup mostly unchanged. The popular Challenger continued mostly unchanged, with the most noticeable difference being a switch from bright body trim to black, including black rear quarter window louvers. Mitsubishi Motors, which built the Colt and Challenger, would begin selling cars in the United States under its own name for the 1982 model year. However, the relationship between Chrysler Corporation and Mitsubishi

Motors, which began in 1970, continued through many financial woes, ownership variations, and the creation of a joint venture company named Diamond-Star Motors in 1985, with an assembly plant in Normal, Illinois. Each company continued selling badge-engineered versions of the other's product into the 21st century.

Aspen 2-Door Coupe with Sunrise package

Aspen 4-Door Station Wagon
with Special Edition Woodgrain package

Challenger 2-Door Hardtop

Colt 4-Door Station Wagon

Colt Custom 2-Door Hatchback

Diplomat 2-Door Coupe with S-Type package

Diplomat 4-Door Sedan

Mirada instrument panel

Mirada 2-Door Hardtop Coupe
with CMX package

St. Regis 4-Door Pillared Hardtop

Omni 4-Door Hatchback
with Custom Exterior package

Omni 024 2-Door Hatchback
with DeTomaso package

1980

Model year production: 259,343, down 26.15% from 1979.
Domestic market share: 3.33% (8th place).
Base price range: $5,151 to $7,125.
Dodge average base price: $6,120, up 13.17%.
Introduction date: October 1, 1979.
Assembly plants: Lynch Road, Detroit, MI (A); Belvidere, IL (D); Newark, DE (F); St. Louis, MO (G); and Windsor, Ontario, Canada (R). *Imports:* Colt — Kurashiki, Okayama, Japan (NA); Challenger — Okazaki, Aichi, Japan (NA).
Data plate identification (VIN): Thirteen digit code read as follows: First four digits indicate series and body style (model number in model charts); fifth digit indicates engine code (see powertrain chart); sixth digit indicates year (A = 1980); seventh digit indicates assembly plant (see list above); remaining digits are sequential with beginning numbers of 100001. *Example:* NL41CAA100001 is a 1980 Dodge Aspen 4-Door Sedan, with 225 CID, 1-bbl. 6-cylinder engine, serial number 100001, built in Lynch Road plant, Detroit, MI.

Powertrains[1]

Engine	Net HP	Engine Code	Transmission Availability[2]		Colt	Challenger	Omni	Aspen	Diplomat	Mirada	St. Regis
86 CID (1.4L) OHC, 2-bbl., 4-cyl.	70	J	4-speed manual		Credit option (HBK)	—	—	—	—	—	—
				MPG:	37	—	—	—	—	—	—
			"Twin-stick" 4-speed manual		S (HBK)	—	—	—	—	—	—
				MPG:	35	—	—	—	—	—	—
				Calif.	31	—	—	—	—	—	—
97.5 CID (1.6L) OHC, 2-bbl., 4-cyl.	77	K	"Twin-stick" 4-speed manual		S (Custom)	—	—	—	—	—	—
				MPG:	33	—	—	—	—	—	—
				Calif.	31	—	—	—	—	—	—
			3-speed Automatic		$ (Custom)/ $ (HBK)	—	—	—	—	—	—
				MPG:	30	—	—	—	—	—	—
				Calif.	29	—	—	—	—	—	—
104.7 CID (1.7L) OHC, 2-bbl., 4-cyl.	70	A	4-speed manual		—	—	S	—	—	—	—
				MPG:	—	—	23	—	—	—	—
				Calif.	—	—	24	—	—	—	—
			3-speed Torque Flite automatic		—	—	$319	—	—	—	—
				MPG:	—	—	24		—	—	—
				Calif.	—	—	23		—	—	—
155.9 CID (2.6L) OHC, 2-bbl., 4-cyl.	77	F	5-speed manual		S (wgn.)	S	—	—	—	—	—
				MPG:	21	21	—	—	—	—	—
				Calif.	—	21	—	—	—	—	—
			3-speed Torque Flite automatic		$ (wgn.)	$	—	—	—	—	—
				MPG:	22	22	—	—	—	—	—
				Calif.	—	20	—	—	—	—	—
225 CID (3.7L), 1-bbl., 6-cyl.	100	C	3-speed manual		—	—	—	S[3]	—	—	—
				MPG:	—	—	—	17	—	—	—
			4-speed manual w/overdrive		—	—	—	$153[3]	—	—	—
				MPG:	—	—	—	17	—	—	—
			3-speed Torque Flite automatic		—	—	—	$319[4]	S	S	S
				MPG:	—	—	—	17/25	17/25	17/25	16
				Calif.	—	—	—	16	16	—	—
318 CID (5.2L), 2-bbl., V8[3]	135	G	3-speed Torque Flite automatic		—	—	—	$535	$429	$	$239
				MPG:	—	—	—	15	15	15	15/23
318 CID (5.2L), 4-bbl., V8	145	H	3-speed Torque Flite automatic	*Calif.*	—	—	—	$590 16	$489 16	$61[4] 16	$61[4] 16

Engine	Net HP	Engine Code	Transmission Availability[2]		Colt	Challenger	Omni	Aspen	Diplomat	Mirada	St. Regis
360 CID (5.9L), 2-bbl., V8[3]	150	K	3-speed Torque Flite automatic		—	—	—	—	—	—	$432
				MPG:	—	—	—	—	—	—	14
360 CID (5.9L), 4-bbl., V8[3]	195	L	3-speed Torque Flite automatic		—	—	—	—	—	$251	—
				MPG:	—	—	—	—	—	12	—

[1]Optional axle ratios may be required on cars sold in California or high-altitude counties. [2]Unless otherwise noted: All manual transmissions are floor-shift. All automatics are floor-shift on Colt, Challenger, and Omni. Floor-shift is available for $35 extra on any Aspen w/3-speed manual transmission. Aspens w/automatic, Diplomat coupes, and Mirada are all available w/floor-shift in combination with specified equipment or packages. [3]Not available in California or designated high altitude areas. [4]Required as standard equipment in California and designated high altitude areas, with appropriate adjustment in price.

Major Options

	Colt	Challenger	Omni[1]	Aspen	Diplomat	Mirada	St. Regis
Air conditioning	$471	$494	$541	$543	$623	$623	$670
Tilt steering wheel	S	S	—	$76	$83	$83	$85
Automatic speed control	—	$107	—	$106	$116	$116	$122
Electric rear window defogger	S	S	—	$97	$106	$106	$113
Tinted glass, all windows	S	S	S	$66	$78	S	S
Power windows[2]	—	—	—	$183	$209	$148	$228
Power door locks[2]	—	—	—	$117	$136	$96	$139
Power front seat	—	—	—	$163	$179	$179	$183
AM radio	$78	—	S[3]	$90	$99	S	$106
AM/FM stereo	$153	$164	$93[3]	$148	$200	$101	$209
AM/FM stereo w/cassette tape	—	—	—	$310	$339	$240	$347
Front bucket seats[4]	S	S	S	$143	$103	S	—
Vinyl top, full[5]	$102	$107	—	$97	$129	—	$162
Landau vinyl top, 2-doors	—	—	—	$178	$176	$141	—
Sunroof, power glass[6]	—	—	$182	—	$871	$787	$1,053
T-Bar roof, w/glass panels[7]	—	—	—	$614	$715	$715	—
Dual remote mirrors, chrome	—	—	$57	$54	$61	$77	$52
Dual remote mirrors, sport	—	S	$69	$68	$76	$77	—
Power steering, std. w/V8	$163	—	$161	$166	S	S	S
Power brakes, w/front disc[8]	S	S	$77	$77	S	S	S
Premium wheel covers	—	—	$44	$81	$138	$92	$91
Wire wheel covers	—	—	—	$150	$308	—	$266
Styled road wheels, w/trim	—	—	$44	$154	$194	$148	—
Forged/cast aluminum wheels	—	S	$254	$287	$380	$334	$336
White sidewall tires, std. size	S	—	$43	$49	$89	$22	$92

Popular Option Groups & Packages

	Colt	Challenger	Omni	Aspen	Diplomat	Mirada	St. Regis
Basic group	—	$650	—	$403	$1,267	$1,034	$1,176
Cabriolet roof package	—	—	—	—	—	$950	—
CMX package	—	—	—	—	—	$1,426	—
Custom exterior package	—	—	$101	$75	—	—	—
Custom interior package	—	—	$112	$162	—	—	—
Custom package	—	—	—	$386	—	—	—
Deluxe insulation package	—	S	—	$51	$110	—	—
DeTomaso package	—	—	$1,575	—	—	—	—
Estate package	$314	—	—	—	—	—	—
Light package	—	—	—	$46	$98	$104	$96
Popular equipment group	—	—	$273	—	—	—	—
Premium exterior package	—	—	$207	—	—	—	—
Premium interior package	—	—	$355	—	—	—	—
Premium package	—	$486	—	—	—	—	—
Premium woodgrain package	—	—	$344	—	—	—	—
Protection group	—	—	—	$64	$70	$61	—

	Colt	Challenger	Omni	Aspen	Diplomat	Mirada	St. Regis
R/T package	—	—	—	$586	—	—	—
"S-Type" coupe package	—	—	—	—	$569	—	—
Special Edition package[9]	—	—	—	$814	—	—	—
Sport appearance package	$[10]	—	$431	$254	$290	—	—
Sport handling/performance package[11]	—	—	$43	$385	$151	$192	$269[11]
Sport Wagon package	—	—	—	$721	—	—	—
Sunrise package	—	—	—	$155	—	—	—
Touring Edition package	—	—	—	—	—	—	$1,904

= Not Available; S = Standard equipment. [1]Note that many of the Omni option group and package prices are lower on the 024 models, which have more standard equipment than the Omni 4-door models. [2]Prices given for 4-Door models. On 2-door models price for power windows on Aspen is $130, and on Diplomat $148. Price for power door locks on Aspen is $83, and on Diplomat $96. [3]For Omni 024 AM/FM radio is standard. AM/FM stereo is $35 extra. [4]Available on Aspen and Diplomat coupes, and standard in certain option packages. Omni has standard bucket seats with optional shift console for $32 and front storage console for $22. Console for Aspen, $51; Diplomat Salon, $109; Mirada, $109. All Colts have standard bucket seats and Colt 4-door has standard console. [5]Not available on station wagons. Canopy style on Challenger. [6]"Tri-Lite" removable sunroof on Omni. [7]For 2-door models only. [8]Standard on Aspen wagons. Colt has manual front disc brakes standard. [9]Special Edition woodgrain group for station wagon is $513. [10]Sport package available for Colt Custom hatchback only. [11]Open Road package for St. Regis.

Paint Colors

Dodge Domestic Models	Code
Spinnaker (or Eggshell) White[1]	EW1
Frost Blue metallic[1,2]	SC2
Nightwatch Blue[1]	SC9
Teal Frost metallic[2,3,4]	SG4
Light Cashmere[1]	ST1
Bright Yellow[5]	SY4
Burnished Silver metallic[1,4]	TA3
Graphic Blue[5]	TB6
Light Heather Gray[2,4,6]	TD2
Light Heather Gray metallic[2,4,6]	TD3
Teal Tropic Green metallic[2,3,4,5]	TG6
Crimson Red metallic[1,7]	TM7
Baron Red[1]	TM9
Graphic Red[3,5]	TR4
Natural Suede Tan[1]	TT4
Mocha Brown metallic[1]	TT8
Formal Black[1]	TX9
Flat Black[5]	X15

Colt and Challenger	Code
Spitfire Orange[8]	073
Bright Blue metallic[8]	B22

Colt and Challenger	Code
Dark Blue metallic & Light Blue metallic[9]	B87
Light Blue metallic & Dark Blue metallic[9]	B88
Bright Gold metallic & Ballast Sand metallic[9]	C59
Ballast Tan metallic[8]	C95
Bright Green metallic[8]	G80
Silver metallic & Black[9]	H03
Silver metallic[8]	H29
Bright Gold metallic[8]	K19
Bright Gold metallic & Ballast Sand metallic[9]	K32
Light Tan[8]	S37
Yellow[8]	Y90

Single tones are coded EW1,EW1. Two-tones are coded on body ID plate as TX9, EW1 where three digits on line 2 are lower body color and three digits on line 3 are upper body color or two-tone color. Two-tone paint packages available: Omni 024 Sport, $137; Omni 4-door Classic, $131; Aspen, $142; Diplomat, $162; St. Regis, $168. [1]Available on all models. [2]Available on Diplomat. Light Heather Gray, Light Heather Gray metallic, Frost Blue and Teal Frost are not available on station wagon. Teal Frost metallic not available w/S-Type package. [3]Available on Aspen. Graphic Red is available only on coupes. [4]Available on St. Regis. Burnished Silver Metallic is only available w/Touring Edition. [5]Available on Omni. Bright Yellow and Flat Black only available on 024 models. [6]Available on Mirada. [7]Not available in two-tone combinations. [8]Not available on Challenger. Y90 Yellow is only available w/RS package. [9]Challenger two-tone combination.

Colt

"It's got everything it needs to make it more than just another little car."

Nameplate year of origin: 1971.
Current bodystyle lifespan: 1979 through 1983 (hatchback); 1978 through 1981 (wagon).
Predecessor to this model: Colt (1971 to 1979).
Replacement for this model: Colt (1984 to 1988).
Primary competition: Chevrolet Chevette and Ford Fiesta.
Notable changes: Minor trim and detail changes.
Major standard equipment: Vinyl front bucket seats w/reclining seat backs, full-floor carpeting, fold-down rear seat, two-spoke steering wheel, trip odometer, tinted glass, flipper rear quarter windows, rear window

Measurements

	HBK	Wagon
Wheelbase	90.6"	99.0"
Length	156.9"	179.3"
Width	62.4"	65.2"
Height	50.6"	52.4"
Legroom — front	40.6"	41.7"
Legroom — rear	29.7"	32.3"
Headroom — front	36.8"	37.2"

defroster, door and quarter window reveal moldings, front and rear rubber bumper guards, locking fuel filler door, power front disc brakes, and 6.15 × 13 WSW tires. Custom hatchback adds: Cloth-and-vinyl bucket seats w/reclining seat backs, floor console, rear shelf security panel, rear wiper/washer, sports steering wheel, remote hatchback release, custom tape stripes, and 155SR × 13 WSW tires. Wagon: All-vinyl reclining front bucket seats, fold-down rear seat, full floor carpeting, clock, sports steering wheel, tilt steering column, tinted glass, rear window defroster, bright belt line and drip rail moldings, locking fuel filler door, power steering, power front disc brakes, styled color-keyed road wheels, and 165SR × 14 WSW tires.

Measurements (cont.)

	HBK	Wagon
Headroom — rear	36.0"	36.2"
Cargo capacity (cu. ft.)	6.5*	59.0
Fuel capacity (gals.)	10.5	13.2

*With rear seat down, 27.4 cu. ft.

Models Available

	Model No.	Base MSRP	Change from LY	Shipping Wt. (lbs.)	Model Year Sales	Change from LY
Colt 2-Door Hatchback	4M24	$4,430	+0.11%	1810	NA	NA
Colt Custom 2-Door Hatchback	4H24	$4,792	+1.03%	1885	NA	NA
Colt 4-Door Station Wagon	6H45	$5,906	+5.63%	2635	NA	NA
TOTALS	Avg. price	$5,043	+8.52%	Production	54,313*	-10.44%*

*Total and comparison to LY based on estimated model year sales.

Challenger

"Designed to put a lot of distance between you and the competition."

Nameplate year of origin: 1970.
Current bodystyle lifespan: 1978 through 1983.
Predecessor to this model: None.
Replacement for this model: Dodge Conquest (1984 to 1986).
Primary competition: Buick Skyhawk, Ford Mustang, Mercury Capri, and Oldsmobile Starfire.
Notable changes: Minor trim and detail changes.
Major standard equipment: Plaid cloth and vinyl front bucket seats w/reclining seat backs, color-keyed carpeting, two-spoke sports steering wheel, tilt steering column, sports car instrumentation, trip odometer, AM/FM stereo, tinted glass, rear window defroster, remote deck lid release, overhead console w/reading light, digital clock and 3-way dome light, deluxe sound insulation package, dual power remote control mirrors, black drip rail, windshield, and rear window moldings, black quarter window louvers, front and rear rubber bumper guards, dual horns, locking fuel filler door, power front disc brakes, cast aluminum road wheels, and 195/70SR × 14 BSW tires.

Measurements

Wheelbase	99.0"
Length	183.1"
Width	65.9"
Height	51.8"
Legroom — front	41.7"
Legroom — rear	31.3"
Headroom — front	36.8"
Headroom — rear	35.0"
Cargo capacity (cu. ft.)	10.9
Fuel capacity (gals.)	15.3

1980

Models Available

	Model No.	Base MSRP	Change from LY	Shipping Wt. (lbs.)	Model Year Sales	Change from LY
Challenger 2-Door Hardtop	2H29	$6,502	+0.23%	2675	13,059	-22.82%
TOTALS	Avg. price	$6,502	+0.23%	Production	13,059	-22.82%

Omni

"If it seems light-years ahead of the
competition, there's good reason for it."

Nameplate year of origin: 1978.
Current bodystyle lifespan: 1978 through 1990.
Predecessor to this model: None.
Replacement for this model: None.
Percentage of division's sales volume: 45.89%.
Corporate siblings: Plymouth Horizon.
Primary competition: Chevrolet Chevette, Chevrolet Monza, Ford Fiesta, and Pontiac Sunbird.
Notable changes: Minor trim and detail changes.
Major standard equipment: Vinyl front bucket seats, color-keyed molded headlining, color-keyed carpeting, door armrests, three-spoke steering wheel, door armrests, fold-down rear seat, folding rear shelf security panel, trip odometer, electric rear window defroster, AM radio, day/night inside rear view mirror, bright liftgate window accents, bright aluminum front and rear bumper face bars w/rub strips, manual front disc brakes, steel road wheels, and P155/80R × 13 WSW tires. 024 adds: Cloth upholstered headliner, simulated woodgrain I/P inserts, four-spoke sport steering wheel, AM/FM radio, remote hatchback release, bright sill and wheel lip moldings, wheel trim rings, and P175/75R × 13 BSW tires, and deletes electric rear window defroster.

Measurements

	2+2 HBK	4-door HBK
Wheelbase	96.7"	99.2"
Length	173.3"	164.8"
Width	66.7"	65.8"
Height	51.1"	53.4"
Legroom — front	42.5"	41.8"
Legroom — rear	28.5"	33.0"
Headroom — front	37.5"	38.3"
Headroom — rear	34.7"	37.4"
Cargo capacity (cu. ft.)	10.7*	10.5*
Fuel capacity (gals.)	13.0	13.0

With rear seat folded down, 2+2 HBK is 33.9; 4-door HBK is 35.8.

Models Available

	Model No.	Base MSRP	Change from LY	Shipping Wt. (lbs.)	Model Year Production	Change from LY
Omni 024 2+2 2-Door Hatchback	ZL24	$5,526	+13.61%	2135	51,731	+10.58%
Omni 4-Door Hatchback	ZL44	$5,681	+27.12%	2095	67,279	-5.98%
TOTALS	*Avg. price*	$5,604	+20.08%	*Production*	119,010	+0.57%

Aspen

"Likable, capable, affordable."

Nameplate year of origin: 1976.
Current bodystyle lifespan: 1976 through 1980.
Predecessor to this model: Dart (1967 to 1976).
Replacement for this model: Aries (1981 to 1989).
Percentage of division's production: 25.96%.
Corporate siblings: Plymouth Volaré.
Primary competition: AMC Concord, Buick Skylark, Chevrolet Citation, Ford Fairmont, Mercury Zephyr, Oldsmobile Omega, and Pontiac Phoenix.
Notable changes: Restyled front end and minor trim and detail changes.
Major standard equipment: Cloth-and-vinyl front bench seat (coupe and sedan), all-vinyl front bench seat (wagon), front door armrests, color-keyed carpeting, two-spoke steering wheel, two-speed electric windshield wipers and washers, front ashtray, color-keyed bumper filler, roof drip rail molding, quarter window moldings (coupe and wagon), windshield and backlight moldings, front disc brakes, hubcaps, and P195/75R14 BSW

Measurements

	Coupe	Sedan	Wagon
Wheelbase	108.7"	112.7"	112.7"
Length	200.3"	204.3"	204.3"
Width	72.4"	72.4"	72.4"
Height	53.6"	55.3"	55.5"
Legroom — front	42.7"	42.7"	42.7"
Legroom — rear	32.6"	37.8"	36.6"
Headroom — front	37.6"	39.3"	39.2"
Headroom — rear	36.2"	37.7"	38.7"
Cargo capacity (cu. ft.)	16.4	16.4	73.1
Fuel capacity (gals.)	18.0	18.0	18.0

tires. Wagon adds: Rear liftgate and fold-down second seat. Special adds: Automatic transmission, power steering, bodyside tape stripes, wheel lip moldings, deluxe wheel covers, and WSW tires.

Models Available

	Model No.	Base MSRP	Change from LY	Shipping Wt. (lbs.)	Model Year Production	Change from LY
Aspen Special 2-Door Sport Coupe	NE29	$5,151	NEW	3155	9,684	NEW
Aspen Special 4-Door Sedan	NE41	$5,151	NEW	3210	14,854	NEW
Aspen 2-Door Sport Coupe	NL29	$5,045	+14.69%	3110	9,454	NA*
Aspen 4-Door Sedan	NL41	$5,162	+14.30%	3165	20,938	NA*
Aspen 4-Door Station Wagon	NL45	$5,434	+12.32%	3340	12,388	-62.56%
TOTALS	Avg. price	$5,189	+13.18%	Production	67,318	-44.53%

*Comparison to LY is not possible due to production of coupes and sedans being kept combined for 1979.

Diplomat

"New elegance in the mid-size class."

Nameplate year of origin: 1977 (previously used as designation on Dodge Coronet 2-door hardtops, 1950–1953, and as an option package on Royal Monaco Brougham 2-door hardtops, 1976–1977).

Current bodystyle lifespan: 1980 through 1989.

Predecessor to this model: Diplomat (1977½ to 1979)

Replacement for this model: Monaco (1990 to 1992).

Percentage of division's production: 11.71%.

Corporate siblings: Chrysler LeBaron.

Primary competition: Buick Regal, Mercury Cougar, and Oldsmobile Cutlass Supreme.

Notable changes: Restyled.

Major standard equipment: Cloth and vinyl front bench seat,

Measurements

	Coupe	Sedan	Wagon
Wheelbase	108.7"	112.7"	112.7"
Length	201.2"	205.2"	205.5"
Width	74.2"	74.2"	74.2"
Height	53.4"	55.3"	55.5"
Legroom — front	42.7"	42.5"	42.5"
Legroom — rear	32.6"	36.6"	36.6"
Headroom — front	37.6"	39.2"	39.2"
Headroom — rear	36.2"	37.5"	38.7"
Cargo capacity (cu. ft.)	14.8	15.6	71.8
Fuel capacity (gals.)	18.0	18.0	18.0

door pull straps, color-keyed carpeting, one-piece cloth headliner, windshield header mounted reading lamps and sculptured cavities to store sunvisors (coupe only), simulated woodgrain I/P cluster and glove box door appliqué, stand-up hood ornament, power steering, power brakes, wheel covers, and FR78 × 15 BSW tires. Wagon adds: All-vinyl front bench seat and fold-down rear seat. Special adds: Automatic transmission, power steering, bodyside tape stripes, wheel lip moldings, deluxe wheel covers, and WSW tires. Salon adds: Cloth and vinyl high-back front bench seat w/fold down center armrest, wide body rocker panel sill moldings w/front and rear extensions, bright roof drip rail and quarter window moldings (coupes), bright upper door frame moldings (sedan), full vinyl padded top (sedan), bright belt molding, rear bumper guards, lower deck panel stripe (sedan), and deluxe wheel covers. Salon wagon adds: Marine teak woodtone appliqué on front fenders, doors, quarter panels and liftgate w/light woodgrain overlay stripe. Medallion adds: Cloth 60/40 front split-bench seat w/ fold-down center armrests and dual recliners, fold-down rear seat armrest, bright pedal trim, map reading lamp, courtesy lights, upper assist handles (sedan), B-pillar assist straps (coupe), rear pillar vanity lamps and mirrors (sedan), trunk dress-up package, LH remote control outside rearview mirror, dual chrome quarter window stripes (coupe), bodyside accent tape stripes coordinated w/body color on coupes and vinyl top color on sedans, deluxe sound insulation package (w/o undercoating and hood pad), and premium wheel covers.

Models Available

	Model No.	Base MSRP	Change from LY	Shipping Wt. (lbs.)	Model Year Production	Change from LY*
Diplomat Special Sport 2-Door Coupe	GL22	$5,995	NEW	3130	2,597	NEW
Diplomat 2-Door Coupe	GM22	$6,048	+15.55%	3220	4,213	NA*
Diplomat 4-Door Sedan	GM41	$6,202	+16.23%	3300	5,671	NA*
Diplomat 4-Door Station Wagon	GM45	$6,346	NEW	3455	1,569	NEW

	Model No.	Base MSRP	Change from LY	Shipping Wt. (lbs.)	Model Year Production	Change from LY*
Diplomat Salon 2-Door Coupe	GH22	$6,372	+16.23%	3230	5,778	NA*
Diplomat Salon 4-Door Sedan	GH41	$6,501	+13.77%	3325	4,251	NA*
Diplomat Salon 4-Door Station Wagon	GH45	$7,041	+14.92%	3485	2,104	-72.97%
Diplomat Medallion 2-Door Coupe	GP22	$6,931	+16.17%	3285	2,103	NA*
Diplomat Medallion 4-Door Sedan	GP41	$7,078	+14.20%	3400	2,086	NA*
TOTALS	Avg. price	$6,502	+13.62%	Production	30,372	-41.24%

*Comparison to LY is not possible due to production of coupes and sedans being kept combined for 1979.

Mirada

"Total performance in a personal car."

Nameplate year of origin: 1980.
Current bodystyle lifespan: 1980 through 1983.
Predecessor to this model: Charger SE (1975 to 1978) and Magnum XE (1978 to 1979).
Replacement for this model: Daytona (1984 to 1993).
Percentage of division's sales volume: 11.04%.
Corporate siblings: Chrysler Cordoba.
Primary competition: Chevrolet Monte Carlo, Ford Thunderbird, Mercury Cougar XR-7, and Pontiac Grand Prix.
Notable changes: All-new model.
Major standard equipment: All vinyl high-back front bucket seats, color-keyed carpeting, brushed aluminum appliqué on I/P, padded door trim panels, two-spoke steering wheel w/brushed aluminum appliqué, trip odometer, AM radio, tinted glass, inside day/night rearview mirror, two-speed windshield wipers w/washers, bright trim moldings (windshield, side windows, quarter window vertical appliqué and front bumper rub strip), non-functional front fender louvers, power front disc brakes, power steering, premier wheel covers, and P195/75R15 WSW tires. "S" adds: Cloth and vinyl 60/40 bucket seats and bodyside tape stripes.

Measurements

Wheelbase	112.7"
Length	209.5"
Width	72.7"
Height	53.3"
Legroom — front	NA
Legroom — rear	NA
Headroom — front	NA
Headroom — rear	NA
Cargo capacity (cu. ft.)	16.7
Fuel capacity (gals.)	18.0

Models Available

	Model No.	Base MSRP	Change from LY*	Shipping Wt. (lbs.)	Model Year Production	Change from LY*
Mirada S 2-Door Hardtop Coupe	XS22	$6,645	+10.03%	3280	1,468	-94.21%
Mirada 2-Door Hardtop Coupe	XH22	$6,850	NEW	3280	27,165	NEW
TOTALS	Avg. price	$6,748	+11.73%	Production	28,633	+12.87%

*Comparisons made to 1979 Magnum XE.

St. Regis

"Stylish. Sensible. Luxurious."

Nameplate year of origin: 1979 (also used as 1955 Chrysler New Yorker DeLuxe 2-door hardtop designation).
Current bodystyle lifespan: 1979 through 1981.
Predecessor to this model: Monaco (1974 to 1976) and Royal Monaco (1977).
Replacement for this model: None.
Percentage of division's sales volume: 5.40%.
Corporate siblings: Chrysler Newport and New Yorker and Plymouth Gran Fury.
Primary competition: Chevrolet Impala/Caprice, Ford LTD, and Pontiac Catalina/Bonneville.

Measurements

Wheelbase	118.5"
Length	220.2"
Width	77.6"
Height	54.5"
Legroom — front	42.3"
Legroom — rear	38.2"
Headroom — front	38.6"

Notable changes: Minor trim and detail changes.

Major standard equipment: Verdi II cloth split-back front bench seat w/fold-down center armrest, color-keyed long-pile carpeting, molded color-keyed headliner, two-spoke steering wheel w/woodgrain trim, gauges (fuel, temperature and alternator), tinted glass, LH and RH manual outside mirrors, two-speed windshield wipers w/washers, drip rail, beltline and wheel lip moldings, front and rear bumper rub strips, dual horns, power front disc brakes, power steering, deluxe wheel covers, and P195/75R15 WSW tires.

Measurements (cont.)

Headroom — rear	37.4"
Cargo capacity (cu. ft.)	21.3
Fuel capacity (gals.)	21.0

Models Available

	Model No.	Base MSRP	Change from LY	Shipping Wt. (lbs.)	Model Year Production	Change from LY
St. Regis 4-Door Pillared Hardtop	EH42	$7,129	+9.14%	3565	14,010	-59.31%
TOTALS	Avg. price	$7,129	+9.14%	Production	14,010	-59.31%

FORD

"Better Ideas for the 80's."

1980

To a typical consumer entering a Ford showroom to view the new models, it probably appeared that Ford had little new to offer, as most lines were carry-overs from 1979. Continuing the pattern of the past 15 years, Ford stressed comfort and quietness in its advertising of the large cars and even the smaller Granada. This year's advertising had subtle glimpses of a Rolls-Royce sitting behind an LTD, and another ad showed a profile of a Mercedes-Benz in the shadows behind a Granada — not terribly exciting, but of interest to many consumers. However, there was some excitement generated by the debut of the newly downsized Thunderbird, as the mid-size platform it was formerly built on disappeared. Ford also recognized the Thunderbird's 25th anniversary year with a special Silver Anniversary edition released at mid-year. For Ford Motor Division, the 1980 model year was all about fuel economy and meeting the new 20 mile per gallon CAFE requirements, and to that end much of the news for the year was to be found under the hood. However, it is important to note that by 1981, every Ford model was replaced or redesigned since the 1978 model year, with much more modern and efficient cars, both in fuel economy and emissions output. Though the replacements were done largely with just three platforms, it was still quite a feat for a large company to create this much change in such a short time frame.

An important development for the Thunderbird and LTD was the introduction of a lock-up torque converter, in a new automatic transmission with overdrive. The new 4-speed automatic overdrive was paired with the 302 CID and 351 CID V8 engines for 1980, and would expand to other installations in the future. The new transmission in a full-size LTD could improve fuel economy by 10 to 20 percent. Also making its first appearance for 1980 was a smaller version of the ever-popular 302 CID V8, the new 4.2 liter, 255 CID V8 engine. Available in the Mustang, Fairmont and Granada, and standard in the new Thunderbird, the engine was a welcome addition to the Fairmont and Granada series, but enthusiasts were disappointed with it in the Mustang, as the 302 CID V8 engine had so much more performance potential. To their credit, Ford would return the 302 CID, 5.0L V8 to the Mustang for 1982.

The new Thunderbird was a third variation on the "Fox" platform, first used on the Fairmont and then the Mustang. The resemblance was most easily seen in the greenhouse area with the design of the squared off windshield and framed door windows. While the wheelbase was stretched slightly from the Fairmont, the new design put the Thunderbird squarely up against the Chevrolet Monte Carlo in terms of size, equipment and price. As a sign of the times, as compared to the 1976 Thunderbird, the 1980 edition rode on a foot shorter wheelbase, was two feet shorter in overall length, weighed 1,600 pounds less, and was powered by a 118-horsepower, 255 cubic inch V8 engine rated at 18 miles per gallon in city driving, as opposed to the standard 1976 engine of 202 horsepower and 460 cubic inches, rated at 12 miles per gallon in city driving. Base price in 1976 was $7,790, while the 1980 version cost about $10,000 similarly equipped.

Styling of the new Thunderbird maintained the theme established with the 1977 through 1979 vintage T-Birds, combining hidden headlights and brightly chromed crosshatch grilles up front, full-width taillamps at the rear, and a wrap-over roof band on upper level models. At the front, a chrome strip with the Thunderbird logo affixed ran through the middle of the headlight closures, and wraparound parking/turn signal lamps and optional cornering lights extended the line around the front fender edge. The grille was of a chromed horizontal crosshatch style, six rows high and eight columns across, with an additional section within the body-colored front bumper, below the bright rub strip. Along each side of the grille and across the top was a heavy band of chrome, with the Thunderbird name in block letters above the driver's side of the grille. A stand-up Thunderbird logo hood ornament completed the front-end look. At the rear, full-width taillamps that dipped to a slim band across the center were a new spin on the Thunderbird rear end treatment that began with the 1967 models. Horizontal backup lamps were placed in the center of the large outer taillamps, and had the Thunderbird logo embossed in them. A body-colored rear bumper carried the license plate mounting below the bright rub strip.

The bumper rub strips were connected on the bodysides by the full-length bodyside moldings with partial wheel lip moldings. The greenhouse area was much like the Fairmont 2-door sedans, except in the rear quarter window area where the B-pillar slanted slightly forward, and small rectangular fixed rear quarter windows left a large C-pillar area, creating rearward blind spot issues, especially on any model or option package having a half vinyl roof and opera windows. Inside, the instrument panel design was horizontally themed with rectangular gauges directly in front of the driver, an optional clock in the center, and a flat panel to the right with the Thunderbird name. Ventilation and radio controls were set in a tall center section below the horizontal section with the clock. Seats and other interior components retained the luxury look of preceding Thunderbirds. In fact, the Silver Anniversary and Town Landau interiors with real leather could rival the look of a Lincoln or Cadillac in most appointments and features.

The use of electronics was more extensive than in any previous Ford this year, with the Thunderbird adding an optional digital instrument cluster, as well as expanding the electronics already used within the powertrain systems such as with the automatic overdrive transmissions. Advertising claimed, "These new Thunderbird features make it a world of electronic marvels," and promoted just how much was available. For example, the "Electronic Instrument Cluster," a $313 option, included a digital speedometer, a switch to change from MPH to KPH (miles to kilometers), a "bar graph" fuel gauge, and an electronic digital clock. With the headlamps on, the "Thunderbird" lettering on the far right

of the dashboard was "softly" illuminated. For an additional $50, diagnostic warning lights could be added above the instrument cluster in the upper portion of the two-tiered panel, much as Cadillac had offered since 1975. Warning lights included such things as door ajar, temperature, washer fluid level, headlamps on, low beam out, brake lamp out, taillamp out, low fuel, and low oil pressure, as well as turn signal indicators. Finally, a keyless entry system, newly available on several Ford models, and for $119 on the Thunderbird, used five small "calculator-type" buttons on the driver's door above the exterior door handle to enter a code that would unlock the doors or decklid.

The smaller Fords experienced only modest downturns in sales, but the rest of the line dropped like an anchor. These smaller Fords included the new-for-1979 Mustang, which returned with minor changes like a repositioned interior door handle. Of most significance to performance enthusiasts were the additions made to the Mustang 3-door with optional Cobra package. The revised package took on the front spoiler, fog lamps, and rear deck spoiler from the 1979 Mustang Indianapolis 500 Pace Car, as well as a rear-opening, non-functional hood scoop and a new three-slot grille design for 1980. Ford's most popular 1980 model, the Fairmont, added a new turbocharged 4-cylinder as an option in any model except the station wagon. Also added in January 1980 was a Fairmont Futura 4-door sedan. The new sedan shared the frontal styling of the Futura sport coupe, including its dual headlamps and its grille, and the higher level of standard equipment, but otherwise had no styling differences from the base Fairmont 4-door sedan. While Pinto sales dropped slightly in its final season, with the ongoing recession and higher fuel prices, the Pinto actually increased its share of total Ford sales by nearly 50 percent, quite a remarkable feat for a ten-year-old design in an age of more modern, front-wheel-drive subcompact competitors. It is equally remarkable that with the one basic design, the Pinto sold over three million cars during its ten-year lifespan with only three basic models, and never sold fewer than 180,000 units in a single model year.

The popular Granada was also entering its final model year on its original platform, which dated from 1971, as used on the Maverick 4-door sedan, and received few changes from the 1979 model. With the LTD II gone, the Granada theoretically assumed the position as Ford's mid-size car beginning with the 1980 model year. For 1981, the Granada would remain as Ford's mid-size car but move to the "Fox" chassis, essentially becoming an upscale and slightly larger version of the Fairmont, and sharing some of the Thunderbird's features.

The full-size LTD had had a successful if not completely impressive first model year as a downsized car. For 1980, a lower-priced "S" subseries was added in 4-door sedan and station wagon body styles, intended to help capture sales that might have been lost due to the discontinuation of the traditional mid-size LTD II, and also to further expand the LTD into a price-leader status against its "Big Three" full-size competitors, which now included a newly designed Plymouth Gran Fury. The new LTD S used the same front end styling as the 1979 LTD, while the 1980 LTD picked up the front end styling of the 1979 LTD Landau and its newly renamed replacement, the 1980 LTD Crown Victoria. However, the full-size regular line Ford ultimately recorded its worst production year since the war-shortened 1942 model year. The entire Ford Division line had its worst season since the recession year of 1958.

Fairmont 2-Door Sedan

Fairmont 4-Door Station Wagon

Fairmont Futura 2-Door Coupe
with turbocharged engine option

Fairmont Futura 4-Door Sedan

Fiesta 3-Door Hatchback with Ghia option

Granada 2-Door Sedan with ESS option

Granada 4-Door Sedan with Ghia option

LTD 4-Door Sedan

LTD 4-Door Station Wagon

LTD Crown Victoria 2-Door Sedan

Mustang 3-Door Sedan with Cobra package

Mustang 3-Door Sedan with
turbocharged engine option

Pinto 2-Door Station Wagon with
Cruising Wagon and graphic options

Pinto 2-Door Station Wagon
with Exterior Décor group

1980

**Pinto 3-Door Runabout
with Exterior Décor group**

Pinto Pony 2-Door Sedan

**Thunderbird Silver Anniversary
Edition 2-Door Sedan**

Thunderbird Town Landau 2-Door Sedan

Model year production: 1,167,028, down 36.07% from 1979.
Domestic market share: 15.27% (2nd place).
Base price range: $4,117 to $12,172.
Ford average base price: $6,302, up 13.93%.
Introduction date: October 12, 1979.
Assembly plants: Atlanta, GA (A); Oakville, Ontario, Canada (B); Mahwah, NJ (E); Dearborn, MI (F); Chicago, IL (G); Lorain, OH (H); Kansas City, MO (K); San Jose, CA (R); Metuchen, NJ (T); Louisville, KY (U); Wayne, MI (W); and St. Thomas, Ontario, Canada (X). *Fiesta:* Cologne, Saarlouie, Germany (C).
Data plate identification (VIN): Eleven digit code read as follows: First digit indicates year (0 = 1980); second digit indicates assembly plant code (see list above); third and

fourth digits indicate model number (model number in model charts); fifth digit indicates engine code (see powertrain chart); remaining digits are sequential with beginning numbers of 100001. *Example:* 9F02Z100001 is a 1979 Ford Mustang 2-Door Sedan, with 170.8 CID, 2-bbl. V6 engine, serial number 100001, built in Dearborn, MI. 1980 Fiesta uses an eleven digit code read as follows: First digit indicates country of origin (G = Germany); second digit indicates assembly plant code (C = Cologne); third and fourth digits indicate model number (model number in model charts); fifth digit indicates production year code (W = 1979); sixth digit indicates production month code; remaining digits are sequential with beginning numbers of 00001.

Powertrains

Engine	Net HP	Engine Code	Transmission Availability[1]		Fiesta	Pinto	Mustang	Fairmont	Granada	Thunderbird	LTD
97.6 CID (1.6L) OHC, 2-bbl., 4-cyl.	66	W	4-speed manual w/overdrive		S	—	—	—	—	—	—
				MPG:	28	—	—	—	—	—	—
				Calif.	25	—	—	—	—	—	—
140 CID (2.3L) OHC, 2-bbl., 4-cyl.	88	A	4-speed manual		—	S	S	S	—	—	—
				MPG:	—	24/38	23/38	23/38	—	—	—
				Calif.	—	21	21	21	—	—	—
			5-speed manual		—	—	$156	—	—	—	—
				MPG:	—	—	22/37	—	—	—	—
			3-speed Select-Shift automatic		—	$340	$340	$340[2,3]	—	—	—
				MPG:	—	22/32	22/31	22/32	—	—	—
				Calif.	—	21	21	21	—	—	—
140 CID (2.3L) OHC, 2-bbl., Turbo 4-cyl.	150	A	4-speed manual		—	—	$481	$481[2]	—	—	—
				MPG:	—	—	18/30	18/30	—	—	—
				Calif.	—	—	18	—	—	—	—
			5-speed manual		—	—	$637	—	—	—	—
				MPG:	—	—	NA	—	—	—	—
				Calif.	—	—	18	—	—	—	—

Engine	Net HP	Engine Code	Transmission Availability[1]		Fiesta	Pinto	Mustang	Fairmont	Granada	Thunderbird	LTD
			3-speed Select-Shift automatic		—	—	$821	$821[2]	—	—	—
				MPG:	—	—	19/26	19/26	—	—	—
				Calif.	—	—	19	19	—	—	—
200 CID (3.3L), 1-bbl., 6-cyl.	91	B	4-speed manual w/overdrive		—	—	$169	$169[2]	—	—	—
				MPG:	—	—	21/30	21/30	—	—	—
			3-speed Select-Shift automatic		—	—	$509	$509[2]	—	—	—
				MPG:	—	—	20/27	20/27	—	—	—
				Calif.	—	—	18	18	—	—	—
250 CID (4.1L), 1-bbl., 6-cyl.[4]	90	C	4-speed manual w/overdrive		—	—	—	—	S[4]	—	—
				MPG:	—	—	—	—	19/28	—	—
			3-speed Select-Shift automatic		—	—	—	—	$340[4]	—	—
				MPG:	—	—	—	—	17/23	—	—
255 CID (4.2L), 2-bbl., V8	118	D	3-speed Select-Shift automatic		—	$628	$628[2]	$378	S	—	—
				MPG:	—	—	18/26	18/26	NA	18/26	—
				Calif.	—	—	18	18	17	18	—
302 CID (5.0L), 2-bbl., V8	131	F	4-speed manual		—	—	—	—	$188[4]	—	—
				MPG:	—	—	—	—	NA	—	—
			3-speed Select-Shift automatic[3]		—	—	—	—	$566[3]	$150	S
				MPG:	—	—	—	—	17/25	17/25	17/26
				Calif.	—	—	—	—	16	17	15
			4-sp. Automatic Overdrive		—	—	—	—	—	$288	$188
				MPG:	—	—	—	—	—	17/29	16/27
				Calif.	—	—	—	—	—	17	—
351 CID (5.8L), 2-bbl., V8	140	G	4-sp. Automatic Overdrive		—	—	—	—	—	—	$338
				MPG:	—	—	—	—	—	—	16/27
				Calif.	—	—	—	—	—	—	16

[1]Unless otherwise noted: All manual transmissions are floor-shift. All automatics are column-shift, except on Fiesta, Pinto and Mustang. Floor-shift is available for $38 extra on Fairmont and Granada with optional bucket seats and automatic. Floor-shift w/bucket seats and console is also available on Thunderbird. [2]Requires optional power front disc brakes on wagons w/3.3L and 4-speed manual, or any Fairmont w/automatic transmission or turbo engine. [3]Requires optional power front disc brakes on Granada w/5.0L engine and on Fairmont wagons when ordered with power windows or air conditioning. [4]Not available in California.

Major Options

	Fiesta	Pinto	Mustang	Fairmont	Granada	Thunderbird	LTD
Air conditioning[1]	$475	$538	$538	$571	$571	$571	$606
Tilt steering wheel	—	—	$90	$90	$78	$78	$78
Fingertip speed control	—	—	$129	$129	$129	$129	$116
Electric rear window defroster	$96	S[2]	$96	$101	$101	$101	$103
Tinted glass, all windows	$55	S[2]	$65	$71	$71	$71	$85
Dual remote-control mirrors	—	$58	$58	$60	$60	$69	$56[3]
Power trunk lid release	—	—	$[4]	$25	$25	$[4]	$[4]
Power windows, 2-dr./4-dr.	—	—	—	$135/$191	$136/$193	$136	$140/$208
Power door locks, 2-dr./4-dr.[4]	—	—	$[4]	$88/$125	$89/$125	$[4]	$89/$120
Power seat, 4-way w/std. seat	—	—	—	$111	$111	$111	$168[5]
Front bucket seats w/console[6]	—	S	$166	S	$110	$176	—
Leather upholstery	—	—	$345	—	$277	$349	—
AM radio	—	S[2]	$93	$93	$93	S	$93
AM/FM stereo[7]	$183	$103	$183	$183	$183	$90	$183
AM/FM stereo w/8-track tape	—	—	$259	$259	$259	$166	$259
AM/FM stereo w/cassette tape	—	$191	$271	$271	$271	$179	$271
Vinyl top, full[8]	—	—	$118	$118	$118	$133	$145
Moonroof, power-operated	$219[9]	$219[9]	$219[9]	$219[9]	$998	$219[9]	—
Power steering	—	$160	$160	$165	$165	S	S
Power brakes, w/front disc	—	$78	$78	$78	$78	S	S
Deluxe/Luxury wheel covers	—	—	—	$41	$46	$88	$70
Turbine wheel covers	—	—	$43	$43	—	—	—
Wire wheel covers	—	$104	$121	$158	$119	$138	$138
Styled Steel wheels w/trim ring	—	$56	$104	$133	$138	—	—

1980

	Fiesta	Pinto	Mustang	Fairmont	Granada	Thunderbird	LTD
Forged/Cast aluminum wheel[10]	—	$225	$321	$351	—	—	$310
Cast aluminum lacy wheels	—	$225	—	—	$321[10]	—	—
White sidewall tires, std. size	$70	$50	$50	$50	$50	$50	$50

Popular Option Groups & Packages[11]

	Pinto	Mustang	Fairmont	Granada	Thunderbird	LTD
Appearance protection group	$40	$41	$53	—	—	—
Cobra package[12]	—	$1,482	—	—	—	—
Convenience group	$118	—	$51	$108	—	$98
Cruising Wagon package[13]	$606	—	—	—	—	—
ES option	—	—	$378	—	—	—
ESS option	$313	—	—	—	—	—
Exterior accent group	—	$63	$95	—	—	—
Exterior décor group	$44	—	$260	—	$359	—
Exterior luxury group	—	—	—	—	$489	—
Futura Sports group	—	—	$114	—	—	—
Ghia option	—	—	$566	—	—	—
Interior accent group	$50	$134	$115	—	—	—
Interior décor group	$238	—	$346	$243	$348	—
Interior luxury group	—	—	—	—	—	$741[14]
Light group	$41	$41	$48	$51	$35	$43
Luxury interior group	—	—	—	—	$975	—
Power Lock group, 2-dr./4-dr.	—	$113	—	—	$113	$114/$166
Protection group	—	—	—	$53	$43	$58
Rallye package[13]	$625	—	—	—	—	—
Sport option	—	$186	—	—	—	—
Sports package	$118	—	—	—	—	—
Squire wagon option	$315	—	$458	—	—	—

— = Not Available; S = Standard equipment. [1]Air conditioner w/automatic temperature control is available for $634 on Granada and Thunderbird, and $669 on LTD. [2]Standard on all except Pinto Pony. Defroster includes tinted rear window. Pinto Pony prices: Defroster, $96; tinted glass, $65; AM radio, $80; AM/FM stereo, $183. [3]LH remote is standard on LTD Landau w/RH being $39. [4]Available only in Power lock group. [5]6-way power seat on LTD. [6]Bucket seats only on Pinto and Fairmont; console not available. Bucket seats standard on Mustang; price shown is for console. Requires interior décor group on Granada. [7]Signal-searching AM/FM stereo available for $333 on Granada and LTD, and for $240 on Thunderbird. 40-channel CB (Citizens Band) radio available for $316 on Thunderbird and LTD. [8]Not available on wagons. Half-vinyl roof for Fairmont Futura w/flip-up open air roof is $90; half-vinyl roof for Granada 2-doors w/o moonroof is $106; padded rear ½ vinyl roof standard on LTD Crown Victoria 4-door. Thunderbird has half-vinyl roof only. [9]Manually operated flip-up open-air sunroof on Fiesta, Pinto, Mustang, Fairmont, and Thunderbird. [10]Granada has cast lacy aluminum spoke wheels. Mustang offers Forged Metric Aluminum wheels for $355 and requires TRX tires at extra cost. [11]Fiesta option groups: Décor group, $389; Ghia group, $735; Sport group, $562. [12]Cobra hood graphics available for $78 with Cobra package. [13]Cruising package available on Pinto runabout for $355; Rallye package for $369. Delete option of the standard stripe/panel appliqués on wagon for $70 credit. [14]Available on LTD Crown Victoria models only. Available on Country Squire wagon for $693.

Paint Colors

All except Fiesta	Code	All except Fiesta	Code	Fiesta only	Code
Light Gray	12	Pastel Sand	6D	Light Green	E
Anniversary Silver[1]	14	Bright Yellow	6N	Gold metallic	H
Black	1C	Dark Pine metallic	7M	Bright Red	O
Silver metallic	1G	Dark Chamois metallic	8A	Light Beige	P
Medium Gray metallic	1P	Medium Bittersweet glow		Venetian Red	R
Bright Red	27	metallic	8D	Light Blue	T
Bright Bittersweet	2G	Dark Cordovan metallic	8N	Strato Silver metallic	V
Red glow metallic	2H	Chamois glow metallic	8W	Midnight Blue	X
Candy Apple Red	2K	White	9D		
Dark Blue metallic	3D				
Medium Light Blue	3F				
Medium Blue metallic	3H	Fiesta only	Code		
Bright Blue	3J	Light Blue metallic	1		
Midnight Blue metallic	3L	Signal Yellow	9		
Pastel Pine glow metallic	4E	Diamond White	B		
Bright Caramel	5T	Light Green metallic	C		
Sand glow metallic	6B	Terra Cotta	D		

In two-tone combinations, first two digits are lower color and second two digits are upper color. Metallic glow paints are $45 extra on Pinto and Mustang, $54 extra on Fairmont and Granada, $60 extra on Thunderbird, and $65 extra on LTD. "Tu-Tone" paint/tape treatment available for $80 on Pinto, $56 on Fairmont w/ES option, $180 on Granada, $163 on Thunderbird, and $75 on LTD. A lower body "Tu-Tone," in black only, for Mustangs is available for $88; and for Thunderbird in a variety of colors and with other trim for $106. ¹Available on Thunderbird only. Thunderbird specific paint combinations for the Silver Anniversary edition are as follows: Anniversary Silver glow, Black, Light Gray, or Black and Anniversary Silver glow two-tone body colors, with silver wrap-over band and black vinyl roof; or (on all but two-tone combination) black wrap-over band and silver vinyl roof; Red glow with silver wrap-over band and red vinyl roof; or Midnight Blue metallic with silver wrap-over band and midnight blue vinyl roof.

Fiesta

"Front wheel drive Fiesta ... Wundercar!"

Nameplate year of origin: 1978 (U.S.; 1976 in Europe).
Current bodystyle lifespan: 1978 through 1980 (1976 to 1983 globally).
Predecessor to this model: None.
Replacement for this model: Escort (1981 to 1985).
Primary competition: None.
Notable changes: Minor trim and detail changes.
Major standard equipment: All-vinyl high-back front bucket seats, color-keyed passenger compartment carpeting, brushed aluminum I/P appliqué, two-spoke steering wheel, open glove box, fold-down rear seat, overhead courtesy light w/door switches, concealed under load floor storage compartment, black window moldings, painted drip rails, rack-and-pinion steering, manual front disc brakes, argent road wheels, and 145SR × 12 BSW tires.

Measurements

Wheelbase	90.0"
Length	147.1"
Width	61.7"
Height	52.3"
Legroom — front	40.1"
Legroom — rear	34.3"
Headroom — front	37.6"
Headroom — rear	36.8"
Cargo capacity (cu. ft.)	6.8*
Fuel capacity (gals.)	10.0

*With rear seat folded down, 29.0 cu. ft, plus 0.6 cu. ft. under floor storage.

Models Available

	Model No.	Base MSRP	Change from LY	Shipping Wt. (lbs.)	Model Year Sales	Change from LY
Fiesta 3-Door Hatchback	FB	$5,032	+12.00%	1726	68,841	-11.44%
TOTALS	*Avg. price*	$5,032	+12.00%	*Production*	68,841	-11.44%

1980

Pinto

"Compare Pinto. It may be the best small car value of 1980."

Nameplate year of origin: 1971.
Current bodystyle lifespan: 1971 through 1980.
Predecessor to this model: None.
Replacement for this model: Escort (1981 to 1985).
Percentage of division's production: 15.86%.
Corporate siblings: Mercury Bobcat.
Primary competition: AMC Spirit, Chevrolet Chevette, Dodge Colt, and Plymouth Champ.
Notable changes: Minor trim and detail changes.
Major standard equipment: Choice of crosshatch pattern cloth-and-vinyl or wicker weave all-vinyl high-back front bucket seats, color-keyed carpeting, AM radio, tinted glass, electric rear window defroster, bright front and rear window moldings, bright drip and belt moldings, deluxe bumper group, rack-and-pinion steering, manual front disc brakes,

Measurements

	Sedan	Runabout	Wagon
Wheelbase	94.5"	94.5"	94.8"
Length	170.8"	170.8"	180.6"
Width	69.4"	69.4"	69.7"
Height	50.6"	50.6"	52.1"
Legroom — front	40.8"	40.8"	40.8"
Legroom — rear	30.7"	30.7"	30.7"
Headroom — front	37.3"	37.3"	37.9"
Headroom — rear	36.2"	36.2"	39.3"
Cargo capacity (cu. ft.)	8.2	6.1*	31.3*
Fuel capacity (gals.)	13.0	13.0	14.0

*With rear seat folded down, Runabout, 29.0 cu. ft.; Wagon, 57.2 cu. ft.

hubcaps, and A78 × 13 BSW tires. Runabout adds: Black rubber load floor mat, fold-down rear seat, and rear liftgate. Station wagon adds: Pivoting rear quarter windows, bright window moldings, counterbalanced liftgate, and liftgate "open" warning light. Pony deletes: Color-keyed I/P and steering wheel, AM radio, tinted glass, electric rear window defroster, deluxe bumper group, bright drip and rear window moldings, and bright belt molding.

Models Available

	Model No.	Base MSRP	Change from LY	Shipping Wt. (lbs.)	Model Year Production	Change from LY
Pinto Pony 2-Door Sedan	10	$4,117	+19.89%	2377	NA*	NA*
Pinto Pony 2-Door Station Wagon	12	$4,627	+18.67%	2545	NA*	NA*
Pinto 2-Door Sedan	10	$4,605	+16.91%	2385	84,053	+10.90%
Pinto 3-Dr. Runabout (hatchback)	11	$4,717	+16.33%	2426	61,842	-10.87%
Pinto 2-Door Station Wagon	12	$5,004	+15.35%	2553	39,159	-27.28%
TOTALS	Avg. price	$4,614	+17.32%		Production 185,054	-7.02%

Production kept as combined totals for Pinto Pony models and Pinto models.

Mustang

"A sports car for the 80's."

Nameplate year of origin: 1964 (also used on a 1963 show car).
Current bodystyle lifespan: 1979 through 1993.
Predecessor to this model: Mustang (1974 to 1978).
Replacement for this model: Mustang (1994 to 2004).
Percentage of division's production: 23.25%.
Corporate siblings: Mercury Capri.
Primary competition: Chevrolet Camaro, Dodge Challenger, Plymouth Sapporo, and Pontiac Firebird.
Notable changes: Minor trim and detail changes.
Major standard equipment: All-vinyl high-back bucket seats, deluxe cut-pile carpeting, door panels w/padded upper panel and bright moldings and carpeted lower panels, full-width woodtone I/P appliqués, deluxe steering wheel, courtesy lights, gauges (including tachometer, trip odometer, fuel, oil pressure, ammeter and temperature), black LH rearview mirror, bright windshield and rear window molding, bright drip rail and side window moldings, color-keyed louvers behind rear quarter window, color-keyed door and window frames w/bright molding, soft color-keyed urethane covered front and rear ends w/black rub strips on bumpers, full wheel covers, and B78 × 13 BSW tires. 3-door adds: Sport steering wheel, fold-down rear seat, liftgate, black louvers behind rear quarter window, black painted door and window frames, black belt and rocker panel moldings, full wraparound wide black bodyside moldings w/dual accent stripe inserts and 13-inch sport wheels. Ghia adds: Crinkle-grain vinyl low-back bucket seats, color-keyed deluxe seat belts, luxury cut-pile carpeting, Ghia door trim w/badge, soft inserts, map pockets and carpeted lower panels, sport steering wheel, roof-mounted assist grips, light group, RH visor vanity mirror, Ghia sound package, carpeted luggage compartment (2-door), Ghia insignia on decklid/liftgate, color-keyed window frames and louvers, dual remote control color-keyed mirrors, bright belt and rocker panel moldings, pinstripes, full wraparound wide black bodyside moldings w/dual accent stripe inserts, Turbine wheel covers, and BR78 × 14 BSW tires.

Measurements

Wheelbase	100.4"
Length	179.1"
Width	67.4"
Height	51.5"
Legroom — front	40.9"
Legroom — rear	29.8"
Headroom — front	37.2"
Headroom — rear	36.3"
Cargo capacity (cu. ft.)	10.0*
Fuel capacity (gals.)**	11.5**

3-door is 33.3 cu. ft. w/rear seat folded down.
**12.5 gallons with air conditioning or optional engines, 11.9 gallons on 2.3L turbo w/automatic.*

Models Available

	Model No.	Base MSRP	Change from LY	Shipping Wt. (lbs.)	Model Year Production	Change from LY
Mustang 2-Door Sedan	02	$5,338	+18.78%	2497	128,893	-17.73%
Mustang 3-Door (hatchback)	03	$5,616	+16.32%	2531	98,497	-18.28%
Mustang Ghia 2-Door Sedan	04	$5,823	+14.99%	2565	23,647	-58.04%
Mustang Ghia 3-Door (hatchback)	05	$5,935	+13.78%	2588	20,285	-44.25%
TOTALS	Avg. price	$5,678	+15.87%		Production 271,322	-26.66%

Fairmont

"Engineered for 1980 and beyond."

Nameplate year of origin: 1978.
Current bodystyle lifespan: 1978 through 1983.
Predecessor to this model: Maverick (1970 to 1977).
Replacement for this model: Tempo (1984 to 1994).
Percentage of division's production: 27.63%.
Corporate siblings: Mercury Zephyr.
Primary competition: AMC Concord, Chevrolet Citation, and Plymouth Volaré.
Notable changes: Minor trim and detail changes.
Major standard equipment: Helix-pattern all-vinyl low-back front bucket seats (w/2.3L 4-cylinder) or Crosshatch cloth-and-vinyl front bench seat (w/3.3L 6-cylinder or 4.2L V8 engines), color-keyed cut-pile carpeting, integral door armrests w/door pull assist handle, two-spoke color-keyed steering wheel, simulated woodgrain I/P appliqué, inside hood release, bright windshield and rear window

Measurements

	2-Door	Futura	4-Doors	Wagon
Wheelbase	105.5"	105.5"	105.5"	105.5"
Length	195.5"	197.4"	195.5"	195.5"
Width	71.0"	71.0"	71.0"	71.0"
Height	52.9"	51.7"	52.9"	54.2"
Legroom — front	41.8"	NA	41.8"	NA
Legroom — rear	35.4"	NA	37.7"	NA
Headroom — front	38.5"	NA	38.5"	NA
Headroom — rear	37.7"	NA	37.7"	NA
Cargo capacity (cu. ft.)	16.8	16.1	16.8	79.5
Fuel capacity (gals.)*	16.0	16.0	16.0	16.0

14.7 gallons with 2.3L turbo engine. Early production models have a 14 gallon capacity on all except wagon, and 12.7 gallon with 2.3L turbo engine.

moldings, bright drip rail moldings, front bumper guards, manual front disc brakes, modified strut front suspension, hubcaps, and BR78 × 14 BSW tires. Wagon adds: Fold-down rear seat, carpet on load floor and rear seat back, cargo area light, bright quarter window and liftgate moldings, "liftgate-open" warning light, and CR78 × 14 BSW tires. Futura adds: Pebble grain vinyl front bucket seats (w/2.3L 4-cylinder) or Crosshatch cloth-and-vinyl front bench seat (w/3.3L 6-cylinder or 4.2L V8 engines), deluxe door trim panels, color-keyed safety belts, high gloss simulated woodgrain appliqué on I/P, bright LH manual mirror (2-door), dual remote control mirrors (4-door), wrap-over roof design w/accent paint stripes (2-door), wraparound taillights (2-door), bright door window frames and belt moldings, lower bodyside protection molding w/vinyl insert and wheel lip moldings, deluxe sound insulation package, unique front end appearance, and turbine wheel covers.

Models Available

	Model No.	Base MSRP	Change from LY	Shipping Wt. (lbs.)	Model Year Production	Change from LY
Fairmont 2-Door Sedan	91	$4,102	+13.19%	2491	54,798	-30.44%
Fairmont 4-Door Sedan	92	$4,220	+13.75%	2544	133,813	-2.22%
Fairmont 4-Door, 5-p. Station Wagon	94	$4,497	+10.68%	2674	100,691	-21.57%
Fairmont Futura 2-Door Coupe	93	$4,463	+8.77%	2546	106,065	-9.32%
TOTALS	*Avg. price*	$4,321	+11.50%	*Production*	395,367	-14.23%

Granada

"A modern American classic."

Nameplate year of origin: 1975.
Current bodystyle lifespan: 1975 through 1980.
Predecessor to this model: None.
Replacement for this model: Granada (1981 to 1982).
Percentage of division's production: 7.75%.
Corporate siblings: Mercury Monarch.
Primary competition: AMC Concord Limited, Chevrolet Malibu, Dodge Diplomat, and Pontiac LeMans.
Notable changes: Minor trim and detail changes.
Major standard equipment: Pebble grain vinyl "Flight Bench" front seat w/fold-down center armrest, 10-oz. cut-pile carpeting, burled walnut I/P appliqués w/Granada script, two rear seat ashtrays, luggage compartment mat, bright front and rear window moldings, bright belt moldings, bright drip rail and wheel opening

Measurements

Wheelbase	109.9"
Length	197.8"
Width	74.5"
Height	53.3"
Legroom — front	41.1"
Legroom — rear	36.0"
Headroom — front	38.5"
Headroom — rear	37.6"
Cargo capacity (cu. ft.)	15.4*
Fuel capacity (gals.)	18.0

Ghia models have 1.6 cu. ft. less capacity, and ESS models have 1.1 cu. ft. less capacity.

1980

moldings, opera window w/bright moldings (2-door), hood ornament, manual front disc brakes, stainless steel full wheel covers, and DR78 × 14 BSW tires. Ghia adds: Pebble grain all-vinyl "Flight Bench" front seat w/fold-down center armrest and seatback map pockets, 18-oz. cut-pile carpeting, deluxe door trim w/burled walnut trim and carpeted lower section, deluxe steering wheel, digital clock, Ghia interior ornamentation, day/night rearview mirror, deluxe color-keyed seat belts, rear door courtesy light switches (4-door), bright LH remote control mirror, opera window Ghia interior and exterior ornamentation, wide vinyl insert bodyside moldings w/integral bright wheel lip moldings, brushed aluminum rear panel appliqué w/concealed gas cap, dual horn, deluxe luggage compartment trim, deluxe sound insulation, color-keyed wheel covers, and ER78 × 14 BSW tires. ESS adds: Chain-pattern vinyl front bucket seats w/European style headrests, 18-oz. cut-pile carpeting, leather wrapped steering wheel, deluxe door trim w/lower carpeted section, day/night rearview mirror, deluxe color-keyed seat belts, rear door courtesy light switches (4-door), dual color-keyed remote control sport mirrors, louvered opera windows appliqué (2-door), black trim (window frames, wipers, grille, back panel appliqué and rocker panels), black bodyside moldings w/bright inserts, luggage compartment trim, sound package, deluxe bumper group, ESS ornamentation on front fenders, hood and decklid paint stripes, heavy-duty suspension, color-keyed wheel covers, and FR78 × 14 BSW tires.

Models Available

	Model No.	Base MSRP	Change from LY	Shipping Wt. (lbs.)	Model Year Production*	Change from LY*
Granada 2-Door Sedan	81	$5,541	+18.50%	3063	60,872	-20.79%
Granada 4-Door Sedan	82	$5,664	+18.44%	3106	29,557	-71.99%
Granada Ghia 2-Door Sedan	81	$5,942	+17.64%	3106	NA*	NA*
Granada Ghia 4-Door Sedan	82	$6,065	+17.61%	3147	NA*	NA*
Granada ESS 2-Door Sedan	81	$6,031	+15.74%	3137	NA*	NA*
Granada ESS 4-Door Sedan	82	$6,154	+15.74%	3178	NA*	NA*
TOTALS	Avg. price	$5,900	+17.23%	Production	90,429	-50.42%

*Model year production and change from LY is not available due to production totals being kept by body style and model number, and not by trim level.

Thunderbird

"Spread your wings."

Nameplate year of origin: 1955.
Current bodystyle lifespan: 1980 through 1982.
Predecessor to this model: Thunderbird (1977 to 1979).
Replacement for this model: Thunderbird (1983 to 1988; restyled in 1987).
Percentage of division's production: 13.44%.
Corporate siblings: Mercury Cougar XR-7.
Primary competition: Chevrolet Monte Carlo and Pontiac Grand Prix.
Notable changes: Completely redesigned.
Major standard equipment: Tweed cloth-and-vinyl "Flight Bench" front seat w/fold-down center armrest, 10 oz. cut pile carpeting, two-tier I/P w/high-gloss black appliqués, simulated woodtone door panel trim, full-length door armrest, electric clock, AM radio, trip odometer, bright moldings (rear hood edge, drip rails, windshield, back window), rocker panel and wheel lip moldings, full quarter windows, full wheel covers, and P185/75R × 14 BSW

Measurements

Wheelbase	108.4"
Length	200.4"
Width	78.5"
Height	52.8"
Legroom — front	41.6"
Legroom — rear	36.4"
Headroom — front	37.1"
Headroom — rear	36.3"
Cargo capacity (cu. ft.)	17.7
Fuel capacity (gals.)	17.5

tires. Town Landau adds: Velour cloth split front bench seat w/individual fold-down center armrests and dual recliners, six-way power driver's seat, color-keyed deluxe seat belts, RH illuminated visor vanity mirror, engraved owner's name plaque on RH side of I/P, woodtone I/P trim, SelectAire conditioner w/manual control, AM/FM stereo w/search radio, electronic instrument cluster, tilt steering wheel, power windows, power lock group, interior luxury group, convenience group, light group, tinted glass, dual remote-control sport mirrors, brushed aluminum wrap-over roof molding, tape stripes (bodyside, hood, and decklid), hood ornament w/Thunderbird logo, Town Landau script on lower front fender, front cornering lights, cast aluminum wheels, and TR-type 200/55R × 14 BSW tires. Silver Anniversary edition adds to Town Landau features: Patterned luxury cloth split front bench seats w/individual fold-down center armrests in dove gray only, door and front seatback assist straps, power driver's seat, luxury cut-pile carpeting, leather covered I/P pad, leather-wrapped steering wheel, LH and RH visor vanity mirrors, fingertip speed control, power radio antenna, bright pedal trim accents, trunk carpeting and molded deck lid liner, padded vinyl roof w/wrap-over band and coach lamps, exclusive paint schemes and turbine-spoke cast aluminum wheels.

Models Available

	Model No.	Base MSRP	Change from LY	Shipping Wt. (lbs.)	Model Year Production	Change from LY
Thunderbird 2-Door Sedan	87	$6,816	+7.71%	3118	156,803	NA*
Thunderbird Town Landau 2-Door Sedan	87	$10,424	+12.83%	3357	NA*	NA*
Thunderbird Silver Anniversary 2-Dr. Sdn.	87	$12,172	+10.05%	3225	NA*	NA*
TOTALS	*Avg. price*	$9,804	+10.46%	*Production*	156,803	-44.82%

Town Landau and Heritage production is included with base Thunderbird; therefore comparisons are not available. Silver Anniversary edition is compared to 1979 Heritage edition.

LTD

"Rides as quiet as a Rolls-Royce."

Nameplate year of origin: 1965 (Crown Victoria subseries, 1956).
Current bodystyle lifespan: 1979 through 1991.
Predecessor to this model: Custom/Galaxie/LTD (1971 to 1978).
Replacement for this model: Crown Victoria (1992 to 2008).
Percentage of division's production: 12.08%.
Corporate siblings: Mercury Marquis.
Primary competition: Chevrolet Impala/Caprice, Plymouth Gran Fury, and Pontiac Catalina.
Notable changes: New Crown Victoria subseries, and minor trim and detail changes.
Major standard equipment: Dual-tone striped cloth-and-vinyl front bench seat, 10 oz. color-keyed cut-pile carpeting, black I/P appliqués, woodtone door appliqués, deluxe four-spoke soft-rim steering wheel, interior courtesy lighting,

Measurements

	2-Doors	4-Doors	Wagons
Wheelbase	114.3"	114.3"	114.3"
Length	209.0"	209.0"	215.0"
Width	77.5"	77.5"	79.1"
Height	54.5"	54.5"	56.8"
Legroom — front	NA	42.0"	NA
Legroom — rear	NA	40.5"	NA
Headroom — front	NA	38.0"	NA
Headroom — rear	NA	37.3"	NA
Cargo capacity (cu. ft.)	22.4	22.4	89.7*
Fuel capacity (gals.)	19.0	19.0	20.0

Additional 9.9 cu. ft. of below deck storage on 2-seat wagons, and 5.7 cu. ft. on wagons w/DFRS.

bright moldings (front and rear window, belt, drip rail, wheel lip, and rocker panel), front bumper guards, deluxe wheel covers, and P205/75R × 14 BSW tires. LTD S Wagon adds: All vinyl bench seat, fold-down rear seat, color-keyed removable load floor carpeting, power tailgate window, and P215/75R × 14 BSW tires. LTD and LTD wagon add: Woodtone I/P and door appliqués, LH remote control mirror, bright window frame and hood rear edge moldings, color-keyed vinyl insert bodyside moldings, brush-finish accent panel on lower decklid, front bumper slot grilles and distinctive plated grille w/ dual rectangular halogen headlamps and wraparound parking lights, decklid (tailgate on wagon) accent tape stripes, dual note horn, and luxury sound insulation package. Crown Victoria adds: Triple line knit cloth-and-vinyl front bench seat w/fold-down center armrest, 18 oz. cut-pile carpeting, color-keyed deluxe seat belts, electric clock, deluxe door trim w/ carpeted lower panel, high-gloss woodtone I/P appliqué w/LTD Crown Victoria nomenclature, rear door courtesy light switch, unique sound insulation package, padded rear half vinyl roof w/ LTD Crown Victoria nomenclature and color-keyed backlight moldings, wide wrap-over roof molding w/brushed aluminum insert and crown ornament, dual accent paint stripes on hood and bodysides, black rocker panel moldings, bright lower bodyside moldings w/rear extension, hood ornament, and luggage compartment light. Country Squire adds to LTD wagon: Simulated woodgrain exterior bodyside and tailgate vinyl paneling w/surround rails, 18 oz. cut-pile carpeting, color-keyed deluxe seat belts, electric clock, deluxe door trim w/ carpeted lower panel, high-gloss woodtone I/P appliqué, rear door courtesy light switch, cargo area light, hood ornament, and LTD style front-end styling.

Models Available

	Model No.	Base MSRP	Change from LY	Shipping Wt. (lbs.)	Model Year Production	Change from LY
LTD S 4-Door Sedan	61	$6,875	NEW	3464	19,283	NEW
LTD S 4-Door, 2-Seat, 6-p. Station Wagon**	72	$7,198	NEW	3707	3,490	NEW
LTD 2-Door Sedan	62	$7,003	+13.24%	3447	15,333	-71.61%
LTD 4-Door Sedan	63	$7,117	+13.26%	3475	51,630	-56.15%
LTD 4-Door, 2-Seat, 6-p. Station Wagon**	74	$7,463	+13.94%	3717	11,718	-69.13%

	Model No.	Base MSRP	Change from LY	Shipping Wt. (lbs.)	Model Year Production	Change from LY
LTD Crown Victoria 2-Door Sedan*	64	$7,628	+14.09%	3482	7,725	-81.74%
LTD Crown Victoria 4-Door Sedan*	65	$7,763	+13.98%	3524	21,962	-70.56%
LTD Country Squire 4-Door, 2-S., 6-p. Wagon**	76	$7,891	+12.63%	3743	9,868	-67.03%
TOTALS	Avg. price	$7,367	+11.85%	Production	141,009	-60.45%

*Comparison of LTD Crown Victoria is made to 1979 LTD Landau, as they are equivalent model numbers.   **Wagons available w/removable DFRS (dual facing rear seats) for $146 extra.

LINCOLN

"A standard by which other luxury cars are judged."

As Lincoln's 60th year of building luxury cars neared, executives at Ford Motor Company must have been holding their breath, much as GM execs did in 1977, as the first ever, downsized 1980 Lincoln models were introduced. Both the Continental and Continental Mark VI were downsized, and for the first time ever, all Lincoln models shared chassis, powertrains, and many basic body components with both Ford and Mercury. Lincoln had previously shared the 1949–1951 "small" series Lincoln bodies with Mercury, and had also shared powertrains with both Ford and Mercury. Of course, the Versailles, introduced at mid–1977, shared virtually everything with its Ford and Mercury counterparts, but alas this would be the last year for the Versailles, which never met with the success of its main competitor.

Literally looking as if they had shrunk, the new Continental coupe and sedan were purposely designed to continue the now familiar Lincoln look. Similarly, the newly designated Continental Mark VI also looked like a modern variation of the recent Mark III, IV and V models. What was completely different was that the Mark VI added a first ever, and short-lived, four-door sedan model, and that all models were about a foot shorter and up to 700 pounds lighter than their immediate predecessors, and were powered by the smallest displacement V8 engines in traditional Lincolns since the 1941 engine, with a new electronic fuel injection system installed on Ford's popular 302 CID V8 engine.* While the fuel injection system did not immediately show promise as a power boost, it definitely helped to improve fuel economy, which was now nearly double what Lincolns had achieved just five years earlier.

As previously stated much of the exterior design and chassis were built around the one-year-old Ford LTD and Mercury Marquis design. In fact, the Mark VI coupe rode on the exact same wheelbase as the Ford and Mercury, while the Mark VI sedan and Continental coupe and sedan rode on a three-inch stretch of the same chassis. The stretch was made between the wheels and is most noticeable by the wider B-pillars and longer rear doors on the sedans. Also while the 302 CID V8 engine with electronic fuel injection was standard, the 351 CID V8 engine, providing slightly more horsepower, was available on all four models.

Front end styling for the Continental received the greatest change with the use of dual rectangular headlamps, which were exposed for the first time since 1969. The now traditional vertical bar grille design with chrome surround continued although it did not extend into the bumper on the Continental. Parking/turn signal lights continued to be vertically mounted in the front fender end caps. All design features were very sharp and angular, with only the wheel openings using full round cutouts, unlike the flattop wheel openings of the prior generation. At the rear, taillamps continued to be vertical units mounted in the rear fender end caps. In between, and below the decklid opening, was a full-width red "reflex" reflective trim molding that was divided into three sections, and the backup lights were mounted along each side of the license tag housing in the center of the rear bumper. The greenhouse area used more aerodynamically shaped and sloped windshields, and nearly upright rear windows, while all side windows were angular, except that the rear quarter window on the coupe had rounded corners. Being on a longer wheelbase than the Mark VI coupe, the Continental coupe looked awkward in comparison, having to use an extended and angular roof. Four-door models used a thin, vertical, forward slanting opera window immediately behind the rear door.

Inside, the Continentals retained all the room of their

*Because of casting problems with the enlarged 1942 engine, some 1946–1948 Lincoln models used the 1941 engine.

predecessors, even adding more space in some areas, such as rear seat legroom and trunk. Instrument panels retained a familiar horizontal theme with simulated woodgrain trim inserts and larger brushed aluminum instrument facings. The new electronic instrument cluster, described below, was available as an option on the Continental for $707. Upholstery materials and craftsmanship continued to maintain Lincoln's tradition of a luxurious and quiet cabin. Equipment levels of the new Continentals remained about the same as in the recent past, to help ease the transition of customers into the smaller models. The rarely ordered fixed moonroof option was dropped for 1980, as customers definitely preferred the power operated glass moonroof.

The new Mark VI sedan would be the only four-door model to appear in the Continental Mark series, excepting of course the 1958 through 1960 Mark III, IV, and V series, which are not considered to be of true Continental Mark series lineage by either Ford or enthusiasts. Much of the new Mark VI styling was shared with the Continental with several exceptions. To look like a modern Mark series car, the new Mark VI had the requisite long hood/short deck theme, and used hidden single round headlamps with a vertical bar grille that extended into the lower front bumper. The grille this year was divided into eight sections vertically by a slightly larger bar. Vertically mounted front fender end parking/turn signal lamps continued as did front fender louvers, which were no longer functional. The rear end styling continued the "Continental" spare tire design on the trunklid, which sloped downward to the rear bumper, and still used vertical taillamps in the angled rear fender end caps. The Mark VI decklid met the bumper, and red "reflex" reflective strips were on the lower edges on each side of the spare tire "hump." All Mark VI models were distinguished by their use of an oval opera window in the C-pillar, except on coupes equipped with the optional simulated convertible top, known as the Carriage roof.

Interiors were more similar to the Continental than in years past, but were not totally unlike previous Mark series cars. A popular new feature was the standard electronic instrument cluster. The new cluster consisted of three square pods housing on the left a bar graph fuel display, at center a digital speedometer, and to the right a trip log and message center. Using soft blue-green backlighting, the fuel display gave a graphic representation of the amount of fuel remaining. The speedometer could be changed from miles per hour to kilometers per hour at the touch of a button on the row of control buttons to the right of the steering wheel. The trip log and message center showed the time, day, date and month unless overridden by a warning message, or by the user selecting a different function. Available functions included digital readouts of elapsed trip time, estimated time of arrival, distance traveled, average speed, distance to destination, and average miles per gallon. The long row of control buttons surely prompted many owners to take their eyes off the road more often than they should. As this was a new technology, customers could opt for a regular analog instrument panel at no cost. A new Mark VI Signature Series option was available from the start of the model year, but was so popular that by mid-year it became a full-fledged part of the Mark VI series, with model numbers of 95 for the coupe and 96 for the sedan. Details of the contents of the Signature Series can be found in Appendix IV.

The mid-size Versailles was in its fourth and final season and received very few changes. The small Lincoln would temporarily disappear from the Lincoln lineup after 1980. Its replacement came along in 1982 and was named the Continental, as the current model of that name would be renamed the Town Car. The 1982 Continental was styled with a humpback sedan look, much like the newly restyled 1980 Cadillac Seville, and it would share its underpinnings with the 1984 Mark VII.

1980

Continental 2-Door Coupe

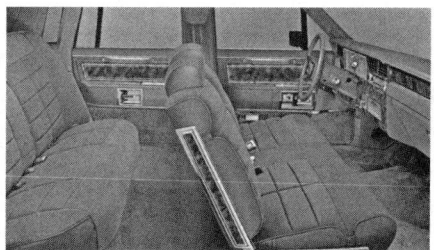

Continental 4-Door Sedan interior

Continental 4-Door Sedan
with Town Car option

Continental Mark VI 2-Door Coupe

Continental Mark VI 4-Door Sedan
with Signature Series package

Continental Mark VI electronic instrument
panel with detail of clock and trip log buttons

Versailles 4-Door Sedan with Dual
Shade paint and Coach roof

Model year production: 74,908, down 60.48% from 1979.
Domestic market share: 0.98% (12th place).
Base price range: $13,251 to $16,691.
Lincoln average base price: $15,098, up 17.28%.
Introduction date: October 12, 1979.
Assembly plants: Wayne, MI (W), and Wixom, MI (Y).
Data plate identification (VIN): Eleven digit code read as
   follows: First digit indicates year (0 = 1980); second digit

indicates assembly plant code (see list above); third and
fourth digits indicate model number (model number in
model charts); fifth digit indicates engine code (see powertrain chart); remaining digits are sequential with beginning
numbers of 600001. *Example:* 0Y82F600001 is a 1980 Lincoln Continental 4-Door Sedan, with 302 CID, EFI V8 engine, serial number 600001, built in Wixom, MI.

Powertrains

Engine	Net HP	Engine Code	Transmission Availability		Versailles	Continental & Mark VI
302 CID (5.0L), 2-bbl., V8	132	F	3-speed Select-Shift automatic		S	—
				MPG:	15	—
302 CID (5.0L), EFI, V8	129	F	4-speed Automatic Overdrive		—	S
				MPG:	—	17/24
				Calif.	—	16/24
351 CID (5.8L), 2-bbl., V8	140	G	4-speed Automatic Overdrive		—	$160
				MPG:	—	15

Major Options

	Versailles	Continental	Mark V
Air conditioning, Auto-Temp	S	S	S
Tilt steering wheel	$81	$83	$83
Automatic speed control	S	$149	$149
Electric rear window defroster	$109	$109	$109
Tinted glass, all windows	S	S	S
Power windows	S	S	S
Power front vent windows	—	S	S
Power door locks, 2-dr./4-dr.	$[1]	$103/$143	$103/$143
Illuminated entry system	S	$67	$67
Keyless entry system, 2-dr./4-dr.	—	$253/$293	$253/$293
Power seat, 6-way w/dual recliners	S[2]	$312	$139
Leather seating upholstery	$416	$435	S

	Versailles	Continental	Mark V
RH remote-control mirror, LH std.	S	$44	$44
Intermittent windshield wipers	S	$43	$43
AM/FM electronic stereo w/search[3]	S	S	S
AM/FM electronic stereo, w/search and 8-track tape	$81	$81	$81
AM/FM electronic stereo, w/search and cassette tape	$95	$95	$95
Vinyl top, full[4]	N/C	S	S[4]
Moonroof, power-operated & tinted	$1,128	$1,128	$1,128
Power brakes, four wheel disc	S	—	—
Wire wheel covers	N/C	$255	$255
Cast aluminum turbine-style wheels	S	$396	$396
Cast aluminum lace-style wheels	—	$396	$396
Wide-band WSW tires	S	$36	$36

Popular Option Groups & Packages

	Versailles	Continental	Mark V
Appearance protection group	$88	—	—
Bill Blass designer series	—	—	$1,825[5]
Cartier designer series	—	—	$2,191
Color luxury group[6]	—	—	$1,044
Defroster group	$132	$132	$132
Emilio Pucci designer series	—	—	$2,191
Fashion Accent series	—	$600	—
Givenchy designer series	—	—	$1,739
Headlamp convenience group	—	$141	$141
Power Lock convenience group	$169[1]	—	—
Reclining Bucket seat group	$416	—	—
Signature series	—	—	$5,485[7]
Town Coupe/Town Car package	—	$1,089	—

— = Not Available; S = Standard equipment.   [1]Power door locks require optional Power Lock convenience group, and include remote trunk release.   [2]Four-way power seat on Versailles.   [3]Citizens Band (CB) radio available for $356, and includes multi-band power antenna.   [4]Valino grain landau vinyl roof standard on Mark VI. Landau vinyl roof w/frenched seams and rear window available on Continental Mark VI for $311; Carriage roof available for $984 (Carriage roof is simulated convertible top). Fully padded coach vinyl roof is available on Continental w/Town Car or Town Coupe option for $296; and with Continental coupe or sedan for $367. Coach vinyl roof includes wide vinyl padded roof bow molding, coach lamps, and fully padded custom half-vinyl roof w/ frenched rear window and side quarter windows.   [5]Price given is with full vinyl roof; price with carriage roof is $2,809.   [6]Color luxury groups available: Bittersweet, Black, Caramel, Champagne, Dark Red, Light Gold, Medium Pine, Medium Vaquero, Midnight Blue, Pewter, and White.   [7]Price on coupe is $5,516.

Paint Colors

	Code		Code		Code
Light Gray[1]	12	Dark Pine metallic[3]	4F	White	9D
Black	1C	Pine Opolescent[2,3]	4G		
Light Pewter moondust metallic[2,3]	1J	Dark Champagne metallic[3]	54		
Medium Pewter metallic[3,4]	1K	Medium Fawn moondust metallic[2]	56		
Medium Gray metallic[1]	1S	Light Fawn moondust metallic[2]	57		
Silver metallic[1,5]	1Y	Light Fawn[3]	5E		
Dark Red moondust metallic[2]	23	Chamois moondust metallic[2,3]	5K		
Bright Red[6]	2K	Dark Cordovan metallic	5R		
Maroon[3]	2L	Pastel Rattan[6]	6M		
Diamond Blue moondust metallic[2]	38	Medium Rattan (two-tone only)[6]	6Q		
Dark Blue metallic	3Q	Dark Chamois metallic[3]	8B		
Medium Beryl metallic	4C	Bittersweet moondust metallic[2]	8E		

In two-tone combinations, first two digits are lower color, and second two digits are upper color. "Dual shade" two-tone paint available only on Versailles for $80 extra plus required bodyside molding for an additional $83; available on Continental for $360. [1]Available only on Versailles. [2]Moondust metallic paints available for $232 extra. [3]Available only on Continental and Mark VI. [4]Available only on Mark VI with Cartier Designer series option. [5]Available only on Mark VI Signature series. [6]Available only on Mark VI. Bright Red and Pastel Rattan available only on coupe.

Versailles

"Engineered to provide total driving pleasure in the Lincoln tradition."

Nameplate year of origin: 1977½ (1975 as a Continental option package).
Current bodystyle lifespan: 1977½ through 1980.
Predecessor to this model: None.
Replacement for this model: Continental (1982 to 1987).
Percentage of division's production: 6.39%.
Corporate siblings: Ford Granada and Mercury Monarch.
Primary competition: Cadillac Seville.
Notable changes: Minor trim and detail changes.
Major standard equipment: Continental body cloth "Twin Comfort Lounge" front seat w/four-way power adjustment, folding center armrests in front and rear seat, deep-pile carpeting, simulated wood appliqués on I/P, steering wheel and doors, leather steering wheel and I/P pad, rear passenger and front passenger side roof rail assist straps, package shelf w/Kasman fabric, Cartier-signed digital clock, power windows, automatic speed control, electronic AM/FM stereo w/electronic search and w/power antenna, automatic temperature control air conditioning, LH and RH illuminated visor vanity mirrors, LH and RH remote control rearview mirror, tinted glass, power deck lid release, interior lighting (ashtrays, courtesy, glove box, luggage compartment, dome/map, and rear seat reading), 18-oz. color-keyed carpeted luggage compartment floor w/14 oz. carpeted decklid liner, full vinyl roof, coach lamps, illuminated entry system, cornering lights, high luster bodyside molding w/vinyl insert, bumper protection group, forged aluminum wheels, and FR78 × 14 wide WSW tires.

Measurements

Wheelbase	109.9"
Length	201.0"
Width	74.5"
Height	54.1"
Legroom — front	40.7"
Legroom — rear	35.6"
Headroom — front	38.2"
Headroom — rear	37.6"
Cargo capacity (cu. ft.)	14.6
Fuel capacity (gals.)	19.2

Models Available

	Model No.	Base MSRP	Change from LY	Shipping Wt. (lbs.)	Model Year Production	Change from LY
Versailles 4-Door Sedan	84	$15,664	+13.81%	3661	4,784	-77.23%
TOTALS	*Avg. price*	$15,664	+13.81%	*Production*	4,784	-77.23%

Continental

"Everything a Lincoln has always meant. And more."

Nameplate year of origin: 1940 (1961 as a regular series).
Current bodystyle lifespan: 1980 through 1991.
Predecessor to this model: Continental (1970 to 1979).
Replacement for this model: Town Car (1992 to 2010).
Percentage of division's production: 41.70%.
Corporate siblings: Ford LTD, Lincoln Continental Mark VI, and Mercury Marquis.
Primary competition: Cadillac deVille.
Notable changes: Completely redesigned.
Major standard equipment: Luxury cloth "Flight Bench" front seat w/six-way power adjustment, folding center armrests in front and rear seat, 18 oz. cut-pile carpeting, simulated wood appliqués (on I/P, door panels, seat side trim, and steering wheel), electronic quartz analog clock, roof rail assist straps, retractable coat hooks, power windows, power front vent windows, AM/FM stereo w/search and w/power antenna, automatic temperature control air conditioning, visor-mounted vanity mirror, LH remote control rearview mirror, tinted glass, power deck lid release, interior lighting (ashtrays, courtesy, glove box, luggage compartment, dual beam dome/map, and rear pillar), fully lined and carpeted luggage compartment w/tire cover, Valino grain full vinyl roof, cornering lights, full-width decklid Reflex molding, bright rocker panel and wheel lip moldings, front and rear bumper guards w/pad and rub strips, deluxe wheel covers, and P205/75R15 WSW tires.

Measurements

	Coupe	Sedan
Wheelbase	117.3"	117.3"
Length	219.1"	219.2"
Width	78.1"	78.1"
Height	55.4"	56.1"
Legroom — front	42.1"	42.1"
Legroom — rear	43.3"	43.3"
Headroom — front	39.0"	39.0"
Headroom — rear	38.0"	38.1"
Cargo capacity (cu. ft.)	22.4	22.4
Fuel capacity (gals.)	18.0	18.0

Models Available

	Model No.	Base MSRP	Change from LY	Shipping Wt. (lbs.)	Model Year Production	Change from LY
Continental 2-Door Hardtop Coupe	81	$13,251	+11.65%	3843	7,177	-55.54%
Continental 4-Door Sedan	82	$13,593	+12.40%	3919	24,056	-68.54%
TOTALS	Avg. price	$13,422	+12.03%	Production	31,233	-66.27%

Continental Mark VI

"A car befitting its illustrious heritage."

Nameplate year of origin: 1956 (Continental Mark II).
Current bodystyle lifespan: 1980 through 1983.
Predecessor to this model: Continental Mark IV (1977 to 1979).
Replacement for this model: Continental Mark VII (1984 to 1992).
Percentage of division's production: 51.92%.
Corporate siblings: Ford LTD, Lincoln Continental, and Mercury Marquis.
Primary competition: Buick Riviera, Cadillac Eldorado, and Oldsmobile Toronado.
Notable changes: Completely redesigned.
Major standard equipment: Continental Mark body cloth "Twin Comfort" lounge seats w/six-way power adjustment, folding center armrests in front and rear seat, simulated rosewood appliqué (on I/P, door panels, seat side moldings, and steering wheel), 18 oz. color-keyed cut-pile carpeting, visor vanity mirror, roof rail assist straps, retractable coat hooks, electronic I/P w/message center, power windows, power front vent windows, AM/FM stereo w/search and w/power antenna, automatic temperature control air conditioning, LH remote control rearview mirror, tinted glass, door panel courtesy lights, power decklid release, fully lined luggage compartment, full vinyl roof w/opera window, dual custom pinstripe, non-functional fender louvers (three per side) w/bright molding, cornering lights, front bumper guards w/pads and rub strips, luxury wheel covers, and P205/75R15 WSW tires.

Measurements

	Coupe	Sedan
Wheelbase	114.3"	117.3"
Length	216.0"	219.1"
Width	78.1"	78.1"
Height	55.4"	56.3"
Legroom — front	42.0"	42.1"
Legroom — rear	38.0"	43.3"
Headroom — front	38.0"	39.0"
Headroom — rear	37.8"	38.0"
Cargo capacity (cu. ft.)	22.4	22.4
Fuel capacity (gals.)	18.0	18.0

1980

Models Available

	Model No.	Base MSRP	Change from LY	Shipping Wt. (lbs.)	Model Year Production	Change from LY
Continental Mark VI 2-Door Coupe	89	$16,291	+18.30%	3892	20,647	-72.81%
Continental Mark VI 4-Door Sedan	90	$16,691	NEW	3988	18,244	NEW
TOTALS	Avg. price	$16,491	+19.75%	Production	38,891	-48.79%

MERCURY

"Presenting the 1980 Mercury fine car collection."

Coming off the highest model year production in its forty year history, Mercury would enter the 1980s with high hopes for the new model year. An all-new Cougar XR-7 was being introduced, the new-for-1979 Capri was doing well, and the recently introduced Zephyr and downsized Marquis were holding their own. However, by the end of the model year, Mercury found itself in a position quite similar to how it began the 1970s, despite the recent successes. In terms of market share, the 1980 figure of 4.55 percent was slightly higher than the 1970 mark. The difference for 1980 was that the market had shrunk. With rising competition from imported cars, especially in Mercury's price range with Volvo, Audi and BMW ramping up their sales, and with the U.S. being in the middle of a second fuel crisis and ensuing recession, the U.S. automakers' portion of the market was beginning to dry up. The result for Mercury would mean that the model year production total for 1980 would end at its lowest point since 1970.

The Cougar XR-7 was "all-new" in appearance, but not below the surface as it was based on a version of the Ford "Fox" platform which it shared with the equally new Thunderbird. Styling maintained cues from recent Cougars, including a vertical bar grille up front and a fake "Continental" spare tire outline on the trunk lid. A half-vinyl roof with louvers on the rear quarter window seemed a half-hearted attempt to emulate the prior XR-7's landau roof and opera windows. The vertical bar grille at the front was divided into eight sections, with a thicker center bar, and within each section were three thin bars. The grille appeared to extend into the body-colored front bumper below the chrome rub strip. Dual halogen rectangular headlights set along each side of the grille shared a bezel with the turn signal and side marker lights on the fender side. Parking and turn signal lamps were centered below each pair of headlamps within the area of the bumper rub strip. The hood was raised slightly in the center with a line running from the grille back to the cowl, and the grille was surrounded by a large chrome trim piece.

Bodysides of the new Cougar XR-7 were very similar to the Ford Thunderbird's, with a single main feature line running end-to-end between the tops of the bumpers, and arching over the flat-topped wheel openings. At the rear a raised center decklid section of a square design created the illusion of the previously mentioned "Continental" spare tire impression. Alongside the trunklid was a square-style wrap-around taillight divided into three sections vertically, with a fourth section on the rear quarter edge. Small backup lights were on the bottom of the inward section, and the license tag mounting was located in the bumper below the rub strip. The new Cougar also used louvered rear quarter windows and a standard half-vinyl roof. Louvered rear quarter windows were used in differing ways on the three main Cougar option packages, the Décor group, Luxury group and Sports group, along with unique looking two-tone combinations.

Inside the Cougar XR-7 had all the latest in electronic gadgetry, with an optional electronic instrument panel available in the Luxury group or as a separate option. The instrument panel itself was in two "tiers," with a horizontal section running the full width of the car, and a center stack holding the ventilation controls and optional radio. Standard instrumentation was two square pods housing the speedometer and

other gauges using black lettering on white faces, and lined in brushed aluminum trim, much like that used on the Marquis. Seats were essentially better padded and trimmed versions of those used in the Zephyr, which shared the "Fox" platform with the XR-7, although sporty Recaro bucket seats were available. The new Cougar was available only in the XR-7 version this year, and only as a 2-Door Sedan, as the base Cougar was dropped, and the Monarch took over the mid-size Mercury reins for the 1980 model year. Unfortunately for Mercury, the new XR-7 sold poorly, losing nearly two-thirds of 1979's production. The Cougar name would return for a brief two-year stint as the Monarch's replacement.

The standard Cougar XR-7 powertrain was the new, and smaller, 255 CID V8 engine, also optionally available on the Capri, Zephyr and Monarch. The 118-horsepower engine seemed anemic, even in a car of this size, but fortunately for Cougar buyers, the popular 302 CID V8 engine was still available as an option. When the 302 CID V8 engine was ordered in the Cougar, a new automatic transmission with overdrive was available that helped to improve highway fuel economy. The new transmission was also available on any Marquis model.

The rest of the Mercury line was mostly a carry-over from 1979. The subcompact Bobcat was in its final season, due to be replaced in 1981 by a new front-wheel-drive "world car" to be named the Lynx. The only changes to be found for the Bobcat were a new optional "Tu-tone" paint treatment and a new sport option, with optional front air dam and rear spoiler. The popular glass third door was still available for $31. Also in its final year was the Monarch, which would be replaced by a new Cougar line, the fourth Mercury series to be built from the "Fox" platform. The only changes to the Monarch included the previously mentioned change to the optional 255 CID V8 engine, and new paint colors with new "tone-on-tone" combinations.

The new-for-1979 Capri and Marquis lines were mostly unchanged aside from the aforementioned automatic overdrive for the Marquis, and the 255 CID V8 replacing the 302 CID V8, if only temporarily, in the Capri. The new-for-1978 Zephyr series was supposed to have the turbocharged four-cylinder engine from the Capri available in the Z-7 sport coupe at the start of the year, but according to most records it did not make it to production until very late in the model year. Some references suggest that none were ever built, but there are records of Ford Fairmont Futuras with the turbocharged engine built, and it seems likely at least a few Z-7's were built. One other change for the Zephyr line was that the Euro-style ES package was dropped. Finally, new features added to the Capri, Zephyr, and Marquis series included revised taillight lenses, standard halogen headlights, and standard P-metric size tires.

Bobcat 2-Door Station Wagon
with Villager option

Bobcat 3-Door Runabout with Sports option

Capri 2-Door Hatchback with Turbo RS option

Capri interior with optional cloth upholstery

Cougar XR-7 2-Door Sedan with Décor group

Cougar XR-7 2-Door Sedan
with Sports group and Tu-Tone paint

Cougar XR-7 electronic instrument panel

Grand Marquis 4-Door Sedan

Grand Marquis 4-Door Sedan interior

Marquis Brougham 2-Door Sedan

Marquis Colony Park 4-Door Station Wagon

Monarch 2-Door Sedan with ESS package

Monarch 4-Door Sedan

Zephyr 2-Door Sedan
with turbocharged engine option

1980

Zephyr 4-Door Sedan with Ghia package

Zephyr 4-Door Station Wagons
with Villager option at front

Zephyr Z-7 2-Door Sports Coupe

Model year production: 347,711, down 48.04% from 1979.
Domestic market share: 4.55% (6th place).
Base price range: $4,764 to $8,824.
Mercury average base price: $6,552, up 14.69%.
Introduction date: October 12, 1979.
Assembly plants: Atlanta, GA (A); Lorain, OH (H); Kansas City, MO (K); San Jose, CA (R); Metuchen, NJ (T); Wayne, MI (W); St. Thomas, Ontario, Canada (X); and St. Louis, MO (Z).
Data plate identification (VIN): Eleven digit code read as

follows: First digit indicates year (0 = 1980); second digit indicates assembly plant code (see list above); third and fourth digits indicate model number (model number in model charts); fifth digit indicates engine code (see powertrain chart); remaining digits are sequential with beginning numbers of 600001. *Example:* 0K31D600001 is a 1980 Mercury Zephyr 2-Door sedan, with 255 CID, 2-bbl. V8 engine, serial number 600001, built in Kansas City (Claycomo), MO.

Powertrains

Engine	Net HP	Engine Code	Transmission Availability[1]		Bobcat	Capri	Zephyr	Monarch	Cougar XR-7	Marquis
140 CID (2.3L) OHC, 2-bbl., 4-cyl.	88	A	4-speed manual		S	S	S	—	—	—
				MPG:	24/38	23/38	23/38	—	—	—
				Calif.	21	21	21	—	—	—
			5-speed manual		—	$156	—	—	—	—
				MPG:	—	NA	—	—	—	—
			3-speed Select-Shift automatic		$340	$340	$340[2,3]	—	—	—
				MPG:	22	22	22	—	—	—
				Calif.	21	21	21	—	—	—
140 CID (2.3L) OHC, 2-bbl., Turbo 4-cyl.	NA	T	4-speed manual		—	$481	$481[2]	—	—	—
				MPG:	—	NA	—	—	—	—
				Calif.	—	18	—	—	—	—
			5-speed manual		—	$637	—	—	—	—
				MPG:	—	18/30	—	—	—	—
				Calif.	—	18	—	—	—	—
			3-speed Select-Shift automatic		—	$821	$821[2]	—	—	—
				MPG:	—	17/26	17/26	—	—	—
				Calif.	—	19	19	—	—	—
200 CID (3.3L), 1-bbl., 6-cyl.	91	B	4-speed manual w/overdrive		—	$169	$169[2]	—	—	—
				MPG:	—	21/30	21/30	—	—	—
			3-speed Select-Shift automatic		—	$509	$509[2]	—	—	—
				MPG:	—	20	20	—	—	—
				Calif.	—	18	18	—	—	—
250 CID (4.1L), 1-bbl., 6-cyl.[4]	90	C	4-speed manual w/overdrive		—	—	—	S[4]	—	—
				MPG:	—	—	—	19	—	—
			3-speed Select-Shift automatic		—	—	—	$340[4]	—	—
				MPG:	—	—	—	17	—	—
255 CID (4.2L), 2-bbl., V8	118	D	3-speed Select-Shift automatic		—	$628	$628[2]	$378	S	—
				MPG:	—	18/26	18/26	NA	18/26	—
				Calif.	—	17	18	17	18	—

Engine	Net HP	Engine Code	Transmission Availability[1]		Bobcat	Capri	Zephyr	Monarch	Cougar XR-7	Marquis
302 CID (5.0L), 2-bbl., V8	131	F	4-speed manual		—	—	—	$188[4]	—	—
				MPG:	—	—	—	NA	—	—
			3-speed Select-Shift automatic[3]		—	—	—	$566[3]	$150	S
				MPG:	—	—	—	17/26	17/26	17/26
				Calif.	—	—	—	16	17	15
			4-speed Automatic Overdrive		—	—	—	—	$288	$188
				MPG:	—	—	—	—	17/29	17/27
				Calif.	—	—	—	—	17	—
351 CID (5.8L), 2-bbl., V8	161	G	4-speed Automatic Overdrive		—	—	—	—	—	$338
				MPG:	—	—	—	—	—	16/27
				Calif.	—	—	—	—	—	16

[1]Unless otherwise noted: All manual transmissions are floor-shift. All automatics are column-shift, except on Bobcat and Capri. Floor-shift is available for $38 extra on Zephyr and Monarch with optional bucket seats and automatic. Floor-shift w/bucket seats and console is also available on Cougar XR-7. [2]Requires optional power front disc brakes on wagons w/3.3L and 4-speed manual, or any Zephyr w/automatic transmission or turbo engine. [3]Requires optional power front disc brakes on Monarch w/5.0L engine, and Zephyr wagons when ordered with power windows or air conditioning. [4]Not available in California.

Major Options

	Bobcat	Capri	Zephyr	Monarch	Cougar XR-7	Marquis
Air conditioning[1]	$538	$538	$571	$571	$571	$606
Tilt steering wheel	—	$78	$78	$78	$78	$78
Automatic speed control	—	$129	$129	$129	$129	$133
Electric rear window defroster	S	$96	$101	$101	$101	$103
Tinted glass, all windows	S	$65	$71	$71	$71	$85
Dual remote control mirrors	$60	$36[2]	$60	$68	$60	$60
Pivoting front door vent windows	—	—	$50[3]	—	$50	$50
Power windows, 2-dr./4-dr.	—	—	$135/$191	$136/$193	$136	$140/$208
Power door locks, 2-dr./4-dr.	—	$113	$88/$125	$88/$125	$[4]	$[4]
Power seat, 4-way w/std. seating	—	—	$111	$111	$111	$168[5]
Front bucket seats w/console[6]	S	$156	S	$93	$176	—
Leather interior trim	—	$313	—	$313	$303	$303
Dual facing rear seats (wagons)	—	—	—	—	—	$199
AM radio	S	S	$93	$93	$93	$93
AM/FM stereo	$103	$103	$183	$183	$183	$183
AM/FM stereo w/tape[7]	$191	$191	$259	$259	$259	$259
AM/FM stereo w/auto-search	—	—	—	$333	$333	$333[7]
Vinyl top, full[8]	—	—	$118	$118	S	$145
Moonroof, power-operated[9]	$219[9]	$219[9]	$219[9]	$923	$219[9]	—
Power trunk lid release	—	—	$25	$25	$[4]	$[4]
Power steering, variable-ratio	$160	$160	$165	$	S	S
Power brakes, w/front disc	$78	$78	$78	$	S	S[10]
Deluxe wheel covers	N/C	—	$41	S	S	S
Sport or Luxury wheel covers[11]	—	N/C	$46	$46	$88	$94
Wire wheel covers	$40	$89	$120	$120	$138	$138
Styled steel wheels w/trim rings	S	$68	$99	$125	—	—
Cast aluminum sport wheels	$185	$279	$310	$310	$530	$310
Forged aluminum wheels	$185[11]	$279[11]	—	—	—	—
White sidewall tires, std. size	$50	$50	$50	$50	$50	$50

Popular Option Groups & Packages

	Bobcat	Capri	Zephyr	Monarch	Cougar XR-7	Marquis
Appearance protection group	$41	$41	$53	$53	$46	$61
Convenience group, 2-dr./4-dr.	$111	—	$31/$55	$40	—	$98
Décor group	—	—	—	—	$516	—
ESS option group	—	—	—	$516	—	—

	Bobcat	Capri	Zephyr	Monarch	Cougar XR-7	Marquis
Ghia option group	—	—	$499	$476	—	—
Grand Marquis decor group[12]	—	—	—	—	—	$581
Interior Accent group	$50	$120	$100	—	—	—
Interior décor group	—	—	—	$234	—	—
Light group	$36	$33	$48	$51	$35	—
Luxury exterior décor group	—	—	$126	—	—	—
Luxury group	—	—	—	—	$1,987	—
Luxury interior package	—	—	$370	—	—	—
Power lock group, 2-dr./4-dr.	—	—	—	—	$113	$90/$164
RS option package	—	$204	—	—	—	—
Sports Accent group/trim option	$263	—	—	—	—	—
Sports group	—	—	—	—	$1,687	—
Sports Instrumentation group	$111	—	$85	—	—	—
Sports Package option	$206	—	—	—	—	—
Turbo RS option package	—	$1,185	—	—	—	—
Villager option package	$113	—	$226	—	—	—
Visibility or Visibility/Light group	—	—	—	$71	—	$48

— = Not Available; S = Standard equipment. [1]Air conditioner w/automatic temperature control is available for $634 on Monarch and Cougar, and for $669 on Marquis. [2]LH remote standard on Capri. [3]Available on any model except the Zephyr Z-7. [4]Available only as part of the Power Lock group. [5]Power six-way seat on Marquis. [6]Bucket seats only on Bobcat; console not available. Capri has bucket seats standard; price is for console only. Zephyr does not include console, and is a $72 option on any model not powered by the standard 2.3L 4-cylinder engine. For Monarch, bucket seats require décor, Ghia, or ESS option. For Cougar, available only on 2-doors. [7]Price for eight-track tape; cassette tape is $12 higher. Citizens Band (CB) radio available on Monarch, Cougar XR-7 and Marquis for $313 extra. Price for auto-search radio on Cougar and Marquis with eight-track tape is $409; w/cassette is $421. [8]Not available on station wagons. Landau vinyl roof is standard on Cougar XR-7. [9]Manually operated, flip-up/removable type. [10]Power four wheel disc brakes available for $197 on Marquis. [11]Sport covers for Capri and Zephyr, Luxury covers for Cougar and Marquis. White forged aluminum wheels available on Bobcat for $200. Forged TRX type only for Capri. [12]Available only on Marquis Colony Park station wagon.

Paint Colors

	Code		Code		Code
Light Grey[1,2]	12	Bright Blue[4,6]	3J	White	9D
Black[3]	1C	Midnight Blue metallic[1,2]	3L		
Medium Grey metallic[4]	1D	Dark Pine metallic[5]	4D		
Silver metallic	1G	Pastel Pine Glamour metallic[5,7]	4E		
Light Grey[5]	1N	Pastel Sand[5]	5P		
Medium Grey metallic[5]	1P	Bright Caramel[4,6]	5T		
Bright Bittersweet[4,6]	2G	Sand Glamour metallic[1,5,7,8]	6B		
Medium Red Glamour metallic[4,6,7,8]	2H	Pastel Sand[1,2,8]	6D		
Candy Apple Red[1,2,5,8]	2K	Bright Yellow[4,6]	6N		
Bright Red[4,6]	2P	Dark Pine metallic[2,6,8]	7M		
Dark Blue metallic[5,8]	3D	Dark Chamois metallic[10]	8A		
Light Medium Blue[9]	3F	Medium Bittersweet Glamour metallic[3,7]	8D		
Medium Blue Glamour metallic[2,4,5,7]	3H	Dark Cordovan metallic	8N		
		Chamois Glamour metallic[1,4,7,8]	8W		

In two-tone combinations, first two digits are lower color, and second two digits are upper color. Two-tones available on Bobcat for $113, Capri for $56 (black lower body only), Zephyr sedans for $88, Zephyr Z-7 for $106, Monarch for $138, Cougar XR-7 for $119, and Marquis for $131. [1]Monarch. [2]Cougar XR-7. [3]Not available on Bobcat. [4]Capri. [5]Marquis. [6]Bobcat. [7]Glamour paints available for $46 extra on Bobcat and Capri, $54 on Zephyr and Monarch, and $65 on Cougar and Marquis. [8]Zephyr. [9]Not available on Cougar XR-7. [10]Not available on Marquis.

Bobcat

"The Lively and Reasonable Little Cat!"

Nameplate year of origin: 1975.
Current bodystyle lifespan: 1975 through 1980.
Predecessor to this model: None.
Replacement for this model: Lynx (1981 to 1985).
Percentage of division's production: 9.68%.
Corporate siblings: Ford Pinto.
Primary competition: AMC Spirit, Dodge Omni 024, and Pontiac Sunbird.

Measurements

	Runabout	Wagon
Wheelbase	94.5"	94.8"
Length	170.8"	180.6"
Width	69.4"	69.7"
Height	50.5"	52.0"

Notable changes: Minor trim and detail changes.

Major standard equipment: All-vinyl low-back front bucket seats, color-keyed cut-pile carpeting, carpeted cargo area, fold-down rear seat, simulated woodgrain parking brake lever handle, shift knob, and I/P appliqué, deluxe two-spoke steering wheel, deluxe safety belts, AM radio, tinted glass, electric rear window defogger, bright window and belt moldings, B-pillar bright molding, rack-and-pinion steering, power front disc brakes, bumper protection group, styled steel wheels w/trim rings, and BR78 × 13 BSW tires. Wagon adds: Flip-out rear quarter windows, "Liftgate Ajar" warning system, and cargo area lamp.

Measurements (cont.)

	Runabout	Wagon
Legroom — front	40.2"	40.2"
Legroom — rear	30.3"	29.5"
Headroom — front	36.9"	37.7"
Headroom — rear	35.8"	38.8"
Cargo capacity (cu. ft.)	6.1*	57.2
Fuel capacity (gals.)	11.7	14.0

*With rear seat folded down, 29.0 cu. ft.

Models Available

	Model No.	Base MSRP	Change from LY	Shipping Wt. (lbs.)	Model Year Production	Change from LY
Bobcat 3-Door Runabout (HBK)	20	$4,764	+16.08%	2445	28,103	-21.21%
Bobcat 2-Door Station Wagon	22	$5,070	+14.97%	2573	5,547	-39.17%
TOTALS	Avg. price	$4,917	+15.50%	Production	33,650	-24.86%

Capri

"A driver's car with the look of Europe."

Nameplate year of origin: 1971 (originally used on 1952 Lincoln Capri).
Current bodystyle lifespan: 1979 through 1986.
Predecessor to this model: Capri (1971 to 1977, imported from Ford Europe).
Replacement for this model: Capri (1991 to 1994, imported from Ford Australia).
Percentage of division's production: 23.00%.
Corporate siblings: Ford Mustang.
Primary competition: AMC AMX, Chevrolet Camaro, Dodge Challenger, Plymouth Sapporo, and Pontiac Firebird.
Notable changes: Minor trim and detail changes.
Major standard equipment: Vinyl high-back bucket seats, fold-down rear seat, 10-oz. cut-pile carpeting, carpeted luggage area, soft vinyl door panels w/lower panel carpeting, color-keyed garnish moldings, woodtone I/P appliqués, full instrumentation including tachometer and warning lights, AM radio, sport steering wheel, LH remote control mirror, dual bodyside paint stripes, bright windshield and side window moldings, black wraparound wide bodyside moldings w/dual color-keyed center stripes, black cowl grille, rack-and-pinion steering, manual front disc brakes, semi-styled wheels w/trim rings, and P185/80R13 BSW tires. Ghia adds: Luxury cloth low-back bucket seats w/European-style headrests, deluxe color-keyed seat belts, door map pockets, passenger assist handle on roof rail, passenger visor vanity mirror, four-spoke luxury steering wheel w/woodtone inserts, Light group, black dual remote control rearview mirrors, deluxe sound insulation package, power front disc brakes, sport wheel covers, and P175/75R14 BSW tires.

Measurements

Wheelbase	100.4"
Length	179.1"
Width	69.1"
Height	51.4"
Legroom — front	40.9"
Legroom — rear	30.1"
Headroom — front	37.2"
Headroom — rear	35.5"
Cargo capacity (cu. ft.)	10.0*
Fuel capacity (gals.)**	11.5**

*33.3 cu. ft. w/rear seat folded down.   **12.5 gallons with air conditioning or optional engines except Turbo. Turbo has 11.9 gallon capacity.

Models Available

	Model No.	Base MSRP	Change from LY	Shipping Wt. (lbs.)	Model Year Production	Change from LY
Capri 3-Door Hatchback	14	$5,672	+16.42%	2547	72,009	-22.10%
Capri Ghia 3-Door Hatchback	16	$5,968	+13.96%	2632	7,975	-54.97%
TOTALS	Avg. price	$5,820	+15.14%	Production	79,984	-27.38%

Zephyr

"Energy-engineered for today's driver."

Nameplate year of origin: 1978 (previously used on 1936–1942 Lincoln-Zephyr series).

Current bodystyle lifespan: 1978 through 1983.

Predecessor to this model: Comet (1971 to 1977).

Replacement for this model: Topaz (1984 to 1994).

Percentage of division's production: 26.23%.

Corporate siblings: Ford Fairmont.

Primary competition: AMC Concord, Dodge Aspen, and Pontiac Phoenix.

Notable changes: Minor trim and detail changes.

Major standard equipment: All-vinyl low back front bucket seats, cut-pile carpeting, integral door armrests w/door pull assist handle, two-spoke color-keyed steering wheel, simulated woodgrain appliqué around instrument cluster, inside hood release, upper bodyside dual paint stripes, bright windshield and rear window moldings, bright drip rail moldings, bright rocker panel and wheel lip moldings, manual front disc brakes, rack-and-pinion steering, modified strut front suspension, deluxe wheel covers, and B78 × 14 BSW tires. Wagon adds: Carpeted load floor area and second row seatback, cargo area light, liftgate "open" warning light, and BR78 × 14 BSW tires. Z-7 sport coupe adds: Pleated vinyl low-back bucket seats, deluxe door trim panels, color-keyed safety belts, high gloss simulated woodgrain appliqué on I/P, deluxe steering wheel, bright LH manual mirror, wrap-over roof design w/accent paint stripes, bright door window frames and belt moldings, lower bodyside protection molding w/vinyl insert, and deluxe sound insulation package,

Measurements

	Sedans	Z-7	Wagon
Wheelbase	105.5"	105.5"	105.5"
Length	193.8"	195.8"	193.8"
Width	71.0"	71.0"	71.0"
Height	53.5"	52.2"	54.8"
Legroom — front	41.7"	41.7"	41.7"
Legroom — rear	35.3"	32.6"	35.3"
Headroom — front	38.3"	37.1"	39.0"
Headroom — rear	37.4"	35.9"	39.0"
Cargo capacity (cu. ft.)	16.8	16.1	79.5
Fuel capacity (gals.)	16.0	16.0	16.0

Models Available

	Model No.	Base MSRP	Change from LY	Shipping Wt. (lbs.)	Model Year Production	Change from LY
Zephyr 2-Door Sedan	31	$5,041	+18.53%	2605	10.977	-31.05%
Zephyr 4-Door Sedan	32	$5,158	+18.03%	2647	40,399	-2.22%
Zephyr 4-Door Station Wagon	36	$5,364	+15.43%	2769	20,341	-19.34%
Zephyr Z-7 2-Door Sport Coupe	35	$5,335	+18.45%	2644	19,486	-54.60%
TOTALS	*Avg. price*	$5,225	+17.58%	*Production*	91,203	-27.26%

Monarch

"A precision-size car with more than you'd expect."

Nameplate year of origin: 1975 (used on Canadian Ford brand from 1946 to 1961).

Current bodystyle lifespan: 1975 through 1980.

Predecessor to this model: None.

Replacement for this model: Cougar (1981 to 1982).

Percentage of division's production: 8.78%.

Corporate siblings: Ford Granada and Lincoln Versailles.

Primary competition: Buick Skylark, Dodge Diplomat, and Oldsmobile Omega.

Notable changes: Minor trim and detail changes.

Major standard equipment: Corinthian vinyl "Flight Bench" front seats w/fold-down center armrest, cut-pile carpeting, simulated burled walnut I/P appliqué, locking glove box, cigar lighter, luxury sound insulation package, bright window moldings, full-length upper bodyside molding, stand-up hood ornament, manual front disc brakes, full wheel covers, and DR78 × 14 BSW tires.

Measurements

	2-door	4-door
Wheelbase	109.9"	109.9"
Length	197.8"	197.8"
Width	74.5"	74.5"
Height	53.4"	53.4"
Legroom — front	40.7"	40.7"
Legroom — rear	33.9"	35.6"
Headroom — front	38.0"	38.2"
Headroom — rear	36.5"	37.6"
Cargo capacity (cu. ft.)	16.2	16.2
Fuel capacity (gals.)	18.0	18.0

Models Available

	Model No.	Base MSRP	Change from LY	Shipping Wt. (lbs.)	Model Year Production	Change from LY
Monarch 2-Door Sedan	33	$5,628	+18.86%	3093	8,772	-68.99%
Monarch 4-Door Sedan	34	$5,751	+18.80%	3134	21,746	-54.31%
TOTALS	*Avg. price*	$5,690	+18.83%	*Production*	30,518	-59.78%

Cougar XR-7

"A totally-new breed of cat."

Nameplate year of origin: 1967.
Current bodystyle lifespan: 1980 through 1982.
Predecessor to this model: Cougar XR-7 (1977 to 1979).
Replacement for this model: Cougar XR-7 (1983 to 1988; restyled in 1987).
Percentage of division's production: 16.69%.
Corporate siblings: Ford Thunderbird.
Primary competition: Buick Regal, Chrysler Cordoba, and Oldsmobile Cutlass Supreme.
Notable changes: Completely redesigned.
Major standard equipment: Cloth "Flight Bench" front seat w/fold-down center armrest, cut-pile carpeting, simulated woodgrain I/P appliqués w/brushed aluminum trim, electric clock, trip odometer, four-spoke color-keyed steering wheel, courtesy lights, half-vinyl roof w/louvered side quarter windows and frenched backlight, bright LH rearview mirror, bodyside accent stripes, black door frames, bright window trim, bright belt and windshield moldings, wheel lip moldings, rocker panel molding, Cougar stand-up hood ornament, power rack-and-pinion steering, power front disc brakes, modified MacPherson strut suspension, XR-7 wheel covers, and P185/75R14 BSW tires.

Measurements

Wheelbase	108.4"
Length	200.4"
Width	74.1"
Height	53.0"
Legroom — front	41.6"
Legroom — rear	36.4"
Headroom — front	37.1"
Headroom — rear	36.3"
Cargo capacity (cu. ft.)	17.7
Fuel capacity (gals.)	17.5

Models Available

	Model No.	Base MSRP	Change from LY	Shipping Wt. (lbs.)	Model Year Production	Change from LY
Cougar XR-7 2-Door Sedan	93	$7,045	+9.56%	3191	58,028	-64.56%
TOTALS	*Avg. price*	$7,045	+9.56%	*Production*	58,028	-64.56%

Marquis

"The most scientifically designed Marquis in history."

Nameplate year of origin: 1967.
Current bodystyle lifespan: 1979 through 1991.
Predecessor to this model: Marquis (1971 to 1978).
Replacement for this model: Grand Marquis (1992 to 2010).
Percentage of division's sales volume: 15.62%.
Corporate siblings: Ford LTD.
Primary competition: Buick Electra 225 and Estate Wagon, Chrysler Newport, Oldsmobile Ninety-Eight and Custom Cruiser, and Pontiac Bonneville and Grand Safari.
Notable changes: Completely redesigned.
Major standard equipment: Cloth-and-vinyl "Flight Bench" front seat w/fold-down center armrest, cut-pile carpeting, simulated woodgrain I/P and steering wheel appliqué, color-keyed four-spoke steering wheel, dome light, LH manual

Measurements

	2-Doors	4-Doors	Wagons
Wheelbase	114.3"	114.3"	114.3"
Length	212.0"	212.0"	218.0"
Width	77.5"	77.5"	79.3"
Height	54.5"	54.5"	56.8"
Legroom — front	42.1"	42.1"	42.1"
Legroom — rear	40.5"	40.5"	39.4"
Headroom — front	37.9"	37.9"	38.7"
Headroom — rear	37.2"	37.2"	39.2"
Cargo capacity (cu. ft.)	22.4	22.4	99.6*
Fuel capacity (gals.)	19.0	19.0	20.0

Includes 9.9 cu. ft. of hidden cargo space.

1980

rear view mirror, sound insulation package, bright window moldings, rocker panel molding, front bumper guards, full wheel covers, and P205/75R14 BSW tires. Wagon adds: Removable load floor carpet, cargo area light, lockable stowage compartment, three-way tailgate w/power tailgate window, rear bumper step pad, and P215/75R14 BSW tires. Brougham adds: Deluxe cloth "Flight Bench" front bench seat w/fold-down center armrest, seatback side shields, 18-oz. two-piece carpeting, luxury door panels w/lower carpeted panel and door pull assist strap, electric analog clock, LH remote control mirror, courtesy lights, power windows, luggage compartment light, vinyl roof (landau on two-door, and full on four-door), and hood and deck lid paint stripes. Grand Marquis adds: Luxury cloth individually adjustable Twin Comfort Lounge seats w/individual fold-down center armrests, rear seat center armrest, digital clock, luxury steering wheel, visor vanity mirror, carpeted luggage compartment, dome/dual map reading light, tinted glass, bodyside, hood and deck lid paint stripes, front fender louver accent stripes, B-pillar mounted coach lamps, spare tire cover, and deluxe wheel covers. Colony Park adds to wagon: Brougham level carpeting and door panel trim, electric clock, power windows, door gate courtesy light switch and cargo area light, LH remote-control mirror, simulated rosewood appliqué on bodysides and door gate w/simulated woodtone/bright surround rails, and deluxe wheel covers.

Models Available

	Model No.	Base MSRP	Change from LY	Shipping Wt. (lbs.)	Model Year Production	Change from LY
Marquis 2-Door Hardtop	61	$7,075	+12.44%	3450	2,521	-74.88%
Marquis 4-Door Pillared Hardtop	62	$7,185	+12.49%	3488	13,018	-59.68%
Marquis 4-Door, 6-pass. Station Wagon	74	$7,583	+13.16%	3697	2,407	-59.84%
Marquis Brougham 2-Door Hardtop	63	$7,860	+12.51%	3476	2,353	-77.86%
Marquis Brougham 4-Door Pillared Hardtop	64	$8,057	+12.28%	3528	8,819	-64.27%
Marquis Colony Park 4-Dr., 6-p. Station Wagon	76	$8,477	+13.10%	3743	5,781	-57.98%
Grand Marquis 2-Door Hardtop	65	$8,631	+11.79%	3504	3,434	-68.97%
Grand Marquis 4-Door Pillared Hardtop	66	$8,824	+11.57%	3519	15,995	-50.55%
TOTALS	Avg. price	$7,962	+12.40%	Production	54,328	-61.41%

OLDSMOBILE

"We've had one built for you!"

From the moment the all-new Omega arrived in the spring of 1979, Oldsmobile was hoping for another "million plus" production year. Not only was there a new compact line, but also in the fall of 1979, the full-sized models received a styling facelift making them more aerodynamic from nose to tail, which helped improve fuel mileage further. And to top it off, the Cutlass sedans were finally given notchback styling, which greatly improved their appearance and popularity. With the Cutlass Supreme and Calais coupe models receiving a front-end update that included dual headlights, only the new-for-1979 Toronado and the Starfire, which was in its final season, were left relatively unchanged. But the recession that began in 1979 took a deeper foothold on the U.S. economy, and for the first time since 1976, Oldsmobile failed to produce over a million cars. On the bright side, while most other makes slipped more, Olds was able to increase its market share for the year, even while slipping to fourth position as Buick climbed into the third place spot for one year.

The new Omega, a member of the front-wheel-drive GM X-car family, followed the formula of the prior downsizing exercises by dropping nearly 20 inches in length, while maintaining or even increasing interior space, and dropping about 600 pounds in weight, thereby allowing the use of smaller, more fuel efficient engines to provide nearly a 50 percent boost in fuel economy in base models. Of the four basic X-body styles introduced, Oldsmobile wisely chose the notchback coupe and sedan versions, after the problems it had selling fastback versions of the Cutlass. Powering the new Omega was a standard transverse-mounted 151 CID 4-cylinder engine and built by Pontiac, or an optional 173 CID V6 engine built by Chevrolet, a newcomer for this year. Either engine came with a standard 4-speed manual floor shift or an optional column-shift automatic transmission.

Styling of the Omega fit into the three box design, typical of the era, that allowed for maximum interior space and minimum exterior size, with squared off front and rear ends and an upright roofline. The grille of the Omega was pure

Oldsmobile, with a center body color divider panel, and a vertical bar grille on each side that wrapped over the top edge of the header panel slightly. Single square headlights with vertically mounted rectangular parking/turn signal lights to the inward side were set into the ends of the grille. The center panel of the grille, which carried the Oldsmobile logo ornament, curved over the top of the header onto the hood to form a slightly raised center section on the hood. Bodysides carried two feature lines, the lower of which ran between the mid-points of the front and rear bumpers creating a slight flare as it ran around the wheel openings. An upper feature line was a forward extension of the top edge of the rear quarter panel across the C-pillar of the roof, ending at the rear door edge on sedans. On coupes, the feature line turned downward about thirty degrees as it met the side window, the bottom rear corner of which paralleled the line. The feature line then faded away as the rear quarter window leveled out. At the rear the Omega's vertical taillamps wrapped over onto the top of the rear end slightly, and a body color panel between the trunk lid opening and the rear bumper had a cutout for the license plate mounting.

Inside the compact Oldsmobile was more luxurious than its predecessor, even in basic trim, with more refined upholstery materials, brushed aluminum accents on the door panels that had "European style" built in door-pull handles, and on the Brougham, brushed knit fabrics that rivaled the Ninety-Eight in luxurious appearance. Lessons learned from the downsizing of the Cutlass included providing for opening rear door windows, the lack of which many consumers saw as a problem with GM's mid-size sedans. (Coupes did have a fixed rear quarter window, however.) The Omega was available with a flip-up sunroof for the first time this year. The sporty SX option, now on either coupe or sedan. Over the course of about a 16-month-long model year, production of the new Omega was twice the amount that the former Omega had in its best model year of 1977.

The mid-size Cutlass line received a new body for the sedans, which went a long way towards putting the Cutlass at its highest percent of total Oldsmobile production since its peak during the 1976 and 1977 model years. The new sedans received a formal roofline notchback design, with rear doors containing opening quarter windows, the same as used on the Cutlass Cruiser wagons. Sales more than doubled with the new design. The model line was restructured with this change to integrate the new sedans with the Supreme coupes and the Cruisers, leaving the fastback style two-door Cutlass Salon models to continue until the end of the model year. The new sedans came in a base version paired with the Salon coupe, an LS sedan with the same trim level as the Supreme coupe, and a Brougham sedan aligned with the Supreme Brougham coupe. The sporty 4-4-2 option package returned one last time before taking a hiatus, this time on the Calais coupe, and remained similar in appearance, but not in fea-

tures, to the 1979 Cutlass Calais H/O coupe. There were 886 Calais coupes produced with the W-30 4-4-2 appearance and handling package.

While interior appearance was not greatly changed, all Cutlass models did receive a freshening of the front end. Cutlass sedans and Cruisers all had a new horizontal crosshatch grille design in a five by five configuration, while retaining the body-color center panel and square headlights and vertical parking/turn signal lamps set to each end. The Salon coupes had a four-column grille on each side, with nine horizontal slats filling each column. Supreme models carried a vertical bar grille with about 25 bars per side. While the Calais used a crosshatch grille similar in design to the Cutlass Sedans and Cruisers, it used the new rectangular dual headlight setup also new on the Supreme coupes, with the parking/turn signal lights set in the bumper directly below the headlights. The Cutlass was still the top selling line in the country, a position that Oldsmobile relished, but its popularity would lead to the overuse of the Cutlass name through the new decade, as Olds tried to capitalize on the success of the name. The proliferation of Cutlass lines eventually confused consumers, which led to the phasing out of the name in the nineties.

Full-size Oldsmobiles benefited from an exterior redesign to make them more aerodynamic, but were still based on the same basic platforms. Hoodlines were lowered, deck lids were raised, bodysides were tucked in and smoother, and coupes had a more upright rear window creating a more formal roofline. The Ninety-Eight series even reverted to using rear wheel opening fender skirts to smooth out the airflow. Along with new grille designs, the new "aero" intentions were noticeable in that the headlights were brought forward and made nearly flush with the plane of the grille. Also, all models had the parking and turn signal lights moved to the bumper directly below the headlights, and side marker lights were incorporated into the headlight bezel. The Delta 88 and Custom Cruiser wagons had a vertical bar grille in four sections per side, with about eight thin vertical bars within, while the Ninety-Eight used a large egg-crate pattern grille four rows high and five columns across with the center section of the header panel again being chrome, rather than body colored. Around back the Delta 88 and Custom Cruiser adopted variations of a square wraparound style taillight, with the Delta 88 having vertical rectangular backup lights placed separately next to the center license plate mount below the trunk lid opening, and the Custom Cruiser's being horizontal on the lower end of the taillamp bezel separated by a body color strip. Taillamps on the Ninety-Eight were still vertically mounted in the rear quarter end panels, but slightly wider than last year. The Delta 88 coupe still offered the sporty Holiday coupe package that included bucket seats and console, and a new Regency Brougham series was added, which no doubt contributed to a sales drop for the Ninety-Eight

LS sedan and discontinuation of the slow-selling LS Coupe before the model year began.

The 403 CID V8 engine was dropped after a three-year run, as it was deemed to be inefficient and unneeded with the more aerodynamic bodies. The new-for-'79 Toronado was still selling well into the new model year, and while its official name became the Toronado Custom Brougham, in nearly all Oldsmobile sales literature it was referred to as the Toronado Brougham. A new horizontal bar grille ran the full width of the front end to cover the parking/turn signal lamps under the headlights. Also new was a sporty XSC option package that included bucket seats, landau vinyl top, and unique two-tone paint features. At the opposite end of the Oldsmobile price spectrum, the only change to the Starfire hatchback was the discontinuation of the five-speed manual transmission option on the inline four and V6 engines, and of the 305 CID V8 engine as an option. Otherwise everything was the same as in 1979, even the pictures in the 1980 Oldsmobile sales brochures. This would be its last model year of production before an early introduction of the Starfire's replacement, the 1982 J-bodied Firenza.

Custom Cruiser 4-Door Station Wagon

Cutlass Brougham 4-Door Sedan

Cutlass Cruiser Brougham 4-Door Station Wagon with woodgrain exterior option

Cutlass LS 4-Door Sedan

Cutlass Salon Brougham 2-Door Coupe

Cutlass Supreme 2-Door Coupe

Delta 88 2-Door Coupe with Holiday Coupe package

Delta 88 Royale 4-Door Sedan

Ninety-Eight LS 4-Door Sedan

Ninety-Eight Regency 4-Door Sedan

Omega 2-Door Coupe interior

Omega 2-Door Coupe with SX package

Omega 4-Door Sedan

Omega Brougham 4-Door Sedan

Omega instrument panel

Toronado interior with optional XSC trim

Starfire 2-Door Hatchback line
with Firenza package (front),
GT package (center), and base (rear)

Toronado Brougham 2-Door Hardtop Coupe

Model year production: 910,306, down 15.02% from 1979.
Domestic market share: 11.91% (4th place).
Base price range: $4,750 to $11,361.
Oldsmobile average base price: $6,696, up 17.87%.
Introduction date: October 11, 1979; Omega introduced April 19, 1979.
Assembly plants: Doraville, GA (D); Linden, NJ (E); Framingham, MA (G); Lansing, MI (M); Arlington, TX (R); Kansas City/Fairfax, KS (X); Willow Run, MI (W); St. Therese, Quebec, Canada (2) and Lordstown, OH (7).
Data plate identification (VIN): Thirteen digit code read as follows: First digit indicates division (3 = Oldsmobile); second through fourth digits indicate series and body style (model number in model charts); fifth digit is engine code (see powertrain chart); sixth digit indicates model year (A = 1980); seventh digit indicates assembly plant (see list above); remaining digits are sequential with beginning number of 100001. *Example:* 3L69RAX100001 is a 1980 Oldsmobile Delta 88 4-Door Town Sedan, with 350 CID, 4-bbl. V8 engine, serial number 100001, built in Kansas City/Fairfax, KS.

1980

Powertrains

Engine	Net HP	Engine Code: VIN/GM	Transmission Availability[1]		Starfire	Omega	Cutlass	Delta 88	98 & Custom Cruiser	Toronado
151 CID (2.5L), 2-bbl., 4-cyl.	85[2]	5/LX6	4-speed manual		S	S	—	—	—	—
				MPG:	24/35	24/38	—	—	—	—
				Calif.	21	24	—	—	—	—
			3-speed Turbo		$320	$337	—	—	—	—
			Hydra-matic	MPG:	24/32	21/33	—	—	—	—
				Calif.	22	22	—	—	—	—
173 CID (2.8L), 2-bbl., V6	115	7/LQ1	4-speed manual		—	$225	—	—	—	—
				MPG:	—	20/29	—	—	—	—
				Calif.	—	18	—	—	—	—
			3-speed Turbo		—	$562	—	—	—	—
			Hydra-matic	MPG:	—	20/29	—	—	—	—
231 CID (3.8L), 2-bbl., 6-cyl.	110	A/LD5	3-speed manual[3]		—	—	S[4]	—	—	—
				MPG:	—	—	18/25	—	—	—
			4-speed manual		$225	—	—	—	—	—
				MPG:	15/23	—	—	—	—	—
				Calif.	16	—	—	—	—	—
			3-speed Turbo		$545	—	S[5]/$358[4]	S	—	—
			Hydra-matic	MPG:	19/26	—	20/27	18/24	—	—
				Calif.	19	—	19	19	—	—
260 CID (4.3L), 2-bbl., V8	105	F/LV8	3-speed Turbo		—	—	$180[5]/$538[4]	—	—	—
			Hydra-matic	MPG:	—	—	19/25	—	—	—
				Calif.	—	—	18	—	—	—
265 CID (4.3L), 2-bbl., V8	120	S/LS4	3-speed Turbo		—	—	—	$180	—	—
			Hydra-matic	MPG:	—	—	—	17/25	—	—

Engine	Net HP	Engine Code: VIN/GM	Transmission Availability[1]		Starfire	Omega	Cutlass	Delta 88	98 & Custom Cruiser	Toronado
305 CID (5.0L), 4-bbl., V8	155	H/LG4	3-speed Turbo Hydra-matic		—	—	$295[5]/$653[4]	—	—	—
				MPG:	—	—	17/25	—	—	—
				Calif.	—	—	14	—	—	—
307 CID (5.0L), 4-bbl., V8		Y/LV2	3-speed Turbo Hydra-matic		—	—	—	$295	S	S
				MPG:	—	—	—	17/25	17/25	17/25
350 CID (5.7L), 4-bbl., V8	160	R/L34	3-speed Turbo Hydra-matic		—	—	$425[6]	$425	$130	$130
				MPG:	—	—	15/22	15/22	15/22	15/22
				Calif.	—	—	—	15	15	15
350 CID (5.7L), Diesel-FI, V8	105	N/LF9	3-speed Turbo Hydra-matic		—	—	$960[5]/ $1,318[4]	$960	$860	$860
				MPG:	—	—	22/34	21/32	21/32	21/32
				Calif.	—	—	23	22	21	21

[1]Unless otherwise specified: All 3-speed manuals are column shift. All 4-speed manuals are floor shift. All automatics are column shift, except on Starfire. Floor shift automatic is optional on Omega, Cutlass and Delta 88 2-doors with other required equipment at extra cost. [2]Horsepower rating for Omega is 90. [3]Not available in California. [4]Cutlass Salon and base Cutlass Sedan. [5]Except Salon and base Cutlass Sedan. [6]Only available on Cutlass Calais with W30 package.

Major Options

	Starfire	Omega	Cutlass	Delta 88	Custom Cruiser	Ninety-Eight	Toronado
Four-Season air conditioner[1]	$531	$564	$601	$647	$647	S	S
Tilt-Away steering wheel	$68	$75	$81	$83	$83	$83	$83
Tilt-and-Telescope steering wheel	—	—	—	$131	$131	$131	$131
Cruise control	—	$105	$112	$118	$118	$118	$118
Electric rear window defroster	$95	$101	$107	$109	$109	$109	$109
Tinted glass, all windows	$60	$73	$78	$92	$92	$92	S
Power windows, 2-dr./4-dr.	—	$133/$190	$143/$202	$149/$210	$221	S	S
Power door locks, 2-dr./4-dr.	—	$87/$1	$93/$132	$95/$135	$175[2]	$95/$135	S
Power front seat, 6-way w/std. seat	—	$165	$175	$179	$179	$148[3]	S
Leather upholstery	—	—	$330[4]	$359[4]	—	$330	$330
Front bucket seats, w/console	S	$	$[5]	$[5]	—	—	—
Third row seat (wagons)	—	—	—	—	$208	—	—
AM radio	S	S	$97	$99	$99	$99	—
AM/FM stereo	$101	$101	$192	$195	$195	$195	S
AM/FM stereo w/tape[6]	$182	$182	$273	$276	$276	$276	$81
AM/FM stereo w/CB radio[6]	—	$413	$525	$533	$533	$533	$290
Twilight sentinel, light control	—	—	$50	$50	$50	$50	$50
Woodgrain exterior panels (wagons)	—	—	$250	—	$260	—	—
Vinyl top, full	—	$116	$124[7]	$155	—	$174[8]	$207[8]
Vinyl top, landau (coupes only)	—	$175	$185	$199	—	$213	$213
Hatch roof (T-top)	—	—	$695[9]	—	—	—	—
Sunroof, power operated, metal	—	—	$561[10]	$770	—	$848	$848
Astroroof, power operated, glass	$193[10]	$240[10]	$733[10]	$981	—	$1,058	$1,058
Power steering, variable ratio	$158	$164	$174[11]	S	S	S	S
Power brakes, w/front disc	$76	$76	S	S	S	S	S[12]
Deluxe wheel covers	—	$	$	$	$	$	S
Wire wheel covers	—	$140	$151	$140	$140	$140[13]	$140[13]
Chrome "Custom sport" wheels	—	—	—	$	—	—	—
Super Stock III (Rallye) wheels	S	$	$[13]	$	—	—	—
WSW tires, std. size	$36	$38	$40	$40	$40	$40	S

Popular Option Groups & Packages

	Starfire	Omega	Cutlass	Delta 88	Custom Cruiser	Ninety-Eight	Toronado
Firenza Sport package	$427	—	—	—	—	—	—
GT package	$644	—	—	—	—	—	—
Holiday Coupe package	—	—	—	$295[14]	—	—	—
"Renaissance" interior package	—	—	$181	—	—	—	—

	Starfire	Omega	Cutlass	Delta 88	Custom Cruiser	Ninety-Eight	Toronado
SX package	—	$303	—	—	—	—	—
W29 4-4-2 package	—	—	$1,255	—	—	—	—
XSC package	—	—	—	—	—	—	$331

—= Not Available; S = Standard equipment. [1]*"Tempmatic" air conditioner with automatic climate control is available for $50 additional on all except Starfire and Omega.* [2]*Includes power tailgate lock.* [3]*Standard on Ninety-Eight Regency.* [4]*Available on Cutlass Supreme Brougham and Delta 88 Royale Brougham only.* [5]*Bucket seats are standard on Cutlass Calais. Console is available for $80 on Cutlass Calais. Bucket seats are available on any Cutlass coupe except Brougham models. Available on Delta 88 coupes with Holiday package only.* [6]*Tape player is choice of 8-track or cassette. Includes power antenna with CB radio.* [7]*Not available on Cutlass Cruiser. Simulated convertible top for Supreme coupe available for $800.* [8]*Full padded vinyl top on Toronado. Full padded vinyl top is also available on Ninety-Eight for $207.* [9]*Available on Supreme, Supreme Brougham and Calais coupes only.* [10]*Manual removable glass roof on Starfire and Omega. Available on Cutlass coupes only.* [11]*Standard on all models except Cutlass Salons, base Cutlass Sedan, and base Cutlass Cruiser.* [12]*Power four-wheel disc brakes available for $222.* [13]*Special cast aluminum wheels available on Cutlass, and wire-spoke wheels available on Ninety-Eight and Toronado.* [14]*Available only on Delta 88 2-Door Coupe.*

Paint Colors

	Code		Code
White[1]	11	Light Camel metallic	63
Silver metallic	15	Medium Camel metallic	69
Gray metallic (two-tone only)	16	Red[2]	72
Black[1]	19	Claret metallic[3]	75
Light Blue metallic	21	Dark Claret metallic	76
Medium Blue metallic	22	Cinnabar	77
Dark Blue metallic	29	Vapor Gray	85
Dark Green metallic	44	Medium Brown Firemist metallic[4]	97
Yellow	50	Charcoal Firemist metallic[4]	98
Gold metallic (two-tone only)[1]	55	Dark Brown Firemist metallic[4]	99
Beige	59		

In two-tone combinations, the first two digits indicate lower color and the next two digits are the upper color. Specific two-tone paint schemes available for $181 extra on Omega, Cutlass Salon and Salon Broughams, Delta 88, Ninety-Eight and Toronado. Firemist paints available for $165 extra. [1]*White/Gold metallic and Black/Gold metallic paint combinations used on W30 4-4-2 package.* [2]*Available only on Starfire and Omega.* [3]*Available on all models except Starfire and Omega.* [4]*Available only on Ninety-Eight and Toronado.*

Starfire

"Nifty little road machines built for the long and winding."

Nameplate year of origin: 1954 (as designation for 98 convertible); 1961 (as series).
Current bodystyle lifespan: 1975 through 1980
Predecessor to this model: None.
Replacement for this model: Firenza (1982 to 1988).
Percentage of division's production: 0.90%.
Corporate siblings: Buick Skyhawk, Chevrolet Monza, and Pontiac Sunbird.
Primary competition: AMC Pacer and Mercury Capri.
Notable changes: No changes.
Major standard equipment: High-backed vinyl bucket seats, folding rear seatback, plush-pile carpeting on all floor surfaces and rear seatback, floor console with shifter, sport steering wheel, door panel map pockets, simulated woodgrain I/P and door appliqués, I/P gauges including tachometer, AM radio, chrome window surround and belt molding, rear stabilizer bar, manual front disc brakes, rallye wheels, and A78 × 13 BSW tires. SX adds: Choice of velour brushed knit or soft vinyl high-back bucket seats, chrome front and rear wheel lip moldings, bodyside striping, and BR78 × 13 BSW tires.

Measurements

Wheelbase	97.0"
Length	179.6"
Width	65.4"
Height	50.0"
Legroom — front	43.0"
Legroom — rear	29.6"
Headroom — front	37.7"
Headroom — rear	35.3"
Cargo capacity (cu. ft.)	27.8*
Fuel capacity (gals.)	18.5

With rear seat folded down.

Models Available

	Model No.	Base MSRP	Change from LY	Shipping Wt. (lbs.)	Model Year Production	Change from LY
Starfire 2-Door Hatchback Coupe	T07	$4,750	+11.11%	2656	NA*	NA*
Starfire SX 2-Door Hatchback Coupe	D07	$4,950	+10.61%	2668	NA*	NA*
TOTALS	*Avg. price*	$4,850	+10.86%		*Production* 8,237	-59.42%

*Production kept as combined total for both models; therefore comparison to LY is not possible.

Omega

"The Oldsmobile of small cars. You gotta drive it. You're gonna love it."

Nameplate year of origin: 1973.
Current bodystyle lifespan: 1980 through 1984.
Predecessor to this model: Omega (1975 to 1979).
Replacement for this model: Calais (1985 to 1991; renamed Cutlass Calais in 1988).
Percentage of division's production: 14.76%.
Corporate siblings: Buick Skylark, Chevrolet Citation, and Pontiac Phoenix.
Primary competition: Dodge Aspen and Mercury Monarch.
Notable changes: Completely redesigned.
Major standard equipment: Choice of cloth or vinyl front bench seat, cut-pile carpeting, simulated butterfly walnut woodgrain I/P and steering wheel appliqués, door-operated courtesy lamps, AM radio, chrome window surround moldings, chrome front and rear wheel opening moldings (sedan only), rocker panel molding (sedan only), hubcaps, and P185/80R13 BSW tires. Brougham adds: Brushed knit fabric Custom Sport front bench seat w/fold-down center armrest, deluxe steering wheel, carpeted lower door panels, wide wheel opening and rocker panel moldings, hood windsplit molding and stand-up front-end panel ornament, and wheel covers.

Measurements

	Coupe	Sedan
Wheelbase	105.0"	105.0"
Length	181.8"	181.8"
Width	67.4"	67.4"
Height	53.5"	53.5"
Legroom — front	42.2"	42.2"
Legroom — rear	34.5"	35.5"
Headroom — front	38.2"	38.2"
Headroom — rear	37.4"	37.4"
Cargo capacity (cu. ft.)	14.3	14.3
Fuel capacity (gals.)	14.0	14.0

Models Available

	Model No.	Base MSRP	Change from LY	Shipping Wt. (lbs.)	Model Year Production	Change from LY
Omega 2-Door Coupe	B37	$5,100	+21.98%	2400	28,267	+488.16%
Omega 4-Door Sedan	B69	$5,266	+23.01%	2427	42,172	+623.86%
Omega Brougham 2-Door Coupe	E37	$5,380	+22.64%	2432	21,595	+1,903.25%
Omega Brougham 4-Door Sedan	E69	$5,530	+23.24%	2459	42,289	+1,871.52%
TOTALS	*Avg. price*	$5,319	+22.67%	*Production*	134,323	+806.91%

Cutlass

"Any wonder why it's America's best-selling mid-size?"

Nameplate year of origin: 1961 (as F-85 Deluxe sport coupe designation); 1962 (as F-85 subseries); and 1965 (as series designation); also used on 1955 Oldsmobile show car.
Current bodystyle lifespan: 1978 through 1988 (restyled in 1981).
Predecessor to this model: Cutlass (1973 to 1977).
Replacement for this model: Cutlass (1988 to 1997).
Percentage of division's production: 53.28%.
Corporate siblings: Buick Century/Regal, Chevrolet Malibu/Monte Carlo, and Pontiac LeMans/Grand Am/Grand Prix.
Primary competition: Dodge Diplomat and Mercury Cougar XR-7.
Notable changes: New front-end treatments, and minor trim and detail changes. Notchback sedans replaced fastback-style sedans.
Major standard equipment: Choice of cloth or vinyl front bench seat, cut-pile carpeting, two-spoke steering wheel, simulated butterfly walnut grain I/P panel, bright window surround moldings, rear door fixed window w/opening quarter vent window (4-door models), bright roof drip moldings, rocker panel molding, hub caps, and P185/75R14 BSW tires. Cutlass Cruiser adds: All-

Measurements

	Salon Coupes	Supreme & Calais	Sedans	Wagons
Wheelbase	108.1"	200.4"	108.1"	108.1"
Length	198.7"	200.1"	198.7"	197.0"
Width	72.2"	72.2"	72.2"	72.2"
Height	53.3"	54.2"	54.0"	54.5"
Legroom — front	42.8"	42.8"	42.8"	42.8"
Legroom — rear	35.1"	36.3"	38.0"	35.9"
Headroom — front	37.9"	37.9"	38.7"	38.8"
Headroom — rear	38.2"	38.1"	37.7"	38.8"
Cargo capacity (cu. ft.)	16.1	16.1	15.9	71.8
Fuel capacity (gals.)	18.1	18.1	18.1	18.2

vinyl front bench seat, cut-pile carpeting on passenger and cargo floors, fold-down rear seat, rear window liftgate w/drop-down tailgate and P195/75R14 BSW tires. Salon Brougham adds: Choice of cloth-and-vinyl or all-vinyl custom sport front bench seat w/fold-down center armrest, door panels with door pull straps, wide rocker panel moldings w/front and rear extensions, B-pillar appliqué and wheel opening moldings, stand-up hood ornament, and P195/75R14 BSW tires. Cutlass Supreme, LS sedan and Cutlass Cruiser Brougham add: Choice of cloth-and-vinyl or all-vinyl custom sport front bench seat w/fold-down center armrest, deluxe steering wheel, bright roof drip moldings, bright wheel lip moldings, and rocker panel molding. Supreme Brougham and Brougham sedan add: "Loose cushion" look velour with vinyl bolster 55/45 divided front seat w/fold down center armrest, wide rocker panel moldings, belt reveal molding w/B-pillar appliqué, power steering, and deluxe wheel covers. Calais adds: Choice of brushed velour w/vinyl trim or soft all-vinyl reclining bucket seats, custom sport steering wheel, full gauge instrumentation including tachometer, special ride and handling package, and special body-color painted wheel covers.

Models Available

	Model No.	Base MSRP	Change from LY	Shipping Wt. (lbs.)	Model Year Production	Change from LY
Cutlass Salon 2-Door Coupe	G87	$5,372	+16.20%	3065	3,429	-59.17%
Cutlass 4-Door Sedan	G69	$5,532	+17.13%*	3069	36,923	+82.19%*
Cutlass Cruiser 4-Door, 2-Seat Station Wagon	G35	$5,978	+20.04%	3263	7,815	-81.81%
Cutlass Salon Brougham 2-Door Coupe	J87	$5,662	+15.39%	3065	965	-73.32%
Cutlass Supreme 2-Door Coupe	R47	$6,252	+23.48%	3190	169,597	-38.98%
Cutlass LS 4-Door Sedan	R69	$6,353	+26.25%*	3179	86,868	+364.19%*
Cutlass Cruiser Brougham 4-Dr., 2-S. St. Wgn.	H35	$6,377	+15.59%	3300	22,791	+111.91%
Cutlass Supreme Brougham 2-Door Coupe	M47	$6,691	+21.83%	3201	77,875	-43.29%
Cutlass Brougham 4-Door Sedan	M69	$6,776	NEW	3206	52,462	NEW
Cutlass Calais 2-Door Coupe	K47	$6,716	+22.31%	3201	26,269	-40.00%
TOTALS	Avg. price	$6,171	+21.19%	Production	484,994	-13.97%

*Comparisons of Cutlass and LS sedans made to 1979 Cutlass Salon and Brougham sedans.

Delta 88

"Our American family car is in great shape."

Nameplate year of origin: 1965 (88 series began in 1949).
Current bodystyle lifespan: 1977 through 1985.
Predecessor to this model: Delta 88 (1971 to 1976).
Replacement for this model: Delta 88 (1986 to 1991).
Percentage of division's production: 16.33%.
Corporate siblings: Buick LeSabre, Chevrolet Impala and Caprice, and Pontiac Catalina and Bonneville.
Primary competition: Chrysler Newport and Mercury Marquis.
Notable changes: Restyled exterior, with some interior trim and detail changes.
Major standard equipment: Choice of cloth or all-vinyl front bench seat, cut-pile carpeting, cut-pile carpeting on lower door panels, door pull assist straps, deluxe steering wheel, simulated butterfly walnut I/P woodgrain trim, courtesy and glove box lights, bright accents on accelerator and brake pedals, bright drip rail moldings, bright front and rear window moldings, bright wheel opening and rocker panel moldings, front and rear bumper vinyl impact strips, stand-up hood ornament, full wheel covers, and P205/75R15 BSW tires. Royale adds: Velour Custom Sport front bench seat w/fold-down center armrest, simulated woodgrain trim on door panels, Royale ornamentation on C-pillar, wide rocker panel moldings w/front and rear extensions, and bodyside protective moldings. Royale Brougham adds: Lombardy and Lansdale velour trimmed divided front bench seat w/fold-down center armrests front and rear, belt reveal moldings, and B-pillar opera lamp (coupe).

Measurements

Wheelbase	116.0"
Length	218.4"
Width	76.3"
Height	54.7"
Legroom — front	42.2"
Legroom — rear	39.1"
Headroom — front	39.5"
Headroom — rear	38.2"
Cargo capacity (cu. ft.)	20.8
Fuel capacity (gals.)	20.7

Models Available

	Model No.	Base MSRP	Change from LY	Shipping Wt. (lbs.)	Model Year Production	Change from LY
Delta 88 2-Door Coupe	L37	$6,457	+11.67%	3325	6,845	-57.75%

	Model No.	Base MSRP	Change from LY	Shipping Wt. (lbs.)	Model Year Production	Change from LY
Delta 88 4-Door Sedan	L69	$6,552	+11.39%	3358	15,285	-39.88%
Delta 88 Royale 2-Door Coupe	N37	$6,716	+11.39%	3333	39,303	-35.24%
Delta 88 Royale 4-Door Sedan	N69	$6,864	+11.54%	3336	87,178	-42.88%
Delta 88 Royale Brougham 2-Door Coupe	Y37	$7,079	NEW	3333	NA*	NEW
Delta 88 Royale Brougham 4-Door Sedan	Y69	$7,160	NEW	3336	NA*	NEW
TOTALS	Avg. price	$6,805	+14.14%	Production	148,611	-41.71%

*Production kept as combined total with Delta 88 Royale models.

Custom Cruiser

*"The luxurious, smooth-riding, full-size Oldsmobile
that works like a wagon — whenever you want."*

Nameplate year of origin: 1971 (1940 as a designation on 90 series cars).
Current bodystyle lifespan: 1977 through 1990.
Predecessor to this model: Custom Cruiser (1971 to 1976).
Replacement for this model: Custom Cruiser (1991 to 1992).
Percentage of division's production: 1.87%.
Corporate siblings: Buick Estate Wagon, Chevrolet Impala and Caprice, and Pontiac Catalina Safari and Bonneville Safari.
Primary competition: Mercury Marquis Colony Park.
Notable changes: Restyled exterior, with some interior trim and detail changes.
Major standard equipment: Choice of velour or all-vinyl front bench seat w/fold-down center armrest, cut-pile carpeting on floors and cargo compartment floor, door pull assist straps, lower door panel carpeting, deluxe steering wheel, simulated butterfly walnut grain I/P trim, courtesy and glove box lights, cargo area light, bright drip rail and window moldings, bright wheel opening and rocker panel moldings, three-way tailgate w/power window, full wheel covers, and P225/75R15 BSW tires.

Measurements

Wheelbase	116.0"
Length	219.4"
Width	79.8"
Height	56.6"
Legroom — front	42.2"
Legroom — rear	37.8"
Headroom — front	39.6"
Headroom — rear	39.3"
Cargo capacity (cu. ft.)	87.2
Fuel capacity (gals.)	22.0

Models Available

	Model No.	Base MSRP	Change from LY	Shipping Wt. (lbs.)	Model Year Production	Change from LY
Custom Cruiser 4-Door, 2-S. Wagon	P35	$7,443	+10.40%	3910	17,067	-53.43%
TOTALS	Avg. price	$7,443	+10.40%	Production	17,067	-53.43%

Ninety-Eight

*"Of the world's great luxury cars, this
could be your most logical choice."*

Nameplate year of origin: 1941.
Current bodystyle lifespan: 1977 through 1984.
Predecessor to this model: Ninety-Eight (1971 to 1976).
Replacement for this model: Ninety-Eight (1985 to 1990).
Percentage of division's production: 8.09%.
Corporate siblings: Buick Electra, Cadillac deVille, and Cadillac Fleetwood Brougham.
Primary competition: Chrysler New Yorker and Mercury Grand Marquis.
Notable changes: Restyled exterior, with some interior trim and detail changes.
Major standard equipment: Velour knit fabric w/vinyl trim front bench seat w/fold-down front and rear center armrests, two-way power front seat, cut-pile carpeting,

Measurements

Wheelbase	119.0"
Length	221.4"
Width	76.3"
Height	55.3"
Legroom — front	42.2"
Legroom — rear	41.9"
Headroom — front	39.5"
Headroom — rear	38.1"
Cargo capacity (cu. ft.)	20.8
Fuel capacity (gals.)	25.0

carpeted lower door panels, door pull straps, driver's door armrest console, power windows, four season air conditioning, simulated butterfly walnut woodgrain I/P trim, deluxe steering wheel, electric clock, wheel opening moldings, rocker panel molding, bright roof drip moldings, stand-up hood ornament, bumper impact strips, front and rear bumper guards, rear wheel opening fender skirts, wheel covers, and P215/75R15 BSW tires. Regency adds: Velour 60/40 front seat button-tufted w/"loose" cushion look, six-way power adjustment for driver's side, digital clock, AM/FM stereo radio, door-mounted entry courtesy lights, and sail panel opera lamp.

Models Available

	Model No.	Base MSRP	Change from LY	Shipping Wt. (lbs.)	Model Year Production	Change from LY
Ninety-Eight LS 4-Door Sedan	V69	$9,113	+18.77%	3789	2,640	-60.71%
Ninety-Eight Regency 2-Door Coupe	X37	$9,620	+22.16%	3811	12,391	-58.65%
Ninety-Eight Regency 4-Door Sedan	X69	$9,742	+20.82%	3832	58,603	-36.21%
TOTALS	Avg. price	$9,492	+22.07%	Production	73,634	-43.64%

Toronado

"Our state of the art in personal luxury cars."

Nameplate year of origin: 1966.
Current bodystyle lifespan: 1979 through 1985.
Predecessor to this model: Toronado (1971 to 1978).
Replacement for this model: Toronado (1986 to 1992, restyled in 1990).
Percentage of division's production: 4.77%.
Corporate siblings: Buick Riviera and Cadillac Eldorado.
Primary competition: Lincoln Continental Mark VI.
Notable changes: New grille and minor trim and detail changes.
Major standard equipment: Velour "loose-cushion" look 50/50 split front seat w/fold-down center armrest and 6-way power driver's seat, rear seat fold-down center armrest, cut-pile carpeting, simulated butterfly walnut woodgrain I/P trim, power windows, power door locks, two-spoke steering wheel, digital clock, AM/FM stereo radio w/power antenna, chrome-accented floor pedals, Four-Season air conditioning w/side window defroster system, tinted glass, dual remote-control rear view mirrors, upholstered trunk and spare tire cover, bright window opening surround moldings, bright rocker panel and wheel lip moldings, front bumper guards, front and rear bumper rub strips, automatic ride level control, chrome wheel covers, and P205/75R15 WSW tires.

Measurements

Wheelbase	114.0"
Length	205.6"
Width	71.4"
Height	53.5"
Legroom — front	42.8"
Legroom — rear	38.9"
Headroom — front	37.9"
Headroom — rear	37.9"
Cargo capacity (cu. ft.)	15.2
Fuel capacity (gals.)	21.0

Models Available

	Model No.	Base MSRP	Change from LY	Shipping Wt. (lbs.)	Model Year Production	Change from LY
Toronado 2-Door Hardtop Coupe	Z57	$11,361	+12.35%	3627	43,440	-13.22%
TOTALS	Avg. price	$11,361	+12.35%	Production	43,440	-13.22%

1980

PLYMOUTH

"Quality, performance and value."

The 1980 model year brought a return of a full-sized Plymouth with the introduction of the new, smaller Gran Fury. The Gran Fury was based on the "new"-for-1979 R-body Chrysler corporate platform that was derived from what used to be known as the M-body mid-size cars (e.g., Plymouth Satellite), introduced in 1971. This year also brought a freshened look to the Volaré just as it was entering its final model year. With the new and freshened models, Plymouth hoped to increase sales and production. However, the second oil crisis, a mild recession and the government bailout hanging over Chrysler Corporation conspired to produce a down year. Only the subcompact Horizon saw an increase, while the facelifted Volaré fell to half of its 1979 volume and the renewed Gran Fury barely got off the ground. The necessity for better fuel economy meant that the 360 CID V8 engine was no longer available on the Volaré, and the 225 CID, 2bbl. "Super Six" was no longer available in any series. This left the dependable old 225 CID 1bbl. "Slant Six" to carry on in rear wheel drive Plymouths for the new decade.

Chrysler's decision to bring back the Gran Fury for 1980 was mostly to satisfy fleet buyers wanting a lower-content, lower-priced full-size sedan, comparable to the Chevrolet Impala or Ford LTDs. The styling of the Gran Fury was nearly identical to the slightly more expensive Chrysler Newport, with even the grille being the same, except that on the Gran Fury the insets of the crosshatch design grille were blacked out, and a slightly different pattern was used on the taillight lenses. Interior accommodations also were shared, with vinyl front bench seat standard on the base model and cloth-and-vinyl seating for the Salon model. There were no split seat options or luxury door trim panels, so a buyer who wanted more luxury would have to choose the Chrysler Newport, which started at only $600 higher. Unfortunately the new R-bodied Gran Fury was not successful, selling only 22,319 copies over its abbreviated two-year life span.

For its final year the Volaré received a facelift that found the popular line of cars sharing hood and front fenders with the restyled Dodge Diplomat and Chrysler LeBaron, as well as its twin, the Dodge Aspen. This change was made to save Chrysler Corporation money as it struggled to stay afloat. Because of the changes, the front fender lines were more angular and the hood was flatter, with a slightly raised center section. The new front-end styling consisted of a blacked out egg-crate style grille with chrome highlights, five rows high and twenty columns across. It sat directly under the raised portion of the hood, and had chrome strips across the top and bottom, with the Plymouth name in block letters across the upper strip. Inboard of the new rectangular headlights in a separate chrome bezel were vertical parking/turn signal lights. On the outer side of the headlight bezels were amber colored parking/turn signal lights and side marker light. The rear end styling had the taillights reconfigured again, this time with taillights and backup lights using larger horizontal lenses side by side, and inset between an outer vertical turn signal lens and an inner vertical taillight lens. Wagons continued to use the same taillight as when introduced in 1976. Coupes with the optional landau top had a new opera window design with angular corners, rather than the former rounded corners.

Two new Volaré models were introduced this year as well, another strange move considering this car was in its last year. Known as the Volaré Special, these were specially equipped coupes and sedans with some of the most popular features as standard equipment, priced below comparably equipped regular Volaré models. Also most of the previous year's option packages were still available, although the formerly separate interior and exterior Custom and Premier packages were combined into a single package format of either Custom or Premier. Still available were the Duster Coupe package, the Sport Wagon package, and the Road Runner package. The Duster name would appear again for the 1984 model year as an option package on the Turismo, which would be the name applied to the Horizon TC3 line for 1983, and it would resurface again as a subseries for the 1992 Plymouth Sundance. However, this was the swan song for the Road Runner name, which is not entirely disappointing to Road Runner enthusiasts, as the 1980 edition was available on the Slant Six powered Volaré coupe this year, making it truly an appearance package, and by no means a performance car. This is evidenced by the installation of only 496 Road Runner packages, while the Duster package was installed on 5,586 coupes, or more than a third of Volaré coupe production.

The Horizon 4-door and TC3 2-door hatchbacks entered the 1980 season with few changes, as they became the top selling Plymouth models. The TC3 was actually the only Plymouth model with a sales and production increase. New options were added such as intermittent windshield wipers and automatic speed control, as well as a new Turismo package for the TC3 coupe. The Turismo option gave the

TC3 a sporty, more European appearance, an approach that Chrysler would follow through the 1980s on various series. Full details of the Turismo package content are included in Appendix IV.

Few changes were seen in the Plymouth captive-import models for 1980. The Arrow was in its final season and was barely mentioned or advertised, other than the sport Fire Arrow model. The new-for-1979 Champ continued unchanged, as did the Sapporo luxury sport coupe.

The future looked bleak for Plymouth, as Chrysler Cor-poration struggled internally with finances, and externally customers were seeing no difference between the Plymouth and Dodge lines. By the mid–1980s, sales would start to pick up, but market share would never recover, and a third place finish behind Chevrolet and Ford was a long forgotten memory. Chrysler would finally pull the plug on the Plymouth brand in 2001, just as Chrysler was introducing the highly popular PT Cruiser that was based on a Plymouth concept car, and could possibly have kept the Plymouth name alive, at least for a few more years.

Arrow Fire Arrow 2-Door Hatchback

Gran Fury instrument panel

Horizon 4-Door Hatchback with Custom exterior package

Sapporo 2-Door Hardtop

Champ 2-Door Hatchback with Arrow pickup in rear

Gran Fury Salon 4-Door Pillared Hardtop

Horizon TC3 2-Door Hatchback with Turismo package

Volaré 2-Door Coupe with Premier package

Gran Fury 4-Door Pillared Hardtop

Gran Fury Salon with Sacony cloth trim

Horizon TC3 interior

Volaré 4-Door Sedan with Custom package

Volaré 4-Door Station Wagon
with Custom package

Volaré 4-Door Wagon with Sport Wagon
package (top) and Volaré 2-Door Coupe
with Road Runner package

Model year production: 249,941, down 21.72% from 1979.
Domestic market share: 3.24% (8th place).
Base price range: $5,033 to $7,116.
Plymouth average base price: $5,663, up 22.85%.
Introduction date: October 1, 1979.
Assembly plants: Lynch Road, Detroit, MI (A); Belvidere, IL (D); Newark, DE (F); St. Louis, MO (G); and Windsor, Ontario, Canada (R). *Imports:* Arrow and Champ — Kurashiki, Okayama, Japan (code 1 through 9); Sapporo — Okazaki, Aichi, Japan (code 1 through 9).

Data plate identification (VIN): Thirteen digit code read as follows: First four digits indicate series and body style (model number in model charts); fifth digit indicates engine code (see powertrain chart); sixth digit indicates year (A = 1980); seventh digit indicates assembly plant (see list above); remaining digits are sequential with beginning numbers of 100001. *Example:* HL41CAF100001 is a 1980 Plymouth Volaré 4-door sedan, with 225 CID, 1-bbl. 6-cylinder engine, serial number 100001, built in Newark, DE.

Powertrains[1]

Engine	Net HP	Engine Code	Transmission Availability[2]		Champ	Arrow	Sapporo	Horizon	Volaré	Gran Fury
86 CID (1.4L) OHC, 2-bbl., 4-cyl.	70	J	4-speed manual		Credit option (HBK)	—	—	—	—	—
				MPG:	37	—	—	—	—	—
			"Twin-stick" 4-speed manual		S (HBK)	—	—	—	—	—
				MPG:	35	—	—	—	—	—
				Calif.	31	—	—	—	—	—
97.5 CID (1.6L) OHC, 2-bbl., 4-cyl.	77	K	"Twin-stick" 4-speed manual		S (Custom)	—				
				MPG:	33	—	—	—	—	—
				Calif.	31	—	—	—	—	—
			5-speed manual		—	S	—	—	—	—
				MPG:	—	29	—	—	—	—
				Calif.	—	27	—	—	—	—
			3-speed automatic		$240 (Custom)/ $ (HBK)	$240	—	—	—	—
				MPG:	30	29	—	—	—	—
				Calif.	29	27	—	—	—	—
104.7 CID (1.7L) OHC, 2-bbl., 4-cyl.	70	A	4-speed manual		—	—	—	S	—	—
				MPG:	—	—	—	23	—	—
				Calif.	—	—	—	24	—	—
			3-speed Torque Flite automatic		—	—	—	$322	—	—
				MPG:	—	—	—	24	—	—
				Calif.	—	—	—	23	—	—
155.9 CID (2.6L) OHC, 2-bbl., 4-cyl.	77	F	5-speed manual		—	$62	S	—	—	—
				MPG:	—	22	21	—	—	—
				Calif.	—	22	21	—	—	—
			3-speed Automatic		—	$302	$240	—	—	—

Engine	Net HP	Engine Code	Transmission Availability[2]		Champ	Arrow	Sapporo	Horizon	Volaré	Gran Fury
				MPG:	—	22	22	—	—	—
				Calif.	—	22	20	—	—	—
225 CID (3.7L), 1-bbl., 6-cyl.	100	C	3-speed manual		—	—	—	—	S[3]	—
				MPG:	—	—	—	—	17	—
			4-speed manual w/overdrive		—	—	—	—	$153[3]	—
				MPG:	—	—	—	—	17	—
			3-speed Torque Flite automatic		—	—	—	—	$340[4]	S
				MPG:	—	—	—	—	17/25	16/24
				Calif.	—	—	—	—	16	—
318 CID (5.2L), 2-bbl., V8[3]	135	G	3-speed Torque Flite automatic		—	—	—	—	$555	$233
				MPG:	—	—	—	—	15	15/23
318 CID (5.2L), 4-bbl., V8	145	H	3-speed Torque Flite automatic		—	—	—	—	$606	$295[4]
				Calif.	—	—	—	—	16	16
360 CID (5.9L), 2-bbl., V8[3]	150	K	3-speed Torque Flite automatic		—	—	—	—	—	$457
				MPG:	—	—	—	—	—	14

[1]Optional axle ratios may be required on cars sold in California or high-altitude counties. [2]Unless otherwise noted: All manual transmissions are floor-shift. All automatics are floor-shift on Champ, Sapporo, and Horizon. Floor-shift is available for $35 extra on any Volaré w/3-speed manual transmission. Volarés w/automatic are available w/floor-shift in combination with specified equipment or packages. [3]Not available in California or designated high altitude areas. [4]Required as standard equipment in California and designated high altitude areas, with appropriate adjustment in price.

Major Options

	Champ	Arrow	Sapporo	Horizon	Volaré	Gran Fury
Air conditioning	$555	$555	$555	$541	$543	$670[1]
Tilt steering wheel	—	S	S	—	$76	$85
Automatic speed control	—	—	$116	$101	$106	$122
Electric rear window defroster	S	$95[2]	S	S	$97	$113
Tinted glass, all windows	S	S	S	S	$66	S
Dual remote control sport mirrors	—	—	S	$69	$68	$52
Power windows, 2-dr./4-dr.	—	—	—	—	$130/$183	$228
Power door locks, 2-dr./4-dr.	—	—	—	—	$83/$117	$139
Power seat, bench	—	—	—	—	$163	$183
AM radio	$86	$86	—	S	S	$106
AM/FM stereo	$185	$185	S	$93	$93	$164
AM/FM stereo w/8-track tape	—	—	—	—	$166	$209
Front bucket seats w/console[3]	S	S	S	$33	$209	—
Vinyl top, full[4]	—	—	—	—	$97	$162
Sunroof, removable	$191	$191	—	$182	—	$1,053[5]
T-Bar roof	—	—	—	—	$614	—
Power steering, standard w/V8s	—	—	S	$161	$166	S
Power brakes, w/front disc	S	S	S	$77	$77	S
Deluxe wheel covers	—	—	—	$44	$44	$49
Premium wheel covers	—	—	—	—	$81	$93
Wire wheel covers	—	—	—	—	$150	$315
Rallye road wheels	—	—	—	$83	—	—
Styled spoke road wheels	—	—	—	—	$154	—
Cast aluminum road wheels	$265	$265	$320	$254	$287	$385[6]
White sidewall tires, std. size	S	S	S	S	$49	S

Popular Option Groups & Packages

	Champ	Arrow	Sapporo	Horizon	Volaré	Gran Fury
Basic group	—	—	—	—	$403	$1,203
Custom exterior package	—	—	—	$101	—	—
Custom interior package	—	—	—	$112	—	—
Custom package	—	—	—	—	$386	—
Deluxe Insulation package	—	—	—	—	$51	—
Duster Coupe package	—	—	—	—	$155	—

	Champ	Arrow	Sapporo	Horizon	Volaré	Gran Fury
Light package	—	—	—	—	$46	$87
Popular equipment group	—	—	—	$273	—	—
Premier package	—	—	—	—	$513[7]	—
Premium exterior package	—	—	—	$207	—	—
Premium interior package	—	—	—	$355	—	—
Premium woodgrain exterior pkg.	—	—	—	$344	—	—
Premium package	$503	—	—	—	—	—
Protection group	—	—	—	—	$64	—
Road Runner package	—	—	—	—	$586	—
Sport package	—	—	—	$431	$254	—
Sport Wagon package	—	—	—	—	$721	—
Turismo package	—	—	—	$1,227	—	—
Two-tone paint package	—	—	—	$137[8]	$148	$168

—= Not Available; S = Standard equipment. [1]Air conditioning with automatic temperature control is $720. [2]Electric rear window defroster is standard on Fire Arrow. [3]Available on Volaré coupe and wagon. Bucket seats without console are standard on Horizon with price shown being for floor shift console only. Bucket seats and console are standard on Champ Custom, Arrow Fire Arrow, and on Champ and Arrow models bucket seats are standard, but without an available console. [4]Volaré Landau top on 2-door models is $178. Not available on station wagon. [5]Power glass sunroof on Gran Fury. [6]Forged aluminum wheels on Gran Fury. [7]Price shown is for coupes and sedans. Price for wagons is $831, and includes exterior woodgrain trim, formerly part of the Premier exterior woodgrain package. [8]Price is for Classic two-tone package on Horizon 4-door. Sport two-tone package on TC3 is $131.

Paint Colors

Plymouth Domestic Models	Code	Champ, Arrow & Sapporo	Code	Champ, Arrow & Sapporo	Code
Spinnaker White	EW1	Bright Blue metallic—Champ	B22	Dull Black & White[7]	X86
Frost Blue metallic	SC2	Light Blue metallic—Arrow	B39		
Nightwatch Blue[1,2,3]	SC9	Dark Blue metallic—Sapporo	B84	*Single tones are coded EW1,EW1. Two-tones are coded*	
Teal Frost metallic[2,4]	SG4	Dark Blue metallic & Light Blue		*on body ID plate as TX9, EW1 where three digits on*	
Light Cashmere	ST1	metallic[7]	B87	*line 2 are lower body color, and three digits on line 3*	
Bright Yellow[1,5]	SY4	Light Blue metallic & Dark Blue		*are upper body color or two-tone color. Import model*	
Burnished Silver metallic[1,2,5]	TA3	metallic[7]	B88	*two-tones use a different code as listed above. [1]Avail-*	
Graphic Blue[1,5]	TB6	Bright Gold metallic & Light		*able only on Horizon. [2]Available only on Volaré.*	
Light Heather Gray[3]	TD2	Tan metallic[8]	C59	*[3]Available only on Gran Fury Salon. [4]Available only*	
Light Heather Gray metallic[3]	TD3	Light Tan metallic—Champ	C95	*on Gran Fury. [5]Available in combination with Flat*	
Teal Tropic Green metallic	TG6	Silver metallic—All	H29	*Black paint on TC3 w/optional sport package.*	
Crimson Red metallic[1,2,3]	TM7	Bright Gold metallic—Sapporo	K19	*[6]Available only on Volaré coupe. [7]Available only on*	
Baron Red[1,2,3]	TM9	Bright Gold metallic & Ballast		*Fire Arrow. [8]Available only on Champ Custom with*	
Graphic Red[1,5,6]	TR4	Sand metallic[7]	K32	*premium package.*	
Natural Suede Tan	TT4	Light Tan—Champ	S37		
Mocha Brown metallic	TT8	White—Champ	W61		
Formal Black	TX9	Black—Champ	X15		

Champ

"The little car that's been designed to stay out front."

Nameplate year of origin: 1979.
Current bodystyle lifespan: 1979 through 1983.
Predecessor to this model: None.
Replacement for this model: Colt (1984 to 1988).
Primary competition: Chevrolet Chevette and Ford Fiesta.
Notable changes: Minor trim and detail changes.
Major standard equipment: Vinyl front bucket seats w/reclining seat backs, full-floor carpeting, fold-down rear seat, two-spoke steering wheel, trip odometer, tinted glass, flipper rear quarter windows, electric rear window defroster, front and rear window moldings, door and quarter window reveal moldings, LH rear view mirror, front and rear rubber bumper guards, locking fuel filler door, power front disc brakes, and 6.15 × 13 WSW tires. Custom hatchback adds: Cloth-and-vinyl door

Measurements

Wheelbase	90.6"
Length	156.9"
Width	62.4"
Height	50.6"
Legroom—front	40.6"
Legroom—rear	29.7"
Headroom—front	36.8"
Headroom—rear	36.0"
Cargo capacity (cu. ft.)	6.5*
Fuel capacity (gals.)	10.5

*With rear seat down, 27.4 cu. ft.

trim and bucket seats w/reclining seat backs, floor console, rear shelf security panel, sport steering wheel, assist grips, remote hatchback release, custom tape stripes, and 155SR × 13 WSW tires.

Models Available

	Model No.	Base MSRP	Change from LY	Shipping Wt. (lbs.)	Model Year Sales*	Change from LY
Champ 2-Door Hatchback	1M24	$4,430	+0.11%	1810	NA	NEW
Champ Custom 2-Door Hatchback	1H24	$4,792	+1.03%	1885	NA	NEW
TOTALS	Avg. price	$4,611	+0.59%	Production	39,756	+47.08%

*Model year sales by trim level is not available.

Arrow

"Our seventies' sizzler outdoes itself for 1980."

Nameplate year of origin: 1976.
Current bodystyle lifespan: 1976 through 1980.
Predecessor to this model: None.
Replacement for this model: Champ (1979 to 1983).
Primary competition: AMC Spirit and Chevrolet Chevette.
Notable changes: Minor trim and detail changes.
Major standard equipment: All-vinyl front bucket seats w/reclining seatbacks, full-floor carpeting including cargo area, folding rear seat, woodtone I/P trim, tilt steering column, two-speed electric windshield wipers, cigarette lighter, heater and defroster, tinted glass, black painted grille, argent painted bumpers, front and rear window moldings, drip rail moldings, power front disc brakes, and 165SR13 WSW tires. Fire Arrow adds: Cloth-and-vinyl bucket seats w/reclining seatbacks, floor console rally gauge cluster w/tachometer, engine-turned I/P and floor console appliqués, rear window defroster, flipper-style rear quarter windows, soft-rim sports style steering wheel, dual body-color racing mirrors, two-tone paint and body stripes w/hood decal, and chrome bumpers except on black and white model which has black painted bumpers.

Measurements

Wheelbase	92.1"
Length	169.9"
Width	63.4"
Height	50.4"
Legroom — front	41.7"
Legroom — rear	28.0"
Headroom — front	36.8"
Headroom — rear	34.4"
Cargo capacity (cu. ft.)	17.3
Fuel capacity (gals.)	13.2

Models Available

	Model No.	Base MSRP	Change from LY	Shipping Wt. (lbs.)	Model Year Sales*	Change from LY
Arrow 2-Door Hatchback Coupe	7H24	$4,588	-1.27%	2095	NA	NA
Arrow Fire Arrow 2-Door HBK Coupe	7P24	$4,987	-12.45%	2135	NA	NA
TOTALS	Avg. price	$4,788	-6.42%	Production	15,718	-27.99%

*Model year sales by trim level is not available.   **Change from LY for Fire Arrow is compared to 1979 Arrow GT with same model number.

Sapporo

"Your own class transit system."

Nameplate year of origin: 1978.
Current bodystyle lifespan: 1978 through 1983.
Predecessor to this model: None.
Replacement for this model: Conquest (1984 to 1989; sold under Chrysler name, 1987–1989).
Primary competition: Chevrolet Monza, Ford Mustang, Mercury Capri, and Pontiac Sunbird.

Measurements

Wheelbase	99.0"
Length	183.1"
Width	66.9"
Height	51.8"
Legroom — front	41.7"
Legroom — rear	31.3"

1980

Notable changes: Minor trim and detail changes. Sold also as the Dodge Challenger.

Major standard equipment: Cord velour cloth front bucket seats w/reclining seatbacks and lumbar support, easy entrance passenger seat w/memory, color-keyed cut-pile carpeting, center floor console, door armrests w/integral door pull, assist grips, dome and interior spot lamps, overhead console w/ digital clock and warning lights, chime warning system, vanity mirror, AM/FM stereo w/four speakers, two-spoke sport steering wheel, tilt steering column, I/P cluster w/trip odometer, tachometer, temperature, fuel, oil, and electrical gauges, tinted glass, rear window defogger, dual power remote mirrors, drip rail and belt moldings, front and rear window moldings, decklid moldings, bright and black vinyl bodyside moldings, front and rear bumper guards, color-keyed road wheels w/bright trim rings, and 195/70SR × 14 BSW tires.

Measurements (cont.)

Headroom — front	36.8"
Headroom — rear	35.0"
Cargo capacity (cu. ft.)	10.9
Fuel capacity (gals.)	15.3

Models Available

	Model No.	Base MSRP	Change from LY	Shipping Wt. (lbs.)	Model Year Sales*	Change from LY
Sapporo 2-Door Hardtop	3H29	$6,429	-0.88%	2675	10,311	-16.32%
TOTALS	Avg. price	$6,429	-0.88%		Production 10,311	-16.32%

Model year production is not available.

Horizon

"Soaring you to new Horizons ... and beyond."

Nameplate year of origin: 1978.
Current bodystyle lifespan: 1978 through 1990.
Predecessor to this model: None.
Replacement for this model: None.
Percentage of division's sales volume: 58.12%.
Corporate siblings: Dodge Omni.
Primary competition: Chevrolet Chevette and Ford Fiesta.
Notable changes: Minor trim and detail changes.
Major standard equipment: Vinyl front bucket seats, color-keyed molded headlining, color-keyed carpeting, door armrests, three-spoke steering wheel, door armrests, fold-down rear seat, folding rear shelf security panel, electric rear window defroster, AM radio, day/night inside rear view mirror, LH chrome mirror, bright liftgate window accents, vinyl bodyside molding, bright aluminum front and rear bumper face bars w/rub strips, manual front disc brakes, and P155/80R × 13 WSW tires.
TC3 adds: Cloth upholstered headliner, cargo compartment carpeting, simulated woodgrain I/P inserts, luxury three-spoke sport steering wheel, glove box lock, AM/FM radio, LH aerodynamic sport mirror, quarter window louvers, remote hatchback release, bright sill and wheel lip moldings, wheel trim rings, and P175/75R × 13 BSW tires; deletes rear bumper rub strips.

Measurements

	2-door HBK	4-door HBK
Wheelbase	96.7"	99.2"
Length	172.8"	164.8"
Width	66.7"	65.8"
Height	51.1"	53.4"
Legroom — front	42.5"	42.0"
Legroom — rear	28.6"	33.0"
Headroom — front	37.5"	38.3"
Headroom — rear	34.7"	37.4"
Cargo capacity (cu. ft.)	10.7*	10.5*
Fuel capacity (gals.)	13.0	13.0

With rear seat folded down, 2+2 HBK is 33.9; 4-door HBK is 35.8. Additional hidden cargo volume of 1.6 cu. ft. on TC3, and 3.6 cu. ft. on 4-door.

Models Available

	Model No.	Base MSRP	Change from LY	Shipping Wt. (lbs.)	Model Year Production	Change from LY
Horizon TC3 2-Door Hatchback	ML24	$5,681	+16.80%	2135	59,527	+9.73%
Horizon 4-Door Hatchback	ML44	$5,526	+23.65%	2095	85,751	-0.54%
TOTALS	Avg. price	$5,604	+20.08%		Production 145,278	+3.43%

Volaré

"Value at its best."

Nameplate year of origin: 1976.
Current bodystyle lifespan: 1976 through 1980.
Predecessor to this model: Valiant (1967 to 1976).
Replacement for this model: Reliant (1981 to 1989).
Percentage of division's production: 36.03%.
Corporate siblings: Dodge Aspen.
Primary competition: AMC Concord, Chevrolet Citation, and Ford Granada.
Notable changes: Restyled front end and minor trim and detail changes.
Major standard equipment: Cloth-and-vinyl front bench seat, color-keyed carpeting, three-spoke steering wheel, AM radio, two-speed electric windshield wipers and washers, front ashtray, bright grille surround molding, roof drip rail molding, quarter window reveal moldings, windshield and backlight moldings, front sway bar, and P195/75R14 BSW tires. Wagon adds: Rear liftgate w/liftgate ajar warning light, cargo area stowage bins, power front disc brakes, and heavy-duty suspension. Special coupe and sedan delete AM radio, and adds: Automatic transmission, power steering, bodyside tape stripes, wheel opening moldings, deluxe wheel covers, and WSW tires.

Measurements

	Coupe	Sedan	Wagon
Wheelbase	108.7"	112.7"	112.7"
Length	200.3"	204.3"	204.3"
Width	72.4"	72.4"	72.4"
Height	53.6"	55.3"	55.5"
Legroom — front	42.5"	42.5"	42.5"
Legroom — rear	31.7"	36.6"	36.6"
Headroom — front	37.4"	39.2"	39.2"
Headroom — rear	35.9"	37.5"	38.7"
Cargo capacity (cu. ft.)	16.4	16.4	73.1*
Fuel capacity (gals.)	18.0	18.0	18.0

*An additional 0.6 cu. ft. in rear quarter panel bin storage.

Models Available

	Model No.	Base MSRP	Change from LY	Shipping Wt. (lbs.)	Model Year Production	Change from LY
Volaré Special 2-Door Sport Coupe	HE29	$5,151	NEW	3155	12,334	NEW
Volaré Special 4-Door Sedan	HE41	$5,151	NEW	3210	20,613	NEW
Volaré 2-Door Sport Coupe	HL29	$5,033	+14.73%	3110	14,453	NA*
Volaré 4-Door Sedan	HL41	$5,150	+14.34%	3165	25,768	NA*
Volaré 4-Door Station Wagon	HL45	$5,422	+12.35%	3325	16,895	-61.68%
TOTALS	Avg. price	$5,181	+13.32%		Production 90,063	-49.63%

*Comparison to LY is not possible due to production of coupes and sedans being kept combined for 1979.

Gran Fury

"A matter of family pride."

Nameplate year of origin: 1956 (Fury); 1975 (Gran Fury).
Current bodystyle lifespan: 1980 through 1981.
Predecessor to this model: Fury (1974 to 1977; renamed Gran Fury for 1975 to 1977).
Replacement for this model: Gran Fury (1982 to 1989).
Percentage of division's production: 5.84%.
Corporate siblings: Chrysler Newport, Chrysler New Yorker, and Dodge St. Regis.
Primary competition: Chevrolet Impala and Ford LTD.
Notable changes: All-new model.
Major standard equipment: Cloth-and-vinyl front bench seat, color-keyed carpeting, two-spoke steering wheel, two-speed electric windshield wipers and washers, front and rear ashtrays, tinted glass, LH and RH manual rear view mirrors, bright front and rear window moldings, bright belt and door moldings, bright upper door frame moldings, dual horns, hubcaps, and P195/75R15 WSW tires. Salon adds: Saxony cloth-and-vinyl front bench seat w/fold-down center armrest, bright wheel opening and rocker panel sill moldings, protective bumper rub strips, and deluxe wheel covers.

Measurements

Wheelbase	118.5"
Length	220.2"
Width	77.6"
Height	54.5"
Legroom — front	42.3"
Legroom — rear	38.2"
Headroom — front	38.6"
Headroom — rear	37.4"
Cargo capacity (cu. ft.)	21.3
Fuel capacity (gals.)	21.0

1980

Models Available

	Model No.	Base MSRP	Change from LY	Shipping Wt. (lbs.)	Model Year Production	Change from LY
Gran Fury 4-Door Pillared Hardtop	JL42	$6,741	NEW	3520	12,576	NEW
Gran Fury Salon 4-Dr. Pillared Hardtop	JH42	$7,116	NEW	3545	2,024	NEW
TOTALS	Avg. price	$6,929	NEW	Production	14,600	NEW

PONTIAC

"More Pontiac excitement to the Gallon."

Pontiac's start to the 1980s began in April 1979, when the all-new downsized compact Phoenix was introduced. It was followed in the fall by completely restyled full-size Catalina and Bonneville models that were more aerodynamically efficient and achieved greater fuel mileage, and the rest of the Pontiac line was given minor updates, with one notable introduction being Pontiac's first ever turbocharged V8 engine available on the Firebird. Sales of the new Phoenix quickly soared in an economy facing a second fuel shortage and impending recession, as the new front-wheel-drive compacts were lighter and roomier than before, yet powered by drivetrains quite similar to their predecessors, allowing them to feel more powerful while achieving impressive fuel economy. All of these features contributed to making positive first impressions.

All of the right elements were in place — fuel economy, front wheel drive, roominess and modern styling — but it was not long before rumors of problems with quality surfaced, and some consumers backed off. Due to an extended 16-month production year, the new "X-car" would be deemed a success. However, in reality, the Phoenix was something of a disappointment. Among the four GM X-car variants, Phoenix had the lowest percentage increase in year to year production and came in a distant third in sales to a wildly popular and newly named Chevrolet Citation, which by itself outsold all Pontiac lines combined, and a very popular Buick Skylark whose sedan models pushed it to second spot, while Phoenix only marginally outsold the Oldsmobile Omega. It was not a promising start. In fact, by the 1981 model year, the Phoenix would be at the bottom of the pile among the four sister cars.

Pontiac's performance image hurt the division's sales during the fuel crisis. Even though Pontiac was down less than the average for the overall market this model year, a resurgent Buick captured third place, overtaking both Pontiac and Oldsmobile, which was now in fourth position. Though only a one-year anomaly for Buick, Pontiac's fifth place industry ranking for 1980 and its uncomfortable fourth place corporate ranking behind Buick and Oldsmobile would remain through most of the eighties, and in fact through much of the remainder of the performance division's lifespan, which ended with the 2009 model year.

Like the other X-body cars, Phoenix featured front-wheel-drive and a transverse mounted engine and transaxle combination. The Pontiac-built 2.5 liter 151 CID 4-cylinder was standard equipment, with the new Chevrolet-built 2.8 liter, 173 CID V6 engine being optional. Pontiac designers chose a unique combination of body styles giving the Phoenix a formal roofline two-door coupe and a sporty four-door hatchback. Styling of the Phoenix was typical for Pontiac, having a two-piece grille split by a vertical chrome bar carrying the Pontiac emblem, and horizontal crosshatch grille inserts three rows high and three columns across, with each of the nine openings per side having three horizontal slots within. Single square headlights placed at the outer edges of the front end were paired with vertical parking/turn signal lights on the inboard side. Urethane body-colored bumpers front and rear wore bright plastic chrome rub strips in keeping with the latest Pontiac trends. Bodyside styling included two feature lines, the upper of which ran from the top corner of the headlight bezel to the end of the rear quarter window, being slightly raised across the center to run about an inch below the side window line. The lower feature line ran between the lower corners of the bezels, creating flares over the wheel openings as the line crossed through. At the rear, taillights were horizontal rectangular units, divided by two horizontal chrome strips and three vertical ones. The innermost section, adjacent to the center-mounted license plate housing, was the backup light.

As mentioned, the greenhouse areas of the Phoenix differed by model. The coupe had a formal roofline with angular widow corners on all sides. A fixed rear quarter window was a continuing feature. The four-door hatchback sedan had a sloping rear hatch lid with fixed rear window, and also had angular window lines, but used a six-window configuration, with a triangular rear quarter window, much like the failed design used on the 1978 to 1979 Buick Century and Oldsmobile Cutlass four-door sedans. Inside the Phoenix, a prominent center pod on the instrument panel trimmed in brushed aluminum housed eight pods. The top row of four pods housed gauges such as fuel and oil pressure, while the four pods below were round air vents. In the lower portion of the center pod were radio and ventilation controls. To each side of the pod was a recessed area out to the ends, with a round speedometer and warning lights housed in a square pod inset over the steering column. An extended section of the instrument panel to the left of the driver, next to the door opening, housed controls for lights and wipers. Interiors appeared more luxurious than ever with new fabrics, full color-keyed interiors, built-in door pull handles, brushed aluminum trim, and standard features such as an AM radio. With base and LJ (luxury) models offered, and an optional SJ (sporty version) package available, the Phoenix profile fit the Pontiac image, but unfortunately it was not accepted by consumers as well as management had hoped.

The full-size line received a complete restyling to make them more aerodynamically efficient. This was accomplished by lowering the leading hood line, raising the rear deck lid, and on coupes adding a more formal, upright roofline. Overall styling was new yet familiar, with both the Catalina and Bonneville incorporating dual rectangular headlights separated by the parking/turn signal lights, as used on the current Grand Prix. Both Catalina and Bonneville shared the same grille this year, a vertical bar design with five openings per side, with all extending into the lower bumper area. Each of the five openings had three vertical bars inset. Bodysides were smooth and mostly unadorned this year, with wheel opening flares eliminated, although Bonneville models used rear wheel opening fender skirts with a small lip along their length. At the rear, larger wraparound taillamps continued a horizontal three row configuration. Powertrain choices were pared back again, making the 301 CID V8 engine the largest available in the 49 states, while the Chevrolet 350 CID V8 engine was available in California. The Oldsmobile diesel V8 engine became available this year, and increased fuel by mileage by more than 50 percent. The standard Catalina and Bonneville 231 CID V6 engine also was made standard on the Bonneville Brougham around mid-year. As the year wore on it became apparent that the Catalina would soon be gone, as production had not been above 100,000 units since 1974, and the Bonneville would outperform the Catalina in sales and production by nearly nine to one during the 1980 model year. It would only get worse for Catalina before the plug was pulled on all full-size Pontiacs at the end of the 1981 season. The Bonneville name would return for 1982, but on a

revised version of the LeMans, which itself was discontinued at the end of the 1981 model year.

The mid-size LeMans, Grand Am and Grand Prix all received new grilles and other detail changes. The LeMans line introduced a five horizontal bar grille design, with seven vertical bars set behind. Larger wraparound taillamps were also introduced this year. The Grand Am four-door model was gone, but the surviving coupe received a new grille with three sections per side, each having sixteen horizontal slats inset. The Grand Am two-door coupe would also be gone by the end of the 1980 model year, but the name would return for the 1985 model year on a compact, front-wheel-drive replacement for the Phoenix. The lack of interest in the second generation Grand Am signaled that the era of the powerful European-style muscle sedan was clearly gone. The Grand Prix's new grille was a classic vertical bar affair with a thick center bar and ten vertical bars per side. Around back, new taillight lenses were set in chrome bezels, with the Grand Prix logo mounted in the center of the lens.

Pontiac's smallest car, the Sunbird, was in its final season as an H-body car and relegated to the back pages of the sales brochure, yet the current fuel crisis made it Pontiac's most popular model, accounting for one quarter of 1980 Pontiac production. Part of its success could be attributed to an extended season that ran into the beginning of the 1981 model year, until the new GM J-car replacement, initially known as J2000 and eventually Sunbird, appeared in May 1981 as a 1982 model. From the start of the model year, the Sport Safari wagon was gone, but after the start of the season, a lower-priced hatchback coupe was added to the line to pick up sales lost from Buick and Oldsmobile dealers, as production of the related H-body Skyhawk and Starfire was discontinued on December 21, 1979. This allowed for increased production of the lower-priced and more popular Chevrolet Monza and Pontiac Sunfire in the Lordstown, Ohio, plant while other GM plants geared up for the start of J-car production.

The Firebird line entered the new decade with the same body styling and only minor interior changes, including a center console becoming a standard feature. The black Special Edition Trans Am continued to be available with 6,094 sold for 1980. However, there were several noteworthy changes for 1980. A new "YellowBird" appearance package continued the "color" series of Firebird Esprit models, while a new turbocharged 301 CID V8 engine stole all the headlines. Based on an idea taken from Buick engineers, who had added a turbocharger to their popular 231 CID V6 engine to gain power while maintaining fuel efficiency, the Pontiac engine oddly came along at a time when Pontiac-built V8 engines were being phased out. In fact, the 1981 model year would be the end of the line for the Pontiac V8, after twenty-six years of production. Regardless, Pontiac proudly declared the 301 CID V8 engine was "the World's Only Turbocharged V8." Pontiac described the new engine as operating like a

1980

conventional engine under normal circumstances, "but when extra power is needed ... the turbo-charging unit kicks in quickly and evenly to boost the power output." As summarized in the sales brochure, the boost was "...accomplished by a turbine driven by the engine exhaust gases. The turbine powers a compressor, which forces a dense air/fuel mixture into the engines' cylinders, producing more power. The process is constantly monitored by an Electronic Feedback Control that provides the most efficient spark advance during boost conditions." The engine was available on Formula or Trans Am models, with a total of 16,476 Trans Ams and 1,245 Formulas receiving the turbo V8. Additionally 5,700 Trans Ams were built with the engine as Indianapolis 500 pace car replicas, as a turbocharged Trans Am was selected as the official pace car of the Memorial Day running of the 1980 Indianapolis 500 race. It was only the second time that Pontiac had been selected to perform pace car duties, with the first being back in 1958. The 1980 (Y85) option) Turbo Trans Am pace cars were similar to the 1979 10th Anniversary Trans Am in their paint scheme, although they were painted in white with charcoal upper body, with tri-color body accent stripes separating the colors. This year also marked the first time

ever that the same car was pace car for both the Indianapolis 500 and the Daytona 500 in the same year. Pace car decals used a larger five-color hood bird and the "Turbo 4.9" logo on the bulge of the hood, offset to the driver's side to accommodate the turbocharger and hood-mounted three-light system for the turbo-boost light gauges. This hood bulge and light system was used on all models equipped with the turbo V8 engine. For the Trans Am pace car replicas, the Indy 500 emblem was located on the side fenders and the rear tail spoilers, while "Indy 500 Pace Car" or "22nd Annual Daytona 500 Mile Race" door decals were an extra cost option. The interior was trimmed in custom Oyster vinyl bucket seats with hobnail inserts and the Firebird "bird" was embroidered on the center of the rear seats and on the front portions of the door panels. The rest of the interior was an Oyster white with charcoal grey dash and center console. A special extended tuning range (ETR) AM/FM stereo with cassette-tape and seek-and-scan features used a digital display with red lights. All gauges on the instrument panel were lit in red, a feature that would be standard in most Pontiac models by the end of the decade. The pace car models came fully equipped, and package details are listed in Appendix IV.

Bonneville Brougham 4-Door Sedan

Bonneville 2-Door Coupe interior with optional bucket seats and console

Bonneville Brougham 2-Door Coupe

Bonneville Safari 4-Door Station Wagon

Catalina 4-Door Sedan

Firebird Esprit 2-Door Hardtop Coupe with Yellow Bird package

Firebird Formula 2-Door Hardtop Coupe with turbocharged engine

Firebird Trans Am 2-Door Hardtop Coupe with Special Edition package and turbocharged engine

Grand Am 2-Door Coupe

Grand Am interior

Grand Prix LJ 2-Door Hardtop Coupe
with double two-tone paint option

Phoenix LJ 2-Door Coupe

Sunbird 2-Door Hatchback Coupe

Grand LeMans 4-Door Sedan

Grand Prix SJ 2-Door Hardtop Coupe

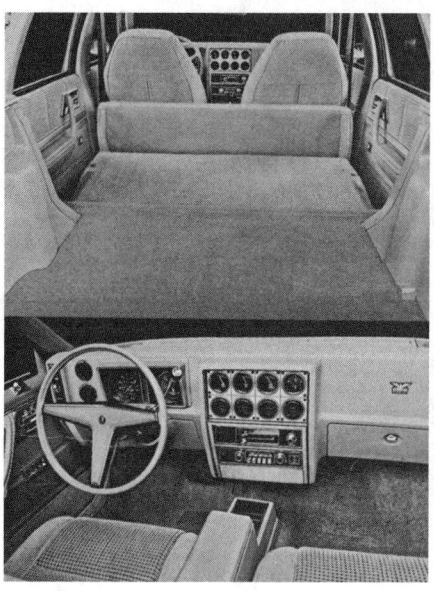

Phoenix LJ 5-Door Hatchback interior

Sunbird Sport Hatch 2-Door Hatchback
Coupe with Formula package

Grand LeMans Safari 4-Door Station Wagon

LeMans 2-Door Coupe

Phoenix LJ 5-Door Hatchback Sedan

Sunbird Sport 2-Door Coupe

1980

Model year production: 775,218, down 14.57% from 1979.
Domestic market share: 10.14% (5th place).
Base price range: $4,623 to $8,157.
Pontiac average base price: $6,453, up 11.98%.
Introduction date: October 11, 1979. Phoenix introduced on April 19, 1979.
Assembly plants: Baltimore, MD (B); Van Nuys, CA (L); Norwood, OH (N); Pontiac, MI (P); Tarrytown, NY (T); Kansas City/Fairfax, KS (X); Oshawa, Ontario, Canada (1); Ste. Therese, Quebec, Canada (2); Oklahoma City, OK (6); and Lordstown, OH (7).

Data plate identification (VIN): Thirteen digit code read as follows: First digit indicates division (2 = Pontiac); second through fourth digits indicate series and body style (model number in model charts); fifth digit is engine code (see powertrain chart); sixth digit indicates model year (A = 1980); seventh digit indicates assembly plant (see list above); remaining digits are sequential with beginning number of 100001. *Example:* 2D35UAB100001 is a 1980 Pontiac Le-Mans 4-Door Safari station wagon, with 305 CID, 4-bbl. V8 engine, serial number 100001, built in Baltimore, Maryland.

Powertrains

Engine	Net HP	Engine Code: VIN/GM	Transmission Availability[1]		Sunbird	Phoenix	Firebird[2]	LeMans & Grand Am[3]	Grand Prix	Catalina & Bonneville	Bonneville Brougham & Safaris[3]
151 CID (2.5L), 2-bbl., 4-cyl.	86	V/LX8	4-speed manual		S	—	—	—	—	—	—
				MPG:	22/35	—	—	—	—	—	—
				Calif.	21/34	—	—	—	—	—	—
			3-speed Turbo Hydra-matic		$320	—	—	—	—	—	—
				MPG:	24/32	—	—	—	—	—	—
				Calif.	22/33	—	—	—	—	—	—
151 CID (2.5L), 2-bbl., 4-cyl.	90	5/LW9	4-speed manual		—	S	—	—	—	—	—
				MPG:	—	24/37	—	—	—	—	—
				Calif.	—	24	—	—	—	—	—
			3-speed Turbo Hydra-matic		—	$337	—	—	—	—	—
				MPG:	—	21/33	—	—	—	—	—
				Calif.	—	22	—	—	—	—	—
173 CID (2.8L), 2-bbl., V6	115	7/LE2	4-speed manual		—	$225	—	—	—	—	—
				MPG:	—	20/26	—	—	—	—	—
				Calif.	—	NA	—	—	—	—	—
			3-speed Turbo Hydra-matic		—	$562	—	—	—	—	—
				MPG:	—	20/27	—	—	—	—	—
				Calif.	—	18	—	—	—	—	—
229 CID (3.8L), 2-bbl., V6[4]	115	K/LC3	3-speed manual		—	—	—	S (cs)	—	—	—
				MPG:	—	—	—	20/27	—	—	—
			3-speed Turbo Hydra-matic		—	—	—	S (s)/$358 (cs)	—	—	—
				MPG:	—	—	—	19/26	—	—	—
231 CID (3.8L), 2-bbl., V6	110[5]	A/LD5	3-speed manual[4]		—	—	S (F & FEs)	—	—	—	—
				MPG:	—	—	NA	—	—	—	—
			4-speed manual		$225	—	—	—	—	—	—
				MPG:	15/25	—	—	—	—	—	—
				Calif.	16/26	—	—	—	—	—	—
			3-speed Turbo Hydra-matic		$545	—	$358 (F & FEs)	S (s)[6,7]	S (GP/LJ)	S	—
				MPG:	20/27	—	20/27	20/27	20/27	18/24	—
				Calif.	19/26	—	19	19	19	15/22	—
265 CID (4.3L), 2-bbl., V8[4]	120	S/LS5	3-speed Turbo Hydra-matic		—	—	$538 (F & FEs)	$180 (s)/$538 (cs)	$180 (GP/LJ)	$180	S (BB only)
				MPG:	—	—	19/25	19/26	19/26	NA	NA
301 CID (4.9L), 4-bbl., V8[4]	140	W/L37	3-speed Turbo Hydra-matic		—	—	S (FF)/$663 (F & FEs)	$295 (s)/$663 (cs)	$295 (GP/LJ)	$295	S (s)/$115 (BB)
				MPG:	—	—	16/23	17/25	17/25	16/24	16/24

Engine	Net HP	Engine Code: VIN/GM	Transmission Availability[1]		Sunbird	Phoenix	Firebird[2]	LeMans & Grand Am[3]	Grand Prix	Catalina & Bonneville	Bonneville Brougham & Safaris[3]
301 CID (4.9L), 4-bbl., E/C*V8[4]	155	W/L37	3-speed Turbo Hydra-matic		—	—	S (TA)/ $150 (FF)	S (GA)	S (SJ)	—	—
				MPG:	—	—	NA	17/25	17/25	—	—
301 CID (4.9L), 4-bbl., Turbo V8[4]	210	T/LU8	3-speed Turbo Hydra-matic		—	—	$350 (TA)/ $530 (FF)	—	—	—	—
				MPG:	—	—	14/22	—	—	—	—
305 CID (5.0L), 4-bbl., V8[6]	150	H/LG4	3-speed Turbo Hydra-matic		—	—	S (FF & TA)/ $663 (F & FEs)	S (GA)/ $295 (s)/ $663 (cs)	S (SJ)/ $295 (GP/LJ)	—	—
				MPG:	—	—	—	—	—	—	—
				Calif.	—	—	14	15	15	14	14
350 CID (5.7L), 4-bbl., V8[4]	155	X/L77	3-speed Turbo Hydra-matic	MPG:	—	—	—	—	—	—	$130 (s) 15/22
350 CID (5.7L), 4-bbl., V8[6]	160	R/L34	3-speed Turbo Hydra-matic	Calif.	—	—	—	—	—	—	S (s) 15
350 CID (5.7L), FI Diesel, V8	105	N/LF9	3-speed Turbo Hydra-matic		—	—	—	—	—	—	$860 (s)/ $915 (BB)
				MPG:	—	—	—	—	—	—	22/34
				Calif.	—	—	—	—	—	—	23

*E/C = Electronic Spark Control. [1]Unless otherwise noted: All manual transmissions are floor shift. All automatic transmissions are column shift except in Sunbird and Firebird. Floor shift w/automatic is available on specific Phoenix, LeMans, Grand Prix and Bonneville models in combination w/optional bucket seats and console. [2]F = base Firebird, FEs = Firebird Esprit; FF = Firebird Formula; TA = Firebird Trans Am. [3]cs = Coupes and Sedans (except Grand Am); s = Safaris; GA = Grand Am; BB = Bonneville Brougham. [4]Not available in California. [5]Horsepower rating in Sunbird is 115. [6]Available only in California or designated high altitude areas. [7]Standard on LeMans coupe and sedan in California.

Major Options

	Sunbird	Phoenix	Firebird	LeMans & Grand Am	Grand Prix	Catalina & Bonneville
Custom air conditioning[1]	$531	$564	$566	$601	$601	$647
Tilt steering wheel	$73	$75	$81	$81	$81	$83
Automatic cruise control	—	$105	$112	$112	$112	$118
Intermittent windshield wipers	$37	$30	$41	$41	$41	$42
Rear window defroster, electric	$95	$101	$107	$107	$107	$109
Dual sport mirrors, remote-control	$43	$43	$46	$73	$73	$74
Soft-Ray tinted glass, all windows	S	$70	$68	$75	$75	$90
Power windows, 2-dr./4-dr.	—	$133/$189	$143[2]	$143/$202	$143	$149/$221[3]
Power door locks, 2-dr./4-dr.	—	$87/$125	$93	$93/$132	$93	$95/$135
Power front seat, 6-way w/std. seat	—	$165	—	$175	$175	$179
Front bucket seats, w/console[4]	$64	$80	S	$177	$177	$235
Third row seating (wagons)	—	—	—	—	—	$199
AM radio	S	S	$97	$97	$97	$99
AM/FM stereo	$101	$101	$192	$192	$192	$195
AM/FM stereo w/8-track tape	$188	$188	$272	$272	$272	$276
AM/FM stereo w/cassette tape	$188	$188	$272	$272	$272	$289
AM/FM stereo w/CB radio	—	$413	$525	$525	$525	$533
Remote trunk release	—	—	$	$26	$26	$27
Vinyl top, full[5]	—	$116	—	$124	—	$155
Vinyl top, padded landau[6]	$165	$180	—	$239	$239	$248
Sunroof, removable[6]	$193	$240		—	—	—
Sunroof, power steel[6]	—	—	—	$561	$561	$770
Sunroof, power glass[6]	—	—	—	$773	$773	$981

1980

	Sunbird	Phoenix	Firebird	LeMans & Grand Am	Grand Prix	Catalina & Bonneville
Hatch roof, glass panel T-tops	—	—	$695	—	$695	—
Power steering, variable-ratio	$158	$164	S	$174[7]	$164	S
Power brakes, w/front disc	$76	$76	$81[7]	S	S	S
Custom finned wheel covers	—	—	—	$60	$60	$65
Wire wheel covers	$92	$156	$171	$171	$125	$130
Rally II wheels[8]	$94	$114	$114	—	—	$120
Rally IV wheels	—	$90	$114	$114	$114	—
Cast aluminum "snowflake" wheels	$162	$242	$245	$245	$245	$245
Wire wheels	—	—	—	$540[9]	$540	—
WSW tires	$18	$45	$51	$45	$45	$51

Popular Option Groups & Packages

	Sunbird	Phoenix	Firebird	LeMans & Grand Am	Grand Prix	Catalina & Bonneville
Custom exterior group	—	$123	—	$107	—	—
Custom trim group	—	—	$80	$305[10]	—	$435
Exterior appearance package	$78	—	—	—	—	$180
Indy 500 pace car replica package	—	—	$3,665	—	—	—
Lamp group	$27	$30	$40	$60	$33	$54
LJ appearance package	—	—	—	—	$499	—
Luxury trim group	$195	$324	—	$271	—	—
Rally RTS handling package	$227	$219	S	$228[11]	$157	$45
SJ option package	—	$502	—	—	—	—
Special Edition Trans Am package	—	—	$784	—	—	—
W50 Formula appearance package	—	—	$100	—	—	—
W66 Formula appearance package	$674	—	—	—	—	—
WS6 Special performance package	—	—	$481	—	—	—
YellowBird appearance package	—	—	$550	—	—	—

—= Not Available; S = Standard equipment. [1]Automatic climate control is available for $700 on LeMans, Grand Am, and Grand Prix, and for $738 on Catalina and Bonneville. [2]Other optional equipment required at extra cost (i.e., console). [3]Standard on Bonneville Brougham. [4]Front bucket seats standard on Sunbird, with console available. Available on any Grand LeMans model, but not available on LeMans. On full-size models, available only on Bonneville coupe. Leather Viscount bucket seats are available on Grand Prix LJ for $349, and on SJ for $319. [5]Canopy style vinyl roof on Firebird, Esprit, and Formula. Vinyl roof is not available on any Safari wagon model, or on Sunbird hatchback models. [6]Available only on 2-door coupe models. [7]Power brakes standard on Firebird Formula, and Trans Am. Power steering standard on Grand Am. Power 4-wheel disc brakes available on Firebird Formula and Trans Am for $162 extra. [8]Body-colored Rally II wheels also available. [9]Available only on Grand Am. [10]Available on LeMans Safari wagons. [11]Price is $45 on Grand Am.

Paint Colors

	Code		Code
Cameo White	11	Fremont Gold metallic[3]	63
Platinum	15	Barclay Brown metallic[8]	67
Dark Charcoal metallic[1]	16	Castilian Bronze metallic[7]	69
Starlight Black	19	Francisco Red[9]	72
Sterling Silver metallic[2]	20	Bordeaux Red metallic[10]	75
Baniff Blue metallic[3]	21	Montreux Maroon metallic[11]	76
Tahoe Blue metallic[4]	24	Agate Red[3]	77
Nightwatch Blue metallic[5]	29	Carousel Red[8]	79
Accent Yellow[6]	37	Fiero Bronze metallic[4]	80
Piedmont Green metallic[7]	44	Ontario Gray metallic[4]	84
Mariposa Yellow[7]	50	Richmond Gray[7]	85
Tahitian Yellow[8]	51		
Yellow Bird Yellow[6]	56		
Solar Gold metallic[4]	57		
Stetson Beige[4]	59		

In two-tone combinations, the first two digits indicate lower color and the next two digits are the upper color. Colors without footnotes are available on all models. Two-tone colors available only on LeMans and Grand Prix, for $180. Two-tone lower body accent paint standard on Grand Am. Double two-tone on Grand Prix is $288. Trans Am "Bird" hood decal available at $100 extra cost. [1]Available as two-tone or accent color in combination with Richmond Gray only. [2]Used only on Grand Prix with optional Sterling Silver Edition package. [3]Available on all models except Firebird. [4]Available on Firebird models only. [5]Available on all models except Grand Am, and Firebird Formula and Trans Am. [6]These colors used on Firebird w/Yellowbird option package. [7]Available on all models except Grand Am and Firebird. [8]Available only on base Firebird and Firebird Esprit. Also an accent color on Firebird Formula. [9]Available only on Sunbird, Firebird and Phoenix models. [10]Available only on LeMans, Grand Am, Catalina, and Bonneville models. [11]Available on all models except Grand Am. [12]Available on all Firebird models except Formula.

Sunbird

"Sunbird offers new thrills for the thrifty."

Nameplate year of origin: 1976.
Current bodystyle lifespan: 1976 through 1980.
Predecessor to this model: None.
Replacement for this model: J2000/Sunbird (1982 to 1993).
Percentage of division's production: 24.25%.
Corporate siblings: Buick Skyhawk, Chevrolet Monza, and Oldsmobile Starfire.
Primary competition: AMC, AMX, Dodge Omni 024 and Plymouth Horizon TC3.
Notable changes: Minor trim and detail changes.
Major standard equipment: All vinyl front bucket seats, cut-pile carpeting, floor shifter and floor-mounted parking brake w/mini-console, deluxe cushion three-spoke steering wheel, simulated rosewood appliqués on I/P, distinctive door and quarter panel trim, AM radio, tinted glass, bright front and rear window moldings, roof drip rail moldings, LH outside mirror, Sunbird exterior identification, argent colored grille, manual front disc brakes, hubcaps, and A78 × 13 BSW tires. Sport models add: Custom all-vinyl bucket seats, padded door trim, body-colored door handle inserts, dual body colored sport mirrors w/LH remote, acoustical insulation package, bright windowsill moldings, bright wheel opening moldings, bright rocker panel moldings, bright rear end panel trim, chrome grille trim, custom wheel covers, and BR78 × 13 WSW tires. Hatchback adds: Fold-down rear seat, load-floor and rear seat back carpeting, and beltline molding.

Measurements

	Coupe	Hatchback
Wheelbase	97.0"	97.0"
Length	179.2"	179.2"
Width	65.4"	65.4"
Height	49.8"	50.2"
Legroom — front	43.1"	43.1"
Legroom — rear	29.2"	29.6"
Headroom — front	37.6"	37.7"
Headroom — rear	37.2"	35.3"
Cargo capacity (cu. ft.)	6.6	27.8*
Fuel capacity (gals.)	18.5	18.5

Capacity with rear seat down.

Models Available

	Model No.	Base MSRP	Change from LY	Shipping Wt. (lbs.)	Model Year Production	Change from LY
Sunbird 2-Door Coupe	E27	$4,623	+15.11%	2603	105,847	+160.96%
Sunbird 2-Door Hatchback Coupe	E07	$4,808	NEW	2651	NA*	NEW
Sunbird Sport 2-Door Coupe	M27	$4,885	+14.30%	2609	29,180	-3.01%
Sunbird Sport Hatch 2-Door Hatchback Coupe	M07	$4,996	+14.09%	2657	52,952	+118.62%
TOTALS	*Avg. price*	$4,828	+13.67%	*Production*	187,979	+92.27%

Production of Hatchback coupe, model E07, included with Sport Hatch coupe, model M07.

Phoenix

"Practically everything about Phoenix was reengineered, including the way it drives, turns and stops."

Nameplate year of origin: 1977.
Current bodystyle lifespan: 1980 through 1984.
Predecessor to this model: Ventura (1975 to 1977); and Phoenix (1977 to 1979).
Replacement for this model: Grand Am (1985 to 1991).
Percentage of division's production: 23.00%.
Corporate siblings: Buick Skylark, Chevrolet Citation, and Oldsmobile Omega.
Primary competition: AMC Concord, Dodge Aspen, and Mercury Zephyr.
Notable changes: Completely redesigned.
Major standard equipment: Cloth-and-vinyl front bench seat, cut-pile carpeting, color-keyed deluxe cushion steering wheel, black I/P trim with simulated brushed aluminum center stack trim, front and rear door armrests and ashtrays, AM radio, door-actuated dome light switches, bright

Measurements

	Coupe	HBK Sedan
Wheelbase	104.9"	104.9"
Length	182.1"	179.3"
Width	69.1"	69.6"
Height	NA	NA
Legroom — front	42.0"	42.0"
Legroom — rear	34.6"	35.5"
Headroom — front	38.2"	38.2"
Headroom — rear	37.7"	37.5"
Cargo capacity (cu. ft.)	13.9	40.9*
Fuel capacity (gals.)	14.0	14.0

Cargo capacity for hatchback with rear seat folded down.

1980

front and rear window moldings, bright side window reveal moldings, bright window sill moldings, bright bumper rub strips, manual rack-and-pinion steering, manual front disc brakes, hubcaps, and P185/80R13 BSW tires. Hatchback adds: Fold-down rear seat, load floor carpeting w/carpeted sidewalls, bright wheel opening moldings, and bright narrow rocker panel moldings. LJ adds: Luxury cloth front notchback seat w/fold-down center armrest, carpeted lower door panel trim, color-keyed luxury cushion steering wheel, LJ crest on I/P, removable cargo cover (hatchback only), added acoustical insulation, bright wide rocker panel moldings, body-color door handle inserts, bright roof drip rail moldings, LJ identification, stand-up hood ornament w/hood windsplit molding, and deluxe wheel covers.

Models Available

	Model No.	Base MSRP	Change from LY	Shipping Wt. (lbs.)	Model Year Production	Change from LY
Phoenix 2-Door Coupe	Y37	$5,465	+33.65%	2496	49,485	+435.96%
Phoenix 5-Door Hatchback Sedan	Y68	$5,656	+35.02%	2539	72,875	+589.78%
Phoenix LJ 2-Door Coupe	Z37	$5,936	+29.35%	2531	23,674	+1196.50%
Phoenix LJ 5-Door Hatchback Sedan	Z68	$6,127	+30.67%	2591	32,257	+1270.89%
TOTALS	Avg. price	$5,796	+32.97%	Production	178,291	+616.03%

Firebird

"A new age of performance for those fabulous Firebirds."

Nameplate year of origin: 1967.
Current bodystyle lifespan: 1970 through 1981.
Predecessor to this model: Firebird (1967 to 1969).
Replacement for this model: Firebird (1982 to 1992).
Percentage of division's production: 13.85%.
Corporate siblings: Chevrolet Camaro.
Primary competition: Ford Mustang and Mercury Capri.
Notable changes: New turbocharged engine and minor trim and detail changes.
Major standard equipment: All-vinyl front bucket seats, console, cut-pile carpeting, deluxe cushion steering wheel, simulated rosewood I/P appliqué, ashtray light, bright front and rear window moldings, Endura front and rear bumpers, trunk floor mat, variable-ratio power steering, manual front disc brakes, RTS package, hubcaps,

Measurements

Wheelbase	108.2"
Length	196.8"
Width	73.0"
Height	50.4"
Legroom — front	43.9"
Legroom — rear	28.4"
Headroom — front	36.9"
Headroom — rear	35.7"
Cargo capacity (cu. ft.)	7.1
Fuel capacity (gals.)	20.8

and 205/75R15 BSW tires. Esprit adds: Custom all-vinyl front bucket seats, distinctive door trim panels w/integral assist strap, I/P assist straps, luxury cushion steering wheel, custom pedal trim plates, rear quarter ashtray, added acoustical insulation, dual body-colored mirror w/LH remote, body-colored door handle inserts, bright roof drip rail and belt reveal moldings, bright rear hood edge molding, bright wheel opening and rocker panel moldings, and deluxe wheel covers. Formula adds: Luxury cushion steering wheel, machine-turned I/P trim plate, rally gauges w/quartz clock, blacked-out grille, dual body-colored mirror w/LH remote, Formula identification, steel hood w/dual simulated hood scoops, power brakes, Trans Am front and rear stabilizer bars, Rally RTS package, Rally II wheels w/trim rings, and 225/70R15 BSW tires. Trans Am adds: Formula steering wheel, machine-turned I/P trim plate, rally gauges w/quartz clock and tachometer, dual body-colored mirror w/LH remote, blacked-out grille, front center air dam, rear deck spoiler, wheel opening air deflectors, front fender air extractors, Trans Am identification, shaker hood scoop, power brakes, power flex fan, Safe-T-Track differential, firm control shocks, dual chrome splitter tailpipe extensions, Rally RTS package, Rally II wheels w/trim rings, and 225/70R15 BSW tires.

Models Available

	Model No.	Base MSRP	Change from LY	Shipping Wt. (lbs.)	Model Year Production	Change from LY
Firebird 2-Door Hardtop Coupe	S87	$5,948	+13.08%	3269	29,811	-22.85%
Firebird Esprit 2-Door Hardtop Coupe	T87	$6,311	+11.94%	3304	17,277	-44.00%
Firebird Formula 2-Door Hardtop Coupe	U87	$7,256	+10.54%	3410	9,356	-62.35%
Firebird Trans Am 2-Door Hardtop Coupe	W87	$7,480	+8.67%	3429	50,896	-53.57%
TOTALS	Avg. price	$6,749	-3.49%	Production	107,340	-49.24%

LeMans

"Roominess stays in style with Pontiac's new mid-size cars."

Nameplate year of origin: 1961 (as a Tempest subseries).
Current bodystyle lifespan: 1978 through 1981.
Predecessor to this model: LeMans (1973 to 1977).
Replacement for this model: 6000 (1982 to 1991).
Percentage of division's production: 10.63%.
Corporate siblings: Buick Century, Chevrolet Malibu, and
    Oldsmobile Cutlass.
Primary competition: Dodge Diplomat, Ford Granada, and
    Mercury Monarch.
Notable changes: New grille and minor trim and detail
    changes.
Major standard equipment: Dover II cloth-and-vinyl front
    bench seat, cut-pile carpeting, deluxe cushion steering
    wheel, cockpit style instrument panel design, simulated regal

Measurements

	Coupes	Sedans	Wagons
Wheelbase	108.1"	108.1"	108.1"
Length	198.6"	198.6"	197.8"
Width	72.4"	72.4"	72.6"
Height	53.5"	54.1"	54.5"
Legroom — front	42.8"	42.8"	42.8"
Legroom — rear	35.1"	38.0"	35.9"
Headroom — front	37.9"	38.7"	38.8"
Headroom — rear	37.8"	37.7"	38.8"
Cargo capacity (cu. ft.)	16.6	16.6	72.4
Fuel capacity (gals.)	18.1	18.1	18.1

walnut vinyl accents on I/P, door panels and steering wheel, bin-type glove box, bright front and rear window moldings, bright roof drip rail and rear quarter window trim, wheel opening moldings, trunk mat, power front disc brakes, hubcaps, and P185/75R14 BSW tires. Wagon adds: All-Morrokide vinyl front bench seat, textured steel cargo floor painted w/vinyl paint, swing-up tailgate window and drop-down tailgate, stationary rear door glass w/swing-out rear quarter vents, power front disc brakes, and P195/75R14 BSW tires. Grand LeMans adds: Choice of all-vinyl or cloth-and-vinyl notchback bench seat w/fold-down center armrest, luxury cushion steering wheel, padded upper door panels w/pull straps and carpeted lower panels, door lamp switches on all doors, added acoustical insulation, bright rear hood edge molding, bright wheel opening moldings, black rocker panels, bright window sill moldings, body color door handle inserts, lower bodyside protective molding, and stand-up hood ornament w/hood windsplit molding. Grand LeMans Safari adds: All-Morrokide vinyl front bench seat, Grand LeMans interior door and I/P trim, side window reveal moldings, choice of woodgrain exterior vinyl appliqué panels w/wide woodtone trim or two-tone paint, and simulated woodgrain door edge guards (with woodgrain trim selection only).

Models Available

	Model No.	Base MSRP	Change from LY	Shipping Wt. (lbs.)	Model Year Production	Change from LY
LeMans 2-Door Coupe	D27	$5,652	+12.34%	3024	9,110	-35.83%
LeMans 4-Door Sedan	D19	$5,758	+12.15%	3040	20,485	-24.01%
LeMans 4-Door, 2-Seat Safari Station Wagon	D35	$6,257	+11.99%	3232	12,912	-53.08%
Grand LeMans 2-Door Coupe	F27	$5,947	+12.17%	3050	6,477	-50.25%
Grand LeMans 4-Door Sedan	F19	$6,120	+12.71%	3089	18,561	-35.05%
Grand LeMans 4-Door, 2-Seat Safari Wagon	F35	$6,682	+12.66%	3265	14,832	-28.63%
TOTALS	*Avg. price*	$6,069	+12.34%	*Production*	82,377	-37.14%

Grand Am

"One exhilarating road machine that's designed to seat families in comfort."

Nameplate year of origin: 1973.
Current bodystyle lifespan: 1978 through 1980.
Predecessor to this model: Grand Am (1973 to 1975).
Replacement for this model: 6000 STE (1983 to 1989).
Percentage of division's production: 0.21%.
Corporate siblings: Buick Century, Chevrolet Malibu, and Oldsmobile Cutlass.
Primary competition: Dodge Aspen R/T, Ford Granada ESS and Mercury Monarch
    ESS.
Notable changes: New grille and minor trim and detail changes.

Measurements

Wheelbase	108.1"
Length	198.6"
Width	72.4"
Height	53.5"
Legroom — front	42.8"
Legroom — rear	35.1"
Headroom — front	37.9"
Headroom — rear	37.8"

1980

Major standard equipment: All-vinyl front bucket seats w/center floor console, cut-pile carpeting, custom sport steering wheel, padded upper door panels w/pull straps and carpeted lower panels, cockpit-style instrument cluster w/brushed aluminum I/P trim and custom-stitched outline appearance, bright front and rear window moldings, bright drip rail moldings, body color door handle inserts, lower bodyside protective molding, distinctive two-tone lower body and bumper paint treatment w/accent stripes, black-out taillamps, power steering, power front disc brakes, rally RTS suspension with front and rear stabilizer bars, Rally IV wheels, and 205/70R14 BSW tires.

Measurements (cont.)

Cargo capacity (cu. ft.)	16.6
Fuel capacity (gals.)	18.1

Models Available

	Model No.	Base MSRP	Change from LY	Shipping Wt. (lbs.)	Model Year Production	Change from LY
Grand Am 2-Door Coupe	G27	$7,504	+35.70%	3299	1,647	-59.04%
TOTALS	Avg. price	$7,504	+35.71%	Production	1,647	-72.02%

Grand Prix

"An uncommonly good year for Grand Prix luxury."

Nameplate year of origin: 1962.
Current bodystyle lifespan: 1978 through 1987.
Predecessor to this model: Grand Prix (1973 to 1977).
Replacement for this model: Grand Prix (1988 to 1996).
Percentage of division's production: 14.80%.
Corporate siblings: Buick Regal, Chevrolet Monte Carlo, and Oldsmobile Cutlass Supreme/Calais.
Primary competition: Dodge Mirada, Ford Thunderbird, and Mercury Cougar XR-7.
Notable changes: New grille and minor trim and detail changes.
Major standard equipment: Choice of cloth-and-vinyl or all-vinyl front notchback bench seat w/fold-down center armrest, cut-pile carpeting, deluxe cushion steering wheel, simulated regal walnut inlay trim on I/P, padded upper door panels w/lower panel carpeting and door pull straps, I/P courtesy lights, electric quartz clock, bright front and rear window moldings, bright side window sill and drip rail moldings, bright rear hood edge molding, stand-up hood ornament w/bright hood windsplit molding, bright wheel opening moldings, wide rocker panel moldings, trunk mat, front and rear bumper rub strips, power steering, power front disc brakes, RTS package, hubcaps, and 195/75R14 BSW tires. LJ adds: Velour "loose-pillow" look notchback front bench seat w/fold-down center armrest, custom stitched instrument panel, luxury cushion steering wheel, luxury carpet, bright hinged door pull handles, pedal trim plates, velour door panel inserts, dual body-colored sport mirrors w/LH remote control, LJ identification, wide rocker panel moldings w/extensions, and deluxe wheel covers. SJ adds: All-vinyl front bucket seats w/center floor console, custom color-keyed seat belts, custom stitched instrument panel, custom sport leather-wrapped steering wheel, brushed aluminum I/P trim, pedal trim plates, rally gauge cluster w/trip odometer, electric clock, lamp group, added acoustical insulation, dual body-colored sport mirrors w/LH remote control, wide rocker panel moldings w/extensions, bodyside accent tape stripes, RTS package, and custom finned wheel covers.

Measurements

Wheelbase	108.1"
Length	201.4"
Width	72.7"
Height	53.3"
Legroom — front	42.8"
Legroom — rear	36.3"
Headroom — front	37.6"
Headroom — rear	37.8"
Cargo capacity (cu. ft.)	16.1
Fuel capacity (gals.)	18.1

Models Available

	Model No.	Base MSRP	Change from LY	Shipping Wt. (lbs.)	Model Year Production	Change from LY
Grand Prix 2-Door Hardtop Coupe	J37	$6,621	+21.40%	3139	72,659	-41.97%
Grand Prix LJ 2-Door Hardtop Coupe	K37	$7,000	+6.79%	3279	34,968	-42.84%
Grand Prix SJ 2-Door Hardtop Coupe	H37	$7,597	+11.49%	3291	7,087	-70.54%
TOTALS	Avg. price	$7,073	+12.72%	Production	114,714	-45.39%

Catalina

"Discover a new dimension in full-size affordability:
the exciting new Catalina from Pontiac."

Nameplate year of origin: 1950 (as hardtop model designation), 1959 (as series).
Current bodystyle lifespan: 1977 through 1981.
Predecessor to this model: Catalina (1971 to 1976).
Replacement for this model: Parisienne (1983 to 1986) and Safari (1987 to 1989).
Percentage of division's production: 2.15%.
Corporate siblings: Buick LeSabre, Chevrolet Impala/Caprice, and Oldsmobile Delta 88.
Primary competition: Dodge St. Regis and Ford LTD.
Notable changes: Completely restyled.
Major standard equipment: Cloth-and-vinyl front bench seat, cut-pile carpeting, deluxe cushion steering wheel, simulated walnut I/P accent trim, ashtray w/light, glove box light, trunk mat, brushed aluminum B-pillar appliqué (coupe), bright windshield and rear window moldings, bright quarter window and roof drip rail moldings, bright wheel opening moldings, front and rear bumper rub strips, rear bumper guards, stand-up hood ornament w/hood windsplit molding, RTS package, hubcaps, and 205/75R15 BSW tires. Safari wagon adds: All-Morrokide vinyl front bench seat, three-way tailgate w/power-operated rear window, and 225/75R15 BSW tires.

Measurements

	2-door	4-door	Wagon
Wheelbase	116.0"	116.0"	116.0"
Length	214.0"	214.0"	216.7"
Width	76.4"	76.4"	79.9"
Height	54.5"	54.9"	58.0"
Legroom — front	42.2"	42.2"	42.4"
Legroom — rear	38.4"	39.0"	37.7"
Headroom — front	38.8"	39.4"	39.6"
Headroom — rear	38.2"	38.2"	39.3"
Cargo capacity (cu. ft.)	21.1	21.1	87.9
Fuel capacity (gals.)	25.0	25.0	22.0

Models Available

	Model No.	Base MSRP	Change from LY	Shipping Wt. (lbs.)	Model Year Production	Change from LY
Catalina 2-Door Coupe	L37	$6,703	+11.35%	3394	3,319	-38.65%
Catalina 4-Door Sedan	L69	$6,761	+11.27%	3419	10,408	-62.99%
Catalina Safari 4-Door, 2-Seat Station Wagon	L35	$7,362	+10.19%	3929	2,931	-78.05%
TOTALS	*Avg. price*	$6,942	+10.91%	*Production*	16,658	-64.47%

1980

Bonneville

"Pontiac announces a whole new dimension to full-size enjoyment."

Nameplate year of origin: 1957.
Current bodystyle lifespan: 1977 through 1981.
Predecessor to this model: Bonneville (1971 to 1976).
Replacement for this model: Bonneville "Model G" (1982 to 1986).
Percentage of division's production: 11.12%.
Corporate siblings: Buick LeSabre, Chevrolet Impala/Caprice, and Oldsmobile Delta 88.
Primary competition: Chrysler Newport and Mercury Marquis.
Notable changes: Completely restyled.
Major standard equipment: Choice of cloth-and-vinyl or all-vinyl notchback front seat w/fold-down center armrest, cut-pile carpeting, luxury door panels w/lower door panel carpeting, door pull straps, deluxe cushion steering wheel, simulated walnut vinyl I/P accents, courtesy light switches on all doors, ashtray w/light, glove box light, sunburst medallion on B-pillar appliqué (coupe) or C-pillar (sedan), luggage compartment mat and light, bright windshield and rear window moldings, bright hood rear edge molding, fixed rear quarter window, wide rocker panel moldings w/rear extensions, bright wheel opening moldings, stand-up hood ornament w/hood windsplit molding, rear

Measurements

	2-door	4-door	Wagon
Wheelbase	116.0"	116.0"	116.0"
Length	214.0"	214.0"	216.7"
Width	76.4"	76.4"	79.9"
Height	54.5"	54.9"	58.0"
Legroom — front	42.2"	42.2"	42.4"
Legroom — rear	38.4"	39.0"	37.7"
Headroom — front	38.8"	39.4"	39.6"
Headroom — rear	38.2"	38.2"	39.3"
Cargo capacity (cu. ft.)	21.1	21.1	87.9
Fuel capacity (gals.)	25.0	25.0	22.0

fender skirts, RTS package, deluxe wheel covers, and 205/75R15 BSW tires. Safari wagon adds: All-Morrokide vinyl front bench seat, door pull straps, three-way tailgate w/power-operated rear window, simulated woodgrain Safari siding and tailgate appliqués, and 225/75R15 BSW tires; deletes rear fender skirts. Brougham adds: Velour "loose-pillow" look luxury trim 60/40 split front seat w/fold-down center armrest, custom door panels w/pull straps and lower panel carpeting, luxury cushion steering wheel, RH visor vanity mirror, electric quartz clock, power windows, rear quarter courtesy lights, custom pedal trim plates, chrome LH remote-control mirror, added acoustical insulation, bright window sill moldings, and velour luggage compartment trim w/spare tire cover and cargo lamp.

Models Available

	Model No.	Base MSRP	Change from LY	Shipping Wt. (lbs.)	Model Year Production	Change from LY
Bonneville 2-Door Coupe	N37	$7,038	+6.75%	3431	16,771	-50.86%
Bonneville 4-Door Sedan	N69	$7,167	+6.68%	3478	26,112	-63.69%
Bonneville Safari 4-Door, 2-Seat Station Wagon	N35	$7,958	+12.88%	3949	5,309	-68.63%
Bonneville Brougham 2-Door Coupe	Q37	$7,888	+6.67%	3571	16,771	-57.10%
Bonneville Brougham 4-Door Sedan	Q69	$8,080	+6.54%	3639	21,249	+22.37%
TOTALS	Avg. price	$7,626	+7.90%	Production	86,212	-51.95%

Appendices

I. Minor Makes and Replicars

A few small, independent automakers operated through the 1973–1980 period, ranging from specialty carmakers to manufacturers of replicars that were becoming more popular. This appendix will cover both replicars and specialty cars, which were produced in much smaller numbers than the regular production cars of the four major manufacturers that are fully covered within this book.

Replicars

There were many manufacturers of replicars, which became big business during the 1970s as the value of vintage collector cars began to rise. The following is a list of some of the better-known replicar companies between 1973 and 1980, showing the years of production during this period and the products that they offered:

- Auburn-Cord-Duesenberg Co., Broken Arrow, Oklahoma, 1973–1980: Auburn Roadster and Phaeton and Auburn 886 boattail speedsters.
- Auburn Speedsters Co., Buffalo, New York, 1973: Auburn speedsters.
- Duesenberg Corp., Inglewood, California, 1973–1980: Duesenberg Roadsters and Model J speedster.
- Glassic Motor Car Co., Palm Beach, Florida, 1973–1976: Model A Ford roadsters, and Romulus Auburn Speedster (1975–1976).
- Replicars, Inc., West Palm Beach, Florida, 1977–1980: Model A Ford roadsters, phaetons and sedans.
- SS Automobiles Inc./Excalibur Automobile Corp., Milwaukee, WI, 1973–1980: Excalibur roadsters and phaetons, based on 1930s vintage Mercedes roadster.
- Stutz Motor Car of America, Inc., New York City, NY,

1973–1980: Blackhawk coupes, powered by Pontiac engines.
- Williams Corp., Tulsa, OK, 1973–1975: Blackhawk coupes, based on Pontiac Grand Prix chassis.

Minor Makes

Aside from the Checker, these cars will not be covered in full detail, but the more notable are mentioned here for reference. Checker, best known for its cabs, continued to produce the Marathon line of cars for the general public through 1982. The Checker automobiles are covered at the end of this section of the appendix.

Avanti II, 1973–1980

On December 9, 1963, Studebaker announced the end of car and truck manufacturing in South Bend, Indiana, and the consolidation of all vehicle manufacturing in its Hamilton, Ontario, Canada plant. At that point, the company dropped the Avanti, the Gran Turismo Hawk, and all pickups and trucks in order to focus on sedans, coupes and station wagons. Only 4,643 Avantis, both 1963 and 1964 models, had been produced by the time Studebaker closed the South Bend factory on December 20, 1963. The Avanti model name, body molds, tooling and plant space were sold to two South Bend Studebaker dealers, Nate Altman and Leo Newman. They introduced a slightly modified version of the car in 1965 under the brand name "Avanti II," but neither it nor subsequent models assembled by a succession of entrepreneurs had any further association with either the Studebaker Corporation or the Studebaker brand name. The two dealers who purchased the Avanti rights would continue making the car under the Avanti II name, but lacking an engine they chose to purchase 327 CID V8 engines used in the Chevrolet Corvette. Each car was meticulously hand-built to order in very small numbers. The Avanti II's engine evolved from the 327 to the 350, the 400, and finally the 305, all sourced from Chevrolet Motor Division of General Motors. All Avanti IIs were built on leftover Studebaker chassis until 1987, though the Avanti II name remained only through 1983 when the company was sold to Steve Blake.

Styling of the Avanti II was nearly identical to that of the original Studebaker Avanti of 1963 and 1964. Changes made by the time the 1973 models were introduced included larger bumpers with black rub pads, and square headlight surrounds among the more noticeable features. Under the hood from 1973 through 1976 was a Chevy-built 400 CID V8 engine, and from 1977 to 1980 a Chevy-built 350 CID V8 engine. The two-door sport coupe remained the only body style available, though in later years there would be sedans and convertibles. Overall dimensions during this

period stayed true to the originals 109-inch wheelbase and 192.5-inch overall length. Prices and estimated production are as follows:

	1973	1974	1975	1976	1977	1978	1979	1980
Base MSRP	$8,145	$8,645	$9,945	$12,195	$13,195	$15,970	$17,670	$18,995
Production (est.)	106	123	125	175	180	190	195	190

BRICKLIN, 1974–1975

Malcolm Bricklin, who made millions in the hardware and plumbing supply distributorship business in Florida, and who set up the first Subaru distributorship for the United States, known as Subaru of America, in 1971, had set up his own company by 1973 in New Brunswick, Canada, to build 2-seat plastic-bodied "sports-safety" cars as they were called,

Top and bottom: 1976 Avanti II   *Top:* 1975 Bricklin SV1. *Bottom:* 1975 Bricklin SV1 interior

due to their high content of standard safety features. High costs, production quality problems, and assembly line issues led to receivership in September 1975. The first year was the 1974 Bricklin SV-1 two-door gullwing sport coupe. It used an American Motors 360 CID, 220-hp, 4-barrel V8 engine, and sold for $7,490. The 1975 version was nearly identical, but was equipped with a Ford 351 CID, 175-hp, 2-barrel V8 engine, mated to a Ford 3-speed automatic transmission, and sold for $9,775. A total of approximately 2,850 were built over the two-year period of production. Basic specifications are as follows: Wheelbase, 96"; Length, 178.6"; Width, 67.6"; Height, 48.3"; Weight, approximately 3,450 pounds.

CitiCar, 1974–1977

Sebring Vanguard, Inc., based in Sebring, Florida, built the most successful electric car of the period. "Tomorrow's transportation here today" is how the company advertised their fully electric commuter car, a small two-passenger runabout with a boxy appearance and flat sloping nose. The electric car used a GE six volt motor with a range of about 50 miles, and its batteries were advertised as being capable of recharging more than 500 times. Approximately 2300 CitiCars were sold during their four-year lifespan. The cars had a 65.5" wheelbase, a 94" overall length, a height of 60", and a width of 54". The base price of the 1974 model was $2,988.

1975 CitiCar

Checker

As mentioned above, the Checker is covered in detail similar to the major manufacturers, to the extent possible. A brief overview of the company's history is in order. Checker Motors Corporation's history began in 1908 with the Deschaum Motor Car Company. Over the next fourteen years,

through a series of buy-outs and mergers, the company had a variety of names and owners. Sometime during the 1910s Checker Taxi of Chicago, Illinois, was formed, and after subjecting its cabs to years of use and thousands of miles of wear and tear, the company found that it needed more durable and longer lasting taxis. In 1920 Checker Taxi found a solution and contracted with the Commonwealth Motor Company to assemble taxicabs on the stronger Commonwealth chassis, with bodies supplied by the Markin Auto Body Corporation of Joliet, IL. This leads up to May 1922, after a merger was formed late in 1921 between a faltering Commonwealth Motor Company and the Markin Auto Body Corporation owned by Morris Markin. The new company became the Checker Cab Manufacturing Company. Feuds with rival companies were escalating, and as sales were quickly expanding to New York and other far-away destinations, the growing Checker Cab factory needed to expand or move, so it was moved to Kalamazoo, Michigan, in April 1923.

Checker took over the former Handley-Knight Company factory and the Dort Body Plant, and by June 18, 1923, the first Kalamazoo-built Checker rolled off of the assembly line. A variety of sales and production companies were started up, sold or bought over the next 35 years — including a short-lived cooperation with the Yellow Cab company, manufacturer of both cars and trucks, and owned by General Motors at the time, and a sale to E.L. Cord of Auburn-Cord-Duesenberg fame which was similarly short-lived — but soon Markin would be back at the helm and in control of his taxicab empire. Through all of this period up until 1959, Checker built cars for taxi, fleet and commercial use almost exclusively. However, they would build a car for a private consumer if requested.

The success of the Checker cabs and the public perception of durability and economy from these sturdy sedans persuaded Checker to enter the consumer market in 1959. The official introduction was made at the 1960 Chicago Auto Show on February 8, 1960, with the showing of a Checker Superba. The Superba, which was otherwise known as the A9 sedan, was introduced for the 1959 model year, and was an updated version of the A8 introduced in 1956, adding new fenders to accommodate quad headlamps, and revised front and rear end restyling. The Superba would be offered in two body styles, an eight-passenger, four-door sedan, and a six-passenger, 4-door station wagon. Each was available in a base or Special series. The Special had Superba script on the bodyside, along with additional exterior trim and nicer décor on the inside. Both models had very large cargo spaces, and the station wagon could carry 4' × 8' sheets of building materials flat and with the tailgate closed.

For the 1961 model year, the Superba Special name was changed to Marathon, and by 1964, the Superba name was dropped, and all models were known as Marathons. Through the years various limousine and other stretched models would be introduced. Also, for the 1964 model year, Checker switched from Lycoming Continental 6-cylinder engines to Chevrolet sixes and V8 engines exclusively. Checker would continue to use Chevrolet engines through its final cabs built in 1982.

For the 1973 model year, new aluminum bumpers replaced the former chromed bumpers, which helped to cut down on weight. Another small change was to add side marker lights where formerly reflectors had appeared. These were the last major visible changes to the bodies that Checker made. For 1974, the specially built eight-door Aerobus was discontinued, but it was later re-introduced for 1978 in a slightly different configuration, and then promptly discontinued again at the end of the 1978 season. For 1975, catalytic converters were added to keep up with federal emission standards. Also during the 1970s, Checker began using the full-size Chevrolet steering column assembly, including the steering wheel, shift lever and ignition switch. The fold-down rear jump seats were also eliminated due to failing required safety tests.

Reduced to its original four models, Checker suffered falling sales through the recession that began in 1979, and was struggling with all of the new government regulations being imposed on passenger vehicles. Extremely poor fuel mileage due to the Checker's tall, boxy shape and heavy weight made more modern sedans such as the Chevrolet Impala, Ford LTD and Plymouth Gran Fury more suitable taxi cabs. During 1979, V6 engines from Chevrolet were used, but their poor fuel economy in the heavy cabs left many companies no alternative but to convert the V6 to run on propane gas. Finally

1974 Checker Marathon 4-Door Station Wagon

with the body stamping dies being worn out after 20 years of continuous usage, many parts were not fitting properly, and repairs and replacement of fenders and doors became a problem. Lacking the resources to develop a new Checker model, and mindful of the evaporating market, Checker decided to end its auto manufacturing business. On July 12, 1982, after 60 years of production, the last Checker taxi rolled off the Kalamazoo assembly line in its original Chicago Checker Cab company colors of light green and cream.

For many years prior to 1982 and thereafter, Checker was in the business of stamping, blanking and manufacturing welded assemblies for many industries including the automotive business. On January 16, 2009, the company filed for Chapter 11 bankruptcy, and on April 3, 2009, Checker Motors Corporation announced to its employees that the plant would be closing on June 30, 2009, thus ending the history of a company once known as the "Rolls-Royce of taxis."

CHECKER

"Uncomplicated. Unpretentious. Honest."

Anyone who ever visited an American city of any size with taxi service, prior to 1985, most likely has seen or ridden in a Checker cab. Beginning with the 1960 model year, Checker built and sold cars to the public.

The design of the Checker cab sold between 1973 and 1980, first introduced in 1956 as the Model A-8, was given a slight facelift including its familiar dual headlights and horizontal crosshatch style grille before going into production for sale to the public in 1960. High roof and door lines aided ease of entry, and a six-window design for the sedan

combined with a high, upright seating position gave the car outstanding visibility in all directions. Interiors were spartan as could be expected in a car designed to be a taxi, but that lineage also meant that the Checker was tough and built to last. Much as the Volkswagen Beetle's advertisements proclaimed through the 1960s and early 1970s, Checker never made changes just for the sake of change. Throughout the Checker's lifetime, nearly every change made was to help the car meet federal requirements. Chevrolet engines had been employed since the 1965 model year, which helped when the changes required to meet emissions and fuel economy mandates came along. To meet the 1974 federal bumper requirements, heavy-duty argent colored shelf-style bumpers became standard, replacing the prior chrome bumpers. From 1974 onward, the bumpers were interchangeable from front to rear, saving not only initial assembly costs, but also replacement costs.

Many of the details that follow are based on the 1974 model year, including the advertising slogan shown. The format of information is similar to that used throughout the rest of this book, with changes made where appropriate to accommodate eight years worth of production. Prices for optional equipment are given for a variety of years, to show how inflation played a role in Checker's ultimate demise. Also note that a 129" wheelbase Marathon DeLuxe sedan was offered for the 1973 and 1974 model years, known as model A12-E, though specific sales numbers are unavailable for these models. Pricing for the extended sedan ran $200 higher than regular Marathon models for 1973, and $678 higher for the 1974 model year.

1974 Checker Marathon 4-Door
extended-wheelbase sedan

1974 Checker Marathon 4-Door Sedan

1974 Checker Marathon
4-Door Sedan interior

1974 Checker Marathon
4-Door Station Wagon interior

Introduction dates: Model year changes generally occurred during October, with no specific dates available.

Assembly plants: Kalamazoo, MI.

Data plate identification (VIN): Three sets of codes read as follow: First three to four digits indicate model (model number in model charts; A12E indicates 1973–1974 extended wheelbase sedan); second set of three to four digits indicates sequential production number; third set of five to six digits indicates sequential chassis number with first digit indicating model year (3 = 1973, 4=1974, etc.) and the next four digits indicating sequential number. If a sixth digit is included it indicates a V8 engine installed (*ex:* A = 350 CID V8 engine); otherwise it is assumed to be a six-cylinder engine. *Example:* A12W-2662-32598A is a 1973 Checker Marathon 4-Door Station Wagon, serial number 2662, chassis number 2598, with a 350 CID, 4-bbl. V8 engine.

Powertrains

Engine	Net HP	Engine Code	Transmission Availability		1973	1974	1975	1976	1977	1978	1979	1980
229 CID (3.8L), 2-bbl., V6	120	—	3-speed Turbo Hydra-matic		—	—	—	—	—	—	—	S
				MPG	—	—	—	—	—	—	—	NA

Engine	Net HP	Engine Code	Transmission Availability		1973	1974	1975	1976	1977	1978	1979	1980
250 CID (4.1L), 1-bbl., 6-cyl.	105	E	3-speed Turbo Hydra-matic		—	—	—	S	—	—	—	—
				MPG	—	—	—	17/23/19	—	—	—	—
250 CID (4.1L), 1-bbl., 6-cyl.	110	E	3-speed Turbo Hydra-matic		—	—	—	—	S	S	S	—
				MPG	—	—	—	—	NA	16/22/18	16	—
				Calif.	—	—	—	—	—	15/20/17	15	—
250 CID (4.1L), 2-bbl., 6-cyl.	100	E	3-speed Turbo Hydra-matic		S	S	S	—	—	—	—	—
				MPG	NA	NA	16/20	—	—	—	—	—
267 CID (4.3L), 2-bbl., V8	120	A	3-speed Turbo Hydra-matic		—	—	—	—	—	—	—	$237
				MPG	—	—	—	—	—	—	—	NA
305 CID (5.0L), 2-bbl., V8	145	C	3-speed Turbo Hydra-matic		—	—	—	—	$145	$179	$201	—
				MPG	—	—	—	—	NA	NA	NA	—
305 CID (5.0L), 4-bbl., V8	155	C	3-speed Turbo Hydra-matic		—	—	—	—	—	—	—	$214
				MPG	—	—	—	—	—	—	—	NA
350 CID (5.7L), 2-bbl., V8	145	A	3-speed Turbo Hydra-matic		$109	$109	$145	$145	—	—	—	—
				MPG	11.0	11.0	12/17	13/17/14	—	—	—	—
350 CID (5.7L), 4-bbl., V8	170	A	3-speed Turbo Hydra-matic		—	—	—	—	$211	$322	$322	—
				MPG	—	—	—	—	NA	12/14/13	12	—
350 CID (5.7L), 4-bbl., Diesel V8	125	—	3-speed Turbo Hydra-matic		—	—	—	—	—	—	—	$
				MPG	—	—	—	—	—	—	—	NA

Major Options

	1973	1974	1975	1976	1977	1978	1979	1980
Air conditioning	$355	$329	$362	$	$460	$474	$520	$579
Rear window defogger	$	$22	$28	$	$	$	$50	$54
Tinted glass	$	$23	$39	$	$	$	$52	$69
Auxiliary underseat heater	$	$46	$53	$	$	$83	$90	$98
Auxiliary rear seats (sedan only)	$	$31[1]	$53	$	$	$75	$84	$99
Carpeting, front	—	—	$	$	$	$	$45	$49
Carpeting, rear	$	$18	$	$	$	$	$48	$53
Inside day-night mirror	$	$7	$7	$	$	$	S	S
Power door locks, rear only	$	$47	$55	$	$	$75	$77	$92
Power door locks, all doors	—	—	$	$	$	$138	$141	$171
AM radio	$69	$69	$80	$	$	$99	$102	$114
AM/FM radio	$125	$125	$151	$	$	$165	$171	$192
Vinyl top	—	$121	$145	$164	$179	$194	$209	$230
Closed-in rear quarter windows[2]	—	$132	$132	$132	$132	$132	$132	$132
Rooftop carrier (wagon only)	$250	$250	—	—	—	—	—	—
Spot light, LH	$33	$33	$42	$	$	$	$63	$68

	1973	1974	1975	1976	1977	1978	1979	1980
Power steering	S	S	S	S	S	S	S	S
Power brakes, w/front disc	S	S	S	S	S	S	S	S
Stainless steel wheel covers	$15	$15	$16	$	$	$	S	S
Radial tires, HR78 × 15 BSW	—	$104	$134	$	$	$	S[3]	S[3]
White sidewall tires	$30	$30	$33	$	$	$	$50	$79

—= Not Available; S = Standard equipment.
[1]Requires HR78 × 15 tires: BSW for $104, WSW for $164.
[2]Requires vinyl top.
[3]1979–1980 standard tire size is P215/75R15 BSW.

Paint Colors

Available in 94 different color choices of DuPont Acrylic Enamel.
Two-tone paint available for $22 (1974); $30 (1975); $46 (1979); $55 (1980).

Marathon

Sedan — "The Practical Car."
Wagon — "The Little Giant."

Nameplate year of origin: 1961. (Checker Motors Corporation began in 1922, and public sales post–World War II began in 1960).
Current bodystyle lifespan: 1960 through 1982.
Predecessor to this model: None for public sale.
Replacement for this model: None; company ceased auto production in July 1982.
Major standard equipment: Choice of black nylon and vinyl interior or all-vinyl interior (in choice of five colors for 1974), padded door armrests, black instrument panel, black steering wheel and column, undercoating, black rubber rear fender guard molding, power steering, power front disc brakes, and G78 × 15 BSW tires. Deluxe adds: 129" wheelbase.

Measurements

	Sedan	Wagon	Deluxe
Wheelbase	120.0"	120.0"	129.0"
Length	205.0"	205.0"	212.0"
Width	76.0"	76.0"	76.0"
Cargo capacity (cu. ft.)	14.0	92.2	14.0

Models Available

	Model No.	Base MSRP	Change from LY	Shipping Wt. (lbs.)	Est Year	Model Sales*	Change from LY
1973 Marathon 4-Door Sedan	A12	$3,955	+5.38%	3622		900	+5.88%
1973 Marathon 4-Door Station Wagon	A12W	$4,211	+5.04%	3825		**	**
1973 Marathon Deluxe 4-Door Sedan	A12E	$4,612	+6.96%	3822		**	**
1974 Marathon 4-Door Sedan	A12	$4,453	+12.59%	3720		900	0.00%
1974 Marathon 4-Door Station Wagon	A12W	$4,710	+11.85%	3925		**	**
1974 Marathon Deluxe 4-Door Sedan	A12E	$5,394	+16.96%	3920		**	**
1975 Marathon 4-Door Sedan	A12	$5,394	+21.13%	3774		450	-50.00%
1975 Marathon Deluxe 4-Door Sedan	A12E	$6,215	+15.22%	NA		**	**
1976 Marathon 4-Door Sedan	A12	$5,749	+22.06%	3775		400	-11.11%
1977 Marathon 4-Door Sedan	A12	$6,156	+14.13%	3775		335	-16.25%
1978 Marathon 4-Door Sedan	A12	$6,814	+18.52%	3765		300	-10.45%
1979 Marathon 4-Door Sedan	A12	$7,314	+18.81%	3740		270	-10.00%
1980 Marathon 4-Door Sedan	A12	$8,118	+19.14%	3680		225	-16.67%

*Estimated sales of non-taxi models.
**Accurate records are not available by body style.

II. History of Captive Imports, 1973–1980

What follows is a brief history of each of the captive imports sold in the 1973 through 1980 model years. They are presented in the order of their appearance on the American market.

1973–1980 Opel

Built in Russelsheim, Germany (1973–1975)
Built in Fujisawa, Kanagawa, Japan (1976–1980)

The Adam Opel AG company, founded in 1863 and producing automobiles since 1899, has been GM's German subsidiary since 1929. In 1958, observing the growing tide of imported cars entering the U.S. market, GM decided to import both the Opel and the English-built Vauxhall. The Opel was sold through Buick dealerships, and the Vauxhall through Pontiac dealerships.

Although the Vauxhall never really found its niche in America and was no longer imported after the 1962 model year, the Opel had slowly gathered a loyal following, partly as an effect of the owner loyalty Buick dealers had earned and partly as an acknowledgment of Opel's quality. It didn't hurt that the early Opels had a 1950s Buick look. During the mid-sixties, when Volkswagen Beetles were rapidly rising on the sales charts, the Opel models were restyled, and the much more stylish and modern looking Kadett series was introduced. Sales quickly improved. In 1968, a stylish sports coupe, the Opel GT, was introduced and quickly earned the nickname of "mini 'Vette," for its similarities to the new-for-1968 Chevrolet Corvette with its new "Mako Shark" styling.

In the early 1970s, Opel was holding its own, and for 1971 it introduced a mildly restyled Kadett as well as a new model named the 1900. The name, derived from the 1.9 liter 4-cylinder engine, was not new, but this was a new stand-alone series added alongside the Kadett and GT. The Opel 1900 came in two- and four-door sedan variations as well as a two-door station wagon model. This was the largest Opel line ever available in the United States. Introduced at the same time was a stylish coupe based on the new Opel 1900 platform, known as the Manta, but not officially labeled as such until the 1973 model year. This new model was developed as a direct replacement for the outdated Rallye Kadett model. Two versions of the new Manta were offered, standard and Rallye. The latter sported a racy matte-black hood finish, twin upper-bodyside tape stripes running up and over the trunklid, fog lights, dual-tip chrome exhaust extension on a single tailpipe, a full complement of gauges (tachometer, oil pressure, ammeter, and clock), and exposed-lug wheels with chrome trim rings. Aside from its stylish good looks, the Manta was generally regarded as one of the better handling cars of its day, nearing the capabilities of period Porsche and BMW automobiles. The Kadett series was dropped at the end of the 1972 model year, and remaining Opel models were relatively unchanged.

By 1973, the U.S. automotive market was beginning to see a turn away from sporty cars and towards luxury cars, and the Manta followed suit with a new Luxus version. Luxus, meaning "luxury" in German, was a new name used by Buick in nearly all of its 1973 series to denote the high end, luxury model. For the Manta, the Luxus was color coordinated in blues, silvers, or maroons, and fitted with corduroy upholstery. As always, the Manta and all Opels were well equipped for economy cars of their day. The only options available were tinted glass, electric rear-window defroster, whitewalls, radio, dealer-installed air conditioning, and vinyl roof.

A strong German Deutschmark was causing prices to rise rapidly in the U.S. market, and by 1974, inflated prices were hurting sales. The 2-seater Opel GT was gone from the 1974 lineup. The remaining 1900 and Manta lines carried about 160 pounds more weight and five inches greater length, thanks to the new 5-mph bumper standards. Changes included a redesigned instrument panel, reclining front seats, optional radial tires, Luxus wheels as an option on standard models, and a new Sportwagon package that added most of the Manta Rallye model's equipment to the small station wagon. The base Manta coupe was the lone surviving Manta model for 1975, but it gained an impressive new fuel-injection system for the 1.9L 4-cylinder engine, helping Opel regain some of its sporty image lost in 1971, when its engines' power outputs were cut back under General Motors' mandate that all engines be fitted to run on regular, low-lead, or no-lead fuel. By this time, as prices continued to rise, General Motors decided to end the two-decade importation of German-built Opels, and move to a new model for Buick to import as the Opel.

In 1976, American Buick/Opel dealers began marketing a new "Opel by Isuzu" produced by Isuzu in Japan, a company in which GM had purchased a 34.2 percent share of in 1971. Initially only 2-door coupes were available, but by March of 1977, a 4-door sedan was added to the line. For the 1978 season, the car was rebadged as the "Buick Opel." The new Isuzu-built car had its roots in Germany as one of General Motors' first "global" platforms, development of which began in 1970. Known as the T-car, the new Opel started life on the road in Germany for the 1973 model year as the third-generation Opel Kadett, which was not imported to North America. The T-car platform spawned many cars around the world, to include the Opel Isuzu (a.k.a. Buick Opel) and the Chevrolet Chevette, both introduced for the 1976 model year. More details on the T-car are at the end of this Opel section.

Isuzu-built Opels never quite reached the popularity of the German-built cars — in spite of, or possibly as a result of, a 1977 marketing campaign that gave weekly updates on the performance of the Opel Isuzu in a variety of competitions with its main rivals, the VW Rabbit, Toyota Corolla and Honda Civic. Ultimately the Opel came in second place to the Rabbit but handily outscored its Japanese competitors. Sales of the Buick/Opel built by Isuzu ended with the 1980 model year, as Isuzu wanted to complement its truck line with a return to the U.S. car market after a long absence. So, for 1981, the Opel Isuzu was slightly restyled and rebadged as the Isuzu I-Mark, and sold through a new Isuzu dealer network, which at the beginning largely consisted of Buick dealers. As a historical note, Chevrolet had sold rebadged Isuzu KB pickups in the United States from 1972 through 1980 as the LUV (light-utility vehicle).

Originally, plans for the T-car did not include producing or selling the car in the United States or Canada. Then the 1973 oil crisis created a dramatic shift in the marketplace. Suddenly, the large V8 powered cars that were so popular among American consumers were sitting unsold on dealer lots. Chevrolet Motor Division investigated ways to quickly bring a new car to market that would meet the rising demand for economical cars. In early 1974, GM management approved plans to produce a version of the T-car in America, to be marketed as the Chevrolet Chevette. The exterior of the U.S. Chevette was similar to the Vauxhall Chevette 2-door hatchback, with changes to meet U.S. regulations such as 5-mph front and rear bumpers and sealed beam headlamps. It was determined that the Chevette engine would be based on an Opel overhead cam 4-cylinder design, instead of the Vauxhall's cam-in-block engine. In an attempt to meet the tastes of American customers, several "upscale" options were made available on the Chevette, including a vinyl top, tilt steering wheel, and a Custom Exterior Trim Package with various chrome trim pieces. There was even a "Woody" version, which had exterior vinyl wood appliqués similar to many station wagons of the era.

In September of 1975, Chevrolet unveiled the Chevette in Washington D.C. This location was chosen in part because the U.S. Congress has just recently passed legislation mandating Corporate Average Fuel Economy (CAFE) standards for automotive manufacturers. The Chevette went on sale in October 1975 as a 1976 model, after being rushed into production in only 18 months. All North American Chevette gasoline engines were produced at the Chevrolet engine plant in Flint, Michigan. The Chevette became the best selling car in America for 1979 and 1980,

1973–1975 Capri and 1976–1977 Capri II

Built in Cologne, Saarlouis, Germany

Originally developed as a "Mustang for the European market," the Ford Capri was a sportily styled 2-door with traditional American pony car long hood/short deck proportions. In the United States, the Mustang had a counterpart in the Mercury Cougar, but it had grown to be quite a large car by the early 1970s, and Ford was looking for a way to market the Capri in North America. The decision was made to bring the Ford Capri to America under the name of "Capri," and it was imported for Lincoln-Mercury. Thus it was available for order, and could be serviced through any Lincoln-Mercury dealer.

The first cars were sold in the U.S. during April 1970, fitted with a British designed 1.6 liter 4-cylinder engine; for the 1971 season, a 2.0 liter 4-cylinder engine (the same as used in the Ford Pinto) became standard. Late in the 1972 model year, a 2.6 liter V6 was offered, so for 1973, models equipped with the 2.0 liter engine became known as the Capri 2000, and those with the V6 engine were tagged the Capri 2600. The 1973 models were also given a facelift to meet the new front bumper standards and also received a new interior, revised grille, and larger taillights. For 1974, the Capri adopted the new German built 2.8 liter V6, which replaced the German-built 2.6 liter V6 design, as well as new rear bumpers to meet the mandated 5-mph crash test requirements. Beginning in 1974, the bumpers were covered in body colored plastic. Technically there were not 1975 models, though Ford listed them in its catalogs. It is assumed that Capris sold in the 1975 model year were leftover 1974 models.

The Capri was restyled to become a hatchback model, debuting in the United States as an early 1976 model with the new name Capri II. This naming convention aligned with the Mustang's 1974 rebadging as the Mustang II. Engine choices continued with the Cologne, Germany–built V6 engine and the 2.3 liter 4-cylinder built in Lima, Ohio. The last Capri II models were shipped from Europe at the end of the 1977 model year, and remaining cars were sold as 1978 models. Special "Black Cat" models were sold in 1976, and other colors were added for the special edition in 1977 such as Crimson and White. The 1979 model Capris were built in America on Ford's new "Fox" chassis, which was shared with Ford's Mustang as well as the Ford Fairmont and Mercury Zephyr. Within the next few years, the "Fox" chassis would be the platform for numerous Ford and Mercury models, including the Thunderbird.

1973–1974 Pantera

Built in Modena, Italy

The Pantera was first sold by Ford in the U.S. in 1971, after Ford Motor Company reached a purchase agreement with Italian manufacturer DeTomaso Automobili. DeTomaso had earlier purchased the Ghia design and coach-building company to manufacture its then new Mangusta as a high performance GT to compete with Ferrari, Lamborghini and Corvette both on the racetrack and on the street. Under the Ford agreement, DeTomaso would provide the chassis and body of their new mid-engined GT model, and it would be marketed through Ford's Lincoln-Mercury division.

The Pantera utilized a full monocoque chassis and was powered by Ford's new 351 CID "Cleveland" V8 engine, rated at 310 gross horsepower. All of the expected race-in-spired components were included, along with a race-inspired cockpit design. The front compartment housed the brake booster, master cylinder, battery and tool kit; the rear trunk unit, easily removable for engine access, held a considerable amount of luggage. In late 1972, the "L" model was introduced, which featured black safety bumpers front and rear, improved cooling and air conditioning systems and other enhancements. For 1973, the "L" model continued with a revised dashboard and instrument layout. The last Panteras constructed for the U.S. market were built in late 1974, and included approximately 150 GTS models. The GTS featured fender flares and additional blackout paint trim. At the end of the 1974 model year, Ford and DeTomaso Automobili dissolved their business arrangement, and importation of the Pantera to the U.S. ceased. Between 1971 and 1973, 6,128 Panteras were produced. DeTomaso continued to produce the Pantera, steadily increasing its performance capabilities while retaining the Ford engine, until 1991.

1973–1980 Dodge Colt

1976–1980 Plymouth Arrow

1977–1980 Dodge Challenger and Plymouth Sapporo

1979–1980 Dodge Colt and Plymouth Champ

Built in: Kurashiki, Okayama, Japan (Colt, Arrow and Champ)
Okazaki, Aichi, Japan (Challenger and Sapporo)

Chrysler bought a 15 percent stake in Japanese manufacturer Mitsubishi in 1971 and immediately began importing rebadged Mitsubishi automobiles. Mitsubishi had itself just completed a reorganization to set up a separate automotive division to concentrate on automobile sales separate from its truck line. The Dodge Colt, the first car to be imported for 1971, was based on Mitsubishi's Galant, which was then a two-year-old design. The Colt came in a full line of two- and four-door models, as well as a station wagon, with standard four-cylinder powerplants and rear wheel drive. A restyle came for 1973. In 1977 the Colt Coupe and sedan (only) moved to Mitsubishi's smaller Lancer platform. The wagon remained on the Galant platform, receiving a 1978 redesign. The Galant-based hardtop model remained in the line through 1978. The Plymouth Arrow was a hatchback model also derived from the Mitsubishi Lancer line. The 1979–1983 front-wheel-drive Dodge Colt and Plymouth Champ hatchbacks were twins to the Mitsubishi Mirage in Japan. The 1978–1983 Dodge Challenger and Plymouth Sapporo both came from the Mitsubishi Galant Lambda hardtop.

1973 Plymouth Cricket

Built in Ryton-on-Dunsmore, England

Seeking to have a European branch as did its chief rivals Ford and GM, the Chrysler Corporation had taken a substantial stake in Simca of France in 1958, and later Barreiros of Spain, and finally the Rootes Group of the United Kingdom in 1967. The new company became known as Chrysler Europe. At that time the Rootes Group built the Hillman, Humber and Sunbeam, which Chrysler had gradually withdrawn from the market. In 1970, the redesigned Hillman Avenger was introduced. Chrysler had wanted the Avenger to be a "world car," so a badge-engineered car named the Plymouth Cricket was introduced to North America, as well as other countries, for the 1971 model year. The car featured modern lines and American-influenced "coke-bottle" body-side styling. The main changes to Americanize the car included a more powerful 1.5 liter, 4-cylinder engine, side marker lights, and front disc brakes being added as standard equipment. A single barrel carburetor and manual choke combination was also standard. The Cricket came in only a 4-door sedan for 1971, and a station wagon model was added for 1972. Beginning in 1972 the single carburetor with automatic choke, a two-barrel carburetor, and air conditioning were all options. The two-door Hillman Avenger did not appear until the middle of the 1973 model year, by which time Chrysler had decided to pull the Cricket from the U.S. market, as the similarly sized and priced Dodge Colt was selling much better. Chrysler Europe was sold in 1978 to Peugeot for $1, and in return Peugeot acquired their two factories and all of Chrysler Europe's enormous debt. The Cricket name lived on in Canada, though, as Chrysler Canada replaced the British-built Plymouth Cricket with a rebadged Dodge Colt during the 1973 model year.

1978–1980 Ford Fiesta

Built in Cologne, Saarlouis, Germany

The Ford Fiesta, a front-wheel-drive subcompact available only as a 2-door hatchback, was launched in Europe for the 1976 model year. It would make its way to the United States for the 1978 model year with slightly different specifications and equipment. Fiestas sold in the United States were built in Germany; European-market cars were also produced in England and Spain. The Fiesta's three year run in the U.S. market, from 1978 to 1980, brought very little change. All U.S. models featured the more powerful 97 CID (1.6L) four-cylinder engine that was optional in Europe, fitted with a catalytic converter and air pump for U.S. emissions requirements, and paired with a four-speed manual transmission. Also added specifically for the U.S. market were energy-absorbing bumpers, side-marker lamps, round sealed-beam headlamps, improved crash protection (i.e., side door impact structure), as well as optional air conditioning which was not available in Europe. The Fiesta continued as part of Ford's European line and has gone through six generations to date.

In the summer of 2010, Fiesta returned to the U.S. market as a 2011 model.

1974–1980 Volkswagen Rabbit

Built in: New Stanton, Pennsylvania

While not a captive import, Volkswagen has several ties to American manufacturers during this period, so this tidbit of history is worthy of a brief note.

Volkswagen of America operated an assembly plant in the city of New Stanton, Pennsylvania, from 1978 to 1988. The facility built the original Rabbit, and later its replacement, the Golf. Originally built as a Chrysler factory in the 1960s, the unfinished buildings were well suited for the purpose of building cars. It had been fifty years since a foreign manufacturer had built automobiles in the U.S., but the VW plant was to be the first of many foreign nameplate plants to be built over the next thirty years. Chrysler had some other ties to Volkswagen during this period, buying a VW designed engine and modifying it with Chrysler heads for use as the standard powerplant in the 1978–1980 Dodge Omni and Plymouth Horizon front-wheel-drive hatchbacks. American Motors also purchased a four-cylinder Volkswagen engine which was offered in the 1977–1978 Gremlin and the 1979 Spirit, before switching to a Pontiac-built four-cylinder engine for 1980 and beyond.

III. Pace Cars and *Motor Trend* "Car of the Year" Winners

Pace Cars

By the 1973 through 1980 period, pace cars for the Indianapolis 500 mile race on Memorial Day weekend were a nearly sixty year tradition. And another tradition had begun by the mid–1960s, as manufacturers started offering pace car replicas for sale on dealer showroom floors. At first a few hundred a year might be sold, but by the seventies, sales of pace replicas usually ran into the thousands. Following are a listing of the pace car for each year with a picture of the actual pace car and one of the pace car replica when there is a visible difference. For the 1973 Cadillac Eldorado, there is not a difference, and some historians dispute whether any replicas were built, but it is believed that at least a hundred or so were available through dealerships.

1973 Cadillac Eldorado 2-Door Convertible

1974 Oldsmobile Cutlass S 2-Door Colonnade Hardtop Coupe
1975 Buick Century Custom 2-Door Colonnade Hardtop Coupe
1976 Buick Century Custom 2-Door Colonnade Hardtop Coupe

1973 Cadillac Eldorado Convertible Indianapolis 500 pace car

1977 Oldsmobile Delta 88 2-Door Coupe
1978 Chevrolet Corvette Coupe
1979 Ford Mustang 2-Door Hatchback Coupe
1980 Pontiac Firebird Trans Am 2-Door Coupe

1977 Oldsmobile Delta 88 Royale Indianapolis 500 pace car

1974 Oldsmobile Hurst/Olds Cutlass Indianapolis 500 pace car

1978 Chevrolet Corvette Indianapolis 500 pace car

1975 Buick Century Custom Indianapolis 500 pace car

1979 Ford Mustang Indianapolis 500 pace car

1976 Buick Century Custom Indianapolis 500 pace car

1979 Ford Mustang Indianapolis 500 pace car

1976 Buick Century Custom Indianapolis 500 pace car

Opposite: 1980 Pontiac Firebird Turbo Trans Am Indianapolis 500 pace car

Car of the Year

"Car of the Year" selections began with *Motor Trend* magazine back in 1949. By 1973, many other automotive magazines were issuing similar awards. However, the *Motor Trend* award was the most highly coveted award of the period. Below is a list of annual winners with a representative picture of each winner.

1973 Chevrolet Monte Carlo
1974 Ford Mustang II
1975 Chevrolet Monza 2+2
1976 Dodge Aspen and Plymouth Volaré
1977 Chevrolet Caprice
1978 Dodge Omni and Plymouth Horizon
1979 Buick Riviera S-Type
1980 Chevrolet Citation

1973 Chevrolet Monte Carlo

1977 Chevrolet Caprice

1974 Ford Mustang II

1978 Plymouth Horizon and Dodge Omni

1975 Chevrolet Monza 2+2 V8

1979 Buick Riviera S Type

1976 Plymouth Volaré and Dodge Aspen

1980 Chevrolet Citation

IV. OPTION GROUPS AND PACKAGES

The following is a detailed content list for the groups and packages listed in the yearly manufacturer "Option Groups and Packages" price listings. This appendix, arranged alphabetically by make, lists most if not all of the features included in each group or package. Unless otherwise noted, it is assumed that the features listed are in addition to or in place of otherwise standard features. See the model year price chart for model availability. Features often differ by model, trim level and year, and this is noted whenever possible; however, space limitations prevent every detail of every variation, or variations in price, from being included. Not all option group or packages available in a given year are included in this appendix or in the model year price charts. This list is intended to encompass the most popular, most distinctive and occasionally the most basic from the wide variety of option packages offered. Not listed are the emissions equipment packages typically required for cars to be sold in California or designated high-altitude areas, bodyside molding packages, most handling and suspension packages, and trailer towing packages.*

AMC

"360 Go" package: 360 CID V8, 4-bbl. engine, hood "T" stripe decal, black paint in rear panel, Rally-Pac instruments, handling package, cowl-air carburetor induction system, heavy-duty engine cooling, twin-grip differential, power disc brakes, E60 × 15 Polyglas® tires w/raised white letters, slot-style steel wheels w/Space-Saver spare tire.

"401 Go" package: 401 CID V8, 4-bbl. engine, hood "T" stripe decal, black paint in rear panel, Rally-Pac instru-

ments, handling package, cowl-air carburetor induction system, heavy-duty engine cooling, twin-grip differential, power disc brakes, E60 × 15 Polyglas® tires w/raised white letters, slot-style steel wheels w/Space-Saver spare tire.

AMX custom interior package: Reclining vinyl bucket seats, custom door panels, split rear seat back, day/night mirror, courtesy lights, and I/P package shelf.

AMX decal package: Black and orange decals on hood and liftgate (orange and gold on black cars).

AMX package: *(Requires 258 CID 6-cyl. or 304 CID V8 engine and 4-speed manual transmission. Automatic transmission can be ordered for difference in cost.) Interior:* Front floor console, rally instrumentation, tachometer, custom interior door trim panels w/assist straps, lower back panel molding, door and quarter window belt moldings, brushed aluminum I/P overlay, "AMX" interior graphics, and "Soft-Feel" sports steering wheel. *Exterior:* Front and rear painted bumpers with bumper guards and nerfing strips, front air dam, front and rear fender flares, rear window louvers, "AMX" bodyside, and rear body graphics, roof band w/ special insignia, LH remote and RH manual flat black rearview mirrors, blacked out features (grille, headlight bezels, door and quarter frames, lower back panel, and license plate depression), front sway bar, styled road wheels, and DR78 × 14 BSW tires

Barcelona package: Individual reclining seats in tan or black Knap knit fabric w/matching fabric on upper door panel, color-keyed 24 oz. cut pile carpeting w/matching inserts on lower door panels, color-keyed door pull straps and headliner, unique Barcelona hood ornament, nameplate on hood and deck lid, unique red/yellow pinstriping, and Barcelona medallion on glove box and front fenders. With tan

---

*Nearly all models in all years during the 1973–1980 period offered some type of trailering package, but the variations are so numerous that space prohibits including them. As an example, trailering packages could range in price from $12 for a light-duty version on a 1974 Ford Pinto to $146 for a Heavy-Duty Class III trailer-towing package on a 1979 Mercury Marquis. Prices may be higher on other makes. Additionally, other optional equipment may be required such as heavy duty cooling systems or larger tires.

interior: Tan color-keyed wheel covers, tan accents around grille, rear license plate area and in headlamp bezels. *1978 models only:* Individual reclining seats in velveteen crush fabric w/woven accent stripes, custom door trim panels, 24 oz. carpeting, Barcelona emblems on glove box and fenders, black trunk carpet, body color front and rear bumpers (coupe), two-tone paint (Golden Ginger/Sand Tan, or Autumn Red metallic/Claret metallic), landau padded vinyl roof w/opera quarter windows (coupe), full vinyl roof (sedan), dual remote control mirrors painted body color, standard bodyside scuff moldings deleted, rear sway bar, color-keyed slot styled wheels, and GR78 × 15 WSW tires.

Body protection group: Scuff moldings w/vinyl inserts, and nerfing strips for front and rear bumpers.

Brougham package: *Interior:* Individual reclining seats (1976 — Hunters plaid fabric in coupe, Custom Hyde Park fabric in sedan, and Sof-Touch vinyl in wagon), custom door trim panels w/assist straps and inserts, simulated woodgrain I/P overlay, and carpet floor covering throughout including trunk or cargo compartment. *Exterior:* Wheel discs, "Brougham" script on C-pillars, tailgate air deflector and roof luggage rack (wagon), hood paint stripes, bumper nerfing strips (coupe), rocker panel moldings (ex. wagon w/woodgrain), and back panel overlay on sedan. For coupes only, roll-down rear quarter windows, full-length bodyside scuff molding, grille perimeter and rear hood moldings, and license plate surround molding.

"Cardin" interior package: "Cardin" fabric trim on seats, door panels, and headliners, plus front fender emblems.

Convenience group: Dome/reading lamp (1973–1978), lighted visor vanity mirror (Spirit, 1979–80 AMX, Concord, and 1978-up Pacer), intermittent windshield wipers (Spirit, 1979–80 AMX, Concord, and 1978-up Pacer), electric clock (1973–1978), litter stowage container (1973–1977), dual horns (1973–1977), and headlights-on warning buzzer.

Custom trim package: Custom door panel and seat trim in pleated vinyl, carpeting, cargo area insulation, custom steering wheel, wheel opening moldings, and drip moldings.

Decor group: Wheel opening moldings, drip moldings (Gremlin and Hornet 1973–1975), hood rear edge molding (1975–1976 Matador), rocker panel moldings (Gremlin and Hornet 1973–1975), bumper nerfing strips (1975–1976 Matador coupe), grille moldings (1974 Matador X, 1975–1976 Matador coupe), and wheel covers (1976 Gremlin & Matador coupe).

"D/L" package: *(Not available with "X" package.)* Interior: Individual reclining front seats w/custom fabric (Hornet — tan fabric on sedans), Basketry fabric upholstery (Pacer 1975–77), specific "D/L" instrument panel trim (Pacer and Hornet sedans: woodgrain overlay), Custom padded steering wheel (Pacer), Custom door trim (Pacer: fabric inserts, door pull straps and lower door carpeting; Hornet: same, excluding fabric inserts), carpeted cargo area (Pacer), trunk mat

(Hornet sedans). Exterior: Wheel covers (Pacer and Hornet Sedans), color-keyed bodyside scuff moldings (Pacer), bumper nerfing strips (Pacer), front sway bar (Pacer), "D/L" ornamentation Pacer and Hornet Sportabout), Extra Quiet Insulation package (Hornet), woodgrain paneling (Hornet Sportabout: sides and rear), roof rack and air deflector (Hornet Sportabout), Exterior Décor Package (Pacer).

Eagle sport package: *(Available on 2-door and wagon only.)* Dual remote control mirrors, black grille insert, low gloss black Krayton flares and rocker panels, black bumpers w/nerfing strips, black taillamp treatment, black windshield and liftgate moldings, halogen headlamps and foglamps, "4 × 4" silver decal on lower front edge of front door, and P195/75R15 Goodyear Tiempo steel-belted radial tires.

Exterior décor package: Wheel opening moldings, rear hood edge moldings, upper door edge moldings, bright license plate moldings.

Extra Quiet insulation package: Undercoating, hood insulation. 1974-up also includes (except Gremlin and Javelin): cowl side panel insulation pads, rear wheelhouse absorption pads, asphaltic foam tape, cargo floor deadener and roof insulation.

Gauge package: Electric tachometer, ammeter, oil pressure gauge, water temperature gauge, (Pacer), manifold vacuum gauge (Spirit), and electric clock.

GT package: *(Requires 258 CID 6-cylinder engine.)* Black full-length console w/integral center armrest (Spirit), black leather-wrapped sport steering wheel and column (Spirit), black I/P w/Walnut Burl woodgrain overlays (Spirit), tachometer (Spirit), Extra Quiet sound insulation package (Gremlin), fiberglass front spoiler and front/rear fender flares (Gremlin); body colored front and rear bumpers (Gremlin), black bumpers w/nerfing strips and bumper guards (Spirit), "blacked-out" grille, headlight bezels, mirrors, wiper arms, door and quarter window frames, black rear panel area (Spirit), front stabilizer bar (Gremlin), five-spoke wheels w/trim rings, and DR70 × 14 BSW tires.

GT Rally-Tune suspension package: Heavy duty front and rear sway bars, heavy duty front disc and rear drum brakes, adjustable "Strider" shock absorbers, heavy duty strut rod bushings, heavy duty rear spring iso-clamp pads, heavy duty Hi-control rear leaf springs, and unique steering gears.

"Gucci" interior package: Multi-colored vinyl interior appointments, individual reclining seats, and "Gucci" emblem.

Interior appointment package: Instrument panel parcel shelf, glove box lock, glove box light, cigarette lighter.

Interior décor/convenience group: Dome/reading lamp, floor mats w/carpeted inserts, clock, storage/litter containers, "headlights-on" warning buzzer, and lighted visor mirror (non-lighted on Gremlin and Hornet).

Interior décor package: *(Gremlin Custom only.)* Interior appointment package, carpeted cargo area, and Extra Quiet insulation package.

Handling package: Heavy-duty springs and shock absorbers. Also includes a front sway bar on Gremlin, Hornet and Javelin 6-cylinder models, or rear sway bar on Matador and Ambassador.

LEVI'S® custom trim package: Spun nylon version of traditional blue denim LEVI'S® trim with LEVI'S® buttons, door panel, door mounted storage/litter container in blue denim, blue headlining and sun visors, and front fender LEVI'S® decal, plus carpeting, cargo area insulation and custom steering wheel, Extra Quiet insulation package (1974-up).

Light group: Trunk (or cargo area) light (except Gremlin), two courtesy lights, map light (except Gremlin & Hornet), glove box light (except Gremlin), parking brake warning light, headlights-on warning buzzer (1973–1978), liftgate switch for dome light (Hornet HBK and Sportabout, Concord HBK and wagon, Pacer, AMX, and Spirit Liftback), ashtray light (Matador), rear door dome lamp switches (Concord and Matador), engine compartment light (1978–1980).

"Oleg Cassini" package: *Interior:* Individual front seats w/black trim and copper buttons, Cassini Crest on head restraints, black door trim w/fabric inserts and buttons, black headliner, black instrument panel and steering wheel w/copper dials and overlays, and Cassini identification on glove box door, black carpet on trunk floor and spare wheel cover. *Exterior:* Copper accented grille and headlamp bezels, front fender medallion, vinyl roof, scuff moldings w/vinyl inserts and custom wheel covers w/copper accents.

Opera window-roof package: Padded vinyl roof with stationary opera window.

Performance package: Includes 258 CID 6-cylinder engine, 4-speed manual w/floor shift, heavy-duty springs and shocks, front sway bar, soft-feel sports steering wheel, I/P overlay, and gauges (clock, tachometer, amp, oil pressure, and coolant temperature, except on Gremlin and Hornet).

Protection group: Stainless steel door edge guards, color-keyed vinyl floor mats (front only for Gremlin), color-keyed vinyl floor mats w/carpeted inserts (1974-up Matador and Ambassador, except Wagons, and 1978-up Pacer w/D/L trim), and front and rear bumper nerfing strips (1976–1980).

Rally-Pac instrumentation package: Ammeter gauge, oil gauge, tachometer/clock "tick-tach" and 140-mph speedometer. Engine turned dash panel on AMX only.

Rally package: Tachometer, oil pressure gauge, ammeter gauge, manual front disc brakes, front sway bar (6-cyl. only), power steering (1974), black leather wrapped sports steering wheel, black steering column and instrument panel cluster.

Rear visibility package: Rear window defogger and rear window wiper/washer.

Silver Anniversary package: (Concord DL 2- and 4-Door sedans only.) Special Quick Silver and Arrowhead Silver metallic two-tone paint treatment, special wire wheel covers, black or russet corduroy interior w/individual reclining front seats, and Silver Anniversary instrument panel and exterior nameplate plaques.

Sport package: Front bucket seats in soft-feel vinyl, custom door trim panels (Concord), sports steering wheel (std. on Concord HBK), brushed aluminum I/P overlays (Concord), Extra-Quiet insulation package (Concord), wide rocker panel moldings (Concord), lower bodyside tape stripe (Concord), two-tone lower bodyside paint (Pacer), bodyside scuff moldings deleted (Concord), slot styled wheels, and DR78 × 14 tires.

Touring interior package: Individual reclining seats in tan "Sof-Touch" vinyl, matching tan headliner and sun visors, sports steering wheel, simulated woodgrain I/P overlay, carpeted lower door panels, tan door pull straps, and Extra Quiet insulation package.

Visibility Group: Remote-control outside LH mirror (chrome for 1973–1974 and all Matadors, color-keyed 1975-on), remote-control outside RH mirror (1977–1978 Matador, 1979–1980 Spirit and Concord), visor vanity mirror (1973–1976), 12" day/night inside mirror, intermittent-action windshield wipers (1973–1978, ex. 1974 Javelin), inside hood release (1973–1975), dual horns (1973–1974 Gremlin and Hornet), electric clock (1973–1975, except Gremlin) or fuel economy gauge (1975 Hornet), and cargo-net (1973 wagons).

"X" package: *(Not available with D/L package.) Interior:* Vinyl bucket seats, floor shift (Pacer), special "X" instrument panel (Pacer: woodgrain overlay; 1976 Gremlin and Matador: engine-turned finish; 1976 Hornet, Gremlin and Matador: "X" ornamentation), sports steering wheel (1976 Pacer, 1973–1974 Gremlin, 1973–1974 Hornet and 1976 Matador), custom door trim (1975–1976 Pacer—vinyl inserts, pull straps and lower door carpeting), Extra Quiet Insulation Package (1974–1975 Hornet Sportabout, 1976 all), interior appointment package (1973–1974 Gremlin), cargo area insulation (1973–1974 Gremlin). *Exterior:* Painted grille (1973 Gremlin) or black highlights on grille (1976 Hornet and Matador), specific tires (1976 Pacer: D78 × 14 BSW; Gremlin, 1974–1976 Hornet: D70 × 14 BSW; 1973 Hornet Sportabout: C78 × 14; 1976 Matador: FR78 × 14 BSW), slot-styled wheels (Pacer, Gremlin, 1973 Hornet and 1976 Matador), space saver spare tire, color-keyed bodyside scuff moldings (Pacer), bumper nerfing strips (Pacer), front sway bar, "X" ornamentation (1974–1978 Gremlin, 1976 Pacer), rally stripe (Hornet), full-length body stripe with "X" decal (1973 Gremlin and 1976 Matador), "Hockey Stick" side decals (1974–1978 Gremlin).

Buick

Accessory Group: *(For 1976 available only on Skyhawk and Skylark S models.)* Trunk/cargo area and courtesy lights, license plate frame, electric clock (1973, 1977–1980), electric digital clock (1974–1976), rear door jamb switch (1973–1976 Estate Wagon only), day/night rear view mirror (1976–1977 Skylark), cigar lighter (1976–1977 Skylark), and sunshade map light.

Acoustical package: Special insulation added to roof, floor, dashboard, doors, and between the cowl and fenders.

Appearance package: Wheel opening moldings, left-hand sport mirror (1976–1977 Skyhawk), bodyside stripes (1976–1977 Skyhawk), and roof drip moldings (1973–1975).

Century 350 package: (Excludes roof drip moldings) Gothic cloth and Madrid-grain vinyl bench seat, front and rear ashtrays, and "350" front fender tip identification.

Convenience Group: Day/night mirror (Skyhawk only), engine compartment light, glove box light, and "headlamps-on" indicator, rear compartment lighting (wagons), and sunshade map light (1976–1977 Century Custom and Regal).

Décor package: *(Sport Coupe only)* Blackout trim moldings (windshield, wipers, door pillars, license plate surround, taillamps, and rocker panel molding), blacked-out grille, dual sport mirrors, Designers' Accent paint treatment, and turbine wheels.

Designers' Accent option: *(Skyhawk only.)* Choice of bright red or bright yellow exterior, flat black accent along and below belt line, "Hawk" decal on hood, rear spoiler, specially-tuned exhaust system, and deluxe wheel covers.

Exterior molding package: Rocker panel molding (wide molding available), wheel opening moldings, roof drip and rear end moldings, belt reveal and window frame moldings, hood ornament and windsplit moldings.

FE2 Rallye ride and handling package: Rear stabilizer bar, and fast-ratio power steering.

(F40) Firm ride and handling package: Rear stabilizer bar (Skyhawk only), larger diameter front stabilizer bar (1973–1976), heavy-duty shock absorbers, springs and wheels.

F41 Rallye ride and handling package: Larger rear stabilizer bar and heavy-duty struts and shocks.

Free Spirit package: Exterior tape stripes and "Free Spirit" logo w/eagle.

Gran Sport package: Oxen-grain and Madrid-grain vinyl bench seat (1973–1974), instrument gauges and electric clock, glove compartment light, courtesy light, ashtray light, specific rallye firm ride and handling, wheel opening moldings, GS-specific blackout grille and headlamp treatment, GS accent stripes, and GS ornamentation.

GS ride and handling package: Firm ride and handling suspension, and specific GS ornamentation.

GSX package: Special blacked out grille, distinctive bodyside paint striping, dual sport mirrors (driver side remote, passenger side manual), special GSX emblems inside and out, red or white exterior finish w/white bucket seats and red interior accents, and wire wheel covers.

Indianapolis 500 pace car replica package: *1975 Century Custom 2-Door Colonnade hardtop coupe:* White vinyl bucket seats w/Glacier Blue interior trim and carpet, Hurst

1975 Buick Century Custom Indianapolis 500 pace car replica

1975 Buick Century Custom Indianapolis 500 pace car replica

1976 Buick Century Custom Indianapolis 500 pace car replica

1976 Buick Century Custom Indianapolis 500 pace car replica

Hatch (T-tops), white exterior paint, white rally wheels w/ trim rings, blackout trim, "Free Spirit" Indy 500 decal package, and 350 CID, 4bbl. V8 engine. *1976 Century Custom 2-Door Colonnade hardtop coupe:* Silver exterior paint, stainless steel wrap-over roof band, rear spoiler, "Free Spirit" Indy 500 decal package, and 231 CID Turbocharged V6 engine.

Light group: Engine compartment light, trunk/cargo area light, ashtray light, sunshade map light (Century models, N/A w/sunroof), courtesy lights, glove compartment light, and I/P flood lights (1977-up LeSabre, Electra, Estate Wagon and Riviera).

Limited package: *1973 Electra 225 Custom:* Oxengrain expanded vinyl and Madrid-grain vinyl bench seat with fold-down center armrest, "Limited" nameplate affixed to rear quarter sail panel, wide rocker panel moldings w/front and rear extensions, and WSW tires. *1977–1979 Estate Wagon:* Electra front-end styling including four-porthole fender ornament and Electra grille, custom 60/40 notchback front seat w/fold-down center armrests, power windows, power door locks, tilt steering wheel, quartz-crystal clock, map light, luggage rack w/air deflector, remote control outside mirrors, exterior bodyside woodgrain appliqué, chrome-plated road wheels, bumper guards, acoustic package, and special "Limited" ornamentation.

Luxus ride and performance package: 455 CID, 4-barrel V8 engine, steel-belted radial WSW tires, specially tuned front and rear suspension, special exterior moldings and trim, custom steering wheel, sunshade map light, and LH litter container (mounted on kick panel).

Park Avenue deluxe package: *(1975–1976.)* Lombardy cloth 40/40 split seats w/6-way power adjustment, velour covered front center floor console (non-operating) w/armrest, power door locks, climate control air conditioning, and padded full vinyl top w/halo moldings, and all other options not otherwise standard on the Electra.

Park Avenue trim package: *1975–1976:* Lombardy cloth 40/40 split seats, velour covered front center floor console (non-operating) w/armrest, and full vinyl top w/halo moldings. *1977:* Cloth 50/50 front seats w/individual fold-down center armrests, door-mounted entrance courtesy and warning lights, and C-pillar mounted coach side lights.

Rallye ride and handling package: See FE2 Rallye ride and handling package.

Riviera GS handling package: Firm ride and handling suspension and specific GS ornamentation.

Riviera LXXV (Buick 75th anniversary) package: Gray 50/50 leather seats, gray carpeting and seat belts, Designer accent paint in silver w/black accents, special LXXV badging inside and out.

Road Hawk package: Oyster white vinyl bucket seats w/"hawk" accents, silver w/gray accent paint and striping, black-painted windshield wipers, window reveal moldings,

grille, headlamp trim, front air dam, deck lid spoiler, bumper trim, special handling package, and BR70 × 13 BSW tires.

Somerset package: Dark blue and Somerset tan exterior two-tone paint, and interior trim décor, roof-mounted front passenger assist strap, wire wheel covers, specific ornamentation, dual exterior sport mirrors, and umbrella pouch in front seatback w/matching umbrella.

Sport coupe or Sport sedan package: *(NA on hatchback.)* Four exterior colors (silver, dark gold, yellow or bright red), black styling accents (on grille, headlight bezels, all window surrounds, bodyside moldings, "porthole" trim, wheel opening moldings, windshield wipers, name badges, and taillight and rear panel area), black bodyside pinstripe, black rocker panel appearance group, dual black sport mirrors, FE2 rallye/ride handling suspension, fast ratio steering (when power steering is ordered), and ER78 × 14 BSW tires.

Sport package: *(Coupe and Sport Coupe only.)* Cloth front bucket seats, full-length operating console, and dual remote control sport mirrors.

Sport Wagon package: *(Custom wagon only.)* Black-painted special headlamp and grille trim, windshield wipers, window reveal moldings, center pillar, wide rocker treatment, wheel opening moldings, air deflector, sport mirrors, Hawk decal, specific two-tone paint including bodysides, rear tailgate area and rear bumper, FE2 rallye ride/handling package, steel-belted radial ply P205/70R-14 W/O BSW tires and Designer Sport wheels.

S/R coupe package: Ribbed velour reclining front bucket seats (Regal), Velour 40/40 front seats (Riviera), full-length center floor console, rallye steering wheel (Regal), headlight dimmer on turn signal stalk (Regal), special S/R nameplates, and FR78 × 15 WSW tires (Regal).

Turbo Coupe package: *Century Sport Coupe:* Flat black trim around grille, headlamps and window/body moldings, front fender "Hawk" decal, Designers' sport wheels, FE2 handling package, fast-ratio steering (when power steering is ordered), sport mirrors, and rear spoiler. *LeSabre Sport Coupe:* Special exhaust system, Turbine wheels, "Turbo Coupe" identification on deck lid. 3.8L Turbocharged V6 and automatic transmission required.

Cadillac

Brougham d'Elegance: Padded elk grain vinyl roof with "Brougham d'Elegance" script set in sail panel, choice of 4 deluxe interior trim combinations (1973–1975, including Sierra leather in 9 colors, shirred stitch Medici crushed velour in 4 colors), contoured pillowed seats trimmed in Mansion knit upholstery with 50/50 dual comfort front seating (1976), contoured pillowed seats trimmed in velour upholstery with 50/50 dual comfort front seating (1977–1980), roof-mounted assist straps (1977–1980 sedans), driver and passenger reading lamps, opera lamps, deep pile carpeting and turbine vaned wheel discs w/wreath and crest ornamentation.

Cabriolet package (aka Custom Cabriolet): Elk grain vinyl covered rear roof section w/sheer chrome accent strip.

de Ville d'Elegance: Stand-up crest hood ornament, opera lights (1976 coupe), accent striping on hood, bodyside, and rear deck lid, "d'Elegance" script on sail panel (Coupe only), Mardi Gras two-toned velour upholstery w/leather trim (1974), Manhattan crushed velour upholstery w/leather cushion bolsters (1975), pillowed seats trimmed in Mansion knit upholstery with 50/50 dual comfort front seating (1976), hinged door pull handles (1975), front seatback storage pockets, plush deep pile carpeting, and color-coordinated carpeted floor mats.

Custom Biarritz: Contoured pillow-style 50/50 Dual Comfort front seats, limousine style rear window and rear quarter windows, padded elk grain vinyl roof (rear portion), black-accented brushed stainless steel belt molding surrounding the upper body from the rear window to the hood terminating in a spear-like design, bodyside accent paint stripes, passenger side remote control mirror, opera lamps, color-coordinated wheel discs, and five select color combinations — Mediterranean Blue Firemist, Cotillion White, Carmine Red, Colonial Yellow, or Ruidoso Saddle.

Custom Biarritz Classic: Similar to Custom Biarritz with two-tone paint scheme.

Deluxe trim package: Deep-pile two-tone shag carpeting, rubber-backed front and rear floor mats, and shirred elastic pockets on front seat backs.

deVille d'Elegance: Random velour 50/50 Dual Comfort front seats, upper doors and front seatback assist straps in random velour, high pile carpeting on floor and lower doors, hinged door pull handles, roof mounted assist straps on sedans (except above driver's door), "deVille d'Elegance" script on glove box door and top behind rear quarter window, opera lamps (coupes), crest with "V" emblem (sedans), side moldings with vinyl inserts, and pinstriping on hood, door and deck-lid.

Elegante package: 40/40 Dual Comfort front seats w/suede-like trim and perforated leather inserts, fold-down center armrests w/functional console, seatback storage pockets, duo-tone exterior finish (available in Platinum and Sable Black, or Western Saddle Firemist and Ruidoso brown), brushed chrome full-length bodyside molding, and chrome-plated wire wheels.

Fleetwood Talisman: Medici crushed velour upholstery, individual seats front and rear w/fabric trimmed console front and rear including an illuminated and locked storage compartment and provisions for writing pad w/pencil & pen, reclining front passenger seat, seat back pockets, sculptured door panel moldings, lighted vanity mirrors, deep-pile carpeting w/carpeted floor mats, padded elk grain vinyl roof,

special wheel discs, stand up wreath and crest hood ornament, and "Fleetwood Talisman" script on the sail panel.

Indianapolis 500 pace car replica package: *(Eldorado convertible only.)* Cotillion white exterior with red leather interior, special dash plaque engraved to note the car is a limited edition replica of the pace car for the 1973 Indianapolis 500, special red tape stripes, Indianapolis Motor Speedway logos on both front fenders and the trunk, and pace car lettering in red and black for the doors.

Phaeton: Convertible-like roof treatment, Phaeton script at each rear quarter panel, wire wheel covers, bodyside accent striping, 45/55 dual comfort front seating, leather upholstery and steering wheel trim. Three color combinations available: Cotillion White w/dark blue roof and white leather seating, Slate Firemist w/black roof and Antique Slate Gray leather seating, or Western Saddle Firemist w/dark brown roof and Antique Saddle leather seating.

Chevrolet

25th Anniversary paint package (B2Z): Distinctive two-tone silver paint treatment (silver metallic upper w/charcoal silver lower body), pinstripes on upper fender profiles, wheel opening, front fender vents, hood, and rear license plate cavity.

Auxiliary lighting package: *1973–1975:* Ashtray light, glove compartment light, courtesy lights, underhood light, and luggage compartment light. *1976–1980:* Time delay for dome reading light (ex. Chevette), under hood light, ashtray light, glove compartment light (Chevette), right front door dome light switch (Chevette Scooter), rear dome reading light (wagons only), rear compartment light (Chevette), courtesy lights, and headlight-on reminder buzzer (1978–1980).

Cabriolet equipment package: *(Notchback coupe only.)* Padded vinyl roof w/opera type rear quarter windows, special Cabriolet B-pillar emblem, Décor group, bright windshield and side window moldings, bright wheel lip moldings, bodyside moldings, and deluxe wheel covers.

Convenience package: *(Corvette.)* Time delay for dome and courtesy lights, RH visor vanity mirror, headlights-on reminder buzzer, low fuel indicator, engine compartment light, intermittent windshield wiper control, and color-keyed floor mats.

Custom appearance package: Details of package are not available.

Custom exterior package: Bright wheel opening moldings, lower bodyside moldings, black-finished body sill, body-colored door handle accent, belt molding (Hatchback), and bright side window moldings (Notchback).

Custom interior package/group: *Chevette:* Custom seat and sidewall trim (all-vinyl or cloth-and-vinyl), day/night inside rearview mirror, passenger assist grip on I/P, load floor and seat-back carpeting, and added acoustical insulation. *Vega:* Choice of luxury cloth/vinyl or solid vinyl contoured Custom front bucket seats, custom trim on door panels w/woodgrain vinyl accent moldings, color-keyed carpeting w/ choice of matching or contrasting colors, additional sound insulation, I/P assist handle, two rear seat ashtrays, day/night rearview mirror, adjustable driver and passenger seat, and carpeted load floor area (Hatchback). *Caprice:* 50/50 front seat w/reclining passenger seat back, Special Custom cloth on seats, upper door panels, and door pull straps, carpeting on rear package shelf and lower door panels, dual center armrests, deluxe color-keyed safety belts, and special bright interior accents. *Corvette:* Genuine leather seating w/vinyl trim, woodgrained vinyl accents on door panels and console, and deep cut-pile carpeting.

Décor group: Bright side window moldings and passenger seat sliding adjustment.

Deluxe appointment group: Quiet sound package, auxiliary lighting package, electric clock, and day/night rearview mirror.

Deluxe exterior package: Side window reveal moldings, front and rear wheel moldings, and rocker panel moldings.

Econominder (Gage) package: *(Caprice/Impala.)* Temperature gage, trip odometer, and fuel economy gage, and round dial cluster (1979).

Estate equipment package: *(Available only on Caprice Classic or Malibu Classic wagons.)* Woodgrain vinyl panels on bodysides and tailgate w/specific surround trim, and special exterior nameplates.

Exterior décor package: Side window reveal moldings, wheel opening moldings, and wheel covers.

FE7 gymkhana suspension package: Heavy-duty front and rear shock absorbers, larger diameter front stabilizer bar, rear stabilizer bar added, and higher rated front and rear springs.

F40 suspension: Special front and rear springs and shock absorbers.

F41 sport suspension: Large front stabilizer bar, rear stabilizer bar, special springs and shocks, special steering linkage, 7" wide wheels, and GR70 × 15 tires.

GT package: *(Hatchback or Kammback wagon only.)* Two-position adjustable driver's seat back, woodgrained accents on I/P, special instrumentation package, four spoke steering wheel, passenger side I/P assist handle, body-color door handle accent, black finished grille and lower body sill, parking lights w/clear lens and amber bulbs, GT nameplates on front fenders, belt molding (Hatchback only), 140 CID two-barrel four cylinder engine, front and rear stabilizer bars, 13 × 6 GT wheels, and A70 × 13 RWL tires.

Gymkhana package: *Camaro:* Special front and rear sway bars, specific shocks and steering gear, 15 × 7" wheels w/bright lug nuts, special center caps and trim rings, and

E60 × 15 R/WL tires. *Corvette:* Higher rate front and rear springs, larger diameter front stabilizer bar, and rear stabilizer bar. Recommended only for off road competition driving.

Indianapolis 500 pace car replica package: Choice of silver leather or silver leather/gray cloth thin shell design bucket seats w/lumbar support, power door locks, power windows, rear defogger, air conditioning, AM/FM stereo w/choice of eight-track tape or CB radio, sport mirrors, tilt/telescope steering wheel, glass T-tops, alloy wheels, heavy-duty battery, front air dam, rear spoiler, black over silver metallic paint w/red pinstripe, pace car decals, and choice of 4-speed manual or Turbo Hydra-matic transmission.

1978 Chevrolet Corvette Indianapolis 500 pace car replica

Instrumentation (Gage) package: Tachometer (Camaro), voltmeter, temperature gage, oil pressure gage (Malibu & Monte Carlo), and electric clock (Camaro & Malibu).

Interior décor/quiet sound group: *(Camaro & Nova.)* Glove compartment light, additional I/P lighting, woodgrain I/P accent trim, additional body insulation on floor and cowl, inner roof panel insulator, and full molded hood insulator.

Medalist package: Special gold metallic paint and "Medalist" nameplates.

Millionth Vega package: *(Available on Hatchback with GT option only.)* Neutral color custom vinyl interior trim w/all-vinyl door panels, orange accent color carpeting, "Millionth Vega" door handle inserts, bright orange exterior paint, white sport stripes, and power steering.

Off Road package: Gymkhana package and heavy-duty power disc brakes.

Quiet sound group: Additional acoustical insulation around passenger compartment, and under hood.

Rally equipment package: *Chevette (requires 1.6L engine):* Passenger assist grip, sport steering wheel and shifter, special instrumentation w/ tachometer and temperature gauge, black rocker panels, special suspension w/rear stabilizer bar, and rally-style sport wheel covers. *Nova:* Diamond-pattern chrome-plated grille and black headlight bezels w/bright trim, horizontally mounted parking lights (1977–1978), triple band striping on bodysides, triple band striping on rear panel (except Nova Custom), special "Nova Rally" identification on grille and front fenders, and color-keyed (except w/gold stripes when wheels would be gold) Rally wheels w/bright trim rings, lug nuts and center caps.

Rally Sport equipment package: *1973:* Special crosshatch style black grille w/silver accents, grille surround of resilient fiberglass composite w/small "bumperettes" on each side, front license plate mounting under right bumper, parking/turn signal lights moved from under bumper to area between headlights and grille, and Rally Sport nameplates on front fenders behind wheel wells. *1975–1977:* Low-gloss black paint treatment on hood, front header panel, grille, headlamp bezels, top of fenders, front part of roof, upper portion of doors, rear end panel and license plate opening, tri-color decal (separates black paint from body color), tri-color rally sport decals on front fenders and deck lid.

Sand Piper package: Custom interior w/patterned "Reef" cloth-and-vinyl upholstery in tones of yellow, cream and gold, full-floor carpeting, instrument panel and seat belts in yellow gold, deluxe door trim, brushed aluminum accents, sport steering wheel, day/night rearview mirror, carpeted cargo area, added acoustical insulation, "Sandpiper" striping and graphics, and choice of Cream Gold or Antique White exterior.

Special Custom interior package: Special knit cloth trim "European" style front bucket seats w/two-position driver's seat and w/matching trim on the lower door panel, foam headliner, additional woodgrained accents, thicker floor carpeting, color-keyed seat belts, color-keyed steering wheel and column, and color-keyed instrument cluster.

Special instrumentation package: (Vega) Tachometer, amp meter, temperature gauge, and electric clock.

Spirit of America package: *Vega hatchback:* White custom vinyl front bucket seats and interior trim, red accent carpeting, Antique white exterior paint, white vinyl top, blue and red bodyside, hood and rear-end panel striping, Spirit of America identification on front fenders and rear panel, white Vega "GT" wheels w/trim rings and Chevy logo center caps, and A70 × 13 R/WL tires. *Nova Custom coupe:* White custom vinyl front bucket seats and interior trim, red accent carpeting, red, white and blue trim on doors (replacing woodgrain appliqué), black instrument panel, black steering wheel and column, red, white and blue insert on center of steering wheel, Antique white exterior paint, red, white and blue body striping and decals (on hood, front fender and door, rear quarter panel and roof, and around top and sides of taillamps), "NOVA" name decal on hood (replacing diecast nameplate), "NOVA" w/Eagle motif decals on front fenders and deck lid (replacing die-cast nameplates), black painted grille and side window treatments, black painted dual sport mirrors, white painted Rally wheels w/trim rings and "SS"-style center cap (with red, white and blue insert), and WSW tires. *Impala Sport Coupe:* White vinyl bench seat, choice of red or blue carpet with color-keyed seat belts and other trim such as floor mats, special badge on instrument

panel, Antique white exterior paint, white vinyl top, choice of red or blue exterior pinstriping, white bodyside protective molding, dual remote control sport mirrors, special fender badges, and special wheel covers. Rally wheels painted white available at extra cost.

Sport equipment package: Choice of knit cloth and vinyl or all vinyl high-back front bucket seats, quiet sound group, bright windshield and rear window moldings w/black trim, black B-pillar appliqué w/argent edges in front of rear quarter window, body-colored finned wheel covers w/argent painted edges, and front sway bar.

Sport front-end appearance: *(Available on Town Coupe only w/sport equipment package only; same appearance as 2+2.)* Resilient urethane front end with dual rectangular headlights, and front and rear bumper rub strips w/rear bumper guards.

Sports décor package: *Camaro:* Dual body color sport mirrors, body color insert on door handles, and body color vinyl appliqué on the lower front and rear bumpers. *Vega:* Bodyside tape stripes w/wrap over stripe on decklid surface, and bodyside protective molding set in stripe. *Chevette:* Lower bodyside sport stripes, and black accent moldings.

Spyder appearance package: Body color front air dam, rear spoiler, Spyder identification and emblems, black sport mirrors, lower bodyside stripe, Spyder hood decal, and the following black trim or black painted parts — Rally II wheels, headlight openings, parking light openings, body sill, door and center pillar louvers, windshield, rear window and side window moldings, rear end panel and taillight openings.

Spyder equipment package: *(Requires Sport Equipment package on Towne Coupe, and available only with 5-speed manual or Turbo Hydra-matic transmission, 1976; available only on Sport 2+2, 1977–1979.)* Sport steering wheel, console, inside day/night rear view mirror, stitched instrument panel w/woodgrain trim, distinctive Spyder identification, wheel opening moldings (if not ordered w/Spyder Appearance package, 1978–1979), dual tailpipe system (1979), F41 sport suspension, and steel-belted radial ply BR70 × 13C BSW tires. *1980 only:* Spyder ID on horn button, dual black sport mirrors w/LH remote and RH manual, black moldings (windshield, rear window, belt and side window), black painted door and center pillar louvers, black painted taillight frames, black headlight frames, black front and rear bumper rub strips, body color front air dam and rear spoiler, Spyder emblem on front header panel and rear lock cover, rear spoiler and bodyside stripes w/Spyder lettering outlined in accent body color, Spyder hood decal, sport suspension, black-painted Rally II wheels w/bright trim ring, and BR70 × 13 BSW tires.

SS package: *1973 Chevelle Malibu coupe and wagon:* SS emblems on door panel and steering wheel, special instrument cluster w/full gauges, LH remote and RH manual sport mirrors, bright roof drip moldings, SS emblems on front fenders and rear deck panel (tailgate on wagon), black finished grille w/ SS emblem, black accented taillight framing (coupe), lower body and wheel opening striping keyed to body color, rear stabilizer bar, 14 × 7 inch Rally wheels w/special center caps and trim rings (coupe), Turbine I wheels (wagon), and G70 × 14 RWL tires (coupe). *Nova:* Color-keyed deep-twist floor carpeting, SS emblem on steering wheel, dual sport mirrors w/LH remote control and RH manual, bright roof drip rail molding, black accented grille and back panel w/SS emblems on grille, decklid and front fenders, bright parking and taillight accents, tapered bodyside striping (1973), hood and decklid striping (1974), "Nova SS" front fender decals (1974), 14 × 6 inch rally-type wheels w/special center caps and bright lug nuts, and special front and rear suspension.

Style trim group: *(Camaro.)* Bright moldings for roof drip, side windows, rear hood edge and belt line, body colored insert on door handles, and bright-accented parking lights.

Value appearance group: *Impala:* Bodyside moldings, wheel opening moldings, and full wheel covers. *Nova:* Bright side window moldings, bodyside protective moldings, wheel opening moldings, and full wheel covers. *Monte Carlo:* Side window sill moldings, color-keyed pinstriping, Rally wheels (wire wheel covers on Landau), bright body sill moldings, and body-color dual sport mirrors.

Woody package: Custom interior w/woodgrain vinyl accents on instrument cluster, sport steering wheel, day-night rearview mirror, bright window moldings, deluxe grille w/bright accents, wheel trim rings, and woodgrain vinyl exterior bodyside trim.

X11 Sport equipment package: *(Available on Club coupe and 2-door hatchback coupe.)* Sport steering wheel, "X11" identification, decal stripes, rear spoiler, bright side window moldings, body-color dual sport mirrors, bodyside pinstripe, body belt line accent stripe, bumper rub strips, and black-accented bright radiator grille, headlight bezels, taillights, rocker panel molding, B-pillar, rear quarter and license plate pocket, sport suspension, rally wheel trim and P205/70R13 white-letter tires.

Z28 special equipment package: Dual sport mirrors w/LH remote control, front and rear spoilers (optional), Z28 stripes (optional), 350 CID, 4-bbl., V8 engine, High-Energy ignition system, dual-snorkel air cleaner, dual exhaust, variable-ratio power steering, power front disc brakes, posi-traction rear axle, special sport suspension, special 15 × 7 inch wheels with center cap and trim rings, and F60 × 15 R/WL tires.

Chrysler

"300" option package: Bucket seats in red leather, engine-turned I/P dash appliqués, leather wrapped steering wheel, tachometer, specific "300" blacked-out crosshair grille w/"300" medallion, Spinnaker White exterior paint, red/white/blue bodyside and decklid stripes, white dual remote sport mirrors, front fender louvers, "300" quarter-window decals w/decorative bar below, white bumper guards and rub strips, special handling suspension, aluminum wheels w/"300" medallion on center hub, and GR60 × 15 OWL tires.

Accessory group: Floor mats, carpeted spare tire cover, RH manual outside mirror, and door edge guard protectors.

Basic (accessory) group: *LeBaron:* TorqueFlite automatic transmission, AM radio, day/night rearview mirror (1979), dual horns (1979), WSW tires, LH remote-control outside mirror, Light package, air conditioning, tinted glass (all windows), deluxe wiper/washer package, hood silencer pad (1979), undercoating, Landau vinyl roof (2-door only), and deluxe wheel covers (1979); *Newport & New Yorker:* AM/FM radio, RH remote-control outside mirror, Light package, manual air conditioning, intermittent windshield wipers, vinyl bodyside molding, and undercoating.

Brougham package: Crushed velour cloth-and-vinyl front bench seat w/center armrest, hood and deck paint stripes, trunk carpeting and spare tire cover.

Cabriolet Roof package: White or cashmere simulated convertible roof or unique beige with Corinthian Edition package in designers two-tone exterior, dual remote control outside mirrors. Available with these paint colors only: Nightwatch Blue, Crimson Red metallic, Baron Red, Mocha Brown metallic, Natural Suede Tan, White and Black.

Cabriolet Roof Two-tone package: Dark blue bench seat w/fold-down center armrest or at additional cost optional dark blue vinyl buck seat w/fold-down center armrest and center seat cushion (Cordoba only), Dark blue 60/40 split bench seat w/fold-down center armrest or at additional cost optional dark blue or white leather bucket seat w/fold-down center armrest and center seat cushion and dark blue accents (Crown only), two-tone paint treatment with white upper body, blue and white tape strip and Nightwatch Blue lower body, white simulated convertible roof, and dual remote control outside mirrors.

Corinthian Edition package: *(Cordoba Crown only.)* Cashmere 60/40 leather and vinyl seat, leather-wrapped tilt steering wheel, intermittent windshield wipers, dual chrome remote control mirrors, specific "Corinthian" identification, wire wheel covers, and P205/75R15 Goodyear wide WSW tires. Available in choice of Black Walnut metallic exterior paint w/gold accent stripes and black walnut reptile-grain padded landau vinyl roof, or Designer's Cream-on-Beige exterior paint w/medium beige accent stripes, and light beige Laredo-grain landau vinyl roof,

Crown Coupe package: Padded vinyl canopy roof, with a stationary rear quarter opera window replacing the regular rear quarter window. *1974 50th anniversary only:* Gold

Fawn exterior with Gold padded vinyl canopy roof, with a stationary rear quarter opera window replacing the regular rear quarter window.

Crown Roof package (also Crown Landau package): Padded Laredo-grain vinyl landau roof, "Frenched" rear window and opera window treatment, illuminated roof band, and bodyside and upper-deck tape stripes.

Crown Roof Two-Tone package: Crown roof package, low-contrast two-tone paint treatment (see Paint Colors chart), front bumper filler painted two-tone to match body color, black nerf strips and bumper guard cushions front and rear, and bodyside, upper and lower deck lid stripes.

Deluxe insulation package: Undercoating, trunk dress-up (LeBaron), underhood pad, rear wheelhouse and luggage compartment floor insulation pad (Newport and New Yorker), and additional body sound insulation.

Deluxe wiper/washer package: Deluxe windshield wipers w/intermittent wipe, and windshield washer fluid level indicator.

Easy Order package: Air conditioning, tinted glass, Basic group (ex. Cordoba), Landau (2-dr. only) or full vinyl roof (4-dr. only), AM radio (LeBaron), AM/FM radio w/rear speaker (ex. LeBaron and Cordoba), rear seat speaker, luxury steering wheel (ex. LeBaron and Cordoba), tilt steering wheel (Cordoba), power windows (1976–1977 Town & Country), power driver's seat (1976–1977 New Yorker and Town & Country), LH and RH remote control mirrors (LH only on Cordoba), deluxe wiper/washer package, electronic digital clock, deluxe insulation package, illuminated vanity mirror (New Yorker), light package (LeBaron), rear bumper guards (ex. Cordoba), trunk dress-up (ex. LeBaron and Cordoba), and WSW tires (LeBaron).

"Fifth Avenue Edition" package: *(New Yorker.)* Interior: Unique champagne environment including seats, garnish moldings, instrument panel crash pad, package shelf, headlining and C-pillar trim, light champagne leather 60/40 split-bench seat and door trim panels, driftwood appliqué on instrument panel and door trim panels, unique 20-oz. cut-pile carpeting, Light package, unique pentastar steering wheel center for standard leather-wrapped tilt steering wheel. *Exterior:* Unique two-tone paint, Designer's Cream upper/Designer's Beige lower (1979–1980), solid Black Walnut metallic (1980), medium beige accent stripes on hood center form and two-tone paint break, light beige Laredo-grain padded vinyl landau roof, quarter window appliqué and roof moldings, Special edge-lighted quarter window w/"Fifth Avenue" nomenclature (std. New Yorker opera lamps deleted), special front fender louver appliqué, unique pentastar hood ornament and trunk lock cover, color-keyed bumper guards and bumper protection rub strips, wire wheel covers, and Premium P205/75R15 Aramid-belted radial tires w/white sidewalls and gold accent stripe.

"Fifth Avenue Edition" Special Edition package:

"Fifth Avenue Edition" package features, plus automatic temperature-control air conditioning, dual remote control mirrors, and power-operated glass sunroof.

Fifth Avenue package: *(LeBaron.)* Velour interior upholstery, formal rear roofline with vinyl padded carriage roof and covered rear door quarter windows, frenched rear window, wrap-over roof band on leading edge of top w/ opera lamps on each end where quarter window front edge would be located, and wire wheel covers.

Light package: Fender mounted turn signal indicators, trunk light, glove box light, map courtesy light (std. LeBaron Medallion), ignition switch light w/time delay, headlight & wiper switch light w/time delay, low fuel, temperature and electrical systems warning lights, door ajar warning light, headlights-on warning buzzer, low windshield washer fluid indicator (1975–1978 Newport and New Yorker), and left-side courtesy light under instrument panel (std. LeBaron Medallion).

LS coupe package: Cloth high-back bucket seats, bright brushed-finish instrument cluster bezel, door trim panel with cloth inserts and brushed-finish moldings, painted dual remote control mirrors, unique LS quarter window ornamentation, front fender louvers (non-functioning), unique classic wire grille texture w/integral LeBaron medallion in grille frame, and P205/75R15 WSW tires.

LS Limited coupe package: LS coupe package plus center floor console, three-spoke steering wheel, color-keyed dual remote control mirrors, painted quarter and back window moldings, deck lid skid strips, trunk dress-up, unique two-tone paint treatments w/accent stripes, and P205/75R15 wide WSW tires. *Two-tone paint treatment choices:* Dark Heather Brown/Light Heather Gray metallic; Brown/Light Heather Gray metallic; Baron Red/Light Heather Gray metallic; Natural Suede Tan/Light Cashmere; and Nightwatch Blue/Burnished Silver metallic.

Navajo package: White bench seats w/unique Navajo cloth inserts, Navajo Copper metallic exterior paint, orange paint stripes, and vinyl roof.

Open Road handling package: Heavy-duty front stabilizer bar, torsion bars and shock absorbers, rear stabilizer bar, heavy-duty rear leaf springs and shocks, special "Firm Feel" power steering, extra-wide wheels, and P225/70R15 BSW steel-belted radial tires.

Roadability package: Rear anti-sway bar, and extra-wide 15 × 7 inch wheels.

St. Regis package: Padded canopy boar-grain vinyl roof w/unique color-keyed molding trim (Seneca grain vinyl used for 1977–1978), unique trim moldings, and formal opera window. *1974 50th anniversary only:* Gold Fawn exterior with Gold padded vinyl canopy roof, w/unique color-keyed trim molding, and a stationary rear quarter opera window replacing the regular rear quarter window.

Salon package: *(Requires optional trunk dress-up, rear* *fender skirts, rear window defroster and JR78 × 15 tires.)* Silver Crystal coat metallic paint with special "clear coat" treatment, silver "Elk" grain vinyl roof, red accent stripes for bodyside and deck lid, standard 50/50 bench seat in red or dove gray crushed velour, padded leather tilt/telescope steering wheel, and aluminum fascia road wheels w/red accent stripes.

Special Appearance package: Unique two-tone paint treatment (Dove Gray/Nightwatch Blue, or Dove Gray/Formal Black), accent stripes, square-cornered opera window design, exclusion of front and rear sill molding extensions, black nerf strips front and rear, dual remote-control outside sports styled mirrors color-keyed to lower body paint, leather-wrapped 3-spoke steering wheel, premier wheel covers, and Goodyear American Eagle Aramid-belted radial tires w/gold and white sidewall treatment.

Sport Appearance package: Dual remote-control sport styled mirrors, luxury 3-spoke steering wheel, and sport road wheels.

Sport Handling package: Special Firm-Feel power steering, rear sway bar, heavy-duty shock absorbers, and extra-wide wheel rims.

Town & Country package: Luggage rack and rear assist handles.

Dodge

Basic group: *Challenger:* Power steering, power 4-wheel disc brakes, 2.6 Liter Silent Shaft engine, and 195/70HR × 14 RWL tires. *Charger, Magnum XE and Diplomat:* Air conditioning, TorqueFlite automatic transmission (std. on Charger and Magnum XE), tinted glass, Landau vinyl roof (2-doors only), AM radio, LH remote-control mirror, light package, deluxe intermittent wiper/washer package, liftgate wiper/washers (Diplomat), vinyl roof (1979–1980 Diplomat), black vinyl bodyside molding (Charger only), undercoating, hood pad (Magnum XE), and WSW tires (except Magnum XE). *Monaco:* TorqueFlite automatic transmission, power steering, AM radio, LH remote-control mirror, undercoating w/hood silencer pad, dual horns, deluxe windshield wiper w/intermittent wipe, deluxe wheel covers and WSW tires. *St. Regis:* Manual airconditioning, AM radio, LH remote-control mirror, light package, deluxe windshield wipers, vinyl bodyside protective molding, undercoating and WSW tires.

Brougham package: *1973–1974:* Cloth-and-vinyl 50/50 front seat w/passenger-side recliner, fold-down center armrests front and rear, vinyl roof w/ "Brougham" nameplate, cornering lights, carpeted trunk and spare tire cover, and rocker panel moldings w/rear extensions. *1975-on:* Crushed velour cloth-and-vinyl or cloth-and-vinyl front bench seat w/center armrest, color-keyed shag carpeting, simulated woodgrain I/P trim, deluxe sound insulation package, deluxe steering wheel, hood and deck paint stripes, trunk carpeting,

deluxe wheel covers, stand-up hood ornament, and spare tire cover.

Cabriolet roof package: Simulated convertible roof, dual remote control mirrors, offered in seven exterior colors only (Nightwatch Blue, Crimson Red metallic, Baron Red, Mocha Brown metallic, Natural Suede Tan, White and Black).

CMX package: Up-and-over roof accent molding, color-keyed bumper protective rub strips w/bright insert, CMX front fender nameplates, dual remote control outside mirrors, color-keyed door handle accents, unique bodyside tape stripes, offered in four exterior colors only (Baron Red, Nightwatch Blue, Frost Blue metallic, or Burnished Silver metallic), color-keyed 10-spoke forged aluminum road wheels, and P205 wide WSW tires.

Custom exterior package: *Omni:* Bright trim accents on hood, fender, wheel lip, door sill and roof drip rail. *Aspen:* Color-keyed full-length bodyside molding w/vinyl insert, belt moldings, rear deck lower appliqué (sedan and coupe only), and upper door frame moldings (wagon only).

Custom interior package: *Omni:* Choice of cloth or all-vinyl high-back bucket seats, custom door trim panels, glove box lock, and simulated woodgrained I/P appliqué. *Aspen:* Custom seat and interior trim, rear armrest w/ashtray, simulated woodgrained I/P appliqué, cigarette lighter, day/night inside mirror, molded cloth headliner, hood silencer pad, and Custom exterior nameplates.

Custom package: *Dart sedan:* Exterior décor group, interior décor group, and Custom nameplate. *Aspen:* Combines features of Custom exterior package and Custom interior package, plus wheel opening moldings.

Dart Sport Hang 10: All-vinyl front bucket seats w/center floor console, multicolored woven door trim and seat inserts, orange-painted I/P w/simulated woodgrained appliqué instrument cluster, eggshell white paint, Wave Crest side, grille closure panel, and hood tape stripes.

Daytona package: *Charger SE:* All-vinyl front bucket seats w/color-keyed carpeting and matching vinyl door panel inserts, two-tone exterior colors w/special body taping, color-keyed dual sport mirrors and bodyside moldings, Charger Daytona decals on door to front fender area, blacked out grille w/bright accents, rear sway bar, and WSW tires.

Décor package: Carpeted cargo area w/bright rub strips, vinyl cargo area side trim, soft-rim three-spoke sports steering wheel, roof luggage rack, and WSW tires.

Decorator trim package: *(Dart Sport.) Interior:* Low back cloth-and-vinyl seat w/Boca Raton inserts, door trim panels w/Boca Raton inserts and unique silver accent tape stripe w/lower door panels carpeted in shag material, shag carpets (black loop-pile when ordered w/floor-mounted manual transmission), rear seat armrests w/ash receiver, deluxe steering wheel, all in dark red. *Exterior:* Paint choices of Silver Cloud metallic, Vintage Red metallic, Eggshell

White or Black, bodyside and lower deck tape stripes in silver and black, or red and black, and wheel-lip moldings.

Deluxe insulation package: Undercoating w/hood silencer pad, noise reduction package (firewall and wheel wells), trunk dress-up (Diplomat only), and special body sound insulation (floors, roof and rear seat).

Deluxe package: *(Base Coronet only.)* Drip moldings, wheel-lip moldings, vinyl bodyside moldings, carpeting (std. on hardtop), and bright armrest bases.

DeTomaso package: Black vinyl bucket seats, DeTomaso I/P plaque, DeTomaso front floor mats, leather-wrapped steering wheel and shift knob, rallye instrument cluster, DeTomaso windshield tint band, wheelhouse flares, front air dam, rear spoiler, black rear quarter window louvers, bright brushed transverse roof band, black front and rear protective bumper rub strips, black painted lower bodyside, black windshield and belt moldings, black taillamp and door handle accents, black dual remote control sport mirrors, DeTomaso decals on quarter panels and rear spoiler, sport suspension, 3.5:1 performance axle, black-accented cast aluminum road wheels, and P185/70R13 BSW tires.

Diplomat package: *(Royal Monaco Brougham hardtop only.)* Padded landau vinyl roof, formal opera windows, framed-in back window, and five-inch-wide over-the-top stainless steel band.

Easy (E-Z) order package: Air conditioning, Fuel Pacer system, tinted glass, AM radio, electronic digital clock (Diplomat), rear seat speaker, light package, Landau vinyl roof (Charger SE), 3-speed windshield wipers (through 1976), wipers w/intermittent wipe feature and low washer fluid level indicator (1977-on), undercoating and hood insulation pad, outside LH remote mirror, outside RH remote mirror (1977-on), WSW tires (Diplomat), and protective bumper strips.

Estate package: Luxury vinyl interior trim (1977), cloth and vinyl houndstooth interior trim (1978), carpeting on lower door trim panels (1978), sport steering wheel (1977), front seat adjustable lumbar support (1977), assist grips (1977), carpeted cargo area w/bright metal skid strips, vinyl-trimmed interior pillars and garnish moldings, electric clock (1977–1978), simulated woodgrain vinyl side and tailgate trim, and A78 × 13 WSW tires (1975 to 1976).

Exterior décor group: Drip rail and wheel lip moldings, and vinyl bodyside protective molding.

Fold-down rear seat package: *(Aspen Custom coupe and Aspen coupe w/ R/T package and bucket seats only.)* Fold-down rear seat, carpeted trunk floor and seat back, and trunk dress-up.

Freeway Cruise package: *(Sedan M/M only.)* Velour cloth trim w/adjustable lumbar supports in front seatbacks, assist grips, electric clock, simulated woodtone appliqué and lower panel carpeting on door panel trim, ammeter and oil gauge, tachometer, "Silent Shaft" 1.6L engine, 5-speed manual overdrive transmission, black upper door frames, and hood tape stripe.

Gran Touring "GT" package: Engine turned I/P appliqués, three-spoke leather-wrapped steering wheel (two-spoke w/optional tilt steering wheel), color-keyed polyurethane fender flares, GT front fender medallion, heavy-duty shock absorbers, firm-feel power steering, seven-inch wheels w/functional air slots and deep-dish trim rings with bright lug nuts and center hub, and GR60 × 15 RWL tires.

Handling package: *(Requires GR70 × 15 steel-belted radial tires.)* Front and rear sway bars and 15" chrome-styled road wheels.

Interior Décor group: Deluxe bench seat, full-floor carpeting, rear armrests w/ash receiver, simulated wood-grained I/P and door and rear quarter panel trim, deluxe steering wheel, and cigarette lighter.

Light package: Ashtray, glove box and trunk (or cargo compartment) lights, ignition switch light w/time delay, map and courtesy lights (Aspen, Diplomat, Coronet and St. Regis), door ajar warning light (Diplomat), decklid ajar light (St. Regis), rear-door courtesy light switch (4-drs., except Aspen), headlight-on warning buzzer (except Aspen), low battery/high temperature light-emitting diodes (St. Regis), low washer fluid light (St. Regis), illuminated hood and parking brake releases (St. Regis), and fender-mounted turn signal indicators,

Luxury equipment package: *(N/A base Coronet or '74 base Monaco.)* Air conditioning, tinted glass, electric clock, vinyl bodyside moldings, deluxe or luxury steering wheel, tilt steering wheel (1976–1978), power windows, AM/FM radio, rear seat speaker, automatic speed control, E-Z order package, power tailgate window (wagons), cargo compartment carpeting (wagons), assist handles (Monaco wagons), air deflector (Coronet wagons), and auto-lock tailgate (wagons).

024 Sport package: Black paint accent stripe w/reflective red accents at taillamp area and paint-break demarcation stripe w/lower bodyside black paint treatment, deleted drip rail molding, louvered quarter window appliqué, black bumper rub strips, black windshield, backlight and rear quarter window moldings, black belt moldings and taillamp accents, black and bright door handles, black dual remote sport style aerodynamic mirrors, rally instrument cluster w/tachometer, clock and trip odometer, body-color wheels w/bright trim rings, hub covers and lug nuts, rear air spoiler, and large 024 decals on rear quarter panels in front of the rear wheel opening and on spoiler.

Open Road handling package: Firm-feel power steering, firm-feel suspension w/heavy duty sway bar, shock absorbers, springs and torsion bars, extra wide wheels, and P225/70R15 wide WSW tires.

Popular equipment group: Dual horns, power steering, light package (1979–1980), LH remote-control mirror

(Omni, 1979–1980), dual remote-control sport mirrors (Omni 024), day/night inside rear view mirror (Omni 024), and wheel trim rings.

Premium exterior package: *Omni 4-door hatchback:* Custom exterior package plus bright door frame accents, bright belt and center pillar moldings, full-length bodyside and liftgate moldings, and Rallye wheel hubs w/bright acorn lug nuts. *Omni 024:* Bright side window and drip rail moldings, louvered quarter window appliqué, black and bright bumper rub strips, and deluxe wheel covers.

Premium interior package: All-vinyl or suede-like cloth bucket seats w/passenger-side recliner and adjustable head restraints (all-vinyl only on 024), three-spoke wood-grained steering wheel, color-keyed shift lever console, passenger-side visor vanity mirror, and premium door trim panels w/carpet, soft uppers and premium front armrests w/integral door pull handles.

Premium package: *(Requires Basic package.)* AM/FM stereo w/8-track tape system and four speakers, power windows, and intermittent wipers w/wipe feature.

Premium woodgrain package: Premium exterior package plus simulated woodgrained vinyl bodyside and lower liftgate appliqué.

Protection group: Door-edge protectors, color-keyed floor mats front and rear (1978–1980), inside hood release and glove box lock (std. on Aspen SE).

Rallye package: *Dart:* 318 CID V8, 4-speed manual transmission, power steering, special suspension w/front sway bar, E70 × 14 RWL tires, Rallye wheels, "Tuff" steering wheel, deluxe vinyl bench seats, and Dodge lettering on lower rear quarter panel. *Challenger:* Performance hood w/dual air scoops, fender scoops w/gradated stripes, Rallye instrument cluster, Rallye suspension w/front and rear sway bars, and F70 × 14 WSW tires (1974); requires 340 CID V8 engine (1973). *Charger:* (available w/V8 only) Rallye instrument cluster w/speedometer, ammeter, oil, temperature and fuel gauges, black bodyside tape stripes, G70 × 14 RWL tires, power bulge hood, and hood tie-down pins. *Coronet and Coronet Custom hardtops:* Bodyside tape stripes, G70 × 14 RWL tires, Rallye wheels w/bright trim rings, rear sway bar, bright exhaust tip, and black grille accents.

Red & White Special package: *(Custom Coupe M/M only.)* White interior trim, red carpets and seat accents, red tape stripes on rear and side, dual racing mirrors, white vinyl bodyside moldings, black door frame and center pillar, and red vinyl roof.

R/T décor group: *(Coupe only — requires R/T package.)* *1976–1977:* Dual remote-control sport-style chrome rear view mirrors, wheel lip moldings, and Rallye wheel trim rings. *1978-on:* Belt molding and Rallye wheel trim rings.

R/T handling performance package: *(Requires V8 engine and R/T package.)* Extra heavy-duty suspension w/HD shocks and rear sway bar, and FR70 × 14 OWL tires.

R/T package: *(Coupe only.)* *1976–1977:* Bodyside and deck tape stripe, R/T decals and medallion, grille blackout treatment, heavy duty suspension, Rallye road wheels less trim rings, and E70 × 14 RWL tires. *1978-on (requires V8 engine):* R/T multicolored bodyside, hood, and rear tape stripes, red-painted grille, R/T decals and grille medallion, sill molding w/black finish paint below, dual remote control racing mirrors (body colored w/tape stripe), heavy-duty suspension, Rallye wheels less trim rings, and FR78 × 14 BSW tires.

R/T Sport Pak package: R/T package, front air spoiler, wheel flares, quarter window louvers, rear deck spoiler, tri-color stripes on white or black exterior.

R/T "Super Pak" package: *(Aspen coupe only — requires R/T package and dual sport mirrors.)* Front spoiler, wheel flares, louvered quarter windows, rear deck spoiler w/orange/red stripe, and R/T Super Pak stripe.

"S-Type" package: Cloth high-back bucket seats w/o center cushion, door trim panel w/cloth inserts and brushed-finish moldings, bright brushed-finish I/P cluster bezel and glove box door panel, three-spoke luxury steering wheel, unique S-type quarter window glass ornamentation, painted or chrome dual remote control mirrors, halogen headlamps, hood, deck and bodyside stripes, painted styled steel road wheels w/trim rings, and P205/75R15 WSW tires.

Special Edition exterior package: Custom exterior package, hood ornament w/windsplit molding, hood tape stripe, bodyside accent tape stripes (only on coupe w/option landau vinyl roof), upper door frame moldings (sedan), and wheel lip moldings.

Special Edition interior package: Premium all-vinyl bucket seats or choice of all-vinyl or cloth-and-vinyl 60/40 front bench w/passenger recliner, rear armrest and ashtray, shag carpeting (w/automatic transmission), LH remote-control mirror, simulated woodgrained I/P and glove box door appliqués, luxury steering wheel (requires power steering), cigarette lighter, day/night inside mirror, pedal dress-up, molded cloth headliner, deluxe insulation package, Special Edition exterior nameplates, and DR78 × 14 BSW tires.

Special Edition package: *(Dart sedan and Swinger.)* *Interior:* Choice of luxury crushed-velour cloth front bench seat, vinyl front bench seat, velour front bucket seats, or vinyl front bucket seats, shag carpeting, luxury door trim, luxury steering wheel (when ordered w/optional power steering), simulated woodgrain I/P trim with black cluster, trunk dress-up including black carpet, deluxe insulation package, cigarette lighter, and day/night inside rear view mirror. *Exterior:* Chrome-plated grille, bright headlamp doors, hood ornament, windsplit molding, lower deck appliqué, "Special Edition" nameplate on C-pillar, vinyl bodyside molding, vinyl roof, hood and deck tape stripes, bright belt and wide rocker panel moldings, bright drip rail and wheel lip moldings, bright upper door frame and B-pillar moldings (Dart sedan), and deluxe wheel covers. *(Aspen.)* Combines features of Special Edition exterior package and Special Edition interior package, plus deluxe wheel covers.

Special Edition Wagon interior package: Custom vinyl bench seat, rear armrest w/ashtray, simulated wood-grained I/P cluster, cigarette lighter, day/night inside mirror, cargo compartment carpeting and covered lockable storage bins, hood silencer pad, and Special Edition exterior nameplates.

Special Edition Wagon wood-grained group: *(NA w/Custom exterior package.)* Simulated woodgrain bodyside and rear exterior panel trim, hood ornament w/windsplit molding, belt moldings, and upper door frame moldings.

Sport Appearance package: Luxury three-spoke steering wheel, dual remote-control sport styled mirrors, and sport road wheels (color-keyed on Diplomat).

Sport handling/performance package: Special firm-feel power steering, rear sway bar, heavy duty shock absorbers, P215/70R15 RWL tires (Mirada), and 15 × 7 inch wheels (Diplomat and Mirada).

Sport "Lite" package: Aluminum hood and decklid inner panels, aluminum bumper reinforcements, and aluminum intake manifolds with a modified engine block.

Sport package: *(For Colt Custom hatchback only.)* Special black and yellow cloth-and-vinyl houndstooth check bucket seats, large floor console w/oil and amp gauges, tachometer, day/night inside rearview mirror, dual electric remote outside mirrors, cargo lamp, yellow exterior paint w/special black bodyside tape stripes, black rear window opening moldings, blackout bumpers, cast aluminum road wheels, and 175/70 HR × 13 W/L tires.

Sport wagon package: Premium vinyl bucket seats w/center cushion and armrest, "Tuff" steering wheel, cargo compartment carpets, wheel-opening flares, front air dam, yellow and orange tape stripes for front air dam, upper bodyside wheel openings, and liftgate, blackout grille treatment, dual body-colored sport mirrors, and 5-spoke styled road wheels w/bright trim rings.

SS package: Vinyl bucket seats w/center cushion and fold-down center armrest (console not available), and tricolor bodyside striping.

Street Kit Car package: *(Requires power steering, power brakes and automatic transmission.)* Super Coupe package equipment (less the dark brown and black paint scheme), door and roof number decals ("43," for NASCAR racing legend Richard Petty's number), large rear spoiler, fender flares with "bolt-on" look, two-tone red paint, and race-inspired wheels without center caps.

Sunrise décor package: *(Requires Sunrise package.)* Lower bodyside two-tone paint treatment w/tape accent at paint break, and 5-spoke styled road wheels w/bright trim rings (requires ER78 × 14 tires at extra cost).

Sunrise package: Plaid cloth-and-vinyl high back bucket seats, multi-colored bodyside tape stripes (in red, yellow and orange tones 1978–1979), rear deck lower panel "strobe" stripes (1978–1979), belt moldings, and louvered rear quarter windows w/tape accent stripe (1978–1979), deluxe wheel covers (1980), and D78 × 14 WSW tires.

Super Coupe package: *(Requires 360 CID, 4-barrel V8 engine.)* Dark brown body color w/contrasting black finish (on hood, front fender tops, headlamp bezels, wiper arms, front and rear bumpers, and remote-control racing mirrors), bodyside and over-the-roof paint striping, black wheel flares, black front and dark brown rear spoilers, quarter window louvers, heavy-duty suspension, rear anti-sway bar, 15 × 8 inch special GT wheels, and GR60 × 15 RWL tires.

Touring Edition package: Leather and vinyl 60/40 seats, unique door trim panels, leather-covered steering wheel w/tilt column, featherwood appliqué on I/P and all associated woodgrain areas, power windows, dual remote control chrome mirrors, wide sill molding rear extension, Touring Edition nameplate on rear pillar, padded full vinyl roof w/formal rear window, unique upper bodyside pinstripes, forged aluminum road wheels color-keyed in red or gold, and P205/75R15 wide WSW tires. Available only in Nightwatch Blue, Mocha Brown metallic, Baron Red, Burnished Silver metallic and Eggshell White.

Two-tone paint package: *Aspen coupe:* Main body color is on hood, roof, decklid and bodysides, and secondary color surrounds side windows continuing to top of front fenders, and lower bodyside including over wheel openings. Available in varying color combinations depending upon model year. As an example, 1976 choices: Yellow Blaze and Harvest Gold w/white, black and gold tape stripes, or Silver Cloud and Black w/silver, bright red and black tape stripes, or Spitfire Orange and Black w/orange, white and black tape stripes. *Magnum XE:* Two-tone paint treatment available in Nightwatch Blue upper and Pewter Gray metallic lower, or Black upper and Pewter Gray lower, front and rear bumper filler painted two-tone to match body color, color-keyed outside dual sport mirrors to match upper body color, and accent stripe at paint break. *Omni:* Two-tone paint break at upper bodyside feature line on 4-door hatchback with chrome accent strip, and at lower bodyside feature line on 2+2 hatchback with tape stripe at paint break. *St. Regis:* Two-tone paint in gray, blue, teal or red colors with tape stripe at paint break.

Utility package: Fold-down rear seat, security panel, and trunk dress-up trim.

Ford

Accent group: *(Standard with Luxury Décor group; requires color-keyed carpeting on Pinto sedan.)* Bodyside protection molding w/vinyl insert (Pinto), bright window trim

(Pinto sedan & HBK), wheel covers (Pinto), dual accent bodyside paint stripes (1974 base Torino cars), passenger compartment carpeting (1973 base Torino), and full wheel lip moldings (1974 base Torino cars).

Appearance décor group: *(Not available on Mustang II Ghia or Mach I models or with Cobra II package.)* All vinyl or cloth-and-vinyl seat trim, brushed aluminum I/P appliqués, lower body two-tone paint treatment, pinstripes, and four styled steel wheels w/trim rings; wheel lip moldings are deleted.

Appearance protection group: Floor mats, spare-tire lock, bright license plate frames (Torino), and door-edge guards.

Brougham luxury group: *(Available only on LTD Brougham models.)* Split bench seats w/manual passenger recliner, crushed velour cloth trim, door trim w/velour inserts, door pull straps, 25 oz. cut-pile floor carpeting, auxiliary ashtray in right front door armrest, cigar lighters in rear door armrests, increased sound packaging, luggage compartment trim, Convenience group, and Deluxe bumper group.

Cobra option: *(Includes 2.3L turbocharged engine— 5.0L engine is available at no cost.)* Interior: Sport steering wheel, engine turned I/P and RH appliqué, Cobra emblem on RH appliqué, and on Ghia level door insert panels. *Exterior:* Color-keyed quarter louvers, black paint and tape treatment on grille, lower bodyside, and below front and rear bumpers, Turbo hood scoop w/bright "TURBO" nameplate, dual remote control mirrors, bright tailpipe extension, dual color-keyed inserts on bumper, wraparound bodyside molding w/ rub strip extensions w/dual color-keyed inserts, black window moldings, tape treatment with "COBRA" identification, Michelin TRZ tires, forged metric aluminum wheels, special suspension tuning, sport tuned exhaust, aluminum brake drums, and semi-metallic front brake linings.

Cobra II package: *(Available only on 2+2 model. Requires power front disc brakes w/2.3L 4-cylinder engine.)* Brushed appliqué door panel trim and I/P with Cobra II identification, Cobra II exterior emblems, dual racing mirrors, pivoting rear quarter windows w/louvers, blackout grille (grille horse emblem eliminated), w/bright periphery molding, bright parking lamp bezel w/yellow lens, styled steel wheels w/trim rings, and BR70 B/WL wide oval steel-belted radial ply tires (195R/70 B/WL tires when ordered with V6 and air conditioning or with V8 engine).

Convenience group: Automatic seat back release (Granada 2-drs. except w/bench seat), LH and RH chrome remote control outside mirrors (color-keyed on 1974–1975 Mustang II, LH only on Maverick and Elite, NA on Granada), visor vanity mirror (NA on Maverick and Granada), inside day/night mirror (Mustang II and Maverick), color-keyed deluxe safety belts (1975–1977 Maverick, std. on Granada Ghia), luggage compartment light (1973–1974 Maverick), cigar lighter (1973–1974 Maverick), interval

windshield wipers, electric trunk lid release (full-size Fords), power tailgate lock (full-size Ford wagons), parking brake boot w/ashtray (1974 Mustang II), automatic parking brake release (Granada, 1975-up Torino & Elite, and full-size Fords), and spare tire extractor (Torino wagons).

Convenience/Light group: Under hood, glove box, ashtray, and cargo area lights, interval windshield wipers, cigar lighter, day/night rear view mirror, visor vanity mirror, parking brake warning light, "headlights on" warning buzzer, passenger door courtesy light (Pinto), map light (N/A with sunroof), flipper rear quarter windows (Pinto), and bright window moldings.

Copper luxury group: *(Not available w/optional sunroof.)* Interior: Unique copper color w/velour or leather seat upholstery, copper trim components, and copper luggage compartment trim. *Exterior:* Copper starfire or white paint, deep dish aluminum wheels, unique hood, bodyside and decklid tape stripes, unique gold Thunderbird ornament in opera window, padded Odense grain half vinyl roof in copper (full vinyl roof required w/optional moonroof), and color-keyed wide vinyl insert bodyside moldings.

Crème and Gold luxury group: *Interior:* Crème and gold leather or gold velour seat trim, gold passenger side instrument panel appliqué and luggage compartment dress-up. *Exterior:* Gold starfire paint on bodyside, and crème color on the hood, roof and trunk, unique belt line and hood tape stripe, gold half vinyl roof in odense grain, color-keyed border moldings, gold opera window emblem, crème colored wide bodyside molding and deep dish forged aluminum wheels.

Cruising package: Load floor carpet, charcoal grille/ headlight doors, black dual sport mirrors, white painted styled steel wheels w/trim rings, blackout treatment on door frames and B-pillars, black windshield molding, and Sports package. Runabout adds: all-glass third door and multi-color paint/tape treatment on lower body. Wagon adds: Inner and outer quarter filler panels, quarter filler panel carpet, porthole on quarter panel, multi-color bodyside quarter panel and tape/paint liftgate treatment (can be deleted for $55 credit), black liftgate louvers, blackout treatment on rear window moldings, rocker panel moldings, and forward portion of upper quarter panel.

Cruising wagon option: *(Available with or without tape/paint treatment. Also available with optional special tape/paint treatment.)* Mini "panel truck" with round, tinted, bubbled porthole windows on rear steel-side panels, front air dam spoiler, dual sport mirrors, styled steel wheels w/trim rings, Sports Rallye package, carpeted hardboard inner panels and load floor carpet.

Décor group: *Interior:* Low-back fully reclining front bucket seats w/houndstooth cloth-and-vinyl or all-vinyl trim, deluxe door panel trim, Ghia armrests, simulated woodgrain I/P including glove box lid, carpeted load floor, day/night inside rearview mirror, interval windshield wipers with electric washers, electric rear window defroster, and cigar lighter. *Exterior:* Black rub strips on bumper, bright belt and window surround moldings, bright windshield and rear window trim, black rocker panels, black bodyside paint stripes, and bright LH outside rearview mirror.

Deluxe bumper group: Front and rear bumper guards w/rubber inserts, and full-width horizontal rub strips on bumpers (except Pinto).

Deluxe equipment group: *(Not available on Ghia or Mach I or w/Cobra II package or Sports Performance package.)* Four-way manual driver's seat, AM/FM monaural radio, power front disc brakes, and BR78 × 13 BSW tires (WSW tires on 2+2).

ES option group: *Interior:* Black instrument panel package tray, grey engine turnings on I/P and cluster appliqués, black sport steering wheel and column, black carpeting, armrests and door trim, and choice of black or chamois on all other interior components. *Exterior:* Blackout grille, Deluxe bumper group, black cowl grille, bright belt moldings, black window frames, quarter window ventilation louvers and lower back panel, vinyl insert bodyside moldings, black dual sport outside rearview mirrors w/LH remote control, turbine-styled wheel covers, and handling suspension.

ESS option: Charcoal grille and headlight doors, black window moldings, black dual sport mirrors, all-glass third door w/black hinges on Runabout, premium bodyside moldings, black wheel lip moldings, Sports package, styled steel wheels w/trim rings, ESS identification, blackout paint on roof drip molding, lower back panel, lower side window and rocker panel area.

Exterior Accent group: Bright belt moldings, window frames, wheel lip moldings and rocker panel moldings, deluxe wheel covers, hood ornament, and LH bright style outside rearview mirror.

Exterior Décor group: *(Not available on Grabber.)* Vinyl insert bodyside moldings (ex. LTD II; std. Granada; unique wide molding w/padded vinyl inserts on Thunderbird), vinyl roof (Granada; Thunderbird 1977–1979; choice of front or rear half-vinyl roof on LTD II), bright window frames (std. Granada & LTD II), belt moldings (std. Granada & LTD II), rocker panel moldings (Pinto 77–80), accent paint stripe (Fairmont, Maverick & LTD II), lower back panel appliqué (Granada), partial wheel lip moldings (Thunderbird through 1976), Exterior accent group (Fairmont), front cornering lamps (Thunderbird through 1976), WSW tires (LTD II), dual sport mirrors (Thunderbird 1977–1979), styled road wheels (Thunderbird 1977–1979), turbine style wheel covers (Fairmont), and standard wheel covers (ex. Thunderbird; deluxe on LTD II).

Fashion accessory package: Fresno cloth seat inserts, driver's side illuminated visor vanity mirror, door panel convenience pockets, coin tray, 4-way manually adjustable

driver's seat, Appearance protection group, pinstripes, stand-up hood ornament, illuminated entry system, and rear seat ashtray.

Futura Sports group: B-pillar tape stripe, charcoal argent grille, and turbine style wheel covers. Standard hood ornament and accent stripes are deleted.

Ghia group: *Interior:* Low back fully reclining front bucket seats w/velour cloth trim, Ghia door panel trim w/Ghia armrests, carpeted package tray, simulated woodgrain I/P and glove box lid, cigar lighter, tachometer, trip odometer, 4-spoke steering wheel, loop-pile carpet in passenger compartment, full wheelhouse trim cover in cargo area, interior surfaces of roof pillars trimmed in vinyl, visor vanity mirror, day/night inside rearview mirror, ceiling mounted grab handles, seatback strap, seatback map pockets, door storage pockets, interval windshield wipers w/electric washers, Ghia sound insulation package, and electric rear window defroster. *Exterior:* Black rub strips on bumpers, bright belt and window surround moldings, bright windshield and rear window trim, black rocker panels, bodyside protection trim moldings w/black vinyl inserts, bright LH outside rearview mirror, third door twist lock, and 155SR × 12 Michelin steel-belted radial BSW tires, w/bright bolts and trim rings on wheels.

Ghia luxury group: *(Available only with Silver metallic, tan glow, or silver-blue glow exterior paint.)* Media velour cloth trim, console, half vinyl roof, full-length bodyside tape stripe, color-keyed rear window molding, and standup hood ornament.

Ghia option: *(Not available on wagons, with other décor or accent groups, ES option or Futura sports group. Requires automatic transmission. Price on 1979 Futura is $207.)* *Interior:* Choice of all-vinyl or cloth-and-vinyl luxury "Flight Bench" seat, deluxe door panel trim w/bright accents and simulated woodgrain w/carpeted lower area, deluxe carpeting, simulated high gloss woodgrain I/P trim, luxury steering wheel, upgraded sound insulation package, visor vanity mirror, day/night inside rearview mirror, color-keyed cloth headliner and sun visors, deluxe safety belts, luggage compartment trim, cigar lighter and inside hood release. *Exterior:* Bodyside accent stripes, vinyl insert lower bodyside moldings with partial wheel lip moldings (full on Futura). The following items are also included, but standard on Futura: Bright belt and window moldings, hood ornament, hood ornament, dual bright LH-remote/RH-manual mirrors, and deluxe wheel covers.

Ghia Sports group: *Interior:* Chamois color Ghia seat trim with black upper straps on seat backs (1978 adds black interior choice), black engine-turned appliqués on I/P, console tray and door trim panel inserts, console, leather-wrapped sport steering wheel, black shift lever knob w/manual transmission (bright w/automatic), and black parking brake handle. *Exterior:* Black or tan exterior paint (1978 adds

Midnight blue paint choice), chamois or black half-vinyl roof, chamois or black vinyl insert bodyside molding, chamois or black Ghia pinstripes, luggage rack w/chamois or black vinyl luggage hold-down straps w/bright buckles, cast aluminum lacy spoke wheels w/chamois painted spokes and blacked out grille.

Glamour paint option group: Color-keyed wheel covers, dual bodyside and paint stripes.

Harmony Color group: *(LTD Brougham and LTD Landau.)* Two-tone upper bodyside tape stripes (replacing dual accent paint stripe on Brougham and fender peak molding on Landau), contrasting paint tones w/darker body color above tape stripes and lighter color below them, and darker body color below the bodyside molding (Landau only). Full vinyl roof available at no extra cost and recommended on 2-door models.

Indianapolis 500 pace car replica package: *(Available only on 3-door sedan.)* 5.0L, 302 CID V8 engine, sport tuned exhaust, and Michelin TRX tires with forged metric aluminum wheels, specially tuned suspension, power steering and power brakes. *Interior:* Recaro front bucket seats w/special cloth trim, padded/net head-restraint, adjustable seat back and thigh supports, floor console, Cobra I/P w/Indianapolis Motor Speedway badge, color-keyed deluxe seat belts, leather wrapped sport steering wheel, intermittent windshield wipers, AM/FM stereo with cassette tape and premium sound system, flip-up open air roof, light group, and Ghia level deluxe sound package. *Exterior:* Black greenhouse moldings, special front fascia w/fog lamps, special hood scoop, Mustang nomenclature on hood, special rear spoiler, black lower back panel, Special Pace Car tape treatment, rubstrip/bodyside molding accent stripes color-keyed to tape treatment, Cobra black lower bodyside treatment, dual remote control sport mirrors.

1979 Ford Mustang Indianapolis 500 pace car replica

Instrumentation group: *(Available only on V8 equipped cars.)* Tachometer, trip odometer, engine gauges (oil, amp, temp and fuel), and electric clock (Torino only).

Interior accent group: Pleated all-vinyl seat trim, door trim w/bright accents, interior color paint on doors at upper edge, deluxe steering wheel hub, simulated woodgrain I/P, and sound insulation package.

Interior Décor group: *(Not available with high-back bucket seats or Luxury Décor group.)* Choice of deluxe cloth (ex. Elite), luxury knit cloth (Elite) and vinyl or pleated vinyl seat trim (pleated vinyl on Grabber, all-vinyl on Granada and Fairmont, super soft vinyl bench or bucket seats with console on Elite), cut-pile carpeting (ex. Granada), carpeted trunk (Fairmont sedans), deluxe door trim panels (ex. Elite), bright instrument panel molding (ex. Fairmont, Granada and Elite), woodgrain I/P cluster appliqué (Elite and Fairmont), deluxe steering wheel, rear seat ashtray (Maverick), color-keyed seat belts (Maverick and Elite), dual note horn (Elite), and sound package (Maverick and Fairmont).

Interior luxury group: Split bench seats w/dual front seat center armrests and dual manual recliners (passenger only on Thunderbird) w/choice of velour or super soft vinyl seat trim w/unique sew style, unique door panels, door assist straps, seatback map pockets and assist straps, 18 oz. color-keyed cut-pile carpet, high gloss I/P and door appliqués, luxury sound insulation package, courtesy lights in quarter trim panels (Thunderbird only), rear seat center armrest (ex. wagon), luggage compartment trim (ex. wagons), luxury steering wheel, deluxe color-keyed seat belts (Thunderbird only), seat side shields (LTD only), package tray trim (ex. wagons), trip odometer, digital clock, low fuel warning light, low windshield washer fluid warning light, Convenience and Light groups (Thunderbird only), and safety belt warning chime.

Jade luxury group: *(Not available w/optional sunroof.)* *Interior:* Choice of two-tone jade/white leather interior trim or jade velour cloth trim, and jade luggage compartment trim. *Exterior:* Jade starfire or white paint, padded half-vinyl roof, dual bodyside and hood paint stripes, vinyl clad rear window molding, color-keyed border molding, wide bodyside moldings, silver opera window ornament, and simulated wire wheel covers.

King Cobra: Unique King Cobra trim, 5.0L V8 engine, power steering, power front disc brakes, Rallye package, unique lacy sport cast aluminum wheels, and 195R/70 steel-belted radial wide oval B/WL tires.

Landau luxury group: Split bench seats w/dual front seat center armrests and manual passenger recliner w/luxury knit cloth or super soft vinyl seat trim w/unique sew style, unique door panels, shag carpeting, simulated burled walnut inlaid I/P appliqué, super sound package, rear seat center armrest (ex. wagon), door assist straps, seatback assist straps, padded rear pillar appliques on vinyl roof (1975 4-door), rear seat cigar lighters (1975–1976 4-drs. and wagons w/optional power windows only), Light group, luggage compartment trim (ex. 1975–1976 wagons), Deluxe bumper group, and luxury steering wheel. *1975 Country Squire adds:* Convenience group, front cornering lights, rear door courtesy light switches, RH door armrest ashtray, and bright seat side shields. *1978 LTD wagon adds:* Wheel covers, dual accent paint stripes, color-keyed deluxe seat belts, carpeted under-cargo-floor stowage well, and rear door courtesy light switches.

Light group: Under hood (engine compartment), glove box, and ashtray lights, cargo area light, illuminated visor vanity mirror (Thunderbird), parking brake warning light (ex. Fairmont & Granada), low fuel warning light (Thunderbird), door ajar warning light (Mustang II & Thunderbird), headlights "lights-on" warning buzzer (ex. 1975–1977 Maverick), auto lamp on/off delay system (Thunderbird), dome/dual beam map lamp (ex. Pinto), I/P courtesy lights (1975–1977 Maverick & full-size Fords), rear door courtesy light switches (Fairmont, Granada, Torino, LTD II, & full-size Ford 4-drs. when not standard), and passenger-side door courtesy light switch (Pinto).

Lipstick luxury group: *Interior:* White leather or vinyl seat and door trim w/lipstick red carpeting and Mylar® insert and luggage compartment dress-up. *Exterior:* Lipstick red paint, lipstick red Normande grain half vinyl roof, color-keyed border and rear window moldings, lipstick red wide bodyside moldings, white hood and bodyside paint stripe, and simulated wire wheel covers.

LTD wagon Brougham option: Squire Brougham option plus wheel covers, front and rear rocker panel extensions, cargo area light, dual accent paint stripes, electric clock, deluxe color-keyed safety belts, and dual note horn.

Luxury Décor group: *(Not available on Grabber or with other décor groups.)* *Interior:* Vinyl trim w/choice of cloth or pleated vinyl inserts (Pinto), super soft vinyl interior trim (Maverick), red or tan ribbed velour cloth and super soft vinyl reclining bucket seats w/unique door trim and large door armrests (Granada Ghia 4-dr.), console w/warning lights (Granada Ghia 4-dr.), deluxe door panel trim, rear seat armrest (Granada Ghia 4-dr.), 14 oz. cut-pile carpeting (1973–1975 Pinto), 25 oz. cut-pile carpeting (Maverick, 18 oz. beginning in 1975), deluxe, luxury or custom steering wheel (depending upon model), multi-directional air vents (1973–1974 Pinto), cigar lighter w/front and rear ashtrays (std. Granada Ghia), passenger door courtesy light switch (Pinto), inside day/night mirror (Maverick), dome/dual beam map light (Maverick & Granada Ghia), instrument panel simulated woodgrain appliqués and bright bezels (ex. Granada), bright parking brake handle w/simulated woodgrain grip (Pinto), color-keyed shift boot (Pinto), shift lever w/simulated woodgrain accents (Pinto), and upgraded sound package (1976 Pinto). *Exterior:* Vinyl roof (Maverick), bright B-pillar appliqué w/vinyl insert color-keyed to roof (Maverick 4-dr.), C-pillar padding and ornament (1975–1977 Maverick 4-dr.), Accent group (1973–1975 Pinto), bodyside protection molding (Pinto and Maverick), bright metal exterior trim including window reveal and drip moldings (1973–1974), choice of two-tone or single-tone exterior paint w/Ghia badge on C-pillar (Granada Ghia: gold/black, tan glow/black, or silver/black), LH remote-control mirror

(Maverick), chrome plated grille (Maverick), color-keyed wheel covers (Maverick), chrome wheel covers (Pinto), spoke-type cast aluminum wheels (Granada), rocker panel molding (Pinto), wheel lip moldings (1976 Pinto), lower back panel appliqué w/bright surround (1973 Pinto and all Maverick), deluxe gas cap (1973–1974 Maverick), front and rear bumper guards w/rubber inserts (Maverick and Granada), WSW radial tires (Maverick).

Luxury interior group: *(Standard on 1976 Ghia models.)* Super soft vinyl seat (or cloth and vinyl on 1976), and door trim, large armrest, reclining front seats (Maverick), deluxe rear seat quarter trim, deluxe steering wheel (Maverick), door courtesy lights, dome/dual beam map lamp (Maverick), I/P with woodgrain appliqué (Maverick), deluxe color-keyed seat belts, 25 oz. cut pile carpeting (18 oz. for 1976 and Maverick), trunk mat (Maverick), parking brake boot w/rear ashtray (ex. Maverick), and super sound package. *Mustang II only:* (standard on Ghia) Super soft vinyl seat and interior trim, super soft vinyl door trim w/large armrest, deluxe rear seat quarter trim, door courtesy lights, deluxe safety belts, 25 oz. cut pile carpeting, parking brake boot w/rear ashtray, and super sound package. *Granada (available on 4-door Ghia or ESS models only):* Deluxe Flight Bench seat, unique seat/door trim, large front and rear door armrests, rear seat center armrest, power windows, dual beam dome/map light, illuminated visor vanity mirror, and luxury steering wheel.

Maintenance group: Five bulbs, 9-inch channel locking pliers, reversible screwdriver, 14 oz. fire extinguisher, three flares, red plastic flag, maintenance manual, five fuses, tire pressure gauge, bunge cord, lubrication kit, 12V trouble light, and 6-inch crescent wrench.

Mirror group: Inside day/night mirror, outside remote control color-keyed dual mirrors, and visor vanity mirror.

Power lock group: Power door locks and power trunk lid or liftgate release. Includes power tailgate lock on LTD wagons for $15 additional.

Protection group: Front floor mats (NA on Mustang, front and rear w/carpeted inserts on full-size Fords and Thunderbird), spare-tire lock (NA Pinto and Mustang II), door-edge guards (deleted on Mustang II Mach I, & Gran Torino Squire, std. on Granada Ghia), bodyside moldings (1973–1974 color and wide/narrow styles vary by model), rear bumper guards (1973 Pinto), front and rear bumper guards (1974–1980 Pinto), locking hood release (full-size Fords), locking gas cap (NA Pinto, Elite, LTD II and Mustang II), and license plate frames.

Rallye appearance package: *(Available only on Pinto sedan and Runabout, or Mustang II 2+2.)* *Interior (Mustang II only):* Black or white vinyl seats w/gold cloth inserts and gold vinyl piping, and black or white vinyl door trim panels w/gold accents. *Exterior:* Dual gold tape stripes, dual sport mirrors, front air dam (spoiler), black upper body and window moldings, black window frames, black windshield wipers, styled steel wheels w/trim rings, and all glass third door on Runabout.

Rallye equipment group: 351 CID 4-bbl., V8 engine, four-speed manual transmission, competition suspension w/rear stabilizer bar, G70 or H70 wide-oval belted B/WL tires with 6" rims, and instrumentation group.

Rallye package: Competition suspension, extra cooling package, sport exhaust w/dual bright tips, CR70 × 13 B/WL tires or 195R/70 B/WL tires (depending upon year), traction-lok differential, digital clock, dual remote control mirrors, styled steel wheels w/trim rings, and leather-wrapped steering wheel.

Silver luxury group: *(Not available w/optional sunroof.)* *Interior:* Unique red leather or red velour upholster, and red luggage compartment trim. *Exterior:* Silver starfire paint, deluxe wheel covers, dual bodyside and hood paint stripes, padded Odense grain silver half vinyl top (full vinyl top required w/optional moonroof), and color-keyed wide vinyl insert bodyside moldings.

Sport coupe package: *(Granada 2-door sedan only.)* *Interior:* Reclining bucket seats, deluxe door trim w/simulated perforated vinyl inserts (available in tan, white or black), leather wrapped steering wheel and floor shift. *Exterior:* Choice of black, white or dark brown metallic exterior colors, half odense-grain vinyl roof (gold, black or white), lower back panel appliqué color-keyed to body color, rocker panel molding, dual outside color-keyed mirrors, styled steel wheels w/gold accents and trim rings, gold hood, bodyside and decklid paint stripes, and heavy-duty suspension.

Sport group: *Interior:* Low back fully reclining front bucket seats w/cloth-and-vinyl or all-vinyl trim, deluxe door panel trim w/Ghia armrests, non-carpeted package tray, brushed aluminum I/P and glove box lid, cigar lighter, tachometer, trip odometer, 4-spoke steering wheel, interval windshield wipers w/electric washers, upgraded sound insulation package, and electric rear window defroster. *Exterior:* Black rub strips on bumpers, bright belt and window surround moldings, bright windshield and rear window trim, black rocker panels, bodyside tape stripe w/"S" near taillight, bright LH outside rearview mirror, sport suspension including rear stabilizer bar, and 4.5" wide wheels w/bright bolts.

Sport option: Black window frames, black belt moldings, black rocker panel moldings, full wraparound bodyside molding w/dual accent stripes, dual accent stripes on bumpers, semi-styled steel wheels w/trim rings and black sport hub covers, and sport steering wheel.

Sports Accent group: *Interior:* Deluxe cloth seat and door panel trim, cut pile carpeting, deluxe steering wheel (all aforementioned in orange or avocado color), multi-directional air vents, front and rear seat ashtray, passenger door courtesy light switch, instrument panel and quarter-trim panels w/simulated woodgrain appliqués, bright parking brake handle w/simulated woodgrain grip, color-keyed boot, deluxe seat belts. *Exterior:* Orange or avocado vinyl roof and "tu-tone" lower bodyside tape/paint, 175R × 13 steel-belted WSW tires, wheel lip moldings, wheel covers, bright side window moldings, B-pillar cap, drip moldings and belt moldings.

Sports appearance package: Broad tri-color bodyside tape stripes, sporty grille badge, Magnum 500 styled steel wheels w/trim rings, and HR78 × 14 B/WL tires. Hood ornament, opera windows, rocker panel molding and wheel lip moldings are deleted.

Sports décor group: Chamois vinyl roof w/color-keyed rear window molding, dual accent paint stripes, hood and fender louver paint stripes, chamois trunk lid straps, chamois vinyl insert bodyside moldings, styled road wheels w/chamois accent paint, dual sport mirrors and blackout vertical grille bars.

Sports instrumentation group: Color-keyed luxury steering wheel, alternator, oil pressure and engine temperature gauges, tachometer, clock, and trip odometer.

Sports interior option: *(Available only on SportsRoof and Mach I w/V8 engines.)* Knitted vinyl high-back bucket seats with accent stripes, door trim panels w/integral pull handle and armrest, color accented deep embossed carpet runners, deluxe instrument panel black appliqué w/woodtone center section, instrumentation group, bright pedal pads, and rear seat ashtray.

Sports package or Sports Rallye package: *(Standard w/Cruising wagon option.)* Tachometer, ammeter, temperature gauge, front stabilizer bar and sport steering wheel.

Sports Touring package: Tu-tone paint/tape treatment, sporty grille badge, Magnum 500 styled steel wheels w/trim rings, and HR78 × 14 B/WL tires. Hood ornament, opera windows, rocker panel molding, wheel lip moldings, and lower back panel appliqué are deleted.

Squire Brougham package: *(Available only on Country Squire wagons.)* Includes most features of the Brougham luxury group as well as color-keyed deluxe seat belts and rear door courtesy light switches. *1973 only:* in addition to above includes high-back split bench seats w/manual passenger recliner, vinyl Brougham trim scheme, cut pile carpet, and front door courtesy lights, but excludes Convenience group and Deluxe bumper group.

Squire Luxury group: Includes most features of the Brougham luxury group with the following changes or additions: tan super-soft vinyl upholstery w/horseshoe-shaped saddle accent stripe, unique door trim, color-keyed deluxe seat belts, and tailgate window washer.

Squire option: *Pinto:* Simulated woodgrain on bodyside and tailgate, load floor carpeting, low-back bucket seats w/deluxe cloth or cloth-and-vinyl trim, deluxe door trim, custom steering wheel, simulated wood trimmed interior items, color-keyed seat belts, cigar lighter, passenger door courtesy light switch, rear seat ashtray, and deluxe sound insulation package. *Fairmont:* Simulated woodgrain bodyside appliqué and surround moldings, deluxe wheel covers, bright window frames and belt moldings, hood ornament, bright LH outside rearview mirror, Squire script, and Interior accent group.

Stallion group: Black windshield and window frame moldings, black wiper arms, black grille (with bright periphery trim on Mustang II), bright parking lamp bezel w/amber lens (Mustang II), black lower back panel (Pinto), black lower bodyside tape treatment (Pinto), black outside dual remote control mirrors (Pinto), black rocker panel, bumpers, lower fenders, doors and rear quarters (Mustang II), "Stallion" decals, competition suspension (Pinto), styled steel wheels, and A70 B/WL wide oval tires (Pinto).

Turnpike group/Turnpike convenience group: Fingertip speed control, manual reclining passenger seat, and trip odometer.

Visibility group: Outside LH remote control mirror, outside RH remote control mirror (Granada), inside day/night mirror (Granada), visor vanity mirror (Granada), headlights "lights-on" warning buzzer (ex. Granada), and the following lights (except Granada): ashtray, dome/map, glove compartment, luggage compartment, I/P courtesy, engine compartment, rear-door courtesy switch, parking brake warning, and headlight switch.

Wagon Brougham option package: *(Available only on LTD wagon.)* Includes all features of Squire Brougham package plus wheel covers, front and rear rocker panel extension moldings, cargo area light and dual accent paint stripes.

Lincoln

Appearance protection group: Door-edge guards, license plate frames (Continental), spare tire cover (Continental coupe & sedan), front and rear floor mats w/carpet inserts, front and rear bumper guards w/horizontal bumper rub strips (Continental), and dome/dual beam map light (Continental).

Collector's series: (Available only on Continental 4-door with Town Car option, and Continental Mark V 2-door) choice of luxury cloth or leather-and-vinyl midnight blue seat trim, unique midnight blue door trim panels, luxury cloth-wrapped garnish moldings and sunvisors, plush midnight blue carpet on passenger compartment floor, umbrella, tilt luxury steering wheel, electronic AM/FM stereo search radio w/quadrasonic 8-track tape, Interior light group, Power Lock Convenience group, automatic speed control, interval windshield wipers, RH remote control rear view mirror, remote control garage door opener, Headlight Convenience group, Defroster group, illuminated entry system, power

mini-vent windows, Appearance protection group, midnight blue trunk carpet, leather-bound tool kit, leather-bound owner's manual, choice of white or midnight blue clearcoat metallic exterior paint, unique bodyside paint stripes, premium lower bodyside moldings color-keyed to exterior paint, color-keyed half-vinyl roof, gold-painted vertical grille bars, and six-inch wide turbine-styled cast aluminum wheels w/midnight blue paint accent. *Mark V adds:* Choice of standard six-way power split bench front seat w/seat back assist straps and map pockets, or six-way power bucket seats w/passenger recliner and driver's power lumbar adjustment (also includes leather covered padded console w/storage compartment for umbrella), miles-to-empty fuel indicator, color-keyed bumper guard pads and bumper rub strips, rocker panel moldings, coach lamps, and unique bodyside paint stripe w/owner's initials on doors.

Color luxury groups: Cordovan and Gold/Cream group includes leather-and-vinyl or velour interior in unique sew style for 1977, and in 1978–1979, all colors are offered with these two choices. All others for 1977, and for 1976, include leather-and-vinyl interior in unique sew style. For 1980 all were in leather with carpet on door and quarter trim panels, dual floor well lamps, seat-back robe cords and map pockets, plus choice of full or Landau vinyl roof. All include 6-way power passenger seat and grey carpeted luggage compartment, and are color-coordinated in the following color groups:

- Bittersweet (1980) — Bittersweet moondust metallic with Champagne interior trim and vinyl top.
- Black (1980) — Black exterior with choice of Pewter, Dark Red or Champagne interior trim, and vinyl top.
- Blue Diamond (1975–1976) — Blue Diamond Fire exterior paint and interior upholstery and trim
- Caramel (1980) — Details unavailable
- Chamois (1978) — Choice of white, midnight blue, or cinnamon gold moondust metallic exterior paint and interior upholstery and trim
- Champagne (1978–1980) — Choice of white, dark champagne or light champagne moondust metallic (1979) exterior paint and interior upholstery and trim
- Cordovan (1977–1979) — Choice of cordovan, white, or light chamois (1979 only) exterior paint, and interior upholstery and trim
- Crystal Blue (1979) — White exterior paint w/blue interior trim
- Dark Jade/Light Jade (1976–1977) — Dark jade metallic or light jade Diamond Fire exterior paint and interior upholstery and trim
- Dark Red (1980) — Dark red moondust metallic paint with choice of dark red or pewter interior upholstery and vinyl top
- Dove Grey (1978–1979) — Choice of dove grey or light

silver moondust metallic exterior paint and interior upholstery and trim

- Gold/Cream (1976–1978) — Choice of yellow-gold Diamond Fire or cream exterior paint and interior upholstery and trim (1977); choice of white, cream, or light gold moondust metallic exterior paint and interior upholstery and trim (1978); choice of white, cream, or jubilee gold moondust metallic exterior paint and interior upholstery and trim (1979).
- Gold (1973–1976) — Gold Diamond Fire metallic exterior paint, tan interior leather w/brown leather accents, and gold Levant grained vinyl roof.
- Jade/Light Jade (1978) — Choice of white, midnight jade or light jade moondust metallic exterior paint and interior upholstery and trim
- Jade/White (1976) — Choice of white, or dark jade metallic exterior paint and white w/dark jade interior upholstery and trim
- Light Gold (1980) — Details unavailable
- Lipstick/White (1975–1976) — Choice of white or lipstick red exterior paint, white or lipstick red Normande grain vinyl roof, white leather interior w/lipstick red accents, lipstick red cut-pile carpeting, and dark red cut-pile carpeting in luggage compartment
- Medium Pine (1980) — Pine opalescent moondust exterior paint with medium pine upholstery and vinyl top
- Medium Vaquero (1980) — Details unavailable
- Midnight Blue (1980) — Dark blue metallic with midnight blue upholstery and vinyl top
- Midnight Blue/Cream (1977) — Choice of midnight blue or cream exterior paint and interior upholstery and trim
- Pewter (1980) — Light Pewter moondust metallic with choice of pewter or dark red upholstery and vinyl top
- Red/Rose (1976–1979) — Choice of dark red moondust metallic or rose Diamond Fire exterior paint and interior upholstery and trim (1977); Choice of dark red moondust metallic or white exterior paint and interior upholstery and trim (1978); Choice of dark red moondust metallic, light red moondust, dove grey, or white exterior paint and interior upholstery and trim (1979)
- Saddle/White (1975–1976) — Choice of dark brown metallic or white exterior paint, saddle or white Normande grain vinyl roof, white leather interior with saddle leather accents and trim, saddle cut-pile carpeting, and luggage compartment carpeting
- Silver (1973–1976) — Silver moondust metallic exterior paint paint, silver Levant grained vinyl roof, silver or red leather (1974 and up), or cranberry velour interior
- Turquoise (1979) — Choice of white, dark turquoise metallic, or medium turquoise moondust metallic exterior paint, and interior upholstery and trim
- Wedgewood Blue (1978–1979) — Choice of white, midnight blue, wedgewood blue or ice blue moondust metallic exterior paint and interior upholstery and trim (1978); Choice of white, diamond blue moondust, or wedgewood blue exterior paint and interior upholstery and trim (1979)
- White (1979–1980) — Choice of white, black, wedgewood blue, dark turquoise metallic, cream, cordovan metallic, dark champagne metallic, dark red, diamond blue moondust, light red rose moondust, dark red moondust, medium turquoise moondust, light champagne moondust, light chamois moondust, jubilee gold moondust or light red moondust exterior paints with white interior upholstery and trim

Defroster group: Electric rear window defroster and heated outside LH remote control mirror.

Designer series options: *(The following features are common to all models.)* Six-way power passenger seat, Interior light group, carpeted luggage compartment, forged aluminum wheels (1976), turbine-styled cast aluminum wheels (1977–1980), custom paint stripes, owner's name engraved on I/P plaque, and designer's signature on opera window. Specific to model features:

- Bill Blass (1976) — Dark blue exterior, cream-colored Normande grain Landau vinyl roof, choice of cream colored leather or Versailles cloth interior, cream or dark blue bodyside molding.
- Bill Blass (1977) — Midnight blue exterior, chamois-colored pigskin texture landau vinyl roof, chamois-colored pigskin texture leather-and-vinyl interior, chamois or bright blue bodyside molding.
- Bill Blass (1978) — Midnight cordovan exterior, light champagne landau vinyl roof, midnight cordovan leather-and-vinyl or ultra-velour interior, champagne bodyside molding.
- Bill Blass (1979) — Midnight blue metallic and white tutone exterior, white carriage vinyl roof, and custom paint stripes, midnight blue w/white accents or white w/midnight blue accent leather-and-vinyl interior, white vinyl insert bodyside molding.
- Bill Blass (1980) — Dark blue metallic w/white upper body exterior, white carriage vinyl roof, and dual gold paint stripes on bodyside and decklid, midnight blue w/white accents or white w/midnight blue accent leather-and-vinyl interior, blue vinyl insert bodyside molding, and color-keyed lacy spoke aluminum wheels.
- Cartier (1976–1977) — Dove grey exterior, bodyside moldings and landau roof, dove grey leather-and-vinyl, Versailles cloth (1976), or Majestic velour interior, and Cartier logo on trunk lid.
- Cartier (1978–1979) — Light champagne exterior, bodyside moldings and landau roof, dark red bodyside

stripe, champagne leather-and-vinyl or media velour interior w/red accents, and Cartier logo on trunk lid.

- Cartier (1980) — Medium pewter upper body with light pewter lower body exterior, light pewter bodyside moldings, medium pewter landau roof, dark red bodyside and decklid tape stripes, light pewter/dark pewter leather-and-vinyl or cloth interior, and Cartier logo on trunk lid.
- Emilio Pucci (1976) — Dark red moondust exterior w/silver Normande grain landau vinyl roof, dark red cloth or leather interior, silver and lipstick red bodyside tape stripes, and choice of red or silver bodyside moldings.
- Emilio Pucci (1977) — Black Diamond Fire exterior w/white landau vinyl roof, white leather-and-vinyl interior w/black components, and black bodyside moldings.
- Emilio Pucci (1978) — Light silver Moondust metallic exterior w/black landau vinyl roof, black bodyside moldings, dove grey leather-and-vinyl interior w/red accents, and Pucci logo on trunk lid.
- Emilio Pucci (1979) — Medium turquoise Moondust metallic exterior w/midnight blue full vinyl roof and bodyside moldings, tri-tone bodyside, hood and trunk lid stripes, white leather-and-vinyl interior w/midnight blue accents, and Pucci logo on trunk lid.
- Emilio Pucci (1980) — Light Fawn metallic and Medium Fawn metallic exterior w/Light Fawn landau vinyl roof and bodyside moldings, tri-band bodyside, hood and trunk lid stripes, light champagne leather-and-vinyl interior w/medium champagne inserts, and Pucci logo on front fender louvers and trunk lid.
- Givenchy (1976) — Aqua blue Diamond Fire metallic exterior w/white half-vinyl roof, choice of white or aqua blue bodyside moldings, choice of aqua blue cloth or leather interior and trim.
- Givenchy (1977) — Dark jade metallic exterior w/chamois-colored front half-vinyl roof, bodyside moldings, dark jade leather-and-vinyl or Majestic velour interior trim.
- Givenchy (1978) — Midnight jade exterior w/chamois-colored front half-vinyl roof, light chamois bodyside moldings, chamois hood, bodyside and trunk lid stripes (hood and trunk stripes terminate in double "G" Givenchy logo), jade leather-and-vinyl w/chamois accents on seats.
- Givenchy (1979) — Crystal blue moondust metallic exterior w/crystal blue front half-vinyl roof, dark crystal blue bodyside moldings, dark crystal blue hood, bodyside and trunk lid stripes (hood and trunk stripes terminate in double "G" Givenchy logo), dark crystal blue leather-and-vinyl w/broadlace inserts on seats.
- Givenchy (1980) — Light Fawn metallic exterior w/Bittersweet bodyside accent, Light Fawn full vinyl roof,

Bittersweet bodyside moldings, Bittersweet hood and trunk lid stripes (stripes terminate in double "G" Givenchy logo), Bittersweet leather-and-vinyl interior, and wire wheel covers.

Diamond Jubilee Edition: Choice of diamond blue metallic or jubilee gold metallic exterior paint, unique landau vinyl roof, coach lamps, color-keyed turbine-styled aluminum wheels, unique paint stripes, bucket seats with 6-way power driver's seat w/power lumbar adjustment and passenger side recliner, luxury cloth trim, cut-pile carpeting in trunk, miles-to-empty fuel indicator, garage door opener, Defroster group, Interior light group, interval windshield wipers, Power Lock convenience group, power vent windows, RH remote control mirror, speed control, tilt steering wheel, Appearance protection group, illuminated entry system, rocker panel moldings, AM/FM stereo radio w/quadrasonic 8-track tape player, dual wide WSW tires, personalized nameplates, special keys, umbrella, tool kit, and leather-bound owner's manual.

Headlamp convenience group: Automatic headlamp dimmer and autolamp on/off delay system.

Interior light group: Dual beam dome/map light, and illuminated visor vanity mirrors for both driver and passenger.

Lock convenience group: Power electric door locks, and power trunk-lid release. On 2-door models, also includes automatic seat-back release.

Majestic velour luxury group: Unique interior w/soft down-filled appearance in blue, red, jade or dove grey, velour finished seats, door panels, headliner and other interior components, 6-way passenger seat, Interior light group, carpeted luggage compartment, and paint stripes on bodyside, hood and trunk lid.

Reclining bucket seat group: *(Requires optional floor shift for 1977½.)* Bucket seats w/leather-and-vinyl trim, leather covered floor console w/warning lights for low windshield washer fluid, "headlights on," "door ajar," and low fuel level.

Security Lock group: Locking gas cap, and inside lockable hood release.

Signature series: *Interior:* Choice of leather or Signature Body Cloth Twin Comfort Lounge front seats w/dual 6-way power adjustment and recliners, Allure floor carpeting on floor, lower doors, cowl side trim panels, and lower rear quarter trim areas, personalized signature I/P nameplate, speed control w/resume feature, illuminated visor vanity mirrors, tilt steering wheel w/woodtone insert and ornament, I/P appliqués, woodtone key inserts, control knobs and door switch plates, woodtone door and quarter trim, 6-speaker Premium Sound System w/power amplifier, power door locks, keyless entry system, illuminated entry system, remote control decklid release, intermittent windshield wipers, Defroster group, Headlamp Convenience group, cloth glove box liner, rechargeable glove box light/flashlight, automatic garage door opener control, dual luggage compartment lights, leather-bound courtesy kit (pliers, 4-way screwdriver, 12-volt trouble light, fuses, first aid kit, jumper cable, tire gauge, disposable coveralls, Swiss army knife, safety light tubes, and holders). *Exterior:* Dark maroon or silver metallic paint, two-tone accent stripes on bodyside and hood, Valino grain vinyl landau roof w/integrated coach lamps, Valino grain vinyl decklid accent w/bright edged molding, ID script, owner's monogram, RH remote control mirror, color-keyed bumper rub strips and license plate frames, and color-keyed turbine spoke cast aluminum wheels.

Town Car package: Unique corduroy velour seat trim, woodgrain appliqué garnish moldings, front seatback assist cords, carpeted front seat back, 25-oz. cut pile carpeting in passenger and luggage compartments, glove box vanity mirror, power front door vent windows, cavalry twill vinyl roof, license plate frames, and Town Car exterior identification. Wide-stripe WSW tires added for 1976.

Town Coupé package: Same as Town Car package less power front door vent windows, and with Town Coupé exterior identification.

Versailles luxury group: (1975): Apricot velour cloth interior trim, seat-back map pockets, illuminated visor vanity mirrors, color-keyed luggage compartment trim, bodyside and decklid tape stripes. Available with all paint colors except aqua blue Diamond Fire. (1976): Crushed majestic cloth w/unique "loose pillow" effect available in four colors (blue, red, tan and jade), door trim panels w/cloth inserts, simulated walnut appliqués, door pull strap and carpeted lower section, seat-back map pocket trimmed in distinctive cloth, LH and RH illuminated visor vanity mirrors, and color-keyed cut-pile carpeting in luggage compartment.

Williamsburg Limited Edition: Silver or cordovan color scheme in unique dual shade paint finish, full-vinyl roof, twin Comfort Lounge seats w/passenger recliner, power vent windows, carpeted luggage compartment, custom paint stripes, luxury wheel covers (1977–1978), heavy-duty maintenance-free battery (1979), and Interior light group.

Mercury

Appearance protection group: Front floor mats w/carpeted inserts, spare-tire lock, door-edge guards, and license plate frames.

Brougham décor group: Twin Comfort Lounge seats w/passenger recliner, luxury steering wheel, deluxe color-keyed safety belts, luxury carpeting, wide color-keyed bodyside moldings (ex. Villager), and rear quarter armrests pads on 2-doors.

Brougham option: Deluxe Flight Bench front seat w/fold-down center armrest, deluxe interior trim, deluxe steering wheel, electric clock, deluxe sound insulation, full-length bright bodyside moldings w/integral wheel lip moldings (replaces rocker panel and wheel lip moldings), bright wide door belt moldings, opera windows, full-vinyl roof (4-door only), and deluxe wheel covers.

Bumper protection group: Front and rear bumper guards w/rubber inserts (rear only on Comet and Montego wagons) and full-width horizontal rub strips on bumpers.

Colony Park option: Brougham-level vinyl Flight Bench seat, cargo area light, rear door light switch, courtesy lights under I/P, deluxe steering wheel, deluxe safety belts, electric clock, Grand Marquis door trim panels, LH remote control mirror, Brougham-level wheel covers, and full-length woodgrain appliqué on bodyside and tailgate.

Convenience group: LH remote control outside mirrors (except Bobcat), RH outside mirror (1977–1979 Cougar), RH visor vanity mirror (Bobcat, Montego & Zephyr), deluxe seat belts, luggage compartment light (Comet), dual beam dome lamps (Comet), I/P courtesy light (Comet), inside day/night mirror (Zephyr & 1973 Comet), automatic seat back release (1977–1979 Cougar, 1980 Monarch & 1974–1976 Montego 2-drs.), cigar lighter and rear seat ashtray (Zephyr), glove box lock (Zephyr), spare tire extractor (Montego wagons) trip odometer (1977–1979 Cougar), interval windshield wipers (1977–1979 Cougar & 1980 Bobcat), and automatic parking brake release (1977–1979 Cougar & 1980 Monarch). *1979 & 1980 Marquis only:* Interval windshield wipers, visor vanity mirror (std. on Grand Marquis), electric decklid lock (tailgate on wagons), trip odometer, and warning light cluster.

Custom interior option: Reclining vinyl bucket seats, higher level door trim panels, color-keyed cut-pile carpeting, higher level sound package, deluxe safety belts, leather wrapped steering wheel, simulated woodgrain I/P appliqué, day/night rear view mirror, rear door ashtrays (4-door), glove box light, and dual beam dome/map light.

Custom option: *Interior:* Cut-pile carpeting, unique front bucket seats w/reclining seat back and individual head rests, vinyl seat trim, color-keyed instrument panel w/simulated woodgrain appliqué and bright bezel, bright lower instrument-panel molding, color-keyed seat belts, day/night rear view mirror, rear door ashtrays (4-dr.), glove box light, dual beam dome lamp, leather wrapped steering wheel, and WSW tires. 1973 Comet adds: DR78 × 14 steel-belted radial WSW tires, Montego deluxe wheel covers w/color-keyed inserts, dual bodyside paint stripes, exterior bright moldings, and full-length stainless steel bodyside and wheel opening moldings.

Custom trim package: *(1974.) Montego MX Brougham:* Deluxe wheel covers, door pull assist straps, 25 oz. carpeting, visor vanity mirror, Levant grain or Odense grain Embassy vinyl roof, luxury steering wheel, simulated cherry wood cluster cover, and I/P appliqué w/simulated teakwood inlays, Comfort Lounge seats w/velour seating surfaces and super soft vinyl facings, door trim panels w/velour inserts, and trunk side lining boards. *Montego MX Villager:* Door pull assist straps, 25 oz. carpeting, visor vanity mirror, luxury steering wheel, simulated cherry wood cluster cover, and I/P appliqué w/simulated teakwood inlays, Comfort Lounge seats w/velour seating surfaces and super soft vinyl facings, and door trim panels w/velour inserts. *(1975.)* Twin Comfort Lounge seats w/velour cloth trim and super soft vinyl, door pull assist straps, 22-oz. carpeting, visor vanity mirrors, luxury steering wheel, Levant grain full (4-door) or Odense grain ¾ (2-door) or Embassy grain full (2-door) vinyl roof, luggage compartment trim, and deluxe color-keyed wheel covers. *Villager Wagon:* Twin Comfort Lounge seats in super-soft vinyl, unique door trim panels w/door pull assist straps, 22-oz. carpeting, visor vanity mirror, and luxury steering wheel.

Décor group: *Cougar:* Rocker panel moldings, deluxe steering wheel, deluxe wheel covers, custom door and quarter trim, door pull-straps, bright pedal trim, and choice of two-tone woven vinyl or upbeat cloth-and-vinyl trim. *Cougar XR-7 (1977–1980):* Twin Comfort Lounge seats (1980), deluxe seat belts and door trim (1980), luxury steering wheel (1980), passenger visor vanity mirror (1980), full-length bodyside moldings w/color-keyed vinyl inserts, styled road wheels (1977–1979), dual color-keyed mirrors (bright for 1980), hood paint stripes, *Capri:* Console w/integrated clock, contoured rear bucket seats, simulated leather steering wheel and shift knob, reclining front seats, adjustable map light, dual horns, and electric rear window defroster. *Monarch:* Deluxe door trim, deluxe steering wheel, and Flight Bench or reclining bucket seats.

ES option group: *Interior:* Black instrument panel package tray, grey engine turned I/P and cluster appliqués, black sport steering wheel and column, black carpeting, armrests and door trim, and choice of black or chamois on all other interior components. *Exterior:* Blackout grille, Deluxe bumper group, black cowl grille, bright belt moldings, black window frames, quarter window ventilation louvers and lower back panel, vinyl insert bodyside moldings, black dual sport outside rearview mirrors w/LH remote control, turbine-styled wheel covers, and handling suspension.

ESS option group: *(Sedan models only.)* *Interior:* Flight Bench seat or reclining bucket seats w/seat back map pockets and European-style headrests, luxury padded door trim panels including carpeting on lower portion, luxury trunk carpeting, luggage compartment trim, leather-wrapped sports steering wheel, deluxe color-keyed seat belts, bright periphery moldings deleted from I/P, Ghia level sound insulation package, day/night inside rearview mirror, and rear door courtesy light switches. *Exterior:* Hood and trunk lid paint stripes, ESS block letters on front fender, black vinyl insert bodyside moldings, black-out grille texture, black windshield wipers, wide wheel lip moldings, black rocker panel paint, black window frames and B-pillars, dual racing outside rearview mirrors, Bumper protection group, louvered opera window appliqués (2-door), black rear door division bars (4-door), dual note horn, color-keyed wheel covers, heavy-duty suspension, and FR78 steel-belted radial BSW tires.

Ghia option group: *Interior:* Deluxe Flight Bench seat or reclining bucket seats w/seat back map pockets, luxury padded door trim panels including carpeting on lower portion, simulated woodgrain I/P appliqués (Zephyr), deluxe trunk carpeting, grey cardboard quarter panel sides and lower back trim panel in trunk (Monarch), deluxe steering wheel, day/night rearview mirror (Zephyr), deluxe color-keyed seat belts, deluxe sound insulation package, and rear door courtesy light switches (Monarch). *Exterior:* Hood paint stripe, wide (or deluxe) color-keyed vinyl insert bodyside moldings, wire wheel covers (Monarch), upper bodyside paint stripes, front fender ornament (Monarch 2-door), C-pillar ornament (Monarch 4-door), trunk lid paint stripe, dual note horn, and ER78 steel-belted radial BSW tires.

Grand Marquis décor option: Twin Comfort Lounge seats (non-reclining) w/unique sew style in leather-and-vinyl upholstery, seatback map pockets and assist straps (1979–1980), upgraded door trim w/pull straps and quarter trim panels (1979), seat belt warning chimes (1980), luxury steering wheel, digital clock, dome/dual beam map light, and tinted glass.

Grand Marquis luxury trim group: *(Requires Twin Comfort Lounge seats and power windows.)* Leather and vinyl or leather and velour seat trim, RH I/P appliqué, dome map/reading lamp, luxury steering wheel, passenger assist handles, digital clock, carpeted luggage compartment, and hood and decklid paint striping. Wagons have the following additions and deletions: unique headrests and door trim panels, 25 oz. cut-pile carpeting, Brougham wheel covers, visor vanity mirror, Brougham sound package, and under I/P lights are added; leather and velour seat trim, and hood and deck lid paint striping are deleted. Colony Park adds to wagons: Brougham split bench seats and door trim panels, front door courtesy lights, door pull straps, and rear door cigar lighters.

GT package: High-back bucket seats, deluxe door trim panels, blackout instrument panel w/bright molding, hood scoop, dual racing mirrors, hubcaps w/bright wheel trim rings, body tape stripes, blackout grille and headlamp doors, deluxe sound package, improved rear seat trim pads, color-keyed seat belts, leather wrapped steering wheel, and 14 oz. cut-pile carpeting. Standard upper bodyside molding and rocker panel moldings are deleted.

Instrumentation group: *(Available only on V8 equipped cars and Capri.)* Tachometer, trip odometer, engine gauges (oil, amp, temp and fuel), and electric clock.

Interior accent group: *Bobcat:* Deluxe seat and shoulder belts, day/night inside rear view mirror, LH remote control mirror, and deluxe 2-spoke color-keyed steering wheel. *Capri:* Sound insulation package, low-back bucket seats, inertia seat-back release, deluxe seat belts w/tension reliever, and visor vanity mirror. *Comet & Zephyr:* All-vinyl seat trim (pleated on Zephyr), deluxe door trim (w/bright accents on Zephyr), interior color paint on doors at upper edge (Comet), deluxe steering wheel hub, simulated woodgrain I/P appliqué, and deluxe sound insulation package.

Light group: Adjustable or dual beam dome map light (depending upon model and year), engine compartment light, glove box lights, ashtray light, luggage compartment light (Zephyr coupes and sedans), headlamps-on warning buzzer (ex. Capri & Zephyr), rear door and passenger door courtesy light switches (Zephyr), and third door courtesy light switch (Bobcat Runabout and Capri).

Light/Convenience group: Deluxe color-keyed seat belts, passenger-side visor vanity mirror, day/night rear view mirror, interior lighting (glove box, ashtray, map, and cargo area–wagon), headlights-on warning buzzer, underhood light, and dual remote control racing mirrors.

Lock convenience group: Power door locks, trunk-lid release (ex. wagons), LH remote control outside mirror, automatic seat-back release (2-drs. only), and power tailgate lock (wagons).

Luxury exterior decor group: Bright door window frames and quarter window moldings, deluxe bodyside protection moldings, hood accent paint stripes, and dual bright outside rearview mirrors w/LH remote control (RH remote also for 1980).

Luxury group: Twin Comfort Lounge seats w/luxury trim, luxury door and quarter panel trim, electronic instrument panel, diagnostic warning light module, luxury half vinyl roof, electronic warning chimes, power windows, light group, 18 oz. carpet, luxury steering wheel, passenger illuminated visor vanity mirror, rear quarter courtesy lamp, luggage compartment trim, dual remote control rear view mirrors, color-keyed bodyside molding with bright rub strip extension and integral partial wheel lip moldings, hood and decklid accent stripes, TR type radial WSW tires, and cast aluminum wheels.

Luxury interior trim package: *(Pre–1977 Marquis and Colony Park wagons, and 1978–1980 Zephyr.)* Brougham split bench front seat and door trim, luxury level non-reclining Flight Bench seat w/deluxe trim (Zephyr), interior accent group (Zephyr), cut pile carpeting, visor vanity mirror, sound package, front door courtesy lights, rear door armrest cigar lighters (ashtrays only on Zephyr), Marquis Brougham wheel covers (Marquis), door-pull straps, day/night inside rearview mirror (Zephyr), and lights under I/P (Marquis and Colony Park).

Midnight/Chamois décor group: *Interior:* Deluxe Tiffany carpeting in passenger compartment, bucket seats w/cloth inserts, vinyl side facings and formed bright buckles, cloth-and-vinyl door trim w/pull straps, console lid w/ cloth on top surface, and deluxe color-keyed seat belts. *Exterior:* Rear half-vinyl roof w/vinyl cross-over strap, black louvers, padded continental tire deck, straight-through paint stripe, color-keyed rear window molding, styled road wheels w/chamois accent paint, upgraded sound insulation package, and color-keyed vinyl insert bodyside molding.

Power lock group: Power door locks, and electric trunk (or hatch) release (power tailgate lock on wagons).

RS option package: Ghia soft door trim appliqué, engine-turned I/P and RH appliqué, black window frame moldings, tape treatment, color-keyed hood louvers, hood scoop, dual black remote control outside rearview mirrors, "RS" identification, sport wheel covers, BR78 × 14 BSW tires, and radial sport suspension.

Runabout Woodgrain group: *Interior:* Deluxe low back bucket seats, deluxe door trim, deluxe color-keyed seat belts, deluxe steering wheel, and sound package. *Exterior:* Simulated woodgrain appliqué on bodyside and lower back panel, and deletes wheel lip and rocker panel moldings.

"S" option group: *Bobcat and Capri II:* Bodyside, hood, third door surround and lower back panel dual gold color tape stripe, blackout treatment for windshield wiper arms, windshield, side windows, rear window, lower back panel surround area, center pillar and belt areas, body color wheel lip and rocker panel areas, styled steel wheels w/gold accents, dual color-keyed remote control racing mirrors, handling suspension, and (on Capri II only) black and gold décor level interior w/gold cloth inserts, black interior moldings, I/P, and sports steering wheel. *Monarch:* Bucket seats, deluxe vinyl insert door trim, leather wrapped sports steering wheel, floor-mounted shift lever, landau vinyl roof, bodyside, hood and trunk lid paint/tape stripes, rocker panel molding, dual remote control color-keyed racing mirrors, styled steel wheels w/trim rings and gold accents, heavy-duty suspension.

Security Lock group: Spare tire lock, lockable hood release (Montego), and locking gas cap.

Special Value package: LH remote control mirror, full-length bodyside moldings w/color-keyed vinyl inserts, deluxe color-keyed wheel covers, upper bodyside dual paint stripes, bright belt moldings, vinyl appliqué on B-pillar, full vinyl roof, front and rear bumper guards, and WSW tires.

Sports accent group: *Bobcat:* Leather-wrapped sports steering wheel, gold bodyside accent tape stripes (Villager only), lower bodyside and lower back panel paint/tape treatment (Runabout only), sound insulation package including carpeted load floor, deluxe low back bucket seats, deluxe door and seat trim, and deluxe color-keyed seat belts. *Comet:* Custom wide bodyside molding, lower back panel paint, dual racing mirrors w/left-hand remote control, belt moldings, lower bodyside paint, styled steel wheels w/trim rings, and WSW tires.

Sports accent trim: *(Cougar XR-7 only.)* Individually contoured cloth-and-vinyl front bucket seats in blue/silver blue, or saddle/tan color combinations.

Sports appearance group: *(Requires SelectShift transmission.)* Sporty hood, dual racing mirrors, black hub caps w/bright trim rings, lower body tape/paint stripe, B/WL G70 × 14 tires (H70 with 460 CID 4-bbl. engine), lower back panel blackout paint, leather-wrapped steering wheel, bright pedal pads, and instrumentation group.

Sports group: Recaro bucket seats w/console, décor rear seat w/luxury trim, luxury door and rear quarter trim appliqués, power windows, 18 oz. carpet, Tu-tone paint treatment, dual bright remote control mirrors, wide door belt molding, hood and decklid accent stripes, and TR type radial WSW tires w/cast aluminum wheels.

Sports Instrumentation group: Sports instrument panel (ex. Bobcat, Capri & Zephyr), luxury steering wheel w/engine-turned insert and black deluxe trim (ex. Bobcat, Capri & Zephyr), sports steering wheel (Bobcat), ampere, oil pressure and engine temperature gauges, tachometer, clock (ex. Capri & Zephyr), and trip odometer.

Sports Instrumentation/Handling group: Sports Instrumentation group less clock, plus front stabilizer bar and performance rear axle ratio.

Sports option: Sports steering wheel, front air dam, dual racing mirrors (black), rear spoiler, white styled steel wheels/trim rings, argent painted grille/headlamp doors, black windshield moldings, all-glass third door, black domed hood, and lower bodyside/rear end tape treatment w/Bobcat name on front doors. Requires power front disc brakes.

Sports package option: Tri-color bodyside tape stripes w/stylized Bobcat head on each front fender, tri-color hood and lower back panel (Runabout only) tape stripes, styled steel wheels, dual color-keyed remote control racing mirrors, black paint on wiper arms, drip rail, window frames, belt areas, and windshield reveal moldings, and black painted rocker panels.

Turbo RS option package: Includes features of the RS option package with the following additions or changes: dual black rearview remote control mirrors, low-back bucket seats w/inertia seat back releases, "Turbo RS" identification, 2.3L turbocharged engine, TRX forged aluminum wheels, Michelin TRX tires, rally suspension, and sports-tuned exhaust w/bright extension.

Villager option: *Zephyr:* Cherry wood tone bodyside appliqué; bright wood tone surround rails, lower bodyside molding, and partial wheel lip moldings, all with wood tone inserts; bright door frame/quarter window moldings; wood tone appliqués on liftgate; and Villager script on liftgate.

Visibility group: LH and RH remote control mirrors (requires LH remote option if not standard), day/night inside mirror, and RH visor vanity mirror, and visibility light group (1973 full-size Mercurys).

Visibility light group: Underhood (engine compartment), glove box, and ashtray lights, cargo area light, parking brake warning light, headlights "lights-on" warning buzzer, dome/dual beam map lamp, I/P courtesy lights, and rear door courtesy light switches (Montego and Monterey 4-drs.).

Visibility/Convenience group: Deluxe safety belts, dual outside remote control mirrors, lighting package (includes ashtray, dual beam map, glove box, I/P, trunk and under hood lights), "headlights-on" warning buzzer, day/night rear view mirror, rear door light switch, and visor vanity mirror.

XR-7 décor group: Choice of twin Comfort Lounge seats w/passenger recliner or bucket seats w/console and floor shift, luxury steering wheel, deluxe door trim, deluxe color-keyed safety belts, luxury carpeting, wide color-keyed bodyside moldings, rear quarter armrest pads, dual remote control racing mirrors, hood paint stripes, and styled road wheels.

Oldsmobile

Brougham interior package: Choice of Oxen-grain vinyl or Laredo cloth 60/40 divided front seat w/fold-down armrests front and rear, and rear compartment assist straps and courtesy lights.

Compaticolor option package: Blue, cranberry or saddle interior color with white vinyl seats. Selected color includes instrument panel, carpeting, door panels, console (if ordered), seat belts, and all other interior trim.

Convenience group: Visor vanity mirrors, map lights, rear door courtesy light switches, and cargo compartment light. *Omega adds:* Trunk light, glove box light, and under dash courtesy lights.

Convenience light package: Map lights, rear door courtesy light switches, and cargo compartment light.

Crown Landau package: *(Delta 88 Royale two-door only.)* Stainless steel roof bar and padded landau roof (eliminates rear quarter window), stand-up hood ornament, and color-keyed wheel covers.

Firenza Sport package: Front air dam, functional rear spoiler, blackout window trim, blackout bumpers, tri-color stripes on bodysides w/lower body blackout paint and "Firenza" name on front doors, blackout hood dome with stripes and "Firenza" name at cowl, special design star-spoke rally wheels, and BR70 × 13 R/WL tires.

GT package: Four-spoke slotted steel padded steering wheel (1976–1978), full gauges including tachometer (1976–1978), electric clock, wide hood and side stripes w/Starfire GT name on front door (in black, white or gold metallic), rear stabilizer bar (1976–1978), special design star-spoke chrome rally wheels, and BR70 × 13 R/WL tires.

Holiday Coupe package: *(Delta 88 coupe only.)* All-vinyl front bucket seats, floor console w/T-handle shifter, padded rim sport steering wheel, dual sport mirrors, special Holiday C-pillar insignia, and body-colored custom wheel covers.

Indianapolis 500 pace car replica package: *1974 Cutlass 2-Door Colonnade Hardtop Coupe (requires W25 or W30 H/O package):* White w/Hurst gold and black exterior trim, black leather interior, and official pace car decal package. *1977 Delta 88 Royale coupe:* Red velour bench seat, sport steering wheel, body color dual sport mirrors, specific two-tone silver paint with black center hood paint, black painted bodysides between the upper and lower feature lines and on the C-pillar, red pinstriping, flat black side window and door frames, flat black grille and headlight trim on bezels, aluminum hood, red-painted sport (Super Stock III) wheels, GR70 × 15 R/WL tires, and 403 CID V8 engine.

1974 Oldsmobile Hurst/Olds Cutlass
Indianapolis 500 pace car replica

1977 Oldsmobile Delta 88 Royale
Indianapolis 500 pace car replica

LS package: *(Available on Omega Brougham only.)* Four-season air conditioning, AM/FM stereo radio, electric clock, power windows, full tinted glass, special two-tone exterior paint treatment, power steering, power front disc brakes, Turbo Hydra-matic automatic transmission, and ER78 × 14 WSW tires.

Regency LX package: *(Available on Ninety-Eight Regency only.)* Leather interior trim, air conditioning, tilt-and-telescope steering wheel, cruise control, rear window defogger, tinted glass, power door locks, dual remote control mirrors, power trunk lid release, padded canvas vinyl top w/formal rear window, wide rocker panel and window sill moldings, wire wheel covers, and wide WSW tires. Exterior color choices of medium beige, black, silver metallic or dark carmine metallic.

"Renaissance" interior package: *(Available only on Cutlass Supreme Brougham models.)* Shades of blue and camel velour upholstery on seat back and seating surface inserts with a "bold contemporary" "zigzag" pattern.

"S" sports package: *(Available only on coupe and hatchback.)* Custom sport steering wheel, bodyside stripes and decals, sports mirrors, Rallye suspension, and Super Stock III wheels.

Salon package: *(1973 Cutlass Supreme sedan only.)* Choice of ribbed-velour or perforated vinyl reclining contoured front seats, Salon specific interior and door panel trim, deluxe steering wheel, center console w/floor-shifter, deluxe front and rear armrests, "Salon" name and flag plaques on exterior, bright rocker panel and wheel lip moldings, ride and handling package, front disc brakes, wheel discs w/body-colored centers, and GR78 × 15 WSW tires.

SX package: *(Not available on sedans 1976–1979.)* Padded sport steering wheel, dual sport mirrors w/LH remote control, lower body paint stripes with SX logo on front door, and FE2 rallye suspension. *1980 base Omegas only:* Dual sport mirrors, monochromatic body stripes with SX logo on front door, blacked-out window surround moldings, blacked-out grille and bumpers, and functional front air dam.

V6 Sports pack: *(Available only on coupe or hatchback.)* Buckskin or white front bucket seats, sports gauge group, Super Stock wheels, and raised white letter tires, plus Custom sport steering wheel, dual outside sport mirrors, SX lower body racing stripe, rocker panel and wheel opening moldings, and Open-Road FE2 suspension.

(W/25) H/O option package: *(1973–1974 Cutlass S 2-Door Colonnade Hardtop Coupe.)* White or black exterior paint w/gold Hurst striping and decals, 350 CID V8 engine, dual exhausts, Hurst Dual-Gate shifter w/Turbo Hydramatic transmission, FE2 rallye suspension, Super Stock III wheels, and 15" RWL tires.

(W29) 4-4-2 appearance and handling package: *1973–1974 Cutlass and Cutlass S coupes; 1975–1977 Cutlass S coupe only:* Special 4-4-2 grille, hood louvers (1973–1975), specific 4-4-2 bodyside and decklid decals, FE2 rallye suspension package (includes heavy-duty front and rear stabilizer bars, heavy-duty rear-suspension upper control arms and 14" × 7" wheels), and rocker and wheel lip moldings. *1978–1979 Cutlass Salon coupe only:* 4-4-2 interior emblems, contrasting striping along the rocker panels and lower doors, and over both wheel wells, 4-4-2 decals on the rear trunk edge and lower front edge of the door, black-out grille, and FE2 rallye suspension.

(W30) 4-4-2 appearance and handling package: *(1980 Calais coupe only.)* Gold velour or vinyl reclining front bucket seats, sport steering wheel, full instrumentation including tachometer, sport console, digital clock, gold sport mirrors, B-pillar appliqué molding, 4-4-2 emblems on sail panel and deck lid lower edge, black and gold or white and gold exterior paint w/painted grille, taillamp and rear window moldings painted to match body color, W-30 logo on front fender above side marker light, 350 CID V8 L34 engine, dual outlet exhaust, FE2 rallye suspension, special gold cast aluminum sport wheels, and P205/70R14 R/WL tires.

(W30) H/O option package: *1973–1974 Cutlass S 2-Door Colonnade Hardtop Coupe:* White or black exterior paint w/gold Hurst striping and decals, 455 CID V8 engine, dual exhausts, Hurst Dual-Gate shifter w/Turbo Hydra-matic transmission, FE2 rallye suspension, Super Stock III wheels, and 15" RWL tires. *1979 Calais 2-Door Coupe:* Gold velour or vinyl reclining front bucket seats, sport steering wheel, full instrumentation including tachometer, sport console w/Hurst shifter, digital clock, gold sport mirrors, B-pillar appliqué molding, black and gold or white and gold exterior paint w/painted grille, taillamp and rear window moldings painted to match body color, W-30 logo on front fender above side marker light, 350 CID V8 L34 engine, dual outlet exhaust, FE2 rallye suspension, special gold cast aluminum sport wheels, and P205/70R14 R/WL tires.

(W45) Hurst/Olds option package: *(Coupes only—1973–1974 Cutlass S; 1975 Cutlass Supreme.)* Choice of black or white vinyl swivel front bucket seats with Hurst/Olds interior logo, sport console, Hurst console-mounted Dual-Gate shifter w/specially calibrated automatic transmission, FE2 rallye suspension, Cameo White or Ebony Black exterior paint with specific gold exterior striping and with Hurst/Olds logos, white or black vinyl landau roof w/opera window, dual sport mirrors, custom hood ornament, dual exhaust w/chrome tailpipe extensions, power disc brakes, Super Stock III wheels, and G60 × 14 radial tires.

XS custom package: Power-operated silver-tinted glass "Astroroof," unique wraparound rear window styling with angled corners, and specific "XS" nameplates.

XSC option package: Contoured front seats w/center floor console (shifter on column), leather-wrapped sport steering wheel, instrument panel gauges, dual remote-control sports mirrors, exterior accent tape stripes, "XSC" emblems, ride and handling suspension package, painted wheel discs (matching body color), and GR70 × 15 WSW tires.

Plymouth

Arrow Jet package: *(Arrow 160 only.)* Two-tone orange and black body paint, black bumpers, orange grille, dual black racing mirrors, chrome road wheels, and 165 × 13 R/WL tires. An assortment of twelve different decals available as a separate option, and include lower door side "ARROW JET" name decal, fuel door "FUEL" decal, directional arrow decals around door locks, "30 PSI" with arrow above each wheel opening, "AIR INTAKE" on front pan below grille, "NO STEP" on front pan below headlights, "CAUTION restricted area" for hood, and "HOT EXHAUST" above rear bumper and exhaust pipe.

Basic group: AM radio, three-speed electric windshield wipers w/washers, remote control chrome LH rearview mirror, power steering (Barracuda), and deluxe wheel covers. *1978–1980 Volaré:* AM radio, left remote-control mirror, deluxe intermittent wipers, hood silencer pad, dual horns, TorqueFlite automatic transmission, power steering, deluxe wheel covers, and WSW tires. *1980 Gran Fury:* Color-keyed deluxe seat belts, air conditioning (manual), AM radio, LH remote mirror, Light package, full vinyl roof, vinyl bodyside molding, deluxe windshield wipers, and undercoating.

Basic package: Trunk dress-up, power steering, 4-wheel disc brakes, and 2600cc engine.

Brougham package: Plush velour bucket or bench seating (Valiant/Scamp), cloth-and-vinyl 50/50 comfort seat w/power left adjustment (Fury Gran 4-doors), cloth-and-vinyl bucket seats w/armrest type center cushion (Fury Gran coupe), fold-down center armrest (Fury Gran), reclining front passenger seat (Fury Gran), luxury door trim panels, shag carpeting, simulated woodgrain instrument panel inserts, carpeted trunk, day/night rearview mirrors, sound insulation system, accent stripes on hood and deck (Scamp), Brougham nameplate on sail panel (Valiant/Scamp), on trunk lid (Fury Gran), or tailgate (Sport Suburban), and hood ornament (Valiant/Scamp).

Custom exterior package: *Horizon:* Bright trim accents on hood, fender, wheel lip, door sill and roof drip rail. *Volaré:* Color-keyed full-length bodyside molding w/vinyl insert, belt moldings, rear deck lower appliqué (sedan and coupe only), and upper door frame moldings (wagon only).

Custom interior package: *Horizon:* Choice of cloth or all-vinyl high-back bucket seats, custom door trim panels, glove box lock, and simulated woodgrained I/P appliqué. *Volaré:* Custom seat and interior trim, rear armrest w/ashtray, simulated woodgrained I/P appliqué, cigarette lighter, day/night inside mirror, molded cloth headliner, hood silencer pad, and Custom exterior nameplates.

Custom package: *Valiant:* Simulated woodgrain interior appliqués and accent trim (1976), color-keyed carpeting (1973–1974), cigarette lighter (1973–1974), drip rail moldings (1976), and wheel lip moldings. *Volaré:* Combines features of Custom exterior package and Custom interior package, plus wheel opening moldings.

Décor package: *(Cricket sedan.)* Deluxe seats, deluxe door trim panels w/storage pockets in front doors, deluxe trim carpet, rear door armrests, high style instrument panel pad w/trim plate, instrument panel light rheostat, voltmeter, oil pressure gauge, glove box light and lock, no-draft vent windows, dual horns, bright upper door frame moldings, rocker panel sill moldings, and wheel covers.

Decorator Special package: White vinyl bucket seats w/plaid cloth insert, red vinyl trim around cloth, white floor console w/woodgrain trim, and red carpeting on the floor and fold-down rear seat back.

Deluxe sound insulation package: Undercoating w/hood silencer pad, noise reduction package (firewall and wheel wells), and special body sound insulation (floors, roof and rear seat).

Duster Coupe package: *1979 Coupe only:* High-back plaid cloth-and-vinyl bucket seats, quarter window louvers w/tape accents, belt and center pillar moldings, color-keyed upper-side tape accent stripe, color-keyed deck lower panel "Strobe" tape accent stripe, "Duster" fender nameplates, and D78 × 14 WSW tires. *1980 Coupe only:* Combines features of Duster Coupe package and Duster décor package into a single package.

Duster décor package: *(Requires Duster Coupe package—1979 only.)* Lower bodyside two-tone paint and tape break stripe, and five-spoke styled road wheels with bright trim rings.

Easy order package: AM radio, Light group, three-speed electric windshield wipers w/washers, inside day/night rear view mirror (Valiant), LH remote control mirror, vinyl roof, bumper guards, luggage rack (station wagons), inside hood release, undercoating w/hood insulation pad, Torque-Flite automatic transmission, power steering, power front disc brakes, deluxe wheel covers, and WSW tires.

Feather Duster fuel economy package: Lightweight aluminum components such as intake manifold, hood inner panel, and decklid inner panel, along with engine modifications and economy axle ratios.

Funrunner décor package: Belt moldings and rallye wheel trim rings.

Funrunner package: Rear quarter window louvers, specific bodyside and decklid tape stripes, and body-colored 5-spoke rallye wheels.

Gold Duster package: All-vinyl bench seat, three-spoke steering wheel, front and rear bumper guards, deluxe sound insulation, distinctive bodyside moldings or tape stripes, canopy vinyl roof, full chrome deluxe wheel covers, and WSW tires.

Gran Coupe package: *Some sources mention this as an option for the 1978 Fury Sport, but no details of the package could be found in corporate literature.*

Light group: Ashtray, glove box and trunk (or cargo compartment) lights, ignition switch light w/time delay, map and courtesy lights (Volaré, Fury and Gran Fury), decklid ajar light (1980 Gran Fury), rear-door courtesy light switch (4-drs., except Volaré), headlight-on warning buzzer (except Volaré), low battery/high temperature light-emitting diodes (1980 Gran Fury), low washer fluid light (1980 Gran Fury), illuminated hood and parking brake releases (1980 Gran Fury), and fender-mounted turn signal indicators,

Light package: Map/courtesy light, glove box light, ignition switch light w/time delay, ashtray light, headlights-on warning buzzer, luggage compartment light, and fender mounted turn signal indicators.

Luxury equipment package: Air conditioning, auto-matic speed control, electronic digital clock, power windows, tinted glass, vinyl bodyside moldings, deluxe or luxury steering wheel, tilt steering wheel, Easy order package, cargo compartment carpeting (Suburbans), air deflector and assist handles (Suburbans), and auto-lock tailgate (Suburbans)

Popular equipment group: Dual horns, power steering, light package (1979–1980), LH remote-control mirror (Horizon, 1979–1980), dual remote-control sport mirrors (Horizon TC3), day/night inside rear view mirror (Horizon TC3), and wheel trim rings.

Premier exterior package: Custom exterior package, hood ornament w/windsplit molding, hood tape stripe, bodyside accent tape stripes (only on coupe w/optional landau vinyl roof), upper doorframe moldings (sedan), and wheel lip moldings.

Premier interior package: Premium all-vinyl bucket seats or choice of all-vinyl or cloth-and-vinyl 60/40 front bench w/passenger recliner, rear armrest and ashtray, shag carpeting (w/automatic transmission), LH remote-control mirror, simulated woodgrained I/P and glove box door appliqués, luxury steering wheel (requires power steering), cigarette lighter, day/night inside mirror, pedal dress-up, molded cloth headliner, deluxe insulation package, Premier exterior nameplates, and DR78 × 14 BSW tires.

Premier package: Combines features of Premier exterior and Premier interior packages. For 1980 wagons, also includes the Premier wagon woodgrained group features.

Premier Wagon interior package: Custom vinyl bench seat, rear armrest w/ashtray, simulated woodgrained I/P cluster, cigarette lighter, day/night inside mirror, cargo compartment carpeting and covered lockable storage bins, hood silencer pad, and Premier exterior nameplates.

Premier Wagon wood-grained group: *(NA w/Custom exterior package.)* Simulated woodgrain bodyside and rear exterior panel trim, hood ornament w/windsplit molding, belt moldings, and upper door frame moldings.

Premium exterior package: *Horizon 4-door hatchback:* Custom exterior package plus bright door frame accents, bright belt and center pillar moldings, full-length bodyside and liftgate moldings, and Rallye wheel hubs w/bright acorn lug nuts. *Horizon TC3:* Bright side window and drip rail moldings, louvered quarter window appliqué, black and bright bumper rub strips, and deluxe wheel covers.

Premium interior package: All-vinyl or suede-like cloth bucket seats w/passenger-side recliner and adjustable head restraints (all-vinyl only on TC3), three-spoke wood-grained steering wheel, color-keyed shift lever console, passenger-side visor vanity mirror, and premium door trim panels w/carpet, soft uppers and premium front armrests w/integral door pull handles.

Premium package: *Champ:* Red and white cloth-and-vinyl bucket seats w/reclining seatbacks, cargo lamp, day/night inside rear view mirror, oil pressure and battery gauges, tachometer, rear window wiper/washer, dual electric outside rear view mirrors, Canyon Red exterior paint, white tape stripes (on grille, bodyside and decklid), cast aluminum road wheels, and 175/70HR × 13 RWL tires. *Sapporo (requires Basic package):* Power windows, intermittent windshield wipers, and AM/FM stereo w/tape player.

Premium woodgrain package: Premium exterior package plus simulated woodgrained vinyl bodyside and lower liftgate appliqué.

Protection group: Glove box lock, inside hood release, and door edge guards.

Rallye equipment group: Rallye instrument cluster w/tachometer, clock and trip odometer, sport steering wheel, Horizon TC3 name decals, rear deck spoiler, rallye wheels painted body color w/bright hubs, lug nuts and trim rings, and 185/70R13 OWL Aramid tires.

Rallye instrument panel group: Electric clock, tachometer, oil pressure gauge, trip odometer, 150 mph speedometer, and three-speed electric windshield wipers w/washers.

Road Runner décor package: *(Coupe only; requires Road Runner package.) 1976–1977:* Dual remote-control sport-style chrome rear view mirrors, wheel lip moldings, and Rallye wheel trim rings. *1978-on:* Belt molding and Rallye wheel trim rings.

Road Runner "Front Runner" Super Pak: *1977:* Black cloth-and-vinyl front bench seat, Spitfire Orange exterior paint, Road Runner multi-colored tape stripe orange/yellow/flat black, front air spoiler, wheel opening flares, quarter window louvers, and rear deck spoiler with tape stripe. *1978 (Road Runner package and dual remote control racing mirrors required; various colors available):* Front air spoiler, wheel opening flares, quarter window louvers, rear deck spoiler, and Road Runner tape stripe applications.

Road Runner package: *(Coupe only.) 1976–1977:* Bodyside and deck tape stripe, Road Runner decals, grille blackout treatment, heavy duty suspension, Road Runner "beep-beep" horn, Rallye road wheels less trim rings, and E70 × 14 RWL tires. *1978–1979 (requires V8 engine):* Road Runner decals, black-painted grille, sill molding w/black finish, dual remote control racing mirrors (body colored w/tape stripe), Road Runner "beep-beep" horn, heavy-duty suspension, Rallye wheels less trim rings, and FR78 × 14 BSW tires. *1980 (available with six-cylinder or V8 engines):* Vinyl bucket seats, "Tuff" color-keyed steering wheel, dual color-keyed remote sport mirrors, black painted grille, black painted headlamp doors and park/turn signal surrounds, black anodized windshield and rear window trim, black drip rail and quarter window surround moldings, black windshield wiper arms/blades, bright rocker panel sill moldings w/black surround, body accent stripes (hood, cowl, mirrors, wheel openings, side window perimeters, and rear spoiler), unique gas filler cap, rear spoiler, "Road Runner" decal on front fenders and rear spoiler, heavy-duty suspension, eight-

spoke painted road wheels w/stainless-steel ornamentation and trim rings, and P195/75R14 BSW tires.

Salon package: All-vinyl 50/50 split bench seat w/passenger side recliner, vinyl roof, color-keyed bodyside molding w/vinyl insert, and Salon exterior identification.

Silver Duster package: Burgundy "Boca Raton" cloth-and-vinyl front bench seat, burgundy interior trim, Silver Cloud metallic exterior paint, unique bodyside and rear panel stripes, and wheel opening moldings.

Space Duster package *(Duster, 1974–1975): see* **Spacemaker Pak.**

Spacemaker Pak/Space Maker Pak: *Duster (1976):* Fold-down rear seat, security panel and trunk dress-up trim. *Volaré:* Fold-down rear seat and carpeted trunk dress-up.

Spectrum decorator trim package: Black cloth and white vinyl bucket seats and door panel trim with multicolor (yellow, orange, red) vinyl inserts.

Sport appearance package: Sport 4-spoke steering wheel, rallye instrument cluster w/tachometer, black windshield and rear window moldings, black paint graphics on lower bodyside, black dual aerodynamic mirrors, black belt moldings, black door handle accents, black taillamp accents, black body tape stripes w/reflective red accents at taillamp area, TC3 name decals on quarter panels, rear deck spoiler w/TC3 decal, black front and rear protective rub strips, and color-keyed rallye wheels w/bright hub and lug nuts, and P175–75R13 WSW tires.

Sport package: Black 4-spoke steering wheel, rallye instrument cluster w/tachometer, clock and trip odometer, blackout moldings, mirrors and accents, louvered rear quarter window appliqués, black lower body paint, TC3 decals, rear deck spoiler, and painted rallye wheels.

Sport wagon package: Premium vinyl bucket seats, "Tuff" steering wheel, cargo compartment carpets, storage bins w/covers and locks, wheel-opening flares, front air dam, dual color tape stripes for front air dam, upper bodyside wheel openings, flares and liftgate, black painted park and turn lamp surround, black painted headlamp doors, blackout grille treatment, dual body-colored remote control sport mirrors, and eight-spoke styled road wheels w/stainless steel ornamentation and trim rings.

Sports décor group: Body sill rocker moldings, wheel lip moldings, bodyside tape stripe and sport hood.

Street Kit Car package: *(Requires power steering, power brakes and automatic transmission.)* Super Coupe package equipment (less the dark brown and black paint scheme), door and roof number decals ("43," for NASCAR racing legend Richard Petty's number), large rear spoiler, fender flares with "bolt-on" look, two-tone blue paint, and race-inspired wheels without center caps.

Super Coupe package: *(Requires 360 CID, 4-barrel V8 engine.)* Dark red body color w/contrasting black finish (on hood, front fender tops, head lamp bezels, wiper arms, front and rear bumpers, and remote-control racing mirrors), bodyside and over-the-roof triple-color tape striping, black wheel flares, black front and dark brown rear spoilers, "Super Coupe" insignia, quarter window louvers, heavy-duty suspension, rear anti-sway bar, 15" × 8" special GT wheels, and GR60 × 15 RWL tires.

Super Pak: *(Base coupe only.)* Louvered rear quarter window, flared wheel openings, front chin spoiler, and rear decklid spoiler.

Turismo package: Popular equipment group, premium interior package, deluxe color-keyed seat belts, sport steering wheel, rallye instrument cluster, AM/FM stereo radio, black windshield and rear window molding, black door handle inserts, black belt molding, black bumper rub strips front and rear, halogen headlamps, power front disc brakes, 3.5:1 performance axle, Turismo decal nameplates on bodysides and rear deck spoiler, rear deck spoiler, cast aluminum road wheels, and P185/70R13 Aramid-belted BSW tires.

Twister package: Lower decklid and bodyside tape stripes, blackout hood paint treatment (1973 only), dual hood scoops (1973 only), dual racing mirrors (1974), drip rail moldings, wheel lip moldings, front sway bar, rallye road wheels, and wheel trim rings.

Two-tone décor package: *Volaré coupe (1976–1978):* Main body color is on hood, roof, decklid and bodysides, and secondary color surrounds side windows continuing to top of front fenders, and lower bodyside including over wheel openings. Available in varying color combinations depending upon model year. As an example, 1976 choices: Yellow Blaze and Harvest Gold w/white, black and gold tape stripes, or Silver Cloud and Black w/silver, bright red and black tape stripes, or Spitfire Orange and Black w/orange, white and black tape stripes. *Volaré (1979–1980):* (Requires two-tone paint package) Hood ornament and center windsplit molding, upper door frame moldings (sedan and wagon only), belt moldings, rocker panel sill moldings, and rear appliqué (coupe and sedan only).

Two-tone paint package: *Volaré:* Two-tone paint, w/lower color including wheel lip moldings. *Horizon:* (Classic two-tone) Two-tone paint break at upper bodyside feature line on 4-door hatchback with chrome accent strip, and (Sport two-tone) at lower bodyside feature line on TC3 2+2 hatchback with tape stripe at paint break.

Pontiac

Basic group: *(Firebird, 1973.)* AM radio, dual horns, power steering, Turbo Hydra-matic transmission, wheel trim rings, and WSW tires.

Brougham package: Plush velour bucket or bench seating, luxury door trim panels, shag carpeting

Can Am appearance package: *(LeMans Sport Coupe*

only.) Unique Can Am interior nameplates on I/P, full-width rear deck spoiler, tri-tone colored (yellow-orange-red) accent tape stripes (on hood, front fenders, doors, sport mirrors, and rear deck spoiler), black lower bodysides w/accent stripes; tri-tone "Can Am" identification on front header panel, front fenders, and rear decklid, blacked-out moldings (windshield, rear window, door window and beltline), and Trans Am-style shaker hood scoop w/tri-tone "T/A 6.6" or "6.6 Litre" identification and accent stripes.

Can Am option package: *(LeMans Sport Coupe only.)* Grand Prix-style instrument panel w/rally gauge cluster, electric clock, dual body-colored sport mirrors w/LH remote-control, front and rear bumper rub strips, blacked-out grille inserts, Cameo White exterior paint, power front disc brakes, power variable-ratio steering, space saver spare tire, T/A 6.6 Litre 400 CID, 4-bbl. V8 engine (6.6 Litre 403 in California or designated high-altitude areas), Turbo 400 heavy-duty automatic transmission Turbo 350 in California or designated high-altitude areas), Rally RTS package, body-colored Rally II wheels, and GR70 × 15 radial tires.

Catalina Custom package: *(Catalina only.)* Custom cloth or all-Morrokide 60/40 front seat w/fold-down center armrest, custom cushion steering wheel, bright window reveal moldings, bright wheel opening moldings, bright rocker panel molding, quad rectangular headlamps, and deluxe wheel covers.

Custom exterior group: Belt reveal and side window moldings, rocker panel moldings, body colored door handle inserts, and wheel opening moldings.

Custom interior group: *Astre:* Custom upholstery, cargo floor carpeting, custom door trim w/ door pull straps and map pocket, courtesy lights, and rear seat ashtray. *LeMans:* Custom front notchback seat w/fold-down center armrest and custom interior upholstery and trim, and color-keyed exterior door handle inserts.

Custom Safari package: Custom cushion steering wheel, lower body and liftgate woodgrain vinyl exterior trim, and 350 CID V8 engine.

Custom trim group: *Astre:* Luxury front and rear seats, RH door dome lamp switch, day/night rearview mirror, I/P assist strap, rear ashtray, luxury door trim w/map pocket, and load floor carpeting. *Catalina:* Custom upholstery and door panel trim, front seat center armrest, and chrome seat trim; (1976 only) adds rectangular headlights. *Firebird:* Custom interior upholstery and trim, bright pedal trim, and color-keyed exterior door handle inserts. *LeMans (1974) and LeMans four door (1975–1976):* All-Morrokide front bench seat w/fold-down center armrest.

Décor group: Custom cushion steering wheel, custom pedal trim plates, bright hood rear edge molding, bright window sill and bright wheel opening moldings.

Firm ride and handling packages: *(Two separate options sold together, unless specifically ordered individually.) Firm Ride package:* Firm shocks, and high rate springs. *Handling package:*

Power steering, large front and rear stabilizer bars, firm shocks, 15" × 7" wheels, and G60 × 15 BSW tires.

Formula appearance package: *Astre & Sunbird (1976–1978):* Rally gauges, tachometer, black lower body w/harmonizing stripes, blacked-out grille, front air dam (Sunbird only), rear deck spoiler (wind deflector on Safari), blacked-out rear panel (except Safari), Formula identification, RTS package, body-colored Rally II wheels, and BR70 × 13 BSW tires. *Firebird Formula:* Specific striping and graphics on lower body, rear panel and hood, blacked out lower body and grille (1977–1978).

GT option package: *Astre (1975–1976):* Adjustable driver's seatback, rally gauge cluster, custom cushion steering wheel, dual body color sport mirrors, window sill moldings, wheel opening moldings, body color door handle inserts, special suspension w/front and rear stabilizer bars, 140 CID 2-bbl. 4-cylinder engine, rally wheels w/trim rings, and BR78 × 13 BSW tires. *LeMans or Lemans Sport coupes (1974–1975):* Body-colored dual sport mirrors, wheel opening moldings, vinyl body stripes, GT identification, heavy-duty three-speed floor shift transmission (Turbo Hydra-matic in California), dual exhausts w/chrome extensions, Rally II wheels, and G70 × 14 R/WL tires. *LeMans Sport Coupe (1977):* Grand Prix-style instrument panel w/rally gauges, dual body-colored sport mirrors, blacked-out grille, Rally RTS package, two-tone color treatment w/body accent stripes, and Rally II wheels.

GTO option package: *LeMans or Lemans Sport coupes (1973):* Blacked out grille, specific body striping w/GTO identification, dual air scoop hood, rear sway bars, three-speed manual transmission w/floor-mounted shifter, 400 CID, 4-bbl. V8 engine, dual exhausts w/chrome extensions, moon-style hubcaps and G60 × 15 BSW tires. *Ventura (1974)*:* Blacked out grille, special grille-mounted parking/turn signal lights, rear-facing "shaker" hood scoop, firmer shock absorbers, computer-selected springs, front and rear stabilizer bars, power steering, dual exhaust w/splitter type extensions, 3.08:1 rear axle ratio, Rally II wheels, and E70 × 14 BSW tires.

Indianapolis 500 pace car replica package: T-top roof, air conditioning, limited-slip differential, white-painted alloy wheels, AM/FM ETR stereo w/cassette tape and seek-and-search functions, power windows, power door locks, and the WS6 Performance Handling Package, which included four-wheel disc brakes and stiffer suspension components. Pace Car replicas were available only in Cameo White with gray accents. Decals were optional.

Lamp group: *Astre & Sunbird:* Glove box light, RH door courtesy light switch, and luggage compartment light. *Firebird:* Instrument panel courtesy lights, glove box light, and luggage compartment light.

LJ luxury appointment package: Choice of Lombardy cloth or genuine buffalo calf leather interior, exclusive two-tone exterior with special striping, and Cordova top in either full or landau styling.

**1980 Pontiac Firebird Turbo Trans Am
Indianapolis 500 pace car replica**

LJ option package: *(Available on base Grand Prix.)* Velour interior trim, plush cut-pile carpeting, door pull straps, dome reading lamp, visor vanity mirrors, litter container, power windows, power door locks, body-colored dual remote-control mirrors, added acoustical insulation, velour trunk trim, spare tire cover, special two-tone paint treatment w/accent tape stripes, and Cordova (landau) vinyl top.

Luxury appointment package: *Astre:* Doeskin Morrokide luxury level interior upholstery, plush cut-pile carpeting and additional sound insulation. *Sunbird:* Plush cut-pile carpeting, custom seat belts, glove box light, dual sport mirrors w/LH remote, spare tire cover, exterior accent stripes, and rear panel molding.

Luxury trim group: Luxury bucket seats w/Doeskin Morrokide or knit cloth trim, luxury door trim w/map pocket and lower door panel carpet, rear seat ashtrays, luxury cushion steering wheel, body-colored door handle inserts, doorsill moldings, and bright wheel opening moldings. *Sunbird:* Luxury seats in cloth or vinyl, luxury door trim w/map pockets, luxury carpeting, luxury cushion steering wheel, custom seat belts, non-glare inside rearview mirror, wood-grain appliqué on RH I/P, and rear seat ashtrays.

Protection group: Bodyside protective moldings, door edge guards, and front and rear bumper rub strips.

Rally gauge cluster package: *Grand Prix and Firebird (1973–1974):* Oil, temperature and ammeter gauges, tachometer, and electric clock. *Ventura (1973–1974):* Console mounted ammeter, fuel, oil pressure and temperature gauges, I/P mounted tachometer, and electric clock. *Astre (1975–1977):* Tachometer, temperature and voltmeter gauges, and electric clock.

Rally RTS package: *(Features vary by model; these are general features.)* Larger front stabilizer bar, rear stabilizer bar, and specifically tuned suspension components.

Red Bird appearance package (W68): Red cloth interior trim (available in vinyl for $42 less), red Formula steering wheel, red custom seat belts, gold accented engine-turned I/P trim plates, two-tone red exterior, dark red accent on lower body w/ gold tape striping, Red Bird decals on sail panel, gold grille liners, and red cast aluminum wheels.

RTS (Radial Tuned Suspension) package: *Firebird:*

Larger front and rear stabilizer bars, Pliacell shock absorbers, higher rate springs, jounce restrictors, and steel-belted radial tires (in standard size for specific model). *Ventura:* Front and rear stabilizer bars, Pliacell shock absorbers, specific springs, and FR78 × 14 WSW or R/WL tires. *LeMans:* Rear stabilizer bar, Pliacell shock absorbers, specific rate springs, and GR78 × 15 WSW tires. *Catalina, Bonneville and Grand Ville:* Front and rear stabilizer bars, Pliacell shock absorbers, specific springs and rear control arm bushings, jounce restrictors, RTS identification on I/P, and HR78 × 15 WSW tires.

SJ Golden Anniversary package: Hurst Hatch (T-top) removable glass roof panels, and special anniversary identification on hood ornament, deck lid ornament, and instrument panel.

SJ option package: *Grand Prix:* Rally gauge cluster, dual body-colored rear view mirrors, bodyside pinstriping, rear stabilizer bar, unitized ignition system, 250-hp, 455 CID V8 engine, maintenance free battery, custom finned wheel covers, and GR78 × 15 BSW tires (1973), GR70 × 15 BSW tires (1974). *Phoenix (1980):* Black painted grille and headlight bezels, black painted side window frames, "Phoenix" bird emblem on center B-pillar, black accented door handles, black accented front and rear window moldings, bright roof drip rail moldings, additional acoustical insulation, rear deck lock cover, black tail lamps, dual sport mirrors w/LH remote and RH manual, wheel opening moldings, black rocker panel molding, accent color on lower body and bumpers w/lower body accent stripe, black bumper rub strips, "SJ" decal on front fender, and emblem on I/P, dual horns, rally suspension (includes larger stabilizer bars, specific shocks and springs, P205/70R13 tires, and requires optional power steering), and Rally wheels.

Sky Bird appearance package (W60): Blue velour interior trim (available in vinyl for $31 less), blue luxury cushion steering wheel, blue custom seat belts, two-tone blue exterior, dark blue accent on lower body w/gradient blue tape stripe, Sky Bird decals on sail panel, blue grille panels, and medium blue cast aluminum wheels.

Special appearance group: *(Two-door models only.)* Special body striping on hood, deck lid and lower body, and black window frames.

Special edition Trans Am package: *1976–1977:* Choice of black or buckskin interior in either standard or custom trim, gold interior accents including gold swirled aluminum I/P facing, Starlight Black exterior with specific gold accents and striping, gold grille liner and headlamp bezels, and GR70 × 15 BSW tires. Hurst Hatch (T-top) roof is available as an option. *1978–1980:* Choice of black or buckskin interior trim, choice of Starlight Black exterior with specific gold accents and striping, or Solar Gold metallic exterior with specific black accents and striping (Gold paint for 1978 only), T-top removable glass panels, gold interior accents including gold swirled aluminum I/P facing, gold Pontiac crest on header panel (w/gold color only), and GR70 × 15 BSW tires.

Sprint option package: *1973 Ventura 2-door:* Custom cut-pile carpeting, Custom Cushion steering wheel, body-colored sport mirrors, specific blacked-out honeycomb style grille, and bodyside tape stripes w/Sprint name on rear quarter panel. *1974 Ventura 2-door:* All 1973 features plus, LH remote control sport mirror, and Rally II wheels. *1975 Ventura 2-door:* Body colored dual sport mirrors w/LH remote control, bright wheel opening moldings, black lower body, black side window frames, hood and decklid stripe in black, gold or white, Sprint identification on front end panel, rear deck lid and fenders, blacked-out grille, road-style parking/turn signal lamps, and special Rally II wheels.

W50 Formula appearance package: *(Firebird Formula only.)* Rear deck spoiler and "Formula" lettering on lower door and rear deck spoiler.

W66 Formula appearance package: Rally gauges and tachometer, blacked-out grille, body colored sport mirrors, Black lower body paint w/Formula lettering and accent stripes, black window moldings (Sport Hatch only), black rear end panel w/accent stripes, front air dam and rear spoiler, Rally RTS handling package, black rally wheels, and BR70 × 13 BSW tires.

WS6 Trans Am performance package: Heavy-duty suspension, cast aluminum "Snowflake" wheels, power front and rear disc brakes (1978–1980), and 255/70R15 R/WL tires.

Yellow Bird appearance package (W73): Camel Tan velour interior trim (available in vinyl for $45 less), tan/gold luxury cushion steering wheel, tan custom seat belts, two-tone yellow exterior, darker yellow accent on lower body w/gold tape stripe, Yellow Bird decals on sail panel, yellow taillight grille panels, and yellow cast aluminum wheels.

V. General Motors Engine RPO and VIN Codes

After the 1977 lawsuit over GM installing Chevrolet engines in Oldsmobile Delta 88s, part of the settlement agreement was that General Motors would disclose information regarding the source of all GM engines in its marketing material and in its dealerships for the next three years, which would include 1978 through 1980. Below is a list of GM engine RPO (regular production option) codes and their related VIN codes. Each engine is listed with its displacement and fuel delivery system, as well as the GM division and engine plant producing the engine. The engine RPO and VIN codes are also listed in the model year powertrain details for GM cars, except Cadillac, which was not a part of this program for the 1978, 1979 and 1980 model years. Details of the issues that led to the lawsuit are in the Introduction of this book.

GM engine RPO Code	VIN code	Engine size and fuel delivery	Producing engine plant location
LX3	1	85 CID (1.4L) 4-cyl., 1-bbl.	GM-Chevrolet Motor Division, Flint, MI
LY5	E	98 CID (1.6L) 4-cyl., 1-bbl.	GM-Chevrolet Motor Division, Flint, MI
LW5	J	98 CID (1.6L) H.O. 4-cyl., 1-bbl.	GM-Chevrolet Motor Division, Flint, MI
L11	A,B	140 CID (2.3L) 4-cyl., 2-bbl.	GM-Chevrolet Motor Division, Flint, MI
LS6/LS8	V	151 CID (2.5L) 4-cyl., 2-bbl.	GM-Pontiac Motor Division, Pontiac, MI
LX6/LX8	1,5,9	151 CID (2.5L) 4-cyl., 2-bbl.	GM-Pontiac Motor Division, Pontiac, MI
LE2	7	173 CID (2.8L) V6, 2-bbl.	GM-Chevrolet Motor Division
LC9	C	196 CID (3.2L) V6, 2-bbl.	GM-Buick Motor Division, Flint, MI
L26	M	200 CID (3.3L) V6, 2-bbl.	GM-Chevrolet Motor Division, Tonawanda, NY
LC5	G	231 CID (3.8L) Turbocharged V6, 2-bbl.	GM-Buick Motor Division, Flint, MI
LC8	3	231 CID (3.8L) Turbocharged V6, 4-bbl.	GM-Buick Motor Division, Flint, MI
LD5	C	231 CID (3.8L) V6, 2-bbl.	GM-Buick Motor Division, Flint, MI (1977–on)
LD7	C	231 CID (3.8L) V6, 2-bbl.	GM-Buick Motor Division, Flint, MI (1975–1977)
L22	D	250 CID (4.1L) 6-cyl., 1 bbl.	GM-Chevrolet Motor Division, Flint, MI
LV8	F	260 CID (4.3L) V8, 2-bbl.	GM-Oldsmobile Motor Division, Lansing, MI
LS5	S	265 CID (4.3L) V8, 2-bbl.	GM-Pontiac Motor Division, Pontiac, MI
L27	Y	301 CID (4.9L) V8, 2-bbl.	GM-Pontiac Motor Division, Pontiac, MI
L37	W	301 CID (4.9L) V8, 4-bbl.	GM-Pontiac Motor Division, Pontiac, MI
LU8	T	301 CID (4.9L) Turbocharged V8, 4-bbl.	GM-Pontiac Motor Division, Pontiac, MI
LG3	U	305 CID (5.0L) V8, 2-bbl.	GM-Chevrolet Motor Division, Flint, MI
LG3	U	305 CID (5.0L) V8, 2-bbl.	GM-Chevrolet Motor Division, Tonawanda, NY
LG3	U	305 CID (5.0L) V8, 2-bbl.	GM of Canada engine plants
LG4	G	305 CID (5.0L) V8, 4-bbl.	GM-Chevrolet Motor Division, Flint, MI
LG4	H	305 CID (5.0L) V8, 4-bbl.	GM-Chevrolet Motor Division, Tonawanda, NY
L14	Y	307 CID (5.0L) V8, 2-bbl.	GM-Oldsmobile Motor Division, Lansing, MI
L30	H	350 CID (5.7L) V8, 2-bbl.	GM-Pontiac Motor Division, Pontiac, MI
L76	P	350 CID (5.7L) V8, 4-bbl.	GM-Pontiac Motor Division, Pontiac, MI
L34	R	350 CID (5.7L) V8, 4-bbl.	GM-Oldsmobile Motor Division, Lansing, MI
L48	L	350 CID (5.7L) V8, 4-bbl.	GM-Chevrolet Motor Division, Flint, MI
L77	J	350 CID (5.7L) V8, 4-bbl.	GM-Buick Motor Division, Flint, MI
L82	K	350 CID (5.7L) V8, 4-bbl.	GM-Chevrolet Motor Division, Flint, MI
LM1	L	350 CID (5.7L) V8, 4-bbl.	GM-Chevrolet Motor Division, Flint, MI
LM1	L	350 CID (5.7L) V8, 4-bbl.	GM-Chevrolet Motor Division, Tonawanda, NY
LM1	L	350 CID (5.7L) V8, 4-bbl.	GM of Canada engine plants
LF9	N	350 CID (5.7L) V8, Diesel	GM-Oldsmobile Motor Division, Lansing, MI
L78	Z	400 CID (6.6L) V8, 4-bbl.	GM-Pontiac Motor Division, Pontiac, MI
W72	Z	400 CID T/A (6.6L) V8, 4-bbl.	GM-Pontiac Motor Division, Pontiac, MI
L80	K	403 CID (6.6L) V8, 4-bbl.	GM-Oldsmobile Motor Division, Lansing, MI

VI. Tire Sizes, Identification and Recalls

During the 1973–1980 time frame, several changes occurred in the numbering, ratings, and construction of tires used on American automobiles. For the past decade, numbers such as 8.25–14 designated tire size. This system was a modification of the numbering convention that had been used since the 1930s. In the example, 8.25 refers to the tire section width in inches, and the 14 indicates the nominal rim diameter in inches. The higher the first number, as in 8.55 compared to 8.25, the wider the tire. A wider tire of the same rim diameter can carry more load at a specified pressure. This is the reason that station wagons generally use a larger, wider tire. With the advent of Wide-oval and Super-wide-oval tires, new size designations were added.

Beginning in 1970, most tires began using a combination letter and number system, which replaced the numbering system. The letter replaced the number system of width, and a new numbering system indicated the aspect ratio. The definition of aspect ratio is determined by the relationship of the tire section height, divided by the tire section width. With this calculation, the wider the tire section is, the smaller the aspect ratio will be. As an example, an aspect ratio of 78 (as in D78 × 14) is considered standard, while an aspect ratio of 70 indicates a wide-oval tire, and an aspect ratio of 60 indicates a super wide-oval tire. Later metric tires were manufactured in 50, 60, 65, 70, 75, and 80 series (aspect ratios).

Along the way, various types of tire construction were developed. In the early 1960s, most tires were of a bias-ply construction, with various plies, or layers. A ply could be made of nylon, rayon or polyester. The definition of bias-ply is that the cords of the ply run diagonally to the circumference of the tread, usually at less than a 45-degree angle. In the mid–1960s, belted tires became more commonplace. Belted tires were at first of bias-ply construction, with a belt of material underlying the tread around the circumference of the tire. The material could be of glass fiber, rayon or woven steel. By the late 1960s and early 1970s, the steel-belted radial-ply tire came into increasingly widespread use on American cars. More durable and more fuel-efficient, radial ply tires use plies that run perpendicular to the tread, completely around the tire from lip to lip.

With radial-ply tires becoming more common by 1975, an additional change was made to the identification system by adding "R" after the tire width designation, such as DR78 × 14. The R stands for radial ply, while tires with no markings would be of bias-ply or belted bias-ply construction. As imported cars became more popular, and as more American cars were being sold with radial tires, yet another tire size designation came into existence in the U.S. marketplace during the late 1970s, the metric designation. The only difference with the metric designation is that it uses the nominal tire section width measured in millimeters, instead of the letter system; for example 175 × 13, where the tire section width is 175 millimeters. Then in 1978, the P-metric designation was adopted for tires manufactured in North America.

The chart below shows the old numbering system with the letter that replaced it and then the newer P-metric size that replaces the letter. Equivalencies are approximate and based on 75 and 70 series (aspect ratio) tires. Smaller aspect ratios will increase the P-metric equivalent size.

One of the most famous tires of the 1973–1980 period, or infamous in reality, was the Firestone 500 radial. Firestone Tire and Rubber Company was one of the last major tire manufacturers to introduce a steel-belted radial tire. Unfortunately, immediate problems were seen with the Firestone 500 that resulted in the separation of the belts at high speeds. After 41 deaths, a federal investigation, and congressional hearings, the presumed cause was determined to be the type of glue or bonding material used between the belts. Another theory was that radial tires had better wear characteristics and lasted so much longer than bias-ply tires that they were often driven longer than they should have been. In October 1978, Firestone recalled more than 7 million tires. The tire they replaced them with was the new Firestone 721, famously advertised as having "a steel structure of seven cords wrapped by two cords, wrapped by one" spiral-wound cord to hold the bundle together. Despite its problems, the Firestone 500 was the best selling of the early U.S. radial tires. Many years later it was stated that all companies had faced similar problems when they first started production of radial tires, and it was a problem each company had to resolve on its own due to varying construction methods. In the end, a rigorous testing program was developed by the industry for all new tires.

Tire Size Equivalents Comparison Chart for 1973 to 1980 Cars

Up to 1978 Bias-ply Numeric	1973 to 1978 Bias-ply Letter	1973 to 1978 Radial Letter	1978 Onward Radial P-metric size*
6.00-13	A78-13	AR78-13	P165/80R13
6.45-13	B78-13	BR78-13	P175/80R13
6.45-14	B78-14	BR78-14	P175/75R14
6.95-13	C78-13	CR78-13	P185/80R13
6.95-14	C78-14	CR78-14	P185/75R14
6.95-15	C78-15	CR78-15	—
—	D78-13	DR78-13	—
—	D78-14	DR78-14	—
7.35-14	E78-14	ER78-14	P195/75R14
7.35-15	E78-15	ER78-15	P195/75R15
7.75-14	F78-14	FR78-14	P205/75R14
7.75-15	F78-15	FR78-15	P205/75R15

Up to 1978 Bias-ply Numeric	1973 to 1978 Bias-ply Letter	1973 to 1978 Radial Letter	1978 Onward Radial P-metric size*
8.25-14	G78-14	GR78-14	P215/75R14
8.25-15	G78-15	GR78-15	P215/75R15
8.55-14	H78-14	HR78-14	P225/75R14
8.55-15	H78-15	HR78-15	P225/75R15
8.85-14	J78-14	JR78-14	—
8.85-15	J78-15	JR78-15	P225/75R15
9.15-14	L78-14	LR78-14	—
9.15-15	L78-15	LR78-15	P235/75R15

*Sizes shown assume "standard" 78 series and "75 & 80" series aspect ratios. See text for other aspect ratio information.
**Some of the captive import models used a "Euro-metric" size rather than the number or letter system from 1973 to 1980. See text.

VII. Aftermarket Convertible Conversions*

The following is a list of companies that built aftermarket convertible conversions during the 1973 through 1980 model years, and the models that they converted. Most would continue to build convertible conversions into the mid-eighties, while a few would assist in designing and building the first of the "factory" convertibles as they returned to the market beginning in 1982. Some are still building conversions for both American and import brands into the 21st century. Accompanying this list are a variety of pictures and advertising materials depicting some of the convertible conversions available for the 1973 to 1980 period.

This list has been compiled through company advertising flyers and brochures as well as magazine advertisements, and is a representative sample. The list may not be complete as to all manufacturers who did conversions, or as to all the products converted by a given company. It is also possible that a few of these companies may not have actually built more than one prototype of a given model, or even have advanced beyond the design and concept stage of production.

- **A.H.A. Inc.**, Belleville, Michigan: Lincoln Continental coupes, 1977–1979; Mercury Capri, 1979–1980; Mercury Cougar, 1977–1979; Mercury Monarch, 1977–1980.
- **American Custom Coachworks**, Hollywood, California: Cadillac deVille, 1977–1979; Cadillac Eldorado, 1979–1980; Cadillac Seville, 1980; Chrysler Cordoba, 1977; Ford Thunderbird, 1977–1979; Lincoln Continental Mark V coupe, 1977–1979; Lincoln Continental Mark VI coupe, 1980; Mercury Cougar, 1978–1979.
- **ASC** (American Specialty Cars, formerly American Sunroof Corporation), Los Angeles, California and South-

THE ALL NEW ROADSTER

MONARCH ROADSTER COUPE CONVERSION .... LIST $895

COUGAR ROADSTER COUPE CONVERSION .... LIST $895

Please call collect regarding substantial dealer discount and to place an order. Limousines, convertibles, funeral coaches and custom conversions are our speciality.

Lincoln Continental Conversions

A. H. A., Inc.   510 SAVAGE ROAD • BELLEVILLE, MICHIGAN 48111 • 313-697-7129

1978 Monarch convertible by AHA

gate, Michigan: Cadillac Eldorado, 1978. ASC invented the glass-panel "moonroof" and the inward-folding convertible top first used on GM's full-size convertibles.
- **Armbruster/Stageway**, Fort Smith, Arkansas: Cadillac Eldorado, 1980.
- **Coach Builders Limited**, High Springs, Florida: Lincoln Continental Mark V coupe, 1977–1978.
- **Coach Design Group**, Westlake Village, California: 1979–1980 Cadillac Eldorado.
- **Custom Coach**, Lima, Ohio: 1979 Cadillac Eldorado.
- **Emess Coach Builders**, Largo, Florida: Chrysler Cor-

*Information on some of the manufacturers mentioned in this appendix is drawn from the Wikipedia article "Coach convertible," http://en.wikipedia.org/wiki/Coach_convertible.

doba, 1977; Ford Mustang II coupe, 1977–1978; Lincoln Continental Mark V coupe, 1977–1978.

- **Global Coach & Armor Manufacturing**, Florida: Cadillac Eldorado, 1979–1980; Cadillac Seville, 1980; Chrysler Cordoba, 1980; Lincoln Continental Mark V coupe, 1978–1979.
- **Greenwood Corvettes**, Apopka, Florida: Chevrolet Corvette, 1980.

1977 Mustang II Classic II convertible by Emess

- **Hess & Eisenhardt**, Cincinnati, Ohio: Buick Electra coupe, 1980; Cadillac deVille (Le Cabriolet), 1978–1980; Cadillac Eldorado, 1980; Lincoln Continental coupe, 1977; Lincoln Continental Mark V coupe, 1978; Oldsmobile 98 coupe, 1980.
- **National Coach Engineering**, Port Sanilac, Michigan: Chevrolet Camaro, 1979–1980; Pontiac Firebird, 1979–1980.
- **Silcco** (Southern & International Lincoln Custom Center), Miami, Florida: Lincoln Continental coupe and sedans, 1977–1979.

In addition to convertible conversions, the National Coach Corporation in Los Angeles built an unknown

THE CLASSIC II...

A LIMITED EDITION HANDCRAFTED CONVERTIBLE MODEL ON THE CHRYSLER CORDOBA CHASSIS

Top up, or top down, the Classic II has the lines of a modern classic automobile. Spacious rear seat allows full comfort for two or three passengers.

Features of The Classic II

- Full double strength folding convertible top in choice of black or white
- Top boot matching interior of car
- Fully carpeted trunk area
- Top is fully electro-hydraulically operated
- Opera windows are an integral part of the top assembly and retract when top is folded
- Fully reinforced body with frame added
- All bright work stainless steel or polished aluminum
- Rear windows with zip out

WARRANTY

All work is guaranteed for a period of 12 months or 12,000 miles from date of delivery.

Sold & Serviced Exclusively By

1977 Cordoba Classic II convertible by Emess

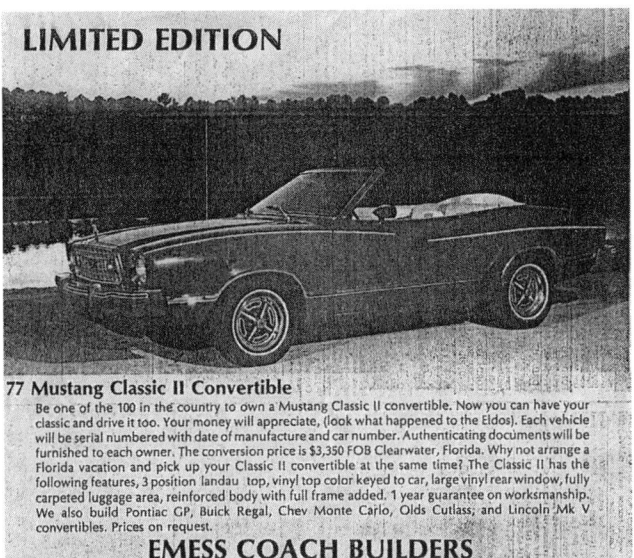

LIMITED EDITION

77 Mustang Classic II Convertible
Be one of the 100 in the country to own a Mustang Classic II convertible. Now you can have your classic and drive it too. Your money will appreciate, (look what happened to the Eldos). Each vehicle will be serial numbered with date of manufacture and car number. Authenticating documents will be furnished to each owner. The conversion price is $3,350 FOB Clearwater, Florida. Why not arrange a Florida vacation and pick up your Classic II convertible at the same time? The Classic II has the following features, 3 position landau top, vinyl top color keyed to car, large vinyl rear window, fully carpeted luggage area, reinforced body with full frame added. 1 year guarantee on workmanship. We also build Pontiac GP, Buick Regal, Chev Monte Carlo, Olds Cutlass, and Lincoln Mk V convertibles. Prices on request.

EMESS COACH BUILDERS

1977 Mustang II Classic II convertible by Emess

1979 Coupe deVille LeCabriolet by Hess and Eisenhardt

1979 Eldorado convertible by Hess and Eisenhardt

Right: 1979 Ninety-Eight convertible by Hess and Eisenhardt

A new dimension in personal luxury.

1979 Eldorado convertible by Hess and Eisenhardt

Oldsmobile 98 Regency Luxury Convertible

THE HESS & EISENHARDT MFG. CO.
Blue Ash Avenue
Cincinnati, Ohio 45242
513 / 791-8888
The Best Since 1876

Buick Electra 225 Luxury Convertible

THE HESS & EISENHARDT MFG. CO.
Blue Ash Avenue
Cincinnati, Ohio 45242
513 / 791-8888
The Best Since 1876

1980 Electra convertible by Hess and Eisenhardt

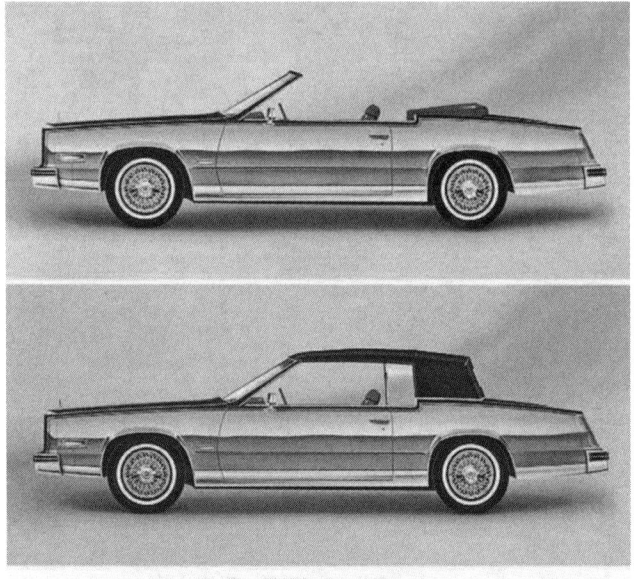

The Hess & Eisenhardt Company
Blue Ash Road, Cincinnati, Ohio 45242
Phone: 513/791-8888

The Best Since 1876

1980 Eldorado convertible by Hess and Eisenhardt

number of Fairmont Durango pickup truck conversions. The idea was based on the Ford Ranchero, which was discon-

1977 Continental Town Coupe convertible by Silcco

The All New
FORD MUSTANG CONVERTIBLE
By SILCCO

After a seven year wait the MUSTANG CONVERTIBLE is back!

With beautiful European styling, an efficient, trouble-free mechanical top and great gas mileage, the SILCCO Mustang is what the public has been awaiting.

Any 1979 or 1980 2 door Ford Mustang, including the exciting high performance Ghia, can be turned into the best looking convertible on the road today. Any resemblance to a $30,000 Mercedes is quite intentional.

SILCCO, already building a full line of luxury limousines and convertibles, felt a true American sport convertible was long past due.

NOW IT'S HERE!

NOTE: All Mustangs will be built in Florida, at either our Ft. Lauderdale or Ocala plant. Arrangements must be made in advance for drop-off as directed, at which time a delivery date will be set.

FOR MORE INFORMATION
CONTACT:

SILCCO
Southern & International Lincoln Custom Center, Inc.
Builders of "The World's Most Beautiful Cars"

Main Office
6600 N.W. 53rd Terrace, Suite 124
Miami, Florida 33166
(305) 592-4990

1979 Mustang convertible by Silcco

tinued after the 1979 model year. The Fairmont-based pickups essentially were slightly lengthened Futura sport coupes with a fiberglass bed inserted in place of the rear deck-lid and rear seating area. They were sold by Ford dealers nationwide between 1979 and 1982 after undergoing the conversion process.

VIII. Concept Cars

Concept and experimental cars had drawn great attention in the 1950s and early 1960s, particularly with General Motors' Motorama shows, but during the 1970s only a few concept cars truly caught the public's attention. Some would go on tour with annual new car shows. Part of the reason for the decline in popularity most likely had to do with the earlier cars being all about new styling, new power and futuristic new features, whereas most concept cars of the 1973–1980 period were centered on safety, fuel economy and aerodynamics, or merely gave glimpses of cars of the immediate future to gauge consumer reaction. These types of concept cars were typically based on existing cars and lacked the glamour of their predecessors. It would not be until the mid–1980s that futuristic styling and features crept back into concept cars, putting them back into the spotlight and capturing the public's attention. Some of the better known 1973–1980 concept cars are listed below, with a short summary description of each vehicle.

- **1973 Ford Experimental Safety Vehicle (ESV).** Built around the design of a Galaxie 500 sedan, the ESV was Ford's version of a "safe" family vehicle. Added features included a heavier frame, aluminum bumpers with 10 mph impact capability, a roll cage, and four built-in airbags. General Motors had also built a 1972 model ESV, and both were shown to the federal government's Department of Transportation as examples of what cars would be like to meet proposed requirements for passenger safety.

1973 ESV (Experimental Safety Vehicle)

- **1973 Ford Pinto Sportiva.** Fashioned from a Pinto Runabout two-door hatchback, the Sportiva was a two-seat roadster concept with an integrated roll bar and removable roof panel. Painted in pearlescent paint and wearing special wheels on the outside, the car featured leather bucket seats with plaid black-and-white cloth inserts, and red piping. All other interior trim was in silver leather with pewter shag carpeting on the floor and rear package tray.

1973 Pinto Sportiva

- **1974 AMC Gremlin XP.** For the smallest of Detroit's four major automakers, funds were always short, so concept cars from AMC were almost always based on an existing car line or a rework of a prior concept car. The Gremlin XP, based on a regular Gremlin, featured a three-piece wraparound rear window and hardtop side window styling with a reverse-angle C-pillar. The concept was a unique take on the Gremlin's production styling and probably could have made it to production if it had been about three years earlier, when AMC had more funds available for adding body styles.

1974 Gremlin XP

- **1974 AMC Gremlin G/II.** Also based on the Gremlin hatchback, this new idea for a hatchback featured a Hornet front end with a special grille, along with a fastback roofline. In retrospect, it turned out to be the

1974 Gremlin GII

basis for the 1979 Spirit hatchback, as the greenhouse area is almost identical.

• **1974 Chevrolet Vega with Wankel rotary engine.** This drawing was a projection as to the appearance of the Chevrolet automobile that would be using the rotary engine that General Motors was working on for a 1974 introduction. Though the rotary engine did not make production, and a restyled Vega appeared for 1974, it was not even close to looking like this sketch from an early 1974 car preview magazine, which has the characteristics of the design that became the 1975 Chevrolet Monza 2+2 Hatchback.

1974 GM Chevrolet Vega with Wankel Rotary engine

• **1974 Pontiac Banshee III.** The first Banshee concept appeared in 1966, as a fastback style two-seater and forerunner of the production Firebird for 1967. A second Banshee, also known as Fiero, was introduced for 1968 as a two-seat open cockpit sports car. The third version seen here for 1974 was based on the existing Firebird platform complete with a 455 CID Super Duty V8 engine, and this time around was a four-passenger fastback coupe. This version would get a makeover and appear again as the 1979 Banshee.

1974 Banshee III

• **1976 Chevrolet Monza Super Spyder II.** Based on a

Monza 2+2 hatchback coupe, the Spyder II was a conceptual successor to the 1962 Corvair Monza Super Spyder concept car. The Super Spyder II had an aerodynamically efficient sloping hood and wheel opening flares, with a unique fluorescent headlight system.

1976 Monza Super Spyder II
(courtesy Chicago Auto Trade Association)

• **1976 Chrysler Research Safety Vehicle (RSV).** Designed and built in cooperation with the National Highway Traffic Safety Administration and Calspan Corporation, the RSV was another project to improve vehicle safety. Based on a Simca 1308 from Chrysler's French subsidiary, the body received modifications that included up to 50 mph impact protection, and run-flat tires. Interior features included airbags and energy absorbing trim panels.

1976 RSV (Research Safety Vehicle)

• **1977 Chevrolet Aerovette.** Originally built to explore design and features of the next generation Corvette with a mid-engine powertrain, the XP-882, as it was first known, was designed in the late 1960's, and later to be powered by two rotary Wankel engines mounted behind the seats. With a lightweight steel and aluminum cage-type structure, and fiberglass body, the car was lightweight and strong. The main visual features were gull-wing style doors, a "V"-shaped windshield and collapsible bumpers. In 1973, the XP-882 was re-fitted with four transverse-mounted rotary Wankel engines, and added the "Aerovette" name. For the 1977 auto show season, the car became known simply as the Aerovette, but also lost the Wankel engines in favor of a traditional Chevrolet 350 CID engine, due to GM discontinuing the rotary engine development program.

- **1977 Chevrolet Corvette Mulsanne.** Powered by a Chevrolet LT1, 350 CID V8 engine, the modified Corvette was a running and driving concept car, unlike some concepts. A mild front-end restyling was the main visual change, and it featured a periscope-style rear view mirror, with the periscope mounted on the rear edge of the roof.
- **1978 AMC Concept Electron.** For 1978, AMC came up with several concept cars as part of its "Concept 80" program. Several "minivan" style concepts based on the Pacer wagon were introduced, as was the Concept Electron. Concept Electron was based on the 1968 AMC Amitron concept, which was to be a battery powered electric three-passenger runabout. The 1978

1978 Concept Electron

version was not greatly changed, other than a new paint scheme and interior changes. In either case it did not become a viable concept car, as both were missing their powertrains, so being able to actually drive and evaluate the AMC electric was not possible.

- **1978 Chevrolet Malibu Black Sterling.** A modestly modified Malibu two-door coupe served as the basis for the Malibu Black Sterling. Custom features included a front air dam and rear spoiler, special wheels, two-tone black and silver paint and a red interior. This car was mainly built to draw attention to the new-for-1978 Malibu coupes.
- **1978 Chrysler LeBaron Turbine.** A LeBaron two-door coupe with custom front-end styling was one of the last Chrysler turbine engine concept cars to be produced. The LeBaron version was done with financial help from

1977 Corvette Mulsanne's unique front-end styling
(courtesy Chicago Auto Trade Association)

1977 Corvette Mulsanne with roof-mounted, periscope-style rear view mirror (courtesy Chicago Auto Trade Association)

1978 Malibu Black Sterling
(courtesy Chicago Auto Trade Association)

1978 Malibu Black Sterling on display
(courtesy Chicago Auto Trade Association)

1978 LeBaron Turbine

the U.S. Department of Transportation to explore powertrain possibilities for the future. A slanting front end design with an upright center grille and fender end caps, and a T-bar roof with vertical rear quarter windows marked the exterior features of what would be the last Chrysler turbine car to have custom bodywork.

- **1978 Pontiac Firebird Trans Am Type K.** First proposed by Chevrolet on its Camaro in the early 1970s, the Kammback wagon design was picked up by Pontiac and combined with its highly popular Trans Am, resulting in the Trans Am Type K. A fixed roof extension and rear window were constructed with a pair of gullwing doors for access to the rear storage area. Two concepts were built, one silver and one gold, and both were crowd pleasers wherever they were shown. In fact they were so popular that both of the cars were updated with the new-for-1979 front-end treatment and shown for a second season.

- **1978 Pontiac Grand Am CA.** Considered for a return

1978 Firebird Trans Am Type K 2-Door wagon
with gullwing cargo doors open

1978 Firebird Trans Am Type K, profile view

1978 Grand Am CA 2-Door Coupe with T-tops removed
(courtesy Chicago Auto Trade Association)

1978 Grand Am California Special, rear two-thirds view

to the Pontiac lineup was the Can Am, or CA, prototype built on the new for 1978 Grand Am two-door coupe. Features included front air dam and rear deck spoiler, wheel opening flares, T-tops, blackout trim, Trans Am "snowflake" wheels, and a Trans Am–style hood scoop. It had the looks to be the next GTO, especially had it been a 1980 version with a 4.9L, 301 CID V8 turbocharged engine.

- **1978 Pontiac Grand Am California Special.** Using much the same design concept as the Grand Am CA, the California Special Grand Am had the same style Trans Am hood scoop and wheels, blackout trim, and a front air dam. From there, it differed in having a Grand Prix leather bucket seat interior and differing paint stripes. Also missing from the California Special

1978 Grand Am California Special 2-Door Coupe

were T-tops, wheel opening flares and rear decklid spoiler. It appears that this car could have been much closer to production than the Grand Am CA.

- **1979 Ford Probe I.** The first of a series of five Probe concept cars to be released over the next six years, the Probe I was built to push the limits of aerodynamics. This first concept was a coupe design that achieved a

drag coefficient of 0.22, far lower than any production car of the time. Each of the successive Probe concepts would achieve an even lower coefficient of drag, with the 1985 Probe V achieving .137.

- **1980 Ford Probe II.** The Probe II was the second of the aerodynamic concept series, built in a four-door sedan format.

1979 Probe I

1980 Probe II

IX. Model and Body Style Codes

Throughout automotive history, manufacturers have used codes to identify their different models and body styles. The wide variety of models and body styles available between 1973 and 1980 can create confusion as to how the codes were used. Of the four major manufacturers, all but Ford Motor Company followed a fairly well defined set of rules to determine these codes. Ford was using a system it had developed many years prior, and on most models, only the first digit of the model number was linked to a specific series. The second

digit could be used on differing body styles within the same model year, such as in 1973 when the second digit of "3" could identify a convertible, a two-door sedan, a four-door wagon or a four-door pillared hardtop. The huge number of combinations prevents detailing them within this section, and only the first digit is deciphered except on a few specific models where it did not change through the eight-year period covered by this book.

American Motors

Model #	Model Name	Body code	Body styles	Trim code	Trim level
0	Hornet, Concord, AMX (78)	3	2-Door Hatchback	0,3	Economy
1	Matador (73–74), Matador coupes (75–78)	5	4-Door Sedan	4	Gremlin 4-cylinder
3	Eagle	6	2-Door Sedan or 2-Door Coupe	5	Base
4	Gremlin, Spirit, AMX (79–80)	8	4-Door Station Wagon	7	Mid-level
6	Pacer	9	2-Door Hardtop	8	Specialty
7	Javelin			9	High-level or Sport
8	Ambassador, Matador 4-Doors (75–78)				

Example: 05-7 = Hornet 4-Door Sedan.

Chrysler Corporation

Model #	Model Name	Trim code	Trim level	Body code	Body styles
B	Plymouth Barracuda	L	Base	21	2-Door Coupe

Model #	Model Name	Trim code	Trim level	Body code	Body styles
C	Chrysler Newport, New Yorker, Town & Country (73–78)	M	Mid-level	22	2-Door Coupe (Coupe w/thin or no door window frames)
D	Dodge Polara, Monaco	H	High-level	23	2-Door Hardtop
E	Dodge St. Regis	P	Premium	24	2-Door Hatchback
F	Chrysler LeBaron	S	Special	29	2-Door Sport Coupe
G	Dodge Diplomat			41	4-Door Sedan
H	Plymouth Volaré			42	4-Door Pillared Hardtop (Sedan w/thin or no door window frames)
J	Dodge Challenger (73–74)			43	4-Door Hardtop
J	Plymouth Gran Fury (80)			44	4-Door Hatchback
L	Dodge Dart			45	4-Door, 2-seat station wagon
M	Plymouth Horizon			46	4-Door, 3-seat station wagon
N	Dodge Aspen				
P	Plymouth Fury (73–74), Gran Fury (75–77)				
R	Plymouth Satellite (73–74), Fury (75–78)				
S	Chrysler Cordoba				
T	Chrysler Newport, New Yorker (79–80)				
V	Plymouth Valiant				
W	Dodge Coronet, Charger (73–74)				
X	Dodge Charger SE (75–78), Magnum, Mirada				
Y	Imperial				
Z	Dodge Omni				
1	Plymouth Champ				
2	Dodge Challenger FWD				
3	Plymouth Sapporo				
4	Dodge Colt FWD				
6	Dodge Colt RWD				
7	Plymouth Arrow				

Example: NP41 = Dodge Aspen SE 4-Door Sedan.

Ford Motor Company

Ford

Model #	Model Name
0	Mustang, Mustang II
1	Pinto
2	Torino, Elite, LTD II S
3	Gran Torino, LTD II
4	Torino wagons, LTD II wagons
5	Custom 500, Galaxie 500
6	LTD
7	Full-size Ford wagons
8	Granada
9	Maverick, Fairmont
87	Thunderbird
F	Fiesta

Lincoln-Mercury

Model #	Model Name
0	Montego, Montego MX
1	Montego MX Brougham, Capri (79–80)
2	Bobcat
3	Comet, Monarch, Zephyr
4	Monterey
5	Monterey Custom
6	Marquis
7	Full-size Mercury wagons
9	Cougar
81	Continental 2-Door
82	Continental 4-Door
84	Versailles
89	Mark series 2-Door

Model #	Model Name
90	Mark VI 4-Door
96	Mark VI Signature Series

General Motors Corporation

Model #	Model Name	Body Code	Body Style
B	Apollo/Skylark, Omega, Fleetwood 60 Special Brougham, Chevette	07	2-Door Hatchback 2+2 Coupe
C	Malibu, Calais, Skylark Limited (80), Astre (75 'S')	09	4-Door Sedan, fastback roofline
D	Malibu Classic, Century, deVille, Skylark Sport (80), Starfire SX, LeMans	11	2-Door Notchback Sedan
E	Laguna, Century Special and Century wagon (78–80), Omega Brougham, Ventura S (75), Sunbird base coupes (78–80)	15	2-Door station wagon
F	Century Wagon (73–77), Fleetwood 75, LeSabre Sport Coupe, LeMans Sport Coupe (–77), Grand LeMans (78–80)	17	2-Door Hatchback Coupe
G	Malibu Classic Estate, Cutlass (base, S and Salon), Century Sport coupe, Luxury LeMans/Grand LeMans (73–77), Grand Am (78–80)	23	4-Door Sedan, 8- or 9-passenger
H	Citation, Monte Carlo, Century Luxus/Custom, Century (78–80), Cutlass wagon, Grand Am (73–75), Grand Prix SJ	27	2-Door Coupe
J	Regal, Cutlass Supreme, Vista-Cruiser, Chevette Scooter (or base), Grand Prix	29	4-Door Colonnade Hardtop Coupe
K	BelAir, Century Luxus wagon, Grand Prix (73–75) Grand Prix SJ (76), Grand Prix LJ (77–80)	33	Limousine
L	Impala, Eldorado, Delta 88, Century Limited, Catalina	35	4-Door, 2-Seat station wagon
M	Monza, Regal Limited, Cutlass Supreme Brougham, Sunbird	37	2-Door Hardtop and 2-Door Colonnade Hardtop Coupe
N	Caprice Classic, LeSabre, Delta 88 Royale, Bonneville (73–74, 77–80)	39	4-Door Hardtop
P	LeSabre Luxus/Custom/Limited, Grand Ville, Grand Safari, Bonneville (76)	45	4-Door, 3-Seat station wagon
Q	Camaro and Z/28, Custom Cruiser, Bonneville Brougham (77–79)	47	2-Door Hardtop Coupe
R	Monza 2+2 HBK, Estate Wagon, Custom Cruiser, Bonneville Brougham (80)	49	4-Door Hardtop Sedan
S	Camaro Type LT/Berlinetta, Skyhawk, Omega F85, Firebird	57	2-Door Sport Coupe and 2-Door Colonnade HT Cpe-specialty
T	Malibu (78–80), Electra 225, 98, Skyhawk S, Starfire, Firebird Esprit	67	Convertible
U	Firebird Formula	69	4-Door Sedan
V	Vega, Electra 225 Custom, 98 Luxury, Electra Estate Wagon, Astre (75-), Firebird Trans Am	77	2-Door Hatchback Coupe
W	Malibu Classic (78–80), Electra Park Avenue, Toronado XSR, Firebird Trans Am	87	2-Door Hardtop Sport Coupe
X	Citation, Nova, Electra 225 Limited, 98 Regency, Astre SJ, Phoenix (77),		
Y	Nova Custom/Concours, Ventura/Phoenix, Riviera, Toronado		
Z	Corvette, Monte Carlo (78–80), Riviera (79–80), Toronado Brougham, Ventura Custom/SJ, Phoenix LJ		

Example: J57 = Buick Regal, Oldsmobile Cutlass Supreme or Pontiac Grand Prix 2-Door Hardtop Coupe.

X. Manufacturer Logos, 1973–1980

The following is a selection of logos used by the manufacturers through this time period.

American Motors Corporation 1954–1979
25th anniversary emblem

American Motors logo, 1973–1980

Left: Buick logo, 1973–1974. *Right:* Buick logo, 1975–1978

Buick 75th anniversary emblem, 1978

Left: Buick/Opel logo, 1973–1974. *Right:* Buick/Opel logo, 1975

Left: Cadillac crest, 1973–1974.
Right: Cadillac wreath and crest, 1975–1980

Checker Motors

Chevrolet logo, 1973–1976

Left: Buick logo, 1979–1980

Left: Chevrolet Spirit of America logo decal, 1974.
Right: Chevrolet Nova Medalist badge, 1976

Chevrolet logo, 1977–1980

Chevrolet Chevette Sandpiper logo, 1977

Left: Chevrolet Corvette
25th Anniversary em-
blem, 1978. *Above:*
Chrysler logo, 1973–
1980

Chrysler Newport and New Yorker hood ornament, 1975

Left: Chrysler Motors Corporation logo, 1973–1980.
Right: Chrysler-Plymouth logo, 1973–1980

Dodge logo, 1973–1980

Dodge Street Fleet logo, 1978

Left: Chrysler Cordoba hood ornament, 1975

Ford line emblems, 1973

Ford Mustang II emblem, 1974

Ford Division and Ford Motor Company logo, 1973–1980

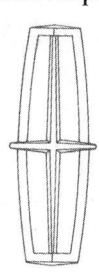

Left: Ford Motor Company 75th anniversary logo, 1978.
Right: General Motors Corporation logo, 1973–1980

Lincoln-Mercury logo, 1973

Lincoln-Mercury logo, 1974–1975

Lincoln-Mercury logo, 1976–1977

Lincoln-Mercury logo, 1978–1980

Left: Lincoln emblem, 1973–1974. *Right:* Lincoln emblem, 1975–1980

Lincoln-Mercury logo, 1978–1980

Left: Oldsmobile logo, 1973–1975. *Right:* Oldsmobile logo, 1976–1980

Above: Plymouth logo, 1973–1980.

Right: Plymouth Fury hood ornament, 1975

Pontiac logo, 1973–1980

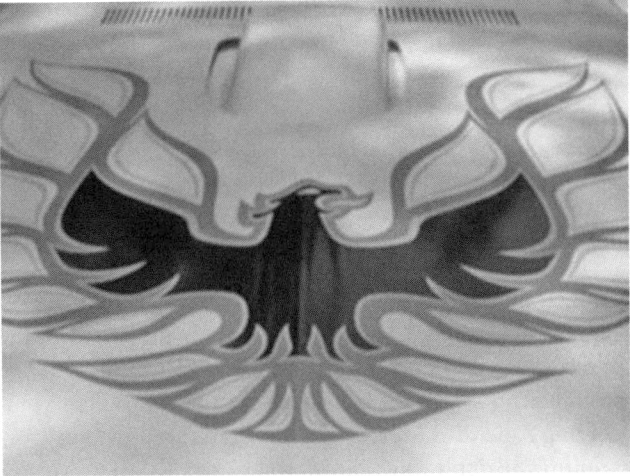

Pontiac Firebird Trans Am hood decal, 1975

Pontiac 50th Anniversary hood ornament on 1976 Pontiac Grand Prix SJ

Pontiac line emblems, 1978

Bibliography

The principal sources for advertising slogans, pictures, powertrains, paint colors, equipment features and pricing information were original corporate sales literature, dealer and corporate product information, and advertising and historical records from the companies featured in this book, including American Motors Corporation, Avanti Motor Corporation, Bricklin Vehicle Corporation, Checker Motors Corporation, Chrysler Corporation, Ford Motor Company, General Motors Corporation and Sebring-Vanguard, Inc. (CitiCar).

Additional pricing, coding and VIN information was obtained from the following sources:

AUTO '73 (*Consumer Guide* special annual issue), 1973, pp. 111–140.

AUTO '77 (*Consumer Guide* special annual issue), 1977, pp. 121, 124, and 152–161.

Buyer's Guide Reports, New Car Prices—1975. Milwaukee, WI: DMR Publications, Inc., 1974.

Buyer's Guide Reports, 1976 New Car Prices. Milwaukee, WI: DMR Publications, Inc., 1976.

Buyer's Guide Reports, 1979 New Car Prices. Milwaukee, WI: DMR Publications, Inc., 1979.

Car Prices Magazine, 1978. Compton, CA: People's Publishing, Inc.

Changing Times, December 1972, December 1973 and December 1974.

Edmund's 1974 New Car Prices. Great Neck, NY: Edmund Publication Corporation, 1973.

N.A.D.A. Official Used Car Guide. McLean, VA: National Automobile Dealers Used Car Guide Co., various issues from October 1973 through January 1981.

Passenger Vehicle Identification Manual. Palos Hills, IL: National Automobile Theft Bureau, 1975 and 1981.

Production Color Book. Ditzler Automotive Finishes PPG Car Color List, 1984.

Additional information was obtained from the following sources:

1975 Car Previews. Los Angeles: Argus, 1974, p. 73.

Ford Motor Company, Technical and Product Information Department.

Mechanix Illustrated, April 1973, "We test the Chrysler Imperial" by Tom McCahill, pp. 54–56.

Flammang, James M. *Standard Catalog of American Cars, 1976–1999.* Iola, WI: Krause Publications, 1999. This book was used to cross-reference and confirm production information obtained through industry records and publications, as there were often discrepancies in record keeping. Note that the information found in the present book does not always coincide with what is found in other references for this period, including *Standard Catalog of American Cars, 1976–1999.*

Index

*Page numbers in **bold italics** refer to photographs.*

8-9-13